EXCESSIVE FLASHPOINTS, SOLITARY DEMANDS, DARKEST CORNERS: IAN CURTIS, JOY DIVISION, CRITICAL THEORY, AND ME

BOB NOWLAN

SAN DIEGO, CA:
LEFT EDGE BOOKS,
2025

Left Edge Books
San Diego, CA
Copyright © 2025 by Bob Nowlan

Nowlan, Bob
Excessive Flashpoints, Solitary Demands, Darkest Corners: Ian Curtis, Joy Division, Critical Theory, and Me

ISBN (Hardcover): 9798218512378
ISBN (Ebook): 9798218512385

ABOUT THE AUTHOR

Bob Nowlan worked for 38 years as a university-level faculty member, concentrating in critical theory and in critical studies in literature, film, television, popular music, and popular culture, including 27 years as a professor at the University of Wisconsin-Eau Claire where Bob is now professor emeritus. Bob has maintained an absolutely immense passion concerning Ian Curtis and Joy Division, Bob's all-time favorite musician and all-time favorite music group, for more than 45 years. Bob is producer and dj host of the weekly show Insurgence with WHYS Community Radio in Eau Claire, Wisconsin, and of the weekly show Left Edge Radio with KNSJ Community Radio in San Diego, California. Bob lives with his husband and life-partner, Andy Swanson, and their two dogs, Aidan and Patrick, both pugs, in San Diego, California.

For Andy

TABLE OF CONTENTS

Chapter 1: 9-102. Introduction.

Chapter 2: 102-312. Listening to, Describing, Analyzing, and Interpreting the Lyrics and Music of Ian Curtis and Joy Division//In depth consideration of "Disorder," "Transmission," and "Twenty Four Hours."

Chapter 3: 312-443. Encounter and Dialogue: Ian Curtis and Joy Division Meets Karl Marx's *Economic and Philosophic Manuscripts of 1844*, Emile Durkheim's *Suicide: a Study in Sociology*, and Sigmund Freud's *Civilization and Its Discontents*//In depth consideration of "Shadowplay," "Isolation," "Means to an End," and "Love Will Tear Us Apart."

Chapter 4: 443-623. Encounter and Dialogue: Ian Curtis and Joy Division Meets Max Weber's *Protestant Ethic and the Spirit of Capitalism*, Louis Althusser's *On the Reproduction of Capitalism: Ideology and Ideological State Apparatuses*, and Michel Foucault's *Discipline and Punish*//In depth consideration of "Insight," "New Dawn Fades," "Atrocity Exhibition," and "The Eternal."

Chapter 5: 623-846. Encounter and Dialogue: Ian Curtis and Joy Division Meets Aimé Césaire's *Discourse on Colonialism*, Edward Said's *Representations of the Intellectual*, and Trinh T. Minh-ha's *Woman, Native, Other: Writing, Postcoloniality, and Feminism*//In depth consideration of "Day of the Lords," "Colony," "Heart and Soul," and "Autosuggestion."

Chapter 6: 846-1121. Encounter and Dialogue: Ian Curtis and Joy Division Meets Robert McRuer's *Crip Theory: Cultural Signs of Queerness and Disability* and *Crip Times: Disability, Globalization, and Resistance*, Ann Cvetkovich's *Depression: A Public Feeling*, and Avery Gordon's *Ghostly Matters: Haunting and the Sociological Imagination*//In depth consideration of "She's Lost Control," "Dead Souls," "Atmosphere," and "Decades."

Chapter Seven: 1121-1194. Conclusion//Reflection on the Journey Writing This Book Has Been Along with In depth consideration of issues of Insecurity, Loneliness, Fear, Fascism, Utopia, and Hope.

PREFACE AND ACKNOWLEDGMENTS

In *Excessive Flashpoints, Solitary Demands, Darkest Corners: Ian Curtis, Joy Division, Critical Theory, and Me* I inquire into issues of fundamental and ultimate concern: the meaning, value, and purpose of existence; our responsibility to and for others; human beings as complex, multiple, contradictory, and dynamic; the challenge of intimacy and the power of love; the quest for authenticity and the struggle for integrity; what it means to be included and excluded along with how as well as why this occurs; how social change happens along with what can be the contribution of artistic and cultural work toward this transformation; and the ethical responsibility to confront myriad metaphorical 'darknesses' in our individual and social lives, despite how challenging, difficult, and painful such confrontation can so often be. I pursue this inquiry by staging a dialogue between critical theory and popular music. I explore how intelligent, sensitive popular music engages the same issues as does critical theory and can help us to better understand and especially better feel how vital, urgent, concrete, and relevant critical theory can be. I use the music as art of pioneering post-punk musician Ian Curtis and his band Joy Division as my vehicle in so doing, drawing upon my experience teaching five upper level undergraduate university classes focused on Ian Curtis, Joy Division, and Critical Theory, at the University of Wisconsin-Eau Claire: English 484, Seminar in Theory and Criticism: Ian Curtis and Joy Division in (Historical and Cultural) Context, Fall 2011; English 484, Seminar in Theory and Criticism: Ian Curtis, The Myth and The Music, Fall 2014; Honors 304, Ian Curtis and Joy Division: Critical Theoretical Perspectives, Fall 2016; Honors 337, Ian Curtis and Joy Division: Critical Theoretical Perspectives, Fall 2017; and English 484, Seminar in Theory and Criticism: 'Let's Take a Ride Out, See What We Can Find': Popular Music, Issues of Fundamental and Ultimate Concern, Empathy and Solidarity–Ian Curtis, Joy Division, and Critical Theory, Spring 2019.

The work my students have done in these classes, and their enthusiasm for what we have explored together, inspires me to write this book–as does my now 45+ years' immense passion for Ian Curtis and Joy Division, life and work, and, especially, music as art. Joy Division has been my persistently all-time favorite musical group and Ian Curtis my persistently all-time favorite individual musician, and the work I have done in teaching the aforementioned classes, and on this book, represents my attempt to account for how and why that might be. Accordingly, and following advice of colleagues who attended two public presentations concerned with my work teaching and writing about Ian Curtis, Joy Division, and critical theory, this book is a part personal memoir. As a part personal memoir, I make reference to diverse areas and periods of my life-experience but I concentrate on my 38 years as a university teacher, and in particular as a teacher of critical theory and of critical studies in literature, film, television, popular music, and popular culture.

Chapter one provides a comprehensive introduction to and overview of what I am doing in this book, how, and why; establishes and elaborates my personal connections with this work; and sets forth my overall argument.

I turn next, in chapter two, to introduce a model for listening closely to Joy Division music in the course of a multi-stage process of careful description, analysis, and interpretation of three Joy Division songs–"Disorder," "Transmission," and "Twenty Four Hours." I precede specific engagement with these three songs by explaining the paper assignment I have used in multiple classes I have taught on popular music as cultural studies, which I am in effect assigning to myself three times in this second chapter. Here I greatly ramp up what I expect in response to this assignment. I do so by extrapolating from theoretical writings concerned with how to make sense of and respond to what we hear, in listening to, thinking about, and feeling music, especially popular music. I make use of concepts, methods, and approaches from these theoretical writings to explain how the music of Joy Division, and by no means just Ian Curtis's lyrics, conveys meaning and exerts impact.

In chapters three through six I carry out a series of encounters, or, in other words, dialogues, among 'Ian Curtis and Joy Division' and three to four works of critical theory in each case. My aim in chapters three through six is for each encounter, for each dialogue, to contribute to the production of knowledge and understanding–to serve, in other words, as an instance of theorization and critique, not simply an 'application' of theory, through critique, from one set of texts 'upon' another. In chapter three I take up Karl Marx's *Economic and Philosophic Manuscripts of 1844*, Èmile Durkheim's *Suicide: a Study in Sociology*, and Sigmund Freud's *Civilization and Its Discontents* in relation to Joy Division songs "Shadowplay," "Isolation," "A Means to an End," and "Love Will Tear Us Apart."

In chapter four I take up Max Weber's *Protestant Ethic and the Spirit of Capitalism*, Louis Althusser's *On the Reproduction of Capitalism: Ideology and Ideological State Apparatuses*, and Michel Foucault's Discipline and Punish in relation to Joy Division songs "Insight," "New Dawn Fades," "Atrocity Exhibition," and "The Eternal." In chapter five I take up Aimé Césaire's *Discourse on Colonialism*, Edward Said's *Representations of the Intellectual*, and Trinh T Minh-ha's *Woman, Native, Other:Writing, Postcoloniality, and Feminism* in relation to Joy Division songs "Day of the Lords," "Colony," "Heart and Soul," and "Autosuggestion." And in chapter six I take up Robert McRuer's *Crip Theory: Cultural Signs of Queerness and Disability* and *Crip Times: Disability, Globalization, and Resistance*, Ann Cvetkovich's *Depression: A Public Feeling*, and Avery F. Gordon's *Ghostly Matters: Haunting and the Sociological Imagination* in relation to Joy Division songs "Dead Souls," "She's Lost Control," "Atmosphere," and "Decades."

In chapter seven, in conclusion, I reflect back on my intellectual and emotional journey in writing this book, in what has changed in my life and in larger social and political contexts surrounding and influencing my life-experience over the course of this writing, as well as take on issues of insecurity, loneliness, fear, fascism, utopia, and hope, in depth, in relation to the lyrics of Ian Curtis and the music of Joy Division–and beyond.

I write this book for a specialized audience maintaining advanced familiarity with critical theory, critical studies in popular culture, and critical studies in popular music, as well as for a general audience of readers much like the students I have taught at UW-Eau Claire in five classes focused on Ian Curtis, Joy Division, and critical theory who are ready and willing to take on a considerable challenge. These latter are upper level undergraduate English and Honors university students, who in most cases have taken some courses offering basic introductions to and overviews of critical theory previously, but in most cases no more than that. These are people who are interested in and receptive to the possibilities a more advanced engagement with critical theory can offer, without approaching embarking on the experience maintaining sharply defined expectations concerning what this will be like. These are people who are, in turn, akin to those among the more specialized audience I am also addressing in writing this book, keenly attracted to work concerned with critical studies in popular culture, and in particular critical studies in popular music. These include people maintaining prior knowledge of and interest in Joy Division–other Joy Division fans–but that kind of knowledge and experience is unnecessary in order to derive benefit from this book, just as has been the case with the students in the aforementioned classes I have taught, less than half of whom maintained any prior knowledge of or interest in Joy Division before we started our work together. This is a book, in sum, for anyone who loves popular music, who cares to think and talk about 'big issues', who believes in the importance of empathy, and who would like to help contribute toward forging a substantive culture of solidarity–especially by engaging with what popular culture, and in particular popular music, has to offer in that quest. I hope this book will show readers that critical theory can be concrete, relevant, and urgent–especially in sustained dialogue with popular culture and in particular popular music–and that popular culture, notably popular music, can, in turn, contribute meaningful and impactful ways of helping make sense of, along with meaningful and impactful modes of helping engage with, issues of ultimate and fundamental importance.

I wrote *Excessive Flashpoints, Solitary Demands, Darkest Corners: Ian Curtis, Joy Division, Critical Theory, and Me* between August 2020 and August 2024. Writing this book has proven to be the most difficult and demanding intellectual work I have ever done. The process, and the result, have not only felt massive but also often monstrous. In starting out I imagined this book as 'career-culminating' work; now I conceive of it as a 'life-culminating' work. I am sending if forth into the public domain as quickly as possible because I am eager to share this work with others, and not keep it to myself, so it can contribute to ongoing conversations and debates, concerning the array of issues the book addresses.

In final editing and proofreading I kept in place a dimension of this book I argue is crucial. As I stage encounters, and dialogues, between 'Ian Curtis and Joy Division' and work in critical theory, and especially as I closely listen to, and carefully describe, analyze, and interpret the lyrics and music of Ian Curtis and Joy Division, I make concrete connections with precisely where I precisely am at, in my life, as I stage these encounters and dialogues, and as I listen to, describe, analyze, and interpret this music–including connections with larger social and political issues that are matters of concern for me *right then and there, in that immediate time and place.* In other words, I have deliberately *not* revised the book so as to suggest it was all written in one fell swoop, at one single moment. My life changes, culture and society changes, and the world changes, as the book proceeds. This is important because I argue the value that comes from closely listening to and carefully describing, analyzing, and interpreting lyrics and music like this, in relation to what this process prompts one pursuing it to think (about) and feel, depends upon making exactly those kinds of highly specific, precise, and concrete connections.

I acknowledge the support of two successive grants from the Cignet Trust, from 2020-2021 and 2021-2022, made the writing of this book possible. I thank the Unitarian Universalist Congregation of Eau Claire, the English Department of the University of Wisconsin-Eau Claire, and the Office of Research and Sponsored Programs of the University of Wisconsin-Eau Claire for inviting me to make public presentations of early versions of small portions of what has become this book, and for offering me considerable encouragement to push forward. I thank the students in all five of the aforementioned classes I taught focused on Ian Curtis, Joy Division, and critical theory for inspiring me to want to write this book and to believe it to be of value to do so. I thank family and friends over the course of my life, far too many to name individually here, without overlooking someone important, for contributing indispensably toward making me whom and what I have been, and have become, at my very best. I thank colleagues and especially students throughout my career as a professor and university-level faculty member for providing me the opportunity to live a fantastic life in what I experienced as a genuine calling and where I felt I could and did, frequently, make a meaningful difference–for the good. I thank everyone associated with Joy Division and Factory Records for all of their contributions and achievements, and everyone else who I cite in this book who has otherwise previously written extensively about Ian Curtis and Joy Division. I thank Peter Hook, Stephen Morris, Bernard Sumner–and Ian Curtis. Above all else, I thank the one person who had done by far the most, and by far the best, to make everything in my life possible, and continues to do so every day, all the time, in countless ways, the love of my life, my husband and life-partner, Andy Swanson, to whom I dedicate this book.

Chapter One

One

In this book I inquire into issues of fundamental and ultimate concern in modern to contemporary critical theory: issues concerning the meaning, value, and purpose of existence; our responsibility to and for others; human beings as complex, multiple, contradictory, and dynamic; the challenge of intimacy and the power of love; the quest for authenticity and the struggle for integrity; what it means to be included and excluded along with how as well as why this occurs; how social change happens along with what can be the contribution of artistic and cultural work toward this transformation; and the ethical responsibility to continue to confront and find a way to work through myriad metaphorical 'darknesses' in our individual and social lives, despite how tremendously challenging, difficult, and painful this can so often be. I pursue this inquiry by staging a dialogue between critical theory and popular music, and in particular by exploring how, I contend, intelligent, sensitive popular music engages the exact same issues as does critical theory and can thereby help enable us to better understand and especially *feel* how vital, urgent, concrete, and relevant critical theory can be. I use the life and work of pioneering post-punk musician Ian Curtis and his band Joy Division as my principal vehicle in so doing, drawing upon the work I have done in researching, preparing for, and teaching five upper level undergraduate university classes focused on Ian Curtis, Joy Division, and Critical Theory, at the University of Wisconsin-Eau Claire: English 484, Seminar in Theory and Criticism: Ian Curtis and Joy Division in (Historical and Cultural) Context, Fall 2011; English 484, Seminar in Theory and Criticism: Ian Curtis, The Myth and The Music, Fall 2014; Honors 304, Ian Curtis and Joy Division: Critical Theoretical Perspectives, Fall 2016; Honors 337, Ian Curtis and Joy Division: Critical Theoretical Perspectives, Fall 2017; and English 484, Seminar in Theory and Criticism: 'Let's Take a Ride Out, See What We Can Find': Popular Music, Issues of Fundamental and Ultimate Concern, Empathy and Solidarity–Ian Curtis, Joy Division, and Critical Theory, Spring 2019. The work my students have done in these classes, and their enthusiasm for what we have inquired into and explored together, inspires me to write this book–as does my now 40+ years' passionate interest in Ian Curtis and Joy Division, life and work, and, especially, music as art. Joy Division has been my persistently all-time favorite musical group and Ian Curtis my persistently all-time favorite individual musician, and the work I have done in teaching the aforementioned classes, and on this book, represents my attempt to account for how and why that might be. Accordingly, and following advice of colleagues who attended two public presentations concerned with my work teaching and writing about Ian Curtis, Joy Division, and critical theory, I am writing this book in part as a personal memoir, and here I want to especially commend Jack Bushnell, now University of Wisconsin-Eau Claire English Professor Emeritus, for pushing me to conceive of what I write with this book as a personal memoir. As in part a personal memoir, I will continue to make reference to diverse areas and periods of my life-experience but I will concentrate increasingly, in moving forward, on my 35+ years as a university teacher, and in particular as a teacher and faculty member concentrating in critical theory as well as critical studies in popular culture.

Two

Let's begin with me introducing myself. You may reasonably wonder why I do so. I admit I feel strange doing so. This is not customary for me, as someone trained to do scholarly writing, and, more specifically, in 'critical studies' as opposed to 'creative writing' (although in my teaching of 'critical studies' I favor synthesizing the 'critical' with the 'creative', and I design class project assignments enabling my students to do the same). I feel uneasy about it, as I am unsure 'I' am all that interesting. Yet, 'I' am writing this book in part, following colleagues' strong advice as a personal memoir. I hope as I share about myself my doing so conveys to you a clearer sense of 'who is this person' represented by the 'I'–and, at times, as part of the 'We'–in this book, where is he is coming from, and what is he about. I am writing this book inspired by my experience teaching five classes with the same focus, and in all my teaching I do, in all my classes, right from the start of the semester on day one, I strive to help students draw personal connections with what we are studying by sharing frankly about myself. Students appreciate my openness, and honesty, as well as getting to know me, while anecdotes and stories I draw from personal experience help students make sense of texts and topics and of positions, concepts, and arguments we engage. Colleagues who advised me to treat this book as a personal memoir also encouraged me to write as if I am writing for people like my students, so I will try do so.

Don't worry–don't throw the book down after reading that preceding sentence. I treat my students with great respect; I value them as people whom it is my privilege, and my honor, to get to know and with whom to collaborate. I prize active and interactive learning, discussion over lecture, and student- as opposed to instructor- centered classes. As much as I can, I avoid delivering any formal lectures, at all, during any class time, preferring to make any necessary 'lectures' available in print for students to read outside and prior to class discussions. I also prefer teaching classes in which we reach the point where students sharing and discussing work they done together individually, in groups, or in teams, becomes the primary focus of what we deal with during class time. I am eager to learn with and from my students, and I am eager to learn with and from you, in imagining who you might be, where you are coming from, and what you are about, and in striving to communicate with you, including by sharing with you my personal background, experience, and outlook. I do not consider myself 'unique', so I expect everything I share about myself will overlap with other people's backgrounds, experiences, and outlooks–and, even if not with yours, or with those of others you know well, then I hope you will find, as my students and I continually do, that it helps us better understand ourselves to learn about people who are, or seem, different from us.

Allow me to begin as I do with my students. I tell my students they can call me Bob and it is in fact what I most prefer of the various modes of address they could logically come up with, in addressing me. I am an informal person, in my teaching I aim to be welcoming and inclusive of everyone. I want all the students I teach to feel they can relax enough to open up and share with and around me, as well as not feel intimidated by me. At the same time, as I tell my students, I understand why they might prefer to address me in a more formal fashion, at least until they get to know me better, and in that case, of the three ready options, I prefer Professor Nowlan as opposed to Doctor Nowlan or Mr Nowlan. The reason why so is I conceive of Professor Nowlan as referencing the work I do, in teaching; in my current research, scholarship, and creative activity; and in my current institutional, professional, and community service. Doctor Nowlan I conceive as referencing what I spent many grueling years as a graduate student struggling to achieve. Mr Nowlan strikes me as what students use to refer to high school teachers without terminal graduate degrees, and otherwise is how I am addressed most often when someone is trying to sell something to me. But students are welcome to address me otherwise as well–such as simply 'Professor' and, as many commonly prefer, 'Professor Bob' or 'Doctor Bob'. I do draw the line, I tell them, at 'B' as 'Bob' is short enough, and I am not really their 'coach', so 'Coach Nowlan' feels strange–and strained.

My full name is Robert Andrew Nowlan, although I will add my saint's name from my confirmation is 'William', which I chose in honor of my maternal grandfather, William J. Lyons. Also, my 'dj name' is Sean Murphy (I chose this name to honor my Irish background–with one of the most common Irish male first names and one of the most common Irish last names). I chose my own middle name early in my young adult life because I didn't want to be my father's namesake–especially since he could never clearly decide whether I was Robert Anthony Nowlan II or Robert Anthony Nowlan III. The roman numerals did not sit well with me; I didn't like the regal connotations. So I legally changed my middle name. In Irish my name would be Riobárd Andriú Ó'Nuallain. My last name, Nowlan, is pronounced exactly the same as 'Nolan'; it is simply a less common variant. It is *not* pronounced 'now-land', and it does not begin with a 'k' or end with a 'd'. I pronounce it as 'No-luhn' with the accent on the 'No' although I accept if people want to pronounce is as 'No-len' or 'No-lahn'. If students misspell my last name, I prefer they misspell it Nolan, not Noland or Knoland or Nowland or Knowland. I often wish my family shared the most common form of the spelling of 'Nolan' without the confounding 'w', but it has at least given me the opportunity to call attention to myself, when people might otherwise be inclined to dismiss or ignore me, by pointing out they are misspelling my last name. I even, in graduate school, posted in our English Department newsletter an explanation of 'N-o-w-l-a-n' which suggested it is spelled that way as it is closer to the sound of its original Irish language antecedent, but that was just a made up story, which, remarkably enough, most people found believable–and from then on, no one in that department ever misspelled my last name. Up through the end of high school, I acquired many nicknames–'Cousin Bob', 'Uncle Bob', 'Buddy Kid', 'Einstein', 'Little Einstein', 'Doc', and those are only the ones I can remember–but few since.

I was born on May 6, 1961 in Belvidere, Illinois; my mother, Marilyn Lyons Nowlan, tells me since then that she hoped I would be born on May 5, the same day as Karl Marx and that tells you much about my family right away (May 5, 1961 was also the day of the first manned US space flight, by Alan B. Shepard Jr., which my mother also conceived would make for an impressive common anniversary–but it was not to be). We lived in Marengo, Illinois at that time, right near Belvidere; both towns are approximately twenty miles south of the Illinois-Wisconsin border. My parents also informed me early on in my still young life that I had been conceived in Madison, Wisconsin, at the end of a great summer they spent in the capital city of the state I would eventually come to live and work in for by far the longest stretch of my life–so I readily tell students, and colleagues, that when I was hired to work at the University Wisconsin-Eau Claire I came full circle, back to where I started–just 175 miles North by Northwest. At the age of one year old, my parents and I moved to South Bend, Indiana, where we lived for the next seven years. During that time, my brother Phil was born on November 27, 1963; my brother Ed on March 24, 1965; and my sister Jennifer on January 14, 1968. We moved to Wallingford, Connecticut in 1969, where I lived until I moved to Middletown, Connecticut to attend Wesleyan University. I have subsequently lived in Syracuse, New York; Tempe, Arizona; and Eau Claire, Wisconsin.

I like to play around a bit with what I identify as my hometown, as I figure I might as well choose a favorite place as my hometown, not necessarily where I am currently living, so I have cited Edinburgh, Scotland or Manchester, England as 'my hometown'–leading a number of people on social media to assume I am a British ex-pat. That assumption I perceive as similar to the surprising number of people who think my natural hair color is red–or even 'ginger'–because I have been dying it to look that way for nearly thirty years now (a combination of reddish blonde dye and dark brown hair, now increasingly gray, with a slight reddish tinge, produces that result). My eyes are green although they have shifted in color notably from much closer to emerald green when I was younger to gray green, and even at times largely gray. I am 5'11" tall and weigh between 140 and 145 pounds; I have been slender almost my entire life. I wear one ultra-thin, small, rose gold men's hoop earring in each ear, and I have no tattoos. I've worn multiple different rings and studs in the past, but the two piercings struck me as sufficient, and while I have no problems at all with anyone else's tattoos I've never wanted any myself. My length of hair has varied wildly, over the course of my life, but at present, with COVID-19 enforcing a highly restricted existence, my partner has been cutting my hair, 'Peaky Blinders style', primarily because I thought this would look interesting, it would be easy to do, and because I'm a fan of Cillian Murphy.

Because, unlike my students, you don't get to see me and interact directly with me in the same physical space at the same moment in time, I will share yet a little more about my appearance–and my 'presentation'. I tend to dress according to what I only learned indirectly, years after the phrase circulated widely, is a 'smart casual' fashion, with more of a tendency toward the 'casual' than the 'smart'. Whether true or not I can't say, but both colleagues and students often tell me I possess an impressive 'sense of style' in how I dress. That seems difficult to credit, for me, as shorts are one of my favorite kinds of clothing. I can't match some of my male students in the extremes to which they feel comfortable wearing shorts, but for me, once the temperature outside is over 50 degrees Fahrenheit, I prefer shorts over long trousers, especially if it is not cold and rainy (but even then I am not too bothered). I am unsure precisely where this preference comes from, but I suppose I do like to dress 'smart casually' and the combination of being gay, coming from a punk background, and loving sports all contribute. I am comfortable wearing shorts 'to work', while teaching and participating in meetings on campus, and this never has struck me as odd, although I suspect some might think so. But, then again, I haven't felt much pressure, fortunately, in the work I do as a university faculty member here in the US, to conform to any stifling norm, or normative range, for how I present and conduct myself. I can be serious, professional, and dressed in a comfortable and casual–albeit, I suppose, 'smart casual'–manner all at once. I do like to dress in a color coordinated fashion, even to the extent now, in the midst of COVID-19, of selecting facemasks that match the rest of what I am wearing, and since I am mentioning color I might as well add my favorite colors are green, red, and black–although I like many other colors too, including Ian Curtis's favorite shade of light blue.

***

From as early as I can remember, and well before kindergarten, I gravitated toward intellectual interests, which my parents strongly encouraged me to follow, even by peppering me with questions and challenges concerning obscure matters in history, politics, and philosophy, as well as sitting me down for lengthily impassioned lectures on the same, even well before I first started school. Reputedly, upon first seeing me, my father quizzed me with 'what were the causes of the Peloponnesian War?' I cried. But my mother helped me find, and memorize an answer, via Thucydides, to impress him with, when he came home from work, one evening when I was still yet three or four years old. My parents were certainly ambitious for me, and worried about making sure they were sufficiently so. Later on my parents told me at one point after I had first started talking I went for a short while without doing so, causing them to fret about something potentially being wrong until I offhandedly spoke my first full sentence: 'It's dark outside'. (I like to think that first sentence foreshadows my life-long compulsive attraction to 'the noir', including in the form of post-punk music.) I knew, entering school, I would be highly engaged and strive to excel in every academic subject area. I also knew, again encouraged and prepared by my parents, I needed to be ready to question and challenge my teachers because they did not know everything I wanted and especially needed to know.

I read voraciously, especially literature, history, and biography, and much more besides. That inclination prepared me well for my eventual choice of career, but, more important, has carried through as one of my persistently favorite activities. My favorite reading today, and in fact for many years now, other than in critical theory and critical studies in popular culture, both of which are more directly related to 'my work', is crime fiction, especially from England and Scotland, and I am currently also writing another book, once again based on five classes I have taught, titled *21st Century British TV Crime Drama: a Critical Guide*. By this point in time, my husband Andy and I have watched virtually every extant British crime drama, are are venturing onward to follow crime dramas from Ireland, Australia, New Zealand, Belgium, France, Spain, Italy, Germany, Austria, Finland, Denmark, Norway, Sweden, the Netherlands, and South Africa. Whenever I have 'free time' (and I have learned the value of making room for this every day, after making myself sick by not doing so), I am usually involved with fictional crime drama, whether in book form or on the screen.

From early on in life, again while still a small boy, I grew to love sports and music too, as well as television and film–and travel. We traveled when I was boy when we had the chance, but unfortunately this was not often, other than to visit my maternal grandparents in Lostant, Illinois, although I have more than made up for that since. But intellectual work was my principal focus of time and energy. I routinely, at least in relation to classes in English and social studies, pursued interests far advanced of what was expected for my grade–or my 'track'–such that teachers at first found it hard to believe I was reading–and writing about–what I was. Teachers nevertheless quickly developed ready ways of accommodating me, by enlisting me to help compliment the knowledge they, along with our textbooks, shared with fellow students. They frequently invited me to help teach my fellow students, and my Advanced Placement English teacher, during my senior year in high school, turned over the entire second half of the year to me to teach my classmates, under her supervision. The highlight: sharing my enthusiasm for William Faulkner's *The Sound and The Fury* with the class. I also taught my AP senior English classmates about existentialism and literature as well as about James Joyce and modernism. I loved to write too–although I cannot, in retrospect, attest to its quality–including by creating elaborate imaginary states and societies, that I detailed precisely, down to street maps of cities and to statistics concerning sports leagues, teams, seasons, and games. I did write many poems and short story sketches replete with dark romantic adolescent angst, especially focused on themes of loneliness and non-conformity, but when I tried something else, like a love poem, I did a poor job at it. My sophomore year high school English teacher, Mr. Goldstone, with whom I worked closely, as, respectively, the faculty advisor and student editor of our literary magazine, frankly told me 'you should not write about what you know nothing about'. He was right.

During my childhood years my greatest struggles had to do with having been labeled 'shy', well before I first started school, by my parents and other adults, which was made all the worse by me being encouraged to regard this 'shyness' as a deficiency for which I was personally responsible and which I could, and should, *will* my way past (or at least this is how I internalized labeling of 'my shyness'). In retrospect it seems absurd–and even worse, damagingly self-fulfilling–to label a toddler shy, make him feel like this was his fault, and then keep reinforcing this thereafter, but I am sure my parents were simply following what was commonsensical at the time in so doing.

What made me resent this label, for as long as I can remember, besides being made to feel as if 'it was my fault' on account of 'my having done something wrong', was the fact I wasn't all that, universally, shy. I was certainly one of the most talkative students in all my classes, and willing to take risks few others ever would, in questioning and challenging my teachers, as well as offering alternative takes on whatever they set forth. And, in terms of political views, fellow students and teachers all readily recognized me as positioned far to the left of everyone else–for instance, I was the only student in my sixth grade class in 1972 to vote for George McGovern for president (as opposed to Richard Nixon, in a class poll), and from early on I developed a keen attraction to democratic socialism, as represented by the likes of Norman Thomas and Eugene Debs. What's more, I willingly engaged in wilder forms of behavior than the conventional norm, at least among 'honors students', that periodically surprised and disturbed my friends. I valued being a non-confomist, from as early as I can remember, and the same with being a rebel–although, yes, I certainly valued being 'a rebel *with* a cause' far more than without. In high school I was one of the few male students to grow and wear a mustache, while I was also receptive to and interested in a variety of alternative and counter-cultural practices, including, late in my high school years, punk, that few others shared any interest in. But I was undoubtedly mostly 'a good kid', 'a smart kid', and someone who managed to get along with people from diverse cliques, including by recognizing how to keep myself out of trouble–or stay away from the prospect of trouble. My father once told me if I ever get into a fight, I should make sure to win the first one, which to my shock, I did, knocking out the boy I fought. After that I didn't get into

14

any of the numerous fights that routinely broke out in hallways and the grounds surrounding my middle and high schools.

I recall, in my senior year, being frustrated with friends who voted me 'shyest boy' because, as I told them, 'you know I'm not really all that shy'. But they told me they wanted to make sure I earned that 'award' as it was clear Steve Ackerman was going to be voted 'most likely to succeed'. It's odd, but back then at Lyman Hall High School, seemingly just about everyone knew class rank, at least at the top–Steve was #1 and I was #2. As these friends attested, 'we couldn't vote for the really shyest boy, because he would be so shy we wouldn't even know him'. It rankled me nonetheless. I was determined to break with what I found to be lazy labeling that followed people throughout their K-12 school years by enrolling at a university no other Lyman Hall student would be attending–Wesleyan University.

***

Early on in my life, in part due to how seriously my parents pushed me to be intellectually–and politically–engaged, and I do thank them for that, no matter what I might have previously suggested, I did develop a strong tendency toward what I have come much later to recognize as serious anxiety. I always wanted to do the right thing (or to do things right, which is not necessarily identical with doing the right thing), I wanted to support the right position, and I wanted to make a meaningful difference for the good. When I didn't do so, I felt badly–about myself–and I worried, excessively, about falling short. But I learned quickly from 'mistakes'. For example, after reading a biography of Andrew Carnegie, which painted him in a most flattering guise, my parents directed me to read Matthew Josephson's *The Robber Barons* to counter this misleading portrait–which I immediately did (and you should keep in mind this happened when I was still in elementary school).

One of the saddest experiences of my young life occurred when I was still only around four or five years old. This happened when my parents decided to force me to confront my shyness by telling me I had to go out and make a friend and I couldn't come back home until I did. I wandered around aimlessly before eventually returning home, not having made any friends, but my parents relented, emphasizing 'at least I tried'. Likewise, when I was six years old, my parents insisted I was old enough to go by myself to buy groceries at a nearby convenience store, across a busy street where we then lived in South Bend, Indiana–and I needed to do this to help overcome my shyness. I managed to purchase the items before I froze crossing the street as a speeding car barreled down and hit me, breaking my leg, while my father, who had come to watch out for me, saw me get hit right in front of him.

My parents were not really mean, despite what I might have suggested, and in fact they provided all of us with a great deal of encouragement and support. My mother and I became especially close and shared a great deal together–including when I was still in middle school beginning to take me to many stage plays, across Connecticut and in New York, on a regular basis. Some of these were daringly 'adult' plays (for example, Edward Bond's *Saved*, including a climactic collective stoning of a baby in a baby carriage) and I certainly recall being the youngest in attendance among those visibly part of the audience on many an occasion. Attending plays with my mother encouraged a lasting love of drama and theatre, which I have followed upon by focusing on plays whenever I teach Introduction to Critical Studies, formerly Introduction to Texts, including by means of an assignment involving students working in three separate teams, over the last approximately four and one-half weeks of the semester, to compose, produce, rehearse, and ultimately perform, for the rest of the class, a short play, approximately 35 minutes long, inspired by plays we had previously read and discussed together earlier in the semester. Students thrive with this assignment, and I am gratified that even the ostensibly 'shyest' of students excel, often by taking on leading roles in these plays. I empathize for anyone who has internalized an identification with the label 'shy', and especially who finds this frustrating. I delight in helping show these ostensibly 'shy' people they are not necessarily–or need not remain–as 'shy' as they too often think they are destined always to be.

I owe yet much more to my mother. For example, my mother is an amazing reader–no matter how lengthy, dense, or difficult the reading, she readily takes it on, is not intimidated to give it a go, and routinely reads through many books, on widely diverse subjects, all at the same time. My mother also gave me an incredible present, to celebrate my graduation from Wesleyan University with my bachelor's degree: a trip to Ireland, which we took together, my first trip outside of the US, other than briefly in Canada. We followed up that trip with two more to Ireland, each two years after the last, the second time with my sister Jennifer and my then girlfriend Stef. Although I only traveled beyond the US once in many years after that, to Canada for a conference in Ottawa, our early trips to Ireland piqued my interest in doing so yet again once able to afford to do so.

My mother has always been keenly interested in what I was reading, and later on, teaching, in my classes, and has always then readily pursued the same herself. She and I, together with various socialist friends of mine from Syracuse, traveled for over a decade each spring to attend the annual Socialist Scholars conference in lower Manhattan, and whenever she came to visit we often held long and increasingly loud conversations prompted by our shared support for socialism and radical politics. My Wesleyan friends I recall being surprised and impressed that when my mother came to visit she would take me out to dinner and we would end up drinking and talking literature, politics, music, and much more besides before bringing me, slightly tipsy, back to our dorm or rental house. At Syracuse (where I was a graduate student) my mother joined my Marxist friends at brunches and for coffee, at local diners, readily joining in the intellectual and political conversation and debate, never hesitating to ask pointed questions of any of us, and firmly requesting an explanation 'why' to any assertion to which she did not already consent.

Well before that point in time my mother stood out among friends of mine, late in high school, as she was entirely at ease asking if visiting friends of mine 'would like a beer'. In my family we learned about social drinking early, so getting drunk never held much, if any, appeal. I got that out of my system quickly one summer working food service at Choate-Rosemary Hall private preparatory school in Wallingford (we, the workers, were the 'townies' who went to the 'lower caste public school', from the vantage point of many students enrolled at Choate), when I attended a party among fellow workers where I drank too much Jim Beam, and threw a glass in the face of a cook who was much bigger and stronger than me, before my friend Jim got get me out of the party, took me home, and tossed me through the front door, where I landed unceremoniously in front of my mother and siblings, who were still up, sitting and talking in our living room. I was not only greatly embarrassed but also suffered such a terrible hangover that the next day I determined I would never drink like that again–and I haven't. My limit is no more than three alcoholic drinks maximum in 24 hours and I stick to it, even as I continue to enjoy drinking–these days especially a variety of reds, dry German and Austrian white wines, and single malt Scottish whisky. When my husband Andy and I visited Islay for four days we toured all eight distilleries then open, as well as walked all about the island–a beautiful place, dramatically different than anywhere else I had ever been, which later I immediately felt as well about Orkney and Shetland, in four-day visits to each of those archipelagos.

I maintain fewer memories of me and both of my parents spending 'quality time' all together, but I do vividly recall several shared television experiences with my parents, from my early childhood and initial adolescent years–the presidential election season of 1968, the Apollo 11 moon landing a year later, *Creature Features* (a series of classic horror films–which my parents made more frightening by insisting I go to bed immediately afterward, and, no, I could not leave the door open or a light on), and the Saturday night CBS comedy line-up of *All in the Family, MASH, The Mary Tyler Moore Show, The Bob Newhart Show*, and *The Carol Burnett Show*. My father and I did spend some time when I was thirteen seeking to more closely 'bond'–I recall him taking me to my first R-rated film, *Carrie*, and teaching me how to golf. I appreciated the effort, but I never became as close to my father as I did to my mother, although I will add he was always patient in helping me with math homework assignments and, although at the time some of his teasing felt relentless, as we were rooting for opposing sports teams, in retrospect I recognize this was jovial and well intended. After all, it was I who decided to choose different favorite baseball and football teams than my parents, symptomatic of a rebellious streak I've displayed from early on, so it was not the Chicago Cubs and Bears for me, but rather the Cincinnati Reds and the Green Bay Packers.

My siblings and I have got along well, by and large, all my life. My role as their long-term babysitter/surrogate parent made it harder to develop as close a relationship back when we all lived together as kids than might otherwise have been the case, but they are all fine people whom I deeply appreciate. I remember my younger brother Ed visiting me at Wesleyan on several occasions which I enjoyed, and felt proved impactful bonding experiences for us both. My sister Jennifer and I have long enjoyed the ability to talk easily, even after a considerable gap in close communication, while we share experience living with recurrent tendencies toward serious mental health challenges, in particular depression. In Jennifer's case this started in her early adolescence, and has periodically proven quite severe, but she has also shown impressive resilience–and her dedication, in working first for many years as a teacher of in-patient autistic adults, and then as a community health nurse, including for patients with severe mental health challenges of their own, are only two examples of many I could cite of her demonstration of great commitment toward helping others and to being actively compassionate. Jennifer's struggles with depression distracted me from my own tendencies for many years, as I tried to deny what I was experiencing by telling myself I couldn't be suffering the same as my sister and that I was sure whatever she had dealt with and was dealing with was far worse than anything I was and had been confronting. Not the case. Yet accepting that recurrent tendencies toward serious to severe anxiety, including panic attacks, and depression, are intrinsic to whom I am–to my identity–required swimming through miles upon miles of denial before owning these tendencies and claiming them as a deliberate and conscious basis from which to engage–i.e., as a crucial standpoint for my own critical and creative practice. My brother Phil and I have become steadily closer after I had the chance to live together with him, while we were both adults, during the year (1996-1997) I spent between working at Arizona State and then UW-Eau Claire, and as a result of Phil, his wife Crystal, and my mom sharing multiple trips with Andy and me to Dublin, Manchester, and Edinburgh. I do have four nieces and nephews, all my brother Ed's children, together with his now ex-wife Amy: Ally, Tom, John, and Cate. Unfortunately, living far away for so much of the time they grew up meant I haven't had the chance to get to know them all that well, but I did appreciate spending time with Ally when she joined us during one trip to Manchester and with John when he joined us during one trip to Dublin. Other members of my family include Pete Golanski, my sister's husband, and Christine Nowlan, my brother's Ed's wife. Although geographically far distant from family members, most of the time, they all retain my love and respect. We haven't needed to live close together in order to achieve and maintain that bond.

***

My parents did experience a breakdown in their relationship, which continued in that state for many years before they finally divorced when I was seventeen. Undoubtedly the long delay was due to the fact divorce carried greater stigma then than it does today–as indicative of a 'broken family'–and because it was going to be financially costly, for both of them, especially my mother. My parents often fought, quite loudly, when my father returned home from work, and they both became highly emotional in so doing, with this repeatedly spilling out onto the street in front of our house. I learned how to stay out of the way, and avoid becoming the spark for yet another outburst, but I felt sad and scared, for all of us, especially for my mother, whenever these fights happened–and that was all too often. By the time they did agree to divorce I still worried about what this would mean but I definitely felt relieved at the same time as it meant the fights would stop.

My mother had obtained a master's degree in English while my father had obtained a master's degree in mathematics, both by their mid-20s, and they then both went on to teach high school, but once my mother became pregnant with me she was expected, as a matter of what was then the conventional norm, to quit and focus on being a housewife and mother. She tried, pouring enormous energy into doing both jobs extremely–even excessively–well, but she grew frustrated with the constraints of that life. As a result, she took a real estate course, passed the test for a license, and acquired a job as a realtor. I remember my dad was furious because he didn't expect she was pursuing an interest in real estate in order to get a job, and I recall as well, in the midst of the fight that followed, my dad angrily declaring my mom doing this embarrassed him because it would seem to others like he couldn't take care of his wife and children by himself, as expected. Yet my mother could be every bit as stubbornly determined as my father, if not more so, which meant she was undeterred.

I was assigned the job of taking principal responsibility, as a virtual surrogate parent, over five years, to care for my three younger siblings, while my mother worked up to 75 hours a week in real estate and my father continued his full-time job as a university professor of mathematics. My mother has joked since then that these days my parents would be arrested for putting someone as young as I was–starting between 10 and 11 years old–in charge, like that, for so much of the time, of my three younger siblings, but at the time it seemed to us all like the logical response to the fact that neither of my parents would be home all that often. I was already well familiar with the expectations of the oldest child, including to 'set an example for', and even, yes, 'to be responsible for' my younger siblings, so this seemed like a mere extension of what was already well established. Nevertheless, looking back years later, it remains a striking feature of my upbringing at a pivotal age, as well as a striking dimension of what consumed a considerable amount of my focus at that same period of time.

I needed to 'grow up quickly' and I did. Fortunately, I still found it easy to play, while my parents were not at all the kind who felt the need to closely monitor or supervise what I was doing. Free play was fine; this made ready sense to them. My siblings and I spent hours exploring away from home without our parents worrying about us. Pick-up games were commonplace, as were adjusting and inventing the rules to compensate for deficiencies of field and equipment as well as due to disparities in skills of players. I liked to use toys and miscellaneous items from a wide variety of collections to meticulously construct these into what I envisioned as an imaginary community before I then instituted a 'war' and everything came crashing down. I'm not proud of that memory, but for kids back then, and of course, especially boys, playing 'war games' was commonplace and rarely provoked condemnation.

As I already mentioned, I have loved sports from as long as I can remember, and likewise, from as long as I can remember, I have been an avid fan–especially of baseball, football, and basketball, although as I have grown up, and grown older, this fanaticism has embraced soccer, rugby, Gaelic football, hurling, Australian rules football, tennis, track, and cross country. Unfortunately I am extremely near-sighted, and have been ever since age six, wearing glasses, or, while in my 20s to mid-30s, contact lenses. My eyesight limited my ability easily to play a number of sports, while reinforcing others' perception, prevalent when I was young, that I couldn't be all that good at sports, because I was someone who wore glasses. Nevertheless I went through the expected rite of passage of trying out for Little League baseball, at the knee high level, but I had a terrible experience with that tryout due to the fact, in practicing earlier that same day, my father threw a fastball at me that I misjudged and which hit me square in the face, leaving my entire face bloodied from below the eyes down. I didn't feel like spending hours trying out, on what turned out to be miserably cold, wet day, and I felt even worse over and over again needing to explain 'what is wrong with my face' by telling those questioning me 'I was a hit by a baseball'–right as they were attempting to judge whether I was qualified to play baseball. I got called back for a subsequent tryout but after that I insisted, more vehemently than usual, I would not do it, I absolutely refused, and my parents relented. I felt humiliated, and I wanted nothing to do with playing baseball.

Perhaps because of this experience, I tended subsequently not to like games involving me needing to catch any kind of ball, or hit it as it is coming toward me (such as in volleyball–back in middle and high school, kids acted more viciously versus each other's failings in volleyball than any other sport), preferring to get out of the way, run after the ball, and then throw it back. In volleyball I could serve well but that was it. In basketball I could play defense well but that was it. I was better at football, including flag football, and floor hockey. For a short while I participated on a YMCA swim team and did reasonably well at that. But my favorite athletic activity I only discovered near the end of high school and that was running. In taking a President's physical fitness test I learned I ran one of the fastest times in our high school (of approximately 3000 students), and I was pleased–but also surprised. I never expected that ability. Subsequently, as an undergraduate and graduate student, I ran regularly, four to six miles on average five to six days a week, including in occasional road races, as well as developed strong interests in biking and especially hiking. These days I love to walk, fast, for up to three to four hours at a time, especially throughout major cities, and will turn to a treadmill when the weather makes it harder to walk long, and far, outdoors. This COVID-19 spring and summer of 2020 I have walked nearly every day, for two and one-half to four hours at a time, outdoors around Eau Claire, and, yes, ever since mid-March I have worn shorts all day every day.

What saddens me, nonetheless, about the time and place I grew up, in connection with playing sports, has to do with the total absence of soccer–shockingly, in comparison with what is commonplace today, we did not have varsity soccer teams at our high school, nor play soccer during physical education classes, nor did soccer leagues exist anywhere else in the larger Wallingford, Connecticut community. I expect I would have enjoyed playing soccer, at least running up and down the field attempting to do so, and maybe in that game found a kind of ball I would have felt at ease not running from but running with.

My parents, like a great many since, did insist I try out for a wide range of activities, from piano lessons to basketball as well as swim classes at the YMCA to little league baseball to cub scouts to religious education at the Roman Catholic Church we attended but from which they had both grown alienated well before the time of my confirmation as a 'soldier for Christ'. Ironically, they promised me I could quit attending mass if I agreed to go through confirmation, although my mother did insist afterward that I give 'high school of religion' a try, which infuriated me because she had promised I need not do so. I went to one meeting, morosely, that confirmed my feeling of alienation, as we sat around in a circle and introduced ourselves, telling everyone who we were and what we liked to do while then repeating the name of everyone who had come before us and what they each liked to do. With appalling cheerfulness everyone in turn simply repeated and 'then there's Bob who doesn't like to do anything'. I was unfair to them, yes, but I found the whole activity disturbingly robotic–and I had no interest in the lecture Father Liddy offered us on how to continue to be 'good Catholic boys and girls', as we entered high school, which, above all else, so it seemed, involved avoiding the temptations of sex.

One of my favorite masses, I recall, happened when Father Liddy responded with fury, during a prolonged sermon, to the published results, in a local newspaper, of a 'sex survey' of local high school students, reporting a seemingly vast array of sexual experience. Father Liddy fumed that this was a terrible slander on the good Catholic youth of the community–and that it *better be so*. I also recall, with relish, another priest who periodically visited another nearby church we periodically attended, who came from a military background and loved to deliver booming 'fire and brimstone' sermons that were so over the top I could barely stop myself from laughing–this priest loved to solemnly warn parents about the dangers of approaching summer, especially around swimming pools, which, he proposed, led inexorably to kids having sex, if they were not continuously monitored. By this time, though, I knew enough myself about 'sex surveys' to recognize no one told the truth on them, and in fact kids exaggerated to fantastical extremes. In middle school, whenever the teachers left the classroom for extended ad hoc conferences with each other, out came the sex survey, from one precocious student. I was smart enough to recognize right away all I needed to do to continue to 'look cool' was simply to lie with a straight face, so, yes like most of the boys, I claimed 'to have done it' 10-15 times or more in the presence of nearby farm animals (just to cite one ridiculous question about which we were surveyed). I am not denying we were sexually curious or that puberty was not happening. In fact, at that same period of time I recall an unspoken competition developed among the middle school boys not only to skip wearing undershirts under button-down shirts, but also to unbutton the latter down steadily further and further. I can remember my mother recommending I wear a t-shirt but me rejecting this, even with the cold weather, because 'none of the boys were doing that'. The trend followed its logical trajectory when one especially daring student, Pat, entered class with no buttons buttoned. This provoked a furious response from Mr. Lion (yes, that was his name), who took Pat out into the hall and repeatedly threw him against the locker while yelling at him that he, Mr. Lion, was far more of a man than Pat would ever be, and he, Mr. Lion, was wearing four layers of clothing over his torso. That mini-fad then ended quickly. If you think that's weird, remember this was the 1970s and we were just imitating larger adult trends.

I run the risk, given what I've written so far, of suggesting my teachers and my experiences with the Roman Catholic Church were largely negative, but they were not. I liked my teachers a great deal, and, by and large, they liked me; they found it encouraging to work with a student as intellectually passionate–and 'advanced'–as I was. I did find it disappointing to encounter multiple teachers who sought to motivate other students by offering laborious accounts of what poor students they themselves were back when they were our age, and, likewise, I found it disappointing when teachers were not prepared for class and instead played films for us, with no direct connection to anything we were learning in that class. I remember teachers screening a film about the lead up to the making of and dropping of the atomic bombs on Hiroshima and Nagasaki so often I could memorize the lines, including J. Robert Oppenheimer citing *The Bhagavad Gita* with tears streaming down his face. Sometimes they even screened this same film more than once in the same class during the same semester. Nevertheless, many of my teachers were most supportive and encouraging of me, and offered me additional reading recommendations as well as alerted me to scholarship opportunities when the time came to prepare for university. At the same time, my guidance counselor seemed baffled that I would want to pursue a university education, and recommended I instead take courses in typing, shorthand, and 'adult living'. Well, after all, the test he administered to determine what would be my ideal career ended up identifying, I kid you not, 'private detective'.

With Catholicism, my parents' left liberal attitudes influenced my skepticism well before confirmation, and because they talked with us about their own disillusionment with the Church I maintained good reasons to feel alienated. It helped support my parents' case versus the Chruch that she had attended a Catholic college as an undergraduate, and, like all students at the school, studied theology during that time (while majoring in English). My mother challenged reductive understandings of Roman Catholicism, but both of my parents were ready to move far beyond Vatican II. Nevertheless, my relatively brief experience as a practicing Catholic did encourage lasting respect for the value religion provides to many people, and for the importance of spiritual striving, broadly conceived, as well as for ethical commitment, actively lived. My grandmother, Ellen Cecilia Lyons, was a highly devout Catholic–even as she was always feisty enough to declare, when we argued with her, that 'I don't care what the Pope says; he is wrong'. The latter had to do with many issues, such as divorce, birth control, abortion, homosexuality, and so on. My maternal grandparents were both fantastic story-tellers, each in their own distinct way, and tremendous influences upon me. They loved us dearly, as they did my aunt and uncle, and my cousins, and were exceedingly generous to us, always. My grandmother loved to spark tension, and to argue about a host of issues, while pretending not to do so, and was restlessly curious, about what other people were up to, including what they sought to keep private. One amusing example I can recall happened one time my grandmother came to visit us. My mother placed our copy of the Bible next to *The Sex Book*, which my grandmother clearly found objectionable, so she snuck that latter book to another location but my mother then snuck it back, and this continued back and forth throughout the duration of the visit. My parents advocated us learning about sex early–I remember being given *Boys and Sex*, *Girls and Sex*, *The Sex Book*, and *Our Bodies, Ourselves* while still in elementary school, instructed to read them all, and invited to discuss questions I had following that reading. It was overwhelming but I was better informed than other kids about sex, which was an advantage, although I also recall what happened in third grade when one girl called another girl 'a faggot' and I interrupted to say that could not be the case because 'faggot' was a 'derogatory term for male homosexual'. In response, the first girl immediately replied, 'only a faggot would know that'. Ah, well.

My grandmother was not as conservative as the last anecdote might lead you to believe. Even later on in life, when we as a family collectively decided it would be too difficult for her to accept I was gay, she knew–and was fine with it. She did at one point (when I was staying with her, and my ex-partner, who was helping me move from Tempe, Arizona back to Wallingford, Connecticut), urge me to keep in mind that 'don't ask, don't tell' could be wise and useful advice. She brought this up, as I suspect my ear piercing served as a prompt for her to do so. Years later, when my now husband visited her for her 94th birthday, the first time Andy met my family, she emphasized with him the importance of taking care of me–'you make sure he eats right; I'm worried he's too thin'.

My grandfather, William J. Lyons, was quieter in large groups than my grandmother but he loved to take us away, preferably one or two at a time, and regale us with elaborate stories from his personal experience or related to Illinois history. It was a gift when he shared a story with us. I recall vivid accounts of his experiences being hired as a teacher when those who hired him only found out after they had offered him the job, and after he had accepted it, that he was a Catholic–as well as incredible encounters with the Ku Klux Klan. When he visited one of my elementary school classes to share with us his experience visiting and traveling across Japan, he became an instant celebrity–more due to his demeanor than to what he was sharing concerning Japan, as he amplified accounts of what he encountered on this trip with stories from other experience and knowledge. I felt heroic to be connected with him as a result. My teachers told him and me he should feel free to come back any time to share more with all of us. My grandparents were farmers who owned and ran their own small farm, including through the Great Depression, which, of course, they shared many harrowing stories concerning. Although I found it most daunting and humbling to be asked to do so, I treasure being the one who delivered the eulogies at each of their funerals.

My grandfather's experience as a teacher–before he returned to farming–as well as my father's and mother's experience as the same, along with that of my aunt and uncle as well, meant I grew up amidst people who loved to teach and regarded being a teacher as a preeminently important vocation. All of these relatives were fantastic teachers. They were all enthusiastic, impassioned, creative, diligent, conscientious, and charismatic. My father and I have never been anywhere near as close as my mother and I, but our best conversations have always been about teaching, including about continually searching for innovative ways to make classes interesting and appealing to students, while insuring students learn what we consider most important (regardless of otherwise prevailing standards or popular trends). My father always insisted 'why' was a far more valuable question to explore than 'how' in mathematics, and he consistently argued as well that mathematics was more an art than a science. My mother's commitment to teaching has carried over toward voluntarily working with students in prison as well as teaching multiple classes, recurrently, often of her own design, at Goodwin University, while also serving as library director.

***

I learned from my parents it is almost always worth giving something a try, and giving it a chance, before deciding not to pursue it. Since this book focuses centrally on a musician and a band, I think it is worth sharing my own experience with music, and how those admonitions from my parents have influenced this experience. I grew up loving my parents' record collections, which in fact were diverse, inclusive of jazz, folk, show tunes, rock, and classical. My mother played the piano and started me doing so early on in my elementary school years, but I grew frustrated with lessons and after three years she allowed me to quit. I do regret that since, as although I can still play keyboards I mostly just manage to play one hand at a time–and not too difficult melodic lines at that. Because my mother owned a french horn which she had played when young, she insisted I play the french horn as well. So, once the time arrived in school to start learning to play a musical instrument, for me the french horn it was. I continued at it, all the way through the end of high school, although I never liked playing the french horn and didn't feel strongly motivated to work hard at it, even when my mother paid for a year for private lessons. Our middle and especially high school bands were large–a strategic decision such that our size would overwhelm any other limitations in our collective sound–and the french horn rarely made itself heard above the other instruments while generally providing only basic rhythmic accompaniment. I longed to play the trumpet, and admired those who did, especially those who did so well, while I also dreamed of playing the drums. But it wasn't to be. So I routinely carried an awkward french horn case back and forth every day to and from school all the way through the end of my senior year of high school, even oddly enough long after I had stopped practicing at home. When I began my first year as an undergraduate university student at Wesleyan I entered relieved at thinking I was finally done with the french horn but my mother insisted I at least try out for a musical ensemble at Wesleyan, even though I knew doing so would be a disaster. My lips were completely out of practice so I could not generate a single sound. The instructor politely recommended I start beginner's lessons if interested. That however was it for me and the french horn. I do accept, as my mother frequently declared, that the french horn can be a beautiful instrument, and I appreciate her trying to tempt me to want to excel at it by playing the overture from the Who's *Tommy* for me, to appreciate the french horn in that piece of music, but I never became convinced to do so.

Subsequently I have messed around, and that is the apt phrase for it, with playing drums–'freestyling' as I like to call it–as well as a little with electronic keyboards and teaching myself the bare bones of how to play a guitar, but my engagement with music is overwhelmingly as a listener, as a dj, and as someone who has taught music as cultural studies. I've attended a vast number of gigs, concerts, festivals, and other musical events–revving up ever since my years at Wesleyan and working at Wesleyan's student-owned and student-run radio station WESU-FM–as well as for a great many years, as often as I could manage, dancing at gay and mixed gay-straight clubs, for hours on end, late into the early morning hours. I didn't ever need much encouragement to get out on the dance floor, and I never needed drugs or alcohol to loosen any inhibitions. I liked to get ever more ambitious, creative, and frenzied as I danced, while I was one of those gay guys who was always ready to take his shirt off right away. Not at all shy. Nevertheless, my greatest musical connection is undoubtedly with my radio show Insurgence at WHYS Community Radio, Eau Claire, now well into my 16th consecutive year, over 800 consecutive weeks' running, on which I feature post-punk and new wave; indie rock, pop, folk, folk rock, and electronica; and progressive music of protest, struggle, resistance, rebellion, revolt, and transformation of diverse styles and from diverse genres–especially from the British Isles and in particular from England and Scotland. I love doing–producing and dj-ing–my show; every week it is a highlight of that week, and often indeed an ecstatic moment that lifts my spirits and keeps me going when I am otherwise feeling like I can't. Searching out and finding, reading about, listening to, and preparing to introduce music for Insurgence each week is wonderful. Immersing myself in music, live or on record, and sharing it with others, is most definitely a favorite personal experience. Sometimes students ask me about my favorite live music experience, and I reply I've accumulated far too many to choose one, but I will add here on numerous such occasions I've felt uplifted physically as well as spiritually in the moment, viscerally interconnected with the music, the musicians, and fellow audience members in ways that provided me an immensely greater 'high' than any drug I've ever taken. I'm continually listening to music, have been my whole life, and I turn to music to accompany a host of everyday activities as well as a means of focusing and clarifying thinking and feeling. I was one of those people who routinely recorded and shared mixtapes as means of initiating and solidifying friendships throughout my undergraduate and graduate student years.

It took me awhile to find my favorite forms of music, but by high school I identified the Kinks and the Who as my two favorite bands; I never felt any kinship with friends' enthusiasm for the likes of Boston, Kansas, Styx, Rush, Led Zeppelin, Jethro Tull, Yes, or Emerson, Lake, and Palmer. But punk was my breakthrough music, and, soon enough, post-punk much more than punk. My mother showed remarkable interest in my favorite music, and often listened to my radio shows with WESU, and has done since then as well with WHYS in Eau Claire. My mother even volunteered to work as a summer substitute classical music dj at WESU. The only time I can recall some tension between us concerning my musical interests occurred when my mother and I went together to a screening of *Quadrophenia*. My mother was appalled by the random anti-social violence, while I was far more interested in the musical soundtrack, but I know my mother wondered if–and why–I might be confusedly identifying with any of the mods depicted in the story. I wasn't.

***

My parents worked hard to provide for us, especially my mother; they loved us sincerely; and they always meant well in whatever they did for us. We scraped by with little money throughout my high school years, and continuing throughout my college years. My mother paid half of her yearly earnings to help cover the cost of my tuition, room, and board, even as I received federal financial aid grants, Wesleyan financial aid grants, federal student loans, federal work study payments for multiple jobs I did while at Wesleyan, along with working an additional half-time job at a local bank, as a marketing and purchasing clerk and delivery driver, and full-time summer jobs, including at a printed circuit board factory as well as a circulation department assistant at Olin Library on the Wesleyan campus. In fact I worked jobs for pay since I was eight years old, starting as a newspaper carrier (a job I continued all the way through the end of high school and then did again later, as one of many, to supplement my meager income as a graduate student while living and pursuing my PhD in Syracuse). I come from a family that prizes the value of working hard and working a lot. My maternal grandparents, and especially my maternal grandmother, proudly identified the Irish who came to the US as, above all else, 'hard workers' who 'built this country'–and I learned to regard stereotypes of Irish as loving most of all to drink and fight as offensive. My mother herself is a remarkable example of a hard worker. For years she took on multiple jobs in addition to work as a realtor, then pursued a masters of library science degree, and after earning that degree became head librarian at Goodwin University where she worked full-time until age 80, while continuing to work part-time afterward. My mother has long demonstrated an extraordinary ability to need no more than three to four hours of sleep each night and even to compound that amazing ability by arising with the break of dawn and proceeding on long walks before moving onto the rest of her daily activity. Growing up as I did, working hard and not having a lot of money to work with, I do recall every day, for years on end, always eating the same breakfast of oatmeal with honey sprayed on top out of a bear-shaped container as well as the same packed lunch of a peanut butter and jelly sandwich. Periodically for lunch I also enjoyed an orange or an apple, and with breakfast I also had a glass of orange juice and once I arrived at high school age a cup of coffee. Holidays and in particular Christmas were difficult times for my parents because they felt the commercial pressure to spend more than they could afford on toys for us. As a result, they both ended up nervous wrecks right before. This often involved my mother breaking down in tears while playing the piano and singing Christmas carols, and then driving off for hours, while my father cursed the difficulty of putting up and decorating the Christmas tree as well as getting us to settle while he read the Bible to us: 'god damn it, you little sons of bitches, get over here while I read the fucking Bible to you'. I think we understood why they felt so stressed, but it took us awhile before we actively discouraged them from feeling the need to spend more on us than made good sense.

Well before high school, I developed an intense identification with the values of a liberal arts education, as I came to understand these, and was thrilled to attend what was at the time widely recognized as the consensual number one undergraduate liberal arts university in the United States, Wesleyan University. I loved my experience at Wesleyan. Beyond classes, including majoring in English and doing substantial studies as well in economics, history, and philosophy, along with writing a senior honors thesis titled *Alienation and Incarceration in James Joyce's Dubliners and Sherwood Anderson's Winesburg, Ohio,* my passion for popular music became a central area of concentration, in particular via our student-owned and student-run campus radio station WESU-FM, where I worked as assistant station manager, music director, program coordinator, news and sports anchor, and, most importantly, punk and hardcore as well as post-punk and experimental new music disc-jockey.

By the time my four short years at Wesleyan had neared their end, I was uncertain what to do next with my life, but I knew I had barely begun to pursue interests in intellectual fields I was just discovering as a junior and a senior–interests in critical theory. So, after briefly considering law school, I opted to continue as a graduate student in English, this time at Syracuse University, where I enrolled in pursuit of a terminal master's degree, in order to give me a chance to decide whether I eventually wanted to pursue a PhD. At Syracuse, as a master's student, I was on fellowship so I was able to finish my degree quickly (in just three semesters) while simultaneously exploring interests beyond classes for my degree, including in film, theatre, and performance art; in training and working as an art museum docent; in electronic music composition; in the Irish language; and, especially, in progressive to radical politics. I concentrated in Irish Studies, while also pursuing further knowledge concerning critical theory, especially Marxism. After my master's degree, I took a year and one-half off before beginning studies for my PhD, again at Syracuse, and during that eighteen months I used the time to learn all the more about Marxism, to deepen my own direct involvement in progressive to radical politics, to take classes in computer science and in German and French, and to teach at the university level for the first time, at Southern Connecticut State University, as an adjunct English Department faculty member.

When I returned to Syracuse I became highly involved in the work of successive Marxist collectives, as well as in studying critical theory, increasingly in connection with cultural studies, and ultimately concentrating in queer theory and queer cultural studies, while also doing advanced work in 20th Century American literature and culture, 20th Century British literature and culture, and Marxist theory of ideology, subjectivity, culture, and the state. My PhD dissertation was titled *Cultural Studies, Queer Theory, Marxism*–a Marxist critique of the place of queer theory within cultural studies. During that period of seven and one-half years, I taught many classes, both as a graduate student instructor and as an adjunct at multiple local colleges and universities, along with founding and serving as principal teacher for a Free University, where a group of graduate students and I offered courses for free, on a variety of topics, to interested members of the wider Syracuse and Central New York communities. During this period of time I also came to terms with my own sexuality, accepting I was gay, and I came out everywhere almost immediately, even when this was risky to dangerous to do, and even when I was not prepared for what I would face as a result.

26

I could write a lengthy book just recounting my experiences teaching and working–not to mention just living, or striving to live–as someone who has been, for nearly thirty-five years now, out as gay. Suffice it to say, the social climate has improved, overall, during this period of time. In the past I have been physically and verbally attacked, experienced weekly threats of death and dismemberment, and been fired and not rehired on account of being gay. Friends and comrades have died tragic deaths, at the least aggravated if not in fact perpetrated by hostility toward their sexual and gender identities. Many students, faculty, staff, administrators, parents and relatives, and community members have at times been overtly hostile as well as passively aggressively indirectly hostile on account of me being gay. I've run up against an agglomeration of demeaning stereotypes as well as been exhausted by being positioned as the 'native informant', supposedly able to testify on account of all LGBTQIA+ people about what we all think, feel, believe, and have experienced. Yet I have persisted. I have believed I can help contribute to changing how gay–and LGBTQIA+ people more broadly–are perceived and treated, and I have believed I can contest damaging misconceptions, thereby helping improve conditions for LGBTQIA+ people following me. I am proud of improvements that have taken place: when I started work at UW-Eau Claire I was the first openly gay faculty member in the history of this university, and many greeted my being so as a bizarre novelty, even a frightening and disturbing aberration, but by this point in time, 24 years later, UW-Eau Claire is yearly touted as one of the best universities for LGBTQIA+ people in the US. I am proud to have played a small but vital part in enabling that scope of change.

As I conceive of it, our sexualities are complex modes of being and relating in society, and they affect the ways in which we engage in all other forms of social relations, exercising a significant impact on our outlook on life and our everyday engagement in the world. I believe we all are in varying, shifting degrees both gay and straight. I associate my own understanding of gayness with a radical theorization and practice of gayness conceived and promoted by revolutionary gay liberation in the late 1960s and early 1970s. I am a staunch opponent of any and all forms of discrimination, harassment, prejudice, and abuse directed against gay, lesbian, bisexual, transgender, and gender non-binary people, and against homosexuality, bisexuality, and transgenderism even more broadly conceived. I take a positive, affirmative stance versus the beauty, value, and necessity of a substantially liberated human sexuality in general; I oppose sex-negative positions, whether religious-based or otherwise.

Yet, perhaps above all else, I am happy to invite and encourage people who might not initially approach 'people like me' in this way, to recognize that gay and straight people share much in common. As I often shared early on at UW-Eau Claire with straight students who interviewed me for class projects, in other classes, 'I am a lot like you, other than the fact my sexuality has often represented a focus of oppression and yours has not'. I am especially pleased to have made serious dents in a long frustrating false notion that gay and bisexual guys tend neither to be any good at sports nor take much interest in sports. I am pleased to report recent students are not at all fazed by a gay professor teaching classes on 'Sports, Politics, and Society'–as I do.

***

After finishing my PhD, I obtained a position for two years as a visiting assistant professor at Arizona State University, principally responsible for teaching classes in critical theory and cultural studies. After a year in between, working as an adjunct in New Haven, Connecticut and New York City, and living back at my mother's crowded house (my mother, my brother Phil, my sister-in-law Crystal, two further adult lodgers, three dogs, two cats, and me) in Wallingford, Connecticut, I obtained a position, in 1997, as a tenure-track faculty member in English at the University of Wisconsin-Eau Claire, where I have lived and worked ever since, principally responsible for teaching classes in critical theory; critical studies in cinema and television; critical studies in popular music and culture; modern to contemporary British literary and cultural studies; and rhetoric and composition.

During my time living and working in Eau Claire I met my life-partner and husband, Andy Swanson. Andy came to Eau Claire the same year I did, initially as a one-year medical leave replacement adjunct faculty member with the Department of Physics and Astronomy (his PhD, from Cornell, is in applied and engineering physics, which builds on interests he began to pursue in earnest before that, as an undergraduate student, at California Institute of Technology). After having his contract renewed for several years with the Department of Physics and Astronomy, Andy needed to find a more stable long-term position at UW-Eau Claire, and due to the kindness of a number of people at our university, including my then department chair, Marty Wood, Andy became a lecturer in the Mathematics Department, where he has worked ever since, much of that time including as director of our Math Lab, our mathematics tutoring center at UW-Eau Claire. Andy and I married, at the Unitarian Universalist Church in Eau Claire, on June 17, 2000, although our wedding was not yet then legal, officiated by the Reverend Virginia Wolf, who later became the lead plaintiff in the lawsuit that eventually led to the legalization of marriage for same-sex couples in Wisconsin. We also married, legally, on December 20, 2013, in Manhattan, New York City.

So Andy and I celebrate two wedding anniversaries–as well as the day of our first date, October 31, 1998 (yes, it was Halloween, when we ventured to Minneapolis together, and besides running through a museum as it was on the verge of closing and visiting several shops, stores, and walking widely about, we recall spying vampires at ATM machines). Andy has been a tremendous partner, and husband, incredibly kind, generous, supportive, and understanding, while also a wonderful companion, notably in us traveling widely and often–on many visits to the UK and Ireland, including over 23 times to Scotland and nine times to Manchester and Greater Manchester, as well as to France, Germany, Austria, and fifteen times to Hawaii. We love to take walks together, and since COVID-19 struck that has meant many long walks about Eau Claire. We love to watch crime fiction (along with a variety of other kinds of series, especially gay and queer fiction, stand-up comedy, situation comedy, game and reality competition and make-over shows). We currently have three pets: Casey, a black Chinese pug, who has been with us since a tiny puppy in June 2011, and Star and Jet, black domestic shorthair cats, who have been with us since tiny kittens in July 2017, when we adopted them from the Eau Claire County Humane Association. Earlier we shared our lives with Brendan, a chocolate point Siamese cat, for thirteen years, and with Bogart, a fawn pug, for fourteen years–Bogart came with me to Eau Claire, from Wallingford, in July 1997.

Three

My intellectual training, and my intellectual outlook, is principally rooted in critical theory. "Critical theory" refers to a series of pathways for intellectual inquiry that first emerged with the end of the 18th century European Enlightenment and in particular with the initial widespread waning of intellectual confidence that the newly dominant capitalist society would succeed in realizing Enlightenment ideals. In short, critical theory represents the intellectual articulation of the conviction that modern capitalist society cannot–at least not without significant reformation or substantial transformation–realize the Enlightenment ideal of an enlightened–that is, a rational, just, and humane–society. According to Enlightenment consensus, this ideal society is to be one which will genuinely embody the highest values of human civilization, and which will thereby insure steady progress in the attainment of liberty, justice, prosperity, and contentment for all of its citizens. Critical theory begins by inquiring into what prevents the realization of this Enlightenment ideal. In doing so, critical theory questions and challenges the seeming obviousness, naturalness, immediacy, and simplicity of the world around us, and, in particular, of what we are able to perceive through our senses and understand through the application of our powers of reason. Critical theory therefore concentrates upon discovering and uncovering, as well as describing and explaining *"mediations."*

I approach Ian Curtis and Joy Division in line with this conception of critical theory. I interpret Ian Curtis and Joy Division as engaged in much the same processes of exploration and inquiry as I associate with critical theory. I might even stop right now (although of course I won't) by summing up Ian Curtis's lyrics and Joy Division's music as all about exploration of and inquiry into *mediations*. Again and again, these songs zero in on the 'in between', on the _distance between_. Always seeking, striving, venturing, pursuing, or hesitating about doing so yet feeling the strong compulsion to do so nonetheless.

I conceive of and approach critical theory as concrete, relevant, and urgent. Because I conceive of and approach critical theory as concrete, relevant, and urgent I connect this with cultural practices and social activities exercising influence, impact, and power in many people's lives. In my own life, and that of countless others, engagement with popular music has proven extraordinarily compelling. I have actively participated in a significant number of popular music subcultures and scenes. I enjoyed a great undergraduate experience at Wesleyan University but by far the most memorable and fulfilling dimension of this time was my work with our campus radio station, WESU, where I dj-ed many different music shows, and served as music director, station manager, program coordinator, as well as a news, sports, and public affairs reporter and anchor. Many years later I was thrilled to join the effort to establish a community radio station here in Eau Claire, and I have absolutely loved the experience I have had working as part of WHYS Community Radio, ever since the beginning, including as the founder and first coordinator/facilitator of our board of directors, and, especially, as producer and host of my weekly show, Insurgence. I could add many further examples of the significance of music in my personal life-experience, but I will stop with those two and simply transition, or segue, to my next point.

The first chance I gained to teach English 484, Seminar in Theory and Criticism, in the spring 2008 semester, I chose to focus on popular music–'Critical Studies in Contemporary Popular Music Cultures'. I subsequently taught English 484 with this focus once again, in the fall 2009 semester, while, in between, in the fall 2008 semester, I taught English 372, Studies in Popular Culture, with a focus on 'Music, Protest, and Resistance'. All were excellent classes, with fantastic students, who, overall, did most impressive work–especially in final projects, in the case of English 484, exploring genres, styles, and scenes of particular individual interest, and in devising elaborate activities during the sessions in which groups of students took the lead for teaching our class in the case of English 372. Yet, in each of those three classes, we surveyed a wide range of different musicians, musical styles and genres, and musical scenes and subcultures from a wide array of historical times and geographical locations. I wanted next to focus much more narrowly, precisely, and intensively. I chose to focus on the life and work of Ian Curtis and Joy Division because no other individual musician and no other musical group have come anywhere close to matching what Ian Curtis and Joy Division have meant to me. It was a risk–I did not know how students would respond, especially to a course centered around a musician and a musical group from so long ago, and one with so many understandably bleak associations. From what I have been able to ascertain, no one, anywhere else, has yet taught a university course with this explicit focus–connecting Ian Curtis and Joy Division, as cultural phenomenon, with critical, and especially social, theory. Yet students have responded amazingly well. I have taught at the university level for over 35 years, but I have never supervised student work more impressive than what students have produced in the five classes I have taught to date focused on Ian Curtis, Joy Division, and critical theory.

Four

Ian Curtis and the rest of Joy Division started as self-taught rock musicians from a broadly working class milieu in Greater Manchester, England, from the late 1950s through the end of the 1970s (and up until Curtis's suicide on May 18, 1980). All eventually found formal schooling, by their secondary school years, unsatisfactory and unappealing; none demonstrated any inclination to pursue a university or other form of post-secondary education; and all turned to music as an alternative to leading lives concentrated upon working civil service, clerical, warehouse, and sales jobs. These might well have turned out to be reasonably comfortable lives but they struck the youthful members of Joy Division as uninspiring and unfulfilling avenues through which to pursue their interests and ambitions. While their active run ended all too soon, and all too tragically, they left an extraordinary legacy that continues to exponentially increase, ever since the mid-2000s. Ian Curtis and Joy Division anticipated and signally contributed to the renaissance of the great city of Manchester with Manchester becoming a robust center of internationally renowned cultural creation, exhibition, and performance in the 21st century. At this point in time, Ian Curtis and Joy Division have, amazingly enough, achieved the status of high, or fine, art.

As indicated on the back jacket of Paul Morley's book, *Joy Division Piece by Piece Writing About Joy Division 1977-2007*, "Joy Division are the perennial cult post-punk band. Four young men with weight on their shoulders, the drama and the tension of their music remains unsurpassed." Paul Morley, aptly described on the back jacket of his book about Joy Division as "one of Britain's foremost cultural commentators for 30 years," well demonstrates the kind of obsessive interest Joy Division can elicit. Morley has frequently written about Joy Division, and Morley has continually found Joy Division stimulates his thinking about–and his feeling in relation to–a wide array of substantial issues (especially questions and considerations of 'the ultimate', interestingly enough, what Mircea Eliade famously argues represents the core concern of all religions, and, implicitly as well, all spiritualities). Morley has frequently written about Joy Division, ever since they first formed, and as he explains,"Everything they make me feel–or suggest I feel–is a central metaphor for everything I feel, about myself, the world, music, emotion, love, death, time, God . . ." (236).

Joy Division's posthumous achievement is remarkable, even as they did break through, winning critical as well as popular recognition as a band of major importance, prior to Ian Curtis's death. Only near the end of their less than four years together did it become possible for Ian Curtis (vocalist, lyricist, and frontman), Peter Hook (bass guitar), Bernard Sumner (guitar and keyboards), and Stephen Morris (drums and percussion) all to stop working full-time at other jobs while also making and playing music. Joy Division only recorded two studio albums, *Unknown Pleasures* and *Closer* (as well as multiple singles, eps, and a limited array of demos, unfinished takes, and live performances). Although they gigged extensively, Joy Division left, by early 21st century standards, a paucity of video performances, as well as few live performances on radio, and few interviews, through any venue. Yet, by the beginning of the 21st century, not only did serious writers begin to produce steadily more articles and books about Joy Division, and Ian Curtis, but also three feature-length films have been made in which the band, and especially Curtis, represent a principal focus: *Twenty Four Hour Party People*, directed by Michael Winterbottom, released in 2002, a Factory Records biopic; *Control*, directed by Anton Corbijn, released in 2007, an Ian Curtis biopic; and *Joy Division*, directed by Grant Gee and released in 2007, a Joy Division biopic. Images of Joy Division, and again especially of Ian Curtis, now enjoy iconic stature, and continue to influence new trends in fashion and design. Numerous, first, 'alternative' and then, second, 'indie' bands, emerging from the early 1990s onward, frequently cite Joy Division, and, often enough, in particular, Ian Curtis, as major influences on their own music, and on their own ethos and aesthetics. *Pitchfork* retrospectively rates *Unknown Pleasures* and *Closer* as each a perfect 10 out of a possible 10.

In Macclesfield, Ian Curtis's hometown, the 30th anniversary of his death sparked a summer-long festival of exhibitions, tours, tribute compositions and performances, and workshops, lectures, and symposia. Brian Gorman debuted his stage play about Joy Division, *New Dawn Fades*, in 2013, in conjunction with this anniversary, and the same play has toured in subsequent theatrical runs once again in 2015, 2016, and 2018; Gorman also published *New Dawn Fades: a Graphic Novel About Joy Division and Manchester* in September 2018. In February of 2015, long-time Ian Curtis and Joy Division fan Hadar Goldman bought Ian Curtis's Macclesfield home in order to transform this house into an Ian Curtis museum. Goldman was inspired by an internet crowd-funding campaign devoted to the same end. Today, in Manchester, Peter Hook is re-using the famous Factory name for musical and related kinds of artistic projects (Factory Records was the independent label, led by the late Tony Wilson, that played a huge role in Manchester music and culture from the late 1970s through the mid 1990s, with Joy Division the first and possibly still the most famous of the bands Factory recorded). Hook and partners opened FAC 251 in 2010; he has also revived use of the Haçienda trademark (the most famous and influential center of the mid 1980s to mid 1990s 'Madchester' club scene, including the birthplace of acid house, was the Haçienda, which closed in 1997, and which was demolished and replaced by apartments in 2002). Hook published his account of Joy Division in book-length form (*Unknown Pleasures: Inside Joy Division*, 2012). Bernard Sumner then published his own biography shortly thereafter (*Chapter and Verse: New Order, Joy Division, and Me*, 2014), with over 1/3 of this book devoted to Sumner's recounting and reflecting upon his experience within Joy Division. Later that same year, Deborah Curtis and Jon Savage released an edited collection of Ian Curtis's lyrics and notebooks (*So This is Permanence: Joy Division Lyrics and Notebooks*, 2014). Jon Savage published *This Searing Light, the Sun, and Everything Else*: *Joy Division, an Oral History* in April 2019 while Stephen Morris' published his book-length memoir, *Record Play Pause*: *Confessions of a Post-Punk Percussionist, Volume I*, which covers his life through the end of Joy Division and the beginning of New Order, in May 2019. On the occasion of the 40th anniversary of the release of *Unknown Pleasures*, many tributes followed, including a series of video re-imaginings of each of the songs comprising this album, along with a book of new fiction titled *We Were Strangers: Stories Inspired by Unknown Pleasures*. If not for the impact of COVID-19 and the general impression it is an even much more somber album, the 40th anniversary of *Closer* would have likely inspired similar efforts, but, even so, Warner is, as with *Unknown Pleasures*, offering a *Closer* 40th anniversary reissue 'package' in 2020.

In October 2020 a mural depiction of Ian Curtis covering the full side of a building at 75 Port Street in Manchester's Northern Quarter was unveiled to coincide with World Mental Health Day. Starting in November of 2020 the podcast series, *Transmissions*, narrated by famous, Manchester native actor Maxine Peake, began, recounting the history of Joy Division and New Order, including interviews with many subsequent musicians who identify Joy Division and New Order as major influences. On Facebook alone, even though I am the obverse of a heavy user, and rarely post to any of these sites, I myself am a member of more than fifteen groups focused on discussions and sharings among fans of Ian Curtis and Joy Division; undoubtedly more dedicated users of social media are aware of a great many more similar sites.

In 2016 Headpress published a book-length collection of critical writings edited by Jennifer Otter Bickerdike, titled *Joy Devotion: The Importance of Ian Curtis and Fan Culture*. Bickerdike earlier wrote her PhD dissertation (in urban anthropology) about visits and visitors to Curtis's gravesite, and she has in addition written and published yet another full-length book about Ian Curtis and Kurt Cobain. Most significantly, in October of 2018 Rowan and Littlefield published *Heart & Soul: Critical Essays on Joy Division*, edited by Martin J. Power, Eoin Devereux, and Aileen Dillane: a collection of fifteen substantial scholarly contributions, addressing Ian Curtis and Joy Division in relation to a broad range of contemporary critical theoretical concepts and approaches, notably hauntology and psychogeography. In relation to the latter connections, *Heart & Soul* follows the late Mark Fisher, aka K-Punk, who wrote repeatedly about Joy Division, notably as collected in *Ghosts of My Life: Writings on Depression, Hauntology and Lost Futures* as well as in *K-Punk: The Collected and Unpublished Writings of Mark Fisher*. A rapidly growing array of scholarly work connects 'Ian Curtis and Joy Division' with intersecting issues of performance, disability, spirituality, and fandom. *Heart & Soul*, what's more, readily testifies to the fact scholarly work engaged with Ian Curtis and

Joy Division has reached the stage where this is not only rapidly burgeoning but also a multiply contested field. I myself have not only taught the five aforementioned classes, the only university classes I have yet to come across focused on Ian Curtis, Joy Division, and Critical Theory, but also designed, organized, and led a church service on 'Spiritual Considerations in the Life and Work of Ian Curtis and the Music of Joy Division' at the Unitarian Universalist Congregation of Eau Claire in November 2014 as well as given a University of Wisconsin-Eau Claire English Department colloquium presentation in the spring of 2017 and a University of Wisconsin-Eau Claire Office of Research and Sponsored Programs faculty forum presentation in the fall of 2018, both once again concerning interrelations among Ian Curtis, Joy Division, and Critical Theory.

Five

I will now summarize a series of articles and book chapters to illustrate something of the considerable extent of critical writing that has developed in recent years surrounding Ian Curtis and Joy Division as well as some of the conversations and debates this has encompassed. To begin I will highlight some of the selections from *Joy Devotion* (2016) and *Heart & Soul* (2018) I have found particularly useful in my classes.

In the former book, Jennifer Otter Bickerdike's subtitle to "Introduction: My only friend, Joy Division," sums up the importance of her personal relationship with Joy Division early in her life and in particular how Joy Division's music and notably Ian Curtis's lyrics, and voice, provided her with a sense of empathetic identification, and, more precisely, consolation for personal losses and psychic troubles as well as inspiration to pursue a daring path for a PhD dissertation focus. Mike Grimshaw's "Transmission in the Colony: On exported Englishness and the secular religion of the axis mundi" likewise is readily summed up in its title, as Grimshaw attests to the importance of the music of Joy Division, and of "Transmission," in particular, growing up in rural New Zealand in the early 1980s, via the radio, for forging his own sense of identity in connection with a strongly felt affiliation with an imagined Manchester, while, like Bickerdike, Grimshaw recounts his relation to the music of Joy Division as akin to a devotee to a secular religion. Jamie Stewart's "New Dawn Fades" describes how extraordinarily valuable, as comfort and release, this Joy Division song, and again Ian Curtis's lyrics and vocals, have felt to him, as someone who, like all too many, has known suicidality and who has needed an outlet to be able to express and share this experience while finding all too few through which to do so. Jason Whittaker's "The Pornography of Science: Curtis, Ballard and Burroughs" argues for a substantive connection among the three artists, in terms of preoccupation and outlook, including a shared critique of 'scientific and technological pornography' as well as a shared attraction to 'occuculture', hidden cultures and subcultures, which is, once again, strikingly reminiscent of more recent popular ventures in psychogeography and especially hauntology.

In *Heart & Soul*, Michael Goddard's "Missions of Dead Souls: a Hauntology of the Industrial, Modernism, and Esotericism in the Music of Joy Division" finds substantial resonances between Joy Division and industrial music insofar as "both were haunted by postindustrial cityscapes, modernist literature . . . and a shared interest in esotericism and the occult," including an intensely vividly felt sense of being extremely alienated from the time and place one mundanely inhabits (3). Giacomo

Bottà's "Trying to Find a Clue, Trying to Find a Way to Get Out!: The European Imaginary of Joy Division" argues Joy Division "cannot be read in any way as inspired by far-right-wing ideologies, despite their early ingenuities. Joy Division were trying to build cold and austere musical and visual aesthetics, coercing an umbrella of heterogeneous cosmopolitan influences that can be labelled European" and as the result of their "dialogue with Europe" "made them a cosmopolitan *Gesamtkunstwerk*: a total work of art" (44). Tiffany Naiman's "In a Lonely Place: Illness and the Temporal Exile of Ian Curtis," argues Curtis exemplifies what she identifies as "ill style," modifying Theodor Adorno's conception of "late style," in particular by means of a careful discussion of Curtis's vocals with "Love Will Tear Us Apart," showing how "Curtis's experience of being ill and being suicidal is aestheticized through his music" while proposing approaching Curtis's musical performance with a conception of ill style as a guide offers the "potential to expand listeners' understanding of illness as a state of being inherent to the human condition and to consider alternative temporalities . . . . desegregating illness from the realm of so-called normal human experience" (95). With "This Is the Crisis I Knew Had to Come: Revisiting Ian Curtis's Suicide," Eoin Devereux, Walter Cullen, and David Meagher perform a psychological autopsy to examine and explain Curtis's suicide, concluding "there was nothing *inevitable* about Ian Curtis's suicide. Seeing it as inevitable is to do considerable disservice to Curtis's legacy in that such a position simply rehearses the well-worn and overly romanticized trope of the 'tortured artist' for whom suicide is the *only* final outcome" (116). Devereux, Cullen, and Meagher further contend Curtis's suicide was, using categories famously devised by sociologist Emilé Durkheim, "all at once, *egoistic*, *altruistic*, *anomic* and *fatalistic*" (127) and that a careful analysis of what contributed and led to his suicide can provide useful knowledge for addressing "psychache" today, especially as experienced among young men. Robin Parmar's "Joy Division in Space: The Aesthetics of Estrangement" provides a precise and thorough examination and explanation of the stylistic and technical means by which Joy Division, including Martin Hannett, achieved an "aesthetics of estrangement," with detailed attention to "Digital," "Glass," *Unknown Pleasures*, and "Transmission." Gay Jennifer Breyley, in "'I Hung around in Your Soundtrack: Affinities with Joy Division among Contemporary Iranian Musicians," spotlights how a strikingly large number of contemporary Iranian musicians experience keen affinities with the music of Joy Division and the figure of Ian Curtis in particular, especially in opposition to what they experience as a repressive as well as oppressive cultural and political regime in power–affinities "encompassing notions of communality; concern with the forgotten, absent, or 'drowned out'; irony and humour combined with disarming sincerity and intense personal emotions; an appreciation of the pleasures of sound itself; and multifaceted imaginaries that can be simultaneously idealistic, even utopian, and deeply pessimistic" (209).

Continuing next through a series of disparate articles and book chapters, Mark Fisher's "No Longer the Pleasures: Joy Division" (2005) argues Joy Division effectively anticipated and in turn perfectly captured "the depressed spirit of our times" (50)–and that no other music more uncompromisingly expresses and communicates what a depressive position, as a vantage point from which to make sense and engage, and not as a merely disabling affliction or abnormal aberration, is truly like.

David Church's "'Welcome to the Atrocity Exhibition': Ian Curtis, Rock Death, and Disability" (2006) inquires into how ableist values, and ableist mindsets have problematically impacted the ways audiences have made sense of Ian Curtis's 'performance of his own disability'.

Atte Oksanen's "Hollow Spaces of Psyche: Gothic Trance-Formation from Joy Division to Diary of Dream" (2007) delves into the Gothic sensibilities of Joy Division and German 1990s darkwave group Diary of Dreams.

Mitzi Waltz and Martin James, in "The (re)Marketing of Disability in Pop: Ian Curtis and Joy Division" (2009), follow David Church by focusing on problematic appropriations of Ian Curtis's disability, in performance, and especially marketed as testimony to a romanticized–and romanticist–notion of 'authenticity'.

Graham White's "The Ians in the Audience: Punk Attitude and the Influence of the Avant-Garde" (2011) discusses how Ian Stuart Donaldson also attended the celebrated Sex Pistols gigs at Manchester's Lesser Free Trade Hall in 1976, and was likewise influenced by modernist avant-gardism, but ventured onward to become a leading figure in British 'nazi punk' music. White aims to show the avant-gardist influences upon punk and post-punk do not inherently lead in a necessarily politically 'progressive' direction.

In "Kids're Forming Bands: Making Meaning in Post-Punk" (2012) Theodor Gracyk argues post-punk makes far more sense as a movement as opposed to a style, given the diversity of styles influential writers such as Simon Reynolds have identified beneath a post-punk umbrella, while suggesting Joy Division might better be characterized as exemplifying a mode of 'new romanticism'.

Benjamin Fraser's and Abby Fuoto's "Manchester, 1976: Documenting the urban nature of Joy Division's musical production" (2012) develops the connection proposed in the film *Joy Division* (2007) between Joy Division and Manchester by connecting Joy Division to a range of urban theories–theories of 'the modern city' (including from Georg Simmel, Henri Lefebvre, Walter Benjamin, Michel de Certeau, Friedrich Engels, Andy Merrifield, Marc Augé, Jane Jacobs, David Harvey, Guy Debord/The Situationists, and Jacob Riis).

Matthew Boswell's "Post-Punk: Joy Division, *Closer*" (2012) argues, far from sympathizing with the Nazis, Joy Division in their music, and notably in *Closer*, pursue the same paradoxical task as Holocaust literature in appreciating such horrors "cannot be conveyed if one somehow confronts the extremity that dictates *why* they cannot be conveyed"–i.e., that this indeed is exactly what Ian Curtis and Joy Division do in dramatically enacting a "necessary encounter" (120), which implicates us within 'the atrocity exhibition'.

In *Shakin' All Over: Popular Music and Disability* (2013), George McKay considers Ian Curtis at length while demonstrating overt concern with disability is pervasive throughout popular music, "Whether in its focus on bodies perfect and deviant alike, the romantic appeal in rock tropes and rock lives to tropes of suffering or cognitive impairment, its damaged or what I call *mal canto* voices, its continuing status as expressive vehicle for emotional autobiography (from artists and audience members), its intermittent fetishing of enfreakment, its industrial carelessness and destructive appetites, or in the place of pop repertoires in music therapy or disability arts and advocacy" (28).

With "When Performance Lost Control: Making Rock History Out of Ian Curtis and Joy Division" (2013) J Rubén Valdés Miyares examines connections between Joy Division, in performance, and performative writing about Joy Division, notably from Paul Morley, arguing the latter effectively enables those who never knew Ian Curtis during his lifetime, or Joy Division when they were active, to continue to find meaning and value in their music, without seeking to control or close down to where this pursuit of meaning and value might lead. In "Liminoid Joy Division: The Sublime Performance of a Rock Star's Identity" (2013) Miyares argues Joy Division music, and especially Ian Curtis's role within and contribution to this music, involves an exploration of a "liminoid" project, a liminoid environment, which involves a convergence of the beautiful and the sublime, and extremes of agony and Lacanian *jouissance* (roughly equivalent to a suberabundant vitality, an extreme of orgiastic enjoyment that becomes so ecstatic it is simultaneously painful and verges upon the deadly).

Jennifer K. Otter, in "My Affair with Ian" (2014), anticipates her later writings on Ian Curtis and Joy Division (as Jennifer Otter Bickerdike), and her editing of *Joy Devotion* (2016) by describing what her infatuation with Ian Curtis and Joy Division meant to her, through tough times growing up, including in helping her deal with hardship and loss, up until her first visit to Curtis's gravesite.

Clayton Crockett, via "In the Colony with Joy Division" (2014) surveys a range of possible interpretations of how Joy Division's music, and Ian Curtis's lyrics, relate to Kafka's "In the Penal Colony" and histories of colonization, concluding Joy Division's song "Colony" offers "us not only hope but weapons with which to fight our own colonization and self-colonization" in what is "a religious task, a sacred combat waged against God as judge and the justice rendered in his own name" (35).

Alex Ogg's "For you, Tommy, the war is never over" (2014) documents how far from uncommon fascination with World War II, Nazi Germany, and the Holocaust was among punk, and early post-punk, musicians–and in particular with boys born in the generation immediately following that which came of adult age during World War II itself, and experienced the War, including the Blitz, directly. It was in fact exceptionally rare for a British boy of the initial punk and early post-punk generation not to play with toys and models from World War II nor to collect magazines as well as watch numerous TV shows and films likewise obsessed with World War II, Nazi Germany, and the Holocaust.

In "'But we remember when we were young': Joy Division and new orders of nostalgia" (2014) Catherine Strong and Alasdair Gray argue for a complex, multifaceted understanding of "nostalgia," in which "ersatz nostalgia" linked with Joy Division, by those whose fascination with Joy Division and the Greater Manchester in Joy Division's time came much later, adds greater interest to

Joy Division and provides enhanced avenues for listeners to find useful meaning and value through Joy Division, including in critical relation to their own lived experiences.

Paul Crosthwaite, in "Trauma and Degeneration: Joy Division and Pop Culture's Imaginative Historicism" (2014) critically examines tendencies among pop critics, notably Paul Morley and Jon Savage, to engage in imaginative historicism when discussing Ian Curtis and Joy Division, eschewing empiricism, deliberately mythologizing, and making use of the ambiguity of meaning within Ian Curtis's lyrics and Joy Division's music, as well as the bandmembers' reluctance to offer their own interpretations of what this might mean–and their seeming inarticulacy when invited to do so–as enabling writers such as Morley and Savage to take liberties in how they in turn connect meanings of these lyrics and this music with historical situations, events, trends, and tendencies.

Mia Tuft, Berljot Gjelsvik, and Karl O. Nakken, in "Ian Curtis: Punk rock, epilepsy, and suicide" (2015) use Ian Curtis as a case study to explore some of the problems and limits of treatments for epilepsy in Curtis's time as well as the lack of effective understanding, at that time, of how widely prevalent "comorbid recurrent depression and suicidality" tends to be among "the epilepsy population" (220).

With "Closer from a Distance: Auras of Factory Records in Music, Place, Film and Historiography" (2015) James McGrath locates the development and refinement of Joy Division's "aura" in more precise relation to Factory Records' greater praxis.

James Ingram, with "Factory records and the situationist influence on urban space" (2016) discusses in detail specific avenues through which Situationism directly shaped Factory's praxis, as well as resonant connections between Factory and Henri Lefebvre's theories of the everyday.

J Rubén Valdés Miyares, with "Breaking Joy Division's 'Glass': Reading Song Lyrics as Literature" (2016) exemplifies an increasingly popular direction in critical writing concerned with Ian Curtis and Joy Division, and that is performing close reading of specific songs, and/or song lyrics. In the course of so doing Miyares explores a broad array of intertextual connections between images of 'breaking glass' in this song and other significant moments in Curtis's personal experience as well as 20th century history–notably *Kristallnacht*, the "Night of Broken Glass" in 1938 Nazi Germany, involving a sweeping attack on Jewish owned shops. Miyares here makes notable use of the theory of conceptual metaphor, traceable to George Lakoff and Mark Johnson (*Metaphors We Live By*, 1980), as well as Derridean deconstruction, in the form of "grafting" of one text onto another, and as exemplified yet further through Jacques Derrida's formally as well as conceptually daring book *Glas* (1974).

In April 2017 Philip H. Kitching submitted his book-length study, *Understanding Suicide: a Psychobiographical Study of Ian Kevin Curtis* in fulfillment of the requirements for his PhD in heath services at the Nelson Mandela Metropolitan University. Kitching provides an elaborate psychobiography explaining what specific factors led to Curtis's suicide, while making use of

Thomas Joiner's interpersonal-psychological theory of suicide as well as Alfred Adler's theory of individual psychology.

James Rovira's "Introduction: Theorizing Rock/Historicizing Romanticism" to the 2018 anthology *Rock and Romanticism: Post-Punk, Goth, and Dark Metal* delves into deep level connections between classic 19th century Romanticism and the three genres of music this book title references. Caroline Langhorst's "A Northern 'Ode on Melancholy': The Music of Joy Division," from the same book, draws this connection more precisely, with Ian Curtis and Joy Division, considering links with Byron, Keats, Coleridge, Wordsworth, and Shelley, as well as numerous subsequent Gothic writers.

And in "'She expressed herself in many different ways': Hypothetical substitutions in Joy Division's 'She's Lost Control'" (2019), Liam Maloy conducts a musicologically close reading of three different versions of this song–Joy Division both on record and live as well as by Grace Jones. Maloy originally submitted this essay for his MA degree in Popular Music Studies at Liverpool University in 2007.

In sum, this, again, is only an illustrative sampling of critical writings produced and published on Ian Curtis and Joy Division over the course of the past 15 years. I could easily extend this summary much further, especially if accounting for numerous reviews and critiques of the films *Joy Division* and *Control*–in particular *Control*. What this short survey nonetheless demonstrates is Ian Curtis and Joy Division have definitely become a 'cultural phenomenon' not only among 'popular music fans' but also writers working from academic and quasi-academic vantage points. My aims with this book do *not* include providing a comprehensive documentation of all 'critical writing' concerned with Ian Curtis and Joy Division, let alone all 'popular writing' concerned with the same (even if it were always possible clearly to distinguish these two kinds of writings, which it is not, especially when writing about a 'popular musician' and a 'popular musical group'). Many others have already been engaged and continue to engage in such efforts. One long-standing online source of considerable influence and repute, for 'all things Joy Division', is Joy Division Central: http://www.joydiv.org. Two other useful sites include Joy Division Official: http://joydivisionofficial.com and Joy Division–The Eternal: http://www.enkiri.com/joy/joy_division.html. Many websites, especially run by devoted fans, do of course come and go, as those responsible cannot always maintain them, or keep them meticulously up to date, but interest in Joy Division is persistent so multiple others have undoubtedly emerged by the time you are reading this book. Joy Division fans often become obsessed with collecting and detailing, so these sites can prove widely interesting and useful.

Six

Peter Hook has toured across Britain, Western Europe, and North America while playing the entirety, first, of *Unknown Pleasures* (2010) and then, second, of *Closer* (2011), with his latest band, Peter Hook and the Light. Hook and the Light have then repeated the same performances in worldwide tours in subsequent years. New Order, which Hook, and fellow surviving Joy Division bandmembers Sumner and Morris formed shortly after Curtis' death (and who were soon joined by Morris's partner, Gillian Gilbert), rarely played Joy Division music. Sumner and Morris have sharply criticized Hook for his recent actions, suggesting Hook is exploiting Joy Division's and Factory's legacy, and nothing can provide a legitimate semblance of what either Joy Division or Factory were like in their heyday. As a result, Hook is now even further alienated from Sumner and Morris, increasing the already considerable extent of estrangement that exists today among these former New Order–and surviving Joy Division–bandmates, but that's another story. Although I will add here, New Order, post-Peter Hook, is now including Joy Division songs in their public performances; at a major event in July 2017 in Manchester, New Order played a series of five two-hour concerts in collaboration with conceptual artist Liam Gillick and the 12-member Royal Northern College of Music 'synthesizer ensemble', in Old Granada Studios–the concert I attended included three Joy Division songs, while Bernard Sumner shared with us, directly, how tremendously proud he is of the work he did as part of Joy Division.

I write the last comment, though, because Joy Division and New Order strike me, and indeed many others who have long followed both, as ultimately more discontinuous than continuous phenomena. Central in explaining this discontinuity is Ian Curtis. All members of Joy Division contributed enormously to the band's collective achievement, and the band would not exist without all of their contributions. Likewise their manager, Rob Gretton, their producer, Martin Hannett, their graphic designer, Peter Saville, and their promoter, publicist, and mythologist, Tony Wilson (to name just a few of the other most prominent figures in the yet larger group that truly made Joy Division what it was) all provided indispensable contributions. But, to borrow words from the man himself, Ian Curtis was–and is–the heart and soul of Joy Division. His lyrics, his vocals, his sensibility, his style, and his presence set the pace. And it is undoubtedly due to the tragic complex of multiple difficult tensions he suffered, and his ultimate suicide, that the band has achieved the kind of historic aura it has. As Morley writes: "And so Ian Curtis. He gave Joy Division their life and their death. He gave Joy Division his life and his death . . . He was under crisis and he passed this sense of crisis . . . right into the bloody, unstable body of the music. Right into its heart and soul. He was fighting mad . . . You can hear the fight that went on between the steady common sense that stabilises this life in this time, and the ferocious senselessness that constantly threatens the balance of life, that wobbles life, that rocks it, and rolls it, until it shakes itself apart" (272).

Commonly, many identify the music of Joy Division, certainly encouraged by Curtis's suicide, as 'depressing', but this characterization, I contend, vastly oversimplifies both the music and Curtis's life. Curtis, like so many of us in fact do, fused myriad contradictions. As those who knew him best frequently attest, he often acted like 'just an ordinary bloke' of his age coming from the place and time in which he lived. He was friendly, considerate, fun-loving, outgoing, and playful; he was rakish and laddish; he was kind and generous; he was shy and sensitive; he was intense, ambitious, driven, troubled, wild, and disturbed; he was obsessive, compulsive, self-absorbed, and egocentric; he was lonely and vulnerable; he was loving and romantic; he was cold and distant; he was physically exuberant and mentally voracious; he was intellectually curious and adventurous; and he was physically and mentally ill. In *Unknown Pleasures: Inside Joy Division* Peter Hook writes repeatedly about how Ian Curtis could readily behave as multiple considerably different kinds of people, of his remarkable shape-shifting quality, and that he was in fact all of these diverse people, all at once. Yet Curtis's lyrics and Joy Division's music transcend the details of Ian Curtis's own individual life–and death–even if this connection marks one significant direction for making sense of what these lyrics, and this music, can mean. The music of Joy Division and the lyrics of Ian Curtis invite, encourage, and enable listeners to situate this music, and these lyrics, in contexts far removed from any direct connection with the life, or death, of those responsible for initially creating it, so listeners are able to make compelling sense and use of this music in ways its initial creators could never have dreamed. The sheer fact the music of Ian Curtis and Joy Division continues to attract new fans and to exert significant impact on new listeners long after Curtis's death, and long after the end of Joy Division's time together as a band, underscores how far this music engages with thoughts, feelings, convictions, ideals, perceptions, and sensations that surpass and supersede the merely autobiographical.

I'd like to add a further more personal response to the characterization of Joy Division's music as 'depressing' because not only do many serious commentators on this music find it demands this kind of personal openness and honesty, but also because I myself do not find it ultimately depressing, in my own experience, as much as I understand and respect that kind of response. Here's how I summed up this point at the time of the 30th anniversary of Curtis's death, in commenting on my weekly radio show, Insurgence:

> Ian Curtis was a great lyricist and a powerful singer and frontman; together with the rest of those involved in Joy Division, he fearlessly explored intensities, extremities, subliminalities, and liminalities that many others never would or could, and his music, while often extremely dark and somber, is never simply that–it is about seeking, struggling, reflecting, examining, and opening one's self up to sensation, perception, emotion, and understanding that presses past familiar layers of protective mediation toward not only intense vulnerability and emptiness but also intense clarity and insight. Joy Division's music fuses the intellectual with the emotional with the spiritual with the somatic–in terms of exploration and questing, in both passionate and dispassionate terms, and in relation to a striving for and imposition of control meeting up with the absolute limits and sheer impossibility of meaningfully striving for and seeking to impose control– all with a seamlessness, and a brilliance, rarely matched in popular rock music. Ian Curtis himself was certainly a highly–and multiply–troubled, often highly confused, and often highly difficult man, but he was also a brilliantly intuitive, driven, committed, impassioned, thoughtful, and serious lyricist and musician.

***

Ian Curtis and fellow members of Joy Division eschewed overt reference to immediately topical issues in their music. As a result, in my classes focused on Ian Cutis and Joy Division we investigate the often complexly mediated ways that intelligent, sensitive popular musical productions reflect, respond to, draw upon, rework, transform, impact, and influence larger social-historical conditions and relations. Curtis maintained limited direct interest in the most immediate form 'politics' takes, for most people, and, the same with many immediate cultural trends. Curtis, and following his lead, the rest of Joy Division as well, made music focused on phenomenological, existential, mythical, spiritual, metaphysical, psychological, aesthetic, fantastical, romantic, and dystopian dimensions of human experience. Nevertheless, political and cultural forces did affect Curtis and Joy Division, but those that exerted the greatest impact are deeper and longer, encompassing dimensions of human experience extending beyond merely what directly and uniquely pertained to a life lived in Greater Manchester, England from 1956 through 1980. If politics is ultimately about relations of power–and if culture is ultimately about creativity, productivity, expression, communication, activity, and interactivity–then matters of politics and culture consumed Curtis, even, often enough, overwhelming him, pulling him to an extreme edge.

The powerful appeal of Joy Division's music long after Curtis's death and the band's end, as well as far away from Manchester itself, demonstrates making sense of Ian Curtis and Joy Division as 'cultural phenomenon' directs us to explore widely, and to test out connections superficially maintaining little to do with the specific places and times in which Ian Curtis spent his life, and in which Joy Division came together to make their music. For this reason, I have found readings in critical and in particular social theory ranging from the classic tradition through modernism to post-modernism and beyond provide useful lenses, or frameworks, that better enable us to come to grips with the meaning, value, and significance of Ian Curtis's and Joy Division's music (and with the life and death of both Curtis and his band) than concentrating solely on studying unique peculiarities of British, especially English, and in particular Greater Manchester, culture and politics from 1956 through 1980. I don't altogether ignore those latter kinds of contexts, yet I don't limit myself to working only with them, and I certainly don't uncritically privilege them over other possibilities.

In line with the last point, we need not limit ourselves to accepting interpretations and perspectives offered by surviving contemporaries of Curtis, including his fellow Joy Division bandmates; their interpretations and perspectives are hardly necessarily automatically 'truer' or 'more accurate' than ours, when we can argue compellingly in support of different takes. Often, in fact, those closest to an individual or a group of people can be too close, thereby missing what makes the creative work the former do matter the most to those who never had and never will have any personal connection with that individual or group. Besides, creating music, like creating any kind of art, is not identical with interpreting what it means–and, certainly, the meaning of any musical composition, like any achieved work of art, is by no means necessarily identical with what its 'author intended'. We, as listeners, recreate the work of art, in making sense of what it means, by situating it in contexts that may well not be the same as those its 'authors' had in mind, or knew (anything) about. To recast this last point in other (more theoretical) terms, the initial 'writer' (such as a musician) of a 'cultural text' (such as a piece of music) 'encodes' it so as to invite and encourage particular kinds of 'decodings'–i.e., particular kinds of readings–by its 'readers' (in the case of music, these readers are, of course, listeners), yet these readers may well 'decode' the text differently: ignoring, refusing, or contesting the direction the writer suggests readers should follow in reading the text this writer has written. Furthermore, the writer of a cultural text is often not fully conscious of what kinds or varieties of 'encodings' the writer is giving the text the writer writes; readers may well be in better positions to recognize these encodings for what they are.

I work here, in this book, just as I have in all five classes I have taught on this same topic, with 'Ian Curtis and Joy Division' *as a point of departure, and as a point of reference.* This means I ultimately explore larger critical and theoretical, as well as larger cultural and historical, issues–periodically taking us a considerable distance from specific details of Curtis's and Joy Division's life and times. I make use of Ian Curtis's and Joy Division's music as a lens, or a framework, to explore critical and theoretical positions, concepts, and arguments, as well as cultural and historical events, relations, tendencies, and trends–in addition to doing the reverse, i.e., using theory and criticism, and historical and cultural texts, as lenses, or frameworks, to make sense of Ian Curtis and Joy Division. And I keep in mind the contexts within which we can, and should, usefully situate 'Ian Curtis and Joy Division' include historical times before Curtis was born as well as before the band formed, along with historical times after Curtis's death and after the band ended. Likewise, I keep in mind the contexts within which we can, and should, usefully situate 'Ian Curtis and Joy Division' include cultures (along with subcultures and countercultures) outside of, and even far away from, those concentrated in Greater Manchester, England, from 1956 through 1980. I, in sum, read the life-experience and life-work of Ian Curtis 'symptomatically', engaging with 'Ian Curtis and Joy Division' as a 'cultural phenomenon', and the sheer fact that recent students ask me whether, if anything, Ian Curtis and Joy Division have been 'overly hyped'–along with the corollary fact it has become futile to strive to keep up with the range of discourse continually newly produced by yet ever new fans, worldwide–underscores that 'Ian Curtis and Joy Division' has indeed become exactly that.

Nevertheless, I would like to call attention here to a few important Manchester contexts I think are crucial in enabling an appreciation of what 'Ian Curtis and Joy Division' has become–and of why, indeed, it is most appropriate to identify 'Ian Curtis and Joy Division' as a 'cultural *phenomenon*'. Manchester was 'the original modern' city–the birthplace of the modern industrial revolution and modern capitalism as well as the birthplace of modern communism (Friedrich Engels' wrote his famous early work, *The Condition of the Working Class in England*, about Manchester, while Engels and Karl Marx also wrote *The Communist Manifesto* in Manchester). Numerous major movements for social change originated in Manchester–for workers and union rights, for women's rights, for LGBTQIA+ rights, the cooperative movement, for pacifism, for postcolonial racial integration and the struggle to create a multiethnic and multicultural variety of postmodern society, and yet much more besides. Manchester was long one of the world's largest, one of its leading, industrial cities, while numerous famous scientists and inventors hailed from Manchester (often working at one or more of Manchester's famous universities), such, as just to name a single figure who has become well-known once again, in recent times, Alan Turing. Yet during the time Joy Division was active, and throughout much of the mid 1960s to mid 1980s, Manchester experienced a period of tremendous, and hugely unsettling, transformation. This was the period in which Manchester moved from being a city dominated by large-scale industrial manufacturing, toward a highly uncertain future. It was a period replete with social tension and unease. Everything everywhere felt in upheaval. Yet visionary figures like Tony Wilson, who over his lifetime became widely and affectionately known as 'Mr. Manchester', firmly believed in and staunchly advocated for Manchester's renaissance–as a center of art and culture. At the heart of this vision, at a time when it seemed the most preposterous, Wilson established Factory Records. The most famous initial band, as part of Factory Records, was Joy Division. As indicated in the documentary film *Joy Division*, written by Jon Savage and directed by Grant Gee, Joy Division created art that so powerfully captured the spirit of the city in this period of tremendous tension and unease that it also paved the way forward, anticipating and inspiring the 'rebirth' of Manchester as the city of art and culture it has since become.

Joy Division, Factory Records, and Tony Wilson created the impetus for an outstanding festival of art and culture, the Manchester International Festival, which began in 2007 and takes place in Manchester for eighteen consecutive days, mid-summer, every two years. I have been fortunate to attend every Manchester International Festival since 2009 (including the entirety of each of the 2011, 2013, 2015, 2017, and 2019 festivals). I have never experienced anything more truly 'awesome' in my whole life. At the 2017 Manchester International Festival, definitely the best yet, Ian Curtis and Joy Division, along with Tony Wilson, Factory Records, New Order, and others maintaining strong connections with Curtis and Joy Division, took center stage. A major exhibition at the Manchester Art Gallery titled *True Faith*, sharing, commemorating, and celebrating the art of Joy Division and New Order, as well as art inspired by Joy Division and New Order, became the principal focus. In many allied events Ian Curtis and Joy Division were acclaimed as producers of truly great–and indeed high and fine–art, while their legacy for the city, for the region, and for multifarious worlds of art and music was repeatedly applauded. A series of tall banners bearing a famous image of Ian Curtis appeared all over Greater Manchester. Curtis would have been amazed. I expect he would have been grateful and appreciative yet also embarrassed by all that prominent attention. Repeatedly, in recent years, those who knew Curtis when he was alive stress that he was, often enough, and most commonly, a kind and even 'sweet' person–even if he was, as Stephen Morris repeatedly underscores in his recent memoir, and as Deborah Curtis's harrowing account of her marriage to Ian, *Touching from a Distance*, make abundantly clear, certainly by no means anything approaching 'a saint'.

What this all attests is, yes, it remains a tragedy Curtis killed himself (I myself often enough feel saddened about it, and wish he could have got the help he needed), but Curtis nevertheless did produce great work in his all too short life, and leave a great legacy–one that burns brighter all the time. As I interpret it, this is by no means simply a sad story, a story of failure and defeat; it is, in fact, ultimately much more the story of the exceptionally transformative power, achievement, and impact of art. And it is a story that, yes, proposes this can indeed be art created by young people from poor, working class, and lower middle class backgrounds who were not initially taken at all seriously by those maintaining positions of cultural authority in their communities. For example, Bernard Sumner writes movingly in his autobiography of how, despite from an early age maintaining a passionate love of art, he was actively discouraged by his teachers from studying or doing art, because art wasn't something people from his socio-economic background were 'supposed' to be interested in or talented at. Another huge lesson concerning what 'Ian Curtis and Joy Division' has come to mean, following yet again from the long-term *success* of Ian Curtis and Joy Division, is resonant throughout Manchester–and Greater Manchester–today. Greater Manchester is at present the second largest urban area, behind London, in the United Kingdom. Over 3,000,000 people live in Greater Manchester. Manchester today has its share of major problems (homelessness, a highly limited supply of quality housing available at prices affordable for people living on low incomes, and a significant extent of yet greater and even more far-reaching socio-economic inequality), but it is a city fighting to take these problems on (for example, *Manchester Street Poem*, at the 2017 Manchester International Festival, took over an entire former shoe warehouse to depict the stories of Manchester homeless people, in large white paint on cardboard-covered walls, while advocating for secure housing on behalf of all who need it). What's more, Manchester today (as epitomized by the Manchester International Festival) is an enormously vibrant, dynamic center of artistic and cultural innovation–and collaboration (many attest what made Joy Division ultimately so exceptional is how effectively those involved worked together–and collaboration is indeed a preeminent Manchester value). Manchester is especially notable for producing and sponsoring creative work that mixes, reworks, and shakes up boundaries between conventionally distinct genres and media. And Manchester is likewise especially notable for stressing artistic and cultural events should be immersive, interactive, and sensitively attuned to as well as sensitively designed for the times and places in which they are set. To my mind, and undoubtedly to that of a great many Mancunians, Manchester is as thriving a center of artistic and cultural achievement as any other city in the UK today, including London.

I will nonetheless add a major caveat to those last series of comments and that is the impact of COVID-19, and the enormous economic fallout this has encompassed, threatens to exercise an especially devastating impact upon artistic culture–and 'creative industry'–across the UK. Manchester after COVID-19 is not likely, at least not immediately, to closely resemble the Manchester exemplified by the 2019 Manchester International Festival. Yet Manchester has rebuilt and come back before, multiple times throughout its storied history, and I remain at least cautiously hopeful this will once more prove to be the case.

Seven

I first encountered the music of Joy Division during my freshman year, 1979-1980, at Wesleyan University in Middletown, Connecticut. At the time I identified strongly with punk, from the likes of the Sex Pistols and the Clash. I even was proud to be told, as a freshman university student, that I looked like Johnny Rotten, and later deliberately sought to make myself look even more like him. Listening to Joy Division, I heard the same freshness, urgency, and intensity that attracted me to punk, yet also something transcending the immediacy and directness of punk, conveying, in contrast, a richly resonant sense of both distance and precision, a controlled fury emanating from a fiercely passionate yet also agonizingly vulnerable exploration of emotional, psychological, physical, and metaphysical extremes. I knew, if Joy Division would tour in the United States, I would do whatever I possibly could to see them live. I learned they did plan to come to the US shortly before I was shocked and saddened to read an account, in an independent music zine I subscribed and contributed to at the time, of the death of Ian Curtis, lyricist, vocalist, and frontman for Joy Division, by suicide, on May 18, 1980, at the age of 23. Ever since, I frequently listen to the music of Ian Curtis and Joy Division; it travels with me, persistently.

Joy Division songs, for me, dramatize introspection as fiercely determined and fully committed struggle. What makes this struggle all the more fraught and challenging is it transpires in a mysteriously otherworldly realm where comfortably reassuring borderlines break down. These are borderlines between interior and exterior, subject and object, self and other, protagonist and antagonist, friend and foe, help and hindrance, solidarity and betrayal, complicity and responsibility, hope and despair, health and illness, movement and stasis, past and present, history and myth, the psychological and the sociological, the sacred and the profane, the beautiful and the sublime, the close and the distant, the private and the public, the familiar and the strange, and the living and the dead. Joy Division songs end not with tension resolved, but merely temporarily suspended. The only definite answer they offer us is we need to join this struggle, and seek what we can find, for ourselves. As Morley writes, Joy Division's music "made everything seem as if it were about to happen even if it had already happened. Their music made it seem as if time itself was building up tension, always building, always flowing forward, always about to happen, in order to open up space, and liberate the future" (112).

From early on, listeners noted an unusual amount of space, of separation, within this music, appropriate for a multidimensional exploration of isolation, and it is these elements of space and separation Martin Hannett considerably augmented in his production work–adding significant amounts of digital delay and echo, as well as filtering and treating each sound source to narrow and concentrate its timbre, while combining the contributions from Ian Curtis, Bernard Sumner, Peter Hook, and Stephen Morris with studio effects designed to accentuate the trancelike movement into a liminal, preternatural space, a surreal yet proximate realm rarely engaged so unrelentingly. In the process of composing their music, each of the four principals approached the task as if they were performing the lead, but Curtis took the lead in selecting and arranging–Curtis chose which riffs and grooves, which lines and passages, which registers and which styles of playing, including at what pace and what volume, to use, and where to use these, according to how this all fit with ideas he had in mind for sounds to accompany his lyrics.

I don't want to overemphasize the last point, however, because, as I will argue throughout the course of this book, the songs need to be made sense of by taking into account all the sonic constituents involved, and by recognizing that each member of the band took charge of his own instrument, 'composing' his own contribution to the overall, composite sound–and this includes Martin Hannett, who took charge of the elaborate extent and array of production studio processes and effects he invested in this music. Joy Division's music is far more complicated than Ian Curtis's self-expression not only because that is an unsatisfactorily narrow form of autobiographical reductionism, that does not respect the possibility that Curtis, however much he drew upon what he personally experienced and felt, was an artist who was creating art that he sought to make meaningful and impactful to others, not simply producing a confessional autobiography, but also because this music encompasses far from just Ian Curtis alone expressing, communicating, prompting and provoking thoughts and feelings.

I commend Curtis and other members of Joy Division for what many found frustrating and upsetting, at the time–a refusal to interpret the music for their audiences, often by suggesting they didn't know what it means or where it came from. The music belongs as much (I am tempted to argue even more) to Joy Division's listeners, as it does to the members of Joy Division themselves–and these listeners are co-creators, with Curtis, Sumner, Hook, Morris, and Hannett, of what the music means and how it can be put to use.

Ian Curtis was both a conscious and an unconscious mythmaker. Inquiring into 'Ian Curtis, the Myth and the Music' involves inquiring into metaphorical 'darknesses' in human history and society, and in the condition of being human, especially that of the human social being living in the advanced capitalist, (post)modern world. This involves facing, without resorting to self-protective blinders or sentimentalizing illusions, often extraordinarily disturbing incidences of cruelty and violence, as well as of anxiety and alienation. It involves inquiring into intensity and extremity as well as into the complexities of distance and connection in human social relations. It involves inquiring into anxious to traumatic dimensions of the human quest for meaning, purpose, value, satisfaction, fulfilment–and especially love–in this late capitalist, (post)modern world, and it involves inquiring into *inter*relations *between* life and death, between living and dying, between being and nothingness, between self and other, and among past, present, and future. It involves inquiring into surfaces and depths, mysteries and enigmas, complexities and contradictions, and fluidities and variabilities in modes of individual identity, personality, and character. It involves inquiring into what it feels like to struggle and strive for authenticity and integrity, in relation to the pull of ambition, popularity, success, and fame. It also involves, on the flip side, inquiring into effective meanings of compassion, empathy, and solidarity. Inquiring into when and where these qualities are under threat, in danger of collapse, on the verge of eclipse, or altogether absent, we recognize, and appreciate, how indispensable they truly are.

As Morley writes, Joy Division's music "suggests infinity and confronts squalor," while it offers "dreams that shout for a better world and a deeper understanding." "The songs never avoid loneliness, cruelty, suffering; they defy those things." These songs register "the horror of the times" yet

> The very act of confronting the void or continuing to confront it is an act of affirmation. The blacker the situation and the deeper the background of despair against which this affirmation is made, the more complete and the more triumphant must be the victory that it constitutes. The uglier the reality that is confronted, the more exhilarating will be its sublimation into symmetry, rhythm, movement and noise. (256)

As Morley continues, "the very best rock music," of which Joy Division is exemplary, "is part of a fight, part of a larger decision, a widespread perception, something that can actively remove prejudice and restriction":

> Rock's greatness is its emotional impact on the individual. Joy Division's worth is immense to every individual who relishes their strange awareness . . . Ian Curtis decided to leave us, and yet he leaves behind words of such strength they urge us to fight . . . [T]he moods and the insight . . . inspire us, excite us, challenge us. The value of Joy Division is the value of love. (158)

At the spectral center of Joy Division's music, and all the more uncannily so when witnessed playing live, was–and is–Ian Curtis. In response to the question posed in 2003 by Manchester magazine *City Life*, 'Who Was Manchester's Greatest Ever Front Man?', Morley writes:

> If rock and roll is serious, and it's all about the serious things that happen to you as you grow up, and get old, and deal with life, and death, and falling in love, and falling apart, then Ian Curtis is the greatest frontman . . . because he was very serious, he took things very seriously, his life was serious, the love in his life was very serious, his death was serious, and he showed us things through his music about how serious life can get, up to the point it falls apart . . . If rock 'n roll is about having your own dance, dancing in your own world, dancing for an audience to know just how much you're in control of being out of control, dancing on top of your dreams, dancing through your nightmares, then Ian Curtis is the greatest . . . If rock 'n' roll is loneliness fired into belonging, Ian Curtis is the greatest . . . Ian Curtis is the greatest . . . not because he died, but because he lived, and packed that life into song, as if he knew the songs would last longer than he would. If rock 'n' roll is a look, then Ian Curtis wins whatever this battle is, because he looked inside everything, which takes some doing, and he had a hell of a look . . . Ian Curtis was the greatest . . . because when he was on a stage, on his toes on his edge, he was as out there as anyone has ever been. (310)

Notoriously, Curtis derived the name 'Joy Division' for his band from the name given by the Nazis to concentration camp victims forced to serve as sex slaves for their captors. At times this association, and other oblique references to Nazi Germany at gigs and in promotional materials, led observers to imagine a connection between Joy Division, the band, and Nazi-style ideology. But, aside from representing typical, punk-style, critical appropriation and resignification of what a dominant culture finds most frightening and disturbing, and which it has worked the hardest to marginalize, even to repress, in choosing the name 'Joy Division' Curtis identified himself, and his band, with the victims, and with the humiliation and pain these victims suffered, as well as with their desire to escape and their fear escape is impossible.

One of Ian Curtis's favorite books was John Heartfield's *Photomontages of the Nazi Period*. Heartfield's photomontages relentlessly expose and condemn the *monstrosity* of Nazism. Curtis's and Joy Division's *anti*-fascism follows in Heartfield's path. The back jacket of my copy cites German novelist Oskar Maria Graf who comments, concerning Heartfield's photomontages–he "has 'disturbed the sleep of the world' more than anyone else in our time." The music of Ian Curtis and Joy Division, I suggest, likewise conjures 'a disturbed sleep', a restless refusal to accept 'the way things are'–or 'the way things seem'–is the natural, desirable, or necessary way they 'should' or 'must' be.

In the classes I teach, focused on Ian Curtis and Joy Division, we always do, despite the distance in time and space, find multiple points of connection, recognition, and sympathetic to empathetic understanding with what life was like for people like Ian Curtis, Bernard Sumner, Peter Hook, and Stephen Morris, growing up and coming of age in Greater Manchester in the 1970s, a time–and a place–experiencing a deep sense of socio-economic, and socio-political, anxiety and insecurity as well undergoing a likewise rapid and often highly unsettling extent of technological and cultural change. In addition, we discover and explore points of connection, recognition, and sympathetic to empathetic understanding with Ian Curtis's struggles striving simultaneously to assume multiple, highly divergent, kinds of lifestyles and to maintain multiple, ultimately incompatible, kinds of relationships. We, likewise, discover and explore points of connection, recognition, and sympathetic to empathetic understanding with Curtis's simultaneous drive and ambition, on the one hand, and his fear and worry, on the other hand, not only about where this drive and ambition might take him, but also about what it might cost. And we discover and explore points of connection, recognition, and sympathetic to empathetic understanding in relation to Curtis's increasingly fraught struggles with epilepsy and depression (or with how difficult it was for his fellow bandmembers, and other friends, to know how best to respond). Many of us further discover and explore points of connection, recognition, and sympathetic to empathetic understanding vis-a-vis Ian Curtis's interest in, as well as Joy Division's lyrical and musical resonance with dark romantic, experimental modernist to postmodernist, and avant-garde literature and art, especially dystopian, and especially manifesting pronounced iconoclastic, miserablist, and/or shock elements (even more precisely, we do discover and explore significant points of connection, recognition, or sympathetic to empathetic understanding, in relation to Curtis's attraction to writers such as William S. Burroughs, J.G. Ballard, Franz Kafka, Nikolai Gogol, Fyodor Dostoyevsky, Herman Hesse, Søren Kierkegaard, Friedrich Nietzsche, Antonin Artaud, Jean-Paul Sartre, H.P. Lovecraft, and Michael Moorcock). Many other areas of connection, recognition, and sympathetic to empathetic understanding emerge and develop as well, such as Curtis's attraction to glam rock, kosmiche rock, and, certainly, punk rock (along with the love for listening to and especially playing music all four members of Joy Division shared). Although my classes and I frequently enough move away from concentrating upon details of Curtis's and his bandmates' personal life-situations and life-experiences, and although Curtis was in retrospect, a strikingly enigmatic and, indeed, shape-shifting, figure, yes, we do indeed consider ways in which we know, or have known, 'people like Ian Curtis', including, perhaps, people like ourselves. The same holds true for the rest of the members of the band as well. We engage with 'Ian Curtis and Joy Division' as point of departure for symptomatic inquiries into a wide array of issues in modern to contemporary critical theory, and social experience, yet we simultaneously respect Ian Curtis and his bandmates as the human beings they were, and for the concrete relationships they forged with people who knew them personally, and who were personally close to them, back when Curtis was alive and his band was still actively making new music. But it also means taking him seriously as an artist, as someone who has given us a great gift, a profoundly beautiful and indeed inspiring repertoire of creative work that helps us to live–as people actively engaged in and seriously committed to a free and responsible search for truth and meaning; as people actively engaged in and seriously committed toward striving to understand what is, what can be, what should be our place, our purpose, our role, our contribution, our destiny, and our legacy in this all too short and all too precarious existence we experience. As Morley writes, "Ian kept trying to answer the question we must constantly be asking ourselves, who do we think we are and what do we think we are doing?" (338).

Respecting Ian Curtis requires his life and work not be reduced to one long suicide note. Ian Curtis, as I see it, was a cultural resistance fighter: he confronted metaphorical darknesses–in his society and its culture, in the conditions of modernity and postmodernity–and he did so because he cared, deeply, passionately. Deborah Curtis observed "all Ian's spare time was spent reading and thinking about human suffering," and she worried he was becoming unhealthily obsessed "with mental and physical pain" but she nonetheless appreciated he was "looking for inspiration for his songs," and through his music–through his art–he was striving to dramatize the felt experience of, and thereby protest against, callousness, cruelty, violence, pain, exploitation, alienation, and dehumanization. As Deborah Curtis writes, further,

> Ian's art was crucial to him and he did not consider songwriting a mere commercial endeavour. So it was unsurprising that he turned to darker, more serious subjects to inspire him. Not specifically the Holocaust but war itself: any war would have been the perfect vehicle for Ian's interpretation of the world. In conversation he would touch vaguely on his Irish family history and on his father's subsequent service in World War II. It's debatable whether he drew on these stories to fuel his creative process or whether he turned to writing because speaking out was frowned upon. Ian was compassionate, empathetic and kind, never ostentatious or materialistic. His ability to immerse himself in the thread of another life was easily demonstrated when he read to me, whether it was lyrics or prose, and that passion continued into his stage presence. (ix)

Curtis's art resonates with many directions in critical theory and many focal concerns of critical theory. His art can readily be conceived as an exploration of and inquiry into the following two sets of fundamental questions:

1.   Why do I exist? What is the meaning, value, and purpose of my existence? To what extent can I exercise any influence, and any control, over what this meaning, value, and purpose becomes? How can, and how should, I attempt to do so?

2.   In what ways, and to what extent, am I responsible for others? For the suffering, hardship, and pain others experience? For the violence and cruelty as well as the injustice and unfairness in the world? What can and what should I do about any of this?

Curtis's art can be readily conceived of, as well, as an exploration of and inquiry into the sense and meaning of alienation, isolation, and loneliness; the position and experience of being a stranger, an outsider, and an outcast; vulnerability, entrapment, anxiety, and fear; and the need to connect, especially intimately, along with the simultaneous difficulty of doing so. Here, once again, the resonance with major directions in modern to contemporary critical theory is enormous. Curtis's art makes sense, moreover, in somewhat more specific terms, as an exploration of the extent to which (and the consequences following from recognition that) the self is an imaginary construct, the subject is simultaneously overwhelmingly unconscious and ineluctably other, desire and anxiety are persistently intrinsically interconnected, the symbolic order and the law of the father are oppressively authoritarian, jouissance is far more terrifying than the common translation as 'enjoyment' can possibly suggest, and intimations and irruptions of the Real are recurrently traumatic. At the same time, Curtis's art also makes sense, again in somewhat more specific terms, as the staging of a dramatic encounter with the shocking resilience and metamorphic resurgence of fascist tendencies, after the end of World War II and the Holocaust, at the heart of ostensibly 'democratic', advanced capitalist, Western society, including in the guises of 'friendly fascism' and 'the fascism of everyday life'. Ian Curtis and his bandmates, in choosing their name, Joy Division, whether consciously, deliberately, intentionally or not, propose fascism lives on after the defeat of Nazi Germany and the liberation of the survivors from the concentration camps–and it lives on, most insidiously, as an integral dimension and recurrent tendency within the very same societies so frequently and routinely celebrating their victory over fascism. It is a daring proposition, but one continuing to inspire and enable a ruthlessly critical, and ruthlessly self-critical, anti-fascist praxis. Assuming that name–Joy Division–demanded an exceptional seriousness of responsibility, purpose, and commitment; otherwise the band would have shortly fallen into disgrace and lost all credibility. As Paul Morley attests, the band changed dramatically quickly upon assuming the name, moving from a largely forgettable and derivative group, innocuous and all too tediously familiar, to become a band standing out as highly distinct, exceptionally serious, and incredibly edgy.

Contrary to an initially prevalent and still common tendency to reduce Ian Curtis to merely a stereotypical 'tortured artist', and as ultimately simply a troubled and confused young man, such that the tragic circumstances of his death provide, in retrospect, sufficient explanation for all he attempted and accomplished in his life's work, including in his art, Ian Curtis continues to compel new audiences, long since his death, because his work strongly resonates with major lines of inquiry engaging interconnections among estrangement, entrapment, madness, and resistance pursued by modern to contemporary critical theorists–as well as writers of literature and producers of other serious works of art. As Jon Savage comments, summing up Curtis's motivation, accomplishment, and ultimate legacy:

> Curtis felt himself emerging into a hostile world outside his control: "We're living by your rules/That's all we know." A powerful strand that weaves through the songs is the idea of "forgotten youth" in a degraded, hostile society: in the late seventies, young people were at the sharp end of the neo-liberal economic and social experiment. As he wrote: "corruption–music biz, government business–everything. Dual standards hypocrisy restrictions those with no choice–social or intellectual position holds no bright prospects for the future. Trapped in corners–solitary" . . . Ian Curtis's great lyrical achievement was to capture the underlying reality of a society in turmoil, and to make it both universal and personal. He felt the economic and social restructuring that was occurring in the late seventies–and that still casts its malign shadow today. Distilled emotion is the essence of pop music and, just as Joy Division are perfectly poised between white light and dark despair, so Curtis's lyrics oscillate between hopelessness and the possibility of, if not the absolute need for, human connection. (xxvii-xxviii).

Ian Curtis's life and his work transcend the circumstances of his death. Even when moving toward elegy, lament, exhaustion, confusion, and resignation, the lyrics and the music propose the need to continue, to endure, and to persist. And to do so even when this seems altogether impossible. Curtis's art is not simply a prolonged suicide note. Curtis was not destined to die young. His suicide was not inevitable. He had family, he had friends, he had a community. And so he had support. Yet he needed more, even much more. In his personal life he faced multiple extreme pressures, all of which taken together would have been enough to completely overwhelm just about anyone. And, at the same time, he was a fiercely committed artist, who maintained extremely high standards and extremely high ambitions, for what he sought to come to grips with, to convey, to realize, and to achieve through this art–an art requiring him to face up to, and to symbolically relive, the worst horrors human beings are capable of perpetrating against each other. That is a noble cause, one we must carry on, but it needs to be a genuinely collective one. Curtis ended up a victim of the very society he was protesting against, a society that forces us, all too often, to resist its injustices, in whatever ways we can, but at the same time to need to do so individually, isolated and alone, even when ostensibly surrounded by many other people. A society all too often complacent about, distracted from, numbed by, or otherwise indifferent to human suffering, including the suffering of those who are yet further suffering on account of their extraordinary extent of empathetic identification with and solidaristic support for the suffering of others. As Paul Morley declares, "it is his refusals which animate his legacy with an incandescent rage, a passionate and profound fury that does not cry out for death–but for just the opposite" (366).

***

In this book, closely following Paul Morley's prior example, I approach Curtis as focus of myth not by way of anti-romantic demythologization (where myth is effectively dismissed by identifying it with primitive reaction and irrational mystification) but rather by way of what Laurence Coupe theorizes as "radical typology" (84). Here myth is critically engaged through a process of progressive "remythologization" (84) that respects myth as socially symbolic action–as a mode of imaginative liberation, revelation, and disclosure–and which works *with* myth, approaching myth as malleable and open-ended, in a process of convergent exploration and inquiry. From this vantage point, "reading myth (mythography) and making myth (mythopoeia) are complimentary activities" (84). Paul Morley certainly exemplifies such an approach to Ian Curtis and Joy Division, and this approach is, as Morley shares repeatedly throughout his book, quite deliberate. Indeed, Joy Division and, especially, Ian Curtis, were already mythopoeic figures before Curtis's death and the band's end, while an elliptically yet persistently mythopoeic current runs rampant throughout the band's music and, in particular, Curtis's lyrics. What's more, Curtis's ritualistic obsession with the ultimate and the extreme resembles the quest to wrestle with Mircea Eliade's famous "dialectic of the sacred and profane" by means of "a rage for purifying disorder" that Laurence Coupe recounts in interpreting Jim Morrison as "neo-shaman" (50)–an interpretation Coupe devises to illustrate the power and uses of a radical typological approach to contemporary, popular myth (even as Curtis embarks upon his own quest with far less self-assurance, and far less certainty over what the desired end might be, let alone anything like Morrison's level of confidence that success in achieving this end might be at all possible).

Years ago, when I first began to pursue sustained intellectual work focused around Ian Curtis and Joy Division, I appreciated and respected Curtis as an artist, but did not imagine he and I were the slightest bit similar. And yet, this process has proven unexpectedly complicated because, as I have proceeded, I have recognized multiple uncanny connections. For instance, I have struggled, for a long time, with multiple serious, debilitating physical illnesses, and, recently, I have also recognized, uncannily enough, this includes epilepsy. Nothing like what Ian Curtis suffered, but even so–a striking connection. I have also struggled, off and on, with serious mental illness as well–depression, anxiety, and, even, post-traumatic stress disorder. Engagement with this topic hasn't 'aggravated' either kind of illness for me, but it has made me all the more acutely aware of what I have so often not been able to do as a result of struggling so hard and so often with each. I perceive, from Ian Curtis, as I listen to his recorded voice, and as I read his written words, while trying to write this book of my own, a tremendous anguish, emanating from a guilty recognition of a persistent uncertainty, hesitation, and doubt, and, when I recognize this in Curtis' voice and words, doing so does aggravate, and accelerate, my own uncertainty, hesitation, and doubt. As a result, at times I feel like I owe a debt of personal responsibility to Ian Curtis, to carry on with what he could not. This troubles me; it certainly is a weight. But I keep trying, and this book is my greatest affirmation to date of my commitment to continue to do so.

***

My own experience of living on an epileptic continuum, or spectrum, has been remarkably strange. I credit my colleague Joel Pace, one of a striking number of colleagues of mine, or family members of colleagues, with personal experience of epilepsy, for directing me to think about epilepsy in terms of a continuum, or spectrum, of disparate kinds and intensities of experience of 'disrupted consciousness'. Early in my life, especially during my adolescent middle and high school years, I experienced periods of repeated 'fainting spells' (often, oddly enough, while in church), or so that is what my family assumed these were (or preferred to assume these were), as well as on occasion other kinds of sudden yet short blackouts accompanied by further disturbing physical responses, including mild shaking, or, yes, mild tremors. Upon coming back to consciousness I often felt incredibly bewildered, unable to understand how I had got to where I was, even if I had only lost consciousness for seconds, because I had also felt during that short interval as if I had traveled far away, in time and space, and, indeed, I did frequently experience a powerful 'aura', a feeling of virtually ecstatic calm and contentment, during that short moment. Unfortunately, the shock of coming back to consciousness, and feeling as bewildered as I then did, made me often subsequently feel severely anxious. We visited doctors several times who discouraged us from even considering this might be epilepsy, given the stigmas associated with epilepsy as well as the restrictions likely to be imposed upon what I could do–and, I assume as well, the risks of side effects likely to occur from standard drug treatment. One doctor I recall suggested he preferred to identify what I was experiencing as a 'psychomotor disorder' (but not epilepsy) and encouraged me to do so as well.

As an undergraduate I experienced several what I now recognize and accept were seizures, but I was able to pass these off as having nothing to do with epilepsy because I proposed they either had to do with working too hard with too little sleep, including frequently 'pulling all-nighters' as well as simply finding waking life at Wesleyan University far too diversely fascinating, and intensely demanding, to spend much time sleeping–or, alternatively, as resulting from me taking drugs, such as LSD. I was never much of a drug user, but I 'experimented' when friends encouraged me to do so, and I concluded, early on, I was likely simply more susceptible to strong reactions than average. For example, on my first acid trip I remember vivid hallucinations of rows filled with dead geese across all the pews of our campus chapel my girlfriend took me to at the time. Subsequently, in graduate school, I frequently experienced 'events' involving temporary loss of consciousness, or a feeling of bizarrely altered and confusedly dazed consciousness, but again dismissed any notion these events might be connected with epilepsy, treating them as nothing more than an idiosyncratic personal quirk. I recall instructing multiple friends, shortly upon meeting me, that I have a tendency recurrently to need to lie down, because I will be on the verge of passing out, which may or may not happen, and if this were to happen while they were with me, just to make sure I don't hurt myself, and be sure to get me two Snickers bars, some water, and two tablets of aspirin. I also recall several of these friends pressing me after these events, suggesting what they witnessed was disturbing, and recommending I see a doctor, or seek medical treatment, but again I brushed that off.

I recall one time passing out, due now, I accept, to a fit, in a restroom cubicle, and coming back to consciousness with someone outside the cubicle earnestly inquiring whether I was all right. To which, you can recognize the pattern by now, I responded, 'yes, I am fine'. But I wasn't. I had outstanding bumps on my head, scratches and cuts on my arms, and for over a month afterward I frequently felt like, multiple times throughout every single one of those days, that I was on the verge of 'passing out'. Nevertheless, by this point in time, I had learned, largely unconsciously, to anticipate, prepare for, and respond appropriately whenever I felt the approaching onset of any such 'event', and that meant carefully, and, I imagine now and then mysteriously, retreating and withdrawing to various relatively 'safe spaces' for the duration.

Afterwards, in Eau Claire, working as a faculty member, I experienced a number of instances where I found myself on the floor, even once falling down the stairs, without knowing what had happened, but it was only once I started to live with my partner, and husband, that it became harder to deny or ignore what I was periodically experiencing. This gradually prompted me to reflect back upon and to recall numerous instances of 'psychomotor disorder' I had simply blocked or dismissed from conscious memory. Among the most striking seizures Andy has witnessed are when I suddenly, or at least apparently suddenly, lose consciousness, including in public, with my eyes glazing over so that even as they remain open I clearly am not seeing anything and I start to snore loudly in a deep register–which is most surprising because I rarely snore, so I am told, and when I do, it is much softer. Otherwise I have noticed times in which I have felt extremely dizzy, shaky, and spacey, sometimes leaving me feeling as if my perceptual experience along with my mental state has dramatically transformed into something much more ethereal–and that I am bouncing, gliding, and drifting, for hours thereafter. On a few rare occasions I've even experienced troubling dissociative moments, at worst passages, in which I've carried on interacting with those around me but have been oblivious to whom I was or what I was saying or doing.

Among the more frightening and dangerous seizures I've experienced in recent times are ones triggered by muscle cramps which have culminated not just in loss of consciousness but actual convulsions–or, at least, rapid hyperventilating. Within approximately five years' time, starting in the summer of 2016, the number, intensity, and variability of these events significantly increased, although they have receded somewhat in recent months. On November 2, 2018 I suffered a major epileptic seizure which left a huge impact upon me afterward, requiring a considerable effort over more than four weeks' time from which to fully recover: I now well know, if I didn't as clearly before, how the impact of that kind of 'event' can leave one incredibly exhausted in the aftermath.

It is amazing Ian Curtis was able to do what we did, while he could, given the severity of the seizures he frequently experienced. I even experienced a 'sympathetic seizure' in direct connection with rescreening *Control* for myself, prior to discussing this film with my students in class, in the early Spring 2019 semester. Immediately as the closing credits began to run, I felt a seizure overwhelmingly take over–take control of–my body, triggered by Sam Riley's performance of Ian Curtis's seizures. This was odd as I had viewed this film many times previously and never previously experienced that reaction. I live now at a time in which understanding of epilepsy has advanced considerably–as has treatment–since what was the case for Ian Curtis in the last years of his life–but, even so, I am familiar with how much pressure continues to persist to ignore or deny this condition is real. Even more recent visits to neurologists (than those from back in high school) concluded with these doctors recommending putting off seeking an official diagnosis, and official treatment, if at all possible, because 'it would be better' to 'wait and see' if the condition will subside by itself, and remain mild enough such that it can just be 'left to itself'. It has been easy enough to convince me to do exactly that–undoubtedly all too easy.

***

Although I certainly do greatly admire and respect Ian Curtis as a talented and accomplished artist, and I further sincerely respect him as a highly complicated person who was indeed deeply passionate and committed, and with whose sufferings and struggles I do maintain a considerable amount of compassion, sympathy, and, yes, certainly empathy, my aim in my work with Curtis is not 'hagiographical'. Ian Curtis was, as I have previously stated, not a saint. His life-story includes major mistakes and major mis-steps, which left him feeling incredibly guilty and deeply ashamed. He was ultimately exceedingly troubled and confused. He needed help, a lot of it, but, tragically, he wasn't able to obtain the help he needed. He didn't live long enough to think and work through many contradictions in his own outlook and understanding. And, as contradictions swirled about him, which he found himself increasingly unable to navigate, he became increasingly dishonest, most notably with his wife, whom he treated in ways clearly demonstrating, for all his sensitivity, expressed in his music as art, that he hardly surpassed conventional patriarchal sexist norms for men relating to women, prevalent at the time.

I certainly find Deborah Curtis's bitterness at and resentment of Ian for striving to control and restrict her, and, increasingly, her access to him and what he was thinking, feeling, and otherwise experiencing, while being unable to tell her the truth about what he knew would infuriate her, especially the intimate relationship he developed with Annik Honoré, as his 'soulmate', to be entirely understandable. As Deborah Curtis also recounts, Ian flirted with extreme positions that included overtly politically reactionary ones, seemingly as poses to provoke her, and others like her, while he romantically identified with the myth of the tortured, and especially tragic, artist, destined to die young. He could be impossible to live with, especially, it seems, for the one person who conventionally might be expected to be the one with whom he felt it the easiest to live–his wife. Deborah Curtis compellingly describes how much she tried to be helpful and supportive, and how much she certainly was, while Ian at the same time, and again increasingly so, cut her off, and blocked her off, from doing what might well have helped save him from an early death. His ability to lie convincingly (seemingly often motivated by a desire to avoid confrontation and argument, both of which he seemingly found most difficult to face) as well as his craving for attention, to an extent that seemingly never could be satisfied, are both further off-putting tendencies Deborah Curtis repeatedly recounts, and, even though less judgmental about this, she also adds a further plausible suggestion, based on her ample direct experience of 'taking care of him', that Ian was, even at the age of 23, as yet emotionally immature, far from fully grown up.

I acknowledge all that, readily, while also noting well it continues to be striking the range of diverse personae Ian Curtis seemingly adapted and conveyed, in his interactions with those who knew him, and reasonably well, during his lifetime. My interest in 'Ian Curtis' is ultimately not with any of those personae but rather with the personae he crafts and projects within and through his music as art. I acknowledge the real Ian Curtis was undoubtedly many different, even vastly different, kinds of people, many of whom I may well not have found personally compelling and many of whom I might even have actively disliked, but knowing about those Ian Curtises is by no means all that interesting to me. It makes no sense for me to become involved in judging his character, in his personal life; I am in no position to do so. Besides, his suicide makes it evident he judged himself harshly enough, and if even Deborah Curtis can conclude it is impossible to "be angry with someone who is dead" ("An Interview with Deborah Curtis" 2008) because the argument with that person is over, no matter how otherwise inclined you might be to remain angry with them, then why should I, or anyone else for that matter, need to carry on such an argument?

I am uninterested in this avenue for making sense of Ian Curtis as well because I think it is largely exhausted by now. Those who knew him personally have, most of them that is, those who lived long enough to do so, enjoyed the opportunity to share their perspective on his life and his character, at length. And, the summary result is many of those who 'knew' Ian Curtis knew him, and remember him, *differently*. For example, *Torn Apart: The Life of Ian Curtis*, by Mick Middles and Lindsay Reade, draws heavily upon Ian's family and childhood friends, as well as Annik Honoré, to convey a much different–even frequently diametrically opposing–impression of what Ian Curtis was typically like, at various stages of his life, than Deborah Curtis's account, in *Touching from a Distance,* communicates. A comparable array of differences pervade the accounts offered by Hook, Sumner, and Morris, as well as within *24 Hour Party People*, *Control* and *Joy Division* (the film) as well as via numerous other scattered recollections and interpretations. It is unnecessary to tie 'Ian Curtis' down and fix the memory of whom he was, and of what he was like, to any single one of these takes–and it is especially unnecessary to do so in order to engage in a critically appreciative collaboration with the music, as art, he contributed to making–forty years after his death. He does not need to have been perfect, not at all, in order to be recognized for having contributed to the accomplishment of a body of music resonant far beyond Greater Manchester and long after his death. And after all, the one account we do not have, of whom Ian Curtis was, of what he was like, and of how to interpret and explain this, is from Ian Curtis himself.

In this sense, I respectfully disagree with Deborah Curtis: Ian Curtis did *not* enjoy the last word. I also respectfully contend the breakdown of their marriage, and the estrangement they experienced from each other, is not something I can reasonably attribute solely to Ian, solely that is to his responsibility–or lack of responsibility. Like many people who marry quite young and whose subsequent lives pull them in divergent directions, they found their marriage a site of tension. I respect Deborah Curtis's vantage point, but I suspect it is possible Ian felt she wanted a kind of life, and a kind of husband, he was increasingly uncertain he also wanted, while it is possible he also thought she did not adequately understand and respect the seriousness of what he was attempting through his music, as art, and was inclined to interpret it in a too literal manner as well as to judge it too much according to normative standards of cultural value, including of 'taste', he was challenging.

What's more, to be fair to Ian, it is entirely natural and common to find one's self sincerely in love with more than one person at the same time, in different ways and for different reasons and to feel like you shouldn't need to have to choose to be with only one of these people, but 'open marriage' and polyamory were undoubtedly foreign concepts for both Ian and Debbie, given their cultural and class backgrounds, while, at the same time, divorce also carried a greater stigma, of failure and blame, for people from their backgrounds, than is common today. I have personally known quite a few people, especially in more politically radical circles, who have created polyamorous families and other kinds of networks, and made them successful and lasting, often by investing highly intentional, conscientious effort into making that happen–but this is not always by any means easy to achieve in the face of a dominant culture that still privileges serial monogamy (even in the age of Tinder–and Grinder), along with the persistent prevalence as well of the socially dominant perception that a person can only 'truly' love one person, in the 'romantic' sense, at a time.

In addition, 'the age of maturity' is an arbitrary marker, and most people remain a complex of 'mature' and 'immature' for much of their adult lives–while becoming 'fully grown up' and 'leaving the child fully behind' can be stifling forms of domination by and subjection to cultural norms and expectations that harmfully limit people's opportunities, and capacities, for self-actualization and self-realization. I have known too many adults, including too many young adults, who have felt an oppressive socially imposed burden to abandon their more playful younger selves, and who have suffered considerably as a result.

But, again, I am only taking the space here to address these issues at all because this is one reductionist trap discussions of Ian Curtis, as musician, and as artist, continually struggle to escape–i.e., that his life, his marriage, and his death collectively prove capable, in and of themselves alone, of adequately explaining the powerful resonance and appeal of his music.

Likewise, I also find the need to endlessly speculate about what precise configuration of factors explains his suicide, and what precisely could or could not have been done, when, where, and by whom to prevent it, to be further tiresome. This will always remain speculation. And it is too late–far too late now, for Ian Curtis. This kind of attention to Ian Curtis's suicide is only interesting and useful, as I see it, at this point in time, if it helps people better understand suicidality in general and how to prevent suicide among people who live after, now long after, Ian Curtis has died.

To conclude this point, I hear Joy Division's music as offering Curtis every reason to live–as providing an avenue to create, to perform, to share, and even, yes, both to escape from and to work through 'personal demons' by recasting them in artistic forms. Even if Ian Curtis's health necessitated him doing something else, beyond continuing as frontman for Joy Division, and even if this would have been exceedingly hard for him to accept, it could have been possible–the same talents could have found other avenues, including other musical avenues, where he could have drawn upon what we was able, initially, to bring to bear, within Joy Division, as a basis for proceeding in a nonetheless dramatically different direction. This could have been as an experimental and avant-garde musician, this could have been as a performance artist, this could have been as a writer, bookstore owner, and publisher–the point is, however, we don't know, and never will; this will always remain nothing but speculation. What lives on is the music–and that continues to offer an incisive source and stimulus for important meaning and powerful impact.

Otherwise, my inclination, always, is to be generously understanding of and even forgiving with people, especially concerning what cannot be known with indisputable certainty, and especially with someone who ended up as ill as Ian Curtis was and who perceived suicide as the only viable solution to the pain he felt–who now no longer can account for, and defend, himself. In my own life-experience I have known sadly too many people who have killed themselves, and I always appreciate my mother teaching me early on in life to approach suicide as indicative of someone experiencing pain so extreme that it is unimaginable unless one has been in the same position one's self–as a position from which death is the only recognizable way to put an end to a severity of pain that is unbearable. As a result I feel terribly distraught, of course, in response to people I know and care about ending their lives, or attempting to do so, but I don't feel inclined to blame them or to otherwise judge them negatively for what they have done.

I myself attempted suicide once. It is incredibly painful even to write this here, a great many years later, because I felt totally crushed at the time, with no way out, and no way forward. I am lucky–and grateful beyond words–I did not succeed, but I remember that Bob Nowlan and I feel deep compassion for him, as well as for so many others who all too often find themselves in similar straits.

What this all means for me is I am wary, yes, because, despite the strong connections I experience with Ian Curtis, uncanny and otherwise, we are also extremely different people–my background and experience is in many respects extraordinarily different from his as is my personality and character. Nevertheless a large part of what makes Ian Curtis especially compelling to me, and seemingly the same to a great many others, is that he was–and remains–a striking combination of the ordinary and extraordinary, he communicates incredibly powerfully through his art yet so much of his art is obsessively focused on the difficulty of communication, and because an empathetic engagement with his life-experience, his artistic accomplishment, and his fierce sense of artistic mission and purpose is richly rewarding–such engagement can help us in efforts to forge a genuinely and indeed systemically caring culture, a culture of compassion, empathy, and solidarity. Curtis's life-story, his life-achievement, and his life-legacy all attest to how important it is to strive to grasp the myriad ways in which we are all far more complex, multiple, contradictory, and dynamic than commonly recognized. Curtis reminds us of how all too many people's critical and creative potential is routinely discouraged, dismissed, and denigrated, and how this in turn leads all too many people all too readily to internalize a powerful tendency to do the same, to themselves.

Insofar as Curtis's own life-story, his biography, is useful to the kind of exploration and inquiry I am embarking on here it has much to do with how thoroughly and multiply flawed he obviously was. It is an important lesson my students and I have repeatedly grappled with–that someone that thoroughly and multiply flawed can nonetheless achieve great things. In my own teaching I strive not to give up on people, and to continually believe in the best they can possibly be, even when students often appear not to believe they are capable of all that much, when they have seemingly given up on themselves, and even when they have already decided to try to fix and limit who and what they are about in ways that are damagingly confining. My students repeatedly demonstrate the ability to astound–themselves as much if not more than me–in terms of creative and critical projects they are able to accomplish, in terms of insights they are able to generate, and in terms of growth in understanding as well as notably in sensitivity, compassion, and empathy. That does not mean precociousness evades or escapes bouts of immaturity, laziness, selfishness, apathy, disinterest, unconcern, callousness, anti-intellectualism, and even more politically reactionary tendencies. People are complicated; they don't add up to fully coherent and smoothly cohesive singularities. Teaching students who have been, most often, much the same age as Ian Curtis was during his time with Joy Division through the end of his life, has taught me that lesson, over and over again.

Eight

Since critical attention to Ian Curtis and Joy Division has accelerated, beginning in the mid 2000s, this has included a number of lines of what I identify as 'backlash criticism'–in other words, criticism that amounts to a backlash versus taking Ian Curtis and Joy Division as seriously as many have come to do, and, especially, against crediting them, and their music, with as much insight and achievement as has often been the case. Certainly, from this 'backlash' vantage point, what I am doing, with this book, is symptomatic of exactly such a problem. I will next proceed to respond to what I perceive as the main lines of backlash criticism.

One main line of backlash criticism is not worth addressing in much detail here, because it is has been largely discredited and perceived as reactionary for 40+ years–and that is dismissal of the value of taking so-called popular culture seriously. Popular culture encompasses the culture within which, through which, and according to which the vast majority of people in late capitalist, (post)modern societies largely live out their lives, find meaning and purpose, establish identity and secure belonging, and carry out ordinary and extraordinary practices central to defining whom and what they are about. For that reason alone popular culture is worthy of sustained critical inquiry.

A second line of backlash criticism contests any attempt to align the music of Ian Curtis and Joy Division with progressive left positions and practices by referring to the bandmembers' flirtation with Nazi images and references, as well as because of Ian Curtis's reputed support for the Conservative Party, and even Margaret Thatcher. Again, I have already responded to this line of criticism at some length, but I want to address it once more, beginning by stressing Joy Division's music, as art, is my focus, and this music, as art, was made by young men who were complex, multiple, contradictory, and dynamic, so what I–and a great many others–hear, in listening to this music, and what it prompts us to think (about) and to feel, as well as what frames of intelligibility, structures of feeling, and directions for interpretation it invites and encourages us to bring to bear, in making sense of and responding to this music, need not line up perfectly with everything these young men said and did everywhere else throughout their lives. The bandmembers' keen interest in World War II, Nazi Germany, and the Holocaust was far from unusual–and in fact commonplace–among members of their generation of British boys, and subsequently British young men, who became punk and early post-punk musicians in the mid-70s through the early 80s. At times, yes, Joy Division bandmembers' flirtations with Nazi references and imagery was certainly naive and even stupid, with Rob Gretton famously calling them out for this in exactly those terms, but these gestures are mostly representative of an attempt to appropriate and resignify what was widely perceived as disturbing and offensive to the mainstream, to thrust it forward, and to shock and discomfort, which was a commonplace punk and post-punk move, drawing upon a long history of similar such moves within modernist avant-garde movements, such as Dada and Surrealism, which, along with Situationism, bear particular strong affinities with, and influences upon Joy Division's–and Factory Records'–aesthetics.

This is in fact not only a classic avant-gardist but also a classic subcultural strategy–as part of many historic subcultures' persistently ongoing resistance and struggle versus the dominant. The Situationist practice of 'détournement' is especially directly influential, in this specific connection, in Manchester circa 1970s: détournement involves an immanently implosive critique of the hegemonic society and culture by means of hijacking, rerouting, derailing, re-situating, re-prizing, and actively un-forgetting and un-burying elements drawn from the hegemonic society and culture or from what the hegemonic society and culture has sought to repress, deny, forget, and/or otherwise marginalize–with these elements then re-worked and made to re-signify, in a challengingly to disturbingly critical direction. From these kinds of avant-gardist and subculturalist vantage points, in 'late capitalist society' the dominant culture is always appropriating from subordinate cultures, and especially from cultures of the social margins and the social fringes–i.e, from subcultures–and in so doing working simultaneously to tame anything that is at all even potentially seriously threatening to the dominant. Subcultures must engage in a constant 'war of position' with the dominant by not only continually imagining and inventing alternative identities, relations, and practices but also through strategies like détournement and other forms of critical appropriation and resignification–or critical un-forgetting and un-burying.

Interest in WWII, Nazi Germany, and the Holocaust is understandable given the time and place in which Curtis, Sumner, Hook, and Morris grew up and came of age, considering the closeness of the war, merely one generation preceding, with many visible signs and audible echoes abounding across Britain yet which all too often previous adult generations, who had lived through and fought in the war, sought to distance themselves from and to which they no longer closely attended. Curiosity about the recent past, especially a past so extraordinarily massive and horrific, including physically immediately within and across Britain itself, and about how that past continues to influence the present, is again, a highly understandable position–and one that members of Joy Division shared widely with many British punk and early post-punk musicians. Magazines, toys, movies, and TV shows replete with representations of WWII, including of the Nazis and of the Holocaust, were pervasive as these young men grew up, and popularly marketed to British children and young adults, especially British boys and young men.

The notorious reference to the Hitler youth image on posters for the *An Ideal for Living* EP (1977) recalls *The Tin Drum* (1959), an overtly anti-fascist novel by Günter Grass which later inspired an equally overtly anti-fascist, widely popular and critically acclaimed film of the same name, directed by Volker Schlöndorff (1979). Fascists and anti-fascists both find cause to evoke this kind of imagery–and long have done so. As aforementioned, John Heartfield's *Photomontages of the Nazi Period* is one classic instance of such anti-fascist critical appropriation. The same anti-fascism is undeniably the case with Bertolt Brecht and his work, reputedly the inspiration for Bernard Sumner's briefly identifying himself as Bernard 'Albrecht'. What's more, fascination with Rudolph Hess likewise makes sense in light of the contemporary best-selling popularity of Eugene K. Bird's *The Loneliest Man in the World: The Inside Story of the 30-Year Imprisonment of Rudolph Hess* (1974). Again, curiosity about how such a once powerful figure, near the top of the command hierarchy maintained by Britain's greatest modern enemy, can be largely forgotten, is likewise understandable as by no means necessitating any identification with Hess's Nazism. In fact, such interest is continuous with anti-fascist inquiry into 'the banality of evil' and of how close to 'normal', 'normal seeming', 'normal acting', and 'normal experiencing' even those responsible for the most horrendous historical crimes can simultaneous still be, anticipating a major focus within Joy Division's music–that is, confronting complicity and assuming responsibility while venturing across tenuous, nebulous, fluid and permeable borderlines between what is conventionally socially familiar and comfortable, on the one hand, and what, on the other hand, constitutes its frightening opposite. Yes it is naive to identify Hess as 'a figure of peace', but *The Loneliest Man in the World* does recount a supposed attempt of Hess to make peace with Britain, without Hitler knowing, supposedly as a result of Hess's disillusionment with Nazism, and even though such a peace agreement might well have meant abandonment of solidarity with all others continuing to fight back against Nazi domination, it partially explains the otherwise bizarre throwaway line, at an early gig, about Hess being a figure of peace. Still, the song "Warsaw" (1977) (which references Rudolph Hess in some detail) is an early pre-Joy Division song and hardly indicative of what the band would go on to achieve, musically or lyrically. And, yes, the cover image for *An Ideal for Living* shows little promise of doing much beyond mimicking well-worn gestures at *épater les bourgeois* (shocking the bourgeoisie). If Joy Division had continued making music like "Warsaw," and as Warsaw, they would have certainly been long forgotten.

Curtis's reputed support for the British Conservative Party appears a position he had not elaborately thought about because neither he nor any other bandmembers were involved in any direct work for or displayed any direct interest in any political party, while their music does not reference any narrowly specific political issues, or campaigns, let alone any specific political figures or movements from their time. This reputed support likely amounted, at best, to nothing more than a vague sense of patriotic affiliation, again, in not so paradoxical opposition to supposed Nazi sympathy, with the party that had led the British government during and won WWII. However, it is important, once again, to recognize Curtis and other members of Joy Division were still quite young, naive, and impressionable, which means, like many young people I have taught for 35 years, still searching for and coming to grips with their precise political party (or anti-political party) allegiances in their own contemporary social-political conjuncture. Nevertheless, I propose it is also credible to read this largely token identification as again representative of an least intuitive interest in keeping live the memory of the struggle against fascism in WWII, and of Britain's critical role in so doing, while, yet again, manifesting an at least intuitive concern about incipient fascist tendencies in contemporary Britain, especially enabled by complacency over what kind of society Britain supposedly was and had become.

It is worth noting here British welfare state social democracy reached its reforming limits quickly while giving rise to the fierce desire to achieve much more, and to do this much better. Too much of post-WWII British welfare state social democracy was top-down, benevolently paternalistic, and insufficiently inclusive of working and lower middle class people in their own self-determination. Fearful concern over authoritative control over working class and lower middle class Britons' lives as drifting toward the positively authoritarian, especially when denied by the British establishment as impossible, given the triumphalist perspective this establishment championed concerning the successful end of WWII, again makes compelling sense, in the Britain of the tumultuous 1970s, experienced then and remembered since as a decade of incessantly proliferating socio-economic and socio-policial crises.

With reference to Curtis's reputed support for the Conservative Party and even reputed enthusiasm for Margaret Thatcher, even insofar as this was true, and the evidence here is fleeting and contested, involvement in party politics was clearly not a significant focus of interest and involvement in his life at any point, to any degree. What's more, the overall thrust of the kinds of music he found appealing, compelling, and inspiring, and which he made himself, was not focused on directly aligning with any specific mainstream political party and that party's platforms, campaigns, or policies. Alienation from the dominant political sphere that he and his bandmates' felt and registered, in their music, is far too clearly overwhelming for any ideological alliance with Conservatism, and especially Thatcherism, to make sense. The vision articulated through the music, including the lyrics, does not align with Thatcherism and with what Thatcher promoted and celebrated. This is not music made in the interest or spirit of privatization of social welfare and public goods, of deregulated markets and rampant multi- and trans- national capital accumulation, and of promoting the positive value and necessity of individual entrepreneurialism along with classically conservatively repressive and punitive social morality over social empathy, inclusion, and solidarity. This is not music that endorses the Thatcherite notion 'there is no such thing as society' as idyllic, but rather depicts such a social world, decimated by fragmentation, alienation, isolation, violence, callousness, and cruelty, as a nightmare. Curtis's music does not suggest choosing among the options available to vote for in parliamentary general elections offers anything even approaching a conceivable way of engaging with, responding to, moving past, and moving beyond the dilemmas with which this music is most centrally and persistently concerned.

***

Another major line of 'backlash criticism' proposes that serious interest in and claims for the achievement of Ian Curtis and Joy Division manifest an exploitation of Curtis's disability, and of his suicide. I certainly agree this is possible to do, in both instances. Yet much critical attention to Curtis's epilepsy and his suicide rejects romanticization of either, and fully respects how tremendously painfully debilitating the former was and how terribly sad the latter was, while firmly rejecting any facile notion Curtis was 'destined for suicide', or that his suicide is decisive in accounting for what makes his life–and his music–as powerfully appealing as it has been and continues to be. Curtis's struggles, in fact, are helpful to those in similar positions, in gaining the support and assistance we need, and which Curtis did not find, vis-a-vis epilepsy, depression, and suicidality. I interpret Curtis's contributions to Joy Division music as by no means simply all about himself, in a superficially far too obvious form of confessionalism, but rather as a site through which he engaged in struggling with demons he recognized he shared with a great many others. Curtis himself may have occasionally, even from his teenage years, romanticized dying early, but in my interpretation of *his music*, this offers by no means an unambiguous endorsement of such a romantic myth.

A fourth line of 'backlash criticism' follows closely from the preceding and that proposes images and other representations of Ian Curtis and Joy Division have become overly commercialized, and overly commodified–risking reducing Ian Curtis and Joy Division to nothing more than advertising, publicity, promotion, and hype. Again, I recognize how and why this line of criticism makes sense, but I also argue for interpreting consumption within late capitalist society more critically, and, especially, more dialectically. It has been more than four decades now since subculture studies, such as those popularized by Dick Hebdige, have shown youth subcultures often, in practices of self-(re)presentation, appropriate and resignify elements drawn from capitalist commercial production and commerce. Youth subcultures incorporate what they so appropriate and resignify within individual and collective modes of stylistic self-fashioning–and they certainly can do so in *critical*, including critically subversive, directions. I contend no one need apologize for being a *fan* of Ian Curtis and Joy Division because fandom is by no means simply reactionary, or purely indicative of total cooptation by capital. Fandom can provide substantial support for fashioning individual identity and for securing and sustaining participation within a collectively shared social identity, both of which need not by any means simply support the maintenance and reproduction of the socio-economic and socio-political status quo, essentially unchanged. Marketing images and other signs, discourses, and texts can serve as 'a way in' for exploring and inquiring into what makes a body of music powerfully meaningful and impactful–and to what this music can contribute to enable and enhance the quality of the listener's life. Of course, in a capitalist society capital is in continuous quest for ever new sources of profit and accumulation, and will capitalize on whatever opportunity it can find, but that does not mean consumers, as fans, need simply be 'dupes' of capital, and simply identify their passion for a particular music, musical group, or body of music, as merely equivalent with what capital promotes. On the contrary, fans can and do create meanings, values, and uses, themselves–as well as communities working together in so doing, and these certainly can and do include communities of resistance versus capitalist normativities. Even simply wearing an *Unknown*

Pleasures T-shirt in Manchester and Greater Manchester has opened up numerous conversations with many local people, in my visits to the city and region, while those I've met responded by indicating how pleased they were to recognize and embrace a shared enthusiasm for Joy Division, even inviting me in to show me 'hidden places', of interest to a Joy Division fan, I might never have gained the chance to visit without establishing that connection. In this book I am proceeding to elaborate a range of meanings, impacts, insights, and perspectives, that the music, as art, of Ian Curtis and Joy Division can offer, in dialogue with major works in critical theory, and in so doing I am demonstrating one pathway among many further possible pathways for keeping this music alive, and full of yet unrealized potential, that will not be exhausted by the hype.

***

Finally, I want to address the critique of 'imaginative historicism' as argued by Paul Crosthwaite and subsequently picked up by a number of others. Crosthwaite warns against the potential dangers of using songs, and notably lyrics, as open to interpretation as Joy Division's and Ian Curtis's are, as the basis for imagining elaborate connections with historical movements and tendencies, and as demonstrating remarkable insights concerning the same, on account of the fact this music, and these lyrics, do not precisely specify how they can and should be interpreted. Crosthwaite worries about the lack of empirical justification in interpretations such as those advanced by Paul Morley and Jon Savage, and about making the music fit the pop critic's own positions without needing to prove this fits with how the musicians themselves conceived, approached, and interpreted their music. Crosthwaite worries about this form of criticism being overly impressionistic, mythologizing, and occultist. Crosthwaite references how this form of pop criticism is reminiscent of new historicism as opposed to classic historicism. Crosthwaite is not entirely dismissive of imaginative historicism as he does credit major contributors for being highly self-conscious and he does attest to its allure but he is clearly nonetheless troubled, because otherwise seemingly inarticulate musicians are credited with creating music that inspires elaborately and densely articulate interpretations, and reflections.

To respond to Crosthwaite, none of the members of Joy Division were necessarily as inarticulate as he suggests, and has often been ascribed—or was, at the time. All three memoirs by surviving members demonstrate Hook, Sumner, and Morris are all voluble people who all likewise convey a compellingly distinct voice along with a powerful ability to tell a story that can sustain rapt attention. All three readily and frankly admit shortcomings, failures, and embarrassing, silly, and even stupid behaviors. All three write in thoughtfully reflective and self-reflective ways about own experiences—including, again, impressively, their own limitations and mistakes. All rebelled against how a conventionally normal life for people like them would have been most likely expected to turn out, and did so from early on—as did Ian Curtis too. In interviews circa 1977-1980 bandmembers' suspiciousness versus interviewers makes better sense not as inarticulateness, but rather skepticism versus why their music should not be allowed to speak for itself, and of how their words could be used against them, especially in the then cutthroat world of popular music publicity with new bands' status rising and falling rapidly and continuously—and with music critics exercising much greater influence than today over whether a band would succeed or fail. Also, as all three surviving

63

bandmembers' memoirs attest, at the time Joy Division was emerging they faced a highly competitive struggle to arrange, maintain, and sustain gigs–in trying to win over enough interest and support to keep going. They worked hard, and had to be persuasive, in order to get to play at all.

What's more, Joy Division's music is challenging and disturbing music, and that easily carries over to how the bandmembers were at least perceived to come across in interviews, especially immediately following performances. Yet, at the same time, the historical record is full of contradictory reports, as at times Ian Curtis in particular is cited as highly forthcoming, talkative, and friendly. Actually, it was smart for Joy Division not to attempt to explain the source and meaning of their lyrics, or their music; this would almost inevitably prove reductive–the music, and the lyrics, need *to be experienced* and the listener needs to determine for themself what to make of them, including by drawing upon connections the listener themself finds makes the greatest sense to bring to bear.

It further makes sense that Curtis didn't like to talk about his work because it was not fodder for casual conversation and he aimed to put it all into his music, and into his performance of this music. It would have been too horrifying for most to feel comfortable talking about all that easily–but composed and performed, musically, it could be powerfully impactful, and indeed transformative, as art. I think, contrary to earlier arguments that suggest Curtis's life-experiences outside of his art overdetermined his art, what he took on and attempted to accomplish with, and through, his art–at such extraordinary extremes, and largely by himself alone–instead overdetermined his life-experiences outside of his art; he drove himself over the edge in significant part because he was trying to take on far more, artistically, than one person alone could readily, healthily, handle. The fact he pushed himself, night after night, to the point of a grand mal seizure, by the end of gigs, shortly after gigs had ended, or before going to bed (for only a few hours sleep) is incredible.

This alone undoubtedly exercised a devastating impact on his mental and physical health. I cannot imagine myself surviving at all for all that long, in attempting myself to do something like that (I have experienced a few grand mal seizures and it took me weeks to fully recover–if I had experienced these night after night for months on end it would have been monstrous; I don't know how I possibly could have gone on at all). Yet, Ian Curtis reminds me of many an activist, including of myself in extended periods of my life, who have been animated by a sense of the cause we were obsessed with, and who believe it is urgent we give everything we have to this cause because people are in desperate need and the issues we are confronting are momentously important such that 'taking time for one's self' seems selfish. I have had advisors who strongly encouraged me 'to go without sleep' and to 'risk everything' and 'take on everything' in order to do all I can to make a real impact in support of the kind and scope of progressive to radical social change I have advocated and supported–and often enough I did indeed attempt to do exactly that. It boomeranged, of course, but this is an understandable temptation–and one I readily recognize a great many activists, artists, and intellectuals do experience (and even many others too–often the 'hero' of TV detective fiction is the detective who sacrifices literally everything in pursuit of obtaining justice for those who have suffered a grievous loss, such that the detective's life subsequently becomes virtually entirely identical with pursuit of resolution concerning the case this detective is pursuing).

Most importantly, however, the critique of 'imaginative historicism' misses the point that this is what music often invites and encourages us to do–to imagine, including to imagine connections, including with histories that shape and constitute who we are and what we are about. Music often addresses specific historical conditions, situations, relations, figures, and events highly elliptically at best, and what is most important here, at least as I perceive it, is what music makes listeners think (about) and feel, and what frames of intelligibility, structures of feeling, and directions for interpretation listeners bring to bear because these respond well to, and fit well with, what these listeners hear the music proposing and making possible. It is not Ian Curtis and the rest of Joy Division who are consciously and deliberately setting out to draw forth all of these precise connections, especially as thorough arguments, but rather us as listeners and interpreters who are able to collaborate with what they have created in order to make this meaningful in relation to history, including history's continuing and profound impact within and upon our experiences of the present. Paul Morley, in particular, is explicit in explaining he writes about what Joy Division makes him think (about) and feel, and this in turn has much to do with who he is, and has been, and with what he has experienced in his own life.

Morley, what's more, overtly explains his mode of writing about Joy Division as an attempt to convey, in words, a parallel equivalent to what he hears in Joy Division music and what this music, again, makes him think (about) and feel, as he listens to it, and as he reflects on the connections he makes with what he knows about the members of Joy Division, where they come from, and what they have experienced. As I will discuss in chapter two, critical musicology has developed a strong emphasis upon seizing the challenge of interpreting music in words, and finding the words that can do justice to the sounds, which in turn requires considerable imagination and creativity. If the pop critic can make a credible argument for how the critic interprets the music, and why, in relation to what intertexts and contexts this critic brings to bear, then it contributes usefully to ongoing conversation, and debate, over what this music can–and should–mean.

***

Since Crosthwaite draws connections between imaginative historicism and new historicism it is worth taking space here to recount tenets of new historicism, which has been a prominent and influential direction of theory and criticism within contemporary English literary and cultural studies. According to new historicism, the meaning of history is not naturally self-evident, and it is not simply 'inherent' within some essential core of 'facts about the past'. How we interpret the meaning of historical 'facts' depends upon the contexts within we situate these facts, and the perspectives we bring to bear to examine these facts in these contexts. The same facts can and will mean differently when situated in different contexts and examined from different perspectives. History itself is constructed through–and is contingent upon–the ways people interpret material evidence from the past; what we recognize as history thus varies according to what frameworks, lenses, or perspectives we bring to bear, and according to what contexts we situate evidence from the past within. Doing history is far from simply finding out and then merely recounting a singularly incontestable truth of 'what happened in the past'. History includes a multiplicity of actual and possible ways of interpreting what happened. History is a field of actual, and possible, arguments over how to interpret the meaning of the past (including in relation to the present). New historicism does not deny the existence of facts, or their importance, but focuses on how facts are connected with values, and interpretive frameworks, which extend beyond facts alone.

According to new historicism, history and literature are far more alike than commonsense suggests–and the same with the interpretation of history versus the interpretation of literature. Literature and history are both made up of many texts and many discourses that require interpretation. Literary texts can be and often are historical documents. And historical documents can be and often are very much 'literary' texts insofar as these documents represent past people's creative and imaginative responses to their life-experiences, to the conditions of their existence, and to dominant as well as alternative ways of making sense of their life-experiences and of their conditions of existence. History encompasses both 'what happened in the past' and *narrative* accounts of 'what happened in the past'. Again, new historicism does not deny the distinction between fact and fiction, but rather emphasizes the importance of paying critical attention to the importance of narrative and interpretation in both fiction and non-fiction. In this connection it is worth noting well that Stephen Greenblatt, often credited as one of the principal founders of new historicism, preferred to identify what he is doing as 'cultural poetics'.

According to new historicism, we can never know the past in itself, as it was directly experienced by those living in the past, but what we can know is the past in relation to our vantage points, interests, and concerns in the present. In engaging with history we should *not* pretend we can approach history, or speak and hear about it, read and write about it, and work with and make use of it in an entirely 'unbiased' fashion. What we need to do instead, in interpreting and otherwise working with history, is to openly foreground our biases, and to account for them–i.e., to identify them upfront, and to argue for them. This involves directly indicating, for example, historical event X means A when situated in context G and examined from perspective M–rather than indicating historical event X simply means A. It involves openly identifying and arguing for the bias that one inevitably brings to bear in interpreting history, not pretending one can interpret history in an unbiased fashion (and this includes acknowledging, forthrightly, the ways one's vantage point in the present inevitably shapes how one makes sense of the past, while not pretending one can ignore or escape from that vantage point). Recognizing all of this does not mean new historicists believe all accounts of the historical past are equally valid–not by a long shot. Nor does it mean new historicists are unable or unwilling to distinguish between fact and lie (or 'alternative fact'), concerning what happened in the past, when, where, how, or why. New historicism relies on rigorous standards of evidence and scrupulous modes of reasoning in making sense of what happened in the past, when, where, how, and why–but also pays careful, critical attention to how much needs to be reconstructed, based on incomplete evidence, which in turn involves interpretation and judgment, and which is therefore not strictly and completely identical with solely what history was like, as direct lived experience, by those participating in it (in the past). Problems come, new historicists contend, with accounts of the past that pretend to be entirely neutrally disinterested, and which pretend, moreover, to represent no vantage point, no perspective, or no angle of vision, and which pretend, yet further, to maintain no connection with any interest or agenda in the present, whatsoever. It is these kinds of approaches toward making sense of history that in turn tend to be the least careful, the least cautious, and the least judicious in recognizing the limits of their interpretations and accounts–and it these kinds of approaches toward history that tend at the same time to lack a self-critically self-reflexive self-awareness as well as to lack accountability to the truth.

According to Michel Foucault, a major influence upon new historicism, knowledge often constructs what it purports to know; knowledge is not, in actuality, always knowledge of something that stands outside of the discursive forms in which knowledge is represented, something that simply precedes discourse. For the sake of simplicity here, 'discourse' and 'the discursive' refer to ordinary written and spoken language as well as all other systems of signs people make use of in rendering things intelligible–that is, in the course of making sense of, and in expressing and communicating, meaning. For Foucault, discourses bridge, or connect, ideas and actions, or practices–discourses involve making use of signs, and articulations of relations among signs, as social practice. Signification is embodied and materialized, in other words, when it becomes discourse. Knowledge takes shape in discourse, and discourse often produces what it purports merely to represent. An object of knowledge–for instance, the nature of gender or sexual identities and differences–is given form and substance within the discourse that offers us 'knowledge of or about' this object (again, for instance, the nature of gender or sexual identities and differences). The particular ways we use language and other sign-systems in talking and writing about gender or sexual identities and about gender or sexual differences in turn lead us to construct what we understand gender or sexual identities and differences to mean in line with these ways of talking and writing. What we commonly take as naturally objective facts are often, on the contrary, constructions according to prevailing cultural conceptions, principles, ideals, values, norms, perspectives, frameworks, lenses, and the like. Knowledge is never neutrally disinterested, but rather is always caught up within the operation of power. This encompasses, more precisely, the power to construct what people understand to be real and unreal, true and false, right and wrong, valuable and not valuable, significant and insignificant, desirable and undesirable, necessary and unnecessary, possible and impossible, and so on. Social institutions make use of power, operating in the form of knowledge, communicated through discourse, to regulate, discipline, police, and exercise surveillance over people's behaviors and beliefs. The key here is the institution's control over the definition of what is real and unreal, true and false, right and wrong, valuable and not valuable, significant and insignificant, desirable and undesirable, necessary and unnecessary, possible and impossible, and so on–and the ability of the institution to compel people to act in accord with this control over definition. When an institution maintains dominant control over these kinds of definitions, that institution tends to maintain dominant control as well over the ways people participating within the same institution think, understand, and act. This often, Foucault proposes, leads these same people to regulate, discipline, police, and exercise surveillance over themselves (because doing so is what they have come to identify with as what is expected or required of them).

Foucault, again, does not deny the existence of objective facts, at all, but he at the same time proposes much of what many people routinely assert or take to be simply 'naturally' objective fact is instead interpretation and, yet more than that, socially interested construction: i.e., what particular social interests have gleaned from and glommed onto supposedly 'naturally' objective fact. Even further, Foucault is directing us to consider another key dimension of 'objectivity' that is often overlooked, beyond what supposedly 'naturally' exists: human social power and human social power relations, including, notably, relations of domination and subjection, themselves create a significant extent of what is objectively real. Objective reality includes what nature provides *and* what humans produce beyond and on top of what nature itself provides. For example, the power to define and delimit, and to classify and regulate, what counts as criminality, mental illness, sexual deviancy, and so on helps in turn produce a vast amount of discourses, practices, and institutional procedures and processes committed toward making sense and taking care of these 'social problems'. Particular definitions and delimitations, and classifications and regulations, create vast institutions, a great many jobs, and a large extent of structures of social relations (governing relations between, for example, those identified as criminal, mentally ill, or sexually deviant–and those identified as not so).

Objective reality includes the entirety of social reality created by human beings who are always caught up in relations of power with each other, and this web of power in turn influences what kinds of *social* reality are created (and recreated) as well in the interests of whom (or, in other words, the existing array of relations of power determines who benefits and who suffers). 'Madness', for example, has been understood in a radically diverse array of shifting ways over the course of Western European (and North American) history since the Middle Ages, and the production of knowledge, supposedly simply 'about' madness, has exercised a powerful influence over how madness is perceived and engaged–as well as over who is viewed and treated as mad, how, and why. In this respect, 'knowledge is power' because knowledge directs how madness is engaged, in society, and with what consequences for everyone, 'mad' and 'not mad'. Different ways of making sense of and understanding 'madness' lead to different ways of engaging with madness, including different ways of drawing distinctions and relations between 'mad' and 'not mad' (as well as among diverse 'kinds' of 'madness'–and diverse kinds, for that matter, of 'sanity'). As Foucault has chronicled in his *History of Madness,* who and what have been interpreted and judged to be mad, what factors are interpreted and judged to be responsible for madness, what variety of kinds of madness are recognized as existing, what is understood to distinguish the mad from the 'not mad', and what is accepted as right and proper to be done about (or with) madness and 'the mad' have all changed dramatically and frequently since the Middle Ages through modern times, and continue to change, with different discourses rising and falling in predominance, and each of these discourses in turn motivating particular kinds of social practices as well as particular kinds of social institutions (concerned to engage with madness and 'the mad'). I use 'engage' here because even the notion that madness is a 'condition' requiring 'treatment' is a relatively modern conception, so it would be a mistake to imagine 'madness' has always been conceived of as equivalent with what we today, most often, identify as 'mental illness', and that the proper response, in turn, is to 'treat' this illness through psychological, and especially psychiatric, means.

Within contemporary cultural studies, which has ultimately proven larger and more widely influential than new historicism per se, yet which shares much common ground with new historicism, many theorists and critics tend to perceive people as maintaining an ability to engage critically with dominant, mainstream, mass culture–i.e., with the products and productions of 'the [entertainment] culture industry'. According to these cultural studies theorists and critics, people don't always make sense or use of the products and productions of the culture industry all in the same way–and people don't always make sense and use of these same products and productions according to how they are invited and encouraged [that is, how they are told] to do so. According to these same contemporary cultural studies theorists and critics, people can and do come up with alternative, resistant, and oppositional interpretations and uses of products and productions of the culture industry. What's more, subcultures often provide elaborate and substantial alternatives to dominant, mainstream, mass culture–and the culture industry–including ways of living out one's life, and of making sense of what one experiences in doing so, that do not simply conform to the demands and expectations of dominant culture. Often, subcultures appropriate from, resignify, and transform the meaning and use of elements of mass culture. Cultural studies has often tended toward taking so-called 'popular culture' highly seriously (as well as, indeed, often, highly positively), arguing people engaging with the products of so-called 'popular culture' (even that which is mass produced for mass consumption by powerful corporate interests) tend to make sense and use of these products in ways far more complicated than as mere dupes of dominant ideology. Mass culture can and does tend to commodify popular culture, including by commodifying individualism and rebellion, but people often, so cultural studies theorists and critics tend to suggest, can and do resist, disrupt, subvert, and otherwise oppose and undo such efforts. At the least, cultural studies theorists and critics tend to suggest, people's mindsets and outlooks are often much more complicated, and more contradictory, than, again, that of mere 'dupes of dominant ideology' (or pure 'victims of false consciousness').

New historicism views historical accounts as narratives, or stories, that are inevitably biased according to the point of view, conscious or unconscious, of those who write them. Bias, again, however, is not equivalent with falsehood–bias is equivalent with having a vantage point, an interest, a stake, or an angle from which one approaches 'the past'. Biases can be enabling as well as disabling. Historical analysis and literary analysis are not altogether distinct but interlinked, new historicists contend, as history is a text that can be interpreted (and argued over) much the same way literary texts can be interpreted (and argued over) while literary texts are often important cultural artifacts that can provide useful knowledge about the interplay of discourses, or the web of social meanings, operating at the times and places these literary texts are written. This, once more, does not mean 'anything goes' or 'everything is equally valid' but it does focus attention, nevertheless, on how important is the mode of *recounting* what happened in the past, involving whom, when, where, how, and why, as well as how important is *interpretation* of the evidence that we do have from the past in attempting to make sense of–that is, to explain and draw lessons from–the past.

For example, back when I was in high school, as I have previously alluded to, whenever teachers had conferences during class time, or were otherwise unprepared to teach us, they would show us movies, often not directly connected to what we were studying in their classes. On multiple occasions, in multiple classes, I watched a film on the making of the atomic bomb, which was an historical account, but was also constructed so as to emphasize the suspense, the action, the drama, and the internal as well as external conflicts and struggles among lead characters–who were actual historical figures. It was much like watching fiction. The film emphasized the difficulty and pain of those making the decision to create, and then drop, the atomic bomb–on Hiroshima and Nagasaki–but at the same time clearly argued this was a sad necessity, and it ultimately ended up saving more lives and aiding and abetting the US and its allies in the 'Cold War', just beginning to emerge, with the USSR and its allies. And the film did not focus on the devastation suffered by the victims and survivors of these attacks. Of course, many highly divergent accounts and interpretations of these same series of events, including in film form, have been produced and circulated. And many others, like this one, while also claiming the status of non-fiction, emphasize as well the suspense, the action, the drama, and the internal as well as external conflicts and struggles among lead characters, just as if these were works of fiction. Certainly, the atomic bombs were dropped, and the extent of the damage they did is calculable, but why these bombs were dropped, and whether this was necessary or not remains subject to debate. Different accounts of the same historical event can and do cast it in considerably different lights–and the same is true, for example, of divergent documentary accounts of other military actions, or wars, in which the U.S. has been involved, such as in Vietnam, Iraq, and Afghanistan. To take another example, while visiting Cuba in 1991 we, North American guests (I was an invited guest as part of a conference of 'North American and Cuban philosophers'), were shown a lengthy chronicle, with abundant artifactual evidence, of an almost incessant campaign, over the course of the preceding 30 years, on the part of the U.S. government, the U.S. military, and leading U.S. intelligence agencies, to overthrow the Castro regime, including by means of assassination, and to otherwise undermine the stability of the regime's hold within Cuban society. An account in the U.S. of the same series of events would likely cast them in a considerably different light, and even substitute a considerably different array of artifactual evidence.

On the other hand, many works of fiction can prove indispensable in helping us better understand and appreciate many eras in the non-fictional past. F. Scott Fitzgerald's *The Great Gatsby*, for example, can help us better understand many issues, and many ways of thinking, feeling, believing, acting, interacting, and behaving during the so-called Roaring Twenties. Graeme Macrae Burnet's *His Bloody Project* can help us better understand many issues, and many ways of thinking, feeling, believing, acting, interacting, and behaving in the late 1860s and early 1870s in the Scottish Highlands. And readers here can undoubtedly name many works of 'fiction' that offer considerable insight into 'non-fictional' history–perhaps by giving us a clearer, more vivid, more graphic, more visceral, and more richly detailed portrait of the felt experience of people living at past times and in past places. My UWEC English colleague, Professor Molly Patterson, in 2018 published an enormously critically acclaimed historical novel, *Rebellion*, which contributes significantly and powerfully toward knowledge of the felt experience of women in China, at the turn of the 19th to 20th centuries, in rural Illinois in the 1950s, and in China once again, at the turn of the 20th to 21st centuries. After all, many writers of historical fiction do extensive research into the non-fictional histories of the times and places they recount in their fiction. At the same time, fictional texts are often powerful elements of and contributors to the cultures of the time and place out of which they emerge–especially if they have been highly popular or otherwise significantly influential. Often enough, fictional texts do make a substantial difference in contributing toward social change. Several years ago I served on a master's thesis committee at UW-Eau Claire for a student writing his master's thesis on Upton Sinclair's *The Jungle*, which is well-known for exerting a substantial impact upon social change–and which this thesis writer, subsequently a PhD student in English concentrating on critical theory, at Purdue University, argues can and should continue to do so.

Just as the aforementioned works of literature, as well as countless others, helpfully enable us to make sense, and use, of history, so can popular music–including the music of Ian Curtis and Joy Division.

***

As a university level teacher for 35 years I well recognize how young adults can be extremely smart, even coming from relatively underprivileged backgrounds; can be quite savvy and indeed precocious; and can make rapid leaps in intellectual growth and understanding, as well as come up with highly impressive achievements in the course of 14 weeks that they never imagined they were capable of accomplishing. Often students achieve and share extraordinary insights, especially through working collaboratively, and collectively, once they feel ready and able to trust and share relatively openly and fearlessly. I am one who is always prepared to listen to and learn from young people, and also believe I can and should do so even when they are troubled and confused, even multiply troubled and multiply confused, because sometimes the greatest and most useful insights come as result of feeling, and working with feeling, troubled and confused. Those times, and struggles in those times, can indeed be the most powerful in terms of the insights they generate. I extend the same receptive inclination to take seriously what Ian Curtis, and the other at the time likewise still young adult members of Joy Division, created–in relation to what this continues to offer of use and value to me, and to a vast number of people of many different ages.

Yet more than enough has been written about Curtis's life, and about its prospective influence upon the music to which he contributed, especially in light of his suicide–and it is ultimately inconclusive, a tissue of disparate accounts, and disparate interpretations, with no decisive consensus conclusion. It is time, I contend, to put a stop to limiting the power of Joy Division music, as art, and Curtis's central role in, and contribution to this, from being continually conflated with and reduced to mere (auto)biography, and that includes abandoning excessive worry whether interpretations of Joy Division music, made by listeners far removed in time and space from Greater Manchester, circa 1977-1980, can possibly make convincingly good sense.

Listeners attracted to this music undoubtedly will explore and learn about Curtis and the other members of the band, where they came from, what their lives were like then and there, and what were significant influences within and upon these lives. And that will add to and reshape how listeners make sense of this music, what it means, what is its value, what it can and does contribute, and what it can and does exert. However, listeners need not, and should not, be bound by that particular contextual direction because it can be misleading and counter-productive; it can prevent the music from meaning as much as it possibly can to the listener in connection with the listener's own life, the listener's own life-experiences, the listener's own philosophical and political outlooks, the listener's own foremost convictions and values and principles and ideals–with what truly matters most to the listener in their own life, in the social, historical, cultural, political, economic, and spiritual contexts which most directly impinge upon and most decisively impact (define, enable, and constrain) the listener's own life. This music is powerful not because the story of Ian Curtis's life, and especially not because his death, is so exceptionally distinctively compelling in and of itself, but rather as

71

music–and as music that can express, communicate, mean, and impact far beyond the immediate details of that individual life-experience.

Ian Curtis's life-experience, in all of its dimensions, undoubtedly influenced–even prospectively at least partially 'overdetermined' the life he lived as one who contributed to making and sharing music, as art–and it is readily possible to speculate, virtually endlessly, about which specific dimensions exercised what relative degrees of influence, yet ultimately that is simply too obvious a course to follow–and a dead end for further useful interpretation of this music, as art. The music needs to be brought into connection with meaningful contexts, with enabling intertexts, so as to bring forth its power as art, as capable of offering substantial meaning and impact beyond merely rebounding back to the specific time and place in which Curtis individually lived. The meaning of the sounds, and the patterns of sounds, comprising these songs, and the words of the lyrics as part of these songs (but not their totality), are only meaningful by way of connection with other expressions, communications, and efforts at accomplishing and providing (opportunities for) meaning and impact. Meaning comes from making connections–by bringing texts into connection with each other and by bringing texts into connection with contexts, or, as I have previously described, frames of intelligibility, structures of feeling, and directions for interpretation.

Curtis as multiply divided, confused, troubled, flawed, and disturbed is interesting on that account–not in and of himself uniquely alone but rather because these are all too humanly relatable qualities of experience. Too many accounts of Curtis's life, and death, and its supposed translation into his music attempt, even seemingly without recognizing they are doing so, to render Curtis coherent–to force him into coherence–when perhaps the most interesting insight we can gain from studying his life, through the web of accounts and interpretations of what this was like, and what he was like, is that he was incoherent, he was not singular, everything does not all add up neatly together, and no precise structure of carefully arranged lines of cause and effect, or even a carefully crafted matrix of vectors of relative determination, explains it all, conclusively, totally, and puts it all, finally, once and for all, to an end. Too many of these accounts and interpretations are unable, and unwilling, to leave their accounts and interpretations of Curtis open-ended and unfinished, and to not attempt to make everything within and about whom and what he was fit together as precisely as a completed jigsaw puzzle. My interest is why do we do this to people–why do we experience a strong need to do so? Why do we feel we must do so, and that nothing else is satisfactory? Why can't we accept people as multiple, complex, contradictory, and dynamic–and as maintaining a perpetually residual and indeed usefully mysterious supplementarity to what can be known and of what remains always beyond the reach of the fully knowable?

To make the most of Ian Curtis's legacy, we need to strive to make contemporary connections. Likely only partially consciously he perceived he was confronting long-running and deeply entrenched dimensions of modern to contemporary social existence–these are our concerns every bit as much as, and all the more than, they were his. Neo-liberalism has become much stronger, more powerful, and more pervasive since Ian Curtis's death, when it was first emergent, and many of the worries his work engages are all the more powerfully and pervasively real today (i.e., he may have vaguely anticipated where neo-liberalism was leading but he did not live to directly experience that).

What *today* creates and sustains sharp divisions and brutal alienations among people, what *today* keeps people constrained in their ability to move and experience life at its richest and most fulfilling, what *today* fosters subjective fragmentation and frustrates subjective integration, what *today* makes people feel like they are floundering in a world that is overwhelming and all too often totally out of and totally beyond control, and what *today* makes it difficult to impossible for us all too often genuinely to take care of, to show empathy, and to show solidarity to 'other' people? How are *we* responsible, and indeed complicit, today–with any and or all of that? What kinds of deep anguish, pain, suffering, and other horrors are all too many people experiencing *today* that are too often not adequately acknowledged, let alone seriously addressed? I recommend not continually returning just to recycle the same biographical details–especially since the principals themselves, those who have survived, have long moved beyond that. Even *Control* is a work of fiction deliberately conceived and executed to evoke and capture an atmosphere–a tone and mood–more than anything else. It was made not because we all want and need a fictional look into what the specific individuals Deborah and Ian Curtis were like, but instead because a dark romantically mythical transduction of this source material can communicate something powerful in the present, something transcending particular details of their actual life-experiences.

In past classes I have taught focused on this same nexus (Ian Curtis, Joy Division, and Critical Theory) students have written critical and creative works engaging directly with what they themselves have identified as among the worst 'horrors' of *our* age, attempting to follow Curtis's lead, and attempting to make use of Curtis as a model in so doing. Unfortunately, all too many possibilities for such a project all too readily suggest themselves to us. In the spring of 2019 we specifically addressed the horrific massacre of Muslims, at worship, in mosques, in Christchurch, New Zealand, and all of what, and all of whom, has enabled this to seem in any way legitimate and justifiable to anyone extremely virulent and frighteningly widespread Islamaphobic racism, as well as a great many related forms of brutal 'othering' and 'abjectification' rampant today, across the so-called 'West' (which extends to encompass Australia and New Zealand as well as North America and Western Europe)–and we collectively argued these are exactly the kinds of horrors Ian Curtis felt compelled to confront in his own art. The decimation wrought by COVID-19 and how states, and governments, have mismanaged the response to this pandemic, leading to horrific numbers of deaths, many dying painfully and alone, along with equally terrifying numbers of those who have not died suffering long-term disabilities, even in the course of their 'recoveries', provide yet another current source of prospective connection with the worst horrors human beings perpetrate against each other, the worst extremes of violence and cruelty, as well as the pervasion of insecurity, disconnection, indifference, neglect, complacency, and passive as well as active abuse–institutionally, structurally, and systemically as much as interpersonally. Ian Curtis's and Joy Division's music provides us one useful avenue through which to reflect deeply upon how most usefully to confront all this, and how terrifying it feels to attempt to do so, while at the same time striving to confront its interior as well as exterior impact–in other words, how all of this violence, cruelty, alienation and more besides shapes and constitutes our minds, our psyches, and our internal emotional experiences as we are living within and as part of such a social world; it challenges us to engage with complicity and responsibility, without shirking and without pretending these are problems perpetrated entirely by 'bad others' completely unlike ourselves.

Nine

In this section I will introduce and explain a further series of theoretical concepts that will prove important in order to understand what I am doing, how, and why as I proceed in this book, especially in the chapters subsequent to this introductory one.

Let's begin with "critical," in relation to "critical studies"–including, for example, critical studies in popular culture, critical studies in popular music, critical media studies, and more. *Critical*, here, sum, does *not* mean 'finding fault' or 'putting down' but rather questioning, examining, exploring, inquiring into, scrutinizing, discerning, and, especially, thinking beyond the readily familiar and the superficially apparent. Critical studies engages the "writing" and "reading" of all "texts" of culture (and not just conventional "literary"–or print or verbal–varieties of texts). According to critical studics, we *"read"* whenever we interpret what something "means," and we *"write"* whenever we create something which others must interpret so as to determine what it means. This leads us to approach all products of culture as "texts" insofar as they are written and read, insofar as they are understood as possessing or bearing meaning. "Texts," in this sense, include everything from the seemingly most "profoundly meaningful" to the seemingly most "mundanely meaningless" (as, after all, to be considered insignificant, or of little or no meaning, is to be judged to mean in a particular way as well). Critical studies thus focuses on making sense of "texts" such as films, television shows, music and video productions and performances, paintings and drawings, sculpture and architecture, sports teams and games, trends in clothing and fashion, commercial advertisements, individual dreams and plans, shopping lists and checkout receipts, buildings and rooms, kinds of food and drink, roads and vehicles, manners and gestures, ceremonies and rituals, personalities and personal relationships, and individual actions and specific incidents. Critical studies focuses on making sense of the *meaning* of human products and practices–as well as of the *meaning* of the social relationships humans form in the course of interacting with each other. Critical studies further inquires into the ways meaning often, in fact, changes over time, from one period to another, and varies across space, from one location to another. Likewise, critical studies further inquires into the ways meaning, even at one place and in one time, is often multiple, complex, and contradictory. Critical studies attempts to explain what accounts for meaning–and especially what accounts for the ways it emerges, develops, and changes, as well as for the ways that it is complex and contradictory, in particular as site, and stake, of conflict and struggle among social groups representing different social positions, maintaining different social interests, and striving toward different social ends. A *"text"* is any entity (of any kind, in any form, and in any medium) that people interpret as meaningful–i.e., anything that people "read" as meaningful and anything that people "write" so others can and do "read" it as meaningful. "*Textuality*" refers, in turn, to the operations of meaning in textual form–to how, in short, texts provide means and medium for expression and communication, and for interpretation and understanding, of meaning.

Critical studies works on the basis of critical theories, which I have discussed earlier in this chapter. Yet I want next to explain why working with critical theories, and doing critical studies, is worthwhile. Throughout the everyday lives of each and every one of us, our ability to make sense of the world around us–and to orient ourselves to engage in relation to it on the basis of how we make sense–means that we are continually working with "theories" of one kind or another. At the same time, because our everyday lives also demand we make numerous judgements according to various standards and criteria and that we then proceed according to the judgements we have made, we are also continually thinking and acting in ways which are at least rudimentarily "critical" as well. Nevertheless, in our everyday lives most of us do not all that often reflect upon precisely what theories are guiding and sustaining us, how so, and why so, nor do we frequently examine how and why we think and act critically in the ways we do. Moreover, if asked to produce a rigorous intellectual explanation, precisely accounting for and meticulously justifying the theoretical and critical influences upon and determinants of our everyday ways of thinking, understanding, feeling, believing, interacting, communicating, acting, and behaving, most of us would have a very difficult time.

Because the theories that guide and sustain us and the ways in which we think and act critically in our everyday lives are rarely simply the result of our own uniquely individual creation and rarely a matter simply of our own autonomously free choice–especially when we either are not conscious of their effects upon us or are unable to explain, account for, and justify these in a sustained and rigorous fashion–we are always working according to the influence and the determination of theoretical and critical approaches which are much larger than the space "inside" of our own "heads" or "minds": we are always working according to theoretical and critical approaches which occupy particular places within particular societies and cultures and which are formed as particular products of particular histories and politics.

Working with critical theories, and doing critical studies, enables us not only to learn about the theoretical and critical approaches of what might often at least initially seem like an elite caste of distant and specialized others–specific, and frequently famous, named "theorists" and "critics"–but also to reflect upon how and why all of us work with the kinds of theoretical and critical approaches we do; where these come from and what gives rise to them; where they lead and what follows from them; which such approaches predominate in what areas of everyday life today, in what places within what societies and cultures, with what uses and effects, toward the advancement of what ends and toward the service of what interests; and what alternative approaches are possible, what alternatives are desirable, what alternatives are necessary, and how do we get from here to there.

Proceeding on the basis of this understanding of critical theory, and of critical studies, we can understand and appreciate why social theorist Charles Lemert, in "Introduction–Social Theory: Its Uses and Pleasures" to the anthology he has to date edited in six successive editions, *Social Theory: The Multicultural, Global, and Classic Readings*, contends "Social theory is a basic survival skill" (1) and why my colleague David Shih indicated, when discussing a presentation I was to make for an English 711, Introduction to Critical Thinking, Reading, and Writing class, that I should tell the students "critical theory will save their lives." Critical theories are not simply theories developed by an academic elite; far from it–critical theories, and critical cultural studies enabled by critical theories, enable people to make sense of the conditions of their own, and others' life-experiences, in ways that combat alienation, exploitation, oppression, dehumanization, and ecological destruction. Critical theories, including brought to bear in critical cultural studies, provide people with frameworks and modes of orientation that enable people to reject and oppose the dominant ideological claim that 'the way things are is the way they have to be'. For a great many groups of people, finding means and avenues to resist their own domination and subjugation, as well as their own marginalization and exclusion, along with their own disenchantment and disaffection, is crucial to their bare survival and minimal subsistence, let alone their ability to flourish and prosper. This resistance encompasses resistance to social forces that crush body and spirit.

Even as many groups of people need to develop their own critical theories "organically," within the lived conditions of their existence, without the chance to study and learn from noted critical theorists, the latter's contributions can prove immensely empowering. However, this work can also be most challenging to take on, especially in the beginning, in large part because critical theories break with commonsense (commonsense is often identified by critical theories as highly problematic), in seeking to provide modes of explanation, judgment, and active engagement that don't simply lead to the "naturalization" and "eternalization" of an historically and socially specific status quo. Commonsense ways of making sense are implicated within the reproduction and maintenance of that status quo and need to be contested as a result.

***

Let's turn next to "the intentional fallacy," originating with the American New Critics, who were most widely influential in the late 1940s through the early 1960s. Today, even long past the heyday of New Criticism, acceptance of the intentional fallacy is a matter of broad consensus among critical theories active within English literary and cultural studies as well as within critical media studies and critical studies in popular culture. The intentional fallacy occurs when a reader equates the meaning of a text with what its author intended. Many problems arise from doing so: this effectively ignores the text actually executed and realized, which may have little to do with what the author intended; it is often extremely difficult to know what authors have intended, while often enough they don't know this themselves; and the text can and will be read differently by different readers regardless of what the author intended. The only intention that matters, for New Critics, is the one *realized in the text itself*. Subsequent directions in theory and criticism have rejected New Critics' formalism, and their refusal to consider texts as always meaningful in relation to other texts–and especially contexts, including specific historical, cultural, social, and political as well as supposedly distinctly artistic or aesthetic contexts–yet share New Critics' rejection of the commonsense notion that the meaning of a text is simply equal to its author's intention. So, in other words, the meaning of the lyrics and music of Ian Curtis and Joy Division is by no means simply and entirely equivalent with what they themselves 'intended' these to mean.

A great deal of work in cultural studies, including critical studies in popular music, accepts and works with–and off of–Stuart Hall's famous theory of "encoding" and "decoding" of meaning. Cultural texts, including popular music songs, albums, performances, and even images and iconographies, mean what they do as a result of an interactive process. The creators of these shows encode them to invite and encourage one set of interpretations of what they mean while audiences may or may not accept this invitation and encouragement to decode their meanings in the same way they have been encoded. Preferred or sympathetic decodings decode in line with how the text has been encoded. Negotiated decodings decode partly in line with how the text has been encoded and partially not. Oppositional decodings decode in opposition to how the text has been encoded. Neither encoding nor decoding is simply a matter of deliberate will and intent. Most of the time much of what any of us encode in the messages we send and the texts we create is the product of our cultural positioning and cultural experience, and the same is true most of the time of much of what any of us decode. Codes are socially shared frameworks people draw upon to convey and interpret meaning. These can come in a variety of kinds. For example, in relation to music, including popular music, musicians and audiences approach making sense of the meaning of music in relation to shared and distinct artistic and technical codes related to matters such as texture and structure, pitch and timbre, rhythm and volume; intertextual codes related to matters such as reference and allusion; and ideological codes related to matters such as social norms as well as ways of thinking about and relating to how existing society is–and should be–organized.

Elaborating slightly more precisely, it is worth noting here Hall developed this theory in attempting to make sense of how audiences interpret television, and to account for how and why television does not necessarily serve as a seamlessly non-contradictory means of communicating dominant ideology–even when TV shows appear to explicitly endorse or implicitly align with dominant ideology. Dominant ideologies are themselves often fractured, contradictory, and even incoherent, while these ideologies are usually opposed by other ideologies, or at least by social positionings, and social experiences, that lead social subjects to question, challenge, critique and oppose dominant ideologies. A broad conception of what encoding and decoding can encompass (beyond alignment, or not, with dominant ideology) is useful, especially if we keep in mind that we encode and decode as social subjects, as participants within cultures that shape and constitute–and multiply and complexly determine, even 'overdetermine'–our predominant ways of perceiving, thinking, understanding, feeling, believing, expressing, communicating, acting, and interacting. So working with the concept of encoding and decoding of meaning does not lead us simply to contend the members of Joy Division in, of, and by themselves alone 'chose' to encode their music to mean in one way and that we in, of, and by ourselves alone simply 'choose' whether to decode in line with that encoding, negotiate with it, or oppose it. Ultimately, in both cases, they encode and we decode as social subjects, as participants in culture, working with the codes, the discourses, the texts and contexts with which we are respectively familiar and with which we identify, largely unconsciously, to co-create the meaning of this body of music.

***

Continuing, next, it is important as well to offer an at least preliminary understanding of how I am making sense of 'culture', especially in relation to 'popular culture'.

To begin I will offer a simple way into understanding what 'culture' can be usefully understood to mean, and then complicate–and especially 'thicken'–this explanation. 'Culture' = a particular socially shared way of life and 'culture' refers to everything human beings have created ourselves beyond what nature itself provides us. Beyond the latter definition of 'human culture in general', 'specific cultures' refer to what human beings create and use within specific societies, communities, and groups throughout the course of living their lives as part of these societies, communities, and groups–to the specific socially shared ways of living they carry out and pursue. But what then is a 'society'? A society equals the systematic organization of a totality of relations among a large number of people living in a discrete expanse of space and over a discrete duration of time. Societies include institutions which human beings make use of to give structure to, and to help facilitate, their relations with each other. Cultures, therefore, refer to the specific, practical ways people engage as part of the relations that make up a society, including as part of the institutions of a society. Cultures refer to the ways people live as members of societies–the ways they think, feel, believe, communicate, act, interact, and behave. Within any one society, moreover, many 'cultures' are likely to exist. These cultures correspond to 1.) specific locations within the larger society, 2.) specific relations within the totality of relations that make up the larger society, and 3.) specific institutions within the totality of institutions that structure and facilitate individuals participating in all of these many relations. So, a society is likely to contain as many 'cultures' as it does relations among groups of people, and as it does institutions (including counter-institutions) that structure and facilitate these relations.

As pioneering cultural studies theorist Raymond Williams famously wrote, "culture" is "one of the most complicated words in the English language" (87). Williams discusses multiple historic conceptions of culture, but those maintaining the greatest bearing in relation to the critical studies of popular culture define culture as a particular socially shared way of life, whether corresponding to a particular group of people, a place, or a period, with particular emphasis on the means and media through which people derive, ascribe, express, and communicate meanings. Popular culture has historically been defined widely and diversely as well, but again, within critical studies of popular culture, popular culture is not the opposite of fine, high, or elite culture, nor is it equivalent to folk culture in the sense of opposition to mass culture, nor is it equivalent merely with whatever culture is popular with a great many people. Instead, popular culture represents the site and stake of ongoing conversation and debate, cooperation and contestation, negotiation and consensus, and conflict and struggle over what nexus of discourses and practices form and constitute the particular ways of living, or the particular modes of lived experience, that provide meaning, purpose, identity, and community for a substantial number of people at a particular place and time, as well as concerning what specific meanings, purposes, identities, and communities are derived, ascribed, expressed, and communicated by means of this nexus of discourses and practices.

In order to flesh out the preceding explanation somewhat further and, again, somewhat more rigorously, I will turn to a number of passages from the writings of Stuart Hall, one of the founding figures in the field of cultural studies, whose work with the Centre for Contemporary Cultural Studies at Birmingham University, from 1969-1979 and with the Open University from 1979 through 1997 proved especially widely influential. As Hall indicates, cultural studies, influenced by Richard Hoggart as well as Raymond Williams, came to conceive of culture as "primarily a matter of *meaning*: not meanings as free-floating ideas or as ideals embodied in texts but as part of lived experienced, shaping social practice" (40). In turn, Hall suggests, "To put it metaphorically, 'culture' refers us to the arrangement–the *forms*–assumed by social existence under determinate historical conditions . . . if the term 'social' refers to the *content* of the relationships into which we involuntarily enter in any social formation, then 'culture' refers to the forms which those relationships take" (301). Drawing from a long Marxist tradition, Hall likewise refers to culture as "second nature," that which human beings have created out of and beyond what nature in and of itself provides, while identifying the problem of "ideology" as arising given "the fact that, in the realm of ideas, meaning, value, conceptions, and consciousness, men can 'experience' themselves in ways which do not fully correspond to their real situation" (303). And yet, for Hall, "it is of critical importance to understand that ideologies are not simply the 'false understandings' of individuals; nor can the individual subject be conceptualized as the source of ideology" (315). Instead, "ideology as a *social practice* consists of the 'subject' positioning himself in the specific complex, the objectivated field of discourses and codes which are available to him in language and culture at a particular historical conjuncture" (315). Culture represents, in this sense, a complex field replete with "maps of meaning" and "fragments of ideology" (315) that inflect, reflect, refract, condense, displace, concentrate, disperse, fuse, divide, limit, delimit, constrain, and afford various ways of living. For Hall, "popular culture" exists in continuing tension with "dominant culture" as a complex, contradictory, multifaceted, and dynamic site of "cultural struggle," including "incorporation, distortion, resistance, negotiation, recuperation," and more (356-357). It is a field of myriad at least potentially *multiaccentual* signs, images, codes, discourses, texts, practices, traditions, habits, rituals, and other modes of social engagement in the quest for meaning, purpose, identity, and community–and where, in turn, political hegemony arises, where it is secured, where it is contested, where it is countered, and where it is undone.

In sum, popular culture is a crucial arena for critical studies because of the immense power it exercises in shaping and constituting people's lives, which includes ways of questioning, challenging, critiquing, resisting, opposing, and striving to transform the social and political status quo as well as ways of consenting, conforming, submitting, obeying, trusting, and identifying with the social and political status quo. Interpretation itself represents a commitment toward engagement in this struggle–over the uses, the ends, and the interests cultural activities and cultural productions will facilitate, advance, and serve.

This leads, logically, to what is "interpretation"–or, more precisely, what constitute the aims of interpretation. Lawrence Kramer, in *Interpreting Music* (2011) as well as in *Expression and Truth* (2012) and *The Thought of Music* (2016) offers useful ways of conceiving of what interpretation involves, what it aims to do, especially in relation to music. Kramer supports a conception and practice of hermeneutics, "the art of interpretation," as "open interpretation" that treats the object of an interpretation "more as an event than as a structure and always as the performance of a human subject, not as a fixed form independent of concrete human activity" (2). As Kramer elaborates in considerable depth and detail, music is "the exemplary object of interpretation. Its relative lack of explicit referential force renders transparent both the conditions of possibility for interpretation and the character of interpretation as act and experience" (7). What's more, "we actively impart the expression we understand" and "meaning is the outcome of interpretation. Music both provokes this movement and enacts it" (7). Kramer's conception and practice of interpretation fits well with theories of interpretation advanced by Paul Ricoeur, who likewise proposes a theory and practice of interpretation "as event" (92). At the end of *Interpretation Theory: Discourse and the Surplus of*

Meaning (1976) Ricoeur sums up what he has arrived at in explaining what interpretation involves, what it does, and how and why it is important. Interpretation involves an appropriation of the meaning of a text that is "nothing other than the power of disclosing a world that constitutes the reference of the text," which is in turn "the disclosure of a possible way of looking at things" (92): "I say that interpretation is the process by which disclosure of new modes of being . . . or new forms of life–gives to the subject a new capacity for knowing himself. If the reference of the text is the project of a world, then it is not the reader who primarily projects himself. The reader rather is enlarged by receiving a new mode of being from the text itself" (94). This is not, in other words, simply a subjective imposition of the reader's preceding interests and concerns upon the text but rather an encounter with the text that is sensitive enough to what the text itself can disclose that it "initiates a new self-understanding" (94). So, in sum, interpretation is a process in which the reader and the text engage in an interactive encounter, resulting in the collaborative generation of meaning that is neither equivalent with what the text nor the reader brings to bear prior to or outside of this encounter. Interpretation is sensitive to what the text can make possible–what it can disclose, what it can enact–by situating this in relation to texts and contexts that will enable it to do so. Multiple interpretations are possible, depending on what connections are brought to bear, but these must be supported by what the text itself affords.

***

Next, I turn to "myth," which I have discussed previously, but which I will address here in somewhat further detail. Myths are not simply illusions, falsities, or superstitions. Myths are powerfully socially shared stories that many people identify with, relate to, and depend upon to help them make sense of their lives and the world in which they live. Myths help explain what is, what is desirable, and what is possible–as well as the opposite. Myths are often combined and reinforced by means of rituals, which, again, can and do assume a variety of forms. People live by myths; myths are the stories we tell that give meaning, value, and significance to our lives; and myths can be understood, and made use of, in multiple, and indeed multiply opposing, ways. Myths cannot be easily reduced to a question of whether they are simply "true or false"; people identify with myths as a matter of belief and of faith. A better set of questions to ask, in critically examining a myth, are as follows: for whom, when and where, do people identify with this myth *as if it is true*; what in particular about it do they so identify with and why so; and what are the consequences that follow for how these people live out their lives, as they are influenced and impacted in doing so by their identification with this myth? Cultural myths operate like religions: people readily identify with and follow cultural myths without requiring anything approaching absolute logical proof or incontrovertible scientific evidence of their "truth"; the "truth" people find in cultural myths, just as is the case with religions, is of a fundamentally different order. In sum, as I have previously indicated, I favor contesting problematic myths with counter-myths rather than seeking to de-mythologize and de-mystify, and these counter-myths can be produced through critical intervention within problematic myths to appropriate, resignify, and rearticulate their key constituent elements.

***

80

Finally, I want to briefly discuss "phenomenon" in the sense I am using this word to refer to Ian Curtis and Joy Division as a "cultural phenomenon." Here I am not using "phenomenon" in a classic phenomenological sense as that which appears to a subject within that subject's perceptual consciousness as the immediately perceptible object of that consciousness. Rather I am using "phenomenon" in the sense of that which is remarkable or extraordinary, roughly equivalent to a "sensation." Referring to Ian Curtis and Joy Division as "cultural phenomenon" prompts me to engage with Ian Curtis and Joy Division not simply as a "cultural text" but rather as one that has provided, continues to provide, and promises long further to provide a remarkable, an extraordinary, and even a sensational extent of interest, appeal, attachment, identification, meaning, value, insight, and impact.

Ten

Before concluding this chapter by addressing for whom I am conceiving I am writing and why, as well as what the subsequent chapters will discuss, I next return to autobiography in reflecting on some of my further personal interests in issues of fundamental and ultimate concern; empathy and solidarity; chronic illness, invisible disability, and mental health; understanding people as complex, multiple, contradictory and dynamic, and confronting obstacles to so doing; and anti-fascism.

To begin, issues of fundamental and ultimate concern connect with my emphasis, throughout my teaching, and which I learned to take to heart long preceding teaching, in my own studies, to concentrate on what is fundamentally and ultimately at stake in issues under consideration, whatever the range of texts and topics we are addressing. Likewise, my emphasis on approaching what we do with urgency, in teaching and learning, as if we are concerned with matters that maintain life-and-death consequences, no matter through what an elaborate chain of mediations, between precisely where we are at, and those consequences, has definitely shaped my proclivity to foreground issues of fundamental and ultimate concern. As I perceive it, these kinds of issues are at stake for us, who are advantaged enough not to need immediately to be directly concerned every day with whether we will be able to survive to the next; we are interconnected, interdependent, and we are responsible for as well as complicit with disadvantage. For me, this kind of emphasis responds to a spiritual commitment that is deeply rooted, even if this is not so much a religious form of spirituality, and certainly not a theistic form of spirituality.

When I visited UW-Eau Claire as a finalist for a position as tenure-track assistant professor of English, one of my many meetings, presentations, and events during that visit involved a discussion with then Dean of the College of Arts and Sciences Carl Haywood, in which we both asked questions of each other. I asked Dean Haywood what he considered to be the foremost aim of the work we are doing, and should strive to do, working in the liberal arts and sciences, at UW-Eau Claire and beyond. Dean Haywood responded: 'to stop us from killing each other'. Dean Haywood elaborated at some length concerning all the many ways human beings, worldwide, were responsible for killing and related forms of destruction, and how ominous and tragic this was, while asserting we all bore responsibility to intervene to reverse this course and put a stop to this state of affairs. I recognized what he was addressing, and I agreed; what I am doing as a university professor, and as an engaged citizen and human being, encompasses much more than merely going about the perfunctory tasks most readily identifiable as part and parcel of my job or of daily life.

In this connection I likewise am continually inspired by our UW-Eau Claire mission statement, devised by English Department colleague Professor Emeritus Jack Bushnell, which includes this integral commitment: "We foster in one another creativity, critical insight, empathy, and intellectual courage, the hallmarks of a transformative liberal education and the foundation for active citizenship and lifelong inquiry." All four of these values are crucial and 'fostering in one another' is as well, but the commitment to empathy, in particular, I find especially powerfully compelling. Throughout my teaching as well as throughout my research, scholarship, and creative activity, as well as my institutional, professional, and community service, this commitment to fostering empathy is something I persistently strive to foreground and which I persistently strive to remind myself. As I frequently indicate to students I teach, this mission statement is one we all need to work deliberately, conscientiously, and aggressively in order to realize–to amount to more than words alone, more than empty promises that remain substantively unfulfilled.

Commitment to actively fostering a culture of solidarity, on campus and beyond, is likewise something I consider of preeminent importance, and which inspires my efforts in all the work I do. Throughout my life, from early age, I have recognized strategies and tactics of 'divide and conquer' do enormous damage to groups of people who are already suffering and struggling in far too precarious positions, and are already extremely socially alienated and largely altogether excluded from the heights of social power. My commitment toward active engagement in progressive to radical to socialist politics, from my middle and high school years onward, and even before that by means of my parents raising my consciousness concerning the Black Civil Rights, Black Power, and Anti-Vietnam War movements as well as in the presidential campaign year of 1968, when I can remember canvassing for Eugene McCarthy and later leaning toward supporting Robert Kennedy, has long been inspired by wanting to contribute as best I can toward fostering a genuine, substantive, inclusive culture of solidarity, overcoming divide and conquer as well as alienation and marginalization. For a great many years I was an active, dues-paying member of Solidarity, the US democratic socialist-feminist organization, whose name sums up the heart of what that organization has long proposed socialist politics involves–working in solidarity with and building solidarity among the diversely exploited and oppressed. Within numerous other organizations I have actively participated in and contributed to, on the progressive to radical left, socialist and a-socialist, the same has been the case. Involvement within my local campus faculty and academic staff union, United Faculty and Staff of UW-Eau Claire, AFT Local 6481, as a member of the Executive Council, including as College of Arts and Sciences Representative and Vice-President, along with serving as principal organizer for our Labor Film Series and our Empowerment Through Solidarity Film Series have followed this line of commitment as well. Here, I want to credit UFAS-UWEC President Peter Hart-Brinson for coming up with the phrase 'culture of solidarity' and making it central to our lived mission as a union local on our campus.

The same commitments, to empathy and solidarity, have inspired other notable efforts in which I have engaged: as a founding member, responsible for creating and heading up the initial

Board of Directors, and drafting our mission statement, at WHYS Community Radio–progressive community radio; as executive director for the Eau Claire Progressive Film Festival; as member of the Board of Directors of the American Civil Liberties Union of Wisconsin Chippewa Valley Region Chapter; as a member of the Unitarian Universalist Congregation of Eau Claire, including as a lead presenter, worship associate, and program assistant; as long-time faculty advisor for Progressive Students and Alumni (formerly Progressive Students Association) at UW-Eau Claire, as founding faculty advisor for National Alliance on Mental Illness at UW-Eau Claire, and as faculty advisor for more than fifteen other student organizations at UW-Eau Claire along with contributing to numerous other faculty/staff, college/university, and community committees, organizations, and initiatives; as the founder and principal teacher of a Free University in Syracuse, NY and similar initiatives in Tempe, AZ and Eau Claire, WI; as a member of Marxist collectives as well as diverse LGBT organizations committed to activism and intervention; and much more than makes sense merely to list here.

***

One of my favorite assignments, which I have included in every instance of Introduction to Theory and Criticism I have taught since the Spring 2005 semester, asks my students, as their final examination assignment, to prepare a five minutes' long presentation to share with the rest of the class, at our last meeting of the semester, in which they address the following questions:

1.)   What do you (truly) value? What (really) matters to you? Why?

2.)   Where are you coming from in relation to what you, today, strongly value? How have these values developed and changed over the course of your life to date?

3.)   What do you aspire to be and do in your life ahead? Why is this important–to you? What would you like to accomplish and to contribute, in your life ahead, thinking about this from where you are at here and now? Why is this important–to you?

As I make clear in the assignment, we have been working with these kinds of questions, and toward students thinking about how they might answer these questions for themselves, all semester. I tell the students that they may focus their answers on any one or more of the preceding sets of questions; they do not need address them all. I indicate this assignment, moreover, only asks them to answer (some of) these questions as they are inclined to do so *at present*, recognizing they likely will answer them differently in the future, and likely would have answered them differently in the past. At the same time, and most importantly, I make clear I will not interpret these questions for them, specifying a particular way I want them to answer these questions–or even what I am looking for in how they address them, other than asking them to take an approximate average of five minutes to address these questions, and to do so *honestly and sincerely*. As I elaborate, following the last point, I do mean honestly and sincerely here; one of the conventions of many classrooms, including at the university level, and in many kinds of courses, is to put people in situations where they are virtually always pretending, virtually always playing, virtually always voicing or acting what they have no necessary stake in and what could just as easily be a position that they entirely disagree with and that they're just trying out, or trying on, for aesthetic–or libidinal–effect. In short, I instruct these students they are *not* to 'play the devil's advocate' with this assignment; not only is this ultimately self-protective in a way that runs counter to the aim of the assignment, but also students regularly purporting to do this is a clichèd way of engaging with far too many assignments. It's all too easy for engagement with every course, and every class, to become just another game, just another way of going through the motions, just another place where nothing really important ever is expressed or exchanged–and where we all, always, protect ourselves from ever actually taking the risk of committing ourselves to anything of substance, or anything that entails any kind or degree of risk. That's *not* the aim with this assignment; on the contrary, as I stress with the students, with this assignment we aim for the opposite.

Overwhelmingly, students greatly appreciate this assignment, and frequently become highly emotional in responding to it as well as in sharing what they have come up with, with the rest of the class. They share in often excruciatingly honest ways, while also manifesting a remarkable amount of idealism that many of them are surprised to recognize they do maintain. It helps I have consistently, throughout the semester, demonstrated I believe in, have confidence in, and respect them, for all they can be, as well as where they are at, and for what they have traveled through to get to where they are at.

In order to help the students think about how they will answer these questions with this final examination assignment I share some of how I answer the same. I don't expect them to look to me as a model. I understand, appreciate, and respect these students maintain many considerably different positions, and perspectives, than my own. However, just to give them some spark toward thinking about how they might address this assignment themselves, I share some of my own responses to the same kinds of questions. I do so as well simply to be open, honest, and forthcoming with them, as I strive to be from day one in every class I teach every semester, about whom I am, where I am coming from, and what I am about; I consider it important I do so, and that I be so accountable, especially if I want them to share with me, and each other, what I am asking them to share in this final examination assignment.

To begin I share a statement I composed, titled "What Progressives Believe," as a guiding set of principles–and, especially, values–to enable the activities of multiple organizations I have been involved with locally, from the Eau Claire Progressive Film Festival to WHYS Community Radio to the Progressive Media Network to *Progressive Outpost* (and more):

1. Progressives believe that we are all ultimately deeply interconnected, that the public good should always come before private gain, that we should work together to take care of each other, that we should work together to make a better future for those who come after us, and that we have a responsibility to do so for those who will succeed us.

2. Progressives believe we maintain a responsibility to serve as genuine stewards in relation to our larger natural environment while progressives at the same time respect and value the 'wisdom' of nature as well as all the 'wisdom' of what nature has created and provided.

3. Progressives respect and value the wisdom of genuinely popular, or folk, cultures, subcultures, and their customs and traditions as well as their achievements and contributions; progressives support and defend the right of the oppressed and exploited to fight back against their exploiters and oppressors; and progressives seek to assist the relatively disprivileged and disempowered in raising themselves up through their own efforts.

4. Progressives believe in genuine, substantive, materially concrete expression of fairness and equality for all, and progressives sincerely, actively care for those who are relatively disprivileged and disempowered.

5. Progressives believe in working actively to overcome exploitative and oppressive disparities in social wealth, social privilege, and social power.

6. Progressives believe in the inherent dignity, worth, and natural equality of all people, regardless of race, ethnicity, or nationality.

7. Progressives believe in the inherent dignity, worth, and natural equality of all people, regardless of sex or gender.

8. Progressives believe in the inherent dignity, worth, and natural equality of all people, regardless of sexual orientation.

9. Progressives believe in the inherent dignity, worth, and natural equality of all people, regardless of age or of physical and mental ability.

10. Progressives respect and value the contribution of labor, and of laborers, in producing and reproducing social wealth; progressives reject, oppose, and seek to overcome exploitative and oppressive forms of class difference, and hierarchy, especially that realized through the exploitation of labor, and the private ownership and control of the means, processes, and ends of social wealth; and progressives are ultimately, in essence, anti-capitalist and pro-socialist as well as pro-communist.

11. Progressives believe in social responsibility and accountability–and especially in holding those who exploit, and oppress, as well as those who maintain complicity with exploitation and oppression responsible, and accountable, for this wrong, while progressives simultaneously believe in active civic participation, in citizens taking responsibility for our own government, for governing ourselves, and for making government truly the people's servant and truly serve the people's interest.

12. Progressives believe that genuine community requires that everyone within the community enjoy the freedom to realize their full human potential, and progressives believe that realization of our full human potential as members of a genuine community is in fact only possible for each and every one of us when freedoms can actually be exercised and opportunities are in fact available.

13. Progressives fight against social alienation, and especially against the forces and conditions which generate this alienation, while progressives at the same time reject, oppose, and seek to overcome cynicism, apathy, disengagement, and despair.

14. Progressives reject, oppose, and seek to overcome selfish individualism, and progressives reject, oppose, and seek to overcome the commercial cooptation of human culture and the commoditization of human social relations.

15. Progressives reject, oppose, and seek to overcome reification and compartmentalization in thought and action, and progressives likewise reject, oppose, and seek to overcome desensitization, callous indifference and lack of concern for others, as well as processes of 'othering', and especially 'abjectification', in general.

16. Progressives strongly oppose militarism and imperialism—economic, political, and cultural.

17. Progressives strongly oppose fascism, neo-fascism, proto-fascism, and post-fascism, in all varieties, as well as all other forms of genuine totalitarianism.

18. Progressives commit themselves toward working actively to advance the causes of human emancipation, collective equality, social justice, ecological sustainability, and a peaceful world.

19. Progressives believe that real social progress ultimately requires real social transformation—and not mere social reformation.

20. Progressives believe in the value, and indeed necessity, of forceful, creative, determined, persistent, and even at times relentless engagement in questioning, challenging, critiquing, resisting, rebelling, and revolting versus established power and authority in order to advance progressive ends and serve progressive interests.

As I comment on, in elaborating this list, these are values to which continually to aspire; no one will fully measure up to any of them, not by a long shot, not even in conscientiously aiming to do so. I readily admit I certainly fall short, even way short, again and again, despite by best efforts to aim to live these values. But these values can prove useful in reflecting critically upon where we are at, and upon where we need to go and what we need to do from where we are at. It requires ongoing work, and struggle, to do the best possible to represent these values, in practice, even partially, even limitedly, and even in 'small' ways (ways that, nevertheless, are not necessarily inconsequential). Nothing any individual does by themself to represent these values ultimately matters anywhere near as much as what many people do together, but what individuals do, even all by themselves, can still matter, as a contribution—however 'small'—toward a greater collective effort.

Next, I share that Unitarian Universalists (of which I am one) agree upon the following seven principles:

1. The inherent worth and dignity of every person;

2. Justice, equity and compassion in human relations;

3. Acceptance of one another and encouragement to spiritual growth in our congregations;

4. A free and responsible search for truth and meaning;

5. The right of conscience and the use of the democratic process within our congregations and in society at large;

6. The goal of world community with peace, liberty, and justice for all; and

7. Respect for the interdependent web of all existence of which we are a part.

What's more, I cite, as we frequently say, in our congregation, 'love is the spirit of this church, and service is its law'–i.e., we are committed toward striving to lead our lives guided, everywhere, by love, to foster love throughout human social relations, and to do so at the same time cognizant of a persistent responsibility to serve others, to serve our communities, and to serve the well-being of the world in which we live and which gives us so much. I make clear I recognize my students may well maintain exceedingly different kinds of religious/spiritual convictions, or none at all for that matter, but I suggest this list might nevertheless also be useful just to give them something to think about, to work off of, in trying to identify a short statement of something particularly meaningful and/or valuable, as they see it.

Continuing on to another example of 'what matters to me', I share in recent years I have become deeply concerned about declining political support for the value of public education, and in particular for public higher education. Given the fact the public now only pays for approximately 15 to 20% of the total cost of 'public higher education' in the state of Wisconsin, it is, moreover, questionable it should continue to be referred to as 'public higher education' at all. During my 24 years at UW-Eau Claire, we have faced cut after cut, while the percentage of our budget paid by student tuition and fees versus state funding has dramatically increased. Students today pay significantly more for less. Our total staff on this campus is between 20 to 25% less in size than it was five years ago. We simply cannot do as much as we used to do, and as much as we want to do, for our students. I know I have worn myself out by striving to do more than I could, and have had, however reluctantly, to cut back significantly. Throughout the University of Wisconsin system, major and minor programs (as well as individual courses and other educational experiences) have continually been cut, even substantially. At UW-Superior and UW-Stevens Point local administrations proposed eliminating a sweeping array of major programs, including to a significant extent in the arts, humanities, and social sciences, which required a coalition of a great many people, led by students and alumni, to fight back hard to forestall and reverse. Recently retired UW-System President Ray Cross proposed, shortly before his term ended, a blueprint for the UW-System beyond COVID-19 calling for rewriting mission statements in order to reduce and consolidate course offerings and opportunities for concentrations across the UW-System's regional comprehensive universities, effectively eliminating the 'comprehensive' dimension of their identity as well as our continuing collective commitment to the Wisconsin Idea, according to which the boundaries of the University of Wisconsin will be equal to those of the state of Wisconsin–i.e., every Wisconsin resident will have access to affordable, quality, comprehensive higher education within their region of the state. I worry the trends I have just mentioned are being accompanied, on a much larger, national scale, by a de-valuing of the liberal arts, and especially the humanities and the arts, as areas 'no longer worthy of significant investment'. As I have cited earlier, our mission statement at UW-Eau Claire declares: "We foster in one another creativity, critical insight, empathy and intellectual courage, the hallmarks of a transformative liberal education and the foundation for active citizenship and lifelong inquiry." We can't make any serious contribution toward realizing this mission if we do not take seriously, and maintain genuine respect for, work in the arts and humanities; this has to be a substantial, materially real commitment, and not just lip service. At the same time, the intellectual, ethical, and professional responsibility of professors has, historically, long been to commit ourselves, first and last, fearlessly, to 'the search for truth', whatever this might mean and wherever this might lead, in our particular fields of expertise, regardless of what might be otherwise immediately or widely popular–or practical–and that responsibility is being significantly de-valued as well. I value the kind of work I and my colleagues do, and I certainly admire my courageous junior colleagues, but I think the relative societal value of this kind of work has dropped significantly since I first seriously considered the prospect of pursuing a career as a professor. Submit, conform, and obey–that has too often been what is expected of us all, in all that we do. And that is deeply concerning, on multiple levels. 'The Wisconsin Idea' is, and has been, multifaceted, but one key dimension, from the beginning, has been to welcome, invite, and encourage University of Wisconsin faculty to contribute, on the basis of our expertise, significantly and continuously to social service, community welfare, the public good, and even to local, county, and state governance. Recently, it has too often seemed like this contribution is, on the one hand, not welcome, invited, or encouraged–and, on the other hand, ignored, dismissed, and disparaged. Moreover, I think pursuing a career as a teacher, or as a professor, is admirable, and should be applauded, but I worry the disincentives for doing so have grown all the more huge–and that our state, and our nation, will suffer seriously damaging long-term consequences as a result. It is quite possible in the not too distant future that the prospect of pursuing graduate degrees will be largely unaffordable for people coming from socio-economic backgrounds like mine, and that fewer people will be able and willing to devote the amount of time, energy, effort, care, and indeed money it takes to be a teacher, and especially an effective teacher, on any level. Our state and our nation will suffer severely if this turns out to be the case.

Yet further, as I share with my students, I believe we face dangerous fascist tendencies within our nation today. We addressed this head-on throughout my Spring 2017 English 359 class, Studies in British Literature After 1790–Dystopian Imaginings Since Orwell's *Nineteen Eighty-Four*. For now, however, I will only point to two quick summaries of 'fascist' tendencies that have proven highly influential, which I shared with my English 359 class, right at the start of our work together. In 2003, Lawrence W. Britt published a brief article, in *Free Inquiry*, that rapidly became a meme, identifying 14 characteristics of fascist (and, implicitly also, proto-fascist) societies: 1. Powerful and continuing nationalism; 2. Disdain for the recognition of human rights; 3. Identification of enemies and scapegoats as a unifying cause; 4. Supremacy of the military; 5. Rampant sexism; 6. Controlled mass media; 7. Obsession with national security; 8. Religion and government are interrelated; 9. Corporate power is protected; 10. Labor power is suppressed; 11. Disdain for intellectuals and the arts; 12. Obsession with crime and punishment; 13. Rampant cronyism and corruption; and 14. Fraudulent elections. (For more detail, see: https://www.secularhumanism.org/index.php/articles/2710.) Earlier, in 1995, Umberto Eco identified a similar list of 14 characteristics of fascist societies (including, again, also implicitly, proto-fascist societies) in *The New York Review of Books* (Eco referred to a collective fascist mode, past and present, as 'Ur-Fascism', or 'Eternal Fascism'): 1. The cult of tradition; 2. Rejection of modernism (or the modern) in favor of traditionalism (or tradition); 3. An irrationalist cult of action for action's sake and a concomitant scorn for intellectuals and intellectual culture (especially for careful deliberation prior to and guiding of action); 4. Intolerance for disagreement and suppression of dissent; 5. Fear of and hostility toward diversity (especially along racial lines); 6. Roots in experiences of individual or social frustration, including economic crisis, resulting in feelings of social and political humiliation, or in experience of competition with and pressure from the rising aspirations of historically subject and oppressed social groups; 7. Nationalism, xenophobia, and jingoism; 8. Exaggeration of the privilege, power, and capability (especially, the supposed 'devious capability') of perceived 'enemies'; 9. Aversion to compromise, especially with all those perceived as 'enemies' and a commitment to social life as a state of virtually constant war; 10. Populism that is ultimately mobilized in support of the interests of a narrow economic, social, and political elite; 11. A cult of individual heroes and individual heroism ultimately linked with cults of sacrificial death and killing; 12. Hyper-masculinity (toxic masculinity), patriarchal sexism, heterosexism, cissexism, homophobia, and transphobia; 13. Distrust, disregard, and dismissal concerning the rights of individuals and discrete social groups in favor of those of an amorphous 'mass'; and 14. A persistent reliance on what George Orwell, in *Nineteen Eighty-Four*, famously described as 'Newspeak', a simplistic, irrational, impoverished and illogical discourse functioning as 'the official language' of those in charge, at the heights of power (I've reworked and updated these tenets, in summarizing from the original, which also contains more detail–see: http://www.buildinghumanrights.us/task/multimedia/dox/umberto-eco-on-fascism/). I leave it to my students themselves to decide how relevant these 'warnings' from Britt, and Eco, are to what we face in the US–and worldwide–today. But I myself find them seriously concerning.

Continuing, with yet another illustration of 'what matters to me', I share excerpts I have already included in this chapter concerning my interpretation of what Ian Curtis's artistic mission ultimately concerns itself with, especially in direct connection with matters of empathy and solidarity. I proceed from there to elaborate on some my own struggles with physical and mental health before concluding by adding the following to what I have already elaborated concerning what I most value and what matters most to me. First, I cite the tremendous efforts of all kinds of people, past and present, all over the world, continually working in myriad ways to make the quality of my life possible–and often giving so much, of themselves, to make this happen, even, in most cases, without ever even imagining someone like me, in particular, might be the beneficiary of their efforts. Second I recognize and pay respect to those who have been and continue to be especially close to me (including many who have died)–friends, family, comrades, colleagues, associates, lovers, partners. What I have gained from them, and continually do, every day, is absolutely enormous. Third I simply state the following: Compassion. Humility. Integrity. Passion. Intensity. Creativity. Honesty. Fairness. Responsibility. Fourth, I turn to the fragility of life–and the fragility of health and well-being. Once again I comment on the fact I have faced many serious health issues in my own life and I have learned as a result to treasure every moment of good health as exceedingly precious. At the same time, I add, I won't ever give it up without a fight to the end–life is worth living, is worth fighting for. I have, in particular, faced my share of serious chronic illnesses, invisible disabilities, and mental health challenges, and they have been tough for me (over the course of this last four years especially), but I value life and living–it's great to be alive, and I am deeply grateful to be. Fifth, I pay tribute to the excitement of discovering the new and of growing–changing–as a result of this experience. Sixth, I return to what I identify and describe as my principal interests, hobbies, and passions in my initial introduction of myself: Music. Film. Travel. Reading. Sports. Seventh, I mention Love–especially as I have experienced this for over twenty years with my life-partner, Andrew Craig Swanson. Andy is a fantastic person who is an amazing companion and constant source of support and resilience. I have been tremendously fortunate in my relationship with this wonderful man. And then one ultimate addition: I underscore I love teaching and working with students. I care, sincerely, about the students I work with about–about these people's intellectual growth and development, as well as about their overall well-being. I emphasize I aim to manifest this care in how I engage in teaching and working with students. And I mention recently I was asked to reflect on what kind of legacy I would like to leave. I am unsure if that's a question I myself should answer, as it will be up to others to decide, if I do leave any kind of legacy at all, but I did indicate in response if I am remembered as someone who loved teaching and working with students, and who genuinely cared about students' intellectual growth and development, as well as students' overall well-being, and who made this the center of much of his adult life, I would be extremely proud to leave that as my legacy.

***

I have earlier discussed my experience with epilepsy, along with mentioning struggles with mental health, including anxiety, depression, and even suicidality. Here I want to elaborate on chronic physical health conditions, that amount to substantial albeit invisible disabilities, which have greatly impacted much of my adult life. Ever since I was 31 years old, I have struggled with a serious to severe chronic digestive disorder. Over the course of the many years since, I have undergone every conceivable examination, procedure, test, treatment, and regimen medical doctors, including specialists, have been able to come up with, and ultimately we concluded, over seven years ago, that I am in the best position to do the best possible to attempt to manage and control this condition, recognizing and accepting this will be a constantly, and virtually daily challenge, as this condition metamorphosizes periodically and varies significantly dependent upon a large range of contingent factors. In short, I live with a chronic dysmotility disorder which involves, most painfully, a proclivity for my digestive system to seize up, to spasm and cramp, and to send waves of sharp pain cycling throughout the system. It feels much like the digestive system is attacking itself. Since this condition is extremely difficult to manage and control, while all conventional remedies and regimens are at best limitedly effective, I need to be vigilant, on guard, throughout every day, for signs that an attack is about to develop, or might develop, or has begun to develop, and then to experiment with an ever-evolving array of methods to try to bring this condition back under control. Throughout the 28 years I have lived with this condition I have frequently needed to go about work, and other life activities, as if nothing were happening despite extreme pain and discomfort, while I have often needed to take time away from any work or other life activity, if and when I could, to try to attend to the problem and bring it back under control. Often I have thought about the enormous amount of time and effort I have devoted to just striving to deal with this condition that could have been focused productively elsewhere and otherwise. It took me a long time to feel confident enough to be forthcoming about this condition, and the severity of its impact upon me, because I felt the pressure to pretend to be healthy, and fully able-bodied, as well as the embarrassment, frustration, and uncertainty about how to explain this condition to others in a way that would do justice to it without placing any undue burden upon anyone else, and without seeming to suggest I am incapable of functioning at all. And all of this is compounded by the fact mine is an *invisible* disability. It's most unfortunate that although this condition is somewhat similar in its symptoms to Chron's Disease, Inflammatory Bowel Disease, and Ulcerative Colitis, it is none of these diseases, and even though loosely classifiable as a form of Irritable Bowel Syndrome, that classification, as my doctors themselves have readily admitted, is largely unhelpful as it a highly nebulous category ascribed to a broad array of conditions not otherwise easily identifiable or treatable and it encompasses extreme variations in intensity and severity of diverse symptoms. Unfortunately, my condition has often been serious to severe.

Beyond this digestive condition, I have dealt with a number of other partially disabling conditions, that have tended to emerge and worsen as I have grown older, but none of these have approached the overall impact of my digestive condition. Nevertheless, in sum, for me, 'being healthy' has long been something I have been unable to take for granted, and is in fact often requires exhausting struggle even partially to achieve. I need to work around many of the routines of daily life, and to seek and find accommodation as best I can, so I am sensitized to what life can indeed be like for many other people with other kinds of visible and invisible disabilities. I prefer to conceive of these as impairments, as opposed to disabilities, and to conceive as well of all of us as existing on an able-bodied to disabled-bodied continuum, across which we all can and will move, multiple times and in multiple directions, over the course of our lives—and that if we are fortunate enough to live long enough, all of us are going to become steadily more 'disabled'. Yet, being 'disabled'—or, again, preferably, living with significant physical and/or mental health impairments—does not mean we are less than fully and equally worthwhile, and does not mean we are incapable of impressive achievements and of leading fulfilling lives. At least it *should* not, and as someone who has grown confident with and comfortable forthrightly sharing my experience living with chronic illness, invisible disability, and mental health challenges, I do accept it as my responsibility to advocate for more fair, just, equitable, and inclusive accommodation for people living, and working, with significant physical and/or mental health impairments.

***

Why do I personally find it so crucial to argue people are complex, multiple, contradictory, and dynamic? Already in this chapter I have suggested many reasons why. For example, I have been shy and not shy, even the opposite of shy, all at once. For example, I am gay but I am not a stereotype, and what this gayness means to me and how this interrelates with other dimensions of whom I am and what I am about is by no means the same as with a great many other gay people. For example, I struggle with chronic illness, invisible disability, and mental health challenges, but I can and do lead an active life, replete with many major accomplishments. I can be strong and fast yet also sick and tired. As a teacher I am flexible, patient, relaxed, calm, accommodating, compassionate, informal, and casual yet simultaneously also serious, challenging, and demanding. And throughout my life I continue to grow, to develop, and to change–certainly I am continually learning, especially what I don't know, and often most of all from the people I teach. I could easily elaborate much further, but I will simply add I intensely dislike being reduced to a one-dimensional being, based on quick and especially quickly dismissive judgment that attempts to deposit me within a single closed container category–and I intensely dislike this happening to and with other people as well. As a teacher I *must not* engage in any of that kind of judgmentalism, or I am doing serious harm–and greatly missing out.

In recent semesters I have employed weekly check-ins, online, in which every student in my class shares with me, in confidence, at least once a week something about themselves, where they are coming from and what they are about, as well as how they are doing, with our class and otherwise, along with questions or comments about what we have been dealing with, in our class. I greatly appreciate this opportunity, and I do respond to every post, because it helps me all the further get to know the people I am teaching and what is happening within their lives. It helps me make empathetic connections–which, again, I consider a crucial aim of the work we are doing together, in our classes and at our university. You will struggle to be empathetic if you do not assume other people, just like yourself, are complex, multiple, contradictory, and dynamic. That's why, especially as I've grown and matured as a teacher, I find it easy to work with, relate to, and respect students whose political positions are dramatically different from my own, not to mention students with dramatically different kinds of life-experiences, because I am confident not only can and will I learn from–and with–these people, but also that whom they are, and what they are about, cannot be reduced to simple and obvious lines of difference from me.

So many students I work with at present, and for many years now, have struggled with serious to severe mental health challenges. Many become easily unsettled by disappointments, mistakes, and setbacks; I understand how they feel. I strive to make them feel none of these disappointments, mistakes, or setbacks sums up the totality of whom they are, what they are about, and what they can and will be–i.e., they can find means to persist and to overcome. As someone who knows all too well how crushing anxiety and depression can feel, I also know these experiences at their worst are not the totality of whom I am, have been, and can and will be. Yet I also well know people may be suffering and struggling with extreme pain while nonetheless not obviously showing this, and, insofar as they do, what they show might represent symptoms that can be unfortunately dismissed by others as reflecting these people's essential characters or core personalities when that is by no means the case. A great many of my students worry at the start of semesters about matters such as how posture, facial expressions, gestures, bodily movements, and so on, of theirs, might appear 'strange' and lead to negative judgments, by people like me and fellow students, before they have a chance to explain what is actually going on in these cases; it is sad they fear this as much as they do, and that so many others fear much the same as well.

In sum, the inability to recognize and appreciate people as complex, multiple, contradictory, and dynamic all too often results in dehumanization–it results in treating 'other people' as if they are of inferior worth and if their lives can and should be disposed of with callous indifference or cruel malevolence. I've experienced this in my own life, in those who have attacked me on the account of me being gay, or because of my being a progressive, a leftist, a socialist, and a Marxist, or on account of my experience living with chronic illness, invisible disability, and mental health challenge. I've experienced this in my own life as well even in relation to simply coming from another region of the country, and from a different kind of upbringing. When this has happened, those doing the attacking have not only judged me to be decisively different from themselves–such that we could seemingly draw a clear line separating 'all of what they are like' from 'all of what I am like'–but also judged 'what I am' to be simple, singular, homogeneous, and static. Too often, likewise, I have recognized the same dangerous tendencies in relation to how other people are identified and treated. For example, in my early experience as a teacher, I was appalled on multiple occasions to talk with other, more experienced, senior faculty who dismissed their students as altogether uninterested in and incapable of learning, and suggested I was naively idealistic not to recognize the same. What I did recognize were the damaging consequences of approaching teaching with this mindset–damaging, in particular, to the students not given the chance to achieve what they were in fact capable of achieving. To take another example, students have sometimes complained about other students, seemingly 'totally different' from themselves, as impossible to work with, for widely varying reasons, but almost always, with sufficient effort to try to find a way to do so, the initially reluctant students have succeeded and gained from this experience–including doing so as part of major collaborative projects with people they initially dismissed as impossible to work with. Being a teacher for three and one-half decades has taught me I can't give up on people–I've got to keep struggling to find ways to reach my students and that means engaging with their complexity, multiplicity, contradictoriness, and dynamism for what it is; within that crucible the necessary connections can be found, drawn forth, and made to work. I was fortunate the teachers with whom I worked most closely throughout my undergraduate and graduate studies were people who never gave up believing in what I was capable of achieving, even when I was most definitely ready to do so–in particular, my principal advisors during my PhD years most certainly pushed me, or, as they would prefer to describe it, pressured me, relentlessly, yet they did so because they believed I was capable of meeting the challenge, and ultimately that confidence in me inspired me to keep striving to do so.

***

And now, one more comment, in this section, related to my personal commitment to anti-fascism. For as long as I can remember I have registered the presence of fascistic tendencies in late 20th to early 21st century advanced capitalist society, perceiving fascism as by no means simply a relic of the past, but as an evolving mode of and response to capitalism in crisis that affects far more than the state alone, as it requires the pervasion of forms of consciousness–and unconsciousness–that I identify as 'everyday fascism' and which manifest themselves in how people relate, including in ordinary, everyday, immediately interpersonal ways, with groups of people they perceive and treat as 'other' than them. As a sophomore student in a political science class focused on 'State and Society', we were assigned to write a paper addressing what we perceived were the prospects for a successful

93

socialist revolution in the United States within the foreseeable future. Reflective of what Wesleyan was like at the time, most of the students were strikingly optimistic about this prospect, but I was not, as I argued the opposite was far more likely, and already underway. The professor was so impressed with my paper he embarrassed me by reading aloud from it to the rest of the class, and, while not ready to agree with me, suggested my argument was compelling. This, however, is only one of many experiences I could readily cite as prompting me to worry about recurrent tendencies toward fascism. I have witnessed the hatred people have directly at other people simply on account of those people being gay, lesbian, bisexual, transgender, or gender non-binary–or merely suspected of being the same–with a vehement determination to stamp out and eliminate us, and I have witnessed the same intensity of hatred and the same vehement determination to engage in extermination directed at Black people and other people of color, at Jewish and Muslim people, and at people who have been actively engaged in campaigns for social justice, and social transformation, as progressive and radical organizers and activists. Often enough I have been directly targeted this way myself. In these instances I recognize a frightening refusal to grant us a common humanity, and a conception of us, instead, as subhuman and even as alien and evil. Whenever this hatred can be and has been whipped up to the point where it starts to embed itself within social institutions–or where social institutions increasingly accommodate it, not only harboring but cultivating it–we face incipient fascism at work.

For many years one of my most vivid recurrent dreams involved a fascist uprising, with the dream focused on a fascist takeover of a small Upper Midwest US city, and the consequences that followed as those perceived to be enemies, or prospective enemies, of the new regime, were targeted for punishment and elimination. During the 2006-2007 academic year I worked together with James Boland, on James's senior capstone project at UW-Eau Claire, supported by a student-faculty collaborative research and creative activity grant, to co-write a fictional feature-length screenplay, *Faceless Fascism*, based on my dream and elaborating the scenario my dream suggested. Unfortunately, we were only able to complete the entire rough draft before James graduated, and moved onto other commitments elsewhere, but I cite our collaborative effort here simply to underscore how important a concern anti-fascism has been with me, for a long time. And I have perceived a great many aspects of Donald Trump's presidency as at least 'objectively fascist', while I recognize similar serious concerns in many other countries worldwide as well, including in the UK and elsewhere in Continental Europe, as Liz Fekete, in *Europe's Fault Lines: Racism and The Rise of the Right* (2019), along with a number of others like Fekete, have recently persuasively argued.

Eleven

In conclusion, I am writing this book for readers like the students I have taught at UW-Eau Claire in five classes focused on Ian Curtis, Joy Division, and critical theory. These are upper level undergraduate English and Honors university students, who in most cases have taken some courses offering basic introductions to and overviews of critical theory previously, but in most cases no more than that. These are people who are interested in and receptive to the possibilities a more advanced engagement with critical theory can offer, without approaching embarking on the experience maintaining sharply defined expectations concerning what this will be like. These are people who are, in turn, attracted to these possibilities in relation to work concerned with critical studies in popular culture, and in particular critical studies in popular music. These include people maintaining prior knowledge of and interest in Joy Division–other Joy Division fans–but that kind of knowledge and experience is unnecessary in order to derive benefit from this book, just as has been the case with the students in the aforementioned classes I have taught, less than half of whom maintained any prior knowledge of or interest in Joy Division before we started our work together. At the end of each semester, especially in the last two classes I taught on Ian Curtis, Joy Division, and Critical Theory, I offered students the opportunity to share culminating presentations on individual musicians or musical groups they themselves have found especially meaningful, valuable, and significant in their own lives, explaining how and why this has been the case. Students responded by sharing passionate connections with a diverse array of different popular musicians, and different popular musical styles and genres. If any popular musician or musical group has exercised this kind of profound and passionate impact within your life, and upon whom you are and have come to be, no matter how different from Ian Curtis and Joy Division, then this book is for you, as I invite you to imagine staging a series of similar dialogues between that musician or musical group and various critical theorists and critical theories. In addition, I am writing this book for a readership that includes both people with knowledge and experience as musicians and many others maintaining no such knowledge and experience. This is a book for anyone who loves popular music, who cares to think and talk about 'big issues', who believes in the importance of empathy, and who would like to actively contribute toward the forging of a substantial culture of solidarity–especially by engaging with what popular culture, and in particular popular music, has to offer in that quest. I hope this book will show you that critical theory can be concrete, relevant, and urgent–in sustained dialogue with popular culture and in particular popular music–and that popular culture, in particular popular music, can contribute helpfully in engaging with issues of ultimate and fundamental importance.

This first chapter provides an introduction to and overview of what I am doing in this book, how, and why; establishes and elaborates personal connections with this work; and sets forth my overall argument. I turn next, in chapter two, to develop and deploy a model for listening closely to Joy Division music in the course of a multi-stage analytical description cum synthetic interpretation of three Joy Division songs–"Disorder," "Transmission," and "Twenty Four Hours." I precede specific engagement with these three songs by explaining the paper assignment I used in multiple classes I taught on popular music as cultural studies, which I am in effect assigning to myself, three times, in this second chapter, as well as by summarizing a series of writings on how to make sense of and respond to what we hear, in listening to and thinking about–and feeling–music, especially popular music, from writers whose contributions in this area have proven most influential to me, and from whom I am drawing concepts, methods, and approaches in carefully explaining how the music of Joy Division conveys meaning and exerts impact.

Then, in chapters three through six, I stage a series of encounters, or, in other words, dialogues, between 'Ian Curtis and Joy Division' and specific works of critical theory–all in relation to the same array of questions and issues of ultimate and fundamental concern I introduced in this chapter. My aim in chapters three through six is for each encounter, for each dialogue, to contribute to the production of useful knowledge in relation to that array of questions and issues–to serve, in other words, as an instance of theorization and critique, not simply an 'application' of theory, through critique, from one set of texts 'upon' another. In chapter three we take up Karl Marx's *Economic and Philosophic Manuscripts of 1844*, Èmile Durkheim's *Suicide: a Study in Sociology*, and Sigmund Freud's *Civilization and Its Discontents*. In chapter four Max Weber's *Protestant Ethic and the Spirit of Capitalism*, Louis Althusser's *On the Reproduction of Capitalism: Ideology and Ideological State Apparatuses*, and Michel Foucault's *Discipline and Punish*. In chapter five Aimé Césaire's *Discourse on Colonialism*, Edward Said's *Representations of the Intellectual*, and Trinh T Minh-ha's *Woman, Native, Other: Writing, Postcoloniality, and Feminism*. And in chapter six Robert McRuer's *Crip Theory: Cultural Signs of Queerness and Disability* and *Crip Times: Disability, Globalization, and Resistance*; Ann Cvetkovich's *Depression: A Public Feeling*, and Avery Gordon's *Ghostly Matters: Haunting and the Sociological Imagination*. In these four chapters 'Ian Curtis and Joy Division' will be represented by the following sixteen songs: "Atmosphere," "Atrocity Exhibition," "Autosuggestion," "Colony," "Day of the Lords," "Dead Souls," "Decades," "The Eternal," "Heart and Soul," "Insight," "Isolation," "Love Will Tear Us Apart," "Means to an End," "New Dawn Fades," "Shadowplay," and "She's Lost Control." Finally, chapter seven, provides a conclusion.

Ian Curtis and Joy Division are even more popular and widely respected today than in 1977-1980: new generations of music listeners–and new generations of musicians–repeatedly, ever since the band's end in 1980, discover Ian Curtis and Joy Division, and discover for themselves meaning, value, and significance in Ian Curtis's Joy Division's music. My aim here is to share further ways of doing so, and to encourage more of the same.

Works Cited

24 Hour Party People. Feature-length Fictional Film. Directed by Michael Winterbottom. 2002.

All in the Family. US Television Situation Comedy Show. Developed by Norman Lear and Bud Yorkin. CBS Network. 1971-1979.

Althusser, Louis. *On the Reproduction of Capital: Ideology and Ideological State Apparatuses.* 1971, 1995. G.M. Goshgarian, trans. London: Verso, 2014.

Anderson, Sherwood. *Winesburg, Ohio.* New York: B.W. Huebsch, 1919.

Bhagavad Gita. Hindu Sacred Text. 2nd Century BCE.

The Bible. Jewish and Christian Sacred Text. From the 9th Century BCE.

Bickerdike, Jennifer Otter. *Fandom, Image and Authenticity: Joy Devotion and the Second Lives of Kurt Cobain and Ian Curtis.* Basingstoke: Palgrave MacMillan, 2014.

_____. "Introduction: My Only Friend, Joy Division." *Joy Devotion: The Importance of Ian Curtis and Fan Culture.* London: Headpress, 2016, 12-15.

_____, ed. *Joy Devotion: The Importance of Ian Curtis and Fan Culture.* London: Headpress, 2016.

Bird, Eugene K. *The Loneliest Man in the World: The Inside Story of the 30-Year Imprisonment of Rudolph Hess.* London: Secker & Warburg, 1974.

Boston Women's Health Book Collective. *Our Bodies, Ourselves.* New York: Simon and Schuster, 1973.

The Bob Newhart Show. US Television Situation Comedy Show. Developed by David Davis and Lorenzo Music. CBS. 1972-1978.

Boswell, Matthew. "Post-Punk, Joy Division, *Closer*." *Holocaust Impiety in Literature, Popular Music and Film*. London: Palgrave MacMillan, 2012, 114-123.

Bottà, Giacomo. "Trying to Find a Clue, Trying to Find a Way to Get Out!: The European Imaginary of Joy Division." *Heart & Soul: Critical Writings on Joy Division*. London: Rowan & Littlefield, 2018, 33-45.

Burnet, Graeme Macrae. *His Bloody Project*. Salford: Contraband Books, 2016.

Breyley, Gay Jennifer. "I Hung Around in Your Soundtrack: Affinities with Joy Division among Contemporary Iranian Musicians." *Heart & Soul: Critical Writings on Joy Division*. London: Rowan & Littlefield, 2018, 209-228.

Britt, Lawrence W. "Fascism Anyone?" *Free Inquiry*, Vol. 23 No. 2, 2003. https://secularhumanism.org/2003/03/fascism-anyone/ Accessed 21 August 2020.

The Carol Burnett Show. US Television Sketch Comedy-Variety Show. Bob Banner and Joe Hamilton, Executive Producers. CBS. 1967-1978.

Césaire, Aimé. *Discourse on Colonialism*. 1955. John Pinkham, trans. New York: Monthly Review Press, 1972.

Church, David. "'Welcome to the Atrocity Exhibition': Ian Curtis, Rock Death, and Disability." *Disability Studies Quarterly*, Fall 2006, Volume 26, No. 4. DOI: http://dx.doi.org/10.18061/dsq.v26i4.804

Control. Feature-Length Fictional Film. Directed by Anton Corbijn, 2007.

Coupe, Laurence. *Myth*. 2nd Edition. New Critical Idiom. London: Routledge, 2009.

Creature Features. Miscellaneous US Television Fictional Horror Film Broadcasts, 1960s-1970s.

Crockett, Clayton. "In the Colony with Joy Division." *The Counter-Narratives of Radical Theology and Popular Music: Songs of Fear and Trembling*, edited by Mike Grimshaw. New York: Palgrave MacMillan, 2014, 25-36.

Crosthwaite, Paul. "Trauma and Degeneration: Joy Division and Pop Culture's Imaginative Historicism." *LitPop: Writing and Popular Music*, edited by P. Carroll and A. Hansen. New York: Ashgate, 2014, 125-140.

Curtis, Deborah. "Foreword." Ian Curtis, *So This is Permanence: Joy Division Lyrics and Notebooks*. London: Faber and Faber, 2014, vii-xi.

_____. "An Interview with Deborah Curtis." Jon Savage, 2008. *Disorder & Other Unknown Pleasures*. Tonino Cagnucci, compiler. https://disordertc.wordpress.com/2015/04/09/interview-with-deborah-curtis/ Accessed 21 August 2020.

_____. *Touching From a Distance: Ian Curtis & Joy Division*. London: Faber and Faber, 1995.

Curtis, Ian. *So This is Permanence: Joy Division Lyrics and Notebooks*. Deborah Curtis and Jon Savage, eds. London: Faber and Faber, 2014.

Cvetkovich, Ann. *Depression: a Public Feeling*. Durham: Duke University Press, 2012.

Decision to Drop the Bomb. Feature-Length Documentary Film. Directed by Fred Freed and Len Giovanniti. NBC. 1965.

Devereux, Eoin, Walter Cullen, and David Meagher. "This is the Crisis I Knew Had to Come: Revisiting Ian Curtis's Suicide." *Heart & Soul: Critical Writings on Joy Division*. London: Rowan & Littlefield, 2018, 115-129.

Durkheim, Émile. *Suicide: a Study in Sociology*. 1897. John A. Spaulding and George Simpson, trans. New York: The Free Press, 1951.

Eco, Umberto. "Ur-Fascism." *New York Review of Books*. June 22, 1995. https://www.nybooks.com/articles/1995/06/22/ur-fascism/ Accessed 21 August 2020.

Eliade, Mircea. *The Sacred and the Profane: the Nature of Religion*. 1957. William R. Trask, trans. Orlando: Harcourt, 1959.

Engels, Friedrich. *The Condition of the Working Class in England*. 1845. W.O. Henderson and W. H. Chaloner, trans. Stanford: Stanford University Press, 1958.

Faulkner, William. *The Sound and The Fury*. London: Jonathan Cape and Harrison Smith, 1929.

Fekete, Liz. *Europe's Fault Lines: Racism and The Rise of the Right*. London: Verso, 2019.

Fisher, Mark. *Ghosts of My Life: Writings on Depression, Hauntology and Lost Futures*. Winchester: Zero Books, 2015.

_____. *K-Punk: The Collected and Unpublished Writings of Mark Fisher*. London: Repeater, 2018.

_____. "No Longer the Pleasures: Joy Division." 2005. *Ghosts of My Life: Writings on Depression, Hauntology and Lost Futures*. Winshester: Zero Books, 2015, 50-63.

Fitzgerald, F. Scott. *The Great Gatsby*. New York: Charles Scribners' Sons, 1925.

Foucault, Michel. *Discipline and Punish*. 1975. Alan Sheridan, trans. New York: Pantheon, 1977.

_____. *History of Madness*. Jonathan Murphy and Jean Khalfa, trans. 1961. London: Routledge, 2006.

Fraser, Benjamin and Abby Fuoto. "Manchester, 1976: Documenting the urban nature of Joy Division's musical production." *Punk & Post-Punk*, Vol. 1 No. 2, 2012: 139-154.

Freud, Sigmund. *Civilization and Its Discontents*. 1930. James Strachey, trans. New York: W.W. Norton, 1961.

Goddard, Michael. "Missions of Dead Souls: a Hauntology of the Industrial, Modernism and Esotericism in the Music of Joy Division." *Heart & Soul: Critical Writings on Joy Division*. London: Rowan & Littlefield, 2018, 3-16.

Goldstein, Martin and Will McBride. *The Sex Book*. New York: Herder and Herder, 1971.

Gordon, Avery F. *Ghostly Matters: Haunting and the Sociological Imagination*. Minneapolis: University of Minnesota Press, 1997.

Gorman, Brian. *New Dawn Fades: a Graphic Novel About Joy Division and Manchester*. Glossop: Invisible Six Books, 2018.

Gracyk, Theodor. "Kids're Forming Bands: Making Meaning in Post-Punk." *Punk & Post-Punk*, Vol. 1 No. 1, 2012, 73-85.

Grass, Günter. *The Tin Drum*. 1959. New York: Pantheon, 1962. Ralph Mannheim, trans.

Greenblatt, Stephen. *The Greenblatt Reader*, Michael Payne, ed. Hoboken: Wiley-Blackwell, 2005.

Grimshaw, Mike, ed. *The Counter-Narratives of Radical Theology and Popular Music: Songs of Fear and Trembling.* New York: Palgrave MacMillan, 2014.\

_____. "Transmission in the Colony: On exported Englishness and the secular religion of the axis mundi," *Joy Devotion: The Importance of Ian Curtis and Fan Culture.* London: Headpress, 2016, 17-23.

Hall, Stuart. *Essential Essays, Volume 1: Foundations of Cultural Studies & Identity and Diaspora.* David Morley, ed. Durham: Duke University Press, 2018.

Heartfield, John. *Photomontages of the Nazi Period.* Karl Hanser Verlag, Trans. 1972. New York: Universe Books, 1977.

Hebdige, Dick. *Subculture: the Meaning of Style.* London: Routledge, 1979.

Hirst, Richard V., ed. *We Were Strangers: Stories Inspired by Unknown Pleasures.* Manchester: Cōnfingō, 2019.

Hook, Peter. *Unknown Pleasures: Inside Joy Division.* London: Simon and Schuster, 2012.

Ingram, James. "Factory records and the situationist influence on urban space." *Punk & Post-Punk*, Vol. 5, No. 2, 2016, 163-179.

Josephson, Matthew. *The Robber Barons: The Great American Capitalists, 1861-1901.* New York: Harcourt, Brace and Company, 1934.

Joyce, James. *Dubliners.* London: Grant Richards, 1914.

Joy Division. "Atmosphere." Recorded Musical Song. 1980.

_____. "Atrocity Exhibition." Recorded Musical Song. 1980.

_____. "Autosuggestion." Recorded Musical Song. 1979.

_____. *Closer.* Music LP. 1980.

_____. "Colony." Recorded Musical Song. 1980.

_____. "Day of the Lords." Recorded Musical Song. 1979.

_____. "Dead Souls." Recorded Musical Song. 1980.

_____. "Decades." Recorded Musical Song. 1980.

_____. "Disorder." Recorded Musical Song. 1979.

_____. "The Eternal." Recorded Musical Song. 1980.

_____. "Heart and Soul." Recorded Musical Song. 1980.

_____. "Insight." Recorded Musical Song. 1979.

_____. "Isolation." Recorded Musical Song. 1980.

_____. "Love Will Tear Us Apart." Recorded Musical Song. 1980.

_____. "Means to an End." Recorded Musical Song. 1980.

_____. "New Dawn Fades." Recorded Musical Song. 1979.

_____. "Shadowplay." Recorded Musical Song. 1979.

_____. "She's Lost Control." Recorded Musical Song. 1979.

_____. "Transmission." Recorded Musical Song. 1979.

_____. "Twenty Four Hours." Recorded Musical Song. 1980.

_____. *Unknown Pleasures.* Music LP. 1979.

Joy Division. Feature-Length Documentary Film. Directed by Grant Gee. 2007.

Joy Division Central: https://www.joydiv.org Accessed 21 August 2020.

Joy Division–The Eternal: http://www.enkiri.com/joy/joy_division.html Accessed 21 August 2020.

Joy Division Official: https://www.joydivisionofficial.com/ Accessed 21 August 2020.

Kitching, Philip H. *Understanding Suicide: a Psychobiographical Study of Ian Kevin Curtis*. PhD Dissertation, Nelson Mandela Metropolitan University, 2017.

Kramer, Lawrence. *Expression and Truth: On the Music of Knowledge*. Berkeley: University of California Press, 2012.

_____. *Interpreting Music*. Berkeley: University of California Press, 2011.

_____. *The Thought of Music*. Berkeley: The University of California Press, 2016.

Langhorst, Catherine. "A Northern 'Ode on Melancholy': The Music of Joy Division." *Rock and Romanticism: Post-Punk, Goth, and Metal as Dark Romanticisms*, edited by James Rovira. Cham, Switzerland: Palgrave MacMillan, 2018, 83-100.

Lemert, Charles, ed. *Social Theory: The Multicultural, Global, and Classic Readings*. 6th Edition. Boulder: Westview Press, 2017.

Manchester Art Gallery and the Manchester International Festival. *True Faith 30 June-3 September 2017*. Exhibition Catalog. Manchester: Manchester Art Gallery, 2017.

Maloy, Liam. "'She expressed herself in many different ways': Hypothetical substitutions in Joy Division's 'She's Lost Control'." Essay Originally Submitted for MA in Popular Music Studies at Liverpool University, 2007. 2019: https://tinyurl.com/y4kh5z97 Accessed 21 August 2020.

Marx, Karl. *Economic and Philosphical Manuscripts of 1844 (The Paris Manuscripts)*. 1844. Martin Milligan, trans., 1961. Mineola: Dover Books, 2007.

Marx, Karl and Friedrich Engels. *The Communist Manifesto*. 1848. Samuel Moore, trans. New York: International Publishers, 1948.

The Mary Tyler Moore Show. US Television Situation Comedy Show. Developed by James L. Brooks and Allan Burns. CBS. 1970-1977.

M*A*S*H*. US Television Situation Comedy Show. Developed by Larry Gelbart and Gene Reynolds. CBS. 1972-1983.

McGrath, James. "Closer from a Distance: Auras of Factory Records in Music, Place, Film and Historiography." *Manchester Region History Review*, 2015: 5-31.

McKay, George. *Shakin' All Over: Popular Music and Disability*. Ann Arbor: University of Michigan Press, 2013.

McRuer, Robert. *Crip Theory: Cultural Signs of Queerness and Disability*. New York: New York University Press, 2006.

_____. *Crip Times: Disability, Globalization, and Resistance*. New York: New York University Press, 2018.

Middles, Mick and Lindsay Reade. *Torn Apart: The Life of Ian Curtis*. London: Omnibus, 2009.

Miyares, J Rubén Valdés. "Breaking Joy Division's 'Glass': Reading Song Lyrics as Literature." *Atlantis*, Vol. 38, No. 2, 2016: 161-180.

_____. "Liminoid Joy Division: The Sublime Performance of a Rock Star's Identity." *Building interdisciplinary knowledge. Approaches to English and American studies in Spain*. Esther Álvarez López, Emilia María Durán Almarza and Alicia Menéndez Tarrazo, eds. Oviedo: KRK, 2014, 237-243.

_____. "When Performance Lost Control: Making Rock History Out of Ian Curtis and Joy Division." *Liminalities: a Journal of Performance Studies*. Vol. 9, No. 4, November 2013, 1-13.

Morley, Paul. *Joy Division Piece by Piece: Writing About Joy Division 1977-2007*. London: Plexus, 2008.

Morris, Stephen. *Record Play Pause: Confessions of a Post-Punk Percussionist Volume 1*. London: Constable, 2019.

Naiman, Tiffany. "In a Lonely Place: Illness and the Temporal Exile of Ian Curtis." *Heart & Soul: Critical Writings on Joy Division*. London: Rowan & Littlefield, 2018, 83-97.

Nowlan, Bob and James Boland. *Faceless Fascism*. Unpublished Fictional Feature-Length Film Screenplay. 2006-2007.

Nowlan, Robert Andrew. *Cultural Studies, Queer Theory, Marxism*. PhD Dissertation, Syracuse University, 1993.

Ogg, Alex. "For you, Tommy, the war is never over." *Punk & Post-Punk*, Vol. 2 No. 3, 2013: 281-304.

Oksanen, Atte. "Hollow Spaces of Psyche: Gothic Trance-Formation from Joy Division to Diary of Dreams." *Nostalgia or Perversion? Gothic Rewriting from the 18th Century until the Present Day*. Isabella Van Elferen, ed. Cambridge: Cambridge Scholars Publishing, 2007, 124-136.

Orwell, George. *Nineteen Eighty-Four*. London: Secker & Warburg, 1949.

Otter, Jennifer K. "My Affair with Ian." *The Counter-Narratives of Radical Theology and Popular Music: Songs of Fear and Trembling*, edited by Mike Grimshaw. New York: Palgrave MacMillan, 2014, 17-24.

Parmar, Robin. "Joy Division in Space: the Aesthetics of Estrangement." *Heart & Soul: Critical Writings on Joy Division*. London: Rowan & Littlefield, 2018, 133-153.

Patterson, Molly. *Rebellion: a Novel*. New York: HarperCollins, 2017.

Pomeroy, William. *Boys and Sex*. London: Penguin, 1970.

_____. *Girls and Sex*. London: Penguin, 1970.

Power, Martin J., Eoin Devereux, and Aileen Dillane, eds. *Heart & Soul: Critical Writings on Joy Division*. London: Rowan & Littlefield, 2018.

Quadrophenia. Feature-length Fictional Film. Directed by Franc Roddam. 1979.

Ricoeur, Paul. *Interpretation Theory: Discourse and the Surplus of Meaning*. Fort Worth: TCU Press, 1976.

Rovira, James. "Introduction: Theorizing Rock/Historicizing Romanticism." *Rock and Romanticism: Post-Punk, Goth, and Metal as Dark Romanticisms*. Cham, Switzerland: Palgrave MacMillan, 2018, 1-25.

_____, ed. *Rock and Romanticism: Post-Punk, Goth, and Metal as Dark Romanticisms*. Cham, Switzerland: Palgrave MacMillan, 2018.

Said, Edward. *Representations of the Intellectual*. 1994. New York: Knopf Doubleday/Penguin, 1998.

Savage, Jon. "Introduction." Ian Curtis, *So This is Permanence: Joy Division Lyrics and Notebooks*. Deborah Curtis and Jon Savage, eds. London: Faber and Faber, 2014, xxiii-xxviii.

_____. *This Searing Light, The Sun, and Everything Else: Joy Division–The Oral History*. London: Faber and Faber, 2019.

Sinclair, Upton. *The Jungle*. New York: Doubleday, 1906.

Stewart, Jamie. "New Dawn Fades." *Joy Devotion: The Importance of Ian Curtis and Fan Culture*. London: Headpress, 2016, 32-33.

Strong, Catherine and Alasdair Gray. "'But We Remember When We Were Young': Joy Division and new orders of nostalgia." *La revue des musiques populaires*. Vol, 11, No. 1, 2014: 1-14.

Sumner, Bernard. *Chapter and Verse: New Order, Joy Division and Me*. London: Bantam, 2014.

The Tin Drum. Feature-Length Fictional Film. Directed by Volker Schlöndorff. 1979.

Trinh, T. Minh-ha. *Woman, Nation, Other: Writing, Postcoloniality, and Feminism*. Bloomington: Indiana University Press, 1989.

Tuft, Mia, Berljot Gjelskvik, and Karl O. Nakken. "Ian Curtis: Punk rock, epilepsy, and suicide." *Epilepsy & Behavior*. Vol. 52, 2015: 218-221.

Transmissions: The Definitive Story of Joy Division & New Order. Produced by Cup and Nuzzle. October 2020->. Podcast series.

UW-Eau Claire Mission Statement. https://www.uwec.edu/acadaff/university-mission/ Accessed 21 August 2020.

Waltz, Mitzi and Martin James. "The (re)Marketing of Disability in Pop: Ian Curtis and Joy Division." *Popular Music*. Vol. 28 No. 3, October 2009, Popular Music and Disability Issue, 367-380.

Warsaw. *An Ideal for Living*. Music EP. 1977. Record Album.

Weber, Max. *Protestant Ethic and the Spirit of Capitalism*. 1905. Stephen Kalberg, trans. Oxford: Oxford University Press, 2011.

White, Graham. "The Ians in the Audience: Punk Attitude and the Influence of the Avant-Garde." *Avant-Garde Performance and Material Exchange*. Mike Sell, ed. London: Palgrave MacMillan, 2011, 188-206.

Whittaker, Jason. "The Pornography of Science: Curtis, Ballard and Burroughs." *Joy Devotion: The Importance of Ian Curtis and Fan Culture*. London: Headpress, 2016, 34-40.

Williams, Raymond. *Keywords: a Vocabulary of Culture and Society*. 1976. London: Fontana, 1983.

Chapter Two

One

My aim in this second chapter is to provide an explanation as well as illustration of how to take into account the sounds as well as the words of the lyrics in listening to, describing, analyzing, interpreting, and entering into a dialogue with, or, more precisely and better put, a co-creative encounter with Joy Division songs. I aim to show how to address the sounds and not just the words of the lyrics in conveying meanings and exerting impacts. I will do so with three Joy Division songs–"Disorder," "Transmission," and "Twenty Four Hours"–by showing how the sounds as well as patterns and deployments of sounds that constitute these songs, and not just the words of the lyrics, account for what I hear these songs expressing and communicating to me, and for what I hear these songs inviting and encouraging me to think (about) and feel. I aim to develop interpretations of song meanings and impacts, as well as dialogues and co-creative encounters with each of these songs, by working through a multi-stage close description, analysis, and interpretation of what I hear, and what these songs invite and encourage me to think (about) and feel, as I listen to each of them–repeatedly–over the course of their duration.

I will, by this means, also provide an introductory explanation and illustration of concepts useful for listening to, and hearing, dimensions of musical sounds, and dimensions of patterns in the organization and deployment of musical sounds, that can enable even those readers, like a great many of the students in the eight music as cultural studies classes I have to date taught at UW-Eau Claire. These are intelligent and capable people but not musicians, and they are not trained in, familiar with, or confident using what is commonly identified as 'music theory', but which I identify, more precisely, as 'traditional, standard, Western formalistically analytical music theory in the form of staff notation'.

I proceed by assigning to myself an elaborated version of a paper I have assigned to my students in five of the eight music as cultural studies classes I have taught at UW-Eau Claire. I would have also included the same paper assignment in the other three classes but the need to include more diverse material in those classes within a tight fourteen-weeks-long schedule, as well as to include room for students to share and critique diverse individual and group projects, in process, precluded doing so. Yet I nonetheless diffused the goals of this same assignment throughout the rest of what we did in those three classes as well.

I ask students to select one recording of one song. I ask them to write a careful description as well as develop an overall interpretation of that song. I ask them to do so based on close listening to the song, taking into account the sounds, and pattern and deployment of sounds, over the course of the song's duration, not just the words of the lyrics. I provide students with multiple options for how they might proceed. No student need consider anything close to a 'comprehensive' array of constituent features (if any such 'comprehensive' account would be possible for even an advanced expert). But I do insist students focus on the sounds and and not just the words of the lyrics. I welcome students using their imagination in coming up with words to characterize the sounds they hear.

I aim to show students they can do this kind of work–they can listen closely and carefully to sounds, sound patterns, and sound deployments in popular music songs, including from Joy Division, and they can develop compelling descriptions, analyses, and interpretations from doing so. I aim to make it clear we can *all* refer to the music, and not just the words of the lyrics, and *all* do so with specificity, precision, and concreteness. Students who can identify notes and chords along with keys and modes by name immediately upon hearing these sounding, and who can also sketch what they hear in terms of conventional staff notation, are welcome, valued, and respected, but these kinds of skills are by no means required.

We precede students' work on this assignment with several days of introduction and overview concerning major concepts commonly invoked in speaking and writing about what we hear when we listen to music–such as pitch, timbre, rhythm, loudness, melody, harmony, song form and structure, notes and chords, intervals and scales, keys and modes, consonance and dissonance, instrumentation and relative density of instrumentation, range and register, ornamentation and improvisation, and instrumental and studio effects devices and treatments. As we do so I illustrate concepts by making use of a variety of songs, including but not limited to Joy Division. I stress I want students not to feel intimidated by this terminology, and associated definitions, but rather to draw from it what they can begin to make work for them–in order to enhance their experience of, and their thoughtful appreciation for, what they hear in listening to music, in particular what they hear music inviting and encouraging them to think (about) and feel, in a co-creative encounter with the song, and with the musicians who initially created it. I stress I want students *not* to aim for '*the* correct interpretation and response' that they suspect 'someone else' 'in authority' might 'be looking for' and 'expect of them'. I stress that they should *not* hesitate to emphasize how this music means to and impacts *them*. I encourage students, if this feels right for them, to interpret and respond to 'their song' as enacting a dramatic scenario, perhaps in a dream or nightmare form, perhaps in an experimental and avant-garde manner, or perhaps as a surreal and hyperreal or fantastical and uncanny experience. I also welcome students describing, analyzing, and interpreting 'their song' in synaesthetic and kinaesthetic terms or as eliciting an abstract expressionist and magic realist take. Whatever students come up with, as long as they can demonstrate how they have arrived at this take, by working closely, carefully, and in a thoughtfully appreciative way with the sounds, patterning of sounds, and deployment of sounds over the duration of the song, and not just the words of the lyrics, they will, I stress, do fine with this paper. And students have done so, over and over again. Often students derived striking insight about themselves by means of their work on this assignment.

As I shared in chapter one, I do not conceive of myself as a musician, despite my passion for music, my tremendous respect and appreciation for a profuse number of musicians, and how central music has been for as long as I can recall in signally contributing toward not only making my life worth living but also in helping me make sense of meanings and respond to impacts of everything I experience and encounter throughout the ordinary and extraordinary moments and passages I traverse in the course of living my life. In preparing to teach classes focused on music as cultural studies I always devoted substantial time studying and reviewing traditional, standard, Western formalistically analytical music theory of staff notation, along with other kinds of theoretical writings focused on what to listen to and for, how, and why in attending closely and carefully to music. In teaching these classes I have strived to be as accurate as possible in explaining and illustrating fundamental concepts. But I am no expert in traditional, standard, Western formalistically analytical music theory of staff notation, and I do not claim to be able to identify specific notes and chords, or keys and modes, by name, simply upon hearing these sound, nor to be able to transcribe what I so hear in conventional staff notational forms. I admire people who do so, and can do so, and I by no means suggest this skill, and talent, is anything less than impressive and beneficial. However, I do not think my limitations undermine my ability to derive valuable meanings and impacts from listening closely and carefully, in a thoughtfully appreciative way, to music. Nor do these limitations undermine the viability of what I find listening to and reflecting on music makes me think (about) and feel. I strive to continually learn about musical sounds, musical patterning of sounds, and musical deployment of sounds–as well as about ways and means of creating and sharing musical sounds. I find this learning stimulating and fascinating. But I don't believe writing about music, in a serious way, needs be restricted solely to professionally trained musicians, or solely to those maintaining professional expertise in traditional, standard, Western formalistically analytical music theory of staff notation.

Undoubtedly if early on in my life I had approached playing first the piano, and second the french horn, with more diligence and commitment; or if I had been able to play an instrument I myself would have much preferred to play, like the trumpet or the drums; or if I had grown up at a time and place in which it was common (and widely encouraged) for kids to pick up and learn to play standard rock instruments such as a guitar or bass guitar, to 'Do It Themselves' (this happened just a little too late for me); or if our classes in music education hadn't continually been cut, or at least cut way back, and otherwise marginalized and denigrated as of far lower value than 'reading, writing, and arithmetic', and especially science; or if I had done more, subsequently, than 'mess about' with teaching myself to 'freestyle' at keyboards, synthesizers, guitars, and drums–then I might have become more adept in working with traditional, standard, Western formalistically analytical music theory of staff notation. But that did not happen. Back when and where I grew up, most of us received little encouragement even to sing, or to learn to sing, or to value striving to sing–other than in the casual ways many people sing along with bits and pieces of favorite songs from favorite musicians and favorite albums. Nevertheless, I value what I have learned from immersion, absorption, and concentration in listening to and reflecting upon listening to music throughout my life. This includes devoting 15 to 20 hours each and every week for now 16 years running preparing and dj-ing my weekly Insurgence show for WHYS Community Radio, just as throughout my time as an undergraduate at Wesleyan University I devoted an average of over 40 hours a week working at WESU Campus Radio, overwhelmingly consumed with music. This includes attending thousands of gigs, concerts, festivals, and other musical performances. And this includes spending many years clubbing multiple days a week for hours on end. Through all of these means, as well as by continuing to read and study intellectually serious writing about music, I believe I have gained in my thoughtful appreciation of, as well as, more important, in my thoughtful appreciation *from* listening and responding to music. I expect many readers of this book share these kinds of experiences–and enthusiasms–with me, and, just as with my students, I encourage you to respect your capacities to think, feel, talk, and write seriously, and compellingly, concerning music–no matter how much experience you might have playing musical instruments; composing, recording, and performing as a musician; or working with traditional, standard, Western formalistically analytical music theory of staff notation. My approach to listening, describing, analyzing, interpreting, and entering into a co-creative encounter with musical songs, including sounds, sound patterns, and sound deployments, and not just the words of song lyrics, is suggestive of what a great many people *can* do, who are not professional music experts, while others who maintain those expert skills can add to and build off of what I share here by bringing to bear what they, in their expert capacities, are confident, comfortable, and skilled at, that extends beyond my own, and many of my students' and other readers', limitations.

Two

In chapter one, at eleven successive internals, I explained what I hear, in listening to and reflecting on Joy Division music, in particular in listening to and reflecting on Ian Curtis's vocals, as well as what I have found this invites and encourages me to think (about) and feel. In this chapter I will explain and illustrate how I make these specific connections in describing, analyzing, and interpreting the sounds, patterns of sounds, and deployments of sounds as well as the words of the lyrics in "Disorder," "Transmission," and "Twenty Four Hours." I will now recall these eleven passages from chapter one, which I will eventually bring to bear in describing, analyzing, interpreting, and entering into a co-creative encounter with each of these songs in the last three sections of this chapter.

#1: I interpret Ian Curtis's lyrics and Joy Division's music as all about exploration of and inquiry into *mediations*. Again and again, these songs zero in on the 'in between', on the _distance between_. Always seeking, striving, venturing, pursuing, or hesitating about doing so yet feeling the strong compulsion to do so nonetheless.

#2: Ian Curtis fearlessly explored intensities, extremities, subliminalities, and liminalities that many others never would or could, and his music, while often extremely dark and somber, is never simply that—it is about seeking, struggling, reflecting, examining, and opening one's self up to sensation, perception, emotion, and understanding that presses past familiar layers of protective mediation toward not only intense vulnerability and emptiness but also intense clarity and insight. Joy Division's music fuses the intellectual with the emotional with the spiritual with the somatic—in terms of exploration and questing, in both passionate and dispassionate terms, and in relation to a striving for and imposition of control meeting up with the absolute limits and sheer impossibility of meaningfully striving for and seeking to impose control.

#3: In listening to Joy Division I hear the same freshness, urgency, and intensity that attracted me to punk, yet also something transcending the immediacy and directness of punk, conveying, in contrast, a richly resonant sense of both distance and precision, a controlled fury emanating from a fiercely passionate yet also agonizingly vulnerable exploration of emotional, psychological, physical, and metaphysical extremes.

#4: Joy Division songs, for me, dramatize introspection as fiercely determined and fully committed struggle. What makes this struggle all the more fraught and challenging is it transpires in a mysteriously otherworldly realm where comfortably reassuring borderlines break down. These are borderlines between interior and exterior, subject and object, self and other, protagonist and antagonist, friend and foe, help and hindrance, solidarity and betrayal, complicity and responsibility, hope and despair, health and illness, movement and stasis, past and present, history and myth, the psychological and the sociological, the sacred and the profane, the beautiful and the sublime, the close and the distant, the private and the public, the familiar and the strange, and the living and the dead. Joy Division songs end not with tension resolved, but merely temporarily suspended. The only definite answer they offer us is we need to join this struggle, and seek what we can find, for ourselves.

#5: Inquiring into the music, as art, of Ian Curtis involves inquiring into metaphorical 'darknesses' in human history and society, and in the condition of being human, especially that of the human social being living in the advanced capitalist, (post)modern world. This involves facing, without resorting to self-protective blinders or sentimentalizing illusions, often extraordinarily disturbing incidences of cruelty and violence, as well as of anxiety and alienation. It involves inquiring into intensity and extremity as well as into the complexities of distance and connection in human social relations. It involves inquiring into anxious to traumatic dimensions of the human quest for meaning, purpose, value, satisfaction, fulfilment—and especially love—in this late capitalist, (post)modern world, and it involves inquiring into *inter*relations *between* life and death, between living and dying, between being and nothingness, between self and other, and among past, present, and future. It involves inquiring into surfaces and depths, mysteries and enigmas, complexities and contradictions, and fluidities and variabilities in modes of individual identity, personality, and character. It involves inquiring into what it feels like to struggle and strive for authenticity and integrity, in relation to the pull of ambition, popularity, success, and fame. It also involves, on the flip side, inquiring into effective meanings of compassion, empathy, and solidarity. Inquiring into when and where these qualities are under threat, in danger of collapse, on the verge of eclipse, or altogether absent, we recognize, and appreciate, how indispensable they truly are.

#6: Ian Curtis's art can readily be conceived as an exploration of and inquiry into the following two sets of fundamental questions:
1.   Why do I exist? What is the meaning, value, and purpose of my existence? To what extent can I exercise any influence, and any control, over what this meaning, value, and purpose becomes? How can, and how should, I attempt to do so?
2.   In what ways, and to what extent, am I responsible for others? For the suffering, hardship, and pain others experience? For the violence and cruelty as well as the injustice and unfairness in the world? What can and what should I do about any of this?

#7: Ian Curtis's art can be readily conceived of, as well, as an exploration of and inquiry into the sense and meaning of alienation, isolation, and loneliness; the position and experience of being a stranger, an outsider, and an outcast; vulnerability, entrapment, anxiety, and fear; and the need to connect, especially intimately, along with the simultaneous difficulty of doing so.

#8: Ian Curtis's art makes sense in somewhat more specific terms, as an exploration of the extent to which (and the consequences following from recognition that) the self is an imaginary construct, the subject is simultaneously overwhelmingly unconscious and ineluctably other, desire and anxiety are persistently intrinsically interconnected, the symbolic order and the law of the father are oppressively authoritarian, jouissance is far more terrifying than the common translation as 'enjoyment' can possibly suggest, and intimations and irruptions of the Real are recurrently traumatic.

#9: Ian Curtis's art also makes sense in somewhat more specific terms, as the staging of a dramatic encounter with the shocking resilience and metamorphic resurgence of fascist tendencies, after the end of World War II and the Holocaust, at the heart of ostensibly 'democratic', advanced capitalist, Western society, including in the guises of 'friendly fascism' and 'the fascism of everyday life'. Ian Curtis and his bandmates, in choosing their name, Joy Division, whether consciously, deliberately, intentionally or not, propose fascism lives on after the defeat of Nazi Germany and the liberation of the survivors from the concentration camps–and it lives on, most insidiously, as an integral dimension and recurrent tendency within the very same societies so frequently and routinely celebrating their victory over fascism.

#10: A large part of what makes Ian Curtis especially compelling to me, and seemingly the same to a great many others, is that he was–and remains–a striking combination of the ordinary and extraordinary, he communicates incredibly powerfully through his art yet so much of his art is obsessively focused on the difficulty of communication, and because an empathetic engagement with his life-experience, his artistic accomplishment, and his fierce sense of artistic mission and purpose is richly rewarding–such engagement can help us in efforts to forge a genuinely and indeed systemically caring culture, a culture of compassion, empathy, and solidarity. Curtis's life-story, his life-achievement, and his life-legacy all attest to how important it is to strive to grasp the myriad ways in which we are all far more complex, multiple, contradictory, and dynamic than commonly recognized. Curtis reminds us of how all too many people's critical and creative potential is routinely discouraged, dismissed, and denigrated, and how this in turn leads all too many people all too readily to internalize a powerful tendency to do the same, to themselves.

#11: I perceive, from Ian Curtis, as I listen to his recorded voice, and as I read his written words, while trying to write this book of my own, a tremendous anguish, emanating from a guilty recognition of a persistent uncertainty, hesitation, and doubt, and, when I recognize this in Curtis' voice and words, doing so does aggravate, and accelerate, my own uncertainty, hesitation, and doubt. As a result, at times I feel like I owe a debt of personal responsibility to Ian Curtis, to carry on with what he could not.

Three

Readers might reasonably ask what is the point of undertaking careful listenings, descriptions, analyses, and interpretations if I aim to demonstrate what I have just identified, because it seems I have already decided how these songs mean and what impact they exert before undertaking the series of listenings, descriptions, analyses, and interpretations I will recount in the last three sections of this chapter. Such an exercise might appear an instance of circular reasoning, a kind of rhetorical fallacy, and simply a contrivance to find 'in these songs' what I already 'expect to find'. I will next address and respond to these concerns.

To begin, the interpretations I just elaborated in section two of this chapter represent the cumulative product of over 40 years of frequent, continuous, and persistent listening to and reflecting on the meaning and impact, for me, of the music of Ian Curtis and Joy Division. These accounts of what I hear as I listen to Joy Division, and what this prompts me to think (about) and feel, result from a vast number of specific instances of listening and reflection, at disparate intervals throughout my own life, across a disparate array of times, places, conditions, and circumstances. In particular, what I identify I hear as I listen to Joy Division, and what this prompts me to think (about) and feel, follows closely from concentrated efforts at inquiring into the meaning and impact of this music, in the course of preparing to teach and then teaching five classes focused on Ian Curtis, Joy Division, and Critical Theory. These interpretations follow closely as well from a vast array of reading, research, and note-taking I have done in preparing for and then delivering multiple public presentations on this topic as well as from traveling repeatedly and at length, in and around Manchester and Greater Manchester, pursuing traces of the real and lasting, albeit mediated, achievement, contribution, and influence of Ian Curtis and Joy Division. So these interpretations arise from myriad preceding instances of much the same as what I once more undertake, and explain, in process, in this chapter.

But I want to respond to the concern I raised at the beginning of this chapter section yet further by explaining how and why I find the famous hermeneutic circle not to be vicious but rather a necessary condition of possibility for any kind of valuable interpretation, and, in other words a virtuous, even a victorious circle–or, as many hermeneutics theorists and critics prefer, a necessarily enabling and virtuous, even victorious spiral, series of loops, or series of arcs.

The concept of the hermeneutic circle emanates from recognition that every interpretation we come up with, of every text we interpret, does so on the basis of unconscious as well as conscious assumptions, presuppositions, and prejudgements concerning that same text, that same object of interpretation. We always approach interpretation from a vantage point, a perspective, a position, or a standpoint, of some kind–or from a nexus of vantage points, perspectives, positions, or standpoints. We are neither neutrally disinterested nor are we blank slates. We interpret on the basis of social and historical positioning, prior and other knowledge and experience, and the codes, discourses, and ideologies with which we identify, again unconsciously as well as consciously (and in fact typically much more unconsciously than consciously). What makes this process circular, or spiraling, or involving an ongoing series of loops or arcs, is not simply that in order to interpret the whole we must interpret the parts that comprise the whole and that in order to interpret the parts we must in turn interpret the whole. Rather, conceiving of interpretation as a circular, spiraling, looping, or arcing process makes sense because we approach what we aim to interpret with tentative, tenuous, preliminary, and provisional anticipations, expectations, and hypotheses, that we in turn modify, alter, and transform, as we bring these to bear in directly considering, meeting, and engaging with the object of our interpretation. And then we return once more to interpret this object yet again on the basis of those now modified, altered, and transformed anticipations, expectations, and hypotheses, continuing to move back and forth between text and presupposition, text and expectation, text and anticipation, text and theory, and text and method, as we learn, understand, and are able and willing to explain and understand more, without necessarily concluding we have thoroughly exhausted, or that we could or should ever thoroughly exhaust, what the text can yet mean and what impact the text can yet convey beyond what we have identified and elucidated. All of our interpretations are always partial and limited, reflective of our own insurmountable partiality and limitedness.

If we approach this task, the art of interpretation, as theorists of hermeneutics advise, we do so receptive to new possibilities, to new horizons of possibilities, for making sense of a text's open range of potential meanings and impacts. We do with the aim of allowing the text to surprise and startle us–and to challenge and change us–and to do so, again and again and again. Interpretation is an active encounter between text and reader, a mutually co-creative moment and process. Our interpretations are mediated by whom we are, from where we are coming, according to what we are about, and in relation to where we are heading, including in relation to what we are seeking. Our interpretations are limited yet enabled by our horizons of understanding and by the confluence of these horizons with others we meet and join up with in the process of interpretation, including those the text itself introduces and proposes to us.

Our challenge, as theorists and commentators on hermeneutics often have written, is not 'how to get out of the circle' but rather 'how to enter into it in the right way'. The latter requires self-conscious attention to our vantage points, biases, assumptions, and presuppositions, especially on matters of fundamental or ultimate concern–on matters of principle, value, conviction, and ideal. Entering the circle the right way, what's more, involves openness to the text, to the rich array of possibilities for meanings and impacts the text represents, and it involves allowing the text to unsettle and disturb as well as to endorse and confirm the notions about what, and how, this text might mean and might impact that we bring to bear prior to the act of interpretation. Entering the circle the right way includes allowing ourselves to be astonished and amazed, including about what we come to recognize and understand, sometimes with a sudden and powerful jolt, concerning our own partiality and limitedness and concerning whom we are, from where we are coming, what we are about, where we are headed, and what we are seeking. Hermeneutics involves interpretation that does not simply apply concepts but rather stages encounters, and welcomes new meanings and impacts, including those that shake up prior certainties and established orthodoxies. Interpretation represents an ongoing dialogue between interpreter and text–and with those historical, social, cultural, political, economic, aesthetic, symbolic, and spiritual forces and conditions that are responsible for forming and constituting both us and the text we are interpreting, and which we allow, and we welcome, interpreting us at the same time as we interpret them.

We approach interpretation on the basis of presuppositions, even provisional and preliminary interpretations, but we also remain open to the process of traveling back and forth between presupposition and new or renewed supposition, ready to learn, understand, and explain more and better about ourselves as well as about the texts we interpret as a result of an accumulation of successive encounters with the text. We approach interpretation ready to believe in the possibility that our encounter with the text can become a moment of illumination and revelation, and that we can make flexible use of preconceptions to guide us as we strive to understand what we encounter such that we will be able to recognize, welcome, respond to, and engage with this encounter as an experience of illumination and revelation. We accept 'our own approaches' are always distilled from shared cultural frameworks and horizons as well as shared social positions and experiences. We don't interpret as unique, autonomous, a-historical, a-cultural, a-political, ultra-individual beings but rather as social subjects. We bring frameworks and horizons, and positions and experiences, to bear, and we make use of these as basis, means, opportunity, and enabling condition of possibility for 'our' interpretations while cognizant 'ours' is never strictly 'ours' alone. As we do so, we allow successive interpretations of the same texts to become deeper, larger, richer, and more complex. We proceed, in interpretation, guided by what we are seeking, yet open to finding what we do not anticipate or expect, including what might shake up our preconceptions concerning what we are seeking, and why.

Lawrence Kramer repeatedly counters common criticisms of hermeneutics that reference the ostensible 'viciousness' of the hermeneutic circle. According to Kramer, in *Interpreting Music*, prejudgement is not only inescapable but also essential to any and all acts of *interpretation*. Interpretation cannot escape subjectivity and, as Kramer contends, should not bother to try. On the contrary, interpretation needs to make positive use of subjectivity. Interpretation comprises "a movement from text to discourse" (5), meaning interpretation situates or re-situates a text in an array of interconnections, including interconnections previous interpreters have not registered, or not drawn forth, and one makes use of one's 'subjectivity' as means and vehicle for doing so. As one works with subjectivity in the process of interpretation, this involves "a constantly mutating practice of negotiation between internal perceptions and worldly conditions" and here it is crucial to grasp subjectivity "is private only insofar as it is also public and historically conditioned; it depends on the power of a symbolic order that in principle it continually seeks to evade" (5). This means the interpretation Kramer hails is not "subjective" in the sense of being strictly individual or merely personal. Interpretation emanates from the intersection of historically specific, socially grounded modes of subjectivity and the contingencies of occasion and circumstance by which these modes are activated and modified in the event of interpretation, even as we feel the experience of this event to be intensely, immediately personal. We ourselves are formed and constituted, as social subjects, on the basis of prior explanations, understandings, and appropriations of meanings and impacts, or, in other words, on the basis of prior interpretations–of myriad texts, including of myriad musical texts. For Kramer, the so-called hermeneutic circle refers not only to the inescapable interdependency of prior and emergent understanding but also to the semantic looping by which music absorbs, transforms, and returns the meanings we ascribe to it (8).

All interpretive statements "leap cognitive gaps," while all interpretations reflect back upon the interpreter, but compelling interpretations do not simply appropriate music as a mirror through which the interpreter merely looks at–and listens to–themself in splendid isolation (47). As Kramer explains, "musical subjectivity" itself is something that "arises in a process of address and reply" where "the music speaks and the listener, in hearing, replies" (48). Music is not so much "a succession of forms, styles, or structures" but rather an array of "performative acts" involving a reciprocal address "between historical subjects and the big Other" (48), with the big Other, in terms drawn from psychoanalytic critical theorist Jacques Lacan, referring to society, or the social order, or major dimensions and institutions constitutive of the same, such as language and the law. Subjectivity, in relation to the interpretation of music, Kramer understands "as a socially constructed position made available by the music and occupied to a greater or lesser degree by the listener." Yes, interpretation does emanate from whom the interpreter is, from where the interpreter comes, from what the interpreter is about, and from where the interpreter is heading, including from what the interpreter is seeking. Yet the interpreter is not a monad but rather a dynamic confluence of social connections and experiences and of cultural affiliations and perspectives.

The interpreter needs "to recognize the force of the address" that the music directs toward the listener and, in particular, "what it seems to be asking" (49). But, at the same time, "we can understand what music 'is' only in light of what we want or need it to be" (81), while "Interpretive language about music does not reproduce meaning but actualizes it. The meaning is neither in nor not in the music. Instead it arises from a complex confluence of activities that include listening, performing, remembering, visualizing, imagining, and commenting. The list is not exhaustive" (89). As Kramer explains, 'music *does* things' but it does so as it is engaged by its users, including its users as interpreters, which means the musical work itself can be thought of as equivalent with "the potentiality of its uses" as "The work is not brought into being once and for all, but periodically, through the abundant variety of its repetitions" (245). This means, in other words, a work, even as a recorded piece of music, "is also a performance–a complex 'speech act' that is never finished . . ." (246) and "the mode of being of the work is a state of perpetual beginning" (246), as we renew our encounter and dialogue with the work each time we listen to it closely and reflect on it carefully.

In *Expression and Truth* Kramer posits "music must be described even before it can be heard . . . Apart from such descriptions, whether potential or actual, there is no 'work' of music, no music itself, though there may be musical sounds in abundance" (13). Music "becomes fully perceptible only when I make, that is, perform, a certain kind of description, a persuasive comparison" (14). This implies the inescapability of 'translation into words', of making sense of the meaning and impact of music via language, without perceiving the inescapability of needing to do so as necessarily reductive. Interpretation of music, in language, using words, does not inevitably limit or diminish our ability to explain, understand, and thoughtfully appreciate music but rather enables and enhances this potential. Putting what we hear music inviting and encouraging us to think (about) and feel in words enables and enhances our ability to come to grips with music as meaningful and impactful. As Kramer elaborates, "Music presents no resistance to language that is not already fully formed in language itself" (19). What, readers might well ask, about respecting the fact that music, comprised of sounds, patterns of sounds, and deployments of sounds, is not equivalent with words, or not equivalent with words alone? This means, in the process of describing music, in words, that "The description . . . has the difficult task of opening up interpretive possibilities without predetermining their outcome . . . . Only a description that grants its own approximateness, its own figurative, conjectural, constructive character, can hope to energize the object and bring it rewardingly close . . . it is precisely the semantic gap between interpretation and the object interpreted that is constitutive of meaning. That gap must be preserved, not closed, to speak effectively of the artwork" (19). And yet, despite recommending careful humility on the part of the interpreter, Kramer simultaneously recommends precipitously balancing this same careful humility with imaginative daring, as "the risk of being too 'subjective' in the sense of eccentric, too 'personal'–is a necessary condition of effective description" (19-20). Because "no interpretation can fully represent a piece of music" (20), we can and should proceed forward, in interpretation of specific instances of music, with the aim of contributing usefully to ongoing conversation and debate concerning how to represent this music, in terms of its actual and potential range of meanings and impacts, doing so in words and making use of all the affordances words offer us, while never seeking to close down the conversation and debate, but rather, always, to do precisely the opposite.

Interpretation is inescapable in engaging with music, as even identifying music as expressing and communicating what supposedly cannot be described, explained, interpreted, and understood in words nonetheless involves offering an interpretation, in words. Yet Kramer persistently rejects interpretation of a supposed inherent ineffability of musical meaning: "We hear music *as* something, as expressing something, because there is no other way to keep hearing it . . . . Music is a sensuous form in which meaning is both inchoate and immanent" (27). The motive and drive to interpret just as understandably and entirely justifiably comes from us, from whom and what we are: "The attachment that we may form to a favorite recording may well involve a desire, a fantasy, a pathos or reanimation that comes as much from ourselves as from the source" (63). Nevertheless, as we proceed in interpretation, even prompted by such a source 'from ourselves', it is helpful, Kramer advises, to hear the music itself as expressing "a way of inhabiting a world" that is not simply already directly and entirely equivalent with how we consciously perceive and conceive we (ourselves, already) do so (66). Music, Kramer proposes, condenses, concentrates, and distills *drama* otherwise experienced, especially intensely, in social life (69). Music is able to "preserve, repeat and intensify" encounters with other people as fellow human beings in the form of 'contours of pitches and rhythms' (74) that constitute the distinctive means by which music dramatizes interpersonal and yet broader interactions and encounters. At the same time, however, Kramer simultaneously advises approaching 'music as drama' as involving a dramatic encounter between us, as listeners, including as individual listeners, and the music to which we are listening. As Kramer explains, when we hear a melody what we "understand" is "what we hear it express"; what happens is, in turn, a "perceptual transformation" to, of, and for us: "What do we do in hearing music express something? The answer turns out to be that–we answer. We express something back" (147). In particular, in the case of music, "What expression expresses is not the hidden but the unobserved, or better put, the unremarked" (162). So it is important to begin, in interpreting music, with what is it we hear the music seemingly expressing to us–perhaps what it seems to be posing of, or asking of, or sharing with, or pleading with, or challenging of us. Then we attempt to inquire into what this expression might be 'about'–to situate the expression in a viable field of plausible interconnections. Next we reflect on how we fit into all of this, including on how has the music, in the course of our engagement with it, brought us, ourselves, into this field of interconnections, and what have we brought with us (which might correspond to specific aspects or dimensions of our selfhood or our subjectivity) that the music has helped us recognize and understand, while also potentially altering and transforming this same accompaniment or companion (which again may well be something intrinsic to 'whom we are'), as we ourselves enter the same field.

In *The Thought of Music*, Kramer responds to the question "Should we interpret when we cannot verify?" by firmly declaring "Of course we should" (28). How then do we proceed with this uncertainty and this lack of definitive answers to 'what is the truth of the meaning and impact of that piece of music'? Kramer recommends we commit ourselves to follow Emily Dickinson's famous advice: "Tell all truth but tell it slant—/Success in Circuit lies" (30) which in this connection translates, he suggests, as "We only interpret music, as we only interpret dreams or the past, by interpreting the stories we tell about it. In so doing we do not distance ourselves from what we address, but involve ourselves with it" (31). We offer the partial and limited truths we can offer, honestly and authentically, by bringing the music and what we hear it inviting and encouraging us to think (about) and feel into connections with what we ourselves are able to cite, to develop, to illustrate, to explain, to narrate, and to dramatize, because of whom we are, from where we have come, what we are about, and where we are headed, including what we are seeking.

Kramer, in *The Thought of Music*, addresses the hermeneutic circle by declaring "hermeneutics must always presuppose what it claims to discover" (91). Proceeding further, Kramer argues: "Meaning may or may not turn in a circle, but it *must* pass through the figural density, associative vitality, and ambiguity of language. Interpretations are not ideas; they are discoveries, extended speech acts. They require reading and rereading and always leave behind an unorganized remainder, not just contrary possibilities of understanding but conceptual dark matter: inert, uninterpreted and uninterpretable material, which serves to mark or testify to the interpreter's necessary interposition" (95). Ultimately key, for Kramer, again in line with 'entering the circle in the right way', is sensitivity to the question of "How, in other words, can we address the musical phenomenon, whatever form it takes, not as a sign or an instance, not as the reflection of a cultural context, but as an event?" (95) More than that, Kramer declares, "The condition of possibility of interpretation is the plurality of interpretations. A text (inter alia) that clearly, decisively, and exclusively meant only one thing could not be interpreted at all; its meaning would preempt or supersede any interpretation . . . Every interpretation is the assertion of possibility, no more–but no less" (98-99). Interpretation "requires that we travel along the famous hermeneutic circle, the principle that no understanding can arise that does not depend on prior understanding, but that genuine understanding must do more than merely reproduce prior understanding" (148).

From this point Kramer proclaims, all the more provocatively,

there is, in fact, no hermeneutic circle . . . The circle is the wrong figure . . . Interpretation does not proceed as mutually correcting loop between part and whole, nor does it proceed as the explication of an existential understanding that precedes its articulation in language. These things may occur in the framing of an interpretation but they occur as events, not as founding forms. One might echo Paul Ricoeur and speak of a movement of detour, but the idea of a detour implies a direct path from which the detour is a departure. There is no such path. If there is a detour here there is nothing *but* detour. Perhaps it would be better to speak of ambling, strolling, wandering, *flanerie*. Interpretation takes us right back to the streets of the imaginary city that Wittgenstein took as model for "our language" . . .

The city models imperfect regulation as the root principle of that culture which is never entirely "ours": one knows the city but not in ways that would show up on a map or an aerial view. One just knows one's way around, one's short cuts, scenic routes, back alleys, and so on. One can move through these streets with purpose or just amble along. But space here must also become time, so we need to give this city scene a soundtrack. One is always *in the midst* of the city. One is in place there the way the ear places itself in the midst of simultaneities of polyphony, counterpoint, harmony, texture, layer–all conducing to a movement of attention in many directions, on many levels, at once. No matter the dimension, space or time, one knows the larger vicinity in knowing, roughly, how to go from here to there. (149)

Continuing along this same line of argument, that the hermeneutic circle is ultimately beside the point in musical interpretation, Kramer proclaims "Interpretation is not a matter of testing hypotheses; it does not simplify but complicates; it does not take reconciliation or integration as an elemental goal, though these things may also happen as events . . . The characteristic actions of interpretation are surmise, suggestion, extrapolation, conjecture, speculation, trope, confabulation, narrative, evocation, coaxing, modeling, imagining. To interpret is to think informally. An interpretation devises a vantage point from which to read, see, hear, and speak, from which to perform and devise and reinvent, and it stands or falls on the results–the rewards, the disappointments, the degree to which the inevitable remainder of the unclaimed understanding provokes another round of interpretation" (150). As Kramer contends, adding yet further to his radicalization of conventional responses to and defenses of the classic challenge of how to conceive and approach the hermeneutic circle, when he listens to music "I hear as the subject I am (or were, or wish to be, or am becoming) even if I do so without thinking about it–even if I do so *in order* not to think about it. The music appears to me (flees from me as it comes to me?) as a form of motion, and my mind has to move faster than the music does, just in order to keep up with it. To listen to the music I have to appropriate it even if my goal is to be appropriated by it or, better, to open myself to its otherness" (170).

Avoidance of subjectivity is not only delusory, but any attempt at doing so is debilitating to genuine engagement with and appreciation for what makes music meaningful and impactful–that includes passionately intense identifications with music and continuous appropriation of and from music to put music to work and to be of use to us, in our own lives. We passionately identify with music and continuously appropriate from music in order to matter, to mean, to impact, to explain, to understand, to think, to feel, to believe, to respond, to engage, to act, to interact, to work, to struggle, to fear, to worry, to dream, to hope, to live, to persist, and to endure. As Kramer consistently reminds us, this need not be solipsistic or egocentric identification and appropriation but rather identification and appropriation that deepens, heightens, advances, expands, and enriches our relations with others, and with what might usefully be conceived of as the simultaneous sameness of others along with the ultimately ineluctable otherness within and about ourselves. As Kramer writes, "Music models the social relationships that inform all acts of understanding–and vice versa" (171). What's more, "Music, whatever kind of music one likes . . . is a loosely bounded neighborhood . . . a place where wandering and knowing one's way about are mutually dependent. The combination of those activities is what I call my response to music. In turn, that response offers the opportunity to find a language suitable to account for it, though not, of course . . . to exhaust or supplant it. In this way music offers a model of responsibility modeled in reciprocity rather than guilt or debt." As Kramer concludes,

To take up that responsibility, to tell that story, means using language in any and every way I can, including musically. It means that I must not be afraid to interpret, resignify, and reimagine the music that arrests my attention, that I must feel free to hear meanings there and to speak personally where doing so can help advance understanding. It means that I must not assume that the music must somehow tell me how to think before I think it, or that it can be circumscribed by a determinate and determining context or historical archive. It means that what I say about music should be understood, not as a thesis or hypothesis based on specialized learning, no matter how much learning may go into it, but as part of a continuum of expressive acts through which we, the neighbor and I, negotiate the hazards and pleasures of proximity and distance. (171-172)

Four

In describing, analyzing, and interpreting three Joy Division songs later in this chapter, I will hardly neglect the lyrics, even while recognizing the lyrics certainly do not equate with the totality of the meaning and impact of the music, or even with the totality of the meaning the vocals convey or the impact they exert. Because I am someone who has concentrated working overtly with words virtually my entire life, including as an English major, as an English master's and doctoral student, and as an English faculty member for more than 35 years, frequently concentrating on teaching students about how to read and write, as well as how to make sense of and appreciate words, it should be unsurprising that words do fascinate and compel me, and this certainly includes the words of song lyrics, especially where these words are as abstract and mysterious yet as simultaneously intense and riveting as Ian Curtis's so often are. Yes, from early on as a rock music fan, including especially as a punk music fan, I have often enjoyed and appreciated songs without immediately paying close attention to the precise words of the lyrics, experiencing vocals as sounds, patterns of sounds, and deployments of sounds just like the rest of the instruments contributing to the song, focusing on the pitch, timbre, phrasing, ornamentation, register, volume, delivery, and so on rather than the semantic content of the words a musician or group of musicians are singing. And I continue to listen to music this way. Only if the songs compel me as complexes of sounds, patterns of sounds, and deployments of sounds, including with the vocals contributing just one musical instrument along with multiple others, regardless of what the content of the words might involve, am I subsequently inclined to pay close attention to and attempt to decipher the precise lyrics. But if this music does so compel me, I do then turn to take the lyrics closely into account. So, what I will offer here, in my discussions to come, of "Disorder," "Transmission," and "Twenty Four Hours," I propose, modestly, amounts to enhanced lyrical description, analysis, and interpretation–in other words, description, analysis, and interpretation of lyrics enhanced by paying careful attention to how these words relate to the entire musical setting in which they are situated, as part of a song. As such, I suggest, all the other elements that contribute to making up the music can prove extremely helpful in making sense of the lyrics, of how and why these lyrics might contribute toward conveying the meanings and exerting the impacts the much larger songs do, for people like me, that is for people who find Joy Division music endlessly resonant with possibilities for meaning and impact.

I begin my process of listening, description, analysis, and interpretation of each song, in stage one, by first attending to the instrumentation and density of instrumentation involved, including in relation to standard functional layers for popular (especially rock) music songs and the soundbox.

This stage involves 1) identifying what instruments show up when and where; (2) identifying what specific roles do different instruments seem to play in contributing to the overall song, as well as how do these roles change—if/as they do—over the course of the song; and (3) identifying the density of the instrumentation as well as changes in this density.

Developing and refining the preceding, I then consider what Allan F. Moore, in *Song Means: Analysing and Interpreting Popular Song* identifies as the four standard functional layers of the popular song: 1. The explicit beat layer, which is the base layer in providing the groove (especially involving the drums and drum kit); 2. The functional bass layer, which further helps establish and support the groove; 3. The melodic layer, responsible for primary and often secondary melodic lines, including the tune, which in turn is the primary melodic line, and this often involving vocals, electric guitar, keyboard of some sort, or other solo instruments, and 4. The harmonic fill layer, which fills between bass and treble layers and can encompass a great range of instruments, from rhythm guitars, organs, pianos, saxophone choirs, voices, brass sections, even entire orchestras, while in many forms of popular song the keyboard is key and in rock the guitar is most often key, with "arguably the construction of this layer and the way it is actualized" exerting "the greatest impact on the attribution of style by any naive listener" (20-21). As Moore suggests, key questions to consider at this stage include: 1."Are all the functional layers employed? How are they constituted?"; 2. "Does the instrumentation that makes the functional layers explicit alter during the course of the track?"; 3."Are any instruments involved in more than one dominant layer? With what effect?"; 4. "How is the harmonic fill layer filled out? How dominant is this layer?"; and 5. "Does the way the layers are disposed help define the track's style?" (331).

Continuing from this point, I proceed next to discuss the soundbox. As Moore indicates, "The soundbox provides a way of conceptualizing the *textural space* that a recording inhabits, by enabling us to literally hear recordings taking space" (30). These can be metaphorical or actual. Key here is "location": "Where, within the soundbox, do particular sounds, or sound-complexes appear to be coming from?" (30). The soundbox "is a heuristic model of the way sound-source location works in recordings, acting as a virtual spatial 'enclosure' for the mapping of source" (31). Location can be described in terms of four dimensions: (1) Time, (2) Laterality, (3) Prominence, and (4) Register or Height. Also worthy of note, in particular, is how echo and reverberation tend to complicate and enhance senses of space and of spacial location (31). Among key questions to consider at this stage Moore suggests the following two I find especially fundamental: 1."How is the soundbox disposed throughout the track?" and 2."Does the way the soundbox is inhabited vary during the track's course?"(331).

Moving on, in stage two, I turn next to attend to pitch, loudness, and timbre.

In relation to pitch my focus is simply on general patterns of movement 'up' and 'down' along with 'staying in place'. These can include patterns of movement across sequences of pitches in terms of general direction, notably up, notably down, or largely remaining in place, along with relative size of intervals, as well as compliments and differences in so doing among different sound sources. And it can include durations of a particular overall direction of movement–or of a particular overall maintenance of stasis. But here I focus primarily only on patterns of pitch I hear as most emphatic and significant.

I approach loudness in much the same way as I do pitch, focusing on patterns in terms of relative loudness versus softness, how along with how quickly do these change, when and where do they change, the relative loudness versus softness of various instruments and other sound sources, and when and where this relative loudness versus softness changes, if it does so, along with how so and how quickly. Also, here it can prove useful to note tendencies toward constancy or stasis in terms of volume, including of specific instruments and sound sources as well as overall. But here, as with pitch, I focus primarily only on patterns of loudness I hear as most emphatic and significant.

Next, I take into account what I can concerning timbre. I here attempt to characterize timbres, and timbral changes, focusing on specific instruments and sound sources both as these sound individually and as they sound combined. In discussing the character, quality, or 'color' of the sound, I aim, as useful, to come up with approximations in words for what this sound is like, feeling free to create similes and metaphors for the sound of Ian Curtis's voice, Bernard Sumner's guitar, Peter Hook's bass, Stephen Morris's drums, and Martin Hannett's production. Many different standard, commonplace terms exist to describe familiar timbres of major instruments, including the voice, and I here will feel free to draw upon these as useful while not necessarily limiting myself to the same. Many music scholars usefully recommend describing and discussing timbre in relation to bodily movements, gestures, expressions, and actions of which timbres and especially means of producing timbres are suggestive. Among questions Alan Moore suggests are particularly useful in consideration of timbre are the following: 1. "Do timbres betray, or disguise, their sources?"; 2."How do timbres line up against the oppositions of modified and natural sources?"; 3. "What class of gestures is implied by the timbres?"; and 4. "How do timbres and gestures pair up, and with what effect?" (*Song Means* 331-332).

In stage three, I turn to a first summary review of what I have come up with so far, reflecting on the implications of what I have discovered in working through these stages, including cumulatively, by posing and reflecting on the following three sets of questions:

1. What do I hear the song expressing and communicating to me? How do I hear this song addressing and engaging me–inviting and encouraging me to enter into dialogue, into a co-creative encounter? What kind of subject, in what kinds of conditions and circumstances and from what position and perspective is here addressing and reaching out to me?

2. What are we, together, grappling with? What is it, more specifically, precisely, and even concretely that we, together, are exploring, inquiring into, pursuing, and confronting?

3. How does this venture implicate and challenge me? What does it call forth from me, from whom I am, from where I come, from what I am about, from where I am headed, and from what I am seeking? How–specifically, precisely, and even concretely–can I respond? What simultaneously creatively

118

imaginative and honestly authentic–even, and perhaps especially, raw and sensitive emotionally felt–response can I here give?

After that, in stage four, I attend to matters of rhythm; structure, in particular of the melody; and delivery, in particular of the vocal.

In considering the rhythm of the song, I focus on elements such as meter and tempo, and what instruments are principally responsible for keeping the beat as well as how so. I note changes in rhythm, especially in terms of meter and tempo, if and when they do occur, and discuss what these changes contribute. Among the questions Allan F. Moore, in *Song Means: Analysing and Interpreted Recorded Popular Song*, recommends for consideration at this stage are the following: 1. "What is the track's basic kit pattern, if it has one?"; 2. "Is the beat tight (a strong single beat), loose (perhaps a shuffle) or does it vary? Where?"; and 3. "How do other instruments contribute to the basic groove? Does it vary?"

In considering the structure of the song, especially of the melody, I examine whether it make sense to conceive of the song as organized according to familiar patterns such as verse/chorus/instrumental bridge, or verse plus refrain/instrumental bridge, or verse/chorus/verse/middle eight/chorus, or verse/pre-chorus/chorus/post-chorus, or, as any of the preceding along with additional separate intro and outro sections. But this process of examining structure also encompasses paying attention to the different contributions to the overall felt mood, or perceived message, that specific parts of the song make. I might find it makes more useful sense to describe the structure of the song in terms such as initiation, exposition, complication, confrontation, conflict, climax, resolution, denouement, conclusion–or moving in, moving out, drawing forward, falling backward, closing down, and emptying out. Moore, in *Song Means*, recommends here paying particular attention to how melodic phrases are structured, while also paying attention to how these phrases are structured in relation to other simultaneous specific lines or dimensions of the overall sound, as well as to what extent the song follows a recognizable outline form, or pattern, and whether its sections are decisively distinguishable, bleed into each other, or remain open-ended (332).

Turning to matters of delivery, I am particularly interested in delivery of the vocal, yet I am also interested in how delivery of the vocal relates, or interrelates, with delivery of the other instruments and sound sources. Moore and Remy Martin, in *Rock: The Primary Text–Developing a Musicology of Rock*, suggest key features of the voice to consider include "register and range," "degree of resonance," "the singer's heard attitude to pitch," and "the singer's heard attitude to rhythm" (45). Other useful considerations here include any embellishing or heightening of features employed in the delivery, including by means of studio production methods, along with ways and degrees to which the voice relates to and departs from speech. Issues for consideration here also include the felt attitude of the singer's expression, via the delivery, to the words being sung, to the immediate context in which these are sung encompassing the other instruments and sound sources contributing to the same song, and to the general suggested or implied content or context of what the singer is singing about.

In stage five, I pause again for summary and review, returning once more to the three sets of questions I engaged in stage three:

1. What do I hear the song expressing and communicating to me? How do I hear this song addressing and engaging me–inviting and encouraging me to enter into dialogue, into a co-creative encounter? What kind of subject, in what kinds of conditions and circumstances and from what position and perspective is here addressing and reaching out to me?

2. What are we, together, grappling with? What is it, more specifically, precisely, and even concretely that we, together, are exploring, inquiring into, pursuing, and confronting?

3. How does this venture implicate and challenge me? What does it call forth from me, from whom I am, from where I come, from what I am about, from where I am headed, and from what I am seeking? How–specifically, precisely, and even concretely–can I respond? What simultaneously creatively imaginative and honestly authentic–even, and perhaps especially, raw and sensitive emotionally felt–response can I here give?

Next, in stages six and seven I attend to what Arnie Cox identifies, in *Music and Embodied Cognition: Listening, Moving, Feeling, & Thinking*, as the eight "avenues of musical affect" (176-199). This process involves assessing the following five technical musical components–pitch, duration, timbre, strength, and location–in relation to eight avenues of musical affect–mimetic participation, anticipation, expression, acoustic impact, analysis, associations, exploring taboos, and engaging with (music's) invisibility, intangibility, and ephemerality. Cox suggests exploring these factors in relation to any one or more of the following possibilities: (1) events within a piece of music, events suggested within a piece of music, or events enacted by a piece of music, (2) structures of and within a piece of music, and (3) narratives suggested by or within a piece of music. Cox advises using these factors all flexibly rather than mechanically, which I will most definitely do. The aim of this approach is to arrive at a better understanding of music as a site through which crucial feelings are engaged, and how these contribute to subjectivity. This includes exploration of feelings otherwise socially discouraged, even socially repressed, or with no other ready or sufficient social outlet for their expression, but which, nonetheless, the music suggests must be expressed–and must be engaged. As Cox proposes, "Affective responses to music most commonly involve feeling something without knowing the precise cause, and without having a name for this feeling" (177). In his approach to addressing the eight avenues of musical affect, Cox focuses on what he theorizes as 'nonmimetic (objective)' and 'mimetic (subjective)' aspects of musical affect in the case of each avenue, which roughly translate into what we perceive 'in' the music versus how we respond 'to' the music (or, perhaps, what we perceive the music, or the musician, feeling versus what we feel in response). Cox defines 'affect' as including "everything that might be described in terms of *feeling*" (177) while "*Musical affect* includes what one feels in performing and in responding to musical stimuli" (177).

It is worth noting well here, in connection with that last quote, that according to Cox, as he argues throughout *Music & Embodied Cognition*, we all always engage with music by way of unconscious as well as conscious imitation, including in indirect and mediated ways, and therefore are always co-performing when we listen to music. Cox proposes this imitation takes place in two general forms. First, "Mimetic motor action (MMA) includes any action performed in imitation of any other person, animal, or inanimate entity or event . . . These actions include limb movements, vocalizations, facial expressions, and poses" (38). Even more prosaically, this can, for example, include humming, tapping one's feet, or clapping one's hands as one listens to music as well as dancing or practicing 'air guitar' as one does so. Second, ""Mimetic motor imagery (MMI) includes brain activity related to such imitative actions, whether or not the actions are actually performed" (38). As the phrase "Mimetic motor imagery" immediately suggests, this includes experiencing conscious, preconscious, subconscious, and unconscious mental images of the actions involved in producing musical sounds, as well as of us, ourselves, imitating these actions.

In stage six, I consider Cox's first four avenues of musical affect: mimetic participation, anticipation, expression, and acoustic impact.

Mimetic participation includes "(1) a sense of effort/ease in the exertion of force, (2) the duration of the exertion, and (3) the complexity of an action or series of actions. (4) Evaluation of the success or failure with respect to the purpose of the exertion(s) is then an additional source of affect. Communal actions, as in the example of ensemble playing, can then add (5) the feeling of mimetically participating with others" (Cox 178). This avenue references "An ordinary part of music listening: physically empathizing with what performers do, automatically and without awareness" (179). In listening we do so, Cox suggests, with three 'partners': performers, 'the music', and other listeners. Cox recommends here focusing on attenuation and non-attenuation of mimetic participation, with the latter involving "the feeling of vicarious exertion and effort, joining in, overtly or covertly" (198).

Anticipation is often unconscious and even automatic and more or less continuous (181) and this includes anticipation of what we will mimetically do as listeners (181). Cox suggests, in terms of nonmimetic (objective) aspects of this avenue of musical affect, taking into account anticipation of "what will happen objectively," such as experienced in the form of "desire (and) dread," which can be objectively negative but "aesthetically positive," along with "successful prediction," which can be again objectively "positive" but experienced as "possibly disappointing" (198). Mimetic (subjective) anticipation, Cox suggests, includes "anticipation of what we will vicariously do" and this in turn involves an 'amplification' of "all nonmimetic (objective) features" of anticipation (198).

Expression as an avenue of musical affect follows, Cox explains, because, as listeners "(1) we simulate the observed behavior or apparent behavior," and "(2) we thereby experience an affective state that, based on our own prior experience, normally correlates with this behavior" (183). Who is it that we hear expressing 'in' or 'through' or 'by means of' the music to which we are listening? Cox allows for multiple possibilities–including multiple imagined personae, the listener themself, the actual composer and performer, and 'the music itself'. Cox identifies nonmimetic (objective) expression with "expression as heard," "the *sound* of various emotional states," as communicated from someone or something else to us, whereas he identifies mimetic (subjective) expression to be "expression as vicariously performed," "the *feeling* of expressing oneself," what we experience and feel we are expressing as we listen (198).

Acoustic impact encompasses "the way sounds 'come at us' or seem to come at us, and enter us" (185). Here the effect in terms of timbre is experienced in terms of "degree of focus" (i.e., concentration as opposed to diffusion) whereas the effect in terms of strength correlates with attack, sustain, and decay while location refers to perceived "proximity" within an imagined 'illusory space' (186-187). Cox identifies nonmimetic (objective) acoustic impact with "Acoustic impact as received," "how sounds come at us and affect us" (185) whereas he identifies mimetic (subjective) acoustic impact with acoustic impact "as vicariously performed," as exerting a "vicarious impact upon others" (198).

In stage seven, I consider Cox's fifth through eighth avenues of musical affect: implicit and explicit analysis, associations, exploring taboos, and invisibility, intangibility, and ephemerality.

Implicit and explicit analysis concerns immediate 'contexts' with which we associate what we hear and feel. Cox suggests this involves analysis at the level of asking and answering questions such as *What is that? What's going to happen next?* and *How does that/this work?*" (187). Cox also suggests analysis here has to do with wanting and seeking to know, and with finding or not finding that which we want and seek to know, as well as feelings we experience in the course of such efforts, while also encompassing the possibility of being "able to 'survive' and even enjoy innocence and confusion without harm" (188). Cox suggests, likewise, but in the opposite direction from the last, analysis also involves perception or anticipation of threats and even reasons for panic (188). In terms of nonmimetic (objective) aspects of analysis under consideration, Cox identifies, for example, experiences of "reward for success" "but possible boredom" and "price of confusion" "but aesthetic pleasure of survival" (198). In terms of mimetic (subjective) aspects, Cox indicates this "always includes analysis of what we vicariously do; the *mere exposure effect* and success/failure go hand-in-hand with musical engagement" (198). Once again, we are attuned here to what kinds of analysis we perceive the music, or the musician, or the musician as persona, engaging in, as well as what kinds of analysis we find the music, musician, or musician as persona compelling us to do.

Associations, Cox proposes, are cultural associations, as the song triggers us to think about and feel outwards and in relation to other horizons of knowledge and experience beyond those explicitly denoted in the song itself. Cox suggests this can include intertextual as well other important kinds of contextual resonances and connections. For example Cox discusses how we culturally conventionally experience sadness, as we hear this within, through, and by means of music–via means such as low pitch, narrow melodic contour, and less distinct articulation, and, as Cox suggests, following his continuous preeminent emphasis on music in relation to embodied cognition, always involving both mimetic motor action and mimetic motor imagery, we 'subvocalize' and 'enact an imitative expression of sadness' even if we do not feel sad otherwise (191). In terms of nonmimetic (objective) aspects of this avenue of musical affect, Cox cites "objective cultural and personal associations" whereas in terms of mimetic (subjective) aspects of this avenue of musical affect, Cox reminds us "associations are always grounded in, and in many cases begin with, mimetic engagement" (198). What the latter suggests is our unconscious as well as conscious mimetic engagement with what we hear in listening to music brings us into a simultaneous engagement, ourselves, with how we experience the same, or similar, or linked kinds of cultural and personal associations that we hear the musician, the music, or the musician as persona indirectly as well directly experiencing and referencing.

In exploring taboos, it is important, Cox writes, to start on the basis of a recognition that "The arts offer ways of exploring various taboos in a normally safe environment" and we can derive "a sense of empowerment" resulting from "'surviving' these artificially negative experiences"–which include being scared, sad, or taking on the subjectivity of a villain (192). Cox here usefully discusses what he identifies as an openness to "aestheticized vulnerability," including to musical means of prompting "chills" that "are a symptom of having made oneself receptively vulnerable" (194). As Cox suggests, sudden changes in musical properties, along lines of pitch, duration, timbre, strength, and location, particularly in terms of strength, represent one especially potent means of prompting chills (193). When we do experience chills within, through, or by means of music we feel these much akin to how we would do in any other encounter with 'that which chills'. As Cox declares, "The chance to make oneself receptively vulnerable to one's environment and to explore and aestheticize the normally taboo experiences of fear and sadness" is a significant avenue of musical affect (195). Through the arts, including music, we can identify, experience, and feel much that would be too threatening or disturbing otherwise–we can enjoy surviving and overcoming or even persisting through and enduring experiences that we would otherwise altogether avoid, fearing these experiences would undo us. We can also feel, through immersion in the arts, including music, as if we are transgressing boundaries, while this needs not even be fully conscious (192) and we can make ourselves open, receptive, and vulnerable in myriad possible ways we, again, would otherwise be reluctant or hesitant to do. Cox suggests nonmimetic (objective) aspects of this avenue of musical affect include "enjoying taboo *sounds*" and "enjoying allowing oneself to be invaded by musical 'spirit'" (198) while mimetic (subjective) aspects of this avenue of musical affect include "enjoying taboo *embodiments* that result from mimetic participation (doing/being something taboo)" (198). The former could, for example, involve experiencing an aesthetic pleasure from immersing ourselves within and identifying with sounds suggestive of sadness and pain while the latter could, for example, involve allowing ourselves experience immense fragility, uncertainty, and desperation–even a shattering of our sense of ourselves as stable selves–that we would otherwise most often retreat from opening ourselves up to, outside of what music, and other arts, make possible for us.

In confronting the invisibility, intangibility, and ephemerality of musical sounds, we also confront matters of invisibility, intangibility, and ephemerality, more broadly, including in terms of haunting experiences of spectral entities and relations neither clearly present nor absent. Central here, once again, is engagement with "aestheticized fear"–with "fear of something we cannot see or touch" (195)–and working this through and working this out, at least in imaginary or symbolic form. Also, we can derive satisfaction from engaging with what is invisible, intangible, and ephemeral via musical means, that once again provide an opportunity to take on what we might otherwise experience as too overwhelming (197). Cox suggests the nonmimetic (objective) aspects of this avenue of musical affect include "experiencing the disempowerment of the eye and the hand and the resulting vulnerability" that emerges when that does take place while the mimetic (subjective) aspects of this avenue of musical affect include "the feeling of being an invisible and intangible entity, moving as music 'moves'" (198). So, in the former case, we experience the limits, but also the powers, of what is invisible, intangible, and ephemeral performing for, addressing, and otherwise engaging with us, while in the latter case, we experience ourselves as becoming invisible, intangible, and ephemeral, or we recognize and reflect on ways in which we always already are, have been, and will be invisible, intangible, and ephemeral.

In stage eight, I once more engage in a summary review of what I have come up, throughout the entire preceding process, reflecting on the implications of what I have discovered, including cumulatively, by exploring the following three questions:

1. What have these features begun to suggest to me, what have they invited and encouraged me to think (about) and feel, as well as to imagine and recollect?

2. How do I hear these features and their accumulation and development beginning to address and position me?

3. What do I hear these features seeking from me as my response and reply?

Finally, in stage nine, I consider in what ways the descriptions, analyses, and interpretations I have just developed, or, better put, have just been developing, in process, through stages one through eight, resonate with and complicate the eleven interpretations of what I hear in Joy Division music, and what this makes me think (about) and feel, that I introduced in chapter one and then recalled in section two of this chapter.

In practice it often proves useful to mix up these stages, and to extract elements from the stages as I have just described them and recombine these in different ways. Likewise, as I have advised my students in the assignment upon which this process is based, it is often the case that only a select number of elements of the musical sound stand out, or that some seem much more useful than others to concentrate on in attempting to account for meanings and impacts we experience. In addition, writing that follows from a multi-stage process of repeated close listening, note taking, and careful reflection does not simply replicate this process. The writing, in other words, follows a logic that fits with how best to convey where this process has brought me rather than methodically recounting it.

It is readily possible to approach each of the three songs I am addressing in this chapter from many viable and compelling directions, while taking into account numerous noteworthy features of the musical sound. I need to be selective, while I explore a range of takes on my way to arriving at what seems like a usefully distilled focus for written discussion of each song. Even though this process culminates with an interpretation, it does so by in fact arriving at multiple interpretations. I am deliberately leaving these interpretations open-ended, while calling attention to their partiality and limitedness. These interpretations are products not only of a specific time and place and of my social background, experience, and positioning as well as my historical and cultural situatedness but also of ongoing dialogues I have engaged in, with this music, and with previous interpretations I have consciously and unconsciously developed of these same songs, over the course of 40 years of listening to them at multiple different times and places as well as in multiple different moments and through multiple different passages in my life-experience. As a further caveat, in my own experience of Joy Division music I most often relate to this music as a body of work that surpasses boundaries demarcating single songs, taken by themselves alone, as discretely separate entities. In other words, I most often experience these songs in terms of their location and articulation across not only specific albums but also the entire repertoire of songs Joy Division created over the course of the band's existence.

Five

Early on in classes I have taught focused on Ian Curtis, Joy Division, and critical theory, I have aimed to help students begin to come to grips with connections and distinctions between punk and post-punk music, as well as provide them with an overview and introduction to distinctive features of the musical sound of Joy Division. In this section of this chapter I will draw upon that work while also introducing an overview of and introduction to some distinctive features of Ian Curtis's vocalization as well, and then proceed to pinpoint key comments from a variety of sources I have found especially useful myself in describing, analyzing, and interpreting the musical sound of Joy Division, including Ian Curtis's vocalization of his lyrics.

Drawing heavily upon the work of Simon Reynolds, notably in his books *Rip It Up and Start Again: Postpunk 1978-1984* (2005) and *Totally Wired: Postpunk Interviews and Overviews* (2009), I draw a series of distinctions between what I suggest might constitute 'classic ideal types' of punk and post-punk music, useful just as a bare beginning, an initial heuristic device, while making clear punk, and especially post-punk, in concrete practice encompass a much wider, more diverse, and more complicated array of sounds, sound patterns, and sound deployments, as well as thematic interests and philosophical-political outlooks and orientations, as one proceeds from one specific punk or post-punk musician or musical group to another. At the same time, both punk and post-punk continue to evolve ever since their initial emergence, while varying substantially according to under what conditions, in what situations and circumstances, specific musicians or musical groups emerge, take shape, convey meaning, and exert impact.

As I begin to discuss relations between punk and post-punk with students born in the 1990s and 2000s, I stress when punk first emerged it was more than just a kind of music–this was music at the forefront of a much larger subculture, a subculture of protest and dissent: punk reflected and responded to a deep sense of alienation on the part, in particular, of working class young people in Britain in the mid-1970s. These young people felt they lived in a regimented society: they felt their destinies were plotted *for them*, without an opportunity to offer their own input and without an opportunity to exercise their own agency. Punks felt disposable. As a result, punk music and culture manifested punks' anger at being treated like garbage. Punk strove to force the rest of mid-1970s British society to face up to what, and whom, it had pushed to the margins.

Punk was frightening to many who maintained much more comfortable, secure, and powerful social positions, and, in fact, when it first emerged, punk provoked moral panic across Britain.

Punk music revolted against the direction rock music had by then taken–rock had become music which, supposedly, only a small minority of exceptionally talented people could really play (well), while everyone else was supposed to listen–and applaud the virtuosity of 'rock stars'. Like my students, readers here may find this hard to believe, but when I was growing up in the mid 1970s, until punk emerged, almost no one in my large public high school class played any rock music, or any rock instrument, because by then the consensus had become widespread that this required exceptional talent to do, and you had, in fact, to be 'born with' this talent. Punk dramatically changed this way of thinking–punk encouraged young people to play music and not just listen to it, and to believe the music they could make, themselves, would be worthwhile. Punk helped break down the boundary between musician and audience, while re-infusing rock music with rebellious energy. Punk is famous to this day for its 'DIY' (i.e., 'do-it-yourself') ethos, which has influenced numerous artistic and cultural movements ever since. So, in sum, back in the mid to late 1970s, punk was, at least briefly, both 'cutting edge' and 'transgressive'. It wasn't perceived, by those passionately invested in it, as *merely* 'simple three-chord music' played 'short, loud, and fast'.

Yet, musicians (and audiences) quickly became tired of the limitations of punk, and wanted to move in more adventurous directions. That leads us to post-punk. The following are some broad 'ideal type' characteristic attributes of post-punk music, from the late 1970s through the mid 1980s, including in comparison and contrast with broad 'ideal type' punk music:

1.   Post-industrial urban life is a key source of inspiration, and a key focus of critique for both. Yet post-punk often focused much more than punk on interior, subjective, introspective, contemplative, and ruminative states as well as on how these are interconnected with exterior, objective, and physically material kinds of conditions and circumstances.

2.   Post-punk frequently mixes intellectually artistic (including literarily and philosophically avant-garde) influences with a 'punk-like' emphasis on the raw, the primitive, and the visceral.

3.   Post-punk incorporates 'alienative' devices and techniques–in the 'Brechtian' sense, where the aim is to compel audiences' thoughtful engagement with what audiences recognize is an interested construction, not simply a 'natural' performance.

4.   Many post-punk bands emphasized jagged, abrupt, herky-jerky, and stop-start riffs as well as parallel kinds of movements by the musicians performing this music. Often post-punk involved a much greater emphasis than punk on a choreographed dramatizing of a rising and falling (or ebbing and flowing) of (diffuse and mysterious) tension.

5.   Post-punk musicians recuperated disco and funk (scorned by many punk bands and punk fans) as well as other pre-punk musical styles, mixing elements of these with elements derived from punk. Post-punk musicians found experimental noise-rock as well as krautrock (aka 'komische rock') particularly appealing. Keyboards and electronic instruments as well as electronic treatments of non-electronic instruments became much more common, prominent, and significant than was the case with punk.

6.   Post-punk spread punk's social critique to target a wider array of institutions and practices (the family, religion, schools, leisure, shopping, consumption, housing, social services, the news and entertainment mass media, and the social construction of normative identities, etc.). Post-punk social critiques focused on capitalist achievement of domination through control of culture, and by means of ideology, as much if not more than on capitalist control of the state and over the economy.

7.   A significant number of post-punk bands produced a sound suggestive of cold, clean, distant, separated, detached, and empty spaces existing within yet larger structures of confinement. At the same time, many post-punk bands paid much greater attention than most punk bands to intricately layering and texturing the multiple constituents (i.e., varied instruments and effects) making up their overall sound.

8.   Post-punk scenes often involved extensive drug use (notably amphetamines, but hardly just that) and often overtly critiqued (the hypocrisies of existing) drug laws.

9.   Frequently, the content of post-punk music focuses on themes of isolation, loneliness, alienation, fear, and panic.

10.   Post-punk musicians often played up elements of the absurd, the grotesque, and even the horrific in their songs–and their performances.

11.   In post-punk music, the bass guitar is often more upfront and distinct than is the case with punk, while often maintaining a more consistent role across the song than the conventionally six-string electric lead guitar. The bass guitar often, in fact, plays principal melodic riffs. The conventionally six-string electric lead guitar is freed thereby to move in and out, playing striking bursts and flares of sound as well as playing off what the bass guitar, the drums, and the vocal (as well as the keyboard) set out and maintain as the dominant thrust of the song, while doing so in freewheeling ways. Use of effects devices with the guitar, when done, are often overt in the case of post-punk (not smoothly integrated into the overall mix so as to readily disappear from conscious attention).

12.   Classic post-punk often deliberately pursued a 'messthetics' (an openness to experimentation–including concerning what instruments are played, when and how, as well as

concerning matters of combination and arrangement, mixing and treating, and producing and recording).

13.   A significant number of post-punk bands emphasized the theatrical, while simultaneously employing a mixture of multiple artistic media. A (dark) romantic, 'cabaret feel' was common. Post-punk often aimed to offer audiences an immersive experience of 'total art'.

14.   Post-punk vocals are often performed in ways strikingly antithetical to much of what was normative for conventional, pre-punk pop rock: for example, snarling, shrieking, screaming, whispering, droning, moaning, spoken as opposed to sung or merging the spoken with the sung [i.e., 'sprechesgang' vocal style]. Often these vocals are exaggerated, inflated, or otherwise electronically treated (especially with use of echo/reverb and similar effects). Post-punk vocals also frequently involve overt (albeit at times subtle) 'playing' with register, volume, timbre, pacing, and intonation.

15.   Tony Wilson famously summed up the difference between punk and post-punk as follows: punk says 'fuck you' whereas post-punk says 'we are fucked'.

This is, again, merely a broad summary of 'ideal type' distinctions, and whenever I have not expressly contrasted post-punk with punk it would certainly be fair to say punk anticipated much of what post-punk became. The boundary between punk and post-punk is far from hard and fast, as the slightness of the '-' between 'post' and 'punk' in 'post-punk' might well suggest.

***

Ian Curtis: vocal, occasionally rhythm guitar and, even more occasionally, percussion. *Peter Hook*: bass guitar and, rarely, guitar. *Bernard Sumner*: guitar and occasionally keyboards, including synthesizers, and, even more occasionally, bass. *Stephen Morris*: drums and percussion. *Martin Hannett*: principally responsible for studio processing, treatment, and effects.

In many Joy Division songs, Peter Hook's bass guitar plays the initial, and most persistent, overarching melody (or, in other words, melodic line). Bernard Sumner's guitar contributes lines or patterns that sometimes coincide with or parallel the melody played by the bass guitar but often stand independent of this line, developing it, complicating it, and even countering it. Hook's bass guitar is often played at a relatively higher than conventional register while Sumner's riffs are often sparser than conventional, with greater use of single notes and less reliance on power chords and distortion, even though generally played quite loudly. Sumner's guitar work is often a much more nuanced, and even abstract, dimension, no matter how fully foregrounded, than was usual in rock, pop, and punk at the time. Morris' drumming tends to follow his experience, his interpretation, of the evolving mood, the emotional process, of the song, rather than maintaining a strictly metronomic, clock-like contribution, with different drum and cymbal sounds taking on distinct roles in developing and elaborating this evolving mood, or emotional process. Curtis's baritone-sounding vocal plays with often slight and subtle yet nevertheless crucial shifts in pitch, intonation, pace, and volume.

Many commentators have suggested each member of Joy Division contributed to the band's music as if he was responsible for the lead. As a result, each contributes a pattern of sound that maintains a pronounced relative autonomy, even as each responds to a common mood and works within a common framework. Characteristically, in composing their music, each of the four would be responsible for coming up with his own pattern of sound, following an initial suggestion or setting of the mood, most often by Curtis, who was also, reputedly, the one who most commonly played the role of coordinating, i.e., of letting others know what worked best in combination, what should be retained, emphasized, developed, and modified–and what should be set aside, even jettisoned. But no one envisioned what he was playing as simply support for or a mere accompaniment to what another was playing.

Joy Division live often sounds considerably different than Joy Division via studio recording. Martin Hannett, as producer, invested considerable effort in working on the band's sound. Much of what Hannett contributed involved adding greater space within the music, especially subtracting and diminishing sound–as well as carefully adding delay and other precisely pinpointed effects. Hannett often foregrounded the vocal–and the percussion, while often considerably transforming the character and individual components of the latter. But Hannett also worked to subtly alter the timbre of the other instrumental components as well as of the drums and cymbals. And he also deployed multiple synthesizer keyboard sounds and miscellaneous sound effects, in addition to the then standard, four-part, vocal-electric guitar-electric bass guitar–and rock drum kit set-up.

Joy Division music, especially as produced by Martin Hannett, has often been noted for it spaciousness, as well as for the clarity and precision of the distinction, separation, combination, and interplay of the separate sources contributing to the overall sound. The songs often, musically as well as lyrically, enact a dramatization of an intense moment of introspection. They often suggest an individual engaged in an elaborate internal dialogue. The overt effect, what's more, has often been described as suggestive of a trance-like state of deep immersion.

Recent accounts, including in Peter Hook's and Bernard Sumner's autobiographies, underscore how Curtis was the principal leader in the process of composition, selecting the riffs, choosing the grooves, and organizing patterns among the musical ideas developed and contributed by the others–i.e., arranging these dimensions to fit with lyrics he had composed and ideas he had in mind for the moods he believed these lyrics should produce when situated within the framework of songs including guitar, bass guitar, drums, and other instrumental features as well as his vocal. Curtis would often ask fellow Joy Division members to play passages they had been working on, listen carefully, and identify which ones he liked because he had written lyrics to work with them, and then he would tell fellow bandmembers how he wanted their individual contributions to work together–when each would come in and play, what they would come in and play, for how long, at what volume, and so on, as well as where he wanted his lyrics to fit. So the process of composition involved a great deal of autonomy and experimentation, along with a great deal of practice and rehearsal, but also considerable coordination and (mental) staging. This care in construction was compounded, all the further, once Hannett reworked these songs in the studio. Still, as Hannett subsequently attested, he contributed what he did to bring out potentials he perceived these songs already demonstrated. Interestingly enough, Hook, Sumner, and to a lesser degree Morris found Hannett, at least early on, frustrating to work with, but Hannett and Curtis quickly developed a considerable and lasting rapport.

The members of Joy Division were self-taught, and they struggled for quite awhile at first to make music virtually anyone found appealing, but soon enough they developed a reputation for being exceptionally hard-working as well as exceptionally serious about their craft. As both Paul Morley and Jon Savage shared, in public discussions in July 2017 in Manchester, musicians like the members of Joy Division did in fact work extremely hard to become highly skilled. Everyone back then could *try* 'doing it yourself', but you had to be unusually fanatical in your commitment to making music in order to reach the level of achievement Joy Division did.

***

Ian Curtis is commonly perceived to have sung his vocals as a baritone, at a pitch register below his normal speaking register, while likewise emphasizing the low or bass end of the baritone range. Others have suggested he achieves his characteristic vocal tone by lowering his larynx, thereby 'darkening' his voice while remaining within a tenor range. Typically Curtis sung his vocals across relatively small intervals, and with an emphasis on ending phrases by moving downward in pitch. Often Curtis's vocals are sung from the chest and with a wider throat and less nasality than common in punk. Curtis's vocals typically exhibit only light breathiness, usually a largely crisp and clean enunciation, and with an emphasis on periodically sustaining notes, typically at or toward the end of a phrase, so that their decay and release is longer than common in punk vocals. As many close listeners have pointed out, Curtis's singing voice conveyed a noticeable 'natural' reverberation that Martin Hannett enhanced in the studio. Likewise, many have detected a distinctly echoing quality in Curtis's singing voice, even in live performances where Hannett was not directly involved, suggestive of Curtis's possible use of digital harmonizing and pitch shifting (especially pitch drop) devices. Although controversy persists concerning how important these kinds of technological devices and treatments were in producing Curtis's characteristic vocal register, resonance, and timbre, and although Hannett clearly did engage in considerable creative manipulation of the sound produced by all four members of the band, the genius of Hannett's contribution to Joy Division's sound ultimately results, again, from Hannett recognizing potentialities within how these bandmembers already played their instruments, or, in Curtis's case, sang his vocals, that constituted extant tendencies already at work in the band's sound, especially notably so in the case of Curtis's singing voice, Hannett could work off of and draw out. Curtis's manipulation of the harmonics within the vocal timbre of his singing voice contributed effectively to accentuate a strong sense of melancholic introspection, of isolated contemplation, periodically punctuated with rebellious bursts of frustration and anguish. Hannett double-tracked Curtis's vocals as well as layered them with synthesizer accompaniment, while also making frequent use of digital delay to significant effect in treating Curtis's vocals, notably by adding pronounced reverberation. Curtis's range is often described as narrow, or limited, but he was able effectively to work within this range by modulating his voice, bending the pitch up and down around the notes he was singing, in what is often identified as singing flat or sharp but is better

130

understood and appreciated, I suggest, as adding subtle nuance and variety within otherwise static or slight intervals.

***

Paul Morley, in *Joy Division Piece by Piece: Writing About Joy Division, 1977-2007*, reviewing Joy Division performing live relatively early on in their active run, in Manchester on 4 September 1978, for *New Musical Express*, already notes Ian Curtis "discovers the scope within tonal limitations" as he "uses his vocals for force; blankly expressed emotions, bitter and angry" in what comes across as "Not tuneless, not tuneful" but rather "Flat and intent, a fourth instrument" (81). Many commentators have followed suit, suggesting Curtis's proved sensitively adept at working with his vocal limitations, readily grasping what he could do especially compellingly with his distinct singing voice. Less than a year later, again for *New Musical Express*, on 31 March 1979, in a review of *A Factory Sampler*, Morley likewise anticipates what many since have come to identify as characteristic features of how Joy Division sound is deployed across the soundbox, by stressing "the separation and interaction of each instrument, their unusually supple positions (high bass, drums to the front, meandering guitar) and the deep, round vocals" (87). In a late live review, of Joy Division performing at the University of London, on 8 February 1980, published in the 16 February 1980 issue of *New Musical Express*, Morley comments further insightfully on how Joy Division songs exhibit "extreme, para-melodies" while, unusual at the time for 'rock' music, "some have no bass, some no guitars," or "Synthesizers and bass with the drums, or two guitars" at the same time as Morley also attests to how "The full new introduction of the synthesizer has not damaged the coherence and balance of the music in any way, it simply increases the amount of mood, atmosphere, ephemeral terror [Joy] Division are capable of achieving" (114). It is difficult today to appreciate how novel the prominent incorporation of diverse synthesizers and additional electronic effects into punk-originating rock music came across at the time; at this point in time it is likely most notable to take this fact into account in appreciating Joy Division music emanates from an openness toward innovation and experimentation. In other words, this is far from 'fearful music' even when it enacts and dramatizes fearful encounters.

Writing about *Unknown Pleasures*, Morley memorably describes the soundbox yet further and its contribution to texture of the sound on this album as follows:

> . . . the way the bass player acted as if he was the obvious leader, and the drummer acted as if the floor would drop away from underneath him if he didn't keep up, and the guitarist introspectively analysed how he was going to deal with the mad, roaming and potentially stupid bass, and outmanouevre the sly, possessed drummer, and he decided to do so by dragging shadows of sound around in violent little circles until people noticed he was there. The singer had all three of them in sight, sort of, and used his fortunate proximity . . . to transform his excessive sensitivity, extreme shyness and outrageous bitterness into something that made sense . . . .

Ian's not really in the room, but he is, he's everywhere, inside and outside at the same time. They were all looking out from different windows. It was Hannett that managed to make it seems as if they were all looking out of–or into–the same window, and he managed to do this with his head in the clouds, his feet on the ground and his back to the wall. (136)

Morley adds, later, to his earlier analysis of Ian Curtis's vocals by suggesting, usefully, concerning Curtis's timbre and delivery, "He sang suffering with an almost tender listlessness. He put the perfect voice to strangled thoughts" (268). Morley perceives Curtis's vocals as involving a kind of awkward crooning that conveys the feeling of the singer plunging into the music, "a transferring himself into the body of the music, stumbling over the line from where the music was for him to where he was for the music" (268-269)–in other words, contributing a vocal whose quality directly suggests and precisely befits that of a persona entering into, embracing, and immersing themself in the "speed and danger of the drama," madness, trauma, and despair (269). In this same essay as well as in multiple other pieces, written before and since, Morley likewise emphasizes the importance of attending to the space that exists in the music of Joy Division, by noting it is characteristic of Joy Division's musical sound that the band and their producer "could leave such emptiness in the middle of their music, and at the edges, without weakening it. It added to the strength, to the resonance" (270). For Morley, this key insight helps lead to another even more crucial one:

And their music is about, finally, isolation. It is about the difficulty of keeping in touch with other human beings as we create for safety's sake a reality around us that works for us as much as it can . . . It's about the mind . . . as the tricks that it plays on itself, the harm it can do itself as it struggles to float in a world containing so much water it can drown you in a second. The songs are about the way the mind can find all sorts of ways to prise apart illusion and reality and then cobble them back together in a way that makes sense if only for the moment . . . .

[Ian Curtis) sung about how close life can be to death. He sang about how the difference between life and death is never more than an instance, a moment, a thought, and he sang about what it's like to get closer and closer to that moment, that thought. (270-271)

***

In his "Introduction" to *So This is Permanence*, in commenting on "Love Will Tear Us Apart," Jon Savage offers us one example of a close description that immediately supports a compelling interpretation of the musical sound of Joy Division, illustrative of one useful way to move directly from describing the sound of this kind of music toward interpreting its meaning and impact:

It begins with a bass pulse: the guitar arrives with a dramatic flourish and the drums clatter, before they resolve into a syncopated drum beat and an instantly memorable synthesizer figure. It's an analogue synth, which conveys warmth and alienation at the same time: the melody is at once uplifting and wistful. Curtis's voice has lost its previous punk bark: it's more nuanced, almost crooned . . .

132

The arrangement is deceptively light and airy, but the sentiments are not. The vocal is mixed up high–in comparison with most of *Unknown Pleasures*, where Curtis is *in* there with the group. It's more a solo rather than a rock vocal, and this forces attention, as was intended, on the lyrics. (xiv)

What's particularly useful here, is emphasis on the instruments as they enter, how they sound as they do, how they relate to and are positioned versus each other, the timbre and location in the soundbox as well as the mode of delivery and the kinds of associations this creates, and how this song maintains sonic features that distinguish it from other Joy Division songs.

***

Mick Middles and Lindsay Reade, in *Torn Apart: The Life of Ian Curtis*, are among many who cite Martin Hannett's pioneering use of an original AMS digital delay device as contributing signally to Joy Division's, and Ian Curtis's, distinctive recorded sound. With this device Hannett was able to alter the pitch and timbre, as well as the timing and placement, of the instrumental components of Joy Division's overall sound, notably by transforming "Steven Morris' rock-based drums" so this "sound became a sharp crisp disco beat when fed through the delay" as well as by producing "an echoed effect on Ian's voice that was as compelling as Ian's onstage performance, and which helped create an intimacy between singer and listener" (98). Hannett's contributions to Joy Division's musical sound are remarkably innovative when compared to common punk musical sounds at the time. As Middles and Reade comment, "what he demanded would have seemed totally alien to any band that had emerged from punk, specifically a total sound separation" (127). As Middles and Reade further note, "This wasn't confined to separating each instrument and voice, however; famously, in the case of Steven Morris's drum kit, the producer isolated each individual drum sound, forcing Morris into the unnatural situation of playing one sound at a time" (127). What's more, Middles and Reade explain, "Hannett's conception was to avoid any trace of 'bleed-through' from drum to drum, instrument to instrument," which helped create "a ghostly ambience" (128). As Middles and Reade aptly propose, "With *Unknown Pleasures* Hannett strived to *contain* the explosion," as here "the twin dominating instruments of the album" become "the voice and the snare drum and it is in that interplay that much of the record seemed so strikingly similar" (128). I can attest as well, that in my experience too, just as Middles and Reade do, with first-time listeners to Joy Division, even decades later, "that prominent snare sound, with lengthy reverb, still occasionally catches the listener unawares," especially as "enhanced by the lovely softened plump of the bass drum" (128). With *Unknown Pleasures*, Middles and Reade recount, Hannett also began to "use various ethereal sound effects, including miking up the elevator shaft with the lift going up and down, and the sound of broken glass" (129).

Middles and Reade are representative of many who cite the feeling of intimacy conveyed in both Joy Division albums, *Unknown Pleasures* and *Closer*, as having much to do with how Hannett deliberately foregrounded Ian Curtis's vocals: "The separation of the instruments drew the listener towards a voice with unusual resonance, giving the impression that the singer was singing to them alone" (130). Likewise, "Hannett's decision to compress the energy levels of the rhythm section and bolster this with Bernard's distorted minor note guitar line placed the focus solely on Curtis's vocals," while listeners, at the time at least, were further struck, and even "unsettled" by the fact that "Hook's bass is reduced to a thin line, and then pushed to the top of the mix" (131). In contrast with this treatment of the bass, Middles and Reade note well how Hannett's treatment of Curtis's voice, in *Unknown Pleasures*, is often "reverb-soaked" and starts lower in the mix while moving steadily upward as the song progresses (133). In contrast, with *Closer* Hannett 'pulls' Curtis's voice "right to the top of the mix" (212). In sum, among other features of Middles's and Reade's discussion of the musical sound of Joy Division, especially as produced by Martin Hannett, the two writers often pay careful attention to where instruments, and other sounds, are located within the soundbox, and how these move as well as change location, when and if they do—while paying particular attention as well, in terms of lines and phrasings, to pronounced movements in pitch and changes in volume as well as pronounced moments of relative stasis and quiet.

***

Peter Hook's *Unknown Pleasures: Inside Joy Division*, Bernard Sumner's *Chapter and Verse: New Order, Joy Division and me*; and Stephen Morris's *Record Play Pause: Confessions of a Post-Punk Percussionist Volume I* offer numerous valuable insights into what each of these members and all of the rest of those involved contributed to developing and refining the musical sound of Joy Division, but I want now to highlight a select number in each case that, again, I find especially useful myself in making sense of what I hear, when I listen to Joy Division, and what this makes me think (about) and feel, in preparation for detailed descriptions, analyses, and interpretations of "Disorder," "Transmission," and "Twenty Four Hours," later in this chapter.

To begin, with Peter Hook, in *Unknown Pleasures: Inside Joy Division*, the story of Martin Hannett's demands upon Stephen Morris have been widely and repeatedly recounted but I find especially notable Hook's recollection that Hannett wanted Morris to play his drum kit, in the studio, so as to sound like a drum machine, and that it is this uncanny convergence of human drummer meets drum machine that contributes, as Hook hears it, to the distinctive sound of Morris's drumming on record (152). In discussing *Unknown Pleasures*, track by track (200-207), Hook shares "Disorder" contains several bum "notes" that were not intended, which turn out being good mistakes, and these include a few instances when it is not Sumner's guitar but actually Hook's bass sounding even if most listeners might imagine the opposite. With "Day of the Lords" Hook indicates Hannett overdubbed the keyboards in a manner bandmembers at the time found disturbing but again this turned out, in retrospect, to be a wise choice. "Candidate," Hook notes, includes not only some recording of Sumner playing his guitar backwards but also Sumner inspired in how he plays his guitar by listening to the previously recorded sound of the track played backwards. With "She's Lost Control," as is well-known, "an aerosol was used to create some of the drum effects–another of Martin's many innovations" while also particularly distinctive here is Morris's use of a Synare drum synthesizer, with Morris being one of the first rock drummers to use this instrument. In relation to "Shadowplay," Hook highlights a common feature of many Joy Division songs, and that is "the lyric doesn't repeat until the end and it has no chorus," while here and elsewhere Hook comments that Curtis deliberately sought to subvert "the normal conventions" of how lyrics are organized in pop and rock music. With

134

"Wilderness," Hook shares this is a Joy Division song he continues to appreciate because of its "fantastic bass line," "A bass line every bass player dreams of and I got it, thank you." Hook also comments on Sumner's "fuzzy guitar playing," which he argues here and elsewhere is quite distinctive, talented, and too often underrated. In the case of "Interzone," Hook recounts he himself sang the main vocal with Ian doing the low, backing vocal, while in the case of "I Remember Nothing," Hook cites Hannett's well-recognized "shattering glass and other effects" as well as Hannett's self-built synthesizer, a modified Transcendent 2000, used often on this track, along with commenting, "One of the interesting things about Joy Division is that people can never tell who's playing what; is it the guitar or bass, keyboard or bass or guitar?" (206).

In his track by track discussion of *Closer* (276-280), Hook begins by noting that "Barney plays bass and I play guitar on 'Atrocity Exhibition'," which also includes Hannett 'melting' the guitar "with his Marshall Time Waster," otherwise known as the Marshall Time Modulator or AMS DMX 15-80, a delay-line musical effects device invented by Hannett that the latter used to contribute chorus and flanging effects, and which, as Hook memorably describes it, made the guitar "sound like someone strangling a cat." With "Isolation," Hook finds this track interesting because of the absence of guitar, and what Hannett "did was take the original drum track, flange it and effect it through his synth, then get Steve to overdub the drums so they were separate; then he could have them really up front in the mix, not buried in a drum mix." What's more, Hannett "used the drums to trigger his synth, which was, again, ahead of its time," while "Barney overdubbed the Arp [keyboard] over the Transcendent [synthesizer], playing the same part, and it sounds current even now." With "Passover," Hook is playing six-string bass, for the first time, together with an Electro-Harmonic Clone Theory effects pedals while "Coupling the chorus with a short eighty-millisecond delay [that] gave me the sound for the next phase of my career." Hook has nothing of particular interest to share concerning precise contributions to the musical sound of "Colony," but does cite it as a song he continues to find especially powerful on an album in which "Every song is confident" and accomplished, with not a one at all "dodgy." "Means to an End" Hook labels *Closer*'s "fucked-up disco song" with a verse containing, unusually, "four ascending notes all next to each other, with no thought to sharps or flats." "Heart and Soul" involves a low bass part transferred to the synthesizer, played by Sumner, with Sumner also in charge of layering and structuring the keyboard and string sounds while Hook plays six-string bass. As Hook notes, this song foreshadows Sumner's ever-increasing movement from guitar to keyboards, accelerating within New Order. In the case of "Twenty Four Hours," Hook has little to offer explaining distinctive contributions to the musical sound but does suggest this song is one that particularly well demonstrates Curtis's abilities as a vocalist, where he uses emotional force and painstaking care in his heartfelt delivery to overcome limitations in his vocal range, and in his ability to remain consistently in key. With "The Eternal," again Hook contributes six-string bass combined with the clone effects pedal while Sumner uses the Transcendant "as a white-noise generator" as he otherwise plays keyboard throughout, and Hannett contributes a notable "echo plate" on Morris's snare. Finally, in the case of "Decades," this song involves Hook "playing low bass and, unusually, playing in sync with the bass drum," which is then followed by overdubbing another bass part, along with "Syndrum sound, loads of echo plate," keyboards played by Sumner that are "layered wonderfully," and "overdubbed guitar melodies."

Sumner, in *Chapter and Verse*, delves into technical detail much further once his memoir arrives at his time with New Order, which is indeed something he is fond of discussing, as I recall from a lengthy public interview conducted by Dave Haslam at a Manchester International Festival, where I was privileged to sit right near the front, virtually within touching distance of Sumner, as the latter at one point expressed relief when asked a relatively rare question, on that occasion at least, concerning technical dimensions of the particular kinds of synthesizers Sumner has most appreciated playing. But, early on, as Hook and Morris also do, in their memoirs, Sumner pays tribute to Curtis's musical ear, and how useful that turned out to be in enabling Joy Division to piece together the individual contributions from each of its members while, as Sumner suggests, Curtis always seemed to have an endless supply of potentially useful lyrics for the band's songs that he could readily draw upon, and that Curtis helped signally in fostering a highly cooperative relationship among the band's members in the process of composition throughout the duration of their time working together (78-79). In the case of "Love Will Tear Us Apart," besides citing how the song "swings back and forth between full-blown power and reflective introspection," deliberately echoing the position of the song's protagonist, as well as its incorporation of "contrasts, peaks, troughs," Sumner notes this song is "quite unusual in that it doesn't conform to a regular structure: it's got no middle eight, for example" (82). In relation to Hannett, Sumner recounts how the latter not only used "wacky overdubs" such as "recording smashing glass and the sound of a building's fork lift," but also introduced Sumner and the rest of the band to sampling, by taking recordings of their playing their instruments, transferring these to keyboards, and in the process manipulating the initial sounds, so these could subsequently be recorded alongside the bandmembers simultaneously playing 'the same' sounds, lines, and patterns of sound on their instruments (110). As Sumner attests, Hannett helped fundamentally change his, Sumner's, understanding of and appreciation for the potential role and contribution of the studio, and of studio production, while Sumner also indicates Curtis was the first to enthusiastically embrace Hannett's innovations, even as Sumner himself remained skeptical for considerably longer (110).

A final noteworthy feature of Sumner's contribution to understanding the musical sound of Joy Division is only elliptically related at best, but still definitely of considerable interest, in attesting to the nature and quality of Curtis's visionary imagination, and that is Sumner's inclusion of the entire transcript of his hypnosis recording of Curtis, late in the latter's life, significant portions of which are included in *Joy Division*, the 2007 feature-length documentary film written by Jon Savage and directed by Grant Gee. As Sumner indicates in a prefatory note, he hypnotized Curtis twice, and startlingly, Curtis, who was easy to put under, repeated the same things both times. Notably these include Curtis first identifying himself, regressing backwards to a seemingly earlier life, and earlier identity, as a twenty-eight year old named John, back in April of 1835, reading and studying law while working for a London office that provides books for shops and schools, and originally from Southampton. Next, Curtis regresses to a yet earlier identity, back in 1642 or 1643, when he is named Justin, is forty-eight or forty-nine, was born in England although grew up and lived in the Netherlands, with a Flemish mother named Cheacott, but is now in prison in France after fighting on the losing side of a war against France, seemingly about to be executed. Regressing yet further one more time Curtis identifies himself next as a priest in 904 AD, or 904 CE, seemingly finding himself at a scene where a bloody battle, even in fact a massacre, has just recently taken place, with Curtis, as that priest, seemingly helping attend to the dead at the scene.

Morris, in *Record Play Pause: Confessions of a Post-Punk Percussionist Volume I*, offers an abundance of useful insights into important details concerning what went into making the sound of Joy Division. To begin, from early on as a yet fledgling drummer, Morris indicates he "liked German drummers best," those associated with krautrock, or kosmiche rock, drummers in bands such as Can, Neu!, Amon Düül II, Tangerine Dream, and Kraftwerk; it is these drummers, and their drumming styles, Morris relied upon as his models and inspirations as he initially learned his craft (91). Later on, Morris shares, it was also these bands' early use of synthesizers that prompted not only his curiosity about but also receptiveness to working with electronic devices. As Morris indicates, he loved using the Synare 3 almost immediately, even as it took some time for him to become dextrous enough to effectively manipulate this machine at the same time as he was playing his drum kit. Early on in Joy Division, Morris confides, "my concept of what drums should do in a band had become distilled down to 'the drummer is the bridge between the bass and the guitar, the thing that glues the two together'" but, as time proceeded, and as Morris became familiar working together with his fellow Joy Division bandmates, Morris stopped playing "too many busy fills," learned "less is more," and recognized his role "was less of a clock because the entire band was the clock." Morris grew to appreciate, in particular, the importance of leaving space within the songs, especially for Sumner and Curtis, while he locked together with Hook on the grooves (170-171). For Morris it is important to note well Joy Division songs typically did not contain choruses but "just a kind of refrain that relieved the wound-up tension of the verses" because the tension, its exploration, its release, and its relief is always pivotal to what these songs are about, which has, as Morris interprets this, much do with wanting to break out and get away but not being sure how well or how far this is possible (209). Morris usefully approaches the verses of Joy Division songs as a "widescreen" "landscape" "that Ian described, Bernard punctuated, Hooky steered and I propelled us through" (209).

Early on, given connotations 'disco' then maintained among 'rock' musicians and fans, especially punk musicians and fans, Morris resisted playing drums in any way suggestive of a disco beat, but eventually, beginning with "Digital," he reports he grew increasingly comfortable doing so, recognizing digital was the future, including percussion incorporating and emulating an overtly digital style (272). Nevertheless, Morris recalls being largely receptive, even excited, right away by many of Martin Hannett's innovations (in contrast with Hook and Morris). Like many commentators, Morris identifies Hannett not only as an early user of the AMS DMX 15-80 Digital Delay device but also as a pioneer who was one of the first, if not the first, to experiment with and reveal how this device could dramatically transform musical sounds (275). In particular, Morris notes the "phasing, flanging, and chorus-type effects" that the AMS DMX 15-80 enabled while also recounting how stunning he and fellow bandmembers found its capability to record snippets of instrumental sound which Hannett could then replace, repair, and rework in a variety of novel ways (297). Morris's own account of Hannett's notorious "deconstruction of the drum kit" (299-302) reinforces others in describing how counter-intuitive and painful this process proved in practice, even as Morris ultimately embraced the virtues of this kind of experimentation. As Morris describes, Hannett required him to separate "the bass drum (boom), the snare drum (crack) and the hi-hat (tsh)" sounds (301), that drummers like him learn to play seamlessly together, so he could only play one of these sounds all the way through a recording of a song at a time. As Morris adds, he did find it fortunate, for all of the value of this particular innovation, that "'Candidate', 'Autosuggestion', 'New Dawn Fades' and 'Day of the Lords' were done in the more conventional manner, by recording the backing track of us all playing together while Ian did a guide vocal" and "Then overdubbing onto that" (302).

Morris attests yet further to Hannett's restless experimentation by describing how in the case of "Atmosphere" Hannett "came up with an experiment using the AMS: a cascading delay, pitch-shift effect. A very short metallic sound was processed, its pitch getting shifted down a semitone, slightly delayed, then fed back in again, and the while process repeated itself over and over again. Until the signal decayed into silence" (312). While this was happening, Morris himself "had the chime off a broken tambourine perched on a scissor blade held very close to the microphone: softly pinging the chime produced the shimmering icy bell effect for the chorus of 'Atmosphere'" (312). As he became more familiar working with Hannett, readily accepting and implementing Hannett's innovations, Morris recalls he became increasingly adept at playing real drums, live and in the studio, augmented by simultaneously playing both the Synare 3 and the SDS4 (Simmons Drums Synthesizer 4) (314). However, he continues to recall it as a startling and uncomfortable experience when Hannett first decided to use aerosol spray as a percussion instrument (famously in "She's Lost Control"), with this decision requiring Morris to squirt the aerosol spray in time with the track (315). Like Hook, Morris attests "Synths were a much bigger part of *Closer* than *Unknown Pleasures*," in particular the ARP Omni-2 that was "polyphonic–you could play more than one note at a time, i.e. chords"; "made lovely ethereal string-type sounds"; "a cool bass synth"; "an OK polysynth"; and "Used on *Low*, so was obviously magnificent even to Ian" (by far the least tech-nerdy of the four according to Morris) (351). Morris lists, among the electronic instruments brought to bear on *Closer*, "Bernard's Transcendent, the Omni-2, Martin's ARP 2600 with sequencer, my SDS4 and trusty/rusty Synare, the AMS DMX 15-80, Martin's new toy the Marshall Time Modulator, and a Lexicon Prime Time"–a full "synth arsenal" yet further complimented by Hook's new Shergold six-string bass and his Electro-Harmonix Chorus pedal (352). As Morris recalls, "Bernard did all the keyboard playing" on *Closer* and even though live performances of a number of later Joy Division songs with Morris doing so required Curtis to contribute, however uncomfortably, via playing Vox Phantom guitar, "in the studio it was often quicker for Bernard to play [all] the [guitar] parts" (352).

What persistently comes across in Morris's memoir is how ready to embrace experimentation and innovation Joy Division was. All the members of the band envisioned themselves deliberately striving, in their music making, to 'go beyond' what was well established, readily familiar, and especially easy, so in this sense, the oft-cited interest of Ian Curtis in making 'extreme art' extends to encompass what they all shared, i.e., a readiness, willingness, and even an eagerness to push what they were doing, and attempting to do, toward extremes.

***

Jon Savage's *This Searing Light, The Sun and Everything Else: Joy Division The Oral History* overlaps considerably with *Joy Division*, the 2007 film he wrote and Grant Gee directed, with many of the same interviews incorporated in that film also included in this book, along with yet further interviews conducted at the same time and also at other times, not directly in anticipation for use in the film. Before zeroing in on passages that offer interviewees' comments particularly focused on describing, analyzing, and interpreting specific dimensions of Joy Division sound, and the precise means by which this was achieved, I want to call attention to several passages that more indirectly concentrate on how these people experienced the musical sound of Joy Division, what it made them think (about) and feel, especially as they first encountered this sound, including live. The book's title comes from Tony Wilson, unsurprisingly as one who demonstrated a recurrent proclivity toward a provocative way with words. Wilson's first memorable experience of Joy Division live elicited this description; this is what Wilson experienced in the moment, as Joy Division's musical sound: "There was this searing light, the sun, and everything else was just dimness throughout the entire evening" (81). Not only is Wilson here exemplary of many others fortunate enough to have attended Joy Division gigs at their peak, finding these stunning such that nothing else seemed immediately comparable or enticing, but also Wilson here illustrates a frequent tendency of many commentators on Joy Division's musical sound to describe this in synaesthetic terms, in particular by referencing visual patterns of light and dark, and especially of high contrast, of what seems strikingly akin to classically noir low-key, chiaroscuro lighting, but here it also complicates a similarly common tendency to translate what listeners hear from Joy Division into visual images that are entirely black, white, and shades of gray. Wilson's phrase, in contrast, suggests an intensely yellow, orange, and red light that piercingly illuminates an otherwise surrounding darkness comprised of a nebulous range of hues ranging across blue, green, violet, and brown to black.

One of the most memorable accounts of Joy Division's musical sound that makes metaphoric use of 'light and dark' is Jean-Pierre Turmel's notoriously mystical essay "Licht und Blindheit," roughly translatable as 'light and blindness', featured in the limited edition March 1980 Sordide Sentimentale label ep of the same name that also featured visual art by Turmel, Jean-François Jamoul, and Anton Corbijn as well as the Joy Division songs "Atmosphere" and "Dead Souls." Thirty-seven years later, in conjunction with the 2017 Manchester International Festival, and more precisely the *True Faith* exhibition at the Manchester Art Gallery, Michael Bracewell released an updated and retrospectively reflective essay again titled "Licht und Blindheit," again exploring Joy Division songs in relation to conceptual metaphors of light and darkness, and vision and blindness. In sum, this direction in interpretation of Joy Division music conceives Joy Division music as enabling perceptions of and insights into orders, or realms, of reality that are conventionally invisible, hidden, and obscured–perhaps because of a fearful refusal even to contemplate venturing into the exploration of such a dangerous unknown territory or perhaps concerned about the potentially overwhelming and destructive consequences of encountering its searing revelatory power. This line of interpretation recalls surrealist theories concerning orders of surreality that surpass and transcend, as well as elide and evade, and even haunt and infuse realms of the empirical and naturalistic, the ordinarily consciously perceptible and tangible, and the culturally normative and conventional.

Beyond reference to conceptual metaphors that translate sounds, patterns of sounds, and deployments of sounds in Joy Division music into a play of light and dark, of shadow and illumination, and of blindness and vision, another common conceptual metaphor invoked in making sense of the meaning and impact of this music includes discussing this music, like so much other music, in terms of 'time as motion', with many commentators attesting to the quality of motion they experience 'within' and as 'conveyed through' Joy Division music. Here, it is useful to note well that a further valuable contribution Arnie Cox makes, in his book *Music & Embodied Cognition: Listening, Moving, Feeling, & Thinking*, involves his schematic analysis of the typical ways listeners conceptualize what we hear, in listening to music, in relation to 'time as motion'–with us doing so, Cox suggests, in first-person, second-person, *and* third-person terms. In other words, we hear, and imagine as we hear that we see and feel ourselves traveling in time, moving, with the music, from the beginning to the end of its duration; we hear, and imagine as we hear that we see and feel the music traveling in time, moving to, by, and past us, from the beginning to the end of its duration; and we hear, and imagine as we hear that we see and feel someone or something else either traveling in time, moving with the music, from the beginning to the end of its duration–or someone or something else experiencing the music traveling in time, moving to, by, and past them or it, from the beginning to the end of its duration. What becomes especially interesting here is what particular complex array of positionings we experience, often simultaneously and interactively, in listening to a piece of music as we make sense of this music in terms of the conceptual metaphor time is motion. In relation to Joy Division, given the elliptical abstractness, the persistent mysteriousness, the recurrent sense of tension that is suspended not resolved, the frequent incorporation of multiple simultaneous paradoxes, along with the ambiguity of references to personages in the lyrics, this can become a quite elaborate puzzle, especially if we experience these songs in first, second, and third person terms all at once.

Yet another commonplace conceptual metaphor frequently invoked in relation to Joy Division music has to do with sound as space, and, more precisely, space as a container. In relation to Joy Division, as I have already suggested, this often involves a sense of considerable empty space, or distance in space, or of space separating distinct entities responsible for distinct sounds, or imaginatively suggested by hearing these sounds and their interplay in this music. At the same time, for all of this emptiness, distance, and separation, the overarching container that this music is conceived, metaphorically, in terms of conjuring a sense of space, and of particular spaces, often still has felt to many listeners as nevertheless confining, claustrophobic, and even incarcerating, leading to an especially fraught circumstance–simultaneously both all too close yet also all too distant from other spaces. Perhaps this is a key paradox in terms of the perception of space that Joy Division song communicates: this is space that contains considerable distance within it, accentuated by use of reverb and echo, but also which feels likes it brings all of the forces operating from within uncomfortably close, as if the space itself is 'closing in'. Paul Morley well exemplifies hearing, and thinking about what he hears, in Joy Division music as conjuring a sense of space, and especially of distance. As Morley writes,

> *Closer* is a soundtrack to distance. The distance between being far away and being incredibly close. The distance you travel to create something out of nothing. The distance between surviving and giving up . . . . the distance between making it all up as you go along, and knowing exactly what you are doing, between turning up for work, and dreaming of something else. It's a soundtrack to the distance between having all the time, ambition and energy in the world, and then suddenly not. Between concentrating on the moment, and

140

thinking about what happens next. Between togetherness and loneliness. Between violence, and peace. Between taking things incredibly seriously, and just getting on with your life. (143)

Here Morley illustrates how powerfully useful thinking in terms of conceptual metaphors can be that equate felt experience with experience of physical distance, with living one's life as traveling a physical distance, of aspiration as projection in terms of physical distance, of restless, alienation, dissatisfaction, and determination as all experiences of physical distance and of traveling physical distances. In other words, emotional, experiential, and existential states are translated into spaces, and, more precisely, distances between spaces, in order to make useful sense of what these feel like, and what they mean, for us. Joy Division, as music that especially acutely conjures a sense of both the perpetual difficulty yet inescapable necessity of striving to move across distances, and of the recurrently distancing effect that life, or, perhaps more precisely, desire encompasses, along with the ever-attendant anxiety that represents the flip side of desire, helps crystalize how we do make sense of emotional states, needs, and wants in terms of distances, movements across distances, and the continuous emergence and development of yet new and renewed distances that we again and again strive to accept and cope with, if we cannot strive to close and overcome.

Returning to *This Searing Light, The Sun and Everything Else: Joy Division The Oral History*, Jon Wozencraft illustrates how complex many impassioned Joy Division enthusiasts find this music to be, while also referencing matters of light and dark, and movement, including movement in space:

So this was a very strong disclosure to me that there's actually a lot of white light happening here, it's not all about death, doom and destruction.

Joy Division's music is very uplifting. It's got nothing to do with sitting in a bedsit being depressed, chewing your fingernails and wondering if you're going to throw yourself out the window. It's about transforming normal lives into something magical and life-affirming. The cliché of Joy Division has been very dark and depressing. For me, that was not the case at all: they were joy-bringer and I felt charged as a result . . . These things are not understood or recognised in our culture, and it's important to acknowledge where we find them in our lives. (252)

As I have indicated in chapter one, I myself strongly identify with this kind of experience of what Joy Division music feels like for me. And, as I also suggest in this same chapter, I suggest, contrary to commonplace interpretations, I interpret Ian Curtis as often likely experiencing his music, and his performance of it, the same way–this was one place where he could experience uplift, and joy, and the possibilities of affirmation and transformation, as well as that which viscerally transcends the ordinary and the mundane, even in singing about and dramatically performing stark and harrowing encounters with multiple metaphorical 'darknesses'.

Late in *This Searing Light, The Sun and Everything Else: Joy Division The Oral History* Mark Reeder shares that Rob Gretton told him what was in Ian Curtis's suicide note, which in sum was about his inability to have to choose only one relationship, only one possible lifestyle, only one possible vocational direction, only one possible dimension of the multiple, complex, contradictory, and dynamic being he experienced himself as–a choice he felt forced upon him that he could no longer refuse or avoid (309-310). This attempt to refuse or avoid what he experienced as unacceptable choices forced upon him spiraled to the point where it rapidly felt well out of and far beyond his control, and where he felt no one was able, or would be able to understand, that he did not want to have to choose, to give up, to narrow, to limit, to confine, and restrain who and what he could be, and that this could, conceivably, all fit together, yet no one else would accept or believe it could. In this connection, it is apropos to mention that Reeder, who later himself became involved with Annik Honoré as his girlfriend, shares with us that Ian and Annik were not involved in a sexual relationship, as she was still a virgin when he, Reeder, and Honoré came together, but her relationship with Ian was as "an intellectual sparring partner," as someone with whom he could address sensitive emotional issues, including concerning fragility and vulnerability, that he was confronting in his art as music, but which working class Britons of the time, and in particular working class British men of the time, rarely talked about directly (312).

'Not talking about it' is a recurrent theme in retrospective accounts of Joy Division, and this included the music itself, as the bandmembers were individually composing and collectively synthesizing their individual contributions, although, again, in *This Searing Light, The Sun and Everything Else: Joy Division The Oral History* Sumner attests that not only did Curtis play a leading role in selecting which lines and patterns of sound to use as part of particular songs but also encouraged Hook to play high (96-97), which Hook also remembers was important affirmation in insuring he continued to commit himself to doing so (99). Sumner adds the effective distribution of roles that developed between him and Hook worked well as "I developed my own style, which was slow and considered. I liked sound, and I used to play on the neck of the guitar where it sounded really nice. I'm more rhythm and chords, and Hooky was melody. He's got a really good talent for melody" (96). As Wilson comments, not only was "Hook's high-fret playing of the bass" something "no one had done before then" but also making this "the core melodic element" freed up Sumner for "Bernard's slash guitar" style, that was also equally distinctive although not always as readily recognized as such (98). As Morris puts it, Sumner "didn't really do big guitar riffs, what he did was not intricate but textural" (99). With Hannett, Wilson suggests he "created the modern drum sound with the digital delay," and what is all the more striking is that Hannett was actually involved in the inaugural vision "behind the delay machine itself," building off Hannett's early recognition of the value of taking away "all the signifiers of the room that the sound is in to render the sound naked, and then apply reverb and echo and the other signifiers of where you're listening to this particular sound" (131).

Although commentators disagree in how precisely to characterize Stephen Morris's drumming, as a result of his collaboration with Martin Hannett, Bob Dickinson offers a useful stab at this by proposing "Joy Division used rhythm in a machine-like way: they could harness rhythm and turn it into something that was unearthly and not quite human, except that human beings were making the rhythm, so there was this interest in interacting with the machine that you got a sense of from listening to their music" (143). At the least, as Sumner attests, "Steve did a lot with electronic drums, which hadn't been used before," while also, together with Hannett collaborating on some even more notable percussion innovations, such as the aerosol spray, and, as Morris also conveys in his own book, what worked to Joy Division's benefit was "One of the strengths of Joy Division's music is that we were in the learning process, and what you can actually hear is someone exploring music and how to play it" (154).

Even so, Sumner suggests the well-recounted tension he and Hook felt versus Hannett had much to do with their punk-originating preference for "screaming in their faces" whereas they, at least initially, heard Hannett transforming this into "whispering into their ear" (154). But here, as well as in many other places, Sumner and Hook both admit, in retrospect, Hannett was right. Audiences did notice, and respond positively, right away, to this difference, as this came across in Joy Division live performances, which were increasingly less diametrically divergent from Joy Division on record than Sumner and Hook initially feared. Dave Simpson attests, describing a Joy Division gig which was the first gig he ever attended, after the release of *Unknown Pleasures*, "The way the drums sound, with this massive, reverb-soaked, pounding, it just sounded incredible. To me, as a kid, it just sounded spookier" (179). Jon Wozencraft, recalling Joy Division live from September 1979, also commends the impact of Joy Division's musical innovation: "Instead of wrapping themselves around the same melodies and configurations, each of them was reversing certain paradigms, so that Hooky, for example, becomes the lead guitarist. Bernard is then freed up to put all kinds of different shades on what a guitar could do, and he was using a lot of distortion and noise in quite a melodic way" (185).

The complexity of what was involved in making Joy Division music, especially later, in working with synthesizers and additional electronic devices, is aptly illustrated by Bernard Sumner in a 1980 interview, reproduced in *This Searing Light, The Sun and Everything Else: Joy Division The Oral History*, where Sumner explains to Alan Hempsall a particular Joy Division rhythm Hempsall finds interesting is the product of "a guitar fed through a synth and that rhythm is created by passing the guitar's signal through a passage in the synth that only lets part of the signal through. So what in effect the synth is doing with the signal is . . . (illustrates by tapping ends of his forefinger and thumb together" (234). Sumner later on explains "Most of *Closer* we pumped out through big speakers, and recorded the speakers to make it sound live. We did more overdubs . . . We actually recorded the instruments separately. Everyone would record together, but then you'd replace your original tape with a better sound . . . We started doing a lot more keyboard then, a lot of experimentation with Martin. We had more synthesizers . . . The great thing about Martin was that he was truly experimental. It made it really fun in the studio" (262-263).

In relation to Curtis, Daniel Meadows comments that "He had a lovely voice. He didn't have fantastic range, but he had a deep baritone" (250). Meadows, as a photographer, found Curtis's voice, and his vocalization of his lyrics, particularly visually suggestive, again attesting to how Curtis was able to make the most of what he could do well while working within his limitations. Interestingly, in one of his later contributions to *This Searing Light, The Sun and Everything Else: Joy Division The Oral History*, Paul Morley interprets Ian Curtis's singing and performance within his music similarly to how I have done so, as not what was exhausting, sickening, and killing him, and not into what he was pouring out how badly he was personally feeling, but rather as "the centre of his existence": as "his life was falling apart" outside of and beyond the music "he would have preferred to stay in the music" (269). Bob Dickinson qualifies this interpretation somewhat by reminding us that Curtis's "vocals and his lyrics are incredibly vulnerable" while at the same time interpreting this as the product of studiously artistic craft and by no means naive confession, because not only was Curtis well aware of and fully ready to make use of his charisma, especially by combining this charisma with "unnerving and unsettling . . . physical things he did on stage," akin to that performance artists like Marina Abramović or Ron Athey where "you didn't know where it was going to take you," but also Curtis deliberately cultivated what Dickinson hears as "a very strange American accent" that also "pitched his voice very low . . . it sounded very ethereal, like a character from a film, something that floats in front of you and isn't quite there" (284-285).

***

In "Trying to Find a Clue, Trying to Find a Way to Get Out!: The European Imaginary of Joy Division," published as part of *Heart & Soul: Critical Essays on Joy Division,* Giacomo Bottà offers a detailed discussion of the strong connections many, including notably Stephen Morris, have also otherwise noted between the musical sound of Joy Division and krautrock, or komische rock. Bottà usefully cites David Stubbs in explaining how Morris's style of playing drums "is an example of the cyclical, looped approach which harks back to Can's Jaki Licherzeit" (quoted 40).

In the same book, with "In a Lonely Place: Illness and the Temporal Exile of Ian Curtis" Tiffany Naiman offers a compelling interpretation of Ian Curtis's vocals by way of her concept of "ill Style," an adaptation of Theodor Adorno's "late style." Naiman proposes "ill style" involves, in this case, Curtis singing in a way that expresses and communicates not only his experience of being chronically ill, and seriously disabled, but also "a sense of exile from normative time," reflective of "premonitions that they will not be contributing to a future or due to challenges faced from disability or illness," which people living with serious disability and chronic illness do experience (85). Naiman contends Curtis's vocals demonstrate a coming to terms with, and at least a partial acceptance, of his illness and disability, offering "an abject performance of ill style outside or normative time," a performance, in other words, "of an exiled, nihilistic bodily experience" (87). Naiman calls attention to the isolated vocal of Ian Curtis singing "Love Will Tear Us Apart," before the addition of studio processing and treatment to this vocal, and separate from the rest of the sounds comprising the song, where Curtis's voice "sounds bare and vulnerable" with his "articulation" sounding "as though it is coming mostly from a tensed jaw rather than muscular control over the cheeks, which here sound especially loose." What's more, "Despite Curtis's attempts to take command of his body, the words are slightly slurred, with lax breath control" as "He nearly runs out of breath throughout," singing "under pitch and with an extreme vibrato," "routinely unintentionally flat," and with yet further "vocal wobble," all of which together "draws attention to his physical vulnerability, anguish and exhaustion," suggestive "of a man not fully present and capable of accomplishing what he sets out to do" (90-91). Naiman indicates Hannett's adding a heavy amount of reverb along with "the elimination of breath and vibrato" to Curtis's vocals partially disguised Curtis's 'ill voice', while at the same time helping define Joy Division's style by making use of reverb to "create the impression of space, and therefore, distance," that includes a feeling of "separating Curtis's voice from his body"

(92). As Naiman explains, in relation to "Decades," use of reverb here "lends a distance to his vocal presence, as is he is singing from the beyond," while also adding "just a touch of echo (the slower delay, rather than the sped-up reverb)" contributes "an untimely repetition that is removed from the act of utterance, taking the vocal out of its time and repeating it as a memory so that it functions as something that is both current and of the past" (93).

Ultimately, Naiman argues for the value of listening for, and learning to hear, the ill style in Curtis's vocals, as well as how this is mediated and elaborated by way of reverb, echo, and further processing and treatment, because, as many others have found likewise in the case of Joy Division, "the producer worked to recreate this uneasiness" (95)–the uneasiness that the chronically ill and seriously disabled feel about their situation, about their bodies, and about their relationship to normative time. As Naiman explains, working with this kind of understanding of Ian Curtis's vocalization can help "expand listeners' understanding of illness as a state of being inherent to the human condition and to consider alternative temporalities." Doing so "desegregates illness from the real of so-called normal experience" (95).

Also part of *Heart & Soul*, Robin Parmar's "Joy Division in Space: The Aesthetics of Estrangement" offers especially precise and illuminating explanations and interpretations of Joy Division's musical sound, with emphasis once again on Hannett's contributions. Among the particular contributions Parmar cites are Hannett departing from convention by assigning the snare drum its own separate track, in order to "isolate this drum from the rest of the rhythmic pulse," while also using digital delay to "thicken the beat, with the timbre reduced to a white noise impulse through extreme equalization" and "Ample reverberation was then applied" (137). With both Sumner's guitar and sometimes Hook's bass, Parmar notes "the extreme dynamic range compression" Hannett implemented. Discussing "Disorder" Parmar focuses on the opening four bars where only the drum kit is present, but while they occupy the center of the soundstage their reverberation "is strangely divorced from the source signal . . . panned to the extreme left and right" which "is an unnatural effect since there is no physical room in which such a sound could be heard" (139). Meanwhile, "The strong articulation of the delay sets up its own counter-rhythm, undercutting the otherwise-propulsive beat of the music proper" (139). And "Though the guitar and bass are more conventionally treated, the vocals have ghostly after-effects in the left channel," while "Knitting together these disparate elements are the noisy 'whoops' from what can be assumed to be a synthesizer" that "acts not as an instrument but as artifice, an unmusical force somewhere between rhythmic accompaniment and environmental effluent" (139). As Parmar aptly sums up, Hannett's use of "the expressive possibilities" of production is no longer designed to create a semblance of a live performance, with instead "Disruptive techniques such as these" "Hannett's stock-in-trade" (139).

In the case of "Digital" Parmar calls our attention not only to "a Joy Division trademark that eschews the usual central place of guitar chords in rock music" but also to a beat that contains "a powerful downstroke and two powerful snare hits, but the third beat is largely missing" so that "Instead of a pulse clearly in 4/4 or 2/4 time, we have the strange count '1 2 [null] 4'" as "there is a space here that creates a moment of suspension" (139). Continuing to discuss "Digital," Parmar notes "Even within his limited vocal range, Curtis is expressive, alternating between three registers" while

"The dislocation" of the refrain "from the other lyrics is marked," as if coming "from some other place, from some other voice," while the "grain of the voice" sonically encapsulates the song's content concerning "the urgent *process* of decision making" with the singer "paradoxically committing to both options at the same time": "'don't ever fade away, and on the other hand 'fade away'" (140). As a song "about the process of its own becoming," the musical sound of "Digital" is crucial, "explicitly acknowledging its spaces and elisions," "with a pulse missing a downbeat," "with delayed and corrupted echoes of the original vocals," "with lyrics that refuse resolution, documenting only the indeterminate process itself" (140). As Parmar elaborates, "The emphasis is on the formation of patterns, not the patterns themselves, which are only adumbrations, tentative shadows of what might be. The emphasis is on the phenomenal *space* in which meaning could (perhaps) form" (140).

In discussing "Transmission" Parmar describes the song as follows:

the reverb is most prominent on the snare. This instrument has been given a distinct echo, placed just off the beat. This would be an unusual decision for a conventional production, as it diminishes the forward momentum of the song. But, as the earlier analysis of "Disorder" demonstrated, this is a Hannett trademark. The unexpected rhythmic complexity is jarring. It increases the listeners' anxiety, reinforcing Curtis's unnerving performance. The signature bass ostinato that introduces the song is joined on bar seven by drums and bar eight by a tight guitar figure from Sumner. The guitar then disappears from the mix, providing a pocket on the spectrum for Curtis's reserved vocal delivery, mixed low, almost to the point of obscurity. The tone of his voice is peculiar, filtered, as though he may be singing through a radio set, from another space or time. (149)

All of this departure from and disruption of the conventional is most apt, Parmar suggests, for a song that involves "a confrontational examination of normative expectations" (149).

In sum, Parmar emphasizes how "Hannett's recording process separated instruments from each other, even from themselves and their recognizable timbres," with "The electric guitar, traditional rock lead instrument . . . relegated to the periphery," as "Resonant noise, sound effects and synthesizer tones supplemented, even supplanted, sounds from more conventional instruments" while "Time-based effects (echo and reverberation) resituated sounds in artificial acoustic spaces" and "The rhythms set up by these delays often conflicted with the inherent musical pulse" (151). Collectively, Parmar contends, "this suite of techniques functioned as an *aesthetics of estrangement*, stripping sounds of their relationships to location . . . and milieu . . . breaking down the ususal functions of musicians in a band . . . and trading the energy and immediacy of live performances for a longevity they might not otherwise have achieved" (151). This 'aesthetics of estrangement' Parmar finds most apt in conjunction with Peter Saville's designs and especially Curtis's lyrics, where the latter "wrote about the distances between people, constraints on movement and experience and the impossibility of constructing an integrated phenomenological reality. His lyrics formed an incomplete web of signification, providing spaces where listeners could insert their own experience and interpretations" (151). As Parmar concludes, "This is the function of Joy Division's music: to fill space with transmissions that must be traced back to an imagined origin, different for every interpolated listener experience" (152).

***

I will cite one final source in elaborating this repertoire of preceding descriptions, analyses, and interpretations of the musical sound of Joy Division: Michael Bracewell's essay "Licht und Blindheit" that offers a close description of what Bracewell hears in listening to "Dead Souls," an account that provides a useful model of what such a close description can be like, and how it can provide the effective basis and support for a compelling interpretation. To begin, "The music manifests from resonant silence. It is as though a sound-proofed door has been opened at the far end of a long corridor. We seem suddenly to be hearing an instrumental exercise that might have been following its course for some time, gradually building in controlled intensity" (21). Continuing onward, Bracewell next indicates, as we listen more closely we hear "Stark and deft, the loosely swinging, echoing beat provides a chassis to carry the interplay of guitar and bass. The guitar sound is metallic, scything. It brings to mind the wind through power lines, or machine parts being sewn from sheet metal" (21-22). Here, "The sound is also plaintive, sinuous and fluid, given depth by the bass running softly ahead, just beneath the surface of the rhythm," as "The drums, guitar and bass configure and entwine like a trio of sonic apparitions" (22). And then, "Fifty seconds in, the accumulating intensity shifts temper" as "The guitar becomes more aggressive, breaking out into four clamorous crescendos, each backed by the tumbling accompaniment of the bass" with "This abrasive package . . . closed with a double beat in the drum, and the rhythm becomes looser, resuming its swinging beat" (22). At this point, "The intensity appears to ease; aerating space opens within the track. The heat of emotion meets the acoustics of absolute zero" (22). But "The calm is short-lived" as "With accelerating urgency, guitar and bass drive the music to a reprise of the harshly metallic crescendo," with the last seeming to "fall neatly into place, its collapse caught by a deft doubling of the drum beat" (22). And then, "at two minutes twelve seconds–a little under half-way through the track–Curtis starts to sing" (22). As Bracewell hears it, Curtis's "deep, faintly transatlantic voice sounds at once frightened and frightening, stentorian yet pushed by gathering panic" (22).

In contrast with "Dead Souls," the other contribution to the original Sordide Sentimentale *Licht und Blindheit* ep, "Atmosphere," Bracewell hears as slower, colder, with "accents of icily glittering beauty," and even though, like numerous others, as "funereal," Bracewell hears this combining with "passages of luxuriant emotional release, building to cathartic crescendo" (23). Both tracks, Bracewell suggest, although seemingly "driven by a compelling sense of tragic destiny," also hold, "in uneasy tension," a "confluence of urgency and exhaustion" (23).

Six

In his contribution to *We Were Strangers: Stories Inspired by* <u>Unknown Pleasures</u>, titled, like the first song on this same album, "Disorder," Nicholas Royle explains his story "is made out of the lyrics to *Unknown Pleasures*, these words and no others. No quotation is used and no word is repeated unless it is represented in the lyrics" (20). In an elliptically atmospheric and overtly anti-

147

realist as well as anti-naturalist fashion, Royle's "Disorder" suggests something akin to an order amidst, or arising out of, or contending with disorder, which only partially succeeds, and only partially aims to succeed. The story, like *Unknown Pleasures*, and like the song that opens this album with the title "Disorder," respects the mysterious; it does not aim to 'cut this down to size', but rather to maintain and even enhance it. Yet Royle's story suggests glimpses of possible elements of order within an otherwise pervasive state of disorder.

"Disorder" commonly signifies in relation to "order"–as, perhaps, the opposite or absence of order; or, perhaps, a breakdown or collapse of order; or, perhaps, an incomplete and imperfect state of order; or, perhaps, a disruption of and even an opposition to and an undermining or subversion of order; or, perhaps, what falls outside of yet remains proximate to and even continually or repeatedly shows up within order, including by infecting or contaminating order or by shadowing or haunting order.

It might seem "disorder" readily conveys negative connotations, as that which is problematic, undesirable, and needs to be vigilantly contested and, as far as possible, forestalled or prevented. And yet this need not be so. What if order, or if *an* order, or if *a* state of order, is oppressive, is repressive, and what if it is linked with an oppressive, and repressive, institution of discipline and punishment, of domination and subjection, and even authoritarianism and totalitarianism? What if disorder signifies resistance to such an oppressive, and repressive order?

Let's consider, more precisely, what "order" might encompass, and what "disorder" might thereby be "dis-ing": i.e., interrupting, unsettling, breaking with, breaking from, and breaking apart. According to my (admittedly dated) *Oxford English Reference Dictionary* (revised 2nd edition, 2002), order involves, first, "the condition in which every part, unit, etc. is in its right place; tidiness." But what is the right place, who determines how and why, and what if this becomes excessive, that *every* part must be so, and what if tidiness becomes obsessive, compulsive, and harmful? Second, order refers to "a usually specified sequence, succession, etc." But, again, if this is "usually" so, then that already suggests the unusual exists, and it also raises the question of specified how, of what, by whom, when, where, and why? Third, order can signify "an authoritative command, direction, instruction, etc." But who exercises this authority, in relation to and over whom, on what basis, and to advance what ends and serve what interests? What prevents authoritative from becoming authoritarian? Fourth, order might reference "a state of peaceful harmony under a constituted authority," which does suggest this might be an authority that is authoritative but the opposite of authoritarian, yet the question remains, constituted how, on what basis, and to advance what ends and serve what interests? Fifth, order can refer to "a social class, rank, etc., constituting a distinct group in society." But what is the relative position of this order to other order*s* within the social whole, and why? On what bases are these distinct, and even separate–or at least separable? To what extent are these distinguishing demarcations among order*s* achieved versus ascribed, and to what extent are they welcome or unwelcome, chosen or imposed, flexible or inflexible, empowering or disempowering?

Sixth, order can refer to, simply, "a kind; a sort." Here, again, in concrete practice this raises the question of what kinds, or sorts, distinguished how, according to what standards or criteria, and in support of what ends and whose interests? Seventh, order might reference "the constitution or nature of the world, society, etc.," in other words some kind of general overarching order. Here questions that arise include how absolute, eternal, inevitable and unalterable is this order–or does it appear to be, or has it been made to appear to be? Is order at this level necessarily singular, or is it possible that the constitution of nature or of the world, of society, and so on might be multiple, plural, continually evolving and transforming, and subject to effective pressure to change? More prosaically, eighth, order could signify "written direction to a manufacturer, tradesman, waiter, etc. to supply something" or "the quantity of goods etc. supplied." But who gives these kinds of directions to whom, under what conditions, in the context of what kinds of relationships, and to what extent is the process of giving and receiving orders, even such as these, always infused with inequitable power relations and embodying inequitable power dynamics?

A further, ninth, signification is "a taxonomic rank below a class or above a family," and, although this seems incontrovertible 'fact' when applied strictly to biology, what are the implications when we think about how these two words are used sociologically, and what connotations have developed with and accrued to each, as well to how we distinguish and relate being a member of each of these versus each other–i.e., a member of a class versus a member of a family? Why are these categories necessarily ranked, moreover, in vertical terms, in terms of height–below and above–and how does this play into conventional associations of those above, or of that which is positioned above, with greater power and those below, or that which is positioned below, with lesser power? Tenth, order can refer to "a fraternity of monks and friars, formerly of knights, bound by a common rule of life," or "any of the grades of the Christian ministry," or "the status of a member of the clergy," or "a Masonic or similar fraternity," or "the insignia worn by members of an order," or "a company of distinguished people instituted especially by a sovereign to which appointments are made as an honour or reward," or "a style of address and equipment" identifying affiliation with a particular order, and even, "in Christian theology, any of the nine grades of angelic beings (seraphim, cherubin, thrones, dominations, principalities, powers, virtues, archangels, angels)." Here we encounter a variety of selective, exclusive, and elevated groups and groupings, that historically at least are traceable to religious and secular authority, and suggestive of an elite company distinguishable from all others not qualified to so belong. Again, this definition raises questions concerning the bases by which distinctions and demarcations, and especially inclusions and exclusions are made, as well as how readily possible, and for whom, and how readily impossible, and for whom else, is elevation to become part of and participant within any of these kinds of orders?

Continuing, eleventh, order can refer to "any style of ancient architecture distinguished by the type of column used" as well as "any style or mode of architecture subject to uniform established proportions," or, in mathematics, "a degree of complexity of a differential equation," "the order of the highest derivative in the equation," "the size of a matrix," or "the number of elements of a finite group." What these definitions add is again a sense of precisely organizing and distinguishing, which again, extended more broadly to consider 'forms of order' more pervasively operative, on what bases, and in support of what ends and in the service of whose interests are precise structures created and implemented, and do they serve to facilitate, regulate, allocate, and distribute? A further, twelfth, definition involves "the stated form of divine service," or perhaps even, more broadly, of any religious service, and "the principles of procedure, decorum, etc., accepted by a meeting, legislative assembly, etc. or enforced by its president," or by any presiding authority. Here, we recognize efforts to insure productivity, effectiveness, and efficiency in how groups of people interact together for an at least ostensibly shared reason or purpose, but we can once again nonetheless raise the question of who determines this form, these principles, and their enforcement, on what bases, and how accommodating, how flexible, and how inclusive are they? In other words, yes these kinds of 'orders' make much possible, but what do they render impossible, or at least less possible? Finally, thirteenth, an order can refer to "a pass admitting the bearer to a theatre, museum, private house, etc. free or cheap as a privilege," and yet once more this raises the question of who receives this order, and who does not, from whom, on what bases, and why?

Human beings, human communities, and human societies need order, and need orders. We are continually striving to create and recreate, to find and establish, and to secure and adhere to myriad different kinds of orders, while every structure we observe and follow, in enabling us to achieve meaning, purpose, value, and fulfillment in our life-practices, including our relations with others, constitutes a form of order, and these range from those that are overarching, such as the order that common measurements of time provide us–in terms of seconds, minutes, hours, days, weeks, months, seasons, years, decades, centuries–and more narrowly precise and culturally specific, such as prevalent patterns of fashionable dress and appearance in a particular place and at a particular time.

It is useful to consider how poststructuralism enables us to engage critically with these and other familiar 'orders'. Poststructuralism refers to an array of theories first emergent in the mid-1960s emphasizing a great deal of suspicion versus structuralists' claims about the stability and coherence of structures supposedly underlying and undergirding human social relations (in particular those structures that structuralists identified as 'universal', 'fundamental', 'ultimate', or 'absolute'). Poststructuralism is especially suspicious concerning the stability and coherence of structures across time and space. Poststructuralism points out that structures are themselves constructed, reconstructed, vary, and change–and that structures are always open to potential deconstruction. Poststructuralism exposes how structures are time- and space- bound, as well as socially and politically interested (rather than natural and neutral).

Yet, even so, poststructuralism readily acknowledges most structures are not easily changed–structural change usually takes considerable effort, by many, over long periods of time, and faces considerable entrenched resistance. Conventions are conventions, after all, poststructuralists readily acknowledge, because they maintain a powerful hold, and are supportive of powerful interests.

The following are some examples of structures, which, on the one hand, poststructuralists argue are not as permanently stable and seamlessly coherent as structuralists are wont to claim, but which are also, on the other hand, hard to dispense with and require time and effort to fundamentally alter: (1) structures of how education takes place in the schools, (2) structures involved in defining relations between labor and leisure, (3) structures affecting the organization of specific duties and operations in the workplace, (4) structures of family relations, (5) structures of family holidays and of extended family get-togethers, (6) structures of church-going and of individual as well as collective worship, (7) structures involved in attending to birth and death, (8) structures involved in weddings, and (9) structures affecting eating and sleeping, etc.

So order, of some kind and to some degree, seems not only necessary and desirable but also inevitable and inescapable. Yet, important questions can and should be raised concerning on what bases an order (or a condition or state or order) is established, to advance what ends and serve whose interests, how exclusively versus inclusively is an order (or condition or state of order) constituted and why so, and how flexible versus inflexible as well as how open to change is an order (or condition and state of order) and why so. Order often depends not only upon inclusion and exclusion, and not only upon arrangement of included constituent elements in organized patterns but also arrangement in terms of hierarchies of importance, value, significance, and power. Order can readily conjure associations with matters such as 'law and order', disciplinary and punitive orders, command or demand and obedience or submission, and conformity with and consent to even that which is alienating, exploitative, oppressive, repressive, unjust, dehumanizing, and otherwise destructive. This in turn suggests disorder, often commonly associated with chaos, anarchy, disorganization, inefficiency, ineffectuality, clutter, mess, and so on might well prove positively necessary and enabling–and empowering and transformative.

Another common association with 'disorder' involves many physical and mental health conditions. Here it is worth paying critical attention to how 'order' and 'ordered' are conflated with 'normal' and 'normality', and how readily the movement is often made from identifying people experiencing a mental or physical health 'disorder' as people who are experiencing an 'abnormal' state of mental or physical health. Even more insidious, people experiencing a mental or physical health 'disorder' are often treated as 'disordered' and 'abnormal' in and of themselves. This way of thinking positions those experiencing what are commonly identified as 'disabilities' as people who live abnormal lives, lives that are lesser rather than different. It can also suggest it is the responsibility of the individual themself for being so disordered that they are in turn disabled. Rather than perceiving everyone as living on a complex continuum, or spectrum, involving multiple and changing kinds and degrees of able-bodiedness (or 'able-mindedness'), thinking in terms of 'disorders' can suggest hard and fast lines separate the normal, the healthy, and the able-bodied (and the 'able-minded') from the abnormal, unhealthy, and disabled.

I live with what is conventionally identified as a digestive dysmotility disorder, that is, according to the latest scientific research, rooted in an overactive and hypersensitive immune system disorder. My condition, and my experience, is marked out, in those terms, as 'not normal', and the impact of this labeling I recognize all too well given how many, many times I've desperately wished that 'my body was normal'–that my digestive system worked 'normally', i.e., that my immune system functioned normally. Likewise, in relation to my experience of epilepsy, even though not usually severe, I too have felt an intense desire to 'be normal', to not suffer from a 'disordered' and 'abnormal' brain and nervous system. And the same with my experience of anxiety, itself commonly identified as 'generalized anxiety disorder', and of depression, also commonly conceived as a result of a disorder in brain functioning, a disordered state of reasoning, a disordered mode of affect, or a disordered series of responses to a history of environmentally traumatizing experiences.

'Disorder' is not neutral in its connotations, when it is associated with a significant, continuing, acute and/or chronic dimension of a person's life-experience. Yes, these impairments present challenges that can be tremendously painful, and even tremendously debilitating, but they are not necessarily insurmountable handicaps in the quest to live a meaningful life–a satisfying, fulfilling, rewarding, and engaged life. And insofar as they do present challenges, should it not be our collective social responsibility to strive to help each other meet these challenges, and to find ways and means to as fully as possible accommodate people facing mental and physical health challenges due to mental and physical health impairments? And should we not attend to, and respect, the insights that emanate from the vantage points of those who live with significant impairments, and thereby significant challenges, to their physical and/or mental health? What can those with *different* physical and mental health vantage points learn, of value, from these people's ways of perceiving, sensing, feeling, thinking about, understanding, imagining, dreaming, responding to, interacting with, and engaging with their bodies, with their selves, with others, and with their communities, societies, cultures, and the greater natural world?

One further common conception of 'disorder' I suggest is worth mentioning here: disorder in the sense of entropy. Again, so as to provide a readily accessible definition, according to my *Oxford English Reference Dictionary*, entropy "represents a measure of the unavailability of a system's thermal energy for conversion into mechanical work," "a measure of the rate of transfer of information in a message," and "the degree of disorder or randomness of any physical system, expressed as the probability of occurrence of its particular arrangement of particles." In turn, "Thermodynamic theory indicates that the entropy of an isolated system can increase but never decrease," and, "Considered as a closed system, therefore, the universe must always increase in entropy, the eventual consequence being a heat death–a state in which structure is absent and temperature is uniform." In common parlance, people use entropy to refer to the inevitable, inescapable tendency of virtually any state of order always to become disordered, such that order, like equilibrium, happens much more rarely, and is a far less stable and lasting state of affairs than disorder, like disequilibrium. What this entropic conception of disorder adds to those I have already identified is attention to a seeming fundamental paradox characteristic of so much of human existence, and especially human activity: our continual striving for order even as disorder always overtakes whatever order we temporarily secure.

The lyrics to "Disorder" provide no obvious clues concerning how the song itself invites and encourages us to make sense of this title–to what sense of, or experience of, or kind of 'disorder' this song references, or which this song 'is about'. Likewise, the lyrics provide no obvious clues concerning what is the position the song is inviting and encouraging us to adopt in relation to whatever sense, experience, or kind of disorder to which the song is alluding. This is where close attention to the sounds, patterns of sounds, and deployments of sounds across the duration of the song can help in directing us to what makes greater versus lesser sense in understanding what disorder–and order–mean in relation to this song. But before proceeding to that point I want to show how the lyrics taken alone raise further challenges as well as offer limited assistance in choosing among multiple potentially viable interpretations of meaning. To begin, though, I need to discuss the title just a little further. The title itself is not directly referenced anywhere else in the song. In an earlier draft of this song, included in *So This is Permanence: Joy Division Lyrics and Notebooks*, we see Ian Curtis initially titled these lyrics "Spirit." As I will discuss further in proceeding through the lyrics, that is hardly the only significant change he made. If anything, the thrust of these changes render the lyrics all the more ambiguous, mysterious, and opaque; it strikes me Curtis aimed for these lyrics to challenge us to work, hard, at making sense of them, and to not make interpretation easy for us by doing this work for us.

"I've been waiting for a guide to come and take me by the hand"–not only begins the lyrics but also introduces us to the singer as the narrator-protagonist of the lyrics. This voice represents the narrator, and protagonist, of the lyrics, but not necessarily of the song as a whole, because it makes better sense, I propose, to conceive of all four principals (and Martin Hannett as producer as well) as all protagonists and as all contributing to the narration of whatever story, including whatever drama, we hear, experience, and interpret this song as enacting and recounting. The 'I' might be close, might be distant, or might bear an indeterminate relationship to Ian Curtis the actual person; we don't know. But what we do have is the 'I' *here*, how this 'I' appears and what it does in these lyrics, and how the 'I' is vocalized by the singer. The first line of the lyrics suggests a striking open admission of need, and for someone to take this 'I' "by the hand" is yet further striking in conjuring up an image of intimacy. This might represent an admission of vulnerability, or of hesitancy, but it also might represent a desire for a teacher or a mentor–or even simply a more experienced and perhaps more immediately confident friend. But it is important to note, right away, the fact the song indicates "I *have been* waiting," which can suggest, as present perfect tense, that the 'I' continues to wait and has been doing so for awhile, but it can also suggest this waiting is now past. At the least, opening the lyrics by declaring 'I' have been so waiting, for an indefinite period of time, for this kind of guide, suggests the waiting has proven significant and exerts present consequences, although these may prove indeterminate.

"Could these sensations make me feel the pleasures of a normal man?" makes us, as listeners, and readers, curious as to what kind of connection might logically or otherwise exist between this question posed here, in this second line, and the statement introduced, that starts the lyrics, in the first line. How are "these sensations," whatever they may prove to be, not only related to "feeling the pleasures of a normal man," but also to "waiting for a guide to take me by the hand"? *"These sensations"* suggests some definite yet in this context indeterminate set or kind of sensations, perhaps in turn suggesting the 'I' as narrator-protagonist is unconcerned to explain to us, or assumes we will intuitively understand what 'he' means, or will connect them with a particular set or kind of sensations that make sense, in this emerging context, to and for us. How a specific set or kind of sensations enable 'feeling' "the pleasures of a normal man" likewise remains mysterious. What kinds of sensations might be capable of this accomplishment? What kinds of "pleasures" does "a normal man" "feel"? What constitutes "a normal man"? By posing the question as this line does, concerning the prospect that "these sensations," whatever they might be, might "make me feel the pleasures of a normal man," the narrator-protagonist, the 'I' of the lyrics, is implying 'he' does *not* "feel the pleasures of a normal man"–and, perhaps, does *not* feel like a 'normal man'. The question perhaps wistfully wonders what it might be like to experience pleasures 'like a normal man'–even perhaps what it might be like, even more generally, to feel and experience 'like a normal man'–from the vantage point of someone who perhaps 'feels' pleasures other than normal, perhaps feels sensations other than normal, and perhaps feels 'himself' as other than normal.

"These sensations barely interest me for another day"–seems to suggest a movement of cancellation, at least in part, of what has been recounted in the preceding two lines, or at least a distancing from the waiting and wondering, and perhaps from the longing, yearning, and hoping that those two lines might reference. Here it seems the 'I' of the lyrics, the narrator-protagonist of these lyrics, is ready to proceed otherwise, although a lingering connection remains with "barely" and "for another day," suggesting vestiges of that previous waiting and wondering, and perhaps longing, yearning, and hoping, are receding but have not yet entirely receded. Whatever the case, it seems like a shift toward a possible new determination to proceed and perhaps engage without waiting for another to serve as the narrator-protagonist's guide in doing so, for another to take the lead instead, and without (any more) desiring to experience the pleasures and sensations, or to identify as and seek the status, of "a normal man."

"I've got the spirit, lose the feeling, take the shock away"–immediately poses another challenge to interpretation, as we need to figure out how we are understanding what "spirit" here signifies, and how this is distinct from and related to whatever sense of feeling is signified by "*the feeling*" here as well as whatever shock is signified by "*the* shock" here. It is notable that the "I" has 'got' the spirit, suggesting perhaps something like the spirit is moving within me, or I am experiencing myself full of and motivated, perhaps even carried and driven forward, by the spirit, or that I have accomplished something potentially most significant in acquiring the spirit, perhaps even in *capturing* the spirit. The spirit here may well, it seems plausible, be embodied in 'me'. However, often when people suggest they find themselves 'inspired' or are praised for their showing of 'spirit' this is indissociably linked with 'feeling'–with 'showing feeling', with being impassioned, which itself is often conceived as manifestation of strong feeling. Here, however, in this line it seems like a distinction is being drawn, or at least suggested, not only between 'spirit' and at least some kind or kinds of 'feeling' but also with at least some kind or kinds of 'sensations'. It is worth noting as well "lose the feeling" might come across as an imperative or at least an invocation–perhaps a suggestion or instruction or command or demand, of 'one's self' to '*lose*' this feeling, perhaps because it is incompatible or contradictory with the spirit and what the spirit encompasses, even with what the spirit requires. Likewise, "take the shock away" might also come across as an imperative or at least an invocation–again, to 'one's self' perhaps, but also quite plausibly to some other, to "*take* the shock away," which again might have to do with the need to do so in order to fully embody and carry forward what the spirit encompasses, represents, expects, requires, commands, or demands. "Lose the feeling," however, could, perhaps, and here I am anticipating later lyrics, also suggest something like 'letting lose the feeling'–or even again an imperative, or invocation, to 'let loose the feeling'. In sum, nevertheless, what this spirit might be, what this feeling might be, what this shock might be, and what these sensations and what these pleasures might be all remain mysterious.

In the earlier draft of these lyrics, published in *So This is Permanence*, Curtis writes, notably differently than in the lyrics he ultimately contributes to and performs as part of this stanza, what looks like "Cure sensation make me feel the pleasures of a normal man/Lose sensation spare the insults leave them for another day/Brand new spirit, touch these feelings, take the shock away." In this earlier version, the lyrics more readily read as suggestive of a definite wish to feel like a normal man, and perhaps be cured of some kind of illness, or the equivalent, that prevents that experience (of feeling like a normal man), while the addition of "spare the insults leave them for another day" suggests a wish, perhaps an inclination and even a determination, to move, at least temporarily, from a situation involving a marked extent and degree of hostility, although it remains ambiguous from whom and toward whom these insults might be directed. In addition, "brand new spirit," although still ambiguous, is less so than simply "spirit," suggestive in this context of a commitment to a new beginning, to a fresh start, to breaking with and leaving behind a problematic situation, while "touch these feelings" reads remarkably differently than "lose the feeling," almost suggestive of a kind of reconciliation with, an embrasure of, and a taking on of feelings as opposed to a jettisoning of them. In this earlier version of these lyrics, "spirit" and "feelings" seem as if they could well be aligned rather than opposed, or at least not problematically misaligned or dis-aligned. And yet, perhaps, "touch these feelings" is part of 'taking the shock away' and enabling the arrival of, identification with, taking over by, and/or carrying forward of the 'brand new spirit'. This earlier version of these lyrics almost seems to suggest a sense of guilt, and perhaps shame, about not being 'the man' that the 'I' of the song would like to be, and perhaps not necessarily relating to or treating others the way this 'I' would like to do.

Stanza two seems like it verges on a more directly concrete depiction: "It's getting faster, moving faster now, it's getting out of hand/On the tenth floor, down the back stairs, it's a no man's land/Lights are flashing, cars are crashing, getting frequent now/I've got the spirit, lose the feeling, let it out somehow." We don't gain much clarity concerning what 'it' might here reference, although 'it' seems like it involves a heightened state of adrenalin, perhaps of excitement, perhaps of anxiety, and quite possibly intense awareness of the close proximinity of an imminent confrontation with the fraught, the precarious, the dangerous, and the threatening. "It's a no man's land" suggests a position of extreme vulnerability, at high risk of exposure to a possible attack, and even to destruction, as well as a borderline territory between sharply contending forces. Interestingly, Curtis changes the line from the earlier version included in *So This is Permanence* referencing "On the fourth floor" to "On the tenth floor," suggestive of an increased emphasis on both how high up 'I' and 'we' along with this 'I' are initially positioned versus what is growing rapidly faster, more frequent, louder, and altogether overwhelming, as well as how far we then must descend "down the back stairs" even if that descent seems like it has little if anything to do with escaping. "No man's land" suggests a war zone, while lights flashing and cars crashing suggest some other but perhaps related, or in some way strikingly similar, kind of 'accident and emergency'–some major destructive, including life-imperiling event. Perhaps an explosion? Perhaps some kind of physical attack? Perhaps this stanza suggests a surge of adrenalin preceding a public performance is likely to prove physically and emotionally exhausting. Perhaps this public performance requires pushing one's body and bearing one's soul. Perhaps this public performance involves invoking and performing as a dramatic persona or as dramatic personae. Perhaps doing any or all of this requires pressing toward, and beyond, an extreme limit. All of that can be both exhilarating and frightening to anticipate.

At the end of this stanza, the concluding line from the first stanza is repeated with a change in the third and final phrase, from "take the shock away" to "let it out somehow," which suggests a need, or at least a desire, to release something held within, perhaps spirit, perhaps sensation, perhaps feelings, perhaps some combination or articulation of all three, but the word "somehow" communicates a sense of uncertainty, perhaps indecision, and, likely a yet further sense that whatever the "I" wants or needs to 'let out' is out of the control of the I to let it out. Or, perhaps, 'I' is still searching for means, or still summoning up the ability, to do so.

A different direction of interpretation might read these lyrics as suggesting the narrator-protagonist is here the target, and the direct victim, of an overt attack, including upon his body, and is striving as best 'he' possibly can to will himself to survive through the course of attack, through what is being done to him–or to do so through the course of what he anticipates soon is about to be done to him–including by striving to leave old sensations behind, to forget relying upon anyone else to come to his aid and help him in this desperate situation, to trust in the spirit (perhaps 'his [life] spirit') to carry him through, and to seek to become numb in feeling, throughout the duration of the attack, while seeking (and this anticipates later in the lyrics) to unite with new sensations, after and as a result of surviving the attack.

"What means to you, what means to me, and we will meet again"–begins the third stanza by introducing another 'character', at least strongly implicit up until now, but not yet directly referenced prior to this point, and that is 'you', which we, as listeners to this song, and readers of these lyrics, are likely inclined to interpret as referring to 'us', just as we are likely to interpret the 'we' as referring to 'us' together with the 'I' (and here 'me') that has been narrating, and simultaneously serving as principal protagonist, in these lyrics. Interestingly, in the earlier version of these lyrics reproduced in *So This is Permanence*, Curtis writes "There's more of me + more of us and we will meet again," which indicates a striking change has occurred since that earlier draft, with the earlier draft suggesting a confidence and assurance about where the venture the lyrics describe, and enact, is headed, that the final version eschews. "Means" (to you and to me) is more ambiguous (than more of me and of you), especially juxtaposed with 'meeting again', while the line is yet further so in suggesting 'means to you' and 'means to me' might not coincide, or not entirely, directly, and immediately. Yet, even if whatever it is that 'means' means differently to 'I'/'me' and to 'you', we will nonetheless "meet *again*," and this suggests we bear some connection to each other, perhaps even some sense of shared fate or destiny, although 'again' is unspecific, and in the context of the rest of the line suggests we each may need to take on whatever challenge this is, each ourselves by ourselves and for ourselves alone, without 'waiting for a guide to take us by the hand', and with the only encouragement we receive being that if we do so, if we enter the fray–perhaps enter the void? perhaps enter the abyss?–we will meet again with the same 'I'/'me' that is nebulously sketching out broad contours of what we are on the brink of taking on.

The next line, "I'm watching you, I'm watching her, I'll take no pity from your friends," changes from the earlier draft slightly but nonetheless significantly, as that earlier draft reads "I'm watching you, We're watching you, We take no pity from your friends." The 'I' here continues to stand at a distance, even as it seems hauntingly close, and here demarcates a distance by declaring this

'I' will be watching 'us', and some 'other' identifiable here only as 'her', which may or may not serve as a stand-in for all those others, like us, who are treading this same path, facing the same challenge, and determining when and if they are ready, as well as how, to enter the fray. And yet the reference in the earlier version to 'We' suggests it is possible it is not the 'I' alone that is watching us, and watching 'her'–perhaps 'we' who are addressed by the 'I' here as 'you' are joining with this 'I' in watching ourselves, and in watching 'her', and perhaps the 'her' is likewise joining with the 'I' in watching us and watching herself.

Perhaps all of these markers–'I', 'me', 'you', 'her'–reference aspects or dimensions within a single albeit complex 'self' or 'subject'. Perhaps they suggest how selfhood or subjectivity is not in fact as singular as commonsense tells us it is, but rather always multiple–inevitably, inescapably, and potentially empoweringly so, even if accessing and exercising this power demands a passage through an experience of 'self-shattering'. This could involve the feeling that who we have imagined (and who we felt safe, content, and comfortable to believe) ourselves to be is being 'shattered' within and without, including in front, behind, along the sides, and all around us.

"I'll take no pity from your friends" is curious, as it suggests, by implication, that whoever these 'friends' might be, they might well be inclined to extend pity. Yet why so is unclear: why would these friends, our friends, be inclined to pity the 'I' of these lyrics, the lyrics' principal narrator-protagonist? What is it about 'him', about whom he is or has been, about what he is or has been like, about what he is doing or has done or is about to do, that makes him a prospective object of pity? The refusal of pity is likewise striking as this suggests a certain amount of pride, a certain amount even of defiance, that the 'I' here will be and do as 'he' must, as he determines he must be and do, or as he is called upon to be and do. Perhaps this refusal of pity, as well as the prospective inclination of others to extend it has to do with the 'I' accepting and identifying–even despite some residual longing or yearning 'to be normal'–with being 'other than normal'. This potentially encompasses no longer wanting or needing to accept and identify with 'being normal', with 'doing the normal', with aspiring to and indeed living 'a normal life', or with being bound by conventional or prevailing norms.

"Who is right, who can tell, and who gives a damn right now"–suggests, at the least, an uncertainty and indeterminacy concerning the question of 'right', by implication not only "who is right" but also, perhaps, 'what is right'. "Who can tell" suggests this is not something that can be determined, at least within this present conjuncture, and perhaps neither 'I' nor we have time to attempt to figure that out, as we need, instead, to act. Perhaps we need to trust in our intuitive intelligence, in our instinctive intelligence, in our embodied experiential intelligence, in our ability to figure out what we need to do in the moment, immediately as it transpires, immediately as we confront the need to do so. Perhaps we cannot afford to wait any longer because the situation is urgent, even desperate, and we need to accept the uncertainty, the indeterminacy, the chaos, and the *disorder* as the terrain upon which we must proceed–and must act. "Who gives a damn right now" reads as if this is a summoning, perhaps an exhorting, to 'give a damn' as seemingly not everyone out there does, or will, but what is required, to meet the demands of the current crisis, are those who do and who will. This phrase feels like a challenge to us, 'to give a damn' and to do so "right now," without waiting, hesitating, or otherwise making excuses not to do so, any longer–and it does seem like 'I' recognizes and understands how difficult a leap, jump, or plunge this can be, as this 'I' has long waited and watched and even attempted to escape and flee. But no longer.

"Until the spirit new sensation take hold, then you know"–repeated three times, as the next three lines, feels like a kind of ritual proclamation that aims to performatively achieve a state of acceptance of the aforementioned uncertainty and indeterminancy, as well as the aforementioned precariousness and danger, along with a readiness to commit to what can be gained, what can be achieved, as a result of this acceptance. "New sensation" seemingly supercedes the sensations previously mentioned, and seemingly rejected and discarded, in the first stanza, and "new sensation" also seems directly interlinked with "spirit," perhaps even constitutes another form or a particular form (of manifestation) of spirit. What is also striking about this wording is "takes hold," which suggests this happens to this 'I' in these lyrics and to 'us', if we are joining and following along, and is not something we make happen through exercise of will–i.e., we don't 'take hold of the spirit' and of 'new sensation' but rather this takes hold of us. Again, this description suggests we have to be ready to 'let ourselves go', to 'lose control', to allow our bodies, and our selves, to be re-made, in the process sketched out for us, and impending right before us. Once so inhabited by spirit, such that new sensation takes hold, then we know, perhaps, 'who is right' and even 'how to tell'.

Complicating what I just described, it is also plausible to interpret these lines as representing a calling upon us, from the 'I' of the lyrics, that has 'got the spirit', to join and follow, and to experience, achieve, and realize what 'he' already has. But at the same time, the need to issue this call, and to sketch out the scene in stanza two, as well as to provide an allusion to a back-story in stanza one, suggests this 'I' needs us to join and follow 'him' if he is to sustain his connection with, his embodiment of, 'spirit'. In the earlier draft of these lyrics reproduced in *So This is Permanence*, Curtis writes "Until this feeling new sensation takes hold, then we know" which not only connects new sensation directly with feeling, as opposed to spirit, but prospectively, as opposed to the final version of the lyrics, suggests a seamless lining up of spirit, feeling, and new sensation that the finished version of the lyrics complicates. The earlier version of the line also suggests then *we* know, as opposed to then *you* know, diminishing the ambiguity concerning where we are by this point in relation to the 'I' of the lyrics and where at this point is this 'I' in relation to us–if the I is with us, or if the I is urging us into the maelstrom without being directly with us, and, if the latter is so, is this I doing so from a position already within or positioned in back, above, or afar from what we are now invited and encouraged to take on?

"I've got the spirit, but lose the feeling/I've got the spirit, but lose the feeling/Feeling, feeling, feeling, feeling, feeling, feeling, feeling"–hardly dispels the ambiguities I've described. The refrain returns, with the addition of "but" and "the" prior to "feeling" in the first and second phrases and the elimination of the third phrase to be replaced by a final line repeating "feeling" seven times. In the earlier draft reproduced in *So This is Permanence* these final three lines do not appear. The reiteration of "I've got the spirit" followed by "but lose the feeling" not only seems to emphasize a quandary, where 'I' has spirit, but not feeling, when perhaps 'I' needs or wants both, but also something of what, perhaps, is most critically at stake here–being able to embody, represent, and carry forward 'the spirit' for a brief flash of time when this occurs and while it lasts

As I suggested earlier, it is possible, in contrast with what I have just written, and especially taking into account the final line, to read "but lose the feeling" as an imperative, a call in other words by the 'I' upon itself to 'lose the feeling', which could even, perhaps, suggest 'letting lose the feeling,' 'letting it out somehow'. With the final repeated emphasis on 'feeling' it can seem like 'feeling' is right at the center, or the heart, of what the lyrics are addressing, even if at earlier points it has seemed as if feelings might represent an obstacle, or a barrier. It can *feel*, ironically enough, given the repeated earlier phase 'lose the feeling', as if the final line insists upon the urgency of feeling and even urgently pleads with us to feel.

At the least, these lyrics suggest complicated questions about distinctions and relations among multiple dimensions of our experience of ourselves–sensation, feeling, knowing, and spirit. And the song suggests a struggle that has not arrived at any definite conclusion in figuring out how best to work with these constituents, especially in their distinctions from and relations (perhaps interrelations) with each other, and in particular in situations that seem urgently to require, even demand, some effort to do exactly this.

***

Listening closely and repeatedly, taking notes, and reflecting on "Disorder," at this present time, in January to February 2021, in Eau Claire, Wisconsin, while on scholarly leave to work on writing two books, and still in the midst of the horrific COVID-19 pandemic, I think about the pandemic's devastating impact, not only in numbers of lives lost and of those impacted by 'long COVID', and not only in terms of the grief many are experiencing for loved ones who have died, but also in terms of the economic fallout that is the worst since the Great Depression beginning in 1929 and extending into the 1930s. I think about how this pandemic has reshaped people's life-experiences, with so much necessary physical social distancing, as well as so many quarantines and lockdowns, and such an enhanced experience, for even those of us in relatively secure and stable situations, of the fragility and precariousness of life, of lifestyle, of lived experience, of lived connection, of community, of belonging, and of participation. In this context, I hear this song inviting and encouraging me to reflect on three sets of issues: 1. Liminalities and Thresholds, 2. Paradoxes and the Paradoxical, and 3. The Complexity, Multiplicity, Contradictoriness, and Dynamism of Subjectivity and Selfhood. As I proceed from this point, I work toward explaining the connections I am experiencing between this song and these issues, while showing how taking into account the sounds, patterns of sounds, and deployments of sounds comprising "Disorder" *as a song* enhances our understanding and appreciation of what we might make of and do with the lyrics–including what we might make of and do with the numerous ambiguities these lyrics include that I have just detailed.

Let's begin with the structure of the song, with particular attention to the melody and how other elements of the composite sound relate to the melody. Here is how I hear this structure, with times representing close estimates:

1.   0:00-0:06: The song begins with Stephen Morris's drums sounding, in particular the snare separate from and given greater emphasis than the others, as I will discuss in further detail, later. The drums introduce and establish the beat. Introduction.

2.   0:07-0:16: Peter Hook's bass enters and joins, introducing and playing the melody, while an initial synthesizer swoosh sound also appears. Initiation.

3.   0:17-0:28 Bernard Sumner's guitar enters and joins, playing a first of three para-melodies, while Hook's bass continues playing the melody. Complication.

4.   0:29-0:49: The first vocal verse unfolds as Ian Curtis's voice enters and joins; this verse ends in line four with what will become a retrospectively recognizable refrain as it is picked up and repeated as line four of the second vocal verse as well. Sumner's first guitar para-melody continues, the swoosh reappears, and Curtis's vocal here takes over the melodic lead while Hook's bass slightly recedes but still accompanies and supports Curtis's vocal in playing the melody. Engagement. Immanent Situation, Imminent Event.

5.   0:50-1:25: The first instrumental bridge occurs, involving an introduction and elaboration of Sumner's second guitar para-melody, while Hook's bass resumes playing the melodic lead, and Morris's cymbal crashes increase. Elaboration, Further Complication, Rising Intensity.

6.   1:26-1:46: The second vocal verse unfolds, as Sumner's second guitar para-melody continues. Curtis's vocal re-enters and re-joins, once more taking over the melodic lead as Hook's bass slightly recedes but still accompanies and supports Curtis's vocal in playing the melody, while the swoosh once again reappears. Confrontation. Immanent Situation, Imminent Event Becoming More Fraught, Urgent, Desperate, Demanding.

7.   1:47-2:20: The second instrumental bridge occurs, as Sumner's second guitar para-melody continues, while Hook's bass resumes playing the melodic lead, Morris's cymbal crashes increase, and the synthesizer swooshes also increase. Near the end of this passage, we hear a switch from a second to third guitar para-melody (which, as Hook has shared in his memoir, *Unknown Pleasures: Inside Joy Division*, is actually his bass playing this para-melody on the recording), and this para-melody then continues into the next section. Elaboration, Further Complication, Rising Intensity.

8.   2:21-2:52: The third vocal verse unfolds as Curtis's vocal re-enters and re-joins, with a concluding three-line refrain, the swooshes appear louder and more prominent as well as more frequent, and Curtis's vocal once again takes over the melodic lead while Hook's bass slightly recedes but still accompanies and supports in playing the melody. Sumner's guitar (or, on the recording, Hook's bass) continues playing the third para-melody. Determination and Commitment. Immanent Situation, Imminent Event Reaching its Peak–No Turning Back.

9.   2:53-2:57: A third extremely brief instrumental bridge occurs, with Sumner's third guitar para-melody (or, on the recording, Hook's bass playing this para-melody) pronounced. Elaboration, Further Complication, Deepening and Fraying of as well as Rising of Intensity.

10.   2:58-3:15: The fourth vocal verse transpires, as Curtis's vocal re-enters and re-joins, but this vocal no longer continues with the previous melody, instead sounding nearly an octave higher, while the swooshes become even more frequent, louder, and more prominent than previously, as do Morris's cymbal crashes, and then this all quickly slows down toward the end. Climax, Fully Entering the Fray. Declamatory Insistence, Pleading/Proclaiming, Agitating/Agonizing.

11.   3:16-3:26: A closing instrumental fade-out takes place, as the swooshes slow down but take over the soundscape while Morris's drums and cymbals rapidly bring the beat to an end. Detaching from and Suspending of Tension.

As this analysis suggests, sections here are distinguishable but not exactly conventional, if convention dictates verses and choruses, as well as, perhaps, clearly distinguishable bridge, middle eight, and solo sections. The sections bleed into each other, especially toward the end of the song. Phrasings, moreover, also tend to suggest sections are left at least in part open-ended, posed yet not settled. The principal melody proceeds with two and one-half measures of sounding, then one and one-half measures of rest, repeated four times. This melodic pattern encompasses an initial pitch sounding through 3/4 of a measure after an opening 1/4 rest, then sounding a pitch down a semi-tone from the immediately preceding pitch for 3/4 of a measure, then sounding a pitch a third up for a quarter of a measure, then sounding a pitch down a third for an eighth of a measure, and then sounding a pitch down a further five semitones for three-eighths of a measure. Adding yet further detail, the principal melodic line begins with a rest and then a series of six eighth notes on an initial pitch in measure one; in measure two follows with a quarter note and four eighth notes (or three eighth notes with one tie between two eighth notes) down one semitone from the initial pitch, and then up a third from this second pitch for two eighth notes; and in measure three proceeds down a third from the third pitch at the end of the previous measure for an eighth note, moving down a further five semitones for a second eighth note, and concluding at this same final pitch for a quarter note. So what we hear with this melodic line is a relatively steady repeated initial pitch followed by a slight drop in pitch followed by a rise of a major third in pitch followed by drop of a third in pitch and then concluding with a drop of nearly two major thirds in pitch. The melody remains closely centered on relatively small intervals and repeated soundings of the same pitch, with a movement that drops slightly, then rises slightly more than the initial drop, and then drops even further than the preceding rise. This is a tightly contained movement that ventures somewhat higher but largely tends lower. What this suggests is even as the song explores what might be involved and what might be required to engage, and commit to engage, in a fraught, urgent, and even desperate venture, and even as it registers the intensity of this contemplation, the song is also doing so in a fashion suggestive of a sense of confinement, of constraint, or at least of recognition of or confrontation with limits, even limitations, and perhaps also with an uneasiness, even a pessimism, about the prospects for success of this venture and of commitment to join it. Alternately, this scale and trajectory of movements might suggest a sense of calm, together with an element of wistfulness, reflective, as the necessity of 'taking

161

the plunge' becomes undeniable, of a yearning or longing for "the pleasures of a normal man" or for the hope and belief that someone else will come as "a guide" to "take me by the hand" or that it will prove a smooth process to sort out distinctions and relations among spirit, sensation, feeling, knowing, and right. But again, this principal melodic line is only one constituent of the larger soundtrack and only ultimately makes sense in relation to the others sounding within and across the duration of the song.

The instruments we hear in this song include Morris's drums–bass, snare, hi-hat, toms, and later crash cymbal, with pronounced delay on the snare, and with the snare separated in its own track and foregrounded versus the rest of the components of the drum kit; Sumner's guitar–which is largely bright, clean, and clear, but does convey the impact of an added element of delay, as well as a filtering and narrowing of the pitch, or more precisely of the harmonic series associated with the pitches being sounded; Hook's bass guitar–which is, as Hook is famous for, here plays higher on the fretboard than commonplace, and concentrates, in playing the melody, on notes as opposed to chords; Curtis's voice, which does resonate with persistent reverberation that becomes increasingly noticeable later in the song; and Hannett's incorporation of a synthesizer responsible for the whooshing sound effect that constitutes a final overt sonic presence. 'Leading' and 'accompanying' seem not only reductive but also unhelpful in describing the roles of the instruments here. Yes, all of the other instruments clear space for the vocal, but all exert their importance, and prominence, including repeatedly and multiply so. The drums carry the beat but also complicate it, injecting elements of an ordered disorder throughout the song. The bass guitar introduces and repeats the melody, with slight variations, especially slight concatenations, adding pronounced elements of persistence and consistency. The guitar plays off of the bass, and the drums, ultimately offering three distinct patterns, that seem best identified as para-melodies, and that are particularly important in complicating, in adding texture and density, to the overall sound, while sending these para-melodies spiraling in three distinct, successive flight patterns. The vocal is clear, direct, forceful, and carries the tune, while seemingly representing the center of the drama, and while also providing the most immediate source of expression and communication from what might be conceived of as *the song's* persona. The synthesizer whooshes add an element of disturbance, of dissonance, that seem to rub against the grain of the rest of the contributing components to the overall sound, while gaining strength over the song's duration, sounding distinctly oddly, and even distinctly at odds with the other constituent sound sources, suggestive of the other lines and patterns of sound eventually being overtaken, and even engulfed, slowly but increasingly rapidly. The song starts with a relatively low density of instrumentation but once the guitar enters, and then the vocals, the song remains at a relatively high level of overall density of instrumentation all the way through, as in breaks between vocal passages the guitar reasserts itself to compensate. At the end of the song the density drops down, but not too much as the increased intensity of the vocal, the addition of further and more frequent cymbal crashes, and the rise in prominence, recurrence, and loudness of the whooshes again also compensate for what otherwise might amount to a marked diminution in overall density. What all of this adds, to the preceding lyrical analysis, is a sense that an inquiry and exploration takes place yet does not arrive at any decisive answers, and, if anything, experiences a heightening of uncertainty, indeterminacy, and mystery. Yet this might, paradoxically, amount to a significant discovery, or significant achievement:

to better recognize, understand, appreciate, and perhaps indeed feel how dark and deep this territory in fact is–or can be.

"Disorder" starts with Morris's drums, with the bass drum on beat one, with double snare hits on beats two and four, with light hi-hat strikes on beats two and four, and with a quick drum roll at the end of the measure. As we proceed through the song we hear a periodically alternating single or double snare hit, sometimes on beat two and sometimes on beat four. Also, periodic cymbal crashes punctuate, especially at seemingly increasingly climactic or otherwise major points (at, approximately: 0:07, 0:55, 1:06, 1:09, 1:12., 1:17, 1:23, 1:51, 2:02, 2:05, 2:08, 2:10, 2:13, 2:17, 2:19, 2:21, 2:53, 2:58, 3:01, 3:04, 3:07, 3:10, 3:12, 3:14, 3:15, 3:16, 3:17, 3:18, 3:19, 3:20, 3:21, 3:22). Again, at 0:07 the bass guitar enters playing a short melodic line that continues throughout most of the song. Again, at 0:17 the guitar enters playing what might usefully be described as a scything pingponging to ricocheting paramelodic figure that develops multiple flourishes as the song proceeds, eventually settling down to make room as at 0:28 the vocal enters. At 0:54 the second guitar line enters, again suggestive of a paramelody, involving less pronounced intervals between chords as well as a seemingly larger number of these sounding until this pattern settles into a swinging movement between seemingly two general pitch locations, while later this movement evolves into a third guitar pattern that becomes deeper, more distorted, and conveys almost a chugging meets chattering effect running until the end (which in fact, as I have suggested, following what Peter Hook has confided, might well be a bass line). So, ultimately, again, we hear three distinct or three seemingly distinct guitar lines arise and unfold over the course of this song. Whooshing synthesizer sounds enter early, and remain relative sparse until they become increasingly frequent, prominent, and loud nearing and at the end of the song, especially with and after the final vocal line. Drum rolls occur at approximately 0:55, 1:06, 1:17, 1:27, 1:50, 2:01, 2:13, 2:19, 2:52, 3:01, 3:06, 3:11, 3:12, 3:13, 3:14, and 3:15, while from 3:12 through 3:22 we hear the cymbal crash on each beat as the song slows down to its end.

The two and one-half measure melodic bass guitar line repeats and then periodically sounds as if it becomes slightly abbreviated in between the second and third measures in conjunction with the second and third set of vocals sounding, while becoming fully elaborated again right as we anticipate the vocal returning after each vocal break. The bass guitar enters clear and definite with the melody right away but becomes less prominent with the entrance of the guitar and the vocal. The vocal follows the melodic line initially introduced and established by the bass. With the third set of vocals the reverb seems more pronounced, while the vocalist allows his vocals to linger and glide yet further. The final three lines of vocals represent a significant interval jump from the earlier vocal pitch range, adding a sense of a more desperate urgency and intensity, that culminates and slow downs in order to stretch out the syllables in the word 'feeling'. The synthesizer whooshes introduced earlier, once we near the end, seem to summon up, or comment on, or conclude the longer final vocal passage. Late in the song these whooshes seem to push themselves to the fore as a major counter-harmonic element, increasingly prominent and moving to take over, displaying a greater range in pitch, as they tend to sweep downward in pitch further and deeper. Elements of delay on the guitar and the snare are also clear throughout.

What all of this adds, to enhance our understanding and prospective interpretation of the lyrics, and, beyond the lyrics, the song as a whole, is a sense of pushing to meet and confront a challenge, but ending without having come close to overcoming or vanquishing this challenge. Instead, the song proposes this venturing must be recurrently ongoing, something many others after us must undertake as well. Like us, they must do so with limited guidance and assistance, with limited preceding mapping of the territory. Like us, they must be ready to accept and welcome confrontation with the unknown, and with the unknowable.

Yes we do in "Disorder" recognize an explicit beat layer, but "Disorder," like many Joy Division songs, both contains and does not contain an entirely conventional kind of functional bass layer, given the role the bass guitar plays in introducing, establishing, carrying forward, and sustaining the melody, together with helping flesh out the groove, in conjunction with the drums. The melody is sounded by the bass guitar and the vocal, with the vocal leading in doing so whenever it is present. In terms of what Allan F. Moore identifies as the harmonic fill layer, here, as in many Joy Division songs, Sumner's guitar plays the principal role in doing exactly that, although again this is complicated, because what I hear Sumner's guitar contributing is, as I have indicated, are 'para-melodies'. At the same time, the synthesizer also contributes to this harmonic fill layer, increasingly so toward the end of the song. This song does introduce, or re-introduce, or clarify Joy Division's style, with a high bass guitar initiating and helping convey the melody, the guitar not playing the melody but rather para-melodies, the drums contributing slight yet nonetheless intricate variations upon and departures from a simply metronomic beat, the vocals clearly foregrounded and carrying the tune, and prominent use of synthesizer as well as production effects on other instruments contributing especially notable elements of reverberation and echo as well as filtered alterations of their timbres. What these observations suggest is this is song is about a carefully conceived embarkation on a venture, even as those embarking recognize it is impossible to adequately anticipate and prepare for what the venture will involve, and what they will encounter in its course. The respective contributions of all the instruments and sound sources involved in the song fit what Matthew Higgs describes as Joy Division's characteristic combination of 'collaboration and autonomy', echoing the lyrics in suggesting 'we' are invited to join and commit to a venture where an 'I' will seemingly be both 'with' and 'not with' us as we do so. This 'I' calls upon us to collaborate, while maintaining 'his' autonomy and our autonomy, as he only shares with us a broad sketch of the urgency of the situation, and the event, that precipitates and necessitates this venture, and he only shares a broad sketch as well of 'his' positioning versus and interest in the same.

In considering the soundbox, the drums seem located on both left and right sides of the soundbox close to the center, slightly low center, with the snare pushed forward and up, the crash cymbals further to the side, the bass drum further down, and the toms and hi-hat further back. The bass guitar seems to be located in the center, mid to low center while the vocal is located in the center mid to high center and closer to the front than the bass guitar. The guitar appears to the left and right sides of the soundbox, higher, running roughly from mid-center to the top. And the synthesizer sounds come from the sides, close to the front. Among especially notable features of the soundbox, the guitar does seem to maintain a significant amount of perceived space in which to move, around the edges and across half the height of the entire imagined scope of the soundbox. Also notable is how clearly separate and foregrounded the snare drum is in the center and to the front versus the other drums pushed further back and to the sides. The bass guitar does seem to recede, moving down and back slightly, as the vocal enters and while the vocal is performing, with the vocal entering and performing just above and in front of the bass guitar. The vocal performs close to the perceived plane also occupied by the snare, as these two sound sources thereby receive the greatest emphasis overall versus all others. It seems helpful here to describe the guitar as sketching lines along the sides, along the entire mid to upper edges of the perceived/imagined soundbox. The whooshes start low and to the sides but not far back, while pushing themselves up and forward as the song progresses. The crash cymbals sound closer to the front than the rest of the drums other than the snare, almost mid-way up the sides of the perceived/imagined soundbox, as the song develops.

In contrast with examining the lyrics in isolation, this analysis of the soundbox suggests a multiplicity of forces proceeding and working together, each instrument including the voice occupying its own position, and assuming its own area of responsibility, all as part of a collective effort to engage with a situation, and an event, that calls for a venture and a commitment to a venture–while inviting and encouraging us to join if we are ready, able, and willing. This analysis of the soundbox also suggests engaging with disorder by bringing to bear an articulated complex of ordered patterns that themselves are tightly defined yet responsive to and open to incorporating elements of disorder as the venture proceeds, indeed already anticipating the need to do so.

The entrance of Sumner's guitar increases the song's loudness although not too much and this volume then settles in relatively quickly with the entrance of the vocal. At times the deeper rumblings of the bass add to the loudness, as do the cymbal crashes, especially in conjunction with the whooshes. The guitar seems to vary much more in pitch than it does in volume. The whooshes do become louder as well as more frequent near the end. The vocal becomes louder at the end as it rises nearly an octave in pitch from where it started earlier in the song and as it verges closer, but not quite, to the point of shouting while yet still singing. Overall, I hear "Disorder" as not loud enough to feel like it is overwhelming me, not loud enough to feel as if it is expressing and communicating past me, but just loud enough to feel as if is addressing me, as if is intimately sharing with me, while variations in loudness among the other instruments besides the vocal repeatedly remind us of their presence, of their crucial contribution to the whole, and the loudness near the end I hear as insistent. The last perhaps suggests, in relation to how this song is addressing and even imploring me, that it has done all it can, and the song is now departing with one last exhortation to me to do my part, to respond, to continue, and to proceed.

The beat, as Robin Parmar discusses in "Joy Division in Space: the Aesthetics of Estrangement," in relation to "Digital," is 1-2-null-4. The bass drum sounds on the first beat, with a relatively soft hi-hat and a relatively loud snare sounding on beats 2 and 4. Rolls and crashes take place at end of runs, but not at precisely consistent intervals. Also notable, as aforementioned, Morris alternates periodically between single and double hits on the snare, either on the 2nd or on the 4th beat. The tempo is brisk, with common estimates for this song ranging between 168 to 172 bpm (my own is 170 bpm). Since the beat varies in a slightly irregular way, this seems neither a tight nor loose beat but rather one in which the backbeat is strongly marked.

Other instruments definitely contribute to the overall rhythm, as rhythm, it is worth keeping in mind, refers to a more broadly encompassing array of patterns of repetition and variation across a song's duration than meter alone, or than meter plus tempo alone. These other instrumental patterns, besides those provided by the drums and cymbals, do tightly align with the beat yet do so by administering periodically successive changes in their patterns. In particular, the rest of the instruments often sound so as to align with drum rolls and cymbal crashes. The bass does help fill in gaps in drum patterns to provide a groove, even as it does so while playing the melody. It does seem like Curtis sings on and with the beat and Sumner's guitar and Hook's bass do seem to chime in regularly with the beat. The key correspondences take places with beats 1, 2, and 4.

As a result of the ordered disorder involved in Morris's playing of the drums and cymbals in this song, the beat at time feels as if it comprises a kind of convergence, or synthesis, of movements of shuffling and strutting. The overall rhythm feels something like a convergence, or synthesis, of movements suggestive of skittering, skipping, and traipsing, while also suggestive of rocking back and forth yet simultaneously continuing to move forward but doing so in steps that vary in length and in force. In fact, the song conveys a sense of considerable movement back and forth, between two pulses, suggestive of movement back and forth between two positions, and also that the time signature here might perhaps be closer to a 2/4 than a 4/4.

In considering the rhythm of this song, it can be useful to apply Morris's conception of the specific roles each of the four principals contributed to Joy Division's songs, which I have referred to earlier in this chapter: he propels, Hook steers, Sumner punctuates, and Curtis describes. In other words, all contribute, importantly, to the rhythm, to the overall sense of patterned movement in time, akin, again following Morris's lead in making this analogy, to the execution of a coordinated collective movement across a widescreen landscape. Another possible way of making sense of these respective roles, and contributions, is to imagine Morris as the engine, Hook as the driver, Sumner as the color commentator who also, in conjunction with Hannett, provides ambient and surrounding effects, and Curtis as the navigator and narrator. Yet another possible analogy, drawing from basketball: Hook contributes as the center/power forward, Sumner as the shooting or small forward, Curtis as the shooting guard, and Morris as the point guard.

Rhythm supports interpreting this song as dramatizing a venture, involving a significant encounter–a venture, and an encounter, that are ultimately inevitable and inescapable. Rhythm supports interpreting this song as dramatizing gearing up for embarkation upon this venture, pumping one's self up, and attending to all the nervous energy as well as all the worries and fears that come to the fore as one verges upon the threshold of a commitment, and as one enters or prepares to enter the fray. Rhythm supports interpreting this song as dramatizing hesitation, and even indeed anxiety, about the imminent arrival of this decisive moment, while simultaneously recognizing and accepting there's no turning back. Alternately, in addressing me, rhythm supports interpreting this song as proposing it is urgent for me vicariously to enter or prepare to enter the fray by aligning myself with the song as it proceeds through the successive stages that I earlier identified in discussing the song's structure.

"Disorder" appears to be in the key of Bb major; the principal guitar chords Sumner plays throughout the song appear to be D#, Gm, and A#; and the principal bass notes Hook plays through much of the song appear to be the 8th fret on the G string (D#), the 5th fret on the D string (G), and the sixth fret on the E string (A#). What is particularly notable about the pitches Sumner sounds, in sum, is their regularity: three chords, involving movements up and down three or five steps. The outro introduces some other notes, as well as reduces the scope of movement while the outro also involves some more quick wavering between chords, that Sumner occasionally anticipates earlier in the song. We do hear variations in terms of how many chords Sumner plays per measure as well as in terms of how long each chord is strummed within a measure. Also patterns of chord progression usually end with a reduction in the number of chords strummed within a measure. Usually Sumner plays three to four chords per measure, except at the end of a section in which he usually reduces this to just one. In addition, Sumner effects the sounding of these pitches by changes (however slight) in how, and especially how quickly, he strums. In relation to Hook's bass, what is particularly noteworthy again is the regularity here as well: Hook plays three principal notes but also incorporates some variation in terms of how long he maintains playing each one within a measure, and toward the end of the song he notably plays a series of notes all on one string, a movement up a chromatic scale. I've already discussed Curtis's vocal singing of the melody, in terms of interval range and sizes, but I will add here with the final three lines Curtis ascends five steps higher in pitch from his initial starting position and then quickly moves up slightly to six steps higher than this initial starting position. What is particularly noticeable throughout is Curtis starting and staying in line at a single pitch, then moving slightly down, then slightly up, then slightly down again, and then slightly further down, as well as one variation: up slightly more, down slightly more, up slightly more, then down slightly more, and down slightly more. With the final three lines Curtis remains largely within a limited pitch range, early on slightly rising and then staying on that pitch through the end.

Curtis's vocal coincides with the bass guitar in sounding the melody, picking this up from the bass and carrying it forward, working in alignment with the beat established by the drum and helping to further elaborate the rhythm, conveying an awareness of and responsiveness to the guitar, and seeming to compete versus the swooshes. Curtis's voice here sounds to me like a lower tenor with perhaps some mild darkening, and, interestingly enough, I detect the lingering presence of a faint yet still noticeable English accent. Curtis's range is actually quite impressive, considering the song as a whole, although he does not move across the full extent of this range at a single time, in any single vocal passage, instead singing across mostly relatively small intervals. Curtis's voice conveys a high degree of resonance–I hear this as deep, full, reverberating, and richly as well as finely textured. To me, Curtis as the singer here does not come across as strictly bound by pitch but rather as inclined to bend it and to sing slightly and gently above and below (or, in other words, slightly and gently sharp and flat). Curtis does so, as I hear it, to add nuance and complexity to a series of notes ostensibly otherwise all on the same pitch. Curtis's apparent felt attitude toward rhythm comes across to me as by no means ignoring or challenging the earlier and other simultaneous contributions to rhythm by the other instruments but rather as inclined to follow and elaborate it. We well know reverb along with echo is used in recording Curtis's voice and quite possibly double-tracking too, and all of this helps define our perception and reception here of his vocal delivery as well as his vocal timbre. I hear Curtis's singing as lightly lilting and gliding, especially toward the end of phrases, while it strikes me, even prior to treatment with reverb and echo, his singing voice seems to suggest it already includes light touches of reverberation, allowing Curtis to linger with and connect one vocal emission to the next with a greater extent of sustain and decay than would be the case in common speech as well as with an often gentle release. Curtis's attack I do not hear as especially pronounced, at least not until the end of the song, and I also do not hear his singing as heightened speech, but rather closer, as multiple commentators have suggested, to a kind of crooning. Curtis's voice comes across to me as paradoxically both simultaneously passionate and dispassionate, calm and intense, defiant yet accepting, and insistent concerning, yet unperturbed about how he might be heard and how we might respond to what we hear from him and from the entirety of the song.

Timbre represents one of the most important as well as most challenging dimensions of musical sound to describe, analyze, and interpret. Before addressing these challenges, and in particular in relation to "Disorder," I am going to detour to discuss the importance of timbre, beginning by drawing upon Daniel J. Levitin's introductory account of timbre in *This Is Your Brain On Music: The Science of a Human Obsession*. As Levitin explains, "timbre is a consequence of overtones," as when we hear the same instrument playing a tone "with an identical fundamental frequency . . . we will (tend to) hear an identical pitch" yet "the instruments all sound very different from each other," and that is because each of these instruments play not just that fundamental frequency but also simultaneously a distinct harmonic series as well (45). As Levitin continues, "These different tones–the overtones–have different intensities, and so we hear them as having different loudnesses." The particular pattern of these loudnesses, as well as the particular extent and array of overtones involved, contributes a distinctive tonal color, or timbre. "Each instrument," Levitin further explains, "has its own overtone profile, which is like a fingerprint," and this proceeds even further than distinguishing different kinds of instruments, such as, for example, a saxophone and a piano, but also particular makes or models of individual instruments: "What distinguishes one particular piano from another is that their overtone profiles will vary slightly from each other, but not, of course, as much as they will differ from a profile for a harpsichord, organ, or tuba" (47). As Levitin adds, briefly describing the initial development of synthesizers as a means to help explain how so, timbre does involve more "than just the overtone series," as it also involves differences in "attack" and "flux" (49), which can be manipulated in a dizzying variety of ways on synthesizers. Even more precisely, this dimension of timbre is often identified in terms of qualities of attack, decay, sustain, and release, all key elements of the "envelope" describing how a sound such as a sounded pitch changes over time. Attack references the amount of time it takes for a sound signal to reach its maximum amplitude, upon emission; decay references the amount of time it reduces in amplitude from this maximum peak until its reaches a kind of amplitude plateau; sustain references the amount of time the amplitude remains at this plateau; and release references the amount of time it takes for the amplitude to reduce from this sustain level to zero. Different instruments, different ways of playing different instruments, different makes and models of different instruments, and different devices, connections, and supports for and elaborations of different instruments, as well as different voices and different ways of using different voices, all can involve significant differences in attack, decay, sustain, and release.

168

Yet much more variety is readily possible too, including concerning the nature of the basic shape or form, and the basic pattern of movement, of a sound wave, such as that extended by a pitch, as well as the introduction of spikes or flares, interruptions or additions, to this same sound wave, as it moves from attack through decay through sustain to release. Levitin prefers to describe attack-decay-sustain-release in terms of attack-steady state-flux, which in the attack phase encompasses an introduction of "energy at many different frequencies that are not related to one another by simple multiple integers," unlike what we commonly associate with the harmonic series responsible for distinctive instrumental timbres, while in the steady state the overtone profile becomes relatively stable and in the flux the sound changes to once more vary in different ways and degrees from this preceding relatively stability (53-54). In other words, following Levitin, we can take into account how a musical pitch sounds initially, with and upon attack, then what it is like in a virtual steady state, and how it fluctuates, and in what ways, as it continues until it ceases. This helps us understand considerable differences we hear between, for example, a cymbal or a gong versus a piano or a trumpet; playing, and especially notably singing, high versus low notes; and singing from or across one or more vocal registers, such as modal, fry, falsetto, whistle, and further variations dependent on how the larynx is used. With electric guitars and bass guitars, not only different constructions of the guitar, including in different shapes and sizes, and using different materials as well as according to different designs, but also the use of different kinds and numbers of pick-ups, effects bars and boxes, amplifiers and amplifier heads, and yet more besides all exercise impact on timbre. The same is the case concerning myriad capacities for effecting tone color and shading that synthesizers offer. And different kinds and placements of microphones, in different kinds and sizes of spaces, along with different kinds and qualities of recording devices and recording materials, and different means of reproduction and transmission of recordings exercise impact on timbre as well.

As an undergraduate student I became increasingly fascinated by electronic music composition, especially emanating from post-punk and new wave, but also in the practices of post-classical new music, and in particular from the likes of Philip Glass, Terry Riley, and Steve Reich. One of my best friends at Wesleyan University while we were both undergraduate students, Greg Lo Piccolo, began working with Alvin Lucier in learning and producing electronic musical compositions, and I enjoyed the opportunity to observe Greg do so and to talk with him about it both in the production studio as well as outside of it. As a master's student on a fellowship at Syracuse University I decided to pursue this interest by taking an additional class, just for fun, outside of my program, in electronic music composition. Unfortunately, the professor was extremely old-school, and not only despised music made by the likes of Glass, Riley, and Reich but virtually all forms of popular music following pre-20th century classical music, and he instructed us to work assiduously with two giant, even then ancient, analog Moog synthesizers to create sounds indistinguishable from the instruments in a classical orchestra and then to combine these in a recognizably classical orchestral form. I found this most difficult to do, and most frustrating to attempt, but I enjoyed playing with the dazzling variety of options for modifying and combining electronic sound signals. Without necessarily focusing on this per se, at the time, what I recognize, in retrospect, that I most enjoyed then was fabricating many differences in timbre.

For all of the technical detail that can be invested in explaining why, for instance, one versus another electric guitar, even from the same maker and from the same period of time, might convey markedly different timbres, or timbral possibilities, words and phrases commonly used to describe, analyze, and interpret timbre, and differences in timbre, often remain remarkably vague and impressionistic. Some of the best student work I have read discussing timbre translates this musical quality into precise visual distinctions in terms of color, hue and shading, saturation and intensity, or into precise motor distinctions in terms of particular kinds of human, machine, and human plus machine forms of movement. Other students have related timbre compellingly to elements of taste and smell, and to aspects of dream, daydream, vision, phantasy, and multiple varieties and degrees of altered states of consciousness. Students have also usefully related specific timbres to subjects and objects from everyday life, or to dramatic moments and passages from literature and cinema. And yet other students have run with my encouragement to come up with impressively elaborate similes and metaphors for specific timbres. Before proceeding to discuss my hearing of timbre, and how I in turn attempt to translate it, with "Disorder," at the present time in which I am writing this chapter, I do want to indicate I am well aware the timbres conveyed by each of the instruments and sound sources contributing to this song, as well as the timbres resulting from their playing and sounding together, have much to do with the particular makes and models of instruments each musician used, including the particular makes and models of the production and recording devices Martin Hannett used. Many others share this information (the precise lineup of musical and studio instruments Joy Division used) in precise detail, through readily accessible locations on the web, for those interested in following it up. I also do want to mention here I am listening to a high quality, slow 'ripped' MP3 version of this song from the 2007 digitally remastered collector's edition CD version of *Unknown Pleasures*, via Itunes on an iMac, a Logitech 5.1 Digital Surround Sound series of speakers, and Beyerdynamic DT 1990 Pro headphones.

Let's begin now, no further delaying, with what I hear in terms of timbre in "Disorder." I hear the timbre of Stephen Morris's drums comprised of a deep booming bass drum, a light booming series of toms, a snare that emits a thin yet precise crack with slight reverberation and slightly longer sustain than the bass and toms, light twinkly hi-hats, and crash cymbals that involve a stronger twinkling and a much sharper attack as well as much longer sustain, decay, and release than the hi-hats. I hear the timbre of Peter Hook's bass as warm but thin with deeper rumbles that almost seem akin to a liquid-like broth slowly heating up with gentle bubbles. I hear the timbre of Bernard Sumner's guitar as overall bright, clean, and thin with a gentle sense of resonating harmonic elements, and then, in the third para-melody this becomes thicker and dirtier (unsurprising, perhaps, if this is actually the bass guitar). I hear the timbre of Ian Curtis's vocal as suggestive of a voice simultaneously close and distant, present and absent, warm and cool, with clear elements of reverberation and echo, clear and clean enunciation, and a slight wavering at the end of phrases even as Curtis allows notes to hold and linger slightly. At the end of the song Curtis sounds like he is close to straining, yet remains in the same vocal register as before. The synthesizer whooshing definitely seems machinic, industrial, and yet also oddly disturbing, startling, unnerving, and unsettling as if difficult to place. It seems, further, suggestive of a machine containing and possibly agitating water or some other liquid.

To add to this portrait, in relation to the timbre of drums I hear snares emitting clearly the strongest resonance, along with the crash cymbals, while the respective resonances of the bass drums, toms, and hi-hat sound relatively diminished. The snare sounds often feel much more like crisp, slightly reverberant hits, and then hits and rides, than cracks per se, or, in other words, involving not so much snap let alone crackle as a kind of 'snip, snip' sound. The bass guitar sounds at times as if its timbre is akin to something suggestive of a sonic palette between, or perhaps fusing, rolling and rumbling. The guitar sounds as if it is moving between soaring and scything, between oscillating and pulsating, while remaining rich yet tight and thin, but later sounds, as I have suggested previously (when this is likely actually the bass guitar) to resemble a chugging meets clattering tone. The vocal sounds as if it least verges upon light crooning, and overall does feel full, rich, and nuanced. Throughout the song, little sounds at all crackly, oddly high-pitched, or dissonant, other than the whooshing.

I hear the timbre of the drums akin to an ambling purposely but somewhat skitteringly, with sudden and unpredictable alterations in numbers of or heaviness of steps; I hear the timbre of the bass guitar akin to a combination of rolling meets rumbling movement, moving firmly yet precisely and carefully, slowly yet purposefully; I hear the timbre of guitar as suggestive of patterned yet rapid movements not just in one direction, but multiply, even proceeding through three phases of patterned movements, much more like a running back and forth and around in an odd but purposeful trajectory; and I hear the timbre of the vocal as suggestive of a fast walk with a gliding step, especially at end of phrases, and with a sense of pressing harder to climb higher near the end.

In terms of connections with, or analogies to, events, I hear the timbre of the drums and cymbals attempting to establish a relative order within disorder, working with a challenge that prevents being able to proceed straightforwardly but requires pressing forward nonetheless; I hear the timbre of the bass guitar as finding, establishing, and repeating almost a mantra, while allowing this to firmly sink in and undergird the effort involved in sustained engagement with the event; I hear the timbre of the guitar exploring the far extensions of the terrain, scouting and mapping it out, while sketching and drawing requisite directional lines that allow further as well as sustained progress in the effort; and I hear the timbre of the vocal carrying and leading the principal charge in this effort. Collectively, these timbres, in relation to such an event, suggest a determined, resolute, but wistful and somewhat anxious, as well as at the end more insistent and yet on the verge of exhausted, perhaps even somewhat despairing, kind and level of engagement. As aforementioned, the whooshes suggests complications–and obstacles. Otherwise, the timbres here, taken together, I hear suggestive of an almost eerie sense of calm in the midst of chaos, or in the midst of impending or surrounding chaos. This in turn suggests a strange detachment, a careful distancing from the self, or from more familiar, comfortable, and conventional senses of the self. At times it seems as if we together, with the music, and the musicians as embodied in the music, are entering into a situation, approaching an event, in an almost ritualistic fashion while the music is also summoning a semblance of efforts at control even while recognizing these efforts might well prove, even are likely to turn out to prove, illusory or fleeting. The timbres suggest a concentration in the moment that despite all of its otherwise fraught character also convey a sense of gently residing, and even gliding, in the moment. The collective nexus of timbres suggests allowing ourselves, together

171

with the music, the musicians as embodied in the music, the music as persona, and the vocalist as persona and perhaps principal narrator-protagonist, to drift, even to spin, as if we are in turn allowing, perhaps even welcoming, a sense of space-iness originating inside our heads to permeate our bodies. This collective nexus of timbres suggests moving beyond ordinarily familiar senses of our body to the point of feeling disembodied or out of our bodies or as both within and without of our bodies or as divided and separated from yet oddly simultaneously attached to and rooted in our bodies but also connected with much more that normally seems to exist far beyond the conventional boundaries defining the limits of our body.

The collective result of the combined timbres at work within and over the course of "Disorder" also conveys a religious feeling, akin to a moment of a prayer or of vigil. This may involve wrestling with uneasiness concerning a contingent and imminent struggle while striving to achieve a state of calm in coming to terms with this uneasiness. Throughout this song, timbres far more often suggest distance than distortion, as well as a paradoxical closing in, near and impending, upon the threshold, at a liminal moment on the advent or verge of entering into and converging with the subliminal. Not just the swooshes, but also the production contribution to reshaping the individual timbres, and collective timbre, likewise suggest a sci-fi/industrial or post-industrial scene that is strange yet fascinating, as well as a consciousness, as theorists in consciousness studies today tend consensually to argue, in opposition to commonsense conceptions, that is embodied, extended, embedded, and enacted. This collective resultant is also suggestive of welcoming absorption, dissociation, and trancing, which music theorist Ruth Herbert argues, notably in her book *Everyday Music Listening: Absorption, Dissociation, Trancing*, are commonplace experiences in listening to music, in the everyday, even while only partially and casually doing so, and can serve multiple positively enabling purposes while existing on a continuum with forms of consciousness commonly identified as 'altered states of consciousness'. In other words, according to Herbert, welcoming and entering into experiences of absorption, dissociation, and trancing, through music, can benefit mental and physical health, psychological and sociological well-being, and spiritual engagement and creative activity.

As a final comment on timbre, in "Disorder," I often find myself, in the process of writing this section of this chapter, listening to and reflecting on what I hear in this song, coming back to the words gleaming, glimmering, glittering, shimmering, and sparkling, especially in relation to Curtis's vocal, with added reverb and echo, but also in relation to the other instruments as well, including the higher-pitched and larger-interval movements of Sumner's guitar and Morris's distinctly separated and clearly defined array of drums and cymbals. I think this timbral element adds to the complexity of the song, and especially of determining what it might mean, as taking what I have described I hear concerning timbre and how this makes me think and feel, the song hardly seems like a straightforward depiction of an anxious moment before plunging into the midst of a fierce and uncertain struggle, with images and sounds of that conflict everywhere surrounding and becoming closer. Something about this gleaming, glimmering, glittering, shimmering, and sparkling quality suggests this may well be a highly introspective moment, engagement, event, encounter, and struggle–one in which what 'we' are wrestling with here, together with the music, the musicians as embodied in the music, the music as persona, and the vocalist as persona and, perhaps, principal narrator-protagonist, is a struggle with 'ourselves', with attempting to figure out whom we are, what we are about, where we are coming from, where we are headed, what we are capable of, with whom and what else we are most intricately interlinked, with what kinds of responsibilities and complicities does this involve, and with what we can and must attempt, strive, and venture to try to do along with what is holding us back.

***

Let's turn now to Arnie Cox's eight avenues of musical affect, beginning with Cox's first avenue of musical affect, mimetic participation. I hear more of a sense of ease as opposed to effort, at least not much straining in the exertion of the force. I do hear more of a pronounced effort with Morris's drums and cymbals because they do not follow consistent, regular patterns of strikes, and with the guitar because it needs to move significant distances in pitch although regularly moving among largely three chords, yet nevertheless sounding as if Bernard Sumner carefully focuses on how many chords he strums within measures, with variations in this number occurring as sequences proceed, and variations also occurring as well, however slight, in terms of his pace of the strumming. Some parallel kind of care in relative duration and frequency of sounded pitches occurs with Hook's bass, although seemingly not as much. With Curtis's vocal, his final vocal lines do feel like a pronounced change from earlier in terms of exertion of force, as if much more is at that point required, to the verge of straining. In terms of the duration of exertion, for Morris it seems like this continues throughout the entire song, for Hook almost throughout the entirety of the song, for Sumner in three (or at least two) principal sequences, and for Curtis in four passages. While sounding, Sumner's guitar feels like he is continuously exerting, and the same with the sounding of Hook's bass in relation to his exertion as well. With Curtis's vocal, it is notable, as aforementioned, that he briefly rests at the end of each line and before the start of the next. With Morris's drums and cymbals, I note the careful attention he must pay toward pauses within the beat, or to null beats, while the exertion feels as if it also varies dependant on whether this is a bass drum strike, a single or double snare strike together with hi-hat strikes, and whether it is a drum roll encompassing the toms and especially with a cymbal crash.

In terms of my felt impression of the complexity of the actions, or series, of actions, with Morris this feels complex because what he is doing is far from simply metronomic, and because of leaving out the third beat, while also varying when to strike the snare once or twice, as well as when to introduce a drum roll, and especially with a cymbal crash, as all of this does not follow a simple repeated pattern, but rather follows and anticipates shifts in the intensity of the flow of the music as whole. With Sumner, my felt impression of complexity comes in relation to him making sure the ringing of his strings is clean and crisp, until the third sequence, and in shifting register, while also paying attention to his pace of strumming and of when within measures to shift from one chord to the next. With Hook, my felt impression of complexity comes in relation to when within measures he needs to shift from one note to the next, and how long he needs to sustain notes. With Curtis, my felt impression of complexity comes in terms of adding his own reverberation while gently bending around the pitch, and with allowing ends of phrases to decay and sustain longer as well as release more slowly than they begin, as well as knowing just how long to rest at the end and before the start

173

of lines. With Curtis's final, higher vocal my felt impression of complexity here comes in relation to him knowing how precisely to pitch his voice nearly but not quite an octave higher than previously, and throughout this sequence how to keep the vocal intervals relatively tightly limited in size, while still adding nuance and texture. Overall. my felt impression is that the bandmembers create multiple interrelated patterns that move at a brisk pace, and over a quick duration, with each of these patterns maintaining or conveying at least a slight element of disorder amidst otherwise pronounced repetition and regularity.

"Disorder" feels to me as if this exertion has succeeded in dramatically enacting a moment, a passage, an introspection, or a contemplation, while exploring some of its principal permutations and implications, and pushing toward resolution while holding back from arriving at it and thereby preserving mystery. This song feels like an exemplary instance of what I earlier referred to as Joy Division's impressive combination of autonomy and collaboration. Each instrument I hear playing a decisive role, each maintains its own space and its own integrity, yet all appear keenly aware, while always relating to and working off, of each other. This feels to me, like I, together with these musicians, am participating in a tight ensemble where we are working together, in a common direction, in a common pursuit, but we maintain independent roles and responsibilities. Exertion seems, overall, largely non-attenuated, until the end, with, if anything, exertion seeming to increase somewhat as the song nears its climax.

I readily imagine myself performing with each of the principals and even switching from one instrument to another as the song proceeds. I imagine imitating drum and cymbal strikes, tapping and clapping along with the beat, singing or humming the melodic pattern, especially with the vocal, in particular the final three vocal lines, and with the guitar I feel a sense of myself imitating its movements up and down and in and out, even of swaying or dancing to these patterns. The music feels like an abstract performative imitation of a rapid process of gathering, collecting, and focusing thoughts, and in conjunction with this impression I feel as if I am moving closer and closer to a point of embarkation, with, on the one hand, excitement, relish, confidence, and purpose, but also, on the other hand, uncertainty, anxiousness, concern, and trepidation concerning what I am facing and will face as well as how prepared I am. I feel I along with other prospective listeners may be called by a witness to ourselves give witness, as well as called by one who has already joined, who has already entered the fray, to follow 'him' in so doing. I feel at the same time the music as persona recognizes not all of us listeners may be able or ready to follow, but I also feel the music as persona is contending it would be for the best if at least a critical mass of us are ready and able to do so.

As "Disorder" proceeds both the music as persona and I as a co-protagonist seem to anticipate a possible resolution or at least clarification by the end of the song yet it feels as if neither of us receives this. However, we also anticipate that might be for the best, as what the song is sketching and summoning concerns a necessarily ongoing effort. It seems like both the music as persona and I as a co-protagonist anticipate joining the fray yet it remains unclear if either of us has done so, by the end of the song. But again it also feels as if we anticipate this might prove a useful ambiguity, sparking valuable further inquiry into and reflection upon what kind of fray this is. It seems as if both the music as persona and I as a co-protagonist anticipate the prospect of working out distinctions and relations among spirit, feeling, sensation, knowing, and new sensation but again I feel like neither of us clearly does, by the end of the song, and again this remains a necessarily ongoing effort. Likewise, it seems as if both the music as persona and I as a co-protagonist anticipate we might figure out who is right, who can tell, along with who gives a damn right now, but once more the song concludes without this rendered at all transparent, and again this feels as if these remain necessary challenges to continually confront. As the song proceeds, it seems as if both the song as persona and I as a co-protagonist anticipate moving beyond waiting and watching but, to continue the same pattern as indicated in the preceding sentences, it remains ambiguous whether either of us have done so, as well as how far we may have done so, but again this might best be accepted as a continuous challenge, and therefore waiting and watching are important, if insufficient. It does seem both the song as persona and I as a co-protagonist desire and dread entering the fray, with this combination remaining consistent throughout the song and lingering beyond the song's end. I anticipate the music as persona and I as a co-protagonist will engage in climactic gestures, and we do, but what these mean, and what if anything they express or accomplish, remains multiply ambiguous. I anticipate as co-protagonist, together with the music as persona, a growing excitement as well as rising intensity, agitation and even a nearing frenzy, but I also anticipate remaining at least partially calm in our determination to proceed. As everything is getting and moving faster, and out of hand, and has been a shock as well as a powerful challenge to feeling, and as we are right on the precipice of a no man's land, it feels like we both, the music as persona and I as a co-protagonist, anticipate a simultaneously precarious yet thrilling confrontation. The song feels as if it dramatizes, for the music as persona and for me as a co-protagonist, an excitement about getting it *out*, about getting *out* what we have been struggling with, or all too often struggle with, and it feels as if we at least in part do succeed in doing exactly this. I early on anticipate the music as persona might function as my guide, might take me by the hand, as we proceed together, and by the end it seems as if the music has guided me and taken me by the hand but only to reveal to me how limited such guidance is in terms of what it can, by itself, offer to me, as the song ends with suspension of tension and no definitive resolution, suggesting I need to make the critical choices and pursue the critical actions, moving forward from here, myself. Finally, as the song proceeds, the music as persona and I as a co-protagonist together anticipate the return, elaboration, and complication of patterns and deployments of sound as we also anticipate these building to a climax.

Conventionally many listeners imagine they hear the actual members of Joy Division, including Martin Hannett, and especially Ian Curtis, expressing themselves here, but I hear an assumption and an enactment of dramatis personae much more than any I hear the explicitly autobiographically confessional. I hear a lead, with a small but capable and committed team, both testifying/taking a stand and challenging us to witness/take a stand. The music feels as if it is moving quickly so I must quickly align with it, or I will quickly miss my chance. I hear expressed in this music a calm assessment of a difficult situation, including of a situation where it is unclear upon whom, if anyone, we can rely, along with a sense of how increasingly desperate as well as rapidly developing this situation is. I hear an expression of someone who has struggled with 'his' readiness to plunge into the fray but is largely now past that, pursuing something that remains nebulous and uncertain yet compelling and appealing. I hear at the same time expressions of struggle recur as the complex interrelationship among constituent features of subjectivity and selfhood the song reflects upon still need to be figured and worked out, with much more yet to be discovered–and to be revealed. Also I hear an expression of alien, and alienative, forces becoming stronger and more disruptive, even increasingly encircling and entrapping. Despite the seeming logical implication of the words early in the lyrics, I feel an expression of powerful compulsion to _feel_, to _feel_ more, to _feel_ passionately, vulnerably, by directly engaging with what is gut-wrenching. I feel an expression of a challenge to make a decisive commitment, and to do so with no guarantees. I feel an expression of aspiring toward transcendence, as well as an expression of struggling considerably in so doing. I feel an expression, finally, of a challenge to me to explore and engage with the mysterious while not eliminating or dissipating its mystery.

In relation to acoustic impact, I hear, and feel, sounds seeming to come at and to enter me, as I discussed in addressing the soundbox, from three dimensions, and from a broad array of positions vertically and horizontally, from directly in front of me, to the sides, from above, and from below. The drums and cymbals seem somewhat diffuse but largely concentrated, the whooshes seem initially diffuse but less so as they grow more frequent and prominent, the vocal and the bass seem concentrated because of the relatively small intervals in pitch across which they move as well as the relatively short and repeated melodic lines they perform, while the last vocal line does, as aforementioned, seem to push at and above me more insistently, and the guitar seems simultaneously concentrated within its spaces yet largely diffused to the sides. In terms of strength, including elements of attack, decay, sustain, and release, the snare offers a pronounced attack, but slightly more decay and sustain than I might otherwise expect, if not treated with delay as it has, and the cymbals decay, sustain, and release more slowly while also communicating a firm attack, but the drum rolls on the toms along with bass drum and hi-hat communicate relatively weak attack, decay, and sustain. With the bass guitar, again the extent and degree of decay and sustain seems more notable than either the attack or release, while the guitar communicates strong attack and decay, with sustain quicker and release difficult to perceive as one strummed chord moves quickly into the next. In the case of the vocal, decay, sustain and release are all more pronounced because of delaying effects, and singing emphases, than attack. And, finally, the whooshes once more offer relatively more pronounced and notable decay, sustain, and release than attack. I feel the impact of the snares and the cymbals as if I am joining in decisively making these moments; I feel the bass guitar as if we are calmly moving together through a tight, short, but prominent, and encouraging melodic sequence; and I feel with the vocal as if I am allowing our own voices and our thoughts and feelings together to gleam, glisten, glimmer, shimmer, glide, drift, and then become more insistent. With the guitar, I feel as if I am joining in adding on elements of urgency, of stretching and straining, and of directly experiencing and even co-participating in causing the flashing, the crashing, the moving faster and more frequently coming at us, including at me, as if I am jointly bringing all this along with us, and at us. With the whooshes I feel these as disorienting.

With "Disorder," the music as persona and I as a co-protagonist feel as if we analyze the situation before us as moving toward some kind of climax, but we are uncertain what this will involve, what this will be like, or how it will affect us, and we speculate this may or may not lead to resolution or clarification of what is at most importantly at stake. Analysis suggests we are facing a situation becoming increasingly fraught, and our confidence about meeting the challenge this increasingly fraught situation presents, as well as our preparedness to do, feel likely to be sorely challenged. Analysis suggests this situation involves some kind of event, some kind of encounter, that must be attended to. Analysis suggests, moreover, we are facing a struggle, internal as well as external, among elements, or forces, pushing us both forward and backward. Analysis suggests we are in a liminal space, and a threshold moment, while precisely where we are headed, as well as precisely when, remain mysterious, although seemingly more so to me than to the music as persona. Analysis suggests we are facing a precarious situation, in which we will be exposed and vulnerable, but which we must confront nonetheless, and we must do so with determination, ready to immerse ourselves in what happens as it happens, allowing ourselves to coincide with the intensity, the speed, and the volume, and even embracing the danger. By the end of the song, analysis suggests we have perhaps been approaching, approaching, and approaching, faster and faster, yet without fully or clearly arriving.

Analysis, especially by the end of the song, suggests the music as persona and I as a co-protagonist have been surveying the terrain we plan to explore more than fully embarking upon of the terrain to be explored, while analysis, again especially by the end of the song, suggests we have been focusing on an internal, subjective, psychological state rather than on the external, objective, physical details of a situation. Analysis suggests by the end of the song we do not find a definite answer, yet this is not necessarily a failure because the process of contemplating pressing to the edge of the precipice can itself prove rewarding, including in the form of taking inventory of sensations, spirit, feelings, and of what we ultimately seek and strive to be and do. Analysis suggests this seem like a threatening situation we have been at least on the brink of confronting, with no turning back, but I feel as if both I as co-protagonist and the music as persona are able to survive and to feel pleasure from doing so, and, even more than that, from losing control, from letting ourselves go, and even from surrendering, temporarily, to a state of frenzy where we can truly relish disorder. Analysis suggests reasons for panic seem imminent, looming, yet nebulous, and it may well be what we are feeling, or are about to feel, or are contemplating feeling, or are imagining feeling is closer to ecstacy than panic–although this feeling may in turn amount to a complicated combination of jubilation, ecstacy, panic, and despair.

Analysis suggests the music as persona is sharing with us where 'he' is at, at a crucial moment, poised right on the brink, and what he is experiencing at this threshold. Analysis in turn suggests what I am vicariously experiencing is rising excitement, curiosity, and concern, but also a fellow feeling of surrendering to the needs of the moment, of being called upon to consider whether I am up to the challenge of joining the music as persona in a mysterious venture, and I do feel encouraged to do so, even as I also feel a sense of the stakes becoming higher while remaining unclear, and of a momentum carrying me forward with an inexorable necessity. Analysis suggests I as co-protagonist together with the music as persona are wrestling with our feelings and of how to get them out, to express them, to release them, to let them loose. Analysis suggests the music as persona is challenging me, insisting to me, and sharing with me, but not completely so. Analysis suggests this persona is testifying and witnessing but it is not precisely clear to or of what. Analysis suggests this persona is urging me to 'join, and come along, if I am up to it' but also suggesting if I am not then this persona will not be bothered by that–not anymore.

I associate what I am hearing in "Disorder" with a situation involving a breakdown of, or possibly a breaking with, (a) social order, of chaos but possibly a welcome chaos, of insecurity and instability but possibly a necessary insecurity and instability, and of the need to move beyond and forget about the possibility of simply resuming or continuing what has been normal, or normative. I associate what I hear with a sense of a venture, a mission, a quest, and potentially even a sacred venture, mission, or quest. I also associate what I hear with reaching a recognition of a point at which both the music as persona and I as a co-protagonist can no longer expect but also no longer need or want to count on others' guidance, leading the way for us, as we instead prepare to do what needs be done by ourselves, for ourselves. I associate what I hear with a resolve to move beyond wavering, hesitation, and uncertainty yet I simultaneously associate what I hear with the persistence and re-emergence of wavering, hesitation, and uncertainty. I associate what I hear with considering, even confronting, the value of experiencing the world at a sharp angle from what is culturally conventionally 'normal', as accepting and embracing one's own distinction and difference from that condition or state of 'normality', while also remaining, again, persistently and re-emergently, wavering, hesitant, and uncertain about doing so. I associate what I hear with confronting anxiety by pushing head on to dare to do what makes me, as well as the music as persona, the most anxious, and about being ready to expose and share vulnerability, while yet once more persistently and re-emergently wavering, hesitant, and uncertain about doing so. I associate what I hear with a call to proceed, driven by a higher purpose than narrow self-interest, and a call to struggle with, through, and past cultural constraints about how best, or how 'properly', or how expectedly, to express, communicate, and share feelings. At the same time I also associate what I hear with the music as persona's struggle with 'his' own feelings and what they are doing to his persona's sense of 'himself'. I yet further associate what I hear with a striving to reconceive and reexperience distinctions and relations among sensation, feeling, knowledge, experience, and 'spirit'. And I associate what I hear with as consideration of the possibility, that with repeated effort, practice, and experience, both this persona, and I as co-protagonist, might become comfortable and confident performing a markedly different version of ourselves–yet I simultaneously associate what I hear with a registration of uncertainty about whether we can, or should, do so, as well as concerning what the consequences might be if we become this new version of ourselves and if we cast aside versions of ourselves with which we have previously been most familiar, if not always comfortable or confident performing.

I hear, in "Disorder," a confrontation with and an exposing of one's vulnerabilities, that I am invited and encouraged to join in sharing, as well as allowing one's self to attend to and inhabit an experience of fragility, uncertainty, precariousness, and even prospective desperation, yet to do from something of a distance, achieving something of a simultaneous distance and detachment from this kind of experience. Opening one's self up to the prospect of deliberately pursuing a shattering of one's sense of one's self certainly seems like a further common 'taboo' engaged here, as the song itself dramatizes at least the beginning and onset of such a process, into pieces such as sensations, feelings, knowings, spirit, new sensations, as well as into pieces such as I/me, you/your friends, and her/them. Another taboo the song invites and encourages an openness toward is, as I have previously suggested, letting one's self go, and feeling calm about doing so, freeing one's self from preestablished inhibitions, welcoming a losing of control and an embracing of the uncertainty, disorder, chaos, and even potential threat and danger this encompasses. This suggests something akin to experimenting with psychotropic drugs; to pursuing action, adventure, or extreme sports; and to putting one's self out there, in a public place, in the context of a public nexus of social relations, risking mockery or pity, and risking being perceived as weird and as crazy, or at least reckless and excessive. A related taboo I hear this song exploring concerns accepting the possibility, while also at least contemplating the trauma that can follow, of dissolution of boundaries between human and machine, accelerated 'cyborgization', and of dissolution of recognizable demarcations among perceptions and experiences of past/present/future. Chills in this song come from the swooshes, from the chugging to chattering third guitar (or bass) line, from the relatively higher pitched and insistent vocal line at the end, from the increasing frequency of drum rolls and cymbal crashes, and even from the brisk tempo and short duration of the song. Overall, in sum, I hear "Disorder" exploring taboos by confronting, even accepting, and even welcoming what threatens to undo what otherwise would seem to represent the adverse of acceptable, welcome, and especially enjoyable–including our most familiar sense, and experience, of being a singularly coherent, secure, and stable self.

In "Disorder" the whooshes suggest a strange, alien presence, while the mystery and ambiguity I have previously detailed suggests something is difficult to see or feel, with any precision, and which may indeed be invisible, intangible, and ephemeral. In effect, the music as persona, and even the voice that sings the lyrics as persona, and as principal narrator-protagonist of the lyrics and perhaps of the song as a whole, feels simultaneously embodied and disembodied, close and distant, present and absent, tangible and ephemeral. Within the drama the song enacts it seems like I as a co-protagonist, along with the music as persona, reach an ephemeral moment when we return climactically to address feeling, and it seems here something has slipped our grasp, something ephemeral as well as intangible and invisible, which we only briefly imagined we had grasped. It feels as if we have been attempting to grasp irruptions of the Lacanian Real–to render these visible, tangible, substantial, and abiding–thus allowing ourselves to feel in alignment with this Real. But ultimately we recognize the impossibility of this goal, of seeking to surpass the Imaginary and the Symbolic through conscious, deliberate effort and according to exercise of powers we can willfully direct and control. And yet the desire to connect, and to sustain connection, with the Real remains intense and strong. In "Disorder" the past, the future, others' and the Other's influences and impacts as well as our interconnections with others and the Other feel as if these all might prove ultimately invisible, intangible, and ephemeral, as do our social position, status, and reputation. Our own subjectivity and even our own selfhood seems as if this might also prove ultimately invisible, intangible, and ephemeral. The liminal in-between, threshold, on the verge position, from which the song emerges and in which it seems to pace about yet linger, feels in addition as if this too might be an invisible, intangible, and ephemeral location, in both space and time. In addition, with all the song's insinuations of being at the verge but not quite there, and not quite past, and with all the nebulousness concerning what this might be a verge upon, clues concerning when, where, and how we must act also seem, prospectively at least, invisible, intangible, and ephemeral as well. Ghostly presences, including of possibilities never realized, or never fully so, as well as lessons, learned and unlearned from history, along with historical memory and historical forgetfulness, and even individual plans, dreams, hopes, and aspirations all yet further verge upon feeling as if these might be ultimately invisible, intangible, and ephemeral.

179

*** *

Let's turn now to consider a merged version of the two sets of summary and review questions I elaborated in section four of this chapter, where I explained the multi-stage approach to listening, description, analysis, and interpretation I am following in addressing "Disorder," "Transmission," and "Twenty Four Hours," in sections six through eight of this chapter:

1. What have these features begun to suggest to me, what have they invited and encouraged me to think (about) and feel, as well as to imagine and recollect? What do I hear the song expressing and communicating to me? How do I hear this song addressing and engaging me–inviting and encouraging me to enter into dialogue, into a co-creative encounter? What kind of subject, in what kinds of conditions and circumstances and from what position and perspective is here addressing and reaching out to me?

2. How do I hear these features and their accumulation and development beginning to address and position me? What are we, together, grappling with? What is it, more specifically, precisely, and even concretely that we, together, are exploring, inquiring into, pursuing, and confronting?

3. What do I hear these features seeking from me as my response and reply? How does this venture implicate and challenge me? What does it call forth from me, from whom I am, from where I come, from what I am about, from where I am headed, and from what I am seeking? How–specifically, precisely, and even concretely–can I respond? What simultaneously creatively imaginative and honestly authentic–even, and perhaps especially, raw and sensitive emotionally felt–response can I here give?

In listening at this present time to "Disorder," I hear myself invited to join a complicated, uncertain, yet urgent venture that the song's persona may have already embarked upon, at least just begun to do so, or may not have already embarked upon but is at the brink of so doing. The song's persona is wrestling with figuring out what this venture involves, or will involve, and how to sort out as well as how to muster all of what commitment to enter the fray in pursuit of this venture will demand. I hear myself called upon to join this venture if I am prepared to accept the uncertainties, the risks, and the dangers, while open to the prospect that the venture may prove not only precarious but also transformative. It seems we, I as co-protagonist and the song as persona, are placing our faith in the hope it might prove so, yet we also are coming to grips with a recognition that everything is already moving rapidly beyond our control, and likely will continue to do so, in terms of both how this venture will unfold and what its impact upon us will be. I am directly implicated by the singer identifying 'you' and 'your friends', but beyond this reference to the lyrics, the music as persona does the same by challenging me to find and not lose my place as I join in what seems like an already ongoing, urgent yet uncertain struggle on a treacherous terrain, leaving us exposed and vulnerable, at an especially fraught yet crucial moment. The song is suggestive to me of heightened anxiousness immediately preceding a public performance, especially one of major importance and likely to require maximum effort. Here I strive to check in with my body, including with my thoughts and feelings, while accepting how much is beyond my control, even far beyond my control. The song suggests to

180

me the anxiousness that can arise in waiting prior to, and in anticipating, the beginning of a performance as part of a major public event, in which I will (need to) take on the lead, as I am called, even summoned, to do so, and in which I must break through, make a difference, and make an impact, with my audience, knowing what I am representing is far more important than myself alone. This is an event where I know I need to challenge my audience as well as encourage them to follow me, and I know nothing guarantees my success in so doing.

In this liminal space and at this threshold moment I need to settle bodily sensations as best I can and keep feelings tightly focused as best I can, letting the spirit guide me. Numerous instances, in my own life, of teaching and of speaking and otherwise presenting publicly come to mind, especially in engaging with sensitive, difficult, disturbing, and controversial texts and topics, including by representing positions I anticipate my audiences are likely to find extreme, or at least extremely divergent from dominant cultural commonsense. These events always involve a performance, while I am always at my best when I approach doing so with a sense of how and why my contribution is not at all about myself alone, or about what is best for me alone. It is crucial in these situations I identify with and accept an intellectual, ethical, and political responsibility to give it my best, while striving to begin and to proceed as relaxed, calm, and confident as I possibly can, maintaining this state throughout the duration of the performance, yet feeling the adverse of relaxed, calm, and confident right before the start. "Disorder" reminds me of many such liminal passages and threshold moments, as I contemplate entering into an uncertain collaboration. I cannot do all that needs to be done, even in this immediate situation, as part of this specific event, all by myself, while at the same time I cannot predict what the others involved will come up with, what they will raise and share, in response to me, including as confusions and misunderstandings, including as objections and resistances, including as fears and worries, and including as hesitancies and uncertainties. But I need to be ready to take all of that on, as it arises, precisely when, where, and from whomever it does arise. I enter this event knowing I can do it, knowing I have done it numerous times before; knowing I have confronted resistance, opposition, skepticism, indifference, lack of preparation, and difficulty understanding many times previously; and knowing I need to continually adapt, shift, and otherwise change what I am doing, and how so, as I proceed, to meet these particular people, in this particular context, at this particular moment, from where they are coming, as what they about, and in relation to where they are heading, and, especially, in relation to what matters most to them. And I know I can do so yet again. But I also know I deal with multiple chronic illnesses and invisible disabilities that continually threaten me, and I worry whether I can continue to keep atop of them, or bear with the pain and discomfort they cause, when I need to push them to the side or proceed within the limits and constraints they impose, in order successfully to perform this lead role, as part of this crucial event.

"Disorder" suggests to me I can't wait for the ideal moment, or for the perfect opportunity, but I must instead intervene when, where, and as needed, which can be exceedingly messy to attempt to do. I can't tell ahead of time if others will be on my side or not, but I also can't wait to determine ahead of time whether this is likely to be so. I am seeking a breakthrough, pushing for transcendence, yet feeling as if this remains highly uncertain. I am recognizing the costs of what needs to be set aside and, even further than that, needs to be overcome, in order to strive to achieve this breakthrough, and this transcendence, while I am nonetheless inspired by its promise to continue to forge ahead, to continue to struggle for its realization, even if I am worried I am pursuing, or about to pursue, an endlessly receding horizon or even a quixotic, futile, and absurd quest.

Over the past 35 years of teaching I have emphasized engagement with controversial contemporary issues, concerning matters of class, race, gender, sexuality, nationality, mental and physical health/illness, ability/disability, religion/spirituality, politics/ideology; of power, privilege, and difference; of equity, diversity, and inclusivity; of oppression, exploitation, alienation, and injustice; and of challenges and oppositions to as well as margins of and exclusions from the normative. Persistently addressing highly sensitive and fraught issues risks provoking resistance, opposition, and even backlash as does taking a strong, clear, open public stand. As does continually challenging students, and seeking to enable them to stretch, not settle. As does challenging students to rethink what they have taken for granted, even what they have regarded as beyond question and what they have previously most strongly identified with–as well as what they have previously most strongly identified *as*. This song invites and encourages me to reflect on this experience of mine, as well as on specific instances where I have felt like I am at the top of my game: where I am meeting every challenge, where my words are flowing and coming to me quickly, neatly, clearly, and precisely; where I am able rapidly and successfully to tie together widely disparate strands of conversation as well as multiple specific activities, texts, and topics; and where I have been able to offer advice and assistance that I recognize has genuinely enabled, genuinely broken through, and been genuinely life-changing. I also think about numerous specific pedagogical relationships where I helped foster students' stepping up in self-confidence and self-belief. I recall further numerous specific meetings and other communications where I did not allow us, my students and I, to rest easily content with an emergent consensus, but instead prompted us to continue to question, unsettle, and open up texts and topics for prospective further new insight. And I think about me sharing my own vulnerability, not just in terms of being out as gay and queer, but also in terms of being out so as to contest and complicate what gay and queer are commonly perceived to mean–as well as doing the same in relation to living with chronic physical illnesses, invisible disabilities, and persistent to recurrent serious mental health challenges.

With "Disorder," a mysterious subject addresses me from a mysterious position with a mysterious challenge and a mysterious sense of urgency. But this subject also comes across to me as if 'he' has already begun what he invites and encourages me to join in doing, or is on the brink of already doing so, and I hear the music as persona suggesting to me that this might be my last chance to catch up and to join in. The song as persona comes across to me as if he is attesting to the lows and highs, or prospective lows and highs, of the experience that has just begun, or will shortly follow, while not being able or willing to offer comfortable reassurance about what this will entail, or cost, either to this persona himself or to me as a co-protagonist. The music as persona seems to suggest if I open myself up to meet this challenge, and accept taking it on, I will discover what it means, and what is it value, as I proceed, but for now I've just got to run with it. I hear the music as persona calling upon me to make a commitment not to be, or no longer to me, a mere bystander, someone who holds back because of fear of what commitment, and engagement, will cost, and of what I might well, even likely, lose as a result–all the while dramatizing exactly that same hesitation, wavering, worry, and fear. It does not seem to me like this subject is inviting me to be the guide, and only partially and limitedly does it seem the subject is extending guidance to me, offering to be my guide, as it seems we both need to lead the way forward ourselves, and not wait for a guide to take us by the hand.

In addition, it seems to me as if the song as persona wrestles with possible responses to the question of why be, why settle for being, normal? Or, in other words, why make 'normalcy', or conformity and submission to normativity, our effective goal in our life-practices? The rising of pitch, ultimately with the vocal but anticipated with the guitar, suggests an urgency, with no time, at least no time any longer, to waste in indecision, even while paradoxically evoking a powerful sense of understanding exactly what that indecision is like and where it comes from as well as of how difficult, and perhaps even impossible, it might turn out to be, to move past, or fully past, such indecision.

The music surrounding and exceeding the vocalization of the lyrics suggests drive, determination, and urgency, but also complication, messiness, disorder, uncertainty, and the presence of competing or countervailing forces at work. The music suggests what it feels like to experience an extreme adrenalin rush in anticipation of what is imminent. It seems as if the music as persona is seeking a way to center 'himself' in embarking on the venture by paradoxically de-centering the self, and by accepting, and even welcoming, the self's formation and constitution beyond the limits of Lacan's Imaginary order, the world of the ordinary ego, as participant within something larger, vaster, and much more powerfully meaningful and vitally important than one's Imaginary perception and sense of one's self, as ego, alone.

I hear this song as persona approaching a paradoxically tightly coordinated, even tightly controlled, state of frenzy, with multiple forces alternating in meeting, joining, separating, and opposing. I hear this song advocating embracing chaos and disorder, even when uncomfortable, and even when doing so risks exposing vulnerability, fragility, and frailty.

What this song calls forth from me is to recognize and accept my limits without necessarily regarding these as impediments. It challenges me to 'get the spirit', to strive for 'the new sensation', and to find a way to 'lose the feeling' that I keep buried within and, that by doing so, undermines my ability to venture forth boldly. This song as persona challenges me to make my openly shared vulnerability a source of strength, and to work to foster such sharing with others, indeed as part of communities founded on shared vulnerability as a source of strength. This song as persona also suggests we only have limited time to make a difference, and the chance does not last or linger very long, so we must be ready to go with it, to go for it, when we experience the call to do so. If the song is about someone sharing 'his' own vulnerability, his own identity as someone who is chronically ill, who is disabled, and who knows he experiences his own life, his own body, his own state of mind, and his own emotional and psychological being at a distance from the normal, and the normative, then it makes sense too that 'he' does not want to take pity from 'my friends', and also that 'he' is moving past lingering desire to be the same, to feel the same, as 'a normal man'.

Spirit might represent the soul, our fundamentally intrinsic interconnection with others, and our participation within the much vaster expanse of nature, the world, the cosmos, and dimensions of the Lacanian Real that exist beyond familiar, comfortable, and assured forms of perception and cognition. Spirit might represent what is of ultimate importance and spirit might represent what links us with the transcendent, with the universal, with the divine, with the eternal, and with the absolute. Spirit, which derives from the Latin word for breath or breathing, might represent life-force, and, as such, might encompass mood, motive, intent, purpose, mission, drive, and capacity for persistence, commitment, and resilience. Spirit might reside, or abide, beyond feeling, because spirit might involve a connection with life and death, as well as with past, present, and future, far beyond what is readily accessible by means of the mundane and the ordinary, including mundane and ordinary sensation, feeling, or thinking.

This song suggests to me it is recounting, it is dramatizing, an effort to work with and through a situation of pronounced disorder, to establish positions and to exercise movements that fit and function with the challenges this kind of situation presents. This song suggests to me taking disorder on, moving into it, exploring it, trying to find one's place within it, while recognizing the difficulties of doing so, and well aware of the limitations we bring to bear in attempting to do so. The song prompts me to think about urgent situations that broadly resemble military conflicts, in which a struggle is ongoing and becoming critical, which we must enter, even if we are afraid, and to which we must contribute our best, because the stakes are too high, and the urgency too extreme, to do otherwise, to hesitate, to merely wait and watch any longer or any further. Such a situation is intensely anxiety-provoking but we need to push past that, guided by the spirit–the mission, the purpose, the cause, the interests and the concerns that are far greater than our immediate individual selves alone. We know we cannot accept or retreat to a normal life; we have turned away from that possibility. We have waited and we have hoped that someone else would take the lead, and be our guide, but we can't wait for that anymore. That time is past. We are pushing toward and for transcendence, toward and for transformation. We are working toward a reconstitution of what feeling can and will mean; we are striving to move beyond feelings that entrap and foreclose toward feelings that will open up and reach out. We are doing this when many others are not ready, able, or willing to do so, and don't even care about the importance of doing so, by instead remaining callously indifferent and unconcerned. The narrator-protagonist is not going to take condescension, or pity, from us or from our friends. He is not going to take this from those who stand detached and judge from privileged positions protected from vulnerability, protected from engagement. We who cannot retreat into 'normalcy' and need to make use of intuition, instinct, faith, trust, and, yes, emotional intelligence in breaking with and rejecting 'normalcy'–we need to fuse emotion with spirit with intellect.

The song suggests a call to ethical, social, and political responsibility in a disordered world. This is a call to abandon pretenses and excuses for not giving a damn. It is a call to embrace possibilities that we can or might experience *through* immersing ourselves within difficulties and uncertainties. We need to accept we will inevitably break off connections from others who won't be able to understand, identify with, sympathize with, and empathize with what we are doing. In the no man's land, there is no way out and no way back. We must accept that we may not be able to persist, endure, and even survive, as we are flawed and limited, and we could all too easily become overwhelmed and engulfed.

184

In sum, I've noted how this song can seem to be about wrestling with how to deal with anxiety, including by making use of this anxiety, by transforming it, to reshape it to make use of it for one's advantage, especially in approaching responsibilities to perform, to engage, to commit, to join and enter, to argue and contest, and to advocate and agitate, in identifying with fraught, sensitive, and even dangerous situations, and with vulnerable and exposed positions that are unorthodox, anti-normative, counter-intuitive, far from readily or immediately popular, controversial, disturbing, provoking, and even extreme. The song seems to be about giving a damn when many others don't or won't. It seems to be about not knowing if we are up to the challenge we are called upon to meet, and aware of what is holding back, but also accepting, however reluctantly, that we maintain no choice but to strive to meet the challenge. The song seems to be about responsibility to something far more important than our self, as a discrete individual. The song seems to be about seeking transcendence, and a higher state or stage of sensation, as well as of feeling, through embarkation into and immersion within a prospectively transformative venture. It seems to be about not being normal, and about being on the verge of accepting this is OK, as well as dispensing with and dismissing judgments of others concerning this seeming 'other-than-normality', including, especially, pity. It seems to be about wanting allies, compatriots, who will experience the fellowship of a shared commitment, but it also seems to be about not being undone by the potential lack or absence of any such allies. And yet, the song also seems to be about trying to get it all together–mind, body, and spirit; intellect, sensation, affect or emotion; and faith, conviction, and vision–but uncertain whether this will prove possible. The song seems to be about needing to express, communicate, share, and connect but also uncertain if it will prove possible to do so.

***

I will turn next to prospective connections between what I have been discussing, in describing, analyzing, and interpreting "Disorder" with the eleven prior interpretations of Ian Curtis's and Joy Division's music, as art, and as cultural phenomenon, that I first introduced in chapter one and then extracted to recount and list in a numerically ordered list in section three of this chapter. I will briefly discuss those that seem especially apt.

#1: I interpret . . . Ian Curtis's lyrics and Joy Division's music as all about exploration of and inquiry into __mediations__*. Again and again, these songs zero in on the 'in between', on the* _distance between_*. Always seeking, striving, venturing, pursuing, or hesitating about doing so yet feeling the strong compulsion to do so nonetheless.* #1 definitely coincides with how I am hearing, and thinking and feeling in response to hearing, this song at present, as the song suggests to me a movement forward but also one caught up with and concentrating on the in between, on a nexus of forces struggling within a liminal space and at a threshold moment.

#2: Ian Curtis . . . fearlessly explored intensities, extremities, subliminalities, and liminalities that many others never would or could, and his music, while often extremely dark and somber, is never simply that–it is about seeking, struggling, reflecting, examining, and opening one's self up to sensation, perception, emotion, and understanding that presses past familiar layers of protective mediation toward not only intense vulnerability and emptiness but also intense clarity and insight.

Joy Division's music fuses the intellectual with the emotional with the spiritual with the somatic–in terms of exploration and questing, in both passionate and dispassionate terms, and in relation to a striving for and imposition of control meeting up with the absolute limits and sheer impossibility of meaningfully striving for and seeking to impose control. #2 makes sense in relation to the song as about seeking contact with a new, higher order or realm of existence, even of being; about the difficulty of achieving this; and about worries and fears concerning what needs be set aside and overcome to get there.

#4: Joy Division songs, for me, dramatize introspection as fiercely determined and fully committed struggle. What makes this struggle all the more fraught and challenging is it transpires in a mysteriously otherworldly realm where comfortably reassuring borderlines break down. These are borderlines between interior and exterior, subject and object, self and other, protagonist and antagonist, friend and foe, help and hindrance, solidarity and betrayal, complicity and responsibility, hope and despair, health and illness, movement and stasis, past and present, history and myth, the psychological and the sociological, the sacred and the profane, the beautiful and the sublime, the close and the distant, the private and the public, the familiar and the strange, and the living and the dead. Joy Division songs end not with tension resolved, but merely temporarily suspended. The only definite answer they offer us is we need to join this struggle, and seek what we can find, for ourselves. #4 coincides well with an interpretation of this song as a dramatic enactment of introspection, as well as in relation to the song embodying a persistent and growing tension that is not resolved, as the slowing down to the end with the whooshings overtaking all of the other patterns of sounds seems much more like suspension than resolution.

#5: Inquiring into the music, as art, of Ian Curtis involves . . . inquiring into metaphorical 'darknesses' in human history and society, and in the condition of being human, especially that of the human social being living in the advanced capitalist, postmodern world. This involves facing, without resorting to self-protective blinders or sentimentalizing illusions, often extraordinarily disturbing incidences of cruelty and violence, as well as of anxiety and alienation. It involves inquiring into intensity and extremity as well as into the complexities of distance and connection in human social relations. It involves inquiring into anxious to traumatic dimensions of the human quest for meaning, purpose, value, satisfaction, fulfilment–and especially love–in this late capitalist, postmodern world, and it involves inquiring into interrelations between life and death, between living and dying, between being and nothingness, between self and other, and among past, present, and future. It involves inquiring into surfaces and depths, mysteries and enigmas, complexities and contradictions, and fluidities and variabilities in modes of individual identity, personality, and character. It involves inquiring into what it feels like to struggle and strive for authenticity and integrity, in relation to the pull of ambition, popularity, success, and fame. It also involves, on the flip side, inquiring into effective meanings of compassion, empathy, and solidarity. Inquiring into when and where these qualities are under threat, in danger of collapse, on the verge of eclipse, or altogether absent, we recognize, and appreciate, how indispensable they truly are. #5 also makes sense here as I hear "Disorder" engaging complicated relations among sensations, feelings, and spirit as well as among I, you, her, your friends and among waiting, making, getting, feeling/not feeling interest, losing, taking

away, moving/moving faster, getting out, getting frequent/more frequent, meaning, watching, telling, giving a damn, taking no pity, taking hold, and knowing.

#6: Ian Curtis's art . . . can readily be conceived as an exploration of and inquiry into the following two sets of fundamental questions:

1.   Why do I exist? What is the meaning, value, and purpose of my existence? To what extent can I exercise any influence, and any control, over what this meaning, value, and purpose becomes? How can, and how should, I attempt to do so?

2.   In what ways, and to what extent, am I responsible for others? For the suffering, hardship, and pain others experience? For the violence and cruelty as well as the injustice and unfairness in the world? What can and what should I do about any of this?
#6 fits with an interpretation of the song as inquiring into what is my responsibility, mission, and purpose; what is going to guide and inspire me; how much needs to come from myself and be done alone yet rapidly; what forces am I aiming to reach and draw upon but can barely grasp; and how much this might all be ultimately about self-overcoming.

#7: Ian Curtis's art . . . can be readily conceived of, as well, as an exploration of and inquiry into the sense and meaning of alienation, isolation, and loneliness; the position and experience of being a stranger, an outsider, and an outcast; vulnerability, entrapment, anxiety, and fear; and the need to connect, especially intimately, along with the simultaneous difficulty of doing so. #7 makes sense insofar as I interpret "Disorder" as concerning itself with something that separates I/you/we from the normal, that not all are able to experience, as well as is nebulous and which those of us who need to face it must do with limited aid while accepting the likelihood of significant cost–and significant loss.

*#8: Ian Curtis's art makes sense . . . in somewhat more specific terms, as an exploration of the extent to which (and the consequences following from recognition that) the self is an imaginary construct, the subject is simultaneously overwhelmingly unconscious and ineluctably other, desire and anxiety are persistently intrinsically interconnected, the symbolic order and the law of the father are oppressively authoritarian, jouissance is far more terrifying than the common translation as 'enjoyment' can possibly suggest, and intimations and irruptions of the Real are recurrently traumatic. #8 makes sense if we interpret this song as an exploration of and an inquiry into self-*overcoming, recognizing the falseness and illusoriness of the ego, and of how much is socially unconscious as well as even beyond the socially unconscious, intimating of a larger Real that is always ultimately beyond our grasp.

#10: A large part of what makes Ian Curtis especially compelling to me, and seemingly the same to a great many others, is that he was–and remains–a striking combination of the ordinary and extraordinary, he communicates incredibly powerfully through his art yet so much of his art is obsessively focused on the difficulty of communication, and because an empathetic engagement with his life-experience, his artistic accomplishment, and his fierce sense of artistic mission and purpose is

richly rewarding–such engagement can help us in efforts to forge a genuinely and indeed systemically caring culture, a culture of compassion, empathy, and solidarity. Curtis's life-story, his life-achievement, and his life-legacy all attest to how important it is to strive to grasp the myriad ways in which we are all far more complex, multiple, contradictory, and dynamic than commonly recognized. Curtis reminds us of how all too many people's critical and creative potential is routinely discouraged, dismissed, and denigrated, and how this in turn leads all too many people all too readily to internalize a powerful tendency to do the same, to themselves. #10 makes sense in connection with an interpretation of "Disorder" as being about getting or moving beyond the normal, while lingering in longing for the normal–in recognizing yet struggling with (recognizing the subject's) own contradictions and its own multiplicity.

#11: I perceive, from Ian Curtis, as I listen to his recorded voice, and as I read his written words, while trying to write this book of my own, a tremendous anguish, emanating from a guilty recognition of a persistent uncertainty, hesitation, and doubt, and, when I recognize this in Curtis' voice and words, doing so does aggravate, and accelerate, my own uncertainty, hesitation, and doubt. As a result, at times I feel like I owe a debt of personal responsibility to Ian Curtis, to carry on with what he could not. #11 is most relevant in relation to the final repeated 'Feeling' that culminates a song dramatically enacting a drive to venture with urgency as well as a contemplation of what must be set aside and overcome as well as what limits in aid and challenges this will involve confronting, along with what pain and suffering are likely to follow.

***

A preeminent focus of modern to contemporary critical theory is making sense of 'the divided self', or 'the split subject', or, more broadly, the complexity, multiplicity, contradictoriness, and dynamism of subjectivity and selfhood, beginning by problematizing commonsense notions, still widely prevalent to this day, that each of us is singular, unique, autonomous, discrete, cohesive, centered, and in full and decisive charge of whatever we choose, decide, and will, as well as of all that we think, feel, believe, and do. Subjectivity and selfhood are overlapping conceptual categories, theorized in multiple considerably different ways, but, it can be useful, as a starting point for engaging with this vast range of theoretical work, to understand subjectivity as referring to how we are formed and constituted via our existence in social relations, in a constellation of diverse social relations exercising many different as well as varying and changing kinds and degrees of shaping impact upon whom we are, and what we are about, whereas selfhood refers to our existence, and our experience of our existence, as individual beings. Modern to contemporary critical theory seeks to understand and explain how and why both subjectivity and selfhood are complex, multiple, contradictory, and dynamic.

In all five classes I have taught on Ian Curtis, Joy Division, and critical theory, students and I have found a considerable, often striking, and indeed startling confluence of interest and concern between Ian Curtis and Joy Division, conceived and approached as art and as cultural phenomenon, on the one hand, and modern to contemporary critical theorists, and critical theories, on the other hand, insofar as both are concerned with this same focus: exploring and inquiring into the complexity,

188

multiplicity, contradictoriness, and dynamism of subjectivity and selfhood. Students and I have considered Sigmund Freud's theorizations of relations between unconsciousness and consciousness; id, ego, and superego; civilization and its discontents; life force and death force; repression and the return of the repressed; neurosis, perversion, psychosis, and the 'normal'; and the uncannily familiarly unfamiliar as well as the uncannily unfamiliarly familiar. We have considered Jacques Lacan's theorizations of relations between Imaginary, Symbolic, and Real, between desire and anxiety, and between symptom and enjoyment. We have considered William James's theorization of relations among the material Self, the social Self, the spiritual Self, and the pure Ego. We have considered Charles Horton Cooley's theorization of the reflected or looking-glass self and its relation to self-idea. We have considered George Herbert Mead's theorization of relations among the self, the I, and the me. We have considered Erving Goffman's theorization of the presentation of the self, including relations among back stage self, off stage self, and front stage self. We have considered Trinh Minh-ha theorization of selfhood in terms of infinite layers. We have considered Donna Haraway's theorization of fractured identities and of cyborgization of identities. We have considered Audre Lorde's theorization of identity in relation to difference and of Patricia Hill Collins's theorization of subjectivity, and especially intersectional subjectivity, constructed through and in relation to the matrix of domination. We have considered W.E.B. DuBois's theorization of double-consciousness. We have considered Peter Berger's and Thomas Luckmann's theorization of interrelations between the making of society and the making of the individual, including processes of externalization, objectivation, and internalization.

And this is just a sampling of theories we have considered, and could easily consider, in this connection. We could also consider Edmund Husserl's theorization of relations between subjectivity and intersubjectivity, between the natural standpoint and the phenomenological standpoint, and between appearances and essences. We could consider Maurice Merleau-Ponty's theorization of relations among consciousness, body, and world as well as between the lived body and the body as lived and between the habit body and the cultural habitus. We could consider Martin Heidegger's theorization of relations among Being and beings as well as between Being-in-the-World and Being-toward-Death and between the I and the They. We could consider Jean-Paul Sartre's theorization of relations among Being-in-Itself, Being-for-Itself, and Being-for-Others. We could consider Gloria Anzaldúa's theorization of subjectivities and identities constructed at and across borderlands. We could consider Kyle White's theorization of collective continuance concerning (inter)relations among humans and nonhumans. We could consider Robert McRuer's theorization of subjectivity and selfhood as constructed in relation to norms of compulsory able-bodiedness and compulsory able-mindedness. We could consider Franz Fanon's theorization of racialized bodies, subjectivities, and identities, as well as George Yancy's conception of confiscated bodies, subjectivities, and identities. We could consider Henri Bergson's theorization of durée and relations among lived time, subjectivity, and identity. We could consider Judith Butler's theorization of the performative construction of subjectivity, and identity, experienced in particular in terms of gender and sex. We could consider Rosemarie Garland-Thomson's theorization of fitting and misfitting, including in relation to matters of embodiment, dependence, and vulnerability. We could consider Linda Martín Alcoff's theorization of relations between public self and lived sense of self. We could consider Kelly Oliver's theorization of relations among witnessing, subjectivity, and sociality. We could consider

María Lugones's theorization of relations among subjectivity, intersubjectivity, traveling, and world-traveling. Again, all of the preceding are merely a small number of examples among myriad theorizations of subjectivity and selfhood that have both challenged and elaborated alternatives to commonsense notions that each of us is singular, unique, autonomous, discrete, cohesive, centered, and is in full and decisive charge of whatever we choose, decide, and will, as well as of all that we think, feel, believe, and do.

What Ian Curtis and Joy Division, conceived and approached as I do, add that is of marked value, to this ongoing, vast intellectual discussion and debate, is a heightened sense of what it feels like to explore and inquire into this complexity, multiplicity, contradictoriness, and dynamism, in one's own experience of subjectivity and selfhood, as well as how treacherous this exploration and inquiry can feel, especially as engagement with this complexity, multiplicity, contradictoriness, and dynamism exposes how much we are, or can be, torn apart and otherwise undone by multiple contesting and potentially irreconcilable forces operating within, upon, and through us. What Ian Curtis and Joy Division have also added, of marked value, to this ongoing intellectual discussion, are powerful glimpses of possibilities of transformation and transcendence of the stifling limitations of confinement to experience of subjectivity and selfhood, conceived and approached within commonsensical terms, that remain widely hegemonic, where each of is, supposedly, always, singular, unique, autonomous, discrete, cohesive, centered, and in full and decisive charge of whatever we choose, decide, and will, as well as of all that we think, feel, believe, and do. What Ian Curtis and Joy Division share here is an encounter with an intense longing to break with and escape these stifling confines, together with a simultaneously intense fear that this will result in disorientation, loss of bearings, and an overwhelming sense of emptiness and desolation as a potentially even crushing experience where we are reduced to a void, or an abyss, of nothingness.

And yet, what Ian Curtis and Joy Division also share with us, in this same connection, is a hesitant yet nonetheless persistent inclination to nevertheless take a leap of faith that the last might not be true, and that, on the contrary, experiencing a shattering of commonsense conceptions of subjectivity and selfhood might enable us to feel, far more thoroughly, vitally, viscerally interconnected: body and mind; heart and soul; self and other; sensation, feeling, and spirit; consciousness and unconsciousness; and multiple inextricably interweaving layers, levels, aspects, and dimensions of individual, interindividual, and social consciousness–embodied, embedded, extended, and enacted. And that 'altered states of consciousness' and 'altered states of being' might prove immensely liberating, in enabling us to let out what needs to be let out, to 'break on through to the other side', and to 'let ourselves go'–even literally so. Yet further, what Ian Curtis and Joy Division also share with us, in this same connection, is a keenly felt sense of how crucial to this entire process are (ad)venturing, engagement, commitment, and struggle, while at the same time communicating a likewise keenly felt sense that none of this is at all easy, or predictable; that we may not succeed in reaching our desired end because there are certainly no guarantees prior to embarkation of success; that whatever guidance, aid, or assistance we will receive in this pursuit is likely to be limited; and, paradoxically enough, in seeking to overcome existential isolation and loneliness, or, paradoxically once more, to use isolation as a means of overcoming loneliness, we may well end up all the more isolated, and especially all the more alone and lonely than previously. All of this leads us, in responding to what Ian Curtis and Joy Division raise for our attention, to inquire into and explore what holds us back from creating, and living, substantively, within social relations, and social communities, that are founded upon and intrinsically structured so as to pervasively manifest genuine empathy and solidarity–social relations, and social communities, that attend, first and last, to ultimate and fundamental concerns, especially for those in the greatest need or who are otherwise experiencing or in danger of experiencing the greatest precariousness, including in spiritual as well as somatic, intellectual, psychological, and emotional terms.

Ian Curtis and Joy Division invite and encourage our attention, with "Disorder," upon those spaces and times that are all too often dismissed as unimportant, or less important, because these are conventionally perceived and understood as 'in between' and 'on the verge' of what is far more important–they are neither here nor there, nor in or out. These liminalities and thresholds are crucial sites at which, potentially at least, we grapple most intensely with the stifling constraints of commonsense notions that each of us is singular, unique, autonomous, discrete, cohesive, centered, and is in full and decisive charge of whatever we choose, decide, and will, as well as of all that we think, feel, believe, and do. These liminalities and thresholds are also crucial sites at which we can and do contend with intense yearning, as well as intense fear concerning what might follow from striving to reach the point where there is no turning back, in striving to achieve a dazzling experience of a decisively alternative sense of whom we are and what we are about (or at least of whom we might or could be and be about). Here we are able to begin to make sense of the ream of paradoxes "Disorder" encompasses–what we fear most may well be what we most desire, what we most need might be what we find most difficult to achieve and secure, what keeps us in alignment with the 'normal' and the 'normative' comforts and reassures us yet warps and damages our scope for vital experience of transcendence, and as we are continually working to create and recreate ordered structures and patterns to navigate our way through perpetual, recurrent disorder we experience this effort as inevitable and inescapable yet also as frustrating and preventing a potentially liberating full and direct alignment of ourselves, of the continuously ongoing dissolution and reconfiguration of our selves (and of our experiences of our selves), with disorder–with processes of radical disorder*ing*, including, most notably, processes of radical *self-disordering*.

Seven

In "Transmission in the Colony: On exported Englishness and the secular religion of the axis mundi," Mike Grimshaw discusses the impact of listening to Joy Division on the radio, growing up in rural New Zealand in the early 1980s, highlighting the influence in particular of Joy Division's song "Transmission." Grimshaw and young New Zealanders like him encountered Joy Division as an overwhelmingly aural presence, in local radio top twenty alternative singles charts. As a band "heard but not seen," for Grimshaw and young New Zealanders like him, Joy Division "truly were an unknown pleasure" (18). Upon this heard but not seen unknown pleasure they imaginatively grafted their own vision of what constitutes 'alternative' 'cool'. The bandmembers' appearances, when Grimshaw and young New Zealanders like him were able to catch glimpses of what they looked like, "so decidedly, determinedly, ordinary looking," only added to the allure of the band, and its music. These appearances suggested possibilities for ordinary, and especially acutely awkward-feeling, boys and girls, and young men and women, from as far from Manchester as rural New Zealand, to also aspire to and become 'alternative' 'cool' as well–i.e, to strive to live as an active part of, participant within, and contributor to an alternative cool counter-culture, one that provided an alternative and a counter to a mainstream culture Grimshaw and young New Zealanders like him experienced as deeply alienating. Grimshaw perceived Joy Division expressing the powerful message to him, and to other rural New Zealand adolescents like him, that the answer to "How do you overcome tragedy, death, and despair?"–as well as, by strong implication, how do you overcome a life otherwise seemingly limited and confined to excruciating banality–was "by movement" (19), by, as Ian Curtis, in "Transmission" proclaims, to "Dance, dance, dance, dance, dance to the radio."

Grimshaw received this 'transmission', and continues to receive it, as representative of "a song about the disparate community of individual listeners united by music" where "Radio provides an aural community of singularity open to be struck by subversive wonder" (20). As Grimshaw elaborates, back when he first heard this song, "'Transmission' sounded like nothing else: it is the sound of post-industrial nihilism and its overcoming, albeit temporarily" (20). Explaining further the precise message Grimshaw receives this song as conveying,

> This is not dancing to the album, not dancing to the DJ, not dancing in the disco. To dance to the radio is a call for all those who are in isolation listening to the radio as the means to engage with a wider world. To listen to the radio is to be open to the event of the unexpected, open to the eruption of difference into our lives. Radio is potentially revolutionary and subversive. Radio, in those pre-internet days, took you out of your context and gave you access to the wider world. (20)

Joy Division, through the radio, for Grimshaw and other young New Zealanders like him, answered the "need of an alternative to the tyranny of distance and suffocating banalities of mainstream conformity." Joy Division, transmitted by the radio, provided those who felt like outsiders, misfits, outcasts, and otherwise perceptually awkward and ill at ease, within the communities where they lived, a means and a medium through which they could, however transiently, experience a reversal of what they 'normally' experienced to be the case: through this music, in this music, with this music they could experience themselves as the true insiders, as those who fit with and who fit with*in* what truly mattered, as those who occupied the true center, and as those who were relaxed, confident, and assured in relationship to that which was most vitally real and truly important. As Grimshaw explains, the bleakness and grimness he and others like him experienced, in hearing Joy Division, including the "haunting, gloomy, sonic shock" they experienced in hearing "Love Will Tear Us Apart," offered a compelling "counter to the prevailing American 'happiness' that seemed so prevalent" otherwise everywhere around–i.e., a compelling counter to an admonition imported from America continually to 'don't worry, be happy'. That admonition didn't work for young people like Grimshaw: "But for adolescents who thought, adolescents who read, adolescents who felt the constraints of provincial life, we wanted and needed more" (21).

What they most wanted and needed was "a place to orient ourselves toward, an axis mundi. A place, a sound, an identity we could bind ourselves with. A place we could re-read ourselves into"

(21). An alternative Manchester, imagined through the music of Joy Division, became this axis mundi. In retrospect, Grimshaw attests, his experience with Joy Division has enabled him to "really understand how popular culture, how music, acts in this way as a secular religion in both senses of the primordial words: religare to bind; relegere to re-read" (21). In other words, music, and in his case the music of Joy Division, furnishes means by which people, especially young people approaching and first entering adulthood, fashion 'bindings' that allow them to feel that their lives are and can be meaningful, that they do and can matter, that they do and can belong, while music does this by enabling them to read themselves into an imagined place, at the crux of a dramatic narrative, together with members of a physically distant yet spiritually united community. As secular religion, music, including the music of Joy Division, binds together those who make sense of and respond to–who 'read'–life-experience in convergent ways, resonant of convergent outlooks and sensibilities. For Grimshaw and young New Zealanders like him, "Ian Curtis became our sacrificial figure, our generation's Jim Morrison, a type of shaman, consumed by his vision, twisting with the power and terror of what he saw, taking us on a sonic journey of the soul through the tensions of late-modern life" (23). Curtis represented "a vision of articulate, awkward Englishness, the embodiment of a young man with too much to say and a body that just couldn't do what it should to be cool." This vision New Zealanders like Grimshaw could all re-read (and re-write), divorced from direct familiarity with actual Manchester and Greater Manchester and thus able to draw what they in turn most wanted and needed from this Mancunian alterity, such that they could use this identification to enable them to persist, endure, and survive otherwise crushing experiences, engulfed within rural New Zealand normality. For Grimshaw and others approaching Joy Division from vantage points akin to his, what made Joy Division appealing ultimately resides with "their proclamation that there is still hope in awkwardness, possibility in despair" (23).

Grimshaw's account of what he hears in "Transmission," as well as what this song makes him think (about) and feel, coincides with much of what I hear in listening to this song and with much of what so doing prompts me to think (about) and feel. As someone with a long-running passion for radio as means of expression, communication, and for establishing and sustaining community, I relish the song's valorization of radio's pivotal role, and of what radio can provide and accomplish. From the vantage point of a radio program producer and disc-jockey, I relish the opportunity each and every week to share my enthusiasms with my listeners, from near and afar, otherwise known and unknown to me, concentrating together on listening to the tones and textures and patterns and deployments of sounds, within songs, across sets, between sets, and within and across my introductions to, comments upon, and reviews of what I am playing, as well as between my voice, what I am saying, and how I am saying it, on the one hand, and the musical cuts, tracks, sets, and shows I am interweaving these introductions, comments, and reviews around on the other hand. I love searching for and finding new, often obscure, frequently independent label and self-released music; learning about this music and about those who have made it along with where they are coming from; familiarizing myself with conversations and debates among critics, reviewers, commentators, and fans concerning how to interpret and evaluate this music; and sharing all of this with my audience–especially music emanating from locations geographically distant from Eau Claire, Wisconsin, yet where I experience an affective affinity, in particular locations in the British Isles, notably in England and Scotland. I love selecting what to play and organizing this over the course of two hours; creating segues from song to song, set to set, and show to show; and determining what to say about the music I play before and after I play it. I craft my shows to address and appeal to an ideal listener, while I always share music I myself find of interest and value, music I enjoy and otherwise respect and admire. I experience working on this radio show, each week, as a high, uplifting me past whatever else I am simultaneously experiencing that is less fulfilling or satisfying, or more worrying or disturbing, or more draining and exhausting. Insurgence keeps me going, and I do feel being a radio dj has saved my life, even that each Thursday night I save my life all over once again. As an undergraduate, working at WESU, my involvement with that station, and especially with music shows I produced and hosted, felt much the same–vitally uplifting.

Likewise, "Transmission" appeals to me as a song that invites and encourages listeners to dance. I love to dance. I love to dance with vigor, and to get wild in doing so. When I used to dance regularly at clubs, I often aimed to dance non-stop for hours upon hours on end, up to four to five hours at a time, only taking short water breaks when thoroughly exhausted, and then getting right back out on the dance floor. In dancing, I loved to experiment, and to play, evolving ways to move my body in relation to the beat, and the groove, and other streams, flares, and bursts of sound. I often moved across a considerable distance in dancing, both feet off the ground at once, intermixing this with patterns of gliding, sliding, rocking, rolling, leaping, jumping, pogo-ing and pulsating while steadily incorporating more of my body into the dance–my feet, legs, ankles, knees, hips, waist, abdomen, chest, shoulders, elbows, arms, wrists, fingers, neck, and head. Whatever I could move, and creatively so, I did. I liked to sustain and shift among patterns of movement throughout the night, trying on a variety while establishing signature moves–at least for that particular night–as points of departure and return. Much of this was not deliberate, but simply what I did in response to the music, to what it made me think (about) and feel, and in relation to what other dancers–and djs–were doing.

I often felt connected with others dancing together with me, in the same time and place, including people I did not otherwise know or whom I had not met until that night, while I always enjoyed dancing with a partner who loved to dance with as much exuberance as me, each of us constructing and enacting our own movements while simultaneously attuned and responsive to, as well as periodically coordinating with, each other. Many nights in many clubs, especially with a packed crowd of exuberant dancers, as we grew hotter and sweatier, shred clothes, and became less inhibited, I felt our collective engagement in dancing together to be highly sensual, and overtly erotic. Many times it did feel as if we were engaged together, however fleetingly, in a euphoric, orgiastic, frenzied collective abandonment of normal, and normative, limits along with a simultaneously euphoric, orgiastic, frenzied collective embrace of counter-normal, and counter-normative, possibilities for liberation, including liberation from the limits and confines of normal, and normative, notions concerning what constitute necessary and proper boundaries seemingly always sharply distinguishing, and always decisively separating, 'self' from 'other'. Yes, I did experience glimpses or glimmers of the immanently utopian as I immersed myself in this activity together with fellow members of these kinds of communities of dancers.

For many years, whenever my husband and I traveled to any city, in the US or beyond, we sought out gay and mixed gay-straight dance clubs, and dance nights. We did so in every city we visited in England, Scotland, Wales, and Ireland, and we did so in every city we visited in the US as well. As a visiting assistant professor at Arizona State, throughout the duration of my two years living and working in the Valley of the Sun, I ventured together with a regular dancing partner, several nights a week, each and every week, to gay and mixed gay-straight dance clubs across the greater Phoenix area. Many times I was happy to be one of the first out on the dance floor–and often enough also one of the last to leave.

I identify with Ian Curtis as someone who loved to dance, who loved to dance even before joining a band and even before dancing while performing as its frontman, who loved to dance with wild abandon, and who created his own distinct dance, while making dancing, his dancing, a central dimension of Joy Division's live performances–even as, yes, his dancing I do experience as both mesmerizing and frightening, with his dancing increasingly, as his epilepsy worsened, not only emulating but eliding into seizures, including grand mal seizures. But despite his illness, and disability, I find it important to recognize Ian Curtis loved to dance, and I strongly identify with this love of his. I do not perceive him dancing because he is *forced* to do so, because *he had no choice but to do so*, or because he is using dancing, first and last, solely as a confessional performance of how much mental anguish and physical agony he is experiencing.

In terms of 'dancing by myself' while 'listening to the radio' 'alone in my own space', or doing the same while listening to music in the form of vinyl records, cassette tapes, CDs, mp3 files, and online streaming, I do this often, both literally and figuratively ('dancing in my own head') and have long done so. I feel an empathetic connection with others through listening to music, ostensibly 'all by myself', including an empathetic connection with others' pain, anguish, suffering, and struggle as well as with others' experiences of a gamut of imaginable sensations, emotions, reflections, experiences, memories, fantasies, yearnings, longings, dreams, hopes, and other pleasures, known and unknown. I have felt this connection with the musicians responsible for making and playing the music, with the music itself as its own persona and with multiple dramatis personae I perceive 'within the music', and with other listeners who find the same music likewise moves and inspires them. I do experience consolation and compensation listening to music. In listening to music I experience compassion extended to me along with me reciprocally extending compassion to what I intuit as the source of this extension of compassion to me. In listening to music I experience solidarity extended to me along with me reciprocally extending solidarity to what I intuit as the source of this extension of solidarity to me. Yes, this happens and has happened while immediately physically alone, while feeling isolated and yes while feeling lonely, including bitterly lonely. And yes this happens and has happened while feeling acutely and chronically awkward within, alienated from, and disaffected by a normative cultural mainstream.

Like many others, I turn to music for reassurance and for uplift, but I also turn to music to experience a shared sense of identity, community, compassion, empathy, and solidarity, when I am feeling down and out, especially worn down and burnt out, as well as when I am feeling excited, hopeful, and joyous, and when I am feeling restless, nervous, uncertain, agitated, and super 'hyper'. I turn to music to suit every conceivable mood and occasion, and as a persistent means of helping me come to grips with where I am at, with what I am thinking (about) and feeling, with what I am doing

195

and with what I need, and want, to do. Even when listening to music as background, I do not ignore it altogether, but rather use it to fill in and fill out the soundscape by adding tone and texture.

I also appreciate 'listening to the silence' or to whatever sounds happen to be immediately around, without choosing to play and listen to any music, fastening mentally instead onto details of what each of these sounds are like, of what precisely I am hearing with each of them, of what patterns each of these involve, of what departures from and variations upon repetitions each of these involve, of what each of these remind me of, and of what each of these suggests about the source, or ostensible or perceived source, of their emission. Listening to music as often, and as often intentionally as I do and long have done, as well as reflecting frequently and extensively about what I am hearing when I am listening to music, and about what this is prompting me to think (about) and feel, helps me appreciate other sounds, patterns of sounds, and deployments of sound, beyond music, including interrelations between sound and silence, in terms of how all kinds of sounds, musical/non-musical/extra-musical, convey meaning and impact, and do so according to the potentialities their sonic qualities afford.

I listen to music to help focus my energy and my concentration before teaching or before making a public speech or other presentation, and before leading or otherwise contributing notably to an important meeting. At any given moment in time I am listening to a current array of favorite musicians, songs, and albums, and I am doing so repeatedly. For example, in the run up to attending a live performance of the Twilight Sad, one of favorite bands, in St. Paul, in October 2018, and in the aftermath of the band's fantastic performance at that gig I attended, I played for myself all of the Twilight Sad's music, all the way through, again and again, for an entire semester. In recent times I have done so as well with albums from another favorite band of mine, Fontaines D.C., both with their first album, *Dogrel* and their second album, *A Hero's Death*. With the initial imposition of physical social distancing, quarantines, and lockdowns, due to COVID-19, last March of 2020, I listened over and over again to all four albums from The Soft Moon. More recently I have done the same with Cabaret Voltaire's *Shadow of Fear*, Trees Speak's *Shadow Forms*, The Blinders's *Fantasies of a Stay at Home Psychopath*, Protomartyr's *Ultimate Success Today*, and IDLES's *Ultra Mono*, just to name a few recent examples of this long recurrent tendency. I also always continue to explore and play songs, and albums, representative of a diverse array of styles and genres.

In sum, often enough interpretations of Joy Division music, and especially of Ian Curtis's contributions to this music, ignore the extent to which these musicians, certainly including Curtis, enjoyed making and performing their music–and how much their making and performing this music involves a sharing of a passionate enthusiasm, of a genuine love. "Transmission" makes sense as a song about the difficult and the disturbing but it also makes sense as a song about an enthusiastic passion, a genuine love, for making, performing, and sharing music; for listening and dancing to music; for identifying with as well as deriving meaning and satisfaction through music; for giving and reciprocally receiving compassion, empathy, solidarity, and community through music; and for mutually and collectively forging vitality and resilience through music.

"Transmission," as a song title, does not initially at least appear anywhere near as multiply ambiguous as "Disorder" is as a title for Joy Division's song of that name. After all, it seems as early as the first word, and the first line, of the lyrics, that the song specifically references 'radio transmission', transmission by radio waves, and in particular transmission through radio broadcasting of music, in which audiences attune themselves solely to the broadcast transmission of sound, especially musical sound, without obtaining access to any directly accompanying transmission of visual images, even though transmission by means of radio waves also occurs in television, mobile phones, wireless networking and satellite communication, radar and other means of radio navigation, and radio remote control devices. Yet titling the song "Transmission" nevertheless indirectly suggests association of this song with multiple definitions of what 'transmission' and 'transmitting' does, can, and might mean. 'Transmission', in general, signifies transferring from one destination to another, or the means that make possible transfer from one destination to another, or the process of transferring and the distance involved in transferring from one destination to another. Transmission is often associated with movements of currents or of waves, or with the entire drive train or a specific central part of the drive train of a motor vehicle, or with an array of mechanisms as part of multiple kinds of vehicles, motorized and non-motorized, that allow for controlled application of power. We often associate the word 'transmission' with communicable disease, notably disease spread through viruses, that can include relatively mild cases of the common cold or seasonal influenza, but also can include sexually transmitted and many other kinds of viral, bacterial, and parasitical infections; poisoning of food and water supplies; and environmental toxins such as those found at industrial waste dumps or in 'sick buildings'. This last use of the word 'transmission' becomes all the more loaded in thinking of transmissions that become widespread and deadly, as with the current COVID-19 pandemic, as well as in relation to radioactive leakage and fallout from nuclear weapons and power plants, chemical and biological weapons, and other historically notorious pandemics such as HIV/AIDS, SARS, ebola, dengue, hand foot and mouth disease, swine flu, avian flu, zika virus, cholera, measles, yellow fever, smallpox, polio, typhoid/typhus, plague, malaria, Spanish flu, diphtheria, and so on. Although "Transmission" with the first two lines of the lyrics–"Radio, live transmission/Radio, live transmission"–encourages us to make sense of the title of the song in relation to radio transmission, and especially, as the song proceeds, to radio transmission of music, the array of common associations with the word 'transmission' I just cited represent possible vectors of interpretation, for readers of these lyrics, and listeners to the vocalization of these lyrics as part of a song with this title. These associations circulate at the edges of awareness, spectral traces of the imprints of further prospective directions for interpreting this song.

Turning directly to the first two lines of the lyrics—"Radio, live transmission/Radio, live transmission"–"radio" references a specific technological and cultural medium, and the role it has played, is playing, and can play as a focus of transmission, while "live transmission" directs attention to what is happening now, immediately, at the present moment, enabling connections among distant locations to be established, and people at these locations brought together, to share a common experience together. "Live" suggests the opposite of pre-recorded and at the same time a broadcast that might be especially significant or noteworthy. As a radio show producer and host, I experience a marked difference between broadcasting live, and preparing a prerecorded show for subsequent broadcast. "Live" suggests the possibility of something surprising, startling, or at least unanticipated happening, perhaps spontaneously or as a result of improvisation. "Live" suggests an immediately intense connection between broadcaster and audience. And yet this 'live connection' is itself nonetheless mediated. Considering "live transmission" as mediated by the radio involves reflecting on how impressions and experiences of perceived 'liveness' and 'immediacy' are rarely simply natural facts but far more often social constructs enabled by and dependent upon cultural and technological mediation.

"Listen to the silence, let it ring on"–begins, with the first phrase, by proposing what initially might seem paradoxical, given the preceding emphasis on radio, and on live transmission, as silence is not usually what people tune in to the radio to listen to or for, and often in fact seems to represent the absence of anything to listen to or hear, yet silences can be eloquently expressive. Just think about how often movies employ silence to underscore pivotal moments–of transition, recognition, anticipation, tension, and suspense. Listening to silence directs us to consider gaps in expression and communication–what is not or cannot be expressed or communicated, or at least not readily or easily so, and why not. Listening to silence might also prove a relief, in the form of an escape from information overload, as we achieve a state of peace, quiet, and calm, and are able to restore, reset, reground, and recenter. Silence resonates with sublime possibilities–wondrous and terrifying. "Let it ring on" suggests attending to the silence as it lingers and lasts–as it slowly decays, sustains, and releases. "Let it" suggests, moreover, not simply allowing this to happen but rather exercising agency to accentuate its duration. Taken together, these two phrases suggest a welcoming of silence. But again, 'the' silence here may not refer to silence in general, and may instead refer to a specific silence, which we have yet to identify. Whatever 'silence' may here represent, it does seem like the lyrics of the song call our attention to a necessary break from sounds that distract from what needs to be attended to, what should be attended to, and what has perhaps been neglected, perhaps even at significant cost, by not attending to 'the silence'.

"Eyes, dark grey lenses frightened of the sun"–conveys an impression of both eyes and specific features of eyes suggestive, perhaps, of wearing eyeglasses and in particular sunglasses, or, in a more overtly metaphoric sense, of hiding from a brilliant source of illumination, frightened of what it might show, what it might reveal, and of what we might then see. More explicitly, this line describes being frightened *of this brilliant source of illumination*, frightened *of the sun*, which leads us to ponder why might this be? Whose eyes are these? What might explain how and why these people are frightened of the sun, or of what 'the sun' here stands for? It is also striking we here move from a previous emphasis on the auditory to an emphasis on the visual–what kinds of relations between listening and seeing are these lyrics suggesting to us, by means of the juxtaposition of these two lines? "Dark grey" is of interest too, suggestive of what approaches but does not quite reach 'black', and it invites us to wonder if this is the color of the iris, because lenses are usually not grey, not even contact lenses, yet it is 'lenses' so identified here and this could suggest cataracts, including in a metaphoric sense. So, vision might be impaired. But that's not all. In these lyrics it seems vision might be impaired not as a result of aging or disease but rather due to fearful hiding. Lenses have darkened, have greyed, due to living life by avoiding the light. The line invites speculation concerning what else might the sun represent, although it might simply represent the literal sun as the source of life, at the center of the solar system. Often, however, the sun metaphorically represents whatever is brilliant and dazzling, even overwhelmingly so. Commonsensically, we are advised not to look directly at sun or we will risk going blind, but what metaphoric 'sun' do we avoid looking at out of fear of metaphorical blindness, yet perhaps we should see, and perhaps we need to see?

"We would have a fine time living in the night" seemingly connects with the previous line referencing being frightened of the sun, and protecting ourselves from confronting our fears by hiding from the sun, with "night" suggestive of the sun as no longer visible, even of the opposite of 'living in the sun'. But "fine time" seems like it could be ironic, given ready connotations associated with acting out of fear–which, in connection with the previous line, may well be why 'we' are living, or could be living, or 'would' be living, 'in the night'. It is notable at this point 'we' is first introduced. This 'we' suggests the narrator-protagonist of these lyrics and 'us', those 'he' is addressing, share this experience–and this perspective (even if this is a problematically limited, and limiting, perspective). 'Would' is interesting because 'would' invites completion of a thought by supplying a phrase beginning with 'if' to do so. We 'would' have such a 'fine time' 'living in the night' *if* what? Under what conditions? According to what circumstances? Those are questions we need to figure out for ourselves because the lyrics provide no explicit answers. "Living in," in this context, suggests something other than conventional associations with the juxtaposition of these two words, as living more often is associated with what most people do during the day rather than during the night, spending more time awake during the day and more time asleep during the night, although of course many groups of people are most active and prefer the night, for myriad reasons. So, again, we remain unsure who precisely 'we' are–what specific kind(s) of people are 'we' in this song? 'The night', moreover, presents another challenge–what might this 'night' metaphorically signify? And once again, the reference here is to 'the' night–is this a reference to night in general, or, given 'the', to a specific night of some specific kind?

"Left to blind destruction/Waiting for our sight"–contributes a paradox, or perhaps irony, typical of Ian Curtis's lyrics, with 'us' "left" to "blind destruction" right as 'we' are "waiting for our sight." Right as, in other words, we are waiting to obtain our sight we are blind to our imminent or impending destruction. Does this destruction follow from us being "frightened by the sun" and "living in the night"? Does this destruction follow from what we refuse or fear to see, and from how 'blind' we have become as a result of habitually not seeing, and not even looking? At the least, it seems odd we are now 'waiting for our sight', given we, in the preceding lines, are depicted as seemingly not wanting to see, especially the sun, because we are frightened of what we might or will see. 'Waiting' moreover to obtain this sight how? From whom? By what means? "Blind destruction" seems to suggest not just destruction, but destruction we don't, or can't, see coming–destruction that overwhelms us before we even realize what is happening, and with no opportunity to prevent. It does seem harshly ironic that we are waiting for means by which potentially to forestall this destruction but we have too long cowered from seeking it out, and now, seemingly, it might well be too late for us.

"And we would go on as though nothing were wrong"–suggests everything is wrong, but we are or have been pretending the opposite, as if we both know and don't know this to be the case. This line prompts questions concerning what might, precisely, be wrong, and why are we evading, refusing, and pretending it is not what it is? How, moreover, are we manifesting this evasion, refusal, and pretense? Again, note well the 'would' here, which invites us to speculate about how we might complete an implicit thought involving an 'if' phrase following this 'would' phrase. It also suggests this situation is conditional, that it might not necessarily be so. In other words, we 'could' go about our lives, or continue to do so, as if nothing were wrong, but we may not have to do so–this might not be the only viable course of action, and, in this connection, "Left to blind destruction/Waiting for our sight" might refer to what follows only if we "go on as nothing were wrong," when we need not necessarily do so, and we need not necessarily face that fate. Again, use of "we" suggests the narrator-protagonist and 'us' share a common vantage point or perspective, a common condition or experience, a common position or situation, yet what, more precisely, might this be? Might it be 'we' have been those hesitant too long to push ourselves forward, to venture forth, to live brilliantly–i.e., to reject and refuse alienation and isolation as inescapable and inevitable? Might it be as 'we' live our lives constantly in fear 'we' in turn constantly hold ourselves back–i.e., 'we' hold ourselves back out of fear of potential failure or fear of potential harm if we don't accept the place to which we are assigned and confined? Might it be 'we' are those expected, by people operating at the heights of economic, political, social, and cultural power, to submit, obey, not cause any trouble, and remain invisible, inaudible, weak, and powerless, as we live out grim lives, grinding away while barely surviving and minimally continuing onward from day to day? If so, it seems as if "Transmission" proposes to 'us' that it is now time to break with (in fact it is past time to break with) this kind of life, and this kind if lifestyle.

"And hide from the days we remained all alone"–suggests these kinds of days have existed, and perhaps been far too numerous, while "all alone" suggests a heightened state of isolation, aloneness, and loneliness, as does "remained," which also suggests not only did no one come to help alleviate 'our' experience of this condition but also we lacked the power, the resolve, the will, the strength, or the courage to get out of and away from this state. "Hide from" suggests, once again, denying or repressing the fact this has been what our lives have been like, and denying or repressing the fact that we have participated in mystifying how empty this state of existence has been. This line yet further suggests to me where a capitalist society ends up putting all too many of 'us', according to its intrinsic logic, and according to how it encourages us to conceive of and relate to others–and ourselves: i.e., as subjects of exploitation only worthwhile as long and as far as we can be exploited, because once that potential has been exhausted we can then be readily discarded, because we are worthwhile solely as mere means for others to generate profit and accumulation. According to this line of interpretation, such exploitation is enabled by success in divide and conquer, and by convincing us to identify 'our' ends and interests with those of capital, acting as if we are, of necessity, ceaselessly engaged in ruthless competition for advantage versus everyone else, while everyone else is also always doing the same in relation to us. Under such social conditions we are indeed left "all alone" with no one to trust, no one we can count on to help pick us up and carry us forward when we fall down and when we can no longer carry ourselves. We learn to manufacture a facade of appearing tough, strong, and in control, while hiding weakness and vulnerability. Only when all alone can we admit weakness and vulnerability, but even then, even all alone, doing so frightens us–what if anyone else were to notice, what if anyone else were to find out? How would they then exploit this knowledge–how would they then exploit us?

"Staying in the same place, just staying out the time"–conveys a connotation of being trapped, of leading a limited and limiting life, of effectively just waiting, and wading, through life until death, with life a temporary stop on the way to dying; of not fully, really, or truly ever living, but rather going through the motions, becoming zombified, as a result of the crushing weight of routinization, habituation, reification, normalization, mediocrity, conformity, and of the necessity to set aside our dreams in order to settle for far less; of never traveling, even imaginatively, all that far, of becoming thoroughly provincial while never contemplating the prospective benefits of cosmopolitanism; and of not taking risks, of not (ad)venturing, and of living life, first and last, according to the dictates of fears and worries. Here "just" is especially brutal, as is "out." Here, again, we face an image of an oppressive 'waiting' that seems to suggest waiting through until the end, and doing little or nothing of any significance as we do so–waiting for the end, waiting to die, and waiting to do so before we have actually lived, before we have begun to truly live.

"Touching from a distance/Further all the time"–is, at least I have long found it, a great line, and I can well appreciate why Deborah Curtis chose the first half of this line as the title of her memoir. This depiction of alienation, and of striving yet failing to overcome it, can suggest deterioration of an intimate relationship, such as a marriage, yet it can also suggest changes that occur in numerous close relationships as time moves on and as people move in different directions, including to different locations, with these relationships becoming more distant and less important as a result, no matter what those involved might have intended. This line can suggest the presence of formidable barriers or obstacles (or what we perceive to constitute formidable barriers or obstacles) to being able effectively to reach out and connect, while it is definitely worth noting that "touching" resonates with suggestion of intimate human contact, and, at the least, of a direct manifestation of care, concern, affection, regard, and, yes, love. This line from the lyrics resonates all too hauntingly with the current COVID-19 pandemic and, in particular, with the forced physical social distancing, as well as the forced physical individual confinement, that this pandemic has necessitated–as well as with a great many people's experience of heightened loneliness and serious mental distress as a result. Also, this line resonates with many people's dissatisfaction concerning their experiences of social media and other internet-mediated forms of social connection. Often, numerous people have attested, social media and time spent on social media leaves them feeling, paradoxically enough, more isolated, more alone, and lonelier than they feel away from social media. Yet further, this line resonates with many people's feeling of increasing inadequacy and awkwardness in situations of direct, face to face interaction within the same immediate physical environment, as they have become more familiar, and ostensibly (or at least this is what they try to convince or pretend to themselves is the case) more comfortable relating to others by way of the mediation of computer screens and networks. This line resonates with long-distance relationships in general and their numerous challenges, and with relationships among otherwise too busy people with too little time for each other. What's more, the line is suggestive of the receding presence and impact of those who have died and who were once extremely important, influential, and central in the lives of those who survived them, but, increasingly, as much as these survivors fight against this becoming so, increasingly are no longer as important, influential, or central. Likewise, this line might well suggest people whose achievements, whose contributions, whose efforts, whose strivings while living are being increasingly forgotten, neglected, and ignored the longer they have been dead. And yes, in relation to a preeminent focus of hauntology, this line is likewise suggestive of possibilities within social environments that were never fully realized yet which persist as ghostly remnants of what could or might have been but was not. This line could even suggest possible past directions for one's own individual activity, one's past dreams and plans, especially bold and audacious ones, that needed to be shelved, abandoned, and jettisoned: i.e., possibilities of whom one could have been, what one could have done, what one might have pursued, and where one might have traveled, literally and figuratively, but all of which never happened. This line might also suggest values, ideals, principles, convictions, and ways of life that once were inspiring, hopeful, and broadly shared, but no longer so. In sum, "Touching from a distance/Further all the time" appears to bring the lyrics from contemplation of regret to the brink of despair.

Let's turn next to the chorus–"Dance, dance, dance, dance, dance, to the radio" repeated four times, and then this chorus itself repeated one more time to end the lyrics. What I find especially striking here is this is worded as an imperative, as well as the repetition of this imperative, suggestive of something between an invocation and an exhortation. These lines I find further interesting because this is not a call to dance to live music, at a venue where live music is performed, or even at a location where recorded music is played by a DJ for many people to dance to, together, but rather is directed toward us, in seemingly separate individual spaces, where we will be dancing to and for ourselves, yet wanting or aiming to dance so determinedly as if our dancing can manifest our spirited commitment to strive with whatever power we can muster to at least imaginatively overcome this separation. These lines might thereby symbolize our commitment to strive, through what mediation makes possible, to overcome alienation and isolation, so as to experience a meaningful semblance of contact, connection, community, empathy, and solidarity. And yet, even so, in the context of the lyrics as a whole, there remains a desperate edge to these lines.

"Well I could call out when the going gets tough"–to begin with is interesting because of the 'Well', which suggests a kind of qualification, hesitation, or anticipation of a contradiction, while what follows seems to suggest 'I could, but that would not be helpful or the right thing or the necessary thing to do'. Here we encounter 'I' for the first time, but who is this 'I'? What does it mean that 'I' is now stepping out from the previous 'we' to announce what 'he' 'could' do? Why, moreover, could he do so? Examining this line yet further, what kind of 'call' might 'he' conceivably make, and precisely about what and to whom? "When the going gets tough" remains vague although it helps somewhat as this phrase suggests perhaps 'I' could call out to extend an offer of what might prove helpful when this going gets tough, and what might be expected from 'him' at such a time–even though doing so won't help. "When the going gets tough" prompts us to ask what specific 'going' and what specific kind of 'getting tough' might be referenced here? What is happening, or might happen, or could happen? How and why is this 'tough'–and, in particular, 'tough going'? Why might 'I' be at all inclined to 'call out' under such circumstances, and why do so, if, seemingly, this won't help?

"The things that we've learnt are no longer enough"–prompts us to ask what things? Learned how, when, where, and from whom? Why were they enough in the past, when was this, and what has changed? 'Enough' suggests these may still be partially helpful, but, if so, where do they now fall short and why so? This line does seem to suggest why 'he' won't call out: because what the 'I' has learned, and what 'we' have learned', that 'he' is most likely to 'call out' 'when the going gets tough' might seem, briefly perhaps, an attempt to reassure but this would not succeed in doing so. It would prove insufficient, and it would not succeed in providing us the help we need. Which then leaves the larger questions of what kind of help do we need 'when the going gets tough', is it in any way possible to obtain this help, and if so how so and from what source and by what means?

"No language, just sound, that's all we need know, to synchronise love to the beat of the show"– suggests powers beyond ordinary written and spoken language, and beyond the visible, perhaps even beyond the tangible (powers of the invisible, intangible, and ephemeral perhaps); it suggests a level of existence beyond ordinary consciousness, or beyond ordinary rational consciousness focused narrowly on cognition; and it suggests kinds and levels of knowing beyond the strictly cognitive, including bodily, emotional, sensory, sensual, intuitive, instinctual, inter-individual, social, collective, natural, and, perhaps even preternatural or supernatural. It suggests a power of music to express and communicate beyond words, as well as to provide means of experiencing bonds, including in the form of love, beyond what words and other systems of signs reliant on visual images and symbols can provide. But 'synchronising love to the beat of the show' might not come across as uncritically celebratory, as it can suggest this is what needs to be done in the absence of what is longed and yearned for, and thereby our dancing all together in time yet distant in space, each immediately physically just with and by ourselves alone, might at best prove transient compensation. 'The show' also suggests a performance that might be nothing but artifice. Yet a paradoxical suggestion remains, and this continues with the next line–"And we could dance"–that the lyrics are referencing a situation in which the ecstatic meets the desperate, or, perhaps better put, the desperate prompts the ecstatic. Concluding with the chorus a second time does not dissipate or even distill preceding ambiguity, paradox, or irony, although it accentuates a movement toward which the song has proceeded from its beginning–to full immersion in this moment of intense if contradictory activity, 'dancing' 'to the radio', giving way to and releasing one's self into this ecstatic moment that might not erase alienation and isolation, might not lastingly overcome distance and lastingly sustain connection, but might, just for this moment, manifest one's determination to do all one possibly can, even in desperate straits and even as the end approaches, to live with passion and intensity, perhaps much akin to 'raging against the dying of the light'.

***

I turn now to begin to discuss, in detail, the sounds, patterns of sounds, and deployments of sounds that make up "Transmission," as I hear them, and in relation to what they prompt me to think (about) and feel, with the aim, once again, of demonstrating how attention to these sounds, patterns of sounds, and deployments of sound can provide an enhanced understanding and appreciation of the song as locus of meaning and impact, beyond what attention to the lyrics alone can provide. As I listen to "Transmission," and as I reflect on what I am hearing, this is my sense of the song's structure, the song's organization into the following successive sections:

1.   Instrumental Intro: Preparation of the Ground; Initiation of the Impetus, of the Drive, to Proceed (0:00-0:38)

2.   First Vocal Verse Passage: Initial Sketching of the Broad Contours of the Scene (0:39-0:50)

3.   Brief Instrumental Passage: Brief Elaboration of the Broad Contours of the Scene (0:51-1:04)

4.   Second Vocal Verse Passage: Initial Detailing of the Scene and Relevant Back Story; Elaborating the Complication and the Challenge, as well as the Central Paradoxes, Confronting the Impetus, the Drive, to Proceed; and Building of Tension (1:05-1:21)

5.   Brief Instrumental Passage: Briefly Reinforcing and Furthering the Building of Tension (1:22-1:29)

6.   Third Vocal Verse Passage: Further Detailing of the Scene and Relevant Back Story; Further Elaborating the Complication and the Challenge, as well as the Central Paradoxes Confronting the Impetus, the Drive, to Proceed; and Further Building of Tension (1:30-1:42)

7.   Extended Instrumental Passage: Accelerating Tension, Moving Toward Initial Climax (1:43-2:06)

8.   Initial Iteration of the Vocal Chorus: Arrival at Initial Climax; Immersive Response to the Challenge and Complication as well as to the Central Paradoxes Confronting the Impetus, the Drive, to Proceed; and the First Seizing Upon, Identifying With, and Channeling Release of Tension (2:07-2:29)

9.   Brief Instrumental Passage: Preparation for Reintroduction, Heightening, and Boosting of Tension (2:30-2:32)

10.   Fourth Vocal Verse Passage, Transition to Second Iteration of Vocal Chorus, and Second Iteration of Vocal Chorus: Reintroduction, Heightening, and Boosting of Tension; Jolt of Rapid Rise in Tension and of Rapidly Heightened Complication and Challenge, as well as Rapidly Intensified Agony Involved in Experience of Central Paradoxes; Immersive Response to the Challenge and Complication as well as to the Central Paradoxes Confronting the Impetus, the Drive, to Proceed; Leading Into and Elaborating Second Chorus and Second Seizing Upon, Identifying With, and Channeling Release of Tension (2:33-3:13)

11.   Final Instrumental Passage: Closing Down, Suspending, and Fading Out of Tension (3:14-3:34)

        In sum, I hear the sounds, patterns of sounds, and deployments of sounds comprising "Transmission" engaging with challenge, complication, and the paradoxical; with a persistent impetus, and drive, to proceed in order to find and deliver a response to the situation, and what it demands, despite the challenge, complication, and paradoxes this impetus, this drive, confronts in seeking to do so; with steadily and rapidly building tension as well as a climactically immersive seizing upon, identifying with, and channeling of the release of tension as a response to what the situation demands; and with a final closing down, suspending, and fading out of remnant tension.

I notice a synthesizer shimmer beginning and extending through the first two seconds of the song; the bass guitar entering by introducing and playing the initial melody, at 0.03; the drums entering with a distinctly foregrounded snare and a pronounced echo effect on the snare, at 0:13; the guitar entering with an initial para-melodic figure, at 0:15; the vocal entering with a second, now itself distinctly foregrounded melody that is not identical to what the bass guitar earlier introduced, yet readily compatible with the latter, while the latter continues to sound its melody in conjunction with the voice performing its variant off of this initial melody, from 0:39-0:50. After this, I hear a first instrumental passage, from 0:50-1:04, with the bass guitar seemingly as well as carrying forward the melody also picking up and reinforcing the initial guitar para-melody; a second vocal passage, extending the same relation between first and second melodic lines as earlier, from 1:05-1:21; a second instrumental passage, with the guitar seeming now to play single extended flares of sound, from 1:22-1:29; and then a third vocal passage, from 1:30-1:42, when once again the vocal takes the lead in performing the melody while the bass guitar compliments. Following this stage, a third instrumental passage occurs, with a higher pitch guitar para-melody entering as well as what seems like a combination of additional bass guitar or guitar flares, perhaps in conjunction with subtle keyboard synthesizer amplification of this sound, from 1:43-2:06; a fourth vocal passage, with a high-pitched twinkly synthesizer sound introduced comes next, from 2:07-2:29; a fifth vocal passage, in which the voice becomes markedly louder, faster, higher, more insistent, and even more desperate-sounding follows, from 2:33-3:13; and a close-out, with the final sound being the initial synthesizer shimmer reintroduced and now slightly elaborated, lasting from 3:14-3:33.

Within "Transmission" the bass guitar introduces the initial melodic line, then continually repeats it, while this repetition becomes somewhat buried and flattened upon the entrance of the guitar, yet picks up and resounds more clearly once again with the entrance of vocal. Later in the song the notes sounded by the bass guitar seem to resonate longer and to move slightly further, especially up, in pitch. The bass guitar continues to rumble beneath the song's increasing instrumental density and the increasing felt loudness of the collective sound while at the end of the song the bass guitar seems to reduce to a final brief single pitch line. As for the drums, I note a 1and2and3and4and pattern of strikes as well as, occasionally, recalling "Disorder," a strike on the bass drum with the first beat, on the snare drum with the second beat, a null third beat, and on the snare drum again with the fourth beat. Periodically, at the end of several measures, constituting a hypermetre for the song, I hear two tom hits culminating the end and bridging the beginning of the next series of measures to follow this hypermetrical pattern. I hear little if any detectable use of ride or crash cymbals, while the hi-hat is backgrounded such that it appears to coincide with and is virtually indistinguishable from the snare. I also note more frequent two tom hits occur nearing the end of the song, but no drum rolls taking place at any point, while also, as the very end, I hear one final pattern, as the tempo slows down: one bass strike on beat one-one snare strike on beat two-two bass strikes on beat three-and one snare strike on beat four. With the guitar its first pattern involves moving among at most three chords, and more likely two, with the first and third, or more likely the first and second, thereby conveying almost a ping-ponging effect. I also notice this initial line then repeated at a lower register that challenges discerning whether this is a guitar or a bass guitar. Later on the guitar performs extended flares of sound in which single chords seem to be pushed to echo and extend, a higher-pitched variation of the initial oscillating pattern, and then a convergence of this pattern with the flares, which themselves in turn also seem to involve some kind of thickening effects, perhaps involving use of chorus, distortion, or overdrive effects devices. Ultimately, the extended and echoing flares of sound take over from and replace the early ping-ponging movement. A synthesizer contributes the song's opening and closing reverberant spacey shimmering meets swooning sound, while it is possible a synthesizer also amplifies the guitar flares, and a synthesizer is further responsible for the twinkly sound that eventually emerges in the middle of the song, that comes across like an awkward percussion triangle or almost as if some small part is loose and lightly rattling while some much larger vehicle moves or some much larger machine works. The vocal sounds deeper and especially darker than on "Disorder," and also as if it has been oddly filtered and distanced. The vocal seems to gently reverberate frequently, especially at the end of phrases, before pausing, and in order to extend words or parts of words including particular syllables within words to give these greater emphasis. The vocal stays within tightly limited pitch intervals throughout even as it rises to begin lines much higher up near the end from where it was pitched previously with the last verse, yet once again, in this last verse, the vocal stays within a limited interval range, despite seeming to become more insistent, desperate, louder, and faster. It is worth noting as well that the last two lines in the four line chorus, at least in its first iteration, are pitched notably higher than the first two. And it does seem as if the voice moves, overall, in the direction of rising pitch. Often it does seem, in the case of this recording of "Transmission" as if the vocals are double-tracked, especially toward the end of the song when it sounds as if Ian Curtis is harmonizing with himself as part of a small chorus of Ian Curtises, while often Curtis's voice does seem to echo, not just reverberate, and that is indeed especially striking in conjunction with the seemingly odd, or strange, filtering of his vocal timbre.

Yes, "Transmission" does contain an explicit beat layer, and yes, it likewise contains a functional bass layer, which it strikes me more thoroughly solidifies the groove, and fills in holes left by the drums, than is the case with "Disorder," yet also, once again, like with "Disorder," introduces and continues to play a principal melodic line throughout virtually the entirety of the song. Yes, "Transmission" contains a melodic layer, which is principally the contribution of the bass guitar, and especially the vocal, with the latter taking the lead from the former whenever the latter is sounding. And yes, although the guitar does once again provide a para-melody, at least initially, it does play a principal role in constituting the harmonic fill layer, by means of an initial para-melody and slight variations, but especially by means of subsequent extended power chord flares. The harmonic fill layer is further embellished by the synthesizer sounds. All functional layers are employed, while the bass guitar is the one instrument here that most readily seems to contribute to more than one layer, although it is possible, by means of contributing an initial para-melody, that it can be useful to conceive of the guitar doing so as well. In relation to what Moore discusses concerning the dominance of the harmonic fill layer in many varieties of popular songs, I perceive this layer as becoming prominent and loud, especially in early instrumental and late vocal passages, but I suggest this layer does not come across, in "Transmission," as singularly dominant but rather as co-dominant.

In terms of style, "Transmission" does seem to epitomize characteristic features of Joy Division's musical sound style, with the bass guitar playing the melody high on the fretboard; the guitar principally playing harmonic fill in the forms of para-melody with variations as well as extended flares; the drums with a separated and foregrounded snare; the vocal with a tightly contained interval range as well as a leaping up toward the end of the song where this vocal sounds more insistent, desperate, faster, and louder; and the incorporation of synthesizer embellishments and oddities along with especially pronounced use of effects that tend to echo and extend the sound of instruments, including the voice, moving from mild reverberation to a seeming longer-delayed chorus.

In consideration of the soundbox, I hear the initial synthesizer sound coming from the back and to the sides; the bass guitar coming from the front and low center; the drums higher up and to the front, especially the snare; the guitar coming from the sides, further back and both higher and lower than the drums and the bass guitar; and the voice coming from the center but further back than in the case of "Disorder." In addition, I hear the toms further to the sides than the snare and bass drums, while the later-entering twinkly synthesizer sound I hear coming from the sides, but not too far back. Especially with the chorus, it seems as if I hear the voice echoed and double-tracked. In terms of the amounts of time these instruments occupy the soundbox, the bass guitar and the drums sound more often and more persistently over the course of the song's duration than any other instruments, with the guitar next, the voice after that, and the synthesizer effects last. In terms of prominence, the bass guitar is prominent early, and remains close to front, so it always remains at least partially prominent throughout much of the song but its prominence diminishes somewhat when the guitar plays simultaneously and especially with the vocal taking the lead in performing the melody, while the drums and especially the snare drum are frequently quite prominent, the guitar persistently makes its presence known but far from overwhelmingly dominates the soundscape, and the same is the case with the vocal as with the guitar. In sum, I hear the bass guitar and vocal to the center, with the bass guitar lower, the voice higher, the bass guitar more forward, the voice the more to the back; I hear the guitar toward the sides, especially higher, and more to the back; I hear the drums toward the sides right near the center and close to the front, especially the snare with the toms further to the sides than the rest of the drums; and I hear the synthesizer effects coming from the sides. In terms of variation, the overall texture of sound becomes steadily denser as each successive main instrument enters, and then at end, with the outro, once again less so. It does seem like the guitar and bass guitar do move somewhat within the soundbox, the former down and up, and the latter back and forward.

What the preceding description and analysis of structure and instrumentation contributes in terms of my interpretation of the song as locus of meaning and impact is a strongly felt sense that "Transmission" embodies an impassioned effort to simulate the delivery of its message: in other words, the song embodies an impassioned effort to simulate making paradoxical use of mediation, with all of the manifest constraints mediation encompasses, to attempt to break through–to cause a disturbance, implosion, and eruption from within–the hold of entrenched structures that suffuse distance, disconnection, isolation, alienation, paralysis, inertia, fear, and witting as well as unwitting blindness throughout individual, inter-individual, and yet more broadly social existence.

"Transmission" first becomes somewhat louder with the entrance of the drums and then that of the guitar. As the vocal first enters, the bass and drums remain as loud as before, but the guitar drops out. The guitar replaces the vocal in contributing to loudness when the vocal next drops out. Then the same occurs once again with the second vocal passage. In the next subsequent instrumental passage, the overall sound becomes slightly louder as the song approaches the beginning of the third vocal passage. Here, this vocal passage seems slightly louder than earlier as well. In the next instrumental passage the overall sound seems, once again, yet further slightly louder. And the same, once more, continues with the next vocal passage all the way through the end of the vocal line. The vocal itself becomes louder toward the end of the song and the entrance of the twinkly synthesizer sound adds slightly to the overall loudness as well. With the vocal, then the guitar, and then the bass guitar dropping out as the song comes to a close the overall sound becomes softer, and this continues once the drums do so as well although the return and elaboration of the initial synthesizer shimmer right at the end partially counteracts this diminution in loudness. This description and analysis of loudness, I suggest, well fits my developing interpretation of this song as embodying a concerted effort, through the course of direct alignment with a movement of steadily building, growing, and accumulating tension, to break through, and, in other words, to embody a piercing from within of the simultaneous cloaking and choking stranglehold exercised by a deadening status quo. This status quo preexists the beginning of the song, while the song ultimately suggests it will continue to persist long after a single playing of the song ends. Yet what the latter in turn implies is it requires successive ongoing iterations of the same piercing efforts in order to be able to contend with what this status quo does to those of us who must live according to its dictates, even while struggling with and under the weight of these dictates, because we can only effectively survive and endure this weight by continually contesting the otherwise seemingly inescapable and unalterable necessity of its deadening impact.

I hear "Transmission" proceeding at a fast tempo, significantly faster than "Disorder." I estimate this tempo, for "Transmission," as 192 bpm. As aforementioned, the principal metrical pattern I hear with the drums is 1and2and3and4and, which means the drums typically follow a pattern of eighth notes, and this pattern involves a clearly syncopated beat. As also aforementioned, it in addition seems as if the drums establish a hypermetrical pattern by punctuating this with tom strikes.

The bass guitar performs three melodic riffs:

Riff #1 proceeds as follows: 1 and 2 and 3 and 4 and (all eighth notes)/1 and 2 and 3 and (all eighth notes) 4 (quarter note)/1 (quarter note) 2 and 3 and 4 and (all eighth notes)/1 and 2 and 3 and (all eighth notes) 4 (quarter note).

Riff #2 then proceeds as follows: 1 (quarter note) 2 and 3 and 4 and (all eighth notes)/1 and 2 and 3 and (all eighth notes) 4 quarter note/1 (quarter note) 2 and 3 and 4 and (all eighth notes)/1 and 2 and 3 and (all eighth notes) 4 (quarter note).

Riff #3 next proceeds as follows: 1 (quarter note) 2 and 3 and 4 and (eighth notes)/1 and 2 and 3 and (all eighth notes) 4 (quarter note)/1 (quarter note) 2 and 3 and 4 and (all eighth notes)/1 and 2 (all eighth notes) and 3 (quarter note) and 4 and (all eighth notes).

The guitar follows a rhythmic pattern of 1 and 2 and 3 and 4 early on and then allows chords to extend and flare across beats later. The vocal, however, follows a somewhat more elaborate series of patterns, as follows:

1 "Radio live transmission/Radio live transmission": Two eighth notes + dotted half note//half note rest + two quarter notes//eighth note tied to quarter notes + tie between two eighth notes and a dotted quarter note.

#2: "Listen to the silence, let it ring on/Eyes, dark grey lenses frightened of the sun/We would have a fine time living in the sun/Left to blind destruction/Waiting for our sight": Opening half note rest + four eighth notes//eighth note + dotted quarter note + four eighth notes//quarter note + eighth note rest + two eighth notes + quarter note + eighth note//quarter note + six eighth notes//quarter note + eighth note rest + four quarter notes//quarter note + quarter note + four eighth notes//two eighth notes + eighth note rest + five eighth notes//quarter note + quarter note + four eighth notes//quarter note plus dotted half note.

#3: "And we would go on as though nothing was wrong/And hide from these days we remained all alone/Staying in the same place, just staying out the time/Touching from a distance/Further all the time": Opening dotted quarter note rest + five eighth notes//two eighth notes + one quarter note + four eighth notes//quarter note + quarter note rest + four eighth notes//quarter note + six eighth notes//quarter note + quarter note rest + two sixteenth notes + an eighth note + two eighth notes//eighth note + quarter note + eighth note + two sixteenth notes + eighth note + two eighth notes//two eighth notes + quarter note rest + four eighth notes//quarter note + quarter note + four eight notes//half note.

#4: "Dance, dance, dance, dance, dance to the radio/Dance, dance, dance, dance, dance to the radio/Dance, dance, dance, dance, dance to the radio/Dance, dance, dance, dance, dance to the radio": Dotted quarter note + eighth note + quarter note + quarter note//eighth note + dotted quarter note + quarter note + two eighth notes//two eighth notes + quarter note. Then repeat three more times.

#5: "Well I could call out when the going gets tough/The things that we've learnt are never enough/No language, just sound, that's all we need know, to synchronise love to the beat of the show/And we could dance": quarter note rest + eighth note rest + five eighth notes//eighth note + quarter note + five eighth notes//eighth note + quarter note + eighth note + four eighth notes//eighth note + quarter note + five eighth notes//eighth note + quarter note + five eighth notes//dotted quarter note + five eighth notes//eighth note + quarter note + five eighth notes//eighth note + quarter note + five eighth notes//eighth note + dotted quarter note + half note rest//half note rest + eighth note rest + three eighth notes//quarter note + two eighth notes + quarter note + eighth notes//dotted half note + quarter note.

#6: "Dance, dance, dance, dance, dance to the radio/Dance, dance, dance, dance, dance to the radio/Dance, dance, dance, dance, dance to the radio/Dance, dance, dance, dance, dance to the radio": Dotted quarter note + eighth note + quarter note + quarter note//eighth note + dotted quarter note + quarter note + two eighth notes//two eighth notes + quarter note. Then repeat three times.

What I find especially notable here is the vocal often carries words across not only beats but also across measures–including by means of many ties. In other words, this not as simple a rhythm as a strict pattern of pulses sounding on all four beats while clearly demarcating the end of one measure from the beginning of the next because, as with the bass guitar melody, the vocal melody incorporates rests and variation in length of notes, while extending pitches sounded, along with words or parts of words sung, across measures. As I've sketched out above, the vocal contributes ultimately five distinct patterns of soundings of pitches within groups and series, and within and across measures, along with several notable repetitions. In terms of suggestions of comparable, including analogous, forms of movement, "Transmission" feels much closer to both running and dancing than does "Disorder." The bass guitar movement feels almost like pogo-ing, but also like a high-kick sprint. The drums feel as if they resemble a quick shuffle and glide movement, yet akin as well to dancing. The vocal feels as if it embarks upon relatively fast initial movements with frequent pauses. The guitar feels like it is releasing flares as well as ping-ponging. The chorus in the song suggests an intense, approaching frenzied dancing, with ever increasingly widening steps and circuits of movement as well as incorporation of arms as well as legs and ultimately the whole body. Again, all of this fits with the developing interpretation of this song I have elaborated at the end of my preceding discussions first of structure and instrumentation and second of loudness.

At this point, I think it will prove useful to introduce some commentary on "Transmission" from two writers more experienced and adept than me at working with formalistically analytic music theory in form of standard notation, as well as in themselves playing rock music instruments. In his blog *The Concrete Void*, Patrick Jenkinson writes, concerning "Transmission," that the bass riff ". . . is made up of only three notes: two long stretches of D and C notes respectively, each one punctuated by a single A note. While the riff undoubtedly possesses punk's trademark simplicity, it also calls bands like Kraftwerk to mind due to its steady, machine-like nature. The first D is a quarter note, and it is followed by thirteen more D's and an A in eighth notes. The pattern is then repeated with C's replacing the D's. The quarter note and fourteen eighth notes pattern gives the riff a super rhythmic quality." Continuing, Jenkinson indicates, "While the song is structured around a verse chorus progression, unlike most songs written in this form," Peter Hook "doesn't change the riff when the song progresses from verse to chorus or vice versa" and, as Jenkinson hears this, "Not altering the riff creates claustrophobic effect; a sensation of being trapped that mirrors the song's lyrical themes," while "having a steady, continuous, rhythmic melody gives the music a strong sense of propulsion." Jenkinson suggests the members of Joy Division counteracted the tendency that could arise, from not including a clear transition from verse to chorus, of running "the risk of having the entire song seem like a unchanging blur" by introducing a slight change in the melodic riff "that only occurs during key moments, such as the transition from verse to chorus." As Jenkinson explains, "This change happens on the fourth and final bar of the riff. During the rest of the song, this bar contains the second half of the C repetitions as well as the closing A note. Instead, Peter [Hook] plays an E - F - E - F - G - G

210

pattern." As Jenkinson concludes, "it is just enough variety to let the listener know that the song has progressed to it's next stage, while retaining enough monotony to maintain the sense of claustrophobia and propulsion."

Jenkinson hears Stephen Morris alternating between "One - Two - Three - and - Four" and "One - Two - Three - and - Four - and" patterns throughout the course of the song, although occasionally adding a "One - Two - Three - and - Four - and" pattern. In relation to Bernard Sumner's guitar, Jenkinson describes Sumner initially playing "an oscillating pattern that meshes very well with the bass" while, as he repeats this pattern a few times, it becomes slightly more complex, increasing tension. Then, "For the verses, in between Ian's singing Bernard will occasionally come back in with either the original oscillating riff or a second riff that has a similar back and forth design," while "When the chorus kicks in, he switches to rhythmic power chords that he plays at the top of every other bar, giving the song a bit of oomph to go along with Ian's call to the dance floor. This power chord accompaniment continues into the final verse, mirroring it's increase in intensity."

Next, I turn to Jono Podmore, writing about "Transmission" for Liverpool-based music webzine *Get Into This*. Podmore ascribes a "brutalist" character to the song on account of the limited number of musical notes the song contains: "This is why 'Transmission' is so special: the melody and the harmony are pared down to the absolute bone. A 2-note bass riff is occasionally decorated but nails down the entire tension of the song between the root note, D, and the tone below it, C. This is reinforced in the guitar lines–sometimes an octave higher, or a fifth, or harmonised, but always just swinging back and forth between those 2 notes, that basic relationship." Meanwhile "The vocal melody again focuses on the same polarity but introduces into the bleak monochrome regime the hopeful warmth of the major third (F#). This tiny chink of light on the bleak horizon seems all the more heartrending in the dour context."

As Podmore explains, "'Transmission' is in D Mixolydian. Joy Division's entire output is in either the Mixolydian or Dorian mode." What this means, more precisely, is these are the notes of the scale corresponding to the key in which Joy Division perform "Transmission": D – E – F# – G – A – B – C. A major third, moreover, involves a movement of four semitones up or down: here, in this mode and this key, it involves possible movements of D to F#, or F# to D, or E to G, or G to E, or F# to A, or A to F#, or A to C, or C to A. The Mixolydian mode involves working with the following sequence of intervals: Tone – Tone – Semitone – Tone – Tone – Semitone – Tone, or Whole step – Whole step – Half step – Whole step – Whole step – Half step – Whole step. Of course it is possible to transpose "Transmission" to another key, and even another mode, and many have done so, but nonetheless it is useful to recognize in what key and what mode "Transmission" is composed and performed by the members of Joy Division themselves.

I will proceed next to identify and then comment on what I have heard in terms of pitch and movement in pitch in "Transmission," beginning with Bernard Sumner's guitar. As I hear it, this involves two chords, in the key of D, D and C chords, more precisely a D power chord and a C power chord, and even more precisely than that D5 and C5 power chords, with D5 played involving just one fretted note, E, on the D string, and C5 played involving just two fretted notes, D, on the B string, and

211

C, on the G string. Sumner's strumming pattern, throughout the song, is 1&2&3&4&. Sumner's contributions involve the following sequences of chords:

(1–Intro): D5, C5, D5, C5; (2-Solo): D5, C5, D5, C5, twice; (3-Verse #1): D5, C5, twice; (4-Interlude): C5, D5, C5; (5-Verse #2): D5 with C5 played later toward the end of the vocal line than previously, and then same in the next three vocal lines with a subsequent D5, C5, and D5 at the end of these lines, along with a final quick C5 D5 and C5 at the end of fourth line; (6–Verse #3): much like Verse #2 except without the final three-chord flourish in Verse #2; (7-Solo): D5 C5 D5 C5/D5 C5; (8-Chorus): D5 then C5 on "radio" at the end of line, and this repeated three times; (9-Bridge): D5 with C5 on the last word of first line, then change to D5 with the last word on the second line, then change to C5 with the last word of third line, then to D5 again with the last word of fourth line, and then to C5 with last word of fourth line; (10-Chorus #2): same as Chorus #1; (11-Outro): D5 C5 D5 C5.

What is especially noteworthy here is a relatively consistent movement between two pitches, a relatively consistent rate of strumming, and a tendency to shift between chords in conjunction with the last word of a vocal phrase. As I hear it, the guitar seems to move a distance relatively a third in terms of an octave between the two pitches, or in other words 3/8 of an octave or 5/12 of an octave in terms of the twelve semitones constituting the chromatic scale. Movements of pitch here oscillate back and forth, throughout, with a suggestion as well of a sliding down one time and a sliding up another one time in terms of where both of the two alternating pitches are located while also varying the playing of these pitches in terms of how long they are allowed to resound, especially as they increasingly extend and flare, further into the song. According to Podmore, as I have earlier indicated, Sumner's guitar sometimes appears to sound an octave higher, sometimes a fifth, and sometimes is harmonized with the bass guitar but always moves back and forth between two pitches.

Peter Hook's bass guitar contributes according to the following riff patterns, as at least I hear this:

(#1): two quarter notes, at the 5th fret on the A string (a D note), followed by six eighth notes, at the 5th fret on the A string (a D note)//six eighth notes, at the 5th fret on the A string (a D note), then a quarter note, no frets on the A string (an A note)//one quarter note, at the 3rd fret on the A string (a C note), six eighth notes, at the 3rd fret on the A string (a C note)//six eighth notes, at the 3rd fret on the A string (a C note), then one quarter note, no frets on the A string (an A note).

(#2) one quarter note, at the 5th fret on the A string (a D note), followed by six eighth notes, at the 5th fret on the A string (a D note)//six eighth notes, at the 5th fret on the A string (a D note), followed by quarter note, no frets on the A string (an A)//a quarter note, at the 3rd fret, on the A string (a C note), followed by six eighth notes, at the 3rd fret on the A string (a C note)//six eighth notes, at the 3rd fret, on the A string (a C note), followed by one quarter note, open string (an A note).

(#3): one quarter note, at the 5th fret on the A string (a D note), followed by six eighth notes, at the 5th fret on the A string (a D note)//six eighth notes, at the 5th fret on the A string (a D note), followed by one quarter note, open string (an A note)//one quarter note, at the 3rd fret on the A string (a C note), followed by six eighth notes, at the 3rd fret on the A string (a C note)//one eighth note, at the 2nd fret, on the D string (an E note), one eighth note at the 3rd fret on the D string (a C note), one eighth note, at the 2nd fret on the D string (an E note), one quarter note, at the 3rd fret on the D string (a F note), and three eighth notes, at the 5th fret on the D string (a G note).

And here's where these riff patterns contribute to the song:

Intro: Riff #1. Then Riff # 2 and then the drums enter. Then Riff #2 X3. Then Riff # 3.

With the Initial Vocal: Riff # 2 X2.

Then With the Following Instrumental Break: Riff #2 X2.

1st Vocal Verse: Riff #2 X3. Then Riff # 3.

2nd Vocal Verse: Riff #2 X2.

Guitar Solo: Riff #2 X4.

Chorus: Riff #2 X3. Then Riff #3.

3rd Vocal Verse: Riff #2 X3.

Chorus: Riff #2 X3. Riff #3.

What I note of particular importance is Hook's bass generally stays a long time on one note, occasionally moves up a note, and occasionally up two notes, contributing a largely tightly confined range of pitch with a slight overall tendency toward an upward movement.

In discussing the vocal in terms of pitch, and especially movement in pitch, I am transposing to the key of C in order to make this easier for myself, but, as I have earlier in this chapter discussed, what is ultimately most important here are how far, and how often, as well as according to what kinds of patterns, does the vocalist move in terms of pitch rather than precisely what pitches he is singing. Here is what I hear in terms of movement and stasis, conjoined with duration in time, of pitches sounded in the vocal lines of "Transmission":

#1 ("Radio live transmission/Radio live transmission"): two eighth notes D and E, followed by one dotted half note F/one quarter note rest, two quarter notes F/two eighth notes D and E, followed by two tied eighth notes E and a dotted quarter note C//Repeat once.

#2 ("Listen to the silence, let it ring on/Eyes, dark grey lenses frightened of the sun/We would have a fine time living in the sun/Left to blind destruction/Waiting for our sight"): one quarter note rest, followed by four eighth notes D/one eighth note D, followed by one dotted quarter note D, followed by four eighth notes three D and one C with the last tied to/one quarter note C, followed by one eighth note rest followed by two tied eighth notes E, followed by one quarter note E, followed by one eighth note D/one quarter note E, followed by one eighth note D, followed by two tied eighth notes E, followed by one eighth note D, followed by one eighth note E, and followed by one eighth note D/one quarter note F, followed by one quarter note rest, followed by four eighth notes D/two quarter notes D, followed by four eighth notes D/two eighth notes D then C, followed by an eighth note rest, followed by two tied eighth notes E, followed by an eighth note D, followed by an eighth note E, followed by an eighth note D/two quarter notes E, followed by an eighth note E, followed by an eighth note D, followed by an eighth note E, followed by an eighth note D tied to/a quarter note D followed by a dotted half note F extending/to a full note F extending/to a full note E.

#3 ("And we would go on as though nothing was wrong/And hide from these days we remained all alone/Staying in the same place, just staying out the time/Touching from a distance/Further all the time"): one quarter note rest, followed by two eighth notes, D, followed by one eighth note, C, followed by a tied eighth note D continuing/to a tied eighth note D, followed by one eighth note D, followed by one quarter note D, followed by three eighth notes D, followed by one tied eighth note E continuing/to one tied quarter note E, followed by one quarter note rest, followed by three eighth notes E, followed by a tied eighth note E continuing/to one tied eighth note E, followed by five eighth notes E, followed by one tied eighth note D continuing/to one quarter note D, followed by one quarter note rest, followed by two sixteenth notes D, followed by one eighth note D, followed by one eighth note C, followed by one eighth note D tied to/one eighth note D, followed by one quarter note D, followed by one eighth note D, followed by two sixteenth notes D, followed by one sixteenth note D, followed by two eighth notes D with a final of these two eighth notes tied continuing/to one tied eighth note D, followed by one eighth note C, followed by one quarter rest, followed by eighth notes E, followed by one eighth note D/two quarter notes E, followed by one eighth note E, followed by one eighth note D, followed by one eighth note E, followed by one eighth note D/one half note F.

#4 ("Dance, dance, dance, dance, dance to the radio/Dance, dance, dance, dance, dance to the radio/Dance, dance, dance, dance, dance to the radio/Dance, dance, dance, dance, dance to the radio"): one dotted quarter note A, followed by one tied eighth and one quarter note A, followed by one tied quarter note A continuing/to one tied eighth note A, followed by one dotted quarter note A, followed by one quarter note A, followed by one eighth note A, followed by one eighth note F/one eighth note A, followed by on eighth note G, followed by one quarter note G, followed by one half note rest/one full note rest. Repeat once. Then: one dotted quarter note D, followed by one tied eighth and one quarter note D, followed by one tied quarter note D continuing/to one tied eighth note D, followed by one dotted quarter note D, followed by one quarter note D, followed by one eighth note D, followed by one eighth note B/followed by one eighth note D, followed by one eighth note C, followed by one quarter note C, followed by one half note rest/full note rest. Repeat once.

#5 ("Well I could call out when the going gets tough/The things that we've learnt are never enough/No language, just sound, that's all we need know, to synchronise love to the beat of the show): one quarter note rest followed by one eighth note rest, followed by five eighth notes D with a final eight note tying/into one eighth note D, followed by one quarter note D, followed by five eighth notes D with one final eighth note tying/into one eighth note D, followed by one quarter note C, followed by one eighth note C, followed by four eighth notes D with one final eighth note tying/into one eighth note D, followed by one quarter note D, followed by one eighth note C, followed by three eighth notes D, followed by one eighth note F tying/into one eighth note F, followed by one quarter note D, followed by five eighth notes D with the last eighth note tying/into one dotted quarter note D, followed by five eighth notes D with the last eighth note tying/into one eighth note D, followed by one quarter note C, followed by one eighth note C, followed by four eighth notes D with the last eighth note tying/into one eighth note D, followed by one quarter note D, followed by one eighth note C, followed by three eighth notes D, followed by one eighth note F tying/into one eighth note F followed by one dotted quarter note D, followed by one half note rest.

#6 ("And we could dance"): one half note rest followed by one eighth note rest followed by three eighth notes D with the last eighth note tying/into one quarter note E, followed by two eighth notes F and E, followed by one quarter note E, followed by one eighth note F, followed by one eighth note E tying/into one dotted half note E followed by one quarter note D. Note well that the last two measures all involves Curtis singing the last word, 'dance' stretched out and modulated over this extended duration.

#7 ("Dance, dance, dance, dance, dance to the radio/Dance, dance, dance, dance, dance to the radio/Dance, dance, dance, dance, dance to the radio/Dance, dance, dance, dance, dance to the radio"): one dotted quarter note D, followed by one eighth note D, followed by one quarter note D, followed by one quarter note D tied/to one eighth note D, followed by one dotted quarter note D, followed by one quarter note D, followed by one eighth note D, followed by one eighth note B/one eighth note D, followed by one eighth note D, followed by one quarter note C, followed by one half note rest/one full note rest. Then repeat three times.

What I find especially worthy of note is that in any one section of vocals the interval range Curtis covers is small, encompassing just one to two notes, or three at most, although over the course of the song Curtis moves more than an entire octave higher in range, while he also moves steadily higher up in his starting pitch with each successive section of vocals as well as tending to move slightly upward in his phrasing throughout. Notably also, in the chorus, at least in the first chorus, Curtis moves up six semitones in pitch from where he begins the first two lines to where he begins the third and fourth lines.

Overall, each of the principal instruments, including Curtis's vocal, involve carefully confined or tightly delimited oscillating and flaring movements in pitch with a general overall tendency to rise in pitch within phrases and sequences as well as from section to section, especially with the vocal. This movement works tightly together to enhance an at least perceived increase in volume and density as the song proceeds. And, again, this pattern and deployment of sound fits well with what I have described earlier, following my discussions of structure and instrumentation, as well as of loudness, as my developing interpretation of what the sounds, patterns of sounds, and deployments of sound contribute to "Transmission" as locus of meaning and impact. To repeat, "Transmission" embodies a concerted effort, through the course of direct alignment with a movement of steadily building, growing, and accumulating tension, to break through, and, in other words, to embody a piercing from within of the simultaneous cloaking and choking stranglehold exercised by a deadening status quo. This status quo preexists the beginning of the song, while the song ultimately suggests it will continue to persist long after a single playing of the song ends. Yet what the latter in turn implies is it requires successive ongoing iterations of the same piercing efforts in order to be able to contend with what this status quo does to those of us who must live according to its dictates, even while struggling with and under the weight of these dictates, because we can only effectively survive and endure this weight by continually contesting the otherwise seemingly inescapable and unalterable necessity of its deadening impact.

Moving on next to consideration of matters of delivery, in comparison with "Disorder" Curtis here, in "Transmission," sounds as if his vocal delivery comes from lower and deeper in the body, and as if this is filtered and distanced, even somewhat strangled, by way of studio treatment and processing, while it also becomes more intense, agitated, and insistent toward end. As with "Disorder," at that point Curtis's singing verges close to shouting while never quite reaching that point. Curtis incorporates ample sliding and gliding about the words he sings, especially at the end of phrases, including even syllables within words, and often extending across measures, allowing words, and syllables, to resonate and modulate but also to gently fade out and disappear before resuming with the next vocal passage. Curtis's singing of 'o' at end of "Radio" is slightly extended as is 'mission' in his singing of 'transmission'. Likewise "on," "sun," and "night" are slightly extended. "Sight" is even further extended while "time" is not extended as much as "sight" yet slightly more than "wrong" and "alone" which are nevertheless slightly extended as well. Once more, in the chorus, the 'o' at the end of "radio" is slightly extended and then in the third full vocal verse "tough," "enough," "know," and "show" are all allowed to move between notes. "Dance" at the end of "And we could dance" is then yet further extended and allowed to modulate across multiple notes. Finally, at least in relation to Curtis's vocal delivery, with "Transmission," it does, again, seem in the chorus sections of this song his voice is double-tracked to in fact suggest we are hearing a chorus of voices, albeit a chorus of multiplied Ian Curtis voices. Curtis's delivery of the vocal, as well as Hannett's collaboration in his doing so, I find especially interesting as it does seem to embody a voice striving toward "touching from a distance" while fighting against forces that result in this at least seeming or feeling as if it is doing so from "further all the time." Curtis's voice here does sound nevertheless as if it is working to immerse itself within, and indeed revel in, the immediate moment, in the process itself of letting go, to "Dance" and to concentrate upon directly aligning solely with sound and movement, so as "to synchronise love to the beat of the show."

In discussing timbre, because of the many challenges involved in doing this, especially as this often becomes highly impressionistic, that I addressed earlier in this chapter, in the section on "Disorder," I am going to make use of comparison with "Disorder" to help flesh out these descriptions somewhat, while acknowledging at the start that it makes logical sense that timbres in two Joy Division songs will share many similarities. Also I am using the same listening equipment myself as I indicated, in discussing "Disorder," while the version of "Transmission" I am listening to is the 2020 digital remastered version of this song.

Let's begin with the drums. I hear the timbre of the snare drum as crisp, again as with "Disorder" like a snip or a snip snip, although on "Transmission" it seems to me the attack stands out more than it does in "Disorder" with relatively little, in comparison with "Disorder," perceptible decay or sustain. I hear the timbre of the bass drum as deep and clear, with something of a notable sustain, with a decisive attack, a quick decay, and a release that is not quite as quick as the toms. With the toms these sound much like extensions of the bass drum at higher pitches, and they contribute a notable resounding effect, especially by means of extended decay and sustain, while their release is quick and sharp as is their attack. The hi-hat as I have earlier mentioned I find difficult to distinguish at all, as I hear this blending with the snare, but this might well have to do with my ears not being as sensitive to as a wide a range of pitches and volumes as I was when considerably younger and prior to attending a great many loud live musical performances. In sum, though, it seems here as if the pitches of bass drum and the snare drum sound closer to each other than is the case on "Disorder" while I do hear a slight element of crackling as part of the timbres of both instruments as they sound. The synthesizer opening and closing timbre feels shimmering and ethereal, while the twinkly sound, again, suggests a small loose part, or two small parts, rubbing up against the movement of some kind of machine, or a slightly awkward percussion triangle.

Turning to the bass guitar I hear this timbre as relatively thin with light reverberation, as a gentle rumble with something of a foggy tone, slightly warm, that also feels somewhat deeper than with "Disorder", has something of a pulsating character to it as well, and does overall feel, more than in "Disorder," as if it is emanating from 'a depths', yet even so this feels like a foundation, a fundamental sustaining force. The timbre of the guitar sounds higher than the bass guitar, as well as moving further in pitch intervals than the bass guitar and the voice. Overall this timbre seems bright and clean while oscillating which happens earlier in the song, and at this point it also seems relatively thin. But as the song proceeds the guitar timbre changes. As it moves deeper, or seems to do so, it also seems to become somewhat muddier and thicker. Yet later it seems, as I have already repeatedly mentioned, like flares of sound that resonate for an extended period, containing a pronounced sustain and a slow release following a quick attack and a quick decay. Once again, with these flares, the sound seems thicker, more overdriven or distorted and more as if sounding in harmony with itself by way of some kind of echoing and delaying effect(s). The guitar timbre definitely sounds crunchier, heavier, and thicker later in the song, as well as more overtly 'chorusy'.

In relation to the timbre of the vocal this does yes sound deeper, darker, lower, more akin to frying than is the case with "Disorder," and also as if more heavily filtered, or otherwise mediated, with pronounced reverberation as well as modulation occurring at and toward the end of lines as well as on key words, with the vocal also at times veering close but not quite to the point of sung speech or sung shouting. The vocal sounds, especially in the chorus, as if pronouncedly echoed and double-tracked. Toward the end of the song, the timbre of the voice seems to shift somewhat as the voice moves closer to straining, to pushing its limits in reaching up to the high end of its register. This vocal, at least as recorded, is not overtly breathy, or nasal, but it is somewhat reedier than on "Disorder." As the voice rises in pitch it seems somewhat less harsh and distant but also sounds more multiplied. Also notable is how swinging between pitches at end of phrases and on key words also calls attention to timbral elements of this voice at these pitches. And again, the voice is produced so it sounds like a chorus of singers singing the vocal in the chorus.

Considering specific characteristics of timbre in "Transmission," overall, beginning with tension/relaxation, I hear the guitar and bass as more relaxed whereas I hear the voice and drums as more tense. In terms of tightness/openness I hear the drums as the tightest, with the other instruments more open, especially in allowing their sound to resonate and resound. In terms of raspiness this is not particularly pronounced although I hear the vocal as slightly raspier than with "Disorder" but raspiness I find hard to apply to the other instruments here. In terms of grittiness I hear the vocal as grittier than in "Disorder" and the guitar as well, especially the guitar later on in the song, and I also detect at least a somewhat grittier timbre with the bass guitar and drums in "Transmission" as opposed to "Disorder." Likewise, I hear the timbre of the voice and guitar as rougher than on "Disorder" while the beat feels somewhat rougher also, especially at ends and beginnings of the hypermetre, as if I can almost feel the physical energy invested to emphasize these points, and in particular on the toms. Similarly, I hear less overall polish, sheen, and cleanness in terms of timbre in "Transmission" than I do in "Disorder" as well as greater dirtiness in the timbres of the guitar, bass guitar, and vocal in the former song than in the latter. The earlier guitar timbres sound bright as do the synthesizer shimmers but not much else does, while distortion seems more noticeable on the guitar than with "Disorder" and perhaps even somewhat more here on the bass guitar as well. In terms of clarity, the voice sounds fairly clear even when somewhat muffled, while the bass guitar sounds clear whenever playing by itself, and the toms as well as bass and snare drums also sound clear. The guitar extends into two registers while the voice demonstrates a relatively expansive register overall, while not moving far across this expanse at any one time. I hear reverberation with the voice and also added reverb on voice, guitar, and drums as well as echo on the voice and the guitar. In terms of coldness/warmth, I hear both from the voice, coldness from the drums, and yet a persistent, recurrent or resurgent warmth, especially with the bass guitar but also occasionally with the guitar. In terms of richness of timbre, overall this does not seem quite as rich as "Disorder," especially the voice, but I hear a certain indirect amount of possibly compensatory richness with the guitar flares. In terms of vigor, I hear this with the guitar, but especially with the drums and with the voice rising and increasing in insistence. In terms of thinness/thickness I hear the bass guitar as relatively thin, and the voice too at the beginning, as well as the same with the snare drum, but the guitar flares feel thicker as does the voice, somewhat, as the song proceeds, while the toms feel thickest among the drums. And, finally, in terms of wetness/dryness, I hear an element of wetness with the drums and with the synthesizer shimmer and twinkle while the guitar feels drier and the same is the case with voice while the bass guitar feels somewhat in between the two.

In terms of timbres suggesting comparable, including analogous, bodily movements, I hear the bass guitar sounding akin to a steady, determined, focused, and purposeful kind of movement; the guitar sounding akin to a more rushing and stop/start as well as skating and, yes, flaring, kind of movement; the voice akin to a running or dancing kind of movement; the drums as well akin to a kind of running or dancing kind of movement; and the synthesizer seems to float or loosely vibrate. Considering common timbral descriptors such as benevolence, potency, naturalness, religiosity, happiness, temporality, stability, and distance, I hear the guitar and the drums sounding especially potent but the bass guitar also does so as well. I hear the synthesizer effects as sounding the opposite of natural. I am unsure benevolence or happiness per se make much sense here. I do hear a secular religiosity, yes. In terms of temporality the song sounds much as if it is immersed within the immediate, the direct moment at hand. In terms of distance, yes I definitely hear this in the timbres, especially in relation to the positioning and treatment of the voice. In terms of stability I hear more the opposite, with any sense of stability here seemingly fragile and precarious at best.

In sum, in terms of timbre, versus "Disorder," "Transmission" sounds harsher, harder, darker, and rougher overall; less sparkling, crystalline, bell-like, ringing, glistening, and glimmering; throatier and reedier; equally resonant while simultaneously grittier; and deeper, drier, and boomier overall. What does all of this, concerning the timbres in "Transmission," including in comparison with the timbres in "Disorder," contribute to my developing direction of interpretation of "Transmission" as locus of meaning and impact? I suggest it contributes a sense that the latter song is more directly and overtly concerned than the former with what makes human connection difficult, and how this difficulty might at least be challenged, if not overcome, and that "Transmission" is less directly and overtly concerned than "Disorder" with introspective examination of the complexity, multiplicity, contradictoriness, and dynamism of subjectivity and selfhood. At the same time, both songs seem much concerned with the precariousness not just of a particular situation, not just of positioning within and responsiveness versus a prospective impending event, encounter, or confrontation, and not just of the background, and backstory, to those two vectors of precariousness. Both songs seem concerned with the precariousness of vitality, of spirit, of 'the' life force in and of itself. Both songs as well seem concerned with the social structures ostensibly designed, paradoxically enough, to facilitate social relations but which all too often and all too extensively exercise effectively 'deadening' impacts, leading all too many people all too often and all too extensively in effect to give up on life, while still continuing to live on–i.e., to give up on life's spirit, life's force, and life's vitality, ending up thereby 'living' as if they are merely dragging themselves along until they are completely dead.

***

I will next discuss my experience of "Transmission" in relation to the eight avenues of musical affect Arnie Cox theorizes in *Music & Embodied Cognition: Listening, Moving, Feeling, & Thinking*, beginning with mimetic participation. In listening to "Transmission" I perceive Peter Hook's bass guitar as involving a relatively steady degree of effort, and the same for the most part with Bernard Sumner's guitar, with no particular section of the song appearing to involve significant straining, pressing, or struggling from either. Stephen Morris's drumming feels vigorous and as if it involves a significant exertion of effort, especially at transitions between one hypermetrical sequence and the next. Ian Curtis's vocal feels as if he needs to press increasingly harder, involving greater effort and less ease in exertion of force as the song proceeds, especially with the final two lines of the first chorus, into the final verse section, and through the transitional line that follows this section and precedes the second chorus. In terms of duration of exertion, I perceive this as almost continuous with Morris's drums and Hook's bass guitar, whereas with Sumner's guitar this rises and falls, as the guitar drops periodically from contributing to the mix, and as Sumner's shifts from an oscillating to a flaring pattern. With Curtis's vocal, again, the duration is discontinuous as Curtis does not sing all the way through, although the duration becomes more sustained as the song proceeds, with, as aforementioned, little break between the last full verse section, the transitional pre-chorus line ("And we could dance") and the second chorus. In my felt evaluation of the success or failure of these exertions in relation to their implicit purpose, with Hook's bass guitar and Sumner's guitar both feel successful, as if both have achieved the patterns of sounds they aimed to achieve, as the bass guitar continues to play a principal melodic line with slight variations among its constituent riffs throughout almost the entire duration of the song, and with the guitar moving from oscillations to flares in what feels like a shift that suits the developing trajectory of the collective sound and its organized deployment. Morris's drums feel persistent, determined, committed, and continually pushing, or propelling, onward but I am unclear what success or failure might mean in relation to this constituent of the overall sound comprising "Transmission," even as the drums do keep up with and on top of the beat all the way through. Curtis's vocal seems both to have achieved its purpose and not, at once, which correlates with what I have already discussed in terms of the combination of exhilaration and desperation Curtis's voice conveys, notably toward the end, with the final full verse section, in the transitional pre-chorus line preceding the second chorus, and, in fact, in both the first and the second chorus.

In listening to "Transmission" I do feel myself moving with the beat, and with variations in the beat, I do feel myself following along closely with the initial bass melody through its slight yet significant variations, I do feel myself swinging and flaring with the guitar, and I do feel myself identifying with the vocal, increasingly so with each chorus, following the vocal's imperative to dance, while I also feel myself stretching my limits as Curtis does in the third and fourth lines of the first chorus, in the third full section of verse, and in the final transitional pre-chorus line prior to the second chorus. Overall "Transmission," with its building, growing, and accumulating tension, and its two climaxes, feels as if exertion of force is largely non-attenuated, although perhaps some attenuation happens as the guitar shifts from oscillations to flares.

I feel as if both the music as persona and I as a co-protagonist anticipate increasing intensity, steady movement toward a climax, and persistently needing and wanting to push harder and reach further. We both anticipate a persistence, or a persistently recurrent reentry, of major constituent lines of sound, with slight variations, as well as all of them increasingly joining together. I as a co-protagonist anticipate moving from taking into account initial backstory to confronting the immediate moment, and, if anything, it feels as if the music as persona is ahead of me here by more clearly perceiving relations between the two as well as by more precisely recognizing where we now are at and what precisely we now need to do. We both anticipate giving way to and joining in with the imperative to "Dance, dance, dance, dance, dance to the radio" and we both anticipate this will be a transient moment that will eventual slow down, dissipate, and disappear, leaving some lingering disappointment concerning departing with a final remnant sense of irresolution. I anticipate as the song proceeds that I will accept the invitation and the challenge to join in vigorously, and by the second chorus I anticipate I will be ready all the most resolutely to do so yet again.

220

I hear this song expressing an impassioned call, an imperative, and an instantiation of a commitment. I hear expression of a desire to feel and to sense vitally. This feels, in turn, as a desire to touch from a distance, no matter how difficult, especially as distance is increasing. I feel I am listening and attending to, as well as sharing and identifying with, an expression of ecstacy meets agony; of a striving to merge with sound and motion, beyond words, and beyond established norms for 'properly' restrained and constrained modes of thinking, understanding, believing, sensing, and feeling. I feel I am listening and attending to, as well as sharing and identifying with, an expression of a desire to experience love through this process of merging. I feel, what's more, as if I am expressing my desire to do so, and sharing this desire with a potentially vast number of others experiencing the same, each at a distance from each other, each in our own separate space, but nonetheless aware of and attuned to each other. In terms of what emotions I hear being expressed to me, I hear not so much fear or sadness, because both seem emotions preceding the present of the song, even as the song acknowledges the past always continues within the present. The song seems committed to 'the now' yet I do hear an expression of a ferocity, of a wildness, and of a wrestling with and striving to break free of restraints and constraints. In terms of what emotions I perceive myself vicariously expressing, in listening closely to and reflecting carefully upon my experience listening to "Transmission," I feel myself expressing a combination of passion and compassion, I feel as if I am expressing a desire as a co-protagonist together with the music as persona to find and sustain a metaphorical light that can penetrate and illuminate a metaphorical darkness, and I feel myself expressing a yet further combination of exhilaration and desperation as I strive both to register depths of alienation and to break free from alienation through pursuit of dis-alienating re-connection.

The sounds comprising "Transmission" feel as if they come at, and enter me, from all sides, from multiple perceptible or imaginable planes, across the soundbox, and they feel as if they increasingly press themselves upon and envelop me within them as the song unfolds. I feel these sounds, collectively, as more concentrated than diffuse, although the guitar flares and the sliding and gliding at the end of vocal phrases feels somewhat diffuse. The bass guitar feels close, the voice feels further back, but both feel close to mid-center; the guitar feels as if it comes from the sides, especially in the top half of a perceptible or imaginable soundbox, while the synthesizer sounds and the drums, especially the snare, feel as if these are positioned close to the front and slightly to the sides, with the toms further to the sides. The voice feels as if it moves closer to me nearing the end of the song, even though throughout the song the voice paradoxically feels simultaneously close and distant. In terms of my perception of the song as a whole, as a movement, "Transmission" feels as if it moves quickly in front and past me, but also it feels as if it pulls me in and sweeps me along.

I feel as if I am vicariously exerting or performing impact, including upon and in relation to others, especially with the first and second chorus as well as with the final full verse section and the single line final pre-chorus. In these passages it feels to me as if both the music as persona, and I as a co-protagonist, are engaging in energetic physical activity involving a simultaneously desperate and ecstatic intensity. In listening to and reflecting on my experience listening to this song, it does not feel to me like we are being quiet, and, even if and when the sound at all resembles whispering in the ear, it nonetheless feels as if it does so with marked urgency. In listening to and reflecting on my experience listening to "Transmission" I feel as if I am joining an effort that involves potentially ceaselessly ongoing effort to invite and encourage more and more others to join and do the same. I readily imagine and indeed directly simulate, as the song proceeds, becoming wilder in my own dancing, making more elaborate moves, extending myself so I spend more time with both feet altogether off the ground, covering wider spaces, indulging in more spins and swirls and spirals and traces, and incorporating simultaneous movements across my body, involving my arms, elbows, wrists, hands, fingers, waist, abdomen, chest, hips, knees, legs, ankles, feet, shoulders, neck, and head.

It feels to me like "Transmission" involves the music as persona sharing with me as a co-protagonist the results of an analysis, outlined most explicitly in the first two full verse stanzas, as we proceed together to respond to their implications. It feels, in other words, as if the situation I enter into has already been analyzed by the music as persona and what is principally now to be done is to move beyond analysis, although it also feels as if the music as persona knows better than I what happens next, although not necessarily how or if this will work, while it also feels as if the music as persona knows better, or at least starts the song by knowing better, what kind of situation this is than I do, perhaps because of the analysis it has already concluded. It feels here as if I am being called to the dance, and that I am being called to dance, but it also feels as if I am being called at the same time to recognize at least the broad contours of a situation in which this dancing is both desperate and ecstatic, absolutely necessary yet prospectively insufficient, that requires me to analyze what this situation might encompass. Analysis I bring to bear here suggests to me I am called to join the music as persona, and other listeners as fellow co-protagonists, in aligning ourselves with the beat of the show, and that we are called to seek and find as well as to give and share love through this means. Analysis, what's more, suggests to me this a full body commitment.

Analysis in "Transmission" suggests we are pushing aside previous knowings and previous quests for knowing, as well as previous illusions and delusions about knowing, as it seems we are no longer embarking upon quests for knowledge per se. Analysis here suggests embracing the circumstances immediately confronting us for what they afford. Analysis here suggests harm has already happened, is now irrevocable; we are and can no longer pretend we are innocent; and we cannot abide any further in paralyzing confusion. We need instead to throw ourselves into the moment without any guarantee concerning to what this will lead or what we might achieve. Analysis here suggests we are aiming to transduce conditions previously experienced in terms of threat and panic while possible rewards for success in this effort might include zeroing in to concentrate on what is ultimately most important, represented by dancing and by synchronizing love to the beat of the show. Yet analysis here also suggests success might just amount to temporary resilience, to temporary survival, and to temporarily casting off illusions, delusions, pretenses, inhibitions, fears, and worries to go with the flow, even in a state of ecstatic desperation—or desperate ecstacy. Analysis here suggests the music as persona, and especially the narrator-protagonist of the lyrics, is testifying and witnessing, is summoning and exhorting, is dancing and reaching across distance with a fervid intensity and compelling us, urgently, to join 'him' and to do the same.

"Transmission" I associate with a call to dance and with dancing, especially simultaneously exuberant, ecstatic, wild, and desperate dancing. I associate what I hear, and feel, in this song with a steady rising and accumulating intensity. I associate what I hear with a feeling of being called upon simultaneously to confront, accept, challenge, and confound limits of mediation. I associate what I hear as pressing back against limits and constraints, and proclaiming that the music as persona and I as co-protagonist are alive, and are striving to live our lives boldly, passionately, and vigorously yet uncertain if we will succeed in doing so. I associate what I hear with the feeling of knowing 'things are fucked', and we are too, but nevertheless refusing to surrender without a fight, as we are going to fight to live vitally as we can for as limited as a time as we might have, we refuse a living death, a life as nought but a slow dragging of ourselves toward our final death. I associate what I hear as striving to discover, access, and exercise resources for vitalization and actualization wherever and however we can, no matter how mediated these may be. I associate what I hear with a desperate desire to live, to feel, to connect, and to love. In terms of yet further associations I make, recognizing these all reflect and respond to my own social background, positioning, and experience, as well as my own historical and cultural situatedness, and are thus far from 'merely personal', I associate what I hear in "Transmission" with rebellion versus all of the following: feeling isolated, alone, and lonely; occupying the position of stranger, outsider, misfit, outcast, and excluded; feeling alienated by means of hypermediatization, mass conformity, oppressive normativity, and zombification; feeling confined by forced mediocrity and forced abandonment of hopes and dreams; living only to die but not in a Heideggerian sense of actually living toward death; and living in situations of precariousness verging on precarity.

I hear this song as exploring the desire to break with oppressive normative restraints and constraints, and I also hear this song as refusing familiar and comforting illusions and delusions, including by refusing any longer to pretend that the situation confronting the music as persona, and I as a co-protagonist, is not desperate. I also hear this song as exploring the taboo of letting one's self crash and burn as well as explode and implode, no longer held back by worry or fear concerning how this will be perceived and how this will forever subsequently mark one, even separate one out, as excessive, extreme, other than normal, bizarre, weird, and even crazy. I hear chills in the sounds of the song with the rising in pitch of the vocal, and with the vocal straining and agonizing, toward the end of the song, as well as with the tight bass guitar, guitar, and drum patterns resolutely recurring with only slight variation, with the guitar flares, with the shimmering and the twinkling synthesizer sounds, and with the pounding of the toms.

In relation to avenue of musical affect eight, confronting the invisibility, intangibility, and ephemerality of musical sounds, as well as matters of invisibility, intangibility, and ephemerality, more broadly, including haunting experiences of spectral entities and relations neither clearly present nor absent, "Transmission" thematizes exactly this as a song directly calls for alignment with sound and motion, beyond knowing, as well as references touching from a distance, even from further all the time, through networks of mediation, in order to align with what can't be directly seen or felt, but can most powerfully be heard, and at the same time to do so in a moment that seems right from its initiation ephemeral. "Transmission" is a song about rejecting, pushing past, and overcoming fears in order to embrace and align with the invisible, the intangible, and ephemeral, and about the powers of sound and motion, of the beat, to be able to provide meaning and value, and in particular a sense of genuinely living, including by discarding protective blinders, breaking out of oppressive chains, and of breaking into a state of oneness with a transcendence of conventional conceptions of self and of boundaries that distinguish self from other–and from others.

***

In summary and review of to where this process of engagement with "Transmission" has led me so far, and in beginning to work toward a conclusion, I will next consider the three sets of questions I have previously indicated I will be coming back to for this purpose with each song:

1. What have these features begun to suggest to me, what have they invited and encouraged me to think (about) and feel, as well as to imagine and recollect? What do I hear the song expressing and communicating to me? How do I hear this song addressing and engaging me–inviting and encouraging me to enter into dialogue, into a co-creative encounter? What kind of subject, in what kinds of conditions and circumstances and from what position and perspective is here addressing and reaching out to me?

2. How do I hear these features and their accumulation and development beginning to address and position me? What are we, together, grappling with? What is it, more specifically, precisely, and even concretely that we, together, are exploring, inquiring into, pursuing, and confronting?

3. What do I hear these features seeking from me as my response and reply? How does this venture implicate and challenge me? What does it call forth from me, from whom I am, from where I come, from what I am about, from where I am headed, and from what I am seeking? How–specifically, precisely, and even concretely–can I respond? What simultaneously creatively imaginative and honestly authentic–even, and perhaps especially, raw and sensitive emotionally felt–response can I here give?

Allow me to begin addressing the immediately preceding three sets of questions by gathering some of the summary thinking I have sketched out to date in relation to discussing various dimensions of musical sound.

1. I hear the sounds, patterns of sounds, and deployments of sounds comprising "Transmission" engaging with challenge, complication, and the paradoxical; with a persistent impetus, and drive, to proceed in order to find and deliver a response to the situation, and what it demands, despite the challenge, complication, and paradoxes this impetus, this drive, confronts in seeking to do so; with steadily and rapidly building tension as well as a climactically immersive seizing upon, identifying with, and channeling of the release of tension as a response to what the situation demands; and with a final closing down, suspending, and fading out of remnant tension.

2. "Transmission" embodies an impassioned effort to simulate the delivery of its message: in other words, the song embodies an impassioned effort to simulate making paradoxical use of mediation, with all of the manifest constraints mediation encompasses, to attempt to break through–to cause a disturbance, implosion, and eruption from within–the hold of entrenched structures that suffuse

224

distance, disconnection, isolation, alienation, paralysis, inertia, fear, and witting as well as unwitting blindness throughout individual, inter-individual, and yet more broadly social existence.

3. "Transmission" embodies a concerted effort, through the course of direct alignment with a movement of steadily building, growing, and accumulating tension, to break through, and, in other words, to embody a piercing from within of the simultaneous cloaking and choking stranglehold exercised by a deadening status quo. This status quo preexists the beginning of the song, while the song ultimately suggests it will continue to persist long after a single playing of the song ends. Yet what the latter in turn implies is it requires successive ongoing iterations of the same piercing efforts in order to be able to contend with what this status quo does to those of us who must live according to its dictates, even while struggling with and under the weight of these dictates, because we can only effectively survive and endure this weight by continually contesting the otherwise seemingly inescapable and unalterable necessity of its deadening impact.

4. "Transmission" is more directly and overtly concerned than "Disorder" with what makes human connection difficult, and how this difficulty might at least be challenged, if not overcome, and "Transmission" is less directly and overtly concerned than "Disorder" with introspective examination of the complexity, multiplicity, contradictoriness, and dynamism of subjectivity and selfhood. At the same time, both songs seem much concerned with the precariousness not just of a particular situation, not just of positioning within and responsiveness versus a prospective impending event, encounter, or confrontation, and not just of the background, and backstory, to those two vectors of precariousness. Both songs seem concerned what's more with the precariousness of vitality, of spirit, of 'the' life force in and of itself–as well as with the social structures ostensibly designed, paradoxically enough, to facilitate social relations but which all too often and all too extensively exercise effectively 'deadening' impacts, leading all too many people all too often and all too extensively in effect to give up on life, while still continuing to live on (i.e., to give up on life's spirit, life's force, and life's vitality and thereby 'living' as if they are merely dragging themselves along until they are completely dead).

"Transmission" conveys to me the suggestion of a situation where circumstances have become grave and in which more and more people are not only unable adequately to grasp how (much or far) this is so but also more and more people are losing or have lost their bearings while flailing about in exceedingly difficult straits (all the while, often enough, pretending this is not the case–denying to themselves as much as to anyone else that this is the case). "Transmission" suggests to me a situation involving a profound experience of deep alienation, especially notably from the life-force, from the spark of vitality that enables us to be truly alive as we live, and the need to seize on what is left of it, what can be held onto, and what we can grasp, with desperate urgency. And yet, in contrast with the preceding, despite what the lyrics otherwise insinuate, and despite claustrophobic elements of the construction and delivery of the song, "Transmission" also suggests to me the song encompasses a powerful expression and performance of vitality, no matter how desperate that is, even so, simultaneously ecstatic.

225

I feel compelled to join in and to dance, while also, more broadly, to strive, passionately, against even seemingly impossible constraints. I feel compelled to revolt. I feel compelled to spread the alarm about the urgency of what is at stake. I feel compelled to want to help raise people from doldrums and inspire them with a like sense of passion and determination. I feel we, the music as persona and I as a co-protagonist, are here grappling, together, with all of the following: alienation and confinement as well as resistance to and revolt versus alienation and confinement; the powers as well as the limits of mediation; lack of but also need for connection and contact; complacency, conformity, submission, obeisance, dejection, fear, repression, and denial–and resistance and revolt versus all of that; and mental, physical, and spiritual pain–as well as resistance and revolt against this pain and its consequent impact upon whom we are and especially what we can and might be and do.

"Transmission" calls upon me to inquire into whether I become complacent; whether I continue to hide, retreat, and settle for illusions and for false hope and reassurance, for convenient bromides, and for being complacently comfortable amidst overwhelming surrounding precarity. "Transmission" challenges me to consider whether I am still passionate, still pressing and pushing as hard as I can against the toughest and most daunting challenges and limits. "Transmission" encourages me to commit to seeking a deeper meaning in, and for, my existence than provided by conventional narratives and dominant explanations of what this could–and should–be. Transmission encourages me to pose, to myself, multiple probing questions: am I feeling intensely, deeply, and vulnerably, and am I able and willing to allow myself to do so, and to share my doing so with other people? Am I able to confront my own weaknesses, blindnesses, worries, fears, anxieties, and traumas, and do so openly and honestly, including with other people as well as with myself alone? What am I contributing to help address and overcome the fact that a great many people, even in relatively wealthy countries like the US and the UK, feel desperately lonely and scared, with the ravages of mental ill health already substantial prior to but only accelerating due to the damage caused by the COVID-19 pandemic and the massive economic fallout it has necessitated? What am I contributing to help address and overcome the multitudinous damages, including in increased precariousness and precarity, caused by decades of neo-liberal hegemony followed by post-2007/2008 global economic crisis austerity politics and by the concomitant rise in power of authoritarian populist neo-fascism? What am I contributing to help address and overcome the destruction of the natural world and the larger ecosystems upon which human life is dependent and to which human beings should be responsible? What am I contributing more specifically in addressing and responding to the devastating impact upon the arts, culture, and the humanities of the pandemic, of neo-liberalism, of the politics of austerity, and of neo-fascism? What am I contributing more specifically in addressing and responding to the devastating impact of widespread demonization and xenophobia surrounding immigration and immigrants? What am I contributing more specifically in relation to finding and securing ways to connect, to unite, to support, and to show solidarity across differences, while respecting differences, and even making use of differences as foundations for coalition, alliance, connection, and bonding?

Most of all, I hear with "Transmission" a striving desperately to connect in extremely alienating circumstances, a striving desperately to feel fully alive, to feel as if one is living with intensity, passion, meaning, and purpose. I hear with "Transmission" a striving to connect with some elemental force that can carry us through, and enable us to survive, persist, and endure despite desperation and alienation. I hear with "Transmission" a striving to find alternative means, beyond those that have clearly failed and are clearly failing all around us, of creating a vital community, because we are desperately, agonizingly in need of just this. "Transmission" conveys to me an impression of dreaming and yearning to be elsewhere and otherwise; of feeling disconnected, alienated, confined, and constrained; and of turning to radio, music, and dance, even by one's self, even in private spaces, as a means of simulating stretching and projecting beyond the limits of mediation and separation. "Transmission" conveys to me a feeling of protesting against circumstances that feel overwhelming while striving not to allow these to annihilate our spirit. "Transmission" conveys to me a refusal to accepting mediocrity and normalcy, and all the blindnesses as well as compromises and concessions this entails. "Transmission" focuses squarely on paradoxes of mediation, that which both registers, reflects, and responds to distance and separation, while in part sustaining this distance and separation, yet which simultaneously facilitates connection, sharing, and even community across distance so that this is not necessarily equivalent with alienation and isolation. I find listening to "Transmission" striking and chilling in the midst of living through a pandemic with forced physical social distancing, as well as resonating strongly with the problematics and discontents of so much of contemporary sociality, even preceding the pandemic, reduced to social media, along with yet further normative modes of distancing all too many of us all too often experience from direct, immediate, physical social interaction, all together at the same place and at the same time—or at least making steadily more of us increasingly uncomfortable participating and reluctant to participate in these kinds of direct, immediate, physically co-present forms of social encounters and social engagements.

At the same time, "Transmission," besides elements of protest, and rebellion, suggests also something of a feeling of ridiculousness, even of absurdity, concerning the position of and the prospects for both the music as persona and I as a co-protagonist, with us experiencing a tremendous amount of angst we need to release yet we can only do so indirectly together as we remain largely physically isolated and alone. "Transmission," even more narrowly, suggests to me striving to deal with and fight back versus the initial emergence of a panic attack, or with the sudden onset of acute depression, or with otherwise feeling gutted. "Transmission," what's more, reminds me of many experiences in my own life in which I retreated to listen alone to music as an attempt to cope with feeling badly, usually as much if not much more about myself as about anyone or anything else, while fervently wishing I did not need to rely on this music alone to provide me solace. "Transmission" reminds me of ways I have attempted in my own life to cover over, hide, and retreat from or compensate for feeling isolated, alone, and lonely, alienated and confined, cut off and left out. "Transmission" reminds me of ways I have experienced myself as an outsider and as a misfit, and feeling doomed inescapably to remain so, including as someone who will always be either unrecognized or misunderstood. "Transmission" reminds me as well of times in which I felt acutely needy yet recognized no one immediately around to whom I could readily turn for help.

"Transmission," with its own striking lyrical reference to love, suggests to me love is an overwhelming human need, yet it is often difficult to obtain and sustain, in part because all too often people enter into relationships in which they love (each other) differently, and these loves prove ultimately incompatible. Also, reflecting on love in this connection, people often also feel as if it is necessary to take love wherever and however they are able to find it, including in highly mediated forms. And, finally, "Transmission" suggests concern with a 'greater love', as all too many of us all too often ignore or deny a vast number of social–and ecological–problems, including critical ones, by pretending these are not really as bad, or as pressing, as they are, or that they do not directly concern us, or there is nothing we possibly can do ourselves to help. In other words, "Transmission" engages a common willingness to overlook and forgive what shouldn't be, including conditions of alienation and confinement and devitalization and dehumanization as well as forces that benefit from producing and reproducing these conditions.

***

In relation to my eleven prior interpretations of the music of Joy Division I first introduced in chapter one, and which I have repeated twice, earlier in this chapter, I do find my latest listening to and reflection upon what this song might mean and what impact it might convey to fits well with many of those. I next address this fit.

 # 1: I interpret . . . Ian Curtis's lyrics and Joy Division's music as all about exploration of and inquiry into mediations. *Again and again, these songs zero in on the 'in between', on the* _distance between_. *Always seeking, striving, venturing, pursuing, or hesitating about doing so yet feeling the strong compulsion to do so nonetheless.* "Transmission" I interpret as overtly and continuously concerned with problematics of mediation, and the song as I interpret it focuses on responding not only to a compulsion but also an urgent need to seek, strive, venture, and pursue, while moving beyond preceding hesitation.

#2: Ian Curtis . . . fearlessly explored intensities, extremities, subliminalities, and liminalities that many others never would or could, and his music, while often extremely dark and somber, is never simply that–it is about seeking, struggling, reflecting, examining, and opening one's self up to sensation, perception, emotion, and understanding that presses past familiar layers of protective mediation toward not only intense vulnerability and emptiness but also intense clarity and insight. Joy Division's music fuses the intellectual with the emotional with the spiritual with the somatic–in terms of exploration and questing, in both passionate and dispassionate terms, and in relation to a striving for and imposition of control meeting up with the absolute limits and sheer impossibility of meaningfully striving for and seeking to impose control. This prior interpretation fits most closely in relation to embracing intensities and extremities as well as pressing past familiar layers of protecting mediation, while risking exposure and vulnerability, as well as about being ready to allow one's self to lose–or to let one's self lose from–control.

#3: In listening to Joy Division I hear . . . the same freshness, urgency, and intensity that attracted me to punk, yet also something transcending the immediacy and directness of punk, conveying, in contrast, a richly resonant sense of both distance and precision, a controlled fury emanating from a fiercely passionate yet also agonizingly vulnerable exploration of emotional, psychological, physical, and metaphysical extremes. Again, focus upon intensity, extremity, passion,

and vulnerability fit well here, as does how much of the song, including in locations and deployments of patterns of sounds, plays with matters of closeness and distance.

#4: Joy Division songs, for me, dramatize introspection as fiercely determined and fully committed struggle. What makes this struggle all the more fraught and challenging is it transpires in a mysteriously otherworldly realm where comfortably reassuring borderlines break down. These are borderlines between interior and exterior, subject and object, self and other, protagonist and antagonist, friend and foe, help and hindrance, solidarity and betrayal, complicity and responsibility, hope and despair, health and illness, movement and stasis, past and present, history and myth, the psychological and the sociological, the sacred and the profane, the beautiful and the sublime, the close and the distant, the private and the public, the familiar and the strange, and the living and the dead. Joy Division songs end not with tension resolved, but merely temporarily suspended. The only definite answer they offer us is we need to join this struggle, and seek what we can find, for ourselves. "Transmission" embodies struggle and, in particular, fiercely determined and fully committed struggle, that is nonetheless uncertain, skeptical, and even worried and fearful that this will lead nowhere, and that whatever escape or transcendence it might secure will be at best fleeting, while the song ultimately suggests the need for persistently ongoing struggle as well as struggle we need to feel more than think our way into.

#5: Inquiring into the music, as art, of Ian Curtis involves . . . inquiring into metaphorical 'darknesses' in human history and society, and in the condition of being human, especially that of the human social being living in the advanced capitalist, postmodern world. This involves facing, without resorting to self-protective blinders or sentimentalizing illusions, often extraordinarily disturbing incidences of cruelty and violence, as well as of anxiety and alienation. It involves inquiring into intensity and extremity as well as into the complexities of distance and connection in human social relations. It involves inquiring into anxious to traumatic dimensions of the human quest for meaning, purpose, value, satisfaction, fulfilment–and especially love–in this late capitalist, postmodern world, and it involves inquiring into interrelations between life and death, between living and dying, between being and nothingness, between self and other, and among past, present, and future. It involves inquiring into surfaces and depths, mysteries and enigmas, complexities and contradictions, and fluidities and variabilities in modes of individual identity, personality, and character. It involves inquiring into what it feels like to struggle and strive for authenticity and integrity, in relation to the pull of ambition, popularity, success, and fame. It also involves, on the flip side, inquiring into effective meanings of compassion, empathy, and solidarity. Inquiring into when and where these qualities are under threat, in danger of collapse, on the verge of eclipse, or altogether absent, we recognize, and appreciate, how indispensable they truly are. "Transmission" emerges out of an experience of systematic alienation and isolation, a collective death in life, and rejects efforts to rationalize or otherwise pretend this state of affairs is not what it is, is not as desperate as it is, while the song embodies a striving through and beyond the ruins to connect, to make contact, and even to experience and share love.

#6: Ian Curtis's art . . . can readily be conceived as an exploration of and inquiry into the following two sets of fundamental questions: 1. Why do I exist? What is the meaning, value, and

purpose of my existence? To what extent can I exercise any influence, and any control, over what this meaning, value, and purpose becomes? How can, and how should, I attempt to do so?
2. In what ways, and to what extent, am I responsible for others? For the suffering, hardship, and pain others experience? For the violence and cruelty as well as the injustice and unfairness in the world? What can and what should I do about any of this? "Transmission" proposes making an effort to reach out, connect, and to both share pain and vulnerability as well as share an effort to strive to escape and transcend it. "Transmission" proposes 'my existence' needs vital connection with 'others' existences' to be worthwhile, to be a genuinely vital existence. My purpose is to live my life as vitally as possible, including in relations with others, as much and for as long as I can.

  #7: Ian Curtis's art . . . can be readily conceived of, as well, as an exploration of and inquiry into the sense and meaning of alienation, isolation, and loneliness; the position and experience of being a stranger, an outsider, and an outcast; vulnerability, entrapment, anxiety, and fear; and the need to connect, especially intimately, along with the simultaneous difficulty of doing so. This interpretation also seems to fit especially well, as "Transmission," according to my developing interpretation of this song, is directly concerned with alienation, isolation, and loneliness; the position and experience of being a stranger, an outsider, and an outcast; vulnerability, entrapment, anxiety, and fear; and, especially the need to connect, notably intimately, along with the simultaneous difficulty of doing so. This interpretation might even stand in, of, and by itself alone, as a compelling interpretation of "Transmission."

  #8: Ian Curtis's art makes sense . . . in somewhat more specific terms, as an exploration of the extent to which (and the consequences following from recognition that) the self is an imaginary construct, the subject is simultaneously overwhelmingly unconscious and ineluctably other, desire and anxiety are persistently intrinsically interconnected, the symbolic order and the law of the father are oppressively authoritarian, jouissance is far more terrifying than the common translation as 'enjoyment' can possibly suggest, and intimations and irruptions of the Real are recurrently traumatic. This interpretation seems to fit most closely with how I have been interpreting "Transmission" in referencing desire and anxiety as persistently intrinsically interconnected, but it is also suggestive in relation to how much of "Transmission" is concerned with attempting to break out of confinement to the limits of an isolated individual self, and to merge with others by merging, together, with sound and motion.

  #9: Ian Curtis's art also makes sense . . . in somewhat more specific terms, as the staging of a dramatic encounter with the shocking resilience and metamorphic resurgence of fascist tendencies, after the end of World War II and the Holocaust, at the heart of ostensibly 'democratic', advanced capitalist, Western society, including in the guises of 'friendly fascism' and 'the fascism of everyday life'. Ian Curtis and his bandmates, in choosing their name, Joy Division, whether consciously, deliberately, intentionally or not, propose fascism lives on after the defeat of Nazi Germany and the liberation of the survivors from the concentration camps—and it lives on, most insidiously, as an integral dimension and recurrent tendency within the very same societies so frequently and routinely celebrating their victory over fascism. This interpretation makes the most sense in relation to my developing interpretation of "Transmission" in relation to consideration of 'the fascism of everyday

life'—in which people are hiding, retreating, confining themselves, and censoring themselves out of fear, while pretending not to do this at all, and as a result are divided from each other, from direct experience of solidarity with each other, from being ready and able to share pain and vulnerability, and to experience life, including social life, at peak vitality.

#10: A large part of what makes Ian Curtis especially compelling to me, and seemingly the same to a great many others, is that he was—and remains—a striking combination of the ordinary and extraordinary, he communicates incredibly powerfully through his art yet so much of his art is obsessively focused on the difficulty of communication, and because an empathetic engagement with his life-experience, his artistic accomplishment, and his fierce sense of artistic mission and purpose is richly rewarding—such engagement can help us in efforts to forge a genuinely and indeed systemically caring culture, a culture of compassion, empathy, and solidarity. Curtis's life-story, his life-achievement, and his life-legacy all attest to how important it is to strive to grasp the myriad ways in which we are all far more complex, multiple, contradictory, and dynamic than commonly recognized. Curtis reminds us of how all too many people's critical and creative potential is routinely discouraged, dismissed, and denigrated, and how this in turn leads all too many people all too readily to internalize a powerful tendency to do the same, to themselves. This interpretation makes the greatest sense in relation to my developing interpretation of "Transmission" in relation to not accepting, or settling for, the place that those at the heights of power, or the prevailing system of social relations, has marked out for you, and to which you then become effectively confined—about striving to communicate, to connect, to make contact, and to share, with passion, even when not having any words that can readily enable doing so, and even when physically distanced from being readily able to do so.

#11: I perceive, from Ian Curtis, as I listen to his recorded voice, and as I read his written words, while trying to write this book of my own, a tremendous anguish, emanating from a guilty recognition of a persistent uncertainty, hesitation, and doubt, and, when I recognize this in Curtis' voice and words, doing so does aggravate, and accelerate, my own uncertainty, hesitation, and doubt. As a result, at times I feel like I owe a debt of personal responsibility to Ian Curtis, to carry on with what he could not. This interpretation makes the most sense in relation to what I have been writing concerning my developing interpretation of "Interpretation" when I elaborate a series of challenges I hear this song as posing to me, as in effect asking of me what am I doing, and am I going to do, about these issues of social—and ecological—concern, and about living my life with passion, commitment, determination, and daring, ready to make myself vulnerable and share my vulnerability as need be, even in the face of myriad worries, fears, and hesitancies concerning what this might risk, whether I'm 'up to it' or not, whether I will be able to do anything worthwhile or contribute anything worthwhile, us, and whether I will not just fall flat on my face and end up a miserable failure.

***

I will conclude this discussion of "Transmission" by bringing this song into a dialogue with selections from *50 Concepts for a Critical Phenomenology*. In so doing I anticipate what I will doing in a more concerted fashion in chapters three through six while also introducing the benefits that can be derived, in interpretation, by creating a dialogue between texts, and in effect, grafting texts together so as to explore what can be learned, and what can be gained, by way of comparing as well as potentially synthesizing their respective focuses and approaches. Texts make sense by situating these in contexts, and these include intertexts, as well as intertexts that might not necessarily be directly suggested by texts themselves.

Let's begin with editors Gail Weiss's, Ann V. Murphy's, and Gayle Salamon's introductory explanation of what is 'critical phenomenology' in "Introduction: Transformative Descriptions" to *50 Concepts for a Critical Phenomenology*. According to Weiss, Murphy, and Salamon, "As a philosophical tradition, phenomenology has privileged wonder, ambiguity, and curiosity over the Cartesian drive toward certainty, determinacy, and indubitability," while "One of phenomenology's most axiomatic methodological commitments is the refusal to accept the taken-for-grantedness of experience" (xiii). Phenomenology inquires critically into experience in order better to understand experience. As Weiss, Murphy, and Salamon add, for phenomenology, "experience can never be understood or described in isolation" (xiii) as it is "always generated from particular places, times, and cultural milieus," which take the form, in relation to individual experience, of "multiple horizons of significance" as well as "sedimented" and "embodied habits" (xiv). *Critical* phenomenology "mobilizes phenomenological description in the service of a reflexive inquiry into how power relations structure experience as well as our ability to analyze that experience" while also seeking "not only to describe but also to repair the world, encouraging generosity, respect, and compassion for the diversity of our lives experiences" (xiv). So far, points of convergence with "Ian Curtis and Joy Division," as represented by "Transmission"–and "Disorder" as well–include privileging "wonder, ambiguity, and curiosity over the Cartesian drive toward certainty, determinacy, and indubitability," although 'Ian Curtis and Joy Division' often focus on the challenge and difficulty of moving from the latter to the former, while in likewise 'refusing to accept the taken-for-grantedness of experience', 'Ian Curtis and Joy Division' often focus on how this refusal can be fraught and dangerous, as it not only risks a sharp break with the comfortably if deadeningly familiar but also marks out those embodying and enacting this refusal as 'other than normal' and as thereby potential objects of suspicion, antagonism, ostracism, and violence. 'Ian Curtis and Joy Division', as represented by these two songs, also calls into question 'embodied habits' while attending to the pull of 'horizons of significance' that remain largely imperceptible and even unintelligible when constrained by normative varieties of 'embodied habits'. In "Transmission"–and also in "Disorder"–the prospect of 'repair' through the generation of active and substantive compassion is proposed as desirable, and the songs enact efforts to move in that direction, yet the songs likewise suggest successful realization of this prospect remains highly uncertain.

In "Being-toward-Death" Mark Ralkowski explains Martin Heidegger's concept of the same name, in which Heidegger argues for living life in awareness and acceptance of how life is always structured by death, and is always proceeding toward death, making our choices and decisions, and authoring our own stories, with the inevitability and inescapability of our death in mind. As Ralkowski sums this up, "*death* is one of our most important educators, because when it is embraced and anticipated, it teaches us *how to live with our ineluctable anxiety* and use it to *make our lives our own*" (43). 'Ian Curtis and Joy Division' are unprepared to go this far, but "Transmission" does propose one path that provides a tenuous and transient opportunity, "to live with our ineluctable anxiety and use it to make our lives our own": by 'synchronizing love to the beat of the show' and 'dancing to the radio' while 'touching from a distance' albeit 'further all the time'. "Transmission" marshals anxiety as energy to bring to bear in living vitally, while accepting one must do so through networks of mediation and while only partially being able to cancel conditions of alienation and isolation.

In "Borderlands and Border Crossing" Natalie Cisneros explicates Gloria Anzaldúa's theorization of borderlands and border crossings, which aside from more direct and explicit connection with matters of race, and of racial difference as well as of complicated varieties of racial identity, also includes a conception of "borders in general as instruments of division that 'are set up to define the places that are safe and unsafe, to distinguish *us* from *them*'" and "are all unnatural boundaries" while 'borderlands' "that are created in their wake are tense, unstable, violent, and even deadly places" (49). This theorization strikes me as perhaps even more usefully suggestive in connection with my discussion of how I make sense of "Disorder" as locus of meaning and impact than in relation to my discussion of how I do the same with "Transmission," yet it nevertheless resonates well with the drive, and impetus, I have described to cross a metaphorical terrain that has been rendered exceedingly difficult to cross, and to thereby make contact, establish connection, and experience love through alignment with sound and motion, and via dancing, together yet separately or separately yet together, to the radio. "Transmission" revolts against conditions of alienation and confinement, against people being impelled and compelled to 'stay in their place' and not to venture at all far or wide, as well as versus fears of the dangers of so venturing–and implicitly versus fears as well of encountering 'others' who live at a distance 'from one's own', who are in turn alienated and confined 'in their places'. Indeed, "Transmission" and "Disorder" both explore, and in part enact, pursuit of "a form of identity that results from crossing over or passing through borders" (49)–all the while registering obstacles that efforts at so doing must confront, as well as trepidation over what can, might, or will happen, in so crossing over or passing through, yet a nevertheless fierce desire to be able to do this, and to transcend the limits and especially the constraints of preceding forms of identity.

Rosalyn Diprose, in "Corporeal Generosity," offers a tantalizing description of Emmanuel Levinas's theorization of intersubjectivity as involving "the nonvolitional opening of the self to another through sensibility 'beyond being' (beyond ontology and politics) in terms of a bond lying in 'the non-indifference of persons toward one another'" as part of a "sociality that 'does not absorb the difference of strangeness'" (85). Although it may seem, in terms of how I have discussed this, that "Transmission" includes a call to 'will' our way into a medium by means of which intersubjectivity can be vitally enacted, it is also worth noting how both in this song, and in "Disorder," an emphasis seems to emerge upon 'allowing one's self' to 'let one's self go' and to let 'spirit' and 'feeling' drive what and how 'I'/'we' will experience, and relate, as well as to do the same in relation to sound and motion, to 'the beat of the show' and in dancing to the music on the radio. At the same time, both songs register a sense both of experiencing alienation and isolation, and of wanting passionately and desperately to find means to move past these states, to experience and relate fundamentally differently, while also suggesting this process cannot be subjected to full, deliberate, conscious control, or to precise prediction, let alone determination, ahead of time, as much inevitably must remain, and is best kept, mysterious. The nebulous guidance the 'I' in each song offers 'us', as well as the nebulous to almost non-existent details provided concerning the personal identities of the various 'characters' that appear in each song suggest we are being called to join and follow but we must do on our own terms, while whatever unity with others we might achieve will not, and should not, by any means 'absorb the difference of strangeness'.

In "Eros" Tamsin Kimoto and Cynthia Willett discuss Audre Lorde's theorization of eros, and the erotic, finding that for Lorde the erotic is a "life-force" and "the locus of the social bond that holds together lovers, friends, and workers in solidarity. It is also the source of resistance to oppressive systems that threaten to appropriate our erotic energy" (117). This represents an interesting avenue of potential connection with 'Ian Curtis and Joy Division' in "Transmission"–and in "Disorder"–as both songs seem to embody and enact a strenuous effort to connect with such a life-force, as well as critical consideration of much that makes doing so difficult, even seemingly impossible. Kimoto and Willett propose "The critical task of an erotic politics," following Lorde, "is resisting the temptation to a heroic and isolated struggle; instead, Lorde urges us to feel ourselves 'part of an ever-expanding community of struggle'" (117). Here we recognize a useful way of identifying a central and repeated locus of angst in Ian Curtis's lyrics, and Joy Division's music, including in both "Transmission" and "Disorder"–a compulsion to break out of a situation in which only heroic and isolated struggle appears possible, and to try to make contact with, to connect with, and to invite and encourage compatriots to join, combined with a foreboding sense this will prove extremely difficult to achieve, even highly uncertain it is possible to achieve. So moving past prior modes of sensing, feeling, thinking, and knowing to dancing frantically in allowing one's self to align with sound and motion might well represent an effort to experience one's self as 'part of an ever-expanding community of struggle' yet it also feels, in this music, as if this is not an end it is easy to imagine readily achieving, let alone readily sustaining.

Helen A. Fielding, in "The Habit Body," draws upon the theoretical work of Maurice Merleau-Ponty to discuss how "our bodies sediment ways of understanding that become habits that anchor us in the world," which are in turn "habits at a cultural and historical level" (156). Connecting this discussion with the theoretical work, in turn, of Frantz Fanon, Fielding discusses "those who live in between worlds, and who are never at home in one world" where nonetheless "the cultural habitus does not recede from view" (157). Yet further, "as Mariana Ortega points out, those who live on the margins and 'in-between-worlds' are denied such ease of movement" as is more readily available to those who live at the center and 'in-one-world'. However, the former experience "a greater possibility for critical reflection" than the latter because "Reflection is demanded only when there is a rupture in that everyday world." Moreover, "those who live-in-between-worlds experience . . . [the] apparently fixed background level against which all things, people, and relations appear . . . as constantly shifting" and as highly unstable (157). These ideas are usefully suggestive in relation to the interpretations I have been developing of what 'Ian Curtis and Joy Division' express and communicate, and how it makes sense to me to understand and use their music, in particular "Transmission" and "Disorder," because both songs fit well with an interpretation of the vantage point from which the music as persona, and the narrator-protagonist of the lyrics, addresses us, as 'on the margins' and 'in-between-worlds' while also addressing and appealing to others who share the same kind of experience and the same kind of positioning. In both songs the normative, everyday world does not feel welcoming or fulfilling, yet nonetheless exercises a looming background presence, ominous and hostile, but seemingly many others do not experience it as such or pretend to themselves they do not. What's more, paradoxically enough, those who do experience this 'background level' of habitualized experience, including as sedimented in the habit body, as oppressive and repressive, are those who also feel both as if it is exceedingly difficult to move and as if movement is urgently necessary.

In "Hometactics" Mariana Ortega discusses when "home is not always what it is supposed to be" (169), and in particular for those who experience what Ortega theorizes as "multiplicitous selfhood." This refers to a self that not only "occupies multiple positionalities in terms of social identities, be it race, class, sex, gender, ability, nationality, etc., and thus lives in various worlds" but also exists as both "being-in worlds as well as being-between-worlds." In turn this results in "this self's constant awareness of not-being-at-home, not-dwelling, a marked sense of not feeling at ease or having a sense of familiarity in many of the worlds she inhabits" (170-171). As I have discussed with "Disorder," it makes useful sense to interpret this song as exploring the complexity, multiplicity, contradictoriness, and dynamism of subjectivity and selfhood, as well as how and why this might be difficult to accept and identify with yet nonetheless desirable and even liberating, while in discussing both "Disorder" and "Transmission" I have addressed an urgently expressed desire to break out, break away, let one's self go, become different and other, even to self-shatter and self-dissolve, which certainly registers a tremendous unease with what conventionally would seem to constitute 'home' or which provides a conventionally comfortable and reassuring sense of 'being at home', with both songs, and especially "Transmission," also strongly rejecting "the ease that comes from mindlessly following everyday norms and practices" (171). In "Disorder" some wistful regret lingers concerning an inability to 'be at home' in this conventional way whereas in "Transmission" none of that continues, as this kind of 'being at home' is instead portrayed as deadening. In response to the latter, "Transmission" mounts an intensive effort to throw one's self into the kind of project Ortega identifies as "hometactics," that in turn involves finding ways of 'making do' and 'creatively constructing', even creatively reconstructing, one's 'everyday dealings' in the midst of otherwise alienating and confining social worlds (171). In dancing, in a frenzied state of desperation cum ecstacy, with the radio, touching from a distance albeit yet further all the time, and in letting one's self go to align with sound and music, with the beat of the show, the multiplicitous subjectivity that "Transmission" embodies and enacts finds an at least partially, temporarily compensatory "breath of fresh air in the midst of confining, suffocating worlds" (173).

Shiloh Whitney, in "Immanence and Transcendence," argues for an embodied conception of intentionality in connection with a synthesis of immanence with transcendence. As Whitney explains, "intentionality is located, not in consciousness as a transcendence of things (including the body), but rather in the body proper: intentionality is not an act of consciousness but an operation of the body as network of sensorimotor and affective relations to the world and others as well as to itself" (190). Furthermore, "If intentionality is embodied, then it cannot be defined as transcendence in opposition to immanence. It is not an intentional *act* at all: it is as much as passion as an action. Embodied intentionality is our inherence in things as much as it is our grasp of them" (191). What follows, further, from such reconceiving of intentionality, as well as of immanence and transcendence, is "as a power to sense, move, and feel rather than merely to be conscious of the world from afar, embodied transcendence *is itself sensed, moving, and affecting*. The body's self-relation to the world and others is itself embodied and experienceable for others" (191). In turn, "*Our intentional relation to the world and to others is visible, moving, and affecting* rather than spirited away in unassailable and unambiguous transcendence" (191). In relation to 'Ian Curtis and Joy Division', as represented by "Disorder" and "Transmission," it strikes me the songs are struggling in this direction while not necessarily being entirely able to escape from the more familiar conception of immanence and transcendence as opposite states. In "Disorder" it seems like the narrator-protagonist of the lyrics is initially attempting to draw distinctions among sensations, feelings, spirit, knowing, and new sensations, while eventually facing a collapsing of this effort, which might also relate to a collapsing of an effort to move from immanence to transcendence, leaving 'him' and 'us' with an overwhelming experience of *feeling*, which might seem a weighty anchor upon us yet which might on the contrary suggest the transcendence that can be achieved, and which is in fact desirable and necessary, to be an 'embodied transcendence'–i.e., an 'immanent transcendence'. At the least, this song and "Transmission" are much more engaged in manifestation of passion than action, or perhaps much more manifestation of passion as a preeminent mode of effective action, while in "Transmission" it does seem as if intentionality is ultimately located in allowing one's self to align with sound and motion, with dancing and synchronizing love to the beat of the show–where an at least tenuous and temporary experience of transcendence appears to take place by means of a passionate investment in immanence.

In "Public Self/Lived Subjectivity" Linda Martín Alcoff discusses relations between "one's public self and one's lived sense of self" (269), including when this is especially fraught because of experiencing a substantial disparity between the two, as "one's lived sense of self" must be "covered over" because it is representative of a marginalized social identity and a non-normative mode of social existence. In this kind of situation "Mediation and coherence may be impossible, and yet the dialectical interplay could induce productive changes" (271). In relation to 'Ian Curtis and Joy Division', as represented by "Disorder" and "Transmission," I suggest the songs can make sense as dramatically as well as introspectively struggling to come to grips with this kind of disparity, as well as to find ways in which such a disparity could prove productive and enabling, including in terms of offering critical insight and in providing an openness toward exploring radically alternative ways of living and being. Both songs reject a preceding normative state of affairs, and both seek to push in challenging new directions that register as simultaneously frightening yet enticing, while both register a sense of wanting and needing to break with preceding modes of identifying, especially publicly, and of letting go what needs to be let go to achieve at least a semblance of freedom.

Perry Zurn, in "Social Death," discusses "a kind of living that feels like dying" (309). Zurn focuses on cultures that have been decimated as a result of slavery, colonialism, ghettoization, impoverishment, and other historically sweeping form of genocidal and ethnocidal forms of obliteration. Yet I suggest it is aalso possible to argue that Cynthia Card's definition of "social death as the theft of meaning and life" could in turn apply to 'the theft of meaning in life' that exists under conditions of alienation and confinement for many people living according to the logic of an advanced capitalist system of social relations: to routinization and habituation of life practices according to this kind of logic, as well as the limited opportunities for other than a privileged few freely and easily to exercise considerable mobility, initiative, imagination, and creativity throughout most of their daily lives, including most often while doing the work that provides them indirect access to a 'means of living', where people fear 'making waves', 'stepping out of line', 'being different', risking condemnation or ridicule or ostracism or some other kind of 'punishment'–and where they end up leading, as I have previously described, 'deadening lives', lives that merely exist as means of dragging themselves along until death. Social death could refer to having given up all significant goals, plans, hopes, and dreams to settle for what is merely readily attainable, and of feeling like life has no vital and uplifting meaning, value, or purpose. Social death could refer to an existence where consumerism represents a shallow substitute for far more meaningful avenues of fulfillment. Social death could refer to an existence where it seems like it is impossible ever 'to get ahead' as one is instead 'always falling (further) behind' and where social existence is becoming steadily more fractured, polarized, mean, frayed, fragile, and precarious. Social death could refer to an existence where overwhelmingly numbing work consumes virtually each and every day. Social death could refer to existences where food insecurity, where homelessness, where lack of ready access to any kind of safe harbor or haven, where experience of abuse and neglect including from within the home, where serious to severe long-term chronic and persistent illness and disability, and where pervasive encounters with discrimination, prejudice, fear, and hatred make every day "a kind of living that feels like dying" (311). In "Disorder" and especially in "Transmission" 'Ian Curtis and Joy Division' suggest an empathetic identification with these kinds of experience of 'social death' and an empathetic engagement with an urgent desire and need to get away from this kind of life, to be able truly to live vitally, to experience transcendence in conjunction with immanence–along with simultaneous worry and fear, and even dread and panic, that none of this will be possible, that even the attempt itself will be beyond one's capacity, beyond one's strength.

Eight

In chapter one I write that many identify the music of Ian Curtis and Joy Division, encouraged by Ian Curtis's suicide, as 'depressing', but this characterization, I contend, vastly oversimplifies both the music and Curtis's life. I argue, beginning in this first chapter, the music of Ian Curtis and Joy Division strikes me as much more about introspection, reflection, contemplation, meditation, exploration, inquiry, confrontation, engagement, struggle, and striving than it is about merely sharing the depressed feelings and depressed outlook from the depressed vantage point of a depressed person. However, I do recognize this latter interpretation makes sense in relation to "Twenty Four Hours," especially in relation to the lyrics of this song, while it also makes sense to interpret *Closer* this way, as this album can, understandably, come across to many listeners as more unremittingly bleak than *Unknown Pleasures*.

This admission presents a challenge to me as I write about "Twenty Four Hours," about what I hear in listening to this song, about what this song makes me think (about) and feel. I tend to deflect questions, from students or others, asking me to identify my single favorite anything–movie, book,

TV show, actor, character, sport, athlete, place, shaping influence, leisure activity, class to teach, personal experience, hero, and even color. Yet I do identify Joy Division as my single all-time favorite band, and Ian Curtis as my single all-time favorite musician. Even so, I usually resist identifying any one Joy Division song as my #1 favorite, and I likewise usually resist expressing a preference in terms of my favorite Joy Division album. However, if any song so qualifies it is "Twenty Four Hours," and in fact this song, from *Closer*, is the most played song in my iTunes library. What's more, I maintain a slight overall preference for *Closer* over *Unknown Pleasures*, if pressed to choose, as I find the former an all the more brilliantly cohesive and bracingly evocative masterwork than the latter. But why so? What appeals to me about "Twenty Four Hours"–and about *Closer*? While I can empathize with depression and suicidality, with related forms of serious to severe mental distress, and with experience of considerable physical pain, I don't believe any of that accounts for why I have experienced this song and this album exerting the impact it has with me, for over 40 years now. As I proceed in this section I aim to share with you what might explain such impact.

A useful place to begin is with Paul Morley. According to Morley, "Some of the things *Closer* is: it's about the end of a life, about feeling out of place in the universe, it's about how rock history changes because of the invention of a new drum sound, it's heavy going in charged pop disguise, and it's a collection of songs imagining all sorts of horrors, melodies and substances made by people who had been big fans of music made by Can, Kraftwerk, the Doors, Love, the Velvet Underground, Black Sabbath, Neu!, Throbbing Gristle, the Sex Pistols, Bowie, Buzzcocks and Brian Eno" (130). To that list, Morley adds, as influences upon Martin Hannett, "Abba and Steely Dan for inspiration, and I suspect Fleetwood Mac, Captain Beefheart and Bonnie Raitt" as well as "Lou Reed's *Berlin*, not just for Reed's monstrous darkness, but for the way producer Bob Ezrin had marshalled the talents of great musicians to give the record rigour and permanence" (130). Yet later, as I cited earlier in this chapter, Morley boldly proclaims:

> *Closer* is a soundtrack to distance. The distance between being far away and being incredibly close. The distance you travel to create something out of nothing. The distance between surviving and giving up . . . . the distance between making it all up as you go along, and knowing exactly what you are doing, between turning up for work, and dreaming of something else. It's a soundtrack to the distance between having all the time, ambition and energy in the world, and then suddenly not. Between concentrating on the moment, and thinking about what happens next. Between togetherness and loneliness. Between violence, and peace. Between taking things incredibly seriously, and just getting on with your life. (143)

In an interview with the surviving bandmembers, Morley cites Bernard Sumner referencing Ian Curtis as "an extreme thinker" (134) who confronted extreme topics in an extreme manner, akin to a novelist, while Morley later suggests, in usefully provocative fashion, that Ian Curtis "sang from the knife edge of doubt with a kind of suave, sordid, middle-of-the-road disconnectedness. He sang about defeat, and a defeated mind, with a dissolved glory, as if there was a kind of triumph in the difficulties of life. He sang suffering with an almost tender listlessness. He put the perfect pitch to strangled thoughts" (268). As Morley adds, yet further, "It was as if Curtis was transferring himself into the very body of the music, stumbling over the line from where the music was for him to where he was for the music. The songs weren't helping him to deal with or recover from the traumas of his life, they were encouraging a fascination with the speed and danger of the drama. They weren't an escape from the madness; they sent him right into the madness. The music was taking him away, from himself, from others, from life. It was taking him over. It needed the drama of his life" (268-269).

It is interesting that Sumner, Hook, and Morris all felt more positive about their contribution and achievement, as well as their relative autonomy versus Hannett in the production process with *Closer* than with *Unknown Pleasures*. In contrast, Curtis, reputedly, was less satisfied and even worried about how *Closer* would be received, how it would stand up versus *Unknown Pleasures*. At this point, late in his life, Curtis clearly felt overwhelmed and overwrought so it is understandable he might have felt unable to contribute his best possible effort, or be able to best judge the quality of his work. Peter Hook offers a perceptive way of making a similar point in discussing Curtis and this song in Hooks's memoir, *Unknown Pleasures: Inside Joy Division*. Here Hook comments "Ian had difficulty singing some of the songs he wrote because he didn't have the range in his key, but I've always felt very, very strongly that a great vocalist can write great music and doesn't have to sing it perfectly as long as the emotion is there" (279). In Curtis's vocal contribution to "Twenty Four Hours," Hook asserts "The emotion comes from the heart, the soul, the passion, which together make a perfect delivery" (279). It is this contradiction that makes Curtis's contribution stunning: "on the one hand, he was ill and vulnerable; on the other he was a screaming rock god" (279).

Hook's comments remind me of what Eric Clarke writes, in "Empathy and the ecology of musical consciousness." In this chapter, Clarke examines the role of the human voice within music, as principal locus of empathy. Drawing upon earlier work by Steven Robert Livingstone and William Forde Thompson, as well as by Roger J. Watt and Roisin L. Ash, Clarke describes how "Music is capable of specifying a 'virtual person'" (76-77). Clarke reports "Studies have found that some listeners can experience the music itself as providing empathy and understanding for the feelings that they are going through, functioning as a kind of surrogate for an empathetic friend" (77). As one participant in a relevant study conducted by Annemieke J.M. Van den Tol and Jane Edwards sums up what these researchers found, "I felt befriended by the music–by this I mean that if you were to pretend the music/lyrics was a real person, with its lyrics of understanding, friendship, comfort and confidence, then surely the song would be your best friend, your soul-mate . . . Music personified is your soul-mate, your trusted secret friend who can empathize with you" (77). According to Clarke, referencing this same study and others like it,

> It appears that music is able to act as a virtual person with whom to empathize, and who (or which) can be experienced as empathizing with the listener's own emotions . . . [music] has attributes either of an idealized person or of an idealized collection or community of people. Musicking can be understood as the enactment of a kind of imagined subjectivity–not associated, or at least not necessarily associated, specifically with the composers or performers who are explicitly engaged in making the music, nor simply as the mirror of the listener's own subjectivity; but in a more abstracted and generic manner" (77).

239

Clarke cites Naomi Cumming in elaborating on this point: "The music *forms* the listener's experience, and . . . creates a knowledge of something that has been formerly unknown, something that asks to be integrated into the mind of the hearer" (quoted, 77). Continuing further, Clarke proposes "Music is . . . both a *medium* for empathetic (or antagonistic) engagement with others, and an *environment* in which to explore and experiment with a range of more or less projected, fantasized, and genuinely discovered subject positions or social formations" (79). Or, in other words, as Clarke cites Ian Cross, Felicity Laurence, and Tal-Chen Rabinowitch theorizing this contribution, music acts as "a scaffold that can help us to acquire the habit of empathizing" (quoted, 79). Illustrating his argument with reference to Janis Joplin, Clarke discusses how "The human voice acts as the primary significant medium of acoustically channelled empathy" (79), while in popular music "the damaged voice" often proves the most evocative of empathy, with what listeners often identify as signature features of famous pop singers' voices amounting to markers of vocal damage (80). Clarke cites Joplin's damaged voice–"strained, raspy, noisy"–as a result of "hard living, social exhaustion, illness, or vocal abuse," while explaining Joplin makes use of what this kind of 'damage' paradoxically enables in her inflection, rhythmic stretching, vibrato, and alteration of the usual melodic line (82-83).

In Joplin's case, as with others like her, manipulation and deployment of a 'damaged voice' has been widely interpreted as indicative of her 'authenticity'. In connection with Ian Curtis, his own limited and damaged voice is therefore not simply a 'unique part of his charm' but rather a significant mode of empathetic connection for listeners with the strain and struggle he expresses and communicates in his singing. Listeners hear this strain and struggle as reflective of Curtis investing his heart, his soul, his passion, and, following Morley, his entire being, into his effort, as a singer, as a frontman, as a performer, as an artist.

And yet, it is hardly Ian Curtis's vocal or lyrical contributions alone that make "Twenty Four Hours" a riveting listening experience. In *Torn Apart: the Life of Ian Curtis*, Mick Middles and Lindsay Reade comment that "Twenty Four Hours" provides "the most heartbreaking moment" in *Closer*, "with Hooky's bass rising to a sudden height and powering the song forward, leaving the singer trailing in its wake. The song, blessed with a captivating ebb-and-flow, was seen by many as the true defining moment of the band's entire career" (213). It is important to note well, as Middles and Reade here suggest, that "Twenty Four Hours" continues to rise and push forward, more than once, even after falling and dropping back, which in turn suggests a musical embodiment of resilience in the otherwise seemingly most desperate to despairing of circumstances.

In "One bleak day gives way to another in Joy Division's '24 Hours'," The A.V. Club's Noel Murray likewise attests to the significance of Hook's bass guitar in explaining the impact of this song: "Peter Hook plays a six-note bass-guitar riff throughout Joy Division's '24 Hours', with slight variations. Sometimes he plays one extra note; sometimes one less. Sometimes the riff walks up; sometimes it starts out in that direction and then suddenly drops off a cliff. It's almost like Hook's writing the music in real time, testing out different combinations to see which one sounds best. As the tempo shifts, Hook stays his course. He knows there's something there: catchy enough to be hummable, yet downbeat enough to make the cheeriest listener feel instantly blue." As Murray concludes,

Musically . . . this is actually one of the rare uptempo songs on *Closer*. The rhythms alternate between funereal and almost punky, recalling some of Joy Division's earliest singles. It bridges every era of the band, in a way that makes it feel all the more final. It's a last hurrah, encompassing all that Joy Division could be, and distilling the despairing themes of so much of Curtis' writing. That's why the bass line is so vital to "24 Hours": It propels the song, but also carries the message, sad as it is. After all the different attempts at the central riff, Hook takes one last crack at it, with six more notes. He ends on a down note—inevitably, conclusively, and inescapably.

As I will indicate, later in this section, I hear the bass line as somewhat more complicated than this, but Murray usefully draws attention to how the musical sounds, patterns of sounds, and deployments of sounds that comprise "Twenty Four Hours" embody ongoing struggle and not surrender.

In *Song Means: Analysing and Interpreting Recorded Popular Song*, Allan F. Moore explains what is commonly identified as "accompaniment" does more than accompany. In fact, "It can explain why the persona is acting in the way the song reports, even to the extent that the persona may be hiding this from themselves" (190). "Accompanimental textures can also set the attitudinal tone of a song" and in doing so help prepare the listener for how to respond to the song (192-193). Musical instruments and other sound sources need not simply compliment, support, and reinforce a message, tone, or mood emanating from the vocal, and the lyrics, because they can also complicate and challenge this same message, tone, or mood.

Moore is wary of simplistic judgments concerning markers of supposed authenticity versus inauthenticity in musical expression, but he does allow this topic a place in analysis and interpretation of recorded popular songs, suggesting it is important to focus on "who it is that a performance authenticates" in assessing authenticity. As Moore explains, "Authenticity of expression, or first person authenticity" authenticates what it is like to be the musician-performer; "Authenticity of experience, or second person authenticity" authenticates what it is like to be you, or to be us; and "Authenticity of execution, or third person authenticity" authenticates an original practice or set of roots–i.e., authenticates what it is or was like to be him/her/them (269). I propose, following Moore, that the lyrics of Ian Curtis and the music of Ian Curtis and Joy Division can be viably interpreted as simultaneously engaging with all three kinds of authenticity, while it is ambiguous to what extent one versus another takes precedence at any given moment. This in turn has much to do with the fact that these songs are not mere accompaniments to Ian Curtis's lyrics.

Moore suggests a key connection with the question of perceived authenticity in listening to music is the ability of music "to articulate for its listeners a place of belonging"–especially versus other music that seems like it offers mere entertainment or casual, transient escapism (270). But with Joy Division this matter is complicated because Joy Division songs characteristically offer listeners a prospective place of belonging, and do extend an invitation, even an encouragement, to respond, join, follow, and embark along the same, similar, parallel, or otherwise comparable path, but these songs at the same time characteristically share agonizing reflections over as well as fraught confrontations with daunting challenges involved in pursuing such a path. Joy Division songs are rife with palpable unease concerning the prospect of maintaining and sustaining any such place of belonging other than 'just for one moment'.

As I have suggested in my earlier discussions of "Disorder" and "Transmission," what I and many others especially appreciate about Joy Division songs, and Ian Curtis's lyrics, are how these songs, and these lyrics, open themselves up to numerous viable interpretations, associations, and connections. I find it crucial to approach a sustained effort at interpretation with the aim of showing how these songs make good sense in multiple and even opposing directions. I find "Twenty Four Hours" compelling because it not only challenges but also undermines interpretations that attempt to wrap the song up neatly into a short synopsis of what, in essence, it supposedly, is 'all about', draining the song of any vestige of lingering mystery.

In *Interpreting Music*, Lawrence Kramer advises us not to identify "musical understanding with the resolution of ambiguity or uncertainty" (196). Kramer proposes "we need not, should not, and in fact do not" do so, when we interpret musical meaning, because we recognize "We are more likely to enjoy music for its freedom from such rigid constructions" (196), and this includes freedom from simple tropes such as movement from equilibrium through disruption of equilibrium to reestablishment of equilibrium. As Kramer further suggests, "A work is also a performance–a complex 'speech act' that is never finished . . ." (246) and "the mode of being of the work is a state of perpetual beginning" (246). Respecting this understanding of what a musical work is–and does–helps us define and refine what musical interpretation aims to do: "Musical hermeneutics is an attempt to account for what the work of music might be heard to do in specific historical and cultural circumstances" (247). While "The essence of this attempt is that it is verbal" (247), "Language becomes the medium in which the musical event *reveals itself* [my emphasis]" (250), and "Interpretation by its very nature is always in excess of whatever facts may be at its disposal. Hermeneutics is the art of semantic excess" (251). In other words, "one of the chief functions of the [musical] work, is precisely to elicit interpretation . . . to unleash interpretation, to let interpretations proliferate" (252), and therefore evaluating interpretations is not a matter of setting up rigid demarcations between objectively true versus objectively false but rather considering new interpretations in relation to preexisting and prospective further interpretations, in terms of what they respectively have to offer, and in particular, as Kramer suggests, what and how these interpretations enable the music, as event, to reveal (253).

In similar terms, Kramer writes, in *Expression and Truth*, "Language brings the distant near but also brings the distance near, and so brings you into proximity to the distance, brings the distance to you. Music does the opposite: It brings you into the distance, brings you to the distance" (159). This conception is useful in contemplating musical meaning in the case of Joy Division, with this music involving considerable attention to matters of distance and closeness. Likewise useful are Kramer's claims that "Music listened to is the ecstacy of distance" (161) and that "Music is distance heard as expression" (161). It is useful what's more, in interpreting music, as Kramer declares, to recognize "Music is perhaps our preeminent means of saying everything in public and yet at the same time keeping it secret if only in the form of fiction. Musical understanding commonly begins with the sense that something significant has been expressed but without the words that would disclose its secret" (280). Or, as Kramer makes a similar point, also in *Expression and Truth*, in discussing relations between expression and meaning: "I express what I mean but always mean more than I (can) express" (83). Likewise, in *The Thought of Music*, Kramer contends "Music offers to demonstrate that experience in the absence of assured knowledge is an entirely livable condition. Listening, enhanced through music, allows us to entertain the possibility of uncertainty and even bewilderment without regret. With music we know by not-knowing, or better, we know surely by not knowing for sure" (16). So, in sum, interpretations of music explore potential meanings and impacts in concert with the music, while aiming to open up room for yet further exploration. And the music might well be 'about' not knowing, uncertainty, lack or absence of assured knowledge, confusion, and bewilderment–and about how none of these states necessarily should be feared as well as about how none of these states can be avoided. Music helps us in living with not knowing, with uncertainty, with lack or absence of assured knowledge, with confusion, and with bewilderment–including by wrestling with, in socially symbolic terms, the frustration, the exhaustion, the pain, and the anguish we often experience simultaneous with not knowing, with uncertainty, with lack or absence of assured knowledge, with confusion, and with bewilderment.

The phrase "twenty four hours" conjures a sense of heightened urgency as opposed to "a day," or "one day," or "a single day," in the sense of an impending–and potentially an inflexible and foreboding–deadline. "Twenty four hours" suggests every hour will be devoted to or consumed with an effort, a cause, a struggle to realize an end–and not just 'normal' waking or working hours.

When I think of what "twenty four hours" connotes to me I think of my love for crime drama, especially TV crime drama, and how often detectives in these shows working to solve an extremely difficult criminal case need to work day and night with next to no sleep to attempt to do so, while frequently running up against formidable deadlines. For example, their superiors may demand our principal detective protagonists achieve a decisive breakthrough in twenty four hours or the case will be closed down, or scaled back, or reduced in priority, or shifted to the responsibility of another team. For example, our principal detective protagonists may need to find a victim of a crime, or prospective victim of a crime, in twenty four hours, because that represents the maximum remaining time this person could still remain alive, if they are not already dead. For example, our principal detective protagonists may need to wait twenty four hours before they obtain crucial forensic evidence, including evidence subject to laboratory processing or more unusual and costly kinds of procedures. For example, our principal detective protagonists may face a deadline of twenty four hours before a prime suspect must be released from custody on bail, or with charges dropped, or with the prospect this suspect will flee the jurisdiction and be much more difficult subsequently to apprehend, or that they will commit yet further crimes. For example, our principal detective protagonists may face a twenty four hour deadline, from their superiors, to 'get their shit together', if, as is so often the case in these kinds of dramas, these detectives are, besides being consumed by attempting to solve crimes, simultaneously confronting unstable personal and family lives, including breakdowns of marriages and other intimate partnerships, alcoholism and drug addiction, and further varieties of self-destructive behavior.

For example, from the opposite end, a suspect may face twenty four hours of questioning, and of incarceration, which may include being cut off from crucial medications as well as other necessary means of maintaining health and well-being, and from family and friends who depend upon this person or upon whom this person depends, all the while fearing the prospect of enduring violent forms of intimidation and abuse during incarceration. For example, such a suspect may face a deadline of twenty four hours to raise bail, or to obtain and secure an alibi witness, or to otherwise provide a convincing account of how and why the suspect is not responsible for a serious crime. For example, a defendant, witness, or victim may face a twenty four hour wait before needing to testify in court, in what are likely to prove traumatic circumstances, where the opposing attorney will exacerbate this trauma–or where such a defendant, witness, or victim will need to endure twenty four hours of providing this kind of excruciating testimony. Or such a defendant, witness, or victim may need to endure listening for twenty four hours to this kind of testimony from someone else whose testimony will reactivate trauma they have already experienced. Or an enterprising group, including an undercover cop or several undercover cops, may face a twenty four hour deadline to arrange a deal, or to make payment on a deal–such as drug deal, or a weapons deal, or another deal in illegal goods–before facing violent retaliation for failure to do so.

The array of possible scenarios can readily proliferate far beyond those examples I have just sketched here but in all these cases, and many more easily imaginable, the common element is how 'twenty four hours' suggests an ominous approaching deadline or duration.

In the work I have done for over thirty-five years as a university faculty member, deadlines are ubiquitous. Students face multiple deadlines continuously, throughout every term, from multiple classes, other academic and extra-academic pursuits, including paid jobs, internships, and as part of sports teams and student organizations. A great many students find themselves working especially assiduously, and often especially desperately, in the last twenty-four hours, to complete a task before the deadline arrives–such as a paper or a project–or in preparing for an event–such as a presentation or an examination. Students also face other significant deadlines–to pay tuition and fees, or to make a necessary deposit toward payment of tuition or fees, to sign a contract for rental housing, to leave rental housing with the expiration of a lease, to apply for financial aid or for a scholarship or for admission into a program, to line up letters of recommendations or other references in applications such as for study-abroad or for a job on or off campus or for graduate study, to register for a required class before it fills, to use up all the remaining money on a cafeteria food plan, to submit an application for a student organization to achieve or maintain official status and be thereby eligible to make use of university resources, and, of late, to test for the COVID-19 virus and, as need be, to quarantine. Again, the preceding list represents only a small sampling of the range of possible twenty-four hour deadlines students face all the time.

Faculty too face many deadlines, including many twenty-four hour deadlines. We often need to work right up to the last moment, and especially intensively within the preceding twenty-four hours, to get ready for classes we will teach, to determine how best to organize and conduct them, to write all materials that will be used to help guide our efforts during that time (I typically prepare detailed outlines and study guides, for every class session, that help students follow what we do together in class as well as assist them in reviewing subsequently on their own), and to select and prepare ancillary materials to use in class, such as clips from films and TV shows, other video links (to interviews, commentaries, performances, and more), musical recordings, and physically illustrative materials (for example, t-shirts, postcards, found objects, and maps and posters). We, university faculty, also often face tight deadlines to work through voluminous amounts of student work that we need to read, comment on, and otherwise respond to, as well as to evaluate and grade. And we face many similar deadlines in order to be prepared for a plethora of 'shared governance' meetings, and to respond to a seemingly endless variety of forms that constitute the bureaucratic normalcy of institutional life. We in addition confront deadlines, often running up against the last twenty four hours to succeed in meeting these, in applying for grants to support research and teaching, and in preparing speeches, public presentations, and public exhibitions and performances, as well as to submit reviews, articles, books, and yet additional kinds of projects for publication. Again, this is just a small sampling of some of the kinds of deadlines university faculty routinely encounter, and indeed these often do become twenty four hour deadlines when we are most busy, and most taxed, attempting to juggle many tasks and commitments all at the same time, and when the need, and the demand, from others is most pressing.

Yet one other possibility readily occurs to me in making sense of what 'twenty four hours' might suggest, and that is how, in 'twenty four hours' time, remarkably enough, a situation can dramatically shift, or at the least how we feel about the situation can dramatically shift in this duration of time. What feels as if it is impossible or terrible right now might, in twenty four hours time, even without any obvious change in the objective dimensions of the situation that at present feel impossible or terrible, subsequently feel, that slight but crucial amount of time later, different and better. I have often reminded myself, and have needed to remind myself, that if I can just manage to hold on for another twenty four hours, if I can just withstand twenty four hours more of whatever I am presently experiencing, no matter how painful, I can make it, I will feel better, and my life will be better. I also find it often does help me to narrow my focus as much and as far as I can, to live directly in the moment, in the immediate present, concentrating on what I need to attend to solely in the next twenty-four hours, and no more than that, not worrying about the future beyond—or the past preceding. Efforts at such mindfulness I find especially helpful when otherwise I am starting to feel as if everything around me, and especially everyone and everything submitting demands upon me, is on the verge of spiraling out of my control, slipping my grasp, and leaving me feeling as if I am being crushed by the weight of what 'I need to do' yet 'I can't do'. Often I have needed, in these situations, to repeat to myself, over and over again, an adage derived from Samuel Beckett, "I can't go on. I will go on." Often I have benefitted from zeroing in, in terms of my conscious attention, on the single day itself, and on its twenty four hour incremental intervals, and in doing so mindfully appreciating I am alive, I am still alive, and I can continue to remain alive, with being and remaining alive enough to carry me through.

At other times, when feeling overwhelmed and overwrought, I have recognized I need to take *twenty four hours away* from what is making me feel overwhelmed and overwrought, from the work I am doing, from the worries I am confronting, and instead do something entirely different, while not thinking about what has driven me to this point. I advise students, when feeling the same, to do this–take time away, go for a long walk, do some other kind of physical activity that you enjoy, reach out to friends and family you know you can trust and who care about you and your well-being, get away and go somewhere else, or do something unusual or different, even seemingly frivolous, just for twenty four hours. And then come back, refreshed. All too often, as I discuss in the "Disorder" section of this chapter, many of our lives feel as if we cycle monotonously through the same rigidly repetitive patterns, while we crave variety versus what we otherwise experience as deadening. When I was a graduate student, and had little to no money, my mother advised me to try shopping at different grocery stores, even if I couldn't buy much, just for variety–or to do anything at all a little different, including wearing a different combination of clothing or my hair in a different style, or taking a walk or a run in a different direction than I usually follow. My mother also advised me to drink Irish whiskey to help with rough patches in my life-experience, but that's another story. I also find crime drama–in the form of literature, cinema, and television–useful in taking me away from my own problems and immersing me in the problems fictional characters experience, while getting me to care about these characters, and especially the desperate struggles they often face, as well as to feel a sympathetic to empathetic identification with how even the ostensible 'heroes' of this kind of fiction are almost always complicated, messy, and flawed.

All of those associations make sense to me in reflecting on what the title of Joy Division's song, and Ian Curtis's lyrics for this song, might mean. But let's proceed with the anticipation that the title might make clearer sense once we have taken into account the lyrics. Line one–"So this is permanence, love's shattered pride"–creates a sense of both mystery and of weightiness, as we are addressing here "permanence," which connotes unchangeable, forever lasting, forever enduring, forever surpassing and persisting and continuing, but we cannot be sure precisely to what 'this' might refer, even if it does seem linked with "love's shattered pride." The last phrase is perhaps the most concrete here, but even so it remains ambiguous: this pride, which is shattered, seems to belong to love, to be an effect or result of love, and yet what might it be about love, or about a particular kind of love, that leads to, or ends up with, "shattered pride"? "Shattered pride" suggests a pride that can no longer, in fact, be so proud, as this pride is, and has been, "shattered," but by what, how, and why? I suggest "love's shattered pride" might suggest what love once made one feel proud about has been shattered, ironically enough, by the vagaries of love itself–by loving too much, or too little, or in the wrong way, or too diversely or diffusely, or not in the same way as that which is loved loves in return, or where that which is loved or has been loved in return does not love or no longer loves, at least not in the same way or to the same degree as was the case before the 'shattering'. How and why this state might prove permanent, and, even more precisely, if one follows the lyrics meticulously, be what *is* permanence, what defines permanence, what might in essence constitute permanence, is by no means readily apparent.

"So" is an interesting way, what's more, to begin the lyrics, as if drawing a logical conclusion and yet doing so in a casual or at least conversational manner, while, at the same time, marking out a sense of hesitation in drawing this conclusion. In other words, think about how 'so' might connote in the following: 'So, you don't really want to go out with me tonight?' 'So, you are not really interested in seeing that movie (or attending that sporting event or joining me at that musical gig or even just going to the grocery store with me)?' 'So, is that your final word on the subject?' In all of these cases, and many others like them, 'so' invites the addressee to contradict the immediately following assertion, and even implies a pleading wish on the part of the addressor that the addressee will or might do so.

Nevertheless, "permanence" introduces a note of solemnity, of gravity, to the immediate situation these lyrics recount, and that we are invited, as the lyrics proceed, to attempt to decipher. And, certainly, the "shattering of love," linked with "permanence," ramps up feelings of solemnity, and gravity, especially as this state of affairs seems extremely stark–i.e., love's pride being shattered, and postulated as equivalent with permanence, which in turn implies love's shattered pride, or the shattering of love's pride, and likely the shattering of love as well, is inexorable, ineradicable, or unsurpassable. It may be that "love" imagines, presumes, or even pretentiously assumes it is capable of achieving far more, by itself alone, than it ultimately ever is, and this then is the nature and destiny of love–to be proud, perhaps even boastful, and to have that pride shattered, permanently. Such an interpretation offers a grim portrait of where love seemingly inescapably leads, that runs overwhelmingly contrary to what the vast majority of people seek and hope to find, in, through, and with love–and also often enough believe they do find and have found. This line might well suggest the vantage point of someone who is feeling bitter about loss of love, or about loss of illusions concerning love, or about previous investment in the comforting notion that finding and experiencing love, and entering into loving relations, can 'take care of' far more than it actually can–or that love, and loving relations, will last far longer than turns out to be the case.

Let's turn to the next line–"What once was innocence, turned on its side." Striking here I suggest is "what once was innocence" is not flipped over on its back, but rather "turned on its side," which could suggest innocence has not simply been punctured or revealed to have been naive and delusory, but has been altered, and twisted, so it remains proximate but no longer exercises the force it once did, while cruelly reminding one, by remaining so persistent yet no longer effectual, of what once was–of what one what once imagined, or believed, or hoped, or dreamed, or even felt confident was the case, but is no longer, and perhaps never really fully was. If we connect this line with the immediately preceding line, it might seem as if this second line elaborates on what has happened to love, and its pride, in becoming shattered. Here it might reinforce the interpretation that the narrator-protagonist is referencing a previous state of innocence, even of naivete and of what turns out to have been reckless and unfounded pretense, now exposed as illusory and even delusory, or which can no longer be sustained because the basis upon which love existed, and for the pride in this love, no longer does. But again, if "this is permanence" suggests once belief in love, and its powers, and what love can give and do is crushed, then what is left in its wake feels like a desolate and barren state of limbo.

"A cloud hangs over me, marks every move"–leads us to wonder what might this cloud be, while also noting that "me" shows up here directly, for the first time, making the lyrics feel now all the more personal, as if the narrator-protagonist is now making clear 'he' is speaking about 'himself', and that, implicitly he was, in the preceding two lines as well. "A cloud hangs over me" suggests a taint of one or another kind, perhaps a shame, perhaps that the narrator-protagonist is the target of blame or is perceived as somehow corrupt or as otherwise 'guilty'. That this cloud hanging over the

247

narrator-protagonist "marks" his "every move" suggests he experiences a weighty indictment–or self-indictment. Or, perhaps, this cloud that hangs over him and marks his every move is the product of his recognition of a fundamental or ultimate existential separation and isolation of each human being from all other human beings, no matter what familiar kinds of bonds he establishes and has established (and, implicitly also, that 'we' establish and have established). At the least the last phrase in this line suggests it is difficult, perhaps even impossible, to escape this cloud and its impact. What's more, if it is "marking every move" it is almost as if "the cloud" is continuing, in relation to each step the narrator-protagonist takes, to repeat the charge, incessantly over and over again: 'Guilty!'

"Deep in the memory, of what once was love"–next brings us back, directly, to love, but also, once again, to love lost, to love that no longer exists, while this line suggests the loss is felt acutely, and, if we connect this fourth line of the first stanza with the third line immediately preceding, perhaps the cloud that hangs over the narrator-protagonist, and marks his every move, *is* the memory of this love that once was, but is no longer, that has been lost, and of which the narrator was proud and yet this pride of his has been crushed. "Deep in the memory" can suggest buried, and perhaps not close to the surface of ordinary, everyday, mundane consciousness, but that interpretation doesn't seem to fit well here, as the narrator-protagonist comes across as all too overwhelmingly aware of this memory, and therefore "deep" on the contrary here suggests this memory cannot be excised, or at least not at all easily, and it has left and continues to leave a profound imprint upon the consciousness of the narrator-protagonist: it is a memory he cannot escape continuing to confront, no matter how painful.

"Oh how I realised how I wanted time" conveys a feeling of heartbreak, of deep sadness for–and with the narrator-protagonist, as right away this line suggests it alludes to what the narrator wanted, and likely needed, but could not obtain, secure, maintain, or preserve. The "Oh" starting the line reads in this context as chilling, as if the narrator-protagonist is sharing confidentially while at the same time on the crux of breaking down in so doing. This "Oh" reminds me of numerous conversations I have had with students where they have shared with me difficulties they have been experiencing in their lives that have undermined their ability to do as well as they hoped in our classes–mental health crises, especially due to anxiety and depression, but also breakups in relationships or deaths of family members; physical and sexual assaults; eating disorders and self-harming behaviors; being kicked out or effectively finding they needed to leave and cut off relations with erstwhile family and friends; or realizing they no longer have the interest or they don't have the academic marks to be able to pursue what they long identified as a desired major or a target career. In many of these situations, these people have been literally all choked up, their voices cracking, their eyes welling with tears, and they often broke down sobbing as well as, even occasionally, hyperventilating. I feel an immense compassion for these people, in these circumstances, and a deep sense of responsibility to do whatever I possibly can to be of help to them, at the least to be sensitive to and supportive of them in what they were dealing with and struggling through. I feel in the most drastic of these occasions like I am presented with the responsibility to help save a life, and that is indeed a tremendous responsibility. Returning, however, to this first line from stanza two of the lyrics, we are invited to wonder when precisely did the narrator-protagonist 'realize' he wanted time,

248

what led him to this realization, and, also, more to the point, what did he imagine he might do with the time–with the further or additional time, perhaps beyond twenty four hours, beyond a twenty four hours' deadline–and why does it seem so strongly implicit he is not going to gain this time (or that he has been rejected or defeated in his efforts to do so)?

"Put into perspective, tried so hard to find"–suggests the narrator-protagonist wanted, and likely needed, time to be able to put into perspective what he is here confronting and has been confronting, as well as what might be responsible for these circumstances, including how *he might be responsible*. This line does suggest a "perspective" is at least hypothetically conceivable that might help the situation, but at the same time exactly what this perspective might be like, what it might involve, the narrator-protagonist cannot say, and, above all else, it seems it is incredibly daunting to find no matter how hard he has tried to do exactly that. In addition, this line suggests the narrator-protagonist has likely been trying out, and trying on, multiple possible perspectives but none, as of yet at least, has provided him what he seeks–and what he needs. These perspectives I suggest might be usefully conceived of as frameworks for thinking, feeling, believing, understanding, communicating, acting, interacting, and behaving–or, in other words, as theories that might offer explanations of what is happening and has happened to the narrator-protagonist, how, and why, as well as what is to be done about this, including how and in what direction it might be possible to move forward. The narrator-protagonist might be suffering because the conditions of his existence, experience, and social positioning don't provide him ready access, or access at all, to those frames of intelligibility that could prove most useful, even urgently necessary, to him–that could even be necessary to save his life.

"Just for one moment, thought I'd found my way/Destiny unfolded, watched it slip away" is heart-breaking in it suggestion that briefly, fleetingly, it seemed to the narrator-protagonist he might have found his way out of the quagmire in which he feels currently trapped, but this proved all the more devastating an experience as it turned out to be a false, or at least illusory, hope. "Finding one's way" suggests aiming to figure out what is one's foremost purpose, even mission, in life–what makes one's life worth living, what can one best offer and best contribute, and what will enable one to feel most satisfied, fulfilled, completed, included, respected, and appreciated.

This is often a fraught quest for so many of us, at pivotal moments in our lives, especially when we need to make crucial choices and decisions, and to engage in crucial actions and practices, manifesting a dramatic break or departure from a previous stage in our lives. Again and again, new university students recount to me how difficult an adjustment it often is, no matter how excited they may be to undertake it, along with numerous fears and worries they bring along with them, as they begin their undergraduate years–will they make friends, will they find their niche, will they find a major, will they like their major, will they find a paid job, will they be able to manage the demands of that paid job (or jobs) together with those of classes, will they get along with a roommate or housemates, will they be able to find a house or apartment they can afford to rent while at school, will they be overwhelmed by homesickness, will the level of expectations for academic achievement prove more demanding than they anticipated and hoped, will they be able to adjust to receiving lower grades than in high school, will they and their families continue to be able to pay the costs of attending university (or the costs of attending full-time), will they be able to find clubs and activities to pursue that they will enjoy, and will they be able to deal with the impact of changing the ways that they think, feel, believe, and act in relation to major social and political issues and in relation to erstwhile fundamental values and ideals?

Returning to the lyrics, "destiny unfolded" suggests the narrator-protagonist perceives forces outside of and beyond his control have propelled him in a direction far beyond a state of affairs where he could take the time he needed, including to find the perspective that would best enable him to make sense of his life, where it had been, where it now is at, and where it might possibly yet go. It seems the narrator-protagonist feels like this is no longer *his* life, in the sense that he is exercising meaningful self-determination, but rather this is a life he is being forced to live, and it's too late to do anything about that. "Slip away" also conveys a mournful image of something that seemingly was within grasp disappearing slowly, gradually, but nonetheless steadily, with the narrator-protagonist 'watching' this as it happens. It appears as if the narrator-protagonist feels paralyzed to do anything as he watches his hope for redemption, or salvation, slip away from him.

"Excessive flashpoints, beyond all reach" suggests that in the distance, perceptible yet impossible to effectively impact, a host of dangerous forces threaten violent eruptions and disruptions, which may refer to numerous possible social problems and conflicts, and numerous possible sources or avenues of social rupture and antagonism, that the narrator-protagonist would like to be able to do something about, to help out in addressing, but which he can't, as he feels not only powerless effectively to do so, but also trapped, confined, and thereby prevented from even attempting to do so. "Excessive" suggests whatever these flashpoints might represent they have become numerous and critical–they represent or are symptomatic of a major crisis, or of major crises, or an imminent major crisis, or of imminent major crises.

"Solitary demands for all I'd like to keep" draws a striking contrast with the immediately preceding line in referencing a narrow locus immediately surrounding the narrator-protagonist, as opposed to distant conflagrations the narrator-protagonist is all too aware of but can do nothing about. Here we are invited to wonder how to take this line–who is making these demands, and of whom? Why "demands"? What is "solitary" about these–are these demands made in a state of solitude, isolation, retreat, confinement? Are these "solitary" in the sense that these are the sole demands being made? And what might constitute that which the narrator-protagonist would "like to keep"? Note well these are demands for *all* he would like to keep, and perhaps this suggests a situation in which someone or something is demanding he give up everything, including everything that matters and has mattered to him, refusing to allow him to keep anything at all afterward. If so, why is this–or why is the narrator-protagonist feeling as if this is the case? Why is he being forced to give up all of this, or why does he feel like he is being so forced?

"Let's take a ride out, see what we can find/A valueless collection of hopes and past desires"–suggests this might well be an entirely introspectively internal drama these lyrics are recounting and enacting, as even in this 'riding out' that involves "us" riding together with the narrator-protagonist what we are finding is the 'stuff' of the subjective: hopes and desires. And yet, why at this point, when it has previously seemed as if the narrator-protagonist can't move, and has lost everything or virtually everything, are we now invited to join him in venturing "out"? And what might "ride"–and 'taking a ride'–connote as the means to do so? The first of these two lines suggests an almost surprising, in the context of what has preceded, openness and curiosity, as if everything has not been all determined, as if everything is not all over and done with, once and for all. But the second line seems to cancel that suggestion by emphasizing what we find, do find, or are likely to find, when we do join the narrator-protagonist, in taking this ride out, is "valueless," and therefore does not seem to redeem the effort invested to seek it out. Since what is "valueless" is a "collection of hopes and past desires" it seems like the narrator-protagonist, and we in joining him, are discovering what once mattered immensely, and what inspired people with a motive and drive, to live, to venture, to seek, to journey, to quest, to create, has all been shown up, as having achieved little or nothing of ultimate or of lasting value. If these represent the aspirations of communities, cultures, and societies, or of initiatives, campaigns, causes, and movements, or of groups, organizations, and enterprises, this passage conveys to us a bleakly dystopian 'revelation'–that so much of all of this, which has meant and mattered the most to so many, has proven futile. If these are the narrator-protagonist's past personal aspirations, and/or our own, it feels likewise exceedingly bleak, as if so much of our previous lives, and what we explained to ourselves were the reasons why we were leading these lives and the goals we were seeking in doing so, were *wrong*. It feels as if we are confronting ourselves in a brutal fashion, refusing any more to deny or pretend, realizing we never were whom we thought we were, or whom we most needed, wanted, and desired ourselves to be.

"I never realised the lengths I'd have to go/All the darkest corners of a sense I didn't know"–to me suggests the narrator-protagonist has taken on an enormously daunting challenge, even indeed mission, in a highly idealist, and undoubtedly overtly romantic fashion, such as to explore the worst evils human beings are capable of committing versus each other, including what it feels like to experience these as a victim and as perpetrator, as well as a bystander and a witness, while wanting to find a way to expose how all of these evils are rooted in the fundamentally flawed nature, the fundamentally flawed systemic structures, of existing society and culture, in terms of how people are organized in what kinds of relations with each other, according to what logics and what principles, facilitated and governed by what institutions, and formed and shaped as what kinds of social subjects–and what kinds of existential beings. This is someone who has embarked on a concerted effort to meet 'the horror' head-on, and not to protect 'himself' from facing up to how thoroughly horrifying it truly is, but who has been devastating by what 'he' has encountered, as well as by what has been required of him in the course of doing so. This effort has required the narrator-protagonist push himself to extreme lengths, and push himself into extreme corners, while discovering, including about himself, an appalling depth and extent of responsibility and complicity. It has proven a monumental learning process, but it has also proven too much–far too much–for the narrator-protagonist to handle, at the least all by himself. He has been badly damaged as result, and is now in desperate need of help to recover, but he is bewildered concerning where to turn to find this help, if such help exists at all.

"Just for one moment, I heard somebody call/Looked beyond the day in hand, there's nothing there at all"–recalls the earlier line "Just for one moment, thought I'd found my way" but as with that earlier line holds out a glimmer of hope to then cancel it in the immediately succeeding line. Here the narrator-protagonist thought he "heard somebody call," as if providing him the help, the direction, and even the answers he wants, and needs, but this turned out to be deceptive, as no one was or is there, nothing but emptiness, a void, an abyss. The two lines almost seem to suggest the narrator-protagonist finds no compelling explanation for the meaning, purpose, and value of his existence, or for that matter ours, or anyone else's, beyond what the immediate moment, in the sheer present, within the current twenty four hours offers, and that hardly seems appealing or satisfying to this narrator-protagonist because it suggests no greater, or grander, reason exists for why we live, or why we die. The narrator-protagonist wants to hear the call of a voice, or of voices, from the past and from the future, from elsewhere and otherwise, to verify to him–to validate for him–that what he is and has been doing matters: that he is making a genuine impact, making a real difference, through what he is and has been doing. But the narrator-protagonist is not hearing this voice, or these voices, and he is likewise failing to willfully project himself into an imagined state of vital connection with these other people, especially those others who have been the victims of the horrific evils he has confronted.

"Now that I've realised how it's all gone wrong/Gotta find some therapy, this treatment takes too long"–again emphatically proposes the lyrics of the song are dealing with something that has failed, that has gone wrong, that has brought with it devastating consequences for which the narrator-protagonist was unprepared. It has taken him time to realize this to be the case, and, if anything, this realization has come too late. The second line is intriguing in suggesting the narrator-protagonist is and has been undergoing "treatment" and that even the process of recounting, and sharing, right here, might be part and parcel of this "treatment," which could signify "treatment" for a modern to postmodern existential human condition of alienation, isolation, precariousness, and desperation, or of acute desire meets acute anxiety. The "treatment" therefore might include confronting all of this head-on, and attempting to work it through, in intellectual, artistic, and performative fashion, but finding this process, of striving to do so, far too draining, with the struggle to work it through 'taking too long', as well being far too hard to maintain 'for so long'. "Gotta find some therapy" is fairly nebulous here–as it at best suggests the narrator-protagonist has no ready idea what kind of therapy he might need, what kind of therapy might help him, or let alone where, and from whom or from what, to access this therapy.

"Deep in the heart of where sympathy held sway/Gotta find my destiny, before it gets too late"–seems to suggest that if this destiny the narrator-protagonist here proclaims he has 'got to find' can be found, then it will be found "deep in the heart of where sympathy held away," which suggests some form, and perhaps some residue, or reservoir, of sympathy might provide what is needed. But, we are prompted to wonder, what kind of sympathy is this, and *whose* sympathy– sympathy *from whom*–is this? And why is sympathy referred to here in the past tense, as what once held sway, but seemingly does not, or might not, anymore? If this sympathy no longer exists–is no longer there–then how might it be at all possible to access and benefit from it? How might it be recovered and restored? Or is this sympathy connected with the love that is seemingly lost, addressed earlier in the lyrics, but which might not remain forever–i.e., permanently–lost? And what does "deep in the heart of" suggest–where might this location be, where seemingly sympathy "held sway"? Does this phrase suggest sympathy held sway deep in the heart of something–or of someone–or does this phrase suggest the narrator-protagonist is referencing 'the deep heart' of "where sympathy held sway," with the latter in effect containing the former? If "where sympathy held sway" contains something 'deep in its heart', what might this be–what might constitute 'deep in the heart', what might be found there, and how does this fit within a metaphorical 'province' of "where sympathy held sway"? Does this line suggest that for all the bleakness preceding, and for all the preceding sense we have gained that these lyrics have been recounting a tale of enormous loss, failure, and defeat, that it might not be all over with–that 'embers' of 'the flame' of an erstwhile sympathy might yet propel resilience, even recovery? If so, this source of renewed vitality seems nevertheless exceedingly tough to reach, and it seems as if it exists, if it does so at all, in a most fragile state.

Nevertheless, the last line suggests the narrator-protagonist has not yet given up entirely, as it indicates he is still conceiving of the possibility of yet finding what he wants, and needs, and still is potentially acting as well to try to find what his destiny might be, albeit "before it gets too late." Clearly, it seems to be late indeed, but perhaps not yet *too* late. Again, though, what might "my destiny" amount to, and how might this be found?

What, moreover, do we make of the fatalistic to deterministic connotations of "destiny"–seemingly something is destined for the narrator-protagonist, perhaps even 'predestined', and therefore, seemingly, he is not referring to what that he chooses, decides, wills, and creates for himself. But the emphasis here both on finding this destiny, and the fear the narrator-protagonist will not find it, suggests that 'he', and seemingly others of us as well, all have destinies that have, in effect, been '(pre-)written for us', by forces outside of and beyond our control, but we have to work long and hard, and with certainly no guarantee of success, to find these destinies, and to fulfill them, which suggests in turn many of us end up never finding, and never realizing, our destinies.

We might translate 'destiny' into 'best possible life' or 'most meaningful and worthwhile existence', and that might help clarify. This is a common quest, and one a great many people all too often feel as if they are failing on, or have failed in, while all too many people also all too often feel as if (or aren't even able to begin to contemplate the fact that) this prospect has been eliminated for them, from the get go, due to the social positions, conditions, and circumstances into which they are born, and from where they grew up–i.e., that real social mobility is extremely rare, and that far more people than often acknowledged lead lives focused overwhelmingly just on the struggle for bare survival, and merely to keep going for a single another day, day to day, twenty-four hours at a time.

***

Let's now discuss the musical sounds, patterns of sounds, and deployments of sounds that comprise "Twenty Four Hours," proceeding through the same stages of description and analysis as with "Disorder" and "Transmission." As with both of those two songs I propose paying close attention to the musical sounds, patterns of sounds, and deployments of sounds that comprise "Twenty Four Hours" will help in determining which possible directions in interpreting this song, as an entire song, and not just a written title and five stanzas of lyrics, make the most compelling good sense.

Here is how I hear the structure of the song, in what I identify as thirteen consecutive sections:

1: Introduction, Initial Establishing and Sketching the Broad Contours of the Introspective Scene (0:00-0:26). Bass guitar introduces initial melodic line, drums and cymbals quickly enter with pronounced emphasis on the hi-hat, and subsequently an initial scratching guitar line follows.

2: Rapid Rise in Intensity as Approach Initial Concentrated Stage of Introspective Confrontation/Examination/Reflection (0:27-0:44). Rise in pitch and volume of bass guitar line, switch of guitar line from scratching to soaring and flaring with rise as well in volume and sustain, drumming adds tom rolls and more frequent snare and bass drum strikes, and the overall tempo increases.

3: Initial Concentrated Stage of Introspective Confrontation/Examination/Reflection–State of High Tension/High Energy Desperation (0:45-1:09). First vocal passage with slight clearing to make room for the vocal, and yet instrumentation, volume, and tempo continues otherwise as in the preceding section.

4: Quieter Introspection, Deeper Mediation, Preparation for Further Concentrated Introspective Confrontation/Examination/Reflection (1:10-1:15). Brief quieter interlude, as guitar drops out, tempo slows down, volume decreases, and bass guitar pitch returns to initial interval range.

5: First More Quietly Meditative/Melancholic/Plaintive Concentrated Stage of Introspective Confrontation/Examination/Reflection–State of Temporarily Lowered Tension/Low Energy Desperation (1:16-1:42). Second vocal passage, guitar switches to scratching pattern, drums and cymbals switch to initial pattern, bass guitar continues resumption of pattern working initial pitch interval range, and overall tempo continues return to initial pace.

6: Rapid Rise in Intensity as Approach Second Concentrated Stage of Heightened Introspective Confrontation/Examination/Reflection (1:43-1:58). Transition to increased density in instrumental bridge, with bass guitar once again rising in pitch and volume, guitar once again returning to soaring and flaring pattern, drums once again returning to adding tom rolls as well as more frequent strikes on the snare and bass drums, as well as the overall tempo, volume, and density of instrumentation also increasing one again.

7: Second Concentrated Stage of Heightened Introspective Confrontation/Examination/ Reflection–State of High Tension/High Energy Desperation (1:59-2:24). Third vocal passage with slight clearing to make room for the vocal as instrumentation including density of instrumentation, volume, and tempo otherwise continues the same from the preceding section.

8: Further Quieter Introspection, Deeper Meditation, Preparation for Further Concentrated Introspective Confrontation/Examination/Reflection (2:25-2:44). Guitar drops out and then returns with a softer chiming as well as scratching meets fluttering pattern, drums and cymbals switch to initial pattern, bass drum returns to initial pitch interval range, overall volume decreases, and overall tempo returns to initial pace.

9: Second More Quietly Meditative/Melancholic/Plaintive Concentrated Stage of Introspective Confrontation/Examination/Reflection–State of Temporarily Lowered Tension/Low Energy Desperation (2:45-3:09). Fourth vocal passage with instrumentation, including density of instrumentation, volume, and tempo otherwise continuing as in preceding section.

10: Rapid Rise in Intensity as Approach Stage of Heightened Confrontation/Examination/ Reflection (3:10-3:12). At end of fourth vocal passage, soaring and flaring guitar pattern returns along with drum pattern involving tom rolls and more frequent strikes on the snare and bass drums, as well as rise in pitch and volume of the bass guitar, and increase in overall tempo, volume, and density of instrumentation.

11: Yet Even Further Rising in Intensity (3:13-3:27) Continuing instrumental bridge, continuing while accelerating patterns (re)introduced in preceding section.

12: Third Concentrated Stage of Heightened Introspective Confrontation/Examination/ Reflection–State of High Tension/High Energy Desperation (3:28-3:53). Fifth and final vocal passage with instrumentation otherwise continuing as in sections 10 and 11.

13: Dropping Off and Closing Out–Suspension of Tension (3:54-4:25). Reduction in tempo, volume, and density of instrumentation as vocal first drops out, then the guitar, a final keyboard figure plays, and the drumming returns to its initial pattern before shifting as does the bass guitar to a final close-out pattern.

What is particularly striking here is the ebb and flow we hear in terms of relative density of instrumentation, loudness, and tempo. This structure helps support an interpretation of this song as enacting an introspective drama that undergoes multiple successive movements, developments, or waves of confrontation, examination, and reflection, as well as multiple successive movements, developments, or waves of rising and falling tension as the music as persona proceeds through this process of introspective confrontation, examination, and reflection. The rise in pitch in the bass guitar line is a key component of each movement from ebb to flow, and it is also worth noting that all of the following instruments alternate between two principal rhythmic patterns, with slight variations in each, that correspond to alternating passages of ebb and flow: the bass guitar, the drums and cymbals, and the guitar. The vocal remains more consistent between these two kinds of passages, although it encompasses some differences as well, which I will describe shortly.

The bass guitar introduces and plays an initial melodic line that it then pushes strikingly up in pitch at the end of each 'ebb' passage, proceeding with each 'flow' passage to sound a second melodic line that represents a close variation upon the initial melodic line, and then moves back and forth between the two patterns before introducing a final variation at the end of the song. In sum, the bass guitar elaborates, sustains, and repeatedly sounds an initial melodic line with one significant and several slight variations over the course of the entire song, and it plays a signal role in marking the switch from ebb to flow.

The initial guitar sound represents a narrow low scratching sound that also might well be described as resembling a sputtering or a stuttering line. Then in 'flow' passages the guitar sounds a soaring and flaring pattern, among a sharply limited number of chords, with long decay, sustain, and release, as well as a slight general downward movement in pitch. Near the end of these denser (flow) passages the guitar introduces a chiming sound in the chords with each of the notes resounding across the strings, leading into the less dense (ebb) passages. And in subsequent denser passages the guitar seems to oscillate or pulsate slightly more although not across any significantly larger pitch interval. Later variations, in ebb passages, repeat or resemble the initial scratching line, although at these later stages this sounds more like plucking and fluttering. Nearing the end of the song it sounds as if the guitar concludes by briefly playing a few scattered notes.

The keyboard figure at the end of the song amounts to a variation on the initial melody, higher in pitch, emphasizing a minor key, which references and reinforces minor chords that the guitar has previously emphasized.

The drums and cymbals patterns are elaborate, with the initial pattern involving a pronounced emphasis on hi-hat strikes, usually twice on each beat, along with alternating snare and bass drum strikes occurring at somewhat odd points within the four principal beats of a measure, including on the up strike with the measure divided into eight eighth notes. The hi-hat strikes are open but a closed hi-hat strike, resembling a light crash, takes place half-way through every second measure. Subsequently, in the 'flow' passages of the song, the drums and cymbals pattern changes so that each hypermeasure begins with sixteenth notes on a high tom followed by sixteenth notes on a mid tom, more regular and frequent snare strikes, and a repeated series of five successive closed hi-hat strikes, as well as additional bass drum strikes following a more regular pattern, nearing the end of these passages. Adding to the elaborateness I just described, a second snare drum joins approximately mid-way through each 'ebb' passage to contribute further complexity to the overall rhythm.

The vocal maintains a relatively short interval range, with a characteristically long sustain and then pause at the end of and before the beginning of lines, along with a tendency to hold and extend words, and parts of words, at the end of phrases and at the end of lines. The vocal pattern pursues a slightly upward movement in pitch followed by a slightly greater downward movement, while often staying for pronounced periods at or close to the same pitch. In less dense sections of the song the vocal sounds as if it conveys a fuller and richer texture, with more delicate nuance than in the denser passages, whereas, in those latter passages, the vocal seems all the more thoroughly drenched in reverb. The vocal sounds as if it has been treated and processed to seem distanced but not quite as far as in the case "Transmission." In 'ebb' passages the vocal conveys a gentle melancholic feeling. The last set of vocals sound as if the vocal timbre has been altered once again, hollowed and echoed even further than previously. And unlike with "Disorder" and "Transmission," we experience no jumping to a higher pitch range, no pushing and straining to reach higher, at the end of the song, although we do hear a roughened emphasis placed on the final word in each of the 'flow' passages.

In "Twenty Four Hours" I recognize an explicit beat layer although this is complicated because of the irregular pattern employed here, in particular in relation to the bass and snare drums, as well as with the hi-hat alternating between predominantly open strikes and periodic closed strikes that occur mid-measure every two measures or five times in immediate succession, and with the drums and cymbals pursuing two principal patterns that each include slight variations. As Allan F. Moore and Remy Martin explain in *Rock: The Primary Text–Developing a Musicology of Rock*, the "standard rock beat" involves the bass drum sounding once on beats one and three, the snare drum sounding once on beats two and four, and a cymbal, especially a hi-hat, sounding twice on each beat, while the beginnings and the endings of verses and choruses are typically marked by a density of events, or fills, especially on the snare (38). In "Twenty Four Hours" the closest to the last is the rolls on the toms that Stephen Morris plays in 'flow' passages, while Morris's snare and bass drums patterns in this song clearly depart from "the standard rock beat."

Continuing, however, with the functional layers, "Twenty Four Hours" contains a functional bass layer with the bass guitar a prominent presence throughout, but once again the bass guitar is also playing the initial melodic line with subsequent slight variations, and thereby the bass guitar contributes significantly to the melodic layer as well, in conjunction with the vocal, which assumes the lead in sounding the principal melodic line whenever it, the vocal, is present.

We do here also recognize a harmonic fill layer, principally provided by guitar, and this is the guitar's entire role in this song, as the guitar does not contribute para-melodies, although the final keyboard figure does. The guitar contributes harmonic fill via two principal patterns, again with slight variations: first, the scratching meets sputtering meets stuttering meets scraping pattern, which as the song proceeds eventually sounds closer to a chiming meets plucking meets fluttering sound, and, second, the soaring and flaring pattern.

I hear these layers as relatively co-dominant while I hear the explicit beat layer as prominent and the bass guitar, as aforementioned, prominent early on and in leading transitions from ebb to flow. With "Twenty Four Hours" the placement and corresponding roles of all the principal instruments throughout the course of song in relation to which functional layer they are occupying and what they are contributing as part of that layer is much that same as with "Disorder" and "Transmission." Key differences are as follows: where the vocal line ends up, rather than rising significantly in pitch near the end of the song; a more prominent hi-hat sound as well as a more irregular bass and snare drum pattern; the lack of guitar para-melodies; and no overt synthesizer oddities. Once again, though, we hear a bass guitar sounding high on the fretboard, playing the melody, and a vocal notably darkened, reverberant, and echoed.

In terms of the soundbox, the bass guitar enters low and to the left. The drums and cymbals enter higher and closer to the center on both sides. The guitar enters low and to the right. The bass guitar and the guitar both seem to rise as we anticipate the vocal, as the guitar and drum patterns shift, and as density, volume, and tempo increase. The vocal enters dead center, but as it quiets down, in 'ebb passages', it seems to resonate both from slightly to the left and slightly to the right of center. The drums feel closer to the front than any other instrument, including the vocal, but the vocal feels positioned higher. The drums come across as more prominent overall than any other sound source in terms of location, both close to the front and the center. The bass guitar appears to be located notably lower down and to the left than in "Disorder" and "Transmission" while the guitar likewise appears to be located notably lower down and to the right than in those previous two songs. I suggest this overall placement conveys to us as listeners a greater sense of confinement and claustrophobia with less imaginable room or hope for escape than with "Disorder" and "Transmission." Echo and reverberation appear most prominent with the vocal, although the soaring and flaring guitar patterns as well as the closed hi-hat strikes decay, sustain, and release relatively slowly. Initially the bass guitar and the drums and cymbals are the most prominent, but then the vocal and the guitar join and assert themselves as roughly equal in prominence to the bass and drums. Change happens, when it does, in terms of perceived positioning of sounds within the soundbox, primarily by means of a slight pushing upward, a slight pushing closer to the center, and a slight movement closer to the front in the denser 'flow' passages of the song.

Depending on the density of the instrumentation, changes in loudness are pronounced in "Twenty Four Hours," corresponding to the previously identified thirteen sections of this song as follows with A, B, C, and D marking out four distinct patterns in terms of relative loudness:

1: Relatively Quieter [A]

2: Quickly Louder [B]

3: Relatively Louder [C]

4: Relatively Quieter [D]

5: Relatively Quieter [D]

6: Quickly Louder [B]

7: Relatively Louder [C]

8: Relatively Quieter [D]

9: Relatively Quieter [D]

10: Quickly Louder [B]

11: Relatively Louder [C]

12: Relatively Louder [C]

13: Relatively Quieter [E]

It is interesting that passages of relative loudness versus relative quiet do not correspond simply with passages where the vocal is sounding or where it is not, as both vocal and non-vocal passages are alternately relatively loud and relatively quiet. Key drivers of increased loudness are the guitar and the drums and the cymbals. But the bass guitar also plays a key role in initiating this increase in combination with a simultaneous increase in tempo. This pattern of variations in terms of overall loudness suggests wavering moments within an introspective confrontation/examination/ reflection that is directly connected with a growing sense of desperation meets despair. The music as persona, the narrator-protagonist of the lyrics, and I myself (insofar as I identify with and join the music as persona, and the narrator-protagonist, as a co-protagonist) increasingly worry that reason for hope may not still exist, that recovery may not still be possible, that what failed previously amounts to a final dead end, and that the situation confronting us has become irremediable. And yet, with this alternating sound pattern, the song comes across as not ready to acquiesce to total defeat: it keeps picking up once again, pressing forward once again, and seeking once more to regain vital–and indeed revitalizing–momentum on the way toward a possible rejuvenation of (the) life-spirit. This alternating sound pattern attests to the dignity and worth of the subject undergoing this experience, and is even suggestive of a kind of grandeur in this subject's experience of suffering and struggling.

"Twenty Four Hours" follows a 4/4 time signature and when the tempo increases, at least according to my estimate, it increases from 132 to 139 bpm, or perhaps slightly faster. Recognizing that all the instruments contribute to the rhythm (the overall patterned movement of repetition and variation across the duration of the song), let's begin, unlike with "Disorder" and "Transmission," not with the drums and cymbals but rather with the guitar. In this song Bernard Sumner primarily follows an eighth notes strumming pattern while he varies over the course of the song how long he continues playing one chord before moving onto the next–1/4 a measure before making a change and then two measures before making a change. Even more noteworthy is Sumner's shift between two distinct patterns: a scratching and scraping pattern on the one hand and a soaring and flaring pattern on the other hand. The former pattern conveying a rapidly oscillating sound while the latter conveys a less rapid but nonetheless perceptively pulsating sound. Sumner affects the sound by how he strums a single chord, which can have something to do with how fast versus slowly he strums as well as whether or not he mutes the sound, likely with his palm, and by where on his fretboard he plays as well as with what effects devices he employs to modify his guitar's sound. The soaring and flaring pattern first enters in the 17th bar and continues to play through the end of 43rd bar; it second enters in the 60th bar and continues to play through the end of the 87th bar; it third enters 3/4 of way through bar 109 and continues to play through bar 137; and then it enters one last time, softer, in bars 142 through 148. The scratching meets scraping sound largely consists of sixteenth notes, while the soaring meets flaring pattern largely consists of eighth notes with occasional whole notes and later, at the very end, quarter notes.

Peter Hook, on the bass guitar, primarily plays eighth notes as well, especially in the parts of the melodic line that resonate most distinctly, although he regularly alternates these with quarter, half, and whole notes, especially at the beginning of measures. It seems like we hear the following bass guitar patterns within the course of a single measure (not in this order, per se, as these seven patterns of length of notes per measure are periodically repeated and intermixed):

1.   One half note + four eighth notes

2.   Two eighth notes + one quarter note + one half note

3.   One quarter note + six eighth notes

4.   One whole note

5.   Three quarter notes + two eighth notes

6.   Two eighth notes + one quarter note + four eighth notes

7.   Eight eighth notes

Hook's bass guitar, moreover, follows what I hear as six hypermetrical patterns, involving combinations of the aforementioned seven per-measure patterns, across a series of anywhere from two to twelve measures. These consist of distinct hypermetrical patterns at the beginning of the song, at the end, for 'flow' sections, for 'ebb' sections, for sections following flow and preceding ebb, and for sections following ebb and preceding flow.

Ian Curtis usually starts singing a vocal passage after an initial rest to open a measure, often extends notes across measures with tied notes included both within and across measures, and usually ends a line with an extended note or sequence of tied notes as well as with a further and longer rest before resuming singing the next vocal line. Curtis often appears to wait until the first beat has sounded before entering. Most often he sings eighth notes, although periodically he sings quarter and sixteenth notes as well, and the final notes in lines he often extends longer than that. Curtis periodically accents the end of phrases mid-way through lines as well as the final word in each stanza, especially in the case of stanzas involving a denser, louder, and faster 'flow' as opposed to the less dense, softer, and slower 'ebb' passages.

Turning, last, to Stephen Morris's drums and cymbals, what I find noteworthy in his contribution to the rhythm of "Twenty Four Hours" is this involves several distinct patterns with the bass drum and snare drum that depart from when and how often these sound as part of a standard rock beat. The bass drum initially sounds on an up eighth note as often if not more than on a down eighth note and the snare initially sounds on beats 1 and 4 with the bass drum initially sounding on beats 2 and 3. Later, in the second drum kit pattern, the snare drum sounds on every beat, including periodically twice on beats 2, 3, and 4, while the toms start these series of measures by playing eight sixteenth notes which the snare then immediately follows with quarter notes on beats 3 and 4. The first pattern incorporates a four-measure hypermetre with a closed hi-hat in the middle of the first measure, and otherwise open hi hat strikes on virtually every other eighth note within this sequence of typically two measures. In the second series, more closed high-hat strikes follow directly in succession after rolls on the toms and the snare, typically five closed hi-hat strikes in a row. Interestingly, both early on and later in the song, Morris adds a side snare strike (likely via an electronic snare drum) to coincide with the hi-hat. Here's something of a mapping out of two principal repeated hypermetrical patterns I detect with // representing the end of one measure and the beginning of the next and with . . . representing a series of beats or partial beats in which the particular drum or cymbal is not sounding:

1.
HH (Hi-Hat): 1 and 2 crash 3 and 4 and//1 and 2 and 3 and 4 and
SD (Snare Drum): 1 . . . 4// . . .
SSD (Side Snare Drum): . . . // . . . 1and, 2, 2and . . .
BD (Bass Drum): . . . 2and . . . 3and . . . //. . . 3 . . . 4and

2.
HH: 1 and 2 and 3 crash crash crash crash crash//1 and 2 and 3 and 4 and//1 and 2 and 3 and 4 and//1 and 2 and 3 and 4 and
SD: 1 . . . 2 2and 3 3and 4 4and//. . . 3 . . . 4//1 . . . 2 . . . 3 . . . 4//1 . . . 2 . . . 3 . . . 4 . . .
HFT (High Floor Tom): . . . //1 ee and uh . . . //. . . //. . .
MT (Mid Tom) : . . . //. . . 2 ee and uh . . . //. . . //. . .
BD: . . . //. . . //. . . //. . .

3.
HH: 1 and 2 and 3 and 4 and//1 and 2 crash 3 and 4 and//1 and 2 and 3 and 4 and//1 and 2 crash 3 and 4 and
SD: . . . //1 . . . 4//. . . //1 . . . 4
SSD: . . . //. . . //. . . 1and 2 2and . . . //. . . //. . .
HFT: 1 ee and uh . . . //. . . //. . . //. . .
MT: . . . 2 ee and uh . . . //. . . //. . . //. . .
BD: . . . 3 4//. . . 2and . . . 3and . . . //. . . 3 4//. . . 2and . . . 3and . . .

In sum, each principal instrument contributes at least two distinctive metrical and hypermetrical patterns, and these are regular and recurrent but also regularly and recurrently alternating as well as encompassing slight variations. Each of these patterns fits well with interpreting "Twenty Four Hours" as involving successive stages of ebb and flow, as well as corresponding waves of confrontation, examination, and reflection, along with multiple likewise corresponding waves of rising and falling tension as the music as persona proceeds through a process of introspective confrontation, examination, and reflection. At the same time, however, even as each of the four principals follow this larger macro pattern, the micro details of how they do so vary as each of the four musicians develops–and elaborates–distinctive sequences of lengths and accents within and across short increments as part of each ebb and flow.

I already pinpointed one of the most dramatic changes in pitch in "Twenty Four Hours," with the bass guitar rising in pitch as the song transitions from 'ebb' to 'flow' and this is, at least as I analyze it, a movement from D to A#. Over the course of the song, the bass guitar plays the following notes: G string 10th fret = F, G string 9th fret = E, G string 7th fret = D, G string 5th fret = C, G string 0 frets = G, G string 12ᵗʰ fret = G, G string 15ᵗʰ fret = A#, and D string 10ᵗʰ fret = C. An initial sequence involves the following movements: slowly steadily rising, then at the end quickly falling, followed by slowly steadily rising, then quickly falling, and then quickly as well as substantially rising. After that the next movements tend to fall slowly but steadily, except at the very end of the song where a slowly steadily rising then quickly falling movement once more recurs. So in sum the initial melodic pattern the bass guitar introduces and repeats ends down in pitch from where it started after rising slowly and slightly but then quickly moving down, while the transition to flow sections of the song involve a dramatic rise in pitch into the next section. Variations in pitch from that point forward include a slightly higher initial rise in pitch and a slightly lower concluding fall in pitch, as well as a falling, twice, in pitch at end of a riff. Peter Hook's bass guitar moves up and then down further, not remaining static in pitch, while frequently starting off each successive riff on the same opening pitch, then rising slightly, and then quickly dropping slightly further down. In transitions to sections involving increased density, volume, and tempo, Hook introduces and carries this transition with a culminating greater movement than over the preceding course of the riff, by rising upward in pitch. Size of pitch intervals is relatively small but significant nonetheless, especially the increased interval size in the risings that transition to denser, louder, and faster sections. Overall the bass guitar pitch is located relatively high within the range of possibilities for the bass guitar–i.e., relatively high on the fretboard.

The hi-hat is pitched higher than the snare and bass drums, while both of the latter sound close in pitch. The toms are pitched lower than the hi-hat although between the hi-hat and the snare and bass, with a notable difference in pitch heard in moving from the high tom to the mid tom. Closed hi-hat strikes, closer to cymbal crashes, allow the pitch to sustain slightly longer, and also seem to rise slightly in pitch as they do so. It also seems as if Stephen Morris (with the assistance of Martin Hannett) is able to incorporate more micro-variations in pitch among hi-hat strikes than in snare and bass drum strikes. The second snare drum helps amplify and echo the pitch of the hi-hat. In terms of noticeable movements in pitch, with the toms through the snare rolls, I hear a marked movement down in pitch while with the most prominent hi-hat series I hear a move slightly up in pitch. I do hear a marked pitch interval difference as well between the open and closed hi-hat strikes with the closed hi-hat strikes adding a punctuating feeling.

Am, Dm, and D7sus2 (D dominant 7ᵗʰ suspended 2ⁿᵈ) appear to be the three principal chords Bernard Sumner plays in "Twenty Four Hours." Movements typically follow between Am and Dm, between Dm and Am, between Dm and D7sus2, and between D7sus2 and Dm. The general pattern of movement is an oscillating, back and forth. The initial scratching meets scraping meets scuttering meets stuttering pattern involves a concentrated pitch interval, although seemingly alternating between two principal locations. The second soaring meets flaring pattern involves a longer sustaining and slower releasing sounding of each pitch, that again moves between two principal pitches, slightly upward, and then slightly down, in the course of a single riff. The chiming meets floating meets plucking pattern, which constitutes a variation on the initial scratching meets scraping meets scuttering meets stuttering pattern, seems more quickly cut off and limited in its decay and sustain, while ultimately tending slightly downward in pitch. In sum, what I hear from the guitar is a general tendency ultimately to move slightly down in pitch but with ample oscillation and persistent risings nonetheless on the way toward doing so, while during the soaring meets flaring pattern the guitar maintains close to the same pitch level for prolonged periods. Especially in climactic moments, I hear a long sustain at a single pitch level, with a greater emphasis, ultimately, downward, although this downward movement is preceded by a movement upward.

In terms of Ian Curtis's vocal, I hear the following:

1st pattern–enters and stays at same initial pitch level, then moves slightly down, then moves back to the initial level, then moves slightly up from the initial pitch level, then moves back to the initial pitch level, then moves into an even slightly briefer rise from the initial pitch level, and then moves down once more to the initial pitch level.

2nd pattern–enters and stays at the same initial pitch level, then moves very slightly up in pitch, then returns to the initial pitch level, then moves very slightly up in pitch, with a suggestion of a very slight dip approximately mid-way through this last movement, and then returns back to the initial pitch level.

3rd pattern–enters and stays at the same initial pitch level, then moves slightly down in pitch, then moves back to the initial pitch level, then moves slightly up in pitch, then moves into an even slightly briefer rise in pitch, and then moves back down to the initial pitch level.

4th pattern–enters and stays at the same initial pitch level, then moves very slightly up in pitch, then returns to the initial pitch level, then moves very slightly up in pitch, with a suggestion of a very slight dip approximately mid-way through this last movement, and then returns back to initial pitch level.

5th pattern–enters and stays at the same initial pitch level, then rises at the end of the phrase; then repeats; then repeats; then repeats; then repeats; then repeats; then repeats; then repeats; and then with the final phrase stays all at the initial pitch level with no final rise in pitch.

So what we have here is a general, slight, recurrent tendency upward in pitch that is always rapidly followed by a return down to an initial pitch level within a tight interval range and a tight overall trajectory of movement across pitches within this range. I hear considerable confinement to an initial pitch level, with a frequent return to this level after slight movements up and down as well as after slightly more pronounced and sustained upward movements. In terms of the relative size of these movements, they amount to a third or a fourth at most, but even more often less than that.

The final keyboard figure moves up and down, between two pitches, but ultimately down, while sounding as if it covers a slightly larger pitch interval range than the soaring to flaring guitar pattern.

Let's proceed next to consider Ian Curtis's vocal delivery in "Twenty Four Hours." Overall it sounds as if Curtis is largely singing low register and, again, across a limited range of pitches, but the degree of resonance of the pitches he sings is high, and even increases as the song progresses, aided by reverb and echo treatment of his recorded voice. As with "Disorder" and "Transmission," in "Twenty Four Hours" I hear Curtis's 'attitude toward pitch' as not strictly bound by it, although always remaining closely around it, yet ready to slide and glide around exact pitches, both slightly sharp and slightly flat, although especially slightly flat, and especially at the ends of phrases and lines. Besides reverb and echo I do detect double-tracking, especially in 'ebb' passages of the song as well as potentially other filtering treatment of Curtis's vocal timbre along with careful attention to where his vocal is positioned within the mix–and within the soundbox. Curtis's voice here comes across most often as a gentle, wistful, tired, yet intensely contemplative crooning. This vocal never ventures all that close to sung speech or sprechesgang, and I would not mistake this vocal for anyone speaking. Curtis's voice is always clearly audible and readily accessible, and he does incorporate a harsher emphasis at the very end of vocal passages. Beyond this, I hear ample characteristic slidings and glidings, especially at the end of phrases and lines.

In terms of what I hear as the singer's felt attitude to the words he is singing I hear him as careful, precise, yet simultaneously involved and detached, while also despairing, numb, bitter, angry, sad, wistful, and residually defiant. I also hear a felt attitude of almost moving past and beyond what the words reference, while continuing nonetheless to feel the intensity, the urgency, and the desperation of the situation at hand yet at the same time able to engage in a contemplative, reflective, ruminative, and meditative stance. In terms of what I hear as the singer's felt attitude to the context of the song as a whole, the other instruments and sound sources involved, and the overall structure and movement of the song, especially in denser, louder, and faster passages, I hear the singer as recognizing, adjusting to, and aligning with this density, loudness, and fast motion.

Otherwise I hear the singer recognizing where space has been cleared for him to enter, while he also allows space at the end and before the beginnings of lines to make room in turn for the other instruments to connect their sounds, and the suggestions these encompass, with the sound of his voice, and the suggestions this in turn encompasses. In other words, I hear the singer claiming his own position within the song while not directly coinciding with the positions of any of the other principal contributors. I hear the singer as almost ready to push the rest to the side while retaining broad awareness of their co-presence as and while he is singing.

In terms of what I hear as the singer's felt attitude to the suggested or implied content of the song I hear a combination of deep investment and slow detachment from investment, and an overarching retrospective feeling, or in other words a feeling as if his time is past and it is now past too late to do anything about what he is describing and to which he is alluding with the future highly uncertain and the present full of foreboding. Again, this attitude comes across to me a wistful, plaintive, sorrowful, and with notable elements of bitterness and exhaustion. And yet I also detect an undercurrent of remnant commitment to continue to struggle.

Allan F. Moore and Remy Martin, in *Rock: The Primary Text–Developing a Musicology of Rock,* discuss resonance as equivalent to the distance from a colorless tone, and this includes vibrato, richness of voice in relation to a vocal register, whether this resonates in the nasal cavity or the chest, and whether sound seems to emanate from the throat or diaphragm, with all of this contributing to what Roland Barthes influentially identifies as "the *grain* of the voice" (45). As Moore and Martin elaborate, "Attitude to pitch is best considered against an abstract norm of tempered pitches (the only ones an in-tune piano can sound), while attitude to rhythm is a factor of both syncopation (anticipation of and delaying behind the beat), and the ways the beat is subdivided" (45). Examples here include sliding up to the pitch and use of audible sighs and intakes of breath (47) as well as a sense of straining in summoning great effort to convey intense emotion (48). As I discussed earlier in this chapter, by way of Tiffany Naiman's "In a Lonely Place: Illness and the Temporal Exile of Ian Curtis," Martin Hannett's production eliminated the breathiness and the sighing in Curtis's singing from recorded versions while also covering that over with reverb and echo, along with filtering and thereby yet further modifying the timbre of Curtis's recorded voice, but we do hear a frequent tendency to slide and glide around pitch, as well as a frequent syncopated relationship to the beat, with Curtis characteristically carrying sounded pitches across beats, and measures, and beginning lines following rests as well as concluding lines with rests. Straining can happen even when, unlike at the end of "Disorder" and "Transmission," Curtis is not pushing to the top of his vocal range at the end of the song but nonetheless struggling forthrightly to express words that carry a heavy emotional weight.

In *Song Means: Analysing and Interpreting Recorded Popular Song* Allan F. Moore discusses a number of further issues to take into consideration when analyzing and interpreting vocals, and these include embellishment, width (i.e. uses of changes of register), melisma, rubato, and glissando (105). Via Jo Estill, Moore, further, identifies "six discreet vocal parameters, with most voices being a combination of these six parameters" (105), and these include opera, twang, belt, speech, falsetto, and sob–as well as 'heightened speech' (107), while what is of principal importance is "appropriateness" of the use of the kind of voice to the expression that is voiced (107). Melisma refers to singing one syllable across a series of multiple notes, a run of notes, such as five or six distinct notes per single syllable. Ian Curtis typically doesn't extend that far, but frequently does sing a single syllable across two to three notes, especially at the end of phrases and in particular at the end of lines. Rubato refers to stretching or compacting beats, measures, and phrases for expressive effect, and again, although not doing this too far, Ian Curtis nevertheless does often stretch words, syllables, and phrases across beats and measures for expressive effect, once more especially at the end of phrases and in particular at the end of lines. He also periodically, and notably in this song, following the overall shifts in tempo the song encompasses, slows down and speeds up his delivery. Glissando refers to gliding from one pitch to another, and once more, although modest, Ian Curtis typically does glide around and between pitches quite often, and, yes, just as with melisma and rubato, especially at the end of phrases and in particular at the end of lines. The 'darkening' that Curtis pursues in achieving a deeper voice amounts to a change in width, and in "Twenty Four Hours" I hear a subtle, yet nonetheless significant difference between 'ebb' and 'flow' vocal passages, with the former more delicately and richly textured, somewhat less 'darkened' than the latter. In terms of the six parameters Moore derives from Estill, I would say Curtis's singing voice, including in "Twenty Four Hours," incorporates elements of belt, twang, sob, and heightened speech but not opera or falsetto. Of the four, twang is perhaps the most pronounced, interestingly enough, but modified sufficiently by belt, as the second most influential of these parameters in Curtis's case, so as to never come across as ever fully 'twanging', as well as yet further conditioned by the relatively equally third most influential elements of sob and heightened speech so as to convey a richer and more complex overall texture.

Turning to timbre, I suggest a useful place to start here is to take into account what Stephen Morris shares in his memoir, *Record Play Pause: Confessions of a Post-Punk Percussionist Volume I*, that with *Closer* the members of Joy Division, together with producer Martin Hannett made use of what Morris describes as a "synth arsenal" (352), which included an ARP Omni-2, a Transcendent, an ARP 2600 with sequencer, an SDS4 and a Synare (both electronic drum machines), the AMS DMX 15-80, a Marshall Time Modulator, and a Lexicon Prime Time (352). What this collectively indicates is, for their time, Joy Division, and Hannett, were able to draw on a cutting edge range of electronic music devices in developing this album and the songs on it. At Joy Division Central (https://www.joydiv.org/eqpt.htm) an even more elaborate list of equipment, including electronic equipment, is listed. Even though, in my preceding discussion of instrumentation in "Twenty Four Hours" I highlighted what I hear from bass guitar, guitar, drums and cymbals, and voice, I also mentioned a synthesizer keyboard shows up at the end, an electronic snare contributes periodically, and multiple sound sources appear to have had their timbres altered, and not just with the addition of reverb and echo, including by means of Hannett's famous and pioneering use of digital delay. It is certainly possible that even more of the distinctive sound qualities I hear, and others hear, from the 'standard' rock instruments in this song are also a result of yet further combinations with electronic instruments and yet further studio effects. It is also worth noting that Peter Hook played a six-string bass guitar as well as a four-string bass guitar on *Closer* and he also began making regular use of an Electro-Harmonix Clone Theory effects pedal. And Bernard Sumner was just as enthusiastic as Hook and Morris about trying out electronic instruments along with elaborate and at the time novel effects devices. So, all in all, a lot of experimentation as well as thought and care is invested in achieving the precise timbres of the instruments we hear in *Closer*, including in "Twenty Four Hours."

As I've mentioned with both "Disorder" and "Transmission," I am listening to a high quality slow ripped mp3 version of "Twenty Four Hours" through iTunes on an iMac, via Beyerdynamic DT 1990 Pro headphones, and with a Logitech stereo surround set of five smaller speakers (front left, front center, front right, back left, back center) and a subwoofer. The version of "Twenty Four Hours" I am listening to comes from the 2007 London Records re-mastered CD version of *Closer*.

Let's turn next to what I previously cited from Allan F. Moore as some useful considerations in analyzing timbre, starting with whether timbres betray or disguise their sources. In "Twenty Four Hours" the initial scratching meets scraping meet sputtering meets stuttering guitar line and its subsequent chiming meets floating meets plucking variation disguise their source, while it also becomes difficult periodically to perceive which specific drums and cymbals are playing, especially in combination, and especially with the addition of an electronic as well as an acoustic snare. The vocal is 'disguised' insofar as it is heavily treated. The bass guitar is not exactly 'disguised' but as I alluded to in describing the equipment Peter Hook uses on *Closer* he is able to reshape the bass guitar timbre from what otherwise would be the case. The final keyboard line, moreover, sounds close to a guitar, which raises the question of whether earlier on we might be hearing a synthesizer keyboard sounding when it at first seems like it has to be a guitar. Peter Hook has commented, in his memoir, *Unknown*

Pleasures: Inside Joy Division, that one of the fond memories he retains from his time within the band has to do with how listeners often couldn't tell precisely who was responsible for what sound, or pattern of sound, within a Joy Division recording (206). At the least, considering Moore's recommendation, in analyzing timbre, that is it also useful to consider how the instruments sound in terms of modified versus natural sources, in "Twenty Four Hours" all of the sounds from all of the principal instruments are modified by use of effects devices and with studio treatments, while electronic sounds are also added to the mix.

In terms of what class of physical gestures or movements is implied by the timbres, I've already identified, with Bernard Sumner's guitar, the following three: (1) scratching, scraping, sputtering, stuttering, and what might also just as readily be characterized as scuttling; (2) chiming, fluttering, and plucking; and (3) soaring and flaring. And the considerable differences among these guitar timbres certainly make a signal contribution to defining distinct differences in the collective timbre we hear in different sections of the song. Ian Curtis's vocal suggests concentrated, slow, careful movements, that repeatedly return to their starting point, along with a marked intensity within and across even slight increments of suggested motion. With Peter Hook's bass guitar I hear an insistent and periodic climbing that at the same time conveys something of a Sisyphean character. And with Stephen Morris's drums and cymbals I hear a propulsive yet often skittering movement as well as a racing and pounding movement that also, as with the physical gestures or movements suggested by Sumner, Curtis, and Hook, changes depending upon whether we are in an 'ebb' or 'flow' passage.

In terms of how the timbres and gestures pair up, and with what effect, especially striking pairings show up in louder, faster, denser passages, suggestive of accelerating and peaking tension. Also, the guitar lines, when not soaring and flaring, give depth and texture to otherwise quieter passages while contributing an element of disturbance at the same time. The bass guitar and drums engage in what often resembles a call and response relationship while I note a pattern of relations as well between open and closed hi hat strikes with the latter offering punctuating effects–while the toms in turn add a rolling effect.

With the drums, the hi-hat involves a longer decay, sustain, and release when closed; the snare and bass drums both are quick strikes where the attack is more pronounced than decay, sustain, or release, and the snare does sound much more like a crack than it did in "Disorder" and "Twenty Four Hours" and as such closer in timbre to the bass drum. The toms convey more sustain than the snare or bass drums, and feel overall more resonant than the latter drums.

With the bass guitar I hear a certain thickness, and I also hear slight elements of muddiness and fuzziness but overall the tone remains fairly clean. The bass guitar's sustain and release I hear as especially notable, in comparison with its attack and decay. Meanwhile, with the guitar the soaring and flaring sounds seem bright yet hard while the other patterns seem strikingly percussive. The vocal sounds dark, often reverberant and echoing, and even hollowed out. It sounds as if much of the force comes from higher in the body, in the upper larynx and the back of throat as well as the roof of mouth, in combination with slight contributions from the chest. The vocal sounds higher in register than in "Transmission," more like a low tenor than in the latter song. Light gliding, sliding, and floating along with pronounced reverberation and extension of vocalization at the ends of phrases and lines also contributes notably to timbre as does hardening around the final word in each vocal passage. In faster, louder, and denser passages the vocal sounds more echoing, and more hollowed out, than in the slower, quieter, and less dense passages where it sounds gentler, softer, and more wistful.

None of the instruments sound to me as gritty as on "Transmission," while neither the voice nor the guitar sound as rough as on "Transmission." The vocal is the harshest at the end of passages, while otherwise not much so; the guitar is harshest with the scratching and plucking patterns; and I don't hear either the bass guitar or the drums and cymbals as harsh. I hear the guitar soars and flares as bright but not much else comes across as bright in timbre in this song. In terms of distortion I may be hearing some, perhaps, on the guitar, but not as much as with "Transmission," while in terms of clarity the vocal is clear even when sounding muffled/hollowed/echoed, the bass guitar is clear whenever playing by itself, and the toms and the hi-hat are also notably clear.

The high register the bass guitar works in, is also a notable timbral element, including in riffs that reach higher, while reverb and echo are likewise so, in relation to the voice. Indeed, more than with "Disorder" and "Transmission," especially in 'flow' passages, it makes good sense to describe the voice in "Twenty Four Hours" as 'drenched' in reverb–and in echo.

I don't hear any of the timbres in "Twenty Four Hours" as cold, although cool makes sense. I do detect elements of warmth here and there with the voice, with the guitar, and especially with the bass guitar. I hear richness in the voice in the 'ebb' passages, while I also hear richness in the timbre of the bass guitar, and across the drums and cymbals. The drums and cymbals sound the most vigorous, with the guitar the next most so.

Considering yet further comments timbral descriptors, the guitar is not as thick as in "Transmission" while the bass guitar is not as thin. The voice sounds thin when also sounding hollowed out–in the 'flow' passages. I hear an element of wetness with the timbre of the drums and cymbals, especially the open hi hat, while the guitar and the voice sound dryer and the bass guitar sounds in between.

In terms of timbre suggesting comparable kinds of bodily movements, and these kinds of bodily movements in turn offering useful ways to characterize what these timbres sound like, the bass guitar's timbre suggests a persistent, intent climbing; the guitar alternatively scratching, scraping, spluttering, stuttering, and spelunking versus chiming, floating, and plucking versus soaring and flaring movements; the voice slow, careful, circular yet intense movements; and the drums and cymbals a steadily propulsive but often irregular movement.

Next, trying something different next versus what I did in discussing timbre with "Disorder" and "Transmission," the visual colors I associate with the timbres of the instruments in "Twenty Four Hours" are as follows: Ian Curtis's voice is burnt orange; Peter Hook's bass guitar is vivid, richly saturated, reddish brown; Bernard Sumner's guitar is alternately metallic gray, a desaturated blend of yellow orange and green, and an evanescent light purple; Stephen Morris's bass and snare drums are shades of darker gray than the metallic gray I associate with Sumner's guitar, his hi-hat is off-white, and his toms are light gray.

In terms of how these timbres might be suggestive of characters, or character types, and of this comparison in turn proving potentially useful, once again, in getting us closer to precisely distinguishing timbres, I hear Ian Curtis's vocal as suggestive of a melancholic and tired yet persistent character, who is continuing to struggle but doing so with limited albeit tightly concentrated energy; I hear Peter Hook's bass guitar as suggestive of a committed, determined, yet also intense and driven character; I hear Bernard Sumner's guitar as suggestive of a wildly and widely inconsistent character who moves around a lot including from the forefront to the background, as he both calls attention to himself and avoids calling attention to himself, and is eccentric, idiosyncratic, and alternately restless and restful; and I hear Stephen Morris's drums and cymbals as suggestive of an impassioned and engaged yet also impatient and demanding character.

Pursuing the last comparison yet further, I hear Peter Hook's bass guitar as suggestive of someone who is insistent as well as persistent, who is not certain he is yet being heard and paid heed, who is trying recurrently to circle around and point to, to remind us of, something of central, crucial, and pivotal importance, that feels like a warning and also like he is indicating at same time he has already been warning us of this repeatedly. This is a character who I also hear as addressing what it is and has been like to bear with and through repeated cycles and spirals of tightly structured and especially tightly regulated activity as well as how confining, constraining, and tiring these can feel, with elements of a compassionate and empathetic recognition of what it is like for many others to endure the same, while also asserting the possibility nonetheless of achieving some at least partial sense of liberation within the limits of what these structures allow. This character resembles a slightly more seasoned or experienced mentor or guardian but also one not far removed from the same position of those for whom he is serving as mentor or guardian, and who indeed continues to experience much the same challenges directly himself. In other words, this character resembles a slightly older and more experienced student, working perhaps as a teaching assistant.

Following this same line of comparison, I hear Stephen Morris's drums and cymbals as suggestive of a character who once again is insistent, who is deliberate but also impatient, who is continually pushing and pressing, and who is persistently calling for more recognition, more respect, and a more just return for what he, and others he is ready also to represent, have given, accomplished, and even sacrificed. He resembles a meticulous but also experimental character who again is ready to push against prevailing constraints in seeking a way to make an impact according to the furthest limits of what these will allow. And he seems like an overtly performative character, for example like a student majoring in the arts.

Turning next to Bernard Sumner's guitar, I hear this as suggestive of a character who likes to operate from the margins, but also to move about and shift a lot in terms of how he presents himself and what he does. This again strikes me as a character interested in asserting his existence/presence, not being easily ignored or forgotten or dismissed, and who likes to throw himself fully into and run with situations he confronts and that he feels are engaging, to the point where he is ready to allow himself to feel as if he is converging with the time and place as well as with the situation and the demands/constraints/opportunities/and affordances at hand. But at the same time, this also seems like a character who displays a distinct element of impatience and of persistently wanting more.

Finally, Ian Curtis's vocal timbre in "Twenty Four Hours" suggests a battered and bruised character, someone who is tired and weakened, but who is still persisting, and who is trying to recreate a self-protective distance at same time as wanting and needing to share intense and extreme vulnerability, while struggling with how these two tendencies feel diametrically opposed as well as with feeling too exposed, or overexposed, yet still wanting and needing to put himself into situations where such raw exposure is inescapable.

***

Let's next proceed in interpreting "Twenty Four Hours" by considering Arnie Cox's eight avenues of musical affect. Let's begin with mimetic participation. Every increase in volume, tempo, and density feels to me like increased effort in exertion of force, especially with every rise in pitch of the bass guitar leading into 'flow' passages. In these 'flow' passages, what's more, I feel increased exertion from addition of the toms, the more frequent snare hits, the more closed hi-hat strikes in succession, and the more rapid tempo. The vocal also conveys a notable feeling of effort in exertion of force by straining with the emotional weight of the words and the larger situation to which they allude, even while not moving very far either up or down in pitch and even while not sounding a particularly elaborate series of notes or shift in volume, register, and overall mode of vocalization.

In terms of my perception of the felt complexity of the actions required to perform these sounds, including what this requires of me to imitate them, the initial guitar line and later variations feel somewhat complicated to me as do both patterns of strikes across the full array of drums and cymbals. In relation to the bass guitar my felt sense of complexity relates to the continuous series of repeated slight variations and recurrent rises in pitch involved, although I recognize these are virtually entirely played all along one string and frequently across very short intervals at that. With the vocal, my sense of complexity comes in relation to the vocal moving against as well as with the beat, finding as well as sustaining its own location within the overall mix of sounds, allowing words and syllables to linger and sustain at ends of phrases and lines, moving precisely and delicately up and down small intervals, and knowing when to shift from predominantly eighth notes to longer notes. Also, in quieter passages, the vocalization sounds different in timbre than in louder passages–less hollowed out, less darkened, and more broadly resonant, involving a greater array of articulating spaces from the front of mouth through the chest and the diaphragm, which in turn involves a certain complexity in being ready and able to incorporate these kinds of shifts, and to do so repeatedly, over the course of the song.

In terms of my evaluation of felt success versus failure of these exertions in achieving their intended ends, the bass guitar feels as if it is persistently pushing toward a goal that it does not quite

270

reach, always falling back to the initial starting point and needing to begin again. But it also feels as if this effort represents a success in itself. The drums and cymbals follow a similar cycle, ramping up and then ramping down. As with the bass guitar I hear this as both success and failure. With the guitar I find the alternating patterns convey a feeling of being caught within an ebb and flow that does not lead to breaking through or moving on but rather involves remaining at least partially trapped. And yet, running with this situation for what it is feels partially cathartic. With the vocal I don't gain the feeling of having achieved much success, as it continues drained, desperate, and even despairing. But some feeling of success follows from not fully or finally giving up, and from maintaining a vestige of stubborn hope.

In terms of physically empathizing with what the musicians are doing in "Twenty Four Hours," with Peter Hook's bass guitar I feel this whenever he embarks on one of the decisive rises in pitch. With Bernard Sumner's guitar I find it hard to say that I feel myself physically empathizing with his playing of the guitar as it seems initially strange and unsettling as well later odd, jarring, and startling, while the soars and flares seem both distant and distanced from me. As Stephen Morris's drums and cymbals patterns feel somewhat complicated and irregular it again feels difficult to physically empathize here, although I can more readily do so with hi-hat hits, especially closed hi-hat crashes, and with the tom rolls. With Ian Curtis's vocal I feel myself physically empathizing because of the narrow pitch range he deploys; because of his lingering over and sustaining of notes, syllables, and words; and because of a straining meets drained quality within his voice. Aside from empathetically identifying or not with lines of sound, in terms of attenuation versus non-attenuation of my mimetic effort, I feel this increase in faster, louder, denser passages and decrease in the slower, quieter, and less dense passages.

I hear the music as persona anticipating waves of rising and falling intensity, density, loudness, and speed, as well as corresponding ebbs and flows of emotion. The music as persona anticipates some kind of impending confrontation but it also feels as if the music as persona experiences the 'present' situation as tragic, reflective of where a life has come to, arrived at, and ended up. Nevertheless, the music as persona and I anticipate a last valiant pushing back and a last valiant and even defiant gesture of self-assertion.

I hear the music as persona, and in particular the narrator-protagonist of the lyrics, expressing exhaustion, feeling drained, feeling isolated, feeling cut off, feeling abandoned, and feeling as if 'he' is now beyond desperation, crossing over into despair. 'He' feels he has suffered multiple devastating losses, and far too many, far too quickly, and of far too monumental a nature to be able to withstand. But I also hear an expression of striving to try to continue, to persist, to persevere, and to find reason to hope, means of survival, and means of recovery even as none are readily perceptible anywhere immediately around.

I feel myself expressing (as my response back to the expression I am receiving from the music as persona) respect, admiration, fear, worry, concern, and a difficult, uncomfortable, yet necessary empathetic identification and self-recognition, along with a prompting toward self-criticism concerning how much, how far, and how well I am recognizing, responding to, and helping address the needs of those who are desperate to despairing, and whose lives are on the brink of complete and final collapse.

It feels to me, as I listen repeatedly and carefully to "Twenty Four Hours," as if the sounds, patterns of sounds, and deployments of sounds comprising this song come at me from a tight space directly in front of me, as well as slightly lower and to the sides of me. I feel as if this is more concentrated overall as opposed to diffuse although I do note ample decay and especially sustain along with notable shifts in pitch, volume, tempo, and density–as these increase, the impact feels as if this amounts to a more aggressive pushing upon me. But otherwise it feels as if I am caught up within the ebb and flow, as if I am enveloped within this.

I feel both compelled to move along with the song and paralyzed by the enormity of the spectacle I perceive this song dramatizing. I feel as if this song dramatizes a critical period of extreme emotion and of difficult to desperate struggle in agonizing conditions along with a deep uncertainty about how this will play out and how I, insofar as I join as a co-protagonist with the music as persona, will be able to manage my way through. I feel this song, and the ways the sounds comprising it operate, encourages me not just to experience sympathetic identification, but also to reach out, to do something. I experience a prompting to recognize and respond to a howl of human pain, and not to deny, dismiss, ignore, or pull away from this when and where it is happening, as well as to consider to what extent I have done and continue to do the latter as opposed to the former.

It feels to me as if the result of the analysis the music as persona has performed has led it to conclude what has happened prior to 'the present' of the song has left it in a grave state. The music as persona conveys to me a feeling of being so familiar with trauma that trauma seems normal–and yet it continues to feel traumatic. At the same time, it feels to me that the music as persona nonetheless continues to affirm *I (still) matter*, or *I _should_ (still) matter*.

I do not hear the music as persona conveying a feeling of earning any reward for successful effort at analysis, or pleasure from being able to continue to survive this far. Instead, I hear a grim determination to strive to survive, endure, and persist while seriously contemplating giving up. It seems to me the result of analysis has led the music as persona to the conclusion that it needs to engage in a series of concerted pushes that will alternate with periods of recovery, and to be prepared to do this repeatedly, akin to running intervals, but in what seems like a race with no definite end.

In terms of what kinds of analysis I feel myself engaging in, in response to what I perceive the music as doing, I experience myself trying to make sense of how bad things are, and why so, as well as what might yet be possible, in response. I feel myself trying to make sense of how desperate are 'we', the music as persona and I as a co-protagonist. I feel myself attempting to make sense of how to ride the crests of the waves within the song. I also feel as if I am analyzing points of connection with my own life-experience in relation to the emotions expressed here and in relation to the felt situation dramatized here. I feel as if I am analyzing this song as enacting a powerful expression of what happens as a result of visceral confrontation with 'darknesses' in how humans have treated and are treating each other.

272

I feel the music making associations with feelings of sadness; experiences of struggle; with ebbs and flows, and rises and falls, from hope to despair, including over the course of 'twenty four hours'; and with occasions and circumstances where it is necessary to keep on striving even when this no longer seems possible. I feel the music making associations with loss of all the following: love, what one loved (to do/to strive to be), opportunities, promises, hopes, dreams, innocence, preceding forms of identity and modes of social interconnectedness, previous outlooks and sensibilities, previous predominant means of explaining and understanding, control over emotional and physical states, sense of one's self and of one's self worth and of one's moral character, and trust that one maintains allies and other possible sources of help.

I associate what I hear, and what this makes me think (about) and especially feel, with situations where I needed to make a difficult decision to undertake a dramatic change, especially at a point of crisis when I was unable to delay or postpone any further. I associate what I hear, and what this makes me think (about) and especially feel, with venturing into the unknown, and not being able to rely upon previous means of support or a previous comfort zone of trusted supporters.

I hear the music as persona in "Twenty Four Hours" confronting taboos concerned with openly sharing despair, depression, and suicidality. I hear the music as persona confronting taboos in challenging conventional advice that we should never give up, or never believe we are incapable of resilience. I hear the music as persona confronting taboos concerning openly admitting failure, illusion, and delusion–including in relation to what one once most cherished or longed for, and including in relation to what is no longer within grasp and even never was. I hear the music as persona confronting taboos concerning dwelling in sadness, such as following the loss of a close and vital relationship–e.g., the loss of a love, or a loved one. And I hear the music as persona confronting taboos in openly sharing the feeling that life might be without meaning and purpose, or that life might have lost (all) meaning and purpose.

I receive chills via the timbre of Ian Curtis's vocal and its restrained/contained/constrained pitch range and movement; from the periodic jumps up in pitch of Peter Hook's bass guitar; from movement into passages of increased volume, tempo, and density, as well as from ebbing into quieter, slower, and less dense passages. In the ebb passages I feel chills by means of the delicate contemplation these moments suggest. In responding to the taboos I hear the song confronting, I feel like I don't want to go there–it's too dark, too shattering, too awful–but that I must. This confrontation with taboos prompts me to recall some of the most painful and traumatic experiences in my own life, as well as how anguished I felt in those times and at those places. This confrontation with taboos makes me think about groups of people who are routinely rendered invisible or less visible, treated as if they exist beyond or are undeserving of sympathy and compassion, and treated as if they exist beyond recognition as persons maintaining inherent dignity and worth. This confrontation with taboos compels me to reflect on my interconnection with all those lives. These are lives we who are fortunate so often distance ourselves from, and which we often ignore or forget. This confrontation with taboos that I hear "Twenty Four Hours" manifesting makes me reflect on when I have not been the kind of person I would most like to be, to aspire to be, to be perceived and recognized for being. This confrontation with taboos pressures me to reflect on flaws in my character, as well as on what delusions and pretensions I maintain, including concerning what I stand for and identify with, how, and why, and including in relation to what I am actually doing–and not–versus what I imagine and represent myself to be doing. I also experience the confrontation with taboos this song enacts as prompting me to re-experience the feelings associated with moments in my life where I felt in crisis, when I suffered physical and mental pain at its most acute, and when I felt desperation becoming despair.

In "Twenty Four Hours" the lyrics do not specify what has led to this seemingly especially bad situation. Whatever this was it haunts the 'present' of the song–as an invisible, intangible, and ephemeral specter. It seems as if hopes, past desires, and love all proved ephemeral as did innocence and pride, as now do memories, as now do others' presence and impact within 'our' lives.

With the scratching and plucking guitar lines it feels as if it is hard to locate these in tangible form. The vocal also seems both close and distant, and thereby also hard to discern from where, and through what, it might be coming. As the drums, cymbals, and bass guitar proceed, through successive patterns with slight variations, they likewise suggest an ephemerality to the structures and frameworks we tend to rely upon, and especially fall back upon, while the slow dissolve of the soaring and flaring guitar lines suggests the same.

And yet, the song also suggests we may be able to survive, endure, and persist by aligning ourselves with the invisible, the intangible, and the ephemeral. We can do so by attesting to what it feels like in the midst of the maelstrom, what this feels like as this ebbs and flows, by making use of sounds to capture and convey what words alone cannot.

In listening closely to "Twenty Four Hours," and reflecting carefully on what this prompts me to think (about) and feel, I contemplate my own inevitable, ultimate disappearance, and of how that inevitable, ultimate disappearance is foreshadowed by my disappearance from previous places, times, situations, relations, institutions, structures, enterprises, organizations, positions, efforts, and campaigns that I once was immersed within but am no longer. I contemplate situations where I have felt invisible, or where I noticed, recognized, or learned others have felt this way, or where I felt like I was not registered and related to as a fully tangible, complex, dynamic presence, or where I have recognized and learned others have felt this. I think about situations in which my voice is the part of me, the manifestation of me, that predominates, and also of what I myself am most intensely aware of, most intensely struggling to bridge, to sustain, to complete, to fill out, to provide sense and meaning to, as well as feel the strain in striving to do so where seemingly everything depends on what I am saying and how I am saying this. I think about experiences in which I have felt awkward hearing the sound of my own voice, even of not even recognizing or feeling like this could possibly be the sound of my own voice. I think about how much is not seen, and not registered, in a tangible way, about myself, or about others, based upon superficial appearances alone or solely by means of what we say or how we say this, and of how often words don't come when, and as, I or others would like them and when we can't think of any 'right words' to adequately express what we are trying to express. And yet I also think about situations where I've felt I do matter, even if I have been unsure how many others felt the same about me.

***

I will now address the three sets of summary and review questions.

1.   What have these features begun to suggest to me, what have they invited and encouraged me to think (about) and feel, as well as to imagine and recollect? What do I hear the song expressing and communicating to me? How do I hear this song addressing and engaging me–inviting and encouraging me to enter into dialogue, into a co-creative encounter? What kind of subject, in what kinds of conditions and circumstances and from what position and perspective is here addressing and reaching out to me? This song invites and encourages me to think (about) and feel, as well as imagine and recollect situations and circumstances where desperation is becoming despair and where depression is becoming suicidality. I hear this song addressing me from the vantage point of a subject experiencing and sharing feelings of painful alienation, isolation, and loneliness. This song invites and encourages me to think (about) and feel, as well as imagine and recollect situations and circumstances at the point of crisis, when a dramatic change is necessary but terrifying to contemplate let alone pursue. I hear this song addressing me from the vantage point of a subject experiencing and sharing the ebbs and flows of emotion characteristic of extreme moments and passages in life-experience, especially genuine crises. This song invites and encourages me to think (about) and feel–to identify and empathize with–the will to continue, even when doing so seems impossible, even when doing so seems absurd, even when doing so seems hopeless. I hear this song addressing me from the vantage point of a subject close to the edge, desperately declaring and sharing 'I (still) matter', 'my life is (still) worthwhile,' yet 'I fear this won't and can't be heard, this won't and can't be attended and responded to, before it will be too late'. In other words, I hear this song addressing me from the vantage point of a subject dramatizing, enacting, witnessing, and testifying to what this position can and does feel like. This song invites and encourages me to think (about) and feel the enduring value of life, and of the life-force, as well as the dignity and worth of the human, at its most vulnerable and precarious. I hear this song addressing me from the vantage point of a subject attuned to the tragic experience of far too many people who are all too easily ignored, dismissed, forgotten, and overlooked, overwhelmed by chasms in social welfare–and by chasms in social recognition and understanding. And I hear this song holding me to moral account in relation to my responsibility for these people, and for their failing to make it through. This song invites and encourages me to think (about) and feel, as well as to imagine and recollect situations and circumstances that manifest how and why self-criticism is necessary yet brutal. I hear this song addressing me from the vantage point of a subject forced to confront and share with me what happens when we realize what we have counted on as essential foundations turn out to be, and to have always been, illusions and delusions. This song invites and encourages me to think (about) and feel the need of a reason, a purpose, and even a mission for living as well as the struggle to find and sustain one, especially after experience of profound (self-)disillusionment. I hear this song addressing me from the vantage point of a subject who has lost and who is sharing with me what it is like to have lost previously crucial bearings, while not recognizing any ready replacement or any ready means to find a replacement.

2. How do I hear these features and their accumulation and development beginning to address and position me? What are we, together, grappling with? What is it, more specifically, precisely, and even

275

concretely that we, together, are exploring, inquiring into, pursuing, and confronting? We are struggling to find reasons to persist, to continue, to endure, and to hope. We are feeling overwhelmed by despair, and by the scale of setbacks and losses we have experienced, without recognizing any clear way forward. We are asserting our inherent worth and dignity, that we matter, and that we are still striving and struggling, even as we are exhausted, to the bitter end. We are confronting accumulating failings, mistakes, losses, setbacks, separations, distancings, and yet further alienating and isolating forces, in the midst of a deep existential crisis, a crisis of identity, a crisis concerning whom we are and how and why we matter, in what ways, when, where, and for whom. We are frustrated with how little is working or is all that helpful in enabling us to pull ourselves out of this desperate situation. We are passionately asserting life matters, and we are proclaiming it matters, in the tragic event where life is on the brink, and when it might seem all too easy to conclude life does not matter–or life no longer does matter. I feel positioned to want to address and alleviate this suffering, to help the sufferer find a way out and a path to recovery. I feel positioned to accept my responsibility and my complicity–and to act accordingly. I feel called upon not to walk away and in effect ignore or forget what I am hearing, and not to repress or otherwise rationalize this away. I feel called upon to wake up and check around me, to take into account the extent and the intensity of suffering that is happening. I feel called upon not to take my relative comfort and security for granted, and to act instead on the basis of a common existential precariousness, to act instead on the basis of what fundamentally unites me with other human beings, including those seemingly most distant and unlike me. I feel my own vulnerability, fragility, and frailty exposed. I am reminded of situations and experiences where I have felt this same way–just as alienated, isolated, lonely, desperate, and despairing–and I feel compassion for as well as empathetic identification with the subject in crisis in this song.

3.   *What do I hear these features seeking from me as my response and reply? How does this venture implicate and challenge me? What does it call forth from me, from whom I am, from where I come, from what I am about, from where I am headed, and from what I am seeking? How–specifically, precisely, and even concretely–can I respond? What simultaneously creatively imaginative and honestly authentic–even, and perhaps especially, raw and sensitive emotionally felt–response can I here give?* I feel called upon to identify and empathize, and not just extend sympathy and compassion. I feel called upon to recall comparable–raw and sensitive–situations in my own life-experience. I feel called upon to recognize desperation around me, especially where it is all too often overlooked, and to try to help save lives. I feel called upon to question my own assumptions and presuppositions, my own values and ideals, and my own kneejerk ways of thinking, feeling, believing, acting, interacting, and behaving. I feel called upon to question inherited and ascribed identities, affiliations, and outlooks. I feel called upon to recognize, own up, and take responsibility for my mistakes and failings and to consider where I have invested in illusions and delusions. I feel called upon to remember and reflect on crisis points in my own life-experience, in which I needed to make a dramatic change and it was frightening to do so. I feel called upon to be honest, open, vulnerable, and genuine. I feel called upon to look and see, to listen and hear, and to sense and feel what others who are frightened, angry, sad, overwrought, and overwhelmed are experiencing, and to try to understand and to try to empathize. I feel called upon to consider what social groups are unseen,

unheard, unfelt, and thereby are not gaining what they need to survive, to persist, to endure, to live on–and of all the potential that is missed, lost, and wasted as a result.

Reflecting yet further, the title of the song, together with what follows as the song, suggest periods of time where I have felt like I am on a perpetual treadmill and, what's worse, can't keep up, as I am constantly repeating the same efforts at the same intensity yet inexorably falling further behind and feeling steadily worse. Also, on the contrary, I recall periods where just one day later a remarkable shift has occurred to a much brighter and happier state, without being able to pinpoint what has changed, but conveying to me the importance of just bearing through the worst times with the faith that I can and will make it even if I cannot readily recognize how, why, or when. And yet I also recall times immediately preceding a major event, which I know is likely to prove fraught, from which I cannot hide and from where there is no turning back.

"Twenty Four Hours" reinforces my conviction that individuals can only do so much, all by themselves alone, and often feel compelled to try to do far more than they can all by themselves alone in taking on what needs to be a collective endeavor. "Twenty Four Hours" reinforces the message that the need for self-care is real, as is the need to be able to give up and let go, to accept defeats and setbacks, and even to accept rejection and dismissal.

We are strengthened when we have others upon whom we can rely to be understanding and helpful to us in these situations, where we are at our lowest and most fragile, but all too many don't have enough people like this in their lives when they most need them. "Twenty Four Hours" prompts me to reflect on what kinds of people do not have this kind of support, and even learn, from early on in their lives, not to expect it, as well as to be distrustful and suspicious of any who offer it.

"Twenty Four Hours" conveys a heady sense of romantic gloom that as understandably appealing as this can be also ultimately needs to be resisted or at least delimited. And yet even when not adopting such a gloomy romantic posture, it is common enough for many of us to struggle concerning desires and needs to want to be, to do, to experience, to identify, and to live our lives differently, even dramatically differently, than we currently are and have been. It is common enough for many of us to experience the desire and the need for a decisive rupture yet to lack the resources, including the confidence in what we ourselves are capable of managing, sufficient to undertake and pursue such a prospect.

I find it useful to interpret "Twenty Four Hours" in relation to crisis moments many people experience at times when and in places where it feels as if it is necessary to shift dramatically, and yet doing so is risky and frightening. This might include moving to a dramatically new place to live, far from where one currently lives and previously has lived, not yet knowing many or any people in the new location, and not knowing much if anything at all about the new location and the local culture. This might include changing jobs, changing careers, or changing what degree to pursue at what institution of higher-learning and over what time-frame. This might include changing what major project to foreground and make central to one's life's activity. This might include ending a previously close and intimate relationship–or beginning a new one. This might include deciding to take time off from a job, a career, pursuit of a degree, involvement in another major activity, or service in a major position within an important (to us) organization. This might include deciding to seek treatment for a mental health issue, an addiction, or a behavioral problem, such as not being able to manage anger. This might include putting one's self up as an applicant, as a candidate, for a major position or it might include withdrawing from, turning down, the prospect of consideration for a major position. This might include ending a long-standing affiliation with a major source of social identity, such as a religious or political affiliation. This might include breaking with erstwhile friends, allies, and family, by identifying openly with what these people consider taboo or at least counter- or anti- normative. This might include admitting one's failings and apologizing as well as otherwise striving to make up, to atone, for these failings. This might include deciding to retire. This might include deciding to give up pursuit of a too long distant and difficult aspiration or dream. This might include admitting limitation, weakness, and vulnerability, especially openly, especially publicly. This might include rejecting a previously pivotal inherited or ascribed social identity and defining oneself as a very different kind of person.

I also think what if we interpret this song, including the 'I' of the lyrics, as not about an individual but rather as about a group, a community, an organization, a movement, an enterprise, an initiative, a cause, a culture, or a society? What if it is the group, the community, the organization, the movement, the enterprise, the initiative, the cause, the culture, or the society that is in a state of crisis, needing to dramatically change yet overwhelmed by the need to do so and bewildered about how to do so, and over whether it will be possible to succeed in so doing? What if this is a group, community, organization, movement, enterprise, initiative, cause, culture, or society that is confronting the possibility that its time may well have run out–that it may indeed face no future? What if we interpret this song as an expression of a *collective* sense of terrible pain and nascent despair yet nonetheless persistent if exhausted struggle?

***

Let's next consider "Twenty Four Hours" in relation to the eleven prior interpretations I first introduced in chapter one concerning what I hear, and what this prompts me to think (about) and feel, when I listen to and reflect on the music, as art, of Ian Curtis and Joy Division.

#1: I interpret . . . Ian Curtis's lyrics and Joy Division's music as all about exploration of and inquiry into mediations. *Again and again, these songs zero in on the 'in between', on the _distance between_. Always seeking, striving, venturing, pursuing, or hesitating about doing so yet feeling the strong compulsion to do so nonetheless.* I find this interpretation less relevant to this song than with "Disorder" and "Transmission." "Twenty Four Hours" does seem to present us with a liminal moment of some kind, a limbo moment even, but this seems one where we are beyond hesitation, and beyond exploring, as we are now fully into, and even beyond, the approach of crisis, and are forced to confront and draw conclusions after the crisis has hit.

#2: Ian Curtis . . . fearlessly explored intensities, extremities, subliminalities, and liminalities that many others never would or could, and his music, while often extremely dark and somber, is

never simply that–it is about seeking, struggling, reflecting, examining, and opening one's self up to sensation, perception, emotion, and understanding that presses past familiar layers of protective mediation toward not only intense vulnerability and emptiness but also intense clarity and insight. Joy Division's music fuses the intellectual with the emotional with the spiritual with the somatic–in terms of exploration and questing, in both passionate and dispassionate terms, and in relation to a striving for and imposition of control meeting up with the absolute limits and sheer impossibility of meaningfully striving for and seeking to impose control. "Twenty Four Hours" does seem to engage extremities as well as intense vulnerability, brutally exposed. And yet the song hardly feels dispassionate, more exhausted than passionate, and, again, as now past struggling with (refusing to accept) limits to and the impossibility of control.

#3: In listening to Joy Division I hear . . . the same freshness, urgency, and intensity that attracted me to punk, yet also something transcending the immediacy and directness of punk, conveying, in contrast, a richly resonant sense of both distance and precision, a controlled fury emanating from a fiercely passionate yet also agonizingly vulnerable exploration of emotional, psychological, physical, and metaphysical extremes. I do hear "Twenty Four Hours" as engaging with agonizingly vulnerable extremes, yes, and also controlled fury makes good sense in relation to the passages of increased density, volume, and speed in this song, as well as the leading up to those passages by way of the rising in pitch from the bass guitar, along with the tightening and hardening of the vocalization of the final word–and note–in vocal passages.

#4: Joy Division songs, for me, dramatize introspection as fiercely determined and fully committed struggle. What makes this struggle all the more fraught and challenging is it transpires in a mysteriously otherworldly realm where comfortably reassuring borderlines break down. These are borderlines between interior and exterior, subject and object, self and other, protagonist and antagonist, friend and foe, help and hindrance, solidarity and betrayal, complicity and responsibility, hope and despair, health and illness, movement and stasis, past and present, history and myth, the psychological and the sociological, the sacred and the profane, the beautiful and the sublime, the close and the distant, the private and the public, the familiar and the strange, and the living and the dead. Joy Division songs end not with tension resolved, but merely temporarily suspended. The only definite answer they offer us is we need to join this struggle, and seek what we can find, for ourselves. "Twenty Four Hours" does make sense as enacting introspection, and struggle does continue, but in this song struggle appears on the verge of stopping and ending. Nevertheless the song does engage borderlines, in particular, between the beautiful and the sublime, the living and the dead, complicity and responsibility, hope and despair, health and illness, movement and stasis, and self and other.

#5: Inquiring into the music, as art, of Ian Curtis involves . . . inquiring into metaphorical 'darknesses' in human history and society, and in the condition of being human, especially that of the human social being living in the advanced capitalist, postmodern world. This involves facing, without resorting to self-protective blinders or sentimentalizing illusions, often extraordinarily disturbing incidences of cruelty and violence, as well as of anxiety and alienation. It involves inquiring into intensity and extremity as well as into the complexities of distance and connection in human social relations. It involves inquiring into anxious to traumatic dimensions of the human quest for meaning,

279

purpose, value, satisfaction, fulfilment–and especially love–in this late capitalist, postmodern world, and it involves inquiring into interrelations between life and death, between living and dying, between being and nothingness, between self and other, and among past, present, and future. It involves inquiring into surfaces and depths, mysteries and enigmas, complexities and contradictions, and fluidities and variabilities in modes of individual identity, personality, and character. It involves inquiring into what it feels like to struggle and strive for authenticity and integrity, in relation to the pull of ambition, popularity, success, and fame. It also involves, on the flip side, inquiring into effective meanings of compassion, empathy, and solidarity. Inquiring into when and where these qualities are under threat, in danger of collapse, on the verge of eclipse, or altogether absent, we recognize, and appreciate, how indispensable they truly are. I think this is the best interpretation for "Twenty Four Hours," out of these eleven, especially as it attests to the impact and the costs of doing the project it describes, in particular pursuing this largely unaided and alone. This interpretation is also useful in drawing our attention to what happens when the artist finds their position becoming identical with what they have been inquiring into and attempting to take into account, recognizing not only how many others are lacking and have lacked the solidaristic support they needed, while having instead been effectively abandoned and left behind, but also that this now has become the artist's own position as well. The artist has taken on more than 'he' can handle all by himself alone, not recognizing how overwhelming this would be, and now it feels like it is too difficult and too late to be able to save himself by pulling himself out.

#6: Ian Curtis's art . . . can readily be conceived as an exploration of and inquiry into the following two sets of fundamental questions: 1. Why do I exist? What is the meaning, value, and purpose of my existence? To what extent can I exercise any influence, and any control, over what this meaning, value, and purpose becomes? How can, and how should, I attempt to do so?
2. In what ways, and to what extent, am I responsible for others? For the suffering, hardship, and pain others experience? For the violence and cruelty as well as the injustice and unfairness in the world? What can and what should I do about any of this? This interpretation is useful insofar as "Twenty Four Hours" seems to express the doubt that the music as persona, and especially the narrator-protagonist, can come up with any good answers to the first set of questions. In relation to the second set of questions, it seems like the 'artist', as alluded to in relation to preceding interpretation #5, has taken on these concerns, and urges others to take them on as well, but is overwhelmed by having done so, by having attempted to do so, while it also seems this artist recognizes and is sharing that this suffering, hardship, pain, violence, cruelty, injustice, and unfairness is far worse, far more searing, than 'he' initially or previously imagined.

#7: Ian Curtis's art . . . can be readily conceived of, as well, as an exploration of and inquiry into the sense and meaning of alienation, isolation, and loneliness; the position and experience of being a stranger, an outsider, and an outcast; vulnerability, entrapment, anxiety, and fear; and the need to connect, especially intimately, along with the simultaneous difficulty of doing so. This interpretation is useful in relation to "Twenty Four Hours" because the music definitely conveys a strong sense of feeling alienated, isolated, and lonely; of being a stranger, an outcast, and an outsider; of vulnerability, entrapment, anxiety, and fear; and of a desperate need to connect along with fear that such connection is impossible, or no longer possible, in the ways and to extents that are needed.

#8: Ian Curtis's art makes sense . . . in somewhat more specific terms, as an exploration of the extent to which (and the consequences following from recognition that) the self is an imaginary construct, the subject is simultaneously overwhelmingly unconscious and ineluctably other, desire and anxiety are persistently intrinsically interconnected, the symbolic order and the law of the father are oppressively authoritarian, jouissance is far more terrifying than the common translation as 'enjoyment' can possibly suggest, and intimations and irruptions of the Real are recurrently traumatic. "Twenty Four Hours" might well make sense as alluding to confrontation with the Real, with the ephemerality of all that the music as persona, and the narrator-protagonist of the lyrics, have built up around sense of self and reasons for self-worth, here encountering the ultimate nothingness of being, and here also experiencing the dominant Symbolic order as far more repressive and punitive than ameliorative and caring.

#9: Ian Curtis's art also makes sense . . . in somewhat more specific terms, as the staging of a dramatic encounter with the shocking resilience and metamorphic resurgence of fascist tendencies, after the end of World War II and the Holocaust, at the heart of ostensibly 'democratic', advanced capitalist, Western society, including in the guises of 'friendly fascism' and 'the fascism of everyday life'. Ian Curtis and his bandmates, in choosing their name, Joy Division, whether consciously, deliberately, intentionally or not, propose fascism lives on after the defeat of Nazi Germany and the liberation of the survivors from the concentration camps–and it lives on, most insidiously, as an integral dimension and recurrent tendency within the very same societies so frequently and routinely celebrating their victory over fascism. Perhaps these are "the darkest corners" that the narrator-protagonist has looked into and perhaps the song responds to the fact that this is what he has discovered and recognized from looking into these corners, as perhaps the song conveys an experience of being overwhelmed by revelation of exactly this resurgent fascist horror.

#10: A large part of what makes Ian Curtis especially compelling to me, and seemingly the same to a great many others, is that he was–and remains–a striking combination of the ordinary and extraordinary, he communicates incredibly powerfully through his art yet so much of his art is obsessively focused on the difficulty of communication, and because an empathetic engagement with his life-experience, his artistic accomplishment, and his fierce sense of artistic mission and purpose is richly rewarding–such engagement can help us in efforts to forge a genuinely and indeed systemically caring culture, a culture of compassion, empathy, and solidarity. Curtis's life-story, his life-achievement, and his life-legacy all attest to how important it is to strive to grasp the myriad ways in which we are all far more complex, multiple, contradictory, and dynamic than commonly recognized. Curtis reminds us of how all too many people's critical and creative potential is routinely discouraged, dismissed, and denigrated, and how this in turn leads all too many people all too readily to internalize a powerful tendency to do the same, to themselves. This interpretation is useful in relation to "Twenty Four Hours" engaging with struggling to communicate, within and beyond words, especially the extraordinary dimensions of all too chillingly ordinary experiences of profound suffering, desperation, and despair. The song, in this connection, impels us think about how commonplace and for what common reasons such discouragement, dismissal, and denigration happens, as well as in particular to whom. Who are those here and now, in the present, and where we

at present are at, who are ignored, forgotten, dismissed, abandoned, and treated as effectively invisible, inaudible, intangible, and worthless, how and why is this happening to them, and what kinds of empathetic and enabling connections might we develop with these groups of people and their experiences, as well as how so?

\   *#11: I perceive, from Ian Curtis, as I listen to his recorded voice, and as I read his written words, while trying to write this book of my own, a tremendous anguish, emanating from a guilty recognition of a persistent uncertainty, hesitation, and doubt, and, when I recognize this in Curtis' voice and words, doing so does aggravate, and accelerate, my own uncertainty, hesitation, and doubt. As a result, at times I feel like I owe a debt of personal responsibility to Ian Curtis, to carry on with what he could not.* In listening to Curtis in "Twenty Four Hours" I do feel like I recognize what it feels like to be in this state, but I also feel like I rarely have got this far down, and rarely have so fully succumbed, while I feel like ways out do exist, and could exist, and that he too maintained real possibilities for further achievement, for further contribution, for further living, for further meaningful interaction with numerous others, for further loving and for further being loved that were all cut off for him, and from him, all too soon (or at least that he felt like the last was the case). But I also do feel inspired by Curtis because it is important to confront the metaphorical and literal darknesses, to not turn away from how bad things are, and for whom, and to remain vigilantly concerned with and focused on the plight of those who are leading the most precarious lives and who are the furthest alienated, isolated, and excluded.

***

To conclude this section, and this chapter, I am now going to stage encounters between "Twenty Fours Hours" and a series of books, in order to further explore, develop, and refine themes that have emerged in the course of my preceding description, analysis, and interpretation of this song.

I begin with Iain Ferguson's *Politics of the Mind: Marxism and Mental Distress* and *Routledge International Handbook of Critical Mental Health*, edited by Bruce M.Z. Cohen. Let's start with Ferguson's book. Ferguson opens his book by sketching the broad dimensions of how "The crisis in mental health has become one of the key 'public issues' of the 21st century" (11). "According to the World Health Organisation, depression now affects 350 million people worldwide and by 2020 will be the leading cause of disability in the world" (11), and "In the UK, one in four people will experience a mental health problem in any given year" (11). Mental distress, Ferguson describes, has been skyrocketing since the global economic crisis and the Great Recession of 2007-2008, as well as in response to the impact of austerity imposed on top of the already damaging impact of neo-liberalism, with people from working class, poor, ethnic and racial minority, and other socially marginalized, socially insecure, and socially disadvantaged populations experiencing greater levels and rates of acute mental distress. Especially worthy of note, "anxiety, which was hardly recognized as health condition fifty years ago, is perhaps the condition *par excellence* in the era of neoliberal capitalism" (19). Yet in response to this state of crisis, mental distress continues primarily to be conceived and engaged as a medical issue, first and last, rooted in individual brain dysfunction–or in irrational forms of individual learned behavior that can be rationally unlearned, and effectively overcome, as people learn better to adapt to existing society rather than work to change and improve it. The overarching capitalist economic and social system, and the prevailing structures of everyday life under capitalism, are rarely conceived as playing a significant role in creating what is commonly identified as 'mental illness', let alone *the most significant role*, but this is what Ferguson indeed argues is the case in *Politics of the Mind*, drawing upon multiple past as well as present critical theories and social movements to support this argument.

Ferguson cites Norman Geras in explaining Karl Marx's conception of what lies at the heart of what it means to be human: "The need of people for breadth and diversity of pursuit and hence of personal development . . . 'all-round activity', 'all-round development of individuals', 'free development of individuals', [and] 'the means of cultivating gifts in all directions'" (quoted, 18). And Ferguson follows up by citing Terry Eagleton proposing a crucial irony, in Marx's view, is that although "self-determination is of the essence of humanity, the great majority of men and women throughout history have not been able to exercise it. They have not been permitted to be fully human. Instead, their lives have been determined for the most part by the dreary cycle of class society" (quoted, 19). In sum, alienation as a result of "denial of our most basic humanity" is a chief source of widespread mental distress, including so-called mental illness, and this is in turn "the consequence of a society–capitalism–based not on human need but on the drive to accumulate profit" (19). The situation becomes all the worse when the so-called mentally ill are identified as themselves 'the problem', or, in other words, as individually deficient and individually dysfunctional rather than responding rationally to the impact of capitalist social conditions and social structures upon their psychic lives and well-being: "In truth, with the (possible) exception of psychoanalysis . . . seriously listening to the voices and experiences of people with mental health problems (as opposed to gathering data to form the basis of a diagnosis) has arguably never been at the forefront of psychiatric practice. The more common patient experience has been one of not being listened to and of views and experiences being discounted or invalidated" (37).

Ferguson cites Jonathan Lear explaining it makes sense to "read Freud as providing the material for a political critique of the conditions of bourgeois modernity. That is, one can read him as making the historical claim that in the social conditions in which he encountered his patients, the discrepancy between the conditions needed for humans to flourish and the demands imposed by society had become too great" (quoted, 55). Likewise, Jacques Lacan's psychoanalytic theories, and clinical practices based on these theories, can also be usefully connected with a Marxist critique of capitalist conditions of possibility and capitalist forces of generation responsible for widespread mental distress. Lacan's Imaginary functions as "a kind of ideology" (71); Lacan's Symbolic functions, as Stpehen Frosh puts it, as "a kind of regulatory *law*" (quoted, 180); and Lacan's Real represents a horizon of awareness concerning possibilities beyond the illusions of the Imaginary and the constraints of the Symbolic. Ferguson remains skeptical, nonetheless, of how useful psychoanalysis can be to a Marxist theorization of mental distress that emphasizes the need to transform capitalism in order to make a substantial impact versus the extent and depth of suffering people experience in the form of mental health challenges.

Ferguson is more positive about the contributions of contemporary, 21st century *critical* psychologists and psychiatrists, whose work is informed by *critical* directions in sociology and that converges with social work and social activism. Among these practitioners, a paradigm shift has occurred that "locates 'madness' and mental distress more generally primarily in people's life experiences" (98). As Jerry Tew explains, from this vantage point, "mental distress may be understood as a meaningful response to life circumstances" (quoted, 99). This means, as Ferguson illustrates, that "cutting and other forms of self-harm would be understood within this framework as coping mechanisms, ways of dealing with emotional pain and releasing intolerable feelings which may be open to negotiation, rather than simply irrational or self-destructive acts" (99). These new directions in engaging with mental distress valorize "the lived experience of people with mental health problems" in locating "the sources of oppression and disadvantage in the structures of capitalist society rather than in individual impairment" (99). From this vantage point, as Richard Bentall explains, "there are myriad adult adversaries" that "contribute to mental ill-health, including debt, unhappy marriages, excessively demanding work environments and the threat of unemployment. Arguably the biggest cause of human misery is miserable relationships with other people, conducted in miserable circumstances" (quoted, 103). Ferguson applauds this direction in engaging with mental distress, because "A model for mental distress which recognises–and provides empirical evidence for–the causal role played by early life experience, poverty, inequality, racism, sexism and other forms of oppression in the genesis of mental health problems is a huge step forward from a model which locates such problems primarily in genes or biochemical deficiencies" (104). This kind of approach, that "emphasises the interaction between our brains and our environments, including the ways in which brain structure is shaped by life experiences" in turn "allows for a much more dialectical understanding of mental distress" (104) that empowers those experiencing mental health problems because it respects what they are experiencing as making sense, as reasonable, given their life-experience, social background, and social positioning.

Ferguson finds some positive value in emergent forms of 'Mad' identity politics, and in 'Mad Studies', that have reclaimed and resignified 'Madness', in challenging the continuing "stigma attached to mental distress" (114). But he maintains reservations about this movement, as although "very large numbers of people will experience periods of mental distress at some point in their lives . . . . A far smaller number . . . would choose to self-define as 'mad', either because the term is generally perceived as too stigmatising or because it does not fit their experience of anxiety, depression or addiction" (115). Ferguson suggests "an approach which stresses the commonality of mental distress is likely to have a greater political impact than one which prioritises difference" (115).

Returning to Marx, Ferguson zeroes in on Marx's concept of 'species being' which Terry Eagleton explains "is really a materialist version of human nature" that stresses "we are needy, labouring, sociable, sexual, communicative, self-expressive animals who need one another to survive, but who come to find a fulfillment in that companionship over and above its social usefulness . . . Because we are labouring, desiring, linguistic creatures, we are able to transform ourselves at the same time. Change in other words, is not the opposite of human nature; it is possible because of the creative, open-ended, unfinished beings we are" (quoted, 121). Our human essence is rooted in our freedom to be able, in concert with others, to change–and to create change–while not only making use

284

of but also controlling how we make use of our capacities and our labor in effecting change. This in turn means "The concept of alienation is also crucial in helping us make sense of mental distress" (106). When we are denied means to cultivate, or outlets to manifest, our creative abilities, we experience alienation that can lead to serious mental distress, and what's more, as Ferguson attests, "a loss of control is a characteristic feature of many forms of mental distress" (116).

Turning to the *Routledge International Handbook of Critical Mental Health*, critical mental health, as indicated in a prefatory note, involves a systematic problematization of "the practices, priorities and knowledge base of the Western systems of mental health," in particular "psychiatric discourse and the work of psy-professionals," while theorizing mental health, in contrast, "as a social, economic, political and cultural project: one which necessarily involves the consideration of wider societal and structural dynamics including labelling and deviance, ideological and social control, professional power, consumption, capital, neoliberalism and self-governance" (iii). For example, in "A constructive antipsychiatry position," Bonnie Burstow argues widespread mental distress not only follows from insufficient and inadequate social services but also requires "a more fundamental social transformation" (36). More precisely, Burstow proposes "With disempowerment and the relentless erosion of community clearly a factor in our current plight, an obvious direction would be predicated on smaller communities wherein everyone has a place, where we see ourselves as connected to every other being and where we grapple with problems together" (36). "How children are raised would be pivotal. Caring–not correction–would need to be prioritised" and this would further require "schools be places of freedom and creativity" (37). "Learning about feelings–one's own and others–would be crucial," and this would include learning "to appreciate the wisdom in states once dismissed as 'mental illness'"; "everyone would learn how to 'befriend' someone in distress, including how to engage in active listening"; and "everyone would acquire the skill to follow thinking processes radically different from their own (including what I call 'mad literacy'–that is being able to follow thought that might initially seem irrational . . .)" (37).

In "Marxist theory" Bruce M.Z. Cohen discusses how neo-liberalism and dominant forms of psychiatric practice converge in exercising social control. Cohen cites Ulrich Beck in explaining how neo-liberalism has led to the "de-politicisation of social and economic inequalities to the point where," to quote Beck, these "have been redefined 'in terms of *an individualization of social risks*'" (quoted, 51). As Cohen adds, "In neoliberal ideology, the self has replaced the group, the community or wider society as the site for reform and change" (51). This means those experiencing mental distress are encouraged both by neo-liberal ideology and 'psy-orthodoxy' to conceive of their selves as not only the sources of the problems they are experiencing but also as encompassing all of what can and must be worked on in order to effectively deal with these problems. Cohen proposes this situation becomes all the more insidious due to what Joanna Moncrieff refers to as "the medicalization of discontent" and what Rachel E. Dubrofsky takes on in discussing how, routinely and normatively, "social, political and economic problems are turned into personal problems" (quoted, 52-53).

In "A critical history of 'mental health care'" Tomi Gomory and Daniel J. Dunleavy conclude their survey of what the title of their article identifies by proposing the result has been the emergence and development "of a biomedical complex beneficial to all but the clients, who have generally been victimized by this contemporary system of operations" (124). At the same time, "The modern term for mad behaviour is the medically encapsulated notion of 'mental illness', but that term really refers to many different hypothesised behavioural syndromes. The term 'mental illness' remains a black box" (124).

In "Neoliberalism and pharmaceuticalism" Emma Tseris follows the previously cited contributors, and especially Cohen, in critiquing dominant psychiatric practice by arguing "psychiatric practices which are able to name as mentally ill those who fail to perform the role of industrious workers, amiable consumers and self-sufficient individuals" perform a significant ideological function, in proposing nothing about capitalism is responsible for the experiences of those who cannot accommodate themselves to capitalist expectations and capitalist normativities. As Tseris further explains, "By focusing on brain-based illnesses that are said to be caused by genetic and chemical vulnerabilities, and treatable via medication, psychiatry emphasises the importance of individual functioning, while shifting attention away from broader social factors." In so doing, "psychiatric discourse is able to sidestep the destructive effects of the social inequalities produced within late capitalism, instead constructing experiences of despair and disenchantment as evidence of disease within individuals" (170). Tseris argues that dominant psychiatric discourses and practices align with and in fact provide a principal vehicle for "additional tactics of overt social control" that neo-liberal societies have made widely commonplace, and those involve "strong notions of self-surveillance as a strategy for managing behaviours and experiences" (172). Once again, as with Cohen and Beck, Tseris charges "With the erosion of notions of collectivist approaches on welfare, self-surveillance obligations in neo-liberal societies reposition individuals as managers of their on risks" (172). Those who don't succeed in this often onerous task, or don't succeed all that well or all that consistently, end up either "at risk of a lifetime of mental health intervention and medication in response to even the slightest of aberrations" or face "the social intolerance" directed against "anyone who conceptualises their experiences outside of a biomedical framework" (173).

China Mills, in "The mad are like savages and the savages are mad: psychopolitics and the coloniality of the psy" further critiques "global mental health as a colonial discourse in that it overlooks the political economy of distress through reconfiguring economic and social crises as individual 'illness' amendable to individualised forms of 'treatment'" (206). This can, in turn, lead to "the pathologisation and individualisation of resistance and suffering" (207), in particular in relation to the combined impact of past colonial histories along with present neocolonial economies and polities. Mills discusses a lengthy history of using illness as a powerful metaphor to discredit social difference and political opposition, as well as to justify repression and oppression, recounting how concentration camps were first deployed and tested in colonial Namibia before being used in Nazi Germany, while the so-called 'insane' along with all disabled people were principal targets for sterilization and extermination by the Nazis (208).

In my preceding discussion of "Twenty Four Hours" I indicate it makes good sense to interpret this song, and not just the lyrics, as representative of the vantage point of a subject experiencing acute mental distress, struggling with it, on the verge of feeling as if no hope exists for anything to get any better, and that it is highly uncertain from whom or what this subject might be able to obtain the help it needs, testifying to what it feels like to be in this situation and at this point, on the brink of desperation become despair become suicidality. "Twenty Four Hours," drawing specific connections with *Politics of Mind* and *Routledge International Handbook of Critical Mental Health*, can make further useful sense as reflective of a vantage point often marginalized as 'mentally ill' and in effect not heard, not listened to, not knowing what it is saying, and in need of 'treatment' because it is problematic, deficient, and dysfunctional. Any kind of valuable insight provided from this vantage point is thereby effectively dismissed. The narrator-protagonist registers the debilitating impact of social stigma associated with mental distress, and especially 'mental illness', as well as dominant ways of making sense of such experience as reflective of, again, individual deficiency and dysfunction, even individual responsibility, and individual failure, which exacerbate guilt, shame, and the feeling of being cut off from and rejected by 'normal' society. And yet 'he' wrestles with this self-understanding, and suggests what he is experiencing is a product of having taken on a massive project, a massive responsibility, that has required more resources than he, individually alone, can provide, and, as a result, has left him drained. It makes sense to connect this state of acute mental distress with what happens to those who inquire critically into the furthest corners of the darkest dimensions of (post)modern capitalist society, including those that reveal fascism is a perpetual danger, and a perpetual threat, from within capitalism, and that reveal capitalist society is structurally dependent upon enormous violence. I am reminded here of what Frederic Jameson famously declares in *Postmodernism or, The Cultural Logic of Late Capitalism*: "this whole global, yet American, postmodern culture is the internal and superstructural expression of a whole new wave of American military and economic domination throughout the world: in this sense, as throughout class history, the underside of culture is blood, torture, death, and terror" (5). Those who work to expose this 'underside of culture', and who immerse themselves in sympathetically to empathetically feeling its devastating weight, as well as recurrently performing a dramatic encounter and engagement with the same for a growing public audience, as a guide for us prospectively to do the same, assume a potentially crushing burden. In this kind of society, when they are unable to bear this weight, and experience acute mental and physical distress as a result, it is easier, and more convenient from a dominant ideological vantage point, to label them as 'sick' than it is to rally in their support and join them in *collectively* pursuing this same vital endeavor.

Recall here how overburdened with sledgehammer prescription medications for epilepsy Ian Curtis was, as well as how doctors told him he needed to give up the kind of life he had worked long and hard for, right as he was reaching a peak of achievement, leaving him projecting that any future life he might lead would be limited and constrained, marked out and perceived by others as indicative of him being fundamentally *unable*—even as a freak, or at least as an object of pity.

"Twenty Four Hours" depicts its entire soundscape as troubled, and not just the subjective state of its ostensible protagonist, which prompts us to consider larger social-historical and political-economic explanations for the distress its central protagonist seems to be experiencing. This protagonist reaches out to others, but the fact none of these others is referred to by a specific name suggests the song addresses shared experiences, and shared affective states, with the narrator-protagonist implying that, as alone as 'he' feels, he recognizes it is not only him who feels this way.

"Twenty Four Hours" provides no answer to the problems it addresses, but emphasizes what it feels like when we refuse to pretend these are not real—especially when we cannot or can no longer pretend that everything is and will be OK.

"Twenty Four Hours" dramatizes what happens to those whose struggles, and sufferings, leave them without meaningful connection with others, including without love that once proved crucial. The individual in crisis, experiencing acute mental distress, is by no means empowered to take charge of their problems, and solve them 'by working on themself', but rather is gravely weakened in their ability to do anything to ameliorate their condition.

"Twenty Four Hours"'s confrontation with, and breaking of, taboos concerning sharing what it feels like, from the inside, to be desperate to despairing to suicidal, encompasses forthrightly sharing vulnerability, and precariousness, more broadly. The agony and anguish testifies to a vital need to express and communicate, to reach out and to share vulnerable emotions and vulnerable emotionality, as well as to how difficult this so often is to do, how limited are outlets in which this is possible, and how stigmatized are those who feel they nevertheless *must* try. Since Ian Curtis's time, we have made gains in reducing stigma associated with 'mental illness', including by 'normalizing' this experience, recognizing how widespread and commonplace this is, and that it makes good sense to conceive of mental health/mental illness as a continuum upon which we are all located, and across which we all move over the course of our lives. Yet predominant treatments continue to include prescription medications to address supposed biochemical sources of mental illness, especially in the brain and the nervous system (such as SSRIs—Selective Serotonin Reuptake Inhibitors), and therapies such as CBT (Cognitive Behavioral Therapy) that eschew inquiry into sources and causes of mental distress (even in an individual history, let alone in social structures and social conditions) by instead advocating 'patients' learn to recognize unnecessary irrational lines of thinking, identify viable rational replacements, and replace the first with the second (or combine this process with practicing relaxation techniques, meditation, and mindfulness). I am not denying these treatments can prove helpful, but, even so, what they leave in place—unquestioned, unchallenged, and uncritiqued—are the social conditions of possibility as well as the social forces of generation of mental distress. It makes sense that people's experiences in the social environments in which they live their lives, in the relations with other people that they maintain and pursue in living their lives, and especially the ways in which these relations are structured, will impact people's mental health—and not just their genetic inheritance, their brain chemistry, and their ability to distinguish 'rational' from 'irrational' kinds of thinking.

After all, 'rationality' and 'irrationality' make sense according to 'modes of (ir)rationality' that correspond to particular forms of social organization, and particular kinds of cultures, with what is commonly identified and marked out and denigrated as 'irrational' at least potentially meaning *irrational according to a currently predominant regime of rationality*. I have often felt frustrated at failure to recognize the material conditions responsible for mental health versus mental illness. Many people maintain good reasons to feel mentally distressed, because many of us live in distressing situations and are well aware of and attuned to other distressing situations which, even if they don't immediately impact us, we recognize we are interconnected with, interdependent upon, and responsible for and complicit with. I hear "Twenty Four Hours" registering not only immediate personal experience of acute mental distress but also awareness of the acute mental distress others are experiencing, and have experienced. I hear "Twenty Four Hours" registering as feelings of distress that follow from recognizing our interconnection with and interdependence upon as well as responsibility for and complicity with the acute mental distress *of others*.

Judith Butler's *Precarious Life: The Powers of Mourning and Justice* and *Frames of War: When Is Life Grievable?* offer major contributions to theorizing precariousness, and precarity, with the latter in particular an increasingly influential conceptual category. Let's begin by drawing out some principal ideas from *Precarious Life* that I posit represent useful point of connection with "Twenty Four Hours." Butler recognizes "That we can be injured, that others can be injured, that we can be subject to death at the whims of another" constitute "reasons for both fear and grief" (xii). Fear and grief can and do motivate war, along with other forms of destructive violence, but Butler raises the question "what, politically, might be made of grief besides a cry for war?" (xiii). Butler suggests "One insight that injury affords is that there are others out there on whom my life depends, people I do not know and may never know" (xii). Accepting "This fundamental dependency on anonymous others" represents a crucial step in working to develop an ethics of non-violence on the basis of "an understanding of how easily life is annulled" (xviii).

Developing an ethics of non-violence involves inquiring into whose lives are grievable and whose are not, as well as, more broadly, what can and cannot be said, what can and cannot be shown: "The limits of the sayable, the limits of what can appear" (xvii). It is useful to consider "Twenty Four Hours" as engaging these limits. Ian Curtis's lyrics refer to and address solely 'anonymous others', while these lyrics and this music confront the invisible, intangible, and ephemeral. This music emphasizes the vantage points of those all too often expelled, or feeling as if they are expelled, to the margins of the visible, the audible, and the recognizable, and as constituting those all too often deemed unworthy of care, concern, compassion, and empathy, but rather treated as objects of suspicion, distrust, dismissal, denigration, mockery, scorn, pity, and callous indifference and disregard. This music represents the vantage point of the injured, the harmed, and those whose existence feels precarious, without advocating violent recompense for this suffering, instead searching desperately, and despairingly, for a means of bringing an end to the violence because its experience is overwhelmingly horrific.

Drawing upon the work of philosopher Emmanuel Levinas, Butler argues "dominant forms of representation can and must be disrupted for something about the precariousness of life to be apprehended" (xviii). This is because "Those who remain faceless or whose faces are presented to us as so many symbols of evil," in turn "authorize us to become senseless before those lives we have eradicated, and whose grievability is indefinitely postponed" (xviii). In the lyrics and music of Ian Curtis and Joy Division, dominant forms of representation are challenged by calling us to come to grips with horrors that the lyrics and music cannot precisely detail for us, but only can suggest to us how frightening these are–along with how urgent must be our own efforts to attempt to look, and see; to listen, and hear; and to sense, and feel.

Butler argues our grieving for others displays our humanness, because in grieving for others whom 'we have lost', whose deaths prompt us to experience grief, "something about who we are is revealed, something that delineates the ties we have to others, that shows us that these ties constitute what we are"–these are "ties or bonds that compose us" (22). Grief displays "the thrall in which our relations with others hold us, in ways we cannot always recount or explain . . . In ways that challenge the very notion of ourselves as autonomous and in control" (23). As Butler declares, "Let's face it. We're undone by each other. And if we're not, we're missing something" (23).

It makes sense, I suggest, to interpret the lyrics and music of Ian Curtis and Joy Division as not only replete with incipient grief, and with foreshadowing of imminent grieving, but also as urging us to recognize we are–or at least should be–undone by each other. And at the same time, I interpret these lyrics and this music as suggesting all too many are indeed 'missing something'–because they have lost the ability to recognize the self within the other and the other within the self, to care enough to grieve, to be willing and able to recognize and share vulnerability, especially vulnerability with and to others, and in particular anonymous others, openly and honestly.

Butler proposes "the primary others who are past for me not only live on in the fiber of the boundary that contains me (one meaning of 'incorporation'), but they also haunt the way I am" (28), while "we all live with this particular vulnerability, a vulnerability to the other that is part of bodily life, a vulnerability to a sudden address from elsewhere that we cannot preempt" (29). Butler suggests as a possible alternative to a social world in which war, and other forms of substantial violence, remain dominant forms of dealing with hurt, harm, grief, and actual or perceived grievance, an ethics of non-violence might involve "demanding a world in which bodily vulnerability be protected without therefore being eradicated"–and this would mean giving vulnerability its due space, recognizing and respecting vulnerability, while at the same time accepting so doing marks a significant change in the nature of vulnerability.

"Twenty Four Hours" makes sense as an effort to call attention to extreme vulnerability, and to demand recognition and respect for vulnerability, even if at times the song seems focused on wanting to overcome vulnerability or on relating to extreme vulnerability as what finally makes it impossible to sustain meaningful and enduring connections with others, rather than as providing the source of a shared humanity in a Butlerian "'common' corporeal vulnerability" (42). In this sense, "Twenty Four Hours" attests to how vulnerability, including vulnerable bodies, are all too often subject to exploitation and abuse, and not conceived as exemplifying what we essentially share in common. And yet, the precariousness depicted in "Twenty Four Hours" and the effort to survive, persist, and endure, including at the brink of desperation becomes despair becomes suicidality, does provide impetus for us, as listeners, to contemplate the fundamental importance, ethically, of striving "to be awake to what is precarious in another life, or, rather, the precariousness of life itself" (134).

If we are (all) ultimately vulnerable, fragile, precarious, and frail, or often are, or easily can be, or inevitably ultimately will be, then we need a system of social relations structured to counteract the limits while continuing to honor the fundamental truth of our ineradicable precariousness. If we realize, and act in accordance with this realization, that our lives, others' lives, and life itself is, above all else, precarious, we will want to do the best we can to enable us to do as much as we possibly can within the limits of what this precariousness allows, while not adding to or exacerbating it, and while vigilantly attending to whatever might render some of us more precarious than others–including attending to forces that alienate and isolate us, and that leave us feeling lonely, helpless, incapable, unworthy, undeserving, guilty, ashamed, weak, failing, desperate, despairing, and suicidal. If our lives are, most of all, precarious, it is all the more tragic when people find themselves in straits where suicide seems the only or the best viable response to how much pain and suffering they are experiencing–because aligned with such a Butlerian ethics we are alert to how easily any life can be snuffed out.

Frames of War: When Is Life Grievable? all the more precisely specifies how Butler proposes we understand precariousness, and precarity, as well as make use of this understanding as the basis for an ethics of non-violence. To begin, "The apprehension of the precarity of others–their exposure to violence, their socially induced transience and dispensability–is, by implication, an apprehension of the precarity of any and all living beings. Since we are also living, the apprehension of another's precarity is implicitly an apprehension of our own" (xvi). And yet, "precarity is distributed unequally," and it is important to pay heed to "the lives whose precarious conditions are suspended or shut out by the frame, or whose traces the frame cannot quite efface," and, what's more to "read the frame as participating in the production of precarity, inducing precarity" (xv).

"Twenty Four Hours" dramatically enacts the felt experience of a precarious life, sketched in terms of broadly ambiguous enough contours to relate to the felt experience of many concrete situations of precariousness, and precarity. It also relates to exploring, inquiring into, and seeking to come to terms with the experiences by others living in extreme precariousness, and extreme precarity. And it further relates to recognition of an intrinsic interconnection, interdependence, responsibility for, and complicity with what happens to others, when they are subject to situations, and corresponding felt experiences, of extreme precariousness, and extreme precarity. This can involve the situations and felt experiences of Holocaust victims in concentration camps, and comparable historic experiences involving victims of genocidal war. It can involve fears of incipient fascist tendencies at work within supposed anti- or post- fascist 'liberal democratic societies', including the post-WWII modestly social democratic UK. It can involve situations and felt experiences of those living on the margins (or what they experienced as the margins) of a 1970s Manchester and Greater Manchester social mainstream and normative culture, due to considerations of class, race, disability, mental and physical health status, age and generation, (counter-)cultural affiliation, philosophical outlook, and aesthetic sensibility. And, for listeners, from other times and places, it can involve connections with many further situations and felt experiences where such an evocation of felt experience of precariousness, and of precarity, makes sense to us, such, as for example, in relation to Butler's *Precarious Life* and *Frames of War*, Palestinian people living in the West Bank, Gaza, and Israel; prisoners in the ongoing 'War on Terror' held at Guantanamo Bay Detention Camp; and Iraqi prisoners of war tortured and humiliated by US soldiers at Abu Graibh. In more recent times, we can think of migrants–from Central America, from the Middle East and in particular from Syria, and from East African nations such as Somalia and South Sudan–including vast number of refugees and asylum seekers, and the hostile environments, including detention centers resembling prisons and concentration campus they face for often protracted and indefinite stays, while often also being harshly separated from families. We can think of victims of abuse and neglect within families, where this is hidden, and where others surrounding, including state authorities, are often reluctant to intervene, and in which psychological violence often equals or exceeds physical violence. We can think of victims of all of the following, and more besides: 'honor killings'; human trafficking; severe drug and alcohol addiction; homelessness; forced inductions into criminal gangs engaged in exceedingly dangerous, and routinely life-threatening work, as still young children; massive numbers of people of color imprisoned for lengthy sentences and otherwise subject to carcereal control for virtually their entire lives on the basis of petty drug crimes; struggling to survive, in the richest nations in the world, needing to rely on food banks, while single families crowd into shared houses with each family living entirely in a single room, just in order to be able to afford the cost of rent; and millions of people worldwide who have died of COVID-19, often isolated, alone, terrified, and in great pain, as well as millions grieving their deaths, and many thousands of others dealing with the debilitating effects of 'long COVID', effectively becoming permanently severely disabled as a result.

And we can certainly think of how many more people are and have been experiencing serious to severe mental health challenges, in the course of this pandemic, adding to an already huge extent of mental distress. In recent years, campaigning to draw attention to the gravity of this issue on my campus, at the University of Wisconsin-Eau Claire, I have repeatedly pointed out that the numbers of students sharing with me they are experiencing, and struggling, with serious to severe mental health issues, or have substantial–and usually quite recent–experience of doing so, has routinely run close to 50% or more in every class I teach, with so many of the people finding it difficult readily to obtain the help they need to get by, suggesting we are confronting 'a mental health epidemic' that is made all the worse by our continuing failure adequately to 'normalize' and 'naturalize' experience of mental distress, to end the stigma, and to treat this as a collective rather than a purely individual concern that requires we create a substantial campus culture of wellness and solidarity, not just increase and make more readily transparent what kinds of counseling services, and other crisis intervention services, people can individually turn to, when and as needed.

Butler raises important questions: How can we make use of heightened and dedicated awareness of our common precariousness, and vulnerability, to engage in an ethically sensitive and responsible manner with other people, especially those seemingly far distant, most unlike, and entirely unknown to us? How can we make use of heightened and dedicated awareness of our common precariousness, and vulnerability, to search out whose lives are hidden, or are distorted and denigrated in terms of how they are represented, such that these lives do not seem worthwhile at all, or substantially less worthwhile, as merely anonymous numbers, and as not worthy of receiving our grief? How can we distinguish common precariousness that exists as a condition of being human, from precarity, which refers to specific conditions and circumstances, where people's lives are at the edge of not being able to continue, to survive, to persist, and endure, and where their extent of deprivation and suffering has rendered it exceedingly difficult for them to experience even partial materializations, even fleeting glimpses of what Marx and Marxists identify as the true essence of being fully human–free, voluntary association with others, in exercising effective control over one's own agency, in laboring, in creating, and especially in laboring to create change, in themselves and their natural and social environments, together with others as part of substantively real communities where everyone is recognized and included?

I suggest it makes good sense to interpret the lyrics and the music of Ian Curtis and Joy Division as inviting and encouraging reflection on and engagement with issues of precariousness, and precarity, where we as listeners draw our own array of connections to specific kinds, sites, and instances of this playing out, inspired by the encouragement to identify with a subject making 'his' own connections, while not specifying these in so much empirical detail that they undermine our capacity to imagine our own, yet which nonetheless conveys the affective contours of such situations and experiences with stark precision and resonant detail. These lyrics and this music continually return us to the situation where we are forced to confront what are we going to do, and what we can do, when it feels as if we are weak, exhausted, overwhelmed, terrified, guilty, numb, desperate, and despairing, while always seeming to be 'in between' something that has catalyzed a fierce introspective state and a future in which we will have to act, somehow, but which we fear will prove most demanding, potentially more than we can handle. And yet these lyrics and this music also continually suggest so acting might prove liberating in ways we cannot yet fathom, but we must out faith it might be so. In doing all that, these songs, including "Twenty Four Hours," delineate a surprisingly precise subject position: that of the subject who wants, and needs, to act; who has recognized and accepted 'his' responsibility and complicity; who has already been acting by inquiring into and exploring what reinforces the conviction that acting is necessary and that there can be no turning back (to illusion, delusion, pretense, complacency, apathy, disengagement, callous disregard and indifference, normalcy, and identifying with and claiming to 'be normal'); who has found the process of acting already devastating, exhausting, shattering, and undoing, and who is, as a result, highly uncertain, fearful, and doubtful 'he' can continue, can survive, can endure, and can persist, but, even while emphasizing hesitation, desperation, and despair, *is continuing*, however unsteadily, nonetheless. Even if 'he' now all the more fully recognizes he has always already been alienated, isolated, lonely, different, even strange in the sense of other than conventionally 'normal' and unable to readily conform to prevailing normativity, he feels this more overwhelmingly now. What 'he' is missing is real, substantial, concrete, collective solidarity in this struggle, and 'he' is desperately reaching out for it. Yet 'he' fears few will understand what he is reaching out for and most will instead respond by viewing and treating him as a grotesque freak–as both excessively needy and pathetically weak.

Butler writes that "Precariousness implies living socially, that is, the fact that one's life is always in some sense in the hands of the other" (14). What's more, "It is not that we are born and then later become precarious, but rather that precariousness is coextensive with birth itself . . . and that . . . survival is dependent on what we might call a social network of hands. Precisely because a living being may die, it is necessary to care for that being so it may live" (14). This in turn means "grievability is a presupposition for the life that matters," and that we cannot adequately celebrate any life, including at its birth, "without an implicit understanding that the life is grievable, that it would be grieved if it were lost, and that this future anterior is installed as the condition of its life" (14-15). "Twenty Four Hours" challenges us to consider whether we are able and willing to grieve for the life at risk in the song–and for others at similar risk that we recognize in reflecting upon, and identifying with, the song, including, prospectively, our own. "Twenty Four Hours" challenges us to recognize how much we are *objectively* interdependent in the ways Butler describes, yet so often imagine *subjectively* that we–and all others–are independent, and that whether we, or they, survive or not, including how well or how badly, is our own and their own *individual* responsibility, and no one else's.

In further elaborating upon how the ethics she is developing is to make sense, Butler contends "Precariousness has to be grasped not simply as a feature of *this* or *that* life, but as a generalized condition whose very generality can be denied only by denying precariousness itself," and it is "on this basis" that "one objects to the differential allocation of precariousness and grievability," while "the very idea of precariousness implies dependency on social networks and conditions, suggesting that there is no 'life itself' at issue here, but always and only conditions of life, life as something that requires conditions in order to become livable life and, indeed, in order to be become grievable" (22-23). According to "Twenty Four Hours," what might such conditions include? As I have suggested earlier, these involve 'finding one's destiny', indeed 'before it is too late', and that makes sense as finding and being able to live out one's life with a sense of meaning, of purpose, even of mission–of living a life that is valuable to one's self and to others, in terms of what it gives and receives, and that entails the subject making full and best use of 'his' capacities, his labor, his creative potential and ability, in concert with others. These conditions also involve experiencing and sharing ample 'love', which can prospectively take multiple forms and involve multiple, including multiple simultaneous, 'loving relationships', because lack and especially loss of love–even if this also involves loss of illusions, delusions, pretenses, and possibly also in retrospect unjustified pride concerning love–leaves the subject of the song weakened and desperate, despairing, even suicidal. In other words, precarious. If, as Butler suggests, "Our obligations are precisely to the conditions that make life possible, not to 'life itself'," it is insufficient to admire and respect the sharing of vulnerability that "Twenty Four Hours" dramatically enacts, and to appreciate the resilience of the life-spirit in this song, but rather we need to focus on what does this precariousness suggest to us concerning conditions of life that this subject has lost, or is lacking, that many others have lost, or are lacking, and urgently need. As Butler herself describes these conditions, "If we take the precariousness of life as a point of departure, then there is no life without the need for shelter and food, no life without dependency on wider networks of sociality and labor, no life that transcends injurability and mortality" (24-25). Beyond recognizing the importance of sociality, as well as shelter, food, and sharing collectively the results of collective labor, as a necessary condition of life, we also here recognize the importance, as conditions that make life possible, of adequate means of anticipating and attending to injurability and mortality, which raises the critical question of how adequately do our present communities, societies, and cultures anticipate and attend to injurability and mortality. Are these shunted off to be dealt with by 'specialists' and 'specialist sectors', while the rest of us only deal with these conditions when and as we absolutely need to do so, are forced to do so, and most of the time avoid doing so, avoid taking any collective responsibility for doing so, avoid making these matters of collective concern rather than issues each individual is responsible for individually taking care of? Do we effectively segregate the injured, the ill, the disabled, and the elderly, even when we think we do not–do we continue to force people, in these circumstances, to feel as if they need to apologize, to feel guilty, for whom they are and where they are at, or would we rather not have to engage with them directly at all and be content if they instead just went away and disappeared, including for example, to nursing homes, hospices, other social care facilities, and to the sole responsibility of social workers, and of doctors, nurses, and health care professionals?

Although "Precariousness and precarity are intersecting concepts" because "Lives are by definition precarious," for Butler "Precarity designates that politically induced condition in which certain populations suffer from failing social and economic networks of support and become differentially exposed to injury, violence, and death. Such populations are at heightened risk of disease, poverty, starvation, displacement, and of exposure to violence without protection" (25-26). What's more, "Precarity also characterizes that politically induced condition of maximized precariousness for populations exposed to arbitrary state violence who often have no other option than to appeal to the very state from which they need protection" (26).

According to this theorization, it seems that subjects in Ian Curtis's precise position, as someone suffering from disabling chronic mental and physical illness but otherwise living a largely stable and secure existence, as well as coming from a happy childhood and a loving, supportive, lower middle class family background, was not experiencing 'precarity' per se as much as extreme precariousness. And, even as Bernard Sumner and Peter Hook came from more impoverished backgrounds and childhoods, and Stephen Morris experienced considerable alienation versus normative pathways toward adulthood, none of these members of Joy Division either, especially as Joy Division itself became more successful, would seem to be experiencing precarity either, with perhaps Sumner and Hook the closest, growing up in complicated and disrupted families also dealing with major deaths and serious disability.

Yet, I don't perceive Joy Division lyrics or music as simply reflective of the specific direct personal experiences of the bandmembers, and I do interpret these lyrics and this music as engaging with affects that engage a much wider array of prospective connections. Ian Curtis, in particular, I interpret as bringing to bear, in his contributions to this music-making, his exploration and inquiry into violence, cruelty, pain, suffering, and hardship that extended far beyond his own immediate experience, with a particular focus on those in the most extreme and desperate of straits, as exemplified by victims of the Holocaust and even more precisely by concentration camp prisoners forced to perform as sex slaves for their captors. As Deborah Curtis herself has suggested, any war would have served as a fruitful source for Ian Curtis's imaginative creation, with war of all kinds representing perhaps the greatest historical locus of induced precarity. Wars destroy many lives, and livelihoods, even among those not killed or maimed, and at the same time destroy social, economic, and political networks essential to insuring fundamental human needs can be met. And wars force vast numbers of people into situations of extraordinary precarity as refugees, and asylum seekers, with no choice but to face a high risk of death, by for example, crossing deserts in the southwest of the United States or the Mediterranean Sea.

But precarity entails another significant dimension, in Butler's theorization, as well, as it refers to "the politically induced condition that would deny equal exposure through the radically unequal distribution of wealth and the differential ways of exposing certain populations, racially and nationally conceptualized to greater violence" (28). In other words, precarity indicates whose precariousness matters, and whose does not. In Joy Division music, including but extending beyond the lyrics alone, it makes good sense to interpret this music as challenging us to notice and respond to those we are normatively encouraged not to notice or respond to–to see, hear, and feel what we would much rather not, which we would much rather ignore or avoid, because this is too shocking, too disturbing, too appalling, too unsettling, and too incriminating, of us, and of what we have to that point failed, or refused, to recognize, acknowledge, and respond to. This certainly can include the kinds of populations Butler references, and it makes sense to interpret Joy Division music as registering an awareness of ongoing fascist tendencies, after fascism seemingly has been vanquished and disappeared, in an otherwise ostensibly anti-fascist or post-fascist nation. In the US, and in fact in many nations in Europe and elsewhere, into the second and third decades of the 21st century, we have witnessed a rise in of what have long been referenced as 'far right movements', as these are now no longer all that far removed from the political center of influence and impact. These movements are objectively fascist, and many, including across the broad left, have been surprised by their recent ascent, while at times wanting to dismiss their impact or pretend they are less extreme, and less fascistic, than they have turned out to be. After the attempted insurrectionary coup in Washington, DC on 6 January 2021, though, even moderate mainstream commentators have identified those involved, and those responsible, as 'fascist'.

But we have to wonder, and Joy Division songs challenge us to do so, why have too many waited or refused for too long to recognize and confront what is happening for what it is? How long will contemporary fascism represent a major threat? How far from defeated is it? Fascism, after all, works hand in hand with racism and xenophobic nationalism, as well as with scorn for and disparagement of intellectuals and academics, artists and the arts, the humanities broadly conceived and practiced, and all populations easily marked out as different, lesser, and other, including on account of gender and sexuality as well as mental and physical health and disability. And fascism scorns and disparages what it perceives as 'weakness', including through openly, publicly sharing vulnerability, especially extreme vulnerability, and through creating communities founded on mutual caring, mutual sharing and nurturing of feelings, collective equality, collective responsibility for individual and communal wellness, and substantively meaningful respect for equity, diversity, and inclusion. An authoritarian populist, neo-fascist society and culture would have no truck with an ethics that, to cite Butler, "reveals me less as an 'ego' than as a being bound up with others in inextricable and irreversible ways, existing in a generalized condition of precariousness and interdependency, affectively driven and crafted by those whose effects on me I never chose" (180). After all, in addition to what I have just previously described concerning what fascism scorns and disparages, fascism champions rugged individualism, albeit at the same time as it champions mass conformity and mass mobilization in support of charismatic individual leadership, and it depends upon being able to define harsh lines of inclusion and exclusion concerning who are supposedly legitimate members of the righteous community versus those whom fascism denounces as insidious 'elites' and 'hordes' of 'scum'. 'Those whose effects on me I never chose' are more likely to be perceived, from a fascist vantage point, as threats and enemies than as beneficiaries and compatriots. What's more, fascism is hardly 'anti-violence' and in fact thrives on the persistent invocation and exercise of violence, including to intimidate, overwhelm, punish, and destroy–even as this is often justified, resentfully, as 'payback' for those betraying o otherwise undermining reactionary norms, values, and modes of identifying, living, and (inter)relating. Fascism would hardly support a Butlerian "critical intervention apropos the norms that differentiate between those lives that count as liveable and grievable and those that do not" (180), as fascism is all about elaborating and even increasing normative differentiations between those whose lives count as more versus less worthy of living and of grieving.

A concluding set of reflections from Butler offers an additional nuance to her theorization and especially to how much of Joy Division music is engaged with violence, and what that might mean, as well as how that might fit with efforts to put into practice an ethics of non-violence. Butler proposes, "In effect, one has to come up against violence to practice non-violence (they are bound together, and tensely so); but, it bears repeating, the violence one is up against does not issue exclusively from the outside" (182). In Joy Division music, we follow a persona that shares with us that "I never realised the lengths I'd have to go/All the darkest corners of a sense I didn't know" who no longer is innocent, or can pretend to be innocent, whose experience of what he has been proudest of is shattered, who experiences "A cloud hangs over me, marks every move," and who has "realised how it's all gone wrong." This is persona who has come up against the violence within, the violence of which he is capable and for which he is responsible, the violence he is guilty of perpetrating (guilty by means of commission) as well as the violence he is guilty of by refusing to intervene and stop (guilty by means of omission). 'He' recognizes the 'violence within', actual and potential–i.e., the incipient fascistic tendencies within an otherwise ostensibly anti-fascist subjectivity. This shock of horrified self-recognition accounts for how and why this song and other Joy Division songs so often suggest we are dealing with a grim to desolate encounter, that the music as persona dreads and has already experienced dread as a result of, while warning us of the same yet exhorting us nonetheless to face up to this for ourselves–to come face to face with these same tendencies *in* ourselves. Butler suggests we need to recognize, accept, and incorporate tendencies toward violence within ourselves into an ethical practice of non-violence, as this is "precisely the dehiscence at the basis of the 'we', the condition under which we are passionately bound together: ragefully, desirously, murderously, lovingly" (183). We need to accept, as Butler indicates, "To walk the line is, yes, to live the line, the impasse of rage and fear, and to find a mode of conduct that does not seek to resolve the anxiety of that position too quickly through a decision" (183).

This last statement resonates with Joy Division songs, so often focused on steadily building, as well as on ebbs and flows of tension, with tension never fully resolved but always ultimately suspended, and with how much these songs address situations where the narrator-protagonist of the lyrics, and the music as persona, are not so much immediately engaged in direct, overt, physically material action, but rather reporting, reflecting on, anticipating, and worrying over this kind of action. All the while, neither quite here nor there but always in between. In "Twenty Four Hours" we encounter a subject in between devastating losses, as 'he' continues to feel the impact of these losses, who is taking stock of where 'he' is at, where he has come to and arrived 'at', and what has happened to him as a result of what he has gone through, anticipating that he cannot long stay in this state, yet uncertain about all of the following: how to proceed forward, if that is possible at all; what this will involve and require if it is possible; what kinds of support and assistance are necessary to do so; from whom and from what to obtain this support and assistance; and where as well as how to find such prospective sources of support and assistance. Still seeking 'my destiny', and seeking it 'in the heart of where sympathy held sway', suggests seeking it in some kind of fellow feeling and real connection with other people, involving an extension and practice of care and concern, but worrying it is getting late, it might be too late, or soon it will be too late to find, obtain, and actualize that destiny. So, here we have a subject far from ready to make a quick decision, and who represents the decision he 'needs' to make as far from simple and easy, even when this matter seems pre-determined or fated, and who is lingering in anxiety that is not resolved by the end of the song, striving to live the line that constitutes 'the impasse of rage and fear'. This seems apt even if much of what is portrayed is bleak and desolate–e.g., "a valueless collection of hopes and desires" or "Looked beyond the day at hand, there's nothing there at all"–and even if this subject seems more sad than angry. This sadness follows from raging against what has resulted in this state of affairs, while fearing what it means and will mean. Here we have a notion of how to approach active engagement with the darknesses that this music concerns itself with, and that is by *not* distancing ourselves from *feeling* what these are like, from the inside, even when these are painful feelings: anger, rage, frustration, disappointment, impatience, restlessness, worry, fear, anxiety, panic, sadness, outrage, agony, anguish, bitterness, desperation, despair, numbness, exhaustion, and resignation. We need to feel the weight of those interior as well as exterior barriers and obstacles toward embracing shared precariousness as basis for confronting and transforming economic, political, social, and cultural conditions that produce precarity in differentially assigning and reinforcing disparity, and that conceal and mystify our responsibility for and complicity with the precarity of others.

Lastly, I will explore connections between, on the one hand, the lyrics and music of Ian Curtis and Joy Division, and "Twenty Four Hours" in particular, and, on the other hand, Darren McGarvey's book *Poverty Safari: Understanding the anger of Britain's underclass* (McGarvey is otherwise well-known, or at least has been in the past, as the rapper Loki). *Poverty Safari* is a memoir, recounting and reflecting on McGarvey's experience born into and growing up in poverty, in the Pollock section of Glasgow, as well as what have been consequences for him, and others like him, in coming from and living this kind of experience; how and why those without such an experience often misunderstand poor people, and offer kinds of assistance that are not helpful, and especially not empowering of those they are supposedly aiming to help; and of changing, himself, as he became convinced of the necessity to reflect critically on past political convictions and inclinations, and to take direct personal responsibility for his own life, for what it is like, and for where it is headed. McGarvey's personal experiences involve a much wider array of vectors of precarity than in Ian Curtis's case, given Curtis's own lower middle class background, and Curtis's lack of comparable experience of the extremes of deprivation–and overt violence–that McGarvey has experienced. Even Sumner's and Hook's upbringings, as harsh as these often and in many ways were, do not appear to be as thoroughgoing instances of precarity as in McGarvey's case. Nevertheless, useful connections can be made, including with what the lyrics and music of Ian Curtis and Joy Division allude to, reference, and suggest, and with how these lyrics and this music do so.

Early on, McGarvey writes about how readily he can identify with the residents of Grenfell Tower, in light of the devastating fire and subsequent prominent revelations of how much was known well before the fire concerning how unsafe the conditions were and of how little respected were the voices of the people living in the Tower. As McGarvey writes, "I know that sense of being cut off from the world, despite having such a wonderful view of it through a window in the sky; that feeling of isolation, despite being surrounded by hundreds of other people above, below and either side of you. But most of all, I understand the sense that you are invisible, despite the fact that your community can be seen for miles around and is one of the most prominent features of the city skyline" (11).

In relation to the lyrics and music of Ian Curtis and Joy Division, including "Twenty Four Hours," I suggest we can recognize a commonality of focus on vantage points, situations, and experiences of felt isolation, even when ostensibly surrounded by many other people, and also of being effectively invisible, where what you are experiencing, and especially struggling with and suffering from, is unnoticed. It makes good sense, as I have previously argued, to interpret "Twenty Four Hours" as reflecting on an encounter with what normally is pushed into "the darkest corners" and which requires "a sense I didn't know" to be able to come face to face with. In "Twenty Four Hours" we meet a subject deeply affected, and seriously disturbed, by what this subject has encountered, is encountering, and expects yet to encounter, in these 'darkest corners' and as a result of previously 'never realizing how far' this subject 'has to go' in order to be able to confront, past self-protective illusions, what it is like–what it feels like–to exist in these spaces. The subject is troubled by recognizing 'his' implication in these conditions of precarity, his responsibility for and complicity with this kind of deprived life. Unlike those McGarvey criticizes–"But most people, despite their best intentions, were just passing through on a short-lived expedition. A safari of sorts" (11)–the subject of "Twenty Four Hours" does not exit unaffected, unchanged, and as secure, stable, and comfortable as before, but rather is shattered, undone, and forever transformed by these encounters, such that 'he' carries the marks of what he has encountered forever onward, not at all inclined to offer glib advice or simplistic solutions.

In chapter 2, "A History of Violence," McGarvey shares how "By the age of ten I was adjusted to the threat of violence. In some ways, violence itself was preferable to the threat of violence" (29). What McGarvey means by the second statement has to do with that fact that "Acts of violence are terrifying, but a sustained threat of violence is sometimes much worse" (29). In order to survive, living amidst continuous and pervasive violence, you need to develop "survival strategies," including learning to "negotiate it," to "become a skillful emotional manipulator," and to respond to violence with violence in kind (29). This situation feels, lived 'from the inside', resistant to any solution, introduced 'from the outside'. 'Outside' alternatives appear nought but illusions, and delusions, akin to "A valueless collection of hopes and past desires." What's more, this situation feels glacially 'permanent', as well as one in which love is absent or meaningless.

McGarvey sharply criticizes those who deny or minimize the importance of class, and especially the divide between middle and working classes in Britain. As McGarvey summarizes, one standard classificatory scheme divides these classes as follows: A, "Higher Managerial, administrative or professional": 1.4 %; B, "Intermediate managerial, administrative or professional": 23%; C1, "Supervisory or clerical and junior managerial, administrative or professional": 29%; C2,

"Skilled manual workers": 21 %; D, "Semi-skilled and unskilled manual workers":15%; and E, "Casual or lowest grade workers, pensioners, and others who depend on the welfare state for their income": 8% (50). ABC1, McGarvey indicates, represent the middle classes, and C2DE represent the working classes. In Ian Curtis's case, his family background is C1 and in his own work as a job referral officer for disabled people is C1, whereas Stephen Morris's family background is A, and his own work for his father, while in Joy Division, is B. Bernard Sumner's and Peter Hook's principal paid jobs, while in Joy Division, even as Sumner's is not manual labor per se, seem closer to D.

The most valuable social resources, McGarvey argues, respond to the needs, interests, and desires of classes ABC1, not classes C2DE. McGarvey challenges those who lament working class and impoverished people's apathy, political disengagement, and failure to identify with and support candidates and parties on the left. The latter claim to serve the interests of working class and poor people, but McGarvey contends working class and poor people know repeated promises and appeals to working class and poor people don't amount to much, don't make much if any real and lasting difference, don't follow from actually listening to what people in these communities have to say for themselves, and don't follow from collaborating with working class and poor people so as to empower the latter to address their own interests, needs, and desires. According to McGarvey, the participation and engagement 'deficit' on the part of the working class and the poor that many lament is the product of "a culture that leaves many people feeling excluded, isolated or misrepresented and, therefore, adversarial or apathetic to it" (55). "It's the belief that the system is rigged against you and that all attempts to resist or challenge it are futile . . . . A belief that you are excluded from taking part in the conversation about your own life. This belief is deeply held by people in many communities and there is a very good reason for it: it's true" (55).

Joy Division emerged from punk that reflected and responded to substantial generational discontent with and rebellion versus being ignored, excluded, and subjugated to an oppressively constrictive set of mainstream prescriptions and proscriptions concerning what constitutes a proper, normal life. And versus how much of post-World War II British social democratic welfare state society was heavy-handedly paternalistic. Such conditions result in feeling left out and left behind. In turn, those who feel left out and left behind feel the need to create an alternative to the dominant culture, one that challenges and critiques the limitations of the dominant, and that emphasizes, in its critique of the dominant, how oppressive and repressive the dominant is as well as on how hard it is to secure space, time, and other resources to create, maintain, and sustain an alternative to the dominant. As McGarvey comments, "being locked out of the decision-making process lies at the heart of a lot of community friction," while "If we can accept that criminality or chronic illness often has its roots in poverty then we must also be prepared to accept that other socially regressive attitudes may too" (170-171). In "Twenty Four Hours" we encounter a repeated effort to try to find, to reach, to secure, to obtain something that seems to slip away, to disappear, or never to have actually existed in the first place. Searching for a meaningful connection, for a fulfilling destiny, for a satisfying perspective, for someone to call out to and for someone to respond to one's own calling out, all represent vital and urgent needs that simultaneously seem virtually impossible to realize.

In chapter 10, "One Flew Over the Cuckoo's Nest," McGarvey discusses how people "in deprived communities" often turn to "comfort eating, smoking, gambling, binge drinking, substance misuse and various cultures of aggression and violence" as means of coping with "lives constrained by emotional stress, anxiety or dread" and as providing "a brief emotional reprieve–and an illusion of control" (80). Explaining why seeking alternatives to these outlets can be so difficult for people living in poverty and from deprived communities, for people from backgrounds like McGarvey's "the simple act of entering a library becomes an immense example of personal courage" (154). People not from this background have a hard time understanding, because "When you don't live this kind of precarious life every day then it's easy to forget that many other people do–and it's bloody hellish" (155).

"Twenty Four Hours" embodies an effort to rise and keep rising; lingering, sustaining, soaring, and flaring; pushing higher, harder, louder, and faster. And it embodies as well a slowing down to contemplate (in quieter, lighter, slower moments), along with an expressed need for perspective, for therapy, for someone else's call, for someone else's response to one's own call, for a modicum of control, for a felt sense of exercising real control and real self-determination for a fleeting instant. Insofar as the song is about struggling to survive, it runs through survival strategies but fails to find any sufficient to insure this end. Nevertheless, as the title of Anton Corbijn's film suggests, and as I have already addressed, major themes throughout the lyrics of Ian Curtis and the music of Joy Division include control, lack of control, loss of control, needing control, confronting how little control we ever can realize or sustain, how much of what we thought we controlled or could control we did not and cannot, and fear of what happens when one is out of or beyond control. Control is important to human beings, yet at the same time many lack control, especially those not occupying socially advantaged positions, such as in terms of class, and it can be crushing to try to survive with no (or next to no) control.

McGarvey critiques programs ostensibly designed to combat poverty and economic insecurity for failing to focus on "improving self-esteem, and not simply employability," because with the latter is "key to cultivating the kind of self-belief and resilience which eludes so many young people in areas like the Gorbals" (99). The lyrics and music of Ian Curtis and Joy Division, including in "Twenty Four Hours," continually foreground issues of fragile self-esteem, or ready and compounding threats to self-esteem. It can be useful, in maintaining and reproducing existing social arrangements, that a great many experience serious self-esteem issues, serious self-doubts and serious worries that they are not capable, talented, or deserving. I often encounter these attitudes among students I teach. Many of these people are hesitant to fearful of 'giving any offense', of 'making any mistakes', of 'getting it wrong', of 'putting themselves out', of risking what they worry might lead to mockery or ridicule, of 'needing to walk on eggshells', and of ever being perceived as 'questioning authority'. All of this is worrisome, and I take it as my responsibility to interrupt and redirect this kind of thinking, and to encourage students to believe in themselves, in what they are capable of, and in what they deserve–not only for their own psychic benefit, but also so they will be capable of making substantial contributions toward needed social change, rather than always, however reluctantly, doing what they are told. When people believe they are incapable of making any meaningful difference to affect any larger social ends, this can become a self-reinforcing prophecy. In relation to people from 'deprived communities', if they are treated solely as victims, as people suffering from deficits, deficiencies, and dysfunctions, they are simultaneously encouraged to perceive themselves as merely passive beneficiaries of help provided from others rather than as people who can, should, and need to learn how to help (raise) themselves (up). In Joy Division songs we confront a persistent wavering between daring assertion, daring performance, daring venture, daring confrontation, and daring engagement, on the one hand, with fear, worry, anxiety, panic, doubt, desperation, and despair over what any of the former can achieve. This music thereby attests to a larger culture leaving many doubting what they are capable of achieving, as well as what they deserve.

In chapter 18, "The Stranger," McGarvey focuses on the need for people in working class and deprived communities to learn "emotional literacy," to be able to open up, share, confront, engage, and work through "painful emotions that drive" so much of the (self-)destructive behavioral cycles, and similar patterns, these people find themselves caught up within–and caught by. In the lyrics and music of Ian Curtis and Joy Division, including in "Twenty Four Hours," what we as listeners encounter is an effort to break the silence, to overcome the stigma, to end the taboo, about openly recounting and sharing messy, disturbing, difficult, and unsettling emotions. As Deborah Curtis has suggested, coming from the background from which he did, her husband learned that doing this was likely to be frowned upon, and, as many have noted, working class to lower middle class males growing up in Manchester and Greater Manchester from the mid to late 1950s onward learned that openly sharing emotional vulnerability was not what boys and men 'normally' did. Music, and the arts more broadly, provided an outlet for what otherwise was difficult to impossible to share–for audience members as much as for the musicians themselves. These constraints on sharing difficult emotions, and especially sharing extreme vulnerability, undoubtedly impacted Ian Curtis in how he minimized or obfuscated when asked how we was doing emotionally, as well as in how limited to non-existent he perceived were available options to share that he was not doing well at all.

To this day it is often hard for many to share intense, disturbing, painful, and vulnerable emotions. As a result many struggle to develop the 'emotional literacy' they need, as well as struggle to respect, value, and make productive use of the emotional intelligence they possess. Many class sessions I have taught where students have shared emotional vulnerabilities, and done so in ways physically attesting to how truly vulnerable they indeed did feel, have proven the class sessions they remembered, and treasured, the most and the longest, with this especially the case when we have engaged in collective sharing. In these class sessions students have felt empathetic and solidaristic connections directly at work, and the idealistic promise of studies in the humanities become immediately tangible.

A culminating emphasis of *Poverty Safari*, as McGarvey proposes, involves "reclaiming the idea of personal responsibility from a rampant and socially misguided right wing that has come to monopolise it" (130). This in turn presupposes greater willingness and more effective ability to engage in self-critique, including to be ready to question fundamental principles, convictions, values, and ideals, as well as to be ready to accept and admit that you can be, and often are and have been, wrong. As McGarvey explains, "For me, getting sober, staying sober and understanding why I was so unhappy has been a profound and life-altering process," which has led to a fundamental shift in his thinking, and "When going through such a fundamental shift in your thinking, everything in your life is on the table for review" (190). The latter includes, for McGarvey, recognizing "that my political principles were not quite the beacon of selfless integrity and virtue I had imagined they were. Quite the opposite in fact" (190). "I'm sure I'm not just speaking for myself when I say that my left-wing beliefs were something I inherited, much like one inherits a title or a religion" (190).

Unfortunately, "Social media has given us a platform to transmit our beliefs" such that "Everyone appears to be very sure of what they believe and that their beliefs are the right ones. But one thing you don't see a lot on social media is people humbly announcing they were wrong about something, or that they have committed the cardinal sin of changing their mind and renouncing a false belief" (191). This criticism coincides with much I find dissatisfying about social media. Social media encourages quick, frequent, and glib assertion–and denunciation–but discourages careful, thoughtful, elaborate, and sustained argument where those engaged always concentrate on arguing and critiquing positions and practices, not attacking and demonizing persons. Social media also too often feels like a location where the same opinion circulates over and over again, and where everyone feels compelled to contribute to this incessant circulation–e.g., to need to comment on every news event as soon as and in immediate reaction to it happening, without taking the time or investing the effort to deliberate carefully before doing so. Because social media becomes an important public face, and normally this face shows most people conforming to a narrow array of what constitute best appearances, with people seemingly in assured control of what they think, feel, believe, and do, sharing being wrong, making mistakes, changing one's mind, or not even being certain what one thinks can feel uncomfortable and unwelcome. Social media operates as a site for social promotion, where one is in effect put in the position of campaigning on behalf of one's self, and it can thereby seem counter-productive to represent one's self as flawed, limited, mistaken, as wrong, hesitant, and uncertain.

McGarvey argues these kinds of spaces, and the dominant modes of discourse they authorize and legitimate, are counter-productive in addressing long-standing, deep-rooted, and multi-faceted problems such as poverty. As McGarvey explains, "By now, I've hopefully established that one of the biggest problems we face as a society is stress" (194). This stress has much to do with how people experiencing poverty respond to their experience, as well as how people not experiencing poverty themselves respond to those who are. Tackling this stress requires recognizing "that the government isn't going to fix this problem any time soon," and "simply attributing responsibility for every ill in society to a 'system' or a vaguely defined power dynamic" is not going to do much good either, even if the latter is "something we lefties have gotten all too good at" (195). Instead, the aim should be "striving to take responsibility" by those who are poor and come from deprived communities, for what they can and will make of their lives (195). This is "not about blame," but rather about "honestly trying to identify what pieces of the puzzle are within our capacity to deal with," guided by recognition that we are all "part of that system and, are, on some level," all "complicit in its dysfunction" (195).

McGarvey provocatively contends, "We are all frauds, copycats, and tricksters" (215), all lying about what we have done, and all supporting beliefs we have done little to nothing, in concrete practice, to substantively embody. McGarvey shares "Much of my own life has been squandered in years of careless or misguided thinking," in which, effectively, "my intent was always to absolve myself of blame–while generously apportioning it to others. If only I had given people I resented as much leeway as I was willing to give myself, what then?" (215). This kind of thinking, "Too much of it, for too long, made me deeply unhappy" (215). Foundational principles in what McGarvey's alludes to as his "new pragmatism" (217) include accepting "while it isn't always easy, sometimes the only solution is to forgive and forget," and that "We are all, to some extent, victims and abusers at different stages of our lives, but we tend only to recall those times when we were harmed. That might be natural, but it's not always the truth" (216). McGarvey admits "I shudder to think how little I knew, precisely at those moments when I thought I knew it all, and how vulnerable such a lack of insight really made me. Which is why I doubt I'll ever be truly certain of anything again–perhaps other than my own capacity to be stunningly wrong" (218-219).

In "Twenty Four Hours" we confront a subject that is recognizing, and accepting, how wrong 'he' was, and readily could be, as well as how little certain he is about what he 'now' knows, and where this can and will taken him–who recognizes all too many "hopes and past dreams" now represent "a valueless collection," and what he once prided himself on is now lost and gone, seemingly forever. But this subject hardly seems inclined to identify with the kind of 'new pragmatism' McGarvey endorses, and in fact, seems to find disillusionment concerning grander dreams, plans, visions, and aspirations to be devastating. He is still searching, albeit desperately, for 'my destiny'. Yes, these lyrics and this music can, like McGarvey does in *Poverty Safari*, challenge us to be more self-critical, including concerning what we have long taken for granted, as self-evident, beyond question, and as 'obviously' right and true, while recognizing how much we don't know, never actually knew, and will never truly or fully know, along with how much we have deluded ourselves, pretended to be what we were not (and even were never capable of), and even that, yes, we all are, more than most of us are inclined to admit, 'frauds, copycats, and tricksters', as well as both victims and abusers.

Yet this kind and extent of exposure, as represented and suggested in the lyrics and music of Ian Curtis and Joy Division, is not an end. Abandoning all prior illusion, and all prior delusion, leaves us with nothing; we 'have got to find' a replacement 'before it's too late'–before the emptiness robs us of our will to live on. In the lyrics and music of Ian Curtis and Joy Division a fierce idealism remains: life must be about something grand, daring, noble, extraordinary, and monumental, if it is to be worthwhile. And if all of what we previously imagined this might involve no longer makes sense, we need something else to do so instead. Yet, in the midst of our disenchantment we worry this 'something else' does not exist, or that it does not exist for us–that we will not be able to find it.

At the end of *Poverty Safari*, McGarvey writes "Today I realise the best contribution I can make to society is to raise a healthy, happy and secure child" and "the most practical way of transforming my community is to first transform myself" (220). In "Twenty Four Hours" the former focus feels far from enough, while effort invested in the latter only seems to expose more pain, longing, yearning, suffering, frustrated desire, desperate need, and greater despair. But "Twenty Four Hours" does not conclude by endorsing suicide as the only logical outcome or the only viable way out. "Twenty Four Hours" raises this as a possibility, but keeps open the possibility of an alternative–and keeps seeking and striving for an alternative, for renewed means and renewed reason to live, and to live with passion and purpose.

Works Cited

Alcoff, Linda Martín. "Public Self/Lived Subjectivity." Weiss, Gail, Ann V. Murphy, and Gayle Salamon, eds. *50 Concepts for a Critical Phenomenology*. Evanston: Northwestern University Press, 2020, 269-274.

_____. *Visible Identities: Race, Gender, and the Self*. New York: Oxford University Press, 2006.

Anzaldúa, Gloria. *Borderlands/La Frontera: The New Mestiza*. 3rd Edition. San Francisco: Aunt Lute Books, 2007.

Barthes, Roland. *Image–Music–Text*. Stephen Heath, trans. London: Fontana, 1979.

Beck, Ulrich. *Risk Society: Towards a New Modernity*. London: Sage, 1992.

Bentall, Richard. "Mental illness is the result of misery, yet we still stigmatise it." *The Guardian*. 16 February 2016. https://www.theguardian.com/commentisfree/2016/feb/26/mental-illness-misery-childhood-traumas Accessed 14 March 2021.

Berger, Peter and Thomas Luckmann. *The Social Construction of Reality: a Treatise in the Sociology of Knowledge*. New York: Doubleday, 1966.

Bergson, Henri. *Bergson: Key Writings*. Keith Ansell Pearson and John Mullarkey, eds. London: Continuum, 2002.

Bickerdike, Jennifer Otter, ed. *Joy Devotion: The Importance of Ian Curtis and Fan Culture*. London: Headpress, 2016.

The Blinders. *Fantasies of a Stay at Home Psychopath*. Music LP, 2020. \

Bottà, Giacomo. "Trying to Find a Clue, Trying to Find a Way to Get Out!: The European Imaginary of Joy Division." *Heart & Soul: Critical Writings on Joy Division*. London: Rowan & Littlefield, 2018, 33-45.

Bracewell, Michael. "Licht und Blindheit." Brown, Glenn, Michael Bracewell, and Lavinia Greenlaw. *Joy Division*. London: Enitharmon Editions, 2017, 21-23.

Brown, Glenn, Michael Bracewell, and Lavinia Greenlaw. *Joy Division*. London: Enitharmon Editions, 2017.

Butler, Judith. *Bodies That Matter: On the Discursive Limits of 'Sex'*. New York: Routledge, 1993.

_____. *Frames of War: When Is Life Grievable?* 2009. London: Verso, 2016.

_____. *Gender Trouble: Feminism and the Subversion of Identity*. New York: Routledge, 1990.

_____. *Precarious Life: The Powers of Mourning and Justice*. 2004. London: Verso, 2020.

Burstow, Bonnie. "'Mental health' praxis–not the answer: a constructive antipsychiatry position." Cohen, Bruce M.Z., ed. *Routledge International Handbook of Critical Mental Health*. London: Routledge, 2018, 31-38.

Cabaret Voltaire. *Shadow of Fear*. Music LP, 2020.

Card, Claudia. *Confronting Evils: Terrorism, Torture, Genocide*. Cambridge: Cambridge University Press, 2010.

Cisneros, Natalie. "Borderlands and Border Crossing." Weiss, Gail, Ann V. Murphy, and Gayle Salamon, eds. *50 Concepts for a Critical Phenomenology*. Evanston: Northwestern University Press, 2020, 47-52.

Clarke, Eric. "Empathy and the ecology of musical consciousness." Herbert, Ruth, David Clarke, and Eric Clarke, eds. *Music and Consciousness 2: Worlds, Practices, Modalities*. Oxford: Oxford University Press, 2019, 71-92.

Cohen, Bruce M.Z. "Marxist Theory." Cohen, Bruce M.Z., ed. *Routledge International Handbook of Critical Mental Health*. London: Routledge, 2018, 46-55.

Cohen, Bruce M.Z., ed. *Routledge International Handbook of Critical Mental Health*. London: Routledge, 2018.

Collins, Patricia Hill. *Black Feminist Thought*. New York: Routledge, 1990.

Control. Feature-Length Fictional Film. Directed by Anton Corbijn, 2007.

Cooley, Charles Horton. *Human Nature and Social Order*. New York: Charles Scribners Sons, 1902.

Cox, Arnie. *Music & Embodied Cognition: Listening, Moving, Feeling, & Thinking*. Bloomington: Indiana University Press, 2017.

Cross, Ian, Felicity Laurence, and Tal Chen Rabinowitch. "Empathetic creativity in musical group practices." *The Oxford Handbook of Music Education, Volume 2*. Oxford: Oxford University Press, 337-353.

Cumming, Naomi. "The subjectivities of 'Erbarme Dich'." *Music Analysis*. 16 (1): 5-44.

Curtis, Deborah. "Foreword." Curtis, Ian. *So This is Permanence: Joy Division Lyrics and Notebooks*. Deborah Curtis and Jon Savage, eds. London: Faber and Faber, 2014, vii-xi.

_____. *Touching From a Distance: Ian Curtis & Joy Division*. London: Faber and Faber, 1995.

Curtis, Ian. "Love Will Tear Us Apart." Isolated vocal recording. 1980.

_____. *So This is Permanence: Joy Division Lyrics and Notebooks*. Deborah Curtis and Jon Savage, eds. London: Faber and Faber, 2014.

Dickinson, Bob. Contributing to Savage, Jon, *This Searing Light, The Sun, and Everything Else: Joy Division–The Oral History*. London: Faber and Faber, 2019.

Diprose, Rosalyn. "Corporeal Generosity." Weiss, Gail, Ann V. Murphy, and Gayle Salamon, eds. *50 Concepts for a Critical Phenomenology*. Evanston: Northwestern University Press, 2020, 83-89.

Du Bois, W.E.B. *The Souls of Black Folk*. New York: A.C. McClurg & Co., 1904.

Dubrofsky, Rachel E. "Therapeutics of the Self: Surveillance in the Service of the Therapeutic." *Television and the New Media*. 8 (4), 2007: 263-284.

Eagleton, Terry. *Why Marx Was Right*. New Haven: Yale University Press, 2011.

Estill, Jo. *The Singing Voice*. http://thesingingvoice.com/about/vocal-technique/jo-estill Accessed 14 March 2021.

Fanon, Frantz. *Black Skin, White Masks*. 1952. Richard Philcox, trans. New York: Grove Press, 2008.

Ferguson, Iain. *Politics of the Mind: Marxism and Mental Distress*. London: Bookmarks, 2017.

Fielding, Helen A. "The Habit Body." Weiss, Gail, Ann V. Murphy, and Gayle Salamon, eds. *50 Concepts for a Critical Phenomenology*. Evanston: Northwestern University Press, 2020, 155-160.

Fontaines D.C. *Dogrel*. Music LP, 2019.

_____. *A Hero's Death*. Music LP, 2020.

Freud, Sigmund. *Beyond the Pleasure Principle*. 1920. James Strachey, trans. New York: W.W. Norton, 1961.

_____. *Civilization and Its Discontents*. Joan Riviere, trans. New York: Jonathan Cape and Harrison Smith, 1930.

_____. *The Interpretation of Dreams*. James Strachey, trans. 1931 Third Revised English Edition. New York: Avon, 1965.

_____. *An Outline of Psycho-Analysis*. James Strachey, trans. 1949. New York: W.W. Norton, 1969.

_____. *The Uncanny*. David McClintock, trans. 1919. New York: Penguin, 2003.

Frosh, Stephen. *A Brief Introduction to Psychoanalytic Theory*. London: Bloomsbury, 2012.

Garland-Thomson, Rosemarie. *Extraordinary Bodies: Figuring Disability in American Culture and Literature*. New York: Columbia University Press, 1997.

_____. *Freakery: Cultural Spectacles of the Extraordinary Body*. New York: New York University Press, 1996.

_____. "Misfitting." Weiss, Gail, Ann V. Murphy, and Gayle Salamon, eds. *50 Concepts for a Critical Phenomenology*. Evanston: Northwestern University Press, 2020, 225-230.

_____. *Staring: How We Look*. Oxford: Oxford University Press, 2009.

Geras, Norman. *Marxism and Human Nature: Refutation of a Legend*. 1983. London: Verso, 2016.

Goffman, Erving. *The Presentation of Self in Everyday Life*. 1956. New York: Knopf Doubleday/Penguin, 1959.

Gomory, Tomi and Daniel J. Dunleavy. "Madness: a critical history of 'mental health care' in the United States." Cohen, Bruce M.Z., ed. *Routledge International Handbook of Critical Mental Health*. London: Routledge, 2018, 117-125.

Grimshaw, Mike. "Transmission in the Colony: On exported Englishness and the secular religion of the axis mundi." Bickerdike, Jennifer Otter, ed. *Joy Devotion: The Importance of Ian Curtis and Fan Culture*. London: Headpress, 2016, 17-23.

Haraway, Donna. *Simians, Cyborgs, and Women: The Reinvention of Nature*. 1985. New York: Routledge, 1990.

Heidegger, Martin. *Being and Time*. 1926. Joan Stambaugh, trans. Albany: State University of New York, 2010.

Herbert, Ruth. *Everyday Music Listening: Absorption, Dissociation and Trancing*. 2011. Abingdon, Oxfordshire, 2016.

Herbert, Ruth, David Clarke, and Eric Clarke, eds. *Music and Consciousness 2: Worlds, Practices, Modalities*. Oxford: Oxford University Press, 2019, 71-92.

Higgs, Matthew. "True Faith." Manchester Art Gallery and the Manchester International Festival. *True Faith 30 June-3 September 2017*. Exhibition Catalog. Manchester: Manchester Art Gallery, 2017, 21-23.

Hirst, Richard V., ed. *We Were Strangers: Stories Inspired by Unknown Pleasures*. Manchester: Cōnfingō, 2019.

Hook, Peter. Contributing to Savage, Jon, *This Searing Light, The Sun, and Everything Else: Joy Division–The Oral History*. London: Faber and Faber, 2019.

_____. *Unknown Pleasures: Inside Joy Division*. London: Simon and Schuster, 2012.

Husserl, Edmund. *Ideas: General Introduction to Pure Phenomenology*. W. R. Boyce Gibson, trans. 1931. New York: Routledge, 2002.

IDLES. *Ultra Mono*. Music LP, 2020.

James, William. *The Works of William James: Principles of Psychology Volume I*. 1890. Cambridge: Harvard University Press, 1981.

Jameson, Fredric. *Postmodernism or, The Cultural Logic of Late Capitalism*. Durham: Duke University Press, 1991.

Jenkinson, Patrick. "Music Criticism–Joy Division–Transmission." *The Concrete Void*. 21 July 2013. https://twistedunkindandnumb.blogspot.com/2013/07/music-criticism-joy-division.html Accessed 14 March 2021.

Joy Division. "Atmosphere." Recorded Musical Song. 1980.

_____. "Atrocity Exhibition." Recorded Musical Song. 1980.

_____. "Autosuggestion." Recorded Musical Song. 1979.

_____. "Candidate." Recorded Musical Song. 1979.

_____. *Closer*. Music LP, 1980.

_____. *Closer*. London Records Remastered Collectors Edition, Music LP, 2007. 2-CD Set.

_____. "Colony." Recorded Musical Song. 1980.

_____. "Day of the Lords." Recorded Musical Song. 1979.

_____. "Dead Souls." Recorded Musical Song. 1980.

_____. "Decades." Recorded Musical Song. 1980.

_____. "Digital." Recorded Musical Song. 1978.

_____. "Disorder." Recorded Musical Song. 1979.

_____. "Disorder." *Unknown Pleasures*. London Records Remastered Collectors Edition, Music LP, 2007. 2-CD Set.

_____. "The Eternal." Recorded Musical Song. 1980.

_____. "Heart and Soul." Recorded Musical Song. 1980.

_____. "I Remember Nothing." Recorded Musical Song. 1979.

_____. "Insight." Recorded Musical Song. 1979.

_____. "Interzone." Recorded Musical Song. 1979.

_____. "Isolation." Recorded Musical Song. 1980.

_____. "Love Will Tear Us Apart." Recorded Musical Song. 1980.

_____. "Means to an End." Recorded Musical Song. 1980.

_____. "New Dawn Fades." Recorded Musical Song. 1979.

_____. "Passover." Recorded Musical Song. 1979.

_____. "Shadowplay." Recorded Musical Song. 1979.

_____. "She's Lost Control." Recorded Musical Song. 1979.

_____. "Transmission." Recorded Musical Song. 1979.

_____. "Transmission." Warner Records Digital Remastered Version. 2020.

_____. "Twenty Four Hours." Recorded Musical Song. 1980.

_____. "Twenty Four Hours." *Closer*. London Records Remastered Collectors Edition, Music LP, 2007. 2-CD Set.

_____. *Unknown Pleasures*. Music LP, 1979.

_____. *Unknown Pleasures*. London Records Remastered Collectors Edition, Music LP, 2007. 2-CD Set.

_____. "Wilderness." Recorded Musical Song. 1979.

Joy Division, Jean Pierre-Turmel, Jean-François Jamoul, and Anton Corbijn. *Licht und Blindheit*. Sordide Sentimentale, 1980. Ep.

Joy Division. Feature-Length Documentary Film. Directed by Grant Gee. 2007.

Joy Division Central. https://www.joydiv.org Accessed 14 March 2021.

Kramer, Lawrence. *Expression and Truth: On the Music of Knowledge*. Berkeley: University of California Press, 2012.

_____. *Interpreting Music*. Berkeley: University of California Press, 2011.

_____. *The Thought of Music*. Berkeley: University of California Press, 2016.

Kimoto, Tamsin and Cynthia Willett. "Eros." Weiss, Gail, Ann V. Murphy, and Gayle Salamon, eds. *50 Concepts for a Critical Phenomenology*. Evanston: Northwestern University Press, 2020, 115-119.

Lear, Jonathon. *Freud*. Routledge Philosophers. Abingdon: Routledge, 2015.

Levitin, Daniel J. *This Is Your Brain On Music: The Science of a Human Obsession*. 2006. New York: Plume, 2007.

Lacan, Jacques. *Écrits*. 1966. Bruce Fink, Héloïse Fink, and Russell Grigg, trans. New York: W.W. Norton, 2007.

Livingston, Steven Robert and William Forde Thompson. "The emergence of music from the theory of mind." *Musicae Scientiae*. 13 (2 suppl), 83-115.

Lorde, Audre. *Sister Outsider: Essays and Speeches*. Berkeley: Crossing Press, 1984.

Lugones, Maria. *Pilgrimages/Peregrinasjes: Theorising Coalition Against Multiple Oppressions*. Lanham: Rowan & Littlefield, 2003.

Manchester Art Gallery and the Manchester International Festival. *True Faith 30 June-3 September 2017*. Exhibition Catalog. Manchester: Manchester Art Gallery, 2017.

McGarvey, Darren. *Poverty Safari: Understanding the anger of Britain's underclass*. Edinburgh: Luath, 2017.

McRuer, Robert. "Compulsory Able-Bodiedness." Weiss, Gail, Ann V. Murphy, and Gayle Salamon, eds. *50 Concepts for a Critical Phenomenology*. Evanston: Northwestern University Press, 2020, 61-67.

_____. *Crip Theory: Cultural Signs of Queerness and Disability*. New York: New York University Press, 2006.

Mead, George Herbert. *Mind, Self, and Society: From the Standpoint of a Social Behaviourist*. 1929. Chicago: University of Chicago Press, 1962.

Meadows, Daniel. Contributing to Savage, Jon, *This Searing Light, The Sun, and Everything Else: Joy Division–The Oral History*. London: Faber and Faber, 2019.

Merleau-Ponty, Maurice. *Phenomenology of Perception*. 1945. Donald A. Landes, trans. New York: Routledge, 2014.

_____. *The Visible and the Invisible*. Alphonso Lingis, trans. Evanston: Northwestern University Press, 1968.

Middles, Mick and Lindsay Reade. *Torn Apart: The Life of Ian Curtis*. London: Omnibus, 2009.

Mills, China. "The mad are like savages and the savages are mad: psychopolitics and the coloniality of the psy." Cohen, Bruce M.Z., ed. *Routledge International Handbook of Critical Mental Health*. London: Routledge, 2018, 205-212.

Moncrieff, Joanna. *The Myth of the Chemical Cure: A Critique of Psychiatric Drug Treatment*. Revised Edition. Basingstoke: Palgrave Macmillan, 2009.

Moore, Allan F. *Song Means: Analysing and Interpreting Recorded Popular Song*. Farnham, Surrey: Ashgate, 2012.

Moore, Allan F. and Remy Martin. *Rock: The Primary Text–Developing a Musicology of Rock*. Third Edition. New York: Routledge, 2019.

Morley, Paul. Contributing to Savage, Jon, *This Searing Light, The Sun, and Everything Else: Joy Division–The Oral History*. London: Faber and Faber, 2019.

_____. *Joy Division Piece by Piece: Writing About Joy Division 1977-2007*. London: Plexus, 2008.

Morris, Stephen. Contributing to Savage, Jon, *This Searing Light, The Sun, and Everything Else: Joy Division–The Oral History*. London: Faber and Faber, 2019.

_____. *Record Play Pause: Confessions of a Post-Punk Percussionist Volume 1*. London: Constable, 2019.

Murray, Noel. "One bleak day gives way to another in Joy Division's '24 Hours'." *The A.V. Club*. 29 February 2016. https://music.avclub.com/one-bleak-day-gives-way-to-another-in-joy-division-s-2-179 8244733 Accessed 14 March 2021.

Naiman, Tiffany. "In a Lonely Place: Illness and the Temporal Exile of Ian Curtis." *Heart & Soul: Critical Writings on Joy Division*. London: Rowan & Littlefield, 2018, 83-97.

Oliver, Kelly. *Witnessing: Beyond Recognition*. Minneapolis: University of Minneapolis Press, 2001.

Ortega, Mariana. "Hometactics." Weiss, Gail, Ann V. Murphy, and Gayle Salamon, eds. *50 Concepts for a Critical Phenomenology*. Evanston: Northwestern University Press, 2020, 169-173.

Oxford English Reference Dictionary. Revised Second Edition. Oxford: Oxford University Press, 2002.

Parmar, Robin. "Joy Division in Space: the Aesthetics of Estrangement." *Heart & Soul: Critical Writings on Joy Division*. London: Rowan & Littlefield, 2018, 133-153.

Podmore, Jono. "Joy Division's Transmission at 40–a watershed moment from team Tony Wilson." *Get Into This: Beats, drones and rock & roll.* https://www.getintothis.co.uk/2019/10/joy-divisions-transmission-at-40-a-watershed-moment-from-team-tony-wilson/ Accessed 14 March 2021.

Power, Martin J., Eoin Devereux, and Aileen Dillane, eds. *Heart & Soul: Critical Writings on Joy Division.* London: Rowan & Littlefield, 2018.

Protomartyr. *Ultimate Success Today.* Music LP, 2020.

Ralkowsi, Mark. "Being-toward-Death." Weiss, Gail, Ann V. Murphy, and Gayle Salamon, eds. *50 Concepts for a Critical Phenomenology.* Evanston: Northwestern University Press, 2020, 39-45.

Reeder, Mark. Contributing to Savage, Jon, *This Searing Light, The Sun, and Everything Else: Joy Division–The Oral History.* London: Faber and Faber, 2019.

Reynolds, Simon. *Rip It Up and Start Again: Postpunk 1978-1984.* New York: Penguin, 2005.

_____. *Totally Wired: Post-punk Interviews and Overviews.* New York: Soft Skull Press, 2009.

Royle, Nicholas. "Disorder." Hirst, Richard V., ed. *We Were Strangers: Stories Inspired by Unknown Pleasures.* Manchester: Cōnfingō, 2019, 15-20.

Savage, Jon. "Introduction." Curtis, Ian, *So This is Permanence: Joy Division Lyrics and Notebooks.* Deborah Curtis and Jon Savage, eds. London: Faber and Faber, 2014, xxiii-xxviii.

_____. *This Searing Light, The Sun, and Everything Else: Joy Division–The Oral History.* London: Faber and Faber, 2019.

Simpson, Dave. Contributing to Savage, Jon, *This Searing Light, The Sun, and Everything Else: Joy Division–The Oral History.* London: Faber and Faber, 2019.

Sumner, Bernard. *Chapter and Verse: New Order, Joy Division and Me.* London: Bantam, 2014.

_____. Contributing to Savage, Jon, *This Searing Light, The Sun, and Everything Else: Joy Division–The Oral History.* London: Faber and Faber, 2019.

_____. Interviewed as part of Morley, Paul. *Joy Division Piece by Piece: Writing About Joy Division 1977-2007.* London: Plexus, 2008.

Tew, Jerry. "Towards a socially situated model of mental distress." *Madness, Distress and the Politics of Disablement.* Helen Spandler, Jill Anderson, and Bob Sapey, eds. Bristol: Polity Press, 69-81.

Trees Speak. *Shadow Forms.* Music LP, 2020.

Trinh, T. Minh-ha. *Woman, Nation, Other: Writing, Postcoloniality, and Feminism.* Bloomington: Indiana University Press, 1989.

Tseris, Emma. "Biomedicine, neoliberalism and the pharmaceuticalisation of society." Cohen, Bruce M.Z., ed. *Routledge International Handbook of Critical Mental Health.* London: Routledge, 2018, 169-176.

Turmel, Jean-Pierre. "Licht und Blindheit." Joy Division, Jean Pierre-Turmel, Jean-François Jamoul, and Anton Corbijn. *Licht und Blindheit.* Sordide Sentimentale, 1980. Ep.

Van den Tol, Anniemieke J.M. and Jane Edwards. "Exploring a rationale for listening to sad music when feeling sad." *Pyschology of Music.* 41 (4): 440-465.

Watt, Roger J. and Roisin L. Ash. "A psychological investigation of meaning in music." *Musicae Scientiae*. 2 (1): 33-53.

Weiss, Gail, Ann V. Murphy, and Gayle Salamon, eds. *50 Concepts for a Critical Phenomenology*. Evanston: Northwestern University Press, 2020.

_____. "Introduction: Transformative Descriptions." Weiss, Gail, Ann V. Murphy, and Gayle Salamon, eds. *50 Concepts for a Critical Phenomenology*. Evanston: Northwestern University Press, 2020, xiii-xiv.

Whitney, Shiloh. "Immanence and Transcendence." Weiss, Gail, Ann V. Murphy, and Gayle Salamon, eds. *50 Concepts for a Critical Phenomenology*. Evanston: Northwestern University Press, 2020, 189-196.

Whyte, Kyle. "Collective Continuance." Weiss, Gail, Ann V. Murphy, and Gayle Salamon, eds. *50 Concepts for a Critical Phenomenology*. Evanston: Northwestern University Press, 2020, 53-59.

Wilson, Tony. Contributing to Savage, Jon, *This Searing Light, The Sun, and Everything Else: Joy Division–The Oral History*. London: Faber and Faber, 2019.

Wozencraft, Jon. Contributing to Savage, Jon, *This Searing Light, The Sun, and Everything Else: Joy Division–The Oral History*. London: Faber and Faber, 2019.

Yancy, George. *Black Bodies, White Gazes: The Continuing Significance of Race in America*. 2nd Edition. Lanham: Rowan & Littlefield, 2017.

_____. "Confiscated Bodies." Weiss, Gail, Ann V. Murphy, and Gayle Salamon, eds. *50 Concepts for a Critical Phenomenology*. Evanston: Northwestern University Press, 2020, 69-75.

Zurn, Perry. "Social Death." Weiss, Gail, Ann V. Murphy, and Gayle Salamon, eds. *50 Concepts for a Critical Phenomenology*. Evanston: Northwestern University Press, 2020, 309-314.

Chapter Three

One

This chapter stages encounters between, on the one hand, Ian Curtis and Joy Division, and on the other hand three significant book-length contributions to critical theory from three classic critical theorists: Karl Marx, with *Economic and Philosophic Manuscripts of 1844*; Emile Durkheim, with *Suicide: a Study in Sociology* (1897); and Sigmund Freud, with *Civilization and Its Discontents* (1930). After this brief introduction I discuss each of these three books in turn, identifying key issues from each that will serve as principal points of connection in the encounters to come with Ian Curtis and Joy Division. Before proceeding directly to those encounters, I sum up points of connection among these books in terms of the key issues I have identified from each. After doing so, I stage four encounters with Ian Curtis and Joy Division, be represented by the following four songs: "Shadowplay," "Isolation," "A Means to an End," and "Love Will Tear Us Apart." In staging these encounters, I consider song title and lyrics; song structure and instrumentation; matters of loudness, rhythm, pitch, vocal delivery, and timbre; Arnie Cox's eight avenues of musical affect–mimetic participation, anticipation, expression, acoustic impact, implicit and explicit analysis, associations, exploring taboos, and the invisibility, intangibility, and ephemerality of musical sounds; and the three sets of summary and review questions I engaged near the end of my descriptions, analyses, and interpretations of "Disorder," "Transmission," and "Twenty Four Hours," in chapter two, as well as the eleven prior interpretations I first set forth in chapter one and then brought back as a focus for detailed consideration in relation to the aforementioned three songs in chapter two.

Marx, Durkheim, and Freud are towering figures who have extensively influenced diverse intellectual fields, while their influence extends far beyond intellectual work alone. Their work has been subject to vast conversation and debate, with each major text itself subject to a host of divergent interpretations and evaluations, and, what's more, their work has often proven controversial. These three critical theorists wrote many books and essays over the course of their careers, and continually developed, refined, and transformed their thinking as they did. In this chapter I am not focused on recounting all of that, as doing so would take me far afield from what I am here focused on doing, while many, themselves lengthy, books have been written, and continue to be written, offering histories of the intellectual and practical development, influence, and impact of Marx, Durkheim, and Freud, as well as of how their theories have been interpreted and put to use–along with how these theories have been challenged and contested. What I am doing here, in this chapter and in the next three chapters, represents an elaborated version of what I have done in teaching five upper-level English and Honors undergraduate university classes on Ian Curtis, Joy Division, and critical theory, where we together staged the same encounters, albeit working with excerpts from these the writings of these three theorists, rather than entire books, and spending less time with each than I do here.

In those classes I assumed responsibility for providing background, context, and perspective concerning the larger works from which the excerpts we were reading were excerpted, as well as for explaining how the ideas we concentrated on, from these excerpts, have consensually been understood along with what have been consensually recognized implications as well as influences of these ideas. I also assumed responsibility for translating positions, concepts, and arguments from these readings into terms with which we could grapple together, as well as for prompting students to begin making concrete connections, and come up with concrete illustrations that test the ramifications that follow from putting these ideas to work, through sharing suggestive illustrations of my own. As we proceeded in staging these encounters, we listened repeatedly to Joy Division songs, to reflect on points of connection–and disconnection too–between, for example, Ian Curtis and Joy Division and Marx or Durkheim or Freud, while drawing connections with current events, contemporary issues, and experiences in students' individual lives and the lives of people they had known well and with whom they had been close.

Two

It is vital, in order to grasp what Karl Marx argues in *Economic and Philosophic Manuscripts of 1844*, to recognize Marx theorizes work and working as fundamental to–i.e., as fundamentally defining and constitutive of–human nature. The ability to work is a fundamental human need because it is through working that we, as human beings, express and realize our humanity. Insofar as we cannot and do not work, in other words, we are not yet human–or at least not yet fully human. We express and realize our humanity by transforming nature and by transforming previous results of what constitutes a 'second nature' for human beings, human culture. We do express and realize our humanity through active and conscious effort, in free and voluntary association with fellow human beings in contributing to a social community, and, more specifically, to a collective project or endeavor that serves social interests and needs.

Alienated labor, in turn, involves alienation of the worker from the worker's human nature, from the worker's human essence, from what Marx identifies as the worker's 'species being'. For Marx, essence is not a super-mundane or rarefied 'core' but rather a collection, an aggregate, a complex, or an ensemble. As Marx and Frederick Engels elsewhere write, in *Theses on Feuerbach*, "The essence of man . . . is no abstraction inherent in each separate individual. It is the ensemble of social relations" (quoted 13).

Under capitalist relations of production, what happens to the worker is that "to an increasing extent his own labour confronts him as another's property" and "he is thus depressed spiritually and physically to the condition of a machine" (24). In other words, the worker is *dehumanized* by means of the worker's activity, in the course of working as a wage laborer for capital, because this work is owned and controlled by another, and, from the worker's vantage point, is a means to an end, not as an end in itself. In the course of successively repeated circuits of capitalist economic activity, accumulation of capital "sets the product of labour against the worker as something ever more alien to him" and "renders him ever more one-sided and dependent" (25). It does so because accumulation of capital represents an accumulation of labor effectively 'congealed' within the products of labor and within what these can in turn realize in monetary terms, which the capitalist has appropriated from the laborer and which in turn increases the capitalist's relative market power both in competition with other capitalists and versus workers who need to sell their labor power to capital in order to obtain means of survival and subsistence. Capital grows larger and stronger at the direct expense of the worker, while the basis of disparity in their relative power is the product of what the worker themself has made possible–has created–but which is appropriated from and turned against the worker.

As Marx explains, "The worker puts his life into the object; but now his life no longer belongs to him but to the object . . . The *alienation* of the worker in his product means not only that his labour becomes an object, an *external* existence, but that it exists *outside him*, independently, as something alien to him, and that it becomes a power on its own confronting him; it means the life he has conferred on the object confronts him as something hostile and alien" (70). In addition, "the estrangement is manifested not only in the result but in the *act of production*–within the *producing activity* itself" (72). This means not only is the product of the worker's labor alienated from the worker but also the worker is alienated from and in the process of working because all of this belongs to another, is ultimately effectively controlled by another, not by the worker themself. As Marx sum up, under conditions of alienated labor,

> labour is *external* to the worker, i.e., it does not belong to his essential being . . . in his work, therefore, he does not affirm himself but denies himself, does not feel content but unhappy, does not develop freely his physical and mental energy but mortifies his body and ruins his

mind. The worker therefore only feels himself outside his work, and his work feels outside himself. He is at home when not working, and when he is working he is not at home. His labour . . . is therefore not the satisfaction of a need; it is merely a *means* to satisfy needs external to it . . . it is not his own, but someone else's . . . it belongs not to himself, but to another." (72-73)

The worker becomes alienated as well from the larger society, from the worker's interdeterminate interdependence on the worker's relations with other human beings as part of a social totality, from the ensemble of social relations that is itself the essence of human being: "estranged labour estranges the *species* from man. It turns for him the *life of the species* into a means of individual life. First it estranges the life of the species and individual life, and secondly it makes individual life in its abstract form the purpose of the life of the species, likewise in its abstract and estranged form" (74-75). Under conditions of alienation, as socially productive life is rendered merely a means to an end for the individual worker, what the worker loses touch with is the fact this socially "productive life is the life of the species. It is life-engendering life. The whole character of a species–its species character–is contained in the character of its life activity; and free, conscious activity is man's species character" (75). So, in sum, under conditions of alienation, "Life appears only as a *means to life*" (75). To put this more prosaically, under alienated conditions we do not live life at its most vital and substantial. We live not by exercising and challenging our powers and capacities to the fullest extent possible, but by doing the least necessary to be able to survive and subsist, even by becoming numb and indifferent as we work.

According to Marx, through our "conscious life-activity" we make our own lives objects for us–in other words, we construct and transform our lives, not merely follow our instincts or merely adapt and react to the demands and constraints of our physical environments. But estranged labor reverses the process, where this life-activity–this capacity for conscious, deliberate, creative, imaginative, and perseverant work–is distorted. We come to crave work environments where we need do as little as possible, and where what we are required to do is simple, easy, and, especially, mindless. We come to crave being told what to do and how to do it without needing to choose or decide ourselves. As a result, the alienated worker experiences is a considerable diminution of what life can and should mean, a considerable diminution of the 'heart and soul' of what life, and living, is–or at least should be–all about. Yes, workers collectively produce great achievements, but these achievements do not belong to the workers, are not subject to their ultimately effective control, and do not directly benefit those who have made them possible. Workers only access these achievements indirectly, as consumers, and according to highly disparate means and opportunities. For example, workers produce a vast array of lines of clothing, but many of those producing these lines of clothing, such as in sweatshops, maintain limited access, if any access at all, to the kinds of clothing they produce for others. And these workers are not in charge of what kinds of clothes they work to make, for what specific customers, and at what specific prices, while the wages they receive from their capitalist employers represent only a small proportion of the total revenue capitalists generate by selling these clothes and investing profits from these sales to make further money.

As Marx explains, human beings produce more and other than what is solely needed for bare survival, which means we as a species are capable of producing from within conditions of freedom, and of producing "in accordance with the laws of beauty" (76). Human beings, Marx contends, express our humanity through our active contribution toward the creation of what enriches the broader social collective as a result of our free and voluntary association in free and voluntary social activity. Again, human beings, through human labor, transform nature to create the 'second nature' that is human culture. As Marx explains, "The object of labour is, therefore, the *objectification of man's species life*; for he duplicates himself not only, as in consciousness, intellectually, but also actively, in reality, and therefore he contemplates himself in a world he has created. In tearing away from man the object of his production, therefore, estranged labour tears man away from his *species life*, his real species objectivity" (76). In sum, therefore, not only does estranged labor estrange the worker from the product and the process of the worker's labor, but also

> Estranged labour turns thus: (3) *Man's species being*, both nature and his spiritual species property, into a being *alien* to him, into a *means* to his *individual* existence. It estranges man's own body from him, as it does external nature and his spiritual essence, his *human* being. [And] (4) An immediate consequence of the fact that man is estranged from the product of his labour, from his life-activity, from his species being, is the *estrangement of man from man*. If a man is confronted by himself, he is confronted by the *other* man. What applies to a man's relationship to his work, to the product of his labour, and to himself, also holds of a man's relation to the other man, and to the other man's labour and object of labour" (77).

Under capitalist relations, human beings become alienated from each other–they become separated from each other, they become each others' mere rivals and competitors. Relations with others becomes increasingly about treating others, first and last, as means to ends rather than as ends in themselves. "The proposition that man's species nature is estranged from him means that one man is estranged from the other, as each of them is from man's essential nature" (84). This includes increasing loss of ability to put one's self in the place of the other–i.e., to empathize with the other. It is hard to recognize what a great loss this is through the prevalent filter that ideological naturalization of these conditions imposes, such that alienated conditions seem simply matters of natural fact, but, in capitalist society "To the man who is nothing more than a worker–and to him as a worker–his human qualities only exist in so far as they exist for capital *alien* to him" (84).

Alienated labor produces the human being, "in keeping with this role as a *spiritually* and physically *dehumanised* being," as "The commodity-*man*" (85). As the worker's labor becomes a commodity, so ultimately, does the worker themself. A commodity, under conditions of generalized commodity production, is something that derives it greatest value as an entity that exists to be sold and bought on a market, with this kind of relation in turn influencing people to approach all kinds of social relations such that we are always competing against others to sell ourselves, for the greatest possible return, and the greatest possible gain, including by taking advantage and making use of whatever we can expropriate from others in order to do so.

316

Marx contends that "Religion, family, state, law, morality, science, art, etc., are only *particular* modes of production," and this means, Marx envisions, in the course of revolutionary socialist transformation of capitalism into communism, "the positive transcendence of *private property* as the appropriation of *human* life is, therefore, the positive transcendence of all estrangement–that is to say, the return of man from religion, family, state, etc., to his *human*, i.e., *social* mode of existence" (103). What Marx here seems to have in mind, in short, is individuality radically transformed so that existence for self becomes existence for the other and vice-versa: i.e., it becomes impossible effectively to distinguish, let alone diametrically oppose, the two. As Marx puts it, in a full realized communist society, "my *own* existence is social activity, and therefore that which I make of myself, I make of myself for society and with the consciousness of myself as a social being" (104). The terrors of death and dying are here transformed as well because of the fully realized unity of the individual with the social totality, such that individuality is only ultimately meaningful in its relation with the social totality, and as formed and constituted by means of identity with the social totality. The dying and death of the individual are not equivalent with the dying and death of the human essence that has animated the individual, that has enabled the individual human being to experience and express their humanity. The human essence lives on–the human essence the individual helped maintain and reproduce, and affirm and realize through the individual's participation in the ensemble of social relations from which the individual's own life derives its meaning, value, and significance. Under these revolutionarily transformed conditions, human beings enjoy positive freedom–freedom achieved with and through relations with others–and not just negative freedom–freedom pursued in separation from and opposition against (relations with others). Senses are transformed and expanded, via the merging of the individual with the collective, and especially as all human beings, and not only those most socio-economically advantaged, enjoy ample means of delight and play. Human beings no longer live one-dimensional, dehumanized, mechanical and machinic existences, as "The *rich* human being is simultaneously the human being *in need of* a totality of human life-activities" (112). Indeed, "for the socialist the *entire so-called history of the world*" is an ongoing struggle for human beings to become human (136). And when this happens, "In so far as man, and hence also his feelings, etc., are *human*, the affirmation of the object by another is likewise his own enjoyment" (136)–or, in other words, empathetic and solidaristic relations become not only materially substantial but also structurally foundational and systemically pervasive. This state of affairs is the antithesis of life under capitalism, where money "transforms fidelity into infidelity, love into hate, hate into love, virtue into vice, vice into virtue, servant into master, master into servant, idiocy into intelligence and intelligence into idiocy" (141).

Alienation from nature is also a major concern of Marx in *Economic and Philosophic Manuscripts of 1844*. As Marx declares,

> *Man* is directly a *natural being*. As a natural being and as a living natural being he is on the one hand furnished with *natural powers of life*–he is an *active* natural being. These forces exist within him as tendencies and abilities–as *impulses*. On the other hand, as a natural, corporeal, sensuous, objective being he is a *suffering*, conditioned and limited creature, like animals and plants. That is to say, the *objects* of his impulses exist outside him, as *objects*

independent of him; yet these objects are *objects* of his *need*–essential *objects*, indispensable to the manifestation and confirmation of his essential powers. (156)

A natural being is a being that is actively engaged in a network of interconnections with nature that exist within and beyond the limits of that being's individual organic body, because the supposed boundary between the two is permeable:

> A being which does not have its nature outside of itself is not a *natural* being, and plays no part in the system of nature. For as soon as there are objects outside me, as soon as I am not *alone*, I am *another*–another reality than the object outside me. For this third object I am thus an *other reality* than it; that is, I am *its* object. Thus, to suppose a being which is not the object of another being is to presuppose that *no* objective being exists. As soon as I have an object, this object has me for an object. But a *non-objective* being is an unreal, nonsensical thing–something merely thought of (merely imagined, that is)–a creature of abstraction. (157)

And yet "man is not merely a natural being: he is a *human* natural being. That is to say he is a being for himself. Therefore he is a *species being*, and has to confirm and manifest himself as such both in his being and his knowing. Therefore, *human* objects are not natural objects as they immediately present themselves, and neither is *human sense* as it immediately *is*–as it is objectively–*human* sensibility, human objectivity" (158). Human history, in turn, is the coming-to-be of man. And in sum, the "Positive humanism" Marx advocates involves "the annihilation of the *estranged* character of the objective world" (164).

So, in sum, in *Economic and Philosophic Manuscripts of 1844*, Marx discusses how estrangement (or, in other words, alienation) arises under conditions in which people do not 'own', in the sense of 'exercise ultimately effective control over', their own labor:

1.   They do not exercise ultimately effective control over what they produce by means of their labor (they are alienated from the product of their labor),

2.   They do not exercise ultimately effective control over how they labor to produce what they do (they are alienated from the process of their labor),

3.   They do not exercise ultimately effective control over the relationships they maintain with other workers who are working together with them as part of the same production process or in allied or related production processes (they are alienated from their fellow laborers), and

4.   They do not exercise ultimately effective control over in what ways they are contributing, by means of their expenditure of labor, toward serving a greater social good–i.e., they do not exercise ultimately effective control over how they are contributing anything of useful value toward the reproduction and enhancement of the well-being of the human species (they are alienated from their 'species-being'–they are alienated from their intrinsic interest in, connection with, and capability of

actively contributing toward the well-being of their community, their society, and humanity as a whole).

In the course of theorizing these modes of estrangement (or in other words, alienation), Marx also discusses how people are alienated:

5. From nature, including the nature that they are a part of, and the nature that is a part of them.

6. From their ability to create and transform, by means of the labor, or work, they are able to do, individually and in concert with others (i.e., from their self-perception, and self-recognition, that they are people maintaining creative, and transformative, capacities–and powers).

7. Versus the products of their labor, and those of other human beings' labor–products that confront them, in the form of commodities, as objects maintaining an independent, and hostile, power over and against them.

I will now offer a more concrete illustration of how people are alienated, as part of the jobs they do, working within capitalist societies, along the lines Marx theorizes in *The Economic and Philosophic Manuscripts of 1844*. These are jobs where workers sell their labor-power to a capitalist who maintains ultimately effective control over what kinds of labor these workers do, how they do this labor, in what kinds of relations with other workers, and toward what ends as well as in whose interests. For this illustration, let's take a hypothetical individual, and let's call him Aidan, and let's examine how might Aidan experience alienation from the product of his labor, from the process of his labor, from his relations with fellow workers, and from his species being, as a wage-worker for various kinds of capitalist firms and enterprises.

Aidan is 24 years old and has worked a considerable number of different jobs for pay since a young boy, devoting successively increasing time to so doing in moving from middle school to high school to adulthood. Aidan has worked in a warehouse, where he has been responsible for loading and unloading packages, and for maintaining and inventorying stock; he has worked in grocery stores, where he has performed numerous jobs from cashiering, bagging, collecting and returning carts, unloading foods and other goods from trucks, organizing these goods in storage, transferring and arranging these goods onto shelves, preparing and maintaining fresh food displays, taking inventory, and handling customer service; he has worked in restaurants in roles from dishwasher to bussing tables to waiting to hosting to helping behind the bar to assisting in food preparation; he has worked as an office clerk responsible for data entry, record keeping and record checking; he has worked as part of ground maintenance and landscaping crews that have taken care of these concerns for individual homeowners, commercial businesses, private and public institutions, and owners of apartment and condominium complexes; and he has worked in other retail settings, such as clothing stories, where he has been responsible for preparing and maintaining racks and other displays, as well as helping customers and again serving as a cashier. These comprise only a sampling of the total number of different kinds of jobs Aidan has worked in his life to date. Yet in every case, Aidan has *not* been an owner, or even part owner of any of these companies, and he has *not* been responsible for or included in determining what specific goods the company makes or what specific services it provides, in what quantities and of what qualities, for whom, in what forms, along what lines, and at what prices.

Aidan has appreciated work environments where his bosses have allowed him some leeway in terms of how he has performed his duties, as well as some opportunity to use his own intelligence and ingenuity in determining how best to do so, but in all cases he has *not* been responsible for or included in determining what are the overarching rules and expectations governing the jobs he has been hired to do, and Aidan has often been directed to follow highly precise and meticulous orders for exactly how he is–and is not–allowed to attend to specific tasks, as part of these jobs, including over what periods of time and with what outcome targets he is required to meet per interval of time, in order to keep his job, let alone to be eligible for possible promotion. Periodically Aidan experiences some limited autonomy and some freedom of maneuver on the job but most of these work environments have been tightly regimented, and a significant number have kept tight scrutiny and even close surveillance of employees in the interest of making sure they do precisely what they are expected and required to do, precisely as they are expected and required to do, and as efficiently as possible. Aidan has enjoyed relations he has developed with a number of his co-workers, at various of these jobs, and even appreciated some of his bosses as well who have been friendly with and respectful of and encouraging of him, but he has *not* been in charge of determining with whom he would work, when, where, how, for how long, doing what, according to what rules and expectations, and for what ends, while fellow workers in these jobs have often come and gone, have not always been able to work the same shifts with Aidan even when they both would have liked to do so, and, while working, Aidan and these co-workers have not always enjoyed much opportunity to develop close relationships. If anything, Aidan and his co-workers have more often developed close relationships, when they have formed them, by getting together and spending time together outside of work.

What has proven especially challenging, and often highly frustrating, for Aidan is so many of these jobs have been undependable as sources of secure and stable employment; frequently he has not been able to obtain or keep the number of hours he has wanted, and needed, at times being offered less and at times more while being forced to accept these offers in order to keep the job. At other times, Aidan has been abruptly let go because his services were no longer needed, as the company has shifted its focus, and its employment profile, without concern to find him another place, and another opportunity, to continue as part of the company. Aidan has been seeking to obtain a university degree, but has needed to work for pay in order to afford the cost of a university education, because his family, even while doing what they can, have been able to offer him little help in this direction. Yet, given the amount of paid work he has needed to do, Aidan has often had to drop out of and even fail classes, as well as cut back to going to university part time, or stop attending for a semester, in order to manage at all. Even though some bosses have accommodated his commitments to his university education, others have required him to work shifts that conflicted with classes or with other important meetings at school, even when they have been previously aware of the latter commitments, on the condition he must do so in order to keep his job.

Aidan's earnings from all of these paid jobs, once he has paid for the cost of education, for his living expenses, and for maintaining his car, which he needs to travel to work and school, and back home to help take care of his aging parents, grandparents, and younger siblings, has left him in a hole, and he has not only borrowed from friends but also made payments using credit cards that have left him in serious debt. He has needed to do so despite the fact he has recently moved into a small house together with his brother, who is a year younger than him, and three friends, where they all share the rent together. Aidan's girlfriend Janice is growing increasingly impatient with how busy Aidan is at work, at school, and with his family at home, as well as with how little money and how much debt he has acquired, especially as it seems Aidan is left with little quality time to spend with Janice and as she would like the two of them to move into their own place together, without needing to share the space with other housemates.

Aidan is further troubled, because, even though he is a hard worker, sometimes he has been too outspoken for his bosses's liking, too ready to ask questions concerning what he is asked to do, how so, and why so on the job, as well as too ready to offer his own suggestions for better ways to accomplish these same ends, which on several occasions has led to him being dismissed from jobs, and this has left at least a partial black mark on his employment record. What's more, Aidan's long-time best friend Alex recently killed himself in the city where Alex attended a different university and where Alex continued to live and work subsequent to Alex's graduation. Aidan was unaware Alex was feeling this badly, and as a result Aidan is not only devastated by the suicide of his best friend but also feels extremely guilty he did not see Alex's suicide coming and didn't do anything to try to prevent it. Aidan also wonders, given how close he long was to Alex, if he faces the same tendencies himself, especially as Aidan has recently experienced growing anxiety, and a number of panic attacks, and worries he himself is on the edge of depression.

All of these stresses are compounded by the fact that Aidan maintains no idea what kind of job, and career, he might want to pursue, or be able to realize, long-term–only that he doesn't want this to be anything like any of the jobs he has worked in his life to date. At university Aidan began his studies intent on majoring in a business field and minoring in a STEM (science-technology-engineering-and-mathematics) field, but he soon found out he most enjoyed working in the field of critical studies in literatures, cultures, and film, to which he has, after considerable agonizing, switched his major. But Aidan is worried concerning what this major will qualify him to do, especially given how long it is taking him to finish his degree, the fact that a number of past failing grades has kept his GPA relatively low, and because he comes from a family background that is relatively poor while he is now in serious debt himself. The last includes student loans Aidan has taken out to help pay the cost of attending university.

Aidan is a hard worker, but other than the work he does in the classes he most enjoys, and on the rare occasions he has sufficient time to engage in leisure pursuits he likewise enjoys (which also require that he expend energy and effort, that he imagine and create as well as plan and execute, and thus involve 'work' as well, although much different work than what he does in the form of paid labor), most of the work he does throughout his everyday life feels as if it belongs to another. It feels as if this paid labor drains him of the capacity to be able to do work that is truly meaningful to and for himself, and where he experiences the sense he is making a meaningful contribution to others' lives, helping satisfy their needs and enabling their well-being.

Aidan often feels like his life is not his, and that he is in effect forced to live as like a machine, like a robot, perhaps even like a zombie, while the alienation he experiences as a result of the work he does, and as a result of how little this work leaves him with, in turn makes Aidan feel increasingly alienated from other people–from those he maintains personal connections with, and from others with whom he doesn't maintain these kinds of connections but whose lives are nevertheless interdependently interconnected with his. At times, at his worst, Aidan feels hugely isolated, alone, lonely, frightened, cut off, and even altogether rejected, discarded, and forgotten. But he also feels guilty about feeling these ways because he perceives the conditions of his life, and of his work as part of this life, as simply 'normal', as simply what is to be expected–what a great many others like him, including people who have lived and worked long before him and people who will live and work long after him, have had to put up with, and will have to put up with. This guilt means Aidan further feels upset at himself for being so 'weak' as not be able to take these difficulties and challenges in stride.

Although this is a hypothetical example, Aidan's situation, and Aidan's straits, represent a composite of situations and straits faced by many university students I have known over the course of the past thirty-five years. Beyond what I just recounted, Marx would also stress that even in all of these jobs, which are generally regarded as relatively low-skill and low-status jobs, and which receive correspondingly relatively low rates of pay, the value Aidan generates by means of the work he does, in these jobs, always greatly exceeds the value equivalent of the wages he receives, and in fact always significantly exceeds the value equivalent of the cost of all the means of production Aidan works with to perform these jobs (these means of production Aidan's employers own, they pay to put in place and to keep up, and, as with Aidan's labor, they own the results of what these means are able to generate). Aidan does not exercise ownership over what is done with the *surplus value* that is generated as a result of the labor he does in these jobs (i.e., the value that exceeds that which is *necessary* to cover the cost of his wages), together with that generated in collaboration his co-workers–neither Aidan nor these co-workers exercise ownership over what uses to which this surplus value is put. This surplus value is instead the source of profit for the capitalist owners of the companies for which Aidan has worked, and is invested by these capitalists to generate yet further capital to enable their successful competition on the market where their growing accumulation of capital augments their market power. Aidan is investing a substantial portion of his life, of his humanity, to contribute toward the production of goods and provision of services to meet social needs and wants, but this fundamental dimension of Aidan's life is not under his control. What's more, so much of Aidan's wage labor is one-sided (or, in other words, one-dimensional) work, work that does not allow him to make use of more than an extremely limited array of his capacities for contributing to the social good–and for creating social value.

In my own life I have worked many jobs that were highly alienating, much like those Aidan has worked. I worked at many food service jobs where we were routinely short-staffed, and as a result we were always required to make up for this by working more and harder than we had been told we needed to do when hired, while we were often employed for indeterminate numbers of hours that were frequently extended or cut with little if any prior notice; where job responsibilities were often both nebulously defined as well as constantly shifting and especially constantly expanding; and where low-level and front-line employees were made scapegoats for mistakes perpetrated by or failings following from decisions made at higher levels–as well as in response to any and all customer complaints. In a few of those environments managers demanded I follow ridiculously precise formulas for exactly how to perform job tasks, such as how to sweep or mop a floor–and how not to do it–with adherence to their preferred formula considered far more important than the result, with any deviation prompting criticism, and even docking of pay.

I also worked in a printed circuit board factory where health and safety conditions were appalling, including exposure of workers to toxic fumes due to inadequate ventilation and us not being able to wear goggles or gloves, even as we needed to retrieve circuit boards from vats containing sulfuric acid solutions prior to running these boards through printing machines. At this same factory, managers routinely came by within the last five to ten minutes of a shift to ask workers to 'voluntarily' work another eight-hour shift, with no consideration given to what workers might have planned–and indeed needed to do–in that next eight hours, let alone how tired we might be. In this same factory we were not provided an overview of the entire production process, so that we would be able to understand what happened at different stages as well as how our particular contribution fit into the larger process, but instead confined to our single station, where we were expected monotonously to perform the same limited mechanical task over and over again for eight to sixteen straight hours.

I have, in addition, worked in multiple libraries, which although far more pleasant environments overall than the kinds of jobs I just previously described, often involved considerable monotonous work, such as typing catalog numbers of books into forms all day long, or reading through the call numbers of books on rows and rows of shelves for hours at a time just to see if any book might be misfiled. In these library jobs I most enjoyed challenges–where, for example, I was called upon to try to find a missing book, or where I was called upon to try to determine which faculty members might find newly acquired books of particular interest, or what new books from regular suppliers might make the most sense to purchase, or where users of the library asked questions and needed help finding resources and my job was try to answer these questions and help them find what they needed. Even so, I well recall, in working in one library acquisitions and cataloging department, that long-term, regular, full-time employees spent virtually all of their time talking about what they would do once work ended, on evenings and weekends, and especially in their once-a-year two-weeks-long vacation. Here it clearly seemed these workers approached their library jobs as a means of obtaining what was required to truly live their lives, which they conceived themselves as doing when not working at the library. They did not conceive the work they did, in their library jobs, as representing an end in itself, because they clearly did not feel truly alive, and most fulfilled, doing this work.

I have worked a great many other paid jobs too, but I will shift here to discuss experiences I have had teaching at the university level. As an adjunct faculty member, I almost always was hired at a sub-minimum wage rate of pay, with no paid benefits, and no job security–i.e., no commitment to rehire me beyond a single semester, or at most a year, at a time. In many of these situations I was simply thrown into a set of teaching assignments, given next to no instruction, guidance, or preparation, especially concerning what was expected of me, after being hired often days before the start of the semester. And then afterward, as I made use of my academic and intellectual training to teach my assigned classes, I often ran into suspicion and hostility from supervisors who expected me, above all else, to 'keep the customer satisfied' such that they never received any complaints and where we never did anything at all challenging, let alone at all provocative. Teaching writing classes with an emphasis on writing about controversial contemporary issues, and engaging with current conversations and debates concerning matters of class, race, gender, sexuality, and nationality, which I did, proved especially taboo, as these supervisors preferred I teach students that writing is a series of empty forms that equally well serve an endlessly interchangeable array of different kinds of content, along with teaching students how to master the rules of Standard Written English concerning grammar, usage, punctuation, and mechanics. Everything that could be turned into a mechanical set of rules was, and this was all we were supposed to teach. I was even instructed to spend whole class periods focused on teaching students how to recognize and avoid split infinitives and comma splices–in university-level classes!–by 'drilling' them in the same ways that had not succeeded prior to these students entering the university. In one conversation with one supervising 'director of undergraduate studies' I was told by this man that 'my problem' was I falsely imagined it was possible actually to teach 'these students' anything. This director of undergraduate studies contended 'these students'–i.e., *his* students, at *his* university–were simply uninterested in and incapable of learning, but instead only interested in partying, in social life, and in moving through as quickly, easily, and painlessly from class to class, credit to credit, as possible on their way to what this man openly disparaged as their objectively worthless undergraduate degree. This director of undergraduate studies told me 'I once was like you but I quickly learned better' and 'now what I do is teach in a way that requires the least of me so I can concentrate my real interest and energy on my scholarship'. Sadly, all too often, throughout my teaching career, at multiple different institutions, I have encountered colleagues, and administrators, who have repeatedly insisted their students were incapable of doing all that much, or doing all that well, as compared with students at X,Y, or Z universities, and as a result these people performed a grave disservice to their students.

The relevance of these last examples, in connection with Marx, is that in many environments adjunct faculty perform highly alienated labor, where adjuncts exercise limited control over what they do how, and why, with any resistance adjuncts offer to constraints imposed upon what they teach, how, and why leading to punishment, including in the form of mandatory meetings with and observations by supervisors as well as by being sanctioned and not being rehired. At the same time, assuming students not only enter classes thoroughly alienated from learning but also will always remain so becomes a self-fulfilling prophecy. Yes, often students develop and carry with them a sense that school is a place of entirely alienated labor, where the goal is to jump through hoops, without being able to question *why these hoops* or why jump through them in the ways demanded, and where the best approach is simply to do exactly what one is told to do while always striving to find ways to sneakily get away with doing as little as possible at the same time. And yes when students have become accustomed to classes like this, as the overwhelming norm, they are likely, at least at first, to feel uneasy and uncomfortable in classes that actually take them seriously, that actually care what they think and feel and believe, and that proceed on the basis of the presumption that education should deal with issues that genuinely matter in the world everywhere around them. But in the long run students tend to much prefer, and to benefit far more, from exactly the latter kinds of classes–and this especially includes classes where students are challenged, because their teachers believe students are capable of meeting these challenges, and where teachers are ready and willing to work with students to help them meet these challenges.

Not all my experiences as an adjunct faculty member were like this, and in some places I did receive support, appreciation, and encouragement from supervisors. When this happened students themselves tended to respond all the more positively, and quickly so, to what I was teaching them, how, and why, because they no longer worried that because my teaching was unfamiliar and unexpected it might be 'wrong'–'wrong' in the sense not only of unsanctioned by the department or the university but also 'wrong' as supposedly inappropriate and unhelpful in qualifying them to succeed in future classes and in life beyond. In fact, in my teaching as an adjunct of introductory university-level writing classes I anticipated the direction the field would eventually follow–as most of what I did then is now considered standard best practice.

However, a larger point I am proposing here is, in comparison with adjunct faculty, tenure-line faculty, and especially tenured faculty, and above all else, full professors, maintain greater ownership, in the sense of ultimately effective control, over their labor–not just in terms of what, how, and why we teach but also in terms of the kinds of scholarship and creative activity we pursue, how, and why, as well the kinds of institutional, professional, and community service we contribute, how, and why. Certainly tenure-track and adjunct faculty take risks in the teaching, scholarship and creative activity, and institutional, professional and community service they do, all the time, but these are greater risks for them than for tenured faculty and especially for full professors. People in adjunct and tenure-track positions face real risks in receiving pushback from taking on anything that might be perceived or responded to as 'controversial'. Some departments, colleges, and universities are more supportive and protective of academic freedom than others, but regardless of this variation, you always do occupy a significantly different kind of position when you are hired year to year or semester to semester, with, as contracts at UW-Eau Claire for long officially included, 'no intent to renew', versus, in contrast, serving in appointed positions, which are expected to continue over many years, even over multiple decades, as long as you continue to receive satisfactory periodic performance reviews.

One of the great appeals of working as a university professor is the high degree of freedom that someone like me enjoys, versus what people enjoy (or better put do not enjoy) in many to most other jobs. This refers to being able to determine what I am working on, how, and why, as well as to be in charge of the process of so doing, and to be able to make use of advanced critical and creative skills and abilities while focusing on what I consider of greatest social value as well. One of the reasons I teach as I do, emphasizing active and interactive learning, discussion over lecture, and individual, group, and team projects, is I want to provide my students as much opportunity as possible to make the work we do together their own, to make it feel as if this is work that is challenging and engaging of them, and in which they feel like they can and do achieve something satisfying and of value, to themselves and to others, as a result of the process as well as by means of the product of this kind of labor. Again and again, from day one, I emphasize, with the students I teach, this is not 'my class'; it is 'our class'–the work we do together, and what they contribute and provide, is what matters, and, if anything, it is far more about, and for, them than it is for me. I am our leader but I lead so as to provide the students I teach something and somewhere to follow, to help the students I teach proceed with growing confidence and to accomplish meaningful results–including in terms of personal as well as intellectual growth–as they do. My role is to help these students figure out what they themselves aim and desire to accomplish, as we proceed, as well as why they aim and desire to do so. I also readily recognize students learn differently, and this means not everyone will be as interested and excited by the same texts or topics in the same ways or to the same degrees, and not everyone will be able to make the most meaningful connections with the same texts or topics–but I want to work with *everyone* to make it possible for *everyone* to find a way to make the class meaningful and valuable to them.

As I repeatedly emphasize with students, I am compelled to grade you, even though I despise grading because I find students' obsession over grades tends to distract students from what is far more important, yet I grade students in response to the outcomes that matter the most to me, and which are, ultimately, always as follows:

1.   You learn something of significant value, and demonstrate to me you are doing so.

2.   You work hard and aim seriously to learn, and demonstrate to me that you are doing so.

3.   You learn something of significant value you will be able to make productive use of after and beyond the time we spend together as a class, and demonstrate to me you will be able to do so. Students meet these outcomes in numerous ways but what's most important to stress here is that when students meet these three outcomes they end up doing extremely well, in terms both of their overall grade, and, ultimately, more importantly, in what and how they learn. I don't always succeed, certainly not always with every student, but I have become steadily better at sticking to these objectives, in all my classes, especially as I have felt freer to do so, with less prospective risk to my job from so doing (in moving from adjunct faculty to tenure-track faculty to tenured faculty to full professor).

One of the biggest challenges I face as a university teacher reflects how normalized conditions of alienation have come to be, not only in capitalist society at large, but within the consciousness and the unconscious of individual members of this society. This impacts how students make sense of and especially initially approach what classes can and should be like. Frequently I need to work extremely hard to convince students to trust me; that I am sincerely interested in what they themselves truly think, feel, and believe; that I do welcome them being honest and forthcoming, as well as being open and vulnerable in sharing; and that I welcome as well a diversity of positions and perspectives concerning all of the texts and topics we take on. Students tend to worry all too often about the least important matters, because they have been encouraged–they have been effectively taught–to do so, and this means again and again, for example, I must reassure them that I am not a stickler for nitty-gritty matters of formatting and style in students' writings, because I am concerned instead, first and last, with substance and engagement. Students often worry as well about offending others, or about disagreeing with others, and especially about doing so with me or with writers of texts we read, and this likewise requires considerable work on my part to emphasize such fear is unnecessary–and unjustified. But I recognize where this fear comes from, because over and over again, in all too many social environments, students learn from an early age that those in authority expect to be obeyed, without question or challenge, and that these authorities are the ones who tell others what to do, how to do it, when and where to do it, and why do it, without these being reciprocal relationships, so others' responsibility is, in turn, to follow orders and to show those in authority they can and will do exactly what they are asked to do and exactly as they are asked to do it. Students can and do overcome these tendencies, and come to relish opportunities to do so, but the fact this amounts to one of the greatest challenges I face, as a university teacher, every semester in every class, testifies to how strong the societal impact of alienation is: people living in capitalist society, immersed in pervasive networks of social relations founded on extensively as well as routinely alienated labor, learn from early age not to value–that is, to devalue–their own work, and their own capacity for work, as well as not to value–that is, to devalue–their own prospective worth as human beings whose lives matter, to and for others.

What is further crucially important, and I have also become steadily better at doing this with experience, is taking into account the fact that what students bring to bear and how well they are able to engage and succeed as part of a class is overdetermined by what else is going on in their life at the same time, and not just by where they are coming from and what have been their principal preceding shaping influences. If anything, it has become easier for me to respond effectively to the student as a whole person the more secure my position has become, within the university. The less I have needed to be unduly concerned about being punitively judged for even the slightest possible failing–or what could be misinterpreted as a failing–the less I feel compulsion to insist on standards of conduct and performance that don't allow sufficient flexibility to accommodate the diversity of different students, and different student needs, represented across a full class of students. I have always aimed to be patient and flexible in my teaching, and to be willing to stretch and modify our de facto 'rules' and de jure expectations as need be, even quite far at that, while often giving students lot of opportunities to make up for earlier work in which they did not do so well, to earn extra credit, and to pursue alternative kinds of assignments more directly suitable to their own strengths and interests. But I accept, at the same time, that I can always strive to be more sensitive, patient and flexible–even as I have become steadily better, over time, in doing so. What this last observation suggests, in connection with Marx, is the less alienated my labor, the more enabling and empowering I can be of others' labor–i.e., the labor of others with whom I am most closely working and where it is my express aim to so enable and empower.

Let's consider another hypothetical illustration, this time of how people can, and do, experience alienation from nature, including the nature they are a part of, and the nature that is a part of them; from their ability to create and transform, by means of the labor, or work, they are able to do, individually and in concert with others (i.e., from their self-perception, and self-recognition, that they are people maintaining creative, and transformative, capacities–and powers); and versus the products of their labor, and those of other human beings' labor–products that confront them, in the form of commodities, as objects maintaining an independent, and hostile, power over and against them. For this illustration, let's take a hypothetical individual and call her Kim, discussing specific ways that Kim experiences these forms of alienation.

Kim has been working customer service jobs for close to twenty years now, and considers this line of work to represent the kind of paid job for which she is best qualified and has acquired the greatest expertise. In this kind of job, however, even as employers, and managers, have often assigned Kim considerable responsibility, including negotiating with customers concerning a broad range of different types of inquiries and complaints, in seeking to find solutions that satisfy both customer and company Kim has had to endure a lot of displaced hostility from people who are actually upset not at Kim personally but at the company she represents, and for decisions and actions over which Kim has had no influence. Kim needs to maintain a calm, patient, and friendly demeanor throughout these interactions, no matter how much the customer manifests the exact opposite. She has to work hard to try to help impatient customers find answers that are not always easy for Kim to find, and often Kim needs to disappoint customers because the company is unable or unwilling to do anything further to help, to respond any further to the customer's grievance or perceived grievance. When she can help customers find satisfying answers and solutions, Kim experiences considerable satisfaction herself, but when she can't do so Kim struggles to resist feeling dissatisfied not just with her job but with herself. Kim also struggles between feeling more loyal to the company versus feeling more loyal to the customer in the midst of a dispute, while accepting she must always represent and serve the company's interest above that of the customer if it comes down to a choice between the two.

This kind of work, over many long hours, weeks, months, and years, involves a considerable investment of emotional labor, and Kim often feels tired, anxious, and restless after working, and, as a result, Kim does not pay close attention, or invest much effort, in taking care of her mental and physical health. In fact, Kim has been growing sicker, in multiple ways, while she largely tries to push off thinking or doing much about these illnesses. Kim is neglecting her body, and her mind as well, as this is inextricably interlinked with the rest of her body–i.e, she is neglecting the nature that makes up whom she is–and she also pays less and less attention to nature that exists outside of and beyond herself, as her working life has grown ever more cumulatively stressful. Kim has become so numbed to her surroundings, beyond her job, that she no longer visually or auditorily registers what she passes by on the way to and from her job, or in the process of doing routine errands. Kim has, in addition, felt increasingly less inclined to pursue intimate relations with others, believing she has become old and unattractive and has little of interest or value to offer prospective romantic and sexual partners, while she doesn't reach out all that far, in other forms of social interaction, beyond a small number of long-standing close friends and a few close relatives. These social interactions have also become increasingly formulaic and predictable with the passage of years, especially as Kim's social network has not changed. Kim is in a rut but isn't able or willing to face up to and accept that, and, in fact, on an unconscious level Kim fears there is no way out from these straits, so it is best to pretend to herself this is not where her life is at.

What makes Kim feel all the more dissatisfied, and worn down, however, is the fact that even when she manages to achieve successful results, for the company, she gets limited acknowledgment, with higher-ups most often taking all of the credit; it seems like her labor is taken for granted, and is unappreciated. Kim feels like she is just an object the company has bought and paid for, and with which the company in turn can do whatever and however it wants, not respecting her as a human being. At the same time, Kim's salary has remained stagnant, and as she grows older and increasingly dissatisfied with her life, while not able to fully understand how and why this happening, she finds herself craving the acquisition of material goods, especially luxury goods, that she imagines would make her feel better about herself if she could acquire them, but she cannot afford to do so. The same is the case with the luxury trips she fantasizes about taking, but can't afford to take, and is, moreover, uncertain if she wants to do so by herself, alone, even if she could afford to do so, yet she doesn't know anyone she would like to bring along with her. Because Kim does not own or do much maintaining a high status, in terms of what are consensually perceived to be the most desirable kinds of commodities, Kim increasingly feels like she has achieved little in her life, that she has little to show for herself.

Again, as with Aidan, although Kim represents a hypothetical illustration, Kim's experiences with alienation represent a composite of experiences common to many people I have known over the course of my life. In relation to my own experience, even though I have been most fortunate in the career I have been able to pursue and to realize, and it has provided me far greater satisfaction than Kim's career has done for her, I have felt the pressure to overwork myself to the point not only of exhaustion but also serious illness, because it has seemingly been expected that this is what people do in jobs like mine. For example, it has felt to me whenever and if ever a student, any student, in any one of my classes, is experiencing any kind of difficulty it is always my responsibility to do everything I possibly can to address and overcome this difficulty. This has included being available to contact at any time of day or night, and on weekends as well as throughout the weekday, while preparing elaborate study guides, and helpful commentaries, as well as responding at length to students' written work. Frequently enough I've failed to maintain an effective balance between work as part of my job and the rest of my life, including not enough time to exercise regularly or for other forms of stress relief and release. At times I have felt as if I cannot ever work hard enough, and that if I don't keep pushing myself constantly to work ever harder I won't be successful, and won't be recognized, respected, and appreciated as successful. During the course of my current extended scholarly leave, in which I am working on writing two books, I have resumed running regularly, which is something I have long love doing, and which I derived great satisfaction from doing as well as also contributed substantially to my mental as well as physical good health, and it feels great to be doing this again, after nearly 25 years not doing so. But why did I stop? I stopped because it struck me the demands of my job as a professor of English at UW-Eau Claire did not allow time for that, and, once I had stopped doing so for a significant duration of time, I felt it would be too hard, and take too much time away from other necessarily priority commitments, to get myself back into the kind of running shape I had once maintained.

I've also often enough felt that no matter how sick I have been, due to acute or chronic illnesses, I owe it to my job, and especially to my students, but also to my colleagues, not to take time off from work, even refusing to do so has made my illness last longer and caused greater damage. Much of this emphasis on always working, working, and working I learned through my family, where doing so has been highly prized and strongly encouraged–and where to be identified as a 'hard worker' or as 'having worked hard' is the highest praise one can earn. I learned from my maternal grandparents, and especially my grandmother, that what principally distinguished the Irish in America has been our capacity for and devotion to hard work. I became determined, from an early age, to carry on this legacy, while internalizing the conviction that I had nothing else–no other qualifications–to offer any role I might aspire to fill other than my readiness to work extremely hard at it, and, as need be, harder than anyone else. It has been difficult for me to recognize being over-committed, and not to get involved, and especially not to volunteer for, more than I can realistically handle, while I have felt guilty in needing to withdraw and pull back when overcommitted. I have done increasingly better with this, as time has passed, and as I have grown older and more accepting of myself, including my limitations, but this has been a struggle. Letting go, and moving on, have not proven easy for me to do.

Like Kim I have at times been so consumed with work commitments that I have moved through life largely oblivious to my surroundings, not paying attention to changing seasons, other than when and as I needed to take account of temperature and precipitation. Another gain from the time I have spent writing this book, and the other book I am writing as well, has been taking many long walks around Eau Claire, and paying close attention to and registering details of the natural and cultural environment in the city I have made my 'home' for the past 24 years. It is easy to neglect this, just as it can be easy to neglect paying close attention to others immediately around one's self as well, when one is 'busy'–or 'too busy'. Yet further, for many years I felt I was not making the best possible use of my time, energy, interests, and passions if I did not travel frequently during breaks from semesters. But with the COVID-19 pandemic, even as I have missed traveling, I have not missed it as much as I imagined I would because I have grown to more fully appreciate where I am at, and opportunities immediately around me, even doing simple, ordinary things–such as sharing in the cooking of meals together with Andy, playing with our pets, reading books and magazines, listening to music and watching television and film, walking through local parks, running four to six mile circuits out from our house and back, and stopping at local ice cream stores in the midst of walks to buy an ice cream cone. Travel that I have been lucky enough to experience has often proven amazing–genuinely life-transforming and immensely enjoyable–but I have often felt I could only justify travel if I was using travel to learn what I could put directly to use in subsequent teaching, scholarship, and service.

Yet another point of useful personal connection involves the pressure I have at times felt to keep up with and to do as much as departmental colleagues of mine, which is neither realistic nor necessary, as we represent different areas of responsibility and expertise, and as judging myself comparatively in this way can be counter-productive, even irrational, while not helping me in accomplishing what I am best equipped to accomplish. The same happens in feeling as if so many worthwhile social and political causes are in demand, and in need, even urgent demand and urgent need, that I 'should' be more directly active concerning more of them than I currently am. At times I have felt, wrongly, or at least not all that helpfully, as it turns out, that I cannot justify time and energy devoted to involvement in other kinds of social groups beyond those directly engaged in progressive to radical forms of social and political activism–and I have neglected, even ignored, my multi-dimensional social needs. Especially when I was an undergraduate and graduate student, yet for awhile after as well, I became highly restless at times and in situations where I was ostensibly supposed to relax, during holidays and on vacations, at the end of and in between semesters. Students in classes I taught early on at Syracuse and other places in Central New York commented on how 'hyper' I often seemed, and came across, as if I had mainlined caffeine into my body right prior to class–or even a stronger drug than that. It took me awhile to take this kind of comment seriously and to reflect on the fact that I did need to find a way to adjust–and to relax–much more readily and easily than I tended to do. If living with a serious chronic digestive dysmotility disorder has taught me one thing above all else, that is how important it is I take time every day to tune into and check in with my body, with how I am feeling across my body. Still, when I have experienced the effects of acute and especially chronic illness, perpetrated or exacerbated by overwork and by stressing over the perceived need always to work all the harder, I have felt as if my life is spinning out of control, and if my body, and its 'weaknesses' (due to chronic illness) don't belong to 'me' but rather exist as alien opponents versus 'me' and my potential for successful achievement.

Three

Emile Durkheim's *Suicide: a Study in Sociology* provides a theorization of the social causes of suicide, or, more precisely, the social causes of *rates* of suicide, as well as of how different types of suicide, explained in social terms and on social bases as reflecting and responding to social causes, are distinct from as well as related to each other. Durkheim theorizes the social types of suicide as egoistic suicide, altruistic suicide, anomic suicide, and, briefly in a footnote, fatalistic suicide, along with demarcating multiple subtypes and combined or hybrid types as well.

Significant elements of Durkheim's theorization are reflective of dominant social norms, in his time (the late 1890s), which have been superseded, or at least strongly challenged and substantially undermined, especially when he focuses on differences between men and women, but also in his discussions of race. Yet for all of his focus on the preeminent importance of society as moral force, Durkheim carefully avoids moralistic theorizing and is often critically self-reflexive, as well as highly deliberate in working through refutations of a wide panoply of other explanations for suicide, suicidality, and trends as well as differences in instances and rates of suicide that he finds unsatisfactory, because these efforts are unable adequately and effectively to explain what they purport to explain.

My engagement with Durkheim's *Suicide* will *not* focus on making use of Durkheim to explain Ian Curtis's suicide, by attempting to classify it in terms of Durkheimian types, but rather to engage with how the *art* of Ian Curtis and Joy Division engages with matters of suicide, suicidality, social integration and cohesion versus social disintegration and 'dishesion', egoism, altruism, anomie, fatalism, and more–as itself a contribution toward a critical theoretical understanding of the same.

According to Durkheim, as editor George Simpson indicates in an introduction to the 1951 English translation of this book, republished once again in 1979 by the Free Press, "Suicide, like crime, is no indication of immorality *per se* . . . it is symptomatic of the breakdown of the collective conscience, and of a basic flaw in the social fabric" (16-17). Indeed, "For Durkheim, all ameliorative measures must go to the question of social structure"–i.e., to effectively reintegrate individuals into a strong alignment with a collective conscience (17). Durkheim's proposed solution, in his last chapters, is that in modern (advanced capitalist) society, work or occupational groups should serve as the vehicles by which to do so–what Simpson describes as "compact voluntary associations based on work-interests" (17). This, to my mind, resembles a cross among a union, a guild, and a syndicate.

Whatever the preferred response, "suicide for Durkheim shows up the deep crisis in modern society" (17), with Durkheim highlighting the emergence along with a rising rate of anomic suicide. Simpson, as I do as well, proposes that Durkheim's sociological theorization, despite its critique of prominent psychological explanations of suicide, is nonetheless compatible with psychological and in particular psychoanalytic theories. As Simpson suggests, it makes sense, drawing from psychoanalysis, to posit that "every individual has what we may call a suicide-potential" (23). To connect this with Durkheim, of key concern is what factors are mostly likely to increase and decrease this potential, to cause it to become acute and realizable, especially on a social scale, within a particular social community at a particular historical moment. Simpson also proposes as likewise compatible with Durkheim's sociological theory of suicide the psychoanalytic argument that "Suicide is an ego-manifestation even though it is an annihilation of the ego . . . [and that suicide represents] the utmost in going 'beyond the pleasure principle'" (24)–in other words, the utmost in going *with* what Freud theorizes as 'the death drive'.

An important argument Durkheim makes throughout his book is that society is more than the sum total of the individuals that participate within society and their relations with each other. Society constitutes a "collective reality" not reducible to the former (38). Distinctly societal influences exercise materially determinate impacts upon individuals (39). Durkheim introduces his theorization of social causes and social types of suicide by proposing it is crucial to determine these causes and types not by referring to superficially or "preliminarily described features" but rather by seeking to determine "the social conditions responsible for them." What Durkheim is concerned with is an "aetiological" as opposed to a "morphological" means of classification (146-147), in which the motives commonly "attributed to the suicide, whether rightly or wrongly, are not their true causes" (149). Durkheim contends "The reasons ascribed for suicide, therefore, or those to which the suicide himself ascribes his act, are usually only apparent causes . . . they express the general state very unfaithfully" and they fail adequately to get at "the social concomitants of suicide" (151). This in turn leads to "Disregarding the individual as such, his motives and his ideas," as "we shall seek directly the states of the various social environments . . . in terms of which the variations of suicide occur" (151).

In discussing his first principal type of suicide, egoistic suicide, Durkheim sets forth an important general conclusion resulting from his research and analysis: "suicide varies inversely with the degree of integration of the social groups of which the individual forms a part" (209). What this means, more precisely, is "The more weakened the groups to which he belongs, the less he depends on them, the more he consequently depends only on himself and recognizes no other rules of conduct than what are founded on his private interest. If we agree to call this state egoism, in which the individual ego asserts itself to excess in the face of the social ego and at its expense, we may call egoistic the special type of suicide springing from excessive individualism" (209). Elaborates further:

> As collective force is one of the obstacles best calculated to restrain suicide, its weakening involves a development of suicide. When society is strongly integrated, it holds individuals under its control . . . But how could society impose its supremacy upon them when they refuse to accept this subordination as legitimate? It no longer possesses the requisite authority to retain them . . . . For they cling to life more resolutely when belonging to a group they love, so as not to betray interests they put before their own" (210-211).

In sum, egoistic suicide, its prevalence, and especially attention to where and when it increases, leads toward recognition of the key role of "mutual moral support, which instead of throwing the individual on his own resources, leads him to share in the collective energy and supports his own when exhausted" (211).

In a stirring passage Durkheim writes, "Life is said to be intolerable unless some reason for existing is involved, some purpose justifying life's trials. The individual alone is not a sufficient end for his activity. He is too little. He is not only hemmed in spatially; he is also strictly limited temporally. When, therefore, we have no other object than ourselves we cannot avoid the thought that our efforts will finally end in nothingness, since we ourselves disappear" (210). The individual needs to be integrated into society, and to feel wanted and needed by society, or he can feel as if he has nothing of worth, and is nothing of worth. It is, after all, "The influence of society" that "has aroused in us the sentiments of sympathy and solidarity drawing us toward others; it is society which, fashioning us in its image, fills us with religious, political and moral beliefs that control our actions" (211-212), and this includes our sense of sympathy and solidarity with the preservation and perpetuation of our own individual life. However, for this influence, and for these sentiments and beliefs "to have a raison d'etre in our eyes, the purpose they envisage must be one not indifferent to us" (212)–but, for the egoistic suicide, the latter is the subjective perception and in fact, what's more, often the objective reality. "In the same measure as we feel detached from society, we become detached from that life whose source and aim is society" (212). As a result of this detachment, the individual becomes "a mystery to himself, unable to escape the exasperating and agonizing question: to what purpose?" (212)–a question, moreover, which seemingly becomes ever increasingly impossible to satisfyingly answer other than 'for no (good) purpose'. Durkheim argues, yet further,

> If, in other words, as has often been said, man is double, that is because social man superimposes himself upon physical man. Social man necessarily presupposes a society which he expresses and serves. If this dissolves, if we no longer feel it in existence and action about and above us, whatever is social in us is deprived of all objective foundation. All that remains is an artificial combination of illusory images, a phantasmagoria vanishing at the least reflection; that is, nothing which can be a goal for our action. (213)

This is, indeed, tragic because "this social man is the essence of civilized man; he is the masterpiece of existence" (213).

In sum, in relation to egoistic suicide, the social cause is clear, if nonetheless paradoxically so: "Thus, at the very moment that, with excessive zeal, he frees himself from the social environment, he still admits to its influence. However individualized a man may be, there is always something collective remaining–the very depression and melancholy resulting from the same exaggerated individualism. He effects communion through sadness when he no longer has anything else with which to achieve it" (214).

In the case of altruistic suicide, converse social factors are at work: not only, Durkheim contends, can extreme individualism (and, more precisely, again, a society that promulgates and valorizes extreme individualism) lead to suicide, but also insufficient individuation can do the same (with again this referring to a society that promulgates and valorizes the opposite of extreme individualism–or, in other words, insufficient individuation). Altruistic suicide is more common in societies and social groups where the weight of society overwhelms the individual, and the individual maintains little place or meaning in collective life *as an individual*; this is a society, or social group, involving massive cohesion and often including constant collective supervision (220-221). As Durkheim explains, "While the egoist is unhappy because he sees nothing real in the world but the individual, the intemperate altruist's sadness, on the contrary, springs from the individual's seeming wholly unreal to him. One is detached from life because, seeing no goal to which he may attach himself, he feels himself useless and purposeless; the other because he has a goal but one outside this life, which henceforth seems merely an obstacle to him" (225). Altruistic suicide often follows in societies and social groups where killing one's self can be conceived of as acting responsibly to the society, or the social group; as fulfilling a duty; or as reflecting a heightened state of "impersonality" among individuals "trained to renunciation and an unquestioned abnegation" (223). Durkheim cites the army as one modern social institution in which this type of suicide remains commonplace, as Durkheim otherwise argues altruistic suicide tends to be more common in 'premodern' societies. Even if Durkheim is perhaps too quick to advance this last argument his explanation of what constitutes the mode of altruistic suicide, and especially its relationship to the collective–and to the force of the collective–remains useful for explaining multiple modern to contemporary varieties of the same.

In situations of anomie (or anomy as it is also spelled), societal norms fail to exercise an effectively regulating influence over individual aspirations and behaviors. Normatively, Durkheim suggests, individuals accept the moral legitimacy of societal norms, "But in times of crisis or transition, especially abrupt," society "is less capable to incapable of exercising this influence" (252). When preexisting social conditions, and preexisting positions or stations within society, especially differentially hierarchized stations and positions, are rapidly destabilized, and no new moral scale is yet in place that can explain and justify this new state of affairs, suicides tend to rise: "The limits are unknown between the possible and the impossible, what is just and what is unjust, legitimate claims and hopes and those which are immoderate. Consequently, there is no restraint on aspirations" (253). In conditions of anomie, people are "no longer resigned" to their "former lot" as "with increased prosperity desires increase" (253). Traditional rules "have lost their authority" and promises of greater possibilities have stimulated desires while making these "more contingent and impatient of control" (253). What's more, "The state of de-regulation or anomy is thus further heightened by passions being less disciplined, precisely when they need more disciplining" (253). Eventually this can lead to the situation where "Nothing gives satisfaction," "the race for an unattainable goal can give no other pleasure than the race itself," and "the struggle grows ever more violent and painful, both from being less controlled and because competition is greater" (253). Modern society has yet to find a sufficient replacement for religion as a principal means and medium for exercising a compelling moral force throughout society, with Durkheim highly skeptical of the capability of the state, in itself, to be able to step in and do so. The challenge is compounded, because in modern (late 19th century, advanced capitalist, Western European) society, elements of what might be identified as 'the anomic character' have become widely accepted, and even widely positively valued: "Yet these dispositions are so inbred that society has grown to accept them and is accustomed to think them normal. It is everlastingly repeated that it is man's nature to be eternally dissatisfied, constantly to advance, without relief or rest, toward an indefinite goal. The longing for infinity is daily represented as a mark of moral distinction, whereas it can only appear within unregulated consciences which elevate to a rule the lack of rule from which they suffer" (257).

Although egoistic and anomic suicide share notable features and can and do fuse to create an especially prevalent mode of suicide, in modern society, it is important to understand that even as egoistic and anomic suicide both "spring from society's insufficient presence in individuals . . . In egoistic suicide it is deficient in truly collective activity, thus depriving the latter [individuals] of object and meaning. In anomic suicide, society's influence is lacking in the basically individual passions, thus leaving them without a check-rein" (258). In relation to the latter, as Durkheim adds, "We may offer society everything social in us, and still be unable to control our desires" (258). To further help explain anomic suicide, Durkheim explains that when one "aspires to everything and is satisfied with nothing," when one is driven by a "morbid desire for the infinite," and "when one is no longer checked" such that "one becomes unable to check one's self," one is likely to be experiencing anomie, as is the case when one "happens almost to have exhausted the range of what is possible," and as a result "dreams of the impossible" and "thirst[s] for the non-existent" (271). In this kind of situation what develops "is a state of disturbance, agitation, and discontent which inevitably increases the possibilities of suicide" (271).

Durkheim's fourth type of suicide, identified in terms of social causes, is sketched out briefly as follows: "the suicide deriving from excessive regulation, that of persons with futures pitilessly blocked and passions violently choked by oppressive discipline"–i.e., "excessive physical or moral despotism"– is what Durkheim labels "fatalistic suicide" (276n).

After introducing and explaining each of these types of suicide, and connecting them precisely, with, as is the case throughout his book, extensive statistical data and analysis of this data to support his claims, Durkheim addresses further complications by taking into account multiple individual forms of these broad social types, while acknowledging that "Each victim of suicide gives his act a personal stamp" (277). Of particular interest here, Durkheim associates one common form of egoistic suicide with excessively and obsessively reflectively focused individuals, and with individuals prone to high degrees of melancholy, and in particular, melancholic detachment from the social, as well as corresponding, in general, to "a high development of knowledge and reflective intelligence" (281). As Durkheim elaborates on this connection, "A mind that questions everything, unless strong enough to bear the weight of its own ignorance, risks questioning itself and being engulfed in doubt" (282). Explaining further the difference between forms of egoistic versus anomic suicide, Durkheim suggests it is useful to conceive that "The former is lost in the infinity of dreams, the second in the infinity of desires" (287). Nevertheless, often types are combined, and do not exist in pure and isolated form, but rather in partial and hybrid form. Egoism and anomie commonly fuse, "where depression alternates with agitation, dream with action, transports of desire with fleeting sadness" (288).

In summing up, and clarifying what he is theorizing in *Suicide*, Durkheim explains that "At any given moment the moral constitution of society establishes the contingent of voluntary deaths. There is, therefore, for each people a collective force of a definite amount of energy, impelling men to self-destruction. The victim's acts which at first seem to express only his personal temperament are really the supplement and prolongation of a social condition which they express externally" (299). Here Durkheim stresses the importance of recognizing "the existence of a collective inclination to suicide from which individual inclinations are derived" (302). Even as individuals making up a society continually change, as long as a society remains essentially the same its rates of suicide tend to do so also. Once again, "Collective tendencies have an existence of their own," and the same is true of "forces external to individuals" (309). These are a material reality: "a totality of forces which cause us to act from without, like the physico-chemical forces to which we react"–they are "objective social facts" (310). Individuals combine together and in so doing create more and other than the mere sum of their individualities. Society includes materially tangible and empirically identifiable things, collective representations, and much more–including collective currents, collective crystallizations, and collective demarcations and distinctions. The individual and the collective are inextricably intertwined, interdependent, and interconstitutive. We are all representations, in various ways, forms, degrees, directions, of the social collective–of what Marx theorizes as the ensemble of social relations.

Why the particular individuals who take their own lives–what explains why these specific individuals as opposed to others are the most influenced by the social factors Durkheim has theorized? Durkheim proposes at least the beginning of an answer, as follows: "If, in a given moral environment . . . certain individuals are affected and certain others not, this is undoubtedly, in great part, because the formers' mental constitution, as elaborated by nature and events, offers less resistance to the suicidogenetic current" (323). As both editor Simpson and Durkheim himself discuss, it is possible to make sense of suicide as existing on something like a continuum of self-destructive tendencies, and actions, including those of which the individual is consciously aware and those which the individual is unconscious–and, anticipating a yet further connection with psychoanalysis, which the individual may repress, deny, disavow, displace or project onto someone, or something, else.

Because Durkheim perceives that high numbers of suicides in modern society "manifests the deep disturbance from which civilized societies are suffering, and bears witness to its gravity," this requires concrete actions directed toward "lessening the collective malady of which it is sign and a result" (391). Durkheim proposes forming collectives organized outside and independent of the state, centered around the occupational group, that will serve as preeminent locations through which social integration can be most effectively achieved and social aspirations most effectively regulated. Durkheim believes individuals strongly, even urgently, need social unity and solidarity, as well as moral discipline exercised through collective means. The occupational group "sufficiently dominates individuals to set limits to their greed; but sees too much of their life not to sympathize with their needs" (384). Durkheim advocates for substantial social decentralization so as to effectively empower these locally based social groups concentrating social energies at this level, with again, "occupational decentralization" involving the making of "the occupational group the base of our political organization" (390).

In sum, according to Durkheim, a society must regulate (i.e., moderate) people's desires, by convincing the members of the society it is right and necessary they limit what they can and should aspire to obtain. If society does not do this people will constantly desire more, including what is impossible to obtain, and end up extremely unhappy as a result. And yet, a society can only successfully exercise this regulating power if its dominant institutions are widely accepted as morally legitimate. This is especially important when a society must encourage its members to accept it is right and necessary that some obtain more while others obtain less. "But when society is disturbed by some painful crisis or by beneficent but abrupt transitions, it is momentarily incapable of exercising this influence; thence comes the sudden rise in the curve of suicides . . ." (252). Sudden, rapid losses in wealth, power, status, freedom, access, or opportunity can lead to this end, but so can situations in which it becomes suddenly, rapidly possible for some people (but not all) to greatly exceed previously socially accepted limits.

According to Durkheim, 'anomie' is a major problem throughout modern society. Anomie refers to 'de-regulation' of desires and the concurrent rise and spread of 'normlessness'. In other words, society and its dominant institutions are no longer able effectively to convince people to limit their desires, or to convince people that different groups of people's different levels or degrees of success are right and necessary. People no longer accept social norms as legitimate, and feel little inclination to accommodate themselves to these norms. Durkheim argues, in modern society, "the dogma of economic materialism" (255) has supplanted religion such that people lead their lives increasingly motivated by greed (and, seemingly, by greed alone). Anomic suicides result from the acute frustration individuals feel that they must always seek, and acquire, more, and better, yet nothing they do seek, or acquire, ever satisfies them. These kinds of anomic suicides result, as well, from loss of any sense of greater purpose in life than the constant pursuit of material gain; anomic suicides result from individuals internalizing a sense that their self-worth is entirely equivalent with their success in competition for material gain. Egoistic suicide, in contrast, results from isolation, from lack of an effectively supportive and sustaining community–from feeling, in other words, as if one is 'thrown back [entirely] upon one's self', as if one is an outcast, a misfit, permanently marginalized and ostracized. Altruistic suicide results from sacrificing one's self for a greater good, so the greater good can live on even as one who kills themself dies. Fatalistic suicide results from the sense that everything is so thoroughly over-regulated and decided for them that they maintain little to any room left for real autonomy and effective individual agency, while their sense of their own individual identity, and its value, has not been subsumed within and conflated with that of the collective in the same way, or to the same extent, that is the case with altruistic suicide.

As a more concrete illustration of how to make sense and use of Durkheim's theorization of suicide, while recognizing Durkheim is concerned with social causes that show up in *social rates* of suicide, let's nonetheless consider the suicide of a hypothetical individual, who we will call Danny, and what social factors might suggest this is, variously, an instance of egoistic suicide, altruistic suicide, anomic suicide, and fatalistic suicide.

Let's imagine Danny has come from a family and community background in which no particular religious, political, or broadly philosophical doctrine held sway, and above all else he learned, and was diversely encouraged, to approach all such doctrinal outlooks as problematic, such that he has tended to be skeptical of such affiliations. Danny has also developed a skeptical to suspicious outlook concerning identifying what he thinks, feels, and believes with any kind of group mindset, and instead has preferred to always maintain a critical distance between completely identifying with the implicit as well as explicit mission and purpose of every organization of which he has been apart. These tendencies on Danny's part have not only led him to lead a highly individualistic life but also to develop and maintain few if any strong social links as part of social groups. As Danny has become older he has felt increasingly more distant from what other people immediately around him are about, what motivates and concerns as well as interests and excites them, and as a result he also feels not only increasingly isolated and alone but also increasingly lonely and abandoned. He feels like his society, as represented in the communities to which he has the readiest access, has nothing to offer him, and it doesn't–and can't–understand and appreciate what a person such as him is like. He also feels as if somewhere there should be a community within which he could fit, feel at ease, and feel at home, but he has no idea where such a community might be and doubts it does exist. Given these factors, Danny's suicide is likely to fit into the category of what Durkheim theorizes as 'egoistic suicide'.

Let's imagine, in contrast, Danny is someone who comes from a family maintaining a military background, and has dreamed from an early age of also becoming a soldier, which he does. He identifies strongly with an army ethos, and is happy readily to subordinate markers that might reference his individual uniqueness and difference–as far less important, and far less meaningful, than his identity as part of the collective identity he experiences, within and as part of the army, and in particular his platoon, squad, and team. On the front lines, his platoon becomes involved in a battle that leads to the majority of members of this platoon being killed, including all of the other members of his team and his squad besides Danny. Despite these major losses, the platoon holds it own and the efforts of all involved, especially those who died in this combat, are lauded by others throughout the army for demonstrating great bravery, including heroically being ready to make 'the ultimate sacrifice'. Yet because of the size of the losses, the surviving members of his platoon are scheduled to be split up and reassigned to other platoons. Danny's suicide not only reflects and responds to the death of those with whom Danny has developed extremely close bonds, and with whom he has forged a strong collective identity that overrides any sense of individual identity for Danny, but also because the loss of the platoon, the squad, and the team means Danny faces the loss of any remaining basis for this collective identity that has come to be of preeminent, and even overriding importance, in giving Danny's life a satisfying sense of meaning and purpose. Given these factors, Danny's suicide is likely to fit into the category of what Durkheim theorizes as 'altruistic suicide'.

Let's imagine, again in contrast with the preceding, that Danny has grown up inspired by the belief, widely promoted within his family and community, as well as the greater society, that he can be and do whatever he wants, as long as he sets his mind to it and is willing to work hard at it. Danny is inspired by stories of entrepreneurs who have started their own businesses from scratch, seemingly with limited resources, going on to achieve great success with their businesses earning large profits, employing many people, and exercising considerable market influence. Danny believes he has come up with an exceptional idea for a unique business of his own, which he believes many people will want to pay for, and he works hard to get started, seeking out assistance wherever he can find it. But after repeated efforts at starting this business end up failing, and people are increasingly less inclined to offer him support in getting started, given this track record, Danny feels frustrated and embittered, because he maintains insufficient resources by himself alone to try one more time. Danny feels he has given everything of himself to try to realize his idea, which he feels is more impressive than that offered by many other start-up businesses he knows about, yet people keep telling him it is time now he give up pursuing what has been his dream and work instead for someone else. Danny feels like what has happened to him is hugely unfair, and that his society has effectively promised him a success that it has then not provided, and, if anything, undermined–or simply ignored–his idea and his effort to bring it to fruition. Given these factors, Danny's suicide is likely to fit into the category of what Durkheim theorizes as 'anomic suicide'.

And let's consider one further hypothetical scenario involving this hypothetical individual Danny. Danny is arrested and convicted, early on in his adult life, for possession and dealing of illegal drugs and is given a stiff prison sentence. After managing to survive life in prison, Danny eventually is paroled and released from prison. But Danny has never had a chance, before his arrest and sentence, to develop qualifications for other than low-skill, low-wage, often temporary, and often transient and precarious kinds of jobs. Unfortunately, his prison record makes him even less readily employable, and because he has served a significant prison sentence he no longer enjoys close connections with family members or previous friends, while he has no one whom he knows he can trust and rely on as a mentor or a guide. Danny quickly becomes involved with dealing illegal drugs once again, and is eventually caught, charged, and tried once more, receiving a longer prison sentence than earlier. Danny previously found prison virtually unbearable, as a location in which his life was thoroughly constrained, where explicit and implicit regulations on what he could and could not do he experienced as crushing. Given these factors, Danny's suicide right before he is set to begin his second prison sentence is likely to fit into the category of what Durkheim theorizes as 'fatalistic suicide'.

As with Aidan and Kim, hypothetical individuals I used to illustrate key ideas from Marx earlier, Danny is a composite of multiple real people I have known. In relation to further personal connections with Durkheim's four types of suicide I will add it is easy to recognize signs of all of the kinds of social factors Durkheim proposes are responsible for these types of suicide among many individuals I have known, most of whom have not killed themselves but who have nevertheless suffered considerable anguish in their lives. Many students I have come to know and work with have often found it challenging and difficult, at least at first, to find their niche at the university, and to make new friends, while often worrying they are too different from other people around them for these others to want to be close to them, to become their friends. At times these students have also felt seriously conflicted about what they now believe and with what they now identify, as this has been in the process of rapidly and substantially changing, in uncomfortable and confusing ways, as they have become university students, versus what they previously believed and identified with, prior to coming to the university. The latter they no longer experience as convincing and appealing to them–meaning, in many cases, they now feel estranged from those with whom they previously shared those kinds of beliefs and identifications.

Imagine a student whom I will name Sam who comes from a culturally, politically, and religiously conservative family and community background who not only increasingly distances themselves from acceptance and identification with these kinds of conservative positions but also increasingly feels unable to relate to or tolerate close relations with family and community members they were close to for much of their previous life. On top of this Sam has started to identify as gender non-binary at the university, while suspecting family and others Sam has known well from their hometown would experience considerable difficulty accepting this new identity of Sam's. At the same time, Sam's conservative background continues to be a significant shaping influence and this means Sam doesn't always feel welcome, at ease, understood, and appreciated by fellow students (including fellow lgbtq+ students) who don't bring that kind of background with them.

At other times students I have met and worked with have shared with me they felt a limited sense of the importance of their own individual selves, and of their own distinct individual identities. These students have instead derived a much more meaningful and fulfilling sense of importance as part of an extremely close social group, whether this be a family, a neighborhood, a religious community, a sports team, a musical outfit, or a nexus of best friends.

Let's consider a hypothetical student, whom I will call Kyle, who was a multi-sport star athlete back in high school. The bonds Kyle developed and maintained with his teammates were overwhelmingly the most important, the and satisfying, sources of identity Kyle has ever experienced. Now, at university, Kyle not only misses those teams and those teammates, but also struggles to find a new social group that offers him the same strong sense of collective identity–and feels in desperate need of finding this.

Likewise, a significant number of students have evinced plenty of frustration about what people in positions of power in society, and in smaller communities as part of society, are and have been doing with the power they maintain. These students have felt they did not trust or respect these ostensible 'leaders' yet at the same time felt they could do little effectively themselves to challenge and displace those in such leadership positions. These students have not found the norms of conduct and behavior exhibited or promoted by those in such leading positions compelling let alone worthy of identification and emulation. As a result, these students have felt adrift and uncertain concerning what kinds of ethical standards they could and should adopt themselves as well as troubled by having to accept and conform to what those they do not trust or respect require these students do.

Let's imagine a student named Michaela who is extremely concerned about the impact of climate change, ecological destruction, and the looming threat of ecocide. Michaela wants to do all she can to help combat these emergencies but perceives social and political leaders failing to treat these issues with the seriousness and urgency they demand, and even blithely proceeding to make the situation all that much worse. Michaela feels as if these people don't care what kind of world they leave behind once they are dead and that she and others of her generation will have to cope with, as best they can, beyond the point of no return.

I have also worked with students who have felt their lives everywhere around them excessively regimented and controlled by institutional mandates and expectations such that they have felt they maintained virtually no freedom, and no power, to determine for themselves what they might try to do with–try to make of–their own lives.

Let's consider here a hypothetical student who I will name Paul, who is a first-generation university student and who hails from a locality, a region, and an ethnicity where obtaining a university degree at a comprehensive, four-year, liberal arts institution remains rare. Paul feels an overriding sense of deep responsibility to his family, community, region, and ethnic group that he always be successful, but this in turn means Paul feels like he needs to choose what he concentrates on, and what he otherwise spends his time doing while attending university, according to what others, from the places where he comes and the groups he feels compelled to represent, expect from and want of him–not what he himself might, independent of that influence, freely choose for himself. Paul feels like he must do precisely what he is expected, even seemingly 'called upon', to do, and that he has no room for exploration and experimentation let alone for experiencing any setbacks and failures–which yet further means Paul feels as all those counting on him expect he always will receive the highest possible grade, and maintain the highest possible grade point average, for all of the academic work he does.

In my own life I have despaired when I have felt marginalized because others where I was at could not and would not accept and include me, on account of my differences from prevailing norms, whether on account of my being gay and queer, Marxist and socialist, concentrating in critical theory and critical studies in popular culture, intellectually oriented, registering the shaping impact of living and growing up in the Northeast, suffering from serious chronic illness that I have found impossible easily to explain and that represents a substantial yet largely invisible disability, and as someone who can be shy, serious, intense, and initially wary among people I don't yet know but at the same time who also can be someone who is friendly, loyal, kind, caring, wild, funny, silly, and exuberant once I feel like I can trust being these ways with people I have come to know. I have also despaired at times when romantic and sexual partners have broken up with me while I was still in love with them, and when I have had to accept that other people I had fallen in love with did not feel the same way about me although they loved me nonetheless as a good, and even as a best, friend. I have felt similar anguish in situations where I needed to venture out on my own, into a new job in a new community, with all those who have been close to me, and who have known me, cared about me, and supported me no longer directly with me, especially when I have had little money to help me survive and subsist in this yet unknown and potentially hostile to indifferent new territory and when I agonized because I recognized even the smallest accident or emergency under these circumstances would drain my resources and leave me in a precarious state. I have lived in situations where I have had to cut back on how much food I ate, along with how often as well as in what kinds and varieties, because of lack of means to afford otherwise. In these straits I worried about being able to continue to pay the rent for the housing in which I lived, to maintain my car in running order, to keep up with other bills, as well as about postponing, delaying, and abandoning seeking medical assistance for health problems I was experiencing because I could not readily pay any of this.

I have lived through times when I felt like I would never manage to obtain a job as a tenure-track professor, and would need to give up altogether working as a teacher and pursuing the kinds of scholarship and creative activity I prized, turning to who knows what as an alternative life direction. In the year I spent living back at my mother's crowded house, with my mother, my brother, my sister-in-law, two additional lodgers, four dogs, and several cats, between Arizona State and UW-Eau Claire, I recognized this was my last shot to obtain a position teaching and working as a university professor, and if I did not succeed in that round of applications I planned to give up and move to San Diego, California, where I knew no one and maintained no ready job prospects, simply because I liked San Diego the one previous time I had spent visiting the city.

Four

In *Civilization & Its Discontents* Sigmund Freud attempts to explain how and why human beings will always experience considerable unease as part of 'civilized' societies and cultures, and what are some of the actual and potential consequences of these discontents. Freud here theorizes aggression as just as fundamental to human nature as he has long argued is 'the pleasure principle', and continues work he began in *Beyond the Pleasure Principle* (1920), theorizing relations between Eros and Thanatos, or life and death drives, while here considering how these drives might play out as part of societies and other social groups and not just within individuals' psychic lives. The consequences of internalized aggression directed inward and that is essentially incessant and unstoppable represent especially striking dimensions of what Freud in this book engages.

After beginning by sharing his personal skepticism about people reporting 'oceanic experiences', contending he himself has never experienced anything of that kind, and relating his skepticism to his staunchly atheistic dismissal of religious belief, Freud relents somewhat by admitting he has come to support the position "that nothing once formed in the mind could ever perish, that everything survives in some way or other, and is capable under certain conditions of being brought to light again, as, for instance, when regression extends back far enough" (15). What's more, "the fact is that a survival of all the early stages alongside the final form is only possible in the mind" (20). The oceanic is, for Freud, an example of such a survival of an earlier stage, or moment, in psychic development, but the oceanic will not constitute a significant focus of Freud's attention in this book. Nevertheless, Freud shares his acceptance, despite how religious faith exerts no appeal for him, and never has, of why it exercises appeal to others: "Life as we find it is too hard for us; it entails too much pain, too many disappointments, impossible tasks. We cannot do without palliative remedies. We cannot dispense with auxiliary constructions . . . [We need] powerful diversions of interest, which lead us to care little about our misery; substitute gratifications, which lessen it; and intoxicating substances, which make us insensitive to it. Something of this kind is indispensable" (25). Freud suggests religion has proven further useful to many by providing a seemingly satisfying answer to "the question, 'What is the purpose of human life?'"

Freud's principal interest lies with "what the behaviour of men themselves reveals as the purpose and object of their lives, what they demand of life and wish to attain in it. The answer to this can hardly be in doubt: they seek happiness, they want to become happy and to remain so" (27). This is Freud's famous "pleasure-principle" which Freud reaffirms yet broaches the difficulty with is that "its programme is in conflict with the whole world . . . It simply cannot be put into execution, the whole constitution of things runs counter to it" (27). Freud proposes it is "much less difficult to be unhappy" (28) than it is to be happy. Unhappiness make sense in response to disease and decline with age and toward death; pain and anxiety concerning disease, decline, and death; and many further impingements on the pursuit of happiness from the outer world along with multiple forces of destruction that come likewise from this same source, and from relations with other human beings, which is "perhaps more painful than any other" source (28). Happiness is, therefore, in actuality, a relatively rare, limited, temporary, and fleeting phenomenon.

Participating in society requires modification of "the pleasure-principle" by means of "the reality-principle" which insures "a certain degree of protection against suffering is secured" at the cost of "an undeniable reduction in the degree of enjoyment obtainable" (32). What Freud is referring to here is accepting limits on what kinds and extents of happiness can be pursued, and what kinds and extents of unhappiness can be avoided, as part of a human society in order that society can effectively function. This requires redirecting pursuit of pleasure, as well as avoidance of suffering, in line with socially acceptable wants and needs–wants and needs that can be socially accommodated. Sublimation, for example, is useful in adjusting to the inevitable and necessary constraints of (social) reality where instincts and phantasies are converted and transformed into intellectual and artistic pursuits.

Freud contends not all people are capable of pursuing this path, and of making it work for them, while sublimation remains limited in preventing unhappiness: "Yet art affects us but as a mild narcotic and can provide no more than a temporary refuge for us from the hardships of life; its influence is not strong enough to make us forget real misery" (35). Work, likewise, can have similarly partially diverting and compensating benefits, but only "when it has been selected by free choice" whereas "The great majority work only when forced by necessity" (35n).

Freud describes one form of madness as involving the attempt to create an imaginary world rid of all the obstacles to the pleasure-principle in which the mad person attempts to live, but the mad person "usually finds no one to help him in carrying through his delusion" (36). Nevertheless, Freud suggests, "each one of us behaves in some respect like the paranoiac, substituting a wish-fulfillment for some aspect of the world which is unbearable to him, and carrying this delusion through into reality" (36). What's more, "The religions of humanity, too, must be classified as mass-delusions of this kind. Needless to say, no one who shares a delusion recognizes it as such" (36). At the same time, the pursuit of love, beauty, and sex all face the same limits–in and of themselves they cannot fully overcome the discontents that humans experience as members of societies in which limits are necessary, and often substantial.

In sum, "The goal towards which the pleasure-principle impels us–of becoming happy–is not attainable; yet we may not–nay, cannot–give up the effort to come nearer to the realization of it by some means or other. Very different paths may be taken towards it . . ." (39). But, again, none can achieve what we [ultimately] desire. Even in conscious pursuit of what we accept as a limited, constrained, and curbed degree or extent of happiness "Success is never certain" (41). And this in turn means two last paths follow as common modes of achieving "substitute-gratifications" in attempts at doing so–neurosis and psychosis.

Yet Freud suggests all of the preceding is common knowledge that does not answer the far more challenging question of *why* happiness is impossible. As a beginning of an answer Freud proposes "We shall never completely subdue nature; our body, too, is an organism, itself a part of nature, and will always contain the seeds of dissolution, with its limited powers of adaptation and achievement" (43). And yet, he suggests, this seems as if it should not be too disheartening because within civilized society–i.e., for Freud, late 19th to early 20th century modern European capitalist society–means of mitigating and compensating for these impacts are continually being developed and deployed. However, Freud is concerned with *why* is civilization itself nevertheless a source and focus of hostility for so many–what explains the "profound, long-standing discontent with the existing state of civilization" (45). After all, scientific and technological advancement has not increased human happiness: "all this newly-won power over space and time, this conquest of the forces of nature, this fulfilment of age-old longings, has not increased the amount of pleasure they can obtain in life, has not made them feel any happier" (46).

For Freud, "culture" is equivalent to "the sum of the achievements and institutions which differentiate our lives from those of our animal forebears and serve two purposes, namely, that of protecting humanity against nature and of regulating the relations of human beings among themselves" (49-50). Culture includes "all the activities and possessions which men use to make the earth serviceable to them, to protect them against the tyranny of natural forces, and so on" (50). Culture has reached an amazing state where humans now possess powers once only imaginable as those of gods, or in fairy tales, but nevertheless "the human being of to-day is not happy with all his likeness to a god" (53). Elaborating further, Freud discusses how civilization, and the culture of civilization, requires more than the immediately practically useful, including beauty, cleanliness, order, and the pursuit of intellectual, scientific, and aesthetic achievement as ends in themselves.

Civilization further requires just forms of relations of people with each other as part of a society, including just forms of regulation and governance of these relations. All of this, as desirable as it is, nonetheless requires in return restrictions upon individuals' pursuit of gratification so that what is accessible to whom, when, where, how, and why is determined according to standards of justice–where all contribute and receive fairly, and all make fair sacrifices and achieve fair recompense for what they do sacrifice. In Freud's words,

> Liberty has undergone restrictions through the evolution of civilization and justice demands that these restrictions shall apply to all. The desire for freedom that makes itself felt in a human community may be a revolt against some existing injustice and so may prove favourable to a further development of civilization and remain compatible with it. But it may also have its origin in the primitive roots of the personality, still unfettered by civilizing influences, and so become a source of antagonism to culture. Thus the cry for freedom is directed either against particular forms or demands of culture or else against culture itself. (60)

Yet, Freud admits this is still common knowledge so it is necessary to inquire further concerning what are the influences to which culture owes its origin, how did culture arise, and what has determined its course (64). The culture of modern society, Freud argues, tends to put substantial restrictions on sexual life. This includes forbidding or stigmatizing most ways of expressing love, in the form of sex, with "the only outlet not thus censored, heterosexual genital love . . . further circumscribed by the barriers of legitimacy and monogamy" (75). In short, "The sexual life of civilized man is seriously disabled, whatever we say"–even "atrophied" as extensive restrictions are imposed on sexuality "as a source of pleasurable sensations" (76). In a long footnote Freud proposes that humans are 'by nature' both bisexual and likely, originally at least, 'hermaphroditic'. He also proposes "we far too readily identify activity with masculinity and passivity with femininity" and this is not justified by reference to the animal world. Yet further, Freud proposes "each individual has both male and female desires which need satisfaction in his sexual life" and these may not be satisfied in the same object, or through the same means, and may well even interfere with each other (77n). But most important, for the purposes of the developing argument of this book is recognition that development of civilization, through its culture, requires extensive sexual repression (78n)–which can readily result in extensive unhappiness.

And yet Freud also calls our attention to the fact that "Culture demands other sacrifices besides that of sexual gratification" (79). Freud discusses how the moral commandment that 'thou shalt love thy neighbour as thyself' is illogical and the moral commandment to 'love thine enemies' even more so. These demands run contrary to 'human nature'. As Freud sees it, "men are not gentle, friendly creatures wishing for love, who simply defend themselves if they are attacked" because "a powerful measure of desire for aggression has to be reckoned with as part of their instinctual development" (85). Freud adds that the proverb 'homo homini lupus' (man is a wolf to another man) is clearly all too true given massive evidence, throughout human history, in support of this proverb. Even in supposedly civilized societies and cultures, "Aggressive cruelty" is widespread and commonplace (85). The key implication here is "The existence of this tendency to aggression which we can detect in ourselves and rightly presume to be present in others is the factor that disturbs our relations with our neighbours and makes it necessary for culture to institute its high demands. Civilized society is perpetually menaced with disintegration through this primary hostility of men towards one another" (86).

Freud contends a principal problem confronting civilized society and culture is what to do with and about this aggressive instinct, which, recognized as such, cannot be denied and cannot be overcome by creating more egalitarian and inclusive forms of society, but in fact needs outlets for release and relief. Freud argues modern society has failed to take this adequately into account by providing outlets which prevent this aggression from turning against the larger society, groups within society, other individuals, and the individual themself. Too much restriction upon the pursuit and realization of pleasure ramps up dissatisfaction yet further, increasing the strength of the aggressive drive. Happiness sacrificed for security promotes discontent. Freud is especially skeptical of social forces of cohesion that "consist predominantly of identifications of the individuals in the group with one another" without adequately accommodating distinctions among individuals, in terms of differential inclinations and abilities, as well as the need of individuals for separation from the group and from others comprising it (93).

Freud cites his earlier book *Beyond the Pleasure Principle* as already drawing "the conclusion that, besides the instinct preserving the organic substance and binding it into ever larger units, there must exist another in antithesis to this, which would seek to dissolve these units and reinstate their antecedent inorganic state. That is to say, a death instinct, as well as Eros; the phenomena of life would then be explicable from the interplay of the two and their counteracting effects on each other" (97). Nevertheless, here, in *Civilization and Its Discontents*, Freud stresses the importance of "the universality of non-erotic aggression and destruction" and criticizes himself for overlooking this universality for too long (99). As he now recognizes, a propensity for evil is just as much human nature as a propensity for good, and the two are in practice rarely clearly distinct and entirely separable. After all, "The instinct of destruction, when tempered and harnessed (as it were, inhibited in its aim) and directed towards objects, is compelled to provide the ego with satisfaction of its needs and with power over nature" (101). Therefore, "In all that follows I take up the standpoint that the tendency to aggression is an innate, independent, instinctual disposition in man" and "it constitutes the most powerful obstacle to culture" (102).

After all, culture principally depends on uniting, and binding together, whereas "The natural instinct of aggressiveness in man, the hostility of each one against all and of all against each one, opposes this programme of civilization. The instinct of aggression is the derivative and main representative of the death instinct" (103). As he concludes section VI of *Civilization and Its Discontents*, "now, it seems to me, the meaning of the evolution of culture is no longer a riddle to us. It must present to us the struggle between Eros and Death, between the instincts of life and the instincts of destruction, as it works itself out in the human species. The struggle is what all life essentially consists of and so the evolution of civilization may be simply described as the struggle of the human species for existence" (103).

Freud begins Section VII by asking "What means does civilization make use of to hold in check the aggressiveness that opposes it, to make it harmless, perhaps to get rid of it?" (105). His answer: it is "introjected, 'internalized'"–it is "directed against the ego" as "a superego," which "in the form of 'conscience', exercises the same propensity to harsh aggressiveness against the ego that the ego would have liked to enjoy against others as "The tension between the strict super-ego and the subordinate ego we call the sense of guilt; it manifests itself as the need for punishment" (105). Elaborating upon this last point, Freud explains that the super-ego takes advantage of the deepest or our human fears, and even our deepest dreads–"of losing love," of being "threatened with the loss of love"–and this in turn shows up in the form of "bad conscience" (107) and social anxiety, with us blaming ourselves as responsible for these prospective losses. Notably, for Freud, conscience tends to be stricter and harsher the more righteous someone is, and it is the righteous who tend to reproach themselves the furthest–even if, perhaps, they deserve reproaching the least. All the more disturbing, in Freud's account of how culture combats the human instinct for aggression by turning it back against the individual, "every impulse of aggression which we omit to gratify is taken over by the super-ego and goes to heighten its aggressiveness (against the ego)" (114). For Freud, what's more, "guilt is the expression of the conflict of ambivalence, the eternal struggle between Eros and the destructive or death instinct. This conflict is engendered as soon as man is confronted with the task of living with his fellows" (121). What Freud here is insinuating is humans maintain a fundamental ambivalence about relations with other humans–we are continually both pulled toward and away from others, we both want and need others and we want and need to reject, dismiss, oppose, or simply distance ourselves from others, but we experience guilt concerning the latter inclination, guilt in response to this manifestation of our instinct for aggression.

In his concluding section, Section VIII, of *Civilization and Its Discontents*, Freud declares it has been "my intention to represent the sense of guilt as the most important problem in the evolution of culture, and to convey that the price of progress in civilization is paid in forfeiting happiness through the heightening of the sense of guilt" (123). Freud finds an unconscious experience of guilt to be pervasive within 'civilized' society, not just conscious remorse. As Freud puts it, "At bottom the sense of guilt is nothing but a topographical variety of anxiety, and . . . in its later phases it coincides completely with the dread of the super-ego . . . Somewhere or other there is always anxiety hidden behind all symptoms" (125). Key here is that this "sense of guilt produced by culture is not perceived as such and remains to a great extent unconscious, or comes to expression as a sort of uneasiness or discontent for which other motivations are sought" (126). It often shows itself in the form of anxiety, with "the anxiety that lies behind all these relations, the dread of that critical institution, the need for punishment," representing "an instinctual manifestation on the part of the ego, which has become masochistic under the influence of the sadistic super-ego" (127). In short, Freud believes a key discovery of his here is that of the enormous power exercised by "an aggression that has been turned inward" (130). As Freud moves toward his conclusion, he advances the claim that "In our investigations and our therapy of the neuroses we cannot avoid finding fault with the super-ego of the individual on two counts: in commanding and prohibiting with such severity it troubles too little about the happiness of the ego, and it fails to take into account sufficiently the difficulties in the way of obeying it–the strength of individual cravings in the id and the hardships of the external environment" (139). What's more, "Exactly the same objections can be made against the ethical standards of the cultural super-ego. It, too, does not trouble enough about the mental constitution of human beings; it enjoins a command and never asks whether it is possible for them to obey it" (139). The presumption in place, in other words, is to the contrary: that the id can be easily suppressed and external reality can be easily engaged. The super-ego, both in its individual and cultural variants, imagines people can much more readily and easily be and do 'good' than they actually can.

This leads to a final looming question whether, akin to what happens to individuals, if "many systems of civilization–or epochs of it–possibly even the whole of humanity–have become 'neurotic' under the pressure of the civilizing trends?" (141). Freud right away acknowledges he is dealing with analogies here and these can be highly problematic. It can as he himself indicates be hard, for instance, to identify what might constitute a state of 'normalcy' for a civilization–what is, in other words, *not* a neurotic form of civilization. And it is likewise just as hard, if not harder, he indicates, to imagine what therapy might mean in this connection. Still, Freud proposes it is plausible that civilized communities can suffer from pathologies.

Ultimately, Freud declares he has no consolation to offer for the discontents that accompany and follow from civilization (143). But he does conclude that

> The fateful question of the human species seems to me to be whether and to what extent the cultural process developed in it will succeed in mastering the derangements of communal life caused by the human instinct of aggression and self-destruction. In this connection, perhaps the phase through which we are at this moment passing deserves special interest. Men have brought their powers of subduing the forces of nature to such a pitch that by using them they could now very easily exterminate one another to the last man. They know this–hence arises a great part of their current unrest, their dejection, their mood of apprehension. And now it may be expected that the other of the two 'heavenly forces', eternal Eros, will put forth his strength so as to maintain himself alongside of his equally immortal adversary. (144)

Civilization and Its Discontents is often interpreted as Freud commenting obliquely on the rise of fascism as well as concomitant destructive forces emergent in early 20th century modern (advanced capitalist, Western European and North American) society, by suggesting these reflect serious problems intrinsic to 'the project of civilization' itself and in particular to the norms and normativities of so-called 'civilized culture(s)'. At the same time, this book offers a further development of his already long-standing theories of relations among the id, the ego, and the super-ego, and of his preexisting theory of distinctions and relations between Eros and Thanatos, or life-drive and death-drive, first addressed at length in *Beyond the Pleasure Principle*. According to Freud these two drives are continuously acting within and upon us, sometimes in opposition, sometimes in cooperation, sometimes with one or the other maintaining the upper hand. It's important, here, to keep in mind the 'life drive' refers to all our instinctual tendencies to reach out, extend, connect, and interact with a larger and more expansive social–and natural–world, whereas the 'death drive' refers to all our instinctual tendencies to retreat, withdraw, pull back, disconnect, and separate ourselves from a larger and more expansive social–and natural–world. In other words, these drives are not simply about 'seeking to live' and 'seeking to die' in literal terms–the death drive, as Freud indicates, can be destructive, even highly destructive, but it can also be necessarily and usefully destructive as well as valuably reparative and restorative. Libido refers to the psychic energy associated with Eros. It is both mobile and tends to attach itself, to fixate upon, particular objects, and even can be thought of, at least so Freud proposes, as arising from particular erotogenic zones in the body. The death instinct maintains no directly comparable kind of psychic energy but it nonetheless seems to involve similar kinds of mobilities and fixations.

What *Civilization and Its Discontents* most forcefully raises, however, is a challenge, for modern societies, and their dominant cultures, especially as these are articulated in the forms of regulative norms and normativities, and elaborate arrays of legal and moral limits and restrictions, to take into account the discontents this kind of imposition creates and aggravates along with what destructive consequences follow, including for these societies, and cultures, themselves. How can modern societies, and their dominant cultures, afford greater scope, greater opportunity, and greater resource for human freedom to pursue and experience pleasure–and more precisely pleasures of diverse kinds and in diverse ways–while minimizing restraints and constraints as far as possible? How can societies, and their dominant cultures, convey genuine love to and for the individuals that make up these societies, and enable them to feel so loved as well as free to love? How much of this is ultimately impossible, in any kind of society, especially in a civilized (modern, industrially and technologically highly developed, as well as densely and elaborately structured) society, and what happens when means of destruction available to these societies, and to leading members of these societies in powerful positions of authority, become massive and threaten the sheer survival of human society and human culture, as well as of nature and the natural world? How can the aggressive instinct be necessarily contained as well as effectively diverted and compensated at the same time that opportunities for the pursuit of happiness are maximized yet in ways that are as fair and just as possible to all of the diverse members of a large and complex society?

In order to further illustrate Freud's theorization of the ego as needing to strive to balance among the competing demands of reality, the id, and the superego, let's imagine a commonplace situation in which an ego might well experience these competing demands. Let's consider a hypothetical individual who I will name Gray (whose pronouns are they, their, and them). What different, and opposing, demands might reality, id, and superego make on Gray's ego in this situation? Let's start with Gray's id. This id might push Gray to seek pleasure at all times, and in all places, including through socially forbidden means, at others' expense, and in terms not only of sexual pleasure but also many possible sources of consumption that Gray might find pleasurable and which Gray's id might push them to pursue by means of theft, hoarding, or skipping out of and refusing to show up at work or for other social commitments and responsibilities. This id might suggest to Gray that they deserve to go kite surfing or wakeboarding rather than show up for a scheduled work shift at Gray's paid job, or to stay home and play video games and watch TV while pretending to be sick and therefore not able to come into work, or by indulging in eating and drinking too much and including by paying more than Gray can afford to do so, or by paying for someone else to write their paper, or by cheating on an exam for class. At the same time, Gray's external reality suggests to them they can only do any of this so long and so far, without being found out and without creating complications for themselves: running out of money, being fired from a job, arrested for committing a crime, or suspended or expelled from school. Gray's superego insists to Gray, even further, that not only are these kinds of actions and behaviors risky to Gray but they are also morally wrong, deserving of severe punishment, and that in even feeling a vague attraction to do any of these things Gray should feel guilty about their own immoral inclinations and tendencies. Gray's super-ego directs Gray to punish themselves by means of and in response to this guilt. Not only, moreover, should Gray feel badly about themselves, and horrified by the inclinations and tendencies for which they 'deserve' to feel guilty, but also Gray should feel compelled to 'make up for' maintaining these inclinations and tendencies by pushing themselves to work all the harder and all the more conscientiously on the job, in school, and in response to what others elsewhere request and demand of them, while readily accepting the 'need' to make even many more self-sacrifices so as to re-establish, and to manifest and display, their good moral character.

Let's next consider another hypothetical example, in the case of an individual who I will name Wilson (who again uses they, their, and them as pronouns), of how this individual struggles with their instinctual tendency toward aggression and especially with social and cultural constraints and limitations upon how this can be acceptably expressed. Let's imagine, more specifically, what might be a concrete example of how this aggressive instinct has been internalized in the forms of Wilson's super-ego, and shows up in Wilson experiencing significant anxiety and guilt, especially concerning Wilson's actual and potential involvement in relations with other people, and with wider social communities. Wilson recognizes they maintain a strong tendency to become aggressively bossy, and to rush to take charge and to give orders to others, in group situations, while often also becoming quickly impatient, and even quickly angered, when others in these same groups aren't ready or willing to follow their lead. Wilson feels a strong drive to assert themselves in these ways, and even to overpower others' objections to what Wilson proposes and advocates, but at the same time Wilson recognizes, and accepts, that these aggressive inclinations and tendencies are problematic, and suggestive, once again, of a failing in their moral character, so Wilson feels guilty and even ashamed at how readily they keep falling back into this pattern of behavior. As a result they become increasingly anxious in social situations, and in anticipating social situations, while at the same times increasingly frustrated by and indeed hostile versus themself, to the point they start to pursue reckless behaviors: self-harm through cutting, not eating, drinking excessive amounts of alcoholic beverages, and using addictive and mind-altering drugs that are also illegal but which Wilson manages to pay for by committing crimes of burglary and theft. Wilson feels further guilty about turning in these directions and becomes all the more embittered versus and hating of themself, and what they have become, to the point where they experience a compulsion to lash out violently at others, putting others' lives at risk, and, if they cannot bring themselves to do that, then turn this violence against themselves, putting their own life at risk.

Let's also consider a few additional examples from my own experience, with which many others can likely relate, of the struggles between life and death drives. On numerous occasions I have felt tremendously excited in anticipating delivering a major upcoming public presentation, while simultaneously feeling as if this is the last thing I want to do, I want instead to get far away all by myself, and I want to get it all over with as soon as possible so I can quickly retreat. I have also felt eager and excited in anticipating hosting or participating as a guest at many parties and social get-togethers while at the same time feeling as if I would rather not, hope just to get through it, and can't wait to get it over with and retreat into a 'safe place'. At other times I have felt both on the one hand happy to move about in public and to encounter many people I know, and who know me, spending short periods catching up and chatting with each of these various people, and on the other hand wishing I could be anonymous, and that I could disappear into the crowd or away from the crowd. In attending professional conferences I have both been both thrilled at the prospect of sharing my own work, and of attending and participating in sessions with colleagues from a great many diverse institutions, many of whom I would be meeting, at least in person, for the first time, while at the same time feeling like the intensity of social interactions at and as part of the conference are so overwhelming I prefer to spend significant blocs of time, during the conference run, away from the conference site, visiting, touring, walking about, and acquainting or reacquainting myself with the city at which the conference is taking place, where I hope not to encounter anyone from the same conference.

Five

The key issues Marx addresses in *Economic and Philosophic Manuscripts of 1844* that provide the basis for the ensuing encounter with Ian Curtis and Joy Division are as follows: 1. the nature, and source, of alienation/estrangement, and its principal avenues; 2. the human essence as comprised of the ensemble of social relations, as well as of the capacity for and engagement in free, voluntary association and constructive activity both for and as part of a larger social totality, and 3. the proliferating impacts of capitalism on human character and experience, including in forms such as commoditization, hyper-competitiveness, hyper-individualism, and a one-sided or one-dimensional relationship with not only culture and society but also with the human being as a natural being and with the rest of the natural world.

The key issues Durkheim addresses in *Suicide: a Study of Sociology* that provide the basis for the ensuing encounter with Ian Curtis and Joy Division are as follows: 1. types of suicide and social causes of suicide; 2. problems and difficulties in social integration and regulation; and 3. relations between society and the individual, and the social group and the individual, as well as what constitute the social needs and interests of the individual.

The key issues Freud addresses in *Civilization & Its Discontents* that provide the basis for the ensuing encounter with Ian Curtis and Joy Division are as follows: 1. what explains unhappiness, especially when this might seem illogical given social and cultural as well as scientific and technological progress; 2. the demands of culture in civilized society and the hardships these cause the individual, chiefly in forms of anxiety and guilt; and 3. aggression and destructiveness as instinctive and primal.

What principally connects these three critical theorists, in these three books, is common consideration of the nature of relations between individual and society and of problems and difficulties in these relations as part of modern society; of what constitute preeminent human needs and to what extent and for what reasons does modern society *not* adequately provide for the satisfaction of these needs; and of what accounts for human pain and suffering in modern society.

Six

"Shadowplay," the seventh song on *Unknown Pleasures*, I experience as a brilliant creation that continues to convey the same combination of thrill and chill every time I play the song, even after thousands of listens. Even when listening solely by myself, at home, I feel compelled to stand up and applaud. This is one of my favorite Joy Division songs to share with others, especially students, for them to hear for their first time. I have played and discussed "Shadowplay" not only in classes I have taught focused on Ian Curtis, Joy Division, and critical theory, as well as on other topics in popular music studies, but also in classes to illustrate expressionism and the uncanny–and "Shadowplay" often becomes a favorite for students among the songs I share in the classes I teach.

The title "Shadowplay" references a form of puppet theater involving puppeteers performing between a light source and a screen where the audience focuses on the projected shadow images of the puppets rather than the puppets themselves. "Shadow plays" date back many centuries and have proven popular and influential in Southeast Asia, the Middle East, Europe, and the Americas. The title of this Joy Division song also suggests, in close association with shadow puppetry, theatrical performances involving pronounced emphasis on play of light and shadow, cast by human actors. "Shadowplay" in addition might make sense as alluding to Plato's allegory of the cave, where Plato proposes human beings normally engage with shadowy reflections of what is, in essence, real and true, not reality and truth in itself, and, what's more, most humans prefer illusion and deception to reality and truth. But "Shadowplay," more broadly, to me at least, suggests play or playing in and among 'the shadows', with all the connotations 'shadowy' tends to convey of the uncertain and insubstantial as well as of the clandestine and illicit. Along these lines "Shadowplay" can readily suggest, moreover, underground, avant-garde, counter-cultural, critical-oppositional, and other modes of resistant and subversive practice. With the title of this song being "Shadowplay," not "Shadow Play," I also tend to interpret the title as much a verb as a noun, inviting us, as listeners, to question what kind of 'shadow playing' might be suggested here involving what kind of 'shadow players'. As with most of Ian Curtis's lyrics, these are and remain multiply ambiguous, allowing for a wide array of diverse associations.

"To the centre of the city where all roads meet, waiting for you" suggests a direction and destination of movement while complicating this suggestion by referencing 'waiting', in contrast with an earlier version of the lyrics that referred in this first line to 'looking' instead of 'waiting'. This final version of the opening line implies already having traveled and already having arrived, with the narrator-protagonist waiting, perhaps at this centre of the city, for someone else to make the same journey 'he' already has. Significant as well are the details included of this destination, representing both 'the centre' and of 'the city'–notably not just *a* city–as well as comprising a location where 'all roads meet'. This city centre seems a location that brings together–perhaps unites–multiple avenues, with these avenues interpretable in figurative as well as literal terms. Contemporaries of Ian Curtis connected this line and the rest of the lyrics of this song with experiences of what it was like to travel to, arrive at, and participate in late night music gigs in mid to late 1970s Manchester. Figuratively, however, this 'centre of the city' could easily represent many possible memorable locations for many possible memorable encounters. Yet we also need to take into account the introduction of 'you' in this first line, which invites us to speculate on to whom this 'you' refers, including to what extent and in what way 'you' might refer to us–i.e., the song addressing *us*, with the narrator-protagonist waiting *for us*.

"To the depths of the ocean where all hopes sank, searching for you," further complicates what the opening line has introduced by taking us to a seemingly radically different location, and destination–'the depths of the ocean'–albeit one the lyrics directly parallel with 'the centre of the city', just as they do 'where all hopes sank' with 'where all roads meet'. With this second line we appear to be moving into even more fraught territory, as 'where *all* hopes sank' suggests an apotheosis of despair. But what is also worth noting in this second line is the lyrics now shift from 'waiting' to 'searching', from a seemingly more passive to a seemingly more active stance, while we remain none the clearer precisely who or what this 'you' might represent, whether 'us' or some other 'you', let alone why the narrator-protagonist of the lyrics waits for 'you' in the centre of the city or searches for 'you' in the depths of the ocean.

"I was moving through the silence, without motion, waiting for you," line three, brings back waiting, but introduces one of the most challenging paradoxes in the entire song–'moving' 'without motion', and 'through the silence' (again notably *the* silence–a precise, specific silence–and not just 'silence' or 'a silence'). What kind of movement happens without motion? What kind of movement without motion happens by 'traveling' through 'the silence'? Perhaps this best makes sense as an introspective journey, or at least as an imagined journey, as opposed to a physically material one.

"In a room with a window in the corner I found truth," line four, is as puzzling as the previous lines, because this room is only distinguished by maintaining a window in a corner, and we are left to speculate on precisely what kind of room within what larger building this might be, and why in 'a window' by 'the corner' of this room 'I' was able to find 'truth'–what is it about this place that makes this finding, this discovery, perhaps this revelation possible, and who, more precisely, might 'I' be as well as what, more precisely, might be the relationship between 'I' and 'you', past, present, and future?

"In the shadowplay, acting out your own death, knowing no more," suggests an intimate yet frightening performance–a kind of ritualized invocation of murder, or suicide, but also perhaps a metaphoric 'death-in-life', such as an instance of extreme performance art that edgily engages, incorporates, and even embraces serious harm, and especially serious self-harm. "Knowing no more" is curious, but perhaps suggests we are provided no gloss to help interpret this performance–the shadowplay. Perhaps the meaning is *in* the performance, in the moment of the performance, in what it feels like at that precise moment.

"As the assassins all grouped in four lines, dancing on the floor/And with cold steel, odour on their bodies made a move to connect," seems to continue to reference the aforementioned shadowplay, while filling in details of what this piece of theater involves, offering a striking image of 'assassins' 'dancing' in a tightly choreographed fashion–'grouped in four lines'–along with further sensory appeal, via reference to 'cold steel' and 'odour', perhaps a 'cold steel odour', that seems simultaneously mysterious and menacing. 'Made a move to connect' could reference making a move to culminate the act of simulated assassination but also suggests the possibility these actors are striving 'to connect' by breaking past social barriers that normally separate people from each other, and that keep people alienated and atomized.

"But I could only stare in disbelief as the crowds all left," does not make it any easier for interpretation, as why 'I' is 'staring in disbelief'–at, or in response, to what–remains nebulous, as well as does the qualifier 'only' and the introductory 'but', although the 'but' and the 'only' do suggest 'I' responds differently to what has just transpired than the 'crowds' that have now 'all left'.

"I did everything, everything I wanted to/I let them use you, for their own ends," is further challenging because 'everything, everything' feels loaded yet open-ended, while what the 'I' wanted' and why so, in relation to what has been done to 'you' is likewise at best elliptically suggestive, only hinting at responsibility for or complicity with some kind of exploitation or other form of abuse. And this is further complicated by 'I' allowing 'you' to be subject to such exploitation or other abuse, perhaps even 'desiring' this, while also feeling guilty about allowing, and perhaps desiring, it to happen.

"To the centre of the city in the night, waiting for you/To the centre of the city in the night, waiting for you," as the closing two lines, brings us full circle, perhaps suggesting this is an endlessly recurrent process, and at the least that we are right back where we were at the beginning of the song, with desire–and perhaps need–as strong as ever, regardless of what might have just transpired. One pivotal detail changes from the beginning of the lyrics, however, and that is the addition of 'in the night'. This addition suggests more precisely when this scenario is occurring, and perhaps also that time has passed since the song began with the light dimming since then. This added detail accentuates the visceral intensity of the confrontation with an object of simultaneous attraction and repulsion, fascination and fear, prospectively over and over again, with no possible return to a prior more 'innocent' state, and no possible escape from an endlessly recurrent nightmare.

In discussing "Shadowplay" with students in classes focused on Ian Curtis, Joy Division, and critical theory, I have used this song as an opportunity to test out what we can do with David Machin's semiotic method of lyrical analysis, from Machin's explanation of this approach in his book *Analysing Popular Music: Image, Sound, Text*–Chapter 4, "Analysing Lyrics: Values, Participants, Agency." I will now do the same here.

Machin introduces concepts for analyzing popular music lyrics by beginning with "the activity or discourse schema that underlines the song." Here we focus on deep narrative structures involving common kinds of character roles and narrative functions. For example, as Machin suggests, we might have "Boy loves girl"–>"Love is unrequited"–>"Girl uses boy" (84). In this example we have two character roles and three narrative functions. Character roles and narrative functions can of course be much more elaborate and complex than in this simple example. In the lyrics to "Shadowplay" we find characters traveling, waiting, searching, finding, using/abusing, allowing use and abuse, and returning to repeat the process.

After identifying the underlying activity or discourse scheme, Machin proposes analyzing participants in lyrics more closely and carefully, focusing on who is represented and what they do. He suggests we can analyze participants in lyrics along the following lines (88):

1. Personalized/impersonalized. How personalized are these participants?

2. Individualized/collectivized. How individualized are these participants?

3. Nominalized. Are these participants named?

4. Funtionalization. What roles or functions do they play, or are they identified with?

5. Anonymous. Are participants implied/suggested/inferred but not directly represented?

6. Aggregated. How are participants identified as members, or parts of, a larger group?

7. Objectivated. How are they represented by attributes of their appearance or behavior?

Let's analyze the participants in the lyrics from Joy Division's "Shadowplay" according to these criteria. The participants are personalized-I, you, they–but this remains nonetheless abstract personalization. In terms of individualization versus collectivization the participants are distanced yet intimate, with sketchy, elliptical, and ambiguous details provided concerning (the basis of or reason for) their connection. They are not nominalized, in the sense that they are not named, except as assassins and crowds. In terms of functionalization, the assassins are identified in terms of their function, while 'I' seemingly is identified as a subject and 'you' seemingly is identified as an object, but exactly what is happening in terms of this subject-object relationship remains, again, sketchy, elliptical, and ambiguous. 'I' is potentially the subject of its own objectification–potentially, complicit in or responsible for what is happening to 'you'–as 'you' and 'I' might represent two dimensions of a single self. The participants in these lyrics are anonymous, as beyond reference to the assassins and the crowd, we only obtain a hazy intimation of the existence of others within a yet greater population of 'the city', and of its 'centre'–i.e., of a prospectively yet greater anonymous 'they'. Participants are aggregated as them, as assassins, and as crowds, and they are objectivated in terms of reference to body odour, acting, dancing, waiting, using and being used.

After the preceding stage of lyrical analysis, concerned with who are the participants and what are they doing, Machin proposes next analyzing what the participants are doing yet further, by considering which of the following process types they are involved in (and how):

1.   Material (Doing Something to the World)

2.   Behavioral (Acting Without Outcome)

3.   Mental (Thinking, Evaluating, Sensing)

4.   Verbal (Saying)

5.   Relational (Being Like or Different to Something Else)

6.   Existential (Existing, Appearing)
(89)

Let's analyze the participants in the lyrics to "Shadowplay" along these lines. In each of these process types we will follow Machin by considering relations among "actor," "goal," "process," and "circumstance." Let's also consider tone, and note well these process types can be overlapping. Material processes include relations between 'I' and 'you', seeking and finding, in the centre of the city, and at the shadowplay, as well as a dance of death involving ritual killing cum suicide in front of a crowd. The principal behavioral process involves waiting: 'I' for 'you' in a place where a connection, however fleeting, might happen and might happen again. Mental processes involve implicitly hoping, wanting, knowing, imagining, and then explicitly knowing no more in relation to 'I' of 'you', and of the interconnection between 'I' and 'you', especially as the two come together at a climactic destructive cum transcendent moment. Verbal processes consist of saying nothing, but thinking, waiting, seeking, and allowing to happen, with a further striking emphasis on silence, suggestive of a silence that communicates what speech cannot. Relational processes encompass how 'I' and 'you' appear intricately interconnected, and also 'I' and 'you' with 'them', as if we all have our precise roles to play in a theatrical piece, roles that are predetermined, and as if we mean–as if we make sense–only in relation to how we perform our roles in relation to each other as part of this same shadow play. Existential processes include waiting, being at, feeling the night, feeling the tension, feeling at once both the ominous and the enticing, you and I together, I for you, and you for me. In sum, we end up with something like the following:

Actor–> I   Goal–> You   Process–> Seeking, Finding, Doing To
Circumstance –> In center of city, in a shadowplay, at a ritual killing/suicide

In his fourth stage of lyrical analysis Machin recommends examining settings and circumstances, noting specific details and considering what kinds of associations these details are most likely to elicit. Let's identify all of the settings and circumstances we can find in the lyrics of "Shadowplay." Here they are: centre of city; all roads meet; depths of ocean; all hopes sank; moving

356

through silence without motion; in shadowplay acting out own death; assassins grouped in four lines dancing on the floor; cold steel; odour on bodies; move to connect; crowds leave; did everything, let everything be done, let use for own ends; center of city in night. In initially discussing these lyrics I have already identified a number of possible associations with these settings and circumstances so here I will just emphasize the potential value of breaking these down into this kind of list and paying attention to patterns that emerge in terms of what kinds of connotations rise to the forefront of attention in reflecting on such a series.

Finally, in the last section of his fourth chapter, Machin considers lyrics where no–apparent–activity schema exists, which seem highly abstract. Here Machin introduces an idea from Tzvetan Todorov that these kinds of lyrics may well represent an "ideological narrative" as opposed to an "action narrative," and that they therefore might be communicating about, or commenting on, abstract rules, general ideas–or, perhaps, broadly philosophical, political, sociological, psychological, spiritual, and/or metaphysical issues. Ian Curtis's lyrics with Joy Division fit exceedingly well with this idea–i.e., that they are dealing not so much with a concrete set of physical actions, or a particular chronicle of a precise sequence of events in the physical world, as they are exploring more abstract ideas, emotions, issues, and concerns. Let's analyze the lyrics to Joy Division's "Shadowplay" in these terms. To begin, it readily appears we are working with an abstract focus here: relations between 'I' and 'you', identified no more specifically than that, and with an equally nebulous concern with acting upon and letting being acted upon, while subject and object seem, plausibly, overlapping and interconnected. As a result, it seems plausible as well to interpret these lyrics as reflecting on matters of betrayal, guilt, futility of resistance and/or failure of honor, romance with death, as well as waiting, seeking, and finding along with waiting and seeking yet again. This scenario seems yet further plausibly suggestive of living through a nightmare of eternal recurrence. These lyrics seem, in addition, plausibly suggestive of a subject reflecting on the difficulty of connecting, breaking past barriers, and reaching true intimacy, as well as on what might need to be destroyed, and with what painful consequences, in order for this to happen. What's more, it also seems plausible to interpret this scenario as suggestive of a subject reflecting that in order to feel life at its most intensely meaningful one must live at the precipice of its imminent annihilation.

Connecting "Shadowplay," so far represented solely by its title and lyrics, to Marx, Durkheim, and Freud, it does seem the song engages problems and difficulties in relations between individual and society, or between the individual and the social group, as well as divisions within the individual and how these multiple dimensions of whom the individual in total is are far from neatly or smoothly reconciled with each other, even while the individual desires and strives to realize such a state of reconciliation. It does seem the song references the existence of barriers that complicate and frustrate the achievement of intimate connection, a connection of the kind that can provide a sustaining sense of purpose and belonging–while insinuating that attempting to evade these barriers, however enticing, involves venturing into not only unfamiliar but also dangerous territory. It does seem, according to the lyrics of this song, likewise, that destruction, and especially self-destruction, exercise powerful appeal. And it does seem, further, as if the need to imaginatively create and to collectively share in so doing, boldly, is vital in order for those who identify with the spirit of the lyrics to feel genuinely alive.

"Shadowplay" suggests what it can feel like to live within an alienated social world, a passionate striving to break through this alienation, and a confrontation with how elusive and even illusory the prospect of succeeding in doing so is likely to prove. At the least, any concerted effort at breaking through requires the subject identify with the position of an outsider, accepting this means letting go of what shields insiders from confronting an omnipresent risk of (self)destruction lurking everywhere about. The lyrics reference a relationship suggestive of commoditization, where other people are engaged as means to ends and not as ends in and of themselves; responsibility for or at least complicity with exploitation, of people using others to extract from others what they can gain for themselves; and even internalized identification with the logic of an overarchingly dehumanizing social system. "Shadowplay" does, nonetheless, suggest that along the edges, and in the shadows, of the socially dominant social order, it is possible to experience intimations of an alternative, of some kind of transcendence of the oppressive constraints imposed by the dominant; in "Shadowplay" the prospect of venturing into this realm comes across as irresistibly, albeit treacherously, alluring.

"Shadowplay" offers none of the confidence Marx does in *Economic and Philosophic Manuscripts of 1844* that a way out and beyond a thoroughly and multiply alienated existence is conceivably, let alone practically, possible. At the same time "Shadowplay" attests to the desire and need of those who, again, identify with the spirit of the lyrics, to nevertheless pursue such a prospect. Or to pursue whatever might approximate or anticipate it. Even while expecting to fall short and remain entrapped in an endless loop of seeking, waiting, briefly glimpsing, what has been briefly glimpsed quickly fading away, and then beginning this quest all over once again. The extent of disconnection the lyrics portray among its anonymous participants resonates with Marx's emphasis in *Economic and Philosophic Manuscripts of 1844* on the impact of estranged labor extending beyond the workplace to alienate human beings from the human essence, from the human species-being, from the ensemble of social relations. And here it is worth introducing another possibility in interpreting these lyrics and that is the 'you' represents a human potential not yet realized, with which the 'I', the human still in the process of becoming human, might eventually successfully unite, but which the 'I' at present is complicit in forestalling, preventing, and even prematurely destroying–i.e., acting as an interpellated agent of relations of alienation and exploitation–while nevertheless yearning for exactly this kind of supersession. This is yearning for supersession of social relations overdetermined by the pervasive logic of alienation and exploitation at the basis of the capitalist economy as this logic works its way throughout the entire nexus of social relations in capitalist society.

In relation to Durkheim, in "Shadowplay" we witness what might amount to a fantasizing of suicide, and in this case it seems as if such a suicide is most suggestive of either an anomic or a fatalistic type of suicide. In relation to anomic suicide, it appears, in the social imaginary sketched out by the lyrics of "Shadowplay," that any moral force exercised from a larger society, by means of any larger social institution, is non-existent in the location at the heart of the song (in the centre of the city at night, at the scene of the shadowplay), with travel to this location in turn representing rejection of the authority and appeal of that kind of moral force. In this 'shadowplaying' counter-social world no alternative social center, let alone no alternative moral force, appears yet substantially operative, as the only developed relations involve attending to and participating within an intricately mediated performance of killing or self-killing. In relation to 'fatalistic suicide' it can make sense to interpret this shadowplaying counter-social world as a dystopian location where individuals and groups alike fall in line in response to an overpowering social imperative that doesn't require specification and elaboration but rather merely submission, obedience, humiliation, and self-annihilation. Either way, it is certainly plausible to suggest "Shadowplay," as represented by title and lyrics, represents a desire to achieve some form of satisfying social integration, along with pursuit of such a possibility, at the same time as doubt this is possible remains pervasive. Given the need to seek this possibility at the edges, limits, and extremes of existing society, it seems this same existing society, in its currently dominant forms, including in its currently dominant institutions, is not exercising that integrative kind of authority and appeal, and is, what's more, incapable of exercising either for the kinds of people represented by, alluded to, and addressed through this song. It seems, according to the lyrics of "Shadowplay," that the human need for a social group, for social connection, and for social belonging is as fundamental as Durkheim theorizes this to be, in *Suicide: a Study in Sociology*, but the song also attests to wanting and needing what is not readily and immediately available in ordinary, normal, everyday life–and, again, doubt this might be anywhere possible, other than in such oblique and fleeting forms that they seem fantastically unreal.

In connection with Freud, the lyrics to "Shadowplay" seem to attest to the influence of something close akin to Freud's 'death drive'; to how human beings are and can be multiply and antagonistically divided within and against themselves; to how tendencies toward aggression and self-destruction are intrinsically interconnected with what is learned in relations with others and the external world, in particular the culture of modern society; and to the internalization of conscience, and guilt, in the form of the super-ego. We here encounter, akin to what Freud theorizes with life and death drives, a yearning and a reaching to connect along with an attraction to and fascination with destruction–and even an attraction toward experiencing connection by way of and through destruction. It makes sense to interpret "Shadowplay" as attesting to an experience of unhappiness living in a social world where desire is endless, yet endlessly unsatisfied, and where we both want and need to reach out to connect with other people as well as to withdraw from and disconnect with other people, and where it is only at the edges, the limits, the extremes, and in direct confrontation with what is taboo that it becomes closest possible to experience the kinds of shadowy pleasures we crave but which society, and which conscience, all too often restrict, condemn, and forbid.

In terms of song structure, "Shadowplay" opens with an initial bass guitar melody, and a rapidly growing intensity even in the first few measures as we so far just hear the bass guitar and the drums. One of the most memorable features of the song involves the smashing first entrance of the guitar, followed shortly thereafter by the vocal entering and assuming the principal melodic role in the song's first vocal passage. Next follows an instrumental passage, with the guitar continuing loud and prominent and with drum rolls and cymbal crashes sounding at pivotal points as the bass guitar carries on with the initial melody. After this, with the return of the vocal, in the second vocal passage, the guitar's role sounds as if it works to compliment and extend what has already been established, while the vocal seems slightly louder and closer to the front of the mix and again we hear decisive cymbal crashes and tom rolls periodically. Following this, we proceed to a brief instrumental passage featuring a flaring guitar sound that veers to the edge of becoming dissonant. And then we move to the third and final vocal passage, accompanied by now familiar patterns from bass guitar, guitar, and drums. Here, the vocal, in common Ian Curtis fashion, rises notably in pitch at the end. In the concluding instrumental passage, the guitar once more plays an especially prominent role, sounding the same pattern introduced in the second vocal passage with this now becoming further elaborated, rising in intensity and pitch, while resounding around a more limited sequence of chords toward the end. This contribution approaches the sound of a guitar solo but even so the guitar is largely elaborating upon the previously established melody.

What the structure of "Shadowplay" suggests, as I listen to and reflect upon it, is a dramatic yet mysterious encounter that becomes increasingly forceful and intense yet at the end of which the mystery surrounding what this encounter has involved, and what this has meant, remains tantalizingly opaque. The structure of the song conveys the allure of entering into, engaging with, and experiencing the mystery, head on, as a source of prospective insight, in the form of revelation. What this encompasses remains coded, and shrouded, but its opacity also remains indispensable to its allure. The song does not feel as if it is either referencing or enacting an unmitigatedly negative experience, in large part because the constituent sound sources suggest a social collective engaged in a common venture, with relations among each of the individual performers coming across as tightly coordinated, as if they are each playing closely and attentively off of and in response to each other.

Considering the instrumentation more directly, Peter Hook's bass guitar is responsible for the initial melody, and also for establishing the song's initial rhythm together with Stephen Morris's drums and cymbals, with the hi-hat a notable presence in the opening instrumental passage and then becoming less prominent thereafter. Bernard Sumner's guitar picks up the first melody but also introduces a second melody, close to that of the initial melody first sounded by Hook's bass guitar, adding slight variations and elaborations, as well as slight extensions and developments. After the opening instrumental passage, the most prominent sounds among Morris's drums and cymbals involve the regular single, quarter note, bass drum strikes on beats 1 and 3 as well as snare drum strikes on beats 2 and 4; double, eighth note, hi-hat strikes on beats 1, 2, 3 and 4 are quieter and less prominent, but periodic tom rolls and cymbal crashes punctuating hypermeasures always make their presence felt. Ian Curtis's vocal carries the principal melody in the vocal passages but not as far backgrounding other sound sources' contributions to the overall melodic line as happens in a number of other Joy Division songs. With these instruments sounding collectively and in response to each other, the song is recurrently chilling and thrilling at once. If anything, the instruments working together conveys a feeling of unity, of cohesion, if only for a short expanse of time, as if the music as persona has indeed found a significant truth, a truth discoverable only in the process of actively pursuing and deliberately conjuring it through such a concerted, collective effort. What is especially striking here is how much the instrumentation of this song suggests the transcendent power of what a group can achieve collectively versus that of an isolated individual, and of how solidarity within and as part of a group engaged in a common endeavor adds immeasurably to the confidence, determination, and courage needed to push far and hard. This in turn suggests the value of 'positive freedom'–freedom with, freedom obtained by working with others and with what working with others in turn makes possible–in contrast with that of 'negative freedom'–freedom from, freedom obtained by separating and getting away from others.

With the instruments in "Shadowplay" taking on multiple interlocking roles in terms of the song's functional layers, picking up from and playing off of each other neatly and efficiently, I do feel, in listening to "Shadowplay," as if I am transported to the centre of the city at a moment of peak intensity, where I am ready, alert, and anxious, yet excited, even if I am also, somewhat nervously and impatiently, positioned as one who is waiting and observing. The construction of the song as an organized complex of textured sounds does not convey any feeling of alienated disconnection or antipathy among the principal sound sources in their contributions to the song as a whole.

Taking into account the soundbox, we hear the bass guitar enter from low to our left while the drums and cymbals enter higher to our center right. The bass guitar then climbs somewhat higher as its gets louder. The guitar is positioned both high left and right while slightly off center in each case. The vocal is positioned to the center, slightly back, and slightly higher than dead center. The vocal does seem to move slightly forward and become most prominent as the song proceeds, while the drums are fairly prominent throughout and as song proceeds seem to position themselves slightly off center to our lower left and right, and as the guitar moves further to the edges during solo parts without ever losing its prominence. What I suggest all of this contributes is an insinuation of the enactment of an intense dramatic moment in which the multiple constituent instruments all play indispensable and overlapping roles. This moment makes sense as one involving the reception of an elliptically oracular revelation, or as a fantastical projection akin to a dream wish-fulfillment involving simultaneously uniting with and destroying, where the dreamer observes themselves, or their stand-in, from a distance, as this stand-in seeks to become other/to become another, to find a fulfilling place and identity in a shadow counter-social world, experiencing this possibility tantalizingly within reach yet ultimately slipping from their grasp.

Taking the structure and instrumentation into account, it thereby seems "Shadowplay" becomes less about lament and despair over alienation but rather more about confronting and engaging alienation, and seeking to push through, past, and beyond it, all the way toward capturing at least a glimmer, if not an even a more brilliant glimpse, of what arrival at such a post-alienated destiny might be like. The song enacts the desire to find a meaningful basis for social connection and a striving to do so; this is a mode of connection that can overcome estrangement. The song does so even as it intimates a subject just beginning this process, just beginning to explore the treacherous terrain such a path must traverse, while not wanting to do all this work for us, not only because the music as persona is hardly in control of what this process means for 'himself' but also because doing so would make it impossible for us to begin to embark upon the same path–a path we must take up and pursue by and for ourselves. Taking into account the song's structure and instrumentation helps in appreciating how it makes sense to interpret "Shadowplay" as resonating with a strong sense of the necessity of inclusion and belonging, yet doing so from a vantage point on the social margins where the specifications of what might constitute the basis for the recreation of a compellingly socially cohesive moral force, in present times and present circumstances, appear barely embryonic. Again, taking into account the structure and instrumentation of "Shadowplay," it makes sense to interpret the song as representing a fusion of life and death drives, and even of seeking each by means of the other, seeking both on the one hand to connect and on the other hand to delay, forestall, or prevent connection. Nevertheless, "Shadowplay" sounds as if the song, as a complex of patterned interconnected sounds, conveys less the oppressiveness of social command, although suggestions of aggression and guilt remain clear, but rather the power of desire, including desire for what Freud likely would argue is ultimately impossible in terms of social integration.

"Shadowplay" starts soft, grow slightly yet steadily louder until the guitar enters, suddenly and blisteringly loud, while the guitar remains thereafter throughout the song by far the overall loudest instrument, with the vocal always notably louder than the bass guitar when the vocal is sounding and the drums and cymbals also most often at least slightly louder than the bass guitar. Only in transitions between sections, when the bass guitar riff becomes most prominent, does the overall loudness of the song notably drop yet again. In further instrumental passages, the guitar becomes all the louder as it reaches and extends further in pitch. Loudness increases in movement across vocal lines and stanzas as well. Overall, however, "Shadowplay" conveys a largely considerable constancy in terms of volume with several notably different passages, such as near the beginning, and preceding the initial entry of the guitar. What loudness contributes to the developing sense of possible meanings of this song, I propose, is once more suggesting we are thrown into the middle of an encounter, or other kind of event, that is briefly yet decidedly intense.

"Shadowplay" follows a 4/4 meter, employing a persistent 1and2and3and4and pattern of notes with the bass guitar and the vocal, and in the strumming of the guitar chords. Throughout the song, we hear principally eighth and sixteenth notes, other than with drums where quarter notes, from the bass drum and the snare drum, are also frequent. The song's tempo is 140 bpm, which makes it a song that is neither among the fastest nor the slowest of Joy Division songs. The guitar typically moves across four to six chords per hypermeasure, and most often approximately two per measure. Overall, the rhythm contributes a sense of a persistent, cohesive, coordinated propulsive movement–one that is confident, determined, precise, and steady, even if this might seem paradoxical in a song containing lyrics that reference moving in silence, and without motion.

What is most striking concerning matters of pitch in "Shadowplay" is its regularity, its consistency, and its often moving for relatively long periods along only slight intervals. Pitch in this song generally tends first to rise and then to fall back, with later passages suggesting pushing higher but still then falling back once again. Throughout we hear ample rumbling about close to or along the same pitch, with the intervals the bass guitar traverses smaller than those of the guitar yet each only sounding a limited array of pitches over the course of the song, albeit with various embellishments. In terms of vocal delivery Ian Curtis's voice sounds somewhat darkened, yet not excessively so, and he sounds as if he periodically strains slightly with upward movements in pitch, but these also emphasize a more emphatic sense of yearning meets striving. Curtis's vocal sounds as if it might be double-tracked, although it sounds as if less reverb and echo is added than in many other Joy Division songs. Curtis's register seems to come from somewhat lower in his body than in a number of other Joy Division songs, while even without substantial added contributions his voice maintains considerable resonance, and natural reverberation, as he also, characteristically, allows notes to slightly linger at the end of phrases and especially at the end of lines while resting at the end of each line before beginning the next.

What these observations concerning pitch and delivery add to my developing reflection on possible meanings that make sense for "Shadowplay" is a further leaning toward an interpretation of this song as enacting a confident engagement with what many others might normally altogether avoid, and even a welcome embracing of and relishing in the simulation of danger, risk, threat, uncertainty, and, indeed, the uncanny–the simultaneously familiarly unfamiliar and unfamiliarly familiar. "Shadowplay" is ready to take on the taboo, to try it out, to test it out, to identify with it, and to admit doing so, without sounding as if wracked by guilt, or shame, for so doing–and this in turn suggests a song emphasizing confrontation and struggle with what is all too often rendered culturally as well as individually unconscious, as a result of repression that acts within and upon social groups, communities, and societies as well as individuals. This song makes sense in turn as supportive of a need for greater socially viable outlets to exercise instinctually aggressive tendencies, as well as of the need to accommodate both death and life drives along with the ways the two drives influence and impact each other. The song also makes sense as registering a need to find, establish, maintain, and sustain avenues for non-alienated and non-anomic social connection that address and respond to the interests, needs, and concerns of people pushed to, or otherwise identifying with, the margins of the currently predominant social order.

Elements of studio polish come through here and there in "Shadowplay" but use of sound effects, synthesized noises, and keyboard parts do not emerge as a foregrounded major contributor here, unlike with later Joy Division songs. In terms of gestures and movements suggested by timbres, Morris's drums and cymbals suggest motoring, driving, undergirding and punctuating; Curtis's vocal periodically suggests reaching and stretching, while otherwise moving briskly with some rocking back and forth but nevertheless steadily forward as well as periodically briefly resting; and Hook's bass guitar sets the stage and maintains the focus and the emphasis along with the consistency and unity–the bass guitar part feels like an essential fulcrum to the song. Sumner's guitar at times suggests movements in terms of circles, spirals, and other comparable figures but also suggests forceful thrusting and soaring. Overall these timbres suggest a marked feeling of confident and cohesive movement toward, into, with, and at.

In "Shadowplay" hesitation feels less pronounced than in many other Joy Division songs, and it almost feels as if the song challenges the listener to decide if they are so shocked by what it depicts, suggests, and proposes that they cannot or will not follow–or, in contrast, if they too are ready to join a subversive and transgressive venture. With its constituent sound elements and their deployment taken into account, "Shadowplay" suggests a collective endeavor in which the individual transcends limitations of 'his' ordinary, isolated, individual self through participation in this collectivity, as it is this collectivity that enables the exploration the song describes. The sounds, patterns of sounds, and deployments of sounds echo the lyrics in suggesting a process of seeking, questing, striving, and yearning but also underscore this same process with a more confident and determined feeling than the lyrics, taken by themselves alone, tend to convey. The song feels self-aware of its embracing a meeting of what thrills and chills, or of what thrills because of how it chills and chills because of how it thrills. This kind of 'dark romanticism' does not easily coincide with critical theory devised in support of social revolution, as represented by Karl Marx, in *Economic and Philosophic Manuscripts of 1844*, or in support of social reform, as represented by Emile Durkheim, in *Suicide: a Study in*

Sociology. The song, and its persona, recognizes, broadly, some of the same social concerns Marx and Durkheim address in these two books, and imagines some ways of confronting, engaging, and struggling with them, but identifies primarily with the process of so doing, and with the uncertainty of to what, if anything, this might lead. With "Shadowplay" it seems at best highly uncertain if any kind of substantial difference or change is possible, or even if it is possible to make any significant progress, and it also seems possible attempts to push in this direction lead to destruction. Nevertheless, the song, and its persona, seem to advocate the attempt, as a means of striving to live as authentically as possible versus pressures and constraints that make an inauthentic existence otherwise unavoidable.

It can make sense, however, in contrast, to interpret "Shadowplay" as highlighting where, and how, a process–a long, difficult, and treacherous process–of working toward substantial social transformation begins, at the present time, in present circumstances, or at least in one location where and through one means by which this might begin. Following this line of interpretation, first it is necessary to turn away from the socially dominant and normative to find spaces where it becomes possible to begin to imagine and create anticipations of alternatives, as well as to find and make connections with others who experience themselves as likewise marginalized and alienated–and anomic–within the lifeworld carved out for, and imposed upon, them. What next follows is a process of actively working through symbolically to undo, ritualistically exorcizing by subversively performing–and in so doing shockingly displaying and revealing–the cruelty, the callousness, the indifference, the exploitation, the abuse, the violence, the destruction, and the killing that the socially dominant and normative routinely perpetrates, and routinely perpetuates, yet also routinely conceals, denies, and mystifies.

Considering "Shadowplay" in terms of avenues of musical affect, "Shadowplay" feels as it builds, rises, pushes, seeks, and strives while ultimately attesting most of all to this investment and accumulation of effort, to this process and not to any conclusive result other than to provide the basis for renewed investment of the same effort along the same paths. Together with the music as persona I feel as if we are desiring, pursuing where our desire takes us, experiencing combined chills and thrills in so doing, and reflecting on what we have been doing by the time we reach the end of the song.

"Shadowplay" offers an apt example of a song that conveys an aesthetically positive anticipation of desire and dread, or even more precisely desire fused with dread. Here the song anticipates going on, no matter how fraught the circumstances, and that we may arrive, may discover, and may meet with some tangible outcome, yet may well not, while also anticipating it might not matter whether this happens, because the process we are engaged upon remains what is most meaningful, in and of itself. "Shadowplay" suggests anticipation of a briefly flashing moment of illumination at a peak of heightened intensity, that will quickly pass yet leave an indelible impression in memory as well as trace kinesthetic effects that will stimulate yet further and renewed desire. In listening to "Shadowplay" I feel as if I am embarking upon a quest that might lead to some kind of connection following a movement to connect, including perhaps involving an integration of disparate dimensions of myself as well as of myself with others. And it feels as if this movement contests pervasive alienation and anomie, yet the song nevertheless leads me to anticipate at best partial and limited success, so what I will end with, above all else, will be the persistence of desire. I register an anticipation of grasping at contact with essential forms and not solely apparent contents, in striving to gain insight, through revelation, yet I also anticipate that engaging in this paradoxical movement, in and of itself, through silence and without motion, is what is, in this instance at least, most urgently at stake.

I hear "Shadowplay" expressing longing, yearning, needing, and desiring but also confidence, determination, commitment, persistence, and a readiness to plunge into the unknown and confront the unknowable, to take risks and seek out dangers, while also watching, observing, and reflecting on the powerful appeal and impact of engaging in such a pursuit. I feel myself, along with the music as persona, expressing excitement becoming exhilaration, awe that borders upon terror, contemplation of responsibility and guilt, and an energized confidence concerning our capacity for resilience, our ability to endure and persevere.

The initial entrance of Bernard Sumner's guitar feels as if it slams right into me, and then subsequently soars above and around me. Otherwise, in "Shadowplay" the acoustic impact enhances the concentrated nature of a brief yet acute moment of intense perception, feeling, and experience–as if this kind of forceful yet tightly cohesive acoustic impact is a necessary enabling condition for an introspective exploration to proceed as deep and far as this song portends, and to do so as rapidly as the song compels.

I perceive the music as persona analyzing relations between 'I' and 'you', and contexts in which to make sense of these relations, but it seems unclear what if any conclusions the music as persona reaches concerning this focus by the end of the song. It strikes me that 'I', 'you', and the social contexts alluded to here are involved in murkily diffuse relations with each other. With the title 'Shadowplay', and the reference to a specific 'shadowplay' in the lyrics, I analyze the song as engaging problematics of mediation, especially in seeking to come close to at least making contact with what is unknown and unknowable but simultaneously compels us to want and to seek to try to know it. Also, with this same title and lyrical reference, I analyze the song as concerned with problematics of performance, and of performativity, in relation to social positions, roles, identities, and relations in the form of the multiple guises, masks, facades, and theatrical stagings of our identity we all of necessity engage in all the time.

I associate what I hear from "Shadowplay" and what this prompts me to think (about) and feel with the thrill of night life, especially late night life, in particular dancing at night clubs, as well as attendance at festival events featuring artistic performances that are dazzlingly immersive and interactive. I associate the song with meeting strangers in situations where we are compelled to interact in physically intimate and passionately intense ways, as can happen in all-night or at least late-night dance clubs, parties, and raves. And I associate "Shadowplay" with longing for viscerally intense and vitally engaging experiences that sharply contrast with boredom and emptiness of mundane experience. I associate the song with questing, with seeking, and with desperately hoping, wanting, and needing to find–especially hoping, wanting, and needing to find another, someone with whom a powerful connection can be achieved–as well as with how draining this pursuit can so often feel even simultaneous with it feeling stimulating, exciting, and hopeful. I associate this song with manifestation of excruciating desire to be able viscerally to feel one's own complexity, multiplicity, contradictoriness, and dynamism, as well as one's interconnections and overlappings with others–to viscerally experience the collapsing of rigid boundaries between self and other as well as between different and all too often antagonistic dimensions of the self.

Taboos "Shadowplay" engage include imagining one's own death, one's own murder, one's own suicide–or watching the killing of another, as a spectator at a form of entertainment–and finding this appealing, even alluring, to envision and contemplate. Taboos engaged here also involve traveling past familiar definitions of whom one is, where one is coming from, and what one is about, to explore the possibility of becoming someone else involved in relations with others previously unknown. Taboos engaged further include admitting and acknowledging one's own deep-seated aggressive, violent, destructive, and self-destructive tendencies as well as one's undeniable complicity with and responsibility for destruction of others. Taboos engaged in addition include giving open expression to feelings of desperation in terms of longing, needing, and wanting. And taboos engaged involve imagining a whole other life might be far more meaningful and fulfilling than our most familiar life, or our most familiar lives, and what might happen if we were to abandon–even to jettison–the latter. Certainly as well another taboo engaged in "Shadowplay" involves actively pursuing and openly embracing the prospect of self-shattering.

"Shadowplay" feels as if the song continually alludes or gestures toward what cannot be fully or adequately rendered in empirical form. The moment itself, the moment of the song, is ephemeral, and those who meet up briefly, at the centre of the city, at the shadowplay, seem ephemeral as well, while movement seems invisible and intangible–again movement, through silence, without motion. Travel of some kind nonetheless seemingly happens or we attend to an account of it seemingly having happened, but precisely to where and involving what and whom remains ephemeral. "Shadowplay" suggests the presence of powerful forces acting all around us, including upon and within us, of which we are normally unconscious and unaware–and especially of these being sources of profound attraction and repulsion. "Shadowplay" likewise suggests we ourselves maintain invisible, intangible, and ephemeral resources, powers, and capacities.

Returning to lines of connection with the foregrounded concerns of Marx, Durkheim, and Freud, "Shadowplay" emphasizes a compulsion to connect and to interact, as well as to find truth and to seek understanding, suggesting these pursuits remain worthwhile, even if risky and dangerous, and even if they end up leading, most of all, to many more questions, and many further uncertainties. "Shadowplay" suggests it is worthwhile to confront and engage with what shadows our everyday normative and commonsensical modes of recognition and understanding in order, at the least, to begin to grasp what limits, binds, and constrains us–as well as how substantial the latter tend to be.

I experience "Shadowplay" calling me to venture to the centre of the city, at night, for an intense experience, where I can anticipate at least the prospect of discovering something powerfully affecting, perhaps powerfully disturbing concerning myself and my own vulnerability, that nevertheless may provide me with startling yet valuable insight. Together the music as persona and I share an experience of attraction not only to danger and risk, but also to violence directed against ourselves and others, even if this is vicariously represented, by means of a fictional mediation–such as in a shadow play or other kind of stage drama but also such by means such as a crime novel, movie, or TV show. As someone who loves crime fiction, and who not only reads crime fiction novels frequently but watches crime fiction movies, and crime fiction TV series on a daily basis, I share the song's fascination with fictionally dramatic renderings of the impacts of violence, in a suspenseful framework where matters of life and death are immediately and persistently foregrounded, and I maintain this fascination even as someone who is far from personally violent, who actively practices non-violence, and who principally identifies, in crime fiction, with the pursuit of knowledge, truth, and justice, as well as with how crime and its detection function as symbolic means by which to engage with socially shared fears, anxieties, traumas, hopes, and dreams along with philosophical questions of ultimate concern related to the meaning of existence and interconnections between being and nothingness.

"Shadowplay" offers me a wager that it might be possible to collaborate with the music as protagonist in imagining and creating something that engages, however elliptically, with what we both have up to this point in time found difficult to imagine, let alone create, because we have experienced this as not only too threatening and too disturbing but also as seemingly unknowable and unrepresentable. In order to accept this gamble we need to enter into a shadow counter-social world enfolded into the gaps and seams of our familiar visible, tangible, and perdurable social world. Because what we discover in this shadow realm amounts to elements suggestive of possibilities not yet fully (or at least not visibly, tangibly, and perdurably) realized–of alternatives to what is normatively, commonsensically, and dominantly recognized to exist and persist–these will appear to us only as fragmentary shards and evanescent traces. We can engage with these elements by attempting to further substantiate and elaborate them, at least in terms of how they might make sense for us in terms of our own individual situatedness, but we must remain keenly aware and respectful of the mysterious and the sublime we encounter within this shadow counter-social world no matter how we take up and respond to this encounter.

"Shadowplay" suggests to me a calling to strive to connect with others, and even with the dimensions of one's self one normally represses, denies, or otherwise disavows and attempts to ignore, displace, and project, in ways that push beyond conventional normative limits–to connect so closely, so intimately, that this feels, and is, dangerous because it threatens to undermine boundaries between self and other and between parts of the self that are much easier to keep discrete and distinct. Perhaps this is because collapse of distinction and division between 'I' and 'you' involves a kind of dying, or a kind of killing off, or an allowing to die or be killed off of what has long felt necessary to insure self-survival.

Yet another possible interpretation is "Shadowplay" references what tends to happen, and perhaps inevitably must happen, to a popular performer, split between whom 'he' conceives 'himself' to be prior to, outside of, and independent of 'his' performance, and the persona, or personae, he must adopt, and over which 'he' loses control, as the crowds of those who attend to 'his' performance take ownership of this persona, or these personae, and effectively force him, as this persona, or this personae, to do what they want, what they demand of 'him'. All the while this performative dimension of the individual remains a fundamental proportion of the totality of whom he is, because it has drawn significantly from the totality of whom he has been, is, can and might yet be, extracting a great deal of the total capacity he maintains for what he could be and do, and especially, referencing Marx, his capacity to labor, his capacity to act within and upon nature and culture to transform and create anew. Insofar as this portion of the individual performer's capacity becomes increasingly lost to and out of his control, he becomes increasingly alienated, increasingly estranged, from a substantial dimension of whom he has been, is, and can be, as well as from a substantial dimension of what he has done, is doing, and can do. In this context "I did everything, I did everything I wanted to/I let them use you for their own ends" makes sense as referencing an ambiguity involved in the pursuit of success, and even fame, as a performing artist, because this is both what 'I' wanted, with the achievement of success corresponding to the realization of ambition, but it also involves allowing a significant portion of one's self–i.e., 'you'–to 'be used' by others 'for their own ends'–and this could resemble a ritualistically simulated performance of one's own death the more and more the process spirals beyond control of the individual who initiated it, and who now has lost, who has now sacrificed, who has now given up, who has now surrendered that much of himself, including that much of what he otherwise might yet have become.

Interpreting "Shadowplay" as grappling with relations between 'I' and 'you', with these as subject positions that all of us continually move between, suggests a focus of interest and concern broadly aligned with what sociologist George Herbert Mead theorizes as the dimensions of the self Mead identifies as the 'I' and the 'me', as well as what multiple other modern to contemporary critical theorists have proposed to explain the self as multiple and divided. "Shadowplay" grapples with, on the one hand, wanting, needing, pursuing, and seeking and, on the other hand, *not* or *not yet* doing so, or not knowing precisely how or where to go in doing so, or not being sure what to make of what one finds in the course of so doing, and this certainly could involve attempting to make sense of relations among multiple and divided *selves* we share and do not share with others, as well as among yet further multiplications and divisions constitutive of whom 'we are'. "Shadowplay" suggests grappling with borderlines between knowledge and ignorance, knowing and not knowing, distance and connection, responsibility and complicity, using and being used, and activity and passivity. "Shadowplay" commonly feels to me as if I am invited to join in seeking sensation as well as insight, and especially insight by way of sensation. It also feels to me as if I am here invited to join in seeking the experience of seeking–as an introspective quest that never aims to arrive at a definite end. Nonetheless, such a pursuit resembles taking the time and investing the effort to attempt to get in touch with and understand one's self, how one has been socially constructed, including constructed as what, with what kind and extent of gaps, holes, aporias, fissures, cracks, and even chasms or abysses in this construction. This in turn seems less an effort at self-care than self-understanding.

Most of all "Shadowplay" seems to call on me to respond–and to engage. This means not sinking back into, or slinking back into, a comfortable detachment. I experience "Shadowplay" eliciting from me a commitment to strive to contribute, as I can, toward breaking with strictures and structures that keep people alienated from each other, from the essence of whom we are as comprised of the totality of our prospective relations with other humans, from our full human potential.

368

"Shadowplay" elicits from me a commitment to contribute, as I can, toward doing the same versus that which all too often holds most of us back, fearful of even trying what might fail, or worse backfire, and versus what keeps us caught up within ourselves in separation and isolation from others, from the social collective. "Shadowplay" elicits from me a commitment to contribute, as I can, toward generating a moral force that can justly, fairly, and equitably bind us together while respecting our differences as sources of strength. And "Shadowplay" summons me to strive to at least begin to confront and work through some of my own contradictions, some of the divisions and oppositions that form and constitute me, while striving to resist oppressive social constraints and internalized guilt concerning my right to enjoy pleasurable experiences, and especially not to need to do solely in line with what is socially normative.

Since the titular reference to a shadow play in itself suggests we are dealing with a form of mediation, it makes sense to interpret this song as inviting us to reflect on what mediation makes both possible and impossible. In particular, in "Shadowplay" we are invited to inquire into what mediates between us and mutually meaningful, fulfilling, enabling, and empowering connections with others; what mediates between what we are conscious of and what we are not concerning ourselves, whom we are and what we are about, and what forms and constitutes us; and what mediates between possible and actual forms of social community. Here, it is important to note well that to mediate involves both connection and separation: mediation enables connection but at the same time stands between, enacts a separation between, what it connects. If we think of mediating a dispute we think of a mediator coming between disputing parties to enable them to work out a settlement, one which enables these disputing parties to reconcile, or reunite, but which does so by way of the mediator standing between, and by means of this intervention restoring, preserving and improving the relationship between the erstwhile disputing parties by means of what the mediator helps fashion *in between*. What might it mean, though, to long for, and to press for, a connection beyond all mediation, and what kind and scale of destruction might this encompass? What might it mean to long for, and to press for, a meeting with another that becomes a merging with another to the point that the distinction between the two dissolves, or collapses, and how dangerous might this be, while how desirous might it nevertheless be, even aware of that danger?

It makes sense thereby to consider "Shadowplay" as inviting us to venture past common forms of protective mediation, yes, including past what prevents us from meeting, connecting, and experiencing real contact with others, including with the other that is (that exists within and is fundamentally constitutively contributive to) ourselves. "Shadowplay" invites contemplation of possibilities for transcending and superseding these and allied varieties of normative distinctions and separations yet the song nevertheless seems reluctant to serve as a conventional guide, let alone as a role model, even as it invites us to join in an ongoing quest and an ongoing struggle.

Perhaps it makes good sense to interpret "Shadowplay," in Lacanian terms, as recounting an experience of jouissance provoked by way of an encounter with intimations as well as irruptions of the Real. Certainly the notion of the self as singular and precisely delimited and confined appears to be confronted and challenged here. At the same time, "Shadowplay" makes sense as alluding to an attempt at evasion or escape versus a social situation in which social authority is overwhelmingly oppressive. Yet "Shadowplay" also make useful sense, as I hear and reflect upon the song, as registering the angst experienced by those who feel like freaks and outsiders, on the social margins, even feeling much like they are–like we are–sacrificial objects set up for ritual execution. Perhaps indeed one feels the most freakish when one feels intensely aware of and deeply disturbed by how estrangement in social relations appears to have become pervasively normalized yet most others seem blithely unaware or indifferent. When you cannot feel the other, when you cannot feel the other's actual and potential suffering and pain, when you cannot identify and empathize with the other, are we already well on our way into a fascist state of collective (un)consciousness? What kind and extent of defamiliarization might prove necessary to puncture this state of unawareness and indifference?

Seven

"Isolation," the second song on *Closer*, exemplifies an apparent contradiction multiple students in classes I have taught on Ian Curtis, Joy Division, and critical theory have registered: if we listen carefully to the music and not just concentrate on the lyrics alone it becomes difficult to equate the meaning of what we hear with merely the autobiographical expression cum confession of one young man's struggle with depression and suicidality. If we set aside the title, and the lyrics, would this song immediately suggest to us it concerns isolation, and it involves wrestling with what isolation can consist of as well as feel like? After all, in this song, keyboard synthesizers entirely replace the guitar while sounding unlike any traditional instrument dependent upon a directly correlative relationship between a human application of mechanical force and the resultant sound. This involves an overtly machinic set of timbres that closest resemble strings, especially violins, but more precisely a group of violins irregularly tuned as well as playing slightly out of tune with each other at the top of their pitch register: producing narrow, virtually shrill, verging on brittle, tones that shimmer yet bristle, propelled forward by a jaunty cadence that nonetheless at the same time feels awkwardly unsettled and unsettling.

The composite texture of sound in this song, as well as its driving pattern of movement, feels as if it represents the adverse of what I would either recommend to another or select myself as music for meditation, relaxation, stress relief, and to counter insomnia (which I have personally experienced as a serious health concern and for which I have been recommended musical therapy). In our bedroom my husband and I make use of a device that incorporates a series of channels that play patterns of sounds meant to help insure relaxed sleep–rainfall, ocean, waterfall, brook, white noise, fireplace, and so on, with the least relaxing of all these channels identified as 'meditation', but even that pattern consists of a prolonged series of drone sounds, all along a narrow frequency range, while also maintaining a carefully calibrated array of overtones. All of these sounds on this sleep enhancement device maintain a narrow and consistent frequency as well as a predictably calming regularity. "Isolation" does not convey a feeling of calm. At the same time, "Isolation" does not necessarily convey a feeling of distress and suffering, if one sets aside the title and the lyrics, and indeed the song has often been cited as an instance of a Joy Division dance song as well as anticipating the electronic dance music of New Order, and Peter Hook even suggests it could have easily been released as a single.

The patterns of sounds emanating from each principal sound source in this song, nonetheless, do feel isolated, even if proceeding in parallel with each other, as if they might not so much be pushing in different directions but rather embodying different moods as they proceed in the same direction. As a result, taking into account the song as much more than its lyrics alone, "Isolation" embodies a feeling of splintering or fragmenting of identification and association. This might make sense, given the prominence of synthesizer keyboards, synth-drums, and additional electronic studio treatments and effects in this song, all of which sound and feel coldly machinic, and as such inhuman, as representing a splintering and fragmenting of perspectives concerning the pace and direction of technological development, following the third industrial revolution involving the emergence and rapidly sweeping impact of digital electronics. "Isolation" might make sense as exploring how this revolution is in turn transforming and in turn might yet further transform human social relations and cultural practices.

These synthesizer sounds, generated at a time when it was still unusual for such sounds to be featured so prominently, at least in popular rock music originating within and evolving out of punk, might register both delirium and bewilderment concerning this new mode of technology, and especially at how these machines can perform spectacular achievements that surpass what humans can do, and which no longer directly correlate, in terms of what they are able to achieve, with precisely specific inputs of mechanical force from a directly and immediately co-present human source. In more contemporary terms, "Isolation" resonates with living in a social world where internet and especially social media means of relating to others have become inextricably part and parcel of everyday life, thoroughly naturalized as normal and simply to be expected, yet despite what extraordinary possibilities these technologies can and do enable in terms of social connection they are nevertheless often experienced as sites of profound alienation, and isolation, as inadequately substituting for, and even preventing, the kinds of social contact people often feel they need and value the most.

Yet, as one especially precocious student aptly noted, in connection with this particular Joy Division song, isolation does not necessarily carry negative connotations, as isolation is not necessarily equivalent, in itself, with loneliness or alienation. What's more, isolation does not necessarily result in loneliness and alienation nor do loneliness and alienation necessarily bring about, do they cause, or even can they explain isolation. Many satisfying activities benefit from and can even require isolation: reading, writing, meditating, watching a movie or a TV show or listening to a song or an album, doing a host of different kinds of demanding work requiring concentrated attention, spending time in nature or otherwise just 'getting away' to experience stress relief and to seek rejuvenation, and even multiple kinds of physical exercise. Writing this book, and the other book I am writing simultaneously, has required me to spend many hours, for days, weeks, months, and now two successive years in succession, isolating myself from others so I won't be distracted and so I can focus my thinking as I write. For extended periods of time, I close my door, so that I am isolated, alone, with my writing, in my study. Preparation to teach classes, which I have done for over thirty-five years now, often requires considerable isolation throughout and well prior to the start of each and every semester. Recovery from illness, or from fatigue, also often benefits from, and indeed requires, isolation.

In response to COVID-19, a great many people worldwide have been compelled to experience significant isolation, and although many have found this experience lonely, alienating, and even seriously mentally distressing, many have attested to how this enforced isolation has provided them unexpected opportunities to reflect on what matters most to them in their lives, on what is necessary and what is not, and on what changes they can and need to make, moving forward. Many people have discovered new hobbies, new interests, and new passions, as well as come to greater appreciate where they are at, and with whom they are at, than they did previously. Many people have felt more grateful for what they have, and have had, and less inclined to feel like they can never have enough, and have never had enough. My husband and I used to travel extensively every winter, spring, and summer break, often overseas, and especially to the British Isles, but during the past year and one-half we have traveled far less than in our entire previous twenty-three years' together. Even so, we have not missed doing so as much as we initially expected we would because we have come to appreciate where we are at, including experience of simple pleasures, walking for hours about Eau Claire, stopping for ice cream cones, playing with out pets, reading, listening to music, and engaging in healthful physical activity. I have resumed running regularly, up to four to six miles at a time, three to four times a week, after 24 years of not doing so. Andy and I have created new meals, which we prepare and cook together, and we are more consciously attuned to what we see, and hear, immediately around us, in the spaces we normally inhabit throughout the bulk of both our days and our nights than previously was the case.

Isolation, in the context of COVID-19, has come to be widely associated with what people need to do, what they are requested or required to do, when they have been exposed or potentially exposed to the virus, while quarantine has come to be widely associated with what people need to do, what they are requested or required to do, when they have contracted the virus, yet these terms have been used loosely interchangeably so that it has been prevalent throughout discourse concerning life under pandemic conditions to propose most of us have, of necessity, experienced a significant increase in isolation, or in the extent and degree of isolation, versus what often was the case prior to the pandemic, as close physical contact with many other people became risky. People have needed to change habits, often drastically, while many remain hesitant about changing back–include about once again participating in indoor activities close together with many other people, or returning to shaking hands, hugging, dapping, kissing and further forms of greeting. At the same time many people, including me, have missed this kind of contact, and felt saddened at the prospect that people will no longer feel comfortable or safe in so greeting each other. Likewise, even as I have assiduously followed recommendations for wearing face masks, as directed, throughout this pandemic, I have also felt saddened that people were not able to see as much of each other's faces as was commonplace prior to the pandemic, missing how much is often conveyed by way of people's mouths, teeth, and muscles in the lower parts of their face, in their jaws, such as when smiling. With increased barriers erected between us, even as these have proven necessary to protect ourselves and others in the face of a terribly destructive and highly contagious disease, it has felt as if I, and a great many others, have been compelled to live, and lead, more isolated lives than we optimally would have chosen for ourselves if the pandemic had not happened.

Yet COVID-19 also helps explain what is responsible for different experiences of isolation, including many experiences beyond those specific to this historical moment and this particular pandemic. My husband Andy and I have not needed worry about getting by, about being able to pay the rent and other bills, about being able to afford basic life necessities, about being confined to too cramped and crowded quarters with too many other people all at once, about being compelled to isolate together with other people who are abusive or otherwise hurtful to us, about not having the resources available to engage in major projects that make us feel like we are continually involved in doing something worthwhile and fulfilling, about being at high risk of contracting the virus by needing to work jobs where we are vulnerable to exposure and we can't effectively isolate, or about being forced directly to confront the worst impact of COVID-19 as have many doctors, nurses, and other health care workers. Since Andy and I successfully avoided contracting the virus, before becoming fully vaccinated this March of 2021, Andy and I also avoided running the risk of ending up isolated from family and friends while seriously ill or dying in a hospital, not being able to be directly in touch with loved ones at those perilous moments, as has been the case for a great many people who experienced severe cases, and often died from, COVID-19. Yet, at the same time, despite how relatively well off we have been, and continue to be, Andy and I, like others in our position, have nevertheless missed social interactions and social ventures we normally would pursue, and enthusiastically enjoy, and while teaching under pandemic conditions Andy indicates he has often felt as if teaching into a void.

How people experience isolation depends upon how extensive, how total, how complete, and how long-lasting this is, as well as where one is isolated, under what conditions, including according to what further restrictions, and including with what extent of access to resources of diverse kinds. How isolation is experienced depends upon for what purpose one is isolating, and to what degree this is at all freely chosen or at least freely welcomed. Isolation certainly can feel lonely and alienating, even extremely lonely and alienating, as well as make one feel precarious, fragile, sad, desperate, and despairing. But isolation can also happen in the midst of being surrounded by other people, especially when one is perceived and treated, or one feels one's self perceived and treated, as different from others, from most or from all others with whom one is in at least ostensibly extensive contact–and this can be exacerbated yet further when one's difference effectively marks one as lesser, leading other people to perceive and treat one as a person of lesser value (or of lesser intelligence, lesser talent, lesser skill, lesser moral character, lesser capacity and potential, as well as lesser deserving), even when they are not consciously, intentionally, or deliberately doing so. And isolation can be exacerbated yet further when no one can identify with, understand, and appreciate where one is coming from and what one is about–or where seemingly no one else can do so. In White-dominant spaces, Black and Brown people can all too readily, and all too often do, feel isolated, even in the midst of and surrounded by many other people. The same is the case with women in spaces dominated by men, or with LGBTQIA+ people in spaces dominated by straight people, or with disabled people in spaces dominated by able-bodied people, as well as in many more cases where one's identity, experience, and outlook, as well as one's values and one's affiliations, and even one's principal interests and passions, are not shared by others immediately around one, by those with whom one most extensively interacts and is compelled to interact–especially where these others are unable to understand and appreciate what any of this means to the one experiencing intense feelings of isolation.

This experience of isolation is not merely subjective, because the person who is isolated is objectively unable to draw upon the same array of resources available to those who are not isolated because their differences do not so distinguish and separate them from others within the social group. If, for instance, you cannot share with your co-workers or with members of the public you interact with, in doing your job, what is most important to and about you because these other people would not be able to understand, appreciate, respect, and support you if you did, then you are objectively isolated. Many gay people have not been able to share with others with whom they worked or otherwise closely interacted, or with family members and best friends, that they are gay, and, as a result, they have not been able to be fully present in these relationships, nor have they been able to experience others as fully present in relations with them, and they did not thereby enjoy the same kind and extent of camaraderie, intimacy, solidarity, and trust as straight members of these social groups have been able to do. As another example, when you know others will exhibit an unconscious bias in responding to and judging whatever you say, whatever you do, however you look, and however you speak, according to demeaning stereotypes applied to your racial identity, you are objectively isolated from these others, you are not fully and equitably included among them, and you do not enjoy the same kind and extent of belonging, of integration in Durkheim's terms, as they do within the same social group.

I myself have been participant on numerous occasions in social groups where I readily recognized the others with whom I was participating were unable to relate to me beyond reductive assumptions and demeaning prejudgments concerning people like me, limiting my inclusion within and effectivity as part of the group, leaving me isolated within the group–a stranger among those with whom I am ostensibly closely connected and with whom we are all, supposedly, quite familiar. This has happened to me on account of being gay as well as on account of being 'openly gay'; on account of being someone who struggles with serious chronic illness, invisible disability, and mental health challenges; on account of being intellectually oriented and invested; on account of coming from a background where I spent a significant amount of my previous life in the Northeast of the United States; on account of concentrating in critical theory and in critical studies in popular culture; on account of being a socialist and a Marxist; on account of being an activist and an organizer; and on account of being a progressive and a leftist. It has happened on account of more trivial matters related to the way I dress and wear (especially dye) my hair, on account of my ear piercings, and on account of the specific kinds of recreational interests and activities I most like to pursue (such as for example, my enthusiasms for crime fiction, spectator sports, and, yes, post-punk music, critical theory, and critical studies in popular culture). I have felt isolated at times at social gatherings, such as parties, where it seemed like the rest of those in attendance maintained no common interests with me, and no recognition or understanding of where someone like me might be coming from, as well as no inclination to attempt to find this out. I have also felt isolated at times when I have been the only one to speak up and raise uncomfortable issues, ask difficult questions, and advance challenging arguments and critiques–especially when others in these same situations clearly did not want me to do any of this. And I have also felt isolated after breakups with romantic and sexual partners, or when friends I have developed a romantic and sexual attraction toward made clear they 'loved me too' but 'not in that way', or when I first moved to start up in a new job in a new community (such as here in Eau Claire) where I barely yet knew anyone, or when family members and friends left after we had enjoyed great visits together or when they moved elsewhere to take up new lives in new locations after we had been sharing closely together for many years and I had come to depend upon these relationships to sustain me. When younger I felt isolated, as I wrote in chapter one, on account of being shy, on account of being perceived and identified as shyer than I actually was, and on account of being made to feel guilty and ashamed of shyness.

As a master's student at Syracuse University I felt isolated because I was attending and pursuing my degree supported by a fellowship while the vast majority of my fellow graduate students were doing so supported by scholarships combined with teaching assistantships, and their common engagement in teaching served as the basis for them developing close bonds with each other. I did make a few good friends but it was harder to do so in my position and I also felt further isolated because my housemate and I, during my first year as a master's student, did not get along, which prompted me to spend as little time as possible in our shared apartment, doing virtually all of my work and spending up to 20 hours every single day outside of the apartment. As a doctoral student I developed great friends but I felt isolated when they went away for long periods during summer or other breaks, or when they graduated and began to pursue new lives far from Syracuse. I felt isolated when I first came to accept that I was gay; I felt my being gay separated me from and marked me out as different from others such that fewer people would want to be my friend and more people would fear and even hate me because I was gay. Even among straight friends who were highly accepting and supportive I still felt isolated at first as I yet knew only a few other gay people.

I have felt isolated at professional conferences where it seemed as if others attending have long known each other and developed such close relationships that I was effectively totally excluded and where it seemed my positions and perspectives were different and even at odds from those represented by virtually everyone else in attendance. I felt isolated after I reached the final cut before a decision was made to choose another candidate for a position as a tenure-track assistant professor at Arizona State University, having just spent two years as a visiting assistant professor in the same department at the same university where I was chiefly responsible for the same areas as this new tenure-track position would take on, losing out in my candidacy for a job I not only wanted but believed I had won. And I felt all the further isolated when it turned out the decision not to choose me had been highly contentious and divisive. I felt isolated after I moved back from Arizona to Connecticut to live in Wallingford, at my mother's house, for a year before obtaining a position at UW-Eau Claire, coming back to live at that place full-time for the first time in over ten years and knowing virtually no one still around other than immediate family members.

I felt isolated after moving and starting my new job and new life in Eau Claire, until Andy and I started our relationship, because Eau Claire initially felt like a foreign environment for me in comparison with everywhere I had previously lived and as I initially struggled to become used to subtle features of Upper Midwestern US regional and local culture. The latter include tendencies toward a polite combination of friendliness and reserve; toward preferring to address serious and sensitive issues indirectly, as well as often to speak apologetically, and in self-deprecating fashion, when compelled to address these kinds of issues; toward considerable emphasis on 'family' locations and gatherings and venues and experiences; and toward considerable common interest in hunting, fishing, camping, home repair and home improvement, and for visiting and staying at cabins in remote rural areas.

I felt isolated whenever people around me, students or colleagues, evinced suspicion and discomfort about me, or identified and treated me as if I represented some exotic other with whom they maintained no significant commonality. I remember on more than one occasion early on having fellow employees working for UW-Eau Claire tell me, upon just meeting me, and without even introducing themselves, that I must be 'a very different kind of professor'. I remember more than one student during those years telling me, in front of the rest of the entire class, that their religion instructed them that people like me represented an abomination and should be put to death–and even that homosexuality represented the greatest moral evil in the world today. I felt isolated in visiting classes throughout my early years at UW-Eau Claire where my role was simply to talk about what it was like to be an out gay faculty member, and even to be an out gay person, answering questions from groups of students who in many cases acted as if they had never encountered an out gay person before. A number of these students clearly perceived me as representing something to be feared, as a significant number put their heads down on their desks so they did not need to look directly at or talk directly with me, seemingly out of risk of contamination, during the course of these visits. Otherwise I encountered many students who glibly referenced 'people like me' supposedly leading '*the* gay lifestyle', which rarely contained any positive associations. At times they proposed 'people like me' were guilty for spreading a deadly virus 'throughout the general population', callously infecting 'innocent people'. Or 'people like me' were voracious sexual predators. Or 'people like me' were diabolically immoral and criminally deviant in a vast number of ways far beyond the biological sex of those with whom we experienced sexual attraction and desire and with whom we preferred to pursue sexual relations. Or 'people like me' maintained our own elaborate and distinctive 'gay language' while we all knew each other and were secretly colluding to shock and scandalize as well as cause a host of other troubles for straight people. I felt isolated as the only openly gay faculty member at my university ever, when administrators objected to me being open with students about my being gay, and when I met closeted gay and lesbian faculty who made emphatically clear they felt terrified at the prospect any of their students might ever learn they were gay or lesbian. I felt isolated bearing the burden of needing to represent all LGBTQIA+ people, as if I could possibly speak for all such others, when faculty across campus continually sent students to interview me in writing papers and doing research projects about 'gay topics' focused on how different we supposedly were from everyone else. I felt isolated when I even needed, in one such interview, to tell one student who had taken multiple classes with me, and who clearly liked and respected me a great deal, that what principally distinguished me from him was simply the fact I had experienced oppression on account of the nature and direction of my sexual attraction and desire while he had not, yet in virtually every other way I could think of we were far more alike than different.

These are merely a few examples among many more I could cite, in my life-experience, where I felt–and was–isolated, lonely, and alienated. Because I teach classes where I work to encourage students themselves to feel comfortable and confident sharing, including what is and has been difficult and painful for them, I have encountered many arresting stories from these people's life-experiences of being in the same or comparable 'isolating' positions, and feeling 'isolated' in much the same ways. Isolation combined with loneliness and alienation is far from an uncommon experience, even if it remains often uncomfortable to acknowledge and address, and even if it remains often much easier to pretend is not the case.

Yet I also have encountered numerous stories from many students who have shared they appreciate some kinds of isolation, and indeed seek these out. A significant number of students have attested to needing periodically to get away from all other people in order to reset and regroup. Others have recounted interests, hobbies, and passions they enjoy pursuing on their own, they prefer pursuing on their own, and that they tend to work best, academically and otherwise, on their own. And certainly many students, just as in my own case, when working on major projects, academic or otherwise, have deliberately isolated themselves from others in order to concentrate intently, and to avoid distraction.

Isolation comprises one dimension of what Marx, in *Economic and Philosophic Manuscripts of 1844*, discusses as alienation, or estrangement, but the latter also involves something which was one's own, or which otherwise has belonged or should belong to one, not only separated from but also opposed to the person from whom it emanates, and to whom it has belonged and should belong. Alienation involves a hostile form of objectification, where what is alienated originates within the one who is alienated, and then becomes a power operating antagonistically against this same person. Alienated labor is not only labor that isolates the laborer from the means of their labor, from the process of their labor, from the ends of their labor, from fellow laborers, and from their capacity to labor so as to express and realize their human essence, but also labor that turns the means of the laborer's labor, the process of the laborer's labor, the ends of the laborer's labor, the relations of the laborer with fellow laborers, and the laborer's capacity to express and realize their human essence into antagonistic phenomena that oppose and undermine the vitality of the laborer.

In relation to Durkheim's *Suicide: a Study in Sociology*, isolation can anticipate and accompany suicide, and suicidality, in the forms of egoism and anomie, but isolation is insufficient to cause suicide, or suicidality; this needs to be isolation carried to an extreme and felt as an extreme, where the gap between individual and society, or between an individual's aspirations and what society renders possible becomes extreme, where it is no longer possible to reconcile the two, where the individual exists effectively outside of and at odds with society or outside of and at odds with social means and opportunities, codes and norms, and regulations and constraints. And yet, as Durkheim's categories of altruistic and fatalistic suicide indicate, insufficient isolation of the individual from the group or from dominant norms and regulations of society, can also fuel increasing tendencies toward suicide, and toward suicidality.

With Freud's *Civilization & Its Discontents*, isolation seems something the individual both wants and needs, and does not want and need, with Freud's emphasizing how difficult it is for the individual to isolate themself from the repressive and oppressive demands of dominant culture, and dominant cultural norms, especially as the individual internalizes these demands in the form of the super-ego. The death drive tends toward isolation. And the same with the aggressive instinct. But isolation also shows up, with Freud, in a different sense as well. The individual can feel painfully isolated from satisfactory and effective means to pursue, and realize, their needs and desires, especially for happiness and pleasure, while the countervailing pressures of the id, the super-ego, and external reality can prove so overwhelming as to leave the ego feeling painfully isolated. Neurotic and psychotic symptoms attest to the individual's struggle to deal effectively with severe pressures operating within, upon, and through their psyche, by attempting to isolate these. At the same time, however, doing so isolates the individual from what has led them to neurosis, or psychosis, and from what they truly most desire and need.

Ian Curtis's lyrics for "Isolation" begin, in line one, with "In fear every day, every evening," which suggests we here confront a negative experience, of isolation, characterized by recurrent fear, but we do not yet know of what or why this fear is so overwhelming. Line two adds "He calls her aloud from above," which suggests a character, a 'he', whom we are logically led to assume is the one immersed in fear, as well as a second character 'her' to whom 'he' calls. He calls her from a location positioned above where she otherwise spends her time–perhaps suggestive of a room where 'he' is confined, in isolation, due to the fear he experiences. "Carefully watched for a reason," line three, seems, logically, to correspond to the 'her' doing the careful watching of the 'he', while 'a reason' leads us to expect we might find out what this is as the lyrics proceed further. The lyrics so far suggest a man confined to an upstairs room, where he is struggling with overwhelming fear, while watched over by a woman who visits and takes care of him, by ascending from below. The lyrics suggest this man needs to be carefully watched because his condition is grave, and because he might deteriorate or harm himself, perhaps in attempting to escape from fear. But who has confined him, and why, as well as who has decided he needs to be carefully watched, and why, remain uncertain. "Painstaking devotion and love," line four, seems logically to correspond to how the 'her' of this stanza attends to the needs of the 'he' of this stanza, while suggestive of a high level of care, one that extends beyond the conventional relationship between, for example, a nurse or a doctor and a patient, instead characteristic of two people who maintain a much closer bond, as spouses or romantic-sexual partners who are not married, or as other kinds of family members or close friends. The line also suggests self-sacrifice on the part of the one who is manifesting this painstaking devotion and love, although another possibility is that painstaking devotion and love works both ways, between in this case the 'he' and the 'her' of this stanza–i.e., they both are painstakingly devoted to and loving of each other, even if in distinct ways, from distinct vantage points, and with distinct capacities for how to manifest this devotion and love. "Surrendered to self preservation/From others who care for themselves," lines five and six, seems to further reference the situation, and perhaps the plight, of the 'he' of this stanza, although perhaps simultaneously that of the 'her' of this stanza as well. These lines prompt speculation concerning what kind of self preservation is necessary, for what reason, and in the face of what threats to it, as well as why this involves a 'surrendering to', with that opening to line five suggesting this situation may have been effectively forced upon the 'he' (and perhaps the 'her' as well), with alternatives eliminated, or rendered too treacherous, yet by what, how, and why remains uncertain. 'Surrendered to self preservation' seemingly involves some kind of response or reaction, perhaps in the form of a retreat, escape, or hiding 'from others who care for themselves'.

It is tempting in relation to this last line to mentally insert 'only' before 'care for themselves', and perhaps this is implied, yet perhaps not, and perhaps what this line suggests is a preference for or a higher valuation of people engaged in caring for others, perhaps caring for each other, versus people caring (only) for themselves. Yet why those who 'care for themselves' might constitute a threat, enforcing a retreat to concentrate on self-preservation for the 'he' of this stanza, and perhaps the 'her' as well, is nebulous at this point. Perhaps those who care for themselves have harmed this 'he', and possibly also harmed this 'her', leaving the he petrified with fear and the her needing constantly to attend to that fear.

"A blindness that touches perfection/But hurts just like everything else," lines seven and eight, the last two lines of the stanza, seem to project the lyrics onto another set of considerations, as it is not immediately easy to imagine how to connect this blindness with what has preceded, but logically it does seem to be associated with the relationship, and the situation, of the he and the her in the stanza, and, if so, perhaps this is a blindness because it means effectively not seeing, or not being able to see or not interested in seeing, what transpires outside of the context of this isolated relationship of caring for the other. Perhaps, in contrast, because of how painstakingly devoted it is, while pushing everything else aside, this relationship represents an image, or model, of perfection. Yet, as line eight adds, whatever might be 'perfect' about it, or more precisely close to or 'touching perfection', does not eliminate, or seemingly even significantly alleviate pain, as even in this blindness that touches perfection, which may relate to the painstaking devotion and love, it hurts. It hurts, moreover, 'just like everything else', so as 'touching' as this form of care for the other, perhaps this form of social care, is, it cannot overcome the pain, and perhaps can't help but add to it as well. Yet why is this hurt, just like fear in line one, seemingly so pervasive–what has led to this situation, what accounts for and explains it, and who or what is ultimately responsible?

"Isolation, isolation, isolation," as the chorus, certainly emphasizes the word itself and a plethora of possible associations in terms of what 'isolation' can and might mean, while reiterated three times serves to underscore this is the precise situation, this is the precise experience, this is the precise feeling this song recounts, confronts, and engages: isolation.

"Mother I tried please believe me/I'm doing the best that I can/I'm ashamed of the things I've been put through/I'm ashamed of the person I am" I find a heartbreaking stanza. In response I want to reassure the narrator-protagonist I believe 'him' and that even though 'he' feels ashamed, and I respect this feeling, he is, has been, and can and will be much more and other than what he feels ashamed about; we all maintain reason to be ashamed yet opportunity exists to make up for and overcome what has caused us to feel ashamed; it may indeed be the case that 'he' need not feel ashamed, or as ashamed as he does; and he does not deserve to take this on as he is. What's more, addressing this stanza to 'Mother' is potentially highly significant. Imagine how differently we might interpret these lyrics if they addressed 'Father', or 'Son' or 'Daughter', or '(My) Friend' or '(My) Best Friend', or '(My) Lover' or '(My) Comrade', or '(My) Partner' or '(My) Wife' or '(My) Husband', or '(My) Fans' or '(My) Followers', or 'God' or 'Jesus' or 'Spirit', or 'Music' or 'Manchester' or 'England' or 'Britain', or someone specific, named, for instance, 'Owen' or 'Olivia'.

Whatever connotations we associate with 'Mother', 'I've tried, please forgive me, I'm doing the best that I can' seems to make ready sense, and not be as multiply ambiguous as many of Ian Curtis's lyrical lines, with this kind of sentiment one many of us can easily identify with, remembering times and places in which we have been working hard, yet struggling, feeling tired and overwhelmed, not succeeding in meeting our goals or the goals others need or want us to meet (or which we believe they need or want us to meet), and feeling, even though we have given all we have felt capable toward this end, that we regret it is not enough and that we wish we were stronger and more capable than we are. Writing is one place where I and many others, including a great many students I have taught, experience this feeling: we pour everything we can muster into the task and yet feel disappointed in the result, frustrated and ashamed we have not done better–agonizing that we *should* have been able to do better, and feeling we have let others down and not just ourselves. When students combine tendencies toward perfectionism and procrastination the two reinforce and exacerbate each other, leading students to feel badly about themselves, about what they seemingly are and are not capable of, and about how they seemingly have let down and disappointed others who were counting on them, to the point where this response becomes a vector for serious mental distress. I have worked meticulously with such students to strive to reassure them, and to help them with strategies to begin to overcome their writers' blocks that are amplified by self-doubt, guilt, and shame. I have felt great compassion for these people which has been tinged with heartbreak when they have shared with me that part of their shame in terms of what they seemingly were not able to do, or do well enough, had to do with their feeling they had let *me* down. In those cases I make emphatically clear this is not the case.

"I'm ashamed of the things I've been put through/I'm ashamed of the person I am" is more complicated than the preceding two lines. This is so because this line challenges us to reconcile being on the one hand ashamed of 'things I have been put through' and being on the other hand ashamed of 'the person I am'. Is this person who 'I am' the result of what 'I have been put through', is this person who 'I am' more or other than just such a result, and, if the two are not immediately causally related, how are they nonetheless connected? What might constitute that which the 'I' here has been 'put through' that caused 'him' to feel 'ashamed', and who or what could be responsible for 'putting him through' these 'things'? Why is the 'I' here ashamed of 'the person I am': what is it about who 'he' is, or who he perceives he is, or who he has become, or who he perceives he has become, perhaps caused by or influenced by what he has 'been put through'? What is shameful about him–about the *kind* of person he is? Also, how is this stanza, and what it describes, related to the first stanza, and what it describes? Is the 'I' here, who is ashamed, and who is addressing 'Mother' in expressing this shame, the same as the 'he' in the opening stanza? Or, perhaps, this persona is the same as the 'her' in the opening stanza, or the 'others who care for themselves' from that stanza? Assuming this is the same persona as the initial 'he', and this is someone who has both retreated into isolation and is being confined in isolation, for their own good, for their own protection, because this person is overwhelmed by fear, to the extreme of panic and dread, and this has something to do with not being able to cope with, or accept, the social world dominated by 'others who care for themselves', and who has experienced grave harm while participant in that world, what precisely has this person been put through to make 'him' feel such fear 'every day, every evening'–to require such isolation for the sake of 'self preservation'–and why does this make him feel 'ashamed'? Does he feel 'ashamed' because he has proven too 'weak' to be able to stand up to, to withstand, what has left him forced to retreat, and isolate, out of fear? Does he feel 'ashamed' because he cannot cope, cannot manage, cannot follow along with those 'who care for themselves' and the social world in which they flourish? Does he feel 'ashamed of the person I am' for the same reasons–because of this weakness and inability? Or does he feel ashamed because he has not demonstrated moral strength to which he has aspired or which he has felt he 'must' demonstrate in order to be a 'good person'? If the last, what constitutes this supposed moral failing–what did 'he' fail to do that he feels he should have done, or should have done differently and better?

I myself have felt guilty, and at times, yes, ashamed by the chronic illness, invisible disability, and mental health challenges I struggle with, and have struggled with throughout most of my adult life. I have felt guilty, and even ashamed, that 'this is me', and about how it often feels like 'this is me' limits me, even prevents me, from doing much I want–and need–to do. Even though 'I know better' I can't always dismiss the feeling that 'I should be better than this' and that these 'weaknesses' are 'my fault', are indices of something deficient in my 'strength of character'–as compared, and especially as contrasted, with others, who seemingly are capable of doing, and giving, much more. I have felt this way when, despite herculean efforts versus allowing acute flare ups to undermine the effectiveness of what I was doing, and how, in teaching, or in institutional and community service, it has nevertheless felt to me that this 'undermining' has nevertheless happened. I have felt this way even when others have reassured me it did not, that they had no idea based on how I engaged that I was feeling that badly. I still have not been able easily to shake off disappointment in myself. I have felt this way when I have needed to turn down opportunities to take on significant roles, including leadership roles, or to continue actively and prominently participating within organizations where I have been doing so, and have been assuming leadership roles–even when stepping down and stepping away has been necessary for my own health and well-being. For many years I denied my experience of chronic illness was as serious as it is, frequently euphemizing what I was experiencing, frequently pretending it was not chronic and especially it was never all that acute. I also struggled for a long time resisting accepting what I experience represents a genuine, and substantial, albeit largely invisible disability. I internalized 'shame' that our larger society and its dominant culture has promoted, and still continues to promote, about being unhealthy, about being sick, about being ill, about being weak, about being vulnerable, about being fragile, and about being frail–and especially about openly identifying myself as any of these things. I internalized 'shame' about identifying myself as a person who lives with recurrent tendencies toward serious to severe anxiety and depression, about episodes of both I experienced, to the point of denying these and pretending this was not at all the case with me. Even for years after first sharing with others I had been experiencing serious anxiety and depression I claimed these were conditions I could readily work through and overcome to the point where I would never again experience serious anxiety or depression. I internalized shame at the prospect others would 'pity' me 'if they knew the truth', or they would find my condition so disturbing they would want to create distance from me, or they would assume I was entirely incapable or 'unstable', thereby untrustworthy and undependable, and even potentially representative of a threat of violence. I have spoken, at length, with many individual students and groups of students who have wrestled with much the same kinds and degrees of shame, in particular due to their own struggles with mental illness, but also due to their own dealings with other chronic illnesses and long-term disabilities as well. It has proven helpful for us to be able to share, empathetically and in solidarity, but to this day opportunities to do so are far too limited, or altogether absent, for all too many who desperately need them.

All of these associations with 'shame' make sense in relation to what Ian Curtis writes here, and in relation to 'things I have been put through' this could represent what it has felt like, when unable to manage and control one's own mental and physical health and well-being, as well as one's ability to as easily move about and interact in a larger social world than many others can. It can also feel as if something else is doing this to–imposing these restrictions upon–'me'. And it can also suggest pressure to put on a front to cover over one's illness and disability, which compounds the 'isolating' effects of these dimensions of one's experience, as a result of the continuing social circulation of insidious notions communicating to the ill and disabled person that they are and will always be lesser, including always less free.

Then again, as I have also suggested, this is only one possible line of interpretation here, as these two lines could suggest being put through a plethora of different possible situations and experiences that result in feeling ashamed and that could cause or influence one to feel 'ashamed of the person I am'. If, for example, one aspires toward success as a performing artist, and rapidly achieves considerable fame and acclaim, one's life can feel as if it has just as quickly escaped one's control, and that one is being 'put through' all kinds of things in order to capitalize on this success and to coincide with the emergent and developing persona associated with this rising fame and acclaim, leading the person to act differently versus, even to lose touch with, other people, including people with whom 'he' was close prior to achieving this degree of fame and acclaim, as well as in relationship to how 'he' otherwise behaves privately–and, perhaps even worse than that, to lose touch with 'his' values, convictions, principles, and ideals, and with living, or striving to live, in accord with the same.

After the second stanza, the chorus of "Isolation, isolation, isolation" is repeated once more and then in the third and final versa stanza we encounter another seemingly abrupt leap with "But if you could just see the beauty/These things I could never describe/These pleasures a wayward distraction/This is my one lucky prize." The opening line not only points toward a vision of beauty that might compensate for, or transcend, hardships previously referenced, but also suggests 'you' might not be able to see this beauty, because otherwise the line would not include 'but', 'if', and 'just'. This 'beauty' seems to be of a sublime character, and thereby not easily represented, if available to representation at all, in words, in what the narrator-protagonist is capable of 'describing'–this is a beauty that seemingly has to be directly experienced in order to be appreciated. Nonetheless, it seems as if the narrator-protagonist is, however paradoxically, striving to point 'us' in the right direction and to give us a helping hand in approaching the vantage from which we too might also see this beauty. I connect this evocation of sublimely transcendent beauty with what can occur by means of a mesmerizing live musical performance. In such a concert it can seem as if the performance not only alludes to and touches upon but also summons and conjures, even enacts and conveys a direct encounter with sublimely transcendent 'beauty'. The same can happen by way of a theatrical performance of a stage play, or of a dance production, or even by way of a movie, a dramatic reading, or a speech. What this line references is whatever feels as if it transports us beyond our ordinary, everyday, mundane selves, and lives–into a marvelous alternative. We might also imagine a visionary imagining of what could or might be, but is not yet, in relation to existing forms of social relations and varieties of cultural practices, even in relation to how we might be able to live our lives, such as, for example, through curing cancer or all forms of coronavirus, or through eliminating poverty and homelessness, or through stopping and reversing the effects of climate change. We might well associate this line of these lyrics, in other words, with George Bernard Shaw's famous adage, adopted memorably as the theme of Robert F. Kennedy's ill-fated 1968 US presidential campaign: "Some men dream dreams of things as they are and ask why. I dream dreams of things that never were and ask why not." This line in these lyrics could gesture toward an infinitely receding horizon of possibility for grasping what it means to be in the world, perhaps corresponding to an infinitely persistent to recurrent experience of desire; perhaps corresponding to what does in fact constitute the 'ensemble of social relations', the essence of the human, the human 'species-being'; perhaps corresponding to a society that can achieve a fair and just balance between individual and society, maintaining a sufficient but not excessive force of moral cohesion, integration, and regulation; and perhaps corresponding to a society that achieves a fair and just balance among the needs of id, ego, super-ego, and the culture of modern 'civilization', as well as between life and death drives and among instinctive tendencies to pursue pleasure, manifest aggression, and maintain as well as sustain the health and strength of social community.

"These pleasures a wayward distraction/This is my own lucky prize" yet further complicates attempts to make sense of these lyrics, however, as we must speculate here to what 'these pleasures' refer–are these coincident with the experience of beauty previously mentioned, and with the attempt to share it, and if so what then makes them a 'wayward distraction'? What are they 'distracting' the 'I' and the 'you' (possibly 'us') from? What makes them wayward, in the sense of uncontrollable, unpredictable, ungovernable, and even capricious, wanton, and perverse? Perhaps this kind of pursuit, this kind of longing, this kind of aspiration, makes little sense in a coldly pragmatic world, a world following the logic of a capitalist business, a world in which people relentlessly pursue a narrowly conceived self-interest in perpetual competition with each other, seeking first and last to take care of themselves alone, over all other ends and interests, and in particular by exploiting what they can from others, and using the proceeds garnered through exploitation of others as the basis to generate profit, and accumulation, including not just in the form of economic capital but also in the forms of social and cultural capitals as well. Perhaps pursuit of a sublimely transcendent beauty runs contrary to instrumentalist logics, and defies positivistic modes of understanding and explanation–and can seem irrational and esoteric. Perhaps this line reflects a hostile valuation of artistic practice: that such practice represents a fringe interest and concern, that is ultimately merely aleatory, ludic, and ephemeral.

And yet, for the narrator-protagonist the pursuit of or indulgence in these pleasures, in this wayward distraction, appears to represent 'his' 'one lucky prize'. This suggests 'he' finds these pleasures to be of exceptional value, yet is otherwise bereft of much he does experience of value, while what he here values so highly seems to come to him in the form of a gift, that he has secured by means of luck, without 'him' necessarily being directly responsible for bringing it about. Here we can think of many possible connections, imagining situations where we or others feel, or have felt bereft of much conveying or representing significant value in our lives, other than one thing that is especially precious to us–one material object, one animate being and our relationship with the same, or one particular interest. And we can think of people in these situations feeling as if this is a matter of luck that they have this one prize that they do–this one prized thing, pursuit, relationship, etc. in their lives.

At times in my life where I have felt most isolated, alone and lonely, it has felt to me that my own 'one lucky prize' has been the music of Ian Curtis and Joy Division or other favorite music or favorite books by favorite authors or video copies of favorite films and TV shows or some other favorite material object–and especially a pet. As I write this section of this chapter Andy's and my beloved dog Casey, who for us has been a best friend and close family member, is dying of cancer, and this is heartbreaking but it also reinforces for us how much Casey has meant to us, how much joy and comfort he has provided, especially when we have felt most isolated, alone, and lonely. In the context of these lyrics it seems like the quest for contact with some form of transcendently sublime beauty is the one lucky prize, providing pleasures even in the form of wayward distraction, and this could well involve continually seeking after what appears just beyond the horizon of empirically tangible embodiment but which is all the more dazzling as such, as a fantastical entity, as an experience of the surreal and especially of surreality, and as powerfully uncanny in impacting with a jolt, or another kind of shock–both intimately familiar and strangely unfamiliar at once.

Ending the lyrics with the chorus repeating the word 'isolation' five times once again underscores the centrality of that word, and associations with what it can and might mean, as well as emphasizing that these lyrics testify to a situation, experience, and feeling of isolation, from a vantage point of isolation, that the narrator-protagonist never escapes–that the isolation is finally all-enveloping, for better as well as for worse. Yet in a song titled "Isolation," and with a chorus consisting entirely of reiterations of this word, it is alternatively possible that each of the three stanzas is concerned with three distinct situations, experiences, and feelings of isolation, involving three distinct characters who are isolated from each other by way of the intervening chorus and instrumental passage.

Isolation breaks down, more specifically, into the following sections:

Opening instrumental passage (through 0:34)

First vocal verse passage (from 0:35 through 0:59)

Brief instrumental passage (from 1:00 through 1:01)

First instance of the vocal refrain (1:02 through 1:09)
Brief instrumental passage (1:10 through 1:15)

Second vocal verse passage (from 1:16 through 1:27)

Brief instrumental passage (from 1:28 through 1:30)

Second instance of the vocal refrain (1:31 through 1:38)

Brief instrumental passage (1:39 through 1:43)

Third vocal verse passage (1:44 through 1:56)

Instrumental bridge (1:58 through 2:24)

Third instance of the vocal refrain (2:25 through 2:39)

Closing instrumental passage (2:40 through 2:52)

If we conceive of relatively extended instrumental passages as section type A, vocal verse passages as section type B, relatively brief instrumental passages as section type C, and vocal chorus passages as section type D, we have the following structure: A-B-C-D-C-B-C-D-C-B-A-D-A, or, in other words, three verse passages, three chorus passages, three relatively extended instrumental passages, and three relatively brief instrumental passages. This structure does suggest a situation involving tight and close confinement, in a limited space, and yet one that offers at least potential portals into other kinds of unusual–perhaps metaphysical–spaces. The song structure reinforces a sense suggested by the lyrics of a constrained and a strange space, that could, because of these characteristics, evoke powerful insight.

In terms of instrumentation we hear Peter Hook's bass guitar; Stephen Morris's drum kit which includes a bass drum, a snare drum, at least one electronic (synthesizer) drum, and hi-hat cymbals; Bernard Sumner's seemingly two distinct keyboard synthesizers; various periodically prominent studio effects supplied by Martin Hannett; and Ian Curtis's vocal. Whenever Curtis is singing, his vocal plays the principal role in carrying the melody, but the synthesizer keyboards and the bass guitar also contribute to the same, and, as is characteristic of Joy Division, the bass guitar initially introduces the melody. Sumner's synthesizer keyboards also contribute harmonic fill, or textural density, as do Morris's drums and cymbals as well as Hook's bass guitar but the drum kit's principal role is representing the explicit beat layer while the bass guitar's principal role, besides initiating and continuing to play the melody, is to represent the functional bass layer. At the beginning, the drum kit is quite prominent, then the bass guitar, and then the synthesizer keyboards, with each instrument in turn becoming slightly more prominent than those preceding. During the vocal passages the drum kit and bass guitar are more prominent than the synthesizer keyboards, and even as the vocal is the most prominent the drum kit and bass guitar do not fade all that far to the background. In between, in short instrumental intervals, the synthesizer keyboards become especially prominent. Before the last vocal verse passage the hi-hat enters for the first time and is here recognizably prominent. Toward the end we hear more noticeable studio effects as well as the effects of treatments added to the synthesizer keyboards and the bass guitar, with these sounds coming prominently to the fore in the brief false ending as well as in the return and then subsequent true ending. Curtis's vocal feels heavily treated as well throughout, much more so, for instance, than in "Shadowplay."

Morris's drum kit enters from low and primarily to the left, Hook's bass guitar from higher and to the center, Sumner's first synthesizer keyboard yet higher toward the top and to the right, Sumner's second synthesizer keyboard in much the same position, and Curtis's vocal from the center. The synthesizer keyboards then bounce between upper right and left, while the bass guitar sounds from somewhat lower, and the hi-hat enters, when it prominently does, from the lower right. Listening through headphones, the synthesizer keyboard sounds seem all the more prominent than listening without. Finally, fading sound toward the end of the song emerges from the lower left and then reemerges from the lower left and right, moving up and forward quickly before then abruptly dropping out. Every third measure we hear a single percussive strike to the left, and this sound definitely feels like it is produced by a synth drum. The early eighth notes also sound like synth drum strikes, while the initial drum pattern involves conventional bass strikes on beats 1 and 3 and snare strikes on beats 2 and 4. The bass guitar follows a persistent 1and2and3and4 pattern, and its general direction of movement in terms of pitch is largely along the same line while trending slightly down. The synthesizer keyboard patterns involve movement over larger intervals but these also seem to move in much like a circle nonetheless. The vocal rises notably at the end of phrases and lines while not ever falling lower than the initial starting pitch. The prominence of the synthesizer keyboards and studio effects along with the absence of the guitar are especially notable. The instrumentation here supports a sense of being caught up within an uncertain but nonetheless determined movement, of some kind, toward some end, within a tightly confined space, yet as part of an ensemble in which the individual constituent members of the group maintain something of an awkward, even jarring relationship with each other, and as if the tone, in the sense of the mood, is not consistent, not identical, among all of these constituent contributors, with some more eager and some more playful than others.

"Isolation" moves in 4/4 time, approximately 150 bpm, with a rhythm that feels tight and consistent, potentially complicating the sense conveyed by the lyrics of a song referencing being at odds with a greater social world, coming from a vantage point of isolation, and oriented toward another dimension of reality that is normally difficult to impossible to perceive and engage. Taking the rhythm into account, the song suggests concerted effort, and indeed struggle, to find a place beyond constraints, that even if partially necessary and partially welcome, feel too confining even while this effort, and this struggle, never escape an enveloping sense of confinement. Ian Curtis's vocal range spans one octave in total, with a relatively limited number of notes sounded by the bass guitar, more by the synthesizer keyboards, and a number in between by the vocal, yet overall all of the patterns in terms of movement in pitch of this song tend to be regular and consistent, with the synthesizer keyboards and the added studio effects the least so. This combination of sounds, and especially timbres, accentuates a feeling of being in a constrained space, and in seeking to engage with, to make contact with, to be able to glimpse and convey a felt impression of what it feels like to glimpse a much stranger kind of space.

In *Torn Apart: the Life of Ian Curtis*, Mick Middles and Lindsay Reade cite Tony Wilson as identifying the beat coming from the keyboard in "Isolation," which is not quite how I hear it, but does emphasize an important point, and that is all of the instruments contribute to defining the rhythm of a song, and not just the drums, nor just the drums and bass guitar. Middles and Reade themselves describe the synthesizer keyboard sound on this song as "ice-cold" and as pushing Curtis's vocal "to a lonely, soulless fringe" (213). Middles and Reade suggests the song's "detached prettiness–like an ice maiden–lost in solitude" makes it seem "as if Ian is gathering his thoughts." They also cite *Sounds* critic Dave McCullough's take, that "Isolation" reminds him of Kafka's "Metamorphosis," as a result of Hannett bringing "the tone down a step," while "synths flower" and "the song is short and bursts with action, though typically, for the entire album [*Closer*], at the very last moment ebbs away incomplete just as the very reverse seems assured," and "That, too adds to the hopelessness." In *Unknown Pleasures: Inside Joy Division* Hook reveals that the famous false ending of "Isolation" resulted from an error made by an editor assisting Hannett in the production of the song, but Hook suggests this turned out to be a useful accident. Hook also shares "What Martin did was take the original drum track flange it and effect it through his synth, then get Steve to overdub the drums so they were separate," so this way "he could have them really upfront in the mix, not buried," while he used "the drums to trigger the synth, which was, again, ahead of his time. Barney overdubbed the Arp over the Transcendent, playing the same part, and it sound current even now" (276-277).

"Isolation" feels easy to move with, even to dance with, especially in conjunction with the drums and the bass guitar as well as the vocal, although for me the synthesizer keyboards sound off-putting enough not for me to identify and move with them as readily as with the drum kit, the bass drum, and the vocal. It does feel like each instrument moves both together and in isolation. It feels like the music as persona is uncertain what it anticipates other than persistence or recurrence of isolation. I anticipate movement toward a possible climax as well as the ready possibility that no distinct climax will take place. Expression, in turn, is a difficult avenue of music affect to analyze because "Isolation" feels as if it is expressing the impossibility of expressing what is most meaningful–what is most prized. The brittle jauntiness of the sound here feels reflective of someone whose state of mind is out of sync with what is conventionally identifiable as normal, and who is both reconstructing performances of self as well as deconstructing the same while calling overt attention to the artificiality as well as the constructedness involved in being able definitively to identify one's self as one's self, conveying a feeling that the music as persona incarnates a fragile complex all too easily split apart and all too prone to dissociation. Acoustic impact feels relatively diffuse yet it is notable that across the array of constituent instruments contributing to "Isolation" attack feels consistently more pronounced than sustain and decay. The song feels more overtly focused on traversing a movement and contemplating this movement, than attempting to analyze and explain it, even if this is, as in the case of "Shadowplay," a movement through silence without motion, or perhaps a movement within an all-enveloping state of isolation.

The vocal, by way of the lyrics, feels as if it has been engaged in the process of some analysis and yet its relative, if even tenuous conclusions, are not easily assimilated into a crystal clear state of coherence. The other instruments feels as if they have analyzed the situation at hand as something of a playful one, but also as one requiring a jarring form of unnerving and disconcerting playfulness. I analyze this situation as representing a series of fragmentary impressions and reflections upon impressions combining feelings both of belatedness and of being ahead of one's time, along with feeling a wistfulness concerning the likelihood, to reference another memorable Ian Curtis line (from "Heart and Soul"), that 'the present is well out of hand'.

I associate what I hear in "Isolation" with cyborgian trends in technological development as well as with how strange these can initially feel. I also associate what I hear in "Isolation" with the kinds of awareness and insight that can accompany illness, injury, and disability, requiring of isolation and confinement. I associate this song as well with testimony to a visionary experience arising from a vantage point located beyond priority focus and immersion in conventionally practical kinds of interests, needs, and concerns. Since what is happening here does not seem to correspond to an image of directly physically mechanical movement, action, and interaction, but rather contemplating, reflecting, and sharing contemplation and reflection while giving voice to regret as well as to something that at the same time seems hardly like regret, I imagine someone in their own room, a bedroom or a study, weakened and disabled but radiating a brilliance this person is attempting to share, yet not able to find the words to do this full justice. This is a person in tune with something of transcendent value, who has experienced and is experiencing something that may be too difficult to relate in a way that makes sense to others who have not undergone or are not undergoing the exact same experience–and who have also not arrived at the same conclusions concerning what to make of this same experience.

It certainly can be taboo to admit and identify with shame, with victimization, with isolation as a simultaneously necessary and enabling as well as sad and painful state, and with experience of what cannot be expressed and shared in words. It can be taboo to bridge boundaries distinguishing human, non-human, other than human, inhuman, and even post-human. It can be taboo to propose in order to engage most effectively with a larger public world, and to do so in the least selfish, least self-centered, and least self-absorbed way it is necessary to withdraw from direct social contact into a space of isolation. It can be taboo to imagine we exist in an elaborately multi-dimensional reality, encompassing far more than is empirically perceptible, much if not most of which we normally are unable to recognize or relate to at all, at least not consciously. It can be taboo to project a sense that one identifies more strongly with a sublime, uncanny, and surreal order of reality than with an order of reality that can be empirically grasped and represented. It can be taboo to suggest we exist in realms and dimensions beyond ordinary and common ways of knowing, and relating, that are immensely powerful and exist far beyond our ability to exercise any deliberate, conscious control, let alone mastery over. The synthesizer keyboards and other electronically synthesized sounds in "Isolation" further suggest the taboo of giving way to, accepting, and making room for the prominence and dominance of artificial intelligence.

The lyrics in the final stanza feel as if they are focused intently on what is invisible, intangible, and ephemeral, while throughout "Isolation" the instrumental sounds and sound patterns feel as if they resist ready translation into sonic correlatives of physically concrete entities. It feels, moreover, uncertain what precisely might be separately suggested by each of the constituent sound sources. But this might itself testify to an experience where one stops trying to make visible, tangible, and perdurable and is instead receptive to and accepting of what cannot be engaged in that kind of form. What's more, "Isolation" conveys a feeling of the inexorable tendency toward growing invisibility, intangibility, and ephemerality of all of the following: our individual existences, our public identities, our dreams and plans, our relations with others and with our selves, successive stages in our unfolding personal histories and how these interconnect, moments when it seemed possible to exercise a modicum of truly effective control, moments when it seemed possible to know and communicate with confidence and certainty, and being able clearly to distinguish between being a victim and being a victimizer as well as between one who has suffered and one who has caused suffering.

As I listen to "Isolation" in writing this section of this chapter and as I reflect on what this song prompts me to consider I think about meanings and experiences of isolation, including those where isolation is not accompanied by loneliness and alienation. I think about what at least seems as if it cannot be readily expressed and shared in words, when words feel inadequate. I think about when and where it might prove worth acknowledging and accepting that one's own self is a messy complex, incoherent and not just contradictory, that one cannot, one's self, ever fully know and understand as much as one often feels intensely driven, even pressured, to attempt to do, and to feel as if one absolutely needs to do. I think about how confusion can anticipate and prepare the way for clarity, of moments and experiences of epiphany and revelation, of moments and experiences where everything seemingly has clicked or where everything has not for no precise reason that can be readily pinpointed. I feel as if this music as persona is addressing me from a position in which it feels uncertain if it can possibly reach me, even as it feels the need to attempt to do so, but is increasingly at peace either way, whether I can be reached or not–as the music as persona is accepting of its isolation. I think of situations of illness and recovery, and of disability and acceptance. I think of not being able to know how to get across to others what it's like to be me, to have gone through what I have, or to be undergoing what I am. I feel as if "Isolation" invites me to try to find a comparable beauty myself, and experience this as my own one lucky prize. I experience this song as grasping at finding, experiencing, and holding on to an ephemeral beauty as a reason for living. I experience this song as struggling with being able to accept one's self as someone who has been both a victim and a victimizer. I experience this song as appreciating giving and receiving care but finding existing society frustrating of both. I experience this song as prompting me to contemplate connections with and distinctions between my own individual existence and other beings, human and otherwise, currently living as well as now dead, the inorganic world, and the technological world.

In addition, I also contemplate how I respond to my own maleness, my own whiteness, my own cisgenderness, and the advantages these identities offer me, without me always being cognizant of them doing so, to how I have been constructed and positioned in these terms, and to how the positions and experiences of those unlike me along each of these same lines might be and have been radically different than my own. How much of my social constructedness am I attuned to, and how much not? How much do I not recognize because of advantages I am not always cognizant of, and how much in consequence do I take for granted? How much, what's more, do I fail to appreciate, and even attempt to understand–concerning my distinction from and relation to others, especially those at least seemingly in significant ways different from me? In what ways, and in response to what, do I back away because I don't want to face up to what I might feel disturbed about–even guilty and ashamed about?

When I think of regrets concerning what I have done, and not done, and where I at least verge upon feeling guilty and ashamed, or where I did feel that way at the time, I do recall feeling badly that I was not always as calm, generous, and kind as I ideally would have liked to have been in intimate (romantic-sexual) relationships when I was the one who decided it was time to end the relationship, when others decided to end the same kinds of relationships with me, and when I sought to create these kinds of relationships with others who did not want these kinds of relationships with me. In relation those experiences, from a retrospective vantage point, I now forgive my own emotionality, but I also do not forget how overwrought I became and how I felt guilty and ashamed about becoming so overwrought.

Most often I tend to regret, and at least to verge upon feeling guilty and ashamed, if I feel I have not been as kind as I could–and should–have been, and if and when it feels to me as if I am acting in opposition to my own foremost values, of which aiming to be kind is of crucial importance. I long have identified with the importance of being ready, willing, and able to speak, write, and act forthrightly by openly associating myself with and strongly advocating for positions that I sincerely believe, as a matter of principle, are right, necessary, and urgent–including where these positions have been controversial and unpopular. Yet I have also long sought to maintain a firm commitment, at the same time, not to demonize other people, those who associate themselves with and advocate for different, including opposing, positions, always striving to distinguish between support for specific positions and entire persons, as well as between engagement in specific practices and entire persons, respecting that all people are multiple, complex, contradictory, and dynamic, and that even when we may disagree fiercely on one or more major issues we still likely maintain common ground on other issues and in other directions–and that everyone maintains an intrinsic dignity and worth, as a human being, no matter how horrific might be the history of the positions they have supported and the practices they have pursued. Of course I have not always lived up to this commitment. One area in which I recognize I have not has to do with internet sites for discussion and debate. Although I learned, relatively early, that little of value can be accomplished by means of entering into prolonged arguments on social media, on listservs, and in online comments sections of newspapers, magazines, blogs, and so on, and at present scrupulously avoid all such engagement, I did participate in one chastening experience nearly 25 years ago now which I continue to regret.

At the time I may have maintained a partially justified grievance in a dispute over whether my term as a caucus chair had ended or not, although in fact neither I nor my predecessor had carefully paid attention to the organizational rules in place governing the length of terms and the procedures for succession in these roles. Nevertheless I worked hard in my capacity as caucus chair, and had just arranged the greatest number of panels, workshops, screenings, and other sessions in our caucus' history when other members of the caucus challenged my understanding that my term as chair ran for one further year. I did feel these people represented a clique of institutionally and professionally prominent academics, especially within the organization and the field, and that they distrusted me, and made me feel unwelcome, as an 'outsider'. Still, when this controversy spilled over to our caucus listserv, and when supporters of mine, representative of a Marxist community I had been closely involved with, became vociferously engaged in this controversy, it all too quickly seemed to me that posts moved into attacks back and forth, and indeed in multiple directions, that did not remain concentrated upon critique of specific positions and practices. And when I attempted to introduce a 'reasonable tone' into this argument, my 'allies' vehemently rejected this and demanded I stop doing so if they were to continue to ally with me at all, because my opponents here were, supposedly, according to my allies, unrepentant and unredeemable bourgeois reactionaries, who were working to ostracize me and others like me because they did not want to engage honestly with the political positions we represented. Before too long my major interest became finding a way to extricate myself from this ongoing exchange and bring it to an end as soon as possible. Once that happened I left determined never to become caught up in anything like this, in these ways, ever again. My take is no one made any impact with those they were contesting in this exchange; those my 'allies' attacked remained convinced they were dealing, simply, with extremist sectarian interlopers who represented nothing of value, while my 'allies', as I have suggested, scorned these opponents as nothing more than duplicitous gatekeepers of a repressive and oppressive status quo.

This was a difficult situation for me because I was becoming increasingly aware of significant lines of divergence that distinguished me from Marxists with whom I had worked closely at Syracuse, including my principal faculty mentors and advisors. The latter were tremendous teachers and scholars as well as tremendous mentors and advisors, incredibly stimulating and usefully provocative–intellectually rigorous, politically principled, and exceptionally generous and helpful to me, over and over and over again. Their impact upon me has been indelible, but at the same time they always insisted they did not want any of us simply to emulate them, as we needed to find and define our own paths, even if and when this led us to diverge from where they, these same mentors and advisors, had traveled and were traveling themselves. Even so, I felt guilty in experiencing this divergence, and struggled with how to effect and explain it, especially to myself, for a long time. In sum, my principal Marxist mentors and advisors at Syracuse firmly adhered to Marx's dictate to ceaselessly engage in ruthless critique of everything that exists, and for them this kind of critique did not equate with mindful engagement and thoughtful appreciation but rather with relentlessly demonstrating precise connections, however elaborately mediated, between, on the one hand, virtually all texts, discourses, positions, and practices existent within contemporary capitalist society and culture, and, on the other hand, the reproduction and maintenance of capitalist relations of exploitation. In contrast, my own tendency has been to seek out contradictions, and contradictory tendencies within texts, discourses, positions, and practices, existent within contemporary capitalist society and culture, that, yes, can and do contribute and lead to the reproduction and maintenance of capitalist relations of exploitation, but also can and do, at least potentially, provide support, or source and means of support, to question, challenge, critique, oppose, and transform capitalist relations of exploitation. I tend to emphasize that it is out of the contradictions within capitalist society itself that the basis for the transformation and supersession of capitalism will and must be found–and that anti-capitalist and pro-socialist intellectual and activist work seeks out and engages these contradictions, and the concrete balance of forces manifest in these contradictions, to try to intervene within and as far as possible seize upon what can be derived from these contradictions to support progressive ends, including, ultimately anti-capitalist and pro-socialist ends. From a certain kind of Marxist vantage point, represented by the likes of my Syracuse mentors and advisors, my tendency here is insufficiently radical, and especially insufficiently revolutionary, too compromising and too reformist, and too ready to invest in and accept mystifications produced and disseminated by capitalist ideology that render capitalist society, and capitalist culture, seemingly much more diverse, heterogeneous, fluid, and open than it actually is. This Marxist vantage point might well, at its most generous, identify my tendency as having become theoretically idealist and practically utopian.

In connection with this same difficult developing divergence from those with whom I worked most closely, and who were my principal teachers, mentors, and advisors as a PhD student, I also struggled for many years unhappy with the state of my PhD dissertation that I was rewriting for publication as a book. Even though I had received a contract, and the publisher's expectations for revision were not all that substantial, I myself was not satisfied, and spent a good number of years massively revising, reconceiving, and recasting this book-in-progress, generating thousands of pages but not ever feeling as if it was ready. My book claimed to offer a Marxist theory of queerity, or of queerness, in a wide array of forms, and not just in relation to lesbian-gay-bisexual-and-transgender forms of identity and experience, in part but not entirely through a critique of queer theory's relation to cultural studies. I was not satisfied that the critique in and of itself equated with the theorization. I also felt I needed to engage contradictions within queer theory and cultural studies more meticulously and elaborately, and with greater nuance and complexity, than I had done in my PhD dissertation. But I nevertheless felt bound as well by the imperative, driven home by my dissertation advisor, that I needed to reference the full range of leading publication in both cultural studies, and queer theory, vastly burgeoning fields, while I was in no position to be able to keep up with all that reading and at the same time do any other work or lead any other life. Even so, I did struggle for a long time with a sense of guilt, verging on shame, that I just could not finish this book, could not write it to my satisfaction, and could not satisfy the expectations of my publisher and especially my Syracuse mentors and advisors.

I find many people's experience with internet online exchanges, discussions, and debates, notably as part of internet social media, represents a source of frustration, guilt, and shame for them. This dissatisfaction can and does happen because people feel undue pressure to manufacture a narrow, reductive, and in many respects limited and false front that presents themselves solely in the best possible light, while forgetting all too often that this is what many other people are doing themselves on social media and that these other people are by no means necessarily as active, happy, successful, beautiful, on top of everything, keeping it all together, and maintaining as many close friends as might seem to be the case based solely on what they post and share—or that these other people always, and even easily, are able to develop and share the sharpest, wisest, most apt, and most compelling kinds of reactions to and comments upon current events and contemporary issues. But this dissatisfaction also comes from the kinds of attacks that occur all too easily on these kinds of sites.

In the 17 July 2021 edition of *The New York Times* writer and activist Roxanne Gay usefully addresses this issue in an article titled "Why People Are So Awful Online." Gay writes that initially "Online is where I found a community beyond my graduate school peers" and where she made many friends, shared valuable experiences, and learned productively in dialogue with diverse others. Yet,

"Something fundamental has changed since then. I don't enjoy most social media anymore. I've felt this way for a while, but I'm loath to admit it." For Gay, "Increasingly, I've felt that online engagement is fueled by the hopelessness many people feel when we consider the state of the world and the challenges we deal with in our day-to-day lives." As Gay explains,

> After a while, the lines blur, and it's not at all clear what friend or foe look like, or how we as humans should interact in this place. After being on the receiving end of enough aggression, everything starts to feel like an attack. Your skin thins until you have no defenses left. It becomes harder and harder to distinguish good-faith criticism from pettiness or cruelty. It becomes harder to disinvest from pointless arguments that have nothing at all to do with you. An experience that was once charming and fun becomes stressful and largely unpleasant. I don't think I'm alone in feeling this way. We have all become hammers in search of nails.

> One person makes a statement. Others take issue with some aspect of that statement. Or they make note of every circumstance the original statement did not account for. Or they misrepresent the original statement and extrapolate it to a broader issue in which they are deeply invested. Or they take a singular instance of something and conflate it with a massive cultural trend. Or they bring up something ridiculous that someone said more than a decade ago as confirmation of . . . who knows?

What's more, as Gay writes, online becomes the location in which many leap to attack as well as to fight over attacks directed at anyone who has become prominent, influential, and successful–in terms of how far from perfection this person falls short: "If a mistake is made, it becomes immediate proof of being beyond redemption. Or, if the person is held mildly accountable for a mistake, a chorus rends her or his garments in distress, decrying the inhumanity of 'cancel culture'." In this context, "Every harm is treated as trauma. Vulnerability and difference are weaponized. People assume the worst intentions. Bad-faith arguments abound, presented with righteous bluster." And added on to all of that are the viciously bigoted, experiencing free reign to engage in blisteringly racist, sexist, homophobic, transphobic, xenophobic, and similar kinds of verbal assaults, along with trolls who just like "gleefully wreaking havoc." In thinking yet further about what might explain these online tendencies, Gay concludes that "Online we want to be good, to do good, but despite these lofty moral aspirations, there is little generosity or patience, let alone human kindness" as what online manifests, above all else, "is a desperate yearning for emotional safety," "a desperate hope that if we all become perfect enough and demand the same perfection from others, there will be no more harm or suffering." This desperation in turn emerges from and reflects people's sense of overwhelming powerlessness, with online providing a location where we can attempt to compensate for this powerlessness, and feel like we are doing something worthwhile, in fighting the good cause–and where whomever we can readily target online becomes the vehicle for us to do so, and for feeling as if we are doing so. I agree with Gay that social media and similar online forums can readily lead in these problematic directions, but what I also notice is how extremely unsatisfied many people are, as a result of having participated in online verbal fights, how empty and unhappy these fights make them feel, and indeed how guilty and ashamed they feel on account of what level of discourse they have stooped to employ. Social media and similar online sites can certainly provide means, and even serve as arenas, for stalking and bullying, but they also can leave people feeling too often as if they are all too frequently harshly judged as well as expected to engage in continuous harsh judgment of others.

"Isolation" resonates with many people's decisions to end or cut way back on their involvement with internet social media, and other similar internet sites. "Isolation" resonates with many people's experience of feeling like what transpires in these locations is frightening and seems to manifest a lack of genuine effort and investment in caring about others, rather than just about one's self. "Isolation" resonates with many people's experience of these locations as places where people get pulled into exchanges that leave them feeling ashamed of what they have been put through and ashamed of the people they are (or have become). And "Isolation" resonates with many people's experience of these locations as places where it is impossible to describe and share experiences of fragile, precarious, yet profound and transcendent beauty.

"Isolation" engages mediations between on the one hand wanting to express, communicate, and share and on the other hand not being able or knowing how to do so, as well as mediations between intimacy and distance, between care and lack of care, between suffering and having caused suffering, between past and present positions and circumstances, between present and future positions and circumstances, between the real and the more than or other than real, between the mystical and the concrete, between the organic and the inorganic, and between the human and the non- or other than human. "Isolation" suggests a highly introspective engagement with borderlines as well as with both liminalities and subliminalities in a paradoxically simultaneously passionate and dispassionate way. In reference to metaphorical 'darknesses' "Isolation" seems concerned with limits to and failings of care–potentially limits to and failings in care for people struggling with serious health and disability issues, mental and physical, even according to what a social democratic welfare state offers, while becoming all the more resonant in the aftermath of neo-liberalism, the global economic crisis following the credit crunch and the Great Recession, austerity, and COVID-19. For example, in Britain today, and for quite some time for that matter, many have warned the NHS is extensively overburdened while, if anything, in Britain today social care provision suffers from even much greater deficiencies than does health care provision. Too many people suffer painfully in isolation, at least relative isolation, waiting far too long for too limited help–in desperate need of care that is not available. And those with chronic illnesses and substantial disabilities, mental and physical, especially those who are otherwise highly vulnerable on account of their class, race, gender, sexuality, or nationality, tend to suffer by far the most painfully within a contemporary British society that continues riven with inequality.

In terms of questions concerning what is the meaning of my existence and what is the nature of my responsibility to and for others, "Isolation" likewise suggests care once again, and how best to give and receive this, is of crucial importance. "Isolation" prompts contemplation concerning what to make of and to do with one's own fragility, even frailty, or, in other words, with how to make any meaningful difference when feeling weak and exhausted as result of trying one's best yet nonetheless failing. "Isolation" connects an experience, or a series of experiences, of isolation closely with experience, or experiences, of vulnerability and entrapment as well as of uncertainty and inadequacy. And "Isolation" makes sense as registering intimations and irruptions of the Real, that lead in turn to an experience of jouissance, but also, in further Lacanian terms, to oppressively authoritarian power of the Symbolic, and, indirectly 'the Law of the Father', by way of a pleading appeal for forgiveness, or at least understanding, to 'the Mother'. In reference to 'fascism of everyday life' "Isolation" can make sense as calling attention to a serious problem, arising due to in a growing inability or refusal to care about and for others, and to take care of one's self without at the same time hurting others or yielding to the coldness and harshness that public life and public exposure seem all too often to demand.

"Isolation" reaches, near its end, to finds words that are adequate and effective, while burdened by guilt, shame, uncertainty, hesitation, and doubt as well as fatigue and exhaustion. The music as persona appears to have reached a limit, an end, a blockage, or an impasse but nevertheless has not given up, and continues to struggle, even to do so with lines and bursts of emphatically energetic reaching towards the infinite.

Eight

"A Means to an End," the fifth song on *Closer*, right from its title addresses issues of central to concern to Marx. Commoditization of human relations involves relating to and treating other people as a means to an end, rather than as ends in themselves, while estranged labor is labor where the labor becomes a means to an end, and not an end in itself.

When work becomes a means to an end, especially a *mere* means to an end, and not an end in itself, it can readily lose any sense of satisfaction, pride, and joy that might otherwise arise from work that comprises an end in itself. This work can feel like drudgery, as something that simply must be endured, with the worker mentally focused on just getting through working, while feeling 'I can't wait to be done with this work' in order to move on to 'my real life', my life 'that truly matters to me'. Work experienced as a means to an end, and again especially a *mere* means to an end, and not an end in itself, is work which the worker does not control, work to which the worker cannot bring to bear their own creative and critical input, work which has been imposed upon them, according to a structure and design, and in relation to an end and interest, which the worker has little to no influence over.

In terms of relating to others as a means to an end and not as ends in themselves, this happens where someone develops a relationship with someone else only because of and for as long as that relationship with the second person can be used to generate economic, social, or cultural capital. The relationship can be traded away or discarded once it no longer serves such ends, once all of what can be usefully extracted from the relationship has been exhausted and especially when other relationships are now more profitable. This can happen not only in relationships among business partners but also among friends, colleagues, associates, comrades, lovers, spouses, siblings, and parents and children. When this kind of relationship becomes socially predominant, and seems necessary in order to be able to succeed in a hyper-competitive social world, the quality of human relations diminishes. People end up increasingly isolated, alone, and lonely; unable to trust in or rely on others, especially as they feel weak or vulnerable; and afraid their weakness and vulnerability will be exploited by those to whom they turn for help. Every relationship becomes transactional: I determine whether I want to enter into this relationship based on what can this relationship offer me, that I can in turn use as a means effectively to 'purchase', 'invest', and 'accumulate' yet more wealth, status, and power, and so does the other who is determining whether they want to enter into this relationship with me. Every relationship must be continually assessed, and reassessed, according to its 'return on investment', and if that return is positive it can be continued and extended, while if it is not that relationship needs to be reduced or ended.

This logic can be insidious. For example, when I was in graduate school I recall one phone conversation with my mother, an otherwise highly progressive person, where she exhorted the importance of recognizing that everywhere we go, in everything we do, with every other person we meet, and in relationship to every opportunity we pursue, we are always and continuously 'selling ourselves', while if we forget this, even for one moment, we are liable to fail such that instead of 'buying us' those to whom we are 'selling ourselves' will 'buy someone else instead'. I told my mother I rejected the necessity of this way of thinking, and acting, but I recognize where she was coming from in advocating this position. This is a message we all receive as members of a capitalist society, and with which we need to negotiate terms as best we can. This logic impacts all of us even as we strive *not* to relate to other people solely in accord with what we can get from these other people, what we can extract from our relationships with them to trade in for some greater gain. This logic impacts all of us even when we strive to relate to other people as ends in themselves. In a capitalist society, it can become all too easy even unintentionally to fall prey to treating others, including others we like, care for, and appreciate, even people we love, as solely means to an end and not as ends in themselves. It can be easy to feel like this is what we simply have to do, what people naturally do, as we move on with our respective lives in divergent directions. For example, colleagues retire or move away to other positions and we no longer maintain close connection with or direct interest in them. For example, as semesters end and students move on to take other classes with other faculty members, or graduate and pursue lives in other communities, we no longer maintain close connection with or direct interest in each other's lives, even if we had forged tight collaborative relationships while working directly together, and even if we shared with each other our respective vulnerabilities. In a capitalist society, it becomes all too easy to assume that others around you are always all right, or always OK, unless these others foist themselves upon you in asserting they are far from all right, far from OK, and desperately need your help. It becomes easy to ignore others, or never seek to get to know or learn all that much about others, including neighbors living in nearby houses or apartments, or colleagues working in nearby departments and offices, or people you encounter often, working to provide you with customer service in venues you frequently visit, such as at coffee shops and cafes, restaurants and take-out food shops, grocery stores and pharmacies, and in providing health care provision or mail and package delivery.

In relation to Durkheim, social integration weakens the more people experience themselves treated within the social group as means to an end and not as ends in themselves, or, in other words, where their value to the group is solely what the group can extract from them. When a social group discards people once they no longer provide profitable sources of such extraction, this leaves people feeling detached from these social groups, thrown onto themselves, with their value to themselves, as individuals, at odds with their value to the social group. This increases tendencies toward egoistic suicide. At the same time, when it seems like the social group represents no moral position that exercises an effective force in supporting integration, and no effective regulation of its individual members' desires and passions, or ambitions and aspirations, because the social group is only united around the common pursuit of self-interest, defined in terms of the acquisition and accumulation of economic, social, and cultural capital, then a situation of anomie, including an increased tendency toward anomic suicide, readily arises. This is especially the case if it seems the social group values achievement of ends through whatever means are necessary to achieve them far greater than it does adherence to any kind of 'proper and appropriate means'.

With Freud, it seems fundamental to human nature that individual human beings will treat other people as means to an end, rather than ends in themselves, according to our instinctual drives to pursue pleasure and to manifest aggression. The culture of modern 'civilized' society works to contain and divert these instinctual drives, including by means of the super-ego, which works as part of the individual psyche to limit and punish even inclinations to act in ways contrary to cultural norms, and does so by inducing anxiety, guilt, shame, neurosis, and psychosis. Freud advocates a loosening and a liberating of the intensity of constraints imposed upon instinctual drives, as well as accommodating both the death drive and the life drive, because human beings need to pull from as well as connect with each other. For Freud the challenge is how to accommodate these instinctual tendencies, and needs, within the culture of modern 'civilized' society, so that excessive repression does not lead to a 'return of the repressed' in highly destructive form because instinctual needs have been provided insufficient outlet for far too long.

Stanza one of "A Means to an End" begins as follows: "A legacy so far removed/One day will be improved/Eternal rights we left behind/We were the better kind/Two the same, set free too/I always looked to you/I always looked to you/I always looked to you." Key in this first stanza is a relationship indicated between 'I' and 'you' who appear to have been proceeding together, with 'I' 'looking to' 'you', and 'always' having done so. Perhaps 'I' has followed 'you''s leadership, or mentorship. Perhaps 'I' and 'you' have been equals, with I looking to you because 'we are in this together' and 'I know I can trust you' and 'I know that I need you, and we need each other' to succeed in our shared mission. "A legacy so far removed" suggests a considerable distance in time, and quite possibly space as well, something that may yet come at a distant time, and in a distant place, perhaps what will follow after the mission has been realized, after it has come to an end, in terms of what kinds of effects it has achieved and how it is remembered and valued by those who do remember it. Alternately, this line might suggest 'you' and 'I' are not concerned with 'our' legacy as we pursue this mission, as that is a matter for another, distant time and place. Perhaps the kind of mission 'I' and 'you' are pursuing, and what 'we' are achieving, or hope to achieve, is not something people in this immediate time and place are likely to appreciate, but others will, elsewhere and subsequently. "One day will be improved" suggests this mission is focused on a long-term objective, and will not reach its goal quickly or easily, but promises to result in meaningful progress, even if how long it will take and what will be required to achieve this progress remains uncertain.

"Eternal rights were left behind/We were the better kind" suggests this mission represents a bold departure as it is ready to 'leave behind', to 'move beyond', reliance or adherence to 'rights' which have previously been accepted as of fundamental importance, seemingly from time immemorial–or as otherwise representing the height of human imagination and achievement in terms of defining what kind of society and perhaps also what kind of polity comes closest to embodying the ideal of European Enlightenment aspiration toward perfection–or, for example, the United Nations 'Universal Declaration of Human Rights'. As such a bold departure, these lines, especially "We were the better kind" suggest pursuit of a decisive alternative, and might suggest, in Nietzschean terms, a refusal to be bound by the constraints on individual freedom imposed through 'leveling' in the form of egalitarian democracy. "We were the better kind" could suggest 'you' and 'I' are especially well equipped to set aside, to leave behind, the protections and securities offered according to existing forms of society, and existing recognitions of human rights, in pursuit of a transcendence of the limitations of existing forms of society, and existing social codes and statutes, where, for instance, despite proclamations of formal equality, rampant inequality persists, along with considerable deprivation. In modern capitalist societies, people are formally free and equal, in terms of 'life, liberty, and the pursuit of happiness', but nonetheless relatively more versus less free and equal according to socio-economic as well as socio-political position, and according to kind and extent of market power maintained in terms of social and cultural as well as economic capital. Even at the heights of the post-WWII social democratic welfare state phase of British history, prior to Thatcherism and neo-liberalism, a major critique directed at this form of society was it was far too 'top-down', with its 'beneficiaries' among the working class and the poor maintaining insufficient influence over 'the help' provided them, for example, in the form of social housing.

"Two the same, set free too" suggests 'I' and 'you' were equals, or at least equally shared and equally invested to the mission they pursued together, and that they developed such a close bond, in the course of this pursuit, that they became a single unit, representing a fusion and transcendence of their individual identities. This in turn may have been what enabled them to experience the 'setting free' alluded to here but even if not it seems the pursuit in itself involved an experience of freedom, of being freed, that implies a setting aside or breaking with prior constraints. The repetition of "I always looked to you" across lines six through eight emphasizes the importance of that relationship, how much it has meant to 'I', while because this is in the past tense suggests being let down, betrayed, and even abandoned. That is not necessarily the case because the song might suggest a kind of testimony, and more precisely a tribute, on the part of 'I' to 'you' for what 'you' has meant to 'I' and to what they experienced and accomplished together. However, with the title "a means to an end," and the ready connotations that phrase conjures, it seems more likely some kind of rupture has developed in this relationship, and that 'I' now feels as if 'I' was taken advantage of by 'you', who seemingly embraced 'I' as an end in 'himself' but who eventually revealed this was not the case–or who changed such that this was no longer the case.

Stanza two declares "We fought for good, stood side by side/Our friendship never died/On stranger waves, the lows and highs/Our vision touched the sky/Immortalists with points to prove/I put my trust in you/I put my trust in you/I put my trust in you." The first line of this stanza elaborates on what has already been suggested in the first stanza, that the mission in which 'you' and 'I' previously

398

engaged was one that involved fighting, directly together, for good. Although not specifying what this 'good' might be, it seems reasonable to imagine an ethical or political good, possibly a way of addressing and redressing something that was 'bad' or at least 'not good enough', something requiring substantial reform or transformation, where the situation in place was causing hardship and suffering, perhaps on account of alienation and exploitation, perhaps manifesting itself in the form of inequity and injustice. 'Good' might also represent what had not yet been realized, or even envisioned, in the form of social and political progress, or artistic and cultural achievement, or moral and spiritual value. This stanza, like the first, emphasizes the bond between 'I' and 'you', the 'friendship' the two shared, that 'never died', persisting across 'stranger waves' and through 'lows and highs', suggestive of finding an ideal comrade, a soulmate, someone who would be with one, literally and figuratively, 'all the way', inspiring and enabling one to feel like it makes sense to pursue ambitious goals: "our vision touched the sky." This fourth line of this second stanza suggest a transcendent vision, perhaps a vision of transcendence, while emphasizing this bond between 'I' and 'you' involved more than collaboration in action alone, as it also involved collaboration in imagination. Perhaps this bond involved a successful uniting of theory and practice as well as of 'I' and 'you'.

"Immortalists with points to prove" suggests seeking something that can and will enable immortality, or at least enable contact with that which might be immortal about the human despite the mortality of the individual, something that will allow a legacy to live on, and burn bright, long after the individuals directly responsible have passed on. "With points to prove" suggests this mission was driven by a commitment to make a difference, to break through, to express and communicate, to shape and impact–that this is not just a quest that empowers 'I' and 'you' as they pursue it, but rather aims to 'prove points', to secure results, to compel and convince others. The repetition of "I put my trust in you" once more emphasizes how deeply invested in and committed to this relationship with 'you' 'I' was or has been, as well as suggesting, again given the past tense and the title of the song, that 'I trusted you but you betrayed my trust', which likely seems to have been the result of 'you' effectively relating to 'I' as a means to an end and not an end in 'himself', or perhaps 'I' engaging in this relationship in an idealistic way whereas 'you' engaged in the same relationship, in contrast, in a cynical way.

It certainly can feel devastating if someone with whom one has not only shared a great deal, of extraordinary value, to whom one also looked up–in the sense of admired, perhaps even idolized–and in whom one invested immense trust, has not been and was not deserving of any of that, has perhaps used and abused you and also took advantage of how much you have admired, idolized, invested in, and trusted this other person. One connection I draw with these lyrics follows from an experience many students have shared in autobiographical essays, and that has to do with finding out an erstwhile best friend has been acting to undermine them, has been secretly spreading malicious gossip and damaging rumors about them with others–or has actually been bullying them in ways it took considerable time, and considerable suffering and struggle, to recognize. Yet another ready connection involves the time when young people first recognize their parents or guardians, or older siblings, or other close relatives, or other influential adult mentors and role models, are not as perfect as previously imagined, and in fact exhibit disturbing flaws. Many students I have taught have shared with me, and with our classes, stories of this kind as well. In "A Means to an End," we confront what happens between comrades, in fighting long and hard together for a great cause, which unfortunately has ended with the narrator-protagonist experiencing profound disillusionment about their comrade, and as a result about what they actually did share together.

Stanza three declares "A house somewhere on foreign soil/Where ageing lovers call/ Is this your goal, your final needs/Where dogs and vultures eat/Committed still I turn to go/ I put my trust in you/I put my trust in you/I put my trust in you/I put my trust in you/In you. In you. In you/Put my trust in you, in you." The opening lines here suggest a location where 'you' has ended up, which the line "Is this your goal, your final needs" appears to question, as if this destination represents a disappointing end, and perhaps 'I' is especially disappointed that 'you' has given up on the quest they shared, given up on their mission, and is content to turn away and accept a life now akin to a living death instead, even while 'I' remains 'Committed still'. 'I' could remain committed still to the mission, the cause, the quest–or 'I' could remain committed also to the friendship, the comradeship, even if 'you' has made clear that 'you' no longer deserves this commitment, and perhaps never did. 'I' in this sense will not follow 'you's betrayal by in turn betraying 'I'–even though 'I' is 'turning to go', turning to leave 'you' behind, at this "house somewhere on foreign soil." That description is vague enough to open itself to many imaginations of precisely where this might be and precisely what it might look like, even though "Where ageing lovers call" somewhat limits and focuses such imaginings. This might seem like some kind of retirement community, some mode of elder care, or some place of exile to which one turns when one's will and ability 'to fight numerous battles' has been exhausted. It is possible that 'I' and 'you' are ageing lovers and this 'house somewhere on foreign soil' is where 'I' calls upon 'you' before turning to go.

It is again, possible, as I suggested in relation to the first stanza, that despite the connotations suggested by the title, that the lyrics do not criticize the 'you', do not call the 'you' out for any kind of betrayal, or for misusing and abusing their friendship, but instead rail against, or elegize, life itself, how quickly it passes, and how soon one starts to decline as well as how rapidly death comes, even to those who live relatively long lives. This last line of interpretation suggests reaching a point late in life, in old age, where one looks back at one's previous life and reflects on how much one strived to do, and believed one could or would do, but never did–how many dreams and plans were never fully realized, or never even partially realized, as well as how much had to be given up as the effects of aging became difficult to ignore and withstand.

Yet "Where ageing lovers call" is also interesting in suggesting that the entire lyrics might be about a relationship between 'lovers', and especially a relationship that many romantically dream of experiencing where your lover is not only your best friend, and your soulmate, but also your closest companion–your collaborator in the most important work you do. In this connection I myself think of forms of gay desire for it to be readily possible to move easily across a homosocial to homoerotic to homosexual continuum, where it would make intuitive sense that your best friend of the same sex, with whom you share the most in common, in terms of interests, hobbies, and passions, and with whom you also share the most in common in terms of outlook and sensibility, even personal style and manner of behavior, would also be someone whom you would love 'all the way', including as a sexual partner. For example, your best friend with whom you like to play sports, or to make music, would also be someone with whom you like to have sex, and you would move readily, back and forth, between having sex and engaging in these other pursuits.

Nevertheless, returning more directly once more to the lyrics, in the third stanza, "Where dogs and vultures eat" adds a further disturbing twist, suggesting this final destination is a place for scavengers, waiting to feast upon the dying and quickly consuming the dead. "Where dogs and vultures eat" might, metaphorically, suggest human beings that prey upon others, especially those who are weak and vulnerable, or who are in weak and vulnerable positions, which could include those who have mistakenly invested their trust in people who in effect do not deserve this trust and who are ready to exploit it by turning on those who have trusted them, in effect preying and scavenging on those who have opened themselves up to the point where they are exposed and vulnerable before those they mistakenly trusted. And yet this line might also suggest arrival at a point where death, or the effective death of the mission, is imminently at hand. Perhaps the entire mission appears in retrospect to reduce itself to this final dispiriting summation, as ultimately all a means to this sad end.

Yet the final six lines, repeatedly emphasizing 'I' 'putting my trust' 'in you' suggests, once more, that the sadness here more likely follows from putting trust in someone who has revealed themselves as not having deserved it, or who has betrayed this trust, while, at the same time emphasizing how devastating arrival at this point is, for the 'I here', because the 'I' invested so much trust, concerning so much of preeminent importance, so much of what was most important within and about 'I''s life in this relationship. The 'I' cannot help but remain paradoxically 'committed' even after it is effectively impossible to be committed to 'you' any more because the 'I' has so little, perhaps even nothing, left. In this connection I think of what happens when an intimate interpersonal relationship between two people comes to an end, and where they break up, after having forged such a close relationship that they have virtually become one person, such that it feels impossible to conceive of themselves as existing other than in relationship with that other person, because the two created an 'us' that superseded and transcended the 'you' and the 'I' within an 'us' such that 'you' and 'I' feel as if they are only constituent dimensions of the larger relationship.

Here it seems as if Durkheim's conception of 'altruistic suicide' might make sense. In this kind of suicide, the individual means little to themselves as an individual outside of their place, their role, their membership and participation within the social group that they experienced as overwhelmingly central to defining and explaining not only their most important focus of identity, but also their entire reason and purpose for existence. In the context of this kind of identification with a social group, no point exists in going on not actively involved with the group, and any sacrifice that might benefit or pay tribute to the supreme value of the social group, and for what it stands, is worth it. However, the lyrics to "A Means to an End" don't quite reach the point where they clearly suggest that 'I' can't go on without 'you' and if 'you' must come to an end then so must 'I'.

As is often the case with Joy Division music, "A Means to an End" as an entire complex of sounds, patterns of sound, and deployments of sounds hardly seems as bleak as the lyrics taken alone might suggest, and emphasizes less a feeling of resignation and despair and more that of resolution and determination–to persist, and especially to persist in struggle. The tightly cohesive coordination of all the constituent elements of these songs, with every contributor working carefully to closely compliment each other while at the same time offering their own distinct signature, conveys a strong sense of collectivity, and indeed of solidarity, in action. As I cited in chapter two, Jon Wozencraft, in *This Searing Light, The Sun and Everything Else: Joy Division–The Oral History* aptly challenges conventional interpretations of Joy Division music too focused on the lyrics alone, and especially not conceiving these lyrics as complex and contradictory, as engaging a multiplicity of thoughts and feelings in elliptically ambiguous and paradoxical ways:

> So this was a very strong disclosure to me that there's actually a lot of white light happening here, it's not all about death, doom and destruction.

> Joy Division's music is very uplifting. It's got nothing to do with sitting in a bedsit being depressed, chewing your fingernails and wondering if you're going to throw yourself out the window. It's about transforming normal lives into something magical and life-affirming. The cliché of Joy Division has been very dark and depressing. For me, that was not the case at all: they were joy-bringers and I felt charged as a result . . . These things are not understood or recognised in our culture, and it's important to acknowledge where we find them in our lives. (252)

Likewise, as I cite in chapter one, Paul Morley has also aptly argued that Joy Division's music "suggests infinity and confronts squalor," while it offers "dreams that shout for a better world and a deeper understanding" (151). These songs register "the horror of the times" yet

> The very act of confronting the void or continuing to confront it is an act of affirmation. The blacker the situation and the deeper the background of despair against which this affirmation is made, the more complete and the more triumphant must be the victory that it constitutes. The uglier the reality that is confronted, the more exhilarating will be its sublimation into symmetry, rhythm, movement and noise. (256)

As Morley declares, "the very best rock music," of which Joy Division is exemplary, "is part of a fight, part of a larger decision, a widespread perception, something that can actively remove prejudice and restriction":

> Rock's greatness is its emotional impact on the individual. Joy Division's worth is immense to every individual who relishes their strange awareness . . . Ian Curtis decided to leave us, and yet he leaves behind words of such strength they urge us to fight . . . [T]he moods and the insight . . . inspire us, excite us, challenge us. The value of Joy Division is the value of love. (158)

I suggest Joy Division's music makes it viable to engage the topics Ian Curtis's lyrics broach, because of the support that music provides to do so. What's more, for Peter Hook, Stephen Morris, and Bernard Sumner, participating and contributing as members of Joy Division was clearly enormous fun and frequently exhilarating. Martin Hannett, Rob Gretton, and Tony Wilson also found much about their involvement with Joy Division powerfully vitalizing, and, I contend, so to a great extent did Ian Curtis as well. In and through his music, as art, he could partially distance himself versus what was leading to deepening depression and suicidality. Through this music he could not only confront his demons, and do by sublimating rather than merely confessing them, but also, however fleetingly, transcend being dragged down and defeated by these forces, instead reaching toward the light and continuing to struggle through the darkness.

The structure of "A Means to and End" divides into sections as follows:

1. 0:00-0:27: Instrumental opening passage. Immediate initiation. Right away this opening passage elaborates a clear, strong, pronounced melodic line with a steady beat followed quickly by a para-melodic line higher pitched and with suggestion, at the edges, of this latter line involving some discordance meets dissonance. The melodic pattern conveys a clear feeling of moving back and forth and up and down according to a series of small yet precise and steady steps.

2. 0:28-1:40: First two verse + refrain passages. Elaboration and focus. Especially notable here is in this song no break occurs between the first and second verse stanzas, with an only slight rest between verse and refrain in each case as well as within the refrain. The vocal picks up the melody from the bass guitar as the latter continues to play it as well. The vocal lingers on notes mid-way through and especially at ends of lines, and adds further sustain and decay before release as well as further reverberation.

3. 1:41-2:40: Instrumental bridge passage. Heightened and intensified concentration. The same complimentary, para-melodic contribution from the guitar is here especially pronounced and both the bass guitar and the guitar vary their patterns somewhat from what they sounded earlier.

4. 2:41-3:37: Third verse + refrain passage. Moving toward climax. At the end in the refrain we hear a further rising in pitch, suggest of further and higher reaching, yet this does not suggest straining and remains mellifluous.

5. 3:38-4:03: Instrumental closing passage. Denouement: moving toward suspension and dissolution. At the end, we hear a notable slowing down in tempo toward a final abrupt stop.

This structure accentuates the song as a tightly cohesive and closely integrated whole, as does each of the principal instruments following highly regular, repeating patterns. A general tendency across this song is to move closely along the same pitch, to rise slightly higher, and then to fall somewhat further–with general overall movement ultimately down in pitch. Nevertheless, what we also encounter is continuously recurrent slight back and forth and up and down movements, much like walking on a treadmill or a stair climber, or literally up and down a series of stairs, or around a maze, or pacing around a confined space, but also, strangely enough, as if while doing so we are slowly marching at the same time. Peter Hook, in *Unknown Pleasures: Inside Joy Division* describes "A Means to and End" as "a fucked-up disco song" (278), perhaps referencing something of this same feeling of a strange combination of distinct types of movement. Because of its regular, recurrent, and consistent patterns of sound, "A Mean to and End" does convey a feeling of containment yet also a feeling of determination to persevere. If this song engages an experience of profound disappointment, disillusionment, and disenchantment, it nonetheless does so by suggesting this disappointment, disillusionment, and disenchantment follows from gaining a critical consciousness in being able to diagnose a relationship previously not experienced and understood as alienating and exploitative to have in fact been so. "A Means to an End" conveys a combination of, on the one hand, deep sadness and bitter regret, and on the other hand, stark revelation and critical insight.

As a concrete connection with what I have just proposed, let's imagine a hypothetical worker named Patrick, who has worked for many years for a company to which he feels he has devoted his life, and indeed he has long been not only content but also proud to do so, making his work for the company a major constituent dimension of his own identity. Yet recently Patrick has come to the realization this company never has been interested in Patrick as a human being, as an end in himself rather than as a means to an end, only in what the company is able to get out of–to extract from–Patrick for as long as Patrick can offer more valuable labor at a more affordable rate of compensation than others who could be hired in his place. This company maintains no long-term loyalty to Patrick, who has just been abruptly let go as the company is replacing Patrick's labor with labor from several workers who can be compensated at a lower combined wage than Patrick and who can at the same time to be pressured to give more to the company, for less. Patrick's long-term fellow employee Angela has also loved working for this company, and like Patrick has made her work as part of this company central to her own self-identity and her own sense of self-worth, but she has now been forced into a premature early retirement, her only choice to avoid Patrick's fate, as the company is now downsizing, outsourcing, and restructuring so that long-term employees paid relatively high rates of compensation, and who have come to expect a certain relative autonomy in how they do their job as part of the company, can be jettisoned in favor of those who can be more easily and extensively exploited. Patrick and Angela realize now that they should have foreseen this development as just last year another long-term fellow worker for the company, Henry, who had been widely known and frequently praised as one of the hardest, most dedicated, most talented, and most accomplished workers for the company–and who had won employee of the month and of the year awards more than anyone else–was dismissed over what seemed only the slightest infraction, trumped up to provide an excuse to get rid of him, bewildering fellow workers such as Patrick and Angela. Henry's dismissal likely had much, in fact, to do with Henry's interest in unionizing the workforce within the company. Patrick, Angela, and Henry all feel as if they have been betrayed by this company that they had 'looked to', 'fought with', 'stood side by with', devoted themselves to helping realizing its furthest goals and achieve its greatest outcomes, regarding the company's owners and managers as friends and the entire company as family, trusting the company appreciated them for all they had invested and would stand by and continue to take care of them for as long as they wanted and needed to work before they chose to retire. But this was never really the case.

However, as devastated as Patrick, Angela, and Henry all feel, they also recognize that in the nearby community of Adeline, the situation confronting former workers at what was long the largest employer in that community, and with which that community had come to virtually totally identify

404

itself, has proven even far more devastating because their company abruptly closed down altogether, laying off thousands of workings in order to pull out entirely and transfer their production to a far distant location where they could more easily and thoroughly exploit the workforce, as well as gain far greater concessions from local and regional governments, in order to significantly increase their profit, even though they had always been making a decent profit in Adeline. Because Adeline is a relatively small community, virtually a company town, the closure of this company's production facilities and the end of employment in Adeline by that company is exerting a massive downward multiplying effect on the rest of the economy of Adeline, with many other smaller businesses needing to close and public services needing to be slashed while the level of poverty, along with related forms of acute distress, have sharply risen. The workers for this company in Adeline, and the entire community of Adeline, feel betrayed–as they always looked to and trusted in the company, believing they were united together, stood side by side, joined together in a common mission, and shared a common commitment and common fundamental values and objectives, that the company was the town's friend and family, but now Adeline realizes this was never really the case.

The preceding hypothetical connections suggest convergent focuses of concern between "A Means to an End" and Marx's *Economic and Philosophic Manuscripts of 1844*, but ready links can also be drawn with Durkheim's *Suicide: a Study in Sociology* and Freud's *Civilization & Its Discontents*.

In relation to Durkheim, "A Means to an End" is suggestive that one significant factor in accounting for deficient social integration follows from the larger society, or social group, failing to demonstrate sufficient loyalty to individuals participant within the society, or social group, and who all too often experience a sense that this society, or social group, is indifferent to and unconcerned about their well-being, and will do little to nothing to insure they are taken care of, but rather casts individuals aside so that they are thrown entirely onto their own limited resources and, as a result, struggle, badly. As such, this kind of society or social group communicates to the individuals participant within it that it does not share a commitment to common principles, ideals, convictions, and values, and that it is in effect an a- or even anti- moral entity. As a result it cannot persuade individuals to adhere to and respect formally abstract yet practically irrelevant norms and regulations concerned with 'proper' and 'appropriate' ambitions and aspirations, or 'proper' and 'appropriate' means to pursue these.

In relation to Freud, "A Means to and End" is suggestive of what happens as a result of societal failure adequately to provide sufficient outlets for individuals to engage in selfish pursuits, both pleasurable and aggressive, and of what can follow when social relations are romantically idealized as capable of transcending and superseding these fundamental human drives and needs. Also, "A Means to an End" can suggest how, in psychoanalytic critical theorist Jacques Lacan's terms, the social oe in other words 'the big S' (society, the social group, the social regime) can appear to have betrayed, to have taken advantage of, to have used and abused, and to have effectively abandoned and discarded 'the small s' (the individual) despite all the small s has done in terms of identification with and conformity to the norms, mores, rules, laws, and other dictates of the big S.

Peter Hook's bass guitar initiates and continues to sound the melody, as is common in Joy Division songs, while proceeding according to a 1and2and3and4and pattern of eighth notes throughout the song. Bernard Sumner's guitar contributes a para-melodic extension, elaboration, and compliment to the melody initially introduced by the bass guitar, and follows a somewhat more diverse array of patterns, yet most often also follows a 1and2and3and4and pattern of strummed eighth note chords. Ian Curtis's vocal is clear, central, rich, deep, and strong, and poised equidistant between sprechesgang and crooning. Martin Hannett's studio effects and treatments of principal instruments don't ever take center stage but enhance the texture and precision. Stephen Morris's drumming incorporates a sliding, syncopated strike, with bass drum hits on beats 1 and 3, snare drum hits on beat 2, and hi-hat hits on beat 4 the most pronounced, as a limited total number of drums and cymbals is brought to bear in this song while Morris follows a repetitive hypermetrical pattern of successive strikes with limited variation. All four functional layers are disposed and well-balanced. The guitar makes the principal contribution to the harmonic fill layer but also contributes to the melodic layer by means of para-melody while in its contribution to the harmonic fill layer it feels as if it enriches, compliments, fills out and fills in more than takes over.

In terms of the soundbox, Hook's bass guitar enters slightly off center, midway between bottom and center, and slightly more to the left, while Morris's drums and cymbals enter slightly lower than Hook's bass guitar, slightly more to the right, and with the hi-hat sounding slightly higher than the bass drum and the snare drum. Hook's bass guitar also feels slightly closer to the front than Morris's drums and cymbals. Sumner's guitar is positioned higher in the soundbox, to both sides, slightly more to the right at first although this does shift over the course of the song with Sumner's guitar sounding alternately from the left and from the right. Sumner's guitar also moves somewhat up and down closer to the center and to the top, but especially to the center while remaining further back overall from the front of the soundbox than either the bass guitar or the drums, especially the bass guitar. For much of the song Sumner's guitar is nevertheless closer to the center, albeit on the sides, than is often otherwise the case in Joy Division songs. Ian Curtis's vocal comes from dead center, and is positioned close to the front, while seeming to resonate across the full range of a slightly extended central circular space, and toward the end of the song Curtis's vocal feels as if it presses against the edges of this space, both upward and to each side. The soundbox in "A Means to and End" feels fully occupied while allowing limited but precise movements around each of a series of distinct positionings.

Taking these dimensions of instrumentation into account, "A Means to an End" need not reference a case of individual disappointment, disillusionment, and disenchantment, but could reference a group experiencing and responding to the same, and the song manifests some degree of protest and resistance versus being left victimized, even if it remains unclear how to push beyond current confines in order to carry this protest and resistance further forward. To take another hypothetical example, the song makes sense in connection with what happens when a community, such as let's say Rallin, is betrayed and abandoned by an owner of a sports team, let's say the Rallin Rovers, moving the franchise out of the community and thereby severing the Rovers' long-term association with Rallin. The Rovers have played a pivotal role in the local economy and culture for multiple successive generations and long comprised a major source of collective identity, cohesion, and pride among the residents of Rallin. These people, and especially the most devout and passionate fans of the Rovers, feel betrayed by the owner, as they looked to and trusted in the team, believing its owners and managers valued the association between the Rovers and Rallin as much as they did, and believing that they were united together, fighting side by side, pursuing common goals and common dreams–i.e., that the Rovers and the team's players were friends of the community and its citizens, and that they were in fact a united 'family'. But the citizens of Rallin, including the most devout and passionate fans of the Rovers living in Rallin, have now been forced to recognize the ownership of the Rovers never shared such a mutual commitment. As much as the Rovers have long felt to the people of Rallin as if they were Rallin's team, belonging to the city and its residents, in fact, legally and practically at least, that is not so, and never has been.

"A Means to an End" remains largely consistent in terms of loudness while no one of the principal instruments is ever all that much softer or louder in the mix than any of the others–resulting in a balanced sound in terms of relative volume. "A Means to an End" does not begin softly and subsequently increase in volume, as in this song the entrance of each successive instrument does not contribute a jolt of increased loudness. Rises in pitch feel as if they combine with at least slight increases in volume, but that is deceptive. The vocal feels as if it increases slightly in volume when rising in pitch, and the guitar also feels as it does so as well in higher pitched sequences along with what it contributes during the bridge passage. But what loudness contributes in terms of meaning potential is the suggestion that the protagonist in the song, the 'I' of the lyrics, remains faithful to the commitment that had seemingly been well established and long followed, even after the 'you' of the lyrics has abandoned this or shown that the you never really maintained this same commitment.

The rhythm in "A Means to an End" supports much the same suggestion, as this too is consistent with little variation. The basic kit pattern is initiated, established, and scrupulously reiterated from beginning to right near the end, right before the final slowing down to an ultimate abrupt stop. The beat is tight except with the hi-hat that feels as if it slides as it strikes, or slides into its strike. The regularity of other lines contributed from the other instruments further reinforces a combined sense that the song as a whole follows a consistent rhythm. The time signature is 4/4 with a 1and2and3and4and pattern of notes and chords the most common, especially as initiated and perpetuated by the bass guitar. The tempo is 130 BPM, making this song slower than average for Joy Division. Taken together, this time signature and tempo suggest a pattern of movement between the martial and the funereal, as well as between the restless and the contained.

"A Means to an End" can be and has been transposed, or modulated, to many different keys for guitar and keyboard, but here sounds as if played in a minor key, possibly A minor. In terms of patterns of pitch movement, working with this song in A minor, the bass guitar travels back and forth between A10 to G12 for two measures, then A9 and G7 for two measures in what I will designate 'riff 1'; the bass guitar travels across D5 for one measure, then between A9 for half a measure and A8 for half a measure in what I will designate 'riff 2'; and the bass guitar travels across A5 to A7 for 1/16th of a measure then across A7 for the rest of the measure, then across A5 for the next measure, then A0 for the following measure, and then following an opening eighth note rest between A7 and G9 for the rest of the measure in what I will designated 'riff 3'. These riffs show up in the song as follows: Riff 1 X 4 [Instrumental Opening]; Riff 2 X3 then Riff 1 [Verse 1]; Riff 1 then Riff 2 X3 then Riff 1 X3 [Verse 2]; Riff 3 X4 then Riff 2 then Riff 1 [Instrumental Bridge]; Riff 2 X3 then Riff 1 X2 [Verse 3]; and then Riff 1 X3 then Riff 3 X2 [Instrumental Closing]. According to more than one prominent transcription, the guitar moves between D5 and D7 and A7, rises to a ringing high E0 and B0, and falls to a simultaneous low E0 and A2, and then repeats. Next, with the verse, the guitar simultaneously plays E3 and A5 for one measure and then E2 and A4 for half a measure followed by E1 and A3 for half a measure. Then the guitar returns to reiterate the pattern and repeats all of what has proceeded so far. With the bridge the guitar plays an E12, A14, and D14 chord followed by an E10, A12 and D12 chord followed by an E5, A7, and D7 chord, followed by an E10, A12, and D12 chord, followed by an E5, A7, and D7 chord, followed by an E12, A14, D14, and G13 chord, followed by an E12, A14, and D14 chord, followed by an E10, A12, and D12 chord, followed by an E5, A7, and D7 chord, followed by an E12, A14, D14, and G13 chord. Then a 'guitar solo' portion of the bridge moves between G7 and G9 and between D7 and G9. And after that the guitar returns to earlier patterns.

What we have here, in sum, is a denser array of sounds in the bridge along with an overall repeated tendency to move back and forth between two or across three notes or chords and at most four chords within a measure as well as a recurrent strumming of one note or chord across a measure, once again generally following a 1and2and3and4and strumming pattern. Movements in pitch tend to stay close to the same pitch for pronounced durations, then rise in pitch, and then fall further in pitch.

As best I can determine, making use of available tabs for graphically representing what happens in as well as how to play this song, it seems like what is most distinctive about Morris's drumming pattern throughout the song is an open, loose, and hard hi-hat strike at the end of measures. In terms of Curtis's vocal, meanwhile, this tends to follow a circumscribed interval at the beginning of lines with a subsequent rise in pitch and then a falling again near the end, especially notably in the refrain.

Overall, patterns of stasis and movement in pitch, in "A Means to an End," suggest an of effort to make a point precisely, forcefully, clearly, and succinctly, in order to drive the point home, to emphasize where it feels as if the protagonist has–and has not–traveled as a result of what 'he' recounts and as a result of where 'he' travels yet further in the course of this recounting.

Curtis's vocal delivery is clear, rich, deep, strong, and resonant, with a tendency to glide and linger at end of phrases and especially lines. Curtis's range in the course of the song covers approximately an octave but this is not attempted all at once. His vocal sounds as if it aligns with the established rhythm neatly and precisely while his pitches are regular and consistent. Curtis's voice conveys something of an elegiac tone, almost funereal, a hardened to resigned form of lamentation meets accusation, but even more simply a suggestion of attesting to while simultaneously registering sadness concerning what he is attesting to and what has transpired. I hear some slightly lingering longing for what could have been but wasn't, yet largely Curtis's delivery such such longing has passed. Words are enunciated so they are clearly and precisely identifiable, and it does seem like Curtis's voice comes from further down in his body, not just emanating from his throat and his mouth, although in this song he definitely sounds as if he is deliberately darkening the timbre through manipulation of his throat. Curtis's overall attitude toward the words he is singing and the subject of these words feels more somber than angry, with sadness and regret more pronounced than bitterness and spleen.

Sumner's guitar conveys the widest range of timbres, including occasional elements of squeakiness verging upon the discordant and dissonant, with a somewhat harsher edge than the timbre of the bass guitar, and the guitar sounds reverberate longer and in messier tones than do those of the bass guitar. Occasionally we also hear the guitar sounding as if sending out flares, as well as alternating between timbres suggestive of lightly chugging and of slightly soaring. It seems plausible these different timbres correspond to distinct emotions within the affective complex of the song–some registering resolution and persistence, some resignation and acceptance, some sadness and lament, and some bitterness and resentment.

Because "Means to and End" is so regular and consistent, it is easy to follow along with, and to identify in particular with the melody, through its variations, starting with the bass guitar, shifting to the vocal, and complimented by the guitar, as well as with the drum kit as the latter defines and executes the beat. In so identifying it can feel oddly akin to marching up, down, and around in a confined space. But these sound elements also convey a feeling of forcefully imprinting an indelible impression. This in turn emanates from drawing a sharp contrast between what 'I' in the past imagined its relationship with 'you' to be versus what 'I' now recognizes that relationship to have been, and where 'you', 'I', and 'you' and 'I' have now ended up.

Early on the music as persona and I as a listener anticipate persistence and recurrence, as well as movement to some kind of climax, along with some kind of dissolution and suspension of tension at the end. The music as persona feels as if it anticipates these reflections will come to an end before it becomes decisively clear where to go, and how to proceed, from here, as well as what might yet be possible that is also desirable.

Although the song expresses deep sadness it nonetheless does also recall past idealistic enthusiasm. The song expresses a feeling as if the music as persona is at present operating from within a tightly enclosed space, but not necessarily trapped, yet again with nowhere clear to proceed outside or beyond this space even as the commitment to what the 'I' believed it shared with the 'you' remains for the 'I'.

The music as persona seems here to be reporting and reflecting on the results of an analysis it has completed prior to the song, while this analysis prompts me, as a listener, to analyze to what extent the 'you' here might be 'me' and to what extent have I participant within the same kind or a similar kind of relationship myself, in the position of either 'I' or 'you'.

In terms of comparable situations, again using hypothetical examples, one possibility is what happens, in an individual fan's or a community of fans' relationship with a sports team, that does not involve the team moving out of its erstwhile home city, but otherwise leaving the fans and the community feeling betrayed, because, for example, ownership raises ticket levels to the point where it is difficult for those who are not wealthy to attend games live, or where it forces followers to pay for expensive subscriptions to obtain premium broadcast access to games, or where the team does not spend sufficient money to do well, in competition, and makes decisions concerning signing and resigning, or trading, players in accord with costs savings rather in concern with winning, including by allowing fan favorites to leave the team or by trading these players away.

Another, similar, connection follows from players with whom fans and the community have developed strong bonds deciding they wish to leave and play for another team, even when their contract is not yet up and even when their current team provides ample opportunity, if they stay, to do well in competition. A devout fan, Nick for instance, has known about Mark since Mark grew up in the community of Strebahn and was a star player at the youth league level. Back then Mark repeatedly proclaimed his dream was to play professionally for the Strebahn Strikers, and he did achieve this goal. Yet now Mark leaves the Strikers right as they are on the edge of breaking through as a top tier team and competing for the championship. Mark leaves to play instead for a richer team in a larger city, despite having frequently declared his foremost goal is to win a championship with the Strikers for the community of Strebhan and all fans of the Strikers. Fans like Nick and the city of Strebahn feel they have been treated as a means to an end, not an end itself, because despite looking to and trusting in Mark, and seeming to be committed to fighting together, together pursuing a shared goal, it turns out Mark never maintained this same commitment.

Other reasonable associations involve the experience of betrayal that citizens of a community, of a society, and of a nation feel when in critical need, and especially in a time of major crisis, as the government is unprepared or underprepared to help, effectively allowing a great many people to suffer without adequate relief. This can happen in response to major storms, such as hurricanes, aggravated by the impact of climate change, or in response to pandemics, such as COVID. The Grenfell Tower disaster revealed that building owners and contractors, as well as designers of building materials and state agencies responsible for regulating these materials in the ostensible interest of public safety, all betrayed the trust of those who lived in this building, because the latter were being forced to live, and die, in a building that was unsafe. Similar examples occur in many other situations where corporations cut corners, or deliberately sell shoddy materials or engage in shoddy practices of construction and implementation, while the state does not call them to account, and even facilitates these corporations getting away with this–again, to the point of getting away with murder. People feel betrayed when corporations they have implicitly trusted manufacture and market goods or design and promote services that are incapable of doing what they claim these are capable of doing, and which cause damage to health and well-being as well as lead people to waste money paying for damaged goods and delinquent services. People likewise feel betrayed when police services they have implicitly trusted engage in systemically racist practices against people like them and their communities, causing them harm and putting them at risk, rather than protecting their safety.

Let's consider some further hypothetical examples, beginning with Monica. Monica worked hard for a great many years, earning just enough to get buy and take care of her family at slightly above poverty level, always paying her taxes, always obeying the law, and always 'playing by the

410

rules'. Monica feels betrayed when she loses her job, through no fault of her own, and it becomes exceedingly difficult to obtain financial support, from the state, during her term of unemployment and even less help in jobseeking. Monica finds, to her chagrin, not only that these resources are hard to access and take too long to kick in (if available at all), but also that she is treated as a scrounger, a skiver, someone who it seems it is official policy to further discourage and humiliate.

Monica's friend Wanda likewise feels betrayed because her disability is the result of an injury on her job, but Wanda cannot afford to sue for recompense, while the company denies it had anything to do with her injury. This injury, what's more, leads to Wanda losing her job, yet Wanda struggles to obtain disability benefits. What makes this situation all the worse for Wanda is she is forced over and over again to struggle to prove how disabled she is and that because of her disability she cannot perform many prospective future jobs. Social service officials treats her as suspect, as someone who must be faking or exaggerating her disability. Wanda, like Monica, thought the welfare state, which she also supported through her taxes, and by being a responsible citizen, existed to help people like her, in need, but it now seems to Wanda as if it primarily exists to punish her for her condition, treating her as if she is somehow guilty of having caused her current straits in order to 'trick the system'.

Jordan, meanwhile, is in a comparable plight because he has temporarily lost his job, and despite government relief support, is still falling steadily further and further behind in paying his bills, including his rent, with his landlord ready to evict him. Other companies are ready to dispossess him of material possessions he is paying for on installment, including his car, which he needs to use to find a new or at least a transitional job, and likely to commute to and from a new job once he has secured one. Jordan keeps trying, but the only job offers he is getting pay far below what he was previously making, and he already paid half of his monthly wages on rent, before losing his immediately preceding job, while too many prospective employers tell him he is either underqualified or overqualified. Jordan feels betrayed and let down by the state, and the larger society, with no one seemingly wanting to help him do what he needs to get back on his feet, but instead everyone appearing to work together to push and pin him down all the further. Jordan feels like companies he has worked for, politicians he has voted for, and companies he has bought and paid for goods and services from, as well as his landlord, are treating him entirely as a means to an end and not as an end in himself.

Many people expect elected officials to lead the way in taking care of members of communities experiencing acute needs, especially in times of crisis, and feel betrayed when it seems those elected and serving in government office did say one thing to get elected and are now doing something entirely different after they have been elected. This is the case when elected government officials suggest they can do little to help people they promised to help, or otherwise come across as unconcerned, uninterested, unresponsive, out of touch, self-serving, and unaccountable, other than to a wealthy elite. Frank, for example, has experienced a major crisis in his family, following a rapid succession of tragically unfortunate major health problems, and is looking for assistance from the state, or through the state, but is repeatedly advised by state officials that he and his family do not quality for available forms of assistance, and that he should instead turn to private charity, including privately initiated fundraisers. Frank feels betrayed.

Louise feels the same as austerity budget cuts have devastated her community, with few public facilities open and accessible nearby any more, including those that meet her health and social care needs, and not even erstwhile free spaces–public libraries and neighborhood recreational centers. Public transit has also been drastically reduced. At the schools in her community, Louise's children are forced into larger and larger classes with more limited and antiquated class materials, while curricular offerings are being eliminated–notably art, music, theater and dance, foreign languages, and physical education.

Frank and Louise are also disturbed that their national government is spying on it own citizens, amassing huge collections of data on people who have broken no laws and who represent no actual threat to 'national security', while large private corporations are harvesting and selling massive amounts of data concerned with individuals' internet search histories, as well as by seeking to manipulate people into buying products they otherwise would not, and do not need, on account of information they have obtained about people's internet search interests and preferences. Frank and Louise are only two among many who feel betrayed by their nation state, and by these corporations, on account of this kind of intrusion and manipulation.

Jill feels betrayed because she has learned that the community activist organization she has invested considerable time, effort, care, and even money toward supporting has been infiltrated by state agents who have not only secretly gathered information about the organization and its members but also plotted to subvert and sabotage the organization from within, and in particular by fomenting artificial tensions and divisions among members. Jill feels betrayed because this organization has been working on behalf of social groups who all too often experience far more injustice than justice within existing society, and because Jill only wants her nation to live up to its express ideals, in practice, fairly and equitably. Yet Jill and this organization have been treated like enemies in war–as 'the enemy within'.

Brock is upset, and feels betrayed, because he recognizes how he, family members, and friends have all been deceived, and in effect treated as fodder for exploitation as opposed to being treated as people who maintain intrinsic dignity and worth, by multiple companies that have advertised and marketed products that have proven not only dangerous and unhealthy. It turns out these companies knew this was the case all along, while not admitting it and pretending otherwise. It also turns out that these companies have caused extensive environmental pollution and other environmental damage in producing the goods they sell, which, once again, these companies have worked assiduously to conceal and deny.

Margaret is upset that her daughter Stephanie and her son Luke have both been harmfully influenced by widespread, even pervasive commercial advertising that plays on weaknesses, insecurities, and sensitivities, in relation to body image, with both of her children developing serious eating disorders because both of them have felt their physical shape fell short of the ideal they encountered in prominent advertising imagery.

Marshall agreed to a second mortgage to refinance his home, at what seemed like a welcome rate, but did not understand this rate was deceptive, and was not in fact 'the real rate', while the second mortgage also required that he pay multiple substantial fees he didn't recognize or fully understand when he signed the agreement. Marshall has been offered this mortgage by a financial lender who recognized Marshall would not be able to pay back what he has been leant, but plans simply to bundle Marshall's loan and a number of others like it into a package to sell off to someone else who will then in turn do the same through a lengthy chain of subsequent sellers and buyers. When Marshall is forced into bankruptcy and has to give up his home and move into a small shared apartment, he feels betrayed, especially since the company that offered him the second mortgage seemed so solicitous, so warm, and so friendly.

Robin, meanwhile, has found herself in a comparable position because she has spent a large amount of money on a service that has not provided her anything approaching what she was promised but, without realizing it, has signed away her rights to sue for compensation, or remediation, and is left with no option but the company-controlled arbitration process that sides in favor of the company more than 95% of the time. Robin feels betrayed and not just by this company, but also by her elected representatives in government who have failed to impose regulations preventing or at least restricting this kind of corporate (mal)practice.

Natasha has long idolized a celebrity performing artist, a musician and actor, whose most prominent personae in his public appearances have suggested he is a gentle, kind, humble, sensitive, sweet, and caring person. Many of his leading roles in movies and on TV as well as many of his songs and records, have been Natasha's favorites, which she has turned to over and over again, and frequently touted to numerous others. But Natasha has just learned that this same celebrity performer is and long has been extremely difficult for others to work with, hated by co-workers on sets and in locations as well as within bands, and frequently engages in overtly abusive behavior versus co-workers, deliberately denigrating and humiliating them. What's worse, this celebrity performer, let's call him Ron, also appears to be guilty of sexual harassment and abuse within and beyond the workplace, with multiple women now accusing him of rape and two former girlfriends accusing him of committing serious domestic violence against them while they were living with him. Natasha feels devastatingly betrayed by Ron–deeply disappointed, disillusioned, and disenchanted–and shudders to think how often she felt the two were alike, sharing a common sensibility.

Lateesha is an adjunct faculty member at a university. She has strived hard to be generous, patient, flexible, and accommodating to all her students, including to the most needy and demanding, and to those who have proven most skeptical to resistant to learning from her, but she is teaching subject matter requiring, as a matter of intellectual honesty and ethical integrity, that she and her classes directly confront sensitive issues subject to considerable controversy. Lateesha believes it is crucially important that she, and her students, engage these issues, these conversations and debates, taking the time and investing the effort to carefully consider who and what is involved, when and where, and how and why. She believes in fostering engaged, critical citizens by way of her teaching, and while she refuses to pretend she is neutrally disinterested, and is open and honest about where she stands, makes emphatically clear again and again that what she is interested in, from her students, is not *what* positions they align with and support on any of these issues but *how* well they are able accurately to represent and thoughtfully to contend with those with whom they do not agree. Yet Lateesha is a young Black woman, who is also open about her lesbian identity, and about experiences she has had with serious issues of physical and mental health, employed on a one-year contract with no guarantee or renewal. Lateesha is teaching considerably more credit hours–primarily consisting of large, lower-level, and writing-intensive classes–in order to be considered 'full-time' than do tenure-line colleagues in her same department, while her adjunct status means she has to submit to thorough performance reviews every semester, including multiple observation visits to her classes from tenured faculty each semester as well. Colleagues who observe Lateesha teach express admiration for how impressively organized and prepared she is, as well as how thoughtfully and sensitively she conducts class discussions, welcoming and respecting a diversity of views. Tenured colleagues also find her teaching materials demonstrate considerable mastery of the field as well as a marked ingenuity in finding ways to make this accessible for first and second year university students. But, nevertheless, Lateesha's student evaluations of instruction report lower average scores on so-called 'objective' criteria for assessment, with a larger than average number of students disagreeing or strongly disagreeing that Lateesha explained assignments and criteria for evaluating assignments clearly, that her approaches to teaching the course material helped them better understand it and incorporated a useful variety of methods, and that she treated everyone in the class with respect. Student comments amplify this pushback in terms that some members of the Department Personnel Committee recognize exemplify coded forms of racism, sexism, homophobia, ableism, and ageism, but other senior colleagues of Lateesha do not recognize–and refuse to recognize–this. Lateesha knows she put in a great deal of thought and care into explaining precisely how she designed assignments, and why, as well as precisely what their aims and benefits were, for students, along with precisely how she would be evaluating student work in response to these assignments as well as why so. And Lateesha also knows she tried to incorporate different classroom practices, and modes of engagement, every week, welcoming student input on what was working and what was not, while bending over backwards to be fair and respectful, in particular, to those who evinced the greatest skepticism and even hostility toward her, and versus what they at least imagined her to represent. But it doesn't matter: as much as Lateesha tries to make a case for herself, and as much as tenured colleagues appreciate other elements of her performance review, they decide they cannot recommend renewing her contract because of the lower than average scores and the greater than average number of negative comments in her student evaluations of instruction. Lateesha feels betrayed by the students, but even more by her colleagues among the tenured faculty and by the department and the institution. She feels she was exploited and then quickly discarded when it became inconvenient and uncomfortable to support her.

Lateesha's example illustrates one way faculty members can and do feel betrayed in doing their jobs, including in doing them well, by their students and by their colleagues, where they feel like their commitment is not matched by those with whom they are working, despite these others initially claiming or otherwise feigning to do so, and where such faculty members feel as if they have been treated as a means to an end and not as an end in themselves. Similar feelings follow when students cheat, or do not show up to class, or do not give back anywhere near the equivalent to what the teacher gives in terms of time and effort and care and seriousness, or when students act in ways that are otherwise lazy or indifferent, or where they shirk their share of responsibility that the class demands of everyone for it to succeed at its best, notably as part of group and team projects. Yet students also can and do feel comparably betrayed, treated as mere means to an end and not ends in themselves, by teachers. When teachers arbitrarily and capriciously change standards for evaluation and expectation without justification, and when they come down harder on some individuals because they don't seem to like or trust them–where they have prejudged these students, including as supposedly needing or requiring harsher treatment in order to learn effectively at all–then students can and do feel used and abused.

Jeremy felt this way when he mustered the courage to approach a teacher to ask for an extension on a project because he had been experiencing a period of severe depression, a long-running tendency for him, but which he hates to admit to others, and feels badly about doing so when he does because he feels as if he is asking for special treatment and also admitting in so doing that he is someone who is lesser and deficient in terms of his worth. But Jeremy proceeded anyway because he respected and admired his teacher and wanted to be open and honest with her, while he also wanted to find any possible way he could to complete the assignment and give it the best he possibly could, under difficult circumstances for him. However, in meeting with this teacher and explaining his situation, Jeremy was shocked and disturbed, feeling let down and betrayed, when the teacher coldly dismissed his depression was 'not an acceptable excuse' and refused to consider any workaround the assigned deadline, other than to propose if Jeremy's condition was that serious he should probably just withdraw for the semester and not return until he had 'got himself under control'.

As with every preceding hypothetical example I've introduced in this section of this chapter, and elsewhere in this chapter as well, Jeremy's experience is a composite of what multiple real people I have known have actually experienced themselves. I've also known a disturbing number of teachers who have sarcastically mocked or otherwise relentlessly derided their students' supposed ignorance, or indifference, or laziness, or lack of ability, or lack of commitment, without justification–usually as a result of prejudging these students and by assuming the worst without needing to do so. Other instances I've encountered in which teachers have left students feeling betrayed, feeling used and abused, have happened when teachers have withdrawn offers they previously made for some students to work closely with them on independent projects and then instead offered the same opportunities to other students, as well as when teachers have at first agreed to write letters of recommendation and then changed their mind–and even when teachers went ahead and wrote negative letters of recommendation for students without telling these students ahead of time that this is what they would be doing, not offering these students the chance to seek more favorable letters of recommendation from other faculty members instead.

It can feel like taboo to openly share experience of having overestimated and overinvested in another. It can feel taboo to admit much of one's life has been caught up in the pursuit of what seemed to be one thing and turned out to be something much different, and, what's more, something seriously disappointing, disillusioning, and disenchanting. It can feel taboo to claim much of one's life has been squandered due to someone else's exploitation of one's investment and trust in that other. The resemblance of "A Means to an End" to a cross between a martial and a funereal song in itself suggests a potential taboo or an least uncomfortable combination.

In terms of invisibility, intangibility, and ephemerality, the 'you' of the lyrics in "A Means to an End" feels invisible, intangible, and ephemeral, even as the ostensible addressee of these lyrics, while the same also seems to characterize where the relationship between the 'I' and the 'you' has ended up. From the present vantage point it seems what is further invisible, intangible, and ephemeral are the goals, the hopes, the dreams, the ambitions, and the aspirations the 'I' long believed constituted the crux of this relationship, as well as what it felt like engaged directly together in pursuit of the same, especially with that now seemingly, in retrospect, not truly to have been what it then seemed to be.

"A Means to an End" feels as if it is addressing me from a location where I am invited to join in registering and reflecting on an experience of great disappointment and disillusionment, on an experience of disenchanted idealism. If I am 'you', on the other hand, I am enormously challenged–to find some way to make up for what seems beyond the possibility of making up for, to try, desperately, to counter the I's profound disappointment in me. The song feels like it summons me to recognize moments in my own life-experience of deep disappointment and disillusionment, and of seeming hopelessness, and yet to recognize as well how I was able to pick up, move on, keep going, and even go forward.

Sometimes I have experienced comparable feelings when encountering fellow teachers, or administrators, or other college and university staff who have taken the position that 'our students' simply are not capable of or in need of X, Y, or Z, unlike students at some supposedly superior campus, and that we cannot and should not expect all that much from them or need not offer all that much to them. This position is most dangerous among high-level administrative and elected officials who dismiss the value of a liberal arts education–especially in the humanities, the arts, and the social scientists–for any other than the wealthiest of students, while also claiming that most students cannot handle being presented with all that many choices in terms of what to study, and what to concentrate in, but instead need to be corralled into a limited array of concentrations. I experience comparable feelings when it seems like the university has come to operate like a for-profit business more concerned with manufacturing a public relations image of supposed success than enabling true learning and growth, when it is more concerned with buildings than with people, and when it pays lip service to rather than doing the hard required to make equity, diversity, and inclusion real and substantial. I experienced comparable feelings as well when members of 'university communities' face prejudice, discrimination, and hostility on account of historical oppressed forms of social identity. I experience comparable feelings, what's more, when the same people are not taken seriously and even criticized for 'complaining too much', for being 'troublemakers', for being 'too angry' or otherwise 'too emotional'. All of these instances feel to me like betrayals of what had, ostensibly, represented a shared mission.

"A Means to an End" is concerned with mediation insofar as this involves mediation between past and present, between a past idealism and a present disenchanted idealism, between in the past looking to, putting trust in, and sharing closely with another versus in the present experiencing disappointment and disillusionment concerning that other and what one's relationship with that other has meant and to where it has led. The song is concerned with mediation between ambition and aspiration on the one hand versus what is actually possible and what actually does happen on the other hand. Yet the song is also a manifestation of not being ready, at least not yet, to altogether give up the fight, as the narrator-protagonist announces 'he' is 'committed still' and is 'turning to go', even if how he will now actualize that commitment and in going where remains unclear. Even as "A Means to an End" attests to how friend can become foe, solidarity can become betrayal, hope can become despair, and movement can become stasis, tension remains unresolved. The song reaches the point of being nearly ready to give up struggling any further, yet ultimately refuses to do so. And despite focusing on disappointment, disillusionment, and disenchantment, "A Means to an End" also apotheosizes the powerful appeal of solidarity and comradeship by way of emphasizing the starkness of the devastation that is felt when solidarity and comradeship is betrayed. The song continues to attest to the need for such bonds while emphasizing how difficult it is to achieve and sustain them. "A Means to an End" exemplifies assumption of responsibility to speak the truth, openly, honestly, forthrightly, even when it hurts to do so, hurts badly, and when one feels vulnerable and damaged by what one is attesting to as well as by the need to attest to it.

"A Means to an End" makes sense in reflecting on a relationship that felt for a long time like a relationship among intimates that turns out to have represented a relationship among strangers, and this raises the related challenge of how difficult it can be to truly know and genuinely connect with another. If 'I' and 'you' are interpreted as representing dimensions of the one self, this song could also be interpreted as expressing profound alienation not so much from but rather *from within* one's self.

In addition, and to close, when people are used and abused as means to an end, and cruelly led to imagine the opposite for a long time while investing an enormous amount of themselves into what is using and abusing them, this is suggestive of fascist demagogues who develop cult followings among masses of people they exploit and betray.

Nine

"Love Will Tear Us Apart" I find daunting to write about–the most famous and widely covered Joy Division song, a great pop song and ready chart-topping single, and one that many commentators, including Deborah Curtis herself, have associated with difficulties Ian and Deborah Curtis experienced in their marriage, as well as the tensions created by Ian Curtis's simultaneous relationships with Deborah Curtis and Annik Honore. Many interpretations conceive of the song as focused on the strain in a relationship between two individuals, in a romantic-sexual relationship, such as a marriage, although I suggest the song, starting with the title and the lyrics, opens up room for other viable interpretations as well.

To begin with the title, what has undoubtedly struck many is how this title seems, at first, counterintuitive, as love is ideally at least what is supposed to bring and keep people together–colleagues of mine have even joked with me that "Love Will Tear Us Apart" represents the flip side of the Captain and Tenille's "Love Will Keep Us Together." Yet, when we think about it, it is easy to recognize many ways love can and does tear people apart. Throughout human history love has often been conceived as a kind of madness that involves people feeling and acting excessively, obsessively, and irrationally–putting themselves and others, including those they love, at risk, as a result. Love, in other words, can lead people to feel and act in ways that endanger their own and others' well-being. Love, what's more, can be overwhelmingly distracting of concentration and as such can run counter to productivity. Love can be overpowering, for both the one who loves and the one who is loved. Love can tear apart when people involved in a relationship do not feel, or do not continue to feel, the same equally intense devotion to and passion for each other. Love can tear apart when someone feels pulled in multiple, potentially incompatible or at least normatively unacceptable directions because of loving too many people, or too many other things, all at once, and is thereby unable to give all of what is needed to simultaneously sustain a strong and lasting connection in all of these directions, or even in any one of them. Love can be so extreme that it can become possessive, jealous, suspicious, and even smothering, isolating, and abusive. Love can be what tears people apart when they need to move in different directions from each other yet because of the intensity of the love they experience with and for each other this becomes extremely painful to do. Love can tear people apart when they worry to an anxious extreme about those they love, and about potential harm that might befall those they love. Love can tear people apart when they give enormously of themselves to people or things they love to the extent that they exhaust themselves of the capacity to do much of anything else–or to be, to identify as, much of anything else. Love can tear apart because it can lead people to feel they need to be more critical of those they love than others because they care that much–even that, with those they love, they need 'to be cruel to be kind'. Love can tear apart because when the beloved moves or passes away, it feels, to the lover, as if they are torn apart. Different kinds and degrees of love can be incompatible or grow to be incompatible, and thus tear apart, while love, because it can be experienced as an extremely powerful emotion, can readily overlap and fuse with other extremely powerful emotions, including hate. Love can tear apart because the word is used in practice in so many ways for so many different kinds of things, so many different kinds of experiences, that people feel one or another kinds of attraction to or likeness for, which can lead to misperceptions and misunderstandings. Think about all these common expressions of 'love': 'I love your smile', "I love that outfit', 'I love that show', 'I love that flavor of ice cream', 'I love that sunset', 'I love that smell', 'I love to take long walks', 'I love running on a warm and sunny day', 'I love playing basketball with Maya and Elin', 'I love getting together and making plans over coffee', 'I love her accent', 'I love the first snowfall of the season', 'I love Halloween', 'I love a good night's sleep', 'I love that musician', 'I love that album', and 'I love that song'.

Love has long been recognized as of preeminent spiritual and religions value. For instance, in *I Corinthians 13* of *The Bible* (New King James edition), a passage which has influenced and inspired many non-Christians as well as Christians, love is extolled as follows:

Though I speak with the tongues of men and of angels, but have not love, I have become sounding brass or a clanging cymbal. And though I have the gift of prophecy, and understand all mysteries and all knowledge, and though I have all faith, so that I could remove mountains, but have not love, I am nothing. And though I bestow all my goods to feed the poor, and though I give my body to be burned, but have not love, it profits me nothing.

Love suffers long and is kind; love does not envy; love does not parade itself, is not puffed up; does not behave rudely, does not seek its own, is not provoked, thinks no evil; does not rejoice in iniquity, but rejoices in the truth; bears all things, believes all things, hopes all things, endures all things.

Love never fails. But whether there are prophecies, they will fail; whether there are tongues, they will cease; whether there is knowledge, it will vanish away. For we know in part and we prophesy in part. But when that which is perfect has come, then that which is in part will be done away.

When I was a child, I spoke as a child, I understood as a child, I thought as a child; but when I became a man, I put away childish things. For now we see in a mirror, dimly, but then face to face. Now I know in part, but then I shall know just as I also am known.

And now abide faith, hope, love, these three; but the greatest of these is love.

I well recall how Jo Clifford cited this passage in the program notes for the debut, in March 2010, of her play, *Every One*, a fantastic drama concerned with love, death, and grief, which I enjoyed the tremendous good fortune to catch at its Royal Lyceum Theatre Edinburgh premiere. I've taught this play in many Introduction to Critical Studies classes since, where students have also drawn upon it as source and stimulus for plays they have composed, produced, and performed. As allusion to *Every One* suggests, love can feel the most tearing in relation to the death of someone one loves, and this suggests, logically as well, that love can feel comparably tearing with the death of a relationship, previously founded and built on love. Love maintains the same preeminent place within all leading world religions, and among many critical theorists, with Marxist philosopher Alain Badiou one prominent example–Badiou has written frequently extolling love, including in his book *In Praise of Love.*

I myself quoted philosopher Georg Wilhelm Friedrich Hegel, from his *Philosophy of Right,* in my statement at my wedding ceremony on 17 June 2000, at the Unitarian Universalist church in Eau Claire:

Love means in general terms the consciousness of my unity with another, so that I am not in selfish isolation but win my self-consciousness only as the renunciation of my independence and through knowing myself as the unity of myself with another and of the other with me . . . The first moment in love is that I do not wish to be a self-subsistent and independent person and [recognize] that, if I were, then I would feel defective and incomplete. The second moment is that I find myself in another person, that I count for something in the other, while the other in turn comes to count for something in me. Love therefore is the most tremendous contradiction; the Understanding cannot resolve it.

As I added, at that time, the kind of love Hegel here discusses involves both the losing and gaining of an independent identity: at one level love means living for another and ceasing to be preoccupied with oneself and one's own interests, but at the same time this relationship gives one a fuller and deeper sense of identity in so far as this is objectified and confirmed by the other person.

What do the lyrics of "Love Will Tear Us Apart" communicate concerning love, and how it can and does 'tear us apart'? Let's starting with the first stanza: "When routine bites hard/And ambitions are low/And resentment rides high/But emotions won't go/And we're changing our ways, taking different roads." 'Routine biting hard' feels painful and suggests routine that is or has become oppressive. 'And ambitions are low' suggests, moreover, a situation in which the force required to overcome hard-biting routine is lacking or deficient. 'And resentment rides high' implies what force remains is exhausted elsewhere and otherwise–on resentment. 'But emotions won't grow' suggests whoever the narrator-protagonist is referencing is experiencing great difficulty transforming the current state of the relationship by infusing it with a renewed positive energy. This is seemingly yet further the case when we consider the final line of the first stanza, suggesting those involved in a relationship are moving in different directions, are each changing 'their ways' and pushing off along different paths, no longer united, perhaps no longer compatible. It seems plausible to imagine the first stanza references people still staying in a relationship even as it is no longer working. Those involved in this love relationship have changed, have become different from and versus each other, and their divergences have caused considerable tension. Although efforts have been made to address these divergences, these efforts have not succeeded. Those involved in the love relationship continue together, despite their growing alienation from each other, because they can't muster the will to end the relationship. Perhaps this is due being worn down due to how draining the stress and strain involved in this relationship has become. But more likely this is because it is hard to end the relationship given how much it has meant to those involved, and how much those involved continue to love each other, even as much about their relationship is not–is no longer–working.

Following this opening versa stanza is the first iteration of the chorus: "Then love, love will tear us apart again/Love, love will tear us apart again." Seemingly, it is when all of these pressures upon a relationship build up that loves 'tears' 'us' 'apart again'. Here it is striking the emphasis is not on people involved in a relationship no longer loving each other that leads to this critical point, not on people 'falling out of love with each other' that does this, but rather on love itself as responsible for making this situation what it is, so hard and so painful. Perhaps because love is and has been so strong, and so powerful, it is not easy to accept 'we've become different and are interested in different things so it is only right and necessary that we move on now in different directions'. Perhaps because of the love involved in this relationship it is not easy to identify with the position that 'there's no hard feelings' as the partners to the relationship end the relationship serenely at ease with sincerely wishing each other well as they move away from each other. It is because of the intensity of the love involved that this increasing divergence has been experienced, and is being experienced, as 'tearing'.

The fact that love tears us apart 'again' further suggests that the present moment represents only the latest in a cumulative history of such moments, in which love, as strong and powerful as it was and is, has made it repeatedly difficult for those involved to pursue divergent ends and interests. These are not readily compatible differences; these are differences that tear apart because they pull people toward different priorities, values, ideals, principles, convictions, aspirations, lifestyles, standards of living, aesthetic and cultural affiliations, political and philosophical identifications, and modes of social relating and interrelating.

The second verse stanza reads as follows: "Why is the bedroom so cold?/You've turned away on your side/Is my timing that flawed?/Our respect runs so dry/Yet there's still this appeal that we've kept through our lives." This stanza readily suggests a relationship, between romantic-sexual partners, perhaps a spousal relationship, in which sex is no longer working, perhaps because those involved have become out of sync with each other sexually and perhaps because bitterness, resentment, or 'respect that has run dry' in relation to other dimensions of their relationship with each other, and what they now think and feel about and in relation to each other, makes it difficult to impossible to engage in satisfying sexual relations anymore–while sex cannot, in and of itself, renew the bond between those involved in the relationship. However, the last line is also crucial because it suggests despite the growing alienation the first four lines have, once again, described, the relationship continues to be one those involved value, perhaps even treasure–exercising an 'appeal' they've 'kept through their lives'. This is an appeal they've kept with and part of them, even as they have become increasingly estranged. So as the next iteration of the chorus indicates–"But love, love will tear us apart again/Love, love will tear us apart again"–this becomes a painful tearing, because love is still present, still strong and powerful, and it hurts to experience estrangement from and hostility versus someone one has loved and continues to love, dearly.

Verse stanza three appears to continue in the same time and place as suggested by verse stanza two: "You cry out in your sleep/All my failings exposed/And there's a taste in my mouth/As desperation takes hold/Just that something so good just can't function no more." Within a relationship forged through love, the at least perceived need has emerged for one party to sharply and even unsparingly criticize the other–'all my failings exposed'. Since this appears to happen in response to 'you crying out in your sleep', it may be a result of the narrator-protagonist here recognizing, to 'himself', that 'he' is failing and has failed, because 'he' is hurting and has hurt his partner, who is 'crying out in their sleep', and perhaps this narrator-protagonist feels 'he' cannot comfort 'his' partner because 'he' is responsible for why 'his' partner is crying out. 'The taste in my mouth' is undoubtedly unsavory, perhaps dry and acrid, a physiological manifestation of how painful this experience of estrangement from someone 'he' has loved and continues to love has become, and perhaps because of how much 'he' feels responsible for what has happened. "As desperation takes hold" accentuates how the narrator-protagonist appears to be feeling, as 'he' recognizes no way out, not wanting alienation to worsen further but perceiving no way to stop this from happening, and as a result feeling desperate because "something so good just can't function no more." This relationship has worked well, has felt good, in the past, which makes what has happened to it feel as if it is 'tearing' the narrator-protagonist apart with sadness and grief, and perhaps also with guilt and shame. This in turn yet further explains why the final iteration of the chorus makes sense. "But love, love will tear us apart again/Love, love will tear us apart again/Love, love will tear us apart again/Love, love will tear us apart again": what we have here is a relationship that greatly mattered to those involved, and certainly to the narrator-protagonist, as it is increasingly unraveling, feeling as if it is tearing apart, and tearing out, a significant dimension of whom those involved have become as a result of this relationship they created with each other. They are losing what has felt precious, vital, and even indispensable. This is not a simple and easy moving on in different directions among casual friends, colleagues, or associates; this is a rupture in a relationship that has been perceived, and felt, to be of ultimate importance to those involved.

'Love tearing us apart' often is interpreted as referencing the tearing apart of the relationship itself, so that the two who were together are no longer and are now instead apart, but it could as easily make sense as referencing what happens to each of those involved in a love relationship once it reaches this stage of alienation and antagonism: each partner feels as if they are individually being torn apart. Love is a preeminent mode by which individuals grasp their interdeterminate interconnection with other human beings, where individuals feel as if they are transcending or have transcended boundaries that throw individuals back onto themselves, as isolated monads, as separate entities who remain distant from each other. Love in contrast creates a shared identity that supersedes the sum of the identities of the individuals in love with each other, and where empathy and solidarity are experienced as tangibly real. For alienation and antagonism to set in, in this kind of relationship, can understandably feel as if it is tearing thse involved apart, in Marx's terms, from the human essence, the ensemble of social relations, the human species-being.

Estranged labor, under capitalism, can readily make love relations more difficult to achieve and sustain. This effect follows due not only to how draining of energy estranged labor can prove but also due to how estranged labor can lead to a numbing, and a desensitization, in order to be able to survive, and cope, over a prolonged period of time, that those so estranged carry over into the rest of their lives. Estranged labor also discourages those who experience it routinely from developing more than limited to minimal expectations concerning other areas of their lives, given how hard it can be just to get by in maintaining a bare existence. Estranged labor can discourage people by leading them to believe they possess little of value to offer to others, including as part of love relations. Experiencing a strong sense that not only what one does but also who one is, is out of one's control, is beyond one's capacity significantly to determine, can undermine capacity for love as well as confidence that love may be possible. Likewise, in a social system arising out of a dominant mode of production in which so much continually represents a means to an end and not an end in itself, and pressure is pervasive to always be prepared to compete with others, and, yet further, to exploit what you can from others because they will undoubtedly be striving to do the same with you, makes it further difficult to forge relations in which it becomes possible sufficiently to trust another in order to truly love that person. All of these connections with Marx's *Economic and Philosophic Manuscripts of 1844* make sense, as does Marx's sketching out of what socialism and communism will be like, involving a substantial qualitative enhancement of positive freedom, such that people will be able to experience a fusion of their individual interests with that of the social group, and where "the free development of each will serve as the condition for the free development of all" as Marx amd Engels declare in *The Communist Manifesto*.

In a society that is fundamentally unloving or anti-loving, love relationships can readily feel, and be, precarious, with their loss or endangerment all the more painful, all the 'more tearing apart', on this account. Love relationships under capitalism often serve as a haven from or bulwark against the stresses and strains of economic and social life, and when these become frayed, and unravel, it can feel–and it can mean–that a vital constituent element of the supportive network required to enable people to keep going falls apart. In my own life-experience I've met many people who have talked, or written, about seeking a love relationship where they felt they could be fully honest, open, trusting, and vulnerable, and where they could be confident the other is not lying to or deceiving them, is genuinely committed to them, is not simply using them or playing games with them, and is interested and appreciative of them as a 'whole person' and especially as a person who is multiple, complex, contradictory, and dynamic–including not at all perfect, who makes and will make mistakes, including serious ones, and who will not remain constantly the same. It can be difficult to find love like this. And that has much to do with how capitalist relations of production influence a broader array of social relations, contributing strong incentives always to be wary, hesitant, suspicious, and distrusting of other people.

In relation to Durkheim, egoistic suicide at first glance seemingly references a different experience of love than that described in "Love Will Tear Us Apart." In this case the individual's relationship as part of a social group, including as part of a love relationship, becomes much less meaningful than the individual's relationship with themselves. In this situation the individual can readily feel as if no one else truly loves them. But perhaps "Love Will Tear Us Apart" depicts what happens in seeking to create and especially sustain a love relationship in the face of egoistic social pressures that detach people from each other, even when they ostensibly are seeking the opposite.

In the case of altruistic suicide it would seem a crisis occurs when the individual's close identification with a social group, including a love relationship, has proven fundamental to that individual's sense of what makes their life at all meaningful and worthwhile. If this bond is threatened the individual needs to take drastic action, out of desperation, to prove they remain fully committed to and totally aligned with the ethos of the social group, or the love relationship, and that they cannot and will not bear the prospect of this link being severed.

Fatalistic suicide seems harder to connect, as this would make more sense in relation to at least the lyrics of "Love Will Tear Us Apart" if a love relationship were overwhelmed by an oppressive burden of normative expectations, and demands, such that it became impossible to experience any freedom or autonomy within this relationship. This would render an ostensible love relation seem like a fraudulent simulation of what love, ideally at least, is supposed to involve–akin to the sterile socially sanctioned relationships that exist in dystopian novels like *Nineteen Eighty-Four*, where all genuinely substantial love is required to be devoted to Big Brother.

In the case of anomic suicide, connections are more promising. Anomie can result from changing and uncertain norms concerning what kinds and variety, including numbers of, love relationships are socially acceptable, at the same time, and with people increasingly following multiply divergent paths in terms of what they imagine can and should be possible concerning love, and love relations. Under such conditions, no larger social force effectively tells people what they can and cannot, or should and should not, do in terms of love and love relations. This results in confusion, anxiety, and even stumbling about and being torn between different conceptions of what love, and love relationships, can and should mean. For example, should love be focused on someone with whom you can marry, raise children, buy a house and settle down to live and work a stable, comfortable, secure, dependable, regular job in one community, for the foreseeable future? Should love be about pursuing your passions and interests, wherever these might take you, exploring multiple possible kinds and numbers of intimate relationships as well as lifestyles, while not being tied to any one place? Should love be about finding a 'soulmate' with whom you can relate to and share principally in terms of common intellectual and artistic interests and sensibilities? Should love be centered around a long-term, monogamous, state-sanctioned, and even religiously sanctified, union of two people of the opposite biological sex? Or should love be open to multiple other possibilities besides that? Is it possible, or should it be possible, to love more than one person at once, love more than one person intimately and not need to choose among these multiple loves? Or is this not possible, and perhaps should not be possible? Is it possible or should it be possible to love an avocation, a calling, a commitment to and involvement in artistic creation and performance equal to (even perhaps more than) that of your love for your romantic-sexual partner(s)? Or is this not possible, and perhaps should not be possible? What moral force offers effective guidance in answering these questions, especially in secular society, and, especially, if as Durkheim suggests, neither the state nor anything else has replaced religion and the family in effectively doing so in modern society? Following Durkheim's proposal that the occupational group provide the source of moral cohesion, this would mean that the occupational group would be responsible for guiding those participating within this group in recognizing what kinds of love relations they should pursue, how they should pursue these, what they should do to sustain them, and what they should not do in order to prevent these relations from being harmfully torn apart. In Ian Curtis's case, this would mean the entire ensemble constituting Joy Division would need to represent this kind of force, for him. But that was hardly how those involved with Joy Division conceived of their role concerning each other's relationships with intimate partners, seeming to conceive these as matters best left to the individuals involved to determine for themselves.

For Freud, it is important to recognize and support the individual human being's innate tendency, and inclination, to love themself, with other love relationships always best sustained when they are built off of and closely relate to that self-love, rather than requiring the individual to renounce or sacrifice self-love, and especially not to feel guilty, ashamed, and driven to punish themselves on account of self-love. Love that requires too much self-renunciation, too much repression and too much conversion and redirection away from fundamental human inclinations, tends to cause serious problems, Freud argues, both for individuals and for larger societies. Limiting normatively acceptable forms of sexual behavior as severely as did the Western European culture within which Freud was directly situated and most familiar, Freud found excessive and unnatural, leading to the return of the repressed in distorted and damaging form. A Freudian framework brought to bear in relation to "Love Will Tear Us Apart" would likely read this song as registering the impact of unrealistic cultural expectations, and especially unrealistic cultural demands, upon individuals, such as represented by the narrator-protagonist in this song, where these people end up punishing themselves for not being able to maintain and sustain what is not all that readily possible to maintain and sustain. At the same time a Freudian framework might interpret this song as representative of a psyche that faces multiple serious issues to work through, with the lyrics symptomatic of a neurotic mindset, one that adheres to perfectionist standards of what a love relationship can and should mean as well as tends to sabotage the relationship by acting to undermine it out of a sense of internalized self-hatred, in the form of an internalized self-punishment–or a hatred and punishment projected outward onto another, in this case the other person in the love relationship. *Love will tear us apart*, in Freudian terms, because we are internally divided, not only between conscious perception and unconscious desire, or among id, ego, and super-ego, or between life drive and death drive, or between instinctual pursuit of pleasure and instinctual manifestation of aggression, but also between on the one hand our participation within the culture of modern (civilized) society, and alignment with its norms, and on the other hand our resistance to and discontent with this participation and alignment.

Before turning to consider the song, more directly, as far more than just title and lyrics, I will next address one other direction for interpretation worth considering. Although these lyrics seem less ambiguous and less open to a widely divergent range of viable interpretations than many others Ian Curtis wrote, it still is possible that listeners to this song might associate experiences of 'love' 'tearing apart' having to do with relationships other than between two or at most a small number of romantic-sexual partners. When it seems as if another affiliation with what one has passionately loved–such as a job, a performance ensemble, a sports team, a political organization, a social movement, or a community where one has lived–is coming to a sad end, it can feel much akin to what happens for people involved as romantic-sexual partners when they break up. Imagine being laid off and let go, or forced into early retirement, from a job you loved doing, and which you made a major part of your self-identity. Imagine being dropped from a performing ensemble or a sports team which you loved being a part of and contributing to. Imagine being forced to move from a community you loved being a part of, and participating within, because you have been priced out, you can no longer afford the cost of housing (such as due to gentrification), or because your company is moving out of the community (in the quest for readier profits or more promising markets), or because of human tragedy (such as a mass shooting) or natural disaster (such as a hurricane, an earthquake, a tornado, severe flooding, severe drought, or severe fire).

The version of "Love Will Tear Us Apart" I have listened to, in writing this section of this chapter, comes from the 2001 *Heart and Soul* 4-CD box set, with booklet, from London Records, which is also the same version as on the 1985 Factory/Qwest/Warner compilation CD *Permanent*. As I hear it, the structure of the song, in this version, divides into the following sections:

1.   Initiation and Initial Exposition: 0:00-0:25. Instrumental opening, leading up to and preparing the way before the synthesizer keyboard plays the principal melodic line for the first time in the song. Starts with bass guitar playing an initial pre-melodic riff, then some quick guitar stabs add further to the sense of rapidly building up to a decisive initial introduction of the melody, then the drums and cymbals establish the beat, and finally the synthesizer keyboard introduces the principal melody with the bass guitar joining in a closely corresponding pattern.

2.   Elaboration and Concentration: 0:26-0:57. First verse stanza followed by first chorus in the form of a culminating refrain, with the bass guitar continuing to play a melodic accompaniment beneath the vocal carrying the tune, while the synthesizer keyboard moves to become primarily involved in contributing harmonic fill, except in the chorus where it once again clearly sounds the melody. The pattern pursued by the drums and cymbals includes notable quick double strikes, but overall sounds close to a standard rock drum pattern, although this is deceptive because in actuality hi-hat strikes occur four times per beat while the bass drum sounds on each beat along with the more standard snare drum sounding on beats two and four; periodically on beat three the hi-hat switches to an open hit followed by a quick hit on a ride cymbal.

3.   Further Elaboration and Concentration: 0:58-1:37. Second verse stanza and second chorus with the instrumentation same as the preceding, in section two.

4.   Rising to Climax: 1:38-2:02. Instrumental bridge, with synthesizer keyboard playing principal role in sounding the melody here, accompanied and supported in so doing by the bass guitar.

5.   Climactic Elaboration and Concentration: 2:03-2:48. Third verse stanza and third chorus, closely similar to sections two and three with some heightening of the tension appropriate for a climactic section.

6.   Denouement and Conclusion: 2:49-3:23. Instrumental closing, with a notably different pattern of movement in the synthesizer keyboard line culminating in a final fading out.

The song is tightly executed. Throughout we hear repetition and amplification of the melody via multiple instruments, albeit with slight variations in numbers of notes and chords and in timing and size of pitch intervals. The song conveys a pronounced sense of energetic propulsion, moving along at 192 bpm (which I myself timed and counted just to make sure). Because of this rapid movement the song feels more energetic than the lyrics taken alone might suggest. I interpret this pace as contributing a performative distance versus the subject of lyrics, with the song reflecting and commenting on this subject rather than directly confessing from the immediate midst of the experience and associated emotion referenced in the lyrics. What this larger sonic context further contributes is a sense of putting this experience and associated emotion into a larger explanatory perspective. Such perspective involves awareness and acceptance that everything emerges, develops, grows, changes, declines, ends, and passes on to become the basis for something else, and that even as painful as love inevitably can and will be, love is inescapably necessary for all of us and we will seek it out and all it encompasses, including it tearing us apart, endlessly over and over again. As we recognize and accept that love will tear us apart _again and again_, we manifest our ability to survive, endure, and persist, even when we feel we cannot. I hear this manifestation supported by the extent to which the sonic texture of the song as well as its regular and consistent structure along with its propulsive beat suggests a certain equanimity in the face of what the vocal is recounting. The tone here feels as if the song is testifying to something beautiful, albeit tragically beautiful, about the agonies of love, that represents a fundamental dimension of what it means to be human and especially to be truly, fully, and vitally alive as a human being: opening one's self up to intense experience that will involve wrenching, tearing, fracturing, and breaking–i.e., agony as well as ecstacy, with often enough the two closely interlinked.

Peter Hook's bass guitar prepares the way for the melody and then keeps resounding a variation of and compliment to it throughout, as well as adding to, sustaining, and supporting the groove; the brief opening guitar–from Ian Curtis live and Bernard Sumner on record–adds initials sparks of rapidly heightening intensity; Bernard Sumner's synthesizer keyboard contributes initial and frequently prominent sounding of the principal melody as well as serving as the principal constituent of the harmonic fill layer; Stephen Morris's drums and cymbals–including bass drum, snare drum, hi-hat and ride cymbal–provide the beat as well as establish and sustain the groove, giving the song its speed, force, and direction of felt movement; and Ian Curtis's vocal carries the tune, as well as adding further texture to the melody.

In terms of the soundbox, the bass guitar enters below center, stronger to the left than the right although sounding from both sides, and then remains below center but not too far below, close to the front although not as close as either the drums and cymbals or the vocal. The guitar enters from the upper right and the synthesizer keyboard sounds seem to come from nearer the top to both sides, especially to the left, while tending to glide across the top as the song progresses. The vocal sounds from close to directly mid-center and near the front, although leaning slightly more to the right than the left of center, and overall sounding slightly off-center to the right. The drums and cymbals sound from higher in the soundbox than the bass guitar and closer to the front, while seeming to sound from both sides of the center as well as further to each of these sides than the bass guitar.

What might these features contribute in terms of meaning? "Love Will Tear Us Apart" is an instantly recognizable, infectiously hook-laded pop song, which supports an interpretation of the song as enacting a performative commentary, by means of a performative distance from the subject of the lyrics, and, in so doing, attesting to the capacity to survive, endure, and persist by taking stock and engaging in introspective reflection. It makes sense as well to interpret the song as registering a complex of emotions with different instruments corresponding to different ways of dealing with and responding to the experience identified in the lyrics, as well as to what this might mean–emotions ranging from remnant hurt and pain to sadness and regret to wistful and bittersweet recollection to dogged persistence and calm acceptance. "Love Will Tear Us Apart" as an entire complex of patterned sounds, and not just a set of lyrics, evokes the famous Gramscian commitment toward maintaining a simultaneous 'optimism of the will and pessimism of the intellect'. "Love Will Tear Us Apart" does not readily suggest an existing form of organization of society, corresponding to an existing dominant mode of production, itself responsible for alienation and estrangement, in work and beyond, is the root cause of the travails of love, of the fragility and transience of love, and of how what once was so good no longer functions anymore, as what once was a preeminent source of intimacy, affection, care, and support has now become a site itself of profound estrangement. "Love Will Tear Us Apart" suggests the 'tearing' it addresses is instead intrinsic to what love means. Likewise, "Love Will Tear Us Apart" does not suggest this tearing follows from problems in social integration, or of the effectivity of social regulation, such that if both of these were improved then relationships of love would less often experience this 'tearing'. And even though it might seem

Freud's suggestion that human beings will always struggle with discontent in 'civilized' society, and that social constructions of what love relations should be about place undue burdens upon individuals—demands that run contrary to instinctual human nature—"Love Will Tear Us Apart" is more romantically idealistic, much more willing to surrender to suffering than to seek ways to minimize or alleviate it. "Love Will Tear Us Apart" even suggests a Nietzschean commitment toward acceptance of eternal recurrence. The song might seem to embody a masochistic desire, in not turning away from and rejecting love, but remaining with it, continuing to accept and turn toward it, all the while fully acknowledging and identifying love with what brings about immense pain, such that this tears those who love apart, and will do so again and again.

"Love Will Tear Us Apart" starts loud and remains fairly consistent in volume throughout, although it does fade out at the end, with what is of greater note in terms of volume in this song being the relative loudness of instruments, with the synthesizer keyboards sounding softer while the vocal is sounding than when not, especially in verse passages, and the drums and cymbals sounding slightly louder than the bass guitar even as overall none of the instruments sound all that much louder or softer than any other but instead are closely balanced in terms of relative volume. The beat conveys a slight shuffling or syncopated feel, especially due to periodic double strikes and quick crashes on the third beat. With the hi-hat striking sixteen times per measure and the bass drum four times per measure, this comprises a denser rhythm than in a standard rock beat but what is also worth noting here in terms of rhythm, in relation to all of the instruments, is these are consistent, repeated patterns with only slight breaks and variations. Seemingly, the bass guitar principally plays eighth notes, following a 1and2and3and4and pattern, throughout most measures of the song, principally consisting of chords of two to three notes at a time, although occasionally the bass guitar will play one or two quarter notes in a measure along with five or six eighth notes. The synthesizer keyboard tends to play five notes or chords in each measure, while the vocal tends to sound principally quarter notes, with ties extending notes across measures at the end of vocal phrases and lines. The guitar, that has a slight role here, in the opening plays five fretted notes on five strings and moves from doing so once per measure to three times per measure to eight times per measure, while at the end of the song returns to play eighth notes, alternating between notes and chords.

In terms of pitch "Love Will Tear Us Apart" has been transposed into many different keys, both major and minor, as well as into many different tempos, but in the recording I have listened to, in writing this section of this chapter, what I hear as most noteworthy is the opening bass guitar riff stays largely in place, and then the synthesizer keyboard, the bass guitar, and the vocal gently rise from a repeated starting pitch before falling back, while the keyboard pitch, in providing harmonic fill, seems to rise somewhat higher. The vocal melodic line seems to consist of a sequence of eight pitches in verses and six in choruses, the bass guitar melodic line seems to consist of a sequence of five pitches, and the synthesizer keyboard melodic line seems to consists of a sequence of six pitches. The bass guitar, the synthesizer keyboard, and the vocal all contribute melodic lines that closely parallel each other yet maintain slight variations, not only in terms of what pitches they are sounding but also how many per measure, and per hypermeasure, as well as in number of steps and length of steps. However, the general pattern in terms of pitch I hear is to begin by staying in place, then to move as follows: down, down again, then up, and then down once more. The most prominent direction of movement, therefore, is down in pitch, and I detect all of the following patterns in terms of direction of pitch movement over the course of this song: (1) Start–Down-Down-Up-Up-Down-Down; (2) Start-Up-Down-Up-Down-Down-Down; (3) Start-Up-Up-Down-Down; and (4) Start-Start-Up-Up/Start-Start-Down-Down//Start-Up-Start-Down.

Ian Curtis's vocal delivery in "Love Will Tear Us Apart" sounds gently melancholic. His voice is resonant and reverberant, dark and concentrated, clear and precise, while he does sound as if he is singing from his own distinct and separate space, broadly aware of the other instruments sounding from their locations yet focused on carrying out his own task. The timbre of the synthesizer keyboard is brightly, cleanly shimmering, and ethereal, with a gently sweet quality to it, much warmer and more mellow than in "Isolation." The timbre of the bass guitar conveys notable warmth as well while the drums and cymbals convey a narrow, thin, yet clear and precise timbre, all with limited decay and sustain, but a decisive attack and a quick release. The synthesizer keyboard sounds in contrast convey pronounced decay and sustain, while the vocal does so as well although not as much as the synthesizer, yet both also offer a slow release. The bass guitar offers a strong and clear attack yet also a pronounced decay and sustain, and, when prominently sounding the melody, also offers a slow release. The timbre of the components of the drum kit contribute to a feeling of moving quickly and decisively along, with limited sense of side to side movement, while the bass guitar also feels like it is following a similar pattern of movement even as the vocal and the synthesizer keyboard seem to glide and drift.

As the song proceeds the music as persona itself seems to anticipate repetition, movement across the same pattern with each successive verse + chorus section, and that the process itself is the end goal here, which again supports an interpretation of this song as enacting a commitment to carry on, anticipating that even as we come to understand that love tears us a apart, and will again and again, we will nevertheless continue to pursue, embrace, and suffer love. We can't help it, and we don't want to help it, no matter how painful love inevitably ends up being. Even though all good things come to an end, and this will feel wrenchingly painful, we will not, we cannot, avoid entering into love relationships. We will and cannot dictate that we will protect ourselves from being hurt by love. To love is to make oneself vulnerable to being hurt, and even to being hurt badly. To love it to make oneself vulnerable to heartbreak. In other words, following the popular adage, derived from Alfred Lord Tennyson, it is 'better to have loved and lost than not to have loved at all'. "Love Will Tear Us Apart," as a song, and not just a detached set of lyrics, expresses this kind of recognition and acceptance along with a determination to persist, no matter how hard, even in the face of expecting one will suffer the same all over again, with no means available of escaping doing so.

"Love Will Tear Us Apart" evokes recollection of wistful and bittersweet experiences that involve some kind of feeling of love tearing us apart, including but not limited to love ending, love declining, and love leading to estrangement and antagonism. I think of the love I experience for teaching and working closely with classes of students, and with particular students, that always means so much to me, always proves an immense joy even while involving an exhausting investment of effort, in which we get to know, share with, and care about each other as we engage vital texts and topics. But I also think about the fact each of these classes eventually comes to an end, and its distinctive collective character and personality fades into memory, as we proceed along our separate paths, once the semester has ended. I feel the pain of recognizing and accepting it has been incredibly life-affirming to teach these classes of students, and these individual students, but now that the semester has ended, I will never teach that exact group of people focused on the same array of texts and topics at that same time and place, ever again, and, what's more, may never hear from or see many of the students again. This includes many wonderful people who it has been an immense delight to meet and work with. I face this at the end of every semester, every year, with every class. I always feel, at the end of each semester, proud of what my classes and I have accomplished together as well as sad this has now come to an end. But nonetheless I am always ready to do it once again and I do not want to protect myself from that bittersweet feeling at the end of the semester because this feeling reflects the extent to which I have truly cared about and deeply invested in what we were doing together, and in these students, individually and collectively. I've poured a significant part of myself into these classes, and when they come to an end, it can indeed feel as if that part of myself is being torn apart.

I have also felt this sense of love tearing me apart in relation to experience of particular places, and events at these places–magnificent performances, great trips, wonderful nights, sublime occasions, meetings up after a long time with family and close friends. In Manchester, especially at the end of the Manchester International Festival, I have felt that sense of profound wistfulness, in relation to the coming to the end of what has been a fantastic experience, and in fact a multitude of fantastic experiences, that I have eagerly and excitedly looked forward to for a long time preceding. At MIF 17 I felt notably saddened after visiting and touring the *True Faith* exhibition focused on Joy Division and New Order one last time, as well as 'saying goodbye' to the statue of Friedrich Engels installed right outside the HOME complex in an elaborate and moving event just days preceding. Every time I visit Manchester I feel sadness visiting favorite locations all across the city and the region one last time, before returning home. At MIF 19, among many outstanding events, one, titled *Tao of Glass*, involved a combination of music, story-telling, puppetry, and theatre, at the Royal Exchange Theatre, in which performer-director Phelim McDermott paid tribute to how inspiring and deeply meaningful the music of Philip Glass had long been for him, ultimately joined in the performance by Philip Glass himself, playing his own famous *Glassworks* music. This was, for me, an immensely moving and enchanting evening, that meant as much as it did to me because I readily felt a keen sense of a parallel between McDermott's relationship with Glass and my own with Ian Curtis. *Tao of Glass* was a wonderful event, and I will long treasure having experienced it, but yes I was sad when it came to an end.

Over the course of my life I can say the same about numerous artistic performances and events I have attended–theatrical stage plays, musical gigs and concerts, films, performance art pieces, immersive and interactive productions, museum and gallery exhibitions, street art happenings, and much more besides: I loved these experiences, and often felt a rush of feelings of love for what I was a part of, for all who were involved in making it possible, and for all who were sharing this with me, in the midst of the experience, as well as a sadness, even a painful sadness, once it all came to an end. In the spring of 2019 I had been struggling with depression for the first half of that semester but then we took a trip, Andy and I, to London for spring break. I felt rejuvenated–I *loved* walking extensively all over Central London, through many parks; visiting many bookstores, libraries, record stores, and other cultural venues; and attending two outstanding theatrical performances: *Grief is a Thing with Feathers*, directed by Enda Walsh and starring Cillian Murphy, based on a novel by Max Porter, as well as *Come from Away*, a musical composed by Irene Sankoff and David Hein. That trip was so wonderful that Andy and I planned to travel again to London in both the spring and summer of 2020, to explore further and learn all that much more about London, even to consider the possibility of eventually retiring and moving to London–but COVID-19 forced us to cancel those plans, and indeed out of love for all of the many fantastic experiences we have had, especially with festivals and other special events, in the British Isles, we determined we will not return to visit until it is safe to do so and people like us are widely welcome once more to do so.

I also readily recall the excitement mixed with trepidation preceding many speeches and other public presentations I have given over the course of my life, that I anticipated and looked forward to contributing, and then felt sad these ended so quickly, even after a strong positive reception from those listening to me. I recall the same bittersweet feelings at the end of putting on each Eau Claire Progressive Film Festival I led. I felt the same after leading a Unitarian Universalist service concerning 'Spiritual Reflections on the life and work of Ian Curtis and the music of Joy Division' in which I felt thrilled to be able to share this passion of mine with a large audience of people, many of whom had never heard of Ian Curtis or Joy Division before, yet who responded overwhelmingly highly positively, and in which it was wonderful to hear a small band just formed for this particular service play a series of Joy Division songs along with me playing others on tape. I have felt the same following the conclusion of collaborations with students as senior teaching assistants and in collaborative research projects. I've felt comparable experiences on myriad occasions coming to the end of reading a great book, even books I felt compelled to read all the way through in one setting, and the same with many great movies and TV shows, especially at the end of the run of a TV show where I've developed an emotional attachment such that I've come to care about the characters and to *love* familiar features of the show. This last is especially sad when the makers of a show kill off a beloved lead character at the end, such as in *Inspector George Gently* and *Unforgotten*.

I also feel the same bittersweet feelings following the death of a performer whose work has meant a great deal to me, forcing to accept no further new contributions will be forthcoming from the same performer while compelled to recall the performer's previous work and what this has meant to me. Frequently on my radio show I've paid tribute to musicians who have just died who have meant a lot to me, including Lou Reed, David Bowie, Leonard Cohen, Alan Vega, Scott Hutchison, Pete Shelley, Scott Walker, and Andy Gill. When people like this die I also feel as if I am mourning for the passing of my younger self, recognizing how much time has passed since I first became an enthusiast for the music these people created, for how much this music has been intertwined with my life, and for how much closer I am to my own eventual death. The same bittersweet feelings accompany the closing of a beloved establishment where I've enjoyed a great many happy experiences. I think here of many examples but I will just cite one–the traditional Scottish restaurant Dubh Prash, on the Royal Mile in Edinburgh, that always served the best food we ever tasted in that capital city, and which for years, until its proprietor retired, we made sure to book once every time we visited that capital city, usually reserving it for our last or next to last night in Edinburgh. I also think of many retired colleagues who have been wonderful mentors, advisors, and friends as well as inspiring teachers, scholars, and engaged citizens, recently including Tess Onwueme, Jack Bushnell, and Jenny Shaddock. I feel happy for them, and for the years we have spent as colleagues, but sad that our time together, and their direct contributions as part of the same department, have now come to an end. People like that–colleagues at all levels–as well as the students who make great strides and demonstrate considerable accomplishments, while sharing their multi-faceted personalities, are what make a place where one works feel like a place one *loves*, as I often indeed have loved working as a faculty member in the Department of English at UW-Eau Claire. Yes, it feels 'tearing' when great people leave, when they move on, when it feels as if one is left behind, now without them–retiring, graduating, transferring, or finding a position elsewhere that provides them better professional opportunities or the chance to live and work closer to family and directly with a partner or spouse–even as one is happy for them. It is even more 'tearing' when great people die, especially unexpectedly and prematurely–and here I can think of colleagues such as mathematics professor Eberth Alarcon and psychology professor Barbara Lozar, just to name two.

The death of people with whom one has been close, and/or whom one looked up to and admired, as has happened to all too many I knew, or knew of, during the worst ravages of the first long wave of the AIDS pandemic here in the US–especially dying far too young, in incredible pain, estranged from family, and with medical professionals wary and distant as well–has been incredibly 'tearing'. It would not be so if I did not love these people–and/or what they were about, what they represented, what they accomplished, what they shared, what they contributed. I've known people who have killed themselves and this has felt incredibly 'tearing' too for much the same reasons, and I've felt much the same for people I've known who have suffered deaths due to motor vehicle and other kinds of accidents. Whenever a close friend or family member has died, no matter if after a long life and relatively peacefully, I've felt this 'tearing' sadness and pain. I feel badly they will no longer be able to contribute more and anew not just to my life, but to life in general and to many others' lives, and that we will not be able, any more, to share meaningful experiences directly together. I've felt this way with the death, and with the approaching death, of a beloved pet. This summer of 2021 Andy and I have felt this 'tearing' as we have pursued all available possibilities of helping our dog Casey combat cancer yet finding ultimately nothing can save him. I cried when I ordered Casey's funeral urn and drafted the inscription for it. And, finally, I've also felt this kind of 'tearing', yes, in an intimate romantic-sexual relationship, when it has reached the point where it clearly is coming to an end, and in which one or the other or both of us decides we must end it, despite continuing to love each other, because we are no longer working as a couple, and the same too in situations where I've fallen in love with men who cannot love me in all of the same ways as I can them, because they are straight and I am gay. I could, at the end of any one of these numerous experiences I have just summarized, determined 'that's it, I don't want to be hurt like that and feel this badly ever again, so I will never put myself in a position where I will ever be at risk of it ever again happening to me', but I did not, I could not–love is too valuable, love is too necessary, even as love indeed can be, all too often, at least eventually, painfully 'tearing'.

"Love Will Tear Us Apart" confronts a common cultural taboo about admitting, accepting, and especially embracing the notion that love can and will be painful–that the more one loves the more one is likely, at least eventually, to suffer, even if only due to the inevitable passing of all things, but also due to the prospect that any and all moments of happiness will be fleeting. It remains counter-intuitive to seek out and pursue love relationships with full awareness and acceptance these will these end up, eventually, tearing one apart. It remains taboo to concentrate on the end of a relationship, rather than the beginning, the peaks, the high moments, of the relationship. It remains taboo to concentrate on the loss, the pain, and the suffering, that the end, the ending, and the troughs, the low moments, in a relationship involve rather than trying to avoid thinking about these. It remains taboo to openly identify with the position that happiness is not our destiny, is not 'owed to us', and is certainly never guaranteed, because no matter what we might try to do to make it so we cannot exercise ultimately effective control over the conditions of possibility or the forces of generation–and preservation and perpetuation–of happiness.

This 'darkly romantic' position leads "Love Will Tear Us Apart" some distance from Marx in Economic and Philosophic Manuscripts of 1844, Durkheim in *Suicide: a Study in Sociology*, or Freud in *Civilization & Its Discontents*. Marx, Durkheim, and Freud would all undoubtedly critique this position as mystifying. All would undoubtedly critique this position for its inability adequately to explain, let alone even tentatively suggest, an explanation of why love must always–will always–lead in this direction and end with this result. And they each might suggest the links I elaborated with 'love tearing us apart' in the various examples of my own experience do not necessarily all add up to the same thing. They might argue these experiences of mine do not deserve to be identified as 'tearing apart' because sadness over the coming to the end of an event one has looked forward to experiencing for a long time, and thrilled while experiencing–such as a gig or a concert, or a play, or a movie, or an exhibition, or a sports contest, or a festival, or a book, or a TV series, or even a class one has taught–does not necessarily 'tear' one apart, in the same way the lyrics of this song seem to suggest: one may feel saddened but also uplifted as a result of having participated in this kind of experience, and often one is in the position to anticipate pursuing much more of the same.

I agree love can be powerfully uplifting and transformative, and that leading one's life with passion, throwing one's self into experiences and relationships, plumping the depths of all they have to offer, ultimately makes life-experience feel all the more satisfying, fulfilling, intense, meaningful, and *real*, while I also agree I learn and otherwise gain from these relationships and experiences, carrying this forward with me, even when those relationships and experiences end. But I do recognize these endings can and do feel sad and painful, even wrenching and tearing, while life does impose choices and decisions that mean I often do need to give up on, to not pursue or no longer pursue, relationships and experiences I once did, and which have meant an enormous amount to me, even simply on the account of growing older. I am not entirely identical with the Bob Nowlan who has proceeded me here and now, and that means I have lived many lives, many successive lives, while in each of these lives multiple possible directions for future lives remained possibilities, yet I have always needed to select among and thereby eliminate many possibilities in moving forward. In terms of writing, for example, at various points in my time at UW-Eau Claire, and throughout my time from graduate study onward, I have contemplated and begun work on many potential writing projects of multiple different kinds on multiple topics, many of which I have ultimately needed to set aside, chiefly because I did not have time to devote to carry these all the way through. Even as a PhD student I wrote over 200 single-spaced pages three times on three differently focused prospective dissertations that my principal advisor rejected before we agreed on the fourth focus that I did carry all the way through. I've also proposed and initiated plans for many initiatives I did not garner sufficient support from others to be able to carry through, such as creating a website along with a series of podcasts and streaming broadcasts focused on progressive music of protest and resistance; a Free University of Eau Claire, offering university-level classes on diverse topics, free of charge, in person, to members of the Eau Claire and Chippewa Valley communities; and an interdepartmental, transdisciplinary emphasis area in sports, politics, and society at UW-Eau Claire. I've been fortunate in what I have been able to accomplish but that hasn't been everything I ever hoped to accomplish. In our culture it is commonplace to prefer that other people not overburden you by sharing with or emphasizing too much what they regret and feel they did not succeed at; what makes them feel sad, pessimistic, and resigned; and what they feel guilty and ashamed about. It is also taboo to foreground this dimension of life-experience as explicitly and relentlessly as Ian Curtis does, in his lyrics, even if the accompanying songs complicate and redirect the message so it feels like a call to struggle onward, to persist and endure.

In listening to and reflecting on "Love Will Tear Us Apart," as well as on what this song compels me to think (about) and feel, I interpret the song as proposing it is important to come to grips with how the great times in our lives, including the wonderful moments when a relationship or experience of love feels overflowing with fabulous possibilities, are ultimately fleeting. We can recollect these in memory but we can no longer render them directly present, as they are all too often impossible to re-experience once again, in precisely the same shape or form. Love itself, "Love Will Tear Us Apart" suggests, is an invisible, intangible, and ephemeral phenomenon. As love passes on, so does our life, and we mourn for our younger days, for our childhood and our youth, for seemingly more innocent times, and for hopes, dreams, and plans that never materialized but we once were determined to bring about. Our past selves, or, perhaps better put, our selves in past situations, in past relationships, at past locations, and in past circumstances, with distance in time and space, can come to seem unreal to us, feeling as if, or almost as if, these happened to an entirely different person leading an entirely different life. It can feel hard to believe, hard to fathom, that was once us, back then and over there. Or it can, alternately, feel hard to believe, hard to fathom, how much time and how much space has come between ourselves here and now and ourselves then and there. "Love Will Tear Us Apart" invites us to reflect on how quickly everything moves on, or seems to move on, especially as one grows older.

In her "Foreword" to *So This is Permanence: Joy Division Lyrics and Notebooks* Deborah Curtis writes, memorably, about this song as follows:

How did I feel when told by Rob Gretton that 'Love Will Tear Us Apart' was about me? Angry; humiliated; I scoured his manuscripts looking for evidence it wasn't so. *Your bedroom, this bedroom, the bedroom*: he played with these variations. Was he trying to depersonalise the lyrics or did he genuinely not know which bedroom he was referring to? Of course, now I can see that it was another situation he could draw on and not that different to writing about a tragedy he might see on the news; but the burden of finding a way to displace what was happening in his life must have twisted him to the core. (x)

Deborah Curtis also comments, in relation to this song, "When I read the lyrics now I hear the music in my head, I hear his voice, I see him" (x). For fans like me ours is a considerably different kind of experience, because what I hear and what I see is Ian Curtis as I have heard him, overwhelmingly in his music, and as represented through various mediated accounts of what he looked and sounded like that make the 'Ian Curtis' I hear and see not identical with the 'Ian Curtis' Deborah Curtis sees and hears. It would be impossible for this difference not to be the case. It is important to learn about the actual person who once lived, and what his life meant to those who knew him personally, especially closely, taking into account and respecting their interpretations and evaluations of his music. But when I hear "Love Will Tear Us Apart" I do not think about Ian and Deborah Curtis's marriage, or the difficulties they experienced in their marriage, and this is certainly not what makes listening to the song, and reflecting on it, meaningful to me. I feel tremendous excitement as I listen to the instantly recognizable opening bass guitar and guitar prelude to the first entrance of the synthesizer keyboard playing the principal melody for the initial time as this directly precedes the first vocal passage. The beat and the tempo also feel as if I am being carried forward on an energetic venture, albeit a complicated one, concerned with what is decidedly bittersweet. I connect what I hear with my own knowledge, experience, background, and social positioning; with issues that matter to me and with multiple other texts that have and continue to prove influential to me; and with principles, values, convictions, and ideals as well as with outlooks, sentiments, and sensibilities which I most strongly identify.

In the same book, in his "Introduction," Jon Savage begins by discussing "Love Will Tear Us Apart," referencing the song as a top twenty hit single, a song that has been covered numerous times by a great many diverse musicians, and a song that is well-known and beloved even by many who don't pay much attention to popular music and know little else by or about Joy Division. Savage then focuses on "Love Will Tear Us Apart" as a new song, when it first arrived, in 1979, one that "heralded a shift in the group dynamic" with Bernard Sumner playing synthesizer keyboard and Ian Curtis playing guitar (xiii). Savage argues "The appeal of 'Love Will Tear Us Apart' lies in its melody, arrangement, performance and message," and, as I previously cited in chapter two, takes note, in detail, of the following features of the song:

> It begins with a bass pulse; the guitar arrives with a dramatic flourish and the drums clatter, before they resolve into a syncopated drum beat and an instantly memorable synthesizer figure. It's an old analogue synth, which conveys warmth and alienation at the same time: the melody is at once uplifting and wistful. Curtis's voice has lost its previous punk bark: it's more nuanced, almost crooned–an echo of the Frank Sinatra record supplied by Tony Wilson as a stylistic guide.

> The arrangement is deceptively light and airy, but the sentiments are not. The vocal is mixed up high . . . It's more a solo rather than a rock vocal, and this forces attention, as was intended, on the lyrics. There are three verses. The first states the situation that gives rise to the chorus .

435

. . while the next two plunge you into the roiling emotions at the end of something that is more than just a love affair: a marriage, or a long-term partnership.

The second verse has lines of starting intimacy . . . Curtis kept on returning to themes of blame, shame and guilt throughout the three or so years he wrote lyrics, but here he applies these themes to a readily identifiable, human predicament . . . (xiv)

Savage adds "At the core of the song is the paradox that love and intimacy . . . can destroy as well as uplift" and "it will continue to do that as long as two people keep on coming back for more, as long as they fail to find a resolution" while although "There is a tiny glimmer of hope . . . by the end, it has been distinguished" (xv). Savage's interpretation is largely compatible with how I have been interpreting the song, yet I suggest, partly because of Savage's literal closeness to Curtis and Joy Division, not quite the same as Deborah Curtis, but close enough, he is more inclined to interpret this song as definitively focused on a marriage, or long-term partnership, and on the two people involved as coming back again and again in seeking resolution yet ultimately not finding it, while I accept this interpretation but also interpret this song in relation to a broader array of kinds of loves, and love relationships, and of drawing at least tentative conclusions concerning the nature of love and love relationships more broadly.

In *Torn Apart: the Life of Ian Curtis*, Mike Middles and Lindsay Reade declare that "Love Will Tear Us Apart" "was born from pain," and "That much was always obvious," while despite how "addictive" the sounds comprising the song, outside of and beyond the song, continue to be, from the "rising opening chords" onwards, these are "profoundly personal lyrics" (206). And yet Middles and Reade also contend that "Part of the success of 'Love Will Tear Us Apart' was its omnipresent capacity to reach all those who'd experienced" much the same kind of situation as the lyrics here suggest, with "a touch of irony in the song's title insofar as it could be seen as a dark antidote to the Captain & Tenille hit, 'Love Will Keep Us Together', a fluffy confection by Neil Sedaka that had stuck like a globule of pink bubblegum to insipid radio play lists since emerging in 1975" (206). For Middles and Reade, right away, despite the song being profoundly personal, and seemingly directly reflective of Ian Curtis's own experience, it also is a song that reaches out and provides a source of connection, even sympathetic to empathetic connection, to all those who have not found their experience of love to be as simple and easy as the Captain and Tenille celebrate.

Bernard Sumner, in *Chapter and Verse: New Order, Joy Division and Me* describes the making of "Love Will Tear Us Apart" as exemplifying the band's common way of composing their material, with Curtis spotting what he liked from what the others had come up with and directing the arrangement of these constituents around lyrics he had already written, yet with each individual entirely separately responsible for devising their respective parts, of what these would consist and of how they would be played. Sumner declares "I think 'Love Will Tear Us Apart' is one of the most beautiful love songs ever written. It's not love for the sake of it, it's no vacuous paean to pretend heartbreak or anything like that, it's genuine, it's real, it swings back and forth between full-blown power and reflective introspection, because that was exactly what was happening to the person writing the lyrics" (81-82). Sumner further adds "It's unquestionably a great song . . . with its contrasts, peaks, troughs, and it's quite unusual in that it doesn't conform to a regular structure: it's got no middle eight, for example, but it's a great song to play live, an absolute stunner" (82). Besides highlighting a distinctive feature of this song, and a number of other 'late' Joy Division songs–the second vocal stanza immediately follows the first vocal stanza while in each case the chorus, much more here like a refrain than a more conventional chorus, immediately follows each verse passage–Sumner usefully underlines that this is a song that engages with a challenging paradox, concerning experience of love, *and struggle concerning love*, while, like Deborah Curtis, Savage, and Middles and Reade, both relating the song closely to Ian Curtis's personal experience and suggesting it reaches considerably beyond merely attesting to that personal experience alone.

In *Joy Division Piece by Piece: Writing About Joy Division 1977-2007*, Paul Morley includes an interview conducted with the surviving bandmembers at time of the release of a repackaged version of *Closer* in which Peter Hook explains that the band wrote "Love Will Tear Us Apart" in three hours once Ian Curtis shared lyrics he that written to fit the central melodic riff, and "When he sang it to us, we didn't think, oh that's about Debbie and Annik, we just thought, that is fucking great–'Love Will Tear Us Apart', rock on. Ian's done it again" (139). Morley himself, in this same book, expresses his characteristically hyperbolic appreciation for this song more than once, identifying it as one of multiple Joy Division songs that stands as "The greatest song ever written," and as exemplifying a remarkably daring effort "to make a game out of human time" (229). What this suggests, as I understand Morley's argument, is Morley interprets "Love Will Tear Us Apart" as both embracing and defying the heartache, and the heartbreak, as well as the strong suggestion of eternal recurrence, in line with his assertion, concerning what Ian Curtis and Joy Division are doing within and through their music, that

> the very act of confronting the void or continuing to confront it is an act of affirmation. The blacker the situation and the deeper the background of despair against which this act of affirmation is made, the more complete and the more triumphant must be the victory that it constitutes. The uglier the reality that is confronted, the more exhilarating will be its sublimation into symmetry, rhythm, movement, and noise. (256)

Morley proposes that "The songs weren't helping him [Ian Curtis] deal with or recover from the traumas of his life, they were encouraging a fascination with the speed and danger of the drama. They weren't an escape from the madness; they sent him right into the madness. The music was taking him away" (269). Morley adds "the music needed the drama of his life" (269), which suggests to me that in and through his music Ian Curtis was able to transform the drama of his life into something other than merely just another reiteration of the same, which explains why, when Morley writes, "In the end, 'Love Will Tear Us Apart' is 'about' its melody" he immediately follows by declaring "With the passage of time, it will become more and more beautiful" (365). This melody is, I have suggested 'infectious', others have suggested 'addictive', and it is foregrounded throughout the song, rendering the lyrics that Curtis sings feel beautiful even if their subject matter is sad and painful. With the passage of time 'the meaning of song' has to do with how it embodies this paradox and provides a site for sympathetic to empathetic identification among others who experience love, in their own lives, as encompassing both ecstacy and agony, both exhilaration and dejection, and both uplift and disintegration.

In *This Searing Light, The Sun and Everything Else: Joy Division–the Oral History*, Bernard Sumner, like Paul Morley, proposes Ian Curtis "seemed to get carried away by the music" and because he was carried away, without his fellow bandmembers being able to anticipate precisely how, when, via what, and to where he would be so carried away, "He was a very charismatic frontman . . . people never knew what was going to happen with him next–we didn't–and it just worked" (115). In being so 'carried away', Curtis was doing far more than merely confessing his personal confusion, sadness, depression, and suicidality. As Malcolm Whitehead argues, in the same book, it seemed clear to him, and to others attending live Joy Division gigs, that Joy Division represented a critical response to fascistic currents prevalent at the time, such as embodied by then Manchester Police Chief Constable James Anderton: "That was the idea to get across: this was resistance through art and culture, and that will someday be bigger than all these right-wing politics, because it's more human than that is, so it will win" (146). Committing to and engaging fiercely in this kind of artistic and cultural resistance, motivated ultimately by love, paradoxically can prove alienating and isolating, and entail a considerable cost, especially when the fight is being waged by attempting to dramatize an encounter and engagement with 'the heart of the darkness' in an attempt at something akin to a ritual exorcism. This involves seeking to find the light, at least anticipatory glimmers, by journeying all the way through the deepest and harshest folds of darkness. As Steve Taylor writes, in a 1979 *Melody Maker* concert review, also cited in *This Searing Light, The Sun and Everything Else: Joy Division–the Oral History*, "Joy Division speak of apocalypse hopelessness and fragmentation, yet their music acts as an exorcism of passivity and neglect, as near a revitalisation of the spirit of primeval rock 'n' roll as I've experienced in a long while" (172).

And that love can be necessary as well as complicated, Deborah Curtis recognizes, as further cited in *This Searing Light, The Sun and Everything Else: Joy Division–the Oral History*: "I don't blame Ian. I think most people need a partner, and if you exclude that partner you have to find somebody else. It's only natural. He must have been very lonely" (212). It is not uncommon and it is far from an unnatural experience to want and need multiple partners that respond to multiple dimensions of whom one is, what one is about, what one is interested and invested in and passionately concerned with and devoted to. And it is likewise far from uncommon and far from unnatural to find that someone whom you initially turned to and expected to be your partner in areas that matter most to you is not going to be the kind of person who will be able to fulfill that role in those areas, or in all those areas, or even in those that are increasingly becoming most important to you. After all, as Peter Hook suggests, in this same book, "'Love Will Tear Us Apart' . . . is so heartfelt and obviously so painful, because I think [every] adult is going to go through a relationship or an episode like that where you feel cut off and a stranger to a lover" (268). And as Bob Dickinson adds, yet later in this oral history, Ian Curtis's combination of vulnerability and charisma is both "unnerving and unsettling," like that of many great performance artists, but at the same time powerfully compelling because of how profoundly it feels as if Curtis is doing this, is sacrificing himself, for 'you' (284-285). In the case of "Love Will Tear Us Apart" this observation makes sense when interpreting the 'us' here as 'us' the listeners, as well as 'us' the listeners and the performer–where the music as persona is implicitly willing to tear itself apart *for us*, as a manifestation of love *for us*, as an expression of love *to us*, and this challenges us to determine how we will match this love, what we will offer back in return.

I hear "Love Will Tear Us Apart" challenging me to intensely *feel*, and to *continue to feel*, the complex of emotions emanating from recognizing and accepting what I once passionately loved is no longer directly with me, may never be again, or may well have always only truly existed for an a brief passing moment. The song challenges me to reflect on whether I continue to seek out relationships and experiences that not only can be demanding, but also likely will lead to me, at least eventually, feeling sad and painful, even immensely so, when they come to an end, or whether, on the contrary, I hesitate or refrain from risking that kind of emotional fallout. How much am I willing to risk my own vulnerability and fragility? How much am I willing to put myself out there? How much am I committed to acting out of love, even when I expect this will not be met with love in return? How honestly do I accept responsibility for bringing to an end, or allowing to come to an end, something which I and others involved deeply and passionately invested in and cared about, that in fact did not necessarily need to end? Do I adequately recognize and understand that love can be extremely hard, and am I willing to persist in loving when and where it becomes extremely hard? Am I willing to invest so deeply of myself that I will be hurt when an experience or relationship based in love comes to an end, yet do so despite the pain because that means I am making this experience or relationship something that truly matters, and into which I am pouring myself? This song feels to me as if it attests to what *will* continually repeat itself, and which we cannot prevent from doing so even if we aim to do so–this will be painful, it will wrench and tear us–but we *must* experience this, we *must* experience this wrenching and pain, in order to truly live. To live life truly, fully, and deeply, "Love Will Tear Us Apart" proposes, *will* involve experiencing grief, loss, and pain, *because* we cannot fix and freeze forever what we love, it never remains constant, and in fact, like all else that exists, like all matter in motion in all modalities of matter in motion, emerges, develops, grows, changes, declines, ends, and passes on to contribute to the formation of the elemental basis for something else, something other and beyond, that will itself emerge, develop, grow, change, decline, end, and pass on in turn. The song encourages me to reflect on experiences in my own life when I have loved someone, or some place, or some thing, and felt torn apart, as I needed to recognize and accept my direct, immediate, and intimate connection with what I loved was coming to an end, and nothing I could do could prevent this from happening. It was ending, and I wished, desperately, it was not, and that I could do something, myself, to keep it going, to keep it as it was, at its peak–forever–but I could not. The song encourages me to reflect on loves of these kinds that I can recall wistfully, and in bittersweet terms, appreciating how much they have meant to me, and even more than that, have become important parts, important dimensions, of me, of whom I am, which I now maintain contact with by way of memory, memorabilia, and the lasting influence and impact they continue to exert in what, how, and why I think, feel, believe, and act as I do.

Like so many Joy Division songs, "Love Will Tear Us Apart" makes sense as centrally concerned with mediations. Unlike with Marx, these are not, at least seemingly not directly, capitalist relations of production and capitalist social relations or broadly. Unlike with Durkheim, these are not, at least seemingly not directly, structures of modern society that create problems in terms of the strength, cohesion, and effectivity of moral integration and regulation concerning relations between individuals and social groups. And unlike with Freud, these are not, at least seemingly not directly, fundamental constitutive divisions within the individual human psyche, or between competing instinctual needs and drives, or between the needs and demands of the social and the needs and demands of the individual. Mediation here comprises all of what creates alienation within erstwhile love relations, and it seems here that distance, in time and space, is a major contributing factor, but it certainly is plausible to argue that estrangement of people from the means and conditions of their labor, from the process and ends of their labor, and from their fellow laborers and from their place within nature and their distinctly human species-being, collectively undermine people's capacity to create and sustain love relationships, or at least to avoid these themselves becoming sites of alienation, exploitation, and commoditization. It certainly is plausible as well to argue that conditions of widespread anomie as well as further forms of rupture with nominal sites of prospective social integration and moral cohesion, such as in a hyper-polarized society where large groups of people do not trust each other and live instead according to sharply opposed perceptions of what exists, what is desirable, and what is possible, can likewise further undermine people's capacity to create and sustain love relationships. And it is certainly possible to argue that frustrated instincts to seek pleasure and indulge aggression, as well as overburdening individual conscience with excessive and unrealistic demands that lead all too readily to guilt, shame, and self-blame–or to agonized outbursts when that becomes too much to take–all likewise further undermine people's capacity to create and sustain love relationships. But it is not necessarily easy to draw a direct line between any of these conceptions of mediating forces and what "Love Will Tear Us Apart" most readily suggests. Since, like many Joy Division songs, "Love Will Tear Us Apart" offers us, in conclusion, no easy answers, and no easy way out, this song does seem like it suggests we need to find these for ourselves, by joining and following in the spirit of the song, *in struggle*. The reality and necessity *of struggle* is, if anything, all the song ultimately has to offer us in the form of something like an 'answer' to how to engage with the dilemmas it addresses. *To suffer yet also to struggle. To feel pain and yet to persist and to be ready to begin the process all over again, leading in the same direction. To accept what cannot be controlled.* To try to scrutinize and take responsibility at the same time for what is one's responsibility *and to try to control what one can, however little this might be.*

Works Cited

Badiou, Alain with Nicholas Truong. 2009. *In Praise of Love*. Peter Bush, trans. New York: The New Press, 2012.

The Bible. "I Corinthians 13." New King James Version. https://www.kingjamesbibleonline.org/new-features.php Accessed 8 August 2021.

Captain and Tenille. "Love Will Keep Us Together." Written by Neil Sedaka and Howard Greenfield. First recorded and released in 1975. Popular song.

Clifford, Jo. 2010. *Every One*. London: Nick Hern Books, 2016.

Collins, Phil, Mica Levi, Demdika Stare, Gruff Rhys, Florian Stirnemann, and more. *Ceremony* (Friedrich Engels's statue comes home to Manchester). NCP Bridgewater Car Park and Tony Wilson Place, Manchester, 16 July 2017.

Cox, Arnie. *Music & Embodied Cognition: Listening, Moving, Feeling, & Thinking.* Bloomington: Indiana University Press, 2017.

Curtis, Deborah. Contributing to Jon Savage, *This Searing Light, The Sun, and Everything Else: Joy Division–The Oral History.* London: Faber and Faber, 2019.

_____. "Foreword." Ian Curtis, *So This is Permanence: Joy Division Lyrics and Notebooks.* Deborah Curtis and Jon Savage, eds. London: Faber and Faber, 2014, vii-xi.

Curtis, Ian. *So This is Permanence: Joy Division Lyrics and Notebooks.* Deborah Curtis and Jon Savage, eds. London: Faber and Faber, 2014.

Dickinson, Bob. Contributing to Jon Savage, *This Searing Light, The Sun, and Everything Else: Joy Division–The Oral History.* London: Faber and Faber, 2019.

Durkheim, Émile. 1897. *Suicide: a Study in Sociology.* John A. Spaulding and George Simpson, trans. New York: The Free Press, 1951.

Freud, Sigmund. 1920. *Beyond the Pleasure Principle.* James Strachey, trans. New York: W.W. Norton, 1961.

_____. 1930. *Civilization and Its Discontents.* James Strachey, trans. New York: W.W. Norton, 1961.

Gay, Roxanne. "Why People Are So Awful Online." *New York Times.* 17 July 2021. https://www.nytimes.com/2021/07/17/opinion/culture/social-media-cancel-culture-roxane-gay.html Accessed 8 August 2021.

Glass, Philip. *Glassworks.* New classical chamber work of six movements. Composed in 1981 and first released on record in 1982.

Glass, Philip and Phelim McDermott. *Tao of Glass.* Manchester International Festival, 11-20 July 2019.

Gramsci, Antonio. 1929-1935. *Prison Notebooks.* Joseph A. Buttigieg and Antonio Callari, trans. New York: Columbia University Press, 2011.

Hegel, Georg Wilhelm Friedrich. 1821. *Philosophy of Right.* T.M. Knox, trans. Oxford: The Clarendon Press, 1952.

Hook, Peter. Contributing to Jon Savage, *This Searing Light, The Sun, and Everything Else: Joy Division–The Oral History.* London: Faber and Faber, 2019.

_____. Interviewed as part of Paul Morley, *Joy Division Piece by Piece: Writing About Joy Division 1977-2007.* London: Plexus, 2008.

_____. *Unknown Pleasures: Inside Joy Division.* London: Simon and Schuster, 2012.

Inspector George Gently. Created by Peter Flannery and starring Martin Shaw, Lee Ingleby, Simon Hubbard, Lisa McGrillis, Tom Hutch, and Helen Coverdale. TV crime drama, BBC, 8 Seasons: 6 April 2007–30 October 2017.

Joy Division. *Closer.* Music LP, 1980.

_____. *Closer.* Warner Classics Remastered Collector's Edition CD Package, 2007.

_____. "Disorder." Recorded Musical Song, 1979.

_____. *Heart and Soul.* London Records 4 CD box set with booklet, 2001.

_____. "Heart and Soul." Recorded Musical Song, 1980.

_____. "Isolation." *Closer.* Warner Classics Remastered Collector's Edition CD Package, 2007.

_____. "Isolation." Recorded Musical Song, 1980.

_____. "Love Will Tear Us Apart." *Heart and Soul*. London Records 4 CD box set with booklet, 2001.

_____. "Love Will Tear Us Apart." Recorded Musical Song, 1980.

_____. "A Means to an End." *Closer*. Warner Classics Remastered Collector's Edition CD Package, 2007.

_____. "A Means to an End." Recorded Musical Song, 1980.

_____. *Permanent*. Factory/Qwest/Warner Compilation CD, 1985.

_____. "Shadowplay." Recorded Musical Song, 1979.

_____. "Shadowplay." *Unknown Pleasures*. Warner Classics Remastered Collector's Edition CD Package, 2007.

_____. "Transmission." Recorded Musical Song, 1979.

_____. "Twenty Four Hours." Recorded Musical Song, 1980.

_____. *Unknown Pleasures*. Music LP, 1979.

_____. *Unknown Pleasures*. Warner Classics Remastered Collector's Edition CD Package, 2007.

Kennedy, Robert F. Campaign Slogan, US Presidential Campaign, 1968.

Lacan, Jacques. 1966. *Écrits*. Bruce Fink, Héloïse Fink, and Russell Grigg, trans. New York: W.W. Norton, 2007.

Machin, David. *Analysing Popular Music: Image, Sound, Text*. London: Sage, 2010.

Manchester Art Gallery and the Manchester International Festival. *True Faith*. Exhibition. 30 June-3 September 2017.

Marx, Karl. 1844. *Economic and Philosphical Manuscripts of 1844 (The Paris Manuscripts)*. Martin Milligan, trans. Mineola: Dover Books, 2007.

Marx, Karl and Friedrich Engels. 1848. *The Communist Manifesto*. Samuel Moore, trans. New York: International Publishers, 1948.

_____. 1844. *Theses on Feuerbach*. As cited in "Translator's Note on Terminology." *Economic and Philosphical Manuscripts of 1844 (The Paris Manuscripts)*. Martin Milligan, trans. Mineola: Dover Books, 2007.

McCullough, Dave. Cited in Mick Middles and Lindsay Reade, *Torn Apart: The Life of Ian Curtis*. London: Omnibus, 2009.

Mead, George Herbert. 1929. *Mind, Self, and Society: From the Standpoint of a Social Behaviourist*. Chicago: University of Chicago Press, 1962.

Middles, Mick and Lindsay Reade. *Torn Apart: The Life of Ian Curtis*. London: Omnibus, 2009.

Morley, Paul. *Joy Division Piece by Piece: Writing About Joy Division 1977-2007*. London: Plexus, 2008.

Nietzsche, Friedrich. 1888, 1900. *Ecce Homo*. Project Gutenberg. https://www.gutenberg.org/files/52190/52190-h/52190-h.htm Accessed 8 August 2021.

_____. 1882, 1887. *The Gay Science (The Joyful Wisdom)*. Project Gutenberg. https://www.gutenberg.org/files/52881/52881-h/52881-h.htm Accessed 8 August 2021.

_____. 1883. *Thus Spake Zarathustra: a Book for All and None*. Project Gutenberg. https://www.gutenberg.org/files/1998/1998-h/1998-h.htm Accessed 8 August 2021.

Orwell, George. *Nineteen Eighty-Four*. London: Secker & Warburg, 1949.

Plato. 375 BCE. *Republic*. Benjamin Dowett, trans. The Internet Classics Archive. http://classics.mit.edu/Plato/republic.html Accessed 8 August 2021.

Sankoff, Irene and Davie Hein. *Come From Away*. Phoenix Theatre, London. March 2019.

Savage, Jon. "Introduction." Ian Curtis, *So This is Permanence: Joy Division Lyrics and Notebooks*, edited by Deborah Curtis and Jon Savage. London: Faber and Faber, 2014, xxiii-xxviii.

_____. Contributing to Jon Savage, *This Searing Light, The Sun, and Everything Else: Joy Division–The Oral History*. London: Faber and Faber, 2019.

_____. *This Searing Light, The Sun, and Everything Else: Joy Division–The Oral History*. London: Faber and Faber, 2019.

Shaw, George Bernard Shaw. 1949. *Back to Methuselah*. The Internet Archive. https://archive.org/stream/backtomethuselah13084gut/13084.txt Accessed 8 August 2021.

Simpson, George. "Editor's Introduction." Émile Durkheim, *Suicide: a Study in Sociology*, John A. Spaulding and George Simpson, trans. New York: The Free Press, 1951.

Sumner, Bernard. *Chapter and Verse: New Order, Joy Division and Me*. London: Bantam, 2014.

_____. Contributing to Jon Savage, *This Searing Light, The Sun, and Everything Else: Joy Division–The Oral History*. London: Faber and Faber, 2019.

Taylor, Steve. 1979 *Melody Maker* concert review. Cited in Jon Savage, *This Searing Light, The Sun, and Everything Else: Joy Division–The Oral History*. London: Faber and Faber, 2019.

Unforgotten. Created by Chris Lang and starring Nicola Walker, Sanjeev Bhaskar, Peter Egan, Jordan Long, Lewis Reeves, Pippa Nixon, and Carolina Main. TV crime drama, ITV, 4 Seasons, 8 October 2015-29 March 2021.

United Nations. *Universal Declaration of Human Rights*. https://www.un.org/en/udhrbook/pdf/udhr_booklet_en_web.pdf Accessed 8 August 2021.

Walsh, Enda. *Grief is a Thing with Feathers*. Starring Cillian Murphy and adapted from the book of the same title by Max Porter. Barbican Theatre London. March 2019.

Whitehead, Malcolm. Contributing to Jon Savage, *This Searing Light, The Sun, and Everything Else: Joy Division–The Oral History*. London: Faber and Faber, 2019.

Wozencraft, Jon. Contributing to Jon Savage, *This Searing Light, The Sun, and Everything Else: Joy Division–The Oral History*. London: Faber and Faber, 2019.

Chapter Four

One

I have repeatedly taught Max Weber's *Protestant Ethic and the Spirit of Capitalism*, Louis Althusser's *On The Reproduction of Capitalism: Ideology and Ideological State Apparatuses*, and

Michel Foucault's *Discipline and Punish: the Birth of the Prison* in dialogue together with Ian Curtis and Joy Division. Students readily draw connections among readings of excerpts from these books, the life and death as well as the music as art of Ian Curtis and Joy Division, interests and concerns in their own lives, and broader social and political issues. We have found these three works of critical theory useful in inquiring into how oppressive power is maintained, in modern capitalist societies, especially without the need for use of directly physical coercion, as well as in seeking to make sense of dimensions of lived experience under capitalism often taken for granted as self-evident, beyond question, natural, normal, and even trans-historically and trans-culturally eternal and unalterable, when that is, in fact, far from the case, while belief that it is so results in pernicious consequences.

I discuss *Protestant Ethic and the Spirit of Capitalism* in section two, *On The Reproduction of Capitalism: Ideology and Ideological State Apparatuses* in section three, and *Discipline and Punish: the Birth of the Prison* in section four. In section five I identify key ideas from these books to serve as points of contact in encounters to come with Ian Curtis and Joy Division. In sections six through nine I stage these encounters, in section six with Ian Curtis and Joy Division represented by "Insight," in section seven represented by "New Dawn Fades," in section eight represented by "Atrocity Exhibition," and in section nine represented by "The Eternal." In staging each encounter I consider song title and lyrics; song structure and instrumentation; matters of loudness, rhythm, pitch, vocal delivery, and timbre; Arnie Cox's eight avenues of musical affect–mimetic participation, anticipation, expression, acoustic impact, implicit and explicit analysis, associations, exploring taboos, and the invisibility, intangibility, and ephemerality of musical sounds; and the three sets of summary and review questions I first engaged near the end of my descriptions, analyses, and interpretations of "Disorder," "Transmission," and "Twenty Four Hours," in chapter two, as well as the eleven overarching interpretations of what the music, as art, of Ian Curtis and Joy Divisions means, in response to what I hear when I listen to it, and what this makes me think (about) and feel, that I first set forth in chapter one.

Two

As Weber scholar Stephen Kalberg explains in an extensive introduction to his new, 2011, English translation of the revised 1920 edition of *Protestantische Ethik und der Geist des Kapitalismus*, written by Weber in German, and originally published in 1904-1905, Weber's principal thesis is as follows: the 'spirit of capitalism' originates in the realm of religion and not solely in that of economics, and this spirit exists in the form of an ethic or an ethos (9). As Weber himself concludes, near the end of *Protestant Ethic and the Spirit of Capitalism*, "Our analysis has demonstrated that one of the constitutive components of the modern capitalist spirit and, moreover, generally of modern civilization was the rational organization of life on the basis of the *idea of the calling*. It was born out of the spirit of *Christian asceticism*" (176). In subsequent elaborations upon this argument in *Protestant Ethic and the Spirit of Capitalism*, Weber explains the emergence and development of modern capitalism depended on, as compliments to economic forces, "the rational frame of mind, the rationalization of the organization of life, and a rational economic ethic" (253). The latter amount to a "methodical application of science to *practical* purposes" that maintains a Protestant religious origin. In *Protestant Ethic and the Spirit of Capitalism* Weber traces both the emergence and development of this ethic as well as its diffusion beyond its originally religious basis in shaping a new kind of human being who internalizes identification with the same ethic.

Kalberg insists Weber's argument has often been misunderstood. In fact, Kalberg emphasizes, the spirit of capitalism "has *many* origins; *PE* [*Protestant Ethic and the Spirit of Capitalism*] constitutes simply its major *religious* source" (63 n51). In other words, although Weber rejects Marxist explanations of the spirit of capitalism as arising (solely) from the economic interests of bourgeoisie, and as operating as a form of ideology (20), Weber does not deny that economic factors played a causal role. But Weber stresses the spirit of capitalism precedes modern capitalism, tracing a major dimension of its essential character to an historical origin in still early Protestantism.

As Weber recounts, despair over uncertainty concerning election versus damnation could not be long tolerated, within dissenting Protestant denominations influenced by yet modifying the teachings of 16th century Protestant theologian John Calvin. The doctrine of predestination asserts, in sum, that an elect few are predestined to be saved, for everlasting life, while the vast majority are predestined to be damned, for everlasting death; who has been chosen and who has not is unknowable; and nothing humans do can effect whether they are chosen or not. God's ways surpass human understanding, God knows all and (pre)determines all, and, as Weber paraphrases, God's "grace cannot be lost once granted and cannot be attained once denied" (119).

Weber describes the resulting effect of this Calvinist doctrine as "a feeling of unimaginable inner *loneliness of the solitary individual*" (119). Melancholy arises because no one can intercede on anyone's behalf; no one can guide others in leading a life that will lead to salvation. The roots of Puritan distrust of the sensuous and the affective lie here as both are useless for salvation while offering false hope and sentimentalizing illusion. Following Calvin, the logical impetus, for Puritans, is to live life without any such hope or illusion, while the orientation to work, to word hard, and to do little else but so work, within Calvinist-influenced Puritanism, is all about paying tribute to the glory of God, not because doing so will effect whether one is elected or damned, and not because this can influence or enable personal salvation.

Post-Calvinist Protestant denominations found ways to overcome despair over uncertainty concerning election versus damnation by emphasizing the virtue of devotion to work and working, and especially the virtue of success in so doing. Such dedication, and especially such success, gradually became accepted as a preeminent sign that an individual is chosen for salvation. As Weber puts this, more precisely: "*Work without rest in a vocational calling* was recommended as the best possible means to *acquire* the self-confidence that one belonged among the elect. Work, and work alone, banishes religious doubt and gives certainty of one's status among the saved" (125).

Kalberg explains the spirit of capitalism that originates with Post-Calvinist Protestantism, beginning with the Puritans, is equivalent to "a configuration of values that implied the individual's duty to view work as an end in itself, to labor systematically in a calling, to increase capital, to earn money perpetually (while avoiding enjoyment of it), and to comprehend material wealth as a manifestation of [what Weber cites as] 'competence and proficiency in a vocational calling' [81]"

(39). Weber proposes Benjamin Franklin, in his renowned popular advice on how to live a productive, successful, and indeed virtuous life, is a quintessential early modern representative of this spirit of capitalism. What Weber finds most significant in the advice Franklin offers is "the idea of the *duty* of the individual to increase his wealth" becoming "an *ethically* oriented maxim for the organization of life" as a whole (79), along with the fact that "all virtues, for Franklin, become virtues *only to the extent* that they are useful to the individual" (80). By Franklin's time (in the mid to late eighteenth century), the ethic from which this spirit emerged has become secularized. As Kalberg puts it, this ethic had been "routinized into maxims, community norms, a particular demeanor, and familiar customs and traditions" (40). Yet, even when divorced from direct links with religious belief and practice, historical links to the same remain traceable, especially to the 'idea of a calling'–that is, pursuing a calling in one's job, career, and profession.

Weber is interested in the origin and evolution of the commonsensical notion that work, working, and especially hard work and working hard, are of fundamental importance in defining identity and worth, both for one's self and for others, and are, what's more, evidence of good moral character. Weber proposes this remains a highly influential Puritan legacy. As Kalberg sums up Weber's point, "Many people define self-worth according to their success in a profession" and in so doing demonstrate the persistent impact of this 'ethic', representing "secularized legacies of ascetic Protestantism" (10).

To this day, it remains commonplace in the US, and other similar countries, at the beginning or early in an acquaintance, for us to ask the other person what they do for work, as their job, and for us in turn to regard this dimension of their identity as highly significant. In chapter three I discussed the influence of this same work ethic upon me, through my family, and how powerful this was for me, even though we were Catholic. I also discussed much the same impact upon multiple hypothetical individuals, representing composites of multiple real people I have known, including many students I have taught and otherwise worked with closely. It remains common in our dominant culture, and others like it, routinely to ask young people what they plan to 'be', and not just 'do'–conflating job/career/profession with identity– when they grow up or when they finish school. Likewise, many students, along with others whom students interact with, treat 'being a student' as 'their current job', even their current profession or career. It is common for someone in that position to respond to the question 'what do you do?' by indicating, for instance, 'I am a business management major at UW-Eau Claire'.

Students commonly identify themselves with their major, or likely or prospective major. It often strikes me that more students' email signatures share their major and other areas of concentration than faculty or staff share the equivalent. Students often feel guilty if they have not yet chosen a major, if they are still undecided among multiple possible majors, or if they are dissatisfied with their current choice of major. For students, a major, just like having a job, is important in defining their identity, and their worth, while without it they can feel lacking in identity and worth. I consider this guilt-inducing pressure unfortunate because I believe an undergraduate education should be foremost concerned with exploring, including multiple possible areas of concentration. I believe an undergraduate education should prioritize learning widely and diversely, including ever more about one's self, about one's interests and capabilities. And I believe an undergraduate education should emphasize learning how to be a knowledgeable, sensitive, concerned, and engaged citizen, who is multi-dimensional, and neither whose identity nor whose worth can be reduced to solely what paid job they do.

Another common way the pervasiveness of this influence upon what one does 'for work' shows up is in the form of embarrassment in being out of work, even temporarily so, or about the social status of the kind of job one does. In my own life, from early on, even while far from adult age, I met many others, adults and people who were still kids, who felt their life was less meaningful, and they were being irresponsibly lazy, in intervals between jobs, even during breaks on weekends or for vacations, and when 'only' working 'part-time'. At UW-Eau Claire, as well as at other colleges and universities where I've taught, peer pressure has led many students to feel they 'need' to obtain a paid job, or multiple paid jobs, as well as take a maximal load of classes, in order to feel good about themselves, so that neither they themselves nor others will judge them as lesser or lacking in worth, on account of being irresponsibly lazy.

Peer pressure has done this, in fact, to many students who did not 'need' such a job, or jobs. Many students have likewise felt an implicit peer pressure to sign up for more classes, involving more credits, than they can reasonably handle, and then ending up, almost inevitably, needing to withdraw from one or more classes and not doing as well, or not learning and gaining as much, from any of their classes as they would have had they chosen a less demanding schedule. What's more, in weekly check-ins as well as through numerous other conversations, I frequently find students experience a need to explain and justify what, as well as how much, they are doing in their lives, especially how much and how hard they are working, and even to seek my implicit approval for them 'to take a break' now and then, when they are becoming exhausted or overwhelmed, because they, again, would not want to be perceived, including by themselves, as lazily irresponsible. I empathize, as I myself often continue to struggle, even though I certainly 'should' 'know better', with feeling guilty if I am not prioritizing 'work', of one kind or another, and if I cannot indicate that I have been 'productive' in 'accomplishing' 'important tasks' and 'meeting important goals' each and every day.

Another useful connection that comes to mind here follows in noting well how many Black athletes and artists, achieving success in sports, music, film, and television, have fought, along with their fans and supporters, to be respected, equally to White athletes and artists, *for how hard they worked* to achieve success, and *for how hard they continue to work* 'at their craft', challenging racist assumptions that Black people who succeed in these fields do so on account of 'natural' talent, on account of innate physical predispositions, while White people who succeed in these fields do so by working hard to cultivate their skill and talent, and 'by using their brain'. This is an important challenge to make, without a doubt, but what is also evident here, once more, is the social valuation of working hard as worthy of greater respect and acclaim than doing anything that seems easy or 'comes naturally'.

Reviews and critiques of popular musicians often rank considerably higher those perceived as working hard, consistently working hard, and indeed evidencing this hard work by continuing to innovate as well as to push themselves to their limits, and beyond, to 'give everything they have and more' to the composition, recording, and especially performance, in particular 'live', of their music. At the same time, when it seems to reviewers and critics that musicians are 'not taking risks' and 'not pushing themselves' but are 'resting content' to 'follow the same established formula' they are sharply criticized on this account–and the same happens with musicians who reviewers and critics judge as not working sufficiently hard to cultivate an impressive, and imposing, performance of their music live. Musicians who come across as working especially hard, and who are willing to put on exceptionally demanding live shows, routinely receive high praise for so doing.

Paul Lafargue, Karl Marx's son-in-law, wrote a famous short book, *The Right to be Lazy*, first published in 1883, yet the impact of Lafargue's argument and of others like it continues to be much less influential than reiterations of, and variations upon, what Weber identifies as 'The Protestant Ethic'. A corollary contribution of this ethic is it makes being poor appear indicative not only of laziness but also of an even poorer moral character.

In *Poorly Understood: What Americans Get Wrong About Poverty*, Mark Robert Rank, Lawrence M. Eppard, and Heather E. Bullock offer a persuasive argument, backed by substantial factual evidence, that Americans maintain many false beliefs about poverty and 'the poor', including about what causes people to become–and to remain–poor. As Rank, Eppard, and Bullock document, "between the ages of 20 and 75 years, nearly 60 percent of Americans will experience living for at least 1 year below the official poverty line, while three-fourths of Americans will encounter poverty or near-poverty" (10). Yet, "The conventional image of welfare use is one of social deviancy" as "few behaviors are as stigmatized in American society," with Americans all too often, and all too predominantly, perceiving poverty as "something that happens to others," and especially to those less capable and in particular less deserving (12-13).

As Rank, Eppard, and Bullock extensively illustrate, poverty "can happen to any of us" (26) for a great many different reasons, and in fact economic insecurity in America is widespread (27). What *is* 'abnormal', the authors contend, is not poverty per se, but the fact that in the United States "we have chosen as a society to punish" "normal life events" that lead to poverty (28). In comparison with other OECD (Organization for Economic Co-operation and Development) countries (including 38 of the world's overall richest countries, primarily in Europe and North America, but also including Japan, South Korea, Australia, New Zealand, Chile, Costa Rica, Columbia, and Mexico), the US provides far less support for people in poverty or at risk of poverty, including far less help for people to get out and stay out of poverty, by means of collective investment in provision of social welfare. As a result, "poverty is a much more normal and systemic feature of the American experience than it is in many other wealthy countries" (28).

Since our dominant culture in the US tends to deny that poverty is a "normal consequence of structural arrangements guaranteed to produce economic insecurity," this same culture likewise tends to "to undermine our empathy" with those commonly perceived, again, as 'others' essentially 'unlike us' and as less capable and less deserving than us (30). In one of the 'expert appraisal' sections included at the end of chapters in *Poorly Understood: What Americans Get Wrong About Poverty*,

Alice O'Connor, Director of the Blum Center on Global Poverty Alleviation and Sustainable Development at the University of California at Santa Barbara, sums up what is, contrary to prevailing misconception, at the crux of explaining poverty in the US today: "Economic hardship is a problem of the vast inequity not just in terms of low wages, but also in the fact that individuals do not have any control over the economy or jobs and wages" (38).

As Rank, Eppard, and Bullock reiterate, "The myths surrounding" the question of 'why is there poverty' "have generally centered on the belief that poverty is the result of individual failing" which dovetails with American idealization of "rugged individualism and self-reliance" (39). Yet, as numerous individuals struggling with poverty share, in Mark Rank's book *Chasing the American Dream*, they "have worked extremely hard their whole lives but have struggled to get ahead financially," many needing to work much harder in poverty than not. As one contributor sums up what this experience has been like for her and others she has known in comparable circumstances, "living in poverty is exhausting!" (42-43). Rank, Eppard, and Bullock explain "there is simply a lack of decent-paying jobs to support all Americans," at least above and beyond poverty-level income, because "approximately 40 percent of jobs currently in the United States" are "low-paying jobs" while "Many of these jobs are lacking in benefits such as health insurance" (44-45). Many "low-paying jobs" are "structured as part-time work, allowing employers to forgo benefits to their employees" (45). Rank, Eppard, and Bullock maintain Michael Harrington's argument in his renowned 1963 book *The Other America* continues prescient: "The real explanation of why the poor are where they are is they made the mistake of being born to the wrong parents, in the wrong section of the country, in the wrong industry, or in the wrong racial or ethnic group. Once this mistake has been made, they could have been paragons of will and morality, but most of them would never even have had a chance to get out of the other America" (quoted 46).

The Protestant Ethic Weber theorizes is insidious in encouraging people to found their sense of their own and others' identity and, especially, worth on what kind of job they do, and on how hard they ostensibly work at that job and beyond, with success in so doing typically measured in terms of how much income and wealth they earn through that job. This same ethic is equally insidious in encouraging people to believe hard work leads inexorably to success, that hard work will always bring rewards, and even, paradoxically enough, that 'hard work is its own reward'. Rank, Eppard, and Bullock contest the "prevalent myth that poverty is largely the result of bad decision-making" by showing how, pace Harrington, "the social and economic class that one finds oneself in is extremely important in shaping the types of decisions that are made" and that it is important not only to identify "those who lose out at the game" but also "why the game produces losers in the first place" (56). Rank, Eppard, and Bullock argue the latter is not necessary, not inevitable, not natural, and therefore an ethic rooted in the supposedly divine predestination of a minority who will be saved versus a majority who will be damned contributes to mystifying what can be done to overcome poverty, suggesting 'the poor will always be with us' and they will always be considerable in number.

The example of other wealthy countries put the lie to this belief, while poverty and economic insecurity have significantly increased in the US over the past forty years: during this period of time "the American economy has increasingly produced larger numbers of jobs that do not pay well, do not provide benefits, and only offer part-time hours" (58). Indeed, "nearly twice the proportion of full-time American workers" work "in low-wage work relative to average workers in comparison countries" and contrary to moralistic demonization of 'the poor' as people who simply no not want to work, or work hard, poverty is most common among people doing 'part-time work' because they cannot find full-time work that they can do while also managing "caregiving responsibilities and school" (58).

"Underlying the bad decision-making myth is the belief that each of us has near-total control over determining the shape of our lives," which as Rank, Eppard, and Bullock explain is far from the case, but this belief is a legacy of the Protestant Ethic, and aptly illustrated in the advice proffered by Benjamin Franklin, who persistently contends individuals are themselves responsible for their success or their failure, according to how hard and how well they work. Franklin's position lends ready support to a commonplace division between the 'deserving' versus the 'undeserving' poor, with the former distinguished from the latter according to their ostensible greater willingness to work, and to work hard. As Rank, Eppard, and Bullock counter, poverty is not traceable to individual failure and lack of deservedness, but rather to a "structural" failure and "an injustice of a substantial magnitude" (93) due to insufficient opportunities to survive and subsist above poverty in the US today. And even though cumulative evidence overwhelmingly demonstrates that welfare helps people in poverty, including to get out and remain out of poverty, many Americans believe the exact opposite to be true, despite welfare fraud being rare.

Welfare can help in the face of the 'uneven playing field' in the US, one mystified by meritocracy. According to meritocratic belief, people are more versus less successful–including in avoiding or overcoming poverty–entirely according to their own merits, according to whether they have earned and thus deserved this success–or not. Rank, Eppard, and Bullock illustrate how meritocracy is mystification by asking readers to imagine a more 'realistic' game of Monopoly: "the players start out with quite different advantages and disadvantages, much as they do in life. Player 1 begins with $5000 and several Monopoly properties on which houses have already been built. Player 2 starts out with the standard $1,500 and no properties. Finally, player 3 begins the game with only $250" (136). In this version of Monopoly player 1 maintains substantially greater chances of winning than players 2 and 3 while player 3 maintains substantially greater chances of losing than the other two: "given the advantages or disadvantages at the start of the game, the result is additional advantages or disadvantages as the game progresses" (137). "This analogy illustrates the concept that Americans are not beginning their lives at the same starting point" while "the cumulative process" further "compounds advantages or disadvantages over time" (137).

This analogy reminds me that considerable popular and not just scholarly or activist attention has been devoted recently to highlighting how systemic racism, from slavery to Jim Crow and 'the new Jim Crow' of mass incarceration, in particular for low-level drug offenses, has left Black and Brown Americans, especially Black Americans, with far less equity, on average, to pass on to their children than White Americans maintain. This disparity follows racist barriers that have long limited as well as often prevented Black Americans from owning their homes, or from owning homes located in neighborhoods with high property values. As a result, Black Americans start off 'the game', on average, with considerably fewer assets than White Americans.

What makes this situation even worse Rank, Eppard, and Bullock illustrate by way of analogy to another game: musical chairs. Again Rank, Eppard, and Bullock modify the set-up of this game to better correspond to the social reality Americans actually face. Not only are an insufficient number of chairs available for all seeking to find one to sit in, 'once the music stops', but also participants are positioned at unequal distances from the chairs that are available. Insufficient resources are available, at present, for all Americans to live beyond poverty, no matter how long and hard people work, and no matter how deserving their moral character. Some people start from positions that make it much easier for them to be successful, without having done anything to earn this. Some people starts from positions that make it much more difficult for them to be successful, without them having done anything to deserve this. As Rank, Eppard, and Bullock elaborate,

> Seventy-eight percent of African Americans grow up in highly disadvantaged neighborhoods, compared with only 5 percent of Whites. The schools that Whites and Blacks attend today are still segregated and unequal. Environmental burdens disproportionately threaten Black communities. African Americans are treated unequally at every stage in the criminal justice system. The list goes on and on; wherever one looks in American society, the playing field is not level. (142)

This "enormous inequality commits structural violence" on social groups such as Black Americans, "who carry a higher risk of hardship than other groups because of forces that are largely outside of their control" (143). "We decide as a country how much inequality we will have" as the resources exist in the US today to overcome and end poverty, for all Americans, but these are currently invested elsewhere (143). Imagine, for instance, spending the billions of dollars devoted every year of the twenty years the US spent waging the War in Afghanistan toward instead combating poverty in the US–imagine what a difference that might have made.

But why do myths concerning poverty and the poor persist as they do? Among other factors, Rank, Eppard, and Bullock cite the influence of "Individualism, meritocratic beliefs," other beliefs that the world is always already inherently just as is, and "the Protestant Work Ethic" in explaining "the persistence of stereotypes about people experiencing poverty" (158). But "who benefits from the existence of these myths?" and "what functions might they play in the wider society?" (163). According to Rank, Eppard, and Bullock, politicians "of various stripes have used the myth of the welfare freeloader" to their advantage to insinuate the 'lazy poor' relying on social welfare support, provided through the state, are solely Black people–or solely Black, Latinx, and Native American people, or solely yet other people of color, or primarily recent, and undocumented, Black and Brown immigrants. This insinuation facilitates dividing working class Americans along racial lines by reactivating what W.E.B. Dubois first theorized as the 'psychological wage' poor White Americans earn on account of being White in a White-dominant society (163). In addition, if poverty is understood as a matter of individual failure, for which the individual themself is responsible, this undermines inclination for low-income people to organize collectively to work to change their common conditions, and to build coalitions and alliances among low-income and low-wealth groups of people coming from different kinds of (ethnic and racial) backgrounds.

Yet another key beneficiary of this state of affairs is "the affluent" because the "myth that poverty is the result of individual inadequacies rather than structural failings provides a convenient justification for the status quo of rising inequality" (163). I contend this same myth provides a convenient justification for private appropriation and accumulation of vast amounts of wealth by a small few while a great many struggle to barely get by at all. This myth provides a convenient justification for massive socio-economic inequality in the US today, as, after all, according to this myth, the rich 'deserve their riches, because they have earned it', whereas the poor 'deserve their poverty' because 'they have not earned anything more or better'.

In *Protestant Ethic and the Spirit of Capitalism* Weber finds one of the most important contributions of the Protestant ethic to the spirit of capitalism involves associating the acquisition and accumulation of wealth with God's blessing–in other words, as a sign of God's hand at work in making this happen. As Weber proclaims, summarizing the implicit logic of this position: "And since the success of work is the surest symptom that it pleases God, capitalist profit is one of the most important criteria for establishing that God's blessing rests on the enterprise" (226). Kalberg elaborates by declaring, "Indeed, because the devout could acquire a psychological certainty of salvation only by an ethical *surpassing* of the utilitarian calculations of everyday routines" this meant "God's glory deserved nothing less than . . . 'mastery of the world'" (36). Such mastery, those originally identifying with this position quickly conceived as only achievable by means of a thoroughly "methodical-rational organization of life" (37), including the 'life' of the firm or enterprise, readily leading from that point toward production on an expanded scale founded in the exploitative appropriation of value generated by means of others' labor, along with amassing steadily greater profit and accumulation from so doing. According to the logic of this position, those who are the most industrious, those who work the hardest, those who make the greatest sacrifices, and those take the greatest risks are those who, as a result, 'naturally' as well as 'logically', obtain the greatest success–which they fully deserve.

This position remains common in capitalist societies like the US today. Many continue to believe, and even to insist, the rich are rich because they have earned their riches, including by means of their hard work, and by their exceptional devotion to and skill at this work. Those identifying with this position do *not* believe the rich are rich because of how they are advantageously positioned in capitalist relations of production, and in the capitalist marketplace, often beginning with huge advantages over those who must sell their labor-power to capital in order to obtain the means to survive and subsist, because the latter maintain no capital themselves, or little of it, that they can make use of to enable this survival and subsistence. What's more, the prevalence of this ideological position shows up in how often people refer to the capitalists who maintain ultimate control over capitalist enterprises as if they are the sole producers of the goods or providers of services these companies produce or provide, neglecting the work of an often vast number of employees who work to produce these goods and provide these services.

It is often assumed those working for a wage as employees do not assume risks, unlike their employers, but those who are poor must take many risks in order to find ways to survive and subsist. Just working in a company for another who determines whether you are hired or not, whether your employment is renewed and continued or not, on what terms and at what rates of compensation, in what kinds of relations with fellow workers and with the means of production the company provides, puts workers at risk in ways the owners of these companies do not face. This risk includes being dismissed from or not rehired to do your job, and it includes being forced, in order to do your job, to accept working conditions that lead to illness and injury, not to mention alienation from being unable to bring more than a small portion of the capabilities you maintain. Control of the means of production through accumulation of capital, and the wealth it provides, protects capitalists from facing the kinds of risks that come from the economic insecurity working class people all too commonly face.

Weber recounts how Post-Calvinist ascetic Protestantism proposes all that is wrong with acquisition of wealth is enjoyment of and indulgence in it, or resting content with what one has achieved in what ideally should be a life devoted to ceaselessly generating, acquiring, accumulating, and investing ever greater wealth–i.e., never wasting opportunities to further attest to God's glory by means of how much wealth one can amass. After all, the purpose of life is to work ceaselessly at your calling, and the more successful you are in so doing the clearer this is is indeed your calling, the clearer you have been called by God to this path. Logically, success at work of this kind should lead toward generation and concentration of considerable wealth in your hands. Wealth is only problematic if it tempts one away from continuing to work hard, and productively, at one's calling. As Weber explains, "Ascetic Protestantism shattered the bonds restricting all striving for gain–not only by legalizing profit but also by perceiving it as desired by God," effectively investing the the pursuit, acquisition, and accumulation of wealth with a religious sanction (169-170). This sanction in turn "gave to the employer the soothing assurance that the unequal distribution of the world's material goods resulted from the special design of God's providence" (174).

From early on, as Kalberg summarizes Weber's argument in this connection, Puritan and post-Puritan Protestant religious sects "*directed* believers in a systematic manner toward profit, the accumulation of wealth and work in a vocation" (199). According "To Weber, only the rigorous organizing of life that occurred in 'the ascetic sects could legitimate and put a halo around the economic "individualist" impulses of the modern capitalist ethos' [226]" (199). As Weber further comments, "The development of the concept of the calling first gave to the modern entrepreneur a fabulously clear conscience–and also to industrious workers" the same, with erstwhile ascetic Protestantism moreover increasingly identifying "ethical fitness" with "business responsibility" (255).

Weber conceives of capitalism and modern capitalism as significantly distinct entities. For Weber, capitalism has existed universally since early on in human history but modern capitalism develops in the 18th and 19th centuries in 'the West'. As Kalberg explains, Weber conceives of capitalism as, in essence, "involving the exchange of goods and calculations of profit and loss balances in terms of money" (14). What is, in contrast, distinctive about "modern capitalism," again as Kalberg explains Weber's conception of this difference, is "a relatively free exchange of goods in markets, the separation of business activity from household activity, sophisticated bookkeeping methods, and the rational, or systematic, organization of work and the workplace in general. Workers are legally free in modern capitalism rather than enslaved. Profit is pursued in a regular and continuous fashion, as is its maximization, in organized businesses" (14). Further key to distinguishing modern capitalism, and directly connected to his central thesis, is, as Weber puts it, "the organization of economic activity in terms of an 'economic *ethic*'" which principally involves "the idea of the *duty* of the individual to increase his wealth" (79) and the further idea that labor is "an absolute end in itself" (86).

This 'modern' conception and valuation of work and working represents a break from a dominant ethic in preceding 'pre-modern' times where work was more often regarded as drudgery or what was to be engaged in only sporadically and unsystematically. Economic traditionalism (predominant before modern capitalism) did not involve the continuous pursuit of more and more money, through more and more work. Yet modern capitalism not only involves this continuous pursuit of and emphasis on the preeminent importance of work, but also has greatly increased the intensity of human work. Key is the contribution of an ethic that valorizes "the capacity to feel an 'internal dedication to work'" along with "a dispassionate self-control and moderation" so as to incite the worker to concentrate effectively on striving to steadily increase productivity in and through work, in order to generate not only the source of profit but also the source of the expansion and growth of capital accumulation (87). In the emergence of modern capitalism the ideal type of capitalist employer is ruthlessly dedicated toward 'his' enterprise, and toward running it in a highly rational way, while ascetically eschewing what distracts 'him' from this end–i.e., 'his' calling effectively consumes his attention, interest, and concern.

Ascetic Protestantism made a vital contribution to the primitive accumulation of capital which made it possible for modern capitalism to 'take off'–i.e., to *the formation of capital through asceticism's compulsory saving*" (170). Ascetic Protestants enjoyed a significant competitive advantage versus non-ascetic business owners, Protestant or not, because ascetic Protestants were not inclined to spend their profits on themselves or to take time off from continuing to make more money. They were instead motivated to invest the vast bulk of their profits back into the enterprise, in order to expand and strengthen it, including in competition with others, and to work relentlessly and continuously toward achieving these ends. So, in sum, for Weber what distinguishes modern capitalism from pre-modern capitalism is not a drive to acquire goods, or to pursue profit, or to seek any other form of material gain, because all of these are commonplace long before modern capitalism, but rather that all of these ends are pursued "in a rational and continuous manner" (236-237).

What stands out as especially central to Weber's overall argument is, as Kalberg describes this, Weber's discussion of how Puritanism "called methodical work, the pursuit of wealth, and virtuous conduct to the forefront" and identified these as "providential" as opposed to purely "utilitarian" activities (27). In other words, "*Methodical* labor in a *vocational calling*" is "'commanded to all' by God" (27) while, once again, "Unceasing work in a calling . . . enables the faithful simply *to consider* themselves among the chosen" (28) and thus "labor as a vocational calling acquired a *religious* significance" (28). Work that leads to the generation of wealth, and especially in abundance, both testifies and contributes to God's glory–because God is, supposedly, the ultimate true source of this wealth and the human being who ostensibly takes charge of it is merely God's vehicle, or vessel.

Emphasis on the importance of 'the calling' is crucial for Weber and it is easy to recognize the continuing influence of this notion, as an ideal, because a great many people attest they experience the greatest satisfaction doing work that feels to them as if this represents a calling, while a great many people aspire to find a vocation that is 'their calling'. If not by means of a paid vocation, many people also seek 'their calling' in what they do elsewhere in their life. Finding and pursuing a 'calling' means finding and pursuing something that truly matters, deeply fulfills, and of which people can feel proud as well as receive praise from others because it allows people to pursue what they believe they are best at and even destined to do. The last sentiment is commonly alluded to by many people doing jobs they love: 'I feel like I was made to do this job', 'I feel like this is the job I was born for', and even 'I feel like this job is me' or 'I feel like this job enables me to show who and what I am, at my best, at my most capable'.

Many students I have taught have shared with me that they aimed for a well-paying job that would enable them to lead a secure and comfortable life, yet many others have contended this goal was not of the greatest importance to them because they wanted instead to lead their life being a particular kind of good, valuable, useful, accomplished, or contributing person, regardless of what paid job they might do. In both cases students identified their ideal job, and career, to be one where they could do work they would greatly enjoy doing, that would fulfill needs beyond providing a liveable wage, and where they could bring to bear their greatest strengths, skills, talents, interests, and passions.

Students often ask me when as well as why I decided to become a professor. I tell them I did not know what I wanted to do as a job, as a career, as a profession, by the time my undergraduate education was nearing its end. I only knew I was eager to learn more in areas with which I was just beginning to become familiar–notably critical theory. So I decided to go to graduate school to do the latter and in effect postpone my decision about what I would do once I had 'finished school'. But I also already knew I enjoyed teaching, and expected I would enjoy doing this, while I also loved pursuing an intellectual life, so I was strongly inclined toward becoming a professor. Once I decided a master's degree was insufficient to satisfy my steadily growing interests in, and indeed passions for, a number of fields of English Studies, I decided to pursue a PhD. From early on as a doctoral student I determined, especially as I gained experience teaching, that I indeed did want to become a university professor. But I also wanted to become a university professor because I felt through this kind of job, in this kind of career, and as part of this kind of profession, I could do work in pursuit of what would feel akin to a calling for me–this would be work where I would draw upon and bring to bear my greatest strengths and pursue my foremost passions.

Perhaps the unspoken to unconscious sense that I approached this prospect akin to pursuit of a calling also had much to do with how I accepted the challenge involved in obtaining such a position. This challenge is even more formidable today because far fewer tenure-line faculty positions exist in humanities fields such as English Studies than the number of people qualified for and interested in these kind of positions. That disparity illustrates one of the problematic dimensions of the continuing influential notion that the best kind of work, the truly most 'exalted' kind of work, is work that one can experience and pursue as 'a calling', because at the same time, and traceable all the way back to John Calvin, few are ever so 'called' while a great many more never are.

Yet further problematic, the pursuit of massive profit and accumulation no longer appears greedy or self-interested but rather as duty and testimony to the glory of God. An initially religiously motivated imperative prepared the way for thoroughly secular successors. As Weber wryly observes, "At a practical level, this doctrine basically means God helps those who help themselves" because "the [post-]Calvinist creates for himself the *certainty* of his salvation"–not through good works, unlike with Catholicism, but rather through application of "*systematic self-control*" in dedication to a calling (127). The ostensible aim becomes to "increase God's glory on earth" through those means humans are able to bring to bear (129). What happens, significantly, in the course of this emphasis, is a movement toward concentration entirely on this-worldly as opposed to other-worldly phenomena.

What ascetic Protestantism contributed is "the psychological *motivation* that arose out of the conception of work as a *calling* and the means best suited–and in the end often as the *sole* means–for the devout to become certain of their salvation" (175). The legacy of this position is that "For the modern worker, the view of work as a 'vocational calling' became just as characteristic as the view of acquisition of money as a 'vocational calling' became for the modern employer" (175).

So a developing thread throughout the course of post-Lutheran Protestantism is the development of the position that a state of grace "could only be acquired through a *testifying to belief*" and this requires "specifically formed conduct" and more precisely that the individual follow an imperative "to *methodically supervise* his or her state of grace" (156-157). What this led to, logically, and here's where we begin to recognize how fully this imperative blended with the rise of modern capitalism and its distinctive 'spirit', is "*rationalization* of the conduct of life–now in the world yet still oriented to the supernatural" as "the effect of ascetic Protestantism's *concept of the calling*" with this in turn showing up in "a new task: to saturate mundane, *everyday* life with its methodicalness" (157).

Weber concentrates near the end of his book on what has transpired since Franklin's time, in what Weber identifies as "victorious capitalism." This stage of modern capitalism, Kalberg explains, involves a "*routinization* of the motives behind economic activity from value-rational to means-end rational" (49). In turn, an originally singularly religiously rooted motive becomes almost totally sublimated. By Weber's time, the capitalist economic order has become, as he puts it, "a vast cosmos into which a person is born. It simply exists, to each person, as a factually unalterable casing . . . in which he or she must live. To the extent that people are interwoven into the context of capitalism's market forces, the norms of its economic action are forced onto them" (81).

Victorious capitalism and its routinization are useful concepts, which can be readily linked to recent and present times, where if anything it is often all that much harder for most to imagine any form of organization of social relations beyond capitalism, a position Mark Fisher has influentially theorized as 'capitalism realism'. Capitalist realism leaves even harsh critics of capitalism finding it easier to imagine the end of the world than the end of capitalism. Fisher conceives of capitalist realism as a powerful dimension, and effect, of dominant capitalist ideology, under late 20th to early 21st century conditions of neo-liberalism, that needs to be combated and overcome. In connection with Weber, capitalist realism suggests continuity with what had already become widely predominant a century previously, and that is the notion that capitalism represents the furthest possible achievement in human history, in terms of the systemic organization of social relations. Although Weber maintains, as Kalberg indicates, a more ambivalent position concerning the positive value of capitalism than Fisher, Weber's entire theoretical work resonates a strong sense of 'foreboding', in response to the perceived pace, scope, and direction of changes within modern capitalist society at the turn of the 19th into the 20th century and on into the early 20th century.

Weber is particularly concerned with an erosion in the importance of moral values, because, as Kalberg explains, these "Values alone . . . offer dignity and a sense of self-worth" and because Weber fears the "spirit of capitalism, which assisted the birth of the new economic order" has become, in early 20th century 'victorious capitalism' a "'steel-hard casing' devoid of compassion" (13). For Weber, "the rational work ethic of Puritans, and their style of life generally, gave a strong boost to the development of modern capitalism" especially with profit and property conceived not as strictly utilitarian ends but as testimony to worth and ability. Eventually, however, the initial religious trappings of this ethic faded and disappeared to the point where "'victorious capitalism' now sustains itself on the basis of *means-end rational* action alone" (42). At this point, in Weber's own time, "Whether employees or entrepreneurs, people born into this 'powerful cosmos' are coerced to adapt to its market-based, functional exchanges in order to survive. The motivation to work in this 'steel-hard casing' involves a mixture of constraint and means-end rational calculation" (42). Moreover, by Weber's time, modern capitalism had evolved in the direction of hyper-specialization, to the point that Weber worries people are being reduced in their total capacities, especially dangerously in their capacities for strong feelings, for ethical values, and for moral living. As Kalberg declares, "to Weber the dignified life–the life directed comprehensively 'from within' . . . now appears endangered. Amid the dependency of most persons upon a modern economy characterized by sweeping coercion, practical rationalism, impersonal exchange relationships, and narrow specialization, a cultivation on a broad societal scale of the life organized by reference to ethical values seems utopian. The person unified by core values–'the personality'–will soon disappear, Weber fears" (43). Instead, modern capitalism in its 'victorious' form, functions, as Weber puts it, as a "grinding mechanism" (177) that wears people down until they effectively lose their distinctly and genuinely human personality and character.

Weber contrasts "The Puritan" who "*wanted* to be a person with a vocational calling" with 'us', who "*must* be" (177). This means the drive for material gain is no longer a 'light cloak one can throw off at any time' but rather "a steel-hard casing" in which we recognize how "the world's material goods" have "acquired an increasing and, in the end, inescapable power over people–as never before in history" (177). Victorious capitalism, "ever since it came to rest on a mechanical foundation, no longer needs asceticism as a supporting pillar" (177). Optimism concerning life devoted to productive work, in work conceived a a calling, has declined and is fading, as "the idea of an 'obligation to search for and then accept a vocational calling' now wanders around in our lives as the ghost of past religious beliefs" (177).

This last contention suggests an increasingly large number–even an increasingly large majority–of people living in modern capitalist societies recognize, however resignedly, that they will *not* be able to pursue a vocation as a calling, and they must simply settle for whatever can best provide for their survival and subsistence. Finding a job, a career, and a profession ends up more often, in practice, a matter of "economic coercion" than a means of realizing "the highest spiritual and cultural values" (177). Especially in the United States, according to Weber, work, and in particular striving to find and define what work is best for each individual, has increasingly come to be "associated with purely competitive passions," involving "the character of a sports event" far more than that of a religious practice (177).

One of the most famous phrases from Talcott Parsons's previous English translation of *Protestantische Ethik und der Geist des Kapitalismus* is that of 'the iron cage'. Kalberg explains why he has changed the English translation of *stalhartes Gehäuse* from Talcott Parsons's "iron cage" to "steel-hard casing" by indicating the latter is a more literal translation, and it also more overtly characterizes "the 'hardness' of the constraining casing, as emphasized in the mechanistic images" Weber uses in the same paragraph "to describe this new 'powerful cosmos'" (397). What's more, Kalberg contends, his translation more effectively links up, than Parsons's does, with the preceding 'lightweight coat' metaphor of something that "has now hardened" (397). This now "encases persons and cannot be thrown off," at least not easily, unlike what was the case previously (397). As Kalberg elaborates, "'Steel-hard' conveys a theme crucial to Weber . . . the massively impersonal, coldly formal, harsh and machine-like character of modern public sphere relationships whenever they remain uninfluenced by traditions or values" (397). Yet, 'steel-hard casing' also suggests a contingent situation rather than something absolutely inescapable and irreversible in contrast to 'cage' which "implies great inflexibility and hence does not convey this contingency aspect as effectively as 'casing' (which, under certain circumstances, can become less restrictive and even peeled off)" (398).

Although I do find Kalberg, overall, convincing here, it is worthwhile to take into account, nonetheless, the fact that Parsons's translation as 'iron cage' has exerted considerable influence. Whether 'steel-hard casing' or 'iron cage' this is a striking metaphor and one that does suggest a seriously disturbing state of affairs. Weber is referring, no matter how this is translated, to people becoming trapped in needing to lead a life in pursuit of material acquisition, profit, and accumulation, in continuous competition with others, where work toward these ends takes over one's life and becomes life's primary effective purpose. People are encased, or encaged, by being caught up in a ceaselessly ongoing pursuit of money and what money can buy. Weber fears people living in the age of 'victorious capitalism' correspond to Nietzsche's 'last humans' who have become "narrow specialists without minds" and "pleasure-seekers without heart" (178). "Mechanized ossification" threatens to destroy the human within the human (177).

Weber warns against what is not yet inevitable, unpreventable, and irreversible, but nonetheless it is unsurprising this section of Weber's *Protestant Ethic and the Spirit of Capitalism* has proven especially memorable and influential, as it speaks directly to late modern capitalism and what might be substantially problematic within and about late modern capitalist society and culture. This warning resonates with contemporary pressures to spend and buy more and more, to continually 'upgrade' one's lifestyle by means of what one can purchase, by means of what one can pay for and what one cannot in fact afford (such as, for example, by 'maxing out' credit cards), and to feel like one must always make choices in terms of what one does for a job, career, and/or profession, as well as what kind of major or other field of concentration one chooses at university, in accord with what will enable one to be able to buy and spend the most freely, easily, and extensively, including on 'big ticket' and 'luxury' purchases.

People's well-being is often, in contemporary capitalist society, closely interconnected and even rooted in what they own, in their material possessions, and in what they can display by these means, including in terms of how they are able to display themselves through these means. Meanwhile, even unconsciously, people often judge others' worth, and certainly others' attractiveness and appeal, in terms of what these others are able to afford, and what these others are able to buy with the means they have to spend on material goods and material services.

Facing an overpowering imperative to participate in this constant pursuit, it can become easy to lose touch with other kinds of ends, and especially with other kinds of values. I have known many university students who have decided they need to major not in the field they found most interesting and appealing, or even where they were most successful, but rather what they believed would enable them to earn the most money and lead the most successful life defined in terms of what they would be able to afford to buy with the money they earned.

Advertisers bombard us continuously by appealing to what we supposedly 'need', but often don't 'need' as much as 'want', while planned obsolescence leads us to 'need' frequently to update models of what we use–from our clothes to our personal computers to much more besides. Frequently we are urged to 'treat' ourselves to what we 'deserve' by spending money. Even when not often inclined to respond to these kinds of appeals, we nevertheless frequently believe, if we have experienced a tough time, that we 'deserve' to 'treat' ourselves by 'spending' on what can help compensate for this tough experience.

Almost everywhere one goes, it is necessary to pay for access to social resources as neo-liberalism has privatized housing, education, transport, communication, energy utilities, social care, and increasingly health care as well–while eliminating many neighborhood and community centers, sports and recreational facilities, and park and wilderness areas that were previously freely or inexpensively publicly accessible and publicly shared, to make room for privately owned, for-profit, businesses and enterprises. It remains jarring for me to witness massive commercialization of seemingly every dimension of sports venues, courts and fields, broadcasts, and player uniforms, but for most of my much younger students, it is hard for them to understand why I might feel this way and to imagine how things might be different.

Even when and where we are not consciously aware of advertisers and marketers, and even when and where we imagine we have successfully 'blocked' them, they are still frequently able to access the histories of our internet activity, including in particular our web browsing and web searches. Companies such as Google are notorious for their elaborately thorough and meticulous accumulation and analysis of this data, as well as for developing and selling predictive means of influencing how and what we will buy as a result. In societies like the contemporary US and UK it becomes extremely difficult for many not to spend considerable time every day attending to internet sites, especially social media as well as apps and games purchased and played on internet-connected smart phones and other kinds of computers, where we can be readily tracked, and where information about what we do, and like to do, including what we might buy as well as how we might be best encouraged to buy, can be extensively and continuously harvested.

Once this all seems to be simply what is entirely normal and natural, with no alternative conceivably possible or desirable, we are left in a position where it becomes questionable whether we are still learning how to make critical connections as opposed to engaging in narrowly reified forms of thinking, to appreciate the value of general knowledge as opposed to narrow specialization, and to be concerned with actively extending care, compassion, and empathy, as opposed to concentrating on commodified forms of pleasure, comfort and security.

Kalberg proposes Weber's critique of capitalist society in his time, at the end of the 20th century and early in the 21st century, resonates with "a generalized 'McDonaldization'" of late 20th to early 21st century capitalist society and that the 'McDonalization of society' thesis "flows directly out of *PE*'s last chapter" (58). As George Ritzer and Steven Miles explain in "The changing nature of consumption and the intensification of McDonaldization in the digital age" Ritzer's book

> *The McDonaldization of Society*, first published in 1993, dealt at one level with the nature of contemporary consumer society, but at another addressed the fact that society is increasingly characterized by processes of rationalization as originally discussed in the work of Weber (1968 [1921]). The book represented an attempt to investigate the changing character of contemporary social life. McDonald's was presented as being symbolic of broader aspects of social change, the "paradigm case" if you will of "the process by which the principles of the fast food restaurant are coming to dominate more and more sectors of American society as well as the rest of the world" (Ritzer, 1993: 1). The argument then was that the focus on McDonald's provided a metaphorical means of highlighting the change toward a more highly controlled, bureaucratic, and dehumanizing society.

In other words, the McDonalization thesis proposes that capitalist society as a whole has increasingly come to operate much like this same fast-food restaurant chain: carefully prescribing and closely regulating what is produced for consumption, quickly and uniformly, according to a monotonously methodical mode of rationalized design, production, and delivery, even while packaged as if it represents something much different: fun and friendly, and even unique and novel, while simultaneously familiar and dependable. According to this thesis, blandness pervades a 'soulless' mass culture where people are increasingly unable cognitively to recognize the former and devoid emotionally of the capacity to feel the latter.

Kalbeg touts Weber theorizing culture's causal capacity, rejecting Marxist economic determination of culture, including in last instance (46), while strongly emphasizing the shaping impact of history–of long history: what Kalberg succinctly identifies as "interpenetration of past and present" (47). For Weber, as Kalberg interprets his theoretical work, "the domains of religion, law, rulership, and the economy develop at uneven rates" and society is "an array of multiple, dynamically interacting spheres, each potentially endowed with an autonomous causal thrust and unfolding along its own pathway" (47). Weber encourages taking culture seriously as exerting considerable social impact–and this certainly logically would seem to include not just religion but also the arts, including 'the popular arts', including popular music such as the music of Ian Curtis and Joy Division.

Three

Louis Althusser's "Ideology and Ideological State Apparatuses: Notes Towards an Investigation" has proven enormously influential in critical studies. I have taught this essay or excerpts from it in numerous classes since working as a graduate student instructor onward, while Althusser's essay made a signal contribution to my own thinking about how to conceive of ideology, and to engage in ideology critique, in Marxist terms, even as I have diverged from accepting the concepts and articulations of relations among concepts that Althusser proposes in exactly the terms and along exactly the lines Althusser proposes. Many students in classes I teach frequently find Althusser's conception of ideological interpellation, as well as his conceptions of ideology as an imaginary representation of an individual's relation to the individual's real conditions of their existence and the materiality of ideology to be compelling, while they are likewise frequently intrigued by Althusser's conceptions of Ideological State Apparatuses (ISAs), of specific ISAs such as in particular churches and schools, and of relations as well as distinctions between the ISAs and the Repressive State Apparatus (RSA). Students usually find it easy, prompted by me sharing initial illustrative examples, to come up with examples of their own demonstrating how each of these dimensions of Althusser's overall theory can be usefully explanatory.

Yet, "Ideology and Ideological State Apparatuses: Notes Towards an Investigation," best-known in English via a translation by Ben Brewster that was initially published in 1971 in *Lenin and Philosophy and Other Essays*, is actually a condensed selection of two extracts from Althusser's much larger, and ultimately unfinished, book *Sur la reproduction*. This larger book was only published for the first time in French in 1995, and then in an English translation, by G.M. Goshgarian, with a preface by Etienne Balibar and an introduction by Jacques Bidet, in 2014, as *On the Reproduction of Capitalism: Ideology and Ideological State Apparatuses*. The larger book helps considerably in elucidating Althusser's theory, as well as emphasizing exigent and kairotic dimensions of this work–i.e., the precise historical context out of which the book emerged and into which Althusser is seeking to intervene. Notably, in *On the Reproduction of Capitalism: Ideology and Ideological State Apparatuses* Althusser explains how he conceives of this book as only the first part of a two-volume work, with the complete theory he is developing in volume one ultimately dependent upon what the second, never written book would have taken up.

As Balibar indicates in his preface, with *On the Reproduction of Capitalism: Ideology and Ideological State Apparatuses* Althusser aims to re-found or as necessary re-construct Marxist theory of history and society–historical materialism–by means of his innovative theorization of ideology and Ideological State Apparatuses, thereby strengthening the effective influence of Marxism, as revolutionary theory and practice, at a time when many Marxism*s* were proliferating along with much distancing from and breaking with orthodox Marxism among other prominent 'leftists' likewise committed toward active struggle for revolutionary social change. Althusser felt a strong sense of loyalty to the French Communist Party, of which he was a long-time member, while at the same respecting the contribution and value of new social movements, in particular the promise of the Paris 1968 Uprising in placing socialist revolution on the agenda as a practical possibility–positions many members of the French Community Party did not share. As Althusser declares: "The time is ripe" (4) and "the moment is propitious" (5) for the kind of theorization he sets forth in *On the Reproduction of Capitalism: Ideology and Ideological State Apparatuses*, because "We are entering an age that will see the triumph of socialism across the globe . . . *the revolution is already on the agenda*" (6). Althusser foresees the world dramatically changing within 50-100 years, and is optimistic concerning the prospects for revolutionary socialist transformation of capitalism on a global scale. This is especially striking to note well given the fact that one of the most common critiques of Althusser's "Ideology and Ideological State Apparatuses: Notes Towards an Investigation" is it is 'functionalist', meaning it suggests societies, and in particular capitalist societies, are structured to insure every major constituent dimension of these societies functions to insure its reproduction. According to this critique, Althusser's theory is effectively pessimistic about the possibility of substantial, let alone revolutionary change, because it closes off all viable ways to account for the latter happening. *On the Reproduction of Capitalism: Ideology and Ideological State Apparatuses* in fact conveys a strong sense of revolutionary optimism, written in the immediate afterglow of the Paris 1968 Uprising. Althusser aims to equip socialist revolutionaries with insight he believes they will need in what he imagined would soon become a pivotal stagee in revolutionary socialist struggle.

As Althusser declares, in "To My Readers" at the beginning of *On the Reproduction of Capitalism: Ideology and Ideological State Apparatuses*, in the two-volume theorization he plans volume one focuses on the reproduction of capitalist relations of production while volume two will focus on class struggle in capitalist social formations. It is important to take this entire plan, never fully realized, into account, in order to understand that Althusser always aimed, in volume two, to complicate the theory he sets forth in volume one, the only volume he was able to complete (because of challenges Althusser faced due to severely disruptive and debilitating experiences of what is now recognized as bipolar disorder). Nevertheless, Althusser's principal focus of concern in *On the Reproduction of Capitalism: Ideology and Ideological State Apparatuses* continues relevant, significant, and indeed urgent.

Jacques Bidet sums up what Althusser is tackling in terms of the following question: "under what conditions, in a society that proclaims its devotion to the ideals of freedom and equality, is the domination of some people over others endlessly reproduced?" (xix). I suggest this formulation is imprecise. Althusser is concerned not simply with explaining the domination of 'some people' by 'other people' but rather the domination of the few over the many, and even more precisely, proletarians and members of other subordinate social classes by capitalists closely aided and abetted by capitalists' principal agents and functionaries. What's more, for Althusser, exploitation, not simply domination, is fundamental. This means Althusser conceives of the few securing means of domination by way of what they are able to extract from the many. Also, for Althusser, the domination with which he is concerned is by no means necessarily always easily reproduced. As Althusser repeatedly stresses, this is a complex process, rarely entirely smooth and seamless, always subject to contradiction and resistance, and comprising many areas of potential–and actual–vulnerability. Althusser takes pains to meticulously elaborate his theory of the reproduction of capitalist relations of production, in particular by way of the contributions of ideology and the Ideological State Apparatuses, because, he argues, this is an intricate process, in which every stage is, at least prospectively, a site–and stake–of class struggle.

According to Althusser himself, what he, in sum, is theorizing in *On the Reproduction of Capitalism: Ideology and Ideological State Apparatuses* is as follows: "The system that ensures the reproduction of the relations of production is the system of the state apparatuses: the repressive state apparatus and the ideological state apparatuses" (1-2). Even though this process of reproduction often works remarkably well, it is a process that must be materially enacted, continuously, over and over again; human agents are what enable this process to happen, not inhuman structures. In particular, individuals interpellated as subjects of ideology materially embody ideology and carry out the work of ideology. Because this is a process that needs to be carried out continuously, and because it requires human beings to materially enact it, ample room exists for other outcomes beyond reproducing the social status quo entirely unchanged.

In order to lay the groundwork for understanding what is involved in the reproduction of relations of production, Althusser first revisits classic Marxist economic theory, beginning with the proposition that "Every concrete social formation is based on a *dominant* mode of production" even as multiple modes of production exist within every social formation, and not just a single dominant mode–i.e., "dominated modes," especially residual, vestigial, or archaic modes as well as emergent or anticipatory ones (19-20). For Marxism, a mode of production is a unity of productive forces and relations of production. This is always a contradictory unity, not only in the sense of comprising a site of tension and struggle–within and among the forces, within and among the relations, and between the forces and relations–but also because it is a unity effected by other modes of production existent within the same social formation. What's more, every social formation in turn encompasses an even more complex unity between all of its forces of production in all of its modes of production and all of its relations of production in all of its modes of production (20). Within a mode of production it is the relations of production that play the dominant role versus the forces of production, although the relations of production do so–dialectically conceived–on the basis of and within the limits set by these forces.

463

Let's review these classic Marxist concepts further. A mode of production equals a particular way of articulating forces of production with relations of production. Forces of production include means of production plus labor-power. Means of production include such things as plant, equipment, tools, machinery, raw materials and supplies, and the overall organizational structure of the process of production. Labor-power includes not just the sheer ability to labor, but also the skills, training, knowledges, and other kinds of competencies laborers acquire and are required of them in order to perform particular kind of productive tasks. I myself find it helpful in explaining what are forces of production, in Marxist terms, to identify these as including all relations IN production: all relations among all inputs involved in the process of production itself. I suggest in turn it is helpful in explaining what are relations of production, in Marxist terms, to identify these as including all relations FOR and FROM production; i.e., relations PRIOR TO and FOLLOWING UPON the actual, direct process of production.

The major kind of relations of production involve ownership and control. In other words, the term relations of production covers two things of key importance. First, relations of production covers who holds what inputs required in the production process, prior to the production process, as well as to what extent, and who controls what inputs are employed in the production process itself, as well as in what ways. Second, relations of production covers who appropriates what outputs from the production process, to what extent, and in what ways. Note well that Althusser is leery about use of 'ownership' in this context: Althusser does not focus here on who 'owns' inputs into and outputs from the process of production because 'ownership' suggests a legal relationship rather than a strictly economic one. Althusser argues what is of concern, in strictly economic terms, is who 'holds' the means of production; who 'holds control over' the process of production, including the labor invested in this process; and who 'takes hold of' the product of production. Yet, to reconnect more directly with Althusser's developing theorization in *On the Reproduction of Capitalism: Ideology and Ideological State Apparatuses,* what accounts for the priority Althusser gives to the relations of production over the forces of production is the fact that the relations of production precede and exceed production proper–these relations determine relative roles in relation to the process of production proper, as well as who gains versus who loses as a result, in what relative proportions, and who is able to do what as a result of what their positions in production enable and as result of what the process of production generates.

Within the productive forces, "in which people figure as agents of the labour process, *the means of production are the determining element*" (23). This is so because those who hold these means of production also hold significant advantage over those who do not in terms of relative power, control, and ability to appropriate from and through the process of production. This difference also accounts for the effectively unequal market power capitalists and workers maintain in the market where the capitalist buys the worker's labor power and the worker sells this labor power to the capitalist. Key here is that the means of production are held not by those who dispose of their labor-power directly in the immediate process of production but rather by those who operate outside of the direct labor process–the "capitalist exploiters" (25). This difference in position versus the means of production helps explains how in turn relations of production prove pivotal in determining what type of unity is involved with forces of production, and even more precisely how and for what–for what ends and in whose interests–these forces are mobilized. In other words, those who hold the means of production and appropriate from the process of production the products of production without contributing directly to this process and its creation of the product–"without providing anything 'in return'"–are positioned so as to be able to "appropriate a share of surplus labor" (27). They maintain hold of the means of production before production and appropriate the product after production, conceding a share to the workers (28). This constitutes "a relation of the one-sided *distribution* of the means of production between those holding them and those without them" (27).

In order better to understand Althusser's mobilization of classic Marxist economic theory I find it useful to provide further background concerning classic Marxist theory of history and society, as well as concerning classic Marxist economic theory. According to Marxism, social classes are not permanent and eternal, but correspond to a historically specific–albeit lengthy–stage of human history. Humans produce means of survival deliberately, collectively, including a social product that divides between a necessary social product and a surplus social product. The necessary social product, conceived from the vantage point of the laborer, refers to the equivalent in value necessary to provide for the survival and subsistence of this same laborer; under capitalism the necessary surplus product refers to the value equivalent of the worker's wage. The surplus social product refers to the equivalent in value of everything else that is produced beyond what is required to compensate the laborer for their labor sufficient that they will be able to continue to labor, so that they will be able to survive and subsist. The social surplus product is important and valuable, it is by no means necessarily at all problematic in itself, but what is so, from a Marxist vantage point, is its appropriation by a small minority from what is generated by a vast majority to primarily serve the independent interests of this small minority and only secondarily serve the collective interests of the whole of society. And what is yet further problematic is chief among these independent interests is securing the means to insure that such exploitative appropriation will repeat and continue, including on an expanded basis.

In class societies, the class that holds the means of social production, and thereby controls the processes of social production, typically appropriates the social surplus product for itself; under capitalism, this is the capitalist class. Under capitalism, workers own nothing of value sufficient to support and sustain themselves other than their own labor-power, whereas capitalists maintain considerable wealth beyond this, and in particular, hold the means of social production which the workers need to engage in order to put their labor-power to use. Workers sell their labor-power to capitalists in order for this to transpire. Capitalists buy labor-power but make use of labor, and they depend on being able to set labor to work to create value substantially greater than the cost of the labor-power they paid for. Members of ruling classes, such as capitalists under capitalism, do not *need* to work themselves in order to support and sustain themselves, even if they often choose to do so, because they are able to use their hold and control over the means, processes, and ends of others' work to appropriate, accumulate, and invest wealth sufficient to support and sustain themselves, including often in considerable luxury. It is this latter hold and control, furthermore, that not only enables the capitalist ruling class to support and sustain itself but also to dominate throughout society.

The cost of labor-power, paid for in terms of wages, includes what Marx identifies as both a biological-physiological minimal component as well as a moral-historical maximal component, where the size and nature of the latter is affected by the relative balance of power between capital and labor in the course of class struggle, as well as by the size of the reserve army of labor (the unemployed and underemployed). The cost of education, skilling, and training, as well the money needed to cover the cost of various secondary and tertiary needs of workers and their families along with their consumer desires all become parts of the moral-historical component of the cost of labor-power. The laborer must be paid a wage sufficient to enable them to take care of themself such that they will be physically able to return to their work and to continue to be able to work. This constitutes the biological-physiological component of the cost of labor-power. Yet, the cost of labor-power also includes what it takes to compel the laborer to be willing to return to work and to do this work in a satisfactory fashion. This means the laborer will press to be paid sufficiently to provide for more than minimal basic needs, and the cost of labor-power will include what is necessary to pay for the standard of living that a given society at a given period in time regards to be necessary to function adequately, and satisfactorily, as a member of the working class of that particular society–i.e., to be morally just and fair. For instance, as Marx himself wrote, the moral-historical cost of labor in France included the cost of enabling workers to buy and consume wine, whereas in England it included the cost of enabling workers to buy and consume beer. Capital always strives to keep this moral-historical component down while labor always strives to keep it up, and this explains one crucial dimension of the ongoing class struggle between capital and labor that is centered directly around the workplace.

But let's return now to Althusser. What is key for Althusser here, in his revisiting of classic Marxist economic theory, is emphasizing that capitalist relations of production are relations of exploitation, and that this exploitation resides in the control by capitalists of the 'surplus product' along with the 'surplus value' it represents, as "the value conceded to the individual worker in the form of a wage by no means represents the 'value of his labour', but only the value required to reproduce his individual labour-power" (32). Exploitation, once again, is more precise than domination: exploitation involves the ability of one to take from another, to take what another has produced and make it one's own without having produced this oneself and without fairly and adequately compensating the other for what is taken from them. Exploitation enables the exploiter to make use of what the exploiter takes from the exploited to strengthen the exploiter's position relative to that of the exploited by turning what the exploiter has taken from the exploited into profit, accumulation, and investment in expanded means of exploitation so as to in turn further advance the exploiter's hold and control over what the exploited is able to produce and which the exploited will yet again take from them. This all leads, as Althusser stresses, to a point that is crucial to recognize before it is possible to proceed further in attempting to explain the reproduction of capitalism: "Capitalism is a mode of production whose overriding objective is to produce, not objects of social utility, but surplus-value and capital itself . . . the driving force of capitalist production is the 'profit motive'," production of surplus value "*by means* of the production of objects of utility," and that will enable uninterrupted growth of exploitation an on extended scale (33). In other words, capitalism is a mode of production that creates use-values mediated by and subordinate to exchange-values where the generation and appropriation of surplus value can be turned into private profit and accumulation–for capitalists.

As Althusser frequently urges his readers never to forget, class struggle is rooted in production itself, and is constantly ongoing, given the fact that production is in fact the locus of relations between exploiters and exploited–it is where they meet up as exploiters and exploited and where exploitation happens (36). The frequent employment by capitalists of extensive surveillance and repression in the workplace, designed to insure the smooth operation of the generation of maximal surplus product, representative of maximal surplus value, which the capitalist appropriates and converts to private profit and accumulation, is one ready testament to how the workplace itself is a prime locus of class struggle (39). Capitalists engage in class struggle by frequently expecting, if not demanding, that workers work long(er) and hard(er) on the job, including by requiring workers to do significant portions of their work away from their direct workplace, without offering additional compensation for workers doing this. Capitalists make greater profits through these means, as well as by other means of waging class struggle such as hiring 'flexible' labor, used only when, where, and as long as absolutely needed, often 'part-time' and compensated at a lower wage on account of this status alone. Capitalists can make greater profits in waging class struggle by changing their operations so as to employ cheaper labor in areas where they can manage to pay lower wages and offer fewer (or no) paid benefits, as well as increase the intensity of labor demanded during work shifts–e.g., this includes moving operations to different localities, regions, or countries to achieve these ends. Many profitable capitalist firms wage class struggle in striving to increase profits by getting fewer laborers to do the same amount of work as previously performed by a larger number of laborers (without increasing wages) and by increasing the pace and extent of demand placed on workers at the workplace so that the same number of workers produce more in the same amount of time (again without increasing wages). Other comparable efforts included keeping close tabs on what workers do and don't do on the job, including on precisely how much and for how long they are working according to how they are directed to work on the job rather than doing anything else. Capitalists wage class struggle by prompting workers to feel so enthusiastic about their work, and their workplaces, that they readily give more of themselves to the job, and this includes encouraging workers to conflate their own identity and their own interest with that of the company as well as to think of themselves and their fellow workers as all part of the company 'team' or 'family'. Ironically, pressure to function as part of a 'team environment' within a capitalist firm often involves encouragement for workers to compete against each other, and even to spy and report on each other, and this dividing of workers against each other effectively conquers their collective resistance before it begins, yet further optimizing conditions for capitalists to maximize profits.

Many workers who do not consciously or deliberately organize in opposition to their exploitation are nonetheless at least partially aware they are exploited, and through various 'everyday forms of resistance', such as taking more time for themselves than directed, taking home goods from the workplace, ignoring or otherwise defying specific orders or mandated procedures, etc. they engage in class struggle. Likewise, when workers do jobs where they attempt to do right by customers and give them what they truly want and need, at the same time that the company tells these workers not to be so honest, or not to be so helpful, these workers are also engaging in class struggle–by resisting identification with capitalist values (that what ultimately matters most is always, first and last, the bottom line). Workers engage in class struggle as well when they exhibit pride in their work, and aim to give it their best, no matter how cost-effective this may or may not turn out to be; in so doing they are effectively attempting to take back control of their labor from the companies they work for, to exercise control over how they exercise this labor, for what, and in accord with what standards. And workers also engage in class struggle when they fight back by uniting and mobilizing together, to push for higher wagers and better benefits; for improved conditions in the workplace, including increased autonomy concerning and authority over the work they do; for greater security of tenure; for more opportunities for advancement as well as for further training and 'upskilling'. Workers engage in class struggle by fighting back to take greater control over the quality of their lives, within and beyond the workplace, including so they are better able to deal with demands of child care and elder care, or care for disabled members of their households. Workers engage in class struggle by fighting back against efforts to divide and conquer them along lines such as race and ethnicity. And workers engage in class struggle in fighting to secure accommodations for fellow workers with physical and mental disabilities. These and many further possible examples suggest how the workplace functions as a site of class struggle in capitalist society, for both capitalists and workers.

Another important point Althusser makes early in *On the Reproduction of Capitalism: Ideology and Ideological State Apparatuses*, is that, contrary to dominant ideology, social mobility in modern capitalist societies is rare and uncommon, with most people remaining in the same social class into which they are born (37). This claim has been amply supported by many serious studies over virtually the entire history of modern capitalism, including, for example in the United States today, by Mark Robert Rank, Lawrence M. Eppard, and Heather E. Bullock, in *Poorly Understood: What America Gets Wrong About Poverty*, which I referred to in the previous section of this chapter. What is also important to recognize, in this connection, though, for Althusser, is that highly skilled and specialized forms of labor maintained by particular strata of workers provides a significant advantage to these workers, especially when these kinds of skills and specializations are relatively rare and/or costly to produce (38). This helps explain why many workers continually chase means of raising and adding to their qualifications: capitalists tend to pay more and provide better working opportunities for workers bringing these kinds of skills and specializations to bear than they do for those who do not.

Althusser repeatedly proposes that it is useful to think about the classes that exist in modern capitalist societies by identifying these in terms of their functions, both in terms of capitalist production and in terms of reproduction of the conditions of capitalist production. On page 41, for instance, Althusser distinguishes "those who perform only *functions of production*" (proletarians), "those who perform *functions of exploitation* that are always *simultaneously* functions of production (engineers, upper-level technicians, production managers, and so on)," and "those who perform *functions of repression* that may be combined with functions of exploitation (supervisors, from foremen to certain engineers) or may not (the goons expressly recruited in a number of factories to serve as informers and execute, among other tasks, all the police manoeuvres of the gutter-level anti-union struggle." All three of these groups of people work for capital, which means capital is in ultimate control over their labor, yet significant differences show up in terms of the levels and rates of compensation these groups respectively earn as well as even greater disparities often show up in terms of the conditions under which they work.

Yet what tends in practice, 'normally' to unite these groups of people, across these three classes, is a common acceptance of capitalist ideology that effectively justifies and legitimates the compensation they receive for their work, and the conditions they encounter in their work. As Althusser explains, exploitation works because proletarians and others who work for capital must take jobs in which their labor is exploited in order to survive and subsist, as well as due to *"the bourgeois ideology of 'work'"* that insures workers accept what presently exists, in the here and now, is what must be, and is even desirable and beneficial–to them (42). This 'bourgeois ideology of work' consists in fact of a panoply of *"illusions/impostures of bourgeois ideology of work"*–i.e., many distinct way of encouraging identification with work, under existing conditions, as right, necessary, and good, including, for example, Weber's 'Protestant Ethic' and associated kinds of valorizations of a *duty* to work, and work hard, in order to demonstrate ones's upright moral character. So class struggle, on behalf of the proletariat (and potential 'middle class' allies as well) includes struggle against bourgeois ideology and in particular against its hold over proletarians and others (43).

After first explaining how non-human means of production are reproduced, Althusser then turns to discuss reproduction of labor-power, emphasizing an important contribution via what people learn in school. The last includes not just 'know-how' but also "the 'rules' of good behaviour" and "in the final analysis, the rules of *the order established by class domination*" (51). Key here is "reproduction of labour-power's *submission to the dominant ideology*" for workers and for agents of exploitation and repression, in turn involving reproduction of these agents' *"capacity to handle the dominant ideology* properly," so as to take up and perform ther proper roles in ensuring "the domination of the dominant class" (51). Althusser adds that the 'know-how' students learn in school also tends to come wrapped "in forms that ensure *subjection to the dominant ideology*" so it is not only in teaching 'the rules of good behavior' that schools inculcate dominant ideology (52). Whenever teaching at schools suggests to students, directly or indirectly, they are learning so as to become equipped to take up positions within the existing capitalist economy, with this economy essentially unchanged, and with no need, or possibility, of in any way questioning, challenging, and working to transform it, this teaching at these schools contributes toward this ideological end, of insuring capitalist domination through the reproduction and maintenance of capitalism and capitalist society.

Schools often serve as conduits for dominant ideology, encouraging students (along with parents and guardians) to identify the primary purpose of education in school as being that of training students to fit into social roles within existing capitalist society, within capitalist society as it is, and especially to perform jobs within the existing capitalist economy as it is. One often overlooked way that schools, and schooling, contribute to this end arises from accustoming students from an early age, and for a considerable number of years thereafter, to accept hierarchical divisions as natural and normal. The design and shape of classrooms typically physically materializes this implicit lesson, especially when the teacher is always positioned in front, with a large desk, table, or teaching station, while the students are always positioned all in rows, further back in the classroom, looking toward the teacher and not toward each other, and with each student provided only a small desk, table, or other space in which to prop up and store what the student brings with them to the classroom. Likewise, when the default mode of teaching and learning is continually assumed to involve a teacher speaking, at length, primarily by way of lecture, with students listening, at length, and primarily taking notes, along with limited dialogue other than brief question-and-answer exchanges between the teacher and students without students ever talking to and working with each other, this tends to reinforce to students that this is the natural and normal way life is and will always be, in the workplace and beyond. In other words, the implicit lesson here is it crucial to learn how to recognize and accept one's place, obediently submissive to and even entirely directed in terms of what one is to do, when, where, how, and why (for what) by an authority figure who is totally and exclusively 'in charge'.

I myself have struggled continually, throughout 35 years of teaching, to try to convince those in charge of classroom design and maintenance to create more classrooms in which we can all sit, in a conference, roundtable, or seminar-style set-up, so that everyone can readily see and talk with everyone else, and where the teachers sits _with the students_, yet all too often to little avail. I have frequently needed to work with my students to rearrange furniture within classrooms to approximate this kind of setting, as best possible, often enough needing to return everything to its 'default setting' at the end of each class session in order to avoid complaints from others who prefer only ever to teach in line with this default arrangement, primarily by lecturing to the students, accompanied by powerpoint presentations, through the vast majority of class time in all meetings of all classes they teach.

Returning, however, once more, directly to Althusser, he next identifies a major contribution of schools involves directing students into different class positions following their time in school, and we can witness how this happens via means such as tracking (in my high school, for example, we had separate basic, general, academic, honors, and advanced placement tracks for five separate groups of students, often overtly identified as heading onto five different kinds of jobs–and lifestyles) as well as through separating different groups of students within a single community (or even separating students between adjacent or nearby communities) by directing students to attend schools of different 'quality', 'rank', or 'stature', which in turn tends to lead to these students subsequently positioned in different quality, rank, and stature jobs–and lifestyles. We can witness this process at work as well in the ways schools help sort out which students are directed toward a university education versus which students are not, and between those directed toward more versus less prestigious universities, including on account of respective (in)ability to pay. And we can witness this process at work, once more, in terms of whether students are directed toward more overt kinds of vocational training early on, as well as in terms of what kinds of training for what kinds of vocations–while similar distinctions happen with students who are designated, even early on, as poor learners, or as troublemakers, or as students needing of 'special' (remedial) assistance and support, as well as with students designated as 'gifted and talented'.

According to Althusser, schools help train students to take up their proper positions and perform as expected within the following social classes: "the exploited (the proletarians), the exploiters (the capitalists), the auxiliaries of exploitation (supervisory personnel)" and "the high priests of dominant ideology" as well as yet other of dominant ideology's "'functionaries', and so on" (52). In sum, what people learn in and through school, according to Althusser, involves a contribution to the reproduction of labor-power needed for capitalist production not just in terms of people's qualifications to labor in positions as part of discrete production processes, but also in terms of subjection to dominant ideology, which means people learn not to question, challenge, critique, and work to transform capitalist society and thereby not to undermine let alone displace the dominance of the dominant capitalist class (52).

In order to proceed closer toward explaining how ideology and the Ideological State Apparatuses contribute to reproducing the relations of production, moving beyond focus on reproduction of the forces of production, it is important to understand the classic Marxist concept of 'base and superstructure'. Although Althusser finds this concept limited because it represents a descriptive and analogical form of theorization, he does not reject Marx's famous analogy but accepts it while seeking to build upon it so as to enable it to prove more fully explanatory. I will now address this concept first by explaining it in classic Marxist terms and second by explaining what Althusser adds to it.

Marx posits that in the course of producing their material life humans enter into definite relations of production, and these in turn determine the shape of the economic basis (or base, or infrastructure) of human society (and this economic sphere includes, strictly speaking, not only production, but also distribution, exchange, circulation, accumulation, and consumption). For Marxism the economic refers to the entire social sphere of production, distribution, exchange, circulation, and consumption of all goods and services necessary for human survival and subsistence and for the satisfaction of all human needs and the fulfillment of all human desires. This includes the totality of all relations among human beings–and all of the materials, instruments, and supplies–necessary to carry out these social processes, as well as all of the ways–or modes–of organizing and conducting these processes. Therefore, Marxism conceives of the economic sphere of social life, as well as of economics, the study of what transpires within this sphere, in much broader and more inclusive terms than is otherwise commonly the case. When Marxists argue, as Althusser does, that the economic is ultimately determinant, in the last or final instance, this means it is necessary to provide means of survival and subsistence, as well as to reproduce the conditions prerequisite for the production of these means, in order that everything else human beings do will be possible. Marxism contends, moreover, that the ways we work together to take care of these needs–and to provide means for the satisfaction of subsequent needs and desires–condition what else we as human beings are able to do as well as how we will pursue what else we do. The economy functions as the terrain upon which we carry out our life-practices; according to the nature of the terrain we pursue these life-practices in different ways, just as we would operate differently in desert, tundra, grasslands, forest, marshlands, etc.

The economic sphere of a social formation, as Marxism conceives it, functions akin to the foundation, including the basement, of a house or other building, whereas the other spheres of social life function akin to the higher floors of this same house or other building. We spend the vast majority of our time living our lives in these higher floors, and relatively little time in the basement. Yet without the foundation the higher floors could not stand up and we would not be able to live within them. The economic sphere serves, analogously, as the foundation for the rest of the life of a society. In short, if people as part of a society are not able to insure their material survival and subsistence, and are not able to reproduce the conditions according to which they work to provide this, they cannot do anything else; economic imperatives must be addressed, first and last, and how these imperatives are addressed ultimately conditions how the rest of social life operates. For example, if one must spend the vast majority of one's time and energy working to obtain means just to barely survive and subsist, this leaves little room left over for much else, and whatever that else might be cannot be too taxing. In contrast, if one's ability to survive, subsist, and even flourish is not dependent on spending the vast majority of one's time and energy working to obtain means to insure this is, barely, possible, then one enjoys ample opportunity to do many other things, including many other things that can and do require a considerable amount of time and energy, and that can be highly demanding and challenging–while, in fact, one can lead most of one's life focused on exactly these kinds of interests and concerns.

Althusser argues the economic is determinant 'in the last instance' along the lines I have just explained, and this means the economic base maintains the ultimately greatest determinate force of any social sphere, but the constituent domains of the superstructure maintain determinate force as well, force that is relatively autonomous from and reciprocally determinant of the economic base. Another way of putting this that Althusser also employs is to indicate all these distinct dimensions of the social totality maintain different 'indices of effectivity' (54). Althusser suggests, following Marx and classic Marxist theory, that the superstructure in fact contains both "the legal-political superstructure (law and the state)" and "the ideological superstructure (the various ideologies)." So 'the superstructure' thereby maintains 'two levels' (or 'two floors') (55). However, what Althusser finds lacking in Marx and classic Marxism is an adequate theoretical explanation of precisely how the superstructure relates to the base, what precise roles it plays in relation to the base, and what precisely distinguishes as well as unites the contributions of the legal-political superstructure and the ideological superstructure.

Althusser recalls that Marx explicitly theorizes the state as a repressive apparatus, and one that works as such to serve the collective interests of the dominant social class. But Althusser suggests it is important to theorize more precisely what this state apparatus involves, and how it works, as well as to distinguish state apparatus from state power. Althusser explains what he is getting at by drawing his readers' attention to the prospect that the same state apparatus can be held and controlled, or dominated over, by different social groups and especially by different classes, and what this means is it is state power, not the state apparatus in and of itself, that is ultimately the object of revolutionary class struggle. This position likewise implies that state power can be exercised on behalf of the same dominant group, or class, in different ways through different kinds of state apparatuses.

In classic Marxist theory, the state apparatus equates with what Althusser theorizes as the Repressive State Apparatus (the RSA) but Althusser argues Ideological State Apparatuses (the ISAs) are also critically important. The RSA, for Althusser, includes the police, the courts, the prisons, the military, the security and intelligence services, the government, and all those departments and agencies that work expressly as part of what is commonly perceived and designated as the state, including those departments and agencies responsible for providing and administering social services, such as social welfare payments and similar kinds of benefits, and those departments and agencies responsible for facilitating and regulating the activities of capitalist firms and industries, ostensibly in 'the public interest' but often enough, in practice, so as to represent the long-term collective interests of the capitalist class as a whole versus the immediate and short-term interests of individual capitalist firms, and industries, engaged in competitive relations with each other.

Althusser includes among the ISAs the following examples: the scholastic, familial, religious, political, associative, informative and news, publishing and distribution, and cultural apparatuses, although as Althusser indicates this is just a sampling of a multiplicity of possibilities and he is concerned in this book not with a detailed analysis of any specific ISA and precisely how it uniquely functions but rather with theorizing the ISAs in general and how they work broadly in common (75). Nevertheless, Althusser specifies that each ISA maintains its own distinct array of institutions, organizations, and practices, and that all of these operate together in a systemic way that is also distinct for each ISA. Each ISA is relatively autonomous versus all of the others in terms of how it serves the interests of dominant ideology but all of the ISAs serve this interest. And another important point Althusser makes early on in his detailed discussion of the ISAs that has often been overlooked is these are rooted, or anchored, not in particular kinds or arrays of ideas but rather in material practices, and ultimately, in the material reality of class struggle, including, again ultimately as well, day-to-day economic activity in and around the workplace.

Yet more precisely, Althusser proposes "*An Ideological State Apparatus is a system of defined institutions, organizations, and the corresponding practices. Realized in the institutions, organizations, and practices of this system is all or part (generally speaking, a typical combination of elements) of the State Ideology. The ideology realized in an ISA ensures its systemic unity on the basis of an 'anchoring' in material functions specific to each ISA; these functions are not reducible to that ideology, but serve it as a 'support'*" (77). 'Anchoring' ISAs in material functions specific to each ISA is a useful point to make—as this more precisely suggests how each ISA connects up with the economic base, and specifically with relations of production. The RSA functions primarily by direct or indirect use of physical violence, whereas the ISAs, in contrast, function primarily by means of ideology. In particular, Althusser highlights a significant dimension of dominant ideology in modern capitalist society involves encouraging individuals to freely choose to identify with and accept positions of domination and subjection, including positions of exploitation, including without conceiving or recognizing these as positions of domination, subjection, or exploitation—or, alternately, to do so maintaining the conviction that domination, subjection, and exploitation (including their own domination, subjection, and exploitation), is necessary, inevitable, and even desirable and good (78).

Readers encountering Althusser's theory for the first time, as has been the case with many students I have taught, often wonder why Althusser identifies both the RSA and the ISAs as *state* apparatuses, given the fact that much of what Althusser claims as constituents of the ISAs represent *private* as opposed to *public* institutions, organizations, and enterprises. The answer, according to Althusser, is this difference between 'private' and 'public' is a distinction internal to bourgeois law, while Althusser is theorizing *beyond bourgeois law*–i.e., theorizing what precedes, exceeds, and conditions the law as well as what the law ultimately enables and serves. What concerns Althusser is *how* these apparatuses, and their corresponding institutions, organizations, and practices, function, as part of and in relation to what, and in particular what and how they each individually and all collectively contribute to the reproduction of the relations of production, which is what Althusser here theorizes the State, in this large sense, to be all about–what is, in sum, the state's precise role in capitalist society. In other words, all apparatuses that contribute to ensuring the reproduction of the conditions of production by means of either coercion or ideology, or a combination of both, are, for Althusser, constituents of the state (79-81). As Jacques Bidet writes in his introduction to *On the Reproduction of Capitalism: Ideology and Ideological State Apparatuses*, Althusser does recognize the state plays a number of significant roles in capitalist society, but in this book Althusser focuses on the contribution of the state in reproducing capitalist society, or, more precisely, in reproducing capitalist relations of production.

According to Althusser, the ISAs do not *produce* the ideologies corresponding to them, but rather "*certain elements of an ideology (the State Ideology) 'are realized in' or 'exist in' the corresponding institutions and their practices*' (82). More precisely, certain forms of ideology are in fact produced within the ISAs, that is certain forms of what Althusser identifies as 'internal ideology', but it is important to distinguish between "on the one hand, the determinate elements of the State Ideology that are realized in, and exist in, a determinate apparatus and its practices, and on the other hand the ideology that is 'produced' in this apparatus by its practices . . . we shall call the former ideology the 'Primary Ideology', and the latter–a by-product if the practice in which the Primary Ideology is realized–the 'secondary, subordinate ideology'" (83). Althusser thus does recognize the existence of ideolog*ies*, even while focusing on dominant ideology, and even more broadly 'ideology in general'.

The important point here is that "The Ideological State Apparatuses are the realization, the existence, of the ideological formations dominating them" (85), as Althusser is greatly concerned to emphasize that ideology not only always only exists and operates in material form but also that ideology always only exists and operates according to how it is shaped and constituted as a result of the unfolding of class struggle ultimately rooted in economic relations. Again, the economic is determinant in the last instance–it exercises the ultimately greatest determinate force, in the long term–even as the RSA and the ISAs exercise relatively autonomous and reciprocally determinate force that can or may take precedence in the short and medium terms. ISAs and the realm of ideology as a whole are complex, elaborate, and messy phenomena, encompassing 'secondary' or 'subordinate' ideologies both supporting and opposing the reproduction and maintenance of the social status quo, that circulate within and even originate from within each ISA or sections of each ISA, as well as what Althusser variously refers to as 'primary' ideology or 'state ideology' or 'dominant ideology' (all, in essence, for Althusser, meaning the same).

Contrary to many of his leading critics, however, Althusser does include room for resistance and opposition within his theorization of ideology, ISAs, and social reproduction, as he expressly indicates contradictions always exist within the ISAs and within how along with how well they do the work of dominant ideology, with "in particular, the *ideological sub-formations* 'produced' in the apparatuses" periodically inevitably tending to "'make the gears grate and grind'" (88). The ultimate end of the dominant class, as exercised through state ideology, is "above all the reproduction of the relations of production in which" exploitation takes place, since the dominant class depends on exploitation in order to acquire and secure the means of its dominance (93). But the process through which state ideology works to achieve this end is always complicated, always subject to the prospect of internal disruption within state ideology itself, as well as always subject to the prospect of external pressure from alternative, secondary, subordinate, resistant, critical, and oppositional ideologies.

State ideology represents a systemic means of ensuring that the exploited, the agents of exploitation and repression, and the agents of ideologization all act in ways to ensure the reproduction of the relations of production and this ideology can assume forms, such as, Althusser suggests, Nationalism, Liberalism, Economism, and Humanism (138-139). Others I will add to this list, include Pragmatism, Reformism, Cynicism, Fatalism, 'Rugged Individualism', Meritocracy, 'Toxic Masculinity', Neo-Fascism or Authoritarian Populism and interconnections of this last with Racism, Sexism, Xenophobia, Heterosexism, Homophobia, Cissexism, Transphobia, Ableism, and Ageism.

In discussing, more precisely, how ISAs contribute to social reproduction, Althusser indicates, once again, that "*All* Ideological State Apparatuses without exception contribute to the same end: the reproduction of the relations of production, that is, of capitalist relations of *exploitation*" while "*Each* of them contributes to this single end in its own way" (144). But what Althusser stresses even more precisely here is that at different moments in history different ISAs are more versus less powerful and once more he argues that the schools have displaced the churches and comparable religious institutions as the most powerful ISA at the time he is writing this book. Why schools? Althusser argues this is because of power schools maintain over people through a long and pivotal formative stage where they are able to pump into students knowledge that is either packaged in dominant ideology or dominant ideology in its pure state (145). No other ISA, Althusser claims, exerts a comparable extent of control over people at and throughout such a critical period–with students representing in effect a captive audience (146). Althusser apologizes to teachers who valiantly struggle to counter dominant ideology, but suggests these people are rare, and it is much easier to serve interests of dominant ideology in teaching, even unaware of so doing, because the system can and will overwhelm and crush efforts to teach otherwise (146-147).

Frequently, in teaching Althusser's "Ideology and Ideological State Apparatuses: Notes Towards and Investigation," I have questioned this claim of Althusser's, and invited students to consider whether they might as well, by proposing, contrary to Althusser, that today mass culture is a more powerful ISA than the schools, and this ISA inserts itself even more thoroughly and pervasively throughout people's lives from an early age, in numerous diverse forms, with the computer and internet revolution–notably accelerating with the rise of the world wide web, social media, smart phones, and numerous other incentives to be engaged online virtually all of the time–ramping up the influence of mass culture in people's lives far beyond what was the case in late 1960s France. Mass culture refers to all of the constituents of culture that are mass produced for mass dissemination and mass consumption by capitalists engaged in culture industries–including, notably, advertising and marketing as well as news and entertainment industries.

Nevertheless, contrary to Max Horkheimer and Theodor Adorno, in their famous chapter, of *Dialectic of Enlightenment*, ""The Culture Industry: Enlightenment as Mass Deception," where Horkheimer and Adorno witheringly dismiss mass culture as altogether reactionary, I find the ISAs, including that pertaining to mass culture and the productions of culture industries, much more open to prospective resistance, opposition, resignification, reappropriation, recasting, redefining, disruption, subversion, and counter-hegemonic imagination, creation, articulation, expression, communication, and practical struggle–and certainly the same for popular culture productions that tend to blend with or at least maintain complicated intersections and overlaps with mass culture, and mass culture industries, such as popular post-punk music of the likes made by Ian Curtis and Joy Division.

Althusser, in *On the Reproduction of Capitalism: Ideology and Ideological State Apparatuses*, theorizes the RSA as "the hard core" or "last bastion" (152) of the state while simultaneously theorizing the ISAS as "infinitely more vulnerable" (153). The ISAs realize State Ideology but "piecemeal and in disorganized fashion (for each of them is relatively autonomous), and since they function as ideology, it is *in them* and their forms that much of the protracted class war represented by the class struggle takes place" (153). After all, Althusser reminds us, as Marx theorized, "people become conscious of their interests and fight out their class struggle *in ideology*" (153). It is thereby in the ISAs where people will often most consciously and deliberately engage in class struggle, or the close equivalent, and this is also a register of the greater vulnerability and fragility of the ISAs. In this connection Althusser is suggesting that alternative, resistant, and oppositional, or at least partially alternative, resistant, and oppositional kinds of positions and practices, can carve out space for themselves from within the ISAs.

Before even beginning to theorize possibilities for resistance and opposition that can lead to social transformation, it is necessary to understand how social reproduction takes place, and through what principal means. In his planned but never written second volume, Althusser aimed to show "that the *class struggle goes far beyond the Ideological State Apparatuses*" and to enable readers "to understand the *limits* of class struggle in the Ideological State Apparatuses, our subject here" (153n), but in *On the Reproduction of Capitalism: Ideology and Ideological State Apparatuses* Althusser is focusing principally on these ISAs because their contribution to social reproduction has often been unrecognized, or underrecognized, as well as inadequately misunderstood, even by revolutionary Marxist socialists and communists. It is worth noting well here how State Ideology unifies the state as a whole, internally, because this can help explain why the state in modern capitalist societies often presents itself as independent of private economic interests and concerns in its exercise of power.

The state plays a highly useful role in capitalist society by serving as a preeminent target of popular discontent within the larger society, functioning as a shock absorber that helps protect the capitalist interests the state ultimately serves, including by concealing how the state is serving these interests or mystifying to what extent it does so. In the US today, as well as in comparable countries, the state is often the target of popular fear, suspicion, and antagonism while corporate power is often simultaneously accepted without question or criticism. For example, when people are experiencing heightened socio-economic precariousness, as well as ample socio-economic precarity, the state is often targeted not only as responsible for addressing this problem but also as having caused it. The state, and in particular the government, are commonly held solely responsible for the overall state of a national, regional, or local economy, including for who benefit/who win versus who suffer/who lose–*rather than* the activities of the capitalist firms and industries that dominate within the economy. Capitalist firms and industries are often applauded when they show themselves as behaving in at least seemingly socially and ecologically responsible ways, but at the same time it is rarely expected this is something they 'naturally' should do–when they operate this way it is considered exceptionally generous, and to their credit, that they do, but it is not widely perceived as fundamentally wrong, to their discredit, if and when they do not do so. It is widely accepted it is entirely legitimate for a capitalist firm–and even an entire industry–to do whatever it takes to earn and increase profits. The state is expected to deal with any fallout, even while the state is not supposed to interfere too far, or regulate too extensively or intensively, whatever a capitalist firm–or an entire capitalist industry–chooses to do, in pursuit of profit and expanded profit.

Althusser's central proposition is "Ideology 'functions' at its most concrete level, the level of individual 'subjects'" (176). 'Subject' here maintains a dual meaning, referencing 'subject of' and 'subject to'. 'Subject' represents a positioning in social relations. According to Althusser, this happens by means of, within and through, ideology: i.e., ideology = the formation and constitution of subjects, and subjects are the essential bearers or representatives of ideology. Althusser, as he indicates in "Ideology and Ideological State Apparatuses: Notes Towards an Investigation," is taking advantage of "the ambiguity of the term *subject*" which "In the ordinary use of the term" means: "1) a free subjectivity, a centre of initatives, author of and responsible for its actions; and 2) a subjected being, who submits to a higher authority, and is therefore stripped of all freedom except that of freely accepting his submission" (269). What Althusser does with this ambiguity is effectively sublate it by proposing that ideology 'interpellates' individuals as free subjects who freely submit to authority, and freely accept their subjection. We will get to interpellation shortly, but we need first to recognize what Althusser is seeking, most importantly to explain, with his theory of ideology and the ISAs, is precisely how ideology works to make "individuals 'act all by themselves', without there being any need to post a policeman behind each and every one of them" (177).

The answer to how this works begins with "*THESIS I*: Ideology represents individuals' imaginary relation to their real conditions of existence" (181). It is important to note well the precise wording of this thesis. To begin, this thesis suggests ideology is both illusory and allusive, referencing what does not directly coincide with individuals' real conditions of existence but nevertheless always alludes to this. What is important next, and in particular versus prior, including prior Marxist, theories of ideology, is addressing why people need an "imaginary transposition of their real conditions of existence in order to 'represent' their real conditions of existence" (182). Althusser rejects as failed explanations theories of ideology that 1) equate ideology with what happens when "priests or despots" concoct "Beautiful Lies" that they manipulate people into believing, or 2) equate ideology with what follows from people's experience of alienation within their real conditions of existence such that this experience of alienation leads people to mistake what is imaginary or illusionary for what is real and true. What prior theories of ideology, even from Marx, have missed, Althusser contends, is "'people' do not 'represent' their real conditions of existence in ideology . . . but, above all, their *relation* to those real conditions of existence" (183). In other words, "every ideology represents, in its necessarily imaginary distortion, not the existing relations of production (and the other relations deriving from them), but, above all, individuals' (imaginary) relations to the relations of production and all the relations deriving from them. What is represented in ideology is therefore not the system of real relations governing individuals' existence, but those individuals' imaginary relation to the real conditions in which they live" (183).

Ideology, and in particular dominant ideology, leads people to imagine they are free in conditions where they are not, or that they are unique individuals when they are not, or that they live in a democracy when they do not, or that they are in charge and control of their own destiny–and even over their thoughts and feelings–when they are not, or that 'other' groups of people are fundamentally different from 'people like me' or 'people like us' when they are not, or that their lives and what they do within them are not interdependently interconnected with the lives of many others ultimately reaching across the globe.

It is crucial to recognize Althusser's first thesis involves a *representation*, a representation of an *imaginary* (more precisely, as Althusser is suggesting this, in French, an imagined) relationship, and it is a representation of an imaginary (i.e., an imagined) *relationship* of individuals to their real conditions of existence. Ideology is *not* a representation of individuals' real conditions of existence, but rather an least partially *distorted* representation, and a representation, moreover, not of these conditions per se bur rather of individuals' *relations* to these conditions. For anything to be an instance of ideology, in other words, a *position* has to be offered to us *in relation to* something we take to be real for us.

For example, ideology may represent to us, again, that we are 'free' when we are not, or that we are much 'freer' (or more entirely 'free') than we actually are. To take another example, ideology might represent to us, again as previously suggested, that we are 'unique' selves when we are not–when we actually share our subjectivity with many others with whom we participate together as part of a larger society. For example, ideology may represent to us all kinds of things that people commonly say, without thinking and accept without question as if these are unquestionably true, when they are not–"there's always two sides to every issue," "everyone will always make sense of every text in their own individual way," "no two people are ever truly alike," "you can never truly know another person," "if you have the right attitude, you can be content in virtually any kind of situation," "everything was always more primitive in the past," "everything was always simpler in the past," and "racism, sexism, classism, etc. continue to be problems today but things are much better today than they were in the past." Identifying *truisms* like these is a useful way to begin to recognize the power and impact of ideology in the sense that Althusser here theorizes. Yet, in so doing, in order to insure one is grasping what Althusser is theorizing, it is necessary in each case to be able to connect each truism with a position from which it is possible for people to act as *subjects* of the truism–as bearers or representatives, in practice, of what the truism identifies exists, is good, and is possible.

This bring us, logically, to Althusser's "*THESIS II: Ideology has a material existence*" (184). This means "Ideology always exists in an apparatus and in the practice or practices of that apparatus" and these are different modalities of matters versus that of "a paving stone or rifle" (184). Matter exists in multiple different modalities, "all rooted, in the last instance, in 'physical' matter" (184). Key here is that the imaginary relation at the heart of ideology "is itself endowed with a material existence" (185). An individual who believes "in God, Duty, Justice, or the like" *always manifests this belief in material practices*. If the individual does not do so that suggests the individual does not wholly believe in, or identify with, a particular ideology–or ideological notion–and instead believes in, or identifies with others (185). In short, Althusser proposes people's alignment with ideology, or with specific ideologies, must be understood in terms of what they do, in terms of what practices they actually engage in, and with the ideas that explain, rationalize, and justify what they do, what they practice, not with what they might merely think, speak, write, or otherwise express and communicate to be the case but never act upon. Either you act on what you believe in–or in accord with what you believe–or you don't truly believe.

"A human subject's 'ideas' exist in her acts or ought to; and, if they do not," ideology critique "ascribes to her other ideas corresponding to the acts (even perverse) that she does perform" (186). For example, when people identify with the ideological position that contends 'if people work hard and play by the rules they will succeed and be happy', they then act in accord with this position, not only by 'working hard' and 'playing by the rules' themselves but also by actively attributing other people's success and failure to their having done or not done so. This in turn influences, for instance, opposition to taxes on the wealthy and paying welfare benefits for the poor, because people 'make their own success' and 'people who fail have no one to blame but themselves'. To take another example, if people identify with an exceptionally rare and difficult to achieve physical appearance as what is 'truly beautiful', even when they cannot attain this appearance themselves, they act in ways that make this 'ideal' a real, material force to contend with by always in practice equating true beauty with the same standard and by always assessing their own and others' appearance in terms of degree of deviation from the same. They might push themselves to attempt to emulate this standard even when it is impossible or dangerous to attempt to do so, and they might dismiss, mock, disparage, and otherwise effectively exclude and ostracize those whose appearance verges far from this standard. People may internalize, and act in accord with such internalization, that they are unattractive–and undesirable–if they do not at all resemble this standard of beauty, and they may also experience a lack of self-confidence, and self-esteem, on this account, that holds them back from pursuing opportunities they would be qualified to take on, and to do well with. People in this position may experience significant physical and mental health damage on account of their identification with this ideological position.

Althusser theorizes acts are "inserted into practices", "practices are regulated by rituals," and these take place within an apparatus or "just a small part of that apparatus"–such as "a small mass in a small church, a funeral, a minor match at a sport club, a school day or a day of classes at university, a meeting or rally of a political party" (186). The ideological subject's "ideas are his material acts inserted into material practices regulated by material rituals which are themselves defined by the material ideological apparatus both from which (hardly by accident!) his ideas derive. Naturally, the four inscriptions of the adjective 'material' in our proposition have to be endowed with different modalities" (186).

Althusser does here add as a brief yet important comment that the ritual practices of a primary ideology can produce secondary ideologies, including critical and oppositional ones, and "thank God, since, otherwise, neither revolt nor the acquisition of revolutionary consciousness nor revolution would be possible" (187). Althusser frequently asserts 'counter-interpellation' happens, is viable, and is important, but unlike the case with 'interpellation' does not, here in volume one of an intended two volumes, show precisely how this might come about. Ideology might be a site of tension between full identification with this position, partial identification and partial disidentification with this position, and even total rejection and complete disidentification with this position.

Yet Althusser does not theorize this prospect, even though others who have followed Althusser have done so. Michel Pecheux for example (in *Language, Semantics and Ideology*) has theorized distinctions among identification, counter-identification, and dis-identification with interpellation into dominant ideological positions. For example, in relation to the ideological dictate that you should 'do as your told and you will be a good person who will be justly rewarded', the 'good subject' accepts and follows this position, the 'bad subject' rejects and refuses to follow this position, and the 'critical subject' critiques, challenges, and works to disrupt, subvert, and transform this position. Also highly useful, modifying Althusser, and which I have incorporated repeatedly throughout this book already is Goran Therborn's *Ideology of Power and the Power of Ideology* in which Therborn proposes that ideology, and dominant ideology in particular, provides answers to three fundamental questions: 1) what exists? 2) what is good? and 3) what is possible?

In my own teaching of ideology, especially for students initially learning to work with ideology, I often elaborate on this set of questions by proposing that ideologies, and again in particular dominant ideologies, provide answers to the following array of fundamental questions:

1) What exists? What does not exist?

2) What did–in the past–exist? What did–in the past–not exist?
3) What will–in the future–come to exist? What will–in the future–not come to exist?

4) What should–in the future–come to exist? What should–in the future–not come to exist?

5) What is true? What is false?

6) What is right? What is wrong?

7) What is good? What is bad?

8) What is desirable? What is undesirable?

9) What is necessary? What is unnecessary?

10) What is possible? What is impossible?

11) Who is the same/who is like us? Who is different/who is unlike us?

12) What connects us to people like us? What separates us from people who are different from us?

All of this departs from Althusser's theorization, although it is based upon and inspired by Althusser, and we don't know how Althusser himself might have theorized different kinds and degrees of identification with–and against–dominant modes of ideological interpellation.

Althusser's second thesis is focused upon insisting that "ideology does not exist *in ideas*," in the sense of these ideas existing as independent and ultimately determinate entities. For Althusser, ideas are important as 'embodied' in discourses and especially practices. Ideology only exists as ideology in terms of its material effectivity. Ideology is material practice, and this means the ideas that people commonly associate with what ideology is comprised of are reconceived in Althusser's theory as constituent dimensions of material practices. Ideology only exists, according to Althusser, insofar as it is actively lived. This can prove most useful in learning how to make use of ideology in critical studies because initially people often start with a notion of 'ideology = idea' or 'ideology = a group or set of ideas'. Althusser's theory enables us to distinguish ideology from idea, and even from a group or set of ideas, in terms of what must be in place for something to function as ideology, and what precisely ideology does do as ideology that is not at all simply identical with what an idea does as an idea or a group or set of ideas does as a group or set of ideas.

After discussing 'THESIS I' AND 'THESIS II' Althusser is almost ready to fully explain his "central thesis," but first proposes two "conjoint theses" that have directly followed from his explanations of 'THESIS I' AND 'THESIS II': "1) There is no practice whatsoever except by and under an ideology" and "2) These is no ideology except by the subject and for subjects" (187). Althusser's argument here is dialectical, and a useful way to begin to grasp it is to recognize that people's practices are always guided by at least implicit and unconscious 'theories' of what it is they are doing, and why, while, again, these 'theories' only become *ideologies* insofar as they are materialized in practices that give these ideas substance and enable these ideas to exercise impact. Ideologies represent subjects acting in practices, according to rituals, as part of apparatuses, and their consciousness as well as their unconscious is ultimately only important isofar as it is inscribed in "the acts of practices regulated by rituals defined in the last instance by an ideological apparatus" (187).

Althusser's "central thesis" is: "IDEOLOGY INTERPELLATES INDIVIDUALS AS SUBJECTS" (188). This means, to begin, "Every ideology has the function (which defines it) of 'constituting' concrete subjects" (188) and it also means that everyone of us is so constituted, including the Louis Althusser writing this book and the readers of his book. We all *live within* ideology, and all the time at that, and we do so, seemingly most often, "'spontaneously' or 'naturally'" (188). This means characteristically those living within ideology, aligning with and representing ideology, as both subject of and subject to ideology, do not consciously recognize this to be the case.

Althusser identifies the "primary 'self-evident fact'," for those living within (dominant, capitalist) ideology is that we are who we perceive ourselves and others to be: "free, moral, responsible, and so on." Our acceptance that the way things seem to be is the way they are and in particular the way we and others seem to be is the way they and we are, Althusser claims, is not only "an ideological effect," but also "the elementary ideological effect" (189). The reason why is "it is characteristic of ideology to impose self-evident facts as self-evident facts (without in the least seeming to, since they are 'self-evident') which we cannot *not* recognize and before which we have the inevitable and eminently natural reaction of exclaiming (aloud or in 'the silence of consciousness'): 'That's obvious! That's right! That's true!'" (189). Key here is to recognize "What really happens in ideology thus seems to happen outside it. That is why those who are in ideology, you and I, believe that they are by definition outside ideology: one of the effects of ideology is the practical *denegation* of the character of ideology by ideology. Ideology never says 'I am ideological'" (191).

This dimension of Althusser's theory of ideology explains how and why ideology works most effectively when it is unconscious. Once we start consciously reflecting on what are we doing, and why, as well as what positions could possibly explain and justify so doing, we are all the more likely to start questioning what we are doing, and why, while prospectively responding in turn to this questioning by changing what we are doing, to do something different. In so doing, according to Althusser's theory, we are shifting positions. We may be shifting positions within–while remaining within–dominant ideology, by identifying with and supporting dominant ideology in different ways (or by imagining we are breaking with or opposing when we actually are not). But we may be shifting positions from dominant ideology to non-dominant or counter-dominant ideology. We might for example at first identify with the position that 'our nation is always a force for moral good in the world' and it is important for me to support what our nation is doing in other countries. We might subsequently shift to support the the position that 'our nation is a force for serious damage and destruction in the world' and it is important for me to oppose what our nation is doing in other countries. Someone might begin by believing, for example, that wars fought by the United States in Vietnam, Iraq, Afganistan–or to reach back to Althusser's time, by France in Algeria–are just wars, where their country is fighting on the side of what is right, in the interest of what is good, and then, with experience, including, as has often been the case, on the front lines of these wars, change their position to believe instead that their country is in fact causing serious harm and not doing good, not enabling what is right, and is engaged in this war for reasons contrary to what has been and continues to be claimed by those who advocate for and lead efforts in waging war. When such a person changes from an uncritical supporter of their nation's military efforts to a critical opponent of the same, as 'imperialist', we witness a shift from a dominant ideological position to a counter-dominant ideological position.

Often students initially find this easy to understand by considering many historically prior 'self-evident' beliefs: for example, men are naturally physically stronger and more physically and intellectually capable of leading roles in public life while women are naturally physically weaker yet also more physically and emotionally capable of leading roles in private life, White people are naturally intellectually superior to Black people, those who engage in homosexual relations are sick

482

and deranged, disabled people are fundamentally incapable of participating actively and extensively in public life, people who suffer or who have suffered from serious mental illness including anxiety and depression are not capable of performing sensitive jobs or other kinds of roles where others will be counting on them, human beings will never be capable of flying, the world will never run short of oil and natural gas, pandemics like the early 20th century 'Spanish flu' will never again exert that extent of impact across Western Europe and North America, the United States of America will never lose in war, and so on. Recognizing these and other such beliefs that long seemed self-evidently true to many should lead us to question whether what we 'prefer' to believe today, as seemingly similarly self-evident, is necessarily true: for example, fascism will never triumph in America and the United States of America is and always will be a free and democratic nation, or, in a contrary direction, the poor will always be with us and it is impossible ever to overcome and eliminate poverty, or it is impossible to convert entirely from fossil fuels to renewable energy, or communities will always need police forces.

Althusser explains that "*All ideology hails or interpellates concrete individuals as concrete subjects*" (190) and this process begins even before we are born, and continues relentlessly onward, over and over again, all the days of our lives. Ideology recruits and transforms all of us (from individuals into subjects). Ideology operates much like an imaginary 180 degree response to someone hailing us on the street 'by name' with us turning around to acknowledge 'yes, that's me'. When we recognize and accept that is us who are being so addressed we effectively become subjects of and to ideology (191). Althusser's imaginary piece of street theater provides an analytic distinction while "In reality, however, things happen *without succession. The existence of ideology and the hailing or interpellation of individuals as subjects are one and the same thing*" (191). In other words, we do not wait outside of ideology to be hailed by ideology, or take our time to turn around and acknowledge this hailing, and we do not maintain a lengthy or otherwise extensive existence as individuals who are not yet subjects. As Althusser explains, *"individuals are always-already subjects"* so "individuals are 'abstract' with respect to the subjects they always-already are" (192) and "Ideologies never stop interpellating subjects as subjects, never stop 'recruiting' individuals who are always-already subjects" (193-194).

Althusser offers a useful concrete illustration of what he is getting at here, using himself as an example:

When religious ideology begins to function directly by interpellating the little child Louis as a subject, little Louis is already-subject–not yet religious-subject, but familial-subject. When legal ideology (later, let us suppose) begins to interpellate little Louis by talking to him about, not Mama and Papa now, or God and the Little Lord Jesus, but Justice, he was already a subject, familial, religious, scholastic, and so on. I shall skip the moral stage, aesthetic stage, and others. Finally, when, later, thanks to auto-heterographical circumstances of the type Popular Front, Spanish Civil War, Hitler, 1940 Defeat, captivity, encounter with a communist, and so on, political ideology (in its differential forms) begins to interpellate the now adult Louis as a subject, he has always already long been, always-already been, a familial, religious, moral, scholastic and legal subject . . . and is now, lo and behold, a political subject! This political subject begins, once back from captivity, to make the transition from traditional Catholic activism to advanced–semi-heretical–Catholic activism, then begins reading Marx, then joins the Communist Party, and so on. So life goes. (193)

A few further illustrations will prove useful at this point. Many times students find it helpful to grasp ideological interpellation by thinking about how advertising and marketing pitches invite and encourage their target audiences to identify with how they are hailed, often by flattering these audiences or by associating products and services with idealized images of what they expect many people will already find desirable and appealing. Think about advertisements again that suggest to us, in effect, that 'we deserve to splurge on ourselves', that 'we want to be part of a cool, fun group of people doing cool, fun things', or that we want–we need–to be being stylish, or practical, or rebellious, or efficient, or even lovably quirky. Advertisements offer us idealized images of all of these kinds of desires, and associate, directly or indirectly, their product with the same. These advertisements in effect hail us, for instance, as follows: 'Hey you, you are a cool, fun person who likes to do cool, fun things with cool fun people, and would like to do more of this more often'. When we in effect accept that address we simultaneously accept interpellation into the position of good subject of–and for–the advertisement.

Students also often readily recognize how movies and TV shows interpellate us as audience members into positions of identification with the visual and auditory vantage point of specific characters as well as sympathetically and empathetically with what these characters seems to be experiencing and how they seems to be responding. Likewise, students readily recognize how novels, short stories, plays, and poems do the same in relation to specific vantage points with which we feel ourselves sensing, feeling, identifying, sharing, sympathizing, and empathizing. Both fictional and non-fictional texts also often interpellate us into positions of antagonism versus various characters or real people. Speeches do the same–or attempt to do so. Politicians' speeches often seek to interpellate us into positions where we accept and identify with a position 'as one of us' versus 'them' who are *not* 'us', not like 'us', and who are our opponents, even our *enemies*.

In relation to being always-already interpellated, think about how, even before we are born, we are interpellated to take up (particular kinds of) positions, as soon as we are born, within particular families, neighborhoods, communities, social classes, localities, regions, nations, genders, races, religions, and so on. We are often named ahead of being born, and most often interpellated into alignment with family surnames before we are born. And from the moment we are born we are continually subject to hailings from many diverse social sources inviting us to identify. For example: 'you want to play baseball, don't you?', 'you want to do well in English, don't you?', 'you want to be honest and responsible, don't you?', 'you want to be a role model for your younger brothers and sisters, don't you?', 'you want to be someone others will find it easy to get along and will readily want to play with, don't you?', and 'you want to grow up and be __ like your dad/mom/grandmother/grandfather/older brother/older sister/aunt/uncle/family friend, etc. don't you'? And this can also take forms such as: 'boys don't cry, and you don't want to be made fun of as a sissy for crying, do you?' or 'you love your country, as a patriot, and support __ politician or ___ party, because that's what true patriots do, don't you?'

These examples could be multiplied virtually endlessly because not only are we all *"always already* subjects and, as such, constantly practice the rituals of ideological recognition, which guarantees for us" that we are who we think we are (189), but also ideologies never stop interpellating–and re-interpellating–us. For example, every time we are addressed as a member of prospective member of a religious faith, or congregation, and we identify with this address–indicating, in effect, 'yes this me', 'yes I am one of you'–we are being re-interpellated into a position as a subject of this religion. For example, every time we are addressed by a political party and we identify with this address, by for example voting for that party's candidates for elective office in government–we are being re-interpellated into a position as subject of that political party. All of us continually accept common subject positions over and over again: parent, child, sibling, spouse, citizen, taxpayer, resident, employee, patient, client, customer, teammate, committee member, student, teacher, graduate, holder of a terminal degree (such as a PhD), holder of a specific position and rank within a profession (such as professor), and so on.

Althusser further theorizes the nature of the relation of ideological interpellation of subjects by proposing that in all ideology subjects always find their place in relation to a central Subject. Althusser uses the example of 'Christian Religious Ideology' to introduce 'the Subject'–which in this instance is God. As Althusser explains, in ideology "the interpellation of individuals as subjects presupposes the 'existence' of a unique and central other Subject" or "the Subject *par excellence*" (195). This means "the structure of all ideology, interpellating individuals as subjects in the name of a Unique and Absolute Subject, is *speculary*, in other words, a mirror-structure," and, in fact, "*doubly* speculary" (196). In other words, "all ideology is *centered* . . . in a doubly specular relation such that it subjects the subjects to the Subject, while giving them in the Subject in which each subject can contemplate its own (present and future) image the *guarantee* that this is really about them and really is about Him"–i.e., we see ourselves in the Subject and the Subject in ourselves (197).

Ideology ultimately offers "the absolute *guarantee* that everything is so" and this enables subjects to act 'properly', to take up their positions and follow along with what these positions expect, require, or demand of them within the much larger overarching system of social reproduction, and thereby the process of social reproduction can go on in effect by itself, as these subjects in acting as the subjects they are interpellated to be effect what is needed to reproduce the social system, and in particular the relations of production (197). In ideology, subjects "recognize that 'it's really me', that 'this is the way it is', not some other way . . . The subjects go, since they have recognized 'all is well' (or the way it is), and they say, for good measure: *So be it!* (197). In identifying with the position that the way things are is the way they have to be, "*the reproduction of the relations of production* is ensured, every day, every second, in the 'consciousness', that is, the material behaviour of the individuals holding the posts that the social and technical division of labour assigns them in production, exploitation, repression, ideologization and scientific practice" (198).

As Althusser further explains this same point in "Ideology and Ideological State Apparatuses: Notes Towards an Investigation," "The Absolute Subject occupies the unique place of the Centre, and interpellates around it the infinity of individuals into subjects into a double mirror-connexion such that it *subjects* the subjects to the Subject, while giving them in the Subject in which each subject can contemplate its own image (present and future) the *guarantee* that this really concerns them and Him, and that since everything takes place in the Family (the Holy Family: the Family is in essence Holy), 'God will *recognize* His own in it', i..e, those who have been recognized God, and have recognized themselves in Him, will be saved" (268). So the mirror-structure of ideology interpellates individuals as subjects, subject to the Subject, with mutual recognition of subjects and Subject, subjects' recognition of each other, and subjects' recognition of themselves, along with the absolute guarantee that all is really as it appears to be (268-269).

The importance of the ideological 'guarantee' is this helps account for the power of ideology–that what ideology represents as so is so, and that ideology maintains a position for the subject, a position from and according to which the subject can know who they are, what they are about, and how they fit in, as well as in what way as part of what. This is, in other words, a position in which the subject knows who they are, what they are about, and how they fit in, as well as in part of what *because of* the relationship ideology provides between subject and Subject. Believers in God, or Jesus Christ, or the Father, Son, and the Holy Spirit, maintain positions as subjects in relation to God, Jesus Christ, or the Father, Son, and the Holy Spirit as Subject. Comparable kinds of subject-Subject relations exists in other religions. But the Subject need not be a divine or sacred entity, as it might, instead, be the Nation, the Family, the Institution (whatever institution this might be), the Community, the Political Party, or even a particular nexus of foremost convictions or fundamental principles such as those defining what it in essence means to be a good citizen, a good neighbor, or a good human being, or to live the good life/live a good life.

We have this kind of ideological relationship as long as an implicit center provides a focal point according to which the Subject is able to define and orient what the subject is about. The subject identifies with this Subject, accepting that the subject is called upon to live in reflection of and response to the Subject, and that the Subject will manifest its presence in the subject's actions and practices. For example, if one is successfully interpellated as subject of the Nation, the subject recognizes themselves in, as part of, the Nation, in what the Nation is all about, in what the Nation stands for, and recognizes this in turn in themself. If the Nation is 'the land of the free and the home of the brave', then the subject recognizes themself as a member of a free and brave nation, a nation which provides for them free opportunity– opportunity to act freely–and brave inspiration–inspiration to act bravely. Or the subject imagines they are acting freely and bravely. Or the subject imagines they are always ultimately capable of acting freely and bravely. Or the subject imagines acting freely and bravely is what they need, must, and should be like in to order to live up to what the Nation expects of them and to be worthy subjects of the Nation.

Althusser follows his discussions of relations between subject(s)-Subject by emphasizing that we are always all subjected to multiple, at least relatively independent ideologies at once, as part of multiple ideological apparatuses, and we live across these in highly complex ways (199). This combination does not always simply smoothly function 'all by itself', and people often need to move across disparate ideological positions, while implicitly at least, for Althusser, it is in this complex of tensions and contradictions that openings for resistance, opposition, revolt, and transformation can and do emerge and grow (200). It is always desirable for a dominant social class that ideology, as exercised through the Ideological State Apparatuses, will prove sufficient, or largely sufficient, to interpellate exploited and oppressed individuals into positions as subjects where they do not recognize they are being exploited and oppressed, or where they accept that even if this is indeed exploitation and oppression, nothing can be done to overcome it. In this kind of situation, exploited and oppressed social groups do not need to be forcibly coerced into accepting, into submitting to, their positions as exploited and oppressed. But when ISAs fail to get people who are exploited and oppressed *not* to resist, *not* to rebel, *not* to revolt, and *not* to actively work and fight for transformation, the RSA backs up the ISAs and brings coercive force to bear (201). As Althusser comments, "When nothing is happening, the Ideological State Apparatuses have worked to perfection" (206). When they are not, 'events' happen, such as the Paris 1968 Uprising (206).

Althusser's planned focus for the second volume was to theorize social classes, the class struggle, ideologies, sciences, philosophy, the proletarian class standpoint in philosophy, and revolutionary philosophical intervention in scientific practice and in the practice of the proletarian class struggle, all of which would make expressly clear how Althusser did in fact strongly believe the social reproductive effectivity of the ISAs can be successfully challenged and overcome (207). As Althusser adds, in "Note on the ISAs," written in response to critics of his theory of ideology and of the ISAs in "Ideology and Ideological State Apparatuses: Notes Towards an Investigation," versus the charge of functionalism: this is an anti-dialectical reading of what he is arguing and he has always asserted the primacy of the class struggle. Here Althusser insists reproduction is always shaped by the current state of the ongoing class struggle. "It is also because of the *materiality and diversity of the practices* whose 'spontaneous' ideology must be unified" that "This huge, contradictory task is never completely accomplished" (219). In other words,

> The dominant ideology *can never completely resolve its own contradictions*, which are a reflection of the class struggle–although its function is to resolve them. That is why we can derive from this thesis *of the primacy of the class struggle over the dominant ideology* and *the Ideological State Apparatuses* another thesis, its direct consequence: the Ideological State Apparatuses are necessarily both the site and stake of a class struggle that extends the general class struggle dominating a social formation into the apparatuses of the dominant ideology. If the function of the ISAs is to inculcate the dominant ideology, the reason is that there *is* *resistance*; if there is resistance, the reason is there is struggle. (220)

Althusser is critical of a tradition within Marxism that he finds 'economistic' and 'reformist', and which he contends has been and continues to be prone to cooptation by capital, in suggesting that so-called 'objective' developments, such as the 'inherent' contradictions between capitalist forces of production and capitalist relations of production, will virtually automatically, by themselves, eventually lead to successful socialist revolution, to successful revolutionary socialist transformation of capitalism into communism. Althusser is critical of Marx's famous "Preface" to *A Contribution to the Critique of Political Economy* for lending support to that interpretation. According to this interpretation, socialists can effectively 'sit back' and wait for socialism to happen, naturally, by itself, as capitalism, naturally, by itself, disintegrates because its fundamental contradictions inevitably grow impossible to reconcile, and impossible to overcome. Althusser, in contrast, strongly aligns with the position that 'subjective forces' are absolutely necessary, in combination with 'objective conditions' for socialist revolution to be successful.

In *On the Reproduction of Capitalism: Ideology and Ideological State Apparatuses*, Althusser stresses a principal fiction at the heart of capitalist ideology is the notion that everyone is fundamentally, essentially, ultimately free–and that capitalist societies are fundamentally, essentially, ultimately free societies (223-225). In other words, ideological mystifications of real unfreedom abound, while highly limited and unequal forms and varieties of freedom mask an enormous extent and depth of unfreedom. As Althusser suggests, the reason why proletarians work proletarian jobs has to do, one, with the fact they need to do so, of necessity, in order to obtain means of survival and subsistence, and, two, due to force of legal, economic, and religious ideologies of work. Likewise, capitalists act as capitalists, one, because competition among capitals requires them to do so if they are to survive and persist, and, two, because of how ideology has encouraged them to conceive of themselves and what they are about (such as, for instance, common in our times, in the US recently, as 'job creators', as those 'who make the economy run', and whose control over the generation of wealth will benefit all as it 'trickles down') (204).

What Althusser offers is a theory that recognizes, supports, and gives encouragement to the importance of ideological struggle, of committing to and engaging in such struggle, but with important caveats, starting with emphasizing that the predominance of class struggle in and through ideology, and in and through the ISAs, tends to long precede the point where a society is even close to a genuinely revolutionary situation. Ideological struggle is important and useful but limited and insufficient. What's more, it is necessary, in order to engage in this struggle most effectively, to pay close and careful attention to–as well as to be able to accurately and effectively analyze–what is the state of class struggle, represented in the economic base, that is being addressed, in mediated form, in ideological struggle. For example, in order to wage ideological struggle most effectively, we would need, following what Althusser is here cautioning, carefully to consider how any and/or all of the following economic developments have shown up within and reshaped the terrain of ideological struggle in late 20th and early 21st century Western European and North American capitalist societies: rise of the precariat and the proliferation of new forms of precarious labor; impact of hegemonic neo-liberalism and the crises it encountered with and since 'the Great Recession' of 2007-2008; long-term decline of unions and union power, as well as of socialist and communist parties where they were once substantial and powerful; rise of a substantial and powerful neo-fascist 'right' and linked forms of 'far right' authoritarianism populism, including their impact upon and appeal to exploited and oppressed social groups; globalization and its discontents; struggles surrounding so-called 'flexible' employment of labor (such as what in the UK are referred to as 'zero hour contracts'), especially in relation to 'flexible' for whom, and 'flexible' to the benefit of whom; impacts on jobs, industries, living and working conditions, poverty, and overall well-being (i.e., on the reproduction of labor power) due to ecological overreach and looming ecocide; impacts of the COVID-19 pandemic on people's working conditions and job status; divide and conquer efforts as well as efforts in contrast of solidarity and resistance, between white working people and Black and Brown working people, between recent immigrants (especially recent immigrants of color and including refugees and asylum seekers) and not so recent immigrants (i.e., longer settled residents of nations), and between groups of working people suspected of being 'terrorists' or sympathetic to 'terrorists' versus 'everyone else'.

Also, in the same connection we would want, usefully, to consider the impact, upon the terrain of ideological struggle of recent and current struggles over minimum and living wages, over access versus lack of access to other paid benefits, over job security versus lack thereof, and over workplace conditions that make whole categories of jobs unappealing or less appealing (or as Eyal Press has written about in *Dirty Work: Essential Jobs and the Hidden Toll of Inequality in America*, doing 'dirty work' that the larger society requires, even depends upon, yet hides from because this kind of work is morally disturbing–and often leaves those who do it damaged by the impact of them of needing to do this kind of work). Also, we might well want to consider the impact, on the terrain of ideological struggle, of what kinds of jobs have recently been expanded versus what kinds have recently been contracting, and why, as well as what kinds of current training and other varieties of education, at various educational levels, are orienting people in what directions toward what kinds of vocations.

Four

Michel Foucault's *Discipline and Punish: The Birth of the Prison* (*Surveiller et Punir: Naissance de la prison*) is one of Foucault's works, along with *Madness and Civilization* and *The History of Sexuality*, most commonly taught in undergraduate English Studies classes, and I have taught this book, and in particular the chapters "Panopticism" and "The carcereal" often, while students have found this work usefully provocative. Foucault begins by tracing what accounts for the historical change from one predominant mode of punishment of crime to another: from the public spectacle where the body of the condemned is subject to elaborate torture to the modern prison. Foucault indicates the change he is focusing on transpires over the 'classical period', approximately 1750-1820, or beginning somewhat earlier, even as early as the mid to late 1600s, encompassing the so-called Ages of Reasons and Enlightenment through the end of the (first) Napoleonic Era up to the beginning of the so-called Age of Romanticism. In modern practice, punishment is hidden, not put on public display. More precisely, with modern punishment shame over what it involves leads to it being hidden but this "does not always preclude zeal" in practicing it (10).

The latter is an important point, given incarceration rates in countries throughout much of the advanced capitalist Global North, and in particular the United States, as well as the United Kingdom; the recurrent popularity of pledging to 'get tough' and 'crack down' on crime; and recurrent moral panics concerning 'out of control' forms of crime 'running roughshod' over public safety and social order. However, even in nations like the US where the death penalty remains legal in a number of states and for some crimes at the federal level, most people 'prefer' not to engage directly with what happens in the punishment of 'criminals': not to watch, not to listen to, not to know or learn about precisely what this involves, and what it is like, what it feels like and what it does to those subject to punishment (or to those directly responsible for administering punishment). Many people likewise maintain considerable ignorance, and even indifference, concerning how criminal law works–for suspects, victims, witnesses, and those convicted and sentenced with punishments for crime. Much of the zeal directed at crime, 'criminals', and 'criminality' is, moreover, directed at whole populations of

489

people who are relatively considerably disadvantaged versus the 'criminal justice system', on account in particular of their race and class positions, or on account of the challenges they face due to mental health issues.

Foucault does allow that "the practice of the public execution haunted our penal system for a long time and still haunts it today" (15). Traces of that 'pre-modern' practice remain, akin to "shadows lurking behind," or as constituents in a proximate "shadow play" (17). I suggest we recognize these 'shadows' and their 'play' at work in periodic demands for crackdowns on 'deviants' and 'delinquents'; in systemic practices of police brutality, including police violence and murder, as well as political complicity with the perpetuation of these practices; in harsh sentences imposed for minor, such as small-scale drug, offenses; in huge disparities in terms of who–what kinds of people, from what races and classes–are more often sentenced and more often sentenced for much longer; in demagogic posturing concerning supposed 'enemies of the nation'; and in demonization of whole groups of people in desperate need as criminals or criminal suspects, such as immigrants, including refugees and asylum seekers.

Foucault emphasizes modern, 'disciplinary' power is productive as opposed to repressive while connecting the rise of disciplinary power with the birth of the human sciences. For Foucault it is indeed crucial to recognize that punishment is linked to "a whole series of positive and useful effects, which it is their task to support" (24). Among the most 'positive and useful' of these effects are *productions of* 'normality'. One ready example of what Foucault is proposing here is modern psychology and psychiatry, which often overtly focuses on attending to a vast array of psychological forms of supposed 'abnormality' (various 'diseases' and 'disorders', or in classic Freudian terms, various 'neuroses', 'perversions', and 'psychoses').

Another crucial point of emphasis Foucault also makes early on, dispelling any misinterpretation of where he is headed in contrasting punishment of crime through torture as public spectacle versus punishment of crime through imprisonment, is that, even as punishment evolves and transforms, "it is always the body that is at issue–the body and its forces, their utility and their docility, their distribution and their submission" (25). Punishment of crime, under the modern 'carcereal regime', is always focused on and impacts the body, but what changes, with the exercise of disciplinary power, is "The body become a useful force only if it is both a productive body and a subjected body" (26). Discipline encompasses careful study and ascertainment of knowledge of the body that enables mastery of the forces of the body. Foucault theorizes disciplinary power operating in, on, and through the body as "a network of relations, constantly in tension" that most importantly exists in its exercise rather than in its possession, and is widely disseminated and diffused as opposed to narrowly centered and concentrated (26).

Foucault contends that "power produces knowledge" and in fact "power and knowledge directly imply one another"–i.e., fields of knowledge are traversed with and by power relations, in what might be better defined as "'power-knowledge relations'" (27). Foucault argues that acquiring detailed knowledge concerning an individual or a social group is coterminous with exercising power in relation to that individual or social group. Ultimately, Foucault declares, his interest in the prison and its historical antecedents is concerned with "its very materiality as an instrument and vector of power" (30)–and with, in particular, power that exercises *disciplinary* effectivity throughout society.

Returning to the earlier historical period in which punishment of crime as public spectacle was commonplace, and even dominant, Foucault emphasizes it is important to understand what such punishment did and did not do: it "did not re-establish justice; it reactivated power" (49). In other words, punishment of crime as public spectacle, and especially by torture and public spectacle, operated as a manifestation of the power of the sovereign. Foucault argues what we in modern times likely would characterize as the 'atrocity' of this mode of punishment represented, from a vantage point rooted in that time, a theatrical display of the atrocity of crime coupled with a ritual recharging of the power of the sovereign through this means of public display. This included demonstrating the far greater power of the sovereign than that of the criminal, as well as how far the sovereign could trump in the atrocity the atrocity the criminal committed.

Yet problems arose, Foucault recounts, as masses of spectators did not always, and increasingly less often, respond to these displays with terrified submission. In fact spectacular punishments increasingly provoked resistance and revolt that threatened those at the heights of social and political power. Especially problematic, from the latter's vantage point, performances of the public punishment of criminals became carnivalesque occasions that led to mocking and ridiculing of authority while often transforming criminals into heroes, which in turn could and did lead to serious social disturbances. As early as the end of the 18th century, "It was evident that the great spectacle of punishment ran the risk of being rejected by the very people to whom it was addressed" (63). Especially concerning was a rise in solidarity among the spectators with the condemned, while "the executions did not, in fact, frighten the people" (63). Convicted criminals became folk heroes, sources of resistant to rebellious identification, and even sources for mobilization of opposition.

In response, punishment of crime increasingly eschewed performative public displays. Crime also was changing in its dominant forms with the rise of modern capitalism, and this in turn proved a major incentive toward the development and deployment of means of more intensive scrutiny and surveillance, including via professional police, with a notable emphasis upon a "new severity towards the poor" (77). What emerged is "a tendency toward a more finely tuned justice, towards a clear penal mapping of the body" (78). So, criticism ostensibly directed at the 'atrocity' of the punishment of crime as public spectacle, including in particular by means of torture as public spectacle, "was directed in fact not so much at the weakness or cruelty of those in authority, as at a bad economy of power," or, even more precisely, versus "a badly regulated distribution of power" (79). In sum, the effective aim of reform, in practice, was "not to punish less, but to punish better," "to punish with more universality and necessity," "to insert the power to punish more deeply into the social body" (82). Reform worked toward punishing crime more subtly, less visibly, and as much by way of a focus on the mind and the soul as upon the body, while punishment of crime became concerned with more effectively serving larger interests, and advancing larger ends, than merely punishing those overtly identified as 'criminals'.

Capitalist societies increasingly criminalized traditional peasant and worker rights as theft (85). What Foucault refers to here as 'illegalities' are tolerances for peasant and worker appropriation that were traditionally accepted in pre-capitalist societies. As Mark Neocleous explains, in *A Critical Theory of Police Power*, 'customary rights' or 'perquisites' included right of "the thresher . . . to some of the harvest, "the coal worker" to "some of the coal he handled," "ships carpenters . . . to some of the spare timber," and "dock workers . . . to any sugar or other commodities that were spilt" (154). With modern capitalism, these same 'ancient entitlements' in the form of partial payment in kinds become "redefined as engaging in 'theft'," with "all forms of non-monetary 'income', 'payment' or subsistence" facing "criminal sanction" (155).

As Neocleous notes, "The increasingly dominant bourgeois class felt that the customary rights in question jarred with the fundamental purpose of labour, which was to earn a wage, and raised a fundamental question: are those who labour entitled to appropriate the products of their own labour, other than through the wage received?" (156). Unsurprisingly, "The answer given by capital was increasingly a firm 'no'. What had previously been seen as *custom* was gradually reconceptualized as *crime*" in an "historical process" that "paralleled that of the enclosures movement" (156). As a result, a host of "Traditional activities which labour used to eke out an existence–casual labour for payment in kind, grazing cattle on public byways, pilfering wood, picking fruit and vegetables for either consumption or sale, poaching, fishing from rivers without a license, hawkng, peddling and street selling–all became targets for police action" (161). As Foucault observes, "Although the new criminal legislation appears to be characterized by less severe penalties, a clearer codification, a marked diminution of the arbitrary, a more generally accepted consensus of the power to punish (in the absence of a more real division in its exercise), it is sustained in reality by an upheaval in the traditional economy of illegalities and a rigorous application of force to maintain their new adjustment" (89).

What develops at this historical moment is "a new economy and a new technology of the power to punish" (89), which at the level of theory is organized around "the contract" (89). This theory posits that every citizen or resident agrees to obey the law and adhere to the norms of a society. That means even "The least crime attacks the whole of society" (90). According to law, the whole of society is now invested in criminal punishment: "The right to punish has been shifted from the vengeance of the sovereign to the defence of society" (90). Simultuaneously emerging is a new conception of crime that proclaims "the injury that crime inflicts upon the social body is the disorder that it introduces into it," which means punishment of crime increasingly becomes conflated with enforcing and reinforcing social order (92). We can recognize the continuing prevalence of this position in many places, such as for instance in the prevalent logic of many superhero comics, films, and TV shows, in which criminals are overwhelmingly represented as threats to the entire community, to society as whole, and superheroes are in turn represented as protectors of the same.

At the same time, fabrication of an increasingly "exhaustive, explicit [criminal] code" works hand in hand with encouragement of "individualization." What Foucault is getting at here is "Individualization appears as the ultimate aim of a precisely adapted code" (99) with a corresponding emphasis on modulating the individual, in terms of "his nature . . . his way of life and attitude of mind" which in turn requires and makes considerable use of "psychological knowledge" (99). This means that gradually "criminality, rather than crime, became the object of penal intervention" (100). Foucault is addressing the development of what he later refers to as a 'carceral society' that is enabled to exercise it carcereal effects because of how it distinguishes and isolates subjects, while also seeming at the same time to address everyone as a unique individual with their own uniquely individual place in that society, even as 'individuals' learn to define and express their 'individuality' in socially prescribed or allowed terms that are broadly shared with many other fellow 'individuals'.

A key dimension of the reform of criminal punishment, over the course of the 'classical period', involved transforming punishment so that this becomes directed "at all others, at the potentially guilty" and not just at the overtly identified criminal offenders, the definitively guilty, while punishment of the latter becomes reconceived as "a retribution the guilty man makes to each of his fellow citizens, for the crime that has wronged them all" (108-109). In effect what arises is a new kind of display–in form of a moral lesson, with punishment now become a schooling in what is right versus wrong rather than a festival exalting the power of the sovereign (110-111) . The criminal becomes "a source of instruction" while punishment of crime must "teach a lesson" such that "each punishment should be a fable" (112-113).

Although we recognize continuities with this conception of crime and punishment to this day, Foucault describes this as a transitional stage, maintaining the emphasis on public display while changing what is displayed and to what precise end. At this stage, the prison continues as only one among multiple familiar means of punishment of crime. Yet the building of prisons and the focus on imprisonment as punishment for crime is nonetheless growing. Prisons are becoming privileged sites for isolating, observing, and generating knowledge. The ultimate aim of 'correction' becomes the production of "the obedient subject, the individual subjected to habits, rules, orders, an authority that is exercised continually around him and upon him, and which he must allow to function automatically in him" (128-129). Prison becomes less important in terms of what is done to those imprisoned and more important in terms of its place and role within a much larger system, or network, of disciplinary practice, focused everywhere on inculcating submission, obedience, and conformity.

According to Foucault, "A body is docile that may be subjected, used, transformed and improved" (136). This kind of body is created by means of "subtle coercion" as well as "uninterrupted, constant coercion," through a series of "disciplines" (137). In fact, one of the principal effects of the exercise of disciplinary power, for Foucault, is the production of 'docile bodies', and, as readers can likely readily imagine, when a subject is produced by disciplinary power as docile, this can be highly useful in maintaining and reproducing that same disciplinary power and the nexus of discourses and practices through which it operates. Although Foucault is well-known for arguing 'wherever there is power there is resistance', for Foucault this is hardly a mechanically formulaic phenomenon such that power and resistance to power are always balanced and evenly matched, or even operate over the same temporal duration and the same spatial expanse. The production of docile bodies makes it all the more difficult for resistance to emerge that can prove effective in challenging power that works by means of domination and subjection.

Coercion acts upon the body by way of "a machinery of power that explores it, break it down and rearranges it" (138). Our bodies develop in line with social conceptions, scripts, programs, and ideals concerning what the body should look like and be capable of, in order to participate within and contribute to what. We learn as part of our society, and its dominant culture, what kinds of bodies are required, and what kinds of bodies are affirmed, even prized–for what, when, where, how, and why. Social institutions and relations within which we participate provide us structure and guidance to shape our bodies along these lines. Docile bodies are those that can accommodate the demands of doing what they are supposed to be doing in the various areas of life where people spend extended periods of time, while being submissive and obedient, while adhering and conforming to dominant norms and normativities, as well doing this repeatedly. According to Foucault, we witness this process of the production–and reproduction–of 'docile bodies' in schools, in the military, in the workplaces, and in a great many more social environments.

Discipline represents a particular mode of the exercise of power modeled on that of the punishment of crime, in particular via incarceration, but which operates throughout the institutions of society, and through the discourses and practices of culture. More precisely, 'discipline' acts as plethora of 'disciplines'. All make use of enclosure, confinement, and other means of restricting temporal and spatial movement–practices Foucault cites as commonplace in schools, the military, and workplaces as well as literal prisons. Also commonly allied with the aforementioned elements in disciplinary exercise of power is "partitioning" into "cellular" micro-spaces (143), which includes, for example, "the individual fragmenting of labour power" in workplaces where workers are assigned discrete individual tasks and responsibilities to perform in discrete individual micro-spaces, such as stations on an assembly line or cubicles in an office (145). Aside from those more obvious examples, it is worth reflecting on to what extent many workplaces–even those that today involve remote work performed from home–separate the work each individual worker does as a contribution to the collective whole, to the collective product the workers, together, are producing. This can indeed happen by means of 'a global assembly line' or the equivalent, where workers across many different countries are all individually contributing pieces to a larger product that results from the labor power of all involved.

Discipline also works by assigning distinct ranks and by systematizing this assignment, and here we recognize it can be useful for a company, for instance, to be able to give workers within the same enterprise a wide variety of different titles, corresponding to different ranks and statuses, with different rights and privileges, including as incentive for workers to strive for promotion in rank and status–and the same with competing for awards that recognize high achievers and likewise enhance status. Foucault argues that discipline "made the educational space function like a learning machine, but also a machine for supervising, hierarchizing, rewarding" (147), and this calls to mind how much of teaching, at least as mandated by the central administration and by larger authorities, such as the state, is concerned with evaluating students, especially hierarchically differentially, in terms of letter grades, numeric proportions out of a total of 100 possible points, or grade point averages.

Foucault suggests that in social environments subject to the exercise of disciplinary power people learn to recognize and accept their 'proper place'. Foucault also calls attention to how activities within these environments are typically tightly controlled and regulated, in precise temporal increments. Everything, Foucault suggests, must be organized and directed toward productive use of time, with wasting of time to be avoided as far as possible. In relation again to schools, it is worth reflecting here on the typical division of the school day into discrete time periods, and of a student's life into multiple classes in different fields, moving throughout the day from one to the other, as well as the further organization of the schedule into weeks, units/modules, and semesters/terms, all in line with a series of deadlines by which papers/projects/homework assignments/quizzes/tests/exams are due. This tight regulation of time takes over the life of the teacher as well as the student–and comes to overwhelmingly structure it.

The same tends to happens at many other workplaces in terms of how shifts are set up and organized. But in the classroom we also recognize this effect in a common practice, among many teachers, which I certainly have made use of from time to time as well, of specifying particular proportions of time in each single class period be devoted to a particular activity, while students often expect they will be told precisely how long they should spend on each particular task as well as precisely how long each segment of each class period will last. Meetings among faculty too are often regulated in these terms as well, with each item on an agenda assigned a corresponding amount of time the chair of the meeting expects to spend on that item–or is willing to spend on that item. Students become so used to observing consistent patterns in terms of particular increments of class time that departures provoke uneasiness, while students are often closely attuned to when each class session ends, and will break off automatically when the time comes, no matter if they are midway through a particularly enthusiastic, engaged, and provocative discussion. We also witness a comparable phenomenon at work in terms of space, as even when teachers do not assign seats, students characteristically tend to sit in the same seats, even without ever being told to do so and even when encouraged not to do so. Once any other pattern concerning how class sessions will proceed seems established, students come to expect it and are startled when that is not how the teacher organizes and conducts a subsequent class session. This happens even when students claim to prefer 'variety' in terms of teaching and learning methods, and in the organization and conduct of class sessions.

Eventually, according to Foucault, "Discipline is no longer simply an art of distributing bodies, of extracting time from them and accumulating it, but of composing forces in order to obtain an efficient machine" (164). What happens is "The individual body becomes an element that may be placed, moved, articulated on others" with "an insertion of this body-segment in a whole ensemble over which it is articulated" whereby "The body is constituted as part of a multiple-segmentary machine" (164). As Foucault suggests, chronological series are "also pieces of machinery" (164). What all of this leads to, moreover, is organization that follows "a precise system of command" (166).

Foucault is referencing many kinds of social environments in which the default practice is to over and over again follow the same process in the same methodical way, with again each individual taking up their own individual place and making their own individual contribution, as part of what not only feels like but also effectively becomes a machinic mode of operation. This effect shows up in 'zombification' where people learn to act much akin to zombies, not needing to pay much attention or think all that hard about what they are doing, or how, and especially why, as they do the same thing over and over again. This effect shows up in many jobs where people on the front lines need to repeat the same lines over and over again, so much so that they often stop paying close attention to what they are saying and are startled by even small unexpected developments or changes in this familiar form of dialogue with customers.

Consider 'Did you find everything you were looking for?', 'What kind of bags do you want–paper or plastic?', 'Are you sitting inside or outside?', 'What brings you out tonight?', 'Are you all right?', 'Would you like a copy of your receipt?', 'Would you like to also make a donation to ___?', 'Do you have any big plans ahead?', 'What are your plans for the weekend?', 'Would you fill out this customer satisfaction survey for me?', 'Do you have a ___ card, and if not would you like to fill out the application for one?', 'Can I bring you anything else?', 'How is your food so far?', 'Can I help you find anything?', 'Have a nice day', 'Thanks for coming', 'Thanks for shopping at ___ ', and 'Thanks for dining at ___ ', etc. I myself think about how those staffing registration desks where patients check in at Mayo Clinic Health Systems Eau Claire so often repeat the same sequence, over and over again, day in and day out: 'Your name?', 'Your date of birth?', 'You have an appointment today with ___ at ___ time?', 'Your primary care physician is _____?', 'Your address is still _____?', 'Your phone number where we can reach you is still _____?', 'Your insurance is still _____?, 'You have ____ listed as your emergency contact?', 'You haven't fallen within _____?', 'You haven't taken anything today which will make you drowsy?', and 'You know where you are going from here?'

What also strikes me as indicative of the validity of Foucault's point is that many times I have checked in with the same person only days after just checking in and they still insist on running through the exact same array of questions. This reminds me of workplaces where I've suggested ways of taking shortcuts, or that I could do something easier or faster to save some time for a fellow worker, but this has been rejected because my fellow workers have become so accustomed to proceeding in one rote manner that it would be too upsetting to try anything different. Also, the whole notion of 'jumping through hoops' which is often used, disparagingly, to characterize requirements to obtain a degree–or, in contrast, to suggest this is *not* how students should conceive of what they are doing when required to take courses outside of their major and other areas of concentration–also fits with this same sense of human beings becoming akin to mere cogs in a machine, or zombies who are acting as if they are effectively dead as they live out their lives participant within such tightly regulated and methodically structured kinds of disciplinary social environments.

Foucault declares "It might be said that discipline creates out of the bodies it controls four types of individuality, or rather an individual that is endowed with four characteristics: it is cellular (by the play of spatial distribution), it is organic (by the coding of activities), it is genetic (by the accumulation of time), it is combinatory (by the composition of forces)" (167). In turn, "Four great techniques" are involved: drawing up tables, prescribing movements, imposing exercises, and arranging tactics (167). What's more, "It may be that war as strategy is a continuation of politics. But it must not be forgotten that 'politics' has been conceived as a continuation, if not exactly and directly of war, at least of the military model as a functioning means of preventing civil disorder. Politics, as a technique of internal peace and order, sought to implement the mechanism of the perfect army, of the disciplined mass, of the docile, useful troop, of the regiment in camp and in the field, on manoeuvres and on exercises" (168). What is particularly noteworthy here, I suggest, is this position coincides with how readily people learn to submit to authority, and not to question, challenge, or critique it, at least not openly and directly, virtually ever, while at the same time learning, even from an early age, to identify all figures in positions of authority as effectively interchangeable and therefore all of these as needing to be related to in the same–submissive–way.

Foucault asserts "The chief function of the disciplinary power is to 'train'" and "Instead of bending all its subjects into a single uniform mass, it separates, analyses, differentiates" in the course of so doing (170). Grades in school do this as do all constituent components of grades, and follow up amalgamations from grades, such as GPA. Students, according to the logic of the educational institution, *must* be differentiated and ranked–they *must* be distinguished and analyzed in order to do so. This is only one example of what Foucault here is proposing is a 'multi-disciplinary' training not only in docility but also in accepting the naturalness of hierarchizing forms of differentiation, ranking, and evaluation, such that these should be expected to be imposed everywhere.

One illustration of how this is the case is how commonplace it is to take the system of letter grades used to evaluate performance in school and transpose this into many other areas of cultural life–with, for example, sports' teams, players, and coaches often evaluated in terms of letter grades in relation to their performance for specific games and over particular seasons. Strikingly, sports fans and other commentators who readily turn to such a system of letter grades tend to use them more harshly than is commonplace these days in many if not most schools. But my larger point is it seems 'natural' always to be distinguishing according to a hierarchical system of letter grades, and to evaluate and rank as many kinds of social and cultural phenomena as imaginable according to such as system.

"Discipline," Foucault declares, "'makes' individuals; it is the specific technique of power that regards individuals both as objects and as instruments of its exercise" (170). Another way of putting this: individuals become individually distinct according to the terms defined by discipline, according to how discipline proposes individuals are in fact individuals, how discipline proposes individuals are individually distinctive from–and in relation to–each other. Different 'disciplines' distinguish individuals and define what constitutes individuals' individuality in at least slightly different ways, which means at least slightly different modes of individuality, and at least slight different ways of 'making individuals', operate in schools, churches, the military, before the law, as part of sports and recreational teams, as citizens and residents of a community and of nation, as members of political parties or other political organizations, and in relation to different kinds of workplaces such as factories, retail establishments, call centers, grocery stores, warehouses, shipping companies, trucking firms, banks and other financial services institutions, social welfare services, medical care provision, and police, fire, and ambulance services. But Foucault's larger point is, nonetheless, that what we commonsensically imagine is our autonomous free choice–we freely determine and freely control, by ourselves, for ourselves, who we are as individuals–is not so, but is instead a social construction, enabled by discourses and practices operating through various social institutions, and other nexuses of social relations, in the interest of the exercise of disciplinary power. Foucault proposes the individual is "a reality fabricated by this specific technology of power that I have called 'discipline'"(194).

Foucault contends "The success of disciplinary power derives no doubt from the use of simple instruments; hierarchical observation, normalizing judgement and their combination in a procedure that is specific to it, the examination" (170). In particular, Foucault highlights the uses of 'the examination' and it is worth noting here, in this connection, how much is so often oriented toward and depends on success in examination, in terms of how well students do in school, as well as how far and along what lines they are able to proceed in school, while a major ongoing focus of critique of the involvement of the state as well as of corporate institutions pushing their agendas in schools has to do with education becoming dominated by teaching toward the taking of tests, and examinations, with little time left for any other kind of education, including what best enables the development of students' critical and creative capabilities. Yet in many other areas of life tests and examinations are also routine–in many workplaces, including as requirements to obtain and retain jobs; in order to obtain many rights and opportunities of citizenship, from status as a citizen to driver's licenses; and in medical settings, where examinations are such routine practices that many if not most people find it hard to fathom how these might operate, in such settings, as instruments of power, and in particular of disciplinary power. Foucault contends the examination epitomizes "a normalizing gaze" and "is highly ritualized" to further authorize its authority (184), while, with the rise to dominance of disciplinary power, "The school became a sort of apparatus of uninterrupted examination" (186).

A major constituent of Foucault's theory of disciplinary power follows his proposition that in the course of the exercise of disciplinary power it is often important to make use "of eyes that must see without being seen" (171). In other words, a principal effective aim of disciplinary power is "to render visible those who are inside" and even more precisely "to provide a hold on their conduct, to carry the effects of power right to them, to make it possible to know them, to alter them" (172). As Foucault adds, moreover, "The perfect disciplinary mechanism would make it possible for a single gaze to see everything constantly" (173). Foucault identifies military camps as models for these much more socially pervasive varieties of 'observatories', but what he is particularly attuned to highlight, across military and non-military 'observatories', is they typically involve a "spacial 'nesting' of hierarchized surveillance" (171-172). These cellular structures enable the exercise of disciplinary power through prospectively continuous surveillance, and this, Foucault contends, is commonplace across disparate social institutions. Foucault cites modern capitalist workplaces as locations maintaining "intense, continuous supervision" throughout the labor process (174). As the labor process within the single capitalist firm became larger and more complex, the need for supervision and surveillance increased in direct correlation, while tight regulation according to the clock became crucially important–to insure efficiency of production and optimization of profit.

Foucault argues the same kinds of precise supervision and surveillance shows up in teaching: "A relation of surveillance, defined and regulated, is inscribed at the heart of the practice of teaching, not as an additional or adjacent part, but as a mechanism that is inherent to it and which increases its efficiency" (176). Foucault's contention, akin to that of Althusser, is teaching is much more a site of domination and subjection, of social control and social normalization, as well as of the pathologization of the different and 'abnormal', than it is a site for what educational institutions idealistically proclaim teaching to be about.

Reconnecting 'discipline' more precisely with 'punishment', Foucault explains that disciplinary power requires penal mechanisms, and that these penalties will be imposed for many different kinds of violations, including small violations and passive 'crimes' of 'omission' as well as 'active' crimes of 'commission' (178). In particular, Foucault finds that disciplinary power emphasizes penalizing what does not observe or conform 'to the rules' (178-179). Punishment, what's more, is often closely interlinked with gratification, as discipline simultaneous rewards some practices while penalizing others (180). Ultimately, the preeminent effective end of the exercise of disciplinary power is to ensure that each "might all be like one another" (182), which means "In short, the art of punishing, in the regime of disciplinary power, is aimed neither at expiation, nor even precisely at repression" as most crucially what it aims and accomplishes is "it *normalizes*" (182-183).

Foucault argues that "Normalization becomes one of the great instruments of power at the end of the classical age" (184) in schools at all levels, in relation to all matters of health, and in industrial and other kinds of work. "Degrees of normality" of which there exist "a whole range" (184) are what matter most in determining relative social status and standing. "The power of normalization imposes homogeneity," yet does so by simultaneously individualizing normalization in terms of these degrees of normality that makes "it possible to measure gaps, to determine levels, to fix specialties and to render the differences useful by fitting them to one another" (184). As a result, "It is easy to understand how the power of the norm functions within a system of formal equality, since within a homogeneity that is the rule, the norm introduces, as a useful imperative and as a result of measurement, all the shading of individual differences" (184). Foucault here portrays a social environment where a formal equality loosely prevails in conjunction with individually differentiated yet normatively homogeneous differences, as disciplinary power effectively polices difference by transforming difference into a range of acceptable gradations among slightly distinct shades of normality. Social institutions effectively teach people how to be normal, how to fit in as normal, and what range and kind of deviation is acceptable and permitted while still remaining acceptably normal. Social institutions teach people what constitute allowed, or allowable, forms of rebellion, including what constitute 'normal' modes, forms, stages, and phases of rebellion.

Another ready connection with Foucault's theory here follows in terms of people's aspirations to be perceived, accepted, treated, and included as normal. If 'the normal', if 'being normal', if being perceived and treated and respected and included as 'normal' did not maintain considerable positive sanction and reward, considerable privilege and advantage, versus 'the abnormal', 'being abnormal', being perceived and treated and disrespected and excluded as 'abnormal', then so many people, and so many groups of people, would not so often aspire, even indeed often desperately, toward being perceived, treated, respected, and included as 'normal'. I well know that pull, as someone who has felt the oppressive weight quite severely at various times and over extended intervals of my life, in being perceived, treated, disrespected, and excluded as 'abnormal'–on account of being gay and queer, on account of being a Marxist and a socialist, on account of being a leftist intellectual and activist, on account of being academically and intellectually oriented, on account of being a person who lives continually with chronic illness and invisible physical disability, and on account of being a person who lives continually with mental health challenges. I have at times wished, even fervently so, that 'I could be (more) normal', and that I could be perceived, treated, respected, and included as (more) 'normal'. Yet, at other times, I have felt a strong pull in the opposite direction–as the slogan common on buttons, bumper sticker, and posters proposes, 'Why Be Normal?'–as I have *not* wanted to fit in with what is normal, or passes for normal, especially when that regime of normality appears to runs counter to my foremost principles, convictions, and values. Nevertheless, it can be extremely difficult to identify with being 'abnormal'–or 'other than normal'–and to live confidently and forthrightly in terms of that identification, even if doing so marks a major focus of both critical queer and critical disability forms of praxis, showing up for example among those who positively identify with labels such as 'faggot', 'dyke', 'pervert', 'crip', and 'mad'. Much of that difficulty has to do with how limited is the 'safe space' within which to exist in openly identifying in these ways–with how limited is social tolerance for this kind and extent of 'deviation' from 'the norm'.

Foucault argues in his famous chapter "Panopticism" that "Disciplinary power . . . is exercised through its invisibility," while "at the same time it imposes on those whom it subjects a principle of compulsory visibility" (187). As Foucault explains, "In discipline it is the subjects who have to be seen. Their visibility assures the hold of the power that is exercised over them. It is the fact of being constantly seen, or being able always to be seen, that maintains the disciplined individual in his subjection" (187).

What Foucault is getting at here is to be subjected to discipline involves being constantly visible to an authority that maintains the power to punish. Foucault's theorization along this line is if anything all the more apt in what Shoshana Feldman has theorized, in the early 21st century, as the age of 'surveillance capitalism', with not only the state but also powerful capitalist corporations implementing extraordinary means by which they are able to monitor all kinds of things people do in all kinds of times and places, while gathering and analyzing massive amounts of information about people's preferences and behaviors, to the point where they are able not only to predict what these will be but also to manipulate them in desirable directions. We have in fact reached the point in time where many people are not troubled by how much of their personal information can be readily tracked via their mobile smart phones, or through other networked computers they regularly use, and I have taught a number of students who have declared they are not at all bothered by the prospect that the state might be watching and listening to everything they do, every day, because, if 'I am doing nothing wrong I have nothing to worry about'. Alternately, many others are somewhat bothered by this, but rationalize it as nonetheless necessary to insure 'the bad guys'–such as 'terrorists'–are thwarted.

A similar collective ethos has developed within many social media platforms, or sections of social media platforms, where people routinely share, and now have done so for decades by this point in time, a great deal of highly sensitive, and indeed often embarrassing personal information–information that can be readily used against them by any inclined to do so. At the same time, the collective ethos in these sites encourages people to present themselves, and engage, along a limited array of common lines, which become the de facto 'normal' ways to so operate. Much critical commentary has been devoted, for instance, to how people's tendencies on many of these platforms to present themselves in the best possible light, emphasizing their achievements and successes at their happiest and otherwise most conventionally attractive moments, while also coming across as consistently self-confident and certain about what they think and believe as well as how and why so, can intimidate as well as provoke anxiety and unease among others who feel comparably inadequate–and unattractive–because it is harder for them to identify and fit with what these social media sites at least appear to posit as the limits defining and surrounding what is 'normal' versus what is not.

Jeremy Bentham's *Panopticon* represents, for Foucault, an exemplary "architectural figure" of the preeminent effective exercise of disciplinary power (200). The Panopticon is set up such that all prisoners can be simultaneously visible, within their separated cells, by a single guard watching them from a central tower, while at the same time this guard is always invisible to all of these prisoners and all of the prisoners are always invisible to each other. Within the Panopticon "visibility is a trap" as the subject of the disciplinary power "is seen, but he does not see" while he cannot see either who is observing him, or if anyone is, or the others being observed, how they are being observed, and by whom: "And this invisibility"–this "lateral invisibility"–"is a guarantee or order" (200). With the Panopticon, "The crowd, a compact mass, a locus of multiple exchanges, individualities merging together, a collective effort, is abolished and replaced by a collection of separated individualities" (201). Yet "The major effect of the Panopticon" is "to induce in the inmate a state of conscious and permanent visibility that assures the automatic functioning of power" (201). The Panopticon's design insures that "surveillance is permanent in its effects, even if it is discontinuous in its action" (201), because prisoners never know if or when a guard is actually watching them from the tower, while this design likewise establishes the principle that disciplinary "power should be visible and unverifiable," or at least is most effective when this is so (201).

As Foucault explains, the beauty of the Panopticon is it provides a general model that can be put to diverse uses by many diverse interests–and is effectively interchangeable in its operations and effectivities across these: "It is in fact a figure of political technology that may and must be detached from any specific use" and "It is polyvalent in its applications" (205). Once more, Foucault cites hospitals, workshops, schools, and prisons as examples of the Panoptic exercise of disciplinary power, while quoting Bentham as asserting the Panopticon it is "applicable 'to all establishments whatsoever'" (as quoted 205). Foucault in turn contends panopticism can be and increasingly is exercised throughout society (208), as "the general principle of a new 'political anatomy' whose object and end are not the relations of sovereignty but the relations of discipline" (208). Within the Panopticon, "A real subjection is born mechanically from a fictitious relation" (202), which means, in gist, that it is not necessary to actively force the subject to submit, because the subject internalizes the need to submit and submits by themselves, aware that they always might be watched and they might always be punished if they do not so submit (202). The Panopticon efficiently reduces the number needed who exercise power while increasing the number over whom power is exercised (206). This effect of the Panopticon (or the panoptic form of the exercise of disciplinary power) closely resembles that of ideology, according to Althusser, in interpellating individuals into positions as subjects such that they 'freely choose' to accept and effectively enact their own submission, acceptance, obedience, and conformity within the reproduction of the relations of production such that they continue exploited and otherwise dominated.

Again, a larger focus of concern for Foucault, over the course of *Discipline and Punish: The Birth of the Prison*, is how disciplinary power developed, from its panoptic capacity for generalized surveillance, into a host of associated "techniques for making useful individuals" (211). As Foucault explains, and here we recognize a key difference versus Althusser, and versus Marxism more broadly than Althusser alone, "'Discipline' may be identified neither with an institution nor with an apparatus; it is a type of power, a modality for its exercise, comprising a whole set of instruments, techniques, procedures, levels of application, targets; it is a 'physics' or an 'anatomy' of power, a technology" (215). As such, discipline may be used by a wide variety of different institutions in different ways and to different extents, yet what is of ultimately greatest interest for Foucault is "the formation of a disciplinary society" where disciplinary power has not necessarily replaced all other modes of power but nonetheless infiltrated all of these others, and is widely as well as generally disseminated (216).

At the end of his "Panopticism" chapter, Foucault queries "Is it surprising that prisons resemble factories, schools, barracks, hospitals, which all resemble prisons?" (228). Foucault has made it clear he does not think so because of the common reliance on a disciplinary mode of the exercise of power in all of these institutions. Yet what is the precise role of the prison within this overall nexus of multiple sites of the exercise of disciplinary power? Prison seems self-evidently useful for punishment of crime in modern times, including in both Foucault's time and ours, but this has not always been so and in fact from a critical vantage point hardly seems at all so. Why then are prisons dominant instruments for the punishment of crime in modern societies?

According to Foucault this is not just because deprivation of liberty increasingly came to be recognized as punishment *par excellence* but rather because prison allows for precisely differentiating punishments, in terms of different lengths of sentences, and this correlates nicely with the idea of 'paying one's debt' to society as a whole. But what is even more important for Foucault is the role of prison in relation to disciplinary mechanisms at work throughout the larger society. Prison does maintain multiple recognizable advantages as a site for the exercise of disciplinary power including total control over prisoners' lives, or at least the capability of exercising this extent of control, along with isolation, coercive individualization, and a systematic machinization of daily life. As Foucault declares, "The theme of the Panopticon–at once surveillance and observation, security and knowledge, individualization and totalization, isolation and transparency–found in the prison its privileged locus of realization" (249).

Yet it is important, Foucault advises, to note well that prisons do not lower the crime rate while they also lead to recidivism (265). In fact, "The prison cannot fail to produce delinquents" and this suggests its social usefulness has to do with *the production of delinquents*: "The prison makes possible, even encourages, the organization of a milieu of delinquents, loyal to one another, hierarchized, ready to aid and abet any future criminal act" (266). So what is going on here, when prisons seemingly fail to achieve their ostensible end, to serve their ostensible purpose? Foucault rephrases that question as "Is not the supposed failure part of the functioning of the prison?" Foucault answers this question by theorizing the role of the prison is less important in what it does to literal prisoners than what is its place, and function, within a larger carcereal system operating coterminous with society as a whole (271). Key, Foucault advises, is to study "what is served by the failure of the prison" (272), and this means "The prison, and no doubt punishment in general, is not intended to eliminate offences, but rather to distinguish them, to distribute them, to use them . . . it is not so much that they render docile those who are liable to transgress the law, but that they tend to assimilate the transgression of the laws in a general tactics of subjection" (272).

As Foucault explains, proliferation of forms of criminality and varieties of crimes, along with the perpetuation of offenses committed by recidivist criminals, support social fear of crime, criminals, and criminality, and of those groups of people, especially from 'lower' social positions, judged to be particularly liable or prone towards the same (275). As Foucault explains yet further, "For the observation that prison fails to eliminate crime, one should perhaps substitute the hypothesis that prison has succeeded extremely well in producing delinquency" and more precisely "producing the delinquent as a pathological subject" (277). This is the subject *against which the normal can be and is defined. Controlled delinquency* can be and is socially useful in multiple ways–including on account of many criminal activities being of benefit to those at heights of social power, as well as giving rise to along with helping maintain and reproduce a vast criminal justice system. Prison and incarceration function as a means of simultaneously exoticizing and taming rebellion while forestalling revolt by transforming rebellion into 'crime'.

In his final chapter, "The carcereal," Foucault argues modern society encompasses a "carceral archipelago" (297) or "a great carceral continuum" or a "carceral net" linking exercises of discipline across an array of institutions (297). This carcereal system works to "produce bodies that are both docile and capable" (294) and its key focus is upon "the supervision of normality" through a proliferation of apparatuses working to do so, leading to "the normalization of the power of normalization" (296). Techniques developed in relation to "the penal institution" are "transported" "to the entire social body" (298) with the focus of discipline, and punishment, moving from sole concern with transgression of the law to even "a slight departure from a rule, an average, a demand, a norm" (298). As the carcereal became more pervasive and more entrenched, the focus "was no longer the offence, the attack on the common interest, it was the departure from the norm, the anomaly; it was this that haunted the school, the court, the asylum or the prison" (299). What transpired was "The social enemy was turned into a deviant who brought with him the multiple danger of disorder, crime and madness" (299-300). Delinquency is produced from within the carcereal, as necessary in order to naturalize and legitimate punishment (301).

With the carcereal coterminous with society as a whole,

Prison continues, on those who are entrusted to it, a work begun elsewhere, which the whole of society pursues on each individual through innumerable mechanisms of discipline. By means of a carcereal continuum, the authority that sentences infiltrates all those other authorities that supervise, transform, correct, improve. It might even be said that nothing really distinguishes them any more except the singularly 'dangerous' character of the delinquents, the gravity of their departures from normal behaviour and the necessary solemnity of the ritual. But, in its function, the power to punish is not essentially different from that of curing or educating. (303)

The carcereal "'naturalizes' the power to punish" and "By operating at every level of the social body," the "universalizing of the carcereal" enables it to seem "natural and acceptable" to punish a vast plethora of different kinds of behavior, including even slight departures from the normative (303). The power of the normative, and of the instruments of normalization, once more, is at the heart of what the carcereal is all about: "it has become one of the major functions of our society. The judges of normality are everywhere" (304). In sum, the specific place and function of the prison within the larger carcereal system is as "the relay in a general network of disciplines and surveillances" (305).

Drawing from what the Panopticon reveals about the nature of disciplinary power and its operation, Foucault contends "Our society is not one of spectacle, but of surveillance" in which "the individual is carefully fabricated" in the course of the operation, in the course of the exercise of power, as an effect of, and a bearer of, this power, and as an essential "part of its mechanism" (217). Contrary to the Situationists, and especially Guy Debord, who identify mid to late 20th advanced capitalist society in the Global North as 'the society of the spectacle', this is 'the society of surveillance', 'the society of discipline', and 'the society of normalization'. Disciplinary power produces subjects who becomes means of (or instruments of the yet further) production and reproduction of disciplinary power (219), while at the same time working to "neutralize the effects of counter-power" and all allied forms of resistance, opposition, disruption, subversion, and transformation (219), even as the latter are already hard to mobilize in opposition to disciplinary regimes because the disciplines simultaneously laterally partition and vertically hierarchize individuals and groups of people (220). Foucault proposes, chillingly, reminiscent of Kafka, that

> The ideal point of penality today would be an indefinite discipline: an interrogation without end, an investigation that would be extended without limit to a meticulous and ever more analytical observation, a judgement that would at the same time be the constitution of a file that was never closed, the calculated leniency of a penalty that would be interlaced with the ruthless curiosity of an examination, a procedure that would be at the same time the permanent measure of a gap in relation to an inaccessible norm and the asymptotic movement that strives to meet in infinity. (227).

In such a circumstance, and even in those approaching it, 'counter-power' is extremely hard to conceive, even if, akin to Althusser in *On the Reproduction of Capitalism: Ideology and Ideological State Apparatuses*, Foucault is theorizing the exercise of disciplinary power in the interest of enabling it to be well understood so that counter-power can prove most viable and effective, so that counter-power can recognize what formidable obstacles it faces in this quest.

Foucault maintains significant differences versus Marxists such as Althusser. Foucault does identify, in terms that Marxists such as Mark Neocleous would find readily compatible with Marxist theory of the same, "the police," in modern, capitalist society as encompassing far more than 'the police proper' or 'the police per se'– as in fact encompassing "an apparatus . . . coextensive with the entire social body" and operating (that is, exercising power) "over everything'" (213). Yet even as Foucault argues that "The organization of the police apparatus in the eighteenth century sanctioned a generalization of the disciplines that became co-extensive with the state itself" he simultaneously argues "it would be wrong to believe the disciplinary functions were confiscated and absorbed once and for all by a state apparatus" (215). Foucault proposes "There is not the 'centre of power', not a network of forces, but a multiple network of diverse elements" (307).

Foucault nevertheless does theorize this diverse and diffuse ensemble as sharing an important commonality: linkage to and reliance on "a whole series of 'carcereal' mechanisms that seem distinct enough–since they are intended to alleviate pain, to cure, to comfort–but that all tend, like the prison, to exercise a power of normalization" (308). What we have here is the operation and exercise of "complex power relations, bodies and forces subjected by multiple mechanisms of 'incarceration'" as well as to "the power of normalization" that is inextricable from "the formation of knowledge in modern society" (308).

Five

Now it is time to distill from what I have addressed at length in the preceding three sections to summarily identify what are principal issues Weber, Althusser, and Foucault each respectively address, as well as what are principal lines of convergence and divergence among these three critical theorists, as represented by *Protestant Ethic and the Spirit of Capitalism, On The Reproduction of Capitalism: Ideology and Ideological State Apparatuses*, and *Discipline and Punish: the Birth of the Prison*. These issues will serve as principal points of contact in the encounters to come, in sections six through nine, with Ian Curtis and Joy Division, represented, in turn, by the songs "Insight," "New Dawn Fades," "Atrocity Exhibition," and "The Eternal."

In *Protestant Ethic and the Spirit of Capitalism* Weber emphasizes:

1. The substantial formative impact upon the spirit of capitalism of a post-Calvinist, originally Puritan-based Protestant ethic that valorizes living life in accord with a preeminent dedication to hard work, pursued in a methodically rational manner, as part of a commitment conceived and approached as a calling.

2. As a result of the impact and influence of the Protestant ethic on the spirit of capitalism with the rise of modern capitalism, people's identities, and their worth, coming to be increasingly defined in accord with the work they do, the kind of work they do, how hard they work, and how successful is their work–especially in terms of generating material wealth.

3. The most desirable vocational and/or avocational endeavors coming to be perceived as those that can feel for those so engaged as indicative of a 'calling', with everyone encouraged to strive to find and pursue their own proper 'calling'.

4. The impact and influence of the Protestant ethic on the spirit of capitalism contributing to not only a rationalization but also a glorification of the generation, acquisition, and accumulation of massive wealth, with this in turn perceived as testimony to the talent, skill, hard work, and just desert of those who succeed in so doing.

5. The impact and influence of the Protestant ethic on the spirit of capitalism insinuating that those who do not succeed in competition for substantial material gain are themselves responsible, because they have not worked hard enough and do not deserve any better than where they end up.

6. Steady erosion and eventual virtual elimination of the originally ascetic dimension of the religious source of the spirit of capitalism with working to generate and accumulate wealth no longer conceived and approached as either testifying to the glory of God or as evidence of one's providential salvation.

7. In the 'victorious' stage of modern capitalism life conducted in continuous pursuit of material gain becomes increasingly in effect 'a steel-hard casing' or an 'iron cage' that is exceedingly difficult to escape, and that focuses people's prime interests and concerns upon purely instrumental ends, according to a means-end ethic, resulting, simultaneously, in an increasing loss of people's capacity to experience life in aesthetically vibrant and sensuous as well as affectively compassionate and empathetic terms–i.e., as motivated by humane values that transcend making money and spending on what money can buy.

In *On The Reproduction of Capitalism: Ideology and Ideological State Apparatuses* Althusser emphasizes:

1. The crucial importance of understanding and explaining how society, and in particular, capitalist society is reproduced, with this requiring, most fundamentally, reproduction of the relations of production, and with the state playing a central role in enabling and insuring the reproduction of capitalist society by means of the contributions of both the Repressive State Apparatus and the Ideological State Apparatuses.

2. The Ideological State Apparatuses, or the ISAs, contribute to social reproduction by way of ideology while ideology provides an imaginary representation of individuals' relations to the real conditions of their existence and is always manifest, and effective, through material acts as part of material practices, governed and regulated by material rituals, and conducted within a material apparatus.

3. Ideology interpellates individuals into positions as subjects to and of ideology, and in so doing ideology interpellates individuals into positions where they 'freely' choose not only to identify with the positions ideology sets forth for them as subjects but also 'freely' choose to act in such ways that they become the direct bearers, the direct representatives, of ideology in carrying out the activities required to maintain and reproduce the existing social status quo.

4. Individuals are always-already interpellated by ideology, even before they are born, and they are continually interpellated and re-interpellated by ideology throughout their lives.

5. Ideology is the site and stake of class struggle, and it is through the contradictions within dominant ideology, and its workings through the ISAs, that possibilities and opportunities for resistance and opposition, aligned with counter-dominant ideologies, arise.

6. Even as it does not appear so, from a vantage point within dominant ideology, the specific content of the dominant ideology, as well, for that matter, of counter-dominant ideologies, is always rooted in the current state of, including the current balance of forces within, the economic class struggle.

7. Multiple ideologies always exist within any social formation, including within the ISAs, but these ideologies tend, as long as an existing society is smoothly reproducing itself and it is not necessary to forcibly coerce people into accepting and conforming with subject positions as members of the exploited and the oppressed, to be dominated over by the power of dominant ideology.

8. Ideology works, especially effectively, when it is largely if not completely unconscious; when it does not appear, for those operating within it, as ideology at all, but rather simply what is natural, obvious, self-evident, to be taken for granted, impossible to conceive otherwise, or as corresponding to what appears to represent the best possible system of social arrangements; and when it seemingly works 'by itself' with little to no supplemental coercive force needed to insure identification, submission, acceptance, and conformity, and where subjects proceed to do what ideology directs them to do by in effect declaring 'so be it!'

9. Ideology works, yet further, by providing subjects a guarantee, in relation to an explicit or implicit central Subject, that the social world, including their place within and purpose as a part of it, makes sense, and that they are doing what and as they should in alignment with what the Subject expects of and from them.

In *Discipline and Punish: the Birth of the Prison* Foucault emphasizes:

1. The birth of the prison, and its rise to predominance as the most influential form of punishment of crime in modern society has much to do with the emergence and development of discipline, and, in concrete practice, 'the disciplines', as a preeminent mode of exercise of power throughout modern society.

2. Discipline exercises power over subjects by measuring, assessing, analyzing, classifying, differentiating, ranking, and maintaining careful surveillance of and scrutiny over behavior, as well as of and over prospective behavior, while working to shape subjects so they will proceed to enact their own subjection in alignment with prescribed norms, including in distinction from and opposition versus various proscribed kinds and directions of abnormality.

3. The prison serves as a crucial anchor, or relay, within a larger carcereal continuum that operates coterminous with the whole of modern society, where human beings are subject to the impact of disciplinary power throughout virtually all social institutions.

4. Discipline works at the level of the body to produce docile bodies, while also fabricating individuals, and in particular what individuals understand their individuality to mean as well as the modes according to which they exercise this individuality, while at the same time limiting, by defining, what precise kinds and degrees of rebellion are socially tolerated and accepted.

5. Jeremy Bentham's Panopticon provides a preeminent architectural model for how discipline often works, at its most effective, within modern society, with panopticism in turn referring to the broad dissemination of the influence of this same panoptic model across social institutions such that people learn repeatedly, and persistently, to submit, obey, and conform because they are seemingly always visible to an authority maintaining the power to punish them for failure to submit, obey, and conform, while this authority is itself by no means equally visible, and where people are continually separated and divided from each other so as to make it possible that they will be all the more easily and thoroughly subjugated.

6. The production of the criminal, and even more significantly, the production of the delinquent and the deviant (as the always-already incipiently criminal) by means of, and through, the operations of disciplinary power, serve as especially crucial and effective means of 'policing' the rest of the population, in enforcing and reinforcing normalization, and in disabling and stifling discontent and resistance.

7. Knowledge itself, and especially as practiced, as mobilized, and in particular as amassed through the human sciences, or in other words the social sciences, becomes a preeminent contributing instrument in the effective exercise of disciplinary power.

Weber, Althusser, and Foucault share in common:

1. Serious concerns with how and why people within modern (capitalist) societies are effectively caught up in 'freely' choosing and acting to identify with, and to submit and conform to, their own confinement, limitation, exploitation, and subjugation.

2. Serious concerns with what people do *not* by and large commonly perceive, recognize, and understand, according to dominant frames of intelligibility, concerning how modern (capitalist) societies and culture operate, along what lines, in accord with what ends and interests, and following what have been the precise historical sources and trajectories resulting in the current state of affairs.

3. A focus of attention on problematic dimensions of modern (capitalist) society because these theorists are interested either in preventing the further deepening and entrenchment of these same problematic dimensions or because they are interested in resisting, challenging, disrupting, subverting, overcoming, and transforming these same problematic dimensions.

Major lines of difference among Weber, Althusser, and Foucault, as represented by these three books are as follows:

1. Weber is less thoroughly critical, in this book at least, of modern (capitalist) society than Althusser and Foucault are, and is instead more overtly concerned with strictly tracing an historical influence that is often unrecognized and unappreciated.

2. Weber's concerns are with excessive methodicalism, rationalism, and instrumentalism, as well as with uncritical glorification of material gain and the accumulation of material wealth, as well as of work and working becoming ends in themselves, as prime (moral) goods.

3. Althusser's concerns focus often upon how people come to perceive and experience themselves as free and in control when and where to a great extent this is not the case at all.

4. Foucault's concerns keep coming back again and again to emphasize the problematic impacts of norms and normativities, of processes of normalization, as well as of what are the social and political uses and the consequences of the production at the same time of 'the abnormal', including the abnormal in the more specific forms of the criminal, the delinquent, and the deviant.

Six

"Insight" is well-known for Martin Hannett's famous opening use of a recording of an old broken-down elevator shaft. It is also one of Peter Hook's favorite songs, and contains one of his favorite bass guitar riffs. For Hook, "Insight" exemplifies "the great thing about Joy Division was that we used the bass to write the songs" (*Unknown Pleasures: Inside Joy Division* 202). Hook praises the lyrics of the song as "wonderful" while noting, appreciatively as well, the fact that, even more clearly so than in a number of other Joy Division songs, "there's no chorus" (which Hook elsewhere also cites as one among many indices of how Joy Division were not content to do what was most readily expected and commonly done). As Hook recalls, "That sound at the beginning is the creaky old freight lift in Strawberry [Studios] that Martin had mic'd up and recorded, adding fantastic atmosphere to the track" (202). Hook also commends "Steve's snare" as this "has such great presence" (202). Hook uses the rest of the space he devotes to commenting on "Insight" to highlight Hannett's use of "echo plate and digital delays" throughout *Unknown Pleasures* as well as to suggest the often "distorted sound" (or at least distorted-seeming sound) of Curtis's recorded vocal likely resulted from Hannett 'pumping up' the vocal–that is, double-tracking it. Indeed a notable feature of "Insight" is the prominent overdubbing by Hannett of electronically generated studio effects in addition to the recording of the elevator shaft.

In teaching "Insight" in connection with Althusser's "Ideology and Ideological State Apparatuses: Notes Towards an Investigation" I have proposed it makes sense to interpret this song as sharing Althusser's *critique* of the function of (dominant) ideology. The way I interpret the song, in line with this Althusserian conception, is it represents an 'insight' into how ideological messages directed at the young, of what to anticipate and look forward to, as you grow up, if you follow the pathway laid out for you, are false (are misleading). For awhile, the song suggests, even while

509

recognizing these ideological messages as illusions, people cling to them out of fear–fear of what it might mean to attempt to live life differently. Nevertheless, at this point in time, the point in time in which the song is addressing us, the narrator-protagonist is "not afraid anymore." Going against the dominant ideology–against the grain of what the larger society tells you that you should do–is scary, is likely to prove costly, and is in no way guaranteed to end successfully, but the narrator-protagonist is ready now, and [he] cannot and will not turn back. The sound of the song, moreover, suggests leaving a sheltered space that is, nonetheless, effectively a prison cage, to enter upon a dangerous battlefield, with little support in so doing other than a melancholic yet resolute sense that emergence to confront the danger is necessary.

"Insight" bears interesting prospective connections as well with Weber's *Protestant Ethic and the Spiritual Capitalism*, starting with references in the lyrics to wasting time. Earlier in the narrator-protagonist's life and that of others with whom 'he' maintained close relationships in the past they innocently imagined they enjoyed more time ahead (perhaps even seemingly endless time) than they in fact did. This past remains "a special moment in time," in memory, even as the narrator-protagonist has become distanced from that time and his mental outlook at that time. References to those with "habits to waste" as well as "Their sense of style and good taste" suggest a critical position akin to the Protestant Ethic Weber theorizes as making a crucial contribution to the spirit of capitalism, as well as to Weber's reservations concerning the 'steel-hard casing' or 'iron cage' that results from becoming consumed with the pursuit of money and what it can buy. Reference in the lyrics to "all God's angels," and "all you judges," admonished to "beware," in conjunction with the refrain "I'm not afraid anymore" resonates with moving past fear concerning one's destiny, as either saved or damned, and past agonizing over what is impossible ever to know with any certainty and which one cannot do anything to affect. The ideal position, for the true believer, is to accept this uncertainty with grace and humility. Curtis's lyrics, however, seem to more closely support living defiantly–no longer afraid–in rejecting the necessity of living according to normative standards and expectations. Yet the song registers sadness at what must be abandoned to arrive at such a position, in coming to grips with where this leaves one versus both what must be left behind and what little might yet still be possible.

"Insight" also connects usefully with Foucault's *Discipline and Punish: The Birth of the Prison,* in particular with Foucault's emphasis on normalization as central to the exercise of disciplinary power, throughout modern society, as well as with how difficult it is to resist exercise of this power. This is especially so when forced to do so from the vantage point of what disciplinary power marks out as 'the abnormal'. It makes sense to interpret "Insight" as suggesting what in the past seemed a position of freedom, and of ease and content, now appears, with the benefit of critical insight, to have been a position subject to constraints of life lived from within a carceral continuum operating across the institutions of modern society. The wasting of time the lyrics reference makes sense as referring to remaining unaware of one's own submission to and conformity with processes of normalization that disciplinary power relentlessly imposes.

According to *The Oxford English Dictionary* (online), "insight" primarily refers to: "The fact of penetrating with the eyes of the understanding into the inner character or hidden nature of things; a glimpse or view beneath the surface; the faculty or power of thus seeing." The word also maintains multiple now, the OED claims, obsolete and rare meanings: 1) "Internal sight, mental vision or perception, discernment; in early use sometimes, Understanding, intelligence, wisdom"; 2) "A mental looking *to* or *upon* something; consideration; respect, regard"; 3) "A view of a subject; a conspectus"; 4) "Sight (of the bodily eyes); looking; looking in, inspection; a look." In addition, the OED adds, in psychological "studies of behaviour and learning," insight refers to "the sudden perception of the solution to a problem or difficulty," while "applied to animals" offers "an indication of their capacity for ideas and reasoning," and in psychoanalysis insight refers to "perception of one's mental condition." 'Insight' in sum suggests knowledge that derives from an ability literally or figuratively to 'see into' what this is knowledge concerning–literally or figuratively to 'see beyond' the seemingly readily apparent and obvious that is generally taken for granted. Those with 'insight' mentally perceive, recognize, and understand (or at least grasp and grapple with) what those 'lacking insight' do not. Insight tends to be prized, and is often sought from people who have 'inside information' and 'inside connections' as well as from people who have highly developed, trained, and otherwise acutely sensitive capacities for making sense. Important 'insight' can also come from those occupying positions 'outside' because such 'outsider' positions can at times recognize of what those 'inside' are incapable of perceiving, on account of how their 'insider' position 'blinds' them. A song with the title "Insight" suggests something *not* readily apparent, obvious, and taken for granted. This title suggests the song is either offering us such insight, or alluding to such insight, or seeking such insight. Perhaps it is doing all three. If, however, we are engaging in this song with an understanding derived from 'penetrating into the inner character or hidden nature of things' we need to ask what specific 'things' does this song, and in particular do these lyrics, suggest we are 'looking into'–perhaps as we are simultaneously being shown what to see when we do 'look into' these 'things' as well as how to do so? What 'inner character' or 'hidden nature' is here revealed, concerning what, if only partially and obliquely, and why is this character, or this nature, otherwise hidden and unknown?

Let's proceed to the first stanza: "Guess your dreams always end/They don't rise up just descend/But I don't care anymore/I've lost the will to want more/I'm not afraid not at all/I watch them all as they fall/But I remember when we were young." 'Guess' is a striking way to begin, as this seems to suggest uncertainty about what follows–as if the narrator-protagonist is 'hazarding a guess' that what 'he' is about to describe likely is the case, but he cannot declare with absolute confidence this is so and it might indeed be otherwise. 'Your dreams always end' is yet further striking as a blunt and bleak assessment, because it is common enough for many to identify with the position that 'without your dreams, you are nothing', or as Alan Vega famously sings in "Dream Baby Dream," "dreams are all you have." If your dreams always end, that implies they stop, and the line insinuates as well they fail in so stopping, which certainly suggests a precarious state, if we equate 'dreams' with 'desires' and if we accept, following Jacques Lacan, that human beings, above all else, are desiring beings, who desire, ceaselessly, throughout the course of our whole lives, and who, in fact, desire above all else to keep on desiring. However, what Curtis suggests here might not be that thoroughly annihilating–not that entirely nihilistic–as it makes sense to interpret the line, somewhat more narrowly, as referencing someone, or some group of people–'you' here–as always dreaming dreams that come to a stop and fall short of achieving their aspired ends. This leads us to wonder what kind of person, or what kind of people, might experience this kind of situation, dreaming of what always ends and is never realized–and to wonder what accounts for why their dreams always end.

The lyrics continue by indicating these dreams "don't rise up just descend" which in turn suggests not just that the 'you' of the lyrics experiences dreams that repeatedly stop, and fail, but also that these dreams don't uplift the 'you'. In fact they bring the 'you' down, implying the 'you' experiences dreams that leave this 'you' feeling worse about themself, about their capabilities, about their prospects, about their situation, about their status, about their stature, about their value, and about their significance. This might indeed involve the you's dreams, and especially how they turn out, or play out, leaving the you feeling depressed and despairing. These dreams that "don't rise up just descend" may well be nightmares.

What comes next complicates where we are by this point seemingly at, with the introduction of the 'I' who 'doesn't care anymore'. Starting line three with 'But' does suggest a relationship with the preceding two lines, as seemingly the 'I' here does not care anymore that 'your dreams always end' as they do–that is, descending not rising. This third line, with 'anymore', suggests 'I' may have cared about this in the past, and may even have shared an identical position with that of 'you'–as a dreamer whose dreams always ended disappointingly, and even hauntingly so. But why is 'I' now like this? The fourth line seems to offer at least the beginning of an answer: "I've lost the will to want more." This makes sense as implying that to dream requires maintaining the will to want more, and not just the belief–i.e., it requires aspiration 'to want more'. Yet, what has caused the 'I' to so lose this 'will'? That remains unclear.

Next, in line five, comes the first iteration of the refrain–"I'm not afraid anymore"–which in the context of what the lyrics so far provide suggests the investment the 'I' maintained in the past in likewise dreaming of wanting more was conjoined with 'fear', because once more 'I' declares 'he' is "not afraid *anymore*," implying he was afraid in the past. But what has happened to this 'I' to change him so he is now 'not afraid'? Might this change moreover be at least partially problematic if while now no longer afraid 'he' is also one who no longer cares, as well as no longer dreams, aspires, or desires? Does this self-characterization suggest someone problematically dissociating himself from life, and from living, even perhaps from commitment to continue to persist, and endure, in so doing?

"I watch them all as they fall," line six, suggests a spectatorial position versus a series of entities–people or something else–identified as 'them' and as 'all' 'falling'. This 'falling' hearkens back to 'descend' in line two, and may insinuate watching a host of others as their dreams–their aspirations–stop, fail, and turn into nightmares. Yet the line is cryptic enough to suggest multiple other possibilities, depending on whom or what we associate with 'they'.

It might make sense to interpret the lyrics so far as reflecting a narrator-protagonist commenting on the process and result of his detachment from illusion, and delusion, while the 'they all' that 'fall' might be various, for example, ideological notions, even perhaps positions into which individuals are interpellated by (dominant) ideology. Or these might be the discourses and practices through which disciplinary power promotes normalized modes of docile behavior. Or these might be pretenses that attempt to justify relentless pursuit of material gain as innocuous, innocent, and good–even as divine will.

The last line of the first stanza, line seven, "But I remember when we were young," seems to at least qualify what has preceded, or immediately preceded, by way of 'But', which could thereby suggest that, even though 'I' no longer identifies directly with a position he has described himself as becoming detached or dissociated from, he remembers–and remembers well–what it was like to 'occupy' this position, what a hold it maintained with, for, and over him, as well as what satisfaction it provided him. If we interpret these lyrics as sharing Althusser's critique of ideology, and of how ideology works, this line recalls Althusser's emphasis on what accounts for the power of ideology–and that is the power of ideology to convince the subject that the subject's life makes sense, that the place the subject occupies in society makes sense, that the subject is welcomed and included within the social whole, and that the way things appear, within and through ideology, is all that exists, all that is good, and all that is possible. When one is able to identify with the dominant social center, with dominant ideological common sense, and with positions that are most dominantly promoted as sensible, desirable, right, good, and necessary, this tends to be more readily reassuring and comforting versus not being able to do so–versus identifying instead with positions at the social margins, positions resistant as well as opposed to dominant ideological common sense and to interpellation of individuals into positions as unquestioning 'good subjects' of dominant ideology. Ideology is immensely powerful because those living within ideology feel like this is not ideology but rather what is simply natural, normal, right and necessary.

Turning to the second stanza, we encounter the following: "Those with habits of waste/ Their sense of style and good taste/Of making sure you were right/Hey don't you know you were right?/I'm not afraid anymore/I keep my eyes on the door/But I remember." Lines one and two reference a 'they' the narrator-protagonist seems to be judging negatively as well as distancing 'himself' from; these are people who are 'wasteful' 'by habit' or 'as a matter of habit'. This suggests a blithely indifferent outlook, an outlook that ignores (or does not recognize or care about) the consequences of one's actions. It may be these are people consumed with the pursuit or money, and with what money can buy, or with, even more precisely, what 'class' authorizes one to manifest and display. This might be on account of the social and cultural as economic capital their class position enables them to draw upon, and it may show up in terms of concern with social status as much as with possession of material wealth. "Of making sure you were right" seems to link a 'you'–perhaps the same 'you' as addressed in the first stanza, and perhaps not–with the preceding 'they', concerned to 'make sure they were right', which in this context suggests emphasis on looking, or seeming, or appearing 'right' according to socially dominant standards for defining what 'right' is supposed to look, seem, or appear like. This could be a hypocritical, shallow, and empty pretense–and it could involve being more concerned with 'looking right' than with 'doing right', or more concerned with how others perceive one (including perhaps to what extent others envy one) versus what one is doing for others, what one is doing on behalf of others' needs and others' well-being.

If we follow this logic, "Hey don't you know you were right?"–line four–comes across almost as taunting, and at the least as proposing those caught up with "habits of waste," "sense of style and good taste," and of "making sure you were right," are insecure, fearful of being 'exposed' for being 'fraudulent'–or, alternately, fearful of losing out in competition to 'keep up' one's social position by always to 'keeping ahead' of those around one. Line five, with the refrain–"I'm not afraid anymore"–further underscores a feeling of the narrator-protagonist marking a clear distance between 'himself' and 'his' current position versus that of the people he has just referenced in the preceding four lines: the narrator-protagonist is no longer caught up in those kinds of insecurities, and those kinds of fears. The last two lines in this stanza however accentuate the complexity of the narrator-protagonist's position by first indicating 'he' is ready to leave–"I keep my eyes on the door"– as he is no longer interested in even bemusedly observing the social scene he has just disparagingly described, but at the same time he remembers, and with a certain persistent sense of loss, what it was like to feel as if he belonged, as if he was included, as if the structure and organization of his society was exactly as it represented itself to be, and as if his social place and social purpose was readily discernable.

In stanza three this last melancholic note continues: "Tears of sadness for you/More upheaval for you/Reflects a moment in time/A special moment in time/Yeah we wasted our time/We didn't really have time/But we remember when we were young." If 'tears of sadness' are coming from anyone, here, it would seem, logically, they are coming from the narrator-protagonist, who, if so, has perhaps contradicted himself, because he clearly *does care*. And yet what he might not care about anymore is participating in 'the competition for success' that leads to becoming trapped in 'a steel-hard casing' that is exceedingly difficult to throw off, and which threatens one's capacity to sense and feel, and especially to be able to relate compassionately and empathetically with others. So it might well be the case that the narrator-protagonist does not care anymore about how he is perceived and judged according to that normative standard of what success means, in modern capitalist society, because he does in turn care much more about the suffering of others, including those who are beaten down, and beaten back, in their quest for success, in their attempt to realize their dreams–these are the people, here addressed as 'you', experiencing continually "more upheaval."

The last five lines of this stanza appear to suggest the narrator does maintain a strong sense of persistent identification with 'you' in terms of shared memory, and indeed in terms of lasting impact of what he shares a memory concerning, even if he now has obtained 'insight' that leads him to view that past experience more critically, and less idyllically, because he continues to recall it as 'special'. The sentiments here suggest multiple viable interpretations, not necessarily easily reconcilable, such as: 1) We all waste our time when we are young on many foolish things, we look back upon this youthful time later in life and realize yes that this was and we were wasteful, and yet that retrospective revaluation nevertheless does not negate how precious those memories continue to be and how vital that experience was in shaping us to be whom and what we are; 2) As we get older we realize we let slip, because we did not know better, an opportunity, that would not last, a proverbial open door that would close all too soon, where we could have done something that would have been highly desirable and make an important difference, which we cannot do now, because the time has passed and the opportunity is now long gone; and 3) We live in time, yet we don't know *how* to live in time, to adequately appreciate our being *as a being in time*–as constructed, defined, and realized in time–and we are only able to grab at evanescent glimpses of what time means in shaping and constituting who and what we are.

Stanza four further complicates what has preceded: "And all God's angels beware"/"And all you judges beware"/"Sons of chance, take good care"/"For all the people not there"/"I'm not afraid anymore"/"I'm not afraid anymore"/"I'm not afraid anymore"/"Oh, I'm not afraid anymore." The first two lines come across as a challenge, even a warning, and a most daring one at that, directed toward two powerful collectives–"*all* God's angels," and "*all* you judges." The admonition here is to 'beware' but it is not readily apparent 'beware of what', or 'beware why'. However, these two lines, especially in connection with what follows, might plausibly warn against judgmentalism–i.e., judging in a harshly moralistic and righteously condemnatory sense– directed against those who make mistakes, who fall short, who don't recognize or understand what they are missing, or even what they are wasting. Versus the notion that everyone should follow Benjamin Franklin, Weber's quintessential representative of the classic 'spirit of capitalism', in always striving to maximize the efficiency of every lived moment in order to not 'waste' any possible opportunity for successful gain achieved through hard work conducted in a methodically rational manner (or face condemnation as 'lazy' and 'undeserving', as shirkers, scroungers, skivers, or chancers), the lyrics align in sympathy with the latter versus the former: "Sons of chance, take good care." This line, interpreted as I just have, connects with a experience many face as they worry about being judged negatively for deciding to 'do things differently', to pursue an unconventional path, to change their lifestyle, to choose a job or career (or a university major) for reasons other than how much money they can earn, to take time out 'from the rat race', to try out what others tell them they have no chance in succeeding at, and to be ready and willing to break with the normal as well as face derision and retribution for doing so.

"For all the people not there" makes sense as referencing people who didn't make it, or who were forgotten, and especially who were not only disciplined but also punished for their deviation from the normative. This line makes sense thereby in relation to groups of people who have been scapegoated and otherwise targeted for abuse, even extermination, to further the interests of those at the heights of social power, including by means of division and conquest of prospective opposition. These targets included, for the Nazis (worth citing given Ian Curtis's interest in Nazi Germany and the Holocaust), Jews, Roma and Sinti, people with mental and physical disabilities, Poles and other Slavic people, homosexual men, Jehovah's Witnesses, communists, socialists, anarchists, various supposedly 'asocial' groups of people, and Christian resisters and objectors to the regime. But we might associate these targets with other groups, such as, in the US and the UK today, immigrants (including refugees and asylum seekers) of color (and especially from Central America and the Middle East), Muslims, Blacks, Asians and Pacific Islanders, Latinx people, Native Americans, prisoners, LGBTQIA+ people, people with mental and physical disabilities, the working class and the poor, the homeless, drug addicts, the young, and the elderly. What Curtis makes me think of, with this line, are people who have disappeared, or who have effectively disappeared, or who have been made to disappear or to effectively disappear (and 'effectively disappear' refers to those living at the margins of society who are ignored and neglected by those living at or close to the social center). In connection with Foucault, this same line calls to mind those who actively 'refused to be normal'–who resisted, defied, opposed, and fought back against attempts to force them to submit, and surrender, through the exercise of normalizing discipline, to subjection–and who were punished on account of so doing. The final four lines of the song seem to propose the narrator-protagonist is ready, or at least on the verge or brink of being ready, to align 'himself' with exactly this last group of people, and he is here seemingly ritualistically attempting to interpellate himself into such a counter-dominant ideological position.

In sum, the lyrics of "Insight" plausibly support diversely divergent takes. Is this a song ~ouncing a retreat, a withdrawal, a distancing, a detachment, or a dissociation from past relationships, and past communities, and even from life and living? Is this a song manifesting sadness, or resignation, or emptiness, or numbness, or bitterness, or defiance, or wistfulness, or dogged persistence? Is the narrator-protagonist sympathetically and even empathetically identifying with others he references in this song, or is he not? Is this song nostalgic for the past or is it suggesting it is better to not be caught up in the illusions and delusions of the past? Is the song supportive and encouraging of breaking with and opposing the dominant or is it defending, by explaining their position, those who do not do so? Is the song judging or it warning against judging? Is the song announcing a decisive departure or is it indicating the narrator-protagonist is too inextricably tied to what 'he' describes and recounts to ever, at least ever fully and entirely, move on from? Does the song suggest it is good to dream or that is it bad to dream? Is the narrator-protagonist condemning or forgiving waste and 'wasting'? Does the song suggest remembering is enough or does the song suggest it is not? Is the narrator-protagonist truly 'not afraid anymore'? In reference to most of these questions I suggest the most compelling answer is not one or the other, but some combination of both because the lyrics of the song register, reflect upon, examine, and respond to a complex of emotions concerning a range of perplexing issues. My developing take on this song, as I've already suggested, is it discusses insight achieved, that is crucially important and changes one's life-direction, yet comes at a significant cost because it forces a painful reevaluation of and rupture with past experiences and past connections. The song is sharing this insight with us, including what it costs to *not* simply 'go along to get along', to *not* simply identify and follow along with what is expected and applauded, and to *not* simply do what is safe while avoiding risks. These include risks of becoming cut off from one's most important past relationships, and one's most important past communities, because these no longer feel 'right' for you while neither do you feel 'right' anymore to them.

Taking into account the musical sound of the song, beyond the lyrics, helps more precisely pinpoint where the emphasis ultimately lies in terms of what kinds of meanings it makes the best sense to interpret the song conveying or enabling. The structure of the song proceeds as follows:

1. First Opening through 0:30: soft ambient drone sound followed by sound of elevator shaft. Initial Preparation/Gathering.

2. Second Opening through 0:55: shimmering hi-hat followed by bass guitar playing the initial melody accompanied by studio-synthesized sound effects. Initial Leading In/Commencing.

3. First Vocal Passage through 1:51: vocal carries the tune while the bass guitar continues to contribute to the melody in accompaniment with vocal, while the guitar adds a soft, subdued harmonic fill, and the drum kit proceeds according to a persistent, slightly syncopated rhythm with prominent snare. Exposition and Elaboration.

4. Instrumental Bridge through 2:33: Notably loud and prominent studio-synthesized effects, like video and pre-video arcade game sounds, evoking sci-fi/space travel connections, in what feels like a fighting sequence, which then subsides into a reassertion of the bass guitar melody as preparation for and transition into the next stage. Dramatic Diversion/Counterpoint followed by Return/Re-initiation.

5. Second Vocal Passage through 3:31: Closely similar to the first vocal passage, but with straining upward in pitch and accompanying increased loudness and intensity near the end, as is often the case with Ian Curtis's vocals. Further Exposition and Elaboration Toward Initial Climax.

6. Instrumental Closing through 4:21: Dramatic Diversion/Counterpoint and Procession Toward Final Climax and Closeout with distinct guitar, bass guitar, drum kit, and studio-synthesized sound effect lines and figures.

Each instrumental section of the song in fact encompasses two sections, or subsections, with a different instrumental density, a different organization of relatively foregrounded versus relatively backgrounded lines of sound, and a different rhythm and purpose. It is notable the song takes its time to get started as well as to close out, and that the two vocal passages seemingly comprise two verses, yet the verses follow each other with no break, and this also, again, involves no chorus but rather a refrain that varies in placement and duration across the verses. If we conceive of this song as enacting an introspective drama, it is one marked by 1) a slow, careful gathering and preparation followed by 2) a gradual leading into and commencing of the process of reflection upon and sharing of insight, which is in turn followed by 3) an exposition and elaboration of this insight, followed by 4) a passage of heightened emotive intensity amounting to a figurative battling with the implications and consequences of what this insight implies and to where it leads, then 5) resettling and transitioning to a prelude to the next phase, followed by 6) yet further exposition and elaboration of this insight that culminates in an initial climax, which after that moves next into 7) another passage of heightened emotive intensity, again amounting to a figurative battling with the implications and consequences of what this insight implies and to where it leads, ending with a second climax, and followed by 8) a slow dropping away and suspending of the tension and the entire moment of dramatic introspection.

This structure accentuates the careful distancing required, as well as the combination of passionate and dispassionate investment required, in order to accept a critical insight concerning what is difficult to break from, to the point of following the logic of this critical insight in seizing upon a partial opening, a small gap or tear in a much larger all-enveloping fabric, at a single, tenuous seam or other kind of join. The same challenge can apply both to what is required to obtain critical insight and to what is required to follow the logic of where this insight leads. This might involve critical insight concerning 1) the extent to which a dominant ethic driving the spirit of modern capitalism in its victorious stage in fact leads to life lived within a figurative steel-hard casing, or iron cage; 2) the extent to which interpellation by dominant ideology, through Ideological State Apparatuses, leads to individuals freely choosing to occupy positions, and carry out practices, as subjects of and to this dominant ideology, working thereby to reproduce capitalist relations of production, and, in so doing, working simultaneously to insure the reproduction as well of their own domination and subjection, and their own oppression and exploitation; and 3) the impact of disciplinary power, exercised across an array of discrete yet interconnected disciplinary fields and agencies, as part of a carceral continuum manifesting the impact of pervasive panopticism, to shape and reshape individuals so they willingly subject themselves to the oppressive constraints of the normative.

Instrumentation in "Insight" includes: an initial quiet, ambient drone sound; early and subsequent recorded elevator shaft sounds; bass guitar that contributes to the melody and together

517

with the drum kit to the groove; studio-synthesized effects that sound like video and pre-video arcade games, especially suggestive of sci-fi and space travel interests; a softly muted, backgrounded guitar; a drum kit that supplies a steady beat and with the bass guitar the groove, with a pronounced emphasis on the snare, although we can also hear the bass drum and the hi-hat throughout most of the song along with two toms in the first part of the instrumental bridge section of the song; and the vocal that maintains an overall limited pitch range and what sounds like a notably filtered timbre yet carries the tune and leads in sounding the melody during the vocal passages. In terms of instrumental density this is sparse at the beginning, then picks up in the second part of the instrumental opening, increases with the first vocal passage, and sounds even denser in the two subsequent instrumental passages, especially the first part of the instrumental bridge. All four standard functional layers are present, but as is typical with Joy Division the bass guitar introduces and continues to reiterate the melody throughout as well as playing the lead role in the functional bass layer. Atypical, at least before *Closer*, the guitar is relatively quiet and considerably backgrounded, much less prominent than the studio-synthesized and recorded sound effects while those latter are not only more prominent but also strikingly varied. In the instrumental bridge and initial closing passages these sound effects take on a dominant role, hardly simply contributing harmonic fill, even seeming to contribute a virtual counter-melody. The drum kit is more complex than an initial listen might recognize, but other than the snare is relatively backgrounded in this song as well. The vocal is clear and prominent, overtly foregrounded, when it sounds, although, again, tightly contained in both range and timbre.

The initial ambient drone sound enters from slightly below center on the right of the soundbox, while the recording of the elevator shaft and the initially plopping sounding studio-synthesized effect both enter just slightly higher than the intitial drone. The bass guitar enters from below center, and slightly to the left along the horizontal axis of the soundbox, and then continues to sound from both sides as well as in a low-middle position along the vertical axis of the soundbox. The drumkit enters somewhat higher in the soundbox than the bass guitar, while positioned slightly further to the sides and slightly closer to the front versus the bass guitar. The periodic recurrences of the elevator shaft sound subsequently come from both sides, especially from the left. The plopping, popping, zinging studio-synthesized sound effects come from both sides, slightly above the center, and closer to the front in the instrumental passages, while the guitar throughout is back and to the sides and, in passages where the studio-synthesized effects become more prominent, the guitar sounds as if it is coming from even further back and slightly down in the soundbox. The vocal comes from higher in the soundbox than the bass guitar and the drums and cymbals, and is forward and close to the front. What we hear, in terms of the soundbox, for the recorded version of "Insight," on *Unknown Pleasures* (and I am listening to the 2007 London Records remastered double-CD edition of this album), consists of somewhat more movement within or across to different positions in the soundbox than is average for a Joy Division song, while this soundbox sounds as if it is stretched out further horizontally than vertically.

The notable studio-synthesized and recorded sound effects, and their prominence as part of this song, are especially worthy of consideration, I suggest, in considering how the song conveys and enables meaning. These sounds add suggestions of both industrial and post-industrial connections, as well as of being poised on the cusp of technological revolution, excited yet worried concerning to where this will lead, and with what larger consequences. These sounds also contribute to a feeling of being uneasily torn between the playful and the serious, the nostalgic and the detached, the energized and the enervated, and the determined and the uncertain. The initial sounds of the elevator shaft suggest a movement into a space, yet their subsequent recurrence suggest a creaky unreliability, as if it might be difficult to leave this space, while the space itself feels as if it serves as the location for an introspective drama, involving moments of frenzy as well as moments of calm, as the music as persona grapples with an insight that is likely to prove, and is already proving, simultaneously empowering and disempowering. This insight prompts a strange new orientation toward the present and future as well as the past while increasing estrangement from both the past and the position the subject of the song occupied in the past, at the same time as this insight also prompts recollection of and meditation upon the past and the position the subject of the song occupied in the past. The drum kit and the bass guitar emphasize persistent determination to proceed through, to push through, this introspective drama, to resecure one's bearings as one proceeds, even after being knocked off balance, while the studio-synthesized and recorded sound effects represent what knocks the subject of the song off balance. The vocal articulates precise contours of the thoughts and feelings involved in the introspective drama, concerning both on the one hand how painful, sad, and tiring this process is, and on the other hand how inescapably necessary it is nonetheless. As is the case with many other Joy Division songs, the song as a whole, taking into account the contributions of all the instruments and other sound sources, as well as the vocalization and not just the words of the lyrics, conveys an overarching sense of being ready to continue to struggle onward, even in the face of great uncertainty and considerable loss, while registering the blows that come and the damage done in continuing this struggle.

"Insight" starts soft, with an unnerving, almost silent opening, before we first hear the drum kit and the bass guitar. It is also worthy of note that the sound effects vary in loudness, softer during vocal passages and louder during instrumental passages, especially in the bridge, while it is striking that the guitar is generally quiet throughout. The bass guitar, the drum kit, and the vocal seem relatively consistent in loudness, although in the final vocal passage as Curtis pushes upward in pitch the sound of his vocal becomes louder. The guitar sounds also do seem louder near end of the song in the final close-out section. Also notable, in terms of relative loudness, when it is sounding the vocal is the most prominent including relatively loudest sound source and when it is not it is either the bass guitar or the studio effects that tends to come across as the loudest.

The tempo of "Insight" is just slightly slower than average for Joy Division: 131 BPM. The time signature is 4/4, and as is typical of many Joy Division songs eighth notes are especially common and pronounced in melodic lines. Stephen Morris most often strikes seven out of eight times each measure, typically following a 1-2-3-X-5-6-7-8 pattern, with 1-2 and 5-6 on the bass drum and 3 and 7-8 on the snare drum. At the same time, Morris hits the hi-hat via the floor pedal twice with each beat in conjunction with that preceding bass drum and snare drum pattern. At the beginning of the song Morris starts off his contribution with soft shimmering sixteenth notes on a closed hi-hat cymbal, for four measures. In the first half of the instrumental bridge Morris plays the following pattern: two sixteenth note strikes followed by one eighth note on one tom, one eighth note strike on a second tom, one sixteenth note followed by one eighth note strike followed by one sixteenth note strike on the first tom, followed by three eighth note strikes on the second tom. And then Morris returns in the second half of the bridge to his initial rhythmic pattern, involving the bass drum, snare drum, and hi-hat. Morris contributes a slightly shuffling syncopated effect to the beat by leaving out one otherwise expected eighth note snare strike per measure and then via a more elaborate movement among sixteenth and eighth notes between the toms in the bridge and the outro. In so doing the drum kit lends the song a pronouncedly jumpy kind of feeling even while simultaneously feeling tightly contained.

Hook's bass guitar guitar primarily moves across all eighth notes in a measure while varying this regularly with a measure involving five eighth notes and a tie with a dotted quarter note leading into the next measure consisting of all quarter notes. Tabs constructed to help those interested in playing this song, such as available on UltimateGuitar.com, suggest Hook in this song incorporates three riffs, or three patterns, and primarily just two, as the first is only played in the intro to the song. Hook follows the same alternation between patterns across both vocal passages. Consistency but with precise variation is notable here.

The same previously mentioned tab site includes the suggestion that Hook plays all the notes he does in this song on the G string of his bass guitar, while another suggestion is he simultaneously hits the open D string while playing these notes on the G string. But what I notice most distinctly is the bass guitar melody moves closely around the starting pitch at the beginning and for a notable initial duration in the bass guitar riffs, then slightly up and then slightly down. The vocal picks up this pattern yet tends to emphasize slightly upward movements in pitch more than downward movements, with few of these except near the end of the song spanning more than a small interval. At any given place in the song the movement in pitch from the bass guitar as it sounds the melody is primarily no more than one to three notes distant from the start, and especially down in pitch. The studio-synthesized sound effect pitches do seem to bounce up and down over larger intervals as does the accompanying guitar harmony. "Insight" to me sounds as if this song is performed and recorded in a minor key although transcriptions and transpositions vary widely, with many recommending a major key. Nevertheless, in terms of pitch, the song feels tightly contained, with moments suggestive of slight uplift and slight downturn, but with a persistent reassertion of the starting point, the ground, the tonic–as well as juxtaposition with a set of movements and locations of pitch, as well as of timbre, that seem to offer a striking counterpoint, involving synthesized patterns of sound coming across as both complimentary and contestatory versus patterns of placement and movement of pitch followed by the more conventional instruments.

Ian Curtis's vocal delivery in "Insight" involves singing within a limited range and across primarily small pitch intervals, although with repeated slight pushes upward and then one final larger upward push near the end. As is typical with Curtis, he extends sounds at the end of phrases, and especially lines, here at times even longer and more noticeably than usual. At the same time, Curtis's vocal delivery in "Insight" conveys a sense of a more emphatic attack quality than often otherwise is the case while the reverberation and echo surrounding his voice does not seem as pronounced here as in many other Joy Division songs. Curtis's voice comes across as dark and deep, and as narrowly filtered and somewhat roughened, which amplifies the extent to which his singing conveys a sense of combined distance and detachment on the one hand together with sadness, wistfulness, and bittersweet recollection on the other hand. Peter Hook's bass guitar timbre is smooth and warm, while the studio-synthesized sound effects offer a weird yet playful arcade games meets sci-fi feel,

Sumner's guitar is so backgrounded it is hard to make a lot of its timbre, and of the timbres conveyed by Morris's drum kit the snare is especially clear, crisp, pronounced, distinct, and separate. What strikes me as most important concerning timbre in "Insight" is how the timbres of the various instruments and other sound sources line up, intersect and combine, and here again the contributions made by the studio effects are especially notable in stretching and adding color to the full timbral array.

Overall, I propose these elements of loudness, rhythm, pitch, vocal delivery, and timbre in "Insight" contribute a combination of wistful sadness and a tired reflectiveness combined with a resilient persistence and bursts of determination to push forward, and fight, even to engage in ongoing contest. These elements of the sound of "Insight" contribute a sense of having moved through and past a period of innocent lack of awareness while now entering an 'in-between' position, a liminal space, uncertain where the music as persona is headed or with what prospects of success. The music as persona is also unclear what success might now and in the future mean, with continuing survival itself at risk, yet is determined nonetheless to keep trying. The music as persona cannot and will not hold back from recounting and sharing what insight has been arrived at while oscillating between commitment and detachment, a longing for the past and a determination to leave the past behind. A shaft of light illuminates new possibilities, including new ways of being and remembering, amidst an otherwise overwhelmingly muddy darkness that clouds judgement concerning where one is at, what has led to where one is at, and where to go as well as what is to be done from here.

The nearly thirty seconds delay before we first hear the hi-hat and then the bass guitar enhances my readiness to participate together with each of the latter in following the initial sounding of the melody as well as the tempo established as part of the beat. I feel myself rocking with the snare drum and picking up as I do on the alternation between single and double snare strikes. I also feel myself compelled to join in with Ian Curtis as he sings the lingering ends of vocal lines, and when he rises in pitch, especially toward the end of the second and final vocal passage. The volley of studio-synthesized sound effects in the bridge and near the end of the song in the final instrumental closing section of the song elicit from me a feeling of wanting to engage in a parallel form of physical accompaniment, such as dancing that simulates fighting or perhaps dancing about as I workout on punching bags. With those instrumental passages, in particular, I feel an increased sense of exertion in my own mimetic participation.

As I listen on through "Insight" I along with the music as persona anticipate surprises given the opening recording of the elevator shaft, its recurrence during the first vocal passage, and the early and repeated prominence of studio-synthesized sound effects. I anticipate, in other words, despite the regularity of the beat, and of the melodic lines, that this song will involve shifts in what I will hear as relatively foregrounded versus backgrounded patterns of sound. I anticipate the return of the second vocal passage, throughout the instrumental bridge, and I anticipate this will closely coincide in form with the first vocal passage. After its key initiating role I continue to anticipate the periodic return to the forefront of the initial bass guitar melody. As I listen to the initial instrumental passage, and through its two subsections, I anticipate the eventual entry of the vocal, and I also anticipate, after the reiteration of the refrain as the final five lines of the second verse of the second vocal passage, that the following section will involve a final close out, leading ultimately to a slowing down and dropping out of sound. I along with the music as persona anticipate periods of heightened intensity in both the second and third instrumental passages. We anticipate a combination of desire and dread in our confrontation together with a situation involving a flash of insight, as we seek to discern the contours of where we are at, and what pathways to follow as we try to ascertain where we are left, given what we have left behind, and what is now altogether past. As I listen onward in "Insight," I anticipate a deepening identification with a position the song will set forth for me and invite me accept. I anticipate this will be a position closely if not indeed directly aligned with that of the music as persona as the song enacts an introspective drama concerning gaining of insight that prompts meditation upon how to respond to what insight calls forth, in terms of change in perspective and orientation versus past identities, relations, communities, and outlooks.

I hear "Insight" expressing a feeling of being in a strange, and estranged, place, as well as a complicated mix of feelings in this location: wistful sadness and fatigue combined with resilient persistence and determination, even a relishing of a fight akin to psyching one's self up to commit to what the lyrics propose will from here on prove necessary. I hear an expression of defiance mixed with mournfulness, as well as an attempt to move beyond the latter while not being yet able to do so. I hear an expression of striving, but not yet being fully able to believe in this striving, to 'not be afraid anymore'. And I hear a combination of critical judgment and distancing together with sympathy and empathy–especially sympathy and empathy for those not yet in this position, who have not yet gained the insight the song concerns. In my own expression, responding to the expression of the song, and of the music as persona through the song, I feel especially compelled by the final vocal stanza, and inclined to join in uttering this warning as well as to extend this sympathy and ritually invoke a determination myself not to be afraid anymore.

Even so, my expression here divides between identifying and sympathizing with that determination versus not sharing what it overtly declares, reflecting my own conviction that I need not eliminate fear, but rather refuse to allow fear to hold me back from acting as I need, in facing up to what I am afraid of, especially when others are counting on me and when this is a matter of principle–a matter of living up, in practice, to my foremost values. Fear, I believe, is best engaged by making use of fear, even running with it, not seeking altogether to transcend it. In other words, it can be most courageous to act even when and as one is afraid to act. I suspect the music as persona is also not really past fear, and is still afraid, but now is striving not to allow fear to hold 'him' back from doing what he must do–what 'he' conceives as right and necessary that he do.

The sounds comprising "Insight" feel as if they come at me from across a horizontal sweep that moves across my body, past it, to its sides, and ultimately surrounds me. These sounds, what's more, seem to come at me from periodically startling places and in periodically startling forms. Even in quieter, less dense, and slower passages I feel the impact of the sounds upon me as insistent, and I feel the music as persona sounding, variously, dispassionately detached, wistfully sad, and passionately determined. My response to this impact is complicated, but I sympathize, and empathize, with an introspective grappling concerning whether one is ready–and how one becomes ready–to embrace the position of the outsider, of the abnormal or 'other-than-normal', of the critic of dominant ideology and the representative of counter-dominant ideology, and of refusing to allow a steel-hard casing or an iron cage to solidify about me, or about others for whom I care and about whom I am concerned, such that we can never escape.

In my own analysis of what I hear, with "Insight," the recorded sounds of the elevator shaft along with the other studio-produced sounds represent a potentially threatening or at least likely challenging force coming from a bizarre, even weird, source. Together with the music as persona I feel our shared analysis leads us to in effect pose these questions as we proceed through the song: 1) how are we going to get through this, what will we meet along the way as we seek to do so, and how often will what we meet keep coming back to confront us yet again, in what form, and with what strength? 2) Where are we? 3) What has happened? 4) What are our prospects and what might success mean as we face up to the challenge before us? Together the music as persona and I analyze what we confront to be a situation of considerable uncertainty and likely irresolution that nevertheless requires our engagement.

I associate what I hear in this song with arcade games, both in video and pre-video form, with early electronic contributions to punk-derived rock music, and with a fascination concerning science fiction along with real-life space travel. The last includes curiosity about what exists beyond this planet in 'outer space' and especially curiosity concerning possibilities for the existence of other forms of intelligent life beyond this planet. It also includes curiosity concerning possibilities for gaining new perspectives on our existence from imagining a vantage point beyond one entirely confined to this planet. I associate what I hear in "Insight" as marking a meeting point between the industrial and the post-industrial. I associate what I hear in "Insight" with prominent hopes and dreams as well as worries and fears surrounding what the computer, internet, and larger electronic technological revolution would bring about, at an earlier historical moment when this revolution was still yet new. I associate what I hear in "Insight" with junctions and disjunctions between childhood and adulthood, with complicated feelings concerning how the two continue to be linked as well as distinct. I associate what I hear in "Insight" with recognizing one's perspective and outlook has significantly changed, that an insight one has gained has changed one's perception of and judgment concerning one's past and one's own place within and relationship to that past. I associate what I hear in "Insight" with a mixture of wanting to be ready to push forward, without fear, combined with feeling exhausted, drained, and uncertain if one is up to the challenge. I associate what I hear in "Insight" with wistfully remembering what one at the same time recognizes from now on is only broachable as memory, and that what was 'special then and there' cannot ever be 'special' in the same way in the form of memory.

I associate what I hear, in short, in this song, with how critical insight–with how critical understanding, especially motivated by critical theory–dramatically changes us, and can lead us to feel, initially at least, at a considerable loss when so much of what we previously thought and believed no longer makes sense to us in that way, and as we recognize we cannot go back and think or believe the same, innocently the same, as we once did, anymore. We can readily feel this way if and when 1) we begin to recognize and begin to accept that much of what we previously imagined flowed from our own independent free choice in fact follows from the working of dominant ideology and interpellation into positions as subjects of and to dominant ideology; 2) we begin to recognize and begin to accept that what we previously imagined was unquestionably natural, obvious, self-evident,

523

and to be taken for granted is not at all so, but in fact the result of the successful functioning of ideology *making it appear to be so*; 3) we begin to recognize and begin to accept the positions we occupy that are most powerfully constitutive of us, of our individual and social identities, are positions into which we have been interpellated to do the work of dominant ideology, to materialize dominant ideology, and to reproduce an economic and social system founded upon relations of exploitation; 4) we begin to recognize and begin to accept that much of our subjectivity has been shaped and is continually being reshaped by the exercise of disciplinary power upon and through us, including at the level of our physical bodies, so that we submit and conform to prevalent notions of normality, including of what is–and is not–normal behavior; 5) we begin to recognize and begin to accept the whole of our larger society is coterminous with a larger carcereal system, and that the fear, and threat, of punishment continually constrains our lives, including by way of pervasive panopticism; and 6) we begin to recognize and begin to accept that the larger capitalist system that we most often take for granted, and most often consciously ignore, as simply the way things are and the way they have to be, is itself in significant part the legacy of a distinctly religious imperative, the initial spiritual dimensions of which have now so far dissipated that we are compelled to participate in amoral or anti-moral relations with each other.

"Insight" explores taboos concerning giving up on dreams, and of no longer caring as well as of no longer being afraid–including giving up being afraid of what might happen to one's self, and including giving up caring about or fearing the prospect of one's demise. Other taboos explored in "Insight" concern breaking with what was, has been, and remains far easier to accept and identify with, at the price of accepting considerable loss–in the form of self-initiated and self-implemented exile. A yet further taboo "Insight" confronts concerns remembering "all the people not there," and especially, implicitly, all the reasons why they 'are not there'. Within the music, taboos confronted include starting off virtually silently for a protracted period and beginning with a sampled sound, as well as giving prominence to studio-synthesized sound effects while rendering the conventional lead guitar a minor, backgrounded presence; not including any chorus; mixing up the placement and duration of the refrain; and not breaking between vocal verses. Confronting these taboos reinforces the sense conveyed by the title and the lyrics that this song represents a significant moment concerning a major change, a decisive break, and how fraught this feels.

The studio-synthesized sound effects in "Insight" convey a sense of strangeness or weirdness that in turn suggest invisibility, intangibility, and ephemerality due to a lack of conventional physically material correlatives for the sources of these sounds. References in the lyrics repeatedly concern what is no longer–and which thereby is now invisible, intangible, and ephemeral–while precisely what the song, and especially the music as persona, is breaking with, moving past, and proceeding to take on feels likewise invisible, intangible, and ephemeral. "Insight" proceeds ahead with what cannot be fully understood, at least not yet and quite possibly never, while accepting that any kind of critical/resistant/oppositional position is itself always implicated within what it is critiquing/resisting/opposing, and, even more pointedly, is always distorted and damaged by the same. The past invoked in this song also feels ephemeral, and increasingly invisible and intangible as well: the past when the narrator-protagonist enjoyed an easier, happier, more innocent time, when 'he' felt at one with those he now feels distanced from, when all the people who are no longer there were still yet there, when it was still possible to believe in dreams that would rise up and not just descend, and when it was not necessary to feel sad for others facing repeated upheavals–'before the fall'. What it was that the narrator-protagonist once feared and the time and place in which it made sense to be so afraid feels ephemeral, and increasingly invisible and intangible. And, finally, invisibility, intangibility, and ephemerality all usefully characterize what it feels like in recognizing one has been constituted by forces that constrain and confine, as well as what it feels like to begin to break with, warn versus, and gather strength to contest enclosure within a steel-hard casing or iron cage, dominant ideology, or a carceral continuum.

"Insight" challenges me to critical awareness, while registering the costs of critical awareness–in particular, the cost of accepting and taking this on, seriously and sincerely, in active practice. "Insight" challenges me to reflect on how I have used and been used by time, indeed how I have been shaped and constituted by time. "Insight" challenges me to reflect on crucial junctures in my own life, where my attitude/outlook/point of view/conviction/and belief has dramatically shifted, and especially where I've come to accept that what I previously invested in was illusion/delusion. "Insight" challenges me to reflect on my own relations with socially dominant normativities, including with how much I have been subjected by normalizing forces and pressures, notably as I have felt myself longing for and aspiring to be recognized and treated as 'normal'. In listening to and reflecting upon this song, and on what it makes me think (about) and feel, I envision this song coming to me from a subject who has passed through on 'his' way to another side but who remains acutely aware of and focused upon what 'he' has just passed through and especially upon what he has left behind. I hear 'him' as simultaneously uncertain yet determined about facing what comes next. "Insight" challenges me to recall, and reflect on, moments in my own life-experience when I have felt much that same way. And the song challenges me to recall moments in my life-experience when I felt defiantly determined to meet my fears, to not let these hold me back from doing what I recognized and believed was right and necessary that I do–as well as to consider when and if I have in fact moved from a position of being afraid to one of not being afraid anymore. "Insight" suggests to me the importance of remembering precisely what it is that motivates me to act as fearlessly as possible, as well as to find ways to respond to major challenges and major changes in my life-experience with more and other than fear alone, especially when I am doing so out of responsibility to those who "are not there," those who are no longer there, those who cannot so represent and act directly on their own behalf and in their own interest but who are counting on me to stand in and stand up for them.

As I have already discussed in this book, on numerous occasions in my past I felt the responsibility to be 'out' about my sexuality, about my philosophical and political positions, about my own experiences with chronic illness and invisible disability, and about my own experiences with mental health challenges, and frequently I have done so, despite experiencing fear, often great fear, concerning being exposed, vulnerable, at risk, yet feeling this was necessary because I was representing many more people than myself alone, including many people not in the position where they were able, or yet able, to be so open, honest, and forthright. I have felt it necessary to persist in so doing even when attacked, physically as well as verbally, and even when I have felt physically ill on account of what I was taking on. I recall, when I was still first beginning to accept I was gay, deciding I would attend a screening of a film at a local neighborhood community center, in Syracuse, in honor of 'pride month', walking to this event all by myself; feeling terrified every step of the way that everyone around knew what I was doing and why, that everyone around was likely to disparage and even assault me because I was gay; and feeling even more terrified concerning how guilty and ashamed I would feel if I stopped and turned back–which I did not. I recall, early on in my first semester at UW-Eau Claire, bursting into tears, in recounting to a friend living far from Eau Claire, how much pressure I felt as 'the first openly gay faculty member in the history of UW-Eau Claire'–feeling always on display as someone representative of the adverse of what almost everyone around would most readily identify as 'the normal'.

On my profile page on my UW-Eau Claire people's pages website I indicate that in my scholarly pursuits I work from a *Humanist* Marxist position, and I conceive of Marxism as a philosophy and politics of *freedom*. I indicate, further, that socialism, as I see it, represents the international revolutionary movement of *self*-emancipation of the exploited working class (the vast majority of the world's population), and that Marxism represents the critical theoretical framework that can best explain the problems and limitations of global capitalism that not only make possible but also viable, necessary, and urgent this eventual, ultimate process of transformation. I also indicate I support an independent, non-sectarian version of Marxism that rejects both ultra-leftism and right-opportunism, and I align myself with independent socialist organizations and movements welcoming of involvement of Marxist and non-Marxist socialists, and famously associated with two of my childhood heroes, Eugene Debs and Norman Thomas. I declare I am a *democratic* socialist, rejecting authoritarian, statist, Stalinist and Maoist variants I believe have falsely claimed to be "socialist" and "communist," and in actual practice were neither genuinely "socialist" nor "communist." I further declare I am a strong opponent of fascism and totalitarianism, in all forms and guises, including fascist and totalitarian currents at work in everyday life of contemporary capitalist societies and cultures.

In this location I undoubtedly come across as bold and confident, and although indeed these are principled convictions and commitments that I worked long and hard to arrive at, I have often felt fear concerning how I will be understood and engaged, as a result of this identification with Marxism and socialism, and even with this particular kind of Marxism and socialism, given a long history of demonization of Marxism and socialism in this country, which persists long after the Cold War, despite a substantial rise in identification with socialism among younger Americans recently. I have felt fear that suspicion and hostility versus what many are convinced Marxism and socialism 'must' mean, or what support for and identification with Marxism and socialism 'must' mean, would leave me always marginalized, always excluded, never trusted, and never welcome, including as a tenure-line university faculty member at any institution for higher learning anywhere in the US. In a time of rising fascist currents in US politics and culture I have experienced fear that someone like me will be readily marked out as a target–just as has been the case in classic fascist regimes–on account of the fact that I am a Marxist and a socialist, I am gay and queer, and I am a person who lives with mental and physical disabilities. After all, one of the most frequent charges from the Trumpist right in the US today versus Black Lives Matter, critical race theory, and the Green New Deal is that this is all thinly disguised Marxism–and, for a great many in the Trumpist right, 'socialism' and 'Marxism' continue to be among the most ostensibly dangerous 'bogeymen'.

Nevertheless, I have not hidden my philosophical and political positioning, but instead worked to demonstrate, in practice, with students, colleagues, and members of community organizations in which I have been actively involved, by how I conduct myself, what this positioning does–and especially does not–actually mean. Still, I recognize I am always potentially vulnerable on account of these identifications, and periodically that can generate real, even considerable, fear–but, as I have mentioned, I seize upon this fear and strive to put it to work to motivate me to act, guided by a conviction that this fear testifies to how important it is that I act as if I am fearless even when I continue to remain afraid. For many years I displayed a poster prominently on my campus office wall that contained a photo of Audre Lorde along with this inspiring quote from her: "When I dare to be powerful, to use my strength in the service of my vision, then it becomes less and less important whether I am afraid." I have aimed to be like this, as best as I can. In my teaching I aim to encourage students to treat fears, their own and others, with respect and kindness, and to share theirs openly as means of forging empathetic and solidaristic connections, while I have certainly often done the same myself.

"Insight" I also hear inviting and encouraging me to reflect on what kinds of insights I have gained, when, where, how, and why, from whom, and into what–as well as where these insights have taken me, what they have enabled me to do along with what they have enabled me to become. I think about insights I have gained through cultivation of and reliance upon intuition and emotional intelligence as well as other sources or varieties of insight that many are not wont to identify as such. I also think about how careful I have become not to imagine I have gained greater insight than I have, or even any insight at all when I have not, along with what specific insights have led me to insist upon deliberately aiming to respect others with whom I interact, always, as complex, multiple, contradictory, and dynamic–and to eschew quick judgments, especially quick dismissive judgments, concerning whom they are, where they are coming from, what they are about, where they are headed, what they are capable of, and how similar as well as how different they are versus me. "Insight" certainly invites and encourages me to reflect on the role of fear, as I have just mentioned, in my own life-experience, on what I have feared and continue to fear as well as how this fear does hold me back, and has held me back, along with what might it mean for me no longer to be afraid–along with when have I felt that way, *no longer afraid*, and when I have, even while continuing to experience fear, not allowed this to hold me back.

As I reflect on "Insight" I also contemplate what it might mean *not to care anymore*, especially concerning dreams that fail, and ambitions that fall short, and to maintain no further interest in 'wanting any more'. I reflect on times in my own life when it seemed I had so much time yet ahead, as well as how quickly it feels I have grown steadily older. I reflect on times from my past that are now distant, but which I vividly recall and find startling to recognize date so relatively far back in time. I reflect on the lives of people now distant from me whom I knew well and who were close and important to me in the past, including many whom I have lost touch with. I reflect on 'special' moments, special situations, and special experiences from my past life that I cannot recapture, return to, or reprise. And I reflect on all the people I have known who are now 'not there', not just no longer in my own life, but who have passed out of life, and of how fragile, precarious, and treacherous life can all too often prove to be, along with when and where I have felt most acutely reminded of exactly that.

"Insight" repeatedly engages 'in between' states, especially 'in between' past and future, in a highly uncertain present, but also states 'in between' being a child and an adult, and 'in between' being young(er) and old(er). Memory in "Insight" mediates between what is and what was, as well as among moments, stages, and phases in life-experience, as well as among the multiple lives that a singular living being can live over the course of their lifetime. And memory in "Insight" mediates between 'me now' and 'me then', as well as between 'us then' and 'me no longer with or part of us now'.

I recall multiple students over the course of my now many years teaching sharing ambivalent feelings concerning having 'grown up' and 'becoming an adult', with many of these same students writing of or speaking to their determination not to lose touch with elements of their childhood, especially delight in and wonder at play, that they fear losing. Many times students and I have engaged in lively discussions concerning pressures to act and conform to expectations surrounding a certain age, or stage, in life, and how constraining these can be as well as how liberating it can feel to be able to break free of those constraints along with how fearful people often are of even attempting to do so. Students and I have often engaged in similarly lively discussions concerning how chronological age is only one dimension of age, and not necessarily always the most important one, as well as explored what it might indeed mean to actually embrace, and directly feel, we are other than simply one singular being but instead multiple complex and contradictory beings that develop and change as our life proceeds and through our interactions with others and with new situations and new experiences. Students likewise have often found it fascinating to reflect on–and indeed begin themselves to experience–how time makes sense, is experienced, and can and should be recognized and appreciated, in other than merely linear-sequential or chronological terms. Similar conversations have explored how our experience of time, including its pace and duration, depends on situation, context, social background, social positioning, ability to move within and across space, and ability to move from one space to multiple other spaces–in other words, examining how space mediates our experience of time, as well as how time mediates our experience of space.

"Insight" comes across as simultaneously both passionate and dispassionate, although somewhat more dispassionate than passionate if primarily focused on the lyrics and vocals. Yet the furious intensity of the bridge and closing instrumental sections at the same time suggest ample passion. The song engages with a great deal that the music as persona, or at least the narrator-protagonist of the lyrics, now recognizes can't be controlled that 'he' seemingly once thought/imagined/took for granted he could control. And the song amply engages with feelings of loss/disconnection/rupture/break/and distance versus situations, experiences, relationships and communities that were once pivotal, and remain 'special' but only in memory, as well as with uncertainty where all of this leaves one now/what is now left.

I have participated in many thoughtful, far-reaching conversations with classes of students concerning our own experiences of the need for control, of social imperatives directing us to feel this need and to seek to exercise it, of what we cannot control or not all that well or all that far, and of fear concerning lack or loss of control. A great many students readily identify the last as a particularly powerful, even overpowering, fear they have experienced and do experience. Likewise, many students have found it somewhat amazing, as well as unsettling and disorienting, to reflect on how much distance has developed, and even seem rapidly so, between these students' lives at present, including their present focuses of interest and concern, versus their past and even recent past lives, including what were their chief focuses of interest and concern then along with whom were the most important people for them then who are not so anymore. Many times students evince a determination *always* to remain close to family and best friends, while sharing worry, even fear, they might not be able to control whether this happens. Many students also recount, in detail, experiences where they needed to let go of what was hard, what was painful, to let go of–such as romantic-sexual relationships, including 'first loves', friendships once close that no longer were working or otherwise mutually enabling, dreams and plans of pursuing one kind of major and career or of actively participating in one kind of competitive sport or performance art, previous beliefs and belief-systems that once felt foundational, and family members, friends, and pets who have died.

The music as persona in "Insight" admits and shares vulnerability, and uncertainty, but conveys no immediate sense of panic. Yet the repeated reference to not being afraid anymore nevertheless suggests having been so, even having been considerably and often frightened, along with a persistent uncertainty that the 'I' of the song is truly "not afraid anymore" no matter what 'he' asserts.

It certainly can happen that we do reach this state where we are not afraid anymore versus what once made us afraid–and I recognize and work to help enable this with students who experience real fear, or at least considerable hesitancy and worry, about speaking forth in class, especially as part of a 'whole class' discussion or in final project presentations. Many students do attest they are developing and have developed greater confidence as we proceed and are no longer afraid, or as afraid, as they once were. I myself long ago moved past the point where I experienced fear in teaching or in other kinds of public presentations, but I do feel an adrenalin rush, and a certain heightened nervous meets excited energy at the beginning of new semesters, in first classes, or before especially important public presentations. The decline and virtual disappearance of fear, for me, in these situations, has come as a result of experience. However, tinges of fear are always present in moments when I share my own vulnerabilities and when I identify myself, openly and decisively, with positions that are not socially dominant–and versus which I know many maintain suspicion and even antagonism.

"Insight" suggests taking stock of where one is at, in connection and especially disconnection with one's past, yet hardly feels as if it reaches resolution by the end of the song. The song conveys to the listener a feeling of gaining insight concerning what once was and is no longer, yet insight concerning where we are at or next headed, and even of what is yet possible ahead, appears far less apparent.

This recalls for me how, in response to my final examination assignment in Introduction to Theory and Criticism classes, students are far more often inclined to address what matters most to them, what comprise their foremost values and convictions, by referencing the past, and especially traumatic experiences in the past, than the future and what they aspire to be and do in the future. When referencing the latter they tends to do so broadly by emphasizing striving to live according to idealistic principles while not being at all clear through what means they will strive to do so. For many students, making progress in overcoming past tendencies they now recognize were debilitating, and which held them back, is far easier to address, confidently and concretely, than any form of speculation about the future.

In manifesting solidarity, the repeated express commitment in "Insight" to remember, and that 'I do remember' is key, as is alignment with 'sons of chance' who are urged to 'take care' and versus 'all God's angels' as well as 'all you judges' who are admonished to 'beware'. Solidarity is also manifest by reflecting on dreams that fade and die, those who tend repeatedly to experience these kinds of dreams, times that in retrospect seem to have involved a wasting of time, sad and repeatedly sad upheavals, and the people not there who are seemingly those who have experienced much of this kind of hardship and deprivation. Solidarity requires remembering what people have experienced, what they have gone through, what has been important in shaping and defining them, and it requires being able actively to stand with and stand up for those with whom one is declaring solidarity. Solidarity requires being able to empathize but also to respect and appreciate when and where people's experiences have been distinctly different from one's own. Solidarity is most impressively meaningful as well as most crucially needed when this is solidarity manifested in support of people 1) who have been, like those referenced in "Insight," repeatedly beaten down and beaten back; 2) who are excluded or forgotten; 3) who are judged and condemned by those in positions at the heights of power, and 4) who experience repeated painful upheavals, dreams that always descend and never rise up, and who cling to illusions and delusions rooted in a past that was much more replete with waste–with wasted opportunities and wasted prospects–than they are readily inclined to recognize.

"Insight" suggests it is difficult to pinpoint in what ways 'I' am responsible for others; for the suffering, hardship, and pain others experience; and for the violence and cruelty as well as the injustice and unfairness in the world. "Insight" also suggests it is even more difficult to pinpoint what 'I' can and should do about any of this. But "Insight" nonetheless suggests I *am* so responsible, and I am obliged to try to figure out what I can and should do, no matter how daunting that prospect clearly is. Likewise, in terms of what is the meaning, value, and purpose of my existence, and to what extent I can and cannot exercise any influence or control over any of that, "Insight" seems to suggest these are also extremely difficult questions to answer, no matter how important they nonetheless are to take on, but a starting point in beginning to do so involves grasping how much develops beyond 'my' control, how much of what I think and believe to be the case may well and even likely will not be so, how much loss and distance will necessarily accompany and inevitably mark my life-experience, and how much incentive I along with all the rest of us regularly experience to invest in illusions and delusions.

Students I have taught have often found it painfully difficult to imagine, and especially accept, that much of what they have learned to think, feel, believe, and do might well be the product of forces outside of their control, and that they are not as 'free' and 'in control' of themselves and their own destinies as they would ideally like to be. Yet often students also gradually come to appreciate the value of inquiring into the sources of what and how they come to think, feel, believe, and act (as they most often have tended to do), what ends are advanced and whose interests are served as a result, and what alternatives might be preferable–especially deliberately, consciously, and critically chosen.

530

Alienation, isolation and loneliness all feel immediately relevant states, in connection with "Insight," while the song seems to emerge from the vantage point of one who is, now at least, a stranger, an outsider, and even an outcast. "Insight" explores when and where it might be possible, as well as how so, through what means, to press past being held back by vulnerability, entrapment, anxiety, and fear–and, especially at what point of and involving what extent or degree of marginalization this might be. "Insight" grapples with how difficult it is to meaningfully connect, and especially meaningfully stay connected, with other people, given overwhelming transience and lack of control, yet memory remains an important aid in the quest as we proceed to do however little this of might be nonetheless possible.

In classes I have taught focused on Ian Curtis, Joy Division, and critical theory, students have often been intrigued by theories of the stranger, the outsider, the outcast, and the exile, finding this helpful in making sense of the position they identify Ian Curtis as occupying, and as taking on, through his music as art, and even in his own life beyond–with this especially intriguing when conceived as a position that offers critical insight unavailable to those on 'the inside', with those on 'the inside' in fact *needing* these 'outsiders' to offer them exactly this. Likewise, in classes focused on a broad array of topics, I have found it common for many students to identify with the position of the outsider, citing their own experiences of feeling exactly like this, such as, all too sadly commonplace, due to bullying, or because their particular interests or passions were not widely shared, respected, and valued where they come from (such as writing weird forms of fantastic fiction or being heavily into esoteric kinds of comics, graphic novels, and other animated productions). The near panic many new university students share with me concerning finding friends, and especially 'good friends' or 'true friends', as well as finding their niche where they can 'be themselves' and be respected and appreciated for being themselves, testifies to how many commonly experience the preeminent value–in order that life feels at all bearable–of meaningful connections with other people as well as the simultaneous difficulty of achieving and sustaining these kinds of connections.

Perhaps "Insight" does manifest and share exactly these Lacanian insights I have identified in the eighth of my overarching interpretations concerning what the music, as art, of Ian Curtis and Joy Division makes me think (about) and feel as I listen to and reflect upon it: "the self is an imaginary construct, the subject is simultaneously overwhelmingly unconscious and ineluctably other, desire and anxiety are persistently intrinsically interconnected, the symbolic order and the law of the father are oppressively authoritarian, jouissance is far more terrifying than the common translation as 'enjoyment' can possibly suggest, and intimations and irruptions of the Real are recurrently traumatic." If so, what the song is sharing with us is a harsh, jarring, displacing, and disrupting series of insights that include recognizing and accepting that one is not and has never been what one has been led to believe one is, while one's supposed 'own self' is always other than 'one's own self' and always ultimately beyond one's control.

"Insight" may make sense as exploring how it might be possible to move past anxiety, and it seems here, which from a Lacanian advantage is a dead end, that doing so requires simultaneously moving past, or at least bracketing off, desire. "Insight" may also make sense as suggests a coming to awareness that oppressively authoritarian forces are at work throughout life much more pervasively and much more intimately than is often realized, especially when one is young(er). And in relation to terrifying flashes of the Real this might, in connection both with "Insight" and the theories of Althusser and Foucault I have discussed in this chapter, suggest an 'insight-provoking' encounter with flashes of what exists beyond what is constructed according to dominant ideology or by the exercise of disciplinary power across a carcereal continuum.

In terms of intimations of fascism, past, present, and prospective future, reference in "Insight" to all the people who are no longer there represents one plausible point of connection. This reference conjures images of people who thought and believed they were safe and that they maintained a comfortable sense of whom they were and within what they fit, when this was actually not the case. In so doing, this reference conjures up further connections with frequently confidently asserted convictions, in countries like the US and UK, that fascism 'could never happen here', meeting up with the disturbing recognition, in contrast, not only that it could so happen here but also it already has happened and is happening here.

Seven

In *Torn Apart: The Life of Ian Curtis*, Mick Middles and Lindsay Reade write that "the first half of *Unknown Pleasures* simply had to conclude with 'New Dawn Fades', another immensely poignant track, given the course in which this story moves" (133), and here Middles and Reade are referring to the story of Ian Curtis's life and especially death, which includes the all too short but nevertheless dazzling active run of Joy Division. As Middles and Reade describe, "The trudging guitar rose through the scale before allowing Ian Curtis total and utter command in what is his best performance on the album," while noting that "Like Mark E. Smith, Ian had the knack of catching the imagination with one line from a pack of lyrics, and, in 'New Dawn Fades', the delicately sung 'A loaded gun won't set you free . . . so *you* say', would echo down the years" with ample "hints that the writer believed it could, perhaps, set you free" (133-134).

In *Unknown Pleasures: Inside Joy Division* Peter Hook indicates "'New Dawn Fades' is the track that most people say is their favourite" on *Unknown Pleasures* but "This seems an odd choice to me, because it's very, very simple and very economical, certainly from my point of view, because the bass is pretty much constant all the way through" (202). I think this preference, which Middles and Reade appear to share, that puzzles Hook, attests to how simplicity can enable profundity if what is simple is nonetheless done just right. Brian Gorman must have felt so because he decided to title his stage play and graphic novel that chronicles Joy Division's active run, from its hopeful beginning through its tragic end, the same as this song: *New Dawn Fades*. In this stage play and graphic novel Gorman, like the film *Joy Division*, portrays the story of Joy Division as a story about the city of Manchester, and, more broadly, a story about the emergent post-industrial post-modern city fighting through a process of cultural survival to cultural resistance to cultural renaissance. Joy Division provides not only a fitting soundtrack but also a vital spark to that transformation. If this is so, then 'New Dawn Fades' becomes at least partially ironic, as the 'new dawn' has not faded and disappeared once and for all, but risen again, reappearing brighter, more vivid, and more enduring than before.

My favorite take on this song, however, comes from Jamie Stewart, frontman for experimental musical group Xiu Xiu, who writes, in a short essay with the same title as the song, about the tremendous impact this song has had, and continues to have, for him, as someone, who like Ian Curtis, has personally experienced suicidality. Stewart opens by confessing he sometimes feels he should be embarrassed to admit "the lyric in all of modern music that has touched me the most deeply and for the longest time" is "a loaded gun won't set you free, so you say" (33). Yet this line Stewart has "hung onto as a vine of clarification, that has given what is a profoundly muddled clod of an internal life" the possibility it might "make some small sense" (33). Stewart shares he has been a passionate fan of this song, and of Joy Division, since he was 17 years old, and "Without fail, those lyrics [in 'New Dawn Fades'] cause me to weep quietly, just a little. It is happening now as I listen to it while I am writing this" (33). Tears flow all the more copiously on occasions where Stewart experiences "the honour to play" this song publicly (33). "New Dawn Fades" vanquishes Stewart's embarrassment over crying as he is performing, including singing, the song publicly, because "New Dawn Fades" communicates to Stewart, and to others like Stewart, "I am so intensely not alone in feeling this way" (33). Even while sobbing as he plays and sings, "all uncertainty is swept aside by collective emotion," the collective emotion shared by Stewart and listeners who 'get' the song (33). As Stewart explains, "Knowing that there is a line, a song, a band that allows the question of suicide to be so bold, so revealed, so confrontational, is such an incredible comfort and release" (33). Suicidality does need to be addressed directly, openly, honestly, compassionately, and empathetically if we are seriously and sincerely interested in preventing suicide. If people feel too guilty and ashamed to share suicidal thoughts and feelings, this compounds the likelihood suicidality will result in suicide. As Stewart declares, "To hear someone you admire as a musician sing, essentially, 'you think that having had enough of life is wrong, but it is you who are wrong', is an unfettered and true relief" (33).

With songs like "New Dawn Fades," "The oppressiveness of a hidden shame dims slightly" and "It loosens the shackles just enough to get through one more day of staying and seeing what else unfolds" (33). Stewart admits suicide can be a 'selfish act', and when "Ian Curtis screams 'ME! It was ME! Waiting for ME again!" this can seem so. But 'selfishness' needs to be reconceived as at least prospectively indicative of painful need. As Stewart observes, "Selfishness is as embarrassing as suicidal ideation but it is only made that much worse by not articulating it," and this is why the song "New Dawn Fades" is important: "'New Dawn Fades' takes this bold leap into what cannot be said and probably what should not be said to anyone except for the specific people whose stars are so unaligned as to need to hear this again and again to keep their place in this dimension" (33). People experiencing inclination toward suicide benefit tremendously from engaging with open, honest, and vulnerable sharing from others of their wrestling with the same suicidal inclination. In sum, "In its seething bed of the most starkly moving, perfectly wrought and artfully unadorned guitar, bass and drums, no one else has ever expressed to me the acceptance of a lack of meaning better. No one else has as directly. No one else has as believably. No one else has as essentially" (33). In a final line that always bring tears *to my eyes*, Stewart writes: "Thank you, Ian. I am sorry there was no one to sing this song to you" (33).

That final line hits me so hard because at my worse, in moments of greatest confusion and deepest despair, what I most want and need is someone to reach out to me, to comfort me, to support and assist me, who truly understands and genuinely respects what it is like for me to think and feel this way, to be in such terrible straits, and who is able and willing to care for me, without judging me, without condemning me. This is someone who will not approach me as a freak, as weird, as abnormal, as sick, as shameful, as pathetic, as ridiculous, or *as merely selfish* because I feel suicidal. For a person to reach the point where that person seriously contemplates not wanting to live any longer, having become convinced it would be better not to do so, better for one's self and for others, and where one feels one simply cannot take it any longer, that person must be experiencing excruciating psychic pain.

In my own experience, when I attempted suicide I felt at that moment in time as if I was overwhelmingly incapable of meeting the expectations of what I myself believed I needed to be and do, to be a worthwhile person, in order to live honorably and to deserve respect. I perceived myself instead as pathetically weak and incapable of being and doing what I believed I needed to be and do. I felt I was incapable of manifesting the strength and the courage required of what I conceived an ethically and politically upright person needed to manifest. At the same time, I felt I could not turn to anyone for help because that would be too embarrassing, too humiliating, and too shameful, while I also felt no one else deserved to be burdened with having to deal with me and my troubles, for how little of worth I was, for how little of consequence I was, while I also felt I was beyond the possibility of anyone in any way being able to help.

In retrospect I recognize I was terribly wrong about what I, in essence, was *doing to myself*, what kinds of cruel judgments I was imposing on myself, and what horrific standards I was setting for myself that I *must* be capable of meeting, *and exceeding*, if my life was to be worth living. It was, ironically, incredibly egotistical of me even as I was filled with self-loathing because I expected from myself far more than I would ever have expected from anyone else. I had internalized a notion that I must be capable of 'the superhuman', or at least of 'the exceptionally human', or that I was not worthwhile. Doing so meant, without me then realizing it, that I was not respecting and appreciating the value of 'the merely human', of 'the all too human', of human vulnerability, fragility, and frailty. My thinking was suffering from a 'macho' illusion, or, in other words, an indication of the deleterious impact upon me, even as a gay and queer man, of 'toxic masculinity' and, more precisely, of 'salvationist masculinity', where I somehow felt as if I was not worthwhile unless I was doing enough to help, to enable, to uplift–to save–a great many others around me, and even a great many others distant from me in need of *me* doing all of this *for them*, and in need of *me* giving all of this *to them*.

I was young then, not that much older than Ian Curtis was when he killed himself, and I learned from that experience. I learned to be much more humble about myself and about my expectations of myself. I learned to be much more accepting and forgiving of myself. I learned to be much more inclined to support others by showing solidarity to others' efforts to help, enable, uplift, and when and as necessary save *themselves*–respecting, appreciating, and valuing the importance of other people acting *as agents on their own behalf*, and in the interest of their own advancement and salvation. I learned to reconceive 'weakness', fragility, frailty, and vulnerability as sources of far greater and more valuable strength than efforts at repressing, denying, or superceding weakness, fragility, frailty, and vulnerability. I learned to be compassionate toward myself, toward my own discomfort and pain, toward my own confusion and insecurity, toward my own sadness and grief, toward my own worry and anxiety, and even toward my own depression and despair. I learned that being able to extend this compassion toward myself enabled me to be much more genuinely compassionate and empathetic with others. This learning was hard; it took time, effort, and struggle. And none of that denies how excruciating was the psychic and indeed also physical pain I did feel at the time of my suicide attempt, nor the same kinds of pain I have subsequently felt at other points, and over other intervals, when my experience of anxiety and depression has been the most extreme.

Back when I was younger, at the time I did attempt suicide, I found it next to impossible to feel so, but now I feel compassion *for that Bob Nowlan*, and I feel, yes, it would have made a difference back then if I had someone "to sing this song"–"New Dawn Fades"–directly to me. This would be someone who understood and respected the situation I was in because they themselves had personally experienced suicidal thoughts and feelings. I don't know why I didn't listen to "New Dawn Fades" then but I am confident if I had done so I would have felt much like Jamie Stewart–that by means of Ian Curtis sharing his own experience of suicidality I would experience solace, and reassurance, that I was not as alone as I had imagined I was, and at least a glimmer of hope remained to keep on trying to last until at least the next 'new dawn'. I have worked with students who have written they themselves learned, long prior to the time in which they were writing, based on their own experiences, that 'a loaded gun won't set you free', seemingly suggesting that contemplating the opposite is what people do when they have not yet arrived at emotional maturity. But I think this take on this lyric falls back on the judgmentalism that makes it still uncommon for public figures like Curtis to share what and as he does in "New Dawn Fades." After all, people do kill themselves at all ages, for a vast array of reasons, while, as I discussed in the previous chapter by way of the work of Emile Durkheim, suicide responds to substantive social causes and modern societies provide ample incentives for many to turn toward suicide.

Although yes Ian Curtis did eventually kill himself, this does not mean it is necessary, or by any means makes the best sense, to interpret "New Dawn Fades" as a 'suicide note', where Curtis announces this is what he is going to do. Suicidal ideation is far more common than acknowledged, and those who experience this are much larger in number than those who ultimately die by suicide. In "New Dawn Fades" the narrator-protagonist of the lyrics, and the music as persona, explore what it feels like to experience suicidality, what it feels like to be deeply unsatisfied and disappointed with one's self, and what it feels like to contemplate a future that appears bleak, with few if any apparent opportunities that might lead to feeling better about one's self, or to be and do differently so as to enable this feeling better, with all such possibilities fading away. But that does not mean "New Dawn Fades" 'endorses' suicide as 'the only way out'. The song contemplates this possibility, including, as Stewart's essay suggests, *in order to counter it* by bringing it 'out into the open', by addressing it forthrightly, and by performatively sublimating–and, especially, by performatively sublating–it. The word 'sublate' suggests simultaneously lifting up, canceling, and suspending, or simultaneously abolishing, preserving, and transcending. What this means, more precisely, is through sublation what is sublated is in part negated, abolished, canceled, rejected, or denied; in part maintained, preserved, carried on, and carried forward; and in part transcended and superseded. In relation to "New Dawn Fades," suicidal thoughts and feelings, as well as suicidal inclinations and tendencies, do not remain the same but become different, become something else, something other, as a result of addressing them directly, in this way, in this song. Through the composition and especially the shared public performance of "New Dawn Fades," suicidal thoughts and feelings are acknowledged, understood, and respected; they are sympathetically, compassionately, and empathetically engaged and shared. Doing so helps *reduce* and *prevent* suicidality from becoming suicide.

'New Dawn Fades' suggests the promise of a hopeful, inspiring, transformative new beginning has faded and is fading–that this 'new dawn' people have eagerly anticipated seems likely not to arrive. This 'new dawn' seems, now, in contrast with an implicit preceding moment in time when the opposite seemed the case, likely not to be realized–or not to be realizable. A 'new dawn fading' certainly could reflect an individual's personal life-experience but this title also suggests the possibility of something much larger than that. As a progressive leftist, and even more precisely as a Humanist Marxist and a democratic socialist, I have experienced many instances of what has felt like a prospective 'new dawn fading', in the broader social world. For example, in the immediate aftermath of the police killing of George Floyd with the nationwide and indeed worldwide protests in support of Black Lives Matter, it seemed possible we were collectively on the brink of a 'new dawn' in recognizing and responding to systemic racism, and to the damage it does and long has done, but the backlash that has since developed, accompanied by attacks on 'Critical Race Theory' as a convenient stand-in for all theories of systemic racism, accompanied by concerted efforts to legally forbid or otherwise intimidate teachers from teaching about systemic racism, suggests this prospective 'new dawn' has all too rapidly faded. Over the course of my lifetime I have experienced moments in which, for example, it seemed possible a 'new dawn' was on the horizon in terms of broad collective support, here in the US, for ending imperialist 'forever wars', eliminating nuclear weapons, enacting substantial gun control so as to sharply reduce gun violence, taking climate crisis and ecological overreach seriously enough to make major changes in relations between human beings and the larger natural world, respecting women's legal right to choose concerning abortion, and accepting the equal worth and dignity of same-sex as well as opposite-sex relationships. Yet in each of these cases I have often felt, subsequently, as if this 'new dawn' has faded, or is fading.

In Britain, by late in the 1970s, at the time of Joy Division's active run, it undoubtedly seemed to many Britons that the promise of 'the new dawn' inaugurated in the immediate aftermath of World War II, with the social democratic welfare state, in what British independent socialist filmmaker Ken Loach has identified as 'the spirit of '45', had faded and was fading in a time of seemingly perpetual crisis. Both Alwyn W. Turner's history of Britain in the 1970s–*Crisis? What Crisis?: Britain in the 1970s*–and Andy Beckett's history of the *same–When the Lights Went Out: Britain in the Seventies*–depict the cultural phenomenology of Britain in the 1970s in terms of exactly this feeling: feeling part of a nation and society in perpetual crisis, with a preceding feeling of promise concerning the nation's and society's future faded. I myself felt cautiously hopeful, in much the same way, as *The Spirit of '45* documents Britons felt in the early years of the post-WWII British social democratic welfare state, following the impressive showing of the Labour Party behind its then 'socialist left' leader Jeremy Corbyn in the 2017 UK general election for parliament. But in the aftermath of the 2019 UK general election, following the decisive defeat Corbyn and the Labour Party suffered, this prospective 'new dawn' appeared to have faded–and it feels to me as if it has continued so with the Labour Party under Keir Starmer's leadership seemingly determined to force out socialist left members and turn its back on prior socialist left commitments. For many people, undoubtedly, hopes, dreams, plans, and goals they imagined they would pursue, and achieve, along with the figurative 'new dawn' they imagined that so doing would bring, as a result, in their own lives, faded with the arrival of COVID-19 and the ravages this pandemic has wrought. 'The new dawn' represents hopeful possibilities for 'a new day'–a better, more enabling, more fulfilling, more inspiring, and more uplifting day than 'the day that has passed'. "New dawn fades' represents disappointment, disillusionment, and disenchantment because 'new dawn' has never arrived and seems will never arrive. As a result, we are thrown back upon 'the old day' we fervently longed to move past.

The first stanza of "New Dawn Fades" reads as follows: "A change of speed, a change of style/A change of scene, with no regrets/A chance to watch, admire the distance/Still occupied, though you forget/Different colours, different shades/Over each mistakes were made/I took the blame/Directionless so plain to see/A loaded gun won't set you free/So you say." The opening line–"A change of speed, a change of style"–suggests the approach and prospective arrival of a metaphorical 'new dawn', or the pursuit of and aspiration to experience this 'new dawn'. This represents, perhaps, a necessary *change* in life's tempo, or in 'lifestyle', involving a 'shaking up' of what has become routine, even deadening routine, even 'carcereal' routine. "A change of scene, with no regrets," line two, suggests, following the implications of line one, this change involves moving to, or relocating within, a 'new scene', a new space in which to focus and carry out life-activity. The line also suggests embracing this opportunity by leaving behind an 'old scene' with "no regrets." These opening lines suggest a welcoming, even an eager welcoming, of 'the new dawn', a strong identification with what it promises to make possible, and a ready joining in efforts to bring this about. This 'new' and 'changed' situation offers, seemingly, the promise of *renewed* energy, *renewed* vitality, *renewed* enthusiasm, and *renewed* hope. And yet, line three, "A chance to watch, admire the distance" qualifies the preceding by suggesting 'the new dawn' to which the lyrics here allude might be something the narrator-protagonist is primarily enjoying by contemplating it as a prospect, and doing so not only by noting its 'admirable' 'distance' from the present state of affairs, from the existing status quo, but also *from a distance*. "Still occupied, though you forget," line four, suggests, next, as the image dims, that whatever the narrator-protagonist has admired, at a distance, and from a distance, representative of a positively appealing change of speed, style, and scene, may well be something unavailable to 'him', or to 'people like him', because it is "still occupied," it is already occupied by others, even if, in the moment of longing for this 'new dawn', 'he forgets' this is so. In this sense, "still occupied" might suggest no room exists for 'him' in this scene, for him to experience the change of speed and of style it encompasses, even as much as 'he' wishes and has tried to pretend it did.

'You', however, might, in contrast, suggest some other figure, some other individual or group, and perhaps 'us' listening to this song and being addressed by it, as the people forgetting this change of scene, with its change of speed and style, is still occupied by others. Perhaps 'still occupied' implies this is not the change it initially appears to be, as it is still effectively 'occupied territory', still territory occupied by dominant ideology, by the work of the Ideological State Apparatuses, in conjunction with the work of the Repressive State Apparatus, and in conjunction as well with the dominance of the dominant capitalist class over the economic infrastructure of the social formation. Perhaps 'still occupied' implies this is not the change it initially appears to be, as it is still effectively 'occupied territory', still territory occupied by agents of the exercise of disciplinary powers, including by means of pervasive panopticism, across a carcereal continuum, enforcing self-subjection of docile bodies to compulsory normalization. Or perhaps 'still occupied' implies this is not the change it initially appears to be, as it is still effectively 'occupied territory', still territory where an instrumentalist means-ends ethic prevails and the competitive pursuit of material gain trumps all other interests and concerns, especially aesthetic sense and sensibility and feelings of compassion and empathy.

"Different colours, different shades/Over each mistakes were made," lines five and six, suggest, perhaps, that both the envisioned 'new dawn' as well as pursuit of this new dawn may have involved coming at it in multiple distinct ways, from multiple distinct directions, yet in all of these "mistakes were made," mistakes that undermined the prospect of achieving the desired end. These lines suggest the method of approach in seeking to reach, to realize, 'the new dawn' matters considerably, which might, by way of connection with Weber, Althusser, and Foucault, suggest in turn this is likewise the case concerning method of approach in 1) attempting to critique, and successfully challenge and counter, dominant ideology, 2) resisting and undermining the workings of disciplinary power as exercised through panoptic discourses and practices as part of a carceral continuum enforcing subjection to normalization, and 3) finding a 'true calling' that enables one to live out one's life devoted to this 'calling' and by making the best out of what one can distinctly bring to bear and offer through one's life activity. In case #1, 'failure' can lead to cooptation and containment by dominant ideology, even to the point of becoming a resource that strengthens the hold of dominant ideology, such as through diversion into allowed or allowable forms of rebellion–rebellion for example more focused upon 'appearing different' than 'making a difference'. In case #2, 'failure' can lead likewise to yet other forms of allowed or allowable resistance that do not threaten or disrupt disciplinary power, let alone its operations across a carceral continuum and in the form of compulsory normalization, but rather enact only slightly modified self-subjection before the panoptic gaze. In case #3, 'failure' can lead to becoming 'a narrow specialist without a mind' and 'a pleasure-seeker without a heart', equating success *in living a good life* with success *in living the good life*, and with the latter defined according to how much money one earns, and accumulates, as well in terms of what one can buy with this money.

These last two lines, in conjunction with the preceding four, also support the following interpretation. One forms a post-punk band that composes, records, and performs original music, conceiving of what one is doing as creating and sharing something that matters, in artistic terms, or as providing a means for musicians and audiences together to break free of subjection to normative convention and expectation by participating in a collectively fashioned counter-public space. This space operates in opposition to, or at least separation from, what transpires in public (and private) spaces thoroughly subject to the exercise of socially dominant forms of power. Yet this creation eventually escapes one's control, and becomes increasingly driven by commercial pressure, the influence of normative convention and expectation, and the impact of socially dominant forms of disciplinary power. In this reading, the next line–"I took the blame"–makes sense as taking the blame for what happened to this post-punk band, perhaps by not foreseeing cooptation could happen and not doing enough to prevent cooptation from happening. Yet "I took the blame" can also suggest 'taking the blame' for failures to reach and to realize other 'new dawns', for failing to recognize and contribute what was needed to overcome obstacles and defeat opponents in this quest. If the new dawn referenced in the title represents a desirable goal for the narrator-protagonist, as it seems it does, or at least as it seems it has, 'he' 'taking the blame' suggests 'he' feels he has let down everyone else sharing this common aspiration, to reach and to realize this desired end, because 'he' was seemingly in a crucial position to be able to determine what would–and what would not–happen, yet failed to do (all of) what was necessary.

"Directionless, so plain to see/A loaded gun won't set you free/So you say," lines eight through ten begin by describing a lack of direction, that seems in striking contrast with what the opening lines of this stanza sketch out concerning 'changes'–in speed, style, and scene–and even with what was watched and admired. The first of these three lines suggests the narrator-protagonist imagined 'he', and perhaps those together with 'him', thought they had a 'map' that would guide them to where they sought to go, but in fact this turned out not to be the case, and at least now, with that 'new dawn fading', 'he' is 'directionless', or *feeling* directionless. He feels as if he now has nowhere to go, nothing to turn to or to fall back on, and, what's more, this is "so plain to see," which in turn suggests the narrator-protagonist himself, in this moment, seems convinced 'he' is clearly now without direction, and perhaps long was, even back when he imagined the opposite to be the case. He is also confronting the prospect that he was never 'the leader' *or the kind of leader* he previously imagined himself to be–or that he was never actually capable of being the (kind of) leader he aspired to be. Perhaps the narrator-protagonist feels he was never actually capable of being the kind of leader required in this specific historical moment and in this specific social conjuncture. Perhaps even if he was, ostensibly, so capable, he nevertheless has clearly, in other words 'plainly', failed to deliver this kind of leadership–the kind of leadership needed to successfully 'seize the day'.

I've already discussed the famous lines "A loaded gun won't set you free/So you say," but in the context of developing possible interpretations of these lyrics from attending to them closely from line to line I will add an inclination toward suicide might make sense here as a response to feeling guilty and even ashamed at failing to live up to what was required of the narrator-protagonist in this specific historical moment and social conjuncture, in response to his failing (or perceiving himself as failing) to provide the leadership needed to lead the way in reaching and realizing 'the new dawn'. These last two lines of this first vocal stanza suggest a dialogue of some sort, that might be an internal dialogue. 'One part of the self' inclines toward suicide in order to free 'himself' from the burden of guilt, shame, and self-loathing, while 'another part of the self' argues against this inclination, that it will not achieve what it seems to offer. The latter might mean if one is genuinely responsible for letting others down, for failing effectively to lead the way in the pursuit of an end others were counting on, for failing to lead the way toward the successful realization of 'the new dawn', then killing oneself will not 'free' one, at least not in the memory of others, and not in the legacy that will follow, even after one is dead, because what one 'failed' at, and was responsible for 'failing at', will live on.

Stanza two of "New Dawn Fades" reads as follows: "We'll share a drink and step outside/An angry voice and one who cried/"We'll give you everything and more/The strains too much, can't take much more."/Oh, I've walked on water, run through fire/Can't seem to feel it any more/It was me, waiting for me/Hoping for something more/Me, seeing me this time, hoping for something else." The first line appears straightforwardly descriptive, but in relation to the developing possible interpretations I have set forth, in relation to the first stanza, poses further complication. Who is the 'we' here–is it the narrator-protagonist and those who, seemingly, have been together with him through the experience that has seemingly now brought him to the brink of suicide? Is this 'him' and 'himself', with these lines in an effect conveying an internal monologue, as the narrator-protagonist ruminates over what he once aspired toward, as well as over feeling all that has slipped away and he is responsible for this happening? Or are these characters 'sharing a drink and stepping outside' new figures, not the same as those who appear in the first stanza, and even a new grouping identified by means of the 'we' in this instance? Either way, why share a drink–of what–and why step outside–from where and into what? If this is the narrator-protagonist 'wrestling with himself', it seems he is commenting on his own tendencies in crisis to turn to what allows him a fleeting escape, such as drink–alcohol–that provides temporary numbing of pain. This also involves temporarily retreating from deciding what to do next.

"An angry voice and one who cried" could represent two dimensions of the narrator-protagonist's emotional experience of the present situation, one angry and one sad, including angry with and sad about himself, about his own perceived failing, about what he feels responsible for, about what he takes the blame for, and about what is leading him to contemplate suicide as a result. Yet these lines could also correspond to two different personages, or characters, who represent two kinds of emotional responses to what has transpired and is transpiring–the fading of the new dawn. Both of these characters vent how upset they are, but in different registers, yet both had, seemingly, invested substantially in being able to reach, to realize, the new dawn. Seemingly, if we read these as two characters other than the narrator-protagonist, they are both upset with the narrator-protagonist, for letting them down, for failing to lead them to the new dawn.

"We'll give you everything and more/The strains too much, can't take much more," lines three and four are notable, to begin with, because they are quoted, which might suggest these are spoken, shouted, or screamed, by someone else or by more than one other character in this drama, perhaps *at* the narrator-protagonist. Perhaps the first of these two lines implies a kind of pleading with the narrator-protagonist to resume efforts to reach and realize the new dawn that is now fading, suggesting this character believes the narrator-protagonist *has not yet done all he is capable of*, and needs further encouragement to do so. Alternately, this character might be suggesting that 'we', all of 'us', who have been united together with the narrator-protagonist in striving to reach, to realize, the new dawn, are ready once more to recommit ourselves to another attempt, and are in effect pleading with the narrator-protagonist by exclaiming 'we' are ready to give all we have to give, to follow his leadership once again, in making this yet further attempt. The second of these two lines, if this represents another 'character' than the narrator-protagonist 'himself', seems not to be the same as the 'character' voicing the first of these two lines, as this character suggests the attempt, even the repeated attempt, and, logically as well, the failing of the attempt or the failing of repeated attempts, has left them feeling so battered and bruised they "can't take much more"–they doubt they 'have it in them' to undertake a renewed attempt to reach, to realize, the desired end. But both lines could come from one character who feels torn between these two directions–wanting to continue and give everything possible to pursue the desired end yet feeling as if they can't do so anymore because of the strain involved. If both lines are part of the narrator-protagonist's internal monologue, it seems 'he' feels as if he has given everything he has to give to this quest, even while recognizing it has not been enough, and he is insisting if he possibly could he would 'reach deep down into himself' but he doubts he has any more to offer after he has 'pushed himself over the edge' and he has felt his limits

–and his limitations–overwhelming him. He is extremely disappointed in himself, in what he is *not* capable of–*not* further capable of–but he recognizes, however agonizingly, that these are indeed his limits, and, if anything, he has already pushed himself to the point he is breaking down.

Before continuing with explication of further lines of these lyrics I will comment here that I can readily identify with exactly what I have just described, with the nexus of feelings I have just described. Many times in my life I have felt called upon, as a matter of intellectual, professional, ethical, and political responsibility–and integrity–to give and to keep giving more and more of myself to causes I passionately believed in, and where I passionately wanted to contribute everything I possibly could to help reach, to help realize, collectively shared desired ends, but in the course of doing so I reached limits beyond which I found I could not go, as much I wanted to do so, and as much as I felt desperately that I needed to do so, but I could not because I was breaking down. Even so, I felt furious at myself as well as despairing that I was limited as I was–wishing I could be more and better than I was, wishing I was someone different and other than myself, someone more capable of being and doing what I aspired to be and so. I felt this way when I attempted suicide, and I have felt this way enough since while needing to fight hard against this kind of feeling bringing me back to the brink of suicide.

Often as a university faculty member, it has felt to me that I must insure every student in every class I teach gains from this experience, and that it is, what's more, my duty to reach all of them, with any problem they might confront along the way my responsibility to help solve. Often, when it has seemed students have been unclear I have felt it is my responsibility to make things clear. Often when students have not understood or done well, I have felt it is my responsibility to make up for that and insure subsequently they understand and do well. I've needed to frequently remind myself this is a collaborative venture that depends equally upon both what I and students bring to bear, and if it is a question of responsibility when students are experiencing problems in learning, or lack of clarity concerning or difficulty in understanding what we are learning, or of students not doing well in work as part of our class, both of us–students and I, as the teacher–are together responsible not just me alone.

In addition, I have also needed to frequently remind myself that no matter how hard I try I am not always going to reach everyone. I have needed to remind myself that these people are their own independent agents who are also responsible for their own learning, and who make their own choices and decisions concerning how hard they strive to learn, while, like me as well, they are subject to influences neither they nor I can control that affect how well they are able to do the work they are doing at any given moment in any given class in any given semester. Yes, I do believe it is my responsibility to provide extra help to students who enter the classes I teach less well-prepared to learn and succeed than others I teach, including to show people who have never recognized and believed in their capacity to learn and succeed they can do so. But, again, I must also recognize and accept my limits, and my limitations, aiming to be kind to myself and not just to the students I teach.

Returning, however, to lines five and six of stanza two, "Oh, I've walked on water, run through fire/Can't seem to feel it any more," suggests, again, the narrator-protagonist has pushed himself extremely far and hard, and he has internalized and followed an expectation that he 'perform miracles', yet he is worn down and worn out, emotionally as well as physically exhausted by this effort, and especially by where this effort has ended up–and not ended up–such that now he "can't seem to feel it any more." One reason I title my own blog "There Will Be No Miracles Here," inspired by the Nathan Coley-designed large sculptural scaffolding of the same name that sits outside the Scottish National Gallery of Modern Art in Edinburgh, is to counter my own tendencies to expect miracles of myself, and then to 'punish myself' for failing to produce these. Another, corollary, reason for embracing this title is to counter common tendencies among many who expect teachers should regularly and routinely perform miracles in what they are able to achieve, through their own powers alone. I am countering the expectation teachers will, all by themselves, according to their deployment of their own miraculous powers, inspire previously or otherwise uninspired and uninterested students to learn, to want to learn, and to work hard to learn, as well as to make leaps and bounds in what they are able to understand and accomplish over the course of a single semester, while, what's more, doing this, performing this same miracle, for all students in all classes in all semesters. Teachers are also often expected to miraculously deal with all other issues and problems students can and do bring to bear, from their lives lived outside of and beyond class, so that none of this undermines their ability to fully succeed in class. And teachers are also commonly expected to represent their fields honestly and forthrightly, while simultaneously being always sensitively inclusive and respectful of all possible philosophical and political positions, such that all students will always feel entirely at ease in engaging with any controversial topic the class might ever even touch upon.

Yet teachers are hardly the only kinds of workers to experience and internalize the sense that they much accede to these kinds of pressures, to function as miracle workers. All too often many of us treat workers, in many jobs, as if we expect these workers to perform miracles. As a result, people who conscientiously want to do everything they can to help, serve, assist, enable, and empower those for whom they produce useful goods and provide useful services, through the work they do, in paid jobs and otherwise, tend to push themselves extremely hard, and indeed to the breaking point where they end up feeling they have 'walked on water, run through fire' but that hasn't been enough, while they also end up feeling they are wearing down so badly from having done so that they 'can't seem to feel it anymore'. If you give everything you've got, even to the point of making yourself sick, and that is still not enough, not enough to satisfy those who seem to always want yet more of and from you, you are likely to reach a point where you need to stop, you can't take it any more, and you can't feel any further incentive, let alone sufficient strength, to keep pushing yourself ever harder.

Think about how commonplace it is, in many areas of learning, in many areas of practice, as part and parcel of developing many a skill or talent, such as an athletic ability, to accede to the implicit if not explicit demand that you keep pushing yourself harder and harder, that you keep *expanding your limits*, that you keep *exceeding your limits*–that you keep realizing you are capable of being stronger, faster, tougher, more savvy, more skillful, more dextrous, and more accomplished than you previously imagined, than you previously believed, you could. Yes, doing this is in part necessary, because virtually any kind of growth in knowledge and ability requires such a push, and this certainly includes musicians pushing themselves to keep coming up with new music by experimenting with new subjects, techniques, and styles. But eventually one reaches limits that cannot be surpassed without doing serious damage to one's self–and prospectively others too. This is especially the case when one identifies with the romantic ideal of striving toward infinity, striving toward an always receding horizon, and not being satisfied unless attempting what is conventionally assumed to be impossible.

Those who, supposedly at least, have pursued what has been conventionally assumed to be impossible are those who often receive exceptional acclaim for their exceptional accomplishments, and this acclaim often touts their unwillingness to accept the impossibility of what conventionally seemed impossible–changing the course of history and effecting major transformations in culture and society because of this 'great refusal'. As a PhD student, my dissertation advisor often exhorted me to conceive of my dissertation and the subsequent book it would become as 'boundary-reshaping', and to settle for nothing less than this, which meant my aim should be to write a work that would reshape and redefine the intellectual fields within which it would intervene. This would mean all subsequent work in those fields would need to take into account and work off of and in response to the terms I had established for what this work can and should be–and do. My dissertation advisor also repeatedly exhorted me 'to go without sleep' as necessary in seeking to do so. I did try, and I do respect the value, at least in part, of pushing one's self this hard and this far, for a most important cause, but eventually I did need to face up to and accept my limits, and that was difficult to do without, for a long time at least, feeling badly that these were my limits.

It is a challenging determination to make: how hard and how far can and should one reasonably push one's self. It is likewise challenging to determine how hard and how far can and should one reasonably push others. "New Dawn Fades" implies this needs to stop before one is ready to kill one's self because one has become so frustrated and disappointed, and so guilty and ashamed, at how much harder and how much farther one cannot yet push one's self, or be pushed by others. The last three lines–"It was me, waiting for me/Hoping for something more/Me, seeing me this time, hoping for something else"–also imply this needs to stop before reaching the point where one no longer is at all satisfied with, or more precisely no longer wants to be, one's self. These last three lines imply the narrator-protagonist turns, in seeking to find some source, some means, of being able to reenter the fray, to resume the quest, to make up for failure and for guilt and shame over failure, in order to pursue the new dawn once more before it has completely faded away, but all he finds is 'himself', with all of what he has grown to feel frustrated, disappointed, bitter, and angry about–even to hate–concerning himself. He sees himself, and he can't get past seeing himself, as replete with weakness and incapacity, and he feels he wants, and needs, instead to see something else, something more and different, in place of himself.

When one is 'with one's self' but can't get past wishing one was not, instead wishing one was with someone or something else, instead wishing that one was oneself someone or something else, this can be an exceedingly bleak state to be in. Most of us feel something like this, now and then, wishing or imagining we were more or other than we are, that we were able to be and do more and other than we can, but often such feelings are not riven with deep self-loathing. In fact they can derive from curiosity, and curiously fantasizing, about what it might be like to be someone and even something else, which can be life-affirming, and life-enhancing, as we feel we have been imaginatively transported out of our familiar lives when we identify with alternative possibilities we experience in reading a book, watching a movie or a TV show, attending a stage play or a live musical performance, or listening intently to recorded music. As Ruth Herbert reports, on the basis of research she has done, in *Everyday Music Listening: Absorption, Dissociation and Trancing*, even when not making listening to music one's sole or primary focus of attention, it is common enough for many people, over the course of their everyday life, to become so absorbed in the music they are listening to partially dissociate from their surroundings and from their sense of whom and what they otherwise are, even entering partially into the equivalent of a trance.

It can be immensely invigorating, and reinvigorating, to fantasize about being someone or something else, someone or something radically different from and what one is. A vast extent of diverse forms of play involves doing exactly this. These much more uplifting forms of dissociation, projection, identification, and fantastic imagination, about being someone or something else, nonetheless exist along a continuum with the far more dispiriting longing the final three lines of the lyrics of "New Dawn Fades" proclaim. Again, suicidality is more common than often acknowledged, and many people who feel this way don't feel able to share they do. Many people who never reach the point of feeling suicidal nonetheless experience occasions in which they are deeply dissatisfied and unhappy with themselves concerning whom they are and what they are doing, as well as concerning whom they are not and what they are not, with these feelings also existing on a continuum with low or lack of self-esteem, self-harm, depression, suicidality, and suicide.

The structure of "New Dawn Fades" includes the following sections:

1.   Opening 1: Prelude (0:00-0:07).

2.   Opening 2: Initiation, Lead-In, and Build-Up (0:08-1:18).

3.   First Vocal Passage: Exposition and Elaboration (1:19-2:04).

4.   Instrumental Bridge: Reflection and Transition (2:05-2:31).

5.   Second Vocal Passage: Heightened Intensity, Pushing Toward Climax, Arriving at Climax (2:32-3:29).

6.   Final Instrumental Close-Out: Reflection and Transition, Leading-Out, Run-Down, and Drop Out (3:30-4:43).

It makes good sense to interpret "New Dawn Fades," like many Joy Division songs, especially when we pay close attention to Ian Curtis's lyrics and his vocalization of these lyrics, as enacting an introspective drama. The narrator-protagonist is imagining possibilities that initially appear distinct but then merge. The narrator-protagonist is imagining a detached vantage point from which to contemplate, yet the focus of this contemplation is what he is seeking to detach himself from. This reencounter prompts him to contemplate possibilities of escaping further, and for good, while anguishing over his inability, so far at least, to get out of and beyond himself.

The song, by way of the total complex of sounds it incorporates and deploys, registers multiple tones and moods in response to what this introspective drama engages, including contemplative, wistful, and agonized. The arrangement of the total complex of sounds enables "New Dawn Fades" to convey both an embodiment of suicidality, as well as a tribute to the human spirit at a moment of existential crisis. "New Dawn Fades" invites and encourages empathetic identification with the troubled figure at the center of its implicit narrative. At the verge of ending 'his' life, we hear, and feel, the vitality of the human life-spirit, as it desperately struggles to survive, endure, and persist. The song honors the dignity that resides in human suffering and struggle–in humans suffering and struggling with painful guilt and shame as well as with painful anguish and despair.

"New Dawn Fades" opens, for the duration of the initial prelude, with a sample of a snippet of a guitar line from "Insight" that is played backwards as well as further modified to render it all the stranger. "New Dawn Fades" is likewise distinctive for incorporating two guitars–one overdriven and one clean–as well as a bass guitar. After the prelude featuring the sampled backwards guitar, first the drum kit beginning with the hi-hat, second the bass guitar, third the overdriven guitar, and fourth the clean guitar enter. In this early section, before the first entry of the vocal, the overdriven guitar and the bass guitar play the initial melodic line in opposing directions together, the former ascending in pitch and the latter descending in pitch, doing so in a manner overtly suggestive of moving up and down steps. The hi-hat and the bass drum are initially clearly and prominently audible, not just the snare drum, unlike in many other recorded Joy Division songs.

Stephen Morris also periodically plays tom rolls followed by a cymbal crash at the ends of phrases in this song, which is also not commonplace among later Joy Division songs. Yet as the song proceeds, as is typical from *Unknown Pleasures* onward, the recorded sound of the snare drum becomes the clearest, loudest, most distinct, and most prominent sound played by Morris on his drum kit.

Once Ian Curtis's vocal enters, we detect a gentle amount of added reverb and perhaps echo as well, perhaps via digital delay, enabling Curtis in effect to harmonize with himself. Curtis's vocal timbre I hear as richer and fuller than in a number of other Joy Division songs, and as if he is ranging across multiple vocal registers. At the beginning, Curtis's vocal comes across as somewhat softer, lighter, higher, and even breathier than is the case later in the song. His enunciation is precise and clear throughout, while, as is characteristic, he holds and extends words and syllables at the end of phrases and especially lincs, and here does so emphatically, especially with the final three 'me's in the third to last and last lines of the lyrics.

In "New Dawn Fades" the primary role of the bass guitar is contributing together with the drum kit to the the groove, rather than also playing a lead role in sounding the melody throughout the song. The melodic layer in "New Dawn Fades" involves contributions from, first, the bass guitar; second, the overdriven guitar; third, the clean guitar; and, fourth, the vocal. The vocal and the clean guitar take the lead in sounding the melody from the first vocal passage onward through the end of the song. The guitars contribute harmonic fill as well as supporting the melody led by the vocal during the vocal passages. The bass guitar also contributes harmonic fill, notably in the instrumental bridge. In the final instrumental section, the clean guitar is chiefly responsible for carrying the melody while we also hear some notable descending arpeggios from the bass guitar.

The backwards guitar comes from low down, to the sides, and more prominent to the left than the right, of the soundbox. The drums and cymbals are also positioned below center, to the sides, somewhat higher than the backwards guitar while as the song moves on tom rolls and cymbal crashes seem to move from left to right. The bass guitar is positioned down, to both sides, yet not as far down or as far to the sides as the backwards guitar or the drums and cymbals, but as the song proceeds it seems to move further back. The overdriven guitar is positioned higher up, and rises slightly, to above the center, while coming from both sides. The clean guitar is positioned yet further higher up, above center, and comes from both sides, indeed periodically bouncing between sides, in terms of which side is more dominant. This guitar sound alternates between sides rather than sounding simultaneously from both sides. The vocal comes from above center, close to the front, and pushes higher. Collectively, what this constitution of the soundbox conveys is a feeling of sound rising from below and sweeping upward, as well as surrounding, supporting and even, ironically enough, 'uplifting' a central subject.

When I reflect on how the structure and instrumentation of "New Dawn Fades" helps me in staging an encounter with Weber's *Protestant Ethic and the Spirit of Capitalism*, Althusser's *On the Reproduction of Capitalism: Ideology and Ideological State Apparatuses*, and Michel Foucault's *Discipline and Punish: The Birth of the Prison*, I come up with the following. In relation to Weber, I hear a sense of a calling gone wrong, a calling out of control, a calling not providing or continuing to provide the satisfaction ideally imagined and fervently sought–which is expected in response to what is pursued as a 'calling'. I hear a sense of recognition that investment in and commitment toward what had been perceived as a calling has turned out to be problematic, and has led to failure, including letting others down and suffering remorse as a result. The song thereby raises the question of whether the ideal of living life by finding and pursuing a calling becomes an oppressive mystification of what is necessary to lead a good life. Emphasis in this song on working extremely hard, ending up failing even so, and feeling one is 'to blame' for failing, to the point of contemplating suicide in response, suggests the Protestant work ethic can be dangerous. "New Dawn Fades" elicits an image of writhing within Weber's steel-hard casing, feeling damagingly alienated from sense and sensibility as well as compassion and empathy, yet unable to cast this off while fearing being nakedly exposed if one is able to do so. Perhaps the subject in this song is already too damaged by life lived within the steel-hard casing to be able survive outside of it.

In relation to Althusser, "New Dawn Fades" conveys a sense of struggling to break from and find a counterpoint to dominant ideology, yet with little confidence this will be possible and considerable fear the harm endured as a result of the attempt will be too damaging to survive. "New Dawn Fades" worries one will be left with little sustainable sense of whom one is, what one is about, and what one can and should seek to be and do without the support of dominant ideology, without the 'guarantee' dominant ideology offers of a place that makes sense and an orientation that 'centers' how to make sense. "New Dawn Fades" suggests ideological interpellation may be much messier than Althusser describes, with individuals interpellated in disparate degrees in various subject positions, and with individuals interpellated into disparate positions that do not smoothly coincide, leaving the subject feeling torn in irreconcilably opposing directions. "New Dawn Fades" makes sense as registering an experience of disenchantment with dominant ideology, and with dominant ideological interpellation, while at the same lacking access to any substantial and sustainable alternative. The song's enactment of a straining to get out of and beyond one's self can be interpreted, in Althusserian terms, as straining to get out of and beyond the subject one has been interpellated to be by dominant ideology, all the while doubting this is possible, and feeling isolated and cut off in not being 'at home' in either dominant ideology or in any counter-dominant ideology.

In relation to Foucault, "New Dawn Fades" conveys the sense of struggling to get away from and resist what is expected, required, and demanded as a result of the exercise of disciplinary power. The subject has registered the costs of this exercise, the destruction and the damage it has caused, and desires to break with compulsory normalization. Yet, again, the subject is doubtful of 'his' ability to be able to do so. It feels 'too late' to escape from or evade the oppressive hold of disciplinary power to become a different kind of subject. "New Dawn Fades" registers a desire to be more and other than the individual shaped by discipline–and, more precisely, by disciplines–through subjection to what they call forth, according to a pervasive carcereal logic, yet at the same registers an anguish that he cannot find any way out–and especially beyond–other than self-annihilation.

In sum, it can make sense to interpret "New Dawn Fades" as testifying to the destructive impact of 1) the Protestant work ethic and the spirit of capitalism, 2) dominant ideology and dominant ideological interpellation, and 3) disciplinary subjection and carcereal normalization. "New Dawn Fades" emphasizes what it is like *to feel* this destructive impact.

"New Dawn Fades" highlights how each of these theories well explains 'the problem' yet only obliquely allude to 'the solution'. In other words, Weber does not offer much useful advice for even beginning to imagine how to cast off 'the steel-hard casing', or to counter what the Protestant Ethic and the Spirit of Capitalism have become in the 'victorious' stage of modern capitalism, or to break with and construct alternatives versus problematic mystifications of the supposed preeminent virtues of work and working, acquisition and accumulation of material wealth, and life lived in pursuit of a 'calling' (especially a calling one is supposedly 'predestined for'). In other words, Althusser does not offer much useful advice concerning how to break with and counter interpellation as subject of and to dominant ideology, nor how to break with and counter acting as an effective agent in the reproduction of capitalism. In other words, Foucault does not offer much useful advice concerning how to resist exercise of disciplinary power, pervasive panopticism, the carceal continuum, and compulsory normalization. In each case, all three theorists staunchly oppose voluntarism; in other words, they do not conceive of effective resistance and opposition, on the scale they are interested in, as something that can be generated as a matter of merely willing this to be. Yet they offer little advice *for what to do*, and especially *how to do it*, to those who experience themselves at odds with the dominant, not able and willing to accept and identify with the dominant, even passively and resignedly so. "New Dawn Fades" suggests what it feels like to be a subject in such a position: the social and political status quo is no longer compelling and no longer serves as an acceptable locus of identification, yet no intelligible alternative appears viable–especially in the aftermath of the 'fading' of 'the new dawn'. This new dawn that has faded and is fading makes sense as representing an alternative that once seemed viable, and was indeed desirable, yet has proven unrealizable.

The opening prelude, consisting of the sample of the guitar snippet from "Insight" played backwards, wobbles slightly in terms of loudness. The drum kit enters softly but the bass guitar followed by the overdriven guitar enter comparably loudly, with each of these instruments successively contributing a step up in the song's overall volume. The clean guitar entrance does not add much to loudness because the overall volume adjusts to include this sound source, and with the first vocal passage the same happens in respect to the entrance of the vocal. As "New Dawn Fades" proceeds, the clean guitar, the drums and cymbals, and the vocal are the loudest contributors. The vocal in stanza two is notably much louder than in stanza one, and in fact becomes exceedingly loud, while the rest of the instruments seem to increase in volume in parallel, in the final section of this stanza. The closing instrumental section maintains a consistent loudness until this drops down together with instruments dropping off and the song slowing down and fading out.

"New Dawn Fades" is among the slowest of Joy Division songs in terms of BPM, with common estimates ranging from 78 to 118. What helps complicate that tempo, and make the song feel faster than it is, has much to do with the predominance of sixteenth notes along with periodic thirty-second notes played on the drums and cymbals, even as the time signature remains, as usual, 4/4. Typically the snare strikes decisively on beats 2 and 4, while the bass drum, interestingly, strikes on 1, 1 and, and 1 uh out of 1-ee-and-uh; on 3, 3 and, and 3 uh out of 3-ee-and-uh; on 2 and 4 out of 2-ee-and-uh and 4-ee-and-uh–or just 2-ee and 2-uh/4-ee and 4-uh. In short, the bass drum strikes more frequently than just once on beats 1 and 3, departing from the standard rock beat. Tom rolls are 32nd notes, and right after these rolls end we next hear the cymbal crash once. Curtis starts singing quarter notes, then mid-way through vocal passage one switches to singing eighth notes, with vocal passage two begins with eighth notes, and then finally extends his singing of 'me' over half and whole notes in the last three lines of the second vocal passage. The overdriven guitar starts with a combination of quarter and half notes and then moves to sixteenth notes in the opening instrumental section right before the first vocal passage. This is followed by resting throughout the first vocal passage and the bridge, then starting with a series of chords, two per measure, in the second vocal passage followed by a series of eighth notes and combinations of quarter, eighth, and half notes. A comparable combination of the last length of notes shows up in the final pattern played by the overdriven guitar in the concluding instrumental section. Typically the clean guitar plays eighth notes along with one ringing quarter note per measure, usually on the third or fourth beat. With the start of verse two this line shifts to chords and then back to notes. The bass guitar line involves a pattern of regularly repeated combinations of quarter, eighth, and sixteenth notes, often within the same measure.

The website UltimateGuitar.com identifies "New Dawn Fades" as played in the key of E minor which seems more apt to me, in relation to what I hear, than what many comparable sites recommend, and that is D major. The general direction of movement in pitch of the bass guitar line is ultimately downward, at most two to three steps at a time, after starting and repeating on each successive pitch in the course of the full extent of this movement. As Peter Hook attests, this relatively simple pattern does repeat with limited variation other than a few notably higher pitched descending arpeggios near the end. The location of the pitch is relatively low, overall, and lower than it often is when Hook is playing a more prominent and consistent role in sounding the melody.

Curtis's vocal involves considerable singing closely at or around the same pitch, with periodic downward followed by upward movements to return to the same pitch as at the start of a phrase and then otherwise to stay down in pitch. Curtis's vocal generally covers intervals no more than one to three steps in pitch. What is impressive here is that while remaining within a limited interval range Curtis is able to convey a marked feeling of distinction and movement across these pitches nonetheless, due to intonation and slight modulations of standard pitches. Bernard Sumner's overdriven guitar moves upward from its initial starting pitch and then back down before moving then back up once more, spanning a total of seven steps, while later alternates between two pitches two steps apart. Chord progressions with this instrument move downward, upward, downward, upward, and downward, while a late variation on the first pattern moves overall slightly downward but again these are relatively small intervals covered. Sumner's clean guitar typically sweeps upward in pitch, rising a significant number of steps, and then descending less than half way back down in pitch before rising again. The opening backwards guitar oscillates in pitch with an ultimate movement down. The opening bass guitar line moves primarily down in pitch with the opening overdriven guitar line playing a parallel upward movement to coincide with this downward movement, before then moving downward itself and from that point oscillating back and forth right before the clean guitar joins, with its most pronounced movement up in pitch before, again, returning down but less than half as far as its initial starting point.

All of these initial movements in pitch feel overtly like stepping downward or upward. As the song proceeds, upward movements in pitch, especially from the clean guitar, receive notable emphasis although the descending arpeggios near the end are emphasized as well. My sense of what pitch contributes to meaning, by way of the fact that the most pronounced and emphatic movements here are upward, yet always feeling as if they never quite reach their desired destination, always falling back and then needing to start up again, is suggestion of a surprisingly undaunted, resilient determination.

Curtis's vocal delivery sounds as if it makes use of a wider extent of vocal registration than in many other Joy Division songs, while emphasizing a wider range in terms of attack, decay, sustain, and release than also is often the case. Especially notable, again, is his increase in volume and 'push' throughout the second vocal passage as opposed to the first, and his holding as well as extending the word 'me' across multiple notes encompassing multiple pitches near the end of this second vocal passage. Curtis's resonance is strong and vibrant, enhanced by Martin Hannett's studio treatment, yet also sounds as if what we hear at least in part corresponds to the natural reverberation of Curtis's singing voice. Curtis becomes vehement in his vocal delivery in the second vocal passage, in voicing his felt relationship to the words he is singing, as well as to what they reference and suggest. Here it sounds as if he is leading the other instruments in simultaneously pushing louder and harder as well. Throughout "New Dawn Fades" Curtis performs intense emotion while suggesting this is not necessarily entirely emotion arising immediately in the moment of performance, but rather emotion mediated by way of performance, as well as by way of recollection and reflection.

In her 2017 doctoral dissertation in music at the City University of New York, *A New Approach to Analysis of Timbre*, Megan Lavengood offers a useful focus on a limited series of binaries, associated with the sustain and attack dimensions of the attack, hold, decay, sustain, and release 'envelope' as well as in relation to pitch, that I will draw upon loosely here to describe what I hear, in terms of timbre, related to each of the distinctive sounds sources in "New Dawn Fades." Sustain can be characterized as bright or dark, pure or noisy, full or hollow, rich or spare, beatless or beating, steady or wavering, or harmonic or inharmonic; attack can be characterized as noisy or pure, percussive or soft, and bright or dark; and pitch considered strictly in terms of contribution to defining timbre can be characterized as low or high and as steady or wavering.

Let's map out the instruments as follows:

1. Backwards guitar:
a. Sustain: hard to characterize as either bright or dark, noisy, full, hard to characterize as rich or sparse, beating, wavering, and inharmonic.
b. Attack: noisy, soft, and hard to characterize as either bright or dark.
c. Pitch: hard to characterize as low or high, and wavering.

2. Drum kit:
a. Sustain: bright, especially the snare while the bass might be dark, the hi-hat bright, the toms might be dark, and the crash is bright; pure, especially the snare, toms, and hi-hat; full; rich; beating; steady; and harmonic.
b. Attack: pure, percussive, and bright.
c. Pitch: both low and high but more pronounced low, and steady.

3. Bass guitar:
a. Sustain: dark, pure, between full and hollow, closer to sparse than rich, closer to beating than beatless, closer to steady than wavering, and harmonic.
b. Attack: pure, percussive, and dark.
c. Pitch: low, and closer to steady.

4. Overdriven guitar:
a. Sustain: dark, noisy, closer to hollow than full, closer to sparse than rich, beating, closer to wavering than steady, and closer to inharmonic than harmonic.
b. Attack: noisy, percussive, and dark.
c. Pitch: low, and wavering.

5. Clean guitar:
a. Sustain: bright, pure, full, rich, beatless, steady, and harmonic.
b. Attack: pure, soft, and bright.
c. Pitch: high, and steady.

6. Vocal:
a. Sustain: bright, a mixture of pure and noisy, closer to full than hollow, rich, between beatless and beating, both steady and wavering, and both harmonic and inharmonic.
b. Attack: pure, soft, and bright.
c. Pitch: both low and high, and both steady and wavering.

It is conceivable someone with much greater aptitude in this area than me might be able to draw precise conclusions by inserting all of these answers into a matrix, giving them numeric representatives, and then analyzing the collective results, but I will simply note what this analysis suggests is even this song, that Hook, understandably, describes as 'simple', involves a diversity of timbral constituents with notable variations along timbral parameters, and if each instrument itself offers a particular timbral 'fingerprint' in relation to this song, the entire combination offers an elaborate 'handprint'.

I hear the timbre of the backwards guitar as conveying a warbling meets wobbling quality; I hear the snare drum conveying the quality of a crisp snap with a slight echo; I hear the bass drum conveying a deep rumbling quality; I hear the hi-hat cymbal conveying a light glittering tink/tink quality; and I hear the crash cymbal conveying a slight, quickly contained ringing meets glittering quality. I hear the vocal conveying a swaying, crooning quality that pushes toward shouting, with a harsh edge when pushing but otherwise tightly contained yet finely textured. I hear the clean guitar conveying a bright, clean, rich, long sustaining, resonantly ringing quality. I hear the bass guitar conveying narrow, precise, rumbling and cascading qualities. And I hear the overdriven guitar conveying harsh, dirty, and somewhat thick and hollow qualities.

In terms of analogies with physical movements I hear the timbre of the backwards guitar suggestive of spinning awkwardly in a close space without in fact moving much if any distance. I hear the drum kit suggestive of a slow, steady, firm, confident, determined, and precise walk. I hear the overdriven guitar suggestive of a paradoxically controlled rambling. I hear the clean guitar suggestive of a careful ascent. I hear the bass guitar suggestive of a careful descent with some variation between rumbling downwards across several steps relatively quickly and some more precise movement down single steps at a time. And I hear the vocal suggestive of a pushing to sweep into a space and then move forward front and center within the space while projecting forcefully outward, as if on a stage.

In terms of perceptual or behavioral qualities as well as colors I associate the timbre of the backwards guitar with awkwardness, unease, uncertainty, being out of joint, waking suddenly and not being entirely clear where one is and how one got there, and a visual image of a faded or fading pastel mix. I associate the timbre of the drum kit with decisiveness, bluntness, crispness, sharpness, and fixation, conjuring a visual image of a clean-lined and sharply-contrasting black and white mix. I associate the timbre of the overdriven guitar with tightness in the throat, pressure in the sinuses, hoarseness, and a straining meets striding to proceed and carry forward, conjuring a visual image of a mix of gray meets brown. I associate the timbre of the clean guitar with a rich, smooth, elegant serenity meets subliminality, conjuring a visual image involving a mix of bright and deeply saturated golden yellow with a vibrant as well as again richly saturated kelly green. I associate the timbre of the bass guitar with a visual image maintaining a rich yet dark rust color. And I associate the timbre of the vocal with a sense of engaging at the forefront of a theatrical stage performance, including making use of theatrical staging to pierce illusions concerning the supposedly 'natural', non-performative quality of the everyday and of everyday interaction, conjuring a visual image comprised of elements of deep purple turning to fierce red.

In terms of how these preceding dimensions of the musical sound of "New Dawn Fades" (loudness, rhythm, pitch, vocal delivery, and timbre) contribute to the meanings I hear the song suggesting to me, they collectively convey a more measured and confident engagement with the subject of the lyrics than the lyrics taken alone otherwise suggest. The relative slowness of the tempo is especially notable as this does seem to offer a 'change of speed' that provides an opportunity–an opening–for contemplation concerning what precisely we here confront. Taking the entire complex of sounds, sounds patterns, and sound deployments into account suggests this song is hardly a raw outpouring of unfiltered emotion but rather a deliberately reflective evocation and examination of emotion, and of constituent elements of it. Yes, we do hear intense emotion expressed but we also hear commentary on this emotion, with the song seeming to suggest we need pay heed to this emotion and to what it signifies, by treating it with compassionate respect and by aiming to empathetically understand. The musical sound of "New Dawn Fades" suggests an emotional experience that pushes and pulls in multiple directions and is comprised of multiple inclinations and tendencies–that suicidal ideation, and suicidality, are themselves like this, encompassing *struggle* among different pushes and pulls. The musical sound of "New Dawn Fades" suggests a sublime quality to this situation, something simultaneously majestic and terrifying, awesome and appalling, dazzling and bewildering, repulsive and compulsive, in recounting and reflecting on what it might mean, and feel like, to reach this edge between continuing to struggle to live on versus no longer wanting to do so.

It is by no means a simple decision to 'commit' suicide. Instead it makes far better sense to interpret the suicidal individual as overwhelmed such that they feel they have no choice other than to kill themself, and that, in effect, the decision has already been made for them. At the point of killing themselves they are acceding to this decision. What contributes to the sublime sensation I just mentioned is recognizing this is a life at a pivotal moment between life and death, a moment that prompts all of us attending to it to become aware of our own mortality, along with that of others close to us. Attending to this moment prompts us to reflect on what is it about life, and about living, we most value–as well as what is it, most of all, that makes life *worth living*, and *worth continuing to live*. Why value life? What do we value in it? To what extent is how we make sense of life, and its positive value, inextricably interconnected with how we make sense of death, and its negative value? How can and how should we live life, aware of death, including that 'death comes to us all', eventually, and often unexpectedly, such that we are not always able to anticipate and prepare for death well ahead of death's arrival? How do we relate, in life, in living life, in living our life and in living our life in relation to others' lives, with those who are dead, to those who have died and to what they have taken with them, in dying, as well as to what they have left behind, from the lives they led, after they have died?

As I listen to "New Dawn Fades" I feel the stress and strain *together with* the vocal in the second vocal stanza, in particular toward the end with Curtis extending his singing of 'me' across successive beats and alternating pitches. The melody compels me to follow along closely, especially in conjunction with the clean guitar and the vocal. Exertion increases, for me together with the song as persona, in the second vocal passage. I feel as if my exertion, together with that of the music as persona, peaks here, and then gradually diminishes over the course of the closing instrumental section. "New Dawn Fades" conveys strength, ironically, in confronting what appears, in the lyrics at least, to represent a feeling of weakness.

The music as persona anticipates a meeting of desire and dread, in the lead-up to and especially over the course of the second vocal passage, and the music as persona anticipates this will prove aesthetically satisfying while psychologically traumatic. The music as persona seems to know what is coming even as the lyrics represent a narrator-protagonist who doesn't seem to know what is coming until it arrives. The music as persona, and I along with it, anticipate honoring this emotional experience.

I hear "New Dawn Fades" expressing suicidality in terms of a complex of emotion. I feel an expression of sadness, and I feel sad in response, yet I also feel an expression of sadness rendered beautiful moving. The slowness of the tempo and the careful layering of the respective instrumental voices in terms of how they relate to the melody, the parallel and complimentary movements in pitch, and the array of convergent and divergent timbres allow the song to feel it engages in an aesthetically and emotionally sensitive, respectful, compassionate, and empathetic way with suicidality–and with closely related forms of depression, despair, and dissatisfaction and unhappiness with one's self.

The sounds of "New Dawn Fades" come at me from a full array of positions across the soundbox and this feels balanced. The voice is especially prominent, with the clean guitar and then the drum kit the next most prominent. I feel as if the sound is structured to sweep up and in toward the center, to direct the way toward it, along diagonal lines. I feel myself compelled to sing along with the vocals, and to sing, or hum, or otherwise emulate the melody as played by the clean guitar. I can't resist singing along with the final three lines and giving extended emphasis to the 'me' in each of those lines together with Ian Curtis. These lines feel as if they are propelling themselves right into me, penetrating past any protective boundary separating myself from the music. I feel the impact of this song as riveting me in place and as wrenching an emotional response from me.

"New Dawn Fades" contemplates suicide at the edge of despair, and it feels uncertain which direction the narrator-protagonist of the lyrics will proceed–following the advice that 'a loaded gun won't set you free' or following the contrary prospect that 'a loaded gun will set you free'. By the end of "New Dawn Fades" this dilemma does not feel settled. Analysis, as implicitly exercised by the music as persona, suggests pushing toward this edge, toward this brink, registering what it feels like, in order to achieve insight that might provide impetus to continue and persist, but it remains unclear whether this happens. The song may make sense as enacting the aesthetic pleasure of surviving an immersion in symbolic suicidality, especially in following along with the music as persona as this music as persona initially anticipates contemplating suicide dispassionately yet finds in moving from the first vocal section to the second vocal section it cannot remain dispassionate.

I associate what I hear in listening to and reflecting on "New Dawn Fades" not just with suicidality, or closely related forms of depression, despair, and deep dissatisfaction with one's self, but also, pointedly, with striving to reach out to share with others that I care and others care about them, their lives matter, and we want and need them to continue to be with us–we love them, and it hurts us terribly to know they are feeling so badly and are at such a desperate point. I associate what I hear in this song with wanting to be part of the solution to taking mental health more seriously and responding more effectively, especially more compassionately and empathetically, than we still often, collectively, do, to this day. I want to help change the status quo affecting people with serious mental health problems. These people represent major percentages of those who are homeless, addicted to alcohol and other drugs, in prison, and regularly in contact with the police and the courts. People with serious mental health problems disproportionately suffer the worst damage as a result of economic crisis, austerity cuts to social welfare, and how underprepared even the wealthiest nations have shown themselves to be in responding to the COVID-19 pandemic.

"New Dawn Fades" confronts a continuing taboo concerned with addressing suicidality from a position of overt identification with this inclination. "New Dawn Fades" confronts a continuing taboo concerning acknowledging how common, how widespread, this kind of emotional experience is, and how these inclinations and tendencies *are normal and natural.* "New Dawn Fades" confronts a continuing taboo that makes it difficult if not impossible to talk about and attend to people's experiences of suicidality, other than by automatically treating this as reason to panic and to expect a suicide attempt is inevitably imminent. "New Dawn Fades" confronts a continuing taboo that involves recognizing suicidality is interlinked across a mobile continuum with a broad range of states and experiences of dissatisfaction and unhappiness, sadness and pain, guilt and shame, and depression and despair.

"New Dawn Fades" confronts a taboo about engaging artistically with the topic of suicide, or suicidality, because to do so runs too great a risk of 'triggering' suicidality and suicide–or, at the least, too great a risk this will leave audiences feeling so overwhelmingly pained and saddened they will be unable to derive anything else from the encounter. "New Dawn Fades" offers comfort, solace, and indeed encouragement to carry on, for those who feel or who have felt the same as the narrator-protagonist here identifies 'himself' as feeling. In its sharing of sadness and pain "New Dawn Fades" aids in moving past sadness and pain.

What if we accept Dan Goodley's challenge, in his book *Disability and Other Human Problems* and centered disability in *reconceiving* what it means to be human–as well as in confronting problems in how being human has been predominantly conceived? What it we define what being human means in terms of being disabled as normal and natural, and identify the so-called able-bodied as always only 'temporarily able-bodied', and also always only 'partially able-bodied'? What if, as Goodley argues, we value dependence, and dependency, far above and beyond valuing independence, and what if we recreate a culture that responds to everyone as dependent, in need of assistance and support from others–active, extensive, and continuous assistance and support from others–in order to live our best possible lives? Suicidality can be thought of as representative of a disability, or at least as a form in which a disability manifests itself. What can we learn from it? What would happen if we were to center suicidality–if we were to imagine it is normal and natural to reach this point and to feel this way, and it is abnormal not to do so? What different, what more, and what better would we do, collectively, to prevent suicidality from becoming suicide?

"New Dawn Fades" engages the invisibility, intangibility, and ephemerality of the borderlines between life and death, living and dying, and being and nothingness. In so doing "New Dawn Fades" suggests consideration as well of the invisibility, intangibility, and ephemerality of what if anything lies beyond life. And "New Dawn Fades" invites consideration of invisible, intangible, and ephemeral dimensions of convergences between life and death, such as experiences of 'living as if dead', of 'barely living', of feeling as if one is dead even as one continues to live, of feeling as if part of one's self is dead even as one otherwise continues to live, and of experiencing a form 'social death' where one is effectively dead to the larger community and society because one is confined, removed, excluded, ignored, and forgotten. "New Dawn Fades" invites consideration of ghostly traces, residues, remnants and vestiges of what once was yet are no more, as well as haunting signs of never realized possibilities or of what never was but could have been or of what is not yet but still yet could be.

"New Dawn Fades" invites consideration of the idea, as notorious critical psychiatrist RD Laing takes on, in books such as *The Divided Self* and *The Politics of Experience*, that those conventionally labeled as 'schizoid' and 'schizophrenic' may exist on a continuum with those labeled 'normal' in relation to experiencing a division, a separation, a disjunction between a perceived true inner self and a perceived false outer self–or a constellation of perceived false outer selves versus a perceived true inner self. Consider also, as Laing does in *The Politics of Experience*, that our ordinary experience of empirically perceptible reality accessed while fully awake, and while overtly conscious, might be significantly limited in comparison with many further domains of the real that also exist.

Consider, along these lines, that Jacques Lacan's order of the Imaginary might represent exactly that, a small slice, and a highly distorted slice at that, of the much greater order of the Real. Consider that the order of the Real, beyond the orders of the Imaginary and the Symbolic, is ultimately invisible, intangible, and ephemeral–at least to us, at least by what means the Imaginary and Symbolic provide. Consider the same might be true of spiritual forces that impact, shape, and perhaps animate us 'from within' as well as 'from without'.

Ultimately what comes across as especially pointedly invisible, intangible, and ephemeral in "New Dawn Fades" is the 'me' that wants to be 'other than me', as well as what is blocking access to that other than me, what is standing in the way of accessing that other than me. Remember, this is an 'other than me' the narrator-protagonist in the lyrics keeps hoping to see, beyond the 'me' that he does keep seeing–i.e., it is an invisible, intangible, and ephemeral 'other than me'.

In Weber's terms, this 'other than me' might represent a calling to be someone or something else that one cannot get at, that one cannot access, and it may be too late even to try. It might represent, given the tenor of this song, a calling to promote respect for the value of the emotional experience of the suicidal. It might represent a casualty of the Protestant Ethic and the spirit of capitalism, but it might also represent a testament to the possibility of sensations, emotions, and values that exist beyond the frames this ethic and this spirit render intelligible, accessible, and viable.

In Althusser's terms, this 'other than me' might represent what one desires to be in seeking to break with whom one has been interpellated to be, and with how one has been so interpellated, and yet, "New Dawn Fades" represents a continuing failing to break with the 'me' to reach, to realize, the position of the 'other than me', because the power of dominant ideology is too formidable. Yet, also in Althusserian terms, "New Dawn Fades" feels as if it pays tribute to the desire and the effort of those not able to abide how they have been interpellated.

In Foucault's terms, this 'other than me' might represent reconceiving what normality means, and especially breaking with subjection to carcereal normalization. In Foucault's terms, longing to see–to find, to reach, to realize, to become–this 'other than me', as well as not succeeding in this longing, represents agony that can follow from not being able to accept, follow, and meet standards, expectations, requirements, and demands brought to bear by disciplinary power–and ultimately not wanting to do so–yet finding no way out, no way beyond, no way to effectively resist.

"New Dawn Fades" prompts me to think about what social factors make US society today, and its dominant culture, and others like ours, deficient in caring, compassion, and empathy–and whether these tendencies have worsened, as well as, if so, why so–and what might be done about this. I think about why is it remains taboo so often to share vulnerability–to admit weakness, fragility, frailty, and dependence on others. The subject I hear addressing me in and through "New Dawn Fades" is troubled, uncertain, and multiply divided in terms of what 'he' thinks and feels. This subject I hear sharing 'his' emotional experience with me for two purposes, intentional or not: 1) to connect with others who can recognize, understand, and identify with this kind of emotional experience, thereby engaging in a socially symbolic act of extending empathy and contributing toward the forging of solidarity, and 2) to elicit a response from someone who can see, hear, and feel what he is going through, how tough this is, how desperate he is, and how much he needs help.

As a total complex of organized sound "New Dawn Fades" suggests a subject that validates this kind of emotional experience, and challenges listeners to break with judgmentalism as well as from silence (and thereby complicity) concerning the prevalence of suicidality. "New Dawn Fades" conveys a striking impression of engaging with something tragically beautiful. In listening to and reflecting on this song I experience myself invited to become an intimate interlocutor of a subject sharing 'his' emotional experience of giving everything he has to give, of pushing himself to his limits and beyond, of not succeeding in reaching his goal, and of feeling responsible for falling short. I feel compassion, but I also feel concern–as I recognize a great many people share this emotional experience.

I feel I bear my share of responsibility as part of my society, and participant in its dominant culture, where it is too common, and too easy, effectively to ignore or dismiss this kind of psychic pain and what prompts it, especially when this is the experience of those whom we have been encouraged to regard as 'other than' or 'different from' or 'far away from' or 'disconnected from' us. As Goodley discusses in *Disability and Other Human Problems*, it remains far too easy to effectively cast others aside, and to act as if we only bear responsibility for our individual lives and those of immediate family members, while unconsciously and unintentionally supporting and sustaining divisions between those judged and treated as more versus less worthy–and as more versus less truly and fully human. I think about what I can and should attempt to do, in response.

What I have done, and what I will continue to do, is to be open, honest, and forthright about my own experience of chronic illness, invisible disability, and mental health challenge, including my own recurrent to persistent tendencies toward serious to severe anxiety, including panic attacks, and including depression, as well as my own experience of suicidality and attempted suicide. This sharing has helped others and will help others, especially when it has prompted sharing back and collective work on thinking through what we might each and all do try to make a positive difference, to better help each other in need, even to better anticipate that others will need our help and when they will need our help. I have joined larger collective efforts involved in extending resources, raising awareness, and changing the culture concerning in particular mental illness/mental health, but also chronic physical illness and physical as well as mental disabilities, visible and invisible–to help *normalize* all of these. At the same time, as Goodley discusses in relation to identifying with 'the posthuman', as well as in relation to Foucault's critique of normalization in *Discipline and Punish: The Birth of the Prison*, I feel compelled to contest the seemingly inescapable need to constantly uncritically fall back upon and adhere to prescriptions for what is normal along with proscriptions against what is abnormal.

This direction for critical praxis follows classic queer theory in promoting a radical mode of queerness that breaks with and intervenes versus normativities by embracing being 'other than normal', 'abnormal', and 'against the normal'. This critical praxis requires continually identifying and contesting oppressive impacts of expectations, requirements, and demands for conformity with 'the normal', along with unintentional as well as intentional and non-deliberate as well as deliberate exercise of disciplinary normalization.

This critical praxis requires I continue to examine limits beyond which I have not yet, and even have been reluctant yet, to consider my own alignment with dominant ideology. What do I tend to accept as self-evident, obvious, beyond question, natural, inexorable, inalterable, and so on *that is not necessarily so*? What do I tend to accept as limits concerning what is 'realistically' desirable or possible? How do I accept this, in practice, and in deed, even if I don't do so in thought and in word?

Commitment toward this critical praxis prompts me to reflect on the following questions as well. To what extent does the legacy of the Protestant Ethic continue to effect me, and in what precise form? To what extent is this ethic still normalized and naturalized, and still problematically operative, around me as well as within and upon me? To what extent have I identified with and even helped promote and reinforce the idealization of the notion of 'a calling' and to problematic effect? To what extent have I been caught up within a steel-hard casing of life organized and oriented in terms of valuing the obtaining of money and especially what money can buy–valuing in monetary terms, in terms of price of exchange rather than social utility, including by discounting social and ecological harms? How hard have I worked and how far have I succeeded in casting off this steel-hard casing?

"New Dawn Fades" seems less concerned with mediation per se, than with division, although sites of division represent prospective sites of mediation. These include between past and present, ambition and aspiration versus failure and guilt, present and future/present and no future, suicide and no suicide, and the 'me' the narrator-protagonist perceives himself to be and the 'other than me' 'he' would rather be.

Unlike Weber, Althusser, and Foucault, this song does not theorize what is responsible for these divisions in need of mediation–the song offers no equivalent to a steel-hard casing or an ethic and spirit that have degenerated and ossified, the song offers no equivalent to ideology and ideological interpellation, and the song offers no equivalent to a carcereal continuum and a pervasive exercise of disciplinary power that becomes especially insidious in the form of compulsory normalization. It might make sense, therefore, to propose "New Dawn Fades" represents a 'pre-theoretical' or a 'proto-theoretical' raising of issues, questions, and challenges for theorization.

If so, it is especially worthwhile considering what challenges this song raises for these three theorists. "New Dawn Fades" suggests, contrary to Althusser, at least contrary to what Althusser chooses to highlight as illustrations, that dominant ideology may work not so much by interpellating individuals into positions as subjects where they feel free, at ease, as if everything works and makes sense, and as if they recognize they are included and that they maintain a rightful place within what includes them, but rather by interpellating individuals into positions where they feel they maintain extremely limited opportunity, extremely limited options, to be or do much of anything; as if they don't matter and they can't make themselves matter; and as if they are close to or entirely powerless.

In this connection it is important, I suggest, to theorize 'dominant ideology' as a complex field of dynamically shifting and differentially weighted constituent discourses and practices, which can involve interpellating people into more disparate kinds of positions than Althusser suggests, including, for example, concerning how 'free' in the sense of unique, discrete, autonomous, independent, and in control people experience themselves to be. As I have already suggested, it also makes sense to propose individuals are interpellated in varying degrees of identification with a single subject position, and the impact of this interpellation is in turn always affected by what other subject positions individuals are interpellated into and in what varying degrees in these other instances. "New Dawn Fades" does *not* represent a subject experiencing himself as 'free', or with everything making sense to 'him', including how he fits in, as part of what, and concerning what kinds of social roles he assumes as well as what he contributes in inhabiting these social roles.

It is possible this subject comes across as bearing a closer resemblance to what Foucault theorizes, because even though Foucault posits resistance always exists and is always possible, in any location within a decentered nexus of power relations, Foucault nonetheless theorizes the carceral as continuous with the whole of modern capitalist society, and disciplinary power as maintaining extraordinary capabilities, such as via panopticism. Yet again, like Althusser, even though Foucault theorizes disciplinary power as enforcing subjection, where people willingly accept or resign themselves to considerable limits upon the extent of their freedom, this happens largely uncritically, even largely unconsciously, as does obedience to and conformity with imperatives of normalization, such that most people in these positions do not recognize themselves as so subjected, and as unfree. Weber as well warns against ossification in terms of a steel-hard casing because he believes all too many people are oblivious to this happening. But "New Dawn Fades" represents a subject who is *not* so accepting, resigned, or oblivious.

Another area where 'Ian Curtis and Joy Division', as represented by "New Dawn Fades," does not neatly coincide with the theories of Weber, Althusser, and Foucault, follows from considering how the introspection enacted by this song might make sense in Weberian, Althusserian, and Foucaultian terms. Althusser theorizes ideology in terms of an imaginary representation of an individual's relation to their real conditions of existence, such that what individuals interiorize, identify with, and experience in conscious form they tend to imagine is uniquely theirs, but in actually, this is not only socially shared but also socially produced and socially imposed. Such a theorization suggests the realm of introspection is rife with difficulty, likely proving misleading and mystifying, because it has been shaped by dominant ideology. Foucault suggests much the same, as disciplinary power induces self-subjection and identification with normativity, so what people are introspecting is shaped by disciplinary power and by the normativity that disciplinary power promotes. Weber also focuses upon how predominant forms of socially shared consciousness and common belief maintain deep-rooted influences that are not widely recognized, or understood, and how it has become more difficult to act as subject rather than an object in relation to the spirit of capitalism and the continuing power in relation to it of the Protestant Ethic. Certainly Althusser, Foucault, and Weber all are thinking, and writing critically, resistantly and oppositionally, so it makes sense in turn to imagine many other instances of people doing the same, yet all three propose this is exceedingly hard to do, and might further seem it is all the harder to do so as one who is as troubled, uncertain, resigned, despairing, and indeed suicidal as the subject of "New Dawn Fades" represents 'himself' as being.

Marxist and non-Marxist socialists (and communists) have needed, frequently, to attempt to explain how and why capitalism has proven as incredibly resilient as it has, and Althusser is in significant part joining in that effort with *On the Reproduction of Capitalism: Ideology and Ideological State Apparatuses*. Likewise, in *Discipline and Punish: The Birth of the Prison*, Foucault strives to explain the incredible resilience of the exercise of disciplinary power, the prison, the carcereal, and the drive to normalize. Likewise, in *Protestant Ethic and the Spirit of Capitalism*, Weber focuses similarly on an ethic and a spirit that persists, even through considerable changes in form, as well as on a hardening an ossifying–as a result what these changes have wrought. Althusser nonetheless comes across as more optimistic than "New Dawn Fades," confident in the long-term prospect for success of revolutionary socialist transformation of capitalism into communism. Weber come across as more optimistic as well, because Weber remains hopeful capitalism can be successfully reformed while insistent it maintains many positive features. Foucault in contrast seems to suggest resistance versus the operations of oppressive power is and must be constantly ongoing, while not proposing any telos concerning where resistance can and should lead. Nevertheless, all three critical theorists write out of an at least strongly implicit sense that they can enlighten and in doing so contribute usefully, offering insight that can be put to use in enabling practical engagement and effective efforts at reform, resistance, and transformation. "New Dawn Fades" performatively engages, by dramatically enacting, an encounter that likewise suggests the possibility of struggling onward even when struggle feels hopeless and one is strongly tempted to give up.

Weber, Althusser, and Foucault all focus primarily on processes they are theorizing when and as these work well, including to produce passive, submissive, conformist, and untroubled good subjects, but in "New Dawn Fades" Ian Curtis and Joy Division highlight a much different kind of subject. Perhaps the emergence of this kind of *troubled and alienated subject* is symptomatic of a time in which dominant ideology is experiencing difficulty in winning consent, due to aggravation of contradictions rooted at the level of forces and relations of social production, as in the mid to late 1970s when Britain was experiencing a crisis that preceded the shift from social democracy to neo-liberalism with the election of Margaret Thatcher's government and the beginnings of Thatcherism. In relation to Foucault, the subject in "New Dawn Fades" might likewise make sense as reflecting and

559

responding to a difficulty, even possibly a crisis, in the exercise of disciplinary power and normalization, requiring the development of new modalities to replace outmoded and ineffective modalities, that themselves might have at least in part been exposed and undone in response to growing resistance, just as Foucault recounts happened to the earlier dominant mode of punishment involving torture as public spectacle. For both Althusser and Foucault, the emergence of such a troubled subject might be an at least tenuously positive development and with Weber it might well seem all the more clearly positive, as representing the beginning of what he implicitly calls for near the end of his book: recentering aesthetic and moral values, especially compassion and empathy.

Eight

The song title "Atrocity Exhibition" alludes to JG Ballard's 1970 experimental dystopian science-fiction novel *The Atrocity Exhibition*. In a 2014 interview Ballard accepts Travis Elborough's characterization of his fiction, *The Atrocity Exhibition* and otherwise, as concerned "to explore the fragility of civil society" and as evincing a "preoccupation with social re-gression, de-evolution even" (185) Ballard explains to Elborough he conceives of himself, in his fiction writing, as "an investigator and a sort of early warning system" (188). As Ballard elaborates, "A large part of my fiction tries to analyse what is going on around us, and whether we are much different people from the civilized human beings we imagine ourselves to be" (188). Ian Curtis's lyrics in "Atrocity Exhibition" and elsewhere indicate Curtis shares these thematic interests, and this conception of himself, working through his lyrics and his music, as an investigator and early warning system.

As Hari Kunzu explains, in his introduction to the 2014 edition, *The Atrocity Exhibition* "presents fragments or avatars of a traumatized man," identified by multiple different names, "who is conducting some kind of spun-out scientific experiment, which also takes the form of a lecture or media spectacle," and this same protagonist "is both a researcher and an experimental subject" (xiv). *The Atrocity Exhibition* is particularly disturbing because "It is clinical when, for decency's sake, it should feign emotion" (xiv). According to Kunzu, Ballard is thereby contending proposing that reliance on cultural codes of 'decency' cannot protect readers from facing up to their investment in, responsibility for, and complicity with multiple interconnected forms of violence.

Kunzu interprets *The Atrocity Exhibition* as a warning concerning dangers following automatization, as well as concerning the emergence and development of new "technologies of control" (xvii). According to Kunzu, *The Atrocity Exhibition* is ultimately "fixated on something terrible it can't let go," and as Kunzu quotes Ballard, in a 2007 interview: "To some extent *The Atrocity Exhibition* is an attempt to explain all the terrible violence that I saw around me in the early sixties . . . I think I was trying to look for a new kind of logic that would explain all these events" (quoted xviii-xix).

As I have argued over the course of this book, it makes good sense to interpret the music, as art, of Ian Curtis in particular, within and as part of Joy Division, as sharing this same focus of concern and pursuing this same end. Curtis perceives terrible violence, as well as potential for terrible violence, all around, and is deeply troubled that many if not most others seemingly do not share his perception, or his concern. Curtis interprets lack of perception, ignorance, denial, indifference, callousness, and turning away from even beginning honestly to face up to the pervasiveness of actual and potential terrible violence all around as constituting a yet further form of terrible violence.

In "The Pornography of Science: Curtis, Ballard and Burroughs," Jason Whittaker argues that Ian Curtis, JG Ballard, and William S Burroughs share a common ethos. Not only did Ian Curtis experience an attraction to, and enjoy reading, "'offbeat literature'" of the kind that Ballard and Burroughs wrote, but also their writing "resonated with Curtis's experience living in postwar Macclesfield" (35). Whittaker cites Christopher Partridge's concept of 'occuculture' in exploring this connection among Curtis, Ballard, and Burroughs, with occuculture referring "to hidden cultures and subcultures" that 'offbeat' writers and other artists seek to make contact with through their art. Whittaker interprets Curtis sharing a common concern over the impact of "scientific and technological pornography"–i.e., scientific and technological mediations that produce clinically detached and affectively numbed engagement with 'terrible violence'. As Whittaker explains, "This detachment is frequently encountered in the numb, eerie sound of Joy Division" (39). The music of Joy Division does not uncritically replicates this detachment and desensitization, because this music instead exposes it and subjects it to critical scrutiny: "what Curtis catches in his own *Atrocity Exhibition*, like Ballard, is the pathos that the pornography of science fails to uncover in its strangely blind vision" (40).

Following David Church, Whittaker reminds us "Curtis often referred to himself as an atrocity exhibition, 'speaking like a sideshow barker inviting audience to the spectacle', demonstrating the tensions between a freakish rock star and incidences of his own disability' (40). In other words, Curtis was well aware of how his disability became an object of spectacularly 'pornographic' fascination for audiences, as he publicly performed self-harm in his losing and loss of control, with audiences all too often uncritically enjoying him falling apart right in front of them, for their pleasure, as they remained unaware and unconcerned about the pain he was experiencing–and to which he was testifying. This is how, Whittaker proposes, Curtis makes use of the notion of 'atrocity exhibition' as a means of critique: "An understanding of this atrocity exhibition, the inability to connect to that other, is what Curtis shares with Ballard and, indeed, Burroughs, that in our search for something to stimulate us we are content to watch any act, however despicable–and that this is a condition of the modern, technological world" (40).

The music as art of Ian Curtis and Joy Division challenges us to recognize our complicity, and to take responsibility for what we are complicit with. This means striving to find a way, well aware of how difficult this will be, to break with and move past remaining trapped in an endless cycle of repeatedly doing nothing, or repeatedly doing far too little, or repeatedly doing what little we do far too late to make a meaningful transformative impact–instead only reestablishing, reenforcing, and re-entrenching our complicity alongside our growing guilt and shame over what we keep failing to do.

In "Literary Influences on Joy Division: J.G. Ballard, Franz Kafka, Dostoevsky," Sara Martinez interprets "Atrocity Exhibition," along with other Joy Division songs, as concerned with "four motifs that are recurrent both in the literary texts and in the lyrical compositions" (51). These include first, "'power; with respect to a succession of allusions that emphasize the state's authority over society and the individual"; second, "'control', where there are certain inner forces that overtake an individual's impulses"; third, "the 'trauma', which is a consequence of certain personal situations"; and fourth, "an emotional condition that is inherently related to the rise of a 'psychological dislocation' in which the individual experiences a series of mental deviations that constitute a dissociative disorder" (51-52). "Atrocity Exhibition" Martinez interprets as a song that "exposes some of the most irrational forms of violence that are present in the contemporary word (represented in terms of psychological, emotional or cultural violence)–a series of actions that create an 'atmosphere' that corresponds to Ian's inner state of mind" (58). Curtis's reading shows up as "a vehicle whose main purpose was catharsis through telling powerful stories," while his music, as art, explores an "existent parallelism between the 'fiction' he read and the 'reality' he was living in" (59).

Uwe Schütte, in "'Possessed by a Fury That Burns from Inside: On Ian Curtis's Lyrics," proposes Curtis's lyrics, vocalizations of these, and his performances on stage all suggest a kinship with The Theater of Cruelty of Antonin Artaud. This theater involves the production and performance of an 'atrocity exhibition' as an attempt to exercise a 'shocking' impact upon the audience, to call audiences' attention to "human existence as precarious and fraught with senselessness," and to prompt audiences' attention to experiences of "bodies in pain," violent death and dying, and people, notably young people, suffering acute "distress or confusion" (78).

Mick Middles and Lindsay Reade, in *Torn Apart: The Life of Ian Curtis*, cite "Atrocity Exhibition" as exemplifying how in *Closer* "Hannett pulled Ian's vocals right to the top of the mix, enhancing the intimacy," while also noting the song "featured a hot, exotic Moroccan beat, perversely reminiscent of Can's *Tago Mago*, which rose and fell behind a Curtis voice that beckoned the listener towards the album; a warm, welcoming command: 'This is the way, step inside'" (212-213). Peter Hook's comments on "Atrocity Exhibition," in *Unknown Pleasures: Inside Joy Division*, meanwhile reveal that he and Bernard Sumner switched instruments for the recorded version of this song, with Sumner playing bass guitar and Hook playing guitar. Yet Hook felt shocked and outraged, initially at least, by what Hannett did to his guitar riff: "Martin had fucking melted the guitar with his Marshall Time Waster [Marshall Time Modulator]. Made it sound like someone strangling a cat" (276).

In *Record Play Pause: Confessions of a Post-Punk Percussionist Volume I*, Stephen Morris recalls himself as more immediately enthusiastic about the use of electronic instruments to produce *Closer*, including the song "Atrocity Exhibition": an ARP Omni-2 polyphonic synthesizer, a Transcendent synthesizer, an ARP 2600 synthesizer with sequencer, SDS4 and Synare synth drums, an AMS DMX 15-80 digital delay device, a Marshall Time Modulator (an analog delay-line musical effects device), and a Lexicon Prime Time digital delay device. In a 2011 interview, Morris comments that of all the unusual sounds he contributed as part of Joy Division, "The unusual noise that I like the best is on 'Atrocity Exhibition'. By then, I had a Synare III and a Simmons SDSVI so we got the Synare out and put it through this horrible fuzz box . . . we used to do a track of stuff and not listen to the music. There's noises like a pig being slaughtered . . . that was me!"

Other interesting comments on "Atrocity Exhibition" include musical sound blogger Lex Flexican characterizing the song as "sounding relatively sparse and ambient with almost mechanical drumming," while citing Simon Reynolds as noting, while the bass guitar carried the melody, the guitar "left gaps rather than filling up the group's sound with dense riffage" and that "Steve Morris's drums seemed to circle the rim of a crater." Flexican also finds it worthy of note that "The guitars on Atrocity Exhibition are very sharp and distorted and sit above Ian's vocals." Elsewhere, writing about Ballard's influence upon popular music, Stephen Dowling indicates that although Curtis had already written most of the lyrics to the song prior to reading the entirety of Ballard's book, nevertheless "the song– anchored round the oppressive chorus 'this is the way, step inside'–is still heavily informed by Ballard's tale of a man restaging world events in his mind."

I find this song, and especially its lyrics, reminiscent of Franz Kafka's short story "A Hunger Artist." In this story the protagonist identifies being a hunger artist as an art form that maintains a long, noble tradition. Hunger artists present themselves on display, as public spectacles, while they fast for up to forty days in a row or more. The hunger artist of this story resides, throughout the duration of his fasts, inside a cage that spectators stop by and stare into, occasionally engaging in dialogue with him, while watchers monitor overnight to insure he does not 'cheat', even as he finds the idea insulting that he might do so. Interest in hunger artists declines, however, as the story proceeds, with hunger artistry no longer a fashionable attraction. Even after the hunger artist arranges his transportation to the front of a circus, crowds rush by him to attend the spectacle of a menagerie of animals they now find far more interesting. Eventually the hunger artist is forgotten, and no one updates the sign on his cage indicating the number of consecutive days he has fasted. Attendants one day spy what seems to be an empty cage in front of the circus that could be usefully re-purposed. The hunger artist makes his presence known, even as he barely continues to exist at all. The attendants indicate they admire what he has been doing, and what he has accomplished. But the hunger artist responds they should not do so because he had no choice other than to be a hunger artist. In short, he became a hunger artist because he could never find a food he liked. The hunger artist dies immediately after sharing that self-denigrating comment and is replaced in the cage by a young panther, full of vitality, and the panther becomes a major popular attraction.

"A Hunger Artist" conveys a disturbing portrait of a public numbingly detached, and callously indifferent, to the spectacle of a fellow human being starving himself to a state at which he is severely enfeebled, all the while doing so ostensibly for their entertainment, with what the hunger artist suffers excusable as what he himself has chosen, what he himself desires, his way of creating and sharing 'art'. "A Hunger Artist" portrays not only the fickleness but also the cruelty of taste and fashion. Yet the hunger artist is complicit with his self-presentation as an 'atrocity exhibition', while he shares, in his final statement about how he has lived his life, that what he had been applauded for, before this kind of performance fell out of fashion, was him simply being and doing what he had to be and do because nothing else–no other direction, outlet, vocation, no *calling*–was viable for him. "A Hunger Artist" adds an extra layer of horror in conceiving of an 'atrocity exhibition' where those exhibited seek out and identify with the performance of atrocity upon themselves. The hunger artist's reason for existence becomes starving himself to the point such that he barely exists. "A Hunger Artist" portends a social situation where the only possible escape from spectacular performance of one's own repeated self-harm as entertaining spectacle is self-annihilation.

The title "Atrocity Exhibition," aside from the readily recognizable allusion to Ballard's novel, connotes what continues to seem like what *should not* be brought together: 'atrocity' and 'exhibition' in the form of an 'exhibition of atrocity'. To 'exhibit' is to put on display for others–to attend to, learn from, appreciate, and enjoy. Here we might readily think about exhibits at museums and art galleries, professional conferences, trade shows, and public meetings and official events. 'Exhibition', moreover, tends to connote a larger public display than an 'exhibit' alone, consisting of a multiple constituent 'exhibits'. An 'atrocity exhibition' is disturbing because this implies a curated collection of atrocities is what is put on public display.

According to the online Oxford English Dictionary, 'atrocity' can mean: 1) "Savage enormity, horrible or heinous wickedness"; 2) "Fierceness, sternness, [and] implacability" [a now archaic meaning]; 3) "An atrocious deed; an act of extreme cruelty and heinousness"; and 4) "A very bad blunder, violation of taste or good manners, etc." An atrocity represents something *extremely* bad, and this often is on account of of how far it departs, or seemingly departs, from what is *normally* identified as welcome, desirable, and even acceptable. Once 'atrocity' becomes the focus of 'exhibition', this means the erstwhile *extremely* bad is now *normally* accepted, even now normally *valued*. It means 'savage enormity, horrible wickedness' and 'extreme cruelty and heinousness' are put on display for public consumption–for public enjoyment and entertainment.

Stanza one of "Atrocity Exhibition" proceeds as follows: "Asylums with doors open wide"/"Where people had paid to see inside"/"For entertainment they watch his body twist"/"Behind his eyes he says, 'I still exist'." This opening stanza conjures association with the former predominance of asylums as the places to which 'the mentally ill', 'the intellectually disabled', and 'the seriously to severely physically disabled' were long consigned and confined. Revelations of routine and systematic atrocity committed within these 'total institutions' (as sociologist Erving Goffman characterizes them), sparked protest movements that led to their closure and to release of their 'prisoners'. 'Outpatient treatment' replaced 'inpatient treatment' as the predominant norm with 'care in the community' becoming the new normative ideal. Yet because 'care in the community' has all too often been inadequately funded and otherwise insufficiently supported, people with mental and physical disabilities have often struggled to find the assistance they need to get by. Many have ended up, by default, in prison.

This result has led to criticism of reformers who played leading roles in advocating for closure of asylums and 'liberation' of those 'imprisoned' in asylums, with critics charging reformers with responsibility for the troubles mentally and physically disabled people suffer today. Yet those critics too conveniently forget–or too conveniently ignore–the atrocities commonplace in asylums when these were predominant. And they at least imply fellow human beings are better off living lives confined and controlled by others, maintaining little to no room for autonomy and self-determination, excluded from involvement and participation in the 'normal life' of the greater society; precluded from accessing and exercising resources consensually considered indispensable to living decently–and especially well–within this greater society; and stigmatized and ostracized as inferior, deficient, and unworthy. It is not reformers, and not reforming movements, that are responsible for the inadequacies of assistance and accommodation provided people with mental and physical disabilities today, but rather national, regional, and local governments, state agencies at all levels, and the greater public as well as those in positions at the heights of power in private firms and enterprises. All of the latter are responsible for not providing 'care in the community' sufficient to meet the extent of the need for this care.

This opening stanza calls upon us to envision being welcomed as spectators to venture inside asylums where the 'freaks' confined within provide entertainment for spectators by displaying, and acting out, their 'freakish' 'deviation' from 'the normal', including, as explicitly here suggested, in the form of epileptic seizures or in response to ECT (electroconvulsive therapy–long a routine form of psychiatric treatment for a a great variety of mental, and physical, health conditions in 'asylums'). The last line of this opening stanza–"Behind his eyes he says, 'I still exist'–is especially haunting, as it insinuates these spectators are complicit in dehumanization of fellow human beings, with the latter people treated as objects not subjects, who do *not* exist as people deserving the right to self-determination, self-control, and self-agency. These lyrics imply a spectator would need to be unusually perceptive–as well as unusually sympathetic–to look "Behind his eyes" to recognize what he is, from this location, silently saying.

Next follows the initial iteration of the repeated refrain, here in the form of a chorus: "This is the way, step inside"/"This is the way, step inside/"This is the way, step inside"/"This is the way, step inside." This refrain conjures the image of someone much like 'a carnival barker', or perhaps an agent of sex shop in a red light district, seeking to attract potential customers to 'sample the wares' within. Those eliciting attendance at strip clubs and gun shows represent other comparable examples this invitation calls to mind. Once more, inviting those addressed to 'step inside' underscores their relative mobility, freedom of choice, and freedom to exercise self-determination versus those they will meet, on display, when they step inside.

"This is the way, step inside" resonates with Althusser's illustration of how we might analogically conceive of ideological interpellation as a form of hailing that Althusser invites us to consider in terms of an imaginary piece of street theater. Ideology hails us by telling us 'to step inside', to step inside of ideology, and by showing us 'this is the way', this is the direction to follow in order to accept the position ideology sets forth for us. Ideology is what we hear, and follow, via the ISAs–and in particular via their concrete agents and specific representatives, who function as the equivalent of 'the carnival barker' in these lines. Likewise, with Foucault, the disciplines effectively communicate this message–'This is the way, step inside'– to individuals as we learn to identify with disciplinary power, and in particular to subordinate ourselves to what we internalize as the expectations of a panoptic authority, chiefly consisting of prescriptions concerning how to act and behave normally and proscriptions concerning how not to act and behave abnormally. In addition, with Weber, the spirit of capitalism that continues infused with the persistent influence of the Protestant Ethic also effectively invites individuals to follow and enter–'This is the way, step inside'–as we identify with the need to work, and work hard, at 'a calling', and especially at a calling to increase our material wealth, measured in monetary terms. Individuals follow this 'beckoning', Weber warns, to the point where we accept enclosure within 'a steel-hard casing' such that we become 'narrow specialists without minds, pleasure-seekers without hearts', exemplars of a 'mechanized ossification' of the human spirit into a degenerative state of empty 'nothingness'.

Stanza three reads as follows: "In arenas he kills for a prize/Wins a minute to add to his life/But the sickness is drowned by cries for more/Pray to God, make it quick, watch him fall." This stanza recalls gladiatorial combat in Ancient Roman times, but also comparable recent situations, including in sports today, where athletes endanger their health. For example, considerable attention has recently focused on how many contact sports lead to serious brain injury, in particular in the form of CTE–Chronic traumatic encephalopathy–and how this already develops at young ages. Many contact sports, over centuries now, have involved not only the high risk but also the virtual certain result that many so engaged will suffer serious physical–and mental–harm, yet spectators have often applauded the most aggressive and destructive kinds of violence, such as 'wicked hits', knocking the opponent out of the game, leaving blood on the field or court, and literal fights breaking out among players–and fans.

We might also here recognize other jobs, careers, and professions that are extremely dangerous, and that involve major risk to health and well-being. Military soldiers and others engaged on the front lines in war; police officers; firefighters; nurses, doctors and medical technicians (especially under conditions such as what COVID-19 has brought about); factory and warehouse workers spending considerable time around dangerous chemicals or in situations where they are pressured to meet output targets in ways that result in damage to their health; prison guards; and many further categories of workers fit this characterization. Just as with gladiators, it is often the case that employers, managers, and others exercising authority over these workers in the work they do, as well as customers, clients, and the general public applaud those who take the greatest risks, including to their own health and well-being, while pressuring other workers to do the same.

The following two stanzas reiterate the refrain, once again in the form of a chorus, the first repeating it four times in a row and the second beginning with four iterations solely of "This is the way" before following that with four iterations of "This is the way, step inside." The extensive repetition of this line and especially the initial phrase reinforces a sense of an overwhelming incentive to follow, such that the process feels increasingly automatized. Here I am reminded of how ideology works, at its most effective, as Althusser portrays, and that is when it is not perceived or recognized as ideology at all but rather 'the way things are' or 'what has to be'. The ideal situation, for the dominant class, transpires as individuals virtually automatically 'follow the way' to 'step inside' of ideology and thereby become subject of and to ideology. It is unnecessary to force people into identification with positions where they are subjugated, oppressed, and exploited. Foucault likewise theorizes disciplinary power works best when those subject to it in effect agree to subject themselves to it, internalizing its expectations and requirements, while always acting as if they are being observed by an authority with the power to punish them if they don't go along and fall in line, even if they have no idea precisely when this is happening. Foucault also theorizes the process becomes productive as it operates within and across major social institutions, combining together to form a carcereal continuum. And Weber proposes that by the time of the victorious stage of modern capitalism, the spirit of capitalism, including the continuing influence of the Protestant Ethic within and upon this spirit, has become something most people largely resign themselves to and with which they passively identify, because no alternative social system is imaginable. At the same time, work is increasingly less often pursued as a 'calling' and more often instead as an inescapable necessity.

Stanza six continues next as follows: "You'll see the horrors of a faraway place/ Meet the architects of law face to face/See mass murder on a scale you've never seen/And all the ones who try hard to succeed." In this stanza the lyrics expand their scope of reference, suggesting atrocities of imperialist conquest. This stanza resonates with Althusser's theorization of the law as an instrument of repression *and* ideology that serves to maintain and reproduce exploitation; genocide; lack of social mobility; and perpetual precarity among those positioned at or near the bottom in class terms. Spectators are nudged closer to recognizing we are at risk of joining those on display as victims of atrocity for the entertainment of others, and, perversely enough, for our own entertainment–i.e., entertainment derived at the expense of our own humiliation. What seems all too often like an 'atrocity' that happens in 'a faraway place' in fact happens to people in many respects much like 'us'. When we falsely imagine, as Ballard warns, that we, where we are at, are safe from ever experiencing 'atrocity' ourselves, we are poorly prepared to deal with the impact when this happens where we are at.

What made the terrorist attacks on 9/11 so shocking for many Americans is it seemed hard to believe this kind of tragedy could ever happen 'inside' of this country, even as many of these same Americans readily accepted the same was all too likely to happen, even to happen often, elsewhere 'far away'. Despite how extensive mass shootings, and mass killings, continue to be in the US, many Americans still find it hard to imagine this ever happening in their community, at their workplace, in their schools, and in their streets–especially if they come from relatively privileged social positions along lines of race and class. The same is the case when someone close by is revealed to be guilty of sexual violence–or guilty of domestic neglect and abuse. When people are sheltered from what is happening, even right near them, they tend to remain oblivious to what others' conditions of existence are like, and find it hard to believe others in their own community are suffering, for instance, from food insecurity, homelessness, inability to afford rent or mortgage payments, lack of means to pay for health care for themselves and their family, and insufficient funds to pay fees required so their children can participate in school activities and club sports.

The lyrics to "Atrocity Exibition," however, depict spectators looking at disparity and deprivation not with guilt, shame, and a determination to overcome it, but rather with delight, finding it entertaining. These lyrics resonate with so-called 'poverty porn', exploitation of images and stories of 'other people' in situations of hardship–including media productions that make fun of people who are poor, working class, or who have otherwise not enjoyed opportunity to access and exercise social resources such as quality higher education, the ability to travel to other countries, and direct experience of multicultural diversity.

The lyrics in this stanza further call to mind how often many people readily think in terms of 'us versus them' concerning those suspected, charged, and convicted of crimes, demanding anyone fitting these categories be punished severely, rejecting any sympathetic concern about atrociously inhumane conditions prevailing within many US and UK prisons, or about atrociously inhumane lack of assistance ex-prisoners receive to do anything other than turn to crime once again to be able to survive and subsist.

These lyrics also call to mind how many people readily support their country going to war without themselves needing to be directly involved, to risk or sacrifice anything as part of this war effort. Such people may enthusiastically support tactics such as drone attacks because these appear 'surgically precise' in limiting casualties 'on our side' while in fact resulting in death and destruction far beyond 'taking out' only clearly identifiable 'targets' 'on the other side'.

These lyrics ask us to imagine taking delight, taking pleasure, in looking head on, at these sites of violence in action, and not just supporting them because we don't have to look at them and because, as Eyal Press chronicles in his book *Dirty Work: Essential Jobs and the Hidden Toll of Inequality in America*, other people are 'taking care of this dirty work'–this morally unseamly work–such that we don't have to face up to what this work actually is like.

These lines in the lyrics of "Atrocity Exhibition" prompt us, yet further, to think about movies, TV dramas, popular songs, and even video games where no critical context is hinted at in representations of violent destruction, especially massive killing, and where we are invited, even encouraged, to identify uncritically with the agents of this violent destruction, including with the agents of massive killing. As controversy surrounding how to interpret and evaluate fictional works such as Ballard's *The Atrocity Exhibition* illustrates, a fine line often distinguishes an explicit portrayal of extreme and pervasive violence consumed as source of obscene pleasure, versus portrayal of the same that provokes critical reflection on what it might indeed mean to arrive at this state of obscene enjoyment as well as what if anything can and should be done about it. "Atrocity Exhibition" communicates awareness of this fine line, even as the song identifies with a classic avant-gardist aim of shocking audiences by representing extreme violence–and by representing consumption of extreme violence as entertainment. The latter callousness is itself part and parcel of 'atrocity', and especially of the 'exhibition of atrocity', that pervades late capitalist society.

After another stanza once more reiterating the refrain four times, as a chorus, the final–eighth stanza–proceeds as follows: "And I picked on the whims of a thousand or more/Still pursuing the path that's been buried for years/All the dead wood from jungles and cities on fire/Can't replace or relate, can't release or repair/Take my hand and I'll show you what was and will be." These lines are more elliptical in terms of what they suggest we make of them, than what has preceded, but these lines suggest the narrator-protagonist is stepping back from his 'pretend role' as a greeter or usher, or host or master of ceremonies, of an atrocity exhibition. Here he is revealing this was a 'pretend role' and he now explains he has been seeking to show us a continuity of atrocity across an extensive duration of time and expanse of space, that is all too often not recognized as such. The aim is to prompt us to become cognizant of this scale of atrocity, and shake us out of complacency. This is one way I make sense of how to interpret the final line–"Take my hand and I'll show you what was and will be." The narrator-protagonist here assumes the role Ballard identifies as his, in his fiction: scout, investigator, and early warning system.

Yet these lyrics also suggest the narrator-protagonist conceives it might be too late to act as a warning system. "Can't replace or relate, can't release or repair" suggests the narrator-protagonist can't turn away from facing up to the sweep of violence he has recounted and alluded to, but he offers no confidence he, 'we', or anyone might be able to counter it, because what has been destroyed can't be replaced or repaired. Nonetheless he still can't release himself, or 'us', from facing up to what has happened, is happening, and will happen. This is a bleak conclusion, suggesting we must look into the face of horror, unflinchingly, registering it for as horrific as it is, knowing all the while that the horror cannot be overcome. Alternately, the "path that's been buried for years" and which seemingly is being here unburied by 'picking on' "the whims of a thousand or more" suggests struggling on,

568

however daunting, against the perpetuation, and the magnification, of atrocity, as well as against its promotion and celebration.

"Atrocity Exhibition" is one of Joy Division's longer songs, running at over six minutes. The song contains eight vocal passages, four verse sections and four chorus sections, in line with eight corresponding stanzas of written lyrics, and six instrumental sections, including an opening instrumental section, three instrumental bridge sections, and a closing instrumental bridge section. More specifically, the song divides into sections as follows:

Section 1. Opening instrumental section: 0:00-0:45. The drums sound first with a single-measure pattern that is repeated continuously from this point forward throughout the song followed next by the 'strangled' guitar (the heavily modulated and altered sound of Peter Hook's guitar) and then the bass guitar joins. Studio-synthesized electronic and other innovative effects suggest a jungle or other wilderness setting, or perhaps a remote setting just outside of, just at the edge of, a larger urban center–perhaps a rural fairgrounds where a carnival or circus is taking place. Eventually, as this opening section proceeds, the strangled guitar introduces the melody, shortly before the beginning of the first vocal section, and then continues playing this melodic pattern in accompaniment with the vocal in that section. This section establishes the atmosphere: distorted, discordant, dissonant, strangled, frazzled, buzzsawed, but with a strong and incessantly repetitive beat and groove. This section contributes toward initially defining the parameters of the situation and contours of the location in what feels like an imaginary transportation to a situation and location involving a clash of the familiar and the unfamiliar that enables a defamiliarization of the familiar simultaneous with a refamiliarization of the unfamiliar.

Section 2. First vocal verse section: 0:46-1:00. The vocal picks up the melody from the strangled guitar and takes the lead in sounding it. The vocal, like the strangled guitar right before it, does not traverse a wide interval range nor does in vary much in terms of register or other qualities of vocal delivery but rather conveys an insistently repetitive melodic line with pronounced emphasis on upward movements in pitch and on extending the singing of words, and syllables, across multiple beats and notes at the end of phrases and especially the end of lines. This section feels as if it begins to sketch the scene and to detail the canvas.

Section 3. First vocal chorus section: 1:01-1:17. This section follows immediately without a break from the preceding section. The chorus takes the form of a built-up refrain that in terms of its melodic line follows closely, in terms of sequences of pitches and note lengths, with the melodic line in the immediately preceding verse section. But in this chorus the vocal emphasizes a rising in pitch as well as a holding and extending of the singing of single words, and single syllables, at and across subsequent pitches, at the end of phrases, and especially at the end of lines–all more so than in the verse. This section feels as if it involves the vocalist pretending to assume the guise of a carnival barker in beckoning us to follow, enter, and witness the exhibition of atrocity 'he' will show us 'within'.

Section 4. First instrumental bridge section: 1:18-1:46. This section involves lots of variation in the modulation and 'strangulation' of the guitar sound while the bass guitar and drum patterns remain steady, and additional studio-synthesized electronic and other studio-fabricated sound effects add increasing color and texture. The guitar continues to sound strangled–highly distorted/discordant/dissonant. Again, the guitar sounds combined with studio effects suggest a jungle or another kind of wilderness, or a remote location at the edge of an urban center, suggestive of carnival or circus situated in a setting that conveys to audiences a palpable feeling of strangeness, even before they 'enter the tent'. And this coincides, yet again, with preparation for confronting a clash of the familiar and the unfamiliar that enables a defamiliarization of the familiar simultaneous with a refamiliarization of the unfamiliar. The feeling here supports the suggestion of the lyrics that what we are here invited to witness, as we follow our guide and 'enter' by 'stepping inside', is something that already has been widely visible, audible, and tangible, if we have been paying attention, and which seemingly many have been but without registering shock, let alone horror, but rather responding to as entertainment. This section reestablishes the parameters of the situation and the contours of the location into which the song calls us to imaginarily project–or introject–ourselves.

Section 5. Second vocal verse section: 1:47-2:02. This section incorporates and follows sonic patterns much the same as the first vocal verse section, and contributes a further sketching of the scene and detailing of the canvas.

Section 6. Second vocal chorus section: 2:03-2:18. This section, likewise, incorporates and follows sonic patterns much the same as the first vocal chorus section. Here again we hear the vocalist pretending to assume the guise of a carnival barker in beckoning us to follow, enter, and witness the exhibition of atrocity 'he' will show us 'within'.

Section 7. Second instrumental bridge section: 2:19-2:40: This section, again, incorporates and follows sonic patterns much the same as the preceding instrumental bridge section. And again this section reestablishes the parameters of the situation and the contours of the location into which the song calls us to imaginarily project–or introject–ourselves.

Section 8. Third vocal chorus section: 2:41-3:09. Notably this section is twice as long as other chorus sections, and in the initial four vocal lines only the first phrase of the refrain is sung, with more emphatic intent yet closer to an intimately whispering mode of beckoning appeal. The vocalist pretending to assume the guise of a carnival barker takes on a more insinuating edge, that can be interpreted in multiple ways, including mocking or shaming the spectator while suggesting the opposite more intently beckoning the spectator to follow 'his' lead and step inside.

Section 9. Third instrumental bridge section: 3:10-3:17. This section offers a short interlude that briefly reestablishes the parameters of the situation and the contours of the location into which the song calls us to imaginarily project–or introject–ourselves.

Section 10. Third vocal verse section: 3:18-3:33. This vocal verse section largely incorporates and follows the same sonic patterns as the previous vocal verse sections. Again, this section contributes by sketching the scene and detailing the canvas, but with a heightened intensity and an exaggerated motion.

Section 11. Fourth vocal chorus section: 3:34-3:50: Again, this section contributes much the same as with previous vocal chorus sections, and once again we hear the vocalist pretending to assume the guise of carnival barker, who invites us to follow 'him' and 'to step inside'.

Section 12. Fourth instrumental bridge section: 3:51-4:33. This section lasts longer than previous instrumental bridge sections and involves a notable change in density of instrumentation with the guitar dropping out eventually as the section proceeds, and then reemerging from the background. This section once more, and yet further, contributes toward defining the parameters of the situation and the contours of the location in what feels like an imaginary transportation to a situation and location involving a clash of the familiar and the unfamiliar that enables a defamiliarization of the familiar simultaneous with a refamiliarization of the unfamiliar. And in this section we hear sounds and sound patterns suggestive of additional nuance–and menace.

Section 13. Fourth vocal verse section: 4:34-4:52. This section varies in terms of the sonic patterns it incorporates and follows versus the preceding vocal verse sections. Here the vocal comes across as more distanced and more overtly critical concerning what we have encountered so far, and with elements of sadness and despair more pronounced. Here it feels as if the vocalist is stepping back and away from 'his' previous assumption of the guise of carnival barker in order to comment critically on what has transpired, on what is happening, on what it might mean, and on what it might portend.

Section 14. Final instrumental section: 4:53-6:03. This section is longer yet again, with lots of emphasis on strangled guitar, complimentary sound effects, and the steadily repeated drum and bass guitar patterns. The overall sound mix gradually drops down to what we hear as a slow snaky whispering meets whistling electronically synthesized sound emerging prominently near the end. This section once more contributes toward defining the parameters of the situation and the contours of the location in what feels like an imaginary transportation to a situation and location involving a clash of the familiar and the unfamiliar that enables a defamiliarization of the familiar simultaneous with a refamiliarization of the unfamiliar. Eventually in dropping down and out the sound mix continues nonetheless to suggest the listener remains enveloped–implicated and complicit to the point of being trapped–within much the same situation and at much the same location as has been introduced and elaborated over the course of the preceding sections of the song.

The sound of Stephen Morris's drumming in "Atrocity Exhibition" is frequently characterized as 'Moroccan-style', although Morris does not use traditional Moroccan clay drums. Morris has shared he made use of five toms and two synth drums and collectively these contribute, along with Martin Hannett's production, to the drum sound on "Atrocity Exhibition." What is especially notable is the repetition of the same pattern across every measure throughout the song, and this pattern involves a feeling of a rolling sequence of successive strikes that sounds much like Morris is playing hand drums, such as bongos and tablas–or Moroccan clay drums. On an initial listen it sounds to me as if beats two and three receive three strikes versus beats one and four receiving one strike, or that beats two and three receive three times as many strikes as beats one and four. Songsterr.com offers a drum tab for "Atrocity Exhibition" that suggests emulating Morris's drumming on this song by following this pattern: One eighth note followed by two sixteenth notes followed by two eighth notes followed by four sixteenth notes on a first drum followed by four sixteenth notes on a second drum, and then repeating this same pattern throughout every measure of the song. But since, as Morris indicates, in an interview with *Drum Magazine*, he worked with five toms and two snares to create the distinctive drum sound on "Atrocity Exhibition," what we are hearing on the recorded version of this song with *Closer* is an array of drums, as well as likely a pattern of strikes across these drums, more elaborate than even Songsterr.com's drum tab suggests. Nevertheless, the same pattern is contained within a single measure and repeated in every measure of the song. Moroccan-style drumming does, according to multiple sources, involves a swinging, circling, hypnotically repetitive quality, and we do hear that quality with Morris's drumming on "Atrocity Exhibition," with this drum pattern standing out as notably different than others he plays on other Joy Division songs.

Bernard Sumner's bass guitar sounds relatively quiet and contributes primarily by supporting the drums in establishing the groove. The bass guitar here feels as if it noodles quietly along, following a repeated, short, counter-melodic pattern, that involves only a slight movement in pitch. Peter Hook's guitar does sound heavily modified in pitch and tone, resembling yes, as Hook suggests, a strangled sound, that is distorted, discordant, and dissonant, while also sounding, as Morris suggests, like a buzzsaw. But this guitar is a prominent contributor throughout the song to both the melodic and harmonic fill layers. Ian Curtis's vocal does not sound overly treated and is most notable for its tight interval range and close use of a single register, as well as for common features of Curtis's vocalizations–notably lengthening, holding, and extending at the end of phrases and especially lines while periodically and at pivotal moments incorporating an insistent reaching up in pitch with a combined increase in volume. The vocal carries the melody when sounding, supported in accompanying roles by the guitar and bass guitar. Studio-synthesized electronic effects and other studio-fabricated sound effects add to color, and texture–to harmonic fill.

Different listeners, working with different recorded versions of this song, using different playback resources, will hear the constitution of the soundbox differently, and this also will be affected by people's training and experience in doing this kind of listening, as well as according to age and condition of their hearing, but I will share what I hear, again working with the same playback resources I described in chapter two, and in this case, once more, working with the 2007 London Records remastered CD version of *Closer*, while also taking into account differences in what I hear listening through headphones versus listening without headphones. I hear the drums enter from both sides, slightly below center, to the edges of the soundbox, but close to the front. The guitar sound seems to come from somewhat closer to the center than the drums, yet slightly further back than the drums in the soundbox, close to the same horizontal location within the soundbox, and from both sides, as well as shifting positions from side to side, up and down, and nearer versus further to the front. The bass guitar sounds as if it comes from yet further back and lower down as well as pushed to the sides. The vocal sounds as if it is located higher, at the center, and close to the front of the soundbox. This seems like a strikingly narrow soundbox, with all of the principal instruments other than the vocal seemingly situated close together along a lengthy horizontal line. The drums and the vocal are quite prominent yet the guitar is also certainly nearly as prominent as well, and in instrumental sections equally prominent to the drums. The bass guitar sounds closest to a backgrounded and complimentary instrument, yet remains essential to the texture, especially without the overall sound mix including a conventional bass drum–or a conventional snare drum and hi-hat.

The structure and instrumentation in "Atrocity Exhibition" work together to suggest we are encountering a defamiliarization of what is in many respects already familiar to us–or should be already familiar to us–as well as a refamiliarization of something that remains unfamiliar to us, perhaps because it is difficult and disturbing to face up to, directly and honestly, yet is always already closely proximate to us and with which we are always already inextricably interlinked. The structure and instrumentation in "Atrocity Exhibition" forces us to confront the regularity and persistence of atrocity, and especially its exhibition, which underscores our implication–including by emphasizing how messy and ugly the perpetuation of atrocity and the clamor for its exhibition is, has been, and will continue to be.

With Weber, a point of connection here involves his at least tentative suggestion that valorization of work, working, working hard, pursuing work as a calling, pursuing work and working as ends in themselves, and earning one's just deserts entirely according to how hard and how efficiently one works, in the 'victorious' stage of modern capitalism, has become increasingly mendacious, increasingly a lie. Under these conditions, this valorization exhibits–and celebrates–what runs the serious risk of becoming an atrocity through stultification of what it means to be a human being, especially in terms of sense and sensibility, as well as in terms of affect and morality. "Atrocity Exhibition," however, extends beyond Weber's culminating misgivings, concerns, and even fears to suggest all of these *have been realized*, and with even far more deleterious ramifications than Weber posits near the end of *Protestant Ethic and the Spirit of Capitalism*. Weber is more overtly concerned with what the relentless pursuit of money and what can be obtained through money does to those engaged in that pursuit than he is to the impact on those who are victimized in the course of such pursuit, exploited as mere means to ends. Nevertheless, it is plausible to argue that atrocities can emerge and develop as manifestations of perverse consequences from identifying with and adhering to the Protestant Ethic as this infuses the spirit of capitalism–leading, at its worst, to methodically rationalized confinement and constraint, and injuring and killing of people, with many acting if they have been 'called' to do this kind of work. The Nazis remain notorious for bringing to bear a methodically rational approach to how they treated prisoners in concentration camps. But many other examples of methodically rational approaches toward commission of atrocities readily apply as well, such as: workplaces where workers are subject to constant surveillance and relentless pressure to go faster and not allowed toilet breaks; overpolicing of target neighborhoods and communities, among people of color, where residents are subject to frequent stop and search, and where criminal charges are issued frequently for even the smallest incidences of perceived 'disorder'; drone strikes in war zones that make use of sophisticated technology to determine targets according to the observations made by military officers monitoring screens located thousands of miles away; and decisions by major capitalist corporations to streamline, cut corners, and effectively write off the prospective cost of 'externalities' in the form of environmental damage, damage to workers' health, and even damage to consumers from unsafe products, when doing so enables higher profits.

"Atrocity Exhibition" leads us to consider another direction in which dominant ideology works, in modern capitalist society, beyond the specific examples Althusser himself offers, and this involves interpellation of individuals as subjects who not only identify with commission of atrocity, recast to appear otherwise within ideology, but also who willingly carry out the work of committing atrocity, of perpetrating and perpetuating atrocrity, including on massive and expanded scales. In other words, individuals are interpellated as subjects who participate within the commission of atrocities, versus other human beings, and versus other forms of life and the larger natural environment, including in the jobs they do, including in the lifestyles they lead, including in the products they buy and consume, including in the waste they generate and how they dispose of it, and including in their indifference to and unconcern about what is being done in their name to support and sustain their material position.

Foucault's theorization of the carcereal, continuous with the entirety of modern society, where virtually all of social life is continuous with life in prison, resonates with "Atrocity Exhibition" insofar as Foucault suggests atrocities are everywhere around us, and many of us are both victims and perpetrators. In connection with *Discipline and Punish: The Birth of the Prison*, "Atrocity Exhibition" emphasizes how people can and do become effective jailers, guards, and wardens of others, and become, as Eyal Press characterizes actual prison guards in *Dirty Work: Essential Jobs and the Hidden Toll of Inequality in America*, 'the other prisoners'. In contrast however with Foucault, "Atrocity Exhibition" makes sense as closer akin to Guy Debord's Situationist theorization of late capitalist society as a 'society of the spectacle', where individuals experience social life as a concatenation of spectacles, spectacular images and spectacular displays for purposes of consumption–and especially entertaining consumption. Likewise, "Atrocity Exhibition" makes sense, in contrast with the idea of a panoptic society, as suggesting a state of affairs closer akin to one in in which people are fascinated with *looking at power and at the powerful*, and also deliberately publicly display themselves for others to look at through social media and elsewhere on the internet. In other words, with exhibition of atrocity, produced for purposes of popular entertainment, power makes itself visible, audible, and tangible in its exercise, in its display and performance, as we are invited to applaud this exercise, as its spectators, suggesting a circumstance closer to the torture as public spectacle Foucault describes in detail at the beginning of *Discipline and Punish: The Birth of the Prison* yet proceeds to argue has been superseded in modern practices of criminal punishment.

"Atrocity Exhibition" increases in volume at the beginning of the song as the bass guitar and the guitar join the drums. Throughout the song the guitar varies in degree of loudness, in relation to flashes, sparks, flares, and bursts added to sequences of notes and chords, while it occasionally drops out or drops down, moving to a softer position in the background, yet tending to become louder in instrumental as opposed to vocal sections. The vocal feels louder as it rises in pitch and in chorus as opposed to verse sections. The bass guitar is the softest of the principal instrumental sound sources while the drums remain steady in volume and always loud enough to make their presence felt. The culminating hissing electronic noise varies in loudness. What we have here are striking variations in loudness, helping contribute toward conveying an unsettling feeling, or a feeling of being unsettled, on account of being forced to re-experience the familiar and that which is often accepted largely unconsciously, or at least largely unquestioningly, in unfamiliar terms. Increases in volume contribute a feeling of threat, and when volume decreases, this is also feels ominous because it feels uncertain how long the decrease will last and what it portends.

The time signature is, as is commonplace, in Joy Division and most other rock music, 4/4. The tempo is between 126-131 bpm, depending on whose estimate you accept, which makes this song slower than average for Joy Division. "Atrocity Exhibition" maintains a highly regular rhythmic foundation established by the drums and supported by the bass guitar, and with the repeated drum pattern involving a series of rolling sixteenth notes, it feels like a sweeping, swinging, or circling rhythm. The guitar works closely with and off of the beat as does the vocal, which reinforces a feeling of regularity amidst what otherwise, especially by way of the sounds of the guitar and studio effects, as well as by way of the content of the lyrics, accentuates disturbance. With the drums, given the number involved in conveying the sound here, it is not surprising the sweeping rolls encompass slight movements up and down in pitch, moving first up and second down. The guitar pitch often feels as if it is staying in place, or oscillating somewhat wildly about the same pitch, while periodic melodic lines convey a sense of regularly patterned movement. With the vocal the most pronounced movements in pitch are up at ends of phrases and lines, especially in chorus sections, although these are typically preceded, especially in verse sections, by an intervening dip down in pitch even as pitch subsequently rises higher than the starting point at the beginning of the line, by the end of the line, and even as the vocal stays in place to a significant degree, especially in the last verse section. The bass guitar line tends to move upward, more pronouncedly, before dropping down and out quickly at the end.

Curtis's vocal delivery in "Atrocity Exhibition" is clearly foregrounded at the top and to the front of the soundbox, and includes his characteristic lengthening/holding/extending of sung words and syllables at the ends of phrases and especially lines, including doing so across successive pitches. He does vary intonation as he adopts a more intimate tone in the third chorus, closer but not quite reaching that of whispering into an ear while continuing to sing and not speak. With the fourth vocal verse passage not only do we hear less notable movement in pitch but also a quieter and more distant-sounding delivery. Curtis's vocal sounds somewhat darkened while we also always hear this as singing that little resembles speaking or sprechesgang even if he never comes close to belting or soaring.

The most interesting timbre in "Atrocity Exhibition" is that of the guitar, which elides with that of studio sound effects. I have already described the timbre with a number of analogies, including as suggested by Peter Hook and Stephen Morris, but I will add here in terms of sustain, the timbre is dark, noisy, hard to characterize as either hollow or full, hard to characterize as either rich or sparse, beating, wavering, and inharmonic; the attack is noisy and dark; and the pitch is wavering as well.

Variations in loudness add to a sense of the song engaging in defamiliarizing what it confronts, which might make sense, in relation to Weber, as calling into question blind spots and dangerous trajectories in the victorious stage of modern capitalism, especially concerning what the spirit of capitalism has become and what has happened to the continued yet transformed influence of the Protestant Ethic within it. If we are attending to what is encased or encaged in this song we are also attending to the exhibition of encasing/encagement for the purposes of entertainment, or a similar kind of fascinated consumption. Here, we might be reminded of how drivers often tend to slow down, to 'rubberneck', to catch a glimpse of a traffic accident, both wanting and not wanting to see it, or how often many people feel compelled, even again while in part not wanting to do so, to stand outside to witness, from a relatively safe distance, a fire in progress or another 'spectacular' disaster. And we can think of how many people become obsessed with scenes, and stories, of killings, including mass killings, or the killing of someone famous–or the suicide of someone famous–as well as with conspiracy theories involving elaborate diabolical plots supposedly involving commission of enormous atrocity. The ups and downs of celebrities struggling with addiction, relationship breakdowns, and various other kinds of strife also become focuses of considerable popular attention and interest. But even 'hard luck' stories, and stories that depict people seemingly 'heroically overcoming' substantial obstacles, are related to what I am addressing here, as many are strongly attracted to accounts of people struggling against figurative encasings, or encagings, finding ways to break free. War itself, and crime–especially violent crime, and in particular murder–are and long have been staples of entertainment, in literature, film, television, music, theater, and other art forms. Moreover, pushing the boundaries in representing atrocity often leads to greater attention and interest. Another connection has to do with how much of 'the news', at least 'mainstream news coverage', no matter in what form or what level or through what medium, tends to focus on violent impacts and tragic losses, so much so that 'human interest stories' provide virtually the only 'relief' from what can feel like a relentless depiction of atrocity upon atrocity.

Yet many atrocities are, in effect, 'hidden in plain sight', such as the extent of poverty in the US, that I discussed earlier in this chapter, and such as violence all too many Black and Brown individuals and communities face on a virtual daily basis, especially from representatives of the state; homelessness and hunger; inadequate resources to help people suffering from serious mental distress; mass incarceration, in particular of poor Black and Brown people; sexual violence and the threat of sexual violence all too many girls and women need to contend with, every day; lack of accessible and especially affordable care for elderly as well as disabled people, especially in the home, along with low rates of compensation for care workers; interns working full-time jobs for no pay while struggling to survive this process in order to minimally qualify to pursue a career in many vocational and especially professional fields; 'gig economy' workers who despite being identified as independent contractors maintain little to no control over the rates they charge, and who must cover the total cost of insurance and maintenance for the vehicles they drive in doing their work; people who must work 'part-time' jobs with low pay, no benefits, and no security–or people working zero hour contract jobs; and people living in war-devastated regions of the world or forced to flee in desperation from these regions, or from regions otherwise suffering from social and political instability, natural disaster, and inadequate resources to support the numbers of people attempting to live in these regions–and who then face considerable hostility, after exceptionally dangerous journeys, from people in wealthier countries to which the former turn in seeking refuge and asylum. These become 'atrocities' because of the extent of precariousness people in these situations all too often face, because the numbers of these people in these situations are as high as they are, and because these situations become entrenched and persistent to the point where they tend to be accepted as impossible to overcome.

"Atrocity Exhibition" suggests all too many people, even if they would not recognize or admit this, enjoy or at least benefit from others' encasing/encagement, and especially the harder, the more rigid, and the more entrapping this is–representing the obverse of a genuine culture of empathy and solidarity. The song makes sense as challenging dominant ideological promotion of the notion that we are all fundamentally free subjects, in total charge of our own destinies, as in this case, in terms of what the song's lyrics suggest, we are all too often caught up in attraction to the exhibition of atrocity, and thereby implicitly to its commission, while exercising little power to escape this trap even when we pretend or deny we are attracted to exhibition (and commission) of atrocity. "Atrocity Exhibition" suggests many people are interpellated into positions of victims of atrocity, and into positions as exhibitors and performers of their own victimization–while many others are 'secondary victims' because of what their effective enjoyment of this spectacle does to their humanity, as people who are attracted to exhibitions of others as victims of atrocity. As with differences in terms of ideological interpellation, including into what kinds of subject positions, defined in relation to situations, events, incidents, and especially exhibitions of atrocity, it makes sense in this connection, with "Atrocity Exhibition," to propose differences exist as well in the kinds of positions different people experience as part of the carcereal continuum, and this may not just extend to the difference between literal and figurative 'prisoners' and literal and figurative 'guards' but also to those who design and supervise atrocity versus others who 'follow orders' and carry this out.

Pitches in "Atrocity Exhibition" add a palpable sense the song conveys to us of being compelled to confront what we are caught within but have been content, or preferred, to make sense of in mystifying terms–as these pitches emphasize regularity and persistence as well as wildness and strangeness, even an awkward and unsettling degree of the bizarre and the macabre. Timbre, especially of guitar, adds to this sense of encountering a messy, strange, distorted, jarring, and both highly unfamiliar as well as simultaneously disturbingly all too familiar situation. The vocal delivery adds further to the complexity of what is plausibly interpretable as happening here, identifying and alluding to what precisely we are invited to follow the narrator-protagonist to 'step inside' to witness, as well as what this means, with it increasingly seeming, as the song proceeds, that we are beckoned to look critically at ourselves previously uncritically (or pre-critically) looking, and to recognize what we have been previously uncritically (or pre-critically) looking at, from what vantage point, and toward what effective end and interest.

"Atrocity Exhibition" I experience as a song that challenges, and even disrupts, readier forms of mimetic participation, as I do not find myself able easily to participate along with the guitar, because of how strange its strangled sound is, or with the sound effects, because they add a complimentary wildness to the sound of the guitar–nor to the drums either because the rolling effect, while hypnotic, does not seem like it is eliciting a ready invitation to join in. The bass guitar, moreover, is so backgrounded that it is hard to emulate. I do experience myself most pronouncedly mimetically participating in conjunction with the vocal, especially with the chorus, but doing so leaves me feeling uneasy, and it feels harder to do this unthinkingly, unreflectively, than with many other popular song choruses, including from other Joy Division songs. I experience "Atrocity Exhibition" as, overall, *not* inviting or encouraging one to lose one's sense of one's independence from the song by identifying with the music as persona but rather as enforcing a distance between the song and me in the interest of provoking self-critical self-awareness. It is compelling to question too easy modes of sympathetic identification that can in fact conceal how much we are responsible for the conditions according to which those we are sympathetically identifying with are struggling against. If I am empathizing with what I hear, in listening to and reflecting on "Atrocity Exhibition," I am empathizing with the challenge, and the effort required, to break past layers of distancing, obfuscation, denial, projection, and convenient justification as well as complicit sentimentalization–and the yet even greater challenge required to show others this is what *they also* are doing and have been doing.

As I listen to "Atrocity Exhibition" I anticipate both repetition of a repetitive pattern as well as jolts of surprising movement–in the former case by way of the drums, bass guitar, and vocal and in the latter case by way of the guitar and studio effects. I anticipate early on what the drums will incessantly do, but since this is a relatively unusual 'rock' music drum pattern it remains startling. The vocal I shortly also expect will follow a repeated pattern and I am thereby especially alert to variations, including in chorus stanza three and verse stanza four. Little here, within this song, feels as if it directly appeals to desire despite the explicit lyrical invitation to follow and enter, because the song feels much more as an occasion in which desire is being exposed and critiqued. "Atrocity Exhibition" suggests we are too far in, too deeply implicated, and too desensitized already for this desire to be fused with dread, and, if anything calls our attention to dissipation of dread along with disconnection of dread from desire.

I hear "Atrocity Exhibition" expressing challenge and critique. I hear expression of a layered invitation, one that is ironically commenting on what it superficially seems to involve. And although I've already, in relation to my discussion of the soundbox, covered much of what acoustic impact involves, I will simply add, as a composite, the sounds that make up "Atrocity Exhibition" come at and impact me as disrupting comfort and ease. Meanwhile, in terms of analysis as an avenue of musical affect, this is complicated because in "Atrocity Exhibition" I hear an emphasis on identifying, on showing/revealing, on sketching/detailing, and on insinuating/implying much more than on analyzing per se. The song offers no sense of surviving without harm, and in fact feels as if it suggests we have already been seriously harmed *by and through seriously harming*. So this song conveys little sense of anticipating an aesthetic pleasure of, or through, survival. It does feel as if we are being encouraging to look, listen, feel, and think critically, especially about our own implication, complicity, and responsibility, which does require analysis, but it feels as as if the music as persona, and especially the narrator-protagonist, have already analyzed the parameters of the situation and the contours of the location that they are compelling us to confront and consider.

The complex of sounds collectively comprising "Atrocity Exhibition" conjure associations with a jungle, wilderness, or other remote area paradoxically right at the edges and closely interconnected with a larger urban environment, comprised of both what feels simultaneously strangely unfamiliar and unsettlingly familiar at once. In terms of atrocities, and their exhibition, many ready possibilities come to mind, many I have already mentioned, and undoubtedly readers here, in listening to and reflecting on the lyrics and the music of this song, will come up with further associations of your own. But I myself am thinking of atrocities on massive scales, including all of the following: slavery and the slave trade; Jim Crow and 'The New Jim Crow'; colonial conquest and occupation; genocides of indigenous populations; brutal crackdowns, retaliations, and mass executions in response to rebellions by slave and colonized populations; mass incarceration, especially of the poor, of people of color, and of people experiencing serious mental illness or other forms of disability that the so-called 'war on drugs' accelerated; systemically racist police brutality and deaths after police contact; 'forever wars', most notably the so-called 'war on terror'; decimation of coral reefs and rain forests; mass species extinction; famine induced by forced conversion of formerly self-sustaining bio-diverse agricultural economies into monocultural, export-focused agricultural economies; sexual violence perpetrated against and suffered by girls and women, leading to horrific percentages of girls and women experiencing harassment, abuse, and even far worse; lack of equitably affordable and responsive access to justice before the law experienced by groups of people not maintaining substantial reserves of economic, social, and cultural capital; neo-liberalism creating a substantial 'precariat', experiencing far more precarious conditions of existence than the 'traditional proletariat' and constituting what social scientist Guy Standing refers to as 'the new dangerous class'; and reemergent to resurgent fascist movements spreading widespread hate and division while undermining and overturning already too limited and weakened vestigial forms of representative democracy in capitalist society.

In terms of 'exhibition' here I associate this addition to 'atrocity' with all too many of these aforementioned atrocities being 'hidden in plain sight', and tacitly tolerated, if not overtly encouraged and even celebrated. I think about how much of the wealth held by the richest nations in today's world, and the richest classes in today's societies, is rooted in exploitation of natural and cultural resources, and in the value created by exploited labor, and that much of what those who are relatively better off enjoy throughout life as their material possessions, as their worldly goods, are 'not innocently acquired'. The last includes clothing produced via sweatshop labor; minerals such as cobalt required to run mobile phones that is extracted by miners subject to horrific abuse as well as extremely dangerous workplace conditions; food staples made available via the work of farm laborers paid subminimum wages, without additional benefits, with little to no regulation protecting their health and well-being on the job, and with little to no job security as well as often in constant danger of arrest and deportation.

A principal taboo "Atrocity Exhibition" confronts is putting atrocity on display. A corollary taboo the song confronts is proposing this is already happening, and has already been happening, with many people benefitting from and enjoying what commission of atrocities enable. A related taboo the song confronts is that of calling attention to how widespread and commonplace commission of atrocity has been, is, and is likely to continue to be in the foreseeable future. This runs counter to the notorious Whig theory of history that interprets history as one of constant progress, where everything, by and large, is always getting steadily better, and where human civilization is always becoming steadily more advanced, enlightened, and humane. It is especially taboo to suggest, as the conclusion of the lyrics do, that no way out or beyond may be possible, that what stands for–what continues to assume the mantle of–civilization is already too far gone, already too invested in and committed to the commission and exhibition of atrocity, and that both are indispensable to the 'normal' workings of 'civilized' human society and culture. It often remains taboo as well to honestly face up to looking at, listening to, feeling, and taking responsibility for the extent of abuse, mistreatment, and destruction of other human beings we are implicated in and complicit with, given how much easier it is to become desensitized to this abuse, mistreatment, and destruction as well as to our responsibility in relation to it. And in terms of invisibility, intangibility, and ephemerality, "Atrocity Exhibition" compels us to see and feel what has been all too often, too easily, and especially too conveniently and too comfortably, rendered invisible and intangible, while confronting the perdurability of what we are simultaneously all too often invited and encouraged to effectively disregard as merely ephemeral.

Connecting how the preceding avenues of musical affect make sense in "Atrocity Exhibition" with Weber's *Protestant Ethic and the Spirit of Capitalism* it is worth recalling, once more, Weber's final concern in this book emphasizes how much he values affect, and worries that in the victorious stage of modern capitalism this is waning in influence and impact, that its continued effectivity is endangered. In addition, a further connection concerns how much of ascetic Protestantism was long distrustful and dismissive of the value of emotions, including of intuitive and emotional intelligence, while not recognizing or anticipating dangerous consequences that can follow from promulgating such a distrustful and dismissive position. These dangerous consequences can include an inability emotionally to register, object to, or experience any substantial response when confronted with atrocity, and with exhibition of atrocity, other than to treat this as an object of consumption, including enjoyable or entertaining diversion, and as what one can afford to purchase access to according to the wealth one earns through one's work–and one's control over what is involved in and that follows from others' work.

In relation to Althusser's *On the Reproduction of Capitalism: Ideology and Ideological State Apparatuses*, a relevant connection with how "Atrocity Exhibition" makes sense in terms of Arnie Cox's avenues of musical affect concerns the mystification and self-justification that dominant ideology invites and encourages, such that atrocities, and exhibitions of what atrocities make possible and bring forth for those of us positioned to benefit from their commission, are perceived as matters of distant unconcern that can be readily rationalized and excused away. Also, a closely related connection concerns not recognizing how we are interpellated, into what, and as responsible for what–as beneficiaries and as consumers of atrocities.

In relation to Foucault's *Discipline and Punish: The Birth of the Prison*, a relevant connection with how "Atrocity Exhibition" makes sense in terms of Arnie Cox's avenues of musical affect concerns the insidious dimensions of operations of oppressive power concealed through normalization, including by means of pervasive punishment, or threat of punishment such that 'atrocities' do not appear as 'atrocities', and 'exhibition of atrocities' does not appear as 'exhibition of atrocity', but rather what is normal, natural, right, necessary, and especially more advanced, enlightened, and humane than in pre-modern times in which overt exhibition of atrocities was normal, unlike what is reputedly the case now.

"Atrocity Exhibition" certainly references and alludes to many 'darknesses' in human history and society, and definitely comes across as calling upon us to confront, without resorting to self-protective blinders or sentimentalizing illusions, extraordinarily disturbing incidences of cruelty and violence. And the song makes good sense as engaging the question of how much am I responsible for suffering, hardship, pain, violence, cruelty, injustice, and unfairness, with the answer seeming to be I most definitely am, while not proceeding further to suggest what if anything I can and should do to do about this responsibility, other than to stop pretending I am not.

Perhaps, in Lacanian terms, "Atrocity Exhibition" makes sense as, like Lacan, proposing the Imaginary is self-protectively distorting and illusionary, the Symbolic is harsh and cruel, and the Real is wilder and more disturbing than brief flashes of contact with it tend to suggest. In relation to the persistence of fascism, and the threat and danger of fascism, "Atrocity Exhibition" makes sense as suggesting this threat and danger has long preceded and long exceeded that of Nazi Germany alone, with atrocities happening all around us here and now, and poised to continue so throughout the foreseeable future, while we are becoming all the more inclined to prefer attending to these as exhibitions put on for our consumption.

"Atrocity Exhibition" prompts me to face up to what I am implicated in, complict with, and yes responsible for that I have not recognized and acknowledged, or which I would prefer not to recognize and acknowledge as such. This raises, in connection with Weber, Althusser, and Foucault as well, the question 'what is to be done?' Weber, Althusser, and Foucault all share with "Atrocity Exhibition" an emphasis upon the crucial importance of developing critical–including self-critical–awareness, recognizing who and what we are produced to be is neither innocent nor what simply follows from our own unique, autonomous and independent will, choice, and effort. But none of these theorists, in these three books, offer much if any guidance, either concerning how we might find ways to resist, oppose, contest, counter, and imagine as well as pursue transformative alternatives.

Emphasis instead resides with what we don't commonsensically readily recognize and understand concerning the sources of what we think, feel, believe, and do, or the implications and consequences of what we think, feel, believe, and do–including the largely unconscious theories and modes of criticism that orient us, and which we rely upon the most often and the most extensively. We are subjects of and to victorious capitalism and its ossifying tendencies, including in the form of a metaphorical steel-hard casing/an iron cage, by way of what the Protestant Ethic has contributed to the driving spirit of capitalism; of dominant ideology and the State, as well as to our places/positions within the relations of production; and of disciplinary power and its exercise, across a carcereal continnuum, most insidiously by way of compulsory normalization. But what might, should, and can we become, as well as how do we get from here to there?

"Atrocity Exhibition" challenges me to step inside, to look, to listen, and to feel–including to look at, listen to, and feel myself as I have previously been uncritically, and even often largely unconsciously, attending to and interacting with the results of atrocities that I have at least seemingly tacitly accepted with callous equanimity. This challenge I interpret as coming to me from a subject who has already begun to do what 'he' is challenging me to do likewise, and this is, therefore, a knowing subject, a knowing guide, but one who offers me no way out or beyond, while even suggesting a way out and beyond might not–or no longer–exist, but who nevertheless continues to encourage me to join 'him' in not only developing but sharing critical–including self-critical–awareness. This subject wants me, and others like me, to join 'him' in recognizing the unfamiliar within and in relation to the familiar, including previously familiar comfort zones.

But again, this prompts me to press beyond the limits of the song to reflect on what can be done with such critical awareness. This is what I experience as the response I can give, I want to give, and I need to give, to what this song challenges me with and calls upon me to recognize and acknowledge: to reflect seriously on what I might possibly be able to do to respond to this implication, complicity, and responsibility. I do accept, however, that it is important to begin by reflecting critically on what atrocities around me in the world today I have not paid adequate heed to, along with how I am connected to these, to what extent, and in what ways do I benefit from their commission and exhibition.

I am thinking in particular here about what Eyal Press's *Dirty Work: Essential Jobs and the Hidden Toll of Inequality in America*. Drawing the concept of 'dirty work' from sociologist Everett Hughes, Press explains that 'dirty work' refers to "something foul and unpleasant but not wholly unappreciated by the more respectable elements in society" (5). For example, "Ridding Germany of 'inferior races' was not unwelcome even among educated people who were not committed Nazis" with the latter preferring that the Nazis do this 'dirty work' on their behalf, rather than having to do it directly themselves and allowing them to dissociate themselves from such work, from responsibility for it, even to the point where they can profess repugnance concerning it (5). Dirty work is "unethical activity" that is "delegated" to other "agents" and which can be "conveniently disavowed" (5). Or, as Press cites James Baldwin declaring, in the epigraph to *Dirty Work: Essential Jobs and the Hidden Toll of Inequality in America*: "The powerless must do their own dirty work. The powerful have it done for them." Indeed throughout *Dirty Work: Essential Jobs and the Hidden Toll of Inequality in America* Press makes the case that this continues to be a key dimension of dirty work–it corresponds to a clear discrepancy between those who must do dirty work because of their relative lack of social power versus those who can afford to have others do dirty work for them because of their relative surfeit of social power.

Press proposes 'dirty work' involves four dimensions: "First, it is work that causes substantial harm either to other people or to nonhuman animals and the environment, often through the infliction of violence"; "Second, it entals doing something that 'good people'–the respectable members of society–see as dirty and morally compromised"; "Third, it is work that is injurious to the people who do it, leading them to either feel devalued and stigmatized by others or to feel they have betrayed their own core values and beliefs"; and "Last and most important, it is contingent on a tacit mandate from the 'good people', who see this work as a necessary part of the social order but don't explicitly assent to it and can, if need be, disavow responsibility for it" (11-12). Press also cites sociologist Norbert Elias's critical discussion of 'civilization', akin to Sigmund Freud's critical discussion of the same in *Civilization and Its Discontents*, according to which "The distasteful is *removed behind the scenes of social life*" (quoted 13).

As one of multiple examples of this kind of 'dirty work' in the US today, Press describes how abuse of prisoners by prison guards follows logically from how 'cheaply' prisons are run and how poorly paid guards are for the jobs they are required to do, with 'nobody needing to instruct guards to get brutal' as "It was enough to pay them modest salaries to enforce order in overcrowded, understaffed prisons that were neither equipped nor expected to much else" (53). A "spectacular boom" in prison sentences at the same time as a previous "rehabilitative ideal crumbled," turning prisons entirely into warehouses for those punished according to increasingly "draconian policies" that involve supposedly 'cracking down on crime', including petty drug crime as well as many other relatively small-scale forms of disorder (53). Laws were passed with widespread popular support, and then 'the good people' did not need to think about the consequences–especially those affecting all the new 'criminals' sentenced to prison terms, even to long prison terms, or the guards and the psychological and other health care workers responsible for dealing directly with this massive influx of prisoners imprisoned, all too often, 'on the cheap'.

Those working the latter jobs, especially as guards, often turned to these positions out of necessity, as in all too many poor and especially poor rural communities, "working at a prison soon became the best employment prospect around, offering benefits unavailable at fast-food restaurants or in the mills and factories that had long ago left down," yet these jobs "tended to be reserved for people with limited options who lived in struggling backwaters" (56). Since the 1970s, "when the number of correctional facilities tripled" (57), these have increasingly been located in what Press cites sociologist John Eason describing as 'rural ghettos', where factories had closed and family farms had gone bankrupt, with continuing residents of these communities desperate to attract any source of employment to these locations (57). Location of prisons in remote, depopulated areas also means few people will come into contact with what happens inside, and this becomes easier to ignore–'out of sight, out of mind'.

But within prisons, including due to the overwhelming percentage of prisoners suffering from serious mental health conditions, atrocious conditions are standard and atrocious acts of violence, especially suffered by prisoners themselves, are frequently recurrent. These are not put widely on display, and in fact are hidden from wide exhibition, but the consequences are nonetheless 'on display', especially among populations, and in communities, from which a disproportionate percentage of prisoners are drawn: notably poor urban Black and Brown communities. When reports of atrocities committed in prisons do receive prominent public attention, typically it is solely the immediate perpetrators of these actions who experience condemnation: "In prisons as elsewhere, dirty workers performed another essential function, shouldering the blame for inhumane systems within which they ultimately had little power and thus deflecting attention from other social actors with far more sway" (65).

Correction officers act as "the agents of a society that was home to the world's largest prison system," as for example, "Between 1970 and 2010, Florida's prison population grew by more than *1,000* percent" (65). Elected government officials create laws that ramp up the extent of punishment of crime by prison sentences, while authorizing police and courts to arrest and convict many more people as criminals who will then be sentenced to prison, with a great deal of public support for doing so, yet they all–elected government officials, police officers, prosecutors, judges, and the general public–fail to take responsibility for the consequences of this ramping up, while approving outsourcing of punishment of crime to private for-profit firms that seek ever cheaper ways to run the prisons they manage. The consequences remain largely hidden. Press cites professor of law and sociology David Garland, drawing upon Norbert Elias's critical theory of what 'the civilizing process' involves, who explains: "Routine violence and suffering can be tolerated on the condition that it is discreet, disguised, or somehow removed from view" (quoted 78). Press also cites professor of law and sociology John Pratt, drawing as well upon Elias's theory of 'the civilizing process', proclaiming "the civilized prison became the invisible prison" (78).

In discussing the dirty workers responsible for drone killings in war zones such as Afghanistan, Press notes Americans objected, with horror, to images of torture from Abu Graibh, reacting against the immediate perpetrators with outrage and condemnation, because what these people did left many of us feeling 'dirtied' by what they did 'in our name'. Yet, it has seemed "The pilots and sensor operators in the drone program, by contrast, carried out 'precision' strikes on video screens, an activity that seemed a lot cleaner" (102). What's more, despite its rapid acceleration as a priority mode of fighting America's wars, "drone warfare scarcely registered in public discourse," following a long-running trend, as "since the Vietnam era and the end of the draft, Americans had grown increasingly disengaged from the wars fought in their name" (104). With drone warfare: "the opaqueness was convenient, sparing citizens from having to think too much about a campaign of endless war to which many were tacitly resigned. As Everett Hughes might have noted, remote-control killing had an 'unconscious mandate' from the public, solving a problem in a nation that had grown disillusioned with the 'war on terror' but didn't necessarily want real constraints placed on America's use of force" (105). As Press adds, "Tuning out the drone campaign was all the easier because no U.S. soldier risked dying in it" (105).

Yet these drone strikes have killed tens of thousands of 'other people', including thousands of civilians. And 'secondary victims' here, just as with the prison guards and prison psychological counselors Press discusses earlier in his book, those responsible for analyzing video images to determine when and where drones should attack, suffer on account of "the emotional toll of killing," in particular in the form of 'moral injury', where they feel guilty and ashamed for causing serious harm that runs counter to their foremost moral values and convictions (110). The reality of drone warfare is it is far from surgically precise and results in numerous ostensibly unintended casualties and concomitant ostensibly unintended destruction. What makes the moral injury worse is this kind of warfare feels "bereft of honor," not benefitting from "the warrior ethic" that has traditionally reassured soldiers their killing as part of waging war is honorable because in doing so they have also put their life directly on the line (116). Press contends 'we' are, once more, allowing these 'dirty workers' to experience this 'moral injury' while shielding ourselves from any responsibility for the immorality of their actions: "Drone operators who killed from afar were very much the agents of a society that, after the protracted conflicts in Iraq and Afghanistan, which squandered hundreds of billions of dollars and thousands of lives, wanted to have the military conduct its business at a minimal cost in blood and treasure, at least for our side" (117). The moral injury drone analysts and operators have suffered "was exacerbated by society's growing disengagement from war," leaving those affected all the more isolated and alone in struggling with this injury (122).

Press cites political philosopher Michael Sandel challenging his students in his "immensely popular course at Harvard, 'Justice'," where after first ascertaining from his students their overwhelming preference for an all-volunteer military as opposed to a military populated by means of a draft, and second that these students likewise agreed it was unjust for affluent Americans to have paid for poor Americans to take their place in fighting on the Union side in the American Civil War, then poses the question: "If the Civil War system was unfair because it let the affluent hire other people to fight their wars, doesn't the same objection apply to an all-volunteer army?" (132). Following Sandel's lead, Press documents that in fact American soldiers today come in disproportionately larger numbers from socio-economically relatively poorer versus socio-economically relatively affluent communities, with poorer Americans assuming the burden of fighting America's war on behalf of all Americans, and in the place of more affluent Americans. As Press points out, "just one in one hundred percent has actually served in America's more recent wars," and those who do are serving in what popular surveys rank as one of the worst jobs in America today (134-135).

Similar to the military, a high percentage of those working as U.S. Border Patrol officers come from relatively poorer backgrounds and communities, often based close to where they do this work, with this job offering better compensation than most others available in these locations. Press discusses examples of border patrol officers who have experienced moral injury from doing this work, sharing what they experienced and what this has done to them, only to be met with little to no sympathy, along with strong condemnation for being perpetrators of immoral abuse versus people seeking to immigrate to the US. This condemnation, as directed against other dirty workers sharing their experiences and the damages they have suffered, is connected with the contention these workers had a choice, and made a choice, to do this kind of work, and therefore should be held accountable. While Press acknowledges this is in part true, he also argues these workers are too often expected to take the entire responsibility, all of the blame, for what is in fact a systemic injustice that people who never need to 'dirty their hands' are implicated in, and this implication is increased to the extent that too many people ignore evidence that is "hiding in plain sight" of what is being done in their name, and effectively to their benefit, such as ample discourse that is not at all difficult to discover revealing what drone warfare is actually like (150-151).

In slaughterhouses Press finds a high percentage of recent, including many undocumented, immigrants are the ones who do these dirty jobs. Not only can these immigrant workers be paid less and expected to put up with harsher workplace conditions because of the lack of alternatives available to them, the status of this work is "diminished by the hiring of foreign-born workers," resulting in "downward pressure on the wages and the bargaining power of all employees" (162). Just as with "picking vegetables" and "cleaning hotel rooms," the hiring of predominantly recent, including undocumented, immigrants to do these jobs has made these jobs appear "harsher and less appealing" on that account alone, which enables super-exploitation of workers doing these jobs, because those left to do them maintain far less recourse to resist and oppose how they are treated than do other workers. This in turn yet further 'validates and confirms' the "unattractiveness," the "dirtiness," of these kinds of jobs and this kind of work "to native-born Americans" (162). In tandem, "Immigrants thus acquired a kind of social dirtiness that was tinged with racism and exacerbated by class anxiety as low-skilled Americans feared that more pliant foreigners were displacing them" (162-163). Moreover, Americans tend to register much greater concern about the brutality directed toward the animals killed and processed as sources of food than they do about the brutality experienced by those who do this 'dirty work' in these plants. Yet the conditions are brutal for these workers, causing many serious and lasting injuries and other health problems, including due to pressure to work faster than is safely manageable and not to take toilet breaks.

Far from the days in which these kinds of plants were located in large urban centers, like Chicago, "America's slaughterhouses has gone the way of prisons, relocating to the 'unobtrusive margins' of society, both to take advantage of business-friendly environments and to be removed from sight" (172). This means that even further damages can occur without challenge: for example, Sanderson Farms, "one of the world's largest poultry producers and the only Fortune 1000 corporation in Mississippi" is also "the state's leading polluter of water" while, according to a 2018 Environmental Integrity Project study, "the typical slaughterhouse discharged 331 pounds of nitrogren a day, roughly the amount contained in the untreated sewage of a town of fourteen thousand people" (173). While companies "routinely violated pollution limits," "The dirty by-products (blood, fecal waste) of the meatpacking industry leached into the streams and rivers of the same communities where the people who did the dirty work inside the slaughterhouses lived" (173). Here we confront multiple interconnected atrocities: the conditions under which animals are killed for meat in these plants, the conditions according to which workers in these plants carry out their work, the pollution of waterways as a result of what is discharged from these plants, and the racist and classist disparity in terms of who suffers the most versus the least as a result of environmental pollution.

As with the other kinds of dirty work Press discusses in *Dirty Work: Essential Jobs and the Hidden Toll of Inequality in America*, workers in slaughterhouses also report experiencing moral injury due to all the killing they need to do, due to how disturbing it is too kill frightened and trusting animals, and due to how literally bloody and dirty so much of this work is. As one of these workers contends, in talking with Press, those who bear the greater moral responsibility for what transpires in these workplaces are not "the workers who shock and kill the animals (and whom some PETA activists have advocated charging with criminal felonies)" but rather "the consumers who eat meat without ever thinking about the costs," and who remain largely oblivious to the fact they have effectively delegated responsibility to "those with the fewest opportunities in society" to carry out this dirty work (191). What's more, as Press argues, all too many 'locavores' and other ethical consumers are "far more attuned to the welfare of the animals in the food system" than they are "to the welfare of the workers" (207). According to Press, seemingly 'virtuous consumption' "can reduce politics to a market transaction whose main purpose is to make individuals feel better about themselves": they "often care more about their own health and a certain kind of purity . . . than about fair wages and labor abuses" (208). In addition, focus on 'ethically consuming' "risks diverting attention from structural issues like the conditions of production in the food industry" (208). What results is "a virtue divide that all too often mirrors the class divide" as 'ethically responsible' avenues of food consumption tend to be more costly and less readily accessible than those that are not, so those who with greater means can more readily afford the former and those with lesser means often have little choice but to turn to the latter. In other words, "As in so many other areas of life, virtue correlates with privilege, enabling affluent consumers to buy their way out of feeling complicit in the impure, dirty practices that go on inside factory farms and industrial slaughterhouses," while altogether ignoring the working conditions of the 'dirty workers' often forced out of economic necessity to work in these farms and slaughterhouses (208).

What dirty workers also lack is what Press cites economist Albert Hirschman theorizing as 'voice', and that means, in essence, the power to insure they are heard and those who hear them need to attend and respond to what they have to say. It is their *absence* of power that made these people vulnerable to being stigmatized, saddled with a 'spoiled identity' that hampered their life choices" (255). As Press argues further, drawing again upon the work of philosopher Michael Sandler, meritocracy and "meritocratic hubris" have not only led those who are socially successful to believe they have earned and deserve their success, with those who are not successful in turn *not* having earned or deserved their relative lack of privilege, but also "to diminish the dignity and self-esteem of working-class people who do not have degrees from top universities and whose fortunes have declined or stagnated in recent decades" (255).

Disparity in power that shows up in disparity in 'voice', disparity in likelihood to be burdened with unshakeable stigma and 'spoiled identity' (another critical concept introduced by sociologist Erving Goffman), along with meritocracy and meritocratic hubris, are forms of atrocity in themselves, and insofar as they are visible from a critical vantage point, represent, 'atrocity exhibitions'. Yet again, as is the case with the horrific conditions Press describes by *creuseurs* (diggers) in cobalt mines in the Democratic Republic of the Congo, who produce the cobalt necessary for laptops and smartphones, remains invisible to most, often atrocity *requires* exhibition to generate critical awareness and critical pressure for substantial change. This particular atrocity involves extensive child labor, 12 to 14 hour workdays, frequent and often horrible deaths, as well as torture, by means such as flogging, perpetrated by overseers.

At the end of *Dirty Work: Essential Jobs and the Hidden Toll of Inequality in America* Press confronts common reasons why many people don't want to acknowledge the extent to which dirty work might "be necessary to society," and in particular the extent to which it is necessary to support their own standard of living: it is too "unsettling" and for this reason alone "Most of us don't want to hear too much about such work. We also don't want to hear too much about the people who do it on our behalf, not least because what they tell us might stir discomfort, maybe even a trace of culpability" (266-267). What's more, many people feel that even if they acknowledge the reality of this dirty work, how extensive it is, the damage it does to dirty workers, and our dependence upon this work and the workers doing what we need but don't want to do—or even to face—ourselves, we are powerless to do anything to change these conditions. Press responds "individually, we *are* powerless to change them . . . But collectively, we are not powerless to alter these things" (267). Press cites as examples of the latter a growing movement uniting people of diverse political views to reduce the extent of incarceration in America's prisons and to change laws so fewer crimes require imprisonment for those found guilty. Press acknowledges much more needs to be done, especially in caring about the conditions experienced by prisoners in prisons—and by those who do their jobs as prison workers—in particular, about "warehousing mentally ill people in jails and prisons" (267). But another reason for hope is steadily more people support phasing out fossil fuels and replacing these with renewable sources of energy, even if too little concern remains focused on the conditions, and the risks, experienced at the front lines of extraction and production of sources of energy.

Press also provides the beginning of an answer concerning what we can do with the kind of critical awareness "Atrocity Exhibition" is urging us to obtain: recognize "how susceptible we all are to collaborating with power" and appreciate "the circumstances that lead relatively powerless people to be pushed into such roles" (268). In addition, we need to recognize and appreciate that socio-economic inequality works in tandem with moral inequality, and this increases the likelihood those in lower class positions will suffer not only socio-economic but also moral injury (268). Furthermore, we need to recognize and appreciate that in fact, as "Atrocity Exhibition" suggests, evidence of atrocity *is* on display, it is available: "The problem is not dearth of information but the fact that so many choose to avert their eyes," and the latter is what the lyrics to "Atrocity Exhibition" are effectively and repeatedly challenging us *not* to do. In relation to dirty workers, Press argues "At minimum, it seems to me, we owe them the willingness to see them as our agents, doing work that is not disconnected from our own daily lives, and to listen to their stories, however unsettling what they tell us may be" (269).

Following what psychiatrist Jonathan Shay recommends in *Achilles in Vietnam*, Press argues "The most effective way to help people overcome moral injury is to communalize it" and that means *embracing* dirty workers by taking responsibility for what we have effectively required them to do as well as what they have suffered as a result (270). This notion of communalizing moral injury counters remaining stuck feeling guilty, ashamed, powerless, and thus despairing. When we share these feelings with others, in disparate yet interdependently interlinked positions, confronting the source of our guilty and shame collectively together, we are not so powerless and need not be so despairing, because we have the collective capacity to begin to make the changes needed to overcome the conditions that have led us to this precipice. In fact, Weber, Althusser, and Foucault all suggest much the same. Weber remains committed to the conviction that reform within capitalism is viable, and that the Protestant Ethic fused with the spirit of capitalism maintains historically retrievable 'progressive' potentialities that if successfully recovered, reinstated, and reasserted, while combined with adequate respect and appreciation for a more holistically encompassing array of and basis in moral values, especially those involving caring, compassion, and empathy, it will be possible to throw off the steel-hard casing, to break loose from the iron cage. Althusser firmly believes that working class people, as well as allies and supporters in other classes, do maintain a strong interest in and have demonstrated a strong inclination to mobilize in resistance and opposition to the limits of capitalism, ready to begin the long and difficult revolutionary socialist journey to communism. This too requires concerted collective action, based upon far-reaching collective organization and on a broadly inclusive critical consciousness. And Foucault recognizes that popular resistance, all the more effective the larger the number of those collectively involved and the more diversely situated and engaged the members of this larger collective in so resisting, has repeatedly historically compelled substantial changes in modes of exercise of power, opening up at least temporary spaces to imagine and pursue directions that undermine the necessity of power always operating as domination and subjection.

Nine

Uwe Schütte makes use of a line from "The Eternal" in the title of his contribution to *Heart and Soul: Critical Writings on Joy Division*: "'Possessed by a Fury That Burns from Inside: On On Curtis's Lyrics." Schütte cites Ian Curtis's response to Mick Middles's question in a 1978 interview concerning what his lyrics are about: "Various things really. I tend not to write about anything in particular. If something strikes me. I tend to write very subconsciously sometimes. Like, well, I don't know what they are about. It depends really . . . I like to leave it open to interpretation. It is pointless writing about specific things then it's going to be dated" (quoted 74). As Schütte adds, in another interview Curtis responded similarly, claiming his lyrics "are open to interpretation. They're multi-dimensional. You can read into them whatever you like" (quoted 74). I myself interpret Curtis as recognizing, on at least intuitive level, that he himself is by no means in definitive charge of what his lyrics can and will mean, that he may not be in the best position to interpret them, and that these lyrics will mean more to many people if they are highly elliptical. As Schütte suggests, the lyrics of "The Eternal" are a case in point, illustrating Curtis, like David Bowie, preferring to write lyrics that "hinge on the poetic surplus of language," reflecting "a strategy of willful ambivalence," and that do "not lend themselves to an easy reading and an unequivocal interpretation" (74).

This is true of "The Eternal" despite the fact that, as Schütte recounts, and many other have as well, Curtis did share a source of inspiration in his writing of these lyrics. As Schütte summarizes: "This song was inspired by a mentally impaired boy who lived in Curtis's neighbourhood. The child was never allowed to leave his family's garden. When Curtis, many years later, walked past the house he found the boy was now a man but still confined to his small domestic world like a prisoner" (74). Even though many have run with this account in their interpretation of "The Eternal," as Schütte points out, "Looking at the text, however, there is hardly any evidence that relates it to the original inspiration. Only small units of text allow for a retrospective hinting at the real model" (74). As Schütte notes, "the frequency of liminal terms like gate, fence and wall also conjures up associations of existential imprisonment," that encompass a broader array of individual–and collectively shared–situations and circumstances (74). Yes, these references can make sense in relation to the story of the intellectually disabled boy become man effectively imprisoned throughout his life within the confines of the yard surrounding his house, because "Curtis's sentiment that the 'imprisoned' boy had, in a sense, remained at the same age 'for eternity', while he himself has grown older in the meantime, can be recognized in the line 'Cry like a child, though these years make me older'" (74). Yet this is far from the only viable interpretation of these lyrics, and as Schütte suggests, if anything, the lyrics to "The Eternal" are less tied to the influence that inspired to write them than in the case of "She's Lost Control," which I will discuss in chapter six. Both songs reflect Curtis's sympathy for and indeed empathy with disabled people, which Curtis also demonstrated in his job as an Assistance Disablement Resettlement Officer, where he helped find paid work for disabled people experiencing a range of disabilities. As disabled studies theorist and disabled rights activist Tom Shakespeare comments, it is worth noting Curtis did this job, and by all accounts took it seriously and was dedicated to doing well by his clients, "in an era which was even less open to disability employment than today."

Schütte proposes, as is the case with many of Curtis's lyrics, the "beautiful, touching, enigmatic words of" the lyrics for "The Eternal" might well make sense as "a poem in their own right," while the "slow-paced funeral music" in turn "evokes the scene of a funeral procession" that "makes the song an uncanny anticipation of Curtis's premature death, a major factor in his 'eternal' glory as the singer of Joy Division" while seeming to closely correspond to the cover illustration with *Closer* of an ornamental tomb (75). Here Schütte outlines what is another leading direction in making sense of these lyrics, beyond interpreting them as 'about' the disabled boy become man remaining 'eternally imprisoned' within the yard surrounding his house, and that is "The Eternal" is a song about death, and more precisely, about a funeral following a death, which alludes to the vantage points of both those attending the funeral service as mourners as well as that of the dead person being mourned who is taking stock of where 'he' is now at, and eternally will be, as well as what profound limitations 'he' must now assume from where 'he' is at, in terms of the severance of 'his' ability anymore directly to express and communicate further with those who are living, limitations that will continue eternally.

In *Torn Apart: The Life of Ian Curtis*, Mick Middles and Lindsay Reade cite Curtis's close friend and confidant, Vini Reilly (guitarist, frontman, and the one constant center of fellow founding Factory Records musical outfit The Durutti Column), explaining the meaning of the lyrics for "The Eternal" as inspired by the same source Uwe Schütte recounts, but with Curtis also insisting his lyrics, in this song and otherwise, maintained quite specific, and important, meanings for him. Also, details of the story representing the source that inspired Curtis to write these lyrics are different:

> That song is about this guy he used to see near where he lived in Macclesfield who, at that time, we would call him mentally retarded . . . a grown man who had the mental age of about four or five . . . This man hung out with the children in the park near where Ian lived. Ian used to watch this guy with the kids. The song was a description of this guy who he used to see quite regularly. This guy couldn't communicate with any other grown-ups, he could only communicate with children. Basically what Ian was saying was that every song, every single line or phrase had a specific meaning for him. It was actually about something very specifically. It wasn't a general vibe–they were very specific his lyrics and people didn't understand that . . . . He said that every lyric in every song was basically multi-layered and had many meanings and could be applied to either him or sometimes it was inspired by describing another person but most of time, in fact a lot of the time, he was describing himself. (238-239)

As Reilly shares, Curtis wrote lyrics in response to experiences that mattered to him. It is, I suggest, due to *how much* these experiences mattered to him, and how effectively he is able to bring to bear what matters to him while allowing room for these lyrics to be perceived as open to diverse interpretations that they are able to resonate as powerfully as they have. Because Curtis responds to experiences that mattered a great deal to him, he is able to invest these words with potency. A song with a title like that of "The Eternal" suggests the lyricist and singer is addressing something he personally considers of spiritual significance. Annik Honoré recalls, as she shares with Mick Middles and Lindsay Reade in *Torn Apart: The Life of Ian Curtis*, experiencing "a sacred quality" as Curtis sang the lyrics of "The Eternal" and those of "Decades" privately, alone, to her, with "his eyes closed and his hands on his head," which led her to feel if she was witnessing "some kind of inner, Holy Communion taking place" (213).

In an interview with *GQ* magazine, Stephen Morris recalls, with the lyrics for the "The Eternal," "[Ian] did actually tell us what it's about. A lad that he knew, I knew him as well, when he worked at the labour exchange who had Down's syndrome. He used to go and see him at the labour exchange, but you'd also see him playing in the park and he never seemed to age. He just always stayed the same. I thought that was really a very moving song." Peter Hook, in *Unknown Pleasures: Inside Joy Division*, likewise attests, in relation to "The Eternal," that "This is a great song. My favourite lyric. So dreamlike. Any band would die to have this under their belt, in their arsenal" (279).

Ultimateguitar.com's rundown of the "28 Darkest Songs of All Time," with "The Eternal" ranked #21, shares the common summary account of the source inspiration for the lyrics to this song: "Ian Curtis wrote this about a mentally impaired boy who lived down the street from him when he was growing up. The boy was never allowed to leave his family's yard. Many years later, Ian returned to the neighborhood to find that the boy was now a man, and was still confined to his family's yard. Ian was struck by the fact that this man's entire world was confined just to the yard, hence the song." On the website Song Meanings, where anyone who wants to do so is able to post and share their interpretations of the meaning of popular songs, the first contributor recounts much the same source: "from what I understand, Ian wrote this about a mentally impaired boy who lived down the street from him when he was growing up. The boy was never allowed to leave his family's yard. Many years later, Ian returned to the neighborhood to find that the boy was now a man, and was still confined to his family's yard. Ian was struck by the fact that this man's entire world was confined just to the yard–hence the song." Another contributor responds they are familiar with this account of the origins of the lyrics as well, and likewise find this to be helpful in explaining what they mean, while adding usefully further to an interpretation that focuses on reading these lyrics as responding to Curtis's experience of a mentally impaired boy become mentally impaired man, and his situation, as follows:

I've heard the story about Ian writing it about a mentally disabled neighbour as well . . . I have always interpreted this song as representing the frustration of mentally disabled people at being unable to express themselves. Lyrics like "tried to cry out in the heat of the moment/possessed by a fury that burns from inside" and "no words can explain, no action determine" imply that this person has emotions, thoughts and desires like everyone else, but is unable to articulate them and make people understand him. The tragedy of the lyrics is how this person seems fully aware of his own disability. How "burdened" and "cursed" he is to spend his life "wastefully with children", looking out "from the fence to the wall" doing nothing but watching things go by for the rest of his life. An incredibly sad song . . .

A third contributor to this same discussion offers the following interpretation:

This song just digs down into the deepest, most dank and dark recesses of tortured, unyielding depression. It almost sounds like Ian Curtis is issuing this personal testimony of his inner demons from beyond the grave. I wonder if anything could have saved him at this point. If he had received treatment would his art be compromised? Does art even matter when a person's life is at stake? The tortured artist suffering for his art certainly can be a cliché, but in this case it was never more true.

A fourth contributor interprets "This song is about Ian Curtis's own funeral." This contributor cites lines from the lyrics as "Clearly describing a funeral and the 'after party' that people have when someone dies to celebrate their life," while with this contributor it "Makes me cry almost just listening to it," as it is "So dark and so horribly sad that he really meant it." The same contributor proposes "I think he's standing at his own funeral as a spirit . . . He's standing amongst the crowd watching his burial (maybe he didn't know he would be cremated.) He tries to cry out to them, possessed by the fury of his decision, but alas he is just a disembodied soul who can never reach them again. It's terrifying." Focusing on later in the lyrics, this contributor adds "I love this: 'Cry like a child . . .With children my time is so wastefully spent'. He's honestly saying he's wasting his own time just by living. Fuck." At the end of their contribution, the same contributor interprets the final stanza as follows: "His view stretches out from the fence to the wall. He's dead. This is a cemetery. I need not say more."

The moderator of this discussion of "The Eternal" on Songs Meanings then closes with the following summary interpretation:

The first verse describes watching a procession. It could be a funeral, wedding or war memorial event such as armistice day. After the event, participants gather round tables–this could be a wake. Either way, the focus is on passing away, summed by flower petals washed away by rain.

In the second verse, we hear about the narrator. This may be a learning disabled boy or man. It could be an echo of the character Benjy in William Faulkner's novel *The Power and the Glory* [actually *The Sound and The Fury*], who is confined by his family to a yard after committing a rape. Through the remaining two verses, the viewpoint seems to shift between childhood and adulthood–the narrator has to spend time with children even though he has grown up. The lyrics express his powerlessness, sadness and awareness of his condition.

A further interpretation is that the garden is a cemetery and the lyric describes Ian Curtis' own funeral and confinement for ever to the grave. There may be a bit of hindsight in this but it would fit the song's title.

Of course, there's no right and wrong interpretation. Ian Curtis may have been thinking about some or none of these things when he wrote and sang it. But coupled with the elegiac music, this is a very sad song about feeling like an outsider, the passing of time and the futility of existence. For me, certainly the most powerful track on *Closer*.

Other readily available interpretations of "The Eternal" are much the same. For instance, *Hot Press* offers the following commentary concerning this song:

Has melancholy ever been so devastatingly expressed than on Closer's penultimate track? All traces of anger and resentment have been removed, with Ian Curtis recounting in a resigned, even neutral fashion, what is seemingly the aftermath of a funeral ('No words could explain, no actions determine/Just watching the trees and the leaves as they fall'). Immaculately produced by Martin Hannett, the genuinely otherworldly music–sounding like it's coming direct from the afterlife–makes for an unforgettable backdrop.

And in "Why It Mattered: Joy Division–*Closer*," James Peppercorn, writing for Happy Media, an Australian youth culture publisher and 'flagship channel', declares:

The album's final one-two punch should be regarded as one of the most powerful final chapters of any artist's career. Much like the Beatles' *The End*, Joy Division's career is summed up in the final 10 minutes of *Closer*. *The Eternal's* funeral march eerily signifies Curtis' own death. However he has lost the words to describe everything he sees. *"No words could explain, no actions determine/Just watching the trees and the leaves as they fall,"* Curtis's baritone haunts the song to its very last note.

Peppercorn offers a less commonplace and more distinctive take when he argues, much as I often have, "The album [*Closer*] shouldn't be seen as the depths of gloom. Its message is one of release, escaping the constraints which hold each individual down." As Peppercorn elaborates,

Closer is more than darkness. Its darkness is so powerful because it seeks light. It searches for hope, for love, for goodness and happiness. These are all thing people strive for in life. Curtis strived to achieve all these things, however, he was shrouded by a vale. *Closer* is life and death. It is an album that strips itself bare and wants you to understand that through this eternal struggle there is some life. All the while, you're experiencing music that has reverberated through time, becoming timeless.

All of the interpretations I have cited illustrate how powerfully meaningful and impactful Ian Curtis's lyrics and the music of Joy Division has been and continues to be. This conversation concerning interpretations of meanings for "The Eternal," and in particular for the lyrics of "The Eternal," recalls for me what students in classes I have taught on the same subject come up with, and share, in our discussions concerning how we interpret this song, and especially its lyrics, as well as other lyrics written by Ian Curtis and other songs by Joy Division.

With a title such as "The Eternal," an interpreter right away is confronted with how to make sense of first what is, or might be, that which is 'eternal' here, as well as, second, what is the significance of titling this song "*The* Eternal" as opposed to "Eternal." 'Eternal' readily suggests God, or another comparable kind of divinity–or divinities, perhaps 'spirit', 'soul', or 'the sacred'. 'Eternal' can imply what exists outside of and beyond time, even if it exercises influence and impact within time. 'Eternal' might differ from 'everlasting' with the latter connoting existing throughout time yet nonetheless within time. 'Eternal' might, and a number of the interpretations of "The Eternal" I have already cited would seem to support this, suggest 'death'–i.e., life is finite, but death is infinite; we are alive a short period of time and then ever after we are and continue dead. 'Death' might moreover be a phenomenon that is so absolutely enduring that it transcends normal experiences within and according to time. Death is everlasting but no longer makes sense, from the vantage point of 'being dead', as measured within and through time. 'Death', in other words, might suggest a phenomenon ultimately unknowable from the vantage point of being alive, and of living, such that it is impossible to comprehend 'what this is like', especially if one accepts any and all forms of consciousness end with death. Therefore, to describe people who have died as continuing to be dead, and as subsequently always continuing to be yet further dead, does not make sense from the vantage point of being dead. 'Eternity' is hard, if not impossible, to fathom, from the vantage point of life in which everything seems to have a beginning and especially an end, even when it feels as if this is not the case, even when it feels like we are trapped eternally in the same place doing the same thing over and over again.

'Eternal' conjures association with the idea of 'eternal recurrence', which both Friedrich Nietzsche and Albert Camus propose as a foremost existential challenge: would we be willing to accept living our lives repeated endlessly over and over again, without being able to change anything? Would we be content if we were in a position akin to Sisyphus such that we knew the stone we spent the entire day rolling up the side to the top of a mountain would then fall all the way down to the bottom and this same pattern would repeat itself ceaselessly forever after? 'Eternal recurrence' or 'eternal return' also suggests belief, or at least speculation, that existence–ours and that of other forms of life, as well as other forms of inorganic matter too–takes place within endlessly recurrent cycles, or spirals, or loops. 'Eternal return' might suggest Mircea Eliade's interpretation of ritualistic religious practices in which those involved experience a literal return such that they are able to participate within, or at one with, a mythical past, a connection that is made possible by and exists in 'sacred time'. And we might also think of 'eternal inflation', the notion that the universe is endlessly inflating, or expanding, possibly from its initial point of origin in a 'big bang', and possibly becoming multiverses as it does so.

'Eternal' most often is taken to imply unchanging, and unchangeable, but it is at least conceivably possible to imagine 'eternal' in contrast as the opposite, endlessly changing and endlessly changeable. But what about "*The* Eternal"? The definite article implies reference to some kind of entity, and makes it at least somewhat more complicated to associate the title of the song with experience of what feels like it is 'eternal', in the sense that it never changes, including that it never changes no matter how hard you work, struggle, and fight for change, and no matter how desirable this change might be. '*The* eternal' nonetheless could reference the latter kind of feeling—with this being, in and of itself, what constitutes *the* eternal, and especially what follows from deep disillusionment and despair concerning the possibility of ever being able to realize change that is wanted and needed. '*The* Eternal' might, however, represent a space, beyond life, in death, where all such agitation and anguish concerned with working, struggling, and fighting for change—as well as concerned with failing to bring it about—ceases, and no longer exercises any relevance. '*The* Eternal' might reference 'eternal life', 'eternal salvation', 'eternal damnation', or even eternal entrapment in limbo that is neither heaven nor hell. 'The Eternal' might reference endlessly ongoing reincarnation of life, including in multiple different, and dramatically changing, forms. '*The* Eternal' might reference the preservation of some kind of (supra-)consciousness that exists far beyond its experience within the individual minds of finite beings. '*The* Eternal' might represent the persistence of matter in motion, even as this changes form, even in multiple forms of organization and at multiple levels of development, even in multiple modalities, and even as every discrete material entity is always inextricably caught up within, and formed and constituted by its interrelations within a vast dynamic totality. It might represent, likewise, as an eternal pattern, that all things emerge, develop, further grow and further change, decline, and end, passing on not to disappear altogether but rather so as to provide the material source of new things to come, which will in turn emerge, develop, further grow and further change, decline, and end as they pass on to provide the source for yet further new things to come—in a ceaselessly ongoing process.

Let's turn to examine the lyrics to "The Eternal," considering what sense of 'eternal' and '*the* eternal' they convey. Stanza one reads as follows: "Procession moves on, the shouting is over/Praise to the glory of loved ones now gone/Talking aloud as they sit round their tables/Scattering flowers washed down by the rain/Stood by the gate at the foot of the garden/Watching them pass like clouds in the sky/Try to cry out in the heat of the moment/Possessed by a fury that burns from inside." It seems plausible that one way of making sense of 'eternal' and '*the* eternal" is to imagine these kinds of situations described in these lyrics are eternally recurrent, which could involve funeral processions, funeral wakes or receptions, and what is spoken at these events, including concerning those who have died. Following the logic of this interpretation, what is being addressed here is the continuously ongoing process, through various ritual forms, of attending to and paying tribute to the dead. Yet elements of this description suggest a troubled take on this process. First 'the shouting is over' might suggest a shouting at an earlier point in the ceremony but this is not commonly how many of us

594

imagine people engage at a funeral. We likely more readily expect crying, even loudly and persistently so. 'Shouting' might however reference the preceding life which, summarily characterized as 'the shouting', in turn suggests this was a life of one who struggled to be 'heard', who experienced difficulty being heard, requiring of 'shouting'. This life might well have been that of one who struggled to make an impact, to make a difference, to achieve an end, but experienced great, and even grave frustration, indeed anger, at not being able to so succeed. Second, 'watching them pass like clouds in the sky' suggests those attending this funeral, if that is what we conceive is here referenced, spend a relatively short time so focused before they 'move on with their lives', and before the dead person is gradually, even quickly, forgotten. If the song is referencing an eternally recurrent pattern, it suggests this is what commonly happens, as the dead are all too soon largely forgotten. Third, if the narrator-protagonist is aligned with the person who has died, and whose funeral has just taken place, and is watching those in attendance, 'he' hardly seems 'at peace', as 'he' 'tries to cry out in the heat of the moment'–a 'heat' he may be the only one in attendance to feel–and as 'he' is "possessed by a fury that burns deep inside."

What other interpretations I previously cited have not delved into is what might make this now dead person–this ghost–so furious: what is 'he' furious at or over, and why, even in death, even after death, does this fury continue to 'burn deep inside'? Whatever might explain this feeling, it seems, for the person who is now dead–who is now a ghost–'the shouting' may not be entirely over, or at least 'he' is not at all 'over' what the shouting was focused on and all about. It is plausible here to suggest this stanza represents the perspective of someone who feels bitter and angry that others have effectively accepted defeat in a struggle, in a fight, that has deeply mattered to 'him', especially that they are able to do so with complacency and equanimity when he thought they were as passionately committed to and invested in the same struggle, the same fight, as 'he' was, but that now seems not to have been the case. In addition, this fury makes sense as reflective of the perspective of one who is forced 'himself' to accept the failure of a struggle, of a fight, because all those he relied upon and whose active and persistent solidarity in struggling, and fighting, united together, have given up and he is left with no one but 'himself' to carry on, and that is now impossible. Further embittering, this narrator-protagonist feels as if it is futile for him to vent this fury, it will do no good, it will result in no useful effect, and therefore 'he' needs to hold it within, and allow it to 'burn inside'. The whole stanza can make sense as an expression of combined sadness and anger concerning how often and how readily efforts and endeavors to achieve important ends fail because too many people give up too easily and too soon–and how our interdependence on others results, yes, in our being able to do a vast amount more than we possibly could by ourselves alone but also that we are going to be let down, even let down badly, by other people who we must depend upon, who we must count on.

The second and concluding stanza reads as follows: "Cry like a child, though these years make me older/With children my time is so wastefully spent/A burden to keep, though their inner communion/Accept like a curse an unlucky deal/Played by the gate at the foot of the garden/My view stretches out from the fence to the wall/No words could explain, no actions determine/Just watching the trees and the leaves as they fall." If we accept these lyrics depict the situation of an intellectually disabled person–or the specific intellectually disabled man that Ian Curtis cited as his direct inspiration for these lyrics–what is striking is the sympathetic and even empathetic identification the lyrics invite, and encourage, with this person's vantage point. This person is depicted as feeling, acutely, how 'he' has been confined and constrained, immensely sadly, in large part because 'he' is unable effectively to communicate with other people, perhaps because of these other people's unwillingness to make the effort to attempt to understand 'him', to engage with 'him' as a person maintaining equal human worth and dignity, and as possessing thoughts, feelings, impressions, reactions, insight, and even perhaps some wisdom that these others are unable and unwilling to imagine 'he' does. 'He' is different, but not lesser, and it requires effort to attend to that difference 'on its own terms' and to be able to 'translate' respectfully–yet few are extending or have extended that kind of effort.

If the lyrics in this stanza are not necessarily representative solely of the specific disabled man Ian Curtis knew, or even solely of intellectually disabled youth and adults, but rather of people living with many different kinds of disabilities that mark their experience of the world, of social life, of community, of relationships with other people, as decidedly 'different' in a wide variety of ways than that of fully able-bodied people, then the lyrics might express how challenging it so often is and long has been for disabled people's 'voices to be heard', for their humanity to be respected, for their worth to be appreciated, and for their prospective contributions to be welcomed, supported, and enabled. Recalling the lyrics of the first stanza, it can be all too commonplace for disabled people to feel like others are not listening to them, and are incapable of and disinclined to listen to them. These others have constructed elaborate filters that translate whatever disabled people have to offer into terms that fail to do justice to what disabled people are striving to get across. As a result, disabled people feel they have to settle for being furious at their exclusion yet unable to channel this fury into action that can bring about the change needed to be equitably included.

A yet further interpretation of the lyrics of the second stanza I suggest fits well with the entire lyrics of the song, and with how the song affects the ways in which listeners are invited to make sense of and respond to this song. As the narrator-protagonist suggests 'his' time with children is "so wastefully spent," it makes sense to interpret this as indicating he no longer feels he has anything of value to get across to people who are younger than him, who might follow him, who might look up to him, who might relate to him as a model or a mentor or other source of inspiration. Even more specifically, it seems the narrator-protagonist feels he maintains no way of effectively communicating what he most importantly would like to communicate, in particular to these children–he is lacking the words to do so–and must maintain 'the burden' 'inside' that he 'keeps to himself' of what he has gained insight concerning but cannot find ways to render intelligible, meaningful, and convincing to those who need access to this insight, and who it would most benefit. The narrator-protagonist experiences an 'inner communion' with this audience, but it is a communion he cannot actively share with these others, not something he can physically materialize so they even recognize this commonality–of feeling, sentiment, sensibility, interest, or concern–with 'him'. 'He' is effectively reduced to a position of passivity, and of immobility. "No words could explain, no actions determine" suggests 'he' experiences 'himself' as now, and potentially forever more, incapable of activity, and mobility.

What these lyrics suggest to me, as do the lyrics of the first stanza, is a representation of what it feels like from the vantage point of serious depression. I will be discussing depression further in chapter six, in conjunction with Ann Cvetkovich's *Depression: a Public Feeling*, but I do want to address this now because "The Eternal" feels to me even more thoroughly representative of what depression can and does feel like–and lead to–than most Joy Division songs. On psy.com Sherry Amatenstein, LCSW, a New York City-based therapist and author, shares a series of representative quotes from people living with depression to explain what depression is like, for those who remain hazy about the difference between experiencing full-fledged depression versus feeling sad and down, frustrated and dissatisfied, and unhappy with themselves and their lives. I will cite some highlights here: 1) "It's like drowning, except everyone around you is breathing," and as Amatenstein indicates, this quote well illustrates "how absolutely alone and terrifying it is to be imprisoned inside the inescapable bog that comprises serious depression"; 2) "When you're depressed you don't control your thoughts, your thoughts control you"; 3) "Depression is feeling like you've lost something but having no clue when or where you last had it. Then one day you realize what you lost is yourself"; 4) "My lips say, 'Fine, thanks', but my eyes tell a different story, my heart sings a different tune, and my soul just weeps," and as Amatenstein adds, "Someone in the midst of a deep depressive episode feels like he or she is walking around in a shroud–suffering the torment of being physically alive while emotionally lifeless"; 5) "Depression is the constant feeling of being numb. Being numb to emotions, being numb to life," and as Amatenstein elaborates, "it is darkness 24/7," "A clinically-depressed person is often beyond sadness–his or her feelings hidden deep beneath a throbbing wall of numbness"; 6) "depression is so insidious–and it compounds daily–making it impossible to ever see the end," "That fog is like a cage without a key"; 7) "When you suffer from depression, 'I'm tired' means a permanent state of exhaustion that sleep doesn't fix," and "Sleep just isn't sleep anymore–it's escape"; 8) "The only thing more exhausting than being depressed is pretending that you're not," and as Amatenstein amplifies, "severely depressed people feel they have no choice but to put on an Academy Award-worthy performance of someone who is enjoying his or her time on the planet," yet "Each time you lie and say you are fine, you die a little more inside"; and 9) "Having anxiety and depression is like being scared and tired at the same time"; "It's feeling everything at once, yet being paralyzingly numb."

Depression, in my experience, is a state where one 'feels' 'beyond feeling', as if one no longer feels much of anything, and as if it pointless to feel sad, angry, or even frightened, because one instead feels numb, empty, virtually non-existent, and incredibly exhausted and enervated. Yes, lingering connections exist with 'the shouting', but the time and place for that feels as if it is now distant and faded, while it also feels impossible to manage the strength to engage in any such 'shouting' anymore, and, what's more, futile do so even if one could.

Typically, to this day, depression is not something most people feel comfortable talking–or writing–about, especially not their own experience of depression, or that of someone with whom they are directly in contact. Typically, this is 'supposed' to be what is addressed with certified counselors, therapists, psychologists, and psychiatrists, and not what anyone not so credentialed can or should take on. Depression remains widely feared, so that in effect, in conversation outside of clinical contexts, it is often in effect 'batted away' or condemned as 'abnormal'. People who are depressed are 'people with problems' they need expert help to address–and to 'fix'. This right away implies people who are depressed are deficient, or lesser, versus people who are not depressed, and that something is sufficiently 'wrong' with these people that whatever they might share and contribute is tainted, is contaminated, by their depression, and is likewise of lesser, or little, and even of no value.

But what if we fundamentally reconceived our socially dominant approach to depression, and actually did accept depression as a position, as a perspective, that everyone should take the time, and invest the effort to try to understand, and appreciate, 'on its own terms', because it can offer valuable insight, even valuable wisdom, which can benefit all of us? What if we fundamentally reconceived socially dominant approaches to depression and refused to individualize, and privatize it, but instead *communalized* it–where we created ample spaces, and opportunities, for people to share their emotional experience of depression, by working through it together, and by attending to what it might have to offer as well as to what needs to be done to overcome it? Yes, depression offers a partial and limited perspective, but so do all others, and yes, depression can be extremely painful and dangerously self-destructive, which most definitely needs to be engaged, but depression is far from uncommon while the extent of its commonality may well attest to something other than merely a large mass of individuals all experiencing depression solely on account of deficiencies in their individual psychologies, in their individual brain biochemistry, or in their individual capacity and readiness to engage in rational as opposed to irrational forms of thinking and behavior.

In "A Future with No Future: Depression, the Left, and the Politics of Mental Health," Mikkel Krause Frantzen, author and member of the faculty of the Department of Arts and Cultural Studies at the University of Copenhagen, forthrightly addresses the last issue, arguing

Depression makes manifest the contemporary subject's alienation, in its most extreme and pathological form. As such, the psychopathology needs to be related to a world of capitalist realism, where there really is no alternative, as Thatcher triumphantly declared, and the future seems frozen once and for all. The crisis embodied by depression thus becomes a symptom of a historical and capitalist crisis of futurity. It is a kind of structure of feeling, as Raymond Williams would say. Consequently, any cure to the problem of depression must take a collective, political form; instead of *individualizing* the problem of mental illness, it is imperative to start *problematizing* the individualization of mental illness . . .

Frantzen cites the late Mark Fisher, aka K-Punk, as "The best political thinker of depression," with "His whole oeuvre" representing "an ongoing meditation on depression as a personal experience *and* a social and political experience." Of particular note is how Fisher, in his 2009 book *Capitalist Realism*, relates depression to capitalist realism, with the latter, as Fisher theorizes it, referring to "the widespread sense that not only is capitalism the only viable political and economic system, but also that it is now impossible even to imagine a coherent alternative to it." In *Capitalist Realism*, Frantzen argues, "depression becomes a paradigm case of how capitalist realism operates, a symptom of our blocked and bleak historical situation." Frantzen further cites Fisher's 2011 essay "The Privatisation of Stress," as reprinted in 2018 as part of *K-Punk: The Collected and Unpublished Writings of Mark Fisher (2004–2016)*, where Fisher distinguishes between sadness and depression as follows: "while sadness apprehends itself as a contingent and temporary state of affairs, depression presents itself as necessary and interminable: the glacial surfaces of the depressive's world extend to every conceivable horizon." What's more, Fisher identifies what Frantzen labels as "a strange resonance" between, in

Fisher's words, "the seeming 'realism' of the depressive, with its radically lowered expectations, and capitalist realism."

Frantzen argues that the sense of the self that people experiencing depression develop, where they are, in Fisher's own words concerning himself, "good for nothing," corresponds to what capitalist society promotes, as we come to conceive of ourselves as discrete, distinct, unique, coherent, autonomous, self-contained, self-determining, sovereign, and transcendent beings who are ultimately always individually responsible for everything having to do with our individual success, happiness, and well-being, which means when we experience ourselves as failing, as unhappy, and suffering in our well-being it is our own individual fault. We likewise learn, as members of capitalist society that we are engaged in continuous competition with everyone else and where all instances of unity, cooperation, solidarity, and empathy are of secondary weight and impact in defining life-experience than a much more powerful and overarching state of ceaseless competition. When replicating this individualizing logic, psychiatric treatment reinforces the conditions that generate the need for ever more psychiatric treatment. What is instead needed is to combat "the neoliberal ideology of focusing on subjects, not structures; personal responsibilities, not collective ones; chemistry, not capital." As Frantzen makes clear, he is by no means denying depression is "hell on earth," or that it causes immense damage, which means anything and everything that can help in any way and to any degree is welcome, but nonetheless, "As Mark Fisher writes in *Capitalist Realism*: It goes without saying that all mental illnesses are neurologically instantiated, but this says nothing about their causation."

Frantzen touts the work of artists like Claire Fontaine for whom "the problem of depression" is "always already *political* and must be understood in relation to its real basis in social conflicts within a capitalist economy of debt and financial speculation." As Frantzen explains, further, failure to confront depression as a social and political phenomenon tacitly reinforces neo-liberal ideology. Here is it worth keeping well in mind, Frantzen writes,

> If the individual is responsible for her own happiness, then she is also responsible for her own *un*happiness. If the keys are in our own hands, each of us is personally responsible for almost everything. Success or failure, and health or illness are a matter of subjective willpower, lifestyle, and choice alone. While we may not be able to change other people, or the world for that matter, we certainly can work on changing ourselves and our selves. Structural change, a change of the system, is abandoned in favor of subjective change, a change of the self. Every problem, however social, political, or economic in nature, is personalized and even criminalized, the subject is made responsible for its own unhappiness, and made to suffer alone and to feel guilty, at the same time, for feeling unhappy, for not being a good and productive citizen, for not coming to work, for not getting out of bed.

The upshot is "Depressed people are encouraged to feel and believe that their depression is their fault and their fault only," yet "the autonomous, self-determining, competitive individual" is 'the fiction of capitalist subjectivity." We are all fundamentally interdependent, and we are all socially formed and constituted, from the very beginning throughout the very end of our lives. We can benefit when we are able to embrace this dimension 'of whom and what we are' openly, consciously, actively, and fully. Yet this is the opposite of what capitalism teaches us to do. As Frantzen observes, "Capitalism . . . inflicts a double injury on depressed people. First, it causes, or contributes to, the state of depression. Second, it erases any form of causality and individualizes the illness, so that it appears as if the depression in question is a personal problem (or property). In some cases, it appears to be your own fault." In other words, "Capitalism makes us feel bad and then, to add insult to injury, makes us feel bad about feeling bad." In response, Frantzen exhorts, "The *personalization* of depression must be answered by a *politicization* of depression." Depression needs to be related to its social and political conditions of possibility and forces of its generation: "It should be connected to our brutal, neoliberal culture of competition . . . And to the concomitant ideology of happiness, which forces all of us to smile and be happy nonstop, even or especially when we are fighting among each other, fighting to make ends meet and just get by another day."

In particular, Frantzen identifies "the economy of debt" as what "causes deep distress as indebted people, students and otherwise, are forced to pawn their own future," all the while "the psychiatric and public discourse remain bent on treating depression as a personal problem devoid of context." Likewise, "ecology and mental health stands in an intimate relation." What is needed, in response, is to "collectivize suffering, externalize blame, communize care," to reconceive "Therapy as resistance, not as reactionary obedience to the given order," "Therapy as a collective project, not an individual one," and "Therapy as the overcoming of alienation." This work can begin through the creation, Frantzen proposes, of "alliances of care" that "destroy the material conditions that make us sick, the capitalist system that destroys people's lives, the inequalities that kill."

Returning to "The Eternal" and the song's representation of depression–indeed the song's representation of depression from the vantage point of the depressive–what we are faced with here is the choice between treating this depression as solely an individual crisis, in an individual's internal psychology, or solely as a result of an individual's unique personal experience, or as symptomatic of the psychological impact of social and political forces. These forces Weber identifies as seriously disturbing tendencies of modern capitalism in its 'victorious stage', again, as I indicated earlier in this chapter, much akin to Fisher's 'capitalist realism' insofar as in this stage of capitalism it seems to a great many as if there is no alternative to capitalism, nothing can possibly succeed or supersede capitalism, and triumphant capitalism in effect represents 'the end of history'. For Weber, the seriously disturbing tendencies of victorious capitalism result in people who live according to a capitalist logic, in line with 'the spirit of capitalism', becoming confined within a 'steel-hard casing'–or, as Talcott Parsons translates Weber, trapped within an 'iron cage'. The same social and political forces at the roots of individual experiences of depression Althusser theorizes as capitalist exploitation, and the combination of repressive and especially ideological means by which individuals are produced as subjects who take up their properly assigned places in reproducing capitalist exploitation. The same social and political forces at the roots of individual experiences of depression Foucault theorizes as the pervasion of a carcereal logic continuous with modern society over which the disciplines instill domination and self-subjection, including most nefariously by means of normalization.

Notably, although none of these three critical theorists are inclined to draw significantly on autobiography in their critical theoretical work, all experienced their own substantial struggles at and over significant periods of their lives with various forms of what we conventionally identify as 'mental illness': in Weber's case severe depression, in Althusser's case severe bipolar disorder, and in Foucault's case serious depression as well. Foucault elsewhere focuses considerable attention on critiquing modern psychoanalysis, psychology, and psychiatry, notably in his major work *History of Madness*, where Foucault theorizes these 'psy' fields as 'disciplines' that work to dominate, subjugate, limit, control, and especially 'normalize'.

Joy Division's song "The Eternal" hardly rises to the position of elaborating or even initiating an explanation of social and political causes of depression, or critiquing individualizing responses to individual experiences of depression, but the song does provide source material that can prove useful in critically reflecting on what it feels like to be depressed, and what kinds of patterns of thinking are connected in what ways with what patterns of feeling from a depressed perspective, as well as of what these might be symptomatic, in terms of larger sources and broader resonances. As I hear this song, the predominant emotional mood is one of resignation, where the narrator-protagonist of the lyrics, and the music as persona, come across as expressing what it is like to feel as if one has given up continuing to work, struggle, and fight, at least outwardly so, and therefore no longer outwardly express, no longer vent, any agony, anguish, angst, sadness, grief, worry, fear, anxiety, terror, anger, bitterness, or outrage.

The lyrics of the song–and the totality of organized sound that makes up the song as well–communicate the same message commonly conveyed through many Joy Division songs and especially many Ian Curtis lyrics: 'I have struggled with all I had to give, and pushed myself to my limits and beyond, but I have failed. I do feel guilty and ashamed I was not capable of achieving more and better. Yet I also feel it is most likely that nothing I could possibly have done, or especially could yet possibly do, would come anywhere near close to sufficient in strength to overcome the obstacles and opponents I have been facing. Those are and always have been overwhelmingly overpowering'. As I have suggested previously throughout this book, dramatically enacting this emotional state, this emotional experience, is more complicated that simply announcing 'the meaning of this song is this is what I feel'. By performatively embodying and enacting this experience the song pushes back against it, the song makes a concerted effort to challenge the conventional individualization of depression that marks off experience of depression as indicative of an individual deficiency that needs be addressed by means of prescription drugs and standard forms of talk therapy administered by a certified 'psy-professional. "The Eternal" as a song that is written to be shared, to be recorded and performed, for a potentially wide public audience, contributes toward 'communalizing' depression, to breaking the silence and the taboo surrounding openly sharing precisely what this feels, looks, and sounds like, and with whom and under what conditions this 'should' be shared. As audience members, far and wide, identify with the emotional state, the emotional experience, of depression expressed and communicated by and through "The Eternal," they begin to recognize they are far from alone, and that this kind of emotional state, and experience, may indeed be far from uncommon. This in turn can lead people to begin, at the least, to wonder why might that be? What factors–what social and political factors–might account for how widespread depression is, in modern life?

I find it makes sense to analyze the structure of "The Eternal," given its overtly funereal character via a modification of common elements drawn from the order of service for Church of

England funeral services (the Church of England being the religious denomination with which Ian Curtis and his family was affiliated). The song incorporates five sections, an opening instrumental section, a first vocal verse section, an intervening instrumental bridge section, a second vocal verse section, and a closing instrumental section. "The Eternal" contains no chorus, and no refrain. It is also a relatively long song, lasting over six minutes, and each section last for over a minute in length, with the concluding section lasting close to a minute and one half in length. Here is my breakdown of the structure of "The Eternal":

1. Instrumental Opening: 0:00–1:08. Slow processional gathering; setting the scene and establishing the pace, tone, and mood. Initiation of the service. Invocation of the gathered to give attendance to the spiritual and of the spiritual to attend to the gathering.
The song begins with a highly distinctive hissing, shaking, snaking electronically synthesized sound. This is followed by entry of the bass guitar, introducing the melody. Next comes a synthesizer keyboard tuned to a piano tone as well as the drum kit, with the snare drum by far the most prominent, along with a yet further synthesizer keyboard tuned to a much lower pitch range, primarily organized in terms of minor chords, sounding akin to an organ meets a chorus of stringed instruments involving an oscillating, warbling, and droning quality.

2. First Vocal Section: 1:09-2:16. In 'the order of service': reading fused with homily/eulogy/testimony that involves a reflective consideration of the meaning and significance of the occasion, in particular concerning relations between the dead and the living, the nature and tenor of the life and the death of the one who is now passed on, whose funeral this is, and of what as well as how we who are here gathered will remember the now deceased. In this section the vocal is overtly foregrounded and carries the melody with the array of synthesizer keyboard sounds providing substantial harmonic fill, the drum kit continuing to maintain the beat according to the same pattern introduced in section one, and the bass guitar coinciding with the drum kit to establish the functional bass level and facilitate the beat becoming a groove while also replicating and seconding the sounding of the melody.

3. Instrumental Bridge: 2:17-3:28. In 'the order of service': hymn fused with prayer. Further reflection on and testimony to the meaning and significance of this occasion and to what is now lost along what remains from and beyond what is lost; to what was achieved and what was not within the life of the one now passed on, the one whose funeral this is; and to what we are to make of this loss, and this remainder, including concerning what and how we will carry the latter forward with us from here. In this section we hear a notably emphatic convergence, coincidence, or direct paralleling of drum strikes and bass guitar notes, emphasizing the attack in both cases while we also hear a prominent return of the hissing, shaking, snaking electronically synthesized sound from the song's beginning. We also hear a striking new piano figure.

4. Second Vocal Passage: 3:29-4:36. In 'the order of service': further reading fused with homily/eulogy/testimony that involves a reflective consideration of the meaning and significance of the occasion, and concerning relations between the dead and the living, the nature and tenor of the life and the death of the one who is now passed on, whose funeral this is, and of what as well as how we

who are here gathered will remember the now deceased. The instrumentation here is much the same as in section two.

5. Closing Instrumental Section: 4:37-6:04. In 'the order of service': commendation, farewell, committal, and final dismissal of those gathering to attend the funeral. This section encompasses a commending the now dead, the now deceased, to the spiritual forces attending to 'his' subsequent eternal state/status; a final farewell to our last direct ties with a lingering embodiment of the now dead, the now deceased; a committal of the now dead, the now deceased, to 'his' eternal state/status, with the hope this will involve 'resting in peace' yet with no guarantee or even confidence that this will necessarily turn out to be the case; and a final dismissal of the mourners in attendance at this funeral to go forth as they will. Once again we hear a striking new piano figure. We also hear the return of the insistent convergent/coincident/directly parallel drum strike and bass guitar note pattern, with the accent on the attack, from the instrumental bridge section. And we hear as well the return of the hissing, shaking, snaky electronically synthesized sound which becomes even louder, more prominent, and pervasive across the soundbox than previously. At the same time, the lower-pitched, minor chord-oriented, organ meets chorus of strings resembling, oscillating, warbling, and droning keyboard sound becomes more pronounced as well, with some slight yet nonetheless striking developments in its timbre. After a final iteration of the hissing sound we hear a brief sampled snippet of unrecognizable recorded speech followed by a few random sounding piano notes.

Multiple commentators suggest the PowerTran Transcendent 2000 synthesizer is most likely responsible for the hissing, shaking, snaking sound, while the Arp Omni synthesizer is likely responsible for the lower-pitched, minor chord-oriented, organ meets chorus of strings resembling, oscillating, warbling, and droning keyboard sound. Each of these synthesizers maintained, even at that time, multiple features that allowed for considerable play with electronically synthesized sound as well as considerable play with sounds from more conventional electric instruments plugged into these synthesizers. What I hear in terms of distinct sounds sources, or distinct lines of sounds, in "The Eternal" are as follows: 1) Curtis's vocal; 2) Hook's bass guitar; 3) Morris's drums and cymbals, with the snare most prominent but often sounding in striking yet jarring unison with a cymbal, possibly a ride cymbal; 4) the hissing, shaking, and snaking electronically synthesized sound, most likely Hannett's creation and contribution; 5 and 6) *two* piano tone or piano voice synthesizer keyboard lines of sound played by Sumner, while likely involving a significant contribution from Hannett, at least on record; 7 and 8) *two* lower pitched, minor chord-oriented, organ meets chorus of strings resembling, oscillating, warbling, and droning keyboard lines of sound, played by Sumner, while once again likely involving a significant contribution from Hannett, at least on record; 9) a series of rattling electronic noises resembling a distorted version of the sound that might be produced by a baby's toy rattle, most likely Hannett's creation and contribution. All functional layers are deployed, while the harmonic fill layer here is particularly interesting with all the electronically synthesized lines of sound contributing to this layer, and it is worth noting that besides the vocal the bass guitar and at least three different lines of keyboard sound also contribute to conveying the melody.

The hissing sound enters the soundbox from low and to the left, then spreads across the soundbox so it is positioned low on both left and right sides. The odd rattle sound enters from higher along the vertical axis of the soundbox later on and is most prominently positioned toward the left.

Later in the song the hissing sound also moves higher along the vertical axis of the soundbox, toward the center along the horizontal axis of the soundbox, and close to the front of soundbox. The bass guitar enters and positions itself within the soundbox low and toward the back yet closer to the center than the hissing sound. The array of keyboard sounds enter and position themselves higher, with the piano keyboard sounds in turn positioned higher and further to the sides than the drone keyboard sounds, and in the latter case close attention to the soundbox leads me to detect the fourth synthesizer keyboard line of sound in the bridge, playing a melodic riff, slightly down from the center and to the sides, and especially pronounced to the left. The vocal enters and positions itself at the top and to the front of the soundbox. The drums and cymbals enter and position themselves from the sides, yet near the center along the vertical axis of the soundbox, with the snare drum and the ride cymbal foregrounded. The final recorded speech sample comes from low to the left, while the final random piano notes come from low to the right.

"The Eternal" involves an intricately layered instrumentation that involves notable movement within as well as across the soundbox with this entire perceptual space well filled. With "The Eternal" comprised of nine major sound sources, or nine major distinct lines of sound, I interpret the song as involving an expression and communication suggestive of or perhaps even directly corresponding to multiple nuances of what the song dramatizes is happening, has happened, and will happen. This multiplicity conveys to me a more complicated and especially a more troubled and unsettled emotional experience than might otherwise seem to be the case, if we only take account of what the lyrics alone suggest.

If "The Eternal" makes sense as an introspective contemplation of what it might mean to reach a state where feelings of surrender and resignation become powerfully compelling yet these continue to contend with resistant feelings that are restlessly troubled and unsettled by the prospect of fully, finally, and forever giving up, the song registers an element of protest at the same time as it pays witness to what its subject seemingly has been driven to experience.

This interpretation of "The Eternal" might resonate well, in Weberian terms, with continuing to wrestle with the clasps that enable the steel-hard casing to envelop, all the while feeling the steely hardness of the casing is too tough to free oneself from, and that repeated efforts to do so have failed, leaving the subject on the verge of deciding it is impossible to escape and all such effort must be abandoned as futile. If this connection makes sense, this nonetheless means the subject has sought to break free, and therefore is consciously and critically aware this is a steel-hard casing, rather than remaining oblivious to that fact–rather than identifying uncritically with the spirit of capitalism and in particular as it has evolved into an instrumentalist means-end logic almost entirely focused on the pursuit of money and of what money can buy.

This interpretation of "The Eternal" might resonate well, in Althusserian terms, with struggling to find a vantage point from which to contest, and counter, the operations of dominant ideology, through the Ideological State Apparatuses–including, for example, from within a specific Ideological State Apparatus, such as the educational or scholastic ideological state apparatus–yet not finding this vantage point, and finding it extremely difficult not to be continually re-interpellated into the position of subject of and to dominant ideology. Again, the individual here might well feel strongly inclined to give up, by concluding this effort is futile, and no such vantage is realizable, but the individual nonetheless has consciously and critically registered what is happening as domination and subjugation, as oppressive and repressive, and as leading to the reproduction and maintenance of conditions and relations of exploitation.

This interpretation of "The Eternal" might resonate well, in Foucaultian terms, with seeking to find a position from which effectively to resist the exercise of disciplinary power–again perhaps in relation to one particular prominent institutional arena through which this power operates, such as the schools–yet finding it extremely difficult, and seemingly virtually impossible, to locate and take advantage of such an opening, while at the same feeling continually overwhelmed by the carcereal force exerted through the exercise of disciplinary power, including via ubiquitous panoptic means and toward pervasive normalizing ends. But once more, although strongly inclined to give up, by concluding such resistant effort is futile, the individual here is nevertheless consciously critical of what exercise of disciplinary power involves, to what it leads, and what it produces, as well as how continuous and extensive is its hold. This individual does not simply uncritically identify with the position that disciplinary power impels them to identify with, and thereby does not uncritically engage in self-subjection aligned with the normative.

Variations in loudness in "The Eternal" are especially notable with the hissing sound, and also in the passages involving a coincidence of the bass guitar notes and the drum strikes, as well as with the drone synthesizer keyboard sounds, especially in the bridge and in particular in the concluding section. The vocal remains largely constant in terms of volume but increases slightly in volume together with movements upward in pitch and when extending notes as well as singing words, or syllables, across successive beats–and measures. At the beginning of "The Eternal" the hissing sound is louder than the bass guitar, but the bass guitar grows slightly louder relative to the hissing sound, and then the initial synthesizer keyboard sounds are even louder than both while the snare is by far the loudest sound from the drum kit. The vocal always sounds distinct and clear, but does not sound as if this involves Curtis singing deliberately loudly but rather the volume of his voice is managed by means of the prominent position Curtis's recorded singing voice occupies within the mix.

The time signature for "The Eternal" is 4/4 while the meter is, relative to the average for Joy Division songs, notably slow, with my estimate being 110 bpm. This is appropriate for simulating a funeral, and in particular a funeral procession. The drum sequence is uncluttered and almost sounds as if it consists of a pattern of soft strikes/loud strikes/soft strikes/loud strikes, all involving quarter notes–or quarter notes and quarter rests. In actuality, the drum pattern is slightly more complicated and not as precisely aligned with the standard rock beat than this but it nonetheless consists of a one-measure-long pattern that is consistently repeated virtually throughout the entire the song. The vocal pattern consists of two lines, which each contain the same two sequences of notes, each lasting slightly over two measures in length–and this is continuous throughout the song. The bass guitar likewise involves two riffs, each comprised of the successive repetition of a sequence that covers two measures. The piano keyboard lines are highly consistent too, comprised of repeated patterns of one to three measures in length while the drone keyboard lines cover six measures yet involve limited variation in chords and are also repeated over and over again. The same is further true with the hissing and rattle sounds, as they involve a limited number of successively repeated pitches. The rhythm contributes a feeling of slow, steady, regular movement.

"The Eternal" is recorded in the key of A minor. Minor chords are pronounced with the droning keyboard lines of sound. Translations of the song into tabs for guitar recommend no more than four to five chords, while following a highly regular pattern of movement among these chords, playing clean and with no reverb while translation of the song into tabs for bass guitar recommends playing a limited number of notes all along one string, the E string. The vocal follows a pattern in terms of pitch of moving gradually slightly down in line one followed by moving gradually slightly up in line two, over the course of a narrow interval range, no more than three steps at most. With the bass guitar, the pattern in terms of movement of pitch tends down, and across a small interval as well. The various keyboard and other synthesized sounds cover somewhat larger interval ranges, although they tend to oscillate among pitches, and also tend to move ultimately down after rising slightly up. The collective location and movement of pitch in "The Eternal" suggests quiet contemplation and introspection, albeit quite possibly while "Possessed by a fury that burns from inside"; some continuing exploration of possibilities meeting up with a pervading sense of tight confinement; and some limited persistence in dedication toward yet ongoing and further inquiry meeting up with a pronounced sense of the demonstrated futility of so doing.

Ian Curtis's vocal delivery in "The Eternal" is light, clear, ethereal, and gentle; it is not at all riven with manifest expression of overtly furious emotion but rather much the opposite. Curtis's vocal register sounds as if this is not confined, as if he is making full use of his diaphragm through his chest through his throat through his mouth without pushing his voice, without harshly darkening it, and without excess of exertion. Curtis's range here is limited but he lands on notes strongly and consistently. His vocal resonance is marked, with a slight reverberation that does not suggest heavy use of studio treatment, other than perhaps to disguise some of the limitations of his singing voice due to illness, as Tiffany Naiman suggests ("In a Lonely Place: Illness and the Temporal Exile of Ian Curtis"). Curtis's enunciation is precise. He sounds as if he is not tightly bound by but fully aware of pitch, while ready to modulate slightly around, slightly sharp or slightly flat. Curtis sounds as if he is following the rhythm, as if he is always first allowing other instruments or sound sources to initiate the rhythm and then to follow in line with what they have set forth, as always opening each vocal line with an extended rest suggests. It does not however sound as if his vocal lands off of or departs from close and consistent coincidence with the beat. Curtis's voice here sounds more distinctly like a natural baritone and less artificially darkened, as well as, ironically enough, given the subject matter of the song–or perhaps not so, if this song marks at least the beginning of coming to peace with 'an end', a decisive and final end–more fully at ease and less overtly filtered than in many other Joy Division songs. Curtis here does not ever sound as if he is pushing all that hard to be heard, and in fact, as Annik Honoré describes from her own direct experience of Ian Curtis doing this alone with her, as if he is singing to a single other person or even to himself, from within a small and intimate space.

In terms of timbre, the contributions of the hissing, shaking, snaking electronically synthesized sound, and that of the low-pitch, minor chord-oriented, organ meets chorus of strings resemblant, oscillating, warbling, and droning synthesizer keyboard sounds are especially interesting and add depth and complexity to the overall texture here that remains striking, even long after this extent of fusion between conventional rock instruments and electronically synthesized sources of sounds has become commonplace. Using once more the categories for analyzing timbre drawn from Megan Lavengood's *A New Approach to Analysis of Timbre*, I hear the following:

Vocal–Sustain: between bright and dark, more pure than noisy, more full than hollow, between rich and sparse, more beatless than beating, more steady than wavering, more harmonic than inharmonic. Vocal–Attack: more pure than noisy, more soft than percussive, and between bright and dark. Vocal–Pitch: between low and high, and more steady than wavering.

Drums and Cymbals–Sustain: between bright and dark, between pure and noisy, between full and hollow, between rich and sparse, beating, steady, and harmonic. Drums and Cymbals–Attack: more pure than noisy, percussive, and between bright and dark. Drums and Cymbals–Pitch: more low than high, and steady.

Bass guitar–Sustain: dark, pure, full, between rich and sparse, beatless, steady, and harmonic. Bass guitar–Attack: pure, between soft and percussive, and dark. Bass guitar–Pitch: low, and steady.

Hissing sound–Sustain: more bright than dark, noisy, hollow, sparse, beating, wavering, and inharmonic. Hissing sound–Attack: noisy, between percussive and soft but more soft, more bright than dark. Hissing sound–Pitch: higher than lower, and wavering.

Drone keyboard sound–Sustain: dark, noisy, hollow, sparse, beating, wavering, and inharmonic. Drone keyboard sound–Attack: noisy, between percussive and soft, and dark. Drone keyboard sound–Pitch: low, and wavering.

Rattle sound effect–Sustain: dark, noisy, hollow, sparse, beating, wavering, and inharmonic. Rattle sound effect–Attack: noisy, soft, and dark. Rattle sound effect–Pitch: low, and wavering.

Piano keyboard sound–Sustain: bright, pure, full, between rich and sparse, between beatless and beating, steady, and harmonic. Piano keyboard sound–Attack: pure, between percussive and soft, and bright. Piano keyboard sound–Pitch: high, and steady.

Collectively this series of timbres combined with tempo and the precise arrangement of the density of the instrumentation contribute an overall somber feeling to the song. Yet they encompass a notable variety, while the relatively foregrounded sound sources contribute a more decisive attack than the relatively backgrounded sound sources. This variety also effectively conveys elements of continuing disturbance, unrest, and of feeling not fully and finally settled intermixing with a pronounced feeling of resignation. So this seems, if this is a funeral, it is not at all an easy funeral–not one that feels as if it is attended by any comforting sense the deceased is likely 'resting', or will likely 'rest', 'in peace'. The sounds convey a strong sense that we are attending a funeral following a tragic death, a death of a life that cried out for more, a death of a life that was cut off unfinished. Even the snare drum strike sounding together with the cymbal crash echoing the snare feels unsettling–harsh and not just hard. Timbres help convey an approximation of a slow, deliberative, formal march–a slow, deliberate, formal procession–combined with a quietly burning, inward barely contained intensity bordering on fury. Timbres convey an approximation of feeling still too tightly contained and too uncomfortably restless, even to an unnatural extent, while seeking to find peace.

Timbre, together with vocal delivery, pitch, rhythm, and loudness conveys a sense of feeling defeated, feeling as if it is impossible effectively to escape or evade, to counter and contest, and to resist and oppose, yet maintaining a residual restlessness, a residual discontent, a residual refusal, even as otherwise inclined to resign and surrender, to give up and give in. This, once more, attests to an at least *initial* rupture–with the steel-hard casing/iron cage, with the power of dominant ideology and of interpellation as subject of and to dominant ideology through the ISAs, and with the exercise of disciplinary power across a carcereal continuum employing panoptic instrumentalities toward normalizing ends. The subject in this case cannot accept, cannot identify with, whom and what 'he' is overwhelmingly called upon to accept and identify–even if 'he' cannot recognize any viable alternative avenue by which he can persist. The challenge this song raises for Weber, Althusser, and Foucault, as well as for all critical theorists and social and political activists committed toward the need for progressive reform, radical dissonance, and revolutionary transformation, is to show other people *how* it might be possible to proceed in leading, living, and especially being able to carry on a life so committed–how to do without ending up all the more alienated and isolated, all the more rejected and defeated, and all the more suffering and hurting.

As I listen to "The Eternal," and especially as I do so over and over again, I feel myself imitating multiple elements of this song quite consciously and deliberately: 1) the vocal, especially in the middle and at the end of lines, especially as Curtis extends syllables and words across multiple beats while moving between multiple notes; 2) the opening bass guitar riff and the strong hits on the snare drum; and 3) the melodic sequences played by the various keyboards. I feel this involves a complex if not strenuous exertion of force while the duration of exertion feels persistent. I also feel the exertion of force accomplishes what it needs to do. It feels to me as if all of the sound sources function as if aware of each other even as they carry out and play their distinct parts, while they do frequently directly line up, converge, coincide, and parallel each other.

I find it difficult to interpret "The Eternal" in terms of anticipation as an avenue of musical affect, as it feels to me as if the song, and more precisely the music as persona, is past anticipating, and at least directly at the edge of abandoning 'anticipation' forever, launching itself into an eternity of non-anticipation, or post-anticipation. If this song does follow a structure close to an order of service common in Church of England funerals, this would be an order familiar to many if not most attending which means, in turn, they–we–will anticipate each successive stage in the service. The unsettled and troubled tenor of this funeral also leads to anticipation that this event is important to conduct, and to carry through, but it will prove insufficient by itself alone as 'healing' and 'peace' will not come easy. Perhaps the music as persona anticipates an eternity of disquiet.

With "The Eternal" I feel expression of resignation combined with a residual troubled and unsettled remnant resistance to and refusal of resignation. I feel expression of elements of other emotions as well, at least small remnants: bitterness, anger, fury, disappointment, disillusionment, condemnation, frustration, and alienation. Collectively the song expresses a sense of mourning with a persistent edge of unquiet upset. It feels as well expressive of a warning–i.e., that this is what is happening and this is what will happen if decisive action is not taken to prevent ending up like this: dead, which could apply as well to a cause as to a life.

Overall, the acoustic impact of "The Eternal" feels intimate, almost uncomfortably so. The music as persona feels as if it might be analyzing where 'we' are now at, and how are those present and participating engaged at this present moment. It feels also as if the music as persona might be analyzing what it means to be in this kind of extreme state. The song prompts considerable analysis, especially but not exclusively of the lyrics, which suggests to me is it is useful to analyze in turn what connects interpretations of this song that many people have commonly shared, as well as what kind of overall 'message', to all of us, does this song offer.

"The Eternal" suggests associations with what a funeral might feel like from the vantage point not only of the mourners, but also of the dead person watching and listening to their own funeral. And the song suggests associations with what it feels like to be forced to live as if dead, as if partially dead, as if not fully or truly human. As Dan Goodley writes, in *Disability and Other Human Questions*, disabled people are often and long often have been excluded from being acknowledged and included as 'human'. This includes not only due to lack of accommodation and access, but also due to the influence of meritocratic ideology, according to which people gain what they deserve according to how hard they work and how much skill, talent, and savvy they bring to bear. But disabled people often are unable, or unequally able, to succeed in this kind of pursuit. In many workplaces, working extremely hard, up to and far beyond 'ordinary' limits–i.e., giving 110% or always pushing one's self to go faster, higher, harder, etc.–is uncritically acclaimed as a model everyone should follow. Yet for many disabled and chronically ill people this becomes effectively possible because their disability and their illness places substantive limits on how far they can push themselves to keep doing steadily more and more.

As Goodley explains, 'humanism' (or at least 'liberal humanism') conventionally valorizes qualities–including the capacity for supposedly fully independent, autonomous, and rationally determined choices, decisions, and actions–that can and do exclude many disabled people, including people with intellectual disabilities or people with serious to severe mental health challenges. Many other groups of people are often not treated as if they are equally and fully human, such as immigrants including refugees and asylum seekers, people of color in general in White-dominant societies, people living in poverty, working class people, members of 'the new dangerous class'–the precariat, women in general (just think about how women routinely do not on average maintain the effective right to move freely in public without fear of being harassed and assaulted as men do, while even, as is the case with the notorious murder of Sarah Everard in London, have ample reason to fear they will be victimized by men working jobs, as police officers, supposedly committed toward protecting the safety of members of the public), LGBTQIA+ people (just think about how many transgender people, especially transgender people of color continue to be murdered in the US on an all too routine basis), homeless people, and prisoners and ex-prisoners.

In considering how "The Eternal" confronts taboos–and invites and encourages confronting taboos–once again I hear, and feel, this song confronting a continuing major taboo by communicating from the perspective of someone experiencing major depression. Likewise, "The Eternal" confronts, at least as I interpret the song, a common taboo against imagining one's own death, one's own funeral, and what it might mean to exist–or to not exist, to no longer exist–after death, including throughout eternity while confined, immobile, and consisting of nothing. I hear "The Eternal" confronting another common taboo: identifying with the situation and vantage point of people who are and long have been extremely marginalized, whom many others don't like to come into any contact with ever because doing so makes them feel highly uneasy–notably intellectually disabled children and especially intellectually disabled adults. And "The Eternal" also makes sense as exploring a taboo by identifying with the position that failure is inevitable and cannot be overcome, eschewing more popular positions that suggest 'there is always hope', and resources–and regimens (such as Cognitive Behavioral Therapy, or CBT, likely the most common form of psychotherapy in the US today) are available to help us through and beyond every problem we might experience.

In listening to "The Eternal" it can be difficult initially to pinpoint precisely how many distinct sound sources, or distinct lines of musical sound, are involved and precisely where and how they separate as well as precisely where and how they blend. And it likewise continues to challenge commentators, even those with musical production and performance expertise, to determine precisely how all of the sounds contributing to making up this song were arrived at. Also, some familiar 'rock' sounds are absent–that of the six (or twelve) string electric guitar as well as the bass drum and hi-hat. Yet what is most invisible, intangible, and ephemeral may be the music as persona, including the narrator-protagonist of the lyrics, as this life feels at the cusp of ending, and disappearing. In a broader sense, the value of an individual self and of this individual's lived existence feels exposed as always destined to end, to disappear, and to become invisible, intangible, and ephemeral, with the passage of time, and even more to the point, from the vantage point of 'the eternal'. As aforementioned, depression tends to leave the depressed feeling virtually non-existent, as no longer truly living–and this song strongly resonates with the vantage point of one who is severely depressed. When one is severely depressed one feels as if one is barely alive, far more dead than alive, more like a ghost of a person than a person who is fully visible, tangible, and perdurable.

As I listen to and reflect on "The Eternal" I draw connections with a feeling that I and undoubtedly many others have experienced, at least from time to time. This feeling maintains multiple components. First, we feel struggles we are and have been deeply invested in seem to be endlessly ongoing, and endlessly in need of repeating, yet without substantial and especially sustainable progress ever being achieved. Second, we feel this is the case no matter how long and hard we struggle. Third, we feel the forces marshaled against us always prove more powerful than we are. Fourth, we feel it is futile to continue to try over and over again while constantly failing to realize and sustain our desired end. Fifth, even as it feels like the consequences of our efforts always seems to involve the equivalent of two steps backward following every one step forward, and we feel exhausted and despairing, we also feel as we have suffered a grave loss not only in committing so much of ourselves to this failed effort but also because we perceive nowhere else to which we can turn that can even come close to filling the emptiness we feel in deciding we need to give up and abandon struggling any further. Many of us can readily relate to feeling this way, at various points and over various intervals, even if if we do not give up and abandon struggling further.

Over the course of my life I have supported and contributed to many social and political struggles where I have at times felt exactly as I have described above, that we are always falling short, always failing, always losing, nothing is ever enough, and the forces against us always prove too strong–and it may be too late. I have felt this way about struggles concerning all of the following: 1) ecological overreach and prevention of ecocide; 2) resurgent fascism, and even more specifically the resurgent and persistent popularity of Trump and Trumpism, as well as the recurrent appeal of populist demagogues and populist demagoguery; 3) substantial levels and rates of poverty, homelessness, and hunger, and especially within one of the world's overall wealthiest–if not indeed the world's overall wealthiest–nation; 4) right-wing populist attacks on and broader collective erosion of support for the value of a liberal arts education, for students from all socio-economic and not just wealthy backgrounds; 5) dismissal of and hostility toward the public value, the value as signal contribution to the public good, of teaching and learning and of intellectual work and cultural production in humanities, arts, and social science fields; 6) lack of available positions for tenure-line faculty, in particular in humanities fields, at the college and university level, for all those qualified for these positions; 7) excessive reliance on, and super-exploitation, of adjunct faculty at colleges and universities, especially in humanities fields; 8) toward anything like socialism, even reinvigoration of post-WWII welfare state social democracy; 9) equitable access to and exercise of resources–full accommodation–for the disabled, including people with both mental as well as physical disabilities and including people with 'intellectual disabilities'; 10) racial profiling, racist police discrimination and racist police violence, and insidiously systemic racism operant throughout social institutions even when and where overt forms of expression of racist bigotry are taboo; 11) reparations in response to the massively damaging impact and legacy of major historical forms of systemic racism, including African slavery and imperialist conquest and colonial subjugation throughout what subsequently became known as 'The Third World'; 12) involvement of the US state–and its familiar allies, such as the UK–in 'forever wars', wars of imperialist aggression, and 'the war on terror' specifically; 13) attacks on 'critical race theory' as code for attempts to ban teaching about systemic, structural, and institutional patterns of inequity and injustice along lines in particular of race–but also of sex, gender, and sexuality; 14) ever-recurrent attacks on the academic freedom of teachers and students–to freely teach and learn, to freely explore and inquire; 15) meaningful gun control in the US that can put a decisive end to or at least greatly reduce the numbing extent of gun violence that all too regularly takes place in this country, in the form, especially, of what feels like countless mass shootings and mass killings; 16) genuine and substantial welcome, acceptance and inclusion of immigrants, including refugees and asylum seekers, predominating over xenophobic suspicion and hostility; 17) reducing socio-economic inequality, and especially ending its seeming continuous rise; 18) the COVID-19 pandemic; and 19) ending systemic violence, especially sexual violence, directed versus women and girls, with girls and women still unable to enjoy the same freedom to move, to engage, to exist, in the same array of public spaces, as boys and men. Yes, in relation to every single one of these issues–every single one of these fights–many concrete gains have in fact been made, the struggle does continue, and I do continue to support this struggle, but in relation to every single one of these concerns I have at times felt despair that the struggle is endlessly ongoing, it never succeeds, it always fails, while the obstacles and opponents always remain too vast and too powerful to overcome.

I certainly have felt, at times, tempted to despair, that none of this has improved in my lifetime, and, if anything, it has in every instance, worsened, with nothing I have attempted to do, individually or together with many others sharing the same commitments and the same objectives, making any positive difference. In order for me, and others for that matter, to empathetically understand, appreciate, and productively respond to what a song like "The Eternal" expresses and communicates, we need to be able to draw connections, in our own emotional experience, with instances, and intervals, in which we also have felt that no matter how long and hard we work, struggle, and fight, or no matter how long and hard groups and movements of people we are a part of work, struggle, and fight, what is truly needed is never achieved, and will never be achieved. When we feel this way we feel the eternal result of all our efforts always has been, always is, and always will be the same: never enough, never enough to succeed in bringing about what needs to be. We don't necessarily need *believe* any of this, but just at any point in our lives to have *felt* this way. This includes feeling we have participated in working, struggling, and fighting for what is right and necessary; giving everything we had to give; and yet it hasn't been enough and instead feels like it never will be enough because, again, the obstacles and opponents we face always have been, always are, and always will be, too overwhelmingly powerful.

I relate manifestation of depression in and by "The Eternal" with the same feeling I have just elaborated. I experience this song as challenging me to keep working to advocate on behalf of the need for us to develop a more fully empathetic understanding, respect, and appreciation for what depression is like, what it *feels* like, at its most extreme and precarious, and especially for the social and political factors that can and do give rise to depression. In order to do so we need to be able to recognize continuities in feeling with those experienced by people in depression, people who are depressed, in order to push toward communalizing engagement with depression, and especially communalizing engagement with its social and political sources, while actively striving toward transforming vulnerability, and precariousness even more broadly conceived, into sources of collective strength. In so doing, we are–we will be–working collectively to enhance the prospect of many who otherwise will reach the point where they feel they cannot persist past their feelings of failing and of failure, even of utter failing and total failure. We need to be able collectively to help each other recognize and accept these feelings are exemplary of all too human imperfection, especially when we are individually isolated, alienated, atomized, fragmented, and fractured. In communalizing engagement with depression, and the social and political sources of depression, while taking depression seriously and treating it with respect, including as a source of potentially valuable insight and indeed wisdom, we can help each other persist even with what feels Sisyphean–not by 'getting over' or 'getting past' depression, but rather by transforming it–by sublating it. In other words, this involves a process of sublation in relation to depression: canceling, preserving, and transforming at once.

In my own more immediately personal life I have felt the same sense of deep despair and futility. I felt this way at Arizona State University, when I lost out as a finalist, as the 'inside candidate' for a tenure-track position in the areas I had been responsible for, for the preceding two years as a visiting assistant professor, after I thought I had done everything well and was the leading candidate, and then experiencing shock in recognizing that my candidacy for this position, and the result, had been and would continue to be the focus of bitter division within the department for the rest of my remaining time at Arizona State. I felt this way after Governor Scott Walker and the Republican Party-dominated Wisconsin State legislature passed Act 10, which ended legal collective bargaining, finally just won the year before for university faculty and academic staff, for all but a narrow few public sector unions on other than a minor array of issues, leading to a rapid decline in union membership. I felt this way after the same state government enacted legislation to erode tenure rights and protections as well as the power of shared governance, while attempting to jettison the substance of the Wisconsin Idea and imposing a massive cut in the budget for the University of Wisconsin System. I have felt this way often on social media, such as Facebook, where it can feel much more like duty to periodically post and respond than providing much if any real pleasure and satisfaction. I have felt this way in writing this book, and the other I am simultaneously writing.

Each semester in my 35 years of teaching I have reached a point where I have felt overwhelmed, as if I am steadily falling further and further behind such that I will never be able to catch up. Even as I always do eventually catch up, that does not negate the impact of that feeling–of how hard a weight I experience it to be–and how much I must rely on stubborn faith I will make it, because precisely how I will do so seems, at its worst, impossible to fathom. Throughout my years teaching and working as a university faculty member, it has frequently felt as if a seemingly endless series of administrative initiatives always takes precious time and energy away from teaching, scholarship, genuinely valuable community service/civil engagement, and necessary/healthful work-life balance. It often feels as if trying to achieve anything approaching a healthful work-life balance is a futile quest, because the implicit as well as explicit pressure in this job always to excel in one's performance, and always to aim to do so by continually working more and more, and harder and harder, feels palpably omnipresent.

For someone such as myself living with serious chronic illness, and substantial disability, however largely invisible, this has often proven excruciating. But I never have wanted to accept that I, because of my illness and disability, am 'lesser'–of lesser capability, of lesser worth. I never have wanted to accept that I, because of my illness and disability, am less truly or fully human, less truly or fully welcome and included, within the province of what my society and culture effectively defines as what human beings are–and should be–capable of being and doing.

In chapter one I advance the following argument:

Ian Curtis's life and his work transcend the circumstances of his death. Even when moving toward elegy, lament, exhaustion, confusion, and resignation, the lyrics and the music propose the need to continue, to endure, and to persist. And to do so even when this seems altogether impossible. Curtis's art is not simply a prolonged suicide note. Curtis was not destined to die young. His suicide was not inevitable. He had family, he had friends, he had a community. And so he had support. Yet he needed more, even much more. In his personal life he faced multiple extreme pressures, all of which taken together would have been enough to completely overwhelm just about anyone. And, at the same time, he was a fiercely committed artist, who maintained extremely high standards and extremely high ambitions, for what he sought to come to grips with, to convey, to realize, and to achieve through this art–an art requiring him to face up to, and to symbolically relive, the worst horrors human beings are capable of perpetrating against each other. That is a noble cause, one we must carry on, but it needs to be a genuinely collective one. Curtis ended up a victim of the very society he was protesting against, a society that forces us, all too often, to resist its injustices, in whatever ways we can, but at the same time to need to do so individually, isolated and alone, even when ostensibly surrounded by many other people. A society all too often complacent about, distracted from, numbed by, or otherwise indifferent to human suffering, including the suffering of those who are yet further suffering on account of their extraordinary extent of empathetic identification with and solidaristic support for the suffering of others.

What "The Eternal" prompts me to think about is the *urgency* of finding ways to better enable people to engage in this or similar kinds of struggle *collectively*, to be able to draw and rely upon the kinds of support they need to be able to proceed and persist in this effort, and this begins by recognizing how insufficient such forms of support so often are in capitalist society. A beginning of a necessary response is to refuse to pretend the problem is not as serious and substantial as it is, and also to refuse to compromise with and concede to ideological norms that pull people away from cooperation, collectivity, unity, solidarity, and empathy by instead emphasizing and promoting individualism, competition, suspicion, distrust, hostility, bigotry, cynicism, solipsism, and callous dehumanization and nihilistic destructiveness.

"The Eternal" engages mediations in particular between life and death, the living and the dead, finitude and infinity, and ephemerality and eternity. Despite its marked funereal form and content, "The Eternal" conveys more of a sense of the persistence of struggle than at first might seem the case. The song certainly is vividly sketched and pointedly reflective while it definitely focuses intently on desire for control meeting up with limits to, and even the impossibility, of exerting control. And at the same time "The Eternal" suggests at the furthest extremes of vulnerability and emptiness we might experience valuable clarity and find valuable insight. This song epitomizes Ian Curtis's, and together with Ian Curtis the whole of Joy Division's, interest in, focus on, and attraction toward contemplation of and engagement with 'the extreme'–with extremes or extremities–and it also epitomizes not only representing but also conveying a controlled fury that involves a paradoxical synthesis of the passionate and the dispassionate. Chillingly, the song might make sense as imagining attendance at one's own funeral is the last instance in one's ghost will be able to move anywhere at all as then forever after, for all of eternity, this ghost will be confined, while remaining conscious, to the space of burial, such that 'he' will spend eternity "Just watching the trees and the leaves as they fall," as "My view stretches out from the fence to the wall." Aside from that imagined scenario, the song also makes sense as an instance of introspective introjection in the form of an empathetic identification with the vantage point of those who in life are unable to express and communicate in 'normal' fashion and who are thereby effectively 'unheard'–such as intellectually disabled youth and adults–feeling similar to 'the ghost' just described.

"The Eternal" conjures up ready association with many 'metaphorical darknesses' in human history and society, and in the condition of being human, especially that of the human social being living in the advanced capitalist, (post)modern world. These include the situation and treatment of disabled people. And these also include the situation and treatment of those who are exceptionally highly idealistic and who thereby experience disenchantment concerning what they are idealistic concerning as an exceptionally devastating blow. Depression and its weight and impact, along with how much about it remains misunderstood and feared rather than helped and supported is another. As are how numerous and powerful are forces committed toward preservation and perpetuation of the social and political status quo even when and where this status quo is virtually crying out in desperate need of urgent transformation. As is how easy and how commonplace it is not to really know people one thinks one knows, and how easy in turn it is not to care, or care all that much, about other people, especially when they are in need of care, even in desperate need of care. As are the consequent impacts of a hyper- or supra- individualized society and culture–cold and hostile, fragmented and atomized, and alienative and incarcerative.

"The Eternal" suggests incredible frustration over meeting up with severe limits to one's own effective individual agency while experiencing a keen sense of responsibility that one _should_ be able to exercise much greater, much more effective individual agency, yet the structural barriers to doing so have proven overwhelming. "The Eternal" also definitely feels like the song identifies with a position as alienated, isolated, and lonely; as a stranger, outsider, and an outcast; as one who has suffered ample vulnerability, entrapment, anxiety, and fear; and as one who feels efforts to connect with others at levels and to degrees one desires have failed, despite desperately wanting and needing to break through.

In "The Eternal" the domination of the Subject, within Lacan's order of the Symbolic, feels closer to fabricating an experience akin to a constantly ongoing funeral than otherwise often is represented to be the case. Intimations of Lacan's order of the Real here come across as are deeply traumatic, deeply traumatizing, to the point of registering feelings akin to those of PTSD.

"The Eternal" alludes to the fascism of everyday life, in ostensibly non- and even post- fascist society and culture, in the form of widespread inability of all of us all too often to be able substantially to care for others, even for others only slightly distant from or seemingly even slightly different from ourselves, even for ourselves, and of how many of us get effectively pushed to the social margins, becoming de facto social 'losers'. "The Eternal" resonates with theories of fascism that conceive of fascism as representative of particular mode of capitalism, capitalism in crisis, that nonetheless carries forward fundamental elements of the logic and spirit of capitalism–perhaps to their indeed furthest logical conclusion.

"The Eternal," as is often the case with Ian Curtis's lyrics, and Joy Division music in which these lyrics play a signal part, conveys a sense of struggling to express and communicate beyond what words can do, while nonetheless registering and attending to the limits of what words can do. And even though the song initially at least feels fully and finally resigned, remnant uncertainty, hesitation, and doubt remain–even persist.

Weber's *Protestant Ethic and the Spirit of Capitalism* traces roots of the spirit of capitalism in an ethic developed by post-Calvinist Protestant religion in need of some way of overcoming a sense of lack of any control, and even any clear direction, for how to live life in the face of predestination for either eternal salvation or eternal damnation that cannot be known. The book ends at the point where the evolution of the response to this dilemma has become increasingly problematic, and is threatening to impose a closing down, even elimination, of the possibility of exercising meaningful control, and of pursuing a meaningful direction, in life, as this is all rigidly defined in continuous terms of pursuit of material gain, within a steel-hard casing that prevents one from doing much of anything else, and from even recognizing it might be desirable to conceive of doing much of anything else. For those recognizing this state of affairs yet recognizing no way to break free, even after trying repeatedly to break free but also repeatedly failing, it can feel as if one is doomed to a state of virtual 'eternal' torment–with one's critical consciousness only making this situation feel all that much worse.

Althusser's *On the Reproduction of Capitalism: Ideology and the Ideological State Apparatuses* suggests contrary to a dominant perception within late modern capitalist society that we are individually free agents, freely in charge of what and how we think, feel, and believe, as well as freely in charge of what we choose, decide, and do, this is far from the case–as our 'freedom' is a freedom that is always already constructed for us within constraints that overwhelmingly define and determine us, as subjects to and of ideology, and as active participants in the forces of reproduction of a social system rooted in, founded upon, and driven by exploitation. If and when we develop a critical consciousness of this situation, and if and when we are not fully interpellated into a completely successful identification with positions as subjects of and to dominant ideology, we can indeed once more feel despair, because even though we cannot abide by the illusions and delusions that comfortably satisfy others, we can't recognize any other way to proceed, from where we are at. If socialist struggle to transform capitalism into communism remains unreal to us, and if we cannot establish any enabling connection with any other more immediate, local, and narrow forms of struggle that inspire us with a sense that we are making and can make a necessary and meaningful positive difference (including, as Althusser recommends, through union activity, directly focused at and around workplace issues), then we are likely, once again, to feel as if we are in effect doomed to a state of what feels like virtually eternally ongoing powerlessness and alienation, with our critical consciousness, once more, only making this experience all that much worse.

Foucault's *Discipline and Punish: The Birth of the Prison* does address how popular responses to dominant exercises of punitive power have historically coopted, resignified, and reoriented what this means, with 'the people' no longer accepting and serving in their positions as expected. Yet the bulk of this book recounts how disciplinary power surpasses preceding forms of punishment of crime, criminals, and criminality, working all the more effectively and extending its reach much further, including much further over virtually everyone, far beyond literal prisons alone. Normally, according to the successful exercise of disciplinary power, individuals are produced not to conceive of themselves as 'produced by disciplinary power', and not as confined or constrained by disciplinary power, even not to be conscious of their self-subjection in response to pervasive panopticism, and certainly not to regard the whole of society, and the whole of social life, as a carcereal continuum. Yet if and when they do develop a critical awareness of this, and no longer can rest content to identify uncritically with the operations of disciplinary power, and in particular oppressive normalization, they need to find means and spaces according to which and from which they can resist. Otherwise, once more, the weight of their lived conditions of existence are likely to feel all the more eternally unbearable, because they cannot invest in and identify with the illusions, and delusions, of a commonsense that cannot recognize the exercise of disciplinary power as such–and their critical consciousness increasingly becomes an unbearable weight.

In sum, "The Eternal" challenges the theorizations developed by Weber in *Protestant Ethic and the Spirit of Capitalism*, Althusser in *On the Reproduction of Capitalism: Ideology and the Ideological State Apparatuses*, and Foucault in *Discipline and Punish: The Birth of the Prison* to attend, further, to how it becomes possible, effectively, sustainably, and perdurably to break with and from, to contest and counter, to resist and oppose, and to reform and transform alienative, oppressive, exploitative, dehumanizing, and destructive structures, relations, norms, and institutional exercises and operations of power–and to do for the long haul, while also attending to the psychic weight and ready risk of major psychic damage of so doing–such that collective struggle can fuse with collective care, and collective repair, of the all too vulnerable, fragile, and precarious individual self.

Works Cited

Althusser, Louis. "Ideology and Ideological State Apparatuses: Notes Toward an Investigation." *Lenin and Philosophy and Other Essays*. 1970. Ben Brewster, trans. New York: Monthly Review Press, 1971, 121-176.

_____. "Note on the ISAs." 1977. *On the Reproduction of Capital: Ideology and Ideological State Apparatuses*. 1995. G.M. Goshgarian, trans. London: Verso, 2014, 218-231.

_____. *On the Reproduction of Capital: Ideology and Ideological State Apparatuses*. 1995. G.M. Goshgarian, trans. London: Verso, 2014.

Amatenstein, Sherry LCSW. "Quotes About Depression & What Depression Feels Like." Psycom.net. Https://www.psycom.net/depression-what-depression-feels-like#slide Accessed 14 October 2021.

Balibar, Etienne. "Foreword: Althusser and the 'Ideological State Apparatuses'." Louis Althusser, *On the Reproduction of Capital: Ideology and Ideological State Apparatuses*. 1995. G.M. Goshgarian, trans. London: Verso, 2014, vii-xviii.

Ballard, J.G. *The Atrocity Exhibition*. 1969. London: Fourth Estate, 2014.

_____. "Author's Note." *The Atrocity Exhibition*. 1969. London: Re/Search, 1990, vii.

_____. "An Investigative Spirit: J.G. Ballard Talks to Travis Elborough." 2006. *The Atrocity Exhibition*. London: Fourth Estate, 2014, 185-188.

Baldwin, James. As quoted in Eyal Press, *Dirty Work: Essential Jobs and the Hidden Toll of Equality in America*. New York: Farrar, Straus and Giroux, 2021.

Beckett, Andy. *When the Lights Went Out: Britain in the Seventies*. London: Faber and Faber, 2009.

Bentham, Jeremy. *The Panopticon Writings*. 1787-1791. London: Verso, 2011.

Bickerdike, Jennifer Otter, ed. *Joy Devotion: The Importance of Ian Curtis and Fan Culture*. London: Headpress, 2016.

Bidet, Jacques. "Introduction." Louis Althusser, *On the Reproduction of Capital: Ideology and Ideological State Apparatuses*. 1995. G.M. Goshgarian, trans. London: Verso, 2014, xix-xxviii.

Burkhart, Kira et. al. "Water Pollution from Slaughterhouses." Environmental Integrity Project. 2018. Https://environmentalintegrity.org/reports/water-pollution-from-slaughterhouses/ Accessed 14 October 2021.

Camus, Albert. *The Myth of Sisyphus*. 1942. Justin O'Brien, trans. London: Hamish Hamilton, 1955.

Church, David. "'Welcome to the Atrocity Exhibition': Ian Curtis, Rock Death, and Disability." *Disability Studies Quarterly*, Fall 2006, Volume 26, No. 4. DOI: http://dx.doi.org/10.18061/dsq.v26i4.804

Church of England. "An Order for the Burial of the Dead (Alternative Services: Series One)." Https://www.churchofengland.org/prayer-and-worship/worship-texts-and-resources/common-worship/death-and-dying/order-burial-dead Accessed 14 October 2021.

_____. "Funeral service step-by-step." Https://www.churchofengland.org/life-events/funerals/funeral-service-step-step Accessed 14 October 2021.

Coley, Nathan. "There Will Be No Miracles Here." Sculpture outside the Scottish National Gallery of Modern Art (Modern Two) in Edinburgh, Scotland. Created 2007-2009.

Conrad, Anna. "How Joy Division made Closer: 'We were really tight as a band; there was a lot of telepathy going on'–Drummer Stephen Morris talks through how each track on Joy Division's *Closer* came together." *GQ Magazine*. Https://www.gq-magazine.co.uk/culture/article/joy-division-closer-album Accessed 14 October 2021.

Cox, Arnie. *Music & Embodied Cognition: Listening, Moving, Feeling, & Thinking*. Bloomington: Indiana University Press, 2017.

Curtis, Ian. *So This is Permanence: Joy Division Lyrics and Notebooks*. Deborah Curtis and Jon Savage, eds. London: Faber and Faber, 2014.

Cvetkovich, Ann. *Depression: a Public Feeling*. Durham: Duke University Press, 2012.

Du Bois, W.E.B. *Black Reconstruction in America, 1860-1880*. First published in 1935.

Debord, Guy. *Society of the Spectacle*. 1967. Freddy Perlman and Friends, trans. Detroit: Black and Red Press, 1970.

Dowling, Stephen. "What pop music tells us about JG Ballard." *BBC Magazine*. 20 April 2009. Http://news.bbc.co.uk/2/mobile/uk_news/magazine/8008277.stm Accessed 14 October 2021.

Durkheim, Émile. *Suicide: a Study in Sociology*. 1897. John A. Spaulding and George Simpson, trans. New York: The Free Press, 1951.

Eason, John. As quoted in Eyal Press, *Dirty Work: Essential Jobs and the Hidden Toll of Equality in America*. New York: Farrar, Straus and Giroux, 2021.

Eliade, Mircea. *The Myth of the Eternal Return: Or, Cosmos and History*. 1949. William R. Trask, trans. Princeton: Princeton University Press, 1971.

_____. *The Sacred and the Profane: the Nature of Religion*. 1957. William R. Trask, trans. Orlando: Harcourt, 1959.

Elias, Norbert. *The Civilizing Process: Sociogenic and Psychogenic Investigations*. 1939. Edmund Jephcott, trans. London: Blackwell, 1994.

Elborough, Travis. "An Investigative Spirit: J.G. Ballard Talks to Travis Elborough." 2006. *The Atrocity Exhibition*. London: Fourth Estate, 2014, 185-188.

Faulkner, William. *The Sound and The Fury*. London: Jonathan Cape and Harrison Smith, 1929.

Fisher, Mark. *Capitalist Realism: Is There No Alternative?* Winchester: Zero Books, 2009.

618

_____. *K-Punk: The Collected and Unpublished Writings of Mark Fisher*. London: Repeater, 2018.

Flexican, Lex. "Joy Division–Atrocity Exhibition." *Sound: all things audio and media related*. 11 December 2016. Https://snava2snava.wordpress.com/2016/12/11/joy-division-atrocity-exhibition/ Accessed 14 October 2021.

Fontaine, Claire. Https://www.clairefontaine.ws Accessed 14 October 2021.

Foucault, Michel. *Discipline and Punish*. 1975. Alan Sheridan, trans. New York: Pantheon, 1977.

_____. *History of Madness*. Jonathan Murphy and Jean Khalfa, trans. 1961. London: Routledge, 2006.

_____. *History of Sexuality*. Four Volumes (*An Introduction, The Use of Pleasure, The Care of the Self*, and *Confessions of the Flesh*). 1976, 1984, 1984, and 2018. Robert Hurley, trans. New York: Penguin/Random House, 1978, 1985, 1986, and 2021.

_____. *Madness and Civilization: a History of Insanity in the Age of Reason*. Richard Howard, trans. New York: Random House, 1965.

Frantzen, Mikkel Krause. "A Future with No Future: Depression, the Left, and the Politics of Mental Health." *Los Angeles Review of Books*. 16 December 2019. Https://lareviewofbooks.org/article/future-no-future-depression-left-politics-mental-health/ Accessed 14 October 2021.

Freud, Sigmund. *Civilization and Its Discontents*. 1930. James Strachey, trans. New York: W.W. Norton, 1961.

Franklin, Benjamin. "Advice to a Young Tradesman." Originally published in 1748.

Garland, David. As quoted in Eyal Press, *Dirty Work: Essential Jobs and the Hidden Toll of Equality in America*. New York: Farrar, Straus and Giroux, 2021.

Goffman, Erving. *Asylums: Essays on the Condition of the Social Situation of Mental Patients and Other Inmates*. New York: Anchor Books, 1961.

_____. *Stigma: Notes on the Management of Spoiled Identity*. 1963. New York: Simon and Schuster, 2009.

Goodley, Dan. *Disability and Other Human Questions*. Society Now. Bingley: Emerald Publishing, 2021.

Gorman, Brian. *New Dawn Fades: a Graphic Novel About Joy Division and Manchester*. Glossop: Invisible Six Books, 2018.

_____. *New Dawn Fades*. Stage play. Written and first performed in 2013.

Harrington, Michael. *The Other America: Poverty in the United States*. New York: Simon and Schuster, 1962. As quoted in Mark Robert Rand, Lawrence M. Eppard, and Heather E. Bullock. *Poorly Understood: What Americans Get Wrong About Poverty*. New York: Oxford University Press, 2021.

Herbert, Ruth. *Everyday Music Listening: Absorption, Dissociation and Trancing*. 2011. Abingdon, Oxfordshire, 2016.

Honoré, Annik. As quoted in Mick Middles Mick and Lindsay Reade, *Torn Apart: The Life of Ian Curtis*. London: Omnibus, 2009.

Hook, Peter. *Unknown Pleasures: Inside Joy Division*. London: Simon and Schuster, 2012.

Horkheimer, Max and Theodor Adorno. "The Culture Industry: Enlightenment as Mass Deception." *Dialectic of Enlightenment: Philosophical Fragments*. 1947. Edmund Jephcott, trans. Stanford: Stanford University Press, 2002, 94-136.

HotPress.com. "Songs To Inspire You: 'The Eternal', by Joy Division." 30 September 2019. Https://www.hotpress.com/music/songs-inspire-eternal-joy-division-22790460 Accessed 14 October 2021.

Hughes, Everett. As quoted in Eyal Press, *Dirty Work: Essential Jobs and the Hidden Toll of Equality in America*. New York: Farrar, Straus and Giroux, 2021.

Joy Division. "Atrocity Exhibition." Recorded Musical Song, 1980.

_____. "Atrocity Exhibition." *Closer*. London Records Remastered Collectors Edition, Music LP, 2007. 2-CD Set.

_____. *Closer*. Music LP, 1980.

_____. *Closer*. London Records Remastered Collectors Edition, Music LP, 2007. 2-CD Set.

_____. "Decades." Recorded Musical Song, 1980.

_____. "Disorder." Recorded Musical Song, 1979.

_____. "The Eternal." Recorded Musical Song, 1980.

_____. "The Eternal." *Closer*. London Records Remastered Collectors Edition, Music LP, 2007. 2-CD Set.

_____. "Insight." Recorded Musical Song, 1979.

_____. "Insight." *Unknown Pleasures*, London Records Remastered Collectors Edition, Music LP, 2007. 2-CD Set.

_____. "New Dawn Fades." Recorded Musical Song, 1979.

_____. "New Dawn Fades." *Unknown Pleasures*, London Records Remastered Collectors Edition, Music LP, 2007. 2-CD Set.

_____. "She's Lost Control." Recorded Musical Song, 1979.

_____. "Transmission." Recorded Musical Song, 1979.

_____. "Twenty Four Hours." Recorded Musical Song, 1980.

_____. *Unknown Pleasures*. Music LP, 1979.

_____. *Unknown Pleasures*. London Records Remastered Collectors Edition, Music LP, 2007. 2-CD Set.

Joy Division. Feature-Length Documentary Film. Directed by Grant Gee. 2007.

Kafka, Franz. "A Hunger Artist." 1922. *The Penal Colony: Stories and Short Pieces*. Willa and Edwin Muir, trans. New York: Schocken, 1948.

Kalberg, Stephen. "Introduction to *The Protestant Ethic*." Max Weber, *Protestant Ethic and the Spirit of Capitalism*. 1905. Stephen Kalberg, trans. Oxford: Oxford University Press, 2011, 8-63.

_____. "Introduction to the Translation." Max Weber, *Protestant Ethic and the Spirit of Capitalism*. 1905. Stephen Kalberg, trans. Oxford: Oxford University Press, 2011, 3-7.

_____. "Notes for *The Protestant Ethic*." Max Weber, *Protestant Ethic and the Spirit of Capitalism*. 1905. Stephen Kalberg, trans. Oxford: Oxford University Press, 2011, 284-400.

Kunzru, Hari. "Introduction." J.G. Ballard, *The Atrocity Exhibition*, London: Fourth Estate, 2014, xi-xix.

Lacan, Jacques. *Écrits*. 1966. Bruce Fink, Héloïse Fink, and Russell Grigg, trans. New York: W.W. Norton, 2007.

Lafargue, Paul. *The Right to be Lazy*. First published in 1883.

Laing, R.D. *The Divided Self*. 1960. London: Penguin, 1969.

_____. *The Politics of Experience*. New York: Pantheon, 1967.

Lastingpost.com. "An example of an Order of Service for a Funeral (an example of an Order of Service for a traditional Church of England funeral)." Https://www.lastingpost.com/wp-content/uploads/2014/07/pa_f_order_service.pdf Accessed 14 October 2021.

Lavengood, Megan L. *A New Approach to Analysis of Timbre*. PhD dissertation, in Music. City University of New York, September 2017. https://academicworks.cuny.edu/gc_etds/2188/ Accessed 14 October 2021.

Martinez, Sara. "Literary Influences on Joy Division: J.G. Ballard, Franz Kafka, Dostoevsky." Martin J. Power, Eoin Devereux, and Aileen Dillane, eds. *Heart & Soul: Critical Writings on Joy Division*. London: Rowan & Littlefield, 2018, 47-61.

Marx, Karl. "Preface." *A Contribution to the Critique of Political Economy*. First published in 1859.

Middles, Mick and Lindsay Reade. *Torn Apart: The Life of Ian Curtis*. London: Omnibus, 2009.

Morris, Stephen. *Record Play Pause: Confessions of a Post-Punk Percussionist Volume 1*. London: Constable, 2019.

Naiman, Tiffany. "In a Lonely Place: Illness and the Temporal Exile of Ian Curtis." *Heart & Soul: Critical Writings on Joy Division*. London: Rowan & Littlefield, 2018, 83-97.

Neocleous, Mark. *A Critical Theory of Police Power*. 2000. London: New Left Books/Verso, 2021.

Nietzsche, Friedrich. 1888, 1900. *Ecce Homo*. Project Gutenberg. https://www.gutenberg.org/files/52190/52190-h/52190-h.htm London: Plexus, 2008. Accessed 8 August 2021.

_____. 1882, 1887. *The Gay Science (The Joyful Wisdom)*. Project Gutenberg. https://www.gutenberg.org/files/52881/52881-h/52881-h.htm Accessed 8 August 2021.

_____. 1883. *Thus Spake Zarathustra: a Book for All and None*. Project Gutenberg. https://www.gutenberg.org/files/1998/1998-h/1998-h.htm Accessed 8 August 2021.

Nowlan, Bob. *There Will Be No Miracles Here: Bob Nowlan's Blog*. Https://bobnowlan.net Accessed 14 October 2021.

O'Connor, Alice. "An Expert Appraisal," Mark Robert Rand, Lawrence M. Eppard, and Heather E. Bullock. *Poorly Understood: What Americans Get Wrong About Poverty*. New York: Oxford University Press, 2021, 37-38.

Oxford English Dictionary Online. https://www.oed.com Accessed 14 October 2021.

Partridge, Christopher. *The Re-Enchantment of the West: Volume 1 Alternative Spiritualities, Sacralization, Popular Culture and Occulture*. London: T and T Clark International/Continuum, 2004.

Pecheux, Michel. *Language, Semiotics, and Ideology*. 1975. Harbans Nagpal, trans. London: MacMillan, 1982.

Peppercorn, James. "Why It Mattered: Joy Division–'Closer'." 18 May 2020. *Happy Mag TV* https://happymag.tv/why-it-mattered-joy-division-closer/ Accessed 14 October 2021.

Power, Martin J., Eoin Devereux, and Aileen Dillane, eds. *Heart & Soul: Critical Writings on Joy Division*. London: Rowan & Littlefield, 2018.

Pratt, John. As quoted in Eyal Press, *Dirty Work: Essential Jobs and the Hidden Toll of Equality in America*. New York: Farrar, Straus and Giroux, 2021.

Press, Eyal. *Dirty Work: Essential Jobs and the Hidden Toll of Equality in America*. New York: Farrar, Straus and Giroux, 2021.

Rand, Mark Robert. *Chasing the American Dream: Understanding What Shapes Our Fortunes*. New York: Oxford University Press, 2016.

Rand, Mark Robert, Lawrence M. Eppard, and Heather E. Bullock. *Poorly Understood: What Americans Get Wrong About Poverty*. New York: Oxford University Press, 2021.

Reilly, Vini. As quoted in Mick Middles Mick and Lindsay Reade, *Torn Apart: The Life of Ian Curtis*. London: Omnibus, 2009.

Reynolds, Simon. *Rip It Up and Start Again: Postpunk 1978-1984*. New York: Penguin, 2005.

Ritzer, George and Steven Miles. "The changing nature of consumption and the intensification of McDonaldization in the digital age." December 2018. *Journal of Consumer Culture*, Volume 19 Issue 1, February 2019, 3-20. Https://doi.org/10.1177%2F1469540518818628 Accessed 14 October 2021.

Ritzer, George. *The McDonaldization of Society*. Thousand Oaks: Pine Forge Press, 1993.

Saint John's Anglican Church, Toorak. "Church of England Order of Service–Funeral." Https://www.saintjohnstoorak.org/funerals/order-of-service/ Accessed 14 October 2021.

Sandel, Michael. *Justice: What's The Right Thing To Do?* New York: Farrar, Straus and Giroux, 2009.

_____. *Tyranny of Merit: Can We Find the Common Good?* New York: Picador/Farrar, Straus and Giroux, 2021.

Schütte, Uwe. "'Possessed by a Fury That Burns from Inside'." Martin J. Power, Eoin Devereux, and Aileen Dillane, eds. *Heart & Soul: Critical Writings on Joy Division*. London: Rowan & Littlefield, 2018, 63-79.

Shakespeare, Tom. "Ian Curtis." *Disabled Lives Collection*. https://farmerofthoughts.co.uk/collected_pieces/ian-curtis/ Accessed 14 October 2021.

Shay, Jonathan. *Achilles in Vietnam: Combat Trauma and the Undoing of Character*. New York: Simon and Schuster, 1995.

SongMeanings.com. "The Eternal–Joy Division." Https://songmeanings.com/songs/view/59129/ Accessed 14 October 2021.

Songsterr.com. "Joy Division Atrocity Exhibition tab." Https://www.songsterr.com/a/wsa/joy-division-atrocity-exhibition-tab-s39992t0 Accessed 14 October 2021.

The Spirit of '45. Directed and written by Ken Loach. 2013. Feature-length documentary film.

Standing, Guy. *The Precariat: The New Dangerous Class*. 2011. London: Bloomsbury, 2016.

"Stephen Morris: Joy Division to Bad Lieutenant." *Drum Magazine*. Https://drummagazine.com/stephen-morris-a-bad-lieutenant/ Accessed 14 October 2021.

Stewart, Jamie. "New Dawn Fades." *Joy Devotion: The Importance of Ian Curtis and Fan Culture*. London: Headpress, 2016, 32-33.

Therborn, Goran. *The Ideology of Power and the Power of Ideology*. London: New Left Books/Verso, 1980.

Turner, Alwyn W. *Crisis? What Crisis? Britain in the 1970s*. London: Aurum, 2008.

Ultimate-Guitar.com. https://www.ultimate-guitar.com Accessed 14 October 2021.

_____. "'Insight' guitar pro tab by Joy Division–interactive version." Https://tabs.ultimate-guitar.com/tab/joy-division/insight-guitar-pro-2024650 Accessed 14 October 2021.

_____. "'Insight' tab by Joy Division." https://tabs.ultimate-guitar.com/tab/joy-division/insight-tabs-544115 Accessed 14 October 2021.

_____. "'Insight' tab by Joy Division–version 2." Https://tabs.ultimate-guitar.com/tab/joy-division/insight-tabs-1742328 Accessed 14 October 2021.

_____. "'New Dawn Fades' official tab by Joy Division." Https://tabs.ultimate-guitar.com/tab/joy-division/new-dawn-fades-official-1960983 Accessed 14 October 2021.

_____. "Top 28 Darkest Songs of All Time." Https://www.ultimate-guitar.com/articles/features/top_28_darkest_songs_of_all_time-42636 Accessed 14 October 2021.

Vega, Alan and Martin Rev/Suicide. "Dream Baby Dream." 1979. Popular music song.

Weber, Max. "Appendix I: Weber's Summary Statements on '*The Protestant Ethic Thesis*'–The Development of the Capitalist Mind (1919-1920) and A Final Rebuttal to a Critics of 'The Spirit of Capitalism' (1910). *Protestant Ethic and the Spirit of Capitalism*. 1905. Stephen Kalberg, trans. Oxford: Oxford University Press, 2011, 251-271.

_____. *Protestant Ethic and the Spirit of Capitalism*. 1905. Stephen Kalberg, trans. Oxford: Oxford University Press, 2011.

_____. *Protestant Ethic and the Spirit of Capitalism*. 1905. Talcott Parsons, trans. London: George Allen and Unwin, 1930.

Whittaker, Jason. "The Pornography of Science: Curtis, Ballard and Burroughs." *Joy Devotion: The Importance of Ian Curtis and Fan Culture*. London: Headpress, 2016, 34-40.

Winitzi, Sergei. *Eternal Inflation*. Singapore: World Scientific, 2009.

Chapter Five

One

Over the course of my long fascination with, and unapologetic fandom for Ian Curtis and Joy Division, I have acquired considerable materials associated with the two–not only numerous books but also multiple editions of CDs and LPs, enough t-shirts to wear every day for an entire semester if I chose to do so without duplicating myself once, and framed posters hanging throughout the walls of our house, along with further posters attached to large black poster boards that I have used as visual displays to accompany public presentations on Ian Curtis, Joy Division, and critical theory. My aim with these visual displays is to highlight the visual influence and visual appeal of Ian Curtis and Joy Division. I loved the *True Faith* exhibition at the Manchester Art Gallery that I toured multiple times while attending the 2017 Manchester International Festival. This exhibition included visual images of and tributes to Ian Curtis and Joy Division, as well as New Order, along with videos of Joy Division and New Order performing live along with further videos inspired by and otherwise connected with Ian Curtis, Joy Division, and New Order.

One of my most recent acquisitions is a hardcover copy of an updated and expanded edition of the book *Joy Division * Juvenes ** ("Juvenes" means, roughly, 'becoming or being young or youthful'), primarily consisting of a collection of by now famous photographs of Joy Division taken by Kevin Cummins. Along with Peter Saville and Anton Corbijn, Cummins has likely played the most influential role in contributing to the visual aura that continues to be associated with Ian Curtis and Joy Division–even as Tony Wilson and everyone involved with Factory were all quite savvy about the power of the image and of the value of constructing and emphasizing a distinctive look. Cummins writes in his introduction to the 2021 edition of *Joy Division * Juvenes ** that he originally published the book in a limited edition of only 200 copies, but because this book has since acquired "a mythical status," he decided to republish an expanded and updated version of *Joy Division * Juvenes ** "for a wider audience" (10). In this new edition, Cummins reflects on what his photographs capture and convey, while including essays from surviving bandmembers and other commentators, all of whom maintain close personal connections with Joy Division or are well-known fans of Joy Division. Expanded from 192 to 256 pages, the 2021 edition of *Joy Division * Juvenes ** Cummins describes as the equivalent of "a director's cut" (10).

Cummins' accounts of the various photos, and in particular photo shoots, he took of Joy Division are by now themselves legendary and have been repeated in many places. When Cummins first met the members of Joy Division they were just beginning to learn how to pose for the camera, while he was was just beginning to learn how to pose subjects for the camera. Given that combination as well as due to the fact that Cummins worked, of necessity, with far more limited stock than readily available today, many of his memorable photos of the band are the result of happy accident. These largely black and white photos do suggest, as Cummins recalls, that "Manchester in the 1970s was a dismal, post-industrial Victorian city," while reminding us this was Manchester "20 years before its decaying warehouses were transformed into lofts and hotels" (11). In the late 1970s the latter "were filthy, dilapidated and mostly abandoned" (11). The city still closely resembled JB Priestley's notorious description of Manchester, from his 1934 book *English Journey*, as "a turgid sooty gloom that was neither day nor night" (quoted 11), and well fit many others' characterization as perpetually gray.

Yet I find these photos expressive and communicative, most of all, of the complexity, multiplicity, contradictoriness, and dynamism of the band, and in particular of its frontman–at once serious and playful, mysterious and down to earth, distant and intimate, exuberant and subdued, luminous and opaque, and canny and uncanny. Cummins at least in part recognized what he was on to, right from the start, because he and Paul Morley, responsible for interviewing Joy Division while Cummins took photos, "were both amazed at how serious they [Joy Division] were about their art"

(11). In turn, whether fully intentionally or not, Cummins photographed Joy Division to emphasize this 'seriousness'.

Fellow contributors to the 2021 edition of *Joy Division * Juvenes ** likewise interpret these photos in 'serious' terms. For example, Scottish writer Ian Rankin, renowned for his 'tartan noir' series of Inspector Rebus crime novels and short stories, writes that,

> In the posed portraits, Joy Division appear elusive, drained of emotion. They stand in shadows, or against brick walls, or framed by windows, producing images which say just about all that needs saying about their music: bleak, beautiful, and 'out there', by which I mean the band weren't about to explain themselves. They left meaning and interpretation in the ear of the listener, the eye of the beholder. (8)

Rankin's take coincides with how I make sense of these photos, and how I make sense of the lyrics of Ian Curtis and the music of Joy Division. These photos, like these lyrics and like this music, invite us to make use of what they share as source in seeking meaning, as spark in pursuing interpretation, but without the band itself, including its frontman, doing this work for us. These are images are redolent, simultaneously, of bleakness, elusiveness, edginess, the beautiful, the sublime, heightened affect, and distanced affect.

According to Bernard Sumner, in his interview with Cummins for the 2021 edition of *Joy Division * Juvenes *,* membership in Joy Division involved "acting as if you don't take things too seriously, even though we were a serious group" (28). This combination comes across in the photos Cummins took: photos of young men enjoying being in band, making and sharing music, leading lives that provided them with thrills of satisfaction and pleasure, yet who are at the same time serious about their music and who are making serious music suggestive of serious matters. These contrasting dimensions follow from the bandmembers being all too aware of the limited opportunities, or indeed lack of opportunities, otherwise available to pursue the kind of life they were experiencing within, and as, Joy Division. As Sumner explains, "I think some of the inspiration came from not wanting to grow up and become a normal, nine-to-five guy, working my balls off to become an unhappy person, getting married at 22 and settling down, and leaving your mates and not having any fun any more, having a job where you get two weeks of holiday a year. It just seemed like crap" (29).

But I also think the drive to be different, and to live differently, comes across, with Joy Division, as inspired not just by rejecting 'the normal' but also by being attuned to how difficult it is to escape from 'the normal', to avoid being pulled back into the normal even after you have temporarily escaped, and to not fall subject, at least eventually, to the enormous pressure to make your peace with and find your place in relation to 'the normal'. Joy Division manifests a fierce desire not to be so coopted and constrained by the normal, not to be coopted and constrained by the power of the normal, as well as a fraught recognition and a fearful concern that the normal, and its power, cannot easily be evaded, and indeed is always lurking proximately, already ready to pull you back in—or to push you so far out that you find it difficult to survive at all.

In his interview with Cummins for the 2021 edition of *Joy Division * Juvenes *, Stephen Morris shares his recognition of how the appeal of Joy Division, and indeed interest in and infatuation with Joy Division, has not only endured but exploded, such that it has become bigger than with New Order, even though New Order has lasted much longer and released far more recorded music. Morris is proud of being a part of Joy Division; he appreciates and is humbled by how much Joy Division means to so many other people. But he resists speculating on precisely why this might be. According to Morris, it is not for him to interpret what Joy Division means to all of those for whom Joy Division means so much. But Morris is willing to offer clues to why this meaning, and impact, continues to be as powerful as it is. Morris notes that everyone in Joy Division shared a keen "interest in weirdness" and in particular in 'dark weirdness'. Morris also considers it significant that Ian Curtis was strongly interested in language, in its power and its possibilities, in language in the form of and as poetry, and in literature and philosophy that defied the conventionally 'normal'.

Morris proposes that 'Joy Division's story' "will never let you down" because the music remains great, it is not confined to a specific time and place, and in particular because the music offers a powerful exhortation to listeners to use "your imagination" (45). Morris proposes the meanings associated with the music of Joy Division are "all about *your* imagination. *You* made it up. And the story of Joy Division is something *you* could identify with. It said something to *you*. It fed the imagination" [my italics] (45).

Peter Hook interprets the enduring appeal of Joy Division in much the same way. As Hook comments in his interview with Cummins, as part of the 2021 edition of *Joy Division * Juvenes *, "every new generation that's come along has found a way to relate to the music, to relate to Ian and to relate to the group" (60). Much of this is because "great music . . . lasts forever" and it was never "our right to bury Joy Division because we were sad" (60). Hook interprets the enduring appeal of the lyrics of Ian Curtis and the music of Joy Division as emanating from the fact that "it completes the rock 'n' roll story, every myth in rock 'n' roll," and because "the music's fucking fantastic, and Ian's lyrics are amazing" (62). As Hook elaborates, "Every band member was equally represented, which is very unusual in a group–the bass, the drums, the guitar, the singer . . . It was the perfect vehicle for every musician to shine and excel" (62).

For Natalie Curtis, Ian's daughter, Cummins's photos of her father and of the rest of the band offered an important compliment to the music, as she listened to it, in growing up. These photos conjured "an alternative reality. The idea of this other world was thrilling and yet it left me uneasy" (70). These photos, as well as the music of Joy Division, felt uncanny; they "did not sound or look as if they belonged to the past," but rather of a perpetual present (70). What she registers most today, in viewing these photos once again, is the bandmembers' "youth and the now unfamiliar landscape they inhabit" along with "an unexpected tenderness" that provides at least partial answers "to the multitude of questions" that are, have been, and continue to be raised by all who have experienced themselves "compelled by the fantasy" Joy Division created, shared, and continues to offer as its ongoing legacy (70).

For Pat Nevin, a now retired yet formerly prominent Scottish footballer, the *Joy Division * Juvenes * photos reinforce his long-standing interpretation of Joy Division as "the antithesis" of a "vapid and self-congratulatory aspect of society" he has long despised and from which he has long felt alienated. These photos convey to Nevin the impression of an artistic critique of just that kind of smug complacency.

Journalist, author, and literary critic Nicholas Lezard likewise interprets these photos as intrinsic to the 'total package' of what Joy Division has meant for him since he was a boy, offering Lezard "all that needed to be said about hope, fellow-feeling and all those other delusions whose tenacity mystified and outraged me" (166). Lezard does not identify Joy Division as cynical or nihilistic but rather as advocating the difficult work of transformation in opposition to settling for the easy comfort of delusion. After all, as Lezard comments, in remembering Ian Curtis, performing live, "You can't watch someone move onstage like that and not come away impressed. You realized instantly he wasn't faking it; his dancing was an ecstacy of sincerity, dancing proof that he was a real thing" (166). This "esctacy of sincerity" attests "that Curtis's vision saw beyond bleakness, or at least knew there were other things out there that were not bleak" (166). As such, Curtis and Joy Division continue to offer Lezard what seems like a more realistically hopeful possibility of a radical alternative to what exists than Lezard has derived from virtually any other source. Curtis knew one needed to fight past, through, and beyond 'ugliness' to find 'beauty', and his lyrics, his music, and his dancing all embody this quest.

Matthew Higgs, meanwhile, perceives in Cummins's photos a reaffirmation of what he experienced in attending Joy Division rehearsals while still a boy, and that was the bandmembers' "unfailing generosity, good humour, and, it probably should be said, patience" (186). Higgs touts Joy Division (and finds the rawness, intimacy, and vulnerability of the photos reinforcing this impression) as establishing "a far more fluid relationship between artist and audience than I had previously imagined and considered possible" (187).

Musician and journalist Cath Carroll in turn connects the photos Cummins took of Joy Division with her interpretation of Joy Division's music as "the sound that explained the new city, the one they keep trying to lay over the old city," the sound of Manchester, and in particular of Manchester in transition. In short, this music "mapped a series of pathways through the ruminative Victorian city" (217).

Writer David Peace adds that the photos Cummins took compliment the sound of Joy Division, cementing Peace's personal bond with the only music he has continued to listen to over and over again, across multiple decades of his life: "Only Joy Division has remained, still; this is the only music I've played year after year, month after month, week in week out, day in day out, for 25 years" (232). The reason why is "this band, their songs, make me feel a little less lonely, a little less lost . . . And that is more than I can hope for . . . Certainly more than I deserve . . . So, thank you, Joy Division" (232).

The now iconic visual imagery associated with Ian Curtis and Joy Division represents a positive mythic force that powerfully adds to the persistent appeal of this music. I experience this music and everything that contributes to the 'cultural phenomenon' that is Ian Curtis and Joy Division as encouraging me to use my imagination to explore and engage connections with what I hear, and with what I think (about) and feel, as I listen. Ian Curtis and Joy Division enable me to perceive glimmers of 'light' that might yet someday and somehow illuminate and redeem 'darknesses' I struggle not to hide from or pretend are not as 'dark' as they are.

Undoubtedly many others feel much the same powerful sense of connection with visual images of Joy Division, and especially of Ian Curtis, as attested by the creation of two large-scale outdoor mural portraits of Curtis, first in Manchester in 2020 and then in Macclesfield in 2022. In relation to the former, as described by Chris Greenhalgh for ilovemanchester.com:

> A mural paying tribute to the late Ian Curtis has been unveiled in the Northern Quarter just in time for World Mental Health Day (today, Saturday 10 October). The legendary musician, who was the lead singer and lyricist of post-punk band Joy Division, took his own life aged just 23 during a long struggle with depression. The artwork was heartfully revealed by the late singer's former Joy Division bandmate Peter Hook (also The Light). The artist, Manchester-based Akse P19, says Ian Curtis was the perfect subject to try to create a conversation around mental health: "It was a pleasure meeting Peter Hook this week at the mural of Ian Curtis," says Akse. "It's based on a photo by [photographer] Philip Pecarly. "It's hoped this striking homage to a Manchester music legend will encourage people to continue to speak out and seek help if they need it."

This mural was commissioned in connection with the Headstock festival that aims to raise money in aid of Help Manchester Musicians and Manchester Mind, both charities responding to people in crisis and especially in facing serious mental health challenges. Headstock aims to become the UK's largest music and mental health festival, so as "To use the power of music to change the conversation around mental health, whilst raising money for mental health projects and services that will help people from all corners of society."

Subsequently, earlier this year, 2022, as Will Lavin reports for *The NME*:

> Peter Hook helped unveil a new mural of Joy Division bandmate Ian Curtis in Macclesfield town centre this afternoon (March 26).

> The bassist and co-founder of New Order cut the ribbon alongside Akse, the Manchester-based street artist who painted the mural, telling those in attendance: "I am actually very honoured to be here, and to do this, because to me it's about time Ian came home."

> The mural, funded by Cheshire East Council, is based on an original photograph taken by Kevin Cummins at The Factory/Russell Club in Hulme, Manchester on 13 July 1979. It adorns a building on Mill Street opposite Macclesfield bus station . . . .

> Councillor Nick Mannion, chair of the authority's economy and growth committee, said: "Before today, I spoke about how perhaps this beautiful mural has been somewhat overdue but now that I'm here seeing it for myself for the first time, I can say without any doubt that it has truly been worth the wait."

"I am a huge fan of Joy Division–the cultural significance of the band and Ian stretches well beyond my home town of Macclesfield. This is such a proud moment, I'm feeling very emotional about it right now."

I felt much the same way throughout my visit to Manchester and Greater Manchester in conjunction with the 2017 Manchester International Festival in witnessing prominent appreciation of Joy Division, and especially Curtis, with Curtis's image festooned on Manchester International Festival banners all over the conurbation, specifically referencing the *True Faith* exhibition.

***

In this fifth chapter I push my exploration of and engagement with broad and diverse connections, emotional and otherwise, a considerable distance, and I do so in substantial part by staging encounters, and dialogues, between 'Ian Curtis and Joy Division', here represented by the songs "Day of the Lords," "Colony," "Heart and Soul," and "Autosuggestion," with Aimé Césaire's *Discourse on Colonialism*, Edward W. Said's *Representations of the Intellectual*; and Trinh T. Minh-ha's *Woman, Native, Other: Writing Postcoloniality and Feminism*. Section two focuses on providing a summary introduction to and overview of Césaire's *Discourse on Colonialism*; section three does the same for Said's *Representations of the Intellectual*; and section four offers a summary introduction and overview of Trinh's *Woman, Native, Other: Writing Postcoloniality and Feminism*. Section five draws out the principal positions, concepts, and arguments advanced by each of these three books that will serve as key points of contact, in the encounters, and dialogues, with the lyrics and music of Ian Curtis and Joy Division to come in the following four sections. Section six focuses on "Day of the Lords," section seven on "Colony," section eight on "Heart and Soul," and section nine on "Autosuggestion."

Two

As Robin D.G. Kelley writes, in his introduction to the 2000 Monthly Review Press English language edition, Aimé Césaire's *Discourse on Colonialism*, originally published in French in 1955 as *Discourse sur le colonialisme*, "might best be described as a declaration of war" as it is "primarily a polemic" (7) against European colonialism and the European colonial order. Césaire wrote and initially published this book in the midst of the transition, after the end of World War II, from European colonialism exercised by means of direct rule–throughout much of Africa, Central and South America, and Asia–toward formal political independence. Yet Césaire is equally critical of the continuation of *neo-colonial* domination by the nations of the global North over nations of the global South through primarily economic means. *Discourse on Colonialism* argues "The instruments of colonial power rely on barbaric, brutal violence and intimidation," with "the end result" being "the degradation of Europe itself" (9). *Discourse on Colonialism* "helps us locate the origins of fascism within colonialism itself" while revising Marx by proposing "the anticolonial struggle supersedes the proletarian revolution as the fundamental historical movement of the period" (10).

Césaire, born on 26 June 1913 in Martinique, in the Lesser Antilles of the Caribbean, grew up at the time in which Martinique was a direct French colony. For Césaire, occupation of Martinique by the forces of the Vichy collaborationist regime during World War II made expressly clear how thoroughly racist France was. The Vichy regime stationed large numbers of French military personnel in Martinique who treated Black native residents of Martinique as distinctly lesser beings. But Césaire's animus versus colonialism more broadly, and not just French colonialism, began to develop much earlier than this and is influenced by multiple sources, notably other Black intellectual critics of colonialism. The journal *Tropiques* that Césaire founded and edited, as well as the Negritude movement of which he was a principal leader, drew on diverse constituents within Modernism as well as a "deep appreciation for pre-colonial African modes of thought and practice" (14). Kelley notes the significant contribution of Suzanne Césaire, wife of Aimé Césaire, a leading surrealist in her own right, citing Suzanne's definition of surrealism "not as an ideology as such but a state of mind, a 'permanent readiness for the Marvelous'" (15). Suzanne Césaire interprets surrealism as a call to embrace "the strange, the marvelous and the fantastic" as well to seek a state of mind and imagination sufficiently free–or freed–to enact "inversions of the old order" (15). In turn, Aimé Césaire makes overt use of surrealism, with Kelley identifying *Discourse on Colonialism* as a surrealist text: "a dancing flame in a bonfire" (10).

Both Aimé and Suzanne, Kelley is careful to stress, were innovators within surrealism, not mere copiers of White European models, who developed and deployed surrealism for their own ends. Surrealism enabled Aimé Césaire to imagine possibilities beyond colonial domination and subjugation, possibilities immanent and proximate as well as vestigial and emergent, providing a source of joyful revelation. Césaire embraces the power of poetry as itself a prospectively 'revolutionary' mode of practice, as "a method of achieving clairvoyance," with *Discourse on Colonialism*, as Kelley characterizes the book, becoming "a kind of historical prose poem" (17). In a 1967 interview conducted by René Depestre, included in the 2000 Monthly Review Press English language edition of *Discourse on Colonialism*, Césaire explains that throughout his writings "I have always striven to create a new language, one capable of communicating the African language," even when working in French: "an Antillean French, a black French that, while still being French, had a black character" (83). In doing so, "Surrealism provided me with what I had been confusedly searching for. I have accepted it joyfully because in it I have found more of a confirmation than a revelation" (83). Through surrealist means Césaire is able to shake up the established and the normative, especially in pressing past conventional limits concerning imagination of what is possible. For Césaire, the unconscious forces surrealism helps him get into contact with represent "a call to Africa" and, what's more, as Césaire declares, "if we plumb the depths, then what we find is fundamentally black" (84).

From the beginning of *Discourse on Colonialism* Césaire condemns European civilization as decadent, sick, and dying: decadent because it is "incapable of solving the problems it creates," sick because "it chooses to close its eyes to its most crucial problems," and dying because it "plays fast and loose with its principles" (31). European civilization is hypocritical in what it claims to stand for, in what it claims are its fundamental principles and values, given its undeniable responsibility for the devastation wrought by means of colonialism. As Césaire boldly proclaims, "Europe is indefensible"–it is "morally, spiritually indefensible" (32)–because no justifiable defense for colonialism is possible. All attempts to do so are lies. Colonialism *is* domination and subjugation: it *is* brutal and destructive violence. Colonialism is *not* mutually enabling 'contact' between different cultures. Césaire rejects attempts to justify colonialism as beneficial to the colonized, because of the colonizer supposedly 'raising up' the primitive colonized, and because of the colonizer supposedly 'gifting' the colonized with 'modern' science and technology as well as 'modern' art and culture. *Discourse on Colonialism* is not only a discourse *about* and *against* colonialism, but also a fierce critique of *discourse on* colonialism written by influential intellectual figures who Césaire cites in arguing against their attempts to justify colonialism.

Césaire turns the tables on these apologists for and defenders of colonialism, who characterize the colonized as uncivilized and barbaric. Césaire proposes that 'decivilizing the colonizer' means 'brutalizing the colonizer' as colonizing not only makes the colonizer a perpetrator of horrific violence against the colonized but also makes the colonizer greedily covetous, willing to relativize all moral principles, and outrageously lie to attempt to cover up what the colonizer is actually doing (35). Césaire theorizes fascism as the result of a "terrific boomerang effect" with the same *barbarism* previously perpetrated *versus the colonized* now perpetrated against fellow Europeans. As Césaire explains, "before they were its victims, they were its accomplices," and "they tolerated that Nazism before it was inflicted on them"; they "absolved it, shut their eyes to it, legitimized it, because, until then, it had been applied only to non-European peoples" (36). Césaire charges "the very distinguished, very humanistic, very Christian bourgeois" with harboring, "without his being aware of it," "a Hitler inside him," and, even more than this, "that Hitler *inhabits* him, that Hitler is his *demon*" (36). Therefore, if the White European Christian bourgeois,

> rails against him [against Hitler], he is being inconsistent . . . at the bottom, what he cannot forgive Hitler for is not *the crime* in itself, *the crime against man*, it is not *the humiliation of man as such*, it is the crime against the white man, the humiliation of the white man, and the fact that he applied to Europe colonialist procedures which until then had been reserved exclusively for the Arabs of Algeria, the 'coolies' of India, and the 'niggers' of Africa. (36)

Because of this massive hypocrisy, Césaire condemns European humanism as a 'pseudo-humanism' because it is a racist humanism, distinguishing among how human beings are recognized, respected, valued, and treated, on the basis of race, with only White people fully admitted into the category of the human (37). In other words, a prevailing state of mind within ostensibly liberal humanist Western democracy is far from true humanism because it does not take seriously and value equally people of all races, and is either directly or indirectly responsible for brutal violence perpetrated against the colonized and the neo-colonized (73). Césaire broadens his condemnation by insisting, further, "At the end of capitalism, which is eager to outlive its day, there is Hitler. At the end of formal humanism and philosophic renunciation, there is Hitler" (37). Hitler, in sum, represents the consequence of European racist pseudo-humanism, and of capitalism that makes use of the former as a preeminent constituent of dominant bourgeois ideology, carried to its furthest logical conclusion. Fascism is not an aberration, therefore, but rather, as Kelley characterizes Césaire's position, "a blood relative of slavery and imperialism, global systems rooted not only in capitalist political economy but racist ideologies that were already in place at the dawn of modernity" (20). Césaire emphasizes, in making this argument, that no atrocity perpetrated by the Nazis against fellow White Europeans was not previously perpetrated by European colonizers on non-European colonized Black and Brown people. Making the connection once more explicit, Césaire declares "No one colonizes innocently . . .

a civilization which justifies colonization–and therefore force–is already a sick civilization, a civilization which is morally diseased, which irresistibly, progressing from one consequence to another, one denial to another, calls for its Hitler, I mean its punishment" (39).

After all, as Césaire demonstrates by citing examples from a variety of prominent writers supportive of and as advocating for colonialism, no matter if overtly or covertly racist, no matter if outwardly bigoted or outwardly patronizing, colonialism is in essence "based on contempt for the native and justified by that contempt," which in turn "inevitably tends to change him who undertakes it" (41). Versus all attempts to whitewash colonialism as a form of mutually enabling 'contact' between different societies and cultures, Césaire memorably asserts that "Between colonizer and colonized there is room only for forced labor, intimidation, pressure, the police, taxation, theft, rape, compulsory crops, contempt, mistrust, arrogance, self-complacency, swinishness, brainless elites, degraded masses . . . . colonization = 'thingification'" (42). Rejecting defenses of what colonialism ostensibly brings to or gives to the colonized, that ostensibly benefit the colonized, Césaire counters "*I* am talking about societies drained of their essence, cultures trampled underfoot, institutions undermined, lands confiscated, religions smashed, magnificent artistic creations destroyed, extraordinary *possibilities* wiped out" (43). Césaire in turn cites all those taken into slavery, all those who suffered and died during 'the middle passage', and all those who suffered and died as a result not only of the conditions of their enslavement but also due to being forcibly cut off from the communities and cultures from which they were taken. Césaire also writes about the many "millions," as a result of colonialism, "in whom fear has been cunningly instilled, who have been taught to have an inferiority complex, to tremble, kneel, despair, and behave like flunkeys" (43). Césaire extends his polemic by declaring, what's more, "*I* am talking about natural *economies* that have been disrupted– harmonious and viable *economies* adapted to the indigenous population" violently transformed into economies overwhelmingly focused on production of agricultural goods solely for export to colonizing countries, with those in formerly self-sufficient agricultural economies in turn suffering from famine, starvation, malnutrition, other forms of deadly disease, and the need to import necessary food at enormous local expense (43).

Césaire at the same time lambastes indigenous authoritarian leaders of now politically independent former direct colonies who continue primarily to serve the political and especially economic interests of colonizers turned neo-colonizers: "in general the old tyrants get on very well with the new ones" (43). For Césaire the formal end to direct colonial rule is not equivalent with the end of colonialism. Colonialism continues, not only throughout the economy and politics of the newly independent nation, but also throughout its national culture–and in particular, by means of what Césaire characterizes as, in what has proven subsequently to be a massively influential conception, 'the colonization of the mind'. Césaire calls for a fundamentally new way of thinking in order to achieve true liberation. This new way of thinking requires decisively breaking with a colonialist and neo-colonialist ideology of progress founded on violence, destruction, and genocide (27). In his interview with Césaire, Depreste proposes "it is equally necessary to decolonize our minds, our inner life, at the same time that we decolonize society," to which Césaire responds "Exactly," while adding, further, that Black people have been "doubly proletarianized and alienated: in the first place as workers, but also as blacks, because after all we are dealing with the only race which is denied even the notion of humanity" (94).

In making "a systematic defense of the societies destroyed by imperialism," versus those who pretend that nothing but 'barbarism' preceded, Césaire proclaims:

They were communal societies, never societies of the many for the few.

They were societies that were not only ante-capitalist, as has been said, but also *anti-capitalist*.

They were democratic societies, always.

They were cooperative societies, fraternal societies. (44)

To this blazon, Césaire elaborates, "The great historical tragedy of Africa has been not so much that it was too late in making contact with the rest of the world, as the manner in which that contact was brought about; that Europe began to 'propagate' at a time in which it had fallen into the hands of the most unscrupulous financiers and captains of industry; that it was our misfortune to encounter that particular Europe on our path; and that Europe is responsible before the human community for the highest heap of corpses in human history" (45). In response to a common rejoinder, from supporters of colonialism, that pre-colonial African societies and cultures were not all egalitarian utopias, Césaire counters: "Colonialist Europe has grafted modern abuse onto ancient injustice, hateful racism onto old inequality" (45). In addition, versus those who argue, yet again, that the colonized have benefitted substantially from the introduction of 'modern' science and technology, Césaire argues no one knows "at what stage of material development these same countries would have been if Europe had not intervened," and, yet further, that the colonized could have eventually, even readily, engaged in substantial technological innovation and material development on their own, by and for themselves, if they had been left to be able to do this (45).

Césaire critiques not only those who trumpet 'Western civilization' as triumphant, virtuous, and superior, but also those who attack it from within while doing so from unacknowledged positions of privilege, and doing nothing effectively to undermine its perpetuation, such as "chattering intellectuals born stinking out of the thigh of Nietzsche" (54). Césaire critiques all who defend capitalist society, and capitalist conceptions of progress, because this necessarily means these people are all, at the same time, "openly or secretly, supporters of plundering colonialism, all of them responsible, all hateful, all slave-traders, all henceforth answerable for the violence of revolutionary action" (55). It does not matter "whether personally these gentlemen are in good or bad faith, whether they have good or bad intentions" (55), because what matters are the effects of their actions and inactions, the effective implications and consequences of the positions and practices they themselves carry out and which they otherwise support.

Césaire notes well an important dimension of colonialism is "based on psychology" with this principally involving, more specifically, cultivation and promotion of "a dependency complex" (59). Césaire here accuses both psychoanalysis and existentialism with complicity in support of the notion that some races are necessarily inferior to and dependent upon those who are superior to them (59). This insinuation repeats itself again and again, Césaire suggests, via "the old refrain: 'The-Negroes-are-big-children'," with such a way of thinking showing up in numerous characterizations of Black cultures as 'primitive' and 'pre-modern' (60). As such supposedly perpetual children, it becomes 'the White man's burden' to lead them, and in effect to save them from themselves, from their intrinsic limitations (60).

Césaire also critiques those who profess to appreciate indigenous colonized cultures yet at the same time support colonialism and neo-colonialism: Césaire accuses people like this of "smug self-satisfaction," "secret contempt," "racism, admitted or not," and maintaining the "delights of vanity"–vanity concerning how seemingly important it is, to the colonized, that these people show the colonized condescending recognition (71). According to Césaire, it would be much better if museums in both colonizing and colonized countries were never needed to preserve artifacts of colonized cultures and he is unimpressed with White Europeans who want to help save these as relics of what they tend to imagine as an exotic primordial past.

As Robin D.G. Kelley explains, for Césaire "The very idea that there was a superior race lay at the heart of the matter," with this idea mystifying what in fact has amounted to "the massive destruction of whole societies," those which Césaire pointedly characterizes as not only 'ante-capitalist' but also 'anti-capitalist' (21). Throughout *Discourse on Colonialism* Césaire is at pains to reverse the commonplace: Césaire argues Africa was civilized, the Europeans who conquered and subjected Africans to colonialism were barbaric in doing so, and that this has in turn infected European civilization 'at home' with barbarism. Césaire and collaborators developed Negritude to deliberately contest commonplace notions of the 'barbaric Negro'. As Césaire explains in his interview with Depestre, the thrust of the Negritude movement emphasized:

> That we are black; that we were black and have a history, a history that contains certain cultural elements of great value; and that Negroes were not, as you put it, born yesterday, because there have been beautiful and important black civilizations. At the time we began to write, people could write a history of world civilization without devoting a single chapter to Africa, as if Africa had made no contributions to the world. Therefore we affirmed that we were Negroes and that we were proud of it, and that we thought that Africa was not some sort of blank page in the history of humanity; in sum, we asserted that our Negro heritage was worthy of respect, and that this heritage was not relegated to the past, that its values were values that could still make an important contribution to the world. (92)

Despite Césaire's defense of pre-colonial African societies and cultures, as well as his condemnation of what colonialism has done to these and imposed in their place, what he advocates for Africa and the rest of the post-colonial global South is 'a new society', not an attempt merely to return to, to revive, or to recapture a pre-colonial past. For Césaire this new kind of society will of necessity include new spiritual values and not just new material practices. As Césaire answers, in response to the question he poses to himself, in *Discourse in Colonialism*, concerning what, precisely, is he calling for, after colonialism:

> Not to make a utopian and sterile attempt to repeat the past, but to go beyond. It is not a dead society that we want to revive. We leave that to those who go in for exoticism. Nor is it the

present colonial society that we wish to prolong, the most putrid carrion that ever rotted under the sun. It is a new society we must create, with the help of all our brother slaves, a society rich with all the productive power of modern times, warm with the fraternity of olden days. (52)

This is an urgent task, because, Césaire contends, the barbarism of Western Europe is being "surpassed" and even "far surpassed" by "the barbarism of the United States" (47). Again it is 'the respectable American bourgeois' who Césaire here most forcefully condemns, including those Americans who associate themselves overtly with 'Christian virtues' but in effect practice, sanction, and otherwise allow for the opposite (47). Césaire likewise blasts cynical forms of resignation–that nothing can be done, because those at the heights of power will always do whatever they want to do and we can't stop them. Césaire avers that "Bourgeois swinishness" is everywhere "the rule" (49), even at a time in which Stalinism and Maoism seemed to many to represent substantial alternatives, with the entire world becoming ever increasingly more thoroughly dominated by capitalism. Yet because of capitalism's inescapable contradictions and capitalism's reliance upon periodic economic, social, and political crises to maintain and renew itself: "The bourgeoisie is condemned to become every day more snarling, more openly ferocious, more shameless, more summarily barbarous" (64). As a still in many respects orthodox Marxist, despite his contention, as he explains to Depestre, that "Marx is all right, but we need to complete Marx," and in particular his argument that Black emancipation cannot simply be taken care of by means of proletarian emancipation (86), Césaire also professes it "is an implacable law that every decadent class finds itself turned into a receptacle into which there flows all the dirty waters of history; that it is a universal law that before it disappears, every class must disgrace itself completely, on all fronts, and that it is with their heads buried in the dunghill that dying societies utter their swan songs" (64). In other words, "Whether one likes it or not, the bourgeoisie, as a class, is condemned to take responsibility for the barbarism of history" (67)–i.e., for the barbarities perpetrated throughout its history of dominance, and a reckoning is coming. Yet, in the meantime, Césaire warns that American imperial domination might well prove to be the most dangerous to have ever existed–with American might threatening the entire world. Césaire recognizes a long-standing American hubristic ambition to 'lead'–i.e., dominate over–the rest of the world at a time that America is now able to do so, yet Césaire defines this assumption of 'global leadership' as a victory above all else for American capitalists, not Americans of all classes, let alone Americans of all races. Césaire warns newly politically independent nations of the global South that so-called aid and investment, from American and American-dominated multinational as well as transnational institutions, comes with a steep price: the setting up, in effect, of a "factory for the production of lackeys" in the nations and among the peoples receiving this aid and investment (77). What is crucial, in contrast, is self-determination in the development of these new societies, and of their new economies, polities, and cultures.

In teaching *Discourse on Colonialism* I have found this book of particular use in discussing what is the crux of the relationship between colonizer and colonized, how and why this relationship is and has been often mystified, and, especially, the concept of *colonization of the mind*. Ready connections with 'Ian Curtis and Joy Division' not only involve shared interest in and influence of surrealism but also common concern with cruelty and violence, as well as anxiety and alienation; resorting to self-protective blinders or sentimentalizing illusions rather than confronting cruelty and violence, and alienation and anxiety, for what they are and for how bad they are; responsibility for and complicity with cruelty and violence, and anxiety and alienation; experiencing oneself as a stranger, an outsider, and an outcast within the culture and society in which one must live; understanding fascism, especially where it is not readily marked or identifiable as such, as well as understanding what accounts for, what promotes and reinforces, fascism; and the complexities and challenges of empathy and solidarity across, within, and by means of recognition and acceptance of as well appreciation and respect for difference. Other useful connections involve prompting students to think about and discuss American imperialism, which is something many have often previously not thought much about, or even have not tended previously to associate at all with this country. This includes discussion of to what extent Americans, and in particular US governments and government leaders, often justify American 'interventions' in other nations along comparable lines to those Césaire discusses as defenses, rationalizations, excuses, apologies, and mystifications concerning European colonialism and imperialism that are totally 'inexcusable' and result in those responsible suffering 'de-civilizing barbarism'.

Frequently many students are troubled by any use of 'violence' of any kind in protest and resistance, both versus US forces or interests abroad, and versus, for example, racism within the US. In these instances it is common to overlook state violence, to not recognize the existence of this source and mode of violence at all, and to do the same with the violence of the invader, the aggressor, when this is students' own nation, the United States, with the US representing itself as a supposedly constant champion and defender of freedom, democracy, and human rights. It can be difficult as well for some students to recognize that violence and non-violence are not always easily distinguishable, that violence is not always everywhere always the same, and that those who resort to violence in response to injustice might have already pursued non-violent alternatives, including repeatedly over protracted periods of time, yet found these ineffective, found them steadfastly blocked and ignored. It is also easy to overlook how much violence is routine in daily life in the US today, especially for those in disadvantaged social positions, on account of abuse and neglect, precarity and deprivation, exploitation and dehumanization, as well as social inequality and lack of real opportunity for social mobility and advancement. Certainly the frequency of gun violence, in particular mass shootings, has rendered violence a familiar occurrence in the US, while violence is commonly represented in popular American sports and in many other forms of popular entertainment in this country. Students often attest, themselves, to the considerably violent impact of toxic masculinity–on women, on men, and on those who, in increasing numbers, identify as neither men nor women. At the same time, students often maintain sharply divergent positions concerning to what extent and through what means desensitization to violence, and its impacts, has become a major social problem in contemporary America. And the same divergence of positions arises in engaging the ethical questions I have suggested the music, as art, and the cultural phenomenon of Ian Curtis and Joy Division raises for us to consider: *In what ways, and to what extent, am I responsible for others? For the suffering, hardship, and pain others experience? For the violence and cruelty as well as the injustice and unfairness in the world? What can and what should I do about any of this?* This can be especially the case when we discuss relations between American imperialism versus those subject to American imperialism, and between global North versus global South/'First World' versus 'Third World'. But it can also likewise be the case in discussing, analogously, responsibility for, and complicity with, systemic racism, sexism, classism, heterosexism, cissexism, ethnocentrism, ableism, ageism, and so on–including when we discuss what is, what can be, what might be, what should be, our responsibility to do anything about the existence and persistence of any of these, and similar, 'isms', even if we seek 'small' ways to do so, in our everyday lives and in relation to where, when, and with whom we might maintain any real power to do some good.

Even among those of us who have long considered ourselves to be staunch critics of American militarism, and especially of American imperialism, it can be easy enough, from a relatively distant and advantaged position, to become complacent or to remain ignorant concerning lengthy ongoing exercises of both, and to not always be sharply attuned to how readily American leaders feel justified in interfering with and intervening in the affairs of ostensibly sovereign nations, in ways and to extents that would provoke massive outrage if another country were to do this within the US. We can forget or otherwise remain ignorant of how many US troops and how many US military bases operate throughout the world, or of how active and in what numerous ways our intelligence agencies are in other countries, while glazing over American involvement in waging 'forever war' in Afghanistan as well as American complicity with genocide in Yemen. And the same can also be the case versus the horrors millions of refugees and asylum seekers experience every day, including all too many seeking but denied entry into this country–including those forced into exile as a result of conditions for which the US bears at least partial and indirect responsibility. Lack of historical awareness can affect people like us (self-professed anti-imperialists) too. I well recall, for example, how shocked I was in first learning about the US annexation of Hawaii, wondering how I could have possibly remained ignorant of this until I was in my early 20s. On my one trip to Cuba, in the early 1990s, as an invited contributor to a conference of North American and Cuban philosophers, I expected to face surprises in what I encountered, but I was particularly struck by the appearance of residences and other buildings, which, by comparison with the same in the US, seemed in urgent need of repainting, not anticipating this would be, for me, one of the most immediately visible signs of the effects of the US blockade. At that conference and throughout that visit I also was struck by much else as well: visiting a massive estate consisting of prime beachfront property that once had been the exclusive property of the Du Pont family and to which native Cubans were barred access, by the fact that at the time of my visit the Cuban government was rationing food which meant observing queues to obtain these rations were a common sight at the same time as our food was carefully separated from what was available to residents and thoroughly sterilized because most of us North Americans did not maintain ready immunity versus diseases we could otherwise easily pick up there, and by the fact that on our last night we stayed in a four-star hotel where the room I and my co-presenter Mark were staying was full of cockroaches. The trip included many positive experiences, certainly, as I was, for example, particularly impressed with how open Cuban conference attendees were in discussing issues of gay and lesbian liberation in relation to socialist revolution, as well as in how thoroughly Cuban attendees addressed questions raised of them, by taking time, at length, to situate their responses in historical, political, and theoretical perspective. But my point here in citing this experience of mine is a simple one: despite extensive experience engaged in activist efforts concerned with 'anti-imperialism' and 'Third World solidarity', I still met with surprises, and still needed to reflect self-critically on what these surprises 'said about me', in particular as someone not only 'from', but also who had lived every previous moment of his life entirely within the 'First World' 'global North'.

Another connection I make with Aimé Césaire's *Discourse on Colonialism* concerns widespread ignorance and denial, to this day, in Britain, of what British imperialism involved, what British imperialism was like, and of the extent to which a great deal of what makes Britain what it is today remains intricately interconnected with the ongoing impact of the British Empire. Although Césaire's concrete examples are primarily French, his critique is directed at European colonialism more broadly, so this connection is, I suggest, a fruitful one to explore.

Britain's status as a global power prior to, during, and after World War II has much to do with the history of the British empire–and of British imperialism. Yet the British empire, it can be reasonably argued, in line with Césaire's contention that 'Europe is indefensible', constitutes an enormous moral and social 'crime' perpetrated by the British state, British state agents, British companies such as the East India Company, and many Britons who played leading and supporting roles in extracting enormous wealth via slavery, and the slave trade, as well as through other forms of oppressive domination and exploitative expropriation from colonized nations and peoples–over the course of many centuries. What compounds the egregiousness of British 'crimes of empire' is the fact so many Britons past and present do not recognize them as such, and in fact often have conceived and continue to conceive of the British empire as positively beneficial not just in England, Scotland, Wales, and Northern Ireland, but also in the nations and for the peoples subject to imperial domination.

In *The Blood Never Dried: a People's History of the British Empire*, John Newsinger begins by focusing on how many "contemporary apologists for empire" continue to demonstrate "reluctance to acknowledge the extent to which imperial rule rests on coercion, on the policeman torturing the suspect and the soldier blowing up houses and shooting prisoners" (15). Throughout his book Newsinger recounts an extensive chronicle, in brutal detail, of just such persistent and pervasive violent coercion, throughout the British empire, ultimately encompassing one-quarter of the world's land mass and exerting dominance over one-quarter of the world's population.

Early on, Newsinger declares "British participation in the Atlantic slave trade is arguably the worst crime in British history" (22). As Newsinger explains, British slave traders are responsible for sending more slaves to the Americas than any other slave trading nation, and slavery was an extremely violent and thoroughly dehumanizing process. As is well documented by many historians, profits from the slave trade, and from slave plantations in the Americas, contributed enormously to the wealth of major cities throughout Britain–and this means the wealth and grandeur of British social and cultural life is rooted in a terrible 'crime'.

In response to those inclined to insist the British never stooped to the lows the Nazis did during their reign of terror, Newsinger counters, citing Matthew Edwardes, a former chairman of British Leyland Motor corporation, "that during the Indian Rebellion [of 1857-1858] the English threw aside the mask of civilisation and engaged in a war of such ferocity that a reasonable parallel can be seen in our times with the Nazi occupation of Europe" (75). In this Great Indian Rebellion, but hardly only then and there, the British tortured and then summarily tried, sentenced, and executed prisoners of war, immediately upon or shortly following capture, while British forces killed many others, including many non-combatants, as well as destroyed a vast amount of the physical structures and infrastructures in communities across India, in 'retaliation' for the rebellion. As Newsinger indicates, the British imperial record in India, involving repeated campaigns of "countryside laid waste, cities sacked, civilians robbed, raped and murdered, and tens of thousands of soldiers killed and mutilated," clearly "demonstrates . . . the British Empire, despite the liberalism of its metropolitan rulers, was a predatory empire engaged in continuous warfare" (75). Torture perpetrated by the British "ranged from rough manhandling through to flogging and placing in the stocks and then on to more extreme measures." The last included use, as Newsinger cites Indian historian Rudrangshu Mukherjee describing, of "searing hot irons," "dipping in wells till the victim is half suffocated," "squeezing the testacles," "putting pepper or red chilies in the eyes or introducing them into the private parts of men and women," "prevention of sleep," "nipping with pincers," "suspension from the branches of a tree," and "imprisonment in a room used for storing lime" (78). It is in critical response to the British imperial action versus the Great Indian Rebellion that the phrase 'the blood never dries' originates, as 19th century English Chartist and socialist Ernest Jones famously declared 'the blood never dries' on the British empire, condemning this imperial campaign as "one of the most iniquitous usurpations that ever disgraced the annals of humanity" (90).

Over the course of his book Newsinger cites numerous examples to support his claim 'the blood never dried' on the British Empire, including in Jamaica, Ireland, China, Egypt, Kenya, Malaya, and India, while in the case of Palestine, and in particular in relation to the Palestinian revolt of 1936 to 1939, Newsinger emphasizes what is especially "astonishing is how little it figures in British history books," as both "a pivotal moment in the history of the Middle East and one of the most shameful episodes in the history of the empire" (140). Newsinger cites David Smiley's account of his service as a soldier during this campaign, where he complained that British methods employed versus Palestinians "were the methods of the Gestapo" (146). As Newsinger declares, records of the British response to the Palestinian revolt exemplify "the reality of colonial rule is that it always rests on the shoulders of a policeman or soldier beating a suspect or applying a cigarette to their testicles. This is something that the apologists for the empire, whether they be politicians, academics or journalists, are seldom prepared to confront" (146).

Subsequently, after World War II, as further evidence that little changed throughout the bloody history of British imperialism, "The British campaign to crush the Mau Mau rebellion in the 1950s has become a byword for colonial brutality," with the British, and not for the first time, evincing a particular aptitude for covering up the worst of the atrocities British forces committed–unlike the Americans, who were, Newsinger notes, nowhere near as successful in doing the same, concerning American malpractices in Vietnam (192). As Newsinger adds, "What happened in Kenya was far worse than anything revealed at Abu Graibh or Guantanamo Bay but excited considerably less controversy" (203). In response to the Mau Mau rebellion, British forces not only killed upwards of 100,000 rebels, a great many after they had been captured as prisoners of war, when they were subjected to summary trial, conviction, and execution by hanging, but also employed a considerable array of techniques of torture, rounding up for interrogation and enhanced interrogation many thousands of Kenyans not directly involved in the fighting, and destroying massive numbers of homes and villages, leaving over a million people displaced.

In Danny Dorling's and Sally Tomlinson's *Rule Britannia: Brexit and the End of Empire*, the authors emphasize considerable ignorance among Britons about what the British empire actually was like continues to exercise a damaging impact upon British social attitudes and political positions to this day. At the beginning of their first chapter Dorling and Tomlinson cite Adam Ramsay of Open Democracy declaring:

> The years of the long recession have brought with them a nostalgia for a time when life was easier, and Britain could simply get rich by killing people of colour and stealing their stuff. All of this is made possible by lies: the lies many of us were told about what our great-grandparents were up to in India, the lies we told ourselves when we decided not to look too closely, the lies we told the peoples we subjugated: Britain is a country built so firmly on deceit, dishonesty and backstabbing that the symbol of our national flag is not just a double-cross, but a triple. (21)

What all too many Britons remain oblivious about is how much and in what a great many ways the British empire benefitted, and indeed continues to benefit, Britain–and Britons. For instance, as Dorling and Tomlinson indicated, "Thanks to the British Empire, London is now the most ethnically mixed city in the world. It is the real global melting pot" (43). And yet "celebrations of Britain's multicultural global supremacy are few and far between" while there are "no British national museums devoted to immigration or to the empire and its associated atrocities" (43). Meanwhile, Britons cling to false histories such as "the Conservative myth that their MP William Wilberforce abolished slavery in 1833" when in reality "It was hardly abolished as far as the living conditions of most slaves were concerned, but a lot of slave-holding families became exceedingly rich from the compensation Wilberforce helped to arrange" (43).

As Dorling and Tomlinson bluntly declare, this is only one of numerous instances of the "rubbish we often teach our children" concerning the empire, which still too few learn "began with avarice," and was fueled, from the start, by "greed for gold and the need for food" (48). Although "Britain's formative identity was at the heart of an empire" (50), many Britons remain blithely ignorant about how little actually binds together the four small nations that make up Britain once the empire has ended. What's more, ignorance concerning the history of the British empire and the extensive migration of peoples to and from the British Isles over the course of many centuries leads to a mystification of 'British' as a racially distinct and homogenous category when 'Britishness' has always been the result of "a collection of mongrel invaders and other immigrants" (110). The empire only greatly compounded this actual British heterogeneity–and actual British multiculturalism.

Dorling and Tomlinson call attention to the fact "Almost all of the older buildings of Britain's great universities were built from the spoils of empire," while noting not all Britons from all British social classes benefitted equally from these spoils, yet "a huge amount of our infrastructure, from municipal sewers to royal palaces, can be traced back to financial sources that would not have existed but for the British Empire" (119). As Dorling and Tomlinson later add, "The primary source of wealth for Britain has always been the exploitation of other nations, with the British military occasionally acting as the bailiff, and the Secret Intelligence Service providing industrial espionage" (172).

Beyond ignorance of this imperial contribution to British wealth, Dorling and Tomlinson charge "Britain is such an unequal and unproductive country today precisely because of its imperial legacy, which required the establishment of an elaborate class structure, creating status anxiety and all manner of phobia, including sexual inhibitions, awe of the upper echelons and disdain of the lower classes and the 'natives'" (120). In this respect, "What is still surprising today is how many people educated in the 1960s and 1970s will look back and say 'I was taught nothing about the empire'. They were–but they didn't realize how much has been implicit" (148). As Dorling and Tomlinson here imply, Britons have been taught attitudes and outlooks that have much to do with matters of class and status, as well as affecting norms for polite or 'correct' social interaction and everyday behavior, without realizing how these attitudes and outlooks are products of the empire.

Even more challenging, Dorling and Tomlinson propose, for Britons wrestling with the legacy of the British empire and its continuing pervasive impact upon Britain to this day, is "Britain has not had the reality check that losing a war instills. Countries that better understand their own history are those which were not on top for so long or were never placed high enough" (190). But, at the same time, "Where Britain has done best," in the economic sectors where Britain has been the most productive, and competitive, "it was often the empire that helped," including through allowing British cultural productions, as well as the English language, readily to spread across the world. In reality, "nothing in Britain has been untouched by empire" and this in turn means "A very large part of what Britain is good at was established during the time of empire and would not be here were it not for that empire," but too many Britons, suffering from 'imperial nostalgia', fail to recognize this is "an empire than cannot be replaced or rekindled, but has to be recognised, represented fairly in our histories and relinquished, not constantly re-conjured" (192).

In *Empireland: How Imperialism Has Shaped Modern Britain*, Sathnam Sanghera concentrates on identifying and describing in detail numerous concrete ways British social and cultural life has been shaped and constituted by the impact of the British empire, yet once again too many Britons remain unwilling to face up to this honestly, let alone engage in a careful reflection on how to make sense of and engage with this impact. As Sanghera recalls, "my education in British empire was almost non-existent. In fact, looking back, it's almost as if teachers went out of their way to avoid telling us about it" (16-17). As someone who is Sikh, and who traces his Sikh ancestry to India, Sanghera recounts how shockingly ignorant he long was of the history of Sikh relations with Britain, and of the place of Sikhs in British history and society. Sanghera stresses Britain has long been a much more "multiculturally, racially diverse society" than many, especially White, Britons have been wont to realize, and this has everything to do with the fact that Britain "once had a muticultural, racially diverse empire. Or as the Sri Lankan writer Ambalavener Sivanandan famously put it: 'we are here because you were there'" (69). Or, as British historian David Olusoga aptly remarks, "If you don't want Nigerians in the UK all you need do is go back to the 19th century and persuade the Victorians not to invade Nigeria" (69). Britain, unfortunately, has too often struggled "to acknowledge that brown people are here because Britain, at best, had close relationships with its colonies for centuries, which included millions of the colonized putting their lives on the line for Britain during two world wars, or because Britain, at worst, violently repressed and exploited its colonies for centuries" (77). A continuing major problem with dominant ideology in Britain, therefore, has to do not only with a tendency to deny or ignore this history of violent repression and exploitation, as well as what wealth it enabled in Britain and for Britons, but also to misrepresent Britain as an overwhelmingly and exclusively white and seemingly monocultural nation, when "brown people have lived in Britain for centuries," and indeed as far back as Roman times. As Sanghera quotes, "multiculturalism is, in the words of the Jamaican poet, actor and broadcaster Louise Bennett, just 'colonizin' . . . in reverse" (76-77).

Sanghera, like Newsinger and Dorling and Tomlinson, discusses many avenues by which British wealth was generated through imperial exploitation, summing up this impact by citing Indian politician, writer, and international diplomat Shashi Tharoor arguing "Britain's Industrial Revolution was built on the destruction of India's thriving manufacturing industries," historian Richard Drayton arguing "The wealth of the West was built on Africa's exploitation," London Mayor Sadiq Khan declaring "it's a sad truth that much of our city and nation's wealth was derived from the slave trade," and the famous writer George Orwell pointing out "the high standard of living we enjoy in England depends upon keeping a tight hold on the empire . . . Under the capitalist system, in order that England may live in comparative comfort, a hundred million Indians must live on the verge of starvation–an evil state of affairs, but you acquiesce in it every time you step into a taxi or eat a plate of strawberries and cream" (124). As Sanghera adds, the slave trade

> explains the wealth of cities like Bristol and Liverpool, why Manchester did well, producing cloth from cotton grown on plantations worked by slaves . . . . British empire helped both establish the City of London as a leading world financial centre and to ensure it dominates our national economy, while our slave trade was so deeply entrenched in our economy that even church ministers, abolitionists and people of colour received some of the £20 million (£17 billion [in today's terms]) compensation. Compensation that was so large and significant that we, as a nation, finished paying it off only in 2015. (141)

What's more, "between 1660 and 1807 Britain shipped around 3 million Africans to America, the slaves kept shackled to each other or to the deck to prevent mutiny during the Middle Passage, stacked in tiers, with no space to stand or turn, the dysentery, suicides, epidemics and murders killing so many Africans on the way that sharks frequently pursued slave ships on their journey west" (152). As Sanghera aptly adds, "Britain was dehumanizing black people on a super-industrial scale" (152).

Nonetheless, Sanghera recognizes even as Britain's "dark history of racism . . . influences contemporary psychology and culture," this same history "simultaneously, albeit inadvertently, inspired anti-racism," while "the abolitionist movement arguably laid the groundwork for all sorts of progressive shifts in society" (156). The latter needs to be appreciated, but of fundamental importance is understanding how the history of empire shaped "the distinct brand of racism practised in Britain," including widespread disparities in representation of Black and Brown versus white Britons throughout virtually all major sectors of British economy, society, culture, and politics to this day, along with persistent evidence of institutional racism such as perpetrated by the Home Office in the *Windrush* scandal and as acknowledged by Prime Minister Theresa May (who in her previous role as Home Secretary bears considerable responsibility for that scandal), with May admitting "black people are treated more harshly by the criminal justice system" (164). As Sanghera indicates, because Britain "dominated the slave trade for a significant period, ran one of the biggest white supremacist enterprises in the history of humanity and dabbled in genocide . . . the stain of it has seeped into many aspects of our contemporary culture, from the jobs market to the sinister reemergence of violent white supremacy" (164).

Unfortunately, as Sanghera recounts, a YouGov poll from 2014 revealed 59 per cent of Britons agreed the British empire is 'something to be proud of' and more than one-third 'would like it if Britain still had an empire'. Likewise, in January 2016, another YouGov poll reported 44 per cent of Britons agreed Britain's 'history of colonialism' "was something to be proud of" while 43 per cent agreed the British empire was 'a good thing'. As recently, what's more, as March 2020 one more YouGov poll found 30 per cent of Britons "believe former colonies were better off as part of the British empire" (186). As a result of the popularity of these kinds of positions, it can be difficult for Britons, especially Black and Brown Britons, to criticize the British empire and British imperialism without being accused of being "anti-British" (188). Sanghera identifies as British and is grateful for many things about being British:

> for having had a free education at one of the best grammar schools in the country; for having attended (for free) one of the best colleges at one of the most successful universities in the world; for an NHS that cares for the people I love the most; for a welfare state that saved my family from the most crushing consequences of poverty; for the chance to live in the greatest city on earth and work for two of the greatest newspapers in the world; for British pop music; for the glorious British countryside; for Pizza Express" (189).

Yet Sanghera does "resent being instructed to demonstrate my gratitude whenever I analyse any aspect of British life, when my white colleagues don't get the same treatment" (189). As Sanghera defiantly declares, "*I was born here*, not India, I am British, I am as entitled to comment on my home nation as the next man and the endless insistence that I display my gratitude is rooted in racism. Racism which is, itself, rooted in the fact that the children of imperial immigrants born here are not always seen as fully British" (189).

Sanghera notes well that "in 1914, it was not only Britain which took on the Germans and their allies, but the entire British empire: over 3,000,000 men from across the empire and Commonwealth," while "In the Second World War, the number of imperial soldiers was just as significant, including 1,440,500 troops from India" as well as close to 1,500,000 from other countries (191). Yet, unfortunately, most accounts and depictions, fictional and non-fictional, of both wars ignore this contribution from the empire and the Commonwealth, especially the vast number of Black and Brown people who fought for Britain. And when only "11 per cent of GCSE students are studying modules that refer to Black people's contribution to Britain and less than one in ten are studying a module which concentrates on empire" this kind of ignorance is likely to persist (192).

Sanghera cites former British Museum Director Neil MacGregor commenting "What is very remarkable about German history as a whole is that the Germans use their history to think about the future, where the British tend to use their history to comfort themselves," with this contrast having much to do, as Sanghera explains, with "the fact that we have not, as a nation, been invaded or occupied in modern times," and therefore "we have never been forced to interrogate our behaviour, in the way that the Germans, the Japanese, and the French were forced to do after the Second World War" (197). This behavior, deserving of interrogation that it has not yet adequately received, might well include "records proving ministers in London were aware of the horrors inflicted on Mau Mau insurgents in Kenya" as well as "intelligence reports on the 'elimination' of those opposed to the colonial regime in 1950s Malaya," and "details of how the UK forcibly displaced islanders from Diego Garcia in the Indian Ocean around 1970" (198).

Referring to post-WWII Germany once again, Sanghera points out "Germans have a word–*Vergangenheitsaufarbeitung*–which translates as 'working off the past'–to describe how they have come to terms with Nazism and the Holocaust in a deep and systematic way" (212). Sanghera lists a considerable series of examples which I too can attest are remarkably powerful, right in the center of Germany's capital city: many monuments, memorials, and museums devoted to remembering Nazi tyranny and the victims of this tyranny, including the Topography of Terror, the Memorial to the Murdered Jews of Europe, and the German Resistance Memorial Center among numerous other such sites just in Berlin alone. What Sanghera is proposing here, as do Dorling and Tomlinson, and as logically follows from Newsinger's history of the British empire as well, is the need for a comparable series of monuments, memorials, and museums, as well as regular commemorative events and a serious effort at honest, thoughtfully reflective, and openly self-critical education concerning the impact of the British empire within and upon Britain–and Britons–past and present, including upon widely diverse dimensions of British social and cultural life.

One more worthwhile contribution to helping open up such space for such a self-critical reconsideration of the British empire and its legacy that I propose to discuss here is Ian Sanjay Patel's *We're Here Because You Were There: Immigration and the End of Empire*. In this book Santel argues that the complications and tensions surrounding immigration in Britain since World War II have much to do with how far–and indeed how tenaciously–Britain, and in particular the British state and the British ruling class, strived to maintain the British empire, in a new form, after its ostensible end. Santel proposes that "The British empire never underwent an 'end of empire' moment," a "clean break" at a single time, because on the contrary "the empire was converted into the Commonwealth around the end of the Second World War, and entered a transitional period where the final end was constantly deferred. The Commonwealth was presented as the latest and most constitutionally advanced stage of the British empire" (4). And yet, "as the post-war world developed . . . British political elites enjoyed increasingly less control over it" (4). When Britain attempted "to ensure the Commonwealth remained an imperial project" by means of the British Nationality Act of 1948, which granted British citizenship to people living throughout the Commonwealth, the British government at the time was not motivated by altruistic considerations, but rather seeking to continue to tie these nations, and their people, to Britain, not anticipating large numbers would ever decide to take advantage of this status to immigrate to Great Britain. As a result, British political elites entered into repeated convolutions subsequently to attempt to close the door this Act opened, feigning impositions of restrictions having nothing to with race yet at the same time in fact having everything to do with race, notably by coming up with the new distinction between being 'a citizen' of global Britain and 'belonging' to Great Britain, which made it easy to define many white residents of Commonwealth nations as belonging and many Black and Brown residents as not, even when the latter were nevertheless legally British citizens. As Patel explains,

The imposition of unity, regularity and continuity over British nationality throughout the Commonwealth was a conscious attempt to keep Britain's post-war imperial ambitions intact. Yet this same efforts also had the effect of granting British citizenship, and confirming this right of entry into Britain, to millions of non-white people in the post-war world. In other words, the constitutional unification of Britain with the empire and Commonwealth, and the post-war migrations to Britain that followed it, were [respectively] intended and unintended consequences of a single post-war imperial project. (5)

Throughout Britain's post-WWII history, Patel charts a continuing "reluctance at the level of the British state to fully come to terms with imperial pasts and their relationship to British national identity" (19). Recently, "the Windrush scandal reveals that this particular history is never far away, and remains in thrall to the same historical abridgements, as Britain continues to redefine its relationship to old and new immigrants alike" (19). British imperialism, Patel documents, continued, under cover, through multiple means, long after its ostensible end. For example, in striking connection with Césaire's warning versus neo-colonialism, "'development' itself was among other things an imperial attempt to capture interests after the end of direct imperial rule" (147). As a concrete illustration of this predicament, Patel cites "rising Kenyan politician Tom Mboya," in 1961, again strongly echoing Césaire, addressing "the frustrating irony that, because 'of the lack of trained men and women', independent African states had to 'depend on outside experts to help them run the countries'" and reliance on these outside experts manifests "'the dangers of neo-colonialism'" with Mboya urging "'equality' not dependence'". As Mboya elaborates,

> If we are equal, only help us where we need help; stop being paternalistic. We need a continuing flow of technical, specialist, financial, and other types of aid. We will take it from you and from any nations ready to offer aid with no strings attached. Do not grumble when we take it. We take it because we need it, and we take it because it is given free. Remember, we are also capable of gauging the ulterior motives of all those who offer to help us. (Quoted, 147).

In conclusion, Patel writes,

British nationality remained imperial at the same time as Britain's imperial power was taken away. British officials experienced the twin processes of immigration and the end of empire in ways that were preoccupied with race and maintaining Britain's imperial purchase on the world. The refrain of the so-called immigrant in this period, *we're here because you were there*, spoke to a political, historical and legal reality, no matter how disavowed and denied.

Post-war politics was transnational. Britain could not come to know its domestic identity without reference to its international status. The problem was for many British officials, politicians and various other elites, the only way they knew how to conceive of the international was in imperial terms. The post-2016 debates around Britain's decision to leave the European Union, for instance, betrayed a faith that Britain might effortlessly restore its Commonwealth links, making good on trade and any number of other partnerships within a

Commonwealth realm. Euphemisms for colonialism readily followed. Britain enjoyed a shared history with many states around the world; the possibilities were endless.

Many of these arguments were out of date in 1960. They speak to a historical failure to reckon with an imperial past . . . (279-280).

What we have, instead of these grandiose illusions, is a Britain after World War II struggling, and even more precisely, flailing about, in attempting to maintain and/or recreate some approximation of its erstwhile empire, with these attempts being messily caught up in matters of race and racism. As Patel comments,

The hostile environment created by the 1971 Immigration Act [which restricted 'right of abode' in the UK itself–England, Scotland, Wales, and Northern Ireland– to those who had a parent or grandparent who 'abided' within the UK] has become a rationale for the British state that is every bit as immovable as the refusal to examine its imperial past, still less its post-1945 imperial ambitions. The close relationship between immigration, British identity and the imperial past will not be broken until this reckoning takes place. The experiences of those affected by the 2018 Windrush scandal [when thousands of British citizens, maintaining the legal right to permanently remain in the UK, were nonetheless deported or threatened with deportation, and also lost jobs, housing, social welfare benefits, and more besides] capture with terrible consequence the distorted relationship the British state has long had, and continues to have, to its past. The idea that the Windrush generation were welcomed by governments, and that British traditions of right and law were gifted to colonial populations who then migrated to Britain as so many pupils gone to meet their teacher, are national superstitions exposed by the hostile environments past and present. In the struggle between imperial idealism and a reactionary nativism, so perceptible in British governments in the 1960s, it is a British nativism that has recently made its hostility the more loudly known. (280-281)

Three

Edward W. Said's *Representations of the Intellectual* consists of a series of six lectures he originally presented for the Reith Lecture Series in 1993, given each year since 1948 by a leading intellectual or cultural figure on a theme of the lecturer's choosing. The series was founded by and is named after John Reith, the first Director-General of the BBC. Said (who lived from 1935 through 2003), was at the time a University Professor at Columbia University; a hugely influential intellectual, scholar, and activist; a renowned literary and cultural critic; and a leading contributor to the field of post-colonial studies by way of books such as *Orientalism, Culture and Imperialism, The Politics of Dispossession: The Struggle for Palestinian Self-Determination 1969-1994*, and *Peace and Its Discontents: Essays on Palestine in the Middle East Peace Process*. In this series of lectures Said's thesis concerns "the public role of the intellectual as outsider, 'amateur', and disturber of the status quo" (x). As he proceeds, Said makes a case for what he argues the genuine intellectual should, even must, be like in contrast with, and opposition versus, various other conceptions and practices of intellectual work, as well as for the urgent importance of the kind of intellectual he is here valorizing.

In his introduction to the book-length publication, in 1994, of his Reith lectures, Said begins to explain what this kind of intellectual is about, by noting, early on, that "One task of the intellectual is the effort to break down the stereotypes and reductive categories that are so limiting to human thought and communication" (xi). As he proceeds over the course of his six lectures, Said elaborates not only by identifying additional tasks the intellectual needs to take on but also by comparing and contrasting his conception of the intellectual with other prominent and influential conceptions, past and present. Said's aim is to intervene within a diffusion, cooptation, and taming of the role, and work, of the intellectual, at the end of the 20th century. As such it is crucial, from the start, "to speak about intellectuals as precisely those figures whose public performances can neither be predicted nor compelled into some slogan, orthodox party line, or fixed dogma . . . [and where] standards of truth were to be held to despite the individual intellectual's party affiliation, national background, and primeval loyalties" (xii).

Continuing to define the parameters of his conception of the intellectual steadily more precisely, Said writes,"For me the intellectual appeals to (rather than excoriates) as wide as possible a public" (xiii). This means the real opponent, the real "problem for the intellectual," is not 'the ignorant public' or 'the reactionary public' or even 'the anti-intellectual public' but rather "the insiders, experts, coteries, professionals who . . . mold public opinion" so as to "make it conformist" and so as to "encourage reliance on a superior little band of all-knowing men in power" (xiii). As Said sees it, these 'insiders, experts, coteries, and professionals' are *not* proper intellectuals because "Insiders promote special interests, but intellectuals should be the ones to question patriotic nationalism, corporate thinking, and a sense of class, racial or gender privilege" (xiii). The proper intellectual, according to Said, is not a narrow specialist, not tied to a narrowly specific social and political interest, but one who is focused on and concerned with speaking, writing, creating, sharing, and acting in favor of "universality," which requires being able and willing to push beyond "easy certainties provided us by our background, language, nationality, which so often shield us from the reality of others" (xiv).

Intellectual commitment to and identification with universality requires independence, a refusal to be tied down to merely serving as the mouthpiece of narrowly particular interests. The intellectual, Said declares, should *seek* "independence" and should deliberately *seek*, what's more, to engage as "an exile and marginal, an amateur, and as the author of a language that tries to speak truth to power" (xvi). Yes, "To deliberately not belong" risks powerlessness in the form of an inability to affect change and as a result needing to accept instead "the role of a witness who testifies to a horror otherwise unrecorded" (xvii). But this kind of powerlessness is to be preferred over cooptation and incorporation, while proper intellectual life, of the kind Said is embracing here, and urging other would-be intellectuals likewise to embrace, depends on maintaining, persistently, "a spirit of opposition, rather than accommodation" and of "dissent against the status quo" in persistent alignment with "the underrepresented and disadvantaged" (xvii). This kind of commitment depends on, yet further, as Said cites Michel Foucault, "'a relentless erudition'" as well as "a sense of the dramatic and the insurgent" while being ready to accept that "representations by intellectuals will neither make them friends in high places nor win them official honors. It is a lonely condition, yes, but it is always a better one than a gregarious tolerance for the way things are" (xviii).

In "Lecture I: Representations of the Intellectual," Said starts with Antonio Gramsci's famous distinction between all men as maintaining the capacity for but not the effective social function of being an 'intellectual' (3). Said continues frrom there by addressing Gramsci's distinction between 'traditional' and 'organic' intellectuals (4). Said next discusses Julien Benda's definition of intellectuals "as a tiny band of gifted and morally endowed philosopher-kings who constitute the conscience of mankind," where such intellectuals operate in many respects much like "clerics" (4-5). Benda's intellectuals are willing to be tortured and killed for their convictions and commitments, and this means these are "thoroughgoing individuals with powerful personalities" (7) who are implacably opposed to the prevailing social and political status quo. Despite its romantic excess, Said admits Benda's conception "remains an attractive and compelling one" (7) and especially, despite Benda's deep conservatism, "this figure of the intellectual as being set apart" (8). Strikingly, as Said proceeds, his conception of what an intellectual needs to be like is closer to that of Benda than Gramsci despite Said maintaining philosophical and political positions otherwise much closer to Gramsci than Benda.

Said finds 'today'–in late 20th century, (post)modern, global capitalist society–a proliferation of people functioning in ostensibly intellectual roles, and who do ostensibly intellectual kinds of work, but Said is at pains to distinguish his conception of the intellectual from precisely those kinds of functional roles and that kind of work. Said argues "the intellectual is an individual with a specific public role in society that cannot be reduced simply to being a faceless professional, a competent member of a class just going about her/his business" (11). The intellectual, instead, "is an individual endowed with a faculty for representing, embodying, articulating a message, a view, an attitude, philosophy or opinion to, as well as for, a public. And this role has an edge to it" because the intellectual must accept it is the intellectual's "place to publicly raise embarrassing questions, to confront orthodoxy and dogma . . . to be someone who cannot be easily co-opted" and who aims to represent "all those people and issues that are routinely forgotten or swept under the rug" (11). This kind of intcllectual proceeds "on the basis of universal principles that all human beings are entitled to accept decent standards of behavior concerning freedom and justice from worldly powers or nations, and that deliberate and inadvertent violations of these standards needs to be testified and fought against courageously" (11-12).

In relation to his conception of what the proper intellectual needs to be, Said declares there can be no such thing as a private intellectual (12). Because, after all, "the whole point is to be embarrassing, contrary, even unpleasant" (12). The intellectual, *as an intellectual*, "visibly represents a standpoint of some kind" and "intellectuals are individuals with a vocation for the act of representing" (12-13). You cannot *represent* if you do not engage publicly in *representing*. 'Represent' here means, more precisely, "representative, not just of some subterranean or large social movement, but of a quite peculiar, even abrasive style of life and social performance" (14). Said declares, moreover, that "The intellectual's representations, his or her articulations of a cause or idea to society, are not meant primarily to fortify ego or celebrate status" (20). Instead, "Intellectual representations are the *activity itself*, dependent on a kind of consciousness that is skeptical, engaged, unremittingly devoted to rational investigation and moral judgment; and that puts the individual on the record and on the line" (20). Said approves of C. Wright Mills' conception of "independent intellectuals" (20) and quotes from Mills: "'The independent artist and intellectual are among the few remaining personalities equipped to resist and to fight the stereotyping and consequent death of genuinely living things. Fresh perception now involves the capacity to continually unmask and to smash the stereotypes of vision and intellect'" (21). In other words, the intellectual *must* "dispute" the official and the powerful, and the intellectual *must* challenge "trends of thought that maintain the status quo" (22). "Unmasking" of what this status quo conceals is key as well as is providing "alternative visions" of what could be but is not, at least not yet (22).

Returning to what he has begun to expound in his "Introduction," Said declares "The intellectual always stands between loneliness and alignment" (22). With the then recent Persian Gulf War in mind as well as alluding to other prior US wars as well, Said argues the intellectual's mission, in contrast with a supposedly 'patriotic' suspending of questioning and criticism in support of the nation while at war is "to unearth the forgotten, to make connections that were denied, to cite alternative courses of action that could have avoided war and its attendant goal of human destruction" (22). Challenging broad popular consensus, even at times, such as the nation at war, where it can be risky to dangerous to do so, is absolutely necessary, because for Said the proper intellectual is someone "unwilling to accept easy formulas, or ready-made clichés, or the smooth, ever-so-accommodating confirmations of what the powerful or conventional have to say or do" (23). The intellectual maintains "a state of constant alertness" and, as result, is perpetually facing "a complicated struggle to balance the problems of one's own selfhood against the demands of publishing and speaking out in the public sphere" (23). The intellectual, for Said, just as for Benda, must be ready and willing to subordinate the former interest to that of the latter.

In "Lecture II: Holding Nations and Traditions at Bay," Said recommends, in relation to one's own language and culture, and in relation to one's own background and social identity, including in relation to one's own nationality, that the intellectual abide by the principle "Never solidarity before criticism" (32). The intellectual, in other words, must be willing to raise difficult, uncomfortable, and challenging questions of 'one's own'–especially versus what is otherwise "overlooked or walked past" (33). The intellectual must always be attentive to 'the underside of power' even as this operates within organizations and movements that are representative of counter-hegemonic power in contest with hegemonic power (34-35). Nevertheless, this challenge is particularly acute for those who are tempted to align their intellectual positions and practices within the socially and politically dominant: "I think the major choice faced by the intellectual is whether to be allied with the stability of the victors and rulers or–the more difficult path–to consider that stability as a state of emergency threatening the less fortunate with the danger of complete extinction, and take into account the experience of subordination itself, as well as the memory of forgotten voices and persons" (35).

Notably, while Said increasingly precisely defines what must be the proper intellectual's social position, role, and purpose, he readily accepts and indeed welcomes the intellectual to engage by way of a diverse array of means and media, including not only artistic works but also "ritual performance and acts of worship" (36). Key, through whatever means and media, is the intellectual committing toward "disputing the prevailing norms" (36). In doing so, intellectuals may focus on raising questions, rather than offering and especially detailing 'answers', and they may act, first and last, as agents of "skepticism and contest" (37). Nonetheless, citing Aimé Césaire and Frantz Fanon in support of this particular position, Said urges the intellectual to strive "always to go beyond survival to questions of political liberation, to critiques of the leadership, to presenting alternatives that are too often marginalized or pushed aside as irrelevant to the main battle at hand" (41). Even more precisely, "For the intellectual the task, I believe, is explicitly to universalize the crisis, to give greater human scope to what a particular race or nation suffered, to associate that experience with the suffering of others" like Fanon did in associating the suffering of Algerians fighting the Algerian War of Independence with "similar afflictions of other people" (44). It is crucial, what's more, to keep faithfully in mind that "just because you represent the sufferings that your people lived through which you yourself might have lived through also, you are not relieved of the duty of revealing that your own people now may be visiting related crimes on *their* victims" (44).

"Lecture III: Intellectual Exile–Expatriates and Marginals," offers an especially distinctive and usefully provocative contribution. Exile in pre-modern experience, Said recounts, corresponded to "being a sort of permanent outcast, someone who never felt at home, and was always at odds with the environment, inconsolable about the past, bitter about the present and the future" (47). Said brings up this pre-modern conception in order to recuperate value from it for modern times. Said contests "a popular but wholly mistaken assumption that being exiled is to be totally cut off, isolated, hopelessly separated from your place of origin" because "The fact is that for most exiles the difficulty consists of not simply being forced to live away from home, but rather, given today's world, in living with the many reminders that you are in exile, that your home is not so far away" (48-49). So exile is always 'in between', neither completely at one with either the old or with the new. The intellectual in/as exile, moreover, in the sense Said is discussing, and advocating, "will not make the adjustment" to 'fit in' with the dominant culture of the new society, "preferring to remain outside the mainstream, unaccommodated, unco-opted, resistant" (52). Exile is "a metaphorical condition" which means it includes many people who have been born in and lived out their lives in the same place, and thereby a much wider array of 'outsiders' and 'naysayers' than merely literal exiles (52).

The condition of intellectual exile involves "the state of never being fully adjusted," of experiencing persistent "restlessness, movement, constantly being unsettled, and unsettling others" (53). Intellectual exile involves never feeling fully 'at home' as well as 'never fully arriving' at any destination (53). In fact, "the intellectual as exile tends to be happy with the idea of unhappiness" (53). This can include considerable, even persistent, melancholy. Said considers Theodor Adorno as "the quintessential intellectual, hating *all* systems, whether on our side or theirs, with equal distaste" (55). Adorno *both represents and is representative of* "the intellectual as a permanent exile" (56). For Adorno, "the hope of the intellectual is not that he will have an effect on the world, but that someday, somewhere, someone will read what he wrote exactly as he wrote it" (57). Said quotes favorably from Adorno's *Minima Moralia*: "'It is part of morality not to be at home in one's home'" (quoted 57).

For the proper intellectual, there is no escape from "inbetweenness," from 'remaining suspended', and as Adorno advises, "'Suspicious probing is always salutary'" while "'For a man who no longer has a homeland, writing becomes a place to live'" (quoted 58). Said adds that, nevertheless, there are 'pleasures of exile' including "of being surprised, of never taking anything for granted, of learning to make do in circumstances of shaky instability that would confound or terrify most people" (59). The intellectual as exile is able to perceive what is left behind, overlooked, marginalized, forgotten, not considered, and not pursued–when most others cannot–and as such, "you tend to see things not simply as they are, but as they have come to be that way. Look at situations as contingent, not as inevitable" (60). Moreover, "The intellectual in exile is necessarily ironic, skeptical, even playful–but not cynical" (61).

Exile, therefore, for the intellectual, is a form of liberation, even while simultaneously experienced as social and political marginalization, because this position provides a freedom not available to those living at, in, and for the social and political center. Exile should be embraced in order to resist temptations of "accommodation, yea-saying, settling in" (63). Therefore, "Even if one is not an actual immigrant or expatriate, it is still possible to think as one, to imagine and investigate in spite of barriers, and always to move away from the centralizing authorities towards the margins, where you see things that are usually lost on minds that have never traveled beyond the conventional and the comfortable" (63).

In "Lecture IV: Professionals and Amateurs," Said takes up the question "as to whether there is or can be anything like an independent, autonomously functioning intellectual, one who is not beholden to, and therefore constrained by, his or her affiliations" with social institutions and political organizations (67). Said argues it is absurd to seek total purity through complete independence, and argues against insistence upon such complete independence as necessary in order to avoid 'selling out'. This is not even worthwhile as an ideal, because it is totally unrealistic. According to Said, academia *does* allow ample room for genuinely intellectual work. Also, intellectuals can be artists, who act as intellectuals through their art, and they can make a living through their art even while operating as the kind of intellectual Said is championing (72-73). As Said explains, "The intellectual does not represent a statuelike icon, but an individual vocation, an energy, a stubborn force engaging as a committed and recognizable voice in language and in society with a whole slew of issues, all of them having to do in the end with a combination of enlightenment and emancipation or freedom" (73). As such, the "particular threat to the intellectual today [at the time Said is delivering these lectures], whether in the West or the non-Western world, is not the academy, nor the suburbs, nor the appalling commercialism of journalism and publishing houses, but rather an attitude that I will call professionalism" (73-74).

Said critiques specialization and the cult of the certified expert and of certified expertise, and advocates instead for a kind of 'amateurism' that focuses on 'the bigger picture', on "making connections across lines and barriers," across fields and disciplines (76-77). Especially crucial is to avoid pursuit of intellectual work motivated by the hope to gain in power and authority, according to existing social arrangements and in line with dominant social interests, and it is likewise crucial to avoid tendencies toward complicity with stifling conformism (80-81). "Amateurism," for Said, is "an activity that is fueled by care and affection rather than by profit and selfish, narrow specialization" (82). Thus, when Said urges that "The intellectual today ought to be an amateur" he means the intellectual ought to focus on raising ethical and political questions for and challenges to the existing social and political order as well as of dominant social and political interests (82).

In "Lecture V: Speaking Truth to Power," Said argues "The intellectual, properly speaking, is not a functionary or an employee completely given up to the policy goals of a government or a large corporation, or even a guild of like-minded professionals" (86), and that maintaining 'the attitude of the amateur' is key in "maintaining relative professional independence" (87). In doing so the intellectual must allow one's self to be "moved by causes and ideas that I can actually choose to support because they conform to values and principles I believe in" (88). In other words, "Uncompromising freedom of opinion and expression is the secular intellectual's main bastion" (89).

Said admonishes that "One of the shabbiest of all intellectual gambits is to pontificate about abuses in someone else's society and to excuse exactly the same practices in one's own" (92). He at the same time advises the intellectual not to confine their attention to only addressing issues that are solely relevant to one's own society. What the intellectual needs is "a concept of justice and fairness that allows for differences between nations and individuals, without at the same time assigning them to hidden hierarchies, preferences, evaluations" (94). The intellectual must be prepared to make far-ranging connections while doing so thoughtfully, sensitively, and self-critically. Certainly, Said admits, "No one can speak up all the time on all the issues" (98), yet, in deciding what issues to address and what not, Said urges "there is a special duty to address the constituted and authorized powers of one's own society" (98). This can come with considerable personal risk, as "Yes, the intellectual's voice is lonely" (102), but the intellectual needs to keep in mind, in the midst of loneliness, that their voice "has resonance because it associates itself freely with the reality of a movement, the aspirations of a people, the common pursuit of a shared ideal" (102). This is so even if concrete representatives of this same movement–actual people sharing these same aspirations and engaged in the same pursuit of the same ideal–are not immediately, empirically present right when and where the intellectual is doing intellectual work. The intellectual needs to act on the basis of solidaristic connections with people not necessarily directly part of the intellectual's everyday life-experience–people who may in fact exist at considerable geographic and historical distances from precisely where (and when) the intellectual is at.

"Lecture VI: Gods That Always Fail" offers a further development and refinement of Said's position of "preferring to retain the outsider's and the skeptic's autonomy" as well as that of "critical detachment" (108). As Said explains, "I am against conversion to and belief in a political god of any sort. I consider both an unfitting behavior for the intellectual" (109). Yes, Said urges, be passionately engaged, be an ally, and be partisan, but always retain the basis from which it is possible to offer–and especially to *represent*–critique, including of those with whom one is allied and of that of which one is a partisan. This means maintaining sufficient critical distance so as to avoid ever getting into a situation where one might need to engage in "unpleasant aesthetics of conversion and recantation," as has happened with intellectuals who publicly recanted prior positions in the process of converting into fierce advocates of dogmatic orthodoxies, such as in the forms of Stalinism, radical Islamic fundamentalism, and authoritarian Arab nationalism (113). In contrast with those who reoriented their intellectual identities in these problematic directions, Said submits "The intellectual's representations–what he or she represents and how those ideas are represented to an audience–are always tied to and ought to remain an organic part of an ongoing experience in society: of the poor, the disadvantaged, the voiceless, the unrepresented, the powerless. These are equally concrete and ongoing; they cannot survive being transfigured and then frozen into creeds, religious declarations, professional methods" (113).

The title of lecture six, "Gods That Always Fail," aims to make clear that intellectuals fail when they relate to and treat any cause as if this were a 'religion', including as a secular equivalent of a 'God', in the sense of offering this cause unquestioning and uncritical support, and allegiance, as 'a matter of faith' and of sheer 'trust' in any kind of dogmatic orthodoxy. "The true intellectual," for Said, is always "a secular being," and effectively 'worships no gods' (120). It is important to keep in mind "Those gods that always fail" because they "demand from the intellectual in the end a kind of absolute certainty and a total, seamless view of reality that recognizes only disciples or enemies" (120). Instead, the intellectual must "keep a space in the mind open for doubt and for the part of an alert, skeptical irony (preferably also self-irony)" (120). "Yes, you have convictions and you make judgments" but you must work hard to arrive at these and you must not become complacent about them, which means in turn you need always to test them and be willing to modify, transform, and even jettison them in response to your active engagement in ongoing intellectual conversation and debate as well as in relation to the (re)shaping impact of larger social and political changes (120).

The intellectual cannot become merely a devout follower of a 'sacred' cause, because "The intellectual has to walk around, has to have the space in which to stand and talk back to authority, since unquestioning subservience to authority in today's world is one of the greatest threats to an active, and moral, intellectual life" (121). Said readily admits "It is difficult to face that threat on one's own" and in fact "The hardest part of being an intellectual is to represent what you profess through your work and interventions, without hardening into an institution or some kind of automaton acting at the behest of a system or method" (121). Said offers no easy answers to this difficulty other than to "keep reminding yourself that as an intellectual you are the one who can choose between actively representing the truth to the best of your ability and passively allowing a patron or an authority to direct you" (121).

When I have taught *Representations of the Intellectual*, and especially the third lecture, "Intellectual Exile: Expatriates and Marginals," students have found Said's theorization of the intellectual operating from a critical margin, embracing the position of exile and the status of amateur intriguing, and broadly compelling, while also appreciating Said's contribution toward reconceiving what isolation and loneliness can mean, how the two are not necessarily identical, and how neither is necessarily always entirely negative. In particular students have often found it easy to associate Ian Curtis with Said's position of intellectual exile, especially if we are taking the lyrics and music of Ian Curtis and Joy Division seriously, as serious art, and as conceived and produced from 'a working class intellectual' (or 'lower middle class intellectual') vantage point that is simultaneously that of a non-university educated/non-university credentialed/non-university affiliated intellectual and as part of a social and cultural milieu where people like Curtis and his fellow bandmembers were not generally thought of as likely to be engaged in any significant kind of intellectual activity despite the fact that they indeed were. At the same time, students have also found it makes sense to interpret these lyrics and this music as calling *upon us* to take up and follow through with what the position of intellectual exile demands as theorized by Said.

Yet a great many students I have taught have wrestled with contradictory feelings in response to arguments such as that advanced by Said in this book–on the one hand wishing they could be more like what he exhorts, as exemplary of 'the true intellectual', yet on the other hand doubting they are so capable, fearful of even tentatively attempting to move in that kind of direction. Students often are idealistically attracted to wanting to 'speak truth to power' and to do so from an independently critical position, refusing dogmatic orthodoxy and incorporative alignment with dominant social and political interests; wanting to represent and indeed fight on behalf of the under-represented and the disadvantaged; and wanting to be fully capable of courageously taking the morally right position, and representing this position publicly, even when this position is controversial and unpopular. Yet at the same time the same students often feel as if they are not up to this challenge, and they often evince considerable worry over causing offense in representing any position that might make others feel at all uncomfortable, let alone coming across as being readily prepared to argue forcefully for and forcefully to critique positions represented by, in particular, fellow classmates, by me as their teacher, and by the authors of various texts we have engaged together as part of the collective work of our class. Often I need to invest concerted effort in encouraging, and helping, students to so engage, to begin to develop the confidence or to further increase their confidence in so doing, while extensively modeling this kind of engagement myself, including by suggesting how others might argue against and critique positions I am representing, authors of texts we are engaging are representing, and students in class are representing. And often I have needed to invest concerted effort in showing how all of our positions are situated within ongoing conversations and debates among representatives of many disparate positions–as well as showing, likewise, how positions can and do change dramatically over time and vary dramatically in terms of location.

Yet, throughout 35 years of teaching, always emphasizing the value of learning how to engage in intellectually serious, thoughtful, and respectful argument and critique, where we are focused on positions and practices as opposed to persons and persons' individual identities, I have continually been impressed by a great many students' steadily growing confidence, and indeed daring, over the course of a semester. At the same time, a not insignificant minority of students typically enters every class I teach already prepared to take on these kinds of risks, and meet these kinds of challenges, due to a wide range of factors that have prepared them to do so. What I need to do here is show relatively quieter, shyer, more self conscious, more hesitant, and more reluctant students that their positions matter just as much, that these are equally worthwhile, that these are equally valuable to all of us, as those positions represented by their relatively more readily outspoken classmates, and that the latter students are not necessarily 'smarter' or otherwise more capable simply because it is easier for them, at this point in their lives, to speak forth in class. Over and over again I work with students who respond positively to this encouragement, and who by the end of semesters offer remarkably impressive presentations to, and elaborate articulations in discussions with, the rest of their classmates, as well as who often enough take on leading roles in team projects, including team projects involving extended dramatic performances. Many times students like this find arguments such as those of Said in *Representations of the Intellectual* highly compelling, and sincerely want their own praxis to more closely resemble what Said sets forth in this book as an ethical and political ideal; this desire helps these students in moving closer to realizing that goal, together with the encouragement and support I and the rest of the class offer. And, yes, many students, for many diverse reasons, can and do identify, from direct experience, with feeling like outsiders, and even as exiles, marginals, and outcasts, at least to some degree and in some form, at significant intervals in the course of their lives. Yet many of these students find it hard positively to identify with such positions, wanting to appear and act as 'normal-seeming' while fearing being perceived as 'abnormal' or 'other than normal'.

In my own life-experience I can think of many examples of me identifying with and representing an unpopular position–and identity–including as a representative of critique 'from the margin' 'of the center'. From early on in my childhood I was recognized by classmates as identifying with, sympathizing with, and indeed representing political positions considerably 'to the left', even 'to the far left', of what was average among fellow students in my classes and in the schools I attended. From early on I overtly identified, positively and without hesitation or embarrassment, as one who relished intellectual activity–especially reading–above just about anything else, and I didn't mind the stereotypical ascriptions that came as a result (with 'bookworm', 'nerd', 'brain', and 'doc' being among the most benign). Also, I always spoke extensively in class discussion, more than anyone else for that matter, and frequently questioned, challenged, and even critiqued (even 'corrected') my teachers, who, to their credit, responded positively to me doing so, and in fact encouraged me in this practice. When we discussed and especially debated topical issues I readily took the side of positions I believed in, no matter if these were unpopular, and pushed hard on their behalf. For example, I can recall in a ninth grade class arguing strongly, as the most outspoken 'leader' on our side, that all those who refused to serve in the U.S. military during the Vietnam War, and who sought exile in Canada, should be granted total and unrestricted amnesty. That was not a popular position among my classmates, initially, but by the end of the debate it was, especially in response to the passion I brought to bear in arguing for our side's position, with a great many of my classmates convinced, because of this passion, that I must have an older brother or another close relative who refused the draft and went to Canada. I remember on multiple occasions my teachers told me they showed examples of my writing for their classes to other teachers who were convinced I couldn't have written what I did, that my parents or other older adults must have done so, to which my teachers in turn responded, 'no, that's just Bob Nowlan for you'.

Throughout my kindergarten to twelfth grade school years I gravitated toward the humanities, the arts, and the social sciences, when it was commonplace for most other students to at least pretend to be more interested in the natural and physical sciences, as well as in overtly vocational training. This too set me apart. And even though often still regarded as shy, I was at the same time often recognized as outspoken and even 'wild', not easily confined to conventional expectations of what constituted 'normal'.

I recall I was extremely disappointed when for the first time ever, the year I graduated from high school, administrators at my high school decided it would not be the students ranked #1 and #2 in class who would give the commencement speeches but rather the student ranked #1 and someone else from the National Honor Society of the opposite sex. So, even though I was ranked #2 in my class, on account of the fact that Steve Ackerman, ranked #1, was also a boy, I didn't get to deliver that speech. I was upset because I had been thinking a lot about it, preparing this prospective speech in my mind. I felt compelled to speak against conformity and conformism, and to urge my fellow graduating students to reject and overcome fears of standing out, of being different, and of going 'against the grain'. I felt compelled to argue that this pressure to conform, and our submission to it, represented the gravest danger and indeed gravest threat we faced, and that our larger society faced. What is difficult for me to recall, all these years later, is precisely why I felt so strongly this issue was of such crucial importance, but at the least it indicates I experienced a powerful sense that people all around me, of my same age, were afraid to take risks, were afraid to challenge themselves, and were afraid to be and act as whom 'they truly were'. I shared that fear, without a doubt, but I felt it was essential to confront it and fight back against it. I experienced a powerful sense that conformity and conformism everywhere around me exerted a crushing and even numbing weight that not only I myself but also all of my fellow classmates needed to overcome.

Despite empathetic affinities I experienced with my classmates, including in 'hyper-conforming' out of fear, I felt otherwise like an outsider, someone 'different' from the average and 'the normal', and who was struggling to find the courage to embrace this difference and this 'other-than-normality' rather than fearing and trying to evade or escape from it. At that time it would have been virtually unthinkable for me or anyone else, in my elementary, middle, and high schools, to identify as gay, given how demonized being 'gay' was–with 'fag', 'faggot', 'fruit', 'fairy', and so on thrown about, day in and day out, as epithets versus anyone and everyone for a vast variety of possible (including exceedingly trivial) reasons. But I recall determining that it made absolutely no sense for me to engage in such name-calling or to cast such aspersions on 'people like that', who none of us knew (actually anything about). I determined this was cruel and unjust, and I wouldn't participate, even if that increased the likelihood I would be called 'a faggot' all that much more relentlessly. It may seem, at this point in time, a trifling differentiation, of myself from my classmates, but it was actually a highly unusual stance to take, then and there.

At Wesleyan University, as an undergraduate, the average political leaning among students shifted considerably to the left versus what had been the case back at public schools in Wallingford, Connecticut. At Wesleyan students were also highly enamored with being 'diverse'. I felt like I was beginning at last 'to find my people'. I don't recall acting as a particularly iconoclastic figure during my years at Wesleyan, but I was nonetheless slowly learning a great deal about myself, about whom I was and what I wanted to be, as well as where I wanted to go and what I wanted to do in my life ahead. Increasingly rapidly, subsequent to graduation from Wesleyan, I embraced an overt leftist political identity, as a Marxist as well as a socialist, and became actively involved in many organizations and causes representative of many issues galvanizing leftist interest and concern, including 'anti-imperialist' and 'Third World solidarity' campaigns. I joined a succession of socialist parties and a plethora of social change organizations. During my PhD years my work as part of the Student Marxist Collective, the Postmodern Marxist Collective, and the Marxist Collective at Syracuse University became major focuses of my activity, as did work as part of the editorial collective of *The Alternative Orange*, initiating and leading a local chapter of the US socialist-feminist organization Solidarity, and serving as the principal organizer and lead teacher for 'The Free University of Syracuse', which offered classes, for free, to members of the greater Syracuse community, on Marxism and other topics concerned with radical action and radical critique. I also taught my 'official' classes, for which I was paid and which students paid to take, as a Marxist and a socialist, from a Marxist socialist vantage point, while working to develop theories and practices of pedagogy and scholarship embodying and enacting this kind of political identification and commitment.

All of this kind of political activity, unsurprisingly, set me apart from a great many others, and caused me to face resistance and opposition from those who objected to and opposed my politics, even as I worked in active solidarity with comrades as part of the aforementioned collectives and other leftist political groups, as well as with faculty mentors sharing closely similar political positions. I insisted on teaching introductory college writing and literature courses, as an adjunct, at colleges in the Central New York region, by focusing on controversial contemporary issues, subject to current public discussion and debate, centered around matters of race, class, gender, sexuality, and nationality, and faced significant backlash from so doing, notably from program, department, and college administrators. And during this same period of time I came to identify as gay, first to myself and then rapidly to everyone else around me. I certainly also faced substantial pushback, and indeed significant hostility, as a result of being widely out as gay.

While working as a visiting professor at Arizona State University I was if anything just as unapologetically out as leftist, socialist, Marxist, gay, and queer–'critically queer'–as I had been previously, if not moreso, and I likewise engaged in a significant amount of organizing and activist work, all of which led to a backlash against me and in particular to hesitation and fear concerning what it might mean to choose me for a tenure-track position in a search where I made it as a finalist as 'the inside candidate' but ultimately was passed over. This proved a traumatic disappointment, short-term because I did not expect that result. I did not recognize the extent of opposition to what I represented, and I thought many more of my colleagues respected and appreciated what I represented, and how I did so, than proved to be the case. At Arizona State I gave public presentations that forthrightly argued for the value of philosophically dialectical as well as materialist ways of thinking, while critiquing popular post-structuralist and post-modernist positions from a Marxist vantage point, and in the writing sample I supplied from my PhD dissertation for the tenure-track search included a trenchant critique of Freudian conceptions of phobia, in relation to making sense of 'homophobia'. All of that rankled more than I recognized it did, or anticipated it would, as I, undoubtedly naively, imagined colleagues would disagree with me, in intellectual and political terms, while nonetheless respecting my positions and even finding them usefully provocative. I also witnessed, in the aftermath of this tenure-track decision, how hard numerous people worked to insure that no other position would be available for me anywhere as part of Arizona State University, or at any other nearby Arizona college and university, because my continued direct presence in the area might prove uncomfortable for the person chosen instead of me in the tenure-track search (or uncomfortable for those principally responsible for the choice of this person to fill that position).

At the University of Wisconsin-Eau Claire I recognized from as early as my campus visit, and quite awhile before I started working at this institution, that it would be important for me, as a matter of ethical and political responsibility, to be out, everywhere, including with all my students in all my classes about being gay, and to be ready to face a backlash as a result. I recognized the even greater importance, again no matter what the risk of backlash, of forthrightly teaching texts addressing LGBTQIA+ issues and representing LGBTQIA+ people, along with forthrightly addressing texts and topics focusing on other controversial contemporary issues. I have continually done so at UW-Eau Claire. I have, although decreasingly so over time, faced backlash, complaints, threats, and a certain real amount of marginalization as a result. But I have persisted in representing my political values and commitment, including in working as a founding member and initial president of the initial board of directors of progressive independent community radio station WHYS, as executive director of the Eau Claire Progressive Film Festival, as long-term faculty advisor for the Progressive Students Association and Progressive Students and Alumni, and as a leader within numerous other 'progressive' organizations on campus and in the greater Eau Claire and Chippewa Valley communities, often enough making public presentations and representations on contentious issues. In recent times I have likewise forthrightly identified as someone–in my classes, with my colleagues, and in the larger community–who lives, long-term, with recurrent tendencies toward serious to severe mental health challenges as well as with substantial, albeit often largely non-visible, physical disabilities, and who is committed toward representing these positions on behalf of myself and others who share these positions with me.

So, yes, in my own history, I have, in a number of instances, identified with and taken up a stance broadly akin to that which Edward Said advocates for in *Representations of the Intellectual*, as I have been ready to represent what I have, as a matter of principle, even when doing so has proven unpopular and even when this has led to backlash and marginalization. But it hasn't been easy for me to do virtually any of what I just described, and in fact I often have felt anxious and afraid, even when I didn't allow this anxiety and fear to prevent me from doing 'what needed to be done'. My chronic physical health conditions, and the recurrent tendencies toward serious to severe mental health challenges I face, both have resulted, in part, from acute and prolonged stress I have experienced on account of forthrightly representing unpopular positions, under-represented and disadvantaged positions, and positions that are commonly misunderstood, misrepresented, and subject to hostility. Doing so has left me, often enough, feeling isolated, marginalized, outcast, and lonely, even as I do not regret doing 'what needed to be done'. This praxis has caused significant stress, and that stress has in turn exerted significant impact upon my physical and mental health and well-being.

I chose to write my senior honors thesis as an undergraduate student at Wesleyan on "Alienation and Incarceration in James Joyce's *Dubliners* and Sherwood Anderson's *Winesburg, Ohio*" not only because I admired those two short-story cycles, in aesthetic terms, but also because through much of my life I had felt alienated, as well as constrained, trapped, and confined. I empathized with the lonely characters in both of these books–with these characters' experience of social paralysis, of being misunderstood and marginalized, of feeling like perpetual misfits and 'grotesques'. I have long and often wrestled with doubt about what I am and am not doing in and with my life, as well as concerning my self-worth, and I don't feel entirely at ease all that often in all that many places anywhere, even to this day. When I do what I determine I need to do in standing up to and directly confronting what is unjust I tend not to hold back and I do feel responsible for carrying this effort all the way through, especially when I feel others are counting on me, others are depending on me, but that doesn't mean I am not simultaneously feeling worried, anxious, and afraid. I am. And it feels a cumulative weight. I would not act otherwise, but the cost has been real.

Recently I have been reading about how valuable it can be, in terms of both long-term mental and physical health, to obtain and maintain a maximal amount of 'social capital'. In doing this reading I have recognized, acting as I have, coming from the vantage points I have, that meant the extent of 'social capital' I at this point in my life maintain does not feel all that much. Writing this book and another as well in the midst of an ongoing pandemic at the same time as I am working alone at home on long-term scholarly leave accentuates this feeling. You don't develop lots of social capital by acting from a position of 'intellectual exile', or at least I have not done so, and in my case I think this also has much to do with my inclination always to give everything I have to give, to the point of exhaustion, to my classes, to the students I am currently teaching and otherwise working with, so that over a great many years these people, their needs, their interests, and their concerns have constituted my overwhelming priority focus of time and energy. Often these people have also been my overwhelmingly primary if not virtually exclusive social contacts while working so intensively with them. Yet I am not one to make many requests, let alone demands, upon students I have taught, as the difference in our social positions and our institutional roles does not make doing that easy, and it doesn't feel like the right kind of thing to do, unlike doing the same with colleagues or other peers. So, by default, I have often been forced to be more 'self-reliant', or at least to be solely reliant on my husband and a small number of other friends, than would be ideal, even as I remain consciously aware of how thoroughly dependent as well as interdependent I am upon the contributions of a vast number of other people, worldwide, past and present, in enabling my standard of living as well as my well-being.

As Said advises, and as my intellectual mentors at Syracuse University did as well, I need to conjure up awareness that I am writing, and otherwise working, in connection with, and indeed representing on behalf of, potentially many other people, who *need* me to be doing as I am–other people who I have never met personally and who I likely will never meet. I do this reasonably well, but that does not mean it is easy to do. It requires persistently 'psyching myself up' to believe in the value, even when I am not receiving immediate testimony to appreciation of this value, of what and how I am writing, of what and how I am teaching, of what I am playing and how I am playing this on my weekly radio show, of what I am including and how I am including it as part of film and discussion series I lead, and even of what I am posting and sharing on social media or via my blog. It also means persisting in efforts where I need to imagine that those who can and will appreciate the value of what I am doing, and how I am doing this, exist but do so somewhere else I cannot identify, let alone pinpoint, from where I presently am at–and even that these people might not yet exist.

People are complex, multiple, contradictory, and dynamic, even if it is often difficult to keep this in mind and to relate to people, ourselves and others, in recognition that this is the case. My life has been far from miserable, and in fact, overall, happy, satisfying, and fulfilling. I enjoyed the support, growing up, of a loving family, and of a loving extended family. I never faced long-term, seriously threatening economic insecurity. By the time I was a high school student, and especially during my junior and senior years, I had many good, close friends, especially those who shared classes with me in honors and advanced placement tracks and who worked with me in food service jobs. I got along well with members of all cliques in my high school. My time at Wesleyan University was wonderful and at Wesleyan I met and developed strong friendships, a number of which have lasted a lifetime, with many people, starting with fellow residents of my floor at Clark Hall my freshman year and continuing with many students who like me worked as part of WESU-FM, our college radio station. At Syracuse University as a graduate student I enjoyed great friendships with comrades, fellow graduate and undergraduate students who shared common political and theoretical commitments, along with further fellow activists, along with the invaluable support of extraordinary faculty mentors. At Arizona State University I made an amazing number of close friends in just two short years–among fellow faculty, staff, and students, from across the university, as well as among an impressive number of others in the larger community across the greater metropolitan Phoenix area.

All of those people, once more, gave me invaluable support, assistance, encouragement, and appreciation.

At UW-Eau Claire and in Eau Claire, many people, throughout my now nearing 25 years here, have 'had my back', have been my friends and supporters, even in the toughest times and in the face of the toughest fights, so I most definitely feel blessed–and cherished. Throughout my life I've appreciated how many people have respected my integrity even when they have not shared the same political and theoretical positions. Above all else, I have benefitted beyond measure from the love and support of my husband and life-partner, Andy Swanson, with whom I never feel truly alone or lonely, and who has given me the material and spiritual support necessary to undertake, pursue, and accomplish a vast array of daunting projects.

In the midst of this ongoing pandemic I have been able to work on writing two books, which has been immensely vitalizing, and to explore and learn in a diverse array of new directions while planning and preparing to teach future classes on topics such as Critical Studies of Disability; Critical Studies of Mental Health and Illness; Critical Studies of Crime, Justice, and the Law; Contemporary Black British Experience; and The Aftermath of Empire and (Post)Imperial Legacies. I have taken up running and increased my pace and distance to the point where I can now run up to five to six miles at a time four to five days a week, and where I have been conscientiously succeeding in improving my overall physical and mental health. I have explored, listened to, and been able to share enthusiasms for a plethora of music, on my weekly Insurgence radio show. I have discovered a considerable array of compelling movies and TV series, especially crime series from nations across Europe and beyond. And I have not been at risk of economic hardship while I've been able to count on the doctors, nurses, and medical staff of Mayo Clinic Health Systems Eau Claire for any and all health issues I have faced and might face. I have loved walking far and wide about Eau Claire, when the weather has not been bitterly cold, and even though leading a highly restricted life involving a great deal of physical social distancing I have appreciated a few establishments Andy and I continue to visit regularly, along with the regular staff as well as patrons we meet at these places. I have enjoyed organizing and helping lead our Empowerment Through Solidarity Progressive Film Screening and Discussion Series. And despite the sad death of our beloved dog, Casey, we have welcomed another wonderful dog to our family, Aidan, whose daily company I enjoy, and am grateful for, as I am for that of our cats, Star and Jet.

As I look forward to returning to full-time teaching and institutional service with the start of the Fall 2022 semester, I am excited about the classes I will be teaching this coming 2022-2023 academic year (Introduction to Critical Studies with a thematic focus on Introduction to Critical Studies of Disability and of Mental Health and Illness as well as a concentration on contemporary drama; Introduction to Theory and Criticism; Sports, Politics, and Society; and The Aftermath of Empire and (Post)Imperial Legacies) as well as meeting and learning with and from many new students along with once again interacting with colleagues in the English Department and across our campus. I am nervous about how I will do after two full years' away, and in response to changes that have transpired in this period, including as a result of COVID-19, but I am excited. At the same time I am determined to keep working hard to insure I bring each of the two books I have been writing since the beginning of the summer of 2020 all the way through to the end and get them published. It is and has been a good life.

I also think it is important to raise some critical reservations about Said's theorization of the intellectual, drawing in part on my own experience. First, although Said himself certainly recognized this, as a Palestinian and as a leading global representative of the Palestinian people and of their aspirations for freedom and independence, his theory of the intellectual in *Representations of the Intellectual* can lend support for a voluntarist and individualist conception where whether or not one succeeds in becoming the kind of intellectual he advocates seems to depend on strength of individual character, on individual will and determination, and on a readiness to act as an individual independent of social ties and social groupings. I strongly believe, in contrast, this cannot be simply a matter of intrinsic individual character, or of individual will and determination, as such an implication ignores the material conditions of possibility and the material forces of generation necessary for an individual to be able to occupy and carry out the tasks of 'the intellectual' as Said identifies and explains these. Different people face considerably different degrees of opportunity to become and continue as such an intellectual, dependent on their relative degree of material support, and, more precisely, on their social background, experience, and positioning and especially on the extent of economic, social, and cultural capital they are able to bring to bear. Many people never gain anything close to the opportunities needed to be able 'choose' to become and to follow the path of such an intellectual life, while many people never are able to sustain such activity for all that long or to obtain access to means by which they are able to share their intellectual work with a substantial public audience. And this has nothing to do with them simply not working hard enough to make this happen. I myself have often found it far from easy to find such outlets, no matter how hard I have tried, no matter how persistently hard I have tried.

Second, intellectual work is often the product of collective creation and of direct, immediate, and extended involvement within collective activities and endeavors as part of social organizations and movements; it is these organizations and movements that are ultimately responsible for the generation of innovative ideas and innovative modes of expression and communication of these ideas. Every significant idea, and every significant creation, I have come up with in my own life is traceable to such involvement–especially as part of activist organizations and movements, and as part of communities of learners, of teachers and students, engaged in working closely together in collective intellectual exploration and inquiry. 'My ideas' are never solely mine–they do not simply emerge from 'inside my head' and from anything even vaguely resembling any kind of uniquely individual 'genius' or 'wisdom'; they are always a product of extensive interaction with many other people as well as a tremendous amount of reading and study of what others have come up with and share. In writing this book, my ideas result from working with students in five classes I have taught on Ian Curtis, Joy Division, and critical theory; from working with students in many classes where I have taught closely related topics; from Ian Curtis and Joy Division themselves; from all those who have previously written about Ian Curtis and Joy Division, and especially who have taken the time and invested the care to think seriously about how to make sense of possible meanings of this music; and from many critical theorists and diverse other cultural commentators and social and political thinkers and actors.

661

Third, it can be most important at times closely to align oneself with the positions of an organization, a cause, and a movement, and not to strive to carve out distance from the same, in order to help enable the success of this organization, cause, and movement, while distinguishing carefully between sharing criticism 'internally' versus sharing criticism 'externally'. At the same time, I also believe the most useful 'intellectuals' often include those who operate more akin to Gramsci's 'organic intellectuals', working directly and fully immersively from within an organization, cause, and movement, as opposed to Said's 'intellectuals as exiles'. In the present conjuncture many people in effect act as if 'the truth' corresponds to whatever they want, whatever they prefer, it to be, and that they need provide little to no support for any of their 'truth claims'. At the same time the concomitant rise of rampant 'anti-intellectualism' together within resurgent fascism casts substantial aspersion on scientific experts and expertise, as well as on 'professionally' educated, trained, qualified, and certified K-12 teachers and college and university faculty. I find it problematic to uncritically endorse adopting the position of 'amateur' in opposition to that of 'professional'. I certainly believe non-professionals, and non-experts, bring to bear potentially vital knowledge, often of kinds that professionals, and other experts, do not and cannot, and I certainly advocate questioning professionals, and other experts, calling on the latter to explain, justify, and account for the positions they are advocating, that they are *representing*. But I don't believe that professional, expert knowledge should be discredited simply on account of it being identified as that of people who have obtained professional, expert status.

Today, in multiple states across the US, Republican Party politicians elected to office as governors and in state legislatures are acting to ban teaching of 'Critical Race Theory', which is not directed in actuality at Critical Race Theory at all, as this is rarely taught before students embark on higher education at the college and university level, but rather against any teaching concerning systemic, structural, or institutional racism–and even in a number of cases, against any teaching about any matters of race and racism at all. Some states are proceeding as far as to ban teaching a prospectively wide array of topics that might in any way ever make any student–or that student's parents or guardians–feel at all 'uncomfortable'. Doing so threatens, logically, not only to leave students vastly ignorant, but also to eliminate virtually everything that is most worth studying and learning in every single academic field, while turning schools in these states into bastions of totalitarian suppression that surpass the 'achievements' of even some of the ruling regimes in the most extreme works of dystopian fiction. Efforts to ban such education, and to insist teachers should only teach what parents and guardians agree that they can teach, strikes a decisive blow against any lingering pretense of public education for the public good while disrespecting and devaluing teachers' preparation, dedication, training, knowledge, skill, talent, and, yes, 'professional expertise'. Efforts to ban such education leads those subject to the continuing oppressive effects of racism inclined to feel all the more thoroughly disillusioned, disenchanted, disrespected, excluded, and alienated–with the likelihood of multiple kinds of 'social dysfunction' sure to follow, including sharp increases in mental ill health. Efforts to ban such education leads lesbian, gay, bisexual, transgender, queer, non-binary, intersex, and asexual young people, already at heightened risk of serious mental ill health, and especially of suicide, toward even more extreme risk of the same.

Said's conception of the intellectual *can* authorize forcefully challenging and critiquing this repressive movement, in line with Said's insistence that this kind of intellectual represents in the interests of, on behalf of, the under-represented and the disadvantaged. And Said's conception of the intellectual aligns well with those who, for instance, long refused to accept medicalizing and individualizing models of what 'disability' means, where 'being disabled' was conceived and treated solely as an 'individual tragedy' such that the disabled individual was regarded as fated to lead a miserably sad, lonely, and painful life, and such that they would have been better off never having been born at all. Disabled people have organized and fought to reconceive what disability means, such that disability is commonly, following the rise of 'the social model of disability', identified with what society does to people with impairments, how society limits and fails adequately to respond to, to accommodate, the needs of disabled people, while likewise failing to recognize and respect the quality of life disabled people can and often in fact do experience, as well as how much disabled people have to contribute, to offer, to the greater public good. This kind of transformation required acting from a socially marginalized position to advance a trenchant critique of the social center. And subsequent critiques in turn of the limitations of the social model of disability that have emphasized complex embodiment, careful attention to and consideration of the diversity of different kinds of disabled people's experiences, and of taking impairment and impairment effects seriously while still forcefully advocating for social access, inclusion, respect, understanding, and accommodation, are products of a continuing willingness to challenge and critique the prevailing status quo.

Likewise, a long history of challenging and critiquing medicalizing and individualizing conceptions of mental health/mental illness has led first to massive de-institutionalization and the end of the dominance, in responding to the condition and experience of 'the mentally ill', of 'the insane asylum' in many countries, as well as substantial challenges along with development of substantial alternatives to standard forms of treatment involving prescription of psychotropic drugs as well as psychological counseling that effectively disconnects the individual's experience from shaping social and political contexts, from formative and constitutive social and political influences and determinants. This has taken the form, variously, of anti-psychiatry, critical psychiatry, users and survivors organizations and movements, Mad Pride and Mad Studies, and redefining mental illness as mental distress and as psychosocial disability–among multiple other similar developments. Organizations and movements of people often disparaged and marginalized as 'mentally ill'–and worse–have pushed for and at least partially succeeded in making real gains as a result of their own actions, together with key allies who have likewise been willing to break with and push back against the dominant, the normative, and what has enjoyed preeminent status on account of 'professional expertise'. People involved in these efforts have needed to adopt and work from positions much akin to that of Said's 'intellectual exile'.

As a final connection, I will note here many commentators, across a broad spectrum of the center to far 'left', have been arguing the threat to survival of democracy in America is today so extreme, and so grave, that it is absolutely essential all of us who care about this survival unite together in a common front in support of President Biden and of whatever can insure Democrats maintain sufficient political power, in elected office, so as to thwart efforts at a fully successful fascist takeover. For example, in his scathing attack on resurgent fascism in *The Fascism This Time: And the Global Future of Democracy*, written before the November 2020 US presidential election, and before the January 6, 2021 insurrection at the US Capitol, Theo Horesh passionately exhorts all across such 'a broad left' to do exactly this. At times commentators urging such a united front also suggest 'now is the not the time' to call attention to any differences in the positions we disparately support, or to our respective visions of what our society needs to become and of how we need to proceed to achieve this, as we need to focus everything we have just on 'stopping' the fascist threat. Although compelling, Said's theorization of the intellectual would suggest this is problematic, and that it should, and must, be possible to do multiple things at once–yes, uniting in opposition to fascism, in efforts necessary to prevent fascism from taking over and to defeat fascism once and for all, yet at the same time promulgating competing, and contesting, visions of the future that we would respectively like to see, of what we believe is right and necessary, while not holding back on *representing*, for example, the importance of pursuing and achieving progressive goals. The latter include all of the following. Radical reforms of police and policing, and of the courts and the prisons. Far-reaching reforms in support of fair, equitable, and inclusive voting rights and of honest and responsible adjudication of election results. Empowering working people and especially their organized representatives, in labor unions. A 'Green New Deal' and accelerated as well aggressive measures to respond to ecological emergency. Effectively eliminating child poverty, raising the minimum wage, making college free and canceling student debt, and providing free access to health care at the point of contact for all. Major gun reform involving sharp restrictions upon access and sharp reductions in stockpiles of guns privately held and privately accumulated. Experimenting much further with universal basic income initiatives. Breaking up monopolies and oligopolies. Vastly increasing mass transit options. Nationalizing critical industries, such as energy utilities and those responsible for the manufacture and distribution of pharmaceutical drugs. And drastically cutting back upon the size of the military budget and the extent of US military troops and bases operating throughout the world.

Of course much of the preceding will not achieve immediate approval and implementation, and much of it depends upon building successful popular movements, mobilized for the long-term, to push hard to realize these ends. But that does not decrease the urgency of doing so. Without offering a powerfully compelling vision of what an alternative society can be like, as a result of far-reaching transformation, the fight against fascism continues solely to be a fight against dissatisfaction with the current social and political status quo, leaving all those who have become alienated, disenchanted, and opposed to this status quo continuing to be susceptible to the appeal of fascism.

As Michael Sandel argues, in *The Tyranny of Merit: What's Become of the Common Good*, support for fascism in America responds to the lies of meritocracy and of the lack of social mobility as well as the lack of substantial avenues for other than a relatively narrow elite to achieve substantial social advancement and improvement. Too often supporters of meritocracy have failed to pay attention to how many are losing out, and at what cost, as well as how much resentment this situation has bred and to how it has contributed toward eviscerating any shared sense of a common good. As James Davies likewise argues, in *Sedated: How Modern Capitalism Created Our Mental Health Crisis*, rising numbers of people suffering from serious mental health issues is a direct result of the kind of neo-liberal capitalist society in which we live, and the fallout this routinely entails, such that it is impossible to make a substantial impact in greatly reducing the extent of mental ill health unless we develop a much more humane, egalitarian, genuinely and substantively caring and inclusive society that does not leave so many people suffering from considerable precariousness and precarity. Intellectuals must be willing to challenge and critique the dominant consensus, as Sandel and Davies do, even when this is promoted by people with whom they otherwise share philosophical and political positions in common. This means being ready and willing, for instance, as in Sandel's case, to challenge and critique the seemingly unquestioned value of judging and rewarding people entirely according to a seemingly unquestionable quality of merit. And this means, in Davies's case, to challenge and critique the seemingly unquestioned acceptance of the idea that the best proper response to mental ill health consists of prescription psychotropic drug treatment combined with psychological therapy that places all of the focus on the individual, decontextually abstracted from their social and political background, experience, and positioning, as entirely individually responsible for their own individual mental illness and for their own individual 'recovery' of their own individual mental health.

In conclusion, I propose Said's conception of intellectual exile represents one useful conception of an intellectual ideal, to which people may usefully aspire, while recognizing and accepting many may not be able to take up and live according to what this kind of role demands, and that even those who can do so will periodically fall short of being fully successful in *representing* as Said calls upon *intellectuals* to do. Yet other conceptions are also vital and viable as well, including as I have mentioned, that of Gramsci's 'organic intellectual', involving intellectuals operating from positions directly, immediately, and immersively aligned with and as such directly, immediately, and immersively *representative* of social organizations, causes, and movements. Nonetheless, writing from within a American society recurrently often inclined toward 'anti-intellectualism', and where a great many Americans today, including many Americans occupying powerful social and political positions, continue to disparage the value of many if not most forms of intellectual activity, it is important to make use of and draw upon a book, like Said's *Representation of the Intellectual*, that argues for this value and offers a precisely elaborated articulation of what it consists. It is worthwhile underscoring that intellectual work can occur in many different forms, and that it can be the activity and contribution of people from many different kinds of social backgrounds, experiences, and positionings. This need not be confined to the academy, or to other certified professional experts alone, and it can include working class and poor people, elderly and young people, people of color as well as white people, people who have not benefitted from college and university education as well as those who have, recent immigrants to this country as well descendants of those who immigrated here long ago, LGBTQIA+ as well as straight people, disabled as well as able-bodied people, and people who face and have faced major mental health challenges as well as those who have not. I invite and encourage the students I teach, all of these students, to take themselves seriously as capable of making valuable contributions to ongoing conversations and debates of a serious intellectual nature and with real and important implications for social change and social progress. They all have much of value to offer of benefit to all of us, and I perceive my role as helping nourish this potential as well as inspire them with self-confidence in what they can be and do, even when it is and will be tough and lonely, and even when they will need to operate from positions as outsiders, marginals, and exiles.

Four

Trinh T. Minh-ha's *Woman, Native, Other: Writing Postcoloniality and Feminism* (1989) offers a wide-ranging exploration of and engagement with a host of issues, including relations between language and subjectivity, what it means to write as a woman and in particular as a 'Third

World' woman of color, the problems and limitations of the discipline of anthropology, and the virtues of working past the constraints of dualistic ways of thinking and understanding.

In her opening section, "The Story Began Long Ago . . ." Trinh begins by stressing the importance of attending to process–in particular ongoing, elliptical, and uncertain process–in the kind of critical theoretical exploration and inquiry she is in this book both pursuing and recommending. Right from the start Trinh suggests stories and story-telling can and do make signal contributions to critical theoretical understanding and engagement. Trinh urges recognition, what's more, that "The story never really begins nor ends, even though there is a beginning and an end to every teller" (1). This means being prepared to allow for and respect the value of what might otherwise seem to be tangents, delays, deferrals, indirections, surprises, and shocks. As Trinh declares: "For the heart of the matter is always somewhere else than where it is supposed to be" (1), while "Time and space are not something entirely exterior to oneself" (2). Trinh is committed to the pursuit of knowledge and understanding but distrusts deceptively easy routes, instead embracing confusion, uncertainty, irresolution, incompletion, the indefinite, the undecidable, the multiple, and the heterogeneous in the course of this pursuit.

Section I of *Woman, Native, Other: Writing Postcoloniality and Feminism*, "Commitment from the Mirror-Writing Box," begins by suggesting poetry, like story-telling, constitutes a valuable mode of critical theoretical practice, as exemplified by her own poem, one of the epigraphs she includes to anticipate issues this chapter will consider: "i was made to believe/we who write also dance/yet no dancer writes/(the way we write)/no writer ever dances/(the way we dance)/while writing we bend/and bend over/stoop sit and squat/and can neither stand erect/nor lie flat on our back/whoever pretends to feed/walk skip run while writing/must be flying free/as free as a cage-bird/seeing not lines as lines/bars as bars/nor any prison-yard" (5). Trinh proceeds to discuss challenges involved in writing as a woman and especially as a woman of color, including being forced to choose, to prioritize, among multiple, in fact, intersecting identities. Such a writer, Trinh observes, often finds "herself at odds with language" and at "odds with her relation to writing" (6). Trinh notes, also, that "Writing, reading, thinking, imagining, speculating . . . are luxury activities . . . permitted to a privileged few" (6). As a result, women writers, and especially Third world women of color writers, are prone to guilt concerning their ability to prioritize pursuit of such luxury activities. Yet, "Substantial creative achievement demands not necessarily genius, but acumen, bent, persistence, time" (7). "In the framework of industrial development," this necessitates "a wage that admits of leisure and living conditions that do not require that writing be incessantly interrupted, deferred, denied, at any rate subordinated to family responsibilities" (7).

Historically, and continuing all too often to this day, "the situation of women does not favor literary productivity," at least not without experiencing guilt over prioritizing writing versus other responsibilities. Guilt also arises on account of awareness that such writing "is always practiced at the cost of other women's labor" (7). This guilt, and an associated burden of responsibility to need to write for, on behalf of, many other women who do not maintain the same opportunity, can lead women writers, especially women of color writers, to be so hyper-critical of their writing that they come to doubt the value of their writing, and especially to doubt the correctness of their choice to be writers. What's more, "Every woman who writes and wishes to become established as a writer has known the taste of rejection," with Trinh remarking, in relation to this rejection, that "Accumulated unpublished writings do stink. They heap up before your eyes like despicable confessions that no one cares to hear; they sap your self-confidence by incessantly reminding you of your failure to incorporate" (8). Such sapping of self-confidence and internalization of a sense of failure is more acute for writers who hail from under-represented and disadvantaged backgrounds. As Trinh observes, "If it is difficult for any woman to find acceptance for her writing, it is all the more for those who do not match the stereotype of the 'real woman'–the colored, the minority, the physically or mentally handicapped" (9). The considerable challenge facing those who do not fit this stereotype further undermines self-confidence. It is a considerable challenge not to let rejection "merely haunt you" such that you in effect "die over and over again . . . until you no longer know how to speak . . . not loathing yourself, not burning it, not giving up" (9).

Conventionally a limited array of acceptable options have been available for women writers and especially for women of color writers/Third World women of color writers. Unfortunately, "Whether s/he makes common cause with the upper classes or chooses to disengage her/himself by adopting the myth of the bohemian artist, the writer is a kept wo/man who for her/his living largely relies on the generosity of that portion of society called the literate" (10). A common alternative to these two directions is and has been that of 'the committed writer', the writer overtly and tendentiously engaged in political advocacy, deliberately writing 'to represent', in Said's sense, on behalf of a group of people and a cause. Yet Trinh cautions even this kind of writer is wont to be writing, at least in part, in response to the same kinds of guilt she has just discussed, and is effectively sharing with their readers, readers who comprise their target audience, a common sense of guilt, a common guilty conscience, with this shared guilt potentially leading toward problematically arrogant assertions of power, perhaps as compensation or projection. Yet Trinh is even more concerned, than she is with recognizing and reflecting on the influences and uses of guilt, about the danger of writers, writing as overtly 'committed writers' from the vantage point as members of under-represented or disadvantaged social groups, denying, or otherwise refusing to admit, any weakness, doubt, fragility, and uncertainty–rather than learning from and making positive use of weakness, doubt, fragility, and uncertainty.

Trinh problematizes influential notions of 'freedom in writing' and 'freedom through writing' as well as 'engagement in/through writing', in particular in relation to what has commonly been identified as 'engaged writing'. Trinh is concerned here about "not only a split between the artist and her/his audience–the spectator-consumer–but also a passivity on the part of the latter" in art supposedly created 'for' the masses but not created 'by' them (13). In this respect Trinh suggests 'art for art's sake' is partly salutary in problematizing grandiose claims for the power of writing, in and of itself, to effect social and political change, and to represent in and of itself a spirit or movement of revolutionary change. As Trinh elaborates, key questions to pose, in this connection, include: "On the one hand, can literature be a 'freedom that has taken freedom as its end' (Sartre) and still concern itself with elements like structure, form, and style–whose totality precisely allows literature to take on meaning? On the other hand, can a writing that claims to break down rules and myths submit itself to the exclusive rules of a sociopolitical stand?" (16). After all, Trinh declares, "Nothing could be more normative, more logical, and more authoritarian than, for example, the (politically) revolutionary poetry or prose that speaks of revolution in the form of commands or in the well-behaved, steeped-in-convention-language of 'clarity'" (16). Trinh is insistent that so-called 'clear language' is too readily identical with 'correct language', limiting and potentially eliminating possibilities for diverse and especially experimental and innovative varieties of language use, while, even more precisely, "Clarity is a means of subjection, a quality both of official, taught language and correct writing, two old mates of power" (16-17). 'Clear' language in other words is 'clear' because it conforms to and even serves as a means of enforcing dominant ideology. Language is material practice; it is not a mere transparent and neutral medium that can be simply taken up and put to any and every possible use.

"Women writers" face many difficult challenges, beginning with failing to recognizing how inclined they are "to hide in (their) writing(s) and feel prompted to do so" (19) on account of multiple vectors of guilt, and shame, they have been made to feel as a result of experience of oppression. A further significant problem arises in how to make writing, and language, 'one's own', how not to merely replicate, in lesser form, an alien, and, more precisely, a patriarchal sexist, male-dominated language: "Stolen language will always remain the other's language" (20). This leads to the question "So where do you go from here? where do I go? and where does a committed woman writer go?" (20). Trinh advises, careful not to undermine the value of such advice by rendering this too programmatic or formulaic, let alone too straightforward or simplistic, "Finding a voice, searching for words and sentences: say some thing, one thing, or no thing, tie/untie, read/unread, discard their forms; scrutinize the grammatical habits of your writing and decide for yourself whether they free or repress. Again, order(s). Shake syntax, smash the myths, and if you lose, slide on, *unearth* some new linguistic paths. Do you surprise? Do you shock? Do you have a choice?" (20)

Trinh calls for "a conception of writing that can no longer naively be reduced to a *means* of expressing a reality or emitting a message" (21). Instead, she urges writers recognize that "writing constantly refers to writing, and no writing can ever claim to be 'free' of other writings" (21). Trinh notes, in this connection, "it seems obvious that writing does not express any more than it 'in-expresses' or 'mis-expresses'" (21). In turn, writing "may be viewed as that which does not translate a reality outside itself but, more precisely, allows the emergence of a new reality" (22). In relation to this recognition that "Writing necessarily refers to writing," Trinh proposes an analogous image "of a mirror capturing only the reflections of other mirrors" and as such "I write to show myself showing people who show me my own showing. I-you: not one, not two" (22). Trinh argues that "We persist in trying to fix a fleeting image and spend our lifetime searching after that which does not exist"–that which seemingly essentially 'is' what it precisely, singularly, expresses/represents. We need, instead, Trinh recommends, to recognize that "Writing reflects. It reflects on other writings and, whenever awareness emerges, on itself as writing . . . writing is meshing one's writing with the machinery of endless reflexivity" (23).

Trinh casts a skeptical eye upon commonplace advice concerning what is required of ostensibly 'good writing', underscoring the explicit as well as implicit sexism and racism in much of this advice: "Remember, the *minor*-ity's voice is always personal; that of the *major*ity, always impersonal. Logic dictates. Man *thinks*, woman *feels*. The white man knows through *reason* and logic–the intelligible. The black man understands through *intuition* and sympathy–the sensible. Old stereotypes deriving from well-defined differences (the apartheid type of difference) govern our thought" (28). Trinh follows by then considering feminist theories concerned with 'writing as woman'/'writing in the feminine'/'writing from the body'. Trinh finds 'writing from the body' in practice too often becomes 'writing about the body' and thereby continues to fall in line with the all too conventional notion that "the author exists *before* her/his own book, not simultaneously *with* it" (29). Trinh calls into question the use value for the writer in adopting the position, intentionally or unintentionally, of 'the one who knows'–i.e., the writer as 'Priest-God'/the 'Priest-God scheme' (30).

Anticipating her later, even more elaborate considerations of issues of language and subjectivity, Trinh proposes that "writing, like a game that defines its own rules, is an ongoing practice that may be said to be concerned, not with inserting a 'me' into language, but with creating an opening where the 'me' disappears while 'I' endlessly come and go, as the nature of language requires" (35). Elaborating further, Trinh argues:

> That which emerges from silence may be revealing, but it is revealing in the sense that language is always older than me. Never original, 'me' grows indefinitely on ready-mades, which are themselves explainable only through other ready-mades. Spontaneity-personality in such a context does not guarantee more authenticity than stereotypy. Writing as an inconsequential process of sameness/otherness is ceaselessly re-breaking and re-weaving patterns of ready-mades. The written bears the written to infinity (36).

Returning to *ecriture feminine*, Trinh concludes "If it is a question of fragmenting so as to decentralize instead of dividing so as to conquer, then what is needed is perhaps not a clean erasure but rather a constant displacement of the two-by-two system of division to which analytical thinking is often subjected" (39). In other words, a strategy of mere reversal of binaries as hierarchies is not enough because "the strategy of mere reversal needs to be displaced further, that is to say, neither simply renounced nor accepted as an end in itself" (40). What Trinh recommends, in line with 'displacing further', is writing from the body that "allows each part of the body to be infused with consciousness. Again, bring a new awareness of life into previously forgotten, silenced, or deadened areas of the body. Consciousness here is not the result of an accumulation of knowledge and experience but the term of an ongoing unsettling process" (40). In addition, Trinh urges recognizing, and working with the recognition, that

> Knowledge leads to more openings than to closures. The idealized quest for knowledge and power makes it often difficult to admit that enlightenment (as exemplified by the West) often brings about endarkenment . . . By attempting to *exclude* one (darkness) for the sake of the other (light), the modernist project of building universal knowledge has indulged itself in such self-gratifying oppositions as civilization/primitivism, progress/backwardness, evolution/stagnation. With the decline of the colonial idea of advancement of rationality and liberty, what becomes more obvious is the necessity to reactivate that very part of the modernist project at its *nascent* stage: the radical calling into question, in every undertaking, of everything that one tends to take for granted–without which is a (pre- and post-modernist) stage that should remain constant. No Authority no Order can be safe from criticism. Between knowledge and power, there is room for knowledge-without-power. Or knowledge at rest–'the end of myths, the erosion of utopia, the rigor of taut practice' as Maurice Blanchot puts it. (40)

Trinh proposes that "in-between grounds always exist, and cracks and interstices are like gaps of fresh air that keep on being suppressed because they tend to render more visible the failures operating in every system" (41). This applies to 'doing theory' as much as doing any other kind of writing because "theory is no longer theory when it loses sight of its own conditional nature, takes no risk in speculation, and circulates as a form of administrative inquisition. Theory oppresses, when it wills or perpetuates existing power relations, when it presents itself as a means to exert authority–the Voice of Knowledge" (42). The problem is "it is still unusual to encounter instances where theory involved the voiding, rather than the affirming or reiterating of theoretical categories" and it is still unusual as well to encounter "instances where the borderline between theoretical and non-theoretical writings is blurred and questioned, so that theory and poetry necessarily mesh, both determined by an awareness of the sign and the destabilization of the meaning and writing subject" (42). Theory "as a tool of survival," which Trinh accepts it can and indeed must be, nevertheless "needs to be rethought in relation to gender in discursive practice" (43), and this includes rethinking the process by which theory proceeds. In her own (theoretical) writing, Trinh declares, "I do not write simply to destroy, conserve, or transmit . . . I write in the thrall of the impossible (feminine ethnic) real, that share of the detour of inscription which is always a de-scription . . . the inscription and de-scription of the non-unitary female subject of color through her engagement, therefore also disengagement, with master discourses" (43). Crucial here is "avoidance of fixed meanings" (43) and "making theory in gender, of making of theory a politics of everyday life, thereby re-writing the ethnic female subject as a site of differences" (44). In concluding her first chapter, Trinh, in sum, valorizes accepting and working with/in/through a critical theoretical project of redefining while being redefined in the process of redefining, at the same time inevitably both taking a position and being positioned in taking a position, recognizing and accepting "'no-position' is also a position, for 'I am not political' is a way of accepting 'my politics is someone else's'" (44). All the while seeking to proliferate, complicate, and problematize positions and positionings as far and as much as possible.

Section II, "The Language of Nativism: Anthropology as a Scientific Conversation of Man with Man," advances a withering critique of anthropology, old and new. As she launches this critique, Trinh proclaims:

> We set out here, she and I, to undo an *anonymous*, all-male and predominantly white collective entity named *he*, and we wish to freeze him in his hegemonic variants . . . I have wondered time and again about my reading myself as I feel he reads me and my false encounter with the other in me whose non-being/being he claims to have captured, solidified, and pinned to the butterfly board (48).

In this oppositional practice of undoing, unnaming, exposing, and freezing, Trinh explains, "I never really start or end the trial process; I persist. Constantly changing my point of departure or arrival, I trace, void, retrace with the desire to baffle rather than bring out contours" and "I thereby do not oppose to eliminate. I'd rather make of writing a site where opposites lose their essential differences and are restored to the void by their own interchangeability" (48). Continuing to affirm her commitment to such a a deconstructive critical practice, while distinguishing the mode of critical theorization she follows from that which has dominated and continues to dominate in anthropology, Trinh declares "I undeniably prefer the heterogeneity of free play in a dice game to the unity and uniformity of dissection, classification, and synthesis toward a higher truth. It is with and within the worn codes or, perhaps more precisely, here within the boundaries of what he says he is or does that I intend to play and spin" (49). Following this course, Trinh deliberately does not refer to proper names of specific anthropologists, or other common appellations associated with these figures, attesting to their authoritative credentials. She plays 'this game', this deconstructive game, by 'echoing back' "his [the anthropologist's] words to an unexpected din or simply let them bounce around to yield most of what is being and has been said through them and despite them" (49). For Trinh, contesting the hegemony of anthropology requires an intervention at the level of discursive form and style as well as at the level of discursive content.

Trinh does, however, precisely identify, right away that "By hegemony, I am referring to the authority of certain states over others, of one sex over the other, and to the form of cultural and sexual ascendency that once worked through direct domination but now often operates via consent—hence its pernicious, long-lasting, and binding strength" (49). For Trinh the language used by the anthropologist, in the discourses that comprise the discipline of anthropology, represents a preeminent instrument of oppression, as one of the primary "conceits of anthropology lies in its positivist dream of a neutralized language that strips off all its singularity to become nature's exact, unmisted reflection" (53). Hearkening back to her earlier critique of naively identifying language with direct, and 'clear' 'expression', Trinh finds that, in anthropology, "Meaningful language is confined to 'expression' and what appears significant to him [the anthropologist] is its reduction to pure instrumentality" (53). Trinh exposes, and through such exposure simultaneously contests, denigrative designations by 'the anthropologist' of 'the object' of the anthropologist's investigation, as these designations only mean in relation to their opposite, implicit or explicit, noting that Claude Lévi-Strauss himself admitted "'The barbarian is, in the first place, the man who believes in barbarism'" (quoted 54).

Trinh accepts that modern anthropology does become aware of itself as not simply neutrally describing and thereby 'capturing' the other in language, and in fact as necessarily 'superimposing itself on the other' (60). And modern anthropology has also become aware it is creating a myth of its own in identifying and describing 'others' myths' (61). Yet Trinh keeps up the critical pressure. Even in modern, self-aware anthropology, she contends, "Questions are always loaded with the questioner's prejudices," and this occurs without the anthropologist yet giving adequate attention to how far language is never transparently neutral and never simply instrumental (62). Trinh finds that even with more critically self-reflexive modern anthropology, "The positivist yearning for transparency with respect to reality is always lurking below the surface" (64). Modern anthropology, what's more, continues to be most interested in one specific variety of 'Man': "the Primitive, now elevated to the rank of the full yet needy man, the Native" (64). Modern anthropology continues, Trinh charges, to turn an ostensible "conversation of man with man" into "mainly a conversation of 'us' with 'us' about 'them', of the white man with the white man about the primitive-native man" (65). A key problem, for anthropology, old and new, is lack of adequate critical theorization of what is language, how it works, and what it does.

Trinh continues by criticizing, within anthropology, what she identifies as "The will to annihilate the Other by means of false incorporation," which can include doing so by way of un-interrogated and inadequately interrogated linguistic/discursive constructs, as well as by way of the assumptions/presuppositions so involved (66). As such, "A conversation of 'us' with 'us' about 'them' is a conversation in which 'them' is silenced" (67). 'False incorporation', meanwhile, involves 'allowing' 'them' to 'sit at the table' 'with us' yet needing to proceed entirely according to 'our standards', 'our norms', and 'our rules'. More broadly, Trinh criticizes how 'authority' is achieved in dominant forms of Western scholarship: "The confidence they (re)gain through the ritual citing of all their fellows' (dead or living) names has allowed them to speak with the apathetic tone of the voice of knowledge" (68). Returning more specifically to anthropology, Trinh accuses 'The Great Master' of 'gossiping' about 'the gossip of others' yet not realizing he is doing so (70), thereby, again, displaying lack of critical self-consciousness concerning his own position and the hierarchies of evaluation he employs. What anthropologists fail to recognize, Trinh charges, is

> The search for meaning will always arrive at meaning through I. I, therefore, am bound to acknowledge the irreducibility of the object studied and the impossibility of delivering its presence, reproducing it *as it is* in its truth, reality, and otherness. The dilemma lies in the fact that descriptions of native life, although not necessarily false or unfactual, are 'actor-oriented', that is to say, reconstructed or fashioned according to an individual's [the individual anthropologist's] imagination. (70)

As such, it is not enough to admit that anthropological writings are interpretations, "For although no writing can escape interpretation and ethnocentrism, obviously not all openly interpretive anti-ethnocentric writings are of equal importance" (71). What modern anthropology needs to do, yet Trinh argues it has not yet done, is to "explicitly assume a critical responsibility towards its own discourse, exposing its status as an inheritor of the very system of signs it sets out to question, disturb, and shatter. Very few anthropological writings, however, maintain a critical language and even fewer carry within themselves a critique of (their) language" (71).

Ultimately, Trinh contends, "No anthropological undertaking can ever open up the other. Never the marrow" (76). "The other is never to be known unless one arrives at a *suspension* of language" which involves, more elaborately:

> a process of constantly unsettling the identity of meaning and speaking/writing subject, a process never allowing I to fare without non-I. Trying to find the other by defining otherness through laws and generalities is, as Zen says, like beating the moon with a pole or scratching an itching foot from the outside of a shoe. There is no such thing as a 'coming face to face once and for all with objects'; the real remains foreclosed from the analytic experience, which is an experience of speech. In writing *close to the other of the other* [my italics], I can only choose to maintain a self-reflexively critical relationship toward the material, a relationship that defines both the subject written and the writing subject, undoing the I while asking 'what do I want wanting to *know* you or me?' (76)

This process is, what's more, inevitably linked with "the necessity of an ongoing critique of the West's most confident discourses" and doing so in turn involves attention to the process of how meaning arises *within* [my italics] language and ideology (157).

Trinh begins Section III, "Difference: 'A Special Third World Issue'," by citing Audre Lorde in relation to the matter of 'survival' for people who are members of oppressed social groups, which depends on striving to do more than 'barely' survive: survival *"is not an academic skill . . . It is learning how to take our differences and make them strengths. For the master's tools will never dismantle the master's house.* They may allow us temporarily to beat him at his own game, but they will never enable us to bring about genuine change" (quoted 80). Trinh is concerned in this chapter to explore what might it mean, what might it involve, to 'take our differences and make them strengths', while not relying 'on the master's tools' to 'dismantle the master's house' and not seeking to 'beat the master at his own game' but rather seeking 'to bring about genuine change'.

Trinh notes, initially, "at least the danger of speaking for the other has emerged into consciousness. But it is a very small step indeed since it serves as an excuse for their complacent ignorance and their reluctance to involve themselves in the issue" (80). Trinh is wary of leaping to the opposite extreme, paying no attention to the other and remaining ignorant of and unconcerned about the other, because you accept 'you cannot speak for the other' and you cannot ever fully know what the other's experience has been like as the other has experienced this. Trinh opposes conflating the meaning of 'difference' with that of 'division', where 'difference' is conceived as "no more than a tool of divide and conquer" (82). As Trinh observes, in relation to remaining silent because of not wanting to risk 'speaking for the other' or speaking in such a way that even inadvertently contributes toward reinforcing preexisting relations of domination and subjugation, "Silence as a refusal to partake in the story does sometimes provide us with a means to gain a hearing. It is a voice, a mode of uttering, and a response in its own right. Without other silences, however, my silence goes unheard, unnoticed; it is simply one voice less, or more point given to the silencers" (83). What Trinh advocates, following Lorde, is working with difference conceived as the basis for connection and collaboration: "It is, indeed, much easier to dismiss or eliminate on the pretext of difference (destroy the other in our minds, in our world) than to live fearlessly with and within difference(s)" (84).

Active engagement is necessary, no matter how messy, complicated, and difficult, and this includes active engagement in 're-writing' history: "Historical analysis is nothing other than the reconstruction and redistribution of a pretended order of things, the interpretation or even transformation of documents given and frozen into monuments. The re-writing of history is therefore an endless task" (84). Proceeding in this effort, Trinh acknowledges, "One has to be excessively preoccupied with the master's concerns" at strategic stages in ongoing struggle against the master's power to exert mastery, but this should not be mistaken as "an end point in itself" (85). Trinh eschews seeking an illusory position of 'purity' outside of or protected from the messiness of working within as well as against, and indeed of working within in order to work against: "No matter which side i belong to, once i step down into the mud pit to fight my adversary, i can only climb out from it stained. This is the story of the duper who turns her/himself into a dupe while thinking s/he has made a dupe of the other" (86). It is an illusion, perhaps even a delusion, to believe one can protect oneself from being 'stained' and to stay 'safe' by refusing/avoiding engagement.

Trinh warns as well against thinking of one's self as a special case, representing a special stratum, elevated above the rest of an oppressed group, including when one is ostensibly working on behalf of this same group: "Specialness as a soporific soothes, anaesthetizes my sense of justice; it is, to the wo/man of ambition, as effective a drug of psychological self-justification as alcohol is to the exiles of society" (88). Those who are caught up in seeking specialness, including a special few who imagine they can avoid becoming contaminated and compromised by dominant ideology, Trinh proposes are akin to tourists and anthropologists in search of 'the unspoiled' and who seek what they project upon 'the other' (88). Trinh is likewise critical of 'authenticity', as "Today, planned authenticity is ripe" with the message sent forth thereby being "We no longer wish to erase your difference. We demand, on the contrary, that you remember and assert it. At least, to a certain extent" (89). Performing this difference, in an 'authentic' manner, according to the expectation/demand of the dominant, and especially of 'the authentic' 'in touch with one's roots', is highly problematic; it is no threat to existing relations of domination and subjugation. What then to do? Trinh advises "The difficulties appear less surmountable only as I/i succeed in making a distinction between difference reduced to identity-authenticity and difference understood as critical difference from myself" (89).

This leads to Trinh's crucial intervention within and contribution toward reconceiving subjectivity:

A critical difference from myself means that I am not i, am within and without i. I/i can be I or i, you and me both involved. We (with capital W) sometimes include(s), other times exclude(s) me. You and I are close, we intertwine; you may stand on the one side of the hill once in a while, but you may also be me, while remaining what you are and what i am not. The differences made *between* entities comprehended as absolute presences–hence the notions of *pure origin* and *true* self–are an outgrowth of a dualistic system of thought peculiar to the Occident (the 'onto-theology' which characterizes Western metaphysics). (90)

Trinh here emphasizes:

the differences grasped *both between* and *within* entities, each of these understood as multiple presence. Not one, not two either. 'I' is, therefore, not a unified subject, a fixed identity, or that solid mass covered with layers of superficialities one has gradually to peel off before can see its true face. 'I' is, itself, *infinite layers*. Its complexity can hardly be conveyed through such typographic conventions as I, i, or I/i. Thus I/i am compelled by the will to say/unsay, to resort to the entire gamut of personal pronouns to stay near this fleeting *and* static essence of Not-I. Whether I accept it or not, the natures of *I, i, you, s/he, We, we, they,* and *wo/man* constantly overlap. They all display a necessary ambivalence, for the line dividing *I* and *Not-I, us* and *them,* or *him* and *her* is not (cannot) always (be) as clear as we would like it to be. Despite our desperate, eternal attempt to separate, contain, and mend, categories always leak. Of all the layers that form the open (never finite) totality of 'I', which is to be filtered out as superfluous, fake, corrupt, and which is to be called pure, true, real, genuine, original, authentic? (94)

This conception stands sharply at odds with commonsensical conceptions of ourselves, according to prevalent Western/Occidental/First World standards, where we rely upon "an illusion of continuity" and "search for a genuine layer of myself to which I can always cling" that Trinh contends are always illusions (94).

Trinh rejects the notion of an essential core of either individual or social identity, contending that difference so (mis)understood is "both limiting and deceiving" (95). Trinh acknowledges it undoubtedly seems 'mad' to many to propose there is no invariant, singular, true core of self-identity, or of the self-identity of any particular group of people, and to eschew the quest to find/arrive at what this essentially/ultimately is. How then can identity be more and other than "a 'consistent pattern of sameness'"? Key here, for Trinh, is to grasp that "Difference in such an insituable context is *that which undermines the very idea of identity*, deferring to infinity the layers whose totality forms 'I'" (96). Trinh argues it is important for feminism, and for post-colonial/Third World feminism in particular, "patiently to dismantle the very notion of a core (be it static or not) and identity" (96). This means refusing to be defined in the sense of being pinned down, narrowly delimited, and refusing "to efface difference within oneself" (97). Trinh here is arguing reduction of identity to a supposedly fixed, solid, constant, narrow, and essential 'core' functions as a preeminent dimension of oppression.

Turning to 'Third World' as a designation of a collective identity, conceived in relation to its difference versus 'other worlds'–First and Second–Trinh argues "Whether 'Third World' sounds negative or positive depends on *who* uses it" (97). 'Third World' can, Trinh proposes, represent a useful break with, alternative to, and even threat versus the hegemony of dualistic logic broadly conceived, and can, moreover, "include all non-whites in their solidaristic struggle against all forms of Western dominance" (98). Key, in relation to this counter-hegemonic use of 'Third World', is compelling the First World to become aware of *the Third World within the First World* and for the Master thereby to "recognize that His Culture is not as homogeneous, as monolithic as He believed it to be. He discovers, with much reluctance, He is just an other among others" (99).

Continuing to problematize notions of identities and differences as essentially fixed, Trinh contends "The search and claim for an essential female/ethnic identity-difference today can never be anything more than a move within the male-is-norm-divide-and-conquer trap" (101). Trinh cites Lorde again in critiquing the notion "that all women suffer the same oppression simply because we are women" because this involves mistakenly "losing sight of the many varied tools of patriarchy" (quoted 101). Trinh, further, advocates "a challenge to the notion of (sexual) identity as commonly defined in the West and the entire gamut of concepts that ensues: femininity-femaleness-feminitude-women-womanhood/masculinity-maleness-virility-man-manhood, and so on. In other words, sexual difference has no absolute value and is inferior to the praxis of every subject" (103). Trinh emphasizes, in particular, the importance of grasping that "Difference does not annul identity. It is beyond and alongside identity" (104).

Trinh acknowledges the usefulness of being able to distinguish sex and gender, especially in relation to "one of the most pernicious hegemonic distortions on which nearly every anthropologist's study of the so-called sex division of labor among the 'non-literate' people (and by extension, the 'bi-cultural' natives) has rested: the fundamental assumption that gender is only a (primitive, underdeveloped) form of sex role" (105). In contrast, in fact, "Each culture has its own interweaving of genders" (105). Trinh is open to consideration that, in contrast with the concept of 'sex', "The concept of gender may be said to be alive, open enough to deal with both differences between and differences within entities" (106). Yet Trinh finds Ivan Illich's theorization of gender, which she here cites and discusses at length, too limiting because even as it "bespeaks a fundamental social polarity that varies with times and places and is never the same" (107), Illich remains thereby committed to a 'fundamental social *polarity*', which amounts to a problematic reassertion of dualism. Trinh finds "The notion of gender is pertinent to feminism as far as it denounces certain fundamental attitudes of imperialism and as long as it remains unsettled and unsettling" (116), but this is not where Illich ends up, as instead his conception is too rigid, too fixating, too much concerned with demarcating lines of separation and enclosure. What her rumination on 'gender' by way of this critial reflection on Illich shows, Trinh contends, is "that distinctions need to be made both (1) between the transgression or infraction of gender in a gendered society and the deviation from a sex-determined behavior in a society where gender has disappeared and (2) between gender infringement and the fading of the gender line itself" (116). Where this leads, Trinh contends, is toward recognition that "The story of gender-as-difference is, therefore, not 'the story of what has been lost' (Illich), but the story of what does not readily lend itself to (demonstrative) narrations or descriptions and continues to mutate with/beyond nomenclature" (116).

Section IV, "Grandma's Story," offers a sustained meditation on the value of stories and story-telling. Why value stories and story-telling so highly? Trinh responds: "For understanding means creating" (121). She determines that people's fascination with 'story' "may be explained by its power both to give a vividly felt insight into the life of other people and to revive or keep alive the forgotten, dead-ended, turned-into-stone parts of ourselves" (123). Recognizing the contributions of stories and story-telling to knowledge and understanding usefully challenges a mindset that always wants/needs 'clear-cut' definitions/distinctions. In contrast, through stories and story-telling, it becomes much more readily possible to conceive of human life itself as "a perpetual to and fro, a dis/continuous releasing and absorbing of the self" (128).

Yet not all stories, or all modes of story-telling, are the same, let alone equally valuable in contributing toward this desired end. In particular, Trinh finds, all too often "Men appropriate women's power of 'making material' to themselves and, not infrequently, corrupt it out of ignorance. The story becomes *just a* story. It becomes a good or bad lie" (129). In contrast, Trinh touts another kind of story, and especially another kind of story-telling, where "The story tells us not only what might have happened, but also what *is happening* at an unspecified place and time" (133). This is also connected with the kinds of stories, and the kinds of story-telling, that are passed from generation to generation, as "What is transmitted from generation to generation is not only the stories, but the very power of transmission" (134). When stories and story-telling are approached with this understanding in mind, it becomes all the more readily possible to appreciate that "To preserve is to pass on, not to keep for oneself" (134). Exemplifying what Trinh is getting at, she discusses the work of Maxine Hong Kingston, characterizing Hong Kingston's writing as "neither fiction nor non-fiction" and praising this writing because it "allows us to read between the lines and in the gaps of her stories" with what is "most truthful" here in fact "the very power of her storytelling," not the specific stories told, nor specific details of these stories (135). Trinh's own poem is also helpful in explaining and illustrating what she is here arguing: "I will tell you something about stories, [he said]/They aren't just entertainment./Don't be fooled./They are all we have, you see,/all we have to fight off/illness and death.//You don't have anything/if you don't have stories . . .//He rubbed his belly./I keep them here [he said]/Here, put your hand on it/See, it is moving/There is life here/for the people."

Trinh critiques a common lack of recognition within Western/Occidental/First World commonsensical thinking that:

> What we 'look for' is un/fortunately what we shall find. The anthropologist, as we already know, does not *find* things; s/he *makes* them. And makes them up. The structure is therefore not something given, entirely external to the person who structures, but a projection of that person's way of handling realities . . . . But it is particularly difficult for a dualistic or dualistically trained mind to recognize that 'looking for the structure of their narratives' already involves the separation of the structure from the narratives, of the structure from that which is structured, of the narrative from the narrated, and so on. (141)

Referencing anthropology once again, while also suggestive of a wider array of practices, Trinh observes that "'Looking for the structure of *their* narratives' so as to 'tell it the way *they* tell it' is an attempt at remedying the ignorance of other ways of telling and listening," but in fact this all too often proves an illusory goal, again constituting an 'imposition upon' that becomes all the more insidious when it is unrecognized as such (142).

Elaborating further, Trinh asserts "Life is not a (Western) drama of four or five acts. Sometimes it just drifts along" while observing "The present, which saturates the field of our environment, is often invisible to us" (143). Unfortunately, "Rare are those who can handle it by letting it come, instead of hunting for it or hunting it down, filling it with their own marks and markings so as to consign it to the meaningful and lay claim to it" (143). Returning to stories, and story-telling, Trinh contends "The truthfulness of the story, as we already know, does not limit itself to the realm of facts" (144). Key is to be able to recognize "the difference between truth and fact" (148). Stories and instances of story-telling are accurate when/because they partake "in the setting into motion of forces that lie dormant in us" (148). Trinh valorizes the insights that emerge from cultures where stories are respected as interconnected and ongoing, continually in process, never arriving at a single end and never starting from a single beginning. Trinh champions the power of stories and story-telling to contribute in resistance/opposition to both patriarchal and racist forms of domination/subjugation, and argues for the need to attend more closely and carefully to stories and story-telling in these struggles, as well as to create yet further stories and practices of story-telling in the course of so doing.

In a 1990 interview with Pratibha Parmar for *Feminist Review*, Trinh emphasizes her praxis is concerned with keeping open and not closing down, especially not hardening into the dogmatic and the formulaic. Trinh's critical method involves simultaneous appropriation and expropriation in 'working with the master's discourses'. She argues, here as well, that "theory can relate intimately to poetry" (69), identifying "poetry is also the place from which many people of colour voice their struggle" and proposing poetry "can also be the site where language is at its most radical in its refusal to take itself for granted" (69). For Trinh, language is "an extremely important site of struggle" and for her this means struggle so that "Meaning has to retain its complexities" because "otherwise it will just be a pawn in the game of power" (69). As Trinh elaborates, "For me, the political responsibility here is to offer meaning in such a way that each reader going through the same statements and the same text, would find tools for herself (or himself) to carry on the fight in her (or his) own terms"

(69). In doing so, it is crucial, what's more, to grasp that "a straight oppositional discourse is no longer sufficient" because of the importance of identifying with "a nonunitary notion of subjectivity" (70). Trinh is interested in 'fragments' and in particular in 'the fragment' that cannot, or at least not easily, be recuperated, and of "fragmentation" as "a way of living with differences without turning them into opposites, nor trying to assimilate them out of insecurity" (71-72). Trinh insists both the self and what the self produces are not cores, but rather processes, and in line with self and what self creates conceived as process, as ongoing process, it is important to engage in "always pushing one's questioning of oneself to the limit of what one is and what one it not" (72). For Trinh, embracing "Fragmentation is therefore a way of living at borders," and this is what we need to do (72).

Explaining her reconception of subjectivity yet further, Trinh declares "The reflexive question asked . . . is no longer: *who* am I? but *when, where, how* am I (so and so)?" (72). In a 1988 contribution to *Inscriptions* Trinh once more rejects "the concept of an essential, authentic core" self, revalidating what this conception necessarily excludes as supposedly 'inessential' 'to whom I am'. Here Trinh problematizes commonplace conceptions of the other as "unavoidably opposed to the self or submitted to the self's dominance." According to this commonplace understanding, that Trinh challenges,

> Identity, thus understood, supposes a clear dividing line can be made between I and not-I, he and she; between depth and surface, or vertical and horizontal identity; between us here and them over there . . . The search for an identity is, therefore, usually a search for that lost, pure, true, real, genuine, original authentic self, often situated within a process of elimination of all that is considered other, superfluous, fake, corrupted, or Westernized.

In contrast with a notion of identity defined in terms of a persistent "pattern of sameness within a being, the style of a continuing me that [has] permeated all the changes undergone," Trinh argues in favor of a notion of identity that emphasizes the "infinity the layers of totality that forms I."

Trinh explains how this conception of subjectivity is linked with a political purpose by explaining that "Hegemony works at levelling out differences and at standardizing contexts and expectations in the smallest details of our daily lives." In opposition to hegemony, what is needed is "a different terrain of consciousness . . . in which clear cut divisions and dualistic oppositions such as science vs. subjectivity, masculine vs. feminine, may serve as departure points for analytical purposes but are no longer satisfactory if not entirely untenable to the critical mind." Trinh argues for letting "difference replace conflict" and in her films strives to work with ways of conceiving of difference that don't automatically align with separation and exclusion or repression and domination, or in other words with what she characterizes as "The apartheid type of difference." Opening up difference in this direction also means that "Interdependency cannot be reduced to a mere question of mutual enslavement. It also consists in creating a ground that belongs to no one, not even to the creator."

As Nasrullah Mambrol writes, addressing Trinh's film-making, for *Literary Theory and Criticism*, in 2018,

The most exciting and, at the same time unnerving, distinguishing element of the oeuvre of Trinh T. Minh-ha is an uncanny mastery of those hybrid spaces or borders between categories: between fiction and nonfiction, art and autobiography, between documentary and document, between subject and object, viewer and viewed and identity as subscribed, and identity as self-inscribed.

Trinh's work engages "The space of the borderline, the taboo, the untranslatable." This *is* "the intersubjective space of Trinh's writing and films." Trinh advocates for and exemplifies "a struggle to conjure and write the body in a way that is actively 'articulating this always emerging-already-distorted place that remains so difficult, on the one hand, for the First World to even recognize, and on the other, for our own communities to accept' (Trinh 1992, 139)." Trinh's films "invoke a multiply formed, constantly moving, negotiating identity. This mobile deconstruction and reconstruction of identity repoliticizes difference issues in ways that inform the multiply produced subjectivities."

Patrick Reed, writing for *ArtReview*, in 2020, emphasizes the crucial importance, in understanding all of Trinh's work, of her explanation, in relation to her early, 1982, film, *Reassemblage*: 'I do not intend to speak about; just speak nearby'. In other words, Trinh refers to her position as a visitor vis-à-vis the villagers she met and discloses her position as an *un*-authoritative narrator. Trinh has thereby "upheld the gap between seer and seen by incorporating self-awareness into the very process of filmmaking: 'speaking nearby' is the creed of a conscientious interloper."

Reed also highlights, in addition to 'speaking nearby', Trinh's likewise crucial conception, and practice, of 'reading across'. As Reed explains, "Simply put, to read across is to engage a text in simultaneous operations. It is to engage, for example, poetry as both poetry and philosophy or vice versa." Citing a 2018 interview, Reed quotes Trinh as explaining:

Information can come in many ways, and it doesn't have to be descriptive . . . And this is where resistance comes in, because with theory, the analytical mind, the dissecting mind, is very sharp. With poetry, on the contrary, 'I' is not just this individual, but 'I' is an open space where every 'I' can come in'. Reading across frees a text from its boundaries and frees a person from the limitations of selfhood; it is an extension of 'speaking nearby', wherein selves commingle through the written word, or with the moving image.

To this explanation, Reed adds, further, his own endorsement of the value of this practice:

One reads across the lines of one's own station to express solidarity with, for example, a marginalised community without lapsing into saviourism, lip service or moral superiority. In 2020, such a lesson could not be more relevant to allies of the Black Lives Matter movement whose own lives have not been marked by police brutality; or, in the United States, to those who are counteracting anti-Asian coronavirus racism but who have never known racist mistreatment. (People like myself.) The enduring relevance of 'speaking nearby' is its protest and inherent respect. Its enduring power lies in the human dignity it preserves.

In another interview, with Erika Balsom, published in 2018 in *frieze*, Trinh again usefully explains what 'speaking nearby' involves, and why this is valuable:

> When you decide to speak nearby, rather than speak about, the first thing you need to do is to acknowledge the possible gap between you and those who populate your film: in other words, to leave the space of representation open so that, although you're very close to your subject, you're also committed to not speaking on their behalf, in their place or on top of them. You can only speak nearby, in proximity (whether the other is physically present or absent), which requires that you deliberately suspend meaning, preventing it from merely closing and hence leaving a gap in the formation process. This allows the other person to come in and fill that space as they wish. Such an approach gives freedom to both sides and this may account for it being taken up by filmmakers who recognize in it a strong ethical stance. By not trying to assume a position of authority in relation to the other, you are actually freeing yourself from the endless criteria generated with such an all-knowing claim and its hierarchies in knowledge.

In teaching *Woman, Native, Other*, and especially section three, "Difference: 'A Special Third World Issue'," students have been particularly struck by Trinh's theory of subjectivity as comprised of "infinite layers" and her robust critique of dualistic thinking more broadly. It is worth considering how even many of the most familiar challenges to commonsensical ways of conceiving of subjectivity in terms of a singular, inner 'core' tend to evince dualistic thinking as well: private self and public or social self, conscious and unconscious, George Herbert Mead's 'I' and 'me', Erving Goffman's 'front stage' self and 'back stage' self, Lacan's subject of the enunciation and subject of the enounced, and so on, all continuing in line with even more broadly familiar and commonsensical distinctions such as between mind and body, 'true self' and the masks or personae we adopt in social situations, and our selves as we perceive our selves versus our selves as others perceive us. Trinh's challenge is to push much further in conceiving of our selves as in continuous process of ongoing transformation, and as intricately and especially interdeterminately interconnected with the selves of others.

Students likewise find usefully provocative Trinh's emphasis on taking into account the materiality of language and of recognizing discourse positions and constructs us, as well as how vital it is to intervene at the level of how we are making use of and working with language, and not just at the level of what we are using language ostensibly to 'express', to 'communicate', and to 'represent'. Students are, what's more, often drawn to Trinh's problematization of what it means, of how far from easy it is, to write, to speak, to discourse, and to do so effectively and in particular differently, from the vantage point of the under-represented, disadvantaged, marginalized, and otherwise oppressed–as they are to Trinh's critique of anthropology and her conceptions of writing nearby as opposed to writing about or writing for, and of reading across as opposed to reading within. Students also are intrigued by Trinh's challenge to conventional divisions between ostensibly theoretical versus ostensibly non-theoretical kinds of writing as well as by Trinh's arguments in favor of poetry and story-telling as valuable means, and modes, of theorization.

In relation to the lyrics and music as art of Ian Curtis and Joy Division, Trinh's theories are useful in helping make sense of these lyrics, and the music as well, in exploring the complexity and multiplicity of subjectivity, and in particular concerning relations among 'I', 'me', 'we', 'us', 'you', 'they', 'them', 'she', 'her', 'he' and 'him'. Trinh's theories are also likewise relevant and useful as well in making sense of these lyrics, and this music, as engaging *borderlines* between interior and exterior, subject and object, self and other, protagonist and antagonist, friend and foe, help and hindrance, solidarity and betrayal, complicity and responsibility, hope and despair, health and illness, movement and stasis, past and present, history and myth, the psychological and the sociological, the sacred and the profane, the beautiful and the sublime, the close and the distant, the private and the public, the familiar and the strange, and the living and the dead. Trinh's theories readily connect, yet further, with interpretation of the lyrics and music of Ian Curtis and Joy Division as concerned with exploration of and inquiry into *mediations*, and as zeroing in on the 'in between', on *the distance between*. Certainly also, focus in these lyrics and this music on the position of the stranger, the outsider, and the outcast constitutes another ready point of connection, as does the frequency by which these lyrics and this music represent by not representing–i.e., by suggesting, gesturing, hinting, alluding, and speculating rather than definitively stating, describing, and detailing. And Ian Curtis's attraction to experimentation offers another point of contact as does the challenge involved in interpreting Curtis's performances in terms of how these relate and do not relate to whom Ian Curtis otherwise was.

Trinh's theories resonate with my frustration versus the commonsensical notion that we maintain an inescapable continuity in terms of whom and what we are, across space and time. That is, in part, why I find writing even a partial memoir daunting because I feel on the one hand I am connected with whom I describe myself as, in the past, and on the other hand I feel disconnected from that person, and more precisely from those people, as 'they' represent not simply one continuous, singular 'me' but rather a series of successive versions of and variations upon 'me' over time–as well as across space. I often tell my students, in introducing myself for the first time, that what I am about to recount feels like a convenient fiction as I have lived long enough that it feels as if I have lived many different lives and that each of these correspond to a different person. My students readily recognize we all have tendencies to represent ourselves differently in different social contexts and to different groups of people, and, not only that, but we also tend to become those different people in these contexts and with these groups of people. I find Trinh's emphasis on the shaping power of language, and of discourse more broadly, to be crucial, in paying critical attention to how we are all formed–and constituted–by language, and by discourse more broadly, with language and discourse not a merely transparent, neutral set of tools that we simply pick up and put to any use we choose. Likewise, Trinh's critique of clarity I find especially important, because the work of critical theory often of necessity involves seeking to explain what has not yet been explained, or not yet adequately explained. This requires new articulations to suit new understandings. It requires pushing preexisting ways of making use of language to their limits–and beyond. That is why critical theoretical language is often 'difficult', and that is why critical theoretical work is also creative work. Critical theoretical work requires not just new ideas but new ways of formulating ideas; in other words, the two, the idea and its formulation, are not distinct and separate.

Trinh's critique of dualism challenges me to reflect on how often, especially when unconsciously unaware of so doing, I tend, as someone who is a product of a culture in which dualistic thinking remains commonsensical, to rely upon dualistic ways of making sense, as well as what am I not able to think as a result of this tendency (and dependency). Trinh's theory I find even more challenging in thinking through how to 'do theory differently', 'how to do critique differently', 'how to argue differently', and especially how to 'engage with differently' and 'to represent differently'. As a specific example, I have often taught argument as providing 'precise' reasons and evidence in support of a thesis, 'clearly' defining and explaining one's key terms, anticipating and responding to opposing positions and arguments for these positions, anticipating and responding to prospective critiques of one's own position, and making sure to account for one assumptions and presuppositions as well as for the implications and consequences of one's position carried to its furthest logical conclusion. I have also often taught argument as involving locating one's position, and one's case for it, in relation to the most important ongoing conversations and debates surrounding the issue one is addressing, while paying careful attention to matters of contingency, exigency, and kairos. And I have also taught students not to write introductions as summaries of what they are about to discuss or conclusions as summaries of what they just have discussed, striving for a concrete opening that sparks interest in reading on and a concrete closing that leaves a strong final impression and makes a clinching statement in relation to one's thesis. Even though students accomplish a great deal working with this kind of advice, making use of this model, Trinh prompts me to ponder what can't they accomplish, or as readily accomplish, by means of this approach? Yes, I do often invite students to make use of creative forms of writing, and other forms of creative production (such as videos, paintings, sculptures, comics, musical recordings, and multi-media collages), as ways of addressing issues we are engaging, and I also problematize distinctions between 'creative' and 'critical' forms of writing, while welcoming students' use of stories and story-telling, but, even so, what possibilities are excluded or rendered less viable according to the models I recommend? Are these 'other possibilities' those that cannot be conceived by means of even only implicit reliance on dualistic modes of thinking?

Near the end of section three of *Woman, Native, Other*, Trinh takes up issues of gender in relation to and especially distinction from sex. This is one area where I have recognized considerable gains in recent years, even if these gains continue to meet with significant resistance–and backlash. Not only do steadily more students as well as steadily more among other young people I meet identify as transgender and as nonbinary but also steadily more young cisgender men and women are comfortable with and confident about combining elements of traditionally masculine and traditionally feminine ways of being. Students are no longer as often surprised, let alone shocked, by notions that gender might represent a spectrum of multiple, even myriad, possibilities, and indeed often already think this way about gender.

Trinh's emphasis on paying attention to the differences within and not just the differences between categories is something I have long found crucially important. All too often for far too long I struggled to problematize reductive assumptions about what being gay means as too many others imagined, or wished to imagine, that gay people, all gay people, are far more homogenous than we are. Likewise, I find it important as well to attend to differences within categories such as people with mental health challenges, disabled people, and even people with experience of anxiety or depression or chronic physical illness. I find it important, further, to complicate supposedly clear-cut, hard and fast boundaries between able-bodied and disabled, sick and well, and mentally healthy and mentally ill. I am someone who is both able-bodied and disabled, and who is both chronically ill and exceedingly healthy, and who experiences mental health challenges yet is able to make use of and transform these challenges into means and motives toward mental well-being.

On my UW-Eau Claire people's pages profile page I include the following in my description of myself:

> I am and have long been (for over thirty-five years now) openly gay. As I see it, our sexualities are complex modes of being and relating in society, and they affect the ways in which we engage in all other forms of social relations, exercising a significant impact on our outlook on life and our everyday engagement in the world. I believe we all are in varying, shifting degrees both gay and straight. I am proud to associate my own understanding of gayness with a radical theorization and practice of gayness conceived and promoted by revolutionary gay liberation in the late 1960s and early 1970s.

Being gay for me has always been as much a political identity as anything, and cannot be simply reduced to or conflated with commonsensical notions of 'homosexual sexual orientation'. Early on at UW-Eau Claire I made a conscious effort to intervene versus the latter kind of reductive understanding of what being 'gay' must mean, especially when being 'gay' was something so few people felt at all comfortable being 'out' about:

> When I first came to terms with my own gayness many years ago I talked with an openly gay teacher of mine who gave me what has since proven incredibly enabling advice. He urged me to theorize my gayness–in other words to develop a conceptual understanding and articulation of what it meant for me to be gay, and to live my life as a gay person. He urged me to recognize that my gayness united me with many others past, present, and future, and with a vast, complex, dynamic, rich, moving, and inspiring history, politics, and culture. As I worked to theorize my gayness I came to conceive of it as the manifestation of an ethical and political commitment to dedicate my life working for progressive social change. For me, declaring myself to be gay means declaring that I actively identify with the fight to overcome oppressively unequal forms of intimate and affectional relations, and to create a new mode of human social organization founded upon genuinely mutually enabling, and substantially equal forms of intimate and affectional relations. For me, following the inspirational path of revolutionary gay liberation, the word "gay" continues to represent, most importantly, a social and political identity, a vantage point, that is, from which I seek to intervene against the anti-democratic, unfree, unequal, and unjust configuration of existing power relations in our society. Gayness, as I have come to conceive of it, represents a commitment, furthermore, to feel who I am through my interdeterminate interconnection with others, and to transcend the solipsistic limits of an insular, alienated individuality. For me, gayness is not a single, fixed, static thing; my declaration that I am gay does not therefore mean I simply announce that I have found, rock-solid deep within me, some innately essential, "true homosexual self." I am gay: this means, instead, that I am committed to a practice and a process of becoming in relation to others, toward making myself vulnerable to and trusting of others, toward reaching out and connecting with others, toward tangibly grasping and passionately feeling the inescapable otherness of whom I am and that makes up what I call "myself" (Excerpted from

an introduction explaining how I conceive of what it means to declare that 'I am gay' which I shared with many classes and other audiences during my first years at UW-Eau Claire and in Eau Claire).

I continue to identify with this understanding of what identifying as 'gay' means for me, although I face constant pressure from our larger culture for it to mean nothing like any of that, and to be simply another word for maintaining 'a homosexual sexual orientation'. I mention this as a way of attempting to 'write nearby' or 'write alongside' Trinh's *Woman, Native, Other*, by focusing on where I have needed to think through what a term of identity can and does mean for me, rejecting the easy and the obvious, and focusing instead on this identity as an active and persistent process, as an aspirational horizon, and as a commitment to a continuous and uneven mode of self-critically striving and endlessly redoing, undoing, unbecoming, and rebecoming. I understand and respect many young people today who identify as nonbinary because they do not experience themselves within the broadly recognizable/acceptable range of what a boy/a man or a girl/a woman is supposed to be/to be like, and especially not to have to only be one or the other. But I identify, and have long identified, as a boy/as a man, yet as a boy/as a man who resists patriarchal sexist and hegemonic masculinist ways of defining and delimiting what it must mean to 'be a man', to 'be a true or real or proper man', and who seeks, and strives, instead, to be a different kind of man.

Five

The principal arguments Aimé Césaire's *Discourse on Colonialism* advances, that will serve as points of departure in exploring areas of prospective connection, in encounters with Ian Curtis and Joy Division to come, in the following four sections of this chapter, as represented, in succession, by the songs "Day of the Lords," "Colony," "Heart and Soul," and "Autosuggestion," are as follows:

1. Colonialism is indefensible, nothing can justify colonialism, and colonialism not only devastates the colonized but brutalizes the colonizer.

2. The roots of fascism lie in colonialism, as colonialism is proto-fascism, and proto-fascistic practices conducted under the auspices of colonialism boomerang to become fascistic practices conducted against populations in colonizing countries.

3. Neo-colonialism is as much a problem as colonialism; merely a formal end to direct colonial rule is insufficient to supersede the impact of colonialism; and post-WWII imperialism is prospectively more insidious than pre-WWII imperialism.

The principal arguments Edward Said's *Representations of the Intellectual* advances, that will serve as points of departure in exploring areas of prospective connection with Ian Curtis and Joy Division in the following four sections of this chapter, as represented, in succession, by the songs "Day of the Lords," "Colony," "Heart and Soul," and "Autosuggestion," are as follows:

1. The intellectual must strive for maximum possible independence without ever expecting to achieve an abstract and uncontaminated state of total 'purity', and must deliberately embrace the position of

the outsider, the marginal, the exile, and 'the amateur', as well as the risks, dangers, and costs attendant upon such a position.

2. The intellectual works in the interest of the underrepresented and disadvantaged and of that which might yet be but is not yet.

3. The intellectual works by making connections otherwise ignored or resisted, by unearthing the buried and forgotten, by unsettling and upsetting dogmatic orthodoxy, by combining rational investigation with moral judgment, by using a prospective variety of means and media, and by emphasizing the complex challenges and responsibilities of *representing* in all the work they do.

The principal arguments Trinh T. Minh-ha's *Woman, Native, Other: Writing Postcoloniality and Feminism* advances, that will serve as points of departure in exploring areas of prospective connection with Ian Curtis and Joy Division, as represented by the songs "Day of the Lords," "Colony," "Heart and Soul," and "Autosuggestion," are as follows:

1. Language and other modes of discourse do not provide neutral and transparent means and media of expression, communication, representation, or reflection. In working sensitively with language and other modes of discourse it is crucial to be able to engage with confusion, uncertainty, incompletion, lack of and limits to control, the indefinite and the undecidable, the indirect and the roundabout, the elusive and the elliptical, the multiple and the proliferating, open-endedness and not just closure, perpetual process and not just process always directed toward a decisively finished product, and the in-between, the alongside, the liminal, thresholds, hybrids, taboos, cracks, gaps, fissures, fragments, borders, borderlines, intersections and intersectionalities.

2. Strive to speak, write, and otherwise discourse 'nearby' as opposed to 'about' or 'for' and strive as well to 'read across' and not be confined by generic, disciplinary, or other kinds of normative and conventional expectations of method, procedure, focus, and emphasis. Pressure, and press past, commonplace distinctions and separations between 'creative' and 'critical' as well as between 'theoretical' and 'non-theoretical' forms of writing and other modes of discourse.

3. Pressure, and press past, the hegemony of dualistic thinking, especially in relation to conceiving of subjectivity and of relations between subjectivity and language and in conceiving of subjectivity as formed and constituted within and through language. Reconceive difference as not necessarily identical with conflict, division, or opposition but rather as prospectively constituting a multiplicity, proliferation, and opening *within* as well as *between*, as providing a necessary means of and basis for contact, connection, coalition, alliance, and collaboration. Reconceive the self as comprised of 'infinite layers' and reject notions of identities, individual or social, as involving a constant, continuous, central and centering 'core'.

Six

In my colloquium presentation to the English Department at UW-Eau Claire, consisting of an early, much shorter version of a section of chapter one of this book, I only had time to play one Joy

685

Division song before turning to discussion. I chose "Day of the Lords." I chose this song because I wanted to emphasize how it makes sense to interpret the lyrics and music of Ian Curtis and Joy Division as 'anti-fascist'. "Day of the Lords" resonates particularly emphatically with the following one of the eleven overarching interpretations I introduced in chapter one: *as the staging of a dramatic encounter with the shocking resilience and metamorphic resurgence of fascist tendencies, after the end of World War II and the Holocaust, at the heart of ostensibly 'democratic', advanced capitalist, Western society, including in the guises of 'friendly fascism' and 'the fascism of everyday life'. Ian Curtis and his bandmates, in choosing their name, Joy Division, whether consciously, deliberately, intentionally or not, propose fascism lives on after the defeat of Nazi Germany and the liberation of the survivors from the concentration camps–and it lives on, most insidiously, as an integral dimension and recurrent tendency within the very same societies so frequently and routinely celebrating their victory over fascism.*

"Day of the Lords" resonates with Césaire's argument concerning relations between colonialism, including neo-colonialism, and fascism. "Day of the Lords" resonates with Césaire's argument concerning how colonialism, including neo-colonialism, brutalizes and de-civilizes colonizing nations, societies, and cultures. "Day of the Lords" resonates with Césaire's argument concerning how tolerance, acceptance, and support of colonialism, and in particular discourse on colonialism authorizing, legitimating, rationalizing, and mystifying the nature of the relationship between colonizer and colonized, enable the damaging impact colonialism exerts upon both the colonized and the colonizer. "Day of the Lords" resonates with Césaire's argument concerning how refusal to grant that colonialism is indefensible prepares the way for–boomerangs back as–fascism at home, within colonizing nations.

"Day of the Lords" resonates with Said's argument concerning the intellectual's need to be prepared to assume the position of the outsider, the marginal, and the exile, in order to speak truth to power, in order to be able to work on behalf of and in solidarity with the under-represented and the disadvantaged. "Day of the Lords" resonates with Said's argument concerning the need to be further prepared, in so doing, to face not only isolation and loneliness but also denigration, derision, dismissal, punishment, and, perhaps the most troubling, failure or refusal to heed what the intellectual has to say.

"Day of the Lords" resonates with Trinh's argument concerning how difficult it is to do effectively critically resistant and oppositional work, in recognizing the most readily available and familiar means and media are neither transparent nor neutral. "Day of the Lords" resonates with Trinh's argument concerning how important it is not simply to speak, write, or otherwise discourse directly about or for 'the other' for whom one is concerned because so doing leads all too readily to yet further suppressing, excluding, preventing, and distorting 'the other' from speaking, writing, and otherwise discoursing, for itself, on its own behalf. "Day of the Lords" resonates with Trinh's argument, as well, that doing so risks oversimplifying, too easily 'clarifying', and too easily being contained, tamed, coopted, and integrated by what one ostensibly seeks to dismantle and deconstruct.

"Day of the Lords" resonates with taking deadly seriously the challenges involved in confronting recurrent and pervasive horror; one's own connection with, complicity in, and responsibility for this horror; and one's limited powers, at least by oneself alone, to prevent, stop, and overcome this recurrence and pervasion. "Day of the Lords" resonates with taking deadly seriously the question of what can we possibly do, from where we are at, with limited means at our immediate disposal, in resisting and opposing fascist forces. How do so when these forces have already succeeded in dividing, fragmenting, separating, and isolating us? How do so when we recognize they threaten *us*, when we recognize *we* are already or soon will be their targets? How do so when we recognize it is because of our vulnerability as those perceived and identified as among 'the weak' that makes us especially ripe for victimization? How do so when we recognize it is from our very 'weakness' that we must find 'the strength' to survive, to endure, to persist, and to continue to resist and to oppose?

When I listen to "Day of the Lords" I imagine a space of confinement, more precisely a space of entrapment, where I am held together–and *thereby bound together*–with the music as persona, and especially with the lyricist and vocalist as protagonist. Yet all the others responsible for the other sound sources that comprise the song are right there in this same space as well. This is a circularly spinning room from which no exit is perceptible, no door is apparent, where both the floor and the ceiling are dense and thick, and where we are drenched in dread that we experience synaesthetically and kinaesthetically. This room contains, around its entire circumference, large windows in the form of video screens. We do not have access to any controls we can use to adjust let alone turn off these screens. These screens reveal to us what is happening 'outside'. On every screen we see images and hear sounds emanating from the commission, right near us, of atrocities, of bodies subjected to brutal violation and horrendous violence. The perpetrators are mysterious figures, as their entire bodies, including their faces, are concealed, in full military armor, rendering them anonymously terrifying. Even more precisely, we are presented with close-up and extreme close-up access to the images and sounds of the suffering and the pain experienced by the victims of these atrocities immediately as they experience this impact. We can push up against these windows and we can push these video screens outward, as they can bend outward. We can do so in striving to reach out to, to touch, to attempt to comfort and even to attempt to save these victims. But we can never reach them, because these windows in the forms of screens bend yet do not break. We cannot break them; we cannot break through. We cannot help but want to do so, and we cannot help but strive to do so, but we always fall short, as this barrier remains impermeable between us and the victims who are suffering in pain outside, surrounding the place of our confinement.

In *We Were Strangers: Stories Inspired by Unknown Pleasures*, Jenn Ashworth's "Day of the Lords" recounts the experience of a man, Paul, taking his step-son, Ted, to his weekly visit with Ted's father, Rick, who Paul dislikes, and considers 'a tosser', because Rick, a military veteran, lives in a shabby location, is personally unkempt, abuses alcohol, and doesn't seem to be trying to lead any kind of respectably productive life. Even while Paul accepts that Rick's military experience has contributed to how Rick now is, Paul nonetheless feels Rick is lazy, irresponsible, and not doing as much as he could or should to lead a better life, or to provide a better environment for his son, when Ted visits. Paul also resents the fact that Rick has no room where he lives that would allow Ted to stay over night, as this limits how much time Paul can spend alone with his wife, Kath, Rick's ex-wife. And Paul further resents Kath 'reporting to' Rick about how good Paul is with their son Ted.

Usually Kath is the one who takes Ted to visit Rick and then picks him up, but today Kath is too busy at work to do so. When Paul drops Ted off he is reluctant to leave. Ostensibly he worries about Ted hurting himself, after Ted accidentally smashes a liquor bottle and barely misses cutting himself. But Paul seems to want, and to need, more than that, to question Rick about why he is living this way, about why he is not doing better, about why he is not making an effort to do better, while also seeking to understand how and why Rick and Ted get along so well. Paul, despite diligently striving to be a good step-dad, finds this role uncomfortably exhausting, and neither he nor Ted have yet warmed to each other. Paul is also curious about Kath's prior relationship with Rick, especially before Rick came back from military service so messed up that Kath decided she needed to leave and take Ted with her. Rick never hurt either of them, only himself, yet Kath found she could no longer take living with Rick while he was doing so. As the visit proceeds, Paul begins to recognize Rick may not be the 'total loser'–the 'tosser'–he previously conceived him to be, and that much about Rick, including how and why Rick has become as he is, result from experiences Paul cannot readily understand.

During this visit, Rick and Paul talk with each other for longer than they ever have before. Paul is especially struck, without knowing quite what to make of this, by Rick's reference to the nightmares he regularly experiences and with how these nightmares parallel ones Ted often experiences. Paul begins to feel a reluctant sympathy for Rick, and begins at the same time to experience a slight increase in understanding of Ted, even as both Rick and Ted remain puzzling and in part frightening to him–frightening because Paul cannot understand what it feels like, and what it has felt like, to be either of them, and especially what it feels like, and has felt like, to end up as exhausted, defeated, and haunted as Rick is.

Surrounding this domestic drama, the war is ongoing, seemingly endlessly ongoing, and this includes calling up successive new waves of soldiers to fight in it. But Paul has never been called, and never will be, because he has been medically excused from military service. So the war, and what it is like on the frontlines, remains a distantly unreal phenomenon for him. As a result, Paul is able to get on with life without having the war interfere. But by the end of the story Paul begins to reflect on how this vantage point of his has affected his outlook and his behavior, in ways he never previously considered.

In this fictional story-world, many people like Paul abound, while most of those who return as veterans from fighting in the war end up, like Rick, not doing well. These ex-soldiers find out, when they return, that gratitude for their service is limited, while impatience with the challenges they present to those who have not been damaged is much greater. Even though Ashworth's example of 'writing nearby' or 'writing alongside' "Day of the Lords" is not quite what I think of when I experience and reflect on this song, it makes good sense to me to interpret the song as engaging with the damaging impact on many soldiers after they return from fighting in war, encompassing not only PTSD but also a limited ability, if not indeed a complete inability, to return to lead any kind of socially recognized 'normal life'. It also makes good sense to interpret the song as engaging with how difficult it is for those without this kind of experience to understand, appreciate, and feel genuine sympathy and compassion for those who have. It in addition makes good sense to interpret "Day of the Lords" as engaging with how easy it is for virtually endless war(s) to become normalized, and for those not directly affected, not directly suffering, to become desensitized to their cumulative impact.

As part of a series of music videos commemorating the 40th anniversary of *Unknown Pleasures*, a series of filmmakers offered new interpretations of these songs. For "Day of the Lords," Irish filmmakers Feargal Ward and Adrian Duncan, who are both based in Berlin, created a music video featuring actor Mat Voorter in which Voorter emerges from a wooded area in Berlin's city centre wearing nothing but underpants and a cape of wing-like leaves, as he slowly but purposely walks through a series of urban locations to a performance space. At this space a large audience is already assembled. Voorter proceeds through the crowd to the center, where he begins to perform for them. Voorter moves about stumblingly yet ritualistically while appearing to shout, roar, howl, and chant upward toward the sky. But the musical soundtrack drowns out what precise sounds he might be emitting.

Voorter proceeded this performance on his way to this space by alternately gritting his teeth and opening his mouth wide, seemingly emitting sounds akin to what his eventual performance will suggest. As the performance ends, he slowly moves back through the crowd and at the end of the video we observe him in the backseat of a car, driven by a chauffeur, after first noting feathers like those he has been wearing are attached to the hood ornament and elsewhere in front of this same car.

When Voorter emerges from the wooded area and walks, in slow motion, to the performance space, some onlookers pay attention to him, while some do not, but no one directly approaches, let alone accosts, him. Some who do pay attention seem mildly surprised, slightly startled, or gently bemused, but no one's reaction approaches shock. At the performance the audience does seem to pay close attention, with some in attendance, including those in charge of a bicycle that seems to be connected to a sound system at the center of the performance space, along with a few others, grinning as the performance proceeds, suggestive of either appreciating the bizarrely humorous aspects of the performance, and of Voorter's appearance, or otherwise 'in on the joke'.

This video, while not devoid of intriguing elements, offers an example of 'creating nearby' or 'creating alongside' "Day of the Lords" that doesn't coincide with what I envision when I listen to, and reflect on, the song. The ridiculousness of his costume and the marked sense I derive from the video, by its end, of Voorter's entire performance as little more than a stunt, undercuts the effectiveness of this video as commentary on 'the society of the spectacle', the performativity of authenticity, the cooptation and containment of the artistically avant-garde, or the artificial appropriation of the natural, including in the guise of ostensible ecocriticism. Nevertheless, I cite this video to attest to the fact that "Day of the Lords," like most Joy Division songs, is highly and multiply suggestive, open to a considerable range of plausible interpretations.

Demonstrating such range, on songmeanings.com users suggest "Day of the Lords" is about having "been distorted through childhood" and "given up hope for mankind, even in a wider perspective, as an adult"; "the horrors of WWII"; "being born and the agony of growing up and living"; "all wars, all the pain and horror that we humans like to inflict on each other"; "war atrocities" and "childhood suffering"; "the general agony of life, how it never stops being a fight, and

689

how the weak are defeated by the mercilessness of the world"; "being made fun of" through bullying, especially in childhood; "epilepsy"; "neurosis"; "the view of a non-Jewish Polish migrant watching the horrors of the Holocaust"; "suicide" in the form of a simulated "suicide note"; "how oppressive governments, 'evil' movements or bad times can turn normal, nice people into cold-hearted killers who see nothing wrong in their actions"; "the general agony of life, how it never stops being a fight, and how the weak are defeated by the mercilessness of the world"; "early Thatcher-era Britain when it was written, a time when the country was slashing its social safety net, adopting much harsher attitudes towards the poor, and generally creating a less compassionate society"; and the Biblical *Book of Revelations*.

In his contribution to the '33 and 1/3' series Ed Ott, in his book on *Unknown Pleasures*, interprets "Day of the Lords" as a song that "confronts uncertainty, the onset of childhood and the death of youth's romantic abandon" (66). In *Unknown Pleasures: Inside Joy Division*, Peter Hook identifies "Day of the Lords" as "a great song," while not focusing on 'what it might mean', but instead highlighting Martin Hannett's overdubbing of keyboards in this song, which he at first found objectionable but later admitted was crucial to making the song as powerfully compelling as it is (200). And in *Torn Apart: the Life of Ian Curtis*, Mick Middles and Lindsay Reade highlight how Ian Curtis's voice initially emerges from low in the mix, as Curtis here "attains a faint trace of Jim Morrison, and not for the last time," while "Day of the Lords" "signals the birth of gothic rock" (133).

The title becomes all the more challenging once one acknowledges that a singular "*Day* of the Lord" would be easier to interpret that "Day of the Lor*ds*" because of the fact that both for Judaism and Christianity the former phrase references 'the final day of judgment', commonly conceived as harrowing because on this day God reveals his supreme power; because this day coincides with the end of the world, or at least the end of human life on earth; and because a prospective vast number of human beings will be damned for eternity. Even though for others this will be a day of salvation for eternity, many of the most memorable Biblical and theological accounts stress the horrors this day will bring and the 'vengeance' God will enact upon those who have earned God's 'wrath'. "Day of the Lord" can also suggest the Sabbath, and in this connection connote responsibilities to 'keep this day' appropriately, to distinguish this day and what one does on it as well as how one does what one does on it from what one does and how one does this on the rest of the days of the week. In particular, identifying "Day of the Lord" with the Sabbath connotes the sinfulness and moral turpitude that follow from not marking the distinction between the Sabbath and the rest of the days of the week. Yet Ian Curtis titled this song "Day of the Lor*ds*," so even as both of the aforementioned connections with "Day of the Lord" make sense as associations with the title of this song, it at the same time suggests other, or more, possibilities than those two alone.

An early version that Deborah Curtis reprints along with the final version in the Appendix to *Touching from a Distance: Ian Curtis & Joy Division* offers a more pedestrian, less mysterious, and less widely resonant set of lyrics, that seem to complain about someone, a specific individual, 'a user', who persistently took advantage of others, including the narrator-protagonist of the lyrics, who declares 'we won't forget you' and what this 'you' has done, even if it is now and will seemingly always be too late to do anything about this, to change anything that has already happened as a result of what this 'you' has done–i.e., how this 'you' mistreated 'we', including the narrator-protagonist of the lyrics as well as, seemingly, multiple others. The 'day of the lords' here seems like it might more narrowly allude to 'the end of the world' in 'the final judgment'–or to the Sabbath. Yet this is not the final version of the lyrics, and it to that version I turn next.

The opening phrase of line one of the lyrics, "This is the room," fits with my imagined visual interpretation of where I experience 'us'–the music as persona and I–situated in this song, as I have earlier described. Notably 'this' points to a space close to 'us', right where 'we' are at, or which we can readily perceive, and also designates it as 'the' room, a specific room of seemingly specific importance. "The start of it all," the second phase of line one, completing the line, appears to begin to identify what is that specific purpose, but we don't yet have any clue to what 'it' might refer or what 'it' is as followed by 'all'. We do note 'it all' suggests something multiple, perhaps serial, and quite possibly entailing significant weight and duration.

"No portrait so fine, only sheets on the wall," line two, seems to suggest we are still 'in' or directly witnessing this same room. Reference to the room lacking any fine portrait hanging on the wall but only sheets suggests the sheets cover over where such portraits previously were hung. This room seems to be in a state of transition, with someone having moved out, maybe even passed on, maybe even literally died. It seems like the room may be undergoing renovation, or awaiting renovation. Yet 'sheets on the wall' is also eerily spectral, suggesting this has been the site, the scene, of damage and continues haunted as a result. "No portrait so fine" might also refer to the room itself, as it does not resemble 'a fine portrait', or is not and will not be rendered by means of 'a fine portrayal', but appears a 'blank canvas', an empty space with not only its walls but also its other features separating it from and linking it to adjacent spaces shrouded.

Line three–"I've seen the nights, filled with bloodsport and pain"–introduces an 'I', a narrator-protagonist, who seems to be testifying to what 'he' has seen, and perhaps confessing that this is what he has not only seen, as a witness, an observer, or a bystander, but also as a direct participant. This he describes as what 'he' *has* seen, but the developing atmosphere of the song suggests this is not over and done with. "The nights" might literally refer to when what 'he' has seen transpired, but it is also worth noting these are *the* nights, definite nights, specific nights, nights that stand out from and can be, even need to be, distinguished from other nights. "The nights" also conjures a sense of darkness, metaphorical as well as literal, in association with a time when more daring, and more deadly, acts are wont to take place than during 'the days' when it is easier to hide or obscure what is happening, who is involved, and how.

"Filled with" indicates the narrator-protagonist is not referencing occasional, fleeting, and sporadic events, but ones that happen continuously. "Pain" at the end of the line gives this word, and its ready associations, particular emphasis, but its link with "bloodsport" narrows this range, suggestive of pain that occurs as a result of physical violence perpetrated in the course of a high-stakes competitive activity. "Bloodsport" conjures a sense of the illicit and the extreme. At the same time, this suggests another way of making sense of what licit conflicts, including wars, are all too often perceived *and played as* by those responsible for launching, commanding, and, profiting from them. "Bloodsport and pain" can also suggest what follows from violent assault on those who are physically weaker, who are susceptible to being overwhelmed and defeated by 'superior firepower', and by those who revel in injuring, mutilating, torturing, and killing those they attack, perhaps because they have determined those 'others' *deserve* this, or do *not deserve otherwise*, or are so primitive, dirty, uncivilized, bestial, savage, inferior, subhuman, sinful, evil, monstrous, decadent, or a combination of these qualities, that they need to be 'punished' and 'eliminated'. Perhaps these 'others' stand in the way of what those leading the assault seek for themselves, and perhaps those leading the assault recognize no other way to acquire what they seek other than through violent expropriation and dispossession. Perhaps those leading this assault enjoy this kind of "bloodsport" and attendant "pain" for its own sake, as a source of sheer sadistic pleasure; perhaps they regard it as entertaining, and even find it addictively intoxicating, a kind of spectacle they keep coming back to, again and again, because they can never get enough.

"And the bodies obtained, the bodies obtained," the last line of the first stanza, seems to draw us directly to the final result of this "bloodsport," and the pain it involves, which is an accumulation of "bodies." Referred to as "bodies," we readily imagine corpses, or those who are so seriously injured that they have become immobile, but it is possible to interpret this line as referencing the bodies of those who have been defeated and conquered, and who are now forced to submit to and work for those who have defeated and conquered them, perhaps as their slaves or at least as a superexploited class of workers. "Obtained" does seem to suggest that 'someone' has acquired something, someone has gained something, in the form of bodies; perhaps 'something' has done this, if we are imagining a particular kind of social system or social order as ultimately responsible, and as ultimately benefitting. This system may here have obtained, may have acquired, an accumulation of 'docile bodies', bodies that can be rendered docile in relation to the power of domination and subjection. Repeating the same phrase twice, "the bodies obtained," suggests a lamenting of what this "bloodsport" and "pain" has wrought, while sympathetically identifying, or empathetically manifesting solidarity, with those referenced here as "the bodies" that have been "obtained."

The "And" to start the final line complicates what I have just suggested slightly as it can also suggest what the narrator-protagonist 'has seen', and is here recounting, involves bloodsport + pain + bodies obtained, with all three of these linked, even inextricably interlinked, but nonetheless not collapsible into one single entity. In other words, the 'I' of these lyrics has seen bloodsport, he has seen pain, and he has seen bodies obtained–he has seen all three, which seem to be connected, yet are not identical. If this so, the narrator-protagonist is recounting 'his' observation of a nightmarish, perhaps even an apocalyptic, situation in which one horror follows another, ceaselessly onward, traversing the entire space over which it is possible to proceed in the course of a night, or in the course of a series of nights. This image suggests a military battlefield, in the midst of or immediately following the heat of the conflict, or a comparable kind of space, perhaps in which military, or paramilitary, forces–perhaps armed police forces or other state agents ostensibly functioning as agents of 'law and order', or of 'national security', or of 'defense of the homeland'–mow down people rising in protest against injustice or oppression, perhaps in non-violent ways publicly venting their grievances, 'speaking truth to power', 'demanding their rights', and mobilizing to advocate that 'another world is possible'.

Stanza two offers the first iteration of the choral refrain: "Where will it end?" This question is repeated twice as line one, and then again twice more as line two. These lines suggest what has just

692

been described, and alluded to, has been ongoing for a long time and has extended its damaging impact widely, even pervasively, such that 'it' needs to end, it 'should' end, it would be inordinately better were it to end, but how this might happen, through what means, via what agency, beginning where, and proceeding through what stages beyond this beginning, is not only uncertain but feels hopeless, even impossible. It is and has been far too much to take, but 'there is no end in sight', and the 'I' of the lyrics, as well as 'us' too, seem to be faced with no choice but to have to take what we cannot take, and to keep on taking this. We will keep being overwhelmed with ongoing repetition of violent atrocity, and with this horror becoming all the more horrific as it serves as source of profitable gain along with pleasurable sport for those in positions at the heights of power, supported by all too many others not themselves occupying the heights of power but ideologically interpellated into positions of identification with such cruel and callous ways of conceiving of and relating to the commission and perpetuation of violent atrocity.

Stanza three begins with the line "These are your friends from childhood, through youth," which seems to implicate 'us', if we imagine the narrator-protagonist is not simply rhetorically indicating 'his' own friends, and, in connection with what has preceded, this suggests 'our friends', "from childhood, through youth," may well be among both 'the victims and the executioners'–just as is the case with "the friends from childhood, through youth," of the narrator-protagonist. We cannot pretend innocence, as mere bystanders, as detached and disinterested, given this connection, and especially since these were friends of 'ours' *through* youth, these were pivotal and enduring friends during a formative period of our lives, and we are, logically, likely to continue to bear much in common with them. Even if we have broken or diverged from them, this has likely proven a painful process, and only a partial and limited accomplishment, that has passed and continues to pass through messy 'gray zones'.

Line two clarifies, more precisely, what kinds of friends these were, and what they did 'to us': "Who goaded you on, demanded your proof." "Goaded" suggests tempting us to do something wrong, dangerous, and reckless. The phrasing suggests 'we' accepted this goading, or gave way–gave in–to it, and did what we were tempted to do, which seemingly involved producing or demonstrating some kind of "proof," perhaps "proof" of our willingness to feign a particular image of being bold and brave by doing something that was actually stupid, and even cruel. Scenarios of being goaded into participating in bullying readily occur here, or to participating in otherwise scapegoating people representative of socially marginalized–and socially oppressed–identities, people vulnerable on this account, people who can be readily identified and targeted as 'weak' on this account. Perhaps 'we' were "goaded" into 'proving' our supposed 'strength' by attacking some 'other' 'weaker' than 'us', ostensibly thereby showing, and 'proving', our 'strength'.

This charge to remember these childhood friends, that lasted for us through our youth, and our connection with them, is thus insinuating this is where people begin to become perpetrators or complicit with the perpetration of violence that causes pain, suffering, and humiliation. This may also be where begins the identification of specific people and especially specific groups of people as 'weak', and as thereby ready targets for pain, suffering, and humiliation. In this connection we can imagine many groups of people mocked, taunted, and abused, on account of whom they are–disabled people, especially visibly but also non-visibly physically or mentally disabled people, including people with intellectual disabilities; people of color, in White-dominant societies; old people; lesbian, gay, bisexual, transgender, gender non-binary, intersex, and asexual people, as well as people suspected of being queer; poor people and working class people; and women and girls.

Line three of stanza three, "Withdrawal pain is hard, it can do you right in," seems to mark something of at least slight shift, seeming to imply a painful process of withdrawing from participation in that nexus of close connections that once was so pivotal at such a formative period–from those friends who "goaded you on" and who "demanded your proof." The narrator-protagonist and I no longer identify with that kind of mindset, and no longer pretend to go along with it without truly believing in it. Perhaps we have rejected direct participation in bullying and in related forms of abuse of 'others' who can be readily targeted as victims of such abuse on account of their ostensible 'weakness', and perhaps we have recognized, or begun to recognize, ourselves among 'the weak'. 'Withdrawing" from those connections is nonetheless costly, because it leaves us isolated and alone, feeling exposed and vulnerable.

Yet, in contrast with the preceding line of interpretation, this same line may also suggest that 'withdrawing' from the 'intoxicating high' of being immersed in the play of violence, or from approving spectatorial attendance upon the commission of violence, continues to be painful. "It can do you right in" suggests loss or lack of a place where one has a role, a purpose, within a group or a community. It is possible this line suggests the narrator-protagonist, and 'us', became addicted to violence, perhaps traceable to the goading we experienced from friends in our youth, to prove ourselves, and even as we have been trying to break from that addiction, we are experiencing this as extremely hard to do. This line might suggest addiction to alcohol or other intoxicating drugs, but in the context of the lyrics as whole is principally suggestive of addiction to forms of reckless behavior that involve committing acts of violence against others as well as against ourselves, such as addiction to fighting and addiction to cutting.

Maybe 'addiction' is not quite right here, despite the use of 'withdrawal', as the line may be merely marking the consequences of attempting to work through a change in dominant patterns of behavior and finding this to be tough to carry through. Yet, in connection with the preceding stanzas I suggest it makes the best sense to read this line as reflecting a struggle to find a critical vantage point, a critical distance, from immersion in 'bloodsport and pain', involving the 'obtaining of bodies', even as an erstwhile observer, bystander, or witness–a vantage point from which it is possible to take stock of what all of this violence means, and of what one's own connection with it, one's responsibility for and complicity in it, means in turn.

The final line of the third stanza–"So distorted and thin, distorted and thin"–is especially ambiguous. What is distorted and thin? How and why both? What is the relationship between being distorted and being thin? How much or how far is suggested by means of 'so'? Is this the narrator-protagonist 'himself', and perhaps 'us' as well, together with him, who are "so distorted and thin"? Is this perhaps the process of withdrawal itself that is "so distorted and thin" and not just where 'he' and 'us' are finding ourselves, are ending up? Is going through this process, leaving you "so distorted and thin," what "can do you right in"? Does "So distorted and thin" refer to the present memories of these now past childhood friends, ours throughout our youth, and of 'his' and 'our' past as well as present connections with them, and in particular with what they 'goaded' 'him' and 'us' to do to 'prove ourselves'? Does "So distorted and thin" refer to what follows as a result of what never ends, which leaves us plaintively wondering "Where will it end?" Does "So distorted and thin" refer to "the bodies obtained" seemingly as a result of "bloodsport and pain"–and, more precisely, of "nights of bloodsport and pain"? Does "So distorted and thin" refer to what we can perceive, and how this appears to us, from 'the room', 'where it all started'?

These questions bring us back to an issue I have not yet addressed: how did "it" "start" in "this room," and why in "this room"? What kind of room, more precisely, might this be–what is, and what has been, its purpose, its function? How can the room be the place out of which "nights filled with bloodsport and pain" emerged, and which led to an accumulation of "bodies obtained"? Perhaps this is the room where those in charge, those at the heights of power, or those otherwise exercising determinate or at least influential institutional power, made the decision, set the course, and promulgated the rationalization, the justification, for the "bloodsport and pain," for the accumulation of "bodies of obtained." Perhaps this room stands in for all those rooms in which 'the masters of war' have made their decision, and from which their commands have ensued–and perhaps this is the room in which others in the same or comparable positions have commanded, and commissioned, violence against protestors, dissenters, the oppressed and exploited, the marginalized and excluded, and all those who comprise ready targets, ready scapegoats–as 'weak'. Perhaps this is the room, symbolizing many such rooms, where many people learned to accept the commission and perpetuation of horrible violence, including 'in their name', as right and necessary, as just and inevitable, and even as not horrifically violent at all.

Such possibilities might extend as far as to include the fundamental role and indispensable contribution, as Kehinde Andrews addresses, in *The New Age of Empire: How Racism & Colonialism Still Rule the World*, of genocide, slavery, and colonialism, including in the form of neo-colonialism, in making possible 'Western civilization', 'the entire project of the West', and especially the continuing vast extent of socio-economic inequality distinguishing 'the West' from 'the rest' under conditions of contemporary, global, 'racial capitalism'. Alternately, such possibilities might include becoming desensitized, through technological mediation and bombardment with spectacular images of violence, to the pain, suffering, and devastation this violence causes–and to losing the capacity for empathy, as a result.

The fourth stanza repeats the choral refrain, with again each of the two lines twice posing the question "Where will it end?" The accumulating effect of this choral refrain suggests that each verse passage attests to a dimension of what is the 'it' the questions here are asking concerning, "Where will *it* end?" This method in itself enacts a semblance of confronting an accumulation of horrors, seemingly without end. It is also worth noting the question the choral refrain repeatedly asks is *where* will it end and not *when* will it end, although it is possible to interpret that question as by implication asking both. However, if the lyrics have pointed us to "the room" that represents "the start of it all," this emphasis on asking *where* will it end suggests the lyrics are concerned with what might be the parallel location–the other room, the room to be, the room that is not yet but which might yet be–where 'it' can and will be brought to an end.

Might this be the location, symbolically represented as a room, where a decisive resolution, intervention, and transformation in the conditions that makes possible, the forces that give to, and the interests that benefit from and depend upon the seemingly endlessly ongoing 'nights of bloodsport and pain' leading to an accumulative 'obtainment of bodies' finally takes place? Might this be the location, symbolically represented as a room, where counter-hegemonic power finally overturns hegemonic power and a fundamentally different kind of social order is inaugurated? Might this be the location, symbolically represented as a room, where people are able and willing to face the truth about the systemic violence at the heart of the social order in which they live–and where they face up to their own connection with, their own implication in, and their own responsibility for this violence? Might this be the room where people stop demanding whitewashing, and stop needing to whitewash, history–where people stop insisting on the absolute greatness of their nation, and stop rejecting and opposing any and all attempts to ever call this greatness into question? Might this be the room where people are willing to accept the rightness and necessity of experiencing guilt and shame for what they are connected with, implicated in, and responsible for, even while not content to 'wallow in' guilt and shame? Might this be the room where people are willing to accept that not only 'another world is possible' but also 'another world is absolutely necessary'–a world in which people live dramatically different kinds of lives with each other–in order to preserve the life of this planet, and in order to overcome vast disparities of wealth and power dependent upon systemic violence?

Whatever associations we might make with such a 'parallel room' it is important to note such a room is nowhere directly represented in these lyrics, which throughout offer no answer to the question "Where will it end?" The lyrics imply that as urgent a question as this is it is also one that cannot be easily answered, and, if anything, it up to each of us, through our own life-praxis, to seek such an answer, not to wait for someone else to tell us what it is. Likewise, the lyrics do not suggest 'there is sure to be an answer', someday somehow, and, if anything, imply, intellectually at least, that it is far more likely none will emerge, none is possible or any longer possible, and as much as an answer might be desperately needed it might never arrive, while the pace of destruction will continue endlessly onward, until human beings have completely destroyed ourselves.

Stanza five begins with the line "This is the car at the edge of the road," which continues with reiteration of 'This is' initiated in the first stanza, and is suggestive, by means of this reiteration, of the narrator-protagonist pointing to, or pointing out, a series of signs of violence and horror. A line like this is as close to concrete as Ian Curtis ever gets in his lyrics, while still remaining nebulous. It is, once more, *the* car, a definite, specific car, not just *a* car, and it seems, therefore, intricately interconnected with the passages, and the scenes these have suggested, articulated in the preceding stanzas. Yet why it is *the* specific car? "At the edge of the road," meanwhile, suggests something 'not right', and suggests, more specifically, standing witness to some kind of violence, to some kind of horror. But again we know nothing more about this road or this car, and we have no direct indication of why the car is "at the edge of the road." We do learn a little more, with line two: "There's nothing disturbed, all the windows are closed." This line suggests coming upon a crime scene, or at least the scene of an accident, but one that challenges interpretation because 'nothing' has been 'disturbed' and 'all the windows are closed'. It is unclear if anyone tried to get out or in, and it is unclear what may have transpired that led to the car ending up "at the edge of the road." We don't know, from these lyrics alone, whether anyone remains in the car, and we don't know, if not, whether any signs of anyone having recently been in the car are present. It seems plausible to interpret the car as 'abandoned' "at the edge of the road," but by whom and why? How, moreover, is this "car at the edge of the road" connected with "the room" at "the start of it all," with no "portrait so fine" but only "sheets on the wall," with "the bloodsport and pain" as well as "the bodies obtained," with "the friends from childhood, through youth" who "goaded you on" and who "demanded your proof," with "the withdrawal pain that is hard" and with what is "distorted and thin," and with the overarching nemesis in the form of the 'it' that the lyrics repeatedly question "where will it end?"

Someone or some people may have fled a situation, and a scene, of violence and horror, in seeking to escape themselves becoming victims, but we don't know if they have escaped or if they *can* escape. This image suggests a setting close to the frontlines in war yet also other catastrophic situations as well–perhaps a climate or another kind of ecological disaster, perhaps a nuclear meltdown, perhaps a leak of dangerous chemicals into the atmosphere, perhaps the collapse of stable government and social structures into a chaotic state of anarchy, and perhaps a rapidly spreading, highly contagious as well as highly deadly disease.

The next line, "I guess you were right, when we talked in the heat," offers no ready clarification. It is interesting here that this 'you' seems less ambiguous, as this seems most likely to be addressing 'us', but what 'we' were 'right' about and when it was 'we talked' 'in the heat' we gain no further clue from the narrator-protagonist. We don't know what we might have been 'right' about, and yet that seems prospectively significant–perhaps we anticipated the current situation, or the ongoing and accumulating state of affairs the entire lyrics seem to reference; perhaps we were right in suggesting no ready way out or beyond is available.

"In the heat" suggests a figurative interpretation, rather than we simply were talking on a warm or hot day. Perhaps this implies a time of heightened tension, all around us, for us, and perhaps even between 'us' and the 'I', the narrator-protagonist of these lyrics. Yet it is worth noting the narrator-protagonist only hazards a 'guess' that we were right. This indecision corresponds with what the entire lyrics seem to communicate: that what is happening, has been happening, and will happen, as terrifying as this is, and as urgent as it logically seems to try to understand it in order to change it, cannot be easily understood, let alone readily addressed.

The final line of this stanza, "There's no room for the weak, no room for the weak," suggests this is what 'we' or some other 'you' was 'right' about, which the narrator-protagonist has not fully accepted, until now: that *there is no room for the weak*. In the context of this stanza, and especially of the lyrics as whole, seemingly 'there is no room' *anywhere* for the weak. In reference to the initial 'room', "at the start of it all," this was, it turns out, not a room *for* the weak, either, because it is the room in which the choices and decisions were made that led to a massive and ongoing assault on 'the weak'. "No room for the weak" also implies whoever was in the "car at the edge of the road" almost certainly has not escaped and will not be able to escape–because, simply put, the world as it is offers no 'safe space' for 'the weak', no space in which 'the weak' are safe from being attacked, with the qualities and characteristics that lead them to be classified as among 'the weak' rendering them exposed and vulnerable, ready targets for victimization. The elegiac lamenting of the phrase "no room for the weak," twice once more, strongly suggests the narrator-protagonist identifies 'himself' and 'us' as among 'the weak', even if we ourselves are guilty, at least in our past lives, for not recognizing this is whom and what we are and for acting in ways contrary to experiencing and demonstrating solidarity with all others who, like us, are also among the 'weak'.

Once more, as the next stanza, we come to a reiteration of the choral refrain: "Where will it end? Where will it end?/Where will it end? Where will it end?" The recurrence of this refrain reinforces the sense that 'it' has caused and is causing immense damage. The recurrence of this refrain reinforces the sense that those who 'it' is damaging but who are not yet completely annihilated are desperately wondering 'where' 'it' 'will end'. And the recurrence of this refrain reinforces the sense that any such ending is unlikely, even unimaginable.

The following stanza returns, in the first line, to repeat the opening line of the lyrics, "This is the room, the start of it all," suggesting we are back where we started, and perhaps we never did leave, but were only directed to remember, to imagine, to listen and conjure up an image in our mind of what we are hearing about, and, as I suggested earlier, looking out and listening to video images and recordings from what is happening all around us outside of the room in which we are currently confined and entrapped. If the last is the case, however, and at the same time "This is the room" that represents "the start of it all," we are definitely connected, implicated, and responsible. Indeed, our present situation in this room while all of the horrible violence and destruction is transpiring immediately outside and surrounding us suggests we are experiencing an uncomfortable and unjust comparative privilege. Perhaps we are only being temporarily spared, and perhaps our being forced to confront what is happening and has happened to others–as well as our connection, complicity, and responsibility–is part of the violence that is being perpetrated against, and upon, us. Perhaps, however, we are shaken to recognize that while we live in relative peace, comfort, and security, others with whom we are connected are suffering horribly, and we are implicated in and responsible for this suffering, because we are benefitting from the perpetuation of a social system that has provided us our relative peace, comfort, and security in direct correlation with denying this to and robbing it from others. We may not be the greatest beneficiaries, and we may not be in ultimate control of what is happening or of what has happened, but as long as we imagine we are innocent, unconnected, not implicated, and not responsible, we are very much 'part of the problem'.

In this connection, these lyrics remind me of Kehinde Andrews' charge in *The New Age of Empire: How Racism & Colonialism Still Rule the World* that even the struggles many white working class and lower middle class people face in 'the West', in the so-called 'First World', or in the so-called 'Global North', pale in comparison with the struggles faced by all too many Black and Brown people not within and among 'the West', Black and Brown people from the so-called 'Third World', or the so-called 'Global South'. These lyrics remind me, as Andrews also cites in this book, of W.E.B. DuBois' famous concept of the 'psychological wage' that racial capitalism grants, in White-dominant societies, to relatively poor white people, on account of their Whiteness, providing these white people partial protection and partial compensation from falling into exactly the same position as poor Black and Brown people. As Andrews elaborates upon DuBois's concept, this psychological wage is amplified in relation to the situation of poor Black and Brown people in colonized and neo-colonized countries as well as in relation to de facto 'Fourth World' 'colonies within the colonizing nations' inhabited by poor Black and Brown people.

Line two of stanza seven, "Through childhood, through youth, I remember it all," is not a reiteration of the second line of the opening stanza, but instead connects this current stanza and the first stanza with the focus, and emphasis, in the third stanza, referencing "friends from childhood, through youth." If 'I' "remembers it all," or *now* "remembers it all," this seems to involve remembering what that 'goading' and 'proving' involved, to what it led, as well as how this anticipates and exemplifies the passing down, the passing on, and the passing along of incentives to participate in victimizing others who can be victimized because of their relatively marginalized and oppressed status–as well as of connections interlinking bullying with the commission of mass atrocities. Now the narrator-protagonist remembers–and seemingly, by remembering, also suggests 'he' 'recognizes'–a common pattern he has witnessed throughout childhood, youth, and adulthood and this is, by implication, I suggest, the human capacity for engaging in acts of enormous cruelty versus other human beings, and for doing so callously, without registering much if any sense that this is wrong, and especially without recognizing any essential commonality, any basis for empathy, with 'the other' who is perceived to be among 'the weak' and thereby a ready and justifiable target.

The next two lines of this stanza repeat the last two lines of the opening stanza–"Oh, I've seen the night filled with bloodsport and pain/And the bodies obtained, the bodies obtained, the bodies obtained." This repetition suggests the narrator-protagonist has observed, been aware of, and witness to these nights, this spectacle, and this result throughout the entirety of 'his' life, with no relief and no escape from continually confronting it over and over again. The repetition suggests 'the bloodsport', 'the pain', and the accumulation of 'bodies obtained' all existed long before the narrator-protagonist was born and will almost certainly continue long after the narrator-protagonist has died. We are all caught up within 'it'. Too many of us don't recognize this to be the case, let alone what roles we play. Too many of us don't recognize that we exist 'among the weak'. Too many of us continue directly responsible for as well as indirectly complicit with harm directed against 'the weak' even as we ourselves are weak, in part in the attempt to deny that we exist among 'the weak'.

The closing iteration of the choral refrain–once more "Where will it end? Where will it end?/Where will it end? Where will it end?"–challenges us to recognize what has been transpiring for so long and so extensively with horrific impact, as well as to recognize how we are positioned in relation to the same horror. These final lines challenge us to figure out what we need to do in response. These final lines challenge us to figure out 'where' (as well as 'when' and 'how') 'it' might ever end while at the same time challenging us to act even as we accept that our actions will never be sufficient. 'It' might never end–even 'all of us' acting together in the effort to to bring 'it' to an end might never be enough. Yet this is a final series of questions, not a fnal series of declarations; whether an end is possible–and where, when, and how this might be possible–remains open.

Now having worked my way through the entire of the lyrics I will return to the title, "Day of the Lords." One possible interpretation is 'the Lords' are those who have been lording it over so many, and especially over 'the weak'. These people are empowered as the 'Lords' they are on account of what they have taken from and done to 'the weak', with the lyrics offering a nightmarish depiction of these 'Lords' supremely triumphant. 'The Lords' might represent 'the masters of war'; 'the captains of industry'; 'the establishment elite' and 'the super-rich'; those with vast accumulations of cultural + social + economic capital; multinational and transnational corporations as well as multinational and transnational institutions such as the International Monetary Fund, the World Bank, the World Trade Organization, the United Nations Security Council, and the North Atlantic Treaty Organization; powerful nation-states such as the United States, the People's Republic of China, and Russia; and so on. But another interpretation also makes sense, hearkening back to association of this title with 'The Day of the Lord', and in particular with this 'Day of the Lord' representing a decisive 'Judgment Day' or 'Day of Judgment'. Titling the song "Day of the Lords" suggests multiple 'Lords' presiding over this 'day of judgment', and it is feasible to imagine these might be the 'new lords' representative of the mass of the exploited, oppressed, and abused–of 'the weak'–rising, on a global scale, to seize power from those who hold it now, to judge those responsible for and complicit with all of the immense injustice that has been perpetrated against those who are now in the position to 'turn the tables', and to inaugurate 'the end of one kind of world' and the beginning of a fundamentally different kind of global social order. In line with this interpretation, the question the choral refrain asks–"Where will it end?–refers to inquiring into from where this shift and change-over in power, from where this end and new beginning, will emerge. In other words, from where will 'the weak' rise up successfully in claiming room, in claiming their need for and right to room, and in overcoming 'the strong' by manifesting a 'strength' rooted, paradoxically, in collectively shared 'weakness' that is capable of defeating 'the strong' and thereby of 'turning the world upside down'?

Let's turn now to consider the music beyond the lyrics that makes up "Day of the Lords," inquiring into how these sounds, patterns of sounds, and deployments of sounds, including the *vocalization* of the lyrics, redirects, or at least refines, the interpretations of what this song might mean that I have discussed so far.

One viable way of describing, and analyzing, the structure of "Day of the Lords," by identifying the song as comprised of a series of successive parts, or stages, is as follows:

1. Instrumental Opening 1 (Intro): 0:00-0:19. Initial opening figure, opening cadence, and preliminary melodic line.

2. Instrumental Opening 2 (Pre-Verse): 0:20-0:33. Build-up and lead-in to vocal, first sounding of principal melodic line.

3. First Verse: 0:34-0:49. Vocal takes over melodic lead, continuing same line as in preceding section.

4. Transition: 0:50-0:52.

5. First Choral Refrain: 0:53-1:06. Variation on principal melodic line.

6. Instrumental Bridge One (Pre-Verse): 1:07-1:20. Variation on principal melodic line, closer to variation enacted with the first choral refrain than to that of the melodic line of the verse.

7. Second Verse: 1:21-1:36. Same melodic line as with first verse.

8. Transition: 1:37-1:39.

9. Second Choral Refrain: 1:40-1:53. Same melodic line as with first choral refrain.

10. Instrumental Bridge Two, Part One (Interlude): 1:54-2:26. Different than first instrumental bridge, with much more of a guitar solo here highlighted.

11. Instrumental Bridge Two, Part Two (Pre-Verse): 2:27-2:42. Return to opening build-up and lead-in to vocal.

12. Third Verse: 2:43-2:58. Same melodic line as previously in verse passages.

13. Transition: 2:59-3:00.

14. Third Choral Refrain: 3:01-3:14. Same melodic line as previously in choral refrain passages.

15. Instrumental Bridge Three (Pre-Verse): 3:15-3:31. Reiteration of previous bridge sections except for the guitar solo part from bridge two.

16. Fourth Verse: 3:32-3:48. Same melodic line yet more forceful, insistent vocal delivery, starting and rising higher in pitch as well as increased and increasing in volume.

17. Transition: 3:49-3:53.

18. Fourth Choral Refrain: 3:54-4:06. Same melodic line as previously, but with what sounds like an at least slightly amplified chorus effect on the vocal.

19. Closing Instrumental Passage (Outro): 4:07-4:41. Distinctive sound patterns yet with still recognizably close connections to previous lines, moving toward close-out but no fade-out, and yet nevertheless near the very end involving a drawing down.

The instruments contributing to "Day of the Lords" are as follows:

1. Bass Guitar. The principal role of the bass guitar in this song is to add depth and texture to help provide the groove, but the bass guitar also sounds a condensed variation on the principal melodic line. The bass guitar part is pitched low with limited movement, often staying on the same note throughout a measure, and often sounds as if it is rumbling persistently in the background to middle ground of the soundscape.

2. Electric Six-String Lead Guitar. This guitar is principally responsible for the melody whenever the vocal is not present, while supportive of the vocal carrying the melody by sounding in a para-melodic background to middle ground role during the vocal passages, involving a ringing effect or a rapid strumming with a reverberating/echoing/choral effect. Directions for those seeking to play this song, as proffered by the likes of UltimateGuitar.com, advise frequently letting the sounds of the rapidly

strummed strings ring while also advising occasional palm muting to vary the timbre as well. The guitar often moves beyond chords involving three notes to sound combinations of up to five to six notes at once.

3. Drum Kit. The drum kit involves the bass drum, the snare drum, the hi-hat, and toms. The snare drum sound is by the far the most pronounced and overtly foregrounded, while the sounds of the drum kit are otherwise notably backgrounded overall, except for periodic quick and succinct tom rolls.

4. Vocal. The vocal is definitely darkened, sounding much like a baritone, yet treatment effects are contained so they are not as overt as in a number of other Joy Division songs, even as Ian Curtis's natural resonance is boosted with added studio reverberation. The vocal becomes notably louder, higher-pitched, and more insistent late in the song, at the song's climax.
5. Synthesizer Keyboard. This amounts to a high-pitched, shimmering on the border of shrill sound that extends across a marked series of beats with relatively little variation in pitch, and which adds texture to the choral refrain and to the pre-verse bridge transitions.

All four common functional layers are represented: an explicit beat layer, a functional bass layer, a melodic layer, and a harmonic fill layer. The electric guitar and the vocal are primarily responsible for the melody, with the vocal taking the lead in so doing whenever it is present. The electric guitar and the synthesizer keyboard play key roles in constituting the harmonic fill layer. The bass guitar contributes, in a complimentary and supportive manner, to both the melodic and the harmonic fill layers while also defining the functional bass layer. "Day of the Lords" maintains a persistent, foregrounded melodic line that we hear over virtually the entire course of the song with a number of slight variations. Overall, the musical patterns sounded by the electric guitar are the most varied, while the bass guitar is less so than in many Joy Division songs and also plays a less prominent role in relation to the melody than is often the case in these songs. The melodic layer is the most dominant, closely followed by the harmonic fill layer, while the explicit beat layer is further backgrounded and less prominent than often the case in Joy Division songs.

In terms of the soundbox, the bass guitar enters from low to the left and low to the right. The bass guitar stays down and remains closer to the back than the front but not far back. It is notably positioned on both sides and even though close to the center on both sides the bass guitar also, relatively unusually for Joy Division songs, seems slightly more prominent to the right than to the left. The bass guitar's contribution is persistent throughout the duration of "Day of the Lords" while highly repetitive. The bass guitar does not seem to move much within the soundbox over the course of the song, although right near the end it seems to rise a bit and move just slightly closer to the front and to the center, at a point in the song where the variation on the principal melodic line the bass guitar is sounding is more pronounced than otherwise. The drum kit, meanwhile, is positioned higher and closer to the front than the bass guitar yet also slightly to the right with the snare drum by far the most foregrounded. The hi-hat is the most backgrounded but the bass drum is also relatively quite soft overall; occasional tom rolls are more pronounced, more foregrounded, and higher up in the soundbox. Again, the drum kit does not seem to move much in position within the soundbox over the course of the song. The tom rolls do, however, seem to reach slightly to the left. But, overall, as with the bass guitar, the drum kit follows highly repetitive patterns throughout the duration of "Day of the Lords." The initial electric guitar sound pattern enters from high to the left and close to the front of the soundbox, with a subsequent chattering meets chugging electric guitar sound pattern seeming to come from the left as well further down below the center and not quite as close to the front as the initial guitar line yet closer than that of the bass guitar. The electric guitar sounds seem, overall, to push–or be pushed–further to the left than any other instruments. The soloing guitar sound patterns again comes from high to the left, and close to the front. Later, in the outro, the chattering meets chugging guitar sound pattern moves higher and somewhat further to both sides. The synthesizer keyboard is positioned close to the front, high up and to the right, and especially to the far upper right, of the soundbox, where it consistently remains. The vocal enters slightly low left center yet is closer to the front than the bass guitar and the drum kit. As the song proceeds, the vocal seems positioned close to dead center while with the choral refrain it seems to move higher and even closer to the front. As the vocal rises in pitch and volume near the end of the song, in the last verse and last choral refrain passages, it again moves up in the soundbox and yet closer to the front.

Working with this account of the structure and instrumentation of "Day of the Lords," we recognize the song is more elaborate than might initially seem to be the case yet is relentlessly reiterative and as such can readily feel entrapping. More precisely, it can readily feel as if the music here is enacting a simulation of entrapment that includes desperate yet futile gestures toward attempting to break past, if not out of, this entrapment by pressing up against and reaching beyond the confines in which we, together with the music as persona, are entrapped. "Day of the Lords" feels elegiac and funereal, suggestive of bearing witness and giving testimony in terms of a paradoxical synthesis of the passionate meets the dispassionate. The sounds, patterns of sounds, and deployments of sounds constituting the structure and instrumentation of "Day of the Lords" suggest on the one hand they are addressing us by way of a position at a temporal and spatial distance versus the principal subject matter upon which the song is focused yet on the other hand both the music as persona, and us as listeners, are simultaneously compelled to graphically imagine and viscerally confront the horrors the song evokes while not being able to emotionally distance ourselves from so doing. The structure and instrumentation of "Day of the Lords" feels like the metaphorical equivalent of being confined and entrapped yet not able to forget, ignore, or escape–or even to avoid continuing vividly to perceive and to need to engage with–what we are only in part physically distanced and separated from. The atmosphere the song conjures resembles that of a long, uncertain, and immensely fraught interval between explosions, as if being trapped within a powder keg with a long as well as intermittent fuse that keeps repeatedly exploding and then reassembling out of the shards of each successive explosion to prepare the way on the unpredictable countdown toward exploding yet again–and yet again.

"Day of the Lords" remains consistent in terms of overall loudness. Neither the beginning nor the ending is notably softer than rest of the song. The shrill synthesizer shimmers are especially loud, almost piercing, while the electric guitar is often quite loud, both as a solo melodic and as a harmonic fill instrument. The vocal becomes louder as it becomes higher pitched later in the song. Yet we gain no relief or release by means of variations in loudness.

The time signature for "Day of the Lords" is 4/4 and its tempo, in terms of BPM, is 124 (that is, for the version of this song I am listening to, in writing this section, from the 2007 2-CD 'Collectors Edition' of *Unknown Pleasures*, released by London Records). UltimateGuitar.com identifies the tempo as slightly slower, starting at 108 BPM in the intro section and then in the rest of song proceeding at 115 BPM. According to the drum kit tab provided by UltimateGuitar.com, a pattern involving bass drum strikes on beats one and two and snare drum strikes on beats three and four is fairly common, throughout "Day of the Lords," all of these consisting of eighth notes combined with ample rests between strikes on each of these respective drums. The hi-hat pattern involves two eighth note strikes occurring on every beat except when an eighth-note open hi-hat strike is followed by an eighth note rest and then in turn followed by six closed hi-hat strikes. Tom strikes are sixteenth and thirty-second notes, and occur in the second halves of measures. Notable also, the bass drum does not always strike on the downbeat and the same is the case with the snare drum while sometimes the second snare strike of the measure is left out and the bass drum takes its place. To me this sometimes sounds somewhat different than UltimateGuitar.com transcribes it, as if the snare drum instead quickly doubles, striking twice in rapid succession. This is the most dominant pattern I hear between bass drum and snare drum strikes, across a short two-measure-long hyper-measure: bass drum one, bass drum two, snare drum three, bass drum four/bass drum one, bass drum two, snare drum three, snare drum four. The snare, the most prominent constituent of the drum kit, often sounds to me like X-X-H-X/X-X-H-H, with H standing for a snare drum strike and X standing for no snare drum strike. The vocal tends to sound eighth notes for beats one and two and then quarter or half notes for beats three and four with ties into whole notes and greater in the choral refrain. The guitar sounds anywhere between six to twelve successive notes or chords per measure, with the strumming pattern predominantly involving eighth notes. According to UltimateGuitar.com, the guitar makes use of nine distinct chords in this song, and it does sound to me that both guitar patterns involve a considerable range and variety of pitch combinations. The bass guitar line involves primarily quarter or eighth notes, often quarter notes or eighth notes all the way through measures, or with variations involving quarter notes followed by eighth notes for the last beat, for the third and fourth beats, or for the second and fourth beats–along with some occasional half notes. The synthesizer keyboard tends to stay on roughly the same pitch for one to one and one-half to two measures at a time.

"Day of the Lords," as I hear it, contains a deceptively simple seeming rhythm, with in fact just enough complexity, just enough variety within instrumental lines and between them, to allow the song to feel jarring and disturbing as well as constricting and entrapping. The relatively slow to moderate tempo is belied–and complicated–by the predominance of eighth notes, and the occasional to periodic interruption of this predominance with sixteenth and even thirty-second notes as well as the guitar and the synthesizer adding even further variations in the number of distinct pitches and pitch combinations they sound per measure. Complications arise as well via occasional slowing down and falling back toward quarter notes and to yet longer notes as well, principally in the form of ties across measures, especially with the vocal but also with the synthesizer keyboard.

UltimateGuitar.com identifies "Day of the Lords" as played in the key of E minor, and that makes sense with how I hear the song. The most arresting pitch movements in this song occur with the vocal in the fourth verse and the fourth choral refrain, notably moving up and indeed starting up much higher while reaching up much further than in preceding vocal passages. The pitches of the synthesizer are likewise relatively quite high versus those of the rest of the instruments while the pitches of the bass guitar are relatively quite low. The electric guitar plays two principal lines, one relatively higher pitched and one relatively lower pitched, with the first more sonorous and the second more staccato. The predominant vocal pattern, before the last verse and the last choral refrain, tends to involve moving slightly down in pitch, twice, then up slightly more, then down, then up, and then down, while at the end of verses again rising higher. In earlier iterations of the choral refrain the general movement is lower, except at the end of these passages. The electric guitar involves much oscillating movement up and down relatively quickly, overall not conveying a sense of markedly extended risings or fallings in pitch (i.e., nothing approaching crescendos or decrescendos), even when encompassing a much larger pitch range, overall, than, for instance, the bass guitar. The bass guitar tends to fall in pitch and then return to the starting position to fall yet again, but relatively slowly so, while I hear a rise in pitch near the very end. The pitch of the drums sounds quite consistent other than with the tom rolls seeming to bring a rise in pitch. The synthesizer lines sound as if reaching up while not moving up all that far.

This complex of pitches, and movements of pitches, suggests a struggle that pulls the music as persona, and us with it, in starkly opposing directions, often at once. This complex of pitches and pitch combinations fits well with an interpretation of "Day of the Lords" representing a critical engagement with the persistent recurrence of human beings committing acts of atrocity, acts of horrific violence against other human beings, and especially of 'the strong' incessantly doing so versus 'the weak'. This complex of pitches and pitch combinations fits well, what's more, with an interpretation of this song as representing a vantage point that on the one hand feels implicated in and responsible for the harms committed by 'the strong' versus 'the weak' yet on the other hand identifies and experiences itself as among 'the weak'. The music as persona challenges us not to ignore, forget, deny, or in any way or to any degree downplay (let alone excuse, mystify, rationalize, and legitimate) the horrors it is referencing and alluding to, but instead to recognize these horrors for how horrible they truly are. Yet the music as persona does so from a position that evinces a simultaneous feeling of being trapped, leaving us feeling trapped as well, unable to do much if anything more than face up to horror for how horrible it truly is, as well as face up to our implication within and responsibility for horror along with our ripeness for victimization and destruction, in belonging to 'the weak'. As such, the music as persona casts doubt upon the possibility of ever overcoming this historical recurrence, and feels as if it cannot identify from where a movement capable of such an overcoming might emerge, even as it attests to the urgent and indeed desperate need, nonetheless, for such a breakthrough to take place.

Ian Curtis's vocal delivery in "Day of the Lords" exhibits characteristic features: darkened, sounding as if he is singing as a baritone, and tending to glide across measures at ends of phrases and especially lines while rising in pitch and volume late in the song. Curtis's enunciation is clean and added reverb embellishes rather than overwhelms such that his voice sounds only slightly doubled, amplified, and elaborated to resemble a chorus of the same voice multiplied and recorded so as to resound simultaneously together. Curtis's overall range is substantial but his movement in pitch in any single passage when he is singing covers a tightly confined interval range. Curtis sounds like he is singing, not speaking, and this comes across as evincing an elegiac to insistent quality. Curtis is not strictly confined by pitch but stays consistent in relation to pitch as well as rhythm, although tending slightly flatter as opposed to sharper. Curtis comes across as clearly in command of his vocal line. This vocalization involves the passionate meeting the dispassionate, and is representative of a controlled fury as well as, all at once, a performative distancing from, enactment of, and commentary on emotional registration and reaction. The vocal delivery, along with the delivery of the other instrumental contributions to the music, feel in charge, and not out of control, of what is being expressed and communicated. Curtis here comes across as 'singing nearby,' akin to Trinh's 'speaking nearby'. "Day of the Lords" thereby avoids the pitfalls that Trinh addresses in promoting the alternative practice of 'speaking nearby' rather than directly discoursing for and about, and, as such, usurping the place of 'the other'. "Day of the Lords" alludes to myriad numbers counted among 'the weak' for which 'no room' exists or has existed, but does not simply conflate the music as persona's particular identification and experience as 'weak' with that of all others.

Notable timbres in "Day of the Lords" include the synthesizer keyboard sound that becomes disturbing with its shimmering bordering on the shrill; the staccato chuttering meets chugging guitar pattern and the oscillating, bright and clean, sonorous guitar pattern; as well as the deep, dark, and ultimately soaring vocal. Other timbres include the low, rumbling bass guitar sound as well as the briskly clipped snare drum sound and occasional quick tom rolls. Collectively, the timbres, other than that of the synthesizer keyboard, seem 'natural' yet at the same time as if they are simultaneously attesting to an alienation, distortion, and perversion of the 'natural' that has come to be 'naturalized' as a result of the persistent recurrence and the continuous pervasion of atrocity that has come to be accepted as 'natural' as well as inevitable and inescapable.

I have already discussed "Day of the Lords" in relation to matters of affect but I will now address Arnie Cox's eight avenues of musical affect, keeping in mind in each case this involves what I hear the music itself as doing as well as what I hear myself doing in response. "Day of the Lords" is a persistently repetitive song so in that respect it should be no surprise that I do not detect significant differences in degree of ease versus effort of exertion while the duration of exertion lasts throughout the entirety of the song. Exertions here, as performed by the musicians, strike me as deceptively simple, or in other words more complex than they initially seem, and this is especially so when taking into account how these are integrated into a collective whole. In terms of accomplishment as result of exertion, this song manifests a sense of having done what it set out to do, which is to draw critical attention to, as well as reflect on the difficulties and challenges involved in confronting, a fraught and complicated subject matter. I feel the song succeeds in conveying the range of emotions it aims to convey. The most overt index of increased exertion comes with the vocal in the fourth verbal verse and the fourth choral refrain stanzas.

Insofar as I feel I am mimetically participating, I experience this most readily in connection with the vocal, in particular the choral refrain, and especially in both of the fourth vocal passages, although I also feel inclined to follow the principal melodic pattern throughout the song and to anticipate its persistence, its slight variation, and its return. I anticipate a climax as well as a denouement, and both occur. The music itself, and I along with it, anticipate this climax and denouement will leave us with a feeling of unrelieved desire and dread, yet also feeling we must persist, nonetheless. I have written a great deal already concerning what I hear the music expressing to me, but I will add I feel a strong sympathetic to empathetic connection with the vantage point from which the music as persona is expressing as well as what it is expressing, as I find both what the music as persona references and how it registers and reflects on its connection with what it references, to be highly compelling, while I identify with the urgent importance of honestly confronting the former, for how horrific it truly is, as well as share feelings of uncertainty, frustration, and anguish about what, if anything, we, the music as persona and I, can do about this horror. In terms of acoustic impact, meanwhile, what I experience as especially notable is feeling as if I am brought into the same space as the music, and surrounded by the music, such that I feel closely aligned with not strictly identical with the music, the musicians performing the music, or the music as persona.

As is common with many Joy Division songs, and especially with many Ian Curtis lyrics, "Day of the Lords" feels less as if it is undertaking analysis than it feels as if it is discoursing beyond analysis, after analysis has already happened, where the aim is to identify and describe, to register and reflect, and to protest and lament. The song is not discovering the atrocities it alludes to, in the course of the song itself, but rather pointing them out, allusively gesturing toward a vast number of these, and ruminating over what constitutes the connection with, implication in, and responsibility for these atrocities. I associate the song with a range of emotions, including sadness, grief, pain, worry, unease, fear, frustration, anguish, anger, despair, shock, sickness, revulsion, guilt, shame, and especially panic, dread, and horror. I associate what I feel in listening to and responding to this song with my own experience as a person who lives and long has lived with recurrent tendencies toward serious to severe generalized anxiety, including in the form of panic attacks, as well as depression. I associate what I hear through this song with the anxiety that extends beyond unhelpfully irrationally thinking about what is immediately confronting me in my daily life, such that this can be corrected by learning to replace irrational with rational thoughts. Instead, I associate what I hear with anxiety that takes the form of an overwhelming feeling of massive dread that has no simple, direct, immediate source or even series of such sources in my immediate personal experience, but rather corresponds to the dread I experience from living in the kind of society this is. As James Davies addresses in *Sedated: How Modern Capitalism Created Our Mental Health Crisis*, this is a neoliberal, global, racial-patriarchal-capitalist society. This is a society that not only individualizes experience of and response to mental distress but also a society that causes mental distress by fragmenting and separating people; by polarizing and antagonizing people; by forcing people into competition to survive and subsist; by encouraging people to equate happiness with commercial consumption and material accumulation; by discouraging assumption of shared responsibility of each for all; and by offering little to no institutionally instantiated incentive to practice kindness, caring, sympathy, compassion, empathy, and solidarity.

"Day of the Lords" confronts what feel like a taboo position: to feel trapped, unable to exercise any responsive, let alone reparative, agency, while forced, without being able to turn away, to confront my connection with, implication in, and responsibility for atrocity. The song is persistently as well as recurrently chilling, offering us no aesthetic pleasure from surviving this experience; this song feels nothing like a scary carnival ride, ghost tour, or thrill-seeking form of action sport.

In terms of invisibility, intangibility, and ephemerality of musical sounds, with "Day of the Lords" these qualities suggest a wide array of possible referents, in terms of specific past and present atrocities, as well as a wide array of possible experiences of pain and suffering, shock and horror, and guilt and shame concerning connection, implication, and responsibility. But these sounds also suggest a continuous struggle to bear witness, and to seek some way that we cannot yet fathom to do justice in response to what we are bearing witness.

It makes good sense to connect the relentlessly ongoing succession of atrocities to which "Day of the Lords" alludes with Césaire's characterization of what colonialism always has been, always is, and always will be all about. It makes good sense as well to connect Césaire's insistence that colonialism is indefensible, such that nothing can ever justify it, with the overall tone and mood of "Day of the Lords." The same with Césaire's charge that colonialism not only devastates the colonizer but also brutalizes the colonized, given the interpretation I keep coming back to, that this song represents the vantage point of a subject horrified not only by atrocity but also by their own connection to, implication in, and responsibility for atrocity. And if we take into account this subject's recognition and identification of itself as among the weak, then we encounter a ready source of connection with Césaire's argument that the roots of fascism lie in colonialism, that colonialism is proto-fascism, and that proto-fascistic practices conducted under the auspices of colonialism boomerang to become fascistic practices conducted against populations in colonizing countries, populations all too complacent about these practices when perpetrated 'against others' 'far away' while not anticipating it could all too soon 'be their turn'. Césaire's further argument that neo-colonialism is as much a problem as colonialism, that merely a formal end to direct colonial rule is insufficient to supersede the impact of colonialism let alone bring colonialism to an end, and that if anything post-WWII imperialism is more insidious than pre-WWII imperialism, also resonates with "Day of the Lords" because the song engages what it proposes is ceaselessly ongoing, such that it becomes hard to imagine 'where will it ever end'. The nightmare is real and continuous, it is happening all around right here and now, and it can no longer be ignored, denied, repressed, or otherwise mystified as something of an entirely different kind than it actually is–this is a nightmare from which it is impossible to wake up. If anything, it feels as if the song is suggesting the ever growing accumulation of 'bodies obtained' and the ever continuous refusal as well as elimination of 'any room for the weak' means the situation is worse, more extreme, more desperate, more apocalyptic, at the present moment (feeling as if the day of judgment at the end of the world is imminent) than it ever yet has been. Fascism here is not an anomaly, it is not an aberration, but rather 'business as usual'.

Where "Day of the Lords" diverges from *Discourse on Colonialism* is in foregrounding feelings of hopelessness, of being utterly trapped so as to be unable to contribute in any viable way to bring about positive change. Césaire is more optimistic, while hardly downplaying the enormous difficulties involved. Césaire is confident Africa and Africans as well as people around the world representative of a greater African diaspora maintain the capacity to reclaim and recreate liberated forms of society and culture, by themselves and for themselves. But this divergence between "Day of the Lords" and Césaire makes sense insofar as we identify the subject of the song with the position of the White European who finds themselves at odds with, and feeling threatened by, or at least alienated by and antagonistic toward dominant forces operating within their own European society at the same time as they are intuitively well aware this is a society that has enormous 'blood on its hands' and, as a result of whose impact on the larger world, 'the blood has never dried'. The subject of this song cannot identify with 'the Black political unconscious' that surrealism enables Césaire to make contact with, nor with Césaire's concomitant vision of Black liberation beyond colonialism–because the subject of this song is a White European subject. The subject desires to find a way to act, from where and how they are positioned, among the 'weak', but to their credit they do not imagine this to be at all easy to do. They are focused instead on attempting to confront and take in what they are connected with, implicated in, and responsible for honestly.

In relation to Said, it makes sense to link this song with not only a Saidean intellectual vantage point but also a Saidean mode of praxis. "Day of the Lords" foregrounds discomfort all the way through, as the song emphasizes not only evidence of extensive and incessant atrocity, but also both the music as persona's and the target audience's connection with, implication in, and responsibility for this atrocity. In this sense, "Day of the Lords" follows Said's admonition that the intellectual needs to work by making connections otherwise ignored or resisted, and by unearthing the buried and forgotten–or what is otherwise mystified and euphemized. Doing so risks unsettling, including for example, still widely prevalent British self-understandings concerning what the British empire was about, was like, and who it benefitted as well as how so–among those for whom this empire is judged to have been a triumphal achievement, a collaborative venture among partners, of positive value to all involved.

As a song, "Day of the Lords," what's more, illustrates how artistic means, and media, can make useful, and even distinctive, intellectual contributions. "Day of the Lords" is much concerned with the challenges and responsibilities of *representing*, as the song *represents* indirectly, suggestively, allusively, and through relentless repetition combined with sufficiently elaborate textural depth and complexity, as well as by means of sufficiently slight but crucial variations and developments, to conjure a sense of a complicated relationship between the subject matter of the song, itself multi-dimensional, and the vantage point of the music as persona and us, its target audience. "Day of the Lords" focusing on the impact of what 'the weak' experience, what 'the weak' suffer, while sympathetically and empathetically identifying as among 'the weak', also fits with Said's urging that the intellectual always work in the interest of the underrepresented and disadvantaged.

In relation to working in the interest of that which might yet be but is not yet, "Day of the Lords" comes across as more pessimistic than Said, but can make sense as referencing a prospective future time–and place–in which all 'the weak' will rise up in judgment against those who have been responsible for their victimization while inaugurating a fundamentally different kind of social order. Still, the bleakness of this song, and the sense of hopelessness it accentuates, corresponds more closely with how Said's characterizes Adorno's pessimistic position where the only real 'hope' it that his writing might make sense and use someday to someone who does not yet exist.

"Day of the Lords" does resonate as discoursing from a position as an outsider, as someone who is marginal, who is even an exile, and who lacks 'professionally' respected claims to 'authority', and as such is an 'amateur', in Said's sense, even if this is not a position so much 'embraced' as 'imposed'. Nonetheless, the subject in this song does come across as aware of the risks, dangers, and costs attendant upon this position. The lyrics of "Day of the Lords" come across as less confident of the narrator-protagonist's position than Said is of his, yet if we pay close attention to the music, and not just the lyrics, the song's tight composition and its precise delivery displays a confidence, and a sense of control, over where it is at, over what it is doing, from where it is proceeding, and toward where it is heading, throughout the expanse of its duration. As has been the case with multiple previous Joy Division songs I have discussed in this book, taking into account the music as well as the lyrics in interpreting meaning suggests "Day of the Lords," like many of those others, may be as much if not more about commitment, engagement, and persistence in struggle than about being overwhelmed by obstacles and opponents such that it is impossible to do other than merely attest to and lament failure. So, despite "Day of the Lords" suggesting to me an image of being confined and entrapped, the song also suggests to me a persistence in struggling from within and against the conditions of confinement and entrapment, doing so even when unable (yet) to recognize what might constitute a way out, into a genuinely different kind of space, a genuinely different kind of 'room', as well as *where* any openings into this new space might emerge. Certainly, Said rejects simple solutions to complex problems, and suggests the intellectual's proper role is to be continually questioning, challenging, and critiquing consensual understandings and normative practices, while "Day of the Lords" hardly offers anything akin to the former and keeps raising the question 'where will it end?' while challenging us to seek answers.

In relation to Trinh, the lyrics of "Day of the Lords," and the music as well, as is the case with multiple other Joy Division songs, can make useful sense as seeking knowledge and understanding, like Trinh, by working with and through confusion, uncertainty, incompletion, lack of and limits to control, the indefinite and the undecidable, the indirect and the roundabout, the elusive and the elliptical, the multiple and the proliferating, open-endedness and not just closure, perpetual process and not just process always directed toward a decisively finished product, and the in-between, the alongside, the liminal, thresholds, hybrids, taboos, cracks, gaps, fissures, fragments, borders, borderlines, intersections and intersectionalities.

In this connection, with Trinh, let's review what I have indicated concerning particular features of the music, to start. Despite its relentless regularity and consistency, enough variation exists within the parts played by each instrument, to suggest cracks, gaps, fissures, and other openings may well exist, but these are slippery, are difficult to find. Consider here such seemingly small, even slight, yet not insignificant variations such as the following: 1.) whether the snare strikes once or twice in quick succession the second time we hear from this drum in a measure, 2.) whether the bass drum takes the place of the second sounding of the snare in a measure, 3.) whether the bass drum strike and whether the snare drum strike coincides with the downbeat or the backbeat, 4.) between the initial open eighth note hi-hat strike and the following eighth note rest followed by six successive closed eighth-note hi-hat strikes; 5.) whether a quick tom roll takes place in the second half of a measure; 6.) in the alternation between the two distinct guitar parts as well as in how these parts are played, using what techniques, and the distinctly different pitch locations of each part; 7.) in the alternation among the number of notes sounded within guitar chords over the course of a measure; 8.) between measures filled with eighth notes and measures filled with quarter notes or combinations of eighth notes and quarter notes as played by the bass guitar; 9.) between the movement in pitch within the first and second lines of the choral refrain as sounded by the vocal; 10.) between the pitch locations and movements the vocal performs in the first three emanations (verse plus choral refrain) of the vocal versus the pitch location and movement the vocal performs in the last emanation (verse plus choral refrain); 11.) between the dominant melodic line as sounded by the vocal or by the guitar when the guitar takes the lead versus that sounded by the guitar when it does not take the lead and by the bass guitar; and 12.) between the predominant location within the soundbox the vocal and the bass guitar occupy over the majority of the course of the song versus movements up and closer to the front in the soundbox near the end of the song.

These and other small, even slight, variations contribute to the song conveying a feeling of not being quite certain where we are at, how are positioned, to what extent we can move, and what if anything we might do beyond feeling confined and entrapped. As is typical with Ian Curtis lyrics and Joy Division music, the situation we are confronting, together with the music as persona, maintains a considerable degree of mystery and this mystery makes the music all the more multiply and openly suggestive, allowing it can take on different meanings at different times and places in the same listener's life as well as mean differently for different listeners making sense of their experience of the song, and what it prompts them to think (about) and feel, as a result of their interpreting the song by way of different frameworks and from different vantage points. The suggestive yet nebulous character of the lyrics leaves room for multiple viable interpretations of how to interpret what they mean, while nonetheless also suggesting the lyrics themselves are caught up in reflecting on conditions of uncertainty, undecidability, and indeterminacy. The interpretations I have offered of the song as referencing incessantly recurring and horrifically violent atrocity suggest specific instances, or acts, of atrocity alluded to here are best made sense of as part of an ongoing process rather than as, each, in and of themselves, discrete, discontinuous, and disconnected products of discrete, discontinuous, and disconnected factors. And as is commonplace with many Ian Curtis lyrics and Joy Division songs, it makes good sense to interpret "Day of the Lords" as confronting and reflecting upon lack of control, or limits to control, here in particular from the vantage point of 'the weak' for whom 'no room' exists, no room which might provide a basis for exercising any such control. The image I have described, of what I see when I listen to and reflect on what the sounds, patterns of sounds, and deployments of sounds that constitute "Day of the Lords" lead me to imagine, is certainly as well an in-between, liminal, and borderline space.

It is further useful to interpret "Day of the Lords" as a post-punk parallel to or post-punk approximation of Trinh's conception of speaking, write, and otherwise discoursing 'nearby' rather than 'about' or 'for', because this song, and in particular these lyrics, allude to the experience of victims of atrocity, of 'the weak' broadly conceived, yet don't offer much in the way of specific detail of this experience nor pretend to be speaking 'as' if the narrator-protagonist of the lyrics, and the music as persona, know precisely what these specific victims might themselves 'say' in response to their experience. The concentration, instead, is upon how the narrator-protagonist, and the music as persona, are positioned nearby and on how the narrator-protagonist, and the music as persona, respond to this positioning. At the same time, "Day of the Lords" might usefully be conceived as a post-punk parallel to or post-punk approximation of Trinh's conception of 'reading across' because while a popular music song, ostensibly an instance of entertainment culture, the song alludes to and prompts reflection on extremely serious matters, and at the same time exemplifies pursuing a 'creative' means of engaging in 'critical' practice. It is even further viable, I suggest, to interpret this song as interested in a theoretical end, and that involves attempting to make sense of a long-ongoing history of horrifically violent atrocity as well as of what it means to be both connected with, implicated in, and in part responsible for, in part benefitting from, what has been gained as a result of commission of atrocity, while at the same time recognizing one's self 'among the weak' susceptible to being targeted and victimized by the same destructive forces.

It is more difficult, I suggest, to propose that "Day of the Lords" represents a break with, or a challenge to, problems and limitations of dualistic thinking, of the kind that Trinh emphasizes, but it can be helpful to bring to bear Trinh's theorization of subjectivity in interpreting this and other Joy Division songs. Typically with Ian Curtis's lyrics and in Joy Division's songs we only confront pronouns and collective nouns referencing vaguely anonymous groups. As I have suggested at multiple points earlier in this book and as the students I have taught in classes focused on Ian Curtis, Joy Division, and critical theory often do themselves, even without me prompting them to do so, it makes sense to interpret these entities as corresponding to different dimensions of, and within, an ostensibly singular self, one that is clearly not only divided but multiple. In the case of "Day of the Lords" it seems as if 'we', together with the narrator-protagonist of the lyrics and the music as persona, are both together with a vast many others among 'the weak' yet not identical with these others, and our present self, and present positioning, is both linked with yet distinct from our past self, and our past positioning. The song makes sense as a manifestation of the affective desire to find the basis for a complex form of identification, empathy, and solidarity that respects rather than collapses difference–including conceiving of and working with difference, as Trinh proposes, following Audre Lorde, as necessary basis for connection, and for unity.

Trinh, yes, develops and elaborates theory, whereas "Day of the Lords" 'speaks to' interest in, and need of, theory, but at the same time it is worth recalling for Trinh poetry can serve as a powerful mode of theorizing, as can stories and story-telling, especially story-telling that calls attention to itself as story-telling, and which is as much if not much more about what is happening in the time and place of the story-telling as it is about what ostensibly happens 'inside' these stories. Ian Curtis's lyrics certainly resemble poetry, or represent a kind of poetry, while these lyrics, and, as I have suggested, the songs themselves, as organized patterns and deployments of sound, resemble stories and story-telling, or, in other words, represent a particular kind of story and story-telling.

Notably, these lyrics and this music emphasize the persistence of mystery; they refuse to 'bring the universe down in size'; they confront, wrestle with, meditate upon, over, and indeed agonize and anguish over, but they don't provide singular, decisive, final 'answers' and they do not purport to 'solve' the 'problems' they take up. Likewise, these lyrics and this music tend to invite and encourage us to imagine the immediate moment in which, and the immediate location from which, they are addressing us, even as these lyrics and this music reference connections with other times and other places.

Yet the most meaningful dimension of these songs may well follow from imagining what it might be like to be in the immediate position of the music as persona at the precise time and place from which 'he' is addressing us in the precise, especially affective, terms 'he' is, over the course of the short duration of the song. "Day of the Lords," like many other Joy Division songs, is thereby not so much 'about' other people, and their experiences, in other times and at other places, as much as it is about the music as persona itself, in the time and place from which this is emanating forth, including what 'he' is experiencing, what 'he' is feeling, in mediated connection with other people, and their experiences, in other time and at other places.

I want to turn now to more directly address a series of questions, inspired by Lawrence Kramer's advocacy of critical hermeneutics as an approach to making sense of music's meaning, and which I have already addressed near the end of each discussion of each specific Joy Division song I have previously written about in detail in chapters two, three, and four of this book: *What do I hear these features seeking from me as my response and reply? How does this venture implicate and challenge me? What does it call forth from me, from whom I am, from where I come, from what I am about, from where I am headed, and from what I am seeking? How–specifically, precisely, and even concretely–can I respond? What simultaneously creatively imaginative and honestly authentic–even, and perhaps especially, raw and sensitive emotionally felt–response can I here give?* For me, responding and replying in such a manner involves making connections, which is indeed a principal points of emphasis I make in teaching critical studies. More precisely, to take seriously the challenge I hear this music posing, to me, these connections need to be daring, provocative, uncomfortable, and push me to my limits. I will focus on one source of such connections: Kehinde Andrews' 2021 Bold Type Publications book, *The New Age of Empire: How Racism & Colonialism Still Rule the World*.

The New Age of Empire: How Racism & Colonialism Still Rule the World is, for me, one of the most impactful books I have read in quite some time, and that is saying a lot because in the work I do I read many powerful and compelling books all the time, and especially so over the course of the past 20 months of long-term scholarly leave during which time I have been reading more such books than ever, well over 500 in fact. *The New Age of Empire: How Racism & Colonialism Still Rule the World* stands out, even as I have been, in this same recent period, assiduously reading and re-reading, and assiduously devoting myself to learning and re-learning, about the history of Black experience in the UK and the US, and about the history as well as the present constituent features of anti-Black racism in the UK and the US. I have been doing so not only out of a sheer intellectual interest, and indeed genuine fascination, but also as a matter of ethical and political responsibility, as one way of seeking to rise to the challenge the Black Lives Matter movement rightly poses to someone who identifies and has long identified himself as progressive, leftist, and socialist, and who conceives of empathy and solidarity as preeminent values, yet who at the same time needs to deliberately theorize and continually re-theorize, what it means, as a white person, to so identify, and especially what it means, and what is called for, in acting on the basis of that identification. Andrews excels at making incisive and sweeping connections, and doing so eloquently and persuasively, while not allowing any white reader, no matter how ostensibly 'sympathetic', to ever get comfortable–indeed continually making abundantly clear why we *should* not.

Andrews's introduction begins by declaring: "We urgently need to destroy the myth that the West was founded on the three great revolutions of science, industry and politics. Instead we need to trace how genocide, slavery and colonialism are the key foundation stones upon which the West was built" (xiii). Throughout his book, Andrews advances the argument that *all* of the achievements of Western civilization are rooted in and dependent upon what genocide, slavery, and colonialism have enabled. No such achievement is independent of that connection, and no such achievement is *innocent* of that connection. *All* of these achievements are rooted in and dependent upon massive exploitative expropriation from and horrifically systematic violence enacted against Black and Brown people, cultures, and societies. As Andrews declares, "A central thesis of this book is that White supremacy, and therefore anti-Blackness, is the fundamental basis of the political and economic system and therefore all interactions, institutions and ideas" (xxi). Throughout *The New Age of Empire: How Racism & Colonialism Still Rule the World*, Andrews substantiates precisely how this is so, while taking on, and refuting, every common defense of, and every influential apology for, what the West has done–*and is doing*. Andrews argues he is not here addressing a mere 'legacy' of the past but rather, as the title of his book indicates, 'a new age of empire', where 'racism and colonialism *still* rule the world'. The form has changed but the essence of racist and colonialist relations remains unchanged.

"In the new age of empire, the United States has become the centre of modern colonial power," which Andrews proposes well befits the true historic origins of this nation:

> The country likes to present itself as a victim of British colonialism, which freed itself from tyranny and now looks to do the same for the rest of the world. But this is a delusional fantasy. The United States is in fact the most extreme expression of the racist world order. Not only does the United States have its own history (and present) of colonial possession but its entire existence is based on the logic of Western empire. Built by enslaved Africans on land stolen through the genocide of the native inhabitants, the United States became a Garden of Eden for Europeans looking for wealth and opportunity. (xiv)

As Andrews elaborates, the US today exercises dominant influence upon the "major institutions that manage globalization and maintain the logic of empire under the guise of 'development': the World Bank, International Monetary Fund and United Nations" (xiv). And "This new regime is as effective as the European empires were at maintaining global White supremacy and colonial domination" (xiv).

At the heart of empire, past and present, is racism: "Racism is not only the glue that holds the system together but the material of which it is comprised" (xv). In developing this argument, Andrews follows directly not only from Césaire but in particular from Cedric Robinson, responsible for theorizing 'racial capitalism', as well as a substantial number of other leading Black radical intellectuals, past and present. As Césaire does, Andrews sharply critiques so-called neo-colonialism, including indigenous elites in formally politically independent former colonies who collaborate with West-based neo-colonial interests: "Diversifying those dining on the spoils of empire does not change the menu and there is nothing new about some Black and Brown people taking advantage of a framework designed to exploit them" (xix). "So-called independence in the former colonies has provided for a privileged few to reap financial rewards from access to a slice of the Western imperial pie," and this has included, as a minority fraction of those so benefitting, "A post-colonial elite" that has also "amassed wealth well beyond the dreams of even those doing relatively well in the West" (xix). But the racial capitalist *system*, even as it evolves in form, remains pervasive and predominant. This is a system that employs racism as principal means of enabling a scale and scope of exploitation that insures enormous global inequality between the West and 'the rest'.

714

Andrews proposes the European Enlightenment played a crucial role in authorizing, justifying, and legitimating racial capitalism, and, even more specifically, the genocide, slavery, and colonialism that Black and Brown people have suffered at the hands of Western racial capitalism. Andrews critiques the arrogant presumption of Enlightenment thinkers in equating 'the universal' with 'the European' and in constructing a racial hierarchy that placed White on top and Brown and Black below, and indeed often far down below, such that for many leading Enlightenment thinkers Brown and especially Black people were perceived as barely members of the same species, as 'subhuman' rather than 'human'. Andrews uses, in particular, Immanuel Kant's words against him, at some length, quoting Kant enthusiastically supportive of genocide, slavery, and the use of torture in forcing Black slaves into submission–with Kant clearly convinced that people of different 'races' were fundamentally unlike, and fundamentally inferior, to white people like him, and therefore entirely deserving to be exploited to benefit white people because these Brown and especially Black people were, according to Kant, inherently incapable of accomplishing anything else. But Kant is far from exceptional, as "Racial science was not some marginal concern at the corners of European philosophy, it was an integral component of its intellectual framework," while Enlightenment pseudo-scientific theories of racial difference and of racial hierarchy readily "bled into the Eugenics movement and gave the theoretical basis for the Holocaust" (10). What is especially damning of Enlightenment theory of race is it is founded on ignorance of non-European societies and cultures, and of refusal to recognize "The truth . . . that Europe was not superior to the rest of the world in the fifteenth century. If anything, the only part of the world in a Dark Age during that period was Europe" (11). Andrews chronicles an extensive record of impressive cultural achievement–including mathematical, scientific, and technological achievement–in societies that in fact surpassed, and far surpassed, the comparable achievements of their eventual European conquerors, even as the latter, falsely, labeled those they conquered as 'undeveloped', 'backward', 'primitive', and 'savage'. In fact, so many of the supposedly greatest achievements of Western civilization were long anticipated outside of the West, prior to arrival of conquerors from the West, "It is not an exaggeration to say that Europe is responsible for very few genuinely new ideas and made its advances by building on an inheritance of knowledge derived from other parts of the world" (17).

As Andrews emphasizes, "explorers like Columbus did not 'discover' a new and empty land to be exploited" because "When they arrived, they found millions of people living in complex societies who needed to be erased in order to create the clean slate necessary for Western progress" (26). Pointedly, "The genocide in the Americas is without precedent, wiping up to 99 per cent of the natives off the face of the earth" and therefore, "The bodies of those slaughtered are the foundation of the current social order. Westward expansion was the key that unlocked the bounties of European domination. Slavery, colonialism, industry, science and so-called democracy are all indebted to the tens of millions sacrificed at the altar of 'progress'" (26). What's more, "Although the genocide in the Americas was by far the largest in human history it is rarely commented on" (16). Many if not most Americans remain ignorant of or steadfastly deny that 'genocide' applies to what has happened here, while at the same time condemning the Nazi regime for genocide as well as condemning genocide perpetrated by "supposedly backward peoples in the underdeveloped world" (16), such as in Rwanda. Yet, "In truth, the West was birthed by genocide and relied on the slaughter of millions of Black and Brown bodies to enrich itself," so "You cannot separate genocide and the West, which is by far the most brutal, violent and murderous system to ever grace the globe" (26). It is often overlooked that

715

"the number of people who lived in the Americas when Columbus landed is 72 million" yet this population was rapidly, and deliberately, eviscerated. Just as one example, before Columbus arrived, the population of the Taino people, who lived on the island which is the home to the present-day Dominican Republic, was 8 million but by 1542 only 200 were left (28). Much more of this reduction is the result of deliberate, systematic murder rather than an 'accident' of exposure to disease brought by the Europeans for which the Taino maintained no immunity: "It is impossible to overstate, or even imagine, the scale of violence that Columbus inflicted on the Taino people," with a mere recounting of an accumulation of statistical results of this murderous violence quickly proving so overwhelming these become numbing. What needs, most of all, to be remembered, is "Columbus sparked the deadliest period in human history" (29). Further crucial to note well is:

When Columbus accidentally landed in the Americas, Europe was behind most of the world. Religious dogma, war and a Dark Age had caused European development to stagnate. Europe did not dominate the world in the fifteenth or even the sixteenth century. It was the wealth produced from the Atlantic system that propelled the West to the position it is in today . . . It was the profits from the Atlantic that allowed Europe to come to dominate the globe, leading the way in industry and science. But none of this was possible without the genocide in the Americas. Europe could not spread into the West and allow the indigenous people to remain on the land. They had to be cleared away to create the blank slate on which the West could be built. (33)

As Andrews also repeatedly recounts, again in line with Césaire, all of the main ingredients of the Holocaust were already long anticipated and practiced against Black and Brown populations that Western powers determined 'needed to be cleared way'. In fact, Andrews declares, "The logic of the Holocaust is *the logic* of Western development" (44). In other words, more precisely,

Since 1492 genocide has been a key organizing principle of the rise of Western modernity, from the annihilation of tens of millions in the Americas and the Caribbean, to the almost total eradication of the Aborigines in Tasmania. The Holocaust represents colonial practices coming into play in Europe. Africans, Asians and indigenous people being slaughtered by Europeans did not trouble the psyche of the West, but seeing colonial violence enacted on White bodies meant a complete re-thinking of long-held paradigms of race and power. Jewish people were racialized into a subhuman position using the same racial science that justified colonial brutality. (44).

Indeed, "Nazis justified the Holocaust using the same racial science that legitimated genocide, slavery and colonialism in the colonies" and "Jewish people became subject to the same genocidal logic as natives in the colonies because they were rendered subhuman by racial science" (48). In doing so, "The Nazis were not only influenced but also inspired by the network of Western scholars in esteemed universities who provided 'evidence' that Jews were less than human" and "They even copied the US sterilization laws as one of the first steps to eliminate the backward race" which means, again, "The Holocaust was the logic of race brought to bear within Europe" (49). It should not be surprising the Holocaust happened, *in Europe, within* the West, because "Racism is as essential to the West as water is to human beings so in looking to explain the Holocaust we should not look for

716

reasons outside the system itself" (49). In sum, "The uncomfortable truth is that the Nazis did not undermine the governing principles of the West, they took them to their extreme" (49).

Intricately interconnected with genocide perpetrated by the West against indigenous people in regions of the world conquered by the West, is slavery, which was the crucial linchpin of the 'triangular trade' among Europe, Africa, and the Americas. This was a highly unequal 'trade' between Europe and Africa, because even as this trade provided the impetus for the growth of modern capitalism and the industrial revolution, as well as made many Europeans and many European cities enormously wealthy. It resulted in not only a loss of "at least 24 million people" from the continent of Africa, consisting of Africans become slaves for Western slave-owners, but also African communities as well as African populations "were devastated and had to retreat from coastal areas and set up defensive mechanisms to avoid being stolen into the trade" (76).

Despite the fact "There is no doubt at all that slavery was facilitated by collaboration with Africans," this was very much "a Western system," such that whitewashing the history of slavery by referring to "African collusion, and particularly the narrative that the involvement of Africans somehow mitigates the West's responsibility for the system" is "nonsense" (77). Yes, as with Jewish collaborators with the Nazis, some Africans collaborated with the slavers, but African slavery was driven by Western interests, including by fierce competition among Westerners, and among Western nations, for profitable resources, while "In this system collusion and resistance often blurred together in the impossible situation that the barbaric trade created" (77). In other words, not only was massive enslavement of Africans enabled by Western superiority in weaponry as well as ample readiness of Westerners to put this superiority to use, but also Africans were often forced to trade others in order to free, or to save, family members and further relatives from becoming slaves. Likewise, Africans were often compelled to trade others for guns in order to help protect themselves and members of their communities from becoming slaves. What's more, "It is important to dismiss the notion of so-called African slavery from the start," as "What is often referred to as slavery in Africa is more like serfdom, where people were tied to a lord for a fixed period of time and enjoyed basic human rights," and where they "could rise from their position and eventually take full part in civic life" (78). Given the fact that Africans' experience of slavery in their own communities much more closely resembled serfdom or indentured servitude, "it is likely that Africans had little knowledge of what exactly they were selling people into" (78). Furthermore, no slave plantations existed anywhere across Africa, despite the fact that staple products of plantation slave labor in the Americas, such as sugar and cotton, "could have been cultivated on the continent" (78).

Nevertheless, Andrews also points out, even racism itself, including its use to justify slavery, is not an invention of the West, but rather of Arabs from North Africa. Still, even as "African slavery was endemic in the Arab world," it "was not essential to the political and economic development of that region" whereas "the Atlantic system" that "lasted for over 300 years, with a peak during the eighteenth century" enslaved twice as many people as the Arabs did over a period of time four times as long, while, in contrast with Arab practices of slavery, where slaves were primarily employed for domestic purposes as house servants for the wealthy, the vast majority of slaves acquired by Europeans were employed "to produce commodities on plantations and to power the development of capitalism" (80).

As "the legacies of slavery are all around us" (82), for those living in Western nations today, even when not recognized or not widely recognized as such, it makes sense to propose "that a debt is owed" to "descendant of the enslaved" (82). However, the West could not possibly afford the cost of full reparations for the wealth that slave labor made possible:

> to transfer the wealth necessary to repair the damage would destroy the West, not only because of the money involved, but also because if the Black world had freedom that would mean the end of the Western project. Reparations are due, and tearing down Western capitalism is an utter necessity if we are serious about ending racism. But to realize the revolutionary politics necessary for this transformation we first need to recognize the West can never pay full reparations for slavery without destroying itself. (84).

The wealth generated via the Atlantic system subsequently "enabled European powers to colonize large parts of Asia and to replace slave labor with the inhumane wages we still see in the world" (88), especially in the so-called 'Third World', where workers producing goods made for Western consumption earn a pittance, a literal starvation wage, while multinational and transnational capitalist corporations based in Western nations enjoy massive profits from control over production of these goods. Throughout the vast majority of these erstwhile colonized nations that gained formal political independence following World War II, "Nothing has changed today, except that the countries are now formally free" (91). Today, "Millions of poor people in the underdeveloped world find themselves trapped in work and working conditions similar to those under colonial rule" while "The majority of these workers are not employed on a permanent basis, making them even more insecure" (92). Upon achieving formal political independence, many of the nations of Africa confronted huge challenges because "Europe has not only stolen their wealth but has also prevented the development necessary for them to prosper," and this "put African governments in an almost impossible position because their economies needed mass investment but remained under economic oppresson from the West" (93). As Andrews further explains,

> Colonialism has left the newly independent countries underdeveloped. They lacked basic infrastructure and were impoverished by colonial exploitation. After so-called independence neo-colonial trade practices ensured that even if they were rich in resources, like most African countries, their wealth was in the hands of foreign nationals . . . Most of the underdeveloped nations found themselves in steep debt not long after the mirage of their liberation, and the IMF [International Monetary Fund] was only too willing to oblige them with loans. Unlike lending to Western countries, in the underdeveloped world these loans had strong conditions; they came with strings attached . . . For their economies to prosper and therefore pay back the loans they would have to make structural adjustments to their economic life . . . [including] abolishing controls on imports, imposing austerity to reduce the size of the state, devaluing the currency and opening the doors to private investors. (117)

As Andrews aptly points out, "Reducing public spending is a euphemism for cutting jobs and privatizing services, making them more expensive, in the poorest countries in the world" (117). What's more, "by devaluing the currency, privatizing utilities and opening up the country to foreign direct investment, structural adjustment makes the receiving nations ripe for takeover by Western interests" (118). In the new age of empire, overwhelming control of neo-colonized nations' economies and overwhelming influence over neo-colonized nations' polities by neo-colonizing interests located in the West is what perpetuates the colonial relationship. As Andrews declares, "the West is not rich because of its genius, democracy and capitalism," but rather "It is affluent because it has expropriated wealth from the underdeveloped world: the Rest is poor *because* the West is rich" (119). In sum, "Western imperialism did not end after World War II, it merely evolved" (136), and imperialism depends upon racism as an indispensable enabling condition of possibility. As such, debates over whether 'the existence of the State of Israel is a racist endeavour' miss the much larger picture, not simply because 'of course if it is' but rather on account of the fact that "the United States, Australia, Argentina, Brazil and any other settler colony are all 'racist endeavours'" (136).

In connection with these kinds of debates within 'the left' in the West, Andrews finds those principally involved remain too narrowly focused, concentrating on advocating what would be good for people within their nation, and not taking into account how far the relative advantages their nation enjoys versus many if not most others across the globe is a result of extensive prior and continuously ongoing exploitative expropriation from these other nations. This includes advocates of a Green New Deal, of universal basic income, and of a return to and restoration of post-World War II social democracy. As Andrews contends, "on neither side of the Atlantic," within either the US or the UK today, "is there any real effort to address the problems of global inequality. In keeping with colonial logic, 'equality for all' really means improving the lives of those in the West" (167). In this respect, Andrews proposes that "We have come to expect too much from the left because we have neglected to understand that its intellectual heritage is just as rooted in the progress narratives as neoliberalism's" (170). For instance, "Marx remains at the core of radical Western thought, but he was just as much as product of the Enlightenment as Kant" (170). As Andrews further explains his critique of Marx–and of Marxism:

> Marx thought that the technological progress brought about by capitalism was essential to providing the abundance necessary for human liberation. Ideas of White supremacy and scientific progress led by the West are absolutely integral to Marxism and remain its greatest limitation. Marx's inability to understand that the underdeveloped world was inhabited by fully human people capable of struggle led him to completely misidentify the revolutionary class . . . . history has shown that those who have embraced Marxism and committed successfully to revolution have resided almost exclusively in the underdeveloped world. In Cuba, China, North Korea, Guinea, Grenada, Mozambique, Angola, North Vietnam, and even in beloved Mother Russia the revolution was largely led by the peasantry rather than the workers . . . . It is a paradox of Marxism that the Western industrial workers never managed to produced a communist revolution whilst across the underdeveloped world Marx inspired the overthrow of the state from Cuba to China, via Guinea-Bissau and many stops in between. Marx was so blinded by White supremacy that he was (and far too many of his disciples remain) unable to understand that the most oppressed, the true revolutionary class has always resided outside the West because of the racist nature of capitalism. The new so-called radicals today are no different, presenting alternative visions of the future clouded by Whiteness. (171)

Among these 'so-called radicals today' Andrews includes those involved in the Occupy movement, critiquing the notion that the world today is constituted by "the 99 per cent standing up to the evil 1 per cent who hoarded the wealth," as this represents "a delusional fantasy and a continuation of the universalizing of the White particular that we have seen from both left and right" (182). In reality, Andrews points out, "Global inequality is so stark that those on the poverty line in the United States are still in the top 14 per cent of earners worldwide" while "The average US salary puts you in the top 4 per cent of earners" (182). In sum, "In claiming to represent the 99 per cent, Occupy, perhaps unwittingly, followed in the path of Enlightenment universalism, speaking for the entire world through the very narrow lens of Western privilege" (183).

It is crucial in this connection to recognize, as W.E.B. Du Bois famously first theorized, that Whiteness grants even poor and working class White people in Western, White-dominant societies 'a public and psychological wage' on account of their Whiteness, and this entails real benefits: "Whiteness is not a mirage, there are actual benefits to being in the category that White workers have fought, and continue to fight, very hard for" (193). And this is true even as it is also true that "Whiteness is a tool used by those in power to control poor Whites, to tie them to the project of imperialism" (193). Western welfare state reforms, including in the form of social democracy, worked as long as capitalist interests could afford to tolerate these conditions, but with the rise of neo-liberalism these same capitalist interests succeeded in dividing working class and poor people once more along racial lines in order to attract White working class and poor people's support for privatizing and dismantling much of this erstwhile welfare state because its beneficiaries became increasingly associated with 'undesirable others', not just skivers and scroungers, but in particular people of color and especially immigrants of color.

Andrews concludes by asserting "The bulk of my work is about developing the politics of Black radicalism, which centres on uniting Africa and the African diaspora to create a true revolution, which remains the only solution to the problem of racism" (206), and this in turn for Andrews is intrinsically interlinked with and at the heart of 'the problem of racial capitalism'. Andrews comments on "The question that I get asked the most, and have no answer to, is 'What can White people do?,'" by elaborating more precisely what he means in indicating he has 'no answer' to this question:

The quest for allyship is in itself misguided. The problem is that society is built on a White supremacy that permeates every institution, intellectual framework and interaction within it. If you have come this far and believe that White people offering a meaningful hand of friendship is the solution you have entirely missed the point. It is not the place of the oppressed to suggest a progressive role for those who benefit from their oppression. My hope is that understanding the scale of the problem and the limits of the solutions offered can spark a conversation about how to overhaul this wicked system. In one of Malcolm X's most famous speeches he offered a seeming olive branch to mainstream White society, arguing that America was 'the only nation in a position to actually become involved in a bloodless revolution'. All it had to do was give Black people 'everything they're due', in order to repair the damage done over the centuries. Malcolm did not hold out much hope, and busied himself with organizing the Black masses. If anything should be clear now, it is that we cannot wait for White allies to join the struggle to end their systemic privilege. (207)

In relationship to the kind and scale of transformation that is needed, Andrews does nonetheless perceive a glimmer of hope:

Maybe it is in this moment, standing on the cliff-edge of annihilation, staring into the abyss caused by Western so-called civilization, that the depth of the problem and the scale of the solution can be grasped. Perhaps we can wipe away the illusions of progress based on the distorted vision of Whiteness we are brainwashed into. This is the chance to refuse the next update of imperialism, destroy the hard drive and create an entirely new framework for the world's political and economic system. But make no mistake, whether spurred by revolution or tipped into collapse under its own weight, the West will eventually fall. Malcolm was right when he warned that it will be 'the ballot or the bullet, liberty or death, freedom for everybody or freedom for nobody'. (208)

As a final word, Andrews shares the following: "If you have got this far, then thank you for reading. Another world is possible if we accept the scale of change necessary to build it. Revolution is not just possible, it is essential" (239).

I have already commented several times in this extended summary of Andrews's book on how his arguments coincide with those of Césaire, but I also suggest he is representative of the kind of intellectual Said is promoting in *Representations of the Intellectual*, as Andrews is certainly writing on behalf of–and indeed re-theorizing precisely who are preeminently–the under-represented and disadvantaged, certainly speaking truth to power, and certainly in a way that is deliberately unsettling of orthodoxy and commonsense among many participant in what Andrews would identify as 'the White left', notably versus Marx and Marxism. Andrews does not write in the formally deconstructive way Trinh does, and he does not focus directly on matters of patriarchal sexism or hegemonic masculinity, but the uncompromisingly radical critique he advances of 'the West' as a totality resembles what Trinh advances versus the entire discipline of anthropology, while Trinh's insistence, following Audre Lorde, that 'the master's tools will never dismantle the master's house', and it is necessary therefore to think, speak, write, and act radically differently, and especially to radically reconceive and radically reorient what identity and difference mean, in turn resembles Andrews's insistence that nothing but revolutionary transformation and supersession of the entire 'project of the West' led by those excluded from and marginalized by the West is acceptable. With "Day of the Lords," the connection to Andrews's argument I perceive involves an intuitive recognition that something is fundamentally wrong, and indeed based on a fundamental lie, about the society and culture from which the narrator-protagonist of the lyrics, and the music as persona, are coming. This renders those sharing this position undeniably connected with, implicated in, and responsible for incessant and pervasive perpetration of horrifically violent atrocity, even those in this position who find themselves appalled and frightened by this violence–and even when they feel acutely vulnerable, as themselves recognizably also among 'the weak', to victimization by the same forces and interests that have been leading the way and achieving the greatest benefit from the commission of atrocity. 'Western civilization' itself, as fundamentally rooted in and dependent on genocide, slavery, and colonialism, rises to the apocalyptic scale of what this song references.

I think, contrary to what Andrews argues, that, even as the achievements of Western culture and civilization are undeniably rooted in, dependent upon, and enabled by genocide, slavery, and colonialism, these achievements are not entirely reducible to merely the epiphenomenal reflux of these roots, dependencies, and enablements. I do think 'the West' has been and continues to be a more contradictory entity that Andrews allows, and that Western achievements can and do provide value other than reiterating and reinforcing socio-economic and socio-political inequality between the West and 'the rest'. I think these achievements are partially autonomous while only partially so, and as such never entirely innocent. I also think Marxism is more open to taking into account what Andrews addresses than Andrews perceives. Yes, Marx concentrated on the Western industrial worker, but Marx himself was beginning to take note of, to study, and to attempt to make sense of forms of class struggle in contemporary societies beyond Western Europe, and it is often forgotten or overlooked that Marx conceived what he achieved at the height of his theoretical production as only the beginning, and only an in fact limited proportion, of the theorization of capitalism as a totality that he identified as ultimately needed. Marx was highly attentive to theorizing concretely and to recognizing that theoretical work was of necessity endlessly ongoing because the object of theoretical investigation and explanation was always changing. After all, Andrews himself cites numerous Black and Brown radicals and Black and Brown revolutionary movements, in the supposedly 'underdeveloped' 'Third World' 'global South', who found Marxism so inspiring that they placed Marxism at the center of their own revolutionary praxis, while themselves contributing toward the further evolution and development of Marxism, as theory and practice. Their example again suggests Marxism can–and indeed should–continually develop beyond Marx, that Marxism can and indeed should operate as 'a living science', as a 'dynamic mode of critical praxis', rather than as any kind of dogmatic orthodoxy. Often enough, Marx and Engels both urged exactly the same. What's more, many Marxists have long recognized the central role of other classes in contributing to revolutionary struggle, beyond that of the industrial proletariat alone, especially in conditions of 'uneven and combined' global capitalist 'development'. Yet those kinds of workers, in the classic Marxist sense of what this category encompasses, have in fact mobilized as revolutionary agents–in 1848, at the time of the Paris Commune in 1871, in multiple Western European nations at the end of World War I, and in many other instances since, even where they have not achieved the critical mass to bring the prospect of revolution to the brink.

Western working class people have not always been coopted and contained by capitalism, unable and unwilling to proceed beyond support for reform within capitalism, and not always unable to recognize or seek to undermine the material and ideological basis of White advantage under *racial* capitalism. Cedric Robinson himself, although a staunch critic of the problems and limits of where Marx had ended up and of much of where Marxism since had not yet proceeded, nonetheless identified the theory he was developing as theory drawing considerably from and considerably enabled by Marx and Marxism even while substantially modifying and revising this source, just as Andrews is also doing. Even if it makes sense to charge classic Marxism with inadequately theorizing race and racism, Andrews, like Robinson before him, still draws and relies heavily upon Marxism in theorizing *capitalism. Contemporary* Marxism is well aware of the changes along with continuities in conditions under which people work and otherwise live, in Western and in non-Western societies, including differences and not just commonalities between Western and non-Western situations and experiences. Revolutionary socialist transformation of capitalism into communism must always be reimagined and reinvented concretely, in relation to the precise conditions under which such efforts are taking place and by the precise agents who are leading the way towards such ends.

Nevertheless, I don't want to concentrate here on disagreements with Andrews because I find his argument, overall, highly compelling. I grant it is quite possible, and indeed makes good sense, to propose that any movement sufficient to revolutionarily transform and supersede the current global capitalist system will be led by those exploited and oppressed on the basis of an intersection of race and class, within this system, and who on this account maintain the greatest material interest, the greatest material stake, in such an end. I grant that initiatives such as a Green New Deal, universal basic income, and a revival and restoration of social democracy, conceived and practiced solely within the confines of the wealthiest Western capitalist nations, remain problematic and limited achievements at best–and that we must conceive of poverty and precarity, alienation and exclusion, exploitation and oppression, and ecological crisis and emergency in global terms, not leaving anyone out, and not leaving any nation or region out.

I do grant as well that as a white person my position in relation to struggles for socio-economic and socio-political transformation may well need to be at the margins, doing my best, most of all, not to create, or to perpetuate, problems for those at the center, and indeed rightly at the center, of these struggles, leading the way in these struggles. What can and what should I do? I need continually critically to reflect on connections between what I experience, what I enjoy, and what is possible for me, and others like me, on account of whom I am as a White Westerner, with genocide, slavery, and imperialism, and with ongoing persistence and ongoing virulence of racism and imperialism today. I need to draw out these connections in what and how I teach, as well as in what and how I write, and in what and how I participate in and contribute to community service and civic engagement. I need to keep learning about Black and Brown's people experience, and struggle, past and present, within the US, the UK, and beyond. I need to confront and fight back against the impact of racism and imperialism in everyday life, represented by White-dominated institutions, organizations, and movements. This includes the current backlash against beginning to engage seriously with exactly the kinds of issues Kehinde Andrews writes about in *The New Age of Empire: How Racism & Colonialism Still Rule the World* in attempting to censor, and indeed ban, discussion of any of this in schools–and by attacking so-called 'wokeness', 'political correctness', and 'cancel culture' in the interest of pretending that genocide, slavery, colonialism, and racism are not and have not always been fundamentally shaping forces in the histories of the US, the UK, and the rest of the West. I need to insist that yes it does make sense that white people feel guilty and ashamed of what our ancestors have done, and what this has enabled for us on account of our whiteness, and yes it does makes sense for white people to feel guilty and ashamed at what our whiteness and our Westernness continues to enable for us, at the expense of what the vast majority of the population of the rest of the world suffers. This makes sense, and is indeed even right and necessary, even as we need to push beyond 'wallowing' in guilt and shame, instead striving to find concrete ways in which we can try to make a difference, however small, however partial and limited, from where we are at, in contributing toward dismantling the material and ideological basis of this unfair and unjust advantage.

723

This is likely for many of us to be an extremely messy process, one in which we will have to work hard to determine where and how we can make such a contribution, and it is reasonable to expect we may run into many at least temporary dead-ends in trying to figure this out, not to mention making many mistakes as we proceed. It is crucial, however, to make ourselves vulnerable, and to seek to find ways to engage in solidarity on the basis of where, and how, we are the most vulnerable–not conflating our vulnerability with conditions experienced by others more (even much more) vulnerable than us, not imagining our experiences of weakness are the same or equal to that of others in (even much) weaker positions than us, but instead seizing upon these as a basis from which to try to practice empathy, along lines of what Terri E. Givens advocates in her book *Radical Empathy: Finding a Path to Bridging Racial Divides*.

Givens defines 'empathy' as "the ability to see the world from another person's perspective, in order to understand their feelings and life experiences" (1). Givens in turn defines 'radical empathy' as 'taking this a step further', as "also to be motivated to create the change that will allow all of us to benefit from economic prosperity and develop the social relationships that are beneficial to our wellbeing" (1). In other words, "Empathy allows us to see the humanity in others, and radical empathy moves us to work towards social justice and change that will benefit us all" (1). White Western people can't make much of any useful contribution toward combating, undermining, and overcoming racial capitalism unless we are able to at least try, sincerely, to imagine what it might well be like *not to be us*, to experience the world from the vantage point of being a poor Black or Brown person living outside of the West, or even being a Black and Brown person living within the West yet dealing every day with the impact of racism, including in systemic, structural, and institutional form. If we can really do this, we might begin to recognize precise, specific, and concrete instances in the everyday life experiences we live where these are constructed and conducted in ways that, even if largely unconsciously for most white Westerners, enforce and reinforce racism and imperialism. And from there, on the basis of such recognition, we can seek to try to figure out how any of this might possibly be changed, even if requiring a long process and a long struggle for that change to happen.

Givens stresses radical empathy depends upon "a willingness to be vulnerable" and "becoming grounded in who you are" as well as upon "opening yourself up to the experiences of others," practicing and taking action on behalf of what you profess to believe, and striving to create change while building trust as you work to do so (21). White Westerners need to keep listening and learning, while being alert to avenues and opportunities where we might be able to make a useful contribution toward a needed difference. But we also must not become complacent and self-congratulatory; if what is needed ultimately involves revolutionary transformation and supersession, along lines such as those Andrews advocates, then we are never done until we get there, and this is going to involve dramatic changes in our own positions and relations, our own everyday conditions of existence and our own everyday lived experiences, many of which we cannot readily anticipate let alone fully prepare for, well ahead of their emergence.

Yet, in contrast with Andrews, I believe even those of us enjoying relatively considerable material advantage, as White Westerners, suffer from living under racial capitalism, where we live lives that are highly individualized, atomized, reified, and compartmentalized; where our relations with all too many others are far more competitive than cooperative; where isolation and loneliness is all too commonplace; where vulnerabilities and weaknesses put us at risk of extensive deprivation and exclusion as well as considerable pain and suffering; where many of those qualities that make us the best possible human beings we can be in terms of how we relate to and treat each other are all too commonly identified and treated as vulnerabilities and weaknesses; where happiness and success are not only commonly defined by, but also intricately interconnected with, commercial consumption, material accumulation, and commodity fetishism; and where the intrinsic logic of the Western racial-patriarchal-capitalist-imperialist system continually threatens to undermine and ultimately destroy the common interest, the public good, collective well-being, and even the long-term survival and subsistence of our own and other living species on this planet. We *can* live much better than this, we *need* to live much better than this, we can and we need to live much more humanely and much more humanly, even if for some of us doing so will mean living a relatively far less 'luxurious' lifestyle than that to which we have always, all our lives, been thoroughly accustomed.

Marxism conceives of *socialism* as a form of human society in which the working class (people who contribute through their labor to producing social wealth, and who need to do so, under capitalism, in order to obtain the means by which they can survive and subsist) collectively owns and controls social production, while likewise exercising collective authority over what happens in politics and culture. Marxism conceives of *communism* as fully realized socialism where there is no longer any need for a separate state and where social class divisions have been superseded; individual and group differences persist (and new ones develop) but these are not based on exploitative ownership and control over others' creative and productive powers and capacities. Marxism proposes socialism represents not only the most progressive direction for overcoming the problems and limitations of capitalism but also it develops *from within the contradictions of capitalism itself* rather than as something coming to capitalism entirely from outside of the latter. At the same time, most Marxists believe there is no guarantee socialism necessarily will come after capitalism–an even much worse form of 'barbarism' might succeed capitalism instead (and this is a 'barbarism' that has nothing to do with the 'barbarism' colonizers claimed those they colonized supposedly exhibited, justifying their subjugation, but much more to do with what Césaire charges infects the colonizers, and colonized nations, as a result of colonialism, and which instead closely resembles a supra-fascism, a fascism without compromise or mitigation, and without any outside, exit, or end). Likewise, most Marxists conceive of socialism as a movement of self-emancipation of the *international* working class that will only truly succeed by transcending national boundaries and divisions. *Proto-socialist tendencies within capitalism* show up wherever people engage in cooperative and non-exploitative forms of creative and productive activity, wherever profits are shared among all who work to enable their generation, and wherever the aim of an enterprise is not to produce a profit at all but rather to satisfy a public or communal need. So, in short, within our capitalist society, many proto-socialist tendencies are at work, and long have been.

Finally, in relation to socialist struggle, Marxists actively support all kinds of reform within capitalism that reduce exploitation, alienation, oppression, injustice, and suffering while arguing at the same time these problems will persist, will recur, and will reemerge as long as this is all that happens, and as long as no movement pushing beyond reform toward revolution ever takes place–which ultimately, of necessity, because capitalism is a global social system, must succeed on a global scale. Moving from reform to revolution demands continually pursuing ways of pushing reform beyond reform, including moving beyond the constraining confines of local/regional/national boundaries. Moving from reform to revolution demands continually pursuing ways of turning quantitative changes or accumulating improvements into qualitative changes or fundamental transformations. This is never easy, never guaranteed, full of risk, prone to setback, liable to defeat, replete with contradiction, fraught, terrifying, and exhausting. No abstract blueprints can direct the way. This happens in concrete practice, via direct engagement, with those so involved, in the moment, in the event, in the arena, the ones to find and define the ways forward. Nothing else can be done, in seeking to move from reform to revolution–*this* is what needs to be done.

Seven

In a July 2020 interview with Anna Conrad for *GQ* magazine, in commemoration of the 40th anniversary of the making and release of *Closer*, Stephen Morris declares:

> "Colony" is probably my favourite Joy Division song. Again, it's got a literary reference to Kafka, which Ian was reading and I read a fair bit as well. Whereas all the early songs were punky, thrashy things, we were trying to do stuff that was a bit unsettling. I really thought Ian's lyrics on that one were absolutely fantastic. He'd had it for a while, so it was an easy one to do. There was no messing about, with Martin doing the drums or anything. It was pretty much done more or less live because we all knew exactly how it went.

In a review, for AllMusic.com, meanwhile, Ned Raggett describe the same song, the fourth song on *Closer*, as follows, while touting it as simultaneously both a "straightforward rocker" and "still shot through with the experimental, off-center touch that makes the album such a fascinating listen still":

> Bernard Sumner's choppy then squalling guitar gets matched by an inventive and definitely not straight-up rave-up rhythm from Stephen Morris and Peter Hook–not quite prog rock per se, in that said tempo doesn't change throughout, but a definite sign of the group's interest in looking beyond the obvious even at their bluntest. Ian Curtis's vision of a strange modern urban setting as home of alienation and, to quote Curtis directly, "dislocation" recalls everything from T. S. Eliot and Kafka to J. G. Ballard. The twisted religious mantra concluding the song–"God in his wisdom took you by the hand/God in his wisdom made you understand"–is delivered in an aggressive but pitiless fashion by Curtis, his own crushed, human stance caught in the off-center grind and pull of the music.

And in SongMeanings.com contributors offer interpretations that make sense of "Colony" as about Ian Curtis's marriage, his depression, his epilepsy, and his suicidality, as well as about World War II and Nazi Germany, either attempting to escape from Nazi persecution or feeling guilty about participating in this persecution, along with interpretations that make sense of the song as dealing with the travails of boarding school or living in suburbia, about institutionalization or fear of institutionalization in an asylum, about a struggle with religious faith and doubt, and about Joseph Conrad's *Heart of Darkness*.

The most elaborate interpretations of this song tend to focus on connections with Franz Kafka's "In the Penal Colony." Clayton Crockett, in his essay "In the Colony with Joy Division," a contribution to the 2014 book *The Counter-Narratives of Radical Theology and Popular Music: Songs of Fear and Trembling*, edited by Mike Grimshaw, links "Colony," by way of Kafka's "In the Penal Colony," with both neo-colonialism and an even broader and more diffuse mode of colonization of consciousness, notably through mass media, that "invades private experience and grasps and redirects attention and desire to direct them toward the consumption of commodities in a hypercapitalist economy" (30). Joy Division, in particular in "Colony" but also elsewhere as well, serves "as a witness to this process, and a testimony to the negative effects of this colonization of consciousness, to which Curtis was incredibly sensitive" (30).

In order to understand the connection with Kafka's "In the Penal Colony," Crockett summarizes the story. As Crockett notes, this story is set on "an unnamed island, a penal colony where an unnamed traveler (or explorer) observes the practices of sentencing and judgment carried out on the bodies of criminals using a harrowing machine" (30). More precisely, I suggest, it is worth noting in Kafka's story the principal characters are all identified by function: "the officer, the explorer, the condemned man . . . and the soldier" (Kafka 191) as well the new Commandant and the old Commandant. Also, the explorer only observes one instance of the use of this machine, seemingly its last ever use. The machine that performs the punishment involves, more precisely, the condemned strapped to a bed where the body of the condemned is 'written on' by the harrow, inscribing the explanation for the punishment into the body, proceeding as a slow, torturous process of execution that lasts up to twelve hours. The ideal result, according to the officer, who is in charge of the operation of this machine and a passionate enthusiast on its behalf, is that in the process of execution the condemned, in Crockett's words, "realizes, accepts, and embraces his sentence and his impending death" (30).

Crockett mistakenly identifies the Commandant as the one who operates this machine, demonstrating it to the explorer, which is a problematic error, because much of the dramatic tension of the story involves the officer, increasingly desperately, striving to convince the explorer to use his influence, as an outsider from a prestigious European location, to undermine the new Commandant's inclination to phase out and end this form of punishment. The officer is fiercely loyal not only to the machine, its method, and purpose, but also to the now deceased and disgraced old Commandant, who was responsible for initially conceiving and designing the machine. Yet the explorer, initially reluctant to interfere, becomes increasingly disturbed at recognizing what this process of execution involves, as well as how those condemned to execution by means of this machine are simultaneously judged and punished such that they are presumed guilty, once charged, with no means available for them to attempt to prove their innocence.

The officer complains throughout his explanation of how the machine works that because its use is out of favor with the new regime it has been difficult to secure needed replacement parts and that executions that once were well-attended, popular spectacles, now take place with virtually no one ever watching. But what makes the lead-up to the climax all the more harrowing, beyond the officer's fanatical enthusiasm for this practice of torture, as well as the typically Kafkaesque automatic presumption of guilt, is the condemned man does not know French, the language the officer is speaking with the explorer, and as such appears ignorant of what is about to happen to him.

The officer further complains to the explorer that the new commandant as well as 'his ladies' are both devious and sentimental, in their opposition to this mode of punishment, as he tries to win the explorer to his side, but the further the officer proceeds in his effort at persuasion the further he alienates the explorer. Once the officer recognizes the explorer will not help him with the new commandant, but intends to do the opposite, the officer substitutes himself for the condemned man, as the last person to be punished by means of this machine. As the officer is tortured and executed, while the machine breaks down in the process, his body is inscribed with the words "Be Just!" Yet this does not provide 'poetic justice', because when the explorer looks "at the face of the corpse" of the officer, "It was as it had been in life; no sign was visible of the promised redemption; what the others had found in the machine the officer had not found; the lips were firmly pressed together, the eyes were open, with the same expression as in life, the look was calm and convinced, through the forehead went the point of the great iron spike" (225).

In what amounts to the story's epilogue, the explorer seeks out the burial place of the old commandant, and reads the inscription on the tombstone: "'Here rests the old Commandant. His adherents, who now must be nameless, have dug this grave and set up this stone. There is a prophecy that after a certain number of years the Commandant will rise again and lead his adherents from this house to recover the colony. Have faith and wait!" (126). The explorer then quickly leaves the island, apparently eager to get away; when the soldier and the condemned man attempt to follow him, he violently threatens them away from the rowboat that takes him back to the steamer.

Crockett proposes the Joy Division song "Colony" "refers to school, probably a boarding school" (30). After "The parent packs the unnamed child's bag and sends him off to school" (30), the child suffers from "profound confusion" and "a feeling of dislocation" in this new setting, with "no sense of family life" in an environment full of "confrontations" that Crockett suggests renders this school "a disciplinary institution," in terms of how Michel Foucault theorizes disciplinary institutions, and as such "the school functions analogously to a prison" (31). As Crockett elaborates, "In the colony, or school, educator-judges inscribe their norms into children, which is an extremely long and drawn-out process that eventually kills their spirit" (31). As with Kafka's description of the process of torture cum execution, in which the condemned struggle for the first six hours, and then come to accept and identify with their judgment and punishment over the course of the second six hours, "In a similar way, education appears terrifying and painful to many children at first, but the goal is to have them identify with and coproduce themselves as judged and as normal" (31). So what we have here is a song that critically engages with "the inflicting and inscribing of norms literally and symbolically onto the bodies and psyches of young people" (31). As Crockett elaborates,

A boarding school certainly can be experienced as a penal colony, an exile to a strange place with arbitrary rules and punishments absent the familiar comforts of home. This practice of education, which is now usually deferred until college, should be thought of as neocolonial. Colonialism begins at home, at school, at work, and in prison. Or rather, what we call colonialism as the colonizing of other peoples becomes recursive in late 1970s Britain; it returns or 'comes home' to the motherland, where it all began. (31)

Continuing yet further, Crockett interprets "Colony" as referencing a significant historic moment, in the transition to neo-liberalism, which he proposes not only renews and accelerates colonizing processes abroad but also the same 'recursively' 'at home' 'in the motherland', while more and more people become oblivious to any problem in this form of colonization of their consciousness.

Crockett interprets the "discordant and choppy" rhythm in "Colony" as 'replicating' "in sound the movement of the apparatus in Kakfa's story, with the needles scratching their sentence on flesh in a way that is expressed by the scratching of the stylus on vinyl back in the days when people played records" (32). What the song is insinuating, moreover, by way of its allusion to Kafka's story, is a critical take on processes of socialization as normalization, and even as naturalization, such that alternatives become inconceivable, undesirable, or seemingly impossible. Crockett makes sense of reference to God's wisdom in the lyrics of "Colony" as ironic, where we learn to conflate an existing system of social arrangements with the equivalent of divine will, that cannot or should not be questioned: "We simply replicate this system of divine judgment on a human level with our disciplinary institutions," including through "internalization as self-judgement and self-condemnation" but in order to truly "Be Just!" we would need to reject this conflation of the social status quo with "the idea of God as the guarantee and support," or with a secular equivalent of God (33). "In the Penal Colony" is useful to such a critical position by "making visible the cruelty inherent in the system of judgment itself" and that, in particular, "School is a process of colonization of young people, to discipline their bodies and minds and train them to be savvy exploiters of other humans, good and just capitalists, and ncocolonial masters" (34).

"Colony" contributes to critique of colonization of bodies and minds, Crockett contends, by enabling us "to sublimate our own pain and identify with the revolt of our bodies and minds against the system of judgment that has been inflicted upon us" (34). Aligned with the song, we recognize that "The institutions created in the modern world are not vehicles of transcendence or humane methods to constitute moral persons, but incredible systems of domination and sublime cruelty that depend on the colonization of our consciousness to work" (34). "Curtis's haunting voice is a visceral protest against the injustice of justice" that is not calling for 'better justice' but rather for "help" in exposing and opposing the cruelty involved in normative systems of discipline and punishment (35).

Although not without appeal, Crockett's interpretation of "Colony" misses some of the characteristic ambiguity in Joy Division's songs' meaning, and indeed ambivalence in Ian Curtis's lyrics, that Sara Martínez usefully notes, in "Literary Influences on Joy Division: J.G. Ballard, Franz Kafka, Dostoevsky," chapter four of *Heart & Soul: Critical Essays on Joy Division* (2018). To begin, Martínez highlights that what passes for 'justice' in Kafka's penal colony is 'lack of justice': "There is no justice, no process, no transparency for the prisoner and little more for the observer" (55). Under the guise of justice what we actually confront here is suffering and trauma, with this practice authorized according to 'tradition' represented as akin to that of a God who cannot and should not be questioned. Martínez interprets Curtis, in "Colony," as "speaking through the voice of a convict who remains in a specific settlement mainly characterized by a heartbreaking background," or in other words inspired by the story to imaginarily identify with the vantage point of a convict in a situation akin to that of a 'penal colony," like that featured in Kafka's story, where, as a result of this positioning, "the subject feels both confused and isolated from the rest of the world," pleading desperately with God because nothing else seems able to help and no one else seems able to understand the subject's pain (56-57). Yet, as I will discuss subsequently, Martínez does not adequately take into account the complicating contribution of the music to the song, in making sense of what kinds of meaning "Colony" as a song, and not just a set of lyrics, or even a vocalized set of lyrics, conveys, offering a much greater feeling of determined energy and committed struggle coexisting with this same isolation, confusion, desperation, and fear that no one can understand and nothing can help.

In *Heart & Soul*, Gay Jennifer Breyley, as part of her chapter, chapter fourteen, "'I Hung Around in Your Soundtrack': Affinities with Joy Division Among Contemporary Iranian Musicians," cites David McKenna et. al, as part of a 2017 contribution to *Quietus*, in contrasting the lyrics from "the 'official' [*Closer*] version" of "Colony" with those from "the alternative [Peel] session" version (quoted 215). In the former "Ian Curtis is simultaneously culprit, victim and witness," whereas in the latter "it's more as if he's broadcasting from a human settlement on the far side of a scarred and blasted landscape, in the aftermath of some barely imaginable atrocity" (quoted 215), which, I note, closely resembles how I hear and make sense of what "Day of the Lords" suggests.

McKenna et. al. claim that the Peel session version, where "Sumner chopping at his guitar becomes helicopter blades whirring into life, Hook and Morris absolutely lock in to their metal-snake groove, and a subtle swell of synth at around 2.20 minutes in like a subterranean tremor" was likely "all too apocalyptically glamorous" to "have matched *Closer*'s exquisitely muted palette" (quoted 215). Breyley finds this characterization of the Peel session version of "Colony" analogously useful in explaining the contradictory positioning faced by popular rock musicians from countries like Iran who are struggle to break through on their own terms within popular rock music circles in the United States. It is difficult for many U.S. audiences to interpret the music these Iranian musicians create in other than reductive terms, either as exotically distinct from or as a lesser and inferior version of what American musicians do. As a result, Iranian rock musicians tend to feel trapped, in other words 'colonized', by confinement to restrictive and isolating niche locations (215-216).

Yet, as I previously indicated in reference to Martínez, the version of "Colony" included on *Closer* is a more complexly multi-dimensional song than McKenna et. al. suggest, hardly entirely 'exquisitely muted'. In relation to Breyley's use of McKenna et. al.'s take to comment on dilemmas faced by Iranian rock musicians, I find this less compelling than possibilities suggested by Clayton Crockett's reference to interpretations of Kafka's "In the Penal Colony" that he does not pursue in his specific interpretation of Joy Division's "Colony": "Europeans devise intricate and horrific means of punishment for native peoples who are criminalized in contrast to the European soldiers, judges, and executioners" (30). I would qualify this last point, though, by noting in Kafka's story the explorer is represented as an outsider, coming from far away, from a country that seemingly is more prestigious and more powerful than the island where the penal colony is located. It is difficult to determine whom among 'insiders' within this penal colony, including the officer, the soldier, and both the old and new Commandants, are likewise themselves 'coming from elsewhere', or as descendants of those who at one time did. However, even as the explorer is suggestive of someone who imagines a great distance separates practices of 'criminal justice' carried out in his country versus those carried out in this penal colony, the connection between the two is moreslippery than that. In other words, colonizers travel to and settle in colonies, which become in effect 'penal colonies', even when not literally designated as such, at least for the colonized 'natives', and over time seem to develop an autonomy and a disconnection from the original colonizing country such that when atrocities are perpetrated in the colonies these can seem to have nothing to do with the colonizing countries, and with the ostensibly far more 'civilized' practices of the latter. But colonialism represents the necessary condition of possibility for the invention and perpetration of exactly these atrocities. Given widespread ignorance, indifference, and self-protective belief in clear moral superiority versus what is and has been happening in the colonies, by many natives of the original colonizing countries, it becomes all the more readily possible for these same practices, directed against the colonized, eventually to 'boomerang' back to be perpetrated, to be re-invented and yet further refined, versus these same natives in the colonizing countries.

Matthew Boswell, in "Post-Punk: Joy Division, *Closer*" aptly interprets Joy Division's engagement with the Holocaust and comparable atrocities as drawing "out a paradox whereby one can only appreciate that such events cannot be conveyed if one somehow confronts the extremity that dictates *why* they cannot be conveyed," and, as such, *Closer* "blends an anti-representational ethos with references to a necessary encounter, inciting listeners to follow the singer's lead and, in imaginative terms, to transgress the border marked by the 'circle of fire'" (120). As Boswell elaborates, "The conceit of *Closer* is that the singer is in possession of some hidden or forbidden knowledge that the listener is urged to share" (120). This album, Boswell proposes, "has the feel of a journey through a modern-day hell, with Curtis playing Virgil to the listener's Dante" (121). Yet, Boswell qualifies, "If Curtis begins as a kind of Virgil, as the album goes on he is increasingly figured as a more detached and bewildered onlooker, compelled against his will to watch things he would rather not see" (121). We are not quite at that point yet, with "Colony," but nonetheless on our way. In this connection, throughout *Closer*, "Without ever being referenced directly, there is a sense that the Holocaust is a defining aspect of this underworld of the mind, and for Curtis it seems to have been instrumental in the formation of a world-view that sees the whole of human history *as* Holocaust" (121-122).

This interpretation adds further support for linking this song, as with "Day of the Lords," with the entire indefensible history of colonialism, with what the colonizer does to the colonized, and with colonialism equal to 'de-civilizing' 'barbarism' leading to 'thingification', as Césaire argues, in *Discourse on Colonialism*. It also makes comparable sense, more broadly in line with critiquing the entire 'project of the West' as responsible for doing exactly the same, as Kehinde Andrews argues, in *The New Age of Empire: How Racism & Colonialism Still Rule the World*. Aptly once more, Boswell also here makes explicit a connection I just have made between "Day of the Lords" and "Colony" as well as the rest of *Closer*: "The album as a whole thus expands on a question posed in 'Day of the Lords', from the first album *Unknown Pleasures* (1979), which asked where all the murder and mass suffering that had been inflicted in the twentieth century would end–a question that feels at once political and deeply personal" (122). As I likewise have argued repeatedly throughout this book as

731

well, "*Closer* necessarily addresses the continuity between Fascism and our own capacity for violence" (122).

To this take I add that many Joy Division songs, on *Closer, Unknown Pleasures,* and otherwise, emphasize confronting our simultaneous inclinations toward ignoring, denying, repressing, or otherwise mystifying our capacities for enacting violence (as well as doing the same in relation to our connection with, complicity in, and responsibility for violence that has been committed, is being committed, and will be committed), along with our susceptibility, nonetheless, to becoming ourselves victims of violence too, in particular as those socially marked, or readily socially marked, as among 'the weak' and thereby particularly vulnerable. What Ian Curtis's lyrics often do not find yet desperately seek is a substantively empathetic mode of collective solidarity, uniting 'the weak' in resistance versus allowing 'our weakness' to become the source of our destruction, and instead enabling transformation of what is normatively identified, disparaged, mocked, and targeted as 'weakness', in contrast, to become a paradoxically liberating form of 'strength'. The songs themselves, as music, as organized patterns of deployments of sounds, most often suggest an impetus to persist and endure. These songs, again as music and not just as lyrics, most often likewise manifest a determination to continue to struggle, even to continue to resist and oppose, and even to continue to push toward a radical breakthrough that cannot be grasped on any immediately perceptible horizon, yet which might yet be realizable in times, at places, and under conditions to be determined.

Let's turn now to work our way carefully through the lyrics to "Colony," allowing potential interpretations to arise through a close reading of these lyrics, and then reflect back after that on how it might make sense to interpret the title of the song. Line one, "A cry for help, a hint of anaesthesia," becomes especially interesting in attempting to discern a connection between what each successive phrase suggests. The second phrase serves, perhaps, to more specifically locate from where the opening 'cry for help' is coming and under what specific circumstances. "A hint of anaesthesia" suggests a possible medical setting, such as in surgery or in undergoing a comparable procedure, or perhaps, more disturbingly, in a war zone, at or near a battlefield.

Yet "a hint of anaesthesia" can also suggest ingestion of drugs that numb the senses via other means and for other purposes, whether self-induced or directed by someone else. In symbolic terms 'anaesthesia' can suggest a setting, or a situation, which calls for, or which induces, numbing of the senses and even desensitization–perhaps, as necessary, in order to be able to survive a prolonged ordeal. In connecting the two phrases, it is possible that 'anaesthesia' is applied in response to the 'cry for help', to attend to this need for and thereby to provide 'help', but it is also possible that the 'cry for help' is a cry of protest against the application, even the imposition, of anaesthesia–or against what people are being anaesthetized against being able sensibly to register, and, especially, to be able to deeply feel.

But the second phrase is even more complicated because it indicates "a *hint* of anaesthesia." This suggests application, or imposition, of anaesthesia is not direct, overt, heavy-handed, and obvious, but rather subtle and perhaps, as such, ultimately even more insidious.

Wherever this 'is' that the line refers to, it is a troubled, and troubling, location from which a cry of help comes and where we can also recognize a hint of anaesthesia. People who are hurting cry for help and people whose hurt cannot be attended to otherwise, or who are diverted from facing up to, confronting, and overcoming the source of their hurt, are subjected to anaesthesia, even subject to confinement in environments that are pervasively yet diffusively anaesthetizing.

Line two, "The sound from broken homes," suggests the preceding "cry for help" may well have emanated "from broken homes," may well have been the result of the 'broken' state of these homes, and, as such "a hint of anaesthesia" may represent a gesture toward palliation that is more about quieting the cry than effectively engaging with the source, the cause, of the cry. Then again, it is possible "the sound from broken homes" represents an additional sound, beyond "the cry for help," which adds to, and amplifies, the disturbing effect of the latter. Notable also we here are dealing with homes, and this implies multiple people are experiencing the consequences of the breakings, or breakings down, that have taken place in these homes, perhaps now more erstwhile homes than actual homes anymore given that they have been broken, with the consequence of this breaking likely including significant pain and hurt. "Broken homes" certainly can cause pain and hurt to all involved, but it is especially likely to do so with children–although perhaps also to erstwhile bonds between parents and children, or among parents, other adults living within the home, and children.

"We used to always meet here," line three, notably introduces "we," which implies, perhaps, that an 'I' who is addressing 'us' via these lyrics, together with 'us', are directly connected with and involved in the scene just sketched out. It is possible that 'we' might not directly include us, as listeners, but it certainly is plausible to interpret it as doing so. What we were doing "here," when "we used to always meet" in this place, and why *here*, presents us with a mystery to decipher. As we speculate concerning what this might have involved, we wonder did this transpire within and as a part of the fractured lives experienced in these "broken homes," or was it nearby, in the vicinity, close enough that we could hear, we could be aware, and yet where we were positioned just that slight distance away so as not to be at the center of the breaking and the fallout? Were we involved in emitting cries for help, were we provoking these cries for help, or were we perhaps doing both? Or, once again, were we instead only hearing, even overhearing, these cries–of others? Were we involved, as recipients of anaesthetics, were we responsible for inducing anaesthetics, or were we perhaps involved in both roles? Or did we merely from close nearby catch a 'whiff' of anaesthetics?

'Meeting here' also implies this is a a a location to which we regularly ventured, from somewhere else, for some specific purpose–but for what? And why did we "use to meet here" but do not any longer? What has happened? Are we implicated in causing pain and hurt, and if so, how much and how far so? Are we united as victims of such implication, in our experience of such suffering, and perhaps in its lasting, its shaping impact upon whom we are and what we have become?

"As he lays asleep, she takes him in her arms," line three, suggests moving in, for a closer perspective, even if we are traveling, perhaps in memory, into the past, into our past, where we are closely observing a 'he' and a 'she'. This seems like a comforting image, one in which 'she' is demonstrating care, and even affection, for 'he', and they may be involved in an intimate relationship.

733

Or they may be otherwise close, they may have shared a common experience in a common setting or situation, and they might as a result be readily able to recognize, sympathize, and empathize with what they each have experienced. Perhaps this is a setting where people are crying out for help, where hints of anaestheticization diffusely surround those so involved, and where people are suffering in pain and hurt due to the breaking within or breaking down of erstwhile, or ostensible, 'homes'.

It makes sense to interpret these lyrics as suggestive of a child's perspective on being sent away to boarding school, not wanting to go, feeling shy and scared about going, feeling lonely and homesick at going, and yet at the same time feeling even worse because of recognizing, at least partially, that they have been sent away because their parents or guardians didn't want them, or couldn't take care of them, at home–and in this sense their homes are 'broken'. The "hint of anaesthesia" here might well suggest, as Foucault argues in *Discipline and Punish: The Birth of the Prison*, that modern disciplinary institutions develop a considerable commonality in terms not only of how they operate but also of how we experience them, such that schools, hospitals, and prisons increasingly resemble each other: they all maintain a heavy 'institutional' aura. The "hint of anaesthesia," what's more, could also refer to what Foucault argues becomes the overwhelmingly effective aim of these institutions, and especially the schools: to inculcate subjection to and identification with a dominant regime of 'the normal'. Successful 'normalization' can include not paying sensitive attention to or experiencing any substantial sympathy for, let alone empathy with, the pain and hurt of those who cannot and will not submit and conform to what 'the normal' demands.

Yet this same setting could be many other places as well, including a refugee camp, or another kind of relocation camp within a colonized country, such as a place where 'natives' of this colonized country are forced to do intensive work, in mining or agriculture, to produce exportable goods for the colonizer, and where these workers and their families in turn live on site or right nearby where they are forced to work. The same setting could also be a place of refuge for victims of domestic abuse, and in this connection the 'she' and the 'he' might refer to a mother and her son, forced to flee abuse from her husband and his father. The same setting could refer, once more, to care homes where children are assigned to live when social services and court officials judge their parents, or other legal guardians, unable to take care of them, and where unfortunately these same children often face the adverse of 'care' while becoming stigmatized because of growing up in these kinds of facilities, including because of moving across many different ones and in and out of placements with many foster families as well.

Line five, "Some things I have to do, but I don't mean you harm," invites us to imagine this 'I' and this 'you' are both part of the 'we' from line three, and, if so, we know that 'I' and 'you' maintain a long-standing connection, or at least did maintain such a connection. We now do seem to be in the present, although this is present perfect tense, with the implication that 'I' is acting in the present, or continuing to act in the present in line with how 'he' has been acting for some time now. We don't know what these "some things" might be that 'he' 'has to do' but we gather 'he' feels compelled to need to do them–'he' *must* do them. Mentioning "but I don't mean you harm" suggests that 'he' doing these 'some things' he 'has to do' *will* cause 'you' harm, even if unintended, or, perhaps better put, even as the 'I' here wishes, as 'he' would prefer, that this *harm* were not the case.

734

It is possible, moreover, that these lyrics move in and out of different accents in identifying with the vantage point, the perspective, of the same limited number of distinct characters, such that 'I' and 'you' and 'we' and 'he' and 'she' are all closely interconnected, even that these are all representative of the same subject or of a strictly limited number of subjects. Perhaps this is only a small number of subjects, perhaps just two such subjects, crying for help or hearing cries for help, experiencing the hint of anaesthesia, suffering as a result of coming from broken homes or from what transpired within these homes as they were breaking, meeting repeatedly in the same place, and with the one comforting the other as the other sleeps. Perhaps this is an internal dialogue within a single subject, among multiple dimensions of 'his' subjectivity. If, however, we return, at least briefly, to the interpretation of the song as involving the experience of kids being sent away to boarding school, the last line of the first stanza might suggest the vantage point of a parent, and especially a mother, sending her child, a boy, whom she has earlier comforted while he was sleeping, off to boarding school, because she 'needed' to do so. Perhaps she has done so because the home was not, was no longer, a safe environment, for the child. Perhaps she has done so because she needed to work full-time or even longer than that with no one else around to watch over the child and her unable to afford a baby-sitter. Or perhaps she has done so because she genuinely believed, or wanted to believe, that boarding school, was best for the child, was in his long-term best interests, however much she would miss him.

The first two lines of stanza two seem to fit well with the line of interpretation I sketch out in the preceding paragraph: "A worried parent's glance, a kiss, a last goodbye/Hands him the bag she packed, the tears she tries to hide." This makes sense as what the parent, the mother, is experiencing at the moment of departure of her child, her son, for boarding school. But again further interpretations are plausible as well. This could involve a child leaving for a care home in response to a court order because social services have judged his family unable to take care of him. This could represent a worker in a literal colony who has been ordered, along with many others, to leave home to work at a distant location, employed in intensive manual labor, such as in mining or agriculture or construction. This might involve leaving to serve as a conscript to the colonizer's military forces. Perhaps this involves being taken to a detention center, or a prison facility. Perhaps this involves immigrating to a distant new country because of 'lack of opportunities' in the 'native' country. And this immigration could well have been the result of the devastation of this native country by means of colonialism, robbed of natural resources and with its economy redirected to serve the interests of foreign corporations and foreign consumers while a 'structural adjustment program' imposed by the International Monetary Fund or the World Bank mandates the state severely limit social welfare provision, despite rampant poverty. The scene here might simply call to mind erstwhile children who are now young adults leaving their childhood homes for university or for their first full-time jobs and independent residences in a different and especially distant city.

Yet the third and fourth lines of the second stanza, "A cruel wind that bows down to our lunacy/And leaves him standing cold here in this colony," emphasizes the greater likelihood of less benign interpretations of what is happening here. These lines, taken together, suggest something is wrong, even deeply wrong, about what is here happening–that this is a product of a kind of social 'madness'. The "cruel wind that bows down to our lunacy" suggests this wind, itself "cruel," is in effect acknowledging that 'we', via our 'social madness', have exceeded in terms of 'cruelty' what this wind is itself capable of, or at least is proposing that 'we' are an apt match for what this wind is capable of, on account of our matching exercise of 'cruelty'. Yet this "cruel wind" might also represent a particular manifestation, in the form of an especially acute sensory dimension, of "our lunacy" in action, in practice. This "cruel wind," as representative of "our lunacy," ends up 'leaving him standing cold in this colony', which suggests, to begin, a cause-and-effect relationship between "our lunacy" represented by this "cruel wind" as cause with being left "standing cold here in this colony" as effect. Being 'left standing cold' suggests being left alone, left cut off and disconnected from source of support, comfort, and care. It suggests being left in a hostile environment, or at least one devoid of necessary support, comfort, and care–devoid of the quality and extent of support, comfort, and care that would adequately address and respond to what 'he' genuinely needs, and, likely, increasingly desperately craves. Whatever "this colony" might be, it is a cold place, a place that is the product of cruelty, and clearly a place replete with pain and suffering that is as much psychological as physical and as much spiritual as material.

Stanza three provides some possible further clarification of what might comprise this situation, and in particular what is at stake for the narrator-protagonist as well as, at least implicitly, for 'us', with 'us' encompassing all those he is including in his protest by addressing 'us'. Here are the first three lines of this stanza: "I can't see why all these confrontations/I can't see why all these dislocations/No family life, this makes me feel uneasy." The breaking down and apart of families can certainly involve many confrontations, including many violent ones, as well as many dislocations, and can at the same time leave all involved with nothing to replace what they once had, or nothing but emptiness, uncertainty, and unease. Sending children away to boarding schools, in part because families are unable or unwilling to provide for them living at home and commuting to school, can involve confrontations, especially if the children are reluctant to go, or if parents or other adult family members are divided about the children going, or if it is in large part because of the frequency and intensity of confrontations within the family, at home, among, for example, parents who are constantly fighting, that it has been decided it is in the children's best interest to send them away to boarding school. This certainly involves dislocations, in particular if siblings are sent to different boarding schools, and if at the same time the family is literally breaking up with, for example, parents separating and divorcing, or with other major changes taking place in terms of whom does and does not continue to live as part of one extended family in the same residence at the same location.

Yet all of the other scenarios I have mentioned these lyrics plausibly suggest, including a number in literal colonies, or neo-colonies, also continue to make sense here, as all of these can readily involve many confrontations and dislocations as well as abrupt endings of family life. Colonialism often involves violent conquest and subsequent continuous or recurrent violent suppression, replete with much confrontation and dislocation. The history of colonialism, in particular of European colonialism, is inextricably intertwined not only with the history of slavery but also of genocide, both definitely involving massive confrontations, dislocations, and eviscerations of family connection and of family life. Indigenous people surviving massive genocide, in Western nations formed initially as settler colonies, have long suffered yet further from children being forcibly taken away from their parents to boarding schools in attempts to sever ties with these children's indigenous cultures, including with their indigenous languages and religions, and to assimilate these children into a seamless identification with Western standards and norms. Refugees experience massive dislocation, often fleeing conditions of massive confrontation in their native countries, that indeed causes them to need to seek exile elsewhere. And yet refugees often face further confrontations in the new countries to which they are venturing, in seeking to live new lives, where they are often treated as criminals, or at least as suspects and threats, and, as a result, are often detained, sometimes for many years, in the equivalent of prisons, and where families are frequently separated from each other.

The first three lines of this stanza might even refer as well to the experience, and the vantage point, of someone who has ventured from a culture, or a cultural location, where confrontation and dislocation were not at all commonplace, and where family ties were strong and central, to a culture, or a cultural location, where the opposite is the case. The latter might well suggest hyper-individualistic, hyper-competitive, neo-liberal capitalist culture, where dominant ideology all too often inculcates the notions that 'there is no such thing as society', that everyone is expected to rise and fall solely according to their own efforts, and that no one, and certainly not the collective whole, is responsible for any one else's well-being, or even for their survival.

The fourth and the fifth lines of stanza three bring us back to where we are left at the end of stanza two: "Stood alone here in this colony/In this colony, in this colony, in this colony, in this colony." We now move directly from "cold" to "alone," even with the former already implicitly suggesting the latter, while the repetition of "in this colony" conveys a feeling of this location as enveloped in an atmosphere of overwhelming coldness and aloneness. This repetition suggests that of a total institution, one to which people are consigned and confined, to which they have no power to object, and in which they lose their privacy, their autonomy, and their control over their own lives as others take over and direct all of this for them, ostensibly on their behalf. This kind of total institution is reminiscent of the classic 'asylum', to which mentally ill as well as physically and intellectually disabled people were routinely assigned throughout the 19th and much of the 20th century. But these institutions, as sociologist Erving Goffman (who is responsible for the concept of 'the total institution') indicates in his 1961 book *Asylums*, also include prisons, concentration camps, boarding schools, military barracks, nursing homes, orphanages or other children's care homes, colonial compounds and work camps, and even cloistered centers of religious retreat–among many yet further examples. The lyrics here bear connection with many of these possible kinds of 'total institutions' while, in particular, they express a fear concerning, and a warning about, the omnipresent danger of newly resurgent fascistic forces moving yet new 'suspect populations' into 'internal colonies', or 'sealing off' new suspect populations in internal colonies, that resemble concentration camps, on the one hand, and ghettoes, on the other hand.

As with the internment of hundreds of thousands of Japanese Americans during WWII, it does not require overtly fascist forces in power in government for massive internment campaigns like this to take place. What's more, many refugees to both the US and the UK today, after fleeing tremendous violence and hardship, and after traveling great distances in the course of treacherous journeys, are confined in internment camps for long periods upon arrival where they await the decision of whether they will be granted right of entry, with no guarantee they won't be deported back to the countries from which they fled, and where they would be at grave risk of being killed. The lyrics here remind us that state violence has often been used in many different kinds of societies to target entire population groups from within these societies for forced confinement, including for forced removal and forced re/dislocation. This is a standard practice of colonialism and therefore the title of the song is most apt.

The final stanza introduces a distinctively new concluding element, an appeal to "God in his wisdom": "Dear God in his wisdom took you by the hand/God in his wisdom made you understand/God in his wisdom took you by the hand/God in his wisdom made you understand/ God in his wisdom took you by the hand/God in his wisdom made you understand/God in his wisdom took you by the hand/God in his wisdom made you understand/In this colony, in this colony, in this colony, in this colony." It does make sense to interpret these lyrics as referring ironically to the employment of religion, and in particular reference to God's way, or to divine wisdom, as justification for colonialism–and, especially, as justification for what colonized people experience. Western colonialism has long been aided and abetted by missionary campaigns, with conquest and subjugation of the colonized in turn mystified as what is necessary in order to 'convert heathen savages', and as if the principal aim of colonialism is not for the colonizer to enrich himself at the expense of the colonized, by means of exploitation of the colonized, but rather for the colonizer to bring 'enlightened' 'civilization' to the colonized. Here, it is well worth recalling Kehinde Andrews's trenchant critique of the European Enlightenment as inherently racist in *The New Age of Empire: How Racism & Colonialism Still Rule the World*, a critique that closely aligns with Aimé Césaire indirectly suggesting much the same in *Discourse on Colonialism*, in particular when Césaire quotes from leading French intellectual advocates of and apologists for colonialism.

This particular kind of patronizing mindset remains alive and well to this day. One of the most excruciating kinds of narratives I repeatedly encounter from students writing about shaping experiences in their own lives recounts these students' experiences traveling as representatives of their church to a 'Third World' country, primarily in Central America, to offer short-term assistance on some minor construction project where they gain the opportunity to interact with local residents, and, especially, with local children. These narratives read eerily identical, down to the smallest detail, as if they follow a cookie-cutter formula, with great emphasis always placed on how tremendously thankful 'the natives' were to these contemporary missionaries for spending time with them and helping them out, even how much the natives looked up to their visitors and showed them an almost reverent appreciation, along with how happy these natives were living their lives 'with next to nothing', not needing or wanting any more, in sad comparison, so these student writers also always propose, to 'us' who live with so much all the time and are often nonetheless so miserable. These narratives pick up and reinforce the long insidious colonialist trope of 'the simple, happy darky', ignoring signs of any kind of extensively developed and genuinely complex indigenous culture while at the same time proceeding entirely oblivious of how the relative material disparities between 'our' lives and 'theirs' is no accident, no coincidence, but rather a product of long-standing uneven exchange, overdevelopment enabled by underdevelopment, and exploitative expropriation of natural resources as well as, in particular, the products of forced–including, for long period of time, slave–labor.

On the other hand, however, it is possible that "God in his wisdom took you by the hand/ God in his wisdom made you understand" might reference turning to God for strength, to be able to survive, endure, and persist under conditions of colonial subjection, even to recognize these for what they are–as *evil* practices of *evil* institutions carried about by *evil* forces in support of *evil* ends and to serve *evil* interests. This might involve some kind of loose parallel with liberation theology, in which religious faith and belief, on the one hand, and commitment to struggle against injustice and in the interest of human emancipation, on the other hand, unite, with religious faith helping sustain that commitment through great difficulty and even past many losses and defeats. Yet, in the context of the entire lyrics, and with the final line reading as it does–"In this colony, in this colony, in this colony, in this colony"–it makes better sense to interpret the reference to God as a chilling comment on how use of appeals to God, and to religion, can be and often are employed to justify violence and cruelty, in terms of how one group of human beings treats another group of human beings.

It may seem startling to some readers, but I have, especially years ago now, often encountered students who cited God and their religious faith as justification for condemning whole populations of people as deserving of punishment, and even of (being put to) death. This has included (all) lesbian, gay, bisexual, transgender, queer, gender non-binary, intersex, and asexual people. It has also included Muslim people in general, and entire populations of countries in which the US has been fighting wars–with some students even advocating dropping atomic bombs on Iraq and Afghanistan so as to 'totally take care of the problem'. And it has included broad groups of immigrants, especially Black and Brown immigrants, as well as poor people, anyone who has needed to access social welfare benefits, and anyone sentenced to serve any length of prison term for any crime. Yes, these have usually been, fortunately, minority positions, among their fellow students, but that does not negate the harm that can and does follow when people who maintain these positions act in accord with the logic of where this can lead them. Today, among those who are 'up in arms', increasingly literally, in opposition to so-called 'wokeness' or 'woke culture', and who vehemently reject multiculturalism and cosmopolitanism, are a good number who conceive what they are doing as acting as God's agents, or in accord with what their religious faith calls them to do. What's more, in nations such as Hungary and Poland today social repression of difference is justified in terms of a revival of Christian nationalism.

Another connection that can be drawn here, with these lyrics, given this final emphasis, concerns being compelled by a religious community to renounce a significant dimension of whom one experiences one's self to be, and even to attend camps that involve, for example, so-called 'reparative therapy' for LGBTQIA+ people–especially for young LGBTQIA+ people. In these kinds of settings, and others like them, it is not uncommon for those leading the way to propose those undergoing such reparative processes are allowing themselves to be led (back to the righteous path) by God, by the hand of God, in accepting God's wisdom concerning what they should and should not be or do. At the end of the lyrics, the narrator-protagonist and us, together with 'him', do not seem to have been persuaded because the reiteration in the final line of "in this colony" suggests substantially augmented feelings of being all alone and of being continually punished.

Returning to the title, "Colony," as referenced in and by the lyrics, can plausibly refer to literal colonies, and literal neo-colonies, where one nation, its people, its natural resources, and its economic and cultural processes are subject to rule by another nation, for the benefit of its people, or dominated over by the interests of another nation, or that of a series of other nations, for the benefit of the people of this other nation or these other nations. It can refer to colonialism, past and present, as Césaire discusses in *Discourse on Colonialism*, Andrews discusses in *The New Age of Empire*, John Newsinger discusses in *The Blood Never Dried*, Danny Dorling and Sally Tomlinson discuss in *Rule Britannia*, Sathnam Sanghera discusses in *Empireland*, and Ian Sanjay Patel discusses in *We're Here Because You are There*. And it can also refer to metaphorical colonies in the form of a variety of possible kinds of 'total institutions'. Whatever the case, the crux of the colonial relationship depends on exploitative expropriation along with yet further systematic domination and subjection as well as the ever present threat of punitive violence.

Here it is worth highlighting the conception of 'colonization of the mind', which is often used broadly today, to refer to situations and circumstances where groups of people have learned to think, understand, make sense, reason, interpret, express, and communicate in terms and according to frames developed by other groups of people who have maintained historically oppressive domination over them, including by means of the dissemination of these very same ways of thinking. It means not being able to think outside of frameworks which in effect rationalize, justify, and legitimate this historically oppressive domination–even render it imperceptible as such, seeming instead as simply unquestionably normal and natural. It means identifying with conceptions of whom and what you are and can be that are reductive and diminishing. It means being unable to question, challenge, critique, resist, oppose, and fight for transformation–and through transformation for liberation–because 'the way things are' is 'the way they have to be'. All of this should remind us of the challenges Trinh discusses that confront the Third World woman of color, writing from within 'the master's language', while seeking not simply to serve the master's interests in so doing, but rather to find sufficient difference within, by deconstructing the language and its dominant structures, so as to discourse in effectively critically resistant and oppositional terms. Colonies might therefore refer to a multiplicity of social institutions that work, in Foucault's terms, to enforce and reinforce 'normalization', or, in Althusser's terms, to interpellate individuals as subjects of dominant ideology.

Let's now consider in some detail the music that constitutes "Colony" and reflect on how this effects interpreting what the song might mean. The structure of the song divides as follows:

1. Instrumental Opening: 0:00-0:19. Immediate, Immersive Commencement.

2. First Vocal Passage: 0:20-0:43. Focused Concentration.

3. First Instrumental Bridge: 0:44-1:01. Intensification.

4. Second Vocal Passage: 1:02-1:26. Focused Concentration.

5. Second Instrumental Bridge: 1:27-1:50. Intensification.

6. Third Vocal Passage: 1:51-2:31. Focused Concentration. Heightened Urgency.

7. Third Instrumental Bridge: 2:32-2:39. Prelude to Climax.

8. Fourth Vocal Passage: 2:40-3:21. Climax. Peak Urgency.

9. Instrumental Closing: 3:22-3:51. Perpetuation Toward Suspension.

The principal instrumental sounds here include an opening and repeated muted and overdriven electric guitar sounding a jagged, sawing, staccato riff that provides the crux of the song's melody which is subsequently picked up and elaborated upon by the bass guitar and the vocal; a soaring, ringing, dirtily discordant, higher-pitched guitar line as well as some brief puncturing, flaring, bursts of guitar sound; a gently rumbling bass guitar, which principally sounds a variation on the melody over and over throughout; the heavily darkened, reverberant vocal that becomes increasingly agitated and agonized as the song nears its end; and a largely recursive pattern that is close to yet nonetheless distinctly divergent from a standard rock beat, involving principally the bass drum, an electric snare drum, and a low tom, while occasionally incorporating a floor tom and an open hi-hat.

I hear the electric guitar positioned principally medium to high along the left side, near the left edge of the soundbox, although I also hear this instrument along the right side, and near the right edge periodically, as well. I hear the opening guitar riff and its recurrence primarily remaining in the same location whereas the soaring, ringing guitar sound rises in the soundbox toward the top and the center as well as moving to the right. I hear the bass guitar positioned midway between the center and the bottom of soundbox as well as close to the front; the bass guitar I also hear as sounding closer toward the center along the horizontal axis of the soundbox than the guitar yet also more clearly coming at me from both sides of the center. I hear the drums positioned between the guitar and the bass guitar along the vertical axis of the soundbox with the sound here somewhat more pronounced to the right although the brief rolls and crashes come from the left; the snare is slightly more prominent than that of the bass drum and the low tom but not as much so as is the case in many other recorded Joy Division songs. The vocal I hear occupying a position at the center of the soundbox while seeming to emanate from a space at this location that it has hollowed out, in terms of depth, neither too close nor not far back from the front; the vocal drifts slightly to the right and then later in the song, together with rising pitch and volume, pushes vertically upward. The vocal does seem to come at me from a tight echoing space located slightly to the left of center, right at center, and slightly to the right of center, all at once.

What this structure and instrumentation conveys to me is a feeling of being confronted with a stark, bleak, uneasy, and ever increasingly urgent situation but not one where the music as persona is yet entirely desperate let alone totally despairing. This structure and instrumentation I hear suggestive of onward struggle involving phases, or stages, and even if it is concerned with a situation of isolation and confinement it sounds as one that we, involved with and through the song, are sharing with others, potential allies, as our common experience of isolation and confinement might, paradoxically enough, constitute the effective basis for an empathetically solidaristic alliance as well for collaboration in resistance. The music is both performative in drawing attention to the felt experience of a situation, and exhortative in demanding recognition, attention, and response.

In terms of loudness, the sound begins almost immediately at the level of volume it will maintain for much of its total duration. The instruments are well balanced in terms of relative volume, close to each other in their respective levels, so it is easy to distinguish all of them and to study their relations with each other. Periodically the electric guitar, as much because of matters of pitch and timbre as volume per se, sounds the loudest but not that much louder overall than the rest. The volume does start to increase in the second instrumental bridge, especially by way of the contribution here of guitar, but also after that via the vocal; it then drops down again at the end of third vocal passage; and it rises yet again over course of the fourth vocal passage, marking a steady crescendo in loudness to a peak at the end of this passage extending into the final closing instrumental section and not softening much at all until right at the end. Loudness, in "Colony," suggests an immediately and persistently focused concentration, along with a steady determination, and a steadily increasing urgency.

The tempo of "Colony" is 136 BPM, the song follows a 4/4 time signature, and its dominant rhythmic pattern, initially evoked by means of the choppy, staccato muted guitar, is 1and2and3and4and/5and6X–eleven eighth notes in a first measure followed by a prolonged sustain to release over the next five eighth notes of the second measure before resuming the same pattern. According to Songsterr.com, and this sounds convincing to me, the principal drums involved in "Colony" are the bass drum, an electric snare drum, and a low tom. The most common drum pattern is as follows: bass, snare, snare, low tom, bass, snare, snare, low tom (all eighth notes)/bass, snare, snare, low tom, snare, snare (the first three eighth notes, followed by two quarter notes and then by a dotted quarter note). Rolls include the low and a very low (a floor) tom, as well as possibly a closed hi-hat, while the cymbal crash is on an open hi-hat. Rhythm in this song again feels highly and indeed ritually performative as if invoking a particular kind of situation while simultaneously underscoring the mediative means and process of doing so, akin to discoursing nearby and in empathetic solidarity without subsuming difference and without ignoring the opacity of representation. At the same time, rhythm here is suggestive of struggle, of the push and pull of contending forces, of increasing confrontation, and of impending collision.

The opening and recurrent guitar sound is a muted (or raked) guitar riff, seemingly involving three strings muted, while the guitar sound also involves notable use of an overdrive device. It is likely that Bernard Sumner makes use of some other combination of chorus/flanger, vibrato, echo/delay, and reverb effects devices to shape the pitch and especially the timbre here as well. Notably the bass guitar performs all along the E string, the lowest string, principally back and forth between two notes and an open string. A sharply, jaggedly oscillating movement in terms of pitch is especially notable in "Colony," while the pitch of the vocal also notably rises at end of lines, and in the last two vocal passages. Overall, pitch location and especially pitch movement in "Colony" suggests a heightened state of tension and of urgency, even one that becomes increasingly so, as well as a situation that is not right, not stable, not sustainable, and that provides no ease, no comfort, no release, and no relief. Curtis's vocal delivery is much the same as in many recorded Joy Division songs, keeping within a tight pitch range at any one moment while extending his singing of pitches and of linked, successive pitches at the end of lines as well as starting and moving higher in pitch in the last two vocal passages. His voice is familiarly deep, dark, resonant, and reverberant. Curtis's vocal delivery here comes across as exhortative, yes, and urgent, yes, but not as desperate or despairing, let alone resigned and surrendering–but rather as committed, confident, and determined.

I have already noted a number of features of timbre in "Colony" but I will now elaborate somewhat further. The most notable timbre is that of the opening guitar riff, which has something of a machinic quality, sounding something like an electric saw or similar electric tool: brash, simultaneously bright and harsh, and simultaneously thick and sharp. The attack here is particularly pronounced in comparison with the decay, sustain, and release, whereas with the subsequent ringing guitar sound the decay and especially the sustain are particularly pronounced. The bass guitar offers a warm, low rumbling quality of sound with a gentler attack and more decay and sustain, although with a clean and quick release as well. The vocal maintains a greater sustain and release than any of the other instruments, while the drums and cymbals are most notable for their attack, with decay, sustain, and release all short. As a composite, the timbre of "Colony" involves a dark, sparse, beating sustain; a dark attack; and a low pitch. Timbre adds yet further to a feeling that is not at all glacial let alone elegiac or funereal but rather anxious, in the sense of being on edge, agitated, ready to explode, yet focused and determined.

In terms of the specific eight avenues of musical affect that I have been addressing since chapter two, from Arnie Cox, with "Colony" I feel little if any sense of ease throughout this song, perhaps with the bass guitar the closest and the vocal the second closest, yet in the latter case any semblance of ease disappears as tension increases and with rising pitch and volume. Exertion feels intense, concentrated, and persistent. Exertion does not feel exceedingly complex and it does feel regular and recursive. Feelings of success versus failure of exertion are hard to assess, because it feels to me as if "Colony" does what it sets out to do, yet success in relation to what the song *is about* is something the song in turn makes clear is far beyond the power of the song in, of, and by itself to accomplish. The opening guitar riff, and its recurrence throughout, is mesmerizing and does compel mimetic participation, more so than that of any other constituent of the music except that of the vocal. Meanwhile, "Colony" does feel as if it incorporates some anticipation, of moving from confrontation to collision, and of reaching the point of no turning back. The song also feels as if it anticipates its recurrent patterns, its climax, and its ending with suspension rather than resolution of tension. I feel the song as anticipating beyond dread, as invoking the felt experience of a situation, and the necessary response to this, that involves a fierce desire to transcend dread. In terms of expression, I hear "Colony" expressing, above all else, urgency. This is an urgency that is closely allied with feelings of restlessness, hyperactivity, and anxiety but not in the sense of panic or dread but rather a rush of adrenalin. As far as acoustic impact is concerned, the instruments are well balanced across and throughout the soundbox, leading me to feel enveloped, swept up and along, as well as thrust forward into confrontation on the verge of collision.

When considering the song in terms of matters of analysis it feels to me as if the song is analyzing, insofar as it is doing so, and inviting analysis insofar as it is doing that, from a position that is now more concerned not with identifying reasons for, or causes of, threat and panic but rather with what needs to be done now. I feel an insinuation that analysis has prompted the conclusion that surviving now requires fighting for more than to maintain bare existence. Any sense of pleasure conveyed here feels as if it has to do with seizing upon the urgency of the moment and running with it. I have already identified many associations with what this music invites and encourages me, and others, to think (about) and feel but I will add here the predominant emotions I associate with listening to "Colony" are not sadness, fear, or even anger but rather correspond to feeling shaken, awakened, and driven. In terms of exploring taboos, it remains often taboo to reference colonialism past or present as a practice of systematic cruelty and to emphasize the pain and hurt it causes, while it is likewise taboo to suggest the same kind of situation has been replicated within many social institutions, even to the point of becoming ubiquitously routine. In "Colony" the forces directly responsible for the situation, operating the instruments of the power to dominate and subjugate, feel as if they are here not directly visible or tangible, but rather the effects of this exercise feel overwhelmingly so, while the precise stages involved in the process that resulted in arrival at this point feel ephemeral. What might be possible, what might exist, beyond 'the colony' also feels invisible, intangible, and ephemeral even if tantalizing at the same time.

In listening to and reflecting carefully on what "Colony" calls forth from me, and in what ways I can usefully respond, I think about a range of connections I make with this song, with what I hear it suggesting, and with how I hear it suggesting what it does. With Césaire's *Discourse on Colonialism* I already have addressed how readily it makes sense to relate "Colony" to the former's critique of colonialism as indefensible, as constituting a form of proto-fascism, and as continuing to this day. More precisely, "Colony" emphasizes affective dimensions of the impact of the experience of colonialism on the colonized, and not so much the impact of the experience of colonialism on the colonizer. "Colony" does not focus on how the colonizer is brutalized, even de-civilized, as a result of colonialism, but rather on how colonialism causes the colonized to experience feelings of alienation and isolation. The song also emphasizes the impact, upon the colonized, of the undermining, breaking up, breaking down, and replacement of institutions that at least promised to provide people with systems of support sufficient to enable and sustain their overall well-being, such as family. "Colony" suggests the phrase 'penal colony' is redundant as the experience of colonialism, for the colonized, is equivalent with that of imprisonment. The song also suggests this imprisonment is multi-faceted and potentially all-encompassing, including 'colonization of the mind' by way of identification with ideological positions that both explicitly and implicitly justify colonialism as right, necessary, inevitable, and inescapable–including in religious forms and by religions means. Yet the song also emphasizes a palpable sense of disquiet, unease, and, yet further, continued fervid inclination toward resistance versus mere passive acceptance of and conformity to the dictates of colonial subjection. "Colony" does not offer much if any hope, let alone much if any confidence, that 'a way out' and a renewed life 'after and beyond' might be possible, but it is not ready to give up, or to give in. The song stresses the pain and hurt experienced by the colonizer yet in such a way as to simultaneously suggest this pain and hurt is not, and cannot be, forgotten or forgiven.

Discoursing from the vantage point of the colonized, isolated and confined within the colony, subject to colonial domination, yet refusing reconciliation to this state of affairs, "Colony" does embrace, as Said encourages, the position of the outsider, the marginal, and the exile. Likewise, the song is redolent with awareness, as Said cautions, of risks, dangers, and costs that follow from not submitting, from not identifying with rationalizations, justifications, and mystifications of the conditions of one's own subjection. "Colony" also follows Said's urging that the intellectual must represent the under-represented and the disadvantaged. The colonized who remains steadfastly resistant, at least 'inwardly' or 'subjectively' if not perceptibly 'outwardly' or 'objectively', and who perhaps, as Homi K. Bhabha has theorized, engages in a form of mimicry of the colonizer such that the colonizer is unable to discern when and if this mimicry becomes mockery, occupies an under-represented position because the colonizer opposes such representation as a matter of self-interest while the colonized fears punishment from the colonizer for such representation. Those who occupy this precise kind of position are thereby doubly disadvantaged, both disadvantaged due to colonial subjection and due to placing themselves at heightened risk of even greater punishment by not fully submitting and, as such, remaining an overt threat to the colonizer. "Colony" also follows Said's recommendations in making challenging connections, which multiple interpretations of the song, and in particular of its lyrics, have taken up, between, on the one hand, literal colonies, and what it is like to be literally colonized, and, on the other hand, metaphorical colonies, and what it is like to be metaphorically colonized–such as by way of what happens within the kinds of 'total institutions', such as in schools, that I have earlier mentioned.

As I discussed in chapter three, in relation to Althusser's theorization of ideology and Ideological State Apparatuses (ISAs), I contend that, today, especially in the US but also, although to a lesser degree, in the UK as well, schools are not the most powerful conveyors of conservative and especially of reactionary ideology, but rather popular media and culture do so, including via distinct enclaves within the internet, especially given how much suspicion, distrust, and hostility is directed against schools, in particular by the political right and far right. When, for example, a particular conspiracy theory, such as that of Q or QAnon, provides a comprehensive framework for making sense of what exists, is desirable, and is possible, as well as provides positions from which to engage as a subject, in representing, and thereby in rendering material, this outlook as an ideological position, we witness a contemporary form of an especially influential 'total institution'.

Nevertheless, "Colony" certainly makes good sense as encouraging listeners persistently to question the ostensible 'normalcy' and 'naturalness' of the structures of social relations according to which they are expected to live their lives, and especially to consider whether these structures might advance ends and serve interests dramatically if not diametrically opposed to those people in positions of authority, occupying the heights of power, claim they advance and serve. In particular, "Colony" resonates with the shock one can experience when recognizing the way things have appeared to be is the way things have *been made to appear to be*, that what one accepted as innocent is far from this, and that what one comfortably imagined one freely chose to think, feel, believe, and do, entirely of one's own free will, entirely of one's own free choice, is hardly that at all, but rather what one has been compelled to think, feel, believe, and do, by forces that may well represent interests fundamentally opposed to one's own. To realize that the contents of 'one's own consciousness', and not just the contents but also the codes, frames, structures, and forms according to which these contents provide us means to make sense of and engage with the world, have been 'colonized', are themselves the products of and serves the interests of 'colonization', can be extremely unsettling.

In this regard, it is possible to draw a ready connection with Trinh's insistence that language and other modes of discourse do not provide neutral and transparent means and media of expression, communication, representation, or reflection: that we need to question the seeming neutrality and transparency of the language and other modes of discourse we use, especially those 'ready at hand', 'easily available', and which 'seem natural and normal', because these modes of language use, these modes of discourse, might well constitute crucial dimensions of our 'colonization', of the colonization of what and how we think, feel, believe, and act. It is also certainly viable to argue "Colony" confronts, and even at least in part is prepared to seize upon, following Trinh's recommendation, confusion, uncertainty, incompletion, lack of and limits to control, the indefinite and the undecidable, the indirect and the roundabout, the elusive and the elliptical, the multiple and the proliferating, open-endedness and not just closure, perpetual process and not just process always directed toward a decisively finished product, and the in-between, the alongside, the liminal, thresholds, hybrids, taboos, cracks, gaps, fissures, fragments, borders, borderlines, intersections and intersectionalities. However, "Colony" is not as ready as Trinh to identify all of these as necessarily providing positive opportunities for effective resistance as opposed to perceiving these instead as disempowering effects of subjection to oppressively alienating and isolating colonial conditions. In other words, for "Colony" these are constituent dimensions of the conditions which the colonized finds themselves, as a result of colonial conquest and subjugation, so the colonized will need to resist, if and as the colonized can, according to the constraints as well as the affordances such conditions provide. Nevertheless, "Colony," by addressing experiences of colonialism elliptically and analogously, and by focusing on sympathetic to empathetic connections with felt dimensions of the position of the colonized, does seem to follow a path akin to Trinh's discoursing 'nearby' as opposed to directly 'about' or 'for', and the song does constitute a manifestly 'creative' way of engaging in 'critical' praxis. In connection with Trinh's theorizations of identity, of difference, of selfhood, and versus dualistic thinking, it can make sense to interpret "Colony" as suggesting a broad range of affective connections in the experiences of multiply disparate groups of people in broadly comparable kinds of situations while not collapsing the conditions of these experiences into a reductively singular homogeneity, and relations among 'we', 'she', 'he', 'I', and implicitly 'you' and 'they' as well as at different times and places remain open to multiple possible interpretations of how these might overlap and interrelate.

"Colony" does not dispel mystery, and it does not resolve tension; it performatively enacts mystery and tension so as to highlight it, to underscore it, and even to augment it. Connections and disconnections we bear with 'ourselves' as we existed at different times and in different places, as well as with various others, then and there, and near and far, become subjects of exploration, of speculation, and especially of open-ended uncertainty yet also possibility in "Colony." In other words, I am both continuous and discontinuous with whom 'I' was at different places and times in 'my' life, I both am and am not 'the same person', and I am both distinct from and connected with 'others' I have directly known and interacted with as well as with 'others' I have only indirectly known about and only interacted with by way of extensive mediation. Who and what 'I' am is a dynamic complex involving relations among layers of interconnections with people, places, times, experiences, conditions, situations, and events, layers that become 'infinite' once we take into account the layers that constitute whom the 'other people are' with whom I am intrinsically interconnected. "Colony" is sensitive enough to accommodate this possible direction of thinking about whom 'I', 'you', 'we' and 'they' *are*, and the constituent instrumental components of the sound of this song also fit with such a conception of subjectivity, as "Colony" displays a characteristic Joy Division tendency for each member of the group both to assume their own clear and distinct position while also carefully relating what they are doing in this position to what each of the others are doing in theirs, with every contributor successively working with and off of the initial short riff sounded by the muted electric guitar to subsequently draw forth a series of lines that carry this riff forward, replicating it while

746

developing and modifying it. The song feels as if it represents a singular overarching 'music as persona' yet with this persona maintaining multiple, distinct yet interlocking constituent dimensions.

"Colony" presents a challenge for me personally to strive, vigilantly, to be cognizant, of what it is like for other people, for people *not* like me, who live considerably different and considerably more difficult lives because they do not share a vantage point I have maintained 'inside', all my life, not only what Kehinde Andrews refers to, broadly, as within 'the West' but also within the most powerful nation in the world, the nation that has engaged in the most aggressive and far-reaching imperialist practices during my life-time. As a white person I have also not been subject to 'internal colonialism' unlike many African American, Latinx American, Indigenous and Pacific Islander, and Asian American people living in the United States, past and present, where people's race has limited and confined them so they have not been able readily to access the kinds of social resources and exercise the kinds of social opportunities white people often come to expect as a matter of right and even tend to take for granted. It is important, as I have done, to actively participate within and contribute, in solidarity, to anti-racist and anti-imperialist initiatives, campaigns, organizations, and movements, and to teach not only about but also against racism and imperialism. However, this never erases the stark difference in my position from that of those who are directly subject to racist and colonialist, including neo-colonialist, oppression. Yet it is also important continually to find my own ways of discoursing 'nearby' or 'alongside' so that I can make empathetic and solidaristic connection with what people in these kinds of positions are directly experiencing, including in affective terms, without collapsing the differences between us and without conflating our positions.

A major challenge I recognize is to be able to maintain a critically complex position in times of crisis where it would be all too easy not to do so, such as at this present moment, writing these words, shortly after the beginning of the Russian invasion of and war against Ukraine. Certainly the justification given by Russian President Vladimir Putin for this invasion is grotesque, the death and destruction that has followed and will follow is sickening, and the long-term consequences are gravely concerning, even prospectively terrifying. The invasion is wrong, it is a monumental injustice, and it deserves total condemnation. My sympathy is totally with the Ukrainian people in resistance to Putin's war against them and their country. I consider Putin's Russia as itself bearing close resemblance to that of a fascist society, regardless of his attempt to justify war versus Ukraine as about 'de-Nazifying' Ukraine, and find it unsurprising that he has been popular and admired by objectively fascist right-wing figures and forces in the West, including in the US. I also am helped here by maintaining no illusions about the Soviet Union, which I interpret, throughout the vast majority of its history, as bearing nothing in common whatsoever with either 'socialism' or 'communism', as I instead interpret the Stalinist and post-Stalinist USSR as the product of the rapid bureaucratic degeneration and counterrevolutionary cooptation of an at once embryonic and fledgling yet also multiply contradictory as well as multiply challenged proto-socialist state and society.

Right at the beginning of Putin's war on Ukraine, Eyal Press, a writer whose work I admire, retweeted, from @mkazin, "I see people on the left I respect blaming the US for stoking another Cold War. Look, an undemocratic nation invading a democratic nation that has done nothing at all to threaten it is both wrong and dangerous. Put your skepticism aside long enough to acknowledge that." My position is that @mkazin is entirely right that Putin's war versus Ukraine and its potentially even more horrifying larger implications is both 'wrong' and 'dangerous', and that Russia is indeed an 'undemocratic nation' whereas Ukraine is at least a fledgling 'democratic nation'. I maintain absolutely no sympathy for Putin whatsoever nor any illusions about what kind of regime he heads, and has headed, let alone about his readiness to employ state violence ruthlessly within and without Russia. I suspect he has become infatuated with the goal of recreating the 'Great Russian Empire' that existed prior to 1914 and he might be ready to use nuclear weapons with globally catastrophic results to attempt to get what he wants. Yet the question of whether the US bears responsibility for 'stoking another Cold War' I find to be more complicated than simply proposing 'yes' the US is totally, or even principally, responsible, or 'no' the US is not at all responsible.

To begin, the US has certainly shown little hesitation to use military force in invading many other countries, including in recent times, Iraq and Afghanistan. This history is extensive and long-running, as Evergreen State College Professor Zoltán Grossman documents on his webpage "From Wounded Knee to Syria: U.S. Military Interventions Since 1890." What's more, some of the shocked reaction, even among many on the left, to the current Russian invasion of Ukraine–that it is hard to believe this war can possibly be happening, and that it represents the worst atrocity committed by any one country versus any other country since World War II–betrays a Western, white, Eurocentric bias according to which what happens in wars waged in other areas of the world involving nations comprised overwhelmingly of Black and Brown people, nations and peoples not included among 'the West', seems much more readily 'to be expected', not so shocking, not so atrocious, and not so immediately threatening and concerning. This is, again, not to deny that the Russian invasion of Ukraine is a gross injustice, and indeed a terrible calamity, but it is rather to emphasize the impact of war in countries such as Iraq, Afghanistan, Syria, Lybia, Yemen, Ethiopia and Somalia has been and continues likewise grossly unjust and terribly calamitous. What's more, extending the reach of an antagonistic military alliance, including the location of 'weapons of mass destruction' as close to Russia in Eastern Europe as the Soviet Union was on the verge of doing in Cuba, precipitating the Cuban Missile Crisis in 1962, is and from the beginning has been a dangerous provocation, especially versus an autocratic regime maintaining massive nuclear weapons capability that was already well known for displaying pronounced tendencies toward paranoiac resentment over perceived deliberate humiliation.

In a lead editorial in the 23 February 2022 edition of *The Morning Star* the editors usefully address some of the complexity of how to make sense of and respond to this war, from a socialist vantage point. Certainly doing so begins with staunchly condemning the Russian war against Ukraine along with the prospect that Russian success in this war will in effect transform Ukraine into a 'Russian colony'. Ukraine has long maintained a cultural identity distinct from that of Russia, contrary to Putin's claims, while the Ukrainian people certainly conceive of themselves and have long conceived of themselves, even under periods of extended prior Russian colonization, as constituting a distinct nationality. Ukrainians clearly overwhelmingly do not want to become a Russian colony once more. Therefore, as *The Morning Star* rightly declares: "Vladimir Putin's invasion of Ukraine is a catastrophe with horrific consequences for millions in that country and beyond. Recognition of Nato's aggressive record and the dangerous consequences of dismissing Russian fears about its expansion in no way justifies this terrifying act of war. Nor should it blind us to the self-serving narrative Putin puts forward." Likewise, despite the presence of some fascist groups within Ukraine, including among the Ukrainian National Guard, Putin's "claim to be 'de-Nazifying' Ukraine" is at best "a flimsy excuse for a blatantly expansionist invasion." What's more, Putin falsifies history by claiming the Union of Soviet Socialist Republics (USSR) artificially invented the difference between Russia and Ukraine, when in fact the USSR responded to the preexisting reality of this difference by recognizing Ukraine as one of multiple distinct republics joining together to form this union. Putin, as *The Morning Star* aptly charges, is engaging in this falsification in order "to promote a nationalist revanchism of the crudest kind."

However, the same editorial simultaneously argues Ukraine "is not the 'front line'" of Western "'democracy'." Ukraine's President Volodymyr Zelensky in fact was "elected on pledges to negotiate a peace with Russia" and "on a platform largely opposed to the wave of neoliberal economic reforms" administered by the preceding government. In running for election, Zelensky "attacked the privatising healthcare reforms of US-imported health minister Ulana Suprun and the 'illegal privatisations' of Ukrainian land," but "In power, he has been unable to act on these positions," as "Further land privatisation, opposed by three-quarters of Ukrainians, has been forced through at the insistence of the EU, so giant European agribusiness can buy up farmland and convert it en masse to monocultures, especially sunflower production for oil." Meanwhile, "Ukrainians have got poorer year by year," such that Ukraine "has the highest poverty rates in Europe." As *The Morning Star* adds, it is also noteworthy that Zelensky's "tearful address in his native Russian to the Russian people today included the proud recollection of his grandfather's service in the Red Army," illustrating that Ukraine is not a thoroughly 'Westernized' nation such that Ukraine bears far less in common with Russia than it does with 'the West', even if Putin's war is, perversely, likely to make this so, in the long run. In sum, Ukraine has become "the victim of a tug of war between Moscow and the West." What this means is "It is no apologia for Moscow to point out that by stifling the Minsk peace process, by their annual military exercises from the Baltic to the Black Sea, by rejecting out of hand any idea that Nato might agree to negotiate troop and missile reductions in Europe, Western powers have engaged in a brinkmanship that has now exploded." According to *The Morning Star*, "The way out, however late the hour, is to address that context, commit to Ukraine not joining Nato, and to a dial-down of militaristic showboating by the world's most powerful and dangerous military alliance, of which Britain is a part" because "A war between nuclear-armed Russia and the West does not bear thinking about."

This critical position versus NATO and the West does not mean excusing Putin because "The peace movement must press for an immediate withdrawal of Russian troops" yet it does means challenging "the might is right doctrine Putin has picked up from US attacks on Yugoslavia, Afghanistan, Iraq and Libya." I myself think Putin did not need to learn anything from the US about how to engage in ruthlessly aggressive actions, including in war versus other nations, and I also don't think Putin needed to be able to point to supposed US and greater Western 'hypocrisy' and 'double standards' in order to be able to go ahead with this war versus Ukraine. I suspect he likely would have been able to find other justifications, as need be, with these not even needing to be all that convincing, at least not outside of Russia. However, in times of major global crisis like this one, it is important to keep in mind that powerful players within Western nations, including the US, are unlikely to maintain a purely disinterested position in their support of Ukrainian resistance and in their pressure to isolate and 'punish' Russia.

In a lead editorial in the 24 February 2022 edition of *The* Nation, publisher Katrina vanden Heuvel writes "War is a tragedy, a crime, and a defeat," condemning Putin's invasion of Ukraine as a violation of international law and as risking fueling an even more "dangerous escalation of violence," that could ultimately result in the "unthinkable": "direct conflict between the world's two largest nuclear powers"–the US and Russia. Heuvel argues "Putin's actions are indefensible, but responsibility for this crisis is widely shared," as *The Nation* "has warned repeatedly that the extension of NATO to Russia's borders would inevitably produce a fierce reaction," has also frequently "criticized NATO's wholesale rejection of Russia's security proposals," and has long decried "the arrogance that leads US officials to assert that we have the right to do what we wish across the world, even in areas, like Ukraine, that are far more important to others than they are to us." As Heuvel elaborates,

> NATO expansion provided the context for this crisis–a fact often ignored by our media. There is rank irrationality and irresponsibility in offering future NATO membership to Ukraine–when successive US presidents and our NATO allies have demonstrated that they do not have slightest intention of fighting to defend Ukraine. Instead, Putin's demand that Ukraine remain outside of NATO–essentially that the status quo be codified–was scorned as violating NATO's "principle" of admitting anyone it wanted.

This 'irresponsibility' in turn encouraged 'irresponsibility' on the part of the Ukrainian government, with President Volodymyr Zelensky promising "voters when he ran for Ukraine's presidency in 2019 that he would pursue a path to peace and end the war in the Donbas," yet "Upon taking office, however, his government refused to implement the provisions of the 2015 Minsk Protocols–signed by Russia, Ukraine, France, Germany, and the EU–that essentially would have guaranteed Ukrainian sovereignty and territorial integrity in exchange for Ukrainian neutrality." Because of these parallel acts of irresponsibility–and parallel acts of 'irrationality'–"hawks and armament-mongers" will be 'emboldened' "on all sides," with prominent figures already demanding the US double its military budget, massively bloated as is, and for European nations to do much the same. The costs of this war, even without it reaching the point of nuclear conflict, may prove enormously destructive: in terms of need to provide relief and sanctuary for millions of refugees from Ukraine, in terms of long-term guerilla warfare between Russian occupiers and Ukrainian resistance fighters, in terms of sanctions and counter-sanctions that devastate the poorest in Russia while substantially raising energy (and food as well as other kinds of industrial production) costs in the West and especially in the global South, in terms of incentivizing fossil fuel companies to ramp up production in the West and in areas under Western control regardless of the ecological consequences this will entail, and in escalating cyber-attacks where the relatively weakest will, as always, suffer by far the greatest disruption and the greatest loss. As Heuvel notes, "A revived and more dangerous Cold War will ravage domestic budgets here and in Europe–and sap resources and attention needed to address pandemics, the climate crisis, and debilitating inequality." Heuvel concludes by proposing:

> What is needed is not a rush to arms and to hawkish bluster but a return to intense negotiations–at the UN, at the Organization for Security and Co-operation in Europe, and among the signatories to the Minsk Protocols. It is time to recognize that there remain options that, if pursued in good faith, could bring the current crisis to a peaceful conclusion.

We believe the crisis can and should ultimately be resolved by a declaration of Ukrainian neutrality and the withdrawal of Russian forces from the Donbas . . . NATO or the OSCE [Organization for Security and Cooperation in Europe] might valuably take the initiative to open negotiations on creating a resilient new security architecture in Europe, one that engages Russia rather than threatens it, and reassures its neighbors rather than militarizes relations. That might sensibly include an end to NATO expansion, and a return to the Conventional Forces in Europe and Intercontinental Ballistic Missile treaties.

And, finally, Heuvel reminds, it is important for Americans to keep in mind that "American interests in Ukraine will never outweigh those of Russia; the US and NATO cannot and will not win a war on the ground against Russia in its own backyard; sanctions are unlikely to prevail and may indeed damage the American economy." Again, while I largely agree with Heuvel's argument, I am not entirely convinced Putin is ready to settle for anything less than conquest of Ukraine, and I am also skeptical he can be compelled to negotiate a settlement without exerting pressure upon his country, including in the form of economic sanctions and global unity in isolating the Russian economy, that will lead others in Russia to pressure him. This may take a long time, and it may not succeed, but it is difficult to conceive of what else is likely to induce Putin to negotiate a standing down of the war he has ordered against Ukraine.

In a *Guardian* article published on 26 February 2022 Peter Beinart, professor of journalism and political science at the Newmark School of Journalism at the City University of New York, usefully addresses the challenge many members of the progressive left, who have long maintained a critical position versus US militarism and imperialism, experience in figuring out how to respond to the Russian war on Ukraine. Beinart cites Hungarian-born journalist Arthur Koestler writing, in 1943, that "In this war [World War II] we are fighting against a total lie in the name of a half-truth." Beinart proposes "That's a good motto for American progressives to adopt in the wake of Russia's full-scale invasion of Ukraine." Beinart agrees, to begin, "Saying the US stands with Ukraine because America is committed to democracy and the 'rules-based international order' is at best a half-truth" because "The US helps dictatorships like Saudi Arabia and the United Arab Emirates commit war crimes in Yemen, employs economic sanctions that deny people from Iran to Venezuela to Syria life-saving medicines, rips up international agreements like the Iran nuclear deal and Paris climate accords, and threatens the international criminal court if it investigates the US or Israel." Yet, apropos of Koestler, Beinart reminds his progressive readers:

the alliance that fought Hitler was led by a British prime minister who championed imperialism, an American president who presided over racial apartheid, and Joseph Stalin. Koestler's point wasn't that the US or Britain, let alone the USSR, were virtuous in general. It was that they were virtuous relative to Nazi Germany in the specific circumstances of the second world war, and that these sinful governments were the only ones with the geopolitical heft to stop a totalitarian takeover of Europe.

In relation to Russia's current war versus Ukraine, "Putin's claim that historical and cultural affinity gives Russia the right to bludgeon Ukraine into submission is a total lie" and this "is no less of a lie because the US–by pushing Nato ever-further eastward after 1989–exploited Russian weakness and compounded Russian humiliation." Even if the terms arranged at the Treaty of Versailles ending World War I fueled German resentment that ultimately led to Hitler and the Nazis taking power, "Hitler's murderous revanchism, like Putin's today, was still a crime," and a crime for which Hitler then, like Putin now, bore overwhelmingly preeminent responsibility. And yet, the US and the West are hardly always in the relatively morally superior position: "When Putin opposed the Bush administration's invasion of Iraq, Russia was defending a half-truth against America's total lie. When his government backed UN resolutions condemning Israeli settlements that the US vetoed, Russia supported human rights and international law while the US defied them." This means progressives cannot agree with President Biden's claim, in the immediate aftermath of the invasion of Ukraine, that "America stands up to bullies. We stand up for freedom. This is who we are," because "Claiming the US possesses an inherent inclination to support liberty implies that the United States can be trusted to act outside of the bounds of international law—a logic that leads to the torture chambers of Abu Ghraib and Guantánamo Bay."

Nevertheless, Beinart argues,

As important as it is to recognize that the US is capable of wars like Vietnam and Iraq, it's equally important to recognize that not everything the US does is Vietnam or Iraq. In Ukraine, it was Putin, not Biden, who lied about weapons deployments. It was Putin, not Biden, who defied the UN and international law. It is Putin, not Biden, who is bombing another nation and creating vast numbers of refugees. In Ukraine, the US is sending weapons not to a prop up a dictator but to defend a free nation against one.

This means, although "It's not surprising that American progressives, having lived through the debacles in Afghanistan, Iraq and Libya, would grow skeptical when Washington's military and foreign policy establishments gear up for conflict with a foreign adversary . . . that skepticism must extend to America's adversaries as well." Beinart approvingly cites an unnamed 'socialist' commenting on Twitter who contends that "believing America has a monopoly on being evil is just another kind of American exceptionalism." I agree with Beinart and the unnamed socialist he cites, and I agree as well that "in the current conflict over Ukraine—where the US is a flawed but essential element in the fight against Vladimir Putin's murderous lies—it's a form of American exceptionalism progressives must avoid." At the same time I also believe it is important to resist uncritically accepting that the motives of the US, NATO, and the West are and will be entirely benevolent in their inclination. In contrast with what Beinart is here addressing, it is also easy enough, even for progressives and other leftists, as Said warns, to become uncritical versus the actions of our own governments, and of our own states, as well as versus those of powerful capitalist interests that our governments, and states, work to advance and serve, including in times of major global crisis. Western interest in Ukraine is not likely to be entirely about 'spreading the good news of liberal democracy' to the Ukrainian people but rather much to do about seeking out and exploiting opportunities for economic profit, including by taking control over, even ownership over, profitable resources and industries, while at the same time extending military and geopolitical dominance to the edge of the Russian border.

752

Yet I also find Yale professor of history Timothy Snyder, author of *On Tyranny*, makes important and compelling points in his contribution to the 1 March 2022 edition of *Democracy Now!*, where Snyder indicates it is important to recognize the nations of Eastern Europe were not mere pawns of Washington and the pre-existing West in 'the expansion of NATO', because the impetus for this expansion came from these nations themselves, while Putin's motives in this current war likewise cannot be explained as simply a reaction against feeling threatened by the expansion of NATO:

> in an important and fundamental way, this entire discussion is moot, because now we know, given the way that the Russians are prosecuting this war, that it never had anything to do with the ostensible motivations that they cited in late 2021. Given the way that they're prosecuting this war, we know that it's about the destruction of the Ukrainian state, given what they say and what they're doing. So, I think it's important to also give the Russians agency, to give Mr. Putin agency, to understand that he might have motives which go beyond things that we do or go beyond the things he says, that he thinks we'll understand.

All of the preceding, concerning Russia's war against Ukraine, might seem like a bizarrely lengthy tangent, yet my point in elaborating on this connection, while interpreting "Colony," is it can be difficult to maintain a nuanced position in the face of an enormous atrocity committed by a 'foreign' agent or entity. Yet as Said reminds us, "One of the shabbiest of all intellectual gambits is to pontificate about abuses in someone else's society and to excuse exactly the same practices in one's own" (92). As Said also urges, "No one can speak up all the time on all the issues. But, I believe, there is a special duty to address the constituted and authorized powers of one's own society." Those of us in the West bear particular responsibility to carefully scrutinize and seek effectively to influence what is being done 'in our name', 'on our behalf', by those principally representing and leading our nation, in responding to Russia's war against Ukraine. Seeking and finding ways to bring about a peaceful end to this war, and to create the conditions for a secure and lasting peace, need to be priority goals, even if it is exceedingly challenging to figure out how to accomplish these goals. We should be critical of all those within our own country seeking to exploit this war for other ends and in support of other interests—such as boosting the appeal of fascist demagogues pretending they could be tough enough to intimidate Putin through sheer force of personality, such as ramping up the military budget of the US while slashing social spending to make up for so doing, such as expanding US military bases and operations as well as US military adventurism yet further throughout the world, such as boosting domestic production of fossil fuels rather than expanding and converting to sources of renewable energy, such as price gouging and other forms of grotesque profiteering in the face of shortages in supplies of goods previously dependent upon economic activity in Russia and Ukraine, and, especially, such as threatening direct military conflict with Russia at the risk of global nuclear war.

"Colony," as is characteristically the case with Ian Curtis's lyrics and Joy Division's songs, and even with Joy Division's appropriation of and identification with the name 'Joy Division', does not suggest simply some 'other' is the one who is 'bad' and 'wrong' while 'I' am the one who is 'right' and 'good'. "Colony," as is common with Ian Curtis's lyrics and Joy Division's songs, does not propose anything as simple as some 'other' is acting as a victimizer while 'I' am the victim or 'I' am entirely innocently aligned with the victim. Likewise, neither 'I' nor 'we' remain unaffected in disinterestedly observing relations between a victim and a victimizer from 'a safe distance'. We are thrown into connection with, implication in, and responsibility for victimization, even as we also suffer pain and hurt as victims ourselves, and we cannot evade or escape what we are connected with, implicated in, and responsible for. We are affected, what's more, in terms of the 'colonization of *our* minds'. We need to struggle, but this includes struggle with and against ourselves–and, as always with Ian Curtis and Joy Division, we may wait 'for a guide to take us by the hand' but this is not going to happen, or at least not all the way through, and we are going to need to venture into 'all the darkest corners of a sense I didn't know' while perhaps only ending up feeling all the more uneasy as we do so, overwhelmed by 'our lunacy', by 'all these confrontations', by 'all these dislocations', with no one providing us any ready explanation of 'why' any of this is as it is–no one, again, 'taking us by the hand' and no one 'making us understand'. We can only achieve even the initial semblance of 'answers' by continuing, ceaselessly, to struggle, and by seeking these answers, without any guarantee we will ever find them, in the course of and through what struggle brings about. The struggle will be difficult, and we may well end up defeated, but we cannot turn away and refuse to take it up or refuse to to take it on.

It is extraordinarily difficult to become critically conscious of and to conscientiously critically inquire into the ways and the extents to which colonialism and empire have enabled and continue to enable us to live the relatively advantaged lives we do and to be the kinds of relatively advantaged people we are, as white Westerners, even if we also come from and inhabit poor, working class, or lower middle class positions–and even if we face challenges on account of yet other kinds of marginalized, oppressed, and stigmatized social identities, beyond those of race and class, such as having to do with gender, sexuality, and disability. But if we don't do so, if we don't strive to do exactly this, no matter how massive a challenge it will so often feel, we are all the more likely to experience, with a vengeance, as Césaire argues, the 'boomerang' effects of what we have tended to dismiss or ignore–atrocities supposedly only ever happening to 'other people', 'people unlike us', 'elsewhere' and 'far away'. It is easy not to recognize, or at least not to think about, these 'other people' as people with whom we are always interconnected, and even interdependent, albeit through a dense chain of elaborate mediations. It is easy not to recognize any such interconnection or not to pay much attention to the precise terms of such interconnection. Yet if we don't make this effort to become critically conscious and to conscientiously critically inquire into how we are situated, including by means of what colonialism and empire have made possible for us, we are all the more likely to become, as Césaire argues, brutalized and de-civilized on account of our inability to perceive 'the other' as a fellow human being with needs and desires like ours, with capabilities and potentials like ours, who 'deserves' as we deserve, who has 'rights' as we have 'rights', and who, because we are interconnected with and, even more precisely, yes, interdependent upon them, makes a claim on us. "Colony" does not instruct us on how to respond in grasping this interconnection, and this interdependence; that is up to us, to each of us, to determine, for ourselves. But "Colony" exhorts us to pay attention so we become aware of the existence of this call upon us to respond, and so we begin to imagine how we will do so.

In the 25 February 2022 edition of the *Guardian*, Kevin Power offers an early review of the novel *The Colony,* by Audrey Magee, which will be published this May. Even though I have not myself had the opportunity to read this novel, Power's description of it suggests useful connections with the song "Colony," and with what thinking critically about colonial relationships can mean, especially including when and where we are not always readily inclined to do so. As Magee describes, "an English painter named Mr Lloyd climbs with his luggage into a small, leaky currach and is rowed across the Irish Sea to an island off the west coast of Ireland," while "The island, 'three miles long and half a mile wide', is inhabited by fewer than 100 people," of whom most "are native Irish speakers." Lloyd is interested in painting the picturesque landscape and wildlife of this island, "But what Lloyd sees when he looks at the boatmen in his hired currach are mostly cliches: 'sinewy/agile strength/sun-stained hands'" and "Lloyd's manner is fussy, patronising, curt," leaving "The Gillans, an Irish-speaking family who have rented him a room . . . unimpressed." As the novel explores answers to the questions "Who is Mr Lloyd?" and "What does he want?" Magee interweaves "scenes of Lloyd failing to charm the islanders" with "terse chapters recounting Northern Irish atrocities," all of this happening "in 1979–the year, it is later confirmed in an aside, when the action of *The Colony* takes place," and also one of the bloodiest years in the 30 years' war in Northern Ireland known as 'The Troubles'. In relation to its title,

> *The Colony*'s nameless Irish island stands . . . for all colonies, and Lloyd for all colonisers. He sees with the colonist's eye. The island cliffs are, he says, more "rugged" and "wild" than those in England: a fanciful notion, fraught with dubious politics. Lloyd is fiercely territorial about his temporary home. When another outsider arrives, he is indignant. His fellow visitor also carries colonial baggage: he is Jean-Pierre Masson, a Frenchman of Algerian descent. Masson is popular with the islanders. For one thing, he speaks Irish, being a linguist who specialises in "languages threatened with extinction". But Masson, too, sees with politicised eyes. His Algerian mother was married to a French soldier who abused her horribly. Masson finds in the island's Irish speakers an authenticity, a naturalness, that might bring him closer to his mother's damaged world.

Lloyd and Masson end up in direct conflict, arguing over the island by each claiming to understand, appreciate, respect and value it better, yet both doing so through politically questionable frameworks, such that it appears, from Power's account, as if they uncritically verge beyond discoursing nearby or alongside to discoursing about and especially discoursing for, as if they have taken possession of, and know best, this island. They do so despite coming from foreign countries, and despite their shaping influences as well as shaping mindsets being forged in those countries, England and France, both of which maintain lengthy histories of colonialist practices to extents where it becomes difficult for English and French people to escape being subject to their own form of 'colonization of the mind'. This means, even if they do not intend or want to do so, they approach 'other countries' and 'other peoples' in terms that continue to bear the weight of colonialist thinking as well as apologies, excuses, rationalizations, legitimations, and mystifications of colonial relations.

Joy Division's "Colony" as I interpret it invites and encourages above all else critical reflection on the complexity of our relations with past and present forms of colonialism, including on the complexity of our inclinations toward sympathetic and especially empathetic identification with the vantage point of the colonized. To what extent are we at risk of imposing our ostensibly sympathetic and empathetic take on colonialism, that we have not experienced and not suffered, on top of that of those who have experienced and have suffered the impact of colonialism, such that they are not seen or heard or felt, on their own terms, representing for themselves, and thereby the distinctiveness of their experience, of their suffering, along with the distinctiveness of their concomitant struggle and resistance, becomes conflated with a host of analogous forms of experience, suffering, struggle, and resistance, that 'we', who are white Westerners from nations that have engaged in major imperialist practices, past and present, can more readily relate to, personally, in our own direct experience? "Colony" reaches out, identifying sympathetically to empathetically with experiences of literal colonialism, while drawing solidaristic connections with analogous experiences of metaphorical colonialism. Yet "Colony" also problematizes the basis from which it is doing so, presenting us with a residual uncertainty concerning precisely where subjects referenced in the lyrics are located, doing what, experiencing what, thinking and feeling what, as well how these locations shift and how they interrelate, over time as well as across space.

Eight

"Heart and Soul," the sixth song on *Closer*, has exerted significant influence as evidenced by the fact the phrase has been used as the title of the 1997 London Records Joy Division box set and the 2018 Rowan & Littlefield anthology of critical writings on Joy Division edited by Martin J. Power, Eoin Devereux, and Aileen Dillane, as well as by Sam Riley, performing as Ian Curtis in the 2007 Anton Corbijn-directed feature-length fictional Ian Curtis biopic, *Control*, reading a striking passage from the lyrics of this song both at the beginning and again near the end of the film.

"Heart and Soul" is a quintessential illustration of Joy Division's movement from rock toward electronica, featuring a heavily treated, light, and ethereal Ian Curtis vocal; Curtis himself providing the spare guitar part while Bernard Sumner plays a low bass part via a synthesizer keyboard; Peter Hook playing six-string bass; Stephen Morris contributing by emphasizing his playing of electronic drums; and the impact of Martin Hannett's studio production quite pronounced. In *Unknown Pleasures: Inside Joy Division*, Hook describes "Heart and Soul" as "so seductive, a very sexy song that has many layers" (278). With "Heart and Soul" Hannett shows Sumner "how to layer and structure the keyboards, the strings especially" (278). Yet here Hannett's vision not only involved "moving from guitar to keyboards" and thereby 'taking the heat out of the mix', but also doubling the bass sound by combining low bass via synthesizer keyboard and high bass via Hook's six string bass guitar, with the regular guitar only adding a minimally supportive chord for purposes of texture. Hook resisted Hannett's vision for "Heart and Soul" at the time of the production of *Closer*, but admits, in retrospect, Hannett was right and he was wrong.

In a July 2020 interview with Anna Conrad for *GQ Magazine*, Morris identifies additional distinctive features of the sound of "Heart and Soul" while reflecting on what made these possible:

> It's based around Bernard playing the bass synths and it was going into a hypnotic rhythm that just doesn't stop. I remember in the studio doing it and you go into a bit of a trance while you're just playing the beat over and over because you couldn't just sample it. I honestly couldn't play that drum riff now. It sounds really simple, but when you listen to it's actually impossible to play. It was probably one of the first ones where Hooky is not playing a bass line. Really he's playing the melody, but his bass riff is really complicated. It's really hard,

possibly because we would have punctured it in. You play a riff for a bit and drop another riff in afterwards, so you build it up like that.

We were really, really, really tight as a band. I mean, we could just jam and you'd know what Hooky was gonna do next, you'd know what Bernard was going to do next and you'd know when Ian was going to start singing. Even if you've never played it before, you just sort of instinctively understood that. There was a lot of telepathy going on when we were making stuff on stage. When things broke down we'd do these spontaneous things.

In interpreting "Heart and Soul," on songmeanings.com, contributors emphasize connections with death and suicide, with strife and apocalypse, with religious speculation and doubt, and with the breakdown of pivotal relationships, especially a marriage. I suggest, in interpreting the title, that we begin with how this phrase–'heart and soul'–is commonly understood. As the Oxford English Dictionary (OED) explains, 'heart and soul' refers to 1) "The whole of one's energy and affection; one's whole being," in particular "to put one's heart and soul into (something): to devote all one's energy and enthusiasm to"–or 2) "A person who or thing which forms the vital or central part of something; the essence or core." The OED also suggests this phrase can translate as "With all one's energy and devotion; wholeheartedly" as well as as "Devoted and enthusiastic; committed, wholehearted; (also) that is felt from the heart (and soul), deeply felt."

'Heart', in turn, most commonly refers to 1) a specific organ of the body and its functioning, or, more broadly, the center of the general functioning of a body or of almost anything else for that matter; 2) "the seat of feeling, understanding, and thought" or "The seat or repository of a person's inmost thoughts, feelings, inclinations, etc.; a person's inmost being; the depths of the soul; the soul, the spirit"; 3) "the seat of the emotions generally; a person's emotional nature (often contrasted with the intellectual or rationalizing nature located in the *head*" or "the seat of love, attachment, or affection, or as representing a person's affections, devotion, loyalty, etc."; and 4) "(One's) intent, will, purpose; inclination, desire" or "Disposition, temperament, character" or "the seat of courage or morale." As the title of the song refers to heart *and* soul, this suggests they are not being used redundantly to signify what is overlapping or interchangeable, and therefore it seems as if 'heart' here most likely is associated with affect–with emotion–and in particular with the material center, the material source, the material basis, or the material epitome of emotion, and especially of emotional investment and engagement.

'Soul', according to the OED, most commonly refers to 1) "The principle of intelligence, thought, or action in a person (or occasionally an animal), typically regarded as an entity distinct from the body; the essential, immaterial, or spiritual part of a person or animal, as opposed to the physical"; 2) "Strength of character; strongly developed intellectual, moral, or aesthetic qualities; spiritual or emotional power or intensity; (also) deep feeling, sensitivity"; 3) "a vital or essential part" or a "leader or inspirer . . . a chief agent, prime mover, or leading spirit"; 4) the "spiritual or immaterial part regarded as a person's physical death and believed to be capable of happiness or misery depending on divine judgement" or "The disembodied spirit of a deceased person (or occasionally an animal) regarded as a separate entity and invested with some degree of personality and form." In "Heart and Soul," if we take 'heart' to refer to a material center or source of affect, then 'soul' makes sense as referring to an immaterial center or source of spirit. How to best interpret this phrase as title for this song, however, once again depends upon making sense of the lyrics as a whole and then further considering what the sounds, patterns of sounds, and deployments of sounds suggest.

Stanza one proceeds as follows: "Instincts that can still betray us/A journey that leads to the sun/Soulless and bent on destruction/A struggle between right and wrong." This is a tantalizing and characteristically mysterious opening, but to begin to unpack what might be suggested here I note well these are 'instincts' that 'can *still* betray us', which suggests 'even after' something, or after many things for that matter, this can *still* happen. Even after developing and refining one's instincts they can still betray, or even after learning and practicing successfully working beyond reliance upon instincts these can nevertheless return to 'betray'. 'Betray' suggests undermining us, and our aims, or at least our inclinations, and especially without us being aware of this happening until they have already succeeded in doing so. We don't know what precise instincts these might be, or how precisely they might betray 'us', only that they 'can'–only that they 'still can'. "A journey that leads to the sun" suggests a fantastical or perhaps more precisely science-fictional scenario, but if we interpret this as metaphorical, or symbolic, this line can suggest proceeding on a journey, or even a quest, that leads to a point at which we will be both dazzled and incinerated–we have pursued our way all the way toward what utterly consumes us, even if this has in many respects proven a spectacular journey. It may be that our 'instincts' have led us to this apocalyptic point, they have betrayed us by suggesting we can and should proceed 'all the way', without us at the same time grasping this means 'all the way toward our total destruction'. And, yes, line three does add "bent on destruction," which might indeed be where the journey is objectively headed, even if not subjectively registered as such, at least not until it's too late to turn around and head back. This third line, however, also begins with "Soulless," suggesting that in the course of this journey 'we' have proceeded without soul, forgetting or ignoring of soul, losing touch with the essence of our spiritual being, with our moral character, with our vital connection to the transcendent.

Yet this has not been a simple 'either/or' situation, so it seems, where we have recklessly pursued ambition, in total disregard of fundamental values and matters of ultimate concern, as it has involved, and it may still involve, "A struggle between right and wrong." What, precisely, constitutes 'right' and 'wrong' here remains uncertain at this point, but the fourth line suggests even as 'we' proceeded on the journey we did so from a conflicted vantage point, struggling with what is the right thing to do versus what is the wrong thing to do, and seemingly not able readily to pinpoint either. It is also worth emphasizing in this connection that this opening stanza refers to 'us', which suggests 'we too', we listeners, or attentive and sympathetically inclined listeners, have shared and are sharing in this same experience, and the same dilemmas it throws up.

Stanza two consists of the following lyrics: "You take my place in the showdown/I'll observe with a pitiful eye/I'd humbly ask for forgiveness/A request well beyond you and I." Here we right away are introduced to a departure from the 'us' of the first stanza, such that 'you' and 'I' are no longer in exactly the same position, but rather 'you' is 'taking the place' of 'I' in a 'showdown', which suggests the contribution 'I' can make, is able to make, to this 'showdown' has reached its end, has run its course, and now someone else–'you'–must take on this role instead. We don't know what this 'showdown' might be, and how it might be related to a 'struggle between right and wrong', let

758

alone a 'journey that leads to the sun', and in particular we don't know with whom, or with what, 'I' previously and now 'you' are contending in this showdown. 'Showdown' suggests a fight, or a contest, that has been anticipated for awhile, and which represents a culminating event of some kind. It seems this is something that has to be confronted, and engaged, even if reluctant to do so, and even if worried or fearful of losing, of being overmatched such that one is likely, even destined, to lose.

"I'll observe with a pitiful eye" suggests 'I' who once assumed a place in this showdown, or leading up to it, now will become a bystander, an observer, and with 'pitiful eye' we have multiple possibilities: 'I' will be pitying us and what we must confront and engage in this showdown, or pitying the necessity or inescapability of this showdown, or 'I' might indeed be 'pitiful' and perceive themself as pitiful because they no longer are 'up to' taking on the place 'you' will take on in their stead. 'I' might feel as if they have become 'pitiful', because they are in effect too weak, or weakened, to do anything anymore but observe–even, perhaps, when the stakes are incredibly high. "I'd humbly ask for forgiveness" fits this last possible interpretation, if 'I' is asking forgiveness for not being able to contribute directly to what is demanded, in the showdown, and of in effect compelling 'you' to need to step in, instead. However, this is in turn complicated by the last line, which suggests neither 'I' nor 'you' is in a position 'to forgive', perhaps because both are too much at fault, even too much too blame, and at least too far implicated in and responsible for what has led to the necessity, or inescapability, of such a showdown. Perhaps both 'I' and 'you' as 'us' are implicated and responsible because 'we' have ventured 'too close to the sun' 'soullessly' 'bent on destruction', 'betrayed' by 'our' instincts, and even repeatedly so. It is possible that both 'you' and 'I' have allowed ambition to guide us in directions that have led us to act in morally problematic ways as well as recklessly risking our own, and others', serious harm in so doing.

The third stanza marks the first iteration of the chorus: "Heart and soul, one will burn/ Heart and soul, one will burn." If we think back to what I earlier suggested are the most common associations with and understandings of the phrase 'heart and soul' as well as the words 'heart' and 'soul', it seems here that one of these is set for destruction, for being perhaps 'burned up' or 'burned out' by pushing beyond the limits of what can be sustained. This could suggest that either one's affective or spiritual nature will be so 'burned up' or 'burned out'. It could suggest an exhaustion of one's ability to continue to act on the basis of, in response to, or in manifesting emotion–or it could suggest losing touch with, having exhausted, the possibility of continuing to represent moral character, to uphold and live out moral principle, to be inspired by and to inspire others in moral terms. Yet we don't know which 'will burn', why this 'will' happen, and why only one and not both. What could possibly explain heart but not soul burning or soul but not heart burning? What might it mean for the two to be so divided and separated as a result? What might it mean to be able to show heart but not soul, or to show soul but not heart? What might it mean to be the heart, or at the heart, or in touch with the heart of an effort, a movement, a cause, but not the soul–and what might it mean to be the soul, or at the soul, or in touch with the soul of an effort, a movement, a cause but not the heart?

Another possible way of making sense of these lines follows from considering what happens if one pours "The whole of one's energy and affection," "all of one's energy and enthusiasm," and "one's whole being," into an effort, a movement, a cause, yet burns one's self out as a result, and falls short of realizing what all of this 'heart and soul' aimed to realize. With what then are you left? What happens when you are thoroughly burnt out? Yes, these lyrics can make sense as suggestive of a narrator-protagonist who feels 'he' no longer has reason to continue to live, no longer has the energy or the will to continue to live, and is contemplating suicide, but they can also suggest a narrator-protagonist who needs to 'retire' from a particular kind of vocation or avocation, a particular kind of lifestyle, to do something much different–perhaps because 'he' has given the end in question all 'he' possibly can, by 'himself', and now it is up to 'us' to contribute our part. Perhaps these lines are suggestive that '*one* will burn', that is an individual will 'burn' as a result of pouring themselves into pursuit of an end, with everything they have, and that this 'burning' might not represent solely 'burning down' or 'burning out' but rather 'burning with passion', 'burning with intensity', 'burning with desire', 'burning with emotion', and 'burning with moral concern'.

Stanza four, does, however, suggest a bleaker interpretation of what these lyrics are conveying: "An abyss that laughs at creation/A circus complete with all fools/Foundations that lasted the ages/Then ripped apart at their roots." It is possible we are invited to imagine this is a retrospective critical reflection on what the narrator-protagonist has participated in, not realizing what in effect 'he' was a part of, and that what has been happening is a scope of massively disruptive and destructive change. "An abyss that laughs at creation" suggests a mocking force and one that has the power to undo, and even to transform into its opposite, what was imagined and pursued as positively enabling and productive, turning substance into emptiness and making the effort to achieve and realize seem like nothing but absurd folly. "A circus complete with all fools" suggests something spectacularly chaotic with all agents engaged, again, in actions that effectively amount to absurd folly. These lines could well suggest disillusionment about a quest, about a dream, that once was maintained with an idealistic fervor, but now seems to have been at best a deluded, an impossible venture.

"Foundations that lasted the ages/Then ripped apart at the roots" suggests a situation in which major changes are happening that many could not possibly imagine would ever occur, and perhaps where it seems like disruptive and destructive forces have pressed beyond boundaries that many could not have imagined would ever occur. Certainly this seems apocalyptic, as if conjuring a state of extreme cultural degeneration, or of a total war, or of an ecological catastrophe, or of an abrupt and decisive ending of systems of support and stability that people have counted on and have been highly dependent upon. Perhaps, to connect this stanza with the preceding, the narrator-protagonist is suggesting 'he' and 'we' have been contributing unwittingly to this process of disruption and destruction, or that we have not recognized and done anything to forestall and prevent the triumph of such forces–and now it is too late. It may be, for instance, that we have complacently accepted capitalist modes of thinking, feeling, believing, acting, and interacting, not realizing where these can and will lead, carried out to their furthest logical conclusion–not realizing, for instance, that discontents with conditions of life experienced under post-WWII social democracy will be dwarfed by discontents with conditions of life to be experienced under post-collectivist, re-privatized neoliberal capitalism. It may be, for instance, that reckless disregard for the perdurability of natural ecosystems has led to a point where ecological catastrophe is already happening, and even far worse is imminently looming, to the point where the future of life, including human life, at least in forms according to which many of us have grown comfortably familiar, and taken for granted, might all too soon be unsustainable.

Stanza five reads as follows: "Beyond all this good is the terror/The grip of a mercenary hand/When savagery turns all good reason/There's no turning back, no last stand." Initially here we recognize there has been and may still be 'good', and even considerable 'good'–"all this good." This might support an interpretation of the lyrics according to which they are describing and commenting on a process–a process of disruptive and destructive transformation. 'Beyond' though is nebulous, as we are uncertain 'how far beyond', even if the thrust of the lyrics as a whole tend to suggest this is an increasingly *closer* beyond. And what lies beyond is "the terror" which appears to be identified with "the grip of a mercenary hand" as well as with circumstances such that "savagery turns all good reason." "The grip of a mercenary hand" suggests a force, or a constellation of forces, acting as they are because they are 'being paid for it', and as such they have no other stake in what they are doing than a pecuniary one. This may well suggest a vision of a larger society in which, effectively, more and more people are acting, whether they realize or acknowledge this or not, first and last, always, in the interest of making money, or of gaining in selfish economic, social, and/or political advantage. And indeed they are doing so at others' direct expense, while no longer caring at all about moral concerns, about the harms they can and do cause in putting this pursuit of individual advantage, of individual fame and fortune, above all else. They eschew principle and are willing to work for, and do the bidding of, whomever will offer them the most profitable form of compensation.

This is a vision of a society that is no longer substantively a society at all, but rather a collection of monadic, atomized, antagonistic individuals and small groupings, all competing against each other solely for their own immediate and short-term gain, and with no semblance of collective interest, let alone of collective responsibility, exercising significant influence–anymore. Such a society can be one in which "savagery turns all good reason"–i.e., where it doesn't matter anymore how you treat others, or your community or the natural environment. It doesn't matter what harm you cause, as all that matters is what exercise of 'might' 'can make right'. In other words, the most important effective values and aims of life are 'to compete successfully with others' in order 'to get ahead of these others' by 'taking advantage of others in any and every way possible to do so' so as 'to advance and enhance one's own individual–and familial–material well-being'. Let others 'sink or swim' entirely according to their own efforts, as no one owes anything to anyone else. "There's no turning back, there's no last stand," suggests 'the showdown' alluded to in the first stanza may have proven a mirage, as it is now too late. Powerful forces have moved us all too far in this 'terrifying' 'mercenary' and 'savage' direction such that we cannot undo what has happened, and we cannot make up for, let alone reverse, what has been destroyed. This all happened without 'a last stand' taking place because all too many of 'us' did not recognize what was happening, where the process of change was heading, until it was too late, and therefore we did not put up a defense to attempt to preserve and protect what is now lost.

After stanza six involves a second iteration of the chorus–"Heart and soul, one will burn/ Heart and soul, one will burn"–stanza seven shares the passage highlighted in *Control*: "Existence well what does it matter?/I exist on the best terms I can/The past is now part of my future/The present is well out of hand/The present is well out of hand." Here it seems these lyrics offer a familiarly existentialist response to an existential crisis involving confrontation with the absence of any inherent, essential, immanent, or transcendent reason why 'I' or 'we" exist. The only reason for existence is existence in itself. Beyond, behind, or beneath existence is nothingness. We exist simply to exist. We make whatever meaning we find in life by way of how we carry out our existence. Existing "on the best terms I can" makes sense, therefore, because in the face of a void, or an abyss, of meaninglessness, or of nothingness, all we can do is exist on our own terms as best we can. In this sense 'to exist' partakes of the 'absurd'–we exist without being able to explain or justify doing so as making sense.

At the same time, in relation to the lyrics preceding this seventh stanza, these lines suggest accepting all that is now possible is simply to try just to get by, even just to barely survive–and that grandiose dreams and visions of what one's life might mean and of what one might be a part of and contribute toward need to be abandoned as illusory, even as delusory. These lines also suggest a situation in which a subject feels as if 'he' maintains extremely little, or extremely limited, power to effect virtually anything, even in 'his' most immediate of empirical circumstances. This may well be a subject who recognizes, and who experiences, himself, as 'out of his control'–whose body, and, more precisely, whose physical health and well-being, is 'out of his control'. "The past is now part of my future/The present is well out of hand/The present is well out of hand" can suggest giving into and accepting this lack, or this loss, of control, this annihilation or obliteration of any substantial sense of self, gesturing toward an uncertain legacy beyond the end of 'his' individual life as all that yet remains ahead. These last three lines reinforce an impression of a subject proposing 'his' story has effectively been written, and will be written, now altogether beyond anything more 'he' 'himself' can do about it–and as if 'he' is being carried along and compelled to 'go through motions' over which he has no control, or no longer has any control.

This stanza can read as if suggesting that one's life, and more precisely life's course, is predestined, fated, and totally determined. The final lines of the stanza, in turn, run counter to common popular therapeutic advice that urges 'mindfulness' such that one focuses narrowly upon the present, while not spending too much time and energy caught belaboring the past or worrying about the future. Repeating "The present is well out of hand" at the end of the stanza gives this particular line even greater emphasis, accentuating the contrast with that kind of popular therapeutic advice.

The final stanza offers an elaboration of the chorus: "Heart and soul, one will burn/Heart and soul, one will burn/One will burn/One will burn/Heart and soul/One will burn." This is a haunting conclusion that I suggest is not easily tied down to any singular interpretation. Perhaps, again, pouring one's heart and soul into an effort will lead to 'one' burning–whether 'one' 'burns' with passionate intensity or one 'burns' down and out. Perhaps either 'heart' or 'soul' will 'burn'; either one's reservoir of emotion or one's fount of morality will 'burn'.

I find the lyrics to "Heart and Soul" among the most difficult of Ian Curtis's lyrics to interpret, solely by themselves, and I find I *need* to consider them in relation to the music in order to do much with them that feels satisfying. I am impatient with interpretations that identify 'the meaning of these lyrics' as Ian Curtis confessing he is suicidal and intends to kill himself, or that he is expressing his guilt about the breakdown of his marriage. The lyrics don't strike me as anywhere near that pat, and, if anything, I'd rather leave the question of 'the meaning of these lyrics' open-ended, and instead work *off of* these lyrics by examining and reflecting on *my own* thoughts, feelings, and beliefs concerning matters of instinct, heart, soul, right and wrong, destruction, journeying and questing, engagement and disengagement, control and lack of control, existence and for what does it matter, (inter)relations among past and present and future, mercenary and terrifying and savage forces and tendencies, showdowns and last stands, and burning with and up as well as down and out. I will come to that, but before proceeding to consider how the music influences the way I make sense of what this song might plausibly mean, I will mention that Deborah Curtis includes one earlier version of the lyrics to "Heart and Soul" in *So This Is Permanence* which, while not departing all that much from the version as performed on *Closer*, offers a few instances where we witness Ian Curtis's thinking in process.

In this earlier draft, Ian crosses out "what leads to" in the first stanza, replacing this with "and bent on" indicating the 'us' involved in this "journey to the sun" are prospectively more willfully as well as recklessly responsible for the "destruction" alluded to here than the earlier version suggested. In the second verse stanza Ian crosses out "task" and replaces it with "request" in the line that reads "A request well beyond you and I," shifting the emphasis from suggesting we–'you' and 'I'–are not 'up to the task' of 'asking for forgiveness' toward suggesting instead that we are not in a position, or the position, to make such a request. As a result of this change it makes somewhat greater sense to interpret this lyric as suggesting you and I are too compromised to make such a request, not too weakened to be able to do so. In the third verse stanza, Ian crosses out "A stone" and replaces it with "Foundations," and this change seems quite significant as the latter suggests something of much greater scope and magnitude than the former is being "ripped apart at their roots." In the same stanza Ian crosses out "Hearts torn" and replaces this with "And then." The former suggests a series of successive allusions, with "Foundations that lasted the ages" followed by "Hearts torn at their roots" amounting to two distinct entities: the 'foundations that lasted the ages' *and* the 'hearts torn at their roots'. The latter, the final version, suggests it is the foundations that are torn at their roots *after* having lasted for ages, suggesting a calamitous change in a larger state of affairs, potentially on a broad social scale. These are slight changes, but overall the revision appears to move in the direction of giving greater emphasis to objective and not just subjective changes.

The structure of "Heart and Soul" (the *Closer* version) proceeds as follows:

1. Instrumental opening: 0:00–>0:59. Introduction: Setting the Stage and Leading In. The song begins with a bass guitar line accompanied by drums and cymbals through the first 19 seconds and then two successive shimmering synthesizer lines enter followed by a second gently melodically oscillating bass guitar line.

2. First vocal passage: 1:00–>2:18. Recollecting and Recounting/Identifying and Describing. Here it is worth noting well how this section includes all of the first six vocal stanzas, as in other words they all proceed in succession without a break, or an intermediary 'bridge', between any of these. The vocal here is far less deep, dark, and hard than often is the case with Ian Curtis's recorded singing voice, but is nonetheless highly embellished–sounding ethereally reverberant.

3. Instrumental bridge: 2:19–>3:13. Registering and Reflecting/Absorbing and Enveloping. This section introduces a slightly discordant, slightly chiming minor key guitar line, played live at least by Ian Curtis, involving movement back and forth between just two chords.

4. Second vocal passage: 3:14–>3:57. Further Recollecting and Recounting/Further Identifying and Describing. This section includes both of the last two vocal stanzas, as once again the second directly follows upon the first without a break, or an intermediary 'bridge'.

5. Extended instrumental conclusion: 3:58–>5:46. Further Registering and Reflecting/Further Absorbing and Enveloping/Closing Down and Fading Out. This section reintroduces the slightly discordant, slightly chiming minor key guitar line moving back and forth between just two chords. It also contains a notably prolonged fadeout.

The instrumentation of "Heart and Soul" is comprised of two bass guitar lines, one performed via a synthesizer keyboard, as well as at least the equivalent of one warm synthesizer pad performing three to four different lines, one guitar line involving oscillating repetition among just two chords, the vocal, and the drums and cymbals. "Heart and Soul" begins with the lower bass guitar line accompanied by the drums and cymbals, then the shimmering synthesizer lines join, then the second higher bass guitar line joins, then the vocal joins, and finally in the bridge and the closing sections we hear the guitar as well. The initial low bass guitar line is the first instrument to sound the melody, while the second high bass guitar line offers a variation on the melody, a kind of counter or para melody, and the vocal subsequently takes the lead in performing the melody with support in doing so from the low bass guitar.

'The heat' is certainly substantially reduced in the production of "Heart and Soul" while the space immediately surrounding each instrument and between instruments in the mix is certainly pronounced. The vocal and the drum kit, not unusually, obtain and maintain foreground positions throughout the song although each of the instruments contributing to the sound of "Heart and Soul" are audibly distinct and none comes close to being 'buried' by any others.

With the drums and cymbals I definitely hear a synthesizer snare drum–responsible for a narrow, crisp, as well as clear and prominent sound. The snare and hi-hat sounds here often come close to converging or blending in terms of timbre. I also hear the bass drum quite distinctly as well, along with what sounds like a conventional (non-electronic) snare drum, accenting as opposing to striking, verging on contributing rolls, in periodic brief flourishes. "Heart and Soul" makes more use of open hi-hat (on the fourth or on the third and fourth beats) than is often the case in Joy Division songs, in combination with the closed hi-hat otherwise predominating. The beat often involves a bass drum strike on beat #1, a snare drum strike on beat #2, then a quick bass drum strike followed by a series of snare drum strikes for beats #3 and #4.

"Heart and Soul" contains all four standard functional layers, as expected of a popular (rock) song, and what is particularly notable in this connection is that the electric and electronic bass guitar lines both signally contribute to the melodic layer, along with the vocal. The guitar is only responsible for harmonic fill, yet despite its minimal and simple part makes a significant contribution along those lines, one that complicates the texture, adding a much stronger element of disturbance and unease than otherwise would be the case. The harmonic fill layer is also achieved via contributions from the shimmering synthesizer lines as well as studio embellishments. The explicit beat layer and the melodic layer are both the most dominant other than in the bridge and conclusion where the harmonic fill layer becomes especially prominent, pronounced, and foregrounded.

In terms of the soundbox, the opening bass guitar lines enters from low and to the left, yet close to the front. This line seems to become slightly softer as the song proceeds, and it seems to drift slightly toward the center and slightly back. This bass guitar line also seems to move higher in pitch register later and to later on also add some light flourishes that add variety to the repeated pattern it otherwise maintains. The drums and cymbals enter from higher than the initial bass guitar line, toward the edges of the soundbox as well, especially to the left of the soundbox and again close to the front, seemingly closer to the front than the initial bass guitar line. Again, the positions of the drums and cymbals within the soundbox seem to drift somewhat toward the center as the song proceeds. The vocal contributes from just above center, or center high, while seeming to echo from both sides of center, or, in other words, to reverberate from within and across a central, hollowed out location. The vocal is prominent and foregrounded but hard to precisely pinpoint in terms of depth because of its degree of resonance and especially reverberation, echo, and multi-tracking. The guitar line contributes from the right of the soundbox, slightly down from the center, and fairly close to the front. The shimmering synthesizer sounds emerge from the lower left, far down, and to the back, pushing upward and closer towards yet never too close to the front as the song proceeds. And the second bass guitar line seems to emerge almost parallel to the first bass line except from the right instead of the left of the soundbox. This bass guitar line seems to contribute more harmonic accompaniment and support than melody.

"Heart and Soul" displays an amplification and intensification of Joy Division's innovation in foregrounding the bass guitar, especially as a principal means of carrying the melody and of diminishing, evacuating, and transforming the role of the guitar, as well as of transforming the traditional rock instrumental array into an electronic and hybrid array, adding layers of electronic sounds. 'Layers' is indeed apt here, because with "Heart and Soul" we hear gentle, slightly distant, layers of electronic soundlines, sounding much like shimmering strings. "Heart and Soul" is also notable given a bass guitar line is played by means of a synthesizer keyboard as well as for the prominent use of electronic drums, in particular for the snare sounds. The vocal is distinctive as well, sounding as if it has been treated with the equivalent of a kind of 'wash' that renders it more strangely, icily, spectrally reverberant, echoing, and simultaneously doubling, or multiplied, than usual, while also drawing out and foregrounding more of a tenor register and offering a clean, clear, distinct, even glistening, and, paradoxically enough, complex and full, timbre.

In terms of loudness the most notable variations, or changes, in loudness in "Heart and Soul" (as again represented by the version on *Closer*) come in the bridge and closing sections, especially via the guitar. Otherwise worthy of note in this connection are more subtle matters, such as the shimmering layered synthesized string lines sounding generally quieter overall than most else (except for brief intervals in the opening and closing sections of the song), the snare and hi-hat sounding louder than the bass drum, and the vocal tending to sound slightly louder than the rest when it is present without this involving any evident straining. The higher bass guitar line also tends, over the course of the song, to sound somewhat louder than the lower bass guitar line.

The tempo for the *Closer* version of "Heart and Soul" is 150 BPM, according to my count, somewhat faster than average for Joy Division, especially for *Closer*, and, as is almost always the case for Joy Division and most rock songs for that matter, the time signature is 4/4. Two single-measure drum and cymbal patterns establish and maintain the beat, with each of these patterns repeated successively across a series of subsequent measures, the first more frequent than the second:

Pattern #1: bass drum on beat 1, snare drum on beat 2, bass drum on beat 3, rest, snare drum on beat 3and, snare drum on beat 4, and snare drum on beat 4and–along with closed hi-hat on beat1and, closed hi-hat on beat 2and, closed hi-hat on beat 3, and open hi-hat on beat 4and.

Pattern #2: bass drum on beat 1, snare drum on beat 2, bass drum on beat 3, snare drum on beat 3eeand, snare drum on beat 3eeanduh, snare drum on beat 4, snare drum on beat 4ee, snare drum on beat 4eeand, snare drum on beat 4eeanduh–along with closed hi-hat on beat 1, closed hi-hat on beat 1and, closed hi-hat on beat 2and, open hi-hat on beat 3and, and open hi-hat on beat 4eeanduh. The drums and cymbals perform only these two patterns in "Heart and Soul," contributing a highly regular and consistent explicit beat layer, or rhythmic ground, to the song, yet with just enough departure from the standard rock beat to add interest.

Meanwhile, the lead bass guitar tends to sound a rhythmic pattern of successive notes across two successive measures as follows: quarter note, eighth note, dotted quarter note, quarter note//quarter note, eighth note, quarter note, and three eighth notes. The guitar moves between two chords across two measures, one chord per measure, with each of these two chords strummed five times and in length as follows: eighth note, quarter note, eighth note, quarter note, quarter note. The second bass guitar line performs a pattern involving three chords per measure in respective length as follows: a dotted quarter note, a dotted quarter note, and a quarter note. The shimmering synthesizer lines extend across up to 20+ measures, while persistently wavering closely around the same, single pitch. The vocal seems to follow this rhythmic pattern: eighth note, eighth note, eighth note, eighth note, quarter note, quarter note/quarter note, dotted quarter note. A periodic variation involves the final quarter note from the first measure holding over or tying into the first quarter note of the second measure. A rest occurs between lines of a quarter note to a dotted quarter note in length. The chorus consists of all quarter notes and especially of quarter notes that are held over or tie into quarter notes from a first to a second successive measure. What we find here once more is a considerable degree of regularity and consistency but with just enough variation in patterns of length, as well as emphasis, or accentuation, in successive notes or chords sounded, among the different instruments, to add complexity and richness to the overall sound.

"Heart and Soul" is performed in the key of D minor. The pitch of the vocal line moves slightly upward and then further down, in general, once more in a highly regular and consistent way, involving no more than two to three steps at a time. The pitch of the guitar moves down and then up, yet across an only slight interval, persistently back and forth. The second bass guitar line moves slightly up in pitch, then back down, and following this, with slight flourishes, then quickly slightly further up and then quickly slightly further down. Here, the overall or ultimate direction of movement tends down in pitch. The lead bass guitar lines moves, again, slightly up in pitch but comes back down after that and once more ultimately emphasizes movement back down. The synthesizer strings involve some notable reaching up in pitch but they too also come back down as well. The ultimate emphasis is on a downward movement in pitch despite pushing upward repeatedly in between down positions, because down feels like where we find the home or the tonic pitch. Overall, locations and especially movements of pitch contribute a feeling of being tightly contained, albeit with efforts repeatedly to push upward and against the limits of this containment yet also bearing a strong sense of acceptance of the inevitability and even desirability of returning down and thereby acceding to what those same limits prescribe—and proscribe.

I have already described notable features of Ian Curtis's vocal delivery on "Heart and Soul" but it is worth emphasizing, again, the lack of any evident straining, of any pushing upward and louder later in the song, as is often the case in Joy Division songs, and as such the vocal here feels as if it conveys a gentle distancing and detachment from the ostensible subject of the lyrics, with the vocal sounding far less disturbed than the content of these lyrics might readily imagine one singing them to sound. Curtis's voice is much less darkened, and by no means as deep, as is commonplace, not sounding as a baritone leaning toward a bass in register, but rather as distinctly a tenor, while sounding overtly heavily treated and embellished. The enunciation is clear and distinct and the vocal is prominent and clear, while sounding akin to a gentle yet tightly contained crooning.

Considering matters of timbre in "Heart and Soul" more precisely, the layered string synthesizer sounds again convey a shimmering timbre, involving a mild warmth, and do resemble conventional strings allowed protractedly to ring while played gently. The sustain is long here, while the decay is limited and the attack is weak. In terms of the vocal, the sustain contributes to a timbre that is bright, pure, hollow, between rich and sparse, between beatless and beating yet more beatless, between steady and wavering yet more steady, and harmonic; the attack contributes to a timbre that is pure, soft, and bright; and the pitch contributes to a timbre that is between low and high, and between steady and wavering yet more steady. The vocal timbre is strongly affected by its echoing, reverberating, doubled or multiplied character, and contains an element of a strange warmth even while, paradoxically enough, sounding notably glacial or icy. Perhaps this has to do with the extent to which the recorded vocal sound offers little evidence of overt strain or stress and comes across as eerily calm, smooth, untroubled, and not labored. The timbres of the drums and cymbals, overall, come across as incisive yet thin, narrow, clipped, and pinpoint, especially the snare and hi-hat. The guitar timbre offers a pronouncedly discordant feeling, again as if taking on major responsibility for overtly representing the element of a persistent disquiet in this song. The timbre of low bass guitar line involves a softer, richer, warmer, and almost mellow character, in comparison with that of the timbre of the high bass guitar line that involves something more of an explicit edge.

As a whole, the individual timbres and the collective timbre are clean and clear not dirty and noisy, with only the guitar sounds approaching sounding distorted sounding yet more discordant than distorted. Nothing comes across as particularly breathy. We do hear vibrato with the synthesizer strings. Often the timbres sound reduced, stripped, narrowed, thin, and clipped. Only the guitar timbre sounds close to piercing with the others sounding much the opposite. Nothing sounds particularly nasal or flat. We do hear much in terms of timbre that sounds silky, even approaching, oddly enough, mellow and warm.

The timbre of the deep bass guitar line feels, analogously, as if it corresponds to a determined, brisk, but controlled walking pace. In the case of the shimmering electronic strings an analogous movement feels like that of slow gliding. The high bass guitar line feels like an element of climbing has been added to the movement, yet otherwise is suggestive of a movement much like that of the deep bass guitar line. The drums and cymbals feel like they are moving at a jauntier pace, closer to a jog or a light run, yet regular and controlled at the same time. Movement suggested by the vocal involves gliding as if reaching about, including up and down, in the same tightly limited space as opposed to moving any significant distance.

In order to move closer to speculating on how the preceding elements of the musical sound of "Heart and Soul" might contribute to and influence interpretations of meanings, and, more precisely, of what it makes good sense to propose the song invites and encourages us to think (about) and feel, whom and what it invites and encourages us to imagine is addressing us in what way and toward what end, as well as how it calls upon us to respond as well as why so, it is useful now to consider this song in terms of the eight avenues of musical affect I have drawn from and been making use of since chapter two. Beginning, first, with mimetic participation, "Heart and Soul" conveys much more a sense of ease versus effort in exertion of force, even though this is deceptive because it can require ample effort to achieve a semblance of calm in the midst of and in response to bleak circumstances. The drumming feels as if it involves somewhat greater effort than the other instruments. Again, complexity is deceptive here, because regularity and consistency are not necessarily as easy to achieve as might seem the case–and in fact both Peter Hook and Stephen Morris have suggested the song was a challenge to get right performed live and they often needed to make significant alterations in performing it live as a result. Locking in, tightly together, while each musician follows his own distinct line or lines, sequences of pitch, and relations to the overall rhythm, in turn maintains its challenges, especially over a song lasting nearly six minutes. Nevertheless, exertion does not seem to change much over the duration of the song, although yes the vocal comes and goes and the guitar only shows up in two out of five sections.

Considering this song in terms of success versus failure of exertion seems puzzling to me, because, as is often the case, in relation to this Joy Division song, in listening to it, closely and repeatedly, it feels as if it has accomplished all it set forth to do. I do feel as if each of the musicians, and each of the musical lines, perform distinct yet tightly interrelated contributions, and, as such, are always aware of each other while concentrating on doing their own thing in their own way, as the latter often involves working off of, in response to, and as compliments to each other. "Heart and Soul" is not a Joy Division song in response to which I feel a strong inclination to join in, and participate mimetically, as here I feel more distinctly like an audience attending to others' participation in making this song what it is than as an imagined or vicarious co-contributor to the sounds, patterns of sounds, and deployments of sounds.

Because of a high degree of regularity and consistency in the music, "Heart and Soul" feels as if it anticipates doing exactly that: repeating, varying, and returning, in predictable ways. This includes anticipating instruments and their lines that drop out for awhile will return as well as anticipating when they will return. I hear the music anticipating the first vocal passage, the return of the vocal with the second vocal passage, and its final fading out. I also hear the music anticipating the return of the guitar in the closing section following its contribution to the bridge section. "Heart and Soul" feels beyond desire or dread, as if located in a becalmed position where stress and strain, and struggle and strife, are now largely past. I hear the song as positioned beyond anticipating disappointment because it feels in contrast closer to emphasizing acceptance that disappointment has happened and that this was inevitable and inescapable. "Heart and Soul" almost feels as it is positioned beyond the affective states of resignation and of coming to terms with the need for resignation. It is as if all of that is already over and done with, and now the only question is what if anything at all is still left, is still possible. "Heart and Soul" contains some elements suggestive of unrest and unease, which make the best sense as unsettling reminders of what has in the past been responsible for provoking unrest and unease, as well as reminders of what this unrest and unesase felt like *then*, in moments of peak intensity that have long since diminished and disappeared.

In listening carefully and repeatedly to the music of "Heart and Soul" the song feels to me as if it expresses a strange, eerie state of calm as well as a strange, eerie degree of distance and detachment. It feels as if the affect conveyed by the music, including by the vocal, is no longer directly associated with the words of the lyrics. "Heart and Soul" expresses a feeling of acceptance beyond resignation, and beyond regret and despair, but also makes sense as expressing a conviction that life will continue after the death of a singular being or a limited number of beings–that life itself will and does go on, even after someone dies, even after we ourselves die, and the same is analogously the case after someone retires or otherwise leaves the scene of direct engagement in a particular pursuit. Larger rhythms and larger forces will persist even after we stop and are no more. One individual's or even a small group of individuals' contributions and involvements eventually tend to disappear into a virtual nothingness. Yes, I hear a gentle melancholy in "Heart and Soul" but not a continuation of a commitment to fight, and not even a continuation of a commitment to struggle. "Heart and Soul" sounds as if this is a moment of giving way, and more precisely of stepping away from a life-force within which one will no longer be directly participating. I myself feel uneasy listening to this song, but also as if I am invited into a prayerful space, sharing a moment of incredible intimacy with one who is not agitated anymore even as I feel troubled by 'his' lack of continuing agitation. The music, however, is even more complex than I have just described, in terms of what I hear it expressing, because it also conveys something of a sprightly feeling, given its tempo, and it likewise is suggestive of the aura that accompanies immersion in a dissociative or trance experience. I feel here, more than in most Joy Division songs, as if the music/the musicians and I are operating in different emotional locations, because this song makes me, again, feel uneasy, unsettled, even more than gently melancholic and mildly saddened, as more worried and concerned than that, but I don't feel this is what the music as persona is experiencing.

In terms of acoustic impact, the sounds that comprise "Heart and Soul" come at me from across the soundbox, with this array well organized and well articulated, balanced, distinctly spaced out yet tightly connected. The space conjured as result of this disposition feels ethereal, aleatory, and evanescent. I feel physically close, almost uncomfortably physically close, to the music/the musicians/the music as persona. I feel the sounds are paradoxically both concentrated in their respective locations yet diffused across the soundbox, with the synthesizer strings contributing the most overtly to feelings of diffusion even as the vocal conveys a pronounced element of this as well. Meanwhile, the guitar seems hard to characterize in terms of more concentrated versus more diffuse while the drums and the bass guitar lines feel overall more concentrated.

As is often the case with "Joy Division" songs, "Heart and Soul" feels to me as if it comes (at me) from a position, from a vantage point or perspective, *after* analysis is already done and has already happened. The lyrics convey elements of analysis in process but it is hard for me to make sense of the rest of the song as 'analyzing' per se. It feels much more as if it is attesting or testifying or, even more simply, performing and presenting than it does as if it is analyzing. Likewise, I find it difficult to make sense of this song as offering any kind of pleasure of survival, because survival seems 'well out of hand' by this point, almost 'beyond the point'. Even if some form of survival is (still) happening, this feels not so much pleasurable as merely happening. With "Heart and Soul" it feels as if failure has preceded the setting of the song, the time and place from which it is directly coming at me, and now it is questionable what success versus failure might have meant, or whether that really mattered. The guitar conveys elements of unease that seem as if they might be approaching panic or dread but the rest of the musical components of the song do not. Perhaps "Heart and Soul," especially by way of the vigorous contributions of the drums and cymbals, is *simultaneously* representing *both* calm acceptance of 'the end' and a continuing edge of wanting and needing to press or persist beyond giving way to this 'ending'.

Even at this stage of my listening to and reflecting on "Heart and Soul" it remains a difficult song for me to interpret in terms of what associations the music is invoking as opposed to what the lyrics, taken by themselves alone, seem to invoke. Perhaps I am associating what I hear in and through this song with seeking to calmly accept what can't be helped, can't be stopped, and to try to quiet myself down, to try not to continue to wear myself down by raging against the dying of the light or even against pain, suffering, alienation, loneliness, hardship, worry, and fear while yet still feeling a pull to continue to do so. I associate what I hear in this song with the death drive strongly at work even if I detect at least slight elements of a persistent struggle between the death drive and the life drive. It might even be that the regularity and consistency that is so pronounced in this song is conveying to me a sense that life can and will go on, even when it feels like it cannot, even after suffering a deep blow, a major loss, or a crushing defeat. Even when it seems like things cannot get any better, and bleakness will be now eternally everlasting, this might not turn out to be the case.

Just like with associations that I interpret the song itself as making, as opposed to those I make with the song, I find it difficult to interpret what taboos "Heart and Soul" might itself be exploring and engaging. 'Chills' here, which Arnie Cox suggests are useful evidence of musical exploration and engagement with taboos, come from the guitar as well as the location, treatment, and delivery of the vocal. At the same time, I wouldn't say "Heart and Soul" offers much at all in the way of 'thrills'. The minor chord guitar line is disturbing and unsettling. It feels as if it is perhaps all the more disturbing and unsettling to face up to, to confront, to vicariously experience a giving up and a giving in, of being totally overwhelmed and even more than this totally annihilated by sadness and pain to the point where the ability to experience any further sadness and pain has been exhausted. It is plausible to interpret this song as prompting associations with the self disappearing to the point where the self becomes effectively a living ghost–a mere vestige, trace, or ephemerally lingering cipher. Fragility and uncertainty remain but desperation feels, at least temporarily, as if this is now gone. "Heart and Soul" is suggestive of what happens in opening up one's self, in exposing and performing one's vulnerability and weakness so far, that one effectively disintegrates and disappears–nothing is left; it is all played out. It is commonly taboo to reflect on the loss, the end, the disintegration, and the disappearance of one's self such that one is no longer a being but rather a nothingness.

Yet again, I find it hard to grasp, to imagine, what the precise location might be, or might be like, from which the music as persona is addressing me in "Heart and Soul." In this song it feels as if the voice is disembodied and not just mediated. It feels as if it might, thereby, be invisible and intangible. What the precise emotional state of the song might be is also difficult to grasp and even so seems on the verge of lingering only for an ephemeral instant. The relation between where the music as persona is at, what the music as persona is conveying in relation to what else, what the music as persona is referencing that has happened and is happening, my location versus this, and how I am supposed to respond–all feel highly ephemeral too.

In seeking out possible connections with Césaire's *Discourse on Colonialism*, "Heart and Soul" feels as if it attests to what no longer exists, what has disappeared, and what cannot be recaptured and recreated. This does resonate with the impact of colonialism, with what colonialism effects. Colonialism, as Césaire argues, does result in the reduction and diminution of the human being. Colonialism, as Césaire argues, is, for the colonized, all too often about being crushed into numbingly accepting, out of necessity, a life of just striving to survive day to day and even moment to moment with nothing more to aspire toward–in effect becoming a thing, in effect experiencing what Césaire characterizes as 'thingification'. It makes good sense, following Césaire, to propose that colonialism destroys the heart and soul (or either the heart or the soul) of a people, of a community, and of a culture–colonialism effectively 'burns' all of this up and leaves nothing behind but embers and ashes.

With Said's *Representations of the Intellectual*, the closest possible connections with "Heart and Soul" feel as if they come in relation to Said's description of how isolating and estranging exile, including self-chosen and intellectually as well as politically necessary exile, can be. "Heart and Soul" resonates with Said's discussion of Adorno's discerning no prospect of being able to reach anyone presently living and be understood, heeded, and followed, with all he could hope for being, as a result, that somehow someone in the future might eventually do so, long after Adorno himself is dead. "Heart and Soul" conjures a feeling as if one has been articulating protest and critique from a position so thoroughly exiled as to become unintelligible, even imperceptible, and, most troubling of all, ineffectual in relation to whom one has been striving to reach. Yet "Heart and Soul," given the placidity and serenity that much of the music conveys, might also make sense as suggestive of calmly accepting the limits and constraints of such a position of intellectual exile.

In connection with Trinh's *Woman, Native, Other: Writing Postcoloniality and Feminism*, it feels as if it is hard, in "Heart and Soul," to precisely distinguish let alone delimit positions of I, you, and us, and the same among I, you, and us then versus I, you and us now, and versus I, you, and us to be. In connection with Trinh, it is plausible to suggest that "Heart and Soul" feels as if the song engages layers of diffuse or diffused identities that don't necessarily add up to any clearly or precisely structured totality. In other words, for both Trinh and "Heart in Soul" it seems I may not be, or never was, or never can or will be the I that I have imagined that I was, and the same with you as well as the same with us, while what distinguishes as well as what unites 'I' with 'you' as 'we' might again not be what I and you have imagined this to be. "Heart and Soul" also makes sense in terms of representing an instance, following Trinh, of discoursing alongside or nearby, in particular alongside and nearby what is nebulous and evanescent. Likewise, "Heart and Soul" makes sense as exploring and engaging with limits and ends, as well as exploring and engaging with potentially endless and unlimited loops. Trinh argues for liberating possibilities in embracing the alternative conceptions of subjectivity and relationality she theorizes, but in the case of "Heart and Soul" liberation seems doubtful, if not altogether impossible.

When I consider, with "Heart and Soul," what kind of subject is reaching out to address me, how I am positioned in being addressed by this subject, and how I hear myself called upon to respond, I think in particular of elaborate connections I make with what this song invites and encourages me to think (about) and feel. To begin, in relation to the eleven overarching interpretations of the lyrics and music of Ian Curtis and Joy Division I first set forth in chapter one, I find the following particularly relevant to "Heart and Soul":

(1) *It transpires in a mysteriously otherworldly realm where comfortably reassuring borderlines break down.* With "Heart and Soul" these borderlines, as suggested by the lyrics, include borderlines among past, future, and present, as well as between being and nothingness, between continuing and ending, between resignation and acceptance, and between trauma and the aftermath of trauma.

(2) *Facing, without resorting to self-protective blinders or sentimentalizing illusions, often extraordinarily disturbing incidences of cruelty and violence, as well as of anxiety and alienation.* With "Heart and Soul" this involves becoming so thoroughly empathetically identified with the destructive impact of these kinds of practices as to experience the collapse and dissipation of self and the exhaustion of the capacity to feel any more.

(3) *An exploration of and inquiry into the following two sets of fundamental questions: 1. Why do I exist? What is the meaning, value, and purpose of my existence? To what extent can I exercise any influence, and any control, over what this meaning, value, and purpose becomes? How can, and how should, I attempt to do so? 2. In what ways, and to what extent, am I responsible for others? For the suffering, hardship, and pain others experience? For the violence and cruelty as well as the injustice and unfairness in the world? What can and what should I do about any of this?* With "Heart and Soul," in response to the first set of questions, it seems almost as if the answer is 'there is no answer', and, more precisely, there is no meaning, value, and purpose, as well as no possibility of influence or control over what already is, in and of itself, ephemeral and illusory, while, in response to the second set of questions, it seems almost as if the answer is I am overwhelmingly responsible yet I can do little to nothing about this responsibility.

(4) *An exploration of and inquiry into the sense and meaning of alienation, isolation, and loneliness; the position and experience of being a stranger, an outsider, and an outcast; vulnerability,*

772

entrapment, anxiety, and fear; and the need to connect, especially intimately, along with the simultaneous difficulty of doing so. With "Heart and Soul" it feels to me as if the song explores how extreme this position can be, can feel, and, as a result, how annihilating this can be, even if it is right and necessary, as well as what kind of uncanny serenity can develop in such a state.

"Heart and Soul" I hear as a meditative and even prayerful song, approaching me from a detached space, that is strikingly ethereal and aleatory, spectrally calm and even glacially becalmed, conveying strong elements of resignation and especially acceptance but also glimmering reminders of what once were and what might yet be other possibilities. In "Hearts and Soul" I hear the music as persona having become resigned to and accepting of what has, at least until recently, caused enormous pain and sorrow. In contrast with many Joy Division songs which I hear as emphasizing and even foregrounding persistent struggle, with "Heart and Soul" I hear a subject addressing me from a vantage point where this subject is now past continuing to struggle–and past continuing to suffer.

It may be, however, that the music as persona is proposing it is now up to me to struggle, and to suffer in the course of struggling, taking up where the music as persona is leaving off. In relation to common understandings of the title phrase, the song feels to me as if it represents the expression of a subject who has given 'his' heart and soul to a pursuit, to an endeavor, to a cause, yet doing so has ended up proving insufficient: 'he' has failed to fully achieve what 'he' set forth to do and he has experienced greater setbacks and fallen back further than 'he' anticipated or hoped. But this subject has not given up identifying with and affirming the value of what 'he' has sought to realize, only 'his' own continuing direct and immediate personal contribution, which 'he' is now turning over to me, and to us.

At the same time, "Heart and Soul" conveys, even more grimly, the suggestion of a subject experiencing an acute sense of existential crisis and, perhaps in particular, a 'dark night of the soul'. As popular German spiritual teacher and self-help books writer Eckhart Tolle indicates, a 'dark night of the soul' refers to the experience of "a collapse of a perceived meaning in life . . . an eruption into your life of a deep sense of meaninglessness. The inner state in some cases is very close to what is conventionally called depression. Nothing makes sense anymore, there's no purpose to anything." Many triggers are possible, Tolle explains, but commonly, "you had built up your life, and given it meaning–and the meaning that you had given your life, your activities, your achievements, where you are going, what is considered important . . . for some reason collapses." As Tolle elaborates, "what has collapsed then is the whole conceptual framework for your life, the meaning that your mind had given it." This experience can result in a 'reawakening' to

something deeper, which is no longer based on concepts in your mind. A deeper sense of purpose or connectedness with a greater life that is not dependent on explanations or anything conceptual any longer. It's a kind of re-birth. The dark night of the soul is a kind of death that you die. What dies is the egoic sense of self. Of course, death is always painful, but nothing real has actually died there–only an illusory identity. Now it is probably the case that some people who've gone through this transformation realized that they had to go through that, in order to bring about a spiritual awakening. Often it is part of the awakening process, the death of the old self and the birth of the true self.

Yet, as "Heart and Soul" suggests, this 'reawakening' or 'deeper awakening' does not necessarily always occur, and is by no means guaranteed. As Yochai Ataria, for instance, discusses at some length, in a 2014 article for the *Journal of Humanistic Psychology*, mystical and traumatic experiences bear many similar phenomenological dimensions and crucially "in both cases . . . one faces nothingness." This kind of experience, in other words, can prove liberating or it can prove the opposite. An experience that involves not only a crisis of faith in what one has previously identified as one's foremost convictions and values, but also of one's sense of one's existence, of one's agency, of one's capacity to engage meaningfully and purposefully in life, can be exceedingly difficult to overcome, and especially exceedingly difficult to overcome such that one is, as a result of passing through the experience of such a crisis, renewed, reborn, reanimated, and revitalized.

Let's imagine a hypothetical individual named Corrine. Corrine has dreamed, throughout much if not most of her life to date, of becoming a medical doctor and of a life committed toward the practice of healing. Corrine has even imagined and relished the prospect of working in war-torn regions or other regions of the world where people are suffering from acute deprivation and desperate need. Yet Corrine has repeatedly found herself unable to meet the standards and expectations necessary to qualify as a medical doctor, despite giving everything she had to give in trying to do so–she has given her entire 'heart and soul'. Corinne has worked exceedingly hard, and made many personal sacrifices in pursuit of this dream, but she has run out of resources to continue any further. Meanwhile, everyone around her is urging her to give up on this pursuit and to find another direction in life, perhaps another way in which she can be involved in medical work but not as a doctor. Yet Corrine has identified herself so fully with pursuit of this end and in particular with its successful realization that she feels devastated, humiliated, and as if 'the heart and soul' of whom she is, has been, and has aspired to be, has been destroyed. She feels as if she has no interest in radically redefining her life plans, and even less energy to begin to do so, such that she feels as if there is no point trying to do so. Corrine feels as if she cannot proceed forward in any alternative direction and as if she no longer feels compelled by any reason to live in being where she is at yet she is at the same time unable to move from where she is at.

Let's imagine another hypothetical individual who I will call Mark. Mark has been working his entire adult life striving, with 'all of his heart and soul', to find, to identify, to capture the essence of what is responsible for a rare yet serious health condition that has afflicted many members of his family, as well as what can be done to counteract its impact, by at least preventing it from becoming seriously damaging. Mark has been inspired to make this pursuit not only his vocation but also his mission because of his family history and experience. He has fought and struggled long and hard to become a leading medical researcher, to work as part of a leading medical research institution, and to do so in collaboration with other advanced experts in the same field. Repeatedly, he and his team have come close to achieving a major breakthrough only to find out, each time, this was not the case, and they needed to start over, once again. Yet Mark has persisted, until now, until he himself has become worn down and increasingly seriously afflicted by the same condition he has been devoting his 'heart and soul' toward attempting to understand so as to effectively combat. His condition has reached the point where those with whom and for whom he works are telling him he needs to stand down because he is no longer capable of making an effective contribution and is only accelerating his own physical decline in attempting to continue. But Mark feels devastated as he is only in his mid 40s, and as he feels he has been on the verge of achieving a decisive breakthrough, while he also recognizes his decline, because of a lack of breakthrough in relation to the etiology and treatment of his disease, is almost certain to rapidly accelerate to the point where he will be not only severely disabled but also incredibly weak and sick. Mark feels cheated–as if his body had betrayed him and as if he is reaching a dead end long before he is mentally, emotionally, or psychologically ready to give up in his quest. He feel devastated that he will never figure out what he has strived so assiduously to figure out.

I connect what I hear in listening to and reflecting on "Heart and Soul," as well as what this makes me think about and feel, with my own experience, now thirty years' running, of living with serious chronic illness–centered around a functional digestive dysmotility disorder. This is a condition that continues to elude precise diagnosis and effective treatment. This is a condition that continues to be unstable and unpredictable. This is condition that continues to require constant vigilance and enormous work, day in and day out, just to attempt to manage and control. This is a condition that is largely invisible or 'non-visible' and that is hard for others, including many doctors and medical professionals, to understand and appreciate, in terms of what it actually feels like, to live with, day in and day out, because it is a condition that never goes away, a condition that I likely never will be 'over', and where it is always complicated to indicate whether I am 'feeling better' versus 'feeling worse'. It can be extremely puzzling from 'the outside', from the perspective of one who has never lived with this kind of condition, because living long-term with this chronic condition means being simultaneously sick and well, weak and strong, incapable and capable, while not being able to offer a definitive guarantee how I will feel, and what for me will feel relatively hard versus relatively easy to do, from day to day, and even from hour to hour–or from minute to minute!

Historically, people with conditions like mine have been pejoratively characterized as hysterical, neurasthenic, hypochondriac, excessively sensitive, malingering, and indolent. I long hid and otherwise downplayed my condition, feeling hopeless about being able to explain it such that others with no personal experience of this kind of condition could adequately understand and appreciate what I was going through. I long felt, even if people were able in part to acknowledge my condition, that they would conclude I was simply incapable and no longer want me involved in, or trust me to be involved in, doing anything important, anything at all challenging or demanding. I have often wrestled with feeling guilty that I myself must somehow be responsible for bringing this condition on myself, for perpetuating this condition, and for not doing enough to pursue every possible solution to overcome this condition completely, once and for all. I have felt this way even when I know full well I have strived relentlessly to figure this condition out, to explain it, to treat it, to solve it, to overcome it. Indeed, I have readily embraced a wide array of alternative, unconventional, and newly emergent as well as still experimental tests and treatments, regimens and lifestyles, and medicines and procedures.

I can be and often have been active, engaged, and productive while simultaneously dealing with the impact of disabling chronic illness, including recurrent bouts of excruciating pain that can continue for weeks and even months on end. I have often felt I faced no choice but to proceed as if none of this was happening—i.e., to pretend to others I was not suffering at all from chronic illness. For too long I allowed myself to go along with the commonsense notion that illness is always temporary, always something from which one shortly fully recovers, and even to go along with the further commonsense notion that if 'I look good' 'I must be feeling well'. I want to be active, engaged, and productive and I can be, despite the impact of disabling chronic illness, but this impact is far from negligible. I have now lived with chronic illness, as of yet incurable and barely treatable, for most of my adult life. This condition is and has been seriously disabling. I struggle every day to do my best to keep the worst ravages of this condition under control or at least to manage to contain the worst possible impacts whenever flare-ups occur. The latter happen regularly yet unpredictably and for durations and intensities that cannot be anticipated. Even though I have been active, engaged, and productive, it has often proven tough to be so, and without a doubt I would be much more so if I did not live with such seriously disabling chronic illness.

I believe people like me maintain much of value to offer, as university faculty and otherwise, and I have refused to give up, in large part because I want to make sure this is so, as far as I can help make it so. But I need friends and colleagues to understand and appreciate that for people like me not everything is always as possible, nor as readily possible, as it is for others. For instance, traveling, of any significant distance and for any significant duration of time, causes flare-ups in my condition, and I need always travel with a caretaker when I do. I need time after traveling to recover and I need assistance even once I do. This means it has become next to impossible for me to attend professional conferences, especially in the midst of busy semesters, so I've redirected my scholarly activity elsewhere and otherwise. To take another example, after I became gravely ill in the summer of 2016, I recognized I need every day to set limits to how much of each day I am working, and I cannot simply make up 'for falling behind', or in facing pressing deadlines, by working longer, and by going without sleep. The consequences of attempting to do so are hugely damaging. I also need to make room for regular and extensive physical exercise in my everyday life. I have too often neglected this need when it has seemed to me the demands of teaching and institutional service have left no room for this.

The best book I have read on what it is like to live with chronic illness, one that resonates strongly with my personal experience, is Meghan O'Rourke's *The Invisible Kingdom: Reimagining Chronic Illness*. In *The Invisible Kingdom* O'Rourke shares her own experiences and struggles living with long-term, serious, chronic illness, while offering astute insights, reflections, interpretations, and arguments concerning what this kind of experience and struggle is and can be like for a great many people, as well as how best to make sense of and respond to these kinds of experiences and struggles.

O'Rourke early on declares "My story does not progress in an orderly fashion, because the course of my illness did not; it circled and jumped and skipped. I got sick and better, sick and better" (8). The trajectory of 'O'Rourke's story' is exactly how 'my story' has proceeded. Just like O'Rourke, I've become intimately familiar with "how our culture tends to psychologize diseases it doesn't yet understand," as well as with "how and why our medical system, for all its extraordinary capacities, is ill-equipped to handle the steep rise in this kind of chronic illness" (8). I too have learned a great deal, of necessity, about what it is like "to live with uncertainty and incapacity" (8). I agree wholeheartedly with O'Rourke that 'our stories' need to be understood in terms of "living with, rather than

776

eradicating or defeating, a disease"–in terms of "letting go of the American ethos of overcoming" and instead "confronting our mutual interdependence" (8-9). Absolutely, I have gained first-hand experience of "the structural problems of late-capitalist society that values productivity over health," yet I, like O'Rourke, am also well aware of how relatively advantaged I have been in navigating the challenges involved in living with chronic illness versus where many others experiencing the same are and have been at. I have had access to resources to help me get through that many others are unable to access. I emphatically agree with O'Rourke this disparity 'underscores' "the need for a stronger social safety net" as well as much greater "recognition of . . . interconnectedness" (9).

Recounting early conversations with other people also living with chronic illness, O'Rourke cites one anonymous individual who aptly comments "It's so frustrating that I have such good days, then I wake up and out of no where [sic] I feel like death" (26). This has been my experience often, and the frustration that results is enormous. I implore of myself

> Why? why? I have been doing everything to anticipate and respond to every possible symptom of my condition and I have assiduously followed regimens that have worked well for me in the past. I felt great yesterday such that I was able to be actively engaged all day and all night, and in doing so I felt immensely happy and altogether devoid of stress. But then all of this has come back, out of nowhere, for no good reason. This cycle happens to me over and over, and no matter what I do I am never able to get out of it.

The same anonymous individual I just mentioned O'Rourke citing also refers to their sudden and unpredictable recurrence of chronic illness as feeling like "my 'black hole'" (26). This is again exactly how it feels to me as well. O'Rourke, similarly, shares a snippet of a conversation she had with her friend Gina where she vented "I just want to go for a day without *thinking* about my body" (30). I have often fervently wished this to be possible for me as well, even though it rarely ever is.

Living "in near constant pain" becomes all the more painful when this occurs as a result of "a disease doctors cannot diagnose" (33). At first I was shocked this could possibly be the case, I could not fathom that doctors did not have any clue what was wrong with me let alone what to do about it, but once I gradually overcame that shock, not only did I accept I need to be my own advocate and to take charge of caring for myself, but also I determined I needed to search much further for doctors who might yet be able to diagnose and treat my condition. Yet, afflicted with 'a disease doctors cannot diagnose', I doubted myself, I doubted I was really as sick and in the ways that seemed to be the case, and I worried that something must be wrong with me in terms of what I am doing, or not doing, in how I am living my life, such that I myself am responsible, somehow, even if I can't yet figure out how, for causing my own sickness and pain. Further complicating the experience of living with this kind of condition is the fact that, for a long time, just like O'Rourke, "I didn't know how to explain to others what was going on. I appeared fine, after all. ('You *look* great', people kept saying, almost in disbelief) (34)." I've experienced countless people telling me this, especially in casual encounters. I've not known how to burst out to contradict them, without appearing to 'accuse' them of anything, without appearing to 'condemn' them. Yet I *want* to insist, to the contrary, "I may look that way but that is not at all how I feel."

These kinds of comments reflect a widespread failing of all too many people in contemporary American society and its mainstream culture, and in comparable Western societies and cultures, to be able to comprehend that 'sick' and 'healthy' are not necessarily always discretely distinct conditions, and that neither sickness nor health necessarily ever simply and entirely begins or ends. In fact, "many of us may live in a gray area between health and disease for years, amorphously fluctuating between feeling well and being symptomatic" (44). It certainly has appeared to be true, based upon my experience as well, that "One of the hardest things about being ill with a poorly misunderstood disease is that most people find what you're going through incomprehensible—if they even believe you *are* going through it" (47). Many others I've known and even with whom I've interacted extensively over the course of many years have again and again seemed to 'forget' I suffer from long-term, serious, chronic illness, or to seem to 'want to forget' this to be the case, often seeming not to recognize any signs at all of when I've been experiencing extreme pain and discomfort. Likewise, the same people have seemingly been unwilling, even incapable, of grasping that I might not always be capable of doing everything they are doing, not grasping that I might need any assistance or accommodation whatsoever, and not grasping that it is insulting and demeaning to pander advice to me concerning ways of treating my illness by offering recommendations maintaining no bearing on this kind of illness and that only make any sense in relation to acute illness that is far less severe and far more readily understood and easily treated.

O'Rourke aptly notes that "a terrible anxiety attends chronic illness" (48), and indeed my experience of recurrently struggling with bouts of serious to severe anxiety, including in the form of panic attacks and in the form of feeling overwhelmed with and overpowered by amorphous dread, has much to do with needing to try to live in a body that is out of control, and that 'can and will let me down' over and over again, without me being able to anticipate precisely when or how this will happen, let alone do anything to prevent this from happening. I also readily identify with O'Rourke's description of living with chronic illness feeling as if "you are impersonating yourself. When you're sick, the act of living is more act than living" (49). I have taught numerous classes and attended and participated, even led, numerous meetings while feeling terribly sick, even on the verge of passing out because the pain and discomfort was so extreme, but I needed to act as if none of this was the case, leading me to marvel, afterward, at my 'performance'.

A serious challenge that arises in responding to chronic illness, and to people living with chronic illness, is "In chronic illness, the patient does not have a problem that can be solved quickly but a disease to be managed, physically and psychologically. Such illnesses can be intractable, messy, mysterious. And doctors don't like to manage; they like to *fix*" (63). This challenge is compounded by the fact "that we live atomized, exhausted, late-capitalist lives, running from here to there" and "in thrall to one of the most powerful contemporary Western delusions: namely, the idea that we can control the outcomes of our lives" (79). Unfortunately, "You cannot muscle your way to health when you are chronically ill. Rather, one way of coming to terms with an amorphous systemic disease is recognizing that you are sick, that the illness will come and go, and that it is not the kind of illness you can conquer" (87). This is an arduous struggle made all the more arduous because "People whose illness has no name get little sympathy" (98). When we feel like we are dying, which is a real and common feeling for those living with serious chronic illness, one I most certainly have repeatedly felt as a result of living with chronic illness, and when we share this worry, we tend to be treated as if we are 'being hysterical' or 'overly dramatic' or 'attention-seeking' or 'hypersensitive'. It feels as if, to cite the title of O'Rourke's book, we are "exiled to an invisible kingdom" (99).

A significant cause of the prevalence of chronic illnesses "rising in the West in comparison to traditional cultures" is due to "the pressures of modern life in late capitalism, with its pollution, its overreliance on antibiotics, its endless stressors, and its weak safety nets (in the United States at least). In each generation we compromise our microbiomes and environment and hand them off to our children, whose microbiomes and environment become further compromised by diet and chemicals" (128-129). O'Rourke aptly emphasizes that both stress and trauma encompass significant physical, and more precisely physiological, impacts, increasing susceptibility not only to acute but also to chronic illness.

I don't consider the anxiety and depression I have had to combat as solely caused by living with chronic illness. I conceive of the two as interdeterminate. I have struggled with stress for as long as I can remember, in significant part because I have rejected, as unethical, seeking altogether to avoid or protect myself from stress. I have lived my life, ever since a young boy, convinced of my moral responsibility repeatedly to ask of myself the following two questions: (1) What *should* I be doing with my life–what *should* I be aiming to contribute and to accomplish? and (2) How best *should* I strive to be of use? I have not wanted to become complacent, to become easily satisfied, and to accept that I *should* just keep on always doing the same with this being always enough to justify how and for what I am living my life. In teaching I always strive to approach each class I teach afresh, to incorporate new focuses and emphases, to make use of new texts and draw new connections, to fashion new ways of organizing and conducting class sessions, to develop new assignments and new methods for responding to and evaluating assignments, and to pursue new aims and realize new ends. I continually want to do better, and always believe this *should* be possible.

I fully accept, as Amanda Cawston explains, in "Pacifism as Re-Appropriated Violence," a contribution to the 2019 anthology *Pacifism's Appeal: Ethos, History, Politics*, part of Palgrave Macmillan's Rethinking Peace and Conflict Series, that "the hidden, externalized nature of much modern violence engenders this: we are able to go about our daily lives feeling as if we never harm or wrong anyone" because "Distance makes us less aware of the very violence we do engage in" (52). The latter violence is done 'in our name' and enables us to benefit at the expense of others' deprivation, and others' harm. As Cawston aptly comments, in relation to matters of war, including 'endless war', and including forms of 'conflict' effectively indistinguishable from war yet not commonly identified as war, "Noncombatants divest themselves both of the unwanted business and moral burden of violence onto combatants" while "Delegating our security work to others" (50). In other words, "Civilians are not confronted with the violence that sustains their life and thus form the distorted belief that our daily interactions are naturally sociable and unmediated, when they in fact depend on substantial violence" (50-51). I interpret the lyrics and music of Ian Curtis and Joy Division as registering unease and distress from the vantage point of a subject acutely aware of 'his' connection with, implication in, and responsibility for violence 'far away' and 'close by' as well as 'his' alienation–externalization and distance–from the violence with which we are connected, in which we are implicated, and for which we are responsible. This is a haunting awareness when it at the same time feels impossible to conceive of anything one can do about this connection, implication, and responsibility.

I have felt troubled in my own life about what precisely I *should* do and how best I *should* do this in attending to this kind of connection, implication, and responsibility. I have also felt troubled in perceiving it can be easy, and it can be tempting, to become and remain oblivious to my connection with, implication in, and responsibility for systemic, structural, and institutional forms of violence. Continually critically examining and reexamining my life-practices in relation to these kinds of issues and the two key questions I elaborated in the preceding paragraph has inspired and enabled me in determining what I *should* do and how best I *should* do this. But doing so has also led me to psychologically torture myself–to the point where I have been so consumed with imagining I bear a necessary burden of moral responsibility that I have suffered repeated occurrences of what used to be commonly identified as constituting a 'nervous breakdown'.

I have had to fight this tendency, and fight it hard, so as not to push myself to an extreme beyond what I can bear. I have not achieved a final victory in so doing, and I wouldn't want to do so, because sometimes it is vital that I do push myself way past a preceding 'comfort zone'. But I am not harming myself to the extent I long was. Nevertheless, because of feeling the impact of monumental developments transpiring throughout the times in which I have lived, but also because of refusing to retreat from advocacy on behalf of controversial positions, positions opposed by powerful social and political interests, positions that run counter to dominant ideological commonsense, and because of facing backlash as a result, including in the form of direct physical attacks and death threats, I've experienced trauma as well as stress. Yes, living with trauma and its impact, while at the same time believing I can't and especially *shouldn't* live my life seeking to avoid or protect myself from the risk of experiencing trauma, but rather the opposite is often right and necessary, undoubtedly has at the least exacerbated chronic illness.

Megan O'Rourke cites English Romantic poet John Keats, who himself died at age 25 of tuberculosis after he had witnessed first his mother and then his brother earlier dying of the same disease. Keats, O'Rourke finds, offers a useful understanding of what living with chronic illness is like, including concerning how doing so shapes one's outlook upon and engagement with the larger social and natural world. Keats's conception of 'Negative Capability' involves "being in uncertainties, Mysteries, doubts, without any irritable reaching after fact and reason" (quoted 129). The latter suggests finding ways to persist without needing rationally to explain, and especially not to explain away, the former. O'Rourke proposes Keats's "formulation of negative capability . . . . to be a key to living well in the face of pain . . . a profound insight of the sort that comes from witnessing loss and suffering up close" (129).

I find 'negative capability' compelling in relation to my experience of living with chronic illness, but at the same time I remain uneasy about becoming complacent, and especially about becoming inadvertently callous concerning what I might accept as mysterious and uncertain such that I also accept I bear no responsibility to concern myself with doing anything about it. I have long felt uneasy about philosophical varieties of skepticism, including popular philosophical varieties of the same, because I perceive skepticism as tending too readily toward becoming cynicism. I have frequently argued cynicism represents a major constituent of dominant ideology that renders the ways things are seemingly the way they have to be, or seemingly the best possible way that they ever could be. When people identify with these kinds of cynical positions they identify with maintaining and reproducing existing social arrangements, essentially unchanged–social arrangements rooted in and dependent upon alienation, exploitation, and oppression along lines of race, sex, class, gender, sexuality, nationality, ability and disability, and health and illness.

Nevertheless, I agree with O'Rourke that "the chronically ill" do come to know that "to be alive *is* to be in uncertainty" (130-131), and that this can be a valuable insight, not only in terms of living with one's chronic illness, but also in relation to what the rest of what life brings. Recognizing and accepting limits to what one can control by one's self, through the exercise of one's own power, as well as recognizing and accepting one's massive dependence upon many others, are crucial elements of what indeed merits characterization as 'wisdom'. At the same time, it can be a brutal and exhausting struggle to get to this point, in living with chronic illness, while such recognition and acceptance is unlikely ever to represent the totality of how many if not most experience 'their chronic illness' no matter how serene they may be able to feel from time to time. Not only do I readily identify with Dylan Thomas's 'raging against the dying of the light', and expect this will certainly be me when that time comes for me, but also I readily identify with O'Rourke in writing "I still feel the waves of grief that rose when I accepted that I had a chronic illness–that my life was permanently changed. The hardest part was accepting the uncertainty of whether I would ever know what was wrong with me" (130). It has been excruciating for me to accept 'this is me' as well, and I vehemently resisted doing so for many years. I continue to mourn the life I never had the chance to lead, encompassing all of what I could not do, or could not do as well as would have been the case if I had not been seriously sick as often and for as extended periods of time as I have.

What I find more 'liberating' than accepting 'living with uncertainty' and 'living with what cannot be changed' is the position, as O'Rourke articulates this, and with which I passionately agree, "that it is not our *selves* that are wrong but the very structure of our society, with its failing support systems, its poor chemical regulation, its food deserts, its patchwork health care delivery" (141). This is close akin to the 'liberation' I experience from embracing the major thrust of 'the social model of disability' at the same time as I agree with criticism of this model from the vantage point of advocates of positions of 'complex embodiment' in taking seriously the deleterious impact of impairment, especially for those who are 'sick disabled' as opposed to 'healthy disabled'. The social model of disability argues it is not we ourselves, as autonomous individuals, entirely in charge, all by ourselves, of determining our own health and ability, who are responsible for causing and perpetuating our disabilities, including our chronic illnesses, but rather our society, and how this society is set up that does so. It is our society that transforms our impairments into disabilities. We are disabled by a society that has not yet developed and implemented sufficient means to fully accommodate our kinds of bodies, and our kinds of bodily experiences of and engagements with, and within, the world. This social responsibility for our disability includes lack of understanding and appreciation for what chronic illness involves as well as all the many social factors, part and parcel of the organization of 21st century late capitalist Western society, that foster, deepen, compound, and expand the disabling impact of living with chronic illness. Unfortunately, as O'Rourke's research demonstrates, interviewing many others with chronic illness, frequently people who are chronically ill have "internalized the idea, as I had, that something about *them* was the problem, and that it rested on them alone to fix the inauthenticity that made them stressed-out and unhappy" (142).

Our society encourages internalization of and identification with this kind of position as opposed to focusing on the facts that "In the United States, there are few autoimmune centers, despite the millions of Americans suffering from autoimmune disease. And there is little political action to regulate chemicals or–despite the work of the Black Lives Matters protests–overcome the structural racism that contributes to the wear and tear on bodies known as 'weathering'" (142). What's more, "If neurasthenic sensitivity was the hallmark of nineteenth-century invalidism, a kind of hyperpersonalized concern with wellness is the hallmark of twenty-first-century invalidism–a quality that lets the rest of us dismiss the invalid as fussy or oversensitive while we get back to our frenetic, endlessly connected, productive lives" (143).

I am grateful I have been able to resume running regularly the past fifteen months, and that I am steadily running further, faster, more often, and over more challenging courses, inside and outside, while I am also grateful for all of the encouragement I-fit trainers offer me along with the tips they share about running well, including concerning the physiology of running, as I run indoors on our home treadmill. But I need to resist an inclination to feel as if I was totally responsible, entirely by myself, for mistakenly 'choosing not to run' regularly over the course of the past twenty-five years, despite how much I previously valued doing so. I need to resist imagining that I have now simply chosen to reverse my previous choice in deciding I am going to return to running regularly, to make running regularly a priority, including when I return from extended scholarly leave to full-time teaching and institutional service. I gave up running regularly because I felt overwhelmed when I started work as a professor at UW-Eau Claire.

This happened not just because of the workload but also because the place initially seemed so foreign to me in comparison with all previous experience while not entirely friendly and welcoming. I frequently felt I was implicitly if not explicitly expected to work way past the point of exhaustion, to forget or dismiss any concern about burnout, and even to be willing to make myself seriously ill, while always doing everything I possibly could for our students and in response to constantly new administrative mandates, initiatives, and demands. Or, if I did not, I would not be allowed to continue. I felt all the more compelled to live my life this way because I accepted I bore a greater burden of responsibility, and a heightened risk of misunderstanding, and antagonism, not only on account of being gay and queer but also on account of being a leftist, a socialist, and a Marxist; living with chronic illness, invisible disability, and mental health challenges in the form of persistent tendencies toward serious to severe anxiety and depression; being a highly intellectual person; being in part still 'shy' as much I loathed this label and reacted violently against it for much of my life; and being a person who spent formative years of my life growing up and 'coming of age' in the Northeast as opposed to the Midwest. I felt I maintained limited margin for error, and even less for any failure. So, even though it would have helped greatly with my physical and psychological health and well-being, I turned away from running regularly.

I also am in part troubled by the pervasive messaging from I-fit trainers that insists anyone can run and can run well, anyone can become a steadily better and steadily more successful runner, and what primarily holds any of us back is not physical limitations but rather self-limiting mindsets. This messaging neglects, even ignores, the real-life situations of many people with physical and mental disabilities, including many people with major forms of chronic illness. My advice in response to ongoing conversations about how to make UW-Eau Claire 'a campus of wellness' or 'a wellness community' is that we must work toward being able to take collective responsibility for wellness, of each for all, refusing to individualize every instance of 'lack of wellness' or 'deficiency of wellness' or 'struggle with wellness'. Instead of simply expanding resources or familiarity with resources that can help individuals when individuals are experiencing individual problems, we need to identify and transform conditions that generate and perpetuate these kinds of problems. At the least, as I have increasingly emphasized in all of my teaching, and in all my collegial interactions, let's talk openly, forthrightly, and at length and in depth, together, about disability, visible and non-visible, about mental health, and about chronic illness. Students welcome doing so, and indeed are often thrilled to do so. So let's *all* commit to doing so.

Grasping the interconnections, intervening at the intersections, between chronic illness and mental health challenges is especially crucial, as O'Rourke attests, from her own experience and that of numerous others. O'Rourke assesses "in retrospect . . . it is painfully clear that the *invisibility* of my illness was one of the most challenging parts of my suffering" (188). Indeed, O'Rourke writes eloquently about how important it has been for her, and for many others, to be recognized, affirmed, and cared for, yet how often this has not been and is not the case, notably among still too many doctors and other health care professionals. A key reason for this failure is, in our dominant culture, "We are bad at recognizing the suffering of others unless we are given clear-cut clues and evidence" and unfortunately, for O'Rourke, for me, and for others like me and her, "The illness was severe but invisible. And that invisibility made all the difference–it made *me* invisible, which itself almost killed me" (188).

I have felt overjoyed on occasions where doctors and fellow medical professionals have actually taken the time and demonstrated the care to relate to me with respect and appreciation for the complexity and the seriousness of my chronic illness. I have felt overjoyed on occasions when they have stopped recommending pat, formulaic, pseudo-solutions that in almost all such cases have consisted of recommending to me merely that I try things I had long ago tried and long ago found entirely inadequate and ineffectual. I too have felt overjoyed on occasions when colleagues, and when students, have actually listened to me, taken me seriously, and either offered their own personal connections with my experience or admitted honestly they don't understand what I am going through, and have been going through, but are sincerely open toward attempting to do so. Yet I have also had people, ostensibly friends, suggest I have not worked hard enough, or in the right way or in the right direction, or in seeking out the right expert or taking the right medication or following the right regimen, to solve my problem and that I must therefore 'prefer to be sick rather than to be well'. And I have also had people, ostensibly friends, who have told me as long as I look OK, as long as I look like I'm doing OK, and as long as I continue to show up, at work or otherwise, they have to assume and will assume I must, in fact, be feeling OK.

I likewise have had similar experiences to that of O'Rourke, who once she did undergo treatment for a difficult to detect form of Lyme disease, and this did help, ran up against many others who "would ask if I was 'better'. I was in fact better, but not in the way they meant: I still was dealing with health issues every day" (228). Many people find it baffling when I try to get across to them that I most likely 'will never get over my chronic illness', I most likely 'will never be better' in the sense they understand what 'being better' means, 'after being sick', and that I will most likely continue to struggle with great uncertainty, unpredictability, and frequent enough intense, severe pain and discomfort–even if and when I am working and otherwise actively living my life.

Last week, for instance, I experienced a severe episode at the beginning of the week, that peaked Tuesday evening, which was so tough I was unable to concentrate, constantly on the verge of passing out, and so weak I could barely take the dog outside to relieve himself. But then I felt much better on Wednesday, and on both Wednesday and Thursday I was able to run extensively, while on Saturday I participated in a race, live, for the first time in over 25 years, about which I was extremely nervous. I did well, despite the frigid single degree Fahrenheit temperature, running faster than I had anticipated even without trying to do so, while carefully pacing myself, and not feeling any stress or strain at all at any point in the race. I felt incredibly happy, that this was a truly beautiful day, and one I needed to treasure because I don't know when the next reappearance and resurgence of my chronic illness will occur.

O'Rourke recommends a paradigm shift in medical thinking, in response to chronic illness, and is hopeful the wide prevalence and considerable attention that 'Long COVID' has received offers a realistic opportunity for this to begin to happen. What I agree is needed is to shift "from the model of the specific disease entity with a clear-cut solution to the messy reality shaped by both infection and genetics and our whole social history" and, most of all, to accept that "When we suffer, we want recognition" (229). Doctors and other medical professionals need to understand what it means "for a chronically ill person to heal" might involve experiencing "remission of disease" but it also might mean "the patient is now able to manage the illness with some degree of integrity" (233).

I, like O'Rourke, have embarked on a "quest to find answers about what was happening to my body" that has "taken me far away from standard medical appointments and deep into meditations about what a life should be like, how wounds could be healed, and what to do when they can't be" (235). I have needed to dramatically reimagine what it means, for me, 'to live a good life' and 'to be happy and successful in life'. More narrowly, I have sought out many alternative treatments, and relied on them, feeling often enough it is better to stop mentioning doing this to nurses, doctors, and the like who would only respond with skepticism or warnings, for instance in relation to herbal forms of 'complimentary' medicine, that 'we don't know for sure what is in these formulas and they have not been scientifically proven to work'. Unfortunately, the prescription medications as well as the over the counter supplements and dietary and lifestyle recommendations from mainstream medical professionals that are available to treat my condition have proven woefully inadequate, and I could not have continued at all if I did not find relief, help, and support from 'alternative' sources. I would have been much sicker and much more thoroughly disabled if I had only listened to and followed the advice of my 'regular' doctors and other 'regular' health care providers–and I might even have died long before now if that had been all I did.

As O'Rourke recommends, "If doctors want to help patients heal, they need to take into consideration the things that contribute to a person's well-being, whether it be sunlight, quiet, nature, or something else entirely" (238). They need to be able to understand, respect, and support our need for 'wholeness' and also our interconnectedness, our interdependency, our precariousness, our vulnerability, and our fragility. Yet "in America today," in contrast with seventeenth century English poet John Donne's famous declaration that "No man is an island, entire of itself; every man is a piece of the continent, a part of he main" (quoted 239), we are too often "brought up against the pathology of a culture that denies this fact" (239). As O'Rourke attests, from her own experience, "In the worst moments of my illness, I was alone because of the way that we have allowed ourselves to believe that the self, rather than the community, must do all the healing" (239).

O'Rourke refuses to mystify her experience of living with chronic illness by claiming it has offered her positive benefits that adequately compensate for this experience. I feel the same way. I totally agree that "There is a razor-thin line between trying to find something usefully redemptive in illness and lying to ourselves about the nature of suffering. Until what we mourn what is lost in illness . . . we should not celebrate what is gained in it" (258). As O'Rourke aptly states and as I emphatically agree: "I *would* have it the other way" (259). With chronic illness, "your story is disrupted" and it becomes hard to map according to formats that are generally considered to be ultimately 'uplifting': this is not, for instance, "a restitution narrative," and "It is almost by definition never a story of overcoming, because the disease's trajectory never resolves" (260). This is closer to "chaos" in the form of "anti-narrative" and perhaps the best that can be declared, in attempting to sum up this kind of experience, is, as O'Rourke puts it, "I survived, but it was the nature of the disease to rob me of myself" (261). Whatever peculiar knowledge or insight or even possibly 'wisdom' is gained from living with chronic illness "is born of loss, of resignation to a condition that forces us to give up on aspects of ourselves that we had hoped might develop. Wisdom, in this understanding, is knowledge coupled with the wound that comes from encountering doom" (264).

Because I could only do so much, in response to living with chronic illness, and its chaotic unpredictability, I have needed to choose selectively, reluctantly accepting what I could and could not do in my intellectual and professional life: I chose to prioritize teaching, and I chose to strive to do the best I possibly could by my students, allowing numerous dreams and plans concerning a host of scholarly projects to fall by the wayside, and I also chose, in terms of institutional and community involvements, to prioritize 'service' over 'pleasure', while frequently giving up and backing away from involvements as they became too demanding and as I just couldn't continue any further despite how much I valued being immersed within these kinds of activities.

I too, like O'Rourke, have been fundamentally changed as result of living with chronic illness and I too do "know more," even much more, "about embodiment than I used to" (266). I need to be keenly and vigilantly attuned to my body, and to its micro as well as meso and macro variations and changes, and I am acutely aware I am embodied–that my mind, and my spirit, do not exist separate from let alone independent of my body. It makes total sense to me to conceive of consciousness as 'embodied'. Yet at the same time, this has also been a particular kind of embodiment. I recognize a profound difference. I love feeling well; I love feeling capable of walking, hiking, running, or otherwise actively moving about; and I love feeling the positive impacts of doing so within and upon my body. I hate feeling the opposite, even as I have felt this way frequently and expect I always will. Like O'Rourke, I experience chronic illness as "a travesty," as "shit," as not at all inherently "redemptive" (267). I too "am wary of papering over illness's real ravages with false pieties that allow us to look away from the true price exacted" (267).

I cannot pretend that severe cramping, spasming, and bloating, as well as piercing stabs of trapped gas and reflux, as well as teetering on the cliff edge of losing consciousness because of how painful this all is while finding it exceedingly hard to concentrate, is not, indeed, *awful*. I cannot pretend that needing to come home, get out of my regular clothes, and change into a bathrobe, while I then lie down on a couch, or apply a heating pad, a hot water bottle, an ice pack, or various warming or cooling rubs to my entire abdomen–or have my husband massage my abdomen over and over again while urging him to keep pushing harder and harder–is anything but extremely frustrating and feels, indeed, *awful*. It is *awful* this happens over and over and over again, and that I cannot anticipate when it will recur nor prevent it from recurring. I cannot pretend it is anything but extremely frustrating and feels, indeed, *awful* needing to go frequently to the toilet and then experiencing far too much or far too little or far too loose and messy or far too hard and fractured excremental clearance or passing nothing but gas for many days on end or feeling massive searing or burning or jabbing or cutting pains within and throughout my abdomen. It is *awful* to be unable freely and easily to join in and participate in many social experiences which center around food because I need to be so careful about what I eat and don't eat, when and how much, while what is optimal in this regard continually and unpredictably varies, including day to day. It is *awful* needing to turn down offers of treats or snacks or other sharing of food among colleagues, neighbors, and friends, or deciding it will be too difficult to explain and make me seem too odd, and too unfriendly and inhospitable, so I go ahead and eat, such as at a pot-luck gathering or as a slice of cake at a celebratory gathering, what I know will make me sick. I've often decided I just can't attend these kinds of occasions, and these kinds of get-togethers, even when I wish I could, because nothing I might eat while there will work for me–and, despite the seemingly wide prevalence of food allergies and sensitivities, the fact that my condition is all that much more complicated and difficult readily to understand means I frequently despair that I will inevitably be misunderstood and judged negatively in these circumstances.

Those are only some examples of what are for me, *regular* experiences. I too "feel a black hole for what I lost" and I too "do not think illness is a gift" (269). I too also feel if any 'wisdom' arises from living with chronic illness this "is not a goal but a process" and "As a process, it can always break down" (269). O'Rourke sums up the experience of living with chronic illness in the most powerfully astute way I have yet come across: "To become chronically ill is not only to have a disease that you have to manage, but to have a new story about yourself, a story that many people refuse to hear–because it is deeply unsatisfying, full of fits and starts, anger, resentment, chasms of unruly need" (270).

"Heart and Soul" resonates with me as highly suggestive of what the impact of living with chronic illness can indeed feel like. The song resonates with wanting, with desiring, with aiming to live a rich, full life–to be actively and indeed vigorously engaged in pursuit of ambitious dreams, to give your 'heart and soul' to this pursuit, with this pursuit in turn representing pursuit of what deeply matters to you, which corresponds to your foremost principles, convictions, values, and ideals, and which as such comes to represent the crux, the essence, of whom you identify and experience yourself to be. But then you run up against the brick wall of chronic illness and are forced to withdraw, to contract, to choose among, to limit and to eliminate, to slow down and to step back, to retreat and to retire. "Heart and Soul" resonates with how draining this experience can be, and especially with the draining away of all but vestigial shards of your felt semblance of maintaining any kind of self at all. In other words, more bluntly, "Heart and Soul" resonates with how the experience of living with chronic illness feels like you are losing yourself, and that you are becoming a radically alien and freakish entity, one that only really exists, if it exists at all, exiled to an 'invisible, intangible, and ephemeral kingdom'. "Heart and Soul" resonates with feeling as if you have become 'the living dead', as if you have experienced a 'living death', perhaps as if you have experienced a 'social death' and are now 'socially dead'. "Heart and Soul" resonates with feeling as if your own body, due to overwhelming and overwhelmingly mysterious and intractable limitations, has massively failed you, and is massively failing you, while you cannot and will not be able, ever, to do anything about this–nothing, at the least, that will allow you any longer to live anything close to 'a normal life' or even the kind of 'alternative' and 'rebellious' life you sought to live, and that you valorized as constituting, for you, 'the good life'. "Heart and Soul" resonates with feeling as if your condition is and will always be massively misunderstood while at the same time remaining frequently not visible to others at all–or ignored, downplayed, and euphemized, with you yourself having felt strongly impelled to do the same even though you know you can't continue to do so for much longer. "Heart and Soul" resonates with feeling as if you are striving to reach a state of serene acceptance of you no longer being, you no longer existing, of your being becoming your nothingness, of your life becoming your death, of your presence resembling far more absence than substance, and of your existence, such that it is, far more spectral than substantial. "Heart and Soul" resonates with reaching the point where you feel as if you have been beaten down so badly, and where your life feels now so delimited, so constrained, and so squeezed and emptied out, that you have become effectively a disembodied observer/commentator on what you can no longer directly participate within, and from which you are now forever affectively distanced, detached, and cut off.

"Heart and Soul" addresses me from the eye of the storm, within an existential crisis, within a 'dark night of the soul', and it makes ready sense to connect this with the kind of crisis living with chronic illness can and does provoke. It is possible to rise again, even to find a renewed and redefined sense of whom and what you are and can and will be, but this is by no means guaranteed to happen; you may never rise, and at rock bottom that prospect seems fantastical. It depends on what kinds of resources are available to you, and whether you are able, to begin with, to obtain the necessary assistance even to begin to access and exercise these resources. This 'rising up' doesn't mean you find some miraculous reservoir of residual strength, some remnant modicum of magical resilience, to reach out all by yourself from rock bottom; it means others reaching out to you, to where you are at, at rock bottom. It means sharing a collective responsibility to intervene so as to transform not only people's individual crisis situations but also, ultimately more importantly, the conditions that give rise to and which instigate, aggravate, compound, and worsen the devastation you–and others like you–are suffering, have suffered, and will suffer.

Undoubtedly it will seem to readers we have moved a long way from pursuing a dialogue between Ian Curtis and Joy Division, as represented in this section by "Heart and Soul," and Aimé

Cesaire's *Discourse on Colonialism*, Edward W. Said's *Representations of the Intellectual*, and Trinh T. Minh-ha's *Woman, Native, Other: Writing Postcoloniality and Feminism*. But I suggest, to conclude this section, that we may have not traveled as far distant from this dialogue as it might seem.

With Césaire, colonialism's insidiousness can make sense, metaphorically, and remember here Césaire was a surrealist and a poet as well as a critical theorist, as a form of chronic social and political illness, and as such encompassing the draining of vital potential, rendering all too many people, communities, and cultures racked by experiences of perpetual pain, while suffering the concomitant loss or denial of substantively meaningful, fulfilling, and satisfying opportunities.

Turning to Said, the position of the critical-oppositional intellectual, on the margin and in exile, is a position that involves considerable risks, dangers, and costs. Even if embracing this position is necessary, as a matter of ethical and political integrity, it is also a position from which it can become difficult, even exceedingly difficult, to be recognized, to be seen and heard and felt, to be understood, to be appreciated. This kind of position can be one from which it can become difficult, even exceedingly difficult, to exercise any substantively effective impact, while one's inability to do so can, as a result, lead to feeling incredible anguish, and even to feeling as if one no longer effectively exists at all. Alternately, it can feel as if the rest of the world exists in another dimension from where one is now located, and as if one is forever alienated from that location while, according to the frames of intelligibility most readily available in that location, one will always be perceived and treated, if acknowledged at all, as a radically alien kind of being.

Trinh, meanwhile, as Indiana University Press describes the focus of her book on the back jacket, explores "cultural hybridization and decentering, fragmented selves and multiple identities, marginal voices and languages of rupture," ultimately arguing these represent positive opportunities, but Trinh nevertheless insists the work to make this so is hard, requires great patience, and involves finding ways to resist and break with normative conventions at some of the most challenging conceivable levels of praxis. This resistance and breaking comes in relation to normative (Western) conceptions of whom and what we conceive ourselves to be, as well as in relation to how we conceive of our connection to and difference from others, including the other within the self, or the other that I always am and that is always in me. This resistance and breaking comes, what's more, in relation to normative (Western) conceptions of how we think, how we read, how we write, how we speak, how we listen, how we express, how we communicate, and how we are able to find and use means and media that enable social interaction at all. And this resistance and breaking comes in relation to normative (Western) conceptions of what constitute desirable and successful modes of engagement with historical and continuing situations and experiences of injustice and inequity, subjugation and exclusion, and alienation, exploitation, and oppression. Trinh proposes fundamentally reconceiving dominant Western ways of making sense of what it means to exist, of what it means to be in relation with 'our self' and with 'others', of how we understand and relate to both identity and difference as well as to how identity and difference mean in relation to each other, and of what it means to to make ourselves seen, heard, felt, and known at all. All of this can require passing through a crisis, even a severe existential crisis, where in effect we can feel as if, in transition, we are left with nothing, or nothing stable, or nothing we can readily rely upon, or nothing that is other than ephemeral, and where we ourselves as we have known ourselves must disappear before we can re-emerge, reborn, revived, as, perhaps 'infinite layers', as perhaps now existing in a felt experience of being at 'home' as part of a space-time continuum where previous conceptions concerning distinctions among past, present, and future, as well as between here and there and near and far, between space and time, between you and I, between us and them, between sick and well, between able and disabled, between living and dying, and between life and death have broken down and have been reconstituted fundamentally otherwise, and, in particular, no longer in dualistic and especially binary opposite terms.

Experiencing interconnection, interdependency, intersectionality, and interdeterminacy such that these no longer feel like abstractions that require continuous translation back into 'the normal language' of 'everyday living', such that they no longer feel like mere words, or even like mere concepts, but rather as materially substantive and phenomenologically concrete dimensions of whom and what we always are–this is a daunting, a fraught, a precariously uncertain prospect. But this process may be registered as we pursue it, and even as we begin to pursue it, in perceiving glimmers of recognition of the kind of society, and of the forms of social relations, that are not yet, and have not yet ever truly or fully been, but that could yet be, that might yet be, and that, perhaps, most of all, that must yet be. What kind of society and what kinds of social relations are necessary for us to transform and transcend conditions according to which individuals are extensively atomized, alienated, and continually thrown onto themselves, to sink and swim, to flourish or wither, to live healthy or to live sick, to live 'abled' or to live disabled, to live recognized and understood and appreciated and cared for or to live ignored and misunderstood and unappreciated and discarded, even scorned? How do we get there from here? Is this at all possible? And how much yet greater strife, how much further pain and suffering, how much vaster struggle and how much deeper exhaustion, will be required in the passage from where we presently are at to this prospective social future that is not yet, and yet must yet be–in rendering this prospect a concrete as opposed to abstract utopia?

Nine

"Autosuggestion" was recorded during the studio sessions that produced *Unknown Pleasures* but this song was left off that album and then subsequently released as a Fast Product label ep, together with the song "From Safety to Where . . .?," also recorded as part of these same sessions and also left off of *Unknown Pleasures*. The ep, titled *Earcom 2–Contradiction*, Fast Product released in September 1979, representing one of multiple examples, Peter Hook later remembers, of Joy Division literally 'giving away' their work. In writing about this song I am listening to the version included on *+/- Singles 1978-1980*, a 2010 box set of remastered recordings, from Rhino UK/Warner, as well as from versions included on the earlier compilations *Heart and Soul*, the 1997 London Records box set, and *Substance*, initially released in 1988 and then in a remastered edition by Warner in 2015. I have listened as well, offering a useful contrast, to a recording of Joy Division performing "Autosuggestion" live from the Prince of Wales Conference Centre in London in August 1979, included on *Heart and Soul*.

In a ranking of all of Joy Division's songs published on 17 July 2020 in *The Guardian*, Alexis Petridis places "Autosuggestion" strikingly high, at number 19. In his capsule commentary, Petridis cites Bob Dickinson, as quoted in Jon Savage's oral history of Joy Division, *This Searing Light, the*

Sun and Everything Else, declaring "Joy Division sounded like ghosts." To Dickinson's comment Petridis adds, "Never more so than on *Unknown Pleasures* outtake 'Autosuggestion', six minutes of backwards guitar, echoing drums, and a vocal reliant on long, mournful notes that slowly reaches a frenetic climax, topped by Curtis's repeated invocation: 'Lose some sleep and say you tried'." In a similar compilation by Alan York, published in November 2020 as part of Warner Music's own *Dig!* online magazine, "Autosuggestion" again places number 19 in a ranking of Joy Division's best songs, with York describing "Autosuggestion" as "a hypnotic, six-minute slow burner with a nocturnal, neo-dub vibe." Earlier in 2020, as yet another ranking of all Joy Division songs, commemorating the 40th anniversary of Ian Curtis's death, *Consequence* places "Autosuggestion" lower, at number 43, although Michael Roffman's capsule comment is positive:

> Perception is reality, as they say, and for some, that notion is terrifying. Curtis tackles that fear head on in *Unknown Pleasures* outtake 'Auto-Suggestion', which takes its name from the act of someone repeating a verbal phrase so that an idea may be willed into existence–at least subconsciously. Given the use of repetition throughout Joy Division, one could argue this is a skeleton key of sorts into Curtis' lyrical way of thinking. And that ending? Post-punk bliss.

In a yet earlier article, published by *The Manc Review*, in February 2012, 'the Manc reviewer' touts "Autosuggestion" as "underrated," requiring multiple listenings in order "to appreciate its value." The Manc Reviewer supports this judgment by offering an elaborate appreciation of this song, proposing that "Autosuggestion" is:

> one of those songs whose pensive lyrics translate like a mantra and are delivered in juxtaposition against the erratic Industrial soundscape. Drawing on the psychological technique of "Autosuggestion", I can only guess that this song is about Curtis's attempt to break free from his restrictions and trying to take control over his anxieties. Significantly the intro of "Autosuggestion" sounds like a match is being lit, which could suggest a fuse or that motivation has been ignited in an attempt to self-hypnotise. Although "Autosuggestion" has never been considered one of the great Joy Division songs, I think that it's a song whose lack of structure subtly reflects the chaos and inner turmoil of Curtis. It's also a song, whose musical innovation was ahead of its time, experimenting with cinematic waves, long before the digital age. Interestingly in this song Curtis's vocals sound more confident as if he is applying the "Autosuggestion" technique. With the opening lyrics: *"Here, here. Everything is by design. Everything is by design"*, Curtis sounds like a crooning, meditative Native Indian, likened to Jim Morrison. It's also after the lyric: *"Here, here everything is kept inside, so take a chance and step outside, your hopes, your dreams and Paradise . . ."* that Curtis's vocals become more intimate as if he has moved away from the back of the room and now is standing up close in front of you. What characterises "Autosuggestion" is how the lyrics are almost repetitive, which mimic a central thought or affirmations linked to the process of Autosuggestion. With guitars which tick against the steady base and drums which tap against the emerging back-tracking guitars, "Autosuggestion" is a song whose musical backdrop is a production of steel resistance, interrupted by waves of cinematic screeching, building to crescendo. It's a song whose fractured guitars hold back and penetrate with sharp precision but dilly dally in the shadows of the song. It's after the lyrics: *"Everything is kept inside. So*

take a chance and step outside. Your hopes, your dreams, your paradise. Heroes, idols cracked like ice" the guitars become unhinged or empowered and speed up in tempo as if they are cutting through the reserve veneer. However it's during the final lyrics of *"So lose some sleep and say you tried . . ."* that the guitars scrape against the intense vocals before disappearing against the staggered and abandoning drums.

The Manc Reviewer's take is more elaborate, in addressing both the lyrics and the music, than those available via songmeanings.com, yet the six interpretations listed on the latter site are also thoughtfully articulated. A first reviewer suggests "Autosuggestion" is about the necessity of making choices, in particular choosing actively to pursue your dreams, or else you will be haunted the rest of your life by regret for not having done so. A second reviewer identifies the meaning of this song with striving to get away from being caught up, solipsistically or narcissistically, within one's "own little world," the world of one's "ego." A third rebukes the other interpretations on the page by insisting the title makes clear the song is about the practice of "Auto-suggestive therapy." This same reviewer adds, however, as a flourish, the further comment that "Autosuggestion" is "absolutely masterful": the song consists of "this dark dismal sound that fills the background for its entire duration, and then you can hear the distinct voice of Ian, akin to the faint glow of candle lighting a dark room on a cold winter night." A fourth reviewer offers an interpretation that is commonly proposed of many if not most Joy Division songs, and in particular of many if not most Ian Curtis lyrics: that "Autosuggestion" is about "Being depressed, weary, and having a growing sense of frustration with everyone and everything, no faith in anything." With "Autosuggestion," this reviewer notes, the song further contends that "In trying to remedy" that growing frustration and lack of faith, "it only gets worse." A fifth reviewer likewise identifies the meaning of the song as an an admonition *not* to be unduly optimistic, interpreting the lyrics as arguing "there's no point in 'taking a chance and stepping outside'" because "you will only 'meet frustration face to face'" in doing so. And a sixth interpreter, while once more claiming "Autosuggestion" is "about despair," adds that the song, even more precisely, criticizes "half-assed" efforts at "trying to change (yourself, the world, society, etc.)" solely to salve "just enough of a good conscience" that "we can relieve ourselves of guilt without really doing anything" to substantially change what we recognize requires substantial change. This in turn allows us to "consider ourselves to be 'good people'" solely "because we worried about something, which means that we care." Even if doing so "is more than most people do," this sixth reviewer interprets "Autosuggestion" as arguing the result remains problematic because it leads us to imagine merely caring enough to worry makes us "better than the rest of society, so now we can sleep easy knowing that we are better." In other words, for example, worrying over a backlash directed against teaching and learning about systemic racism, or about the real existence of LGBTQIA+ people's lives, without doing anything other than worrying, is problematic, especially if we excuse ourselves from doing anything more by contenting ourselves with claiming 'at least I care enough to be worried about these matters'.

In a cover story for the February 2007 issue of popular music magazine *Mojo*, written in conjunction with the release that same year of the films *Control* and *Joy Division*, Jon Savage praises "Autosuggestion" because of how accurately the song "reflected the sense of frustration and claustrophobia I felt then," as the song "seemed to replicate the sound of drowning alive," which Savage strongly identifies with from shared personal experience. Savage also commends

"Autosuggestion" for capturing the likewise shared experience that "there was something perversely pleasurable in this," because "As anyone who has lived in Manchester knows, there can be comfort in the murk and the mist: you could feel curiously nurtured" (82). Savage, like others maintaining this shared experience, proposes here as well as elsewhere that Joy Division seemed to maintain an intuitive grasp of how to translate this complicated felt experience of what it was like to live in a particular place and time, Manchester and Greater Manchester in the 1970s, into musical form. Stephen Morris comments, in one of the numerous interviews collected in Savage's later book-length oral history of Joy Division, "'Auto-suggestion' we made up on the spot. It was just me and Hooky soundchecking, and we were just waiting for Martin to do whatever he was doing . . . We were just playing, and it is basically me and Hooky and then a bit of backwards guitar, stick on some lyrics, and it was literally that quick, but still good" (220). As Morris recalls, "That was how we wrote; in fact, it was easier doing it just like that. It's strange to think that for the largest extent, Joy Division just existed in our heads" (220).

Brian Edge, in his book first published in 1984 and then in a revised edition in 1988, *New Order + Joy Division: Pleasures and Wayward Distractions*, contends both "Autosuggestion" and "From Safety to Where . . .?" are "as good as anything from *Unknown Pleasures* itself," yet Edge finds these two songs representative of the band "in a lighter mood" than the rest of the songs that are included on *Unknown Pleasures*: "The tracks are dark green as opposed to sombre black" but "that doesn't mean to say that they're froth" (41). Edge commends "Autosuggestion" in particular for highlighting "Curtis's soulful, crooning style" (41).

Dave Thompson, in the revised, 2017, edition of his book, *A Legacy in Wax: Listening to Joy Division and New Order, 1976-2017*, is not so positive about the quality of achievement that "Autosuggestion" represents, describing the song as "little more than a drum pattern, over which Curtis croons, and ghostly guitars scrape and keen; it has a certain atmospheric quality, mantric to a point, but even the band seem to tire of it after five minutes or so, picking up the pace for one final run through the circuit, and then dribbling out on a dying drumbeat" (39). In relation to the live performance recording of "Autosuggestion" from the Prince of Wales Conference Centre in London, in August 1979, Thompson finds this recording suggestive of "a considerably tamer evening" and "a considerably quieter crowd" than those in attendance then and there recall, an intriguing comment for those of us only listening subsequently to this live version of "Autosuggestion," because here the song comes across as considerably louder, more raw, more raucous, and overall more overtly 'punky' than as produced in the studio.

In yet another early book about Joy Division, *An Ideal for Living: An History of Joy Division*, written by Mark Johnson and published in 1984, Johnson uses "Autosuggestion" as the title for one of the many short essays he includes in this book, each comprised of distilled compilations of commentaries from diverse contributors. In this case Paul Morley's contribution is the longest, as Morley discusses 'masking effects' employed to disguise and complicate the sources of constituent sounds in Joy Division songs, both as these songs are recorded in the studio and as they are performed live. Morley suggests a kind of 'auto-suggestive' process is at work in Joy Division songs. Accordingly, Morley interprets these songs as seeking to unearth what is otherwise normally hidden, perhaps within a cultural unconscious, and to do so broadly akin to practices of hypnotic therapy and surrealist automatic writing. This musical process requires considerable as well as often subtle manipulation, including in the form of double- or multi- tracking, additive effects and subtractive treatments, carefully separating and distinguishing discrete sound sources, de-tuning and re-tuning instruments, playing with and against reverse recordings, and, as Steve Taylor discusses in yet another piece included in *An Ideal for Living: An History of Joy Division*, making use of a vocal harmonizer to change the register and timbre of Curtis's voice, when performing live. "Autosuggestion" thus involves deliberately seeking to break through musically to expose something normally hidden from direct perception, and, in exposing what can be exposed, running the risk of becoming overwhelmed by what will prove impossible to withstand, akin to the sudden release of a blinding light.

"Autosuggestion" is one song for which Deborah Curtis, in *So This is Permanence*, has been able to share multiple drafts of Ian Curtis's lyrics. An earlier version of these lyrics asserts a recognition that "everything is falling, broken down," while proposing "I'm getting through," seemingly in being able to recognize the former. Curtis equates the situation "here," from where he is located, from where is situated, where "everything is by design," with being "Broken down, pounded in/Not brought about from deep within" (170). Curtis appears to be seeking to achieve contact with a surreal order of existence, comprised of "different words that mean much more" than those "I say you've heard before" (170). Curtis emphasizes "We are the product, of what we've made/Stunted growth that can't be saved" (170). As such, what is required is a dramatic transformation of whom and what we are, of whom and what we have been shaped to be, including of how we continually contribute toward maintaining and reproducing this problematic and limited version of what we can be. Even though discouraged by normative convention as well as by those in positions of cultural and political authority from pursuing such a course, it seems potentially enabling to embrace the recognition that "a point of view creates new waves . . . prompting questions" (170). These passages from this early version of the lyrics for "Autosuggestion" imply 'we' are forcibly pressured, even while not recognizing this to be the case, into accepting the way things are, and especially the way things appear to be, as if this is the way things must be, and as if this is in turn a desirable and beneficial state of affairs, for us. 'We' are, further, forcibly pressured not to 'make waves', not to 'ask questions', not to "take a chance," and not to "step outside."

Curtis's earlier draft includes two further stanzas that show up nowhere in the final version of the lyrics of "Autosuggestion." The first reads: "Hollow in their meaning/Hollow in their thinking/Can't you see it's getting harder/Deprived of any vision/Locked in indecision/ Destination getting farther" (171) And then the second stanza proceeds as follows: "European breakdown/No purpose in this showdown/No love of life to take you higher/Burning in a new guise/All you want is a new life" (171). These passages suggest seeking and needing to find a dramatically new way of making sense, and, even more than that, a dramatically new way of living. Perhaps they are seeking a revolutionarily new 'ideal for living', a revolutionarily new ideal for what life can–and what life should–be about. These draft lyrics suggest too many people are effectively compelled to live dreary, empty lives, and to identify themselves with these lives such that they come to imagine this kind of life is what they truly want and need. Too many people live lives designed for them that delimit, that constrict, what they can be and what they can do, depriving and robbing people of genuinely enlivening possibilities. In this connection, 'Autosuggestion' might represent a mantra enacted in the attempt to counter tendencies toward accepting and conforming to the dictates of this denuded state of being, even while recognizing how difficult and challenging it is to refuse what seemingly everyone around insists one must be.

The next two pages, a rambling series of notes, which may or may not have been connected with early ideas for the lyrics of "Autosuggestion," follow in much the same vein. These notes emphasize discontent that noble causes, inspiring pursuits, and revolutionary possibilities all seem to be sharply in decline, at least from a vantage point in 'the here and now'. These notes depict a writer wrestling with desiring a way to break from complacent acceptance of mediocre conformity as constituting the furthest horizon of the possible yet who is also frightened, confused, and uncertain about how to do so, to what end such striving might lead or what end might result from attempting to do so, and even whether it might be possible to do so, at least anymore, and at least from where this writer is himself situated.

In what is likely a yet later draft, positioned adjacent to the final version of the lyrics, Curtis includes a line he subsequently drops, as part of the exhortation these lyrics seem to manifest, urging 'us' or 'himself' or both 'himself' and 'us' "To show the choices they often hide" (60). This line seems to reference living in a society where all too many people are narrowly tracked into limited and limiting pathways designed *for* us, without us being in the position to imagine let alone pursue alternatives. Here it seems all too many people do not even recognize that many ostensible 'choices', for what we might aim to be and do, how, and why, have been rendered effectively unavailable to us, from the get go, as a result of the social positions into which we are born and from where we grow up. All too often people do not even recognize these alternatives as real possibilities: given social conditioning, given how people are socially designed, manufactured, and packaged, these alternative prospects for what, how, and why people might live their lives are rendered effectively unintelligible. As a yet further line that is left out of the final version of the lyrics likewise declares: "We're the product, way we're made" (60).

"Autosuggestion" Curtis chose as the title for these lyrics, and eventually for this song, from early on. In order usefully to speculate about why this might be so, and, more important than that, what this title contributes to this song, in terms of how plausibly to make sense of what it means, let's turn next to discuss to what does 'autosuggestion' commonly refer. To begin, this term references people's attempt to deliberately influence and even direct the course of what they think, as well as how so. Autosuggestion can be loosely connected with the commonsense notion of the exercise of 'mind over matter'. In this sense, autosuggestion suggests invoking a mantra to 'psych one's self up' or to calm one's self, by pushing distracting and disturbing thoughts–and feelings–aside in order to focus on what needs to be done and on centering the belief that one is capable of doing what needs to be done.

I myself do this often enough. Before entering a class or a meeting, or before participating in another kind of event or occasion, in which I know I will be taking on a prominent role, that will make demands upon my capabilities, especially if this is a relatively novel experience–or even for instance, the first meeting of a new class or my first participation in the meeting of a group involved in some form of civic engagement–I remind myself to enter 'relaxed, calm, and confident', assuring and reassuring myself that I am prepared and able to do what I need to do. I remind myself to take some deep breaths and to loosen and relax my muscles as well as to focus on the positive benefit, value, or importance of what I am about to be doing. Frequently, trainers I work with in running and related forms of fitness activity encourage me and others with whom they work to believe in what we are capable of and to narrow and concentrate our focus so we can do our best in the course of this activity, and, for instance, in the case of a road race, remember 'we have already done all the hard work to prepare for this occasion', now is the time to relax and have fun, we are ultimately only ever competing with ourselves, and we can only ever do the best we can according to how well we are feeling on any given day. And yet, as the Oxford English Dictionary indicates, autosuggestion refers, more precisely, not simply to "Suggestion, or a suggestion, arising from oneself" but rather to "the hypnotic or subconscious adoption of an idea which one has originated oneself."

The practice of autosuggestion is traceable to French apothecary Émile Coué, in the early 20th century. As a departure from hypnotic suggestion, Coué found, via his work with his patients, that suggestions of what to think and how so that come from these patients themselves tended to prove more effective and last longer than those that came from others. Coué concluded that patients must use their imagination, must willingly suspend disbelief, must eschew critical judgment, and must stay precisely focused. Coué believed, as a result of his research with his patients, that we maintain resources within our psyche that can enable us to heal ourselves or at the least lessen the unhealthful impact upon us of troubles we experience in our lives.

In "Autosuggestion: a cognitive process that empowers your brain?," written by Kasia A. Myga, Esther Kuehn, and Elena Azanon, and publishjed in a November 2021 issue of the scientific journal *Experimental Brain Research*, the authors aim to explain precisely what autosuggestion can mean, and how it can proceed, as well as to assess its prospective usefulness, while pointing out directions for further research that is needed beforc it can be determined precisely how useful, and for what, autosuggestion can be. Myga, Kuehn, and Azanon identify autosuggestion as "a cognitive process that is believed to enable control over one's own cognitive and physiological states" and they suggest since Coué's time autosuggestive techniques have become "an integral part of our modern life," as evidenced in the widespread popularity of "positive affirmations (i.e., statements of desired outcomes that people reiterate)." But Myga, Kuehn, and Azanon argue autosuggestion needs to be more precisely defined and distinguished from closely related but not identical processes. The authors contribute to this end by proposing "Autosuggestion is a process in which the implementation of an idea results in changes in perceptual and/or brain states."

Autosuggestion, yes, involves 'self-administered suggestion" but it is a particular form of self-administered suggestion because if "alterations in perceptual or brain states cannot be detected" then "autosuggestion did not take place." What's more, "Self-induced suggestion differs from heterosuggestion," and Myga, Kuehn, and Azanon imply the two are too easily conflated. Heterosuggestion "implies that suggestions are reinforced *by another person*, whereas those are reinforced *by the to-be-suggested person* in autosuggestion." More precisely, Myga, Kuehn, and Azanon

define autosuggestion as the *instantiation and reiteration of ideas or concepts* by *oneself* aiming to *actively bias one's own perceptual, brain or interoceptive states, as well as the valence of perceived sensations. This reiteration takes a verbal/linguistic form (internally or out loud) and may be reinforced by employing imagery. Autosuggestion may take both forms: implicit (i.e., adopted and internalized suggestion from external sources) and explicit (applied consciously and volitionally).*

It is especially important to note well that "the word 'actively' indicates that autosuggestion is volitional and intentional." In other words, autosuggestion represents a manifestation of "agency or free will"–which distinguishes it from many familiar practices of hypnosis, as well as from a variety of similar therapies in which another person or persons are in charge or in control.

Autosuggestion is especially effective, or at least promising in its prospective effectiveness, "as a reactive form of cognitive control, because in autosuggestion, one tries to bias or override an *existing* perceptual state into a desired perceptual state." "Autosuggestion is often used as a tool in therapeutic and relaxation methodologies, such as autogenic training" where it is implemented so that "the inner repetition of a thought or sentence" can "trigger" desirable "somatic sensations."

"Autosuggestion is also part of the so-called cognitive behavior therapy intervention (CBT), which aims at alleviating symptoms via challenging and realigning maladaptive thoughts with reality." Autosuggestion fits what is often set forth as an aim of such therapy, in which a therapist initially instructs or leads the way as a patient practices this form of therapy, but the aim is for the patient to be able, ultimately, to do this work themself. What the patient learns to do is to catch counterproductive thoughts and thought patterns when and as they occur, recognize these are not only counterproductive but also unnecessary, and replace them with productive and enabling thoughts and thought patterns. Yet I have often been impatient with CBT, as these techniques seem too obvious and are ones I already pursued, before seeking therapeutic assistance, without me doing so doing much to counter, let alone overcome, my feelings of anxiety and depression.

But for Myga, Kuehn, and Azanon a principal aim, once again, is to distinguish autosuggestion from closely related but distinct kinds of practices. For example, autosuggestion, they argue, is not identical with "reappraisal." In reappraisal, "one can change an emotional response to a situation by thinking differently *about the situation*." This "is related to but also different from autosuggestion." The difference Myga, Kuehn, and Azanon explain as follows: "if one experiences muscle pain after a workout in the gym, in autosuggestion, one would directly target the perceptual state of pain by reducing it, whereas in reappraisal, one has more choices of approaching the painful experience." The latter include changing "how one feels *about* the pain after exercising, for example by accepting the pain but reducing its effect on behavior," or "welcoming the pain as part of a sportive experience," or "Instead of focusing on its unpleasantness and discomfort," striving "to change the emotional impact of the painful experience." Autosuggestion is a more narrowly specific practice, albeit quite powerful, if it works, which again, as with Coué, depends on being able to imagine and believe that self-induced healing is possible, and to be able to achieve a mental state in which one allows this to happen.

"To those who like to be in control, this subjective feeling of self-control but also the actual ability to control oneself are major advantages of autosuggestion compared to hypnosis and heterosuggestion." Yet, as Myga, Kuehn, and Azanon conclude, much more research needs to be done to determine precisely how this practice works. Research is needed in relation to all of the following: 1) what brain networks and primary sensory areas are involved; 2) what methods are more versus less effective (such as "loud or internally reiterated linguistic repetitions"); 3) whether mental imagery is crucial to successful autosuggestion and if autosuggestion is "possible without 'believing' in it"; 4) what expectations and beliefs exercise what kinds of impact over "one's capabilities in performing autosuggestion"; 5) what "individual traits determine autosuggestibility" and if these are "related to high levels of hypnotizability and imagery skills"; 6) whether training is necessary in order for people to be successful in practicing autosuggestion and if so what kind; 7) how effective is autosuggestion as "treatment for physiological or psychological disorders"; and 8) if effectiveness as treatment varies according to disorder and in terms of what kinds of people are experiencing disorders.

It is possible autosuggestion fascinated Ian Curtis because it offered him the possibility of being able to think, feel, and act differently than he otherwise experienced himself pressured to think, feel, and act–and than he otherwise experienced himself as responding to such pressures. This could include seeking ways to heal pain he experienced as a result of anxiety and in response to epilepsy and depression. But it seems more likely autosuggestion attracted his interest as a means of contact with a surreal order of existence: a realm consisting not only of lingering traces but also substantive instantiations. These include hauntological suggestions of possibilities within the past that *might* have become the present and *might yet* anticipate the future. Throughout his lyrics and related writing, as well as in his favorite reading, Curtis is attracted to the idea that what we empirically engage is not the totality of 'the real', and in fact only a slight and all–too-constraining dimension of a much greater expanse.

Although this undoubtedly will seem far-fetched to some readers, I recognize a connection with some fundamental dimensions of Marxist philosophy, which I will recount next not only to draw out this connection but also in order to further explain my skepticism concerning what autosuggestion, in and of itself, is capable of achieving. To begin, Marxism is a *dialectical* theory: this means it approaches objects of theoretical and critical interest (for example, works of literature, film, music, and so on) as 1.) *interdeterminately interconnected* with a vast, complex array of other entities and as 2.) always existing *in history*, thereby always involving (and always subject to) *development and change*, while 3.) paying especially close attention, in studying development and change, to *contradictory* forces and tendencies at work within–and upon–these very same objects of theoretical and critical interest. This suggests that past, present, and future, as well as self and other, us and them, I and you, the subjective and the objective, and so on, are not discretely distinct, but rather interpenetrating, overlapping, and mutually constitutive. It further suggests that we, like everything else, are constantly in process, not static and fixed, and pulled in multiple, often competing or contesting directions, often indeed at once. It suggests 'the meaning of a song' (such as 'the meaning' of "Autosuggestion") is likely to be multiple, contradictory, and changing, and that, even more precisely, 'the song's meaning' is best found in the song's multiple, contradictory, and dynamic *interconnections* with numerous other possible texts and contexts.

Marxism is moreover ultimately concerned with *concrete* analysis: analysis of how things actually are and what they actually do in the real world–not in an abstract, ideal, or purely fantastical realm. So in relation, once more, to a song, its meaning, and better put its meaning*s*, are those that it has exercised and does exercise with, for, and upon actual people, or, in other words, what the song prompts actual people to think (about) and to feel, as well as what kind of response it evokes or provokes from actual people and what place it occupies within actual people's lives. A Marxist analysis of a song is interested in what kinds of meaning*s* the song conveys, or is likely to convey; what kinds of impact*s* the song exerts, or is likely to exert; and how these meanings and impacts vary depending upon what kinds of people are attending to the song, when, where, how, and why. The Marxist critic is likewise interested in how–and why–the meanings the song conveys and the impacts the song exerts can and do change over time as well as vary from place to place.

Marxism is, further, a *philosophically materialist* theory: i.e., for Marxism physical reality exists outside of its representation in human consciousness, and outside of its representation in human language. Material conditions are primary; subjective perceptions, reflections, and experiences are secondary–the former ultimately determine the latter, even as the latter exert a reciprocal impact upon the former. *Philosophical idealism* suggests ideal or spiritual entities are ultimately determinant of what happens in the material world; *philosophical materialism* suggests the opposite is the case. For example, years ago a man who conducted positive thinking seminars as his job picked up a friend and I as we were hitchhiking from New Haven to New York City. We came to a tollbooth crossing from the Bronx into Manhattan and our driver greeted the tollbooth attendant in an effusively cheery way, asking (or perhaps declaring to) the tollbooth attendant "isn't it great to be alive and enjoying this wonderful day?!" To that, the tollbooth attendant replied "fuck you." Our driver, a classic philosophical idealist, declared, immediately afterward, the man was a tollbooth attendant *because* of his 'bad attitude'. But a philosophical materialist reading of the same situation would propose that it is more likely the man's 'bad attitude' resulted from his working all day as a tollbooth attendant (rather than vice-versa).

To take another example, years ago a student argued in a class I was teaching if people would just stop talking or writing about oppression, then oppression would disappear such that noone would be oppressed anymore and noone would be oppressing anyone else anymore. This, again, is an example of a classically philosophically idealist way of thinking. A philosophical materialist would propose, instead, people write and talk about oppression because people experience oppression, because people maintain oppressive relations with each other in the material world–in the world, that is, which exists outside of people's heads.

I likewise remember a notorious example of a keynote speaker at an ostensibly Marxist conference declaring people did not need to get all worked up about capitalism and the damage it can and does do, because capitalism is only a word, as a word it can be deconstructed, and she herself did so every time she took a shower while at the same time also constructing socialism in its place. Marxism in fact argues capitalism is an enormously substantial *material* reality, both a mode of production and form of social organization that has become globally dominant and pervasive, while although continually evolving and always encompassing a great many internal struggles, cannot by any means be easily displaced or replaced, certainly not by merely 'willing' or 'wishing' that this be so.

In sum, philosophical idealism proposes if we successfully change the way we think and speak or write about a social problem (such as homelessness, poverty, war, drug abuse, rape, etc.), the problem will disappear; in contrast, philosophical materialism argues how we think, speak, or write about the problem is itself a product of material conditions, processes, relations, and interests–and those latter need to be tackled in order effectively to solve the problem.

Yet more precisely, Marxism, as a form of *dialectical* materialism, argues human consciousness, and language as a mode of practical consciousness, themselves ultimately exist and exert an impact in the material world as well, because this is consciousness by and shared among materially real beings as part of their material real engagement with each other and with the materially real world in which they exist. But consciousness, and language, are only parts of the larger whole that is material reality: material reality is much larger than just consciousness and language. It's like a Venn diagram, with consciousness and language representing a small circle within the much larger circle that is material reality in its totality.

But to review, 'material reality' = reality maintaining a physical existence outside of (or beyond) its mere *representation* in consciousness and language, while 'ideal reality' = reality purely in the form of its representation in consciousness or language. 'Zebras', the actual animals, are part of material reality, and 'zebras', as words, which we can hear or see, are part of material reality too; 'zebras' as ideas, or concepts, or images that come to mind when we hear or see the word 'zebra' are part of ideal reality. Yet, according to philosophical materialisms, including Marxism, the ideas that come to mind in relation to the word 'zebras' are ultimately the results of human beings' engagement in a world that exists outside of the contents of our minds alone. Even abstract or fantastical ideas are ultimately rooted, from a philosophical materialist vantage point, in human beings' participation and engagement in social relations.

One key addition I need to add here, to avoid common misconceptions following what I have just shared. Materiality, according to Marxists, exists in multiple modes or modalities, which involve processes of transformation in moving from one mode or modality to another. What we think and what we speak operate as specific modes, or modalities, of materiality, as do our physical bodies, and as do our social relations and the products of our social relations with others, at work, for example. Ideality is, in effect, ultimately a particular mode or modality of materiality. For Marxism, all of reality is matter in motion but this encompasses an enormous variety of different forms of organization. What's more, boundaries distinguishing these forms of organization of matter in motion are often highly fluid as well as extensively crisscrossed. What exists in one modality of materiality is interdeterminately interconnected with, or interpenetrating of and interpenetrating by, what exists in other modalities. And all these modes are dynamic–they are frequently and often extensively changing, including as a result of their interactions with each other.

'Objective reality' is far from simple for Marxists–it is not something obvious, fixed, static, and purely 'rock-like' (in relation to what commonsense conceptions of 'rock-like' tend to call to mind). And that further means, although Marxists believe accurate (or at least adequate) knowledge of objective reality is possible, accurate (or adequate) knowledge is by no means guaranteed. In fact, for Marxists, in practice different understandings and different explanations of the complexity and dynamism of various aspects or dimensions of objective reality are, almost always, at best, more versus less accurate, or more versus less adequate–not simply absolutely right versus absolutely wrong. Knowledge is an extremely difficult challenge, and it is often highly partial and limited, reflective in turn of often highly partial and limited bases, or vantage points, in objective reality, from which the prospective 'knower' seeks 'to know'. Knowledge is shaped by the particular complexes of social and natural conditions, forces, relations, and interests that guide its pursuit–by these, in other words, specific aspects and dimensions of 'objective reality'–so that even, if not especially, in attempting to understand and explain its own conditions of possibility, knowledge is often likely to prove partial and limited. To posit that objective reality exists and that it is prospectively possible to understand and explain objective reality more versus less accurately, or more versus less adequately, does not guarantee this can or will happen–and, as aforementioned, this is only possible, at all, as a result of practical engagement with (and within) what one attempts to understand and explain, practical engagement that often involves considerable work and difficult struggle. The test of whether knowledge is more versus less accurate, or adequate, is, for Marxism, always practical–what it enables versus what it disenables. If, for example, one offers a theory of poverty, this theory needs to be tested in practice to discover how well it does and does not accurately (or adequately) explain what it purports to explain, as well as what responses to and interventions within poverty it most readily enables. It is not 'knowledge of poverty', in other words, unless it can prove itself so.

To return to practices of autosuggestion, Marxism would argue that suggesting to one's self that what one is experiencing can and should be better experienced differently runs up against inevitable limits to how far this can prove successful, by itself alone, as merely thinking differently, for example, about one's experience of pain cannot completely overcome or eliminate the material conditions that have made this pain possible and the material forces that have generated this pain on the basis of what those conditions have made possible. Yet, because our mind, and more precisely our consciousness, is itself materially embodied, extended, embedded, and enacted, it can and does exercise a material force, which can in turn prospectively effect how we might register and respond to sensations that cause pain, potentially partially diminishing or redirecting the way we do so. Yet this remains not only partial but also, more importantly, compensatory, as it at best 'overwrites' what is already 'written' or, in other words, at best reimagines and reconceives what the reaction and response can be to what already has been 'triggered'. It does not get to the root of what is ultimately causing the pain, what is ultimately 'writing' the condition, what it ultimately triggering the state. Exaggeration concerning the ostensible reparative and recuperative capabilities of practices of autosuggestion can provide ideological justification for limiting and especially cutting back on provision of resources in the form of social services designed and targeted toward aiding people in processes of repair and recovery, while simultaneously supporting the all too prevalent ideological notion, within capitalist societies, that individuals are in charge, ultimately individually themselves alone, of their own success or failure–and their own happiness or unhappiness–so those who end up struggling and suffering are simply those who have not worked hard enough and who have not through their own merits earned anything better than where they are at, than where they have ended up.

Let's turn now to closely examine the lyrics to "Autosuggestion." To begin, a meticulously precise transcription of the vocals in lyrical form would note that the word "Here," which by itself constitutes the first line, and then the second line of the first stanza, as well as, once more, the first line and then the second line of the second stanza, might better be represented as something like "Hee-ee-ee-ee-eer-eer-rr-rr-rhh-rhh" as Curtis extends his vocalization of this word for a prolonged period, emphasizing every phoneme within this single word. Nonetheless, "Here" does seem to function in some kind of indexical fashion, 'pointing' toward a specific location, perhaps also at a specific time, that seems not only to be the setting for what the lyrics will recount, and address, but also where the narrator-protagonist and 'we' along with 'him' are at, at least at present. However, as it typical with Curtis, we gain few details concerning what this 'Here' appears like–few empirical details in terms of how it looks, sounds, and feels, although more concerning how it sounds and especially feels than how it looks. Still, it seems that we are directed to focus attention to the immediate moment, the immediate situation, and prospectively what is happening, has happened, and can, will, or might happen 'here' or *from here*. In this location, as lines three and four of stanza one reiterate, "Everything is by design," which does not carry a positive or even a neutral connotation, but rather suggests a state of affairs in which room for manoeuver, for exercise of free will and agency, for spontaneity and creativity, for collaboration and innovation, is all severely limited, perhaps even non-existent, as in effect 'we' along with the narrator-protagonist are constrained to do what has been designed *for us* but not *by us*, to an extent that our very subjectivities have been effectively designed so that we are completely overdetermined, completely *subject to* the shaping power of forces over which, or in response to which, we maintain little if any influence, let alone control. In stanza two, the third line suggests a particularly insidious consequence of this state of affairs, as 'here' "Everything is kept inside." That might suggest 'we' cannot share any doubts, hesitations, confusions, uncertainties, and especially objections or misgivings 'we' maintain about what has been designed, because we are strongly encouraged not to do so. We must 'keep these to ourselves', 'do as we are told', and 'live the lives that have been set out for us, according to the patterns that have been prepared for us in living these lives', while not showing any discontent with let alone manifesting any opposition to any of this.

These lyrics evince deep frustration and dissatisfaction in experiencing one's self as socially situated so that one's opportunities for mobility, for advancement, for exploration, for fulfillment, for imagination, for discovery, for invention, and for creation are sharply curtailed, with access to many avocational as well as vocational paths effectively barred, at the same time that one is encouraged to identify with the limits of what has been defined by more powerful social forces and interests as 'one's proper social position' and even to identify with these limits as desirable and good. In this kind of social location, and as part of the culture associated with living life in acceptance of and conformity to its constraints, it is seemingly crucial that people keep 'a tight lid' on open expression and sharing of their emotions, especially troubled and troubling emotions–and this would certainly seem to be especially true for boys and men, at least according to terms of hegemonic masculinity.

And yet, as line four of stanza two proposes, it may nonetheless be possible to resist: "So take a chance and step outside." In other words, you may grow up socially conditioned to assume that you simply cannot do so, but in fact openings may exist, if you do 'take a chance' and are able and willing 'to step outside' of the existence that has been designed, that has been programmed, for you. Yet rarely does it make sense to interpret Curtis's lyrics as offering an unambiguously positively hopeful message, one that is not heavily freighted by the risks, costs, and dangers of pursuing what might otherwise seem right and necessary. Taking that qualification into account can help in making sense of the next two lines: "Your hopes, your dreams, your paradise/Heroes, idols cracked like ice." It is possible the lyrics here urge 'us' to 'take a chance' and 'step outside' in pursuit of our 'hopes' and 'dreams', even in pursuit of our visions of 'paradise' or of what we imagine as constituting 'the ultimate good life'. If so, the lyrics are urging us not to allow our 'heroes' and our 'idols' to degenerate into nothing more than nonsensical childish fantasies that 'crack like ice' in comparison with what 'real life-experience' for us is and inevitably always will and must be like. Alternately, this passage might suggest in 'taking a chance' by 'stepping outside' you find what you hoped, what you dreamed, and what you imagined your heroes, your idols, as representing, in leading you to identify with them, turn out to be mystifications because it is far more challenging, difficult, and even virtually impossible to proceed all that far and do all that much to escape and live out a substantial alternative to the carefully designed and closely constrictive life into which you have been interpellated and are incessantly re-interpellated. No ready outlets exist for realizing these hopes and dreams, at least not 'for people like you', no substantial help or support exists for this pursuit, and your heroes and your idols appear to represent fraudulent models in terms of to what you might aspire to be and for how you might achieve that to which you aspire. What exactly do 'we', the narrator-protagonist and 'us', find when we 'take a chance' and 'step outside'? Perhaps we find we are on our own, and as hugely alienating as our previous existence 'inside' was, this 'outside' world is, at least 'for people like us', equally so–very much 'a cold, cruel world'.

The first four lines of stanza three repeat what has already been stated: "Here/Here/Everything is kept inside/So take a chance and step outside." The repetition is important, as this reinforces interpretation of the vocalization of these lyrics as constituting a kind of exhortation or a mantra. This 'autosuggestion' might represent a mantra one is repeating to one's self, to encourage one's self to confront and push past one's fears, one's metaphorical as well as possibly even literal agoraphobia, to 'dare' to be and to do what one has otherwise convinced oneself, or allowed others to convince one, that one cannot be and cannot do–ever. And yet, in in these lyrics, this appears unlikely to be a glib exercise or an easy indulgence in the 'power of positive thinking', where the immediate follow-up might take the form of something like 'you can do it, it's really nothing at all as bad or as hard as you have imagined it, you've got this, nothing can hold you back but yourself, you can be and do whatever you set your mind to do', etc. Line four, instead, reads "Pure frustration face to face." This line suggests 'taking a chance' and 'stepping outside' leads to meeting up with 'pure frustration face to face', in other words frustration no longer obscured, no longer denied, no longer mystified. When you take a chance and step outside you cannot hide from the reality that what you are experiencing, what you are confronting, and what you have experienced and confronted, is indeed 'frustration', and not just that as this is *pure* frustration'–total, unadulterated frustration. Nothing takes the edge off, nothing palliates, nothing compensates. You are engulfed in frustration.

Why might this be? Perhaps you have tried to be and do something other than what you have been socially directed to be and do, to try to lead a life other than what is expected and commonly denoted as right and proper 'for someone like you'. Yet you have found no support, no assistance, no welcome, no encouragement for such an attempt, and as much as you cannot retreat 'inside' and pretend that you are satisfied with that life, you find that sheer individual will, effort, intent, desire, and so on are not enough in order to enable you to be and do what you aspire to be and do. Doing so depends on material conditions of possibility and material forces of generation that the society of which you are a part does not provide, and in fact denies and refuses, for 'people like you'. Social class is rigidly constraining, and so are other major categories of social identity, as well as intersections among these, including sex, gender, sexuality, race, ethnicity, regionality, locality, generation, age, mental and physical health status, and dis/ability.

Lines five and six of stanza three read "A point of view creates more waves/So take a chance and step outside." This may amount to an encouragement to take a stance, to identify with a position, to represent it openly, honestly, and forthrightly, and to be ready to commit on behalf of something and to act on the basis of this commitment. It may constitute such an encouragement because in developing "a point of view" that "creates more waves" you might be doing what is needed, in order to break past, break through, and at least contribute toward opening up possibilities otherwise denied 'to people like you'. This may indeed be a prerequisite for any kind of positive, and progressive, social change to happen. In order to transform the status quo, in other words, it is necessary "to make waves," to manifest discontent with merely maintaining and reproducing this status quo, essentially unchanged. It may be necessary to refuse to 'stay in one's place', to refuse to remain content with 'what one is told to do', to refuse to keep quiet or to remain silent when that is expected of one–and especially not to do so in the face of injustice and inequity, or in the face of mass conformity, complacency, and passivity. So 'taking a chance and stepping outside' might mean doing what is necessary to exert an impact, by actually manifesting, actually embodying, a meaningful challenge, critique, resistance, and opposition. However, in the context of the lyrics as a whole, and also the entire song as an organized patterning and deployment of sounds, it seems 'making waves' might only redound upon one's self, furthering and deepening one's isolation, alienation, marginalization, and exile, because you now are standing out, alone, with few if any others able and willing to stand with you, in the face of what is 'designed' to punish you in doing so, in 'stepping outside' of where you have been directed to step.

Stanza four reads as follows: "Take a chance and step outside/Lose some sleep and say you tried/Meet frustration face to face/A point of view creates more waves/So lose some sleep and say you tried/So lose some sleep and say you tried/So lose some sleep and say you tried/So lose some sleep and say you tried." And then stanza five follows this up with eleven successive lines, all comprised of "Say you tried." These lyrics convey a sense that doing what you feel strongly compelled to do, as the right and necessary thing to do, by 'taking a chance and step outside', means proceeding not only without any guarantees whatsoever of success but also confronting the likelihood of realizing and accomplishing very little. You will be able to "say you tried" but to emphasize this phrase as much as the lyrics do intimates that this is as much as you will accomplish, or realize–making an effort, standing out in standing up. What you are seeking and supporting, even what you have hoped and dreamed of, what you identify and align with, *will* be defeated, the forces opposed to you are too powerful and you are too powerless. But you have at least, as a matter of conscience, made clear where and for what you stand, acting to represent this, even knowing you will lose.

In relation to interpretations I early cited, suggesting these lyrics are critical of people who imagine merely caring enough about an issue to be worried about it means they have done enough, or that 'half-assed' efforts are sufficient, I suggest the lyrics don't seem to me to be making quite these judgmental points. Instead they seem to suggest no matter how 'full-assed' one's efforts, and how much one converts care and worry into action, into actively trying, it is unlikely to be enough. Nevertheless, it is better to do so than simply to retreat from so doing, returning to lead a 'sleepy', even somnolent, existence, where you aren't bothered about what is wrong in the world, or you have become completely aligned with the cynical position that nothing can or ever will be changed for the better so it is a complete waste to try. The lyrics, and with this song the music even more than the lyrics, strike me as despairing concerning the prospect of making any meaningful difference. Yet this despair emanates from a position unable to settle for a life that pushes aside what is wrong, refusing to pay attention to one's connection with, complicity in, and responsibility for what is wrong. This position manifests a need to do one's best, from where one is at and with what one can bring to bear, to *try* to contribute towards making things better.

Let's turn now to consider *the sound* of "Autosuggestion" in some detail, concentrating on the most distinctive features of each of the elements of musical sound I have been focusing on throughout this book, and in particular those that are most readily suggestive of meaning, in supporting, complicating, and countering meaning suggested by the lyrics. Here let's also consider the avenues of musical affect I have been emphasizing in conjunction with each of these musical elements. To begin, the structure and instrumentation of "Autosuggestion" can be usefully characterized as follows:

1. Instrumental opening. Preparatory, setting the stage, gathering and assembling.

a. 0:00–>0:06. Sampled mechanical sounds–initial opening.

b. 0:07–>0:13. Just bass guitar, initial sounding of a melodic line. Four notes: two quick, one long, and one medium in length. Opening pitch, same pitch, slightly up, and then further up.

c. 0:14–>0:43. Guitar enters–two distinct guitar lines at different pitch registers and maintaining significantly different timbres–and the drum kit joins in as well. Gradual increase in volume and density. One guitar line: higher in pitch register, more of a whine or a stab or a flare. Second guitar line: lower in pitch register, primarily stuttering to chugging in oscillating between two chords. Drum kit involves light, closed, rapidly repeating hi-hat strikes, while the snare definitely sounds as if it echoes due to the use of a delay device. The drum pattern is slightly skittering, involving, between the bass drum and the snare drum, a 1st beat strike, followed by a 2nd beat strike, followed by no strike on the third beat, and then striking just off of the fourth beat twice, once just ahead of the beat and once just after the beat. The bass drum and the snare drum come close to converging in pitch and timbre. This minimal pattern is largely relentlessly repeated with only slight variation throughout the course of the song.

2. 0:44–>1:07. Commencement and Initiation. First vocal passage. Not only are voicings extended longer than typical for Curtis, meandering across successive notes for an extended period of time between breaths, and after longer pauses, but also the temporal duration involved in voicings of

words and voicings of lines is also at least somewhat longer than usual for Curtis. The guitar sounds themselves also here become somewhat more meandering.

3. 1:08–>1:16. Brief break, preparation to continue. Brief instrumental interlude.

4. 1:17–>2:01. Further exposition and elaboration. Second vocal passage.

5. 2:02–>2:34. Complication and disturbance. Instrumental bridge. A jagged to ragged guitar sound is more prominent here than previously and this tends to rise in pitch and slightly in volume across phrases.

6. 2:35->3:19. Return to renew exposition and elaboration with further nuance and detail. Third vocal passage.

7. 3:20–>3:40 Further complication and disturbance. Instrumental bridge. The jagged to ragged guitar moves even further upward in pitch.

8. 3:41–>5:47 Confrontation Moving Toward Climax. Fourth and climactic/culminating vocal passage. This includes a final, pushing and straining vocal, increasing in volume, rising in pitch, and suggestive of a heightened intensity.

9. 5:48–>6:04 Denouement. Instrumental closeout.

The specific sounds sources we hear in "Autosuggestion" include the following:

1. The bass guitar that concentrates on reiterating a short and compact melodic line, and that is highly consistent to persistent in reiterating the same minimal pattern over the course of the song.

2. The vocal, that tends to sustain voicings for extended periods while meandering across pitches, between breaths and pauses, and then heightens in intensity in the final vocal passage.

3. The drum kit, in which the echoing effects achieved through use of digital delay are pronounced and the short and slightly skittering pattern it performs is repeated with only small variation throughout the song.

4. The sampled sound that marks the initial opening.

5. The guitar, which is employed solely for purposes of harmonic fill, of texture, and involves stark patterns that either stutter or stab or flare, that sound emphatically minor key, and that verge on the discordant and the dissonant while all appearing to be considerably processed and especially filtered and reduced. Also, as I have cited via a number of commentators, the guitar sounds are the product of reversing what was initially played and recorded.

All four standard functional layers are represented with the bass guitar a major contributor to the melodic layer along with the vocal, the guitar solely responsible for harmonic fill, and the bass guitar and drums tightly interlocking in connecting the explicit beat layer with the functional bass layer in establishing a groove.

In terms of the soundbox, the initial sampled sound enters from the middle to upper regions along a vertical axis on both the left and right sides while leaning toward the far edges of a horizontal axis. In terms of perceived depth, this sound appears to be coming at us from further back in the soundbox than most of what we subsequently hear. The bass guitar starts from low to the left, and fairly close to the front, while it climbs slightly higher and moves slightly closer as the song proceeds. The drums and cymbals sound from both sides, slightly higher than the bass guitar yet also slightly closer to the edges. Listening on headphones I also detect what seem like occasional tom rolls and cymbal crashes, later in the song. The vocal sounds from slightly below the center in the middle of the soundbox. It seems to move around in this space, including pushing higher as well as drifting leftward and rightward. It is difficult for me to discern its precise position in terms of how close versus far the vocal is located in relation to the perceived front of the soundbox, as this seems to vary slightly yet repeatedly over the course of the song, while the fact that no sound source seems to operate from anywhere close to the same or even an overlapping location in the soundbox–all are well spread out and clearly distinguished from each other–means the vocal can sound prominent without necessarily sounding as if it is close. The guitar sounds come from higher in the soundbox, and further back, from both sides, with distinct lines coming from the left and the right.

The structure and instrumentation contribute an overall eerie feeling, as if the song is emanating from a strange as well as a largely empty or barren space. The structure and instrumentation call to mind, as a potentially useful analogy, a minimal as well as abstract theatrical stage. Emptiness, in the form of space between sound sources and surrounding each constituent sound source is pronounced. At the same time, the organization and deployment of this instrumentation across this entire space contributes a feeling of a slowly gathering and growing unease. The song might represent an interior mental space, an introspective space, in which the music as persona is trying to clear it's head of distracting clutter but not able to do so all that well. Perhaps this is a space in which an attempt at achieving a meditative state is only partially successful. Perhaps this is a space suggestive of a consciousness self-aware that it does not and cannot offer itself refuge, protection, security, and comfort.

Variations in terms of loudness primarily correspond to increases versus decreases in the numbers of instruments, or sound sources, as well as the number of distinct lines or patterns of sound that we hear sounding at the same time. Overall, the song remains largely constant in terms of volume level, although it feels as if this increases with the final vocal passage and in places where guitar sounds are the most stabbing and flaring. Volume also increases in the initial lead-in section of the song and decreases in the final fade-out section.

In terms of rhythm, the time signature, as is typically the case, is 4/4, but the tempo is a matter of some dispute, with a number of commentators identifying this as 130 bpm or more, yet the song feels quite slow to me, and it is only possible to identify the tempo as that fast if one is taking the rapid closed hi-hat strikes as defining the beat rather than the bass drum and the snare drum. If so, then the bass drum and the snare drum contribute accentuation and further complexity, but if one concentrates on the bass drum and snare drum in identifying the beat then the song is much slower in tempo. In general each bass drum strike or snare drum strike is accompanied by four hi-hat strikes. The song sounds as if it increases in tempo somewhat in the final vocal passage, while in the recording of Joy Division performing this song live from the Prince of Wales Conference Centre in London the band abruptly and markedly changes the tempo at several points in the course of their playing of the song. Meanwhile, the rhythmic contributions of the vocal and the guitar both change over the course of the song, involving in sections of peak intensity an increasing number of notes or chords sounding for shorter periods of time as well as a movement more quickly from the one to the next.

In terms of pitch, the bass guitar is steady and consistent, in its short and repeated melodic line, always moving upward twice. The guitar oscillates around successive pitches, while maintaining distinct lines at higher and lower registers. The guitar periodically moves abruptly upward or downward in pitch, in combination with increasing the number of chords sounded within the same duration of time and in moving more quickly from the one to the next. Likewise, the guitar also sounds as if it repeatedly includes bendings and stretchings of pitch while playing the same chord. The vocal is most notable for maintaining the same voicing, without a breath and break, across extended notes, especially at the end of phrases, lines, and with the word 'Here', while also tending most often to move upward in pitch within a single distinct sequence. Because of the pronounced echoing sound, the drums seem to shimmer in terms of pitch.

Curtis's vocal delivery, in the studio recording of "Autosuggestion," seems hollowed or emptied out as well as darkened, but this sound is far less deep and steadily so than in the live recording. Curtis's vocal on the studio recorded version of "Autosuggestion" seems to move freely about in terms of pitch, not concerned with landing flat or sharp, and likewise varying notably in timbre. This delivery demonstrates 'soulful crooning' by extending a single voicing, without a breath or pause, for notable durations, and by emphasizing a pronounced vibrato. Even more notable is a pronounced wobbling quality in the vocal that yet is not breathy.

In terms of timbre, to begin, the opening sampled sound is spectral while the bass guitar is warm and almost mellow. The guitar timbre is stark, harsh, and abstract, combining elements that sound 1) like scratching, sputtering, and stuttering; 2) like chugging and chuttering as well as bursting, stabbing, and flaring; and 3.) like sliding, gliding, rumbling, and grating. The timbre of the vocal, meanwhile, is richer and more elaborately nuanced than in the live recording even while highly concentrated and clearly highly filtered. It definitely reveals pronounced elements of added reverb and echo. And the drums, other than the shimmering echoing dimension of their sound are thin, crisp, and narrow.

With the bass guitar, attack and decay are not as pronounced as sustain and release, which are notably slower and longer; with the drums attack is crisp, sustain is short, and echoing treatment tends to add more to decay and release; with the guitar sustain and release, and especially flux, are particularly pronounced; and with the vocal attack is diffuse and prolonged, while decay, sustain, and release are all slowed and extended. In the live recording, the drum kit sounds a much fuller range of distinct timbres; the vocal sounds much more darkened as well as much thicker, muddier, deeper, harder and even harsher; the guitar is much louder and much less filtered, with more distortion and notably more emphatic stabs, flares, slides, and pulsations; and the bass guitar is further buried beneath the guitar.

In listening to "Autosuggestion" I feel most compelled to mimetically participate in response to the repetitiveness of the vocal, and in response to the sense the song conveys of the vocal part resembling a series of conjoined choruses without involving any verses, or any regular dialogue between verse and chorus. Points at which changes occur in speed and loudness, or where at least it feels as if these change, in particular where this is accompanied by a pressing and straining in pitch, are also times when I feel most compelled toward mimetic participation. Yet otherwise I feel more a spectator. I experience ease of exertion with the bass guitar while I experience the guitar as uneasy, the vocal as if the effort involved in exertion increases and this exertion becomes more difficult as the song proceeds, especially in the final vocal passage, and the drum kit I experience conveying neither pronounced effort nor ease of exertion. The duration of exertion is almost continuous for the bass guitar, while the duration of exertion with the drum kit is largely continuous but with both the guitar and the vocal this varies considerably. In terms of my felt impression of the complexity of duration, the guitar feels the most complex while the drum kit feels somewhat more complex than at first seems to be the case, and the vocal feels complex in terms of frequent shiftings of tone and length of time between breaths. I find it difficult to identify whether exertion has proven successful or not, because despite emphasis, particularly by way of the lyrics and the vocal, as well as the minimal and regular sequences contributed by the bass guitar and the drum kit, upon keeping *trying*, I experience "Autosuggestion" communicating considerable uncertainty. At the same time, "Autosuggestion" does not convey to me a strong feeling of a community of effort due to how far the instruments feel spaced out from each other and how distinct each of the lines of sound feels, as well as due to the frequency and duration of pauses, rests, and breaks in lines, other than with the bass guitar.

"Autosuggestion" is likewise difficult to associate with the music conveying a clear sense of anticipation. Rather than anticipation, "Autosuggestion" emphasizes bare continuation, especially in the form of trying, or at least aiming to do so. Beyond that, nothing feels certain. "Autosuggestion" feels as if it is proceeding from a vantage point beyond direct concern with or direct experience of either desire or dread. "Autosuggestion" feels close to a last gesture, a last effort in response to the compulsion of conscience, combined with a strong sense of likely futility. I do anticipate, and it feels as if the music as persona does as well, that the song will involve considerable repetition, that intensity will rise and peak, and that the song will slowly fade out.

In characterizing what and how I hear the music as persona expressing, in "Autosuggestion," this feels to me as if it comes in an almost deadened, or at least denuded form, despite the semblance of impassioned exhortation, almost as if that seeming impassioned exhortation is an artificially contrived gesture. "Autosuggestion" feels as if expression proceeds from a limbo space, an empty space or a space that has been largely emptied out yet continues haunted by troubling and disturbing remnants. "Autosuggestion" feels to me as if this song conveys the expression of one who is still, minimally, striving, yet not hopeful, just *trying* to assert 'himself' sufficient to attest that 'he' does still exist and 'he' does still maintain a will. The music complicates the lyrics because "Autosuggestion" conveys not so much the enunciation of an impassioned determination 'to step outside' and thereby aim to make a meaningful difference, as much as it expresses a grim resolve to go through the motions of so doing while doubting what if anything this can achieve, to the point where the music as persona almost seems as if it ironically mocks the very notion of making such an attempt.

Because acoustic impact, in the case of "Autosuggestion," involves sounds that feel as if they are widely spaced out and separated, especially as if much of what I am hearing comes from edges or corners, it feels to me also as if much of what I am hearing in the song are the echoing or otherwise secondary effects of what has already happened. Perhaps, however, 'the present' of the song makes sense as happening within 'a head space', and especially a troubled head space, of one who is trying to gather and focus but who is finding this difficult to do.

What happens in "Autosuggestion"? It seems as if a call is sent forth to step outside and to be able to say you tried. It seems as if a movement toward some kind of decision, toward some kind of commitment, is at least introspectively engaged. Perhaps, the music as persona has engaged and is engaging in an analysis that arrives at the conclusion it is better to have tried and failed, than not to have tried at all: it is better to 'lose some sleep', 'step outside', 'make some waves', and 'say you tried', even if it seems unlikely this will make any effective difference, because one's own powers are severely limited, in part due to spending so much time 'inside' and being shaped by that extensive 'inside' experience.

Beyond sadness, exhaustion, feelings of numbness, feelings of having been and continuing to be overwhelmed, I associate what I hear, in "Autosuggestion," with the summoning of one last concerted effort to make one final push. I associate what I hear in this song with introspection, perhaps with attempting an autosuggestive form of therapeutic practice and yet doing so without maintaining any naive illusion concerning its likely success. I associate the song as well with performative simulation of and commentary on such states, as if this is not necessarily what the music as persona is 'himself' directly and immediately going through but rather that 'he' is performing, from a distance, what this might be like in order to spark reflection and interpretation.

Taboo sounds in "Autosuggestion" include the reverse guitar, especially with this in turn further cut up, disjoined, and distorted. Yet in terms of taking on the taboo, the song also does so in representing or performatively presenting a simulation or a semblance of psyching one's self up to do something one otherwise is highly disinclined to do without believing in the process and without maintaining any faith to where this might lead and to what it might achieve. It also verges upon the taboo to convey a musical correlative of a state of mind that is troubled, disturbed, exhausted, worn down, uncertain, and indeed shattering, while nevertheless trying to mobilize one last assertion of will.

Where precisely the music as persona is at, from where it has come, and to where it is headed all remain highly nebulous–highly ephemeral, and at the same time feel largely invisible and intangible. It feels hard to come up with a visual correlative that will adequately correspond to what this song is communicating. It feels perhaps as if this is a state, or a situation, or a vantage point that is much better represented sonically than visually or in tactile form, and perhaps one that can't be represented in visual or tactile form. As such, it feels as if fear and dread make sense in connection with what "Autosuggestion" is conveying because this is fear and dread of what exists beyond the possibility of adequately representing in visually luminous or tangibly substantial form.

As I listen to and reflect on my listening to "Autosuggestion," as I make sense of what kind of subject is addressing me, from what kind of position, expressing and communicating what, inviting and encouraging me to think (about) and to feel what, and to respond in what kinds of ways, I am most compelled to explore extended connections. First, with the repressive and oppressive impact of 'the normal' as well as challenges and difficulties involved in resisting 'compulsory normalization'. Second, with debates concerning how to make sense of and respond to trauma that are taking place within trauma theory and trauma studies. Third, in relation to transformative pacifism, with reference to the current war in Ukraine. And fourth, in relation to the work of Trinh T. Minh-ha, Aimé Césaire, and Edward W. Said.

In *Nobody's Normal: How Culture Created the Stigma of Mental Illness* (2021), Roy Richard Grinker explains exactly what his title indicates, while also addressing challenges to, and prospects for overcoming, this stigma. Grinker begins by observing that "Although 60 percent of people with a mental illness in the United States still receive no mental health treatment, mental illness is fast becoming a more accepted and visible part of the human condition" because "We are acknowledging that mental illnesses are more common than we think, and they affect us all–either individually or because of our relationships with others" (xiv). These changes surrounding the stigmatization of mental illness "show us that we need not surrender to stigma, as if were natural to marginalize otherness and difference . . . Stigma isn't in our biology; it's in our culture" (xiv). Grinker's famous grandfather, also named Roy Grinker, a leading neurologist and psychiatrist, shared with him, from early on in the younger Roy Grinker's life, the elder Roy Grinker's conviction that it would have been much better if the 20th century course of both psychiatry and popular understanding of psychology had followed what Freud wished: for people to understand "emotional distress was universal," and because "we are all neurotic," that people "might eventually feel no shame seeking psychological care for their problems" (xv).

Roy Richard Grinker "was raised in a family that believed everyone has a little mental illness, that emotional pain was a normal part of life, and that mental illnesses existed within a hierarchy of all diseases" (xv). As a result, Grinker was shocked when he first confronted direct evidence of the severe stigma surrounding mental illness. This occurred when he ran into a classmate who was a patient at a psychiatric hospital where Grinker's summer job involved him cleaning and filing. Grinker was shocked by how many people harshly admonished him "to keep her hospitalization confidential" such that "I felt as if I had committed a crime" (xv). From that point onward, Grinker came to recognize "the extent to which our society had made psychiatric conditions frightening and shameful, a double illness: first, the ailment itself, and second, society's negative judgment" (xv). This stigma, despite notable progress in recent years, continues to operate in such a compounding way, despite the wide prevalence of experience of mental illness within the US and worldwide.

Stigma operates in a manner close to what its etymological origin suggests, as "a mark or branding" (xvii). With mental illness this is not so much a literal, physical inscription, but instead, "The stigma of mental illness is when your psychological state defines your identity; when people see you as flawed and incompetent; when you are invisible to others; or when people see you suffering but blame you for it" (xvii). In 1963 sociologist Erving Goffman, a pioneer in the study of stigma, declared "all people will at some point in their lives experience the pain of stigma," except the "young, married, white, urban, northern, heterosexual Protestant father of college education, fully employed, of good compexion, weight, and height, and a recent record in sports" (quoted xvii). Goffman thereby argued a considerable majority of the population was suffering or would suffer from the impact of stigma.

Today we might modify Goffman's description of those likely to escape ever suffering this impact while also noting that even among the seemingly most thoroughly privileged sectors of an overall population it is still common for people to experience mental illness and to need to combat stigmas associated with mental illness. Yet stigma does impact different kinds of people differently, in different ways and to different degress, and this varies according to time and place—in other words, according to culture. Because stigma is a product of culture, not a 'naturally' 'normal' response to what is stigmatized, stigma has changed and does vary, and it is possible successfully to combat it. This has been happening, most notably, in relation to autism as well as anxiety and depression. Grinker commends those identifying themselves as 'neurodiverse' for making productive use of 'the social model of disability', in arguing nothing is wrong with them but rather what is wrong is society's continuing difficulty understanding, respecting, and valuing neurodiverse people, "people who don't conform to society's definition of the normal" (xix). Grinker urges pushing yet further, because "Nobody's normal" (xix); normal is only sensible as a mere statistical average. As Grinker declares, "since we have for so long used the concept of 'normal' to decide who we accept into our social worlds and who we reject, it's about time we recognize that normal is a damaging illusion" (xix).

But what has been and continues to be responsible for the stigmatization of large groups of people experiencing mental illness as not normal? One principal factor, Grinker argues, is capitalism itself. Because capitalism has defined work, the ability to work, and what can be gained through work, including through working hard, as the highest good, and indeed as essential in measuring individual value, including in contributing to social value, mental illness has long been conceived as problematic, "as the sign of the idle," as an index of "a personality incapable of achieving the ideal: producing for oneself and the economy" (xxv). Mental illnesses have come to be stigmatized as "diseases of the failed worker" and as manifesting "diseases of character" (xxv). From this ideologically *normative* vantage point, 'the mentally ill' are judged to be either individually morally irresponsible or individually constitutionally unfit. Capitalism did not 'create psychological impairments', or at least capitalism did not bring psychological impairments into existence for the first time, but "psychological impairments acquired new meanings in capitalism" (xxv). These new meanings arise under capitalism where "the most stigmatized people tend to be those who do not conform to the ideal modern worker: the autonomous, self-reliant individual" (xxv).

As a result of this tendency within capitalist societies to define a person's value in accord with the work they do, the kind of work they do, and with how hard they work, according to their deployment of their individual powers and capacities, "It's not surprising, then, that many people with disabilities that limit their ability to work want to be invisible, and that many don't even seek care" (xxvi). Unfortunately, socialist societies tend to "do no better, since the ideals of independence and productivity fostered by capitalism were in place long before socialism emerged" (xxvi). From early on, capitalism has been closely associated with and strongly reliant on the ideological notion that we must imagine ourselves, and live out our lives, first and last, "as competing individuals," while accepting, yet further, the concomitant false premise that "all people" are "equal from the start," such that we enjoy equal opportunity for success if we work hard in competition with others and if we earn our success through our own hard work (14). Accordingly, capitalism has taught us that "Every individual was accountable for his own misfortunes" (15), or, to put it more bluntly, you have no one or nothing to blame but yourself if you are misfortunate. At the same time, "Doctors came to define mental and physical disabilities in terms of the failure to function properly in the economy" (15). In fact, to this day many treatment programs worldwide, for both the mentally and physically disabled, judge success primarily in terms of how capable those who have gone through these programs or who are going through these programs are able to work at paid jobs, or return to work at paid jobs, thereby rendering themselves 'productive contributors to the economy'.

Grinker also identifies war as a principal influence upon modern understandings of and responses to mental illness, with this influence often proving at least partially positive, because the mental illnesses experienced by large number of soldiers have been hard to dismiss as indicative of 'weakness of character'. Yet not so positive is the third major historical pattern Grinker takes up in his book, "the increasing medicalization of mental illness" (xxviii). Increasing medicalization of mental illness has too often prompted reductive thinking about mental illness, not taking adequately into account the complexity of factors that can and do contribute to mental illness, and what this experience is like, especially social and cultural factors. Among such factors are social and cultural pressures upon people to aspire to 'normality', or to 'normalcy', to want to 'fit in' while not wanting to 'stand out', and to conform, rather than be perceived and treated as 'weird' and, often enough, as 'dangerous' on account of being weird.

Grinker calls attention to David Riesman, Nathan Glazer, and Reuel Denney warning, as early as 1950, via their best-selling book *The Lonely Crowd*, that American people "were becoming . . . motivated to be as much like everyone else–as 'normal' as everyone else–even at the risk of losing their individuality" (126). Riesman, Glazer, and Denney worried about this tendency as well as the linked tendency to conceive one could only "be 'normal' if" one "conformed to" one's "community's ideals" (126). Grinker cites Riesman, Glazer, and Denney as offering strong evidence concerning how "Normal became a powerful ideological tool with which to stigmatize people whose adaptive capacities kept them from 'fitting in'" (126). At roughly the same time, in 1953, Roy Richard Grinker's grandfather likewise told a journalist interviewing him on similar matters that "the desire for 'normalcy' in American society was 'the essence of neurosis'," with Grinker's grandfather claiming "Americans were increasingly neurotic because they were unable to accommodate change and diversity" (126).

In more recent times, the younger Roy Grinker argues, contrary to common belief, medicalization has proven counter-productive in reducing stigma associated with mental illness, because diagnosis of an individual 'suffering from a disorder' due to a 'broken brain' is reductive: the diagnosis, acting just like stigma classically does, "comes to represent a person as a whole" (214), comes to define the totality of their identity and comes to explain the totality of what they are like and how they behave. It is important to recognize in this connection, Grinker contends, that "Medicalization is also an integral component of capitalism" (215). Capitalist "societies organize and make use of–capitalize on–human bodies for political and economic purposes," with the ideal society amounting to "an efficient mechanical organization, like a factory," where all bodies are in their right places doing their right jobs in the right ways. With this at least implicit notion of the ideal society, "it makes sense," in turn, "that the human body itself can be explained in mechanical and utilitarian terms" (215). Medicalization complies, reducing "the body to those aspects that can be observed and measured in biomedical terms" such that "when bodies become sick in capitalism they become vulnerable to technologies like pharmaceuticals and reimbursable diagnoses that shape them for the medical marketplace" (215). These technologies "govern the healing process in order to help bodies return quickly to the labor force and limit the loss of production" (215).

Grinker does "understand the desire for a biological model of mental illnesses in a society in which people think about and act toward medical and psychiatric conditions so differently," recognizing a "seductiveness of simplicity" in being able to explain "one's illness to others in scientific terms" as opposed to "explaining it in psychological or emotional terms," while also being able to claim mental illness is an "illness like any other" with the problem "not *me*, it's my brain" (220). Yet Grinker finds little evidence that this kind of model has "ever succeeded in reducing stigma" (220). What is required, again, needs to push far beyond this–challenging and indeed overcoming the continuing widely influential tendency to valorize 'the normal', and likewise to distinguish as well as rank people in terms of ostensible degree of difference, or deviation, from 'the normal'. The brain, after all, Grinker argues, is much more complex than many if not most medical models tend to suggest in tracing a supposed mental health condition, or 'disorder', to a supposed precise, discrete source in a 'broken brain' and its 'improper functioning'. In addition, "it's problematic even to juxtapose 'physical' and 'psychological' conditions since scientists have repeatedly shown that psychology plays a vital role in worsening or improving outcomes of people with heart disease, cancer, and other medical illnesses," with, "For example, depression, anxiety, and stress" constituting "major risk factors for morbidity and mortality in patients with coronary artery disease" (222). Furthermore, "it's as simplistic, and dehumanizing, to reduce a person to his or her brain as it would be to reduce someone to their genes, their ethnicity, religion, sex, or sexual orientation" and "Given how much we know about the role of social factors in shaping mental illnesses, how could we ever remove culture and experience from the brain?" (223). If we were to do so, "we'd risk overlooking how poverty, trauma, and other kinds of adversities affect us" (223).

A key problem, thereby, in describing "someone with a mental illness as having a chemical imbalance or abnormal brain circuitry" is we "risk providing reasons to fear the person, to see them as permanently damaged; it is the person's brain, and not the social context, that needs to be fixed" (223). Biologically reductionist models of mental illness "mask our complex political, economic, and social lives," and "Just as workers under capitalism are alienated from the products of their labor, so too does the 'illness like any other' model alienate us from the products of our emotional social lives–the good and the bad, the successes and the failures, all the circumstances and all the people other than ourselves that make us who we are" (235).

Grinker endorses the practice of 'cripping' as theorized by 'crip theory', and this "means that we see disability as a viable identity or culture, not a damage or deficit. Cripping also means questioning the norms that societies create to oppress people with disabilities in the first place" (309). In line with such a 'cripping' practice, it is important to note well that "Stigma is not eradicated when someone hides their distinctive personalities, skills, and challenges, or when someone pretends they don't see or don't need to see them," because, to the contrary, "Hiding creates stigma while openness erases it" (317). Grinker further endorses "The emerging idea of the *spectrum*," in relation to mental illnesses, so that these are not categorized as 'disorders' and not reduced to the simple question of whether one 'has' or 'does not have' a specific disorder.

Grinker here is "Echoing social movements such as those for transgender rights and neurodiversity, which view gender as continua rather than binaries and autism as a spectrum" (322). Thinking in terms of "A spectrum" is enabling because it "presents an opportunity for people (and their health care providers) to negotiate perceptions of health over time, as symptoms change or improve" (323). It is crucial to note as well that "The spectrum is an invitation: it asks us to join the rest of the world on a continuum of suffering" and "asks us to say, along with neurodiversity advocates, that both normality and abnormality are fictional lands no one actually inhabits" (323).

"Autosuggestion" makes sense as recounting, reflecting upon, and performatively enacting the simulation of a struggle to *try* to come to grips with what it might mean to reject and to break with the repressive and oppressive power of 'the normal' and a host of 'normalizing' regimes operating throughout the dominant culture of a society–and even more precisely than that to *try* to step outside of and break free from stifling conformity within social relations where everything is designed for you, but not by you, including whom you are supposed to be, and how you are supposed to think, feel, believe, communicate, act, interact, and behave. The song registers how damaging 'normalization' can be, including of the capacity to resist and to strive for an alternative. "Autosuggestion" registers discomfort, unease, alienation, and indeed refusal of and resistance versus acceptance of and identification with the normal, but it also registers how hard it becomes to imagine succeeding in striving to be and do otherwise.

With "Autosuggestion" normalization has emptied out the space 'inside' so far that it has become virtually devoid of viable resources to draw upon in seeking to 'step outside'. Stepping outside, making waves, and living life like the heroes and idols one has romantically idealized because these figures have soared beyond leading empty, shallow, conformist lives seems a fantastically unreal–and fantastically unrealizable–aspiration. Yet from the vantage point of the subject addressing me in the song, retreating inside and pretending that this is all right, and reconciling one's self to living that kind of life, is, impossible, or has become impossible. So the subject of the song is in a desperate position–unable and unwilling to 'fit in' yet lacking in the energy and the conviction necessary to 'break out' and 'push beyond'. 'He' is urging himself, and all like him, to 'try', to at least 'try', to at least 'say you tried', but at the same time suggesting this is as far as he can imagine either him, or us, proceeding. "Autosuggestion," thereby, is representative of not yet finding or being convinced by arguments that 'nobody's normal', that we can and should embrace our differences from whatever constitutes current social and cultural norms, and that we all exist and can all move across spectra, or continua, in terms of how close to or distant we might be in relation to any of these norms.

"Autosuggestion," in relation more specifically to mental illness, represents efforts at striving to at least calm one's mental distress somewhat, to at least try to will one's self into a state of mind where one is not suffering such extreme mental anguish, while at the same time only being able to do so to a limited and still problematic extent, all the while wrestling with whether and how as well as how far one can be open about whom one is, as one who is experiencing and does experience significant mental distress, and indeed mental anguish. "Autosuggestion" represents a subject on the cusp of recognizing that social factors are responsible for 'his' condition, rather than merely his own individual weakness or failing, and that 'his' condition might be indeed symptomatic of 'his' honest response to serious and substantial problems within the kind of society in which 'he' lives, with how this society is structured and organized.

That position 'on the cusp' can include beginning to grasp the extent to which capitalism defines people's value in narrowly economic terms, with emphasis upon people's ability to act ostensibly independently by and for themselves. Capitalism valorizes being able to provide for oneself, and one's family, as well as contributing through one's paid work to the production of goods and the provision of services that are recognizably of significant social value. Capitalism valorizes accepting and conforming to the requirements of the social position where one ends up. This is the position which corresponds, supposedly, to what one's hard work and intrinsic merits, including one's strength of character, has earned them. It is the position which also corresponds to what is supposedly 'appropriate', given one's background and what qualifications this background makes possible 'for people like this'. Capitalism valorizes accepting total responsibility oneself alone for coping with how well one does and especially does not do in the course of life's ceaseless competitive challenges as well as in relation to any and all setbacks or misfortunes one might encounter.

The beginning of 'a *critical* understanding' questions all of the preceding, yet must contend with *the power* of capitalist ideology. It is not only economic conditions of life under capitalism that leave people experiencing distress, anguish, alienation, and trauma, but also how people are ideologically encouraged to make sense of what they experience. Capitalist ideology amplifies the distress, anguish, alienation and trauma experienced by people who cannot 'fit in' with and conform to the demands of the life options that capitalist society makes readily available to 'people like them'. Capitalist ideology encourages these people to conclude that the distress, anguish, alienation, and trauma they experience is, at least ultimately, 'all their fault' and that they are indeed 'freakishly weird' in the worst possible ways–they *are* lesser and deficient, they *are* abnormal and deviant. So "Autosuggestion" *does* represent *struggle*, a struggle between opposing ways of making sense of one's felt difference from 'the normal'–a struggle between (1) an inclination toward critique of and resistance versus capitalist normativity, and (2) the power of capitalist normativity to frighten and intimidate against pursuing such critique and resistance.

"Autosuggestion" makes sense as concerned with trauma experienced from not being able to 'fit in' with what is expected in conformity to 'the normal' as well as from not being confident that one can survive, at least not long-term, living openly as 'other than normal', as breaking with, rejecting of, and departing from 'the normal', in particular because the forces of normality, or of normalization, will punish such 'deviation' if it not carefully circumscribed–and also because one is already 'torn apart' between the pull of the normal on the one hand versus that of resisting and living other than and opposed to the normal on the other hand.

Ian Curtis's lyrics and Joy Division's music has often seemed to many to be concerned with experiences of trauma, and certainly the band's name itself amounts to a provocative association with notorious victims of atrocity and the acute trauma these victims experienced. A useful connection, therefore, to explore, involves debates within contemporary trauma theory and trauma studies. In so doing, in the interest of keeping this within reasonable bounds, I focus on Lucy Bond's and Stef Craps's account, as an introduction and overview of these debates, in *Trauma*, their 2020 contribution to Routledge's New Critical Idiom series. The aim of the New Critical Idiom series of textbooks is to provide "introductory guides to today's terminology" which will, in each instance, offer "a handy, explanatory guide to the use (and abuse) of the term" in question, "an original and distinctive overview by a leading literary and cultural critic" or critics, and connect the term with a "larger field of cultural representation" as well as with leading conversations and debates in that larger field (ii).

A useful place to begin, I propose, especially given Edward W. Said's prominent focus on Theodor Adorno in his *Representations of the Intellectual*, is with Bond and Craps situating Adorno's famous declaration that to "write poetry after Auschwitz is barbaric" (quoted 46) in larger context, explaining that what Adorno is arguing for is not artistic silence but rather "art that bears witness to its own incapacity to represent the unrepresentable" (48), art that "incorporates a self-reflexive awareness of the limits of representation" (49). In other words, Adorno is calling for an art that attests, in form and style as well as content, to the impossibility of adequately representing historical trauma as extreme as the Holocaust, and in so doing, in attesting to the impossibility of adequately representing, comes as close as possible, paradoxically enough, to doing so, and even to artistically simulating key dimensions of what traumatic experience, including collective traumatic experience, is like. This involves an overwhelming experience of dread that cannot be broached by means of merely rational explanation or by means of attempts at merely rational understanding.

Bond and Craps identify trauma theory as 'standing in the tradition' of this kind of "engagement with the ethical and aesthetic dilemmas involved in bearing witness to the Holocaust," with trauma theory "similarly marked by an intense preoccupation with the demands of events and experiences that defy comprehension and narrativization," while nonetheless investing "in the idea that literature and art are uniquely positioned to meet those contradictory demands" (50). According to pioneering trauma theorist Cathy Carruth, as Bond and Craps explain, "Harmonizing narratives, stories that literally make sense of trauma, are inadequate because they fail to capture the unique specificity of a traumatic historical reality" (58). Yet, for Carruth, "[t]he impossibility of a comprehensible story . . . does not necessarily mean the denial of a transmissible truth" (quoted 59). "What we need, according to Carruth, is a kind of speech that does not simply communicate that which is understandable but also that which cannot be understood" and for Carruth, as well as a number of other prominent early trauma theorists, "literature just might be that kind of speech" (59).

For Carruth, the impossibility of adequate representation of trauma, at least in conventional realist or naturalist terms, in fact increases the moral responsibility to attend to trauma and to "the ethical value of bearing witness to trauma" (60). Carruth indeed "argues that trauma can create the grounds for new forms of community by building a bridge between disparate historical experiences" (60). Carruth urges attending to the "plea by an other who is asking to be seen and heard" (quoted 60) while maintaining "a principled refusal to appropriate or impose closure" in how we respond (60).

Carruth and fellow early trauma theorist Geoffrey Hartman find William Wordsworth's poetry useful in modeling what they have in mind. As Pieter Vermeulen describes, in *Geoffrey Hartman: Romanticism after the Holocaust,* Carruth and in particular Hartman find Wordsworth's "poetry instigates a deepened awareness of loss, of the fact that things can disappear" simultaneous with affirming "the reality of something that remains untouched by loss" and as such "makes possible an experience of non-experience" (quoted 64-65). Wordsworth does this, according to Hartman, as Bond and Craps put it, by "giving a reality that we cannot confront directly a form that we can experience and remember" (65).

As fellow early trauma theorist Shoshana Felman likewise writes, literature can "do justice to the trauma in a way the law does not, or cannot," because "Literature is a dimension of concrete embodiment and a language of infinitude that, in contrast with the language of the law, encapsulates not closure but precisely what in a given legal case refuses to be closed and cannot be closed" and indeed "It is to this refusal of the trauma to be closed that literature does justice" (quoted 71).

Yet as trauma theory, and trauma studies, have proceeded to develop beyond the work of these original contributors, "a tension" has arisen "between those who are primarily concerned with doing justice to traumatic repetition as a sign of survival and those who seek to drive home the point that one need to heal from trauma" (73). Dominick LaCapra is a principal representative of and advocate for the latter position, which is also critical of a potential "unhealthy elevation of victimhood" and a de-historicizing extraction of victims, in their experience of victimhood, from the precise historical nexus of events in which they actually did experience victimization (74). As Bond and Craps note, LaCapra's concerns readily connect with "the question of how we might ethically relate to the suffering of others," and in particular when and how is "secondary or vicarious witnessing" ethically responsible and when and how is it not (74). LaCapra is troubled "when the past is uncontrollably relived," as if "there were no difference between it and the present," and where "one experientially feels as if one were back there reliving the event, and distance between here and there, then and now collapses" (quoted 77). LaCapra urges attending to past trauma not so much in an attempt to vicariously relive or reexperience what that was life, but rather, through studiously engaging with past trauma, "allowing openings to possible futures" (quoted 77).

LaCapra is interested, as Bond and Craps describe, in engaging with trauma so as to the pursue "the possibility of overcoming, or at least ameliorating," by "reconnecting knowledge and feeling" as opposed to surrendering to experience of trauma's "endless repetitions"–or endless echoes

817

(77). LaCapra draws upon Freud's distinction between "working-through" and "acting-out," which for Freud, correspond, respectively, to "mourning" and "melancholy" (78). LaCapra advocates shifting from emphasis upon acting out, where "the past is performatively regenerated or relived as if it were fully present rather than represented in history and inscription" (quoted 78) toward working through, which involves "gaining critical distance on [traumatic] experiences and re-contextualizing them in ways that permit a re-engagement with ongoing concerns and future possibilities" (quoted 78).

LaCapra is critical of "the tendency to sacralize trauma or convert it into a founding or sublime event" (quoted 79), running the risk, as Bond and Craps put it, of adopting a stance toward trauma that "makes trauma seem almost desirable" (80). LaCapra is also critical of a concomitant tendency to conflate "loss," as "the product of discrete historical events, resulting from the removal or destruction of a person, place, or thing" (81), with "absence," in the sense of "the lack of foundations (be they referential, ideological, theological, or some other structural component) that *have never existed*" (81). LaCapra finds that "absence converted into loss can manifest as a 'misplaced nostalgia',", and a form of "'endless melancholy' can arise, frustrating any possibility of productive mourning or working-through" (quoted 81-82).

As Bond and Craps underscore, "At stake here is what LaCapra identifies as 'the dubious appropriation of the status of victim through vicarious or surrogate victimage' . . . resulting from an overidentification with the suffering of another person or group," and "'with respect to historical trauma and its representation, the distinction between victims, perpetrators, and bystanders is crucial'" (quoted 82). LaCapra calls for "fostering a *virtual* rather than a *vicarious* relationship to the trauma of others," which "would not preclude the development of ethical forms of empathy and solidarity for victims and survivors, but would refute any kind of appropriation of their suffering" (82). This requires "that 'the attentive secondary witness' should open themselves to the experience of 'empathetic unsettlement', which involves a kind of virtual experience through which one puts oneself in the other's position while recognizing the difference of that position, and hence not taking the other's place" (quoted 82).

Others have followed up on LaCapra's argument, for instance, as Bond and Craps subsequently discuss, by way of the work of Gary Weissman, in critiquing "fantasies of witnessing" (90) such that "non-witnesses," in Weissman's words, "convince themselves and others that they too occupy a privileged position in relation to the [traumatic] event," in relation to experiencing its devastating impact (quoted 91). Weissman is critical of works of art, notably films, concerned with representing historical traumas that pride themselves on enabling those attending to these works of art, and in particular these films, "to 'feel the horror'" (quoted 92).

Yet the earlier trauma theorists are not lacking in compelling ways of anticipating and responding to these subsequent critiques, with for instance, Carruth making use of Freud's *Moses and Monotheism* to develop an elaborate argument in support of the proposition that "history, like trauma, is never simply one's own, that history is precisely the way we are implicated in each other's traumas" (quoted 97). According to Carruth, by way of Freud, we are connected with, implicated in, and responsible for what might otherwise ostensibly seem considerably distant from us, in time and

818

space, such that even as we should be wary of imagining we could possibly identify with what experience of trauma felt like then and there, for those distant 'others', 'our traumas' and 'their traumas' are nevertheless linked, and trauma studies as well as 'trauma art' can involve inquiry into how so, and with what kinds of implications and consequences.

It is viable therefore for trauma studies and trauma art to move beyond initial concentration on White Western European experience. Many contributions in this direction have already been long underway, including, as Bond and Craps mention, Aimé Césaire's *Discourse on Colonialism*. The interlinked traumatic impacts and legacies of genocide, slavery, and colonialism are ripe territory for such engagement, and seeking to do justice to these traumatic impacts and legacies, for as devastating as they have been and continue to be, represent crucial ethical and political tasks for 'the West' as well as for 'the rest'. The ongoing backlashes directed against 'political correctness', 'the woke', and, more recently, teaching and learning about systemic racism as well as about the identities and the lives of LGBTQIA+ people in US public schools, attests to how crucial this work is because of how much resistance it is meeting, how much is invested in repressing and denying present connection with, implication in, and responsibility for historical trauma.

Bond and Craps also cite the important development of work within trauma studies moving beyond "the victim-perpetrator binary by recognizing the specific experiences of various in-between groups with complicated levels of guilt and complicity such as bystanders, beneficiaries, collaborators, forced perpetrators, victims-turned-perpetrators, and people one or more generations removed from those directly involved in violence in one way or another" (124). This can include drawing upon the work of, for instance, Michael Rothberg, who "has recently coined the concept of the 'implicated subject' as an umbrella term identifying some of those various intermediate and alternative forms of involvement," and Primo Levy, who famously theorized the 'grey zone' as "inhabited by victims who compromise and collaborate with their oppressors in various ways and under varying levels of coercion in exchange for material or other benefits" (124).

In conclusion, Bond and Craps themselves argue that trauma theory, trauma studies, and trauma art "can help make visible and intelligible the suffering of individuals and communities, assist us in identifying situations of exploitation and abuse, bring them to a wider public consciousness, and act as an incentive for . . . sustained and systemic critique of societal conditions" (140-141). After all, Bond and Craps declare, "The direct action AIDS movement ACT UP, the Black Lives Matter movement against police brutality in the United States, and the #MeToo movement against sexual harassment and assault, all of which wed mourning to militancy, would seem to be cases in point of how trauma and meaningful activism are not necessarily in contradistinction to each other" (141).

Just this same week as I am writing this subsection of this chapter I am facilitating a screening and discussion of the film *The Lesson* as part of the Empowerment Through Solidarity Progressive Film Series I curate and which is sponsored by United Faculty and Academic Staff of UW-Eau Claire and Leaders Igniting Transformation at UW-Eau Claire. *The Lesson*, filmed over the course of five years by director Elena Horn and her crew in Horn's small hometown, focuses on problems and limitations in teaching and learning about the Holocaust in rural Germany today.

As Horn declares in her "Director's Notes," *The Lesson* "shows that Germany's Holocaust education is unfit for our time." As the synopsis on the film's official website indicates, yet further, "despite Germany's reputation for exemplary Holocaust education," it is "backfiring in rural areas" where "educators encourage middle school students to view the events of World War II from the Nazi perspective." Because "younger generations of Germans lack basic factual knowledge of the subject," knowledge which the curriculum seemingly assumes they do maintain, students "are unintentionally taught to empathize with the fascist point of view through exercises that reap the net effect of desensitizing young people to the nation's dark history." Through "immersion" devices, schools end up, again however inadvertently, "lauding German efficiency, engineering and design" so that "it is the efficiency of industrial murder that is praised" with the curriculum resulting in the "unintended effect of teaching Nazi ideology."

Even though neo-fascist far right movements are on the rise, notably in the same area where *The Lesson* is filmed, the school fails to draw adequate connections between this contemporary development and the rise of the Nazi regime. As Horn notes, in her Director's Notes, "40% of German children today do not even know what Auschwitz means," and in *The Lesson* she deliberately emphasizes "the subtle ways in which fascism self-propagates and lingers within society." Horn is particularly keen to highlight "the powerful truth that 'Mitlaufer' or 'bystanders' enabled the rise of Nazism in the 1930s," and that too many young Germans are becoming 'Mitlaufer' or 'bystanders' in relation to the rise of the neo-fascist far right in Germany today.

What current teaching about the Holocaust fails adequately to do is to convey a powerfully felt sense of the depth and extent of the traumatic nature and impact of the Holocaust, as well as strongly felt bonds of empathy and solidarity with the victims of the Holocaust. It fails as well to draw precise and effective connections between fascism then and fascism now, especially concerning the role of bystanders then and that of bystanders now. Although ostensibly taught as a matter of moral concern, the students are not adequately engaged at an emotional level, and they are too often addressed as if they exist outside of any substantive connection, however mediated, with the Holocaust and Nazism then as well as with the rise of a neo-fascist far right now, while 'free to choose' from a relatively detached position how they will make sense of the meaning of the Holocaust and its legacy. Too little of the sheer horror of the Holocaust is emphasized and too little discussion is focused on how and why Germans and Germany 'must never forget' and must actively commit to do everything possible to insure nothing like Nazism and the Holocaust can recur–'never again'.

As the director indicates, in a voice-over comment, from the time of her initial childhood education about the Holocaust, she has wondered why did this happen in Germany, yet too often the answers offered to this question take the form of proposing 'it could have happened in many other countries across Europe' while not explaining 'but why, then, in Germany, and not in these other countries'. This seems to be another serious problem with 'the lesson' German young people are learning in schools like the one that serves as the focus of *The Lesson*: they are not brought into contact with major intellectual conversations and debates concerning how and why Nazism rose to power in German, and with how and why Nazism in power enjoyed considerable active as well as passive support across Germany. Yet, most telling, 'the lesson' does not enable students to imagine what the Holocaust was like, and what it felt like, from the vantage point of the victim–i.e., how traumatic it truly was–leading a number of students to respond, at their field trip to a concentration camp, that the location seemed like a pleasant place to be and they could not imagine how it could have functioned as a prison.

"Autosuggestion," like much of Ian Curtis's lyrics and Joy Division's music, alludes to experiences of trauma without being overly specific, if not in fact being highly non-specific, suggesting at the same time that the 'event' of this trauma can only be indirectly alluded to and not directly represented. "Autosuggestion," as with much of Curtis's lyrics and Joy Division's music, does seem to be engaged in the paradoxical task of 'representing the unrepresentable' or 'representing the limits of representation'. What precisely has led to the situation from which the music as persona is addressing us, as well as has motivated this address to take the form it does, is gestured toward, but not pinned down. "Autosuggestion" engages trauma, as well as its subsequent lingering and recurrent impact, but does not explain, in the sense of explain away, what precisely causes this trauma or what perpetuates, and indeed recurrently renews, its impact.

It makes compelling sense to interpret "Autosuggestion" as both manifestation of and response to a "plea by an other who is asking to be seen and heard," even if this 'other' represents 'an other' within 'the self' or an 'other' who the self once was or who the self could have been or might yet be. Since the trauma invoked here seems both intimately immediate and elliptically abstract, it doesn't feel like the song is irresponsibly appropriating or conflating 'primary' and 'secondary' experience of trauma, or direct experience of trauma with *witnessing direct experience of trauma*. It feels as if the song, like multiple other Joy Division songs, is not trying to make us see, hear, and feel exactly what it was like to see, hear, and feel at a specific historical time and place–and to immerse ourselves in an identification with the trauma of those who directly experienced this then and there–but rather to draw indirect connections with an array of actual and prospective experiences of trauma, all in the interest of prompting confrontation with "how we are implicated in each other's traumas." What's more, as is typical with Joy Division, the song ends without the source of anguish it addresses resolved, or overcome, refusing reductive forms of closure. It thus makes good sense to interpret "Autosuggestion," like many Joy Division songs, akin to how Vermeulen explains Hartman interprets Wordsworth's poetry: "giving a reality that we cannot confront directly a form that we can experience and remember."

It might seem that "Autosuggestion," like many Joy Division songs, engages in an "unhealthy elevation of victimhood" and a de-historicizing extraction of victims, in their experience of victimhood, from the precise historical nexus of events in which they actually did experience victimization–especially when these victims are not only unnamed but also barely described. Yet, this song, like other Joy Division songs, hardly 'sacralizes' trauma, hardly suggests it is in any way desirable. Trauma is depicted as devastatingly painful, as shattering, and as robbing of one's very being. And even though 'healing' and 'recovery' seem unlikely prospects, "Autosuggestion" is involved in attempting–in trying–a 'working through', in striving to find the means to push toward something like healing and recovery. The latter are clearly desirable ends even if the song laments the lack of adequate means to realize these ends. Because of the song's open-ended refusal to link the trauma it cites with a discrete historical event, and because "Autosuggestion" in turn suggests this trauma is not something that is being merely relived, and vicariously re-experienced, but rather is happening now and promises to continue happening into the future, even beyond the limits of the duration of the song itself, it hardly seems like the song is engaging in "misplaced nostalgia."

Here, as elsewhere in Curtis's lyrics and Joy Division's music, it remains uncertain, or at the least ambiguous whether what is being depicted in fraught terms corresponds to a "loss" or an "absence." This could mean the two are conflated but it also could mean that this music provides means to inquire into not only the distinctions between the two that LaCapra emphasizes but also possible connections which he does not. Structural absences within a society can and in fact do provide conditions of possibility for situations, events, and experiences of loss. In other words, for instance, in a society where 'everything is by design', the lack or absence of room for autonomous self-determination and self-actualization; for freely creative exercise of resources, powers, and capacities; for self-reinvention and for self-initiated social mobility; and for a proliferation of viable ways of being that do not coincide with or conform to limiting conceptions of 'the normal' all can contribute to an immense experience of loss–ultimately loss of sense of self, loss of sense of connection and community with others, and loss of sense of there being meaning or purpose to existence. Ian Curtis's lyrics and Joy Division's songs, in addition, most definitely seem to be "fostering a *virtual* rather than a *vicarious* relationship to the trauma of others," which "would not preclude the development of ethical forms of empathy and solidarity for victims and survivors, but would refute any kind of appropriation of their suffering," and which requires "that 'the attentive secondary witness' should open themselves to the experience of 'empathetic unsettlement', which involves a kind of virtual experience through which one puts oneself in the other's position while recognizing the difference of that position, and hence not taking the other's place."

Again and again these lyrics and this music emphasize the difficulties, if not the impossibilities, of fully coming to grips with what is happening 'outside' and 'elsewhere', even immediately 'outside' and 'elsewhere', as well as with what has happened in the past and what will happen in the future. The lyrics and the music emphasize the enormity of the challenges to interpretation that all of these sites of actual and prospective trauma, and the struggle to find ways adequately to respond to these challenges present, including to what they are calling forth from those who are attentively witnessing and empathetically unsettled by what these lyrics and this music is virtually confronting, and by what they are inviting and encouraging us virtually to confront as well. Rarely do these lyrics and does this music suggest it has come close to offering us any kind of decisive answer to the question of how to make sense of and what to do about what they are alluding to, registering, ruminating upon, and agonizing over, while often enough suggesting the lyrics and the music can only do so much of this, by themselves alone, with much more dependent on us, and with how we then carry forward, in pursuing the same paths, and with how we carry out and carry on the same quests. Neither does "Autosuggestion," nor do most other Joy Division songs, insinuate that the music as persona, or the narrator-protagonist of the lyrics, or us as a sympathetic to empathetic audience, enjoy 'privileged access' to trauma that is alluded to and gestured toward, and if the songs suggest that the music as persona, or the narrator-protagonist of the lyrics, or we as a sympathetic to empathetic audience, are 'feeling the horror', this is not elevating us to a position of moral superiority, simply from doing so, or from being able to do so, because the horror is depicted as overwhelming, as destructive and debilitating. Even if we need to strive 'to feel it', this is not in order, in and of itself, so that we can claim doing so 'makes us better people'.

Bond and Craps offer a most useful frame for interpreting Ian Curtis's lyrics and Joy Division's music, in "Autosuggestion" and elsewhere, in describing work in trauma theory, studies, and art that pushes beyond "the victim-perpetrator binary by recognizing the specific experiences of various in-between groups with complicated levels of guilt and complicity such as bystanders, beneficiaries, collaborators, forced perpetrators, victims-turned-perpetrators, and people one or more generation removed from those directly involved in violence in one way or another." If anything, the various personae identified and suggested within the lyrics of Ian Curtis, and also the music of Joy Division as well, make better sense more often as corresponding to these kinds of positions rather than to that of a direct and immediate victim or a direct and immediate perpetrator. After all, as I have repeatedly emphasized, in this chapter and elsewhere throughout this book, these lyrics and this music are virtually obsessed with confronting *indirect* connection with, implication in, and responsibility for atrocity–and for trauma. Ian Curtis's lyrics and Joy Division's music is virtually obsessed, in other words, with "implicated subjects" operating in "grey zones."

"Autosuggestion" does not encourage complacency, let alone smugness, because the song is about trying, persistently, to do what recognizably needs to be done, as well as exhorting us to do the same, yet without confidence that this is at all possible, at least not anymore (it may be far too late and indeed it may have always been too late, at least 'for people like us'), and without confidence, furthermore, even if we can do what is needed, that doing so will achieve anything that is genuinely substantial and worthwhile. Insofar as it makes sense to interpret "Autosuggestion" as concerned with representing and reflecting on experience of trauma, it makes sense as well to interpret the song as emphasizing how trauma overrides and undermines will, how trauma feels totally enveloping and especially totally eviscerating, so that even if an 'outside' of trauma, and an outside of its persistent return, in the form of 'post-trauma', appears objectively to exist, this feels nonetheless subjectively beyond reach, or as merely ephemeral and even illusory.

And yet the effort must nonetheless be made *to try*. From 'inside' of trauma an 'outside' can seem unreal and impossible, and efforts to 'step outside' can seem pointless and futile, yet it is necessary to make that effort, *to try*, nonetheless, guided perhaps by a stubborn residue of remnant faith that healing and recovery might be possible, that it might be possible to move beyond continually reliving toward working through, and from being swallowed up within melancholy toward turning melancholy into mourning and mourning into action, including action dedicated to intervening at the source of what continues to produce, enforce, and reinforce trauma.

Another connection I make in listening to and reflecting on what "Autosuggestion" prompts me to think (about) and feel, especially at this time, concerns the difficulty of arguing for, and working in support of pacifism, especially at a time of a war that seems as if it cannot have been avoided, and now must be fought, against a horrendous enemy guilty of major war crimes, which is where we are at, in the US and the West, at present in relation to Russian President Vladimir Putin and his regime's war in and against Ukraine. Pacifism can seem, in this context, like a foolishly naive and unrealistically utopian position at best, and at worst as guilty of allowing and encouraging the aggression perpetrated by a figure like Putin and his regime. I think here of what it might mean to 'step outside', 'make waves', 'ask questions', 'lose some sleep' and 'say you tried' in interjecting a pacifist argument into the discussion of what is happening in Ukraine, how and why this has come to happen as it has, and what needs to be done in response, both in the short and long terms. It can seem like no room exists for this kind of position to be heard, and to be taken seriously, as other than absurd or dangerous, yet if one is committed to pacifism as a principled mode of ethical praxis it undoubtedly feels morally irresponsible not to step forth and speak out, even at risk of much worse than merely being ignored or dismissed.

In *Transformative Pacifism: Critical Theory and Practice* (2018), philosopher and leading pacifist critical theorist Andrew Fiala responds to many of the most common critiques of pacifism while articulating an elaborate argument on behalf of what Fiala identifies as "transformative pacifism." Fiala begins by countering those who have turned pacifism "into a straw man" (3). Fiala explains "a variety of pacifisms" exist, have long existed, and even though pacifists oppose the use of violence, "they need not be absolutist in this rejection" (3). Pacifists are always confronted with the question of what would they do in the worst possible situation, such as represented by the notorious 'trolley problem'. Here people are presented with a stark choice: they either do nothing, leading to many being killed, or they do something which means they kill one person or a much smaller number so that a larger number need not be killed. But pacifism (or at least most pacifism), Fiala argues, is not preeminently focused on what must be done in the worst possible situation, or with insisting "that 'violence and killing are always absolutely wrong'" (4). Instead, pacifism "is concerned with a broad critique of violence that includes questioning the social conditions that leave us with the sort of forced choices found in trolley problem scenarios" (4). As Fiala further explains, "Pacifists want to create safeguards against violence. They want to find ways to avoid violence. They want to rescue victims. They even want to find ways to reconcile offenders" (5). Pacifists are focused upon systemic transformation, as much concerned about structural and cultural forms of violence as they are about violence committed in literal wars. Insofar as pacifists do focus on the violence of war they focus on intervening at the level of the conditions that make war not only possible but also seemingly inevitable and necessary, including through celebration of militarism and 'warism'.

Fiala identifies the *ideal* principle of pacifism as follows: "Peace is the highest good. Human beings ought to seek peace, live in peace, and to develop non-violent means of conflict resolution that respect the liberty, rationality, and autonomy of persons" (16). Note well this is an *ideal* principle, a statement of what *ought* to be. In line with this *ideal* principle, pacifists share a *general* critique of violence, arguing that "Violence is limited as a means for promoting peace because it is irrational and negative and thus unable by itself to build a positive and lasting peace" (16). Note well that violence is *limited* in its effectivity because it is *unable by itself* to achieve and secure peace. Pacifists in turn support a third fundamental principle that logically follows from the preceding two: "The preferred means of activity are non-violent. We ought to strive for a coherent system of means and ends. If peace is our end, then the means employed should be non-violent" (16). Once more, note well these are *preferred* means, representative of what we *ought* to strive for, of what *should* be. So pacifists are more concerned with *building peace* and the conditions which will create and sustain peace than they are proscribing what cannot and should not be done in extreme and desperate situations where peace has failed and peaceful means are any longer available.

Fiala accepts that "A common objection made against pacifism is *the atrocity objection*," according to which "pacifism is either foolish because it cannot respond to atrocities such as the Holocaust or that it is immoral because it refuses to do what is morally responsible in the face of atrocity" (22). Fiala finds this objection reductive because pacifism is focused on doing everything it can to prevent violence, including in war, as well as the damage violence causes, short term and long term, rather than focusing on whether violence is acceptable as a last resort when all such efforts fail. As Fiala explains, from a pacifist position far more important than striving always and forever to avoid engagement in any and all forms of violence is advocating that "killing should never be easy nor should it be celebrated and enjoyed," because pacifism accepts "The reality . . . that it is not easy to be a peaceful person in a world that is broken, tragic, and sometimes atrocious" (24). Except for an extremely small number of 'absolutists', pacifists do not deny that at times "Violence may be necessary–as the only means that work," at times it may prove necessary "to fight fire with fire or use efficient means that work to achieve your greater ends," and that at times it is true "Those unwilling to use necessary means will suffer and probably end up dead" (25). Pacifism's emphasis, however, is upon working actively to change the world so that these times are increasingly rare, while pushing to insure these times are always truly representative of a 'last resort'.

In other words, "rather than viewing pacifism as morally necessary and violence as necessarily wrong, a pacifist can view violence as less than optimal and non-violence as better" (30). As Fiala elaborates, "the point is to create a situation in which fires don't erupt–or in which the fires of violence are kept in check and under control," so "Rather than fighting fire with fire, pacifists introduce a new element–dialogue and other forms of cultural transformation–aiming to quench and prevent fire" (31). "*Transformative* pacifism" aims "to criticize and alter the background conditions in which violent responses to violence becomes necessary" (31).

Pacifism, as critical theory, is akin, Fiala argues, to feminism, socialism, critical race theory, and deep ecology because "the goal is to transform the world by offering a critical vantage point on the status quo" (51). This means "while pacifists may grudgingly have to accept some concrete cases where violence can be justified self-defence, the ultimate goal is not to rest easy with those cases–rather the goal is to transform the social scene so that those cases are fewer and farther between," and to make "clear that our dominant ideology's commitment to warism and militarism is an impediment to obtaining that goal" (51).

Pacifism is not equivalent with "*passive-ism*" because "non-violent resistance can be understood as a middle path between passivity and angry violence" (54). Fiala acknowledges that "Pacifism looks absurd to those who live in a culture where violence is routine, normalized, and taken for granted" (81). Yet pacifism is concerned with exactly how and why this has become as it is, such that violence is 'routine, normalized, and taken for granted': "a genuinely self-critical pacifism must also seek to understand how violence structures human experience and our own self-understanding," including that of those who identify as pacifists (81). Indeed, "A self-critical pacifism must try to be aware of the ubiquity of violence" (81).

Fiala continually admits that critics of pacifism, at least of pacifism in absolutist form, offer many reasonable and compelling objections:

1. Peace and non-violence only make sense in an ideal world where there is no war or criminal aggression and in which people are persuaded by arguments and acts of conscience.
2. Pacifism is inconsistent and incoherent since it claims to value life but refuses to do what is necessary to defend life.
3. Pacifism is immoral when it ignores the real-world need to respond to violence with violence and when it thus appears to allow innocents to be killed.
4. Pacifism and the demand for non-violence are defended from within a bubble of privilege that ignores the groans of the oppressed, the demand for revolution, and the violence that undergirds the status quo. (87).

Yet it is important to recognize "Pacifism appears to be inconsistent, immoral, and bourgeois (even reactionary) in a world in which violence is taken for granted as natural and normal, or in a world where structural violence is simply ignored," but transformative pacifism "aims to change the world and our way of understanding ourselves so that violence is no longer taken for granted" (88).

For transformative pacifism, "the real project of peace" is *not* maintaining one's individual moral purity, by personally refusing to directly engage in acts of violence, or by cultivating an escapist form of "inner peace" through retreating from engagement with the violence of the world surrounding one, but rather "to confront the world as it really is, while remaining committed to the ideal of peace," accepting "that the project of peace is one of the most difficult projects of all" (110). This project includes confronting the pervasiveness of "images and evaluations of violence in cultural practices–in the realm of ideology, art, philosophy, religion, symbolism, and so on" that "make it look as if violence is normal, natural salutary, and even heroic" (152). Pacifism counters the prominence and influence of "Violent cultures–or if you will, thug cultures" that are "dominant and aggressive" with the cultivation and promotion of peace cultures that are the opposite (153). In other words, while "*violent culture* is a culture that normalizes and valorizes violence . . . *non-violent culture . . .* normalizes and valorizes non-violence" (154). This means, yet further, "Rather than suppression of violent culture, what is needed is an effort to delegitimate violence and de-normalize it by emphasizing the values of the culture of peace," including by starting with "pointing out the inherent stupidity of the idea that 'might makes right'" (165).

As such, pacifism, while not ruling out fighting in war as genuine last resort, continues to insist "that war is irrational; that war is rarely (or never) just; and that notions such as national pride, patriotic service, and the like must be re-evaluated" (165). When war happens, pacifists argue, this must be conceived as a tragedy, and emphasis must be placed on bringing war to an end as quickly, completely, and justly as possible while learning from this war lessons than can and will be applied to prevent future wars. After all, as Fiala reminds us, "defenders of war often downplay the true damage of war, ignoring the long-term psychological harms, ecological damage, and the larger social cost of militarism" (200). Transformative pacifism, in sum, "dwells somewhere between retreat and radicalism": "Pacifism as a critical theory is melioristic. It seeks to transform the world and improve it" (245). All the while, transformative pacifism fully accepts "that the task of transformation is difficult, complex, incremental, and ongoing" (245).

With Fiala's theorization of transformative pacifism in mind, it might make sense to interpret "Autosuggestion" as reflective of what it's like to feel as if one needs, as a matter of principle, as a matter of conscience, to step forth, speak out, and advocate for a pacifist position, especially at a time of widespread support for the seeming necessity and inevitability of waging war, yet anticipating you will not only struggle to exert an impact but also struggle to be understood. Your position will likely come across as utopian and unrealistic, inconsistent and incoherent, and even immoral and reactionary. The sound of the song suggests a long, lonely effort to psyche one's self up to represent this position, knowing how unpopular it is likely to be, how ineffectual it is likely to prove, and how fiercely it is likely to be condemned. Discordant and dissonant shards of sound echo antagonistic responses to one's representation of a pacifist position in the past as well as anticipate similar antagonistic responses to one's doing so yet again in the future. The sound of the song likewise suggests what it feels like to represent such a position with few others joining in, or likely to join in, while recognizing your efforts may accomplish little to nothing, even as the devastation of war continues, and increases, as does popular support for the necessity and inevitability of war and for the naturalness and normalcy of militarism and warism. But you feel nonetheless compelled to try.

As "Autosuggestion" suggests, it is exceedingly difficult to gain support for this kind of critical understanding in the face of how the current Ukraine-Russia war is being predominantly represented, and thereby understood, as a result of those who maintain by far the greatest power to insure their preferred frames are the ones that reach and compel by far the greatest number of people. It is important to persist in making this case, but the risk of being ignored, dismissed, distorted, trivialized, denigrated, and demonized, are substantial. At the same time, as "Autosuggestion" also suggests, even as you persist, it is immensely dispiriting, from a pacifist position, inclining one toward the brink of despair, to recognize that the war in Ukraine has given a major boost to spending on the military, including on weapons of mass destruction, and including on nuclear weapons, in the US and elsewhere in the West, as well as likewise boosting numbers of troops and sizes of arsenals stationed throughout a great many Western nations and regions, at the same time as militarism and warism again are increasingly celebrated as righteous, necessary, and admirable.

For a final set of connections with "Autosuggestion" I will return one last time to take up the work of Trinh T. Minh-ha, Edward W. Said, and Aimé Césaire. I will begin with Trinh, and in this case focus on her film *Surname Viet, Given Name Nam* (1989). As distributor Women Make Movies summarizes,

> Vietnamese-born Trinh T. Minh-ha's profoundly personal documentary explores the role of Vietnamese women historically and in contemporary society. Using dance, printed texts, folk poetry and the words and experiences of Vietnamese women in Vietnam–from both North and South–and the United States, Trinh's film challenges official culture with the voices of women. A theoretically and formally complex work, *Surname Viet, Given Name Nam* explores the difficulty of translation, and themes of dislocation and exile, critiquing both traditional society and life since the war.

This film, like others Trinh has made, might be reasonably characterized as 'experimental documentary', but also perhaps as 'post-documentary' or even 'anti-documentary', continuous with the 'post-ethnographic' and 'anti-ethnographic' position Trinh advocates in relation to anthropology in *Woman, Native, Other: Writing Postcoloniality and Feminism*. *Surname Viet, Given Name Nam* employs Vietnamese women as actors, primarily Vietnamese women (now) living in the United States, to read words written by other Vietnamese women and to do so in carefully constructed, minimally furnished, and sensitively stylized settings. Yet only gradually does it become apparent this is what we are seeing and hearing. Trinh calls attention to mediation by provoking critical self-reflection on commonsense expectations of and associations with 'authenticity' of 'testimony' from direct and immediate 'first-hand experience'. *Surname Viet, Given Name Nam* calls into question frames audiences are most likely to bring to bear in making sense of Vietnam, war in Vietnam, Vietnamese women, and Vietnamese women's vantage point and experience. As the title of her film overtly suggests, 'Vietnam' is *constructed* to mean by way of and through the imposition of these kinds of frames, and the power relations at stake.

Surname Viet, Given Name Nam contains a plethora of excerpts from a diverse array of archival footage, recorded at times before, during, and after what Americans commonly identify as 'the' Vietnam war, including long before, and from across multiple regions of Vietnam, featuring scenes of people engaged in many kinds of activities, all the while continually emphasizing Vietnamese *women's* vantage points and experiences. We also periodically encounter passages within the film of Vietnamese women engaged in formal dancing as well as a soundtrack that involves Vietnamese women singing notable traditional and more recent Vietnamese songs. Trinh constructs *Surname Viet, Given Name Nam* so that visual framings of figures and of objects such as props surrounding the women actors as they are doing their dramatic readings are often jarring, and this is the case for both static and mobile framings. Parts of faces are cut off both horizontally and vertically, and how this is so as well as how far so changes within and between shots, while figures and objects are often decentered and frames are tighter or closer on the one hand or more distant and opaque than common in more mainstream documentary as well as in realist and naturalist forms of fictional film making. Periodically written text is superimposed, either filling the visual frame all by itself, on an all-black or all-gray background–or directly on top of the women actors engaging in dramatic readings. The words of these written texts are also close but not entirely identical with the words the women actors are speaking.

The women who wrote these words, as well as the women who subsequently dramatically read them, offer critiques concerning women's status, and in particular women's inequitable status, as well as reflecting on women's diverse roles and complex forms of agency, including resistant agency. The film critiques governments, states, and economic and political systems in both South Vietnam and North Vietnam, as well as from the US, France, and China. In particular the women critique patriarchal institutions and patriarchal presumptions, past and present. *Surname Viet, Given Name Nam* recounts stories of numerous Vietnamese women, including from the now relatively distant past, who have engaged in resistant forms of activity, versus patriarchal norms concerning women's 'proper' role and 'correct' behavior, including scandalous kinds of activity. Yet *Surname Viet, Given Name Nam* always resists being reduced to an argument in support of any simple thesis, such as 'Vietnamese women have been and continue to be resistant versus and rejecting of patriarchal norms', as the film also recounts and depicts many Vietnamese women sharing their understanding of the subordinate positions and roles expected of them within in Vietnamese society and culture, along with their conformity to these expectations. The film is even more complex than that, however, as it refuses to characterize these normative expectations as simply and entirely subordinating, restricting and confining, nor identification with and pursuit of alternatives as simply and entirely rejecting, resisting, and opposing such norms. Trinh deliberately strives to render it exceedingly difficult to propose 'Vietnamese women are/have been/tend to be like X' because Vietnamese women, past and present, have been and are extraordinarily diverse, including often enough extraordinarily diverse 'within themselves'.

Surname Viet, Given Name Nam challenges audiences to reflect critically on how they already make sense or are inclined to make sense of 'the Vietnam war', of Vietnamese people, and especially of Vietnamese women–how are each of these already understood, and already *misunderstood*? Trinh exposes and undermines reliance upon frames of understanding that many are wont to turn to uncritically, while at the same time exposing and undermining audience expectation that this film will involve Vietnamese women testifying from first-hand experience to reveal an, let alone *the*, 'authentic Vietnamese women's perspective on Vietnamese women's experience'. The film motivates audiences to keep exploring, to keep asking questions, to keep listening to and to keep learning more, beyond time spent in attending to this film, while approaching with humility their own preconceptions concerning the vantage point and experience of 'others'.

Trinh indicates, in explaining her approach to making films, "The reflexive question asked," in her film-making as well as in her praxis otherwise, "is no longer: *who* am I? but *when, where, how* am I (so and so)?" ("*Woman, Native, Other*: Pratibha Parmar interviews Trinh T. Minh-ha"). We all are, in other words, as I have also repeatedly argued, multiple, complex, contradictory, and dynamic; we are not at all always the same, or always essentially the same. Our own subjectivity is shaped and formed and continually re-shaped and trans-formed in the course of our social interactions, including by way of the discourses that not only mediate but also, indeed, facilitate these interactions. Trinh constructs her films so that they overtly foreground their construction as well as overtly foreground a perpetually ongoing process of critical reflection concerning "the tools and relations of production that define us" ("*Woman, Native, Other*: Pratibha Parmar interviews Trinh T. Minh-ha"). She pays particular critical attention to "how we are constituted through the image-repertoire that insiders and outsiders have historically fashioned and retained of us" ("*Woman, Native, Other*: Pratibha Parmar interviews Trinh T. Minh-ha"). This involves, in relation to *Surname Viet, Given Name Nam*, an 'image-repertoire' that represents who Vietnamese women are and what Vietnamese women are like that both 'insiders and outsiders' bring to bear in engagement with Vietnamese women, and with cultural productions concerning Vietnamese women, that in turn exercise significant influence in affecting, in shaping, how Vietnamese women conceive of themselves and of what they can and should do, as themselves, as Vietnamese women ("*Woman, Native, Other*: Pratibha Parmar interviews Trinh T. Minh-ha").

Another principal aim of Trinh in her film-making as well as her other praxis, which she likewise addresses and begins to theorize in *Woman, Native, Other: Writing Postcoloniality and Feminism*, involves advocating for "difference" to "replace conflict" ("Not You/Like You: Post-Colonial Women and the Interlocking Questions of Identity and Difference"). For Trinh, difference is not merely the opposite of sameness nor is it merely equivalent with separateness. Trinh illustrates by mentioning how women undergoing veiling means different things, depending on context. And the same with women's silence. Trinh, as always, strives not only to avoid but also to problematize resting content with simple assumptions and easy conclusions. For Trinh it is crucial to emphasize that "I is not unitary, culture has never been monolithic" and "Differences do not only exist between outsider and insider" but also "within the outsider herself or the insider, herself" ("Not You/Like You: Post-Colonial Women and the Interlocking Questions of Identity and Difference"). Trinh rejects giving 'the outsider', especially in the contexts of a colonial/neo-colonial relation, what is expected from 'the insider': "a projection of an all-knowing subject that the outsider usually attributes to himself and to his kind" ("Not You/Like You: Post-Colonial Women and the Interlocking Questions of Identity and Difference").

Returning to *Surname Viet, Given Name Nam*, Trinh explains in "'There is No Such Thing as Documentary': an Interview with Trinh T. Minh-ha" that the film's title emphasizes how "a national identity is not given but constructed" and "What is thought to be typically Vietnamese turns out not so typical after all." After all, a country's identity "is, in reality, a multiplicity and an assemblage" while "What is conventionally understood as authentic is highly questionable because you can only be authentic if you confine yourself to locking doors and putting up fences." As a result of being extremely wary of conventional understandings of authenticity, Trinh, as I have emphasized repeatedly over the course of this chapter, advocates 'speaking nearby rather than about and for' and as Trinh explains "When you decide to speak nearby, rather than speak about, the first thing you need to do is to acknowledge the possible gap between you and those who populate your film: in other words, to leave the space of representation open" ("'There is No Such Thing as Documentary': an Interview with Trinh T. Minh-ha"). Foregrounding this gap, as Trinh does over and over again, in multiple different ways, throughout *Surname Viet, Given Name Nam*, is a matter of foremost artistic, intellectual, ethical, and indeed political integrity, and once you accept that "You can only speak nearby," you accept as well this "requires that you deliberately suspend meaning, preventing it from merely closing" and thus you must "leave a gap in the formation process" ("'There is No Such Thing as Documentary': an Interview with Trinh T. Minh-ha"). You must aim not to "assume a position of authority in relation to the other" ("'There is No Such Thing as Documentary': an Interview with Trinh T. Minh-ha"), either explicitly or implicity, either intentionally or unintentionally.

In "The Enduring Power of Trinh T. Minh-ha's Anti-Ethnography," Patrick J. Reed explains that this enduring power comes about because Trinh upholds a gap between seer and seen through deliberate and elaborate, multi-layered means of mediation that are overtly 'antiethnographic', and because Trinh proceeds as far as to reject the fiction/non-fiction binary while continually foregrounding doubt and deconstructive praxis, emphasizing the irreducible complexity of the subject matter she is exploring as well as emphasizing the importance of preserving mystery surrounding the totality of what this does mean, has meant, can mean, and might mean. Allied with 'speaking nearby', Trinh's practice of 'reading across', Reed further explains, means "to engage a text in simultaneous operations" ("The Enduring Power of Trinh T. Minh-ha's Anti-Ethnography") where a text might for example work as both poetry and philosophy at once, and, even more complicated than that, operate as poetry because of/by way of operating as philosophy as well as operate as philosophy because of/by way of operating as poetry.

In "Interview: Forgetting Vietnam," with Lucie Kim-Chi Mercier, Trinh describes her film-making as focused upon "the play between seeing and not seeing; on the work of the invisible within the visible, and vice versa; on how the seen both displays and veils, and how what is necessarily left unseen in each instance of the seen could contribute to bringing about *another seeing*." With *Surname Viet, Given Name Nam*, this play is illustrated by re-translating and dramatically re-narrating a series of interviews originally conducted in French, in Vietnam, that became the basis for an earlier 16 mm film and book, by Mai Thu Vhan. Because of the attention to emphasizing complexity and refusing to adopt a singular stance in relation to this complexity, Trinh recounts that her film received especially strong criticism from the left by people who objected to inclusion of women's critiques of the Communist Party and of revolutionary and socialist Vietnam. But, as Trinh responds, *Surname Viet, Given Name Nam* actually includes women articulating critical positions in multiple directions, from multiple vantage points. Trinh refuses to apologize for how her film calls attention to the limited gains for women achieved under socialism and revolution in Vietnam while pointing out Mai Thu Vhan's original set of interviews, her book, and her film faced similar criticism from the left even though Mai Thu Vhan is a Marxist herself.

"Autosuggestion" makes sense as an exploration of the complexity of a situation, a state of mind, and a prospective decision and action, which registers conflicting emotions as well as an experience of push and pull in multiple, and especially, opposing directions at once. Certainly the song emphasizes doubt–doubt concerning what it might be possible to achieve, doubt about the value of attempting to do so, yet doubt as well about being able to live with one's self if one did not at least *try*. The song might represent the direct and immediate situation of a narrator-protagonist, or a musical persona, or it might represent the indirect and mediated dramatic performance of what it might be like, and might feel like, to be in that kind of situation. The song combines elements of overwhelming constancy, of overwhelming constant reiteration, from the bass guitar and the drum kit, with persistent disturbing to dissonant shards or sparks from the guitar, complimented by the slightly skittering pattern emphasized by the drum kit, while the vocal likewise seems both persistent and meandering at once, both sincere and ironic or even mocking at once, and both calm and detached as well as agitated and anguished at once. The song offers something of an indeterminate range of possible ways of making sense of and responding to a situation, state of mind, and prospective decision and action, without clearly privileging, or preferring, one over the others, while precisely where the music as persona is at, in relation to the pressure, and need, to choose and act, is open to a considerable range of plausible interpretations, as are what has led the music as persona precisely to this point, what has immediately preceded, why there is seemingly no turning back, and why moving forward seems so hopeless.

Relations between the 'I' and the implicit as well as explicit 'you' here are likewise ambiguous, as the 'I' may be addressing the 'you' as another dimension of the self, representative of the self as itself comprised of an array of differences that are not strictly opposite or entirely separate from each other but which nevertheless do not add up to a neat singularity, and it may be addressing 'others', including 'us', as listeners, by way of the implicit as well as explicit 'you' here–and it may be addressing both 'the you within' and 'the you without' at once. It might well be helpful also to interpret "Autosuggestion" as fixated on not so much *'who* am I? but *when, where, how* am I (so and so)?', and in particular 'when, where, how am I' 'inside' versus 'outside' as well 'when, where, how am I' while straddling the border between or caught in limbo among trying versus not trying and versus struggling to determine whether one can and will try.

The song may be alluding to historical situations in which people have needed to make this kind of difficult decision. This is a decision whether to act, whether at least to try to act, while faced with overwhelming doubt about the viability of so doing, overwhelming doubt concerning prospects for success in so doing. Complicating the situation yet further, those confronting this decision might also experience anguish that they are considering acting, or trying to act, not so much for a noble reason, but rather because they are thoroughly estranged from being able to continue to live otherwise.

The song does not attempt to 'speak about or for' any of these precise, specific, concrete, historical instances, but rather 'speaks alongside' in contemplating, and sketching out, a comparable yet distinct situation, and scenario, that might and might not directly involve the narrator-protagonist of the lyrics and the music as persona. In relation to the title, the song is suggestive of a contemplative exploration of and reflection on what practices of 'autosuggestion' might and might not feel like as well as what they might and might not be able to achieve. This is broadly akin to where Trinh leaves her audiences at the end of her films, prompted to explore further, to listen further, to continue further to seek more and greater understanding and appreciation, as well as to be humbly critically self-reflexive concerning the assumptions they bring to bear, along with where these come from and what kinds of interests they represent and serve, in refusing to offer any singular, decisive answer to a reductive question such as 'what has Vietnamese women's experience been like?'

"Autosuggestion" ends without offering us a singular, decisive answer concerning 'what is to be done', as well as how and why, let alone in relation to what. But the song resonates with contemplating multiple possible ways of beginning to address these questions, including wrestling with how one might tentatively and provisionally answer the same. "Autosuggestion" does so in relation to a situation where the need to decide whether or not to act is pressing, and crucial, but where this does not seem at all easy to do, even if choosing to act seems more likely more desirable than choosing to not. The song highlights doubt, especially self-doubt, hesitation, reluctance, and feeling as if one's choices and actions are overdetermined such that one's exercise of 'free will,' 'self-control,' and 'independent agency' are questionable to illusory, yet one needs to 'go through the motions' and at least 'pretend' as if that is not, or might not be, the case. One might be engaging, for instance, in specific practices of autosuggestion while maintaining substantial doubt these can and will work, at all.

In connecting "Autosuggestion" with Aimé Césaire's *Discourse on Colonialism*, yes, colonialism certainly can and does rob colonized people of belief in their own capacities while cutting them off from resources that are empowering, including self-empowering. And, yes, colonialism certainly can and does leave colonized people in situations where they can readily feel like it is intolerable not to resist, and not to rebel, yet at the same time feel that resistance and rebellion will almost certainly be crushed because of the overwhelming power of the colonizer. This also extends to internalizing colonialist notions of the colonized's supposed backwardness, primitivism, and need for 'civilized assistance' to 'rise up' and 'join the modern world', along with learning to identify with the culture of the colonizer as supposedly producing all of the greatest achievements of humankind in philosophy, literature, art, and science. From that last vantage point, it may even feel as if life is overwhelmingly designed, regulated, and controlled in line with the colonizer's dictates, but any realistic alternative might be impossible to achieve, even to imagine at all.

On the other hand, even if the colonized rejects this denigrative view, it certainly would make sense to interpret "Autosuggestion" resonating with a keen frustration at acting in resistance, and even in rebellion, solely to manifest one's conscience, one's principled convictions, while not being able to affect any transformative results in the prevailing colonial, or neo-colonial, situation, and in the prevailing relations between colonizers and colonized. Merely 'trying' as a matter of conscience, and merely 'stepping outside' to identify one's self as a 'conscientious objector' can seem not only futile but also distracting of focus from where it needs to be, and that is developing the resources, powers, and capacities, as well as determining how to deploy these, that can bring about the substantive change that is needed, as opposed to merely attesting to the desire and the need for such change to happen.

Yet at the same time, in contrast with what "Autosuggestion" emphasizes, Césaire is also emphasizing what colonialism does to the people in colonizing countries, in particular the effectively 'de-civilizing' impact upon people in colonizing countries by both passively accepting as well as actively supporting the colonization of others. Césaire is emphasizing the 'de-civilizing' impact upon such people of refusing to recognize and acknowledge that colonialism is totally indefensible, that it is indeed a monstrous practice, and that it cannot and should not be justified in any way. Likewise, Césaire is emphasizing the 'de-civilizing' impact of refusing to recognize and acknowledge what has been gained by way of exploitative expropriation from the colonized. Césaire focuses not only on the devastating impact of colonialism on the colonized but also upon the moral damage done to people from colonizing countries in terms of this fostering desensitization and callous indifference, leading to multiple as well as repeated efforts to justify colonialism as necessary for and beneficial to the colonized, including by continually asserting the colonized are inherently inferior.

Césaire would seemingly have little sympathy with the position of the narrator-protagonist, and music as persona, in "Autosuggestion," people living in colonizing countries, indeed people at the metropolitan center of imperialism, who are as hesitant, about acting, and who, even if and when they do, proceed overwhelmed by doubt. In other words, it might well seem, from a critical vantage point in line with Césaire's principal points of emphasis in *Discourse on Colonialism*, that people like the narrator-protagonist of the lyrics, and the music as persona, in the case of "Autosuggestion," are too caught up with themselves, too solipsistically and even narcissistically self-absorbed, for all their melancholy self-doubt and even self-mockery, and not focused upon the lived conditions of those directly subject to colonialism. It might well seem that all of this hesitation and doubt runs counter to what is necessary, in order to act in solidarity, which includes being ready and willing to take real risks, and not to allow hesitation and doubt to prevent one from doing so.

Also, Césaire seemingly would be critical of the position that regards the prospect of 'stepping outside' as one enveloped in feelings of overwhelming dread rather than imagining doing so as pursuing an opening toward a prospective eventual 'liberation' that will prove immensely uplifting as opposed to inevitably deflating. Perhaps, from such a critical vantage point, allied with what Césaire argues in *Discourse on Colonialism*, this is reflective of a 'sickness' that has affected the European 'at home': no longer capable of imagining a world in which equitable relations might be maintained among people from different regions of the world, people of different ethnicities, people with different cultures, and people commonly identified as of different races. This might mean living long-term from within the metropolitan center of a colonial/neo-colonial nation, especially as a White person with no family background directly connecting 'him' to the peoples and cultures of colonized nations, especially to the peoples and cultures of colonized nations located outside of Europe, has rendered this kind of person in this kind of position effectively incapable of imagining what the end of colonialism, and of neo-colonialism, might bring to, might make possible, for the European. Colonialism might have rendered 'him' unable effectively to grasp how struggles over access to and exercise of resources, powers, and capacities are interdeterminately interrelated: within the colonizing nation on the one hand and within the nations and regions where this colonizing nation has established and maintained colonies on the other hand.

Guilt and shame might indeed be apt emotions to feel as a White European, even from a poor, working class, or lower middle class socio-economic position, in relation to what one's own nation has perpetrated in the form of colonialism, and neo-colonialism, as well as how the colonized has suffered deprivation as a result, with this White European benefitting from this deprivation. And doubt and hesitancy might be apt emotional responses as well, in being careful to avoid inadvertently taking on the role of 'the white savior', or 'the reverse missionary', and speaking for and about rather than alongside the other. Yet if these emotional states amount to all this White European is able to manifest, they would seem to fall short of what is needed, in solidarity with the colonized, in supporting the colonized's efforts to resist and overcome colonialism.

In connecting "Autosuggestion" with Edward W. Said's *Representations of the Intellectual* I want to emphasize once more contrasts between, on the one hand, the positions Said is arguing from and especially for, and, on the other hand the positions "Autosuggestion" seems to be representing. Yes, it makes sense to propose the vantage point from which the song emanates bears resemblance to what Said theorizes as that of 'intellectual exile', and it could make sense as a position that is self-chosen, but "Autosuggestion" offers nothing of what Said proposes this kind of position positively enables, including independence, in being able to perceive insightfully 'from the outside', and to not be confined to making only suggestions and recommendations for improvement that work within the existing system of social relations. From 'outside' one can contemplate the need for an entirely new and much different and better system.

It might well seem "Autosuggestion" does not even offer the equivalent of what Said interprets Adorno as envisioning: an eventual future audience that will be able to appreciate and understand, and thereby make positive and productive sense and use of what he at present is writing. It might well seem "Autosuggestion" is too caught up within a fatalism that verges upon nihilism. As such, it might make sense to interpret "Autosuggestion" as not grasping that this fatalistic to nihilistic perception of what will follow from daring to 'step outside', 'to make waves', and evincing an effort to 'try', itself reflects what people are encouraged to think and feel by forces whose interests depend on the maintenance and reproduction of the status quo.

What's more, a critique in line with what Said argues in *Representations of the Intellectual* might reasonably charge "Autosuggestion" with not recognizing the source of the strength needed to ensure one can try, and this trying can make a difference, while being ready to accept and bear the consequences from trying. This kind of 'strength' must be attained by associating one's own praxis with historical and ongoing struggles for the same ends and in particular with the praxis of others likewise engaged in intellectual exile, past and present. "Autosuggestion" might represent an individual who feels overwhelmed by 'his' experience of alienation and isolation from others, such that 'he' is not able to feel an empowering interdependent interconnection with others, at or over a distance, who are and who have been actively committed toward striving in support of the same ends 'he' 'would like' to *try* to help realize. However, Said, like Césaire, recognizes this a real danger for all working from a marginal position. Sometimes, especially in the bleakest of situations, the marginal figure must rely upon what 'he' can summon forth and pressure 'himself' to attempt to do by drawing upon resources immediately available to 'him', in his isolation and alienation, even if, *even as*, it is precisely *against* those forces and interests that have left 'him', and so many others like 'him', isolated and alienated that he is rallying the will to *try*, once more, to fight.

Works Cited

Adorno, Theodor. "Cultural Criticism and Society." 1949, 1951. *Prisms*. Samuel Weber and Sherry Weber, trans. Cambridge: MIT Press, 1981, 17-34.

_____. *Minima Moralia: Reflections from Damaged Life*. 1951. E.F.N. Jephcott, trans. London: New Left Books, 1978.

Akse. Quoted in Chris Greenhalgh, "Ian Curtis mural unveiled in the Northern Quarter ahead of mental health music festival." ilovemanchester.com. 10 October 2020. Https://ilovemanchester.com/ian-curtis-mural-manchester-mental-health Accessed 16 April 2022.

Althusser, Louis. *On the Reproduction of Capital: Ideology and Ideological State Apparatuses*. 1971, 1995. G.M. Goshgarian, trans. London: Verso, 2014.

Anderson, Sherwood. *Winesburg, Ohio*. New York: B.W. Huebsch, 1919.

Andrews, Kehinde. *The New Age of Empire: How Racism & Colonialism Still Rule the World*. New York: Bold Type Books, 2021.

Ashworth, Jenn. "Day of the Lords." *We Were Strangers: Stories Inspired by Unknown Pleasures*. Richard V. Hirst, ed. Manchester: Cōnfingō, 2019, 23-39.

Ataria, Yochai. "Traumatic and Mystical Experiences: The Dark Nights of the Soul." *Journal of Humanistic Psychology*. 18 December 2014. Https://doi-org.proxy.uwec.edu/10.1177/0022167814563143 Accessed 16 April 2022.

Balsom, Erika and Trinh T. Minh-ha. "'There is No Such Thing as Documentary': An Interview with Trinh T. Minh-ha." *Frieze*. 1 November 2018. Https://www.frieze.com/article/there-no-such-thing-documentary-interview-trinh-t-minh-ha Accessed 16 April 2022.

Beinart, Peter. "Russia speaks total lies. That doesn't diminish America's half-truths." *The Guardian*. 26 February 2022. Https://www.theguardian.com/commentisfree/2022/feb/26/russia-lies-america-half-truths Accessed 16 April 2022.

Benda, Julian. *The Treason of the Intellectuals*. 1928. Richard Aldington, trans. New York: Norton, 1990.

Bennett, Louise. As quoted in Sathnam Sanghera, *Empireland: How Imperialism Has Shaped Modern Britain*. New York: Viking/Penguin Random House, 2021, 76-77.

Bhabha, Homi K. "Of Mimicry and Man: The Ambivalence of Colonial Discourse." *October*. Vol. 28, Discipleship: A Special Issue on Psychoanalysis, Spring 1984: 125-133.

Blanchot, Maurice. *The Writing of the Disaster*. 1980. A. Smock, trans. Lincoln: University of Nebraska Press, 1986.

Bond, Lucy and Stef Craps. *Trauma*. The New Critical Idiom Series. New York: Routledge, 2020.

The Book of Revelation. Final Book of the *New Testament* of the Christian *Bible*.

Boswell, Matthew. "Post-Punk, Joy Division, *Closer*." *Holocaust Impiety in Literature, Popular Music and Film*. London: Palgrave MacMillan, 2012, 114-123.

Breyley, Gay Jennifer. "I Hung Around in Your Soundtrack: Affinities with Joy Division among Contemporary Iranian Musicians." *Heart & Soul: Critical Writings on Joy Division*. London: Rowan & Littlefield, 2018, 209-228.

Carroll, Cath. "On Joy Division: Essays and Memories." Kevin Cummins, *Joy Division * Juvenes **. 2007. Revised and Expanded Edition. London: Cassell, 2021, 216-217.

Carruth, Cathy. "Recapturing the Past: Introduction." *Trauma: Explorations in Memory*. Cathy Carruth, ed. Baltimore: Johns Hopkins University Press, 1995, 151-157.

_____. "Trauma and Experience: Introduction." *Trauma: Explorations in Memory*. Cathy Carruth, ed. Baltimore: Johns Hopkins University Press, 1995, 3-12.

_____, ed. *Trauma: Explorations in Memory*. Baltimore: Johns Hopkins University Press, 1995.

_____. *Unclaimed Experience: Trauma, Narrative, and History*. 1996. 20th Anniversary Edition. Baltimore: Johns Hopkins University Press, 2016.

Carruth, Cathy and Geoffrey Hartman. "An Interview With Geoffrey Hartman." *Studies in Romanticism*. Vol. 35 No. 4, 1996: 631-652.

Cawston, Amanda. "Pacifism as Re-appropriated Violence." *Pacifism's Appeal: Ethos, History, Politics*. Rethinking Peace and Conflict Series. Jorg Kustermans, Tom Sauer, Dominick Lootens, and Barbara Segaert, eds. Cham: Palgrave MacMillan, 2019, 41-60.

Césaire, Aimé. *Discourse on Colonialism*. 1955. John Pinkham, trans. New York: Monthly Review Press, 1972.

Césaire, Suzanne. Quoted in Robin D.G. Kelley, "A Poetics of Anticolonialism," Introduction to Aimé Césaire, *Discourse on Colonialism*. 1955. John Pinkham, trans. New York: Monthly Review Press, 1972, 15.

Conrad, Anna and Stephen Morris. "How Joy Division made *Closer*: 'We were really tight as a band; there was a lot of telepathy going on'." *GQ* Magazine UK. 14 July 2020. Https://www.gq-magazine.co.uk/culture/article/joy-division-closer-album Accessed 16 April 2022.

Conrad, Joseph. *Heart of Darkness*. 1899. Edinburgh: William Blackwoods and Sons, 1902.

Control. Feature-Length Fictional Film. Directed by Anton Corbijn, 2007.

Coué, Émile. *Self-Mastery Through Conscious Autosuggestion.* 1920. New York: Malkan Publishing, 1922.

Cox, Arnie. *Music & Embodied Cognition: Listening, Moving, Feeling, & Thinking.* Bloomington: Indiana University Press, 2017.

Crockett, Clayton. "In the Colony with Joy Division." *The Counter-Narratives of Radical Theology and Popular Music: Songs of Fear and Trembling*, edited by Mike Grimshaw. New York: Palgrave MacMillan, 2014, 25-36.

Cummins, Kevin. "Introduction." *Joy Division * Juvenes *.* 2007. Revised and Expanded Edition. London: Cassell, 2021, 10-11.

_____. *Joy Division * Juvenes *.* 2007. Revised and Expanded Edition. London: Cassell, 2021.

Curtis, Deborah. *Touching From a Distance: Ian Curtis & Joy Division.* London: Faber and Faber, 1995.

Curtis, Ian. *So This is Permanence: Joy Division Lyrics and Notebooks.* Deborah Curtis and Jon Savage, eds. London: Faber and Faber, 2014.

Curtis, Natalie. "On Joy Division: Essays and Memories." Kevin Cummins, *Joy Division * Juvenes *.* 2007. Revised and Expanded Edition. London: Cassell, 2021, 70.

Davies, James. *Sedated: How Modern Capitalism Created Our Mental Health Crisis.* London: Atlantic, 2021.

Depestre, René. "An Interview with Aimé Césaire." Aimé Césaire, *Discourse on Colonialism.* 1955. John Pinkham, trans. New York: Monthly Review Press, 1972, 79-94.

Dickinson, Bob. Contributing to Savage, Jon, *This Searing Light, The Sun, and Everything Else: Joy Division–The Oral History.* London: Faber and Faber, 2019.

Dorling, Danny and Sally Tomlinson. *Rule Britannia: Brexit and the End of Empire.* London: Biteback, 2019.

Donne, John. "No Man is an Island." *Devotions Upon Emergent Occasions and Death's Duel* with *The Life of Dr. John Donne* by Izaak Walton. 1623-1624, 1631, 1640. New York: Vintage, 1999.

Drayton, Richard. As quoted in Sathnam Sanghera, *Empireland: How Imperialism Has Shaped Modern Britain.* New York: Viking/Penguin Random House, 2021, 124.

Du Bois, W.E.B. *Black Reconstruction in America: An Essay Toward a History of the Part Which Black Folk Played in the Attempt to Reconstruct Democracy in America, 1860–1880.* 1935. Oxford: Oxford University Press, 2007.

Edge, Brian. *New Order + Joy Division: Pleasures and Wayward Distractions.* 1984. Revised Edition. London: Omnibus, 1988.

Edwardes, Matthew. As quoted in John Newsinger, *The Blood Never Dried: a People's History of the British Empire.* Second Edition. London: Bloomsbury, 2013, 75.

Fanon, Frantz. *A Dying Colonialism.* 1959. Haakon Chevalier, trans. New York: Grove Press, 1967.

Felman, Shoshana. *The Juridical Unconscious: Trials and Traumas in the Twentieth Century.* Cambridge, MA: Harvard University Press, 2002.

Fiala, Andrew. *Transformative Pacifism: Critical Theory and Practice.* London: Bloomsbury, 2018.

Foucault, Michel. *Discipline and Punish*. 1975. Alan Sheridan, trans. New York: Pantheon, 1977.

Freud, Sigmund. "Mourning and Melancholia." 1917. James Strachey, Alix Strachey, and Alan Tyson trans. *The Standard Edition of the Complete Works of Sigmund Freud*. Vol. 13. James Strachey, ed. London: Hogarth Press, 1953-1974, 239-258.

_____. *Moses and Monotheism*. 1939. Katherine Jones, trans. Mansfield Centre, CT: Martino Publishing, 2010.

Givens, Terri E. *Radical Empathy: Finding a Path to Bridging Racial Divides*. Bristol: Polity Press, 2021.

Goffman, Erving. *Asylums: Essays on the Condition of the Social Situation of Mental Patients and Other Inmates*. New York: Anchor Books, 1961.

_____. *The Presentation of Self in Everyday Life*. 1956. New York: Knopf Doubleday/Penguin, 1959.

_____. *Stigma: Notes on the Management of Spoiled Identity*. 1963. New York: Simon and Schuster, 2009.

Gramsci, Antonio. 1929-1935. *Prison Notebooks*. Joseph A. Buttigieg and Antonio Callari, trans. Three Volumes. New York: Columbia University Press, 2011.

Greenhalgh, Chris. "Ian Curtis mural unveiled in the Northern Quarter ahead of mental health music festival." ilovemanchester.com. 10 October 2020. Https://ilovemanchester.com/ian-curtis-mural-manchester-mental-health Accessed 16 April 2022.

Grimshaw, Mike, ed. *The Counter-Narratives of Radical Theology and Popular Music: Songs of Fear and Trembling*. New York: Palgrave MacMillan, 2014.

Grinker, Roy (Sr). As interviewed in "Cry for 'normal' times stirs warning." *Chicago Daily News*. 17 November 1953, 5.

Grinker, Roy Richard. *Nobody's Normal: How Culture Created the Stigma of Mental Illness*. New York: W.W. Norton, 2021.

Grossman, Dr Zoltán. "From Wounded Knee to Syria: U.S. Military Interventions Since 1890." The Evergreen State University. https://sites.evergreen.edu/zoltan/interventions/ Accessed 16 April 2022.

Hartman, Geoffrey. *The Fateful Question of Culture*. New York: Coumbia University Press, 1997.

Headstock. "Headstock Manchester May 2020." Https://headstock.live Accessed 16 April 2022.

Heuvel, Katrina vanden. "Editorial: Putin's Invasion–De-escalation and negotiation are the only way out of this crisis." 24 February 2022. Https://www.thenation.com/article/world/putin-invasion-ukraine-war/ Accessed 16 April 2022.

Higgs, Matthew. "On Joy Division: Essays and Memories." Kevin Cummins, *Joy Division * Juvenes *.* 2007. Revised and Expanded Edition. London: Cassell, 2021, 186-187.

Hirst, Richard V., ed. *We Were Strangers: Stories Inspired by Unknown Pleasures*. Manchester: Cōnfingō, 2019.

Hook, Peter. "In Conversation." Kevin Cummins, *Joy Division * Juvenes *.* 2007. Revised and Expanded Edition. London: Cassell, 2021. 60-62.

_____. Quoted in Will Lavin, "Joy Division's Peter Hook unveils new Ian Curtis mural in Macclesfield town centre." *NME*. 26 March 2022. Https://www.nme.com/news/music/joy-divisions-peter-hook-unveils-new-ian-curtis-mural-in-macclesfield-town-centre-3190982 Accessed 16 April 2022.

_____. *Unknown Pleasures: Inside Joy Division*. London: Simon & Schuster, 2012.

Horesh, Theo. *The Fascism This Time: And the Global Future of Democracy*. Boulder: Cosmopolis Press, 2020.

Horn, Elena. "Director's Statement." *The Lesson*. Feature-Length Documentary Film. 2020. Http://thelesson.film Accessed 16 April 2022.

Illich, Ivan. *Gender*. New York: Pantheon, 1982.

Indiana University Press. Description, Back Jacket, Paperback Edition, Trinh T. Minh-ha, *Woman, Native, Other: Writing Postcoloniality and Feminism*. Bloomington: Indiana University Press, 1989.

Johnson, Mark. *An Ideal for Living: An History of Joy Division*. 1984. London: Bobcat Books, 1986.

Jones, Ernest. As quoted in John Newsinger, *The Blood Never Dried: a People's History of the British Empire*. Second Edition. London: Bloomsbury, 2013, 90.

Joy Division. *+/- Singles 1978-1980* 10-CD Collection. Rhino UK/Warner Box Set of Remastered Recordings. 2010.

_____. "Autosuggestion." *+/- Singles 1978-1980* 10-CD Collection. Rhino UK/Warner Box Set of Remastered Recordings. 2010.

_____. "Autosuggestion." Live from Prince of Wales Conference Centre, London. Recorded Musical Song, 1979.

_____. "Autosuggestion." Live from Prince of Wales Conference Centre, London. *Heart and Soul* 4-CD Box Set. 2007.

_____. "Autosuggestion." Recorded Musical Song, 1979.

_____. *Closer*. London Records Remastered Collectors 2-CD Edition. 2007.

_____. *Closer*. Music LP, 1980.

_____. "Colony." Castle Records Peel Sessions CD Collection. 1989.

_____. "Colony." *Closer*. London Records Remastered Collectors 2-CD Edition. 2007.

_____. "Colony." Recorded Musical Song, 1980.

_____. "Colony." Recorded Musical Song. Peel Session. 1979.

_____. "Day of the Lords." Recorded Musical Song, 1979.

_____. "Day of the Lords." *Unknown Pleasures*, London Records Remastered Collectors 2-CD Edition. 2007.

_____. "Disorder." Recorded Musical Song, 1979.

_____. *Earcom 2–Contradiction*. Recorded Music EP. 1979.

_____. "From Safety to Where . . .?" Recorded Musical Song, 1979.

_____. "Heart and Soul." *Closer*. London Records Remastered Collectors 2-CD Edition. 2007.

_____. *Heart and Soul*. London Records 4-CD box set. 2001.

_____. "Heart and Soul." Recorded Musical Song, 1980.

_____. *Substance*. Record Album, Music LP. 1988.

_____. *Substance*. Record Album, Remastered CD Edition. 2015.

_____. *Unknown Pleasures*. London Records Remastered Collectors 2-CD Edition. 2007.

_____. *Unknown Pleasures*. Music LP, 1979.

Joyce, James. *Dubliners*. London: Grant Richards, 1914.

Joydivisionofficial.com. *Joy Division Unknown Pleasures Re-Imagined Series*. Https://www.joydivisionofficial.com/reimagined/ Accessed 16 April 2022.

Kafka, Franz. "In the Penal Colony." 1914, 1918, 1919. *The Penal Colony: Stories and Short Pieces*. Willa and Edwin Muir, trans. New York: Schocken, 1961, 191-227.

Keats, John. On 'Negative Capability'. *Selected Letters*. 1817-1818. John Barnard, ed. New York: Penguin Classics, 2015.

Kelley, Robin D.G. "A Poetics of Anticolonialism." Introduction to Aimé Césaire, *Discourse on Colonialism*. 1955. John Pinkham, trans. New York: Monthly Review Press, 1972, 7-28.

Kingston, Maxine Hong. *The Woman Warrior*. 1976. New York: Vintage, 1977.

Koestler, Arthur. Quoted in Peter Beinart, "Russia speaks total lies. That doesn't diminish America's half-truths." *The Guardian*. 26 February 2022. Https://www.theguardian.com/commentisfree/2022/feb/26/russia-lies-america-half-truths Accessed 16 April 2022.

Kustermans, Jorg, Tom Sauer, Dominick Lootens, and Barbara Segaert, eds. *Pacifism's Appeal: Ethos, History, Politics*. Rethinking Peace and Conflict Series. Cham: Palgrave MacMillan, 2019.

Lacan, Jacques. *Écrits*. 1966. Bruce Fink, Héloïse Fink, and Russell Grigg, trans. New York: Norton, 2007.

LaCapra, Dominick. *History in Transit: Experience, Identity, Critical Theory*. 2014. Second Edition. Ithaca: Cornell University Press, 2014.

_____. *Understanding Others: Peoples, Animals, Pasts*. Ithaca: Cornell University Press, 2018.

_____. *Writing History, Writing Trauma*. Baltimore: Johns Hopkins University Press, 2001.

Lavin, Will. "Joy Division's Peter Hook unveils new Ian Curtis mural in Macclesfield town centre." *NME*. 26 March 2022. Https://www.nme.com/news/music/joy-divisions-peter-hook-unveils-new-ian-curtis-mural-in-macclesfield-town-centre-3190982 Accessed 16 April 2022.

The Lesson. Feature-Length Documentary film. Directed by Elena Horn, 2020.

Levi, Primo. "The Grey Zone." *The Drowned and the Saved*. Raymond Rosenthal, trans. London: Abacus, 1989, 22-51.

Lévi-Strauss, Claude. *Race and History*. 1952. Paris: Unesco, 1952.

Lezard, Nicholas. "On Joy Division: Essays and Memories." Kevin Cummins, *Joy Division * Juvenes **. 2007. Revised and Expanded Edition. London: Cassell, 2021, 166-167.

Lorde, Audre. "The Master's Tools Will Never Dismantle the Master's House." *The Bridge Called Me Back: Writings by Radical Women of Color*. Cherrie Moraga and Gloria Anzaldúa, eds. Watertown: Persephone Press, 1981, 94-103.

_____. *Sister Outsider: Essays and Speeches*. Berkeley: Crossing Press, 1984.

MacGregor, Neil (British Museum Director). As quoted in Sathnam Sanghera, *Empireland: How Imperialism Has Shaped Modern Britain*. New York: Viking/Penguin Random House, 2021, 197.

Magee, Audrey. *The Colony*. London: Faber & Faber, 2022.

Mai, Thu Van. *Vietnam: un peuple, des voix*. Paris: P. Horay, 1983.

_____. *Vietnam: un peuple, des voix*. Compiler and interviewer. Documentary film. Precise date unknown.

Malcolm X. "The Ballot or the Bullet." Public Speech, Cory Methodist Church, Cleveland, Ohio. 3 April 1964.

Mambrol, Nasrullah. "Trinh T. Minh-ha and Film Criticism." *Literary Theory and Criticism*. 25 July 2018. Https://literariness.org/2018/07/25/trinh-t-minh-ha-and-film-criticism/ Accessed 16 April 2022.

The Manc Review. "Joy Division." Made in Manchester Feature. 6 February 2012. Https://www.mancreview.com/2012/02/joy-division/ Accessed 16 April 2022.

Mannion, Nick. Quoted in Will Lavin, "Joy Division's Peter Hook unveils new Ian Curtis mural in Macclesfield town centre." *NME*. 26 March 2022. Https://www.nme.com/news/music/joy-divisions-peter-hook-unveils-new-ian-curtis-mural-in-macclesfield-town-centre-3190982 Accessed 16 April 2022.

Martinez, Sara. "Literary Influences on Joy Division: J.G. Ballard, Franz Kafka, Dostoevsky." Martin J. Power, Eoin Devereux, and Aileen Dillane, eds. *Heart & Soul: Critical Writings on Joy Division*. London: Rowan & Littlefield, 2018, 47-61.

May, Theresa (Former UK Prime Minister). As quoted in Sathnam Sanghera, *Empireland: How Imperialism Has Shaped Modern Britain*. New York: Viking/Penguin Random House, 2021, 164.

Mayne, Judith and Trinh T. Minh-ha. "From a Hybrid Place [Interview with Trinh T. Minh-ha]." *Framer Framed: Film Scripts and Interviews*. New York: Routledge, 1992, 137-150.

Mboya, Tom. Quoted in Ian Sanjay Patel, *We're Here Because You Were There: Immigration and the End of Empire*. London: Verso, 2021, 147.

McKenna, David, et. al. "Beyond the Hits of New Order, Joy Division and Warsaw." *Quietus*. 23 July 2015. Https://thequietus.com/articles/18315-new-order-joy-division-beyond-the-hits Accessed 16 April 2022.

Mead, George Herbert. *Mind, Self, and Society: From the Standpoint of a Social Behaviourist*. 1929. Chicago: University of Chicago Press, 1962.

Mercier, Lucie Kim-Chi and Trinh T. Minh-ha. "Interview: Forgetting Vietnam." *Radical Philosophy* No. 203, December 2018. Https://www.radicalphilosophy.com/article/forgetting-vietnam Accessed 16 April 2022.

Middles, Mick and Lindsay Reade. *Torn Apart: The Life of Ian Curtis*. London: Omnibus, 2009.

Mills, C. Wright. *Power, Politics, and People: The Collected Essays of C. Wright Mills*. Irving Louis Horowitz, ed. New York: Ballantine, 1963.

Morley, Paul. From *The NME*, 9 September 1978. As Excerpted and Republished in Mark Johnson, *An Ideal for Living: An History of Joy Division*. 1984. London: Bobcat Books, 1986, 50-51.

The Morning Star. "Editorial: Russia's assault on Ukraine is a catastrophe that could lead to nuclear war. The peace movement is more important than ever." 24 February 2022. Https://morningstaronline.co.uk/article/russias-assault-ukraine-catastrophe-could-lead-nuclear-war-peace-movement-more-important Accessed 16 April 2022.

Morris, Stephen. Contributing to Savage, Jon, *This Searing Light, The Sun, and Everything Else: Joy Division–The Oral History*. London: Faber and Faber, 2019.

_____. "In Conversation." Kevin Cummins, *Joy Division * Juvenes *. 2007. Revised and Expanded Edition. London: Cassell, 2021. 42-45.

Morris, Stephen and Anna Conrad. "How Joy Division made *Closer*: 'We were really tight as a band; there was a lot of telepathy going on'." *GQ* Magazine UK. 14 July 2020. Https://www.gq-magazine.co.uk/culture/article/joy-division-closer-album Accessed 16 April 2022.

Muhkherjee, Rudrangshu. As quoted in John Newsinger, *The Blood Never Dried: a People's History of the British Empire*. Second Edition. London: Bloomsbury, 2013, 78.

Myga, Kasia A., Esther Kuehn, and Elena Azanon. "Autosuggestion: a cognitive process that empowers your brain?" *Experimental Brain Research*. No. 240. 19 November 2021. Https://doi.org/10.1007/s00221-021-06265-8 Accessed 16 April 2022.

Nevin, Pat. "On Joy Division: Essays and Memories." Kevin Cummins, *Joy Division * Juvenes *. 2007. Revised and Expanded Edition. London: Cassell, 2021, 86-87.

Newsinger, John. *The Blood Never Dried: a People's History of the British Empire*. Second Edition. London: Bloomsbury, 2013.

Nowlan, Bob. "Biographical Profile: Bob Nowlan." https://people.uwec.edu/ranowlan/PROFILE_.htm Accessed 16 April 2022.

_____. Excerpt from "What it Means for Me to Declare that 'I am Gay'." Miscellaneous Public Presentations at the University of Wisconsin-Eau Claire and in Eau Claire, Wisconsin, circa 1997-2001.

_____. "Teaching and Writing About 'Ian Curtis and Joy Division: Critical Theoretical Perspectives'." University of Wisconsin-Eau Claire English Department Colloquium Presentation. 28 April, 2017.

Olusoga, David. As quoted in Sathnam Sanghera, *Empireland: How Imperialism Has Shaped Modern Britain*. New York: Viking/Penguin Random House, 2021, 69n.

O'Rourke, Meghan. *The Invisible Kingdom: Reimagining Chronic Illness*. New York: Riverhead Books, 2022.

Orwell, George. As quoted in Sathnam Sanghera, *Empireland: How Imperialism Has Shaped Modern Britain*. New York: Viking/Penguin Random House, 2021, 142.

Ott, Ed. *Unknown Pleasures*. 33 and 1/3 Series. New York: Continuum, 2006.

Oxford English Dictionary Online. https://www.oed.com Accessed 16 April 2022.

Parmar, Pratibha and Trinh T. Minh-ha. "WOMAN, NATIVE, OTHER: Pratibha Parmar Interviews Trinh T. Minh-ha." *Feminist Review*. No. 36, Autumn 1990. Https://www.jstor.org/stable/1395110 Accessed 16 April 2022.

Patel, Ian Sanjay. *We're Here Because You Were There: Immigration and the End of Empire*. London: Verso, 2021.

Peace, David. "On Joy Division: Essays and Memories." Kevin Cummins, *Joy Division * Juvenes *. 2007. Revised and Expanded Edition. London: Cassell, 2021, 232.

Petridis, Alexis. "Joy Division: all of their songs, ranked!" *The Guardian*. 17 July 2020. Https://www.theguardian.com/culture/2020/jul/17/joy-division-all-of-their-songs-ranked Accessed 16 April 2022.

Priestley. JB. *English Journey*. London: Victor Gollancz, 1934.

Power, Kevin. "*The Colony* by Audrey Magee review–an allegory of the Troubles." *The Guardian*. 25 February 2022. Https://www.theguardian.com/books/2022/feb/25/the-colony-by-audrey-magee-review-an-allegory-of-the-troubles Accessed 16 April 2022.

Power, Martin J., Eoin Devereux, and Aileen Dillane, eds. *Heart & Soul: Critical Writings on Joy Division*. London: Rowan & Littlefield, 2018.

Press, Eyal. Retweeting of @mkazin Twitter post. 24 February 2022. Https://twitter.com/mkazin/status/1496846868633907200?cxt=HHwWgMCjgfyS78UpAAAA Accessed 16 April 2022.

Raggett, Ned. "Joy Division 'Colony' Song Review." Https://www.allmusic.com/song/colony-mt0035364786 Accessed 16 April 2022.

Ramsay, David (of Open Democracy). As quoted in Danny Dorling and Sally Tomlinson, *Rule Britannia: Brexit and the End of Empire*. London: Biteback, 2019, 21.

Rankin, Ian. "Foreword." Kevin Cummins, *Joy Division * Juvenes *. 2007. Revised and Expanded Edition. London: Cassell, 2021. 8-9.

Reassemblage. Experimental documentary film. Directed by Trinh T. Minh-ha, 1982.

Reed, Patrick J. "The Enduring Power of Trinh T. Minh-ha's Anti-Ethnography." *ArtReview*. 19 October 2020. Https://artreview.com/the-enduring-power-of-trinh-t-minh-ha-films/ Accessed 16 April 2022.

Riesman, David, Nathan Glazer, and Reuel Denney. *The Lonely Crowd: A Study of the Changing American Character*. 1950. New Haven: Yale University Press, 2001.

Robinson, Cedric J. *Black Marxism: The Making of the Black Radical Tradition*. 1983. Revised and Updated Edition. Chapel Hill: University of North Carolina Press, 2020.

Roffman, Michael, Phillip Roffman, and Dan Pfleegor. "Ranking: Every Joy Division Song in Honor of Ian Curtis. *Consequence*. 17 May 2020. Https://consequence.net/2020/05/ranking-joy-division-songs/ Accessed 16 April 2022.

Rothberg, Michael. "Trauma Theory, Implicated Subjects, and the Question of Israel/Palestine." *Profession*. 2014. Https://profession.mla.org/trauma-theory-implicated-subjects-and-the-question-of-israel-palestine/ Accessed 16 April 2022.

Said, Edward W. *Culture and Imperialism*. London: Chatto & Windus, 1993.

_____. *Orientalism*. New York: Pantheon, 1976.

_____. *Peace and Its Discontents: Essays on Palestine in the Middle East Peace Process*. New York: Vintage Books, 1995.

_____. *The Politics of Dispossession: The Struggle for Palestinian Self-Determination, 1969-1994*. New York: Pantheon, 1994.

_____. *Representations of the Intellectual*. 1994. New York: Knopf Doubleday/Penguin, 1998.

Sandel, Michael. *Tyranny of Merit: Can We Find the Common Good?* New York: Picador/Farrar, Straus and Giroux, 2021.

Sanghera, Sathnam. *Empireland: How Imperialism Has Shaped Modern Britain*. New York: Viking/Penguin Random House, 2021.

Sartre, Jean-Paul. *What is Literature?* 1948. Bernard Frechtman, trans. London: Methuen, 1950.

Sivanandan, Ambalevener. As quoted in Sathnam Sanghera, *Empireland: How Imperialism Has Shaped Modern Britain*. New York: Viking/Penguin Random House, 2021, 69.

Savage, Jon. "The Eternal." With Portraits by Kevin Cummins and thanks to Liz Naylor, Charles Salem, Steve Walsh, Jon Wozencroft, and Max Norman. *Mojo*. February 2007: 74-89.

_____, ed. *This Searing Light, The Sun, and Everything Else: Joy Division–The Oral History*. London: Faber and Faber, 2019.

Schell, Jonathan. *The Fate of the Earth*. New York: Knopf, 1982.

Smiley, David. As quoted in John Newsinger, *The Blood Never Dried: a People's History of the British Empire*. Second Edition. London: Bloomsbury, 2013, 146.

Snyder, Timothy. "Journalist Andrew Cockburn & Historian Timothy Snyder on Ukraine, Russia, NATO Expansion & Sanctions." *Democracy Now!* 1 March 2022. Https://www.democracynow.org/2022/3/1/nato_expansion_ukraine_russia_crisis#transcript Accessed 17 April 2022.

_____. *On Tyranny*. New York: Tim Duggan Books, 2017.

Songmeanings.com. "Autosuggestion–Joy Division." Https://songmeanings.com/songs/view/59697/ Accessed 16 April 2022.

_____. "Colony–Joy Division." Https://songmeanings.com/songs/view/59126/ Accessed 16 April 2022.

_____. "Day of the Lords–Joy Division." Https://songmeanings.com/songs/view/59693/ Accessed 16 April 2022.

_____. "Heart and Soul–Joy Division." Https://songmeanings.com/songs/view/59127/ Accessed 16 April 2022.

Songsterr.com. "Joy Division–'Colony' Tab." Https://www.songsterr.com/a/wsa/joy-division-colony-tab-s39996t0 Accessed 16 April 2022.

Sumner, Bernard. "In Conversation." Kevin Cummins, *Joy Division * Juvenes *.* 2007. Revised and Expanded Edition. London: Cassell, 2021. 26-29.

Surname Viet, Given Name Nam. Feature-Length Experimental Documentary Film. Directed by Trinh T. Minh-ha, 1989.

Taylor, Steve. *Melody Maker*, original publication date not indicated. As Excerpted and Republished in Mark Johnson, *An Ideal for Living: An History of Joy Division*. 1984. London: Bobcat Books, 1986, 36.

Tharoor, Shashi. As quoted in Sathnam Sanghera, *Empireland: How Imperialism Has Shaped Modern Britain*. New York: Viking/Penguin Random House, 2021, 124.

Thomas, Dylan. "Do Not Go Gently into that Good Night." 1947, 1951. *The Poems of Dylan Thomas*. John Goodby, ed. New York: New Directions, 1971.

Thompson, Dave. *A Legacy in Wax: Listening to Joy Division and New Order, 1976-2017*. 2005. Revised and Expanded Edition. Morrisville, NC: Lulu.com, 2017.

Tolle, Eckhardt. "Eckhart on the Dark Night of the Soul." Https://eckharttolle.com/eckhart-on-the-dark-night-of-the-soul/ Accessed 16 April 2022.

Trinh, T. Minh-ha. *Framer Framed: Film Scripts and Interviews*. New York: Routledge, 1992.

_____. Interview with Ute Metta Bauer, California Collage of the Arts Wattis Center for the Contemporary Arts, San Fransisco, November 2019. Cited by Patrick J. Reed, "The Enduring Power of Trinh T. Minh-ha's Anti-Ethnography." *ArtReview*. 19 October 2020. Https://artreview.com/the-enduring-power-of-trinh-t-minh-ha-films/ Accessed 16 April 2022.

_____. "Not You/Like You: Post-Colonial Women and the Interlocking Questions of Identity and Difference." *Inscriptions*. Vol. 3-4, 1988. Https://culturalstudies.ucsc.edu/inscriptions/volume-34/trinh-t-minh-ha/ Accessed 16 April 2022.

_____. *Woman, Nation, Other: Writing, Postcoloniality, and Feminism*. Bloomington: Indiana University Press, 1989.

Trinh, T. Minh-ha and Erika Balsom. "'There is No Such Thing as Documentary': An Interview with Trinh T. Minh-ha." *Frieze*. 1 November 2018. Https://www.frieze.com/article/there-no-such-thing-documentary-interview-trinh-t-minh-ha Accessed 16 April 2022.

Trinh, T. Minh-ha and Judith Mayne. "From a Hybrid Place [Interview with Trinh T. Minh-ha]." *Framer Framed: Film Scripts and Interviews*. New York: Routledge, 1992, 137-150.

Trinh, T. Minh-ha and Lucie Kim-Chi Mercier. "Interview: Forgetting Vietnam." *Radical Philosophy* No. 203, December 2018. Https://www.radicalphilosophy.com/article/forgetting-vietnam Accessed 16 April 2022.

Trinh, T. Minh-ha and Pratibha Parmar. "WOMAN, NATIVE, OTHER: Pratibha Parmar Interviews Trinh T. Minh-ha." *Feminist Review*. No. 36, Autumn 1990. Https://www.jstor.org/stable/1395110 Accessed 16 April 2022.

True Faith. Art Exhibition, Manchester Art Gallery and the Manchester International Festival. Manchester, England, UK. *30 June-3 September 2017*.

UltimateGuitar.com. "'Day of the Lords' Official by Joy Division." Https://tabs.ultimate-guitar.com/tab/joy-division/day-of-the-lords-official-2022057 Accessed 16 April 2022.

Vermeulen, Pieter. *Geoffrey Hartman: Romanticism after the Holocaust*. London: Continuum, 2010.

Ward, Fearghal and Adrian Duncan, directors. "Joy Division–'Day of the Lords'–Official Reimagined Video." *Joy Division Unknown Pleasures Re-Imagined Series*. Https://www.youtube.com/watch?v=l4npQSb7dDk Accessed 16 April 2022.

Weissman, Gary. *Fantasies of Witnessing: Postwar Efforts to Experience the Holocaust*. Ithaca: Cornell University Press, 2004.

Women Make Movies. "Synopsis: *Surname Viet, Given Name Nam*." Https://www.wmm.com/catalog/film/surname-viet-given-name-nam/ Accessed 16 April 2022.

York, Alan. "Best Joy Division Songs: 20 Unknown Pleasures You Need To Hear." *Dig!* 25 November 2020. Https://www.thisisdig.com/feature/best-joy-division-songs/ Accessed 16 April 2022.

YouGov. July 2014 Poll. As cited in Sathnam Sanghera, *Empireland: How Imperialism Has Shaped Modern Britain*. New York: Viking/Penguin Random House, 2021, 186.

_____. January 2016 Poll. As quoted in Sathnam Sanghera, *Empireland: How Imperialism Has Shaped Modern Britain*. New York: Viking/Penguin Random House, 2021, 186.

_____. March 2020 Poll. As quoted in Sathnam Sanghera, *Empireland: How Imperialism Has Shaped Modern Britain*. New York: Viking/Penguin Random House, 2021, 186.

Chapter Six

One

Following this introductory section, I proceed in section two of this sixth, and next to last, chapter to provide a thorough explication of Robert McRuer's principal positions, concepts, and arguments in *Crip Theory: Cultural Signs of Queerness and Disability* (2006) and *Crip Times: Disability, Globalization, and Resistance* (2018) along with some extended, and especially 'personal', connections with McRuer's ideas. In section three I do the same with Ann Cvetkovich's *Depression: a Public Feeling* (2012). And in section four I do the same with Avery Gordon's *Ghostly Matters: Haunting and the Sociological Imagination* (1997, 2008). In section five I draw out what will serve as points of contact and bases for staging encounters and pursuing dialogues, in sections six through nine, between McRuer, Cvetkovich, and Gordon, on the one hand, and Ian Curtis and Joy Division, on the other hand. In section six I proceed with description, analysis, and interpretation of Ian Curtis's and Joy Division's song "She's Lost Control," including by way of encounter and dialogue with the key ideas from McRuer, Cvetkovich, and Gordon I have discussed in sections two through four and precisely pinpointed in section five. I then do the same in section seven with Ian Curtis's and Joy Division's song "Dead Souls"; in section eight with Ian Curtis's and Joy Division's song "Atmosphere"; and in section nine with Ian Curtis's and Joy Division's song "Decades."

Two

In his foreword to Robert McRuer's book *Crip Theory: Cultural Signs of Queerness and Disability*, published in 2006, Michael Bérubé aptly identities McRuer's critical approach as "conjunctural analysis" (ix). McRuer concentrates, in other words, on critical readings of signs and texts as well as situations and events in terms of their implications at the historically specific times (and often also the geographically specific places) in which they are most immediately meaningful and impactful. Conjunctural analysis requires working from a constantly moving critical margin so as to be nimbly responsive to continuous and often rapid changes in object and focus of critical attention. Not only do the precise constituents of particular conjunctures often and rapidly change, but also new conjunctures just as frequently and quickly emerge to replace and displace preexisting conjunctures as those sites that demand the most urgent critical intervention. Accordingly, I will supplement consideration of McRuer's *Crip Theory: Cultural Signs of Queerness and Disability* with McRuer's more recent *Crip Times: Disability, Globalization, and Resistance*, published in 2018.

Robert McRuer, like Michel Foucault in *Discipline and Punish: The Birth of the Prison* and Roy Richard Grinker in *Nobody's Normal: How Culture Created the Stigma of Mental Illness*, is often focused, especially in *Crip Theory*, on critiquing tendencies toward chasing or even racing after inclusion within 'the normal' by members of social groups long subject to oppressive exclusion and denigration as 'abnormal', 'not normal', and 'other than normal'. This chasing or racing after inclusion within 'the normal' often involves distancing from other members of the same social groups who continue to be marked off as 'other than normal', and therefore continue subject to exclusion and denigration, even as 'the normal' expands, 'flexibly', to include, for instance, 'acceptably' 'good gays' ('model gays') and 'acceptably' 'good disabled people' ('model disabled people'). What happens, however, as a result, of this chasing–and racing–after the normal is the problems and limitations concerning how the normal is itself formed and constituted are not (or are no longer) challenged. These include structural and indeed systemic inequities and injustices that define the normal and upon which the normal depends in order to exist and persist. In addition, alternative modes of social existence, and indeed alternative modes of individual being, that members of these historically oppressed groups have fashioned, from positions at the margins of the social and cultural 'center' or 'mainstream', are effectively jettisoned, including those representing the potential for overcoming the problems and limitations, and especially the inequities and injustices, intrinsic to the 'normal'.

For instance, McRuer is critical of divisions arising between 'the good Gay' and 'the bad Queer', in conjunction with the push for legal same-sex marriage, insofar as these unwittingly fall back on "the logic of the poster child," failing to register how this same logic has long been used to divide disabled people between 'the good disabled'–i.e., the ostensibly 'innocent' as well as ostensibly 'attractively appealing' and even ostensibly 'exceptionally deserving' disabled–versus all the rest of 'the bad disabled', who are effectively rendered, in contrast, guilty, unattractive, unappealing, and undeserving (82). McRuer questions whether gay advocacy of inclusion within 'the normal' as represented by focusing on obtaining legal same-sex marriage is predicated upon fear of the normal and, more precisely, fear of stigmatization as abnormal, not normal, and other than normal (82). McRuer argues that unquestioning acceptance of the desirability of legal marriage misses important opportunities for queer people to 'denaturalize' marriage as what is supposedly necessary to maintain and sustain 'proper' forms of family and domesticity (83). McRuer concedes legalized same sex marriage allows gays and lesbians some room to change what marriage means from within this institution but he nonetheless worries about the trend toward emphasizing the pursuit and obtainment of legal marriage as a priority focus of queer concern because "we have already proliferated multiple queer alternatives to straight ways of relating" (82).

Sharon Kowalski and Karen Thompson lived together as lovers and partners in a largely private, closeted, yet very much spousal-equivalent existence prior to Kowalski, in 1983, suffering seriously disabling injuries in a car accident, which led to a long and difficult struggle between Thompson and Kowalski's biological family over who should be granted the right to be her legal guardian, with Thompson ultimately winning, in 1991, after many setbacks and indeed many defeats in this effort. McRuer interprets this famous case as illustrating not only how disabled people (in this instance, Sharon Kowalski) are often thought not to maintain a sexuality, but also, in relation to the question of legal marriage, a significant double bind. On the one hand Kowalski's and Thompson's relationship was effectively discarded, devalued, and ignored because it was not (it could not have been) a legal marriage, yet on the other hand the couple's success in fighting back depended upon resisting traditional notions of domesticity and marriage by uniting within, identifying as part of, and drawing solidaristic strength and support from a much larger queer–including queer and disabled–community. What Kowalski and Thompson eventually discover, as opposed to "a limited (and isolating) understanding of 'family'" that they initially sought to replicate, is "an alternative model of family that would position the couple as connected to–as, in many ways, dependent on for survival–other lesbians" (96). Where Kowalski and Thompson end up is exemplary of living in active embrace of 'interdependency' while also, as McRuer cites Eva Feder Kittay proposing, living in active embrace yet further of recognition that "interdependence begins with dependence" (quoted 101).

As Bérubé writes in his foreword to *Crip Theory*, McRuer's critique of 'the political unconscious of normalization' extends to "problematic rehabilitative logics" affecting a variety of disabilities including those resulting from AIDS, with HIV/AIDS indeed representing a particularly prominent site, in recent times, of intersectionality between queer and disabled [1]. In Chapter 3, "Noncompliance: The Transformation, Gary Fisher, and the Limits of Rehabilitation," McRuer addresses this intersection directly, problematizing normative conceptions and practices of 'rehabilitation', including the ostensible value of 'keeping people alive' under any and all conditions, as well as striving, first and last, always for 'recovery', in terms of what recovery is commonly understood to mean. As McRuer suggests, even good intentions in this direction do not prevent what in practice amounts to degradation (110). Citing Henri-Jacques Stiker in support of his argument here, McRuer is critical of how recovery proceeds on the basis of the "assumed prior normal state" (quoted 111). Stiker warns about making the disabled disappear as whom and what they have been, by rehabilitating them 'so they are no longer disabled', or so they are *seemingly* no longer disabled, and by simultaneously assimilating them into what McRuer theorizes as 'compulsory able-bodiedness' (112). McRuer is critical of social practices that aim to provide 'a place at the table' without transforming 'what kind of table this is', or, in Stiker's words, of "Society's wish to make identical *without making equal*" (quoted 113). Stiker, McRuer approvingly notes, is even more critical of how rehabilitative practices insure that "disability cannot be a confrontational position" (quoted 113). In other words, as McRuer explains, for those designated as 'patients', "Rehab demands compliance or–more properly–makes noncompliance unthinkable" (113). McRuer here also cites the work of David Serlin in recounting how disabled bodies were remade with a virtually exclusive emphasis on (re)enabling workforce productivity in the aftermath of World War II (114-115). McRuer, like Stiker and Serlin, is particularly concerned about the production, including the mass production, of "Identity as generic sameness," with everyone adjusted as far as possible so as to appear to resemble (or aspire to approximate) an able-bodied normative ideal (115).

McRuer uses a detailed analysis of the academy award-winning 1997 film *As Good As It Gets* to introduce his concept of 'heteronormative epiphanies'. These epiphanies involve straight subjects discovering ways to reaffirm heteronormativity by being tolerant and at least limitedly accepting of the other than entirely heteronormative (12-13). Such epiphanies occur as the straight subject works through a personal crisis by making use of their increasingly 'flexible' tolerance, acceptance, and interaction with other subjects whose embodied identities and experiences are different from theirs as a pivotal means of achieving such resolution (16). McRuer questions (1) what precisely is being tolerated, accepted, and included here, by whom and from what vantage point, in enabling what ends and serving what interests; (2) what at the same time is not (what continues not to be) tolerated, accepted, and included; and (3) at the expense of what and of whom is this tolerance, acceptance, and inclusion taking place.

At the beginning of his "Introduction" to *Crip Theory*, McRuer proposes that able-bodiedness even more than heterosexuality has tended, historically, to be invisible, treated as a nonidentity, as simply what is natural, and as such as beyond question and in no need of any critical consideration. As a result, McRuer contends, able-bodiedness exercises even more of a normalizing power than heterosexuality (1). Accordingly, McRuer announces a preeminent aim of *Crip Theory* is to problematize this normalization of able-bodiedness, while highlighting the effect of this kind of normalization in compelling virtually everyone to experience a strong compulsion to define and conduct themselves in relation to an ideal of able-bodiedness. McRuer theorizes "compulsory able-bodiedness" as "thoroughly interwoven with the system of compulsory heterosexuality that produces queerness," with both 'compulsories' contingent upon each other (2). At the same time, and this argument he pursues much further in *Crip Times*, McRuer argues "neoliberalism and the condition of postmodernity . . . increasingly need able-bodied, heterosexual subjects who are visible and spectacularly tolerant of queer/disabled existences" (2). This need for visible and indeed spectacular tolerance is a significant shift concerning *how* dominant ideology in postmodern, advanced capitalist, 'First World', 'Western' society, in 'the global North', privileges straightness over queerness and able-bodiedness over disability (2). In other words, the focus now turns towards coopting and containing as well diluting and destroying resistant, transgressive, and radically transformative potentials among 'the queer' and 'the crip', in significant part by dividing and separating those 'queers' whom are accepted, welcomed, and included 'within', or *close* to, the normal versus those whom are not.

McRuer observes that "Nearly everyone, it would seem, wants to be normal in the able-bodied sense," including many disabled people and many disabled communities. Indeed, it continues commonplace for many disabled people to express the desire–and to be representing as desiring–the opportunity to live their lives as close as possible to what lives are like for able-bodied people (to be able to 'lead a normal life' by 'doing all the things that able-bodied people ['normal people'] do' and to do so as close as possible to how able-bodied people ['normal people'] do so) (7). Yet, as Roy Richard Grinker does in *Nobody's Normal*, McRuer links this 'aspiration' toward able-bodied normalcy with the powerfully persistent and pervasive influence, albeit largely unrecognized, of a long-standing capitalist need for and valorization of 'productively able' bodies to perform wage labor (8).

According to McRuer, "Like compulsory heterosexuality . . . compulsory able-bodiedness functions by covering over, with the appearance of choice, a system in which there actually is no choice" (8). The reason why this is so is because "our culture" continues widely to assume "that we all agree: able-bodied identities, able-bodied perspectives are preferable and what we all, collectively, are aiming for," with the strong insinuation thereby logically following that disabled people would all 'in the end' rather not be disabled/rather be able-bodied (or at least *should* prefer this) (9). From a compulsory able-bodied perspective, disabled bodies do *not* represent different yet equally worthwhile modes of embodiment, modes that ultimately encompass a vast percentage of the overall population; disabled bodies do *not* attest to a larger societal need to provide substantive support so people representative of a plethora of different embodiments can thrive, and contribute; and disabled bodies do *not* attest to the need to fashion a society rooted in effectively responsive attendance toward universal dependency and interdependency.

In "Compulsory Able-Bodiedness," his contribution to *50 Concepts for a Critical Phenomenology*, edited by Gail Weiss, Ann V. Murphy, and Gayle Salamon, and published in 2020, McRuer clarifies what he means with this concept. McRuer derives 'compulsory able-bodiedness from a reworking of Adrienne Rich's famous concept of "compulsory heterosexuality" that Rich introduced in "Compulsory Heterosexuality and Lesbian Existence," first published in 1980. As McRuer explains, Rich contends under patriarchy heterosexuality is naturalized such that it becomes "the unspoken norm," and, as such a norm, in turn marks off "a range of substantialized 'deviations'" (62). Yet, for Rich, "lesbian existence" does not operate solely as what has been marginalized and denigrated as 'deviant', but rather encompasses a broad continuum of diverse "forms of resistance to patriarchal imposition of compulsory heterosexuality" (62). According to McRuer, "able-bodiedness is in many ways even more naturalized and subsequently invisibilized and difficult to analyze in contemporary culture than heterosexuality" (62). Yet it is crucial to undertake this effort because compulsory able-bodiedness exercises hegemonic power. It does so even as "it is essentially founded on a logical contradiction–able-bodiedness is simultaneously assumed to be the supposed 'natural state' of any body *and yet* is a state that all of us are striving to attain or maintain" (62). *Naturalized as what is normal and desirable,* compulsory able-bodiedness both enacts and depends upon 'marginalization, stigmatization, and oppression of disability' (62). McRuer points out that by the end of the 19th century the *Oxford English Dictionary* defined normal explicitly in terms of physical and mental able-bodiedness. McRuer argues "industrial capitalism's need for able-bodied workers" played a pivotal role in 'helping sediment' "the unconscious association of able-bodiedness and normalcy" while neoliberal capitalism has updated and refined this association, "generally through a 'tolerance' or even contained 'celebration' of disabled or queer minorities that nonetheless sustains the subordination of disability and queerness to the desired states of heterosexuality and able-bodiedness" (62).

Yet McRuer's concept involves one significant step further and this depends on reworking Judith Butler's theory of "gender trouble," according to which Butler "famously argues that heterosexuality is constituted performatively through repeated, compulsory acts or citations" that result in the 'materialization' of "a dominant masculinity and femininity" and of "heterosexuality as the supposed foundation or origin of all gender identifications" (62-63). As Butler argues, this is essentially a false "*origin,*" only "established paradoxically, as the *outcome* of repeated acts," and this means in turn that the entire process struggles to mask an ineradicable instability as well as a constitutive deceptiveness. McRuer addresses what he conceives as "a lacuna in Butler's theory: the most successful heterosexual subject . . . compelled to repeat dominant gender identities, *is already an able-bodied subject* . . . just as the most successful able-bodied subject *is already a heterosexual subject,* free from 'deviance' or 'perversion' that might somehow manifest itself on the body" (63). In other words, "Queerness broadly conceived . . . is regularly understood or positioned in contemporary culture as always a bit disabled" while "Disability, likewise, is regularly perceived in contemporary culture as always a bit queer or perverse, as stereotypes of disabled people without or with an excess of sexuality make clear" (63).

850

In *Crip Theory* McRuer notes "If anything, the emphasis on identities that are constituted through repetitive performances is even more crucial to compulsory able-bodiedness" despite the fact that "the ideal able-bodied identity can never, once and for all, be achieved" (9). Just as versus the heterosexual norm, these repetitive performances persistently fail fully to match what is strived after, or only fleetingly achieve a close (re)semblance to this same impossible ideal (10). So Judith Butler's 'gender trouble' is, McRuer claims, matched by 'ability trouble'. The latter includes not only continuous striving after an ultimately impossible yet simultaneously disciplining and delimiting ideal, but also, on the contrary, those forms of embodiment that overtly break with, reject, resist, question, challenge, and critique this ideal as representing the apex of what must be desired and pursued (10). McRuer argues both compulsory heterosexuality and compulsory able-bodiedness "depend on a queer/disabled existence that can never quite be contained," and he further contends "able-bodied heterosexuality's hegemony is always in danger of collapse" (31). *Crip theory* explicitly works "to further the crisis, the inadequate resolutions that compulsory heterosexuality and able-bodiedness offer us" while resisting "delimiting the kinds of bodies and abilities that are acceptable or that will bring about change" (31). This effort requires the kind of concrete conjunctural analysis McRuer practices, moreover, while making use of Raymond Williams's influential theorization of dominant, residual, and emergent modes of production, "to think through the ways in which different forms of compulsory heterosexuality and compulsory able-bodiedness coexist and influence each other" (i.e., dominant, residual, and emergent forms of compulsory heterosexuality and of compulsory able-bodiedness) (n12 212).

Crip theory, according to McRuer, represents, in relation to disability, a parallel to what radical currents in early queer theory initially conceived and practiced as queer theory. Yet McRuer contends this latter conception and practice became steadily less prominent and influential with the burgeoning growth–and flattening spread–of academic queer studies. 'Queer' has lost its earlier association with radical praxis, McRuer suggests, as 'queer' has instead become predominantly used as an umbrella term for all varieties of other than strictly 'straight' kinds of gender and sexual identities–or as merely one among multiple such possibilities, especially as a loose identity marker for those who experience themselves as 'other than straight' but do not recognize or have not yet found a more precise marker to signify the 'difference from straight' with which they feel compelled to identify themselves.

McRuer critiques the original *Queer Eye for the Straight Guy* television show (2003-2007) as indicative of this trend in relation to the meaning of 'queer'. *Queer Eye for the Straight Guy* represents an exemplary instance of commercial commodification, conjoined with ideological dilution by means of reductive trivialization, of what 'queer' means. *Queer Eye for the Straight Guy* is further problematic because the show renders 'queer' and 'queers' as entirely non-threatening while at the same time doing so by suggesting queers and straights are essentially different and distinctly opposite kinds of people. In other words, McRuer interprets the show as proposing straights need fear no threat that permeable or fluid borders might exist between straight and queer, and that it is on these non-threatening terms that it 'finally' become possible for queer guys and straight guys comfortably to get along (174-175). McRuer critiques *Queer Eye for the Straight Guy* yet further because of how it "domesticates camp and other disruptive queer forces" (175), while faulting members of the 'queer cast' for repeatedly indulging in stereotypically denigrative dismissals of multiple forms of disability

(176). Counter to what the show's slogan contends, that 'things just keep getting better', McRuer proposes, for queers like him, *Queer Eye for the Straight Guy* shows the exact opposite (177).

McRuer argues cultural productions such as *Queer Eye for the Straight Guy* illustrate the workings of a 'hegemonic' mode of representation vis-a-vis erstwhile marginalized and oppressed social groups, as this is a mode of representation that "elicits consent to the dominant economic and political ideologies of a particular historical order" (192). In the past, photographs of disabled people predominantly catered to onlookers' need "to constantly reaffirm the difference between 'us' and 'them'," but this kind of affirmation is no longer what is needed today, in representations of either disabled or queer people, as by the end of the 20th century dominant ideology had evolved past requiring such a comforting representation of disabled and queer people as freaks. Instead, dominant ideology has shifted in response to a need for more flexible distinctions and relations between disabled and able-bodied, as well as between queer and straight (192-193). Today priority emphasis falls upon converting disabled and queer into tamely incorporated yet insidiously still 'lesser and unequal' variations upon able-bodied and straight. In opposition to these tendencies McRuer touts transgressive artists such as Bob Flanagan, notorious for performing overtly disturbing forms of sadomasochistic 'self-punishment' while often doing so from a wheelchair as one openly living with cystic fibrosis. McRuer praises Flanagan for continuing to emphasize "crip existence as atypical" and characterizes Flanagan's performances as reaching "for something beyond the current order" while embodying a disturbingly threatening form of virtual seduction of the viewer (194).

McRuer cautions that no such performance remains tranhistorically, transculturally transgressive; every performance is always susceptible to the prospect of eventually being coopted by and incorporated into what it previously resisted, opposed, and critiqued. That is why radical critique, whether by academics, artists, or activists, or by those who engage within, among, and across all three of these avenues, needs to continually shift as well–in terms of location, content, and form. And that is why it is important for me to discuss, as I will do shortly, McRuer's more recent *Crip Times*, because *As Good as It Gets*, *Queer Eye for the Straight Guy*, Gary Fisher, and Bob Flanagan no longer represent priority points of reference for where struggles over what disability and queerness can and should mean are pitched today, in the 2020s.

One concrete focus of McRuer's 'conjunctural analysis' in *Crip Theory* does strike me as continuing to raise relevant questions for and challenges to dominant practices to this day, and this is McRuer's focus in chapter 4, "Composing Queerness and Disability: The Corporate University and Alternative Corporealities." According to McRuer, "I contend that recentering our attention on the composing bodies in our classrooms can inaugurate and work to sustain a process of 'de-composition'–that is, a process that provides an ongoing critique of both the corporate models into which we, as students and teachers of composition, are interpellated and the concomitant disciplinary compulsion to produce only disembodied, efficient writers" (149). Instead of seeking and valuing 'order' in writing, McRuer declares "I argue for the desirability of loss of composure"–which involves prioritizing not only 'composing as process' but also valuing the messiness and complication that happens in process (149). McRuer critiques cultural norms that interpellate students and teachers into performances of 'composing' straightness and able-bodiedness, and that, as such, operate as if by design to significantly limit and exclude, especially the disabled.

McRuer identifies an exemplary instance of this kind of privileging in how "straight composition" concentrates "on a fetishized final product" (151). McRuer argues the finished product is allied with "the composed heterosexual or able-bodied self" while "the composing body, in contrast, is in some way inevitably queer/disabled" (156). Here McRuer links his argument with Eve Kosofsky Sedgwick's famous theorization of queerness as an "open mesh of possibilities, gaps, overlaps, dissonances and resonances, lapses and excesses of meaning when the constituent elements of anyone's gender, or anyone's sexuality aren't made (or *can't be* made) to signify monolithically" (quoted 156). McRuer adds to Sedwick by proposing that "Able-bodied identity, similarly, emerges from disparate features that are supposed to be organized into a seamless and univocal whole," yet are not, so "we might say disability refers to the open mesh of possibilities, gaps, overlaps, dissonances and resonances, lapses and excesses of meaning when the constituent elements of bodily, mental, or behavioral functioning aren't made (or *can't be* made) to signify monolithically" (156-157).

McRuer champions this kind of 'decomposition' class as benefitting *all* students because while we are not all always literally queer/disabled, "there are *moments* when we are all queer/disabled and that *those queer/disabled moments are desirable*" (157). McRuer identifies this desirability as involving a refocusing, in teaching and learning 'composition', back on the bodies doing the composing and on the process involved in composing. Also, "Desiring queerness/disability means not assuming in advance that the finished state is the one worth striving for" (159), but instead striving in line with what Donna Haraway identifies as "permanently partial identities" (quoted 159). McRuer describes his experience teaching this kind of composition class as one where students felt comfortable and encouraged to come out as disabled, where disabled students were able to position themselves as subjects in terms of their disability, and where able-bodied students were able to discover and identify with/on the basis of their own disabilities (161). McRuer identifies this curricular and pedagogical approach as aligned with "radical liberationist" traditions that place "an emphasis on difference and distinction" as opposed to "liberal reformist" traditions that emphasize "sameness" (163).

Despite what eventually happened at George Washington University, where McRuer teaches, as critical cultural studies approaches to teaching 'composition' were first marginalized and second replaced by a safer, mainstream, 'corporate, efficiency and product-oriented', as well as 'vocational preparation-oriented' model, McRuer finds the time spent in creating and pursuing critical cultural studies 'de-composition' classes that he and colleagues taught, overtly centering queerness and disability, of continuing value. McRuer cites Stuart Hall explaining how struggles over hegemony are always about shifting balances in and of power, never about 'pure victory or total domination'. This includes being prepared, as new opportunities arise, to draw upon what has been useful from past efforts while simultaneously devising new strategies and tactics. In relation to the teaching of college composition (first-year writing), McRuer proposes it continues to be important not to cede the right to determine what 'skills' must mean as part of a corporate model that emphasizes students learning and being able to apply 'skills'. In other words, McRuer advocates working subversively to problematize what the category 'skills' do, can, might, and should include (170). In sum, even as a short-term effort, this attempt at George Washington University 'to do composition differently' illustrates that queer theory and disability studies offer strategically useful resources from which to speak back against, and to contest, hegemonic exercise of power in areas where this prospect might not be immediately or readily apparent (170).

McRuer emphasizes activist examples of 'coming out crip' that overtly pressure limits and exclusions of otherwise liberal to progressive organizations and institutions. These include confrontational critiques of organizations and institutions for failing to anticipate the need to accommodate disabilities, and of what these disabilities might encompass, along with confrontational critiques directed at ostensibly well-meaning attempts to be helpful in ways that nonetheless continue always to 'reach down' and thereby maintain strict hierarchical divisions between helper and helped (48-49). McRuer insistently emphasizes 'crip' is not a solely academic development, that it is as much the product of the work of artists and activists as it is academics.

In precisely distinguishing crip praxis from non-crip disability praxis, it is useful to note well that McRuer contrasts a 'critically disabled' from a 'virtually disabled' position, proposing this distinction as a parallel to Judith Butler's contrast between a 'critically queer' and a 'virtually queer' position (with Michael Warner identifying 'virtually queer' as the unnamed other versus Butler's 'critically queer') (30). This means, for example, not pushing for tolerance simply by reiterating the common disability studies and disability activist contention that we will all become disabled if we live long enough, and that we all at least come close to being disabled at multiple points throughout our lives even before reaching old age. 'Crip', in contrast, as a *critically disabled* position, demands a fundamentally different kind of society and culture, not one that accommodates the disabled in relation to a still overwhelmingly pervasive and at least strongly implicitly superior/preferable/normative able-bodiedness (30). Versus the "truism" that "Sooner or later, if we live long enough (so we often say), we will all become disabled" (197), and thereby disabled will become an "identity that each of us will, at some point in our lives, inhabit" (198), McRuer emphasizes, without altogether discarding or denying this 'truism', that "sooner or later, if we live long enough, we will all become normate [making use of a key concept devised by Rosemarie Garland-Thompson]" (198). "Normate" refers to the body that is accepted as 'normal' and against which other types of bodies are defined as abnormal, not normal, or other than normal, and, more explicitly, as Joel Michael Reynolds indicates, in *50 Concepts for a Critical Phenomenology*, "the constructed identity of those who, by way of the bodily configurations and cultural capital they assume, can step into a position of authority and wield the power it grants them" (244).

As a concrete example of how McRuer conceives of crip theory as proceeding beyond 'non-crip disability theory', in line with McRuer's 'cultural materialist' approach toward critical theory, it is worth returning to McRuer's critique of the neoliberal valorization of 'flexibility' in labor, that McRuer aptly notes requires 'flexible subjects'. "The flexible subject is successful precisely because he or she can perform wholeness through each recurring crisis" and this includes being able to manifest the performance of successfully adapting to crisis, even performing as if crisis is not happening, has never happened, or is not and was not all that threatening or disturbing (17). Flexibility for workers means being expected to be able to cope with crisis on or in relation to the job as a matter of routine, and this can also involve being expected to be able to cope with insecurity and precarity, on the job and off. Neoliberalism has made use of this expectation that accepting and coping with perpetual crisis is unavoidably necessary, and even 'natural', in order to facilitate the transfer of enormous wealth from workers to capitalists, considerably increasing disparities in terms of who owns and controls how much social wealth (17). Yet McRuer recognizes flexibility can also be desirable for workers, for LGBTQIA+ people, and for disabled people, so the rise of flexible labor is "double-edged," which means it needs to be examined closely, carefully, and concretely to determine what in practice it means, to the benefit of whom, and at the expense of whom else *in a specific conjuncture* (18).

As a further illustration of such a concrete mode of analysis, McRuer discusses the able-bodied 'home' as representing an impossible ideal that has also, in practice, often been identified and resisted as stifling, notably for women, while noting further how disability and the disabled have virtually always been excluded from this ideal (91-92). Disability was long "firmly linked to ideas of pathology, loss, lack, and isolation and [as such] was opposed to the intimacy and security associated with (heterosexual and able-bodied) domestic space" (93). The place for the disabled, to the contrary, was in a separate and distinct kind of institution (an 'asylum') that ostensibly handled their 'care and treatment' while at the same time keeping disabled people warehoused away from contaminating the sacred space of the home. It is no surprise therefore that the Independent Living Movement and similar campaigns "have generally opposed, implicitly and explicitly, both institutionalization and dominant models of domesticity" (94). McRuer shares this critique and is likewise critical of how the home has been established under capitalism as a privileged location for the reproduction of labor power, and as a privileged locus in terms of how capitalism distinguishes the private versus the public. The home has functioned and continues to function as a key "site for the development of able-bodied identities, practices, and relations" (and not just for heterosexual identities, practices, and relations), that suit the interests and needs of capital (88-89). Even so, McRuer acknowledges a certain amount of positively valuable flexibility has arisen in terms of what kinds of homes, families, and domestic situations and spaces are by now widely acceptable and desirable, suggesting it may in part be possible to intervene critically *from within* 'the domestic' and *from within* 'the home' just as it might also be possible to do so *from within* 'the family' and *from within* 'marriage' (94). Yet McRuer, nonetheless, continues ultimately to lean strongly in favor of imagining and pursuing radical alternatives to home, domesticity, family, and marriage (94).

In sum, according to McRuer, key tenets of crip theory and practice include (1) "Claiming disability *and* a disability identity politics while nonetheless nurturing a necessary contestatory relationship to that identity politics"; (2) "Claiming the queer history of coming out–'out of the closets, into the streets'–while simultaneously talking back to the parent culture"; (3) "Demanding that . . . another world is possible, or that, put differently, an accessible world is possible" while understanding "access" both "very specifically and very broadly, locally and globally"; (4) "Insisting that . . . counterglobalization and other left movements" are failing to conceptualize the kind of other world is possible that needs to be imagined; and (5) Grasping that the movement must continue "beyond ramps," "to questions of how private or privatized versus public cultures of ability or disability are conceived, materialized, spatialized, and populated," highly unequally, among multiple, including multiple intersecting, lines of social identity (71-72).

McRuer cites Judith Butler, in *Bodies That Matter*, as an offering a most useful contribution toward defining what kind of direction crip theory and practice should follow: "It is important to resist that theoretical gesture of pathos in which exclusions are simply affirmed as sad necessities of signification. The task is to refigure this necessary 'outside' as a future horizon, one in which the violence of exclusion is perpetually in the process of being overcome" (quoted 155). Ultimately, crip theory must be alive to the challenge of 'conjuring' "spectres of disability" and in particular of "the disability to come" (5). McRuer urges attendance upon and toward 'the disability to come', by welcoming it, even desiring it (207). He concludes with what he identifies as "a crip promise that we will always comprehend disability otherwise and that we will, collectively, somehow access other worlds and other futures" (208).

McRuer declares "The main contention of *Crip Times: Disability, Globalization, and Resistance* is that the absolute centrality of disability to a now-global politics of austerity has rarely been theorized explicitly or comprehensively, even if large numbers of disabled activists and artists globally are recognizing and calling out the disproportionately negative impact of austerity on disabled people" (13). As McRuer acknowledges, austerity has frequently been referred to as 'crippling' and he accepts this as one dimension of what can be usefully signified by his phrase 'crip times', even as he places greater emphasis on 'cripping the times', in other words on crip modes of contesting, critiquing, fighting back against, and fighting for a world beyond 'crippling austerity' (13).

Austerity, as McRuer explains, is rooted in neoliberalism. Neoliberalism emphasizes "both the centrality of the unencumbered 'free' market and the state's complex role in vouchsafing that centrality" (14). Drawing upon Richard Seymour, McRuer explains, contrary to common misperception, "the neoliberal state is a big interventionist state" (quoted 14) because the neoliberal state intervenes 'in the market' to support the interests of capital, especially the interests of 'big capital'–large-scale monopolistic, oligopolistic, multinational, and transnational capital. Neoliberalism "was consolidated and slowly globalized through the state-driven privatization and deregulation of forces that would block the sacrosanct 'free flow' of capital. In the process, the state was indeed, in one very specific sense, downsized through profound cuts to public social services, but it has been, in some ways paradoxically, deeply interventionist states around the globe that have managed the downsizing" (14). Especially important to note well is "Neoliberalism institutes 'flexible' production, or 'just in time' production, that is often outsourced to locations with cheaper labor costs, usually in the Global South" (15).

At the same time, under neoliberalism "this efficiency of production has been coupled with an 'efficiency' of sorts, of consumption; in and through its flexibility and speed, as neoliberalism has congealed, it has relied on or produced 'new forms of niche consumerism' [with McRuer here alluding to the work of David Harvey], in constructing or hypostasizing target markets or identities–particular, defined groups to whom a streamlined 'just-in-time' production could cater" (15-16). Yet more precisely, "Niche consumerism is one of the ways in which individualism has been reinvented or repackaged for our times (consumption, in other words, has been hyper-individualized). The other dominant way in which individualism has been repackaged is more obviously punitive, as neoliberalism depends not only upon fetishized notions of consumer 'choice' but also upon related notions of 'personal responsibility'" (16). Indeed, "Rhetorics of personal responsibility, perhaps unsurprisingly, have been particularly pronounced in the United States, but they are increasingly central in other locations such as Britain" (16).

In an apt clarification of relations between the two, McRuer explains austerity "is in many ways neoliberalism intensified, even as the fantasy of consumer choice is positioned out of reach for more and more people" (16). Austerity is "characterized by a lowering of government spending, an increasing of labor hours for workers . . . cuts to benefits and social services, and–wherever possible–privatization of those social services" (16). Austerity is induced under the "pretext" of "managing crisis" with the effect of "ongoing (and indeed astronomical) upward redistribution of wealth" (18). Austerity budget cuts, cuts in state spending, especially in providing for social welfare, are "a class strategy, in that the vulnerable bear the brunt of the supposed 'crisis'," while the wealthy are protected from suffering any significant harm and even benefit in the process (103).

McRuer reports as a first-hand witness-participant at multiple sites of protest and resistance versus austerity, including in Spain, Mexico, Chile, and Greece. Yet his preeminent focus throughout *Crip Times* is austerity in the UK. In the UK, the implementation of austerity has severely impacted disabled people. In the Conservative-Liberal Democrat Coalition government's first year in power, 2010-2011, up to 1 in 10 disabled people in the UK ended up living in 'absolute poverty' while 300,000 more disabled people entered into 'absolute poverty' (47). In Britain, austerity has been amply supported and enabled by means of massive demagoguery surrounding ostensible 'benefit fraud' even as such fraud has been vastly exceeded in its cost to the Treasury by corporate tax evasion (48). The notorious 'bedroom tax' has especially punitively 'targeted' disabled Britons (52). The 'bedroom tax' is, more precisely, a benefit cut–a reduction in housing benefits in accord with how many bedrooms, or in other words how many ostensibly 'additional' or supposedly 'spare' rooms, a benefitting household maintains. This tax has ended up unduly penalizing households that include disabled people because disabled people often need additional space to accommodate their needs, and for caretakers to help in so doing. As McRuer reports, two-thirds of those impacted by the bedroom tax have been households that included a person with disabilities (150). Yet the bedroom tax is only one of the most notorious ways that austerity has exercised a devastating impact on a vast number of disabled people in the UK. Another especially egregious instance took place as many disabled people were among those displaced from their residences in constructing the facilities for the 2012 Olympic and Paralympic Games in London (154).

Austerity relies upon, and indeed exploits, "an 'ideology of disability'" that includes and in fact has "long vouchsafed flattened, nonthreatening representations of disability" (56). In other words, an "austerity of representation works to *foreclose* other crip possibilities" (56). To illustrate what he means by this contention, McRuer points out that "Disabled activists, artists, and scholars have long critiqued the ways in which 'inspirational' imagery or messages attach to disabled lives and experiences: as disabled individuals supposedly 'overcome' what has long been put forward as the 'struggle' or 'hardship' of disability, they 'inspire' nondisabled observers or readers, even by carrying out the quotidian activities of an ordinary life" (58). All too often this kind of representation of disability predominates over and obscures others. At the 2012 London Olympic and Paralympic Games this kind of representation of disability was "particularly pronounced" (58). Representing disability in this way, and largely exclusively in this way, proved "especially useful to the neoliberal establishment" (58)–in effectively effacing what neoliberalism was in fact doing, in particular the damage it was causing disabled people and disabled lives, while proposing, insidiously, that in contemporary (austerity neoliberal) British society all are included, and all can aspire toward and achieve success, with sufficient determination and in accord with sufficient exercise of personal responsibility.

McRuer identifies 'official' images of disability circulated by and in support of the 2012 London Olympic and Paralympic Games as quintessential examples of 'cripspiration'. McRuer cites, as one of the most prominent instances of this kind of 'neoliberal propaganda', a photo of paralympic athletes Oscar Pistorius and Ellie Challis with a complimentary quote by Scott Hamilton claiming that 'The only disability in life is a bad attitude' (60). This kind of rhetoric and imagery suggests it is up to disabled people to determine for themselves if and how, as well as how far, they will 'succeed' in life, with 'the good disabled' being those who 'assume personal responsibility' to pursue and achieve success through their own individual effort, whereas 'the bad disabled' are 'scroungers' or 'skivers' who expect 'others' (who expect state and society) to 'take care of them'. As McRuer observes, UK Prime Minister David Cameron at this same time overtly championed the supposed virtue "of overcoming the difficulties you've been handed," suggesting those 'who make the effort to do so' are those of superior moral character versus those who, at least supposedly, do not (quoted 67). McRuer is critical, in particular, of how this form of "Paralympics advertising offered spectacular disability identities but foreclosed or *obscured* what I would call . . . a crip or queer/crip horizon," and of how it was used as a "smokescreen" versus what neoliberalism was otherwise doing, including right thereby, in the immediate vicinity of the Games, directing "attention away from what was happening to disability communities, *not* in the fantastic reality of heaven, but on the ground" (65). McRuer contends this propaganda initiative well illustrates Stella Young's definition of 'inspiration porn': "it's there so non-disabled people can put their worries into perspective . . . It's there so that non-disabled people can look at us and think, 'well, it could be worse . . . I could be that person'" (quoted 66).

As McRuer proceeds further in his critical analysis of austerity and its impacts, he teases out another distinctive feature of 'post-Fordism' or neoliberalism versus earlier Fordist capitalism, by way of Naomi Klein and Kevin Floyd, and that is this form of capitalism no longer needs rely on stability and indeed thrives on instability, becoming, in Klein's terms, 'disaster capitalism' (75). Under neoliberalism "dispossession" becomes more important than "normalization or enforced uniformity" (76). In other words, "global capital has increasingly 'given up' on some earlier forms of normalization or enforced uniformity, installing in place of those forms of control an accelerated (and especially militarized) commitment to dispossession that does not always and everywhere require Fordist uniformity of behavior and identity" (76). What's more, "the architects of neoliberalism have strategically secured this new mode of regulation through a foreclosure or *containment of radical queer sociality and the identities that emerged from it*" (76). Elaborating further, McRuer explains that "What [Kevin] Floyd terms 'identity's glossy normalization' appears to value and integrate difference, but only by privatizing it, attempting to neutralize in the process the more radical forms of collective solidarity that produced some identities or identifications as resistant to isolation and pathologization in the first place" (77). For example, "Neoliberalism thereby takes possession of gay identity (not least by encouraging those with that identity to realize themselves *through* increasing their personal possessions) and forecloses upon the radical potentiality that gay identity at times signaled and signals" (77). According to McRuer, what neoliberalism cannot coopt and contain, and cannot individualize and privatize, it "relocates, displaces, dispossesses, or disappears" with for example traditional "queer communities or collectivities" in many places "being dispossessed and displaced, gentrified out of existence" (78).

McRuer traces the insidious impacts of neoliberalism to its initial emergence in Britain as Thatcherism, noting it was during the time when Margaret Thatcher served as UK Prime Minister, from 1979 through 1990, that major tenets of not only neoliberal political economy but also of neoliberal ideology became entrenched. Since Thatcher's time, for example, "Aspiration has basically been codified" as an "individualist, libertarian concept around personal achievement and merit" (176). McRuer's analysis reveals the rhetoric of Thatcherism as highly ableist, depending a great deal on championing the 'able-bodied', even as McRuer notes this dimension of Thatcherist rhetoric has not previously elicited much critical attention (176). McRuer cites ample evidence directly from Thatcher's own speeches and writings (179), while emphasizing that Thatcher's advocacy of a 'meritocratic creed' is exemplary of how neoliberalism displaces social democratic welfare state emphasis on achieving 'equality of outcome' with emphasis instead on providing 'equality of opportunity'. Instead of assuming a collective responsibility to take care of each other, and to insure that people's needs are met and their well-being is secured, what we have instead, with neoliberalism, is a supposed 'equal opportunity' for people to take care of themselves, of their own needs and of their own well-being, through their own individual initiative, effort, and merit. Even on its own terms, however, this ideal of 'equality of opportunity' is insidious because British people in fact do not all start out with and are not all subsequently able to access and exercise the same resources, powers, and capacities (186-187). Thatcher's valorization of 'striving'–and of 'strivers'–is, what's more, intimately interconnected with her concomitant valorization of strength, and of 'the strong'; for Thatcher and Thatcherism this serves as a key "structuring, able-bodied metaphor" (188).

Indeed, "Metaphors praising able-bodiedness are ubiquitous in contemporary culture and, once you know how to look for them, they are easy to detect" (190). What's more, disability "routinely functions in our cultural narratives to explain something bad" as well as to contribute yet further toward enhancing "able-bodied supremacy and disabled oppression" (191). Yet, as McRuer explains, "Compulsory able-bodiedness, not disability, was one of the forces that allowed for the emergence of Thatcherism and that sustains austerity" (191). Thatcher repeatedly exalted qualities of "health, vigor, and clear-mindedness" while disparaging their opposites, in effect positioning "sick and disabled *figures* in the shadows" (192). Subsequent 'New Labour' (ascending to power during the years of first Tony Blair and then Gordon Brown serving as UK Prime Minister, lasting from 1997 through 2010) has been fully complicit with this ableist aspirational agenda. For example, Blair's culture secretary James Purnell is the person responsible for coining the phrase 'Aspiration Society' (193). Subsequent to New Labour, the same trend continues unabated, with McRuer pointing out the influence, on the British political Right, in relation to Brexit, of "The metaphorical invocation of an able-bodied muscular England defending itself against others" (222). In sum, McRuer contends, "Figurations of disability and contours of ableism have been structural components of neoliberalism and austerity politics from their inception" (194), and, in fact, "austerity and neoliberalism can *make no sense* without disability" (195). In particular, "Neoliberalism conjures up spectacularized identities [such as, for instance, of 'the good disabled' and 'the good gay'] to both dilute the potential critical force of various identities and (more important) to forestall the (antiausterity, antiracist, proimmigrant) alliances that might be generated through and across acknowledged differences" (227).

How can austerity be resisted and how is it being resisted? McRuer is strongly invested in exploring answers to these questions but he admits "*Resistance* has arguably had an uneven history of late in critical cultural theory" because notions of 'resistance'–of what counts as resistance–can be and have been amorphously extended such that it all too often seems resistance is everywhere, with too many working in critical cultural studies falling back on Foucault's famous assertion that 'wherever there is power there is resistance' as a virtual cliché, or even as a virtual mantra. It too often seems, within much of this work, that not only is resistance easy to manifest but also that manifestation readily translates, in and of itself, into effectivity (94). As McRuer comments, "Spotting difference and resistance suggests that there is nothing left to do once it is found; it can, essentially, only be admired. Foucault, himself, however, consistently turned away from the fantasy of simply spotting or naming that which was supposedly or inherently good (and, of course, thereby liberatory) or bad" (97). As a starting point, in avoiding this kind of problematic celebration of the supposed ready pervasiveness and pervasive effectiveness of resistance, McRuer argues, citing the work of Nirmala Erevelles in so doing, in favor of emphasizing *collective* resistance while simultaneously prioritizing resistance in support of 'transformation' over resistance in support of 'transgression' (98).

In line with this wariness, McRuer shares a common critique of the supposed 'supercrip', who is able 'to achieve great things' *'despite* their disability' because not only is this notion of 'the supercrip' typical of problematically 'ableist' 'overcoming' narratives that represent disability an a state of adversity over which one *must* 'triumph'," but also because 'the supercrip' is one who does this by means, typically, of what they are able to bring to bear, on their own, as exceptional individuals rather than as members of mutually supportive and enabling 'crip communities' (20-21). McRuer much prefers the counter-campaign, mounted in response to the austerity neoliberal propagandist image of Oscar Pistorius and Ellie Challis at the time of the 2012 London Olympic and Paralympic Games, with its complimentary quote by Scott Hamilton claiming that 'The only disability in life is a bad attitude', when many diversely disabled people created and publicly shared their own contesting images of "This is what disability looks like" together with slogans that critiqued and challenged the sentiments expressed by Hamilton. Nevertheless, even though McRuer finds this counter-campaign was useful at the time and place it emerged, at that specific conjuncture, he once more cautions that, longer term, nothing is "not *appropriable* about" what those participating in this counter-campaign set forth (89). In other words, this counter-campaign exerted a useful critical impact at the specific time and place in which it was launched and circulated but that does not mean it continues to do since and that it can do the same if merely repeated in another conjuncture.

What McRuer emphasizes most strongly, in referring to the 2012 London Olympic and Paralympic Games, is that "Activists looked toward a crip horizon, toward a world where disabled lives would be genuinely valued rather than tossed away and when the debilitating logic of privatization concentrating wealth in the hand of a few . . . would be unthinkable" but that "crip horizon was foreclosed in August 2012 by an austerity of representation: the global circulation of inspiration porn or cripspiration," as the austerity neoliberal propagandist representation of disability circulated much more widely and thereby exercised a much greater impact, overall, than the 'This is what disability looks like' counter-campaign (68).

Yet McRuer continues to argue in favor of crip resistance "appropriating, inhabiting, theatricalizing, and resignifying the very terms of extravagant abjection used to disqualify," and that specific practices of so doing at specific times and places reveal the impact crip resistance can and does exert (125). In traveling to multiple different countries as a witness-participant at diverse protests against austerity, "I was compelled by the ways in which bodies and bodily imagery emphasizing precarity were being used to send messages of outrage and resistance. Unruly bodies occupying public spaces, bodies–as it were–out of bounds, were challenging the guardians of capital and short-circuiting the official consensus that those guardians urgently needed to forge about the 'necessity' or inevitability of drastic austerity measures" (8). As McRuer elaborates, "Austerity arguably generates extravagant abjection, literally wounding bodies and minds and then metaphorically redoubling that woundedness by pointing to the faded scars and insisting that they *merit* austerity as they have no value and supposedly generate no value. Crip/queer theorizing of *resistance*, I have implied here, is itself a crip tactic that opposes both such austere ways of thinking and austerity as an economic policy" (101). In other words, crip resistance refuses to acquiesce with the pretense, promoted by champions of austerity, that brokenness, wounds, and scars are fading, have faded, and have exercised little to no lasting degree of damaging impact by throwing these back 'in the face' of those who attempt to 'write them off'.

McRuer identifies a 'crip camp' as representing not so much a distinct "physical reality" but rather "a more contingent and ongoing practice of resistance or freedom, to be erected wherever and however necessary" (104-105), and as what takes place in what McRuer cites Petra Kuppers identifying as 'unhinged time' (quoted 104). A 'crip camp' in other words is a temporary and mobile mode of crip resistance that strives to make a meaningful impact within a specific conjuncture. In chapter four of *Crip Times*, "Crip Figures: Disability, Austerity, and Aspiration," McRuer devotes considerable attention to one such instance of what qualifies, in McRuer's terms, as 'a crip camp', artist's Liz Crow 2015 public performance piece *Figures*, ultimately comprised of 650 figures Crow sculpted from river mud representing various kinds of people harmed by austerity, with each figure accompanied by an individual story detailing this harm. McRuer notes that Crow is herself a disabled artist and she in the past spent "one hour on the fourth plinth," at London's Trafalgar Square, in 2009, "wearing full Nazi regalia in her wheelchair" to call attention to Aktion T-4, the infamous Nazi program that involved killing hundreds of thousands of disabled people and that set the stage as well as prepared the way for the greater Holocaust to come (203). McRuer touts *Figures* because it likewise "makes clear that public art can indeed work to bear witness to the experiences of 'the most disadvantaged'" (213). *Figures* usefully provokes critical attention concerning how "Disabled people, under austerity, have been rhetorically figured by the establishment media and politicians across the political spectrum as excess, waste, rubbish, or debris that needs to be cleaned up or moved away; through this rhetorical figuration, they have been essentially positioned and treated as 'drifted accumulation'" (181). Yet McRuer also cautions that public art is by no means essentially aligned with any political vantage point, and indeed can serve diametrically opposing interests, especially in the form of "*monumental* public art," "in the stupefying and awe-inspiring sense" of what this typically involves, and in particular when this same public art is endorsed and championed by an elite social and political establishment (215).

Crow's public art sides with what Marxist philosopher Alain Badiou, as McRuer indicates, refers to as "the *inexistent* of the world," those who "are present in the world but absent from its meanings and decisions" (quoted 113). Another concrete example of the same comes by way of McRuer's discussion of protests against austerity and even more specifically against gentrification that McRuer again directly witnessed, and supported, in Mexico City. McRuer notes well at the same time as the Conservative-Liberal Democrat Coalition government was aggressively imposing and implementing austerity in Britain, it was representing itself in Mexico as progressively inclusive, including, notably, in relation to disabled people. The British government's position in so doing so, in claiming to be doing the opposite of what it fact was doing, McRuer argues, coincided with how Mexican governments, at multiple levels, attempted to represent a gentrified Mexico City center as likewise progressively inclusive, in particular for disabled people, even after a great many poor and working class people, including a great many *disabled* poor and working class people, were displaced in order to enable this gentrification. Superficial improvements in 'accommodation' for those disabled people who can afford life in the gentrified city centre garner support from liberal reformists but do so by 'directing attention away' "from class struggle and class analysis" (132-133). Gentrification, moreover, often incorporates a semblance of paying respect to history and tradition, but in doing so gentrification "preserves the past for those who can afford to buy a piece of it" (143).

In Mexico City, as elsewhere, McRuer finds value in protests that raise key questions in relation to officially dominant representations of a city or of comparable kind of community: 'who is missing', 'where did they go', "whose space is expropriated by whom," and "who might be prohibited from occupying the space" (157). In relation to disability in particular, these kinds of protests help show how "Contemporary states regularly put forward the 'image of the nation as a whole, nondisabled body whose health must be protected from external pollutants . . . including those with disabilities and diseases" (quoting Julie Avril Minich 159), even as "*certain* disabled bodies can actually be flexibly included" (159). 'Cripping' gentrification, McRuer argues, "entails reading beyond the cultural signs of disability we think we know and recognizing displacement and dispossession in the shadow of incorporation" (174). As McRuer explains the difference, "In contrast to incorporation, which is about targeting–even spotlighting–certain individuals or groups for recognition, displacement is always implicated in an inability or even a willed refusal to recognize" (156). 'Cripping' gentrification, what's more, must also, McRuer contends, recognize that "displacements are always crip displacements" because displacement means "unruly bodies are moved elsewhere, evicted, relocated" and in so doing displacement "not only ensnares already disabled bodies or minds, but inescapably produces *more* disability and illness" (174).

Early on in *Crip Times* McRuer proposes that "'Crip times' . . . are obviously harsh times" but also times of "promise and possibility," especially for rethinking subjectivity and reconceiving connections among subjectivities that have been and continue to be marginalized, displaced, and dispossessed (29). Throughout *Crip Times* McRuer places considerable emphasis on conceiving of 'crip times' as times that help foster 'crip collectivities', notably crip collectivities in resistance to austerity and committed to the conviction that 'another (much better) world is possible' (30). McRuer argues these kinds of collectivities are emerging and growing, as is "A crip affective politics" that involves "forms of excessive and flamboyant, activist and artistic, crip resistance" (31).

'Crip times and places' reworks Jack Halberstam's 'queer times and places', and like the latter involves "strange temporalities, imaginative life schedules, and eccentric economic practices" (quoted 5). Also akin to Halberstam, McRuer is interested in "finding *and* describing" (5) "the alternatives to capitalism that already exist and are presently under construction" (quoted 5). He is particularly interested, moreover, in what Sharon L. Snyder and David T. Mitchell identify as "cultural locations of disability"–"locations which represent a saturation point of content about disability" (quoted 6).

For McRuer, "*cripping* means radically revisioning" (22). Even more precisely, "'To crip', like 'to queer', gets at processes that unsettle, or processes that make strange or twisted," while *"Cripping* also exposes the ways in which able-bodiedness and able-mindedness get naturalized and the ways that bodies, minds, and impairments that should be at the absolute center of a space of issue or discussion get purged from that space or issue or discussion" (23). McRuer is insistent that "*Cripping* always attends to the materiality or embodiment at the same time that it attends to how spaces, issues, or discussions get 'straightened'. The critical act of cripping, I argue, resists 'straightening' in a rather more expansive sense than we might think of straightening, at the moment, in queer studies, activism, or art" (24).

McRuer cites Lisa Duggan's argument that a 'new homonormativity' along with a concomitant 'homonationalism' has become prominent over the course of the early 21st century, notably in countries like the US and the UK. This development is indicative, for McRuer, of how neoliberalism has more successfully disarmed, coopted, and contained erstwhile queer resistance than it yet has crip resistance (38-39). In a later endnote McRuer cites Dick Hebdige in identifying "two forms of incorporation that threaten to contain resistant subcultures: a commodity form . . . and an ideological form" (n1, 242), and as McRuer argues in *Crip Times* as he did earlier in *Crip Theory* erstwhile resistant queer subcultures have suffered both of these forms of containment. In relation to this containment and the supplanting of resistant queer subculture by homonormativity and homonationalism, McRuer contends it is useful to recall that anti- or post- identitarian critical theories have long been motivated by critical opposition to how emphasis on identity tends to divide those who are judged as fitting within an identity versus those who are not, those who are acceptable versus those who are not, those who are 'good' versus those who are 'bad', those who are intelligibly recognizable within this category versus those who are not, and especially those who are assimilable versus those who are not (46). McRuer is likewise opposed to identitarian tendencies to continually obsess over questions of 'positive versus negative representation' with what is conceived and defined as positive versus negative always an ultimately highly limited and problematic focus for critical praxis (46). The same kinds of issues arise, McRuer argues, in organizing strictly around struggles for 'rights', where rights for a specific identity group can all too easily be "cordoned off" from attention to structural and systemic problems. Nevertheless, McRuer is willing to support focuses around identity and struggles for rights in strategically partial and critically reflexive ways. Key here, as McRuer explains, is to recognize "identity itself is of course neither necessarily or automatically radical. Identity is, however, at this point both useful for and in many ways necessary to those continuing to execute austerity and neoliberalism" (229).

In *Crip Times* McRuer is most strongly critical of forms of 'identity politics' "that in fact do not offer any political economic critique" (n11, 244). Throughout this book, even much more than in *Crip Theory*, McRuer illustrates how his is indeed a cultural *materialist* approach. For McRuer, cultural materialism recognizes the both constraining and enabling powers of the economic sphere of society but does not accept the economic as fully or finally determinative in, of, and by itself alone (n3, 245). This means it is necessary to pay critical attention to both economic and cultural considerations, and especially to how these are interlinked, for instance in terms of ongoing cutbacks, in nations such as the US and the UK, reducing support for, investment in, and provision of opportunities so that people can participate in and contribute to the arts and the humanities (n3, 245). At the same time, as with mobilizing politically on the basis of identity and in support of rights for those represented under the umbrella of a particular category of identity, McRuer accepts that gaining 'state recognition' of a group's concerns is and can be important, even if insufficient, noting this kind of recognition is often an inescapably necessary aim of political action for people with disabilities or impairments (n21, 247).

What such efforts fail to take on, however, is of ultimately greater interest to McRuer. McRuer is most interested in 'imagining' beyond what currently exists and is readily recognizable as immediately possible, inspired by "a *disabled* sociality that . . . has historically refused the very distinction between the social and the bodies engaged in *a range of intimate practices* that certainly can include sex . . . but that can also include other embodied ways of being-in-common" (93). McRuer cites José Esteban Muñoz theorizing queerness as a haunting phenomenon that is not yet here because 'we are not yet queer', with Muñoz further theorizing queerness as "a structured and educated mode of desiring," specifically of other possibilities, and, as such, "an ideality that can be distilled from the past to imagine a future" (quoted 147)." McRuer conceives of what he is doing as contributing toward theorizing a crip parallel to how Muñoz conceives of queerness. Indeed, McRuer stresses the crucial importance of attentiveness to profound 'yearnings' for something radically other than neoliberal austerity capitalist forms of social existence.

McRuer identifies himself as 'intellectually pessimistic' concerning how readily austerity might be countered, given the power maintained by those in charge of and who benefit from austerity (18). But *Crip Times* continually returns to exactly those kinds of 'countering' efforts. McRuer recommends wariness about overemphasizing the place of 'hope' within the crip politics he is advocating. Yet McRuer asserts that "pessimism need not be austere, and optimism of the will should always keep us pointed toward an inevitable excess, as well as toward the possibilities that excess affords for new connections and coalitions" (232).

A promising example of what is needed, McRuer contends, comes by way of "salvage-Marxism" as advocated by the journal *Salvage*. This form of Marxism "rigorously attends to the bleakness of contemporary neoliberal capitalism and a global austerity politics, to the immense and structural power held by those who benefit from and implement those systems, and to the lack of viable strategies on the Left for constructing real alternatives" (144). Yet it does so while seeking to find what can be usefully drawn forth in opposition, by 'salvaging from the rubble' of all this bleakness and destruction. In doing so, "Salvage-Marxism is actually contingent on projects such as queer theory, queer of color critique, or crip theory, even as many such projects remain more eccentric, eclectic, and compromised than most traditional Marxist projects would ever allow" (n6, 248). For McRuer, neither Marxism nor 'projects such as queer theory, queer of color critique, and crip theory' are sufficient without each other (n6, 248). Supporting this last claim McRuer again cites Muñoz as offering an exemplary indication of the value of "working on and against" (quoted n14, 244), as Muñoz "tries to transform a cultural logic from within," by drawing upon Michel Pecheux's distinction among positions of "identification, counteridentification, and disidentification" (n14, 244). It is notable in this connection that Pecheux's discourse theory synthesizes elements of Marxism, linguistics, and psychoanalysis. As McRuer interprets what Muñoz is proposing, this is a critical praxis that unites support for and involvement in "local or everyday struggle or resistance" with "laboring to enact permanent structural change" (n14, 244).

McRuer finds support for what a more orthodox Marxist likely would critique as problematic 'eclecticism' from Vladimir Lenin himself. McRuer notes well Lenin's critique of the notion of a 'pure revolution' and Lenin's concomitant argument that socialist revolution "cannot be anything other than an outburst of mass struggle on the part of *all and sundry oppressed and discontented elements*" (quoted 129 with McRuer adding italics). McRuer argues, following his interpretation of Lenin, for conceiving of "revolution alongside and beyond a traditionally mobilized working class, revolution somehow *expansively* composed of scroungers, scum, wounded bodies, and 'all and sundry discontented elements'" (129).

In conclusion, it is worth citing a notable contrast McRuer draws with Thatcherist conceptions of 'aspiration': "Our crip aspirations to totality . . . are always necessarily, inescapably, disabled: attend to those who are not you, to those who are different from you (different embodiments, different minds, different behaviors), and attempt in that interdependent attending to apprehend the web of social relations in which we are currently located–social relations that can (of course) be figured, and that can (of course) be changed" (217).

I have not taught Robert McRuer's *Crip Theory*, *Crip Times*, or any other work of his in the five classes I have taught focused on Ian Curtis, Joy Division, and critical theory–although I could readily imagine doing so, because McRuer's work offers the basis for a useful encounter, and dialogue, with 'Ian Curtis and Joy Division', one I will take up in sections six through nine of this chapter, in relation to the Joy Division songs "She's Lost Control," "Dead Souls," "Atmosphere," and "Decades." I have occasionally taught selections from McRuer's critical theoretical work in "Introduction to Theory and Criticism," and it is in light of doing so that I will now draw the first of three connections between *Crip Theory* and *Crip Times*, on the one hand, and matters of personal experience, interest, and concern, on the other hand.

When teaching McRuer's critical theoretical work in "Introduction to Theory and Criticism," I have taught it in relation to, and even as an instance, of 'Queer Studies'. I find McRuer's theorization of crip theory, crip practice, and crip praxis bears a useful comparison with what I have emphasized in teaching students about, and especially in introducing them to, queer theory and queer cultural studies. I identify Queer Studies as overlapping with, yet not identical to either gay-lesbian-bisexual-and-transgender studies or to critical studies in sexuality and gender. As I explain to students, Queer Studies is ultimately interested in "queerness," which includes potentially *all* ways of thinking, feeling, believing, acting, interacting, and behaving marked off as contrary to what is–or what seems or appears to be–"normative." *Normative* refers to conformity with standard social norms for thinking, feeling, believing, acting, interacting, and behaving–especially norms that have become deeply entrenched and widely pervasive, and which have acquired an idealized status.

"Queer" means that which seems or appears "strange" from the vantage point of the normative. It also means that which questions, challenges, critiques, rejects, ignores, opposes, resists, disrupts, subverts, or otherwise undermines the normative. Queer Studies recognizes what is considered normative changes over the course of human history and varies across human cultures and subcultures yet Queer Studies also continually finds that the normative (whatever this happens to be, at a particular place and time) is by no means as fixed and stable, or as natural and necessary, let alone as eternal and unalterable, as it would like to believe itself to be. In fact, according to queer theory, the normative is itself always overlapping and interconnected with what it attempts to distinguish from itself as "queer," while the normative is, moreover, itself quite strange when subjected to close and careful scrutiny from a critical vantage point.

Queer Studies concentrates on instances of normative versus queer that have been and continue to be oppressive–that form, in deconstructionist terms, 'violent hierarchies'. Queer Studies aligns itself directly with the queer position in this hierarchy, and attempts to overturn the hierarchy through a process very familiar to what the second reading in deconstructionist 'double reading' involves. The goal of the queer critique is not to invert the violent hierarchy, but rather to make it difficult to re-impose any kind of violent hierarchy. In place of violent hierarchies, Queer Studies advocates for norms that are relative, qualified, and limited, along with boundaries between normative and non-normative (or other-than-normative) that are permeable and fluid. Queer Studies opposes dividing people into rigidly defined categories of seemingly essentially different kinds, but rather conceives of people as existing and moving across various *continua*, where people are at least potentially much more like those whom they otherwise perceive as different than they often recognize to be the case. For example, I suggest to students, it is worthwhile, from a Queer Studies' vantage point, to consider the following continua: gay<->straight or heterosexual<->homosexual, homosocial<->homosexual and heterosocial<->heterosexual, healthy<->sick, able<->disabled, young<->old, etc. According to Queer Studies, people occupy positions across these *continua*, and they often do *move* among different positions across these continua, over the course of their lifetimes–even sometimes quite extensively within relatively quite short durations of time.

Queer Studies, in sum, has, from the beginning of its emergence, moved to focus beyond LGBT issues and concerns, especially in the areas of health and disease, mental and physical (dis)ability, and youth and age. Many other possible focuses are readily imaginable as well. But in terms of how Queer Studies has engaged with LGBT issues and with matters of sexuality and gender it is worth noting well, to begin with, that Queer Studies builds upon previous work within gay and lesbian studies, and within critical theory of sexuality and gender, to deconstruct, for example, the seeming 'naturalness' of heterosexuality, or, in other words, of heterosexual predominance ('heteronormativity' or, in McRuer's terms, 'compulsory heterosexuality'). In other words, heterosexuality is, in practice, not as thoroughly predominant as many routinely believe, and has not always been so, while the predominance that it does maintain is far from simply 'what comes naturally', but rather what has been rendered effectively 'compulsory' within many cultures, and subcultures, where homosexuality–along with homoeroticism and even substantial homosocial intimacy and affection–is and has been heavily proscribed, even rendered altogether taboo. According to Queer Studies, human sexual desire, and human sexual practice, is much more complex, multiform, and polyvalent than many people are wont to admit–and it is only due to oppressive social institutions that this is not more readily, even extensively, expressed in practice.

Along the same lines, Queer Studies suggests that sexual identities are socially and historically constructed, as opposed to biologically essential. This does not mean people individually 'choose' their sexual identities but rather they work within a range of possibilities that has been historically and socially defined; different ranges exist at different places and in different times. What sexuality means for us is shaped by the cultures and subcultures we inhabit, and by the positions we maintain within these cultures and subcultures. "Straight" and "gay" are mid-20th century Western inventions while "heterosexual" and "homosexual" are late 19th-century Western inventions; before these terms were developed and circulated, people made sense of sexualities in highly different ways. For example, it is only at the end of the 19th century, in the West, that the idea of sexuality as constituting a form of 'identity', as a property pertaining to a person's being, first emerged; before that, sexualities were widely regarded as no more and no less than practices, which any and all might or might not pursue–but which were not rooted in people's individual 'orientations'.

According to queer theorists like Judith Butler, neither gender nor 'sexual orientation' are innate, pre-social, essences, bur rather modes of cultural performance that most people participate within largely unconsciously. As we participate in these performances, and we as we recognize others doing so, these performances take on a semblance of naturalness. Yet repeated performances, even of dominant or familiar models, can and do diverge from these models, albeit to varying degrees. The fact that gender and sexual orientation must be repeatedly and continually performed, by active individuals as part of active relations with many other individuals, shows how ultimately unstable any single model turns out to be concerning what gender and sexual orientation supposedly 'should' be like. It is important, however, to recognize, even when consciously and deliberately attempting to challenge and critique (such as parody or satirize) a dominant mode of performance of gender, or of sexual orientation, that we cannot control the outcome involved in so doing. These challenging and critical performances can and will be made sense of in a wide variety of different ways, depending upon where their audience is coming from, and depending on what interpretive frameworks their audience brings to bear.

Queer readings of cultural texts often focus on ostensibly heterosexual practices and unveil a queerness within them. In short, the queer reading shows that the seeming straightness at work in the text is not as seamless and as unambiguous, not as consistent and coherent, and not as stable and unquestionable as at first appears to be the case. The queer reading may, at the same time, focus on showing how straightness is produced in the text by way of characters' work and effort involved in performing straightness–i.e., that their 'straightness' doesn't simply come naturally–and that it may be a quite difficult and even precarious challenge for some characters striving to manifest straightness. Queer readings also focus on ostensibly cisgender or gender binary kinds of identities, relations, and practices, and seek to unveil a queerness within these. And the same kind of queerly deconstructive engagement happens as well versus other normative kinds of identities, relations, and practices–including, in particular, hierarchies of what is, at least supposedly, normative versus what is, at least supposedly, non-normative or other-than-normative–where the aim is to show the normative is, in fact, far queerer than readily recognized or admitted, and that the boundaries between what is, supposedly normative versus what is supposedly queer are tenuous, diffuse, and unstable.

We can, if we follow queer theory, take "straight" even more broadly here than many commonly do, and extend its meaning to refer to more than merely 'heterosexual': 'straight' can refer to all kinds of attempts to show that one is in full conformity with what is normative, while 'queer' refers to all of the ways in which this is not an easy task or it does not fully succeed. *'Queering' the text involves showing the work and the struggle involved in the effort to conform with the normative, as well as the difficulties and problems involved in attempting to do so.* So any and every passage of, for instance, a novel or a film that shows a character [1] struggling to conform with what is normative, [2] not readily or easily fitting in with what is normative, and [3] finding herself or himself at odds with or different from what is normative, serves as an apt focus for a queer reading. Likewise, whenever characters question, challenge, criticize, reject, ignore, oppose, resist, disrupt, subvert, or otherwise undermine what is normative they also becomes principal focuses of concern for a queer reading. The aim of such a queer reading is, ultimately, to explore how the particular kind of normativities represented in the text (such as a novel or a film) affect people: how these normativities limit, frustrate, and constrain people, as well as what are the costs, along with what are the opportunities, of diverging from or opposing these normativities.

Queer Studies is thoroughly anti-essentializing. This means Queer Studies does not see gay, lesbian, bisexual, transgender, straight, or other kinds of similar identities as meaning the same thing at all places and in all times–and that means Queer Studies does *not* draw transhistorical or transcultural connections between people engaging in seemingly similar kinds of practices by suggesting they share a common identity. These seemingly similar kinds of practices are only, at best, seemingly similar, in many if not most cases, and, what's more, these practices mean very differently across time and space because people make sense of them using very different frameworks or lenses for interpretation of meaning.

Although Queer Studies is, as aforementioned, a wide-ranging field, a significant emphasis, at least early on, has been directed toward understanding, and combating, homophobia, which is often connected, by those engaged in Queer Studies, with homosexual panic. Because a particular society and/or culture has rendered homosexuality–and homosexual attraction and desire–an object of considerable denigration, people experience intense anxiety, indeed even a great deal of fear, concerning their experience of homosexual attraction and desire, and their participation in intimate homosocial, homoerotic, or homosexual relations. They may strike out violently against others because they feel a need to prove that they are not like those others (others known to be, or suspect as, 'homosexual'). At the same time, the fear of being perceived 'to be homosexual' has often proven socially useful, for dominant interests, in inclining people all the more readily to obediently conform to the roles prescribed for them–within the family, on the job, and elsewhere throughout society. Queer Studies, likewise from early on, has likewise sought to understand, and combat, biphobia and transphobia–which are not usually understood as rooted in exactly the same kinds of fears, anxieties, and social interests as homophobia, but nonetheless are likewise often explained as connected with fear and anxiety concerning (perceived) departures from and challenges to normative positions, roles, relations, and behaviors, as well as social interests dependent upon or benefitting from limiting–and policing–options in terms of gender and sexuality (as identity and as practice).

As an illustration of how I have explained what 'queer' means, and especially what *queering* can mean, I have repeatedly shared the following 'queer reading' of the 2012 film *The Perks of Being a Wallflower*, based upon an earlier 'cult' novel of the same title, which I watched while on a transatlantic flight in March of 2013 when I was too tired to read. As I was doing so, it struck me as a useful site of application and illustration for teaching Queer Studies in Introduction to Theory and Criticism. In this film the protagonist and his friends all experience themselves as 'misfits' in relation to what they perceive as the 'normative' 'center' of high school life. In this respect they perceive themselves as 'queer'. And in some ways they do appear to occupy the margins of what is 'central' within that high school, and community, environment. But at the same time, they form their own group that is highly mutually supportive and sustaining, and which reflects and responds to their interests and inclinations much better than would be the case if they were to participate extensively within other groups. They even conceive of their group as more hip than any other, and it seems like a number of people not part of this group perceive that group, and its members, in similar ways. What's more, they interact quite extensively with many people primarily aligned with other social groups, and often participate in social occasions where there is plenty of mixing among members of these ostensibly distinctly different kinds of social groups. In addition, although they deal with a number of 'heavy' coming of age problems, these hardly seem to be exclusive to members of this group. And, no matter how queer they may experience themselves as being versus what they perceive as normative in their high school, and in their community, they are all socio-economically and socio-politically relatively highly privileged. This is clearly an affluent suburban community, with the kids seemingly never needing to worry about money (and even about working for pay), as well as living in large houses with ample space and plenty of luxurious material possessions. They also enjoy a considerable amount of freedom over what they do with their time/they have lots of free time. And they are overwhelmingly white.

So, in sum, in some ways, and in some contexts, they occupy the margin versus the center–they are 'queer' versus 'the normative'–but in many other ways they occupy the center, the relatively dominant and the relatively privileged, or move readily back and forth between margin and center. What this ultimately shows us is that 'queerness' is not only multiply relative but also quite commonplace: it is common for many young people, growing up in even the relatively most socio-economically and socio-politically privileged of upper middle class and upper class suburban American environments, to experience considerable alienation from what they perceive, and what is variously communicated to them, as normative. Many kids, from even otherwise highly privileged environments, deal–at one time or another, or for one period of time or another–with isolation and loneliness, with abuse and addiction, with mental illness and with suicidality, with physical health problems and challenges, with not doing so well in classes or with doing so well that it makes one stick out uncomfortably, and with self-esteem issues and with difficulties finding and sustaining friends and intimate relationships. Most people can identify with what it means to feel like they are 'queer' versus what is 'normative'; the key here is to recognize that some kinds of people are generally conceived and treated as far 'queerer' than most others (traditionally, this has been the case with LGBT people), and to recognize as well that not everyone can or should lead their lives in conformity with dominant norms–that it is OK, and also socially useful and valuable, for many people to live their lives in ways that are 'queer' in relation to dominant standards.

I continue to define, explain, apply, and illustrate 'queer theory' and 'queer cultural studies' widely, including in making sense of relations between disability and able-bodiedness and including in critique of what McRuer theorizes as 'compulsory able-bodiedness'. I understand, respect, and to a significant extent share McRuer's position that in practice, queer theory and queer studies has not been able to maintain its initial 'radical edge', yet I at the same time continue to find it useful to reassert what queer theory and queer cultural studies was initially conceived to be about and what it can still encompass and take on that is not simply identical with LGBT theory and LGBT cultural studies or even with critical theory and critical cultural studies of sexuality and gender. However, I also understand, respect, and to a significant extent share McRuer's position that in light of queer theory's and queer cultural studies' tendency, in practice, overwhelmingly to emphasize matters of sexuality and gender it is important to distinguish queer theory and queer cultural studies from crip theory and crip cultural studies, which give priority emphasis to matters of disability–which, in other words, 'center' disabled subjects and subjectivities, perspectives and experiences, relations and practices, and communities and cultures, and which at the same time push disability studies toward a radical mode of critical praxis, especially as this emphasizes transformation over transgression, beyond where work in line with, for example, 'the social model of disability' or even 'disability as complex embodiment' leave off.

The second matter of personal experience, interest, and concern I find McRuer's *Crip Theory* and *Crip Times* compels me to engage is my PhD dissertation–*Cultural Studies, Queer Theory, Marxism*–as well as the book, based on this dissertation, that I had obtained a contract to write and eventually publish, but which I eventually determined I could not do. My PhD dissertation in sum offers a Marxist critique, in many ways a classic Western and even orthodox Marxist critique, of relations between queer theory and precursor forms of poststructuralist and postmodernist cultural studies. In this dissertation, and especially in the prospective subsequent book based upon the dissertation, I argue for the value, and even necessity, of developing a Marxist theory of 'queerness', as well as a Marxist form of 'queer praxis'. I do so largely by way of critiquing the problems and limitations, from a Marxist vantage point, of non-Marxist and post-Marxist forms of queer theory. I emphasize the need to make sense of 'queerness' in relation to the determinative impact of capitalism, and especially late 20th to early 21st century global capitalism, upon queerness–upon when and where as well as as how and why queerness emerges, along with how and why queerness develops, grows, and changes in the ways that it does. I emphasize the need to make sense in particular of queerness in relation to economic, and political economic, not just cultural, determinants, and propose to develop a Marxist mode of queer theory and praxis that is historically and dialectically materialist. I also emphasize the crucial importance of reorienting queer theory and praxis away from priority emphasis on cultivating, promoting, and proliferating 'dissidence within' capitalism toward priority emphasis in working toward revolutionary socialist transformation and supersession of capitalism.

The challenge I faced in turning my dissertation into a book had much to do with my dissatisfaction in equating development and elaboration of Marxist theory as thoroughly as the dissertation did with critiquing the problems and limitations of non- and post- Marxist queer theory. I was convinced I needed also to articulate a series of precise connections among distinctly Marxist concepts, and on the basis of where this articulation left off develop Marxist theory in relation to an arena of concern that Marxism had barely yet engaged–queerness. In doing so I needed to develop a more precise theory not only of 'late capitalism' but also, especially, of interrelations among 'late capitalist culture', 'the left', and 'the academy'. I needed as well to theorize, concretely, how it might be possible to move from where we were at, at this specific historical moment, toward building an international movement, capable of at least beginning effectively to advance the cause of revolutionary socialist transformation and supersession of capitalism. I needed, further, to theorize how and why this kind of transformation and supersession interests and especially benefits 'queers', broadly conceived. All the while I conceived it to be crucial to continue to track and take fully adequately into account continuing shifts and new developments in the rapidly burgeoning field of queer cultural studies.

This remains a worthwhile project, but it was impossible for me to carry out, and especially to carry through, while working as a tenure-track professor at a teaching-intensive and indeed institutional service-intensive institution like the University of Wisconsin-Eau Claire. I decided I needed to choose, and I chose to concentrate at making the best of, and from, my position as a professor of English at the University of Wisconsin-Eau Claire, not only because of how highly I do and long have valued teaching–and service, especially community service as civic engagement–but also because I simply had no other choice. I did not have any means to support myself in concentrating full-time over the course of several years running if I were to give up my position at UW-Eau Claire, which, again, I would have needed to do in order to be able to concentrate on that book project, in making it what it needed to be–in insuring that it lived up to what it claimed to be. In retrospect I am at peace with this decision, and with the consequences, although it was an extremely tough and indeed genuinely agonizing decision to make, which I only arrived at after trying my best for years to keep writing the book, even drafting multiple hundreds of new pages beyond the dissertation as well as dramatically reframing and reorienting what I was doing in the book versus what I had done in this dissertation.

Despite being at peace with this decision, and with the consequences, I do remain well aware this was not simply a 'personal decision', as the consequences included me not developing theory of a kind and in a direction that could have been highly useful to many others. I don't know if I would have succeeded in creating what my principal PhD advisors urged me to aim for–'boundary-shifting work', work that all those engaged in theorizing interrelations among queerness, cultural critique, social struggle, and social change would need to take into account–but I am aware this is a possibility, even as it is often exceedingly difficult for me to imagine myself as someone capable of that kind of achievement.

Robert McRuer's work does demonstrate a significant and an increasing concern with relations between, for instance, queerness and disability, on the one hand, and the determinant economic and political economic impacts of capitalism, notably neoliberal capitalism and austerity neoliberal capitalism, on the other hand, while in *Crip Times* he does draw extensively upon the queer Marxist theory of Kevin Floyd, as set forth in Floyd's 2009 book, *The Reification of Desire: Toward a Queer Marxism*. Likewise, Marxists such as David Harvey are significant influences upon how McRuer understands neoliberalism and austerity. McRuer yet further touts the project of 'salvage Marxism', favorably cites Lenin in support of McRuer's embryonic conception of what forces might well join together in bringing about socialist revolution, and indeed, as aforementioned, emphasizes the priority of transformation over transgression. McRuer's problematization of 'resistance' as well as his emphasis on exposing and combating dislocation and dispossession, including along lines of class, beyond emphasizing lack of equitably inclusive representation and accommodation of the disabled within a predominantly able-bodied society and culture, and beyond emphasizing the same concerning LGBTQIA+ people within a predominantly straight society and culture, are also significant indications of how McRuer's 'cultural materialism' comes close to Marxism. And McRuer's interest in the critical usefulness of 'the utopian' echoes that of comparable work within Marxism, including that of Ernst Bloch, Walter Benjamin, and Fredric Jameson–as well as, indeed, Vladimir Lenin.

However, McRuer doesn't directly link what he is supporting and advocating with 'socialism', 'socialist struggle', and 'revolutionary *socialist* transformation' per se, and he does not begin to explain how the disparate social groups and groupings that he imagines as sharing a common interest in 'revolution' and 'transformation' might be effectively united together, or how that unity might be sustained over the course of a long and arduous quest, facing and forced to absorb the impact of many setbacks and defeats, even many devastating setbacks and defeats, along the way. At the same time, even in *Crip Times*, McRuer continues to lean toward emphasizing 'the normal', or 'regimes of the normal', or 'compulsory normalization', as representing the preeminent antagonist, which can at the same time tend toward emphasizing, first and last, the value of cultivating and sustaining 'dissident' 'subcultures' that are not focused so much on social transformation as they are on striving not to be coopted and incorporated, able to continue to manifest their 'dissident difference' versus the heterosexual and able-bodied normative, as well as versus already coopted and incorporated varieties of LGBTQIA+ and disabled subjects and subjectivities, while not undermining the perpetuation of this normativity and especially not the material basis for its persistent predominance.

This brings me to my third matter of personal experience, interest, and concern I want to bring to bear in connection with McRuer's *Crip Theory* and *Crip Times*. I definitely do respect and value critiques of the oppressive impact that 'the normal' does and can exert. Yet I also respect and value what recognition and inclusion within 'the normal' can mean for members of social groups who have long experienced this prospect as impossible, unlikely, difficult, and precarious. For me, legal marriage has been important and beneficial, in enabling my husband and I to at least come much closer to maintaining 'equal protection under the law', which I firmly believe we deserve, as so do all same-sex couples, and as do for that matter a host of other kinds of 'families', 'households', and 'shared domestic communities'. Legal marriage is by no means the ultimate horizon of what is needed, or to be desired, but, as long as existing society remains fundamentally as it is, legal marriage provides a crucial means of helping insure my survival and subsistence, including my ability to be able to continue to contribute usefully in even the smallest possible ways toward ends of 'liberation' and 'transformation'–and the same is the case for many others like me.

At our first, non-legal, wedding, within the Unitarian Universalist Congregation of Eau Claire, I shared the following as my personal statement to those gathered to witness and celebrate this occasion with me and Andy:

Thank you all–colleagues, friends, and family–very much for being here today. Andy and I deeply appreciate you joining us to witness and celebrate our public expression of commitment to union in marriage. I *myself* also want to express my sincere gratitude to the Unitarian Universalist Fellowship of Eau Claire for welcoming me here today, even though I am not a member of the Fellowship myself [I was not yet then a member, although Andy was]. I want now to make a few brief remarks about my perception of the meaning and significance of this occasion.

For me, marriage represents a commitment of partners *not only* to love each other *but also* to share a life together. This requires work: it requires that the partners struggle together and it requires that they challenge each other. Marriage represents a commitment of partners to communicate openly and honestly with each other, to rely upon and to trust in each other, to take care of and to maintain responsibility for each other, to learn from and to teach each other, to respect each other's independent as well as interdependent needs, and to nurture each other's foremost aspirations while enabling each other continually to strive toward the realization of new goals. This is *not simply* a commitment that partners make *privately* to each other *but rather* one which they make *publicly*, as members of the interconnected series of social communities within which they carry out their everyday lives.

And yet, I nevertheless also firmly believe that the necessary foundation for a successful marriage is a deep and abiding mutual love. The kind of love about which I am talking is, to my mind, best described in a passage from philosopher Georg Wilhelm Friedrich Hegel's *Philosophy of Right*:

"Love means in general terms the consciousness of my unity with another, so that I am *not* in selfish isolation but win my self-consciousness only as the *renunciation* of my independence and through knowing myself as the *unity* of myself with another and of the other with me . . . The first moment in love is that I do *not* wish to be a self-subsistent and independent person and [recognize] that, if I were, then I would feel defective and incomplete. The second moment is that I *find myself* in another person, that I *count* for something in the other, while the other in turn comes to count for something in me. Love therefore is the most tremendous contradiction; the Understanding *cannot* resolve it."

In sum, the kind of love Hegel here discusses involves both the *losing* and *gaining* of an independent identity: at one level love means living for another and ceasing to be preoccupied with oneself and one's own interests, but at the same time this relationship gives one a fuller and deeper sense of identity in so far as this is objectified and confirmed by the other person.

Obviously, therefore, I strongly believe that gays and lesbians deserve the equal right to pursue this kind of love in marriage, and that *our marriages should receive equal* recognition and protection under the law. And yet, at the same time as a movement toward acceptance of the legitimacy of gay marriage gradually gains greater support in contemporary American society, I also believe it is extremely important to oppose prospective uses of this growing acceptance to divide gay and lesbian communities by sanctioning tolerance for those involved in marital relationships while maintaining, and even increasing, prejudicial discrimination and violent abuse versus those who are not. *All* discrimination, prejudice, and violent abuse directed at human beings on account of sexual orientation and gender identification is *wrong*, and *must* be fought.

Nonetheless, I disagree with those gay radicals who reject marriage altogether, as a monolithically repressive institution, and who conceive of gay marriage as a capitulation to heteronormative values and codes of conduct. As a Marxist I grasp reality as a complex, dynamic, concrete totality. All of reality is interconnected and in motion, and contradictions are the driving force of change, development, and progress, not mere logical fallacies or indices of a breakdown in social or natural order. Marriage, like most major human social institutions, is divided between, on the one hand, a *universal* dimension, which represents the progressive movement of human society toward a state of genuine enlightenment and emancipation, and, on the other hand, an *independent* dimension, independent of this universal progressive movement, which represents that which is thoroughly overdetermined by the functional needs of a particular form of human social organization, and political rule, at a particular stage in the course of human history. At its best, in its ideal form, in its utopian dimension, marriage is one human social institution which anticipates, and prefigures, the organization of human society where *each* gives according to his abilities while receiving according to her needs, the free development of *each* serves as the condition for the free development of *all*, and people relate to each other as *ends* rather than simply as means, as *subjects* rather than simply as objects, and as complex and dynamic *totalities each in our own right* rather than as reified assemblages of compartmentalized roles and functions.

As you can tell, I do *not* enter marriage lightly; I conceive of a commitment to marriage as extraordinarily serious and important, as quite possibly the *most* serious and important commitment I will ever make. I am nonetheless confident here today in making this commitment together with Andy, who has already provided me with an *enormous* amount of love, support, strength, and joy. Andy *is* a wonderful, beautiful, sweet, generous, patient, and vibrant person with whom I consider it to be a *great honor*, and an *humble privilege*, to go forward together as life's partners.

Thank you all very much, once again.

So, I understand and respect Robert McRuer's wariness about and indeed critical take on legal same-sex marriage, but I also offer a counter to that position which I don't find to be all about striving for and obtaining, exclusively for Andy and I, what might be dismissively characterized as 'homonormativity'. I have known many LGBTQIA+ people throughout my life who have lived in, who have chosen and preferred to live, in other kinds of domestic and familial relationships, including with multiple and changing members, including multiple and changing *numbers of* members, and including spanning a variety of ages, genders, sexualities, and, also for that matter, health and ability challenges and complications. I have respected and appreciated what they have formed, and the considerable work and struggle this has often entailed. I do not consider any of those bonds, and especially not the love shared across those bonds, to be less intrinsically worthwhile, let alone less 'real', than the bond, and the love, Andy and I share. I want to contribute toward radically transforming contemporary capitalist society and culture (and for that matter contemporary patriarchal-racial-capitalist-imperialist society and culture) so that more people can readily live within these kinds of domestic and familial relationships, as well as within yet more kinds that have not yet been imagined or invented, and that all of these kinds of relationships are treated as equally worthwhile within, across, and throughout the larger communities and societies of which they are a part.

I myself longed for a life-partner, for someone with whom I could share a deep and abiding love, ever since I was a boy, and I often worried this would never be possible for someone like me. I even, yes certainly, often worried that I was undeserving of such love, and that I was destined to live my life largely, ultimately alone. I have appreciated membership within many collective communities, many of which have provided me considerable support, and some of these have been LGBT or queer communities, but my experience has led me not to idealize what any group of LGBT and/or queer people, brought together, can, in and of itself, mean. Many of these LGBT and/or queer groups have been riven with internal divisions, yes in significant part reflective and responsive to external pressures but these have been serious divisions nonetheless: divisions over whether people's interests were more 'social' or more 'political', over how widely out to be as well as over what being 'out' involves/must or should involve, over whether people were more interested in 'friendship' or 'romance' or 'sex', over what kinds of friendship or romance or sex people were interested in, over how friendship and romance and sex relate to each other or must or should relate to each other, over monogamy versus polyamory versus various 'in-between' positions, between men and women/between gays and lesbians, between gays and lesbians on the one hand and bisexuals on the other hand, between gays/lesbians/bisexuals on the one hand and transgender/gender non-binary people on the other hand, along lines of age, in terms of matters of health and ability, along lines of race and class and nationality, and yet more besides.

In practice, many such groups have been fragile and precarious, as well as loose and diffuse, and many of these so-called LGBT or queer 'communities' have been more a scattershot and disparate array of groupings and scenes. This has been the case not only in smaller population areas where I've lived but also in larger ones as well. And at the same time, I have certainly at times found more meaningfully in common as well as more meaningful support from straight friends, comrades, colleagues, and associates than I have from LGBT and/or queer people that I have simultaneously known and interacted with in the same locations. I maintain long-standing alignment with theorizations of what 'gayness' means, and especially can and should mean, such as that set forth by fellow gay Marxist David Fernbach, in his 1981 book *The Spiral Path*, that conceive 'gayness' as ultimately aiming to offer a contribution toward the revolutionary transformation and liberation of what intimate and affectional relations can mean for *all* people and not just for those who themselves identify, or who are otherwise identified, as 'gay people' (or as lgbtqia people for that matter).

As the last film in the 2021-2022 Empowerment Through Solidarity Progressive Film Series at UW-Eau Claire, co-sponsored by United Faculty and Academic Staff of UW-Eau Claire and Leaders Igniting Transformation at UW-Eau Claire, we screened *Judas and the Black Messiah* (2021), which focuses on the betrayal of Fred Hampton, chairman of the Illinois chapter of the Black Panther Party, culminating in his assassination in his home by the FBI in December 1969. I have long been an admirer of the Black Panther Party, the Black Panther movement, and of Fred Hampton in particular, while appalled at the war the FBI waged against the Black Panthers and the FBI's assassination of Hampton. *Judas and the Black Messiah* is an important film, well made, and deservedly has reached and positively impacted a wide audience while insuring a crucial moment in history is remembered so many can and will draw upon this history in present and future struggles for social justice. An especially crucial lesson the Black Panther Movement offers concerns the preeminent importance of creating substantive cultures of community-based collective self-help. This requires assuming collective responsibility, as communities, to look after and take care of the needs and the well-being of all members of these communities, and not just delegate that responsibility to private families, private extended families, occasional and sporadic charities, and whatever can be begrudgingly and often with extraordinary difficulty and only temporarily at best wrung from the state–let alone delegated to individuals to bear responsibility to take care of themselves, to take care of their individual well-being, by themselves alone.

For almost my entire life this has been a major focus of my own deep discontent with the kind of society and culture that has been and continues overwhelmingly dominant in the US: hyper-individualist, anti-collectivist, alienating and isolating, and where even in institutions that pretend otherwise or 'officially' represent themselves otherwise, the dominant ethos continues, in effect, to be that of rugged individualism, individual self-reliance, individuals 'rising and falling' (or 'sinking or swimming') first and last on their own supposedly distinctly and discretely individual 'merit' (philosopher Michael Sandel's recent critique of meritocracy, *The Tyranny of Merit: What's Become of the Common Good?*, is a helpful point of reference here), and with no one needing actively to care all that much, in genuinely substantive terms, about any others beyond immediate family members.

It's a revolutionary transformation of precisely that kind of society and culture that the Black Panther movement continues to herald, even more than it is a revolution in terms of whom is in charge of the state. One specific example of where we are currently failing in this connection is 'the crisis in mental health' that is by now widely acknowledged to exist, in this country and others much like it, and to have been getting steadily and rapidly worse for some time, even before the pandemic, especially but hardly exclusively among younger people. By far the most common response to this crisis continues to involve judging the crisis to result from a large number of individuals independently experiencing biochemical disorders in their individual brain functioning, and who thereby need to be helped, individually, one by one, in isolation, for their supposedly individually 'personal' and 'private' problems.

In contrast, we could (and in fact I argue we *should*) conceive of and approach a crisis in mental health and well-being as a social, cultural, economic, and political phenomenon, that requires collective address, and collective redress, ultimately by means of social, cultural, economic, and political transformation–and where the harm this encompasses needs to be engaged as a matter of collective as opposed to individual responsibility. How, for instance, can we be serious in claiming commitment toward fostering 'cultures of wellness' when sharing of individual vulnerability continues all too often to be treated, in practice, regardless of superficially 'nice words' here and there to the contrary, as exposure of weakness that can and will be exploited? What happens when we accept a responsibility to proceed beyond merely saying 'I am sorry you feel that way', 'I sympathize/empathize with you feeling that way because I have had experience of feeling the same', and 'I recommend you seek out this or that service provider/institutional or community resource who may be able to help you attend to what you are feeling'? What happens when we take seriously that so many people are experiencing these ostensibly 'individual bad feelings' in the way that they are, and to the extremes that they often are, because of the ways that, for example, their workplaces are set up and operate, as well as because of what is expected, required, and demanded of them in doing their work at/as part of these workplaces, and with what kinds of relations (or lack of relations) they are positioned to be able to maintain with others as well as with their immediate physical and social environments in doing this work at/as part of this workplace?

Several years ago now, a very smart student in a class I was teaching shared his thoughts related to this issue: no one in our society today is in the position realistically to be able (i.e., can realistically afford to be able) to be there for someone else in order to do all that it takes to be of help if and when that other person falls apart and breaks down. That has to change: not by asking that more people individually take on this kind of burden of responsibility, individually by themselves alone, but rather that we do so collectively, within our communities, as communities, and so that we collectively, within our communities, as communities, get at–and intervene at–the roots of what leads so many members of our communities to suffer this kind of damage.

In conceiving of this as a key lesson that I believe the Black Panther movement continues to offer I certainly share McRuer's deep dissatisfaction with and strong critical opposition to neoliberal capitalism's exaltation of individualization and privatization. I have felt this impact personally in my own life, often enough, where, despite the tremendous support I gain from Andy, as well as that I also gain from a small number of other friends and family, it can all too readily and all too frequently feel to me as if I am far more isolated than I want to be, and that in turn this extent of isolation undermines whom and what I am and can be, at my prospective best. However, I also feel the fact that existing capitalist society is structured so as to depend upon, and as such to foster and to augment, individualization, privatization, and isolation, heightens the value of finding love, when and where it is possible, especially among groups of people who still are all too often effectively addressed by this society as unlikely or less likely to be able to find and to experience love, or as needing to suffer and struggle considerable stress and strain in seeking love and in seeking to maintain and sustain loving relationships–as still remains all too often the case for *gay people*.

Just as with marriage, if not in fact even more so, I conceive of 'love' as maintaining 'universal' and 'independent' dimensions, or as maintaining both ideological and ideological critical or critically utopian dimensions. That's why my critical reading of 'young gay romance' in the films *Beautiful Thing* (1996), *Get Real* (1998), and *Edge of Seventeen* (1998), published in *The Journal of Homosexuality* in 2006, makes sense of these as contradictory texts, much as McRuer does *The King's Speech* which he evaluates perhaps surprisingly largely positively, and why I have also found myself powerfully compelled by the much 'darker' and indeed more 'tragic' film *Urbania* (2000), which I taught often in the early 2000s, and wrote about in a chapter published as part of *Coming Out to the Mainstream: New Queer Cinema in the 20th Century* (2010). *Urbania* I judge much more highly on multiple levels than *Beautiful Thing*, *Get Real*, and *Edge of Seventeen*, but the intense and often desperate need of the youthful gay protagonists in the latter films for love, as well as the hardships they experience in striving to obtain and sustain love, I do not find to be, by any means, mere 'reactionary escapism' let alone simply symptomatic of acquiescence in and even surrender to entirely 'heteronormative' conceptions and practices (as exemplifying, thereby, the rise, at the end of the 20th century, of 'homonormativity' in cinema–and television).

Yes, these last three films all represent youthful white gay male characters seeking love without framing their desire, and need, in ways that make sense of how and why they face the hardships that they do, and what it might be about the nature of the society and culture in which they live that needs to be transformed so that love becomes more readily, substantially obtainable and sustainable for the great many who live lives all too devoid of love–change that cannot be achieved by means of micro-individual and micro-interindividual efforts, or by investing hope in 'magical moments' where individuals overcome barriers by simply showing sufficient tenacity to do so, while winning the hearts of increasing numbers of allies and supporters by means of this show of tenacity. But the desire and need for love, especially among those for whom the efforts involved in obtaining and sustaining love remains often treacherous and uncertain, I find compelling because love can be absolutely crucial in enabling quality of life and quality of contribution in terms of how one lives one's life and what one does with, in, and through this life.

While first writing this section of this chapter Andy and I watched the first season of *Heartstopper*, an eight-episode British 'coming of age' romantic TV drama, on Netflix. *Heartstopper* is based on a preceding webcomic and graphic novel by Alice Oseman. The principal focus of the show, in season one, is upon the developing romantic relationship between Charlie Spring, played by Joe Locke, and Nick Nelson, played by Kit Connor. Charlie, Nick, and the other principal characters are all secondary school students, in either their tenth or eleventh years at school. Charlie is universally known to be gay, after having previously been outed, and he has been as well as remains a frequent target for bullying on this account. Nick is the star player on the school's rugby team, who befriends Charlie, and quickly becomes attracted to Charlie, while struggling to figure out what is going on with him, and whom he is, before he decides he is bisexual and is ready to openly share with everyone else who is important to Nick and Charlie that this is so and that they are 'boyfriends'. Their relationship is about romantic attraction, as opposed to sex per se, and their romantic relationship represents an elaboration of and development upon their steadily growing close, 'special' friendship–on their being 'best friends'. Nick steadily realizes he much prefers to spend time with Charlie than his erstwhile friends, and likes Charlie much better than most of these erstwhile friends, especially those associated with his rugby circle. Charlie steadily realizes he is deserving of love and that it is genuinely viable for someone like Nick to really want to be involved in a romantic relationship with him, and to ready to risk alienation from his previous friends in doing so, even though Charlie is used to believing that he simply needs to accept being the object of abuse, even that he himself is responsible for his own abject state, and even that he is at fault whenever 'bad things happen' to other friends of his.

The youthful characters here are all seemingly comfortably middle class, as they do not seem to suffer from any notable economic insecurity or deprivation, and they are able to focus their lives on school and school activities, as well as on personal interests (no one needs to work to earn money to help sustain themselves and their families). At the two closely linked boys and girls schools we do encounter bullying as a commonplace among the students, and this is specifically directed not only at Charlie for being gay but also at Tara Jones (played by Corinna Brown) and Darcy Olsson (played by Kizzy Edgell) for being lesbians, at Elle Argent (played by Yasmin Finney) for being transgender, and at Tao Xu (played by William Gao) for being someone who, although seemingly straight-identifying, rejects hegemonic and especially toxic masculinist ways of being, maintaining a long-term, close, and protective friendship circle with Charlie, Elle, and fellow 'outsider' and the seemingly asexual Isaac Henderson (played by Tobie Donovan). Yet despite the extent of this bullying the schools seem at the same time to be well-endowed with ample resources for their students, including in the arts as well as in STEM subjects and in physical education and athletics. In addition, miraculously enough, despite bullying taking place on account of sexual and gender difference, none is visible in relation to racial difference, despite the overt racial diversity of those attending the two schools, including among the main cast, and despite the prominence as well of interracial relationships. Yes, it is plausible to contend these characters lead relatively socio-economically and even culturally privileged lives while their struggles greatly pale in comparison with those of a great many people in more precarious, including multiply precarious, kinds of situations, but *Heartstopper* is affecting because it treats 'falling in love' with such delicacy and sensitivity, especially 'falling in love' with someone of the same sex. The confusions, uncertainties, doubts, and hesitations in this process, as well as the emotional pain the principal characters register as result of suffering bullying and denigration, or fearing suffering it, along with, at the same time, the joys, and even the exuberances, of coming together, in sharing youthful love, especially with someone you did not imagine you would not long before, are all portrayed in *Heartstopper* in ways that I find compelling, and which resonate with my own experience, even as my situation growing up was much harsher than depicted in this TV show.

As I have previously mentioned in this book, the pervasion of anti-gay slurs was so dense and overwhelming throughout my time in public elementary, middle, and high school that it was impossible for me to even to begin to imagine, then and there, that I might, that I could possibly be, gay. No one was out as such, and anyone who would have been would have suffered much worse than the kind of bullying *Heartstopper* portrays. Even so, anyone who for any reason 'stood out' as 'different' for any reason was readily and relentlessly picked on. I needed to spend considerable effort striving to find ways to avoid becoming the object of physical abuse, including finding ways of avoiding being forced into physical fights, which broke out regularly and routinely on and immediately surrounding school grounds. It was not until afterward, and not until after finishing my undergraduate education at Wesleyan University, as well as after finishing my master's degree studies at Syracuse University, that I first fell hard, headlong, seriously in love–with a man. I realized then, as I came to recognize myself as gay, and to identify myself to others as gay, that I had long been unconsciously yet assiduously and indeed forcefully blocking myself from facing up to my interest in and attraction to other males, and to the fact that I was in fact much more romantically and sexually interested in and attracted to other males than I was to females. I realized as well that I had yearned to enter into a romantic relationship with someone who could be both my best friend, and my lover, and this would be a fellow male of my age. As I proceeded forward, 'out' as gay, I was most interested in finding love, and especially that kind of love. Yet all too often this is not what I found. I fell in love with men who loved me too, and indeed who loved me a lot, yet 'not in that way'. I found men readily interested in having sex with me but not interested in a romantic relationship with me. And I entered into short-term relationships or met up and joined up short-term with men who were seriously damaged by the virulent impacts of heterosexism and homophobia, especially internalized heterosexism and homophobia, or who were otherwise highly confused about and troubled concerning what they wanted and needed, in intimate and affectional terms, with and from whom. As a result, I increasingly doubted I would ever find the love I craved, and I simultaneously increasingly doubted my own value and my desirability as someone worthy of love. So I do viscerally connect with the craving for love, and the fear that they will not be able to obtain or sustain this, the principal characters in *Heartstopper* are depicted as experiencing.

Heartstopper I also find affecting because it suggests despite all the seeming gains in greater tolerance, acceptance, and inclusion of gay people, and of LGBTQIA+ people more broadly, in the US, the UK, and countries much like the US and the UK, in recent times, that bullying continues to be as persistent and as harmful as this show suggests, for many youthful LGBTQIA+ people, and that many youthful LGBTQIA+ people still find it much harder to obtain and sustain romantic intimate and affectional relationships than do straight youth. Among LGBTQIA+ students I have got to know, these struggles continue to be common as well. A TV show like *Heartstopper* resonates yet further at a time in which a major backlash against the extent of tolerance, acceptance, and inclusion that has been achieved is well underway. In the UK, transgender and gender non-binary people bear the greatest brunt of this current backlash but multiple reports document rising attacks on and harassment directed at all kinds of LGBTQIA+ people, or those suspected of being LGBTQIA+, just as multiple surveys document persistent and often increasing anti-LGBTQIA+ discrimination, prejudice, and abuse across many different British workplaces and leisure spaces as well as throughout many different British social institutions.

In the US, the now authoritarian populist, or in other words neo-fascist, MAGA-dominated Republican Party has been mounting a concerted effort to outlaw teaching of subjects related to LGBTQIA+ lives, from kindergarten upward, including by allowing parents and yet others besides to sue teachers and schools for teaching material concerning matters of race, gender, and sexuality that is not 'age appropriate' with what is and is not 'age appropriate' left deliberately and insidiously nebulous. Republicans in power in government have also been pushing to censor public library collections or to otherwise restrict access to materials addressing issues of race, gender, and sexuality that they disapprove of–or suspect they disapprove of without ever taking the time to read these materials. Likewise, legislation has been passed and is being proposed in many states to render it illegal for transgender people to use public restrooms that do not correspond to their biological sex at birth, to likewise bar transgender youth and young adults from playing on school sports teams in alignment with the gender that corresponds with whom they experience themselves to be, and to outlaw gender-affirming medical care, even as far as redefining parents, guardians, and doctors as perpetrating 'child abuse' for seeking and providing this kind of care. At the same time, the recent leak of a draft decision by the US Supreme Court to overturn *Roe v. Wade* and *Casey v. Planned Parenthood*, which provide constitutional protection for women to be able to legally obtain an abortion, after many years of many states chipping away at and doing everything else they possibly could to undermine this protection, not only puts many US girls and women–including lesbian and bisexual girls and women, and many transgender and gender non-binary people–at serious risk, but also, according to the terms of Justice Samuel Alito's draft ruling, threatens constitutional protection for same-sex marriage and for people engaging in mutually consensual same-sex sexual relations in the privacy of their own homes, among numerous other freedoms from being forced to conform to conservative religious dictates or suffer legal punishment.

Right-wing forces have organized to target public school boards across the country, seeking to intimidate members of these boards, and teachers and administrators in these schools, against continuing to teach virtually anything of substance concerning matters of race, gender, and sexuality at all–especially anything that might be in any way critical of this country in terms of its history and continuation of inequity along lines of race, gender, and sexuality, and especially anything that might propose, even further, that this country has been founded on as well as continually depended upon systemic racism, and/or systemic oppression of people along lines of gender and sexuality. This effort recently targeted Eau Claire, and as has been the case in most of these locations it was closely tied to a campaign to elect right-wing candidates to the board of education who agreed parents should be able to dictate what their children are and are not taught in public schools as well as what kinds of services school staff are and are not able offer to their children. In Eau Claire a major thrust of this effort was directed in opposition to teachers and other members of public school staff offering 'safe spaces' where students are able to share their sexual and gender identities, or questions and confusions about their sexual and gender identities, in confidence, such that teachers and other members of school staff are not bound to share this information with students' parents if the students do not want it shared. In response to this charged situation I wrote the following editorial column for the Eau Claire *Leader-Telegram*, Eau Claire's daily newspaper, addressing as much as I could in the limited space the paper is able to make available for this purpose, but nonetheless doing what I could because it struck me my experience and perspective is relevant and useful, and this is something I *should* share, as the least I can do:

> Critical Race Theory is an inquiry into why, despite the gains of the Black Civil Rights Movement, disparities in the social, economic, political, and cultural positions of Black and brown versus white people–in terms of access to and exercise of resources, powers, and capacities–continues, on average, to be as substantial as it is, and, in many instances, to have increased. As a mode of intellectual inquiry, Critical Race Theory not only develops provisional explanations, and provisional arguments for explanations–i.e., hypotheses–but also invites and encourages conversation, dialogue and debate, on these matters. The only intellectually, ethically, and politically responsible position in response to Critical Race Theory is to accept this invitation and encouragement, and to enter into such dialogue and

debate. To seek to ban Critical Race Theory, as well as all teaching and learning about matters of race and racism even remotely connected with Critical Race Theory suggests you are scared of Critical Race Theory because you are convinced even the slightest exposure to any position even indirectly connected with Critical Race Theory will prove overwhelmingly, automatically persuasive, and cannot possibly be answered, because Critical Race Theory is so obviously true it cannot be argued with or against. If this is not the case, show some courage, and some integrity, and actually learn about what Critical Race Theory really argues–for example, Critical Race Theory does *not* argue people are *inherently* racist but rather we all are shaped by the accumulative, ongoing impacts of histories that long proceed and greatly exceed our individual lives, including in terms of disparities along lines of race. Show some courage, and enter into actual dialogue and debate with Critical Race Theory, and its adherents, for what it actually is about. And if you have alternative theories for explaining ongoing disparities, or apparent ongoing disparities, in terms of social, economic, political, and cultural positions, along lines of race, represent, advocate, and argue for these.

The same holds for teaching and learning about (as well as offering confidential support services to) LGBTQIA (lesbian, gay, bisexual, transgender, gender nonbinary, queer, questioning, intersex, and asexual) people in schools, about the fact that such people do exist, that such people do live lives (and not just lifestyles), and that they do develop and maintain relationships that are about living their lives, according to whom they experience themselves to truly be. If a student shares their sexual or gender identity in confidence with a teacher or another member of a school staff they do so because they cannot trust that their parents, guardians, and/or other family members will love them for whom they are. The consequences can indeed be severe. In 35+ years of teaching, many students have shared with me that they have been kicked out of their homes, cut off and disowned by their families, as a result of 'coming out' or of being 'outed' as LGBTQIA. Many others have shared with me they have experienced serious strain and deep alienation, short of this complete a break, with this strain and alienation in turn exercising an extremely negative impact on their well-being and on their ability to succeed both in school and elsewhere. I have known numerous LGBTQIA people who have killed themselves, who have engaged in other forms of serious self-harming, who have suffered eating disorders, who have suffered from addiction to alcohol and other drugs, who have turned to crime, who have dropped out of school and who have lost jobs, and who have suffered major anxiety and depression all on account of hostility they have experienced from parents, guardians, and family members. And I have known many LGBTQIA people whose families have not visited them even when they were dying and who refused to attend their funerals–or refused to acknowledge their lovers and partners at funerals. Banning teaching and learning about LGBTQIA people and banning offering confidential support services to LGBTQIA people in schools will not reduce the numbers of LGBTQIA young people but it will increase the numbers of endangered, at risk, unhealthy, traumatized, harmed, harming, and, yes, suicidal LGBTQIA young people–including prospectively your children and the children of your friends and neighbors. Again, if you have alternative ways to insure that LGBTQIA people's lives are recognized and valued, argue for these, work for these; don't simply seek to ban what you are afraid of because you aren't willing and able to take the time and make the effort to understand–and to help.

Heartstopper along with other films and TV shows like it continue to address a critical need, and respond to what continues a precarious state, concerning LGBTQIA+ people's need to be affirmed, and to find support, appreciation, friendship, and especially love as whom and for whom they are–in the face of still all too powerful forces still all too determined to undermine and prevent this from happening. This need, as well as the threat to it, continues for suburban middle class LGBTQIA+ people too, even if they do not need to contend with many further compounding kinds of needs and threats at the same time, faced by working class and poor LGBTQIA+ people–and by LGBTQIA+ people in countries in the global South where the past and continuing present impacts of imperialism have created and persist in reinforcing vast disparities versus countries in the global North.

Three

Public Feelings is a project within which Ann Cvetkovich has played a founding and leading role, and is part of a larger movement, begun in 2001, representative of 'an affective turn' in critical cultural studies, often referred to as 'affect theory' and 'affect studies'. Inspired by her participation in and contribution to this collective project, Cvetkovich, in *Depression: a Public Feeling* (2012), theorizes depression as a sensible response to what it feels like to live as part of an often highly troubled and especially highly troubling larger world. Cvetkovich explores what living in an often highly troubled and especially highly troubling larger world *feels like* in the form of depression as she theorizes how experience of depression, and especially of learning how to live with depression, can comprise a valuable contribution to critical praxis.

Depression: a Public Feeling includes, as part "Part I: The Depression Journals (A Memoir)," Cvetkovich's account of her personal experience of depression and of how she learned to make sense of and respond to its impact upon her. Here Cvetkovich stresses how the exhausting demands of academic life, of all of its professional obligations, can and do induce depression. Cvetkovich first experienced serious depression as an English PhD student as Cornell University, in the process of completing her doctoral dissertation while embarked on a highly competitive job market in seeking to obtain a rare position as a tenure-track professor of English. This depression continued even after succeeding in achieving the latter goal, at the University of Texas at Austin. Cvetkovich's depression makes sense in response to relocating and setting up anew in beginning to take on the responsibilities of an ambitious new position in an area of the world where she had never lived or worked before, as part of, for her, a new and considerably different institution, while still finishing and anticipating defending her dissertation. Depression makes sense in academia in response to "the harsh conditions of a ruthlessly competitive job market, the shrinking power of the humanities, and the corporatization of the university" that squeezes out space and time for genuine creative engagement and endeavor (17).

Cvetkovich characterizes her depression memoir as recounting "how academia seemed to be killing me" (18). Cvetkovich insists this is not melodramatic exaggeration but rather accurately corresponds to what happens when it feels like "your work doesn't matter" such "that you feel dead inside" (18). Cvetkovich recognizes this is "a condition that is normalized for so many" far beyond academia, yet stresses academia "breeds particular forms of panic and anxiety leading to what gets called depression–the fear that you have nothing to say, or that you can't say what you want to say, or that you have something to say but it's not important enough or smart enough," so within "this particular enclave of the professional managerial class, there is an epidemic of anxiety-induced depression" (18). All of these impacts, Cvetkovich readily admits, are all that much worse for the many more graduate students as well as untenured and adjunct faculty, especially in the humanities, who do not achieve the success that she has in obtaining a tenured position. Thinking in particular of these people, all those unable to finish their pursuit of terminal graduate degrees as well as all those unable to secure long-term employment as college and university faculty, Cvetkovich asks "Why is a position of relative privilege, the pursuit of creative thinking and teaching, lived as though it were impossible?" (18).

Perhaps this impossibility is due to how capitalist society and culture is set up, to the intrinsic nature of capitalist social relations and capitalist cultural practices, to what ends capitalist society and culture advance and to whose interests capitalist society and culture serve, as well as due to what is most beneficial to the reproduction and maintenance versus what is least beneficial and even distracting from or threatening of the reproduction and maintenance of capitalist society and culture. Cvetkovich certainly considers these issues, but her initial aim is to describe the depression-inducing dimensions of contemporary *academia*, notably in the humanities, as the prevailing system of institutional arrangements "often leaves us feeling like we're never doing enough to make a difference" (19), with this especially the case for those whose intellectual work is focused on matters of social justice. This indeed comprises a considerable proportion of those pursuing advanced degrees and professorial positions in humanities fields such as English today. Cognitive dissonance can prove extreme because most working in academia today feel the pressure common to corporate cultures "that demand deliverables and measurable outcomes and that say you are only as good as what you produce" (19). Unfortunately, the projects that turn out to be most valuable as contributions toward social justice, and toward social transformation, are often messy, complicated, take considerable time and effort to realize, and pass through many ups and downs in the process, which means these often do not readily result in 'deliverables' or provide 'measurable outcomes' (19).

Closely related is "a depression-inducing anxiety about separation from real struggles" (160). This happens because of the intrinsic nature of the academic work and how demanding this work is, which often leaves little room for other forms of engagement. Such a state of affairs can become exceedingly upsetting for academics who have committed enormous time and energy in pursuit of a professional life within academia out of the conviction that this path would provide a preeminent means by which they could valuably contribute, using their distinct knowledge, skill, talent, and ability, toward the same ends that drive activist efforts for social and political transformation. These academics imagined they could readily unite academic and activist work; they imagined they would maintain ample time and energy for activist work beyond academic work; and they imagined they would receive respect, appreciation, and indeed commendation for their activist work as representing valuable community service as civic engagement, from those evaluating their performance in their academic position. Yet these academics subsequently find out little to none of that is actually the case.

As Cvetkovich's depression set in, she experienced enormous fatigue, that persisted no matter how long or how often she slept. The panic she felt at the same time she experienced as dread deeply embedded throughout her body, operating as a hostile force that overwhelmed her to the point she felt unable to move about or to attend to basic activities, such as going to the grocery store (35). At its worst, Cvetkovich's depression made getting out of bed in the morning hard to do, as it felt impossible to attend to "ordinary routines of self-maintenance," because all too many ordinary activities became 'excruciating' to undergo (45). In turn, heightened awareness of how seemingly incapable she had become added yet further to her already severe depression (45). Even after her depression temporarily receded, Cvetkovich experienced a second bout of depression that felt all that much worse as it set in because she felt depressed about the return of depression. Panic began as soon as depression showed up once more, as Cvetkovich felt "caught in the downward spiral of feeling bad about feeling bad" (63).

As Cvetkovich indicates, depression can make "people feel small, worthless, hopeless" and, as such, depression constitutes a form of what Lauren Berlant identifies as 'slow death' (13). As Cvetkovich is well aware, from personal experience of losing close friends to suicide following their struggles in living with depression, slow death can and does lead too often to literal death: "Along with worrying about all the adolescent and college-age queers who are more anxious than ever, this book is haunted by the memory of many people for whom growing up didn't necessarily mean getting better, people who couldn't figure out how to wait until things got better, people who are not that different from me" (207). What's more, developing a sophisticated understanding of how depression works, and what it does to you, is by no means sufficient to guarantee survival. Cvetkovich cites novelist David Foster Wallace as keenly attuned to "the deadening power of 'boredom, routine, and petty frustration'" that both induces and characterizes depression. But Wallace's suicide illustrates no matter how sensitively one grapples with these dimensions of depressive experience doing so does not prevent depression from becoming so overwhelming that it feels impossible to continue (207).

Nevertheless, Cvetkovich places greater emphasis throughout her book on strategies for survival and ways of learning from depression in the interest of putting what can be so learned to work to enable intellectual, artistic, and activist praxis. In order to do so, Cvetkovich argues depression must be understood radically differently than is most commonly the case. This means rejecting biologically reductionist explanations that identify the source of depression as strictly equivalent with faulty–or, in other words, *disordered*–individual brain functioning. Cvetkovich characterizes the first part of her book as a *critical* memoir (23) because she writes and shares this memoir as a rejoinder to depression memoirs that embrace prescription drug treatment as 'the solution' and wherein their authors praise psychotropic drugs as exercising a miraculous power in enabling recovery–and salvation. Cvetkovich acknowledges what she refers to as 'the medical model of depression', based on a seemingly clear-cut biologically inherent source, can be appealing because conceiving of depression in this way "relieves people of individual blame or responsibility" (91). But Cvetkovich warns doing so ultimately amounts to a refusal to explore "the overwhelming, diffuse, and messy tendencies of social or cultural analysis," analysis that is necessary in order to understand and explain widespread and rapidly increasing 'prevalence' (91).

Cvetkovich is also critical of dominant medical discourses on depression, including by way of the DSM (The Diagnostic and Statistical Manual of Mental Health Disorders, sponsored and published by the American Psychiatric Association, the APA), for their tendency to "homogenize and universalize a nuanced range of feelings" (157). Cvetkovich argues the dominant medical model is not dominant simply because it offers the 'best possible' 'true explanation' of how to understand and 'treat' depression, or other 'mental health disorders', but due to success in marketing (98). As many other critics of the DSM have likewise pointed out, the DSM is as much if not more a social construction–and reconstruction–of 'mental illness' as it is a description and analysis of the same (99). Cvetkovich recognizes "a growing popular backlash" has been taking place "against the Prozac revolution" (100), but she remains concerned that even leading critics of 'the medical model' "stop short of any real consideration of the social causes of depression or the social transformations that might address it" (101).

Cvetkovich argues that "environmental, social, and familial factors" are responsible for 'triggering' 'biological responses,' and even though she herself has taken Prozac and other anti-depression prescription medicine she is and remains highly skeptical about the value of so doing (15). Cvetkovich makes clear she does not condemn the use of SSRIs (selective serotonin reuptake inhibitors) or other forms of standard prescription drug treatment for depression by those who find this works for them. But Cvetkovich's chronicle of her own experience with depression, and her efforts to combat its damaging effects, reveal Prozac's impact upon her as making her manic to the point where she became erratic and aggressive (54, 59). Cvetkovich acknowledges her father also experienced serious mental health problems, in the form of what was eventually diagnosed as manic-depression, but Cvetkovich rejects interpretation of his story as that of someone who simply suffered from a biochemical imbalance in the normal working of his brain functioning, and which could therefore be effectively addressed and overcome by means of proper prescription drug treatment. Cvetkovich interprets social environmental inheritance, as well as commonality of social experience, not biological inheritance in the form of a genetic predisposition, as what links her experience of 'mental illness' with that of her father (41). As Cvetkovich writes, "My own history of dislocation connects to the histories of immigration and displacement that affected my father as much as any biochemical imbalance" (71).

Cvetkovich's declares "There is nothing wrong with our biology or our intelligence; sometimes we are just stuck" (68). Drawing from Lauren Berlant, Cvetkovich inteprets an 'impasse' as in fact representing an opportunity, following recognition of a need to 'slow down', to approach an endeavor differently, even radically differently, than one has been previously prepared to do (20). An impasse represents "both stuckness and potential," and it is, moreover, from within the 'stuckness' itself that the potential is ultimately to be derived (21). Cvetkovich advocates engaging with "depression as the occasion for an ongoing process of adjustment, interpretation, and new ways of living" (140). In other words, depression is "a form of being stuck" that requires "new ways of living" (26). As such, depression can function as the kind of crisis that leads people to seek out as well as to fashion ways of living that might enrich critical insight, creative acumen, quality of life, and quality of intellectual and artistic as well as social and political contribution.

Cvetkovich does find the "recent turn to neuroscience within cultural studies" promising, including "neurobiological inquiry into the embodiment of emotion" (103). Social and cultural approaches can therefore fruitfully combine with biological approaches in making sense of phenomena such as depression (103). Yet she nevertheless continues to insist "that depression can be known not just by studying the nervous system but by paying attention to what we learn through intuition or spiritual practice" (104). Cvetkovich embraces practices conventionally regarded with skepticism in much of the academy, aiming to "make conceptual space" for "alternative medicine and healing practices" as well as "alternative ways of understanding depression (including other vocabularies) as the product of a sick culture" (102). Cvetkovich is particularly strongly motivated to "create more space for creative thought" in reconceiving depression, as well as in how to respond to depression (22).

Turning from her memoir in part one of *Depression: a Public Feeling*, the first of three chapters of "Part II: A Public Feelings Projects: a Speculative Essay" Cvetkovich titles "Writing Depression: Acedia, History, and Medical Models." In this chapter Cvetkovich not only elaborates her critique of the dominant medical model in explaining and responding to depression but also explores alternative models, especially from writers writing long before this medical model became dominant, that Cvetkovich argues can and should be reclaimed, re-validated, and made productive use of once again today. Cvetkovich finds the fourth-century Christian monastic concept of 'acedia' more useful than many secular historians have, and indeed more useful than currently dominant medical understandings of what is today commonly identified as 'depression'. Acedia, as Cvetkovich explains, can be translated from the writings of fourth century monk and theologian John Cassian as "weariness or distress of the heart," as "the anguish of the troubled heart," and as "spiritual dryness" (88). In contrast with contemporary (mis)understandings of depression, "acedia is characterized not just by lack of affect but by intense feelings," including "disgust," "dislike," and "disdain," that "lead to a powerful urge toward movement or flight" (85). Acedia involves a combination of "restlessness and desperation" as well as an "impatience with things as they are and a desire to be not only in a different place but a different time" (86). Cvetkovich values 'spiritual despair', of the kind of acedia references, which she argues resonates "with both activists, whose political disappointments can lead to a 'loss of faith' in collective ideals and goals, and academics, who often question the solitary life of intellectual work" (86). Notably, this is despair that combines elements of *both* 'restlessness and desperation', and as such suggests reaching the kind of 'impasse' Cvetkovich identifies as potentially productive, the kind of 'crisis' that represents a potentially crucial 'turning point'.

Cvetkovich also argues in support of reclaiming the conceptual usefulness of 'melancholy' (105). The long history of discourse on melancholy offers an opportunity to "return to a time when sadness could be viewed in other ways," other that is than an individually inherent 'disorder' that requires 'treatment' so as to 'cure' the disorder and thereby 'fix' the individual. A deep historical archive of writings on 'melancholy' can reveal multiple contesting ways of making sense of 'sadness', "including as a normative part of cultural experience" (106). Cvetkovich finds these conceptions of melancholy useful in facilitating "understandings of political depression as the loss of hope in how to bring about change," as what Cvetkvovich and others refer to as 'left melancholy' (109). Accepting such loss of hope as an understandable and even inevitable dimension of engagement in long-term struggle for large-scale social change is crucial in learning "how to embrace emotional responses as part of social justice projects" (109). Cvetkovich advocates in favor of "forms of activism that can address messy feelings rather than trying to banish them," and that directly incorporate practices that resemble therapy in the course of activism itself (110).

Cvetkovich interprets her experience of depression as indicative of the need to attend to what can be learned in living with and through melancholy, by attending to it rather than fleeing from it. This includes appreciating "how anxiety and what gets called depression are ordinary feelings embedded in ordinary circumstances" (79). In relation to how depression impacts those committed to a life of activist engagement, Cvetkovich emphasizes it is important "to be honest about the way that activism can sometimes stall out in the routines of daily life" (80). Cvetkovich also stresses that her own experience of depression "seemed to be telling me that a connection to where you are from, especially if it's been denied to you, is crucial; if anything, naturalization covers over the hard process of making home somewhere on the planet" (81). Writing a memoir of one's experience living with and through depression offers, moreover, a useful means of inquiring into "*how capitalism feels* or *how diaspora feels* without screening out nostalgia or sentiment or melancholy" (81). Cvetkovich is here suggesting that capitalist forces unite with diasporic forces to leave a great many people feeling cut off from connection with 'their roots' as well as from anything that feels as if it constitutes a genuine 'home' (81). As Cvetkovich further explains, "Depression, or alternate accounts of what gets called depression, is . . . a way to describe neoliberalism and globalization, or the current state of political economy, in affective terms" (11). In other words, "What gets called depression in the domestic sphere is one affective register of these social problems and one that often keeps people silent, weary, and too numb to really notice the sources of their unhappiness" (12).

Cvetkovich discusses the work of Sharon O'Brien, author of *The Family Silver: a Memoir of Depression and Inheritance* (2004), as compellingly exploring the affective impacts, across multiple successive generations, of poverty and migration in her Irish family history. O'Brien addresses how members of her family experienced these affective impacts prior to, during, and after the process of emigrating from Ireland to the US. O'Brien's memoir attests to "the crushing pressures of the American dream," and especially to 'the link between depression and seeking external approval' (143). Resonant with Cvetkovich's own experience, O'Brien finds "a way out of depression by detaching herself from this capitalist emphasis on the pressure to make one's identity around dissertations, books, and other markers of productivity" (143). O'Brien reinterprets depression as 'an unconscious form of resistance to the work ethic' (143). As O'Brien declares, "This is a struggle in America, a culture that celebrates and practically requires individual achievement, a culture where we don't have enough stories for imagining lives that do not fit, in one way or another, the success plot" (quoted 143).

Cvetkovich also commends the work of Jeffery Smith, in *Where the Roots Reach for Water: a Personal and Natural History of Melancholia* (2001), for likewise writing compellingly about "how the medical and scientific models of depression are linked to industrialization with its relentless demand for labor" (146). Smith identifies the late 20th to early 21st century as an 'Age of Anti-Depression' because of a dominant inclination to want to rush past and quickly put an end to depression. Smith argues that "because depression counters the 'efficiency', 'productivity', 'success', 'networking', and 'optimism' demanded by the modern workplace and culture, it is shunned" (quoted

146). Smith, in contrast with this 'shunning', as Cvetkovich explains, "embraces the possibility, inspired by the psychologist James Hillman, that 'depression is hidden knowledge' and is encouraged by his therapist to consider what depression might be trying to tell him" (146). Depression leads Smith to explore meanings of 'homesickness' in broader terms than commonly associated with this word. As 'homesickness' becomes depression, 'home' represents something much akin to an ancestral home, an ancestral place of belonging, and Smith does not presume "that home can only be found in the place where one is from" (149). Cvetkovich agrees that depression represents 'homesickness' for people who feel sick because of not feeling at home, of not feeling any substantial connection with any place that satisfies their need 'for a home' and 'to be at home'. Cvetkvoch remains cautious about broaching the idea that 'returning home' or 'finding home' will in and of itself be sufficient to 'cure', 'heal', or otherwise enable 'recovery from' depression (152). Yet this kind of quest can provide one dimension of what is needed, especially when those undergoing such a quest recognize that "The connection to land or home need not be 'natural' or in the blood to still be a relation to 'nature' that connects people and places (and it can thus be queer and diasporic)" (152).

Cvetkovich's major focus in chapter two of part two of *Depression: a Public Feeling*, "From Dispossession to Radical Self-Possession: Racism and Depression," is upon how "Epidemics of depression can be related (both as symptom and as obfuscation) to long-term histories of violence that have ongoing impacts at the level of everyday emotional experience" (7). Cvetkovich frames this discussion by posing the question "What if depression, in the Americas at least, could be traced to histories of colonialism, genocide, slavery, legal exclusion, and everyday segregation and isolation that haunt all our lives, rather than to biochemical imbalances?" (115). In beginning to unpack what this might mean, Cvetkovich draws upon Cornell West to distinguish between 'black sadness' and 'white depression'. As Cvetkovich summarizes, West links both "to the failure of the American dream," but for whites "sadness comes when the belief that one should be happy or protected turns out to be wrong and when a privileged form of hopefulness that has so often been entirely foreclosed to black people is punctured" (116). Cvetkovich contends, for both Blacks and whites, albeit in distinct and different ways, 'racial melancholy' is a key source of what is commonly identified as depression. and this key dimension of what forms and constitutes 'depression' deserves careful scrutiny. Cvetkovich cites David Eng and Shin Hee Han as helpfully explaining that, in this same connection, "melancholy's negativity might in fact be a productive corrective to a naive politics of hope" while further citing West as likewise helpfully proposing "the challenge is to dwell in sadness . . . while not giving up a hopefulness that remains stubbornly faithful for no good reason in the midst of despair" (117). In sum, despair represents "a starting point, not an endpoint" (117).

As she proceeds further along this particular line of inquiry, Cvetkovich continues to emphasize the importance of recognizing experiences of 'depression' differ along lines of race as well as the importance of being able to respond to this difference, while arguing nonetheless that all are impacted by racism, past and present, in ways that can and do contribute to depression, including "sometimes in oblique ways that aren't overtly visible" (120). This includes white people "living lives of privilege in the vicinity of the violence of racism" (120). Cvetkovich distinguishes between racism as source of depression versus racism as source of trauma–i.e., racism leads "to more chronic and low-level feelings" of despair as well as to more acute and tempestuous feelings (120). Recognizing both is important because "*long histories* [my italics] of 'dispossession'" are those responsible for exerting psychic damage not only on those who directly dispossessed but also on people whose ancestors have been so dispossessed (120).

In doing justice to this continuing impact it is crucial to take seriously "what it *feels* like for people of color to live in the context of racism" (122). Doing so requires inquiring into "the everyday affective life of racism," including by respecting the value of what Phil Harper characterizes as the 'evidence of felt intuition' as well as the value of what happens within 'the domestic sphere' of everyday life (122). Also crucial in such attending to 'the everyday affective life of racism' is paying due respect to the impacts of so-called "casual forms of racism" (124) and to how "we are all living in an environment steeped with racialized violence" (125).

Cvetkovich argues that "A politics of depression is one in which the 'rupture [is] the story'" (128). This rupture can be found in the form of wounds that remain, wounds that are not healed, and wounds that linger and fester, especially over extended periods of time–wounds that are, indeed, cross-generational as well as more broadly historical and social. As Cvetkovich notes well, past experiences spanning casual forms of racism to the most brutal forms of racial violence as well as racism's systemic pervasion, structural entrenchment, and institutional implementation continue to manifest themselves as living presences within contemporary Black and Brown people's psychic experience (131). This massive impact can be readily recognized, for example, as a "legacy of fear and suspicion even in a respectable Black family" (131). This 'legacy of fear and suspicion' indeed constitutes a preeminent dimension of "the everyday life of affective racism" (131).

Cvetkovich advocates for "A radical theory of depression" that "aims to do justice to questions of dispossession and race in order to build a systemic framework that can be used by all," even as it is multiculturally multivalent, nuancedly sensitive and sensitized to racial differences (139). The distinctiveness of what Cvetkovich here advocates reveals itself in her appreciation for literary and other writings that demonstrate it is possible to find "ways to move forward by coming together around violence and despair," in particular by 'holding on to' "depressive affect" in 'keeping' "despair next to hope" (132-133). The distinctiveness of what Cvetkovich is advocating also shows up in her appreciation yet further for what she identifies as forms of 'spiritual' praxis, with 'spiritual' here broadly conceived–practices "that begin from the premise that all human beings are important and connected" (137).

Cvetkovich extols the benefit of discovering ways to "hold on to forms of 'enchantment' (and other related feelings) rather than demystifying religion as cultural expression" (199). Cvetkovich contends both religious and non-religious forms of spirituality have much of value to offer those who have not previously considered this prospect, or who have been dismissive of it, because "The spiritual can help articulate a politics of feeling that is manifest not just in the overt or visible social movements of conventional politics but in the more literal kinds of movement that make up everyday life practices" (199).

Cvetkovich calls our attention to how social movements organized and mobilized to strive for social change are concerned, even without realizing this to be the case, with what needs to be changed in terms of its harmful impact at the level of ordinary, everyday life practices, and in terms of how it feels to live our daily lives caught up within structures of relations that are so harmful and demand change. It is at this level or the ordinary and the everyday, of the habitual and the mundane, that Cvetkovich locates the spiritual. Yet, spiritual practice represents an *intervention within* the ordinary and the everyday, and the habitual and the mundane, because "Spiritual practice is a way of becoming open to what we don't know," and such an openness is vital in seeking to bring about, to contribute to bringing about, meaningful social and political change (200). Spiritual practice requires "a willingness to encounter impasse or lack of knowledge," representative of profound possibility, and here Cvetkovich notes well kinship between what she is advocating and Buddhist advocacy of embracing fear, anxiety, and the unknown (200).

In describing what amounts to her process of 'recovery', Cvetkovich identifies the positive benefit of bodywork, including but extending beyond physical exercise. Neglecting this kind of activity, as Cvetkovich did for awhile due to the pressures she experienced upon becoming an assistant professor at the University of Texas at Austin, proved costly (65). Indeed pressures that lead people to abandon what is vital to their health and well-being are all too commonplace not only within academia but also many other areas of contemporary capitalist society. But what Cvetkovich is at pains to stress in this connection, when doing so leads people to become depressed, is that "Sometimes saving the day is all it really takes to save a life. If you can hold the despair at bay for just a little bit longer, there's a chance that something will come along to change things. Swimming has saved my life, or at least saved the day, on numerous occasions. When you're depressed, and all you want to do is to sit still or curl up in a ball in bed and never get up, putting the body in motion is a major struggle and a major accomplishment" (50). Cvetkovich now swims regularly and has found this and other physical exercise "becomes an opportunity for sanctioned dissociation" (51).

Cvetkovich interprets perhaps the greatest thematic emphasis in her 'depression memoir' is indeed "on transformative daily habit as an antidote to depression" (76). Writing the journals that became this memoir themselves exemplify this kind of 'transformative daily habit' (76). Cvetkovich found doing this kind of writing on a regular basis helpful in breaking from the constraints exercised by the dominant temporalities of academic life, and more specifically by the kinds of writing required in her scholarship, teaching, and institutional and professional service (76). Cvetkovich conceives of her 'depression memoir' as "making a case for the value of writing that is open-ended and process-based," citing Audre Lorde in support of "forms of truth that are felt rather than proven by evidence" (77). For Cvetkovich, doing this kind of writing manifests "an important pushback against the tremendous pressure to acquire 'discipline' in academia" (77).

"Daily life in all its ordinariness can be a basis for the utopian project of building new worlds in response to both spiritual despair and political depression," Cvetkovich declares, as she discusses what she identifies as "the utopia of ordinary habit" (191). Cvetkovich links 'the utopia of ordinary habit' with "a sensory being who crafts a self through process and through porous boundaries between self and other, and between human and nonhuman (including animals and things)" (191-192). Cvetkovich pronounces "The *utopia of ordinary habit* is forged out of the loss of connection . . . that characterizes depression," that involves a 'remaking', especially an affective and collective 'remaking', and yet in so doing "does not seek to gloss over the dire state of contemporary politics, nor to deny the feelings of sadness, apathy, isolation, or anger that are often manifest in the practice of small daily gestures" (192-193).

I have described what Cvetvovich does in *Depression: a Public Feeling* as theorizing, and in particular as theorizing depression along with how to make sense of and respond to depression in social and political terms, but it is worth taking into account that Cvetkovich sees herself, in *Depression: a Public Feeling*, as, more humbly, demonstrating "ways of bringing new knowledge to the table" while also *resisting a general theory* [my italics] of depression" (160). Cvetkovich is interested in cultivating "reparative" knowledges and reparative practices. She seeks to contribute toward this end by sharing cases and examples that have helped her to come to understand not only is depression 'ordinary' but also so is its 'cure', "which resides not in medical treatment but in the art of daily living" (161). Cvetkovich contends these strategies for survival and persistence are urgent because "Atrocities are happening in our front yards and on our television screens and we need to find ways to react against what is happening without either giving up or exploding" (176).

Cvetkovich extols collective practices of survival and persistence, especially subcultural community practices centered around various forms of art, such as performance art, and including forms of 'folk art' such as 'crafting'. Queer activism in particular is and has long been important for Cvetkovich because queer activism not only aims at and contributes toward valuable social change, or at least carving out space to manifest alternatives to normatively straight ways of being, but also provides Cvetkovich with an affirming culture and a supportive community (60-61).

And yet, Cvetkovich avers, "If depression is a version of Lauren Berlant's slow death, then there is no clean break from it. The bad feelings that hover around daily practices of survival are always there, especially if it's a political depression, which won't end until there is real economic justice and a better reckoning with histories of violence" (206). Still, what Cvetkovich argues throughout *Depression: a Public Feeling* is that feelings of hope and joy can coexist with 'bad feelings' (206). In line with the broad aim of Public Feelings praxis, "to depathologize negative feelings so they can be seen as a possible resource for political action rather than its antithesis" (2), *Depression: a Public Feeling* is a book about depression, yes, including about how depression makes the effort to live one's live arduous, and indeed harrowing, but it is also a book "about hope and even happiness, about how to live a better life by embracing rather than glossing over bad feelings" (3). The Public Feelings project concerns itself with "how to think psychic and social life together" and this requires "rethinking activisms in ways that attend to its emotional registers, including the frustrations that come from trying to keep activism and scholarship together" (7). From a Public Feelings vantage point, no 'magic bullets' are available; what is available is "just the slow steady work of resilient survival, utopian dreaming, and other affective tools for transformation" (2).

Even while 'depathologizing' negative feelings, the Public Feelings project "resists pastoralizing or redemptive accounts of negative feeling that seek to convert it into something useful or positive" (5). But "it also embraces categories such as utopia and hope" (5-6). What opportunities can be gained by working on, with, through, and even beyond depression require considerable *work*, the success of which is far from guaranteed, while what is achieved by doing so is not identical with the pain, sorrow, hardship, and despair of depressive feelings in and of themselves. Depression, after all, according to Cvetkovich, represents a reasonable response to living within 'a sick society', or more narrowly partaking as part of 'a sick institution', a 'sick social situation', or 'a sick social relation'. This 'sickness' is not to be romanticized–it is, as a 'sickness', a site of immense damage. Public Feelings is a "queer project" that "tries to imagine a liberatory version of social and affective relations *beyond* [my emphasis] the liberal versions that have come to dominate the public sphere of gay politics" while also focused, in this same connection, on "finding ways to *survive* [my emphasis] disappointment and to remind ourselves of the persistence of radical visions and ways of living" (6).

In writing her memoir Cvetkovich confides she struggled against an inclination to feel this kind of writing is self-indulgent and not sufficiently rigorously academic, as well as with reluctance to expose her own vulnerability *publicly* (74). Yet Cvetkovich felt empowered to proceed by linking what she is doing in her book with the important role of memoir in queer and feminist subcultures, in particular the riotgrrrl movement and allied kinds of spoken word forums taking place in the early 1990s (75). Cvetkovich nevertheless also struggled to feel justified in doing this kind of work, concentrating so centrally on matters of feelings, and especially in the form of a memoir, because she felt unease that it is a luxury to be able to do so given how many other people never gain such an opportunity. Cvetkovich does prize this opportunity because this kind of 'respite' is, even if a relative 'luxury', 'necessary' in order to be able to continue to do vital critical and creative forms of intellectual work (205). It is important to "protect that privileged position from being eroded by budget cuts and constant slams against not only radical cultural studies but the humanities in general" because academic workers without such opportunities are at all too ready risk of all too rapid "burnout" (205). Indeed, a society that cannot provide people with the material conditions necessary to think, to reflect, to explore, to experiment, to innovate, to create–and which does not provide people with respite from what leads them to 'crash and burn' is indeed, as Cvetkovich suggests, 'a sick kind of society' (205).

Public Feelings, as part of "the affective turn in cultural criticism," not only takes emotion, feeling, and affect seriously but also inspires new ways of doing theory and criticism (3). This is an ongoing endeavor that not only takes into account emotion, feeling, and affect as these take shape in concrete conjunctures but also strives to come up with new ways of connecting emotion, feeling, and affect, on the one hand, with activist practice on the other hand. For instance, in an interview published for *Cultural Studies*, first conducted on May 20, 2022, and then updated in September 2022, Megan Boler and Elizabeth Davis ask affect theorists Lauren Berlant, Ann Cvetkovich, and Deborah Gould to make use of affect theory and criticism in interpreting and responding to the presidency of Donald Trump and the rise in support for authoritarian populism, or neo-fascism, in the US, as well as to do the same in relation to concomitant struggles over matters of race, gender, and sexuality in the US.

As Boler prefaces this discussion, "Since 2016, emotion has come to have a new currency in political discussion" (360). Berlant expresses reservations concerning the mobilizations immediately following the police killing of George Floyd because "'white people reckoning'," finally, with systemic racism, circa 2020, maintains "gross, unfortunate resonances with the abolitionist project of white sentimentalists (of all genders!) in the US nineteenth century" (367). Yet Gould, while respecting the caveats Berlant expresses, declares "I always think it's a good thing when people open themselves to facing what it's easier to turn away from" (367). Gould adds that she also refuses to interpret those who do not vote in elections as displaying 'apathy'. She interprets them as instead manifesting "a political withdrawal that often indicates desire for something beyond what's on offer" (368).

Cvetkovich in turn explains she uses the term 'ordinary racisms' rather than 'microaggressions' because the latter term does not do justice to what these practices actually mean and to the impact they actually exert. Cvetkovich finds it important "in addressing systemic racism" always simultaneously "to account for the combined force of overt or sensational forms of violence and more invisible forms of racism in everyday life" (370). Cvetkovich reads "the moment we're in as one in which the tensions and the conflicts are expanding and becoming more visible–including the pushback and the resentments against gains that have been made around race, around gender, around sexuality" (370).

In explicit connection with affect studies, Cvetkovich mentions she has been "interested in the activist organizing around the category of 'mutual aid' during the pandemic" and that "I've been very interested to see the role of affect in discussions of self-care and mental health within activism" such as in relation to Black Lives Matter (372). Cvetkovich emphasizes that 'affective cultural criticism' is inspired by "Audre Lorde's discussion of care as a revolutionary act" and "as integral to political organizing" (373). In Lorde's words, "Caring for myself is not self-indulgence, it is self-preservation, and that is an act of political warfare" (quoted 373). This assertion of Lorde's fits with Cvetkovich's conviction that "For me, the best work in affect studies is equipment for living, tools for living in the world" (373).

Gould proposes, in relation to right-wing emotionalism, that "we need to wonder about the materialization of those feelings, about what's happening in people's lives, what's affecting them, what's coursing around that makes people feel defeated, resentful, aggressively angry, hateful, violent . . . Those of us on the left need to reckon with the political sources and effects of feelings, that is, we need to attend to the ways political structures become subjectivized . . . and . . . to the ways systemic conditions manifest in our felt experience" (373). In other words, it is too easy and ultimately does not help to dismiss these people as engaging in irrationally nonsensical thinking, and to simply counter emotional 'excess and distortion' with rational fact, because doing so does not get to the root of why these people experience the need to feel in the ways that they do.

In conclusion, Berlant declares "it's our job to be placeholders in the space of contention and to extend it. Because it's very easy to forget that it could have been otherwise, you know? And that it could have been otherwise–this is Adorno's phrase for what politics is, a commitment is a memory that can power futures" (377). In other words, affect theory and criticism is a contribution to an ongoing state of contestation, and its foremost contribution at the present time may well be keeping open the space for continued consideration of what powerful, and especially powerfully reactionary, forces strive to close down. The aim is to insure the survival of the memory of other possibilities so these can live on and be available to inspire and enable forces capable of bringing about substantial transformation when the conditions and circumstances are ripe for this to happen.

As with Robert McRuer's *Crip Theory* and *Crip Times* I have not included Ann Cvetkovich's *Depression: a Public Feeling* as part of prior classes I have taught on Ian Curtis, Joy Division, and critical theory, but I can readily imagine doing so. In sections six through nine of this chapter I show how and why so by exploring connections between *Depression: a Public Feeling* and the Joy Division songs "She's Lost Control," "Dead Souls," "Atmosphere," and "Decades." For now I will add reflections on personal connections with *Depression: a Public Feeling* that come to mind.

To begin, like Cvetkovich, I have suffered from serious to severe depression. My experience of depression has also been shaped and influenced by working in the academic humanities, and by the stresses and strains, as well as the requirements and expectations, of doing this kind of work as part of this kind of institution. Feeling tired all the time, feeling unable to do much beyond what is absolutely necessary, feeling that whatever I do and however I do it will inevitably turn out to be futile and worthless, feeling that I myself am futile and worthless, feeling as if I barely exist at all anymore–all of this I know well. The same with anxiety so extreme that 'anxiety' hardly does justice to what is happening, as massive waves of panic and dread simultaneously envelop me and hurtle throughout my body even as nothing specific has 'triggered' this happening.

I share Cvetkovich's deep dissatisfaction with dominant medical explanations for and treatments of depression, and for me this includes both SSRIs (which did nothing at all for me) and CBT (which I found reductive and trivializing). I likewise am far more compelled by social and political explanations of depression that link depression to the nature of capitalist society (and, even more precisely than that, to the nature of patriarchal-racial-capitalist-imperialist society), and to the enormous extent of violence necessary to create and sustain this kind of society. I agree that 'bad feelings' individuals experience often make 'good sense' in response to living in this kind of society. I agree that an inquiry into the 'politics of depression', from a critical cultural studies vantage point, can, potentially, generate insight useful for persistence, endurance, and survival, including of ongoing struggle for social and political transformation.

I agree it is important to engage with experience of depression *publicly*, by talking and writing about this *publicly*, by openly and honestly sharing experience of depression and by respectfully supporting sharing and discussing this experience. And I agree we need to respond collectively, and to take collective responsibility, in attending to people's individual experience of depression, in particular by critically inquiring into social sources of this depression that do not reside *'inside'* of the individual person, that cannot be explained as the products of inherent, and inherited, biochemical disorder, or malfunctioning, entirely *'within'* the individual's supposedly uniquely discreet and distinct brain and nervous system.

Unlike Cvetkovich, however, I have not arrived at a confident sense of precisely what 'the spiritual' means to and for me, let alone a confident sense of precisely how important spirituality is in my life. I am, therefore, much less likely to recommend specific kinds of 'spiritual practices' to others. For me, 'the spiritual' comes closest to an ongoing seeking after truth and meaning, and as such well fits with Unitarian Universalism. I find elements of prospective value in this quest, as do many if not most Unitarian Universalists, from a wide variety of sources–i.e., from multiple faith traditions as well as from many other forms of knowledge and modes of practice. No single source is sufficient, in and of itself, and I never feel at all inclined to conclude confidently I have now arrived 'close enough' to 'the meaning and truth I have been searching for' that I can and should rest content to seek no more. If anything, I am constantly discovering how little I do know and how much more there is yet to know. But that 'much more' excites me, and it motivates me to keep moving–i.e., to keep seeking.

Nevertheless, I do not cultivate particular habits or rituals in keeping moving, in keeping seeking, that help me in living with and through experiences of anxiety and depression. I live with and through anxiety and depression simply because I *have* lived with and through anxiety and depression in the past; I know it has been possible to do so and I know therefore it can continue to be possible to do so. I live with and through anxiety and depression as well because I continue to maintain interest in and enthusiasm for doing much more yet ahead such that I cannot allow anxiety and depression to annihilate me. As long as I can maintain that interest in and enthusiasm for doing much more yet ahead, I will persist, endure, and survive.

I have found, moreover, when feeling at my worst, that I need to make changes, even small changes, and to try to do different things, even if these amount only to tiny differences, rather than to trust in the habitual and the ritualistic. Too much of my life, like that of all too many of us in contemporary capitalist society, is subject to routinization, to structures that are so incessantly and rigidly recurrent that they can and do feel deadening. I do share Cvetkovich's conviction that literally moving at moments when one is least inclined to feel like one can move at all can be vital–can be crucially revitalizing. But for me this does not necessarily take the form of moving in a habitually or ritually familiar manner–not, for example, turning to the same form of physical exercise, such as swimming in Cvetkovich' case, or walking or running in my case, that I have already frequently pursued.

Undoubtedly, under the influence of orthodox Marxism, I have at times in my past expressed some skepticism about privileging feeling or feelings, and even argued for the necessity of prioritizing thinking over feeling, or for the necessity of always being able to provide a rational explanation of and account for feeling(s), while warning about dangers of 'irrationalism' that can arise from not doing so. Yet I also define critical theory as problematizing European Enlightenment rationalism and empiricism.

In terms of visual and plastic arts I prefer primarily non-, anti-, and post- representational forms, in particular modernist to postmodernist and especially experimental and avant-garde varieties. In training to be a docent at the Everson Museum in Syracuse, New York, my culminating project focused on the 'color field' abstract painting of Helen Frankenthaler, Morris Louis, and Kenneth Noland. I was hugely excited to help visitors, and especially young people, appreciate art like this, to find compelling ways to make sense of and respond to it without needing to compare it to something it empirically resembled or to some linear-sequential narrative it suggested. From my earliest memories of my mother first taking me to visit art museums, galleries, and similar spaces, I always was far more interested in modern to contemporary art than anything else, and to this day I skip everything else when I visit these places. Likewise, from well before my undergraduate years began but then accelerating during that time and over the course of my years as a master's and PhD student at Syracuse University, I developed similarly keen interests in experimental and avant-garde forms of 'post-classical' new music, including diverse currents in early experimental electronica.

In my senior year in high school I taught Faulkner, Joyce, and existentialism to my AP English class, and I loved doing so because I loved this kind of literary and philosophical work. Well before my undergraduate years at Wesleyan University, I developed keen interests in modernist movements such as expressionism and surrealism, both of which I have been delighted to teach on numerous occasions since–and indeed among the most fun classes I have ever taught are the two I taught on 'The Fantastic, The Uncanny, and The Surreal' at UW-Eau Claire. I have also long been enormously compelled by utopian, dystopian, and critical (dys)utopian literature. I have returned again and again to these kinds of literature both in my teaching and in my writing. My initial PhD dissertation focus, towards which I wrote over 200 single-spaced typed pages, I conceived as a critical theoretical examination of ecological utopian, dystopian, and critical (dys)utopian literature. From the moment I first learned about the critical theoretical as well as the dramatic and poetic work of Bertolt Brecht I have been hooked. I love Brechtian-influenced theatre, cinema, music, and literature.

In sum, I maintain considerable respect, of long-standing, for the power of feelings and for the distinct capabilities and contributions of emotional and intuitive varieties of intelligence, even as I also am strongly compelled to inquire into and explore ways of critically theorizing what accounts for the power of feelings and for the capabilities and contributions of emotional and intuitive forms of intelligence. Like Deborah Gould, and others working in 'affect studies', I too am more inclined to want to understand how and why people emotionally invest in what I myself find bizarre, absurd, ridiculous, outrageous, dangerous, and disturbing than in attempting to counter this investment by attempting to show them this is false in comparison with what is true or by attempting to show them this is fallacious in comparison with what is fact. I too am much more interested in seeking to understand *why* people *feel* the desire and even the need to believe falsity is truth and fallacy is fact than to merely contrast the false and the true and the fallacious and the factual.

Cvetkovich's emphasis on the importance of connection with 'home', in the sense of 'roots', and more precisely 'familial' and 'ancestral' roots, I find intriguing but I have not discovered, or rediscovered, that particular kind of connection, for myself, in the same way she has, or some of the writers she discusses have, such as Sharon O'Brien and Jeffery Smith. Yes, to some degree I do feel a sense of connection with Irish ethnicity and ancestry, that has been deepened by explorations and concentrations in Irish Studies, by numerous visits to Ireland, and by attending a good number of Irish-American events, such as Irish Fairs and Irish Festivals, on a semi-regular basis. But it was my great-great-grandparents that came to the US and Canada, in the wake of the Great Irish Famine, or 'Black 47', so my ties, through family, to Ireland are quite indirect.

I have at many points in my life felt 'not at home' in places where I have lived, and at places where I have worked, longing to find 'home' in a considerably different kind of place. Often, indeed, I have felt 'home' in visiting large cities, especially in the UK, in ways I have not in the places where I have lived and worked in the US, including Eau Claire, although I have slowly but surely come to feel more and more 'at home' in Eau Claire in my now more than 25 years living and working in Eau Claire, while living and working here during the course of the COVID-19 pandemic has accelerated that sense of attachment. Nevertheless, I still dream of retiring to live in and start a new life as a resident of a large city, and that yet will happen. I find dimensions of the kind of lifestyle available or more readily available in a large city, and especially within a specific large city, enticing, but not because of particular family or ancestral ties to that kind of location.

I do experience the phenomenon of 'the uncanny' powerfully and often; this may explain why it is hard for me to conceive of establishing or reestablishing connection with familial and ancestral roots that will enable me no longer to feel as troubled as I often recurrently have throughout much of my life by a palpable sense of not being at home or not fully at home in a place that is ostensibly my home. I interpret this feeling as a reflection of and response to my perpetual dissatisfaction and unease living within the kind of society which this is, founded and continually dependent upon a massive and horrendous extent of violent dispossession, expropriation, exclusion, suppression, marginalization, and erasure.

I would like to turn, in concluding this discussion of 'personal connections' that come to mind in reflecting on Ann Cvetkovich's *Depression: a Public Feeling* to other two books: *Mad at School: Rhetorics of Mental Disability and Academic Life*, written by Margaret Price, and published in 2011, and *Ableism in Academia: Theorising Experiences of Disabilities and Chronic Illness in Higher Education*, edited by Nicole Brown and Jennifer Leigh, published in 2020, and involving essays and poems from thirteen different writers. In doing so I want to explore further matters of 'feelings' in connection with how academia is structured and operated and in particular what that does to people whom Margaret Price identifies as experiencing 'mental disabilities' as well as a broader range of disabilities, notably 'invisible disabilities' in the form of 'chronic illness' that the contributors to *Ableism in Academia* emphasize. Although Cvetkovich discusses how academia can contribute to depression, and how restrictive as well as increasingly restrictive are opportunities to pursue a career as tenure-line professor in English or a comparable humanities field today, let alone to be able to flourish in doing so by realizing the dreams one had for 'making a difference' in committing to pursue this career path, she does not focus as directly, as do Price or Brown, Leigh, and fellow contributors to *Ableism in Academia*, on how extremely difficult it can be for disabled people to succeed in academia–including on account of how structurally hostile academia tends to be toward disabled people.

In anticipating writing here about *Mad at School* and *Ableism in Academia* I have felt trepidation even as these are both most compelling and important books. I have recognized I need to address not only how I feel about inequitable access I myself have experienced on account of challenges and complications I face in relation to matters of health and ability but also how I myself have been at least in part complicit in contributing to and reinforcing lack of equitable access for others.

I have grown steadily more sensitively attuned over the lengthy period of time I have been teaching to the diversity of the needs the students I teach bring to bear with them, in relation to matters of access, and in relation to how I design and conduct the classes I teach. I have done well in sensitively and compassionately responding to students' needs and concerns when they have shared these with me, as I in multiple ways strongly encourage them to do, right from the start of our work together–in informational questionnaires where I explicitly invite them to share in confidence with me any matter that might in any way affect how they are able to succeed in our class, in statements that elaborate on the same in my own initial presentation and in our class syllabi, and in repeated similar remarks thereafter. I include this kind of invitation on all assignments I implement, and am ready to work with students to devise alternatives that work better for whom they are and what they are facing, as need be, while I strive to be as expressly clear as possible what are my expectations of students, notably in terms of class conduct and 'civility', as well as in terms of attendance and participation. And I am understanding, patient, and flexible with students who face difficulties meeting these expectations due to matters of illness and disability they share with me.

In openly sharing my own challenges and complications due to chronic illness, disability, anxiety, depression, and even post-traumatic stress disorder as well as personal experience attempting suicide and suicidality, I do prompt many students to feel confident they can share similar issues frankly with me, and to do so from early on and repeatedly thereafter. The fact that I talk precisely about my digestive dysmotility disorder, about my experience of epilepsy, and about other issues concerning illness, injury, and disability I face, when and as I do, also helps, as does my readiness to share with my classes, at least afterward, when I have been impacted, for example, by the approach of an epileptic seizure or by severe pain in my abdominal region.

Making use of weekly check-ins, and giving students credit toward the grade for doing these, has also helped considerably, and I pride myself on responding to every check-in and to doing so in a timely fashion. In these check-in students share with me a wide array of thoughts and feelings, concerning what we are doing in class together as well as in relation to their lives beyond, and in particular challenges and difficulties they face. I tend to be patient and flexible with students who need more time to complete assignments, papers and projects, and who need to come to class late or leave early or make use of assistive technologies and other unorthodox techniques to help them concentrate and do well while in class. The same with allowing young children to attend because parents who are my students cannot afford other means of taking care of these children while class is running. The same with actively encouraging students to feel free to get up, stand up, walk out, lie down, stretch, do breathing exercises, and take short breaks where they leave class and then return–as long as they let me know this is helpful to them that is fine with me. I also welcome students bringing food and drink to class, eating and drinking while class is taking place, if and when this is helpful to them. And I maintain no restrictions on how they may dress in order to feel comfortable. If they need to be making use of cell phones, or notebooks or tablet computers, regularly, and they let me know they need to do, this is fine. If they have problems always appearing directly focused on what is going on, as part of lessons and discussions, or if they need to be moving their hands, legs, or other parts of their body, doing so regularly, 'stimming', to feel comfortable, and they tell me so, this is entirely welcome.

I incorporate a variety of discussion techniques, and indeed activities, so that we can include a range sufficient to work for diverse learning styles, while I evaluate participation in conjunction with 'contribution' that can include many ways of contributing beyond literal participation in classroom discussion, and I evaluate all of this qualitatively and in relation to each individual student doing the best they can, from where they are at and as whom they are, rather than in comparison with others. I do much more besides in aiming to provide maximally inclusive access to diverse students' situations, and their needs, while being ready to listen and talk with them about how we can work together to do better, when and as necessary. And I am eager to learn more and to improve my own habits to always do better.

However, I am not always so good in responding as well as I could to students who are unable and unwilling to share with me, no matter how much invitation and encouragement, and how many avenues and opportunities, I offer for them to do so. And so I have at time tended, especially earlier in my teaching career, to respond in more judgmental and punitive ways to students' whose behavior, and whose presentation, has struck me, working according to institutional commonsense, as disengaged and, especially, as disrespectful, as lazy and apathetic, and as arrogant and capricious. I admit, with regret, at times, especially earlier in my teaching career, I have been too ready to interpret some forms of student behavior as deliberately disrespecting me and our class, as deliberately designed 'to cause trouble' and to deliberately 'test me'. This might be in relation to me as an 'out' gay and queer teacher, as someone from the Northeast, as someone who is highly intellectually presenting and affirming, or as someone who openly identifies with and teaches from a critical theoretical as well as from a left radical perspective. This might be in relation to me as a graduate student instructor, an adjunct faculty member, a tenure-track faculty member, or a tenured faculty member but not yet a full professor.

I have allowed myself to become angry at students repeatedly coming late to and leaving early from class, at showing up not having done the required reading/screening/listening and therefore not being prepared to do class work, at holding 'private conversations' in class while I and other students have been focused on the ostensible direct aims of the class, on reading other materials besides those having to do with class while class is proceeding and in frequently texting or playing with other apps on their cell phone while class is running, at repeatedly interrupting me and other students with questions and comments bearing no obvious connection to what we are talking about or what the class is ostensibly is focused upon, in not showing up to required meetings or to conferences they themselves have requested, in turning in slipshod and careless work which doesn't follow assignment instructions and which doesn't even show evidence of having paid attention to assignments at all, and in seemingly refusing to let others talk without dominating the conversation while also seeming to prefer always to talk solely with me and to ignore or dismiss even the prospect of learning through working with other students.

I know I have become angered for further reasons as well. For example, by students over and over again asking the same questions about page and word targets/limits/minima and maxima when I have repeatedly answered the same questions in stressing none apply, I am interested in writing quality and not quantity, and when I have stressed I am ready to offer *suggested* page or word ranges to those who need these and find these useful but these are *not* 'requirements'. For example, by students who have simply told me, and not asked if this would be OK, that they will miss class to go to a concert or a gig because 'they like the band', to attend a study session or a rehearsal for another class without informing the professor of this other class these meetings conflict with our class meeting time, or to meet with a faculty advisor when faculty advisors always are able to schedule meetings at times that do not conflict with times classes meet. In relation to the last series of examples, I have at times interpreted these behaviors as indicative of students inadequately valuing our time in our class. And the same has been the case at times with students who have asked if they could sign up for a class I was teaching while missing more than half of the time in class we would be meeting due to an overlap with another class they wished to take at the same time. I have also become angered at times as well by with students continually pestering me with questions about how well they are doing, grade-wise, even after I have already answered these questions over and over again with nothing new to report.

I have never raised my voice with, let alone yelled at, students. I have instead become coldly firm, and quietly harsh, often spelling out in a detailed email or other piece of writing how disappointed I have been. In egregious cases I have elaborated what negative consequences I am imposing and will yet follow, while requiring these same students to meet not only with me but also with members of other campus offices to discuss and agree on ways to overcome their problematic and disruptive behavior–or leave our class. The last I have only resorted to when it has struck me these students are clearly undermining the learning experience for other students and/or when they have been making fun of and otherwise deriding and denigrating other students' identities.

All of the preceding instances where I have at times experienced anger, in the course of teaching, might seem reasonable enough. Many other teachers will undoubtedly recall similar occasions when they have felt much the same. And the institution indeed often encourages us to act exactly this way–that is, not to tolerate any of these kinds of '(mis)behavior'. I recognized from early on a normative institutional expectation is that teachers must demonstrate their ability always to maintain 'control' over the classes they teach and to engage in 'appropriate disciplinary practices' when and as necessary to do so. If we don't do so, we suffer in evaluations of our teaching performance, and in the readiness of colleagues and supervisors to recommend that we be rehired or promoted. What's more, for a great many years I taught within institutions where it was abundantly clear to me that evaluation of teaching performance did not acknowledge students tend, on average, to evaluate teachers less positively, even considerably less positively, as women versus men, as people of color versus white people, as LGBTQIA+ versus straight (or 'cis-het') people, and as disabled and older people versus able-bodied and middle-aged or younger people. Referring to any of these markers of identity as influencing student evaluations, and as influencing other means of assessing student responsiveness to teaching, including students' complaints about teaching, I recognized would simply be dismissed as excuses for the teacher not being 'individually good (individually *tough*) enough'.

So I knew I needed to do everything I could to insure not being forced into the position where I would refer to, let alone rely on, any of what would be so dismissed as 'excuses'. This put greater pressure on me, leading me to the conviction that I maintained less room for 'mistakes' in my teaching, ever, than, a number of other colleagues–especially straight white able-bodied cisgendered male colleagues who were neither 'too old' nor 'too young'. I have taught in places where being at all 'out' about being gay, as a teacher and in the course of teaching, was considered 'wrong', irrelevant, counter-productive, and offensive–and the same teaching anything even remotely touching on LGBTQIA+ lives, lived-experiences, outlooks, and perspectives (and my refusal to go along with this valuation has caused me plenty of trouble). In these situations my refusing to 'hide' and to 'suppress' was considered highly problematic. Likewise, approaching the teaching of topics, and fields, according to newer and more recent conceptions and practices of pedagogy as well as in conjunction with newer and more recent directions for intellectual pursuit, than colleagues were familiar with, especially when they were convinced only one or an extremely limited range of 'right' ways to teach these subjects existed, has also required considerable diligence on my part. I needed always to be exceedingly well prepared to explain and justify everything I was doing, for a skeptical to hostile audience (an audience not consisting of the students I was teaching). In these circumstances, I have felt pressure to be less tolerant and accepting than would be ideal versus student conduct I perceived as disrespecting me, whom I was, what I was about, and what I was working to aim to achieve.

But in a number of such instances, it makes sense, in retrospect, to interpret what ostensibly 'disrespectful' students were manifesting as reflecting their own challenges and complications–in particular in relation to mental health and diverse abilities. Admittedly, it has taken me time, and effort, to be more readily understanding than I used to be of students whose neurodiversity, or prospective neurodiversity, shows up in ways that could be interpreted as rude, as insensitive, and even as disruptive. I have been working on this for a good number of years now, and I have improved, but I regret not always having been so understanding. And I regret as well thinking that just because I offer students so much encouragement and so many avenues to share with me complications and challenges they experience in their lives, and concerning whom they are and what they are about, that this is sufficient to guarantee that they will do so.

In Tobin Siebers's "Foreword" to *Mad at School*, he characterizes as a "stunning revelation" Margaret Price's claim that "Rationality, participation, independence, coherence, and collegiality are educational standards" used in academia not only "to measure students and teachers," but also to "serve a medical purpose because individuals who fail the standards are not only considered unfit for the classroom, they are suspected of being unfit for life" (xii). Judgments of these kinds can cause tremendous 'bad feeling', most definitely including depression, including by compounding the depression that already depressed students and teachers struggle with.

Price begins her book by interrogating how such judgments are made, within academia, concerning who are and who are not manifesting indications of 'mental disability' (Price prefers 'mental disability' while acknowledging a plethora of terms that are used by others to signify much the same). According to Price, academia engages in what Benjamin Ross has characterized as "quasi-psychiatric surveillance" (quoted 3), in particular versus student writing, in order to ascertain signs of mental disability, and especially to ascertain threats that this mental disability might represent. Academia tends to de-value "disorderly minds," despite the fact "such minds show up [in academia] all the time in obvious and not so obvious ways," and despite "recognizing their appearance is not a yes-no proposition, but rather a confusing and contextually dependent process that calls into question what we mean by the 'normal' mind" (4).

In relation to faculty and staff, many working within "academe tend to pass much of the time," pretending we do not experience any form of mental disability. This is, as Price aptly sums up, "passing for survival" (7). Doing so, however, reinforces academic ableism. And "Ableism contributes to the construction of a rigid, elitist, hierarchical, and inhumane academic system," with many academics totally oblivious to how exalting academia "as a bastion of reason, the place where one's rational mind is one's instrument," indeed one's priority or even exclusive instrument, represents a signal dimension of exactly this construction (8).

Price frequently discusses the repeated insistence, within academia, that teachers are not therapists, and that therefore they should not engage in anything even indirectly approaching therapy in relation to their students, but instead always refer their students elsewhere for such help–especially to on-campus student counseling services. However, citing Michael Payne's work, Price argues "a teacher's ability in analysis and critical questioning might be more useful than commonly imagined" in relation to students' struggles with the impacts of 'mental disability' (50). As Payne declares, "I think it is important that we, as writing teachers, stop seeing emotion, pain, and trauma as threatening, anti-intellectual, and solipsistic, and instead begin to see how we might, like therapists, feminist theorists, and philosophers, begin to recognize them as ways of knowing, not signs of dangerous pedagogies or teachers who are acting as therapists" (quoted 50). I whole-heartedly agree. I encourage students I teach to share as openly, honestly, fully, and forthrightly as they can what has strongly emotionally impacted them, and continues to do so, in their writing, and in their contributions to class discussion as well as in individual, group, and team projects they prepare for and present to the rest of the class. I urge them to do so because this will enable their writing, and their other work, to prove more meaningful, even much more meaningful, for them and for fellow students, as well as provide the basis for substantial insight and indeed genuine personal growth in better understanding whom they are, where they are coming from, where they are headed, and why so.

I welcome sharing emotionally, and I encourage responding sensitively, respectfully, and compassionately to such sharing. I seek continually to model doing both. When students tell me, in sharing matters of serious emotional distress with me, that they don't want to make me 'their therapist', I reply by asking them to consider me as 'a friend', even as I do talk with them about the availability of licensed therapists to help them, on campus and off, along with other kinds of available resources that can prove helpful as well. Within the National Alliance on Mental Illness chapter I helped start on the UW-Eau Claire campus an early success has been students meeting regularly simply to share how they are doing, in terms of their mental health and well-being, in a mutually supportive environment, and to share with each other strategies and tactics that help them in coping as well as in living the best possible lives, on and off campus, that they can.

Certified psychiatric professionals do not maintain a monopoly, not by a long shot, on helpful ways of dealing with emotional distress. Some of the best first-year student writing that students I have taught have done, and shared with classmates, recounted severely traumatic experiences, including suicide attempts as well as sexual and other forms of abuse. Yes, we needed carefully to prepare ourselves to be ready to trust, share, and support each other, in these instances, but we have done so. And it has made a positive difference. Sharing vulnerability can be immensely empowering. I regularly find the majority of my students have faced serious hardships, and continue to do so, that have caused and are causing substantial emotional pain. Discussing these hardships directly together while drawing connections with relevant social, historical, cultural, and political contexts often proves empowering.

Price discusses many dimensions of how the structure of academic life is and can be difficult for people with mental disabilities, and especially how little of this is organized in line with or compatible with what might usefully be referred to, in contrast, as 'crip time'. These difficulties include when classes are scheduled to run, for how long, in what kinds of spaces, and with what length of break as well as what distance is needed to travel in between. What's more, versus glib assumptions that all students will readily feel at ease, and safe, in classroom environments that are smaller or more discussion-oriented, Price counters that these assumptions ignore many reasons why that is not necessarily the case. Not all students feel at ease talking and sharing in academic settings, no matter how small the size of the group, and students may feel uneasy doing so in the direct presence of certain fellow students enrolled in these same classes, or teachers as well, given prior negative interactions with these people or with people who closely resemble these people. Participation can be tough for students who are highly self-conscious and suffer from acute forms of anxiety in social situations, including classroom social situations, as well as for students who need to take greater time than others to process their thoughts about what they have heard before they are ready to respond.

It takes considerable sensitivity and a great deal of effort to 'create the classroom as a safe space'; it cannot be assumed it readily starts out as such. This kind of 'safety' won't always be possible for all students, no matter what a teacher might do. Indeed some students do feel more at ease, and better able to learn, in large lecture classes, and/or by learning on their own outside of class. Even as "presence is the sine qua non of learning in higher education," such that it is commonly accepted that students either responsibly 'choose' or irresponsibly 'choose not' to attend classes, "disabled students face barriers to attendance," which may be substantial, that cannot be reductively conflated with matters of individual choice (65). It may be, literally, hard for disabled students to get to class, and to get between classes in time, and it may also be hard for disabled students to stay (sitting) in class–or to stay 'properly behaved' in class for the full duration of the time class lasts. All too often faculty, including faculty researchers on students' attendance (or lack thereof), fail to consult students to figure out why, from students themselves, that they don't attend class when they don't. Studies that do take the latter into account demonstrate students' reasons are, on average, far less capricious or apathetic or uncaring, let alone irresponsible, than often assumed. As Price sums up, "what teachers often assume to be 'poor motivation' may in fact be a more complex situation" (71). One helpful way of dealing with this issue that I have increasingly practiced, over time, is to contact students when they miss class sessions, to express concern about how they are doing, in non-judgmental ways, starting by always assuming they have missed for a good reason. And this includes readily accepting it when students let me know they need 'mental health time' or 'a mental health day'.

In conjunction with what is commonly labeled as 'classroom incivility', Price advises considering it is plausible that at least some of what many teachers interpret in these terms, "as an 'annoyance' or 'rudeness', *might in fact be a student participating* in a way that performs, or attempts to accommodate, her own mental disability" (74). As I have grown more knowledgeable about, along with more respectful and appreciative of, neurodiversity, I welcome such students finding ways to contribute as whom they are, with the strengths they can and do bring to bear, and with the rest of us finding and learning ways to work respectfully with the same. This can mean finding roles in classroom activities that these students are well-suited for and especially interested in taking on, and it can mean offering alternative ways of doing assignments, such as holding 'interview conferences' where a student and I talk through the prompts for a written paper assignment rather than the student literally writing a paper. It can include gently encouraging other students to find ways to work with such fellow students, even if and when they find them 'hard to work with' or characterize them 'as not the kind of people I like'. As Price observes, "students with mental disabilities may disrupt conventional agendas of participation not out of laziness or malice, nor even rebelliousness, but through sincere efforts to participate in ways that reflect their own abilities and needs" (76). In working with students who initially found it frustrating to be asked to work at all with other students in groups or teams, I have found it helpful to urge these frustrated students to imagine they are learning by leading these groups and teams or at least by providing a form of leadership to these groups and teams that no one else in the same group or team is able to offer. In response, these initially frustrated to resistant students have often come to relish group or team work.

Beyond seemingly aggressive class participants, it is also worth investing the effort to better understand students whose mental disabilities lead to a manner of engagement with a class that takes the form of "immobility, dread of entering classroom spaces, unpredictability of symptoms, and difficulty concentrating" (76). These attitudes and behaviors often combine with the same students' experience of "being disbelieved" in previously attempting to explain their mental disability. It is important to anticipate and even expect these kinds of students will be among those enrolled in virtually every class a teacher teaches, and the teacher therefore needs to be prepared therefore to consider such students' presentation and behavior may reflect their mental health challenges. The teacher needs in turn to work to win these students' trust, and this can be hard work, in order that these challenges be adequately taken into account and effectively accommodated.

I definitely agree with Price that it is necessary "to move beyond the notion that argument must equal disagreement, and that silence equals nonparticipation" (79). I regularly emphasize silence can be just as if not equally and even more important than listening, while asking students, in papers and other written assignments, to share and reflect on what they have listened to, and heard, from fellow students and from me, as well as what this has prompted them to think (about) and feel that they did not directly respond to in class discussion. And I also strongly encourage discussion that involves people building on and making connections with, and that work off of, what others have shared, while emphasizing that in relation to most issues subject to disagreement, of any complexity and perdurability, more than two positions (for versus against) are undoubtedly extant and worth taking into account, while positions themselves can and do change in dialogue with other positions. At times it is useful to stage 'mini-debates' as classroom exercises, but at times it is useful to do by defining the parameters of the activity so this is not just two sides, arguing either pro or con in relation to a single proposition, and instead multiple groups working to develop different takes that build off of each other in response to a series of interrelated yet distinct propositions.

Price admits that no effort at universally inclusive design will ever completely realize such a goal, while affirming how important it is for every teacher to accept and clearly identify their own limits, in terms of what they themselves require to be able to do their job well; this includes what range of access they can accept and integrate into their teaching along with what range they cannot.

905

Price values attendance, in the form of presence, and often insists on this, and she also values participation, and makes that clear as well. Price urges teachers to "set limits: you are not establishing yourself as a constantly available answering machine, but rather as someone who can respond in different ways at different times–within your own abilities" (90). That means teachers need to be clear that I can't accommodate X, Y, or Z, because doing so would push me beyond my limits, and cause my own mental and/or physical well-being seriously to suffer.

I accept students emailing me at any time, evenings, nights, and weekends, even though I won't always respond right away, but I don't give students my cell phone number to call or text me. I am ready to arrange conferences beyond office hours when and as need be, but I also make clear when I simply cannot because I maintain other commitments, including to doing what is necessary to attend to my own physical and mental health. I do take pains to stress that 'office hours' are 'student drop-in hours', that they are entirely for students not for me, and if students don't come I will not be doing anything else; I stress students are never 'bothering' or 'disturbing' me by coming to my office hours. I find it useful as well to require conferences with students because students will not always voluntarily seek out help on their own–and I offer and accept opportunities to meet with students in other locations that are easier for them to access and where they feel more comfortable than in my office.

In terms of participation, I strive to specify as precisely as I can what counts, what range of ways of doing so count, and to insure everyone has a chance, often working our way around the room, moving in various and shifting directions, so students will all have opportunities to respond to a question or other prompt, not just waiting for volunteers–and I do organize and conduct many small group discussions and small group activities of diverse kinds. Likewise, I use student writing within class and done prior to class as basis for discussion; this helps students who are better able to participate in this way than having to speak without first writing something out. And yes I advise students concerning many techniques for how to study and how to come prepared for discussion, as well as provide elaborate guides for discussion, study, and review, which I usually get to students ahead of the time in which we will be working with these guides so they can anticipate what we will be doing in what order when we are using them in class, even while allowing for ample spontaneous and flexible deviations from these plans as we collectively determine where to go and how to proceed. These guides help students in knowing what to focus most on in preparing for class and help them in knowing what I most recommend they take away from a text, or a topic, in eventually writing about the same. I aim for everything we do to be recursively interconnected and scaffolded.

But I could do better in all the more forthrightly addressing matters of accommodation in my syllabi and in our first class meeting than I do. I like what Price includes in her syllabi:

> I assume that all of us have different ways of learning, and that the organization of any course will accommodate each student differently. For example, you may prefer to process information by speaking and listening, so that some of the handouts I provide you may be difficult to absorb. Please communicate with me as soon as you can about your individual learning needs and how this course can best accommodate them. (90)

Likewise, I appreciate Price "giving examples of my own needs as a learner in order to emphasize that such needs are not a question of needing 'more' support, but needing different kinds of support" and that "Since I began actually speaking about accommodation rather than just pointing to that section of the syllabus, I have noticed an increase in the number of students who discuss their learning needs with me early in the semester–some of which involve documented disabilities, some not" (91). Key, as Prince indicates, in taking this kind of approach, is that it also reduces the inclination for teachers to imagine students who initially present or behave in ways that are disconcerting are likely to be 'problems' but rather recognizing it is teachers' 'perception' of these manners of presentation and behavior as representing that is the 'problem'. The latter is much easier to work out, effectively, for both student and teacher, early on, than the former (91).

In relation to participation, Price also usefully advises thinking from a student's vantage point, in terms of what students want and need to know, which can lead to offering as concrete as possible an indication of what precisely the teacher would like students to do, or to try to do, in participating, as well as in honestly representing what, as a teacher, are "your pet peeves" (92). I do a reasonably good job with this, but I recognize I can strive to do better. For instance, I likely can do even better in specifying the value I place on presence in class, and what I mean by that, which is something Price recommends all teachers do (93). As I anticipate returning to full-time teaching with the Fall 2022 semester, I recognize the need to specify that direct engagement, in the same physical space at the same time, works better for me, is much easier for me to handle and to do well, causes less mental and physical hardship for me, than attempting simultaneously to teach both 'in person' and 'on line' or even to teach entirely 'on line', whether synchronously or asynchronously. Obviously, that means classes I teach will not work as well for some disabled people for whom online classes work far better for them than in person classes, but, as Price urges us to recognize, we all have our limits, and we all have our needs; what is crucial is to be as open, honest, precise, and clear as we can with students about these as possible.

Price offers considerable further suggestions of ways to increase access for disabled students, in terms of participation techniques, many of which I have tried and do incorporate, and the same in terms of providing feedback. Over time I have become more strategic about what kinds and extents of feedback I offer in response to students' assignments, and strived to try more often to balance encouragement with challenge, while eschewing what will be interpreted simply as 'correction'. I have strived to incorporate detailed rubrics indicating precisely how assignments will be graded, in relation to what criteria, and on what kinds of curves, while usually incorporating multiple possible options for each assignment, adding suggestions for how to organize papers along with stages to follow in working to complete assignments, as well as yet further suggestions for 'best practices' or 'good ideas' to keep in mind in seeking to do well.

Price usefully recommends offering "frequent feedback on how well the class as a whole is responding," including in relation to "your concern for participation" while making clear "when students' ways of participating are not meeting your expectations" (96). I do this regularly, now, yet gently, often explaining variations and departures in how I am organizing our class time and how we are proceeding with discussion as efforts designed to help elicit different kinds of responses and dialogues than we have to date. I will often prepare and send messages to whole classes after class sessions to follow up further on useful points raised in class, especially questions, comments, or confusions we did not adequately address in class.

I also welcome students producing work that takes the form of sounds and images and not just words, or via yet other media as well, instead of writing more conventional papers–and doing 'creative' as opposed to 'critical' writing in response to assignments. I don't, unlike Price, do simultaneous in-person and real-time computer chat office hours or conferences with students, because that it hard for me to do at once, and I am not one who 'chats' all that often. But I am receptive to trying new techniques, especially if these can make what we are doing more accessible for more students, within my own limits, and in this connection I agree with Price "True accommodations are not *added on* to a classroom *environment*; they are *built in* to its infrastructure, with flexibility and revision part of its very foundation" (102). That is why I do think about how can I make each class I teach, and how we work together as the class proceeds, as accessible as well as encouraging and helpful to as many students as I possibly can, in preparing each class session, while also stressing with students that the syllabus is not a blueprint we must follow, and from which we cannot deviate. On the contrary, anything and everything can change, as need be, and we will determine together if changes are needed, in what, when and where, how so and why so.

But I also agree with Price that "I cannot anticipate the needs and styles of every student who will walk into my classroom. Nor can I become a fundamentally different kind of teacher than I am" (102). And I also accept as well "not every student will want to be a part of this dialogue," over how we can work together to make our class as accessible and accommodating as possible, and "that some will choose not to so engage for their own reasons, and [I must] respect that" (102). Still, to return to Cvetkovich's *Depression: a Public Feeling*, making this deliberate, intentional, conscientious effort to try, and to keep trying to do more and better, can help combat the extent to which academia can cause many students to feel anxious, depressed, and to otherwise suffer exacerbated distress in terms of mental disability.

In discussing, next, challenges faculty with mental disabilities can and do face in academia, in relation to prevailing understandings of and expectations concerning matters of productivity and collegiality, Price's critique is also most compelling, and dovetails closely with what Nicole Brown, Jennifer Leigh, and collaborators address in *Ableism in Academia*. To begin, I certainly recognize how commonplace the expectation has been and often continues to be that faculty will 'overcome' whatever challenges they face in terms of health and ability, and even 'heroically' bear with and push through 'the pain' in order to meet expectations. I myself have done so, often and repeatedly, throughout most of my academic career. I long recognized no other possible choice. I internalized the conviction that unless I did so I would not be allowed to continue. Countless times I have taught and otherwise participated directly in institutional, and professional, activities, while feeling extremely sick, and in terrible pain, while determining I needed to 'pretend' this was not the case and that I needed 'to pass' as fully healthy and able-bodied. I have incessantly downplayed the severity of what I struggle and suffer with, and what this does to me–as well as what it costs me. I have frequently, for a long time, concluded it would be impossible for most colleagues and supervisors to understand what I routinely go through, let alone respond in a compassionate and helpful way. And I have even all the more frequently concluded nothing is possible that could amount to improved accommodation, and access, for me, in relation to what I struggle and suffer with.

As a result, yes, I have been complicit with the "point of view, which imagines disablement as a personal deficit that must be 'heroically' and 'secretly' borne" (104). And I do recognize, from Price's account as well as from the accounts provided in *Ableism in Academia*, that this has harmed not just me but others by rendering the complications and challenges of chronic illness and disabilities that are not readily perceptible to seem non-existent or largely insignificant or only of limited consequence. In terms of 'feelings', I have felt the gamut of negative emotions both as a result of the impact of these conditions as well as on account of not being able to be honest about this impact. I have in recent years, in particular since first achieving tenure and promotion to associate professor and especially since achieving promotion to full professor, been widely open about what I long downplayed or kept concealed. It has felt liberating to do so, and I think it has proven helpful with colleagues–and certainly with students.

But we are no further along in doing much concretely, *as an institution*, to render this institution, institutional life, and institutional requirements and expectations more accessible and more accommodating for people who suffer, in particular, from chronic illness, mental disability, and other so-called 'invisible disabilities' or complications and challenges in terms of health and illness due to departure from what is most commonplace, or most 'typical'. Like many institutions, at UW-Eau Claire we have an Office of Services for Students with Disabilities, but nothing comparable for faculty and staff–and likewise Student Counseling Services is overwhelmed in responding to student needs and as such is unavailable to do much to help faculty and staff with our needs.

As Price discusses, colleges and universities are often far less comfortable acknowledging let alone helpfully responding to mental disabilities than they are to more readily perceptible and familiar kinds of physical disabilities, while often replicating the same kinds of unease and fear concerning those who might be identifiably 'mad' as is common throughout much of the rest of American culture, notably that people like us are especially prone to violence. As Price recounts, people with mental disabilities usually find it hard, and usually fail, to achieve accommodations in accord with the Americans with Disabilities Act (ADA), and that includes faculty and staff working on college and university campuses. In relation to collegiality, Price aptly identifies many ways in which consensual understandings of what this involves and especially 'what it looks like', 'what it sounds like', and 'what it *feels* like' are not only nebulously insidious but also harder for people with mental disabilities to meet than people without mental disabilities. In fact, as Price discusses, many people with mental disabilities need to invest considerable effort figuring out how 'to perform' what does not at all 'come naturally' to them, in terms of collegiality, where they are most certainly *not* 'being themselves' or 'acting like themselves' in attempting to do so. I have been well attuned to the need to make at least a strongly implicit case in favor of my collegiality, in performance reviews that have determined whether I would be rehired from year to year as a tenure-track faculty member, whether I would earn tenure and promotion to associate professor, whether I would earn promotion to full professor, and whether I would receive a positive post-tenure review. And I have worried about not always being clearly likeable or likeable enough, even if in retrospect it seems, at UW-Eau Claire I have had little reason to worry.

Job interviews, of all kinds, and especially during prolonged 'campus visits', where every moment of time spent with anyone else is actually part of the interview, and where in effect the candidate must represent themselves continuously as always gracious, charming, witty, confident, respectful, energetic, enthusiastic, open, receptive, and so on, can be 'a minefield' for many people who deal with many kinds of mental disabilities. Asking for accommodations as part of such a process is often exceedingly difficult as well, with many candidates understandably worried that doing so will cause them to become stigmatized in the minds of those who will be the ones deciding whether to hire them or not, including simply because they are perceived as likely to represent 'more trouble' to need to take into account and respond to, if hired, than other candidates. I recognized it was crucial to represent myself during interviews and campus visits exactly as I have just described, and I made sure to do so. But what I find even more troubling to consider is how often search and screen committees on which I participated, or departments and programs where I was part of the broader array of people consulted about hiring future colleagues, have relied on matters of perceived 'personality' and perceived 'collegial' 'fit' that in fact had little to do nothing to do with whether the chosen candidate would do their job well, and which in turn discriminated against people with mental and other kinds of disabilities. And I also worry that, despite our best efforts, within the work of our Department Personnel Committee in the English Department at UW-Eau Claire, we have periodically allowed considerations of perceived collegiality, or 'deficiency in collegiality', defined in terms of 'likeability', to play into decisions we have made.

I expect some of the opposition to hiring me for the tenure-track position at Arizona State in the same area where I had been working for two years as a visiting assistant professor had much to do with perceptions that my collegiality was not of the right kind, especially not adequately deferential and instead too earnest, too independent, too aggressive, and too serious. Likewise, at institutions such as Onondaga Community College and State University of New York College at Cortland I expect decisions not to rehire me were in part motivated by the same concerns, especially when I challenged and critiqued supervisors' judgments about the appropriateness of how and what I was teaching, by 'bringing content to bear' in first-year writing classes, especially content dealing with controversial contemporary issues concerning matters of race, class, gender, nationality, and, especially, sexuality.

Price writes at length about the numerous ways standard academic conferences are often problematic for people with mental disabilities. In my own case, as I have previously mentioned in this book, professional conferences have become increasingly problematic for me, because of the complications travel causes me, leaving me often sick as a result, and with this sickness subsequently making it all the more difficult to catch up if I need to do so in the midst of an already busy semester. I need a caretaker to travel with me to help out and when that is not possible I simply can't go. I, like Price, also recognize academic conferences as environments where a heavy emphasis is placed on networking, outside and alongside of actual sessions; where sessions are by default treated as if questioning should always be adversarial; and where masses of people are moving about rapidly and noisily in multiple directions as part of a frenzied overall atmosphere. All of this can be overwhelming. I have often sought out quiet escapes by taking extensive time away from the conference center, visiting sights in the city, or by secreting myself away to practice and be sure I am fully prepared for my presentation(s).

I have, in addition, been on both sides of 'meat-packing' 'assembly-line' style interviews at conferences, where many tables representing many institutions interviewing for many disparate positions are all in the same large room, all relatively close to one another, and candidates navigate through this to find the right table to talk for up to 30 minutes while candidates and interviewers try to ignore interviews taking place at adjacent tables. Even interviews in hotel rooms can be strange experiences, with people coming and going, swirling about, seemingly almost designed to test how comfortable the candidate is with distraction.

I was well prepared, however, by my faculty mentors for adversarial exchanges, and even strongly encouraged to use every conference presentation as an occasion to push boundaries, test limits, set forth provocative arguments and critiques, and even intervene in consensually prevailing understandings. So I was always ready to respond to questions and comments, including highly critical ones, following my presentations. But I have often been frustrated by questions and comments from people who clearly weren't listening at all closely to what I had to say, or who weren't even in the room when I was speaking. However, given the pressures conferences often place on people to try to be in many different places all at once, these kinds of questions are understandable, I recognize, in retrospect. In my own questions and comments in response to others' presentations I have nonetheless tended to be more cautious, usually asking for presenters to consider connecting what they have addressed with what seem to be closely related texts and topics, or to reframe points to make sure I and others adequately grasp what they are arguing, or to elaborate about practical implications–in terms of curriculum and pedagogy and in relation to efforts at and commitments toward social and political change.

Price offers a useful distinction between "accommodation," which, "while helpful, is often used to indicate specific measures intended to 'fix' specific situations for individual 'problems'," and "access," which "means designing spaces . . . in ways that are flexible, multimodal, and responsive to feedback" (130). Both accommodation and access prove complicated in relation to mental disability. As Price cites Heather Clark, "There is no illness, except perhaps AIDS, that bears the shame still attached to mental illness and that is hidden so well in the academy" (quoted 131). In Price's words, "any acknowledgment" of this kind of disability "can be dangerous" (131), and this has much to do not only with how mental disability is commonly perceived as equivalent with being prone to become dangerously violent but also with how mental disability suggests one is unable to think effectively, and especially rationally, in an institution where that is, supposedly, a fundamental, an indispensable, requirement.

Expectations concerning "productivity" also can present extreme hardships for faculty with mental disabilities, as for us it can indeed be hard to be as continuously, uninterruptedly 'productive', working from early morning to late at night, every day of the week, throughout the entirety of the year, as all too often seems to constitute the standard of perfection toward which we are all supposed to chase. Price argues it is unnecessary that all faculty excel equally in teaching, scholarship, and service, and that it would be much more helpful for many faculty with mental disabilities if they did not need to do so and could concentrate in one or two of these areas where they are able to do their best work. I myself, as I have already discussed in this book, have intuited the expectation as part of academic institutions for which I have worked, including UW-Eau Claire, if not indeed especially

UW-Eau Claire, that you must constantly be striving to work harder and harder, to steadily always do more and better, in order to realize exceptionally high standards not only of productivity but also of achievement–and as a result I have been broken down, badly, and repeatedly, as a result. Under these kinds of pressures, to return to *Depression: a Public Feeling*, depression is a high risk, especially for those already maintaining tendencies or inclinations toward depression, and this can all the more likely prove to be an especially severe bout of depression at that. If one is depressed because one feels overwhelmed by expectations, requirements, and even demands of academia, while simultaneously feeling guilty and ashamed at being so overwhelmed, this can be a devastating and even a deadly combination.

It is also worth noting well, as Price does, citing many reputable expert studies and investigators, that 'mentally ill' people are by and large not any more dangerous that anyone else, and if anything far more likely to suffer violence from others than to perpetrate violence against others, while if anything when 'mentally ill' people do resort to violence it tends overwhelmingly to be directed against themselves and themselves alone. But I do wonder sometimes, as I have been 'out' for a good many years now, more than 20 at that–as someone with experience of serious to severe anxiety and depression, even recurrent tendencies toward the same, and one who has suffered post-traumatic stress disorder and from suicidality, including leading to a suicide attempt–if people around me, colleagues at work for instance, are ever worried about my 'madness' taking a threateningly violent form. I hope not, but I admit that is not entirely inconceivable–even though I am, like the vast majority of such 'mad people', one who has been the victim of violence myself as opposed to a perpetrator of violence against others, and who always whenever crushed down by severe depression only imagines committing violence against myself while always feeling horrified about even indirectly effecting violence against anyone else.

Price advocates centering disability as opposed to able-bodiedness and cites how disability studies usefully contests the valorization of 'independence' within academia and beyond by instead championing 'interdependence' over 'independence' (227). As Price quotes Tobin Sievers, "A focus on disability provides another perspective by representing human society not as a collection of autonomous beings, some of whom will lose their independence, but as a community of dependent frail bodies that rely on others for survival" (227). Priority emphasis on "*inter*-dependence," in other words, instead of "independence" could well be, Price contends, "enabling" and "empowering" (228). But academia has a long way to go. Price acknowledges she has often "felt like an outsider," whose disability disqualifies her from full and equitable inclusion, but also "I have felt too much like an insider, someone whose personal history with mental disability might cloud my judgment and make of me an overly biased apologist" (233). It is sad, yet understandable, that Price feels this way. Mentally disabled students, faculty, and staff are often likely to *feel* as if academia does not and cannot and will not welcome them, include them, adequately accommodate them, provide them adequate access, and judge them and what they have to contribute as of equal worth. But as Price recognizes, despite fear "that the attention paid" to what she has written "will wind up reinforcing the powerful forces that wish to expel persons with mental disabilities from academic discourse," she recognizes "the questions I am raising *need* to be raised" and "My hope is that persons with mental disabilities will remain a part of academe, as we have been for thousands of years, and that deeper understanding of our abilities and limitations, our place in the human world, might reshape academic culture" (233).

Ableism in Academia emphasizes the damage that follows as a result of how neoliberalism and ableism work together within the academy. Academic neoliberalism, as editors Nicole Brown and Jennifer Leigh describe, in their "Introduction" to *Ableism in Academia*, involves, in short, "The process of universities turning into corporate businesses" (2). Value is defined in terms of maximal return on minimal investment, on efficiency and speed of turnover, and success in market competition. Brown and Leigh in turn cite Fiona Kumari Campbell's definition of ableism as "a network of beliefs, processes and practices that produces a particular kind of self and body (the corporeal standard) that is projected as the perfect, species-typical and therefore essential and fully human. Disability then is cast as a diminished state of being human" (quoted 4). Ableism promotes "the concept of the perfect academic," and, in particular, pressure to strive to approximate this state of perfection, as close as possible. This pressure works hand in hand with an endemic priority emphasis, as part of the normal workings of academia, exacerbated by neoliberalism, upon "performativity, efficiency, productivity and personal reflectiveness" (or, in other words, in relation to the last, continuous personal reflectiveness on performativity, efficiency, and productivity) (4). Ableism, moreover, "affects more than visible forms of disability," and throughout *Ableism in Academia* Brown, Leigh, and fellow contributors to this anthology emphasize the position and experience, in particular, of people with "invisible disabilities and chronic illnesses, the 'non-normative other'" (4). Put succinctly, "the normative framework of the ever-available and able-bodied academic driven by ambition, and in a climate of university rankings, leaves little room for those who do not conform to this ableist framework" (18).

Ableism in academia "is a structural problem that cannot be reasonably resolved at the individual level, though it is at the individual level that the implications and consequences of ableism are felt most keenly, and already precarious work conditions easily become untenable" (19). Ableism in academia shows up at the latter level, broadly, in intolerance for and exclusion of individuals manifesting fragility, frailty, and feebleness–in either body or, especially, in mind. As a result of how thoroughly ableist academia is, and has increasingly become, disabled people are seriously under-represented within academia–and in contributing to fields of academic knowledge. What's more, because "Ableism is deeply rooted in historical and political ignorance of the material realities of disabled people's lives," and the normative demands of academic life often effectively exclude disabled people, or force disabled people to pretend not to be disabled and to attempt to pass as able-bodied, "there is no incentive to examine such ignorance as there are not repercussions" (25). In marginalizing and excluding disabled people's contributions and disabled people's perspectives from the work of knowledge production and its social circulation, academia "serves to uphold historically and politically dominant knowledge systems, perpetuating systems of domination" that render it impossible to create a genuinely "fairer society" because the latter depends on achieving equitable recognition and inclusion of those who are and long have been unrecognized and excluded (25).

Francesca Peruzzo explains how "Being able becomes a new requirement for being in academia" (39-40). Institutions must do everything they possibly can to make themselves "attractive" in order to win "funding, resources, customers/students and attention," which requires that academics "make ourselves agile . . . marketisable, highly performative and presentable" (40). Academics, as subjects, "are produced by discourses of academic excellence, impact and productivity" (40). Academics are produced as subjects, moreover, in terms of "calcu-*ability*," which defines quality of performance and achievement in line with readily measurable benefits to the institution in terms of its market position and market power (40). In fact, "The only way in which neoliberal academia *enables* subjects to be part of the *academic body* is by being high-performing and marketisable, casting outside subjects that are not 'economic', not calculable enough, not able enough" (41). After all, as Peruzzo identifies, in this kind of institutional environment there is no room for illness, because "sickness slows you down," and there is no room for bodily limits on how much one can produce, through how much labor, because maximal productivity and continuous achievement, even steadily increasing productivity and ever-growing achievement, are baseline expectations for satisfactory performance (41).

In chapter three, "Disclosure in Academia: a Sensitive Issue," Nicole Brown discusses the results of her surveying and interviewing academics suffering from fibromyalgia, a classic form of both chronic illness and invisible disability. This condition is hard to explain because "symptoms typically wax and wane, change and move" and because "The lack of a definite process for diagnosis and the variability of the condition make it a doubtful and contested condition within the medical profession, too" (54). As a result, many do not disclose and instead suffer in silence. Fibromyalgia tends, like many serious chronic illnesses, to be subject to flare-ups and complications that are difficult to anticipate, and to manage, that are often exacerbated by stress, and that means academic life, with all of its tight deadlines and high expectations, can often prove nightmarish. What's more, "Academics, specifically early-career academics, worry about the consequences of being identified as someone dealing with health issues and conditions" and it is often difficult to accept this is the case for one's self "as it means learning to accept chronic illness, neurodiversity or disability as a normal experience of life" which significantly impacts self-identity (60-61).

The process of reaching the point where one is able and willing to accept this dimension of whom one is, and to publicly disclose the same, can be empowering, including in gaining allies and companions, especially with others who likewise maintain health and ability complications and challenges, as well as in no longer needing to invest considerable effort in, and experience considerable worry over, attempting to come up with excuses in the attempt to continue to conceal and compensate. 'Openly' 'owning' one's chronic illness and disability can also enable one to discover ways in which this dimension of one's identity and experience might even prove, at least in part, an 'asset'. However, many academics fear "disclosing fibromyalgia" or a similar condition "would be seen as a weakness," in an institutional environment where 'there is no room for the weak' and as a result, many of these academics "push themselves through episodes of illness, pretending everything is fine" (63).

In sum, "being ill in academia" can prove extremely "taxing and demanding," because "academia is experienced and interpreted as an all-encompassing lifestyle choice and identity," while "Being diagnosed with a chronic illness is in itself life-changing and isolating," and as such exercises a major impact on one's sense of one's own identity as well (65). Brown emphasizes in particular how common it is among those she has interviewed to share feeling isolated, as a result of their condition, while also suggesting the following comment is typical: "At the moment I just feel like I'm just a, a mess. I feel like, like, people are avoiding me from my course, maybe not deliberately but they're so busy and involved with what they are doing. And I think extended illness of this type makes people very uncomfortable. They, they don't know what do say, they don't know what to do" (66).

I have felt exactly like this, myself, repeatedly, and I feel terrible that so many others working in academia feel much the same, and are often thoroughly isolated in feeling this way. This is a major indictment of an institution that often represents itself as maintaining an exalted mission and purpose, and that encompasses many fields ostensibly highly valuing caring in what these fields are about and in what people who work in these fields do. All too often academia is unconcerned with the feelings of those who work within it, especially when these are 'negative' or 'bad' feelings, while yet worse still the way academia is set up and operates is all too often responsible either for causing these kinds of feelings or for making these kinds of feelings much worse than they otherwise would be.

Brown emphasizes the importance of being recognized and accepted for whom one is at one's academic workplace, with one's chronic illness and invisible disability respected and supported. This requires co-workers and supervisors understand that some disabilities are "not continuous" but rather "fluid" and that just because 'you don't look sick' this doesn't mean you are not sick. It also requires convincing people with these kinds of conditions that "there will not be any repercussions," no negative repercussions that is, from disclosure. This in turn requires that academic institutions be actively and recognizably committed toward rejecting and contesting 'stigma' associated with illness and disability while at the same time appreciating people who live with chronic illness and disability, visible and invisible, cannot always do exactly the same, to the same degree and in the same amount, in terms of performance and productivity as those who are healthy and able-bodied (68-69).

It would be a significant gain, I propose, if more people could wrap their heads around the idea that chronic illness is real and its impact can be severe, even if its presence cannot be readily perceived on the surface of someone's body and even if its presence cannot be readily perceived via someone's voice, posture, expressions, gestures, level of apparent energy or fitness, or any other dimensions of how the person superficially presents themself. And it would be a significant gain as well if more people could wrap their heads around the idea that chronic illness is illness that one doesn't 'get over', one that doesn't end, and one that will always be there. In her poem "Fibromyalgia and me," Divya Jindal-Snape aptly addresses this issue: that by no means "does everyone understand that the pain and fatigue are here to stay" (74). I readily identify with Jindal-Snape when she writes "I hope no one has such pain and fatigue," because I do hate to imagine others having to live with the same pain and fatigue that I have, and I further readily identity with Jindal-Snape declaring "What hurts more is that people who don't have a clue/Give me advice on what I should or shouldn't do" because I have experienced this too and it only deepens the pain and fatigue, especially the emotional pain and fatigue, I experience when others do so, however ostensibly well-meaning they are (74-75).

In chapter six, "Autoimmune Actions in the Ableist Academy," Alice Andrews likewise emphasizes that "Living and working with chronic illness, with fluctuating energy and pain levels and uncertainty regarding the future can be isolating," and this is made all the worse within academia, because "The workforce is presumed able-bodied and able-minded until proven otherwise" while "The onus is, therefore, placed on individuals to navigate support through obtuse administrative networks" (106). It feels particularly "risky to identify with a stigmatised form of difference such as being one of the *unhealthy* [my italics] disabled, for here narratives of disability pride are easily overwritten by narratives of overcoming, eradication and cure that continue to oppress disabled people" (108). As Andrews points out, further, it is important to note well that "Metaphors of disability and impairment are deeply ingrained in our language and cultural discourses and have commonly been employed to signify lack of worth, to oppress and exclude already marginalized identities," that is to do so by drawing comparisons between other marginalized identities and 'disability' or 'impairment' (108). Andrews cites Fiona Kumari Campbell's definition of ableism that Nicole Brown and Jennifer Leigh cited earlier, in the "Introduction" to *Ableism in Academia* in order to contrast this with how Campbell also defines 'disableism': "a set of assumptions (conscious or unconscious) and practices that promote the differential or unequal treatment of people because of actual or presumed disabilities" (quoted 116). Attributing this point to Dan Goodley, Andrews adds, in turn, that it is crucial to grasp that "by essentializing certain abilities ableism *produces* disability" (116). Ableism and disability are, in other words, both social constructions not natural facts or states, and because able-bodiedness and able-mindedness are in fact impossible, and impossibly oppressive ideals of perfection, ableism and disableism harm everyone and not just overtly disabled people. Yet because of how ableist academia is, because in other words of how thoroughly ableism is normalized in academia, the result is, overwhelmingly, "disabled individuals being forced either to 'overcome' their disabilities or leave" (116). However, Andrews glimpses the glimmers of a possible alternative in recognizing we all experience imperfection of body and mind: "perhaps by recognising that we are all 'disabled'–*and* privileged–in different ways by different forms of injustice and oppression, we might locate the possibility for forging alliances with a politics of disability justice" (117).

In chapter seven, "'But You Don't Look Disabled': Non-Visible Disabilities, Disclosure and Being an 'Insider' in Disability and 'Other' in the Disability Movement and Academia," Elisabeth Griffiths also refers to Dan Goodley as explaining "the marked identity of a neoliberal citizen is a worker: willing, capable and able" (quoted 125), in order to add to this that "It is often assumed that the 'willing, capable and able' worker can perform to an excellent standard in everything all the time," but this is hardly the case, in fact, and next to impossible for disabled people (125). Yet the expectation continues and is insidious in its impact, certainly including within academia. This expectation is highly problematic for people with chronic illnesses, which "are not fixed disabilities," and which mean that how able one is varies wildly and unpredictably (132). As Griffiths explains, further, "Unseen, hidden or non-visible disabilities, which are not readily seen or immediately obvious to others, also raise many issues about the presentation of self in everyday life" (132). In other words, this is a highly complicated and perplexing challenge–to live with chronic illness that "does fluctuate and 'flare', but is always there, even if I can hide it on some days" (133). Unfortunately, chronic illness and, as Griffiths prefers, 'un-visible' disabilities are still far less readily accepted, let alone understood, including in academia, than, for example, "someone in a wheelchair" (133). It remains hard for many if not most outsiders, including in academia, to understand disabilities that alternate such that some days people feel like they can do virtually anything and other days they feel like they can do virtually nothing. But, as Griffiths argues, people with chronic illness and un-visible disabilities are often helped, long-term, by "slowing down," by being able to slow down, and by rejecting, by being able to reject, a "culture of perfectionism," while the same is, Griffiths suggests, likewise the case, with just about everyone, at least now and then (135). Academia needs to accept that some highly valuable workers might be more consistently 'willing' and 'capable' than they are 'able', while prizing what these workers do offer, do contribute, when and as they are able, and according to how able they are when and as they are such (135). But Griffiths recognize this is far from where academia at present is at, in terms of how a "pervasive culture of perfectionism" defines and assesses "productivity and performance" (137). Griffiths recognizes how many in positions such as hers are tempted, understandably, by "the rewards of being or appearing 'normal'" and that "sometimes it is easier to lie," but "in remaining silent for so long and in this context, I am not facilitating the need for change in academia about how disabled academics are viewed and how much our presence and our research matters" (137).

This is also a prime motive for me as well in contributing to 'breaking the silence' by overtly identifying myself as a person, working within academia for over 35 years and attaining the rank of full professor, who lives with serious to severe chronic illness, invisible–or 'un-visible' disability, and mental health complications and challenges. I belong here, so do others like me, and so do many who have been excluded and who are being excluded from belonging because of chronic illness and because of visible and un-visible disability. "Academia needs to acknowledge this difference," *our* difference, as "It is crucial to acknowledge how much we contribute to academic life and how we see ourselves in the wider society" (140).

In chapter eight, "Invisible Disability, Unacknowledged Diversity," Carla Finesilver, Jennifer Leigh, and Nicole Brown critique prominent advocates for cultivating consciousness of 'embodiment' that fail to acknowledge "if a person is in chronic pain, or disabled by their body not working as it 'should', such awareness . . . is no longer a choice but instead a constant, chronic, unavoidable reality. For those of us who live with chronic pain or disability, our bodies are continually present and reminding us of their presence–they are dys-appearing" (144). "A profession like academia, which is competitive, cerebral . . . and–according to some . . . devoid of emotion, is not conductive to embodied awareness of our bodies," while the nature of much academic work effectively encourages many academic workers to neglect attention to their bodies, concentrating "on the cerebral in our thoughts and outcomes" (144). Yet for those with chronic illness and disability this is not possible because the body continually "makes its presence known and felt" (145). Academia often does not register awareness of those kinds of inescapable bodily impacts. But, what if, Finesilver, Leigh, and Brown ask, a disabled person identifies their disabled body as crucial to their identity, to whom they are and what they are about, to whom and how they want to be recognized and addressed, yet does so in a way that does not treat their body as an inert or static 'thing' but rather a site of multiple and complex and ongoing interactions, as a means or mode of, in Dan Goodley's words, "becoming, reflection and production" (quoted 146). Finesilver, Leigh, and Brown here follow Goodley in raising the question of what might follow if we were to center disability, and disabled bodies, including in academia.

Such a venture cannot begin to proceed, however, until the need is met, first, for "a clear move away from the thought processes of 'I cannot see that, therefore it is not real or true' towards a more empathetic stance of kindness, tolerance and acceptance" (147). For those with disabilities that are both invisible and that fluctuate in their impact and severity, academia constantly presents obstacles and frustrations, including just in getting from one classroom or meeting room to another, from having to carry or otherwise transport what is needed in so moving about, in having to be 'on' for hours on end with limited breaks, and for being "repeatedly scheduled in rooms without adequate accessibility arrangements" (149). In relation to the last, one example I have not mentioned yet in this book is that it often has been frustrating that so many classrooms offer insufficient lighting for me be able to see effectively, in teaching, given cataracts in both my eyes.

Finesilver, Brown, and Leigh summarize the issues that faculty with chronic illness and invisible disability routinely face, even after disclosing and attempting to explain: 1) "Overestimation," where the person is assumed, because their condition is 'invisible', to be essentially able-bodied and as a result "expected to cope with all tasks without appropriate accommodation of needs or differences"; 2) "Underestimation," where the person is assumed, because they are 'disabled', to "be 'too disabled' to cope with tasks that are well within their capabilities"; 3) "Lack of flexibility," where the institution is too rigid and therefore unable to accommodate the fluctuations in the person's condition; and 4) "Disability as an exclusively 'student' issue" where support is available on campus to assist disabled students but not to assist disabled faculty and staff. Finesilver, Brown, and Leigh share many examples from those they have interviewed, as part of their research, including of one academic who was required to attend an all-day conference, for multiple days in succession, in a muti-story building without elevators and with many able-bodied colleagues entirely oblivious to the obstacles this presented. Academics with chronic illness and comparable kinds of disabilities or injuries are forced into constant "internal calculations" concerning what they can do and how so given the pain they face, how much energy they can muster due to the drain on energy their condition encompasses, and how much time they can devote to getting various tasks done and to moving about given the need to take into account how much their condition is likely to slow them down or otherwise interfere with attempts at 'efficiency' (151-152). As Finesilver, Brown, and Leigh rightly highlight: "Chronic pain is tiring . . . Dealing with disability is tiring . . . Academia, particularly within its current managerialist and metric-driven context, is tiring . . ." and these vectors of fatigue intersect with each other, compounding the impact (156). This is "additional labour" that these academics need to put in, and "working in academia has hidden costs for persons who have an invisible disability or chronic condition" (156). It remains largely unrecognized 'additional labor' bearing 'hidden costs' because "Academics living with chronic illness or a disability are being forced to confront their dys-appearing body at every turn, within an environment and culture that is not welcoming to difference and diversity," no matter how much it is likely to claim to be so (156).

As Finesilver, Brown, and Leigh contend, "being inclusive is about being empathetic"; it is about being "compassionate human beings who have consideration for others" (157). It would seem that academic institutions *should* prize doing so, and *should* prize aspiring to do so, while continually striving to insure they are making real and substantial progress in doing so. This *must* encompass disability, visible and un-visible, including in the forms of chronic illness and mental disability. Principles of 'universal design' have already been widely implemented in relation to student learning; therefore, Finesilver, Brown, and Leigh argue, these principles "could be extended to a universal design for research, teaching and learning, so also accommodating staff" (157). This requires rethinking 'productivity and performance', as well as ways of evaluating the same, in line with the "starting assumption" that "there will be diversity," that there *is* diversity, among faculty and staff, in terms of health/illness and ability/disability, and this means people working as part of the academic institution will maintain "many different needs that may not be obvious to others and that might change over time" (157). With this as a 'starting assumption', it becomes possible "to build in accessibility" (157). On "a more individual level," Finesilver, Brown, and Leigh advocate that if "one of our number is not participating in an activity (e.g. shifting chairs, volunteering to take minutes) and it is not obvious why, we should assume it is for a good reason" (157). We should at the same time *not* assume "that because someone has been observed doing something in the past, they necessarily can today" while we should also *not* assume "that because someone could not do something on a previous occasion, it is and will always be impossible" (157). In other words, "We should trust that individuals (staff or students) know best how to 'do academia' in the ways that work best for them–however different these may be from the ways of their colleagues" (157).

Yet again, as Jennifer Leigh and Nicole Brown address further, in chapter ten, "Internalised Ableism: Of the Political and the Personal" none of those ways of thinking are widely commonplace in academia today, and in fact the reverse overwhelmingly tends to prevail. Academia selectively includes those who maintain strongly perfectionist orientations and selectively excludes those who do not–as well as those who, even while identifying with perfectionist orientiations, cannot follow through in "perfectionist strivings" after "perfectionist concerns" (170). Disabled people often are 'excluded' because they do not maintain strongly perfectionist orientations, or because, even if and as they do, they cannot follow through in perfectionist strivings after perfectionist ends. When disabled people do make it into the academy but increasingly realize they cannot continue to pursue a perfectionist standard of performance and productivity, they readily fall victim to "imposter syndrome," convinced that they don't belong and that it has been and continues to be the result of a 'mistake' that they are there at all, a mistake likely eventually if not soon to be discovered–and to be rectified.

In general, Leigh and Brown argue, "There is little space for the body within neoliberal academia" (171). Academia, under the influence of neoliberalism, strongly encourages academics to ignore their bodies, to ignore negative impacts of the kind and extent of work they do on their bodies, and to be willing to suffer and sacrifice bodily health and well-being to achieve desirable ends. At the same time, the neoliberal academia has coopted the notion of 'well-being' as a marketable entity, one that is marketed back to faculty and staff (as well as students) and to the broader public in order to increase the competitive advantage (the relative attractiveness) of the particular institution, but which overwhelmingly relies on promoting the idea, as Leigh has written elsewhere, "that wellbeing is an individual responsibility" (quoted 171). In doing so, faculty, staff, and students are encouraged to learn and develop techniques "of self-management" (quoted 171), that suggest nothing about the institution itself, and certainly nothing *structural*, needs to be changed. At the same time, these neatly packaged versions of well-being as matters of individual responsibility and self-management also fail to recognize that "Wellbeing is not just the absence of illness, but an active and ongoing pursuit of something" (173). This means faculty, staff, and students need active and ongoing pursuits, including those they can pursue both flexibly and collectively, that can enable wellbeing, and institutions need to create and foster such opportunities.

In chapter 12, "The Violence of Technicism: Ableism as Humiliation and Degrading Treatment," Fiona Kumari Campbell, whose definition of ableism fellow contributors have repeatedly cited in prior chapters of *Ableism in Academia*, drives home the thesis the title of her article sets forth. Campbell begins by describing an experience where her needs, as a disabled faculty member, were effectively disregarded and ignored that one last time that she decided 'enough is enough' and she would 'refuse to take it any more'. Again and again, Campbell recounts, she has been put in the position of scrambling by herself to arrange and put in place the accommodations she needs to be able to do her job, and again and again the institution has failed to adequately respond to her requests for assistance. All too often the result is putting disabled people like herself in humiliating positions, where for instance they are not able to access a teaching station on an elevated platform to be able to teach their students. As Campbell indicates, "Microaggressions such as these are experienced by disabled people in our private lives and in our work lives," repeatedly and all too often (203).

Yet Campbell argues "Ableism is everyone's business, not because of some ideological imperative but because we as living creatures, human and animal, are affected by the spectre and the spectrum of the 'abled' body. Therefore, it is critical that ableism stops being thought of as just a disability issue" (203). Elaborating further, Campbell explains "Ablement, the process of becoming 'abled', impacts on daily routines, interactions, speculations and, significantly, imagination. While all people are affected by ableism, we are not all impacted by ableist practices in the same way. Due to their positioning some people actually *benefit*: they become entitled by virtue of academic ableism" (203). People are 'abled' by what social, including technical and technological, means are made available to enable them to 'be able', and these are differentially, even widely differentially available.

In this chapter Campbell shares a revised and updated definition of ableism as a

system of causal relations about the order of life that produces processes and systems of entitlement and exclusion. This causality fosters conditions of microaggresion, internalized ableism and, in their jostling, notions of (un)encumbrance. A system of dividing practices, ableism institutes the reification and classification of populations. Ableist systems involve the differentiation, ranking, negotiation, notification and prioritization of sentient life. (204-205)

In turn, Campbell defines "ablement" as "the ongoing, dynamic process of becoming abled" that readily couples, at least implicitly, with 'disablement' conceived of as the ongoing, dynamic process of becoming disabled (205). Neither ablement or disablement are simply natural or obvious states; they require construction and they require explanation. In her own approach toward understanding 'ableism' Campbell emphasizes, "while not rejecting a discrimination paradigm outright," starting "from a different premise: namely ableism is not simply about ignorance (or even unconscious bias, a concept that is very much flavour of the month)" (207). Instead, "ableism is soma-epistemological, configuring legitimised knowledges concerning normalcy, perfection and intense ontologies of bodies; that is, what it means to be *fully* human" (207). So, from this critical theoretical vantage point, "Ableism moves beyond the more familiar territory of disability, social inclusion, and usual indices of exclusion to the very divisions of life," and, again, especially, what kinds of lives are more versus less valued and valuable, how so and why so (207). From this vantage point Campbell also identifies "compulsory ablement" in relation to "a dynamic promise that suggests ablement is in reach for all," and thereby, for example, "it is possible and indeed desirable to be a 'superhuman' academic" (207). As Campbell further explains, ableism, therefore, "does not just stop at promulgating the 'species-typical, which is assumed to be demarcated, stable, and self-contained,'" but in fact "An ableist imaginary tells us what a healthy academic's body means–a 'normal' mind, the pace and tenor of thinking, energy levels and the kinds of emotions and affect that are suitable to express–all played out in student evaluations, perceptions of what an academic looks like, feedback, ideas of 'objectivity' and scores" (208). In turn, "these fictional characteristics of corporeality are promoted as an ideal," even as they can and do vary slightly in terms of time and place (208). What's more, "An ableist imaginary relies upon the existence of an unconscious, imagined community of able-bodied and able-minded people, who are bound together by an ableist homosocial worldview that asserts the preferability of ableism, norms often asserted by way of the political codes of citizenship, including nation, corporation building and the idea of the 'productivity of the multitude' [alluding to Michael Hardt and Antonio Negri]" (208).

Ableism is a much more powerful, pervasive, and all-encompassing phenomenon than discrimination, and this in turn requires a different way of conceiving and mobilizing on the basis of disability, as "The decision to adopt a minoritizing approach–which sees disability as discreet and insular–keeps the disabled population in its place as an insignificant minority population" (208). Adherence to such "fiction," Campbell argues, "masks the reality that disability could be experienced by at least 40 per cent of the population, which, if accepted, has profoundly different political and legal implications about how governments understand the diversity continuum" (208-209). Such a reunderstanding would represent a profound challenge as well to the "veiled subtext," all too often continually present, "that disability is somewhat unsatisfactory, and that people should make attempts to 'ameliorate' their impairments" (209). What Campbell is working toward encompasses disrupting binary divisions between able-bodied and disabled following in line with similar efforts to do the same in relation to categories of sex, gender, and sexual orientation (209)–and Campbell proposes doing so can in turn enable disruption and reconfiguration of "ableist trajectories" that "erase differences in different cultures and in different situations" (209).

In sum, Campbell argues "able-bodiedness circulates and produces notions within a university environment" that establish parameters, set standards, and define limits concerning matters of health and well-being, productive contribution and responsible citizenship, what is normal and what is typical, what is universally assumed and expected, how different workers and fields of work are conceived in terms of their distinctions from and relations to each other, how this environment itself is to be engaged and appreciated in terms of what kinds of relations prevail among diverse people participating in the same environment, and in relation to what facilities and resources further constitute fundamental dimensions of this environment (209-210). A major feature of ableism that cuts across this array of parameters, standards, and limits has to do with deflecting problems to the level of the individual and solutions to the form of "An obsession with *techne* or procedures" (210) that suggests the only problems that can reasonably be attended to are those that can be met with adjustments in procedures in conjunction with reallocation or reconfiguration of available resources: in other words, solely those problems readily responsive to tinkering with and tweaking technical dimensions of especially physical infrastructures–but not problems that require rethinking the dynamics of how social relations are structured within and across the institution. As the deeper issues disabled members of 'university communities' experience continue to be ignored and disregarded, this amounts to *institutional violence against disabled people*.

To return to Cvetkovich's *Depression: a Public Feeling*, disabled people working in academia are wont to experience considerable 'negative' or 'bad' feelings, and often so, while academia functions as a pivotal locus for engendering and promulgating ableism, resulting, across the larger society and culture, in a vast expanse of emotional damage. Depression, once more, makes ample good sense as part of a society in which success depends, overwhelmingly, upon a thoroughly ableist conception of *ability*. This is *ability* that demands not only continually aspiring toward, but also as close as possible realizing, an impossible ideal of perfection in terms of productivity and performance. This is *ability* yet further that demands striving toward realization of this same impossible ideal over and over again, while always steadily improving and always thereby coming ever closer to arriving at perfection. Even as many of us recognize this is impossible, even absurd, that does not mean we do not continue to act otherwise, subject to the enormous pressure (and often the sheer necessity of following along with the enormous pressure) that ableism exerts upon us–i.e., even if and when we know it makes no good sense to do so and even if and when we know it damages us and others all around us to do so.

Four

In an introduction to the 2008 edition of *Ghostly Matters: Haunting and the Sociological Imagination*, originally published in 1997, Avery Gordon explains "haunting" is the term she invokes "to describe those singular yet repetitive instances when home becomes unfamiliar, when your bearings on the world lose direction, when the over-and-done-with comes alive, when what's been in your blind spot comes into view" (xvi). "Haunting," crucially, "raises specters, and it alters the experience of being in time, the way we separate the past, the present, and the future. These specters or ghosts appear when the trouble they represent and symptomize is no longer being contained or repressed or blocked from view. The ghost . . . is not the invisible or some ineffable excess. The whole essence . . . of a ghost is that it has a real presence and demands its due, your attention" (xvi). "Haunting is a frightening experience," moreover, because "It always registers the harm inflicted or the loss sustained by a social violence done in the past or in the present. But haunting, unlike trauma, is distinctive for producing a something-to-be-done" (xvi). This 'something-to-be-done' is what is ultimately most important: seizing the imperative of recognizing ghostly demands that show up in the form of hauntings and coming to grips with how it is right and necessary to respond (xvii).

In her foreword to the 2008 edition of *Ghostly Matters*, Janice Radway commends Gordon for engaging the sweeping question "How do we reckon with what modern history has rendered ghostly?" (xi), while at the same time provocatively proposing this reckoning "should underwrite all social analysis" (quoted xi). Radway characterizes the 'new sociology' Gordon advocates as requiring "a new way of knowing . . . that is more a listening than a seeing, a practice of being attuned to the echoes and murmurs of that which has been lost but is still present in the form of intimations, hints, suggestions, and portents" (x). This 'new sociology' zeroes in on the gap "between what we only see and what we actually know" while the echoes and murmurs to which this new sociology attunes and attends are those 'ghostly matters' Gordon's title references. These 'ghosts' "haunt us at every turn" (x) because "To be haunted" involves being "tied to social and historical effects'" (quoted x).

As Radway attests, with *Ghostly Matters* Gordon "traces . . . the intricate process by which the reductive and universalizing powers of the market are lived at the level of the conceptual and the intellectual and how the resulting divide between the general and the particular, between the social and the individual, constrains our ability to recognize and to address the profound human costs of a system that is utterly dependent on the repression of a knowledge of *social* injustice" (ix). This line of inquiry leads Gordon to conclude "radical political change will come about only when new forms of subjectivity *and* sociality can be forged by thinking *beyond* the limits of what is already comprehensible" (xiii). Gordon's "desire" is "to reanimate the utopian" (xiii) by welcoming the ghost that 'will allow you to heal', and in so doing "'help you imagine what was lost that never even existed, really'" (quoted xiii). As Gordon herself emphasizes, "That is its [the ghost's] utopian grace: to encourage a steely sorrow laced with delight for what we lost that we never had; to long for the insight of that moment in which we recognize, as in [Walter] Benjamin's profane illumination, that it could have been and can be otherwise" (57).

Radway glosses *Ghostly Matters* as a call for a new sociology designed to "detect how conditions in the past banished certain individuals, things, or ideas, how circumstances rendered them marginal, excluded, or repressed. Sociology must preoccupy itself with what has been lost" (viii). This mode of doing sociology proceeds on the basis of understanding "the lost is only apparently absent because the forced 'disappearance' of aspects of the social continues to shadow all that remains. Because the past *always* haunts the present, sociology must imaginatively engage those apparitions, those ghosts that tie present subjects to past histories" (viii).

Gordon begins chapter one of *Ghostly Matters*, titled "her shape and his hand," with the following striking opening sentence: "That life is complicated may seem a banal expression of the obvious, but it is nonetheless a profound theoretical statement–perhaps the most important theoretical statement of our time" (3). A first key dimension of the profundity at work in this otherwise seemingly banal statement "is that the power relations that characterize any historically embedded society are never as transparently clear as the names we give to them imply" (3). A second key dimension is that "even those people who live in the most dire circumstances possess a complex and oftentimes contradictory humanity and subjectivity" (4). In relation to the latter, Gordon's concept of "complex personhood" means "*all people* [my italics] . . . remember and forget, are beset by contradiction, and recognize and misrecognize themselves and others," "suffer graciously and selfishly," "get stuck in the symptoms of their troubles," and "transform themselves" (4). Complex personhood means "even those called 'Other' are never never that" (4). Recognition of the fact "That life is complicated," and that this shows up, notably, in the form of "complex personhood," "guides efforts to treat race, class, and gender dynamics as more dense and delicate than those categorical terms often imply," while underscoring "We need to know where we live in order to imagine living elsewhere" and "We need to imagine living elsewhere before we can live there" (5).

Making use of Raymond Williams's concept of 'structure of feeling', Gordon theorizes 'hauntings' as socially 'vexatious' phenomena that manifest in the form of "phantoms of modernity's violence" (19). While representative of *shared* structures of feeling, it is crucial, in understanding and engaging with 'hauntings' and 'ghosts', to attend to the 'mediations' between "an institution and an individual, a social structure and a subject, and history and a biography" (19). Even as "the ghost is a social figure" (25), in attending to "What does the ghost say as it speaks" (24), we each need to grapple with what does it say as it speaks *to me*; we each must accept "we are part of the story, for better or worse" (25). We are *disparately* caught up within the violence and the wounds ghost signify, such that in order for any of us to grasp what a particular haunting, and what a particular ghost, means, "the ghost must speak to *me*, in some way sometimes similar to, sometimes distinct from how it may be speaking to others" (24).

Chapter two, which Gordon titles "distractions," begins with Sarina Spielrein. Spielrein is largely forgotten today and to the extent she is remembered at all this tends to be due to her having fallen in love with Carl Jung, as she underwent psychoanalysis with Jung, and for also later undergoing psychoanalysis with Sigmund Freud. Yet Spielrein was a psychoanalytic theorist in her own right who developed a theory of 'the death instinct' ten years before Freud did the same in *Beyond the Pleasure Principle*. Spielrein has been rendered invisible, or at least marginal, in accounts of the time and place in which she was significantly active, and indeed this 'ghostly' rendering of Spielrein began early on, as exemplified by Spielrein's absence from a photograph of ostensibly all the major figures in attendance at the Third Psychoanalytic Congress held at Weimar, Germany in 1911–an event at which Spielrein was nevertheless definitely present and to which she was in fact a prominent contributor. Gordon recounts becoming distracted on her way to present a paper at an academic conference by this photo from which Spielrein was missing. This distraction prompted Gordon to undertake an elaborate detour in developing the argument she was preparing to present. In working on her argument Gordon "was still struggling with acknowledging that sociology and its world of self-confident facts did not always seem more real than its haunting remainders" (38). Gordon recognized she needed to develop her argument via a method itself closely resembling fiction, at least in foregrounding narrative and especially *re-narration*. Re-narrating Spielrein's story thereby proves useful to Gordon in redirecting sociological attention "to what is not seen, but is nonetheless necessarily real . . . to what appears dead, but is nonetheless powerfully alive . . . to what appears to be in the past, but is nonetheless powerfully present . . ." (42).

Consideration of Spielrein's story, and of Spielrein's anticipation of Freud, leads Gordon back to Freud. Gordon recognizes she needs to engage critically with Freud's theories of the unconscious and the uncanny. In developing his theory of the unconscious, Gordon finds that "Freud cannot quite get away from the possibility that the unconscious derives its characteristic force from its role as the place where all the others out there in the world and their life come inside me and unhinge my sense of self as they make what I am, as they live within me" (47-48). Freud early on seriously contemplated theorizing the unconscious as a 'social unconscious', but ultimately turned away from doing so. Glimpses of this alternative that he did not pursue testify to how "vexed" Freud was by "the possibility of conceiving the unconscious as the life of others and other things within us" (48). In this vexation, Gordon avers, "the specter of the social unconscious raises its head" (48).

Gordon argues in favor of following the path Freud does not, theorizing the unconscious as a social unconscious. Freud interprets "all vestiges of animism," and "all the spirits or the hauntings" that "come from the unconscious" as located "inside the troubled individual," inside the troubled individual's troubled mind, even at the same time as this "individual . . . had become increasingly taken with the animation of the commodity world" (48). In so doing, Freud tries "to demystify our holdover beliefs in the power of the *world at large*, hoping to convince us that everything that seems to be coming at us from outside is really coming from this now shrunken inside" (49). Yet Freud cannot convincingly do so, as a critical reading of his famous essay "The Uncanny" makes clear.

Gordon declares "uncanny experiences are haunting experiences" (50). In discussing Freud's "The Uncanny," Gordon seeks to identify what haunts Freud in this essay, and what as a result subsequently hunts Freudian psychoanalysis. Gordon, like multiple others, interprets "The Uncanny" attesting to how 'the uncanny' proved *too uncanny for Freud*. Freud strives to do so but he cannot pin down, fix, and contain the uncanny. He cannot provide a single coherent explanation for all forms of the uncanny. Freud is forced to admit he "is troubled by . . . the presence of uncanny experiences that are not reducible to the acting out of an individual's psychic state" (52). Freud is troubled, in particular, in dwelling on encounters with the uncanny he himself has experienced, by "the recognition of himself as another, as a stranger, the arrival of a person from elsewhere, from the world outside himself, from what we call the social" (54). In response to this troubling recognition, "Freud might have called the primitive or the archaic the social and thereby have supplemented the Marxist notion of estrangement" (54). But Freud cannot bring himself to do so, in what Gordon deems a major loss to psychoanalytic theory because "the social is ultimately what the uncanny is about: being haunted by the *world of common reality*" (54). "Freud is deeply concerned, haunted you might say, by society and its institutions" (55), yet "Freud gets so close to dealing with the social reality of haunting only to give up the ghost and everything that comes in its wake" (57).

Gordon's discussion of Freud enables her to draw a sharp contrast, indeed, between, on the one hand, critical theories that deny, refuse, dismiss, or avoid what manifests in 'ghostly' form, and, on the other hand, critical theories that instead follow the direction she advocates, akin to what Jacques Derrida proposes in *Specters of Marx*: "To exorcise not in order to chase away the ghosts, but this time to grant them the right . . . to . . . a hospitable memory . . . out of a concern for justice" (quoted 58). Gordon arrives at her articulation of this position, and her argument for it, circuitously, by way of indirection and by means of story-telling, because doing so is indispensable to the kind of critical theorization she contends is necessary to sustain this argument: "it would have not been quite the story I wanted to tell if I had just told you that sociology needs a way of grappling with what it represses, haunting, and psychoanalysis needs a way of grappling with what it represses, society" (60). Gordon *shows* us why this proposition is so along with how she has arrived at it, while deliberately leaving us to "ponder the paradox of providing a hospitable memory for ghosts *out of a concern for justice*" (60).

Chapter three, titled "the other door, it's flood of tears with consolation enclosed," centers around Gordon's reading of Argentinian novelist Luisa Valenzuela's 1977 novella *Como en la guerra* (*As in War*), first published in 1979 and translated in English as *He Who Searches. Como en la guerra* takes on "the difficulty of representing what seems unrepresentable, even unthinkable" in relation to 'ghosts that haunt state-sponsored systems of disappearance' (70). In Argentina, lasting from 1976 through 1983, the military junta that then controlled the state 'disappeared' many tens of thousands of people, murdering over 30,000. Efforts to discover what happened to many of those so disappeared have often proven arduous and taken decades. 'The disappearance' meanwhile exercised an intimidating impact on Argentinians who were not disappeared, who were too terrified to protest and resist this exercise of state violence.

Complicity, however, extended further than failure to object and oppose. Gordon finds *Como en la guerra* especially compelling as a critique of "middle-class consciousness . . . engrossed by the personal, the familial, the professional, and the accidental" (133). As Gordon elaborates, "This is a class consciousness that always has something else on its mind: the bills, the errands, the car, the house, the petty tyrannies of administrators, colleagues, relatives . . . This is a class consciousness that escapes public civic life because it is tired or busy or what can you do anyway?" (133). The middle class, moreover,

> always wants things taken care of, done right, and is always complaining about what it is about to lose, as if the whole world would end if the middle class collapses. It fears falling down where the others live and it craves success stories of whatever kind. But it is cowed by the lure of achievement, internalizing an aggressive inferiority it projects remarkably consistently, as it often sits waiting, distracted, while others act in its name. It hates authority and loves authority at the same time . . . . (133).

In other words, in sum, middle-class consciousness not only tolerates but also welcome benefits that accrue by 'going along with' systematic exercise of state violence.

In *Como en la guerra* Valenzuela emphasizes an indictment of the dominant institutional form of psychoanalysis in Argentina during the years of 'the disappearance'. Valenzuela critiques this mode of psychoanalytic theory and practice for 'cultivating' "a depoliticized understanding of trauma . . . a kind of social sedative" for the middle classes to ease their prospective anxiety about what they are complicit in (91). Valenzuela advocates in favor of a radical psychoanalysis that converges with Marxism and which as such would be "capable of treating haunting as an objective force" (97). Yet Gordon interprets *Como en la guerra* as also illuminating problems confronting attempts at mergers of Marxism and psychoanalysis: "The more-psychoanalytic-than-Marxist never quite accept that the subject is a superstructural effect or that the psychic world could really be trumped by the social world" while "The more-Marxist-than-psychoanalytic never quite accept the autonomy of the psychic world and distrust a politics that relies on psychological explanation" (97).

Gordon credits Valenzuela, via *Como en la guerra*, for showing how the Argentinian 'disappearance' exemplifies use of state power in "controlling the imagination, controlling the meaning of death," "haunting the population into submission," and compelling people "To live under the mantle of omnipresent dread" (124). Disappearance is especially useful "From the authoritarian state's point of view" because "the disappeared cannot remain hidden away, but rather must be discernible enough to scare 'a little bit of everyone' into shadows of themselves, into submission. Disappearance is a public secret" (126). Disappearance, moreover, is definitively registered in forms of 'haunting' and 'the ghostly', as disappearance "transgresses the boundaries between the living and the dead" in each of 'two classes of disappeared': "First, there are those who have disappeared and literally return" and "Second, there are those who have disappeared who reappear only as apparitions" (126-127).

Gordon interprets the campaign of the Mothers of the Plaza de Mayo, in particular their use of photographs to call attention to and demand justice for their children, grandchildren, and other relatives who had been disappeared, a campaign that played a pivotal role in bringing the disappearance along with the rule of the military junta to an end, as "potent evidence of what is harrowingly present," in a haunting and ghostly form (109). This "repertoire of counterimages" it itself a key "part of a movement to break the silence" (109) that, in Susan Sontag's words, proceeds to "'lay claim to another reality'" (quoted 109). The Mothers needed to, and were successful in, 'conjuring' "the ghosts" of their family members who had been disappeared as well as "the haunting quality of [their] disappearance" (110).

It is worth noting well that "Disappearance is not only about death"; it "is a thing in itself, a state of being repressed"–and therefore it needs to be addressed on its own terms, on terms aptly befitting its distinctiveness, as the Mothers of the Plaza de Mayo in fact did (115). As Gordon explains, further,

> A disappearance is only real when it is apparitional . . . because the ghost or the apparition is the principal form by which something lost or invisible or seemingly not there makes itself known or apparent to us. The ghost makes itself known to us through haunting and pulls us affectively into the structure of feeling of a reality we come to experience as a recognition. Haunting recognition is a special way of knowing what has happened or is happening. (63)

The Mothers of the Plaza de Mayo evoked their disappeared children and grandchildren as ghosts, that is in ghostly form, to haunt the Argentinian state and the greater Argentinian society. "The ghost," as Gordon underscores, "imports a charged strangeness into the place or sphere it is haunting" and "the ghost is primarily a symptom of what is missing" (63). This is an apt characterization of precisely what the campaign of the Mothers of the Plaza de Mayo did that in turn aptly explains how and why this campaign proved influential in achieving redress after all preceding efforts at protest and resistance had been easily defeated.

It is important, in addition, Gordon contends, to recognize that "From a certain vantage point the ghost also simultaneously represents a future possibility, a hope" (64). The ghost represents what could be, what could yet be, by way of a conjuring of what was robbed of what it could have become. Gordon argues "Societies become haunted by terrible deeds that are systematically occurring and are simultaneously denied by every public organ of governance and communication" (64). The Argentinian 'disappearance' is an exemplary instance of systematic perpetration and denial of terrible deeds, and it is also an exemplary instance of the haunting consequences of so doing in the form of the ghostly remainder and especially the ghostly return of what cannot be completely and forever suppressed. From Valenzuela's novel, "We learn," moreover, "that in order to understand and to transform state power, to fight even the most coercive, threatening, militarized, and violent state, the story must be told in the mode of haunting" (131). Valenzuela's *Como en la guerra* haunts by evoking ghosts of whom and what state violence worked to systematically crush and destroy.

Haunting is "about reliving events in all their vividness, originality, and violence so as to overcome their pulsating and lingering effects. Haunting is an encounter in which you touch the ghost or the ghostly matter of things" (134). Engaging with haunting is often excruciatingly painful yet nonetheless vitally necessary: "To be sure, haunting terrorizes but it gives you *something you have to try for yourself. The madness* and *the feeling for what it at stake . . .* what the encounter is finally about" (135). This is the encounter you experience yourself compelled to engage, in facing up to the haunting impact of historical and ongoing socio-political violence as it resonates in your own life-experience. You are and have been affected by this haunting impact upon your individual everyday life-experience, in line with how the contours of this individual life-experience have been framed and structured on the basis of historical and ongoing socio-political violence. You are and have been so affected even if not consciously attentive to or aware that this is so. But in the 'ghostly encounter' you no longer remain inattentive or unaware. You *need to respond* not by refusing but rather welcoming the ghost, the ghost representative of what has not been satisfied, of what has not received due justice. You *need to do so* in order to begin the process that will eventually exorcise this ghost through attending to what it demands of you–by finally providing it with what it justly requires in order to disappear (135).

"Haunting" is *"the mode by which the middle class, in particular, needs to encounter something you cannot just ignore, or understand at a distance, or 'explain away' by stripping it of all its magical power; something whose seeming self-evident repugnance you cannot just rhetorically throw in someone's face" (131). "Haunting" is "the mode by which the middle class needs to encounter *something you have to try out for yourself, feeling your way deeper and deeper into the heart of darkness until you do* feel *what is at stake, the madness of the passion*" (131). And here is exemplified "The double edge of haunting: the singularity of the loss of my previously held securities and supports, the particular trouble the ghost is making for me; and the sociality of those abstract but compelling forces flashing now (and then) in the light of day, the organized trouble the system is experiencing" (105).

Engaging with haunting is of ultimate value in opening up possibilities for (re)imagining, and on the basis of what can be newly (re)imagined, creating a radically different kind of human society. "What has the state tried to repress?" Gordon queries, and to this question she answers "It has many names that I will call simply, and despite the reputation it has acquired of evasive naïveté, the utopian: the apperception of the fundamental difference between the world we have now and the world we could have instead; the desire and drive to create a just and equitable world. The utopian, the most general subject of the state's repression, makes its appearance too, lingering among the smoldering remains of a dirty war" (127).

In chapter four, titled "not only the footprints but the water too and what is down there," Gordon engages once more with a fictional novel as itself doing the work of social theory, just as she has with Luisa Valenzuela's *Como en la guerra* in chapter three. In this chapter it is Toni Morrison's *Beloved* (1987) that Gordon interprets as doing so. *Beloved* enables understanding of "the lingering inheritance of racial slavery, the unfinished product of Reconstruction," including of what follows once "Slavery has ended, but something of it continues to live on" (139). *Beloved*, in fact, offers "one of the most significant contributions to the understanding of haunting," in general–of how haunting takes place, of what it means, and of how and why it needs to be engaged (139).

Beloved retells the story of the real-life escaped slave Margaret Garner, 'who killed her child rather than see it taken back into slavery' (139). It is the fictional correspondent to Margaret Garner and to Garner's immediate family that the ghost of the child she killed, here identified as Beloved, principally haunts when this child 'returns' as a ghost. In this novel, "This ghost, Beloved, forces a reckoning," but it is important to recognize even as this happens "Beloved, the ghost, is haunted too" (139). Beloved is haunted by all those who died in the course of transport across the Atlantic Ocean from Africa on their way to becoming slaves in the Americas (139). In fictionally invoking these interlinked hauntings, *Beloved* raises the fundamental questions of "What is too much to remember when there is yet more?" (141) and "What is too much to tell, to pass on, when 'remembering seem[s] unwise', but necessary?" (quoted 141).

Gordon reads *Beloved* as subverting and transforming the conventional 'slave narrative'. The latter kind of autobiographical writing wrestled with "The complex articulation" of a "double bind," as the slave narrative needed to "testify to my transformation into a Slave while I testify to the existence of my shared humanity with you" (145). *Beloved* "remembers some of what the slave narrative forgot" (146). Unlike the common trope of slave narratives according to which acquisition of literacy is asserted as decisive proof that the erstwhile slave shares a common humanity with white readers, *Beloved* "refuses the task of having to prove the slave's (and by implication her descendants') humanity" (147). In *Beloved*, "Sethe [Margaret Garner's fictional counterpart in the novel] runs" from slavery, "not when she learns to read and write, but when she learns how she will be read and written" (147). Sethe runs from slavery when she recognizes control over what and how she 'becomes literate' is being used to control how the meaning and value of her life will be understood (147). In *Beloved*, Morrison is not concerned with proving enslaved and erstwhile enslaved Blacks shared a common humanity with Whites, but rather with the questions of "What sort of people were the slaves and the former slaves and their descendants"? and "What sort of people could they be?" (150). Morrison strives "to imagine the life world of those with no names we remember, with no 'visible reason' for being in the archive," but "Morrison does not speak for them. She imagines them speaking their complex personhood as it negotiates the always coercive and subtle complexities of the hands of power" (150).

Gordon illustrates the significant difference in what Morrison does by in turn critiquing abolitionist Levi Coffin's account of Margaret Garner's case. Coffin has long been identified as the authoritative chronicler of this case at the time it was immediately unfolding. Gordon critiques Coffin for not grasping his privilege in comparison with Garner, and as a result not recognizing what is ultimately at stake. Coffin takes pain to establish his authority in offering the account he does by tracing his own lengthy genealogy, oblivious to how this form of authorization has been robbed of slaves and their descendants, slaves like Margaret Garner and the child she killed rather than return to slavery. Coffin, moreover, inserts a lengthy tangential discussion into his narrative of how he refused, as a Quaker, to doff his cap while inside public buildings, during the course of Garner's trial, as a matter of principle, and how he took flack for not doing so, insisting since this hat was his property he maintained the right to do with it as he pleased. All the while Margaret Garner's case, as well as that of the others captured with her, pivot upon whether she and they are recognized as human beings or as property, with their erstwhile 'owners' insisting they were property, not human beings, and as such their owners maintaining the right to do with this 'property' as they pleased, while in turn 'property' maintains none of either the legal rights or responsibilities pertaining to legally recognized human beings. Coffin's account is, moreover, typical of those written and published at the time, even among those coming from positions ostensibly 'sympathetic' to Garner, in that it provides Garner next to no opportunity to speak for herself.

In relation to the specific issues *Beloved* addresses, the presence of the ghost informs us that the over and done with 'extremity' of domestic and international slavery has not entirely gone away, even if it seems to have passed into the register of history and symbol. Haunting the post-Civil War and by allegorical reference the post-civil rights era is the presence of a ghost who is herself haunted, notably in relation to "confronting the trauma of the Middle Passage," and in doing so confronting links between slavery and "the origin of modern American freedom . . . the paradigmatic and value-laded operations of the capitalist market. This is a market whose exchange relations continue to transform the living into the dead, a system of social relations that fundamentally objectifies and dominates in a putatively free society" (169).

The 1873 setting of *Beloved* is, in itself, highly significant, as 'Radical Reconstruction' at that point "had entirely exhausted itself"; "It aims had failed" (171). The era of White Southern 'redemption' was about to begin, involving systemic retribution versus freed Blacks who had sought to take advantage of what Reconstruction, at least in its most 'radical' form, had ostensibly promised them: equitable inclusion in social and political life. 'Redemption' rapidly evolved into the oppressive regime known as Jim Crow that reimplemented and reinforced systemic Black subjugation. As Gordon observes, "Twenty years after the Emancipation Proclamation, the characters in *Beloved* are struggling with the knowledge that 'freeing yourself was one thing; claiming ownership of that freed self was another' [quoted from *Beloved* 172]" (172).

In other words, a form of 'reconstruction' happened but not in line with what 'official' Reconstruction was ostensibly conceived to achieve, but rather, in practice, "Reconstruction ratified a prevailing but limited notion of freedom as the freedom to own property, to sell one's labor, and to not be owned as property," linking "slave labor" with "wage labor" in defining what "freedom" differentially means, for whom, in American capitalist society (173). Gordon interprets *Beloved*'s 'freed Black characters' intuitively recognizing Reconstruction's substantial limitations, as well as what was set to follow: "Smelling the lynchings and the long march of those now possessing 'free' status into the twentieth century. Reconstruction was a failure politically, socially, and economically, and we still live today with the consequences of the great divide between legal right and substantive freedom" (173). As *Beloved* attests, "we should beware forgetting the enslavement or domination that persists and that often masquerades as emancipation or freedom" (184).

What is necessary, that Morrison demonstrates her fictional characters realizing together by the end of *Beloved*, is to 'hospitably' attend to ghosts and their hauntings, responding to "their demanding their due," and in doing so, simultaneously accepting that "the ghost must be *collectively* [my italics] exorcised" (182). As signal contribution toward a social theory of 'haunting' and of the 'ghostly', *Beloved* shows "The ghost cannot be simply tracked back to an individual loss or trauma," "the ghost's desire is not just negative," "The ghost is not other or alterity as such, ever," and "It is (like Beloved) pregnant with unfulfilled possibility, with the something to be done that the wavering present is demanding." Gordon emphasizes

> This something to be done is not a return to the past but a reckoning with its repression in the present, a reckoning with that which we have lost, but never had. The ghost always figures this utopian dimension of haunting, enscapsulated in the very first lines of Jacques Derrida's book on specters: 'Someone, you or me, comes forward and says: *I would like to live finally*" (183-184 and quoted 184).

Before turning from *Beloved*, it is important to highlight several further key points Gordon derives from her reading of this novel. A key question *Beloved* raises for us today is "How can we be accountable to people who seemingly have not counted in the historical and public record?" (187). To begin to do, Gordon proposes we need to critique "the American dream of innocence and clean slates and the future" (187), while for White Americans "It is our responsibility to recognize just where we are in the story, even if we do not want to be there" (188). White readers of *Beloved* often 'prefer' to identify, insofar as they experience themselves inclined or able to identity, with Black characters, but these are not in fact our true historical antecedents. We need to recognize "that white people are in the story too," and that what these characters represent, appalling as this is, is linked with us, on account of our shared whiteness (189). So even as we prefer to identify with the Black characters we must reflect critically on our links with the white characters we don't want to identify with, with what they represent, in critically inquiring into our connections with such white figures, past and present. We need to recognize, "we are in this story, even now, even if we do not want to be" and "you cannot simply choose the ghosts with which you are willing to engage" (190).

For Gordon, "There is something unique about haunting as a structure of feeling. It is 'emergent'"–in terms of Raymond Williams's distinction among dominant, residual, and emergent kinds of social structures; it anticipates a possible future form of society, and culture, that has not of yet been generalized or fully realized (201). Nonetheless, no matter how much haunting might represent an 'emergent' structure of feeling, "We need to know that something is missing in order to even begin to look for it" and it is "The ghostly haunt" that "gives us precisely this notification" (178). In other words, "The ghostly haunt says, Something is happening you hadn't expected. It says, Something is making an appearance to you that has been kept from view. It says, Do something about the wavering present the haunting is creating" (178-179).

Importantly, Gordon insists, "There is no question that when a ghost haunts, that haunting is real" (179) and, again, "When ghosts haunt, that haunting is material" (184). In haunting us, the ghost makes claims upon us: "the ghost is nothing without you" (179), and what this leads to, ultimately, once again, is "the ghost will have to be dispatched" (181) by responding to and satisfying what it calls upon us to give, by responding to and satisfying how it calls upon us to act. Gordon contends that whenever one writes about social-historical "exclusions and invisibilities" one is, of necessity, by definition, writing "ghost stories" (17). What particularly concerns Gordon in this connection is ascertaining *how* "to make contact with haunting, to engage the shadows and what is living there," as opposed to merely registering this existence (18). Indeed, "The wavering quality of haunting often hinges on what sign or image raises the ghost and what it means to our conscious visible attention" (102) while "It takes some effort to recognize the ghost and to reconstruct the world it conjures up" (66).

What kinds of signs or images might these be? Gordon draws upon Roland Barthes's theory of how photography conveys meaning in addressing this question. Barthes refers to "the element of the photograph that 'transforms reality' without doubling it, without making it vacillate," the element without 'duality . . . indirection . . . disturbance" as "the *studium*" (quoted 106, 106). This "studium," Gordon explains, encompasses "the most obvious tableaux of the photograph," the "recognizable and culturally comprehensive signs" that 'generate polite interest' in 'educating and communicating with civility'. Yet even as *the studium* "may shout . . . it does not wound" (106). For Barthes, it is, in contrast, "the *punctum*" that "breaks" or "punctuates" the *studium* (quoted 106). The *punctum* "is the 'off-center detail' that draws one in and around the polite cultural engagement with the historically interesting or the politically poised *studium*" as the *punctum* "causes me to '*give myself up*'" (107, quoted 107). The *punctum* is what "creates a compelling astonishment" (107). It is "what I add to the photograph and *what is nonetheless already there*" (quoted 107). The *punctum* "is the detail that arouses" such that "the photograph and its reference come alive" (107). In sum, "'The *punctum*' is what haunts. It is the detail, the little but heavily freighted thing that sparks the moment of arresting animation, that enlivens the world of ghosts' (108)." This "enchanting detail cannot be predicted in advance or calculated for methodological rigor" (108) but nonetheless even "If you are not looking for it, it can take you to it without your permission" (107).

A ghostly encounter is "An encounter of tremulous significance, a profane illumination" (134). 'Profane illumination' is a concept Walter Benjamin derives from surrealism, and this involves a 'shattering of habit' in "a discerning moment" that provides "a mode of apprehension distinct from critique or commentary" (204-205). A moment of 'profane illumination' takes the form of "Sensuous knowledge" where "Everything rests on not being afraid of what is happening to you" as you accept and begin to explore the implications of accepting "You are *already* involved, implicated in one way or another" (205).

Why is this kind of tremulous encounter, this moment of profane illumination so important? What can be gained? According to Gordon, "Change begins slowly with individuals who are unsettled and haunted by forces that are much greater than themselves and barely visible" (202). And this means "Change cannot occur without the encounter, without the *something you have to try for yourself.* There are no guaranteed outcomes for an encounter; much is uncertain and the results may be very limited. But if you think you can fight and eliminate the systems' complicated 'nastiness' [in Cedric Robinson's words] without it, you will not get very far because it will return to haunt you" (203).

Paying heed to ghosts by attuning and attending to as well as most importantly responding to their haunting is necessary because part and parcel of long ongoing histories of systemic oppression are "The more subtle violations" that "are *unseen* and denied," or at least most commonly so. These violations show up in the forms, among others, of "the wear and tear of long years of struggling to

932

survive," "the deep pain of always having to compete in a contest you did not have any part in designing for what matters and merits," "the sinking demoralization and forlorn craziness of exchanging everything with the invisible hands of a voracious market," and "the virtually unspeakable loss of control, the abnegation, over what is possible" (206-207). In other words, "Today, the nation closes its eyes neither innocently nor without warning. It has a renewed commitment to blindness: to be blind to the worlds of *race, class,* and *gender* . . . What does it mean for a country to choose blindness as its national pledge of allegiance?" (207). Aside from any problematically ableist implications in making uncritical use of 'blindness' here in common metaphorical terms, what Gordon is getting at is a persistent refusal to recognize and respond to–to reckon with–how race, class, and gender function and have functioned as principal and interconnected axes of oppression, by for instance pretending America is, has been, and will always be–or will be once again–exceptionally 'great', with this 'greatness' benefitting us all, or at least all of us who have rightly earned and genuinely deserve its benefits. Yet 'reckoning' requires more than 'refusal of blindness': "Reckoning is about knowing what kind of effort is required to change ourselves and the conditions that make us who we are, that set limits on what is acceptable and unacceptable, on what is possible and impossible" (202).

Gordon highlights the fictional writings of Valenzuela and Morrison as social theory "concerned with change and transformation," and as well aware that "Transformation means something distinct from resistance" (202). Social theory must change, following Valenzuela and Morrison's examples, because if we are seriously committed toward social transformation and not just social resistance, "We must learn how to identify hauntings and reckon with ghosts, must learn how to make contact with what is without doubt painful, difficult, and unsettling" and in order to do so "we will have to change the way we have been doing things" with the latter in particular involving change in how we do the work of social inquiry, analysis, theory, and critique (23). What is needed, more precisely, is a "materialist historiography," in Walter Benjamin's terms, that calls attention, as Benjamin's describes this, to "'Where thinking suddenly stops'," to where a historical materialist "'recognizes . . . a revolutionary chance in the fight for the oppressed past'" (quoted 65). Benjamin proposes the historical materialist in turn "'takes cognizance'" of what is recognized "'in order to blast a specific era out of the homogeneous course of history'" (quoted 65). Benjamin's materialist historiography Gordon finds especially useful in emphasizing the crucial importance of attending to when and where "All of a sudden your thinking is stopped, shocked, as it were, into a configuration or conjuncture that crystallizes the social gist of a dramatic or mundane event" (65). This kind of encounter is necessary in redressing the haunting legacies of "whatever organized violence has repressed and into the process formed into a past, a history," while doing so is dependent upon "remaining nonetheless alive and accessible to encounter" (66).

With a transformative social praxis, "It is essential to see the things and the people who are primarily unseen and banished to the periphery of social graciousness," at the least "because they see you and address you," and you need "to imagine their life worlds" (196). In doing so, it is crucial to take seriously into account what Raymond Williams describes as *affective elements of consciousness and relationships: not feeling against thought, but thought as felt and feeling as thought: practical consciousness of a present kind, in a living and interrelating continuity*" (quoted 198). Gordon adds that, after all, our lives "at any given moment" amount to "a tangle of structured feelings and palpable structures" (201). Attending and responding to haunting and to the ghosts that function as the signs or images of haunting is of central significance for this kind of social theory because "Ultimately haunting is about how to transform a shadow of a life into an undiminished life whose shadows touch softly in the spirit for a peaceful reconciliation. In this necessarily collective undertaking, the end, which is not an ending at all, belongs to everyone" (208).

Gordon advocates focusing on "the living effects, seething and lingering, of what seems over and done with, the endings that are not over" (195), in writing 'histories of the present' that "requires stretching toward the horizon of what cannot be seen with ordinary clarity yet" (195). This necessitates grappling with "the difficulty of imagining beyond the limits of what is already *understandable*," because "To imagine what is beyond the limits of what is already understandable is our best hope for retaining what ideology critique traditionally offers while transforming its limitations into what, in an older Marxist language, was called utopian possibility" (195).

In a September 2020 interview with Verso Books as part of *Revolutionary Feminisms: Conversations on Collective Action and Radical Thought*, Gordon explains "The ambitious problem that preoccupied me in *Ghostly Matters*–and still does to a large extent–was how to understand and write evocatively about some of the ways that modern forms of dispossession, exploitation and repression concretely impact the lives of the people most affected by them and impact our shared conditions of living." 'Haunting' in this connection represents "one way in which abusive systems of power make themselves known and their impacts felt in everyday life, especially when they are supposedly over and done with (such as with transatlantic slavery) or when their oppressive nature is continuously denied (such as with free labour or national security)." Haunting "is an animated state in which a repressed or unresolved social violence is making itself known, sometimes very directly, sometimes more obliquely." In turn, "Spectres, or ghosts, appear when the trouble they represent and symptomise is no longer being contained, repressed or blocked from view." A ghost thereby "has a real presence and demands its due, demands your attention." The ghost does so because "Haunting always registers the harm inflicted, or the loss sustained, by a social violence done in the past or being done in the present, and it is for this reason quite frightening," because "haunting, unlike trauma, by contrast, is distinctive for producing a something-to-be-done." Haunting, in fact, Gordon declares, "refers to this sociopolitical-psychological state when something else, or something different from before, feels like it must be done, and prompts a something-to-be-done." Key in grasping her argument, Gordon underscores, is "Again, for me, haunting is not about invisibility or unknowability, per se; it refers us to what's living and breathing . . . [that is] hidden from view: people, places, histories, knowledge, memories, ways of life, ideas." When the ghost demands your attention and something must be done you arrive at 'an emergent state': "I think this emergent state is also the critical analytic moment. That's to say, when the repression isn't working anymore."

What is especially challenging about Gordon's theorization is "The something-to-be-done is something you have to try/do for yourself." Gordon proceeds beyond articulating that challenge by citing Chuck Morse in making an even further challenging distinction: *"It is the task of the radical critic to illuminate what is repressed and excluded by the basic mechanisms of a given social order. It is the task of the politically engaged radical critic to side with the excluded and the repressed: to develop insights gained in confrontation with injustice, to nourish cultures of resistance, and to help define the means with which society can be rendered adequate to the full breadth of human possibilities."*

At the beginning of the second decade of the 21ˢᵗ century, "Capitalism now lurches from crisis to crisis more frequently, and it is incapable of resolving them without ever increasing financial and military assistance from the state, even as its anti-state ideology sounds louder and louder." What follows, "In this context of enhanced militarism and securitisation," is an "ongoing redistribution of resources from social property to private property" that "has led to more widespread social abandonment and more entrenched inequalities within and between countries." At the present time, "The major capitalist powers in the West seem either not to understand or to be in denial about the decline of Western hegemony and the quiet but definitive eastward shift of the world system." In turn, "The capitalist democratic state–what Ruth Wilson Gilmore calls the 'anti-state state', or most people know by the name of the neoliberal state–is also weakened, internally conflicted to the point of incapacity, nowhere more evident than in the UK's Brexit debacle." That means "The legitimation crisis that besets the viability of a capitalist democratic state is real, and the authoritarian alternative quite further advanced than the notion of a populist surge implies."

Nonetheless, "At the same time, there is widespread, daily, active and open political opposition to all this, at the scale at which people can contest it: protecting this group of migrants from arrest, confinement and deportation; organising this strike among teachers in this city; defending this territory from oil drilling; filing lawsuits against a police department and so on; gathering in public to swear, shout, shake fists, confront the inevitably helmeted riot police." What's more, "There is also widespread, daily, active, infrapolitical and even secret political opposition, which needs and wants to remain hidden." In addition, "there are also so many people, more and more in the Western wealthy countries, looking for ways to think and live on different–better terms–and doing it in small ways, whether in local collectives, or in extended family units, with illegal housing and electricity, alternative currencies, in cities and on old tribal lands."

This is where reactivating and reanimating 'the utopian' becomes valuable although, as Gordon indicates, "I am not invested in the term 'utopian'– and I don't care if it's used or not. I care about what I call . . . 'being in-difference'. Being in-difference is a political consciousness and a sensuous knowledge, a standpoint and a mindset for living on better terms than we're offered; for living as if you had the necessity and the freedom to do so; for living in the acknowledgment, that despite the overwhelming power of all the systems of domination which are trying to kill us, they never quite become us." This is, Gordon declares, "the key challenge politically . . . to promote and develop that being in-difference, to learn to stop appealing to the system itself for redress, to stop believing the forces that are killing you can or will save you." Certainly "This doesn't mean that we don't engage politically in struggle," but "It does mean preparing for being ready and available, possibly at a moment's notice, to live autonomously from the system one wants to abolish." As Gordon urges, "The goal" has to be "not greater participation or assimilation into the given terms of order," but rather "to overturn that order or displace it or live otherwise than within it." Yet "The balance between withdrawal/separation and engagement in social struggle is what has to be determined. And there are, unfortunately, no clear rules for this." Nonetheless, the politically engaged intellectual, *the politically engaged radical critic*, recognizes "There's a reach, or desire, for

935

something else–for a life without racial capitalism, a life in which we are not enclosed by values and modes of being together based on money and exchange values, status hierarchies, violence and force, alienation, racialisation and discipline to externally imposed standards." This reach, or desire, "may be inchoate, underanalysed or inexperienced, but something of what we used to call a revolutionary impulse is more widespread than the authorities would like us to believe." And the fact "That we have to build this life ourselves–it will not be given to us–is also I think partially understood, if not quite comprehended in full," which is a right and necessary discernment, even as it "makes an already enormous job even more complex, difficult and fraught with seemingly overwhelming obstacles and challenges."

In discussing excerpts from Avery F. Gordon's *Ghostly Matters: Haunting and the Sociological Imagination* in classes I have taught on Ian Curtis, Joy Division, and critical theory, we have focused on Gordon's concepts of 'complex personhood' and of 'ghosts' and 'haunting'. In particular we have considered not only what Gordon means by 'complex personhood' and how this differs from more familiar, commonsense understandings of what might be identified as 'simple personhood', but also what might be the advantages of thinking of and relating to personhood as complex, in the ways Gordon advocates, as well as why it might be that this often does not happen and seemingly proves difficult for many to do. We have made sense of Ian Curtis as exemplifying what complex personhood can indeed be like, and not only in Curtis's uniquely individual instance, but also for many if not most of us who are as multiple, complex, contradictory, and dynamic as Curtis, however much retrospective commentary on Curtis often emphasizes seemingly exceptionally enigmatic as well as shape-shifting dimensions of his character. But we have also pushed further than that to consider to what extent it makes sense to interpret Curtis's lyrics and Joy Division's music as engaged with 'complex personhood', however elliptically, in determining what might constitute viable and useful ways of making sense of what these lyrics and this music means. We have explored to what extent it might make sense to interpret the music illustrating a musical group representing a form of 'complex personhood' that simultaneously combines, fuses, surpasses, and transforms elements of the 'personhood' of each of the individuals contributing to the group in fashioning the group's identity–and especially in contributing to fashioning what might be posited as the group's own 'personality' or 'character'.

In relation to Gordon's conceptions of 'ghosts' and of 'haunting', we have discussed how it makes sense to interpret much of Ian Curtis's lyrics and Joy Division's music as engaging ghosts and their haunting impacts, while considering what these specific ghosts and these specific hauntings might represent, might be used to represent–what 'whole social worlds' they might be usefully interpreted as working to help conjure. But we have also discussed many instances beyond direct connections with Ian Curtis and Joy Division of where it makes sense to recognize and identify 'ghosts' and 'hauntings' according to how Gordon has theorized what these mean. Students have proposed that all of us, in the internet age, leave behind numerous 'ghosts' of 'ourselves' that we often forget about and which can come back to 'haunt' us in equally numerous ways–in the form of everything from e-mails to text messages to posts, involving words and images, on social media sites to posts on blogsites. Students have further proposed that in the course of our lives we leave behind many 'ghosts' of our past lives, of whom we were as well as what we were like at past times and places, as well as in past relationships. We do so in relation to a potentially vast number of erstwhile influential dimensions of whom we were but whom we now are not, at least not directly, anymore. Memories too can function like 'ghosts' and these can 'haunt'. As can dreams and nightmares, daydreams and reveries, fantasies and other imaginings–and all of these can themselves be 'haunted' by 'ghosts' in turn. Students and I also have discussed how we can be haunted by ghosts of possible paths we did not pursue in our lives, or of paths which we turned back from pursuing 'all the way through'; these can include 'ghosts' of other kinds of people we might have become, doing other kinds of things in other kinds of places. And we have discussed, all the more directly relevant to Gordon's theorization, how we as individuals are haunted by 'ghosts' of social-historical violence–including violent suppression and subjugation as well as violent expropriation and dispossession. We have considered, even setting aside questions of violence, and of injustice that has not been attended to but needs for this be done, how particular places where we live, work, go to school, and otherwise lead our everyday lives might be 'haunted' by 'ghosts' of what once was happening at these places, especially if that was considerably different from what happens in the same locations now. But we have, again more directly connecting with what Gordon emphasizes, particularly concentrated on discussing to what extent we are haunted, including in disparate ways, by legacies of racism, colonialism, and genocide–as well as by all those who worked extremely hard, and continue to work extremely hard, to make possible the kinds of lives, the kinds of lifestyles, and the standards of living we are able to enjoy today yet often simply take for granted. We have discussed to what extent it makes sense to suggest we are haunted by ghosts of those who have died tragically–such as the vast numbers of those killed by gun violence in the US, all too omnipresent in the US, as illustrated by mass shootings, and mass killings, in Buffalo, New York and Uvalde, Texas recently, just days prior to me writing these words. And we have also discussed to what extent it makes sense to suggest we are haunted by ghosts of people we have known personally who have died tragically prematurely, such as by suicide.

As I myself reflect on *Ghostly Matters: Haunting and the Sociological Imagination*, the principal connection that comes readily to mind for me, in relation to what Gordon in this book theorizes, is with *The 1619 Project: a New Origin Story*, created by Nikole Hannah-Jones and *The New York Times Magazine*. This project provides a new point of origin for the history of United States: the arrival in Jamestown, Virginia in 1619 of the first enslaved Black Americans. *The 1619 Project* argues slavery and the systemic racism it spawned has been, ever since, fundamental in shaping this nation. *The 1619 Project* is, appropriately therefore, dedicated "To the more than thirty million descendants of American slavery" (vi).

In the preface to this book, titled "Origins," Hannah-Jones recalls as a young Black girl growing up she was fascinated with the past but troubled that "Black people . . . were largely absent from the histories I read" (xvii). When Black people did show up, "We were not actors but acted upon" as "The world revealed to me through my education was a white one" (xviii). Enrolled in a one-semester elective, "The African American Experience," during her sophomore year in high school, Hannah-Jones quickly recognized "that Black people had so much history that *could* be learned" (xix). The absence of that history from most teaching and learning of American history, and from most common perceptions and understandings of the same, has long operated as a 'ghost' that 'haunts' those able to perceive something important is missing and that this absence is deeply wrong. Widespread ignorance of what happened in Jamestown, Virginia in 1619, and its subsequent historical significance, leads to a yet greater 'haunting' absence, as "School curricula generally treat slavery as an aberration in a free society" (xx). As a result, "in 2017 just 8 percent of U.S. high school seniors named slavery as the central cause of the Civil War, and less than one-third knew that it had taken a constitutional amendment to abolish it," while the "The majority of high school students can't tell you that the famous abolitionist Frederick Douglass had once been enslaved; nor can they define the Middle Passage, which led to the forced migration of nearly 13 million people across the Atlantic and transformed–or, arguably, enabled–the existence of the United States" (xx). Similar surveys reveal most (especially white) Americans are equally ignorant of the contribution of slave labor to the American economy as well to the design of the American polity, and they are just as ignorant of the long history of systemic "anti-Blackness" that has continued well after slavery's end. Nevertheless, as a hopeful sign, a 2019 *Washington Post* poll "found that despite their meager knowledge of slavery, two-thirds of Americans believe that the legacy of slavery still affects our society today. They can see and feel the truth of this fact–they just haven't learned a history that helps them understand how and why" (xxi). In Avery Gordon's terms, these Americans are vaguely aware of a 'haunting' but unprepared–unequipped–to welcome 'the ghosts', to attend to what these 'ghosts' want and need, and thereby are unable to work to 'dispatch' them.

Black Americans have long struggled to accept "the typical origin story of the United States" that has long dominated in the teaching and learning of American history, as well as in popular understandings of the same, because "Black Americans understand we have been taught the history of a country that does not exist" (xxv). Black Americans are more likely than white Americans, therefore, to recognize the United States has never lived up to its 'mythological' ideals. After all, "How do you romanticize a revolution made possible by the forced labor of your ancestors, one that built white freedom on a Black slavery that would persist for another century after Jefferson wrote 'We hold these truths to be self-evident, that all men are created equal?'" (xxxi). The result of the haunting legacy of slavery and the omnipresence of its ghosts that have not been adequately engaged is "white Americans desire to be free of a past they do not want to remember, while Black Americans remain bound to a past they can never forget" (xxxi).

As Hannah-Jones underscores, "Eight in ten Black people would not be in the United States were it not for the institution of slavery in a society founded on ideals of freedom" (xxxi). Because Black Americans are more apt to recognize a gap, even a chasm, between the nation the US claims to be versus the nation it is, Black Americans can remind white Americans shocked by the attempted coup at the U.S. Capitol on January 6, 2021, "that violent efforts to subvert U.S. democracy were not novel nor unprecedented and that true democracy has been attempted in this country only since 1965, when after a bloody and decades-long Black freedom struggle, Congress passed the Voting Rights Act" (xxxii). *The 1619 Project* and allied efforts can help more white Americans understand substantial shortcomings in 'American democracy', but these people need to work past often tremendous fear about what will follow from facing up to the truth. Yet doing so is urgently needed: "We are the most unequal of the Western democracies" and we need to face the truth of how we got to be so in order "that we can truly become the country we already claim to be" (xxxii). In other words, "If we are a truly great nation, the truth cannot destroy us" (xxxii).

In chapter one, "Democracy," Hannah-Jones recounts it took her a long while to understand why her father, who had experienced persistent and virulent anti-Black racism throughout his life, remained proud of the American flag, which he always flew outside their house. Eventually she realized "My father knew exactly what he was doing when he raised that flag. He knew that our people's contributions to building the richest and most powerful nation in the world were indelible, that the United States simply would not exist without us" (9). Enslaved Africans and their descendants "transformed the North American colonies into some of the most successful in the British Empire" through "backbreaking labor" and by doing the bulk of the work necessary to produce the principal sources of wealth that secured the profits invested to enable the US to grow and expand to become the nation it is today, a nation within which enormous wealth is concentrated (9). Black Americans, what's more, have contributed invaluably not only "to the material wealth created by our bondage," but also have "been, and continue to be, foundational to the idea of American freedom," serving as "the perfectors of this democracy" (9). Black Americans' struggles are and have been central in striving to bring the United States closer to matching its ideals: "despite being violently denied the freedom and justice promised to all, Black Americans fervently believed in the American creed" and "Through centuries of Black resistance and protest, we have helped the country live up to its founding ideals. And not only for ourselves–Black rights struggles paved the way for every other rights struggle, including women's and gay rights, immigrant and disability rights" (11). Black Americans, what's more, have fought in every war since the American revolution and "today we are the most likely of all racial groups to serve in the United States military" (11). In Gordon's terms, Black Americans have always been at the forefront in confronting and engaging the ghosts that represent the tangible signs of the haunting gap that has long persisted between the kind of nation the US ideally claims itself to be versus the kind of nation it actually is. As a result, Hannah-Jones proposes, Black Americans "are this nation's true founding fathers" and "no people has a greater claim to that flag than we do" (11).

The need to justify slavery, Hannah-Jones explains, resides at the root of racist ideas and ideologies and of "a further consolidation of whiteness across class, religious, and ethnic lines," involving "a hardening of the racial caste system" as "Blackness came to define whiteness" (21). The belief, infamously enshrined into law with the 1857 US Supreme Court 'Dred Scot decision', "that Black people were not merely enslaved but a slave race, is the root of the endemic racism we cannot purge from this nation to this day" (22). The devastating impact of the fabrication of racism on the foundations of slavery has led subsequently, even after slavery formally ended, to "The systemic white suppression of Black life" (30). This systemic suppression "proved so severe" in the "period between the 1880s and the early twentieth century" that this same period "became known as the second slavery or the Great Nadir" (30). With the advent of this 'Great Nadir', Black people were forced back "into quasi-slavery" (30). Aptly, Waters McIntosh, who had been enslaved in South Carolina, lamented 'it was the poor white man who was freed by the war, not the Negroes'" (quoted 30). Once the short twelve years of Reconstruction ended, "the radically egalitarian spirit of post-Civil War America evaporated under the desire for national reunification," meaning, in both North and South, that "Black Americans, simply by existing, served as a problematic reminder of this nation's failings. White America dealt with this inconvenience by constructing a savagely enforced system of racial apartheid that excluded Black people almost entirely from mainstream American life–a system so grotesque that Nazi Germany would later take inspiration from it for its own racist policies" (31).

Nevertheless, "Black Americans fought back," even if most often "alone, never getting a majority of white Americans to join and support their freedom struggles" (33). Still, "we never fought solely for ourselves. The bloody freedom struggles of the civil rights movement laid the foundation for every other modern rights struggle" (33). And it is worth noting well that "No one cherishes freedom more than those who have not had it," while "to this day, Black Americans, more than any other group, embrace the democratic ideals of the common good" (33). Black Americans manifest the highest rates of support of any commonly identified demographic group for "universal healthcare and a higher minimum wage" and the highest rate of opposition to government "programs that harm the most vulnerable" (33). Black Americans are also the "most strongly opposed to capital punishment" even as they "suffer the most from violent crime" and Black Americans are the "most likely to say that this nation should take in refugees who others claim will be a drain on American institutions" despite the fact that Black Americans' "unemployment rate is nearly twice that of white Americans" (33). In sum, "For generations, we have believed in this country with a faith it did not deserve. Black people have seen the worst of America, yet, somehow, we still believe in its best" (34). Hannah-Jones then closes this chapter by raising the entirely apt question, in light of Black Americans maintaining this persistent faith despite it being unearned: "What if America understood, finally, now, at the dawn of its fifth century, that we have never been the problem, but the solution?" (36).

In chapter two, "Race," Dorothy Roberts traces the invention of race in America, as well as how 'race' has been conceived and defined to construct an oppressive hierarchy that racist practices in turn have materialized, cementing in place. This oppressive construct has harmed Black Americans in numerous directions. Just to cite a few: "in addition to monumental losses inflicted by enslavement, Black families had been severely disadvantaged by racist housing policies, employment discrimination, inferior schools, exclusionary banking practices, and unjust law enforcement. They were also deliberately prevented from benefiting from the radical government-assistance programs of the New Deal that promoted the well-being of white families" (56). All the while, "many white sociologists blamed unwed Black mothers for creating a dysfunctional family structure by displacing Black men as the heads of households and transmitting a depraved lifestyle to their children" (56). Similar historically prominent forms of 'blaming the victim' include the mythical 'Black welfare queen' living in luxury on the riches welfare payments provided her, the further mythical notion of Black women addicted to crack cocaine giving birth to 'crack babies' biologically destined to become social deviants, and the common tendency, referred to as 'adultification', according to which Black girls are treated as much closer to adults and as bearing much heavier burdens of responsibility and accountability than white girls of the same age (56-57). In connection with Gordon, we recognize all too often Black Americans have been denied recognition of 'complex personhood'. We also recognize all too many Black Americans have been excluded from equal opportunities and have suffered the consequences of this exclusion, but are then blamed as personally responsible for not succeeding 'in a game they were not allowed to play'; these Black Americans end up, at best, 'ghostly reminders' of lives reduced, diminished, prevented, and destroyed–as well as of all these Black Americans were not able to create and contribute as a result.

In chapter three, "Sugar, " Khalil Gibran Muhammad documents how enslaved Black women and men did work foundational to enabling the United States to become an economically wealthy nation, beginning, before cotton, on Southern sugar plantations. As Muhammad indicates, during the antebellum period of US history, "The value of enslaved people alone represented tens of millions of dollars in capital that financed investments, loans, and businesses" Indeed, "None" of the latter "growth was possible without trafficking in human lives," while enslaved Blacks working in jobs throughout the sugar industry, from fields to processing plants, "were some of the most skilled laborers, doing some of the most dangerous agricultural and industrial work in the United States" (82-83). In a terrible irony, "Though Black labor no longer plays a big role in producing sugar, sugar still plays a big role in the lives of Black people. Among all Americans, added sugar has been linked to growing rates of certain chronic illnesses, including those from which Black people suffer the most. African Americans are more likely to eat poorer-quality, processed foods with high amounts of added sugars" (86). This disparity is due to the relatively greater poverty Black Americans experience as well as, in particular, to the widespread segregation of Black people in relatively deprived Black communities across the US, whereby "even low-income white neighborhoods" are "twice as likely to have a food store as Black ones" (86). As Kansas State University researchers discovered, in a 2015 study "of healthful food availability" (86), "Food deserts and food insecurity . . . are perhaps the most important deleterious consequences of residential segregation in the United States" (quoted 86).

Leslie Alexander and Michelle Alexander, in chapter four, "Fear," take up "The deep-seated, gnawing terror that Black people might, one day, rise up and demand for themselves the same freedoms and inalienable rights that led white colonists to declare the American Revolution" and how this terror "has shaped our nation's politics, culture, and systems of justice ever since" (109). As Alexander and Alexander explain, "Modern-day policing, surveillance, and mass criminalization, as well as white vigilante violence and 'know-your-place aggression', have histories rooted in white fear–not merely of Black crime or Black people but of Black liberation. Nothing has proven more threatening to our democracy, or more devastating to Black communities, than white fear of Black freedom dreams" (102). Once more, in Gordon's terms, the US is haunted by the ghosts of all those Black people killed and all those Black communities destroyed as a result of this white fear that has been persistent throughout the five centuries of American history *The 1619 Project* takes into account–yet all too many white people adamantly refuse to recognize and attend to this haunting. Alexander and Alexander recount numerous 'incidents' of horrific violence Black Americans and Black American communities have suffered, including all too many that are by no means as notorious as they deserve to be, and in fact are often forgotten or unknown by many if not most (especially white) Americans.

Black Americans have regularly fought back in response to the violence directed at them and their communities. Alexander and Alexander cite Elizabeth Hinton's *America on Fire: The Untold History of Police Violence and Black Rebellion Since the 1960s* (2021) in which Hinton recounts "Roughly two thousand uprisings occurred between May 1968 and December 1972, nearly all of which were sparked by routine police violence" (117). The protests in the summer of 2020, sparked by George Floyd's police murder, were, therefore, nothing new. And as Hinton emphasizes, like many have needed to do in relation to the protests of summer 2020, "This was not a surge of purposeless criminality, as many white observers claimed; it was a sustained revolt" (118). All too often white people's revolt in America "has been understood as thoroughly political in nature," but all too often this kind of understanding has been denied Black people's revolt, even as Black people maintained ample reason, ample justification, to revolt. At the time of the uprisings Hinton focuses upon, despite himself forming the Kerner Commission to investigate causes of 'Black revolt', President Lyndon Johnson chose to ignore the Commission's conclusion "that severe segregation, poverty, joblessness, lack of access to housing, lack of access to economic opportunities, and discrimination in the job market, combined with police violence and harassment, had created a tinderbox of rage and despair that would certainly result in more uprisings if drastic action were not taken" and "that white people were in denial about the true causes of Black uprisings, but Black people were not" (118). In doing so Johnson anticipated what has become a predominant pattern ever since that principally involves using "law enforcement . . . to achieve law and order," while neglecting the root causes of lawlessness and disorder in Black communities (119). Political leaders have subsequently

> declared wars on drugs and crime, invested billions of dollars in highly militarized police forces, and embarked on a race to incarcerate in Black communities, while slashing funding from education, drug treatment, public housing, and welfare. The result has been disastrous. The United States now has the highest rate of incarceration in the world–the number of people behind bars has quintupled in the past four decades–while the Black-white economic divide is as wide as it was in 1968. (120)

Black families and communities are 'haunted' by the ghostly absences of many erstwhile members of these families and communities sentenced to prison, often for extraordinarily long sentences in response to petty drug crimes, as well as by the ghostly absences of those members of these same families and communities killed by police. But, as Gordon points out, so are we all, even if in different ways, and even if we differ radically in how willing and prepared we are to face up to this, as Alexander's and Alexander's chapter stresses one key way haunting does impact many white people and many white communities: fear of Black people, including especially of Black people rising up in revolt is often extreme. As Alexander and Alexander point out, "anxiety over shifting racial demographics due to immigration" coupled with the election of Barack Obama as the first Black president fueled an unsurprising "rise in white nationalism, hate crimes and vigilante violence, as well as the election of politicians like Donald Trump," with increasing numbers of fearful whites worried about becoming "a racial minority by the mid-twenty-first century" (121). This fear has become a prominent focus of mainstream attention, at least for a short while, after an 18-year old white man deliberately targeted for murder the ten Black people he killed at Tops Friendly Markets on 14 May 2022 in Buffalo, New York. This killer subscribes to 'replacement theory', increasingly widely championed across multiple prominent sectors of the white Right in the US, according to which a nefarious conspiratorial effort is and has been underway to 'replace' white people with Black and brown people in the US; in turn white people thereby must fight back to save 'the white race' and 'white civilization' 'before it is too late'. Beyond that level of extremism, white fear shows up as well among all those white Americans suspicious about, along with resentful concerning, any and all efforts to tackle income and wealth inequality, especially along racial lines, as well as to reformulate what public safety involves, particularly in Black and Brown communities where police have alienated the vast majority of the members of these communities.

Apropos issues of income and wealth disparity, Matthew Desmond's chapter six, "Capitalism," explains how slavery and its legacy in the form of persistently systemic racism accounts for the fact that the United States "stands today as one of the most unequal societies in the history of the world" (166). As Desmond explains, borrowing from Joel Rogers, what the US has pursued is a "peculiarly brutal version of 'low-road capitalism'" (160) traceable to how "slavery shaped our political institutions and founding documents, our laws governing private property and financial regulation, our management techniques and accounting systems, and our economic systems and labor unions" (161). As Demond notes, by the advent of the Civil War, more millionaires per capita resided in the Mississippi Valley than anywhere else in the US while cotton was "the nation's most valuable export"–cotton "grown and picked by enslaved workers" (161). At that same time, denser concentrations of capital were located in New Orleans than New York City. As these and other examples Desmond cite document, in the words of historians Sven Beckert and Seth Rockman, "American slavery is necessarily imprinted on the DNA of American capitalism" (quoted 187). In other words, American capitalism took shape and form on the basis of what slavery made possible, as slavery enabled the profit and accumulation that made possible the successful growth of capitalism in America.

The 'three-fifths compromise' in the US Constitution, according to which each enslaved Black person counted as three-fifths of a citizen for purposes of determining the relative size of states' representation in Congress (and the electoral votes states thereby receive in presidential elections) enabled Southern states to continue to distinguish enslaved Black Americans from human beings, in relation to rights citizens enjoyed, while at the same time counting these enslaved Black Americans as each three-fifth's of a human being in terms of the relative political weight they contributed to the state wherein they were enslaved. This 'compromise' provided Southern states with considerable relative power in the early history of the United States, and in fact virtually ever since, as even today "the fifteen states where slavery remained legal as of 1861 still hold the power to block a constitutional amendment supported by the other thirty-five" (169). As Desmond adds, what's more, "if Washington often feels broken, that's because it was built that way," including the US maintaining the exceptional total, among all long-standing democratic nations, of "four veto points" that are "empowered to block legislative action: the president, both houses of Congress, and the supreme court" (169). This system of 'veto points', more commonly referred to as 'checks and balances', while often also including the relative autonomy of the states versus the federal government, was deliberately designed to protect slavery, yet also "hobbled Washington's ability to pass legislation on a host of other matters" (169), including taxation. For a long time those with the greatest economic and political power in the US preferred the "financially weak and bureaucratically weak federal government" that 'the founders' had deliberately created, in large part to satisfy Southern concerns about any prospective interference with slavery (170). "Progressive taxation remains among the best ways to limit economic inequality," including through "funding public services like schools and healthcare and incentivizing business to work for the common good" (170). Yet in the US doing so has long been exceedingly difficult to achieve and to sustain, with the result that economic inequality is virtually unlimited: "America's present-day tax system . . . is regressive and insipid in part because it was born out of political compromise steered by debates over slavery" (170). In the US large corporations can readily avoid paying "their fair share–or *any* share" (170).

But "Slavery shaped the Constitution in profound and lasting ways" (170) beyond those I have just indicated, as in the words of historian Robin Einhorn, "One consequence . . . may well be the exceptionally powerful devotion to individual property rights that made American business stronger, American labor weaker, and the American welfare state a comparative 'laggard'" (quoted 170-171). Indeed, as Desmond points out, "Article I, Section 8 granted Congress the power to summon the militia to 'suppress insurrections', understood to mean rebellions of the enslaved"; "Article I, Section 9 forbade Congress from ending the slave trade until 1808"; and "Article V, Section 2 prohibited free states from emancipating runaways: human property in the South would remain human property in the North" (171). As Desmond observes, "The framers helped create a doctrine of private property strong enough to justify and enforce human trafficking, so much so that abolitionists publicly burned copies of the Constitution" (171). In connection with Gordon's *Ghostly Matters*, relevant 'hauntings' here include not only those that manifest themselves in the form of 'ghosts' of the vast numbers of those who were trafficked, and who frequently 'disappeared' into even further anonymity than what they already maintained while alive and enslaved, following brutally short and painful lives, but also those that manifest themselves by way of 'ghostly reminders' of all the lives that have been stunted and stifled (white and Black) as a result of the exaltation of the pursuit, acquisition, and accumulation of massive wealth by a privileged few at the expense of a great many forced to struggle to live harsh and precarious lives. Directly related 'ghosts' that 'haunt' us today include 'ghosts' of all those never offered the fair, just, free, and equal opportunities that America so often prides itself offering all of its citizens–and indeed often as supposedly offering all who come to live and work here. These are the 'ghosts' of people who couldn't and didn't 'make it', who couldn't and didn't get by, other than in conditions of perpetual hardship and deprivation, and who represent enormous lost–indeed enormous squandered–human potential, that could well have contributed enormously to the benefit of our larger culture and greater society.

Desmond continues by detailing how the US Supreme Court often 'vigorously defended' human bondage, perhaps most notoriously in the 1857 *Dred Scott v. Sandford* case that ruled Scott's enslaver's property rights trumped Scott's right to freedom, even as Scott had been moved by his enslaver to live and work for extended periods of time in ostensibly 'free states'. Desmond also points out, drawing upon the work of historian Stephanie Jones-Rogers, that "elite white women were particularly invested in securing a jurisprudence that valued (white) property over (Black) freedom because their economic independence and influence depended on it. (Southern parents tended to give their daughters more enslaved hands than land)." As Desmond avers, in relation to these and a host of convergent property interests, "Slavery demanded a legal defense of ownership rights much more far-reaching and severe than would have been necessary to secure, say, a house or a herd of cattle," as, after all, "Houses do not attempt to become non-property by running away" and "Cattle do not stage armed revolts" but "humans treated as property were constantly doing both" (172). To this day, US Supreme Court decisions are strongly influenced by this long tradition of exalting private property rights, especially of the wealth elite, over virtually any and all other 'constitutional rights', such as in *Citizens United v. Federal Election Commission* (2010) which ruled "corporations' political speech . . . was protected by the Constitution" from government regulation (173).

From the earliest years of the fledgling United States of America, the profits generated by employment of slave labor, notably through cotton production, long proved by far the greatest source of wealth generated in, and indeed across, the country. Slavery "also helped mould modern management techniques" (177), including the development of workplace systems that were later generalized and copied in many capitalist industries designed to 'extract' "maximum effort out of each worker" and including by 'paying' "close attention to inputs and outputs" through "precise systems of record-keeping" (178). Slavery also provided the source of techniques for precisely calculating "depreciation" that were likewise copied and generalized far beyond enterprises reliant upon slave labor (178). "Detailed analysis also allowed planters to anticipate rebellion" as "Overseers recorded each enslaved worker's yield" attuned to exactly how much they were doing over what periods of time and with what implements in what ways so that any 'deviation' could be swiftly 'corrected' (179). What's more, "The uniform layout of the land has a logic" as did "complicated workplace hierarchies" so that collectively workers, organized in differential positions across carefully arrayed plantation fields, were positioned to realize the greatest 'output' from their efforts (179). Constant efforts to improve efficiency and productivity of enslaved labor led to results such that by "1862, the average enslaved fieldworker picked not 25 or 50 percent more but 40 percent more cotton than his or her counterpart did in 1801" (180). Indeed, "The cotton plantation was America's first big business, and the overseer was the nation's first corporate Big Brother" (180).

Yet "Slavery, and the racism it nourished, also played a decisive role in weakening the American labor movement" (181). This happened as "Capitalists leveraged slavery and its racial legacy to divide workers–free from unfree, white from Black–diluting their collective power" (181). Yet "Instead of resisting this strategy, white-led unions embraced it until it was too late, undercutting their movement and creating conditions for worker exploitation and inequality that exist to this day" (181). Slavery, moreover, "hastened the development of the factory, an institution that propelled the Industrial Revolution and changed the course of history," as factories initially emerged in response to the need to process and turn into finished goods what slave labor cultivated, most notably cotton (181). In the US, unfortunately, in contrast with most European countries, a politically organized and class conscious labor movement identifying with and supportive of socialism never developed, as slavery along with the racism used to justify slavery proved pivotal in preventing such a development: "White workers viewed Black workers, both free and unslaved, as a threat to their livelihood" (182). Capital has indeed long succeeded in employing race, and especially racism, in successfully dividing and conquering the working class in the US even as "Slavery pulled down all wages" and even as the same has been the case subsequently in relation to maintaining stratified employment opportunities and pay rates for Black versus white 'free workers' while labor unions long remained racially segregated. As Demond comments,

> Closing the door on Black people created a pool of available and desperate men and women who could be used to break strikes and quell unrest. Companies hired Black workers to put down labor militancy in a number of industries, replacing steelworkers, meatpackers, longshoremen, railroad hands, and garment workers. To Black workers, strikebreaking was a means to gain a foothold in an industrial economy and to secure opportunities long denied them. Black leaders even encouraged strikebreaking and began promoting Black workers as safe investments for industrialists. (183)

In the South, moreover, white yeoman operating small farms were gradually squeezed off these farms, even prior to the Civil War, as larger farmers seized steadily more of the potentially profitable land, yet these white yeoman then became overseers and higher ranked and higher remunerated employees on plantations and in factories where, even as they "lost their farms," they "retained their whiteness as consolation" (184). That pattern has been generalized in the form of what W.E.B. DuBois famously theorized as 'the psychological wage' that poor and working class white people are effectively granted solely 'for being white' or, in other words, solely 'for not being Black'. Further 'haunting' both Black and white Americans today are the many specific histories of times and places where Black and white people maintaining common economic and indeed common social and political interests did *not* recognize this to be the case and instead were divided against each other, with poor and working class white Americans perceiving Black and brown Americans as their principal enemies, threatening their livelihood and well-being, no matter how meager and precarious this might be, and threatening their relatively superior social and political standing as 'white people', as 'not Black or brown people'.

Slavery and its ongoing legacy is key in understanding other constitutional issues, including the Second Amendment that has frequently been interpreted to establish the right of all US citizens to stockpile guns and ammunition, including of military caliber that can be used to quickly kill large numbers of people. In chapter nine, "Self-Defense," Carol Anderson discusses how the right to 'self-defense' has been effectively rendered radically different for Black versus white people throughout US history, and by deliberate design. As Anderson indicates, Black people were long barred from legally bearing arms, despite the Second Amendment, including both free and enslaved Black people (251). Yet even more insidious, "Though it did not explicitly say so, the Second Amendment's 'well regulated militia' ["A well regulated Militia, being necessary to the security of a free State, the right of the people to keep and bear Arms, shall not be infringed"] was motivated in large part by a need for the new federal government to assure white people in the South that they would be able to defend themselves against Black people" (252). Fear of uprisings by enslaved Black people was widely shared among many white Americans, in the North as well as in the South, and for good reason, because enslaved Blacks did often resist and strive to free themselves, while the example of the Haitian Revolution, fought between 1791 and 1804, where Haitian slaves successfully freed themselves from direct French colonial rule, further scared many white Americans, especially white Americans in the South who 'owned' slaves, and who secured economic profit as well as social and political power on the basis of what slave labor made possible. State laws have carried forward this tradition by frequently affirming the right of American citizens to bear arms in 'self-defense' but all too often this right has been denied to Black people while Black people have been all too often been killed by white people who are all too ready to perceive Black people as threats. Anderson cites the well-known case of Trayvon Martin's murder by George Zimmerman while also citing the case just two years later where Jessie Murray's claiming the same 'Stand Your Ground' right to self-protection was denied because, as Anderson caustically comments, the judge contended "Murray clearly couldn't have been threatened by the white people who were beating him" (252). Martin did nothing to provoke Zimmerman other than walk through the neighborhood where Zimmerman lived, while in Murray's case a group of white men attacked him in a serious physical assault. Yet Zimmerman was acquitted and Murray convicted. The difference between these two cases "exposes the harsh reality than even in the modern era, the enforcement of self-defense laws varies widely according to race"

(252). Indeed, "Stand Your Ground laws are only the latest form of self-defense legislation to be applied unequally," as "Since the nation's founding, our legal and political architecture has privileged the safety and self-defense of white people over that of Black people" (253).

It is worth underscoring what legal scholar Carl T. Bogus has characterized as "The Hidden History of the Second Amendment" (quoted 257), especially as this amendment is continually the subject of sharply polarized debate in the US today, between those advocating the need for much stricter gun control versus those arguing for virtually none. It needs to be emphasized not only that the history of this amendment links 'the right to bear arms' with the need of states to be able to organize and maintain militias, where implicitly solely as members of these militias does this right apply, but also with the design and creation of this amendment as an instrument of slave control, and in particular as an instrument designed to suppress slave revolts. As Bogus explains, "As a Virginian, [James] Madison knew that the militia's prime function in his state, and throughout the South, was slave control. His use of the word 'security' (in the Second Amendment) is consistent with his writing the amendment for the specific purpose of assuring the Southern states, and particularly his constituents in Virginia, that the federal government would not undermine their security against slave insurrection by disarming the militia" (quoted 257).

Anderson emphasizes, as she discusses the sharply differential history of 'self-defense' for Black versus white people in the US, that "Systemic violence against Black people was not just a Southern phenomenon," and it was the long, relentless enactment of this kind of violence in Oakland, California that prompted the formation of the Black Panther Party for Self-Defense (BPP) in 1966. Although the BPP were, essentially, engaging in their ostensible constitutional right to 'self-defense', as US citizens, even as they not only dressed in "'uniforms' of leather jackets and berets" but also "openly carried rifles and .45s while monitoring police officers making arrests," the BPP doing so frightened and outraged many white people, including many powerful white people. As Anderson notes, "Many white people in America, in fact, saw the Panthers and the uprisings in Watts, Detroit and Newark [happening at the same time as the emergence of the BPP] not as protests against police violence but as indications of dangerous Black pathology" (265). California Governor Ronald Reagan "and other officials quickly realized their was a political gold mine in white fear," which they happily exploited as they popularized "election campaigns steeped in the rhetoric of 'law and order'" while they "successfully fueled 'soft on crime' charges against their opponents" (265). In this continuing climate of white fear, when Bernard Goetz shot four young Black men on a subway in New York City in December 1984, simply because he was afraid they *might* mug him, he was widely hailed as a "a 'hero' to many: the 'subway vigilante'" (265). The Goetz case and that of George Zimmerman both illustrate what the U.S. Civil Rights Commission reported in 2020: "that when a white person kills an African American, it is 282 percent more likely to be ruled a 'justifiable homicide' than a white-on-white killing" and as the Giffords Law Center and the Southern Poverty Law Center jointly comment on the totality of findings included in this report, "the consequences are predictably deadly and unequal" (quoted 266).

In the US we are all haunted, whether we are ready and willing to face up to this haunting, by gun violence, by how widespread and frequent is its devastating impact, and by the 'ghosts' of all those killed or severely injured. That means we are all haunted in turn by the way slavery shaped the

Second Amendment and by long-running white fear of Black people that has resulted in all too many Americans all too easily creating their own stockpiles of 'weapons of mass destruction'. According to Gun Violence Archive, 17,924 people have been killed in the US by guns in just the first five months of 2022, and 241 have been killed as a result of mass shootings and mass murders in the same period of time. As World Population Review reports, "The U.S. endures the most mass shootings in the world," while, that noted, "mass shootings actually comprise only a fraction of the overall gun deaths in the United States." And as the BBC reports, "There were 1.5 million of them between 1968 and 2017 [people killed by gun violence in the United States]–that's higher than the number of soldiers killed in every US conflict since the American War for Independence in 1775"–and the US greatly exceeds the per capita numbers of people killed by guns in all comparably 'wealthy' 'democratic' countries, in both the global North and the global South. In the US we all are 'haunted', again whether we are able and willing to face up to this haunting or not, by the ever persistent effective inability of those in government, especially at the federal level, to enact gun control laws comparable to those found in most other countries–i.e., by the power 'the gun lobby' maintains to override what repeated surveys reveal the vast majority of Americans support.

Not only, however, has the supposed constitutional right 'to self-defense' through owning and using guns to protect oneself radically disproportionally impacted Black versus white Americans, through the history of this country, but also the American legal system likewise has systematically abused the supposed "founding principles of justice and equality before the law" in massively disproportionately punishing Black people versus white people. And this disproportion has been notably increasing. As Bryan Stevenson writes, in chapter ten, "Punishment," over the course of the last now "more than three decades, our country has spent billions of dollars every year not only on constructing prisons and jails but also on policing and funding a carcereal system that has ensnared millions" (276). And, yes, "Disproportionately, those affected by the system are Black" in terms of frequency of arrest, charge, and conviction; in severity of sentence upon conviction; in the application of the death penalty; in how often and how harshly juveniles are punished; and in terms of how prisoners are treated while in prison as well as how ex-prisoners are treated upon parole or release. The same disproportion shows up especially horrifically in Black people being sentenced far more often than white people to serve terms in the most brutal of US prisons, such as Louisiana's Angola prison 'plantation'.

Stevenson traces the "endless list of harsh, extreme, and cruel sentences" enacted across the US today, for "minor and major crimes," and disproportionately punishing Black versus white people, to colonial laws passed in relation to the institution of slavery well before the American Revolution. These included laws that declared all Black people should endure 'hard labor' for life, and that refusal passively to accept this condition in turn justified horrific forms of punishment, including cutting off hands, severing heads, and drawing and quartering bodies. What's more, while "The Thirteenth Amendment" to the US Constitution "is credited with ending slavery," in fact "it stopped short of that," as "It made an exception for those convicted of crimes" (279). This amendment "could not abolish the true evil of American slavery, which was the belief that Black people are less evolved, less human, less capable, less deserving, less trustworthy than white people" and, throughout American history, "The existing racial hierarchy" has been "sustained by myths about Black criminality" (279). Black people in the US have long been treated, before the law, and by those acting as agents of law enforcement, as "presumptively criminal," with this presumption in turn 'cultivating' "a tolerance for employing any level of brutality to maintain the racial hierarchy" (280). The US continues haunted to this day by how poorly this nation has done in respecting Black people's 'complex personhood' equal to that of white people, and by how often as a matter of routine Black people have been treated as so suspicious and so sinister, so threatening and so dangerous, simply on account of the fact they are Black, that they must continually be subject to violent repression–or the ready prospect of violent repression.

Another crucial contribution to *The 1619 Project* comes in chapter eleven, "Inheritance," by Trymaine Lee. Black people have been barred from accessing means and avenues available to white people to provide an inheritance to their children. All too often, as Lee recounts, even modestly successful Black people have met with resentment and violent backlash from white people, including long after the end of legal slavery, with laws frequently allowing white people to appropriate, including through violent means, the material bases of Black people's success, whether this came in the form of land, or a small business, or yet another profitable source of earnings that might otherwise have provided the basis of an inheritance to pass on. "With violence largely sanctioned by state and local governments, Black families, especially in the South, faced poverty coupled with a life in limbo, where safety, stability, access to education, and mental health were always precarious," and that means "Today, Black Americans far removed from slavery and Jim Crow continue to be handed the economic misfortune of their forebearers," such that "as of 207, white households were twice as likely as Black households to receive an inheritance" (301). What's more, "when white people inherit money, it's typically three times the amount Black beneficiaries get" and "Those inheritances help drive the racial wealth gap" as "Receiving an inheritance boosts the median wealth of white families by $104,000 but for Black families it's just $4,000" (301).

In chapter 16, "Traffic," Kevin M. Kruse draws attention to long-standing practices that have worked hand in hand with those Trymaine Lee discusses, to disadvantage Black Americans versus white Americans. Traffic in major American cities such as Atlanta is as 'mired in gridlock' as it is because of how these cities have been divided into racially segregated sections with major traffic projects in turn designed to both maintain and to increase this segregation. As Kruse describes, systematic efforts at achieving and maintaining strict residential racial segregation have a long history in the US. Not only this, but these efforts dovetailed with efforts to achieve and maintain substantial relative deprivation for Black versus white residential neighborhoods. Notably, "During the New Deal, federal agencies like the Home Owners' Loan Corporation and the Federal Housing Administration encouraged redlining that explicitly marked minority neighborhoods as risky investments and, therefore, discouraged bank loans, mortgages, and insurance there," while "other policies simply targeted Black communities for isolation and demolition" (407). In relation to the last, "The postwar programs for urban renewal, for instance, destroyed Black neighborhoods and displaced their residents with such regularity that African Americans came to believe, in James Baldwin's memorable line, that 'urban renewal' meant 'Negro removal'" (407, quoted 407). As the interstate highway system was built, what's more, these highways were "steered along routes that invariably ran right through the neighborhoods of racial minorities" (407). "Planners often argued that they targeted the most 'blighted' regions for bulldozing," yet, due to the long history in this country of where Blacks versus whites were able to live, "the poor residents there," in these supposed 'blighted' areas, as Kruse facetiously remarks, "simply happened to be African American" (407). This practice of targeting Black and other 'minority neighborhoods' as the sites through which the new highways would run happened all over the country, as Kruse documents, North and South, and East and West, while these highways have come to serve as dividing lines between predominantly white versus predominantly Black communities or communities where the population is predominantly comprised of Latinx or Black and Latinx people.

Disparity and abuse continues when we come to the focus of chapter twelve, by Linda Villarosa, "Medicine." Villarosa traces the explanation for why Black people have been 1.4 times more likely to contract COVID-19, 3.2 times more likely to be hospitalized, and 2.8 times more likely to die, in comparison with white people, due to "the many ways America's history of racial violence and inequality is baked into the institutions and structures of society," including medicine and health care provision (317). Even aside from the latter, "Black Americans are far more likely to work in low-wage jobs and to live in segregated, crowded, polluted neighborhoods that lack adequate healthcare facilities and transportation; they are far less likely to live near safe outdoor spaces and have access to healthful and affordable food" (317). In particular, poor Black Americans' relative ill health versus white Americans in terms of respiratory disease is tied to long-standing disproportionate exposure to air pollution (317). But Black Americans of all classes share "the stress of coping with racism, embedded into day-to-day life, which can lead to a kind of premature aging" (317)–what University of Michigan School of Public Health Professor Arline T. Geronimus has identified as "weathering" (quoted 317). Within medical and related forms of health care provision, as Villarosa recounts, repeated studies have documented persistent differential treatment of Black versus white patients, as well as how doctors and other health care providers "are often unaware of their own complicity in perpetrating the internalized racism and the conscious and unconscious biases that drive them to go against their oath to do no harm" (322). As Villarosa sums up, "In reality, it's never been race that predicts the disease and disability that disproportionately afflict Black Americans, but racism" (323).

At the same time, as Jeneen Interlandi discusses in chapter fifteen, "Healthcare," major advances in healthcare in the US, in the form of Medicare, Medicaid, and the Affordable Care Act, have all resulted from the efforts of Black people leading the way, over extended periods, to keep pushing to address urgent needs–of both Black people and of everyone else. For example, the 1964 Civil Rights Act prepared the way for federal funding to help cover expenses in every hospital in the country, for the first time ever, which in fact soon showed up via Medicare and Medicaid: "As has happened so often in our history, Black struggles for equality resulted in greater rights for all Americans" (394).

Five centuries of substantially unequal and often brutally violent mistreatment, along with systematic relative disadvantage in being able to access and exercise vital resources, powers, and capacities has shaped the distinctive nature of Black forms of cultural production that in fact a great many white people tremendously admire without being attuned to that shaping impact–such as music, the focus of chapter fourteen, by Wesley Morris. The 'freedom' that shows up in Black musical forms, as well as in Black modes of performing this music, is reflective of and responsive to how this kind of freedom has long represented the only way in which Black people have been able to experience freedom in America, and is indeed directly traceable to how this was the case under slavery. As Morris characterizes Black music, and Black musical forms, this is "the music of a people who have survived," and, more than that, of a people "who not only won't stop but also can't *be* stopped" (379). This refusal to be 'stopped' is reminiscent of Gordon's valorization of the utopian, of persistent utopian yearning, imagining, and aspiring–of the utopian as a prospective material force of transformation. Reference to the utopian in this connection suggests it is yet possible adequately to come to grips with the haunting legacy of slavery in the US, to how it has shaped every social institution and every sphere of culture, as well as the fundamental nature of the American economy and the American polity. It is yet possible to do so by responding to what all the ghosts that represent this legacy demand of us in order to do so–by atoning for systemic racism and all the damages this has done to Black people in America for now over 500 years.

In chapter seventeen, "Progress," Ibram X. Kendi critiques an especially insidious ideological support for the persistence of racial inequity and for the persistent pervasion of racial violence in the US. This is the commonly shared belief that the US is always moving steadily forward in progressively overcoming all of the problems of its past–and that these are now largely if not entirely 'past matters'. As Kendi puts it, "when seen as the defining narrative of American history, this vision of our past as a march of racial progress is ahistorical, mythical, and incomplete":

> Even as those civil rights victories of the 1950s and '60s were transpiring in the courts and the streets, the unemployment rates of Black Americans were rising. These persistently poor socio-economic conditions–not to mention police violence–led to urban rebellions in 1964, 1965, 1966, and 1967–a year when Martin Luther King, Jr., said "That dream that I had that day [in 1963] has, at many points, turned into a nightmare." (424, quoted 424)

The situation has only worsened, Kendi explains, in the post-civil rights era, as "American society . . . became obsessed with fear of Black criminality," leading to the War on Drugs, mass incarceration, persistent police violence, renewed voter suppression, and "the widest racial wealth gap between Black and white Americans since the government began recording such data" (424).

"When the long sweep of American history is cast as a constant widening of equity and justice," which is indeed how many standard, traditional historical accounts have cast this, the problem is "it overlooks this parallel constant widening of inequity and injustice," which Kendi uses many concrete examples from the post-civil rights era to illustrate (424). In fact, "The singular racial history of the United States is . . . a *dual* racial history of two opposing forces: historical steps toward equity and justice and historical steps toward inequity and injustice" (425). In addition, "This popular construct of racial progress does more than conceal and obfuscate; it actually undermines the effort to achieve and maintain equality" (425). Kendi cites as one notable illustrative example the 2013 decision of the US Supreme Court to strike down "the federal preclearance section of the Voting Rights Act of 1965, which required certain states and counties with a history of electoral racism to receive federal approval before changing local voting laws or practices," with the majority of the court ruling that 'racial progress' since 1965 meant this was no longer necessary (425). Immediately afterward voter suppression efforts, principally targeting Black voters, ramped up in many Republican-dominated states, and, as Kendi contends, these "were crucial to Trump's victory" in the 2016 presidential election (425).

"Inequality lives, in part," Kendi argues, "because Americans of every generation have been misled into believing that racial progress is inevitable and ongoing," and even "That racial progress is America's manifest destiny" (425). Yet, "In fact, this has more often been rhetoric than reality, more often myth than history" (425). Kendi draws the following compelling distinction: "Saying that the nation can progress racially is a necessary statement of hope. Saying that the nation *has* progressed racially is usually a statement of ideology, one that has been used all too often to obscure the opposite reality of *racist* progress." Throughout his chapter Kendi documents a depressingly persistent reiteration of this same mythological notion, over and over again, with each generation of Americans, and in particular each generation of white Americans, nevertheless identifying with the same ideological mystification. In relation to popular accounts of the Black civil rights movement of the 1950s and 1960s that indulge in congratulating the US for its ostensibly great progress in overcoming racism, "what is left out of this story is that this Second Reconstruction was needed because the First Reconstruction, after the Civil War ended in 1865, failed to bring into being and sustain an equitable nation" while 'What is left out of the story of our time is that a Third Reconstruction is needed because the Second Reconstruction failed to actualize King's dream" (436).

The 1619 Project concludes with chapter eighteen, "Justice," in which Nikole Hannah-Jones argues for reparations. Hannah-Jones begins her case for reparations by proposing the familiar "origin story of the United States we tell ourselves," as *The 1619 Project* has demonstrated, represents a "mythology" that "has positioned almost exclusively white Americans as the architects and champions of democracy" and as a result has led to the belief "that white people should disproportionately reap the benefits of this democracy" (452). This familiar origin story "portrays an intrepid, freedom-loving people who rebelled against an oppressive monarchy, won their independence, tamed the West, advanced an exceptional nation based on the radical ideals of self-governance and equality, and heroically fought a civil war to end slavery and preserve the nation" (452). In contrast, "as this book has shown, a truer origin story requires us to place Black Americans prominently in the role of democracy's defender and perfecters" (452). As *The 1619 Project* makes clear, "It is Black Americans who have struggled and fought, when many white Americans were willing to abandon the charge that 'all men are created equal', to make those words real" (452). It is Black Americans "who have consistently made the case, even when they were utterly disenfranchised and forced out of a country founded on a government of the people, by the people, and for the people" (452). "The efforts of Black Americans to seek freedom through resistance and rebellion against violations of their rights have always been one of this nation's defining traditions," even if this has not been a dominant perception or interpretation. Nevertheless, even "Though we are seldom taught this fact, time and time throughout our history, the most ardent, courageous, and consistent freedom fighters *within* this country have been Black Americans" (453).

What is needed, moreover, is a reckoning not only with the true origin story and true history of the United States, one that places Black Americans as well as Black Americans' struggles and Black Americans' contributions front and center, but also a reckoning with the continuing, long-running inequity that persists in the relative positions of Black versus white Americans. As Hannah-Jones summarizes, "the stark reality we must confront" is that "even . . . wide-ranging policing and voting reforms, on their own . . . cannot bring justice to America" (456). Even as "Resolving the police issue would save precious Black lives and help preserve the dignity Black Americans still must fight for," and even as this "would make Black Americans safer and dismantle a tool of social control with a lineage that stretches back to slavery," nevertheless "it would leave wholly intact the primary culprit of Black suffering today" (456). Hannah-Jones exhorts "We must get to the root of it," and this root is "the lack of wealth that has been a defining feature of Black life since the end of slavery" (456). White Americans, on average, maintain considerably greater wealth that can be transferred from generation to generation in the form of inheritance than do Black Americans. Even though many if not most white Americans do not recognize the existence or the size of this wealth gap, its effects are real and substantial, and it is "white Americans' centuries-long economic head start that most effectively maintains racial caste today" (457). As Hannah-Jones explains, "In a country where Blsck people have been kept disproportionately poor and prevented from building wealth, rules and policies involving money can be nearly as effective for maintaining the color line as legal segregation and disenfranchisement" (457). All of this accumulated swath of rules and policies "has worked with impressive efficiency" as "Today Black Americans remain the most segregated group of people in America and are five times as likely as white Americans to live in high-poverty neighborhoods" (457). Even "Black Americans with high incomes are still Black: they face discrimination across American life today" (457). And yet as often as relatively economically better off Black Americans continue to live, on average, in substantially poorer neighborhoods than white Americans with the same incomes, what is key, in this context, is focusing on that fact that for a great many Black Americans, past and present, "it is because their families have not been able to build wealth that they have not been able to buy in more affluent neighborhoods, while white Americans with lower incomes often use familial wealth to do so" (457). Hannah-Jones characterizes the average difference in wealth between Black and white Americans as "nothing other than a chasm," citing research by scholars from Duke University and Northwestern University published in 2020 that shows "the average Black family with children holds just one cent of wealth for every dollar held by the average white family" (458).

What's more, it is all too often all too conveniently 'forgotten' "that the racism we are fighting today was originally conjured to justify working unfree Black people, often until death, to generate extravagant riches for European colonial powers, the white planter class, and all the ancillary white people, from Midwestern farmers to bankers to sailors to textile workers, who earned their living and built their wealth from that free Black labor and the products that labor produced" (458). As such, to this day, "The prosperity of this country is inextricably linked with the forced labor of the ancestors of more than 30 million Black Americans, just as it is linked to the stolen land of the country's Indigenous people" (458). Most of all, "slavery and the hundred-year period of racial apartheid and racial terrorism known as Jim Crow were, above all else, systems of economic exploitation" and, borrowing from Ta-Nehisi Coates, "racism is the child of economic profiteering, not the father" (458). Racism, in ideological form, in other words, has been repeatedly and consistently used to justify this exploitation, and this profiteering, as well as the chasm that it leaves between the relative economic positions, on average, of Black versus white Americans.

As Hannah-Jones proceeds, she traces a long history of many Black people persistently advocating, and fighting, for reparations, in particular but not exclusively on account of slavery, yet most often to little avail. It is on the basis of the legacy left by these efforts that Hannah-Jones makes her case for the same, once more, today, challenging "The inclination to bandage over and move on" that represents "a definitive feature when it comes to anti-Black racism and its social and material effects" (468). As Hannah-Jones observes, "many white Americans love to play up moments of racial progress like the Emancipation Proclamation, *Brown v. Board of Education*, and the election of Barack Obama, while playing down or ignoring lynching, racial apartheid, and the 1985 government bombing of a Black neighborhood in Philadelphia" (468). Many white Americans are especially fond of citing Martin Luther King Jr.'s "I Have a Dream Speech" and in particular King's line from that speech "about being judged by the content of your character and not the color of your skin"–so much so, in fact, Hannah-Jones contends, that this has come to be "used as a cudgel against calls for race-specific remedies for Black Americans" (468). But as Hannah-Jones points out, doing so requires "ignoring the part of that same speech where King says Black people have marched on the capital to cash 'a check which has come back marked "insufficient funds"'" (468, quoted 468-469). Veneration of King since his assassination has been accompanied by "an astounding silence around his most radical demands," and in particular King's insistence "that the true battle for equality, the actualization of justice, required economic repair" (469).

Hannah-Jones cites a speech King gave in 1967 to the Hungry Club Forum in Atlanta where he argued that the struggle "now" was no longer about ending legal segregation, but rather "a struggle for genuine economic equality, on all levels, and this will be a much more difficult struggle" because while "it didn't cost the nation anything to integrate lunch counters," "It didn't cost the nation anything to integrate hotels and motels," and "It didn't cost the nation a penny to guarantee the right to vote," "Now we are in a period where it will cost the nation billions of dollars to get rid of poverty, to get rid of slums, to make quality integrated education a reality" (quoted 469). King both witnessed the beginnings and predicted the considerable growth of "white backlash" (quoted 469), among even erstwhile 'white friends' of the Civil Rights movement, in response to the demand for economic equality of Black and white Americans. King reiterated these same arguments often in his last years, including in Memphis less than a month before he was killed: "Now our struggle is for genuine equality, which means economic equality" (quoted 469). But today, Hannah-Jones indicates, over 50 years later, "the racial wealth gap is in relative terms about the same as it was in the 1950s" as "The typical Black household today is poorer than 80 percent of white households" (470). In a 2020 study by economists Moritz Kuhn, Moritz Schularick, and Ulrike Steins, published in the *Journal of Political Economy*, the authors find "No progress has been made over the past 70 years in reducing income and wealth inequalities between Black and white households" (quoted 470). Even so, "most Americans remain in an almost pathological state of deial about the depth of Black financial struggle" (470). For example, a 2019 Yale University Study "found that most Americans believe that Black households hold $90 in wealth for every $100 held by white households" while "the actual amount is $10" and "About 97 percent of the study participants overestimated Black-white wealth equality," as "most assumed that highly educated, high-income Black households were the most likely to achieve economic parity with white households," even though this is "wrong" because "The magnitude of the wealth gap only widens as Black people earn more income" (470). What's more, "college simply does not pay off for Black Americans the way it does for other groups":

Black college graduates are about as likely to be unemployed as white Americans with a high school diploma, and Black Americans with a college education hold less wealth than white Americans who have not even completed high school. Further, because Black families hold

954

almost no wealth to begin with, Black students are the most likely to borrow money to pay for college and then to borrow more money in total. That debt, in turn, means that Black students cannot start saving immediately upon graduation, the way their less-debt-burdened peers can. (471)

In sum, "Wealth begets wealth, and white Americans have had centuries of government assistance to accumulate wealth, while the government has for the vast history of this country worked against Black Americans' efforts to do the same" (472). "At the center" of what must be done in response are "reparations" (472). As Hannah-Jones makes clear, to begin, in rejecting common objections to reparations, "Reparations are not about punishing white Americans, and white Americans are not the ones who would pay for them," while "It does not matter if your ancestors engaged in slavery or if you just immigrated here two weeks ago," because "Reparations amount to a societal obligation in a nation where our Constitution sanctioned slavery, Congress passed laws to protect it, and our federal government initiated, condoned, and practiced legal racial segregation against Black Americans until half a century ago," so "it is the federal government that must pay" (472). As Hannah-Jones explains, yet further, "Nor is it impossible to figure out who is eligible. Reparations should go to any person who has documentation that he or she identified as a Black person for at least ten years before the beginning of any reparations process and can trace at least one ancestor back to American slavery" (472). Reparations will come in the form of "individual cash payments to descendants of the enslaved in order to close the wealth gap" (473).

And yet, "The technical details, frankly, are the easier part," as "The real obstacle, the obstacle we have never overcome is garnering the political will" (473). But it can be done. The US each year pays "$5 million . . . to help Holocaust survivors living in America," and "This country has also paid reparations to Japanese American victims of internment during World War II and to some Native American nations" (473). Still, "Congress has refused for three decades to pass H.R. 40, a bill introduced shortly after Congress approved reparations for Japanese Americans, which seeks to simply study the issue of reparations for descendants of American slavery" (473).

As Hannah-Jones moves to finish the final chapter of *The 1619 Project,* she turns to W.E.B. DuBois, quoting from his 1903 book *The Souls of Black Folk* in which DuBois argues that Black people are, as Hannah-Jones summarizes, "not this nation's problem, but it's heart" (474). Apropos of dating 'the new origin story' of the US as 'the *1619* Project'', Du Bois challenges white readers: "Your country? How came it yours? Before the Pilgrims landed we were here. Here we have bought our gifts and mingled them with yours . . . . Actively we have woven ourselves with the very warp and woof of this nation . . . Our song, our toil, our cheer, snd warning have been given to this nation in blood-brotherhood. Are not these gifts worth the giving? Is not this work and striving? Would American have been America without her Negro people?" (quoted 474). As Hannah-Jones echoes DuBois: "This is our national truth: America would not be America without the wealth from Black labor, without Black striving, Black ingenuity, Black resistance" (475). So much that is and has long been distinctive about American culture has been created and provided by Black Americans, and represents "Black Americans' legacy to this nation" (475).

In return, "*The legacy of this nation to Black Americans* [my italics] has consisted of immorally high rates of poverty, incarceration, and death and the lowest rates of land and home ownership, employment, school funding, and wealth" (475). What this "reveals" is "that Black Americans, along with Indigenous people–the two groups forced to be a part of this nation–remain the most neglected beneficiaries of the America that would not exist without us" (475). And "This unacknowledged debt, all of it, is still accruing" (475). "Black Americans helped build the economic foundation that has made the United States a global power," but "they have also played an unparalleled and *uncompensated* role in building our democracy itself" (475). What is to be done? No, "We cannot change the hypocrisy upon which we were founded," and, no, "We cannot change all the times in the past when this nation has had the opportunity to do the right thing and chose to return to its basest inclinations" (475). It is impossible "to make up for all of the lives lost and dreams snatched, for all the suffering endured" (475). And yet, "we can atone for it. We can acknowledge the crime. And we can do something to try to set things right, to ease the hardship and hurt of so many of our fellow Americans" (475).

What Hannah-Jones is arguing for here directly resonates with what Avery Gordon theorizes as 'reckoning' with 'ghosts' that make their presence known and felt by means of a 'haunting' that encompasses a challenge, and indeed a demand, to respond to what they need, from us, to atone for historical violence and injustice. They will not go away until we can so 'reckon' with them and we can pay them their due. Only then can they be dispatched. This is a collective effort, but it is also an individual one, in which each individual must experience the haunting impact and the immediate interaction with ghosts directly, palpably, viscerally, and undeniably themselves, determining what their particular role and contribution must be in responding to what these ghosts demand. The United States has not yet reckoned with how pervasively and ubiquitously slavery has shaped and continues to shape the fabric of this nation, as well as how its legacy has continuously advantaged white Americans at the direct expense of Black Americans while simultaneously mystifying the extent to which American economic, social, political, and cultural achievement has been hugely dependent on the contributions, the all too often unrecognized and uncompensated contributions, of Black Americans. What's more, too often this nation and too many (especially white) Americans have denied the presence of these ghosts, refused to recognize and engage with this haunting, and retreated from and rejected even considering the notion of seriously undertaking any such confrontation and any such reckoning.

Other 'origin stories' need to be attended to as well, including those of Indigenous and of Latinx and of Asian and Pacific Islander people, but the 'origin story' that Nikole Hannah-Jones and fellow contributors have put together in the form of *The 1619 Project* is vital and essential. It must be foundational in responding to the state of racial capitalism and how this plays out in the US today, as well as in relations between the US and the rest of the world, in particular to what Gordon identifies, in her interview as part of *Revolutionary Feminisms: Conversations on Collective Action and Radical Thought* as "a reach, or desire, for something else–for a life without racial capitalism, a life in which we are not enclosed by values and modes of being together based on money and exchange values, status hierarchies, violence and force, alienation, racialisation and discipline to externally imposed standards."

Gordon champions Martin Luther King Jr.'s conception of "the indivisibility of justice" in King's famous declaration "Injustice anywhere is a threat to justice everywhere. We are caught in an inescapable network of mutuality, tied in a single garment of destiny. Whatever affects one directly, affects all indirectly." In order to make this kind of 'inescapable network of mutuality' a foundational structural dimension of social life in this nation it is necessary to come to grips with, and atone, for the injustices of this nation's past and their continuing weight in the present. Gordon advocates on behalf of "being-in-difference" which she defines as "a political consciousness and a sensuous knowledge, a standpoint and a mindset for living on better terms than we're offered; for living as if you had the necessity and the freedom to do so; for living in the acknowledgment, that despite the overwhelming power of all the systems of domination which are trying to kill us, they never quite become us." "Being-in-difference" suggests overcoming fears of confronting and reckoning with ghosts, of frankly acknowledging and addressing the impact of past and present differences, while working to transform social relations, and social systems, so that these are equitable as opposed to inequitable differences and so that differences can become the basis for social unity and solidarity, the basis for social strength and genuinely substantive and collectively empowering social diversity, not the locus solely of division, antagonism, conflict, and, especially injustice, inequity, exploitation, alienation, and oppression.

Five

The principal issues I explore in sections six through nine of this chapter, as points of contact and as bases for staging an encounter and pursuing a dialogue between Robert McRuer's *Crip Theory: Cultural Signs of Queerness and Disability* and *Crip Times: Disability, Globalization, and Resistance*, on the one hand, and Ian Curtis and Joy Division, as represented by the songs "She's Lost Control," "Dead Souls," "Atmosphere," and "Decades," on the other hand, are:

1) disability, reconceived in 'crip' or 'cripping' terms, especially in critique of compulsory able-bodiedness, of able-bodiedness as both norm and ideal, including by way of crip approaches to and crip varieties of *art* and/as *activism*; and

2) the damaging effects of neoliberalism, especially upon those who are already, and indeed already often multiply, dispossessed, displaced, and denied.

The principal issues I explore in sections six through nine of this chapter, as points of contact and as bases for staging an encounter and pursuing a dialogue between Ann Cvetkovich's *Depression: a Public Feeling*, on the one hand, and Ian Curtis and Joy Division, as represented by the songs "She's Lost Control," "Dead Souls," "Atmosphere," and "Decades," on the other hand, are:

1) depression–what the experience of depression can be like, what this experience can *feel* like, as well as what conditions makes it possible and what forces give rise to it, what provokes and elicits it, what even *causes* and *explains* it, and, in particular how to interpret depression as a viable reflection of and response to (i.e., as viably symptomatic concerning) larger social and political concerns, rather than as merely an individual instance of a biological and/or psychological disorder; and

2) taking feelings, and especially *bad feelings*, seriously, including as providing a crucial impetus for critical praxis.

The principal issues I explore in sections six through nine of this chapter, as points of contact and as bases for staging an encounter and pursuing a dialogue between Avery Gordon's *Ghostly Matters: Haunting and the Sociological Imagination*, on the one hand, and Ian Curtis and Joy Division, as represented by the songs "She's Lost Control," "Dead Souls," "Atmosphere," and "Decades," on the other hand, are:

1) complex personhood, and

2) hauntings and ghosts–when, where, how, and why do these arise; how to interpret what these mean as well as how to evaluate their significance; and how to engage with them as well as why do so, to what end–i.e., what can be the gains of so doing.

McRuer, Cvetkovich, and Gordon all share common interest in and concern with:

1) interdeterminate interrelations among past, present, and future, as well as with prospective alternative pasts, presents, and futures;

2) the value and even the necessity of the utopian;

3) taking the affective, the sensuous, and the somatic seriously;

4) social transformation, not just resistance, not just disruption, not just subversion, not just transgression, not just separation, not just distancing, not just dissidence, and not just protest–in particular in working out from conditions of (austerity) neoliberal capitalism, and in particular in ascertaining what kinds of contributions toward social transformation can and should be made by means of critical theory, of art and literature, and of social and political activism that connects with yet is not coincident with critical theory, or with art and literature; and

5) intersectionalities along lines of class, race, gender, sexuality, health/illness and ability/disability, and nationality.

In the encounter and dialogue to come with Ian Curtis and Joy Division, as represented by the songs "She's Lost Control," "Dead Souls," "Atmosphere," and "Decades," I also consider these five areas of interest and concern that McRuer, Cvetkovich, and Gordon share in common.

Six

"She's Lost Control," the sixth song, and the first on the second side, or the 'inside', of *Unknown Pleasures*, is one of Joy Division's best-known songs, and its lyrics are well-known, what's more, as inspired by a young woman Ian Curtis knew and worked with as an Assistance Disablement Resettlement Officer, in Macclesfield, a young woman who dealt with epilepsy and who Curtis was shocked subsequently to be told, by the young woman's mother, that the young woman had died of an epileptic fit. According to some accounts, this young woman had previously fitted while meeting with Curtis in his office, and this was one of the first times he witnessed a major epileptic seizure in person. Reputedly this young woman wore a helmet for protection from fits, which was still common for people with epilepsy in the mid to late 1970s in Britain. But "She's Lost Control" is well-known for many other reasons as well, including as one of the most overtly recognizable instances of Martin Hannett's 'deconstruction' of Stephen Morris's drum kit and for asking Morris to make use of unusual additional 'percussion instruments', in this case an aerosol spray can.

In *Unknown Pleasures: Inside Joy Division*, Peter Hook mentions the aerosol as one of "Martin's many innovations," as well as "a Ring Modulator on the real dampened snare" and "Steve's Synare, which was a drum synthesizer with a white-noise generator" (204). About the reputed inspiration for Curtis's lyrics, Hook comments "That must have been terrifying for him," although "The first I knew of it was when Bernard mentioned it on a Joy Division documentary" (204). In relation to Curtis's vocalization of the lyrics to "She's Lost Control," Hook did readily recognize "He delivered his vocals with the perfect amount of passion and spirit, exactly what we wanted," while "Saying that, reading the lyrics now, his use of repetition and onomatopoeic delivery is startling" (205).

In *Torn Apart: The Life of Ian Curtis*, Mick Middles and Lindsay Reade cite "The simplistic disco drum beat intro" as "among the finest moments in rock history" and as "after the guitar build-up to 'Love Will Tear Us Apart', the second most accessible into to the music of Joy Division for future generations of fans" (134). Later in this same book Middles and Reade reproduce a letter Curtis wrote to Annik Honore where he comments on writing a new verse for what has come to be known as 'the extended version' of the song, a version that "sounds completely different from the version on the album," and in relation to which Curtis "can't make up my mind whether it's better or not" (196).

Even later, near the end of his life, Curtis stayed with Tony Wilson and Lindsay Reade at their house, and spent time with Reade as company, although not saying much as he was in an extremely depressed state of mind. Reade recalls she became upset at Curtis for his virtually catatonic silence and immobility, but when Wilson came to drive Curtis away she regretted complaining about Curtis to Wilson, recognizing Curtis could overhear, so she ran out and nearly threw herself in front of Wilson's car. This led Reader subsequently to identify herself as the 'title character' 'who lost control' in the lyrics Curtis wrote for "She's Lost Control" (240). This anecdote illustrates how readily many listeners have been able to identify themselves with the subject in the lyrics 'losing control'–and, as I will discuss shortly, clearly Curtis did so himself as well, especially by the time of writing additional lyrics for 'the extended version'.

In *We Were Strangers: Stories Inspired by Unknown Pleasures*, Zoe Lambert's short story "She's Loat Control" elaborates upon the situation that reputedly inspired Curtis to write these lyrics. Lambert imagines a young woman with epilepsy who has suffered from bullying, rejection, and isolation on account of her condition, and especially her fits, and whose hyper-protective mother insists she 'wear her helmet' even though the young woman hates the helmet. The young woman has been let go from a series of jobs because of fitting, and has now obtained an unpaid job where she reads and types up reports on agricultural materials, eventually accompanying her boss on a visit to a farm with which he is involved. Even as she is now not being paid, her boss and his business partner both accept and accommodate the young woman's epilepsy, so some hope lingers that she can experience some kind of satisfying life with at least a limited degree of autonomous self-determination. Yet overall Lambert's story emphasizes how difficult it is for this young woman and others like her to live anything close to 'a normal life'.

In the '*Unknown Pleasures*: Reimagined' series of short films created to commemorate the 40th anniversary of the release of the album, director Lorraine Nicholson's black and white film depicts a woman living in what seems like a relatively luxurious yet at the same time austerely minimalist, modern to contemporary, artfully designed house, during what might be an earthquake yet more likely is some kind of breakdown on her part, in which the shattered furnishings in her immediate physical surroundings represent the objective correlative of her mental state. This woman, who for most of the film is just wearing a flimsy nightdress, also puts on a series of successively more outlandish wigs and over the top makeup as the film proceeds while displaying an obsessive-compulsive desire for cleanliness and order in an increasingly messy and disordered domestic environment. A male partner leaves near the beginning of the film and then returns near the end, at the end appearing mildly disapproving but patronizingly dismissive and largely unsurprised by what has transpired during his time away. The woman in this film appears trapped in this environment and by the expectations of being a housewife, living in the equivalent of 'a doll's house', as the film echoes Maya Deren's famous experimental feminist film *Meshes of the Afternoon*.

Attke Oksanen, in "Hollow Spaces of Psyche: Gothic Trance-Formation from Joy Division to Diary of Dreams" cites "She's Lost Control" as an exemplary instance of sonically evoking the experience of 'trancing': "singing and drums have a strong throbbing echo," while "In the lyrics the loss of self-control is systematically repeated until the end of the song" (130). As Oksanen adds, "This is even more underlined in the extended version of the song" where "the narrator starts to doubt his own life and loses control of himself too" (130). Mitzi Waltz and Martin James, in "The (re)Marketing of Disability in Pop: Ian Curtis and Joy Division," cite "She's Lost Control" as an instance where Curtis "quietly addressed the experience of epilepsy," likely at least obliquely referencing his sharing of this experience (372). Adam Robson, writing for *Far Out Magazine*, describes "She's Lost Control" "as a sad foreshadowing of Ian Curtis' future," while noting "Lyrically, the song, once understanding its conception, is stark and cold," as "It handles the arresting fear of witnessing such a thing [a major epileptic seizure] with clinical brutalism" in such a way "that would sadly offer a shocking vision of Curtis future." Robson notes the song was actually "Written before Curtis' first epileptic seizure," but nevertheless "the song is a hard reminder of the illness which plagued the singer." Robson also highlights, in "She's Lost Control," that "the snare was actually created by layering the sound of a Syn Drum; an early electronic drum pad, with the sound of an aerosol can tape head cleaner being sprayed." As Robson observes, this was long "Before the days of Pro Tools or even reliable triggers," so "the spray had to be recorded live while being played in time to the initial drum track" and "Due to Hannett's obsession for isolated recordings (a technique used to ensure there is no 'bleed' between instrument tracks) it is rumoured that drummer Stephen Morris had to play the respiratory blocking percussion while sealed off in a small recording booth," which is indeed a rumor Morris has confirmed on more than one occasion. On Songmeanings.com, meanwhile, contributors overwhelmingly identify the song's meaning as about epilepsy, and in particular what it is like to live with epilepsy and to experience an epileptic seizure–or to observe someone else undergoing such a fit directly in front of you. Among the more useful complimentary interpretations a few others propose are the song resonating with experience of panic attacks, dissociative identity disorder, and losing control even more broadly than due to epilepsy or a comparable health condition.

In a detailed close reading of the music of "She's Lost Control," Liam Maloy, writing in "'*She expressed herself in many different ways*': Hypothetical substitutions in Joy Division's 'She's Lost Control," argues that the music itself is 'epileptic', or simulates in sound what it is like to experience an epileptic seizure or other kind of episode. As Maloy describes, the song begins with "an isolated synthesised burst of percussion," and he suggests "This white noise blast" resembles either "an electric cattle prod or the electrical discharge in the brain that precedes a generalised epileptic seizure" (8). As this sound "is left to decay," "the highly-idiosyncratic drum track appears," sounding a pattern that Maloy interprets as "echoing the rigidity of the body during the tonic phase of a tonic-clonic seizure" (8). Because of its "sparseness" and its simultaneous prominence in the mix, as well as its relatively fast pace and the lack of cymbals, the drum pattern sounds "distorted" and overtly "machine-like" (8). This contributes yet further to a sense of being out of balance, or of losing balance. While the bass guitar contributes the primary backup to the vocal in sounding the melody, it does so at a markedly high register, sounding "effectively the highest notes that can be played on a conventional 4-string bass guitar" (9). This is also markedly minor key, and yet further 'thinned out' by "using EQ and playing chords" when the bass guitar shifts "to a lead instrument" (9). Maloy further calls attention to the melodic line in "She's Lost Control" repeatedly refusing 'to resolve', to return to the tonic, and because "The brain expects the music to resolve at key points in the song," but it does not, this creates "a feeling of perpetual tension" (9). Therefore "She's Lost Control" "is decentred and adrift both structurally and sonically" (9). What's more, the song is further complicated by the entrance of a second bass guitar line over two minutes into the song that adds "a minor variation on the melodic riff" performed by the first guitar line. In addition, "On the extended single version," a yet further complication of the initial bass guitar melodic line comes by way of "a ghostly synthesizer" that "plays the same four notes but reordered and shortened to semi-quavers" (10).

Maloy describes "the entire vocal melody" in "She's Lost Control" as yet "further emphasizing the lack of a tonic note," yet "further unsettling the listener" (10). This unsettled feeling is compounded by Curtis's voice as "it sounds damaged, vulnerable and confused," while "The vocals ride high in the mix, isolated from the other instruments and filling the void in the mid-range of the track" (11). Maloy attributes "The close-mic recording technique" as 'ensuring' "Curtis's voice has the listener's full attention," sounding, as Maloy interprets this, akin to "a dark and harrowing confessional" (11). Maloy notes "The lyrics are constructed with a strong emphasis on the rhythm," with quavers matching syllables beat for beat, and "This rhythmic precision is maintained throughout the song," adding a feeling of claustrophobic entrapment (11). At the same time, strikingly, Maloy points out that "Curtis hits each syllable with percussive exactitude; the vocalist is *in* control," and this adds an additional disturbing dimension to the song as a controlled voice narrates the situation and experience of someone who has lost control, and who has done so again and again, from a close-up observational vantage point. Long delays added to the vocal along with manual alteration lending

"The effect of short vocal phrases being randomly speeded up or slowed down" makes the song come across, quite "literally," as "multiply-voiced," suggesting that "Curtis is battling for space in the mix with a host of his own mischievous demons," as Maloy suggests the lyrics may represent an internal monologue (13). More likely, however, Maloy proposes "The song has two protagonists: the narrator 'speaking' in the first-person ('I', 'me') and the female subject (*"I've lost control"*) that engage each other in a "call-and-response" "format," "back and forth between narrator and subject; a gothic gospel spoken in tongues, hideously giddy with the rapture" (13).

Maloy also notes, as is far from uncommon in Joy Division songs, the guitar contributes primarily a sense of "conflict and dissonance," and does so in pitching its chords against the initial bass riff in a manner that sounds "alarming" (14). The guitar is made to sound 'harshly mechanistic' while "Mixed low and ultra-compressed, it fulfills none of the traditional roles of the electric guitar in rock," as indeed "Its harsh stabbing quality conjures up a violent street attack" (14). The guitar becomes increasingly "unhinged" in its relation to the two bass guitar lines, "playing rhythmically out of phase, creating a new level of discordance and disharmony" (15). And all of this "aural mayhem" is punctuated by means of "the use of a bizarre pitch-shifting effect on the snare" (15).

In live versions, Maloy notes further, the band considerably speeds up the tempo while at the end of each chorus Curtis holds a low D, "forcing it rapidly upwards, transforming it into a bloodcurdling roar that overwhelms the pain and confusion of epilepsy and the unpredicatability of the next major seizure" (15). Doing so is all the more hauntingly affecting in its impact upon an audience as Curtis dances his inimitable frenzied dance, which many commentators have observed comes chillingly close to resembling an epileptic seizure in and of itself.

Let's turn now to a close examination of the title and lyrics of "She's Lost Control," beginning with the title. 'Control' attracts immediate attention, even as I am only one of many who have interpreted Ian Curtis's lyrics and the lyrics and music of Joy Division as often centrally focused on issues of control, lack and loss of control, desire for and need of control, and of both inevitable limits of control along with considerable difficulty accepting these limits. After all, the Anton Corbijn-directed, feature-length, Ian Curtis-biopic is titled *Control*, and many commentators have cited the title as most apt in relation to what this film depicts. Certainly, many of us persistently strive to carve out and maintain even tiny areas of life over which we can exercise at least the semblance of control, in the face of so much everywhere surrounding and confronting us that we come to recognize, however reluctantly, and however agonizingly, over which we exercise little to no control. Being able to maintain micro-control in the face of macro-lack-of-control often proves vital to mental health and physical well-being, even if it can often prove likewise useful to health and well-being to identify with the Serenity Prayer in 'accepting the things I cannot change' and 'the wisdom to know the difference' between what I can change and what I cannot. Loss of control, or lack of control, over what one expects to be able to control, including over what one has in the past been able to control without giving this much if any conscious attention, as well as in relation to what seemingly most other people can control, but one cannot (or now cannot), can be highly disturbing, even terrifying. Loss of control, or lack of control, over one's own body, as well as over one's mind, including as a unitary 'bodymind' rather than a Cartesian duality, can be especially disturbing, and even especially terrifying.

From personal experience, I recognize and identify with feeling exactly this disturbance, and terror, in relation to epileptic seizures and other episodes, panic attacks and waves of massive dread, deep depression to the verge of suicidality, and chronic physical illness that is fluctuating and unpredictable while never finally leaving me, never finally 'over' once and for all. I have also experienced the disturbance and terror of confronting violent threats against me in response to which I have felt as if I could do little but hope that somehow I might manage to survive. And I have also experienced the disturbance and terror of being involved in situations and circumstances, and efforts and initiatives, where it has indeed seemed no matter how hard I, and those joining together with me work–no matter how much of ourselves we give in striving to succeed–it is and will always be too little, because we will always end up falling short, even always end up defeated. In these kinds of situations and circumstances, and as participant in these kinds of actions and campaigns, it definitely has often felt like I, and we, lost, or lacked, or were losing or were lacking, the control we needed over what we were aiming to do, how so, when and where so, in relation to and especially representative of and to benefit whom, as well as why so.

The Oxford English Dictionary [*OED*] cites a number of other common definitions of 'control' that are useful in making clear what is at stake in loss or lack of control. The *OED* first cites "holding in check or constraining; constraint." Prison is, after all, a mode of control–and it makes sense as well to argue that the entire system of law, and law enforcement, is also. Such control can be necessary and useful, it can be the opposite, it can be a combination of both, and it can be the site of conflict and struggle. At the same time, 'self-control' involves 'holding in check or restraining', exercising 'restraint', and this can be difficult to do, much more difficult for some people in some conditions than for others. Self-control perhaps needs to be taught and learned, yet it might usefully be argued also needs to be 'un-taught' and 'un-learned', if and when people hold themselves in check or restrain themselves too tightly such that they cannot do what is right and necessary, including in representing and advancing their own interests. 'Control' exercised over people's consciousness, as well as for that matter over their unconscious too, can be particularly powerful, and can be particularly powerfully problematic, even highly pernicious, as exercised by 'others' who do so in order to serve and advance 'their' interests, including at the expense of–in opposition to the interests of–those so 'controlled'. After all, 'ideology' and in particular 'dominant ideology' represent preeminent modes of 'control'.

The next two definitions offered by the *OED* again lean in this direction: "prevention or limitation of the spread of a noxious agent," including "in extended use: the confinement or limiting of a socially undesirable phenomenon or tendency," as well as "the fact or power of directing and regulating the actions of people or things; direction; management; command." And the next series of definitions after those yet further compliment the preceding: "the capacity or power to manage an animal, vehicle, or moving object"; and "a method or means of restraint"; "a measure adopted, especially by a government for the regulation of prices, the consumption of goods, etc." The common emphasis here is on limiting or preventing, and on directing or containing.

In the next series of definitions 'control' is associated with "a person who acts as a check or constraint," "a disembodied spirit who gives messages to a medium," and as "(a code name for) a member of an intelligence organization who personally directed the activities of a spy." 'Control' thereby not only takes on embodied–or disembodied–form but also represents either direction or mediation.

After these definitions, we come to the scientific definition of "an experiment conducted without a factor or variable being tested for in other experiments that are otherwise identical, to enable the effect of this factor or variable to be inferred; an experimental subject in such an experiment." Once again emphasis is placed on 'keeping in check', on limiting, confining, containing, and constraining. Similar implications follow in relation to definitions of 'control associated with the games of whist and bridge, in motor rallying and road racing, in operating machines and vehicles, in sound recording and broadcasting, and even in relation to computing, while the final definition the *OED* crystallizes this common direction of emphasis in striking terms: "The organization or place from which a system or activity is directed, managed, or regulated; a control centre, room, tower, etc., or the people occupying this."

So, in sum, 'control' tends to be both centered and central, authoritative and commanding, governing and regulating, directing and facilitating, as well as, especially, checking, curtailing, limiting, delimiting, isolating, confining, containing, and constraining. It may well be that control is often absolutely indispensable, vitally necessary, and righteously beneficent. But control can also be harmfully and wrongfully repressive and oppressive.

Certainly, common interpretations of "She's Lost Control" identify the loss of control the lyrics and the song take up as disturbing and frightening, as seemingly entirely negative and most unwelcome. But it is at least worth considering, as we proceed to discuss the lyrics and the song closely and carefully, that even many of the most common 'dictionary definitions' of 'control' do not posit 'control' as always so clearly and entirely a positive and welcome state, which means, in turn, that 'loss of control' might not necessarily always be terrible.

It is understandable that of the three words that comprise the title of "She's Lost Control," the last, 'control', attracts the most immediate attention, with 'lost' the second most. At the same time, in relation to "she's," listeners readily interpret the lyrics and the song by connecting this recounting and depiction of having lost control with a variety of situations and experiences in which they themselves, or others they know or know about, have lost control. Despite the well-known real-life inspiration for Curtis's lyrics in this song, and this young woman's and Curtis's own experience of epilepsy, many listeners put themselves in the place of the subject who has lost control, imagining what this might be like, what this feels like in doing so. Listeners experience a sympathetic to empathetic connection with this subject, while feeling simultaneously chilled by the seeming brutal observational detachment and mechanical coldness of the vocals and the rest of the music. But I do want to call attention to the fact that the title of the song is "*She's* Lost Control," and to reflect on how this choice affects the ways in which we are likely to interpret it.

As we have repeatedly encountered, Ian Curtis typically prefers anonymity in identifying 'characters' in his lyrics–by using pronouns such as 'I', 'me', 'we', 'us', 'she', 'her', 'him', 'his', 'them', 'their', etc., not proper names, and also, although less often, by way of their participation as members of equally anonymous groups such as, for example in the case of "Shadowplay," 'assassins'

964

and 'crowds', along with a particular Curtis lyrical favorite, 'bodies'. This *is* significant. Imagine, for instance, if the title of the song were "Joan's Lost Control," or "Harry's lost control," or "The Jones sisters have lost control," or "The people of Warwick have lost control," or "The Chief Constable has lost control," or "The Prime Minister has lost control," or "The Chairman of the Board has lost control," or "Dr Evans has lost control," or "Reverend Grant has lost control," and so on. The difference between the kinds of songs that Ian Curtis and Joy Division created with songs that might have carried titles like these is huge.

Returning, though, to pronouns, it might seem obvious what 'the meaning' of 'she' in "She's Lost Control," must be, given that it was the tragic death of a specific individual young woman with epilepsy that inspired Curtis to write these lyrics–that the 'she' here simply *does* refer to her, and only to her. However, that need not be the only viable way to interpret this 'she', especially for listeners who derive their own meanings from the song by connecting it with knowledge and experience, and matters of interest and concern, to them–in their own lives, as whom and what they are, from where they have come and toward where they are headed. All of the last might be extraordinarily different from the practical, empirical details of Ian Curtis's own individual life-experience. If, for example, it makes sense to interpret this song as dramatically enacting an interior monologue, or a dialogue the narrator-protagonist of these lyrics (and even of the music as persona) conducts with 'himself', 'she' might represent a distinct dimension of 'his' 'complex personhood', of his 'multiple and complex personhood'. Perhaps, because many commentators have interpreted 'Ian Curtis,' as represented in his lyrics and his music, in his performance and his projected image, as a figure who is at least potentially, at least implicitly, 'fluid' in terms of gender, and sexual, identity, 'she' here makes sense as referencing a part of a 'multiple and complex personhood' that encompasses both male and female, or both man and woman, or both masculine and feminine (and even both homosexual and heterosexual) constituents. Perhaps this represents, at least as a composite, an androgynous, bisexual 'personhood' or a gender nonbinary, polysexual 'personhood'. Undoubtedly a number of readers are likely to find this far-fetched, and that suggests the song does not make sense to them in those terms, but among the students I have taught in five classes on Ian Curtis, Joy Division, and critical theory, this kind of interpretation has been commonplace, resonating with how these students made sense of 'the Ian Curtis' represented 'in the music', 'in the performance', and 'in the myth'.

"Confusion in her eyes that says it all," line one of stanza one, strikingly juxtaposes, right at the start, 'confusion' and 'says it all'. 'Confusion', commonly, makes sense in close connection with 'lack of clarity', and with 'uncertainty' concerning something that is being expressed, communicated, and signified. Yet here it is 'confusion' itself that expresses, communicates, and signifies 'it all'–'all' that, perhaps, can or needs be expressed, communicated, and signified. 'Confusion' is of the essence here, or at least it is through 'confusion' that we recognize and come to grips with what is of the essence. 'Confusion' might here constitute the 'meaning' being cited, or referenced, not just in this line but across all the lines yet to come and that collectively comprise the lyrics as a whole. It is notable this is confusion "in her eyes," which indicates that meaning, insofar as confusion here is meaning, or confusion that serves as means and medium through which meaning here takes place, does not come, at least not right away, by way of what 'she' says or by how she otherwise makes uses of words to get across. Not even gestures are the initial source of meaning. Meaning, what's more, does not depend upon any other part of the face to become clear, 'to say it all', as all of what is at stake shows up "in her eyes." "Says it all" is mysteriously uncertain at this point: what is that 'all' that is 'being said'—that 'needs to be said'? And does everyone who 'reads' the expression in 'her eyes' recognize that it is 'in there' that 'all is said'? Or are only some people likely to recognize and understand? If the latter, what kinds of people recognize and understand, and what kinds of people don't? What factors shape, even determine, who will versus who will not recognize and understand this 'all' that is 'said', 'in her eyes'?

Proceeding to line two, "She's lost control," it makes sense logically to interpret this as what the "confusion in her eyes that says it all" in fact is saying—i.e., that she has lost control. With epilepsy, yes, 'confusion in the eyes' is commonly indicative of someone undergoing a seizure, or about to undergo a seizure. I myself know from what others have told me, witnessing seizures I have experienced, that, yes, 'confusion in my eyes' is a prominent clue that this is happening, or is about to happen, or has just happened. Yet again, 'the meaning' of this song, and even just of these lyrics, need not be limited solely to 'it is about epilepsy, about what it is like to experience an epileptic seizure, and about what it is like to not be able to control when, where, or how frequently these seizures happen', let alone 'how severely' they do so. It is plausible to interpret "Confusion in her eyes" signifying "losing control" in many other kinds of situations, relations, or events. In all such circumstances it is plausible that 'she' would register awareness, or begin to register awareness, of this happening to her by means of a show of 'confusion' 'in her eyes' resembling 'fear', or 'panic', especially if 'she' has been counting on this 'control', even without consciously thinking about this need for control at all, in order to meet the demands of the situation, relation, or event.

Line three, "And she's clinging to the nearest passer by," suggests this is what 'she' is doing as 'she's losing control', although it is worth noting the song proposes she *has* lost control, which implies 'clinging to the nearest passer by' is what she does once she *has* lost control, in response to loss of control already having happened, or, perhaps better put, as this is already happening. Yes, epileptic seizures certainly can and do exhibit ample elements of 'loss of control'—loss of control of one's own body, of how one moves one's body and parts of one's body, of what kinds of expressions and gestures one is making with one's body or parts of one's body, and of kinds of sounds one is emitting, among multiple other possibilities as well, in addition to literal loss of consciousness. And, yes, this loss of control can and does often come upon one suddenly and rapidly, bewilderingly so, with the need to reach out to cling to whatever one can becoming quite pronounced in order to protect one's self as one is falling. It makes sense to so reach out in relation to anything or anyone immediately at hand—such as "the nearest passer by." But then again in multiple other scenarios where someone suddenly and rapidly loses control or becomes aware of such loss of control it makes sense to do so as well, especially if one is flailing badly: it makes sense to seek 'stabilizing' support from whomever and whatever is closest at hand. If someone has lost control, for example, over a group of people whom one has been leading, one might feel compelled to reach out for support to whomever is nearest by as one is metaphorically 'falling', as one is losing one's ability to lead and to exercise authority in relation to others through doing so. If one is in a situation where one is charged to accomplish a task that proves beyond one's capacities, at least with the means of assistance presently available, and one as a result 'loses control' over one's performance of the task, yet again one might readily be prompted to reach out and 'cling to the nearest passer by' in desperation—in panic.

After line four reiterates line two–"She's lost control"–line five reads "And she gave away the secrets of her past." "And" logically connects what this line references with what has just preceded. Therefore 'she giving away the secrets of her past' seems logically connected with 'losing control' and 'clinging to the nearest passer by'. Perhaps now that she has lost control, or now as she is losing control, she 'gives away the secrets of her past' to this 'nearest passer by'; perhaps that is what she cannot help but do as a result of losing control, or as part and parcel of the process of losing control. Perhaps this is what happens when she loses control, or has lost control–she 'gives away secrets of her past', even 'to the nearest passer by'–because that's what loss of control means for her, that's what loss of control does to her. Because these are "secrets," it would seem she otherwise would not be sharing them, at least not with 'the nearest passer by'. Yet loss of control leads her to do so, or involves her doing so–or even is equivalent with her doing exactly this. After all, 'normally' most people don't share 'secrets of their past' with 'the nearest passer by', because this would seemingly involve giving up control over these secrets, control over with whom one shared these secrets, and over whether they remain secret at all. Loss of control might mean sharing what you 'normally' would not with those with whom one 'normally' would not. Loss of control might mean acting in a dramatically non-normative, even anti-normative or counter-normative, manner: doing what we are socially conditioned *not* to do.

It might mean, paradoxically enough, *breaking free*–breaking free from constraints that keep people alienated and isolated. It might mean rejecting clear lines between whom is, ostensibly, 'like us' versus whom is not; between whom is, ostensibly, 'close' to us versus whom is not; between whom we can, ostensibly, 'trust' and confide in versus whom we cannot; between whom we can, ostensibly, 'share' with versus whom we cannot; and between whom we maintain interests in common versus whom we do not.

The lyrics do not specify what might comprise these 'secrets' nor do they explain why they are kept or maintained as 'secrets', but line five does identify these as *secrets of her past*, which suggest they are secrets concerning something about whom she was, or has been, in the past–or something about what she did, or did not do, or what was done, or not done, to her, in the past. Perhaps these are secrets of her past that she has kept secret right up to the point of losing control, and perhaps, anticipating where the lyrics proceed, the heart of the mystery here is in fact that 'she has lost control again'–and 'again and again'. In other words, perhaps "the secrets of her past" are the tendencies she maintains repeatedly to lose control and of how many times this has happened to her. Given stigma associated with epilepsy as well as how limiting this condition can be, and especially long has been, until recently, in terms of what it has meant people can and cannot do, are advised and even allowed to do and not do, it makes sense to want, and to need, to keep it a secret. If her condition is known, and not a secret, 'she' might not be able to work the kind of job, and pursue the kind of career, she desires, and, for that matter, which she would 'be good at' if adequate accommodation, and indeed access, was available for someone with her impairment. If her condition is known, not a secret, 'she' might be restricted from moving about as freely as she desires, which she could do if provided adequate accommodation, and indeed access, for someone with her impairment. If her condition is known, not a secret, people might back away from getting close to her, from getting to know her, from becoming her friend, even if they are losing a great deal from not developing and pursuing a close relationship with her.

However, it is certainly plausible to interpret "the secrets of her past" as referencing something else, not having anything to do with a disability she deals with, and has dealt with–not necessarily an 'un-visible disability' such as epilepsy she can often keep secret. Yet what else these 'secrets of her past' might be is, at least of yet, devoid of any overt clue. One final comment on this line is nevertheless worth making: 'giving away' these secrets can suggest an element of volition, and not just being forced, by accident, because she has lost control, and is out of control, to do what she otherwise would not do. Even, indeed, if she would otherwise not 'give away' these secrets, perhaps here, under these conditions, she is effectively deciding to do this–deliberately choosing to do so. Perhaps 'she' acts considerably differently when 'under control', when *subject to control*, versus when not–and perhaps the former state is not unquestionably 'when she is at her best' while perhaps the latter state is not unquestionably 'when she is at her worst'.

The next three lines, the last three lines of the first stanza, deepen the mystery: "And said I've lost control again/And of a voice that told her when and where to act/She said I've lost control again." She now literally *says* "I've lost control," doesn't merely evince this taking place, or having taken place, by means of "Confusion in her eyes"–or by means of "clinging to the nearest passer by" and by 'giving away' "the secrets of her past." Also of significant note here is she says "I've lost control *again*." So this has indeed happened previously, and as the lyrics proceed, it becomes clear it has happened frequently.

The last two lines are especially challenging because it seems 'she' is here sharing 'she' has lost control "of a voice that told her when and where to act," which leads to speculation concerning what might that voice be. Might this be her internalized conception of what is right and proper, her conception of etiquette and decorum? Might this be the result of her socialization, of her social conditioning, of her recognition of and identification with what is not only normal but also normative? Might this be the equivalent of the Freudian superego, or the Lacanian Subject, or the social unconscious Avery F. Gordon advocates for in opposition to the Freudian unconscious? Might this be the equivalent of dominant ideology? It makes sense that this voice represents an internalization of a larger social nexus of instruction concerning what she can and should do, as well as cannot and should not do, when, where, with and otherwise in relation to whom else, and why so. She might, in losing control, be acting contrary to this kind of 'instruction', but the way these lines is worded suggests another possibility as well: she has lost control over how to manage the 'demands' of 'this voice' as they have grown louder, more insistent, and perhaps all the more oppressive. In effect this voice has come to demand more of 'her' than she is able to give without breaking down. 'Her' experience of what she has been telling herself is right and necessary for her to do, as a good and decent person, as an honorable person, as a moral person, etc., had led here to the point where she has 'demanded too much of herself', so much that she feels overwhelmed, and this feeling of being overwhelmed shows up in a corresponding physical manifestation of losing bodily control. Perhaps she has not been able to live up to the demands of the voice 'within her' that has told her what she must do, "when and where to act," as a talented person, as an ambitious person, as a creative person, as a strong person, as an independent person, as a leader, as a free thinker, as an artist, as a rebel, as a lover, etc. Perhaps she has identified herself as being such a person, she has aspired and worked to become such a person, but she has defined what it means to be this kind of person, to be a success as this kind of person, to be genuinely worthy of identifying as and being identified by others as this kind of person, in terms that have proven beyond her reach because these terms are extreme and excessive.

The first four lines of stanza two continue as follows: "And she turned around and took me by the hand and said/I've lost control again/And how I'll never know just why or understand/She said I've lost control again." Here it is significant that 'I' is introduced and that 'she' is 'turning to' this 'I' and sharing with this 'I', albeit sharing what she does not understand and cannot explain, as she has lost control. 'I' may or may not be simply identical with 'the nearest passer by'. Either way here she is 'turning to' 'I' and she is confiding even more than she already has, to 'the nearest passer by': she is confiding not only that she has lost control, and lost control again, but also that she does not understand and cannot explain why this has happened, repeatedly–and will never be able to understand or explain. Yes, even if one knows one 'is (an) epileptic', that one experiences epilepsy, that one receives medical treatment for this condition, and what are currently prevailing medical explanations for what happens in an epileptic seizure as well as why this happens as it does, one can still readily *feel* as if one will never know or understand precisely why these seizures happen when and where, or as often and as severely, as they do–or why 'this is happening to me', 'why I am one who suffers from this condition' while 'so many other people don't'. Seizures can readily *feel* inexplicable, as they are happening, and immediately prior to and immediately after they are happening, even if one is well aware of medical explanations for what is happening and why this is happening.

However, 'she' might be telling 'I' something other than her experience of a condition such as epilepsy is what 'she'll never know just why or understand'. What "she'll never know why or understand" might relate to division and conflict within whom she experiences herself to be, within the multiple and complex person she experiences herself to be, as a nexus of competing and contesting forces resulting in considerable tension, restlessness, unease, and, indeed confusion, uncertainty, and exhaustion. Each of us represent sites at which it is likely that competing and contesting social forces–and social interests–do and will meet, and do and will 'battle it out'. These forces and interests are much larger, and far more powerful, than we are, as individuals, while what they represent is so vast and complex we cannot consciously register all that much of the totality of this impact within and upon us–meaning a great deal is inevitably thereby that of which we are unconscious. We may well never "know just why or understand" precisely whom we are, precisely whom we were, precisely whom we are becoming. And we might "never know just why or understand" no matter how conscientiously we have strived to 'know ourselves'. It can feel incredibly *haunting*–incredibly uncanny–to experience somatic intimations that 'I am other than whom and what I have thought that I am', that 'I don't know myself' and, as such, that *I cannot control myself.*

It is possible here that "And how I'll never know just why or understand," on the contrary, represents the vantage point of the character identified in these lyrics solely as 'I'. In this interpretation 'I' will 'never know just why or understand' what 'she' is undergoing, and has undergone, or what she has been attempting to explain to this 'I' in taking 'him' by the hand and turning to him to speak, in the midst of what is happening to her–loss of control. This is plausible but it is more interesting, and more consistent, as well, to attribute this line to 'she', as part of what she has to 'say' to the 'I'–it is definitely all the more stunning for her to be sharing with the 'I' of the lyrics not only that what is happening is 'I am losing control', as she is losing control, and that this has happened again (i.e., it has happened repeatedly and frequently before), but also to share 'I am not able to explain to you precisely why this is happening and has happened to me, and *never* will be able to do so'.

The second stanza continues from this point, as follows: "And she screamed out kicking on her side and said/I've lost control again/And seized up on the floor, I thought she'd die/She said I've lost control again." These four lines are then followed, in the third stanza, with a chorus that picks up on the already well-evidenced refrain: "She's lost control again/She's lost control/She's lost control again/She's lost control." The last four lines of the second stanza readily suggest an epileptic seizure, how disturbing this can be to witness, and the danger it can represent. But it is worth noting here 'she' seemingly is repeatedly saying, as this is happening, as she is 'screaming out', 'kicking on her side', 'seizing up on the floor', and appearing as if she is about 'to die': "I've lost control again." Emphasizing this line insistently and repeatedly, in the midst of this happening to her, suggests she is haunted by losing control, and by doing so again–and again. Losing control, and doing so over and over again, is what most concerns and most disturbs her, not what else is happening to her body. Exercising control, or aspiring and striving toward exercising control, has been of crucial importance, and it is a crushing blow to have to accept she has 'failed' and 'will always fail' to 'be in control' and to 'stay in control'–of *herself*. These lines suggest she is testifying from the vantage point of abjection, and perhaps, at least implicitly, on behalf of fellow 'abjects' to what is hardest to take about 'abjection'.

At the same time, such an emphasis on how horrible it is to lose control, especially in front of others, of one's body and in ways that seem to suggest even greater loss of control of one's self, when such control is always, even for those who never experience anything like epilepsy, an impossible ideal, a normative fiction, is further testimony to what an oppressive kind of society this is, where one must perform the semblance of complete self-control at all times, or one suffers far worse than 'loss of face'. Indeed one loses *place*, one is effectively sidelined from 'being able to compete', from being able to approximate the ideal of one who is able to be 'self-reliant', self-determining, 'self-actualizing', independent, fully able to take care of one's self completely by one's self as need be, strong, rugged, resilient, undaunted, unintimidated, ready to work tirelessly whenever and as ever need be, and ready to work ruthlessly whenever and as ever need be. This is precisely the kind of capitalist society, and in particular (austerity) neo-liberal capitalist society, that Robert McRuer, Ann Cvetkovich, and Avery F. Gordon all critique, and all argue is in need of transformation because of how destructive it is and long has been, and which lead all to search out 'concrete utopias'. According to Marxist philosopher Ernst Bloch, concrete utopias can be developed out of anticipatory elements, within present capitalist society, of a revolutionarily transformed society, of a society that overcomes and surpasses capitalist alienation and exploitation. Intimations of such a transformed society come whenever and wherever signs present themselves, within existing capitalist society, of social relations founded and structured on the basis of a valorization of substantive interdependence, and indeed of substantive dependence, among all so involved, such that no one is expected, individually by themselves, to always maintain tight control over themselves and where, to the contrary, 'losing control', including losing control 'again and again', is accepted as 'normal', as 'natural', as 'to be expected', and as attesting to how and why those involved are, in fact, always interdependent, and indeed always dependent upon each other.

The third stanza, the first of two choral stanzas, once more emphatically underscores the crux of what is at issue in these lyrics–losing control, and doing so again and again. The fourth stanza then reads as follows: "Well I had to 'phone her friend to state her case/And say she's lost control again/And she showed up all the errors and mistakes/And said I've lost control again/
But she expressed herself in many different ways/Until she lost control again/And walked upon the edge of no escape/And laughed I've lost control again." The first line is noteworthy insofar as 'I' not only needed to phone for assistance, for help, but "to state her case," almost as if "her friend" needed to be convinced, needed to be persuaded, to accept this case, and to act accordingly, even though, as a friend this person would seemingly be aware that 'she has lost control' before and repeatedly so, as well as what doing so is like and what needs to be done in response. It seems even 'friends' would rather deny or distance themselves from the reality of this repeated loss of control. It seems this is something they would rather pretend did not exist, and which they find too troubling to deal with when it does happen. The third line of this stanza is ambiguous insofar as the 'she' who "showed up all the errors and mistakes" could be the friend that 'I had to phone', but it also, and seemingly more likely, continues to refer to the title character. If the latter, then 'she showing up all the errors and mistakes' might refer to 'showing up all the errors and mistakes' of people like this 'friend'. It might refer to all of those who would rather push disabled people aside and treat us as less than human, as better not seen and not heard, and who certainly would not accept anything resembling 'the social model' of disability according to which society causes disability, and creates disabled people, by not providing equitable means of access for those differently embodied and whose impairments are not treated as equally for instance as that of people who need to wear eyeglasses or contact lenses. "All the errors and mistakes" might reference a long and continuing history of social failure adequately to do justice to the needs of people with impairments such as epilepsy.

If, on the contrary, this line references 'the friend' 'showing up all the errors and mistakes', it would seem this friend is acting the converse of a true friend by venting against her friend in need, at the time of her friend's need, by blaming her, the title character, for her neediness. It makes more sense, however, to me, to read this line as representative of what the title character is doing, and in this connection 'showing up' suggests 'putting to shame', which means 'putting to shame' the abuse and neglect disabled people suffer and have suffered.

"But she expressed herself in many different ways" suggests the title character has much to share and that, indeed, she is doing so, in significant part, in embodied form, and in particular by way of, that is through, her impairment and her disability–because this condition 'speaks', and not only of human fragility and vulnerability but also of the value and necessity of human responsibility, in community, of each for each other. This condition 'speaks' of how and why we need to recognize and respond to our actual interdependence, and indeed our actual dependence, by transforming our social relations and institutions so that respect, appreciation, and support for this interdependence, and indeed this dependence, becomes genuinely substantive, foundational, pervasive, and equitably inclusive. Until that happens, people like the title character in these lyrics will continue to 'walk upon the edge of no escape'. This image suggests remaining in a perpetually precarious position, without any realistic hope of improvement, and that, to the contrary, it is only a matter of time before one falls off or over the edge.

The line that reads "And laughed I've lost control" suggests a delirium that sets in once one realizes escape is impossible, and one has no control over one's destiny. But it also suggests a kind of courageous defiance in the face of absurdity: since nothing else is possible, since no reason for hope is available, one might as well laugh at what becomes thereby 'a cosmic joke' rather than merely 'a joke that fate has perpetrated against oneself'. This line might in addition suggest a kind of 'wisdom' only available to, only grasped by, those who recognize and accept 'they have nothing to lose', and perhaps 'never really had anything to lose'. These are people pushed to the social margins as 'the disturbing', 'the shocking', 'the frightening', 'the embarrassing', 'the freakish', 'the grotesque', 'the monstrous', 'the abject', and 'the unwanted'. Their impairments are perceived as rendering them less than fully human, as tragic objects of pity or as comic objects of ridicule.

And then the lyrics conclude with the second and final chorus: "She's lost control again/She's lost control/She's lost control again/She's lost control."

In the extended version, the new final stanza that shows up right after that second and final chorus reads as follows: "I could live a little better with the myths and the lies/When the darkness broke in, I just broke down and cried/I could live a little in the wider line/When the change is gone, when the urge is gone/To lose control/When here we come." Now the 'I' of the lyrics steps to the forefront and adds 'his' own chilling coda. "I could live a little better with the myths and the lies" suggests that this narrator-protagonist recognizes what are 'myths and lies' and that these are hard to live with, perhaps especially hard to live with in recognizing them as 'myths and lies', but at the least likely all the harder to live with because these myths and lies are potent, and they are myths and lies those at the heights of social power use to maintain this position of theirs, including by convincing those with far less and far more limited social power that the latter maintain much greater social power than the latter actually do. At the same time it is puzzling to propose I *could* live *a little better* with these myths and lies, because this implies an 'if' in the sense of 'I could do so, if X were so'. Perhaps 'I could live a little better with the myths and lies' if I encountered some way of convincingly pretending, to myself, that this is actually a genuinely caring society, that takes care of all who need care when and as they need it, but I cannot do so. Instead, in 'my' experience what 'I' have encountered is 'the darkness' that 'broke in' and revealed to me the 'uncaring' truth about this society: it is the kind of society that tolerates people falling down, falling apart, falling to pieces, without doing anything to help them back up and to keep holding them up. 'The darkness' represents the 'dark awareness' that this is what people like the title character do face, and will continue to face, as nothing promises to get any better for people like them in the foreseeable future, while what individuals like this 'I' can do, isolated and alone, amount to extremely little, and are in fact not only too little but also too late.

This is certainly a situation I can identify with experiencing myself: being overwhelmed by a situation of enormous suffering, by a situation that is devastating in the harm it encompasses, yet feeling like nothing can and will be done about it, and I myself can't do anything to make what is needed happen. In the United States today, this is, for example, how I often feel, despite continuing to

972

do whatever I can, for well over forty years contributing as an active support of organized efforts to combat gun violence and implement gun control, in recognizing the Republican Party continues steadfastly to deny guns need to be controlled, let alone restricted and eliminated (with the state buying these back from citizens and then destroying them); that guns do kill far too many people far too often and far too easily; that it is absurd to argue more guns leads to fewer killings as well as that all schools and many other public places should become 'hardened' fortresses; and that it is absurd as well to argue that people, including as young as 18 years of age, 'need' to own military assault weapons.

"I could live a little in the wider line" suggests the 'I' of these lyrics 'could' do so, again, if certain conditions were met that are not being met and which 'he' does not expect to be met. 'The wider line' might refer to the more conventional pathway, or even the more commonsensical way of just calmly (and complacently) going about everyday life and 'not ever getting too worked up' about anything, especially anything beyond one's immediate control, or seeming immediate control–the socially normative way to be. "When the change is gone, when the urge is gone/To lose control. When here we come" can suggest I 'could' accept this if I were provided some convincing reason to 'live a little better with the myths and the lies', to ignore that these are myths and lies, to pretend that they are not myths and lies or only minor and relatively inconsequential, relatively harmless myths and lies. But 'I' cannot do this. 'He' might do this when 'the change' is 'gone', when it is over, when 'the urge is gone to lose control'. But again, this is not so. 'Losing control', and indeed seeking out and embracing losing control, while readily recognizing this as dangerous and frightening, suggests breaking out from, breaking free of, resisting and refusing normative expectations and demands–and being willing to share, including publicly, what one is taught and persistently told again and again 'to keep to one's self', 'to keep private', 'to keep in check', 'to hold within', 'to maintain as secret'. 'I' cannot accede to denial, including self-denial, of how messy and out of control 'I' in fact am. 'Let it out', share it, and in sharing that one is not in control of one's self, that one can't control one's self, that one is fragile and vulnerable and needy and scared, one is contributing to forging the basis for a much different kind of community, and society, even if this will come too late to save the one who is here making this contribution. In response to extreme social repression, and stifling social constraints, the urge to just let go of it all can become immense, and eventually cannot be stopped, even if this appears to lead to chaos.

"When here we come" enlists the listener as joining with the 'I', the narrator and co-protagonist of these lyrics, in 'losing control', in proceeding forward to embrace doing exactly that. We won't be held back, we won't remain inside, we won't hide away, we won't pretend and deny, we won't conform to what we are supposed to be and how we are supposed to present and conduct ourselves. We don't know for sure what will happen to us as a result, although we suspect the worst, but we proceed nonetheless. In order to make a difference, a meaningful difference, an impactful difference, sometimes you need to take the risk of losing control, of not being in control, of not knowing what one is doing and of where one is headed, of not being able to explain and account for one's self–and this can indeed include pushing to the forefront one's own impairments and disabilities, one's own fragilities and vulnerabilities, one's neediness and precariousness, one's own agony and desperation.

One further connection: as someone fascinated with 'extreme' art and determined to make 'extreme' art, Curtis was interested in 'extreme' experiences of multiple kinds. Despite how much damage his epilepsy and his prescribed treatment regime caused him, Curtis was undoubtedly familiar with 'the aura' that can occur in the midst of or preceding an epileptic seizure, and how this can feel as if it represents a transportation to a fantastically different realm, however fleeting and however much afterward one feels terribly confused, unsettled, tired, sore, and sick, including for a long time thereafter. So it is possible Curtis is at least elliptically referencing such an aura, referencing perception and experience of such an aura, and referencing as well connections with other kinds of visions and visionary experiences, many of which have often at least in many religious traditions been considered 'sacred'. Undoubtedly 'auras' can be all too easily and all too problematically romanticized, and I certainly don't want to do that myself, but I can attest that many times, in the midst of epileptic episodes, or in pivotal moments as part of them, this is indeed what I have experienced. I know these vary widely, but for me they typically involve feeling as if I have been transported to a fantastically different realm of being, and that in this brief instant everything becomes completely calm, peaceful, serene, and indeed blissful. I feel safe, protected, sheltered, welcomed, integrated, and strangely 'at home' in ways that do not readily correspond with any other sense of 'home' I have ever experienced. Yes, even so, upon the next shift in my conscious state I feel bewildered and all the more frightened by the contrast, as well as by how much it has felt as if I have been 'well beyond the exercise of any even semblance of control' over where I have been taken, by what or whom, and why so. In sum, however, this can be tantalizing state for those fascinated with 'the extreme' such as Ian Curtis, all too well aware of the risks and dangers that come with this kind of experience–as he knew by way of what happened to the young woman who inspired the lyrics to "She's Lost Control" that it is possible to die from an epileptic seizure or at least to suffer an extremely serious injury.

The structure of the *Unknown Pleasures* version of "She's Lost Control" proceeds as follows:

1.   Instrumental Opening: 0:00-0:21.

a.   Part One: 0:00->0:08. Initiation.

b.   Part Two: 0:09->0:21. Embarkation.

2.   First Vocal Verse Section: 0:22->0:47. Specification.

3.   Early Instrumental Bridge One: 0:48–>1:08. Registration.

4.   Second Vocal Verse Section: 1:09–>1:33. Elaboration.

5.   First Vocal Chorus Section: 1:34–>1:47. Amplification.

6.   Instrumental Bridge Two, Main Instrumental Bridge: 1:48–>2:27. Acceleration and Intensification.

7.   Third Vocal Verse Section: 2:28–>2:53. Complication.

8.   Second Vocal Chorus Section: 2:54–>3:06. Further Amplification.

9.   Closing Instrumental Section: 3:07–>3:52. Climax and Denouement.

The major change, meanwhile, with the extended version of "She's Lost Control" is the insertion of a third instrumental bridge, followed by a fourth vocal verse section, after the end of the second vocal chorus section and preceding the closing instrumental section, as this version of the song in turn lasts approximately four minutes and fifty-three seconds. In this version I describe the third bridge section as contributing by 'Deepening', the fourth vocal verse section as constituting the 'Climax', and the closing instrumental section contributing the 'Denouement'.

In terms of instrumentation, in the *Unknown Pleasures* version of "She's Lost Control" I hear the following:

1.   Drums and Percussion:

a.   Layered synthesizer snare drum sounds that also sound pronouncedly hollow (in an early version of an electronic drum pad), sounding somewhat between a wood block and a wood bell, while also notably affected by significant use of digital delay.

b.   Aerosol spray.

c.   Bass drum (with a thinned out timbre) and later seemingly a conventional snare drum also in an unusual backgrounded role.

d.   Occasional rolls (across toms).
The drum sounds here achieve Hannett's aim of not bleeding together, while the use of digital delay allows them to ping-pong across multiple simultaneous positions within the soundbox.

2.   High pitch register bass guitar provides the initial source of the melody and then continues to play the principal melodic line in accompaniment and support of the vocal once the vocal takes the lead role in sounding the melody, while also moving back to assume the lead role in subsequent instrumental passages. This bass guitar line strikes me as just about the highest in pitch that we do hear from Peter Hook in Joy Division songs, even as he usually plays high.

3.   Vocal provides the second source of the melody and takes the lead in so doing whenever it is sounding. The vocal here is treated with ample reverb, and seemingly an additional chorus effect as well as being double- or even multi- tracked.

4.   Guitar provides a gritty harmonic fill. Commentators have noted Bernard Sumner playing barre chords in this song while some guitar tabs recommend using overdrive to play this song and I

also detect elements approaching para-melody in portions of the main instrumental bridge and the instrumental conclusion.

5.	Low bass guitar in the background provides harmonic fill but also contributes to sounding the melody in the middle portion of the main instrumental bridge as well as in the instrumental conclusion.

6.	Studio synthesized sounds near the end of the song, or sounds that might also correspond to a source from another element of the total percussion set up.

With the extended version of "She's Lost Control," the synth drums sound considerably different, closer to conventional drums, with pronounced echo effect, and with a thicker overall timbre, sounding closer to a hi-hat instead of an aerosol spray while an additional tinkly sound periodically shows up as if from a jingle bell or by lightly tapping cymbals. The vocal sounds different, too, echoed once again but not as elaborately so, and without the voice as radically modulated as in the *Unknown Pleasures* version. The guitar timbre is different as well, not as brutally harsh in timbre, and it does not show up as often, except in instrumental bridges and in the instrumental conclusion. The bass guitar, especially the lower bass guitar line, sounds different in timbre too although closer to *The Unknown Pleasures* version than the preceding instruments do. Here the song adds what sounds like a synthesizer keyboard, that is especially notable when it contributes a high-pitched swirling to careening strings sound, and this seems to correspond to what Curtis himself played when performing this song live.

In terms of the conventional layers of the popular rock song, we do hear an explicit beat layer, a melodic layer, and a harmonic fill layer. It is somewhat difficult to ascribe a functional bass layer to this song, because the bass guitar is primarily providing (and even for significant durations carrying) the melody, while the drums and additional percussion instruments don't thereby lock together with a bass guitar part as much as would be the case if the bass guitar were primarily contributing to the groove. The explicit beat layer's distinctiveness as well as the persistent simplicity and continuous repetition of the melody make those the two most prominent layers. Sharing of the melody between the bass guitar and the vocal is common for Joy Division as is the guitar primarily contributing harmonic fill. The drumming and associated percussion well exemplifies the experimental and innovative characteristics of Martin Hannett's production. In sum, the layers here seem to be principally three, most often: a high bass guitar line either together with or without the vocal contributing the melody; the guitar supported by studio treatments and effects as well as the low bass guitar contributing harmonic fill; and the drums and associated percussion contributing the explicit beat layer. All do feel definitively *layered*, yes, in the sense of clearly distinct and separate although also tightly complimentary. The extended version of "She's Lost Control" is similar in terms of functional layers, although the additional synthesizer keyboard offers a further prominent contribution to the harmonic fill layer, in providing texture.

In terms of positioning within the soundbox, I hear the drum and percussion sounds spread and even 'shooting' across the soundbox although most notably positioned toward the horizontal edges, right and left, approximately mid-height, while the synthesizer snare and aerosol sounds I hear closer to the front than the other drum sounds, which I hear slightly lower down as well as further back. I hear the vocal positioned centrally, in terms of the horizontal axis, mid to high in terms of the vertical axis, and close to the front in terms of perceived depth, or according to location within perceived three-dimensional 'planes'. The guitar seems to come at me from both sides, slightly down from the center in terms of height, as well as somewhat further back in terms of depth than the bass guitar but it does move closer as well as higher along the sides, above the middle, and becomes more prominent in doing so, in the main instrumental bridge and in the conclusion. The principal bass guitar line I hear somewhat below mid-center and the vocal in terms of height, closer to the center along the horizontal axis than the guitar, and fairly close to the front in terms of depth. The final synthesized sound seems high, vertically, and located variously across a singular horizontal expanse, left, right, and center. Overall, it is striking to me how close to the edges, horizontally, the sound feels as if it is pushed, and how much feels as if it is pushed simultaneously to both sides, or simultaneously left, right, and center. The soundbox does feel spacious, and indeed cavernous, as if this is stretched out, an inflated space, while I feel both considerable depth as considerable lateral expanse. A key change, as aforementioned, occurs in the main instrumental bridge and the instrumental conclusion when the guitar becomes louder and more prominent, as it moves upward and closer to the front of the soundbox.

In the extended version I hear the initial drum and percussion sounds close to the center on a vertical axis and fairly close to the front, with the snare drum higher than the bass drum, and more evidently doubled or otherwise echoed symmetrically than is the case with the bass drum. Later on, a light bell, or perhaps light cymbal, manifests further to the sides and down slightly, as well as further back. The principal bass guitar I hear above center, slightly more prominent to the right, and fairly close to the front, but not as close to the front as the vocal. The lower bass guitar comes from somewhat further down and again more prominent to the right. The vocal I hear slightly above center, more prominent to the left, even though it is echoed left, right, and center, as well as closer to the front than the bass guitar. The guitar I hear further back, and lower, especially to the right. The synthesizer keyboard I hear high and principally to the left, and further back than the bass guitar, the snare, and the vocal. The layers do not seem quite as neatly separated here, and the instruments don't seem as multiply positioned across the soundbox, while the soundbox also does not feel as cavernously stretched out and inflated. And the soundbox feels closer to what might be associated with an intimate live performance.

Taking these elements of structure and instrumentation into account in exploring possible viable interpretations of meaning in relation to "She's Lost Control," it makes sense to highlight defamiliarizing dimensions, coming principally by way of innovations in drumming and percussion as well as in further use of electronic instruments and synthesized sounds, as part of a song that is otherwise simple and especially simply reiterative in terms of melody and rhythm. The former add to a feeling of an estranging kind of situation or experience. Further estranging, or attesting to the estranging, is how monotonic the vocal remains overall, how deadpan and cold it sounds, as well as how elaborately echoed to the point of verging on resembling a chorus of voices. The persistently recurrent melodic line and metrical pattern underscore a sense of dealing with something that is happening, has happened, and will happen, over and over again. This seems apt in conveying an uncanny sense of engaging at once with what is both highly familiar and highly unfamiliar. In

977

addition, here it feels as if we encounter virtual vocal and synthesizer 'ghosts' as well as 'ghostly' effects, treatments, and innovations in relation to what has been the previously orthodox rock drum kit.

In order to 'crip', it is necessary to invoke the familiar in a way that exposes what is unfamiliar within the familiar but is commonly not recognized or acknowledged as such, while rendering the familiar all the further unfamiliar–i.e., critically *refamiliarized*, made to appear radically other than what it conventionally appears to be. It is at the same time necessary to expose what is widely accepted without question, widely taken for granted, as natural and normal to be anything but natural and normal; this is instead what has been constructed to appear so, and thereby be accepted as so. Cripping destabilizes what is accepted as simultaneously norm and ideal while at the same time exposing the damaging effects of its establishment and enforcement as such. In "She's Lost Control" both the regularly recurrent melody and meter feel oppressively confining and constraining, while haunted by ghostly accompaniments that accentuate a sense of discomfort, unease, and disturbance. The sounds, patterns of sounds, and deployments of sounds simulate an inescapably monotonous cycle of repetition mixed together with elements accentuating feelings of alienation, anxiety, and dread. At the same time, these sounds, patterns of sounds, and deployments of sounds convey the sense this is not a natural state, but rather one fabricated to serve the interests of an oppressive force, in maintaining and reproducing oppression. The song is defamiliarizing in the sense that is both conjures a sense of enacting the broad contours of a typical day, of the ordinary and the everyday, while showing how unnatural and abnormal this kind of day, and what one does over its course, continues to feel, even if this kind of day recurs over and over again.

Elements of strangeness abound, and these contribute a sense that the subject of the song, or the music as persona, is relentless in following along but at the same time resisting while doing–by failing or perhaps even refusing to go along with a guise that falsifies how oppressive this cycle continuously is, how oppressive it continuously feels. Past, present, and future feel as if they run together, interminably, without meaningful distinction, while alternatives to this state appear only as glimmers of abstract (im)possibility. As such the song feels dystopian while not altogether giving up on the viability of utopian moments of 'profane illumination' and of 'blasting' through this spatio-temporal state of virtual incarceration. Especially by way of the vocal, the song feels as if it recounts reaching a point where it is difficult to feel any more, as if one has been too long and too far strangled of all emotion. Perhaps the song registers what this kind of situation and experience is like, what it feels like, honestly and without pretending it is any better than it is, even if 'feels' here means feeling as if one is being steadily and has been steadily robbed of one's capacity to feel, as if one is losing connection with one's own feeling self, as if this dimension of whom one ostensibly still is has been and is being taken over by, and become subject to the control of, a hostile external force.

Moving on, next, to consider loudness, in the *Unknown Pleasures* version of "She's Lost Control" what is most notable is the guitar becoming louder mid-way through the main instrumental bridge and again in the instrumental conclusion. Otherwise, loudness remains largely consistent, including evenly balanced in terms of the relative loudness of the instruments, although it is also worth noting that the final studio synthesized sound becomes strikingly loud as it enters and contributes. With the extended version of "She's Lost Control," the initial percussion sound seems somewhat louder overall than the high bass guitar as does the vocal, while the guitar volume never increases to the extent it does in the *Unknown Pleasures* version. Again, overall little changes in loudness over the course of the song, but we do hear the synthesizer keyboard sounds and the tinkly percussion sounds, because more space seems to exist for them, oddly enough, than in the *Unknown Pleasures* version, and the former of those two sounds somewhat louder near the end of the song.

The time signature for "She's Lost Control" is 4/4, while I hear the *Unknown Pleasures* version sounding 164 bpm and I hear the extended version sounding 178 bpm. Other commentators typically identify the song as ranging between 140 and 144 bpm, especially the *Unknown Pleasures* version, although we both recognize an even faster pace in live versions, up to 192 bpm or more (along with the latter following a more scattershot and less meticulously precise rhythm). The basic metrical pattern here is 'one-and-two-and-three-four' or 'eighth note-eighth note-eighth note-eighth note-quarter note-quarter note' as played by the drums and associated percussion instruments. Occasionally, when rolls show up, this shifts to measures containing sixteenth note runs consisting of this pattern: 'one-and-two-ee-and-three-ee-and-uh- four-ee-and-uh'. The vocal primarily sounds all eighth notes, with periodic ties mid-way in the second of every two lines, interrupted by rests of typically 1 and 1/4 beats between every two lines in the verses and in the choruses 1 and 1/4 beats between each line. This pattern is highly regular as is that of the bass guitar which principal sounds the following hypermetrical pattern: measure one–quarter note, then six eighth notes; measure two–eight eighths notes with a tie between the fourth and fifth eighth notes. Over and over the bass guitar follows this same pattern, with a slight variation in the instrumental bridges and the conclusion: two measures all eighth notes, first with ties between the second and third and also the sixth and seventh of these eighth notes, followed by a measure of one quarter note and six eighth notes, and followed after that with a measure of eight eighth notes, before then repeating. The guitar meanwhile sounds all eighth note chords.

Liam Maloy, in his careful reading of "She's Lost Control," describes and analyzes pitch more precisely than I do here, and I recommend his article for anyone interested in this dimension of the song. But I nonetheless highlight here a few significant features. The pitch direction of the bass guitar sounding the melody involves a slightly yet steadily downward sweep, while remaining largely at the same pitch, and the vocal involves much the same although the vocal line does move slightly down and then up in pitch while otherwise remaining at the same pitch. It is notable how much the melody stays at the same pitch, or more precisely on the same note, and thereby remains largely constant and closely contained–other than in small intervals, pitch stays in place much more than it moves up or down. We hear no jumping, pushing, or straining in pitch by the vocal in the final vocal passages, as otherwise is common with Curtis in many Joy Division songs. The guitar here likewise seems primarily to move in place, creating a gritty rumbling sound across a relatively short interval range, but when it does verge upon a para-melodic role, the guitar sounds as if it is climbing, step by step, while the studio synthesized sound does much the same when it shows up in the conclusion to the *Unknown Pleasures* version. In the extended version of "She's Lost Control," the synthesizer keyboard sound is high-pitched and indeed swirls upward in pitch. Finally, commentators disagree on which precise key they recommend playing this song, but D minor and B minor are the most common recommendations, and the song clearly does make the best sense played in a minor key.

Curtis's vocal delivery in "She's Lost Control" contains many by now familiar elements, including a deep, darkened tone that is simultaneously both hard and harsh yet not rough. Here a limited range is covered, and the use of reverb, added choral effect, and multi-tracking is pronounced. Also, Curtis's voice is modulated differently across the two recordings. Curtis keeps close to staying on pitch, although trending flat. He is regular and consistent rhythmically. As aforementioned, Curtis's voice feels deadened in the sense of monotonic and drudge-like. Curtis appears broadly aware of the other instruments and the context of song as a whole while narrowly concentrated on his precise role. It is difficult, simply by listening to the qualities of his vocal, to ascertain what his stance versus what he is singing about might be as his vocal seems to give little away, including little in terms of affect, but it makes sense to interpret the way he here sounds as if he is conveying a sense of feeling resigned, exhausted, and numbed.

Timbre is of keen importance in "She's Lost Control." It is as much as ever the distinctive timbres of the instrumental and studio components, as well as their combined timbre, and the difference in timbres in the two versions, that is especially compelling of attention and interest. Yes, the timbres of "She's Lost Control" do contribute a feeling that might be aptly ascribed as a spaced out disco feel while elements suggestive of rumbling, spinning, and climbing yet largely stepping in place are prominent. Timbre in "She's Lost Control" contributes to a sense of moving in a tense fashion, ping-ponging within a close space, as well as an almost martial feel suggestive of a forced march, in response to an externally imposed and mandated pace and meter. The timbres here also are suggestive of gritty, grinding and grating qualities as well as overall of hard, harsh, cold, and brutal ones as well. Overall, attack offers a stronger impression than decay, sustain, and release.

Considering matters of loudness, rhythm, pitch, vocal delivery, and timbre, in dialogue with key ideas from McRuer, Cvetkovich, and Gordon, leads me to suggest the following, beginning with McRuer. In relation to a 'crip' or 'cripping' mode and direction of critique, "She's Lost Control" suggests how representations from disabled vantage points can be strange and disturbing as well as hard to know how to make sense of and respond to from an able-bodied vantage point, or more precisely, a compulsory able-bodied vantage point that posits 'able-bodiedness' as simultaneous norm and ideal. The song is thoroughly anti-sentimental and thus suggests little if anything to do with either pity for the disabled or with 'inspiration porn'. "She's Lost Control" makes sense in relation to recognizing how living as disabled in ableist society and culture feels as if one has lost control, and has done so over and over again, as well as if one is thoroughly and closely controlled. This can include not only control over one's own body and how to make use of it, but also of the opportunity to speak for or to otherwise advocate on behalf of one's self and be recognized and understood in so doing. From this kind of alienated vantage point one can readily feel as if one is overwhelmingly regarded as strange in the sense of embarrassing, disturbing, threatening, and unwanted.

In relation to neo-liberalism this song can suggest gaping holes in an ostensible 'social safety net' and in collective commitment to provide for 'social welfare', as well as suggesting this provision, insofar as it exists at all, is highly uneven and inequitable. This kind of society places individual interests ahead of and sets these against those of the collective, endorsing 'survival of the fittest', 'might makes right', distinguishing between 'good' 'strivers' versus 'bad' 'skivers', meritocracy, and leaving many behind–callously and cruelly neglected, ignored and forgotten.

In terms of depression, "She's Lost Control" can be usefully interpreted as resonating with how living with disabling conditions in an ableist society and culture can readily lead to depression, and in other words how depression and ableism are interlinked. Depression can readily follow when caught in a vicious cycle with no escape where one has lost control over and over again and expects one will continue to do so interminably yet one cannot even begin to explain why this has happened, is happening, and will continue to happen. When badly depressed, moreover, one can often feel as if one exercises no effective control over one's self, even one's body, and that indeed control has been altogether lost, lost again and again, and that there is no way out. Also the song suggests when social responsibility for causing depression is not recognized, or ignored, or rejected, this can make the experience of depression all that much worse. The song, in sounding estranged, controlled, cold, bleak, and detached, embodies a sonic correlative to the visceral impact of what is seriously wrong in such a society, registering the damage at an affective level–again to the point of feeling as if one has altogether lost control, over and over again, of whom and what one is, not to mention whom and what one might have been.

In relation to 'complex personhood, the 'she' of this song comes across as both complex but as difficult to grasp as such given the severe limitations of available frames for understanding 'people like her', even for recognizing 'people like her' at all, because even ostensible friends would rather turn away from facing up to what 'people like her' do have to offer while refusing to offer the kind of help 'people like her' need to be able to share the best they are and can be. At the same time, 'she' conveys a complex response to loss of control, and to a larger lack of any control over what happens as part of a larger community, by acknowledging this for what it is, and that is happens repeatedly and incessantly, while still striving to reach out and share insight, potentially important *critical* insight, that she possesses even as she struggles to render this insight intelligible.

In terms of 'haunting' and 'ghosts', 'she' certainly appears to haunt the 'I' of the lyrics, and us as well as 'I' shares this haunting with us, including how far 'he' has come to recognize and experience a convergence with where 'she' has been at. And it does make sense to interpret 'she' as attesting to more than her own uniquely individual story alone, while challenging us to figure out what this might represent, and challenging us to determine what we can and should do, ethically, in response. The lyrics contain images suggestive of violence, while the sounds, patterns of sounds, and deployments of sound suggest the same, and this could viably make sense as referencing the violence involved in not attending to the needs of those who are all too easily neglected, ignored, forgotten, disparaged, marginalized, and excluded, such as on account of how ableist society and culture treats disabled people.

Turning now to discuss avenues of musical affect at greater length, making use of Arnie Cox theorization of the same, let's begin with mimetic participation. As I listen to "She's Lost Control" I feel the music as persona engaged in persistent exertion. The percussion feels as if this involves somewhat greater effort than other contributing sound sources because of its somewhat unusual constituent features and how these are so precisely separated. Yet this percussion is nonetheless regular and the hypermetrical pattern here is brief. Persistence and consistency of exertion is, overall, pronounced in "She's Lost Control," with no passages standing out as involving markedly increasing or decreasing levels of perceived exertion. Perhaps, if the latter happens at all, it does in the main instrumental bridge and the instrumental conclusion when the guitar becomes louder and moves more prominently to the foreground, but the bass guitar in particular feels constant in terms of level of exertion throughout. Exertion does not feel particularly complex; however, such narrowly recurrent patterns of sound do require a disciplined focus in order to remain that consistent. In relation to success or failure of the perceived exertion, it feels to me as if the song does what sets out to do, and indeed as if it is not aiming for or convinced of the viability of aiming for any kind of 'success'.

It is easy to lock into this song, with each of the major elements, consciously as well as unconsciously mimetically participating: with the melodic line as sounded by the bass guitar and by the vocal; with the regular rhythm of the drum kit; and with the climbing sequence from the guitar. It readily feels to me, in listening closely to "She's Lost Control," that I am co-participating, yet in an eerily self-estranging manner.

In the extended version, the drums come across even more as if the persistent recurrence of the limited pattern they sound nonetheless requires a disciplined effort. The duration of exertion is again persistent, with the guitar contributing less duration of effort than in the *Unknown Pleasures* version and the synthesizer keyboard only showing up to manifest exertion later in the song. This version of the song feels no more versus less complex in terms of the exertion involved, no more or less concerned with success of failure of exertion, and just as readily encouraging of mimetic participation as the *Unknown Pleasures* version.

In listening to "She's Lost Control," I hear the song itself, along with me, anticipate some kind of conclusion yet at the same time a conclusion without any decisive resolution, in the sense of change in situation or atmosphere. I anticipate as a listener that I will continue to repeat the same patterns of imitation of the music all the way through. Once these first show up, I readily anticipate the recurring directions of the climbing pattern from the guitar and from the swirling strings and other odd synthesizer noises in the extended version. The music as persona and I anticipate feeling dread that becomes so enveloping that it feels impossible to imagine a state beyond dread. Perhaps this corresponds to feeling like one is compelled to perpetually reenact performance of one's own 'living death'.

Expression is complicated with "She's Lost Control" because the vocal in particular feels as if it is conveying exhaustion meets resignation. In "She's Lost Control" I hear expression of loss of control as resulting from being controlled *by*, as resulting from having control taken away from one, or, all the more chilling, as if the ostensible 'promise' of control turns out to always have been a lie. "She's Lost Control" feels if it expresses fatalism, nihilism, and inescapable doom.

In terms of acoustic impact, "She's Lost Control" feels close and intimate yet as surrounding me from positions that are spaced out and clearly separated although carefully choreographed in how the sounds from these spaces perform in relation to each other as the song moves briskly along. Overall, the timbres feel concentrated while their strength comes via attack, as opposed to decay, sustain, and release. Everything feels set in place, set in *its* place, which offers a jarring contrast with what the lyrics describe and with Ian Curtis's frentic dancing while singing this song in performing it live.

The song raises more questions *for* analysis than it offers analysis in process. For example: why deadpan, why monotonic? Why relentlessly recurrent, and why constrained? The lyrics evince signs of analysis, as both 'she' and 'I' attempt to analyze, but also attest to limits in being able to do so, to find terms to fit what their analysis might lead them toward. In relation to these characters, questions *for* analysis include all of the following. What is 'she' attempting to get across, and why does she reach out to 'I' in attempting to do so? What explains the connection between 'she' and 'I', and does this connection change as well as how so, in particular as a result of her reaching out as she does and of 'I' attempting to respond? What kind of control did she have, if she ever had any, and why has she lost this, again and again? What secrets does she have to share–and of what value might these be? What force is fighting against 'her', against 'I', and against 'us' in analyzing what is happening, and what has happened, as well as what might this mean along with what might be its significance? Why recount this scenario, concerning this character/these characters, in this form, and with this kind of tone and atmosphere? As a result of my own effort at analysis it makes sense to me to propose she has lost control because this control has been taken from her, perhaps even long ago, almost from the beginning, and likely even back when she imagined she maintained control but did not. My analysis leads me to propose this loss of control is the result of living in a society that prevents particular kinds of people from exercising control–it does not provide necessary accommodation/access, it does not provide necessary support/care, it is ultimately callously indifferent/unconcerned, and it even 'abjectifies' those whose embodiments, and whose bodyminds, depart from the normative sufficient that it becomes hard, if not impossible, to hide these departures and to pretend they can fully conform to the ways people are normatively expected to present and comport themselves, mentally and physically.

I associate what I hear in this song, and what it makes me think (about) and feel, with epilepsy, panic attacks, dissociative episodes/disssociative disorders, and comparable kinds of conditions that repeatedly lead one to feel as if one is losing control of one's body, as if one is losing control of one's mind, as if one is losing control of one's 'bodymind', and as if one is in effect a puppet whose strings are pulled by a powerful external force. I associate what I hear in this song with being caught up in a monotonously recurrent cycle over which one exercises no effective control and which both constrains one and robs one of one's vitality. Perhaps this corresponds to experience working many jobs where this is exactly what conditions are like, and especially *feel* like. It might also refer to feeling bound by overwhelming obligations to something else, such as to family, community, and what is socially dominant and culturally normative. The song is suggestive of what it might feel like to be caught up in an environment that resembles a classic assembly line, or of otherwise feeling like one is compelled to act as an automaton or a robot. This could be any situation where one is told what one must do, when, how, with whom, and for what end, without being able to influence let alone determine any of that one's self, and where one is told the same day in and day out for years on end. The result can be loss of a sense of one's self as independently capable, as maintaining a will of one's own, as being able to determine for one's self what one wants and needs, of being capable of any substantive exercise of creative imagination, and of being able to hope and dream, or even to plan and aspire.

It can be taboo to suggest loss of control happens inexorably over and over again, with no way out, and, all the worse, that it is impossible to explain how and why this is happening, has been happening, and will continue to happen. "She's Lost Control" explores taboo not only by evoking what an epileptic seizure or similar kind of 'episode' or 'event' can be like, for both one experiencing this and one witnessing it, but also treating this occurrence in such a seemingly deadened manner, suggesting nothing can or will be done to help and that others are either incapable of helping or don't care to help. An *aesthetic* pleasure can nevertheless arise from identifying with this taboo, this peak of alienation–identifying with loss of control becoming loss of self. An *aesthetic pleasure* can arise in taking on taboo in imagining being left alone with one's own weakness, precariousness, and frailty as one falls down–and falls apart.

"She's Lost Control" makes use of synthesizer sounds as well as unorthodox percussion sounds to suggest an 'unnatural' state where invisible and intangible forces are at play. Efforts at reaching out and striving to explain what is happening meanwhile feel ephemeral as does the prospect of obtaining and sharing insight. "She's Lost Control" suggests what it is like for another person, even right in front of one, to become effectively invisible, or otherwise imperceptible. "She's Lost Control" suggests losing control of ability to feel, to be able to experience tangibility: one becomes unable to feel, literally–unable to experience tactile sensations 'normally'. Vulnerability is simulated here, what's more, by means of the absence of visual and tactile means of expressing and communicating, and of only relying on sounds, patterns of sounds, and deployments of sounds to express and communicate what it feels like *not* to be able to express and communicate intelligibly at all. "She's Lost Control" suggests a connection develops between 'She', 'I', and 'us', which might indeed represent a spreading and a sharing of loss of control, including over means and modes of signification concerning control and loss of control. This might encompass a spreading and a sharing of loss of control over our lives and over what we aspire to do with or in them. This might encompass a spreading and a sharing of loss of control over whom we are, over whom we experience ourselves to be, and even of ourselves *as selves*. Yet, at the same time, a residual mournful resistance is enacted here by way of testifying to an overwhelming bleakness while pulling no punches in doing so.

In sum, what kind of subject, from what kind of position, do I hear addressing me as I listen to and reflect upon "She's Lost Control"? How do I hear this subject calling upon me to respond? How do I so by making connections with "She's Lost Control" in relation to what the song prompts me to think (about) and to feel? In reflecting on these question it is important, first, to note well that the music as persona is not equivalent with either the 'she' or the 'I' in the lyrics, and if anything is not caught up within the immediate details of the specific drama these characters share. The music as persona embodies a feeling of relentlessly monotonous bleakness in response to a situation, and more precisely a condition, that is both perpetually recurrent and next to impossible to escape–because there is no alternative to which to escape. The music as persona comes across as suggestive of loss of control but even more than this of loss of control due to being controlled, due to having control denied and taken away. Yet a slight undercurrent of resistance remains and even a glimmer of utopian imagination and aspiration, in the face of the otherwise seemingly impossible, enacted through persisting despite ostensibly overwhelming hopelessness and through attesting to precisely how bleak this situation, or condition, is–and, especially, feels like.

"She's Lost Control" prompts me to reflect in what ways and to what extent I am complicit with and indeed even responsible for lack of necessary care, and of necessary caring–of not doing enough to respond to, and even to recognize, those in the most pressing and urgent need of care, and of caring. "She's Lost Control" prompts me to reflect upon my complicity with compulsory able-bodiedness, as norm and ideal, and with marginalization and exclusion of the disabled, despite my own experience, including in the form of internalized ableism and shame concerning my disability. "She's Lost Control," at the same time, however, prompts me to think about the many ways and the considerable extent to which loss of control, over and over again, corresponds with what has been my own experience, as disabled due to 'un-visible disability' in the form of chronic illness. At the same time, "She's Lost Control" prompts me to think about concrete areas of contemporary social life, concrete dimensions of contemporary social institutions, and concrete manifestations of contemporary social interests maintaining and exercising considerable power that are not only effectively indifferent to the condition and experience of those suffering and struggling with loss of or lack of control, including in their intimately immediate personal and interpersonal lives, but also in fact responsible for denying or taking away such control.

I think here about 'everyday fascism', or 'the fascism of everyday life', where cruel and callous detachment and lack of concern becomes, in practice, the ostensibly 'normal' and 'natural' way to relate to others who are suffering and struggling, and to the conditions that give rise to as well as the forces that enforce this suffering and struggling. I think here about the ever increasingly massive numbers of young people facing serious mental health challenges, young people just like my students. I think here of populations at heightened risk of loss of control, and recurrent loss of control, due to long and ongoing histories of subjugation and marginalization–Black, Indigenous, and other people of color; LOGBTQIA+ people; and disabled people, visible and un-visible, including those physically and mentally disabled. I think of the desperate straits facing millions upon millions of refugees and asylum seekers, who exercise little control over their fate even if they succeed in making it to another country because of how suspicious and indeed hostile that new country, and many members of it, are to 'people like this'. I think about the always highly deficient and grotesquely incomplete and unequal welfare state safety net in the US and its steady evisceration over more than four decades as well as similarly drastic diminution of the promise of post-WWII social democracy in the UK. I think here about all the many kinds of people 'who fall through the cracks'–who *are* falling through the cracks– and indeed how wide these cracks are, along with how these have widened to the point that 'cracks' is a misnomer: these have become cavernous 'holes'. I think here about who maintains and exercises greater versus lesser control in and over their own lives, as well as what specific factors determine this. In capitalist society, economic, social, and cultural capital is crucial; the more one has, the greater control one is able to exercise over one's own life (and the lives of others) while the less one has, the less control one is able to exercise over one's own life (and the lives of others). Who is able to–afford to–move about, freely and widely, as well as to be accepted–and supported–in so doing, and who is not? Who is able to exercise greater versus lesser determination, or even influence, upon what they do in their daily lives, when, where, how, with whom, and for what? I think about how far we from valorizing interdependency and indeed dependency, and, as such, substantive empathy and solidarity, in early 21st century neoliberal capitalist society.

I think also about what happens when depression reaches the point where one largely feels numb, beyond feeling badly, and almost as if one no longer feels as if one exists at all. I think about the ghosts that haunt us, or should haunt us, of all those people, and all those groups of people, who have been denied control within and over their lives, or who have had this robbed from them, along with what has happened to these people, to these groups of people, as a result, including what have we have all lost as a result of what they were not able to be and do, not able to create and contribute.

How to respond to all of this–what is to be done?–is incredibly difficult because no easy response makes good sense. Instead, those of us engaged in critical studies need to articulate connections among diverse relations, situations, and conditions encompassing loss or lack of control, past and present–as well as the same in relation to why this loss or lack of control exists and persists, despite the enormous damage it does and it has done, in particular in relatioin to who benefits, how, and why from this state of affairs. We need to commit to empathetic activism, and radical praxis that links critical inquiry with concrete efforts at, and strivings for, social transformation. Such an empathetically activist radical praxis needs to be centered on engaging the condition, situation, and experience of those who lack control, or those whom have lost control, in particular on precisely what this lack or loss feels like and does to those so impacted.

"She's Lost Control" fits well with elements of each of the eleven overarching interpretations I first introduced in chapter one. In this song, something is blocking, something is preventing mediation, even as this is urgently needed. In this song, limits upon what one can control are severe, in particular versus that which is controlling. In this song sharing of vulnerability proceeds as far as to become sharing of emptiness, of being emptied and hollowed out, so that nothing–or, perhaps, only nothingness–remains. In this song clarity and insight appear theoretically existent but practically unreachable because clarity and insight cannot be rendered intelligible and explicable. In this song, 'the compassionate' becomes 'the dispassionate' to a frightening extreme. In this song, simultaneous distance and precision are definitely strongly registered, while acute vulnerability is at the heart of what the song takes on. In this song, introspection transpires yet without any substantive movement or gain, without any substantive breakthrough. In this song borderlines dissolve so thoroughly that it feels as if it is hard to gain one's bearings, let alone to know how or to where to proceed, even as if one at the same time feels compelled to proceed nonetheless. In this song, 'metaphorical darknesses' are engaged in the form of an uncaring society, even when and where claims to care are promoted and circulated, and in the form of the forgetting, ignoring, hiding away, and leaving to rot until death all those who are normatively rendered so disturbing and frightening, and so monstrous and grotesque, as to justify their exclusion. In this song, it seems as if it is impossible to answer the question of what is the meaning, value, and purpose of existence, and that one exercises next to no control over any of that while it seems as if we maintain overwhelming responsibility to and for others yet without any accessible or even intelligible–let alone effective–ways of acting on this responsibility. In this song, engagement with the sense and meaning of alienation, isolation, and of being a stranger, an outsider, and an outcast are central emphases as well as are simultaneous feelings of both vulnerability and entrapment. In this song, we encounter wanting and striving to connect yet not being able to do so. In this song, the Imaginary is collapsing, the Symbolic is brutal, and the Real is terrifying. In this song fascism is alive and well in callous disregard for others, especially those in need and those who are all too readily scapegoated. In this song difficulty of communication is prominently foregrounded as well as is what happens, while communication is what is lost, when this difficulty cannot be overcome. In this song, doubt overrides uncertainty and hesitation, while in this song we encounter testimony to what losing control, over and over again, incessantly, can and does feel like and how doing so makes sense, and is real, yet without broaching any answer to the question of what is to be done about this as well as little hope that an answer can and will be found.

Perhaps the greatest contrast with McRuer, Cvetkovich, and Gordon is that "She's Lost Control" does not suggest control can be regained and reasserted, that control remains and will continue site and stake of ongoing conflict and struggle. McRuer certainly addresses how incorporative and cooptive normalization of both queerness and disability is connected with losing control over the means according to which it becomes possible to define and explain what it means to be queer, and to be disabled–to live as queer, and to live as disabled. And this is connected with losing control in relation to what is in fact controlling of those who have lost this control, and who even have seemingly willingly surrendered such control–who even have desired and welcomed giving up such control. McRuer certainly addresses how austerity neo-liberalism exacerbates lack of control, as well as takes the form of loss of control, and indeed of robbing of control, in particular for disabled people and disabled communities. But McRuer also continually emphasizes the efforts of numerous intellectuals, artists, and activists resisting and fighting back, grabbing what (counter) control they can access and putting this to use in critique and in struggle, while imagining and aspiring toward more than mere resistance–imagining and aspiring toward transformation. Cvetkovich certainly addresses how depression feels like losing control, like having lost control, and indeed, through its duration, often enough like losing control over and over again, seemingly ceaselessly without end and with no way out. But Cvetkovich also emphasizes efforts at overcoming, at regaining and reasserting (counter) control by attending to what can be learned from experiences of depression, of melancholy, and of 'bad feelings', in terms of the social and political causes of all of these, and of all of these manifesting at least the beginnings of resistance to accepting social and political injustice. Cvetkovich, what's more, emphasizes what might be usefully identified as concrete micro-, meso-, and macro- forms of resistance versus allowing depression to rob one of the capacity to exercise any form of meaningful control over what one is able to do and what one is able to create and contribute. Gordon certainly focuses on the loss as well as lack of control of those subject to historic violence, as well as the continuing ramifications of that violence, including in the forms of loss or lack of control, in the present, along with situations involving massive loss or lack of control, and massive robbing of control by an oppressively controlling force, such as within the history of psychoanalysis, and versus what as well as whom it has excluded; over the course of the Argentinian 'disappearance'; and in relation to slavery as well as Jim Crow in the US. But again Gordon also emphasizes contesting loss or lack or robbing of control, by rediscovering, reclaiming, and reasserting counter control, such as happens in Luisa Valenzuela's *Como en la guerra* and Toni Morrison's *Beloved*. And Gordon theorizes hauntings and ghosts in order to enable these to be engaged and their just grievances addressed, which involves finding ways, again, ultimately to discover, claim, and assert significant elements of 'counter-control' over what a haunting and a ghost signify–over what a ghostly haunting demands we strive to control. Gordon's interest is not in perpetuating and proliferating ghostly hauntings but rather in coming to terms with these and doing what needs to be done so ghosts can be 'dispatched' and hauntings 'dispelled'. Likewise, Gordon's conception of complex personhood suggests people maintain elements of prospective (counter) control that they themselves might not recognize or others might not recognize–that they are capable of dynamic and transformative action.

"She's Lost Control," in contrast, renders 'counter-control' seemingly impossible and virtually absurd. However, that does not necessarily put the song and the critical theoretical work of McRuer, Cvetkovich, and Gordon entirely at odds, because the song represents this chasm as a crucial dimension of the violence inflicted by way of social harms that have been done, and continue to be done–i.e., what it *feels* like to have lost, and indeed to have repeatedly lost, control, as well as what it feels like to have lacked and to have been robbed of control. It is indeed because of the severity of this damage, including at the level of what this damage does to sense and to feeling, as well as to selfhood, that resistance, and especially transformation, are absolutely necessary.

As a final reflection on "She's Lost Control," I am struck by how much I do continue to seek, and to need, at least a certain amount of control in, and of, my life, as well as how that need becomes all the more intense as more of my life feels as if it is out of my control. I am struck by this because I have over the course of my life often recognized, and indeed embraced, the value, the necessity, and even yes the wisdom of accepting what I cannot control, and should not worry about being unable to control. In teaching long ago I accepted what students bring to bear is equally if not more important than I what to do, and it is impossible to anticipate all of what this might be as well as how best to respond. What students bring to bear needs to be engaged, as it happens, and to be welcomed as it happens. I have often 'turned over control' of class time to students, in the form of students presenting and sharing numerous projects and leading class discussion as they do. In many semesters student groups met with me before class sessions to plan and strategize how these student groups would lead subsequent class meetings, including three-hour class meetings at that. In Introduction to Critical Studies classes I have turned over the last four to four and one-half weeks to students to work in teams writing, producing, rehearsing, and ultimately performing short plays; students work within parameters I set and I continually observe and offer assistance, including suggestions and recommendations as need be, but these student teams by and large proceed to direct themselves. In my teaching I strive for mutually interactive experiences where students and I learn together. I have accepted that I cannot control how students will respond to any particular text or topic, and I cannot *control* precisely what they will do with this, even as I do exercise *influence* over what this will be. I have accepted that I cannot control how hard students work at a class or how seriously they take what we are doing, let alone what they ultimately make of and especially take away from our collective work, even if again I do exercise influence over all of this. Despite such influence, I don't want to 'control' the students I teach, and I never aim to do so; I want to work together with them, to engage in meaningful conversation and substantive dialogue so as to help them find connections with and value in the work we do–connections and value that may well differ widely from student to student, or class or class, and in relation to what this is for me versus what it is for them.

I also have accepted that limits always exist on how others will make sense of and respond to me, and that I can only do so much to counter, or contest, any of that, including in relation to being gay and queer, living with chronic illness and un-visible disability, living with mental health complications and challenges (persistent tendencies toward anxiety and depression), being intellectual, being a progressive/a leftist/a socialist/a Marxist, coming from the Northeast, being shy, and being what the Myers-Briggs schema for characterizing personality types identifies as maintaining an introverted, intuitive, feeling, perceiving (INFP) type of personality (although I remain skeptical of the validity of the Myers-Briggs personality test I do find it fascinating that I always test as INFP). I have accepted as well, although reluctantly, that I can only exercise limited control over my chronic illnesses–and even as I strive to 'manage' and *control* these illnesses, and in particular their impacts upon me, I can only do so to a limited degree. Likewise reluctantly, I have accepted that aging exercises real consequences and I am not able to do everything I was able to do, or at least not as easily, as I did when younger.

Yet as the COVID-19 pandemic set in and many of us felt, understandably, as if we had suddenly suffered a major loss of control over what we were doing and aspired to be doing with our lives, I felt appreciative of working on two book projects where I was able to exercise considerable control over when and how as well as how much and how hard I worked on these projects. I felt appreciative as well of what I, and Andy and I, were able to 'control' within our household, with the resources available to us, including as activities we could pursue–reading, listening to music, watching movies and TV series, playing with our pets, and physical exercise. Because we were economically secure, we enjoyed greater and less fettered control over our lives, even under conditions of strict physical social distancing, than many others who experienced the pandemic as plunging them into precarity or exacerbating the precarity they were already experiencing. Running appeals to me because it allows me a modicum of control over my body, and indeed over my physical and mental health; it does 'take the edge off' of what otherwise might become unduly worrisome and stressful. Having that to do, regularly, makes a huge positive difference for me, in my life, as does producing and hosting my weekly radio show for the past nineteen years; even when so much else in my life has felt like it was out of or beyond my control this show has felt like something over which I could maintain satisfying control and that has helped 'compensate' for the rest. Pets provide much the same support, and so, even much more so, does my husband, as acting together we are able to exercise considerably greater 'control' in many directions than we would if we were single and living alone.

Nevertheless, every semester, by approximately six weeks in, I begin to feel like the workload has become so excessive that it is out of control, beyond my control, and I worry about being able 'to catch up' and to complete all that needs to be done before the semester ends. Around the same time, because of already feeling that loss of control over what I am able to keep up with myself, I worry about whether I have previously done enough, in the right ways, to make as much of a positive contribution to and impact upon my students' learning as I had set out and as I hoped to do, when the semester started. I also have tended to fret, during the course of registration periods, over the numbers of students registering for my classes and in particular whether as many are registering as I would ideally like, because I always love to teach the maximum number of students in any single class as are allowed to register for that class. I fret whether I've done enough to explain what the class will be about, in ways that are likely to prove sufficiently compelling to registering students, and whether I have 'advertised' widely and effectively enough. I also have tended to fret about book orders through our campus bookstore, especially when due to constraints under which the bookstore has to operate they have not been able to obtain available copies of books I want to order for classes when I can do so–or when they have taken a long time to order these books, or when they have neglected to do so or made mistakes in doing so. In addition, especially before becoming a tenured associate professor, and then a full professor, I tended to fret about students' evaluations of instruction, about how these would be read by those evaluating my performance, and about the entire process of performance evaluation, even after putting together massive portfolios of materials explaining and documenting everything I had been doing in terms of teaching, scholarship, and service.

I felt like I 'lost control' when I was shocked to learn the results of the tenure-track search at Arizona State, that I have described earlier in this book, as I felt I had done everything necessary to be chosen as the clearly best candidate–and I felt like I continued to lose control over and over again when every effort to obtain another teaching position in Arizona, subsequent to that tenure-track search position, was blocked, and when, as a result, I needed to move back to Connecticut to live in my mother's house.

Mostly, however, I have felt this sense of losing control, and doing so over and over again, in trying to deal with my chronic digestive dysmotility disorder, because no matter how much I do to try to exercise control, and how hard I work at so doing, it frequently breaks free of that control and flares out of control. Right as I am writing this section, Andy and I are preparing for our first extended travel experience since the summer of 2019, as we will be traveling for three weeks to the UK. I am at ease, or at least largely at ease, accepting, due to a nationwide rail strike next week, that we have needed to change our initial plans and will be staying longer just in London, while I am likewise at ease about needing to do so again, later in the trip, at a point in time when we hope to travel to Edinburgh, before returning to London to end the trip–if rail travel still is limited or difficult. I am at ease with this because I support the strike, and the strikers; I sympathize with the circumstances the rail workers are in and with what they are asking for. I certainly have no interest in being complicit with 'scab labor' running the trains while the rail workers are on strike. And London offers a vast wealth of opportunities for much to see and do. I am even at ease over the prospect of waiting for hours to pass through customs and immigration at Heathrow and that our checked luggage might be delayed–due to labor shortages at British airports. But I am not at ease over the prospect of becoming sick as a result of flying, which can readily happen; sitting for so long and in that kind of environment can play havoc with my digestive system.

Still, reflecting on this upcoming flight I note well that like most air passengers I accept, without giving it much if any thought, that others are in control of the plane–the flight team on the plane and all those responsible for making sure it is safe and ready to fly. In a great many situations I and most other people readily accept lack of control over what is going on, as we are readily accepting–and grateful to–others who are in control, and who are working on our behalf. Only when something goes wrong do we worry in relation to a situation that we tend to take for granted where we are not in control and indeed exercise little to no influence. We need, much of the time, to trust that as members of a society, we do not need–and we would not want–to exercise control over everything, or even over all that much, of what we take part in.

But also, like many others, and especially many young people I know and with whom I have worked closely, I worry a great deal about climate change and even worse ecological crisis, emergency, and looming catastrophe. We often feel no matter how much we might care, and might try to make a difference, it is too little, too late, while too many others do not care, and are not trying to help. Likewise, I worry concerning gun violence, and the danger of gun violence, especially in the form of mass shootings in the US, that can seemingly happen just about anywhere and just about at any time. Again, no matter how much I care, or do, it *feels* as if nothing will change–as if even together with all those who also support gun control we control little to nothing. Likewise, I worry about the fallout from the war in Ukraine, and the increased risk of nuclear war that has attended the former war, as efforts at reaching a peaceful settlement seem to go nowhere. As much as I want all interested parties to focus on ending the destruction as soon as possible and forging a mutually acceptable compromise, I feel I exercise no control over whether that will happen. Likewise, I worry, despite how despicable as well as dangerous Donald Trump has shown himself to be, that I can exercise no control over large numbers of Americans continuing to support Trump, as well as Trumpist fascism, and I thereby *feel* I exercise no control over whether a subsequent fascist coup, insurrection, or 'revolution within a constitutional crisis' takes place and to what that will lead. Likewise, I worry that try as I might as part of larger efforts, and indeed movements, to fight back against threats to reproductive freedom and to teaching and learning about issues of race and racism–especially systemic racism–and about sexual and gender diversity–especially the real lives of lesbian, gay, bisexual, transgender, gender non-binary, queer, intersex, and asexual people–that I and we can do little to nothing to effect the outcome of these ongoing contests, and certainly little to nothing to do to stop those 'on the other side'.

Despite *feeling* these ways often enough, I remain inclined, along with McRuer, Cvetkovich, and Gordon, to keep believing I can exercise a modicum of control through doing my part, however small this might be, in contributing toward ongoing efforts at critical resistance and, over the long-term, successfully realizing genuinely revolutionary social transformation. Boldly imagining what 'the good society' can and should be like, what kind of society is optimally most desirable, even as this kind of society is seemingly impossible to realize, and from there critically inquiring into what makes it seem so impossible, what currently stands in the way of and as such blocks and prevents meaningful effort toward its realization, along with what forces must be mobilized and how to overcome these obstacles and defeat these opponents–engaging in critically utopian praxis–is necessary in order not to be totally defeated in response to experience of losing control, over and over again, and of lacking or being robbed of control. This must be a deliberate, concerted, and tangible *collective* effort, because alienated and isolated individuals cannot long sustain such radical hope, and because only by working in such collective fashion will it ever be possible to make what we yearn for, as 'the good life in the good society', become what we live.

Seven

Reputedly, according to Mick Middles and Lindsay Reade, Joy Division's and especially Ian Curtis's live performance of "Dead Souls" as the opening number in an August 2 1979 gig in London at the YMCA on Tottenham Road prompted manager Rob Gretton to respond with "explosive enthusiasm," as this performance of this song, "a ferocious number on any given occasion" conveyed "unprecedented levels of intensity" that made it abundantly clear "Joy Division was indeed a happening band and there was no doubt that Ian Curtis was its true star" (Middles and Reade 145). As Middles and Reade share, further, "Dead Souls" remained Gretton's "favourite Joy Division song, not least because it so effectively highlighted the resonance of the Curtis voice" (178). "Dead Souls" at the same time provided a quintessential vehicle for Curtis's powerful physical performance of mesmerizing movement, i.e., for his distinctively frenetic dancing. As Jon Wozencraft recalls, "Once Joy Division really found their seam, they almost always started with 'Dead Souls'" as "That track has a very, very progressive, intensive build-up," that lasts "nearly three minutes before the vocal comes in" (206). As Wozencraft explains, this lengthy instrumental build-up "gives Ian a chance both to calibrate–to position himself to start to read the atmosphere, to feel how the band behind him are locking in with each other on that particular evening–and to decide how far he wants to travel" (206). In turn, "Once he was able to position or balance himself to go out of his body, he would use performance as a way of projecting himself, channelling" (206). In this "stark" yet simultaneously "monumental performance" Curtis became the clear central "point of focus," enacting "incredible movement" that "was very ritualistic" and involved 'amplification' and 'projection' 'to the extreme' (206).

Joy Division recorded "Dead Souls" late in 1979 as part of the limited edition *Licht und Blindheit* single, together with "Atmosphere," released in March 1980 by French record label Sordide Sentimental, in an overtly 'artistic' package with striking visual art by Jean-Pierre Turmel and Jean-François Jamoul as well as a densely philosophical essay on Joy Division in performance by Turmel. "Dead Souls" has subsequently been included in most Joy Division compilations, starting with the 1981 Factory Records *Still*, and even though not part of either *Unknown Pleasures* or *Closer* continues a favorite of many listeners, including myself, as we share Gretton's enthusiasm for this song and what it exemplifies about Joy Division and especially Ian Curtis as artistic performers.

Although "Dead Souls" alludes to Russian novelist Nikolai Gogol's 1842 novel of the same name, most commentators interpret the lyrics and the music as bearing little direct connection with that book and its emphasis on absurdist social satire. Instead, for example, Uwe Schütte relates "Dead Souls" to "the voices of the dead that haunt the singer," and to "the day of reckoning, the doomsday when the world will end and the dead will be redeemed" (75). Caroline Langhorst, meanwhile, identifies "Dead Souls" "as prime example" of Joy Division's "musical style," evincing a "haunting effect" (91) that is overtly gothic, and indeed aptly exemplifying what Langhorst cites Isabella van Elferen classifies as distinctly 'gothic music' that uses "gothic imagery to express feelings of being haunted in an empty world" (quoted 91). This, Langhorst contends, is so as "Dead Souls" amplifies the effect of Gothic imagery by "accompanying musical devices such as Curtis's monotonous voice and musical and lyrical repetition" (91). Langhorst also relates "Dead Souls" to Michael Bibby's account of 'gothic music' because the song, as do *Unknown Pleasures* and *Closer*, exemplifies what Bibby identifies as characteristic of such music: "a world devoid of hope and filled with horror" as well as "a descent into a personal hell" (quoted 92). Langhorst adds, yet further, that "Dead Souls" illustrates how Joy Division's music, and especially Ian Curtis's lyrics and vocals, convey "a feeling of numbness or loss of self" as well as a "musical evocation of melancholy" through "direct confrontation with extreme states of mind, including a prolonged state of painful suffering" (96).

"Dead Souls" aptly demonstrates how "sentiments such as melancholy and anxiety are openly enunciated" through Joy Division's music, "which is also of a rare genuine and poetic nature" (96).

Michael Goddard interprets "Dead Souls" as having "less to do with Gogol's satirical portrayal" of "middle class corruption and spiritual ennui," than it has to do "with being haunted by past lives," which was "an abiding interest" to Curtis. As Goddard interprets it, Joy Division's music, and notably "Dead Souls," is "haunted by the ruins of modernism," and here, as I have previously discussed in this book, especially in chapter two by way of the work of Mark Fisher, Goddard's take suggests "Dead Souls" offers an exemplary instance of music engaged in hauntological praxis. According to Goddard, "Far too much has been made about the links between Joy Division's music and the urban regeneration of post-industrial Manchester," because this music is "less concerned with a specific urban environment than a kind of psychogeographical virtual city of the mind, as much inherited from modernist literary imaginaries as from the often referred to demolition of terraced housing in favour of grim tower blocks." Goddard links Joy Division with Throbbing Gristle, in maintaining "a shared vision of contemporary industrial society as a spiritual wasteland" but, unlike with Throbbing Gristle, for Joy Division 'there is no way out'.

Goddard characterizes "Dead Souls" as expressing "the kind of esotericism experienced by Curtis in the most direct way, as a form of involuntary past life regression." Here, "a type of hypnotic autosuggestion is enacted through a ponderously slow rhythmic guitar riff, that builds for over two minutes before any vocals as if enacting a process of hypnotic regression." Goddard interprets the vocals, once they enter, as conveying the sense that "the vocalist is being taken over and possessed by a figure or figures from the distant past." Although it remains nebulous precisely whom the latter might be, Goddard finds that "Nevertheless, the constant repetitions give a sense of a powerful haunting by an ancient past that overwhelms the present and seems to give spiritual explanation for the lack of the 'will to want more', given the impossibility of overcoming such a powerful mode of possession."

Goddard's interpretation coincides with that of Amanda London, who recalls Ian Curtis "being under the impression that he lived a past life, having walked the Earth previously during the Middle Ages," and with the ability of Bernard Sumner "to extract this belief out of Curtis while the latter was under hypnosis, which many of us understand as a state in which the subconscious comes more to the forefront." London proposes "the lyrics of 'Dead Souls' reveal that Ian, to some degree, obviously held such a conviction consciously also." London identifies Curtis as believing "he existed during the 100 Years War" between England and France in the 11th to 15th centuries, and that his "dreams" of that time are "pronounced"–that he did possess "an alternative personality," remnant from such as past existence. In "Dead Souls," according to London's interpretation, Curtis is recounting and reenacting his visceral experience of graphic emanations from this past, and of 'his' place within it, while "using the opportunity" of this visionary experience elliptically "to criticize the historical powers that be, i.e. European imperialists." Most important, London contends, in appreciating precisely what Curtis is expressing in "Dead Souls," is recognizing that Curtis is not imaginarily projecting himself into a past he has merely learned about from books, but rather is literally "haunted" by "actual spirits" of "dead souls" from the past.

In the songmeanings.com page for "Dead Souls," contributors interpret this song as: 1) conveying Curtis's sense that he has lived a previous life, or previous life, and experiences flashbacks to that life or lives; 2) expressing what it is like to experience an epileptic or even a schizophrenic state of mind; 3.) expressing what it is like to have died temporarily, such as in the course of a surgical operation, and then returned to life, or to have had another kind of near-death experience, or to have had a premonition of what it is like to die and of what comes after; 4) Curtis sharing feelings of being haunted by people he has known in his life whom he has left behind or would like to leave behind, even needs to leave behind, but cannot; 5) Curtis being plagued by something, and not necessarily by someone, from which he cannot get away; 6) Curtis confronting various personal demons; 7) about the end of the world and the final judgment; 8) about the hypocrisy and venality of organized, institutional Christianity and its working hand in hand with imperialistic conquest and subjugation; 9) about nostalgia for a heroic past no longer possible in the postmodern age; 10) about aspiration for greatness combined with trepidation concerning what it might involve to strive to achieve this; 11) about an artistically extreme sensitivity, including in being readily able to listen, feel, and see things from a perspective that is not one's own; and 12) about longing to escape a life of drudgery and monotony but again being uncertain to doubtful that this will be possible. One commentator does link Joy Division's "Dead Souls" with Gogol's book of the same title, indicating that "One of the themes has to do with the irony of the lifelessness of the actual living landowners and characters in the book compared to the dead serfs who are often described [as] lively and talented," while similarly the song is "not dealing with life and death, but the death of life," or, in other words, living life as if one was dead–which as I have argued previously in this book is a critique at least strongly implicit in multiple other instances of Ian Curtis's lyrics and Joy Division's music.

'Dead Souls' might suggest 'dead folk', or 'dead people', and in particular a specific set of such dead people from a specific time and place as exercising a haunting impact on the narrator-protagonist of the lyrics, the music as persona, and us as listeners in identifying with the narrator-protagonist and/or the music as persona. "Dead *Souls*" also might suggest a spiritual dimension of whichever dead beings are referenced here, and 'souls' might refer to spiritual essences, even if 'spiritual' is not necessarily understood in overtly supernatural terms, such as, instead, connoting life-forces or perhaps, in a Marxian sense, 'the ensemble of social relations'. 'Dead Souls' might suggest on the one hand those who are and have been literally dead, or it might suggest on the other hand those who are literally alive, but spiritually dead–whose souls are dead, or whose souls are dying. Yet it seems, in the context of the lyrics, and the song, taken as a whole, that these 'dead souls' are capable of manifesting considerable force, are animated with considerable energy, and so it also seems somewhat less compelling to interpret the song, starting with the lyrics, as lamenting how many people resemble robots or zombies in leading lives of drudgery, misery, and mediocrity.

The lyrics that comprise stanza one proceed as follows: "Someone take these dreams away/That point me to another day/A duel of personalities/That stretch all true realities." Yes, these dreams might be dreams of the apocalypse, or of *an* apocalypse–or they might reference a visionary reliving of an historically past life and past life-situation. Here it useful to note, however, that the narrator-protagonist begins by asking, perhaps pleading, for 'someone' to 'take these dreams *away*', which suggests these are troubling dreams, these are dreams perhaps in the form of nightmares–and yet, since the narrator-protagonist is calling on a vague 'someone' to do so, it seems 'he' does not know who might, and who even can, 'take these dreams away', as these dreams, and their recurrence, might be unstoppable. The dreams may proceed as far as to take the narrator-protagonist out of 'his' present time, and place, but, then again, they *point* 'to another day', which may suggest they don't quite transport 'him' there, but continually and repeatedly verge upon so doing. These dreams may remind the narrator-protagonist of 'another day' of which 'he' would rather not be reminded, but which he cannot repress, and this might represent both a critical situation, perhaps involving a critical encounter, in the past that continues to 'haunt' the narrator-protagonist because he has not been able to, and cannot, work this through–he has not been able to, and cannot, get away from his connection with and in particular responsibility for and complicity in whatever that 'another day' has involved. But these dreams may also remind the narrator-protagonist of 'another day' yet to come which he would like to avoid, or fears encountering, but knows he cannot avoid and knows also no one can make it possible for him to do so, as he will have to face up to what he fears.

"A duel of personalities" might suggest a duel, in the sense of a clash, between two or more distinct, and distinctly different, kinds of personalities maintained by two or more individuals, but this might also represent a duel, in the sense of a clash, between multiple, contradictory, and contesting dimensions of an ostensibly 'single self'–i.e., "dual personalities" that the narrator-protagonist 'himself' maintains. Perhaps so far he has been able to maintain some kind of balance, or equilibrium, among these different personalities, even at the cost of considerable pain, but he recognizes he cannot forever do so, and the duel, or clash, is inexorable–and imminent.

"That stretch all true realities" is challenging to interpret but perhaps suggests 'stretching' common, familiar, dominant, and prevailing notions of what constitute 'true realities' or the bounds and limits that separate what is 'truly real' from what is not. Perhaps this phrase suggests dimensions of 'reality' that are 'true' yet often not recognized or experienced as such–perhaps forms of 'surreality'. Perhaps these are dimensions of 'true reality' akin to the Lacanian Real that cannot be other than intuited because they cannot be represented in the forms of conventional images or symbols. Perhaps these are dimensions of 'true reality' that dominant ideology obscures, or for which readily available frames of intelligibility are lacking. Perhaps it is difficult, next to impossible, to conceive of 'one's self' as multiply divided, contradictory, and even dueling or clashing, yet this *is* a dimension, even a key dimension, of 'true reality' even so. Perhaps it is difficult, next to impossible, to conceive of 'one's self' as not only embodied and enacted, or staged and performed, but also as socially embedded and extended–but again this *is* so, not withstanding the difficulty and even seeming impossibility of conceiving how this might be. Perhaps it is difficult, next to impossible, to conceive of 'one's self' as formed and constituted by 'other people' and not just by relations with 'other people' who exist 'outside' and 'independent', including 'other people' we have never met personally and who lived long ago or who live far away–and yet this *is*, again, a dimension, even a key dimension, of 'true reality', even so. Perhaps it is difficult, next to impossible, to accept we are or at least can be 'haunted' by 'ghosts', including, specifically linking this song and these lyrics with Avery F. Gordon's *Ghostly Matters: Haunting and the Sociological Imagination*, with hauntings, represented in the form of ghosts, that call us to account in relation to our connection with, responsibility for, and complicity in acts of historic violence and their lingering consequences. We may not want to face up to this calling to account, but we may not be able to escape so doing–and if we do not attend to these ghosts and the hauntings they signify, by responding to what they demand of us, we will feel worse and worse, we will be wracked and we will be undone.

The first iteration of the effective chorus in this song occurs as stanza two: "That keep calling me/They keep calling me/Keep on calling me/They keep calling me." These lines enact a semblance of what they indicate—a 'calling' upon 'me' that persists. Again, this is a 'calling upon me' that appears impossible, or increasingly impossible, to ignore. 'They' does suggest specific figures, specific representatives—specific 'ghosts'—are the agents of this calling, and their persistence in doing so conveys 'they want something', or 'they need something', 'from me'. What's more, 'I' will continue haunted as long as 'I' cannot figure out what this is and as long as 'I' cannot provide what they want or need. This could in fact represent 'a calling' 'upon me' 'by me', from one dimension of the complex, contradictory, and dynamic multiplicity that I am, to so respond—and to so act. For example, in more prosaic terms, this might represent 'a calling' 'upon me' in the form of the urging of 'conscience'. But 'calling' here might also suggest 'having a calling', or experiencing one's self as 'having a calling', such as to do a particular kind of work, to live a particular kind of life, or commit to (struggle on behalf of) a particular kind of cause. In the context of these lyrics, and the song as a whole, it seems this might not prove an easy 'calling' to accept, so accepting such a calling might prove risky, even dangerous. It might well leave the one so 'called' 'exposed'—including to ridicule, ostracism, and abuse. Yet again, this calling seemingly cannot be ignored—and cannot be refused.

Stanza three offers the closest to a concrete set of allusions in these lyrics: "Where figures from the past stand tall/And mocking voices ring the halls/Imperialistic house of prayer/ Conquistadors who took their share." It is possible to interpret this stanza in diametrically opposing ways in relation to 'the project of the West' that Kehinde Andrews identifies as a history of genocide, slavery, and empire. 'Conquistadors' specifically alludes, seemingly at least, to 15th and 16th century Spanish and Portugese conquerors of the so-called 'New World' of the Americas in the so-called 'Age of Exploration', but by implication could stand in for many others who have used violent force to seize land and other sources of wealth, establishing and maintaining colonies (and neo-colonies) in the course of doing so. And "house of prayer" does suggest how Christian missionaries worked hand in hand with military conquerors in enacting and especially justifying genocide, slavery, and empire, chiefly by promulgating influential notions of racial hierarchy and of racial destiny. "Mocking voices ring the halls" might allude to 'conquistadors' and their clerical allies mocking those they have judged to be intrinsically inferior, and even 'subhuman', including mockingly pretending to be engaging in conquest for noble reasons while knowing this was a lie, as greed for the acquisition and accumulation of wealth and power was always the true, even sole, motivation. "Where figures from the past stand tall," meanwhile, does seem to suggest being 'transported' into this time and place, to directly see 'those who strode at the head' of these missions of conquest and to directly hear 'those whose voices mockingly resounded through the halls of houses of conquest'. Yet, it is, in contrast, also possible to interpret these lines as evincing an admiration for and identification with these 'great' 'heroic' figures, and with their accomplishments—as evincing a longing to live as part of 'an age of heroes' that seems to have passed, and which is no longer possible in (post)modern society.

At the same time, it is possible yet further to interpret these lines diametrically oppositely, once again, with 'dead souls' representing 'the ghosts' of those massacred and otherwise exploited and abused, calling upon the narrator-protagonist, and upon us, to account for our connection with, responsibility for, and complicity in the continuing, the ongoing, consequences of what the Western project of genocide, slavery, and empire has made possible–of whom it has benefitted and whom it continues to benefit, how, to what extent, and at the expense of whom else. After all, 'they' who 'keep calling me' only seem to be identified here in terms of '*where*' they are calling from–not as necessarily identical with the 'conquistadors' or 'the mocking voices' or those in charge of running the 'imperialistic house of prayer'. In other words, that is the time and place from which the calling seems to be coming, but this calling seems to evince an urgency suggestive of an unsatisfied need, which can make sense as an urgently unsatisfied need of redress. Alluding for the moment to Bernard Sumner's transcript of the 'regression' Ian Curtis underwent, under hypnosis, it is worth recalling that 'Curtis' perceived himself, ultimately, on a battlefront, in the seeming aftermath of a bloody battle, as a seeming priest, attending to the dead and even lamenting how little impact he had been able to exert in preventing this extent of killing.

It is also worthwhile remembering from where the band and especially Curtis obtained the name 'Joy Division' as this name references those forced to serve as sex slaves for their Nazi captors, as victims of horrible atrocity, while, likewise, so many of Ian Curtis's other lyrics again and again, as I have discussed throughout this book, keep returning to scenes of horror, in which the affective impetus is *to feel the overwhelming horror for how horrific this is while simultaneously agonizing over how difficult it is to do anything to put a stop to the horror*, to overcome the horror, or to make up for the horror–as well as yet further agonizing over how attempting to do so, nonetheless, is the only ethically responsible position to take, because one is inseparably connected with, responsible for, and implicated in what such atrocities have made possible, and do made possible, as well as in their ongoing perpetuation.

The final stanza offers an extended iteration of the effective chorus: "They keep calling me/They keep calling me/Keep on calling me/They keep calling me/Calling me, calling me, calling me, calling me/They keep calling me/Keep on calling me/They keep calling me/They keep calling me." The emphasis here is on the relentless persistence of this calling, and in particular upon *me*. In other words, even if I don't want to do so, even if I don't know how to do so, and even if I am afraid that whatever I do will prove pathetically inadequate, I cannot shirk attending and responding to this call, and I need to take this *personally*, to accept and act upon my *personal* stake.

Yes, these lyrics might reasonably coincide with the articulation of a perception that one lives in 'a vast cultural wasteland' where idealistic hopes of a previously ascendant 'modernity' have faded, where widespread disenchantment now rules instead, and where 'there is no way out' because 'there is no alternative'. These lyrics might suggest the future appears immensely bleak and all that can be clung onto as reasons for continuing are no more than vestiges of past possibilities never (yet) realized. But the lyrics also might suggest taking seriously, even deadly seriously, ethical responsibility: that one is 'called upon' to live life for a purpose, for a 'higher purpose', other than 'just to get by' and other than just to enjoy a materially comfortable life one's self, or together with fellow members of one's immediate family. Above all else, in typical Ian Curtis fashion, these lyrics evince a sense of experiencing such a calling as an undeniable imperative that is rendered all the more overwhelming due to uncertainty concerning how best to respond along with doubt one is capable of

997

adequately responding, given the scope of what is needed versus the limits of what one has to offer. At the same time, the song manifests a desperate determination to want and to need to do so, even a vehement insistence on trying to do so–i.e., to attend and respond to what is and has been persistently 'calling of me' while remaining unclear concerning precisely what to do or how, and while maintaining at least residual doubt one is up to the challenge.

In chapter two I identified Michael Bracewell's essay "Licht und Blindheit" as offering an initial model example of an effective combination of close description, analysis, and interpretation of what Bracewell hears in listening to "Dead Souls." As a transition to discussing the music that comprises "Dead Souls," beyond the lyrics to this song, it is worth here repeating my summary of Bracewell's reading. To begin, as Bracewell hears it, "The music manifests from resonant silence. It is as though a sound-proofed door has been opened at the far end of a long corridor. We seem suddenly to be hearing an instrumental exercise that might have been following its course for some time, gradually building in controlled intensity" (21). Continuing onward, we hear "Stark and deft, the loosely swinging, echoing beat provides a chassis to carry the interplay of guitar and bass. The guitar sound is metallic, scything. It brings to mind the wind through power lines, or machine parts being sewn from sheet metal" (21-22). Here, "The sound is also plaintive, sinuous and fluid, given depth by the bass running softly ahead, just beneath the surface of the rhythm," as "The drums, guitar and bass configure and entwine like a trio of sonic apparitions" (22). And then, "Fifty seconds in, the accumulating intensity shifts temper" as "The guitar becomes more aggressive, breaking out into four clamorous crescendos, each backed by the tumbling accompaniment of the bass" with "This abrasive package . . . closed with a double beat in the drum, and the rhythm becomes looser, resuming its swinging beat" (22). At this point, "The intensity appears to ease; aerating space opens within the track. The heat of emotion meets the acoustics of absolute zero" (22). But "The calm is short-lived" as "With accelerating urgency, guitar and bass drive the music to a reprise of the harshly metallic crescendo," with the last seeming to "fall neatly into place, its collapse caught by a deft doubling of the drum beat" (22). And then, "at two minutes twelve seconds–a little under half-way through the track–Curtis starts to sing" (22). As Bracewell hears it, Curtis's "deep, faintly transatlantic voice sounds at once frightened and frightening, stentorian yet pushed by gathering panic" (22). In contrast with "Dead Souls," the other contribution to the original Sordide Sentimentale *Licht und Blindheit* ep, "Atmosphere," Bracewell hears as slower, colder, with "accents of icily glittering beauty," and even though, like numerous others, as "funereal," Bracewell hears this combining with "passages of luxuriant emotional release, building to cathartic crescendo" (23). Both tracks, Bracewell suggest, although seemingly "driven by a compelling sense of tragic destiny," also hold, "in uneasy tension," a "confluence of urgency and exhaustion" (23).

The structure of "Dead Souls" divides into the following successive sections:

1.   Progression: 0:00-2:12. This pivotal section involves an extended, slowly, steadily, yet also emphatically building movement: a progressively climbing instrumental opening, encompassing a series of recurrent, complimentary, alternating yet interlocking guitar and bass guitar patterns that introduce the melody as a variegated series of slightly differential short and simple sequences that are relentlessly persistent nonetheless, accompanied by a supportive, parallel slowly, steadily building drum pattern that is interlaced with a series of quick yet soft tom hits. The music here encompasses a

series of crescendos as well as pauses in that crescendoing movement that feel as if they take the form of arrival at and spreading out across peaks, or plateaus, or, in other words, of almost celebratory yet temporary breakouts that then soon transition into resettling before resuming climbing yet further. The patterning and deployment of sounds here comes across to me as evincing a strikingly confident, determined, and even resolute feeling, with again an almost celebratory constituent element, evoking a sense of alignment with an invincible force or momentum. As such, this feeling I hear conveyed in this extended instrumental passage is strikingly at odds with most common interpretations of the song based solely on the lyrics. Even so, as Bracewell attests, the sound of this extended instrumental opening also conveys a decidedly brutal and chilling feeling at the same time.

2. Initial confrontation: 2:12-2:43. First vocal passage. The vocal sounds more vulnerable than the preceding instrumental combination and at least as edging upon the desperate even while sharing the preceding sense of being intensely driven, even swept along and carried forward–or carried upward (perhaps as if carried out of and beyond the limits of one's body, as this is conventionally understood and especially conventionally delimited). This vocal may well indeed come across as suggestive of being haunted, of being overwhelmed, and, yes, even of being possessed–especially as Curtis slows down and softens slightly to simulate a virtually ghostly incantation of a choral line.

3. Brief pause and regrouping: 2:43-2:51. Brief instrumental break. It is notable here that not much time passes at all before the vocal needs to muster its strength to commit to proceeding forward yet once again.

4. Renewed confrontation: 2:52-3:24. Second vocal passage. If anything, I hear the intensity of the confrontation and of the commitment to pursue it all the way through, to align fully with the process, ramping up at this point, while reaching out to at least allude or gesture toward the sources of the impetus the song enacts.

5. Brief pause and regrouping: 3:25–3:40. Brief instrumental break. This instrumental bridge lasts nearly twice as long as the break between the first and second vocal passages but is nonetheless quite short as a bridge, including for Joy Division. But "Dead Souls" rearranges where such an extended instrumental passage is located by placing it at the beginning of the song before the first vocal section rather than in between vocal sections.

6. Climactic confrontation: 3:41–4:13. Third vocal passage. The vocal here offers an extended iteration and elaboration of the choral refrain, at a point in the song suggestive of arrival at maximum intensity.

7. Denouement and dissolution: 4:14–>4:51. Closing instrumental section. The music eventually drops down and out, finally relatively quickly, suggestive perhaps of a visionary experience coming to an end, or, slightly more prosaically, returning to a state closer to an ostensibly 'normal' state of consciousness at the end of an hallucinatory trip or an hypnotic spell. It remains unclear whether the narrator-protagonist of the lyrics, and the broader music as persona, has fully responded to 'the call' or even if doing so has been (yet) entirely possible. This remains a tantalizing uncertainty, which is suggestive of a need to reenter such a state and resume such a pursuit again, even perhaps over and

over again–until resolution is finally achieved, yet without being able to anticipate ahead of this happening when that will be or what it will encompass.

Notably, the recorded version of "Dead Souls" doubles the guitar lines, so that we are in effect hearing two contributions from Bernard Sumner on guitar at once, both making pronounced use of distortion effects, pitched at different register heights and varying in terms of to what extent these allow strummed strings to deliberately ring as well as in terms of how frequently and how elaborately they make use of barre chords, including rapid movement among barre chords. The guitar, in both instances, contributes to the melodic layer and the harmonic fill layer, at times doing both simultaneously, and, as is the case in many Joy Division songs, often providing the principal contribution toward textural density. Peter Hook's bass guitar contributes both to the melody and the groove while Stephen Morris's drum kit anchors the rhythm by keeping the beat. What is especially notable here in relation to the latter, beyond the relatively greater prominence in the sound mix of the snare over the other constituents of the kit, is the regular use of a tom in place of the hi-hat to contribute sixteenth note strikes over the course of a measure. When Ian Curtis's vocal is present this takes the lead in performing the melody. Even while only moving at any given point in the song across relatively short pitch intervals and even while often repeatedly sounding the same pitch in succession, Curtis's vocal in "Dead Souls" nonetheless encompasses a striking variety of intonations, suggestive, variously, of all of the following: being or feeling haunted and possessed, being or feeling compelled or impelled toward haunting and possessing, worrying and fearing, hesitating and agonizing, longing and yearning, pushing and striving, attesting and proclaiming, and relishing and exalting.

In terms of the soundbox, the guitar initially seems to sound from somewhat further back, slightly more notably to the right, slightly above center, but as the song progresses the guitar becomes positioned and more precisely displaced, or duplicated/multiplied, across the soundbox, as the guitar lines rise in the soundbox, occupying and filling more space throughout the soundbox, and relatively quickly so at that. Listening to the guitar in terms of the soundbox definitely accentuates how the guitar's contribution is split into what come across as two or more yet often simultaneous lines, with some of these tending to be more focused on elaboration of the melody and some tending to be more focused on provision of harmonic fill to contribute textural density. The bass guitar sounds as if if is positioned lower and more to the left than where the guitar appears at least initially to have been positioned, but at the same time the bass guitar sounds as if it is also positioned closer to the front of the soundbox than the guitar. As the song proceeds, and in fact from early on in the opening extended instrumental passages, it feels as if the guitar and the bass guitar take turns in terms of which instrument is principally sounding the melody, at least other than when the vocal is doing so. The vocal enters positioned at the center, slightly high on a vertical axis, but it also sounds as if echoed both left and right of center. In addition, the vocal feels close to the front of the soundbox, even as this feeling is complicated somewhat by the extent of reverberation involved and especially by a pronounced feeling of echoing left and right. With the drums, the snare, again, is the most pronounced, other than with occasional rolls that are punctuated with a brief hi-hat cymbal crash. The drums sound as if they are positioned slightly below center in the soundbox yet further to both sides than the other instruments, and especially to the left. In quieter passages we can hear that the toms are involved throughout the song, but these become especially pronounced, again, in the occasional rolls.

Taking the structure and instrumentation of "Dead Souls" into account, as well as the place of this song at the opening of Joy Division's live sets, what comes across to me is a sense of an energetic vitality, of a building and indeed climbing intensity, of a confidently controlled and asserted force. As a total piece of music, as opposed to a mere set of lyrics detached from the music, "Dead Souls" comes across more as summoning, as conjuring, as evoking, and as mediatively, dramatically, performatively rendering than as directly and immediately experiencing. In other words, "Dead Souls" comes across more as if the song is dramatically narrating and commenting on what it *re*-enacts, what is *re*-presents in performance. So this is not necessarily about 'someone' immediately experiencing 'a calling' but rather a dramatic performance of what that can look, feel, and sound like. At the same time, it is worth stressing that the music comes across as ready to embrace the call, as enthused about taking on what the call comprises. Whatever the lyrics, and their vocalization, are referencing here as constituting the source, the nature, and the purpose of the calling, the music as persona wants this, desires this, and is ready to go to and with it. The music dramatizes effectively merging with or even having already merged with what is or what was calling upon it so that the music now has become itself in turn the principal agency through which this calling is being emitted. The music suggests entering or having entered a mesmeric, trancing, hypnotic state but one the music as persona embraces no matter if risky, if dangerous, if cause for trepidation, and if replete with uncertainty concerning how, for how long, and to where this will proceed as well as what will transpire and what will be encountered along the way.

Taking account the sounds, patterning of sounds, and deployment of sounds that makes "Dead Souls" a song and not just a set of lyrics, this song thus conveys a strong sense of wanting, even needing, to go where called to go, and, even more than this, to become one with what is calling, from when and where this is calling, and on behalf of what ends and interests this is calling. This can indeed feel chilling, at least to us, as listeners, because it feels as if the song enacts, or *reenacts*, casting off a familiar kind of life and a familiar way of living, even a familiar kind or way to exist as a self, in order to to take a radical leap into a considerably different kind of existence, as a considerably different kind of being. This does effectively involve a kind of will to die, even yes a kind of suicide, in the form of a jettisoning of all that is no longer useful, needed, or wanted about whom and what one was, in order to join up and become one with something incredibly different and, seemingly also, incredibly vaster.

The song also makes good sense as offering a sonic simulation of what it might or indeed can feel like to experience 'a calling', especially a *spiritual calling*–that is to feel called upon to a specific path and focus, even a specific mission, and again, especially, to a higher purpose and a special destiny. "Dead Souls" comes across as redolent with an exuberant intensity involved in experiencing this calling and in committing to it: notably with bursts of adrenalin as one affirms 'yes, yes, yes' that is me, that is where I want to go, that is what I want to do, and that is whom I want to be. All of this comes across despite the words of the lyrics seeming to suggest wanting to get away from, to avoid, and to seek and find help so as not to be overwhelmed by what is 'calling me'. As I make sense of this seeming contradiction, yes, the song registers ambivalence, certainly, but it is important, nonetheless, in interpreting the song beyond the lyrics alone, not to discount how enticing the song depicts the calling as feeling, how much the song evinces a desire to respond to this calling with a decisive 'yes!', with the music as persona wanting, and even needing, to follow this calling, embracing the opportunity to become one with this calling and with the source(s) of the call to this calling.

The music of "Dead Souls" is similarly suggestive to me of moments in life when it feels scary but right, necessary, and important to do something that 'puts one's self out there'–moments that comes with clear risks and even considerable dangers. The song comes across to me as making sense in this way especially when this involves 'putting one's self out there' in the midst of a struggle, in the midst of a fight, united with others who are committed to pursuing the same end. Alternately, the music of "Dead Souls" makes sense as suggestive of rare occasions at rare moments in time when one feels as if this moment will prove to be among the most memorably impactful, life-shaping, experiences I will ever have, and of not wanting it to end even as the intensity of 'enjoyment' of the moment, due to this sense of its extraordinary uniqueness, has become excruciating. Indeed, the music of "Dead Souls" makes sense as suggestive of a sublime moment, or a sublime encounter and experience, in which one feels in touch and connected with powerful forces beyond the conventional limits of an individual self 'contained in an individual body'–with forces that extend across vast expanses of historical time and space, with feeling integrated into an historically ongoing movement as it is in motion, and in particular into a movement capable of bringing about substantial transformation. All of these takes involve feeling one's individual self, or one's individual subjectivity, becoming subsumed within a larger collective self, or a larger collective subject. One here feels animated by a driving purpose, mission, and goal united together with a collective host of others striving in the same direction such that 'one is no longer one', 'one no longer feels as if one is one' anymore.

In terms of loudness, "Dead Souls" starts off notably loud, with no slow build-up in volume, as if, as Michael Bracewell suggests, the musicians have already been playing for some time before we are introduced to them playing. The initial extended instrumental section does however involve passages that are relatively louder versus relatively softer depending on the precise contributions of the guitar, in particular, including whether this offers a dirtier versus a cleaner and a denser versus a sparser sound, especially where the doubling of guitar parts is most noticeable. The song is also relatively louder when the guitar takes the lead in principally sounding the melody versus when the bass guitar does so. At points thereafter where the vocal performs the choral refrain the loudness increases in combination with an increase in density of instrumentation and a rising in pitch. As the song proceeds, harmonic fill in support of the vocal, principally from the guitar but also from the the bass guitar as well, periodically becomes more cacophonous than previously. Loudness does finally decline somewhat, as expected, as the song moves toward its dissolution and end. It is further worth noting, what's more, to conclude this discussion of loudness, that the relative loudness of the contributing instruments versus each other depends not only on which recorded version one is listening to, and especially in comparing studio recordings with live recordings, but also how one is listening and supported by what means of apprehending the sounds; listening with headphones I hear the bass guitar and drums as louder versus the vocal and the guitar than I do listening without.

The time signature for "Dead Souls" is 4/4 and the song proceeds at 121 bpm (at the least the version shared on *Still* does so). In terms of the contribution of the drum kit to the beat, and the larger rhythm, it is notable that for much of the song eighth note strikes by the bass drum on beats 1 and 3 and snare drum strikes on beats 2 and 4 are accompanied by sixteenth note hits on a tom, usually four tom hits on beat 1, six tom hits on beats 2 and 3, and either one or two tom hits on beat 4. A two measures long hypermetre based on this alternation proceeds through the first 63 measures, with the 64th measure, right before the entrance of the vocal, changing the proceeding pattern to involve ending with two snare strikes, a tom hit, a bass strike, and a snare hit on beat three followed by a bass strike and four tom hits on beat four. The first vocal section then starts, in measure 65, with a short crash produced either via a closed hi hat or a floor hi hat pedal. Here, in this section, the bass drum strikes twice on beats one and three and the tom twice on beats one, two, and four as well as three times on beat three in one measure followed by a subsequent measure that involves a simultaneous bass drum and tom hit on beat 4 followed by a snare drum hit on beat 4and. This pattern continues until right before the chorus with two more cymbal crashes on beats 4 and 4and along with a bass drum strike on beat four and four tom hits on beats 4, 4ee, 4and, and 4uh. The chorus begins with another short crash produced by a closed hi hat or a floor hi hat pedal. The bass drum then strikes on beats 1 and 3, including twice on beat 1 (on 1 and on 1and), the snare drum strikes on beats 2 and 4, and the tom strikes twice on beats 1, 2, and 4 as well as four times on beat 3, with this then varying after one measure to four hits on beats 1 and 3 as well as an alternation between one or two hits on beat 4. After that the pattern returns, involving four tom hits on beats 1, 3, and 4 right before the brief instrumental interlude, following the first vocal passage. This interlude begins again with a brief crash produced by a closed hi hat or a floor hi hat pedal. And then we confront similar patterns from the drum kit from this point forward all the way through the end of the song.

Of particular note here is incorporation of a tom playing a pivotal role throughout, primarily involving short series of sixteenth note hits, as well as minimal use of cymbals of any kind, except to introduce sections, and variations across short hypermeasures in terms of how many strikes in particular take place on the tom over the course of each of the four beats along with periodic variations of the same kind from the bass drum and the snare drum. Overall, the rhythmic patterns that the drum kit contributes involve considerable regularity albeit with this regularity encompassing nonetheless continuous slight variation from measure to measure.

The bass guitar plays primarily eighth notes up until the third vocal passage where sixteenth notes become more common, and this continues from there on through the concluding section of the song. In the immediately preceding short instrumental interlude, vocal passage three, and the concluding section of the song, more rests are introduced than previously that break up sequences of notes and chords sounded within measures as well as drum strikes. The bass guitar periodically switches from playing single notes to playing two simultaneous notes across two strings, although more often playing a single note at the time on one string. With the lead guitar we encounter periodic bursts in which the guitar plays a series of barre chords, involving four to six strings, albeit most often four strings, while otherwise the guitar usually involves fingered notes as part of chords on one to two strings. The guitar most often plays eighth note chords, while one of the two guitar lines often involves a continuous ringing from the playing of one chord to the next as well as often denser clusters of sounds than the other. The vocal part principally involves eighth notes too, typically with rests preceding and following each enunciation of a vocal line and tied notes enunciated across measures within lines.

It is especially noteworthy that the song involves highly consistent and continuously repeated short rhythmic patterns that always contain slight variation within these short hypermeasures, and it is notable how the precise patterning of the overall composite rhythm as well as that of each contributing instrument changes at least slightly as well in moving from section to section of the song. The fact that the most common length of notes as performed by each of the instruments are eighth notes, and rarely ever shorter than this, along with the sixteenth notes contributed by the tom, means that even as the song proceeds relatively slowly, on average, versus other Joy Division songs, it also involves a feeling of considerable energy, of considerable push, of considerable momentum, within that procession.

Most commentators suggest "Dead Souls" is performed in the key of F major. In terms of movements in pitch, with the vocal in the verse the starting pitch receives significant repeated emphasis, before the pitch then moves briefly slightly lower, next returns to the starting pitch, after that moves briefly slightly higher, before then concluding this pitch pattern by moving down quickly and yet slightly further than previously. In the choral refrain the vocal jumps to a notably higher starting pitch and then moves in successive steps yet higher, back to the start, and yet even higher than previously before finally returning back to the start. With the bass guitar a considerable emphasis occurs on repeating the same starting pitch in each pitch sequence while the bass guitar does move up slightly before then moving down further than it has moved up. Sections involving notes on two strings tend to start higher in pitch while ultimately moving even lower than otherwise. With the guitar the most notable direction of movement in pitch is upward, even after briefly climbing back down, with the upward movements sounding the most emphatic. Overall, it is worth noting that pitch intervals tend to be slight and small, involving typically two to four semitones. Nevertheless, pitch sequences convey a feeling of restlessness and of not being satisfied to remain down or to return and stay at a starting position even when and as this repeatedly happens. A restless aiming upward comes across as most pronounced, and, at many moments, interval movements suggest climbing steps.

Turning to Curtis's vocal delivery, the resonance of his voice here is strong, enough to readily encompass the notable variety of intonations I have previously mentioned even if only for short periods of time. Curtis's apparent attitude toward pitch and rhythm as he sings comes across as confident while not strictly bound in the former case yet markedly consistent in the latter. Again, intervals are short and his overall range is modest but it is notable that choral lines start and push higher. Curtis's voice sounds multiplied and echoed, as if it is allowed to fill out and resound across a significant extent of space at the front and center of the soundbox. Curtis's vocal timbre is neither as harsh nor as dark as in many other Joy Division songs. We hear slight wobbles that combine with reverb to suggest, by way of the vocalization, that the music as persona is simultaneously restless and eager to respond to and unite with 'the call to a calling' yet also maintains some reluctance and trepidation about doing so. Curtis's vocal and its variation throughout this song notably conveys a feeling of richness and of warmth by no means always as pronounced in other Joy Division songs.

Continuing with timbre, the guitar notably involves both ringing and 'dirtied' qualities, elements of pronounced distortion, and the effects of being doubled in the recording. Timbre in "Dead Souls" helps contribute to a feeling of steadily climbing, as the song pushes onward and upward, along with a feeling of periodically breaking out or breaking away from the climbing to relish and even celebrate reaching the plateau upon which the song has just arrived. Otherwise, timbre, notably from the vocal, suggests a reaching out and toward–including a reaching out and toward the listener, as if the music as persona has become the principal agency of 'the call to a calling' and we are now its principal addressee. In "Dead Souls" each individual component of the drum kit sounds as if the attack is sharp and prominent with a quick release and little notable sustain and decay, but the use of the tom does add, collectively, to a sense of the kit as a whole sharing a lengthier decay and release. At the same time, even the loudest constituent of the drum kit and the one in which the attack is the clearest, the snare drum, comes across as combining decisive attack with a nonetheless evident albeit brief sustain. Because of the ringing and the distortion, with the guitar sustain is prolonged while decay and the release are slow. The attack with the guitar is not entirely clean and crisp, with chords blending into each other, often contributing to the feeling that the guitar is continuously resounding without being clearly released or an entirely distinctively new attack introduced, although this changes later in the song where pointed rests are introduced between chords. With the bass guitar the sustain is also relatively long, while the release when it comes is relatively quick as are both attack and decay as well. Turning to the vocal, here sustain and decay stand out versus attack and release. It is also worth mentioning that the use of the sixteenth note tom strikes adds a slight jittery feel to the song. But overall what is most worth underscoring is that timbre contributes to "Dead Souls" feeling as if the music as persona is clearly moving along and not staying in place, even of breaking loose and pushing onward and ahead, while casting aside all that has up until now held the music as persona back. Indeed, the music as persona comes across here as aligned with a relentless power of movement, in and of itself. Excitement here might well be at least in part nervous excitement but this is definitely excitement.

As I listen to "Dead Souls" I feel a sense of exertion of force that is persistent and only increases somewhat in passages that begin at notably higher pitches and with notably upward interval movements as well as in those that involve a greater density of instrumentation. The exertion feels deceptively simple, with a considerable amount of repetition paired with slight variation. It feels as if this duration is, overall, successful in accomplishing what the music as persona seeks to achieve with this song, although perhaps the music as persona never fully reaches the point at which 'he' is completely at one with that which is 'calling upon him'. But this might constitute a recognizably ever receding horizon that is nonetheless an inspiration and a guide in showing the way to proceed as one strives to move steadily closer toward this horizon, as one engages in continuing effort at improvement, at making progress, at self-transformation and even at self-transcendence. As I listen to "Dead Souls," I feel overtly conscious of my mimetic participation. Melodic riffs are short, simple, and easy to follow as well as repeated over and over, making them readily available to mimetic participation. The lyrics likewise are not elaborate and emphasize the choral refrain that Curtis's vocalization of this refrain readily invites me to join in singing along. I experience myself joining in, and as even irresistibly compelled to do so. As I do join in, I physically empathize most directly with the vocalist but not solely so. And as I mimetically participate, I feel my vicarious participation is largely not attenuated, or at least not until near the end, as at no point until right at the end do I feel myself released from the song; I never feel myself positioned to merely stand back and observe dispassionately what the song is performing right in front of but entirely separate from me.

As "Dead Souls" proceeds, the music as persona and I anticipate a continuous reiteration of fundamental patterns with slight variations. We anticipate continuous building, continuous climbing. We anticipate at the beginning of the song and throughout the entirety of the first section the eventual entrance of the vocal, with the long delay before this happens heightening our anticipation of it happening. Subsequently we anticipate the return of the vocal, and especially of the chorus, and in particular the lines 'They keep calling me', 'keep on calling me', and 'calling me'. We also anticipate the eventual climax and the eventual denouement and dissolution. I anticipate I will follow closely along and experience a shared aspiration to respond to the call as well as a shared nervousness and trepidation about doing so, combined with a shared adrenalin rush, a shared burst of excitement, and a shared fervid determination to push on, to push forward, to reach out, and to rise up.

I hear "Dead Souls" expressive of determination, drive, persistence, and, especially notably, of climbing. I hear "Dead Souls" expressive of a reaching out to me as well as responding to a call. I hear an expression of excitement conjoined with some nervousness yet of being largely confident that the music as persona is up to the challenge. I hear an expression of excitement not only concerning the prospect of arriving at where this journey is taking us but also, from the moment of embarkation, in moving away from, in decidedly breaking with and leaving behind the dull and the mundane, the limiting and confining, and the narrowing and stultifying.

In terms of acoustic impact, I feel "Dead Souls" coming at me in the form of an enveloping sweep across the soundbox and especially from close up in the soundbox. I feel a close proximity to the music as persona and I feel swept up and carried along as the song proceeds. The music simulates the feeling of being subject to and compelled to respond to a call that is irresistible.

Analysis, in the song, suggests the call originates from both close at hand and far away, in terms of both time and space, surpassing conventional temporal-spatial boundaries and surpassing conventional temporal-spatial horizons, suggestive of transcending the limits, and the limitations, of a prior existence. Aesthetic pleasure comes in this song, and in listening to this song, via at least imagining giving way to and accepting the call, becoming one with the call, and going with what the call is calling upon us to do–and to become.

I associate this song with what it feels like to experience a powerful calling. I associate this song with a feeling of exuberance so extreme in its intensity that it becomes painful. I associate what I hear in this song with being called past the limits, and limitations, of what has been, of what I/we have previously settled for and as what I/we have previously felt compelled to settle for/to settle as. I associate this song with a feeling of undergoing a vision that involves a transportation, a possession, and an out of body experience, clearly transcending the limits, and again the limitations, of a conventional sense of where the individual self begins and ends. I associate what I hear in this song with entering into a life-changing, a life-shaping, and indeed a life-defining experience.

Certainly, all of the proceeding might seem difficult to reconcile with 'dead souls' 'calling me'. Yes, the song might make sense as an expression of romantic infatuation with and attraction to death and dying, but I propose it makes even better sense to interpret this as a symbolic death and dying, a death and dying of one way of being, of one kind of life, and even one kind of self, in

1006

preparation to become another. If, moreover, it is 'dead souls' that are 'calling me'–calling the music as persona and calling us as listeners aligned with the music as persona–this makes sense as being called upon to take up their cause, to take up their interests, and to respond to what they need, to what must be done on their behalf, perhaps at the least by picking up and carrying on with where they left off, on the basis of what they have been able to achieve and what they have made possible for us. The struggle may be far from finished, and the struggle may have to be renewed and repeated, even again and again, which means these 'dead souls' who previously waged this struggle need us to do our part.

In terms of exploring taboos, certainly it would seem to be taboo to respond with passionate enthusiasm to a call from 'the dead', and even more taboo than that to merge with 'the dead' or allow 'the dead' to take over, to inhabit and possess us, and to allow ourselves to become subsumed within and, paradoxically enough, animated by 'the dead'. It is also often taboo to identify the dead as not fully dead at all but existing as seething presences that exercise a powerfully and even irresistibly compelling force upon us–i.e., of proclaiming that hauntings and ghosts are real and that they are addressing us and demanding of us. It can be taboo as well to welcome self-shattering and transcendence of the conventional confines of the self by allowing one's self to become diffusely united with a mysteriously expansive force. And it can be taboo to pursue and embrace experience of such excruciating pleasure that pleasure becomes pain.

In "Dead Souls" precisely who and/or what is calling, from when and where, along with how and why, remain tantalizingly invisible and intangible yet viscerally present in audible form. We obtain only ephemeral glimpses of when, where, how, and why. And the song likewise conveys a marked feeling of the ephemeral in terms of how close versus how far we are in relation to whom and/or what is calling 'us', as well as how close versus far we have moved in response to this call over the course of the song.

In reflecting on how specifically I make sense of what this song is *calling from me*, I begin by returning to the eleven overarching interpretations of what Ian Curtis's and Joy Division's music invites and encourages me to think (about) and feel that I first introduced in chapter one. And from there I proceed, as I have repeatedly throughout this book, to respond by exploring connections that help me in elaborating what this song prompts me to think (about) and feel as I listen to and reflect upon it.

"Dead Souls" makes sense to me as one of many Joy Division song that involve a strong compulsion to seek, strive, venture, and pursue, despite manifest hesitation about doing so. "Dead Souls" likewise makes sense to me as engaged with extremities as well as intensities, especially in pushing beyond the limits, and the limitations, of the self, in opening one's self up to become one with a force that surpasses these limits and limitations. "Dead Souls" make sense as a song attesting to a readiness to surrender control in order to experience intimate contact with levels of the Real otherwise impossible to so contact, let alone recognize as existing at all, certainly not via means that either the Imaginary or the Symbolic make available. "Dead Souls" makes sense as attesting to a readiness to undergo a visionary experience–an experience of transportation out of body, and out of mind, across time and across space. Whatever 'borderlines' might have previously held us back are falling away in "Dead Souls," even borderlines that conventionally seem impossible to do without, while what precisely is calling us past these borderlines, and toward what, is up for each of us to determine, for ourselves. And, yes, "Dead Souls" feels close to direct an embodiment of Ian Curtis calling upon me to carry on with what he could not, even while I am inspired and enabled by what he leaves to me as the basis from which to do so.

In exploring extended connections, in response to this call, I begin by turning to Nikolai Gogol's *Dead Souls* to consider whether this novel and the Joy Division song share any more in common than previously recognized. As I do so I am working with the Bernard Guilbert Guerney translation, originally from 1942 and then revised in 1948, as updated and revised yet further by Susanne Fusso for a 1996 copyright Yale University Press edition of *Dead Souls*. As Fusso explains in her "Introduction," the most "clear, seemingly mundane referent for the phrase 'dead souls'" in Gogol's novel has to do with the fact that before 1861 in feudal Russia serfs were often referred to as 'souls', "especially when counted for tax purposes" (ix), while "Serfs who died after one of the periodic censuses were, until the next census, still considered taxable property despite their nonexistence" (ix). This inspires the protagonist in *Dead Souls*, Pavel Ivanovich Chichikov, to concoct a scheme where he will buy 'dead souls' from landowners to reduce their tax burdens while mortgaging the 'dead souls' he has bought to make considerable money for himself, notably by pretending these are 'live souls' that he has bought to 'relocate' to other properties he claims to own but does not. Chichikov here appears as a fictional forerunner of much more recent schemes involving the buying and reselling of bundled packages of sub-prime mortgages, not to mention numerous other questionable to nefarious maneuvers involving the continuous 'repackaging' and 'reselling' of steadily less tangibly concrete forms of what Karl Marx famously identified as 'congealed' or 'dead' labor. Yet, as Fusso writes, despite that 'mundane referent' for his use of the phrase 'dead souls', it is worth noting that "Gogol does seem to call into question the worth and even the existence of the human soul" while "Chichikov's day-to-day activity, his obsessive bargaining for 'dead souls', is a constant reminder of the hideous moral ulcer that a society founded on slavery can never hide or heal" (x).

As Fusso recounts, from initial censors onward, many early readers were struck, and especially troubled, by Gogol's use of that phrase within and as the title of his novel, considering this, for instance, as 'blasphemous' in suggesting a 'soul could be dead', or macabre in giving emphasis to the value of the dead. Fusso further traces how subsequent readers, including in the Soviet Union, attempted to recruit Gogol as a champion of social realism, and even of naturalism, although most modern to contemporary readers, including modern to contemporary scholars, regard *Dead Souls* as well as the bulk of the rest of Gogol's fictional writings "not as realist social protest but as a brilliant phantasmagoria," "as a verbal performance, a delirious, nearly surrealistic fantasy" that delights in word play as well as the more broadly witty and humorous, and, especially, the bizarre and the absurd. Fusso contends, moreover, that Gogol was aware that his title and use throughout his novel of the phrase 'dead souls' would be provocative and indeed aimed for this to be so.

Gogol's style and tone presents the most immediate challenge in drawing any kind of connection with Joy Division's "Dead Souls," as the latter is riven with a markedly earnest seriousness and makes no use of levity in the form of satirical humor or otherwise. Yet a possible connection arises in considering that Gogol's *Dead Souls* represents a scathing satirical critique of a middle class milieu and of a middle class outlook. The characters Chichikov meets and swindles, or attempts to swindle, are often stubborn and suspicious, indeed to a paranoic degree, but also often naive and gullible, while, beyond both of those seemingly opposed tendencies, appear to live lives that are shallow and trivial, characterized by mass conformity and pervasive self-delusion, absorbed in vacuous forms of materialistic hoarding and indulgence while continually focused on competition over image and status. These characters are prone as well to collective moral panics. Chichikov is little better, and as the narrator frankly declares, 'a scoundrel', but Chichikov knows these people and what they are like well enough to be successful, at least for a good while, in flattering them, inveigling himself into their good graces, and convincing a good number to collaborate with him on his fraudulent scheme. The connection with Ian Curtis's and Joy Division's "Dead Souls" that I recognize involves interpreting "Dead Souls" as fervently desiring to be somewhere else, do something else, as someone else, that will give life a meaning, a value, and a purpose it otherwise lacks in a social environment where seemingly no room exists for the heroic and for heroes and heroism. Even taking into account the narrator-protagonist's hesitation and reluctance to acknowledge and respond to 'the call', this call exerts the appeal that it does because it seemingly offers the opportunity to break decisively with a previous life that is 'safe' and 'steady' yet also drab, dreary, uninspiring, and unfulfilling.

Implicitly, therefore, "Dead Souls" argues people need to experience 'a calling' and they need to experience a sense of vital connection with forces and movements that exceed restriction and constriction, that enable them to press past limits that separate their individual lives from the lives of others, their individual bodies from the bodies of others, their individual minds from the minds of others, and their individual selves from the selves of others. Both Gogol's novel and Ian Curtis's and Joy Division's song engage with social alienation, while both at least allusively suggest that 'the dead', what they represent, and what amounts to their continuing value, must be taken into account, even in ways that are uncomfortable and disturbing to do, while what this value amount to constitutes site and stake of ongoing social conflict and struggle.

Since I wrote the last section of this chapter, the US Supreme Court overturned *Roe v. Wade* and *Planned Parenthood v. Casey*, which means the right to abortion is no longer protected at the federal level in this country and up to 26 states are likely ultimate to ban or severely limit access to abortion, including in cases of rape, incest, and where the mother's life is at stake. A number of states aim to go so far as to attempt to punish those who seek to obtain an abortion in another state where it remains legal, as well as punish all those who assist the person in obtaining this abortion. Supreme Court Justice Clarence Thomas also indicated in his statement as part of the recent *Dobbs v. Jackson* decision on abortion that he would like the Court to revisit past decisions that have provided for legal same-sex marriage nationwide, federal protection for people to be free to engage in same-sex sexual activity in the privacy of their homes, and prospectively even federal protection for the right of men and women of different races to legally marry. The Supreme Court has this term also issued rulings placing significant limitations on the ability of states to implement gun control measures and for the federal government to regulate environmental emissions that cause pollution and contribute to climate change through global warming. At the same time, the January 6 Committee of the US House of Representatives have made it clear that former US President Donald Trump aided and abetted an attempt at a coup that would have kept himself in office and prevented the peaceful transfer of power to President Biden while that effort came perilously close to succeeding even as fascistic forces inspired by the former president's popular following continue to push for much the same in the not too distant future. In the UK as in the US inflation continues to soar while growth slows and recession looms. In the UK, increasing numbers of unionized workers, beginning with rail workers, are striking or planning to strike, in particular to call attention to the hardships they are facing due to the cost of living, while the response of the Conservative UK government continues to be refusal to talk with unions to try to broker a settlement while condemning their actions and proposing legislation to limit the legal right to strike. And the current Labour Party leadership under right-leaning Labour Party leader Sir Keir Starmer, insists on 'remaining neutral' in labor disputes while condemning Labour Party members of Parliament for standing in solidarity or giving media interviews in support of striking workers and their unions. In both the US and the UK, but notably in the UK as well as across much of the rest of Continental Europe, record highs in temperature, traceable to the impact of climate change, have caused many problems and created many new risks, while the COVID-19 virus continues to mutate and shows little sign of fully disappearing. Those are just some of the most prominent recent reasons why 'doomsdayer' discourse is now popular and influential.

In a 23 July 2022 editorial column for *The New York Times*, Jane Coaston begins by noting at present "the internet is awash with Cassandras," as "being a doomer" in "believing the end is nigh, everything is going to go to hell and maybe we are, too–is big right now," with "apocalyptic thinking" extending "beyond the standard end-times fare of certain sects of evangelical Christians" to encompass a "new political and social doomerism" that "has become mainstream and is definitely unholy." Coaston acknowledges reasons why many are tempted in this direction while criticizing 'doomers' for proceeding beyond the reasonable position that involves "recognizing that things are bad and could get worse," to 'luxuriate' "in the awful," in ways suggestive that all too many 'doomers' "seem unable to get enough of it–the equivalent of rubbernecking at a terrible car accident." Coaston challenges 'doomers' to explain "What's the point of all this?" After all, Coaston contends, "If the idea of doomerism is to use hyperbole to spur readers or listeners to greater action, it's not very effective" and "It seems to make our situation worse." As Coaston elaborates, doomer thinking undermines motivation to try to do anything to tackle problems and bring about solutions, or even to work for any kind of real change and significant improvement. Coaston asserts that she herself is "an increasingly optimistic person," despite being concerned by many if not most of the issues that trouble 'doomers', because she has "found that the best way to spur action is to begin from a place of optimism–a belief that the thing you want really is possible." Coaston urges others to follow her example in maintaining or developing a similar "faith in possibility," as a necessary counter to 'doomerism'.

While I do appreciate what Coaston is urging, I find this argument too simple as Coaston does not address precisely *why* it is that today so many people increasingly believe social and environmental problems are impossible to solve, that little to nothing can be done about them, and that everything is inexorably becoming and will continue to become all that much worse–*why*, in other words, 'faith in possibility' doesn't make sense (anymore). At the same time, I agree with Mike Davis, in an interview with Sam Dean published on 25 July 2022 in *The Los Angeles Times*, who argues 'hope' versus 'hopelessness' is *not* what is most important in responding to current urgent issues. As Davis, author of many notable works of radical left social and political critique, including

Prisoners of the American Dream and *City of Quartz*, explains, "I don't think that people fight or stay the course because of hope, I think people do it out of love and anger." Davis, who is at peace with the fact he is now experiencing terminal esophageal cancer, for which he has stopped treatment, admits to being "a fatalistic Celt" as well as a "neo-catastrophist," which includes "in resonance with Walter Benjamin . . . the belief in the sudden appearance of opportunities to take leaps into an almost utopian future" along with a refusal to downplay the severity of matters such as the impact of climate change, which is proceeding such that we are headed toward "an already anticipated genocide" whereby "A large minority, the poorest people on the planet, are in a sense doomed." Davis, however, believes that people can, will, and must fight, again not motivated by hope but rather by love and anger, while noting well "this generation," the current generation just coming or recently having come of adult age, "is different from any other postwar generation. The combination of seeing rights stripped away on one side and facing declining economic ability on the other has radicalized them and has given struggles over what some people denounce as identity politics a very material force." Davis adds, aptly as well, that "the biggest single political problem in the United States right now has been the demoralization of tens of thousands, probably hundreds of thousands of young activists," which in significant part follows from "lack of organizational structure, particularly of organizations of organizers," as "There's no leadership to give direction," with too much of the broad left for too long exclusively focused on electoral politics and on wanting those they have helped get elected to positions in government to then do all of what is necessary to be done. Davis indicates he too votes for and otherwise supports Democrats over Republicans in elections, "but the movement's more important." According to Davis, "we've forgotten the use of disciplined, aggressive but nonviolent civil disobedience," which means, for instance, in relation to climate change, "We should be sitting in at the headquarters of every oil company every day of the week" and that "You could easily put together a national campaign" with "tons of people who are willing to get arrested, who are so up to do it," but "Nobody's organizing that."

In connection with "Dead Souls," acting out of 'love and anger' as opposed to 'optimism and hope' strikes me as useful in making sense of 'the call to a calling' the song embodies. None of what people on the broad left at present lament as lost, or is being lost, or is in danger of soon being lost, has always, until now, been firmly in place, or was easily won and easily secured in the past. Not at all: not reproductive freedom and bodily autonomy (including not for same sex sexual relations or for 'sodomy' more broadly conceived); not marital equality (whether same sex or interracial); not equitable inclusion of queer representation in public school curricula and public library collections; not access for transgender people to toilets, to health care that enables them to live in line with the gender they experience themselves to be, and to be able to participate on competitive sports teams in line with the gender they identify as; not rejecting and undermining equation of 'homosexuality' with sickness, sinfulness, and criminality, as well as queer people with sexual predators, pedophiles, and groomers; not the right to strike and engage in other modes of collective action on behalf of working people, in particular as members of labor unions; not acceptance that police violence is real and hugely damaging, as are allied police practices that target Black and Brown people and communities for discrimination, harassment, and abuse; not creating and striving to maintain and sustain a substantial social welfare safety net; not recognition of and responsiveness to the reality of scarce natural resources, ecological precarity, and the need of concerted efforts on behalf of ecological sustainability that include reducing pollution and toxic waste as well as converting to renewable energy sources and leading overall less environmentally harmful lives; not struggles to gain people the right to vote, freely and fairly, in elections, for people who have been denied and otherwise prevented from exercising this right; not recognition that unregulated gun violence leads to devastating tragedies and renders entire communities collectively unsafe. People in the past have had to fight, and did fight, long and hard, to address these issues and many more, striving to achieve progress in the form of substantial improvement, including via radical transformation. Their efforts, and their achievements, can inspire and enable us today–and tomorrow. We need to heed their call, and that call is to pick up from and build upon where they left off, and to derive courage from what they demonstrated in terms of their determination and persistence, even when they felt overwhelmed by what they were taking on and aiming to do, even when they felt overwhelmingly scared and overwhelmingly pessimistic.

What is at stake, therefore, is not whether to be more versus less hopeful or more versus less optimistic, but rather how we conceive of precisely where we are at, and with precisely which efforts we are most closely connected, from those who have come before us, as well as with what they, those now 'dead souls', and not just 'future generations' or 'our children and grandchildren', are calling upon us to do. Those 'dead souls' calling us from the past also include, in particular, all those who struggled with and against their own oppression, and who often suffered tremendously on account of this oppression. They have not yet been done the justice they deserve–the violence they faced and the harm they endured has not been atoned for, and its ongoing pernicious legacy has not been eradicated and overcome. We need to identify which particular of these 'dead souls' bear the closest connections with us, in terms of where we are at, and in terms of what we are able to draw upon and make use of, according to what their efforts have made possible for us.

The strongest connection I recognize between Ian Curtis's and Joy Division's "Dead Souls" and Robert McRuer's *Crip Theory: Cultural Signs of Queerness and Disability*, McRuer's *Crip Times: Disability, Globalization and Resistance*, Ann Cvetkovich's *Depression: a Public Feeling*, and Avery Gordon's *Ghostly Matters: Haunting and the Sociological Imagination* has to do with the use value of the utopian. In short, I interpret "Dead Souls" recognizing and responding to a utopian call, and in doing so affirming the use value of the utopian.

In his 2006 article published in *The Irish Review*, "To Stand with Dreamers: On the Use Value of Utopia," Tom Moylan, whose scholarly work concentrates in utopian and science fiction studies, proposes that "Utopia's primary vocation is to tell us what is wrong with the world as it is," and to do so "by evoking a totally transformed society, not by settling for piecemeal repair or reform," which in turn means "The Utopian gaze, therefore, empties the present of its absolute authority–as it imagines how we might better live together–not in some escapist fantasy-land, but in a possible future reality." Moylan cites Marxist critical theorist Ernst Bloch, a major champion of the value of the utopian, in support of this claim and in particular in relation to the necessity, if substantial social change is to be pursued, of being able to conceive of possibilities not (yet) realized from within social reality as this presently exists. Moylan likewise cites leading utopian studies scholars Lyman Tower Sargent identifying utopianism as necessary 'social dreaming' and Ruth Levitas identifying utopianism as setting forth 'dreams to be pursued'. Likewise, as Moylan reminds his readers, Marxist critical theorist Fredric Jameson usefully attests to the value of utopianism in keeping open the possibility of living in a fundamentally different–and substantially better kind–of world than as yet presently exists. Elaborating further, Moylan recounts how advocates supportive of the use value of the utopian share a common conception of utopianism as "a vital process of seeking a better, not a perfect, world," although "some scholars, such as Vincent Geoghegan, argue that even the category of perfection can work productively, not as a form of closure as the anti-utopians aver, but rather as a radical provocation towards that which is not yet lived." From this pro-utopian vantage point, the utopian is "open and developmental, not closed and static," while utopianism provides both a "critique of current ideologies" and "space for radical alternatives," space to imagine and invent what they might be.

In a more recent, 2021, article, published in *Utopian Studies*, Lyman Tower Sargent readily admits that utopias can align with many different kinds of political outlooks and agendas, and that even one who finds positive value in the utopian will recognize that utopias and utopianisms can be dangerous. Interestingly, in surveying a long sweep of conversation in support and opposition to utopias and utopianisms, Sargent cites an interview with Mike Davis where the latter argued that "Utopia in the most profound sense is not the dream of a paradise but the defense of the necessary against the realistic. It's the refusal to accept the triage of humanity implied by the vicious circle of inequality and environmental degradation." As Sargent recounts, Davis adds, further, that utopia "is a huge toolbox from which communities can forge solutions on a participatory scale." Useful as well is the position Sargent cites the late Black feminist critical theorist bell hooks as taking in support of the use value of the utopian: "I found a place of sanctuary in 'theorizing', in making sense of what was happening. I found a place where I could imagine possible futures, a place where life could be lived differently. This 'lived' experience of critical thinking, of reflection and analysis, became a place where I worked at explaining the hurt and making it go away."

In a 2022 article published in the journal *Moral Philosophy and Politics*, E.R. Prendergast likewise argues "In Defense of Wishful Thinking." Prendergast supports this argument with relatively modest yet nonetheless useful claims, including that "those who do not engage in some wishful thinking about the feasibility of political projects they desire to succeed risk moral complicity with what leads those projects to fail" and that "political theorizers' judgments regarding which political projects are politically feasible may sometimes become part of the story that explains why a political project is or is not politically feasible." Prendergast respects the importance of attending to matters of feasibility but also indicates that at many points in time in history what eventually proved possible was judged to be unfeasible, unrealistic, and impossible–such as abolition of slavery. Utopian imagination, Prendergast proposes, needs to be as concrete as possible and as context specific as possible, yet it is nonetheless important to appreciate its usefulness at the same time in extending the horizon of what is conceived and recognized as possible. After all, "Political judgments of citizens as a whole that help determine feasibility are subject to shift, sometimes dramatically, and even quickly," and "Over time, social ideas change, and the range of political policies that are politically feasible changes, expands, or shrinks." Providing due space for the utopian is valuable in enabling perseverance, or 'grit', as one continues to seek out ways to arrive at what is morally desirable yet seemingly not immediately readily practical, while not allowing a narrow focus solely on what seems most immediately readily practical to close off, or close down, efforts to imagine and pursue any kinds of changes that are more far-reaching than that.

But, what specifically, do McRuer, Cvetkovich, and Gordon identify as the use-value of the utopian, and in particular of utopian imagining? Beginning with McRuer, critical disability theory as opposed to virtual disability theory must engage in reimagination and transformation of the public sphere to displace able-bodiedness from its position at the center of and at the top in a hierarchy of what is normative, and this requires that the tasks of intellectual reimagination and practical transformation work in hand in hand. McRuer advocates on behalf of a crip praxis that demands a fundamentally different kind of society and culture, not one that merely accommodates the disabled in relation to a still overwhelmingly pervasive and at least implicitly superior, preferable, and normative able-bodiedness. In order to work in pursuit of an effectuation of these demands it is necessary to be able to imagine that such a society and culture is possible and at least to imagine rudiments of what this might be like as well as how it might be possible to move from 'here to there'. McRuer repeatedly argues in favor of "Demanding that . . . another world is possible," "an accessible world is possible," and that this is another world requiring radical imagination of possibilities "beyond ramps," encompassing radical transformation in turn in terms "of how private or privatized versus public cultures of ability or disability are conceived, materialized, spatialized, and populated" (71-72). McRuer approves of Carrie Sandahl's conception of crip praxis which, notably "clearly connects cripping to alternative worlds and performances," that "allow 'for a multiplicity of imaginary identifications across identities'" (quoted 139).

As McRuer yet further argues, "some of the most important challenges of crip theory, or more simply of progressive queer and disability movements at the turn of the century" include "the challenge of always *imagining* [my italics] subjects beyond LGBT visibility, tolerance, and inclusion" and "the challenge of shaping movements that, regardless of how degraded they are, can value the *traces* of agency, resistance, and *hope* [my italics] that are as legible where identity disintegrates as where it comes together" (145). Drawing upon Judith Butler, McRuer argues further "for continually *reimagining* [my italics] the collective disidentifications" that enable a 'refiguring' of current exclusions as contributing toward the constitution of a 'necessary outside' from which 'the violence of exclusion can be overcome' (145).

In *Crip Times*, moreover, McRuer identifies himself as keenly interested, following Jack Halberstam's work in theorizing 'queer times and places', in, as Halberstam puts this, "finding *and* describing . . . the alternatives to capitalism that already exist and are presently under construction" (5). Here McRuer and Halberstam seem interested in what Ernst Bloch has theorized as 'concrete utopias': utopias that develop out of possibilities inherent within existing realities. Later in the same book, McRuer declares that he aims to contribute toward and is interested in others likewise contributing toward the project of working "to imagine a *disabled* sociality" that overcomes "the very distinction between the social and the bodies engaged in *a range of intimate practices* that certainly can include sex . . . but that can also include other embodied ways of being-in-common" (93). Yet once more McRuer is here endorsing and exhorting on behalf of the work of imagination, and in particular of imagining in a radically far-reaching direction at that. Likewise, McRuer favorably cites the theoretical work of José Esteban Muñoz, in relation to queerness as a haunting phenomenon that is not yet here because 'we are not yet queer', in what amounts, as McRuer interprets this, to "a structured and educated mode of desiring," specifically of other possibilities, of "an ideality that can be distilled from the past to imagine a future" (quoted 147), which McRuer aligns with his own keen

1014

attentiveness to 'yearnings' for something radically other than neoliberal austerity capitalist social existence.

In *Depression: a Public Feeling*, Cvetkovich explains that Public Feelings is a "queer project" that "tries to *imagine* [my italics] a liberatory version of social and affective relations beyond the liberal versions that have come to dominate the public sphere of gay politics" while at the same time "finding ways to survive disappointment and to remind ourselves of the persistence of *radical visions* [my italics] and ways of living" (6). Public Feelings offers no magic bullets but "just the slow steady work of resilient survival, *utopian dreaming* [my italics], and other affective tools for transformation" (2). And again, even as Public Feelings "resists pastoralizing or redemptive accounts of negative feeling that seek to convert it into something useful or positive," Public Feelings "also embraces categories such as *utopia and hope*" (5-6). A major critique Cvetkovich makes, moreover, of academia is that it readily fosters depression by promoting disillusionment versus what those working in academia are otherwise inclined to *imagine and dream*, including in relation to what kind of radically transformed society is desirable and necessary as well as how they can contribute toward helping bring this about (17-18).

In chapter three of part two, "The Utopia of Ordinary Habit: Crafting, Creativity, and Spiritual Practice," Cvetkovich proposes that "Daily life in all its ordinariness can be a basis for the utopian project of building new worlds in response to both spiritual despair and political depression," in particular in the forms of what Cvetkovich theorizes as the "utopia of ordinary habit" (191). For Cvetovich, this *"utopia of ordinary habit* would be a version of Avery F. Gordon's 'usable utopia', a utopia of the 'here and now' that is 'oriented toward the future' but 'doesn't treat the future as either an off-world escape or a displacing fetish'" (quoted 191, 191). As Cvetkovich elaborates, more precisely, "The *utopia of ordinary habit* is forged out of the loss of connection . . . that characterizes depression," and involves an affective and collective project of 'remaking', "But it does not seek to gloss over the dire state of contemporary politics, nor to deny the feelings of sadness, apathy, isolation, or anger that are often manifest in the practice of small daily gestures" (192-193). In her review of Cvetkovich's *Depression: a Public Feeling* for *Kirkus* Cindy Wender gives priority emphasis to Cvetkovich's theorizartion of 'the utopia of ordinary habit," as the title of the review is "Utopia, Every Day." And this is indeed a major emphasis for Cvetkovich, concerning how experience of 'building new worlds', at the least in imagination, can be productively pursued in the course of engagement in everyday spiritual practices.

Avery F. Gordon is even more overtly engaged with the usefulness of the utopian than either McRuer or Cvetkovich. As Janice Radway notes well in her "Foreword," *Ghostly Matters* makes clear Gordon's "desire to reanimate the utopian," and in particular to do so in connection with theorizing haunting as providing a means by which a ghost can allow you to heal–yet, more specifically, as the ghost can "'help you imagine what was lost that never even existed, really'" (xiii). 'The lost that never even existed, really' is strikingly suggestive of 'the no place' that constitutes the literal meaning of 'utopia', a non-existent place that nonetheless can exercise a compelling power as contribution to practices of critique and struggles for transformation. In writing about the Argentinian 'disappeared' in response to the question "What has the state tried to repress?" Gordon answers "It has many names that I will call simply, and despite the reputation it has acquired of evasive naïveté, *the utopian* [my italics]: the apperception of the fundamental difference between the world we have now and the world we could have instead; the desire and drive to create a just and equitable world" (127). Gordon argues that in the course of the manifestly lived dystopian reign of 'the disappeared' "The utopian, the most general subject of the state's repression, makes its appearance too, lingering among the smoldering remains of a dirty war" (127).

As Gordon interprets it, Toni Morrison's *Beloved* also mobilizes the use value of the utopian because Morrison engages in an effort "to imagine the life world of those with no names we remember, with no 'visible reason' for being in the archive" (150). Morrison here *imagines* "them speaking their complex personhood as it negotiates the always coercive and subtle complexities of the hands of power," in other words imagines a utopian counter-history (150). In *Beloved*, what's more, "The ghost cannot be simply tracked back to an individual loss or trauma," "the ghost's desire is not just negative," "The ghost is not other or alterity as such, ever," and "It is (like Beloved) pregnant with unfulfilled possibility, with the something to be done that the wavering present is demanding. This something to be done is not a return to the past but a reckoning with its repression in the present, a reckoning with that which we have lost, but never had. The ghost always figures this *utopian dimension* [my italics] of haunting . . ." (183).

The mode of sociology Gordon brings to bear as well as advocates for in *Ghostly Matters* focuses on "the not there" as "a seething presence," on "the living effects, seething and lingering, of what seems over and done with, the endings that are not over" (195). Gordon argues this is the kind of history sociologists need to write: 'histories of the present' that "requires stretching toward the horizon of what cannot be seen with ordinary clarity yet" (195). This in turn means grappling with "the difficulty of imagining beyond the limits of what is already *understandable*" because "To imagine what is beyond the limits of what is already understandable is our best hope for retaining what ideology critique traditionally offers while transforming its limitations into what, in an older Marxist language, was called *utopian possibility* [italics]" (195). Gordon here is calling for a mode of critical praxis founded upon the understanding that "It is essential to see the things and the people who are primarily unseen and banished to the periphery of social graciousness," at the least "because they see you and address you," and you need "to imagine their life worlds" (196).

Gordon's subsequent work, compiling *The Hawthorn Archive*, represents "a desire to pick up where *Ghostly Matters* ended, with 'those historical alternatives' that 'haunt a given society', as Herbert Marcuse wrote; to find the place where, as Patricia Williams put it, our 'longings' are 'exiled.' In this book, I call that place, after Ernst Bloch, the *utopian margins* [italics] ("Revolutionary Feminisms: Avery F. Gordon")." In this extensive collection Gordon does exactly what she describes: compiling a wide array of disparate and often obscure traces of historical alternatives to modern racial capitalist society that haunt from the margins, that represent what was not but yet might be, what yet might prefigure or contribute usefully toward configuring what might yet be.

In this archive Gordon emphasizes materials representative of "another kind of utopianism" that is entailed by slaves running away, marronage, piracy, heresy, vagabondage, soldier desertion, and other illegible or discredited forms of escape, resistance, opposition and alternative ways of life that continued, of course, to challenge the modern racial capitalist system over time. This 'other' utopianism lends to the term 'utopian' a very different meaning–one rooted much more in the past and the present than in an unrealistic future–and a very different notion of politics–one rooted in ongoing social struggles, in various forms of nonparticipation, and in an autonomous politics hostile or indifferent to seizing state power. ("Revolutionary Feminisms: Avery F. Gordon")

Nevertheless, Gordon declares,

I am not invested in the term 'utopian'–and I don't care if it's used or not. I care about what I call, in the book, 'being in-difference'. Being in-difference is a political consciousness and a sensuous knowledge, a standpoint and a mindset for living on better terms than we're offered; for living as if you had the necessity and the freedom to do so; for living in the acknowledgment, that despite the overwhelming power of all the systems of domination which are trying to kill us, they never quite become us. ("Revolutionary Feminisms: Avery F. Gordon")

As Gordon explains further, the structure of the *Hawthorn Archive* is designed to invite "the reader into a world situated in a liminal place–one we can call *the utopian margins* [my italics], where then, now and soon we are capable of, and are, living on very different terms than the various forms of enslavement, indebtedness and repression that order this one" ("Revolutionary Feminisms: Avery F. Gordon"). Likewise, Gordon touts, versus Marx's and Engels's critique of utopian socialism, the work of Cedric Robinson in offering "A similar and expanded argument . . . in *An Anthropology of Marxism*," where Robinson contends that "Marx and Engels's dismissal of precapitalist forms of socialism, female heresy and rebellion, among other outcomes, 'obliterated the most fertile . . . domain for their political ambitions and historical imaginations' ("Revolutionary Feminisms: Avery F. Gordon")."

"Dead Souls" is suggestive of the call of voices from a comparable archive at 'the utopian margins', an archive of possibilities never fully realized, even never substantively materialized, perhaps rejected and discredited in the past, that have been buried and forgotten, yet nonetheless represent powerful manifestations of 'being-in-difference'. "Dead Souls" is suggestive of these 'dead souls' here and now *resurrected*, here and now staking out and making claims upon those in the present who are able to hear their voices. The latter are those able to overcome trepidation about what these voices might represent and what they might portend, in order to listen to these voices, to attend and respond to them, to join up and unite with them as they 'call me' to a 'calling'. This is a calling *to recall* and *to re-present* visions of radically alternative ways of living in society and with nature, as well as to carry on and carry forward struggle to concretely realize the transformative promise embodied in as of yet ephemerally abstract possibilities.

Eight

Although acknowledging "'Atmosphere' is a massive song" and that "A lot of people say it's their favourite Joy Division song," Peter Hook, writing in *Unknown Pleasures: Inside Joy Division* confides "but it's not mine," as "it reminds me too much of Ian, like his death march or something, and it figures that it's one of the most popular songs to play at funerals" (188). Despite what Hook here writes, undoubtedly due to the *massively mythic* status of Joy Division by this point in time, and especially surrounding what the four principals have done and said about the band and its music, as well as due to Hook's volubility concerning Joy Division, many casual commentators cite "Atmosphere" *as Hook's personal favorite* and as a song he wants to play at *his* funeral. But I trust what Hook writes in *Unknown Pleasures: Inside Joy Division* because this makes sense to me. Although I respect and admire the impressive conception and execution of "Atmosphere," this song is not a personal favorite of mine either, and it is not a song that has sparked the kinds of far-reaching thoughts and feelings, and extended connections, I have recounted and explored in this book. Although I generally am able to dissociate how I make sense of matters of meaning from popular and especially (auto)biographical takes, I find it harder than usual to do so with "Atmosphere," perhaps for similar reasons to those Hook references.

"Atmosphere" was originally released as part of the *Licht und Blindheit* ep together with "Dead Souls" by Sordide Sentimental in March 1980 in a limited run of 1578 copies, frequently cited as attesting to how little attention Joy Division paid to commercial concerns, with the band recognizing the quality and appeal of both songs but deciding they wanted to pursue this niche route for their initial release. Nonetheless, both songs and especially "Atmosphere" quickly attracted considerable attention. As attested on the Wikipedia page for this song, John Peel played "Atmosphere" on his show immediately upon its release, on 11 March 1980, and then "Dead Souls" the next night. "Atmosphere" was subsequently released as a single together with the alternative, extended, version of "She's Lost Control" shortly after Curtis's death, in May 1980. "Atmosphere" reached #1 on the New Zealand singles chart in August 1981 and after a reissue in August 1988 reached #1 on the UK indie singles chart in 1988. "Atmosphere" has been released as part of the *Substance* Joy Division compilation, initially in 1988, and the *Heart and Soul* box set, initially in 1997, including together with an early version of the song in which it remained titled "Chance." But more to Hook's point, and my connection with it, "Atmosphere" serves as a subject of a surrealistic black and white 1988 music video, directed by Anton Corbijn, that depicts a literal funeral march involving, as described by Wikipedia, "characters wearing black cloaks and white burial shrouds carrying around large pictures of the band" while concluding this procession with an apparent bowing to Curtis, via his picture, as having passed on. "Atmosphere" subsequently plays after Curtis's suicide in *24 Hour Party People* and, especially memorably, after the same, over the final credits, in Corbijn's Ian Curtis fictional feature biopic, *Control*. Notably, Peel played this song on his radio show in first announcing Curtis's death and "Atmosphere" was also played at Tony Wilson's funeral in 2007. As Hook attests, "Atmosphere" has undoubtedly also been played at numerous other funerals. Perhaps unsurprisingly, on this account alone, in 2009 *NME* ranked "Atmosphere" #1 of "The 20 Greatest Goth Tracks," according to soundmeaningsandfacts.com.

Also in *Unknown Pleasures: Inside Joy Division*, Hook recounts on the night Annik Honoré saw Joy Division live for the first time the band played "a great gig" that started with "Atmosphere" (220). "Atmosphere" "didn't have the connotations then that it does now that it's sort of Ian's death march," but instead, "Back then it was a good song to start with" because Joy Division "liked to come on and defy expectations by starting with something slow and reflective, before building up to the faster songs" (220-221). Elsewhere in *Unknown Pleasures: Inside Joy Division*, Hook acknowledges "Atmosphere" much improved upon its predecessor "Chance," with this having to do first with the addition of organ and later of synthesizer keyboards as well as Martin Hannett's creative production (160). As Stephen Morris discusses in *Record Play Pause: Confessions of a Post-Punk Percussionist Volume I*, "Atmosphere" represented yet another instance of Hannett refusing to follow a straightforward path. In making this song, "I had the chime off a broken tambourine perched on a scissor blade held very close to a microphone [and] softly pinging the chime produced the shimmering icy bell effect for the chorus on 'Atmosphere'" (312). Morris also notes that Hannett replaced the sound of the song the band previously achieved in live performance via a Bakelite plastic push button reed organ with an ARP-Omni 2 keyboard synthesizer (312).

The aura of innovation, due to the extensive presence within the song of synthesizer sounds, in part accounts for the song's initial appeal, but as Mick Middles and Lindsay Reade write in *Torn Apart: the Life of Ian Curtis*, the 'total package' is even more important:

> Indeed, the first bleak seconds of "Atmosphere" convey an unparalleled intimacy through the close-up timbre of Ian's voice. Lyrics that are awash in ambiguity– "Walk in silence . . . don't walk away, in silence . . ."–suggest the head-in-hands desperation as a lover leaves for the last time; hollow moments of realisation, of a life lost, a killed passion, the final embers of dream. Ian's voice might be the loneliest in the world as it hovers above Hannett's simplistic mix, a flickering candle of truth, a grim realisation. Pop music was never meant to be like this: the fire of youth vanquished and an emotive power so effortlessly believable flowing through the lyrics. And then, slicing through the pitch black like a shard of glass, there's the blinding white light of sound that cuts straight to the heart. (177)

Middles and Reade characterize "Atmosphere" as representative of the atmosphere of Britain, and especially of Manchester and Greater Manchester, at the time the song was written, from the perspective of disenchanted and even further alienated youth: bleak, gray, and riven with angst and anguish. According to Middles and Reade, "Atmosphere" prefigures the Cure's 1981 song "Faith" and the Cure's 1989 album *Disintegration*, as well as "a thousand sub-genres with their roots dangling in that very same moment" (177). Yet "'Atmosphere' is really in a genre all on its own, settling eternally into the more solemn fringes of goth rather than the cartoon version which gather in knots of teenage angst in new Millennium shopping malls," while the moment it captures "came largely from Ian Curtis," because "All the other elements, the Hannett technique, the savage swath of the synth, the velvety sheen, *all* those elements simply exist to bring you closer to Ian Curtis. He was and remains a most shockingly believable singer, touching the places you choose to ignore" (177).

In a 18 March 2021 article on "Atmosphere" for *Dig!*, Alan York begins by crediting a reference to the song, in a recent retrospective by *The Guardian*, as "encapsulating the song perfectly," and that is: "a glacial, glittering masterpiece." York agrees with those who identify "Atmosphere" as among Joy Division's very best, describing the song as a "towering ballad" that is "Sombre, yet spine-tinglingly beautiful." As York recounts, although the melody originates with "Chance," the Hannett-produced version "had evolved into a thing of wonder." With Hannett's input, "The band delivered the lush, keyboard-led backing track with admirable restraint, while Ian Curtis compounded his intensely personal lyrics . . . by delivering one of his richest and most evocative vocal performances." York cites the aforementioned *Guardian* take on the song as "'an unshakeable testament' to Joy Division's brilliance" while also quoting from Peter Hook, interviewing with *Louder* in 2017, that "Atmosphere got voted the favourite rock song to be played at funerals at one stage . . . Which was a very dubious honour. However, it's got a wonderful bass riff and it is very moving and melancholic, which Ian capitalised on with the vocal line and the lyrics. It's a massive song!"

In a 2016 article on "Atmosphere" for *American Songwriter*, Jim Beviglia describes the song as "a piece of music that easily could have worked an an instrumental." According to Beviglia, as the song "builds and builds via Stephen Morris' relentlessly thumping drums, while Peter Hook finds creases for probing bass notes," in turn "Bernard Sumner clears the tension occasionally with sprightly keyboards," such that "The end result" is "of something that sounds like it's trying to claw its way out of the depths of despair." Nevertheless, despite its potential as an instrumental piece, "Curtis' performance meanwhile is unfailingly compelling," as even taking into account the "inscrutable" nature of the lyrics, "the quiver in Curtis's voice makes clear these words are a futile conversation with someone who seems to have already departed the haunted landscape inhabited by the narrator." Although the narrator-protagonist seemingly initially does "want to resolve the issues" between this narrator-protagonist and his now absent interlocutor, "without it devolving into an argument," nonetheless "The 'endless talking' seems to be injuring him," the narrator-protagonist. However, the song is yet further complex, because the narrator-protagonist "also sees this separation as a kind of cycle that must perpetuate itself: 'Life rebuilding'." Eventually, however, according to Beviglia, the argument develops and the break-up happens, although this is perhaps at least in part "mitigated by the lack of effort put into saving the relationship in the first place." After offering this interpretation, Beviglia concludes by agreeing that "'Atmosphere' is the type of song that might elicit a thousand different reactions and interpretations from a thousand different listeners."

Venturing onto the songmeanings.com page for "Atmosphere" appears to confirm Beviglia's concluding point. A number of commentators link the meaning of the song to Curtis's suicide, and his suicidality, or his epilepsy, without adding much more than that. However, many push further. One common take involves difficulty in communication between people, especially in pushing beyond surface impressions, including pushing beyond self-protective or otherwise outward-projective masks, and especially involving people who experience themselves, or whom others commonly experience, as different from 'normal'. Many commentators, focusing overwhelmingly on the lyrics, interpret the song as a troubled account from someone who feels like others can't, and won't, understand 'him', but who hasn't made it easy for these others, and who is torn between blaming himself and blaming them for the isolation and alienation 'he' experiences. Some of these commentators suggest the song emphasizes failure to take the time and make the effort to get to know people, beyond the surface, and failure to devote the time and effort needed to win their trust so they will reveal 'more of themselves'.

The narrator-protagonist seemingly, according to a number of these commentators, has adopted a fierce and off-putting outward persona, that pushes people away, even when 'he' desires the opposite, but 'he' is unable to figure out how to change.

Another strand in the interpretations of "Atmosphere" posted on songmeanings.com centers the meaning of the song on the line "Don't walk away in silence," as urging people not to forget those who have passed on and died, or not to forget those who are troubled and in need. This can relate to the line of interpretation I previously described, having to do with interpersonal relationships, as a critique of people who prefer shallow relationships and who don't want to get to know others all that well or all that far, especially not when they have to confront what can be upsetting and unsettling about others, in particular others' confusions and vulnerabilities.

A further common thread on songmeanings.com is to link "Atmosphere," and again seemingly largely the lyrics alone, with being a kind of person who prefers isolation, and who is more inclined toward introversion than extroversion, but nonetheless is pulled away from isolation and from introversion to extroversion, however uncomfortably. One commentator, meanwhile, proposes the song "is about cyclic existence and the survival instinct that perpetuates it," which includes recognizing "the transitory and insubstantial nature of everything," while at the same time, once more, somewhat contradictorily, the song critiques "people who are content with living on the surface, just floating through their meaningless routines never bothering to look deeply or question anything," because here the narrator-protagonist "wants people to wake up and take a look around."

More specifically, a number of these commentators propose the song deals with stress, strain, and breakdown in a particular kind of relationship: with an intimate romantic-sexual partner, such as a spouse. In this connection, the song laments the emotional distance that has developed in what otherwise, but only superficially, remains a 'close' relationship, where the people in the relationship have effectively stopped loving or even caring about each other but persist in the pretense of maintaining the kind of relationship they once had yet don't any longer. Motivated undoubtedly by knowledge of Curtis's marriage, one commentator extends this interpretation further, focusing on what it feels like to be needy and vulnerable but unable effectively to communicate this, especially with the one to whom one ostensibly should be best able to do so: "To me, this is someone who has trouble expressing themselves and is also overwhelmed by constant noise of the world. He wants this person to stay and be with him, to comfort him, but quietly, without needing to talk. Just being there, and understanding without words. Walking in silence, but not walking AWAY in silence needn't be a contradiction." The last is an apt comment, because yes it can make sense to interpret the lyrics as referencing the need, above all else, for someone who is able to listen and hear, or even just to be there. In this case this could well mean 'to be there' for someone who is suffering painfully. Under these circumstances, yes, it could make sense that the person suffering painfully wants someone to listen to and walk with him without at the same time feeling compelled to tell the person in pain what they *should* do about their situation, and in particular without proposing precisely how they *should* go about seeking to achieve an end to the pain they are experiencing.

Perhaps the resonance here to difficulties in communication applies more generally, as another commentator suggests: "it's about wanting to say something to someone . . . seeing the confusion in their face knowing you've either said to much, or what you said makes no sense." In other words, "Atmosphere" is more simply yet more generally about "Difficulty interacting with people," about difficulty "Connecting with people," and, as such, calls upon us to "Imagine the difficulty, and frustration when someone walks away completely silent," when you have tried, but seemingly failed, to communicate something that is most important, and that deeply matters, to you. As others on this site suggest, this line of interpretation can connect in turn with critique of those who aren't interested in 'deep conversation', 'deep sharing' of an intellectual and emotional kind, or of leading a reflective, including a self-reflective, life.

Other interesting takes shared on this songmeanings.com page include one linking the song to the sentiments expressed in the famous Dylan Thomas poem urging the narrator's father, and us as well as readers as well, 'not to go gently into the night' but instead to 'rage, rage against the dying of the light'. In other words, "don't walk away in silence." An intriguing take from a self-identified deaf commentator links the song with the feelings this person and other disabled people have in dealing with non-disabled people who are too uncomfortable around them to know how to interact and engage with them at all, and who thereby tend either to ignore or avoid contact with disabled people. A further distinctive take comes from a commentator who contends "this song is the only uplifting song Joy Division did apart from 'Ceremony'" as "the song is like Ian or whoever you'd like it to be in this, is saying don't worry" with the reference in the lyrics to "Life rebuilding" suggesting "the song is about life and death but in a good way and that no one should just grieve but be happy that this person had good times and they had a good friend." And as a final, interesting, take, in contrast, many on this page interpret "Atmosphere" as epitomizing a depressive perspective, the perspective of someone who is deeply depressed, and in particular how such a person in turn interprets and evaluates what 'he' experiences as his surroundings, especially other people surrounding 'him'.

Next, I turn to three longer, sustained pieces not expressly focused on "Atmosphere," but rather the music of Joy Division as a totality, that I have not previously addressed in this book, because all prove useful in further exploring how to interpret "Atmosphere." I begin with Helen Pleasance's chapter "Paying more close anxious attention to Joy Division" from *Music, Memory and Memoir*, edited by Robert Edgar, Fraser Mann, and Helen Pleasance, and published in 2019. Pleasance recounts a personal experience, from the last day of her second term at Sussex University in 1984, when another young woman attending the same university at the same time, Maddy, a member of Pleasance's circle of friends, was killed when Maddy was struck by an automobile while attempting a shortcut across a dangerous road that Pleasance and the rest of her friends often crossed. What disturbed Pleasance in the immediate aftermath of Maddy's death, and prompts this chapter, is the response of a young man who didn't know Maddy, or not all that well, but who seemed to experience Maddy's death as prompting "some greater kind of existential angst," that this young man immediately associated with the music of Joy Division, playing the latter music repeatedly on his turntable as, seeming to him at least, an apt response to Maddy's death and what might constitute its 'meaning'. Pleasance found it disturbing that Maddy's death became the occasion for this young man to immerse himself in Joy Division music as "providing a soundscape for what feels like a staged moment of trauma." In other words, this young man's response seemed inauthentic and disrespectful, leaving Pleasance feeling "complete and utter irritation."

That experience with Joy Division, and with how many other Joy Division devotees make sense of and respond to Joy Division music, with 'close anxious attention', has troubled Pleasance as indicative of a tendency toward "a peculiarly masculine mythologization"–not only of specific traumatic events to which one is not directed connected but also in relation to a broader "cultural moment." Pleasance's concern is with how "Joy Division had become a particular kind of 'cultural template' through which to modulate emotional experience." Pleasance finds Paul Morley's writing exemplary of such tendencies, suggesting Morley moves beyond what Paul Crosthwaite problematizes as "imaginative historicism" (which I discuss in chapter two), to become "willfully personal." Pleasance acknowledges Morley is hardly alone in this kind of approach to Joy Division, as she notes it is commonplace among commentators who suggest Joy Division provides a definitive musical correlative to what it felt like to live in Manchester, and Greater Manchester, and even 'the North' of Britain in general, at a specific cultural moment, the late 1970s to the early 1980s, and especially to have done so from the vantage point of 'sensitive' (and in particular sensitive *male*) youth. Pleasance does appreciate some usefulness in Morley's engagement in mythologization: "His process of mythologizing the band is, partially at least, a way of writing a self that acknowledges and transcends the trauma that threatened to consume and destroy him," and "Myth serves a really important function of giving the traumatized subject an identity narrative that gives them a future." For Morley, writing about Joy Division as "displaced autobiography," Pleasance acknowledges, "allowed him to reflect on almost inexpressible, liminal emotional states, especially those of young men, which he saw Joy Division as expressing."

Pleasance respects that this kind of response, when shared among many others, transcends the limits of being entirely personal and represents a kind of "collective history of trauma," in particular in relation to how "writing into history" from "below the level of power" "allows individual listeners to engage with the collective at the level of personal affect" as "each listener *feels* they are inscribed in and actively inscribing a historical moment." But Pleasance remains wary of overextending a tendency to use one trauma, notably Ian Curtis's suicide, "to narrate other traumas" to the point where doing so effectively collapses these 'other traumas' into elaborations of Joy Division's 'enduring' mythic grasp. Pleasance does grant 'close anxious attention to Joy Division' can achieve "something quite staggeringly radical" in putting "something hitherto inexpressible into historical discourse," and in allowing "*something to be done with it*." Problems arise, nonetheless, by conflating achieving of personal agency in finding means and medium through which to transcend trauma, experienced at the personal level, with achieving collective agency in transcending collective trauma, because the former is much "easier to achieve" than the latter.

Bringing her reservations up to date, Pleasance cites how Joy Division was invoked with little explanation of its direct relevance and connection, as seemingly obviously linked with and aptly brought to bear, in processing the impact of the bombing at the MEN Arena in Manchester in May 2017. According to Pleasance, Joy Division was invoked in response to this traumatic event as maintaining a preeminent place within a seemingly seamless continuity of experiences and expressions of trauma, and survival, in Manchester. Pleasance worries about how resort "to the Joy Division myth might produce an overly or inappropriately traumatized response to events" among those who are in fact *not* directly, personally connected, and she also worries that such such "overpersonalization of history" can prevent "other kinds of engagement with events in the public sphere." For Pleasance this can happen with Joy Division in particular because of how gendered she interprets 'close anxious attention' to this music to have been from its beginning and continuing ever since. Pleasance concludes by suggesting Mark Fisher's identification with the music of Joy Division further exemplifies a similarly problematic romantic mystification of depression and suicide that might not have happened if this music did not already bear such an overpowering weight of mythic associations.

Certainly, the entire book you are reading might well make sense as exemplifying 'close anxious attention' to Joy Division, and indeed as making use of this music as a way not only to address and come to grips with personal trauma but also to make broad connections with collective trauma. However, while I respect Pleasance's cautions, it is important to underscore that my listening to and reflecting upon what I think (about) and feel in response to this music prompts me to explore reflections on matters of interest and concern that proceed far beyond the music, in and of itself, while opening up this music to a range of interpretations that counter tendencies to identify it as always all about trauma. At the same time, as I have emphasized throughout this book, I tend to be impatient with interpretations that relate this music solely to depression, suicide, and suicidality, and that are dependent upon direction connections with the 'traumatic' life-experience of Ian Curtis. In addition, my identifications with this music continue to evolve and transform, while I do not identify with straight cisgender masculine white male 'laddishness', circa mid 1970s to early 1980s–or since. On the flip side, the familiar trope of the hyper-sensitive straight cisgender young white male as 'the tortured artist' does not resonate, personally, for me. And in the five classes I have taught on Ian Curtis, Joy Division, and critical theory, women as often as men experienced strong connections with this music, and with what our engagement with this music prompted them to explore, while men just as often as women were among those who struggled to find such connections. What's more, queer-identifying or queer-affiliating students were particularly inclined to experience strong connections, as were students of color and students with personal experience of significant disabilities, physical and mental. In addition, students closest to 'laddish' in their outlook and sensibility found it hardest to draw connections, because Joy Division came across to them as too unremittingly serious, somber, and bleak.

At the same time, moreover, as I have emphasized in these classes and others I have taught focused on popular music as cultural studies, I certainly do not 'prescribe' that anyone else ever 'should' embrace the music of Joy Division as music they find powerfully meaningful to them. I happily accept many people experience the kind and degree of connection I long have with Joy Division in relation to the music of other musicians, including music of considerably different kinds. I myself, while maintaining an affinity for the music of Joy Division and 'classic' early post-punk, am enthralled, regularly, by an ecumenical variety of different music, in numerous styles and genres, and I continually seek out new, recent, and current music, that I pursue quite voraciously (only in part in seeking material to feature on my weekly radio show), and that often sounds nothing at all like Joy Division.

I can readily imagine many people *not* finding the music of Joy Division compelling to them, even being unmoved by and indifferent to it, while preferring much different music–and I am entirely at peace with that. I *love* students sharing what music matters most to them, however different from

Joy Division, as well as their reflections on how and why this music means as much as it does to them along with others who feel the same. I *love* it when they nonetheless, as I do, hold out the *possibility* that others who have not yet become familiar with the music they are sharing, or who have not previously experienced this music as particularly compelling, might yet be persuaded to consider giving it a chance, or another chance, in order to do so. I too, like Helen Pleasance, admire the music of Young Marble Giants, and other punk and post-punk bands from around the same time as Joy Division, in which women were prominent if not indeed leading contributors, and I would not be at all be surprised if someone pursued a similar project to what I am doing with this book in relation to the music of Young Marble Giants. I welcome such efforts.

A problem *can* arise in suggesting the music of Joy Division is automatically, unquestionably right and appropriate, as a means of responding to diverse experiences of collective trauma–and then effectively *imposing* this music on these traumas, or *appropriating* these traumas into Joy Division as myth such that they become most important as mere constituents of this myth. In this respect I don't think "Atmosphere" makes unquestionable sense to be played at funerals (and I definitely do not want this song played at my funeral). What matters, instead, is whose funerals these are, what these people were like and what kinds of music best resonates with what they were like. What matters is what those who have now died, and who are being commemorated at these funerals, meant, and what their loss now means, to those closest to them, to those suffering the most painful bereavement following their deaths. And what matters is who are driven to want, and to need, to celebrate the lives of their now dead loved ones and to treasure the legacy of the relationship they forged with those now dead. Vastly different songs make sense in taking these matters concretely into account. After all, in connecting Joy Division with critical theory as I am in this book I am deliberately challenging thinking that relies upon unquestioned assumptions and that is content with the superficially apparent, the merely commonsensical, the seemingly self-evident, and the already familiar, because critical theory itself deliberately challenges all of this.

The second longer, sustained piece I want to discuss here is titled "Channelling the darkness: Group flow and environmental expression in the music of Black Sabbath and Joy Division," and is an article written by Steve Taylor published in the March 2020 edition of the journal *Metal Music Studies*. Taylor is a senior lecturer in psychology at Leeds Beckett University, UK; the current chair of the Transpersonal Psychology section of the British Psychological Society; the author of five books and numerous articles in scholarly journals; and a musician and a poet. Taylor's major aim with this article is to argue for a close affinity between the music of Joy Division and that of Black Sabbath. That particular comparison is not directly relevant to me here, so I will concentrate on Taylor's description, analysis, and interpretation of the music of Joy Division. Right away Taylor zeroes in on Peter "Hook's mildly distorted bass riffs accompanied with the further distortion of Bernard Sumner's guitar, and the frequent use of tom-toms by drummer Stephen Morris." Taylor notes that, as with Black Sabbath, Joy Division avoids "the brightness of major third notes" as "Seventh notes and chords are also rarely–if ever–used by both bands." Notable as well, Morris makes relatively unusual use of tom-toms in place of the hi-hat, and this is especially apparent on both "Dead Souls" and "Atmosphere," while Sumner embellishes or departs from the melodic riffs played by Hook as opposed to playing along with them. All of this along with Ian Curtis singing his vocal lines primarily in "a staccato style, without vibrato," contributes to a 'channelling of the darkness' simultaneous with conveying a pronounced "sense of distance and emotionlessness," or perhaps, as I in contrast would put it, complicatedly layered and mediated forms of emotional expression. Further notable, for Taylor, again as with Black Sabbath, Joy Division "did not utilize a standard pop structure of verses and choruses (or hooks) with middle eights or bridges" and "Because of this departure from traditional song structure, there is a sense in which both bands' songs do not resolve or even end, which lends a strange sense of incompleteness to the songs." As Taylor elaborates,

> Joy Division songs usually contain one single riff, locked together with a drum rhythm and repeated without variation, in a metronomic and mechanical way. Guitar phrases overlay and intersperse the repeated riff, with a vocal melody on top. Songs such as 'Heart and Soul' and 'Colony' are based on two-bar bass guitar riffs that repeat for the whole duration of the song, and which one could imagine repeating indefinitely, like the endless churning machines of a factory. Live recordings reveal Joy Division songs grinding to a close rather than finishing, almost like a machine being turned off and slowly petering out. Many songs end with each instrument dropping out in turn after the final verse–first the guitar, then the bass and finally the drums. In other words, both bands' songs do not resolve in the same way the highly structured songs of the Beatles or the Kinks–or even tightly structured progressive rock bands such as Yes or Genesis. This is another source of the unease and austerity of both bands, since a resolution usually brings a sense of order and cohesion to a song.

With Joy Division, "there is a regular, mathematical quality to their music that is clearly redolent of industry" as "Drummer Stephen Morris was heavily influenced by 'Krautrock' bands such as Neu! and Kraftwerk and their motoric, repetitive rhythms." In turn, "Morris' motoric rhythms (often providing sixteen beats to the bar hi-hat or tom-tom patterns)," are complimented by Hook's bass riffs that "are almost invariably eight beats to the bar throughout the whole song, while Ian Curtis' vocal lines are also extremely regular, with the same syllabic patterns rigidly repeated (and also, as mentioned before, sung without vibrato)." All of this enables 'channeling of the darkness' and especially of how bleak and brutal such 'darkness' can feel.

Ultimately even more important than all of what I have so far cited, for Taylor, is the fact that both Black Sabbath and Joy Division "created music in a highly collaborative, organic way," which meant that "Unlike most bands, there was not one or two single creative forces, who pre-wrote most of the songs, which were then arranged and rehearsed by the whole group for performance and recording," as instead "The collaborative nature of both bands' creativity is reflected in the fact that–unusually–songwriting credits were shared equally amongst all members." What's more, "Both bands' high level of social flow is also indicated by the unconscious nature of their creativity, involving a lack of conscious deliberation," and "This is a theme that continually crops up in the memoirs of the surviving members of Joy Division." According to "the members of both groups' descriptions, songs almost seemed to be coming through them rather than from them, as if the band members were serving as channels for the music." Taylor finds the disjunction between the music members of Joy Division made, with it predominantly 'dark' tenor, and the way they led their lives, as well as their personalities evidenced elsewhere and otherwise, "again illustrates the quasi-channelled nature of Joy Division's music, as if the music was coming through rather than from them." Taylor concludes by touting the way group "flow manifests itself in the compositional stage rather than just in performance," with Joy Division and Black Sabbath as "quite rare–in pop and rock music," because "it is standard practice for songs to be pre-written by one or two main creative forces," while "Arguably" the former "type of group requires a more intense degree of group flow." As such Joy Division and Black Sabbath are better able than most rock bands "to become pure conduits of environmental influences and unconscious psychological forces." In turn, Taylor proposes that "The music of both bands is so powerful because it carries such a strong imprint of the environment they emerged from," and this "was a spontaneous unconscious outpouring of a particular cultural experience of mid- to late twentieth-century Britain" where "The darkness of their environment became the darkness of their music, in a very pure and primal way, and with a powerful spontaneous creativity that–paradoxically–gave the music an uplifting transcendent quality."

Taylor's argument is useful to keep in mind, pace Pleasance, because it can make good sense to interpret the music of Joy Division as unconsciously 'channeling' elaborate arrays of social 'environmental' influences from the times and places in which they made this music, including social environmental influences that are shared with or maintain close parallels to many other times and places, especially those likewise experienced as bleak, harsh, difficult, and challenging, with social crises proliferating and where a palpable sense pervades of existing in a fraught state of social transition combined with great uncertainty concerning where this transition might lead. "Atmosphere" makes sense as 'channeling the darkness' that resonates with lived experience as part of such a social environment, and it makes sense as doing so in unconscious form, rather than as representing a deliberate comment on a specific kind of personal or interpersonal experience. The 'atmosphere' in question might indeed include this 'darkness' as well as 'shafts of light' that can and do break through, especially when, as Taylor suggests, the darkness is channeled in a "pure and primal way, and with a powerful spontaneous creativity that–paradoxically" gives "the music an uplifting transcendent quality." Interpreting the song along these lines, "Atmosphere" becomes more about the performative recreation and transformation of a shared unconscious experience of a social environment, with the words of the lyrics mattering more in terms of how they sound than about 'what they have to say'. As such, these lyrics, when considered as part of *the song as a song* and not just in and of themselves alone, are abstract prompts toward the elicitation of a felt response to a social atmosphere that is shared among the musicians, and prospectively among many listeners, but which is often experienced unconsciously rather than consciously, and which as such is not often precisely identified, described, and explained in words by those experiencing this kind of response when and as they do experience it.

The third longer, sustained piece of writing I want to discuss before turning to my own close reading of the title and the lyrics of "Atmosphere" is a master's thesis, submitted in 2020 by Logan James Hunter, for a degree in German at the University of South Carolina, and this thesis is titled *Dark German Romanticism and the Postpunk Ethos of Joy Division, the Cure and Smashing Pumpkins*. Here I am not directly concerned with a major aim of Hunter's thesis and that is to compare and contrast Joy Division, the Cure, and Smashing Pumpkins, but I do want to cite what Hunter writes concerning how specifically Joy Division draws upon (or perhaps 'channels') influences from 'Dark German Romanticism'. To begin, the music of all three groups, Hunter proposes, "is dark and Romantic because of the artists' reach beyond finite limits to attain Romantic ideals" (v). In other words,

Each of them fixates upon Romantic ideals stretching beyond the possibility of measurable achievement. Discarding their disillusioned realities for infinite ideals brings these artists face to face with existential despair, and they each face destructive consequence for venturing too far in their pursuits. With their Romantic ideals becoming the all-consuming desire of their minds, they turn to artistic expression in rock as a platform to express their angst-laden yearnings and despairs. (v)

Hunter links his reading of 'the postpunk ethos' with that of Simon Reynolds, from *Rip It Up and Start Again*, where Reynolds declares that shared among postpunk musicians, "Their songs grappled with classic existentialist quandaries: the struggle and agony of having a 'self'; love versus isolation; the absurdity of existence; the human capacity for perversity and spite; the perennial 'suicide, why the hell not'" (quoted 1). But Hunter is interested in pushing further than this and in making more precise connections with a specific historical antecedent. Even though "Postpunk artists are not necessarily aware" of "underlying connections to German Romanticism," nonetheless "they are aware of the role modern society and industrialization served in spawning their disillusions," which is relevant because "German Romantic disillusion dealt with economic and social change in the late eighteenth century," with "The Age of Enlightenment and the French Revolution" acting "as a catalyst for German Romanticism's rise as a form of art" (2).

The 'disillusions' postpunk musicians share with German Romanticism, and especially with *Dark* German Romanticism, center around a "growing divide between the material and spiritual, the past and present, and reality and fantasy" (4). In particular,

Dark German Romanticism arises from disillusion with modern reality, leading to solipsistic withdrawal. Withdrawn into the mind, the artist uses the imagination as a place of inspiration. It serves as a safe haven from the terrors and horrors of modern reality, limitless in its expanse to enrapture the mind with Romantic *ideals*. These ideals can be defined as a desired state or condition conceived within the imagination as a satisfying replacement for the insufficiencies of life. They are *infinite* ideals, because the desired outcome is immeasurable or unachievable within the physical realm. Problems therefore arise when the Romantic artist fixates upon this inward ideal and forgoes the normal sensory foundation of real life. When a Romantic ideal expands into the all-consuming object of desire, the results can be disastrous existentially and artistically. Fantasy, left unchecked, has the potential to consume the artist. (7)

Interestingly, despite these manifest dangers, Hunter argues "The rise of dark Romantic expression within the postpunk ethos exemplifies German Romanticism as a *progressive* force resurfacing well beyond the nineteenth century, continuing its transcendent march into the postpunk ethos" (8). What this means, more precisely, is that "This phenomenon will continue onward, reappearing whenever rebellion, disillusion and despair surface within the artistic soul" as "This dark cataclysm of artistic expression will be found blossoming amidst the gardens of modern industrialization, technological development and social unrest" (8).

In proceeding to discuss Joy Division, Hunter again cites Simon Reynolds warning that "The trouble with demystification . . . is that it strips the world of superstition and sentimentality, but also eliminates intuition and other non-rational forms of perception and awareness" (quoted 9). Hunter is keen to emphasize how much the music of Joy Division is *about* bringing to bear 'intuition and other non-rational forms of perception and awareness' as well as deriving 'insight' from these sources. Hunter finds the postpunk music of Joy Division, like that of many other early postpunk bands making music that departs from merely reiterating prior forms of punk, is suggestive of "Art students seeking an experimental lifestyle outside of school . . . challenging the boundaries of punk by using literature, history and personal experiences for new ideas" (13). In turn, "Postpunk would be predominately apolitical and solipsistic in its message, though their audiences' interest in the music was perhaps political in listening as an act of rebellion against parents and the status quo" (13).

Hunter identifies Ian Curtis as the classic 'dark romantic figure' of "a tortured poet in every way" (14). More to the point, the music Curtis contributed toward creating shared Dark German Romanticism's considerable skepticism, and indeed outright doubt, that existing society is moving in the direction of steadily greater social progress, that 'enlightenment' is everywhere increasingly triumphant.

In relation to the band's name, Hunter agrees with Stephen Morris "that the name has to do with the prisoners rather than the oppressors," while adding "this makes sense from a Romantic point of view" (15). From a critical *Romantic* vantage point "The factory worker, enchained by an industrial oppressor, is reduced to only a number or mechanical unit serving as a means to produce for a master entity. Stripped of their individuality, their purpose is to work for someone else's financial gain. The factory worker functions as a machine in this environment, rather than as a human." In turn, the name "'Joy Division' served as a metaphor for the band's perceived enslavement to ordinary industrial life in Manchester, where the creative elements of the human soul are restrained to working paycheck to paycheck for someone else's prosperity." To quote Morris, "It was the flipside of it . . . Rather than being the master race, the oppressed rather than the oppressor" (quoted 15). In sum, Hunter interprets the band Joy Division, in characteristic 'Dark German Romantic' fashion, as suggesting contemporary "Manchester represented the 'joy division' of industrial progress," with the bandmembers sharing a common yearning, among many living in the city and the region at the time, and in closely comparable locations elsewhere at the same time as well as before and since, "to escape their metropolitan oppressor" (15), even as Curtis ultimately "would yearn for a different type of escape" (15). Hunter contends that "Curtis was a Romantic visionary and intellectual" (15) whose lyrics concerned discontents and longings for a vastly different and better life beyond merely the particular personal difficulties he experienced, such as due to his epilepsy. Ultimately, Hunter asserts, Curtis's yearnings lead him to feel "paralyzed" and "trapped" such that he could not identify any way to realize these, and to feel "paralyzed" and "trapped" yet further because in not being able to identify any such way toward such realization death comes to feel "an inevitable outcome" in response to such 'failing' (21).

Hunter is useful, in connection with "Atmosphere," in suggesting the possibility of interpreting this song as concerned with frustrated aspirations that are broader yet at the same time maintain more specific historical antecedents than other takes that interpret this song as an expression of deep discontent to the point of suicidality. With Hunter, it is possible to propose "Atmosphere," along with yet other Joy Division songs, continues in a long 'dark romantic' tradition of registering and sharing profound discontent with what might be identified as 'the spiritual emptiness' of so much of modern social existence, including the social structures that shape and especially circumscribe this existence, along with the kinds of social aspirations and the forms of social achievement that tend to receive the greatest encouragement and applause in modern societies. This is life subject to the multiply alienative effects of modern capitalism, which continues to resonate with what life feels subject to multiply alienative effects of early 21st century capitalism, in the UK, the US, and beyond. The focus is not so much on the precarity but rather the meaninglessness of existence, and of the lack of access to and opportunity to exercise resources, powers, and capacities necessary to create a meaningful existence. This could be lack of meaning in 'spiritual' terms, of being inspired with a calling. It could be lack of avenues available to pursue such a calling. And it could be lack of social respect and appreciation for the value of pursuing such a calling.

It makes sense here to think about how many people, even if they are able to avoid destitution, live their lives doing jobs they find deeply dissatisfying and unfulfilling, jobs that make little to no use of their foremost talents and abilities, jobs that give them little space let alone encouragement to exercise their creativity or their 'criticality', and jobs that leave them exhausted so that they maintain little time or energy to pursue 'spiritual needs', broadly conceived, elsewhere and otherwise. It makes sense here to think as well about how many people are discouraged and otherwise prevented, under conditions of austerity neoliberalism and neofascist authoritarian populism, from pursuing studies, even from learning at all, in the humanities, the arts, and the social sciences, that might acquaint them with prospectively liberating forms of knowledge, especially in relation to issues of race, gender, and sexuality. It is makes sense yet further to reflect on how far even the supposedly most 'advanced' societies are from providing equitable access and inclusion for people with disabilities, including people with mental disabilities. Still all too often superficially sympathetic gestures are all of what is available, and these ultimately do not make a substantial difference in the quality of disabled people's lives, leaving all too many disabled people, despite this ostensible sympathy, effectively ignored, excluded, and discarded.

I have discussed many useful interpretations of what, and how, "Atmosphere," might mean. Yet few, despite close attention to the lyrics, take into account the prospective meaning of the title of the song, or of the song's earlier title, "Chance," or of what 'it might mean' to move from "Chance" to "Atmosphere." Let's consider this next.

Definitions of 'atmosphere' typically encompass 'a variety of surrounding and enveloping environments', along with the ability to exercise such a surrounding, enveloping, and not just a background influence. "Atmosphere," in the case of of the Joy Division song, combines 'surrounding' and 'enveloping' with 'permeation' such that what ostensibly exists 'outside' is so intermeshed with what ostensibly exists 'inside' that the two become effectively inseparable, even close to indistinguishable.

Many students, in literature classes, learn to conceive of 'atmosphere' as greater than 'tone', with 'tone' a smaller part of a larger 'atmosphere', and with 'atmosphere' often identified as equivalent to 'mood'. But 'atmosphere' is also a kind of 'mood' that seems, often enough, simultaneously to 'come inside' 'from without' and to correspond to the projection of 'what is inside' onto 'what is outside'. 'Atmosphere', as such, connotes something of a breakdown, even a crisis, in the ability sharply to distinguish figure from ground, subject from object, event from situation, text from context, and foreground from background. 'Atmosphere''s power, what's more, often feels nebulous, elusive, and mysterious–yet substantial, often overwhelming.

Definitions of 'chance', meanwhile, typically emphasize what happens or befalls, often unpredictably, or seemingly randomly or accidentally, or according to fate or luck, as well an opportunity, or a prospect, which, while often welcome, also tends to involve risk. In moving from "Chance" to "Atmosphere" as the title of this Joy Division song, therefore, the connotation shifts from denoting a potential opportunity, however risky and however unpredictable and uncontrollable, to denoting what envelops and permeates. For 'chance' to become 'atmosphere' suggests that what happens, or befalls, unpredictably, randomly, accidentally, and uncontrollably, seemingly according to fate or luck, representing a risky opportunity, has become pervasively enveloping and even pervasively permeating as a fundamental felt dimension of life-experience–in particular life-experience 'on the edge'. This amounts to feeling not only immersed in what one cannot control, whether this control has been lost or never actually existed, but also, all the more chilling, that what happens, what befalls, is devoid of inherent meaning, purpose, or value, and is, in and of itself, random and accidental. Perhaps the quest for meaning, purpose, and value comes to appear futile because the 'atmosphere' appears to be what maintains all the power, an atmosphere that surmounts agency. But, once more, as often with Ian Curtis's lyrics, and even more with Joy Division songs as songs and not just lyrics alone, what "Atmosphere" the song emphasizes is persistence, even if this might seem a bitter, anguished, and exhausted persistence. Perhaps this is persistence in the face of apparent impossibility of persisting.

"Walk in silence/Don't walk away, in silence," calls for the seemingly contradictory: to both 'walk in silence' and 'not walk in silence'. But perhaps this isn't as contradictory as it might seem. The second line, after all, includes 'don't walk *away*, in silence'. Perhaps the narrator-protagonist here is calling upon whomever 'he' is addressing to walk, initially, in silence, together with 'him', but to *then, immediately thereafter, not to walk away*, not *from* him–not to do so, that is, without 'breaking the silence'. These lyrics suggest a narrator-protagonist asking 'his' addressee to do the following: 'Walk with me, silently, aligning yourself with me, sympathetically allowing me to be as I need to be, in this moment, while nonetheless dependent upon your presence *together* with me. But *don't* then merely walk away from me, after a short interval walking together in silence, without responding to what I need from you that extends considerably beyond extending me this brief indulgence. What I need from you is you to tell me what you will do *on behalf of* me, what you will do for me, as you experience yourself called upon by me to do. I need you to carry with you what I need from you and to act in good faith in relation to what I am entrusting in you that I need from you.

The narrator-protagonist calls 'his' addressee to share this experience in walking silently together, in its immediacy, and then to act in response to what the addressee has learned, and continues to learn, sparked by the memory and impact of this shared experience. If we recognize ourselves as the addressee here, then while we literally must eventually 'walk *away*', the narrator-protagonist is insisting in a more important sense we must *not* do so. It is as if the narrator-protagonist calls upon us: 'Don't leave and forget me, don't make this one instance of walking in silence with me a single, and especially not a token, gesture of sympathy from which you all too readily detach and distance yourself–as soon as you can. Instead, allow the silence that is at the heart of *the atmosphere* in the immediacy of this moment to show you what and how you need to speak, and act, in following upon what you attend to, listen to, and learn as we move in silence together, neither of us alone and neither of us standing still, even as neither of us *yet* speaks'.

"See the danger/Always danger/Endless talking/Life rebuilding/Don't walk away" continues and completes the first stanza. Here we are directed to 'see' even as we remain silent, and perhaps all the better and more clearly see by remaining silent, in other words alert and attentive to what we might miss if we were talking. The narrator-protagonist, moreover, directs us to 'see' danger, but not just any and all danger, as 'he' identifies this as '*the* danger'. 'He' might, nonetheless, allude to multiple varieties of danger that occur, or recur, in *these kinds of* circumstances. But perhaps this is a singular danger. Perhaps this danger is identified, however obliquely and allusively, by emphasizing it is 'always' so; it is persistent and even perpetual; and it follows as a result, both, of 'endless talking' and 'life rebuilding'.

How might that be so? 'Endless talking' can make sense as referencing talking on and on without ever acting in response to what one talks about. The action forestalled by this endless talking might indeed be action that could reshape the contours of further, future talking. These lyrics might make sense as alluding to dreaming about and planning to do something significant, but never following through. These lyrics might allude to making a promise to stand up and be counted, to show up and demonstrate solidarity with and on behalf of others, yet never doing so. In either case, these lyrics can make sense as referencing 'walking away' from *doing* when and because doing is hard–i.e., harder than expressing an interest in doing, and harder then expressing an intent *to do*. In this context, 'life rebuilding' might mean turning away from responsibility to and for others, from collective social responsibility, to attend solely to one's 'private affairs', to one's personal life, and to one's own individual safety and security, as well as to the safety and security of one's own immediate family. This phrase can also suggest always waiting, or delaying, until 'the right moment', which never comes, because the demands of one's own immediate, personal, private life are constantly in flux, always imperfect, and seemingly continually demand their own constant 'rebuilding'.

It is plausible to interpret the narrator-protagonist as here exhorting 'his' addressee to join, to commit, to a project of 'life rebuilding'. Such a project requires 'taking a chance', with all the risk involved, of confronting 'the danger', which, after all, will always be there, because doing so is necessary in order *to rebuild life*. This latter phrase might suggest to 'rebuild a life' together with another person, or group of other persons, or with and on behalf of a larger community–including in response to what has brought life to the state that it needs be *re*built. 'Rebuilding a life' follows when a life as previously built has crumbled, collapsed, or been wrecked. That destruction might be intrinsically interlinked with the 'danger' the narrator-protagonist has already mentioned. Danger can include forces and interests that demand, that implement, and that profit from this destruction. The life so ravaged might be the narrator-protagonist's life, it might be the life of 'people like him', or it might be the shared life and collective bond 'we' continue to maintain with 'him' or 'them', however precarious this last might be. In reference to the last, destruction might have encompassed division, antagonism, indifference, or disregard among us–among us who have been, or who at least *should* have been and *should* yet be, *united*.

To rebuild a life, even to rebuild one's own life, after it has reached a point where no way forward exists but to *re*build it, from the foundation up, will be hard, will be painful and will be replete with danger. Danger can include how exposed 'we' are as we attempt to rebuild what is no longer safely and securely standing, and thereby all the more vulnerable to 'attack'. Danger might also encompass running out of resources to rebuild, or of means needed to acquire these resources, or of will and stamina to keep trying. Imagine an apartment or a house, or a whole apartment building or residential neighborhood, or an entire city or region devastated by fire, by water, or by wind–or by war or by riot or by the spread of toxic chemicals or by a deadly contagious disease. Imagine how hard it is to rebuild, after all that has been lost, after all those who have been lost, and to do so while the threat of further destruction has not abated. Imagine attempting to rebuild life on this planet in the face of global ecological emergency that is irreversibly upon us: how might we commit to doing so, knowing that severe weather conditions, and not just severe storms, will be all the more widespread and commonplace, everywhere, and that more and more of the planet will become unlivable for human beings, not to mention other forms of life, with those left behind forced to compete desperately for scarce resources just to attain a state of survival in the form of 'bare existence'–especially if we continue merely 'endless talking'. How do we face up to all of that, to the myriad dangers of global ecological emergency, without turning away from doing so because facing up to these dangers is too overwhelming–and 'too depressing'? How do we face up to global ecological emergency without accepting that the future inevitably will end up harsh, brutal, vicious, mean, and desperate, for everyone–and how do we grasp it might still be possible, but time is rapidly running out, to realize a better future?

In our world today, our literal 'atmosphere' is full of danger: Canadian wildfires in the summer of 2023 causing many unhealthful days throughout much of the Midwest and Northeast of the US; PFAS ('forever chemicals') everywhere in our water supplies; rivers and oceans polluted with sewage, plastic, and other rubbish; droughts, deluges, hurricanes, and tropical storms becoming ever larger and more intense; glaciers melting more often and more rapidly than in many centuries; dwindling numbers of animal and plant species along with the rapid eradication of biodiversity. It can readily feel that we are approaching if not already living our 'last days', as a species, and, at the least, 'modern civilization' as we have known it is in its final phase, with those left alive beyond today, especially those young today, offered little choice but to mourn for what they will never be able to experience. Certainly it can readily seem political leaders, and leaders of powerful corporations and transnational institutions, all too often *talk endlessly* about ecological emergency, and the need for urgent action, but do not follow through with the actions that are needed.

Stanza two reads as follows: "Walk in silence/Don't turn away, in silence/Your confusion/My illusion/Worn like a mask of self-hate/Confronts and then dies/Don't walk away." Here it seems, in contrast with where I ended the preceding paragraph, the lyrics are more focused on self-critique and critique of individuals involved in inter-individual relationships as opposed to focusing on those maintaining ultimate authority at the heights of economic and political power in a larger society. "Your confusion/My illusion" suggests that perhaps both 'you' and 'I' bear responsibility for what is

1033

happening–or not happening–here. At the least communication appears to have reached an impasse as 'you' are 'confused' while I am operating, or have been, according to 'illusion'. Perhaps the illusion is that 'I' have made myself clear, already, to 'you', or that 'you' are the kind of person who can understand what I am attempting to express and communicate, rather than being 'confused' by this. Perhaps 'I' have maintained the illusion that, with 'you', 'I' might be understood, by 'you', that 'you' are attuned to nuance and subtlety in how I attempt to express and communicate in ways others are not so attuned. Perhaps 'I' have maintained the illusion that 'you' appreciate the importance in what 'I' am expressing and communicating *between and beyond the words 'I' say*, notably in the gaps and the silences surrounding and enveloping these words–and that 'you' even appreciate what 'I' cannot express and communicate by means of words alone, but can only use words to gesture towards. However, it seems this is not the case, and has not been the case. In that respect, yes, it can make sense to interpret the narrator-protagonist as expressing frustration bordering on bitterness that 'you' cannot understand 'him'–perhaps even insinuating 'you' have not tried hard enough to do so, or that 'you' do not really want to do so, because you regard doing so as too 'dangerous', and because you regard 'people like him', like the narrator-protagonist, as 'too dangerous'.

"Worn like a mask of self-hate" seems to link 'my illusion' with a 'mask of self-hate' but it could instead be 'your confusion' that constitutes such a mask, and it could be both 'your confusion' and 'my illusion' that both do. 'Worn *like*' suggests this isn't literally 'a mask of self-hate', but rather something resembling such a mask, while 'mask of self-hate' suggests it is not directly 'self-hate' at stake here because whomever is presenting as if they are 'wearing something like a mask of self-hate' has assumed a guise that conceals, even misleads. Perhaps 'you' perceive 'self-hate' when that is inaccurate in relation to what 'I' am struggling to get you to appreciate. Perhaps experiencing self-hate is not all of or even most importantly what is going on here. Perhaps presenting 'a mask of self-hate' is the only way 'I' am able to convey complexity that resonates not only 'my' discontent and dissatisfaction but also 'my' yearning and drive for change concerning much more than merely 'how I feel about myself'. Perhaps the problem lies in commonsense separation of 'how I feel about myself' from 'myself as always existing, part and parcel, within a series of successively enveloping modes of existence'. In other words, whom and what 'I' am is embodied, extended, embedded, and enacted within such a series, within *that kind of atmosphere*. Perhaps 'my mental distress' is rooted in 'me' registering, as James Davies argues in *Sedated: How Modern Capitalism Created Our Mental Health Crisis* (2021), that it is the kind of society in which 'I' live that is truly 'sick', while attempts to 'sedate' those of us who are acutely sensitive to the impact of this sickness in the form of damage to our psychological health and well-being are 'symptoms', in this damage we experience, of the same sickness–a sickness that is *not* being addressed by placing responsibility for 'dealing with' 'mental illness' onto 'the individual' while *not* taking into account the kind of society in which 'the individual' must struggle to cope.

"Confronts and then dies" might make sense as 'your confusion' and 'my illusion' confronting each other, with this confrontation including the performative assumption of a guise of 'self-hate', perhaps on both sides. Whatever confronts and whatever is confronted seemingly does not lead, or at least has not yet led, to a transformative breakthrough, because 'confrontation' is here followed, right '*then*', by death. It is as if the confronting leads to the dying. If not the former 'causing' the latter, at least the former anticipates the latter. This passage is followed, however, by a concluding reiteration of "Don't walk away," suggesting the narrator-protagonist persists; 'he' has not given up all hope; and even if this particular confrontation results in 'a dead end', it need not be the final end.

The third and final stanza reads as follow: "People like you find it easy/Naked to see/Walking on air/Hunting by the rivers/Through the streets/Every corner/Abandoned too soon/Set down with due care/Don't walk away in silence/Don't walk away." To begin, it makes sense to interpret line one as chastising others, including whomever the narrator-protagonist is addressing with these lyrics, for not understanding 'people like him' and for not being able to offer 'people like him' much help, because 'people like you' cannot or will not do the work necessary to understand someone as sensitive and complicated as well as someone struggling and suffering as badly as the narrator-protagonist is. 'People like you' may include those insufficiently troubled by the problems of the world for this to upset them, or insufficiently guilty and even ashamed concerning their own responsibility or complicity to feel any need to atone, or to offer anything that could make any modicum of difference. Perhaps 'I', as opposed to 'people like you', feels the enormity of responsibility yet also feels too weak and thus incapable of being able to do so, to do what haunts this 'I' as what *should* be 'his' part.

And yet, the meaning of "find it easy" is not easy to pin down–what, even more precisely, do 'people like you' find so 'easy'? Why do they–or why do we–find it such? Is this an allusion to going about daily life untroubled by horrific violence around us, including what that violence has made possible for us? Is this an allusion to being able, all too readily, to detach and distance ourselves from the violence–to declare, 'that's not my problem', 'those people are not (like) me', '*I* am not personally responsible for any of it', '*I* am not personally responsible for any of them', and that those 'other people' 'have brought it on themselves'?

"Naked to see" could suggest that 'people like you' are easy to read, easy to see through, because they are not interested in complexity, or trouble, let alone responsibility, and let alone facing up to danger. But 'naked to see' could also suggest the problems the narrator-protagonist is urging attendance upon are, in fact, readily apparent–if 'people like you' would only make the effort and care enough to 'take a look'. "Walking on air," meanwhile, makes sense as referring to people riding too comfortably with the relative ease of their lives, accepting without question that they simply deserve what they have, that it is simply their due according to their merits, including in just return for their own hard work. 'Walking on air' might also suggest 'people like this' imagine themselves existing 'above and beyond' the kinds of hardship others experience all the time, not recognizing that they themselves will eventually 'fall to earth'. But 'walking on air" could, yet further, in contrast, suggest what it might feel like if sufficient 'people like you' together with 'people like me' united to tackle the issues that stress and distress so many individual lives and so much of collective life, in working together toward transformation of this sorry state of affairs.

Turning to "hunting by the rivers," who here is hunting by the rivers? Hunting what–or hunting whom? This could, again, be 'people like you' engaged in their own pleasurable pursuits while not questioning the conditions that make these pursuits possible and especially not questioning what makes these pursuits easy to pursue. 'Hunting', moreover, connotes seeking something out, to kill, or at least to seriously harm. Again, these lyrics can make sense as referencing people living individual lives oblivious to the impact of how they live their lives on the health of life on this planet.

People can and do still often proceed as if nature provides an inexhaustible supply of resources, with little to no need to care about whether these resources are 'renewable' or not.

Turning from 'hunting by the rivers' to 'moving through the streets', it can make sense to interpret the latter phrase, again, as referring to what 'people like you' are doing, and have been doing, 'all too easily'. These people enjoy themselves in both 'the country' and in 'the city'; they find ample pleasure in both spaces, and 'easily' move about both as well as between the two. But perhaps 'people like this' pass over everything, in both areas, too quickly. Perhaps they ignore or push away whatever, and whomever, they might find unsettling. Perhaps they don't take time to 'get a good look', to appreciate where they are at, including how what at present came to be versus what this was like in the past. Perhaps they don't register how fragile such places can be. Perhaps they pass by 'every corner' without looking closely at what, and whom, they might see within. Perhaps these kinds of people are those who prefer that homeless people be moved far away, out of sight, so that they do not need to consider let alone confront their presence, nor assume responsibility to help homeless people, and never imagine they themselves could ever become homeless. Homelessness, according to this kind of mindset, results not from lack of affordable housing and due to inadequate restriction on what landlords can can do versus renters, but rather from personal irresponsibility–by, for example, 'the homeless individual' 'choosing' to become an addict, or mentally ill, or physically disabled, or to live in housing they cannot afford or can no longer afford, or to work at jobs where they are not paid enough to afford their cost of living or where they have been let go because their company has reorganized to reduce labor costs–or relocated elsewhere. Certainly, 'abandoned too soon' suggests people in need, whose needs may attract short-term attention, but not enough adequately to address these needs.

If we follow the line of interpretation I have just been proposing, then "Set down with due care" seems potentially contradictory, identifying the same 'people like you' I have been describing as here setting something, or someone, down, with 'due care'. The preceding line of interpretation suggests a failure to recognize and act upon a 'duty of care', and while 'due care' and 'duty of care' are not necessarily identical, the former tends to suggest, especially with 'due' modifying 'care', that something here is being done, and has been done, right. However, 'set down with due care' might mock people who live easy, comfortable, uncomplicated lives, who never have to deal with all that much 'mess' or 'messiness', and who can move easily from one focus to another 'easily', setting the one down before proceeding to the next with 'due care'. In other words, for 'people like this' everything they encounter can be easily 'set down'–too easily.

'People like you' might 'set down' with 'due care' their assumption of responsibility to the 'I' of the lyrics, before all too easily, and all too quickly, 'walking away' and indeed 'walking away in silence'. Again that appears to be exactly what the narrator-protagonist is urging (even pleading with) them, and us, *not* to do. In other words, don't turn away from, don't abandon people, when they become messy and difficult, and when dealing with their messiness and difficulty becomes frustrating and tiring, because that same messiness and difficulty is symptomatic of how much people like the narrator-protagonist do need help. Or, in other words, don't turn away from, don't abandon, your express commitments to help address serious issues, such as concerning ecological emergency, homelessness, lack of affordable housing, and laws that allow landlords, all too easily, to raise rents beyond renters' ability to pay, to evict tenants, and to sell off or transform the housing properties they own into luxury developments where previous tenants can no longer afford to live. The call here is to *not* walk away from the risks involved in doing what is right and necessary, and to persist even when acting, and not just talking, becomes tough. It makes sense to interpret these lyrics as exhorting those of us who recognize ourselves in the position of their addressee to embrace the challenges, risks, and dangers that constitute the very 'atmosphere' itself, in relation to broad social and ecological harms and in relation to individual people who are, at present, seemingly 'messed up' and even seemingly 'out of control'. It certainly can be hard to interact with people in states like this, while keeping in mind they are multiple, complex, contradictory, and dynamic, and, as such, deserving of respect for their intrinsic worth and dignity. But "Atmosphere" makes sense as suggesting this is necessary, no matter how hard. Even if we make sense of these lyrics as Ian Curtis writing about himself, about how badly he himself is feeling, deeply depressed and on the edge of suicidality, it makes sense, simultaneously, to interpret Curtis as here reaching out and calling upon others, as best he can, 'not to abandon him' *to himself*, urging and indeed pleading with others to help him, even as he struggles to be able to communicate what he needs clearly and directly.

An earlier draft of the lyrics for "Atmosphere," included in *So This is Permanence: Joy Division Lyrics and Notebooks*, indicates Curtis previously conceived of what he was writing, as the lyrics for this song, in close alignment with this direction of interpretation of their meaning. In the earlier draft Curtis concludes stanza one with the imperative "Face life's dangers" right after the preceding imperative "Don't walk away," suggesting the narrator-protagonist exhorts 'his' listeners to not walk away from the dangers life bring but to face up to them, and that the narrator-protagonist is concerned too few too rarely do this. Stanza two is even more explicit in supporting this same argument: "Fear and violence/Don't stay away from" followed by "See the danger/Always danger" and then followed by "Rules are broken/False emotions." This passage suggests either a need to break rules and break with presentation of false emotions or that breaking of rules and presentation of false emotions it at the heart of the danger that must be confronted. Again, this stanza concludes, notably different from the final version: "Don't walk away/Face the dangers." Stanza three of this earlier version next adds that "People like you" not only "find it easy" but, all the more explicitly, "find it easy to forget," and that these people are "always in tune" as opposed to "naked to see." Again this version is less ambiguous and more explicit than the final version in critiquing 'people like you' for too easily retreating from necessary confrontation with life's dangers, on account of this being all too easy for these kinds of people to be able to do. What's more, the earlier version proceeds to make this same critique all the more explicit by referring to "Your hunting in packs," suggesting a synthesis of predatory meets conformist behavior as object of critique. The conclusion in the earlier version, yet again, is also more explicit in its condemnation, and less ambiguous than the final version: "But it's over too soon/Then maybe you'll care/And we'll walk away/Face the danger." According to these concluding lines, the escape to what is easy, or at least what is easier, cannot and will not last, and when that opportunity has disappeared, then 'people like you' will be forced to join the 'I' of the lyrics in walking away *together* and in *together facing the danger*. The earlier version of the lyrics in sum is not only more straightforward but also more hopeful as well as more directly critical of 'people like you'. Even so, this earlier version does suggest "Atmosphere" makes sense as lamenting that all too many other people refuse to face life's dangers, because for them it is easier, and indeed all too easy, not to do so. They continue this refusal even though they cannot retreat and escape from 'the danger', nor ignore and deny it for how dangerous it truly is, forever.

The change from the earlier to the final version of the lyrics for "Atmosphere" suggests Curtis revises in order to blur the lines between 'people like you' and 'people like me', including 'himself' in both categories. Indeed Ian Curtis's lyrics, and drafts from notebooks, convey a frequent tension between advancing criticism, ostensibly, of 'others', with precisely whom these others might be left largely ambiguous, versus advancing a criticism of 'one's self," as the borderlines between 'self' and 'other' collapse such that the two, self and other, become difficult to distinguish.

Turning from the lyrics to the sounds that make up the song, once again I will emphasize what I hear that amplifies and especially complicates, even contradicts, meanings derived solely from consideration of the lyrics alone, and as I do so I reference what I hear by way of repeated close listening to the 2020 digital remaster of the single version of "Atmosphere."

As I hear it, the structure of "Atmosphere" proceeds according to the following pattern:

1.   Opening: 0:00->0:25. This section feels as if it situates us in a nebulous location as well as a nebulous position, according to which we, together with the music as persona, proceed to move. A synthesizer wash sound begins the song together with the bass guitar's guitar initial pattern, followed quickly by the drums' initial pattern, then a high-pitched synthesizer sound that verges upon but not does quite reach that of a screech, followed by the bass guitar and the drums settling into their successive interlocking patterns that these two instruments carry forward throughout the rest of the song.

2.   First vocal stanza 0:26->0:59. This section feels as if it continues from the last by elliptically identifying, describing, and elaborating broad parameters of where we, the music as persona and I, nebulously are at, while providing us with a vaguely felt sense, however ultimately opaque, of what might be at stake, what might have brought us here, and what might be possible yet ahead, from where we now are at, in this present situation, at this specific location, and in this present moment. Here the bass guitar and the vocal compliment each other in sounding the melody, with the vocal louder and more pronounced than the bass guitar that contributes in turn by filling in, supporting, and embellishing the vocal in the full articulation of the melody.

3.   First instrumental bridge 1:00->1:29. This section feels as if it underscores and emphasizes, as well as draws out, and elusively comments on, at least prospectively meaningful resonances emanating from existential dimensions of the situation, location, and moment at hand. Here a shimmering meets shivering strings meet bells sound pattern (the combined effect of a keyboard synthesizer and modified tambourine percussion) enters to contribute significantly for the first time in the song.

4.   Second vocal stanza 1:30->2:04. This section once more elliptically identifies, describes, and elaborates where we, the music as persona and I, nebulously are at, while simultaneously providing us with at least some vaguely felt sense, however ultimately opaque, of what might be at stake, what

might have brought us here, and what might be possible yet ahead, from where we now are at, in this present situation, at this specific location, and in this present moment. But this feels more like amplification of what already has been established as otherwise little feels changed versus where we were at in section two.

5.   Second instrumental bridge 2:05->2:34. This section once more feels as if it underscores and emphasizes, as well as draws out, and elusively comments on, at least prospectively meaningful resonances emanating from existential dimensions of the situation, location, and moment at hand. Once more, the shimmering meets shivering strings meets bells pattern of sound is most prominent but an overdriven guitar line of sound first emerges in this section as well. Nevertheless, again this feels like amplification of what has already been established as otherwise little feels changed versus where we were at in section three.

6.   Third vocal passage 2:35->3:15. This section involves reaching toward a climax although not realizing anything as decisive as a climax. In this section the vocal starts higher and moves slightly further upward in pitch than previously, while becoming somewhat more overtly agitated. Ian Curtis's vocalization of words and syllables quivers while also suggesting elements of a bark meets a bite. Taken together, these timbral dimensions of the vocal delivery suggest a state of heightened agitation, and perhaps also heightened anguish, frustration, and bitterness.

7.   Closing 3:16->4:10. This section once more underscores and emphasizes, as well as seems to draw out, and elusively to comment on, at least prospectively meaningful resonances emanating from existential dimensions of the situation, location, and moment at hand. And it does so while moving toward what amounts to a dissolution or suspension, but not a resolution, of tension. Overdriven guitar chords sound clearer and louder than previously, yet the shimmering meets shivering strings meets bells sound pattern also comes across in this section as further spread out than previously. At points in this section the guitar is louder and more pronounced than the synthesizer but the latter regains priority in prominence by the end.

As I listen to "Atmosphere" I detect the following distinctive lines and patterns of sound:

1.   Ian Curtis's vocal, which sounds even deeper, darker, rougher, harsher and more tightly confined and further constrained than usual.

2.   The lead guitar, which commentators often identify as played by Curtis in live performance, although likely not performed by Curtis in the studio recording of this song, and which as commentators also suggest is overdriven. This line of sound performs a short series of ringing chords later in the song.

3.   Peter Hook's bass guitar, which, as common in Joy Division songs, performs a melodic line throughout the song, and which is pitched, overall, high in register.

4.   Stephen Morris's drums, which sound here as just bass drum and toms with perhaps lightly brushing of a snare if and when this shows up at all, while at the same time sounding much like the

toms and the bass drum in terms of timbre. The drums are concentrated so closely in terms of timbre that their respective sounds virtually fuse together. Morris's principal drum pattern also involves a harder strike on what appears to be the bass drum than the strikes that then follow on the toms.

5.   We do know, from Morris's own account, that in this song we also hear "a broken tambourine perched on a scissor blade held very close to a microphone" with "softly pinging the chime" producing "the shimmering icy bell effect for the chorus."

6.   A first keyboard synthesizer pattern, played by Bernard Sumner, that comes across as a wash that approaches a warm glow.

7.   A second keyboard sound pattern, played by Bernard Sumner, that comes across as a high-pitched short, near screeching sound.

8.   A third keyboard sound pattern, played by Bernard Sumner, that comes across as a shimmering meets shivering strings meets bells sound, and fuses with Morris's close-miked pinging of the chime on a broken tambourine that is perched on a scissor blade.

Commentators largely agree that an Arp Omni 2 analog keyboard synthesizer plays a key role in "Atmosphere," in producing the strings as well as the wash sound, while commentators speculate further synthesizers might be employed but disagree which ones these might be. Regardless, synthesizer sounds are more central, and more dominant, than in many if not most other Joy Division songs, even as Joy Division, especially in the studio and in working with Hannett, played a prominent role in pioneering the use of synthesizers as key constituents of punk-originating forms of 'rock' music.

Turning to the functional layers of the classic popular 'rock' music song, an explicit beat layer is present and this layer is steady and persistent. This layer is foregrounded and changes little over the course of the song. In terms of a functional bass layer, the bass guitar interlocks with the drums to establish a groove, while, like the drums, changing little over the course of the song, but the bass guitar also contributes, along with the vocal, to the melodic layer. Once more, in contributing to the melodic layer, the vocal pattern remains highly consistent over the course of the song. The harmonic fill layer is the most important in "Atmosphere," and it results from all of the synthesizer sounds, the modified percussion instrument devised by Hannett and played by Morris, and the overdriven guitar. The harmonic fill layer becomes slightly more elaborate over the course of the song but otherwise once again remains largely consistent. In terms of disposition, these four layers are cleanly separated while precisely balanced.

In terms of the soundbox, here is what I note:

1.   The opening wash sound comes from down low, slightly off center, to the left.

2.   The subsequent screech sound comes from much higher up, but also to the left again.

3.   The bass guitar sound comes from a similar position as the opening wash, low, back, and primarily to the left, but even though this sound is not positioned at the front of the soundbox it remains clear and is never buried.

4.   The drums are positioned to the front of the soundbox, closer than all of the previously mentioned sound sources and sound patterns, but the drums are also positioned primarily to both sides, albeit seeming to move periodically back and forth across the center from both sides. The bass drum sounds from the left, with the light brushing snare as well as the toms sounds toward the right, while movements from left to right and right to left resemble a quick scamping across the center.

5.   The vocal is positioned low, central, and near the front but not as close to the front as the drums. The vocal also sounds as if it moves slightly closer to the front and slightly higher up in the soundbox in the last vocal stanza.

6.   The overdriven guitar sounds emanate from the deep background, low center, while they move slightly upward as they ring out and as we move into the final section of the song.

7.   The shimmering meets shivering strings meet bells sound pattern seems to come from both sides, moving up each side over the duration of each shimmer meets shiver.

All of the instruments sound as if they are distinctly yet closely positioned. The drums and the bass guitar are the most persistent but all other sound patterns are regular and consistent. The sounds move across the full horizontal expanse of the soundbox but not the full vertical expanse with some areas within the soundbox thereby feeling pointedly vacant. The bass guitar sounds high in register but not as high as Hook plays at his most extreme; the vocal sounds low register; the guitar sounds mid register; and the synthesizer sound patterns are high, with the wash lower than the others, but even that sound pattern is high versus the bass guitar, the vocal, and the guitar.

As I listen to these dimensions of the sound of "Atmosphere," I feel the music as persona has reached an impasse without resolution, and, more than that, some kind of significant ending. But, paradoxically enough, the song conveys the impression of persistence, even so. Perhaps the music enacts 'a passing of the torch' from the music as persona to the listener to carry on and take up what needs be done next. But perhaps what the songs enacts cannot be so easily translated. Yes, "Atmosphere" can feel 'icily cold' but "Atmosphere" also feels *magical*, suggestive of movement beyond stasis, continuation beyond stoppage, life beyond death, and being beyond nothingness. Perhaps this song enacts a magical movement emergent out of, and that results from or is made possible by stasis; a magical continuation emergent out of, and that results from or is made possible by stoppage; a magical life emergent out of, and that results from or is made possible by death; and a magical being emergent out of, and that results from or is made possible by nothingness. Perhaps this magical quality of "Atmosphere" makes sense in relation to afterlife, or incarnation. Perhaps this magical quality of "Atmosphere" makes sense in relation to persistence of consciousness beyond death. Perhaps this magical quality of "Atmosphere" makes sense in relation to flashes of memory, to traces and echoes, or to ghosts and hauntings, from the past persisting, or returning, even as the past has ostensibly altogether passed away. Perhaps this magical quality of "Atmosphere" makes sense in relation to 'eternal recurrence'–or in relation to other infinite cycles and spirals of energy and matter. "Atmosphere" sounds as if the song hearkens to the utopian, to a seemingly un-real and im-possible no-place that exercises a nonetheless ecstatic appeal. It may be, in Sisyphean fashion, that "Atmosphere" suggests struggle is worth it, even when and if it fails, incessantly over and over. It may be that "Atmosphere" suggests struggle is worth it even if and when struggle is misunderstood, if and when it not intelligible at all, and if and when one representative agent of this struggle becomes exhausted such that they can no longer continue themself–because the struggle is an ongoing, collective struggle toward a yet distant and unknown destination, perhaps akin to pursuit of an ever-receding horizon that is nonetheless irresistibly compelling.

The mysteriously magical quality of "Atmosphere" suggests a simultaneously terrifying and tantalizing persistence beyond the existence of a subject represented by the lyrics and their vocalization. This dimension of the song can make sense as challenging us to reflect on what here is passing away, what is persisting, and what might be the relation between the two. The song can make sense as echoing Avery F. Gordon's exhortation, in *Ghostly Matters: Haunting and the Sociological Imagination,* to recognize and respond to hauntings of ghosts who represent historical grievances that remain unresolved, and for which we must seek to do what we can to atone. "Atmosphere" can also make sense, as echoing Ann Cvetkovich's argument in *Depression: A Public Feeling,* that depression makes sense in political terms, and, interpreted as such, can offer insight useful not only for individual rejuvenation but also social transformation. "Atmosphere" can make sense, further, as echoing Cvetkovich in proposing that painful emotions, in ourselves and in others, need to be engaged, not 'walked away from', so that we can learn how we need to change social institutions and social discourses, the faults and failings of which show up, in affective terms, as 'bad feelings'. "Atmosphere" can make sense further, as echoing what Robert McRuer argues in *Crip Theory: Cultural Signs of Queerness and Disability* and *Crip Times: Disability, Globalization, and Resistance,* by alluding to modes of social collectivity founded upon shared vulnerability and shared dependency that only begin to be conceivable via a radical cripping of 21st century neo-liberal capitalist modes of living and relating.

I have already addressed ways that loudness, rhythm, pitch, delivery, and timbre contribute to meaning and impact in "Atmosphere," so I will keep further comments on these elements succinct. To begin, loudness remains remarkably consistent and unchanged, throughout the song. The song does become louder when the shimmering meets shivering strings meets bells sound complex enters and as long as this continues before fading, while the entrance of the guitar, especially toward the end, also increases overall loudness. The vocal is slightly louder in the third vocal stanza than previously and also louder at specific points in this third stanza. Loudness does drop down at the end of the song but not just before arriving at the end.

"Atmosphere" follows a 4/4 time signature, approximately 120 PBM, and maintains a 1eeanduh2eeanduh3eeanduh4eeanduh pattern as the beat. Movements in time of each of these instruments are regular and consistent. Little variation occurs and each rhythmic series is short. Drum strikes move in repeated short sixteenth note series; the bass guitar alternates between two short series which both move from relatively long to relatively short notes, often repeating over and over again from as short a distance in time as one measure to the next; the vocal rests significantly between lines while always starting with quarter notes and ending with tied quarter notes, in series that again last only as long as four measures, and even more often only two or three; the synthesizer wash pattern is almost exclusively whole notes, linked across two successive measures; the strings meets bells sound complex involves alternations between simple whole note patterns and quarter note patterns; and the guitar line involves primarily whole notes, linked across two measures.

In terms of pitch, the version of "Atmosphere" I am listening to is in the key of F# major, but producers of tabs and scores recommend people play this song in keys of F# major or A major or C major or C# major or D♭ major. All of these, however, are major keys, encompassing the connotations major key tends to bring, as opposed to minor key, which complicates interpretations of "Atmosphere" as a funeral march. In terms of movements in pitch, the vocal ultimately tends downward in culminating passages while downward movements cover larger intervals than upward movements. This suggest tentative climbing, perhaps representative of yearning, hoping, and persisting, but the weight of obstacles, opponents, failures, and defeats is too heavy to shift. The third vocal stanza, once again, does start higher in pitch and persists higher for longer than previously, but ultimately drops down, and even over a larger interval than previously. All other instruments move differently, however. For example, the bass guitar moves across even shorter intervals, back and forth upward and downward, buts stays up longer than the vocal. Here, perhaps we encounter suggestion of confronting limits that might not mean an ultimate end, let alone a total defeat. The most notable movement with the synthesizer wash sound is slightly upward, while the strings meets bells sound complex moves upward as well; even as both oscillate while they sound, upward movement in pitch is pronounced. The guitar, as simple as the pattern here is, likewise emphasizes moving up in pitch. Even the drums, although primarily remaining at the same pitch, move up periodically too. Overall, again, this combination of movements, and this key, suggest the song is prospectively more complicated than interpretations of it as funereal, or even as elegiac, tend to suggest.

Turning to the delivery of the vocal, beyond what I have already noted concerning Curtis's register and range here, it is also notable that degree of resonance feels more curtailed than in many other Joy Division songs, even as the vocal sounds, characteristically, subject to studio treatment and manipulation. Curtis sounds largely unconcerned about exactitude in relation to pitch but the opposite in terms of rhythm. Still, it here feels as if this is not 'his choice', but as if his voice is confined, against its will, yet resigned to not being able to break out of this state of confinement. It almost sounds as if Curtis's vocal in "Atmosphere" is not particularly concerned with what the other instruments are doing other than allowing them their space and not stepping out of 'his space'. When Curtis's voice agitates in stanza three, this suggests an emission, or admission, of pain, whether this be due to present confinement or or whether this be due to a more decisive kind of end, and even defeat. Curtis's vocal delivery comes across as if acknowledging the surrounding, enveloping atmosphere as overpowering. Yet the vocal suggests some resistance, nonetheless, combined, paradoxically enough, with a suggestion of emotional detachment. The words of the lyrics, taken by themselves, suggest an intensity of emotionality that Curtis's vocalization does not. Indeed, the vocal approaches a droning quality, suggestive of not being able to continue much longer. The third vocal stanza suggests a remnant motivation to persist but this seems to falter. In sum, it sounds as if the other instruments that constitute "Atmosphere" simulate the surrounding, enveloping, and overpowering atmosphere that the vocal expresses may be ultimately indifferent to whether any single individual who is so surrounded, enveloped, and overpowered continues, individually themselves, to keep on going or not.

The composite timbre, in "Atmosphere," suggests human life continues according to regular, persistent structures that are largely external to our individual will or choice, that are largely beyond our individual control, and that individual lives quickly end while something much vaster continues, as it has continued long before. This composite timbre suggests something majestic about what precedes, exceeds, and succeeds us, and that strictly individual cares diminish altogether in comparison with that vast expanse. In terms of how timbre analogously suggests movements, the drums and the bass guitar here suggest a persistent, determined pushing onward; the synthesizer sounds as well as the guitar and the modified percussion suggest allowing the surrounding, enveloping, and overpowering atmosphere to resound within as well as without as this pushing onward continues; and the vocal suggests wearily dragging along. In terms of attack, decay, sustain, and release, with the drums the attack is strongest; with the bass guitar, each of these dimensions are relatively equal in weight; with the synthesizer and guitar, attack is pronounced but sustain is prolonged and release is slow; and with the vocal, decay, sustain, and release stand out versus attack. Overall, the distinctive timbre of "Atmosphere" is primarily due to the contributions of the synthesizer sounds, while the degree of confinement of the vocal also stands out, especially in comparison with other recordings of other Joy Division songs.

In consideration of avenues of musical affect, the relative simplicity of the sound patterns as well as the predictability of their recurrence makes it easy to mimetically participate, yet as I listen to "Atmosphere" I feel positioned at a distance from both the narrator-protagonist of the lyrics, and the music as persona, such that I experience this song inviting and encouraging me to maintain that distance as I reflect upon what I am hearing. As I do so, I anticipate regularity and recurrence, along with movement toward both climax and conclusion without either being fully realized. Expression is difficult to pinpoint, because this involves both an enveloping atmosphere and a singularity enveloped within this atmosphere, while as is often the case with Joy Division, I feel in "Atmosphere" a tension between seeming direct expression of an emotional state versus seeming indirect performance of such expression. The latter feels markedly distanciated, prompting critical reflection on what might prompt that emotional state, and especially what it might mean to experience it. The acoustic impact of "Atmosphere" is, strikingly, not all-enveloping, as sound does not feel like it surrounds me even though it feels as if comes toward me from across from a full horizontal expanse as well as along both sides of a full vertical expanse as well down, front, and center, while timbre feels discretely articulated and precisely combined.

Aside from the lyrics, the sense of analysis I gain from the implicit music as persona is of a continuation beyond an ending, of something far smaller dissolving into something far larger, and of time, space, and the Real greatly transcending and thoroughly superceding the individual. Associations I experience with the music as a whole, and the implicit music as persona, are of the sublime, of what is awesome and terrifying at once. Other associations involve at least the insinuation that opportunities for renewal of aspirations and strivings can and will recur even after we ourselves no longer continue to represent these, and even after we pass on and fade away. In other words, endings in own individual lives are not necessarily equivalent with endings once and for all of what matters most to us.

In terms of engaging taboos, it can feel to taboo to imply, as it feels to me that it makes sense to interpret "Atmosphere" as implying, that one must accept endings, including major endings, and including the ending of life itself, even when and if such acceptance can feel like surrender to defeat. It can be taboo, once more, as it makes sense to me to interpret "Atmosphere" as doing, to represent 'atmosphere' as all-encompassing, all-enveloping, and all-determining, suggestive of the Real that cannot be represented in either Imaginary or Symbolic terms. It can be taboo, further, to suggest, as it makes sense to me to interpret "Atmosphere" as doing, that a larger universe, or larger cosmos, is not so much 'indifferent' to our individual existence but in effect 'knows' precisely where and how this individual existence fits within its far vaster expanse—that it, in effect, has a plan for us, but not one it will ever communicate to us, at the least because we could not comprehend any such attempt. This 'atmosphere' is totalizing yet invisible and intangible while our particular existence and our place within it feels ephemeral. Certainly feeling so can be disturbing, frightening, and at the least overwhelming, especially if this seems simultaneously to suggest that we, as individual human beings, are, in essence, tiny masses of weaknesses and vulnerabilities.

"Atmosphere" prompts me to reflect on how I make sense of what has transpired in my life over the course of the past fourteen months, during which I time I stopped writing this section of this chapter of this book. It has been, for me, a time of massive change, involving significant endings—and new beginnings.

At the beginning of August 2022 I experienced the sudden onset of a cluster of symptoms: pronounced tiredness, faintness, and dizziness; nausea, queasiness, and greater indigestion; muscle aches and pains across multiple and unusual areas of my body; edema (swelling) in my calves and ankles; massively foamy urine; a strange metallic taste in my mouth, and persistent hunger. After many tests and consultations, following early identification that I was suffering from significant anemia and that both blood and protein levels in my urine were concerningly high, doctors and I determined this was most likely a kidney issue. Working with a nephrologist, Dr. Khan, and undergoing a considerable array of additional tests, as well as a kidney biopsy, while consulting advanced specialists working at the Mayo Clinic in Rochester, by early December it became clear I was dealing with lupus nephritis, an autoimmune disease involving my immune system attacking my kidneys. Throughout the preceding four months, after returning to teach and otherwise work full-time as a professor at UW-Eau Claire, I struggled with incredible tiredness. Every day I 'hit a wall' by early evening, right after the end of student drop-in hours and teaching classes, such that I could not do anything demanding mental concentration for the rest of the day, and instead typically collapsed into bed by 9 pm. The biopsy surgery, in turn, caused its own complications. Immediately upon leaving the hospital, I experienced a severe seizure, due to the impact of anaesthesia. Shortly thereafter, I spent most of a night undergoing tests in a hospital emergency room to make sure that I was not experiencing serious internal bleeding. I was not, but biopsy surgery caused muscles surrounding the surgical area to clench tight and not relax for four weeks.

Early in the process of working together Dr. Khan starting me on some prescription medications to deal with the effects of kidney disease, but this was only the beginning, as in December, once the diagnosis of lupus nephritis was confirmed, he added high-dosage prescriptions of six additional powerful drugs, and for many months thereafter I struggled with intense as well as rapidly varying side effects. Among many dimensions of this experience I will long recall I underwent numerous urine and especially blood tests, at times providing more than 40 tubes of blood at once; frequent meetings with Dr. Khan and others, including traveling to Rochester to meet with a specialist, Dr. Gonzalez; and confronting the frank reality that this most serious disease required I conscientiously follow the treatment protocol if I hoped to achieve remission, or I would only likely live five to seven more years.

Among the many lifestyle changes I needed to make I gave up drinking alcoholic beverages entirely. I imagined this would prove harder for me than has turned out to be the case. It has now been more than ten months since I last drank any alcoholic beverage. Although I never drank much at once, I did drink one to two drinks per day, and two to three drinks per day during travels and holidays–especially Scottish single malt whisky, a variety of different wines, and beer, in particular local craft and specialty ales. I had been doing so since I was a kid. I enjoyed it. I enjoyed drinking in pubs; visiting and touring distilleries; trying out local draft ales, different wines, and varieties of single malt whisky. I enjoyed drinks on special occasions and nightly at dinner and before bed. But giving up drinking alcoholic turned out much easier than I worried might be the case. Surprisingly, I have not missed it, virtually at all, and I have found satisfying non-alcoholic alternatives. Other changes, and other impacts, have not always been so easy.

My experience during my first year living with lupus nephritis meant recognizing I simply could not do many things I wanted, and often enough felt I needed, to do–I could not follow through on plans and pursue goals I had previously set. For example, I had to give up running, especially due to the complications I experienced following kidney biopsy surgery, but also due to the fact I was tired more often, and I often struggled with many muscle aches and pains as well as feelings of dizziness, nausea, and weakness. This has been a letdown, as right preceding my contraction of lupus nephritis Andy and I spent three weeks in the UK, fifteen days in London and five in Edinburgh, including highlights, for me, of running regularly widely about Central London, thrilling at weaving in and out as well as all around huge crowds of people and bypassing frequent construction detours, as well as in two organized races, a 5K at Olympic Park and a 10K at Regents Park, after having run in two earlier 5K races and one earlier 10K race in Eau Claire prior to that UK trip. I was in my best running shape in 25 years, and running was making me incredibly happy as well as exercising huge benefit in relieving mental stress and anxiety.

Lupus, moreover, complicated, and indeed compounded, preexisting chronic illnesses with which I already found it arduous to cope. To explain how so I will next undertake a detour, incorporating what I wrote as part of my statement in my post-tenure review, in August 2022. Keep in mind, what I write then preceded awareness that I was beginning to deal with lupus as well.

Perhaps the most striking aspect of my Fall 2016 post-tenure review statement for me, reading this now six years later, is how much I there engage in an euphemistic account of the impact

1046

of living with chronic illness, at best downplaying this impact and at worst ignoring it altogether. It might seem to another reader that I am frank and forthcoming about this matter in that statement. But I am not. Allow me to begin to give you a sense of how not. I wrote that statement early in the Fall 2016 semester. That preceding summer of 2016 I was severely ill for over two months, and I often felt, honestly, as if I was dying or on the verge of dying. I needed to make dramatic changes, or I would die. As a result, I not only turned down an opportunity to serve as the next Academic Policies Committee chair, but also resigned as English Department University Senate representative. I did so before the semester began. I also began to do something I had never previously done: call an end to my working day, and call an end to working every day throughout every week, for the majority of my time awake, throughout the entire semester. Instead of working every night after dinner until late at night on weekdays and all day Saturday and Sunday, I stopped working after dinner and I made sure to carve out at least half a day's time not working on the weekend. I in addition attempted to make sure I kept at least four hours a week available to work on scholarship.

All of that helped. But not enough. My health continued to grow more fragile and more precarious. Not only did I continue to struggle with a functional digestive dysmotility disorder, which I will discuss shortly, but also over the course of the next several years my struggles with anxiety (generalized anxiety disorder) skyrocketed as I experienced numerous physically serious panic attacks and often long periods, even without entering into a full-fledged panic attack, when I became so overwhelmed with amorphous dread I could not concentrate on almost anything at all, other than pacing about, back and forth, over and over again, for hours on end. Within the next few years as well, an epileptic condition that I had experienced, off and on since early adolescence, returned in force. I began to experience more seizures more often, and of far greater intensity and lasting duration, than I ever had previously. Never before had I experienced 'grand mal' seizures. I have since. I have also experienced seizures that have left my state of consciousness severely altered and disturbed for up to four to five hours as well as seizures that have left me feeling physically brutalized, as if I had been beaten up badly in a fight I clearly lost, that lasted for many weeks. All of this resulted from the fact I was striving to do more than I could manage, even much more than I could manage.

What has helped is from the start of the Fall 2016 semester I have openly claimed the identity of a person who lives with chronic illness and who is and long has been most definitely disabled (no matter how invisible–or un-visible this is). I have shared openly and at length, with all my students in all my classes, often engaging in far-reaching conversations about issues of health and illness, which they have been most enthusiastic about pursuing. I have also been every bit as open in sharing that I am a person who lives, and long has lived, with serious to severe mental health complications and challenges, with mental disability, that this is intrinsic to whom I am and what I am about, while, again, being ready to discuss, in detail, my own experiences with anxiety, including in the form of panic attacks, depression, trauma, PTSD, suicidality, and attempted suicide. I have also immersed myself in learning about disability studies, especially critical disability studies, and about critical studies in mental health and illness (often identified in many other ways, such as, for instance, as 'Madness Studies'). Likewise I have immersed myself in learning about and seeking ways to contribute usefully myself toward critical praxis conducted on the part of disabled people and people with experience of 'mental illness' by disabled people and people with experience of 'mental illness' ourselves, collectively. All of this has helped me–and helped me recognize how widely shared much of what I deal with and long have dealt with is, empowering me to refuse to further downplay or disguise what living with chronic illness, invisible/un-visible disability, and recurrent to persistent serious to severe mental health complications and challenges means for me.

That brings me to the functional digestive dysmotility disorder that I deal with, and have dealt with, for over thirty years. What this means is my digestive system does not function 'normally', and in fact often does not function 'correctly' at all. It certainly struggles to work in a smooth and synchronous fashion. Often it breaks down. Often I experience flare-ups that are actually much more aptly characterized as 'attacks'. That's what it feels like: my body is attacking me. It feels like my body is hurting me, and hurting me badly. This can cause considerable discomfort, yes, but much worse than that, it can cause acute pain. I want to stress this last point. This is a painful condition. The pain is almost entirely unbearable. Frequently in the midst of such pain I struggle with great difficulty to maintain consciousness. Yet I have taught far more classes and participated in far more meetings that I could possibly enumerate without almost anyone ever recognizing that I was doing so while experiencing such tremendous pain. I have had to pretend this is not happening, and to feign feeling fine, so often that doing so has long since become automatic. Yet a typical day involves strenuous efforts to get myself prepared so that I can perform being healthy when I need to do so while engaging in any and all subsequent forms of public interaction. For many years, long before we as a department moved from Hibbard Hall to Centennial Hall, I have done the bulk of my work from home, only working on campus during classes and meetings, including meetings in the form of office hours and other conferences with students. I work so much from home because I need to do so. I am constantly engaging in therapeutic efforts at the same time as I do most of my work so that I am able to work at all, and the former efforts are far easier to carry out from home than on campus.

I want to take a little more time to discuss this condition yet further. I do so because one of the hardest parts of living with chronic illness is that a great many others do not recognize this is happening and cannot begin to appreciate what it is like. All too often, I have found, in my reading of many accounts from others working in academia who live with chronic illness, and of studies done surveying and interviewing people like us, that academia is relentlessly and unremittingly ableist, and, not only that, but also unaccommodating of and hostile for people living with chronic illness and other invisible/un-visible disabilities, as well as for people with mental disability. Academia in fact is worse than many other job fields. Much of this has to do with the nature of academic culture and of how performance is defined, evaluated, and rewarded in academia. Too much of this altogether excludes people living with chronic illness and other invisible/un-visible disabilities, including mental disabilities, or renders it far more difficult and far less likely that people in this kind of position, in my kind of position, will be able to succeed at all. All too often people like us decide not to pursue academic careers, or leave these careers, because these careers are impossible for people like us.

My functional digestive dysmotility disorder involves all of the elements experienced by people with Chron's disease and with ulcerative colitis as well as many more besides. Unlike those two conditions, no prescription medicine is yet available that works for my condition. Only one prescription medicine is available that has any useful effect at all, and only occasionally and not consistently, for only one dimension of this condition, while also contributing 'side effects' that are often worse than 'the effect' it is supposedly helping to treat. I have undergone numerous tests, procedures, regimens, and on and on–all to little avail. Medical scientific researchers are still exploring explanations and are still a long way off from finding these, let alone from developing and providing any kind of effective treatment. I keep up with research in this area along with a host of 'alternative therapies' that can or might help. I am ready and willing to try anything. But long ago now gastroenterologists I work with have told me that I am far more expert concerning my health condition than they are, and I should follow whatever works best for me as I determine it does, even expressing their wish they could hire someone like me to help others like me in ways they cannot.

Many times what happens is my digestive system seizes up, cramps, tightens, hardens, spasms, and sends sparks or shoots of pain swirling throughout its expanse. Gas builds up, cannot release, and forms a double seal, or double lock, in places that are already the tightest. Muscles begin to ache and spasm far from the abdomen, I grow light-headed and dizzy, and I start to feel very tired–but I cannot rest or sleep. Nothing I can do, and believe me I have tried everything imaginable, can anticipate when such attacks will happen, how long they will last, or how severe they will be. And nothing can be done to prevent or forestall them from arising. After they occur, I try as I can to ameliorate their effects, but this is as best, always, hit and miss. What seemed to work in the past, and even in the recent past, all too often no longer works in the present. Even though by this point in time I know better, that precise triggers for these attacks cannot be pinpointed, I tend to wrack my brain trying to figure out what might have triggered any particular attack when it does come, especially if this comes at a highly inopportune time, which all too often has been the case. Everything can be going along fine, other than low level disturbance, and then all of a sudden a severe attack takes place. It can happen any time any day, and usually it is a rapid change–a rapid change for the far worse. Yes, stress does not help, but I do engage in a plethora of stress management and stress reduction practices, which only help to a limited degree. Yes, some foods are especially bad, but my condition ultimately has little do with food allergies or intolerances, although I cannot eat chicken, eggs, shellfish, mayonnaise or aioli, soy, kidney beans, or MSG.

I simply cannot do many things, or can no longer do many things, that colleagues, most colleagues that is, take for granted. I cannot travel anywhere without a full-time caretaker with me, which means I cannot travel to attend and present at professional conferences in the course of the regular academic year, in fall or spring semesters. Travel in general takes a toll on me, and I often need a few days to recover, if I have traveled any considerable distance, which I also cannot do on my own. I cannot decide I will go without sleep, and work even longer and harder, than I already do, if and when the need should arise. I also need to be highly conscientious about preserving the best of my health for when and where it is most critically needed, which has meant, in recent years, pulling back from the extent of involvements I had long pursued in the larger community, beyond campus, as well as on campus. It has also long meant not attending many if not most events taking place on and off campus–talks, discussions, workshops, forums, readings, exhibitions, performances, plays, concerts, recitals, games, festivals, and so on. In general, so I can preserve what health is needed to teach, and to teach well, along with do what I need to do in terms of institutional service, I don't do almost any of that–and await to do it during Winter, Spring, and Summer breaks, especially while traveling and visiting elsewhere. I also want to highlight that although specific foods are not, in and

1049

of themselves, the most important factors in contributing to flare ups and attacks, I am exceedingly careful, and indeed immensely cautious, about what I eat and drink, of what kinds, how much, how often, and when—and this of absolute necessity. All too often in the past I have become very sick after eating food at pot lucks, or meals with candidates, or department get-togethers, or snacks shared at meetings or in conjunction with meetings. I mostly don't eat anything at all whenever in these circumstances, but I feel awkward about not doing so, which means I often do not attend. What's more, even though I do love to meet and talk with people, to listen to and learn from and share with others, it is very hard for me to arrange to get together over a meal, or snacks, or even, for that matter, at times, over coffee or drinks, so I don't pursue that. Yes, that means I feel more isolated as a result, but I have no choice.

In conclusion, every day I need to check in, and check in, repeatedly, with my body, and especially with my digestive system. I need to be alert and aware at all times to signs of impending trouble or in response to trouble that has already emerged. I never escape and can never avoid needing to do so. This is something many people do not need to do, and cannot readily imagine others working with them need to do. I remember what it was like to be 'normally' healthy. For my first thirty years I was such a person. I was rarely sick, other than occasional colds, even less occasional flu, and rare digestive upsets. I was able to stay up all night for days on end, as need be, and to eat anything whenever I wanted and wherever I wanted. I had enormous energy, and stamina, or at least it seems so to me now, in comparison, and rarely if ever worried about anything concerning my body and more specifically what it was able or unable to do. The difference between then and now is stark—starkly antithetical.

I can do a great deal, and have done a great deal, as a person who lives with a serious to severe, incurable, barely diagnosable, almost completely untreatable, chronic illness, that constitutes a genuinely substantial disability, but I cannot do everything that able-bodied and healthy colleagues can. I cannot even drive a car very often or very far. All too often people with no idea that this is the case recommend I sign up for and participate in (contribute in or even lead) workshops, or other trainings, or to attend similar events, in Madison or Minneapolis—but I could not possibly do so. I could not drive to and from home to any of these locations, and especially not repeatedly. Andy drives us almost everywhere we need to go by car, and everywhere that is any significant distance, but Andy is not available, all the time, as my personal chauffeur. Ideally, I would be provided tangible, concrete, practical support that would enhance my equitable access to the conditions necessary for me able to do my job, and to do it well, but few if any such means have yet been conceived let alone implemented. As far as this department is concerned, my challenge, in the twilight of my time here, is for everyone moving forward to critically examine their own ableism, especially their unconscious ableism, and in doing so learn about and become sensitive to the real existence, and real challenges faced, by colleagues and students living with chronic illness, other invisible/un-visible disabilities, and mental disability. Resist even unintentionally reinforcing ableist norms and ideals. Don't make life harder for those for whom it already is all too hard.

Returning from that detour, in short lupus has made everything about which I then wrote even tougher. Although epileptic episodes have not been frequent, fortunately, over this past fourteen months, when they have arisen they have been major, and harsh, requiring days to recover before I could begin to return to 'a normal routine'. Dealing with lupus and its impact, as well as lupus treatment and its impact, prompted serious depression. What's more, at the beginning of full prescription medication treatment for lupus, due to an extremely high dosage prescription of prednisone, I dealt with manic symptoms unlike anything I had ever experienced before. I hardly could sleep, and I became highly agitated, making this state feel often excruciatingly emotionally painful.

I do now understand my long-term digestive condition, with help from my primary care physician, Dr. Furlano, and as a result of research I have done, is rooted in central sensitization. This amounts to an overly elaborate development of the nerves that connect my brain and 'my gut', and which thereby produces overreactions to otherwise benign stimuli. That diagnosis has been helpful, even though no precise 'treatment', per se, yet exists for central sensitization. But lupus, and especially full lupus treatment, caused a plethora of digestive symptoms which even I, with my 30+ years' experience of digestive hypersensitivity, was previously unfamiliar. These new digestive symptoms settled down, five and one-half months after beginning full lupus treatment, but I now deal with a lasting impact, as the predominant nature and characteristic tendencies of my hypersensitive digestive system have shifted to the virtual opposite of what they were like for the preceding 30+ years. It's been tough to convince myself this shift is real, in order to make the necessary corresponding changes in what, when, and how I eat, drink, exercise, and supplement prescription with complimentary medicines as well as further alternative therapies. But I have done so, proceeding through a complicated process of ongoing trial and error.

Otherwise, lupus has interacted in problematic ways as well with long-term overactive bladder tendencies. And in April 2023 I underwent bladder surgery to remove 'anomalies', fortunately benign but which my surgeon, Dr. Primley, feared would be malignant because that had previously been the case with the same surgery in January 2021. This surgical procedure, for prospective bladder cancer, felt remarkably minor in comparison with what I had been going through, in relation to lupus.

I also came down, after successfully avoiding doing so throughout the history of the pandemic until then, with COVID-19, in early May 2023. I experienced a severe case, taking four weeks before I began to recover, and needing to take prescription paxlovid to avoid hospitalization. My bad experience with COVID undoubtedly resulted from me being immunosuppressed, by then for nearly six months. I recovered, but the effects of COVID on my body included a subsequent major anal fissure, for which again I needed emergency hospital treatment, and an even further slowing down of what I could manage to do for close to a month and one-half. To this day, even though I wish I did not need to do so, I wear a facemask while teaching and at meetings on campus, and by now am one of the relatively few to still do so on a consistent basis.

The good news is I am making progress. I am on my way to remission. Nearly all elements in all blood and urine tests have returned to normal. Neither blood nor protein shows up anymore in tests of my urine while I am no longer anemic, after having been seriously anemic, for over a year. I will need to continue taking prescription drugs and continue to undergo regular testing for the rest of my life. But I am relieved, and grateful, I am where I now am at.

Nonetheless, living with lupus and with lupus treatment these past fourteen months left me feeling that my life was further reduced and limited than what I described in my August 2022 post-tenure review statement. Throughout the entirety of the 2022-2023 academic year I had no energy left for anything other than teaching and what institutional service I could manage. I had no energy left to work on writing this book, or to do any other scholarship. My physical and especially athletic activity diminished to the point where it became virtually non-existent, and we, Andy and I, ventured out of our house only rarely, largely just to buy groceries and household supplies–or to attend my many medical appointments.

I experienced returning to full-time teaching as both rewarding and challenging. I relished teaching Introduction to Critical Studies in both the Fall 2022 and Spring 2023 semesters with a new thematic emphasis on 'Introduction to Critical Studies in Disability and in Mental Health and Illness', working with four plays I had never previously taught before, and renewing the culminating project I have previously described in this book that involves students working in three teams over the last four weeks of the semester to compose, produce, rehearse, and ultimately perform short plays, of approximately 35 minutes in length, inspired in each case by two plays we had previously read and discussed together as a class. In Introduction to Critical Studies I incorporated a new elaboration of the precise concepts and methods I propose define critical studies, and returned our discussions repeatedly to these, while emphasizing social and political explanations of disability and mental illness in wide-ranging conversations, where students freely shared, at length, many often harrowing personal experiences with major varieties of mental and physical illness along with many major kinds of disabilities, visible and un-visible. Students' readiness to so engage and share, as well as to make and explore connections, I found most impressive. Meanwhile, in both the Fall 2022 and Spring 2023 semesters I taught Introduction to Theory and Criticism by narrowing our focus to six approaches: Feminism, Queer Studies, Marxism, Critical Studies in Race and Racism, Postcolonial Studies, and Intersectionality as Critical Inquiry and Critical Praxis. In this course I also incorporated three new literary texts and many new ways of illustrating ideas, including by way of multiple video connections. And I continued to find great value in having our first class meeting focused on each distinct approach involve students asking me questions, based on a textbook chapter and a print lecture of mine they had read for that class meeting, along with students sharing initial efforts at explaining and illustrating concepts based upon what they were able to grasp from the same two sources.

In the Fall 2022 semester, I taught Sports, Politics, and Society for the fifth time, and I found doing so most satisfying as well. Here I incorporated almost entirely new and more to up to date texts and references versus the last time I taught this class, in the Spring 2019 semester. We engaged thoughtfully with issues of athletes and activism, race and sports, gender and sports, sexuality and sports, disability and sports, mental health/mental illness and sports, class and sports, age/ageing and sports, the economics and politics of sports, and the value, appeal, and use of sports along with trajectories for the future of sports. And in Spring 2023 I taught Contemporary Black British Experience for the first time, focusing primarily on recently published book-length memoirs. In retrospect I wish I had been better prepared and more experienced with this focus than I was, as well as thought through more carefully how best to structure this course as a senior seminar. Yet, overall student response was positive and we engaged many vital issues with students making abundant impressive connections.

Throughout those two semesters my overwhelming priority focus was teaching, as long had been the case, but during this period of time I increasingly realized, with lupus becoming a decisive factor in prompting this realization, that I could not do this work, full-time, for much longer, as it now demanded more from me than I was able to give. In particular, in the Spring 2023 semester, due to the weight of my health issues, I needed to draw back from doing weekly check-ins with all students as well as to stop making myself available for consultation on weekends and evenings. I also needed to streamline and re-orient class plans, notably in Contemporary Black British Experience. And due to onset of COVID I needed to transfer my final examination session in Introduction to Theory and Criticism from sharing together, directly in the same room and at the same time, student's reflections on their foremost convictions and values, as well as on what had shaped them to hold these convictions and values, to an online assignment that worked nowhere near as well.

Another major challenge I faced in teaching, throughout the 2022-2023 academic year, involved getting used to changed student attendance habits, promoted by the pandemic. Students now readily and often do not attend class whenever experiencing any kind of health challenge, mental or physical. I respect students making their health and well-being their first priority. But this does mean, as a teacher, I cannot count on any precise number people being present from class session to class session. That means I as the teacher need to improvise all that much more than I ever previously needed to do to make up for those students not there. This is a major pressure in teaching as I do, by way of continuous discussion as well as by means of related forms of active and interactive student learning, with no lectures or other instructor presentations during class time. This 'new attendance normal' proved stressful for me for many weeks until I learned to accept and adjust to it. At the same time, I now am more flexible than ever before on virtually all 'deadlines' for completing required work. Despite my flexibility I also feel saddened because many students face crises in their lives that I can do little to help them with. It is frustrating to feel like so many are in tremendous need but what I can do, by myself alone, as simply one caring and concerned, sympathetic and empathetic individual, amounts to little.

A yet final challenge I faced in the Spring 2023 occurred with one student enrolled in Contemporary Black British Experience because this student, right from the outset and ever thereafter, did not find the class, or how I was teaching it, revelatory. They complained about this, repeatedly, in brutal terms. I struggled to accept that the tenor of this student's complaints reflected their autism and were not indicative of 'my fault' as much as they were reflective of where this student was at, at that point in their life, as a last-semester, older adult senior. But because I was then as weak and sick as I was, I felt as if this student's dissatisfactions was one additional burden to bear.

At the end of the Spring 2023 semester I did arrive, strikingly, at my own 'revelatory' moment. As I shared on my blog at that time, teachers, at all levels, including at the university, especially at teaching-intensive and teaching-emphasis institutions like UW-Eau Claire, often face the pressure *to perform miracles*. We are often expected to reach every student in every class we reach, such that we enable every student's experience working directly with us to be transformative and for all of them to leave the class firmly convinced that this has been a great class and we have been great teachers. When students don't so respond, and are not so responding, we have intuited the expectation that this is our responsibility and we must do everything we can to make up for it. No semester, in no class, is ever fully a success until it achieves this miraculous standard of perfection. I know I have internalized this expectation and pushed myself hard, and unreasonably and unjustifiably so, to meet this goal. For instance, whenever I am reviewing students' final work for a class, at the end of a semester, if it does not seem all that impressive, I have learned always to accept this is on me, and to come away convinced I should have done better, while I also need to strive, assiduously, to do better in the next semester.

An unfortunate consequence for me, and undoubtedly many other teachers as well, is we thereby neglect taking adequate care of our health and well-being, along with failing in attending to enough diversity, enough balance, in our full life-praxis so as to leave us adequately intellectually, emotionally, physically, and spiritually fulfilled. Sad to say, we are all too often praised precisely on account of how much and how far we neglect all of that to instead 'give everything we have' to our students and to our teaching–praise, for instance, for all the 'sacrifices' we routinely make, and for our willingness to be exceptionally devoted to helping our students, in numerous divergent ways, everywhere and all the time. Yes, I have in part resisted this kind of pressure, as I have often taught by granting students considerable space to take charge of their own learning, and to learn by working extensively and intensively, for protracted periods, with and from each other. And I have often directly acknowledged students do all the time often learn much more from fellow students and much more from the rest of their life-experience than they do directly from me as a teacher in a class they take with me, but I still have all too often acted as if I don't take that acknowledgment seriously. I do think many of the health problems I have experienced that have cumulatively grown more and more serious and substantial over nearly forty years' time result from me pushing myself to strive to achieve the impossible, and so pushing myself yet over and over and over again.

The reflection I just recounted feels rather strange because when I think back to my own experience as a student I often learned a great deal from fellow students, and from the rest of my life-experience, more than I did from teachers and in classes, while many of the teachers from whom I learned the most, and whose teaching left the strongest and most lasting impact with me, were not teachers who exercised that kind of impact with all of their students. Not at all. Many of these teachers were even unpopular with a significant number of their other students. What's more, yes, it is worth *trying* to reach everyone and *trying* to make a learning experience valuable for everyone, but teachers need to recognize and accept this is not often going to happen, and that does *not* mean we have 'failed'. We need to recognize our limits, and recognize students' limits, accepting both for what they truly are.

As aforementioned, in the spring 2023 semester, to recount a specific example, one student early on confided to me that he was highly disappointed in our class as he was not learning anything he found to be valuable, especially anything he found he did not already know. He was looking instead, explicitly, for a 'revelatory' and indeed 'miraculous' experience, but not finding it. Initially I did feel badly about this, and I did feel as if I were failing them. But as time proceeded, I recognized this student's expectations of me, and of our class, were unrealistic and unjustified. I did take into account his positions, and his criticisms, by opening up as much space and creating as many opportunities as I could for him to represent his critical positions in class and to otherwise pursue independent areas of strong personal interest and value–as much space as conceivably possible without fundamentally altering the nature and focus of the class for everyone else. Every other student in the class responded positively to what we were doing together while finding the class to be enlightening and useful. But what I too frequently had learned, through my many years as a teacher, is not to focus on the latter but instead to focus on the former–i.e., not to take any satisfaction from the latter but instead concentrate, entirely, on dissatisfaction associated with the former. Eventually, as the spring 2023 semester proceeded, and sooner than most prior semesters, I reflected on what was happening here, for me, and determined I didn't need to feel this way. In fact, I recognized it is harmful to me to feel this way–and harmful when other teachers likewise learn, routinely, to feel this way, that if they don't successfully reach and fully satisfy ever student in every class they teach, what they have done it not yet good enough, requiring still more and harder work on their part to reach 'perfection'. Institutions need to do a much better job at not encouraging, and not rewarding, this kind of mindset, among teachers working at these same institutions.

In an article I wrote in the Spring 2023 semester for the UWEC English Department website and newsletter, announcing my forthcoming retirement, I concluded as follows:

> It is up to others to determine what my legacy might be, and what kind of impact I might have left. I will simply add that I have worked extremely hard as a professor, I have given it everything I had and often enough much more than I could afford to give; I have strived continually to do better and to be all the more useful to others with whom I work, especially in teaching; I have never become complacent and taken for granted any level of achievement by instead constantly experimenting and innovating as well as pursuing new passions, interests, concentrations, and emphases in new ways as well as new directions; and I have always strived to do what I do as a matter of principle as opposed to pragmatism. I hope I have contributed in some useful ways, through my own actions, while working here at UW-Eau Claire and for nearly 40 years as a university faculty member, in the long and challenging process of creating a genuinely substantial culture of empathy and solidarity; of embracing active responsibility for collective well-being, of each for all and of all for each; and of drawing upon shared vulnerability as a source of, at least prospectively, the greatest strength.

In writing and sharing this brief statement I arrived at an unusual point, for me: accepting that is sufficient, as a useful legacy. But I also believe 'my legacy', as a a teacher and university faculty, functions as 'a warning'–of the damage that can happen if and when as a teacher one internalizes the expectation that nothing short of perfection is ever good enough, and that you can never do or give enough to the work you do as a teacher.

An even more somber reflection that has occurred to me, since initially writing and sharing the immediately preceding, is that I could never have even begun to pursue the prospect of working as a university faculty member, especially at a teaching- and service- intensive institution like UW-Eau Claire, as part of a culture that prizes pushing oneself always to do more and better, and to never be satisfied at anything less than perfection, to the point of actual burnout, *if* I had developed lupus earlier than in August 2022. I could not have met the expectations of this institution, or most others like it, while coping with the ravages of this kind of health condition. Now, in my last semester, in the Fall 2023, I am teaching and working 60%, and that feels reasonable, for me, with where I am at and what I am able to give. Yet, our institution is reluctant to allow faculty to work at less than 100%. I am only 'allowed' to do so because my health has been so bad, and because this is my last semester. The problems with this stance are multiple. After all, like most colleges and universities in the US, and for many decades now, a great many who work to teach within these institutions are adjunct faculty, who often are not hired 'full-time', in part because 'full-time' for adjunct faculty involves a significantly higher teaching load than for 'regular' faculty, but also because hiring this kind of faculty saves the institution, and the state, money. In addition, many people working as faculty and staff at universities like UW-Eau Claire cannot afford to 'choose' to work 60%, at a 60% salary rate, unlike me this semester. And, yet again, as I have previously discussed earlier in this chapter, reluctance to 'allow' faculty to work different workloads shows that academia is *not* equitably inclusive of people with chronic illnesses. In effect academia rejects large numbers of people, not welcoming the talents they can bring to bear, in significant part due to whom and what they are, as people living with chronic illness, while preventing these people from fully actualizing themselves such that they can contribute the best they have to offer to communities in which they are situated and cultures with which they are aligned. All too often, people living with disability, including chronic mental as well as physical illness, are effectively barred from spaces where they might, at least ideally, experience rare feelings of genuinely belonging and genuinely mattering.

All the more stunning, for me, doctors and other health care providers I work with, as well as many people living with lupus, have all recommended I retire as soon as possible while emphasizing people in my situation simply cannot work high demand and high stress jobs of any kind. But we do not live a society where most people enjoy a sufficiently cushioning social safety net such that they can live economically viable as well as socially fulfilling lives without working full-time jobs that pay well yet involve high demand and high stress. I find it hard to imagine any kind of job I could readily have done if I had developed lupus much earlier in my life. I find it hard to imagine how I could have got by at all, without Andy, and without being able to afford health insurance as well without access to quality health care along with flexibility to attend medical appointments at many different times of the day, week after week. Most people cannot manage any of that.

In returning to full-time teaching, at the start of the Fall 2022 semester, I recognized I still valued doing this work. I appreciated teaching is one area where I can and do make a meaningful difference. In teaching I bring to bear talent, skill, knowledge, and experience that matters, and in teaching I produce and perform the most satisfying version of myself. Yet I also recognized I could not continue. I decided to retire at the end of the Fall 2023 semester.

At the beginning of February 2023 I publicly announced my plans to retire, as well as Andy's (at the end of the Spring 2024 semester). I announced we planned to move to San Diego, California, to live, full-time, as of the beginning of June 2024. Andy and I have aimed to live in a large city upon retirement since before we were married in 2000. We want a city that will challenge us, and that will provide us ample opportunity, incentive, and indeed provocation to continue to learn and grow. We want to retire to a city where we can be active, engaged, and contributing members in multiple communities, while at the same time leading less structured lives, according to a more relaxed pace, than has most often been the case in Eau Claire. We determined San Diego offers all of that. Neither of us have lived in San Diego previously, but multiple previous visits to San Diego, and considerable investigation of San Diego, inspired us to make San Diego our top choice. Spending ten days over winterim, December 2022 through January 2023, walking close to 150 miles in total all over Downtown, Uptown, and many other neighborhoods, clinched this decision. Since then, Andy and I bought a house in San Diego, spent five weeks living in San Diego in the summer of 2023, and have undergone considerable preparation to complete our move in early June 2024.

We are aware of many challenging issues San Diego faces; we do not romanticize life living in this city, as much as we do like it. We aim to do our part to help address these issues, which include homelessness and lack of affordable housing; high risk of drought and fire as well as impacts of pollution, climate change, and declining biodiversity; the consequences of a hardened border with Mexico in confrontation with the desperation of many seeking refuge and asylum in the US, often starting in San Diego. Many new opportunities will be available to us in San Diego but I do worry about making such a dramatic change. I am not only leaving what has been the 'heart and soul' of my life's practice for close to 40 years, teaching and working as a university faculty member, but also moving to an area where Andy and I will be starting from scratch in establishing relationships and making connections. And we will be undertaking this adventure even as I deal with multiple, accumulative, serious chronic illnesses, and as I am feeling ever increasingly 'older'. Yet this is a dream we have aspired to experience, so we want to pursue it while we have the chance. How it turns out, and how well it does, we cannot predict or control, but we accept that, even as frightening as that can be.

Acceptance Commitment Therapy (ACT)'s concept of 'radical acceptance' has proven helpful to me in enhancing my ability to accept what I can neither predict nor control. Radical acceptance, as I understand it, does not mean rationalizing what is 'bad' is 'good'. To the contrary, radical acceptance, for me at least, means being able to live with what is 'bad', while accepting how 'bad' it is–by accepting that this 'bad' is where I am at, at present, or that this 'bad' is where 'we' are at, at present. Radical acceptance, along these lines, means accepting that what is, is *not* acceptable, that it is indeed *unacceptable*, but accepting that living with the unacceptable is where I am situated, or where we are situated, at present. Efforts at change begin from accepting where I, and we, are at, at present, for what this is, and from accepting my, and our, limitations, for what they are, as we strive to bring about, or at least contribute to bringing about, needed change. Radical acceptance means accepting that my tendencies toward worry, anxiety, and sensitivity are not solely problematically *disabling* but instead complex, and contradictory, involving prospectively *enabling* dimensions as well.

As with "Atmosphere," I am at present undergoing a series of major endings, but also a series of major new beginnings. As with "Atmosphere," likewise, this is not the final end, altogether, of my prospective contributions toward, or as part of, much greater processes, with which I have passionately identified. Rather, I am, akin to what "Atmosphere" suggests is happening, with the narrator-protagonist, and the music as persona, undergoing a major reorientation of from where, and how, I am positioned in relation to these vaster processes. I do periodically experience profound sadness, and even sheer terror, at reaching this point, and undergoing these changes. But, in contrast with the lyrics of "Atmosphere," I experience no bitterness. I experience no feeling whatsoever that anyone is to 'blame' for me reaching this point, and beginning this change, not even myself.

Yes I worry about many problems in the world today. Many deeply concern and definitely frighten me. These include catastrophic death and destruction in Palestine, leaving well over 30,000 Palestinian civilians killed, virtually the entirety of Gaza reduced to rubble, and Gazans across the board on the brink of dying in massive numbers due to starvation and lack of other life essentials, in the time since Israel responded with massive force to Hamas killing over 1,200 Israelis and taking hostage hundreds more on October 7, 2023. These include little reason to expect an enduringly peaceful settlement to the more than seventy-five years of often violent conflict between the Israeli state and the non-Israeli people of Palestine. These include ecological emergency and impending ecological catastrophe. These include the persistent popularity of fascism, along with the precariousness of ready alternatives. These include dehumanization of homeless people and of immigrants, including refugees and asylum seekers. These include increased intolerance for and hostility directed against LGBTQIA+ people. These include, within public colleges and universities, threats to the preservation of: academic freedom; curricular and extra-curricular investments in fostering equity, diversity, inclusion, belonging, and mattering; and the availability of liberal arts electives and concentrations in the humanities, arts, and social sciences that are free to engage with controversial issues, and controversial takes, in difficult and disturbing conversations.

I worry about not doing enough, and not being able to do enough, to help out, in even the smallest of meaningful ways, to address these issues, and I worry that it will be much less readily possible for me to do so once no no longer teaching and working as a university faculty member. I also do at times wrestle with guilt at being relatively privileged versus where many if not most others are at who are suffering and will suffer the worst impacts of these festering trends. I maintain real fears concerning the prospective advent of major social and political regress, and real grief concerning lost chances and tragic reversals. I do indeed fear even worse catastrophes that might be irreversible. As in many Joy Division songs, and especially many Ian Curtis lyrics, not just in "Atmosphere," I struggle with uncertainty about how I can, and how I much can, contribute to what at the same time feels urgent–and with retirement, with the accumulative effect of increasing numbers of chronic illnesses, and with aging, this can become more painful to contemplate, but just as these lyrics, and this music, proposes, it is right and necessary not to retreat from, or protect myself from, the painful but rather to face up to it, honestly, nonetheless.

The dramatis personae in the lyrics of "Atmosphere," including the narrator-protagonist as well as whomever 'he' is addressing, whomever 'he' is pleading to walk in silence with 'him' but not to walk *away* in silence, need not be as young as Ian Curtis was, when he wrote these lyrics. Indeed, the lyrics make sense in relation to the position of someone older, at the brink of retirement, contemplating the enormity of what that change means, especially as it brings to an end what has served as 'the heart and soul' of that person's life-practice for decades. These lyrics make sense, moreover, in relation to contemplating the need to retire in significant part due to the impact of chronic illness, as well as due to the 'weathering' effects aging has revealed. Intimations of sadness, frustration, fear, worry, bitterness, resentment, desperation, resignation, and ultimately acceptance in these lyrics all make sense from that vantage point.

Yet, as I have analyzed "Atmosphere," the music of the song complicates and indeed counters interpretation of the song as merely evocative of sorrow and grief. For me, work in critical theory as well as in left politics interconnected with critical theory has accustomed me to perceiving and accepting myself as part of larger processes and movements, and as representative of positions and practices where I am at best a partial, limited, and temporary stand-in among a vast array of others who likewise reprssent the same, or similar, positions and practices. This kind of work has accustomed me to think of myself as interconnected with, and representative of, what greatly transcends my individual existence. I have a responsibility to represent interests that I share together with people I will never meet, and never even know about, past and future as well as present. I have thereby realized, and accepted, 'my praxis' is never simply 'my praxis'; it is dialectically and historically interconnected with the praxis of an enormous number of others, individuals and groups, across immense expanses of time and space, so what I do, 'within my own life', and especially *with my own life*, is not, is never really, 'all about me'. The most far-reaching social and political changes I support almost certainly will never happen in my life-time. But that is OK. I accept being a microscopically minute wave-particle within the overwhelming, enveloping, and subsuming 'atmosphere' the Joy Division song "Atmosphere" references–and enacts.

I am likely more familiar thinking in this way, 'about myself', than Ian Curtis was, but I don't want to underestimate Curtis, or Joy Division, even as conduits or channels for more powerful insights that they might not deliberately, consciously set out to arrive at, because I experience considerable affinity with exactly this same direction of transcendent thinking in both Curtis's lyrics and especially the music of Joy Division. I argue these lyrics and this music, in "Atmosphere" and otherwise, make sense in alliance with the proposition that we each maintain a representative connection with vast numbers of people engaged in struggles far beyond our direct acquaintance or even indirect familiarity. Each of us represents these interests in the specific locations, in time and space, where we individually are at. Each of us maintains extremely limited individual agency, but as part of a much larger movement, in time and space, our collective agency can become impactful and transformative. At the same time our differences, as Audre Lorde for example has famously theorized, need not divide and separate us, as they can, to the contrary, prove vital in producing and sustaining a unity that is sufficiently tenacious to persist in continually striving after the 'not yet' that 'yet could be', the 'not yet' that *should* be, and the not yet that is only barely imaginable, as theorized by José Esteban Munoz, in fleeting ecstatic 'queer' interruptions of 'straight time', or, as theorized by Avery F. Gordon, in the ghostly manifestation of past dreams that were never fully realized in the past but which survive in haunting us, in the present, as persistent aspirations toward, and persistent demands for, a future that could yet, and especially should yet, be.

Nine

Late in Jon Savage's and Grant Gee's documentary film, *Joy Division,* Peter Saville declares "There's just the two albums. All the rest is the merchandising of memory." I agree in part with Saville, but I find a number of songs not included on *Unknown Pleasures* or *Closer* important as well, and I conceive of myths surrounding Ian Curtis and Joy Division as not *merely* merchandising of memory, even if that in part is true. The two most prominent of these myths, as I discuss later in this section, surround, first, the transformation of Joy Division into New Order, and, second, Joy Division's and especially Factory Records' relation to Manchester. According to the latter myth, Joy Division provides a quintessential musical evocation of the look, sound, and feel of Manchester at its post-industrial nadir, while Joy Division also both anticipates and sparks a remarkable transformation of Manchester. In other words, Joy Division, ostensibly, provided a crucial impetus toward Manchester becoming the massively built up city it now is, a city that has been reborn following massive capital investment intricately interlinked with promotion and celebration of Manchester as a preeminent center of artistic and cultural creativity, innovation, and achievement. Myths matter, but these two myths do not explain what this music means *to me* and how or why it impacts *me*, in relation to what it prompts *me* to think (about) and feel as *I* listen to and reflect upon it. In the proceeding, I discuss "Decades" in connection with these two myths while exploring how "Decades" can and does make sense, and resonate, beyond those connections.

"Decades," the final song on *Closer*, is one of my favorite Joy Division songs. I agree with Peter Hook, who writes in *Unknown Pleasures: Inside Joy Division*, "It's one of the most beautiful songs we ever did. I think it's more beautiful than 'Atmosphere'" (280). Hook notes that "Decades" "begins with me playing low bass and, unusually, playing in sync with the bass drum; then there's overdubbing of another bass part, on the six-string, very rhythmic so it sounds like guitar" (280). Further notable, "There's a great Syndrum sound, loads of echo plate in use," while "Barney on the keyboards" is "again layered wonderfully" as are, yet additional, "overdubbed guitar melodies" (280). In *Record Play Pause: Confessions of a Post-Punk Percussionist Volume 1*, Stephen Morris highlights the prominent role that a synthesizer drum machine plays in this song, and Morris recalls this didn't bother him because he welcomed such experimentation, and innovation, on account of the effects doing so enabled (349). Bernard Sumner, like Morris, in Sumner's memoir, *Chapter and Verse: New Order, Joy Division and me*, calls attention, in discussing "Decades," to the prominent and successful contributions to the sound of this song from Arp Omni, Transcendent 2000, and ARP 2600 synthesizers.

In the same passage from *Unknown Pleasures: Inside Joy Division*, reflecting on "Decades," Hook writes "I find *Closer* much easier to listen to than *Unknown Pleasures*. I like it as a musical offering and find myself listening to *Closer* simply for pleasure, which I can't really do with anything else that I've done. Definitely not the New Order stuff, sadly. This is actually one of my favourite albums" (280). As Hook shares in an interview with Jonathan Wright for *The Quietus*, on the occasion of the 40th anniversary of the release of *Closer*, when he performed this album in its entirety with *Peter Hook and the Light* he experienced doing so as "perfect," because "To play the album in its entirety was so emotional and so fantastic that, at times, it literally took my breath away." Seemingly, therefore, as much if not more than with any other music he has made, *Closer* prompts Hook to reflect "It's a wonderful thing as a man and as a musician to think, 'You know, I'll be dead and gone and yet, years and years later, people will still be listening to the bass on those records going, "Fuck, this is great."' I'm very happy about that. To leave a mark on the world is something we all dream of, isn't it?"

In an interview with *GQ*, likewise commemorating the same 40 years anniversary, Morris adds the following comment on "Decades":

It was originally called "Euro pop," which it sounded absolutely nothing like. When it started it had a bossa nova beat to it, which Martin absolutely hated. It was probably about the same day we would have done "The Eternal." We didn't have a drum machine at the time, so we hired one and this Roland CR-78. I'd never seen a drum machine before and thought Martin would know how it worked. He's pressing buttons and it plays "In The Air Tonight," all those classic drum machine beats. I said, 'Well it's not really that kind of song, Martin. And he said, 'No. We can program it. They can make it play wherever you want'.

Despite the challenges involved in learning to work with a drum machine for the first time, Morris indicates, in *Record Play Pause: Confessions of a Post-Punk Percussionist Volume 1*, that he agrees with Hook: the song ended up a triumph.

None of the three–Hook, Morris, and Sumner–are much concerned in their comments on offering interpretations of what 'the song might mean', as they focus instead on the quality of the selection, organization, and deployment of sounds and sound patterns the song involves. They don't need do so, as many others have focused on the former. For instance, writing for *Old Time Music* in November 2023, Kelvin Ingram's article addresses exactly what its title indicates, "The Meaning Behind The Song: 'Decades' by Joy Division." Concentrating on the lyrics, Ingram identifies three themes in "Decades": "nostalgia, regret, and mortality." Ingram in turn interprets this thematic emphasis as "influenced by Curtis's own struggles with depression and feelings of isolation," as well as Curtis's "fascination with existentialist philosophy." Ingram interprets the choral refrain, "Where have they been?," as referencing "the passing of time and the loss of youth," with, more precisely, this line offering "an introspective lament for all that has been lost over the years." According to Ingram, "the slow and melancholic instrumental introduction to 'Decades' sets the mood "for the rest of the song," by initiating "a somber and introspective atmosphere" that fits "the song's themes of regret and nostalgia." In sum, therefore, "Decades" amounts to "a poetic meditation on the passing of time and the loss of youth."

Writing in March 2022 for *The Run Out Grooves*, a blog that celebrates the final track on various albums, Mitchell Stirling writes that many people have interpreted "Decades" as "a song about the impact of war on the generations of young men whom their leaders force to pick up arms and fight," and as about experiences of shell-shock or PTSD. According to this line of interpretation, as Stirling describes it, "Decades" conveys the perspective of a man "contemplating his ultimate fate," with the song encompassing "a fast-forward to many years in the future" from which "to look back," and in particular to imagine what it might be like to look back from far into the future upon a life that has now long since passed. Yet Stirling is skeptical of interpreting the song too closely in line with Curtis's suicide. Stirling points out "Decades" "is almost peaceful and melancholic," sounding like an early instance of synth-pop that anticipates later New Order. For Stirling, therefore, while the song is somber it is not necessarily 'depressive'–or 'depressing'.

Contributing to *SMF* (Song Meanings and Facts), George Spencer, writing in August 2022, is more certain that "Decades" is about "the atrocities of war." Spencer interprets "Decades" as reflecting and responding to "the climax of the Vietnam War, which was also around the first time the brutalities of modern warfare were televised to the masses." In addition, Spencer interprets the song as concerned with a yet earlier but not that long distant war, because "the early 1980s wasn't really that long after World War II," which means this remained "a time when many people who witnessed the conflict firsthand were still around." Yet, in the aftermath of the Vietnam War "in particular, this was a time in Western history where normal citizens, like musicians, began to more deeply question why their governments would send them half way around the world, to kill or be killed." Spencer thereby interprets "Decades" "as a poetic portrayal of the psychological ramifications of being a soldier out on the field," that "definitely isn't such that it'd have listeners lining up to join the army anytime soon." According to "Decades," "doing so only results in 'trauma and degeneration' while in action" and "it also births never-ending 'sorrows' afterwards." For Spencer, "Decades" is therefore about both PTSD and the lack of welcome many US soldiers received, at least reputedly, in returning home after fighting in the unpopular Vietnam War.

If "Decades" is about war, and about the impact of war upon those who directly experience its violence, it makes sense for listeners to connect the song, as they interpret it, with those wars that are most immediately resonant with them. Listening to "Decades" over and over again, in early 2024, I think of the war in Gaza that began after October 7, 2023, after Hamas killed over 1,000 Israelis and took hundreds more hostage. This war has resulted in over 30,000 Palestinians killed, along with many thousands more seriously injured, or forced into exiled, while the majority of the buildings in Gaza–including hospitals, universities, and mosques–have been destroyed, and while access to resources vital to sustain human life–food, water, shelter, sanitation, medicine, electricity–have been either cut off altogether or drastically reduced for the well over a million people still remaining. I think as well of the escalation of violence directed against Palestinians in the West Bank and in Israel since this current war started, and especially of the decades of violence–involving massive killing, maiming, deprivation, marginalization, exclusion, and forced displacement–that followed the establishment of Israel in a place where a vast number of other people had long lived and likewise also claimed as their ancestral homeland. I think of how 'violence in the Middle East' centered around 'conflict between Israel and Palestine' or between the government and the state of Israel and the non-Israeli people living in 'Greater Palestine' has been ongoing for decades, and has often seemed intractable, with no apparent prospect of a peaceful, and especially a lasting peaceful, resolution.

Turning, however, from this line of interpretation, focused on war and its consequences, blogger The Socratic Method interprets "Decades" as concerned with all of the following: "the often-overwhelming burdens carried by young people"; "the immense responsibility and pressure they encounter as they transition into adulthood"; "the exploration into the unknown and the willingness to face internal demons in pursuit of self-discovery"; "the fickle nature of life and the constant struggle to find one's place in the world"; "paths being opened and abruptly closed, leading to a profound sense of disappointment and disillusionment"; "despite our efforts to find meaning and purpose, life often appears to be a series of inaccessible doors that tantalizingly beckon, only to be slammed shut upon reaching them"; and "the turmoil of youth, where opportunity and potential can feel both abundant and frustratingly out of reach." The Socratic Method conceives of "Decades" as recounting an introspective reflection, from a young adult's vantage point, upon preceding journeys, and passages, this young adult has already made, as well as upon the consequences that have followed from the choices they made, at previously pivotal points in their lives. This introspection yet further concerns wanting, and needing, these choices and these consequences to make meaningful sense yet struggling to discern what that meaningful sense might be. "Decades," in sum, is about "young individuals striving to find their place in the world" while reflecting on how fraught this quest so often turns out to be.

In songmeanings.com, most of those who share their interpretations connect "Decades" with reflection on experiences of war, and in all cases, with the pain and horror that war can and does involve, as well as long-lasting damaging impacts of war, such as PTSD, along with indictment of the 'masters of war' who are responsible for sacrificing so many young lives to serve their own political interests. Commentators also suggest war is used in this song metaphorically to stand in for other experiences of pain and horror related to social alienation of multiply varied kinds. Further interpretations of "Decades" include the song is about looking back at one's life after death, including after suicide; about how 'it is better to burn out than fade away'; and about what it looks, sounds, and feels like to be immersed in the midst of deep depression.

Michael Goddard, in his contribution to *Heart & Soul: Critical Essays on Joy Division*, "Missions of Dead Souls: a Hauntology of Industrial, Modernism and Esotericism in the Music of Joy Division," while focusing primarily on "Dead Souls," links "Decades" as well as "Dead Souls" with "dyschronia," or "the lived experience of temporal disjuncture or of time being out of joint," as part of a "dystopian imagination of the cancellation of the future" that "has now become the matrix for the twenty-first-century retromanic culture of both the acceleration of everyday life and the exhaustion of cultural innovation" (7). Later in the same book, Tiffany Naiman links "Decades" with her argument concerning Curtis's experience of temporal exile as a result of his serious illness, and with the particular 'ill style' she proposes Curtis develops in response, where the struggle required of Curtis to record the songs on *Closer*, due to how ill he then was, shows up in the style of Curtis's singing, with this style playing a pivotal role in conveying the sense of profound dislocation and isolation that many associate with this album and its constituent songs. As Naiman writes, with "Decades," "Curtis's voice drags behind the music, sounding slightly off time as his baritone trudges through the slow, descending vocal lines in an extremely clear timbre that lacks any kind of vocal embellishment, such as vibrato" (93). Here, instead, "Reverb has once more been added to Curtis's voice" and "This reverb lends a distance to his vocal presence, as if he is singing from the beyond," while "a touch of echo (the slower delay, rather than the sped-up reverb)" contributes "an untimely repetition that is removed from the act of utterance, taking the vocal out of its time and repeating it as a memory so that it functions as something that is both current and of the past" (93). In sum, "the timbre of Curtis's voice is made to sonically reflect the alienation and emptiness it describes" (93).

In considering the contribution of the title, "Decades," to the prospective meaning of the song, beginning with the lyrics, it is notable, first, that the title refers to plural decades and at the same time does not indicate any specific decades. What's more, as is often enough the case with Ian Curtis's lyrics, the lyrics do not directly refer to the title. Nevertheless the title does influence how people intuit what kind of meanings they experience the song as inviting and encouraging them to associate with the song, as well as what kinds of impacts they are likewise invited and encouraged to experience, in listening to and reflecting, subsequently, on their listening to the song. The title "Decades" suggests the song addresses a phenomenon that exists, that lasts, that persists, or at least recurs, over an extended period of time.

Stanza one reads as follows: "Here are the young men, the weight on their shoulders/Here are the young men, well where have they been?/We knocked on the doors of Hell's darker chamber/Pushed to the limit, we dragged ourselves in/Watched from the wings as the scenes were replaying/We saw ourselves now as we never had seen/Portrayal of the trauma and degeneration/The sorrows we suffered and never were free." Let's begin with the first phrase of the first line, noting we are referring to 'young men' and because of 'the' this is seemingly a specific group or set of young men. It also seems the narrator is pointing to these young men, pointing to them right in front of us–or otherwise visibly, audibly, and tangibly nearby–so that we witness their presence and what this looks, sounds, and feels like. The second phrase makes the image slightly more concrete, by depicting these young men as carrying 'weight on their shoulders', suggestive of bearing a burden, perhaps a heavy burden, and as a result, prospectively experiencing pain and fatigue as a result. Line two, beginning with the repetition of the same initial phrase, amplifies its significance, the significance of directing us to note well these young men, and how they appear before us, while raising a question that suggests the narrator either does not know the answer or is not going to answer for us, or for them. The answer to "well where have they been?" seems to be something we need to determine for ourselves, by attending closely to what these young men express and communicate, or indirectly allude to, as that 'from where they have come'. But posing the question does imply 'where they have come from', including both what they experienced there and in the course of the journey from there to here, is what accounts for 'the weight on their shoulders'.

In line three it appears as if the narrator now joins the young men, or reveals 'himself' to be one of them, or at one with them, by starting with "We." Now the narrator-protagonist *is* identifying to us from where these young men, including the narrator-protagonist have come. The narrator-protagonist claims "We knocked on the doors of Hell's darker chamber." So we confront a narrator-protagonist, seemingly at one with an indeterminate number of other young men, who confides to us that they have been to hell in back, and not only that but also to the worst region of hell. This line conjures an image of experiencing great and indeed grave horror, such that it is hard to imagine surviving, and returning, without being severely damaged as a result. The next line, "Pushed to the limit, we dragged ourselves in," suggests these young men arrived at the doors of Hell's darkest chamber because they had been pushed to that location–pushed to the furthest they could possibly be pushed and still survive, if barely survive at that. Yet while external forces compelled them to travel that far, once they arrived at that threshold internal forces took over and carried them across.

These lines makes sense in relation to soldiers' experience of war, where soldiers, at least those on the front lines, are not ultimately responsible for 'pushing' themselves to these front lines, but once there, immersed in a situation that demands 'kill or be killed', the soldiers must 'drag' themselves forward. Similar situations also make sense where external forces demand much of 'us', and push us far and hard, even wear us down and beat us up, with the full extent of this impact showing up most acutely when we surrender to these demands and become their compliant agents, now that we have been broken down–and *broken in*. Expectations surrounding 'normalcy', can, as I have often discussed throughout this book, prove oppressive. As subjects become 'normalized', as they submit and conform to the demands of dominant regimes of the normal, this can include internalizing and identifying with what substantially limits and prevents genuine self-actualization. Perhaps this is what happens, so these lyrics make sense as suggesting, in the passage from childhood to adulthood, in the course of that transition, concerning both what needs to be given up and what needs to be taken on, and in particular in relation to how much loss and pain 'adultification' involves.

"Watched from the wings as the scenes were replaying" moves us together with the narrator-protagonist and the rest of 'the young men' to the position of spectator–spectator of our own past lives, or the lives of many others past, and present, as well as most likely, future, who will follow the same course. This line invites reflection on what it means not only to be worn down and out, and needing to 'retire' from the field of action, but also to recognize that 'we' and others like us–past, present, and future–are used, abused, and discarded, as mere tools, implements, or appendages to a relentless machine. We are interchangeable, and thereby replaceable–for example, as exploited and alienated workers who produce surplus value expropriated by capitalists as source of capitalist profit, the accumulation of which allows for the continuous reinvestment in the same cycle of production, and at successive larger scales, leading to yet further exploitation and alienation. Regardless of what specific direction of interpretation we follow here, it seems the narrator-protagonist, together with the group of young men with whom 'he' is identifying himself, and thereby inviting and encouraging us to do the same, is contemplating scenes from a life, or from a series of lives, akin to the proverbial quick succession of images that many experience as they are dying.

This direction of interpretation gains support from the next lines in this same stanza: "We saw ourselves now as we never had seen/Portrayal of the trauma and degeneration/The sorrows we suffered and never were free." The first of these three lines suggests obtaining an insight into 'ourselves' when examined from this distance. Perhaps 'we' maintain no real continuity across this extent of time, and change, but rather at this stage, in this state, and from this vantage point, we are *not* the same people we were then, we are now strangers to 'ourselves'. Those lives, ostensibly lived by us, that we are observing and reflecting on now, 'from the wings', appear as the 'lives of others', the lives of people whom we now are not, at least not anymore, while feeling as if those lives 'never were ours'. *Those* lives appear akin to the lives of characters in a play performed by actors, actors who are by no means identical with the characters whom they are playing. As such, we are compelled to contemplate whether an individual, or a group for that matter, maintains any singular continuity, any enduring essence or core of being, over time, across space, and throughout the many changes and in response to the many impacts that occur in the course of what is conventionally assumed, perhaps as a merely convenient fiction, to be 'a single life'.

Nevertheless, it fits these lyrics best to interpret them as contemplating forces involved in fracturing, dissolving, and even disintegrating a singularity while also (barely) preserving it, as the last two lines of the stanza suggest that 'we', together with the narrator-protagonist, and together with the young men, are observing and contemplating what now appears to be an overarching life-experience dominated by 'trauma and degeneration', as if, in considering this life-experience from a critical distance, it is trauma and degeneration that comes overwhelmingly to the fore. These lyrics make sense in relation to going to war, fighting in war, and participating in the massive killing and destruction of war, while the lyrics at the same time propose nothing about such experience is worthwhile or in any way redeems it, because war results, above and beyond all else, in trauma and degeneration.

The last line of this first stanza, referencing 'the sorrows we suffered and never were free', suggests that at one point 'we' may well have imagined, or been invited and encouraged to imagine, the sorrows we suffered were necessary in order for us to experience, to obtain, or to realize 'freedom', but it turns out this was a lie. Here we can imagine being called upon to sacrifice ourselves 'because it will be worth it', because the cause is right and just. But, it turns out that it was neither. All of our efforts, and all we sacrificed and suffered in the course of these efforts, have been worthless. These lyrics also resonate with a common experience of many young people in moving from childhood to adulthood: they imagined, while still children, that they would always remain close to the people they were close to, in their childhood years, but those relationships have since faded and ended.

The next, choral, stanza, "Where have they been?/Where have they been?/Where have they been?/Where have they been?," suggests less seeking an answer and more a lament for what is now lost. This may well indeed be a lament for 'the people they once were', including the person the narrator-protagonist 'himself' once was–but is no more. Life-experiences, especially involving pain, hardship, sorrow, suffering, and trauma, change people so they are no longer the people they were before, and such that they cannot return to being these people ever again. Yes, this stanza is suggestive of post-traumatic stress disorder, which many people experience for many reasons, not just as soldiers fighting in war–such as, for example, resulting from violent abuse and callous neglect. Whatever the specific reference point, these four lines call upon us to attend to these people, to their experiences, to what 'they' have gone through, as a result of 'where they have been', and to engage in reparative praxis that begins by not allowing what they suffered to be forgotten or neglected. Ultimately, repair requires getting at the root causes, and intervening therein to prevent trauma and degeneration from endlessly recurring. Yet "Decades" laments the damage done without evincing confidence this can be stopped.

Stanza three reads as follows: "Weary inside, now our heart's lost forever/Can't replace the fear, or the thrill of the chase/Each ritual showed up the door for our wanderings/Open then shut, then slammed in our face." The first line suggests an enormous fatigue that follows from having 'lost our heart' and having done so 'forever'. This makes sense as implying 'we' have now forever lost what has been our life's passion, the central focus of meaning and purpose in our life, what we have loved most in and about the life we have lived. This might be a person, a group, a vocation, an avocation, a cause, a mission, and yet more besides. The second line completes that thought by proposing what is now 'lost forever' cannot be replaced. Nothing, in other words, can take its place, even as, somewhat paradoxically, what is now lost forever, and leaves tremendous weariness in its place, was animated by fear. Connecting fear with 'the thrill of the chase', though, it seems 'we' have lost a passion that involved risk, and danger, but was exciting, even invigorating, and that, in retrospect, is what made 'us' feel truly alive. 'The thrill of the chase' can indeed involve any kind of 'pursuit' in which we believe, and in which we are invested, that requires hard work, and faces significant obstacles, but feels all the more fulfilling as result of doing that work and overcoming those obstacles. Yes, in the course of such pursuit fear takes place–for instance, fear of not being able to succeed in the task or on time or in doing it well. But that fear can nonetheless drive forward the effort to meet the goal.

The next line, "Each ritual showed up the door for our wanderings," is especially challenging to interpret. But this line might reference rituals attendant upon many a social situation, and many a social effort. Rituals provide key elements within frameworks that structure, or guide, how to proceed in terms of a social situation, and a social action, including in relations to others who are co-participants in the same situation, and the same action. Rituals also help render what transpires in the course of a social situation, and a social action, valuable, or at least seemingly valuable. Rituals can, in addition, provide feelings of familiarity, comfort, assurance, confidence, and security. "Showed up the door" insinuates these rituals are what led to 'the door', whether this door be literal or figurative, what made 'the door' appear to exist, with the door appearing to mark a threshold across which we can pass, if not indeed must pass. "For our wanderings" in turn suggests a restless quest to find a door, or perhaps even 'the right door', which could mean the door that opens to the answers we are seeking to find, or to the place we want and need to be, or to arrival at a state or stage where we feel as if we have earned and accomplished something significant and are recognized and appreciated for having done so. This could be where 'we' find a satisfying direction and purpose in life, as part of a community, as well as a direction and purpose that is sustainable long-term. Here, through or beyond this door, we find 'what we have been looking for' and 'those others we have been looking for', with doing so providing us confirmation that all of our efforts–all our wandering–has been worth it.

The final stanza, repeating the chorus–"Where have they been?/Where have they been? Where have they been?/Where have they been?"–suggests on the one hand a lament for all those who are too easily forgotten as well as an exhortation *not* to turn away and ignore these people, what they have suffered, and the damage they have experienced, because doing so–turning away and ignoring–insures the cycle will endlessly repeat itself, with so many, generation upon generation, decade upon decade, ending up in the same position. Too often it is only those who have succeeded according to dominant social conceptions of what 'success' is defined to mean whose stories receive attention, and who are recognized and respected, while those who 'fail', according to the same standards, are too often not represented, let alone remembered. "Decades" not only critiques this disparity but also expresses anguish that the same disparity seems ineradicable.

We seemingly are never allowed entry through the aforementioned door even as it beckons us toward it. This door, seemingly 'open', is quickly 'shut', and, more than that, "slammed in our face." 'We' have been under the illusion we have been promised what in fact we will never be allowed access. 'We' may have been promised that we will live in genuine and extensive freedom, or that we will live as part of a democratic society, or that we will be secure and that our community and society will insure our survival, subsistence, and well-being. Or 'we' may have proceeded under the conviction that we live in a society where opportunities are readily available for all if 'we work hard and play by the rules'. But we find out none of this is true. Those opportunities are disparately available, with many facing precarity through no fault of their own, giving the lie to prevailing meritocratic ideals. Access to and exercise of social resources, powers, and capacities, are not, contrary to dominant ideology, available for everyone, solely dependent on how hard they work and how well they adhere to social expectations, norms, rules, and laws. Society is unfair, and for many of us our predominant social role, and predominant social purpose, is to be exploited, whether in the form of proverbial 'cannon fodder' on the literal battlefield, or on the job in working for a capitalist industry or enterprise, or yet otherwise as well. Institutions, such as academic institutions, or artistic and cultural institutions, that maintain missions proclaiming these institutions prize diversity, equity, inclusion, and belonging—as well as social responsibility and civic engagement—fall short in practice, even far short, of living up to these ostensible commitments. Too many are excluded, marginalized, disparaged, forgotten, and ignored—and in effect thereby treated as unimportant, unworthy, and even as non-existent.

In describing and analyzing the music beyond the lyrics, I am listening to the version of "Decades" from the 2020 digitally remastered, 40th anniversary release of *Closer*, in an AAC audio file format, via the Music program on my Apple desktop computer, a 2023 Apple M2 Pro Mac Mini, using the Sonoma 14.3 operating system, through Beyerdynamic DT 1900 Pro headphones. The sound I hear is remarkably crisp and clean, the distinction and separation of every sound source and especially every specific sound line are precise with no apparent bleed and a virtually undetectable noise floor. In paying close attention to the song, from beginning to end, I detect the following divisions within the song as distinct parts of an overall structure:

1.   Opening Instrumental Section: 0:00–>0:42

a.   0:00–>0:13 Emerging, Stepping Forth

b.   0:14–>0:23 Elaborating, Complicating

c.   0:24–>0:42 Deepening, Sustaining

2.   First Vocal Section–Verse: 0:43–>1:51 Narrating, Reflecting

3.   Second Instrumental Section: 1:52–>2:27

a.   1:52–>2:10 Contemplating, Mourning

b.   2:11–>2:27 Tensing, Resuming

4.   Second Vocal Section–Chorus: 2:28–>2:46 Lamenting

5.   Third Instrumental Section: 2:47–>3:23 Elaborating

6.   Third Vocal Section–Verse: 3:24–>3:57 Narrating, Reflecting

7.   Third Instrumental Section: 3:58–>4:51

a. 3:58–>4:34 Contemplating, Mourning

b. 4:35–>4:51 Agitating, Climaxing

8. Fourth Vocal Section–Chorus: 4:52–>5:09 Anguishing

9. Closing Instrumental Section: 5:10–>6:06

a. 5:10–>5:42 Contemplating, Mourning

b. 5:43–>6:06 Fading, Dissolving

The sheer length of the song and the large number of distinctively identifiable sections, or sections and subsections as I have just marked this out lends an epic quality to what this song recounts and how it does so. "Decades" comes across as tight, even with each contributing constituent carefully demarcated as well as carefully integrated. "Decades" intimates proceeding mindfully in a journey of introspective reflection that requires resolute attendance to the affective nuances of what we, along with the music as persona, engage along the way. The scope of the song enables a calling forth of vivid images, including in the form of powerful memories, while emphasizing feeling intently but at the same time feeling the distance from when events involved directly happened or when situations according to which these events happened were immediately present and initially felt. We are compelled to engage with the meaning and impact of exactly that distance as much as not more with that from which this distance 'takes a distance'. In other words, we are aware we are remembering, and that remembering involves distance, as much as we are aware of what we are remembering.

As far as instrumentation is concerned, with "Decades" I find it challenging to pinpoint precisely what instruments are used, what treatments and effects are applied in production, and what modifications are involved in playing these instruments as well as employing these treatments and effects. Others, including many interested in approximating the sound of Joy Division, on this song and on this record, in their own playing of "Decades," disagree over precisely what sound sources are involved and how so. But let's begin by reviewing what I have already identified from Hook, Morrris, and Sumner, as well as from a few other influential sources. Hook identifies a low bass guitar, a bass drum, another bass guitar part via a six-string that is overdubbed and sounds likes a guitar, a syndrum, an echo plate, layered keyboards, and overdubbed guitar. Morris recalls prominent use of a drum machine, suggestive of more than a single syndrum, and Sumner mentions use of Arp Omni, Transcendent 2000, and ARP 2600 synthesizers. Many others, including on Joy Division Central, cite the use of a melodica, brought to the studio by Curtis, and, as also previously discussed, many commentators note that reverb, in particular applied to Curtis's vocal, is especially prominent here along with some yet further echo, both seemingly produced, at least in significant part, by Hannett's familiar use of digital delay. In addition to those instruments and yet further sound sources, it does sound, at least later in the song, that a standard drum kit is briefly employed. What makes this complex particularly challenging, though, as Hook has suggested, is that sound sources are here employed, modified, and processed to resemble other sound sources, and they are heavily filtered and

1069

otherwise treated to further complicate such identification. So, yes, "Decades" is often identified as one of Joy Division's songs in which synthesizers are especially prominent, even dominant, but the reality seems not to be quite so simple, even setting aside which synthesizers are used, when, where, and how, in what combinations with each other and with what other instruments. What I will do is identify the nine distinct *lines of sound* I hear in "Decades," and describe them in terms of timbre where it is not precisely clear which instrument, or combination of instruments, is responsible.

So here goes. First, and easiest by far to identify is the vocal, with the added effects–reverb and echo. But let's turn, from there, to discuss the rest, in order of their entrance into the song. Initially, and as the source of sound line number two, I hear a percussive sound that resembles a snare but at the same time also sounds like a strike in which the overall tone has been narrowed to the point that it sounds less like hitting a conventional snare with a conventional drum stick than it does a different instrument hitting a different surface, and as a result I hear this as a synthesized 'strike strike-strike' snare-resembling sound. The next sound line to enter the song, and the third I identify in contributing to this song, sounds like a bass guitar, that again has been filtered and perhaps otherwise treated, so that its timbre is likewise thinned and narrowed but comes across as relatively warm if nonetheless maintaining limited decay, sustain, and release. As I hear it, this third sound line quickly becomes somewhat thicker, as if it has been doubled, or as if an overdubbed additional bass guitar sound is fused with the initial bass guitar sound. It does sound to me that it can make sense to compare this bass guitar sound, or bass guitar sound complex, to the sound of a guitar, but overall it sounds closer to me to a bass guitar. Fourth, it does sound to me, in close connection with this bass guitar line of sound, that I hear a bass drum sound, whether synthesized or not, with the two so tightly interlocking into a groove that they again sound as if they fuse together. Fifth, I hear a line of sound involving a jaggedly percussive as well as slightly discordant and chime-like oscillating wave, that sounds as if it is may be produced by way of a keyboard, perhaps a keyboard synthesizer, and perhaps an overdubbed and extensively modified guitar. This fifth sound line sounds, moreover, somewhat akin to an accordion meets a harmonica combined with a warm resonant synthesizer pad. Sixth, I hear a line of sound that even more clearly and decisively resembles a sound produced via a synthesizer, in this case suggestive of a synthesizer string ensemble meets a warm resonant synthesizer pad that conjures a sense of a convergence of floating meets diffusing meets gently rising kind of sound. Seventh, I hear a reedy meets stringy oscillating wave, that to me at least sounds the most likely correspondent to a melodica, although also seeming to sound as if combined again with a synthesizer, and again especially a warm resonant pad. Eighth, I hear a light percussive sound, that resembles a tinkling meet brushing sound, at least in part but not completely suggestive of a conventional hi-hat cymbal, because of the tinkling, triangle-resembling dimension of this song as well as the use of a muting or dampening pad. Ninth, I hear what sounds like a conventional drum kit, with the snare and the hi-hat particularly pronounced. I will, next, in discussing the roles these instruments play by focusing on the soundbox, identify them as sound lines #1-9, corresponding to the first through ninth sound lines I have just identified and described.

Sound line #1 occupies the center of the soundbox while at the same time reverberating so as to carve out an expansive central location, and seemingly lightly echoing slightly left and right, top and down, and front and back, from the center. This sound line remains singularly central as well the most clearly closest to the front of the soundbox whenever it does sound during the song. Sound line

#2 comes to me from the far edges of the soundbox, both left and right, low and near the bottom, yet readily apparent and not at all obscure. Sound line #3, that enters next, comes to me from slightly higher, close to the center of the vertical axis defining the perceived height of the soundbox, if not slightly above the center, while also somewhat closer toward the center along the horizontal axis defining the perceived length of the soundbox, yet still likewise close to both the left and right edges of the soundbox, and roughly the same as sound line #2 in terms of proximity to the front of the soundbox. Sound line #4 follows off of sound line #3 ending and then dropping down below the center, on both sides, while seemingly positioned just above sound line #2, again somewhat further in from both sides than sound line #3 and roughly the same in terms of proximity to the front. Sound line #5 starts again toward both edges, while close to the center along the vertical axis marking out the perceived height of the soundbox, yet slightly closer to the front, and in the climax section of the song moves higher vertically as well as closest to the front of any sound line other than sound line #1. Sound line #6 positions itself higher vertically, along both horizontal edges of the soundbox, than sound line #5, while subsequently, in its second and third manifestations, seeming to emanate from higher still and yet closer to the front. But sound line #7 comes across as positioned even higher than sound line #6, while further in from the edges along the horizontal axis marking out the perceived length of the soundbox, and close to the center, yet not as close to the front as sound line #1. When sound line #8 enters, approximately half way through the song, it does so, once more, toward the horizontal edges, somewhat low vertically, and slightly further back, but also slightly higher than other primarily percussive lines of sounds. And sound line #9 appears just slightly below center along the vertical axis while equally spaced to both the left and right along the horizontal axis yet also relatively close to the front, closer than sound line #8, and seemingly closer than any other sound lines besides sound line #1 and sound line #5 in the climax.

What do I make of the preceding? In sum, I hear most sound lines remaining in the same positions whenever they do sound, but I do hear several small yet significant departures from this overall tendency. It strikes me as worthy of note how expansive horizontally this soundbox feels, as if it maintains ample space horizontally, in terms of perceived length, as well as how much open space the soundbox feels as if it likewise maintains vertically, in terms of perceived height, space not as filled out as much as seems the case horizontally. And it definitely strikes me as notable how decisively front and center the vocal is consistently positioned. In terms of prominence, the vocal, sound line #1, is definitely the most prominent, while all three broadly keyboard-resembling sound lines (sound lines #5, #6, and #7) are also prominent, but sound lines #2 is as well when it opens the song as is sound line #3 when only sound line #2 is also in play, and sound line #9 is prominent too in its otherwise relatively brief appearance. I find it striking that none of these sound lines is buried; all are readily detectable and incisively present. The vocal, line #1, carries the melody while present, while lines #5-#7, all seemingly involving at least a significant synthesizer contribution, most importantly contribute harmonic fill, doing the work the guitar might otherwise, but in each case these lines of sound contribute harmonic fill that also, again resembling what Sumner's guitar often contributes in Joy Division songs, at least verge upon para-melody. Even sound line #2 introduces a precursor to, or an initial anticipation of, the melody, before proceeding as sound line #3 through the rest of the song primarily to perform the role of the functional bass layer in establishing the groove, in conjunction with sound line #4 as well as sound lines #8 and #9, whereas these last three play a principal role in establishing and reiterating the beat. Unlike with a number of other Joy Division songs, it does not make ready sense for me to identify any one of these four standard layers as more dominant than the others, because with "Decades" all come across to me as equal in weight, equal in importance.

What the specific array and deployment of instruments and other sound sources contribute to "Decades" is an immersive feeling, that of a total experience. At the same time this array and deployment provide amble room for a listener to insert themself, while, yet again, as with the structure of the song, directing the listener to attend to distance and separation as well as silence and emptiness via intricate yet tenuous points of connection and interconnection among interweaving lines, and patterns, of sound. Instrumentation, together with structure, contribute to the feeling that accepting an invitation to 'join the song', to identify with the music as persona, requires resolutely facing up to an epic expanse of horrific devastation, respectful of the dignity of all those involved, and appreciative of the beauty in their lives' strivings–akin to perceiving a piercing, dazzling, flood of brilliant light shining forth from amidst and thereby illuminating and otherwise vast darkness.

Turning to loudness, with "Decades" individual sound lines remain largely constant, although sound line #5 becomes louder in section 7b, the song's climax. The vocal line, sound line #1, also becomes steadily slightly louder with each subsequent section, but not as much so as sound line #5 does in the climax. Sound line #6 also increases slightly in loudness right before the climactic appearance of sound line #7. This climactic section is louder overall than previous sections because of the increase in loudness from sound line #7, as well as because of the number of sound lines occurring simultaneously here, including a notable contribution via sound line #9. In section 9b the volume rapidly decreases as the song moves to its end. "Decades" is louder the more lines of sound occur simultaneously. Accordingly, I hear increases in loudness in moving from section 1a to section 1b, from section 1b to section 1c, and from section 1c to section 2. Section 3a is, for the inverse reason, quieter than section 2, but section 3b is, once more, louder than section 3a, while section 4 is again louder than section 3b. Section 5 does not mark a notable decrease in loudness, even though we only hear one sound line, but loudness increases once more in moving from section 5 to section 6. Again, even as only one sound line occurs in section 7a, loudness remains constant, but it does notably increase, as aforementioned, from section 7a to section 7b while immediately after that remaining close to the same, if slightly quieter in section 8, and then continuing much the same in moving to section 9a before the considerable drop occurs in moving from section 9a through section 9b. Variations in loudness, however slight, evoke a feeling of movement, even if this is an entirely introspective movement, as well as evoke a feeling of contemplation upon a significant duration that here becomes the subject of contemplation, while these variations also contribute a dramatic quality to this exercise in introspection.

The time signature for "Decades" is 4/4, and I note the tempo as 107 BPM. The meter frequently exhibits a shuffling, syncopated quality that nevertheless feels 'tight' as opposed to 'loose', in part because of how regular it is and how much repetition it involves. I note the following patterns in the beat, with 'R' indicating a rest, 'S' indicating a quarter note, 'SS' two eighth note strikes, 'ss' two sixteenth note strikes, and a comma indicating a separation between each beat:

29 measures: R, S, R, SS

8 measures: S, S, S, S

7 measures: S, SS, RS, SS

1 measure: S, SS, RS, ssS

3 measures: S, S, S, S

1 measure: S, S, SS, ssS

3 measures: S, S, S, S

1 measure: S, S, SS, ssS

21 measures: S, S, S, S

25 measures: SS, SS, SS, SS

1 measure: SS, SR, SR, SR

2 measures: SR, SR, SR, SR

1 measure: SR, SR, SR, SR

1 measure: SR, SR, SS, SS

1 measure: SR, SR, SR, SR

1 measure: SR, SR, SS, SS

1 measure: SR, SR, SR, SR

1 measure: SR, SR, SS, SS

1 measure: SR, SR, SR, SR

1 measure: SR, SR, SS, SS

1 measure: SR, SR, SR, SR

1 measure: SR, SR, SS, SS

17 measures: SR, SR, SR, SR

1 measure: SR, SR, Sss, SS

1/4 measure: S

Rhythm is elaborated and complicated by way of the contributions of further drums and cymbals, beyond those directly responsible for the beat, and by way of the interweaving patterns of soundings across time emanating from the full array of sound lines. Sound lines 2, 4, 8, and 9, drums and bass, are primarily responsible for and most closely related to the beat. Sound line 1, the vocal, consists primarily of quarter notes followed by half notes or whole notes at the end of phrases with rests often occurring at the beginning of measures. Sound lines 3 and 4, bass guitar, consist principally of eighth notes, while sound lines 5 and 7 also consist principally of eighth notes but with a marked staccato feel, whereas sound line 6 consists principally of half notes and whole notes.

In terms of pitch, I hear "Decades" as played in the key of D minor. Curtis's vocal sound line moves up, then up further, and then down below where it started, in the two chorus sections. In the verse section this sound line remains close to its starting point while always rising then falling back to this same starting point. This vocal sound line covers intervals of no more than three steps or six semitones. With the other instruments and additional sound sources what is especially notable is these mostly involve no more than three to four principal pitch locations, with a tendency to move back and forth, frequently and repeatedly, according to a general pattern of pushing upward before falling back down, all the way back down to where the lines begin, or even further down than that. A few times sound lines push just a bit higher, but never linger for too long in doing so. Sound line #7 seems to move a larger interval distance up and down than sound line #5, even if their overall patterns closely parallel each other, while sound line #6 seems as if it might move further in pitch than it does but largely remains constant. Notably, most available tabs for those interested in playing "Decades" themselves, even in doing so on different instruments than used in the version of this song included on *Closer*, identify only a limited array of principal pitches, such as no more than four chords for a guitar, while for a number of other instruments recommending no more than one to three principal notes or chords. In sum, what we confront here are highly contained interval ranges with relatively short movements, and even though different sound lines start and end at considerably different pitches, these movements closely parallel or otherwise smoothly compliment each other, with the varieties in terms of timbre principally responsible for conveying nuance and texture.

Eirik Askerøi, in "Transmissions: Sonic markers of difference in the sound of Joy Division" identifies multiple characteristic "sonic markers" in Joy Division's studio recorded music. Those I find most relevant in relation to "Decades" include the following: "dynamic play of tension and release" (209) preceded by a long dynamic build-up (214) as well as a highly performative attention to level of intensity and dramatic progression (218); "repetition and intertwining of instrumental motives" (214); totally clean and clear sound separation (210); significant amounts of added reverb or delay (210) in conjunction with considerable use of digital delay (218); in relation, specifically, to Curtis's vocal, pitch modulation, especially downward; a "stylistic suggestion of crooning" (216); and, again in relation to Curtis, communication of "earnestness" in vocal performance (216).

According to Askerøi, "Curtis's temperament alone dictates the dynamic progression of the music" (218), and, more broadly than that, it is Curtis's vocal, its placement and its role in Joy Division songs that is pivotal in defining what is most characteristic about Joy Division's sound.

In "Decades" Curtis's register is baritone, and his tone, in studio recorded form, is clean, clear, and resonant, especially due to the extent of reverb and yet further delay applied. Range required is small but Curtis sounds careful, confident, and consistent in relation to both pitch and rhythm, while he sings the last word of each phrase within each line by gently gliding across successive pitches. Curtis's voice here sounds gently crooning, and while sounding aware of the other contributors to the song as a whole, and of his specific place as part of this while concentrating on the words he is singing and how he is singing these as if he is singing alone. The subject matter that Curtis addresses is exceedingly bleak, but here he sounds as if he is addressing this bleakness from a considerable distance, offering an elegiac commentary on both the bleakness and on how far this distance has separated him from any tangible influence over the same. What is notable here, as I have discussed with multiple other Joy Division songs, is how much of what we are engaging comes across as by no means unmediated, as *not* a direct expression of immediately felt pain and anguish, but rather as a highly mediated performative evocation verging on invocation of the same–a performative evocation verging upon invocation that includes considerable awareness of its distance from what is being evoked, and invoked, while commenting on this distance as much, if not more, than commenting on what this is distant from.

I have already identified a number of features of how I hear timbre in "Decades," in particular in describing the nine sound lines I have identified, as well as in discussing instrumentation, and Curtis's vocal delivery, including in reference to Eirik Askerøi's article. In sum, it is important to reiterate that the inclusion of nine distinct sound lines involves the deployment of a considerable array of timbres. It is also worth reiterating how much timbre is effected by Hannett's insistence on totally clean separation as well as resolutely minimal noise, along with heavy use of reverb, echo, and delay, and that, even beyond all that, Hannett yet further filters and modifies multiple parameters of each sound source, including from synthesizers in the process of transferring sounds to the mix. In "Decades," to refer to common impressionistic descriptors, sound line one's timbre comes across as clean, clear, resonant, and reverberant; sound line two's timbre comes across as harsh, metallic, thin, and artificial; sound line three's and sound line four's timbres come across as deep, resonant, compact, and hollow; sound line five's timbre comes across as sharp, metallic, harsh, intense, ringing, and potent; sound line six's timbre comes across as warm, luminous, shimmering, and floating; sound line seven's timbre comes across as reedy, stringy, thin, and metallic; sound line eight's timbre comes across as tinkly, ping-y, bright, and muted; and sound line nine's timbre comes across as quick, sturdy, strong, and full.

Turning, next, to address avenues of musical affect, it is important to recognize that with "Decades" affect encompasses all of the following:

1.   What is and was felt in the immediacy of the moment, when and where 'the young men' were at, and where 'we' were at as well–when and where they, and we, felt weighted and pushed, shut out and forcibly barred, and when and where they, and we, felt fear, thrill, sorrow, pain, and exhaustion.

2.   What they, and we, have felt since, as a result of what happened then and there, in the forms of weariness, loss, trauma and degeneration.

3.   What we now feel in dramatically evoking, and ritually invoking, the preceding, both #1 and #2, as successive stages in an introspective journey of recollection and revisitation, of offering testimony and bearing witness.

4.   What is felt in confronting what remains irrecoverable–as well as what is felt in confronting what remains inexplicable and un-representable. This includes what is felt in confronting what remains tantalizingly invisible, inaudible, and intangible, despite assiduous efforts to render this visible, audible, and tangible. And this includes what is felt in confronting what remains as yet unanswerable despite assiduous efforts to arrive at answers, concerning 'to where' have 'the young men', and 'to where' have 'we', gone, subsequent to #1, and even subsequent to #2, with 'to where' here involving much more than merely movement from one discrete physical location or even one discrete emotional state to another. What we are striving to recover, explain, and represent does not itself feel ephemeral, because this feels, in sharp contrast, unendingly persistent, or eternally recurrent. However, our efforts to recover, explain, and represent themselves feel ephemeral.

5.   What is felt in confronting the distance between #1 versus #2 as well as between #1 and #2 on the one hand versus #3 and #4 on the other hand.

In "Decades" I experience myself mimetically participating together with virtually all of the sound lines, and this array of mimetic participation, as well as the sense of anticipation I hear within the music enables me to feel all of #1 through #5 above, and especially #3, the journey itself, including each of its successive stages, and movement from one stage to the next–in particular, movement from tension to release of tension. Anticipation, in turn, involves the feeling quality of evocation, and especially invocation, taking place, as if I, together with the music as persona, are participating in a ritual ceremony, including one that we anticipate will eventually climax as well as eventually end. As an avenue of affect in the music of "Decades," expression, next, plays a pivotal role in relation to dimensions of affect in "Decades" #s 1, 2, and 5 I have just described, notably in underscoring that "Decades" not only concerns expression of #1, or even of #1 and #2, but also of #5. As such, "Decades" offers an exemplary instance of the passionate meets the dispassionate in the music of Joy Division. Commentators oversimplify when they interpret this song, and other Joy Division songs like it, as equivalent with either an immediate release of passionate emotion or a dispassionate reflection upon and commentary on passionate emotion, because this song, and those others, accomplishes both–and yet more as well.

Acoustic impact in the music of "Decades" is significant in relation to all five 'dimensions of affect', as we are enabled by means of this impact to *feel* weighted and pushed, shut out and forcibly barred; to *feel* fear, thrill, sorrow, pain, and exhaustion; to *feel* lasting weariness, loss, trauma, and disintegration; and especially, to *feel* distance, to *feel* distance that neither eliminates or overcomes any of the preceding feelings, yet makes it complicated to come to grips with what those feelings might mean. As such, what we feel with "Decades" runs contrary to truisms that proclaim distance makes it possible to 'put things into proper perspective'–or, in other words, distance is what enables us 'to understand what was really going on', versus what we could not 'properly understand' in the immediacy of the moment when and as we are initially experiencing an emotional response, and an emotional impact.

Analysis, as is often the case with music in Joy Division songs, seems not quite the apt word for what is happening with this music, because yes, the music of "Decades" contributes to feeling as if we, the music as persona and I, are exploring, confronting, reflecting, and examining, but the music also also feels as if we, the music as persona and I, are fixated upon *obstacles to analysis*, and upon the dead ends that follow from attempting to analyze complex phenomenon with too much confidence and too little care. Insofar as the music of "Decades" conveys feelings of or by way of analysis this seems to me to involve analyzing what we are engaging no further than to conclude this is both incredibly important and incredibly difficult to engage. Analysis, in other words, conveys the feeling that we are dealing with phenomena that are overwhelmingly undecidable, uncertain, inexplicable, indeterminate, unknowable, and ineffable.

In discussing how others have interpreted 'the meaning' of "Decades," referring primarily to the song's lyrics, as well as in my own close reading of the title and these lyrics, I have already identified many associations this song elicits. Here it is important to add that taking into account the structuring of the nine song lines, their interweaving across twelve successive sections, the song's characteristic pitch and volume movements, and the song's distinct and combined timbral constituents, leads me to feel unsatisfied with interpretations that focus solely on what I have identified as #1 among the five different dimensions of affect in "Decades." In fact, dimensions #s 3-5 feel, if anything, more decisively foregrounded.

The music of "Decades" suggests feelings associated with exploring taboos by way of the slightly discordant timbres of sound lines 5 and 7; by way of the harsh, metallic timbre of sound line 2; by way of the rise in tension in the climax section of the song; and by way of the fading away of sound in the final section without any sense of clear resolution. The extent to which the sound lines interweave, and where instruments and other sound sources mimic and echo each other, as well as become interchangeable in their roles, with major dimensions of their sound quality considerably narrowed, filtered, and otherwise extensively modified, all contributes to a sense of stepping out of 'normal' time, and out of 'normal' space. Likewise, the relative length of the song, together with its extensive repetition, and limited pitch movement, limited rhythmic variation, and limited volume change, can feel unsettling, leading to feeling as if one, together with the music as persona, is exploring taboos. This feeling arises in willingly joining together with these sounds, patterns of sounds, and deployments of sounds while experiencing considerable trepidation in doing so, anticipating both an extremely intense experience but also one that will result in feeling all the more unsettled afterward. It can feel taboo to confront not just grave 'injustice', but also our connection with, complicity in, and responsibility for this injustice, and, even more troubling, profound uncertainty concerning what, if anything, we can and should do in response to this injustice. In other words, it can feel taboo to confront head-on doubt whether we can do anything at all to prevent this injustice from happening, ceaselessly over and over again.

In previously identifying and describing dimension of affect #4 I have already addressed matters of invisibility, intangibility, and ephemerality. But here I add that the structure of the song contributes signally in these terms. In following along with "Decades" it feels as if we keep picking up and trying, repeatedly, through successive stages of an introspective journey, to come to grips with what then repeatedly evades such attempts. The extent to which the vocal only sounds for approximately half of the song's duration means other sound lines need to take center stage in sounding the melody as well as in most overtly suggesting what the song is engaging, but these sound lines, other than following highly delimited patterns of relative small movements in pitch, variations in rhythm, and increases and decreases in volume, accentuate a felt sense of approaching what can at best be gestured toward but never reached (or, in other words, what can only be longed for yet never attained). What's more, Curtis's lyrics are highly elliptical and tantalizingly vague, while the choral refrain of "Where have they gone?" emphasizes how much 'is not here', not in front of us–how much we cannot see, we cannot touch, and we can only gain fleeting impressions concerning.

"Decades" makes sense as concerned with complicated 'mediations'–and tenuous 'borderlines'–between then and there and here and now, as well as among past, present, and future; between 'them' ('the young men') and 'me', or between 'them' and 'us'; between event and impact; between immediate impact and subsequent impact; and between event and impact, immediate as well as subsequent, on the one hand, versus recollection and re-visitation of event and impact, on the other hand. With "Decades" tension is not resolved but rather dissolves, or suspends. "Decades" enacts a fusion of the passionate with the dispassionate. "Decades" alludes to metaphorical 'darknesses' that are clearly extreme, and all the more excruciating as they seem ceaselessly ongoing. "Decades" at the same time is obsessed with problematics of 'distance', from trauma and degeneration, but also from our selves and from others ostensibly immediately around us, suggestive of insidiously fascistic tendencies manifest in the everyday life of ostensibly non- or post- fascist society. "Decades" makes sense as concerned with the overwhelming power of the Real far eclipsing that of the Imaginary and Symbolic, while accepting yes 'we' do maintain responsibility to others–to others' suffering, hardship, and pain–yet doubtful 'we' are capable of meeting this responsibility. So, yes, "Decades" fits well with the eleven overarching interpretations of meaning I introduced in chapter one.

Considering "Decades" in relation to the critical theoretical writings of Robert McRuer, Ann Cvetkovich, and Avery F. Gordon I have taken up at length in this chapter, I recognize the following principal convergences and divergences.

First, with McRuer, it can make useful sense to interpret "Decades" as engaging the long historical experience of all too many disabled people. All too many disabled people have suffered institutional, structural, and systemic violence, not only institutionalization and elimination, but also pervasive barriers to equitable access and inclusion as well as continuing denigration and stigmatization, even in ostensibly 'sensitive' and 'sympathetic' forms–as seemingly always lesser, always deficient, and always deserving of pity. These patterns have persisted across many decades, with many disabled people as result having disappeared, or having been made to disappear, such that we might well insistently inquire, 'where have they gone?' However, in contrast with McRuer, "Decades" does not valorize radical disabled ways of being as the locus of a 'crip' praxis that can provide important contributions toward imagining and inventing alternatives to neo-liberalism capitalism.

Second, with Cvetkovich, it can make useful sense to interpret "Decades" as engaging shared experience of deep depression. What's more, "Decades" can make sense in line with Cvetkovich's critique of reductive ways of explaining depression that ignore its social and political causes, as well as neglect its potential as source of social and political insight. Yet, "Decades" does not, in contrast with Cvetkovich, suggest that rigorously attending to depression, working in community, and participating in subculture can transform depression into a source or spark of hope.

Third, with Gordon, it can make useful sense to interpret "Decades" as engaging 'hauntings' by 'ghosts' that demand 'we' attend to historical injustices, and their shaping impact upon our lives in the present–that we bear an ethical and political responsibility to do so, even if this is a most daunting and indeed frightening responsibility. Yet, "Decades," in contrast with Gordon, does not evince overt evidence of radical utopian conviction.

As I listen to and write about "Decades," in early 2024, I focus on two further, extended connections: first, myths surrounding Joy Division and New Order as well as Factory Records and Manchester along with arguments concerning the politics of post-punk, and second, women and Factory Records.

In relation to the first of these two myths let's begin with John Aizelwood's 2021 book *Decades: Joy Division + New Order*. Aizelwood employs the Joy Division song title 'Decades' as the title of his book to emphasize that 'the story' he recounts is a remarkable one both to have lasted and to undergone the extent of changes and especially tensions it has for now over four decades. As Aizelwood sums up, "It's a tale of love, death, fall-outs, make-ups, hardcore bacchanalia, money gained, money squandered and some of the most remarkable and influential music of the '80s, '90s, and beyond" (11). Aizelwood's account is mostly descriptive and largely anti-mythologizing, especially in relation to New Order. He depicts the latter as a band that persists as long and makes as much critically and popularly successful music as it does, despite itself, despite tensions between Peter Hook and Bernard Sumner that have been omnipresent throughout the band's history, even as these tensions considerably worsened over time and ultimately led to an irreconcilable split. Aizelwood also depicts the bandmembers, again principally Hook and Sumner, other than when focused on making and performing music, as hardcore hedonistic, '24 hour party people', and, as often enough, petty, insensitive, callous, and cruel.

For Aizelwood, "Ian was why Joy Division was great" and both *Unknown Pleasures* and *Closer* come "as close to perfection as popular music can come" (238). According to Aizelwood, what Curtis shared with Sumner, Hook, Morris, and the other principals spanning 'Joy Division + New Order' was a stubborn persistence along with a readiness to work hard. In Aizelwood's account, New Order *needed* to change its characteristic sound from that of Joy Division, even as if New Order could never entirely jettison this connection. As Aizelwood describes it, New Order music becomes not just music *for* partying, but nonetheless music *about* partying, even if not as simple as all about having fun while partying. From this perspective, New Order made many great songs, but even as

Curtis shared pop interests with his bandmates that eventually became New Order, as well as interests in electronica, what is most significant is how far New Order changed from Joy Division. Joy Division ends with Curtis's suicide, after Joy Division creates the quintessential musical representation of 'the wasteland' that late 1970s post-industrial Manchester evidently felt like to all too many living then and there. But then New Order subsequently creates the quintessential musical representation of "the British dance music boom" (back cover blurb) of the 1980s, centered around the Haçienda nightclub:

> If Joy Division were sublime musical darkness, New Order were bathed in sunlight and their globally popular music bridged the chasm between indie and dance and inspired a generation. Having conquered the world while maintaining their credibility, they snatched defeat from the jaws of victory and imploded in a tsunami of recrimination, while still making fabulous music to this day.

According to Aizelwood's take, 'Joy Division + New Order' makes sense in mythical terms because Joy Division's success would seem unlikely if it were not true, Joy Division becoming New Order would seem unlikely if it were not true, and New Order becoming as successful as it was, despite all of its internal drama, would seem unlikely it it were not true. In other words: 'only in rock 'n roll'.

"Decades," the song, as I listen to and I reflect on it, resonates barely at all with the preceding myth, and I find it hard to connect what I think (about) and feel in listening to this song with a phoenix-like rise of New Order from the ashes of Joy Division, and of New Order repeatedly thereafter repeating this phoenix-resemblant trajectory in relation to the latter's band self-destructive tendencies. Likewise, nothing about the music of "Decades" resonates for me with non-stop partying, not even with partying 'on the edge' and to an 'excessive extreme'. If one only references the title of the song and the lyrical query, 'where have they gone?', it might seem plausible to relate this song to the transformation of 'the young men' of Joy Division into the eventual 'no longer young men (and woman)' of New Order, while also finding it remarkable for New Order to last as long as it did, first with both Hook and Sumner together, and then second after Hook left.

Every time I have taught classes on Ian Curtis, Joy Division, and New Order, a few students are always keen to explore this connection. I welcome students doing so, and I respect that many others, such as Aizelwood, are likewise inclined, but I do not share this interest. If anything, reading *Decades: Joy Division + New Order* once again underscores why my degree of interest in Joy Division does not carry over to the same degree of interest in New Order. Yes, I greatly respect the members of New Order, and I am much more interested in their skills, talents, and achievements as musicians than I am in any their personal foibles, and, yes, I enjoy listening to New Order music, as well as playing this music now and then on my radio show. And yes, I definitely found New Order's performance at the 2017 Manchester International Festival most enoyable. But I would never teach a class or deliver a public presentation or construct a religious service, let alone write a book, centered around what listening to and reflecting upon listening to the music of New Order prompts me to think (about) and feel, what this means to me, how I connect this with critical theory, and how I draw extended connections, from there, with matters of social, political, and philosophical significance.

It does make sense to me, nonetheless, to compare Aizelwood's reasons for titling his book 'Decades' with the remarkable continuation and expansion of interest in as well as appreciation for Joy Division's music over the course of more than four decades–especially interest in as well as appreciation for this music as art that exerts powerful impact and provides significant insight. I am writing this section of this chapter while recovering at home in Eau Claire from foot surgery that leaves me with limited mobility for eight weeks, less than two months after retiring following 38 years during which my job as a teacher and a faculty member required an overwhelming amount of priority effort and concentration, in the midst of transition between this life focus in Eau Claire and a new life focus yet to be determined in San Diego, while spending considerable time alone other than with my dog Aidan, and while worrying often about the state of the world. In these circumstances I experience no connection with "hardcore bacchanalia" of the kind *Decades: Joy Division + New Order* highlights. I do not write that as judgmental disapproval. I simply don't relate to this from where I presently am at, and, frankly, I have rarely in my life been in the position where I could do so. That connection, with that kind of lifestyle, does not explain how, or why, I find the music of Joy Division as compelling to me, now, if not in fact all that much more so, at age 62, than I did at age 18.

Nevertheless, I can well imagine the thrill of spending nights at the Haçienda in its heyday. I can readily imagine loving the vastness of the nightclub, its variety of spaces, and its plethora of sensations and pleasures, including via performances of a multiplicity of different kinds, from live performances of bands and other musicians, to djs, to films, to other forms of visual and performance art, to readings and stagings, and yet more besides–as well as sharing these experiences together with widely diverse arrays of people as well as with many people like myself all feeling free to let go, to have fun, and to not have to hide much of whom and what they were about. Because *Decades: Joy Division + New Order* concentrates so much on the sordid dimensions of clubbing, nightlife, and partying, it becomes difficult in reading this book to understand the appeal, while at the same time this concentration also renders it difficult to understand how New Order became as renowned and influential as it the band did. *Decades: Joy Division + New Order* falls short in giving due credit to New Order as comprised of dynamic, not static, individuals, who continually developed and refined their musical skills–notably in relation to electronic instrumentation, composition, production, and performance–and who were highly creative and innovative.

As someone who has spent considerable time on nine different extended visits to Manchester and Greater Manchester, coinciding with six Manchester International Festivals, exploring and experiencing widely throughout each visit, I do find fascinating the multitude of stories that have developed surrounding the city, including those stories that have achieved the status of myth, and in particular the myth crediting Joy Division with a signal contribution to Manchester's 'rebirth'. Manchester has undergone an astounding transformation, over the course of these past four and one-half decades, while according to this mythic account it is popular music that has provided the driving force that has enabled this transformation.

The best account of this history I have read is Andy Spinoza's 2023 *Manchester Unspun: How a city got high on music*. Spinoza moved to Manchester from London to attend the University of Manchester at the cusp of punk becoming post-punk. Spinoza became the founder of influential 'alternative' Manchester magazine *City Life*, subsequent to that a long-time 'gossip' columnist for

Manchester Evening News, and, yet later, founder of his own influential Manchester-based public relations company. Spinoza has interacted frequently with Manchester power players in music, arts, culture, sports, entertainment, journalism, business, and politics over the course of these past four and one-half decades.

Spinoza begins *Manchester Unspun* by adding detail to the mythic image of Manchester in the late 1970s, the Manchester many hear authentically represented in the music of Joy Division: "When I arrived in Manchester, it was sliding into the dustbin of history. It was 1979, and the shattered cityscape all around led to the unavoidable conclusion that the people of Manchester, and much of the North, were second-class citizens" (1). Everywhere around, "Manchester looked like it was locked in a fatal post-industrial tailspin," while "Life in the failed Hulme estate was an in-your-face existence straight from the pages of a J.G. Ballard dystopia" (1). Walking to the Haçienda nightclub from student flats in Hulme, Spinoza and friends experienced a journey involving "a mind-mending meander through concrete underpasses and walkways, past the decommissioned Gaythorn gas works and derelict Macintosh mills complex," through a city center that "seemed vacant–smashed-up, worthless, unloved and unused" (1). In the midst of such ruins, Spinoza and his friends imagined possibilities: "As we revelled in the thrilling immersive aesthetics, it felt for all the world like we owned the place" (1). Since that time, "What changes I have seen . . . the centre has undergone an astonishing transformation, growing outwards and surging skywards" (2). Underscoring how amazing this transformation feels, "In 1982, the year the Haçienda venue opened, only five hundred people lived in the centre. Today that number is 60,000 but the area the officialdom calls the city centre's 'central core' . . . has today over-topped the 250,000 mark thanks to the building boom" (2). Manchester today is on the verge of becoming "one of the tallest cities in Europe, with construction growth rates eclipsing Barcelona and Madrid" (2). In sum, "If the city was on its knees in the early 1980s, the new millennium has seen a remarkable revival, with an astonishing jump in Manchester's success, confidence, investment and importance" (3).

Zeroing in upon the mythic importance of the Haçienda, Spinoza reflects that "It all could never, of course, begin with just one eccentric and experimental building. And yet it did. The skyrocketing city of today began with a bunch of squabbling hedonists, anarchists, musicians and intellectuals opening a ridiculously outsize New York-style nightclub, for an audience that did not yet exist" (3). According to Spinoza, "Factory Records and the Haçienda . . . gave the kiss of life to a dying city, and sparked a chain reaction of hubris, scandal, money and power politics still playing out today" (8). In line with why Peter Saville proposed 'original modern' as a slogan in developing Manchester as a leading international 'city of culture', Spinoza recalls "Manchester has for centuries been more than a place, a shorthand for ideas and ideals" (9). Here we encounter a key dimension of this myth concerning 'the spirit of Manchester': the spirit of the city is restlessly re-inventive, across generations and across decades, recurrently ready to begin again, and, more precisely, to begin again with nothing but ruin, decay, emptiness, and ugliness as the basis from which to recreate the beautiful and the sublime. If Manchester in the late 1970s and early 1980s seemed like an old and dying city, it also seemed like a city open to the possibility of beginning the opposite, such that today not only is Manchester "the fastest growing city in the UK," but also its "population of over 555,000" includes "one of the youngest age profiles in the nation" (18).

Spinoza does wrestle with disbelief concerning the credibility of myth: "That such personal despair expressed through his [Curtis's] lyrics, disturbingly cathartic performances and Joy Division's music could be the source of a city's staggering revival is worthy of detailed examination" (27). Spinoza responds by offering exactly this detailed examination over the course of his book, and his book ultimately endorses this myth: "Manchester's reinvention was made possible by the global sales of Joy Division's music, an austere sound of space and mystery, with high bass guitar, unexpected drum patterns and doomy, open-ended lyrics interpreted with deep retrospective meaning after Curtis's death" (27). Or, more succinctly, "The majestic mystery of the music powered the group's myth, which became a classic emblem of the city in the collective imagination" (27).

Much of the power of this myth, of its resonance with what 'feels true', follows from the readiness of those involved with Factory/Joy Division/New Order to make the most of a classic punk do-it-yourself ethos, and this had much to with feeling as if they had no other choice:

> The explosion of music following the 1976 [Sex Pistols] gigs chimed with the depressing economic downturn of the mid-to-late 1970s. Mancunians who once counted on factory work, it seemed, suddenly had no jobs to follow their parents and grandparents into, a progression on which had been built communities whose identities were formed around the workplace and the local football team, the pub and the church. The nihilism of punk hit a nerve, with the Sex Pistols' 'No Future' slogan holding a highly personal meaning to teenagers on benefits. (43)

Spinoza is alert to many contradictions within this mythic history. For example, as he wrote for *City Life*, as early as 1992, "The Haçienda must take its share of the blame. The best club in pop culture's capital was often, at Madchester's dizzy heights, a deeply unpleasant place, crawling with bimbos and their pistol-packing sugar daddies. We danced on, oblivious–oblivion was where we wanted to be–to the undercurrents: it was hip to be thick, cool to be a criminal . . . Clubbers dressed down and worse, they thought down" (142-143). Likewise, even as "The influence of the Manchester music scene on the changing face of the city was unmistakable," with "the music culture . . . prime-pumping the growth of a new city centre," Spinoza acknowledges that many questioned "how healthy it was for a city to be appearing to remake itself around alcohol consumption" and where in the city centre redevelopment were "the missing pieces" required for sustainable living: "Where were the GP and dental surgeries, schools and grocery shops?" (161). The latter was–and I suggest remains–a serious shortcoming: "the ideal was proving elusive. Instead of a continental-style utopia in which parents could raise their offspring, and for seniors to retire . . . living in Manchester city centre felt more like a Club 18-30 holiday camp with rather less sunshine" (182). Even for many of those in the latter demographic, this hardly seemed like an entirely appealing lifestyle, at least not long-term, as "it has often seemed as if city-centre transformation was being floated on an ocean of booze, its prospect for success swaying precariously on the foundations of an endless bout of rowdy drinking" (162).

For better and worse, nonetheless, as early as the late 1980s, Manchester anticipated the 'third way' championed a decade later by Tony Blair's New Labour in government. This 'third way' has involved cultivating capital investment: "The city had become a snake charmer, adept at snaffling whatever public funding was available–private sector, regional, national or European" (173). City leaders championed large-scale development and growth by embracing the marketing and public relations appeal of Manchester as a city of 'art and culture' in order to secure investment. In this project they often worked closely with Tony Wilson, long a keen advocate for exactly this kind of reimagination and reinvention of Manchester. Spinoza describes Wilson as multiply contradictory and wildly inconsistent, yet it makes sense, nonetheless, Spinoza proposes, to characterize Wilson's politics as both "anarchic libertarianism" (297) and idiosyncratic populism. Manchester's transformation from the late 1970s to the early 2020s is the result, Spinoza suggests, of a collaboration between this precise kind of Wilsonian cultural politics and neo-liberal capitalist modes of urban redevelopment.

Yet even that explanation is insufficient, Spinoza suggests, to capture what the achievement of Factory, Joy Division, and New Order has meant, and why this has attracted the status of myth:

> New music can go from a cult to a cliché in an instant, but Factory Records emerged in the shadows. It felt like a guerilla foothills opposition taking on the fortresses of high culture . . . . [Yet] After the label collapsed, Factory's legend flourished, and today it has an undeniable claim as that rare thing, popular art which also commands the cultural high ground.

> Factory, Joy Division, New Order is an exceptional, self-contained universe: rock and dance music lauded for innovation and originality, record sleeves exhibited in galleries, fine artists commissioned for band videos, the Haçienda globally recognised as a rules-busting redefinition of what a music venue can be like. Factory refused to play by the rules, making exceptional moves . . . (316).

Spinoza identifies the Manchester International Festival (MIF) as "exemplifying" a "clear, direct lineage" with Factory, Joy Division, New Order, and the Haçienda, and doing so even before the recent building of 'Factory International', at the site of the old Granada Studios, as the now permanent headquarters of MIF. Spinoza appreciates the achievements of MIF, including how, "From the off, the MIF programme was militantly avant-garde" as well as "inescapably urban and contemporary, and intentionally risky" (319). But Spinoza shares his concern that MIF has been more focused on 'the international' than on the interests and needs of Manchester communities. As he comments, and not just in relation to MIF, "Despite Manchester's social problems, its unskilled young people, its lack of secure jobs and lamentable health and education outcomes, there seemed an almost improper eagerness to find money for palaces of entertainment" (318).

It has seemed to me that MIF is attentive to its setting in Manchester and is concerned with issues that affect Mancunians, especially those who are the least well-off, notably homeless people and immigrants/refugees/asylum seekers. And it has also seemed to me a great many of the events that have comprised each MIF maintain the basis for ready appeal to a wide array of audiences, while these events have frequently been impressively immersive, interactive, collaborative, and site-sensitive as well as innovative and provocative. Still, the prices required to attend MIF events, even with discounts, can be difficult for poor and working class people to afford, and it remains to be determined what long-term impact MIF will make toward redressing the deepest, most intractable problems in the city, which emanate from vast socio-economic inequality as well as widespread socio-economic precarity.

Yet for me, and seemingly for Spinoza as well, more troubling than any failures of MIF to be adequately sensitive and responsive to the interests and needs of relatively impoverished people living in Manchester, is the building of numerous new skyscrapers, since the mid 2010s, with all too many of these constructed so as to provide 'luxury housing'. As I concluded, wandering about the city in 2019, during my last visit, checking out each of these new skyscrapers, in their respective states of development at that time, more 'luxury housing' is the last thing Manchester needs. To the contrary, more low-income/low-wealth/affordable housing for the working class, the poor, and the homeless, especially in the city center, is the first thing Manchester needs. As Spinoza observes, Manchester today suffers from a "spiralling homelessness crisis, due to the lack of rented homes genuinely affordable to the less well off," along with "the highest rate of people in emergency accommodation outside the capital, except Luton" (335). Yet even more disturbing, there is 'almost nowhere left' to house those who have been left out, because "Manchester is full" (336). This is indeed a major test for Manchester, moving forward, a major test for how socially responsible will this city be, including how socially responsible will be the now abundant array of Manchester arts and culture productions, performances, exhibitions, venues, festivals, scenes, and other events and happenings.

Spinoza admits "It sounded almost preposterous" (340) when Tony Wilson, in Grant Gee's and Jon Savage's 2007 documentary, *Joy Division*, asserted "I don't see this as the story of a rock group. I see it as the story of a city . . . The revolution Joy Division started has resulted in this modern city" (quoted 340). And yet, Spinoza recognizes, "as the years roll on, we can see the links, effects and influences. A slow-motion epiphany reveals itself– the Haçienda founders' intention 'to restore a sense of place' is substantially mission accomplished" (340). As such, "The Joy Division legend is surely a kind of spiritual song-line across Mancunian time and space" (340). In an interview with Spinoza, Peter Saville makes exactly this connection in all the more pointed fashion: "Modern Manchester stands in part on the sacrifice made by Ian Curtis . . . His untimely death was the capital investment in Factory Records and inevitably that which has followed on as the consequence of Factory . . . Much of the aura of Manchester today is founded on the charisma of Factory, and Factory's charisma was founded on Ian" (quoted 341). This take is certainly redolent of romantic myth, and as such has prompted a "perhaps inevitable pushback about the cultural value of the Factory–Haçienda art project" (344). This pushback includes sharp critiques of this same project as the product of "a white-male dominated culture," and includes charging its leading members with "racism and misogyny" (344). Yet Spinoza finds such "revisionism" falls short in its attendance to "context, complexity and nuance" (344). After all, "if we follow the money . . . it is incontestable the Factory directors . . . could have taken their royalties and departed to Cheshire mansions, tax havens or, the most appalling destination of all, London" (344). Instead, despite the Haçienda ultimately losing £18 million, "No grants were applied for, no government forms were filled in. The Haçienda was Manchester celebrating itself, and if culture is in any sense political, then it was the expression of a place starved of power and simply making its own fun" (344).

David Wilkinson does not share Andy Spinoza's take on the positive value of this myth. In *Post-Punk, Politics and Pleasure in Britain*, Wilkinson writes "Tony Wilson's much-mythologised

Factory Records . . . excelled in idiosyncratic pranksterism rooted in regional pride," with "the label's legacy . . . heavily co-opted by the 'municipal entrepreneurialism' adopted by Manchester City Council from the late 1980s onwards" (65). Or, in other words, as Wilkinson argues, "In Manchester, the sensibility of local post-punk independent Factory was drawn on in a move that exhumed the city's musical past to advertise the supposedly sophisticated glamour of city-centre living, surrounded by the trappings of a 'post-industrial' creative economy. It was a myth mostly exploited by out-of-town investors and buy-to-let landlords (192)." In such a situation, post-punk is reduced to "subcultural capital," in the form of "an elitist marker of distinction amongst music fans within a shifting and indirectly acknowledged hierarchy of taste" (192).

Certainly, these tendencies are and have been real, but I don't agree that they represent the totality of the legacy of 'Factory' at present and indeed I think Wilkinson's larger arguments in his book concerning the continuing political usefulness of 'classic post-punk' can be reworked to at least in part include Joy Division plus Factory in ways that Wilkinson does not acknowledge. One of Wilkinson's principal claims in *Post-Punk, Politics and Pleasure in Britain* is that "as a development of the counterculture and the libertarian left of the 1960s and 1970s, post-punk retained a utopianism that contrasted valuably with its crisis-ridden and ultimately pessimistic moment" (vi). For Wilkinson this utopianism is crucial, and, as such it is easy to recognize why he does not focus on Joy Division, but I would argue, as in fact many have and continue to do, that Factory did encompass utopian dimensions, and that these do show up in projects such as the Haçienda, at least in its heyday. After all, the aim with that club as with numerous other projects was to create something remarkably novel and distinct that seemed preposterous to imagine, let alone to realize, at least from where these projects began to take shape and with what means those involved at least initially maintained at their disposal.

What's more, dystopian critique does not necessarily imply that 'the way things are is the way things have to be', and certainly does not imply that the way things are is 'good' or 'desirable' or 'right'. Dystopian critique can suggest that much that many people accept is, in fact, *not acceptable*, or *should not be acceptable*, and much that people accept as good, desirable, and right, is, on the contrary, *bad, undesirable, and wrong*. Dystopian critique can suggest that radical transformation, not moderate reform, is the only viable direction to follow if one is truly committed toward human emancipation, collective equality, social justice, ecological sustainability, and a peaceful world. Yes, dystopian critique can suggest it is extremely hard to imagine how we might 'get from here to there', precisely 'what is to be done' in seeking to do so, and it might indeed at least feel like it is 'too late', but that often is not the whole story.

After all, to survive, persist, endure, and, above all else, to continue to struggle onward, even when it feels impossible to do so, even when it feels absurd to do so, is not surrendering. After all as well, and here the connection with what Wilkinson valorizes becomes all the stronger, to carve out even partial and limited kinds of alternative spaces and alternative modes of being and relating, where people can experience possibilities that 'normal life' suppresses and denies, is what many have experienced as attracting them to Joy Division, and to Factory, including, notably, to the Haçienda. Wilkinson values the contribution of 'leftist post-punk' in relation to 'freedom and pleasure', in particular to imagining ways of experiencing freedom and pleasure that are normatively suppressed and denied as well as in providing avenues for at least partial and temporary experience of liberating alternatives–and this is something that Joy Division, Factory, and the Haçienda certainly have done, for many.

Wilkinson emphasizes, drawing upon Raymond Williams, 'residual' and 'anticipatory' cultural elements, within leftist post-punk, that contrast with and in part counter 'dominant' cultural elements. These residual and anticipatory dimensions of post-punk provide reservoirs of hope, including in the face of what otherwise all too often seems hopeless. Wilkinson finds glimpses "of how things could be otherwise" and even prefigurations "of socialist cultural production" in leftist post-punk (24). For Wilkinson, this does not happen, at least not as usefully so, with post-punk music that emphasizes overwhelming "bleakness," such as Joy Division "and other early Factory Records acts" (49), even though he acknowledges that the relatively early popular as well as critical success of Joy Division, "on the independent label Factory, showed that something was going on," seemingly something suggesting this kind of music resonated strongly with many people. This music resonated I suggest, with many people's perceptions of what life was like for them in late 20th post-industrial capitalist society, including with how limited their experience of 'freedom and pleasure' so often was.

It is likewise, I contend, possible to interpret the music of Joy Division in line with advocacy of "the pursuit of a sensuous reason placing human fulfillment above the instrumentalist pursuit of profit, sexual liberation, and a revaluation of the natural environment motivated by anti-productivist and anti-consumerist critique" (56) if we interpret the 'bleakness' of this music as critically reflecting upon and responding to the dominance of 'productivism', 'consumerism', 'instrumentalism', 'profiteering' such that 'sensuous reason', 'human fulfillment', 'sexual liberation', and 'revaluation of the natural environment' are denied and suppressed. Joy Division's music makes sense as evincing the "acute self-consciousness" Wilkinson agrees with Simon Reynolds is characteristic of leftist post-punk (quoted 57), and, as I have argued throughout this book it likewise makes sense to interpret Joy Division's music as often concerned with "the political implications of everyday actions" (57), if we conceive of 'the political' broadly, as Wilkinson clearly does, in relation to struggles over access to and exercise of resources, powers, and capacities throughout society, and including throughout ordinary, everyday, daily life.

But, from Wilkinson's vantage point, even leftist post-punk bands becomes politically problematic, when, as with Gang of Four, their "lyrics highlight the contradictions of dominant attitudes a rejection of them," but "do not indicate a radical alternative perspective" (97). Likewise, Wilkinson endorses Raymond Williams's distinction between "alternative and oppositional," "that is to say between someone who simply finds a different way to live and wishes to be left alone with it, and someone who . . . wants to change the society in its light" (quoted 105). Here, I do recognize how readily both critiques can apply to Joy Division (and to Factory), but I conceive of the relations between 'highlighting the contradictions of the dominant' and 'indicating a radical alternative', as well as between 'alternative' and 'oppositional' to be more complicated, and at least potentially more fluid, than it seems Wilkinson does. In particular I think what matters is what can be done with this music (and with this associated array of cultural creation), that the immediate creators did not necessarily accomplish all by themselves alone. The music (and the associated array of cultural creation) can provide the site and stake of ongoing struggle, in terms of how to interpret what this music can mean as well as how to put this music to work in contributing to transformative praxis.

In other words, Joy Division does not need to *both* 1) prompt me to think (about) and feel metaphorical 'darknesses' in human history and society, and in the condition of being human, especially that of the human social being living in the advanced capitalist, (post)modern world, or the continuing powerful influence and impact of fascist forces and tendencies in ostensibly non-fascist or post-fascist societies, while 2) at the same time delineating a precise alternative as well as a precise plan or program for how to get from here to there. The latter challenge I must take up. The musicians have done their part, and now I can make use of the music in doing my part.

Engaging directly, and intently with the music, as visceral experience, does, after all, as Wilkinson cites, drawing upon Simon Reynolds once again, at the least provide "an antidote to boredom," "a constructive response to the boredom generated by the dominant expectations of fulfillment under capitalism" (124). Indeed, as I have proposed early on in discussing interpretations of prospective meanings of the lyrics of "Decades," the song reasonably makes sense as lamenting decades of lives lost to such unrelenting boredom, and to a corresponding paucity of available avenues for sensuous fulfillment, for pleasurable experience, for the freedom to feel truly and fully alive. As I will discuss in the next, seventh and concluding, chapter of this book, I myself place a premium value on the utopian, more precisely on radical utopianism, including of the urgent necessity, especially in the seemingly 'bleakest' of times, of hope, but that does not mean I interpret artistic work that is manifestly dystopian as by any means necessarily reactionary, or even as necessarily simply 'defeatist' or entirely 'pessimistic'.

In chapter one I argue in favor of engaging with myth critically not by simply equating myth with falsehood and deception, and not thereby engaging solely in 'demythification' (or 'demythologization'), but rather by intervening within problematic myths to transform them, 'to remythologize'. Doing so respects the power of myth in conveying meaning and exerting impact, the power of myth to provide frameworks that enable compelling explanation as well as affective identification. Myths matter for people. They provide modes of orientation and structures of feeling for engaging with the familiar and the unfamiliar, the ordinary and the extraordinary, the predictable and the unpredictable, and the usual and the unusual–but, especially, in relation to each of these pairs, with the latter, and this includes, notably, with the fantastic, the uncanny, the surreal, the spectacular, the marvelous, and the sublime. Yet, yes, myths certainly can be highly problematic, in relation to what they elide or obscure, and not just what they denigrate or disparage, and in particular in relation to *whom* they elide or obscure.

In her 2007 novel, *Girl Meets Boy: The Myth of Iphis*, part of a series sponsored by Grove Press in which contemporary writers rewrite classic myths, Ali Smith does so in relation to Ovid's 'Myth of Iphis'. In Ovid's version, Iphis is born biologically female, but in order to prevent her husband, the girl's father, from putting Iphis to death immediately following birth, 'because they could not afford a girl', Iphis's mother pretends Iphis is born biologically male and raises Iphis to present publicly as a boy. Iphis and Ianthe fall in love, and become pledged to marry. In turn, Iphis's mother worries that this marriage will ruin everything as Iphis's 'secret' will inevitably be revealed.

So Iphis's mother pleads with the goddess Isis for help, and Isis responds by transforming Iphis from biologically female to biologically male so that Iphis and Iante can live happily ever after. In Smith's contemporary rewriting, the need for such transformation is rejected, and superseded, in a celebration of gender and sexual fluidity, creativity, and mutual self-reinvention. In Smith's novel the same prototypes exist, and a broadly similar set of challenges present themselves, but the protagonists do not need to bow down to the weight of patriarchal sexist, misogynist, homophobic, and cissexist normative expectation. In fact, only by defiantly breaking from this expectation, by defiantly showing it up, are they able to achieve success, happiness, and indeed liberation.

Perhaps the principal problem with prevalent myths that have developed around and become associated with Factory Records is these myths center almost entirely on the suppposedly exceptional contributions of a small coterie of 'leading *men*'. As such, the Factory mythos problematically resembles mythic accounts of historical achievements where those granted credit for these achievements are small numbers of 'great men'. All too often, according to these kinds of mythic accounts, such 'great men' are the ones responsible, themselves alone, for 'making things happen'. These mythic accounts obscure the important contributions of vast numbers of other people while at the same time eliding what is required for historic achievements of note. Such accounts depict historic achievements as the result of the exceptional talent and skill, drive and determination, strength and stamina, and especially genius of these great mean, with everyone else at best contributing solely as 'supporting players', if not in mere 'bit roles'.

The Factory mythos depicts a small coterie of men as virtually solely responsible for Factory's achievement, while depicting Factory as a phenomenal creative success, and enormous shaping influence, despite the 'men in charge of Factory' maintaining little to no interest in running a profitable enterprise because these men were focused overwhelmingly instead upon doing whatever was the most 'interesting', 'daring', 'innovative', and 'provocative', even if this made no conventional 'business sense' at all, and even if this meant losing lots of money. According to this mythic account, Factory's success is miraculous because it strains credibility to believe such a chaotic organization could last as long as it did and flourish in as many forms as it did, as well as prefigure and inspire the dramatic transformation, and artistic as well as cultural renaissance, of Manchester–and *yet it did exactly that, exactly all of that*. According to this mythic account, none of this success makes logical sense, none of it realistically 'should have happened', but it all happened nonetheless. Thereby, according to the prevalent mythic framework, it must have happened because those *men* responsible *made it happen* through sheer 'force of will' and sheer 'brilliance of vision'.

In connecting what I have just recounted with "Decades," I think of the repeated refrain, "where have they gone?" Yet, in contrast with the lyrics that pose this question in relation to "all the young men," I think about all the young, and the not so young, *women*, of Factory–where have *they* gone? Fortunately, in *I Thought I Heard You Speak: Women in Factory* Records, a nearly 500 pages long book published by White Rabbit Books in 2023, organizer, compiler, and interviewer Audrey Golden, along with the eighty-five women she interviews as co-contributors to this book, provide the answer. In the case of Factory Records, the answer to the question 'where have all the women of Factory Records gone?' seems to be to the margins, where these women have been barely recognized and certainly not received acknowledgment or credit for the pivotal roles they played within Factory, and all of its projects. Although these women made crucial contributions to Factory's achievement—to its impact, influence, and legacy—they have remained all too often unseen, unheard, unrecognized, unacknowledged, and unappreciated. Yes, Deborah Curtis has forced, of necessity, public recognition of her indispensable contribution toward making Ian Curtis's artistic achievement possible. But too few other women involved with Factory, at any point in time and in any capacity, have yet received their due. Even Annik Honoré too often remains depicted as little more than Ian Curtis's 'girlfriend', failing to acknowledge her considerable artistic, journalistic, and entrepreneurial talents, including as co-founder of Factory Benelux and as founder of Les Disques du Crépuscule.

As Golden summarizes, in her concluding chapter:

From the beginning of Factory through its legacy in the present, women have been central to the work. Yet the story of women at Factory Records has long been a history on the margins. Intentionally or not, women haven't been captured fully in the existing narratives of the label and, by default, they have been written out of its legacy. The women's voices included in *I Thought I Heard You Speak* reflect on the vestiges of misogyny, and they stand collectively in resistance to preceding chronicles of the label. At the same time, these voices shine a light on stories of indomitable work ethics, massive creativity, laughter, friendship, and the long-lasting inheritance of Factory Records. This is indeed a story of a happening that became a label that became an (inclusive) cultural phenomenon, in spite of itself. (473)

Even though many prior histories of Factory have been produced and disseminated, achieving considerable renown in their own right, none of these call attention to the roles and contributions of women—until Golden and collaborators do, in *I Thought I Heard You Speak*:

Women designers crafted dazzling images and iconography for record sleeves, posters, and other merchandising materials, while women managers and promoters made the bands famous. Women engineered live and studio sound for New Order, Happy Mondays, and other Factory musicians. Running the Haçienda? Establishing a queer space through Haçienda DJing? Getting Factory songs played on the radio? Making video recordings of Haçienda gigs when male videographers deemed them unnecessary? Developing a viable financial model for the label? *Nearly all women.* (3)

Golden divides her book into thematic chapters that focus, in turn, on contributions of women to running Factory Records and its diverse operations, from headquarters first at Palatine Road and second at Charles Street, as Factory label and Factory club musicians and as non-Factory musicians closely collaborating with Factory musicians, in numerous roles at the Haçienda nightclub, in organizing and running live gigs, in organizing and running performances and exhibitions at the Haçienda involving much more than music alone, as djs at the Haçienda and other Factory venues, at Factory New York and Factory Benelux, as Factory engineers and technicians, as Factory filmmakers and videographers, in the management and promotion of Factory musicians and other Factory projects, in Factory and Factory-adjacent art and design work, and yet more besides. For example, as Golden argues, in introducing Chapter 2, "Running the Label at Palatine Road,"

Women ran the Factory Records office at 86 Palatine Road. While their roles were behind the scenes and have rarely been recorded in great detail within existing histories of the label, the administrative skills and keen business minds of women such as Lesley Gilbert and Lindsay Reade were critical to the label's cultural ascendancy during its early years. Tracey Donnelly, Tina Simmons, Tracy Farmer, Alyson Patchett, Lieve Monnens. Jane Lemon, and Seema Saini continued that often unglamorous yet critical labour of keeping an ideas-driven label functioning until the offices moved to a new location in September 1990. (31)

Martine McDonagh seconds this account by asserting that Lesley Gilbert, Tina Simmon, Tracey Donnelly, and Tracy Farmer "were absolutely indispensable" and that, as a result, no story of Factory can ever come close to being adequate, let alone accurate, without taking their contributions fully into account (31). As does Ann Quigley: "What Tina and Tracey did was they worked harder than anyone else . . . it was *them* at the label" (34). As does Rebecca Boulton: "[Tina Simmons] instigated proper accounting and made it into a proper business, and she was quite vocal in her criticism of some things that were going to distract from focus on the music. She made predictions that ultimately came to be true. She knew, and she said, this is what is going to happen if you do this–meaning it would go bankrupt, it would all end–and actually, it did" (35).

At the Haçienda, Teresa Allen worked many different jobs, recalling "We all worked very hard. Every time it rained, the roof would leak, and we'd have to sweep up all the water out the back doors, dodging customers. The cocktail bar toilets used to overflow and we used to have to sweep that out, and that was Penny [Henry] and me in the main. We ruined lots of pairs of shoes!" (124). As Penny Henry shares, adding to Allen's account,

I kept trying to do all this housekeeping: to cut down on the costs to keep it running. It was a boat showroom before, so when it poured with rain, the water would come pouring in, down through the light fittings. That was why I had to go on the roof to try to shove the slats back in, to fix it. You can't have water with electricity! I learnt a lot about buildings by looking after the basic building issues, the roof, the emergency lights. We all put our heart and soul into that place. I worked seventy-hour weeks, and all my relationships broke up over it. I was putting so much time into it. I paid a lot for working there, and I don't think it was particularly appreciated by the people who owned it. I'm sure it must have been a terrible headache for New Order, having to play gigs because we were always running out of money. In the winter, it was a *huge* place to heat. Most clubs aren't as big as that, and the sound wasn't particularly good either . . . the sound was dreadful, actually. (125)

Many of the women working at the Haçienda not only worked long days and nights, but also, like Allen and Henry, worked numerous, changing jobs at the club, as Allen attests:

My role morphed and expanded over time, and I did lots of other things like getting the merchandising started in the early days before other people came on to do it. Everybody just did everything. I'd work in the office in the daytime, go home and have a bath, get changed, come back, and then I'd be the go-to person at night. If anybody needed anything, if there was any trouble, I'd sort that out. If there were bands on, I'd be liaising with them and sorting out the dressing room, getting them onstage, and all that stuff. (127)

One among many especially notable Haçienda women workers was Yasmine Lakhaney, the first woman doorperson at a major English music nightclub. Yet, as Ruth Taylor recalls, Lakhaney was not exceptional, as a woman, in performing a major role at this club: "Women were always there in Factory, weren't they? There were probably more women than men working in The Haçienda . . . women were all over the place. Sure there were blokes on the front door, but even Yasmine [Lakhaney] was on the front door. Because there were women all over the place, it wasn't a patriarchal place–there was no room for patriarchy there. It wasn't a job-for-the-boys kind of place at all" (237). In the same vein, Yasmine Lakhaney's daughter Soraya reflects, "You know, it wasn't perfect, and there's nothing perfect in this world. But she was so proud that she was part of that club and was part of such a strong female team" (237).

Another major woman contributor to the Haçienda was Ang Matthews, who became [the] manager and [the] licensee for the club. As DJ Paulette emphasizes,

Women actually ran Factory, and they ran The Haçienda. Women *ran it*. From the cloakroom to the kitchen to the bars, to managing it. Absolutely not enough is made of Ang Matthews's role in running The Haçienda, and she *ran it* . . . . It was the women who were making sure that the relations with the police were such that it stayed open . . . . [Women served in] all those major roles–they kept it running. Ordering in the beers, wines and the spirits, and making the deals with the distributors. That was Ang. And it wasn't Peter Hook, and it wasn't Tony. The person that was signing the cheques and making the deals was Ang Matthews. (385-386)

Elaborating on Matthews's pivotal role in particular yet further, DJ Paulette insists

You always have to scratch under the surface of what's going on because even if you went to The Haçienda two or three times in its entire existence, you will have seen Ang at the corner of the main bar! It was impossible to miss her. She was there handling everything from the door, to the bar, to the money. She was involved in absolutely *every* step of the organisation, so there's no way you can tell The Haçienda story without giving her that credit. (386)

Strikingly, no matter how indispensable Yasmine Lakhaney's and Ang Matthews's contributions indeed were, these were by no means exceptional as instances of women playing pivotal roles in making Factory what it was–and is. As Golden notes, for example, "Few jobs were more important to the success of Factory than the management and promotion of artists–a role played by women from the label's earliest days to the present" (321). Here, as Golden does, it is important to give credit, to pay tribute, to the contributions of Martine McDonagh, Lindsay Reade, Jane Roberts, Liz Naylor, Rebecca Boulton, Nicki Kefalas, and Jayne Houghton.

Likewise, Georgina Trulio, working for Factory out of the Charles Street headquarters at the time Factory was nearing bankruptcy, makes clear it was women who were on the frontlines dealing with this impending end, while still striving to maintain as much of Factory's operations as possible all the way to the end:

> I think we, the women at Factory and The Haçienda, really held it together. It was the women who made sure everything ran smoothly and got problems solved. A lot of it might have been behind the scenes, but we were there doing it. At the end of the Factory road, we had to fend everybody off while the men were just having a drink and hiding in the Lass O'Gowrie. So the women were very strong. We worked really, really hard to keep things going, and at the end, the women took the brunt of what was going on. We were the infantry, holding the fort for everybody, so we had a huge role there and were never properly acknowledged. (451)

However, as Gonnie Rietveld observes, even as a considerable number of women worked for Factory as sound engineers and as other skilled technicians, both at live events and in studio recording work, yet "when you hear women's stories about becoming sound engineers . . . there are more female engineers than there are female producers because, I guess, that's still a supportive role, comparatively. How many producers are there that are female, in this world?" (282).

How do the women that Golden interviews evaluate their experience with Factory, and in particular how welcome did they feel, how included and how *equitably* included did they feel, how recognized and acknowledged did they feel, how respected and appreciated did they feel, how much did they feel that they belonged as part of Factory and that their contributions to Factory mattered, in relation to the enterprise as a whole, and in particular to the prominent men who maintained ultimate authority and control?

Some of these women evaluate Factory in largely negative terms. For instance, Ann Quigley, part of both Factory label music groups Swamp Childen and Kalima, comments, "That's the thing. It's almost always the boys' story. With Tony Wilson, if you were flavour of the month, he'd do anything for you, but if you weren't flavour of the month, it wasn't very nice . . . because of the success of Joy Division and New Order . . . all the smaller bands found it harder to get attention. You had to work harder to be noticed and stand your ground" (94). Adding to this direction of criticism, Julia Adamson, studio sound engineer and former member of both What? Noise and The Fall charges that "Factory also became a label of white boys, as well. When you look at the catalogue, there are a couple of Black artists there, and there are some women, but that wasn't what was 'iconic' about Factory. Factory could have had stronger female representation, in my opinion. It was labels like 4AD and One Little Indian [now One Little Independent] who took up the baton for that" (95). Along the same lines, Clare Cumberlidge, art curator and responsible for painting the Guy Traitor cocktail bar at the Haçienda, declares: "There was amazing Black music happening in Manchester at that time, but they weren't getting signed by Factory, and I think that made me frustrated. Politically, that's problematic to me" (95).

Adamson "got the impression it was a boys' club with Factory, even from the studio side of things" (477). Liz Naylor, writer of *City Fun*, and also someone who worked on Factory public relations as well as in multiple other capacities, shares the same take: "My bottom line is, I think Factory was a very male environment . . . the built environment, the gig environment, the labour. It didn't feel like there were women around Factory at all . . . It didn't feel like a very welcoming space" (477).

Tony Wilson is the target of especially strong criticism. Naylor, for instance, is blunt, even though as she indicates she would rather not be: "I kind of feel a bit like you shouldn't speak ill of the dead, but my basic take on Tony is that he was a bully, and that's a bit uncomfortable" (343). Carol Morley, filmmaker and musician, although more ambivalent, is still likewise critical of Wilson: "It was extraordinary to have someone like Tony Wilson in your midst because he was so fiercely intelligent. He believed in scenes and thought about how scenes are created always through a place, which is why he created The Haçienda. But as a woman, I don't think you were taken seriously–it felt as if your artistic aspirations weren't as important as, say, the way you looked" (343). Morley also mentions even though, in first viewing *24 Hour Party People*, she thought the film "was fantastic" but at the same time she "also thought the film overlooked women because there were hardly any women's stories that were known about at that time," while, perhaps all the worse as someone who was herself a Haçienda regular, "I mean, I hardly knew many stories of women that had contributed to the times!" (316). Lindsay Reade, author, band manager, and contributor to Factory Records in numerous capacities from the get go, as well as Wilson's ex-wife, likewise recalls with *24 Hour Party People* "I wanted to be listed as a co-founder. They wouldn't do it, and I said, 'Well, all right, you won't do it, but it was our money that started Factory'. The film-makers came back with 'No, no, no. It was Tony's money'. Sorry, we were married–it was *our* money" (315).

In contrast with these takes from Quigley, Adamson, Cumberlidge, Naylor, Morley, and Reade, a number of other women that Golden interviews offer largely positive evaluations of their experiences with Factory. For example, Lesley Gilbert, a major contributor to the company in multiple key roles, especially early on, as well as Rob Gretton's wife, comments:

> The one thing I would say about Tony and Rob, and Rob in particular, actually, was that they just thought women were great and much better than they were. That was the general consensus: 'let's just leave it to the women'. Prior to working for Factory, I worked in various offices, corporate offices, and . . . it could be horrible. The men would treat you badly. I remember once, in particular, this guy in the office–and I had very long curly hair at that point–got hold of a bit of my hair and said something terrible. That would never, never, *ever* have happened at Factory, ever. There was never anything sexist or inappropriate because I think most of the men involved really admired women. (49)

Gonnie Rietveld, musician with Factory label outfit Quando Quango, Haçienda employee in multiple capacities, collaborator on the *The Haçienda Must Be Built* (FAC 351) project, the official commissioned history of The Haçienda, and subsequently a professor of sonic culture, also singles out Rob Gretton, in particular, for praise: "I felt that Rob really supported the women of Factory. I really have to underline that: it's Rob who was always very supportive. I don't think he ever read anything to do with feminism as such. It was just because he was a genuinely nice person" (335). Rietveld adds she perceived Gretton as acting like a generous and caring father to others involved with Factory, while Tracey Donnelly extends this same characterization in declaring "they were the best bosses ever. To work for Tony, Rob and Alan–they were amazing. They changed a lot of things for a lot of people, almost like father figures" (430).

Gillian Gilbert, one of the best-known women involved with Factory, because of her membership in New Order, but someone who was also, as such, a co-owner of the Haçienda and who has worked as a music producer in addition to performing with New Order, and, together with husband Stephen Morris, as The Other Two, shares much the same positive take concerning what it was like to work as a woman with Factory: "It was so good how so many women worked for Factory because in those days, in other industries, it was still 'Benny Hill country' with mother-in-law jokes and men running around making fun of women. But it was *never* like that 'in the bubble' I'd say, the Factory bubble. Other record companies were like that, but not Factory" (96). Gilbert contrasts her positive experience at Factory with her negative experience subsequently at London Records, as, unlike at Factory, label representatives at London refused to take her seriously as a songwriter. As Gilbert reflects on this contrast, "It was only after Factory that I realised how special it was to be an equal, treated the same as everybody else (430)." Gilbert also calls attention to how Factory showed at the time more than typical respect for women employees when they became pregnant: "At Factory, Lesley [Gilbert] left to have a baby, and she didn't go back to work, and it was *her choice*–that's the difference (430)."

According to Alyson Patchett, who, like many others interviewed for *I Thought I Heard You Speak*, worked multiple jobs as a Factory Communications Limited employee, "From the outside, Factory looked very male, I think, especially the time I was there, because it was the Happy Monday laddishness of it that created an image of a very blokey sort of scene. But there were a lot of women . . . So it always felt like a level playing field (477)." Cath Carroll, a member of the group Miaow and a solo musician, as well as a *City Fun* and *NME* writer, shares the same positive take on what it was like for her and other women at Factory: "I never, ever personally got any kind of sexist vibes at Factory or the *NME* . . . I'm hesitant to say, well, it's just a boys' club, because that was what people said about everything then. In most cases it was true, but with Factory I just don't think it was the case (477)."

Chris Mathan, a Peter Saville Associates partner and designer, offers an even more positive evaluation than most other women that Golden interviews: "I will always look back on that period as exceptionally creative. It was all business, [but] we had a lot of fun too. It may not have always seemed that way then . . . the long days, the late nights, not enough sleep, etc. but looking at the design profession today, I'm immensely grateful to have had that experience (364)." Upon leaving Peter Saville Associates,

> I knew I would likely never have the opportunity to work with such an inspiring group of creatives again. It was an exciting time in my life as a designer, having worked almost exclusively for corporate clients before that. I collaborated with amazingly talented people on fabulous music, art, and fashion-related projects. And much of the music was what I was passionate about. It was pretty crazy, too. I never went to sleep before one o'clock in the morning . . . and Peter, despite his eccentricities, had his finger on the culture and was a force of innovation. (374)

Many women that Golden interviews commend the Haçienda in particular for being an exceptionally welcoming as well as dynamic place. As Dian Barton, live sound engineer recalls, "The Haçienda brought a very diverse genre of acts, obviously lots of 'normal' bands, but also a lot from different parts of the world like Africa and South America," and although "These acts often brought traditional instruments, which presented their own challenges, not least in how to mic them up," such as "traditional drums, panpipes and homemade xylophones," often all-acoustic," Barton loved working with these musicians and appreciated that "The chance of encountering this kind of act" was "unlikely anywhere other than The Haçienda" (153).

Yvonne Shelton, musician in Haçienda Classical, praises the club because "It was all different types of music. It wasn't just dance music in the beginning. It was every kind of music, and it would change throughout the night." In relation to dancing the Haçienda was unusually inclusive, and infectiously encouraging: "We were always like, 'If you dance, then I'll dance', then, 'No, I'm not dancing!'. We watched it transform into an electronic dance room because, in the beginning, you'd see the reggae guys and the punk rock guys all in the same venue. The punk rock guys would be dancing to the reggae music, the reggae guys dancing to punk rock, and then it became hard-core dance music in the late eighties and into the nineties. It changed completely" (154).

As Golden comments, one of the advantages of interviewing many diverse women concerning their experiences with the Haçienda is doing so helps counter how the club is "most often remembered," and that is exclusively "as a music venue and dance club," yet the Haçienda "was so much more" (163). Insofar as "Its space gave rise to cultural production that helped to put Manchester on the global map," it did so with "women across various creative industries" serving as "key figures in making it happen," and this included women involved with "Fashion, merchandising, visual art, theatre, literary drama, performance art, gastronomy, hairstyling, design, experimental sound" (163). Indeed, as Clare Cumberlidge adds, "Another aspect of The Haçienda that is not sufficiently spoken about is the way it became an after-hours club . . . . It was a place where you met different creative people and had the kinds of conversations that were generative for cultural production, supporting emerging practices" (189).

Yet the Haçienda definitely played a ground-breaking role in relation to employing women as djs, and in creating nights catering to LGBTQIA+ audiences. As Golden writes, "Women DJed at The Haçienda from the early days through the Madchester years," even though "you might not know it," because "they've been largely written out of the club's histories to date." Golden and others contributing to *I Thought I Heard You Speak* help rewrite that history, by emphasizing, for instance, that "Through DJ culture and themed nights–Flesh in particular–women firmly established The Haçienda as a queer sanctuary in the heart of Manchester. On its dance floors, the club became a safe space for LGBTQIA+ dancers and music lovers who could thwart the hazards of identity politics outside and create their own narratives on the dance floor to the sound reverberating from the DJ booth" (203).

As Haçienda dj Kath McDermott recalls, "I suppose The Haçienda was quite a masculine space, normally, but it also really became a space that opened itself to trans people, to cross-dressers, queer people. There was a real openness, and a sense of inclusion, maybe even in spite of itself, thanks to Flesh" (229). As a woman dj, McDermott found the Haçienda welcoming and supportive whereas that was not her experience elsewhere: "I was having two very different experiences on the decks: at Home, completely not comprehending that a women could DJ, whereas at The Haç, it was like, why wouldn't a woman DJ?" (230).

Haçienda workers Ann-Marie Copeland characterizes the Haçienda as "the place where gay people, Black people could go without discrimination, and there was no misogyny. It was just a completely different place" (404). Corrine Drewery, musician in Swing Out Sister, agrees: "What I noticed when I came to The Haçienda was how no one made a big deal about being Black, white, gay, straight, male, female–it was a collective of people. It was so diverse, and everybody was well represented" (404). Bev Bytheway, curator at the Cornerhouse and responsible as well for programming at the Haçienda, comments that young Black people previously considered Manchester city centre hostile territory, but the Haçienda played a pioneering progressive role as "one of the spaces that pulled Black youth into the city centre," offering "them a space to come into" (405).

Likewise, Stella Hall, co-founder of the Green Room, and also involved with Haçienda and Festival of the Tenth Summer programming, cherishes positive memories of the club, in particular because of how relatively unusually welcomg and inclusive it was:

> In the eighties, The Haçienda felt like a very open space. As the Green Room, we were absolute pioneers in ensuring that queer, disabled, Black artists and audiences were encouraged into that space, and that was the same at The Haçienda then. It was a 'come all ye'. Obviously people choose their particular nights, but it was really an eclectic mix. It's certainly the last club that I ever felt really comfortable in, wandering about. I usually went with my girlfriends, but probably I would have been happy to go in on my own. (405)

As Rebecca Goodwin, Haçienda worker and also involved with FAC 51 productions and Factory promotions, adds, at the Haçienda, at least for quite some time, there was neither an explicit nor an implicit dress code, with people dressing in widely divergent ways, and clubbers spanning the very young to the very old. Like Hall, Goodwin emphasizes the club was a place where women felt much safer than just about anywhere else they could go out at night: "It felt like everybody was equal and you didn't get groped, you didn't get propositioned, you didn't get sexually threatened, you didn't feel remotely vulnerable in The Haçienda" (407). Copeland agrees: "The Haçienda was a different environment. There wasn't anything macho about it. It really felt safe. There was always respect coming from everybody who worked there. It was like family . . . everybody looked out for each other" (405). What's more, Ruth Taylor, Haçienda worker, emphasizes, contrary to popular *mis*representation since, "There was a very, very, very small minority of the bad stuff as The Haçienda, and it didn't impact most people. You hear the stories now and there were a few awful nights, like the horrific day where one of the doormen got stabbed, but that wasn't the norm" (413). Ang Matthews agrees: "I do think that sometimes people focus on that too much–the drugs and the violence–and it was a very small part" (413).

For Clare Cumberlidge, moreover, even as "Factory Records always had a laddie element to it," albeit "Not necessarily macho" but nonetheless "laddie in a kind of northern white boys' culture" way, while "everybody who wasn't a white boy knew that," in contrast "The Haçienda didn't actually *feel* like a Factory space for that reason–because it felt like it was shaped by the communities in it rather than by Factory" (407).

With Tony Wilson mythmaking was a deliberate process, and much of the character of the prevalent myths associated with Factory coincide with how Wilson preferred to operate. Unfortunately, this approach has resulted in marginalizing the contributions of women who played major roles in Factory projects. As Bridget Chapman, who worked for Factory Two, describes, "Tony liked chaos. He never ever liked it when things were running smoothly. He liked a bit of conflict, and if things were running smoothly, he would always drop sort of mental bombs into the situation to disrupt things. I'm not sure that I could live like that permanently, but he made things happen. He really did make things happen" (343). Prevalent myths surrounding Factory and its most famous projects do indeed portray 'creative chaos' as essential to how Factory operated and what enabled Factory to achieve the innovative results it did. However, what this portrayal mystifies is how much sheer hard work, on the part of a great many people, requiring considerable discipline, structure, organization, regularity, consistency, dedication, and accountability–as well as how much collaboration and accommodation–proved vital in order to realize Factory projects, from Joy Division to New Order, from Factory Records to the Haçienda, and much more beside. It further mystifies those who played less 'colorful' roles and who did not maintain the position nor the interest in self-promotion that Wilson did. As Martine McDonagh, manager of James and who also worked for Factory in other public relations capacities, reflects,

> With Wilson, it was all about him. He took credit for everything, but Alan (Erasmus] and Rob Gretton weren't like that. And Wilson didn't just take credit for the women's hard work . . . . There's a lot of mythology, as lot of mythmaking in Manchester about Factory and Tony Wilson and all of that–a lot of it created by him. But it's great that Manchester has so much pride in its culture, and Factory did release some really amazing bands . . . So of course there was going to be some mythology around the Factory bands, and I think Tony Wilson really encouraged that kind of thinking. It might sound like I didn't like him–I did. (344)

Bev Bytheway, curator at Cornerhouse and also a contributor to Haçienda programming offers a similar assessment: "It's always the main story that's promoted, always the 'main characters' that are promoted, even though there's a lot of other stuff which went on around it. Manchester is very good about mythologising itself and mythologising the male leads" (192),

Even at the time, however, some women attempted to produce and disseminate counter-myths, that re-centered women's roles and contributions, notably at the Haçienda. Stella Hall cites Carol Morley's 2000 film *The Alcohol Years*, a 45 minutes long experimental memoir, as encapsulating the Haçienda in its heyday, and in particular the absence of women in the stories that have been told about that era: "Carol Morley was an always-there figure, with so much potential and so much talent, but of course, she wasn't viewed in that way. She's a real illustration of how women are . . . in the shadows" (194). As the British Film Institute summarizes *The Alcohol Years*, with this film "Carol Morley returns to Manchester, where in the early 1980s, five years of her life were lost in an alcoholic blur. *The Alcohol Years* is a poetic retrieval of that time, in which rediscovered friends and acquaintances recount tales of her drunken and promiscuous behaviour. In Morley's search for her lost self, conflicting memories and viewpoints weave in and out, revealing a portrait of the city, its pop culture, and the people who lived it." According to Morley herself, in *I Thought I Heard You Speak*, "Factory created a sense of desire for something–not just the music, but the energy and a way of looking at life. So as a young woman growing up in that context, or with that organisation of Factory Records around you, it was very inspirational, but getting to be truly part of it in one way or another felt almost impossible. As time went on, it felt more and more elusive" (193). In relation to *The Alcohol Years* in particular, Morley explains,

My initial interest was in what I didn't remember and what gets forgotten, and the people within history that get ignored, like the bartenders or the cloakroom people–people that are never asked what it was like but have a really amazing and significant point of view. I was also fascinated by this idea of mythology, and especially the idea of mythologising young women–*The Alcohol Years* covers the time from when I was sixteen to twenty-one. I was interested in how others played into this mythology, but also in a way how I was mythologizing my life and that of others too!

A large part of what I do in my films probably has been triggered from that time in Manchester, at the Haçienda, of feeling somehow misplaced, or an outsider in that world. As a young woman, you weren't necessarily integrated into what was going on–it felt very difficult to know exactly how to be a part of it–and I so wanted to be a part of it! An insider! (292-293)

In sum, Morley declares,

the point is, we were all of us living under a patriarchal system where women globally on the music scene/cultural scene were marginalised in some way, because that's how things were, but within that there were men who were supportive of women as artists . . . It was complicated. But histories are always skewed male because possibly men are better, and more free, to mythologise themselves and those they choose around them. But I definitely think *The Alcohol Years* was a corrective to that! (332)

The overall impression *I Thought I Heard You Speak: Women at Factory Records* leaves is decidedly mixed. In sum, Factory did involve many women, and many women did many important, even indispensable, jobs as part of Factory. These included many jobs where women were doing far more than simply 'assisting' and 'supporting' men. It was by no means simply men who came up with creative ideas at Factory, and it was by no means simply men who exercised leadership and maintained ultimate responsibility. At Factory, in the 1980s and into the 1990s, women did, on average, enjoy relatively more opportunities, greater freedom, and less restriction, as well as less overt disparagement and denigration, than was widespread in many if not most comparable organizations. Yet men held all of the most prominent, leading roles, and men were always the ones in ultimate charge. Likewise, men were the ones who received the attention and the credit for virtually everything Factory did, for all of its greatest successes, its most significant influences, and its most substantial legacies. As Nicki Kefalas, who worked with Factory radio and TV public relations as well as on Out Promotion (FAC 161), summarizes her, and many other Factory women's mixed thoughts about the company, "Factory were . . . sexist in their own way, by which I mean there was a lot of masculine energy. They did not hire me because I was a woman, or make decisions not to hire someone because they were a woman, not like that. But . . . women didn't get credit in the same way . . . There's a thought of 'oh, that's the way it was back then', but that's not good, so let's correct that" (342).

And that is exactly why *I Thought I Heard You Speak* is is necessary. This is especially so as more and more time passes, and more and more of those involved themselves become elderly and are no longer alive. Film-maker Margaret Jailler makes this precise point in her interview with Golden: "It's terrible the way older people become invisible–older women especially–and I do think the struggles of women who challenged gender stereotyping by entering professions which they were not largely welcomed into by their male counterparts *are* worth telling" (473). The last is also key: women at Factory *did* challenge gender stereotyping and they *did* push back against male counterparts who were not entirely welcoming; women at Factory were not mere 'victims' of male domination. But, this pushback did demand a lot from women then and it continues to do so, to this day. In this light DJ Paulette's sobering comment calls attention to another key dimension of what makes *I Thought I Heard You Speak* important, *in relation to the present–and the future–beyond Factory*:

> in the thirty years that I've been [working as a DJ] . . . as much as things have changed a tiny little bit, we've got so far to go. We've got many, many miles to go before even the changes that we're making now will make any difference. But this is why we have to make as many changes as we can. This is why we have to tell as many stories as we can–if we don't tell the stories, whenever and wherever we can, those stories stay closed and 'other'. We have to bring those stories into the canon, bring them into the discussion. (475)

It is striking, for all their compelling criticisms of Factory, that so many of the women contributing to *I Thought I Heard You Speak* emphasize how proud they were, and remain, of their participation within and their contribution to Factory, as well as how this experience provided them with considerable satisfaction and indeed considerable joy. For example, as Jayne Houghton, Factory public relations, founder of Excess Press, and *NME* journalist, summarizes her experience with Factory:

> The whole thing was like a big, dysfunctional family–Factory as a whole. Yeah. Everyone looked out for each other, and obviously it got hideously messy towards the end when it all started going wrong. Coming through it, and having been part of the New Order family for thirty years, I didn't realise until much later how special and privileged that was. I suddenly became a PR after I'd been a photographer. I always felt very heard, loved and encouraged. Whatever mad ideas and schemes, and plans for stories and articles and trips–everything was a blank canvas of opportunity. There were no constraints. (328)

In conclusion, as Teresa Allen, musician with The Wake, comments, in relation to the Haçienda, in particular, "We were paid a pittance, but I think the people who worked there loved working there, and we did it because we loved to be in there. It was the only place to go in Manchester of any none, so I was there twenty-four hours a day" (129). What's more, Allen declares,

"There was nothing else like Factory, there's never been anything like it since, and I don't think there every will be, to be perfectly honest . . . . We all worked incredibly hard and got very little thanks for it, but we did it because *god damn it was fun*" (481).

Where does this bring us, in reconsidering and prospectively *rewriting* the dominant Factory mythos, including in particular how this influences common interpretations of meaning and experiences of impact in listening to, registering, and reflecting upon the lyrics and music of Ian Curtis and Joy Division, in particular as represented by the song "Decades"? Again, "Decades" is much more than its lyrics, or its lyrics and title, alone. It is a sustained series of movements of tension and release that involve processes of interweaving defamiliarization and refamiliarization, and that both involve the feeling of movement according to a trajectory forward through time as well as movements in multiple yet regularly recurrent directions across space as the temporal movement proceeds. Listening to "Decades" I feel compelled to stop what I am otherwise thinking, feeling, and doing–to suspend those concerns–and to instead attend closely to the sounds, patterns of sounds, and deployment of sounds that the song comprises, through its duration. "Decades" calls me out of the 'normal' 'everyday', and compels me to consider my existence from the vantage point and within the scope of a much vaster expanse of history, historical situations and events, and historical struggles and strivings. "Decades" calls upon me to attend to all of this with great and grave respect, with both humility and with awe, and to scrutinize my relationship all the more acutely and painfully in relation to this vast historical sweep. I need to step out from and break with what queer theorists Judith Halberstam and José Estaban Muñoz theorize as 'straight time' in favor of 'queer time', and indeed identification with the music as persona in "Decades" feels as if this involves immersion within a kind of ecstatic extreme that is wrenching and shattering, yet also brilliant and majestic.

Rewriting Factory myth, by way of "Decades," while taking into account *I Thought I Heard You Speak: Women and Factory Records*, means attending to those whose pivotal contributions have been ignored, forgotten, obscured, elided, marginalized, and dismissed in the history of Factory Records. It means re-centering these contributions, and re-articulating Factory as a much more collective effort than commonly represented, as well as one that suffered many messy contradictions, including many problems and limitations, throughout its duration, and whose legacy is similarly messily contradictory, similarly problematic and limited. But what deserves respect and appreciation are the opportunities and the possibilities Factory opened up, and which can still be seized upon as inspiration for striving to create new opportunities and new possibilities in the future, by daring to believe in and to push for what has never yet been, what otherwise seems altogether impossible and indeed absurd, as well as to insist that popular cultural production can be both pleasurable entertainment and serious art, and that this kind of cultural production, and especially diversely sharing and enthusiastically reveling in this kind of cultural production, can and should be 'the heart and soul' of city life. "Decades" suggests a tribute to all of those who have suffered and strived to be artistic cultural producers and not just consumers of what powerful forces and interests have set forth for them to consume. These are people who have suffered and strived to create their own scenes and subcultures, to imagine and invent what has never been imagined or invented previously, to push past boundaries of what has been established as the limits of the conceivably possible as well as the normatively acceptable, and who have done so, even way past the point of exhaustion, while often enough not succeeding in realizing these dreams, no matter how long and hard they pushed to do so, and who indeed have often failed, often been defeated, over and over again, even spectacularly so in such efforts. These are people whose efforts have been, all too often, subsequently ignored, forgotten, elided, obscured, marginalized, dismissed, denigrated and demeaned, so that their legacy only exists, if at all, in the form of spectral traces–haunting ghosts–of what never really was and never truly could have been. But our task, "Decades" proposes, is to intervene versus this ignoring, forgetting, eliding, obscuring, marginalizing, dismissing, denigrating, and demeaning. It is our task to reanimate these ghosts, to attend to and do justice to what they call forth from us, so that we can show that, what really was, even though it most often seems not to have been so, as well as what truly could have been, yet was thwarted and thus not realized, provide essential sparks toward what yet really can, should, and must be.

In attending to artistic cultural productions, performances, exhibitions, spectacles, and happenings, therefore, "Decades" directs us to consider what has been required to make these possible, including all of those people beyond the most readily identifiable 'authors' of this work whose contributions have also been indispensable for any of this work to succeed, even if their contributions have not been recognized at all, including by those same 'authors'. Yet "Decades" also directs us to consider all of those people who maintained the capability to be 'authors' in their own right, in their own name, but who never were able to access and exercise the material resources necessary to do so, including the time and space to be able to create, the time and space to be able to think and to feel–deeply, the time and space to be able to learn and to train, the time and space to develop and refine skills, the time and space to collaborate and interact, the time and space to be able to test out and to take risks, the time and space to share and to receive feedback, the time and space to experiment and innovate, the time and space to work with new tools and technologies, the time and space to be able to make themselves seen and heard, and the time and space to be taken seriously and given due credit.

Today, in the US and the UK, it is extremely difficult for most people to concentrate full-time working as a musician, or as an artist, so much so that even as many try to do be as active in creating music and art as possible, while working other jobs, often multiple other jobs, as a matter of necessity, a great many others turn away from even considering such pursuits, and are left with little time and space in their busy, chaotic, and precarious lives even to pursue such activities as 'hobbies'. And today, in the US and the UK, there are all too few places where 'all are freely welcome' 'as whom they diversely are' that are readily affordable and otherwise readily accessible and where all those so welcomed can feel as if they are not only welcomed but also included, and equitably included in what happens, in what is created, as part of these initiatives and enterprises, such that they are able to attain and sustain feelings of genuinely belonging and that their contributions genuinely matter.

But this has all too often been the case, living within a social system founded upon exploitation of labor, alienation of people's creative capacity as well of their creative exertion, and that depends upon deepening and widening inequality, as well as extensive dispossession and exclusion. The maintenance and reproduction of this social system makes ample use, what's more, of suspicion versus any and all easily perceived as 'threatening' as well as hostility versus any and all easily marked out as 'different' and thereby 'disturbing'. Imagine all of the prospective artistic and cultural contributions we have lost, and continue to lose, due to the vast and rising extent of homelessness in the US and the UK today. Imagine all of the prospective artistic and cultural contributions we have lost, and continue to lose, due to the impact of racism, sexism, homophobia, transphobia, ableism, and ageism. Imagine all of the prospective artistic and cultural contributions we have lost, and continue to lose, due to hate crimes and due to trauma, as well as post-traumatic stress disorder, following decades of abuse and neglect. Imagine all of the prospective artistic and cultural contributions we have lost, and continue to lose, due to the massive numbers of people worldwide forced to becoming migrants, and who all too often, even as refugees and asylum seekers, are met with prejudice and hostility, in the new countries to which they come and to which they could potentially make valuable contributions. Imagine all of the prospective artistic and contributions that have been lost due to decades of such prejudice and hostility. Imagine all of the prospective artistic and contributions that have been lost due to decades of devastating conflict and outright war in Palestine. Imagine all of the prospective artistic and cultural contributions that are being lost and will be lost in towns, cities, states, regions, and nations where teachers are being forbidden from teaching freely, from exercising academic freedom, in relation to any subject that encourages thinking critically concerning historical injustices and socially systemic inequities, or that might be in any way 'controversial', 'disturbing', or 'upsetting'. Imagine all of the prospective artistic and cultural contributions that are being lost and will be lost, by students who only learn about and who are only taught to value, even only to imagine, artistic and cultural work that does not in any way threaten the powers that be, that does not allude to or incite any kind of controversy, and that never questions or breaks with what is normative. "Decades," in sum, encourages reflection on what might happen, and especially who might struggle and suffer–that is, what might be lost and who might be 'disappeared', for *decades* moving forward–if resurgent fascist forces, in the US, the UK, Western Europe, and beyond become all the more powerful and all the more entrenched.

Works Cited

The 1619 Project: a New Origin Story. Created by Nikole Hannah-Jones and *The New York Times Magazine*. New York: The New York Times Company/One World, 2021.

24 Hour Party People. Fictional feature film. Frank Cottrell Boyce, writer, and Michael Winterbottom, director. 2002.

Adamson, Julia. Contributing to *I Thought I Heard You Speak: Women and Factory Records*. Pam Golden, compiler, editor, and interviewer. London: White Rabbit, 2023.

Aizelwood, John. *Decades: Joy Division + New Order*. London: Palazzo, 2021.

The Alcohol Years. Experimental documentary film. Carol Morley, writer and director. 2000.

Alexander, Leslie and Michelle Alexander. "Fear." *The 1619 Project: a New Origin Story*. Created by Nikole Hannah-Jones and *The New York Times Magazine*. New York: The New York Times Company/One World, 2021: 97-122.

Allen, Carolyn. Contributing to *I Thought I Heard You Speak: Women and Factory Records*. Pam Golden, compiler, editor, and interviewer. London: White Rabbit, 2023.

Allen, Teresa. Contributing to *I Thought I Heard You Speak: Women and Factory Records*. Pam Golden, compiler, editor, and interviewer. London: White Rabbit, 2023.

"America's Gun Problem in Graphs." *The BBC*. 23 January 2023. https://www.bbc.com/news/live/world-us-canada-64365251/page/2 Accessed 29 March 2024.

Anderson, Carol. "Self-Defense." *The 1619 Project: a New Origin Story*. Created by Nikole Hannah-Jones and *The New York Times Magazine*. New York: The New York Times Company/One World, 2021: 249-266.

Andrews, Alice. "Autoimmune actions in the ableist academy." *Ableism in Academia: Theorising experiences of disabilities and chronic illnesses in higher education*. Nicole Brown and Jennifer Leigh, eds. London: University College of London Press, 2020: 103-123.

Andrews, Kehinde. *The New Age of Empire: How Racism & Colonialism Still Rule the World*. New York: Bold Type Books, 2021.

As Good As It Gets. Fictional feature film. Mark Andrus and James L. Brooks, writers, and James L. Brooks, director. Starring Jack Nicholson, Helen Hunt, Greg Kinnear, Cuba Gooding Jr., Skeet Ulrich, and Shirley Knight. 1997.

Askerøi, Eirik. "Transmissions: Sonic markers of difference in the sound of Joy Division." *Punk & Post-Punk*. Vol. 3, No. 2 (2021): 201-220. https://doi.org/10.1386/punk_00072_1

"Atmosphere (Joy Division)." Music video. Anton Corbijn, director. 1980.

Badiou, Alain. Cited in Robert McRuer, *Crip Times: Disability, Globalization, and Resistance*, New York: New York University Press, 2018: 113.

Baldwin, James. Cited in Kevin M. Kruse, "Traffic," *The 1619 Project: a New Origin Story*, Created by Nikole Hannah-Jones and *The New York Times Magazine*, New York: The New York Times Company/One World, 2021: 407.

Barthes, Roland. *Camera Lucida: Reflections on Photography*. 1980. Richard Howard, trans. London: Fontana, 1981.

Barton, Dian. Contributing to *I Thought I Heard You Speak: Women and Factory Records*. Pam Golden, compiler, editor, and interviewer. London: White Rabbit, 2023.

Beautiful Thing. Fictional feature film. Jonathan Harvey, writer, and Hettie MacDonald, director. Starring Linda Henry, Glen Berry, Scott Neal, Tameka Empson, and Ben Daniels. 1996.

Beckert, Sven and Seth Rockman. Cited by Matthew Desmond, "Capitalism," *The 1619 Project: a New Origin Story*. Created by Nikole Hannah-Jones and *The New York Times Magazine*, New York: The New York Times Company/One World, 2021: 187.

Benjamin, Walter. Cited in Avery F. Gordon, *Ghostly Matters: Haunting and the Sociological Imagination*, Minneapolis: University of Minnesota Press, 2008: 204-205.

Berlant, Lauren. Cited in Ann Cvetkovich, *Depression: a Public Feeling*, Duke University Press, 2012: 13, 20-21.

Berlant, Lauren, Ann Cvetkovich, Deborah Gould, Megan Boler, and Elizabeth Davis. "On taking the affective turn: interview with Lauren Berlant, Ann Cvetkovich, and Deborah Gould." *Cultural Studies*. Vol. 36, No. 3 (2022), 360-377. DOI: 10.1080/09502386.2022.2040562.

Bérubé, Michael. "Foreword: Another Word is Possible." Robert McRuer, *Crip Theory: Cultural Signs of Queerness and Disability*, New York: New York University Press, 2006: vii-xi.

Beviglia, Jim. "Joy Division, 'Atmosphere'." *American Songwriter*. 2016. https://americansongwriter.com/joy-division-atmosphere/ Accessed 29 March 2024.

Bibby, Michael. Cited in Catherine Langhorst, "A Northern 'Ode on Melancholy': The Music of Joy Division," *Rock and Romanticism: Post-Punk, Goth, and Metal as Dark Romanticisms*, James Rovira, ed., Cham, Switzerland: Palgrave MacMillan, 2018: 96.

Bloch, Ernst. *The Principle of Hope*. Three Volumes. 1954, 1955, 1959. Neville Plaice, Stephen Plaice and Paul Knight, trans. Cambridge: MIT Press, 1986.

_____. *The Spirit of Utopia*. 1918. Anthony A. Nassar, trans. Palo Alto: Stanford University Press, 2000.

_____. *The Utopian Function of Art and Literature: Selected Essays*. 1930-1977. Jack Zipes and Frank Mecklenberg, trans. Cambridge: MIT Press, 1989.

Bogus, Carl T. Cited in Carol Anderson, "Self-Defense," *The 1619 Project: a New Origin Story*, Created by Nikole Hannah-Jones and *The New York Times Magazine*, New York: The New York Times Company/One World, 2021: 257.

Boulton, Rebecca. Contributing to *I Thought I Heard You Speak: Women and Factory Records*. Pam Golden, compiler, editor, and interviewer. London: White Rabbit, 2023.

Bracewell, Michael. "Licht und Blindheit." Glenn Brown, Michael Bracewell, and Lavinia Greenlaw. *Joy Division*. London: Enitharmon Editions, 2017, 21-23.

British Film Institute (BFI). "*The Alcohol Years:* Carol Morley's exploration of Manchester in the early 1980s, and the five years of her life she lost to alcoholism." https://player.bfi.org.uk/rentals/film/watch-the-alcohol-years-2000-online Accessed 29 March 2024.

Brown, Glenn, Michael Bracewell, and Lavinia Greenlaw. *Joy Division*. London: Enitharmon Editions, 2017.

Brown, Nicole. "Disclosure in academia: A sensitive issue." *Ableism in Academia: Theorising experiences of disabilities and chronic illnesses in higher education*. Nicole Brown and Jennifer Leigh, eds. London: University College of London Press, 2020: 51-73.

Brown, Nicole and Jennifer Leigh, eds. *Ableism in Academia: Theorising experiences of disabilities and chronic illnesses in higher education*. London: University College of London Press, 2020.

_____. "Introduction." *Ableism in Academia: Theorising experiences of disabilities and chronic illnesses in higher education*. Nicole Brown and Jennifer Leigh, eds. London: University College of London Press, 2020: 1-10.

Butler, Judith. *Bodies That Matter: On the Discursive Limits of 'Sex'*. New York: Routledge, 1993.

_____. "Critically Queer." *GLQ: A Journal of Lesbian and Gay Studies*. Vol. 1 No. 1 (1993): 17-32.

_____. *Gender Trouble: Feminism and the Subversion of Identity*. New York: Routledge, 1990.

Bytheway, Bev. Contributing to *I Thought I Heard You Speak: Women and Factory Records*. Pam Golden, compiler, editor, and interviewer. London: White Rabbit, 2023.

Cameron, David. Cited in Robert McRuer, *Crip Times: Disability, Globalization, and Resistance*, New York: New York University Press, 2018: 67.

Campbell, Fiona Kumari. *Contours of Ableism: The Production of Disability and Abledness*. Basingstoke: Palgrave Macmillan, 2009.

_____. "The violence of technicism: Ableism as humiliation and degrading treatment." *Ableism in Academia: Theorising experiences of disabilities and chronic illnesses in higher education*. Nicole Brown and Jennifer Leigh, eds. London: University College of London Press, 2020, 202-224.

Carroll, Cath. Contributing to *I Thought I Heard You Speak: Women and Factory Records*. Pam Golden, compiler, editor, and interviewer. London: White Rabbit, 2023.

Cassian, John. Cited in Ann Cvetkovich, *Depression: a Public Feeling*, Duke University Press, 2012: 85-86, 88.

Chapman, Bridget. Contributing to *I Thought I Heard You Speak: Women and Factory Records*. Pam Golden, compiler, editor, and interviewer. London: White Rabbit, 2023.

Clark, Heather. Cited in Margaret Price, *Mad at School: Rhetorics of Mental Disability and Academic Life*, Ann Arbor: University of Michigan Press, 2011: 132.

Coaston, Jane. "Try to Resist the Call of the Doomers." *New York Times*. 23 July 2022. https://www.nytimes.com/2022/07/23/opinion/climate-doomers-possibility.html Accessed 29 March 2024.

Coates, Ta-Nehisi. Cited in Nikole Hannah-Jones, "Justice," *The 1619 Project: a New Origin Story*, Created by Nikole Hannah-Jones and *The New York Times Magazine*, New York: The New York Times Company/One World, 2021: 458.

Coffin, Levi. Cited in Avery F. Gordon, *Ghostly Matters: Haunting and the Sociological Imagination*, Minneapolis: University of Minnesota Press, 2008: 151-153.

Control. Fictional feature film. Matt Greenhalgh, writer, and Anton Corbijn, director. Starring Samantha Morton, Sam Riley, and Alexandra Maria Lara. 2007.

Copeland, Anne-Marie. Contributing to *I Thought I Heard You Speak: Women and Factory Records*. Pam Golden, compiler, editor, and interviewer. London: White Rabbit, 2023.

Cox, Arnie. *Music & Embodied Cognition: Listening, Moving, Feeling, & Thinking*. Bloomington: Indiana University Press, 2017.

Crosthwaite, Paul. "Trauma and Degeneration: Joy Division and Pop Culture's Imaginative Historicism." *LitPop: Writing and Popular Music*. P. Carroll and A. Hansen, eds. New York: Ashgate, 2014: 125-140.

Crow, Liz. *Figures*. Mass-sculptural public performance piece. London, 2015.

Cumberlidge, Clare. Contributing to *I Thought I Heard You Speak: Women and Factory Records*. Pam Golden, compiler, editor, and interviewer. London: White Rabbit, 2023.

The Cure. *Disintegration*. Music LP, 1989.

_____. "Faith." Recorded Musical Song, 1981.

Curtis, Ian. *So This is Permanence: Joy Division Lyrics and Notebooks*. Deborah Curtis and Jon Savage, eds. London: Faber and Faber, 2014.

Cvetkovich, Ann. *Depression: a Public Feeling*. Durham: Duke University Press, 2012.

Davies, James. *Sedated: How Modern Capitalism Created Our Mental Health Crisis*. London: Atlantic, 2021.

Davis, Mike. Cited in Lyman Tower Sargent, "Utopia Matters! The Importance of Utopianism and Utopian Scholarship," *Utopian Studies*, Vol. 32, No. 3 (2021): 464.

_____. *City of Quartz: Excavating the Future in Los Angeles*. London: Verso, 1990.

_____. *Prisoners of the American Dream: Politics and Economy in the History of the US Working Class*. London: Verso, 1986.

Davis, Mike with Sam Dean. "Mike Davis is still a damn good storyteller." *Los Angeles Times*. 25 July 2022. https://www.latimes.com/lifestyle/image/story/2022-07-25/mike-davis-reflects-on-life-activism-climate-change-bernie-sanders-aoc-los-angeles-politics Accessed 29 March 2024

Deren, Maya, writer, and Maya Deren and Alexandr Hackenschmied, directors. *Meshes in the Afternoon*. Experimental film. 1943.

Derrida, Jacques. *Specters of Marx: the State of Debt, the Work of Mourning and the New International*. 1993. Peggy Kamuf, trans. New York: Routledge, 1994.

Desmond, Matthew. "Capitalism." *The 1619 Project: a New Origin Story*. Created by Nikole Hannah-Jones and *The New York Times Magazine*. New York: The New York Times Company/One World, 2021: 165-185.

Diagnostic and Statistical Manual of Mental Disorders. 1952, 1968, 1980, 1987, 1994, 2000. Washington, D.C.: American Psychiatric Association, 2013.

DJ Paulette. Contributing to *I Thought I Heard You Speak: Women and Factory Records*. Pam Golden, compiler, editor, and interviewer. London: White Rabbit, 2023.

Drewery, Corrine. Contributing to *I Thought I Heard You Speak: Women and Factory Records*. Pam Golden, compiler, editor, and interviewer. London: White Rabbit, 2023.

Du Bois, W.E.B. *Black Reconstruction in America: An Essay Toward a History of the Part Which Black Folk Played in the Attempt to Reconstruct Democracy in America, 1860–1880*. 1935. Oxford: Oxford University Press, 2007.

_____. *The Souls of Black Folk*. New York: A.C. McClurg & Co., 1904.

Duggan, Lisa. Cited in Robert McRuer, *Crip Times: Disability, Globalization, and Resistance*, New York: New York University Press, 2018: 38-39.

Edgar, Robert, Fraser Mann, and Helen Pleasance, eds. *Music, Memory and Memoir*. New York: Bloomsbury, 2019.

Edge of Seventeen. Fictional feature film. Todd Stephens and David Moreton, writers, and David Moreton, director. Starring Chris Stafford, Tina Holmes, Andersen Gabrych, Stephanie McVay, and Lea DeLaria. 1998.

Einhorn, Robin. Cited by Matthew Desmond, "Capitalism," *The 1619 Project: a New Origin Story*, Created by Nikole Hannah-Jones and *The New York Times Magazine*, New York: The New York Times Company/One World, 2021: 170-171.

Elferen, Isabella Van. Cited in Catherine Langhorst, "A Northern 'Ode on Melancholy': The Music of Joy Division," *Rock and Romanticism: Post-Punk, Goth, and Metal as Dark Romanticisms*, edited by James Rovira, Cham, Switzerland: Palgrave MacMillan, 2018: 91.

Eng, David and Shin Hee Han. Cited in Ann Cvetkovich, *Depression: a Public Feeling*, Duke University Press, 2012: 117.

Erevelles, Nirmala. Cited in Robert McRuer, *Crip Times: Disability, Globalization, and Resistance*, New York: New York University Press, 2018: 98.

Fernbach, David. *The Spiral Path: a Gay Contribution to Human Survival*. London: Gay Men's Press, 1981.

Finesilver, Carla, Jennifer Leigh, and Nicole Brown. "Invisible disability, unacknowledged diversity." *Ableism in Academia: Theorising experiences of disabilities and chronic illnesses in higher education*. Nicole Brown and Jennifer Leigh, eds. London: University College of London Press, 2020: 143-160.

Fisher, Mark. *Ghosts of My Life: Writings on Depression, Hauntology and Lost Futures*. Winchester: Zero Books, 2015.

_____. "No Longer the Pleasures: Joy Division." 2005. *Ghosts of My Life: Writings on Depression, Hauntology and Lost Futures*. Winchester: Zero Books, 2015: 50-63.

Floyd, Kevin. Cited in Robert McRuer, *Crip Times: Disability, Globalization, and Resistance*, New York: New York University Press, 2018: 75, 77.

Foucault, Michel. *Discipline and Punish*. 1975. Alan Sheridan, trans. New York: Pantheon, 1977.

Freud, Sigmund. *Beyond the Pleasure Principle*. 1920. C.M.J. Hubback, trans. New York: Norton, 1990.

_____. *The Uncanny*. 1919. David McClintock, trans. New York: Penguin, 2003.

Fusso, Susanne. "Introduction." Gogol, Nikolai. *Dead Souls*. 1842. Bernard Guilbert Guerney, trans. Revised, edited, and introduced by Susanne Fusso. New Haven: Yale University Press, 1996: ix-xv.

Garland-Thomson, Rosemarie. Cited in Robert McRuer, *Crip Theory: Cultural Signs of Queerness and Disability*, New York: New York University Press, 2006: 198.

Geoghehan, Vincent. Cited in Tom Moylan, "To Stand with Dreamers: On the Use Value of Utopia," *The Irish Review* (Cork), No. 34 (Spring, 2006): 7. https://www.jstor.org/stable/29736293 Accessed 30 March 2024.

Geronimus, Arline T. Cited in Linda Villarosa, "Medicine," *The 1619 Project: a New Origin Story*, Created by Nikole Hannah-Jones and *The New York Times Magazine*, New York: The New York Times Company/One World, 2021: 317.

Get Real. Fictional feature film. Patrick Wilde, writer, and Simon Shore, director. Starring Ben Silverstone, Brad Gorton, and Charlotte Brittain. 1998.

Gibby, Michael. Cited in Catherine Langhorst, "A Northern 'Ode on Melancholy': The Music of Joy Division," *Rock and Romanticism: Post-Punk, Goth, and Metal as Dark Romanticisms*, James Rovira, ed., Cham, Switzerland: Palgrave MacMillan, 2018: 96.

The Gifford Center and The Southern Poverty Law Center. "'Stand Your Ground' Kills: How These NRA-Backed Laws Promote Racial Violence," July 2020 Study Report. Cited in Carol Anderson, "Self-Defense," *The 1619 Project: a New Origin Story*, Created by Nikole Hannah-Jones and *The New York Times Magazine*, New York: The New York Times Company/One World, 2021: 266.

Gilbert, Gillian. Contributing to *I Thought I Heard You Speak: Women and Factory Records*. Pam Golden, compiler, editor, and interviewer. London: White Rabbit, 2023.

Gilbert, Lesley. Contributing to *I Thought I Heard You Speak: Women and Factory Records*. Pam Golden, compiler, editor, and interviewer. London: White Rabbit, 2023.

Gilmore, Ruth Wilson. Cited in Avery F. Gordon with Brenna Bhandar and Rafeef Ziadah, "Revolutionary Feminisms: Avery F. Gordon," *Verso Books*, 2 September 2020. https://www.versobooks.com/blogs/news/4842-revolutionary-feminisms-avery-f-gordon Accessed 29 March 2024.

Goddard, Michael. "Missions of Dead Souls: a Hauntology of the Industrial, Modernism and Esotericism in the Music of Joy Division." *Heart & Soul: Critical Writings on Joy Division*. Martin J. Power, Eoin Devereux, and Aileen Dillane, eds. London: Rowan & Littlefield, 2018, 3-16.

Gogol, Nikolai. *Dead Souls*. 1842. Bernard Guilbert Guerney, trans. Revised, edited, and introduced by Susanne Fusso. New Haven: Yale University Press, 1996.

Golden, Pam, compiler, editor, and interviewer. *I Thought I Heard You Speak: Women and Factory Records*. London: White Rabbit, 2023.

Goodley, Dan. Cited in Nicole Brown and Jennifer Leigh, eds., *Ableism in Academia: Theorising experiences of disabilities and chronic illnesses in higher education*, London: University College of London Press, 2020: 116, 125, 146.

Goodwin, Rebecca. Contributing to *I Thought I Heard You Speak: Women and Factory Records*. Pam Golden, compiler, editor, and interviewer. London: White Rabbit, 2023.

Gordon, Avery F. 1997. *Ghostly Matters: Haunting and the Sociological Imagination*. Minneapolis: University of Minnesota Press, 2008.

_____, compiler and editor/keeper. *The Hawthorn Archive: Letters From The Utopian Margins*. New York: Fordham University Press, 2017.

_____. "Introduction to the New Edition." *Ghostly Matters: Haunting and the Sociological Imagination*. Minneapolis: University of Minnesota Press, 2008: xv-xx.

Gordon, Avery F. with Brenna Bhandar and Rafeef Ziadah, "Revolutionary Feminisms: Avery F. Gordon." *Verso Books*. 2 September 2020. https://www.versobooks.com/blogs/news/4842-revolutionary-feminisms-avery-f-gordon Accessed 29 March 2024.

Griffiths, Elisabeth. "'But you don't look disabled': Non-visible disabilities, disclosure and being an 'insider' in disability research and 'other' in the disability movement and academia." *Ableism in Academia: Theorising experiences of disabilities and chronic illnesses in higher education*. Nicole Brown and Jennifer Leigh, eds. London: University College of London Press, 2020: 124-142.

Grinker, Roy Richard. *Nobody's Normal: How Culture Created the Stigma of Mental Illness*. New York: Norton, 2021.

Gun Violence Archive. https://www.gunviolencearchive.org Accessed 29 March 2024.

Guskin, Emily, Scott Clement, and Joe Helm, "Americans Show Spotty Knowledge About the History of Slavery but Acknowledge Its Enduring Effects." 2019 *Washington Post* poll results. Cited in Nikole Hannah-Jones, "Preface: Origins," *The 1619 Project: a New Origin Story*, Created by Nikole Hannah-Jones and *The New York Times Magazine*, New York: The New York Times Company/One World, 2021: xxi.

Halberstam, Jack. *In a Queer Time and Place: Transgender Bodies, Subcultural Lives*. New York: NYU Press, 2005.

Hall, Stella. Contributing to *I Thought I Heard You Speak: Women and Factory Records*. Pam Golden, compiler, editor, and interviewer. London: White Rabbit, 2023.

Hall, Stuart. Cited in Robert McRuer, *Crip Times: Disability, Globalization, and Resistance*, New York: New York University Press, 2018: 170.

Hamilton, Scott. "The Only Disability in Life is a Bad Attitude." 2012 London Olympics and Paralympics Games Promotional Campaign. Cited in Robert McRuer, *Crip Times: Disability, Globalization, and Resistance*, New York: New York University Press, 2018: 60.

Hannah-Jones, Nikole. "Democracy." *The 1619 Project: a New Origin Story*. Created by Nikole Hannah-Jones and *The New York Times Magazine*. New York: The New York Times Company/One World, 2021: 7-36.

_____. "Justice." *The 1619 Project: a New Origin Story*. Created by Nikole Hannah-Jones and *The New York Times Magazine*. New York: The New York Times Company/One World, 2021: 451-476.

_____. "Preface: Origins." *The 1619 Project: a New Origin Story*. Created by Nikole Hannah-Jones and *The New York Times Magazine*. New York: The New York Times Company/One World, 2021: xvii-xxxiii.

Haraway, Donna J. Cited in Robert McRuer, *Crip Theory: Cultural Signs of Queerness and Disability*, New York: New York University Press, 2006: 159.

Hardt, Michael and Antonio Negri. Cited by Fiona Kumari Campbell, "The violence of technicism: Ableism as humiliation and degrading treatment," *Ableism in Academia: Theorising experiences of disabilities and chronic illnesses in higher education*, Nicole Brown and Jennifer Leigh, eds., London: University College of London Press, 2020: 208.

Harper, Phil. Cited in Ann Cvetkovich, *Depression: a Public Feeling*, Duke University Press, 2012: 122.

Harvey, David. Cited in Robert McRuer, *Crip Times: Disability, Globalization, and Resistance*, New York: New York University Press, 2018: 15-16.

Heartstopper. TV series. Season One. Alice Osman, Creator. Starring Kit Connor, Joe Locke, William Gao, Yasmin Finney, Corinna Brown, Kizzy Edgell, Tobie Donovan, Jenny Walser, Sebastian Croft, and Olivia Colman. 2022.

Hebdige, Dick. Cited in Robert McRuer, *Crip Theory: Cultural Signs of Queerness and Disability*, New York: New York University Press, 2006: 242.

Hegel, Georg Wilhelm Friedrich. 1821. *Philosophy of Right*. T.M. Knox, trans. Oxford: The Clarendon Press, 1952.

Henry, Penny. Contributing to *I Thought I Heard You Speak: Women and Factory Records*. Pam Golden, compiler, editor, and interviewer. London: White Rabbit, 2023.

Hewitt, Ben. "Joy Division: 10 of the Best." *The Guardian*. 15 July 2015. https://www.theguardian.com/music/2015/jul/15/joy-division-10-of-the-best Accessed 29 March 2024.

Hickner-Johnson, Corey. Review, Ann Cvetkovich, *Depression: A Public Feeling*. *Journal of Literary and Cultural Disabilities Studies*. Vol. 10, No. 3 (2010): 370-374.

Hillman, James. Cited in Ann Cvetkovich, *Depression: a Public Feeling*, Duke University Press, 2012: 146.

Hinton, Elizabeth. *America on Fire: The Untold History of Police Violence and Black Rebellion Since the 1960s*. New York: Norton, 2021.

Hirst, Richard V., ed. *We Were Strangers: Stories Inspired by* <u>*Unknown Pleasures*</u>. Manchester: Cōnfingō, 2019.

Hook, Peter. Cited in York, Alan, "'Atmosphere': The Story Behind Joy Division's Spine-Tingling Classic," *Dig!*, 18 March 2021. https://www.thisisdig.com/feature/atmosphere-joy-division-song/ Accessed 29 March 2024.

_____. Interview with Jonathan Wright. "40 Years Later: *Closer* & The Last Days Of Joy Division." *The Quietus*. 13 July 2020. https://thequietus.com/articles/28578-joy-division-closer-review-40th-anniversary Accessed 29 March 2024.

_____. *Unknown Pleasures: Inside Joy Division*. London: Simon & Schuster, 2012.

Houghton, Jayne. Contributing to *I Thought I Heard You Speak: Women and Factory Records*. Pam Golden, compiler, editor, and interviewer. London: White Rabbit, 2023.

Hunter, Logan James. *Dark German Romanticism and the Postpunk Ethos of Joy Division, The Cure and Smashing Pumpkins*. Master's thesis. University of South Carolina. Fall 2020. Retrieved from https://scholarcommons.sc.edu/etd/6182 Accessed 29 March 2024.

Ingram, Kelvin. "The Meaning Behind The Song: 'Decades' by Joy Division." *Old Time Music*. 29 November 2023. https://oldtimemusic.com/the-meaning-behind-the-song-decades-by-joy-division/ Accessed 29 March 2024.

Interlandi, Jeneen. "Healthcare." *The 1619 Project: a New Origin Story*. Created by Nikole Hannah-Jones and *The New York Times Magazine*. New York: The New York Times Company/One World, 2021: 387-394.

Jailler, Margaret. Contributing to *I Thought I Heard You Speak: Women and Factory Records*. Pam Golden, compiler, editor, and interviewer. London: White Rabbit, 2023.

Jameson, Fredric. Cited in Tom Moylan, "To Stand with Dreamers: On the Use Value of Utopia," *The Irish Review* (Cork), No. 34 (Spring, 2006): 4-5, 9. https://www.jstor.org/stable/29736293 Accessed 30 March 2024.

Jindal-Snape, Divya. "Fibromyalgia and me." *Ableism in Academia: Theorising experiences of disabilities and chronic illnesses in higher education*. Nicole Brown and Jennifer Leigh, eds. London: University College of London Press, 2020: 74-75.

Jones-Rogers, Stephanie. Cited by Matthew Desmond, "Capitalism," *The 1619 Project: a New Origin Story*, Created by Nikole Hannah-Jones and *The New York Times Magazine*, New York: The New York Times Company/One World, 2021: 172.

Joy Division. +- *singles 1979-80*. Warner 10-CD Collection. 2010-2011.

_____. "Atmosphere." +- *singles 1979-80*. Warner 10-CD Collection. 2010-2011.

_____. "Atmosphere." Recorded Musical Song, 1980.

_____. "Atmosphere." Digital Remastered single, Warner. 2020.

_____. "Atmosphere." Recorded Musical Song, *Licht und Blindheit* ep, Sordide Sentimental. 1980.

_____. *Closer*. 40th Anniversary Digitally Remastered Version, Rhino/Warner. 2020.

_____. *Closer*. London Records Remastered Collectors 2-CD Edition. 2007.

_____. *Closer*. Music LP, Factory. 1980.

_____. "Colony." Recorded Musical Song, *Closer*, Factory. 1980.

_____. "Decades." *Closer*. 40th Anniversary Digitally Remastered Version. Rhino/Warner. 2020.

_____. "Decades." *Closer*. London Records Remastered Collectors 2-CD Edition. 2007.

_____. "Decades." Recorded Musical Song, *Closer*, Factory. 1980.

_____. "Dead Souls." *+- singles 1979-80*. Warner 10-CD Collection. 2010-2011.

_____. "Dead Souls." Recorded Musical Song, *Licht und Blindheit* ep, Sordide Sentimental. 1980.

_____. "Dead Souls." *Still*. London Records Remastered Collectors 2-CD Edition. 2007.

_____. *Heart and Soul*. London Records 4-CD box set. 2001.

_____. "Heart and Soul." Recorded Musical Song, *Closer*, Factory. 1980.

_____. *Licht und Blindheit* ep. Sordide Sentimental. 1980.

_____. "She's Lost Control." Recorded Musical Song, *Unknown Pleasures*, Factory. 1979.

_____. "She's Lost Control." *Unknown Pleasures*. London Records Remastered Collectors 2-CD Edition. 2007.

_____. "She's Lost Control: Extended Version." *Heart and Soul*. London Records 4-CD box set. 2001.

_____. *Still*. London Records Remastered Collectors 2-CD Edition. 2007.

_____. *Substance*. Music LP, Factory. 1988.

_____. *Substance*. Remastered CD Edition, Warner. 2015.

_____. *Unknown Pleasures*. London Records Remastered Collectors 2-CD Edition. 2007.

_____. *Unknown Pleasures*. Music LP, Factory. 1979.

Joy Division. Documentary Film. Jon Savage, writer, and Grant Gee, director. 2007.

Joydivisionofficial.com. *Joy Division Unknown Pleasures Re-Imagined Series*. Https://www.joydivisionofficial.com/reimagined/ Accessed 30 March 2024.

Joy Division, Jean Pierre-Turmel, Jean-François Jamoul, and Anton Corbijn. *Licht und Blindheit*. Sordide Sentimental, 1980. Ep package with essay and visual art.

Judas and the Black Messiah. Fictional feature film. Will Berson and Shaka King, writers, and Shaka King, director. Starring Daniel Kaluuya, LaKeith Stanfield, Jesse Plemons, Dominique Fishback, Ashton Sanders, and Martin Sheen. 2021.

Kefalas, Nicki. Contributing to *I Thought I Heard You Speak: Women and Factory Records*. Pam Golden, compiler, editor, and interviewer. London: White Rabbit, 2023.

Kendi, Ibram X. "Progress." *The 1619 Project: a New Origin Story*. Created by Nikole Hannah-Jones and *The New York Times Magazine*. New York: The New York Times Company/One World, 2021: 421-440.

King, Martin Luther Jr. Cited in Ibram X. Kendi, "Progress," *The 1619 Project: a New Origin Story*, Created by Nikole Hannah-Jones and *The New York Times Magazine*, New York: The New York Times Company/One World, 2021: 424.

_____. "Letter from Birmingham Jail." 16 April 1963.

_____. "Speech: 'I Have a Dream'." 28 August 1963. Washington, D.C.

_____. "Speech: 'The Three Evils of Society'." 10 May 1967. Hungry Club Forum, Atlanta, Georgia.

The King's Speech. Fictional feature film. David Seidler, writer, and Tom Hooper, director. Starring Colin Firth, Geoffrey Rush, Helena Bonham Carter, Guy Pearce, Timothy Spall, Derek Jacobi, Jennifer Ehle, and Michael Gambon. 2010.

Kittay, Eva Feder. Cited in Robert McRuer, *Crip Theory: Cultural Signs of Queerness and Disability*, New York: New York University Press, 2006: 101.

Klein, Naomi. Cited in Robert McRuer, *Crip Times: Disability, Globalization, and Resistance*, New York: New York University Press, 2018: 75-76.

Kruse, Kevin M. "Traffic." *The 1619 Project: a New Origin Story*. Created by Nikole Hannah-Jones and *The New York Times Magazine*. New York: The New York Times Company/One World, 2021: 405-410.

Kuhn, Moritz, Moritz Shularick, and Ulricke Steins, "Income and Wealth Inequality in America." *Journal of Political Economy* study (2020). Cited in "Justice," *The 1619 Project: a New Origin Story*, Created by Nikole Hannah-Jones and *The New York Times Magazine*, New York: The New York Times Company/One World, 2021: 470.

Lacan, Jacques. *Écrits*. 1966. Bruce Fink, Héloïse Fink, and Russell Grigg, trans. New York: Norton, 2007.

Lakhaney, Soraya. Contributing to *I Thought I Heard You Speak: Women and Factory Records*. Pam Golden, compiler, editor, and interviewer. London: White Rabbit, 2023.

Lambert, Zoe. "She's Lost Control." *We Were Strangers: Stories Inspired by Unknown Pleasures*. Richard V. Hirst, ed. Manchester: Cōnfingō, 2019: 91-106.

Langhorst, Catherine. "A Northern 'Ode on Melancholy': The Music of Joy Division." *Rock and Romanticism: Post-Punk, Goth, and Metal as Dark Romanticisms*, James Rovira, ed., Cham, Switzerland: Palgrave MacMillan, 2018: 83-100.

Lee, Trymaine. "Inheritance." *The 1619 Project: a New Origin Story*. Created by Nikole Hannah-Jones and *The New York Times Magazine*. New York: The New York Times Company/One World, 2021: 293-305.

Leigh, Jennifer and Nicole Brown. "Internalised ableism: Of the political and the personal." *Ableism in Academia: Theorising experiences of disabilities and chronic illnesses in higher education*. Nicole Brown and Jennifer Leigh, eds. London: University College of London Press, 2020: 164-181.

Lenin, Vladimir Ilyich. Cited in Robert McRuer, *Crip Times: Disability, Globalization, and Resistance*, New York: New York University Press, 2018: 129.

Levitas, Ruth. Cited in Tom Moylan, "To Stand with Dreamers: On the Use Value of Utopia." *The Irish Review* (Cork), No. 34 (Spring, 2006): 4. http://www.jstor.com/stable/29736293 Accessed 30 March 2024.

Lincoln, U.S. President Abraham. "Emancipation Proclamation." 1 January 1963.

London, Amanda. "Joy Division's 'Dead Souls' Lyrics Meaning." *Song Meanings and Facts (SMF)*. 29 April 2022. https://www.songmeaningsandfacts.com/joy-divisions-dead-souls-lyrics-meaning/ Accessed 29 March 2024.

Lorde, Audre. *A Burst of Light and Other Essays*. Ithaca: Firebrand Books, 1988.

_____. *Sister Outsider: Essays and Speeches*. Berkeley: Crossing Press, 1984.

Maloy, Liam. "'She expressed herself in many different ways': Hypothetical substitutions in Joy Division's 'She's Lost Control'." Essay Originally Submitted for MA in Popular

Music Studies at Liverpool University, 2007.
https://www.academia.edu/39583443/_She_expressed_herself_in_many_different_wa
ys_Hypothetical_substitutions_in_Joy_Division_s_She_s_Lost_Control_ Accessed 30
March 2024.

Mathan, Chris. Contributing to *I Thought I Heard You Speak: Women and Factory Records*.
Pam Golden, compiler, editor, and interviewer. London: White Rabbit, 2023.

Matthews, Ang. Contributing to *I Thought I Heard You Speak: Women and Factory Records*.
Pam Golden, compiler, editor, and interviewer. London: White Rabbit, 2023.

McDermott, Kath. Contributing to *I Thought I Heard You Speak: Women and Factory
Records*. Pam Golden, compiler, editor, and interviewer. London: White Rabbit, 2023.

McDonagh, Martine. Contributing to *I Thought I Heard You Speak: Women and Factory
Records*. Pam Golden, compiler, editor, and interviewer. London: White Rabbit, 2023.

McIntosh, Walters. Cited by Nikole Hannah-Jones, *The 1619 Project: a New Origin Story*,
Created by Nicole Hannah-Jones and *The New York Times Magazine*, New York: The
New York Times Company/One World, 2021: 30.

McRuer, Robert. "Compulsory Able-Bodiedness." Weiss, Gail, Ann V. Murphy, and Gayle
Salamon, eds. *50 Concepts for a Critical Phenomenology*. Evanston: Northwestern
University Press, 2020: 61-67.

_____. *Crip Theory: Cultural Signs of Queerness and Disability*. New York: New York
University Press, 2006.

_____. *Crip Times: Disability, Globalization, and Resistance*. New York: New York
University Press, 2018.

Middles, Mick and Lindsay Reade. *Torn Apart: The Life of Ian Curtis*. London: Omnibus, 2009.

Miller, Michael, Gerard Middenhorf, and Steven D. Wood, "Food Availability in the
Heartland: Exploring the Effects of Neighborhood Racial Segregation, Poverty, and
Urbanicity and Its Impact on Food Source Availability in the United States," Kansas
State University researchers study. Cited in Kahil Gibran Muhammad, "Sugar," *The
1619 Project: a New Origin Story*. Created by Nikole Hannah-Jones and *The New
York Times Magazine*, New York: The New York Times Company/One World, 2021:
86.

Minich, Julie Avril. Cited in Robert McRuer, *Crip Times: Disability, Globalization, and
Resistance*, New York: New York University Press, 2018: 159.

Monnens, Lieve. Contributing to *I Thought I Heard You Speak: Women and Factory Records*.
Pam Golden, compiler, editor, and interviewer. London: White Rabbit, 2023.

Morley, Carol. Contributing to *I Thought I Heard You Speak: Women and Factory Records*.
Pam Golden, compiler, editor, and interviewer. London: White Rabbit, 2023.

Morley, Paul. *Joy Division Piece by Piece: Writing About Joy Division 1977-2007*. London:
Plexus, 2008.

Morris, Stephen. Cited (By Logan James Hunter) in Simon Reynolds, *Rip It Up and Start
Again: Post-Punk 1978-1984*, New York: Penguin, 1985: 15.

_____. Interview with Anna Conrad. "How Joy Division made *Closer*: 'We were really
tight as a band; there was a lot of telepathy going on'." *GQ* Magazine UK. 14 July
2020. Https://www.gq-magazine.co.uk/culture/article/joy-division-closer-album
Accessed 30 March 2024.

_____. *Record Play Pause: Confessions of a Post-Punk Percussionist Volume 1*. London: Constable, 2019.

Morris, Wesley. "Music." *The 1619 Project: a New Origin Story*. Created by Nikole Hannah-Jones and *The New York Times Magazine*. New York: The New York Times Company/One World, 2021: 359-379.

Morrison, Toni. *Beloved*. New York: Knopf, 1987.

Morse, Chuck. Cited in Avery F. Gordon with Brenna Bhandar and Rafeef Ziadah, "Revolutionary Feminisms: Avery F. Gordon," *Verso Books*, 2 September 2020. https://www.versobooks.com/blogs/news/4842-revolutionary-feminisms-avery-f-gordon Accessed 29 March 2024.

Moylan, Tom. "To Stand with Dreamers: On the Use Value of Utopia." *The Irish Review* (Cork), No. 34 (Spring, 2006), 1-19. http://www.jstor.com/stable/29736293 Accessed 30 March 2024.

Muhammad, Khalil Gibran. "Sugar." *The 1619 Project: a New Origin Story*. Created by Nikole Hannah-Jones and *The New York Times Magazine*. New York: The New York Times Company/One World, 2021: 71-87.

Muñoz, José Estaban. *Cruising Utopia: The Then and There of Queer Futurity*. New York: NYU Press, 2009.

The Myers-Briggs Company. "Myers-Briggs Type Indicator." https://www.themyersbriggs.com/en-US/Products-and-Services/Myers-Briggs Accessed 29 March 2024.

Naiman, Tiffany. "In a Lonely Place: Illness and the Temporal Exile of Ian Curtis." *Heart & Soul: Critical Writings on Joy Division*. Martin J. Power, Eoin Devereux, and Aileen Dillane, eds. London: Rowan & Littlefield, 2018: 83-97.

Naylor, Liz. Contributing to *I Thought I Heard You Speak: Women and Factory Records*. Pam Golden, compiler, editor, and interviewer. London: White Rabbit, 2023.

Nicholson, Lorraine, director. "She's Lost Control (Official Reimagined Video)." *Joy Division, Unknown Pleasures: Reimagined*. 40th Anniversary Series of Short Films. https://www.youtube.com/watch?v=s4prQ11orEM Accessed 29 March 2024.

Nowlan, Bob. "It Seems to Me: CRT should be fully understood." *Eau Claire Leader-Telegram*. 7 April 2022.

_____. "The Politics of Love in Three Recent U.S. and U.K. Films of Young Gay Romance: A Symptomatic Reading of *Beautiful Thing*, *Get Real*, and *Edge of Seventeen*." *Journal of Homosexuality*. Vol. 50, No. 4 (2006): 141-184.

_____. "Queer Cinema and *Urbania*." *Coming Out to the Mainstream: New Queer Cinema in the 21st Century*. Joanne C. Juett and David M. Jones, eds. Newcastle Upon Tyne: Cambridge Scholars Publishing, 2010, 233-256.

_____. "Retiring after almost 30 years at UWEC." https://www.uwec.edu/news/english/retiring-after-almost-30-years-at-uwec-5647/ Accessed 29 March 2024.

_____. "Statement to the Congregation." Wedding to Andrew Swanson. Unitarian Universalist Congregation of Eau Claire. 17 June 2000.

Nowlan, Robert Andrew. *Cultural Studies, Queer Theory, Marxism*. PhD Dissertation, Syracuse University, 1993.

O'Brien, Sharon. *The Family Silver: A Memoir of Depression and Inheritance.* Chicago: University of Chicago Press, 2004.

Oksanen, Atte. "Hollow Spaces of Psyche: Gothic Trance-Formation from Joy Division to Diary of Dreams." *Nostalgia or Perversion? Gothic Rewriting from the 18th Century until the Present Day.* Isabella Van Elferen, ed. Cambridge: Cambridge Scholars Publishing, 2007: 124-136.

Oxford English Dictionary Online. https://www.oed.com Accessed 29 March 2024.

Patchett, Alyson. Contributing to *I Thought I Heard You Speak: Women and Factory Records.* Pam Golden, compiler, editor, and interviewer. London: White Rabbit, 2023.

Payne, Michael. Cited in Margaret Price, *Mad at School: Rhetorics of Mental Disability and Academic Life*, Ann Arbor: University of Michigan Press, 2011: 50.

Pêcheux, Michel. Cited in Robert McRuer, *Crip Times: Disability, Globalization, and Resistance*, New York: New York University Press, 2018: 244.

Percheski, Christine and Christina Gibson-Davis, "A Penny on the Dollar: Racial Inequalities in Among Wealth Among Families with Children," Duke University and Northwestern University researchers study (2020). Cited in Nikole Hannah-Jones, "Justice," *The 1619 Project: a New Origin Story*, Created by Nikole Hannah-Jones and *The New York Times Magazine*, New York: The New York Times Company/One World, 2021: 458.

The Perks of Being a Wallflower. Fictional feature film. Stephen Chbosky, writer and director. Starring Logan Lerman, Emma Watson, Ezra Miller, Mae Whitman, Kate Walsh, Dylan McDermott, Joan Cusack, and Paul Rudd. 2012.

Peruzzo, Francesa. "I am not disabled: Difference, ethics, critique and refusal of neoliberal academic selves." *Ableism in Academia: Theorising experiences of disabilities and chronic illnesses in higher education.* Nicole Brown and Jennifer Leigh, eds. London: University College of London Press, 2020: 31-50.

Pleasance, Helen. "Paying more close anxious attention to Joy Division." *Music, Memory and Memoir.* Robert Edgar, Fraser Mann, and Helen Pleasance, eds. New York: Bloomsbury, 2019: 25-38.

Power, Martin J., Eoin Devereux, and Aileen Dillane, eds. *Heart & Soul: Critical Writings on Joy Division.* London: Rowan & Littlefield, 2018.

Prendergast, E.R. "In Defense of Wishful Thinking." *Moral Philosophy and Politics* (2022): 1-21. https://doi.org/10.1515/mopp-2021-0041.

Price, Margaret. *Mad at School: Rhetorics of Mental Disability and Academic Life.* Ann Arbor: University of Michigan Press, 2011.

Purnell, James. Cited in Robert McRuer, *Crip Times: Disability, Globalization, and Resistance*, New York: New York University Press, 2018: 193.

Queer Eye for the Straight Guy. TV Series. David Collins and Michael Williams, creators. Starring Ted Allen, Kyan Douglas, Thom Filicia, Carson Kressley, and Jai Rodriguez. 2003-2007.

Quigley, Ann. Contributing to *I Thought I Heard You Speak: Women and Factory Records.* Pam Golden, compiler, editor, and interviewer. London: White Rabbit, 2023.

Radway, Janice. "Foreword." *Ghostly Matters: Haunting and the Sociological Imagination.* Minneapolis: University of Minnesota Press, 2008: vii-xiii.

Reade, Lindsay. Contributing to *I Thought I Heard You Speak: Women and Factory Records*. Pam Golden, compiler, editor, and interviewer. London: White Rabbit, 2023.

Reynolds, Joel Michael. "The Normate." *50 Concepts for a Critical Phenomenology*. Gail Weiss, Ann V. Murphy, and Gayle Salamon, eds. Evanston: Northwestern University Press, 2020: 243-248.

Reynolds, Simon. *Rip It Up and Start Again: Postpunk 1978-1984*. New York: Penguin, 2005.

_____. *Rip It Up and Start Again: Postpunk 1978-1984*. Restored, expanded edition. Faber Greatest Hits. London: Faber and Faber, 2019.

_____. *Totally Wired: Postpunk Interviews and Overviews*. New York: Soft Skull Press, 2010.

Rietveld, Gonnie. Contributing to *I Thought I Heard You Speak: Women and Factory Records*. Pam Golden, compiler, editor, and interviewer. London: White Rabbit, 2023.

Rich, Adrienne. "Compulsory Heterosexuality and Lesbian Existence." *Signs: Journal of Women in Culture and Society*. Vol. 5, No. 4 (1980): 631-660.

Roberts, Dorothy. "Race." *The 1619 Project: a New Origin Story*. Created by Nikole Hannah-Jones and *The New York Times Magazine*. New York: The New York Times Company/One World, 2021: 45-61.

Robinson, Cedric J. *An Anthropology of Marxism*. 2001. Second Edition. Chapel Hill: University of North Carolina Press, 2019.

_____. Cited in Avery F. Gordon, *Ghostly Matters: Haunting and the Sociological Imagination*, Minneapolis: University of Minnesota Press, 2008: 203.

Robson, Adam. "What's That Sound? How Joy Division created the 'hissing' snare drum on 'She's Lost Control'". *Far Out Magazine*. 1 September 2020. https://faroutmagazine.co.uk/joy-division-snare-drum-sound-shes-lost-control/ Accessed 29 March 2024.

Rogers, Joel. Cited by Matthew Desmond, "Capitalism," *The 1619 Project: a New Origin Story*, Created by Nikole Hannah-Jones and *The New York Times Magazine*, New York: The New York Times Company/One World, 2021: 160-161.

Salvage Editorial Board. Cited in Robert McRuer, *Crip Times: Disability, Globalization, and Resistance*, New York: New York University Press, 2018: 144.

Sandahl, Carrie. Cited in Robert McRuer, *Crip Theory: Cultural Signs of Queerness and Disability*, New York: New York University Press, 2006: 139.

Sandel, Michael. *Tyranny of Merit: Can We Find the Common Good?* New York: Picador/Farrar, Straus and Giroux, 2021.

Sargent, Lyman Tower. Cited in Tom Moylan, "To Stand with Dreamers: On the Use Value of Utopia," *The Irish Review* (Cork), No. 34 (Spring, 2006): 4-5, 7.

_____. "Utopia Matters! The Importance of Utopianism and Utopian Scholarship." *Utopian Studies*. Vol. 32, No. 3 (2021): 453-477.

Savage, Jon, compiler, editor, and interviewer. *This Searing Light, The Sun, and Everything Else: Joy Division–The Oral History*. London: Faber and Faber, 2019.

Saville, Peter. Contributing to *Joy Division*, Documentary Film, Jon Savage, writer, and Grant Gee, director, 2007.

_____. Interview in Andy Spinoza, *Manchester Unspun: How a city got high on music*, Manchester: Manchester University Press, 2023: 341.

Sedgwick, Eve Kosofsky. Cited in Robert McRuer, *Crip Theory: Cultural Signs of Queerness and Disability*. New York: New York University Press, 2006: 156-157.

Serlin, David. Cited in Robert McRuer, *Crip Theory: Cultural Signs of Queerness and Disability*, New York: New York University Press, 2006: 114-115.

Seymour, Richard. Cited in Robert McRuer, *Crip Times: Disability, Globalization, and Resistance*, New York: New York University Press, 2018: 14.

Shelton, Yvonne. Contributing to *I Thought I Heard You Speak: Women and Factory Records*. Pam Golden, compiler, editor, and interviewer. London: White Rabbit, 2023.

Siebers, Tobin. Cited in Margaret Price, *Mad at School: Rhetorics of Mental Disability and Academic Life*, Ann Arbor: University of Michigan Press, 2011: 227.

_____. "Foreword." Margaret Price. *Mad at School: Rhetorics of Mental Disability and Academic Life*. Ann Arbor: University of Michigan Press, 2011, xi-xiv.

Smith, Ali. *Girl Meets Boy: The Myth of Iphis*. Edinburgh: Canongate, 2007.

Smith, Jeffery. *Where the Roots Reach for Water: A Personal and Natural History of Melancholia*. New York: North Point Press, 1999.

The Socratic Method. "Meaning of Decades [live At Birmingham University] by Joy Division." Personal Blog. No Date. https://www.socratic-method.com/joy-division/meaning-of-decades-live-at-birmingham-university-by-joy-division Accessed 29 March 2024.

Soghomonian, Talia. "Release The Bats–It's The 20 Greatest Goth Tracks." *NME*. 5 March 2009. https://www.nme.com/blogs/nme-blogs/release-the-bats-its-the-20-greatest-goth-tracks-758985 Accessed 29 March 2024.

Songmeanings.com. "Atmosphere." https://songmeanings.com/songs/view/59696/ Accessed 29 March 2024.

_____. "Dead Souls." https://songmeanings.com/songs/view/50137/ Accessed 29 March 2024.

_____. "Decades." https://songmeanings.com/songs/view/59130/ Accessed 29 March 2024.

Spielrein, Sarina. Cited in Avery F. Gordon, *Ghostly Matters: Haunting and the Sociological Imagination*, Minneapolis: University of Minnesota Press, 2008: 38-42.

Spencer, George. "'Decades' By Joy Division." *Song Meanings and Facts (SMF)*. 9 August 2022. https://www.songmeaningsandfacts.com/decades-by-joy-division/ Accessed 29 March 2024.

Spinoza, Andy. In *City Life*. July 1992. Cited in *Manchester Unspun: How a city got high on music*, Manchester: Manchester University Press, 2023: 142-143.

_____. *Manchester Unspun: How a city got high on music*. Manchester: Manchester University Press, 2023.

Stevenson, Bryan. "Punishment." *The 1619 Project: a New Origin Story*. Created by Nikole Hannah-Jones and *The New York Times Magazine*. New York: The New York Times Company/One World, 2021: 275-283.

Stiker, Henri-Jacques. Cited in Robert McRuer, *Crip Theory: Cultural Signs of Queerness and Disability*, New York: New York University Press, 2006: 111-112.

Stirling, Mitchell. "Here are the young men, the weight on their shoulders: Joy Division - 'Decades' (Closer - 1980)." *The Run Out Grooves*. 24 March 2022.

https://therunoutgrooves.substack.com/p/here-are-the-young-men-the-weight Accessed 29 March 2024.

Sumner, Bernard. *Chapter and Verse: New Order, Joy Division and Me.* London: Bantam, 2014.

Taylor, Ruth. Contributing to *I Thought I Heard You Speak: Women and Factory Records.* Pam Golden, compiler, editor, and interviewer. London: White Rabbit, 2023.

Taylor, Steve. "Channelling the darkness: Group flow and environmental expression in the music of Black Sabbath and Joy Division." *Metal Music Studies.* Vol 7, No. 1 (2021): 85-102. doi: https://doi.org/10.1386/mms_00033_1

Thatcher, Margaret. Cited in Robert McRuer, *Crip Times: Disability, Globalization, and Resistance,* New York: New York University Press, 2018: 176, 179, 186-188.

This is What Disability Looks Like. Counter-Promotional Campaign, 2012 London Olympic and Paralympic Games. Cited in Robert McRuer, *Crip Times: Disability, Globalization, and Resistance,* New York: New York University Press, 2018: 89.

Thomas, Dylan. "Do Not Go Gently into that Good Night." 1947, 1951. *The Poems of Dylan Thomas.* John Goodby, ed. New York: New Directions, 1971.

Trulio, Georgina. Contributing to *I Thought I Heard You Speak: Women and Factory Records.* Pam Golden, compiler, editor, and interviewer. London: White Rabbit, 2023.

Turmel, Jean-Pierre. "Licht und Blindheit." Joy Division, Jean Pierre-Turmel, Jean-François Jamoul, and Anton Corbijn. *Licht und Blindheit.* Sordide Sentimental, 1980. Ep.

Urbania. Fictional feature film. David Reitz and Jon Shear, writers, and Jon Shear, director. Starring Dan Futterman, Paige Turco, Samuel Ball, Josh Hamilton, Matt Keeslar, and Alan Cumming. 2000.

U.S. Commission on Civil Rights, *Examining the Racial Effects of Stand Your Ground Laws,* 2020 Report. Cited in Carol Anderson, "Self-Defense," *The 1619 Project: a New Origin Story,* Created by Nikole Hannah-Jones and *The New York Times Magazine,* New York: The New York Times Company/One World, 2021: 266.

U.S. Congress: Final Report of the Select Committee to Investigate the January 6th Attack on the United States Capitol, December 2022. https://www.govinfo.gov/app/details/GPO-J6-REPORT/context Accessed 29 March 2024.

U.S. Congress: H.R.40–Commission to Study and Develop Reparation Proposals for African Americans Act, Introduced in 2021.

U.S. Constitution Amendment II: A well regulated Militia, being necessary to the security of a free State, the right of the people to keep and bear Arms, shall not be infringed.

U.S. Constitution Article I (Legislative Branch), Section 8 (Enumerated Powers).

U.S. Constitution Article I (Legislative Branch), Section 9 (Powers Denied Congress).

U.S. Constitution Article V (Amending the Constitution).

U.S. Reports: Brown v. Board of Education, 347 U.S. 483 (1954).

U.S. Reports: Dred Scott v. Sandford, 60 U.S. (19 How.) 393 (1856).

U.S. Reports: Dobbs v. Jackson Women's Health Organization U.S. 19-1392 (2022).

U.S. Reports: Planned Parenthood of Southeastern Pa. v. Casey, 505 U.S. 833 (1992).

U.S. Reports: Roe v. Wade, 410 U.S. 113 (1973).

U.S. Reports: Shelby County v. Holder, 133 S. Ct. 2612 (2013).

Valenzuela, Luisa. *Como en la guerra (As in War) [He Who Searches]*. 1977. Helen Layne, trans. Elmwood Park: Dalkey Archive, 1979.

Villarosa, Linda. "Medicine." *The 1619 Project: a New Origin Story*. Created by Nikole Hannah-Jones and *The New York Times Magazine*. New York: The New York Times Company/One World, 2021: 315-323.

Wallace, David Foster. Cited in Ann Cvetkovich, *Depression: a Public Feeling*, Duke University Press, 2012: 207.

Waltz, Mitzi and Martin James. "The (re)Marketing of Disability in Pop: Ian Curtis and Joy Division." *Popular Music*. Popular Music and Disability Issues. Vol. 28 No. 3 (October 2009: 367-380.

Warner, Michael. Cited in Robert McRuer, *Crip Theory: Cultural Signs of Queerness and Disability*, New York: New York University Press, 2006: 30.

Weiss, Gail, Ann V. Murphy, and Gayle Salamon, eds. *50 Concepts for a Critical Phenomenology*. Evanston: Northwestern University Press, 2020.

West, Cornel. Cited in Ann Cvetkovich, *Depression: a Public Feeling*, Duke University Press, 2012: 116.

Widner, Cindy. "Utopia, Every Day." Review of Ann Cvetkovich, *Depression: a Public Feeling*. 12 February 2013. Kirkus Reviews. https://www.kirkusreviews.com/news-and-features/articles/utopia-every-day/ Accessed 29 March 2024.

Wikipedia. "Atmosphere (Joy Division Song)." https://en.wikipedia.org/wiki/Atmosphere_(Joy_Division_song) Accessed 29 March 2024.

Wilkinson, David. *Post-Punk, Politics and Pleasure in Britain*. Palgrave Studies in the Histories of Subcultures and Popular Music. London: Palgrave MacMillan, 2016.

Williams, Patricia. Cited in Avery F. Gordon with Brenna Bhandar and Rafeef Ziadah. "Revolutionary Feminisms: Avery F. Gordon," Verso Books. 2 September 2020. https://www.versobooks.com/blogs/news/4842-revolutionary-feminisms-avery-f-gordon Accessed 29 March 2024.

Williams, Raymond. *Keywords: a Vocabulary of Culture and Society*. 1976. London: Fontana, 1983.

_____. *Marxism and Literature*. Oxford: Oxford University Press, 1977.

Wilson, Tony. Contributing to *Joy Division*, Documentary Film, Jon Savage, writer, and Grant Gee, director, 2007.

World Population Review. Mass Shootings by Country (2024). https://worldpopulationreview.com/country-rankings/mass-shootings-by-country Accessed 29 March 2024.

Wozencraft, Jon. Contributing to *This Searing Light, The Sun, and Everything Else: Joy Division–The Oral History*. Jon Savage, compiler, editor, and interviewer. London: Faber and Faber, 2019.

York, Alan. "'Atmosphere': The Story Behind Joy Division's Spine-Tingling Classic." *Dig!* 18 March 2021. https://www.thisisdig.com/feature/atmosphere-joy-division-song/ Accessed 29 March 2024.

Young, Stella. Cited in Robert McRuer, *Crip Times: Disability, Globalization, and Resistance*, New York: New York University Press, 2018: 66.

Chapter Seven

One

Over the course of the preceding six chapters of this book I have inquired into issues of fundamental and ultimate concern in modern to contemporary critical theory. I have explored issues concerning the meaning, value, and purpose of existence; our responsibility to and for others; human beings as complex, multiple, contradictory, and dynamic; the challenge of intimacy and the power of love; the quest for authenticity and the struggle for integrity; what it means to be included and excluded along with how as well as why this occurs; how social change happens along with what can be the contribution of artistic and cultural work toward this transformation; and the ethical responsibility to continue to confront and find a way to work through myriad metaphorical 'darknesses' in our individual and social lives, despite how tremendously challenging, difficult, and painful this can so often be. I have pursued this inquiry by staging a dialogue between critical theory and popular music, and in particular by demonstrating how it is possible to interpret intelligent, sensitive popular music as engaging the same issues as critical theory and how this music can help us better understand and especially all the more viscerally *feel* how vital, urgent, concrete, and relevant critical theory can be. I have used the music, as art, of Ian Curtis and Joy Division as my principal vehicle in so doing, drawing upon the work I have done in researching, preparing for, and teaching five upper level undergraduate university classes focused on Ian Curtis, Joy Division, and Critical Theory, at the University of Wisconsin-Eau Claire. I have vastly expanded upon the work we did together in those classes, yet students' enthusiasm and accomplishment as part of those classes has inspired me throughout the course of writing this book–as has my passion, now 45 years running, for Ian Curtis and Joy Division, life and work, and, especially, music as art. I have accounted for why Joy Division has been my persistently all-time favorite musical group and why Ian Curtis has been my persistently all-time favorite individual musician. In order to render all the more concrete what that has meant, as well as how to stage a dialogue between critical theory and popular music to generate reflection and insight, I have written this book as a part personal memoir, emphasizing my 38 years-long career as a university teacher, concentrating in critical theory as well as critical studies in popular culture. I have engaged in detailed descriptions, analyses, and interpretations of nineteen songs from Ian Curtis and Joy Division, culminating in each case by drawing extended connections with what listening closely to this music, and carefully reflecting on it, prompts me to think (about) and to feel. I have done so by listening to and reflecting on these songs as I have been writing about them, and by making connections with what has been happening with me, and in the larger world, at the precise time I have been doing this listening and reflecting. As such, this book has often ventured far beyond Ian Curtis and Joy Division, with the latter representing a point of departure, as well as a point of reference and return. My ultimate aim with this book is not, however, to valorize Ian Curtis and Joy Division, but rather to encourage others reading what I have written to stage dialogues between critical theory and instances of popular music *that matter to them* in sparking reflection and insight *useful to and for them.*

In this concluding chapter I revisit my initial introduction of myself, explaining how and why I reintroduce myself differently, as a result of what has changed for me in the course of time that has passed since I began writing this book, including as a result of how writing this book has changed me. I then proceed to draw final connections between the music, as art, of Ian Curtis and Joy Division, and issues of urgent concern. These final connections resonate with the three phrases I select from the lyrics of "Twenty Four Hours" as the title of this book–'Excessive Flashpoints', 'Solitary Demands', and 'Darkest Corners'. I consider matters of insecurity, loneliness, fear, fascism, utopia and hope.

Two

In chapter one I began my introduction of myself by recounting my hesitancy in writing this book as a part memoir. I maintain that hesitancy. I continue to doubt my life is interesting enough to serve as the focus of a memoir that others will want to read. That hesitancy, and that self-doubt, remain prominent dimensions of whom I am and what I am about. Nevertheless, in the course of these past four years I have come to accept this is so to an extent I previously did not. As I have written in chapter six, I have become 'less anxious about being anxious'. I accept I am and always will be an anxious person. Even though anxiety causes me distress, and pain, I accept this is intrinsic to whom I am and what I am about. I cannot change this about myself and I no longer wish I could. I now identify the anxiety I experience as a reasonable response to living in neo-liberal capitalist society. I accept I am attuned to socio-economic, socio-political, and socio-cultural reasons why not only I myself, but also a vast number of others in far more precarious positions than I have ever known, experience insecurity, loneliness, fear, and despair.

I am now retired, and I no longer identify who I am, and what I am about, in relation to work I currently do as a teacher and faculty member. Since retiring, I recognize how much I did identify with this job and the work it involved. I do feel a loss of anchorage. I am working on figuring out who am I now that I am retired. I wrestle with feeling I am now nothing, as I now maintain no purpose. But I *wrestle* with this feeling, resisting it. Still, retirement is not easy. I am not like the man I overheard, a month into retirement, in a local grocery store in Eau Claire, who responded to an acquaintance's question about how he was finding retirement: "I love it . . . I absolutely love it." Nor am like retired colleagues who have told me that "retirement has been the best thing they have ever done" and that they feel immensely freer, happier, more relaxed, and more joyful as a result. I appreciate the new opportunities retirement brings but I gave my job, and especially the work of teaching and the needs of students, everything I had to give. In fact, in retrospect, I recognize I often gave more than was sensible or healthy to do. Yet, as another former colleague reminded me, early in my retirement, I made a difference and that effort mattered.

I hope so. What I am doing now is figuring out what I aim to be, and do, in this next stage of my life. I am learning to embrace new opportunities. I am learning to embrace the unknown. I am learning to embrace what I cannot predict, and certainly not control. Doing so is hard, for me, as a hyper-anxious person. I like to be prepared, anticipating ahead of time what might happen, and how I might respond, by considering prospective scenarios, especially concerning where 'things might go wrong'.

Since I began writing this book my father died. I am thankful Dad and I restored our relationship during the last years of his life such that we communicated regularly, making make clear we did respect, appreciate, and love each other. Our dog Casey died of cancer, but we adopted our dog Aidan around the same time, and Aidan has been wonderful. We gave our cats, Star and Jet, to Andy's brother Eric, and Andy's sister-in-law, Lori, because of Andy's allergies and my immunosuppressed condition.

Contracting lupus nephritis and undergoing an intensive treatment regime in response exercised a huge impact, forcing me to stop writing this book for a year and one-half. This condition also forced me to give up running, after I had reached the point where I ran regularly, five to seven miles four to five times a week, and competed in 5k and 10k races, relishing the mental as well as physical benefits of so doing.

In my earlier introduction of myself, from the summer of 2020, I wrote that I playfully identified 'my hometown', on Facebook and in similar locations, as one of my favorite cities in the U.K., such as Edinburgh, Manchester, or London. I now do maintain a new 'hometown', in a large city, but it is not in the U.K. Andy and I own a house in San Diego, in South Mission Hills that we bought in June of 2023 and which we spent time living in on four successive visits for a total of seven weeks prior to moving in, with Aidan, for good in June 2024. In the summer of 2020 I did not imagine I would soon retire to live in San Diego, but since the summer of 2023 I have increasingly identified San Diego as my 'home city', and now San Diego *feels* like where we live, where our lives are based, and no longer a city we are visiting or dreaming about moving to live in.

I am physically active in San Diego, and that is a major benefit of living here. We walk daily, often long and far, and I am working out two to three times a week with a professional personal trainer at a fitness center. However, running is proceeding slowly. I underwent surgery on my right foot in January 2024 to correct the positioning of both the first and fifth toes, as well as to include an artificial–a mechanical–replacement in the big toe joint where the cartilage had entirely worn away, due to arthritis. Even though I received the green light from my surgeon to run as well as walk again in early April, my progress in returing to running has been slow, especially as I moved to live in an area with many steep hills and little extended flat terrain. But I did run the San Diego Pride 5K all the way through and I ran faster than I anticipated I would.

I continue a fan of Cillian Murphy, but I long ago gave up a 'Peaky Blinders' style haircut, instead favoring a modified version of a French crop that is blended without a sharp fade, and that fits my hair having become shorter and thinner. But I do continue to dye my hair 'reddish blonde'. At present my weight averages 147.5 pounds, so I remain thin. I dress as described in chapter one, with 'smart casual' making sense in describing my 'dress style', although likely more 'casual' than 'smart'. I continue to prefer wearing shorts whenever the temperature is above 50 degrees Fahrenheit, and even often enough when below that. In San Diego, and retired, I wear shorts year round. I don't wear face masks at present, since stopping teaching, even though I continue immunosuppressed, as my lupus nephritis condition has been in remission since July 2023.

I do, much more than I did in June 2020, identify as 'disabled'. I recognize better than I did four years ago that being disabled has shaped my experience, my outlook, and my sympathies and sensitivities. I am more accepting than I was four years ago that chronic illness fluctuates unpredictably, and I cannot 'control', let alone forestall, these fluctuations. I also accept, more readily than in 2020, that many will not grasp what chronic illness of the kinds I experience is like, no matter what I might do in seeking to explain.

Crime fiction remains a favorite pursuit. I finished writing *21st Century British TV Crime Drama: a Critical Guide, Book One–Fearless to The Fall* well before reaching this last chapter of this book and I remain committed to writing *21st Century British TV Crime Drama: a Critical Guide, Book Two–Life on Mars to Line of Duty*. But before doing that latter I am prioritizing finding publishers for 'Book One' as well as for this book. I feel anxious about this pursuit. I feel anxious about meeting harsh criticism from prospective publishers, and from reviewers they commission. I feel anxious about distinguishing between constructive criticism, indicative of publishers able and willing to work with me, versus destructive criticism, or any other form of criticism indicative of publishers maintaining no interest in what I am doing, how, or why. I don't want 'rejection' from others to lead me 'to reject myself', but I know that can happen with me.

Eventually, I hope to write about Continental European TV crime drama, and about the politics of memoir/memoir as politics, starting with recent memoirs from Black Britons. I am interested in trying found poetry as well as fictional writing. I like it when Andy introduces me to people we meet in San Diego as 'a writer'. Writing gives me a sense of purpose, all the more important now that I am no longer teaching. Engaging actively in intellectual work remains crucial. But I am reaching out to become involved with multiple organizations in San Diego, including First Unitarian Universalist Church of San Diego, Democratic Socialists of America San Diego, Activist San Diego and KNSJ radio, The LGBT Center of San Diego, The National Alliance on Mental Illness of San Diego and Imperial Counties, and more. I feel an imperative to help out widely, as much as I feel the need to become involved in order to meet new people, especially people who will become friends.

In chapter one I wrote that being labeled 'shy' frustrated and upset me. In these past four years I let go of that feeling. I accept I am, and long have been, in part 'shy', and 'there's nothing wrong with that'. I don't resist this label anymore even as I continue aware that shyness can lead to misunderstandings and misjudgments that shy people are not able easily to counter or prevent.

I continue to enjoy traveling, but Andy and I plan to spend the first year of our lives living in San Diego by traveling no further than in San Diego County. San Diego presents us with much to explore, discover, and learn about, while it will take at least a year to settle in and feel at ease with what niches we carve out for ourselves in terms of what we do regularly, with whom, and as part of what. I resist ageist views of what it means 'to be old', but traveling takes a toll upon me, and I also respect ecological arguments against frequent flying.

I don't drink alcohol anymore, while I am committed toward eating a healthy diet. Each week we receive delivery of fruits and vegetables from organic farms in San Diego County and we shop at an organic grocery store as well as at farmers' markets. We are focused on 'living healthy'–physically, mentally, and spiritually. This includes reading and writing, along with physical activity of diverse kinds, as well as attending and supporting the arts in the city and region–in particular theatre, as, for example, we have already joined four theatres as season ticket holders.

At a UW-Eau Claire English Department Colloquium Series presentation in 2017 concerning 'Ian Curtis, Joy Division, and Critical Theory', a colleague questioned whether I would reach the point where I would grow tired of Ian Curtis and Joy Division, and no longer want to listen to, let alone write about, this music, because of what writing a book this ambitious and likely to take this long would entail. I responded then I was confident that would not happen, because I maintained a passionate interest in Ian Curtis and Joy Division for four decades without losing interest, and because successive listening and reflection continued to convey new as well as renewed meaning and exercise new as well as renewed impact. However, this book has increasingly felt a monstrous and not just a massive project, while working on it has felt exhausting.

I now recognize what has enabled me to live this long, whereas someone like Ian Curtis could not, is I maintain stronger feelings than Curtis did of hope, stronger affinities with utopian thinking and action, stronger inclinations to identify with Ernst Bloch's theorization of utopia, of distinctions between abstract and concrete utopias, and of the value that can be gained by means of a speculative materialist engagement with wishful images and imaginings ranging from 'little daydreams' to revolutionary visions. Yet I also empathetically identify with what I perceive across *the music* of Joy Division: a determination to survive, endure, and persist, even when this seems impossible, even when this seem pointless, even when this seems absurd–and a determination, what's more, to keep struggling, even when one feels thoroughly worn down and out. 'Determination' and 'persistence' strike me as my two most characteristic traits across my 60+ years of life to date. I am neither especially 'strong', nor especially 'resilient', and I don't experience myself as exceptionally smart, skillful, capable, or talented–not at all. But I do experience myself as determined, persistent, and ready to keep on struggling–while it is the same determination, persistence, and readiness to keep on struggling that I experience dramatically invoked, evoked, enacted, performed, and introspectively scrutinized in the lyrics of Ian Curtis and, especially, in the music of Joy Division. Above all else, it is this commonality of determination, persistence, and readiness to keep on struggling that explains my life-long passion for the music, as art, of Ian Curtis and Joy Division.

Three

In chapter two I write that "Excessive flashpoints, beyond all reach" suggests something happening in the distance, perceptible yet impossible to control. These lines suggest dangerous forces threatening violent disruptions. The latter might refer to numerous possible social conflicts, and, more precisely, numerous possible forms of social antagonism, that the narrator-protagonist in "Twenty Four Hours" seemingly would like to do something about, but which 'he' can't, as 'he' feels not only powerless to do so, but also trapped, confined, and prevented from even trying to do so. "Excessive" suggests, moreover, these flashpoints breaking out all over, indicative of a state of extreme crisis.

In chemical terms 'flashpoint' signifies the temperature at which a substance will spontaneously combust. In common usage 'flashpoint' signifies arriving at a critical point or stage involving the igniting of conflict, especially violent conflict, or which otherwise marks a decisive action or change, especially a dramatic rupture or shift. "Excessive flashpoints" thereby suggest too many of these happening all at once, or in too rapid succession–too many to cope with, even too many to comprehend. "Excessive flashpoints" suggests what appears, and feels, overwhelming, all the more so when these flashpoints are not only "excessive" but also "beyond all reach."

Yet, in listening to Joy Division, and not just to "Twenty Four Hours," I hear a commitment, paradoxically, to strive *to reach what appears, and feels, "beyond all reach."* This means confronting the risk, and the danger, by moving toward and not retreating from it. Engage in order to feel. Feel in order to comprehend. Do so, no matter how terrifying the prospect.

In *World Risk Society* (1999), Ulrich Beck argues in the 'age of second modernity' at the end of the 20th century, "The collective patterns of life, progress and controllability, full employment and exploitation of nature that were typical of the first modernity have now been undermined by five interlinked processes: globalization, individualization, gender revolution, underemployment and global risks (as ecological crisis and the crash of the global financial markets)" while "The real theoretical and political challenge of the second modernity is the fact that society must respond to all of these challenges *simultaneously*" (482). In other words, 'flashpoints' abound: they appear, and they feel, 'excessive'. In this 'age of second modernity', "the very idea of controllability, certainty or security–which is so fundamental to the first modernity–collapses" (482). This is a new age *defined by* "dangers and risks," and these dangers and risks appear, and feel, heightened–i.e., excessive–because they are now global, and can no longer be confined within national boundaries (483). Politics, in turn, increasingly centers on management of risks and dangers, real and perceived. Yet political leaders often fail because they continue reliant on intra-national frameworks rooted in the 'age of first modernity'. Failure amplifies insecurity. What is needed is decentralization as well as collectivization of the exercise of political power. But this is not happening, with centralization and privatization instead increasing.

In her August 18, 2023 opinion piece for *The New York Times*, "Why Does Everyone Feel So Insecure All the Time?," Astra Taylor declares insecurity not inequality to be the most vexing issue of the current historical moment. "Unlike inequality, insecurity is more than a binary of haves and have-nots," with concentration on insecurity revealing a "universality" of "unnecessary suffering" that "is widespread–even among those who appear to be doing well." Nearing mid-way through the second decade of the 21st century, "We are all, to varying degress, overwhelmed and apprehensive, fearful of what the future might have in store." We live our lives "on guard, anxious, incomplete and exposed to risk," doing what we can "To cope," "to scramble and strive, shoring ourselves up against potential threats . . . And yet, for the most part, security eludes us."

Why so? Because "the main mechanisms by which we are told to gain security for ourselves–making money, buying property, earning degrees, saving for retirement–often involve being invested in systems that rarely provide the stability we crave." The problem arises from "intensifying" "manufactured insecurity," not the "existential insecurity" "indelible to being human," as early 21st century capitalism has become *extreme* capitalism, following "the deregulation of finance and business and the decline of the welfare state." Extreme capitalism relentlessly 'capitalizes' "on the insecurities it produces." Now more than ever, capitalism "prods and perpetuates" insecurities, "making us all insecure by design."

Taylor recognizes that capitalism has long 'thrived' "on bad feelings," and that insecurity for the vast majority has been the rule rather than the exception throughout the history of capitalism. But, in early 21st century 'extreme capitalism', the variety and intensity of these feelings have exploded. All these 'vectors of insecurity' make sense, in other words, as 'flashpoints' that have become qualitatively as well as quantitatively 'excessive'.

In her 2023 book *The Age of Insecurity: Coming Together as Things Fall Apart* Taylor details many of these 'vectors of insecurity'. They include:

1.   Increasing need of many workers to work precarious jobs in the so-called 'gig economy' for companies like Uber and Lyft.

2.   Insidious pressure to compare what one 'expected' and feels was 'promised' versus what one feels one does not have and what others (appear to) have.

3.   Evisceration of the erstwhile post-World War II welfare state.

4.   Privatization of the erstwhile commons, such that access to and exercise of erstwhile public resources becomes increasingly costly and exclusively delimited.

5.   The end of realistic hope that 'upward mobility' might be possible, while 'downward mobility' feels all too palpably real for all too many.

6.   The vast number of people now working jobs they would gladly quit, but cannot afford to quit. These jobs they made clear they would quit if they could during the brief period early in the COVID-19 pandemic when limited approximation of universal basic income was implemented.

7.   The pervasive permeation of advertising appeals to turn to commodities as 'surrogates' for the security that people crave, with pursuit of these substitutes leading to vast "spiritual emptiness" (36).

8.   Escalating 'mental illness', especially in the forms of anxiety and depression, with surveys, such as a 2022 Gallup poll, attesting that "anger, stress, sadness, physical pain and worry . . . have reached a new global high" (39).

9.   Stockpiling guns, and in doing so exemplifying the "security paradox," where efforts "to increase one's own security lead to the heightened insecurity of other actors, stimulating strong counterreactions that leave everybody worse off in the end" (42).

10.   Increasing food, housing, health, and economic *insecurity*, including in the wealthiest nations in the world.

11.   Schools, at all educational levels, effectively surrendering to the logic of the capitalist marketplace, by treating education as a competitive zero-sum game, in emphasizing grades, test scores, and 'carrots and sticks' forms of reward and punishment over the fostering of genuine intellectual curiosity and free intellectual exploration.

12.   Massive levels of individual and household debt.

13.   Global ecological emergency and its ravages effected upon both human and other-than-human life.

14.   Panic over perceived threats from 'out of control' crime, 'out of control' immigration, and 'out of control' numbers of homeless people.

All of these factors in turn contribute to the rising popularity of authoritarian–fascist–leaders and movements because those leaders and movements promise 'to take care' of people's insecurities. More than anything else, what they promise their followers is to 'restore their lost security'.

Taylor's anatomy of this 'age of insecurity' resonates with the lyrics of Ian Curtis and the music of Joy Division, even as it is not easy to recognize the equivalent of Taylor's ultimate optimism in the same lyrics and music. In her *New York Times* article Taylor proposes that "Rather than pathologize, I want us to see insecurity as an opportunity." What this means, according to Taylor, is seizing upon shared experience of insecurity as the basis for a radically transformed society centered around a culture of "solidarity." In working toward that end, Taylor advocates beginning with "reweaving the social safety net." This can be the beginning of reclaiming what the concept 'insurance' was originally conceived to mean: "The concept of insurance is rooted in recognition that we all need protection from life's hazards and vicissitudes, whether natural or man-made" (277). In other words, "To be vulnerable and dependent on others is not a burden to escape but the essence of human existence, as well as the basis of what I have called, throughout this book, an ethic of insecurity–a potentially powerful source of connection, solidarity, and transformation" (279). As Taylor elaborates, yet further, "We all need care throughout our lives, from birth to death, not only when we are struck by illness" (284), yet we are suffering from lack of care due to "What the writer Rebecca Solnit has called capitalism's 'ideology of isolation' that encourages us to ignore all the ways we are, in fact, mutually dependent" (285). Working for change, and here I do find what Taylor proposes resonates with the lyrics of Ian Curtis and the music of Joy Division, requires embracing and channeling insecurity. The need for 'radical' change, if change is to make any meaningful difference, also resonates with this same lyrics and music, even as Taylor comes across as more confident that such change is possible, no matter how daunting, than what I hear in listening to Joy Division.

For Taylor, radical change is crucial because the safety net cannot be 'rewoven' so that it merely replicates what it previously was before it was 'unwoven', given the extent of damage capitalist society has done, over multiple centuries, notably in terms of entrenching insecurity.

"Reparation" is what is required, and this must be 'reparation' in response to both natural and social harms, pursued "not as acts of charity but rather acts of solidarity and self-preservation" (278).

Toward the end of *The Age of Insecurity*, Taylor writes "There are no panaceas, only possibilities. I don't believe in utopia, but I can imagine a more hopeful future" (221). Here, once more, it is useful to mark a distinction between Taylor's take and resonances I and others most likely experience with the lyrics of Ian Curtis and the music of Joy Division. Even as Taylor stresses what she proposes as a radical alternative is only a possibility, that depends upon considerable work and struggle to realize, the lyrics of Ian Curtis and the music of Joy Division do not convey the same overtly 'hopeful imagination of the future'. Hope, as I will discuss later in this chapter, is not abandoned in these lyrics and this music, and neither is utopia, but it is highly uncertain.

The lyrics of Ian Curtis and the music of Joy Division resonate more immediately with arguments such as those Owen Jones makes in his April 11, 2024 column for *The Guardian*, "Blood, chaos and decline: these are the fruits of unbridled western hubris." Joy Division, starting with Ian Curtis's lyrics, at least more immediately conjures a sense of registering and reflecting on substantial loss, and defeat, that well may have involved and continue to involve 'blood and chaos' in leading to 'decline'–or, even, *degeneration*–on the scale of what Jones perceives, a 'decline of the west'. Jones argues that those on 'the right' who have proclaimed such 'a decline' are right insofar as this is and has been happening, but they are 'right' *for all the wrong reasons*. According to Jones, "This century has one overarching theme: the fall of the west, that is, the US and its European allies. Every major crisis accelerates the unmistakable trend. The war in Gaza is just the latest manifestation. Western newspapers are now littered with articles full of the panicked realisation that more is buried in the rubble of Gaza than just thousands of unidentified bodies." Jones claims not only has the west failed, militarily and morally, in engagement with the rest of the world, as exemplified in Gaza, but also western capitalism has amounted to a colossal failure within the west:

> Such unrestrained capitalism directly paved the way for the 2008 financial crash, from which the west never truly recovered. Many of its countries then embarked on a ruinous course of austerity, which led to stagnation and decline, the ideal conditions for a rightwing authoritarian surge. The subsequent rise of Donald Trump's far-right movement now imperils the very future of US democracy. Everywhere, liberal democracy is in retreat, increasingly replaced by autocratic regimes such as in Hungary, which the European Union occasionally wrings its hands over but with little action to back it up. In most European countries the far right is surging, a worrying omen of the continent's future.

Emphasis on a tragic lost opportunity and the devastating consequences of this loss unites Joy Division with Jones's argument here:

> Things could have been different. There could have been accountability over previous foreign debacles: instead those responsible–from government ministers to hawkish newspaper commentators–walked from disaster to disaster, splattered with more and more blood, yet continued in their roles with their careers and reputations somehow intact. Meanwhile, rather than being treated with the respect those with insight deserve, the people who opposed these

1129

calamities at the time remain ostracised as fringe extremists or dupes of foreign enemies, despite being repeatedly vindicated.

Just as we could have built an economic model that doesn't hoover up wealth into the bank accounts of the tiny elite, the lessons of the west's disastrous foreign policy history could have been heeded, and thus its catastrophic backing of Israel's Gaza assault avoided. Alas, it was not to be. You may have found these last years of turmoil exhausting. Buckle up: the fall of the west has several more acts to come.

Nevertheless, what unites Joy Division, Jones, *and Taylor* is the manifestation of an at least residual determination, even in the worst of conditions and even in the face of the least immediate reason to maintain hope of success, to keep on trying to make some kind of impact in the midst of and *against* 'the blood, chaos, and decline'.

In 1970s Britain, as historians such as Andy Beckett, in *When the Lights Went Out: Britain in the Seventies* (2009), and Alwyn W. Turner, in *Crisis? What Crisis? Britain in the 1970s* (2008) recount, many Britons felt increasingly insecure, facing a proliferation of simultaneous crises that their social and political 'leaders' seemed unable to redress, let alone prevent, while many felt disillusioned by the apparent structural inadequacies and indeed structural failings of post-World War II social democratic institutions and arrangements. These influences show up, indirectly, in the lyrics of Ian Curtis and the music of Joy Division. For many Britons, living in the 1970s felt like living in a time of 'excessive flashpoints'. The impact of crises of capitalism connects experiences of insecurity in 1970s Britain with experiences of insecurity in 2020s Britain, the United States, and Canada (where Taylor resides). The 1970s mark the beginnings of 'neo-liberal capitalism', which is in essence what both Beck and Taylor address even though they do not identify it as such. In the 1970s people at least vaguely perceived and vaguely felt the initial impacts of neo-liberal emergence, and it makes sense to interpret Joy Division as channeling these vague perceptions and feelings.

Distinctive, however, with the music of Joy Division is an insinuation that the immediate present and the foreseeable future are desperate, extreme, and virtually apocalyptic times, at least for some, if not for many, or at least *feel* as such, and in turn require a matching response. The music of Joy Division insinuates what such a matching response might be, and whether it might be possible, remains uncertain, even doubtful, yet the attempt to find it must be pursued.

Insecurity makes useful sense in explaining many current social trends. Fear of crime has risen across much of the US since the pandemic, even among those whose risk of becoming victims of crime has not increased. Among the most frequent posts on popular media platform Nextdoor are those reporting reputed acts and in particular threats of crime, including reputed sightings, and recordings, of 'suspicious people'–people who are often homeless and/or poor people of color. Discussions that ensue in response to these posts often emphasize the need to be perpetually vigilant concerning omnipresent threats from anonymous criminals inclined to attack people they don't otherwise know, with anyone who might be perceived as in any way vulnerable constituting a ready target. These posters on this site depict their own neighborhoods as frighteningly insecure places in which to live, where they are forced to rely upon what they themselves can muster to protect themselves, and their immediate families, from dangers that lurk everywhere about. Likewise, as has long been the case, prominent and influential discussions of crime, including among other than 'critical' criminologists, continue to represent crime as a reflection of 'deviance', such that criminals are those who engage in crime as a matter of choice, not necessity, because of inherent anti-social tendencies, or because of other personal failings and deficiencies that mark these criminals off as distinctly different from 'non-criminal' kinds of people. The root causes of crime continue to be underemphasized, and unaddressed, in advocating for 'getting tough', or tougher, on crime, in 'cracking down' on crime, and in rendering 'the cost' of crime so onerous such that would-be 'criminals' will be 'deterred' from making the implied 'rational calculation' to choose to commit a crime. But those living in extreme poverty, struggling to survive from day to day, living extremely close to people whose lives are diametrically divergent from this kind of bare existence, are understandably inclined, out of desperate need, to take what they can get, from whom and when and where they can, without the freedom carefully to calculate whether this is 'worth the risk'. These people are the ones living the truly most insecure lives.

Similarly, many object to the increasing prevalence of large numbers of homeless people living in public areas, including in so-called 'encampments', and to how that interferes with unfettered access to the places those who are not homeless want to go and with the things they want to do, while exposing those not homeless to encounters with filth, drugs, and violence–from homeless people. And, yes, these encounters can and do increase feelings of insecurity, but once more homeless people are the ones in far more insecure positions. It is symptomatic of living in an 'age of insecurity' that many find it easy to argue homeless people are themselves responsible for being homelessness because they have 'made bad choices and decisions', including 'choosing and deciding' to become addicted to alcohol and other dangerous drugs, such as fentanyl; 'choosing and deciding' to become mentally ill, not only from anxiety and depression, but also from schizophrenia, dissociative identity disorder, and other 'psychotic' conditions; 'choosing and deciding' to be dismissed from their jobs or evicted from their apartments; 'choosing and deciding' to work jobs that don't pay enough to afford the cost of housing; and 'choosing and deciding' not to rely upon family, friends, or social services sufficient to help them through their hard times. Many refuse to recognize the fact that most Americans are not far removed from precarity, and it would not take much to push them over the edge, where they too became homeless–or where they too needed to turn to crime because of desperate need. The social forces that foster feelings of rampant insecurity leave people less inclined to experience sympathy, and empathy, for others, because it feels all too often as if 'we' must focus solely on looking after themselves, and 'our' immediate families, while others in even 'less secure positions' constitute threats to 'our' tenuous security.

Insecurity makes sense as well in explaining why many Americans, Britons, and members of other European nations perceive 'immigrants', again especially poor immigrants of color, as threats. The latter are commonly perceived, and often represented, as threatening 'the security' of those already living in the nations to which they are immigrating. The latter experience themselves as insecurely reliant on resources that are already too scarce and simply cannot be shared with any more people than is already the case. Even when the facts make clear that immigrants contribute more to the economy than they 'take' from it, and that they do many jobs no one else does or would do, including many essential jobs, while revitalizing communities as well as enriching local, regional, and national cultures, these facts are ignored or rejected. It is easier, when experiencing one's own existence as highly insecure, to scapegoat immigrants as responsible for this insecurity.

Insecurity makes sense as well in explaining why many people in the U.S. and the U.K., as well as other nations too, are threatened by increasing numbers of people, especially young people, identifying and living openly as transgender and gender non-binary. Binary divisions along sex, and gender, have long provided a sense of stability that has felt essential in the face of insecurity otherwise. When it no longer seems gender, or even sex, are necessarily binary, with increasing numbers of others refusing to live according to those terms, it can feel threatening. This is all the more the case for those worried about their 'own children' identifying, and living, as transgender or gender non-binary, and especially these children doing so without telling their parents or guardians.

In an April 3, 2024 opinion piece for *The New York Times* philosopher Alex Byrne and evolutionary biologist Carol K. Hooven argue against use of "sex assigned at birth," declaring there is no such thing because biological sex is simply a matter of fact, with recognition of this fact crucial in terms of attending to people's health concerns. Likewise, on April 10, 2024, Baroness Dr Hilary Dawn Cass, a former president of the Royal College of Paediatrics and Child Health, released her major review of how the National Health Service in the U.K. treats people under age 18 "who are unsure about their gender identity" (Denis Campbell, *The Guardian*). In this review Cass argues in favor of slowing down the process of facilitating changes in gender identification. According to Cass, what is needed instead is to invest more time and effort in consideration of a complex of factors that might cause young people to experience discomfort and distress such that they reach to redefine their gender as 'a quick fix' for problems such a change will not fix but only exacerbate. Both of these arguments reflect concerns that more young people today, in countries like the U.S. and the U.K., are identifying, and living, as transgender and gender non-binary, with seemingly no available biological basis to explain this increase. Unfortunately, Byrne, Hooven, and Cass appear inclined to discount the validity of social-historical factors, and especially of cultural-political ones. In other words, according to Byrne, Hooven, and Cass, the biology of gender remains essentially the same over time, and it not susceptible to change as result of social-historical, and cultural-political, influences. Yet not only do people's ideas about 'people's biological natures' change as a result of the latter influences, but so do people's bodies, while human beings maintain the capability of reshaping our biological beings, including in redefining what sex designates, as well as in identifying distinct 'sexes' and demarcating changing relations between 'sex' and 'gender'.

More relevant to matters of insecurity, however, is why it matters if 10 to 15 to 20% of young people identify, and live, as transgender or gender non-binary–i.e., why is that threatening. Supposedly, a principal concern is transgender and gender non-binary people hurting themselves, but according to the latest, 2024, official "US Trans Survey,"

Nearly all respondents (94%) who lived at least some of the time in a different gender than the one they were assigned at birth ("gender transition") reported that they were either "a lot more satisfied" (79%) or "a little more satisfied" (15%) with their life. Three percent (3%) reported that transitioning gender made them "neither more nor less satisfied" with their life, 1% were "a little less satisfied", and 2% were "a lot less satisfied" with their life.

The results of this survey are hardly surprising, let alone new, as transgender people–and non-binary people–report that the greatest obstacles to their happiness and well-being come from institutions, organizations, and *other people* who refuse to accept them as they are, and who refuse to treat them as equally worthwhile, as maintaining equal human dignity.

Insecurity helps explain what is at stake here. An increasing number of people identifying, and living, as transgender and gender non-binary undermines the seeming unquestionability of notions of sex and gender upon which many people rely to provide the rest of their lives with a solidity, and a stability, that feels indispensable when so much else feels insecure.

But again, it is transgender and gender non-binary people who are the ones living more insecure lives than those who fear them–in societies where suspicion, distrust, hostility, and outright violence is frequently directed against transgender and gender non-binary people. I know a number of gay commentators have expressed concern that 'effeminate boys and men' who might otherwise identify, and live, as gay, are now identifying as transgender and non-binary, thereby 'reducing the numbers of those counting as gay', but this strikes me as, once more, indicative of insecurity–insecurity concerning how many others 'like us' there will be, with the worry that those seemingly 'not like us' cannot be counted on to be our allies. It has been extremely important for me to assert that 'being a man' can encompass a diversity of possibilities, and the same with masculinity. I identify with theorization of 'gay' male masculinity by revolutionary gay liberation in the 1960s and 1970s as intervention versus restrictive conceptions and practices of what it 'must' mean to be, and act, as a man, and to be, and act, as masculine. It has been essential for me to assert I am every bit as much a man as those who deny that I could possibly be a 'real' or 'true' 'masculine' man on account of the fact that I am capable of and inclined toward loving other men sexually. Men loving men, fully, freely, and as genuine social equals, has long been important to me as contribution toward *feminist* ends, because only by transforming what it means to be a man, and to be masculine, can it be possible to enable men and women to live as true social equals, and the same vis-a-vis masculine and feminine dimensions of men's and women's social being. I welcome transgender and gender non-binary people as allies in the same direction of intervention, and transformation, even though I myself do not experience myself as transgender or gender non-binary.

In sum, a radical project along the lines that Taylor proposes–transforming society so that insecurity is collectively shared, and collectively addressed, upon genuinely solidaristic foundations, where we embrace our respective vulnerabilities, along with the considerable vulnerabilities of the rest of life on this planet, as basis for a preeminent commonality of interest–this makes sense, and is appealing, no matter how daunting the prospect appears in aiming to move 'from here to there'. The lyrics of Ian Curtis and the music of Joy Division emphasize what it is about the status quo that makes this kind of radical project necessary, and urgent, along with how exceedingly difficult it will be to achieve, but not on intimating details of what that desired end might be like.

Four

In chapter two, I write that "Solitary demands for all I'd like to keep" draws a striking contrast with the preceding line ("Excessive flashpoints beyond all reach") in referencing a narrow locus immediately surrounding the narrator-protagonist, as opposed to distant conflagrations the narrator-protagonist is aware of but can do nothing about. The line "Solitary demands for all I'd like to keep" prompts many questions in seeking to interpret what this might mean. Who is making these demands, and of whom? Why "demands," and what exactly is "solitary" about these "demands"? Are these demands 'solitary' because they are made in a state of solitude? Is this solitude a state of isolation, or of retreat, or of confinement? Is this solitude chosen or is it forced? Are these demands "solitary" because these are the sole demands being made? And what makes these demands the narrator-protagonist would "like to keep"? How and why so?

In chapter two I observe that this line describes these as demands for *all* the narrator-protagonist would like to keep, with that modifier 'all' suggesting a situation in which someone or something is demanding 'he' give up everything, including everything that matters and has mattered to 'him', thereby refusing to allow him to keep virtually anything afterward. But, if so, why is this–or why is the narrator-protagonist feeling as if this is the case even if it not objectively so? Why is he forced to give up all he seemingly is, or why does he feel like he is so forced?

"Solitary demands" can suggest what it is like to experience loneliness, and loneliness resonates as strongly with the lyrics of Ian Curtis and the music of Joy Division as does insecurity. Yet, as I write in chapter three, particularly in discussing the Joy Division song "Isolation", it makes sense to distinguish loneliness from 'aloneness'. Solitude can be deliberately chosen, and welcomed, whereas loneliness signifies the obverse. However, being alone, living and working in isolation, and experiencing protracted solitude, can lead to loneliness, while the boundary between these kinds of experiences, and what they respectively feel like, can be tenuous.

Insofar as it makes sense to interpret the music of Joy Division as concerned with loneliness, it hardly seems adequate to posit these songs as merely expressing direct feelings of loneliness on the part of the narrator-protagonist of the lyrics, let alone the music as persona, let alone Ian Curtis himself. The songs enact not only a performative engagement with what loneliness immediately feels like, but also with distance from the immediacy of feeling lonely that allows for critical reflection upon loneliness, including reflection upon not only 'our own loneliness' but also 'the loneliness of others'. Despite the space between the instruments and other sound sources that Joy Division songs, in studio-recorded versions produced by Martin Hannett, are famous for, these songs involve tight collaborations among multiple contributors in a collective effort that involves considerable interaction and cooperation, in itself suggesting the antithesis of loneliness. The same holds true in relation to Joy Division creating this music to be shared with other people, in live performance, on record, and beyond. Such sharing can forge and sustain community to counter loneliness, and many have testified that listening to and identifying with the music of Joy Division has done so for them, enabling these listeners to feel part of a community of Joy Division fans, even an imagined community of lonely people feeling less lonely by means of this shared connection with other lonely people. If it makes sense to interpret Joy Division's music as 'about loneliness', it also makes sense, therefore, to interpret this music as about confronting, countering, and even striving to overcome loneliness.

In addition, Joy Division's music is as much concerned with recalling past loneliness and anticipating future loneliness as it is with expressing present loneliness, and this music is likewise concerned with reflecting on the yet further degree of loneliness that arises in the course of, and results from, engaging in such recollection and anticipation. Joy Division's music makes sense as contemplating loneliness not only due to absence of meaningful connections with other people, but also due to being together with other people where these connections are not meaningful or satisfying, where they are inadequate to satisfy what is desired and needed. This includes loneliness experienced in ostensibly intimate relations that are normatively defined as protecting from loneliness, in situations where these ostensibly intimate relations do not, or no longer, so satisfy, but instead feel impoverished and empty. Joy Division's music makes sense, yet further, as contemplating loneliness beyond the interpersonal, including in relation to where and how one fits, and especially does not, within larger communities, cultures, and societies–and even as contemplating existential and cosmic forms of loneliness. 'Contemplation' is key here, because Joy Division's music invokes, evokes, and ritualistically performs what it feels like to be lonely, but it does more than that–i.e., it contemplates what such feeling might mean from a distance, from a *critical* distance. Likewise, Joy Division's music manifests a commitment, albeit haltingly, to carry on, to persist in struggle, to cope with, to survive, to endure, and, if possible, to strive to overcome loneliness.

In a January 2024 article for *The New Statesman*, "From Bowling Alone to scrolling alone: Why loneliness is the defining political crisis in America," Lee Siegel argues loneliness in the U.S. today is massive, and the political consequences are dire. Siegel cites Hannah Arendt explaining that "the sine qua non for totalitarianism" is loneliness: "What prepares men for totalitarian domination in the non-totalitarian world . . . is the fact that loneliness, once a borderline experience usually suffered in certain marginal social conditions like old age, has become an everyday experience of the ever-growing masses of our century (Arendt, quoted)." Because Siegel insists that "loneliness is the cardinal political condition of our time," he worries Arendt's warnings concerning the seeds of totalitarianism could not be more relevant in America today. Yet despite a vast discourse on loneliness as a major social problem, "America still has not plumbed the weird depths that the fusion of its politics with its loneliness could lead. Instead, loneliness is isolated from its multiple contexts and elevated into–or reduced to–an Important Issue that is redundantly talked about in the most general, abstract terms, as an Important Issue." In other words, "There is no real sense that, aside from conditions like old age, the remedy for loneliness is not merely to foster 'little platoons' of companionship, as essential as they are, but to address how a person is made to feel when they are alone."

Siegel advances his own "solitary demands" in response, advocating for "replenishing depths of solitary thinking and imagining" that "have been made to disappear in a maelstrom of rapidly forming and dissolving social relationships." As Siegel conceives it, "In solitude, you divide yourself in two so as to carry on a dialogue with that part of yourself that is linked with other humans; in that way, the solitary operation of your moral imagination leads you back to the company of others." In America today, in contrast, we have lost our way, "more dependent on screens and technology than in any other place on Earth," while "the emotionally blunting effects of almost universally used psychiatric drugs" undermine "the capacity to carry on a dialogue with yourself in the process of making you bearable to yourself." Unable to carry on this kind of dialogue with ourselves, we are all the less able to carry on dialogue with others.

Even more concerning, for Siegel, is increasing prevalence of 'catastrophic thinking': America is now in the grip of an ice-cold algorithm of catastrophic thinking on the left and the right. On the left, rational and humane worry about injustice and climate has devolved into an iron apocalypticism, in which nearly all authority is unreliable and malign, an apocalypticism that is nevertheless cheerfully and lucratively promoted by the liberal media. On the right, rational and humane worry about crime and disorder descends into calls for revenge against unreliable and malign authorities, for violence and even civil war.

Again Siegel cites Arendt as warning that "The famous extremism of totalitarian movements" follows from "'thinking everything to the worst'" (Arendt, quoted). Totalitarian movements exploit catastrophism in offering what feels like "a last support in a world where nobody is reliable and nothing can be relied upon" (Arendt, quoted).

We urgently need, therefore, to transform loneliness into solitude–to restore our capacity to make solitary demands within and as part of a larger community that respects the need for and use of being alone–that is, "A place where it feels safe, and good, to be alone." For Siegel, in sum, a nation experiencing an excess of loneliness is a nation suffering from a dearth of solitude, or in other words, a nation where solitude has degenerated into loneliness.

In a September 6, 2023 opinion piece for *The New York Times*, Nicholas Kristof echoes Siegel's concern, but makes sense of the social problem of loneliness, and how to address it, in more conventional terms. Kristof begins by reciting dimensions of problem: "Loneliness crushes the soul, but researchers are finding it does far more damage than that. It is linked to strokes, heart disease, dementia, inflammation and suicide; it breaks the heart literally as well as figuratively." Loneliness is "more dangerous than obesity" and "as deadly as smoking 15 cigarettes a day and more lethal than consuming six alcoholic drinks a day, according to the surgeon general of the United States, Dr. Vivek Murthy." All the more concerning, "we have been growing more lonely," as "A majority of Americans now report experiencing loneliness," and, "if the researchers are correct, social isolation probably kills far more people in the West each year than terrorists and murderers, and it costs the public enormous sums in unnecessary health costs."

Kristof asserts that "Countermeasures can make a huge difference," citing research suggesting "that social connections increase the odds of an individual's surviving over roughly the next seven years by about 50 percent." According to Kristof, pace Siegel, isolation leads to loneliness, and it is because Americans today are too isolated that they are too lonely: "These pathologies are linked to social isolation. I've seen how old friends self-medicated with meth or alcohol in part because they were disconnected from the community, and then addiction and criminal records left them even more stigmatized and isolated." In contrast with America today, "at the time of the Great Depression . . . there were community institutions–churches, men's clubs, women's associations, bridge clubs, bowling leagues, extended families–that buffered the pain and humiliation of unemployment and economic distress." Yet "Those community institutions have frayed. Now we're on our own, and perhaps that's why so many are also dying alone."

Meanwhile, ostensibly 'social' media makes people feel lonelier–especially younger people. Lonely Americans need better opportunities, as well as real incentives, to engage in direct, physical, sustained social interaction: "little nudges to encourage us to mingle the way we evolved to," that will reinforce acting upon the recognition that "for the sake of our happiness and well-being, we need one another."

Insofar as the lyrics of Ian Curtis and the music of Joy Division resonate with conditions and experiences of loneliness in America and the larger 'West' a quarter way through the 21st century, these lyrics and this music suggest the opportunities and incentives Kristof recommends are, in practice, too often lacking, and even when and where available too often limited and insufficient, while forces and interests opposed to 'making things better' are powerful and insidious. In other words, countering this scope and scale of loneliness is and will be immensely difficult, and painful, with no guarantee of success.

This brings me to three recently published book-length examinations of the current 'crisis of loneliness': *A Biography of Loneliness: The History of an Emotion* by Fay Bound Alberti (2019); *Loneliness: a Social Problem* by Keming Yang (2019); and *The Lonely Century: How to Restore Human Connection in a World That's Falling Apart*, by Noreena Hertz (2021). Let's begin with *A Biography of Loneliness*. In this book Alberti argues what 'we' in 'the West' conceive of as loneliness is a modern phenomenon first emergent "around 1800" that is linked with "the emergence of an all-encompassing ideology of the individual" (10). In short, "The politics and philosophy of individualism" have shaped 'modern loneliness' (xii), especially by "the separating of the mind from the body" (xiii). Neoliberal capitalist society amplifies individualism, to the point where Margaret Thatcher notoriously asserted 'there's no such thing as society'. Neoliberal capitalism also valorizes material acquisition, consumption, possession, and accumulation, but the problem is "Excessive materialism" tends to "make people lonelier" (14), providing "only short-term satisfaction" (185). Loneliness follows from lack as well as from hunger for what is lacking, but this is not lack of or hunger for material goods, because loneliness is a dimension of alienation, involving subjective experience of "powerlessness, meaninglessness, normlessness, isolation, and self-estrangement" (36).

Alberti commends Lars Anderson's definition of loneliness: "an enduring condition of emotional distress that arises when a person feels estranged from, misunderstood, or rejected by others and/or lacks appropriate social partners for desired activities, particularly activities that provide a sense of social integration and opportunities for emotional intimacy" (quoted 5). Alberti stresses, in addition, "Loneliness is not the state of being alone," no matter how often the two are conflated, and "Loneliness is entirely subjective" (5).

Alberti rejects descriptions of contemporary loneliness as 'an epidemic', because doing so mystifies not only how loneliness develops, for whom, when, where, and why, but also what, in essence, loneliness feels like. Spreading "Fear about loneliness creates loneliness" (3), notably among the old and the young, two groups particularly 'susceptible' to becoming lonely, especially when this fear takes the forms of "Fear of a social death" or "moral panic" concerning its ostensibly pervasive prevalence (141).

For Alberti, key in distinguishing loneliness from being alone, or from solitude, is "not whether or not people are *around*, but the recognition that one has nothing in common with others" (49). "Meaningful connections based on a shared understanding" prevent loneliness (185). Without these connections, loneliness readily arises, even amidst a crowd. Yet, loneliness can be useful in prompting reflection and contemplation necessary for creative activity, while quietness and solitude can be valuable, *if temporary and if "chosen"* (221).

Unfortunately, digital culture, and especially social media, offer nothing of the kind. Alberti bluntly declares: "The paradox of social media is that it produces the same isolation and loneliness that it seeks to overcome" (38). It is especially problematic, Alberti contends, when social media induces people to compare their lives with how they perceive others' lives to be, as this leads to loneliness on account of 'fear of missing out'. In addition, online communities often maintain problematic and at least partially obscure power dynamics that are not present in offline communities, while accountability is more easily evaded online than offline (132-133). Likewise, commercialization of contact online increases tendencies toward loneliness due to the limited satisfaction that such commodification of contact entails. In societies where social media use is highest so is loneliness (122). Alberti proposes that social media should not replace but rather supplement off-line relationships (128-129). People need directly physically shared lived experience as well as regular physical 'touch' in order not to become, and not to stay, lonely (136).

Alberti emphasizes the often overlooked "sheer physicality of loneliness" (xiv); loneliness, in other words, is *not* only a mental, emotional, or psychological problem. "Loneliness causes illnesses of the body as well of the mind" (182-183), because people's experience of loneliness is "embodied" and must be attended to as such. Lonely people experience a "craving for physical touch" (161).

Alberti makes clear that loneliness does not impact all demographic groups equally, noting for example, higher degrees of loneliness among lgbtqia+ people, disabled people, people with mental illness, younger people, and older people. Often an increased inclination to loneliness, even more specifically, is linked with experience of 'home' as "an elusive ideal, connected to a sense of safety, of belonging, that one has lost, or never experienced" (163). Unsurprisingly, therefore, homeless people and refugees experience high rates of loneliness, as do other groups of people who experience themselves as 'rootless' (164-165). In fact, experience of "Lack of safety," along with "difficulties of integrating into community, being accepted, and often experiencing mental and physical disabilities as well as economic precarity" are major factors in causing both loneliness and homelessness (176), while loneliness can itself be responsible for homelessness (170).

Effective responses to loneliness continue to fall short because "loneliness is shrouded in shame in the West," still frequently regarded as indicative of "personal failing" (6). At the same time, many pursue unhelpful avenues toward redressing or forestalling loneliness, such as via pursuit of a 'soulmate'. Alberti argues yearning for such a singular 'special other' is symptomatic and reinforcing of loneliness. It is, she asserts, "incredibly limiting," missing out on the need of the lonely for community, not just for one other person (66).

Alberti rejects the notion that increasing loneliness is inevitable in becoming older: "The experience of loneliness in old age is not universal, or inevitable. It is dependent on the dominant ideologies of aging and social care, as well as individual, familial, and societal qualities of experience" (155). A major factor influencing loneliness among older people is that, as modern capitalist society has proceeded, older people have become increasingly viewed as no longer productively capable. As a result, older people are not only treated by the non-elderly as incapable but also internalize this perception of themselves (154-155). It is worthy of note that many of the most prominent and influential ageist notions today "didn't become mainstream until the 1950's" (152), again suggesting association between 'growing old' and 'becoming lonely' are far from 'natural fact'. Yes, "Isolation through illness" and "limited mobility" that can come with older age does increase risk of loneliness (143), while lack of social acceptance of a duty of care for older people does the same (145). The problem is not 'being old'; instead, neoliberal capitalism is at fault for failure in this duty of care (148). Individually and collectively, we must refuse to accept loneliness as an inevitable companion to growing old, as well as reject reductive associations with aging and becoming older (150-151).

Besides its emotional and physical costs, Alberti highlights "the financial cost of loneliness" (4), and not just to the lonely, but to the greater society, because the latter misses out on what the lonely could otherwise contribute while also needing, however reluctantly, to pay the cost of attending to the emotional and physical damages that the lonely suffer. 'We' need to develop a consensual understanding that modern loneliness, and especially loneliness under neoliberalism, requires not a medicalized but rather a societal response—one that proactively arranges for those at high risk of loneliness to access resources they need to counter loneliness—and these include meaningful social relationships based on shared understandings, along with physical activities and physical connections that attend to the embodied nature of what loneliness is and does.

Throughout *Loneliness: a Social Problem* Keming Yang provides statistical analyses of surveys concerning experiences of loneliness in more than twenty, primarily European, nations. But before doing so he takes time to define loneliness. Yang starts with Daniel Perlman and Letitia Anne Peplau's definition: "loneliness is an unpleasant experience that occurs when a person's network of social relations is deficient in some important way, either quantitatively or qualitatively" (quoted 2). Working off this definition, Yang, like Alberti and Siegel, emphasizes loneliness *is not* identical with aloneness (2), while underscoring that loneliness *is* painful (3). Loneliness, Yang stresses, can involve not only "the absence of desired social relations but also the presence of undesired (deficient) ones," but what is most important to take into account is the *perception* and *interpretation* of this lack or deficiency (3). Again, like Alberti and Kristof, Yang emphasizes loneliness causes more than psychological pain: "Involuntary (or forced) severance of social relations, to which loneliness is expected to be a natural emotional reaction, is strongly related to many illnesses" (6). In this connection, Yang cites John Cacioppo on how "chronic *feelings* of isolation can drive a cascade of physiological events that actually accelerates the aging process" (quoted 6). And the psychological impact of loneliness can be severe: "loneliness and depression seem to mutually reinforce each other over time" (7), while loneliness involving loss of purpose and meaning can lead, in turn, to suicide (8). What's more, the risk is real "that transient and mild loneliness could develop into . . . chronic and serious loneliness," so it is incumbent on those concerned about these consequences to identify the key determinants effecting such development (13).

Yang next distinguishes between "emotional loneliness" that "comes from the lack of at least one intimate personal relationship" and "social loneliness" that "refers to not belonging to a wider social network of community" (16). Yang cites a number of sociological forerunners of his work, notably David Riesman and associates who "established the central role of cultural norms in shaping people's sense of loneliness," and Émile Durkheim for his concept of 'anomie' (25). Yang also mentions the concept of 'anomia' from Leo Srole; 'anomia' refers to "the individual's experience of anomie" (26). While discussing these contributions toward theorizing loneliness as a social problem, Yang distinguishes between aloneness and isolation, although he differs from Alberti in identifying aloneness as an 'objective' state whereas loneliness he identifies as a 'subjective' one (26). What's more, Yang later proposes loneliness is a negative state, aloneness is a neutral state, and solitude is a positive state (86).

Loneliness is a social problem for five reasons. First, citing W.A. Sadler and T.B. Johnson, "loneliness is an experience involving a total and often acute feeling that constitutes a distinct form of self-awareness of signaling a break in the basic network of the relational reality of the self-world" (quoted, 27). Second, *the meaning of loneliness is social*" (28). Third, *the prevalence of loneliness is significantly higher among some social groups than others*" (29). Fourth, *loneliness has serious social consequences as well*" (29), with lonely people tending not only to be lonely but also to be more fearful and less trusting than non-lonely people (29-30). This in turn leads lonely people to become "trapped in a vicious cycle of social isolation, more fear, and more isolation" (30). As such, lonely people's loneliness exerts consequential impacts for non-lonely people when lonely people act–that is, act out–in response to isolation, and especially fear, while "the reactions of the non-lonely people to the lonely" play pivotal roles in either reinforcing or countering the experience of loneliness that lonely people feel (30). Fifth, *the remedies and strategies for coping with loneliness must be social too*" (30), or in other words, it is only through *social* remedies and *social* strategies that coping will make a substantial difference.

Yang criticizes "the habit of the focusing on *the immediate, rather than the ultimate* causes of loneliness" (31). In contrast, Yang emphasizes that "*The unpredictability, the uncertainty, and the uncontrollability of social relations are the ultimate sources of loneliness* for the vast majority of members of society" (32). To flesh out what he here means, Yang cites Erich Fromm: "A person who has not been completely alienated, who has remained sensitive and can feel, who has not lost the sense of dignity, who is not yet 'for sale', who can still suffer over the suffering of others, who has not acquired fully the having mode of existence–briefly a person who has remained a person and not become a thing–cannot help feeling lonely, powerless, isolated in present-day society" (quoted 35). And yet, because of social stigma concerning loneliness, leading many to perceive loneliness as an individual failing rather than a social problem, too many lonely people do not admit they are lonely, and do not seek help to deal with their loneliness. Failure to be honest about being lonely leads to what James Lynch identifies as 'loneliness traps' wherein lonely people become trapped because they are "ashamed," regarding being lonely as indicative of personal "weakness" (36). Caught in these 'traps', lonely people fail to recognize that "admission to another human being is frequently the catalyst allowing the other person to admit that he or she is equally lonely" (quoted 36).

Loneliness is shaped by how we are socialized to address the questions of "who am I in relation to a particular group of other human beings? Who are the others in a particular way? Do I see myself as one of them? Do they recognize me as 'one of them'?" (36). Logically, "humans will feel the most severe loneliness at the moment of discovering that they could *identify* themselves *with no one else*" (37). Following Sadler and Johnson, Yang characterizes loneliness as encompassing more than the interpersonal and social; loneliness includes the cultural and the cosmic: feeling like we cannot identify with and do not belong within what is supposedly 'our' culture, or even within the wider world and the greater universe (38).

Yang's research findings indicate that older and younger people are both more likely to experience loneliness than people in ages in between (45). Yet studies reveal no consistent relationship between age and loneliness worldwide; this varies across nations and within nations (48-49). Loneliness, however, always tends lower when mobility is higher (58). Yang writes that while loneliness among older people is unsurprising given life events that commonly occur as people grow older (retirement, children growing up and moving away, and deaths of friends and acquaintances as well as partners and spouses), rendering older people more lonely by reducing the extent of their meaningful contact with others (43), the expectation that older age inevitably leads to loneliness is a self-fulfilling prophecy. This association between growing old and becoming lonely is in part counteracted, what's more, by the fact that older people tend more readily than younger people to share that they are lonely (44).

Although loneliness varies in line with gender, with the gendered direction of these results diverging according to nation and region, there are, Yang stresses, no biological or neurological explanation for gendered differences in experience of loneliness (53). One key factor Yang emphasizes in addressing varying rates of loneliness along lines of race and ethnicity is that those experiencing *discrimination* along these lines experience greater loneliness than those who do not, especially more frequent loneliness (125). Poverty, moreover, contributes to loneliness because it is hard to develop or sustain satisfying social networks when poor (149). Yet self-perception is also influential because the poorer people perceive themselves to be the lonelier they feel (150). Still, "it is definitely the case in every country that income level and the chance of feeling financial difficulties are associated negatively," even as "the exact form of relationship varies noticeably across the national contexts" (153).

Social capital mediates loneliness, with higher social capital countering the effects of low economic capital in influencing loneliness (142-143). Unemployment does not, in itself, directly correlate with increased loneliness, because what matters is "the length of unemployment," with "the longer the unemployment, the higher the risk" (147). This higher risk results from loss of social as well as economic capital (147). In sum, the greater the social capital, the reduced likelihood of feeling lonely, and vice-versa (157). In turn, how people feel about their financial situation tends to reflect the extent and quality of their social capital (160).

Loneliness results "from the perceived discrepancy between existing and desired social relations," with the greater this perceived disparity the greater the experience of loneliness (164). This disparity explains why loneliness is highest in Russia and Eastern Europe, not as high in Western and Southern Europe, and lower still in Northern Europe (165). In other words, loneliness tends higher in nations where dominant cultures maintain high expectations of social relations versus nations where that is not the case (167). "The perceived gap" between what is expected versus what is experienced is what matters, and this is why, contrary to what many others argue concerning the crisis of loneliness in the West today (such as Siegel, Kristof, and Alberti), many relatively more collectivist nations show higher rates of loneliness, including of frequent loneliness, than many relatively more individualist nations (168).

Yet more likely to induce loneliness is "living in economically deprived regions"–or, more precisely, living in *relatively* economically deprived regions (170). Key factors, as sociologist G. Hofstede identifies, include: "the degree to which the less powerful members of a society accept and expect that power is distributed unequally"; the degree to which members of a society tend to prefer relatively more individualist versus collectivist "social frameworks"; the degree to which a society tends to emphasize more classically 'masculine' as opposed to classically 'feminine' values as norms and ideals; "the degree to which members of a society feel uncomfortable with uncertainty and ambiguity"; the degree to which societies "prefer to maintain time-honoured traditions and norms while viewing societal change with suspicion"; and the degree to which society "allows relatively free gratification of basic and natural drives related to enjoying life and having fun" (quoted and paraphrased 171). Yet more influential than all those factors are GDP per capita and the Human Development Index (the latter measures the extent to which members of a nation live long and healthy lives, are educated and knowledgeable, and enjoy decent standards of living).

In line with Alberti and Siegel, Yang's statistical analyses show that aloneness does not necessarily increase loneliness. It is, in other words, an insufficient factor. Aloneness, however, does become problematic when people who struggle to take care of their needs, and who are dependent upon others to be able to do so, are *forced* into aloneness and *do not voluntarily choose aloneness* (72). At the same time, Yang argues living alone is unhealthy for many if not most people, and that societies must provide more opportunities for more people to live with others instead of providing as many incentives as they currently tend to do to live alone (80).

Yang also emphasizes forms of loneliness he characterizes as especially devastating. One is homesickness. Here Yang draws a connection between immigrants' experience of homesickness and their struggles to find their place in a new country, with each factor reinforcing the other (117). Another form of loneliness Yang characterizes as "The most saddening kind of loneliness" is loneliness that comes "not because there is no one around but *exactly because some people are around*" (92). Neglect, abuse, conflict within the family or household, and bullying are all examples of this form of loneliness. Abuse, what's more, happens within many institutions beyond the family or household, causing painful 'loneliness among others'–including within the church, at school, and on the job (100-101).

Lack of trust, including lack of 'social trust' (lack of "trust of people in society at large") (110) and lack of "political trust" (lack of trust in political institutions in one's society and even lack of trust in the entire political system in one's nation) also significantly contribute to loneliness (112). In countries where the degree of trust in the political system is high, loneliness is low, and vice-versa (113-114).

Yang advocates societal-wide changes that will enable members to experience the quantity and quality of social relations necessary to prevent loneliness, even as he recognizes the commitment to make these changes is lacking in most societies today (34). Nevertheless, Yang contends, "Loneliness should not just be a problem for the lonely"; it *should* be the responsibility of the non-lonely and of the larger society (184). Assuming this collective responsibility begins with identifying and responding to the needs of the most lonely. But it must proceed beyond that to address the question "how could we tackle loneliness by stopping people from becoming lonely in the first place?" (213). We need to reconstruct our societies based on the recognition that "what human beings truly want is *being both alone and social at the same time*; put differently, they want to *control when they are alone and when they are social*" (209).

In *The Lonely Century: How to Restore Human Connection in a World That's Falling Apart*, Noreena Hertz does embrace the analogy with an epidemic. As Hertz writes, even before the COVID-19 pandemic, "three in five U.S. adults considered themselves lonely" and "In Europe, it was a similar story" with comparable percentages identifying as lonely in many European countries (6). An even greater level of loneliness prevails in contemporary Japan (7). Among many measures, from a plethora of surveys and other studies Hertz cites, "perhaps surprisingly, the youngest among us . . . are the loneliest" as, for instance, "In the United States, slightly more than one in five millenials say they have no friends at all," while "In the United Kingdom, three in five 18-to-34-year-olds and nearly half of children aged between 10 and 15 say they are lonely often or sometimes" (8). As with all four writers I previously discussed, Hertz argues 'the contemporary crisis of loneliness' "isn't just a mental health crisis. It's a crisis that's making us physically ill." In line with Kristof, Hertz cites research that shows "loneliness is worse for our health than not exercising, as harmful as being an alcoholic, and twice as harmful as being obese" (8). Along the same lines, "If you are lonely, you have a 29 percent higher risk of coronary disease, a 32 percent higher risk of stroke, and a 64 percent higher risk of developing clinical dementia," while "If you feel lonely or are socially isolated, you are almost 30 percent more likely to die prematurely that if you are not" (21). Loneliness leads to unrelieved inflammation–i.e., nothing periodically calms down the body's inflammatory response to stress–while, loneliness, what's more, "is a type of stress that can massively *amplify* the effects of other stresses," including in impacting the immune system (27-28). In addition, "There are over 130 studies that have found a link between loneliness and suicide, suicidal ideation, or self-harm. It's a link that holds true among *all* age groups" (31).

Hertz shares the position Siegel, Kristof, Alberti, and Yang all also maintain–that loneliness is a social and not purely an individual problem, a serious social problem, and one that has worsened notably in recent decades. But Hertz adopts, along with Yang, the broadest explanation of what loneliness today encompasses. Loneliness is "also about feeling unsupported and uncared for by our fellow citizens, our employers, our community, our government. It's about feeling disconnected not only from those who we are meant to feel intimate with but also from ourselves. It's about not only lacking support in a social or familial context but feeling politically and economically excluded as well" (11). Hertz defines loneliness "as both an internal state and an existential one–personal, societal, economic, *and* political" (11). According to Hertz, neoliberal capitalist loneliness "incorporates how disconnected we feel from politicians and politics, how cut off we feel from our work and our workplace, how excluded many of us feel from society's gains, and how powerless, invisible, and voiceless so many of us believe ourselves to be" (11). Hertz posits, therefore, that most of us are lonely, even profoundly so.

Hertz is more direct than Siegel, Kristof, Alberti, or Yang in placing responsibility squarely upon neoliberalism, underscoring that neoliberalism by definition means no government, state, or larger societal responsibility to care for people and to make sure people's needs are met (15). "Under neoliberalism," we are reduced to "rational humans consumed by our own self-interest" while "Collectivist words like *belong*, *duty*, *share*, and *together* have since the 1960s been increasingly supplanted by individualistic works and phrases such as *achieve*, *own*, *personal*, and *special*" (16). Loneliness has spiked "where traditional social support structures have collapsed" (32). The result: "Our culture of self-reliance and hustle, so valorized by neoliberal capitalism, comes at a significant cost. For when neighbors are strangers and friendliness and connection are far from the norm, the danger is that at those times that we most need community it simply isn't there" (64).

Hertz warns that loneliness is easily exploited "by politicians at the extremes," especially by those she identifies as "populists"–politicians, in other words, who pit an ostensible 'people' versus an ostensible cabal of sinister 'elites', while "often portraying their nation as under threat of 'invasion' by immigrants or those of different ethnicities or religions" (38-39). Like Siegel, Hertz cites Hannah Arendt warning against the political dangers of loneliness: "the experience of not belonging to the world at all" is "the essence of totalitarian government, preparation of its executioners and victims" (quoted, 41).

Yet Hertz proceeds further than this by attempting to show *how* right-wing authoritarian populists (neo-fascists) exploit loneliness. These politicians and the larger movements they represent intuitively recognize that loneliness "is not simply about feeling socially isolated or lacking communal ties" but also about "not being heard and understood" (43). Hertz identifies Donald Trump as especially successful in exploiting exactly this kind of feeling (45). Trump along with others like him intuitively grasp not only do many people *feel* they have been forgotten but also in fact "many *had* been forgotten for decades as neoliberal capitalism and deindustrialization was then followed by the 2008 financial crisis and a subsequent recession, coupled with politics of austerity" (47). Trumpian 'populists' cultivate much of their support in response–on the basis of both feeling forgotten and being forgotten. "A sense of diminished status" is particularly significant in explaining the appeal of this politics to "many white, working-class men" (48). 'Populists' like Trump offer groups like this what they crave, what they feel they deserve, and, more pointedly, what they feel has been taken from them–along with, most importantly, a feeling of "belonging" (48-49). Hertz calls attention to how Trump speaks "predominantly in the first-person plural, repeatedly using *we* and *us* to forge a relational bond, though of course he has nothing in common with most of his supporters" (50). Trump has also "repeatedly invoked 'the people': 'the beautiful people', 'the amazing people', 'great people'," with 'people' in fact constituting "the most common word used in his speeches" (50). Trump has succeeded in making many who have experienced themselves as socially and politically alienated feel as if they are now included, that they now do belong and do matter–that they represent the heart of 'the America' he promises 'to make great again'.

Of course, this kind of 'populism' depends on defining 'the people' it claims to represent *versus* many groups of 'others' who are supposed 'enemies of the people'. Yet, the key point here, in relation to loneliness, as a leading European Social Survey documents, is that "people who feel politically disempowered, financially insecure and without social support" are "the most likely to become extremely negative toward migrants" (quoted, 56). Notably, Hertz adds, those same three characteristics "are key drivers of loneliness" (56). In order to prevent fascists from taking power, anti-fascist political leaders must, as a matter of urgency, "find ways to make all their citizens feel that they are heard and seen," while providing opportunities to be actively involved in inclusive communities (58).

Hertz recognizes this is by no means easy to accomplish. The obstacles only begin with the continuing "stigma associated with loneliness" (9), because, even more influential, the ways many of us typically live our lives foster loneliness. For example, high rental costs are a major contributing factor, leading Hertz to admonish that "housing is one area where market forces need to be mediated for our collective good" (68). Simply put, it is hard not to feel lonely when one's housing is insecure. In addition, and in part in contrast with Siegel, Alberti, and Yang, Hertz asserts it is demonstrably proven that people who live alone are, on average, lonelier, including more frequently so (70). "Physically coming together" is important for the cultivation of "democratic skills," and Hertz is concerned that 'coming together' via zoom represents a poor substitute (72-73).

Hertz criticizes many other trends for contributing to greater loneliness such as tendencies toward 'contactless living' that accelerated during the early years of the COVID-19 pandemic; urban architecture designed to discourage social gathering and social interaction; 'broken windows' approaches to policing; and NIMBY (Not in My Backyard) mindsets (78-79). All of these trends both pull and keep people apart–while also making people suspicious of and hostile versus others who do not appear 'like themselves'. In addition, Hertz criticizes closing down or privatizing public spaces, such as parks, playgrounds, other green areas, libraries, and community centers, because doing so also increases loneliness (82-83). As Hertz comments, "For people to feel united there need to be well-funded and cherished public spaces where relationships can develop, evolve, cement, including with people different from us, spaces where we *all* can interact, regardless of race, ethnicity, or socioeconomic background. We can't join together if we don't interact with each other. We can't find common ground if there is no ground to share" (84).

Hertz forcefully critiques "digital distraction" (93). According to Hertz, when focused on screens people tend not to be present otherwise (94). Too often digital devices "estrange us from people we already know, including those we love and care for" (95). Too often, Hertz encounters large numbers of people wandering about in close proximity but absorbed by their devices, indicative that we are increasingly "together and yet alone" (96). Empathy is a vital social need, but its cultivation requires hard work, and regular practice, through focused engagement. Yet digital devices "fragment our attention" such that this kind of work is neglected (97).

According to Hertz, social media tends to make "the world feel more hostile, less empathetic, and less kind" and this occurs not just on account of trolling, doxxing, and swatting (107). Hertz contends that the foundational design of social media renders it useful in the interests of hate and abuse (108). Social media "is making society as a whole meaner and crueler. And a mean and cruel world is a lonely one" (109), because spending too much time in one angry, hostile, and lonely environment carries over to other areas of life where angry, hostile, and lonely people attempt to relieve, or release, their pain by targeting others.

Like Alberti, Hertz calls attention to how social media provokes "*FOMO*–fear of missing out," to which Hertz adds "BOMP . . . a Belief that Others are More Popular" (110). What makes this especially hard to take is it includes belief that you are being "*visibly* ignored," inducing shame (112). Such concern pressures people engaged on social media to feel as if they constantly have "to sell oneself" (113). This leads to inauthenticity, where on social media "we are performing the act of sharing, rather than truly sharing ourselves" (115).

Hertz expends even more attention, across multiple chapters, on loneliness as this arises in relation to jobs and workplaces. For instance,

> Forty percent. That's the percentage of office workers globally who say they feel lonely at work. In the United Kingdom it is as high as 60 percent . . . In the United States almost one in five people do not have a single friend at work, and 54 percent of Generation K feel emotionally distant from their colleagues. All these figures predate the coronavirus and the age of social distancing, which have only exacerbated such feelings. At the same time, 85 percent of workers globally do not feel engaged with their jobs. (125)

Even though Hertz is careful to indicate "we should not romanticize the workplace of yore" (125), she stresses that "so many aspects of modern-day work intended to make us *more* productive and efficient are ultimately having the opposite effect because they make us feel less connected and more isolated" (126). Among examples of this tendency are the 'open-plan office' and 'hot-desking' as well as "The rise of remote working" (131). Hertz admits remote working "is not fundamentally bad," but nonetheless argues this can lead to isolation and loneliness by making it much more difficult to develop and maintain close relations with fellow workers, and with customers or clients. The 'gig economy' Hertz critiques for much the same reasons, because workers doing these jobs experience little to no connection with others doing the same, and thereby suffer from lack solidarity with fellow workers (136).

Hertz cites studies that report most workers prefer 'kind' and 'nice' workplaces, but the problem is "in our neoliberal capitalist system kindness and niceness are . . . traits that are significantly undervalued" (139). Kindness and niceness are hardly characteristic of most workplaces in what Shoshana Zuboff identifies as 'The Age of Surveillance Capitalism', which Hertz cites in addressing how pervasive surveillance at work increases loneliness. Hertz claims, due to the pervasiveness of such surveillance, many of us today work "In the Age of the Panopticon Workplace" (157). Along similar lines, excessive emphasis on measurement of even the most minute possible contributions to productivity not only is self-defeating because it undermines productivity but also leaves workers feeling dehumanized. Dehumanized people are lonely people. Constant measurement of how much the worker does and does not do on the job "incentivizes employees to self-censor and withdraw," with both of these responses tending to increase feelings of loneliness (159), as, after all, when you are hesitant, if not afraid, to represent what you truly think, openly and honestly, and certainly when you withdraw, you are doing the obverse of reaching out to forge meaningful connections with others. Yes, Hertz acknowledges, these practices have long been characteristic of capitalist firms, but what is new about the 21st century neocapitalist workplace is "the *extent* [my italics] to which we are being monitored, the disturbing *levels* [my italics] of intrusiveness that digital technology makes possible, and the *degree* [my italics] to which decision-making powers have been ceded to machines" (160).

Constant ratings of workers, by managers and bosses, and by customers and clients, similarly encourages workers to pursue the safest ways of doing their jobs, so as not to risk low ratings, while also fomenting competition and undermining cooperation among workers (162-163). Automation and roboticization likewise increase alienation and loneliness in relation to work and jobs. Hertz speculates, if current trends along these lines continue unabated, soon many fewer people will work jobs, with those remaining experiencing less human contact on the job, while others will struggle without jobs. Both groups will experience all the greater loneliness.

And yet, "Many of us feel lonely at work because we're lonely *outside* of it" while "one of the reasons we're lonely is the long hours many of us spend working," with this combination amounting to "a vicious cycle" (141). After all, "Working long hours and juggling multiple jobs is increasingly common" (141) as, notably, "Almost one in six U.S. teachers now has a second job, not just in the summer" (141). Burnout and loneliness often go hand in hand. In addition, digital technologies require workers to be "always on" (143), which means they are never able 'to get away from work' to focus instead on developing relations capable of countering loneliness. Even though some countries, such as France, have legislated a 'right to disconnect', this remains uncommon (145), and certainly gig economy workers do not enjoy this right.

Hertz proceeds beyond work and jobs to discuss how many people today turn to robots for friendship, sex, and even love. Many people in fact find such robots indispensable. In Japan, for instance, where "Fifteen percent of elderly Japanese men go two weeks without speaking to a soul" (185), robot companions are highly popular, but their popularity has been rapidly increasing in many other nations too. Hertz worries about AI substitutes for human-to-human connection, arguing that long-term reliance upon such substitutes makes it more difficult for people to learn how to relate to and treat other people with sensitivity, understanding, compassion, and empathy.

Hertz is, in addition, highly skeptical of 'communities' run by for-profit industries that supposedly provide otherwise lonely people opportunities to live and/or work together. As Hertz explains, these enterprises prove problematic when they reinforce individualistic values. Too often these 'communities' allow people to live and work in proximity, but, as Hertz observes, real

"Community is predicated on people *doing* things together, not simply *being* together or bumping into each other as they pass by" (221). Also of concern is that co-living communities, and co-working communities, need to be run from the ground up not the top down in order to prove effective in countering loneliness, as well as not so that people living and/or working in the same space engage with each others solely as exploitable opportunities, as "a potential mark" (223). Real community requires hard work and persistent commitment over an extended period of time, yet too many co-living and co-working enterprises pretend that is unnecessary, and what's more, all too rarely are they diversely inclusive.

Loneliness becomes "a self-perpetuating cycle. This is because in order *not* to feel lonely we need to give as well as take, care as well as be cared for, be kind to each other and respectful of those around us, as well as be treated as such ourselves" (17). But lonely people are often poorly equipped to give. In sum, "Loneliness is not just a subjective state of mind. It is also a collective state of being that has taken a huge toll on us as individuals and society as a whole, contributing to the deaths of millions of people annually, costing the global economy billions, and posing a potential threat to tolerant and inclusive democracy" (228).

The answer to this state of massive loneliness starts with "the antithesis of loneliness–community" (21). Although "It is important not to overly romanticize community" (25), because what matters is the kind and quality of community, Hertz is willing, despite her skepticism of what she identifies as the 'loneliness economy', to endorse the "creation of a new category of business: pro-community enterprises that are eligible for tax breaks, incentives, and grants if they deliver on verifiable metrics of inclusivity and help drive social cohesion" (212). Likewise, Hertz urges the implementation of incentives to "create a workplace of people paid explicitly to help others feel less lonely" (233), and the same with jobs that concentrate on fostering community where this is lacking (232). Hertz also champions the opening of more shops designed to enable people to gather and hang out–as well as the benefit that comes from adopting pets. Even "micro-interactions" with others, Hertz believes, can help (66). Unsurprisingly, therefore, Hertz recommends we all support local businesses and make the conscious effort to be friendly with strangers.

Big or small, what is needed, Hertz proposes, are multiple enhanced opportunities for social interaction, physical touch, and the giving as well as receiving of kindness. One concrete way of working toward these ends might involve following the example of Rwanda, where citizens are now required by law to contribute three hours of public service every month (244). Hertz favors similar requirements, or at least strong incentives, to compel neighbors to get to know each other, especially neighbors 'different from ourselves'. In addition, Hertz urges governments to intervene to stop the abusive impacts of social media on young people, arguing that social media "should be banned for children under the age of adult consent" (118). She insists governments should enforce "zero tolerance" for "the most egregious examples of toxic discourse" (119) on these platforms as well as mandate that tech companies maintain "a statutory 'duty of care' to their customers" (122). Other robust new laws are needed, Hertz advises, to protect the most vulnerable workers, such as those working in the gig economy (236).

Yet Hertz recognizes the need for more sweeping changes, with the nature of what counts as 'work' and as a 'job' needing to be radically reconceived. Here Hertz at least implicitly supports universal basic income. The logical implication of Hertz's overall argument is "neoliberal capitalism" must be replaced. This system is directly responsible for massive loneliness "by redefining our relationships as transactions" and by "recasting citizens in the role of consumers" (230). Although ready to recommend a host of short-term, small-scale responses, Hertz emphasizes the "root causes" of this contemporary 'crisis of loneliness' are what ultimately need to be addressed, not just "the symptoms," with these root causes being "political, economic, and . . . societal rather than simply pharmaceutical" (32).

The lyrics of Ian Curtis and the music of Joy Division resonate strongly with desire to be able to choose to be alone, to pursue and derive positive benefits from solitude, when and as useful, while not being forced into aloneness, especially not for long durations and especially not when one needs others, and suffers painfully without them–without, that is, being able to count on others for help when and as one is struggling, and without being able to interact with others on the basis of shared understandings, sensitivities, and sensibilities. These lyrics and this music resonate as well with the loneliness that follows from working jobs performing alienated labor, and from the spirit-destroying consequences of doing so for decades on end; with the loneliness that follows from the normative expectation that people should not maintain multiple simultaneous intimate relationships; and with the loneliness that follows from experience of violence and trauma. At the same time, these lyrics and this music manifest commitment to strive to find a way out, and to encourage others–especially those of us listening closely and attending carefully to these lyrics and this music–to join this effort. In accepting this encouragement, we nourish a flicker of hope that it might be possible, even when it feels impossible, genuinely to counter, contest, and break past the worst ravages of loneliness.

Five

In chapter two I interpret the lines "I never realised the lengths I'd have to go" followed by "All the darkest corners of a sense I didn't know" as indicative of the narrator-protagonist announcing 'he' has taken on an enormously daunting challenge, in a highly idealist and highly romantic fashion, to confront the worst evils human beings are capable of committing versus each other. This confrontation has forced the narrator-protagonist to feel for himself what it is like to experience these evils as victim and as perpetrator, as well as bystander and as witness. This exploration has, yet further, involved attempting to show how these evils are rooted in the fundamentally flawed nature, that is the fundamentally flawed systemic structures, of existing society and culture, in terms of how people are organized in what kinds of relations with each other, according to what logics and what principles, facilitated and governed by what institutions, and formed and shaped as what kinds of social subjects–and what kinds of existential beings. The narrator-protagonist is devastated by what he has encountered, and in particular by what has been required of him not to retreat from the encounter or otherwise protect himself from feeling the impact of what he encounters. The narrator-protagonist has discovered an appalling depth and extent of responsibility for and complicity in 'evil'–including an appalling depth and extent of his own responsibility for and complicity with 'evil'. The lengths he has traveled, through the darkest corners of what he did not previously register at all, has left him feeling overwhelmed, in desperate need of help to recover, but bewildered concerning where to turn to find such help, if it exists at all.

"Darkest corners" suggest the most *frightening* places, the places we *fear* the most, and the places where we *fear* we will meet the worst possible outcomes. According to the lyrics from "Twenty Four Hours," we cannot understand, let alone appreciate, the 'darkness' within these 'corners' for how 'dark' it truly is until we enter these spaces. It is imperative we do so, yet doing so will leave us devastated. As I have previously written, such a task, while worthwhile, requires a collective effort because individuals attempting this by themselves alone risk being unable to survive the impact.

What specific 'fears' resonate as capable of exerting such overwhelming impact? I begin, in considering this question, by referring to Robert Peckham's 2023 book *Fear: An Alternative History of the World*. Peckham proposes the history of the world, and especially of 'the West', can be recounted by focusing on widely socially shared 'fears', from 'The Great Pestilence' in the Middle Ages through the COVID-19 pandemic. Peckham argues against 'fear of fear', because "Fear isn't always inimical to freedom but may be its corollary, an integral facet of empowerment. Fear has generative potential, even when it appears as a desperate invocation graffitied on a bus shelter. It can be harnessed to change the world, creating new possibilities, even as it forecloses others" (xiv-xv). Fear is multiple, complex, contradictory, and dynamic: "different political regimes are enabled by the production of different kinds of fear, just as counter-fears, often unforeseen, disrupt the smooth operation of those regimes, sometimes shattering them, but often creating pressure upon them to evolve. Viewed like this, fear isn't just the tool and nemesis of power; it's also the reactive agent that can force change" (xxi). The progressive aim, therefore, should not be to eliminate fear, as "It's a mistake to assume that modern freedoms have been won by the abrogation of fear from political life. On the contrary . . . state-sponsored fear has played a crucial role, not only in the ascent of modern freedom but also in the emergence of the economic order on which it has been built" (xxii).

The lyrics of Ian Curtis and the music of Joy Division render fear as terrifying, with fear interlinked with violence experienced as traumatic. Still, it might make sense to interpret invocation of fear within these lyrics and this music as serving the interest of "a social glue and check on power" (8), by encouraging us to keep vigilantly "alert to potential infractions on our rights and attentive to the state's repressive instincts" (12). In this respect, 'feeling the fear' might be crucial for us to realize and respond to the gravity of what is at stake.

Peckham emphasizes fear is not just biological, but socially and culturally mediated, and tends to manifest "in response to uncertainty" (7). Yet fear maintains broadly common features. For instance, 17th century English philosopher Thomas Hobbes relates humans' "perpetual fear" (quoted 54) with, as Peckham summarizes, fear "of the unknown–and in particular fear of death" (54). As Hobbes theorizes, religions use this dimension of fear "to keep the people in obedience" (quoted 54) and, as Peckham paraphrases, "to ensure the status quo" (54). Yet Hobbes also theorizes, as Peckham paraphrases, that "Foresight and prudence . . . arise out of fear" (55). It might make sense to interpret the lyrics of Ian Curtis and the music of Joy Division addressing 'fear' as double-edged, yet with the qualification that if this is 'foresight' and 'prudence' it nonetheless feels closer to 'anxiousness' and 'unease'. In these lyrics and in this music, security obtained through fear feels fleeting, at best.

The lyrics of Ian Curtis and the music of Joy Division make sense as sympathetically to empathetically identifying with the position of social groups 'feared' on account of real and perceived differences, with such fear stoked by demagogues and totalitarians. These lyrics and this music simultaneously register an uncomfortable identification with what it is like to 'fear' 'others' on account of their ostensible 'otherness'. Likewise, these lyrics and this music conjure fear suggestive of pleasure converging with pain, such as in relation to experience of 'the sublime' or by way of intimations of the Lacanian 'Real'. Fear resulting from or attendant on alienation, as well as anomie, resonates as well. As does fear of 'degeneration' due to the machination of everyday life, including, more recently, by way of the influence of digital technology and artificial intelligence. As does fear in relation to economic crisis, including what Naomi Klein has theorized as contemporary 'disaster capitalism' (cited, 165).

All the more readily convergent with the lyrics of Ian Curtis and the music of Joy Division, however, are the kinds of fear that result from experience in war, including post-traumatic stress disorder, as well as comparable experiences likewise involving "mental collapse brought on by fear" (Peckham 180). Similarly, pervasion of fear experienced as a result of living in totalitarian societies, such as Nazi Germany and Stalinist Russia, readily converges with the kinds of fear the lyrics of Ian Curtis and the music of Joy Division invoke. In particular, these lyrics and this music resonate with fear that results from the impact of fascism in everyday life. This kind of fear can be especially insidious: "It's precisely because terror emerges from this jostling, everyday space of mutually reinforcing *angst* that it's so difficult to manage" (194). As Bertolt Brecht aptly comments on fascism and fear: "Fear holds sway not only over those who are ruled, but also/Over those who rule" (quoted 194).

In Nazi Germany the Nazis successfully mobilized fears among the masses, persuading them that Nazism provided the the only way to avoid otherwise inexorable 'social breakdown' (196-197). In this kind of regime, the great leader gives "voice to the people's fears" (196), while exhorting 'pre-emptive' violence as a way of addressing these fears (197). As such, the Third Reich was, in Peter Fritzsche's words, "premised on both supreme confidence and terrifying vulnerability; both states of mind co-existed and continuously radicalized Nazi policies" (197). Likewise, under Stalin, as Peckham describes, "Fear permeated Soviet society," even "to a far greater extent than it did in Germany under Hitler" (198). Here Peckham also cites Hannah Arendt in explaining that totalitarianism works by "dominating and terrorizing human beings from within" (quoted 203), aiming "to monopolise every aspect of the individual's intellectual and emotional life" (quoted 203). Alienation, in the form of "loneliness," provides "fertile ground for totalitarian leaders to exploit" (quoted 203). Totalitarian fears–including both fears of totalitarianism as well as fears exploited by totalitarianism–strongly resonate with fear as invoked in the lyrics of Ian Curtis and the music of Joy Division.

In relation to present fears, Peckham cautions against imagining these are necessarily worse than past fears. Peckham worries that too many, across the political spectrum, have become overwrought with fear:

We've entered a world of illiberal democracy and authoritarian populism. A world in which the right and the left alike are at war with what used to be called the middle ground. The right believes that liberalism is yoked to a progressive politics that is eroding 'traditional' values. For the left, neoliberalism is pushing a free-for-all market economy that has exacerbated inequalities, while right-wing pundits are accused of cooking up a moral panic around illusory fears of the unforgiving 'woke mob'" (313).

Peckham commends "a benevolent fear that prepares us for the challenges of the future without overlooking the possibilities for change in the present–a fear that sees grounds for hope, not despair, in uncertainty" (314). Peckham insists that "fear connects us, as individuals and as societies, in ways that we often don't see" (314), and this can be for good as well as for bad. It is important, what's more, to keep in mind that "the fears we experience in the present are also rooted in the past. Our responses to any crisis are inevitably shaped by earlier crises . . . fear is always intersectional, an unnerving confluence of past, present and future . . ." (316).

Joy Division songs alternate moments of calm with moments of unrest and moments of hope with moments of fear, while both the lyrics and the music call attention to the *distance* between the position from which they are addressing us versus the position of the imagined characters in the imagined situations in the imagined dramas these lyrics and this music stage and perform for us. Yet neither these lyrics nor this music propose that if we carefully attend to intersections among past, present, and prospective future fears will we recognize we can cope with and make positive use of what we fear. Fear in the lyrics of Ian Curtis and the Joy Division is not invoked in order to dampen this down, to lower the temperature, to subject it to rational management and control. To the contrary: according to these lyrics and this music, fear must be taken on, while emphasizing that doing so feels terrifying. According to these lyrics and this music, where fear takes us, how, through what, and with what consequences if we 'make it through' cannot be managed or controlled, let alone predicted or guaranteed.

From early on in my own life I feared that forces representative of fascist tendencies, operant throughout everyday life, were much more persistent and influential than many if not most others perceived. I perceived these tendencies in people all too easily dehumanizing other people on the basis of differences from themselves they ascribed to and associated with those others. I recognized these tendencies when the former people related to the latter people as if the latter were not human at all. I recognized these tendencies when the former people related to the latter people as if the latter deserved ostracism, denigration, and abuse. I recognized these tendencies happening along lines of race, ethnicity, nationality, citizenship and immigration status, gender, sexuality, class, disability, physical and mental health/illness, age, body shape and size, religion, regionality, and locality. I recognized these tendencies immediately around me, among the people living in the same communities where I lived, among people attending the same schools I attended, among people pursuing the same recreational activities I pursued, and among people participating in the same natural and cultural spaces I participated in. I did not encounter these tendencies solely at a distance, far away. I felt frightened in recognizing how callous and cruel people could be, and could become, including others right around me. I felt frightened in recognizing that people received incentives and rewards for being callous and cruel.

I felt frightened in recognizing how easy it is to avoid the 'darkest corners', to keep away and to turn away–even to refuse to recognize, or altogether to deny, that these 'darkest corners' exist at all. I felt frightened in recognizing that 'no one is innocent', certainly not me, and that we are all responsible–and all complicit–with others' pain and suffering. I felt frightened in recognizing that many acted in callous and cruel ways because they feared the others they treated in these ways, and feared, what's more, how they would be treated themselves if they did not respond to those others in indifferent or hostile ways. I felt frightened to recognize how easily we can become absorbed in our immediate individual concerns such that we become oblivious to others, to what they are experiencing, and especially to how they are suffering. I felt frightened to recognize how easily we can determine we cannot do anything to help these others because our own individual concerns seemingly require all of our attention. I felt frightened in recognizing how easy it can be to rationalize and justify what others are suffering as 'not my concern', and, worse than that, as 'what they deserve', as where they have ended up due to their lesser merit or as a result of what they themselves ostensibly have freely chosen. I felt frightened in recognizing that, no, I could not possibly imagine I would automatically act differently, and especially better, than did many Germans who preferred to do and say nothing while the Nazi regime was in power because they feared for their own lives, as well as for those of their immediate family members, and because they feared torture and imprisonment. A number of students in classes where we discussed these issues always voiced the confident conviction that if ever involved in such circumstances they would readily stand up for what is right and never be cowed into submission because of fear. But I recognized I could not possibly say this about myself, and it frightened me to recognize this was so.

In the 'State and Society' class I took as a sophomore undergraduate student at Wesleyan University our professor asked us to write an essay response to the prompt, 'how likely is a socialist revolution in the United States in the near future?' I immediately recognized I judged this to be next to impossible. In my paper I wrote that a fascist counter-revolution was far more likely. My professor was so struck by my response that he embarrassed me by reading from my paper aloud to the whole class, commending me for arguing the far less popular position, because most other students in the class argued a socialist revolution in the United States within the near future was likely, even highly likely.

For decades running, and beginning well before my undergraduate years, one of my most frequent recurrent nightmares involved immersion in the chaos surrounding a successful fascist uprising in the U.S. This uprising begins in small towns, but spreads rapidly to larger cities. The uprising involves frightening violence, notably in relation to the rounding up of large numbers of people for internment in concentration camps, one of whom always is me. Because of the disturbing recurrence of this vivid nightmare, I proposed to an advanced undergraduate student, James Boland, that we use this same dream as the basis for writing a feature-length fictional screenplay as part of a senior honors undergraduate collaborative student-faculty research project. We did so, working together from 2006-2007 to write a screenplay we titled *Faceless Fascism*.

But the fascist takeover James and I imagined did not anticipate imagine Donald Trump's rise to power and influence, nor the principal means by which he has gained support, nor who would constitute the chief constituents of his primary base of support. Nor for that matter did we imagine the rise of similar 21st century neo-fascist figures and movements in France, Italy, Brazil, Hungary, Denmark, Norway, Sweden, Austria, Germany, Ireland, and Britain.

In a November 2023 opinion piece for *The Washington Post*, Robert Kagan argues that "A Trump dictatorship is increasingly inevitable. We should stop pretending." Kagan argues we cannot count on others serving within the executive branch of a prospective second Trump administration, Republicans or Democrats in Congress, the courts, the military or the intelligence services, the media, the states, or even the people organized in protest to prevent a reelected Donald Trump from becoming a full-fledged dictator. Trump and those behind him, those pushing to return him to power, are prepared to prevent any of those forces from acting as effective constraints, and once reelected Trump and those immediately around him plan to push immediately in a dictatorial direction. As Kagan explains,

> It is worth getting inside Trump's head a bit and imagining his mood following an election victory. He will have spent the previous year, and more, fighting to stay out of jail, plagued by myriad persecutors and helpless to do what he likes to do best: exact revenge. Think of the fury that will have built up inside him, a fury that, from his point of view, he has worked hard to contain. As he once put it, "I think I've been toned down, if you want to know the truth. I could really tone it up." Indeed he could–and will. We caught a glimpse of his deep thirst for vengeance in his Veterans Day promise to "root out the Communists, Marxists, Fascists, and Radical Left Thugs that live like vermin within the confines of our Country, lie, steal, and cheat on Elections, and will do anything possible, whether legally or illegally, to destroy America, and the American Dream." Note the equation of himself with "America and the American Dream." It is he they are trying to destroy, he believes, and as president, he will return the favor.

And it is not just those Trump identifies as his own personal enemies that this second Trump administration will target, because

> His administration will be filled with people with enemies' lists of their own, a determined cadre of "vetted" officials who will see it as their sole, presidentially authorized mission to "root out" those in the government who cannot be trusted. Many will simply be fired, but others will be subject to career-destroying investigations. The Trump administration will be filled with people who will not need explicit instruction from Trump, any more than Hitler's local gauleiters needed instruction. In such circumstances, people "work toward the Führer," which is to say, they anticipate his desires and seek favor through acts they think will make him happy, thereby enhancing their own influence and power in the process.

What is likely to make a Trump dictatorship all the more likely to succeed, Kagan warns, is that this "will not be a communist tyranny, where almost everyone feels the oppression and has their lives shaped by it," but rather a "conservative, anti-liberal" tyranny where "ordinary people" will "face all kinds of limitations on their freedoms," but this will be "a problem for them only to the degree that they value those freedoms, and many people do not." In other words, "The fact that this tyranny will depend entirely on the whims of one man will mean that Americans' rights will be conditional rather than guaranteed," which means "if most Americans can go about their daily business, they might not care, just as many Russians and Hungarians do not care." Kagan acknowledges "Americans might take to the streets," and "In fact, it is likely that many people will engage in protests against the new regime, perhaps even before it has had a chance to prove itself deserving of them." Yet Kagan suspects these protests will be suppressed, because

Even in his first term, Trump and his advisers on more than one occasion discussed invoking the Insurrection Act. No less a defender of American democracy than George H.W. Bush invoked the act to deal with the Los Angeles riots in 1992. It is hard to imagine Trump not invoking it should "the Communists, Marxists, Fascists, and Radical Left Thugs" take to the streets. One suspects he will relish the opportunity.

Kagan places little faith in the notion that other political figures will call Trump and his administration to account for acting in this way, and especially not that 'blue states' will serve as effective 'sanctuaries' from the ravages of a Trump dictatorship everywhere else, because

The power shift at the federal level, and the tone of menace and revenge emanating from the White House, will likely embolden all kinds of counter-resistance even in deep-blue states, including violent protests. What resources will the governors have to combat such attacks and maintain order? The state and local police? Will those entities be willing to use force against protesters who will likely enjoy the public support of the president? The Democratic governors might not be eager to find out.

This is a real and imminent danger, and indeed it may well already be too late:
Should Trump be successful in launching a campaign of persecution and the opposition prove powerless to stop it, then the nation will have begun an irreversible descent into dictatorship. With each passing day, it will become harder and more dangerous to stop it by any means, legal or illegal. Try to imagine what it will be like running for office on an opposition ticket in such an environment. In theory, the midterm elections in 2026 might hold hope for a Democratic comeback, but won't Trump use his considerable powers, both legal and illegal, to prevent that? Trump insists and no doubt believes that the current administration corruptly used the justice system to try to prevent his reelection. Will he not consider himself justified in doing the same once he has all the power? He has, of course, already promised to do exactly that: to use the powers of his office to persecute anyone who dares challenge him.

In closing, Kagan declares "We are closer to that point today than we have ever been, yet we continue to drift toward dictatorship, still hoping for some intervention that will allow us to escape the consequences of our collective cowardice, our complacent, willful ignorance and, above all, our lack of any deep commitment to liberal democracy."

In a December 2023 follow-up column, once more for *The Washington Post*, titled "The Trump dictatorship: How to stop it," Kagan indicates, yes, it is still possible to prevent this dictatorship, as "It does not require a miracle, only courage." Yet, the question remains, "will the people do what they need to do? Human frailty being what it is, and ambitious and selfish politicians being what they are, it is probably fanciful to imagine that the right combination of people will turn up and show a wisdom and courage they have not shown for the past eight years." Too many, in other words, have been not only complacent, but also compliant–and complicit–for far too long, so Kagan is "deeply pessimistic," even though "I could not more fervently wish to be proved wrong."

What should prompt many to fear a second Trump administration, including many who do not (yet), is that Trump's backers are much better prepared than in 2016, including to push much further, harder, and faster to implement an elaborate program of radical change. These plans are publicly available, a clear sign of the confidence of the coalition responsible, as 'Project 2025'. Reviewing Project 2025, Global Project Against Hate and Extremism (GPAHE) declares,

> The America that Project 2025 wants to create would involve a fundamental reordering of our society. It would greatly enhance the executive branch's powers and impose on all Americans policies favored by Christian nationalists regarding issues such as sexual health and reproductive rights, education, the family, and the role of religion in our society and government. It would strip rights protections from LGBTQ+ people, immigrants, women, and people of color. It would dismantle much of the federal government and replace our apolitical civil service with far-right partisans it is already training in anticipation of a power shift. It would end attempts to enhance equity and racial justice throughout the government and shut down agencies that track progress on this front. Efforts to tackle issues such as climate change would be ended, and politicized research produced to back the project's views on environmental policy, the evils of "transgenderism," and women's health would take priority.

Numerous aspects of Project 2025 are concerning, inciting of justified fear. An overarching concern, and reason for fear, is that

> The entire project is devoted to aggrandizing executive power by centralizing authority in the presidency, and a key aspect of democratic backsliding is viewing opposition elements as attempting to destroy the "real" community, an essential aspect to quashing dissent. Project 2025 paints progressives and liberals as outside acceptable politics, and not just ideological opponents, but inherently anti-American and "replacing American values." Targeting vulnerable communities is a core tenet of Project 2025. Certain populations, in particular the LGBTQ+ community, are treated as deviants with ill intent rather than humans and Americans, and do not appear to exist within the far right's framework of those deserving of fulsome human rights and protection from discrimination. Perhaps even more frightening, the left, the LGBTQ+ population, and the "woke," are described as subversive elements aimed at destroying the country and its "real values."

Echoing concerns I have addressed at multiple points in this book,

The Project especially demonizes the transgender community, equating "transgenderism" and "transgender ideology" with "pornography." Immigrants are demonized with false claims of inherent criminality, turning them into a national security threat that must be dealt with harshly. And anti-Black racism is evident in the Project's sweeping denunciation of "the noxious tenets" of Critical Race Theory (only taught at the college level and beyond) which it falsely claims is "advocating for more racial discrimination" rather than acknowledging America's history of racism.

Particularly insidious, Project 2025 "rejects the constitutional separation of Church and State, rather privileging religious beliefs over civil laws. Religious freedom is referenced throughout the plan and is seen to trump all other civil rights which should be subsumed to an individual's religious rights. The message that America must remain Christian, that Christianity should enjoy a privileged place in society, and that the government must take steps to ensure this is clear in every section of the plan, as is the idea that American identity cannot be separated from Christianity." Elaborating upon this point, GPAHE explains that

The Project's Christian Nationalist goals are inherent in its dehumanizing language about LGBTQ+ people, putting them in the same sentence as pornography and pedophilia, rabid rejection of "wokeness," its promotion of the "traditional family" writing that, "Families comprised of a married mother, father, and their children are the foundation of a well-ordered nation and healthy society," its certainty that gender identity is binary and that being LGBTQ+ is an ideology rather than a natural state.

Along the same lines, "The Project claims falsely that only heterosexual, two-parent families are safe for children, and that 'All other family forms involve higher levels of instability (the average length of same-sex marriages is half that of heterosexual marriages); financial stress or poverty; and poor behavioral, psychological, or educational outcomes'. (Their data on the length of marriages is false)."

Project 2025 calls for

"deleting the terms sexual orientation and gender identity ('SOGI'), diversity, equity, and inclusion ('DEI'), gender, gender equality, gender equity, gender awareness, gender-sensitive, abortion, reproductive health, reproductive rights, and any other term used to deprive Americans of their First Amendment rights out of every federal rule, agency regulation, contract, grant, regulation, and piece of legislation that exists." And it calls for the Department of Health and Human Services' (HHS) "antidiscrimination policy statements" to "never conflate sex with gender identity or sexual orientation." It demands changes to Title VII, calling for a restriction of Bostock's [Bostock v. Clayton County] "application of sex discrimination protections to sexual orientation and transgender status in the context of hiring and firing" and to rescind "regulations prohibiting discrimination on the basis of sexual orientation, gender identity, transgender status, and sex characteristics." Sex discrimination should be restricted to a "biological binary meaning." Further, it calls on the HHS secretary to "proudly state that men and women are biological realities that are crucial to the advancement of life sciences and medical care and that married men and women are the ideal, natural family structure because all children have a right to be raised by the men and women who conceived them."

In addition, Project 2025 advances "unfounded, hyperbolic claims that 'children suffer the toxic normalization of transgenderism with drag queens and pornography invading their school libraries', repeatedly linking transgender people to pornography." Accordingly, Project 2025 "would abolish the Gender Policy Council, which 'would eliminate central promotion of abortion . . . comprehensive sexuality education . . . and the new woke gender ideology, which has as a principal tenet "gender affirming care" and "sex-change" surgeries on minors'."

Likewise out of ostensible concern for what it identifies as *the* family as well as 'the sanctity of life, Project 2025 mandates that "The next conservative President should work with Congress to enact the most robust protections for the unborn that Congress will support while deploying existing federal powers to protect innocent life and vigorously complying with statutory bans on the federal funding of abortion" (Paraphrase, GPAHE), while proceeding "farther than that," in "calling for a ban on 'abortion pills' and tasking the Department of Justice (DOJ) to criminally prosecute providers and distributors of such medications" (Paraphrase, GPAHE). In sum, "The Project would force all Americans, in contrast with the Supreme Court ruling overturning Roe that left abortion policy to the states, to abide by the wishes of those Americans for whom abortion 'violates the conscience and religious freedom rights'." Meanwhile, Projects 2025 "attacks contraception in many different ways, pushing for example to eliminate the morning after pill, and suggests instead that, 'fertility awareness–based methods of family planning [the rhythm method, which is much less effective than birth control] are part of women's preventive services under the ACA [Affordable Care Act]'." What this means, as GPAHE puts it, is "the Project would restrict as much as is possible any access to services it views as related to abortion, even contraception if necessary, even in those states that have elected to keep the procedure legal."

A major target of Project 2025 are "efforts to improve racial equity," as "The Project calls for an end to 'Racial Classifications and Critical Race Theory (CRT) Trainings'," while it at the same time "advocates for an executive order that would ban CRT training, a new law barring the use of taxpayer dollars to fund CRT trainings, and the elimination of all Equal Employment Opportunity data collection, which is used to assess the diversity of the workforce (Paraphrase, GPAHE)." But the Project envisions yet greater changes than those, because, "A big part of Project 2025" involves "changing the nature of America's public education system to remove elements from the curriculum that are seen as too 'woke' and supposedly 'inject racist, anti-American, ahistorical propaganda into America's classrooms'." What this means, more precisely, is "The Project characterizes public schools as poisoning and indoctrinating children with leftist ideologies and undermining parents' role in their children's education," so it "advocates for private schooling (often religious) paid for by public monies," as well as eliminating "the Department of Education (DOE), which it calls a 'one-stop shop for the woke education cartel'," in order to "return all responsibility for education to the states (Paraphrase, GPAHE)." Yet, even without the DOE, the federal government hardly would abandon involvement in nationwide public education, as it would lead the way in showing that so-called "radical gender ideology" exercises a "devastating effect on school-aged children today–especially young girls (Paraphrase, GPAHE)." And that means "names and pronouns" used in schools "must be based on birth certificates," while, at the least, "no education employee or contractor should be 'forced' to use a pronoun that doesn't match the person's biological sex, as that would be against their religious or moral convictions (Paraphrase, GPAHE)."

Particularly striking, "Project 2025 claims that the Pentagon is teaching 'white privilege' and has 'emphasized leftist politics over military readiness'." Project 2025 calls upon a need to "Eliminate Marxist indoctrination and divisive critical race theory programs and abolish newly established diversity, equity, and inclusion offices and staff (Paraphrase, GPAHE)." It is indeed a sign of the extent of fear motivating Project 2025 that those responsible for putting these plans together are deeply concerned that the U.S. military has supposedly become a central locus of the influence of "cultural Marxism." As GPAHE explains, 'cultural Marxism' is where, reputedly, Marxists "cloak their goals under the pretense of social justice," but in reality "seek to dismantle the foundations of the American republic by rewriting history; reintroducing racism; creating privileged classes; and determining what can be said in public discourse, the military, and houses of worship." Project 2025 avers that "Unless Marxist thought is defeated again," especially in the military, "today's cultural Marxists will achieve what the Soviet Union never could: the subjugation of the United States to a totalitarian, soul-destroying ideology (Paraphrase, GPAHE)." As GPAHE in response aptly points out, "The Cultural Marxism conspiracy theory was originally developed by white supremacists and antisemites, but has increasingly been accepted by the far right."

Since the U.S. military represents a seemingly urgent site for intervention, Project 2025 "would also reverse policies that allow transgender people to serve in the Armed Forces. It would expel 'those with gender dysphoria', likely referring to transgender individuals, and reverse 'policies that allow transgender individuals to serve in the military'." Project 2025 "claims that 'gender dysphoria' is incompatible with military service, and that 'the use of public monies for transgender surgeries or to facilitate abortion for service members should be ended'." What's more, the Project "also obsesses over the idea that mask-mandates and mandatory vaccines have somehow weakened the Armed Forces, even though the requirement to be vaccinated against Covid has been dropped."

This ostensibly 'strengthened' military will be necessary, as GPAHE discusses, because "One of the pillars of Project 2025 is 'Defend Our Borders'," while Project 2025 "demonizes immigrants as a crime-ridden plague." Project 2025 "proposes incredibly harsh immigration policies, including tent cities and restricting asylum for those fleeing gang violence and domestic violence. It would dismantle the Department of Homeland Security (DHS) and place all immigration-related activities across the administration in one agency." Moreover, "Project 2025 wants to restrict asylum, end 'chain migration', and authorize state and local law enforcement to participate in immigration and border security." In turn, "The project advocates for 'the flexibility to use large numbers of temporary facilities such as tents' to house migrants and the restriction of T visas, given to the victims of human trafficking, and U visas, meant to help crime victims suffering from mental or physical abuse, asserting that, 'Victimization should not be a basis for an immigration benefit'. Asylum would become harder, and sanctuary cities banned." In culmination, "The Project also proposes to use the military in border protection operations, meaning it would militarize the border," and use the military "to assist in expanding the border wall."

Project 2025 is, yet further, relentlessly opposed to environmental protection and renewable energy. As GPAHE highlights, "In the world of Project 2025, environmental protections actually hurt the 'aged, poor, and vulnerable' and environmentalism has become a 'pseudo-religion meant to baptize liberals' ruthless pursuit of absolute power in the holy water of environmental virtue. At its very heart, environmental extremism is decidedly anti-human'." Notably, "Clean energy policies are a particular bugaboo. The government should stop any policy making that gets in the way of 'private-sector energy innovation' and the EPA must stop 'strangle[ing] domestic energy production'." Meanwhile, "A reform of the Department of the Interior would remove protections for endangered species, open up many areas to oil, gas, and coal development, and abandon protections for federally-owned lands," while there would "be no government role in promoting 'environmental, social, and governance (ESG) objectives', objectives many corporations and investors adopt to help them effectively manage their impact on the environment and society." Likewise, the Project "advocates rescinding 'all climate policies from its foreign aid programs'."

In order to insure Project 2025 is implemented, and rapidly so, Project 2025 calls for "thousands of properly vetted and trained personnel from across the country who will be ready on January 20, 2025, to begin dismantling our unaccountable fourth branch of government, the administrative state (Paraphrase, GPAHE)." In the section called "The Conservative Promise," these plans for "how to gut the civil service" are detailed. Subsections offer prescriptions for "how to fire supposedly 'un-fireable' federal bureaucrats; how to shutter 'wasteful and corrupt bureaus and offices'; how to muzzle woke propaganda at every level of government; how to restore the American people's constitutional authority over the Administrative State; and how to save untold taxpayer dollars in the process (Paraphrase, GPAHE)." Project 2025 in addition "proposes that any employee that has been involved in diversity, equity and inclusion (DEI) efforts and did not object 'on constitutional or moral grounds' should be subject to 'per se grounds for termination of employment'." The writers of Project of 2025 make all the clearer "The kinds of people" they want "to install in the civil service" by means of the project's proposed "personnel questionnaire." As GPAHE describe, "The application is prefaced, 'With the right conservative policy recommendations and properly vetted and trained personnel to implement them, we will take back our government'." Accordingly, "the survey is filled with leading questions that would clearly screen in candidates who are far right, anti-LGBTQ+, and against international institutions." Examples, which "applicants are asked to agree or disagree with," include: "The federal government should recognize only two unchanging sexes, male and female, as a matter of policy," "The U.N. should have authority over the citizens or public policies of sovereign nations," "The President should be able to advance his/her agenda through the bureaucracy without hindrance from unelected federal officials," "The police in America are systemically racist," and "The permanent institutions of family and religion are foundational to American freedom and the common good (Paraphrase, GPAHE)."

As the Heritage Foundation announced, as of 10 October 2023, the coalition responsible for Project 2025 had reached 75 partners, and the full list is worth citing to emphasis how much power is collectively amassed here, and how important it is to take this Project seriously, including to fear what it foretells: Alabama Policy Institute, Alliance Defending Freedom, America First Legal, American Accountability Foundation, American Association of Pro-Life Obstetricians and Gynecologists, ACLJ Action, American Compass, American Cornerstone Institute, American Council of Trustees and Alumni, American Family Association, American Family Project, American Legislative Exchange Council, American Juris Link, AMAC Action, American Moment, American Principles Project, California Family Council, Center for Equal Opportunity, Center for Family and Human Rights, Center for Immigration Studies, Center for Renewing America, Claremont Institute, Coalition for a Prosperous America, Competitive Enterprise Institute, Concerned Women for America, Conservative Partnership Institute, Defense of Freedom Institute, Ethics and Public Policy Center, Family Policy Alliance, Family Research Council, Feds for Medical Freedom, First Liberty Institute, Forge Leadership Network, Foundation for American Innovation, Foundation for Defense of Democracies, Foundation for Government Accountability, Frederick Douglass Foundation, FreedomWorks, Heartland Institute, Heritage Foundation, Hillsdale College, Honest Elections Project, Independent Women's Forum, Institute for Education Reform, Institute for Energy Research, Institute for the American Worker, Institute for Women's Health, Intercollegiate Studies Institute, James Madison Institute, Job Creators Network, Keystone Policy, Liberty University, Media Research Center, Mississippi Center for Public Policy, Moms for Liberty, National Association of Scholars, National Center for Public Policy Research, Noah Webster Educational Foundation, Oklahoma Council of Public Affairs, Pacific Research Institute, Patrick Henry College, Personnel Policy Operations, Project 21 Black Leadership Network, Public Interest Legal Foundation, Recovery for America Now Foundation, Susan B. Anthony Pro-Life America, Tea Party Patriots, Teneo Network, Texas Public Policy Foundation, The American Conservative, The American Main Street Initiative, The Leadership Institute, Turning Point USA, Young America's Foundation, and 1792 Exchange. Many of these organizations have been developing and pushing for many of these ideas for some time now, but they are now united together in the effort to bring these to fruition in fundamentally reshaping not only the U.S. federal government but also U.S. society and culture more broadly. What's more, as Global Project Against Hate and Extremism makes clear by citing directly from Project 2025, the achievement of such drastic changes requires a dictatorial regime, while the coalition partners do not consider remnant commitment to abstract 'democracy' important in comparison with the *fascist* program the Project details.

Despite what I have just written, and despite my lifelong 'fear' of what I have perceived as a real threat, and real danger, from persistent fascist forces and tendencies in post-WWII U.S. culture, society, and politics, I am not as pessimistic as Kagan. I am not simply optimistic either. But I do recognize people have resisted, opposed, and struggled against repressive and oppressive power throughout history, even in dire circumstances and even with the odds heavily against them. I also recognize contradictory tendencies within the insecurity, loneliness, and fear that lead many to identify with and support Trump, Trumpism, and Project 2025. I know many others share my concerns–and indeed my worries and fears. I appreciate that a great many young people, as has been repeatedly reinforced in my experience teaching, do not want the kind of future America Project 2025 heralds, and in fact staunchly oppose much if not most of what the coalition of right-wing groups responsible advocate. In this connection it is worth citing what University of North Carolina at Chapel Hill Professor of Information and Library Science, and former MacArthur Fellow, Tressie McMillan Cottam discusses, in a 28 March 2024 opinion piece for *The New York Times*. Here Cottam reflects on the results of a just published report by Gallup and the Lumina Foundation investigating "Policies and Laws: How they're impacting college enrollment" across the U.S. today. What is especially striking about this report is "The national debate about so-called woke campuses does not reflect what most college students care about." In fact, in relation to supposedly "'divisive' concepts," the report shows that "Students want them," and that "A majority of students who cared about those issues . . . . said they did not want restrictions on classroom instruction," while "Even 61 percent of Republicans who cared about" a directly related 'divisive issue' "when choosing a college preferred a state that did not restrict instruction on topics related to race and gender" (as "compared with 83 percent of Democrats and 78 percent of independents").

Nevertheless, I agree with Kagan that ignoring or downplaying the seriousness of the threat increases the likelihood that it will come to pass. When I listen closely to the lyrics and music of Ian Curtis and Joy Division, and reflect carefully on what so listening prompts me to think (about) and feel, I likewise experience the same sense of urgency, the same sense that it is no longer acceptable to retreat or hide from what is happening, or from what needs to be done in response, no matter how daunting and no matter how frightening.

It is worthwhile therefore to delve further into how to make sense of the precise nature of fascism today, beginning with how it makes sense and why it is important to characterize this as fascism. In answer to the questions "What exactly is fascism?" and "Where does the word and concept come from?," California State University San Marcos history professor Kimber Quinney answered that fascisms vary, so it is less important to provide a definition that pinpoints what all fascisms maintain in common as 'the fascist essence' than it is to explain how and why fascisms come to exercise power and influence when and where they do. Fascism always arises in times of "major political, social or economic upheaval." And "Because of the dire circumstances in which fascism arises," the ideology characteristic of fascism "is often accompanied by a sense of cultural pessimism." Typically, "This pessimism inspires a claim to renew or remake the nation, with an extraordinary emphasis on ultra-patriotic or nationalist aims." Typically as well, "While the fascist ideology looks forward to a renewal or restoration of the nation, it also looks to the golden years of a past era." This means, in turn, that "Tradition is a prominent theme" as is "Veneration of an authoritarian leader who is seen as a savior who can rescue the country from its decline is another characteristic." None of that is sufficient, however, because "fascism cannot exist without a tide of popular–or populist–support that usually begins with the lower middle classes." In order to build that level of support, fascisms rely upon "Concerted campaigns of propaganda and disinformation, full of bold imagery and symbols" as "necessary tools," with "Manipulation of the media" especially important. In addition, it is characteristic of fascism to "use intimidation and violence to achieve political ends," especially in combination with "intentionally creating a climate of unrest" according to which "only the fascists seem capable of securing the nation from 'unpatriotic' or 'radical' forces."

Even more recently, author, commentator, and former U.S. Secretary of Labor Robert Reich criticizes those who continue to identify Donald Trump and his movement as merely 'authoritarian', because, as Reich asserts, in his 15 June 2023 article, "How do we describe what Trump wants for America? 'Authoritarianism' isn't adequate. It is 'fascism'." Fascism "stands for a coherent set of ideas different from–and more dangerous than–authoritarianism. To fight those ideas, it's necessary

1162

to be aware of what they are and how they fit together." Reich identifies five key elements that fascism and authoritarianism share in common yet which mean differently for fascism versus authoritarianism.

First, fascism and authoritarianism both involve "The rejection of democracy, the rule of law, and equal rights under the law in favor of a strongman who interprets the popular will." While "Authoritarians believe society needs strong leaders to maintain stability," and "They vest in a dictator the power to maintain social order through the use of force (armies, police, militia) and bureaucracy," in contrast, "fascists view strong leaders as the means of discovering what society needs" and "They regard the leader as the embodiment of society, the voice of the people."

Second, fascism and authoritarianism both involve "The galvanizing of popular rage against cultural elites." "Authoritarians do not stir people up against establishment elites," but instead "They use or co-opt those elites in order to gain and maintain power." In contrast, "fascists galvanize public rage at presumed (or imaginary) cultural elites and use mass rage to gain and maintain power." Fascists "stir up grievances against those elites for supposedly displacing average people" and "seek revenge" by forging or coopting "mass parties" as means to do so. In pursuit of revenge, fascists "often encourage violence."

Third, fascism and authoritarianism both involve nationalism founded upon the notion of "a dominant 'superior' race and historic bloodlines." "Authoritarians see nationalism as a means of asserting the power of the state" and are principally concerned "to dominate other nations," "to protect or expand" their "geographic boundaries," and with "worry about foreign enemies encroaching" on their "territory." In contrast, "fascists see a nation as embodying what they consider a 'superior' group–based on race, religion, and historic bloodlines." For fascists, "Nationalism is a means of asserting that superiority." Fascists "worry about disloyalty and sabotage from groups within the nation that don't share the same race or bloodlines," and this leads these "others" to be "scapegoated, excluded or expelled," and "sometimes even killed." "Fascists," moreover, "believe schools and universities must teach values that extol the dominant race, religion, and bloodline," and that "Schools should not teach inconvenient truths (such as America's history of genocide and racism)."

Fourth, both authoritarianism and fascism involve "Extolling brute strength and heroic warriors." For authoritarianism, the goal is is "to gain and maintain state power," with "strength" meaning "large armies and munitions." In contrast, fascism aims "to strengthen society," which for fascism means "to reward those who win economically and physically and to denigrate or exterminate those who lose." "Fascism depends on organized bullying–a form of social Darwinism," and "For the fascist, war and violence are means of strengthening society by culling the weak and extolling heroic warriors."

Fifth, both authoritarianism and fascism involve "Disdain of women and fear of non-standard forms of gender identity and sexual orientation." For authoritarianism this involves imposition of "hierarchies" because "authoritarianism seeks order." In contrast, "In fascism, anything that challenges the traditional heroic male roles of protector, provider, and controller of the family is considered a threat to the social order." In response to this threat, "Fascism seeks to eliminate homosexual, transgender, and queer people because they are thought to challenge or weaken the heroic male warrior."

In sum, "These five elements of fascism reinforce each other," because "Rejection of democracy in favor of a strongman depends on galvanizing popular rage," "Popular rage draws on a nationalism based on a supposed superior race or ethnicity," "That superior race or ethnicity is justified by a social Darwinist idea of strength and violence, as exemplified by heroic warriors," and "Strength, violence, and the heroic warrior are centered on male power." Reich asserts "These five elements also find exact expression in Donald Trump and the White Christian National movement he is encouraging." Project 2025 fits Reich's characterization of fascism versus authoritarianism, and, especially, fascism in 'White Christian nationalist' form.

Broadcaster, author, and political commentator Mehdi Hasan recently shared, in an interview with *Democracy Now!*, much the same position as Reich. Hasan criticizes the mainstream news media in the U.S. for not identifying Trump and Trumpism as fascist: "I believe there is a fascist threat to the United States from the modern Republican Party, and including its standard-bearer, its now official candidate, Donald J. Trump, and we need to speak very clearly about what that fascist threat is. We need to be able to say the F-word, not dance around it, not pretend Donald Trump is a normal candidate, not normalize his extremism and racism and bigotry and authoritarianism." Journalists and commentators must recognize that their own self-interest is itself now clearly at stake:

If Donald Trump wins the election, what do you think is going to happen to our free press? He's not hiding it. He has talked openly about wanting to come after NBC and MSNBC for treason. His allies, like Kash Patel, have talked about going after the media criminally and civilly. One of his allies, Mike Davis, says if Trump makes him AG, he's going to put me in Guantánamo Bay. This is the kind of open authoritarian rhetoric that we're hearing from the Republican side. And the media cannot pretend that this is normal or not a threat to our very freedoms.

Ample evidence abounds of the influence Donald Trump and Trumpism have come to exert in American life. For too long all too many imagined this has not been the case and that Trump was merely a crude entertainer and a temporary aberration while his base supporters constituted a minority of dupes and extremists 'out of touch' with where most of America, and most Americans, are at. But that is not true. After a cargo ship struck the Francis Scott Key Bridge in Baltimore, causing it to collapse, early in the morning of 26 March 2024, Mayor Brandon Scott received considerable disparagement online because he was Black and because of cooptation of 'DEI' (in other words, Diversity, Equity, and Inclusion) as a term of denigration, just as happened previously with 'CRT' (Critical Race Theory), 'woke', and 'affirmative action'. 'DEI' as a term of disparagement refers to a Black or brown person, or a group of Black or brown people, acquiring unearned advantages over a white person or over white people. According to this position, 'DEI' unfairly privileges Black and brown people over white people who are the supposed victims of (reverse) racism. As columnist Eugene Robinson writes, in *The Washington Post*, "'DEI' is shorthand for diversity, equity and inclusion. For decades, since the triumph of the civil rights movement, those concepts have been lauded in our public discourse as virtues. For the unhinged far right, however, 'DEI' has come to mean 'any Black or Brown person who holds a position of authority that we think should have gone to a White man'." Reflecting on the denigration of Scott as a 'DEI mayor', Robinson writes that "It would be wrong to blame all of this on Donald Trump," as "He didn't invent racism," yet "by bulldozing the guardrails that used to delimit our political rhetoric, he has given permission for quiet racism to be shouted from the rooftops." Trump has made it viable, "In the MAGA universe," for people indulging in overt racist comments "to be not shamed but rewarded." Robinson echoes how I feel as well concerning much the same 'reemergence': "Sigh. In my lifetime, we've already fought this battle once–and won. Now, we fight it again."

In a similar column, published the same day, also in *The Washington Post*, Philip Bump discusses how, in his next presidency, "Trump aims to be a fearless warrior for White advantage." Bump cites Trump spokesman Steven Cheung declaring that Trump "is committed to weeding out discriminatory programs and racist ideology across the federal government." As Bump translates, "Here, 'discriminatory programs' refers to those that attempt to address systemic racial disadvantages. It is an evolution of the idea that affirmative-action policies meant to eliminate those imbalances are, in effect, racist against White people." Trump champions this position, as Bump indicates, because he recognizes this is a position with considerable support.

Conditions that lend support to fascism today are hardly limited to the U.S. For instance, in its 2024 annual report, *State of Hate 2024: Pessimism, Decline and a Rising Radical Right*, U.K. Human Rights charity Hope Not Hate finds:

> There is a strong mood of pessimism and declinism amongst the British public. When asked to describe modern Britain, 43% of the public choose 'declining'. Only 6% of people strongly agree with the statement 'the political system works well in the UK' and 79% think that 'politicians don't listen to people like me'.

> 2023 was the year the Radical Right in the UK came of age. The Radical Right is growing in confidence to push divisive, populist, anti-immigration, climate-sceptic policies in British politics. With the mood amongst the public in favour of change, if a new Government isn't able to deliver this could open the door for the Radical Right.

> Anti-migrant activism continues to dominate the far right. Hope Not Hate researchers found that anti-migrant activity rose by 20% compared to 2022, itself the highest year on record. There was an 18-fold increase in anti-migrant demonstrations from 2022, following the riot at the Suites Hotel in Kirkby in February 2022.

> A record number of far-right activists and sympathisers were convicted of terror related offences in 2023. The average age was 32, whilst 4 convicted were teenagers. 19% of people referred to Prevent were considered as 'extreme right wing', higher than the 11% referred for 'Islamist concerns'.

The conflict in the Middle East has led to a huge rise in antisemitism and anti-Muslim hatred in the UK, with the far right divided on the issue. Hardline Nazis like the BNP's Nick Griffin and fascist Patriotic Alternative's Mark Collett have taken pro-Palestinian stances and attacked 'Zionist' influence. Anti-Muslim activists like Stephen Yaxley-Lennon (aka Tommy Robinson) have taken pro-Israel stances.

Reference to the war in Gaza brings us to the greatest obstacle that prevented rallying a popular front in support of the reelection of Joe Biden as President as necessary to prevent the triumph of fascism via election of Donald Trump to a second term. Biden and his administration have maintained and even expanded provision of the military weapons that Israel has used to fight this war. Biden and his administration have denied, ignored, and downplayed evidence Israel has engaged in massive killing of civilians and destruction of virtually everything standing, while severely restricting access to food, water, fuel, medicine, and other basic necessities of life–in violation of international law and consensually agreed human rights standards. Biden and his administration have offered criticism of Israel and sympathy for Palestinians in Gaza but these words have not been backed with deeds. Israel faces no consequences for doing what the Biden administration warns Israel against doing. As a result, Biden lost substantial support among Palestinian Americans, Arab Americans, and Muslim Americans; Black and brown Americans; progressive Americans and young Americans. Many refused to rally behind the reelection of a President they hold responsible for enabling genocide. I sympathize with this position, despite my fear of Trumpist fascism.

As writer Mustafa Barghouti, Palestinian physician, activist and politician, as well as general secretary of the Palestinian National Initiative, calls attention to, in an interview with *Democracy Now!* on 8 April 2024, "[Israeli government Minister of Finance Bezalel] Smotrich and [Israeli government Minister or National Security Itamar] Ben-Gvir are not extremists. They are fascists. And this whole Israeli government does have now a fascist nature. If you look at what they are doing to our prisoners in jail or what they are doing to the people of Gaza or even the West Bank, where more than 460 people have been killed also, it's a fascist approach." This is the paradox we face, those of us opposed to fascism in America today, including via a second Trump presidency: Israeli Prime Minister Benjamin "Netanyahu and his fascist government and the Israeli government cannot continue this war without American supplies of weapons, of bombs." In other words, not only is it plausible to identify the Biden administration as complicit in ethnic cleansing and genocide in Gaza, but also it is plausible to identify the Biden administration as complicit in fascism. As writer and analyst, as well as communications chief at Euro-Mediterranean Human Rights Monitor Muhammad Shedada emphasizes, in the same *Democracy Now!* interview,

> it's not just the mass killing that is the problem. It's the deliberate, intentional targeting of civilians, the disregard, complete disregard, for human life that we're seeing on full display, and the cruelty of the killing itself. We see bodies flattened by Israeli tanks, turned into–literally turned into mush, crushed by Israeli tanks and armored vehicles. We see people hacked into pieces by Israeli missiles and shells. And we see people having their arms bound, their eyes blindfolded, and then executed, especially at Al-Shifa Hospital . . . .
> The other dimension that we see there is the people, the amount of people, the hidden iceberg of about 70,000 to 80,000 people who have been maimed or burned severely or wounded

critically, without basically any appropriate medical treatment or the possibility to go out of Gaza and seek medical treatment. At the moment, it's only very, very meager, very minor numbers of people that are allowed outside Gaza to get medical treatment. And hospitals in Gaza, the majority of them, have been fully compromised by Israel surgically, one after the other, in broad daylight . . . We see also the mass destruction . . . twice the amount of bombs that were used in Hiroshima, as an estimate that it's about 70,000 tons of bombs that were dropped on Gaza. And we recently see Israeli officials admitting in the Israeli newspaper *Haaretz*, saying that "We could have achieved the same military objectives with about 10% of the damage," but, quote, "cruelty was the point" . . .

Treating all Palestinians in Gaza as guilty, as all 'deserving of punishment', either via exile or extermination, while indiscriminately targeting journalists, health care providers, and relief aid workers is chillingly suggestive of what many theorists of fascism identify as leading dimensions of fascism in power, and of fascist exercise of power. Likewise so, is what Shedada describes as

the last dimension of the engineered, systematic starvation throughout Gaza . . . we have about half a million to 700,000 people stuck in the north of Gaza, refusing to leave. Israel is continuing a process of ethnic cleansing in the north . . . They continue to drop leaflets on people, telling them to move south if they want food, if they want safety, although the south is just as ravaged and compromised and devastated as the north. And we see Israel not just preventing aid from going to the north, but targeting anybody–literally anybody–that tries to secure the aid trucks coming through, prevent looting and ensure fair distribution.

What Shedada highlights is disturbingly indicative of fascism in action. And this renders it difficult for Americans concerned about the threat of fascism within this nation to ignore 'what is happening there' because 'it is not happening here', given the links between the support the Biden administration continues to provide the Israeli war in Gaza versus the people of Gaza:

this very deliberate, very engineered starvation process of people in northern Gaza to ethnically cleanse it and force them out, but also to sustain chaos in the entirety of the Gaza Strip, to sustain the loss of civil order and to bring about a societal collapse, in whole or in part, to push it to the deepest conscience of people in Gaza, to the deepest of their minds, the idea of leaving, that it should be their only ticket to survival, to achieve the Israeli goal of population transfer, what they refer to as "thinning the population." They call it "voluntary migration," but in fact it's ethnic cleansing. And we see that process still on full display. And we see a very systematic, deliberate, conscious effort to make Gaza uninhabitable for decades to come.

I support a binational solution, one that aligns with what writers as diverse as Edward Said, in *The Question of Palestine*; Rashid Khalidi, in *The Hundred Years War on Palestine: a History of Settle Colonialism and Resistance, 1917-2017*; and Jonathan Graubart, in *Jewish Self-Determination Beyond Zionism: Lessons from Hannah Arendt and Other Pariahs* all advocate. As I spoke, on my 19 October 2023 Insurgence show, too much official rhetoric from those in positions at the heights of power in the US and other 'Western' nations fails to situate the current war in historical context and fails to acknowledge the horrific conditions under which Palestinians have long been forced to live, in territories occupied and controlled by Israel. What's more, all too often no attention is paid to the history of the establishment of the nation of Israel involving the violent forced removal of vast numbers of Palestinians to make way for this new nation, Palestinian people whose families had lived in this same area for many preceding centuries, indeed for more than 2000 years. Most of those Palestinians currently living in Gaza and the West Bank are already refugees or descendants of refugees from elsewhere in what once all was Palestine but now has become predominantly Israel. Leading human rights organizations worldwide and in Israel as well have long charged the Israeli state, and successive Israeli governments, with violations of international law, commission of war crimes, and the establishment of apartheid conditions worse than in South Africa. The 7 October 2023 Hamas attack on Israeli civilians, killing over a thousand and taking hundreds more hostages, was horrific and deserves condemnation. Yet, the Israeli government has resorted to 'collective punishment' of the Palestinian people as a whole, waging war on Palestinian civilians, and engaging in forced relocation of Palestinians in Gaza that amounts, effectively, to ethnic cleansing and genocide. The Israeli military has already killed many more Palestinians and destroyed vastly more of an already deeply impoverished area, in Gaza where millions of Palestinians up to now have lived, than what Hamas did on October 7.

What is needed is an immediate ceasefire, and a withdrawal of US military support for Israel until Israel is ready seriously to commit itself to forging a genuine peaceful settlement with Palestinians and their chosen representatives so that Israelis and Palestinians can equitably share the land, resources, and opportunities the region offers, ending the Israeli occupation, and enabling both Palestinians and Israelis to freely determine, for themselves, what their collective destinies are to be, in just, peaceful, and mutually respectful relations with each other. The US government should not continue one-sided support for Israel such that the President of the United States sounds as if he is doing nothing, in his public statements, other than reading off of a teleprompter lines written for him by the Israeli Defense Ministry. The US must recognize the historical contexts that explain the conflict, while by no means condoning the killing of any civilians, and the US must recognize, respect, and help to redress the legitimate grievances of the Palestinian people. As long as the US government continues on its current course, not only does it do a grave injustice to the Palestinian people but also it severely alienates the United States from many other nations and peoples worldwide, in the Middle East and beyond. In doing so, the Biden administration is giving excuse to terrorists to target the US and US citizens, which is something Biden and those in his administration should well know by now is what they are doing. Why have terrorists from Arab and Persian Middle Eastern nations targeted the US and US citizens in the past? All too often this has been motivated in significant part by extreme bitterness at the way the US has sided with Israel, against Palestinians, and against the US for supplying Israel, every year, with an enormous amount of military aid. Those aforementioned terrorist actions are horrifically wrong, entirely unjust, and certainly themselves violate international law and amount to major war crimes, but in order to prevent them from arising, and recurring, it is necessary to get at the root of what makes them possible. Too many US governments have refused to do so, often not even recognizing what it might mean to do so.

This past spring, in the U.S. and beyond, university students organized sit-ins, encampments, hunger strikes, and similar protests. These students demanded that their universities divest from companies doing business in Israel until a lasting ceasefire is enacted and the war in Gaza is ended. These protests remind me of earlier protests against apartheid South Africa, back when I was a student, and, earlier than that, in support of free speech and Black civil rights as well as against the Vietnam War. These protests demonstrate how passionate many Americans, especially young progressive Americans, are about what is happening in Gaza, along with how angry they are about the Biden administration's complicity. And this alienation and anger has exacerbated as many university administrations cracked down on these protests by calling upon police to arrest students and clear encampments, as well as by threatening to suspend and even expel students involved in protests, while offering little attempt at dialogue with *their own students* over the issues *their students* were raising, issues demonstrative of students' passionate concern about fundamental human rights, concern directly in line with what most universities' mission statements claim to be foremost aims of the education they purport to offer. As University of Georgia Professor of International Affairs Cas Muddle writes, in a 30 April 2024 column for *The Guardian*:

> Let there be no doubt that the current attacks on US universities are a major political victory for the far right. Not only do they mobilize and unify the conservative base, they also divide that of the liberal opposition. But there are also major lessons for liberal democrats in the country. First, neoliberal universities are no match for illiberal politics. Second, no university is safe: this is not a private versus public university or red state versus blue state issue. And, third and finally, the current attacks are just a small prelude to what the return of Trump will mean for liberal democracy in general and higher education in particular.

It is important to understand why support for Trump and others like Trump is as strong as it is, and why many of those who do support Trump, and 'Trumpism', fear what they imagine these student protestors represent, while also fearing 'cultural elites' and leftists of all kinds, as well as people of color, immigrants of color, and lgbtqia+ people. It is important, likewise, to explain why this version of 'late capitalist fascism' has become prominent and influential, as well as what is distinctive about it.

University of Copenhagen Professor Political Aesthetics Mikkel Bolt Rasmussen's 2022 book *Late Capitalist Fascism* provides an explicitly Marxist theory of fascism today. Rasmussen argues his theory is more rigorous in its explanatory power, and thereby ultimately more politically useful to anti-fascist ends, than what Rasmussen characterizes as a burgeoning number of 'checklist' accounts of constituents of fascism by varied authors who argue what Trump and others like him represent is fascism. Although I find these 'checklist' contributions more useful than Rasmussen does (after all, I have already cited and made use of instances of this kind of analysis from Lawrence W. Britt, Umberto Eco, and Robert Reich in this book), I agree it is important to explain how and why fascism becomes prominent and influential when and where it does in connection with developments in capitalism.

According to Rasmussen, fascism involves "an extreme nationalist ideology intent on rebuilding an imagined organic community by excluding foreigners" (3-4), and that is able to exercise significant power in response to crisis. Fascism today bears broad similarities with fascism yesterday insofar as "Ultra-nationalist parties have emerged protesting against a political system that is in crisis and seems unable to get the national economies going." Fascism today bears broad similarities with fascism yesterday as well, insofar as "These parties protest against the system by gesturing towards an idea of an 'original' ethno-national community that can be remade by targeting people labelled as migrants, Muslims and leftists"–who are, ostensibly, "all enemies of the national community that needs protecting."

Nonetheless, *late capitalist* fascism must be understood, more concretely, as "a protest against the long slow neoliberal dismantling of the Second World War social state, or a certain idea of the world at that time, a better time, before unemployment, globalization and the emergence of new political subjects that threaten the naturalness of the patriarchal order (9)." Late capitalist fascism is, moreover, "*a protest against the protests* [my italics]," because late capitalism fascism amounts to "a preventive cancellation of the emergence of more radical opposition against neoliberal globalization and the capitalism-nation state nexus" (9-10). In other words, instead of targeting capitalist forces and interests as responsible for the insecurity, loneliness, and fear that large numbers of working and middle class people understandably do feel, late capitalist fascism coopts this insecurity, loneliness, and fear, redirecting it against "Migrants, people of colour, Muslims, Jews, women, sexual minorities and communists" as the supposed agents "of a historical and moral decline that the fascist leaders promise to reverse engineer by excluding such unwanted subjects and restoring the original community" (9).

Continuous with what I have argued throughout this book, in relation to what I propose the lyrics of Ian Curtis and the music of Joy Division offer toward critique of fascism, Rasmussen likewise theorizes fascism as *not* disappearing at the end of WWII. After WWII, fascism "actually lived on in the form of fascist zones." In other words, "Fascism never really went away but continued in the margins of the national democratic societies, in prisons, in ghettoes, and, later, in migrant camps, and of course continued full-scale in the former colonies" (12). Rasmussen theorizes fascism as *a persistent tendency within capitalism*. Fascism persists as "a kind of slow violence, a violence that is out of view or not deemed to be of central importance to an analysis of a political situation or an age" (12). "Fascism is a ghost in the machine," with "the machine being capitalism" (13).

Fascism becomes more than a 'ghost in the machine' when needed to serve capitalist interests and save capitalism in times of crisis–crisis, that is, in terms of the legitimacy of existing political institutions, where trust has substantially eroded and where large segments of the population believe the existing system does not work for them, and is either indifferent or hostile to their interests. Late capitalist fascism is "the expression of the decomposition of capitalist society, the expression of a crisis. It is a symptom of a declining economy, intensified competition among large capitalist powers and the slow erosion of political institutions, as well as the replacement of mass and class politics with identity" (22).

Although I am not critical of 'the politics of identity' in the way Rasmussen is because I do not conceive of 'the politics of identity' as necessarily at odds with 'mass and class politics', I find his argument otherwise compelling, especially his theorization of the rise of late capitalist fascism as a result of the consequences of the neo-liberal assault on social welfare, and the end of the post-WWII 'class compromise' between capital and labor: "When the economic foundations of the Fordist class compromise disappeared," that is when the long wave of expansion in the average rate of capitalist profit following WWII ended and a long wave of stagnation and contraction ensued. As a result, "fascism returned" from the global South and the margins of the global North. As Rasmussen recounts, "For a period in the second part of the twentieth century the fascist zone was reserved for the most rebellious subjects, and most people could dissent and protest as they saw fit," but "This is no longer the case" (17).

Rasmussen theorizes the 2007-2008 'financial crisis' as neoliberalism in crisis, and as a crisis, moreover, from which neo-liberalism has been unable to recover. Yet because political leaders regard neo-liberalism as the only game in town, they have responded, since 2007-2008, with the same neo-liberal measures that brought the crisis to a head. Across the spectrum, all political parties have, "since the early 1980s, devoted themselves to implementing the slow dismantling of the post-Second World War welfare state, falsely believing this was the way to restore growth," and, as a consequence of this embrace of neoliberal dismantling of the welfare state, all erstwhile 'mainstream' political parties have become discredited among a growing mass of the population (46). The crux of problem is that neoliberalism has "never managed to solve the fundamental problems of late capitalism, namely overcapacity, overproduction, overaccumulation, and declining profitability" (30). Indeed, the 2007-2008 financial crisis "only aggravated the contradictions and made them more visible" (30).

"The capitalist economy has been contracting for the last fifty years," in a protracted long wave of stagnation and decline (31). Citing Marxist economist Robert Brenner, Rasmussen highlights the fact that "the *lowest* annual rate of profit in the US industrial sector during the period from 1948 to 1973 was higher than the highest rate of profit in the period after 1973. At no time after 1968 did the American economy get close to achieving the results of the previous era" (32). In other words,

> Because the economy was shrinking, capitalism was no longer capable of compromising with labour as it did during the expansionist long wave after the Second World War. Capitalism's health depends on growth, on production expanding and the selling of commodities, but this was no longer possible. The neoliberal period has therefore been one of intense class struggle, but one-sided class struggle, where the ruling class has tried to get rid of more and more workers (33).

Short-term success in this one-sided class struggle has increased precariousness, and especially precarity, while a corresponding rise in inequality has led to further bitterness, resentment, and hostility. Force, meanwhile, increasingly supplants consent in the exercise of state power: "As the state is unable to secure work or welfare, the police take over, and exclusions have to make up for a political programme" (37). However, "There's a limit to the amount of people that can be excluded from the economy, controlled by the police, or kept in prisons and camps"–that is, according, to 'normal' 'democratic' practices, and that is where fascism comes to the rescue (39). Fascism supersedes 'the normal'. Fascism emerges as "a paradoxical attempt simultaneously to confront and to deny" the aforementioned developments that are manifestations of economic, social, and political crisis, "to mobilize a collapsed political sphere through recourse to racist fear and violent exclusions"–in other words to mount "an (ideological) attempt to stop the slow etiolation of (the material basis of) capitalist rule" (40).

Fascism undermines (class) solidarity, turning it on its head, such that those subject to intensified crackdown and punishment are feared and blamed by those not yet subject who in fact share objective interests in common with those they fear and blame. Fascism exploits people's distress in the face of austerity and precarity, turning this against an array of scapegoats, while exploiting people's distrust of 'establishment' politicians and political parties to mobilize support for a reactionary alternative.

As much as late capitalist fascism is indicative of "late capitalism in crisis," late capitalist fascism also succeeds by means of "the fascist spectacle." Rasmussen emphasizes that "fascism today is not isolated in specific fascist parties but is spread out in everyday culture" (15). "Fascism is a cultural logic of an affection that transcends specific political parties" (65) and it is much akin to "a structure of feeling, almost like an emerging *Zeitgeist*" (66). Late capitalist fascism begins as ideology and becomes politics as it grows stronger. "Late capitalist fascism is an arming of resentment caused on the basis of accumulated frustrations caused by a long economic crisis and the general potential for conflict in capitalism" (68). Especially important are "emotions and feelings" in generating identification with and support for fascist politicians and political movements (70). Rasmussen cites Trump's success as illustrative of exactly this dimension of late capitalist fascism (70) in explaining why Trump is a fascist even if he has not deliberately set out to be, and even as Trump maintains little knowledge of or interest in fascist theory and history. Many of Trump's key advisors are fascists in the latter sense, but Trump is a perfect fascist figurehead for our times because of his exceptional ability, above all else, to command attention (72). As Rasmussen comments, "Fascism has always been opportunistic, but Trump has taken this to new heights" (73).

Rasmussen argues Trump is savvier than many of his critics acknowledge, and he has actually been more honest than his opponents in "the admission that things are not nearly as good in the US as the political class and its courtiers continue to claim" (74). Those who have claimed the latter come across as out of touch with the lived experience of many Americans, leaving an opening for Trump: "Trump's primary appeal was his shocking admission that ordinary Americans have in fact been losing for the last forty years" (75). An element of truth exists in what Trump routinely asserts: "Namely that the US economy has been shrinking for a long time and that a select few has been able to amass more and more wealth" (76). This is so even as Trump is clearly one of the latter. Yes, claiming that he, and he alone, can fix the problem is "always the fascist promise" (79), and it may seem risible to those who recognize no quick and easy fix is possible, certainly not due to the sheer will, or exceptional charisma, of a single individual. But "The fascists' advantage is that they admit that there is a problem" (80).

The roots of Trumpism lie in the damage wrought by neoliberalism, as "More and more facets of human sociability have been subjected to the logic of the market," and "The result is deprivation–a psychological crisis that has been intensified by social media" (124-125). This deprivation has proceeded so far that "This is society without any kind of sociality, where 'association' or 'community' have no meaning" (125). In line with what Noreena Hertz cites as examples of people seeking surrogates for their experience of profound loneliness, Ramussen writes that "Fascism is scattered across the social field; it is present in unconscious identifications and expectations" (127). In other words, the collapse of 'the sociality of the social', and of substantive association and community, leaves people bereft, in desperate need of something to make up for what has been lost. Fascism offers a powerful surrogate for feeling insecure, lonely, and afraid, with otherwise little to no fulfilling social life, and otherwise little to no sense of belonging and mattering as part of any substantive community or association. Fascism offers a surrogate by means of identification with 'the strong leader' who will use whatever means is necessary to root out 'the enemies of people' 'deep within' as well as 'at the top' of 'corrupt' and 'decadent' institutions, in order to 'make America great again'– restoring 'traditional norms and values', 'traditional roles and identities', and 'traditional lifestyles and standards of living'. Here, it is useful, as Rasmussen does, to cite Walter Benjamin who wrote, in relation to ascendant fascism nearly 100 years ago: "The masses have a *right* to changed property relations; fascism seeks to give them *expression* in keeping these relations unchanged" (quoted, 134).

It might seem the lyrics of Ian Curtis and the music of Joy Division give 'expression' to desire and need while failing to provide direction or assistance in recognizing what is desired and needed. But Benjamin does not condemn 'expression'; he condemns fascist politics that pretends to address the root of what prompts expression, yet in fact maintains, reinforces, and reproduces what it is ostensibly protests. Fascism provides a pressure valve for release of tension for capitalism in crisis–tension that threatens to reach the point of explosion, that threatens the foundations of capitalism. The lyrics of Ian Curtis and the music of Joy Division resonate with frustration over desires and needs unmet, over spiritual emptiness, over lack and loss of genuine meaning, purpose, and fulfillment–as well as with *fear* that all of this cause for frustration can, and will, lead to ramping up of conflict and especially of violence. Yet the lyrics of Ian Curtis and the music of Joy Division do *not* identify with let alone valorize exercise of crushing strength versus those easily targeted as not only 'different' and 'other' but also as 'weak' and 'vulnerable'. To the contrary: the lyrics of Ian Curtis and the music of Joy Division engage issues of insecurity, loneliness, and fear, including in relation to fascism, from the vantage point of the marginalized, the excluded, and the brutalized–i.e., marginalized, excluded, and brutalized on account of being or perceived as being different, other, weak, and vulnerable. Yes, in identifying with the narrator-protagonist in the lyrics of Ian Curtis and the music as persona of Joy Division one identifies with the vantage point of one who fears 'he' bears responsibility for and maintains complicity with fascism's influence and appeal. Yet 'he' fears this responsibility and this complicity because 'he' simultaneously fears this influence and appeal to be insidious, and because he fears reemergent fascism to be horrific.

Six

Most listeners and commentators associate the lyrics of Ian Curtis and the music of Joy Division with hopelessness as opposed to hope and with dystopia as opposed to utopia. Without denying the validity of either of those associations, I nonetheless propose these lyrics and this music *also* make useful sense as manifestations of striving and struggling for hope, and toward utopia.

In order to conceive of a place, a time, a state of being, a social order, a tendency, a movement, a projection, a hypothesis, a perception, a sensation, a vision, a dream, a scenario, a narrative, an image, a sign, and so on, *as dystopian*, it is necessary, simultaneously, to conceive of the same as *not* what is wanted or needed, *not* what is hoped for and sought after, *not* what is right and good. Even if the dystopian feels inexorable, the dystopian, if it is identifiable *as dystopian*, feels wrong and feels bad. This is why theorists of fictional dystopias interpret these as warnings, and as exhortations to do everything possible to prevent existing tendencies toward the worst imaginable state of affairs from reaching that point. Even when people assert they are 'living in dystopia', that dystopia is no longer 'mere fiction', they conceive what they are living in as wrong and as bad. The dystopian is intrinsically interlinked with recognition of an urgent need for radical transformation, an urgent need for utopian striving, and an urgent need to find–and especially to *found*–reasons for hope. The lyrics of Ian Curtis, and the music of Joy Division, even at their bleakest, challenge *us* to respond to our own experiences of living in dystopia by aligning with utopian striving and for reasons to hope.

In *Everyday Utopia: What 2,000 Years of Wild Experiments Can Teach Us About the Good Life* (2023), Kristen R. Ghodsee writes that "Historically, moments of political uncertainty often give birth to utopian dreaming, which is one reason why it is enjoying such a renaissance today" (3). As Ghodsee elaborates, "Utopian visions of how to build a different future often follow moments of great upheaval" (12), because the latter incline people to become receptive to radical alternatives to the existing status quo. For example, before the COVID-19 pandemic emerged most people regarded universal basic income as impossible but the pandemic showed this not to be the case (13). Nevertheless, "Those who benefit from the way things are have a strong motive for labeling as 'utopian' any ideas that threaten the status quo," in the sense of altogether impossible or absurdly impractical. What's more, all "those steeped in the the ideology of their current existence cannot imagine an alternative to it," and in general "most of us follow along" (12). Unsurprisingly therefore, after the pandemic peaked, governments quickly ended their short-term experiment in providing a universal basic income. Likewise, they quickly ended a similar short-term experiment in eliminating eviction for those unable to pay the cost of rent. But these short-term experiments remain valuable, as models, and as lessons, of what could yet be. As Ghodsee observes, 'utopian demands' "push the limits of what seems politically, scientifically, or psychologically feasible, to boldly go where no one has gone before" (255). And as Howard Zinn advises, "To be hopeful in bad times is not just foolishly romantic. It is based on the fact that human history is a history not only of cruelty, but also of compassion, sacrifice, courage, kindness" (quoted, 258-259). The COVID-19 pandemic has shown us both, and *the utopian demand*, in response, is to seize upon the manifestations of compassion, sacrifice, courage, and kindness the pandemic has shown, in order to build upon, to generalize, to institutionalize, and to systematize these kinds of practices.

The reason why those invested in maintaining existing social, economic, political, and cultural inequities perceive "Utopian ideals and political movements" as "dangerous" is "precisely because they give people hope: the cognitive capacity to imagine that a better world is possible and seek to make it real" (249). A crucial distinction nonetheless must be observed between hope and optimism: "Hope differs from optimism because the latter is just a belief that everything will work out well, whereas hope is an active thought process that affirms our ability to influence the future course our lives or societies will take" (239). Hope represents "militant optimism" where one is prepared to work, struggle, and fight for one's vision, and where one accepts success is not guaranteed: "Without recognizing the possibility of failure and disappointments, hope is little more than wishful thinking" (255). Nevertheless, Ghodsee challenges us to recognize that "historically speaking, real social progress often begins" not only with "hopefulness," but also with "extreme dreaming" and "crazy ideas" (26). We can usefully draw upon past utopian ideas, as well as traces of utopian possibilities in material reality that were not (yet) realized: "When we lose sight of the past, we lose sight of the idea that there were other pathways forward, other roads not taken" (15).

Taking the utopian seriously is difficult because "We have to fight against our own deeply ingrained status quo bias and control the normal defense mechanisms of cynicism and apathy because without social dreaming, progress becomes impossible" (13). For example, in my experience teaching 'Critical Studies in Crime, Justice, and the Law', and in my observation of dominant tendencies since the summer of 2020, it is evident many reject all discourse concerning police and prison abolition as 'absurd'. They do so because for them it seems impossible to imagine a society functioning without either, and especially impossible to imagine how to get from here to there. Those who are so dismissive include many who are otherwise sympathetic to critiques of systemic problems in policing and prisons. It is difficult for many to grapple with the fact that neither police nor prisons have always and everywhere existed, especially not in current forms; that the reasons for their creation and for their systematization have aligned with the political interests of specific social groups as opposed to those of society in general; and that many alternatives are being pursued and have long been pursued. Skeptics question, moreover, why anyone continues to hope for abolition, when the prospect, if at all feasible, is only likely to be achieved as the result of a long, difficult, and uncertain process of transition. But, as Rebecca Solnit reminds us, we need to be able to hope for what the future might bring, and that it might indeed be dramatically better than the present, as indeed "To hope is to give yourself to the future . . . and that commitment to the future is what makes the present inhabitable" (quoted, 26).

Ghodsee explicitly draws upon the work of Ernst Bloch, the Marxist 'philosopher of hope' in articulating what she means by "militant optimism" (234). Bloch "proposes that people actively produce history every day through the collective actions of those living through it as an ever-contingent present" (235). As such, our world is more open to change, and is more continuously changing, than many of us realize, and especially than those at the heights of power often want us to realize. "According to Ernst Bloch, the value of utopian thinking lies in its ability to inspire hope in both of its related but distinct forms: hope as a cognitive capacity and hope as an emotional state" (238).

As translators Neville Plaice, Stephen Plaice, and Paul Knight indicate, Bloch's three-volume, 1500-pages-long *The Principle of Hope* is "a historical and collective statement of hope" against "annihilation," as well as "a practical guide to living in late capitalist society, in cultural decline, where the possibility of a truly human society seems remote and the dominant emotion is fear" (xxxiii). As Bloch avers, "even in a desperate man" consciousness "does not stare into complete nothingness," and has not lost connection with utopian yearning: "Even the suicide still flees into negation as into a womb; he expects rest. Even disappointed hope wanders around agonizing, a ghost that has lost its way back to the cemetery and clings to refuted images" (*The Principle of Hope* 195). In other words, such a 'ghost' manifests a persistent longing for what is *at present* refuted, or at present *apparently* refuted, but nonetheless desperately desired–and indeed desperately needed. The utopian desire, and need, to overcome an alienated life, a life dominated by insecurity, loneliness, and fear, persists even at the edge, even upon the verge, of self-annihilation. After all, as Bloch repeatedly insists, "There is no hope without anxiety and no anxiety without hope" (*The Principle of Hope* 333). Strikingly, this image of 'the desperate man' on the edge, or verge, of the suicidal, overcome with disappointed hope, yet continuing to wander about and agonize restlessly, coincides remarkably closely with the interpretations I have offered of the narrator-protagonists of the lyrics and the music as personae across the nineteen songs of Ian Curtis and Joy Division I discussed in chapters two through six. As does the image of this same 'desperate man' who, even as he 'flees toward negation' and expects or wants rest, nonetheless persists, in ghostly form, in still manifesting an unsatisfied desire for what has seemingly been refuted, denied, and defeated.

As Cat Moir summarizes, for Bloch *hunger* is "the main drive," and this is hunger directed toward rejecting and overcoming "deprivation," which in turn requires "the most important expectant emotion: hope" (*Ernst Bloch's Speculative Materialism: Ontology, Epistemology, Politics* 11). Hope, according to Bloch, as Jack Zipes explains, is

> an inner force we all have and that drives us to seek better working and living conditions. We hope because we are discontent and because we lack what is necessary to endow our lives with meaning. Since most of us cannot control our lives, we must live in hope or use hope to discover what it is that will benefit us and others. Bloch talks about speculative and educated hope. By speculating, we can go beyond limits set for us by civilizing processes that impede our search and curtail our curiosity. Hope spurs us on. By educating or enlightening our hope, we can become conscious of how we must work with other people to obtain our wishes. (*Ernst Bloch: The Pugnacious Philosopher of Hope* 186)

Even when repeatedly running up against 'hopelessness', the lyrics of Ian Curtis and the music of Joy Division continue to evince a 'hunger' rooted in 'deprivation' and redolent of 'discontent' that wants, and needs, reason and ground for hope. If one takes carefully into account the music as well as the lyrics, it makes sense to interpret these songs as more committed to and aligned with struggle than surrender, and with persistence with cessation. Yes, the songs make sense as embodying a fleeting, and fragile, quest for hope. But hope remains, even at the most excruciating extremes, because, after all, to push this far, despite how devastating it feels, requires the outlandish hope that it might yet be possible to reach the light, and that, even at its darkest, glimmers of the light beyond are perceptible.

Zipes characterizes Bloch as "essentially *a critic of utopias* [my italics]" who "sought to grasp why humankind had failed thus far to overcome the obstacles confronting the concretization of utopia on this earth in the here and now." Bloch praises fairy tales and colportage (popular serial fiction) for their *defamiliarizing* contributions, in intimating "the distance between the average misery of existence and the images of hope" they simultaneously depict–i.e., for deriving hope from dejection (392). Utopian dreaming always follows from recognition that 'something is missing' (*The Principle of Hope* 914). As Moir puts this, for Bloch the utopian attests to "something that is fundamentally not (yet) as it should be" (61). And, as Zipes attests, "Bloch places special emphasis on *dissatisfaction* as a condition which ignites the utopian drive" (127). One principal reason the lyrics of Ian Curtis and the music of Joy Division continue to resonate with me, and I argue this to be true with many others, is because of their 'special emphasis' on 'dissatisfaction' as well as their potent expression of yearning for that 'something' that 'is missing', that 'something' that is 'not (yet) as it should be'.

In "Ernst Bloch and The Philosophy (Principle) of Hope," Epoch Philosophy argues Bloch's philosophical work is especially relevant and urgent today, as we seek ways of "salvaging hope in an age of cynical despair." This is because Bloch wrote what he did concerning utopia and hope in "dark times of catastrophe, fascism, and suffering on a global level." Zipes agrees: [Bloch's] "cry for and defense of hope . . . is more urgent than every before" because "We are living in seemingly hopeless times" (177). Today "the major conflicts are all about regaining and retaining hope. Even the rise of fascism can be regarded as a movement based on hope for the fulfillment of people's needs and dreams. Everyone is hungry for hope, longs for hope, and strives for hope" (77). I write these lines after Joe Biden dropped his campaign for reelection and after the Democratic Party quickly united behind Vice-President Kamala Harris, and her running mate, Minnesota Governor Tim Walz, inspired by their embodiment of hope, and joy, with many supporters of Harris and Walz indicating they longed to feel this way, as they felt far too much fear and dread for far too long. Even so, as multiple speakers at the Democratic National Convention caution, it remains uncertain whether a campaign that emphasizes hope and joy will triumph over one that emphasizes fear and hate (i.e., the Donald Trump and J.D. Vance Republican ticket for President and Vice-President). But, as Bloch underscores, fear and hope, and especially anxiety and hope, are closely interrelated, and it is easy to swerve back and forth between the two. Hope requires ongoing work and struggle, which can be exhausting and can end in defeat, short-term and long-term; hope is no guarantee of success, but only recognition of a possibility and a commitment to strive to help enable its realization.

A crucial concept for Bloch is the 'Not-Yet'. As Epoch Philosophy explains, this concept is "a way of understanding that the present is not complete, that there are potentials to existence which have not yet found their fullest expression. To put it in other words, it's a phrase that is designed to focus our attention to the multiplicity of ways that existence is unfinished." Epoch Philosophy cites Wayne C. Hudson as elucidating how Bloch in turn uses 'Not-Yet' to mean all of the following:

> 'Not-Yet' in the sense of not actual now; 'Not-Yet' in the sense of actual, but not yet having reached a future determination; 'Not-Yet' in the sense of not so far; 'Not-Yet' in the sense of still not; 'Not-Yet' in the sense of not yet, but expected in the future; 'Not-Yet in the sense of conceivable now, but not yet possible; and 'Not-Yet' in the sense of present now in a problematic manner, but still to come in its actual realisation. (paraphrased, Epoch Philosophy)

Epoch Philosophy illustrates the 'Not-Yet' by referring to revolutionary moments such as that of The Paris Commune, to illustrate. For Bloch, these are not "naive experiments" but rather "moments out of time" that offer "glimpses of a possible future that has not yet arrived. And yet, traces of utopian possibility don't even have to be as grand as that" because Bloch finds "traces of the Not-Yet" in a wide array of sources, including ordinary daydreams (Epoch Philosophy).

What is crucial to grasp, as Moir explains, is for Bloch, "the material world is utopian in that it is literally not yet 'there' or complete," but it is "rather in a process of desire-driven becoming" (58). Bloch posits "the 'subjective factor'" exists "*in* [my italics] matter" (58). Matter, for Bloch, is *not* the result of a play of forces prior to or beyond itself, but "it *is* the play of forces itself"–it is intrinsically dynamic, it is both objectivity and subjectivity, and it is both actuality and possibility (59). Bloch declares "We have in us what we could become" (927) and, what's more, "There is not one of us who could not also be someone else" (930). These are important dynamic elements because "What we want is always a life which is not driven away from our inclinations and strengths," which, admittedly, "is vague, because most people are not even familiar with their inclinations, above all because nobody can get himself straight when all relations between people are in a mess" (927). Nevertheless, "No one is yet like himself. Our core remains dark and indefinite, does not know its name" (931). Consider the persistent dialogues in Ian Curtis's lyrics among relatively anonymous personae–'I', 'you', 'she', 'they', etc.–and how readily these lyrics often make sense as introspective reflections upon and explorations of not only self-proliferation but also self-dissolution, self-disintegration, self-shattering, and self-transcendence. These attributes attest to a keen interest in seeking out that 'someone else' 'who we could be' as well as a yearning to be that 'someone else' who could live a less alienated and more authentic life, 'not driven away from inclinations and strengths', and, all the more bluntly, who 'could get himself straight' rather than exist 'in a mess'. Likewise, the frequency with which these lyrics and this music broach the limits of the representable, including through struggle at self-understanding and self-overcoming, coincides yet again with Bloch's characterization of 'our core' as something 'dark and indefinite' that 'does not know its name'.

Bloch's conception of utopia "is not teleological" but "rather processual in nature" (Epoch Philosophy). In other words: "Utopia doesn't exist as a place or a program that we will arrive at with the right leader or the right set of mere ideas. Rather, whatever utopia arrives in the future will be the product of the process to get there in the first place (Epoch Philosophy)." Bloch's concept of 'concrete utopia' is

> concrete in the original Latin sense [of] 'con custere'–[i.e.,] growing together of unfolding processes through time, all our interventions in material history, all human culture and struggle to accumulate across history, taking in everything from great seismic revolutionary upheaval to the daydreams of ordinary working people imagining a better life for themselves. All of these things grow together historically, an accumulation of tendencies and possibilities that is utopia. Utopia is thus, for Bloch, an idea that is both speculative and materialist. (Epoch Philosophy)

For Bloch, 'latency' and 'tendency' are further principal concepts. Tendency refers to "the pressures of the objectively-real possible blocked by the actual conditions of the present," while latency refers to "the possible content of the future that is around us" (Epoch Philosophy). In other words, "The subjective latency of the present meets the objective real possible conditions of history which forms the dialectical engine which drives history forward into the mysterious waters of the future" (Epoch Philosophy). As Bloch himself explains, "truth is not the reflection of facts but of processes; it is ultimately the indication of the tendency and latency of that which has not yet become and needs its activator" (quoted, *Ernst Bloch: The Pugnacious Philosopher of Hope* 9). As Moir adds, "The material process comprises, on the one hand, tendency, an intensive quality or drive containing in its core a goal, which, however, is not yet fully determined. In conjunction with this, there is latency, which asserts itself as the outstanding essence, the placeholder of the not-yet-realised goal-content of tendency" (67).

The concrete utopian is, therefore, the possibility within the real of actual movement towards the ultimately desired good. The utopian is concrete insofar as it refers to objectively real possibilities that nonetheless always require substantial subjective action to achieve genuine realization. The concrete utopian function is process, is movement, within history, combining objective and subjective factors, toward the actual realization of possibilities that humans have dreamed of, desired, and hoped for. For Bloch, "Expectation, hope, [and] intention towards possibility that has still not become . . . is not only a basic feature of human consciousness, but, concretely corrected and grasped, a basic determination within objective reality as a whole" (7). As Zipes explains, the concrete utopian requires "constant dialectical interaction" of "Both factors, the subjective and the objective" (148). In other words, "Hope does not just occur. It springs intentionally from the pursuit of a better world in which there is genuine freedom. People must learn to hope from the tendencies and latencies in the world and to cultivate them" (71).

Bloch praises art, literature, and everyday daydreams for the contributions they make toward concrete utopian ends. For instance, as Bloch writes, "As long as man is in a bad way, both private and public existence are pervaded by daydreams; dreams of a better life than that which has so far been given him" (*The Principle of Hope* 5). Daydreams "come from a feeling of something lacking and they want to stop it, they are all dreams of a better life" (76). In turn, art is closely connected with daydreaming. In particular, Bloch praises art that emphasizes a utopian 'venturing beyond' because it is through doing so that art often manifests "the most exact imaginative experiment of perfection possible" (95). Bloch is especially compelled by the 'will to journey' he finds to be commonplace in 'artistic daydreaming', identifying this as a vital form of 'forward venturing'. For Bloch, "*Art is a laboratory and also a feast of implemented possibilities,*" that is possibilities implemented in artistic form, which in turn correspond to "pre-appearance" of what can, or might, yet be realizable otherwise (216). Yet Bloch also salutes 'great art' as that which is not closed, and does not feign completeness, but rather emphasizes its openness and that it is a fragment in a process that is larger and not yet resolved. This kind of art allows ample room for surprise, astonishment, and wonder, all of which are necessary in order to imagine and believe that 'The way things are is not the way they have to be'.

Again and again, we have witnessed how Joy Division songs involve a journey, and even more than this, a *will* to a journey, a compulsion to 'venture beyond', and to 'venture forward', even when experiencing immense trepidation about doing so, even when experiencing grave doubt about the possibility of surviving doing so. Likewise over and over again we have witnessed Joy Division songs concluding not with resolution of tension, of conflict, and of the need to struggle, but rather with only temporary, tentative, and tenuous dissolution or suspension of the same. The songs, in addition, are multiply ambiguous in terms of reasonable interpretations of possible meanings, while

1179

music and lyrics often do not neatly line up in terms of precisely what meanings they respectively suggest, nor do particular instrumental contributions or studio production techniques do so, nor do distinct dimensions of musical sound, such as loudness, rhythm, pitch, timbre, and delivery do so. And even as these songs come across as tightly conceived and executed, as coherently organized and articulated, they suggest collaboration among contributors aware of and attuned to each other who at the same time maintain considerable autonomy such that each contributor follows his own course in his own space. These songs make sense as "*a laboratory and also a feast of implemented possibilities*" in dramatizing a venturing beyond and a pressing to the limits, to the furthest and most dangerously self-destructive extremes, in desiring to get past and beyond, to escape and transcend, the problems and limitations of the present, of the existing status quo, of the normative, of the commonsensical, of the ordinary, of the settled, of the established—of the routinized, fetishized, reified, and alienated constraints of what life, according to existing economic laws, social structures, political imperatives, and cultural mores unite to define, and delimit, as all that supposedly is, as the best that supposedly can (ever) be.

Bloch stresses that "Dreams did not always have to be of things far off to see light" (*The Principle of Hope* 534). It is their "Intention towards a better world" that is and remains most valuable (582). Bloch commends "The work of the genuine social dreamers" versus those content with or otherwise accepting of the social status quo as the best of all possible worlds, and he commends these dreamers for daring to be "different," to be "honest," and to pursue what *might* be "great" (583). As translators Neville Plaice, Stephen Plaice, and Paul Knight write in their "Translators Introduction" to *The Principle of Hope*, "Bloch demonstrates that it is precisely radical thinkers 'venturing beyond' available existence who have extended and humanized the world through intellectual, scientific and artistic innovation" (xxxiii). As Bloch himself attests, those he identifies as quintessentially 'utopian types' are "venturers beyond limits or pioneers" (1055). Bloch in turn relishes "living-life-to-the-full, living to the end," which often requires venturing beyond prevailing normative limits to the point where what one appears foolhardy (1001). Bloch likewise praises restlessness and especially remaining "true to unrest" (1001), while he also praises the quest "to know oneself in action" (1027), even when this comes, as it does with Shakespeare's Hamlet, who Bloch identifies as a 'great dreamer' too', in the form of "the paradox of a great dreamer who does not believe in his hopes and goals; of a venturer beyond the limits who believes that beyond the . . . limits is nothingness" (1029). Readers will likely recognize Bloch's interpretation of Hamlet as a 'great dreamer' who 'does not believe in his hope and goals' and as 'a venturer beyond the limits' who 'believes beyond the limits is nothingness' is suggestive of how many have interpreted Ian Curtis, and how I have repeatedly suggested is at least one valid way of making sense of what the narrator-protagonist in many of Curtis's lyrics expresses, or at the least contemplates. But Joy Division songs, as complex wholes and not just as Curtis's lyrics alone, make even better sense as 'true to unrest', because these songs typically show unrest, despite Curtis's notoriously frenzied dancing, as ultimately the obverse of sheer chaotic 'restlessness'. Instead they show 'unrest' as regular, repeated, and especially as regularly and repeatedly ebbing and flowing, through movements that attest to encountering routine and persistent constraints, while striving to imagine possibilities beyond these constraints as well as to push toward concretely experiencing those same possibilities—possibilities that, paradoxically enough, often seem impossible, at least impossible to articulate or otherwise represent in conventional terms, through conventional means and media, yet which 'keep calling' the music as persona, and us in identification with the music as persona, to come toward them, to venture forward in *restless* pursuit.

Bloch conceives "works of the past contain the premonitory and pre-figurative images of the next stage of society" (Plaice, Plaice, and Knight "Translators Introduction" xxvii). Bloch theorizes a "utopian surplus is carried over into the future" even as "It may lie dormant for centuries before new social conditions recall it and extract its new meaning" (xxvii-xxviii). As Bloch explains, "What has cultural value expresses more than the goal of one age or one class: It speaks for the future . . . great achievements in the superstructure no longer belong completely to their age . . . . What interests us now is its meaning for later generations living under a changed general situation" (quoted, *Ernst Bloch: The Pugnacious Philosopher of Hope* 26-27). In *The Principle of Hope* Bloch theorizes this "cultural surplus" as that which does not fully coincide with the dominant ideology of its time and place of origin (154-155). "And the blossoms of art, science, philosophy, always denote something more than false consciousness which each society, bound to its position, had of itself and used for its own embellishment. Rather, these blossoms definitely can be removed from their first socio-historical soil, since they themselves, in essence, are not bound to it" (155). The critical task must be to ascertain "the anticipatory element" even from within "the false" (155). In contrast with this 'cultural surplus', 'ideology' is what tends to involve a false, or premature, "harmonization of social contradictions" (156). Even so, the desire for, and the drive to, harmonize remains important and must not be peremptorily dismissed (156). After all, much of what seems 'too good to be true' may well be 'ahead of is time', and this means it cannot be realized *under current capitalist conditions*. For example, Immanuel Kant's famous categorical imperative: that we act only in such ways that at the same time we will that how we so act should become universal law.

As Plaice, Plaice, and Knight note well, "Bloch considered music to be the most important of the arts, in which the Not-Yet and the utopian could be most perfectly realized" ("Translators Introduction" to *The Principle of Hope* xxxi). According to Bloch, music, more than any other art, "works explosively, occurring in open space," and, likewise more readily than any other art, transports us to "the level of the beautiful and the sublime" (*The Principle of Hope* 216). In music, "Sound hovers, it is not clear where it is located. Equally it is not very plain what it expresses, completely different words have been set to the same tune. Yet a sound can express better than any colour or words that transition where we no longer know whether it is a lament or a consolation" (827). Music provides "that paradoxical perspective that its objects appear even greater, and therefore nearer the more they move towards the horizon on which music lies and forms hope" (834). Music is best of all the arts in engaging "the unfathomable" that otherwise tantalizes beyond the capacities of verbal and visual modes of representation (834). Indeed, "Music is the supreme art of utopian venturing beyond" (1057) and "There is something overhauling and unconcluded in music which no poetry can satisfy, unless it be the poetry which possibly develops music from itself" (*Subject-Object, Commentaries on Hegel*, quoted *The Principle of Hope* 1058).

All of what Bloch here identifies as among music's distinctive capabilities feature in my descriptions, analyses, and interpretations of Joy Division's music. The frequently remarked extent of felt space and especially of felt distance among the constituent sound lines in Joy Division songs. The characteristic unfolding of the structure of these songs across stages highlighting movements upward and downward across small pitch intervals organized in terms of repeated short sequences that encompass only slight variations. Pushing slowly but inexorably through confrontation, climax, denouement, and dissolution. Regular alternations in total density of sound. Arresting openings that build suspense in leading up to the initial entrance of the vocal as well as, subsequently in the song, to returns and reassertions of the principal melodic line and of the choral refrain. Taken together, all of these dimensions make it possible for Joy Division songs to 'work explosively' and to do so 'in open space'. Students I taught often recounted feeling stunned in first listening to songs like "Shadowplay," or "Dead Souls," or "Disorder," or "New Dawn Fades," or "Transmission," or "Twenty Four Hours," encountering what they experienced as resembling an explosion, or series of explosions, occurring in an open space.

Joy Division songs often suggest a meeting of, even a convergence of, the beautiful and sublime. Joy Division songs frequently suggest a hovering presence. What's more, even as the location of the constituent lines and patterns of sounds responsible for this suggestion can be readily charted within the soundbox, these sounds are nonetheless arranged across the space of the soundbox to enhance the felt perception of their distinction within a composite inter-articulation. Deployment within the soundbox emphasizes perceived space between sounds, and in turn accentuates the impact of those sounds pushed to the front and center, notably Ian Curtis's vocal, rendering the 'presence' of these sounds feel greater, and nearer, if only for the fleeting duration of their sounding within the song. What precisely is expressed in Joy Division songs is almost always multiply ambiguous and elliptically mysterious. These songs straddle the border between lament and consolation, especially when we take into account the interplay among all the lines and patterns of sound comprising the song and not just the lyrics. Joy Division songs illustrate the affective impact music exercises via exploration of taboos and through the invisibility, intangibility, and ephemerality of constituent sounds, which closely aligns with conjuring the unfathomable. These songs make sense as dramatizing striving at, or toward, venturing beyond. And they make sense as performing an 'overhauling' of what is commonly left unquestioned or perceived as too traumatic to take up, and to take on, even as this 'overhauling' ceases without arrival at any definite resolution.

Bloch theorizes that, in music, "the tone expresses in man what is still dumb" (1058). In other words, "The Not-Yet . . . has its most characteristic esistence from the air-roots of sound" (1061). As Bloch elaborates,

It is not self-evident that the tone should be able to indicate anything external and be related to it. For it dwells precisely where the eyes have no say any more, where a different dance begins. Nonetheless, the sound does not only remain within, on the contrary its interior has a subterranean relation to that outwardness which is more than mere outwardness . . . Good music in its tone-painting always reproduces something other than the surface, rather it draws out a sounding and showing which remains over beside the thing which has become (1081).

"Music begins longingly and already definitely as a *call to that which is missing*" (1059). "Something is lacking, the sound at least clearly expresses this lack" (1060). "Precisely the sharp figures of restlessness are unmistakedly tuned in music" (1060). Music is replete with "The figures of venturing beyond" and "all have an especially strong utopian ferment" (1060). And music is capable of even more than that, as music can provide "the answer which is no answer but which contains the unfound answer in the context which the significant pause before the thunder produces in the coda" (1062).

Bloch attributes to music "more than other arts the quality of incorporating the numerous sufferings, the wishes and the spots of light of the oppressed class" (1063). "No [other] art has so much surplus over the respective time and ideology in which it exists," because music is exceptionally replete with "the surplus of hope-material" (1063). Bloch is adamant that "*Social tendencies* themselves have been reflected and have been uttered in sound material" that takes the form of music, and that "No art is as socially conditioned as the supposedly spontaneous, indeed mechanically self-righteous art of music; it teems with historical materialism" (1063). Expression, in turn, is central to music: it is "the terminus a quo [starting or originating point] and the terminus ad quem [finishing or ending point] of music" (1068). Yet musical expression is "ultimately a *vice-regent for an articulation which goes much further than anything so far known*" (1069). In other words, "The expression of music is . . . still fermenting, has not yet come out in complete, definable form" (1070). "The relation to this world makes music, particularly in social terms, seismographic, it reflects cracks under the social surface, expresses wishes for change, bids us to hope" (1088). Not only 'seismographic', as "Music, with its open flow, full of the beginnings of something still indesignable, necessarily posits something extraterritorial at the same time" (1088). Music is redolent not only of fissures within the existing social status quo but also of forms of organization that might yet be possible beyond the existing social status quo.

Bloch touts "*the figures of venturing beyond the limits in tone-spheres*: they are articulations in a developing language of intensity" (1088-1089). These are quintessential manifestations of the spirit of utopia "in a world which has come to itself," a world "which seeks to gain *its entire essence* by hearing its way keenly and expanding" (1088-1089). This quest involves immense *struggle*, as illustrated by "The two traditional musical forms of sonata and fugue," which point "towards *struggle* against fate and towards ultimately intended situationlessness, and therefore struggle towards *fatelessness*" (1096). Music dares to venture as far as it is possible to venture: "Music really does go to face death" (1098). Indeed, "How much deep music has its darkness, indeed its light from this ingredient, the night of death, and from its black there burns a brightness different from that which otherwise already exists" (1098). "All music of annihilation points towards a robust core which, because it has not yet blossomed, cannot pass away either . . . In the darkness of this music gleam the treasures that will not be corrupted" (1101).

The lyrics of Ian Curtis and the music of Joy Division resonate with struggle against alienation and with reaching toward a far horizon where it might yet be possible to realize the dream of life lived beyond alienation. This is so even as these lyrics and this music simultaneously convey enormous doubt that such realization might ever be practically possible, at least 'for us', and even as these lyrics and this music simultaneously register this far horizon as so dimly, barely perceptible it remains easier to believe its existence is an illusion, even a delusion. And yet, the lyrics of Ian Curtis and the music of Joy Division also resonate with striving, even when striving seems pointless, doomed to fail, and altogether absurd, to make contact with what exceeds the capability of existing frames of intelligibility to signify–i.e., to attempt not only to 'represent the unrepresentable', but also to make contact with dimensions of the Real that cannot be represented, at least not according to what existing words and images are able to represent. What's more, the lyrics of Ian Curtis and the music of Joy Division resonates with a willingness to pursue this quest, full of fear and trepidation, all the way through, even if this demands facing death or otherwise risking annihilation. These lyrics and this music make sense as reflective of and responsive to not only anguish and trauma but also protest against anguish and trauma, as well as longing and striving to venture beyond, to overcome, pain and trauma, as this pain and trauma is experienced, in particular, by people who are and have been oppressed, exploited, outcast, and abused.

According to Bloch, the real, concrete utopian goal of human striving, and of human hope, is "the only unchanging thing in history" (1375). Always the same, whatever the name: "Happiness, freedom, non-alienation, Golden Age, Land of Milk and Honey, the Eternally-Female, the trumpet signal in Fidelio and the Christ-likeness of the Day of Resurrection" (1375). Nonetheless, "The goal as a whole is and remains still concealed" (1375). This is so because the utopian most often appears fantastically unreal while effective means of working toward its realization are most often blocked by those with the power to do so, and, especially, by those with the interest in doing so. Yet Bloch insists humans maintain the capacity to pursue *and to realize* utopia. Even well into the 20th century, and undoubtedly Bloch would argue the same for us, living at the end of the first quarter of the 21st century, "Man everywhere is still living in prehistory . . . . But the root of history is the working, creating human being who reshapes and overhauls the given facts. Once he has grasped himself and established what is his, without expropriation and alienation, in true democracy, there arises in the world something which shines into the childhood of all and in which no one has yet been: homeland" (1375-1376).

As Zipes explains, '*Heimat*', or 'homeland', functions as a "symbolic term for the home that we have all sensed but none have ever experienced or known" (32). 'Home' is identical with overcoming alienation, with alienation here conceived along all of the lines Marx theorizes in his *Economic and Philosophic Manuscripts of 1844* that I addressed in chapter three. As Plaice, Plaice, and Knight indicate, for Bloch socialism is equivalent with "humanizing the world," and this in turn implies neither the world, nor humanity itself, are yet truly human ("Translators Introduction" to *The Principle of Hope* xxviii). The homeland Bloch apotheosizes will be a real, concrete place in which true human freedom will finally be experienced (xxviii).

Bloch theorizes God and other forms of the divine as stand-ins for what humans yet can do and be for themselves (1283). Bloch advocates moving "from heaven back to man, so that man is not made in the image of God but God in the image of man, or more exactly of the ideal guiding images of man at any given time" (184). In the concrete utopia Bloch theorizes, God as creator of the world disappears with "the divine as a hypostatized human wishful image of the highest order" turned on its head (1285). Here, Bloch directly follows Marx. For example, in the latter's "Introduction to the

Critique of Hegel's *Philosophy of Right*": "The critique of religion ends with the doctrine that man is the highest being for man, therefore with the categorical imperative to overturn all circumstances in which man is a degraded, a forsaken, a contemptible being" (quoted, 1358). And from Marx's famous "Letter to Arnold Ruge": "It will . . . become apparent that the world has long possessed the dream of a matter, of which it must only possess the consciousness in order to possess it in reality. It will become apparent that it is not a question of a great thought-dash between past and future, but of the *carrying through* of the thoughts of the past," including by means of critical "analysis of the mystical consciousness which is unclear to itself" (quoted, 1363).

In his 1961 lecture "Can Hope Be Disappointed?" Bloch declares "hope never guarantees anything. It is characteristically daring and points openly to possibilities that in part depend on chance for their fulfillment" (quoted, *Ernst Bloch: The Pugnacious Philosopher of Hope* 16). And yet, "Hope can learn and become smarter through damaging experiences" (quoted, *Ernst Bloch: The Pugnacious Philosopher of Hope* 17). Hope persists, even when hopelessness dominates over everyone everywhere around, because "the oldest conscious dream . . . of humankind" is "the overthrow . . . of all conditions in which the human individual is a humiliated, enslaved, forsaken, despised creature'" (quoted, *Ernst Bloch: The Pugnacious Philosopher of Hope* 17).

In my own life, despite often being plagued by anxiety and doubt, and despite often being extremely self-critical, I have maintained a persistently stubborn hope. Again and again I have pulled myself back from the brink to refocus on what can I do, slowly, small step by small step, in carefully delimited stages, in order to begin to respond to a situation, or a set of circumstances, that I experience as stressful, and even overwhelming–and by finding ways to *act*, in response, not just continue to stress out. Often, I have reminded myself that even when everything feels incredibly awful, and I experience no reason to expect any change, that change for the better can and will happen, often suddenly and often where and as I don't expect it. I have persisted when I frequently felt as if I was not at all capable of doing so. What I think about and feel when I listen to Joy Division is ultimately, for me, always much the same, despite the bleakness of the lyrics, and despite Ian Curtis's suicide.

Since moving to live full-time in San Diego, now three months on, even as much about my life here has been wonderful, I have again struggled with anxiety, so much so that once again I am working with a psychologist. For me, anxiety at its most painful assumes the form of successively crashing waves of dread as well as spikes of adrenalin that resemble incessantly peaking in the red on the meter measuring the gain in sound recording. This anxiety often arises without a direct source, or trigger, in my own life, and often enough when everything is fine for me, and I am otherwise personally secure. Fear of fascism, of the re-election of Donald Trump and implementation of Project 2025, exercises that impact, even as I most fear the consequences for others, not myself. Fear of ongoing destruction in Gaza and Palestine, with no end in sight, and of the devastating consequences for many generations to come, exercises that impact, even as I fear these consequences for others, not myself. Fear of ecocide is another major factor. Locally, in San Diego, I experience anxiety in response to substantial disparities in income and wealth, especially as these show up in the paucity of housing available for people with low incomes and limited wealth; the lack of sufficient regulation of landlords, property owners, and developers; and the ever rising numbers of homeless. I experience anxiety in relation the last because while a proliferation of organizations attempt to respond they do so without effectively coordinating among each other, while popular opinion trends more hostile toward homeless people, more supportive of 'clearing them out of the way' by 'any means necessary', and increasingly inclined to conceive of homelessness not as a housing problem but rather a problem of addiction, mental illness, and criminality. Again, I am in a fortunate position, personally, in relation to all of that, but, for me, the ultimate test of how 'good' a community is, is how well the community provides for and takes care of everyone within the community.

Influenced by utopian thinking, coming from the likes of Ernst Bloch and Kristen R. Ghodsee, I find it useful to imagine what the ideal community might be like, starting at the neighborhood level. In my own neighborhood, where I reside in San Diego, in the southernmost end of South Mission Hills, right near Little Italy, I envision extensive, quality social housing; I envision universal basic income; I envision people not working paid jobs more than four days a and 32 hours a week maximum; I envision a large, multi-purpose, multi-venue community center; I envision a vibrant self-managing neighborhood government; I envision a much more extensive array of mass transit options and many fewer cars; I envision a large green space; and I envision substantive incentives toward sharing resources and collaborating on activities along with much less privatization according to which every household operates as an autonomous and virtually entirely self-contained entity.

I have been thinking about that kind of envisioning in relation to the challenge of determining what it means to be a socialist at the present time. Since arriving in San Diego I have become active with the Democratic Socialists of America, for the first time, through the local San Diego chapter, after being an at-large, sympathetic but otherwise non-active member for eight years' preceding. Within DSA many disagree over how to relate to electoral politics, and in particular to the Democratic Party. Recently, the California DSA shared with members two columns, representative of opposing positions concerning the 2024 Presidential election. One writer argued that the Presidential election is a distraction from more important work, which is organizing in local communities at the grassroots level, and training people to be capable of organizing and advocating for themselves, in claiming and exercising power on their own behalf. This writer argued that the Democrats, in elective office, will always need to be pressured, and challenged, no matter who they are, and will often represent obstacles, and barriers, toward accomplishing the far-reaching changes necessary, including by coopting radical ideas so these are compatible with maintenance and reproduction of the status quo. This writer argued socialists will be fighting the same fight, whether Donald Trump or Kamala Harris becomes the next U.S. President.

The second writer, in contrast, while agreeing that Democrats, including a President Harris, will not themselves push a socialist agenda, argued that the threat of fascism represented by Trump, Vance, Project 2025, and the like is so grave it is vital that democratic socialists commit to work as part of an 'Anti-MAGA united front'. This second writer argued doing so is necessary for socialists to develop credibility among many of the groups of people we hope, and need, to persuade, eventually, to align with us. If we don't take seriously where they are at, and what they consider their most immediate and urgent fights, then we will seem out of touch and even, ourselves, obstacles and barriers to what they most need and want.

I think both positions are right and I don't think democratic socialists need to choose one or the other. I think we can do both, with some of us more directly involved in the former and some of us more directly involved in the latter. I have long argued that the most important political activity often occurs outside of, as well as in between, campaigns for election to government positions, especially on the national level, and that what ultimately matters is how continuously organized and how well mobilized groups of people are, and remain, independent of campaigns to elect people to political offices, especially as members of one or the other of the two major political parties in the U.S.–Democrat or Republican–because politicians elected to office often are only likely to go as far as they are pressured to go. All too often, however, in our existing system, most people, if they pay attention to 'politics' at all, only do so in relation to national elections, and expect that politicians elected to office should be the ones who 'take care of everything' all by themselves once elected. In contrast, many lobbies, especially representative of powerful, wealthy interests, know better, and are continuously active, exerting continuous pressure on elected officials, and indeed doing a lot of the work for them, including devising models for legislation and executive action. What's more, given the huge costs of running in even local elections in the U.S. today, those campaigning for political office need to spend inordinate time eliciting and cultivating donations, especially among those in the position to donate a great deal.

For me, socialism, especially democratic socialism, means people collectively taking responsibility for and control over the means and processes of managing their own neighborhoods, and communities, rather than turning this over to elected 'officials', especially in a system that it is far from equitably representative. Not only do those with more money, and the many opportunities money can and does provide, maintain a significant advantage over those with less–or no–money, but also increasing voting restrictions hinder populations who already maintain and have historically maintained the least political power. Meanwhile, the U.S. Constitution itself is not democratic. Founded to reward slave owners and slave states, while severely limiting the franchise, the U.S. Constitution continues to allow the votes of voters in small states, such as Wyoming, to count vastly more than the votes of voters in large states, such as California. The U.S. Constitution continues to maintain a bicameral federal legislature that includes a senate, wherein each state, no matter its population size, is represented by the same number of members. The U.S. Constitution fails to prevent the President from exercising often truly 'imperial' powers, powers that are effectively unrestricted and unaccountable. And the U.S. Constitution continues to authorize a Supreme Court of nine unelected judges serving life terms to render unaccountable judgments that exercise extraordinary impact over Americans' lives.

When Democrats champion 'democracy' and its defense, they are championing a limited form of political democracy, and this does not even begin to address the question of economic democracy. For socialists like myself, it feels nauseating to listen to incessant insistence, from mainstream Democrats, that the United States of America is, was, and always will be 'the greatest' nation on Earth, the greatest democracy ever, the greatest land of freedom ever, and on and on. Yes, a choice between 'America is already and always has been as great as it needs to be' and 'America is no longer great but can be if we "return" America to a fascist state in White Christian Nationalist form" is a limited choice. Yet, the former is superior, it is far less harmful, to a great many groups of people than the latter. And with Democrats in power, as opposed to MAGA Republicans, it is and will remain far more viable for democratic socialists to organize, mobilize, and work slowly but surely to advance a democratic socialist agenda. I have been skeptical since a young boy that 'Socialism in America' will arrive any time soon, but that has not deterred me from identifying as a socialist and advocating on behalf of socialism–for others, yet to come–in part as well because I believe socialist struggle involves pushing for reforms within capitalist society that benefit people in areas where people are neediest. For instance, as we approach this November 2024 election, California DSA in campaigning in support of statewide ballot propositions that make affordable rent-controlled housing much more readily possible at municipal and county levels, and that lower the percentage of votes needing for municipal and county governments to raise and allocate funds for low-income, including social, housing.

I empathize with the extent and intensity of insecurity, loneliness, fear, and alienation a great many people feel, a quarter of the way through the 21st century. Yet I remain, long-term, hopeful, because I recognize we don't want to live our lives like this; we want, and we deserve, so much more and so much better. I believe as long as capitalist society persists that even those living in the relatively most fortunate positions will not be leading their best possible lives, and will not be truly free. I believe we remain, collectively, capable of forging a socialist alternative. I believe we can come, collectively, to embrace the work necessary to get 'from here to there'. I do believe in hope, and I do believe in concrete utopia. I value engaging forthrightly with the violence, meanness, cruelty, callousness, and hatred, on the one hand, as well as the pain, trauma, suffering, grief, desperation, and despair, on the other hand, that is part and parcel of living in capitalist society, and especially living in capitalist society where fascism remains a perpetually insidious subterranean force that can all too quickly break the surface. It is, paradoxically enough, such engagement that sparks hope in me, according to how Bloch theorizes hope, because I don't accept that fascism is 'the fate of humanity', is our inescapable destiny, even if and when I don't recognize how we get past it. But I believe we can, it is worth the try, and it is important for me to contribute as best I can, all the while accepting nothing in this quest is guaranteed, and that includes survival along the way.

Works Cited

Alberti, Fay Bound. *A Biography of Loneliness: The History of an Emotion*. Oxford: Oxford
    University Press, 2019.

Anderson, Lars. Cited in Fay Bound Alberti, *A Biography of Loneliness: The History of an
    Emotion*, Oxford: Oxford University Press, 2019.

Arendt, Hannah. *The Origins of Totalitarianism*. Cited in Noreena Hertz, *The Lonely Century:
    How to Restore Human Connection in a World That's Falling Apart*. New York:
    Currency, 2021; Robert Peckham, *Fear: An Alternative History of the World*, London:
    Profile Books, 2023; and Lee Siegel, "From Bowling Alone to scrolling alone: Why
    loneliness is the defining political crisis in America," *The New Statesman*, 12 January

2024, https://www.newstatesman.com/ideas/2024/01/from-bowling-alone-to-scrolling-alone, Accessed 20 April 2024.

Barghouti, Mustafa. Interview with Amy Goodman. *Democracy Now!* "Killing People Around the Clock": Dr. Mustafa Barghouti & Muhammad Shehada on 6 Months of War on Gaza." 8 April 2024. https://www.democracynow.org/2024/4/8/gaza_update Accessed 25 April 2024.

Beck, Ulrich. Excerpts from *World Risk Society*, Cambridge: Polity Press, 1999. Lemert, Charles, ed. *Social Theory: The Multicultural, Global, and Classic Readings*. Sixth Edition. Boulder: Westview, 2017.

Beckett, Andy. *When the Lights Went Out: Britain in the Seventies*. London: Faber and Faber, 2009.

Benjamin, Walter. Cited in Mikkel Bolt Rasmussen, *Late Capitalist Fascism*, Theory Redux Series, Cambridge: Polity, 2022.

Brecht, Bertolt. Cited in Robert Peckham, *Fear: An Alternative History of the World*, London: Profile Books, 2023.

Bloch, Ernst. "Can Hope Be Disappointed?" 1961 Public Lecture. Cited in Jack Zipes, *Ernst Bloch: The Pugnacious Philosopher of Hope*, Cham, Switzerland: Palgrave Macmillan, 2019.

_____. *The Principle of Hope*. 1938-1947, 1953, and 1959. Three Volumes. Neville Plaice, Stephen Plaice, and Paul Knight, trans. Cambridge: The MIT Press, 1986, 1995.

_____. *Subject-Object, Commentaries on Hegel*. Cited in Ernst Bloch, *The Principle of Hope*. 1938-1947, 1953, and 1959, Three Volumes, Neville Plaice, Stephen Plaice, and Paul Knight, trans., Cambridge: The MIT Press, 1986, 1995.

Brenner, Robert. Cited in Mikkel Bolt Rasmussen, *Late Capitalist Fascism*, Theory Redux Series, Cambridge: Polity, 2022.

Britt, Lawrence W. "Fascism Anyone?" *Free Inquiry*, Vol. 23 No. 2, 2003. https://secularhumanism.org/2003/03/fascism-anyone/ Accessed 21 August 2020.

Bump, Philip. "Trump aims to be a fearless warrior for White advantage." *Washington Post*. 1 April 2024. https://www.washingtonpost.com/politics/2024/04/01/white-advantage-elections-trump/ Accessed 25 April 2024.

Byrne, Alex K. and Carol K. Hooven. "The Problem With Saying 'Sex Assigned at Birth'." *New York Times*. 3 April 2024. https://www.nytimes.com/2024/04/03/opinion/sex-assigned-at-birth.html Accessed 20 April 2024.

Cacioppo, John. Cited in Keming Yang, *Loneliness: A Social Problem*, Routledge Advances in Sociology, London: Routledge, 2019.

Campbell, Denis. "Thousands of children unsure of gender identity 'let down by NHS', report finds." *The Guardian*. 10 April 2024. https://www.theguardian.com/society/2024/apr/10/thousands-of-children-unsure-of-gender-identity-let-down-by-nhs-report-finds Accessed 20 April 2024.

Cass, Baroness Dr. Hilary Dawn Cass. Cited in Denis Campbell, "Thousands of children unsure of gender identity 'let down by NHS', report finds," *The Guardian*, 10 April 2024, https://www.theguardian.com/society/2024/apr/10/thousands-of-children-unsure-of-gender-identity-let-down-by-nhs-report-finds, Accessed 20 April 2024.

Cheung, Stephen. Cited in Philip Bump, "Trump aims to be a fearless warrior for White advantage," *Washington Post*, 1 April 2024, https://www.washingtonpost.com/politics/2024/04/01/white-advantage-elections-trump/ Accessed 25 April 2024.

Clifton, Jon. "The Global Rise of Unhappiness." *Gallup*. 15 September 2022. https://news.gallup.com/opinion/gallup/401216/global-rise-unhappiness.aspx Cited in Astra Taylor, *The Age of Insecurity: Coming Together as Things Fall Apart*, CBC Massey Lectures, Toronto: House of Anansi Press, 2023.

Cottam, Tressie McMillan. "Who Would Want to Go to a College Like This?" *New York Times*. 28 March 2024. https://www.nytimes.com/2024/03/28/opinion/dei-ban-college-students.html?smid=nytcore-ios-share Accessed 25 April 2024.

Curtis, Ian. "Twenty-Four Hours." Song Lyrics. 1980.

Durkheim, Émile. Cited in Keming Yang, *Loneliness: A Social Problem*, Routledge Advances in Sociology, London: Routledge, 2019.

Eco, Umberto. "Ur-Fascism." *New York Review of Books*. June 22, 1995. https://www.nybooks.com/articles/1995/06/22/ur-fascism/ Accessed 21 August 2020.

Epoch Philosophy. "Ernst Bloch and The Philosophy (Principle) of Hope." Premiered May 23, 2022. https://www.youtube.com/watch?v=zBkdHRsay3E Accessed 26 August 2024.

Fritzsche, Peter. Cited in Robert Peckham, *Fear: An Alternative History of the World*, London: Profile Books, 2023.

Fromm, Erich. Cited in Keming Yang, *Loneliness: A Social Problem*, Routledge Advances in Sociology, London: Routledge, 2019.

Gallup and The Lumina Foundation. *Policies and laws: How they're impacting college enrollment*. March 2024. https://www.luminafoundation.org/wp-content/uploads/2024/03/Policies-and-Laws.pdf Accessed 25 April 2024.

Ghodsee, Kristen R. *Everyday Utopia: What 2,000 Years of Wild Experiments Can Teach Us About the Good Life*. New York: Simon and Schuster, 2023.

Global Project Against Hate and Extremism. "Project 2025: The Far-Right Playbook for American Extremism." https://globalextremism.org/project-2025-the-far-right-playbook-for-american-authoritarianism/ Accessed 25 April 2024.

Graubart, Jonathan. *Jewish Self-Determination Beyond Zionism: Lessons from Hannah Arendt and Other Pariahs*. Philadelphia: Temple University Press, 2023.

Hasan, Mehdi. Interview with Nurmeen Shaikh and Amy Goodman. "Mehdi Hasan on the Risk of the Media Normalizing Trump's Fascism & Dangers of TikTok Ban." *Democracy Now!* 14 March 2024.

https://www.democracynow.org/2024/3/14/mehdi_hasan_media Accessed 25 April 2024.

The Heritage Foundation. "Project 2025 Reaches 75 Coalition Partners, Continues to Grow in Preparation for Next Conservative President." 10 October 2023. https://www.heritage.org/press/project-2025-reaches-75-coalition-partners-continues-grow-preparation-next-conservative Accessed 25 April 2024.

Hertz, Noreena. *The Lonely Century: How to Restore Human Connection in a World That's Falling Apart*. New York: Currency, 2021.

Hobbes, Thomas. Cited in Robert Peckham, *Fear: An Alternative History of the World*, London: Profile Books, 2023.

Hofstede, G. Cited in Keming Yang, *Loneliness: A Social Problem*, Routledge Advances in Sociology, London: Routledge, 2019.

Hope Not Hate. *State of Hate 2024: Pessimism, Decline and a Rising Radical Right*. March 2024. https://hopenothate.org.uk/wp-content/uploads/2024/03/state-of-hate-2024-v15.pdf Accessed 25 April 2024.

Hudson, Wayne. *The Marxist Philosophy of Ernst Bloch*. London: Macmillan, 1982.

Jones, Owen. "Blood, chaos and decline: these are the fruits of unbridled western hubris." *The Guardian*. 11 April 2024. https://www.theguardian.com/commentisfree/2024/apr/11/blood-chaos-decline-west-capitalism-gaza-moral-collapse-us Accessed 20 April 2024.

Joy Division. "Dead Souls." Musical Song. 1979.
_____. "Disorder." Musical Song. 1979.
_____. "New Dawn Fades." Musical Song. 1979.
_____. "Shadowplay." Musical Song. 1979.
_____. "Transmission." Musical Song. 1980.
_____. "Twenty-Four Hours." Musical Song. 1980.

Kagan, Robert. "A Trump dictatorship is increasingly inevitable. We should stop pretending." *Washington Post*. 30 November 2023. https://www.washingtonpost.com/opinions/2023/11/30/trump-dictator-2024-election-robert-kagan/ Accessed 25 April 2024.
_____. "The Trump dictatorship: How to stop it." *Washington Post*. 7 December 2023. https://www.washingtonpost.com/opinions/2023/12/07/robert-kagan-trump-dictatorship-how-to-stop/ Accessed 25 April 2024.

Kant, Immanuel. 1785. *Groundwork of the Metaphysics of Morals*. Mary Gregor and Jans Timmerman, trans. Revised Edition. Cambridge: MIT Press, 2012.

Khalidi, Rashid. *The Hundred Years' War on Palestine: A History of Settler Colonialism and Resistance, 1917-2017*. New York: Picador, 2020.

Klein, Naomi. Cited in Robert Peckham, *Fear: An Alternative History of the World*, London: Profile Books, 2023.

Kristof, Nicholas. "We Know the Cure for Loneliness. So Why Do We Suffer?" *New York Times*. 6 September 2023.

https://www.nytimes.com/2023/09/06/opinion/loneliness-epidemic-solutions.html
Accessed 20 April 2024.

Lemert, Charles, ed. *Social Theory: The Multicultural, Global, and Classic Readings.* Sixth
Edition. Boulder: Westview, 2017.

Lynch, James. Cited in Keming Yang, *Loneliness: A Social Problem*, Routledge Advances in
Sociology, London: Routledge, 2019.

Marx, Karl. 1844. *Economic and Philosophic Manuscripts of 1844 (The Paris Manuscripts).*
Martin Milligan, trans. Mineola: Dover Books, 2007.

_____. "Introduction to the Critique of Hegel's *Philosophy of Right.*" Cited in Ernst
Bloch, *The Principle of Hope.* 1938-1947, 1953, and 1959, Three Volumes, Neville
Plaice, Stephen Plaice, and Paul Knight, trans., Cambridge: The MIT Press, 1986,
1995.

_____. "Letter to Arnold Ruge." Cited in Ernst Bloch, *The Principle of Hope,*1938-1947,
1953, and 1959, Three Volumes, Neville Plaice, Stephen Plaice, and Paul Knight,
trans., Cambridge: The MIT Press, 1986, 1995.

Messing, Vera and Bence Ságvári. "What Drives Anti-Immigrant Attitudes?" European Social
Survey. Cited in Noreena Hertz, *The Lonely Century: How to Restore Human
Connection in a World That's Falling Apart*, New York: Currency, 2021.

Moir, Cat. *Ernst Bloch's Speculative Materialism: Ontology, Epistemology, Politics.* Leiden,
The Netherlands: Brill, 2019.

Murthy, Dr. Vivek. U.S. Surgeon General. Cited in Nicholas Kristof, "We Know the Cure for
Loneliness. So Why Do We Suffer?," *New York Times.* 6 September 2023,
https://www.nytimes.com/2023/09/06/opinion/loneliness-epidemic-solutions.htmlAcc
essed 20 April 2024.

Nowlan, Bob. *21st Century British TV Crime Drama: a Critical Guide, Book One–Fearless to
The Fall.* Yet Unpublished Book.

_____. *21st Century British TV Crime Drama: a Critical Guide, Book Two–Life on
Mars to Line of Duty.* Forthcoming Book.

_____ and James Boland. *Faceless Fascism.* Unproduced fictional feature film screenplay.

Peckham, Robert. *Fear: An Alternative History of the World.* London: Profile Books, 2023.

Perlman, Daniel and Letitia Anne Peplau. Cited in Keming Yang, *Loneliness: A Social
Problem*, Routledge Advances in Sociology, London: Routledge, 2019.

Plaice, Neville, Stephen Plaice, and Paul Knight. "Translators Introduction." Ernst Bloch, *The
Principle of Hope*, 1938-1947, 1953, and 1959, Three Volumes, Neville Plaice,
Stephen Plaice, and Paul Knight, trans., Cambridge: The MIT Press, 1986, 1995, xix-
xxxiii.

Project 2025: Presidential Transition Project. *Mandate for Leadership: The Conservative
Promise.* https://static.project2025.org/2025_MandateForLeadership_FULL.pdf
Accessed 25 April 2024.

Quinney, Kimber. Interview with Brian Hiro. "Ask the Expert: Fascism and the Fragility of
Democracy." California State University at San Marcos News Center. 2 November
2020. https://news.csusm.edu/ask-the-expert-fascism-and-the-fragility-of-democracy/
Accessed 25 April 2024.

Rasmussen, Mikkel Bolt. *Late Capitalist Fascism*. Theory Redux Series. Cambridge: Polity, 2022.

Reich, Robert. "How do we describe what Trump wants for America? 'Authoritarianism' isn't adequate. It is 'fascism'." *The Guardian*. 17 June 2023. https://www.theguardian.com/commentisfree/2023/jun/17/trump-republican-party-fascism Accessed 25 April 2024.

Riesman, David and Associates. Cited in Keming Yang, *Loneliness: A Social Problem*, Routledge Advances in Sociology, London: Routledge, 2019.

Robinson, Eugene. "'DEI mayor' insults prove that unapologetic racism is back." *Washington Post*. 1 April 2024. https://www.washingtonpost.com/opinions/2024/04/01/baltimore-bridge-dei-mayor-governor/ Accessed 25 April 2024.

Sadler, W.A. and T.B. Johnson. Cited in Keming Yang, *Loneliness: A Social Problem*, Routledge Advances in Sociology, London: Routledge, 2019.

Said, Edward W. *The Question of Palestine*. 1979. New York: Vintage Books, 1992.

Shakespeare, William. *Hamlet*. Cited in Ernst Bloch, *The Principle of Hope*. 1938-1947, 1953, and 1959. Three Volumes. Neville Plaice, Stephen Plaice, and Paul Knight, trans. Cambridge: The MIT Press, 1986, 1995.

Shehada, Muhammad. Interview with Amy Goodman. *Democracy Now!* "Killing People Around the Clock": Dr. Mustafa Barghouti & Muhammad Shehada on 6 Months of War on Gaza." 8 April 2024. https://www.democracynow.org/2024/4/8/gaza_update Accessed 25 April 2024.

Siegel, Lee. "From Bowling Alone to scrolling alone: Why loneliness is the defining political crisis in America." *The New Statesman*. 12 January 2024. https://www.newstatesman.com/ideas/2024/01/from-bowling-alone-to-scrolling-alone Accessed 20 April 2024.

Solnit, Rebecca. Cited in Astra Taylor, *The Age of Insecurity: Coming Together as Things Fall Apart*, CBC Massey Lectures. Toronto: House of Anansi Press, 2023.
_____. Cited in Kristin R. Ghodsee, *Everyday Utopia: What 2,000 Years of Wild Experiments Can Teach Us About the Good Life*, New York: Simon and Schuster, 2023.

Srole, Leo. Cited in Keming Yang, *Loneliness: A Social Problem*, Routledge Advances in Sociology, London: Routledge, 2019.

Taylor, Astra. *The Age of Insecurity: Coming Together as Things Fall Apart*. CBC Massey Lectures. Toronto: House of Anansi Press, 2023.
_____. "Why Does Everyone Feel So Insecure All the Time?" *New York Times*. 18 August 2023. https://www.nytimes.com/2023/08/18/opinion/inequality-insecurity-economic-wealth.html Accessed 20 April 2024.

Thatcher, Margaret. U.K. Prime Minister. Cited in Fay Bound Alberti, *A Biography of Loneliness: The History of an Emotion*, Oxford: Oxford University Press, 2019.

Turner, Alwyn.W. *Crisis? What Crisis? Britain in the 1970s*. London: Aurum, 2008.

U.S. Trans Survey 2024. "Preliminary Results." https://ustranssurvey.org/ Accessed 20 April 2024.

Yang, Keming. *Loneliness: A Social Problem*. Routledge Advances in Sociology. London: Routledge, 2019.

Zinn, Howard. As Cited in Kristin R. Ghodsee, *Everyday Utopia: What 2,000 Years of Wild Experiments Can Teach Us About the Good Life*, New York: Simon and Schuster, 2023.

Zipes, Jack. *Ernst Bloch: The Pugnacious Philosopher of Hope*. Cham, Switzerland: Palgrave Macmillan, 2019.

Zuboff, Shoshana. *The Age of Surveillance Capitalism: The Fight for a Human Future at the New Frontier of Power*. Cited in Noreena Hertz, *The Lonely Century: How to Restore Human Connection in a World That's Falling Apart*, New York: Currency, 2021.

***

www.ingramcontent.com/pod-product-compliance
Ingram Content Group UK Ltd.
Pitfield, Milton Keynes, MK11 3LW, UK
UKHW051349271224
3870UKWH00008B/72